Who's Who in the Theatre

Who's Who in the Theatre

A Biographical Record of the Contemporary Stage

Volume 1
Biographies

SEVENTEENTH EDITION

Edited by Ian Herbert

with Christine Baxter and
Robert E. Finley

Gale Research Company • Book Tower • Detroit, Michigan 48226

London:

Consultant Editor: Christine Baxter
Assistant Editor: Lindsay Fieldman
Research and Services: Veronica Baxter, Eve Ford, Katy Turnbull

New York:

Consultant Editor: Robert E. Finley
Assistant Editor: Noreen Curtis

First Edition, 1912
Second Edition, 1914
Third Edition, 1916
Fourth Edition, 1922
Reprint, 1922
Fifth Edition, 1925
Reprint, 1926
Sixth Edition, 1930
Seventh Edition, 1933
Eighth Edition, 1936
Ninth Edition, 1939
Tenth Edition, 1947
Eleventh Edition, 1952
Twelfth Edition, 1957
Thirteenth Edition, 1961
Fourteenth Edition, 1967
Reprint, 1971
Fifteenth Edition, 1972
Sixteenth Edition, 1977
Seventeenth Edition, 1981

ISSN 0083-9833

Library of Congress Cataloging in Publication Data

Main entry under title:

Who's who in the theatre.

    Contents: v. 1. Biographies —— v. 2. Playbills.
Includes indexes.
    1. Actors——Biography--Dictionaries. 2. Theater--
England--London--History--20th century. 3. Theater--
New York (N.Y.)--New York (City)--History--20th century.
4. Playbills. I. Herbert, Ian.
PN2208.W5   1981   792'.028'0922 [B]   81-6636
ISBN 0-8103-0235-7 (v. 1)   AACR2
ISBN 0-8103-0236-5 (v. 2)
ISBN 0-8103-0234-9 (set)

Contents

Volume One

Volume Two

Preface to the Seventeenth Edition

At first sight, this seventeeth edition of WHO'S WHO IN THE THEATRE may seem very different from its predecessors. A new format, two large library volumes instead of the one stout handbook of the past, and a feeling of space about the presentation, should all combine to add to the book's attractiveness as well as its utility. There will be those—including members of our own editorial board—who find it hard to adjust to the new 'image'. These purists can be assured that in its coverage and in its aspirations to accuracy the book remains true to its original editor's intentions.

In these pages will be found, as always, career details of those who have contributed significantly to the development of the English-speaking stage, together with supporting records that should have a lasting value for the theatre student, and evoke many happy memories for the theatre enthusiast.

HISTORY AND DEVELOPMENT

John Parker put together the first edition of this book for Pitman in 1912. It was the successor to his *Green Room Book,* whose publisher had gone out of business after its first three editions. As well as 563 octavo pages of English-speaking theatre biographies and a separate 62-page Continental Section, it had a short reference section listing 1911's more important openings of new plays in London, New York, Paris and Berlin, giving noted theatrical family trees, listing working dimensions backstage and showing seating plans for West End theatres.

The second edition, published in 1914, had grown by two hundred pages, a hundred of them devoted to a list of Notable Productions and Important Revivals of The London Stage From the Earliest Times to 30 June 1913, a feature which remained and grew until the fourteenth edition.

Two new sections were added to the 1916 third edition; a listing of London Long Runs, and a separate but bound-in volume entitled WHO'S WHO IN VARIETY—84 pages of biographies with their own Obituary listing and a list of London Variety Theatres.

Six years went by before the fourth edition, to which over 650 biographies were added, although the variety section, with most of its entries, was dropped. Playbills made their appearance for the first time—a short section giving the casts of important London and provincial productions from July-December 1921, and intended as an update to the main biographical section, which was corrected to 30 June 1921. London Playbill listings as we now know them began with the fifth edition, which carried them for January 1922 to July 1925. The Continental Section was now dropped, and most of these entries disappeared, although one or two, such as Diaghileff, Serge, Russian manager, made the main body of the book.

The sixth edition appeared in 1930, later than intended, because a burglar made off with all of John Parker's notes for the year 1925 and much of his manuscript. He manfully rewrote his notes and added 500 biographies. For the first time, entries for inactive names were cut and the reader referred to the previous edition for full details.

The 1933 seventh edition started to pay attention to activities in 'Talking Pictures', a task delegated by John Parker to his son, John Parker, Jr. This continued in the 1936 eighth edition, the first to pass two thousand pages. The ninth edition dipped below two thousand again, and in a preface written in October 1939, John Parker recorded the melancholy fact that all London theatres had been closed by Government order the month before on the outbreak of war—the first time that this had happened since the Great Plague in 1665. They were back in business by the month's end, however, as shown in the tenth edition, which came out in 1947. This was the first edition to list Long Runs on the New York Stage, though American theatre people had been well represented in the biographies right from the first edition.

The eleventh edition in 1952 was the last to be edited by John Parker, who died that year. His son John was responsible for the 1957 twelfth edition, from which the tables of hereditary theatrical families were omitted. Some more sections had to be cut from the 1961 thirteenth edition, and the ballet biographies were taken out for a projected WHO'S WHO IN BALLET AND THE DANCE, which unfortunately never appeared. Nevertheless, the new editor, Freda Gaye, was able to add playbills for the two Stratfords among other useful new sections, including a few pages of photographs; more photographs in the 'fourteenth and jubilee' edition, 1967, covered the fifty-plus years of the book's history, and another new feature was an index to all the playbills in previous editions. Seating plans were dropped for the first time from this edition.

Economy was the keynote of the fifteenth edition in 1972 and although we were able at last to make the book truly Anglo-American by adding Broadway and Off-Broadway to the playbill section, the Notable Productions and Revivals list and the cumulative Obituary, by now occupying nearly two hundred and over a hundred pages respectively, had to be sacrificed. 'Continental' names, too, which had been creeping back in, were consciously omitted in order to retain the book's concentration on English-speaking theatre. The only section to disappear from the sixteenth edition was the cumulative index to playbills. New setting enabled us to keep the book down to less than 1400 pages while increasing legibility considerably—a process which has been taken further in this present edition.

Availability

Today a complete set of editions of WHO'S WHO IN THE THEATRE is very hard to find, but for serious students, very desirable, since as we have seen, every edition contains some valuable information not duplicated elsewhere. The Gale Research Company has done theatre scholars a service by collecting together the last updated biography of everyone who dropped out of the book before the sixteenth edition, and reissuing the collection as WHO WAS WHO IN THE THEATRE, 1912-1976. Naturally, this cut-and-paste job perpetuated any few errors that remained in these biographies, and the only updating Gale's editors were able to do was insert a good few of the known dates of death. Nevertheless, it is a boon to those of us who do not possess a complete set of editions, and even the lucky few who do can look up a figure from the past much more conveniently in these four volumes. It means that complete access to the biographical corpus of WHO'S WHO IN THE THEATRE since its beginning can be had for the price of that compilation, plus the sixteenth and now this seventeenth edition.

COMPILATION

Some of the more common misconceptions about this book may perhaps be removed by a short explanation of some of the work that goes into compiling a new edition.

Playbills

The playbills form the backbone of our research and record-keeping. Programmes have to be obtained for all the major London and New York productions, from which casting details are typed out for the book's playbill sections. Thanks to the excellent co-operation of the main programme producers, Playbill in New York, Stilwell Darby and Theatreprint in London, the first part of this work is easily done, but it can be quite a task to track down a programme which may have existed only as a typewritten sheet from a company playing an obscure venue for one or two nights. Many cast-lists, though not so often in this category, are given in *Variety* and *Plays and Players,* while the three splendid American theatre annuals provide a useful check for earlier seasons, though of course not available for our use for the whole span of research time. For London, however, assembling a reasonably complete set of playbills is no easy task, especially for this edition, where we determined to give more prominence to the many new and significant productions being given on what used to be called 'The Fringe' but is steadily becoming more integral to the fabric of London theatre. We have also tried to expand our New York playbill coverage, now that the distinction in standard between Off- and Off-Off-Broadway has been blurred by a tendency to try out more and more good work in less crippling economic conditions.

Biographies

Once recorded in the playbills, appearances have to be marked up on our records of those people already in the book, and of the ever-growing number of people who look as if they are going to be added to the book one day. To collect London and New York appearances is not enough, so English provincial and US regional programmes have to be scanned regularly, and issues of *The Stage* (which regrettably no longer gives cast-lists) dissected for clues to appearances in remoter theatres. Then we have to keep in touch with Australia and Canada; and so it goes on!

All this gives us a fair base for biography maintenance, but it would not be enough without the collaboration of the subjects themselves. Everyone appearing in the book already was sent a copy of his or her existing sixteenth edition biography by the end of 1979 with a request for update, and such is the respect for the book that a very high percentage of people supplied information. Not everyone keeps perfect records, however, and everything supplied in this way has to be checked as far as possible against our own records.

An especially thorough effort was made in the revision of existing biographies for this edition, particularly since every word set had to be read again. New material has been added to practically every entry, and the additions and corrections, so the printer tells me, average thirty percent of the material—a staggering increase that should be brought to the attention of anyone who thinks they can get by on the sixteenth edition.

New Names

We also made a special effort to locate as many new candidates as possible for this edition. There were consultations with the editorial board in London and with the new editorial board in New York, and suggestions were solicited from all sorts of friends in theatre criticism, theatre research, etc. We finished with a list of over a thousand names, all of whom had some good reason to be included. Questionnaires were sent to all of these—or almost all, since the addresses of some theatre people are almost impossible to find. (Heaven help the compilers of the next edition now that Equity in New York has stopped forwarding their members' mail!) Once again, we were gratified by the very high percentage of people who took the trouble to return their questionnaires, and even more by the high percentage of those returning who had taken a lot of time to give us the very detailed information we sought.

Missing Names

It would be splendid to report that all those thousand names have been added to this edition. The total is in fact just over three hundred—and *not*, it must be stressed at once, the most important three hundred. All the new names included deserve their place, whether because of an outstanding record or simply because their name keeps cropping up and ought to be accessible in a reference book of this kind. Some very significant and well-loved names in the theatre do not appear, however, and this may be for one of several reasons. As with any publication, comprehensiveness must be weighed with timeliness. Although an effort was made to include as much information as possible on each biography, time did not allow a comprehensive listing in every case. Much of the material so generously supplied is still on an embarrassingly high 'pending' pile that may one day be converted into a biography supplement, or perhaps be included in the eighteenth edition—suitably updated, of course. Or it is possible that the material that has been supplied does not really add up to a useful entry, and our own records have been insufficient to supplement it. For a number of biographies, where no information at all was supplied by their subjects, we have been able to construct a very acceptable record, and indeed in some cases we have been able to use this as a means of prising further information out of previously reluctant prospects! Once again, however, time has prevented us from doing this in every case where it would have been desirable.

For a number of biographies, where no information at all was supplied by their subjects, we have been able to construct a very acceptable record, and indeed in some cases we have been able to use this as a means of prising further information out of previously reluctant prospects! Once again, however, time has prevented us from doing this in every case where it would have been desirable.

The last group of absentees is a very curious one, and fortunately also a small one. It is those three or four people who have actually asked not to be included in the book. We take the view that WHO'S WHO IN THE THEATRE is a historical source and should therefore include every major figure if at all possible. What an actor has done on stage is a matter of public record and it seems a useful service to theatre researchers to collate that record; so with reluctant actors and actresses our usual policy is to omit personal details if asked, but to record their career where we have the data. With some other peripheral figures, it is easier to respect their wish for anonymity—but it would be fascinating to know what can prompt such a wish in a profession which gains its existence from exposure to the public.

To those who did send us biographical information which has not been used this time round, an apology is due. As has been stressed, non-appearance, especially in this edition, is not an indication that a person has somehow failed to pass the scrutiny of some know-it-all review body—simply there was not time to include everyone. Each new name who *does* appear was sent a draft of their proposed entry for comment, and again a high percentage came back, usually with very little alteration.

When considering the absence of a particular name from this book, readers might also like to reflect on just how many of the key figures on both sides of the Atlantic, as well as in Australia, do appear. With the total number of biographies close to 2400, and the membership of both US and British Equity in the tens of thousands, the coverage is really quite respectable.

SOME COMMON QUESTIONS

If I have spent a lot of time talking about how biographies are compiled and how new names are chosen, it is because these are the most frequent areas of enquiry, and criticism of course. Some other questions about the book are more easily answered. Why, for instance, do we not give more information about film and TV appearances? Because it is difficult enough to give a full account of theatrical careers in what has always been designated a theatre reference book. Why do we not always give dates of birth? Because dates of birth are not always supplied, and also because we have come across actors who have a fear (unfortunately often well-founded) that managements will reject them for a juvenile lead the moment they pass twenty-nine. Why do we drop entries for living people? Usually because we can find no trace of stage activity for at least ten years, and can see no likelihood of that person returning to the stage. (When they do, as James Mason did recently, we try to reinstate them.) Why do some people appear as alive in the Biography Volume when their death date is recorded in the Obituary? Because the Obituary list was the last item to be prepared, apart from this preface. As a rough guide to dating, although the playbills stop at 31 December 1979, most of the existing biographies are up-to-date to the spring of 1980, and the new biographies to the summer. While London Long Run listings were completed as long ago as January 1980, we have rounded off the totals for shows that closed before 1 July, and for New York we have been able to update most of the Long Run totals to 1 July also.

Ian Herbert
31 July 1980

Volume 1
BIOGRAPHIES

NOTE ON BIOGRAPHIES

As with previous editions, great care has been taken to ensure the complete accuracy of biographical details. In most instances full co-operation has been received from the person concerned, and the Editors are most grateful for the help given. However, where it has not been possible to obtain the necessary information, personal details have been omitted.

WHO'S WHO IN THE THEATRE

A

ABBENSETTS, Michael, dramatist
b Georgetown, Guyana, 8 June 1938; *s* of Neville John Abbensetts and his wife Elaine; *e* Queens College, Guyana, Stanstead College, Canada and Sir George Williams University, Montreal, Canada.

His first play, Sweet Talk, was first performed at the Royal Court's Theatre Upstairs, London, in July 1973, and subsequently at the New York Shakespeare Festival's Public Theatre, Nov 1974; has since written the plays Alterations, 1978; In the Mood, 1980; resident dramatist, Royal Court theatre, 1973–74; television writing includes the series *Empire Road* as well as plays such as The Museum Attendant, Road Runner and Black Christmas.

Address: 4 Caxton Road, London W12 8AJ.

ABBOTT, George, actor, dramatic author, producer, and director
b Forestville, New York, 25 June 1887; *s* of George B Abbott and his wife May (McLaury); *e* Hamburg, NY and Rochester University (BA), and studied playwriting with Professor G P Baker at Harvard University; *m* (1) Ednah Levis (dec); (2) Mary Sinclair (mar dis).

Made his first appearance as an actor in NY, at the Fulton Theatre, 25 Nov 1913, as Babe Merrill in The Misleading Lady; appeared at the 48th Street Theatre, Apr 1915, as the Second Yeoman in The Yeoman of the Guard; in 1916 played in The Queen's Enemies; rewrote some scenes for Lightnin', Gaiety, 1918; served as assistant stage manager for Three Wise Fools, 1918; at the Belasco, Sept 1918, played Henry Allen in Daddies; 48th Street, Nov 1920, played Sylvester Cross in The Broken Wing; toured for some time in Dulcy; Empire, NY, Apr 1923, Texas in Zander the Great; Princess, Oct 1923, Sverre Peterson in The White Desert; Klaw, Jan 1924, Sid Hunt in Hell-Bent for Heaven; Vanderbilt, Sept 1924, Steve Tuttle in Lazy Bones; Garrick, Jan 1925, Dynamite Jim in Processional; George M Cohan, Sept 1925, Dirk Yancey in A Holy Terror; played in Cowboy Crazy, 1926; John Golden, Feb 1930, Frederick Williston in Those We Love; Ethel Barrymore, Jan 1934, John Brown in a play of that name; re-appeared on the stage at the ANTA Playhouse, Aug 1955, as Mr Antrobus in The Skin of Our Teeth; he is co-author or sole author of: The Head of the Family (Harvard Dramatic Club), Man in the Manhole (Boston), 1912; The Fall Guy (with James Gleason), A Holy Terror (with Winchell Smith), 1925; Love 'Em and Leave 'Em (with J V A Weaver), The Ragged Edge (adaptation), Broadway (with Philip Dunning), 1926; Four Walls (with Dana Burnett), Coquette (with Ann P Bridgers), 1927; Ringside (with E A Paramore, Jr, and H Daab), 1928; Those We Love (with S K Lauren), 1930; Lilly Turner (with Philip Dunning), 1932; Heat Lightning (with Leon Abrams), 1933; Ladies' Money, Page Miss Glory, 1934; Three Men on a Horse (with John Cecil Holm), 1935; Sweet River (from Uncle Tom's Cabin), On Your Toes (with Rodgers and Hart), 1936; The Boys

from Syracuse, 1938; Best Foot Forward (with John Cecil Holm), 1941; Beat the Band (with George Marion, Jr), 1942; Where's Charley? 1948; A Tree Grows in Brooklyn (with Betty Smith), 1951; Pajama Game (with Richard Bissell), 1954; Damn Yankees (with Douglas Wallop), 1955; New Girl in Town, 1957; Fiorello! (with Jerome Weidman), 1959; Tenderloin (with Jerome Weidman), 1960; Flora, The Red Menace (with Robert Russell), Anya (with Guy Bolton), 1965; Music Is (Book), 1976; he also directed: Broadway, Chicago, 1926; Four Walls, Spread Eagle, Coquette, Bless You Sister, 1927; Ringside, Gentlemen of the Press, Jarnegan, Poppa, 1928; Those We Love, 1930; Louder Please, 1931; Lilly Turner, The Great Magoo, Twentieth Century, 1932; Heat Lightning, The Drums Begin, 1933; John Brown, Kill That Story, Small Miracle, Page Miss Glory, Ladies' Money, 1934; Three Men on a Horse, Boy Meets Girl, Jumbo, 1935; On Your Toes, Sweet River, Brother Rat, 1936; Room Service, Angel Island, Brown Sugar, 1937; All That Glitters, What a Life, The Boys from Syracuse, 1938; The Primrose Path, Mrs O'Brien Entertains, See My Lawyer, Ring Two, Too Many Girls, The White-Haired Boy (Boston), 1939; The Unconquered, Goodbye in the Night, Pal Joey, 1940; Best Foot Forward, 1941; Jason, Beat the Band, Sweet Charity, 1942; Kiss and Tell, Get Away, Old Man, 1943; A Highland Fling, Snafu, On the Town, 1944; Mr Cooper's Left Hand (Boston), One Shoe Off (New Haven), Billion Dollar Baby, 1945; Beggar's Holiday (redirected), 1946; It Takes Two, Barefoot Boy with Cheek, High Button Shoes, You Never Know (redirected), 1947; Look Ma, I'm Dancin', Where's Charley? Mrs Gibbons' Boys, 1949; Call Me Madam, Tickets Please (redirected), Out of This World (redirected), 1950; A Tree Grows in Brooklyn, The Number, 1951; In Any Language, 1952; Wonderful Town, Me and Juliet, 1953; The Pajama Game, On Your Toes, 1954; Damn Yankees, 1955; Coliseum, London, Mar 1957, author of Damn Yankees; NY, New Girl in Town, 1957; Drink to Me Only, 1958; Once upon a Mattress, Fiorello!, 1959; Tenderloin, 1960; A Call on Kuprin, 1961; Take Her, She's Mine, 1961; A Funny Thing Happened on the Way to the Forum, for which he received the Tony Award; Never Too Late, 1962; Strand, London, Oct 1963, directed A Funny Thing Happened on the Way to the Forum; NY, Fade Out—Fade In, 1964, which closed in Nov owing to illness of star, and which he redirected when it reopened in Feb 1965; Flora, The Red Menace, Anya, 1965; Help Stamp Out Marriage, Agatha Sue, I Love You, 1966; How Now, Dow Jones, 1967; The Education of Hyman Kaplan, The Fig Leaves Are Falling, 1968; Three Men on a Horse, 1969; Norman, Is That You?, Not Now, Darling, 1970; The Pajama Game (revival), 1973; Seattle, Washington, Repertory, Dec 1974, Life with Father; Music Is, 1976; Winning Isn't Everything, 1978; has produced or co-produced Twentieth Century, 1932; Lilly Turner, Heat Lightning, The Drums Begin, 1933; John Brown, Kill That Story, 1934; Boy Meets Girl, 1935; Sweet River, Brother

Rat, 1936; Room Service, Angel Island, Brown Sugar, 1937; All That Glitters, What a Life!, The Boys from Syracuse, 1938; The Primrose Path, Mrs O'Brien Entertains, See My Lawyer, Too Many Girls, Ring Two, The White-Haired Boy (Boston), 1939; The Unconquered, Goodbye in the Night, Pal Joey, 1940; Best Foot Forward, 1941; Jason, Beat the Band, 1942; Kiss and Tell, Get Away, Old Man, 1943; A Highland Fling, Snafu, 1944; Mr Cooper's Left Hand (Boston), Twilight Bar (Philadelphia), One Shoe Off (New Haven), 1945; The Dancer, 1946; Barefoot Boy with Cheek, 1947; Look Ma, I'm Dancin', 1948; Mrs Gibbons's Boys, Touch and Go, 1949; A Tree Grows in Brooklyn, 1951; On Your Toes, 1954; in 1928, directed the film of The Bishop's Candlesticks; also collaborated in dialogue of All Quiet on the Western Front, and has since written and directed many films; on 25 Nov 1963, to mark his fiftieth anniversary in the theatre, he published his autobiography, Mr Abbott; Tony Award, 1976, for distinguished career achievement in the theatre; holder of five other Tonys; hon doctorates from University of Rochester, NY, 1961, U of Miami, Fla, 1974.

Recreation: Golf. *Clubs:* Coffee House, Dutch Treat, Indian Creek Country, The Merriewold. *Address:* 1 Rockefeller Plaza, New York, New York, 10020.

ABEL, Walter, actor

b St Paul, Minnesota, 6 June 1898; *s* of Richard Michael Abel and his wife Christine (Becker); *m* Marietto Bitter (dec); studied at the American Academy of Dramatic Arts.

In Feb 1918, appeared there in Harvest, Nocturne, and A Woman's Way; made his first professional appearance at the Manhattan Opera House, New York, 20 Dec 1919, as 2nd Lieut Vincent Moretti in Forbidden; at the Garrick, NY (for the Theatre Guild), Feb 1922, played Acis in Back to Methuselah; Punch and Judy, Jan 1923, Eugene Huckins in A Square Peg; 44th Street, Apr 1923, Jacques de Bois in As You Like It; Provincetown, Mass, Jan 1924, The Student in The Spook Sonata; Provincetown, Mass, 1924–5, played in Fashion, The Crime in the Whistler Room, SS Glencairn, Beyond, and Michel Auclair, and at the Provincetown Playhouse, Greenwich Village, NY, in Desire Under the Elms, and Love for Love; at Times Square, Oct 1925, played Carl Behrend in The Enemy; Forrest, Dec 1926, Dermot McDermot in Hangman's House; Maxine Elliott, Oct 1927, Henry Bascom in The House of Women; Bijou, May 1928, Wayne Trenton in Skidding; Comedy, NY, Apr 1929, Boris Trigorin in The Sea-Gull; made his first appearance on the London stage at the Apollo, 3 June 1929, as Michael Jeffery in Coquette; on his return to NY, appeared at the Royale, Oct 1929, as Elmer Gray in First Mortgage; Waldorf, Jan 1930, played Vaska in At the Bottom; Times Square, Sept 1931, George in I Love an Actress; during 1932, toured as Orin Mannon in the O'Neill trilogy Mourning Becomes Electra, and appeared in that part at the Alvin, NY, May 1932; Royale, Oct 1932, Jimmie Lee in When Ladies Meet; Royale, Oct 1933, Niko in A Divine Drudge; Shubert, Nov 1933, André Roussel in The Drums Begin; Ethel Barrymore, Apr 1934, Morgan Chadwick in Wife Insurance; Masque, May 1934, Doctor Linton in Invitation to a Murder; Music Box, Sept 1934, Jonathan Crale in Merrily We Roll Along; Empire, Dec 1936, Nathaniel McQuestion in The Wingless Victory; County Theatre, Suffern, NY, Sept 1938, John Shand in What Every Woman Knows; Princeton, New Jersey, Jan 1939, David Hudson in The Birds Stopped Singing; Mar 1939, toured as Cedric Trent in West of Broadway; Playhouse, Nov 1939, Benjamin de Wolfe in No Code to Guide Her; Empire, Nov 1945, Clement Waterlow in The Mermaids Singing; Biltmore, Mar 1947, Charles Burnett in

Parlor Story; Mansfield, Mar 1949, Dr Jay Stewart in The Biggest Thief in Town; went to Elsinore, Denmark, in June 1949, where he appeared as Claudius in Hamlet, and subsequently went to Germany to appear for the American Army of Occupation; at the Martin Beck, NY, Mar, 1950, Gavin Leon Andrée in The Wisteria Trees; Lyceum, Mar 1952, Capt Mike Dorgan in The Long Watch; in Seattle, Washington, 1953, played the title-role in Noah; in NY and Philadelphia, Mar 1953, acted as narrator at the Philadelphia Orchestra's performances of King David; also played the Narrator for the same orchestra in Lincoln Portrait; Kaufmann Auditorium, Feb 1954, appeared in reading performances of Under Milk Wood; Longacre, Oct 1958, played Jim Dougherty in The Pleasure of His Company; Fulton, Dec 1959, Scrooge in A Christmas Carol; Brooks Atkinson, Oct 1962, Lew in Night Life; Fresno State College, Fresno, Calif, Dec 1963, played in Twelfth Night; US tour, 1964, directed The Imaginary Invalid; Papermill Playhouse, Millburn, NJ, Feb 1965, played in Affairs of State; Goodspeed Opera House, East Haddam, Conn, Aug 1966, played in Maggie; Biltmore, Nov 1967, Bill Hastings in The Ninety-Day Mistress; Arena Stage, Washington, DC, Feb 1972, Chief Justice Harry Griffin in A Conflict of Interest; Martin Beck, Nov 1974, Antonio in Saturday Sunday Monday; Vivian Beaumont, Oct 1975, William Gower in Trelawny of The Wells; regularly appears in summer stock seasons in such plays as Inherit the Wind, Our Town, The Skin of Our Teeth, etc; entered films, 1935, and first appeared in The Three Musketeers and has since played in many pictures, including: Fury, 1936, Skylark, 1941, Mr Skeffington, 1944, Dream Girl, 1948, Mirage, 1965, etc; has appeared regularly on television since 1944; Vice President, Episcopal Actors' Guild.

Recreation: Gardening and landscaping. *Club:* Players. *Address:* 167 East 71st Street, New York, NY, 10021. *Tel:* TR 9–9444.

ABRAHAMS, Doris Cole, producing manager

b New York, NY, 29 Jan 1925; *d* of Mark Harris Cole and his wife Florence May (Kleinman); *e* Goucher College, Baltimore, Md and Ohio University; *m* Gerald M. Abrahams, CBE.

Trained for the stage at the Leland Powers School of the Theatre, Boston, Mass; formerly an actress, later a literary and theatrical agent; at the Belasco, NY, May 1945, presented her first production, Blue Holiday; presented an eight-week season of summer stock in Connecticut, 1946; came to Britain and has presented or co-presented the following plays in London unless otherwise stated: Enter A Free Man, Out of the Question, 1968; Enemy, 1969; Child's Play, 1971; Equus (NY), 1974; Travesties (NY), 1975; Wild Oats, Once a Catholic, 1977; Once a Catholic (NY), 1979; member, Society of West End Theatre, League of New York Theatres & Producers.

Recreations: Boating, swimming, antique furniture. *Address:* 246 West 44th Street, New York, NY 10036.

ACKLAND, Joss, actor

b London, 29 Feb 1928; *s* of Sydney Norman Ackland and his wife Ruth (Izod); *e* Dame Alice Owen's School; *m* Rosemary Kircaldy.

Trained for the stage at the Central School of Speech and Drama; first appeared on the stage in 1945 at the Aldwych, in The Hasty Heart; Arts, Nov 1946, appeared as Gans and the Police Constable in The Rising Sun; played minor roles in the 1947 Stratford season; appeared in repertory until 1954 at various towns including Buxton, Hayes, Croydon, Windsor,

Chesterfield and Coventry; also appeared at the Embassy, Q, Watergate, New Lindsey, Boltons etc; Pitlochry, 1951, played Simon in Mary Rose; after various tours, in 1954 left the stage to work as a tea planter in Central Africa; 1955–7, worked in the theatre in South Africa, also as a disc jockey and scriptwriter; returned to England, 1957, joining the Oxford Playhouse company; and playing such parts as Father in Life with Father and Bottom in A Midsummer Night's Dream; joined the Old Vic, 1958, to play Sir Toby Belch in Twelfth Night; subsequent appearances with the company included Caliban in The Tempest, Northumberland in Richard II, Falstaff in The Merry Wives of Windsor (1959), Archbishop of Rheims in Saint Joan, Pistol in Henry V (1960), Aegisthus in The Oresteia (1961); while with the Old Vic toured Russia, the USA, etc; Associate Director, Mermaid Theatre, 1962–4, directing The Plough and the Stars, Sept 1962, and playing, among others, Scrofulofsky in The Bed Bug, Bluntschli in Arms and the Man, Sotmore and later (at Her Majesty's) Squeezum in a revival of Lock Up Your Daughters (1962); Galileo in The Life of Galileo, Kirilov in The Possessed, Long John Silver and Blind Pew in Treasure Island (1963); Herdsman in The Bacchae (1964); Royal Court, Aug 1965, Prof Gilbert Medlin in The Professor; New, Sept 1966, played the title role in Jorrocks; Royal Court, July, New, Sept and Duke of York's, Dec 1968, played Gus in The Hotel in Amsterdam; New, Jan and Strand, June 1970, played four parts in Come As You Are; at the Cambridge, Feb 1971, played Brassbound in Captain Brassbound's Conversion; Duchess, Apr 1973, Sam Brown in Collaborators; Piccadilly, March 1974, Harold Mitchell in A Streetcar Named Desire; Adelphi, April 1975, Fredrik Egerman in A Little Night Music; toured, 1977, as Petruchio in The Taming of the Shrew; Olivier, June 1977, Eustace Perrin State in The Madras House; Prince Edward, June 1978, Juan Peron in Evita; first appeared in films, 1947, in Seven Days to Noon; later films include Too Many Chefs, Saint Jack and The Apple; his numerous TV appearances since 1950 include The Lie, Tinker, Tailor, Soldier, Spy, Constance Kent, etc; is a frequent broadcaster.

Recreations: Painting, writing and his seven children. *Address:* c/o The Garrick Club, Garrick Street, London WC2. *Tel:* 01–836 3846.

ACKLAND, Rodney, actor and dramatic author
b 18 May 1908; *s* of Edward Ackland and his wife Diana (Lock); *e* London; studied for the stage at the Central School of Speech Training and Dramatic Art; *m* Mab Lonsdale.

Made his first appearance on the stage at the Gate Theatre studio, 1924, as Medvedieff in The Lower Depths; played in various repertory companies, including J B Fagan's Oxford Players, The Masque Theatre, Edinburgh (where he played Lubin, Zozim, and the He-Ancient in Back to Methuselah) Southend, etc; in 1929, toured as Young Woodley in the play of that name; Nov 1932, toured in Recipe for Murder; during 1933, toured as Joseph in Musical Chairs; Gaiety, Oct 1933, played Paul in Ballerina; Cambridge, Feb 1934, Tony Willow in Birthday; Embassy, Apr 1934, Tony in Battle Royal; during 1934, toured as Paul in Ballerina; Criterion, May 1936, played Oliver Nashwick in his own play, After October; has written the following plays: Improper People, 1929; Marion-Ella, Dance With No Music, 1930; Strange Orchestra, 1932; adapted Ballerina from novel 1933; Birthday, 1934; adapted The Old Ladies from the novel, 1935; After October, Plot Twenty-One, 1936; adapted Yes, My Darling Daughter, 1937; adapted The White Guard, 1938; Remembrance of Things Past, 1938; adapted Sixth Floor, 1939; adapted Blossom Time, 1942; staged The Belle of New York,

1942; author of The Dark River, which he also directed, 1943; adapted Crime and Punishment, and in collaboration with Robert Newton, was the author of Cupid and Mars, 1945; adapted The Diary of a Scoundrel, 1949; author of Before the Party, 1949; in collaboration with Robert Newton, author of A Multitude of Sins, 1951; author of The Pink Room, or, The Escapists, 1952; author of A Dead Secret, 1957; adapted Farewell, Farewell, Eugene, 1959; Before the Party successfully revived at the Queen's, 1980; publications include an autobiography, The Celluloid Mistress.

Address: c/o Eric Glass, Ltd, 28 Berkeley Square, London W1.

ADAMS, Edie (*née* Edith Adams Enke), actress and singer
b Kingston, Pa, 16 Apr; *d* of Sheldon Enke and his wife Ada (Adams); *e* Juilliard School of Music, 1946–50, Columbia Univ, 1947–8, Traphagen School of Fashion Design, 1956; *m* Ernie Kovacs (dec).

Made her professional début at the Ridgewood, NJ, Chapel Theater, July 1947, in Blithe Spirit; first appeared in New York at the Winter Garden, 25 Feb 1953, as Eileen in Wonderful Town; St James, Nov 1956, played Daisy Mae in Li'l Abner; toured in The Merry Widow, 1959; played in stock editions of Sweet Bird of Youth and Free As a Bird, 1960; played Sadie Thompson in Rain at the Packard Music Hall, Warren, Ohio, July 1963; toured 1974 as Reno Sweeney in Anything Goes; toured 1975 as Lovely Lowell in The Cooch Dancer; has appeared in the films The Apartment (1960), Lover, Come Back (1961), The Best Man (1964), The Honey Pot (1967), etc; has appeared regularly on television since 1949 in *The Ernie Kovacs Show* (1951–6), Cinderella (1959), her own series *Here's Edie* (1962), *The Edie Adams Show* (1963), and many other variety programs; has toured extensively in the US and Canada in cabaret and variety shows.

Recreations: Dressmaking, interior decoration. *Address:* Cleary, Straus, Irwin, and Goodman, 7175 Sunset Boulevard, Los Angeles, Cal, 90052. *Tel:* 462–6486.

ADDAMS, Dawn, actress
b Felixstowe, Suffolk, 21 Sept 1930; *d* of James Ramage Addams and his wife Ethel Mary (Hickie); *e* at fourteen schools in India, England and California; *m* (1) Prince Vittorio Massimo (mar dis); (2) James White; formerly a journalist.

Trained for the stage at RADA; made her first professional appearance at the Piccadilly Theatre, London, 22 Dec 1949, as Amy Spettigue in Charley's Aunt; after a period devoted to films, returned to the stage in Dec 1964, to play the title part in Peter Pan at the Scala; King's Edinburgh, Sept 1966, played Annabelle West in Cat and the Canary; toured, 1967, as Elle in Sleeping Partners; New, Bromley, Mar 1970, Jemima in The Coming-Out Party; Richmond, 1970, Susan in The Little Hut; toured, 1972, as Peter in Peter Pan; has appeared in at least thirty-five films since her first in 1950, including A King in New York, Dr Jekyll and Mr Hyde, and The Unknown Man; TV, since 1960, includes plays and variety.

Recreations: Photography, languages, travel. *Address:* c/o Eric Glass Ltd, 28 Berkeley Square, London W1X 6HD.

ADDY, Wesley, actor
b Omaha, Nebraska, 4 Aug 1913; *s* of John R and Maren S Addy; *e* University of California at Los Angeles; *m* Celeste Holm.

Made his first appearance in New York at the Imperial Theatre, 14 Mar 1935, in the chorus of Panic; Booth, Nov

1935, played in How Beautiful with Shoes; Imperial, Nov 1936, Marcellus and Fortinbras in Hamlet, with Leslie Howard; St James, Sept 1937, Earl of Salisbury in King Richard II, with Maurice Evans, with whom he also appeared in Philadelphia, Nov 1937, as Hotspur in Henry IV (Part I) and at St James, NY, Oct 1938, as Laertes in Hamlet; St James, Nov 1939, Melvin Lockhart in Summer Night; 51st Street, May 1940, Benvolio in Romeo and Juliet; St James, Nov 1940, Orsino in Twelfth Night; served in US Army Field Artillery, 1941–5, achieving rank of Major; reappeared in NY at the Cort Theatre, Feb 1946, as Haemon in Antigone, and Apr 1946, as James Mavor Morell in Candida; Fulton, Feb 1947, succeeded Leo Genn as Benjamin Hubbard in The Petrified Forest; Maxine Elliott, Dec 1947, Old Cardinal in Galileo; National, Oct 1948, Harry in The Leading Lady; 48th Street, Mar 1949, Professor Allen Carr in The Traitor; Lyceum, Jan 1950, The Supervisor in The Enchanted; National, Dec 1950, Edgar in King Lear; Broadhurst, Sept 1953, Ladislaus Oros, SJ, in The Strong Are Lonely; Belasco, Apr 1957, Henry Brougham in The First Gentleman; City Center, Sept 1959, Narrator in the opera Œdipus Rex; same theatre, Apr 1961, Commander W Harbison in South Pacific; Maidman, May 1963, Rakitin in A Month in the Country; toured US summer 1963 in With Love and Laughter; toured US 1967–8 as Dwight Babcock in Mame; Longacre, Apr 1970, James Mavor Morell in Candida;, Studio Arena, Buffalo, NY, Jan 1972, played in the musical Mama; Roundabout, NY, Apr 1973, Pastor Manders in Ghosts; toured summer 1973 in The Irregular Verb, To Love; Woodstock, NY, Playhouse, Aug 1975, Sam Pleasant in And Nothing But; Church of the Heavenly Rest, NY, Jan 1977, Becket in Murder in the Cathedral; first appeared in films in The First Legion, 1951, and has since played in The Big Knife, 1955, Whatever Happened to Baby Jane? 1962, etc; has also appeared on television.

Address: Actors Equity Association, 165 West 46th Street, New York, NY 10036.

ADLER, Jerry, director, producer, and production supervisor
b Brooklyn, 4 Feb 1929; *s* of Philip Adler, general manager for Group Theatre, and his wife Pauline; *e* Syracuse University, NY; *m* (1) Dolores Parker (mar dis); (2) Cathy Rice, dancer/choreographer; studied directing under Sawyer Falk and Erwin Piscator.

His first engagement in the theatre was as ASM for Gentlemen Prefer Blondes at the Ziegfeld, NY, 1 Sept 1950; he has since acted as production supervisor for over 40 productions including Who's Who in Hell, Anna Christie and I Remember Mama, as well as all the Tony Awards telecasts 1967– ; produced Orson Welles's Moby Dick, 1962; Drat! The Cat!, 1965; Broadway productions he has directed include Fun City, 1972; Good Evening, 1973 (tour, 1975); Words and Music, 1974 (tour, 1975–76); My Fair Lady, 1976 (tour, 1977–78); We Interrupt This Program, 1975; Checking Out, Hellzapoppin (pre-Broadway), 1976; at regional theatres and for stock companies has directed more than 30 productions, including Conflict of Interest, 1972; That Championship Season, 1977; California Suite, 1978; member of the executive board of the Society of Stage Directors and Choreographers.

Address: 225 West 44th Street, New York, NY 10036. *Tel:* 212–757 1200.

ADLER, Luther (*né* Lutha), actor
b New York City, 4 May 1903; *s* of Jacob P Adler and his wife Sarah (Lewis); *e* Lewis Institute, Chicago; *m* (1) Sylvia Sidney (mar dis); (2) Julia Roche; studied for the stage under his parents.

Made his first appearance on the stage at the Thalia Theatre, Bowery, NY, 1908, in Schmendrick, and continued as a child actor in the Yiddish Theatre with his parents and later as a juvenile; made his grown-up début at the Provincetown Theatre, NY, 5 Dec 1921, as Joe and Samuel Elkas in The Hand of the Potter; subsequently toured in Sonia; at the Vanderbilt, NY, Feb 1923, played Leon Kantor in Humoresque; Sam H Harris, Dec 1925, Zizi in The Monkey Talks; National, Jan 1926, Sam Madorsky in Money Business; Sam H Harris, Oct 1926, Phil Levine in We Americans; Klaw, Nov 1927, the Old Man in John; toured South Africa and England, 1927, with Harry Green in The Music Master, Is Zat So? and Give and Take; returned to NY and appeared in several plays in his father's repertory with his mother, his sisters, and brothers; Playhouse, Jan 1929, played Sam in Street Scene; Martin Beck (for Theatre Guild), Dec 1929, Piotr in Red Rust; joined the Group Theatre, 1932, and appeared at 48th Street, Mar 1932, as Don Fernando in Night over Taos; Maxine Elliott, Sept 1932, Sol Ginsberg in Success Story; Belasco, Feb 1933, Julian Vardaman in Alien Corn; Broadhurst, Sept 1933, Dr Gordon in Men in White; Morosco, Nov 1934, Emperor Norton and Tang Sing in Gold Eagle Guy; Belasco, Feb 1935, Moe Axelrod in Awake and Sing; Longacre, Dec 1935, Marcus Katz in Paradise Lost; Barrymore, Mar 1936, the Doctor in The Case of Clyde Griffiths; 44th Street (for Group), Nov 1936, appeared in Johnny Johnson, Belasco (for Group), Nov 1937, Joe Bonaparte in Golden Boy; made his London début in this role at the St James, 21 June 1938; returned to NY, and at the Belasco (for Group), Nov 1938, played Mr Prince in Rocket to the Moon; Mansfield (for Group), Nov 1939, Chatterton in Thunder Rock; Broadhurst (for Group), Jan 1940, Lawrence Ormont in Two on an Island; Guild, Dec 1942, Globa in The Russian People; toured, 1943–4, as Mr Rochester in Jane Eyre, which he also directed; in Chicago, Apr 1944, played Harry in Uncle Harry; Fulton, Apr 1945, Captain Angelini in Common Ground; Coronet, Oct 1945, Noll Turner in Beggars Are Coming to Town; Golden, Dec 1945, Miguel Riachi in Dunnigan's Daughter; Alvin, Sept 1946, produced A Flag Is Born, and at the Music Box, Oct 1946, succeeded Paul Muni as Tevya in this play; City Center, May 1952, played Commissar Corotchenko in a revival of Tovarich; in Boston, Aug 1952, appeared in The Play's the Thing; NY City Center, Mar 1953, played Shylock in The Merchant of Venice; Phoenix, Apr 1956, Shpichelsky in A Month in the Country; Playhouse, Nov 1956, Casale in A Very Special Baby; toured, Mar 1960, in A View from the Bridge, which he also directed; Ethel Barrymore, Feb 1964, Lenin in The Passion of Josef D; Morosco, June 1964, Chebutykin in The Three Sisters; Imperial, Jan 1965, took over from Zero Mostel for two weeks the role of Tevye in Fiddler on the Roof; Aldwych (London), May 1965, played Chebutykin in The Three Sisters; Imperial, NY, Aug 1965, took over Tevye in Fiddler on the Roof; toured Jan–Feb 1966, in The Tenth Man; toured US Apr 1966–Oct 1967 as Tevye in Fiddler on the Roof; Ivanhoe, Chicago, Jan 1969, General St Pé in Waltz of the Toreadors; Theatre on the Mall, Paramus, NJ, Mar 1970, Gregory Solomon in The Price; made film début in Lancer Spy, 1937, and since has appeared in many films, notably Cornered, Saigon, The Last Angry Man, etc; on television has appeared in Hedda Gabler, 1954, Billy Budd, 1955, The Plot to Kill Stalin, 1958, The Lincoln Murder Case, The Brotherhood, etc.

Address: Actors Equity Association, 165 West 46th Street, New York, NY, USA 10036.

ADLER, Richard, composer, lyricist, producer, and director *b* New York City, 3 Aug 1921; *s* of Clarence Adler and his wife Elsa Adrienne (Richard); *e* Columbia Grammar School, NY, and University of North Carolina; *m* (1) Marion Hash (mar dis); (2) Sally Ann Howes; served in US Navy, 1943–6, as a Lieutenant (JG).

With Jerry Ross wrote the music and lyrics for John Murray Anderson's Almanac, 1953; The Pajama Game, 1954 (London, 1955); Damn Yankees, 1955 (London, 1957); co-produced The Sin of Pat Muldoon, 1957; wrote the lyrics and music for Kwamina, 1961; produced and staged New York's Birthday Salute for President Kennedy, 1962; Inaugural Anniversary Salute for President Kennedy, 1963; Washington Salutes President Johnson, 1964; and New York Salutes President Johnson, 1964; all four being presented at the National Guard Armory in Washington, DC, and subsequently at the Madison Square Garden, NY; staged the Inaugural Gala for President Lyndon B Johnson, 1965; music and lyrics for A Mother's Kisses, 1968; co-produced a revival of his The Pajama Game, Dec 1973; produced Rex, Music Is (also music), 1976; served as White House Consultant on Talent and the Arts; a Trustee of the John F Kennedy Center for the Performing Arts; received the Antoinette Perry Award, the Donaldson Award, and the *Variety* Critics Award for The Pajama Game and Damn Yankees; films include: The Pajama Game and Damn Yankees; composed the scores for the television productions of The Gift of the Magi, 1957, and Little Women, both of which he co-produced; wrote score and produced Olympus 7-0000 for ABC-TV's *Stage '67*; member of the Council of the Dramatists Guild; member of the Board of Directors of ASCAP; formed a production unit at Duke University, NC, 1977.
Address: 870 United National Plaza, New York, NY.

ADLER, Stella, actress, director, and teacher of acting *b* New York City; *d* of Jacob P Adler and his wife Sarah (Lewis), distinguished actors and producing managers in the Yiddish theatre; *e* NY University; *m* (1) Horace Eleascheff (mar dis); (2) Harold Clurman (mar dis); (3) Mitchell Wilson; studied for the stage under her father, Maria Ouspenskaya, and Richard Boleslavsky at the American Laboratory Theatre, and with Constantin Stanislavsky in Europe.

Made her first appearance on the stage, 1906, at her father's theatre, The Grand, NY, with her father, in Broken Hearts; played continuously in her father's company throughout the US; in her parents' repertory were plays by Shakespeare, Tolstoi, Jacob Gordon, *et al*, as well as other classical and modern plays; made her first appearance in London, at the Pavilion Theatre, Mile End, 1919, as Naomi in Elisha Ben Avia; returned to NY, 1920, and appeared in Martinique, The Man of the Mountains and The World We Live In; for one season of vaudeville appeared coast to coast on the Orpheum Circuit; appeared with the American Laboratory Theatre, Oct 1926, in the role of the Baroness Crème de la Crème in The Straw Hat; Apr 1927, as Elly in Big Lake; and Nov 1927, as Beatrice in Much Ado About Nothing; in 1927, played a season at the Living Place Theatre with Bertha Kalich, and in 1928, with Jacob Ben Ami; in 1929, starred in a repertory of plays in United States, South America, also in Paris, Antwerp, and Brussels; in 1930, played a series of leading parts with Maurice Schwartz and Samuel Golendenberg at the Yiddish Art Theatre, Second Avenue, including: Kiddish Hashem, The God of Vengeance, The Witch of Castile, The Lower Depths, The Living Corpse, He Who Gets Slapped, Liliom, Jew Süss, etc; played over one hundred parts from 1927–31; joined the Group Theatre, 1931,

and has played at the Martin Beck, Sept 1931, Geraldine in The House of Connelly; Mansfield, Dec 1931, in 1931; 48th Street, Mar 1932, Donã Josefa in Night over Taos; Maxine Elliott, Sept 1932, Sarah Glassman in Success Story; same theatre, Jan 1933, Myra Bonney in Big Night; Martin Beck, May 1933, Hilda Cassidy in a play of that name; Cort, Mar 1934 (for the Group Theatre), Gwyn Ballantyne in Gentlewoman; Morosco, Nov 1934, Adah Menken in Gold-Eagle Guy; Belasco, Feb 1935, Bessie Berger in Awake and Sing!; Longacre, Dec 1935, Clara in Paradise Lost; Morosco, May 1943, Catherine Carnick in Sons and Soldiers; Forrest, Oct 1943, directed Manhattan Nocturne; National, Apr 1944, played Clotilde in Pretty Little Parlor; Alvin, Oct 1945, directed Polonaise; Booth (for the Guild) Mar 1946, Zinaida in He Who Gets Slapped; Coronet, May 1952, directed Sunday Breakfast; Carnegie Hall Playhouse, Oct 1956, directed a revival of Johnny Johnson; Lyric, Hammersmith, London, July 1961, Madame Rosepettle in Oh Dad, Poor Dad, Mama's Hung You in the Closet, and I'm Feelin' So Sad; since 1949 directs and teaches at the Stella Adler Conservatory of Acting in NY; was head of the Acting Department under Erwin Piscator at the Dramatic Workshop of the New School for Social Research, 1940–2; was Adjunct Professor of Acting at Yale University, 1966–7; also currently head of Undergraduate Drama Dept, New York University; under the name of Stella Ardler made her film début in 1938 in Love on Toast, subsequently playing in The Thin Man and My Girl Tisa; in 1943 was the associate producer of Metro Studios.
Address: 130 West 56th Street, New York, NY 10019.

AITKEN, Maria, actress *b* Dublin, 12 Sept 1945; *d* of Sir William Aitken MP and his wife Penelope (Maffey); *e* Riddlesworth Hall, Norfolk, Sherborne School for Girls, and St Anne's College, Oxford (M.A.); *m* (1) Richard Durden (mar dis); (2) Nigel Davenport.

First stage experience with the OUDS, 1963–6; first professional appearance at the Belgrade, Coventry, 1967, walking on as a prostitute in A Streetcar Named Desire; in repertory at Northampton, Theatre Royal, 1970–1; made her first London appearance at Hampstead, 1 Mar 1971, as Clara in Ellen; Arts, Cambridge, 1971, played Mrs Honeydew in The High Bid; toured the Far East for the British Council, 1972, as Viola in Twelfth Night and Hermione in The Winter's Tale; Aldwych, June 1974, Gwendolyn in Travesties; Adelphi, Apr 1975, Countess Malcolm in A Little Night Music; Lyttelton, June 1976, for National Theatre Company, Elvira in Blithe Spirit; same theatre, Mar 1977, Susannah in Bedroom Farce; Open Air, Regent's Park, July 1978, Lady in The Man of Destiny; Bristol Old Vic, Sept 1978, Rosalind in As You Like It; Northcott, Exeter, Nov 1979, Millament in The Way of the World; first appeared in films, 1968, in Some Girls Do; subsequently in Mary Queen of Scots; television, since 1969, includes *The Regiment, Quiet as a Nun, and Company & Co.*
Recreations: Cooking, poultry-keeping, arguing. *Address:* c/o Leading Artists, 60 St James's Street, London SW1.

AKALAITIS, JoAnne, actress and director *b* Chicago, 29 June 1937; *d* of Clement Akalaitis and his wife Estelle Mattis; *e* U of Chicago (BA in Philosophy, 1960); *m* the composer Philip Glass (mar dis); trained for the stage at the Actors' Workshop, San Francisco.

First appeared on stage in 1950 in a school spring pageant; since 1970 has worked as actress and director with the Mabou

Mines group, which has presented its productions since 1976 at the Public Theatre, NY; these include The Red Horse Animation, Cascando, 1976; Dressed Like an Egg, 1978; Southern Exposure, 1979; winner of three Obie awards; Guggenheim Fellowship for experimental theatre, 1978; directed the film Other Children.

Favourite part: The Woman in Come and Go. *Address:* c/o Artservices, 463 West Street, New York, NY 10014. *Tel:* 212–989 4953.

ALBEE, Edward (Franklin), dramatic author, director, and producer
b Washington, DC, 12 Mar 1928; adopted *s* of Reed Albee and his wife Frances (Cotter); *e* Lawrenceville, Valley Forge Military Academy, Choate School, and Trinity College.

Author of the following plays: The Zoo Story, 1958; The Death of Bessie Smith, The Sandbox, 1959; The American Dream, Fam and Yam, 1960; Bartleby (co-librettist with James Hinton, Jr), 1961; Who's Afraid of Virginia Woolf?, 1962; The Ballad of the Sad Cafe (adapted from the novella by Carson McCullers), 1963; Tiny Alice, 1964; Malcolm (adapted from the novel by James Purdy), 1965; A Delicate Balance, 1966; Everything in the Garden (adapted from the play by Giles Cooper), 1967; Box and Quotations from Chairman Mao Tse-Tung, 1968; All Over, 1970, which was produced by the Royal Shakespeare Company at the Aldwych, London, 31 Jan 1972; Seascape, which he also directed, 1975; Counting the Ways, Listening, 1976; The Lady from Dubeque, 1980; at the Cherry Lane, Feb 1962, directed The Sandbox; John Drew, Easthampton, NY, 1972, directed The American Dream and The Palace at 4 AM; Wollman Auditorium, Feb 1979, directed three programs of his one-act plays; as part of a Columbia University Course; these productions have also been presented in California, Texas, etc; joined Richard Barr and Clinton Wilder in production, 1963, and has since produced or co-produced the following plays: Corruption in the Palace of Justice, 1963; Play, The Lover, Funnyhouse of a Negro, Two Executioners, The Dutchman, Tiny Alice, 1964; Lovey, Hunting the Jingo Bird, Do Not Pass Go, Happy Days, That Thing at the Cherry Lane, Up to Thursday, Balls, Home Free, Pigeons, Conserico Was Here to Stay, 1965; The Butter and Egg Man, Night of the Dunce, 1966; The Long Christmas Dinner, Queens of France, The Happy Journey from Trenton to Camden, The Rimers of Eldritch, The Party on Greenwich Avenue, 1967; The Death of Bessie Smith, The American Dream, Krapp's Last Tape, The Zoo Story, Happy Days, 1968; The Front Page, 1969; Water Color, Criss-Crossing, 1970; All Over, 1971; Who's Afraid of Virginia Woolf?; received the NY Drama Critics Award and the Antoinette Perry Award of the American Theatre Wing for the best American play of the year; also received the *Evening Standard* Award for Who's Afraid of Virginia Woolf?, 1964; received the Margo Jones Award for encouraging new playwrights 1965; A Delicate Balance was awarded the Pulitzer Prize, 1967; Seascape awarded the Pulitzer Prize, 1975; elected member of National Institute of Arts and Letters, Dec 1966; founded the William Flanagan Center for Creative Persons in Montauk, NY, 1971.

Address: c/o William Morris Agency, 1740 Broadway, New York NY 10019.

ALBERT, Allan, director, producer, and writer
b New York City, 29 Jun 1945; *s* of Irving Shelbourne Albert and his wife Ferda (Praigrod); *e* Miami Beach HS, Amherst College (BA 1968), and Yale School of Drama.

Conceived, produced and directed the improvisational revue The Proposition, which has been seen in colleges and regional theatres in various forms since Sept 1969, including appearances off-Broadway at the Gramercy Arts, Mar 1971; Actors Playhouse, May 1978, etc; artistic director, Charles Playhouse, Boston, 1972; since 1977 artistic director, Berkshire Theatre Festival, Stockbridge, Mass, summer home of The Proposition Workshop, which developed from the original Proposition Group into a permanent company specialising in non-fiction theatre; most of the company's recent productions have been scripted by Mr Albert and these include Corral, The Wanted Wagon, The Whale Show, 1975; The Boston Tea Party, Soap, 1976; The Casino, 1977, etc.

Address: Suite 701, 1697 Broadway, New York, NY 10019.

ALBERT, Eddie (*né* Edward Albert Heimberger), actor
b Rock Island, Illinois, 22 Apr 1908; *s* of Frank Daniel Heimberger and his wife Julia (Jones); *e* Univ of Minnesota; *m* Margo (Maria Margarita Guadalupe Bolado y Castilla), the actress.

Began his stage career as a singer in Minneapolis in 1933, and also as a stage manager; joined a trio called the Threesome and performed on radio and in Chicago, NY, Cincinnati, and St Louis; became the partner of Grace Bradt in an act called The Honeymooners—Grace and Eddie and also performed in it on radio, 1935; made his Broadway début at the Empire Theatre, 25 Dec 1935, in the play O Evening Star; Biltmore, 16 Dec 1936, played Bing Edwards in Brother Rat; Cort, 19 May 1937, played Leo Davis in Room Service; Alvin, Nov 1938, Antipholus in The Boys from Syracuse, a musical; went to Hollywood and made films for many years; reappeared on Broadway at the Imperial, 15 July 1949, as Horace Miller in the musical Miss Liberty; Shubert, Boston, Oct 1955, played Reuben in Reuben, Reuben; ANTA, 1958, took over from David Wayne as Jack Jordan in Say, Darling; Majestic, 1960, took over from Robert Preston as Harold Hill in The Music Man; reappeared on Broadway at the Martin Beck, Apr 1973, as George Bartlett in No Hard Feelings; made his film début in Brother Rat, 1938, and has since appeared in many films, including: On Your Toes, 1939, Roman Holiday, 1953, Oklahoma, 1955, The Teahouse of the August Moon, 1956, The Longest Yard, 1974, etc; has appeared on television in The Chocolate Soldier, 1984, and many of the major series, including his own *Green Acres*, 1972 and *Switch*, 1976; served as a lieutenant in the United States Navy in WWII; was Special World Envoy of Meals for Millions, a philanthropic organization, 1963.

Recreations: Organic gardening, philosophy, guitar playing, making mobiles, glass painting. *Address:* Actors Equity Association, 165 West 46th Street, New York, NY 10036.

ALBERTSON, Jack, actor
b Revere, Mass; *m* Wallace Thomson.

Played in vaudeville before making his New York Début at the Mansfield, 25 Dec 1940, in the revue Meet the People; National, 1942, took over a part in Strip for Action; Adelphi, Apr 1944, played Caswell and Bulbul in the musical Allah Be Praised!; Broadhurst, Jan 1945, Dr Bartoli in A Lady Says Yes; Knickerbocker, 1946, took over a part in The Red Mill; Mansfield, Dec 1947, Yasha in The Cradle Will Rock; Broadhurst, 1948, took over in the revue Make Mine Manhattan; Century, 1948, took over from Joey Faye as Mr Pontdue in High Button Shoes; Coronet, Apr 1950, played in the revue Tickets, Please!; Winter Garden, Nov 1951, Vic Davis in Top Banana; Royale, May 1964, John Cleary in The Subject Was Roses, for which performance he received the Antoinette Perry (Tony) Award; Broadhurst, Dec 1972,

Willie Clark in The Sunshine Boys; Hanna, Cleveland, Ohio, Nov 1973, again played Willie Clark in The Sunshine Boys and subsequently toured; Latin Casino, Philadelphia, Nov 1975, appeared in cabaret; has toured in Girl Crazy, Panama Hattie, Showboat, etc; in California has played in Waiting for Godot, Mother Courage, The Child Buyer, etc; has appeared in many films, including: Justine, Rabbit Run, Willie Wonka and the Chocolate Factory, 1972, The Poseidon Adventure, 1973, and won the Academy Award Oscar for his role in The Subject Was Roses, 1968; has appeared frequently on television, notably in his own series *Dr Simon Locke* and *Chico and the Man* (1974–6), for which he received the Emmy Award, 1976, and in various dramatic and comedy programmes.

ALBERY, Sir Donald (Arthur Rolleston), manager
b London, 19 June 1914; *s* of Sir Bronson James Albery and his wife Una Gwynn (Rolleston); *e* Alpine College, Switzerland; *m* Heather Boys.
Was until March 1978 managing-director of Wyndham Theatres, Ltd; managing- director of Donmar Productions, Ltd, and associated companies; managing-director of Piccadilly Theatre, Ltd; director of Independent Plays, Ltd, and Anglia Television, Ltd; general manager of Sadler's Wells Ballet, 1941–5; presented or jointly presented the following plays: Birthday Honours, The Living Room, 1953; I Am a Camera, The Living Room (New York, with Gilbert Miller), 1954; The Remarkable Mr Pennypacker, Lucky Strike, Waiting for Godot, 1955; The Waltz of the Toreadors, Gigi, Grab Me a Gondola, 1956; Zuleika, Tea and Sympathy, Dinner With the Family, Paddle Your Own Canoe, 1957; The Potting Shed, George Dillon, Irma la Douce, 1958; The Rose Tattoo, A Taste of Honey, The Hostage, The Complaisant Lover, One to Another, The Ring of Truth, The World of Suzie Wong, Make Me an Offer, 1959; Fings Aint' Wot They Used T' Be, A Passage to India, Call It Love, The Art of Living, Irma La Douce (NY), A Taste of Honey (NY), The Hostage (NY), Oliver! The Tinker, 1960; The Miracle Worker, Breakfast For One, Sparrers Can't Sing, Beyond the Fringe, Celebration, Bonne Soupe, Heartbreak House, 1961; Not to Worry, Blitz!, Beyond the Fringe (NY), Semi-Detached, Fiorello, 1962; Oliver! (NY), Le Mariage de Figaro, Licence to Murder, The Perils of Scobie Prilt (tour), A Severed Head, The Time of the Barracudas (US), 1963; The Fourth of June, The Poker Session, Who's Afraid of Virginia Woolf?, A Little Winter Love (tour), Entertaining Mr Sloane, Instant Marriage, Carving a Statue, The Diplomatic Baggage, A Severed Head (NY), 1964; Portrait of a Queen, Entertaining Mr Sloane, (NY), Oliver! (tour), 1965; Jorrocks, The Prime of Miss Jean Brodie, 1966; Mrs Wilson's Diary, Spring and Port Wine, The Restoration of Arnold Middleton, 1967; The Italian Girl, Man of La Mancha, 1968; Conduct Unbecoming, 1969; It's a Two Foot Six Inches Above the Ground World, Mandrake, Poor Horace, 1970; Popkiss, 1972; Very Good Eddie, The Family Dance, 1976; Candida, 1977; Director and Administrator, London's Festival Ballet, 1964–8.
Address: 31 Avenue Princess Grace, Monte Carlo, Monaco.

ALBERY, Ian Bronson, manager, producer and theatre consultant
b 21 Sept 1936; *s* of Sir Donald Albery, the theatre manager, and his wife Rubina (Gilchrist); *e* Stowe and the Lycée de Briançon, France; *m* Barbara Yuling Lee.
His early training was in stage and electrical departments, stage management, box office and TV floor management;

stage or production manager or technical director for over 100 West End productions, including: West Side Story, Irma La Douce, 1958; The World of Suzie Wong, 1959; The Tinker, Oliver!, 1960; The Miracle Worker, Sparrers Can't Sing, Beyond the Fringe, La Bonne Soupe, 1961; Blitz!, Fiorello!, 1962; A Severed Head, The Poker Session, Who's Afraid of Virginia Woolf?, Instant Marriage, 1964; Portrait of a Queen, 1965; Jorrocks, The Prime of Miss Jean Brodie, 1966; The Italian Girl, Hadrian VII, Man of La Mancha, 1968; Anne of Green Gables, Conduct Unbecoming, 1969; Mandrake, Poor Horace, 1970; Popkiss, 1972; technical director, London Festival Ballet, 1964–68; technical director for various Broadway productions including Oliver!, 1963, and Conduct Unbecoming, 1969; managing director, The Wyndham Theatres Ltd, The Piccadilly Theatre Ltd, Donmar Productions Ltd, Omega Stage Ltd; productions he has presented or co-presented in London include Very Good Eddie!, The Thoughts of Chairman Alf, 1976; Vieux Carré, 1978; Oliver!, Last of the Red Hot Lovers, 1979; Piaf, Once in a Lifetime, Accidental Death of an Anarchist, The Primary English Class, 1980; has acted as theatre consultant for a number of studies and projects including the Gulbenkian Auditorium, Lisbon; Camden Theatre, London; Teachers Theatre and National Theatre (proposed), Kuwait; National Theatre and State Theatre (proposed), Athens; Royal Theatre and Palace of Culture, Amman, Jordan; and for the theatres under his management; chairman, Theatre Arts Society; vice-chairman, Association of British Theatre Technicians, 1973–1978; executive member, Society of West End Theatre (president 1977–79, vice-president 1979–   ); member of drama panel, Arts Council, 1974–1976; drama advisory committee, British Council, 1979–   ; Society of Theatre Consultants (founder member, 1964); Trustee of the Theatres Trust, 1977–   .
Address: Albery Theatre, St. Martin's Lane, London WC2. *Tel:* 01 836 1371.

ALDA, Alan (*né* Alphonso D'Abruzzo), actor
b New York, NY, 28 Jan 1936; *s* of Alphonso D'Abruzzo (Robert Alda) and his wife Joan (Browne); *e* Fordham University (BS 1956); *m* Arlene Weiss; attended Paul Sills's Improvisational Workshop.
First appeared at the Hollywood Canteen with his father in imitations of Abbott and Costello (1951); in Barnesville, Pa, summer 1953, played Jack Chesney in Charley's Aunt; Teatro del Eliseo, Rome, Italy, 1955, played Leo Davis in Room Service; first engaged in NY as understudy to Don Murray as Clarence McShane in The Hot Corner at the John Golden, Jan 1956; in stock in 1957 played Wade in Roger the Sixth, Artie in Compulsion, Irwin Trowbridge in Three Men on a Horse, Horace in The Little Foxes; stock, 1958, played Billy Tuck in Nature's Way; Cleveland Playhouse, 1958–9, played in The Book of Job, which he adapted from the Bible; David Williams in Who Was That Lady I Saw You With?, Toni in To Dorothy, a Son; stock, July 1959, Sky Masterson in Guys and Dolls; first appeared on Broadway at the Cort, 19 Nov 1959, as the Telephone Man in Only in America; stock, 1960, title-role in Li'l Abner; Madison Avenue Playhouse, Oct 1960, played in the revue Darwin's Theories, to which he also contributed material; Teatro dei Servi, Rome, Italy, Jan 1961, David in The Woman with Red Hair; stock, June 1961, Fergie Howard in Golden Fleecing; Boston Arts Center, July 1961, Fleider in Anatol; Cort, Sept 1961, Charlie Cotchipee in Purlie Victorious; Compass Improvisional Revue, Hyannisport, summer, 1962; Cricket, Oct 1962, Howard Mayer in A Whisper in God's Ear; Shubert, New Haven, Feb 1963, Willie Alvarez in Memo; toured, summer 1963, as Francis X

Dignan in King of Hearts; Second City at Square East; Oct 1963, played in revue Second City; Cort, Feb 1963, Benny Bennington in Fair Game for Lovers; Martin Beck, Apr 1964, Dr Gilbert in Café Crown; ANTA, Nov 1964, F Sherman in The Owl and the Pussycat; Shubert, Oct 1966, Adam, Captain Sanjar, and Flip, the Prince Charming in The Apple Tree; taught at the Compass School of Improvisation, NY, 1963–; first appeared in films in Gone Are the Days, 1963; recent films include Same Time Next Year, and The Seduction of Joe Tynan; has appeared regularly on dramatic and variety television programs since 1955, notably in the long-running series *MASH*.

ALDA, Robert (*né* Alphonso Giovanni Giuseppe Roberto D'Abruzzo), actor
b New York, NY, 26 Feb 1914; *s* of Anthony D'Abruzzo and his wife Frances (Tumillo); *e* Architectural School of NY University; *m* (1) Joan Browne (mar dis); (2) Flora Marino; formerly an architectural draughtsman.

Made his stage début in vaudeville at the RKO, NY, 1933, as a singer in an act called Charlie Ahearn and His Millionaires, and subsequently toured the RKO circuit in this act; played in burlesque at the Republic, NY, 1935, and toured in burlesque, 1935–40; played summer stock engagements in the Catskills in such plays as Waiting for Lefty, Golden Boy, Of Mice and Men, Men in White, Three Men on a Horse, Love from a Stranger, Tobacco Road, Boy Meets Girl, Room Service, The Jazz Singer, The Postman Always Rings Twice, and The Time of your Life, also 1935–40; La Jolla (Cal) Playhouse, 1947, played in There Goes the Bride; Beverly, Mass, 1948, played in The Male Animal; toured, 1949–50, in A Hollywood Revue; made his legitimate Broadway début at the 46th Street, 24 Nov 1950, as Sky Masterson in Guys and Dolls, and received the Antoinette Perry (Tony) Award, the Donaldson Award, and the *Variety* NY Drama Critics Poll for this performance; Royal Nevada Hotel, Las Vegas, 1955, again played Sky Masterson in a condensed version of Guys and Dolls; toured Italy and Sicily, 1955–6, in La Padrona di Raggio di Luna, playing in Italian and being awarded Italy's Golden Wing Award for his performance; Playhouse, NY, Oct 1956, Chris in Harbor Lights; toured, summer, 1957, in Roger the VI; toured, 1958, in Fair Game and Three Men on a Horse; toured, Jun–Aug 1963, in Can-Can; 54th Street, NY, Feb 1964, Al Manheim in What Makes Sammy Run; Booth, May 1969, Arthur Gordon in My Daughter, Your Son; Ethel Barrymore, 1970, took over as Walter Burns in The Front Page; Westchester Country Playhouse, July 1973, played Benjamin Stone in Follies and subsequently toured; toured 1974–5 in The Sunshine Boys; recent stage work includes musicals and plays in Stock and on tour; entered films in 1945 as George Gershwin in Rhapsody in Blue, and has since appeared in many films including: The Beast with Five Fingers, The Man I Love, Tarzan and the Slave Girl, Imitation of Life, House of Exorcism, I Will I Will . . . For Now, Bitter Sweet Love (1978), etc; appeared regularly on radio from 1934 until 1948; first appeared on television in 1937 in Alda and Henry, a variety program, and has since appeared in *By Popular Demand*, 1950, *The Milton Berle Show*, 1950–1, *What's Your Bid?* 1952, *The Robert Alda Show*, 1953, *Can-do*, 1956–7, and on Italian television and radio; has appeared in clubs and cabaret frequently since 1935; author with his wife of 99 Ways to Cook Pasta, 1980.
Recreations: Reading and writing. *Address:* c/o Buddy Clarke Associates, 305 W 52nd Street, New York, NY 10019.

ALDERTON, John, actor
b Gainsborough, Lincs, 27 Nov 1940; *s* of Gordon John Alderton and his wife Ivy (Handley); *e* Kingston High School, Hull; *m* (1) Jill Browne (mar dis) (2) Pauline Collins.

Made his first stage appearance with the repertory company of the Theatre Royal, York, Aug 1961, in Badger's Green; after a period in repertory, made his first London appearance at the Mermaid, Nov 1965, as Harold Crompton in Spring and Port Wine, later transferring with the production to the Apollo; Aldwych, Mar 1969, played Eric Hoyden in the Royal Shakespeare Company's production of Dutch Uncle; Comedy, July 1969, Jimmy Cooper in The Night I Chased the Women with an Eel; Howff, Oct 1973, Stanley in Punch and Judy Stories; played the same part in Judies at the Comedy, Jan 1974; Shaw, Jan 1975, Stanley in The Birthday Party; Apollo, May 1976, four parts in Confusions; has appeared on TV since 1962, in plays and in series including *Please Sir* and *My Wife Next Door*; first film, 1962; subsequent appearances include Duffy and Hannibal Brooks.
Recreations: Golf, cricket. *Clubs:* Green Room, Lord's Taverners. *Address:* c/o News Management Ltd, 29 King's Road, London, SW3.

ALDREDGE, Theoni V (*née* Theoni Athanasiou Vachlioti), costume designer
b Salonika, Greece; *d* of Athanasios Vachlioti and his wife Merope; *e* The American School, Athens, and Goodman Memorial Theatre, Chicago, 1949–52; *m* Thomas Aldredge.

First designed costumes for the Goodman Theatre production of The Distaff Side, 1950; designed a stock production of The Importance of Being Earnest, 1953; designed for the Studebaker Theatre in Chicago The Immoralist, 1956, and Much Ado About Nothing, A View from the Bridge, Lysistrata, and The Guardsman, 1957; moved to New York and has since designed costumes for Heloise, The Golden Six, 1958; Geraldine Page's costumes for Sweet Bird of Youth, The Nervous Set, The Saintliness of Margery Kempe, Chic, The Geranium Hat, Flowering Cherry, Silent Night, Lonely Night, 1959; A Distant Bell, The Best Man, Measure for Measure, Hedda Gabler, Rosemary, The Alligators, 1960; Mary, Mary, Under Milk Wood, Smiling the Boy Fell Dead, First Love, Ghosts, A Short Happy Life, Much Ado About Nothing, A Midsummer Night's Dream, The Devil's Advocate, 1961; The Umbrella, Rosmersholm, I Can Get It for You Wholesale, Macbeth, King Lear, The Tempest, The Merchant of Venice, Mr President, Tchin-Tchin, Who's Afraid of Virginia Woolf? 1962; Geraldine Page's costumes for Strange Interlude, The Blue Boy in Black, Memo, The Time of the Barracudas, Antony and Cleopatra, As You Like It, The Winter's Tale, The Trojan Women, 1963; But for Whom Charlie, Anyone Can Whistle, The Three Sisters, Hamlet, The Knack, Othello, Electra, Any Wednesday, Luv, Geraldine Page's gowns for PS I Love You, Poor Richard, Ready When You Are, CB!, 1964; Coriolanus, Troilus and Cressida, Minor Miracle, The Porcelain Year, Skyscraper, The Playroom, Cactus Flower, 1965; UTBU, First One Asleep, Whistle, Happily Never After, A Time for Singing, Serjeant Musgrave's Dance, All's Well That Ends Well, Measure for Measure, King Richard III, A Delicate Balance, 1966; You Know I Can't Hear You When the Water's Running, That Summer . . . That Fall, Ilya Darling, Little Murders, The Comedy of Errors, Hamlet, Hair, King John, Titus Andronicus, Daphne in Cottage D, The Trial of Lee Harvey Oswald, 1967; Before You Go, I Never Sang for My Father, Portrait of a Queen, Weekend, The Only Game in Town, Ergo, The Memorandum, King Lear, Ballad for a Firing Squad, Huui, Huui, Henry IV, Parts 1 and 2, Hamlet, Romeo and Juliet, Don Rodrigo (opera), 1968; Zelda, Billy,

The Gingham Dog, Cities in Bezique, Invitation to a Beheading, Peer Gynt, Electra, Twelfth Night, 1969; The Wars of the Roses, Parts I and 2, Richard III, The Happiness Cage, Trelawny of the Wells, Colette, Jack MacGowran in the Works of Samuel Beckett, 1970; Subject to Fits (also London), Blood, Underground, The Basic Training of Pavlo Hummel, Timon of Athens, Two Gentlemen of Verona, The Tale of Cymbeline, The Incomparable Max, Sticks and Bones, The Wedding of Iphigenia, Iphigenia in Concert, 1971; The Sign in Sidney Brustein's Window, Voices, That Championship Season, Older People, The Hunter, The Corner, Hamlet, Ti-Jean and His Brothers, Much Ado About Nothing, The Wedding Band, the Children, 1972; A Village Romeo and Juliet (Delius's opera for the New York City Opera), The Three Sisters, No Hard Feelings, The Orphan, Nash at Noon, As You Like It, King Lear, Boom Boom Room, The Au Pair Man, Two Gentlemen of Verona (London), 1973; Find Your Way Home, The Killdeer, The Dance of Death, Music! Music!, An American Millionaire, That Championship Season (London), In Praise of Love, Mert & Phil, Kid Champion, 1974; A Doll's House, Little Black Sheep, A Chorus Line, Trelawny of The Wells, Souvenir (Los Angeles), 1975; Rich and Famous, Mrs Warren's Profession, The Belle of Amherst, The Baker's Wife (pre-Broadway), Threepenny Opera, The Eccentricities of a Nightingale, 1976; The Dream (Philadelphia), Marco Polo Sings a Solo, Annie, 1977; Ballroom, 1978; The Grand Tour, Break a Leg, The Madwoman of Central Park West, 1979; designed the films Girl of the Night, You're A Big Boy Now, No Way to Treat a Lady, Uptight, Last Summer, I Never Sang for My Father, and Promise at Dawn.

ALDREDGE, Tom (Thomas Ernest), actor
b Dayton, Ohio, 28 Feb 1928; *s* of W J Aldredge and his wife Lucienne Juliet (Marcillat); *e* Univ of Dayton; *m* Theoni Athanasiou Vachlioti, the designer; studied acting at the Goodman Memorial School of the Theatre, Chicago, BFA 1953.

First appeared on the stage at the Belmont High School, Dayton, 1939, as Rip Van Winkle; at the Goodman, Chicago, Jan 1950, played the Messenger in Hamlet; made his professional début as Bud Norton in a stock production of Personal Appearance, 1950; joined the Tower Ranch Tenthouse Theater in Rhinelander, Wisconsin, where he performed in such plays as The Corn Is Green, Death of a Salesman, The Glass Menagerie, Private Lives, Our Town, The Little Foxes, Blithe Spirit, 1951–3; directed there The Fourposter and played in and directed Arms and the Man, The Guardsman, Streetcar Named Desire, The Heiress, Shadow and Substance, etc, 1954; played in and directed I Am a Camera, Sabrina Fair, Mister Roberts, The Rainmaker, etc, 1955; returned there in 1958 and directed A Member of the Wedding, and appeared in various plays, 1958; made his New York début at the Jan Hus House, 9 May 1958, as the Messenger in Electra; Henry Miller's, May 1959, played Danny in The Nervous Set; East 74th St, Dec 1959, Trinculo in The Tempest; York Playhouse, Feb 1960, David in Between Two Thieves; began his long association with the NY Shakespeare Festival Theater at the Belvedere Lake, 29 June 1960, as the Dauphin in Henry V; Premise, Nov 1960, played in the improvisational revue The Premise, which he also played at the Shoreham, Washington, DC, Jan 1962; made his London début at the Comedy, Sept 1962, also in The Premise; Delacorte, June 1965, Boyet in Love's Labour's Lost and, Aug 1965, Nestor in Troilus and Cressida; Helen Hayes, Jan 1966, Eugene Boyer in UTBU; Longacre, Feb 1966, Bernie in The Mutilated in the double-bill Slapstick

Tragedy; Delacorte, July 1966, Angelo in Measure for Measure, and, Aug 1966, A Murderer and A Citizen in King Richard III; Cherry Lane, Oct 1966, Jack McClure in The Butter and Egg Man; American Shakespeare Theatre, Stratford, Conn, summer 1967, Quince in A Midsummer Night's Dream, Chorus in Antigone, Gratiano in The Merchant of Venice, and Macduff in Macbeth; Plymouth, Nov 1967, Gilbert in Everything in the Garden; Anspacher, Mar 1968, Wurz in Ergo; Delacorte, Aug 1968, Tybalt in Romeo and Juliet, and Sir Andrew Aguecheek in Twelfth Night; Wyndham's, London, Feb 1969, Emory in The Boys in the Band; Brooks Atkinson, NY, Oct 1969, Senator Logan in Indians; Helen Hayes, May 1970, Victor Bard in The Engagement Baby; Estelle Newman, Oct 1970, directed The Happiness Cage; Royale, Mar 1971, William Detweiler in How the Other Half Loves; Anspacher, Nov 1971, Ozzie in Sticks and Bones, and transferred with this production to the John Golden, 1 Mar 1972; Delacorte, June 1972, Second Gravedigger in Hamlet; Anspacher, Apr 1973, Calchas in The Orphan; Delacorte, July 1973, Lear's Fool in King Lear; Circle in the Square, Dec 1973, James Cameron in The Iceman Cometh; Circle in the Square, Dec 1974, Mr Spettigue in Where's Charley?; Booth, Oct 1975, Shaughnessy in The Leaf People; Lunt-Fontanne, Apr 1976, The Fool in Rex; Phoenix, Nov 1976, Father in Canadian Gothic; St James, May 1977, Painter in Vieux Carré; Circle in the Square, Dec 1977, Archbishop of Rheims in Saint Joan; New Apollo, Feb 1979, Norman Thayer Jr in On Golden Pond, repeating this performance at the Century, Aug 1979; appeared in the films The Mouse on the Moon, 1962, The Troublemaker, 1964, The Rain People, 1969, Acts of a Young Man, 1979, etc; was producer-director for the Chicago Educational TV Association, 1955–7 and producer and star of The Curious One, 1956; Emmy award, 1978, for Henry Winkler Meets Shakespeare.
Recreation: Sailing.

ALDRIDGE, Michael, actor
b Glastonbury, Somerset, 9 Sept 1920; *s* of Frederick James Aldridge and his wife Kathleen Michaela Marietta (White); *e* Gresham's School, Holt, Norfolk; *m* Kirsteen Rowntree.

Made his first appearance on the stage, at the Palace Theatre, Watford, Aug 1939, as Kenneth in French Without Tears; after the war, made his first appearance in London, at the Garrick Theatre, Sept 1946, as Prologue and the Mechanic in This Way to the Tomb; toured with the Arts Council Midland Theatre Company, from Nov 1946 to July 1948; appeared with the Nottingham Theatre Trust, Nov 1948 to Mar 1949; joined the Birmingham Repertory Company Mar 1949; at the Embassy, June 1949, played the title part in Othello; joined the Old Vic company at the New Theatre, Sept 1949, to play Ferdinand in Love's Labour's Lost; Hastings in She Stoops to Conquer, Valère in The Miser and Horatio in Hamlet, also playing the last mentioned part at Elsinore Castle, June 1950; joined the Bristol Old Vic Company for the 1951–2 season, when he played, among other parts, Macbeth, Launce in Two Gentlemen of Verona, and Lennie in Of Mice and Men; St James's, Jan 1953, played Peter Henderson in Escapade, which ran for over a year; Vaudeville, Aug 1954, appeared in the musical production Salad Days; Savoy, June 1957, played Lord Paul Posthumous in Free As Air; Theatre-in-the-Round, 41 Fitzroy Square, W1, Theseus in Phedre; Lyric, Jan 1958, played Philip Lowrie in Tenebrae (for The Repertory Players); Arts, Jan 1960, played James Tyrone in A Moon for the Misbegotten; Pembroke, Croydon, Oct 1961, Aubrey Tanqueray in The Second Mrs Tanqueray; Pembroke, Croydon, May 1962,

James O'Shaughnessy in State of Emergency; Queen's, Nov 1962, played Lord Steyne in Vanity Fair; Ashcroft, Croydon, Jan 1964, Major Frederick Lowndes in Home and Beauty; Empire, Sunderland, Feb 1964, directed King Lear; Theatre Royal, Stratford, E, May 1964, Gorse in The Man Who Let It Rain; Empire, Sunderland, Mar 1965, played Father Kahn in The Third Picture; 1966 to 1969 appeared in four seasons of the Chichester Festival, playing, in 1966, Baron Henri Belazor in The Fighting Cock and Banquo in Macbeth; Oct 1966, transferred with The Fighting Cock to Duke of York's; in 1967, Churdles Ash in The Farmer's Wife; Hector Hushabye in Heartbreak House and Nonancourt in An Italian Straw Hat; Nov 1967, transferred with Heartbreak House to the Lyric; in 1968, the Enemy Leader in The Unknown Soldier and His Wife, Edward in The Cocktail Party and Stephano in The Tempest; Nov 1968, transferred with The Cocktail Party to Wyndham's and later the Haymarket; in 1969, a Lawyer in The Caucasian Chalk Circle, Capt Vale in The Magistrate and Enobarbus in Antony and Cleopatra; Sept 1969, transferred with The Magistrate to the Cambridge; Haymarket, Sept 1970, Lord Minto in A Bequest to the Nation; returned to Chichester, season 1971, playing Cravatar in Dear Antoine, May, Rufio in Caesar and Cleopatra and Anton Krug in Reunion in Vienna, July, transferring in the latter part to the Piccadilly, Feb 1972; at Chichester, season 1972, played Lockit in The Beggars' Opera, Cutler Walpole in The Doctor's Dilemma, May, and Hebble Tyson in The Lady's Not for Burning, July; Arnaud, Guildford, Sept 1972, Mr Black in Who's Who; Criterion, July 1973, Ronald in Absurd Person Singular; at The Other Place, Stratford-upon-Avon, played Prospero in The Tempest, Oct, and Serebriakov in Uncle Vanya, Dec; Her Majesty's, Apr 1975, played the title role in Jeeves; Albery, Oct 1975, Sir Richard Jackson in Lies!; Lyric, Jan 1977, took over as Victor in The Bed before Yesterday; Haymarket, Oct 1977, Dr Kroll in Rosmersholm; Queen's, June 1978, took over as Duff in The Old Country; Prince of Wales, Nov 1978, Victor in the National Theatre production of Bedroom Farce; first appeared in films, 1946, in Nothing Venture; has appeared frequently on television.
Recreation: Sailing. *Address:* 11 Crooms Hill, Greenwich, SE10 *and* South Bell House, Bell Lane, Birdham, Sussex.

ALEXANDER, Bill, director
b Hunstanton, 23 Feb 1948; *s* of William Paterson and his wife Rosemary; *e* Keele University (BA in English and politics); *m* Juliet Harmer.
Spent six months as an actor with Naftali Yavin's group, The Other Company, 1971; trainee director, Bristol Old Vic, 1971, where he stayed for two years and directed plays at the Little and New Vic; joined the staff of the Royal Court, 1973, where his productions included Sex and Kinship in a Savage Society, 1975; Amy and the Price of Cotton, 1976; Class Enemy, 1978; resident director, Royal Shakespeare Company, for whom he has directed Factory Birds, 1977; Captain Swing (Stratford), Shout Across the River, the Hang of the Gaol (both London), 1978; Men's Beano, Captain Swing (both London), 1979; Bastard Angel (London), 1980; also Betrayal, Tel Aviv, 1980.
Address: 6 Caxton Road, London W12 8AJ.

ALEXANDER, C K (Charles Khalil Alexander Saad), actor,
   director, composer and playwright
b Cairo, Egypt, 4 May 1923; *s* of Alexander Constantine Saad and his wife Marigo (Sabbagh); *e* Fuad University (1938–39) and the American University, Cairo (1940–41); *m* Margaret Frances Kachur.

Made his professional debut in The Merry Widow at the Royal Opera House, Cairo, in 1942; in Egypt he was a member of the New Vic Players and the Cairo Dramatic and Musical Society; made his Broadway debut as Steward in Hidden Horizon, Plymouth Theatre, 19 Sept 1946; directed a season of summer stock at Duxbury, Mass, 1947; for the next two years directed plays and revues in lofts, church halls, coffee shops, clubs etc; returned to Broadway in The Happy Time, Plymouth, Jan 1950; appeared as Karim Effendi in Flight Into Egypt, Music Box, Mar 1952, for which he composed the incidental music; played Fat Boy and Turnkey in Mr Pickwick, Plymouth, Sept 1952; Judge Paul Barrière in Can-Can, Shubert, May 1953–55; Ali Hakim in Oklahoma, Théâtre des Nations Festival, Paris, and tour of Italy, 1955; played Khadja in The Merry Widow, City Center, Apr 1957; toured as Warden Bastiand in The Gay Felons, Feb 1959; took over as the Café Proprietor in Rhinoceros, Longacre, Jan 1961; played the Burgomaster in The Dragon, Phoenix, Apr 1963; Justice Croz in Corruption in the Palace of Justice, Cherry Lane, 1963; toured as Pedro Juarez in Not in the Book, 1964; was Peachum in The Threepenny Opera, Playhouse in the Park, Cincinnati, Ohio, 1964; played Vulturne-Mirabeau in Poor Bitos, Cort, 1964: directed Francesca da Rimini and the Campbells of Boston for The Company of Twelve, Library and Museum of the Performing Arts at Lincoln Center, 1967; directed As Happy as Kings, New, NY, 1968; again played Peachum in The Threepenny Opera, Arena Stage, Washington, DC, 1969; directed Harlequinades for Mourners, New, 1970; played Mandria the Greek in Ari, on tour and at the Mark Hellinger, 1970–71; produced The Justice Box, Theatre de Lys, 1971; directed Love One Another, New Dramatists, 1974; played the Rev. Dr Lloyd in Life with Father, Seattle Rep, 1974–75; Lecturer in On the Harmfulness of Tobacco and Chubukov in The Marriage Proposal, Syracuse Stage, Nov 1975; Peachum in The Threepenny Opera, Vivian Beaumont, Apr 1976; played Pischik in The Cherry Orchard, Vivian Beaumont, Feb 1977; appeared in his own play, The Applegates, Public, 1978; Aki in An Angel Comes to Babylon, PAF Playhouse, Huntington, L.I., 1978–79; directed Viaduct, Bouwerie Lane, 1979; played Harpagon in The Miser, Carnegie-Mellon Theatre Co, Pittsburgh, Pa, 1979; under his own name or using the pseudonyms Mario Quimber or Basheer Qadar, he has composed the music for Francesca da Rimini, The Campbells of Boston, As Happy as Kings, Harlequinades for Mourners, The Justice Box, and Love One Another, and the entire score for The Applegates; numerous television appearances on most of the major dramatic shows, notably in *The Defenders, Hallmark Theatre,* The Adams Chronicles, and The Scarlet Letter.
Address: c/o Jeff Hunter, 119 West 57th Street, New York, NY 10025.

ALEXANDER, Jane (*née* Quigley), actress
b Boston, Mass, 28 Oct 1939; *d* of Thomas B Quigley, MD, and his wife Ruth Elizabeth (Pearson); *e* Beaver Country Day School, Sarah Lawrence College, and the University of Edinburgh.
First appeared on the stage as a child in Boston as Long John Silver in Treasure Island; joined the Arena Stage in Washington, DC, in 1966 and during the next three seasons played some fifteen parts, including: Major Barbara and Eleanor Bachman in The Great White Hope; first appeared on Broadway on 3 Oct 1968 as Eleanor Bachman in The Great White Hope, and received the Antoinette Perry (Tony) Award for this part; rejoined the Arena Stage in 1970 as guest artist and appeared in Mother Courage; at the

American Shakespeare Festival Theatre, Stratford, Conn, summer 1971, played Mistress Page in The Merry Wives of Windsor and Lavinia in Mourning Becomes Electra; Eisenhower, Washington, DC, Jan 1972, and later at the Huntington Hartford, Los Angeles, Cal, played Kitty Duval in the Plumstead Playhouse production of The Time of Your Life; Stratford, Conn, summer 1972, played the title-role of Major Barbara; Helen Hayes, Oct 1972, Anne Miller in 6 Rms Riv Vu; Brooks Atkinson, 2 Jan 1974, Jacqueline Harrison in Find Your Way Home; Eisenhower, Washington, DC, May 1975, Liz Essendine in Present Laughter; Vivian Beaumont, Dec 1975, Gertrude in Hamlet; Broadhurst, Apr 1976, Catherine Sloper in The Heiress; Majestic, Oct 1978, Judge Ruth Loomis in First Monday in October; Manhattan Theatre Club, Sept 1979, Joanne in Losing Time; first appeared in films in The Great White Hope, 1970, and has since played in such films as, The New Centurions, All the President's Men, The Betsy, and Kramer vs Kramer; TV work includes Eleanor and Franklin, Lovey, and A Question of Love.

Favourite parts: Eleanor Bachman in The Great White Hope and Lavinia in Mourning Becomes Electra. *Recreation:* Tennis, birdwatching. *Address:* c/o Arlene Donovan, International Creative Management, 40 West 57th Street, New York, NY 10019.

ALEXANDER, Terence, actor
b London, 11 Mar 1923; *s* of Joseph Edward William Alexander and his wife Violet Mary Patricia (O'Flynn); *e* Ratcliffe College; *m* (1) Juno Stevas (mar dis); (2) Jane Downs.

First stage appearance Dec 1939, at the Opera House, Harrogate as a young journalist in The Good Companions; first London appearance, Princes, Oct 1950, as Tom Williams in Party Manners; subsequent parts include Paul in Mrs Willie, Globe, Aug 1955; Donald Gray in Ring for Catty, Lyric, Feb 1956; Commander Rogers in Joie de Vivre, Queen's, July 1960; Brassac in Poor Bitos at the New Arts, Nov 1963 and afterwards at the Duke of York's, Jan 1964; the Man in In at the Death, Phoenix, April 1967; Henry Lodge in Move over Mrs Markham, Vaudeville, Mar 1971; Jack in Two and Two Make Sex, Cambridge Theatre, Sept 1973; Bill Shorter in There Goes the Bride, Criterion, Oct 1974, transferring to the Ambassadors', April 1975; Whitehall, Aug 1976, Jim Hudson in Fringe Benefits; for Actors Company, Sept 1978, toured as Pastor Manders in Ghosts; Nottingham Playhouse, Feb 1980, Dr Wicksteed in Habeas Corpus; first film appearance, 1947; his numerous subsequent appearances include The League of Gentlemen, The Magic Christian and Waterloo; frequent television appearances since 1951 include the series The Pallisers and Moody and Pegg.

Recreation: Golf. *Club:* Stage Golfing Society. *Address:* c/o ICM, 22 Grafton Street, London W1.

ALLEN, Elizabeth (*née* Elizabeth Ellen Gillease), actress and singer
b Jersey City, New Jersey, 25 Jan 1934; *d* of Joseph Gillease and his wife Viola (Mannion); *e* St Aloysius HS, Jersey City, and Traphagen School of Design, 1952–7; *m* Baron Carl von Vietinghoff-Scheel (mar dis); formerly a fashion designer and model.

First appeared on the stage, 1955, as Julie in The Tender Trap; joined the Helen Hayes Group in New York, 1956, and played Shakespearean parts including Viola, Rosalind, Ophelia, and Portia; Ivy Tower Playhouse, Spring Lake, New Jersey, summer 1957, Jane in The Reluctant Debutante; toured in the Pontiac industrial show, 1957; made her Broadway début at the Plymouth, 10 Oct 1957, as Juliet in Romanoff and Juliet; toured, 1959, as Irene in Say, Darling,

and Kitty in Where's Charley?; Renata, NY, Sept 1959, played in a revival of the revue Lend an Ear; toured, 1960, as Babe in The Pajama Game and Nellie Forbush in South Pacific; Starlight Theatre, Kansas City, Mo, 1961, played Frenchy in Destry Rides Again; Shubert, NY, Nov 1961, Magda in The Gay Life; toured, 1963, as Julie in Show Boat and Nellie Forbush in South Pacific; Civic Light Opera Company, Los Angeles, Apr 1964, Lois and Bianca in Kiss Me Kate, later repeating these roles in San Francisco; 46th Street, NY, Mar 1965, Leona Samish in Do I Hear a Waltz?; Alvin, Mar 1967, Maggie Cutler in Sherry!; toured, 1967–8, as Stephanie in the national company of Cactus Flower; toured summer 1973 in My Daughter's Rated X; San Diego, Cal, 1973, Martha in Who's Afraid of Virginia Woolf?, also toured in Plaza Suite; toured summer 1974 in Mother Is Engaged; toured 1977–78 in California Suite; first appeared in films in 1960 in From the Terrace, and has since played in Diamond Head, Donovan's Reef, The Carey Treatment, 1972, and others; elected National Recording Secretary of the Screen Actors Guild, 1973 and 1975; first woman in 20 years to be elected to the Board of Governors of the Motion Picture Academy of Arts and Sciences; appeared as the Away-We-Go Girl on the *Jackie Gleason Show* on television, 1955–6, and has since played in the major dramatic and variety programs, including *The Twilight Zone*, The Jimmy Walker Story, the serial *Bracken's World, The Paul Lynde Show*, 1972, etc.

Favourite parts: Viola in Twelfth Night, Annie Oakley in Annie Get Your Gun. *Recreations:* Swimming, sailing, guitar playing, cooking.

ALLEN, Jack, actor
b Sandbach, Cheshire, 23 Oct 1907; *s* of Robert Lea Allen and his wife Charlotte Cecilia (Johnstone); *e* Rugby and Clare College, Cambridge; *m* Ruth Dunning.

Formerly engaged as labour manager in Imperial Chemical Industries; made his first appearance on the stage at the Playhouse, Liverpool, Sept 1931, as the Butler in The Swan; at the Playhouse, Liverpool, 1931–3, and Oxford Repertory Theatre, 1933; made his first appearance on the London stage at the Fortune Theatre, 18 Sept 1933, as Oliver Campion in The House of Jealousy; Comedy, June 1934, played the Butler in First Episode; Whitehall, May 1934, Guy Pleydell in No Way Back; appeared at the Malvern Festival, 1934; Wyndham's, London, Oct 1934, played the Hon. Robert Melford in Sweet Aloes; Aldwych, Dec 1935, Apollo in These Mortals; Royalty, May 1936, Henry Meurdough in Marriage Settlement; Comedy, Oct 1936, John Trenton in All-In Marriage; Arts, May 1937, and Ambassadors', Sept 1937, Charles Trent in People In Love; People's Palace, July 1937, Hugh Drummond in Bull-Dog Drummond Hits Out; Garrick, Nov 1937, Roger Baldwin in It's a Wise Child; Embassy, Jan 1938, and Shaftesbury, Apr 1938, Malcolm McLeod in Poison Pen; Embassy, Mar 1938, and Duke of York's, Apr 1938, Stephen Harrington in Three Blind Mice; Kingsway, May 1939, Tony in Uneasy Living; after war service, re-appeared on the stage at the Embassy, Aug 1945, as Tim Smith in Myself a Stranger; Embassy, Sept 1945, played the Hon. George Wimpole in Fit for Heroes; at Brighton, Oct 1945, Tim in It Happened in New York; Whitehall, Dec 1945, again played in Fit for Heroes; Westminster, May 1946, Robert Dawson in Frieda; Westminster, Aug 1946, played Robert Chalcot in Message for Margaret; Strand, July 1947, Lucian Travers in My Wives and I; Q, Sept 1949, appeared as Richard Poole in A Poor Weak Woman; Royal, Stratford, Oct 1949, Capt Oke in The Phantom Lover; Richmond, Nov 1949, John in The Foxes of Kildorgan; Embassy, June 1950, played Tiggy Raseby in Shepherd's Warning; Embassy, Dec 1950, Roger Inglis in Caviar and Chips; Q, Jan 1951, Sir George Constable in High Life; Arts, Sept 1951, Gerald Halstane in Mrs Dot; Garrick, May 1952, played William Meraulton in Meet Mr Callaghan; Royal, Birmingham, Sept 1953, Lloyd Howes in Foreign Field; Q, Feb 1954, Reggie Godber in Life Story, and John Marshall in Local Colour; Westminster, May 1954, Roderick Hudson in The Bombshell; Duchess, Apr 1955, Edmund Royston in It's Different For Men; Saville, Oct 1957, played the Doctor, Strakard, and Mr Bertulet in The Egg; Strand, July 1961, Henry Fordyce in Goodnight Mrs Puffin; Pavilion, Bournemouth, Feb 1965, played the Vicar in Oh Dear! What Can the Matter Be?; Arts, June 1966, Mr Bennet in Pride and Prejudice; Leeds Festival, Aug 1968, Gerald in The Game; New, Hull, Dec 1969, the Major in The Day of the Sabre; Playhouse, Nottingham, Oct 1970, Schon in Lulu; Hippodrome, Bristol, Mar 1974, Henry Slaughter in The Tilted Scales; Albery, Dec 1977, Mr Brownlow in Oliver! has appeared on several occasions for the Repertory Players, and at the Arts Theatre in various productions; has frequently appeared in films and television, and broadcasts.

Favourite part: Robert Browning in The Barretts of Wimpole Street. *Recreations:* Golf, riding, bowls, cricket and darts. *Club:* Green Room. *Address:* c/o CCA, White House, 29 Dawes Road, London SW6 7DT.

ALLEN, John Piers, OBE, educator

b London, 30 Mar 1912; *s* of Percy Allen and his wife Marjorie (Nash); *e* Aldenham and St John's, Cambridge; *m* (1) Modwena Sedgwick (mar dis); (2) Anne Preston (mar dis).

First appeared on the London stage at the Westminster, 7 Oct 1931, as a student in The Anatomist; other acting experience included seasons with the Old Vic, 1933–5, and Group Theatre, 1935–6; from 1936 directed intermittent productions at the Unity; directed Belshazzar, 1937; A Pageant of Music for the People, 1938; war service 1940–5 in RNVR, ending as Engineer Lieutenant; from 1945–51 administrator and producer, Glyndebourne Children's Theatre; BBC Schools Broadcasting, 1951–61; HM Inspector for Schools, with national responsibility for drama, 1961–71; Principal, Central School of Speech and Drama, 1972–8; Chairman, Conference of Drama Schools; member, Council for National Academic Awards dance and drama panels, London University Special Advisory Committee in Drama; chairman of accreditation panels, National Council of Drama Training and Council for Dance Education and Training; Visiting Professor, Westfield College, London; his books include: Producing Plays for Children, Great Moments in the Theatre, Masters of British Drama, Drama in Schools, and An Elizabethan Actor.

Address: Garden Flat, 8 Upper Park Road, London NW3 2UP. *Tel:* 01–722 2293.

ALLEN, Patrick, actor

b Malawi, 17 Mar 1927; *m* Sarah Lawson.

Hippodrome, Apr 1955, played Jesse Bard in The Desperate Hours; Lyric, Hammersmith, June 1959, Capt O'Keefe in The Rough and Ready Lot; joined the RSC at the Aldwych to play Auguste in Ondine, Jan, Jean d'Armagnac in The Devils, Feb, season 1961; Achilles in Troilus and Cressida, Oct 1962; Apollo, Aug 1967, Theo in The Flip Side; Greenwich, Sept 1971, Colin in The Sandboy; again with the RSC, Aldwych, Dec 1972, played Arthur in The Island of the Mighty; Thorndike, Leatherhead, Apr 1973, Garry Essendine in Present Laughter; Hampstead, July 1973, Kurt in Play

Strindberg; Greenwich, Nov 1977, the Captain in The Father; films, since his British début in 1947, include: The Night of the Generals, and Puppet on a Chain; TV includes series such as *The Troubleshooters* and *Brett*.

Address: c/o Bryan Drew Ltd 81 Shaftesbury Avenue, London W1.

ALLEN, Rae (*née* Raffaella Julia Thérésa Abruzzo), actress and director

b Brooklyn, New York, 3 July 1926; *d* of Joseph Abruzzo and his wife Julia (Riccio); *e* St Edmund's Grammar School, St Brendan's Academy, Hunter College, and NY University School of the Arts (MS, 1969, in directing); *m* (1) John M Allen (mar dis); (2) Herbert Harris (mar dis); prepared for the stage at the American Academy of Dramatic Arts, and by Stella Adler, Morris Carnovsky, Harold Clurman, Jerry Grotowski, and Uta Hagen.

First appeared on the stage in NY as a singer and understudy at the St James, 1948, in Where's Charley?; Winter Garden, Jan 1950, appeared in the revue Alive and Kicking; Imperial, Oct 1950, appeared as understudy to Ethel Merman and as a singer in Call Me Madam, touring with this production, 1952–3; St James, May 1954, Poopsie in The Pajama Game; 46th Street, May 1955, Gloria in Damn Yankees; at the Kauffman Concert Hall, May 1956, took part in a staged reading of Pictures in the Hallway in which she also co-produced; Belasco, Sept 1957, appeared in a concert reading of I Knock at the Door; Carnegie Hall Playhouse, Nov 1958, played Lorna in Cock-a-Doodle Dandy; Players, Oct 1959, Pearl Cunningham in Summer of the 17th Doll; Shubert, New Haven, Conn, Dec 1959, Miss Krantz in Sweet Love Remember'd; Martinique, off-Broadway, Jan 1960, took over some roles in the revue USA; Shakespeare Festival, Stratford, Conn, summer 1960, played Ceres in The Tempest and Charmian in Antony and Cleopatra; toured Sept–Dec 1960, as Hippolyta in A Midsummer Night's Dream and Paulina in The Winter's Tale; Cherry Lane, off-Broadway, Dec 1960, took over various roles in the staged reading Drums Under the Window; York Playhouse, off- Broadway, Jan 1961, played the Nurse in The Death of Bessie Smith, playing the same role at the Cherry Lane in May 1961; appeared as Saint Joan with the Princeton (New Jersey) Repertory Company, Oct 1961; Mermaid, Jan 1962, Tekla in Creditors, appearing in the last role with the UCLA Professional Theatre Repertory Company, June 1962; appeared with the same company, July–Oct 1963, playing Hippolyta in 'Tis Pity She's a Whore and Casilda in Peribanez; Orpheum, Dec 1963, took over the role of Miss Frost in The Ginger Man; Shonberg Hall, Los Angeles, June 1964, Goneril in King Lear; ANTA, Sept 1964, played Juliette in Traveller Without Luggage; Theatre de Lys, Nov–Dec 1964, again appeared in I Knock at the Door, and Pictures in the Hallway; Delacorte, summer, 1965, played Rosaline in Love's Labour's Lost; Mark Hellinger, Oct 1965, Mrs Hatch in On a Clear Day You Can See Forever; joined the APA Phoenix Repertory Theatre for 1966–7 season, playing Essie in You Can't Take It With You, Lady Sneerwell in The School for Scandal, and in Right You Are If You Think You Are; Delacorte, June 1968, Doll Tearsheet in Henry IV, Part II; Imperial, 1969, took over the role of Golde in Fiddler on the Roof; Center Stage, Baltimore, Oct 1970, Anne in A Cry of Players; Morosco, Feb 1971, Fleur Stein in And Miss Reardon Drinks a Little; toured the US July–Nov 1971 as the Old Lady in Candide; summer, 1972, directed The Country Girl at the Barter, Abingdon, Va; Broadway, Oct 1972, Reba in Dude; Anspacher, Apr 1973, Clytemnestra 2 in The Orphan; Coconut Grove Playhouse, Miami, Florida, Feb

1974, played various roles in The Trouble with People . . .; Barter, summer 1974, directed Private Lives; Brooklyn Academy of Music, Oct 1974, directed Hot House; Artistic Director, 1975–78 Stage/West, West Springfield, Mass, where she directed Serenading Louie, Ah Wilderness, 1975; The Balcony, You Can't Take It With You, 1976; When We Dead Awaken, The Hot 1 Baltimore, Jacques Brel Is Alive and Well . . ., The Little Foxes, A Christmas Carol (also adapted), 1977; Rib Cage, Three Sisters, 1978; directed The Gingerbread Lady for the Queen's Festival, 1977; Father's Day, 1979; in 1970–1 served on the faculty of the Acting Department of the NY University School of the Arts; first appeared in films in 1958, as Gloria in Damn Yankees and has since appeared in Tiger Makes Out, 1966, Where's Poppa? 1970, RTO, 1971, Taking Off, 1972, etc; has appeared regularly on television in *Look Up and Live, Camera Three, The Untouchables, The Steve Allen Show,* The Little Moon of Alban, *All in the Family, Medical Center,* etc.
Address: 2 West 67th Street, New York, NY 10023.

ALLEN, Ralph G, writer, director, and university teacher *b* 7 Jan 1934; *s* of Ralph Bergen Allen and his wife Sara; *e* Amherst College (BA 1955) and Yale School of Drama (DFA 1960); *m* Harriet Nichols.

Artistic director, 1968–72, Victoria Fair Theatre, BC; artistic director since 1972 of the Clarence Brown company, a professional theatre company in residence at the University of Tennessee, Knoxville, where he was also Chairman of the theatre department, 1972–78; plays he has produced at Knoxville include Everyman, 1974 (also directed); Rip van Winkle (also co-author with Joshua Logan), 1976, transferring to the Kennedy Center, Washington; The Tax Collector (also wrote), 1977 and tour; editor, Theatre Survey, 1965–68; author of two other plays, numerous articles, and of the books Theatre and Drama in the Making, 1964 (with John Gassner); Gaiety: the life and times of the American Burlesque show, 1980; conceived and wrote the burlesque sketches for Sugar Babies, Mark Hellinger, 8 Oct 1979; Fellow, American Theatre Association; Guggenheim Fellowship, 1965.

Recreations: Chess, baseball, detective fiction. *Address:* 2980 Sevier Avenue, Knoxville, TN 37916. *Tel:* 615–577 4582.

ALLEN, Sheila, actress *b* Chard, Somerset, 22 Oct 1932, *d* of William Allen and his wife Dorothy Essex (Potter); *e* Howell's School, Denbigh; *m* David Jones.

Trained at RADA, 1949–51; made her first stage appearance at Covent Garden in The Faerie Queene, followed by repertory seasons with the Garrick Players in Devon and Yeovil; Pitlochry Festival, 1953, played Lucy in The Rivals; 1954–6 appeared with the Arena Theatre Company, Birmingham, in parts including Katherina in The Taming of the Shrew, Beatrice in Much Ado About Nothing, and Alkmena in Amphitryon 38; 1956–7 joined the Rapier Players, Bristol; appeared as a member of the Bristol Old Vic Company, Theatre Royal, Bristol 1957–8, in the following parts: Hippolyta in A Midsummer Night's Dream, Mrs Pearce in Pygmalion, Marfa Zlotochienko in Romanoff and Juliet; Delilah in Sodom and Gomorrah, Miss Ramsden in Man and Superman, and Ba in The Pier; Belgrade, Coventry, Sept 1960, played Nell in The Lion in Love; Richmond 1960, Portia in The Merchant of Venice; Theatre Royal, Stratford, E, Jan 1962, Drusilla in On a Clear Day You Can See Canterbury; Lyric, Hammersmith, Apr 1962, Pat Garnet in The Last Ally; for the Royal Shakespeare Company,

Aldwych, June 1962, played the Daughter-in-Law in the one-act play Playing With Fire; Old Vic, Oct 1962, played Portia in The Merchant of Venice; Comedy, May 1963, played Sister Bonaventure in The Umbrella; Royal Court, Sept 1964, played Liz in Inadmissible Evidence; and Nov 1964, Portia in Julius Caesar; Royal, Stratford, E, May 1965, Stella Herberden in Saint's Day; 1966, joined the Royal Shakespeare Company and appeared in The Hollow Crown at Westminster Abbey, and in the following parts at Stratford: Lady Percy in King Henry the Fourth (Parts I and II), Helen Rawston in Belcher's Luck (Aldwych), 1966; Lady Macduff in Macbeth (also Aldwych, 1968), Lady Capulet in Romeo and Juliet, also touring Finland and Russia in the former part, 1967; Polly Garter in Under Milk Wood (Aldwych only), Goneril in King Lear, Helen in Troilus and Cressida, 1968; in 1969 appeared in Vagina Rex at the Arts Lab, Drury Lane, and Comrade Jacob at the Gardner Arts Centre, Sussex University; founder member of Holocaust Theatre, 1971, appearing at the Traverse, Edinburgh, Apr, as Geriatric in A New Communion for Freaks, Prophets and Witches; Greenwich, June 1973, Lady Brute in The Provok'd Wife; Shaw, Oct 1973, Lady Macbeth and First Witch in Macbeth; played Constance in King John at Stratford, Mar 1974 and the Aldwych, Jan 1975; the Queen in Cymbeline, Stratford, June, and Aldwych, Dec 1974; The Other Place, Stratford, Apr, and The Place, London, Oct 1974, Goneril in Lear; Aldwych, Apr 1976, Sofia in The Zykovs; The Other Place, 1977–8, title part in Queen Christina, Wemwood in The Sons of Light, and Alice in The Dance of Death, transferring in the two latter roles to the Warehouse, and subsequently, in The Dance of Death, to the Aldwych; for the Cambridge Theatre Company, 1979, toured as Beverly in The Shadow Box; first film 1959, and appearances include The Prince and the Pauper, Children of the Damned and Venom; television performances since 1953 include *Shoulder to Shoulder, A Bouquet of Barbed Wire* and *Another Bouquet*; has taught at LAMDA and in US Universities, the latter with the RSC's 'Artist in Residence' project.
Address: 59 Frith Street, London W1.

ALLEN, Woody, actor, playwright, and director *b* Brooklyn, New York, 1 Dec 1935; *s* of Martin Konigsberg and his wife Netty Cherry; *e* City College of NY and NY University; *m* (1) Harlene Rosen (mar dis); (2) Louise Lasser (mar dis).

His play Don't Drink the Water was produced at the Morosco, 17 Nov 1966; at the Broadhurst, 12 Feb 1969, made his Broadway début as Allan Felix in Play It Again, Sam, which he also wrote; played in the film What's New Pussycat? 1965, which he also wrote; played in Casino Royale, 1967; writer, director and star of films including Take the Money and Run, 1969, Bananas, 1971, Sleeper, 1974, Love and Death, 1975, Annie Hall, 1977, Interiors, 1978, Manhattan, 1979, etc; author of the books Getting Even, 1971, Without Feathers, 1975; is also a noted jazz musician.
Address: c/o Mike Hutner, United Artists, 729 7th Avenue, New York NY 10019.

ALLINSON, Michael, actor *b* London; *s* of Adrian Allinson and his wife Joan (Buckland); *e* Ryeford Hall and Wycliffe College, Stonehouse, Gloucestershire, and the Lausanne Univ and Institut Ribeaupierre, Lausanne, Switzerland, 1937–8; prepared for the theatre at the Royal Academy of Dramatic Art, 1940; *m* Judith Lee Schriver; served as a Captain in World War II.

First appeared on the stage at Wycliffe College, Stonehouse, as Mabel Dancy in Loyalties, 1935; first appeared in London at the Little Theatre, 9 Apr 1940, as a Servant in The

Country Wife; after the war reappeared in London at the Granville, 17 Dec 1946, as Robert Brown in Just William; played in repertory in Tunbridge Wells, Watford, and Richmond until Jan 1949; Phoenix, London, May 1949, Hounslow in The Beaux' Stratagem; at the Q, July 1950–Jan 1951, appeared in A Pig in a Poke, Who Goes Home?, Celestial Fire, Quay South, Red Dragon, etc; played in repertory in Leatherhead, Feb 1951–July 1952; Phoenix, London, Sept 1952, waiter in Quadrille, also understudying Alfred Lunt; again played in repertory until Mar 1954; then played with the Bristol Old Vic until Sept 1955; Assembly Hall, Edinburgh, Aug 1955, played in A Life in the Sun; at the Moscow Arts Theatre, Russia, Nov 1955, Francisco and A Captain in Hamlet, and repeated these parts at the Phoenix, London, Dec 1955; toured, July 1956, in Ring for Catty; played in repertory at Leatherhead until Feb 1957; toured, Feb 1957, in Love's a Luxury and concurrently in Mar 1957 in We Must Kill Toni; played in repertory again in Leatherhead, Richmond, and Windsor until Mar 1958; Arts, London, Apr 1958, Bamboo in Imperial Nightingale; came to the US where, in June 1958, he was standby to Michael Evans as Henry Higgins in the touring edition of My Fair Lady; made his New York début at the Mark Hellinger, 10 Feb 1960, when he succeeded Edward Mulhare as Henry Higgins in My Fair Lady; appeared at the Hollywood Bowl at various times in 1960, 1961, 1963 in concert; Madison Avenue Playhouse, NY, Feb 1963, John Worthing in The Importance of Being Earnest; toured, Dec 1963–Apr 1964, as Philip Clair in Kind Sir; Music Box, Feb 1966, Sir Peter Crossman in Hostile Witness; Billy Rose, Jan 1967, Tristram Hawkins in Come Live with Me; Coconut Grove Playhouse, Miami, Fla, 1967, played in Camelot; Ahmanson, Los Angeles, 1968, Lord Melbourne in Love Match; Mark Hellinger, Dec 1969, Charles, Duke of Glenallen in Coco; toured in this part, Jan–June 1971; Royal Alexandra, Toronto, Canada, Oct 1971, Andrew Wyke in Sleuth, and subsequently toured; played the same part at the Garrick, London, Mar 1973; Albery, Sept 1973, Bernard in The Constant Wife; Papermill Playhouse, NJ, Nov 1974, Arthur in Camelot; Manhattan Theatre Club, Apr 1975, Charlie in Staircase; Guthrie, Minneapolis, Oct 1975, Elyot Chase in Private Lives, Lyceum, NY, Dec 1975, Manningham in Angel Street; repeated his role in Sleuth at the Sombrero Playhouse, Phoenix, Ariz, Apr 1976; Cape Playhouse, Dennis, Mass, Jul 1976, appeared in Absurd Person Singular; Chateau de Ville, Saugus, Mass, Sept 1976, Dr Wicksteed in Habeas Corpus; McCarter, Princeton, Mar 1977, Leo in Design for Living; Theatre East, Milwaukee, Oct 1977, Martin Dysart in Equus; First Chicago Centre, Dec 1977, in the revue Compliments of Cole; Atlanta and Palm Beach, Jan 1978, Charles in Blithe Spirit; Studio Arena, Buffalo, Mar 1978, appeared in Coward in Two Keys; Meadow Brook, Mich, Oct 1978, Burgoyne in The Devil's Disciple; same theatre, Feb 1979, again played Charles in Blithe Spirit; Alley, Houston, Mar 1979, title role in Don Juan in Hell; Williamstown Theatre Festival, summer 1979, David Bliss in Hay Fever and Sir Francis Chesney in Charley's Aunt; first appeared on television in England, Nov 1953, as Robert in The Shop at Sly Corner, and appeared on various dramatic shows since, including Macbeth and The Two-Headed Eagle, and in the US since 1961, recently in Love of Life.

Recreations: Ski-ing, swimming, golf, bridge, chess.
Address: William Morris Agency, 1350 Avenue of the Americas, New York, NY 10019. *Tel:* 586–5100.

ALPER, Jonathan, director and actor
b Washington, DC, 14 Sept 1950; *s* of Jerome M Alper and his wife Janet; *e* Amherst College (BA 1971); trained for the stage at the Webber-Douglas Academy.

Made his professional debut as an actor, June 1974, at the Arena Stage, Washington, in The Madness of God; director and literary manager with the Folger Theatre Group, Washington, 1975–78, during which time he directed The Comedy of Errors, 1975; All's Well That Ends Well, Black Elk Speaks, Much Ado About Nothing, 1976; Teeth 'n' Smiles (with Louis Scheeder), 1977; Hamlet, 1978; has since directed Safe House (Manhattan Theatre Club), Rosencrantz and Guildenstern Are Dead (Monmouth, Maine), 1978; The Romance of Shakespeare (Meadow Brook and tour; also acted), Fishing (Actors' Collective, NY), The Eccentricities of a Nightingale (Bergen Stage, NJ), 1979.
Address: 785 West End Avenue, New York, NY.

ALSWANG, Ralph, designer, director and producer
b Chicago, Ill, 12 Apr 1916; *s* of Hyman and Florence Alswang; *e* Goodman Theatre, Chicago Art Institute; studied with Robert Edmund Jones; *m* Betty Taylor.

His first designs were for the production of Revelation, at the Al Jolson Theatre, 1942; Winged Victory, 1943; Beggars Are Coming to Town, Home of the Brave, 1945; I Like It Here, Crescendo (tour), Barnaby and Mr O'Malley (tour), Swan Song, Lysistrata, 1946; The Whole World Over, Darling, Darling, Darling (tour), A Young Man's Fancy, Our Len, The Gentleman from Athens, 1947; Strange Bedfellows, Small Wonder, The Last Dance, To Tell You the Truth, The Play's the Thing, Seeds in the Wind, A Story for Strangers, Set My People Free, Jenny Kissed Me, 1948; Blood Wedding, Me, the Sleeper, S M Chartock's Gilbert and Sullivan Company, How Long Till Summer, 1949; Peter Pan, Tickets Please, King Lear, Julius Caesar, Legend of Sarah, Pride's Crossing, Let's Make an Opera, 1950; Courtin' Time, Out West of Eighth, Peter Pan (tour), Love and Let Love, The Number, 1951; Conscience, The Suspects, The Pirates of Penzance, HMS Pinafore, Trial by Jury, Iolanthe, The Mikado, Two's Company, 1952; Ladies of the Corridor, Be Your Age, The Bat, The Pink Elephant, Anna Russell's Little Show, Sing Till Tomorrow, 1953; The Magic and the Loss (also co-produced), The Fragile Fox, The Troublemakers, The Rainmaker, 1954; The South-west Corner, Deadfall, Catch a Star, 1955; Time Limit!, Affair of Honor, The Hot Corner, The Best House in Naples, Uncle Willie, 1956; The Tunnel of Love, Hide and Seek, The First Gentleman (also co-presented), 1957; Sunrise at Campobello, Love Me Little, Epitaph for George Dillon (supervision), Starward Ark, 1958; A Raisin in the Sun, Detour After Dark (London), The Girls Against the Boys, 1959; Come Blow Your Horn, Impulse (also staged), Nine O'Clock Revue (the last two in Toronto, Canada), 1961; Beyond the Fringe (lighting), Music for Tonight, at the Greek Theatre, Los Angeles and also directed, as well as designed and directed The Harry Belafonte Show, 1962; The School for Scandal (lighting), The Advocate (costumes), Man and Boy (also London), 1963; Rugantino (technical director), Fair Game for Lovers, The Committee, Comedy in Music, 1964; at the Essoldo, Brighton, England, Mar 1964, co-produced and directed Is There Intelligent Life on Earth? in a process devised by himself (*Living Screen*), which integrates live action with motion pictures; The Bernard Shaw Story (co-presented), The World of Charles Aznavour, 1965; Hostile Witness, Come Slowly, Eden (co-produced), Seven Ages of Bernard Shaw, The Effect of Gamma Rays on Man-in-the-Moon Marigolds, Israeli Mime Theatre, Gilbert Becaud on Broadway, At the Drop of Another Hat, 1966; The Hemingway

Hero (also co-produced at Shubert, New Haven, Conn), Halfway up the Tree, 1967; during 1967–8 designed for the Mark Taper Forum, Center Theatre Group, Los Angeles; Gilbert Becaud . . . Sings Love, 1968; Fun City, 1972; Piaf . . . A Remembrance, 1977; The Lesson, 1978; in 1970–1 designed the Uris Theatre in New York; designed the New Orleans Civic Center Theater and Pine Knob Pavilion (New District, Mich), 1972.
(*Died 1979.*)

AMECHE, Don (*né* Dominic Felix Amici), actor
b Kenosha, Wisconsin, 31 May 1908; *s* of Felix Amici and his wife Barbara Etta (Hertle); *e* Columbia Academy, Macquette University, Georgetown University, University of Wisconsin; *m* Hortense Prendergast.
Made his stage début with the Al Jackson Stock Co, in Madison, Wisconsin, Nov 1928; made his New York début at the Waldorf, 9 Sept 1929, when he took over the part of Perkins in Jerry-for-Short; in Greenwich, Conn, 1930, appeared in Excess Baggage; in Chicago, 1930, played Illegal Practice; also in 1930 toured with Texas Guinan in vaudeville; reappeared in NY at the Imperial, Feb 1955, as Steve Canfield in Silk Stockings, and toured in this part in 1956; Longacre, Feb 1957, Robert Dean in Holiday for Lovers; Lunt-Fontanne, Oct 1958, Max Grady in Goldilocks; 54th Street, Mar 1961, Chun in 13 Daughters; toured 1964, in I Married an Angel; Palace, Oct 1967, Henry Orient in Henry, Sweet Henry; toured, 1968, as Oscar Madison in The Odd Couple; State Fair Music Hall, Dallas, Texas, Oct 1972, Jimmy Smith in No, No, Nanette, and toured in this part until Aug 1973; Westbury, Long Island, Music Fair, Aug 1974, again played Jimmy Smith in No, No, Nanette; Country Dinner Playhouse, Austin, Tex, May 1976, appeared in Never Get Smart with an Angel; entered films in 1933 and has since appeared in many films, including: Ramona, 1936, Alexander's Ragtime Band, In Old Chicago, 1938, Swanee River, The Story of Alexander Graham Bell, 1939, Lillian Russell, 1940, Heaven Can Wait, 1943, A Fever in the Blood, 1961, Rings Around the World, 1966, etc; made his radio début in 1930 and appeared on *The Chase and Sanborn Hour*, 1937–9, *The Old Gold Don Ameche Show*, *The Charlie McCarthy Show*, 1940, *The Morgan–Ameche–Langford Show*, 1947–8, *Don Ameche's Real-Life Stories*, 1958, etc; first appeared on television in 1950 and has since appeared in the Frances Langford–Don Ameche Show, High Button Shoes, Junior Miss, 1957, and various dramatic programs.

ANDERSON, Daphne, actress and singer
b London, 27 Apr 1922; *d* of Alan Edward Scrutton and his wife Gladys Amy (Juler); *e* Kensington High School; *m* Lionel William Carter.
Studied dancing under Zelia Raye; made her first appearance on the stage at the Richmond (Surrey) Theatre, Xmas, 1937, in the chorus of Cinderella; first appeared in London, at the Windmill Theatre, 1938, in the chorus of Revudeville; toured 1939–40, as Dora in Funny Face; toured for ENSA, 1940–1; Savoy, Oct 1941, appeared in Sorotchintsi Fair; Cambridge, 1942, with the New Russian Ballet; toured, 1943, for ENSA; at the Scala, Dec 1943, played Father William in Alice in Wonderland and the Walrus in Alice Through the Looking-Glass; toured, 1944, in Gangway; at the Players' Theatre, Xmas, 1944, appeared in the pantomime, and during 1945, in Late Joys; Piccadilly, Aug 1945, in Sigh No More; Players', Apr 1946, played Jennifer in The Cave and the Garden; Windsor Repertory Company, July, 1946, in The Apple Cart; Players' Theatre, 1946, again in Late Joys; Drury Lane, Dec 1946, played Penelope in Pacific 1860; at the Boltons Theatre, Dec 1947, played lead in The Boltons

Revue, also at the St James's, Mar 1948; Boltons, June 1948, Serpolette in Les Cloches de Corneville; Chepstow, Sept and Oct 1948, appeared in the revues Ad Lib, and Encore; Saville, Mar 1949, played Belle Barrow in Belinda Fair; Players', Dec 1949, Beauty in Beauty and the Beast; Watergate, Nov 1950, appeared in the revue, After the Show; Players', Dec 1950, appeared as Morgiana in Ali Baba and the Thirty-nine Thieves; Princes, Mar 1951, played Susan Brook in The Seventh Veil; Players', Dec 1951, Princess Allfair in Riquet With The Tuft; Aldwych, Apr 1952, played Girl and Girl Junior in Under the Sycamore Tree; Players', Dec 1952, Sally in The Babes in the Wood and the Good Little Fairy-Birds!; St Martin's, May 1953, Patty Moss in a revival of The Two Bouquets; Saville, May 1955, Sylvia Crewes in The Tender Trap; St Martin's, July 1955, Kitty Hemming in Twenty Minutes South; Royal Court, Feb 1956, Polly Peachum in The Threepenny Opera, transferring with the production, Aldwych, Mar 1956; Windsor Theatre Royal, July 1956, Elvira in Blithe Spirit; Comedy, Jan 1958, played Mae in Cat On a Hot Tin Roof; Windsor Theatre Royal, June 1958, Verity Croone in Double Take, subsequently transferring to the Aldwych, July 1958, when the play was re-named Three-Way Switch; Phoenix, Nov 1960, played Bichette in Out of This World; Hampstead Theatre Club, Sept 1963, played Mother and Miss B in Cider With Rosie, transferring with the production to the Garrick, Oct 1963; Players', Dec 1963, played Queen Serena in Sleeping Beauty in the Wood; Thorndike, Leatherhead, 1970, played the Mother in Spring and Port Wine; Duke of York's, Feb 1970, Jane Amberley in A Woman Named Anne; Arnaud, Guildford, Sept 1970, Lottie Grady in When We are Married, and at the Strand, Nov 1970; Sadler's Wells, Mar 1972, played Lady Windermere in Lord Arthur Savile's Crime; toured, Aug 1972, as Gwenny in The Late Christopher Bean; Ashcroft, Croydon, Christmas 1972, the Red Queen in Alice Through the Looking Glass; Shaw, Mar 1973, Mrs Summerfield in Only a Game; played Mrs Fairfax in Jane Eyre at the Theatre Royal, Windsor, July 1973; the Queen in The Sleeping Beauty at the Arnaud, Guildford, Christmas 1973; toured N America, 1974, playing Maud Boothroyd in Lloyd George Knew My Father; Theatre Royal, Bath, Oct 1974, Lady Boothroyd in the same play; was standby for Hermione Gingold and Jean Simmons in A Little Night Music, Adelphi, Apr 1975, taking the parts of both; appeared in Late Joys, Player's, 1977–9; also dinner theatre at the Dickens Inne; films include The Beggars' Opera and Hobson's Choice; recent TV includes *Thomas and Sarah* (LWT) and *The Old Curiosity Shop* (BBC).
Recreations: Gardening, reading, winemaking. *Address:* Little Tatton, Upperton, Tillington, Petworth, Sussex. *Tel:* Petworth 2047.

ANDERSON, J. Grant, actor and director
b Glenlivet, Banffshire, Scotland, 20 Apr 1897; *s* of James Anderson and his wife Helen Christina (Grant); *e* Richmond, Surrey.
Made his first appearance on the stage at the Apollo Theatre, 8 June 1914, as Charles Widdicomb in When Knights Were Bold, with the late James Welch, with whom he also appeared at the New Theatre, Dec 1914, in The New Clown; at the New, May–June 1915, appeared with Sir John Martin-Harvey, in The Breed of the Treshams, Armageddon, The Only Way, The Corsican Brothers, The Cigarette Maker's Romance and Hamlet, subsequently touring in the same plays; in the first World War, served with the London Scottish from 1915; was severely wounded 1917, and discharged 1918; played leading parts at Oldham, 1918–20, and

with the stock company at the Princes', Portsmouth, 1920–3; started his own repertory company, 1923, at Gosport; lessee of the Embassy, 1928–9; from 1929–39, toured in the Far East, India, Burma, Ceylon, China and Japan, also taking his company to Kashmir, Afghanistan, Java, and Sumatra, and playing numerous parts, from Tony Perelli in On the Spot to Hamlet, Shylock, Mark Antony, etc; in 1932, founded the Indian National Theatre in Bombay, for the playing of English and Indian classics, in English, with all-Indian casts; in 1934, while in Burma and Siam, appeared as a clown with Hagenbeck's Circus; at His Majesty's Theatre, London, Mar 1938, appeared as Jenner in Operette; again served with the London Scottish, in second World War, from 1939; subsequently served on ENSA Military Staff; toured on all fronts, giving entertainment for the troops; was lessee of the Torch Theatre for six months in 1946; was resident director at the Intimate Theatre, 1947–50, during which time twelve of his productions were presented on television; directed dialogue and mime for the Ice productions of Rose Marie at Harringay Arena, 1950, and at the Empire Pool, Wembley, Dick Whittington, 1951; Robinson Crusoe, 1952; The Sleeping Beauty, Chu Chin Chow, 1953; Humpty Dumpty, 1954; was lessee of the New Cross Empire, with R Colling-Pyper, 1950–5, presenting variety, revue, and pantomime; was lessee of Theatre Royal, Chatham, with Rita Buchan, 1950–5; at the Chelsea Palace, Mar 1955, appeared as Nero in The Sign of the Cross, which he also directed; toured, 1955–7, in Murder at the Vicarage; 1958–60, presented, directed, and played in tours of Love in Idleness, Worm's Eye View, Wanted—One Body, While Parents Sleep; Savoy, Mar 1960, appeared as Mr Thorpe in The Gazebo; Mermaid, June 1961, played General Mott in The Andersonville Trial; St Martin's, July 1962, Mr Hardy in Brush With A Body; returned to active management, 1969, presenting, directing and acting in 36 plays in annual summer seasons at Wimbledon; toured with Witness for the Prosecution, 1971; presented the tour of Fiddlers Five, 1973, playing the Lawyer; Garrick, 1974, took over the part of Ribart in Birds of Paradise; Strand, 1975, took over as Mr Needham in No Sex Please, We're British; Lyric, summer 1977, took over the part of Hawkins in The Kingfisher; author of the play The Wisest Fool, 1946, and an autobiography, Diamond Jubilee Hangover.

Club: Green Room. *Address:* 13 Cypress Road, South Norwood Hill, London, SE25. *Tel:* 01–653 6192.

ANDERSON, Dame Judith, DBE (*cr* 1960), *née* Frances Margaret Anderson-Anderson, actress
b Adelaide, South Australia, 10 Feb 1898; *d* of James Anderson-Anderson and his wife Jessie Margaret (Saltmarsh); *e* Adelaide; *m* (1) Benjamin Harrison Lehman (mar dis); (2) Luther Greene (mar dis).

Made her first appearance on the stage in 1915, at the Theatre Royal, Sydney, NSW, as Stephanie in A Royal Divorce and subsequently toured in Monsieur Beaucaire, The Scarlet Pimpernel, and David Garrick; made her first appearance in New York, in 1918, at the old Fourteenth Street Theatre, playing small parts in the stock company, rising to leading parts there in the following year; during 1920 toured with William Gillette in Dear Brutus; during 1921 played leading parts in stock companies in Boston and Albany, and during Sept 1922 appeared at the Playhouse, billed as Frances Anderson, as Mrs Bellmore in On the Stairs and Crooked Square; at the Sam H Harris Theatre, Sept 1923, appeared as Judith Anderson as Jessie Weston in Peter Weston; she made a substantial success at the Hudson Theatre, Apr 1924, when she played Elise Van Zile in Cobra; at the Empire, NY, Feb 1925, played Dolores Romero in The

Dove; she returned to Australia, Jan 1927, and appeared as Elise in Cobra, the Wife in Tea for Three, and Iris Fenwick in The Green Hat; she returned to America during the same year and appeared at the Cort Theatre, Dec 1927, as Antoinette Lyle in Behold the Bridegroom; Lyceum, NY, May 1928, played Anna Plumer in Anna; John Golden Theatre (for the Theatre Guild), July 1928, succeeded Lynn Fontanne as Nina Leeds in Strange Interlude, and in 1929 toured in the same part; during 1930–1, toured as the Unknown One in As You Desire Me, and appeared at the Maxine Elliott Theatre, NY, Jan 1931, in the same part; in 1932, toured as Lavinia Mannon in the O'Neill trilogy, Mourning Becomes Electra, and appeared at the Alvin Theatre, NY, May 1932, in the same part; Empire, Nov 1932, Karola Lovasdy in Firebird; Plymouth, Feb 1933, Helen Nolte in Conquest; Guild, May 1933, Savina Grazia in The Mask and the Face; Shubert, Nov 1933, Valerie Latour in The Drums Begin; Maxine Elliott, Jan 1934, the Woman in Come of Age; in Pittsburgh, Aug 1934, appeared as Mimea Sheller in The Female of the Species; Ethel Barrymore, NY, Sept 1934, Lila in Divided by Three; Empire, Jan 1935, Delia Lovell in The Old Maid; in the autumn, toured in the same part; Empire, Oct 1936, Gertrude in Hamlet, with John Gielgud; made her first appearance in London at the Old Vic, 26 Nov 1937, as Lady Macbeth, subsequently playing the same part at the New Theatre, Dec 1937; Morosco, NY, Mar 1939, Mary in Family Portrait; on the Pacific Coast, 1939, Clytemnestra in Tower Beyond Tragedy; National, Nov 1941, again played Lady Macbeth; Ethel Barrymore, Dec 1942, Olga in The Three Sisters; National, Oct 1947, the title-role in Medea, and again appeared in this part at the City Center, May 1949; ANTA Playhouse, Nov 1950, Clytemnestra in Tower Beyond Tragedy; City Center, Jan 1952, played The Woman in Come of Age; New Century, Feb 1953, appeared in a dramatic reading of John Brown's Body; Playhouse, Dec 1953, Gertrude Eastman-Cuevas in In the Summer House; toured, Aug 1956, as Miss Madrigal in The Chalk Garden; Ambassador, NY, Nov 1958, Isabel Lawton in Comes a Day; Edinburgh Festival, Aug 1960, appeared with the Old Vic Company as Irina Arkadina in The Seagull, subsequently playing the same part at the Old Vic, Sept 1960; toured the US and Canada, Sept–Dec 1961, in scenes from Medea, Tower Beyond Tragedy, and Macbeth; Sombrero Playhouse, Phoenix, Arizona, Jan 1964, Alice Christie in Black Chiffon; Elder Hall, Adelaide, Australia, 1966, performed excerpts from Medea and Macbeth, and subsequently toured; Ypsilanti, Michigan, Greek Theatre, summer, 1966, Clytemnestra in The Oresteia; New York City Center, Nov 1966, the title-role of Elizabeth the Queen; toured US, winter 1970, and played Carnegie Hall, Jan 1971, as Hamlet; first appeared in films, 1933, in Blood Money, and since has played in many films, including: Rebecca, Jane Eyre, Laura, and A Man Called Horse, 1970; recent TV, The Chinese Prime Minister, 1974; received the title of Dame Commander of the British Empire in the Birthday Honours, 1960.

Favourite part: The Woman in Come of Age. *Recreations:* Riding and reading. *Address:* 808 San Ysidro Lane, Santa Barbara, Calif 93103.

ANDERSON, Lindsay, director
b Bangalore, S. India, 17 April 1923; *s* of Alexander Vass Anderson and his wife Estelle Bell (Gasson); *e* Cheltenham College and Wadham College, Oxford.

Began his career as a documentary film director and film critic; directed his first stage production, The Waiting of Lester Abbs, at the Royal Court Theatre, June 1957 (Without Décor); he has since directed the following plays: The

Long and the Short and the Tall, Progress to the Park (Without Décor), Jazzetry (Without Décor), Dispersal, Serjeant Musgrave's Dance, 1959; The Lily-White Boys, Billy Liar, Trials by Logue, 1960; Box and Cox and The Fire Raisers (double-bill), 1961; The Diary of a Madman (also co-adapted), 1963; Andorra (National Theatre), Julius Caesar, 1964; The Cherry Orchard (Chichester), 1966; Contemporary Theatre, Warsaw, also in 1966, directed the first Polish production of Inadmissible Evidence (Nie do Obrony); Co-Artistic Director of the Royal Court Theatre, 1969–70; Associate Artistic Director, 1971–5; here he directed In Celebration and The Contractor, 1969; Home (also New York), 1970; The Changing Room, 1971; The Farm, 1973; Life Class, 1974 and What the Butler Saw, 1975; the last six productions transferred to the West End; at the Lyric, directed The Seagull (also co-adapted), and The Bed Before Yesterday, in repertory, 1975; The Kingfisher, 1977; has since directed Alices Boys (Savoy), The Kingfisher (Biltmore NY), 1978; The Bed Before Yesterday (Sydney), 1979; Early Days (National Theatre), 1980; Royal Court, Apr 1965, played Reg Parsons in Miniatures (in a Production Without Decor); has also played in Inadmissible Evidence (film), and The Parachute (TV); directed his first film (documentary) Meet The Pioneers, in 1948; subsequent documentaries include Thursday's Children (Hollywood Academy Award 1953), Every Day Except Christmas (Venice Grand Prix 1957); films include This Sporting Life, The White Bus, If . . . (Grand Prix Cannes International Film Festival 1969), O Lucky Man! and In Celebration; first drama production for TV: The Old Crowd, 1979.

Address: LGA (Services) Ltd, 13 Parkfield Street, London N1.

ANDERSON, Robert Woodruff, dramatic author
b New York City, 28 Apr 1917; *s* of James Hewston Anderson and his wife Myra Esther (Grigg); *e* Phillips Exeter Academy and Harvard University; *m* (1) Phyllis Stohl (dec); (2) Teresa Wright (mar dis).

At the Dunster House, Harvard University, Dec 1938, wrote book, lyrics, music, acted in, and directed Hour Town; while serving in the US Naval Reserve overseas, he won the prize (sponsored by the War Department) for the best play written by a serviceman, Come Marching Home, 1945, and this was subsequently produced at the University of Iowa, and at the Blackfriars Guild in NY; on returning to civilian life, he received a Rockefeller Fellowship to write plays, and studied with John Gassner; 1946–50, organized and taught a playwriting class for the American Theatre Wing Professional Training Program; organized and taught Playwrights Unit at Actors Studio, 1955; he is the author of the following plays, The Eden Rose, Love Revisited, 1952; Tea and Sympathy, 1953; All Summer Long, 1954; Silent Night, Lonely Night, 1959; The Days Between, 1965; You Know I Can't Hear You When the Water's Running, which consisted of four short plays, 1967; I Never Sang for My Father, 1968; Solitaire, Double Solitaire, 1971; author of the films, Tea and Sympathy, Until They Sail, The Nun's Story, The Sand Pebbles, I Never Sang for My Father; for television has adapted several plays, including Biography, The Old Lady Shows Her Medals, etc, as well as written various original works; author of the novels After, 1973; Getting Up and Going Home, 1978; member of the Playwrights Company 1953–60, formerly President of the New Dramatists Committee; member of the Council and past President, Dramatists Guild.

Clubs: Harvard, The Century Association, Coffee House.
Address: Roybury, Connecticut.

ANDERSON, Rona, actress
b Edinburgh, 3 Aug 1928; *d* of James Anderson and his wife Evelyn (Thomson); *e* Edinburgh and Ottawa; *m* Gordon Jackson. Trained for the stage at the Glover Turner-Robertson School, Edinburgh.

First appeared at the Garrison Theatre, Salisbury, Apr 1945, as Bennet in Peg O' My Heart; played leading parts, 1945–9, with Glasgow Citizens' Theatre; Edinburgh Festival, 1950, played Venus in The Queen's Comedy; first appeared in London at the Piccadilly, 11 Oct 1951, as Angela in The White Sheep of the Family; Phoenix, Sept 1953, played Joan in Bruno and Sidney; toured, Mar 1955, as Sabrina in Sabrina Fair; toured, Sept 1955, as Mary in All for Mary; Cambridge, May 1957, played Sarah Sylvester in A Month of Sundays; Theatre Royal, Windsor, Oct 1958, played Mary Tufnell in Once A Rake; Garrick, Jan 1968, took over Liz in Let Sleeping Wives Lie; Royal Court, Apr 1973, played Mrs West in Savages, transferring to the Comedy, June 1973; Mermaid, Mar 1978, Mrs Boyle in Whose Life Is It Anyway?, transferring to the Savoy, June 1978; has appeared in numerous films since 1948.

Address: c/o Al Parker, Ltd, 50 Mount Street, London W1.

ANDREWS, Dana, actor
b Collins, Mississippi, 1 Jan 1912; *s* of Charles Forrest Andrews and his wife Annis (Speed); *e* Sam Houston State College, Texas; *m* (1) Janet Murray (dec); (2) Mary Todd; formerly an accountant; prepared for the stage at the Pasadena (California) Playhouse and studied vocal training with Isadore Braggiotti and Florence Russell.

First appeared on the stage at the Pasadena Playhouse, June 1935, as the Frenchman in Cymbeline; toured New England in the summer of 1952 as Tom in The Glass Menagerie; first appeared on Broadway at the Booth, 30 June 1958, when he took over the role of Jerry Ryan in Two for the Seesaw; Playhouse, Jan 1962, played Richard Kohner in The Captains and the Kings; Royal Poinciana Playhouse, Palm Beach, Florida, Feb 1965, Sir Thomas More in A Man for All Seasons and subsequently at the Papermill Playhouse, Milburn, New Jersey; toured, Aug 1965, as Kenneth Higman in A Remedy for Winter; Sombrero Playhouse, Phoenix, Arizona, 1966, Julian Armstone in Calculated Risk; toured the US, 1967–8, as Oscar Madison in The Odd Couple; Bucks County Playhouse, New Hope, Pa, Aug 1971, appeared in Child's Play; Little, Albuquerque, New Mexico, Oct 1971, played Sam Nash, Jesse Kiplinger, and Roy Hubley in Plaza Suite; Golden Palace, Arlington, Texas, Aug 1972, played in Marriage-Go-Round; toured, 1972, in Conflict of Interest; Bucks County Playhouse, 1972–3 season, played Stage Manager in Our Town; made his début in England at the Thorndike, Surrey, playing the same part in Our Town when that production changed places with the Thorndike production of The Rivals; Royal Poinciana Playhouse, Palm Beach, Fla, Jan 1975, played Gil in Janus; toured Jan–Apr 1976 in Together Tonight; first appeared in films in 1939 and has since played in Swamp Water, The Ox-Bow Incident, Tobacco Road, Boomerang, The Best Years of Our Lives, Innocent Bystanders (1973), The Last Tycoon (1975), etc; first appeared on television on 20 Mar 1958, in the drama The Right-Hand Man; Vice President of the Screen Actors' Guild, 1957–63, and President 1964–5.

Recreations: Photography and sailing. *Address:* 4238 Beeman Ave, Studio City, California, 91604.

ANDREWS, Harry, CBE, actor
b Tonbridge, Kent, 10 Nov 1911; *s* of Henry Arthur Andrews and his wife Amy Diana Frances (Horner); *e* Wrekin College.

Made his first appearance on the stage at the Liverpool Playhouse, Sept 1933, as John in The Long Christmas Dinner; made his first appearance on the London stage at the St James's Theatre, 26 Mar 1935, as John in Worse Things Happen at Sea; Whitehall, May 1935, played Christopher in Snow in Summer; at the New Theatre, July, 1935, the Lion in Noah; Oct 1935, Abraham and the Captain in Romeo and Juliet, subsequently playing Tybalt; he made his first appearance in New York at the Empire Theatre, Oct 1936, as Horatio in Hamlet; at the Queen's, London, May 1937, played Francis in He was Born Gay; Lyric, June 1937, the Queen's gentleman in Victoria Regina: Queen's Sept 1937 to Apr 1938, appeared in John Gielgud's company in Richard II, The School for Scandal, Three Sisters, and The Merchant of Venice; Westminster, Sept 1938, Diomedes in Troilus and Cressida; Old Vic, Dec 1938, Demetrius in A Midsummer Night's Dream; Garrick, Jan 1939, Charlie Glover in Hundreds and Thousands; Globe, Mar 1939, John in We at the Cross Roads; Lyceum, June, 1939, Laertes in Hamlet, the last performance given at that theatre, and subsequently played the same part at Elsinore; during the second World War, served from Oct 1939 to Oct 1945, with the Royal Artillery, 15th Scottish Division; re-appeared on the stage at the New Theatre, with the Old Vic company, Dec 1945, succeeding George Curzon in the parts of Sir Walter Blunt in Henry IV (Part I), Scroop in Henry IV (Part II), Creon in Oedipus and Sneer in The Critic; he also went with the company to New York, appearing at the Century Theatre, May–June 1946, in the same parts; on his return to England, appeared at the New Theatre, with the Old Vic company, from Sept 1946 to the end of the 1948–9 season, during which period he played Cornwall in King Lear; Gerald Croft in An Inspector Calls; De Castel-Jaloux in Cyrano de Bergerac, Bolingbroke in Richard II, Hortensio in The Taming of the Shrew, Earl of Warwick in St Joan, Osip in The Government Inspector, Tullus Aufidius in Coriolanus, Orsino in Twelfth Night, Lucifer in Dr Faustus, Mirabel in The Way of the World and Epihodov in The Cherry Orchard; joined the company of the Memorial Theatre, Stratford-on-Avon, Apr 1949, playing Macduff in Macbeth; Don Pedro in Much Ado About Nothing, Theseus in A Midsummer Night's Dream, Pisanio in Cymbeline, Cardinal Wolsey in King Henry VIII; toured Australia with the company, 1949, and on his return, during the 1950 season at Stratford-on-Avon, played Vincentio in Measure for Measure, Brutus in Julius Caesar, Edgar in King Lear, and Benedick in Much Ado About Nothing; remained with the company for the 1951 season, appearing as Bolingbroke (Henry IV); at the end of the year went to NY with Sir Laurence Olivier's Company, appearing at the Ziegfeld, Dec 1951, as Lucius Septimus in Caesar and Cleopatra, and Enobarbus in Antony and Cleopatra; returned to the Shakespeare Memorial Theatre Company for the 1953 season, appearing as Antonio in The Merchant of Venice, Buckingham in Richard III, Enobarbus in Antony and Cleopatra, and Kent in King Lear; appeared with this company at the Princes, London, Nov 1953, as Enobarbus in Antony and Cleopatra; subsequently touring Europe in the same part; again appeared with the Shakespeare Memorial Theatre Company, 1956 season, as Claudius in Hamlet, in the title part of Othello, and as Don Adriano de Armado in Love's Labour's Lost; Phoenix, Apr 1957, played Casanova in Camino Real; Old Vic, May 1958, played the title part in Henry VIII, subsequently appearing in the same production in Paris, Antwerp, and Brussels; Shakespeare Memorial Theatre, July 1959, played Menenius in Coriolanus; Haymarket, May 1960, General Allenby in Ross; Phoenix, May 1962, played Robert Rockhart in The Lizard on the Rock; at the same theatre, Feb 1963, played Ekart in Baal; Haymarket, Jan 1966, Crampton in You Never Can Tell; Royal Court, Sept 1971, played Lear in Edward Bond's play; Haymarket, July 1978, Ivan Kilner in A Family; first appeared in films, 1952, in The Red Beret; subsequent films include The Hill, Entertaining Mr Sloane, The Prince and the Pauper, Equus, etc; TV includes the series *Clayhanger* and recently, Tolstoy in A Question of Faith.

Favourite parts: Bolingbroke, Enobarbus, Brutus, Buckingham in Richard III, The Duke in Measure For Measure, and Kent in King Lear. *Recreations:* Cricket, sailing, tennis, riding and gardening. *Address:* Church Farm Oasts, Salehurst, Robertsbridge, Sussex. *Tel:* Robertsbridge 880429.

ANDREWS, Julie, actress and singer
b London, 1 Oct 1935; *d* of Edward Wells and his wife Barbara (Morris); *e* Beckenham, Kent; *m* (1) the stage designer Tony Walton (mar dis); (2) the film producer Blake Edwards; studied singing under her step-father Ted Andrews, and also with Madame Stiles-Allen.

Made her first appearance on the stage at the London Hippodrome, 23 Oct 1947, singing operatic arias in the *revue* Starlight Roof; she was chosen to appear at the Royal Command Performance, at the Palladium, 1 Nov 1948; at the Casino, Dec 1948, played Humpty Dumpty in the pantomime of that name; Theatre Royal, Nottingham, Dec 1950, Red Riding Hood in the pantomime; Casino, London, Dec 1951, Princess Balroulbadour in Aladdin; Coventry Hippodrome, Dec 1952, appeared in Jack and the Beanstalk; London Palladium, Dec 1953, appeared as Cinderella in that pantomime; Royal Court, Liverpool, May 1954, played Becky Dunbar in Mountain Fire; made her first appearance on the New York stage at the Royale, 30 Sept 1954, as Polly in The Boy Friend, which she played for over a year; Shubert, New Haven, Conn, Feb 1956, created the part of Eliza Doolittle in My Fair Lady, subsequently appearing at the Mark Hellinger, NY, Mar 1956, and playing in that production for two years; Drury Lane, Apr 1958, opened in the same part in the London production, and remained in the cast until Aug 1959; Majestic, New York, Dec 1960, played Guinevere in Camelot; has since appeared in a solo show at the London Palladium Jun 1976, etc; starred in her first film Mary Poppins, 1963, for which she received the Film Academy Award, 1965; subsequent films include: The Sound of Music, Star, Thoroughly Modern Millie and 10; has also appeared on television in London and New York, including *The Julie Andrews Show*; author (as Julie Andrews Edwards) of Mandy, 1971, and The Last of the Really Great Whangdoodles, 1973.

Address: c/o Chasin-Park-Citron Agency, 9255 Sunset Boulevard, Los Angeles, CA 90069.

ANDREWS, Nancy, actress and singer
b Minneapolis, Minnesota, 16 Dec 1924; *d* of James Currier Andrews and his wife Grace Ella (Gerrish); *e* Beverley Hills (California) High School and Los Angeles City College; *m* Parke N Bossart (mar dis).

Formerly a singer and pianist in cabaret, and toured with USO shows 1943–5; prepared for the stage at the Pasadena Playhouse, and at the American Shakespeare Academy; first appeared on the stage at the Beverley Hills Shakespeare Theatre in 1938, alternating as Mistress Page and Mistress Ford in The Merry Wives of Windsor; made her New York stage début at the Broadhurst, Oct 1949, in the revue Touch and Go; toured California in 1950 as Dorothy in Gentlemen Prefer Blondes; Imperial, Oct 1950, was stand-by for Ethel Merman in Call Me Madam; Mark Hellinger, May 1953, took over the role of Laura Carew in Hazel Flagg; La Cienega Playhouse, Los Angeles, Jan 1954, played Sister Bessie in Tobacco Road; toured Europe, Mar–Aug 1954, in the one-woman show Songs and Laughter; Mark Hellinger, Jan 1955, Emma Miller in Plain and Fancy, touring in this role in the spring of 1956; Shubert, June 1956, took over the role of Fauna from Helen Traubel in Pipe Dream; Winter Garden, Mar 1959, played Mrs Brady in Juno; Theatre de Lys, off-Broadway, at various times from Dec 1959, to Mar 1961, played Mrs Peachum in The Threepenny Opera; 46th Street, Apr 1960, Auntie in Christine; Cherry Lane, Feb 1961, Mother Cadman, Madame Spig-Eye, and Irish Washer-woman in The Tiger Rag; toured Mar–Sept 1961, as Madame Liang in Flower Drum Song; Orpheum, Dec 1961, played the title-role in Madame Aphrodite; Lunt-Fontanne, Nov 1962, Belle Poitrine, in Little Me, subsequently touring the USA and Canada in this role, Jan–Aug 1964; Theatre Four, off-Broadway, Nov 1964, Mrs Mister in The Cradle Will Rock; Jan Hus Playhouse, Jan 1965, Mrs Bailie in Say Nothing; toured, 1965, in Little Me; toured US, Oct 1965–Oct 1966, as Mrs Brice in Funny Girl; Gate, Dublin, Aug–Sept 1969, Inez in In the Summer House, for the Dublin International Theatre Festival; Provincetown Playhouse, Apr 1970, Peggy Monash in How Much, How Much?; Alhambra, Jacksonville, Florida, Sept 1970, Sister Bessie in Tobacco Road; Starlight, Kansas City, Mo, St Louis Municipal Opera and Dallas, Texas, State Music Fair, July 1971, appeared in 70 Girls 70 and as Esther in Two by Two; Bergen, NJ, Mall Playhouse, 1975, Mme Armfeldt in A Little Night Music; Jones Beach, NY, June 1975, Aunt Eller in Oklahoma!; Goodspeed Opera House, East Haddam, Conn, May 1976, Mrs Murray in Dearest Enemy; Wilbur, Boston, Apr 1978, Lil in Broadway; since 1950 has made numerous summer stock appearances, notably as Nicki in Break It Up, Julie in Show Boat, Mrs Sally Adams in Call Me Madam, Lavinia in Hit the Deck, Ruth in Plain and Fancy, the title-role of Panama Hattie, Grace in Bus Stop, Mrs Livingstone in Happy Hunting, Mother Grieg in Song of Norway, Amanda in The Glass Menagerie, Bloody Mary in South Pacific, Helen in A Taste of Honey, Emma in Look Out, Sailor, Marian Hollender in Don't Drink the Water, Aunt Eller in Oklahoma, 1977, Miss Tweed in Something's Afoot, 1978; first appeared in London in Cabaret at the Embassy Club in 1951, and in the one-woman show Songs and Laughter, at the Colony Club, 1954; appeared in the films Werewolf of Washington, Summer Wishes, Winter Drama, W.W. and the Dixie Dance Kings, The Night of the Juggler (1978), etc; has appeared frequently on television since 1950 in *The Ed Sullivan Show, The Perry Como Show, Dinah's Diner*, etc; wrote the music and lyrics for Bright Champagne, which was produced at the Melrose Theatre, Los Angeles, in 1943; wrote much of her own material for cabaret in the USA and abroad; member of the Board of Directors of Veteran's Hospital Radio and Television Guild; member, Events Committee of National Academy of Television Arts and Sciences; member, Membership Committee, AFTRA.

Favourite parts: Belle Poitrine, Sister Bessie, and Amanda. *Recreations:* Archaeology, painting, and writing. *Address:* 1766 N Orange Grove, Hollywood, Calif 90046.

ANGERS, Avril, actress and singer
b Liverpool, 18 Apr 1922; *d* of Harry Angers and his wife Lillian Erroll (Woods); *e* in various schools in England and Australia.

Made her first appearance in a concert party, at the Palace Pier, Brighton, 1936; at the Alexandra Theatre, Birmingham, Xmas, 1936, appeared as Cinderella; engaged in light concert work from 1937–44; in 1940, was with The Fol-de-Rols, and was then with ENSA for five years (holder of the Africa Star); broadcast with the BBC, from May 1944; made her first appearance on the West End stage at the Palace, 10 Aug 1944, in the revue, Keep Going; Winter Garden, Mar 1945, appeared in The Gaieties; Duchess, Mar 1946, in Make it a Date; appeared as Guest Artist at the Connaught Theatre, Worthing, 1949, playing Miss Prue in Love for Love, and the title-rôle in Jeannie; at Hayes, Oct 1949, appeared as Madeleine in Don't Listen Ladies; Connaught, Worthing, Nov 1949, as Adeline in Sugar Plum; Gaiety, Douglas, IOM, 1950, as Billie Dawn in Born Yesterday; Strand, Nov 1951, played Dolores in Mary Had a Little . . .; New, Bromley, Mar 1952, Susan Ray in Susan; Wimbledon, Dec, 1953, appeared as Robinson Crusoe; Pleasure Gardens, Folkestone, Dec 1955, again played Robinson Crusoe; Richmond, May 1958, Belle in The Gypsy Warned Me; Lyric, Hammersmith, Feb 1960, Mrs Webster in The Night Life of the Virile Potato; appeared at the Tivoli Theatres, Melbourne and Sydney, Australia, May–Oct 1962, in the revue Paris By Night; Lyceum, Edinburgh, Apr 1964, played Mrs Piper in Busybody; Alhambra, Bradford, Aug 1964, Amy Holroyd in This is Your Wife; Cambridge, London, Nov 1964, played Miss Poitrine in Little Me; Belgrade, Coventry, Aug 1966, Madame Arcati in Blithe Spirit; Alexandra, Birmingham, Apr 1967, played Harriet Humphrey in I'll Get My Man; Derby Playhouse, 1967, Grace Winslow in The Winslow Boy and Mrs Candour in School for Scandal (also Richmond, Yorks); appeared as the Mother in Barefoot in the Park, Guernsey, Sept 1968, and at the Phoenix, Leicester, Aug 1969; Hippodrome, Bristol, Dec 1968, a wicked sister in Cinderella; Watford, Jan 1970, played Mrs Rogers in The Au Pair Man; Pier Theatre, Bournemouth, summer 1971, played Mrs Finney in The Mating Game; Princess, Torquay, Christmas 1971, Dame in Goldilocks; again appeared as Mrs Finney in The Mating Game, Apollo, June 1972; Vaudeville, Dec 1973, appeared in Cockie; toured S Africa, 1974, as Sylvia Bennett in Not in the Book; Phoenix, Apr 1975, Beatrice Charlton in Norman, Is That You?; Billingham, 1975, Eleanor Hunter in No Sex, Please, We're British, Strand, 1975, followed by a tour of See How They Run, playing Miss Skillon; Croydon, Dec 1975, Fairy Queen in Cinderella; Savoy, Mar 1976, took over miss Marple in Murder at the Vicarage; Birmingham Rep, Sept 1978, Mrs Hardcastle in She Stoops to Conquer; toured UK, 1979, as Mme Arcati in Blithe Spirit, followed by tour of Middle and Far East as Miss Smythe in Move Over Mrs Markham; recent pantomime appearances include Richmond, 1977, Bath, 1978, and Eastbourne, 1979; has appeared in cabaret since 1946; has appeared in many radio programmes and on television, in her own series Dear Dotty, Looks Familiar, *The Les Dawson Show, Are You Being Served?*, etc; appeared in the film Skimpy in the Navy, 1950, and has since made numerous pictures including The Green Man, The Family Way, Staircase, A Girl in My Soup, etc.

Hobbies: Cooking and do it yourself. *Recreations:* Swimming, sailing, films, theatre, and TV. *Club:* Arts. *Address:* 12 James Street, London, WC2.

ANGLIM, Philip, actor
b San Francisco, 11 Feb 1953; *e* Yale University (BA).

Made his stage debut at the Yale Theatre, 1970, as Rosencrantz in Rosencrantz and Guildenstern Are Dead; played various roles at the Southbury Playhouse, season

1972; at the Cincinnati Playhouse in the Park, season 1975–76, appeared in What the Butler Saw and The Contrast; American Place, 1976, played Kevin in Donald Barthelme's Snow White; Berkshire Theatre, Stockbridge, Mass, season 1977, Geoffrey in The Lion in Winter; Theatre of St Peter's Church, Jan 1979, John Merrick in The Elephant Man, transferring with the production to the Booth, Apr 1979 and winning several awards for his performance in the role; films include All American Boy, 1970; TV includes The Adams Chronicles, and Tomorrow's Families.

Address: 1160 Fifth Avenue, New York, NY 10029.

ANNALS, Michael, designer
b Harrow, Middx, 21 Apr 1938; *s* of Henry Ernest Annals and his wife Constance Anne (Walter); *e* Harrow Weald County Grammar School and Hornsey College of Art.

First designed the sets and costumes for the Old Vic's production of Macbeth that toured the Soviet Union and its production of Dr Faustus that played at the Edinburgh Festival, 1961; has since designed the sets and costumes for Jackie the Jumper, Saint Joan (Chichester and National Theatre), 1963; Love's Labour's Lost (Bristol), The Royal Hunt of the Sun, Il Tabarro (opera), and Macbeth for the National Theatre of Portugal, 1964; The Chinese Prime Minister, Samson Agonistes (Yvonne Arnaud), The Crucible (National Theatre), and the New York production of The Royal Hunt of the Sun, 1965; A Bond Honoured (National), 1966; Iphigenia in Aulis (New York), Shadowplay (Royal Ballet), Prometheus Bound (Yale University), 1967; Staircase, St Joan, Her First Roman, Morning, Noon, and Night (all NY), The Importance of Being Earnest (London), 1968; H (National), The Satyricon (Stratford, Ontario), The Seagull (Habimah, Tel Aviv), 1969; Beggar on Horseback (NY), 1970; Captain Brassbound's Conversion (London), Hamlet (Prospect Productions), 1971; Long Days Journey into Night (National), 1972; Lorenzaccio (Stratford, Ontario), Richard II (National), Ariadne Auf Naxos (Glyndebourne), The Front Page (National), Macbeth (National), 1973; The Visit of the Old Lady (Glyndebourne), Design For Living, Chez Nous (London), Prodigal Son (London Festival Ballet), Dr Faustus (RSC), 1974; Heartbreak House (National), Shadowplay (American Ballet Theatre), The Clandestine Marriage (London), Engaged (National), 1975; Plunder (National), Frontiers of Farce, The Ghost Train (both London), 1976; Privates on Parade (RSC), Die Schweigsame Frau (Glyndebourne), Pillars of the Community (RSC), The Lady From Maxim's (National), 1977; Barmitzvah Boy (London), 1978; Rookery Nook (London), 1979; in 1966–7 was Associate Professor of Scenic Design at Yale University; film decor includes Joseph Andrews, 1976.

Recreation: Doing nothing. *Address:* 12 Wellington Court, Shelton Street, London, WC2, England. *Tel:* 01–836 1937.

ANOUILH, Jean, dramatic author
b Bordeaux, France, June 23 1907; *e* Collège Chaptal, and University of Paris. *m* (1) Monelle Valentin; (2) Nicole Lançon.

Began his career in the theatre as general assistant to Georges Pitoëff in Paris; author of the following plays: L'Hermine (The Ermine), 1932; Le Bal de Voleurs (Thieves' Carnival), 1932; Mandarine, 1933; Y Avait un Prisonnier, 1935; Le Voyageur sans Bagages (Traveller Without Luggage), 1937; La Sauvage (Restless Heart), 1938; Cavalcade d'Amour, 1941; Le Rendezvous de Senlis (Dinner with the Family), Léocadia (Time Remembered), Eurydice (Point of Departure), 1942; Antigone, 1944; Oreste, 1945; Jézabel, Roméo et Jeannette (Fading Mansion), Médée, 1946; L'Invi-

tation au Château (Ring Round the Moon), 1948; Ardèle ou la Marguerite (Ardele), 1949; La Répétition, ou l'Amour Puni (The Rehearsal), Colombe, 1950; La Valse des Toreadors (The Waltz of the Toreadors), 1952; L'Alouette (The Lark), 1953; Ornifle, 1955; L'Hurluberlu (The Fighting Cock), 1958; Becket, ou l'Honneur de Dieu (Becket), 1959; La Foire d'Empoigne (Catch as Catch Can), 1960; La Grotte (The Cavern), 1961; Poor Bitos, 1963; Le Boulanger, La Boulangère, et Le Petit Mitron, Cher Antoine (Dear Antoine), Les Poissons Rouges, 1969; Ne Reveillez pas Madame, 1970; Tu Etais Si Gentil quand tu Etais Petit, 1971; Le Directeur de L'Opèra, 1972; L'Arrestation, 1975; The Scenario, 1976; films include: Monsieur Vincent, and Pattes Blanches.

Address: c/o Dr Jan van Loewen Ltd, 81/83 Shaftesbury Avenue, London, W1.

ANTHONY, Joseph (*né* Deuster), actor and director
b Milwaukee, Wisconsin, 24 May 1912; *s* of Leonard Deuster and his wife Sophie (Hertz); *e* University of Wisconsin; *m* Perry Wilson; prepared for the stage at the Pasadena Playhouse, 1931–5, and at the Daykarhanova School, 1935–7.

Made his professional début as Rizzio in a West Coast production of Mary of Scotland, 1935, and his New York début with the Federal Theatre Project Company at Daly's 63rd Street Theatre, Apr 1937, as Rolf Mamlock in Professor Mamlock; at the same theatre, June 1938, played David Chavender in On the Rocks; Alvin, 1941, appeared in Lady in the Dark; Shubert, Feb 1941, appeared in Liberty Jones; dance partner to Agnes de Mille, 1941–2; served in the US Army 1942–6; reappeared on Broadway at the Belasco, Feb 1946, under the name Joseph Adams as the Second Man in Truckline Cafe; at the Peterborough, NH, Playhouse, 1947, directed his play Return at Night; Maxine Elliott, Jan 1948, under the name Joseph Anthony, played Richters in Skipper Next to God; Brighton Beach, Apr 1949, Rothschild in Exodus; ANTA, NY, Feb 1951, Solveig's Father and Dr Begriffenfeld in Peer Gynt; Lyceum, 1951, took over the role of Paul Unger in The Country Girl; Music Box, Mar 1952, played Ghoulos in Flight into Egypt; National, Mar 1953, Casanova, A Gentleman of Fortune in Camino Real; Lyceum, Dec 1954, played Prince Bounine in Anastasia; made his NY début as director at the Maxine Elliott, Apr 1948, when he staged Celebration; he has since directed the following plays: Bullfight, The Rainmaker, 1954; Once upon a Tailor, The Lark, 1955; The Most Happy Fella, 1956; A Clearing in the Woods, Maiden Voyage, 1957; Winesburg, Ohio, The Marriage-Go-Round, 1958; The Pink Jungle, 1959; The Best Man, Under the Yum-Yum Tree, 1960; Rhinoceros, Mary, Mary, 1961; The Captain and the Kings, Romulus, 1962; The Dragon, 110 in the Shade, Mary, Mary (London), 1963; The Chinese Prime Minister, The Last Analysis, Slow Dance on the Killing Ground, 1964; The Taming of the Shrew (Stratford, Conn), Mrs Dally, The Playroom, 1965; Happily Never After, Falstaff (Stratford, Conn), 1966; Week-end, The Homecoming (Guthrie, Minneapolis), 1968; Jimmy, 1969; Finishing Touches, 1973; founder member of the American Actors Co, 1937, and directed for it Indiana Sketches, Saturday Night, Minnie Fields, Roadside, and short plays by Horton Foote; teacher at the American Theatre Wing, 1947, and has also taught at Vassar College, Hunter College, and NY University, and is currently (1976) Professor of Theatre Arts at the State University of New York, Purchase, NY; member of the Actors Studio; Member of the Council of Actors Equity Association; Member of the Board of the Screen Directors Guild; elected first President of the Society of Stage Directors and Choreographers; appeared in the films, Hat, Coat, and Glove (1934), She (1935), Joe Smith, American, and Shadow of the Thin Man; since 1956, has directed the following films: The Rainmaker, The Matchmaker, Career, All in a Night's Work, Captive City (Italy, 1963), Tomorrow (1972) etc; first appeared on television, 1940, and appeared regularly in dramatic television programs, 1947–54; directed episodes of the television series *Brenner*, Profiles in Courage, and his play Return at Night was produced on *Lights Out*, 1953.

Recreations: Gardening and landscaping. *Address:* Winding Road Farm, Ardsley, NY. *Tel:* OW 3–3099.

ANTOON, A J, director
b Lawrence, Mass, 7 Dec 1944; *s* of Alfred J Anton, Sr, and his wife Josephine (Saba); *e* Boston College.

Directed his first production, Story Theatre from Chekhov and Tolstoy, at St Clement's, New York, Aug 1971; began his relationship with the New York Shakespeare Festival Theatre when he directed Subject to Fits at the Public, 14 Feb 1971; made his London directorial début on 24 Oct 1971, at the Place, when he directed The Royal Shakespeare Company in Subject to Fits; Delacorte, NY, Aug 1971, directed The Tale of Cymbeline; directed both the off-Broadway and Broadway productions of That Championship Season, for which he received the Antoinette Perry (Tony) Award, and of Much Ado About Nothing, 1972; directed The Good Doctor, 1973; The Dance of Death, That Championship Season (Garrick, London), 1974; Trelawny of the 'Wells', 1975; Nasty Rumours and Final Remarks, The Art of Dining, 1979; directed the television production of Much Ado About Nothing, 1972.

Address: c/o Richard Rosenthal, Esq, 425 Park Avenue New York, NY 10022. *Tel:* 758–0809.

ANTROBUS, John, dramatic author
b Aldershot, 2 July 1933; *e* King Edward VII Nautical College and Sandhurst; *m* Margaret McCormick.

Author of the following pieces: The Bed-Sitting Room (with Spike Milligan, with whom he directed and designed the London production at the Mermaid, Jan 1963, and Duke of York's, Mar 1963); The Royal Commission Revue, 1964; You'll Come to Love Your Sperm Test (which he directed at Hampstead, Jan 1965, playing three parts); The Bed-Sitting Room (revised version), 1966; Trixie and Baba, 1968; Captain Oates' Left Sock, 1969; The Looneys, 1971; Crete and Sergeant Pepper, 1972; Why Bournemouth? and other short plays, 1973; Mrs Grabowski's Academy, 1974; Royal Court, Oct 1969, played Glendenning in The Contractor, transferring with the production to the Fortune, Apr 1970; scripted the film of The Bed-Sitting Room, and has written radio scripts including *The Goon Show.*

Address: c/o Blanche Marvin, 21a St John's Wood High Street, London, NW8.

ARDEN, Eve, actress and singer (*née* Eunice Quedens)
b Mill Valley, Calif, 30 Apr 1912; *d* of Charles Peter Quedens and his wife Lucille (Frank); *e* Mill Valley Grammar School and Tamalpais High School; *m* (1) Edward G Bergen (mar dis); (2) Brooks West; after leaving school joined the Henry Duffy Stock Company, at the Alcazar Theatre, San Francisco, 1928, and remained there eighteen months.

Subsequently appeared at the Pasadena Playhouse, in Low and Behold; toured with the Bandbox Repertory Co, 1933, as Matilda in On Approval and Amanda Prynne in Private Lives; was then engaged by Florenz Ziegfeld and made her first appearance in New York, at the Winter Garden, 4 Jan 1934, in The Ziegfeld Follies; Guild Theatre, May 1935, appeared in Parade; Winter Garden, Jan 1936, in The Ziegfeld Follies; Alvin, Nov 1939, played Winnie Spofford in Very Warm for May; Booth, Feb 1940, appeared in Two for the Show; Imperial, Oct 1941, played Maggie Watson in Let's Face It; in summer theatres, 1950, played Paula Wharton in Over 21; at Olney, Md, June 1951, played Mary Hilliard in Here To-day; toured West Coast in the title-role of Auntie Mame 1958; toured, 1960, as Charlie in Goodbye, Charlie; toured, 1965, in Beekman Place; Shubert (Chicago), June 1966, took over from Carol Channing as Dolly Gallagher Levi in Hello, Dolly!; Atlanta Municipal, Atlanta, Ga, Feb 1967, played Mrs Banks in Barefoot in the Park; Coconut Grove Playhouse, Miami, Fla, 1968, Stephanie in Cactus Flower; Huntington Hartford, Los Angeles, Cal, May 1970, Mrs Baker in Butterflies Are Free, and subsequently toured in Chicago in this part; toured, summer 1971, as Jessica Brandenburg in Natural Ingredients; off-Broadway, San Diego, Cal, Apr 1973, played in Under Papa's Picture; Ahmanson, Los Angeles, Feb 1978, Marion in Absurb Person Singular; first appeared in films, 1937, in Oh, Doctor and has since appeared in numerous pictures, including: Stage Door, The Women, Let's Face It, Voice of the Turtle, Anatomy of a Murder, etc; since 1948 has achieved great popularity by her radio and television comedy feature *Our Miss Brooks*, 1948–56, *The Eve Arden Show*, 1957, and her television series *The Mothers-in-Law*, 1967–70.

ARDEN, John, dramatic author
b Barnsley, Yorkshire, 26 Oct 1930; *s* of Charles Alwyn Arden and his wife Annie Elizabeth (Layland); *e* Sedbergh School, King's College, Cambridge, and Edinburgh College of Art; *m* Margaretta D'Arcy.

Formerly an architectural assistant; author of the following plays: All Fall Down, 1955; The Waters of Babylon, 1957; Live Like Pigs, When is a Door Not a Door? (one-act), 1958; Serjeant Musgrave's Dance, 1959; The Workhouse Donkey (Chichester Festival), Ironhand (Bristol Old Vic), 1963; Armstrong's Last Goodnight (Glasgow Citizens'), 1964; Left Handed Liberty, 1965; Squire Jonathan (one-act) 1968; the Soldier's Tale (translation) 1968; in collaboration with Margaretta D'Arcy has written The Happy Haven and The Business of Good Government, 1960; Ars Longa, Vita Brevis, 1964; The Royal Pardon, 1966; The Hero Rises Up, 1968; Harold Muggins is a Martyr (with others), 1969; The Ballygombeen Bequest and The Island of the Mighty (RSC), 1972; The Non-Stop Connolly Show, 1975; The Little Gray House in the West, Vandaleur's Folly, 1978; is the author of the radio plays Life of a Man and The Bagman and the TV plays Soldier, Soldier and Wet Fish.

Recreations: Antiquarianism and architecture. *Address:* Illaun Faddabeg Island, off Ard Point, Oughterard, Co. Galway, Eire.

ARGENT, Edward, educator
b London, 21 Aug 1931; *s* of Albert Arthur Argent and his wife Clara Beatrice; *e* Mercers School; *m* Christine Tuck; trained for the stage at RADA.

Made his first stage appearance on tour, 1954, as Orderly in The Hasty Heart; first London appearance, Phoenix, 8 Apr 1957, as a Guard in Camino Real; after a stage career including various roles with the Royal Shakespeare Company, 1960–62, a season as actor and director at the White Rose, Harrogate, 1963, and various roles at the Mermaid, season 1964, taught at the Guildhall School of Music and Drama and the Webber-Douglas Academy, 1962–70; from 1970–73 Head of School of Theatre, Manchester Polytechnic; appointed Director, School of Drama, Royal Scottish Academy of Music and Drama, 1974– ; Chairman, Com-

mittee of Heads of Drama Departments in Scotland; Fellow of the Guildhall School of Music and Drama.
Address: RSAMD, St George's Place, Glasgow G2 1BS. *Tel:* 041-332 5294.

ARKIN, Alan, actor and director
b New York City, 26 Mar 1934; *s* of David Arkin and his wife Beatrice; *e* Los Angeles City College, Los Angeles State College and Bennington College; *m* Barbara Dana.
Made his professional début with the Compass Players at the Crystal Palace, St Louis, Missouri, 1959, in improvisations; later joined the Second City group, Chicago, 1960, also in improvisatory theatre; made his NY début at the Royale, 26 Sept 1961, in the revue From the Second City; Cricket, Apr 1962, appeared in Man Out Loud, Girl Quiet, for which he also composed the music; Henry Miller's, Mar 1963, played David Kolovitz in Enter Laughing, for which he received the Antoinette Perry (Tony) Award and *Variety's* New York Drama Critics Poll; toured Mar–May 1964, in Enter Laughing; Second City at Square East, Aug 1964, appeared in the revue A View from Under the Bridge, to which he also contributed sketches, music, lyrics, and photographic slides; Booth, Nov 1964, Harry Berlin in Luv; toured, summer 1972, as Alvin Gold in The Opening; first directed some of the revue material he has performed, and his first direction of a legitimate play was for Eh? at the Circle in the Square, Oct 1966; has since directed Hail Scrawdyke! 1966; Little Murders, 1969; The White House Murder Case, 1970; The Sunshine Boys, 1972; Molly, 1973; Joan of Lorraine, 1974; the double-bill of Rubbers and Yanks 3 Detroit O Top of the Seventh, 1975; The Soft Touch (Boston), 1975; Joan of Lorraine (Hartman, Stanford), 1976; first appeared in films in The Russians Are Coming, The Russians Are Coming, 1966, and since has played in Woman Times Seven, 1967, Catch 22, 1970, Last of the Red Hot Lovers, 1972, etc; first appeared on television in 1962 on the *David Susskind Show.*

ARLEN, Harold (*né* Hyman Arluck), composer
b Buffalo, New York, 15 Feb 1905; *s* of Samuel Arluck and his wife Celia (Orlin); *e* Hutchinson Central High School, Buffalo; *m* Anya Taranda.
Formerly a cabaret pianist, jazz performer and arranger, and singer; his first work in the legitimate theatre was at the Apollo, July 1928, as rehearsal pianist and intermission singer for George White's Scandals, and, at the Cosmopolitan, Oct 1929, for Great Day; his first song for a Broadway musical was Get Happy, which was sung by Ruth Etting in The 9:15 Revue in Feb 1930; since then has composed the music for Earl Carroll's Vanities, 1930; eight separate productions of the Cotton Club Parade revues, 1930–4; You Said It (his first complete score), 1931; Earl Carroll's Vanities Americana, The Great Magoo, 1932; George White's Music Hall Varieties, 1933; Life Begins at 8:40, 1934; The Show Is On, 1936; Hooray for What? 1937; Cabin in the Sky, 1940; Bloomer Girl, 1944; Saint Louis Woman, 1946; House of Flowers, 1954; Jamaica, 1957; Saratoga, 1959; expanded Saint Louis Woman into an opera entitled Free and Easy, which was produced at the Carré, Amsterdam, in Dec 1959; The Harold Arlen Songbook, 1967; House of Flowers (revised), The Wizard of Oz (puppet version of the film), 1968; The Wizard of Oz produced as a pantomime at the Victoria Palace, London, 26 Dec 1972; toured in vaudeville performing his material in 1932–3; first composed for films the song It's Only a Paper Moon, for Take a Chance, 1933, and has since composed the scores for Let's Fall in Love, 1934; Strike Me Pink, The Singing Kid, Stage Struck, Gold Diggers of 1937, 1936; Artists and Models, 1937; Love Affair, The Wizard of

Oz, At the Circus, 1939; Blues in the Night, 1941; Captains of the Clouds, Rio Rita, Star Spangled Rhythm, 1942; Cabin in the Sky, The Sky's the Limit, They Got Me Covered, 1943; Up in Arms, Kismet, Here Come the Waves, 1944; Out of This World, 1945; Casbah, 1948; My Blue Heaven, The Petty Girl, 1950; Mr Imperium, 1951; Down Among the Sheltering Palms, The Farmer Takes a Wife, A Star Is Born, 1954; Gay Purr-ee, 1962; I Could Go On Singing, 1963; Happy with the Blues, a compilation based on his music, presented at the Manhattan Theatre Club Cabaret, May 1978; composed the scores for the television productions Happy with the Blues, 1962, and The Songs of Harold Arlen, 1964; has also composed concert works, notably Minor Graff, 1926; Mood in Six Minutes, 1935; American Minuet, 1939; American Negro Suite, 1940; Blues Opera, 1958–9; Ode, and Bon-Bon, 1960; received the Academy Award for Over the Rainbow from The Wizard of Oz; received *Variety's* New York Drama Critics Poll for House of Flowers.
Recreations: Painting and photography. *Address:* ASCAP, Lincoln Plaza, New York, NY 10023.

ARNATT, John, actor
b Petrograd, 9 May 1917; *s* of Francis Arnatt and his wife Ethel Marion (Jephcott); *e* Epworth College, Rhyl; *m* (1) Betty Huntley-Wright (mar dis); (2) Sheila Tracy.
Studied for the stage at RADA, and made his first appearance at the Arts, 9 May 1936, as Roy Wells in Little Ol' Boy; in 1937 toured as Roger in George and Margaret; at the Adelphi, May 1938, appeared in the revue Happy Returns; subsequently appeared in repertory, 1938–9, at Sheffield, Edinburgh and Glasgow; served in RE and RA during the war; further appearances in repertory, 1946–7, at Kettering and Liverpool; at the King's, Hammersmith, May 1947, played John Neilson in Fly Away Peter, and appeared in this part at the St James's in Aug 1947; in 1949 produced tour of My Mother Said; during 1951–2 was again engaged in repertory, and also appeared as comedian at the Windmill Theatre; at the Arts, Apr 1953, played Dorn in The Seagull; subsequently played Richard Plantagenet in the Birmingham Repertory Company's production of Henry VI, Parts I, II, and III, and in July 1953, appeared in the same part at the Old Vic; with the Bristol Old Vic, played Leonid Gayev in The Cherry Orchard; at the Q, Dec 1953, appeared as John Wilding in No Other Verdict, and played this part at the Duchess, Jan 1954; St Martin's, Sept 1954, Victor Ledwood in The Pet Shop; Q, Oct 1954, Det-Insp Peters in The Case of Dr Ambrose; Q, Dec 1954, David Etheridge in Portrait of a Woman; Strand, June 1957, Lt-Col Stewart in The Last Hero (for the Repertory Players); Piccadilly, Oct 1959, Ross Barnett in The Marriage-Go-Round; Vaudeville, Sept 1960, played Tom Atwood in Horses in Mid-Stream; Apollo, Nov 1960, played Inspector Drew in The Little Doctor (Repertory Players'); Pembroke, Croydon, May 1961, Jacques in As You Like it; Lyric, Hammersmith, Nov 1961, played Jones in A Wreath For Udomo; Theatre Royal, Windsor, May 1962, played George Wharton in Ask Me No More; toured, Aug 1964, as Superintendent Neale in Alibi For a Judge; Savoy, Aug 1965, again played Superintendent Neale in Alibi For a Judge; Royal Court, June 1966, played the Boss in Bartleby in a production without décor; Thorndike, Leatherhead, 1967; Mr Bathwick in The Silver Box; Derby, 1969, Mr Crampton in Spring and Port Wine; Queen's, Aug 1970, took over the part of the Doctor in Conduct Unbecoming; Young Vic, Oct 1971, Lord Sidmouth in Cato Street; Open Space, Nov 1974, Count Von Palen in The Snob; Greenwich, July 1975, played Lafeu in All's Well That End's Well and Escalus in Measure for Measure; Marlowe, Canterbury, 1976, Gayev

in The Cherry Orchard; Basingstoke, 1977, Ronald Alexander in Favourites; Newbury, 1977, Dr Sloper in The Heiress; Greenwich, Mar 1978, Francisco and Don Luiz in Don Juan; Crucible, Sheffield, 1978, Balance in The Recruiting Officer; has also made numerous television appearances.

Address: 3 Warren Cottages, Woodland Way, Kingswood, Surrey. *Tel:* 01–604 2190.

ARNAZ, Lucie, actress
b Los Angeles, 17 July, 1951; *d* of Desiderio Alberto (Desi) Arnaz III, the actor/producer; and Lucille Desiree Ball, the actress; *e* Immaculate Heart HS; *m* Philip Menegaux (mar dis); Laurence Luckinbill, actor.

A regular on her parents' TV show *Here's Lucy* at 16, she played in the series for six seasons before making her professional stage debut at the San Bernardino Civic Light Opera, Mar 1972, in Cabaret; played Gittel Mosca in the national tour of Seesaw, 1974–75; Mark Taper Forum, Los Angeles, 1977, Kathy in Vanities; Jones Beach, June 1978, Annie Oakley in Annie Get Your Gun; other summer show appearances include three seasons for John Kenley Theatres, playing leads in Once Upon a Mattress, Li'l Abner, Bye Bye Birdie, etc; made her Broadway debut in They're Playing Our Song, at the Imperial, 11 Feb 1979, as Sonia Walsk, receiving several awards for this performance; films include Billy Jack Goes to Washington, 1977; and The Jazz Singer, 1980; TV, since *Here's Lucy,* includes The Black Dahlia, 1974; her radio show, Tune in with Lucie, was syndicated nationally in the US.

Favourite part: Gittel Mosca. *Recreations:* Songwriting, photography. *Address:* c/o Nathan Golden, 9601 Wiltshire Boulevard, Beverly Hills, CA 90210.

ARNOLD, Tom, MP (*né* Thomas Richard Arnold) producing manager
b London, 25 Jan 1947; *s* of Thomas Charles Arnold (Tom Arnold, the producer) and his wife Helen (Breen); *e* Bedales School, Le Rosey, Switzerland, and Pembroke College, Oxford (MA).

Productions include the annual Christmas ice pantomimes at Wembley Arena, 1969–78; London seasons and provincial tours of Peter Pan, 1971– ; Danny La Rue at the Palace, 1970; The Sunshine Boys, 1975; The King and I, 1979; Member of Parliament for Hazel Grove, 1974– ; member, Society of West End Theatre.

Address: House of Commons, London SW1A 0AA. *Tel:* 01-219 4096.

ARNOTT, James Fullarton, Emeritus Professor of Drama, University of Glasgow
b Glasgow, 29 Apr 1914; *s* of Hezekiah Merricks Arnott and his wife Susie Willock (Fullarton); *e* Ardrossan Academy, Glasgow U (MA), Merton College, Oxford (M Litt), and Peterhouse, Cambridge; *m* Martha Lawrence Grant; studied at the Royal Scottish Academy of Music and Dramatic Art (Fellow).

After teaching at Hull University, taught at Glasgow U from 1939, where he became first Head of Drama Department, 1966; Reader, 1971; Professor of Drama, 1973; major productions he has directed in Glasgow include Murder in the Cathedral, 1952; Love's Labour's Lost, 1964; The Play of Daniel, Curlew River, 1968; A Satyre of the Thrie Estaitis, 1969; The Forrigan Reel, 1970; Valentine, 1976; member, Arts Council of Great Britain, 1977–79; Chairman of Drama Committee, Scottish Arts Council, 1976–79; trustee, The Theatres Trust, 1980– ; member, UK National Commission for UNESCO, 1980–present; director, Scottish Ballet; Governor, Scottish Theatre Trust; formerly director, Citizens' Theatre; President, 1975–79, International Federation for Theatre Research; editor since 1964 of *Theatre Research,* now *Theatre Research International;* his publications include English Theatrical Literature, 1970.

Address: 1 Huntly Gardens, Glasgow G12 9AS. *Tel:* 041-339 8494.

ARONSON, Boris, painter and stage designer
b Kiev, Russia, 15 Oct 1900; *s* of Solomon Aronson and his wife Deborah (Turovsky); *e* State Art School, Kiev, and trained by Alexandra Exter at the School of the Theatre, Kiev, by Ilya Mashkov at the School of Modern Painting, Moscow, and by Herman Struch, Berlin; *m* Lisa Jalowetz.

Designed his first stage production in 1924, for Day and Night, at the Unser Theatre in the Bronx, New York; Final Balance, Bronx Express, 1925; Tenth Commandment for the Yiddish Art Theatre, 1926; Tragedy of Nothing, and for the Civic Repertory Theatre, $2 \times 2 = 5$, 1927; Stempenyu the Fiddler, Jew Suss, Angels on Earth, 1929; Roaming Stars, 1930; Walk a Little Faster, 1932; Ladies' Money, Small Miracle, 1934; Three Men on a Horse, Awake and Sing, Paradise Lost, Battleship Gertie, The Body Beautiful, Weep for the Virgins, and Radio City Music Hall productions, 1935; Western Waters, 1937; Merchant of Yonkers, 1938; The Gentle People, Ladies and Gentlemen, 1939; The Unconquered, Heavenly Express, Cabin in the Sky, The Great American Goof (ballet), 1940; The Night Before Christmas, Clash by Night, 1941; The Family, The Russian People, RUR, Café Crown, Snow Maiden (ballet), 1942; South Pacific, The Family, The Red Poppy (ballet), What's Up? 1943; Sadie Thompson, Pictures at an Exhibition (ballet), 1944; The Stranger, The Desert Song, The Assassin, 1945; Truckline Café, Gypsy Lady, Sweet Bye and Bye, 1946; The Big People, 1947; Skipper Next to God, The Survivors, Love Life, 1948; Detective Story, 1949; The Bird Cage, Season in the Sun, The Country Girl, 1950; Barefoot in Athens, I Am a Camera, The Rose Tattoo, 1951; I've Got Sixpence, Ballade (ballet), 1952; The Crucible, My Three Angels, The Frogs of Spring, 1953; Mlle Colombe, 1954; Bus Stop, Once upon a Tailor, A View from the Bridge, The Master Builder, The Diary of Anne Frank, Dancing in the Chequered Shade, 1955; Girls of Summer, 1956; A Hole in the Head, Orpheus Descending, The Rope Dancers, Small War on Murray Hill, 1957; The Cold Wind and the Warm, The First-born, This Is Goggle, J B, 1958; Coriolanus (Stratford-on-Avon), A Loss of Roses, Flowering Cherry, 1959; Semi-Detached, Do-Re-Mi, 1960; The Garden of Sweets, 1961; A Gift of Time, Judith (London), 1962; Andorra, 1963; Fiddler on the Roof, Incident at Vichy, 1964; Cabaret, 1966; Mourning Becomes Electra for the Metropolitan Opera Company, Fiddler on the Roof (London), 1967; The Price (also costumes), Zorba, Cabaret (London), 1968; The Price (London), 1969; Company, Fidelio for the Metropolitan Opera's Beethoven bicentennial production, 1970; Follies, 1971; The Creation of the World and Other Business, Company (London), The Great God Brown, 1972; A Little Night Music, 1973; Dreyfus in Rehearsal, The Tzaddik (ballet), 1974; Pacific Overtures, The Nutcracker (ballet), 1976; received a Guggenheim Fellowship in 1950; won the American Theatre Wing (Tony) Award for Stage Designs, 1950–1, also 1966 for Cabaret, 1968 for Zorba, 1970 for Company, 1971 for Follies, 1976 for Pacific Overtures; won NY Drama Critics Award for Fiddler on the Roof, 1964; has exhibited his paintings and designs on many occasions in NY, Paris, and in London; received a Ford Foundation Grant in 1962; served as consultant for the film The Diary of Anne Frank, 1957; designed the Nutcracker ballet for TV, 1977..

Address: 1 West 89th Street, New York, NY.

ARONSTEIN, Martin, lighting designer
b Pittsfield, Mass, 2 Nov 1936; *s* of Milton David Aronstein and his wife Selma Frances (Herman); *e* Queens College.

Has designed the lighting for the following New York productions: Carousel for the Equity Library Theatre, 1959; The Taming of the Shrew, 1960; King Richard II, Black Nativity, Romeo and Juliet, Julius Caesar, Electra, Mister Roberts, 1961; The Tempest, 1962; The Winter's Tale, Morning Sun, 1963; The White Rose and the Red, Cindy, The Milk Train Doesn't Stop Here Anymore, A Severed Head, I Was Dancing, Tiny Alice, Othello, Electra, A Midsummer Night's Dream, Rich Little Rich Girl (tour), 1964; The Impossible Years, The Royal Hunt of the Sun, Cactus Flower, Love's Labour's Lost, Coriolanus, Troilus and Cressida, King Henry V, 1965; Slapstick Tragedy, The Condemned of Altona, All's Well That Ends Well, Measure for Measure, Richard III, The Investigation, Those That Play the Clowns, 1966; Marat/Sade, The Astrakhan Coat, The East Wind, Galileo, The Comedy of Errors, King John, Titus Andronicus, Song of the Grasshopper, Hair, How Now, Dow Jones, Hamlet, 1967; The Education of H*Y*M*A*N K*A*P*L*A*N, George M! I'm Solomon, The Memorandum, Henry IV, Parts I and II, Romeo and Juliet, Her First Roman, Huui, Huui, Morning, Noon, and Night, Promises, Promises, Dames at Sea, Forty Carats, 1968; Cities in Bezique, The Owl Answers, Play It Again, Sam, The Dozens, Invitation to a Beheading, Billy, Peer Gynt, Twelfth Night, The Reckoning, The Penny Wars, Buck White, La Strada, Sambo, 1969; Paris Is Out! The Chinese and Dr Fish, Grin and Bare It, Postcards, The Effect of Gamma Rays on Man-in-the-Moon Marigolds, Park, Mod Donna, The Wars of the Roses, Parts I and II, Richard III, The Happiness Cage, Trelawny of the 'Wells', Jack MacGowran in the Works of Samuel Beckett, The Gingerbread Lady, 1970; Four on a Garden, And Miss Reardon Drinks a Little, The Basic Training of Pavlo Hummel, Charlie Was Here and Now He's Gone, Timon of Athens, The Tale of Cymbeline, The Incomparable Max, Aint Supposed to Die a Natural Death, 1971; Moonchildren, Sugar, Promenade, All! The Little Black Book, Different Times, Don't Play Us Cheap, Hamlet, Ti-Jean and His Brothers, Much Ado About Nothing, Hurry, Harry, Wedding Band, Ambassador, 1972; Tricks, Echoes, Nash at Nine, Smith, As You Like It, King Lear, Boom Boom Room, The Three Sisters, The Beggar's Opera, Measure for Measure, The Au Pair Man, Scapin, 1973; Next Time I'll Sing to You, More than You Deserve, What the Wine-Sellers Buy, Dear Nobody, Once I Saw a Boy Laughing . . ., My Fat Friend, Music! Music!, An American Millionaire, Pericles, The Merry Wives of Windsor, Mert & Phil, Fame, In the Boom Boom Room, 1974; The Ritz, A Doll's House, A Matter of Time, Little Black Sheep, Hamlet, Kennedy's Children, Souvenir (Los Angeles), 1975; The Poison Tree, Hamlet, The Comedy of Errors, Mrs Warren's Profession, I Have a Dream, and the D'Oyly Carte productions of The Mikado, The Pirates of Penzance and HMS Pinafore, 1976; Absent Friends (Toronto), 1977; Hello Dolly!, Players, 1978; The Grand Tour, 1979.
Address: 91–30 84th Street, Woodhaven, LI, NY 11421. Tel: 296–8568.

ARRABAL, Fernando, dramatist
b Mellila, Spanish Morocco, 11 Aug 1932; *s* of Fernando Arrabal Ruiz and his wife Carmen (Teran); studied law in Madrid. *m* Luce Moreau.

Has written over sixty plays in French; plays translated and performed in English include Picnic on the Battlefield, Fando and Lis, Orison, The Labyrinth, The Executioners, The Automobile Graveyard, Guernica and The Architect and the Emperor of Assyria; New York, 1972, directed his own play, And They Put Handcuffs on the Flowers; Arrabal is also the author of several novels and film scripts; awarded the Prix de l'Humeur Noir, 1969.
Address: 32 Boulevard de Strasbourg, Paris 10, France.

ARTHUR, Beatrice (*née* Bernice Frankel), actress
b New York, NY, 13 May 1926; *d* of Philip Frankel and his wife Rebecca; *e* Blackstone College and Franklin Institute of Science and Arts; *m* Gene Saks (mar dis); prepared for the stage with Erwin Piscator at the New School for Social Research.

First appeared on the stage at the Dramatic Workshop of the New School, 1947, in the title-role of Lysistrata; first appeared on the professional stage at the Cherry Lane, NY, 21 July 1947, in the chorus of The Dog Beneath the Skin; at the same theatre, appeared in Gas, and in the title-role of Yerma, 1947; played Inez in No Exit, Kate in The Taming of the Shrew, the Mother in Six Characters in Search of an Author, and the Mother in The Owl and the Pussycat, 1948; the Marchioness in Le Bourgeois Gentilhomme, Constance in Yes Is for a Very Young Man, Tekla in The Creditors, and Hesione Hushabye in Heartbreak House, 1949; played in stock productions of Personal Appearance, Candlelight, Love or Money, The Voice of the Turtle, Gentlemen Prefer Blondes, etc, 1950–3; at the State Fair Music Hall, Dallas, Texas, 1953, played Clotilde Lombaste in The New Moon; Theatre de Lys, NY, 10 Mar 1954, Lucy Brown in The Threepenny Opera; President, Feb 1955, played in The Shoestring Revue; ANTA, May 1955, Mme Suze in Seventh Heaven; Theatre de Lys, Sept 1955, again played in The Threepenny Opera; Shubert, Boston, Apr 1956, and tour, appeared in The Ziegfeld Follies; Theatre de Lys, Jan 1957, Queen Gertrude in Siobhan McKenna's Hamlet; Coronet, Oct 1957, Nadine Fesser in Nature's Way; Rooftop, June 1958, Bella-Bello in Ulysses in Nighttown; Orpheum, May 1959, appeared in the revue Chic; Cherry Lane, Apr 1960, Hortense in Gay Divorce; Walnut, Philadelphia, Pa, Sept 1962, Mrs Miller in A Matter of Position; Imperial, Sept 1964, Yente in Fiddler on the Roof; Winter Garden, May 1966, Vera Charles in Mame, for which she received the Antoinette Perry (Tony) Award; Shubert, New Haven, Conn, Sept 1968, Meg in a Mother's Kisses; first appeared in films in That Kind of Woman, 1959, and has since played in Lovers and Other Strangers, 1970, Mame, 1974; first appeared on television in Once Upon a Time, 1948, and has since played regularly on such programmes as The George Gobel Show, 1958; The Steve Allen Show, The Sid Caesar Show, and in the title-role of the series Maude, 1972–8.
Address: Actors Equity Association, 165 West 46th Street, New York, NY, 10036.

ASHCROFT, Dame Peggy, DBE (*cr* 1956), CBE Hon DLitt, Oxon, 1961; Hon DLitt, Leicester, 1964; Hon DLitt, London 1965; actress
b Croydon, 22 Dec 1907; *d* of William Worsley Ashcroft and his wife Violetta Maud (Bernheim); *e* Woodford School, Croydon; *m* (1) Rupert Charles Hart-Davis (mar dis); (2) Theodore Komisarjevsky (mar dis); (3) Jeremy Nicholas Hutchinson (mar dis); studied for the stage at the Central School of Dramatic Art under Miss Elsie Fogerty, where she gained the Diploma in Dramatic Art, awarded by London University.

Made her first appearance on the stage at the Birmingham Repertory Theatre, 22 May 1926, as Margaret in Dear Brutus; made her first appearance in London at the Playroom

Six, May 1927, as Bessie in One Day More; at the Everyman, May 1927, played Mary Dunn in The Return; at Q, July 1927, Eve in When Adam Delved; Wyndham's, Nov 1927, Betty in The Way of the World; Arts, Jan 1928, Anastasia Vulliamy in The Fascinating Foundling, and Mary Bruin in The Land of Heart's Desire; in the spring of 1928, toured as Hester in The Silver Cord, with Lilian Braithwaite; at Q, Sept 1928, played Edith Strange in Earthbound; Arts, Oct 1928, Kristina in Easter; Lyric, Hammersmith, Nov 1928, Eulalia in A Hundred Years Old; Everyman, Apr 1929, Lucy Deren in Requital; Strand (for Repertory Players), May 1929, Sally Humphries in Bees and Honey; in June 1929, toured as Constance Neville in She Stoops to Conquer; at the Duke of York's, Sept 1929, played Naomi in Jew Süss, with Matheson Lang, making a big success; appeared at the Savoy, May 1930, as Desdemona in Othello, with Paul Robeson; at the Vaudeville, Sept 1930, played Judy Battle in The Breadwinner; Wyndhams, Apr 1931, Angela in Charles the 3rd; Ambassadors', June 1931, Anne in A Knight Passed By; New, June 1931, Fanny in Sea Fever; Haymarket, Sept 1931, Marcela in Take Two from One; Globe (for the Stage Society), May 1932, Stella in Le Cocu Magnifique; Duchess, June 1932, Salome Westaway in The Secret Woman; she was then engaged to play lead for the Old Vic and Sadler's Wells Theatres, and in Sept-Oct 1932, appeared as Cleopatra in Caesar and Cleopatra, Imogen in Cymbeline, Rosalind in As You Like It, etc; at the Kingsway (for Independent Theatre Club), Nov 1932, played Fraülein Elsa in the play of that name; returned to the Old Vic, Dec 1932–May 1933, and played Portia, Kate Hardcastle in She Stoops to Conquer, Perdita, Mary Stuart in Drinkwater's play of that name, Juliet, Lady Teazle in The School for Scandal and Miranda; Shaftesbury, Sept 1933, Inken Peters in Before Sunset; Coliseum, Feb 1934, Vasantesena in The Golden Toy; Little, Oct 1934, Lucia Maubel in The Life that I Gave Him; King's, Glasgow, May 1935, Therese Paradis in Mesmer; New Theatre, London, Oct 1935, Juliet in Romeo and Juliet, and May 1936, Nina in The Seagull; made her first appearance on the New York Stage at the Martin Beck Theatre, 8 Jan 1937, as Lise in High Tor; on her return to London joined John Gielgud for his season at the Queen's, Sept 1937–June 1938, and played the Queen in Richard II, Lady Teazle, Irina in Three Sisters and Portia in The Merchant of Venice; Phoenix, Oct 1938, Yeleina Talberg in The White Guard, and Dec 1938, Viola in Twelfth Night; May 1939, toured as Isolde in Weep for the Spring; Globe, Aug 1939, played Cecily Cardew in The Importance of Being Earnest; Globe, Mar 1940, Dinah Sylvester in Cousin Muriel; Old Vic, June 1940, succeeded Jessica Tandy as Miranda in The Tempest; toured, Jan 1941, as Mrs de Winter in Rebecca; Phoenix, Oct 1942, again played in The Importance of Being Earnest; Whitehall, Oct 1943, Catharine Lisle in The Dark River; toured Aug 1944, as Ophelia in Hamlet, with John Gielgud; Haymarket Theatre, Oct 1944–June 1945, played Ophelia, Titania in A Midsummer Night's Dream, and the Duchess in The Duchess of Malfi; His Majesty's, May 1947, Evelyn Holt in Edward, My Son, in which part she subsequently appeared at the Martin Beck, New York, Sept 1948; Haymarket, Feb 1949, Catherine Sloper in The Heiress; at the Shakespeare Memorial Theatre, Stratford-on-Avon, during the 1950 season, she appeared as Beatrice in Much Ado About Nothing, and Cordelia in King Lear; at the re-opening of the Old Vic, Nov 1950, played Viola in Twelfth Night; also at the Old Vic, Mar 1951, played the title-rôle in Electra, and May 1951, appeared as Mistress Page in The Merry Wives of Windsor; at the Duchess, Mar 1952, played Hester Collyer in The Deep Blue Sea; at the Shakespeare Memorial Theatre, Stratford-

on-Avon, during the 1953 season, appeared as Portia in The Merchant of Venice, and Cleopatra in Antony and Cleopatra; with this company appeared as Cleopatra at the Princess, London, Nov 1953, and subsequently toured the Continent (The Hague, Amsterdam, Antwerp, Brussels, Paris), in the same part; Lyric, Hammersmith, Sept 1954, and at the Westminster the following November, played the title-rôle in Hedda Gabler; scored a great success when she appeared in this part at the New Theatre, Oslo, 16 Mar 1955, in the presence of King Haakon, and for which she was subsequently awarded the King's Gold Medal; at the Palace, London, July 1955, appeared with the Shakespeare Memorial Theatre Company, as Beatrice in Much Ado About Nothing; Haymarket, Apr 1956, played Miss Madrigal in The Chalk Garden, for which performance she won the Evening Standard Drama Award, 1956; Royal Court, Oct 1956, played Shen Te in The Good Woman of Setzuan; Shakespeare Memorial Theatre, Stratford-on-Avon, Apr 1957, Rosalind in As You Like It, and July 1957, Imogen in Cymbeline; Edinburgh Festival, Lyceum, Sept 1958, appeared in a solo recital Portraits of Women; Piccadilly, Oct 1958, played Julia Raik in Shadow of Heroes; toured, Jan 1959, as Eva Delaware in The Coast of Coromandel; Royal Court, Nov 1959, played Rebecca West in Rosmersholm, transferring with the production to the Comedy, Jan 1960; Shakespeare Memorial Theatre, Stratford-on-Avon, June 1960, played Katharina in The Taming of the Shrew, and Paulina in The Winter's Tale; Aldwych, Dec 1960, played the title part in The Duchess of Malfi, with the same company (re-named Royal Shakespeare Company Jan 1961, when she became a long-term contract player with them); at the same theatre, June 1961, appeared in the Anthology The Hollow Crown; Royal Shakespeare, Stratford-on-Avon, Oct 1961, played Emilia in Othello; Aldwych, Dec 1961, Madame Ranevsky in The Cherry Orchard; Belgrade, Coventry, May 1962, appeared in the Anthology The Vagaries of Love; toured Europe, June 1962, with The Hollow Crown, and was chosen as the Best Actress of the Paris Theatre Festival, 1962; Royal Shakespeare, Stratford, July 1963, played Margaret of Anjou in the trilogy The Wars of the Roses (comprising Henry VI, Edward IV, and Richard III), subsequently appearing in the same productions at the Aldwych, Jan 1964; for the English Stage Company at the Queen's, Mar 1964, played Madame Arkadina in The Seagull; Royal Shakespeare, Stratford, July 1964, again played Margaret of Anjou in The Wars of the Roses; Aldwych, June 1966, played the Mother in Days in the Trees, followed by Mrs Alving in Ghosts, June 1967; The Hollow Crown, 1968; Agnes in A Delicate Balance, Jan 1969; Beth in Landscape, July 1969; at Stratford, Oct 1969, played Queen Katherine in Henry VIII, returning to the Aldwych, July 1970 as Volumnia in The Plebeians Rehearse the Uprising; Aldwych, Dec 1970, again played Katherine in Henry VIII; Royal Court, July 1971, Claire Lannes in The Lovers of Viorne; Aldwych, Jan 1972, the Wife in All Over; Savoy, July 1972, Lady Boothroyd in Lloyd George Knew My Father; Aldwych, Oct 1973, played Beth in Landscape and Flora in A Slight Ache; joined the National Theatre at the Old Vic, 1975, to play Ella Rentheim in John Gabriel Borkman, Jan; and Winnie in Happy Days, Mar; appeared as Lilian Baylis in the National Theatre's farewell to the Old Vic, Tribute to the Lady, Feb 1976; returned to the RSC to play Lidya in Old World, Aldwych, Oct 1976; Lyttleton, Sept 1977, played Winnie in Happy Days; in addition, she appeared for the OUDS at Oxford, Feb 1931, as Pervaneh in Hassan, and Feb 1932, as Juliet in Romeo and Juliet; created DBE in the Birthday Honours, 1956; elected to the Council of the English Stage Company, Jan 1957; member of the Arts

Council, 1962–5; President of the Apollo Society, 1964; became a director of the Royal Shakespeare Co., 1968; first appeared in films, 1933; made her first television appearance, July 1959, in Shadow of Heroes; appearances include: Madame Ranevsky in The Cherry Orchard, 1962, Margaret in The Wars of the Roses, 1965, and The Mother in Days in the Trees, 1967; in Nov 1962, she spoke the prologue at the opening production at the Ashcroft Theatre, Croydon, which had been named in her honour.

Address: 40 Frognal Lane, Hampstead, London, NW3. *Tel:* 01–435 4260.

ASHER, Jane, actress
b London, 5 Apr 1946; d of Richard Alan John Asher and his wife Margaret (Eliot); e North Bridge House and Miss Lambert's PNEU.

Began her professional career as a child, in Housemaster at Frinton Summer Theatre, 1957; Playhouse, Oxford, Dec 1958, played Alice in Through the Looking Glass; first London appearance, June 1960, as Muriel Webster in Will You Walk a Little Faster at the Duke of York's; Scala, Dec 1961 and tour, played Wendy in Peter Pan; Theatre Royal, Windsor, Apr 1962, Dinah in Level Crossing; New, Bromley, Dec 1962, played Cinderella in pantomime; joined the Bristol Old Vic Company in 1965; plays she appeared in included Cleo, Great Expectations, The Happiest Days of Your Life and Sixty Thousand Nights; left to appear at the Edinburgh Festival, 1966, for Pop Theatre as Cassandra in The Trojan Women, Aug, and as Perdita in The Winter's Tale, Sept, transferring with the latter production to the Cambridge in the same month; returning to Bristol she played Juliet in Romeo and Juliet and Julietta in Measure for Measure, touring North America with these productions and making her first New York appearance at the City Center, Feb 1967 in the latter part; at the Fortune, July 1968, played Lorette in Summer; Royal Court and Criterion, Oct 1968, Alison in Look Back in Anger; Royal Court, Aug 1970, Celia in The Philanthropist, transferring with the production to the May Fair, Sept and to the Ethel Barrymore, NY, in Mar 1971; Oxford Playhouse, Oct 1973, appeared in the gala performance, Fifty; New Vic Studio, Bristol, Oct 1975, Sally in Old Flames; Royal Court, Feb 1976, Ann in Treats, transferring to the May Fair, Mar 1976; joined the National Theatre Company, 1977, to play Charlotte in Strawberry Fields, Apr, and appear in To Those Born Later, June, both at the Cottesloe; Oxford Playhouse, Oct 1977, and tour, title rôle in Ophelia; Mermaid, Mar 1978, Dr Scott in Whose Life Is It Anyway?, transferring to the Savoy; Shaftesbury, Dec 1978, title rôle in Peter Pan; first appeared on television in 1955; more recent appearances include The Mill on the Floss and Brideshead Revisited; first film, 1952, since when notable appearances include The Greengage Summer, Alfie and Deep End.

Recreations: Music and cookery. *Address:* c/o Chatto and Linnit, Globe Theatre, Shaftesbury Avenue, London W1.

ASHERSON, Renée, actress
b London; d of Charles Stephen Ascherson and his wife Dorothy Lilian (Wiseman); e Maltman's Green, Gerrard's Cross, Switzerland, and Anjou, France; m Robert Donat (dec); studied for the stage at the Webber-Douglas Dramatic School.

Made her first appearance on the stage at the New Theatre, 17 Oct 1935, walking-on in John Gielgud's revival of Romeo and Juliet, and was also second understudy for Juliet; at the Criterion, July 1936, engaged as an understudy in The Lady of La Paz; Ambassadors', Nov 1936 (for the 1930 Players),

Kit Miles in Within Seven Hours, and at the Strand, Feb 1937, Isabella Linton in Wuthering Heights; was for eighteen months a member of the Birmingham Repertory Company, 1937–8; appeared at the Malvern Festival, 1937, as Amanda in The Apple Cart, Maria in The School for Scandal, and Mustascha in Tom Thumb the Great; at the Torch, Jan 1939, played Anna in On a Summer's Day; appeared at Richmond, Feb–Oct 1939, in various plays; at the Tavistock Little Theatre, Feb 1940, scored a success when she appeared as Katheryn Howard in a revival of The Rose Without a Thorn; appeared at the Old Vic, May 1940, as Iris in The Tempest; toured with the Old Vic Company, 1940–1, as Kate Hardcastle in She Stoops to Conquer, Maria in Twelfth Night, Nerissa in The Merchant of Venice, and Blanche in King John; at the New Theatre, July 1941, appeared in the last-mentioned part and then again toured with the company, playing in addition, Herloffs-Marte in The Witch, Ann Page in The Merry Wives of Windsor, and Bianca in Othello; again appeared at the New Theatre, July 1942, playing Bianca and Ann Page; at the Liverpool Playhouse (for the Old Vic), Nov 1942, played Desdemona in Othello; at the Westminster, Dec 1942, Puck in A Midsummer Night's Dream; Mercury, Apr 1943, Henriette Duquesnoy in The Mask of Virtue; Vaudeville, July 1943, Rose in Lottie Dundass; Westminster, July 1945, Millie Southern in The Cure for Love; at the King's, Hammersmith, with the Travelling Repertory Theatre, from Mar 1946, appeared as Juliet, and Una in The Wise Have Not Spoken; Aldwych, Oct 1946, Beatrice in Much Ado About Nothing; Playhouse, Apr 1947, Daisy Sage in The Animal Kingdom; at the New, during the Old Vic 1947–8 season, appeared as Bianca in The Taming of the Shrew, The Queen in Richard II, and Marya Antonovna in The Government Inspector; Aldwych, Oct 1949, played Stella Kowalski in A Streetcar Named Desire; Arts, Feb 1951, Katia in Spring At Marino; Aldwych, May 1951, Irina in Three Sisters; Duke of York's, Jan 1954, Marion Castle in The Big Knife; Connaught, Worthing, June 1955, Marie Balard in The Dazzling Hour; Royal, Brighton, Oct 1955, Jeanne in The Captain's Lamp; Apollo, Mar 1956, Margot Prescott in One Bright Day; Criterion, July 1956, took over Ghislaine in The Waltz of the Toreadors; Arts, Mar 1958, played Theresa in The Catalyst; Duchess, Aug 1958, Laura in The Unexpected Guest; at the Pembroke, Croydon, Feb 1961, played Cora Flood in Dark at the Top of the Stairs; Connaught, Worthing, Nov 1961, played Belle Starkie in Death and All That Jazz; Pembroke, Croydon, May 1962, Milly in The Summer People; St Martin's, Oct 1962, Alice Thomas in Kill Two Birds; Savoy, Oct 1963, Denise Murray in Portrait of Murder; toured Mar 1965, as Miss Jones in Past Imperfect; Birmingham Repertory Theatre, 1966, played Viola in Twelfth Night (April), Isobel Keith in A Boston Story (May), and Amanda in Private Lives; Bristol Old Vic, 1967, played Millamant in The Way of the World (Feb), and Annie Roberts in Strife (March); Chichester Festival, 1969, played Charlotte in The Magistrate (May), Alithea in The Country Wife and Octavia in Antony and Cleopatra (July), transferring with The Magistrate to the Cambridge Theatre, London (Sept 1969); Arnaud, Guildford, Sept 1970, Mrs Parker in When We Are Married; Chichester, May 1971 and Piccadilly, Nov 1971, played Valerie in Dear Antoine; Arts, Cambridge, Feb 1972, Adele in You and Your Clouds; toured, March 1973 as Mrs Cherry in Flowering Cherry; at the Theatre Royal, York, Aug 1973, appeared in All Over; same theatre, July 1976, Catherine in In Good King Charles's Golden Days; Savoy, Aug 1977, Mrs Whitefield in Man and Superman; first appeared in films, 1943, in King Henry V, subsequently appearing in The Way Ahead; she has also appeared in many television plays.

Recreation: Reading. *Address:* c/o Boyack and Conway Ltd, 8 Cavendish Place, London W1.

ASHLEY, Elizabeth (*née* Cole), actress
b Ocala, Florida, 30 Aug 1939; d of Arthur Kingman Cole and his wife Lucille (Ayer); e Louisiana State University; m George Peppard (mar dis); previously a ballet dancer and fashion model; prepared for the stage at the Neighborhood Playhouse and with Philip Burton.

After performing at the Neighborhood Playhouse, 1959, as Esmeralda in Camino Real and Abigail in The Crucible, made her professional début under the name Elizabeth Cole at the Westport Country Playhouse, June 1959, as Louise in Marcus in the High; made her New York début at the Actors Playhouse, July 1959, as Jessica in Dirty Hands; Longacre, Nov 1959, played Jane Ashe in The Highest Tree; Biltmore, Dec 1961, under the name Elizabeth Ashley played Mollie Michaelson in Take Her, She's Mine; Biltmore, Oct 1963, Corie Bratter in Barefoot in the Park, and continued in this part for more than a year; Martin Beck, Apr 1972, Maggie Train in Ring Round the Bathtub; John F Kennedy, Washington, DC, Mar 1973, Isabel in The Enchanted; American Shakespeare Festival, Stratford, Conn, July 1974, Margaret in Cat on a Hot Tin Roof, and repeated this part at the ANTA, Sept 1974; Mark Hellinger, Sept 1975, Sabina in The Skin of Our Teeth, Ethel Barrymore, May 1976, Betsey-No-Name in Legend; Palace, Feb 1977, Cleopatra in Caesar and Cleopatra; Chicago, Mar 1977, Mary in Vanities; received the Antoinette Perry (Tony) Award for her performance in Take Her, She's Mine; entered films in 1964 as Monica in The Carpetbaggers, and has since played in Ship of Fools, The Third Day, The Marriage of a Young Stockbroker, Paperback Hero (1974), etc; first appeared on television in Dec 1960, on the *Du Pont Show of the Month* and since has played in *The Hallmark Hall of Fame*, The File on Devlin, *Prudential On-Stage,* etc.

Favourite part: Abigail in The Crucible. *Address:* c/o Hesseltine-Baker Associates, 119 West 57th Street, New York, NY 10019.

ASHMORE, Basil, author and director
b Sutton Coldfield, Warwickshire, 13 Sept 1915; s of William Gerald Ashmore and his wife Frances Daisy (Shuter).

Formerly an actor and made his first appearance on the stage at the Birmingham Repertory Theatre, 1935; subsequently assistant stage-manager to the Glyndebourne Opera Company and Covent Garden Opera; toured for some time with Donald Wolfit's company; directed his first production, Hassan, at the Midland Institute, Birmingham, 1937; directed The Way Things Happen, Easter, The Watched Pot, Gateway, 1945; Rosmersholm, Exiles, Torch, 1945; The Winter of Our Discontent, The Red Horizon, To-morrow Will be Different, New Lindsey, 1945; Summer at Nohant, Lyric, Hammersmith, 1946; Carmen (with original score), King's, Hammersmith, 1948; he also directed Mozart's Il Seraglio, with a new libretto written by himself, at the Glyndebourne Opera, 1948; The Late Edwina Black, Dear Heart!, Desire Shall Fail, Chepstow, 1949; has since directed The Lonely Heart, Hand In Glove, Tiger Bay, 1951; Here's To Us, The High Bid, The Constant Lover, Desire Shall Fail, 1952; Snow, In Springtime, Portrait of a Gentleman, 1953; Strange Haven (also co-author), 1956; Hurdles to the Moon, 1957; The Triangle (also co-author), 1958; The Bridesmaids, 1959; The Pleasure Garden, 1960; Halka (opera, also adapted); The Cupboard, Our Little Life (also adapted), 1961; Music at Midnight (new version), 1962; The Gulls (also adapted), 1965; The Adventures of the Black Girl in Her Search for

God (also adapted), Aerial Football: A New Game, The High Bid, 1968; The Spoils of Poynton (also adapted), 1969; co-directed his adaptation of The Other House, 1969; directed his translations of On the High Road and Humulous, his adaptation of Darling Mildred and the monodrama Dear Friend, 1973; organised Milton Tercentenary Festival, Chalfont St Giles, Bucks, for which he directed his own plays Milton on Trial by his Peers, Milton Meets Galileo, 1974; subsequently Hon Director of the Chiltern Festival, 1975–, for which he has directed a number of his own works as well as neglected dramatic and operatic classics, including the world premiers of Treemonisha (original version), 1979; has also directed a number of other operas including several British premieres; co-author of numerous plays, including: Where There's a Will, The Threatening Storm, Quintet in A Flat, etc, and author of many translations; has broadcast frequently on various subjects.

Hobbies: Research into neglected music and dramas; music criticism and record reviewing; collecting fairy and folk tales.
Address: Misbourne House, Chalfont St Giles, Bucks; c/o John Hunter, Film-Rights, 113 Wardour Street, London, W1.

ASHTON, Ellis, MBE, 1975, light comedian and theatre historian
b Liverpool, 1 Dec 1919; s of Joseph Ashton and his wife Beatrice; e Holy Trinity, Liverpool and Army Formation College; m Margaret Mitchell, dancer.

First appeared on stage Pavilion, Silloth, as a light comedian in The Silloth Follies, June 1947; subsequently toured in, managed and directed variety and seasonal shows; among many theatrical activities he is Chairman of the British Music Hall Society, a founder member of the Theatres Trust and the British Theatre Institute, and a past President of the National Association of Theatrical, Television and Kine Employees; a member of many theatrical committees, and of associations for the preservation of rare buildings, especially theatres and cinemas; Governor of Ruskin College Oxford; Vice-President, Ruskin Fellowship London; FRSA FLS FZS FRGS; regular contributor to *The Stage.*
Address: 1 King Henry Street, London N16. *Tel:* 01 254 4209.

ASKEY, Arthur Bowden, OBE, comedian
b Liverpool, 6 June 1900; s of Samuel Askey and his wife Betsy (Bowden); e Liverpool Institute; m Elizabeth May Swash (dec).

Formerly a clerk in the Education Offices, Liverpool; was a concert-artist for many years and made his first appearance in the professional theatre at the Electric Theatre, Colchester, in Mar 1924, as a member of the Song Salad concert party; he made his first appearance in London with them, a month later, at the Crystal Palace; he toured with Concert parties in the provinces, 1924–5; was leading comedian at Margate, 1926–9; Shanklin, 1930–7, and Hastings, 1938; he was also engaged in Broadcasting, after-dinner entertaining, and provincial pantomimes during the whole of this period; first claimed notable public attention in the Broadcast feature Band Waggon, which was first broadcast in Jan 1938, and became widely popular; in addition, he has appeared at the Garrick Theatre, Dec 1937, and Cambridge Theatre, Dec 1938, as Miss Tripaway and Mr Teachem in The Boy Who Lost His Temper; Palladium, and Prince's, 1939, in Band Waggon; Palace, Dec 1941, as Big-hearted Arthur in Jack and Jill; the same part, at His Majesty's, Dec 1942; Victoria Palace, Oct 1943, Tony Merrick in The Love Racket, and toured in this, 1944–5; toured, from Aug 1945, as Goofy Gale in Follow the Girls, and appeared at His Majesty's, Oct 1945, in the same part; Casino, Dec 1947, Big-hearted Buttons in Cinderella; Princes, Sept 1948, Arthur Prince in The Kid from Stratford; visited Australia 1950, where he appeared in The Love Racket; re-appeared in London, at the Casino, Dec 1950, as Big-hearted Martha, in Goody Two Shoes; Hippodrome, Feb 1952, played Arthur Golightly in Bet Your Life; Palace, Nov 1953, Bill Brown in The Love Match; Golders Green Hippodrome, Dec 1954, Nurse Martha in Babes in the Wood; Royal, Birmingham, May 1955, appeared in Love and Kisses; Streatham Hill, Dec 1955, Nurse Martha in Babes in The Wood; Golders Green, Dec 1956, Clara Crumpet in Humpty Dumpty; Palladium, Dec 1957, Big Hearted Martha in Robinson Crusoe; Golders Green, Dec 1958, Idle Jack in Dick Whittington; Streatham Hill, Dec 1959, Idle Jack in Dick Whittington; toured, May 1961, as George Millward in What a Racket; Golder's Green, Dec 1961, Buttons in Cinderella; Palladium, Dec 1964, played Widow Twankey in Aladdin; Palladium, Dec 1965 and Wimbledon, Dec 1966, Big Hearted Martha in Babes in the Wood; Palladium, Dec 1967, Mrs Crusoe in Robinson Crusoe and Dec 1968, Big Hearted Martha in Jack and the Beanstalk; Wimbledon, Dec 1969, played the King in The Sleeping Beauty; Opera House, Manchester, Dec 1970, Baron in Cinderella; played the same part at Nottingham, Theatre Royal, 1971; Birmingham, Hippodrome, 1972; Bournemouth, Pavilion, 1974; Richmond Theatre, Dec 1973; Hippodrome, Bristol, Dec 1975, and Palace, Manchester, Dec 1976, Big-Hearted Martha in Babes in the Wood; Richmond, Dec 1977 and Alexandra, Birmingham, Dec 1978, Big-Hearted Martha in Jack and the Beanstalk; has appeared in twelve Royal Variety Performances since 1946; has played variety in summer seasons at Blackpool, Great Yarmouth, Scarborough etc; first appeared in films 1934, and has since appeared in many pictures; has also appeared on television, in *The Arthur Askey Show, Sunday Night at the Palladium, New Faces* etc and on radio in *Does the Team Think?*

Recreations: Music, golf, and motoring. *Clubs:* Savage, Garrick. *Address:* c/o The Grade Organization, 235 Regent Street, London, W1.

ATHERTON, William (*né* William Atherton Knight II), actor
b New Haven, 30 June 1947; *s* of Robert Atherton Knight and his wife Myrtle Robison; *e* Hopkins Grammar, New Haven, Amity HS, Woodbridge, Conn, and Carnegie-Mellon University of Drama; studied at the Aesthetic Realism Foundation, NY, with Consultation with Three, Ted van Griethuysen, Roy Harris, Sheldon Kranz, and with Eli Siegel.

Made his first professional appearance at the Clinton Playhouse, Clinton, Conn, summer season 1964, in The Boy Friend; in 1970 played Kenny in the National company of Little Murders, Civic, Chicago, and Victor in Goodbye and Keep Cold, Loft, NY; Truck and Warehouse, Feb 1971, Ronnie Shaughnessy in House of Blue Leaves; Newman, May 1971, title role in The Basic Training of Pavlo Hummel; Longacre, 26 Jan 1972, made his Broadway debut as David Ragin in The Sign in Sidney Brustein's Window; Forum, Lincoln Center, May 1972, title role in Suggs; Bucks County Playhouse, 1974, Leonidik in The Promise; Kennedy Center, Washington, 1975, Lord Ravensbane in The Scarecrow; Long Wharf, New Haven, 1975, Aubrey in The Show-Off; Public, Feb 1976, Bing Ringling in Rich and Famous; Lake Forest, Ill, Aug 1976, Percival in Misalliance; American Place, Nov 1977, Richard in Passing Game; Wilbur, Boston, Apr 1978, Roy Lane in Broadway; Terrain Gallery, NY, 1978, gave a performance entitled William Atherton: Acting, Ethics, Per-

son; Morosco, NY, Mar 1980, Johnny Case in Happy New Year; first film, The New Centurions, 1972; subsequent pictures include Class of '44, Sugarland Express, The Day of the Locust, The Hindenburg, Looking for Mr. Goodbar; TV work includes Centennial, 1978, and The House of Mirth, WNET.

Address: c/o Becker and London Attorneys, 15 Columbus Circle, New York, NY.

ATIENZA, Edward, actor
b London, 27 Jan 1924; *s* of Alvaro Atienza and his wife Dulce (Laws); *e* Sutton Valence and King's College, London; trained for the stage at LAMDA.

Made his professional debut at the Scala, Dartford, 1949, as the Butler in Up in Mabel's Room; joined the Memorial Theatre Company, Stratford, for seasons 1950–2 and 1954, also a tour in 1953; first London appearance, Mole in Toad of Toad Hall, Prince's, Dec 1954; at Stratford, season 1955; Arts, Dec 1955, played the East Wind in Listen to the Wind; Playhouse, Oxford, Mar 1956, Dromio in a musical Comedy of Errors; Piccadilly, May 1956, the Archbishop in Romanoff and Juliet; Stoll, July 1957, and tour, Clown in Titus Andronicus; made his New York debut at the Plymouth, Oct 1957, as the Archbishop in Romanoff and Juliet; toured US, 1960, as Wash in Destry Rides Again; St James, New York, Oct 1960, the Pope in Becket; Dec 1961–Feb 1962, toured America, Europe and the Middle East with the Old Vic company, playing Mercutio in Romeo and Juliet, Porter in Macbeth, and D'Estivet in Saint Joan; Henry Miller's, NY, Sept 1962, Prof Gay in The Affair; Biltmore, Feb 1963, the Doctor in Andorra; Drury Lane, Nov 1963, the Sorcerer in The Boys from Syracuse; Open Air, Regent's Park, played the Dauphin in Henry V, June 1964, Biondello in The Taming of the Shrew, July 1964, and Touchstone in As You Like It, June 1965; Phoenix, Sept 1964, and Shubert, NY, May 1966, Shabelsky in Ivanov; Hampstead, Oct 1966, and Fortune, London, Nov 1966, Ward V Evans in In the Matter of J Robert Oppenheimer; toured, Apr 1967, as Potter in Brother and Sister; Queen's, Oct 1967, Firs in The Cherry Orchard; Mermaid, Nov 1967, Alfonso Santospirito in Climb the Greased Pole; Piccadilly, Apr 1968, Barber in Man of La Mancha; Arnaud, Guildford, Apr 1969, Foehn in The Eagle Has Two Heads; Gardner Centre, Brighton, Jan 1970, Dr Rank in A Doll's House; at the Chichester Festival, 1970, played Solveig's Father in Peer Gynt and de Quadra in Vivat! Vivat Regina!, May, and Subtle in The Alchemist, July; repeated the part of de Quadra at the Piccadilly, London, Oct 1970; Mermaid, Nov 1971, played General Flanco de Fortinbras in Geneva; in three seasons at Stratford, Ontario, he played Touchstone in As You Like It and the Fool in King Lear, 1972; Gower in Pericles and Grumio in The Taming of the Shrew, 1973; the title role in King John and Boyet in Love's Labours Lost, 1974; at the National Arts Centre, Ottawa, Dec 1973, Malvolio in Twelfth Night and Arturo Ui in The Resistible Rise of Arturo Ui; Shaw Festival, Niagara-on-the-Lake, 1975, Col Pickering in Pygmalion and Caesar in Caesar and Cleopatra; films include Battle of the River Plate; television since 1957, includes Victoria Regina and The Six Wives of Henry VIII.

Address: c/o Peter Campbell, Nems Management Ltd, 31 Kings Road, London SW3.

ATKINS, Eileen, actress
b London, 16 June 1934; *d* of Arthur Thomas Atkins and his wife Annie Ellen (Elkins); *e* Latymers Grammar School, Edmonton; *m* Julian Glover (mar dis); trained for the stage at the Guildhall School of Music and Drama.

Made her first appearance on the stage at the Repertory Theatre, Bangor, Ireland, June 1952, as the Nurse in Harvey; first appeared in London at the Open Air Theatre, Regent's Park, June 1953, as Jacquenetta in Love's Labour's Lost; from 1957–9, appeared as a member of the Memorial Theatre Company Stratford-on-Avon, playing among other parts Diana in Pericles; at the Bristol Old Vic, Mar 1960, played Beattie in Roots; Bromley, Apr 1961, played The Girl in The Square; joined the Old Vic Company, Jan–May 1962, to play Viola in Twelfth Night, Lady Anne in Richard III, and Miranda in The Tempest; Saville, Dec 1962, played Eileen Midway in Semi-Detached; Vaudeville, July 1963, Lady Brute in a revival of The Provok'd Wife; Edinburgh Festival and Royal Court, London, Sept 1963, played Juliette in Exit the King; made her first appearance in the United States at the Ravinia Festival, Illinois, Aug 1964, as Viola in Twelfth Night, and Ophelia in Hamlet; Bristol Old Vic, Apr 1965, played Childie in The Killing of Sister George, appearing in the same production at the Duke of York's, London, June 1965, and making her Broadway début in the same part at the Belasco, Oct 1966; Royal Court, London, July 1967, played Joan Middleton in The Restoration of Arnold Middleton; Henry Miller, New York, Nov 1967, Lika in The Promise; Chichester, May 1968, played Celia Coplestone in The Cocktail Party, transferring, Nov 1968, to Wyndham's and subsequently the Haymarket; Royal Court, Nov 1969, played Joan Shannon in The Sleeper's Den; returned to Chichester, May 1970, as Elizabeth I in Vivat! Vivat Regina! transferring to the Piccadilly, Oct 1970; played the same part at the Broadhurst, NY, Jan 1972; Aldwych, Mar 1973, title role in Suzanna Andler; joined the RSC to play Rosalind in As You Like It, Stratford, June 1973; Old Vic, Feb 1975, Hesione Hushabye in the National Theatre's Heartbreak House; Old Vic, May 1977, played Joan in Saint Joan; Old Vic, Apr 1978, Viola in Twelfth Night and July 1978, Jennet Jourdemayne in The Lady's Not for Burning; Long Wharf, Newhaven, Feb 1980, played the title role in Mary Barnes; first appeared on television, 1959, as Maggie in Hilda Lessways, subsequent performances include: The Age of Kings, The Lady's Not for Burning, Electra etc.

Favourite part: Celia Coplestone in The Cocktail Party. *Address:* c/o Larry Dalzell Associates, 3 Goodwin's Court, St Martin's Lane, London, WC2.

ATKINSON, Barbara, actress
b Manchester, 8 Jan 1926; *d* of Charles Stuart Atkinson and his wife Dorothy Carol (Lyons); *e* Châtelard; trained for the stage at the Birmingham Repertory Theatre.

Made her first stage appearance at Birmingham, Dec 1945, as Mr Fox in Toad of Toad Hall; early work in repertory at Swindon, Wigan, Wednesbury and a number of other theatres; first London appearance, 17 Feb 1955, Garrick, as Mary Williams in Serious Charge; more repertory work followed, including Oxford, Birmingham, Nottingham and the opening production of the Octagon, Bolton, 1967, as Fanny in Annie and Fanny; joined the National Theatre Company, season 1969–70, playing Mincing in The Way of the World; visited the Ravinia Festival, Chicago, 1970, with the Birmingham Repertory Company, playing Mrs Higgins in Pygmalion, and parts in Tonight at 8.30; at Leeds Playhouse, 1971, her roles included Gertrude in Hamlet; Theatre Royal, Haymarket, Oct 1972, Hon Margaret Wyndham in Crown Matrimonial, a part she played for eighteen months; 1975–77 worked at Sheffield, Watford, and Leeds, including the premiere of The Wedding Feast, Jan 1977, and Mrs Malaprop in The Rivals, Feb; Greenwich, 1978, Lady Markby in An Ideal Husband; Comedy, Oct 1978, Eve in Molly; TV work includes *Emergency Ward 10*, Secret Orchards, and The Prince Regent.

Recreation: Travel. *Address:* c/o Roger Storey, 71 Westbury Road, London N12 7PB.

ATKINSON, (Justin) Brooks, dramatic critic
b Melrose, Mass, 28 Nov 1894; *s* of Jonathan H Atkinson and his wife Garafelia (Taylor); *e* Harvard University; *m* Mrs Oriana T MacIlveen.

Instructor of English, Dartmouth College, 1917; reporter for *The Daily News* of Springfield, Mass, 1917; was assistant to the dramatic critic of the *Boston Transcript,* 1918; literary editor of the *New York Times,* 1922–5; dramatic critic *New York Times,* 1926–41; from 1941–6, was acting as war-correspondent, abroad; *New York Times* dramatic critic, 1946–60; critic-at-large, *New York Times*, 1960–71; the author of Skyline Promenades, 1925; Henry Thoreau, 1927; East of the Hudson, 1931; The Cingalese Prince, a travel book, 1934; Broadway Scrapbook, 1948; Once Around the Sun, 1951; Tuesdays and Fridays, 1963; Brief Chronicles, 1966; Broadway, 1970; The Lively Years (with Al Hirschfeld), 1973; was a contributor to the London *Daily Telegraph* on American theatrical topics; in Sept 1960, the Mansfield Theatre, NY, was re-named the Brooks Atkinson Theatre in his honor; received a Pulitzer Prize, 1947, for his reporting on the Soviet Union; received an Antoinette Perry (Tony) Award for distinguished achievement in the theatre, 1962; member of The Players; Fellow of American Academy of Arts and Sciences.

Address: Durham, New York, 12422.

ATTENBOROUGH, Sir Richard, CBE (cr 1967), actor
b Cambridge, 29 Aug 1923; *s* of Frederick L. Attenborough, MA, and his wife Mary (Clegg); *e* Wyggeston Grammar School, Leicester; *m* Sheila Sim; Leverhulme Scholarship to the Royal Academy of Dramatic Art, where he gained the Bancroft Medal, in 1942.

Made his first appearance on the stage at the Intimate Theatre, Palmer's Green, in the summer of 1941, as Richard Miller in Ah, Wilderness!; at the Arts Theatre, May–June 1942, played Ralph Berger in Awake and Sing, and Sebastian in Twelfth Night; at the Q Theatre, Sept 1942, played Andrew in London W1; Piccadilly, Oct 1942, Leo Hubbard in The Little Foxes; Arts, Dec 1942, Ba in The Holy Isle; Garrick, Mar 1943, Pinkie in Brighton Rock, in which he made an outstanding success; joined the Royal Air Force, June 1943; in Feb 1944, seconded to RAF Film Unit; demobilized in 1946; reappeared on the stage at the Westminster, Jan 1949, as Coney in The Way Back; Savoy, Nov 1950, played Toni Rigi in To Dorothy, a Son; Vaudeville, May 1952, Valentine Crisp in Sweet Madness; Ambassadors', Nov 1952, Det-Sgt Trotter in The Mousetrap, which he played for two years; Savoy, Nov 1956, played David and Julian Fanshaw in Double Image; Piccadilly, Dec 1957, Theseus in The Rape of the Belt; first appeared in films, 1942, in In Which We Serve, and has since starred in over forty pictures including Dunkirk, League of Gentlemen, Guns at Batasi, Loot, Ten Rillington Place, and A Severed Head; in 1959, formed his own production company, Beaver Films, and co- produced and appeared in The Angry Silence; produced Whistle Down the Wind; co-produced The L Shaped Room; directed Oh! What a Lovely War; Young Winston, A Bridge Too Far, etc; Best Actor Award, Variety Club of Great Britain, 1959 and 1965; Best Actor, San Sebastian Film Festival, 1961 and 1964; Best Actor, British Film Academy, 1965; Hollywood Golden Globe, 1966, 1967 and 1969; Chairman of the Royal Academy of Dramatic Art; Chairman, Capital Radio; Pro-Chancellor of Sussex University and Chairman of its Arts Centre Board; Member of the

Arts Council of Great Britain, 1970–73; Governor of the National Film School; Member of the Cinematograph Films Council; Vice-President of the British Academy of Film and Television Arts; Council Member of the British Actors' Equity Association 1949–73; Chairman of the Actors' Charitable Trust; President of the Muscular Dystrophy Group of Great Britain; Hon DLitt (Leicester), 1970; Hon DCL, Newcastle, 1974; CBE 1967; Knighted in the New Year Honours, 1976.

Recreations: Listening to music, collecting paintings. *Clubs:* Garrick, Green Room, and Beefsteak. *Address:* Old Friars, Richmond Green, Surrey.

AUBERJONOIS, René, actor
b New York City, 1 June 1940; *s* of Fernand Auberjonois and his wife Laura (Murat); *e* Carnegie Mellon University; *m* Judith Mihalyi; prepared for the stage at Carnegie University.

In 1962 joined the Arena Stage in Washington, DC, and played some twenty roles for that company, including the Witch Boy in Dark of the Moon, Leslie in The Hostage, and Edmund in Long Day's Journey into Night; joined the American Conservatory Theatre in 1965, and played fourteen roles, among them Beyond the Fringe, and the title roles in Tartuffe, King Lear and Charley's Aunt; at the Mark Taper Forum, Los Angeles, 1968, played three roles; made his New York début at the Vivian Beaumont, 7 Nov 1968, as the Fool in King Lear; same theatre, Nov 1968, Ned in A Cry of Players; Longacre, Jan 1969, Marco in Fire!; Mark Taper Forum, summer 1969, played in Chemin de Fer; Mark Hellinger, Dec 1969, Sebastian Baye in the musical Coco, for which he received the Antoinette Perry (Tony) Award; Vivian Beaumont, Mar 1972, Malvolio in Twelfth Night; Alvin, Jan 1973, Scapin in Tricks; Delacorte, July 1973, Edgar in King Lear; Eugene O'Neill, Nov 1973, various parts in The Good Doctor; returned to the ACT, San Francisco, Cal, 1975, and appeared in The Ruling; Brooklyn Academy, Mar–May 1977, played John Karslake in The New York Idea and Solynony in Three Sisters; for the same company, 1978, played Sandor Turai in The Play's the Thing, Feb, and Brutus in Julius Caesar, Apr; Palace, Apr 1979, Johann Schiml in Break a Leg; Metropolitan Opera House, NY, July 1979, Ivanov in Every Good Boy Deserves Favour; first appeared in films in MASH, 1969, and has since played in Brewster McCloud, McCabe and Mrs Miller, Pete 'n Tillie; Hindenberg, King Kong (1976); first appeared on television in 1971 and has played in *Mod Squad* and *McMillan & Wife.*

Favourite parts: Tartuffe and Fancourt Babberley. *Recreation:* Drawing. *Address:* c/o William Morris Agency, 350 Avenue of the Americas, New York NY 10019.

AUBREY, James (*né* James Aubrey Tregidgo), actor
b Klagenfurt, Austria, 28 Aug 1947; *s* of Maj Aubrey James Tregidgo and his wife Edna May (Boxall); *e* Wolmers Boys School, Kingston, Jamaica, Windsor Boys School, Hamm, W Germany, St John's School, Singapore; *m* Agnes Kristin Hallander (mar dis); trained for the stage at Drama Centre, London, 1967–70.

First professional appearance was at the Wilmington, Dela, Playhouse, Mar 1962, as Philip in Isle of Children, in which part he also made his Broadway debut at the Cort, 16 Mar 1962; 1970–72 at the Citizens', Glasgow, his parts included Aguecheek in Twelfth Night and Theridamas in Tamburlaine (Edinburgh Festival, 1972), Flamineo in The White Devil, Pozzo in Waiting for Godot, and Claire in The Maids; London debut, Royal Court, 28 June 1973, as the Constable in Magnificence; toured, 1973–74, with the Cambridge Thea-

tre Company as Aguecheek and as Diggory in She Stoops to Conquer; Theatre Upstairs, Apr 1974, Mick in Bird Child; Stratford, season 1974–75, with the Royal Shakespeare Company as Sebastian in The Tempest, Confessor/Froth in Measure for Measure, and Jeff in Afore Night Come; Bush, 1975, Ralph in Hitting Town; Royal Court, May 1975, Dennis in Loot; Birmingham Rep, Oct 1975, Orlando in As You Like It; Comedy, Mar 1976, Rex in City Sugar; Theatre Upstairs, June 1976, Terry in Amy and the Price of Cotton; Shaw, June 1977, Tom in The Glass Menagerie; Round House, Feb 1978, Ritchie in Streamers; with Prospect at the Old Vic, 1978, played Faulkland in The Rivals, Sept, and Edgar in King Lear, Oct; toured with the Cambridge Theatre Company, 1979, as Mark in The Shadow Box and Tony in From the Greek; Lyric Studio, Hammersmith, Feb 1980, title role in Dr Faustus; first film, 1961, Lord of the Flies; recently The Great Rock 'n' Roll Swindle and Home Before Midnight, 1979; TV, since 1972, includes A Bouquet of Barbed Wire, Danton's Death, and Saint Joan (1979).

Address: 95 Barnsbury Street, London N1.

AUDLEY, Maxine, actress
b London, 29 Apr 1923; *d* of Henry Julius Hecht and his wife Katharine (Arkandy); *e* Westonbirt School, Glos; *m* (1) Leonard Cassini (mar dis); (2) Andrew Broughton (mar dis); (3) Frederick Granville (mar dis); trained for the stage at the Tamara Daykharhanova School, New York, and London Mask Theatre School.

Made her first appearance on the stage at the Open Air Theatre, 27 July 1940, walking on in A Midsummer Night's Dream; appeared in repertory at Tonbridge, Maidenhead and Birmingham, 1940–2; Open Air Theatre, 1942 and 1943, played Nerissa in The Merchant of Venice, Hippolyta in A Midsummer Night's Dream, etc; engaged in war work, 1943–5; CEMA-Old Vic tour, 1945–6, played Raina in Arms and the Man; appeared at the Arts Theatre, Salisbury, 1946–7; Palace, Mar 1948, played Edith in Carissima; Nottingham Playhouse, 1948–9; at the Embassy, June 1949, played Emilia in Othello; at the Shakespeare Memorial Theatre, Stratford-on-Avon, during the 1950 season, she appeared as Goneril in King Lear, Mariana in Measure for Measure, Ursula in Much Ado About Nothing, and toured Germany with this company in the same year; Embassy, Jan 1951, played Melibea in Celestina; St James's, May 1951, appeared as Charmian in Caesar and Cleopatra, and Antony and Cleopatra, and Oct 1951, played Emilia in Othello; Arts, Jan 1952, Eva in Thieves' Carnival; Winter Garden, Mar 1952, Lady Lurewell in The Constant Couple; Aldwych, Aug 1952, played Suzanne in A Letter From Paris; with the Bristol Old Vic company, Jan–Mar 1953, she appeared as Mrs Foresight in Love for Love and Marie in The River Line; Arts, July 1953, played Sara in Tobias and the Angel; Sept 1953, Mrs Fergusson in Penelope; at the Savoy, Feb 1954, played Violet, Comtesse de Chaumont, in Angels in Love; appeared at the Shakespeare Memorial Theatre, Stratford-on-Avon, during the 1955 season, playing Olivia in Twelfth Night, Lady Macduff, and Tamora in Titus Andronicus; Alexandra, Birmingham, Nov 1955, played Marion Field in Love Affair; May 1957, toured Europe with the Shakespeare Memorial Theatre Company, as Tamora in Titus Andronicus, appearing in the same part at the Stoll, July 1957; St Martin's, June 1958, played Annabelle Logan in Speaking of Murder; Strand, June 1959, Maria Marescaud in All in the Family; Strand, Oct 1960, Josephine Barnwell in Settled Out of Court; joined the Old Vic Company, and appeared with them at the Lyceum, Edinburgh, Aug 1961, as Constance in King John, subsequently appearing in the same production at the Old Vic, Sept 1961; during the same season played Lady Macbeth in Macbeth; at the Edinburgh Festival, Lyceum, Aug 1962, played Eleanor in Curtmantle, with the Royal Shakespeare Company, subsequently appearing in repertory in the same play at the Aldwych, Oct 1962; at the same theatre, in repertory, Oct 1962, played Helen in Troilus and Cressida; Haymarket, Apr 1963, Helen Cobb in Who'll Save the Plowboy?; New Arts, Mar 1964, played Maggie in The Formation Dancers, transferring with the production to the Globe, Apr 1964; Queen's, Apr 1965, Joanna in Present Laughter; Watford Palace, Oct 1968, Mrs Gereth in The Spoils of Poynton; Intimate, Palmers' Green, Mar 1969, appeared as Marie Lloyd and others in A History of the Music Hall; Old Vic, Bristol, Apr 1969, played Mrs Hasseltine in Conduct Unbecoming, transferring with the production in July 1969, to the Queen's, where she played the part for a year; Greenwich, Sept 1970, played Marina in The Servants and the Snow; Leeds Playhouse, May 1971, Blanche du Bois in A Streetcar Named Desire; Windsor, July 1971, Ruth in The Time of Departure; at Sadlers Wells, 1972, Kate Keller in All My Sons, Apr and Mrs Malaprop in The Rivals, May; Globe, Oct 1972, Kate Weiner in A Touch of Purple; toured, 1972 as Mrs Baker in Butterflies are Free; Palace, Watford, Oct 73, Mrs Goforth in The Milk Train Doesn't Stop Here Anymore; Forum, Billingham, Oct 1974, Lady Smith in The Grouse Moor Image; Arnaud, Guildford, June 1975, Mrs Marwood in The Way of the World; toured, 1976, in Britain and S Africa, in The First Night of Pygmalion; also toured 1976 as Laura Sinclair in The Edge of Darkness; Strand, June 1977, Amanda Wingfield in The Glass Menagerie; joined the RSC, 1977, to play Volumnia in Coriolanus, Stratford, Oct, and Aldwych, June 1978; Warehouse, Nov 1978, Olive in Look Out . . . Here Comes Trouble; Aldwych, Dec 1978, Mrs Vanderpool in Saratoga; Aldwych, Mar 1979, again played Volumnia; first appeared in films, 1947, in Anna Karenina, and subsequent films include Here We Go Round the Mulberry Bush, House of Cards, The Looking Glass War, Peeping Tom, Running Scared, etc; has made several hundred broadcasts and appeared in numerous television plays.

Favourite parts: Tamora in Titus Andronicus, Amanda in Private Lives, and Blanche du Bois in A Streetcar Named Desire. *Recreations:* Photography, playing the spinet, and swimming. *Address:* c/oBarry Burnett, Suite 409, Princes House, 190 Piccadilly, London W1.

AUKIN, David, producing manager

b Harrow, 12 Feb 1942; *s* of Charles Aukin and his wife Regina; *e* St Paul's and St Edmund Hall, Oxford (BA); *m* Nancy Meckler; qualified as a solicitor.

Co-devised The Young Churchill, presented at Leicester and the Duchess Theatre, 1969; literary adviser, Traverse Theatre, Edinburgh, 1970–73, where he co-produced The Novelist, The Black and White Minstrels, and Caravaggio Buddy; 1974–75, Administrator, Anvil Productions, Oxford, for productions including Happy End (which transferred to London); 1975–present, at Hampstead Theatre as Administrator, later Artistic Director; the productions he has presented here that have transferred to the West End include Dusa, Fish, Stas and Vi, Clouds, Gloo Joo, Bodies, and Outside Edge; in 1978 Hampstead Theatre was given The Evening Standard Drama Award for Outstanding Achievement; has also presented or co-produced shows including Son of Man, 1969; Straight Up, 1971; Le Grand Magic Circus in Robinson Crusoe, 1972, and From Moses to Mao, 1974; much involved in the work of experimental companies such as Freehold (Administrator), Portable Theatre (presenter, Lay By), Joint Stock (co-founder), and Foco Novo (co-founder); Chairman, Oval House Arts Centre, 1970–74.

Hobby: Arsenal FC. *Address:* 36 Parliament Hill, London NW3.

AULISI, Joseph G, costume designer.

Designed costumes for the following New York productions: The Ox Cart, 1966; The Wicked Cooks, 1967; Saturday Night, The Man in the Glass Booth, 1968; Someone's Comin' Hungry, The Transgressor Rides Again, Pequod, The American Hamburger League, Passing Through from Exotic Places, The Burial of Esposito, Sunstroke, The Son Who Hunted Tigers in Jakarta, Seven Days of Mourning, 1969; Nobody Hears a Broken Drum, Whispers on the Wind, Steambath, Happy Birthday, Wanda June, A Dream Out of Time, One Night Stands of a Noisy Passenger, 1970; The Shrinking Bride, The Birthday Party, The Last Analysis, F Jasmine Addams, Inner City, 1971; All the Girls Came Out to Play, The Real Inspector Hound, After Magritte, Ring Round the Bathtub, An Evening with Richard Nixon and . . ., Tough to Get Help, The Kid, The Trials of Oz, 1972; The Enemy Is Dead, Milliken Breakfast Show, 1973; Brainchild (Philadelphia), Thieves, God's Favorite, 1974; Murder Among Friends, 1975; Rockabye Hamlet, 1976; Unexpected Guests, Sunset (Buffalo), 1977; The November People, 1978.

AUMONT, Jean-Pierre, actor and playwright

b Paris, France, 5 Jan 1909; *s* of Alexandre Aumont and his wife Suzanne (Berr); *m* (1) Maria Montez (dec); (2) Marisa Pavan.

Made his stage début at the Comédie Champs-Elysées, Paris, 10 Apr 1934, as Oedipe in Jean Cocteau's La Machine Infernale; Gymnase, 1937, played in Le Coeur; Théâtre des Champs-Elysées, 1938, Pélléas in Pélléas et Mélisande; same theatre, 1939, Orlando in As You Like It; after serving in the Free French Forces, came to the United States to make films; Curran, San Francisco, Jan 1942, Pierre in Rose Burke; Théâtre des Maturins, Paris, Jan 1948, Pierre Renault in L'Empereur de Chine, which he also wrote; Westport Country Playhouse, Conn, 1948, Otto in Design for Living; made his New York début at the Lyceum, 9 Feb 1949, as Pierre Renault in My Name Is Aquilon, which was Philip Barry's adaptation of L'Empereur de Chine; Arena, Arles, France, 1953, played Mark Antony in Julius Caesar; Booth, NY, Nov 1955, Henri and Pierre Belcourt in The Heavenly Twins; Comédie des Champs-Elysées, Paris, 1957, Jupiter in Amphitryon 38; Théâtre de la Madeleine, Paris, 1960, played in Mon Père Avait Raison; Eugene O'Neill, Apr 1960, Farou in Second String; Boston Arts Festival, July 1961, Anatol in The Affairs of Anatol; in Los Angeles, 1962, played in Incident at Vichy; Variétés, Paris, 1962, played in Flora; Broadway, Mar 1963, Prince Mikail in the musical Tovarich; appeared in Los Angeles and San Francisco, 1964, as Emile de Becque in South Pacific; formed a cabaret act and appeared in it at The Persian Room, NY, 1966, and subsequently toured in it in Chicago, Miami, Montreal, Mexico City, etc; Vivian Beaumont, Jan 1970, Jacques Casanova in Camino Real; at the Jules César, Paris, 1970, played Mark Antony in Julius Caesar; Théâtre National Populaire, Paris, May 1971, Dag Hammersjold in Murderous Angels; Playhouse, NY, Dec 1971, Dag Hammersjold in Murderous Angels; Tappan Zee Playhouse, Nyack, NY, July 1972, played in the revue Jacques Brel Is Alive and Well and Living in Paris; Eisenhower, Washington, DC, June 1974, Nicholas Astrov in Perfect Pitch; Royal Poinciana Playhouse, Palm Beach, Fla, Jan 1975, appeared in Janus; Ambassador, NY, May 1976, played in Jacqués Des Journées Entières dans les Arbres; City Center, Apr 1977, Ulysse in La Guerre de Troie N'Aura Pas Lieu, both of these performances in French;

played in stock in Gigi, 1977, and The Sound of Music (tour), 1978; author of the following plays, all produced in Paris: L'Ile Heureuse, 1951; Un Beau Dimanche, 1952; Ange le Bienheureux, 1956; Farfada, 1957; Lucy Crown (from Irwin Shaw's novel), 1958; entered films, 1932, in Jean de la Lune, and has since played in Lac aux Dames, 1936, Drôle de Dame, 1938, The Cross of Lorraine, 1942, Assignment in Brittany, 1943, Lili, 1953, Five Miles to Midnight, 1963, Castle Keep, 1969, Day for Night, 1973, Something Short of Paradise, 1978, and many others; has appeared frequently on television in such plays as Crime and Punishment, The Tempest, Intermezzo, and various series and variety programmes.

Favourite parts: Prince Mikail in Tovarich and Jacques Casanova in Camino Real. *Address:* International Creative Management, 40 West 57th Street, New York, NY 10019.

AXWORTHY, Geoffrey, director of Drama, University College, Cardiff

b Plymouth, 10 Aug 1923; *s* of William Henry Axworthy and his wife Gladys Elizabeth (Kingcombe); *e* Exeter College, Oxford; *m* (1) Irene Dickinson (dec); (2) Caroline Griffiths.

University lecturer in drama, Baghdad, 1951–6; Ibadan, 1956–62; Founder-director of the School of Drama, University of Ibadan, 1962–7; Director of university travelling theatre, 1961–7; Principal, Central School of Speech and Drama, London, 1967–70; appointed Director of Drama, University College, Cardiff, 1970 and Artistic Director of the Sherman Theatre of University College, Cardiff, opened in 1972.

Address: Monkton House, Marine Parade, Penarth, Glamorgan. *Tel:* Cardiff 703360.

AYCKBOURN, Alan, director and dramatist

b London, 12 Apr 1939; *s* of Horace Ayckbourn and his wife Irene Maud (Worley); *e* Haileybury; *m* Christine Roland.

Went into theatre straight from school, 1957, as stage manager and actor with touring and repertory companies including Donald Wolfit and Stephen Joseph; with the latter's Victoria Theatre company, Stoke on Trent, 1962–4, his roles included Starbuck in The Rainmaker and More in A Man for All Seasons; also directed a number of plays including his own Mr Whatnot, 1963; drama producer for BBC radio, Leeds, 1964–70; since 1971 director of productions, Library Theatre (later Stephen Joseph Theatre in the Round), Scarborough; here the following plays written by him received their first production: The Square Cat, 1959; Love after All, 1959; Dad's Tale, 1961; Standing Room Only, 1962 (these four written as Roland Allen); Relatively Speaking (as Meet My Father), 1965 (London, 1967, NY 1970); The Sparrow, 1967; How the Other Half Loves (also directed this and all subsequent Scarborough premieres), 1969 (London 1970, NY 1971); The Story So Far, 1970; Time and Time Again, 1971 (London 1972); Absurd Person Singular, 1972 (London 1973, NY 1974); The Norman Conquests: Table Manners, Living Together, Round and Round the Garden, 1973 (London 1974, NY 1975); Absent Friends, 1974 (London 1975); Confusions, 1975 (London 1976); Bedroom Farce, 1975, co-directing the National Theatre productions in London, 1977,

and NY, 1979; Just Between Ourselves, 1976 (London 1977); Ten Times Table, 1977 (London 1978—also directed); Family Circles, Joking Apart, 1978 (London 1979—also directed); Sisterly Feelings, 1979 (National Theatre 1980); other work includes the children's play Ernie's Incredible Illucinations, 1969; book and lyrics for Jeeves, 1975, and TV plays; his plays are now performed all over the world; in the autumn of 1975 five of them were running in London's West End; awards include three London *Evening Standard* Drama Awards.

Recreation: Music, cricket, astronomy. *Address:* c/o Margaret Ramsay Ltd, 14a Goodwin's Court, St Martin's Lane, London, WC2. *Tel:* 01–836 7403.

AYRTON, Norman, *b* London, 25 Sept 1924; trained for the stage at the Old Vic School under Michel Saint Denis.

Joined the Old Vic Company, 1948; in 1951, after a period in repertory at Farnham and Oxford, returned to the Old Vic School to teach movement; opened his own teaching studio in London, 1952, teaching also at Stratford, Ontario and the Royal Shakespeare Theatre, Stratford; Assistant Principal, LAMDA, 1954–66; CHQ Drama Adviser to the Girl Guide Movement 1960–75; after directing Golden Jubilee Spectacle, Empire Pool, Wembley; first London opera production, Artaxerxes (Handel Society), 1963; Director of Productions, Sutherland-Williamson Opera Season, Australia, 1965; first production in USA Twelfth Night, Dallas, Texas, 1967; Principal of LAMDA, 1966–72; Dean of World Shakespeare Study Centre, Bankside, 1972; guest theatre consultant to Australian Council for the Arts 1973; joined faculty of Juilliard School, New York, 1974; first opera production in Vancouver, Canada, Rigoletto, 1975; first production at Sydney Opera House, Lakme, 1976; has directed many student and professional productions of classic and modern plays, as well as operas at Covent Garden and elsewhere.

Recreations: Travel, reading, listening to music. *Address:* 71 The Avenue, Brondesbury Park, London, NW6 7NS. *Tel:* 01–459 3180.

AZENBERG, Emanuel, producer

b Bronx, NY, 22 Jan 1934; *s* of Joshua Charles Azenberg and his wife Hannah (Kleiman); *e* New York University; *m* Elinor Shanbaum.

At the Gramercy Arts, Feb 1961, co-presented Rendezvous at Senlis; has since presented or co-presented, in New York unless otherwise stated, the following productions: The Lion in Winter, Mark Twain Tonight, The Investigation, 1966; Something Different, 1967; Ain't Supposed to Die a Natural Death, 1971; The Sunshine Boys, 1972; The Poison Tree (Phila), The Good Doctor, 1973; Scapino, God's Favorite, 1974; California Suite, Something's Afoot, 1976; Chapter Two, 1977; Ain't Misbehavin', 1978; They're Playing Our Song, Whose Life Is It Anyway?, Devour the Snow, Last Licks, 1979; Whose Life Is It Anyway? (new production), Children of a Lesser God, I Ought to Be in Pictures, 1980.

Address: (home) 100 West 57th Street, New York, NY 10019; (office) c/o Iron Mountain Productions, 165 West 46th Street, New York, NY 10036. *Tel:* 212-489 6530.

B

BABE, Thomas, playwright

b Buffalo, NY, 13 Mar 1941; *e* Harvard College (BA 1963), St Catherine's, Cambridge (BA), Yale Law School (JD 1972); *mar dis.*

While at Harvard wrote the play The Pageant of Awkward Shadows, 1963; founder and co-director, the Summer Players, Cambridge, Mass, 1966–68; his first play to be produced professionally was Kid Champion, seen at the Public/Anspacher, 19 Nov 1974; has also written Mojo Candy, produced 1975; Rebel Women, 1976; Billy Irish, A Prayer for My Daughter (also Royal Court, London, 1978); Great Solo Town 1977; Fathers and Sons, 1978; Taken in Marriage, 1979; Salt Lake City Skyline, When We Were Very Young (with Twyla Tharp), 1980; fellow in playwriting, Yale Drama School, 1975–76.

Address: 103 Hoyt Street, Darien, CT 06820.

BACALL, Lauren (*née* Betty Joan Perske), actress

b New York, NY, 16 Sept 1924; *d* of William Perske and his wife Natalie (Bacall); *e* Highland Manor, Tarrytown, NY, and Julia Richmond High School, NY City; *m* (1) Humphrey Bogart (dec); (2) Jason Robards, Jr (mar dis); previously a fashion model; prepared for the stage at the American Academy of Dramatic Arts.

Made her NY début at the Longacre, 16 Mar 1942, as a walk-on in Johnny 2 × 4; played the ingenue in a pre-Broadway tour of Franklin Street, autumn, 1942; went to Hollywood where she made films before reappearing in NY at the Lyceum, 16 Dec 1959, as Charlie in Goodbye, Charlie; Royale, Dec 1965, played Stephanie in Cactus Flower, and continued in this part for two years; Palace, Mar 1970, Margo Channing in the musical Applause, for which she received the Antoinette Perry (Tony) Award, and in which she played for more than a year; in Toronto, Nov 1971, Civic Auditorium, Chicago, Dec 1971, again played Margo Channing in Applause, and subsequently toured; made her London début at Her Majesty's, 17 Nov 1972, as Margo Channing; stock appearances include Wonderful Town, 1977; entered films in 1944, in To Have and Have Not, and has since appeared in The Big Sleep, Dark Passage, Key Largo, How to Marry a Millionaire, The Cobweb, Designing Woman, Sex and the Single Girl, Harper, Murder on the Orient Express, The Shootist, etc; has appeared on television in various dramatic roles, notably in Petrified Forest, 1955, Blithe Spirit, 1956, A Dozen Deadly Roses, 1963, The Light Fantastic, 1967, etc; received the American Academy of Dramatic Arts Award for Achievement, 1963; her autobiography, By Myself, published 1979.

Hobbies and recreations: Fashion, tennis, swimming, needlepoint. *Address:* c/o STE Representation, 888 Seventh Avenue, New York, NY 10019.

BACKUS, Richard, actor

b Goffstown, New Hampshire, 28 Mar 1945; *e* Harvard Univ.

Made his New York début at the Booth, 1971, as standby for Keir Dullea as Don Baker in Butterflies Are Free, and occasionally played this part; Alvin, Apr 1972, played Willie, Wesley, Walter, and Wendell in Promenade, All!; appeared with the American Shakespeare Festival Theatre, Stratford, Conn, summer 1973; Ensemble Studio, NY, Mar 1974, played the title-role of Studs Edsel; McCarter, Princeton, Oct 1974, Robert Mayo in Beyond the Horizon; Long Wharf, New Haven, Conn, Dec 1974, Richard Miller in Ah, Wilderness!; Stratford, Conn, summer 1975, King of France in King Lear, George Gibbs in Our Town, and Florizel in The Winter's Tale; Circle in the Square, Oct 1975, Richard Miller in Ah, Wilderness!; McCarter, Princeton, Mar 1976, again appeared in The Winter's Tale; acted at the O'Neill Center, Waterford, Conn, seasons 1976 and 1977; Long Wharf, Oct 1977, Albert Prosser in Hobson's Choice; Brooklyn Academy of Music, Dec 1978, played Kev in Gimme Shelter; appeared in the film Dead of Night, 1974.

Address: c/o STE Representation, 888 Seventh Avenue, New York, NY 10019.

BADDELEY, Hermione, actress

b Broseley, Shropshire, 13 Nov 1906; *d* of the late W H Clinton-Baddeley and his wife Louise (Bourdin); *e* privately; *m* (1) Hon David Tennant (mar dis); (2) Captain J H Willis, MC; at an early age joined Margaret Morris's School of Dancing; then travelled with the Arts League of Service, for three years.

Made her first appearance on the London stage at the Court Theatre, 11 Mar 1918, as Le Nègre in La Boîte à Joujoux; next appeared at the Lyric, Hammersmith, Dec 1918, as Paste in Make Believe; Kingsway, Nov 1920, played Michael in The Knight of the Burning Pestle; Christmas, 1922, played Balk in Balk and the Bighead; Lyric, Hammersmith (for the Stage Society), Feb 1923, played Léa in The Mental Athletes; at the St Martin's, Aug 1923, made a notable success when she played Florrie Small in The Likes of Her; Nov 1923, played Jeanne in The Fledglings; Mar 1924, Amina in The Forest; Duke of York's, May 1924, appeared in The Punch Bowl; Palace, Sept 1924, joined The Co-Optimists; London Pavilion, Apr 1925, appeared in On With the Dance; St Martin's, July 1925, Daisy Odiham in The Show; Little, Aug 1925, played in Nine to Eleven; returned to London Pavilion, Aug 1925, in On With the Dance; Nov 1925, in Still Dancing; Apr 1926, in Cochran's Revue (1926); at the Strand (for the Repertory Players), Sept 1926, played Minetta Huggins in Minetta; Queen's, Nov 1926, Coddles in Queen High; Lyric, Hammersmith, June 1927, Ninetta Crummles in When Crummles Played; Vaudeville, Jan 1928, Clara in Lord Babs; Globe, June 1928, Vera in Holding Out the Apple; Playhouse, Sept 1928, Amélie in Excelsior; Hippodrome, Mar 1929, Susie Snow in The Five o'Clock Girl; Scala (for the Venturers), May 1929, Poppy in The Shanghai Gesture; Duchess, Jan 1932, Faith Bly in Windows; Westminster, Mar 1932, Sara in Tobias and the Angel; Gaiety, Oct 1932, in After Dinner; Comedy, Dec 1932, in Ballyhoo; at the Prince of Wales's, Sept 1933, appeared in Paris Fantaisie; Fulham, Nov 1933, played Polaire in The Greeks had a Word for It; at the Vaudeville, Aug 1934, appeared in Why Not To-Night?; Duke of York's, Nov 1934, again played Polaire in The Greeks had a Word for It; Comedy, Nov 1936, appeared in To and Fro; Saville, June 1937, in Floodlight; Little, Jan 1938, in Nine Sharp, and Apr 1939, in The Little

Revue; Little, Apr 1940, played Margery Pinchwife in The Country Wife; Comedy, June 1941, appeared in Rise Above It; Phoenix, June 1942, in Sky High; Garrick, Mar 1943, played Ida Arnold in Brighton Rock; Winter Garden, Dec 1944, Minnie in Cinderella, and Mar 1945, appeared in The Gaieties; Apollo, June 1946, played Babs Coates and Pinkie Collins in Grand National Night; Savoy, June 1948, appeared in À la Carte; Ambassadors', Nov 1949, played Doris in Fumed Oak, and Julia Sterroll in Fallen Angels; Ambassadors', Aug 1950, Arabella in For Love or Money; Westminster, Apr 1951, Ada in The Martin's Nest; Lyric, Hammersmith, June 1952, Christine Foskett in The Pink Room; Royal, Bath, Sept 1952, and also in the same month at Wimbledon, played Noo-Ga in Pagan In the Parlour; Lyric, Hammersmith, Dec 1953, appeared in the revue At The Lyric, and at the St Martin's, May 1954, played in a revised version of this production entitled Going To Town; Duchess, May 1955, played Mrs Pooter in The Diary of a Nobody; Royal, Newcastle, Aug 1955, played Laura Saintsbury in Postman's Knock!, and appeared in this part at Streatham Hill, Oct 1955, when the play was re-titled Breakfast in Salisbury; toured, Sept 1956, as Mrs Curtis Honey in Your Young Wife; Olympia, Dublin, Dec 1956, played Six-Gun Kate in Adventures of Davy Crockett; Oxford Playhouse, Sept 1958, played Mother in Jezebel; Edinburgh Festival, Sept 1960, Sonia Mann in The Dream of Peter Mann; made her first appearance in New York at the Booth, Apr 1961, when she took over the part of Helen in A Taste of Honey; toured the US Sept 1951–Apr 1962 in the same play; at the Spoleto Festival of Two Worlds, Italy, July 1962, played Flora Goforth in The Milk Train Doesn't Stop Here Anymore, subsequently appearing at the Morosco, NY, Jan 1963, in the same play; Forrest, Philadelphia, Apr 1964, played Bessie Linstrom in Cool Off; Nov 1955, toured India in cabaret, Los Angeles, May 1966, Marty Owen in Anna Christie; St Martin's, July 1966, took over the part of Sister George in The Killing of Sister George; Stage 73, NY, Feb 1968, starred in I Only Want an Answer; Eugene O'Neill, NY, Feb 1969, the Wife of Bath in Canterbury Tales; Richmond, Apr 1970, Mrs Gwynne in Nell; Prince of Wales, Feb 1972, Mrs Peachum in The Threepenny Opera, transferring to the Piccadilly in Apr; Hampstead, Apr 1973, Mother in Mother Adam; her numerous films include Brighton Rock, Room at the Top, and recently The Black Windmill; TV includes Julia, and Maude.

Address: c/o Peter Campbell, 31 King's Road, London SW3.

BADEL, Alan, actor

b Rusholme, Manchester, 11 Sept 1923; *s* of Auguste Firman Joseph Badel and his wife Elizabeth Olive (Durose); *e* Burnage High School, Manchester; *m* Yvonne Owen; studied for the stage at the Royal Academy of Dramatic Art, 1939–41 (Bancroft Gold Medallist).

Made his first appearance on the stage, at the Repertory Theatre, Oxford, Aug 1940, as George in The Black Eye; first appeared in London, at the Mercury Theatre, 18 Aug 1941, as Pierrot in L'Enfant Prodigue, and subsequently toured in the same part; Piccadilly, July 1942, played Lennox and the Servant in Macbeth; served 1942–7, with the Parachute Regiment, 6th Airborne Division; during this time he appeared with the Army play Unit, as Othello, in Egypt and the Middle East, and as Joe Rock in Exercise Bowler, in Germany; re-appeared on the stage with the Farnham Repertory company, Apr–May 1947, as Morgan Evans in The Corn is Green; at the Lyric Theatre, July 1947, played Stevie in Peace in Our Time; St Martin's, Mar 1948, Sandman in

Frenzy, and toured in the same part; joined the Birmingham Repertory company, and from Feb–July 1949, played Everyman in The Modern Everyman, the Fool in The Marvellous History of St Bernard, King Richard in Richard III, The Scoundrel in The Diary of a Scoundrel, etc; Memorial Theatre, Stratford-on-Avon, Dec 1949, played Ratty in Toad of Toad Hall; remained for the Stratford Festival Season, Apr–Oct 1950, playing Claudio in Measure for Measure, Octavius in Julius Caesar, Don John in Much Ado About Nothing, the Lord Chamberlain in King Henry VIII and the Fool in King Lear; Westminster, Dec 1950, the Prince in Beauty and the Beast; Stratford Festival Season, 1951, played Poins and Justice Shallow in Henry IV parts I and II, the Dauphin in Henry V, and Ariel in The Tempest; at the Old Vic, during the 1951–2 season, played Quince in A Midsummer Night's Dream, and François Villon in The Other Heart; during the 1952–3 season, appeared as Romeo; Lyric, Hammersmith, Sept 1954, Eilert Lovborg in Hedda Gabler; Shakespeare Memorial Theatre, Stratford-on-Avon, Apr 1956, played the title-rôle in Hamlet, and subsequently Berowne in Love's Labour's Lost, and Lucio in Measure for Measure; Arts, Oct 1957, played Fouquier Tinville in The Public Prosecutor, which he also directed; Arts, May 1959, played Stephen Dedalus in Ulysses in Nighttown, and also appeared in the same part at the Paris, and Holland Festivals, July 1959; Westminster, Feb 1960, played Kreton in Visit to a Small Planet; Lyric, Hammersmith, Nov 1960, played Alex in The Life of the Party; Globe, Apr 1961, played Hero in The Rehearsal; made his first appearance in New York at the Royale, Sept 1963, in the same production; New Arts, Nov 1965, John Tanner in Man and Superman, transferring to the Vaudeville, Jan 1966; Playhouse, Oxford, 1970, played the title roles in Kean (Sept) and Othello (Oct); Globe, Jan 1971, again played Edmund Kean in Kean; with Lord Furness, entered management, Dec 1957, as Furndel Productions, Ltd, and presented the following plays, The Ark, 1959; Visit to a Small Planet, Roger the Sixth, 1960; also presented the Voodoo Dancers, 1960; first appeared in films, 1941, in The Young Mr Pitt; and television appearances include Pride and Prejudice, The Count of Monte Cristo, The Loner, The Raging Calm.

Favourite part: Richard III. *Address:* c/o Plunket Greene Ltd, 91 Regent Street, London W1R 5RU.

BADEL, Sarah, actress

b London, 30 Mar 1943; *d* of Alan Firman Badel and his wife Yvonne (Owen); *e* Poles Convent, Herts.

Made her debut on a Bristol Old Vic tour of India, Jan 1963, in Hamlet; first London appearance, Lyric, Oct 1964, as Bella Hedley in Robert and Elizabeth; made her New York debut, Oct 1965 at the Billy Rose as Helen in The Right Honourable Gentleman; Chichester Festival, 1966, played Miss Fanny in The Clandestine Marriage, Sophie in The Fighting Cock, and Anya in The Cherry Orchard; returning to Chichester, 1967, played Petronell Sweetland in The Farmer's Wife, Helene in An Italian Straw Hat, and Ellie Dunn in Heartbreak House, reopening in the last part at the Lyric, Nov 1967; again at Chichester, 1970, played Solveig in Peer Gynt, and Raina Petkoff in Arms and the Man; joined the National Theatre Company, Dec 1970, to play Vivie Warren in Mrs Warren's Profession; St George's Playhouse, Islington 1976, played Olivia in Twelfth Night, Apr, and Juliet in Romeo and Juliet, June; first film, Every Home Should Have One, 1970; television since 1962 includes Cold Comfort Farm, King Lear and *The Pallisers.*

Recreation: Gardening. *Address:* c/o Plunket Greene, 91 Regent Street, London W1R 5RU.

BAGLEY, Ben, producer, director, and hustler
b Hardwick, Vt, 18 Oct 1933; *s* of James Bagley and his wife Madeline (Beaupre); *e* Holy Family HS, Hardwick.

Producer and director of The Shoestring Revue, President, 21 Feb 1955; The Littlest Revue, Phoenix, May 1956; Shoestring Revue '57, Barbizon Plaza, Nov 1957; produced and directed a number of revues in clubs and cafes, 1960–63; director, producer and co-author of The Decline and Fall of the Entire World as Seen Through the Eyes of Cole Porter Revisited, Square East, Mar 1965; same theatre, Dec 1965, The New Cole Porter Revue, a second edition; a combination of both shows under the title of the first has since been widely produced, including Criterion, London, Sept 1967; film appearances include Chafed Elbows, and Putney Swope; his record company, Painted Smiles, issues collections of little-known works by George Gershwin, Cole Porter, Rogers and Hart, etc.

Address: c/o Painted Smiles Inc, 116 Nassau Street, New York, NY 10038. *Tel:* 212-964 3140.

BAGNOLD, Enid, CBE, dramatic author
b Rochester, Kent, 27 Oct 1889; *d* of Colonel Arthur Henry Bagnold, CB, and his wife Ethel (Alger); *e* Priors Field, Godalming, Surrey; Marburg, Germany; and Villa Leona, Paris; *m* (Sir) Roderick Jones, KBE, Chairman of Reuters (dec).

She is the author of the following plays: Lottie Dundass, 1943; National Velvet, 1946; Poor Judas, 1951; Gertie (New York), 1952; Little Idiot (re-named from the play Gertie), 1953; The Chalk Garden (NY), 1955; (London), 1956; The Last Joke, 1960; The Chinese Prime Minister (NY), 1964; (London), 1965; Call Me Jacky (Oxford), 1967; as A Matter of Gravity (NY), 1976; her play Poor Judas received the Arts Theatre Prize in 1951; she also received the Award of Merit, American Academy of Arts and Sciences, for The Chalk Garden, 1956; she is also the author of the following books: A Diary Without Dates, 1917; Sailing Ships (poems), 1918; The Happy Foreigner, 1920; Serena Blandish (or the Difficulty of Getting Married), 1924; Alice and Thomas and Jane, 1930; National Velvet, 1935; The Squire, 1938; The Loved and Envied, 1951; The Girl's Journey, 1956; Enid Bagnold's Autobiography, 1969.

Address: North End House, Rottingdean, Sussex, BN2 7HA.

BAILEY, Pearl, actress and singer
b Newport News, Virginia, 29 Mar 1918; *d* of Joseph James Bailey and his wife Pearl; *e* William Penn High School; *m* (1) John Randolph Pinkett, Jr (mar dis); (2) Louis Bellson, Jr.

First appeared on the vaudeville stage at the Pearl Theatre, Philadelphia, 1933, as a singer; continued in vaudeville and then in cabaret, notably at the Village Vanguard, 1941, the Blue Angel, 1942, La Vie en Rose, 1945, etc; made her Broadway début at the Martin Beck, 30 Mar 1946, as Butterfly in St Louis Woman; 46th Street, Feb 1950, played Connecticut in Arms and the Girl; Mark Hellinger, Dec 1950, played in the revue Bless You All; Alvin, Dec 1954, Madame Fleur in House of Flowers; Melodyland, Berkeley, Calif, Aug 1966, Sally Adams in Call Me Madam; St James's, 12 Nov 1967, took over the role of Mrs Dolly Gallagher Levi in Hello, Dolly!; played in this last part until Dec 1969, and then toured in it until May 1970, when her illness forced its close; Circle in the Square at Ford's, Washington, DC, 1970, appeared in Festival at Ford's; toured the US, May–July 1971, in Hello, Dolly!; Coconut Grove, Los Angeles, Cal, Dec 1971, appeared in cabaret; Royal Box, NY, May 1972, in cabaret; Empire Room, Waldorf-Astoria, May 1973, again in cabaret; Talk of the Town, London, Nov 1972, made her London début in cabaret, and appeared here again in June 1973; Madison Square Garden, NY, 11 June 1973, appeared in variety for Weight Watchers; Starlight, Kansas City, Mo, July 1973, appeared in The Pearl Bailey Show; toured the US and Canada, 1975, as Dolly Gallagher Levi in Hello, Dolly!; Minskoff, NY, Nov 1975, again played in Hello, Dolly! and toured in this play in 1976; first appeared in films in Variety Girl, 1947, and since has played in Isn't It Romantic, 1948, Carmen Jones, 1954, That Certain Feeling, 1955, Saint Louis Blues, 1957, Porgy and Bess, 1959, etc; has appeared regularly on television on the principal variety programmes, on a special with Carol Channing in 1969, and on her own series *The Pearl Bailey Show*, 1971, etc; received a Donaldson Award for her performance in St Louis Woman and a special Antoinette Perry (Tony) award for Hello, Dolly!; author of Pearlie Mae, her autobiography, Talking to Myself, 1971, and Pearl's Kitchen, 1973; appointed member of the American Delegation to the United Nations, 1975.

Recreation: Cooking. *Address:* 109 Bank Street, New York NY 10014.

BAILEY, Robin, actor
b Hucknall, Nottingham, 5 Oct 1919; *s* of George Henry Bailey and his wife Thirza Ann (Mettam); *e* Henry Mellish School, Nottingham; *m* Patricia Weekes; was formerly engaged in the Postal Service and the War Office.

Had amateur experience before making his first appearance on the professional stage with the Court Players, at the Theatre Royal, Nottingham, 1938, as George in The Barretts of Wimpole Street, and played a number of small parts with that company, 1938–9; appeared in repertory at the Playhouse, Newcastle upon Tyne, 1940; served in the Army, 1940–4; during 1944–5, was engaged in repertory at the Alexandra Theatre, Birmingham, and also toured in Italy; during 1945–6, engaged in repertory at Worthing; during 1946–7, toured in Europe with the English Arts Theatre, as Horatio in Hamlet and Ludovico in Othello; made his first appearance on the London stage, at the Piccadilly Theatre, 26 Mar 1947, in the last-mentioned part; was engaged with the Birmingham Repertory Theatre company, 1947–8, playing Edmund in King Lear, Peer Gynt, Reggie in The Banbury Nose, Pip in Great Expectations, Faulkland in The Rivals; St James's Theatre, with the Birmingham Repertory company, June 1948, played Faulkland in The Rivals; gained the Clarence Derwent award for this performance; Lyric, Hammersmith, June 1949 and St James's, July 1949, played Robert Lawn in Love in Albania; New, May 1950, Alexander MacColgie Gibbs in The Cocktail Party; Arts, Aug 1950, Terence Sullivan in The Gentle Gunman; St Martin's (for the Preview Theatre), Nov 1950, Ludolph in Otho, the Great; Embassy, Jan 1951, Prof Henry Higgins in Pygmalion; Royal, Brighton, Mar 1951, and in the same month at the Golders Green Hippodrome, played Robin Colquhoun in Winter Sport; Arts, Jan 1952, Gustave in Thieves' Carnival; Vaudeville, May 1952, Henry Winter in Sweet Madness; at the Old Vic, Feb 1953, played Mark Antony in Julius Caesar, and in Mar 1953, the 2nd Knight in Murder in the Cathedral; Arts, June 1953, Sergius in Arms and the Man; Savoy, Dec 1953, Lord Basingstoke in No Sign of the Dove; Cambridge, Sept 1954, Jack Hokinshaw in No News From Father; toured Australia with the Old Vic Company, 1955; playing Lucio in Measure for Measure, Gratiano in The Merchant of Venice and Tranio in The Taming of the Shrew; returned to London, St Martin's, Feb 1956, to play Captain Hawtree in She Smiled at Me (musical version of Caste); Edinburgh Festival, Lyceum, Sept 1956, played Juggins in Fanny's First Play;

Apollo, Apr 1958, Mr Justice Blanchard in Duel of Angels; Her Majesty's Melbourne, Australia, Jan 1959, played Henry Higgins in My Fair Lady, subsequently touring Australia with the production, 1960–1; made his first appearance in New York at the Majestic Theatre, Oct 1963, as Christopher Lawrence Cromwell in Jennie; New Arts, London, Mar 1964, played Gerald in The Formation Dancers, transferring to the Globe, Apr 1964; Criterion, June 1964, took over the part of Martin Lynch-Gibbon in A Severed Head, prior to appearing in a new production of the same play at the Royale, NY, Oct 1964, then touring Australia as Lynch-Gibbon in his own production in 1965; Edinburgh Festival, 1967, played Theseus and Oberon in A Midsummer Night's Dream, later appearing in those parts at the Saville Theatre, Sept 1967; Edinburgh Festival, Aug 1969, played Haakon Werle in The Wild Duck; in 1970 he repeated his performance of Henry Higgins in a further Australian tour of My Fair Lady; Traverse, Sept 1971, played the title role in The Novelist, in the Edinburgh Festival; Nottingham Playhouse, Jan 1972, Mervyn Dakyns in A Life of the General; Globe, July 1972, Harry Branksome in Parents' Day; returned to Nottingham, Sept 1972, to play Don Armado in Love's Labours Lost, Miller in The Deep Blue Sea and Dr Prentice in What the Butler Saw; King's Head, Islington, June 1973, Edward G in Edward G, Like the Film Star; at the same theatre, July 1973, directed Marriages in a double bill; joined the Young Vic, May 1974, playing Dogberry in Much Ado About Nothing and the Player in Rosencrantz and Guildenstern Are Dead, touring Europe in these parts; Theatre Royal, Windsor, May 1975, Dr Wicksteed in Habeas Corpus; Hampstead, Feb 1976, Sir Benjamin Paton in You'll Never Be Michel-Angelo; same theatre, June 1976, appeared in The Script; Manitoba Theatre Centre, Winnipeg, 1977, played Philip in Relatively Speaking, Jan; Mr Justice Danforth in The Crucible, Mar; Mr Hardcastle in She Stoops to Conquer, Apr; on returning to London joined the National Theatre Company at the Olivier Theatre, taking over the parts of Prologue and Sir Politick Would-Be in Volpone, Aug 1977; played Sir Jasper Fidget in The Country Wife, Nov 1977; took over as Firs in The Cherry Orchard, Mar 1978; played Banquo in Macbeth, June 1978; toured, Feb 1979, as Dr Charles Prentice in for Services Rendered, and subsequently played the part at the Lyttelton, also appearing there as Councillor Parker in When We are Married, Dec 1979; first appeared in films, 1948, in Private Angelo, and has since appeared in Catch Us if You Can and Blind Terror; television performances include *The Pallisers*, I Didn't Know You Cared, *Upstairs, Downstairs*, and North and South.

Favourite parts: Peer Gynt and Faulkland. *Recreation:* Tennis, gardening. *Address:* Panton House, 25 Haymarket, London SW2.

BAIN, Conrad, actor
b Lethbridge, Alberta, Canada, 4 Feb 1923; *s* of Stafford Harrison Bain and his wife Jean Agnes; *e* Western Canada High School, Calgary, and Banff School of Fine Arts; *m* Monica Sloan; prepared for the stage at the American Academy of Dramatic Arts, 1948.

First appeared on the stage in 1939 in a high school production of Our Town, playing the Stage Manager; made his professional début at the Ivoryton (Conn) Playhouse, summer 1947, as Albert Kummer in Dear Ruth; toured, 1949, as Alfred Moulton-Barrett in The Barretts of Wimpole Street; played with various stock companies in the US and the Bahamas, 1949–56; made his New York début at the Circle in the Square, 8 May 1956, as Larry Slade in The Iceman Cometh; Longacre, Oct 1956, Dr Peter Hoenig in Sixth

Finger in a Five Finger Glove; Martin Beck, Dec 1956, the King of Hesse, the Captain, and the Old Inquisitor in Candide; Phoenix, Dec 1957, Vitek in The Makropoulos Secret; Carnegie Hall Playhouse, Feb 1958, Smelicue in Dark of the Moon; City Center, Apr 1958, Mark Eland in Lost in the Stars; Stratford, Ontario, Shakespeare Festival of Canada, 1958, Earl of Northumberland in Henry IV, Part I, Antonio in Much Ado About Nothing, and Antigonus in The Winter's Tale; Phoenix, Oct 1958, Dr Warburton in Family Reunion; Provincetown Playhouse, May 1959, Mr Juno in Overruled, the Solicitor in Buoyant Billions, and General Bridgenorth in Getting Married; Greenwich Mews, May 1960, Nicholas in A Country Scandal; Cort, Nov 1960, Senator Winthrop in Advise and Consent; Van Dam, Apr 1962, Mr Norah in It's All Yours and Daddy Jack in A Summer Ghost, in repertory with the overall title A Pair of Pairs; toured, 1962, as Mr Nicklebush in Rhinoceros; Theatre de Lys, Nov 1962, Older Man in Lunatic View; Majestic, Apr 1963, George Higgins in Hot Spot; joined the Seattle, Washington, Repertory Theatre and played, in Nov 1963, the Duke of Cornwall in King Lear and Biedermann in The Firebugs, Feb 1964, Howard in The Death of a Salesman, and, Apr 1964, Rakosi in The Shadow of Heroes; Theatre Four, Feb 1965, Raim in The Queen and the Rebels; Theatre de Lys, May 1965, Doc in Square in the Eye; The American Place, Nov 1965, James Palsy Murphy in Hogan's Goat; Eighty-First Street, June 1966, Max in The Kitchen; Theatre de Lys, Feb, Mr Hopp etc in Willie Doesn't Live Here Anymore; The New, Oct 1967, the Tourist in Scuba Duba; Henry Miller's, Sept 1968, Appleby in The Cuban Thing; Fortune, Mar 1970, George Griffith in Nobody Hears a Broken Drum; Truck and Warehouse, June 1970, Oldtimer in Steambath; Vivian Beaumont, Mar 1971, Aslaksen in An Enemy of the People; Forum, June 1971, Kurt in Play Strindberg; Broadhurst, Nov 1971, Swede in Twigs; Joseph E Levine-Circle in the Square, June 1973, Ilya Telegin in Uncle Vanya; Palm Springs Center, Cal, Apr 1976, F Sherman in The Owl and the Pussycat; has appeared in films in A Lovely Way to Die, New Leaf, Strangers, The Anderson Tapes, Bananas, etc; has appeared frequently on television in various dramatic programs and in the plays Little Women, The Last Dictator, Quartet, The Choice, Twigs, as Arthur in the long-running series *Maude* (1972–78), and in *Diff'rent Strokes* (NBC), etc; founder and President of the Actors Federal Credit Union.

Club: The Players. *Recreations:* Swimming, sculpture, sailing, guitar playing. *Address:* c/o Henderson/Hogan Agency Inc, 200 West 57th Street, New York, NY 10019.

BAIRD, Bil, puppeteer
b Grand Island, Neb, 15 Aug 1904; *s* of William Hull Baird and his wife Louise (Hetzel); *e* State University of Iowa (BA) and Chicago Academy of Fine Arts; *m* (1) Evelyn Schwartz (mar dis); (2) Cora Burlar (dec); (3) Pat Courtleigh (mar dis); (4) Susanna Lloyd; formerly a sign painter, steeplejack and jazz musician.

Joined Tony Sarg, 1927, as principal puppeteer for Ali Baba and the 40 Thieves, remaining with the Sarg company for five years; produced Bil Baird's Marionettes for the Chicago World's Fair, 1933; his marionettes have since been seen in a wide variety of media; in Horse Eats Hat, 1936, and Dr Faustus, 1937, at the Maxine Elliott, NY; in The Ziegfeld Follies, Winter Garden, Apr 1943; Flahooley, Broadhurst, 1951, with Mr Baird as Clyde; in a marionette production, Davy Jones' Locker, Morosco, 1959, and tours of India etc, 1962, and the USSR, 1963; in Man in the Moon, Biltmore, 1963; Baker Street, Broadway, 1965; with his wife Cora, opened the Bil Baird Theater, 1966–   , where productions have included Pinocchio, Alice in Wonderland, etc; the Baird marionettes have appeared on numerous TV shows since 1950, as well as in hundreds of commercials; film work includes The Sound of Music, 1965; night club and concert appearances have also been frequent; author of The Art of the Puppet, 1965, and Puppets and Population, an account of the use of puppetry in lecture tours on family planning, which he has undertaken in India and Turkey.

Recreation: Collecting musical instruments. *Address:* Bil Baird Theater, 59 Barrow Street, New York, NY 10014. *Tel:* 212-989 9840.

BAKER, George, actor, director and producer
b Varna, Bulgaria, Apr 1931; *s* of Francis Pearson Baker and his wife Eva (Macdermot); *e* Lancing College, Sussex; *m* Julia Squire.

First appeared on the London stage at the Haymarket, Aug 1953, when he played Arthur Wells in the revival of Aren't We All?; St James's, Sept 1956, played Nevile Strange in Towards Zero; at the same theatre, May 1957, played Florent France in Restless Heart; made his first appearance on the New York stage at the Henry Miller Theatre, Mar 1959, when he played Phillipe de Croze in Look After Lulu; on returning to England, he joined the Old Vic Company, Nov 1959, to play the following parts: Henry Bolingbroke in Richard II, Page in The Merry Wives of Windsor, 1959; the Earl of Warwick in Saint Joan, David Wylie in What Every Woman Knows, 1960; toured Great Britain, Sept–Dec 1960, with the Old Vic Company, as John Worthing in The Importance of Being Earnest, Third Witch and the Porter in Macbeth, Warwick in Saint Joan, and Antonio in The Merchant of Venice, subsequently appearing in The Importance of Being Earnest, Macbeth, and Saint Joan in the same company's tour of Russia, Jan 1961; Piccadilly, June 1962, played Buddy in The Glad and the Sorry Season; Queen's, Nov 1962, played Rawdon Crawley in the musical version of Vanity Fair; Lyric, May 1963, played Paul Sevigne in A Shot in the Dark; Savoy, Oct 1963, played Eliot Barlow in Portrait of Murder; Yvonne Arnaud, Guildford, Oct 1965, the Gentleman Caller in The Glass Menagerie, prior to appearing at the Haymarket, Dec 1965, in the same production; Aldwych, June 1966, played the Son in Days in the Trees; St Martin's, May 1968, the Regent in The Sleeping Prince, also directed; Duke of York's, May 1970, Gene Garrison in I Never Sang for My Father; toured, Sept 1971, as Thomas Mendip in The Lady's Not for Burning; joined the RSC to play Worcester in Henry IV Part I at the Memorial Theatre, Claudius in Hamlet and Clarence in Richard III at The Other Place, Stratford, 1975 season; repeated Claudius at the Round House, Jan 1976, and Worcester at the Aldwych, Jan 1976; for Prospect Theatre Company, 1978, directed The Lady's Not for Burning; Aldwych, Sept 1978, Austin Proctor in Cousin Vladimir; Riverside Studios, Hammersmith, May 1979, The Duke in Measure for Measure; Artistic Director of Candida Plays, 1966; productions include Charley's Aunt, Ghosts, Private Lives, Gigi, School for Scandal, The Constant Wife, etc; entered films, 1953, and principal pictures include: The Dambusters, Justine, Goodbye Mr Chips, On Her Majesty's Secret Service, The Thirty-Nine Steps, etc; first appeared on television, 1957, and performances include: Death of a Salesman, Medea, Candida, I Claudius, Print Out, etc; has written radio plays, poetry, and schools programmes.

Favourite parts: Earl of Warwick in Saint Joan, and John Worthing in The Importance of Being Earnest. *Recreation:* Horseback riding. *Address:* c/o London Management, 235–241 Regent Street, London, W1.

BAKER, Mark, actor
b Cumberland, Md, 2 Oct 1946; *s* of Francis Tweedie and his wife Aretta Sue Swayne; stepfathers Paul Baker, Al C. Warhaft; *e* Carnegie-Mellon U, Wittenberg U; *m* Patricia Britton, actress and designer (mar dis); trained for the stage at the Neighborhood Playhouse, NY.

Made his professional debut as Linus in You're a Good Man, Charlie Brown, Theatre 80 St. Mark's, off-Broadway, 1970; Mercer-O'Casey, Nov 1971, was the Boy in Love Me, Love My Children; Promenade, 1972, joined the cast of Godspell; Broadway debut, 28 Nov 1972, as Cook in Via Galactica; Chelsea Theatre Center, Dec 1973, title role in Candide, transferring with the production to the Broadway, Mar 1974, where he played the role until Sept 1975; Martin Beck, Jan 1976, took over as Dennis in Habeas Corpus; Public, Aug 1977, Michael in Flux; Pittsburgh, summer 1978, Finch in How to Succeed in Business Without Really Trying; appeared in the film Swashbuckler, and was assistant director to Ken Russell for Valentino; TV appearances include guest spots with Mike Douglas, Merv Griffin, etc.

Recreations: Film making, puppet making. *Address:* 235 West 4th Street, New York, NY 10014.

BALANCHINE, George (*né* Georges Malitonovitch Balanchivadze), choreographer
b St Petersburg, Russia, 22 Jan 1904; *s* of Maliton Balanchivadze and his wife Maria (Vasiliev); *m* (1) Alexandra Danilova (mar dis); (2) Tamara Geva (mar dis); (3) Vera Zorina (mar dis); (4) Maria Tallchief (mar dis); (5) Tanaquil LeClercq; graduated from the Imperial School of Ballet in St Petersburg, 1921.

First appeared on the stage as a student, at the Maryinsky, 1915, dancing Cupid in The Sleeping Beauty; began his career as a dancer, appearing in many ballets; between 1923–4, arranged a number of new ballets at the Milchaelorsky, St Petersburg, and also dances for State Opera productions; left Russia in 1924, and visited Germany, London, and Paris, with his own company; subsequently appointed Ballet Master and choreographer to *Les Ballets Russes de Diaghilev*; Ballet Master to the Royal Danish Ballet, Copenhagen, 1931; choreographer for the *Ballets Russes de Monte Carlo*, 1932; formed the School of American Ballet, New York, from which grew the American Ballet Company, 1934; choreographer to the Metropolitan Opera, NY, 1935–8; with Lincoln Kirstein, founded *Ballet Society*, 1946, which was re-named the *New York City Ballet*, 1948, for which he has since created innumerable ballets, and toured extensively in the US and abroad; London, 1950, 1952, 1965; Lisbon, 1955; Japan, Australia, and the Philippines, 1958; Russia, 1962 and 1972; Europe (including the Spoleto Festival), 1965; US and Canada, 1966, etc; occasionally has danced with his Company, notably Feb 13, 1968, the title-role of Don Quixote; his ballet The Nutcracker has become a regular feature of the Winter holiday season in NY; he has also choreographed the following plays and musical comedies: Wake Up and Dream (London), 1929; Cochran's 1930 Revue (London), 1930; Cochran's 1931 Revue (London), 1931; The Ziegfeld Follies, On Your Toes, 1936; Babes in Arms, 1937; The Boys from Syracuse, I Married an Angel, 1938; Keep off the Grass, Louisiana Purchase, Cabin in the Sky, 1940; Rosalinda, The Lady Comes Across, 1942; Dream with Music, The Song of Norway, 1944; Where's Charley? 1948; Courtin' Time, 1951; On Your Toes (revival), 1954; The Merry Widow (revival), 1957; A Midsummer Night's Dream, A Winter's Tale, 1958; Romeo and Juliet, The Merry Wives of Windsor, 1959; the opera Orphée et Euridice, Paris Opera, Apr 1973; the opera Boris Godunov for the Metropolitan Opera, NY, Nov 1974; he has staged dances for the following films: Goldwyn Follies, On Your Toes, and I Was an Adventuress; he has also served as choreographer for television, including: Stravinsky's The Flood, 1962; for the Ringling Brothers Barnum and Bailey Circus, 1942, he devised a polka for fifty elephants, entitled Circus Polka, with music by Stravinsky.

Address: New York City Ballet, New York State Theatre, Lincoln Center for the Performing Arts, New York, NY 10023.

BALL, William, actor and director
b Chicago, Illinois, 29 Apr 1931; *s* of Russell Ball and his wife Catherine (Gormaly); *e* Iona Preparatory School, Fordham University, and Carnegie Institute of Technology, 1953–5, where he studied acting, design, and directing.

Made his stage début in a student production of Uncle Vanya, later appearing in Candida and Hamlet, Carnegie Institute, Pittsburgh, Pa, 1948; joined the Margaret Webster touring Shakespeare company as assistant designer and as actor, 1948–50; at Ashland, Oregon, 1950, appeared with the Oregon Shakespeare Festival as Mark Antony in Julius Caesar, and subsequently played Feste in Twelfth Night, Lorenzo in The Merchant of Venice, Ariel in The Tempest, and Claudio in Much Ado About Nothing, 1950–3; Pittsburgh Playhouse, 1952, played Richard in Ah, Wilderness!; with the Pittsburgh Symphony Orchestra, 1954, appeared as Puck in A Midsummer Night's Dream and as the Devil in L'Histoire du Soldat; Antioch Shakespeare Festival, Yellow Springs, Ohio, summer, 1954, played Romeo, Trinculo in The Tempest, Old Gobbo in The Merchant of Venice, Puck, Vincentio in The Taming of the Shrew and Montano in Othello, and directed As You Like It; San Diego (Calif) Shakespeare Festival, summer, 1955, played Hamlet; Group 20 Players, Wellesley, Mass, 1955–6, played the Lion in Androcles and the Lion, Gonzalo in The Tempest, and the Witch in Faust; Antioch Shakespeare Festival, 1957, directed Twelfth Night; made his New York début at the Theatre East, 12 Nov 1956, as Acaste in The Misanthrope; Theatre de Lys, Jan 1957, Rosencrantz in Siobhan McKenna's Hamlet; Carnegie Hall Playhouse, Feb 1957, Nicholas Devize in The Lady's Not for Burning; Renata, June 1957, Mr Horner in The Country Wife; toured, 1957, as Conrad in Visit to a Small Planet; Arena Stage, Washington, DC, winter, 1957–8, appeared as Dubedat in The Doctor's Dilemma; Ambassador, NY, Mar 1958, was stage manager for Back to Methuselah; since 1958 has worked principally as a director and administrator and in this capacity directed Ivanov at the Renata, Oct 1958; Once More, with Feeling at the Alley in Houston, Texas, 1958; Henry IV, Part 1 and Julius Caesar for the San Diego Shakespeare Festival, 1958–9; The Devil's Disciple for the Actors Workshop, San Francisco, 1958; A Month in the Country for the Arena Stage, 1959; Six Characters in Search of an Author (opera) and Cosi Fan Tutti for the New York City Opera, 1959; The Tempest for the Stratford, Conn, Shakespeare Festival, 1960; The Inspector General for the New York City Opera, 1960; Under Milk Wood for Circle in the Square, 1961; Porgy and Bess for the New York City Opera, 1962; directed and played Prince Hal in Henry IV, Part 2, for the San Diego Shakespeare Festival, June 1962; Martinique, Mar 1963, directed Six Characters in Search of an Author, and directed his first play in London at the May Fair, June 1963, when he again directed this play; Don Giovanni for the New York City Opera, 1963; ANTA, Washington Square, Jan 1965, directed Tartuffe for the Repertory Theatre of Lincoln Center; founded the American Conservatory Theatre at the Pittsburgh Playhouse, Pitts-

burgh, July 1965, and during this season produced and directed Tartuffe, Tiny Alice, The Rose Tattoo, King Lear, Six Characters in Search of an Author, Antigone, Noah, The Servant of Two Masters, The Devil's Disciple, Death of a Salesman, Uncle Vanya; as General Director of the American Conservatory Theatre in 1966 he toured with six productions to Westport, Conn, East Haddam, Conn, Palo Alto and San Francisco, Calif, and Ravinia (Chicago), Illinois; in 1967 the American Conservatory Theatre (ACT) settled permanently in San Francisco, where it has functioned since, producing both original and classic drama and where it has founded a theatrical school; the company visited NY at the ANTA, Sept–Oct 1969, in The Three Sisters, A Flea in Her Ear, and Tiny Alice, Carnegie Hall, 14 Jan 1971, directed Dame Judith Anderson as Hamlet in his company's production of that play, other plays he has directed for ACT include Hamlet, Oedipus Rex, Twelfth Night, The Taming of the Shrew, Richard III, The Winter's Tale, Cyrano de Bergerac, Three Sisters, Rosencrantz and Guildenstern are Dead, Equus, Jumpers, etc; Cyrano (1974) and The Taming of the Shrew (1976) were televised; ACT visited the USSR in 1976, touring Moscow, Leningrad and Riga, and Tokyo in 1978, the first US company to appear here; ACT has toured to Hawaii 1972–79 inclusive; Mr Ball received an Honorary DFA from Carnegie Mellon University, 1979, and in the same year ACT was given a "Tony" for "distinguished achievement in theatre".

Address: American Conservatory Theatre, 450 Geary Street; San Francisco, Cal, 94102.

BALLANTYNE, Paul, actor
b Moorhead, Iowa, 18 July 1909; *s* of James Carl Ballantyne and his wife Inez Mae (Adams); *e* Lamoni, Iowa, High School, and Sherwood Music School, Chicago, from which he received a teacher's certificate, 1931; studied acting with Mrs Luella Canterbury in Chicago; served his apprenticeship with Eva Le Gallienne's Civic Repertory Company.

Made his New York début, 12 Dec 1932, as the Eight of Hearts in Alice in Wonderland; toured, 1934, in Dark Tower; Cape Playhouse, Dennis, Mass, summer 1934, played Fred in Talent; joined WPA's Federal Theatre Project and played Captain Jack Absolute in The Rivals, Everyman in the play of that name, and Young Marlowe in She Stoops to Conquer, 1935–7; toured, Feb 1937–June 1938, as Bing in Brother Rat; Lyceum, Feb 1939, Heinrich Wertheimer in Mrs O'Brien Entertains; Lyceum, May 1939, Johann in Brown Danube; Biltmore, Feb 1940, a Student in The Unconquered; Biltmore, Mar 1940, Kurt in Goodbye in the Night; toured, summer, 1940, as Kurt in Biography; Morosco, Oct 1940, Charles Owen in Suzanna and the Elders; served in the US Army Infantry, 1940–6, achieving the rank of Major; Brattle, Cambridge, Mass, 1950–1, played Brutus in Julius Caesar, Ferrovius in Androcles and the Lion, Frank in The Little Blue Light, Reverend Davidson in Rain, Northumberland in Henry IV, Part 2, Tchebutykin in The Three Sisters, the Burglar in Heartbreak House, Costard in Love's Labour's Lost, and Cleante in Tartuffe; Cort, NY, Oct 1951, La Hire in Saint Joan; Broadhurst, Sept 1953, William Clark, S J, in The Strong Are Lonely; New York City Center, Dec 1953, Brackenbury in Richard III; toured, Sept–Nov 1954, as de Baudricourt in Saint Joan; for the US State Dept toured Europe, Mar–June 1961, with the American Theatre Guild Repertory Company as Fred Bailey in The Skin of Our Teeth and Mr Keller in The Miracle Worker; toured the USA 1961–2, with the National Repertory Theatre as the Earl of Shrewsbury in Mary Stuart and Sir Walter Raleigh in Elizabeth the Queen; joined the Minnesota Theatre Company,

Minneapolis, 1963, and at the Tyrone Guthrie Theatre played Marcellus in Hamlet, La Fleche in The Miser, and Charley in The Death of a Salesman; Tyrone Guthrie, 1964, Williams in Henry V, de Stogumber in Saint Joan, and the First Avocatore in Volpone, in which he also understudied Douglas Campbell in the title-role; Tyrone Guthrie, 1965, appeared in The Way of the World, Richard III, The Cherry Orchard, and The Caucasian Chalk Circle; in 1966 appeared in The Dance of Death, As You Like It, and SS Glencairn; in 1967, House of Atreus, Shoemaker's Holiday, Thieves' Carnival, Harper's Ferry, She Stoops to Conquer, Tango, and Man with a Flower in His Mouth; in 1968 in Twelfth Night, Serjeant Musgrave's Dance, The Resistible Rise of Arturo Ui, and The House of Atreus; appeared with that company at the Billy Rose, Dec 1968, when he played the Chorus Leader in The House of Atreus and Hindborough in The Resistible Rise of Arturo Ui; Tyrone Guthrie, 1969, in The Beauty Part, Vanya in Uncle Vanya, Gen St Pé in Ardèle; 1970, in The Venetian Twins, The Tempest, Galy Gay in A Man's a Man, and A Play by Aleksandr Solzhenitsyn (world première); also in 1970 appeared in Murderous Angels at the Mark Taper Forum, Los Angeles; Lyceum, NY, Feb 1971, played Crysalde in School for Wives; Tyrone Guthrie, 1971–2 season, played in Misalliance; July 1972, Candy in Of Mice and Men; in 1973 played in The Government Inspector; July 1974, Gloucester in King Lear and Aug 1974, Deputy Governor Danforth in The Crucible; Chanhassen, Minneapolis, Feb 1975, played Andre Wyke in Sleuth; Nov 1975, Arvide Abernathy in Guys and Dolls; Mar 1976 Nat Miller in Ah, Wilderness!; May 1976, Captain Andy in Show Boat; Tyrone Guthrie, season 1977, The Count in La Ronde and Diggory in She Stoops to Conquer; Chanhassen, 1978, Al Lewis in The Sunshine Boys, Merlin in Camelot; 1979–80, Starkeeper in Carousel; appeared in the film The Andromeda Strain, 1971; has appeared frequently on dramatic television programmes, including: *Hallmark Hall of Fame, You Are There, The Play of the Week,* etc.

Favourite parts: Vanya, Gen St Pé, Galy Gay. *Address:* 1912 Dupont Avenue South, Minneapolis, Minnesota, 55403.

BALLARD, Kaye (*née* Catherine Gloria Balotta), actress and singer
b Cleveland, Ohio, 20 Nov 1926; *d* of Vincent Balotta and his wife Lena (Nacarato).

First appeared on the stage in Cleveland, 1941, in Stage Door Canteen in a USO production; made her professional début in vaudeville on the RKO Circuit, 1943; first appeared in New York at the Adelphi, 1946, in the revue Three to Make Ready; toured in stock productions of Once in a Lifetime, Look Ma, I'm Dancin', Annie Get Your Gun, etc, 1947–9; Shubert, Philadelphia, Sept 1948, appeared in the revue That's the Ticket; made her London début at the Prince of Wales's, 19 May 1950, in the revue Touch and Go; toured the USA as Betty Dillon in Top Banana, Oct 1952–June 1953; Phoenix, Mar 1954, played Helen of Troy in The Golden Apple; Shubert, Boston, Oct 1955, the Countess in Reuben, Reuben; Royal Alexandra, Toronto, Canada, Sept 1957, appeared in The Ziegfeld Follies and subsequently toured; Imperial, Apr 1961, The Incomparable Rosalie in Carnival; State Fair Music Hall, Dallas, Texas, 1962, Rose in Gypsy; New York City Center, Feb 1963, Ruth in Wonderful Town; Plymouth, May 1963, played in the revue The Beast in Me; Square East, Mar 1965, played in the revue The Decline and Fall of the Entire World as Seen Through the Eyes of Cole Porter Revisited; Mister Kelly's, Chicago, Jan 1972, played in cabaret; St Regis, NY, Feb 1973, in cabaret; Alvin,

Nov 1973, Molly Goldberg in Molly; First Chicago Center, July 1974, Lola Delaney in Sheba; Hyatt Regency O'Hare, Chicago, Mar 1975, in cabaret; Crystal Palace, Dallas, Texas, May 1975, played in I'll Stake My Life; Persian Room, Hotel Plaza, NY, Dec 1975–Jan 1976, appeared in cabaret; made her film début in The Girl Most Likely, 1956, and recent films include The Ritz, Freaky Friday and In Love Again (1980); made her television début on the *Mel Torme Show*, 1952, and has since appeared frequently including: her own series *The Mothers-in-Law*, 1967–70, *The Love Boat, Fantasy Island,* The Robber Bridegroom, and most recently (1980) a special entitled Hello Kaye Ballard, Welcome to Las Vegas.

Address: c/o Richard B Francis, 328 S Beverly Drive, Beverly Hills, Calif 90212.

BALLET, Arthur H, director and educator
b Hibbing, Minn, 6 Feb 1924; *s* of Aron Ballet and his wife Marie; *e* U of Minnesota (BS, 1947; MA, 1949; Ph D, 1953); trained for the stage at the Max Reinhardt School, Hollywood.

Has directed some two hundred plays at high school, college and professional level; is Professor of Theatre Arts at the University of Minnesota; founder and director, Office for Advanced Drama Research, 1961–77; edited vols 1–13 of Playwrights for Tomorrow for U of Minnesota Press; advisory editor, Theatre Quarterly; has served as dramaturg for the Eugene O'Neill Playwrights' Conference; consultant to the Dept of State and the Ford, Rockefeller and Guggenheim Foundations; Program Director, Theater, for the National Endowment for the Arts.

Address: Theater Program, National Endowment for the Arts, 2401 E Street NW, Washington DC 20506. *Tel:* 202-634 6387.

BALSAM, Martin, actor
b New York City, 4 Nov 1919; *s* of Albert Balsam and his wife Lillian (Weinstein); *e* DeWitt Clinton High School, Bronx, NY, and the New School for Social Research, 1946–8; *m* (1) Pearl L Somer (mar dis); (2) Joyce Van Patten (mar dis); (3) Irene Miller; formerly a mechanic, salesman, radio operator, waiter, usher.

Made his first appearance on the stage in the NYC Playground, 1935, as the Villain in Pot Boiler; made his professional début at the Red Barn, Locust Valley, NY, Aug 1941, as Johann in The Play's the Thing; Daly's, NY, Sept 1941, Mr Blow in Ghost for Sale; joined the US Army and served in the combat engineers and the air force, 1941–5; joined the Town Hall Players, Newbury, Mass, 1947; Princess, Feb 1947, Eddie in The Wanhope Building; for the Equity Library Theatre, 1947, played in A Sound of Hunting; New Stages, NY, Dec 1947, Sizzi in Lamp at Midnight; National, Mar 1948, a Murderer in Michael Redgrave's Macbeth; Belasco, Sept 1948, Merle in Sundown Beach; Empire, Dec 1949, Ambulance Driver in The Closing Door; in stock, 1949, played in Three Men on a Horse, Home of the Brave, and A Letter from Harry; Broadhurst, May 1950, Serving Man in The Liar; Martin Beck, Mar 1951, a Man in The Rose Tattoo; National, Mar 1953, various roles in Camino Real; stock, 1953, played Bernie Dodd in The Country Girl and a Gangster in Detective Story; 1954, again played in The Country Girl and in Thirteen Clocks; ANTA, Feb 1956, Son-in-Law in Middle of the Night; toured, 1955, as Norman in Wedding Breakfast; La Jolla (Calif) Playhouse, 1958, Eddie Carbone in A View from the Bridge; Theatre Group, UCLA, 1961, played in The Iceman Cometh; Winter Garden, NY, Nov 1962, Moe Smith in Nowhere to Go But Up; Locust, Philadelphia, Oct 1965, Jules Walker in The

Porcelain Year; Ambassador, Mar 1967, Richard Pawling, George, and Chuck in You Know I Can't Hear You When the Water's Running, for which he received the Outer Circle Critics Award and the Antoinette Perry (Tony) Award; Walnut St, Philadelphia, Pa, Feb 1974, Willy Loman in Death of a Salesman; American Place, Apr 1977, Joseph Parmigian in Cold Storage, repeating this role in a revised version of the play at the Lyceum, Dec; is a member of the Actors Studio; first appeared in films, 1954, in On the Waterfront, and has since played in many others, including 12 Angry Men, Psycho, Breakfast at Tiffany's, The Carpetbaggers, Seven Days in May, A Thousand Clowns for which he received the Academy Award, 1965, Catch 22, Tora, Tora, Tora, Little Big Man, The Anderson Tapes, Summer Wishes, Winter Dreams, etc; has appeared regularly on television since 1948 in such dramatic programs as *Actors Studio Theatre, US Steel Hour, Mr Peepers, Alfred Hitchcock Presents, Arrest and Trial,* etc.

Recreations: Golf and photography. *Address:* c/o William W Lazarow, 119 West 57th Street, New York, NY 10019.

BANBURY, Frith, actor, director and manager
b Plymouth, Devon, 4 May 1912; *s* of Rear-Admiral Frederick Arthur Frith Banbury, RN, and his wife Winifred (Fink); *e* Stowe School and Hertford College, Oxford; studied for the stage at the Royal Academy of Dramatic Art.

Made his first appearance on the stage at the Shaftesbury Theatre, 15 June 1933, walking-on in If I Were You; after touring, Jan 1934, in Richard of Bordeaux, appeared at the Shaftesbury, May 1934, as Barry Green in The Dark Tower; at the New, Nov 1934, played the Courier in Hamlet; appeared at the Ambassadors', Mar 1935, in Monsieur Moi; Arts, June 1935, in Love of Women; Duke of York's, Oct 1935 in The Hangman, and at the Little, Dec 1935, played the Unicorn in Alice Through the Looking Glass; appeared at the Perranporth Summer Theatre, 1936–8; at the Gate Theatre, Sept, 1936, played Eustace in Oscar Wilde; Victoria Palace, Dec 1936, Gerald Perkins in Adventure; Arts, Feb 1937, Michael in First Night; next appeared at the Players' Theatre, Jan 1938, in Ridgeway's Late Joys; Vaudeville, Oct 1938, Peter Thropp in Goodness, How Sad!; Chanticleer, Nov 1939, in Let's Face It; Apollo, Jan 1940, Quetsch in Follow My Leader; Comedy, Apr 1940, appeared in revue for the first time in New Faces; at Stratford-on-Avon, Oct 1940, played Algernon in The Importance of Being Earnest and Horace Bream in Sweet Lavender; Q, Jan 1941, in Rise Above It; Ambassadors', July 1941, in The New Ambassadors' Revue; St Martin's, Feb 1942, played Peter Blakiston in Jam To-day; Ambassadors', July 1942, appeared in Light and Shade; from Jan 1943, played a season at the Arts Theatre, Cambridge, appearing as Gregers Werle in The Wild Duck, Quex in The Gay Lord Quex, Muishkin in The Idiot, the Actor in The Guardsman, Joseph in The School for Scandal, Sneer in The Critic, Cusins in Major Barbara, etc; Westminster, Sept 1943, played Astrov in Uncle Vanya; appeared at the Arts Theatre, London, May–July, 1944, as Lord Foppington in A Trip to Scarborough and Cyril Beverley in Bird in Hand; Palace, Dec 1944, the White Rabbit and White Knight in Alice in Wonderland; at the Citizen's Theatre, Glasgow, Feb 1945, Hlestakov in The Government Inspector; Piccadilly, June 1945, the Gestapo Man in Jacobowsky and the Colonel; toured on the Continent, Sept 1945, as Colbert in While the Sun Shines; Globe, Dec 1945, took over the same part; Lyric, Hammersmith, Nov 1946, played Capt Hawtree in Caste, and appeared in this part at the Duke of York's, Jan 1947; has since directed the following plays, in

London unless otherwise stated: Dark Summer, 1947; Shooting Star, 1949; The Holly and the Ivy, Always Afternoon, and The Old Ladies, 1950; The Silver Box, Waters of the Moon, All The Year Round, 1951; The Deep Blue Sea (London and Broadway) and The Pink Room, 1952; A Question of Fact, 1953; Marching Song and Love's Labour's Lost (Old Vic) 1954; The Bad Seed, 1955; The Good Sailor, and The Diary of Anne Frank, 1956; A Dead Secret, and Flowering Cherry, 1957; A Touch of the Sun, The Velvet Shotgun, and Moon on a Rainbow Shawl, 1958; The Ring of Truth, and Flowering Cherry (NY) 1959; The Tiger and the Horse, Mister Johnson, 1960; A Chance in the Daylight, Life of the Party (also co-presented), 1960; Big Fish, Little Fish, 1962; The Unshaven Cheek (Edinburgh Festival), The Wings of the Dove, 1963; I Love You, Mrs Patterson (also co-presented), 1964; Do Not Pass Go (co-presented) (New York), The Right Honourable Gentleman (NY), 1965; Do Not Pass Go, 1966; Howard's End, Dear Octopus, 1967; Enter A Free Man, A Day in the Death of Joe Egg (Tel Aviv), and Le Valet (Paris), 1968; On the Rocks (Dublin), 1969; My Darling Daisy (also co-presented), The Winslow Boy, 1970; Captain Brassbound's Conversion, 1971; Reunion in Vienna (Chichester, 1971) 1972; The Day After the Fair (also co-presented), 1972 (London), 1973 (US tour); Glasstown (also co-presented), 1973, Ardèle (also co-presented), 1975; On Approval, 1977 (also S Africa, 1976); The Aspern Papers (US); Equus (Kenya); The Day After the Fair (Australia), 1979; has also appeared in films.

Recreation: Piano. *Address:* 4 St James's Terrace, Prince Albert Road, London, NW8. *Tel:* 01–722 8481.

BANCROFT, Anne (*née* Italiano), actress
b Bronx, New York, 17 Sept 1931; *d* of Michael Italiano and his wife Mildred (Di Napoli); *e* Christopher Columbus High School; *m* (1) Martin A May (mar dis); (2) Mel Brooks; studied for the stage at the American Academy of Dramatic Arts, and Actors Studio.

Began her career on television in 1950, where she played in numerous productions including The Goldbergs as Anne Marno; made her first appearance on the stage in NY at the Booth Theatre, Jan 1958, as Gittel Mosca in Two for the See-saw, for which she received the Antoinette Perry (Tony) Award; she followed this success by appearing (in another play by the same author) at the Playhouse, NY, Oct 1959, as Annie Sullivan in The Miracle Worker, for which performance she received the NY Drama Critics Award for the Best Performance by a Straight Actress, and the Tony Award, 1959; Martin Beck, Mar 1963, played Mother Courage in Mother Courage and Her Children; Broadway, Nov 1965, Prioress in The Devils; Vivian Beaumont, Oct 1967, Regina Giddens in a revival of The Little Foxes; Vivian Beaumont, Nov 1968, Anne in A Cry of Players; Morosco, Nov 1977, Golda Meir in Golda; entered films in 1952, and appeared in Don't Bother to Knock, other films include The Miracle Worker (for which she received the Academy Award), The Pumpkin Eater, The Graduate, Young Winston, Lipstick, and Silent Movie; has appeared on television in *The Bob Hope Show, The Perry Como Show,* and her special Annie, the Woman in the Life of Men.

Address: c/o Howard Rothberg, 1706 N Doheny Drive, Los Angeles, Calif 90069.

BANNEN, Ian, actor
b Airdrie, Scotland, 29 June; *s* of John James Bannen and his wife Clare (Galloway); *e* Ratcliffe College, Leicestershire; *m* Marilyn Salisbury.

Made his first appearance on the stage at the Gate Theatre, Dublin, in the summer of 1947, as the Emperor's Son in Armlet of Jade; joined the Shakespeare Memorial Theatre Company Stratford-on-Avon, 1951, and remained a member of the company for four seasons, which included a year's tour of Australia and New Zealand, 1953; Arts, Cambridge, Nov 1954, played A Customer and The Mayor in Robinson; appeared for the first time in London at the Irving Theatre, Sept 1955 as Captain Rickman in Prisoners of War; Comedy, Oct 1956, played Marco in A View From The Bridge; Royal Court, June 1957, played Lester Abbs in The Waiting of Lester Abbs (in a Production without Décor for the English Stage Company); Arts, Jan 1958, played Hickey in The Iceman Cometh, subsequently transferring with the production to the Winter Garden, Mar 1958; Edinburgh Festival, Lyceum, Aug 1958, played Jamie in Long Day's Journey Into Night, also appearing in the same production at the Globe, Sept 1958; Royal Court, Oct 1959, played Sergeant Musgrave in Sergeant Musgrave's Dance; Piccadilly, Nov 1960, played Julian Berniers in Toys in the Attic; joined the Royal Shakespeare Company, Stratford-on-Avon, Apr 1961, to play the following parts: the title-part in Hamlet, Orlando in As You Like It, Mercutio in Romeo and Juliet, and Iago in Othello; for the same Company at the Aldwych, Jan 1962, again played Orlando in As You Like It; Dublin and Venice Festivals, Sept–Oct 1962, played Cornelius Melody in A Touch of the Poet; New Arts, Feb 1963, Morris Pieterson in The Blood Knot; Royal Court, Nov 1964, Brutus in Julius Caesar; toured, Sept 1965, as Dick Dudgeon in The Devil's Disciple; Arnaud, Guildford, July 1972, played Brig Brown in The Brass Hat; Duke of York's, June 1977, and Edinburgh Festival, Sept 1977, Judge Brack in Hedda Gabler; first appeared in films, 1950; recent films include Station Six Sahara, The Hill, Flight of the Phoenix; The Offence, The Driver's Seat, Bite the Bullet, etc; first appeared on television, Mar 1955; performances include Johnny Belinda, Jesus of Nazareth, and Tinker Tailor Soldier Spy; is also a professional photographer.
Recreation: Swimming, horseriding. *Address:* c/o John Redway, 16 Berners Street, London W1.

BANNERMAN, Celia, actress

b Abingdon, Berks, 3 June 1946; *d* of Hugh Bannerman and his wife Hilda (Diamond); *e* Convents of the Sacred Heart, Hove and Brussels, and Dartington Hall; *m* Edward Klein; trained for the stage at the London Drama Centre.

Made her professional debut at Leatherhead, Aug 1965, as Juliet in Romanoff and Juliet; first London appearance, Haymarket, Jan 1966, as Dolly in You Never Can Tell; at the same theatre, Oct 1966, played Lucy in The Rivals; Palace, Watford, 1967, Portia in The Merchant of Venice; Citizens', Glasgow, 1968, Miranda in The Tempest; joined the Bristol Old Vic company, 1968, where her appearances included Viola in Twelfth Night; Open Air, Regent's Park, July 1968, Silvia in The Two Gentlemen of Verona; Haymarket, Sept 1968, took over Cecily in The Importance of Being Earnest; Royal Court, July 1969, Cynthia in The Double Dealer; New, March 1970, played in the four plays Come as You Are, transferring to the Strand, June 1970; Theatre Upstairs, Dec 1970, Mrs Adams in a Sunday-night production of Pirates; Apollo, Dec 1971, Amy Spettigue in the 69 Theatre Company's production of Charley's Aunt; Open Air, Regent's Park, Summer season 1972, played Miranda in The Tempest and Viola in Twelfth Night; toured, Feb 1973, as Gloria in You Never Can Tell; at the Other Place, Stratford, season 1975, played Lady Katherine Gordon in Perkin Warbeck, Galy Gay's wife in Man is Man, and Lady Anne in Richard

III; Shaw, 1976, Clea in Black Comedy; Vienna English Theatre, season 1977, Elizabeth in The Circle and Sorel in Hay Fever; assistant director, National Theatre, 1978–9, for Lark Rise, The Passion, Strife and The Fruits of Enlightenment; directed Lies in Plastic Smiles, 1979; Birmingham Rep, Feb 1980, played Amanda in Private Lives; television appearances, since 1967, include Pride and Prejudice and Vile Bodies.
Address: c/o ICM, 22 Grafton Street, London W1.

BANNERMAN, Kay, actress and dramatic author

b Hove, Sussex, 11 Oct 1919; *d* of Robert George Bannerman and his wife Chicot (Mowat); *e* Heatherley, Inverness-shire and Tours, France; *m* Harold Brooke *qv*; studied for the stage at the Royal Academy of Dramatic Art.

Made her first appearance on the stage at the Gate Theatre, Apr 1939, when she succeeded Joyce Redman as Emmanuele in Asmodée; at the Q, Apr 1939 played Suzanne in Prison Without Bars; Globe, May 1939, Doreen Pierce in Rhondda Roundabout; Westminster, Oct 1939, Deborah in Music at Night, and Dec 1939, Sarah in Major Barbara; Q, Apr 1940, Virginia Farquharson in Temporary Residence; Phoenix, Mar 1942, Ann Sheldon in Other People's Houses; Q, Nov 1942, Mary Jefferson in One Flight Up; at the New Theatre, Feb 1943, with the Old Vic Company, played Portia in The Merchant of Venice; subsequently toured with the company, also playing Miss Neville in She Stoops to Conquer and Raina in Arms and the Man; at the Lyric, Hammersmith, Apr 1944, played Suzanne in Guilty (Thérèse Raquin); Q, Mar 1945, appeared as Joan Manby in We Are Seven; Embassy, Aug 1945, as Hazel Crawford in Myself a Stranger, and Nov 1945, Polina in The Gambler; Arts Theatre, June 1946, Frau Frühling in The Dove and the Carpenter; New Lindsey, Dec 1946, Diana Temple in High Horse; is the author (with Harold Brooke) of Fit for Heroes, 1945; The Nest Egg, 1952; All For Mary, 1954; The Call of the Dodo, 1955; Love and Marriage, 1956; Once a Rake, 1957; How Say You?, 1958; Handful of Tansy, 1959; Death and All that Jazz, 1961; Don't Tell Father, 1962; There's a Yank Close Behind Me (originally The Call of the Dodo), subsequently re-named Let's be Frank, 1963; The Snowman, 1965; Let Sleeping Wives Lie, 1967; It Shouldn't happen to a Dog, 1970; She Was Only an Admiral's Daughter, 1972; Take Zero, 1974.
Recreation: Work. *Address:* Babergh Hall, Great Waldingfield, Sudbury, Suffolk. *Tel:* Long Melford 361.

BARAKA, Imamu Amiri (*né* Everett LeRoi Jones), playwright, poet, administrator

b Newark, New Jersey, 7 Oct 1934; *s* of Coyt L Jones and his wife Anna Lois (Russ); *e* Newark, Rutgers, Howard Univ, New School for Social Research, Columbia Univ; *m* (1) Hettie Cohen (mar dis); (2) Sylvia Robinson (Bibi Amina Baraka); has taught poetry at the New School, drama at Columbia Univ., literature at the Buffalo, New York, Univ, and was Visiting Professor at the San Francisco State Univ.

Author of the following plays: Dante, 1962; Dutchman, produced at the Cherry Lane, 24 Mar 1964; The Slave, The Baptism, The Toilet,1964; Jello, Experimental Death Unit 1, 1965; Black Mass, 1966; Mad Heart, Slave Ship, 1967; Great Goodness of Life (A Coon Show), 1968; Junkies Are Full of Shh . . ., Bloodrites, 1970; Baraka, 1971; A Recent Killing, 1973; Sidnee Poet Heroical, which he also directed at the New Federal, May 1975; S–1 (also directed); The Motion of History (also directed), 1977; author of the following books, mainly poetry and essays: Preface to a Twenty-Volume Suicide Note, 1961; Blues People, The Dead Lecturer, 1963;

Home, 1965; Black Music, 1967; Tales, 1968; Black Magic Poetry, 1969; In Our Terribleness, 1970; Raise Race Rays Raze, The Life and Times of John Coltrane, African Congress, 1971; The Creation of the New-Ark, Spirit Reach, 1972; Hard Facts, 1976; founded the Black Arts Repertory Theater School, Harlem, 1964, Spirit House, Newark, 1966; entered into political activity in Newark, New Jersey, heading various committees and organizations concerned with Black rights and culture.

Address: Ronald Hobbs Literary Agency, 211 East 43rd Street, New York, NY 10017.

BARDON, Henry, designer

b Cesky Tesin, Czechoslovakia, 19 June 1923; *s* of Jan Bardon and his wife Helena (Peter); *e* Dundee College of Art; *m* Stephanie Bidmead (dec); formerly a painter.

Designed his first stage production, The Firstborn, at Perth Rep, Oct 1950; he designed his first London production, Everything in the Garden, in 1962, and has since designed in London unless otherwise stated: Love's Labour's Lost, 1962; Naked, Much Ado About Nothing, Escape From Eden, 1963; Henry V, The Taming of the Shrew, Games, 1964; Miss Julie, Ride A Cock Horse, 1965; A Midsummer Night's Dream, 1966; Cyrano de Bergerac, 1967; Anne of Green Gables, Phil the Fluter, 1969; Who Killed Santa Claus?, 1970; in addition he has designed for both the Royal Opera and the Royal Ballet, for Glyndebourne and for opera houses in many other countries; costume designer for the film Fathom, 1966.

Recreations: Classical guitar, music, films. *Address:* 16 Meredyth Road, London, SW13.

BARGE, Gillian (*née* Bargh), actress

b Hastings, Sussex, 27 May 1940; *d* of Frederick Augustus Bargh and his wife Dora Clare; *e* Feltham Secondary Modern School, Erdington, Birmingham; *m* Malcolm Reynolds.

Trained for the stage at Birmingham Theatre School; first professional appearance, Dudley Hippodrome, 1958; first London appearance, Her Majesty's, 1966, when she took over the part of Sarah Lord in Say Who You Are; transferred with the production to the Vaudeville, Jan 1967; joined the National Theatre Company at the Old Vic, 1967, where her parts included a whore in Love for Love, guest in A Flea in Her Ear, 1967; Celia in Volpone, member of chorus in Oedipus, Jenny in The Dance of Death, 1968; Narrator in Macrune's Guevara, Vanessa in Pursuit, Dancer in The Way of the World, Lucienne in A Flea in Her Ear, Savvy and Ecrasia in Back to Methuselah, Dr Bird in The National Health, girl at the inn in The Travails of Sancho Panza, 1969; Taylor in Home and Beauty, 1970; Nastasya in The Idiot, neighbour in The Rules of the Game, Julie in Danton's Death, 1971; Arsinoe in The Misanthrope, Varya in The Cherry Orchard, Hesther Saloman in Equus, Isabella in Measure for Measure (mobile production), Kara Massingham in The Party, 1973; toured the US in the National Theatre production of The Misanthrope, as Arsinoe, making her New York début in this part at the St James, Mar 12 1975; toured with Joint Stock, 1976, in Yesterday's News; Royal Court, Feb 1977, played Betty in Devil's Island; Young Vic, May 1977, Vi Sprightly in A Mad World My Masters; Round House, Aug 1977, appeared in Epsom Downs; first film, The National Health, 1972

Recreation: Country Life, *Address:* Wood Cottage, Sibton, nr Peasenhall, Suffolk, *Tel:* Yoxford 397.

BARKER, Clive, actor, director and dramatic writer

b Middlesbrough, Yorks, 29 June 1931; *s* of Samuel Lawrence Barker and his wife Lily (Dawson); *e* Acklam Hall GS, Middlesbrough; *m* Josephine Smith; formerly a civil servant.

First appeared on the stage as the Messenger in the Theatre Workshop production of The Sheep-Well, Theatre Royal, Stratford, Sept 1955; subsequently played various small parts with the company, including the Burglar in The Good Soldier Schweik, Oct 1955, in which part he made his first West End appearance in Mar 1956 at the Duke of York's; Wyndham's, Oct 1958, played the Volunteer in The Hostage; 1964, joined the cast of Oh, What a Lovely War! at the same theatre; Shaftesbury, Dec 1965, played a seer and a Scot in Twang!; Ambiance, April 1970, Foot in After Magritte; made his debut as a director at the Marlowe, Canterbury, Dec 1960, with A Clean Kill; has since directed The Lion in Love (Royal Court), 1960; The Police, 1961; Enter Solly Gold, 1962; The Good Woman of Szechwan, 1964; Coventry Theatre, May 1976, directed Leonard Bernstein's Mass; Festival Organiser, 1960–3, for Centre 42; Director of Courses, National Youth Theatre; Lecturer in Drama, University of Birmingham, 1966–75; Senior Lecturer in Theatre Studies, University of Warwick, 1975–; Vice-Chairman, British Centre of the International Theatre Institute, 1978–; Associate Director, Northcott Theatre, Exeter, 1975–; his productions at this theatre have included Home; co-translated The Days of the Commune for the RSC, and published Theatre Games (Eyre Methuen), 1977; author of a television play, The Queen Street Girls.

Recreation: Cricket. *Address:* 249 Windmill Road, Coventry CV6 7BB. *Tel:* 0203 82315.

BARKER, Felix, drama critic

b London; *s* of Anthony Raine Barker and his wife Patricia (Russell); *e* Felsted, The Choate School, Connecticut (ESU exchange scholar), and in the gallery of the Old Vic; *m* Anthea Gotch.

At age 19 became Fleet Street's youngest dramatic critic with a weekly column in the London *Evening News* on amateur stage under the pseudonym 'The Prompter'; spent the war years as actor/writer i c The Balmorals Concert Party; returned to *Evening News* as feature writer and reporter, 1946; deputy dramatic critic, 1946–58; chief critic, 1958– ; also film critic since 1960; President of the Critics' Circle, 1974; presented a weekly radio programme on the theatre for LBC, 1977–78; his publications include The Oliviers, 1953, The House That Stoll Built, 1957, as well as numerous works on history and archaeology including London: 2000 Years of a City and Its People, 1974.

Recreations: Historical research, dozing in the British Museum, landscape gardening. *Address:* 4 Lindsey House, Lloyd's Place, Blackheath SE3 *and* Watermill House, Benenden, Kent. *Tel:* 01-852 1868 *and* Benenden 637.

BARKER, Howard, dramatic author

b Dulwich, London, 28 June 1946; *s* of Sydney Charles Barker and his wife Georgina Irene (Carter); *e* Battersea GS and Sussex University; *m* Sandra Mary Law.

His first play, Cheek, was produced at the Royal Court's Theatre Upstairs in July 1970; subsequently he has written No One Was Saved, also 1970; Alpha Alpha, Edward, the Final Days, 1971; Private Parts, 1972; Rule Britannia, Skipper, My Sister and I, 1973; Claw, Stripwell, 1975; Wax, 1976; Fair Slaughter, That Good Between Us, 1977; The Love of a Good Man, The Hang of the Gaol, 1978; The Loud Boy's Life, 1980; has scripted films including Made, and Aces High; TV scripts include Cows, Mutinies, and Prowling Offensive.

Address: c/o Judy Daish Associates, Globe Theatre, Shaftesbury Avenue, London W1. *Tel:* 01–734 9261.

BARKER, Ronnie, OBE, actor

b Bedford, 25 Sept 1929; *s* of Leonard William Barker and his wife Edith Eleanor (Carter); *e* Oxford City HS; *m* Joy Tubb; formerly a bank clerk.

Made his first professional appearance as Lieut Spicer in Quality Street at the Aylesbury Repertory Theatre, 1948; first London appearance, Arts, 9 June 1955 as the Chantyman and Joe Silva in Mourning Becomes Electra; Apollo, Nov 1955, played the Farmer in Summertime; Arts, Dec 1955, the Gypsy Man in Listen to the Wind; Savoy, Nov 1956; Mr Thwaites in Double Image; Phoenix, Apr 1957, three parts in Camino Real; Royal Court, Sept 1957, Perigord in Nekrassov; same theatre, Dec 1957, in Lysistrata; Lyric, July 1958, Robertoles-Diams in Irma la Douce; Royal Court, Oct 1960, Nikolai Triletski in Platonov; Phoenix, Apr 1961, and later at the Comedy, appeared in the revue On the Brighter Side; Royal Court, Jan 1962, Quince in A Midsummer Night's Dream; May Fair, Mar 1964, Bob Acres in All in Love; Arts, Aug 1964, Lord Slingsby-Craddock in Mr Whatnot; Theatre Royal, Stratford E, Feb 1966, Alf Always in Sweet Fanny Adams; Criterion, Jun 1968, Birdboot in The Real Inspector Hound; Birmingham Repertory Theatre, Dec 1971, Sir John in Good-Time Johnny; appeared in a stage version of The Two Ronnies, Bristol, May 1978, and subsequently at the London Palladium, also May; Gaumont, Southampton, Dec; and in Sydney and Melbourne, June 1979; films, since 1957, include Futtock's End, and Picnic, which he wrote himself, Robin and Marion, and Porridge; has made numerous appearances on television since 1958, notably in *The Two Ronnies* and *Porridge*; author of four humorous books.

Hobby: Deltiology. *Address:* c/o Peter Eade Ltd, 9 Cork Street, London, W1X 1PD. *Tel:* 01–734 2858.

BARKWORTH, Peter, actor

b Margate, Kent, 14 Jan 1929; *s* of Walter Wynn Barkworth and his wife Irene May (Brown); *e* Stockport.

Made his first appearance on the stage while still at school at the Hippodrome, Stockport, 1942, in For What We Are; studied for the stage at the Royal Academy of Dramatic Art, 1946–8; began his career with the Folkestone Repertory Company, 1948; was for two years a member of the Sheffield Repertory Theatre Company, and also appeared at the Q and Palmer's Green; made his first West End appearance at the Aldwych, Oct 1952, as Gaston Probert in Letter From Paris; Savoy, Feb 1953, played Gerald Arbuthnot in A Woman of No Importance; Aldwych, Apr 1954, Stefan in The Dark is Light Enough; Lyric, May 1955, played Paul Cassagnon in My Three Angels; Lyric, Hammersmith, Feb 1956, Bentley Summerhays in Misalliance; Lyric, Apr 1956, played Captain Christopher Mortlock in South Sea Bubble; at the Phoenix, Sept 1957, played Bernard Taggart-Stuart in Roar Like a Dove, which ran for over 1,000 performances; at the same theatre, Dec 1960, played Victor in The Geese Are Getting Fat; Haymarket, Apr 1962, played Sir Benjamin Backbite in the revival of The School for Scandal, subsequently making his first appearance in New York at the Majestic, Jan 1963, in the same production, also playing the part of Careless; English tour, Mar 1964, David Armitage in Everything Happens on Friday; Globe, May 1965, Oliver in The Chinese Prime Minister; toured, Apr 1967, as Rev Arthur Humphrey in I'll Get My Man; Haymarket, Oct 1972, played Edward VIII in Crown Matrimonial; Globe, July 1976, Headingley in Donkeys' Years; Piccadilly, May 1979, Philip Turner in Can

You Hear Me at the Back?; his films include Where Eagles Dare, Escape from the Dark, International Velvet and Mr Smith; TV, since his first appearance in 1960, includes The Power Game, Crown Matrimonial, Professional Foul and Telford's Change; several of these performances brought him awards from BAFTA, the Royal Television Society, etc; author of the book About Acting, 1980.

Favourite part: Edward VIII. *Recreations:* Walking, gardening, listening to music, looking at paintings. *Address:* 47 Flask Walk, Hampstead, London, NW3 1HH. *Tel:* 01–794 4591.

BARNABE, Bruno, actor

b London, 3 Apr 1905; *s* of Louis Vincent Barnabe and his wife Tina (Bendi); *e* London; *m* Avice Landon (dec); studied for the stage at the Royal Academy of Dramatic Art.

Made his first appearance on the stage at the Royalty Theatre, 4 Apr 1927, as the Wedding Guest in The Dybbuk; toured with Ben Greet's Pastoral Players, 1928, playing Romeo, Bassanio, etc; went to Egypt, Oct 1928, with Robert Atkin's Shakespearean company, and played Orlando, Laertes, etc; appeared at the Gate Theatre, 1929, in Fashion, Twenty Below, 12,000, etc; went to America with Ben Greet, 1929, and first appeared in New York, at Columbia University, as Everyman; during 1930, played in Hollywood, subsequently touring through the Western States, in Bird of Flame; toured in the United States, 1931, with the Shakespeare Memorial company, from Stratford-on-Avon; returned to England, and appeared at Stratford-on-Avon, 1932, as Slender, Lucentio, Launcelot Gobbo, Autolycus, Feste, etc; Kingsway, Oct 1932, played Colonel House in Versailles, and Nov 1932, Paul in Fräulein Elsa; Gate Theatre, 1933, played in Hinkemann, I Hate Men, Peter's Parade, etc; Lyric, Aug 1933, Baron von Düring in The Ace; Apollo, Dec 1933, Butler in Escape Me Never and Playhouse, 1934, took over Emile in Libel; Royalty, 1934, played Carl in As You Desire Me; Shubert, NY, Jan 1935, again played in Escape Me Never; appeared at the Criterion, Oct 1935, for a time, as Schimmelmann in Nina; at the Intimate, Palmer's Green, 1936, played Bolingbroke in Richard of Bordeaux; toured in Australia and New Zealand, 1937–8, with Fay Compton's Company, as Prince Albert in Victoria Regina and in To-night at 8.30, George and Margaret, etc; at the Q, 1938, played Paul in Call It a Day; Streatham Hill, Apr 1940, Godfrey Kneller in In Good King Charles's Golden Days; Apollo, Aug 1940, Baron von Alveston in Margin for Error; during 1940–2, appeared at the Theatre Royal, Windsor, playing Maxim de Winter in Rebecca, Captain Vanbrugh in Viceroy Sarah, Meister in The Ringer, Sergius in Arms and the Man, etc; served in HM Forces, 1942–6; re-appeared in London, at the Arts Theatre, Aug 1946, as Vanhattan in The Apple Cart; Strand, Aug 1947, played Gary Bryce in Separate Rooms; Prince of Wales, Jan 1948, Pablo Juarez in Diamond Lil; Arts, Ipswich, Nov 1948, directed The Rose Without a Thorn; Toynbee Hall, London, Feb 1949, played the title-rôle in Abraham Lincoln; Duke of York's, June 1949, Richard Carling in The Third Visitor; Bedford, Camden Town, Mar 1950, Sir Francis Levison in East Lynne; Grand Theatre, Southampton, 1951–3, played leading parts in four seasons of repertory; toured, 1953, as Romainville in Ring Round the Moon; Arts, London, May 1954, Dan Kempton in The Sun Room; Grand, Croydon, May 1954, Ivan Boroslavic in The Queen of Calabash Island; Arts, June 1954, and at the St James's the following month, played the Leading Actor in Six Characters In Search of an Author; Royal, Windsor, Sept–Nov 1954, Sir Pomeroy Jones in Angels In Love and

Jan Letzaresco in Dear Charles; Stoll, Dec 1954, Mr Bong in Noddy in Toyland; Royal, Windsor, Mar–July 1955, John Williams in The Conscience of the King, William Corder in Maria Marten and Dr Chumley in Harvey; Royal Windsor, 1956–9, played the following parts: West in The Trial of Mary Dugan, Clifford Armitage in Light's O' London, Baron Foehn in The Eagle has Two Heads, Michael Ambrion in Don't Listen, Ladies, Zamario in His Excellency, Dr Grenock in Mr Kettle and Mrs Moon, Mr Wembley in Man Alive, Inspector Bouchard in Hotel Paradiso, John Mallorie in A Day in the Life Of . . .; Duke of York's, June 1962, played Harry in The Cigarette Girl; Leatherhead, 1968, Mr Purdie in Sport of Kings; Theatre Royal, Windsor, played Velasco in Barefoot in the Park and M Maingot in French Without Tears, 1969, Moses in School for Scandal, 1971, and Sidney Redlitch in Bell, Book and Candle, 1978; first appeared in films, 1927, and on television, 1937; subsequently seen in numerous pictures and television shows including Sinbad and the Eye of the Tiger, and Jesus of Nazareth; has also broadcast frequently.

Recreations: Writing, reading, sketching and designing stage-settings. *Address:* 79 Kingston Lane, Teddington, Middlesex. *Tel:* 01–977 5507.

BARNES, Clive Alexander, drama and dance critic
b London, 13 May 1927; *s* of Arthur Lionel Barnes and his wife Freda Marguerite (Garratt); *e* Oxford University (BA 1951); *m* Patricia Amy Evelyn Winckley.

Co-editor of the Oxford dance magazine *Arabesque,* 1950; assistant editor *Dance and Dancers,* 1950–8; associate editor 1958–61; executive editor 1961–5; New York editor 1965–; writer on music, dance, drama, films for the *Daily Express,* 1956–65; dance critic to *The Spectator,* 1959–65; went to the US where he became dance critic for *The New York Times,* 1965–78; drama critic 1967–77; drama and dance critic for the *New York Post,* 1978–; adjoint associate professor, department of journalism, NY University, 1968–; member of the Critics Circle (past secretary); chairman, ballet section, NY Drama Critics Circle (president 1973–5); author of Ballet in Britain Since the War, 1953; Frederick Ashton and His Ballets, 1961; (with others) Ballet Here and Now, 1961; Dance Scene USA, 1967.

Address: New York Post, 210 South Street, New York, NY 10002.

BARNES, Peter, dramatist
b London, 10 Jan 1931; *s* of Frederick Barnes and his wife Martha (Miller); *m* Charlotte Barnes.

Author of the following plays: Sclerosis (one-act), 1965; The Ruling Class, 1968; Leonardo's Last Supper (one-act) and Noonday Demons (one-act), 1969; Lulu (adapted from Wedekind), 1970; co-directed his adaptation of this play at Nottingham Playhouse, Oct 1970; the production subsequently transferred to London; The Devil Is an Ass (adaptation), 1973; The Bewitched (RSC), 1974; directed his adaptations of The Purging (Feydeau) and The Singer (Wedekind) under the title Frontiers of Farce, Old Vic, 1976; co-directed his adaptation of The Devil Is an Ass, Edinburgh Festival 1976 and National Theatre, 1977; directed For All Those Who Get Despondent, a cabaret based on his translations of Brecht and Wedekind, Theatre Upstairs, 1977; Laughter! (Royal Court), 1978; directed Bartholomew Fair (Round House), 1978; co-directed Antonio, his adaptation of Marston's plays Antonio and Mellida, and Antonio's Revenge, Nottingham Playhouse, 1979.

Address: 7 Archery Close, Connaught Street, London, W2.

BARR, Patrick, actor
b Akola, India, 13 Feb 1908; *s* of Alexander David St Clair Barr and his wife Marjory (Birley); *e* Radley and Trinity College, Oxford; *m* Ann Jean Williams; was formerly an engineer.

Made his first appearance on the stage at the Q Theatre, 27 Feb 1933, in Miss Black's Son, and in Mar appeared as Mr Harvey in Francis Thompson, subsequently playing the same part at the Royalty, Mar 1933; Shaftesbury, Nov 1934, played Roberto Cavalcanti in For Ever; Vaudeville, Feb 1935, Tony Cornell in Summer's Lease; Westminster, Mar 1935, and Daly's, May 1935, Robin Phillimore in Chase the Ace; Q, Feb 1936, Guy in Children to Bless You; Old Vic, Oct 1936, Mr Dorilant in The Country Wife; went to the United States, and made his first appearance in New York, at the Music Box, Mar 1937, as Stephen Horka in Young Madame Conti; Lyric, Mar 1939, played Rod Shufflepenny in The Jealous God; Strand, Aug 1939, Mike in Spotted Dick; Q, June 1940, Ronnie Holt in House Party; re-appeared on the stage at the Apollo, July 1945, as Victor Prynne, in Private Lives; Piccadilly, May 1946, played Blake Ritchie in Portrait in Black; Lyric, Hammersmith, Mar 1947, Peter Rossiter in The Rossiters; Wyndham's, July 1947, Howard Merrick in Deep Are the Roots; Arts, Jan 1948, Oliver in Invitation to a Voyage; Cambridge, Aug 1948, Bill Jackson, MP, in Trouble in the House; New Lindsey, Dec 1948, Jason Otis in Jason; Hippodrome, June 1949, played Martin Nash in Her Excellency; Saville, Mar 1950, appeared as Russell Wain in The Platinum Set; Embassy, Feb 1951, played Major Gerald Craven, DSO, in Iron Curtain; Saville, July 1955, Frank in The Shadow of Doubt; Lyric, Hammersmith, June 1958, Danny Corrigan in Honour Bright; Phoenix, July 1958, took over Lord Dungavel from John McCallum in Roar Like a Dove, and played until Mar 1960; Richmond, May 1962, played Hurst in The Clostin Case; Arnaud, Guildford, Oct 1967, Rev Winemiller in The Eccentricities of a Nightingale; same theatre, Jan 1968, appeared in Shadows of the Evening and Come into the Garden, Maud; Feb 1970, became a member of the Royal Shakespeare Company, appearing that season at Stratford as Escalus in Measure for Measure, the Bishop of Ely in Richard III (April), King Hamlet and others in Hamlet (June), and as Alonso in The Tempest (Oct); Ashcroft, Croydon, Feb 1973, James in Nightfall; St Martin's, Jan 1974, George Hamilton in Dead Easy; Hippodrome, Bristol, Mar 1974, Judge in The Tilted Scales; Her Majesty's, July 1977, Judge in Cause Célèbre; first appeared in films, 1935; has made numerous TV appearances.

Address: 1 Coleherne Court, London, SW5. *Tel:* 01–373 7165.

BARR, Richard (*né* Baer), director and producer
b Washington, DC, 6 Sept 1917; *s* of David Alphonse Baer and his wife Ruth Nanette (Israel); *e* Princeton, New Jersey; began his career as an actor with Orson Welles's Mercury Theatre Company.

Made his stage début at the Mercury, New York, Nov 1938, in Danton's Death, and remained with the company until 1941; served in the US Army Air Force, 1941–5; at the City Center, NY, Jan 1948, directed Volpone (also co-adapted), Angel Street, and Feb 1948, The Bear; Booth, Feb 1949, directed Richard III; Arena, 1950, directed Arms and the Man; 1950–2, directed plays for stock companies, and produced and directed package shows with Ethel Waters, Sylvia Sidney, etc; at the Broadway Tabernacle Church, 1954, directed The Boy with a Cart; between 1952–9, co-produced (with Charles Bowden) the following: At Home with Ethel Waters (also directed), 1953; Ruth Draper and

Her Company of Characters, Ruth Draper and Paul Draper, 1954; All in One (triple-bill), 1955; Fallen Angels, Hotel Paradiso, 1957; Auntie Mame (tours), 1958; in 1959, formed a production company, Theatre 1960, with Clinton Wilder, and produced the following plays: Krapp's Last Tape, The Zoo Story, The Killer, 1960; The Sudden End of Anne Cinquefoil, The American Dream (one-act), Bartleby (opera, one-act), The Death of Bessie Smith (one-act), *The Valerie Bettis Dance Theatre,* Gallow's Humor, 1961; at the Cherry Lane, Feb 1962, under the title of Theatre of the Absurd the same company presented the following plays in repertory: Endgame, Bertha, Gallow's Humor, The Sandbox, Deathwatch, Picnic on the Battlefield, The American Dream, The Zoo Story (also directed), and The Killer (also directed); also co-produced Who's Afraid of Virginia Woolf? Whisper into My Good Ear and Mrs Dally Has a Lover (double-bill), 1962; Like Other People, The American Dream, The Zoo Story (also directed), Corruption in the Palace of Justice, 1963; in 1963, Edward Albee joined the partnership, and the company has since produced: Play and The Lover (double-bill), Funnyhouse of a Negro, Who's Afraid of Virginia Woolf? (London), Two Executioners, The Dutchman, The Giants Dance, 1964; Lovey and Hunting the Jingo Bird (double-bill), Do Not Pass Go, That Thing at the Cherry Lane, Happy Days, Up to Thursday, Balls, Home Free! Pigeons, Conerico Was Here to Stay, 1965; Malcolm, The Long Christmas Dinner, Queens of France, The Happy Journey from Trenton to Camden, A Delicate Balance, The Butter and Egg Man, Match Play, A Party for Divorce, Night of the Dunce, 1966; The Rimers of Eldritch, The Party on Greenwich Avenue, Johnny No-Trump, Everything in the Garden, 1967; The Boys in the Band, Private Lives (directed), and, as co-producer of the Playwrights Repertory, Box, Quotations from Chairman Mao Tse-Tung, The Death of Bessie Smith, The American Dream, Krapp's Last Tape, The Zoo Story, Happy Days, 1968; The Front Page, 1969; as co-producer of The Playwrights Unit, Water Color and Criss-Crossing, 1970; All Over, Drat!, The Grass Harp, 1971; at the John Drew, Easthampton, NY, summer 1972, The Long Christmas Dinner and What the Butler Saw, and in New York City, the Last of Mrs Lincoln; Seascape, PS Your Cat Is Dead!, 1975; I Was Sitting on My Patio . . ., 1977; directed Who's Afraid of Virginia Woolf, Buffalo, 1978; co-presented Sweeney Todd, 1979; The Lady from Dubuque, 1980; has also produced tours of the *Paul Taylor Dance Company,* and the *Jeff Duncan Dance Company;* elected President of The League of New York Theaters, Feb 1967, and during his term instituted a number of progressive reforms; as a member of the Orson Welles Company, he broadcast in the radio program War of the Worlds; served as an executive assistant on the film Citizen Kane; in 1947, acted as dialogue director in films in Hollywood, notably for The Voice of the Turtle.

Address: 150 East 50th Street, New York, NY 10022.

BARRANGER, Millie S, educator, and producer
b Birmingham, Ala, 12 Feb 1937; *d* of Clem Slater and his wife Mildred (Hilliard); *e* U of Montevallo (BA, 1958); Tulane U (MA, 1959; PhD, 1964); *m* Garic K Barranger.

Lecturer, Louisiana State U, New Orleans, 1964–69; assistant professor of theatre, Tulane U, 1969–73; associate professor, 1973– ; chair, theatre and speech dept, 1971– ; founding producer of Tulane Center Stage, a summer resident theatre, 1973–77, where plays produced included The Rivals, Cat on a Hot Tin Roof, Blithe Spirit, and The Lion in Winter; officer of the American Theatre Association, since 1975; president, 1978–79; co-editor of Generations: an introduction to drama, 1971; author of Theatre: a Way of Seeing, 1980; and numerous articles in theatre journals.

Address: Theatre and Speech Dept, Tulane University, New Orleans, LA 70118. *Tel:* 504-865 6205.

BARRETT, Leslie (*né* Klein), actor
b Staten Island, 30 Oct 1919; *s* of Cecil Klein and his wife Theresa (Leonhardt); *e* George Washington HS, NY; *m* (1) Diana Newman Barth (mar dis); (2) Ruth W Livingston.

Made his professional debut under the name Leslie Klein at the Guild, 12 Jan 1937, as Bosco in But for the Grace of God; Hudson, Feb 1937, a boy in Enemy of the People; changed his name to Leslie Barrett and succeeded Billy Halop as Tommy in Dead End, Belasco, Apr 1937; Hudson, Feb 1938, Pogriski in Sunup to Sundown; Windsor, Mar 1938, Tommy Hammond in There's Always a Breeze; Biltmore, Jan 1939, Davy Wallace in The Primrose Path; Biltmore, May 1940, Newsboy in At the Stroke of Eight; Mansfield, Nov 1940, Jockey Lane in Horse Fever; Windsor, Oct 1941, Western Union Boy in Good Neighbor; Henry Miller's, Jan 1942, Marco in All in Favor; Royale, Nov 1942, Henry Susskind in Counsellor-at-Law; after Army service attended the American Theatre Wing, 1946–49, and studied with Lee Strasberg; Paper Mill Playhouse, Apr 1947, Lee Brady in The Love Wagon; formed the Actors' Workshop, 1949–50, with Sidney Lumet and Joseph Anthony; formed the American Mime Theatre, 1952–55, with Paul Curtis, performing at Jacob's Pillow, Brooklyn Academy etc; Apr 1955, joined Shakespeare Theatre Workshop, NY, under Joseph Papp, performing in Much Ado About Nothing, As You Like It, etc; at Westport Playhouse, Jul-Aug 1955; Holiday, NY, Oct 1955, Clerk of the Court in Deadfall; Cherry Lane, May 1957, took over as Postmaster in Purple Dust; Jan Hus, Jan 1958, Grigory in The Trial of Dmitri Karamazov; from 1958–61 wrote and performed the biographies of the poets in From the Classics to the Contemporaries, a series of ongoing poetry readings at Donnell Library Theatre, NY, and ELT, LA; directed the first production of Equity Library Theatre-West, The Crucible, in 1959; Longacre, Jan 1961, Old Gentleman in Rhinoceros, also touring; Phoenix, Apr 1963, the Cat in The Dragon; national tour, 1965, as Doc in West Side Story; Longacre, Feb 1966, Henry in Slapstick Tragedy; Playhouse in the Park, Philadelphia, Jun 1966, Waiter in Incident at Vichy; Ambassador, Oct 1966, First and Second Witnesses in The Investigation; Renata, Mar 1967, Padre in Hamp; Jan Hus, Oct 1967, in The Day the Lid Blew Off; Pocket, Jan 1969, Uncle Eugene in Tango; in repertory at the Loretta Hilton Center, St Louis, Mo, Mar 1970; appeared in Canada, Jan 1971, as Jim Heeler in Hobson's Choice; Barter, Va, Jul 1972, Judge Gaffrey in Harvey; Actors Theatre, Louisville, Ky, Oct 1972, de Pinna in You Can't Take It With You; Chelsea Westside, Oct 1973, played matinees as Old Mr Ewbank in The Contractor; Walnut, Phila, Jan 1974, the Pedant in the Taming of the Shrew; Westgate, Toledo, Dec 1974, Mr Wilbur in Once More with Feeling; toured with the Kenley Players, Ohio, Jul 1975, as Herr Schlick in Bitter Sweet; toured, Feb 1976, as Josef in The Student Prince; Hudson Guild, Feb 1977, Maj Brigg in Savages; Studio Arena, Buffalo, Nov 1977, Rosas in Semmelweiss; AMDA Studio, Oct 1978, John of Gaunt in Richard II; Orpheum, Jan 1979, and 22 Steps, Apr 1979, Fineberg in My Old Friends; has appeared frequently on TV and radio.

Recreations: Gallery-going, tennis. *Address:* c/o Actors Equity Association, 165 West 46th Street, New York, NY 10036.

BARRIE, Amanda (*née* Broadbent), actress
b Ashton-under-Lyme, 14 Sept 1939; *d* of Hubert Howarth

Broadbent and his wife Constance (Pike); *e* St Anne's College, St Anne's-on-Sea; *m* Robin Hunter; trained for the stage at the Cone-Ripman School.

Made her first appearance on the stage as a child in the chorus at Finsbury Park Empire; made her first appearance in the West End at the Phoenix, Apr 1961, in the revue On the Brighter Side; Duchess, Mar 1963, appeared in the revue See You Inside; Adelphi, Sept 1963, appeared in the revue Six of One; at the Lyric, 1964, she took over the leading part of Ilona Ritter in She Loves Me; joined the Bristol Old Vic Company, 1964, to play a number of parts in Little by Little, Alice in Hobson's Choice, and Lucy Lockit in The Beggar's Opera; St Martin's, May, 1965, played Bridget in A Public Mischief; Apollo, Aug 1965, played Ellen in Any Wednesday; Palace, Watford, Dec 1967, played the title part in Aladdin and, Mar 1968, Amanda in Private Lives; Sept 1968, toured as Sybil Merton in Lord Arthur Savile's Crime; Johannesburg, Summer 1969, played Sally Bowles in Cabaret, returning to play Dandini in Cinderella at Golders Green (Dec); May 1970, toured in The Mating Game; Richmond, Sept 1970, appeared in Lady Audley's Secret; toured, May 1971, as Jackie Coryton in Hay Fever; Shaw, Apr 1972, played Olive Ashton in Come When You Like; Arnaud, Guildford, Sept 1972, Helen Brown in Who's Who; Bankside Globe, July 1973, Viola in Twelfth Night; Westminster, Mar 1974, Kay in Oh, Kay!; Vaudeville, Jan 1975, took over as Marion in Absurd Person Singular; Comedy, Oct 1975, took over as Alison Ames in A Touch of Spring; Globe, July 1977, took over as Lady Driver in Donkey's Years; Piccadilly, May 1979, appeared in The French Have a Song for It; toured, Aug 1979, as Helen in Ten Times Table; Churchill, Bromley, Dec 1979, title rôle in Aladdin; she has also appeared in the films Carry On Cleo, and I Gotta Horse; first appeared on television, 1956, and recent appearances include: Ooh, La, La and A Midsummer Night's Dream.

Favourite part: Lucy Lockit. *Recreation:* Horse racing. *Club:* Arts. *Address:* c/o Leading Artists, 60 St James's Street, London SW1.

BARRIE, Barbara (*née* Barbara Berman), actress
b Chicago, 23 May 1931; *d* of Louis Berman and his wife Frances Rose Boruszak; *e* Corpus Christi, Tex, public schools and U of Texas, Austin (BFA 1953); *m* Jay Malcolm Harnick, producer-director; trained for the stage with Uta Hagen, Walt Witcover etc.

Lenox Hill Playhouse, Apr 1953, played Sloth in an ELT production of Dr Faustus; several parts at the Corning Summer Theatre, NY, 1953–54; Broadway debut, Booth, 6 Oct 1955, as Janey Stewart in The Wooden Dish; Martinique, Mar 1958, Goody Proctor in The Crucible; American Shakespeare Festival, Stratford, Conn, season 1958, her parts were Player Queen in Hamlet, Hermia in A Midsummer Night's Dream, and Dorcas in The Winter's Tale; Phoenix, Feb 1959, Cherry in The Beaux' Stratagem; again at Stratford, season 1959, played Anne Page in The Merry Wives of Windsor and Diana in All's Well That Ends Well; NY Shakespeare Festival, Aug 1960, Bianca in The Taming of the Shrew; toured Europe and the Middle East for USIA, 1960, as Annie Sullivan in the Theatre Guild production of The Miracle Worker; Eugene O'Neill, NY, Mar 1966, Joan Mills in Happily Never After; Delacorte, Jun 1966, Helena in All's Well That Ends Well; Fortune, Jan 1969, Intellect in Horseman, Pass By; Delacorte, Aug 1969, Viola in Twelfth Night; Alvin, Apr 1970, Sarah in Company; Shubert, Mar 1972, Grace Mason in The Selling of the President; Eugene O'Neill, Jun 1972, took over as Edna Edison in The Prisoner

of Second Avenue; Newman, Mar 1974, Sparky in The Killdeer; Ahmanson, LA, Apr 1976, and Eugene O'Neill, Jun 1976, Millie and Beth in California Suite; Marymount Manhattan, Apr 1979, Lotte in the Phoenix production of Big and Little; films include Giant, 1956, and recently The Bell Jar and Breaking Away; frequent TV work in serials and plays, including recently Roots II.

Favourite parts: Viola, Sparky. *Recreations:* Tennis, antiques. *Address:* 465 West End Avenue, New York, NY 10024.

BARRIE, Frank, actor
b Scarborough, Yorks, 19 Sept 1939; *s* of Arthur Smith and his wife Annie; *e* Archbishop Holgate's GS, York, and Hull University (BA); *m* Maryann Lloyd.

His first stage appearance was in 1959 at the Theatre Royal, York, as Mouldy in Henry IV Part II; after three years of repertory in various parts of Britain, joined the Bristol Old Vic Company, 1965, where he stayed for four years, playing leading roles including the title parts in Alfie, Oedipus Rex, Richard II and Stand Up for Nigel Barton; toured N America and Europe with the company, 1967, as Mercutio in Romeo and Juliet and Lucio in Measure for Measure, making his New York debut in the latter role at the City Center, 14 Mar 1967; with the National Theatre company at the Old Vic, 1969–72, his parts included Hamlet in Rosencrantz and Guildenstern Are Dead, 1969; Bracciano in The White Devil, Ganya in The Idiot, and Mirabell in The Way of the World, 1970; Wendoll in A Woman Killed with Kindness, Barelli in The Rules of the Game, and Camille Desmoulins in Danton's Death (these last two at the New), 1971; Young Vic, Jan 1971, Byron in Byron, the Naked Peacock; Old Vic, 1972, Bassanio in The Merchant of Venice; at the Open Air Theatre, Regent's Park, played Orsino in Twelfth Night and Jacques in As You Like It, season 1973, and Oberon in A Midsummer Night's Dream, season 1974; York, autumn 1974, played More in A Man for All Seasons and the title role in Hamlet; Bristol, appeared in Cowardy Custard, Dec 1974, and played Macheath in The Threepenny Opera, Feb 1975; Thorndike, Leatherhead, Dazzle in London Assurance, Apr 1975, and the Stranger in The Lady from the Sea, May 1976; at Greenwich, played the Count in The Artful Widow, Nov 1976; appeared in the revue The Great Wall, Dec 1976; Second Messenger in The Sons of Oedipus, Feb; Orsino in Twelfth Night, Mar; Crichton in The Admirable Crichton, Apr; Yang Sun in The Good Person of Szechwan, May, all 1977; Arnaud, Guildford, Sept 1977, again played Mercutio; Greenwich, Mar 1978, title role in Moliere's Don Juan; at the Northcott, Exeter, 1978, played the title role in Macbeth, and Jacques in As You Like It, Oct; 1979, Lord Rosebery in Motherdear, Apr, and John Worthing in The Importance of Being Earnest, Aug; in Oct 1979 at this theatre he gave the first performance of his solo entertainment Meet Mr Macready, with which he has since toured including New York, Mar 1980; Theatre Royal, Haymarket, Oct 1979, took over as Major Ross in The Crucifer of Blood; first TV appearance, 1964, in *Emergency Ward 10*; subsequent appearances include The Rehearsal and Coriolanus (for Irish Television); has appeared frequently in poetry recitals and on radio.

Hobbies: Gardening, architecture, furniture restoration. *Address:* Farnham House, 53 Wickham Road, London SE4. *Tel:* 01-692 6502.

BARRY, Michael (*né* James Barry Jackson), director
b London, 15 May 1910; *s* of Archie Jackson and his wife Helen (Callaghan); *e* Haberdashers Askes, Hampstead, and the Hertfordshire Agricultural Institute; *m* (1) Judith Gick

(mar dis); (2) Rosemary Corbett (dec); (3) Pamela Corbett; trained for the stage at RADA, 1929–30.

In repertory as an actor at Northampton and Birmingham before London experience, 1932–34, as actor, designer, SM; directed at Hull Rep, 1934–35, Croydon Rep, 1935–38; joined BBC television as a producer, 1938, and returned as drama and documentary writer/producer after war service with the Royal Marines; Head of BBC Television Drama, 1951–61; Programme Controller, Telefis Eireann, 1961–63; freelance writer/director for television, 1963–68, during which time he was executive producer for The Wars of the Roses, 1966; Professor of Drama and Head of Drama Dept, Stanford University, Calif, 1968–72; Principal, London Academy of Music and Dramatic Art, 1973–78; member, Arts Council Drama Panel, 1955–68; Council of RADA, 1966–69; National Council for Drama Training, 1976–78; Director, Royal Exchange Theatre, Manchester, 1972–   ; awarded the OBE for services to television drama, 1956.

Club: Savile. *Address:* 5 Clarence Gardens, Brighton, Sussex *and* Gilios, Paxos, Greece. *Tel:* Brighton 27728.

BART, Lionel, composer, lyricist, playwright
b London, 1 Aug 1930.

Began his professional career at the Theatre Royal, Stratford, E, Feb 1959, writing the lyrics and music for Fings Ain't Wot They Used T' Be, which was revived at the same theatre, Dec 1959, and transferred to the Garrick Theatre, Feb 1960, where it ran for over two years; he is also the author of the following: Lock Up Your Daughters! (lyrics), 1959; Oliver! (book, lyrics, and music), 1960; Blitz (co-author of the book, lyrics, music, and co-directed), 1962; Merry Roosters Panto (some lyrics, and music), 1963; Maggie May (music and songwords), 1964; Twang! (book, music, and songwords), 1965; Lock Up Your Daughters! was also produced on an out-of-town tour in the United States, 1960, and revived in London, at the Mermaid, Mar 1969; Oliver! (New York, Imperial), 1963, and English tour, Nov 1966; La Strada (music and lyrics), NY, 1969; The Londoners (songs), Costa Packet (songs), 1972; musical supervision, So You Want to Be in Pictures, 1973; he is the composer of the following film scores: The Tommy Steele Story, The Duke Wore Jeans, Tommy the Toreador, Oliver!; composer of the title songs From Russia With Love, and Man in the Middle; he received the Ivor Novello Award for the following: Lock Up Your Daughters! Oliver! Blitz; received the Antoinette Perry Award, for the Best Musical of 1963 and a Gold Disc for album sales, with Oliver!; the musical Lionel (New London, May 1977), was based on his career and works.

Address: c/o Patricia McNaughton, MLR, 194 Old Brompton Road, London SW5.

BARTLETT, D'Jamin, actress and singer
b New York, NY, 21 May 1948; *m* William Bartlett; trained for the stage at the American Academy of Dramatic Arts.

Made her first professional appearance at Ford's, Washington DC, 1971, in Godspell; Broadway debut, Shubert, 25 Feb 1973, as Petra in A Little Night Music; Studio Arena, Buffalo, NY, 1974, appeared in I Got a Song; Theatre Four, May 1975, Liana in The Glorious Age; Edison, Nov 1975, Isabella and Sister Angelica in Boccaccio; Village Gate, Oct 1976, appeared in the revue 2 by 5; Direct, Jan 1977, title role in Lulu; National, Washington, Jan 1978, Holly Beaumont in a pre-Broadway tryout of Spotlight; Pittsburgh Civic Light Opera, 1979, Sally Bowles in Cabaret; has toured or appeared in stock as Eliza in My Fair Lady, 1976, Fastrada in Pippin, 1977; has appeared regularly in cabaret at Reno Sweeney, the Chelsea Encore etc; has appeared on TV panel shows.

Favourite parts: Eliza Doolittle, Sally Bowles. *Address:* c/o Henderson-Hogan Agency, 200 West 57th Street, New York, NY 10019.

BARTON, John, director and dramatic adapter
b London, 26 Nov 1928; *s* of Sir Harold Montagu Barton and his wife Joyce (Wale); *e* Eton College, and King's College, Cambridge; *m* Anne Righter; Fellow of King's College, Cambridge, 1954–60.

Directed his first production at the ADC Theatre, Cambridge, 1949; while at Cambridge directed and acted in many productions for the Marlowe Society and ADC; at the Westminster, July 1953, directed his first London production, Henry V, for the Elizabethan Theatre Company; Shakespeare Memorial Theatre, Stratford-on-Avon, June 1960, directed The Taming of the Shrew; Aldwych, Mar 1961, devised and took part in the Anthology, The Hollow Crown; Sadler's Wells, Nov 1961, directed Carmen; Aldwych, Mar 1962, directed and Narrator in The Art of Seduction; at the Belgrade, Coventry Festival, June 1962, devised and took part in The Vagaries of Love; made his first appearance in New York, at the Henry Miller Theatre, Jan 1963, in The Hollow Crown; RSC, Stratford-on-Avon, July 1963, adapted, edited and assisted in the direction of The Wars of the Roses; RSC, Stratford-on-Avon, 1964, co-directed Richard II and Henry IV (Part I and II), Henry V, and The Wars of the Roses; RSC, Stratford-on-Avon, April 1965, directed Love's Labour's Lost; Aldwych, May 1965, co-directed Henry V; Stratford, 1966, co-directed Henry IV (Parts I and II) and adapted text for The Revengers' Tragedy; 1967–8, directed Coriolanus and All's Well That Ends Well (also at the Aldwych); 1968–9, directed Julius Caesar, and Troilus and Cressida (also at the Aldwych); 1969–70, directed Twelfth Night (also Aldwych) and When Thou Art King (adapted from Henry IV, Parts I and II, and Henry V); April 1970, directed Measure For Measure; Oct 1970, directed The Tempest; 1971, directed Twelfth Night and Othello (also Aldwych 1972); directed Richard II and Henry V for Theatregoround, 1971; co-directed Titus Andronicus, 1972; Stratford 1973 and Aldwych 1974, Richard II; co-directed King John (in his adaptation) and Cymbeline, at Stratford and the Aldwych, 1974; directed his version of Doctor Faustus, Aldwych 1974; co-directed Perkin Warbeck, The Other Place, 1975; Stratford 1976, directed Much Ado About Nothing, and co-directed The Winter's Tale, Troilus and Cressida, and King Lear; Aldwych, season 1977–8, co-directed A Midsummer Night's Dream and Directed Much Ado, Pillars of the Community, and The Way of the World; Stratford 1978, The Merchant of Venice (Warehouse 1979) and Love's Labour's Lost (Aldwych 1979); Aldwych, 1980, The Greeks (his own adaptations from Homer, Euripides, Aeschylus and Sophocles); Drama Lecturer at University of Berkeley, California, 1953–4; Associate Director of The Royal Shakespeare Company since 1964; 1968–74, Company Director of the RSC at Stratford.

Address: 14 De Walden Court, 85 New Cavendish Street, London, W1. *Tel:* 01–636 7031.

BASEHART, Richard, actor
b Zanesville, Ohio, 31 Aug 1914; *s* of Harry T Basehart and his wife Mae (Wetherald); *e* Zanesville public schools; *m* (1) Stephanie Klein (dec); (2) Valentina Cortesa (mar dis); (3) Diana Lotery.

First appeared on the stage with the Wright Players Stock Company in Zanesville, 1932; joined the Hedgerow Theatre,

Moylan, Pa, and played in repertory there, 1938–42; made his New York début at the Windsor, 3 Feb 1943, as Weiler in Counterattack; Belasco, Sept 1943, Sergeant Hauptmann in Land of Fame; Shubert, Oct 1943, joined the cast of Margaret Webster's production of Othello; 48th Street, Feb 1944, Kip in Take It As It Comes; Mansfield, May 1944, Steven Ames in Hickory Stick, Hudson, Jan 1945, Lachlan in The Hasty Heart; Playhouse, Jan 1948, Steve Decker in The Survivors; Belasco, Feb 1958, Charles Morrow in The Day the Money Stopped; American Shakespeare Festival, Stratford, Conn, June 1962, title-role of Richard II; Mark Taper Forum, Los Angeles, 1969, played in Uncle Vanya; received the *Variety* New York Drama Critics Poll for The Hasty Heart; made his film début in Cry Wolf, 1947, and since has made many films including He Walked by Night, Decision Before Dawn, Titanic, La Strada, Il Bidone, Moby Dick, The Brothers Karamazov, The Satan Bug, Rage, Chato's Land, etc; has appeared regularly on television since 1957 in such dramatic productions as So Soon to Die, A Dream of Treason, The Men in White, He Who Gets Slapped, The Light That Failed, the long-continuing series *Voyage to the Bottom of the Sea*, Sole Survivor, The Andersonville Trial, The Bounty Man, etc.

Recreations: Reading, tennis, and swimming. *Address:* Jack Fields Agency, 9255 Sunset Boulevard, Los Angeles, Calif 90069.

BASS, Alfred, actor
b London, 8 Apr 1921; s of Jacob Bass and his wife Ada (Miller); e elementary school, Bethnal Green; m Beryl Margaret Bryson.

He had considerable amateur experience before making his first professional appearance at the Unity Theatre, 1939, as Izzie in Plant in the Sun; at the Arts Theatre, July 1943, scored a striking success when he appeared as Buster King in Buster; Playhouse, Sept 1943, succeeded Harry Ross as Cohen in Mr Bolfry; Playhouse, Liverpool, 1945, appeared with the Liverpool Old Vic company, and played Abel Drugger in The Alchemist; Unity, June 1945, Rooky in Alice in Thunderland; Q, Apr 1947, Morgan in Those Were the Days; Duchess, June 1947, Tilly in He Who Gets Slapped; Embassy, July 1947, Fred Bassett in Headlights on A5; Palace, Oct 1947, Og in Finian's Rainbow; Stratford-on-Avon Memorial Theatre, 1948 season, played Gurney in King John, Launcelot Gobbo in The Merchant of Venice, Second Gravedigger in Hamlet, Grumio in The Taming of the Shrew, Autolycus in The Winter's Tale; Embassy, Sept 1949, Benjamin Brownstein in The Golden Door, and Apr 1950, Philip Anagnos in The Gentle People; appeared in a number of parts at the Embassy, May 1951–Apr 1952; Lyric, Hammersmith, May 1952, played Augustus Colpoys in Trelawny of the Wells; Embassy, Apr 1953, Jimmie Thomson in Starched Aprons; Arts, June 1953, played Fender in The Bespoke Overcoat, and repeated this performance at the Embassy, Jan 1954; Embassy, Jan 1955, appeared in The World of Sholom Aleichem; Duke of York's, Sept 1955, appeared in The Punch Revue; Duchess, May 1956, played Emmett in The Silver Whistle; Her Majesty's, 1968, took over the part of Tevye in Fiddler On the Roof; Greenwich, Sept 1972, Eccles in Caste; appeared in the London Palladium pantomimes Cinderella, 1973 and Jack and the Beanstalk, 1974; first appeared in films 1937, in the Army Film Section, and has since appeared in numerous pictures including The Lavender Hill Mob, The Bespoke Overcoat, Alfie, Death on the Nile and Moonraker; television appearances include *Robin Hood, The Army Game, Bootsie and Snudge, Danger UXB, Are You Being Served,* etc.

Recreation: All-round sports, and gardening. *Address:* c/o Pamela Simons, 9–15 Neal Street, Covent Garden, London, WC2.

BATE, Anthony, actor
b Stourbridge, Worcs; s of Hubert George Cookson Bate and his wife Cecile Marjorie (Canadine); e King Edward VI GS, Stourbridge; m Diana Fay Watson; after experience in banking and hotel work trained for the stage at the Central School of Speech and Drama, 1950–53.

Made his first professional appearance at the Palace Theatre, Bideford, 13 July 1953, as Capt Carlos in the premiere of Ronald Duncan's play Don Juan; in repertory, 1953–56, at Worthing, Durham, Palmer's Green etc; toured, 1954–55, as Lt Cmdr Redmond in Seagulls over Sorrento; toured, 1956, as Sir Wilfred Robarts in Witness for the Prosecution; New, Bromley, Feb 1957, Bob Acres in The Rivals; Mermaid, Dec 1959, Tom in Treasure Island; West End debut, 16 Mar 1960, as Tom Davenport in Inherit the Wind; Hampstead, May 1966, Mark Solstice in Happy Family; joined the Royal Shakespeare Company at the Aldwych, July 1969, to play Rumsey in Silence and Don Pedro in Much Ado About Nothing; Open Space, May 1970, Alan Harrison in Find Your Way Home; toured, 1972, as Charlie Appleby in Eden End; Haymarket, Leicester, 1973, Denis in Economic Necessity; Comedy, July 1976, Ulick Drummond in Getting Away with Murder; toured, 1979, as Brian in the Cambridge Theatre Company's production of The Shadow Box; first film, High Tide at Noon, 1956; frequent TV, since 1955, includes The Seagull, Crime and Punishment, and Tinker, Tailor, Soldier, Spy.

Recreation: Listening to music. *Address:* c/o Al Parker Ltd, 50 Mount Street, London W1Y 5RE.

BATES, Alan, actor
b Derbyshire, 17 Feb 1934; s of Harold Arthur Bates and his wife Florence Mary (Wheatcroft); e Herbert Strutt Grammar School, Belper, Derbyshire; m Victoria Ward; studied for the stage at the Royal Academy of Dramatic Art.

Made his first appearance on the stage with the Midland Theatre Company, Coventry, 1955, in You and Your Wife; first appeared in London at the Royal Court, Apr 1956, as Simon Fellowes in the English Stage Company's production, The Mulberry Bush; as a member of the same company at the Royal Court, he played the following parts: Apr 1956, Hopkins in The Crucible; May 1956, Cliff Lewis in Look Back in Anger; June 1956, Stapleton in Cards of Identity; Dec 1956, Mr Harcourt in The Country Wife; May 1957, Monsieur le Cracheton in The Apollo de Bellac; June 1957 (in a Production without Décor) Dr Brock in Yes—and After; at the World Youth Festival in Moscow, July 1957, played his original part of Cliff in Look Back in Anger in the English Stage Company production; made his first appearance in New York, at the Lyceum Theatre, Oct 1958, in the same part and play; following the successful NY run, he returned to England to appear at the Edinburgh Festival, Lyceum, 1958, as Edmund Tyrone in Long Day's Journey Into Night, subsequently appearing in the same production at the Globe, Sept 1958; he received the Clarence Derwent Award, 1959, for his performance in this play; Arts, Apr 1960, played Mick in The Caretaker, and transferred with the production to the Duchess, May 1960; Lyceum, NY, Oct 1961, again played Mick in The Caretaker; Helen Hayes, NY, Dec 1964, played Richard Ford in Poor Richard; Saville, London, Aug 1965, Adam in The Four Seasons; Stratford, Ontario, 1967, Ford in The Merry Wives of Windsor, and Richard III; Royal Court, Apr 1969, Andrew in In Celebration; Playhouse, Nottingham, Nov 1970, and Cambridge Theatre, Jan 1971, played Hamlet; Criterion, July 1971, title role in Butley; repeating the part in NY, 1972; Stratford-on-Avon, Sept 1973, Petruchio in The Taming of the Shrew; Royal Court, Apr 1974, Allott in Life Class, transferring to the Duke of York's, June 1974; Queen's, July 1975, Simon in Otherwise Engaged, for which he received the *Evening Standard* award as Best Actor, 1975; Derby Playhouse, July 1976, Trigorin in The Seagull, transferring to the Duke of York's Aug; Vaudeville, Nov 1979, Robert in Stage Struck; first appeared in films, 1960, as Frank Rice in The Entertainer, he has since appeared in A Kind of Loving, Zorba the Greek, Far From the Madding Crowd, The Fixer, Women in Love, The Go-Between, Royal Flash, An Unmarried Woman, Nijinsky, etc; has made many television appearances, notably in Look Back in Anger, The Wind and the Rain, and The Mayor of Casterbridge.

Favourite parts: Cliff in Look Back in Anger, Edmund in Long Day's Journey Into Night, Mick in The Caretaker, and Andrew in In Celebration. *Recreations:* Driving, tennis, swimming, riding. *Address:* c/o Chatto and Linnit, Globe Theatre, Shaftesbury Avenue, London, W1.

BATESON, Timothy, actor
b London, 3 Apr 1926; *s* of Dingwall Latham Bateson and his wife Naomi Judith (Alcock); *e* Uppingham and Wadham College, Oxford; *m* Sheila Shand Gibbs.

Joined the Old Vic, 1948, and made his debut with the company at the Opera House, Manchester, Aug, walking on in Twelfth Night; made his first London appearance in the same part at the New, Sept 1948, also playing parts including Ralph in Dr Faustus; went to New York, Dec 1951, with Laurence Olivier's company to play Theodotus in Caesar and Cleopatra and Clown in Antony and Cleopatra at the Ziegfeld, having played the latter part at the St James's, May 1951; at the Old Vic theatre, played Osric in Hamlet, Sept 1953, and Trinculo in The Tempest, Apr 1954; Arts, Aug 1955, Lucky in Waiting for Godot, transferring with the play to the Criterion, Sept 1955; Her Majesty's, Aug 1956, Ben Whitledge in No Time for Sergeants; Aldwych, Aug 1958, Ubaita in Brouhaha; Apollo, Sept 1961, Bellamy in The Fantasticks; Chichester Festival, July 1962, Tecnicus in The Broken Heart; Garrick, Nov 1963, Jerome Pitman in Difference of Opinion; Mermaid, June 1965, de Vesci in Left-Handed Liberty; same theatre, Sept 1965, Joseph Knox in Fanny's First Play; joined the Leeds Playhouse company in its first season, Sept 1970, playing in Simon Says and as Belcredi in Henry IV, the latter also at Edinburgh, Aug 1970; Savoy, Apr 1975, M Canton in The Clandestine Marriage; Oxford Festival, 1976, Nicola in Arms and the Man; Gardner Centre, Brighton, Dec 1979, title rôle in Winnie the Pooh; film appearances include Richard III, Our Man In Havana, and The Anniversary; television, since 1958, includes plays, serials and series; council member of Equity, 1968–70.

Favourite part: Lucky. *Recreation:* Music. *Address:* c/o Ken McReddie, 4 Paddington Street, London, W1.

BAUERSMITH, Paula, actress
b Oakmont, Pennsylvania, 26 July 1909; *d* of William Robinson Bauersmith and his wife Susan (Paul); *e* St Margaret's, Waterbury, Conn, and the Carnegie Institute of Technology; *m* Dr B M Warren (dec); studied for the stage at the Drama Department of the Carnegie Institute.

First appeared on the stage in 1929 while a student; made her New York début at the Forrest, Oct 1931, as Carmen Bracegirdle in Lean Harvest; Belmont, Jan 1932, played Lora McDonald in East of Broadway; Morosco, Mar 1932, played

the First Sergeant in Warrior's Husband; Bijou, Oct 1932, Mary Paterson in The Anatomist; Cort, Mar 1933, Jennie in Three-Cornered Moon; Henry Miller, Dec 1933, Miss Moorhead in All Good Americans; Bijou, Jan 1934, Marge in Mahogany Hall; Broadhurst, Nov 1935, Emma Martin in Let Freedom Ring; Ethel Barrymore, Apr 1936, Martha Webster in Bury the Dead; 48th Street, Nov 1936, Jennie Walters in Two Hundred Were Chosen; New School, Nov 1942, Katya in Winter Soldiers; American Theatre Wing, 1943, appeared in It's Up to You; toured in Paths of Glory, 1947; Educational Alliance (ANTA's Experimental Theatre), May 1948, Augusta Stetson in Battle for Heaven; ANTA, Dec 1950, Dr Johnson in a revival of Twentieth Century; at the Broadway Congregational Church appeared with the Chapel Players in Oct 1956, as Anna in Thor, with Angels, Feb 1957, as Margaret in A Box of Watercolors, Oct 1957, As Anna in Tobias and the Angel, Feb 1958, as Bernoline in The Marvellous History of Saint Bernard, and Nov 1958, as Miss Connolly in The Potting Shed; Phoenix, Jan 1958, The Maid in The Lesson; toured as Hecuba in Tiger at the Gates, 1960; Broadhurst, Oct 1961, played Mrs Sweeney in Sail Away; Theatre de Lys, off-Broadway, 1962, appeared in Sweet of You to Say So; toured with the National Repertory Company in Liliom, as Aunt Julia in Hedda Gabler, and Mrs Hardcastle in She Stoops to Conquer, 1964–5; toured with the same company as Luce in Comedy of Errors and in various roles in John Brown's Body, 1967–8, during this tour performing at the re-opening of Ford's Theatre in Washington, DC; since 1933 has appeared frequently at summer theatres in such plays as You Can't Take It with You, Anything Goes, The Other Devil, Separate Tables, The Mousetrap, Take Me Along, Write Me a Murder, Damn Yankees, Bells Are Ringing, and Tunnel of Love; in 1956 appeared at the Ann Arbor (Michigan) Drama Festival in A Member of the Wedding, Tiger at the Gates, The Chalk Garden, and The Solid Gold Cadillac; first appeared on television in 1948 and has since appeared frequently in the following programs: *Omnibus, The US Steel Hour, East Side, West Side,* etc.

Favourite parts: Martha Webster in Bury the Dead and Jennie Walters in Two Hundred Were Chosen. *Recreation:* Creating crossword puzzles for *The New York Times.* *Address:* 10 Christopher Street, New York, NY 10014. *Tel:* 691 0478.

BAXLEY, Barbara, actress
b Stockton, Cal, 1 Jan 1927; *d* of Bert Baxley and his wife Emma (Tyler); *e* College of the Pacific; *m* Douglas Taylor.

Prepared for the stage at the Neighborhood Playhouse and Actors Studio in New York; toured 1947–8 as Sibyl Chase in Private Lives, making her first NY appearance at the Plymouth, Oct 1948, in the same role; at the Imperial, in 1950, took over the title-role of Peter Pan; Ethel Barrymore, Sept 1951, played Virginia Beamer in Out West of Eighth; at the Empire, 1952, took over the role of Sally Bowles in I Am a Camera; National, Mar 1953, played Esmeralda in Camino Real; Broadhurst, Oct 1953, Virginia Belden in The Frogs of Spring; Henry Miller, 1954, took over the role of Mildred Turner in Oh Men! Oh Women!; Belasco, Dec 1954, played Goldie in The Flowering Peach; Music Box, 1955, took over Chérie in Bus Stop; Cricket, Nov 1957, played Barbara Harris in A Palm Tree in a Rose Garden; US tour, Jan–May 1959, played Cora Flood in The Dark at the Top of the Stairs; Helen Hayes, Nov 1960, played Isabel Haverstick in Period of Adjustment; Theatre de Lys, 1962, appeared in the anthology Brecht on Brecht; Eugene O'Neill, Apr 1963, played Miss Ritter in She Loves Me; Morosco, June 1964, played Natalya in The Three Sisters; Aldwych, May 1965, made her London début as Natalya in The Three Sisters, during the World Theatre Season; University of Chicago, Feb 1966, Célimène in The Misanthrope; Delacorte, NY, for the New York Shakespeare Festival, July 1966, Isabel in Measure for Measure; Trinity Square, Providence, RI, Dec 1966, Dollyheart Talbo in The Grass Harp; for the American Shakespeare Festival, Stratford, Conn, summer 1967, Portia in The Merchant of Venice; Plymouth, NY, in 1968, took over from Maureen Stapleton her three roles in Plaza Suite; Cherry Lane, Jan 1969, appeared in the dramatic revue To Be Young, Gifted, and Black; Theatre de Lys, Nov 1969, Juliet in Oh, Pioneers; Eisenhower, Washington, DC, Aug 1975, Goody Rickby in The Scarecrow; John Golden, Mar 1976, Annie in Me Jack, You Jill; Lyceum, Oct 1976, Carolyn Parsky in Best Friend; Forrest, Philadelphia, Feb 1977, Elaine Thomas in The Dream; Hartford Stage, Conn, Nov 1977, Emily Michaelson in Past Tense; Promenade, 1979, guest appearance as Lillian Hellman in Are You Now or Have You Ever Been . . .?; first appeared in films, in 1954, and notable appearances include: East of Eden, All Fall Down, and The Savage Eye, Norma Rae, and the Last Resort; first appeared on television in 1953, recently in All That Glitters.

Favourite parts: Esmeralda, Peter Pan, Isabel Haverstick, and Miss Ritter. *Recreation:* Reading. *Address:* 150 West 87th Street, New York, NY. *Tel:* SU 7-7156.

BAXTER, Anne, actress
b Michigan City, Indiana, 7 May 1923; *d* of Kenneth Stuart Baxter and his wife Catherine (Wright) the daughter of Frank Lloyd Wright, the architect; *e* The Lenox School, The Brearley School, 20th Century Fox Studio School; prepared for the stage at the Theodore Irvine's School of the Theatre, 1934–6, and studied with Maria Ouspenskaya, 1937–40; *m* (1) John Hodiak (mar dis); (2) Randolph Galt (mar dis).

Made her New York début at the Henry Miller's, 17 Sept 1936, as Elizabeth Winthrop in Seen But Not Heard; Windsor, Mar 1938, Lita Hammond in There's Always a Breeze; Cape Cod Playhouse, Dennis, Mass, summer 1938, played in Susan and God; Cort, Oct 1938, Rosalie in Madame Capet; Cape Playhouse, July 1939, played in Spring Meeting; went to Hollywood, where she made many films; toured US with Raymond Massey in John Brown's Body, 1953; returned to Broadway at the National, 30 Oct 1957, as Mollie Lovejoy in The Square Root of Wonderful; made her London stage début at the Duke of York's, 9 July 1958, as Louise Schaeffer in The Joshua Tree; returned to films, then, at the Palace, 17 July 1971, took over from Lauren Bacall as Margo Channing in the musical Applause; Ethel Barrymore, Feb 1974, Maud Caragnani in Come into the Garden, Maud, and Carlotta Gray in A Song at Twilight in the double-bill Noel Coward in Two Keys, and subsequently toured in these parts; has also appeared at the Huntington Hartford, Los Angeles, in Light Up the Sky; Ahmanson, Los Angeles, Oct 1979, Alma Rattenbury in Cause Célèbre; is President of the Chamber Symphony Society of California; made her film début in 20 Mule Team, 1938, and subsequently appeared in The Magnificent Ambersons, 1942, Guest in the House, 1944, The Razor's Edge, for which she received the Academy Award, 1946, All About Eve, 1950, The Ten Commandments, 1956, Fool's Parade, 1971, etc; has appeared on television on *Playhouse 90, Columbo, Love Story, Banacek, Mannix, Dr Kildare*, etc.

Favourite parts: Maud and Carlotta in Noel Coward in Two Keys. *Hobbies and recreations:* Music, art, travel. *Address:* c/o Lionel Larner, Ltd, 850 7th Avenue, New York, NY 10019. *Tel:* 246-3105.

BAXTER, Jane, actress
b 9 Sept 1909; *d* of Henry Bligh Forde and his wife Hedwig von Dieskau; *e* privately; *m* (1) Clive Dunfee; (2) Arthur Montgomery; studied for the stage under Italia Conti.

Made her first appearance on the stage at the Adelphi Theatre, 6 Feb 1925, as an Urchin in Love's Prisoner; at the Shaftesbury, Dec 1925, played a Brave in Peter Pan; at the Aldwych, June 1926, understudied Winifred Shotter in Rookery Nook; Adelphi, Dec 1926, was again in Peter Pan, and in Jan 1927, played Mrs Darling; Gaiety, Dec 1927, understudied Jean Forbes-Robertson as Peter Pan, and played the part for a week in Jan 1928; in 1928, toured in Thark; at the New Theatre, Aug 1928, played Lady Maud in A Damsel in Distress; Apr 1929, Hermia Wyndrum in Baa, Baa, Black Sheep; Shaftesbury, Aug 1929, Fay Eaton in The Middle Watch; Strand (for Repertory Players), Dec 1929, Madge Wallace in Caught; Shaftesbury, Sept 1930, Eve Halliday in Leave It to Psmith; Apr 1931, Myra in Mr Faint-Heart; Aug 1931, Celia Newbiggin in The Midshipmaid; Comedy, Apr 1932, Madeleine Pelham in Faces; Haymarket, Oct 1932, Bunny Shaw in Once a Husband; Palace, Jan 1933, Dora in Dinner at Eight; Webber- Douglas, May 1933, Martine in the play of that name; Lyric, Nov 1933, Phais in Acropolis; joined the repertory company of the Playhouse, Liverpool, Aug 1935, opening in Youth at the Helm, and remaining until Nov 1935, Embassy, Aug 1936, played Eve Grant in Zero; King's, Hammersmith, Oct, and Daly's, Nov 1936, Giulietta Guicciardi in Muted Strings; Q, Jan 1937, Peggy Harding in To Have and to Hold; Wyndham's, Jan 1937, Frankie in George and Margaret, which ran for two years; Duke of York's (for London International Theatre), Feb 1938, Miriam Ward in No More Music; Piccadilly, Nov 1939, again appeared in George and Margaret; Garrick, June 1943, played Molly Benton in Living Room; Globe, Dec 1943, Lady Elizabeth in While the Sun Shines; made her first appearance in New York at the Royale, 3 Mar 1947, as Cecily Cardew in The Importance of Being Earnest; after returning to England appeared at the Aldwych, June 1948, as Isobel in Ambassador Extraordinary; at the New, Sept 1948, with the Old Vic Company, played Viola in Twelfth Night; Lyric, Hammersmith, Feb 1949, played Rhoda Meldrum in The Damask Cheek; St Martin's, June 1949, Frances Morritt in The Young and Fair; Bedford, Camden Town, Nov 1949, Frances in A Guardsman's Cup of Tea; at the Lyric, Hammersmith, Mar 1950, appeared as Jenny in The Holly and the Ivy, and played this part again at the Duchess, May 1950; Criterion, Dec 1951, Kate Hartley in Indian Summer; Westminster, June 1952, Sheila Wendice in Dial M for Murder, which ran for a year; Haymarket, Aug 1953, played the Hon Mrs W Tatham in a revival of Aren't We All?; Saville, July 1955, played Laura in The Shadow of Doubt; Cambridge, May 1957, played Mary Sylvester in A Month of Sundays; Winter Garden, Dec 1957, Zena Drummond in Be My Guest; Strand, Feb 1960, Jane Loring in The More the Merrier; Cambridge, Apr 1966, played Lady Hibury in A Friend Indeed; Theatre Royal, Bury St Edmunds, June 1967, Mrs Alving in Ghosts; Arnaud, Guildford, June 1968, Miss Orley in Robert's Wife; Chichester Festival, 1971, Gabrielle in Dear Antoine, transferring to the Piccadilly, Nov 1971; Haymarket, Apr 1972, took over as The Mother in A Voyage Round My Father; commenced film career, 1930; television, 1951.

Recreation: Gardening. *Address:* 13 Belvedere Avenue, Wimbledon, SW19. *Tel:* 01-946 2035.

BAXTER, Keith (*né* Baxter-Wright), actor
s of Stanley Baxter Wright and his wife Emily Marian (Howell); *e* Newport High School and Barry Grammar

School; trained for the stage at RADA (Bronze Medallist, 1956).

After appearances in repertory at Oxford and Worthing, 1956–7, toured as Sanyamo in South Sea Bubble, Feb 1957; made his first London appearance, 25 Apr 1957, at the Comedy, as Ralph in Tea and Sympathy; Theatre in the Round, Feb 1958, played Hippolytus in Phèdre; Strand, May 1959, Vasse in Change of Tune; Belfast and Dublin, Mar 1960, played Prince Hal in both parts of King Henry IV; St Martin's, May 1961, Roger Balion in Time and Yellow Roses; Pembroke, Croydon, Sept 1961, David Glyn in Unfinished Journey; made his New York debut at the ANTA, 22 Nov 1961, as Henry VIII in A Man for All Seasons; Henry Miller's, Sept 1962, Donald Howard in The Affair; returning to London, played Gino Carella in Where Angels Fear to Tread at the Arts, June 1963, transferring to the St Martin's; Haymarket, Jan 1966, Valentine in You Never Can Tell; same theatre, Oct 1966, Bob Acres in The Rivals; Booth, NY, Jan 1968, Baldassare Pantaleone in Avanti!; Chichester Festival, July 1969, Horner in The Country Wife and Octavius Caesar in Antony and Cleopatra; St Martin's, Feb 1970, Milo Tindle in Sleuth, playing the same part at the Music Box, NY, Nov 1970; Birmingham Repertory, Oct 1972, played the title role in Macbeth; Greenwich, Jan 1973, Vershinin in Three Sisters; Royal Lyceum, Edinburgh, Oct 1973, Benedick in the theatre's 90th anniversary production, Much Ado About Nothing; Chichester Festival, May 1974, Ricco Verri in Tonight We Improvise; Sherman, Cardiff, Oct 1974, played the Dead Poet, the Preacher and the Politician in Sap; Stratford, Ontario, June 1976, Antony in Antony and Cleopatra; Witwoud in The Way of the World, Vershinin in Three Sisters; Round House, June 1977, co-directed and played King in The Red Devil Battery Sign, transferring to the Phoenix; Chichester, May 1978, Lord Illingworth in A Woman of No Importance and Dorante in The Inconstant Couple; Palace, NY, Mar 1979, Patrick in A Meeting by the River; Kennedy Center, Washington DC, Jun 1979, Bill Cardew in Home and Beauty; films, since 1956, include The Barretts of Wimpole Street, Chimes at Midnight, and Golden Rendezvous; television since 1958, includes Saint Joan, The Miracle Man and The Bonus.

Favourite parts: Gino, Bob Acres, Antony. *Recreation:* The sea. *Address:* c/o ICM, 22 Grafton Street, London W1.

BAXTER, Stanley, actor
b Glasgow, Scotland, 24 May 1926; *s.* of Frederick George Baxter and his wife Bessie (McCorkindale); *e* Hillhead High School, Glasgow; *m* Moira Robertson; began his training for the stage at Glasgow Citizens Theatre.

Made his first professional appearance on the stage at the Assembly Hall, Edinburgh, Aug 1948, when he played Correction's Varlet in The Thrie Estates; Citizens Theatre, Glasgow, 1949, played one of the Broker's Men in a fantasy pantomime, The Tintock Cup; the success of this led to a long contract in radio revue, and seasons of pantomime and revue in Scotland; made his first London appearance at the Saville, 9 Dec 1959, when he played Sydney Green in The Amorous Prawn; Phoenix, Apr 1961, appeared in the revue On the Brighter Side; Whitehall, July 1965, took over the part of Gerry Buss, for four weeks, in Chase Me, Comrade, prior to Australian tour; at the Queen's, Mar 1969, Dr Prentice in What the Butler Saw; Palace, Nov 1969, Phil McHugh in Phil the Fluter; most recent pantomime, Ugly Sister in Cinderella, King's, Edinburgh, 1979 (also book); films in which he has appeared include: VIP, The Fast Lady, Crooks Anonymous, etc; made his first appearance on television, 1951, in the BBC's Shop Window; subsequent appearances include sev-

eral of his own series, including *The Stanley Baxter Picture Show* (SFTA Award, 1975); he also appeared in the television play The Confidence Course.

Favourite part: Elwood Dowd in Harvey. *Recreations:* Reading and swimming. *Address:* 18 Shepherds Hill, London, N6.

BAXTER, Trevor, actor and dramatic author
b London, 18 Nov 1932; *s* of Walter Henry Baxter and his wife Dorothy Maud (Parkinson); *e* Dulwich College; trained for the stage at RADA, 1949–51.

Made his first professional appearance as an American Marine in Rain, County Theatre, Aylesbury, Bucks, Sept 1951; played leads with the West of England Theatre Company, 1953–55, and at Liverpool Playhouse, 1957–60; toured S America for the British Council, 1964, as Solanio in The Merchant of Venice and Philostrate in A Midsummer Night's Dream; toured with Prospect, 1965–67, as Chasuble in The Importance of Being Earnest, Medley in The Man of Mode, and Stephano in The Tempest; Oxford Playhouse, 1967, Tribulation Wholesome in The Alchemist; Mermaid, Feb 1968, appeared in The Adventures of the Black Girl in Her Search for God; made his West End debut at the Phoenix, 21 Mar 1968, as the Knight in Canterbury Tales, playing the role until 1972; Greenwich, Feb 1973, Elector of Saxony in Hans Kohlhaas; Haymarket, Oct 1975, Sir George Coburn in Betzi; Greenwich, May 1976, Bishop of Deptford in Heaven and Hell; same theatre, Apr 1977, Earl of Loam in The Admirable Crichton; Garrick, July 1977, again played Bishop of Deptford, the play now retitled The Bells of Hell; Thorndike, Leatherhead, 1977–78, parts including Dr Wickstead in Habeas Corpus; Greenwich, Nov 1978, Bishop of Lax in See How They Run; toured, 1979, for Cambridge Theatre Company as John Middleton in The Constant Wife; Citizens, Glasgow, 1979 and Lyric, Hammersmith, Feb 1980, Fulgenzio in Country Life; RSC Stratford Season, 1980, Capulet in Romeo and Juliet; is the author of the plays Edith Grove, 1973, performed at the Albery, London, 21 Oct 1975 under the title Lies; The Undertaking, 1979; has been seen frequently on TV in plays, serials and series.

Favourite part: Bishop of Deptford. *Address:* c/o Fraser and Dunlop, 91 Regent Street, London W1.

BAY, Howard, designer, director, teacher
b Centralia, Washington, 3 May 1912; *s* of William D Bay and his wife Bertha A (Jenkins); *e* Universities of Washington and Colorado, Westminster and Marshall Colleges, and also studied at the Carnegie Institute of Technology; *m* Ruth Jonas (dec).

Designed sets for There's a Moon Tonight, Chalk Dust and Battle Hymn, 1936; Marching Song, 1937; first came into prominence for his work with the Federal Theatre, 1937, designing sets for Power (the Living Newspaper), One Third of a Nation, Native Ground, Trojan Incident, etc; he worked for the Federal Theatre until 1939; has also designed sets for Sunup to Sundown, The Merry Wives of Windsor, 1938; The Dog Beneath the Skin, The Little Foxes, The Life and Death of an American, The Fifth Column, 1939; Morning Star, The Corn Is Green; also designed four operas for the National Orchestral Association, 1940; Brooklyn, USA, 1941; Johnny 2 × 4, The Moon Is Down, The Strings, My Lord, Are False, Uncle Harry, The Eve of St Mark, Count Me In, The Great Big Doorstep, 1942; Something for the Boys, The Patriots, The Merry Widow, A New Life, One Touch of Venus, Carmen Jones, Listen, Professor, 1943; Storm Operation, Chicken Every Sunday, Follow the Girls, Ten Little Indians, Catherine Was Great, Franklyn Street, It's Up to You, The

Visitor, Violet, Glad to See You, The Searching Wind, 1944; Marinka, Devils Galore, Deep Are the Roots, Polonaise, Spring in Brazil, Up in Central Park, 1945; The Would-Be Gentleman, Show Boat, Woman Bites Dog, 1946; The Big Knife, Montserrat, As the Girls Go, Magdalena, 1949; Come Back, Little Sheba, 1950; Flahooley, The Autumn Garden, Hilda Crane, Two on the Aisle, The Grand Tour, 1951; Jollyana, Les Noces (Brandeis Univ), The Children's Hour, The Shrike, 1952; Peepshow, A Certain Joy, Mid-Summer, 1953; Show Boat, Sandhog, 1954; Top Man, The Desperate Hours, Finian's Rainbow, Red Roses for Me, 1955; Carmen Jones (revival), A Very Special Baby, Build with One Hand, A Certain Joy, Night of the Auk, 1956; Tevya and His Daughters, Look Back in Anger, The Music Man, 1957; Interlock, Regina (revival), 1958; A Desert Incident, The Fighting Cock (lighting only), Carmen (San Francisco Opera Co), 1959; The Cut of the Axe, The Cool World, Toys in the Attic, Show Boat (Los Angeles Civic Light Opera Co), The Wall, 1960; The Music Man (London), Show Boat and Pal Joey (revivals), Milk and Honey, 1961; Isle of Children, 1962; My Mother, My Father, and Me, Bicycle Ride to Nevada, 1963; Never Live over a Pretzel Factory, Natalya Petrovna (New York City Opera), 1964; Man of La Mancha, Capriccio (opera), 1965; Chu Chem, 1966; Man of La Mancha (London), 1968; Cry for Us All, 1970; décor and lights for Knickerbocker Holiday, Curran, San Francisco, 1971; décor and lights for the tour of Hallowe'en, 1972; costumes with Ray Diffen and décor and lights for the tour of Odyssey, 1975, renamed Home Sweet Homer in NY, 1976; Poor Murderer, 1977; The Utter Glory of Morrissey Hall, 1979; also designed puppets and settings for a puppet-film in technicolor, 1939; directed the production of As the Girls Go, 1949; directed There Are Crimes and Crimes, 1951; again directed There Are Crimes and Crimes (Carnegie Institute of Technology), 1963; directed The Cage (University of Ohio), 1964; at Brandeis University directed Ping Pong, 1966, The Workhouse Donkey, 1967, Colombe, 1968, The Cradle Will Rock, 1976; Pal Joey, 1977; received a Guggenheim Fellowship, 1939–40; President of the United Scenic Artists of America, 1941–6; director-designer with International Pictures, 1946; Antoinette Perry Award for best designer, 1959–60 season and 1965–6 season; has also received two Donaldson Awards and *Variety*'s New York Dramatic Critics poll; National Board Member of the National Society of Interior Designers; Professor of Theatre Arts, Brandeis University, from 1965 and Chairman of the Department, 1966–7; Visiting Critic in Stage Lighting, Yale University Drama School, 1966; production designer for television series Mr Broadway, 1965; Pueblo Incident, 1975; and designed George Balanchine's ballet film A Midsummer Night's Dream, 1966; has lectured at several other universities, including: Michigan, Ohio, Purdue, etc; author of Stage Design, 1975, and the Staging and Stage Design section of Encyclopaedia Britannica III.
Address: 159 West 53rd Street, New York, NY.

BAYLISS, Peter, actor
One of his first appearances was as the Cabman in The Matchmaker, which came from the Edinburgh Festival to the Haymarket, Nov 1954; played the same part on his New York debut at the Royale, Dec 1955; Duke of York's, Nov 1958, Roofie Williams in The Big Tickle; Haymarket, May 1960, Parsons in Ross; Her Majesty's, June 1962, Egon in Judith; Mermaid, July 1963, played Cardinal Barberini in The Life of Galileo; Royal Court, Sept 1963, Guard in Exit the King; Mermaid, Dec 1963, Long John Silver in Treasure Island; Hampstead, Aug 1965, the Colonel, Mr Cross and Mr Scase

in How's the World Treating You?, repeating these parts at the Arts, Jan 1966, transferring to Wyndham's, Jan 1966 and the Comedy, May 1966; Music Box, New York, Oct 1966, again appeared in How's the World Treating You?; Mermaid, Jan 1967, Beamish, Mitchener and Fitz in Trifles and Tomfooleries, a Shaw triple-bill; Open Air, Regent's Park, June 1967, Bottom in A Midsummer Night's Dream; Fortune, Nov 1967, Joseph King in Fanghorn; Ethel Barrymore, NY, Oct 1968, William Butler in Rockefeller and the Red Indians; Queen's, London, Mar 1969, Sgt Match in What the Butler Saw; Vaudeville, Nov 1969, Martin Morley in The Man Most Likely To . . .; Hampstead, June 1970, Police Commissioner in Mr Kilt and the Great I Am; Criterion, Aug 1970, God in Council of Love; at the Haymarket, Apr 1971, played Maitland in The Chalk Garden; Young Vic, Jan 1973, Hobson in Hobson's Choice; Phoenix, Nov 1973, Ernest in Design for Living; Open Space, July 1974, Watson in Sherlock's Last Case; Shaw, Oct 1974, Christopher Sly in The Taming of the Shrew; toured S Africa, Nov 1974, as Pratt in Who Saw Him Die?; toured Japan, 1975, in The Rocky Horror Show; Theatre Royal, Stratford E, Dec 1975, Squeers in Nickleby and Me; Cambridge, June, 1976, Soliony in Three Sisters; Criterion, Feb 1977, played Gerardo in The Singer in the double-bill The Frontiers of Farce; Ambassadors, June 1977, Col Gillweather in Something's Afoot; Round House, Aug 1978, Adam Overdo in Bartholomew Fair; 1979 toured as Alfred Doolittle in My Fair Lady, and played the part at the Adelphi, Oct; has appeared in films and on television, including Martin Chuzzlewit.
Address: 106 Jermyn Street, London SW1. *Tel:* 01–839 5151.

BEACH, Ann, actress
b Wolverhampton, Staffs, 7 June 1938; *d* of Claude Ripley Beach and his wife Rebecca (Van Startup); *e* Cardiff High School for Girls; *m* Francis Coleman; fulfilled her first professional engagement at the age of twelve when she sang in the operetta Hansel and Gretel on the radio; trained for the stage at the Royal Academy of Dramatic Art (scholarship student).
Made her first appearance on the stage at the Streatham Hill Theatre, July 1957, when she played Paquerette in Hotel Paradiso; at the Appollo, Mar 1958, played the title part in Beth; Theatre Workshop, Stratford E, Dec 1958, played Belinda Cratchit and Emily in A Christmas Carol; at the same theatre, Feb 1959, played Rosey in Fings Ain't Wot They Used T' Be; Apr 1959, Franceschina in The Dutch Courtesan; May 1959, Miss Gilchrist in The Hostage, transferring with the last production to Wyndham's, June 1959; after a year's run, she appeared with the Theatre Workshop Company at the Paris Festival, June 1960, as Mistress Bridget in Every Man in His Humour, subsequently playing the same part at the Theatre Royal, Stratford, E, July 1960; Cambridge, Sept 1960, played Barbara in Billy Liar; Royal Court, Dec 1961, played Anna in The Fire-Raisers; Arts, Feb 1962, appeared in the revue Twists; Royal Court, July 1962, played Jenny in Under Plain Cover (in the double bill Plays for England); at the Theatre Royal, Windsor, Nov 1962, played Minnie in Engaged (comic opera); Theatre Royal, Stratford, E, Mar 1963, appeared in Oh What a Lovely War; Aldwych, June 1963, played Hermia in A Midsummer Night's Dream; Queen's, Mar 1964, Masha in The Seagull; Royal Court, Sept 1964, Shirley in Inadmissible Evidence; at the same theatre, Oct 1964, Marguerite Hickett in a revival of A Cuckoo in the Nest; Wyndham's, Mar 1965, again played Shirley in Inadmissible Evidence; Chichester Festival, June 1966, Miss Sterling in The Clandestine Marriage; Players', Dec 1966,

Principal Girl in Whittington Junior and his Sensation Cat; Comedy, Nov 1967, played Hortense in The Boy Friend; Drury Lane, Feb 1969, Agnes Gooch in Mame; at the Shaw, May 1972, Maria in Twelfth Night; Theatre Royal, Stratford, Dec 1975, Mrs Squeers in Nickleby and Me; Arnaud, Guildford, 1976, Isobella in Caroline; Olivier, Nov 1977, Mistress Dainty Fidget in The Country Wife; entered films, 1959, and has appeared in Hotel Paradiso, Never Mind the Quality, Feel the Width and in Under Milk Wood; made her first appearance on television in 1954, in the programme All Your Own, and has since appeared in many television productions, including The Vanishing Army, The Winslow Boy, and Diary of a Nobody; author of Learn to Act, 1970.

Recreations: Music and painting. *Address:* c/o Peter Browne Management, 13 St Martin's Road, London SW9.

BEACHAM, Stephanie, actress
b 28 Feb 1947; *e* St Michael's Convent, Finchley and Queen Elizabeth's Girls School, Barnet; *m* John McEnery; trained for the stage with Etienne de Creux, Paris, 1964, and at RADA 1965–67.

Made her first professional appearance at the Liverpool Everyman, 1964, as Clarice in The Servant of Two Masters; other parts that season included First Witch in Macbeth; Bristol Old Vic, 1967, appeared in Monsieur Barnett; Oxford Playhouse, season 1967–68, parts included Irma in The Madwoman of Chaillot and Louka in Arms and the Man; made her London debut at the Duchess, 17 Sept 1970, as Jane in The Basement; Nottingham Playhouse, season 1972, played Ruth in The Homecoming, Juno in The Tempest, and Nora in A Doll's House; Theatre Royal, Haymarket, 1976, took over as Helen in On Approval; Crucible, Sheffield, 1977, Eva in Absurd Person Singular; New End, June 1978, Hubert Page in The Singular Life of Albert Nobbs; Greenwich, Oct 1978, Berthe in An Audience Called Edouard; Royal Court, Feb 1979, Eugenia in The London Cuckolds; Piccadilly, May 1979, Margery Hartnoll in Can You Hear Me at the Back?; first film, The Games, 1970, subsequently The Nightcomers, Schizo, etc; TV ranges from the series *Marked Personal*, Jane Eyre and A Sentimental Education, to *Call My Bluff*.

Recreation: Making dollshouse furniture. *Address:* c/o Fraser and Dunlop, 91 Regent Street, London W1.

BEAL, John, actor (*né* Bliedung)
b Joplin, Mo, 13 Aug 1909; *s* of Edmund A Bliedung and his wife Agnes (Harragan); *e* Joplin High School and University of Pennsylvania; *m* Helen Craig; studied for the stage under Jasper Deeter of the Hedgerow Repertory Company; while still at school took part in many amateur productions with Mask and Wig Club.

Made his first professional appearance at the Hedgerow Repertory Theatre, Moylan, Pa, May 1930, as Horace in Inheritors, and played several small parts during the season; going to New York, he understudied at the John Golden Theatre, Sept 1930, in That's Gratitude; Lyric, Philadelphia, Feb 1931, played Sample Swichel in Ten Nights in a Bar Room; made his first appearance on the NY stage at the Charles Hopkins' Theatre, 4 Mar 1931, as a Page in Give Me Yesterday, also acting as assistant stage-manager; at the Provincetown, Oct 1931, played young Flint Bailey in No More Frontier; Times Square, Feb 1932, John Duffy in Wild Waves; Booth, Apr 1932, Jerry Hallam in Another Language; 46th Street, Nov 1933, Paul Lawton in She Loves Me Not; Masque, Jan 1936, John Galt in Russet Mantle; Empire, Nov 1938, Jimmy Mimms in Soliloquy; Cort, Feb 1939, Bert Nansen in Miss Swan Expects; Hudson, Nov 1939, Karl

Hedstrom in I Know What I Like; Shubert (for the Guild), Feb 1941, Commander Tom Smith in Liberty Jones; during summer stock engagements appeared in The Petrified Forest, Good-bye Again, and No Time for Comedy; during the War, served with the US Air Force, 1942–5; re- appeared on the stage, at the Morosco, Jan 1946, when he succeeded Elliott Nugent as Bill Page in The Voice of the Turtle; Coronet, Hollywood, Oct 1948, Monsieur Henri in Eurydice; Circle, Los Angeles, May 1949, Chorus in Antigone; Mansfield, Nov 1949, succeeded William Eythe in Lend an Ear, subsequently touring with the same revue; Brattle, Cambridge, Massachusetts, Jan 1952, the title-role in Ivanov; Royale, NY, May 1952, directed sketches in the revue New Faces of 1952; Curran, San Francisco, Aug 1952, Jin-Jan in Jollyanna; toured United States and Canada in 1954 as Michael in The Fourposter; Martin Beck, NY, May 1955, took over from John Forsythe as Fisby in The Teahouse of the August Moon; Saint Louis, Missouri, Sept 1956, John Moore in Heartland, USA; Garden Center, Vineland, Canada, July 1958, the title-role in Mr Roberts; Wooster, Ohio, Nov 1958, Everyman and Everyman's Six Manifestations in Everyman To-day, which he repeated at North Central College, Naperville, Illinois, in May 1960; Fred Miller, Milwaukee, Wisconsin, Jan 1959, Sheriff Hawes in The Chase; Circle-in-the-Square, NY, March, 1959, Stage Manager in Our Town; Biltmore, during the week of 23 Jan 1962, took over from Art Carney the role of Frank Michaelson in Take Her, She's Mine, and played this role on occasions thereafter; Ambassador, Oct 1962, Harrison Bellows in Calculated Risk; toured, 1965, as Sir Thomas More in A Man for All Seasons; Kaufman Auditorium, Jan 1966, played in a concert reading of The White Rose and the Red; White Barn, Westport, Conn, July 1966, played the Narrator in Come Slowly, Eden; Cherry Lane, Sept 1966, played various roles in Wilder Triple Bill; toured, Mar–Sept 1968, as Horace Giddens in The Little Foxes; Cherry Lane, Jan 1969, appeared in the dramatic revue To Be Young, Gifted, and Black; Billy Rose, Mar 1969, Dansker in Billy; Vivian Beaumont, June 1969, Gordon Gray in In the Matter of J Robert Oppenheimer; ANTA, Nov 1969, Simon Stimson in Our Town and in 1970 played the Stage Manager in two productions of this play; Edison, Nov 1970, Tom McGrath in Candy-apple; Promenade, 20 July 1971, succeeded Robert Ryan as James Tyrone in Long Day's Journey into Night; appeared with the Long Wharf Theater, New Haven, Conn, 1971–2 season as Ed Mosher in The Iceman Cometh; has also appeared in numerous stock and repertory productions; first appeared in films, 1933, in Another Language and has since made many films, including: Les Misérables, The Cat and the Canary, Edge of Darkness, The Sound and the Fury, The Little Minister, My Six Convicts, That Night, Ten Who Dared, etc; has appeared regularly on television, recently in The Adams Chronicles; is also a portrait artist, having been formally trained in fine art.

Clubs: Mask and Wig, and Players, New York. *Address:* c/o Robert Longenecker Agency, 11704 Wilshire Blvd, Los Angeles, Calif 90025.

BEAN, Orson (*né* Dallas Frederick Burrows), actor
b Burlington, Vermont, 22 July 1928; *s* of George F Burrows and his wife Marian Ainsworth (Pollard); *e* Cambridge Latin School; *m* (1) Jacqueline de Siboun (mar dis); (2) Carolyn Maxwell.

Was a boy magician; made his first cabaret appearance in New York, at the Blue Angel, June 1952; made his stage début at the Cambridge, Mass, Summer Theatre, 1945, in The Spider; toured, Jan–Feb 1953, as Sonny Dorrance in

Josephine; made his NY début at the 48th Street, Apr 1953, as Edgar Grassthal in Men of Distinction; Theatre de Lys, June 1953, Careless in The School for Scandal; Imperial, Dec 1953, appeared in the revue John Murray Anderson's Almanac; Belasco, Oct 1955, George MacCauley in Will Success Spoil Rock Hunter?; City Center, Dec 1956, Ensign Pulver in a revival of Mr Roberts; Coronet, Oct 1957, Billy Turk in Nature's Way; City Center, Feb 1959, Jack Jordan in a revival of Say Darling; St James, Dec 1961, Charlie Smith in Subways Are for Sleeping; Playhouse, Nov 1962, Charlie in Never Too Late, in which he appeared for eighteen months; Provincetown Playhouse, May 1964, produced and later took over the role of Father Shenanigan in Home Movies; summer theatres, 1964, played Arthur in Warm Heart, Cold Feet; Lyceum, Nov 1964, Tom Considine in I Was Dancing; Shubert, Nov 1965, took over Cocky in The Roar of the Grease Paint—The Smell of the Crowd; Mark Hellinger, Apr 1967, played Homer Thrace in Ilya Darling; Theatre de Lys, Oct 1969, appeared in the revue A Round with Ring; toured Australia, 1970–1, as Chuck Baxter in Promises, Promises; appeared in the film Lola, 1973; Founder and Administrative Director of the 15th Street School in NY, a primary school based on England's Summerhill School; author of Me and the Orgone, 1971.

Address: c/o William Morris Agency, 1350 Sixth Avenue, New York, NY 10019.

BEATTY, John Lee, designer

b Palo Alto, Calif, 4 Apr 1948; s of Shelton Lee Beatty and his wife Caroline (Burtis); e Brown University (BA 1970) and Yale School of Drama (BFA 1973).

Early work includes designs for Baal, Yale Rep, Feb 1973; since 1974 has been particularly associated with the Circle Rep, NY, for whom he has designed a score of productions; has also worked off-Broadway with the New York Shakespeare Festival, with Rebel Women, 1976, Ashes, 1977, The Woods, 1979; Manhattan Theatre Club, with Catsplay, The Rear Column, 1978 etc; first designs for Broadway were those for Knock, Knock, 1976; has since designed The Innocents, 1976; The Water Engine, Ain't Misbehavin', 1978; Whoopee, Faith Healer, Ain't Misbehavin' (London), 1979; Talley's Folly, Hide and Seek, 1980; has worked with regional companies including the Goodman, Chicago, the Mark Taper Forum, LA, Seattle, Indiana, and the Arena Stage, Washington DC, and for the Goodspeed Opera House, Ct, and the Los Angeles Civic Light Opera; TV designs include The Mound Builders, 1975, and Out of Our Father's House, 1979, both for WNET.

Address: 107 West 86th Street, New York, NY 10024.

BEATTY, Robert, actor

b Hamilton, Ontario, Canada, 19 Oct 1909; s of Charles Thompson Beatty and his wife Blanche Sarah (Rutherford); e Delta Collegiate School, Hamilton, and University of Toronto; m (1) Dorothy Anderson Steele (mar dis); (2) Princess Anne Obolensky (mar dis); (3) Rosemary Hall Spencer; formerly a cashier in a gas and fuel company; had much amateur experience in Canada; on coming to London, studied at the Royal Academy of Dramatic Art.

Made his first appearance on the London stage, at the Apollo, 22 Mar 1938, playing the Third Officer in Idiot's Delight, and understudied Raymond Massey in the leading part; at the Kingsway, Feb 1939, played Dave Manford in To Love and Cherish; Criterion, May 1939, Slick McCoy in Grouse in June; during 1939–40 appeared in several productions at Q and Richmond Theatres; at the Duchess, July, 1942, played Larry Oulton in Lifeline; Globe, Dec 1942,

Boze Hertzlinger in The Petrified Forest; Wyndham's, Feb 1944, Private William Mackenzie in A Soldier for Christmas; St Martin's, Feb 1945, Mark McPherson in Laura; Gateway, June 1945, Bruce Lovell in Love from a Stranger; Phoenix, Sept 1945, Major Victor Joppolo in A Bell for Adano; St Martin's, Apr 1949, played Christopher Regan in Twice Upon a Time; Duchess, Dec 1949, Macaulay Connor in The Philadelphia Story; Connaught, Worthing, July, 1951, John Brugiere in The Long Arm; New Boltons, Feb 1952, Francis Drinkwater in Here's To Us; Richmond Theatre, and also toured, May 1957, as Harry Brock in Born Yesterday; Cambridge, Nov 1957, Antony Drexel Biddle in The Happiest Millionaire; Theatre Royal, Windsor, Dec 1959, Gerry Ryan in Two For the See Saw; Queen's, Apr 1960, took over H J in The Aspern Papers, subsequently touring South Africa in the same play; Pembroke, Croydon, Sept 1961, played Simon in The Man Who Played God; Lyric, Sept 1962, Danny Gronshaw in Breaking Point; Ashcroft, Croydon, Feb 1964, played Mark Ellery in The Excursion; Garrick, Sept 1964, took over the part of Anthony Wilcox in Difference of Opinion; toured, July 1970, as Tom Chadwick in Roar Like a Dove; Ashcroft, Croydon, Dec 1970, appeared in Scrooge; toured, Feb 1971 as Charles in The Grass is Greener; Criterion, Dec 1972, played Howard Wheeler in Bunny; toured S Africa, Feb–Aug 1974, in In Praise of Love; toured Canada, Dec 1974, in The Pleasure of His Company; Theatre Royal, Windsor, Feb 1975, again appeared in In Praise of Love; toured UK, Sept 1976, as Max Sinclair in Edge of Darkness; Churchill, Bromley, July 1978, Lord Beaverbrook in The woman Love; first appeared in films, 1938, and recent films include Golden Rendezvous and King Arthur and the Spaceman; has performed frequently on television, recently in Walk with Destiny, Jesus of Nazareth, and Suez 1956.

Recreations: Music, swimming and fixing things. *Address:* c/o Joseph and Wagg, 78 New Bond Street, London W1.

BEAUFORT, John, dramatic critic

b Edmonton, Alberta, Canada, 23 Sept 1912; s of Ernest Beaufort and his wife Margaret Mary (Crawley); e public and private schools in Canada and the United States, and Rollins College, Florida; m Francesca Bruning.

Began his career as a copy boy for *The Christian Science Monitor* and after filling various news and feature assignments, was installed as a member of that paper's theatre and film department; became the *Monitor*'s resident New York dramatic critic in 1939; after serving as the paper's war correspondent overseas, he returned to the *Monitor* NY office as Chief of the News Bureau, 1946–50; Editor of the Arts and Magazine section, 1950–1; resumed position as NY dramatic and film critic, 1951; appointed *Monitor* Arts-Entertainment Editor, 1959; chief of the London Bureau, 1962–5; feature editor in Boston, 1965–70; NY drama critic, 1971–; contributed Broadway reviews for *The Times* (London); elected President of the New Drama Forum Association, Inc, in Oct 1976; Treasurer, New York Drama Critics' Circle, 1971–; has lectured extensively on the theatre for college and community audiences.

Recreations: Playgoing, walking, travelling. *Clubs:* Players, Garrick, Coffee House. *Address:* Suite 3006, 220 East 42nd Street, New York, NY 10017. *Tel:* 599 1850.

BECHER, John C, actor

b Milwaukee, Wis, 15 Jan 1915; s of John Becher and his wife Katherine (Schmidt); e Milwaukee Teachers College (BS 1938) and the Goodman School of Theatre, Chicago (BFA 1941); m Margaret Williams.

First professional appearance, 20 Sept 1946, at the McCarter, Princeton, as Lord Sands in the American Repertory Theatre's Henry VIII; with the same company in 1946–47 played Sands, a Villager in What Every Woman Knows, the Lion in Androcles and the Lion, Brinkerhof in Yellow Jack, and the Queen of Hearts in Alice in Wonderland at the International, NY; Maxine Elliott's, Jan 1948, Mate Meyer in Skipper Next to God; national tour as Mr Lundie in Brigadoon, 1948–49; City Center, May 1951, Dumpsty in Idiot's Delight; Music Box, Mar 1954, took over as Howard in Picnic, also toured; de Lys, Apr 1955, Mr Henderson in Teach Me How to Cry; tour, 1955, as Cliff Snell in The Solid Gold Cadillac; Alvin, Aug 1956, took over as Draft Man in No Time for Sergeants; again played Mr Lundie, City Center, Mar, and Adelphi, Apr 1957; Daddy in The American Dream, and took over Father in The Death of Bessie Smith, in the double-bill seen at the York, Jan, and Cherry Lane, May 1961; Willie in Happy Days, Cherry Lane, Sept 1961; same theatre, in repertory under the title Theatre of the Absurd, Feb 1962, played six parts including Nagg in Endgame; City Center, May 1962, again played Mr Lundie; returned to the role, Jan 1963, after playing Gus in The Dumb Waiter in a double-bill at the Cherry Lane, Nov 1962; Martin Beck, Oct 1963, Stumpy in The Ballad of the Sad Cafe; Ann Arbor, Mich, Mar 1964, and Garrick, NY, Dec., Voyolko in The Child Buyer; in the revue That Thing at the Cherry Lane, May 1965; Cherry Lane, Sept 1965, again played Willie; Winter Garden, May 1966, Mr Upson in Mame; ANTA, Feb 1970, Judge Gaffney in Harvey; Brooks Atkinson, Feb 1973, the Detective in Status Quo Vadis; Winter Garden, Sept 1974, three parts in Gypsy; Music Box, Feb 1975, Abe in The Ritz; first film Kiss of Death, 1946; also seen in Next Stop Greenwich Village, Up the Sandbox, etc; TV work, also since 1946, includes plays and series.

Address: c/o Gage Group, 8732 Sunset Boulevard, Hollywood, CA 90069.

BECK, Julian, producer, director, designer, actor
b New York City, 31 May 1925; *s* of Irving Beck and his wife Mabel Lucille (Blum); *e* Yale University and the College of the City of NY; *m* Judith Malina.

With his wife founded Living Theatre Productions, Inc, 1947, and presented in various places, chiefly in their own home, several avant-garde plays, notably Childish Jokes, in which he played the Regisseur, He Who Says Yes and He Who Says No, in which he played the Teacher, Gertrude Stein's Ladies' Voices, which he directed, and Dialogue of the Young Man and the Manikin, in which he played the Young Man; made his professional début at the Cherry Lane, Mar 1951, by designing The 13th God; since 1951 the Living Theatre has functioned continuously at various theatres in NY and Europe with the following repertory: Dr Faustus Lights the Lights, Beyond the Mountains, 1951; Desire Trapped by the Tail (Pablo Picasso), Ladies' Voices, Sweeney Agonistes, Faustina, Ubu Roi, and The Heroes, in which he played Theseus, 1952; The Age of Anxiety, and played Quant, The Spook Sonata, played the Colonel, Orpheus, played Azrael, The Idiot King, played the title-role, 1954; Tonight We Improvise, which he directed and played the Director, Phaedra, played Theramenes, The Young Disciple (directed), 1955; Many Loves (directed), The Cave at Machpelah (directed), The Connection, Tonight We Improvise, which he again directed and played the Director, Madrigal of War, All That Fall, Embers, Act Without Words, I and II, Bertha, Theory of Comedy, Love's Labors, 1959; The Devil's Mother, Faust Foutu, The Marrying Woman (directed), The Women of Trachis (directed), The Herne's

Egg, Purgatory, A Full Moon in March, The Election, played the Director, In the Jungle of Cities, later playing Shink, 1960; toured in Rome, Turin, Milan, Paris, Berlin, Frankfurt, 1961, in The Connection, Many Loves, and In the Jungle of Cities, and returned to America to produce The Mountain Giants, Many Loves, played Peter, and The Apple, played Ajax, 1961; toured in Switzerland, France, The Netherlands, Germany, and Belgium, 1962, in The Connection, In the Jungle of Cities, and The Apple, and returned to America to direct Man Is Man, 1962; The Brig, 1963; made his London début at the Mermaid, Sept 1964, when he designed and co-produced The Brig; remained in Europe with the Living Theatre troupe, playing at the Academy of Liberal Arts, West Berlin, 1964; moved to Brussels, Mar 1965, where he wrote, produced and directed Mysteries, at the Theatre 140; Brussels, 1966, was co-author and co-director with his wife of Frankenstein; moved to Rome and at the Teatro Parioli, May 1967, produced in repertory Antigone, The Maids, and Mysteries, and subsequently toured in Europe; returned to America and at the Brooklyn Academy of Music, Oct 1968, produced Frankenstein, in which he also acted, Mysteries and Smaller Pieces, The Antigone of Sophokles, in which he played Kreon, Paradise Now, and subsequently toured; in 1971 devised The Legacy of Cain, consisting of 100 or more short plays to be performed in a village over a two-week period at various public sites; Rituals, Rites, and Transformations, first performed in Rio Clara and Embu, Brazil, 1971; Washington Square Methodist Church, Apr 1974, presented Seven Meditations on Political Sado-Masochism; formed a theatre group in Bordeaux, France, Nov 1975; visited the Round House, London, July 1979, with Prometheus; the Living Theatre has received many awards, including the Lola D'Annunzio, 1959; the Obie, 1960; the Page One, and, in Paris, the Grand Prix of the Théâtre des Nations, the Medal for the Best Acting Company, and the Prix de l'Université, the Brandeis University Creative Arts Award, 1961; the New England Theatre Conference Award, 1962, etc; The Brig has been televised and filmed.

BECKERMAN, Bernard, educator, and director
b New York, 24 Sept 1921; *s* of Morris Beckerman and his wife Elizabeth (Scheftel); *e* City College of New York (BSS 1942), Yale Drama School (MFA 1943) and Columbia U (PhD 1956); *m* Gloria Brim; trained for the stage at the New Theatre League.

Joined the teaching staff of Hofstra U, 1947; special lecturer in drama, Columbia U, 1957–60; Fulbright lecturer, Tel Aviv U, 1960–61; returned to Columbia, 1964, where he is now Brander Matthews Professor of Dramatic Literature and Chairman, theatre division; directed the Equity Library Theatre production of The Shining Hour, Nov 1946, and has directed over fifty other productions, including fifteen Shakespeare plays for the Hofstra Shakespeare Festival, 1950–65; President, American Society for Theatre Research, 1973–79; fellow, American Theatre Association; writings include Shakespeare at the Globe, 1962, Dynamics of Drama, 1970, etc.

Address: Redwood Road, Sag Harbor, NY 11963.

BECKETT, Samuel, dramatic author
b Dublin, Eire, 13 Apr 1906; *s* of William Frank Beckett and his wife Mary (Roe); *e* Portora Royal School, Enniskillen, and Trinity College, Dublin.

Author of the following plays: En Attendant Godot (Waiting for Godot), Fin de Partie (Endgame), both plays written in French and translated by the author into English; Krapp's

Last Tape, written in English, 1955; Actes sans Paroles (mime), 1957; La Dernière Bande, Oh, Les Beaux Jours! (Happy Days), 1961; Play, 1963; The Old Tune (one act, adapted), 1964; Come and Go (one scene), 1967; Not I, 1971; That Time, Footfalls (both one-act), 1976; his plays have been performed in almost every country; Waiting for Godot was revived at the Ethel Barrymore, New York, Jan 1957, with a Negro cast and was performed under his own direction in 1976 at the Royal Court, London, where he also directed Happy Days (1979); plays for radio, written in English, All That Fall, Embers and Cascando; he is also the author of two books of verse, Whoroscope, 1930; Echo's Bones, 1935; novels he has written include: Murphy, 1938; Watt, 1944; Molloy, 1951; Malone Meurt (Malone Dies) 1952; L'Innommable, 1953; Comment C'est, 1961; he has also written the following short stories: More Pricks than Kicks, 1934; Nouvelles et Textes Pour Rien, 1955; Lecturer in English at the École Normale Supérieure, Paris, 1928–30; Lecturer in French at Trinity College, Dublin, 1930–2; Prix Formentor, 1959; awarded the Nobel Prize for Literature, 1969.

Address: c/o Faber & Faber Ltd, 3 Queen Square, London WC1.

BEDFORD, Brian, actor

b Morley, Yorks, 16 Feb 1935; *s* of Arthur Bedford and his wife Ellen (O'Donnell); *e* St Bede's School, Bradford; formerly a trainee wholesale warehouseman; studied acting at the Royal Academy of Dramatic Art.

Made his first appearance on the stage with the Bradford Civic Theatre, 1951, as Decius Brutus in Julius Caesar; appeared as a member of the Liverpool Playhouse Company, spring, 1956; first appeared in London at the Arts Theatre, Aug 1956, as Travis de Coppet in The Young and Beautiful; Comedy, Oct 1956, played Rodolpho in A View From the Bridge; joined the Shakespeare Memorial Theatre Company, Stratford-on-Avon, July 1957, to play A Frenchman and Arviragus in Cymbeline, and in Aug 1957, appeared as Ariel in The Tempest, subsequently playing the same part when the production transferred to Drury Lane, Dec 1957; Comedy, July 1958, played Clive Harrington in Five Finger Exercise; following a year's run with the play, he made his first appearance in New York in the same production, at the Music Box Theatre, Dec 1959; on his return to London, at the Lyric, Mar 1962, he played David Roddingham in Write Me a Murder; Royale, NY, Nov 1962, played Derek Pengo in Lord Pengo; Haymarket, May 1963, Louis Dubedat in The Doctor's Dilemma; Wimbledon, Sept 1963, and Morosco, NY, Oct 1963, played Tchaik in The Private Ear (in the double-bill The Private Ear and the Public Eye); New, London, May 1964, Tom in The Knack; Helen Hayes, NY, Jan 1967, James in The Astrakhan Coat; Vivian Beaumont, NY, July 1967, the General in The Unknown Soldier and His Wife; Lyceum, NY, Oct 1968, Edward Chamberlayne in The Cocktail Party; Stratford, Conn, 1969 season, June, played Hamlet in Hamlet and Tusenbach in Three Sisters; Billy Rose, NY, Dec 1969, Elyot Chase in Private Lives; at Lake Forest, Mich, July 1970, played Charles in Blithe Spirit and the Stranger in The Tavern; Lyceum, NY, Feb 1971, Arnolphe in School for Wives (Tony Award for Best Actor, 1971); New London, Jan 1973, repeated the part of the General in The Unknown Soldier and His Wife; toured the USA, fall 1973, as Butley in Butley; Kennedy Center, Washington DC, Mar and Billy Rose, NY, Apr 1974, George Moore in Jumpers; Stratford, Ont, 1975 season, played Angelo in Measure for Measure, and Malvolio in Twelfth Night; toured, 1975, as Martin Dysart in Equus; Ahmanson, LA, Dec 1976, played the Actor in The Guardsman; repeated this

part in the 1977 Stratford Ontario season, also playing the title rôle in Richard III, and Jacques in As You Like It; season 1978 again played Jacques, as well as Leontes in The Winter's Tale, Astrov in Uncle Vanya, and Elyot Chase in Private Lives; also directed Titus Andronicus; toured US and Canada, 1979–80, as Sidney Bruhl in Death Trap; films in which he has appeared include: The Angry Silence, The Pad and How to Use It, Grand Prix, etc; first appeared on television July 1955, and principal performances include: Winterset, The Judge and His Hangman, The Secret Thread, etc.

Favourite parts: Arnolphe and Angelo. *Recreations:* Living in the country, going to the movies and eating. *Address:* c/o STE Representation Ltd, 888 Seventh Avenue, New York, NY 10019.

BELDON, Eileen, actress

b Bradford, 12 Sept 1901; *d* of Albert Beldon and his wife Bertha (Nicholson); *e* Bradford Grammar School, and Hendon County School.

Made her first appearance on the stage, at Drury Lane Theatre, 26 Dec 1917, in the chorus of Aladdin; gained early experience at the Old Vic, where she appeared as Maria in Twelfth Night, Audrey in As You Like It, Mopsa in The Winter's Tale, etc, from 1917–19; at Drury Lane, Sept 1919, played Lucy and Spring Onions in The Great Day; toured as Jocelyn in Sacred and Profane Love, followed by a tour as Kitty Cranford in The Great Day, 1920; Garrick Theatre, Dec 1920, succeeded Edna Best as Lady Sloane in Brown Sugar; Comedy Theatre, Oct 1921, played Araminta Perry in Araminta Arrives; Court, Dec 1921, Constance Neville in She Stoops to Conquer; joined the Birmingham Repertory Company, in Mar 1923, where she played Ellie Dunn in Heartbreak House, Imogen in Cymbeline, Zoo in Back to Methuselah, Donna Louisa in The Duenna, Comtesse Zicka in Diplomacy, Petronel in The Farmer's Wife, etc; appeared at the Court Theatre, London, with the same company, Feb 1924, as Savvy Barnabas and Zoo in Back to Methuselah, and Mar 1924, as Petronel Sweetland in The Farmer's Wife, which ran for three years; at the New Theatre (for the Stage Society), Dec 1924, played The Maid in The Man with a Load of Mischief; Comedy, Jan 1927, Enid Bassopp in The Desperate Lovers; subsequently went to America, and appeared at the Fulton, New York, Sept 1927, as Emma Major in Yellow Sands; 49th Street Theatre, Nov 1927, as Rosie in The Fanatics; Dec 1927, as Saunders in Fallen Angels; on returning to London, appeared at the Court, Feb–Apr 1928, as the Gentlewoman in Macbeth (in modern dress), Savvy Barnabas and Zoo in Back to Methuselah, Aldwych in Harold and Katharina in The Taming of the Shrew (in modern dress); at the Garrick, Nov 1928, played Jessie Borlase in The Runaways; Royalty, Mar 1929, Bertha Beck in The Mayor; Queen's, Sept 1929, Lysistrata in The Apple Cart; Sept 1930, Wilson in The Barretts of Wimpole Street; Jan 1932, Petronel Sweetland in The Farmer's Wife; Apr 1932, Katherina Kling in Caravan; Apr 1932, Ellie Dunn in Heartbreak House; appeared at the Malvern Festival, Aug 1932; Oct 1932, toured as the Nurse in Too True to be Good; Royalty (for G Club), Feb 1933, Ellen in The Synthetic Virgin; Piccadilly, Sept 1933, Lady Todd Walker in A Sleeping Clergyman; Open Air Theatre, May 1934, Audrey in As You Like It; Sept 1934, Helena in A Midsummer Night's Dream; Winter Garden, Sept 1934, Megaera in Androcles and the Lion; Piccadilly, Jan 1935, Wilson in a revival of The Barretts of Wimpole Street; Open Air Theatre, June 1935, Maria in Twelfth Night; Malvern Festival, July–Aug 1935, Cecily Hyering in The Simpleton of the

Unexpected Isles, Lady Wouldbe in Volpone, Avonia Bunn in Trelawny of the Wells; Q, 1937, played Candida, and Grace in The Philanderer; Malvern Festival, July 1937, in Return to Sanity; Royalty, London, Sept 1937, Sally Pratt in I Have Been Here Before; Malvern Festival, Aug 1938, Begonia Brown in Geneva, Miss Newman in Coronation-time at Mrs Beam's and Clotho in Alexander; Guild Theatre, New York, Oct 1938, Sally in I Have Been Here Before; Globe (London Int. Theatre), Jan 1939, Sally in Adults Only; Savoy (Stage Society), Mar 1939, the Bride's Servant in Marriage of Blood; again appeared at the Malvern Festival, July 1939; New Theatre, May 1940, played Nell Gwyn in Good King Charles's Golden Days; New, Feb 1942, Hetty in Goodnight Children; Garrick, June 1943, Maggie Pryce in Living Room; with the Birmingham Repertory company, 1944–5, appeared as Paulina in The Winter's Tale, the Empress in Empress Maud, Juno in Juno and the Paycock, Constance in King John; Arts, Aug 1946, played Lysistrata in The Apple Cart; toured in Australia and New Zealand, 1948, with the Old Vic Company; at the New, with the Old Vic Company, during season 1949, appeared as Mrs Candour in The School for Scandal, Margaret of Anjou in Richard III, and the Nurse in Antigone; Players', June 1949, played Jeanne in From This Day Forward; Lyric, Hammersmith, Jan 1950, Mrs Preen in Shall We Join the Ladies, and also appeared in The Boy with a Cart; New Lindsey, May 1950, appeared as Miss Oakes in The Dark Corridor; at Cardiff, and Golders Green Hippodrome, Feb 1952, played Edith Parsons in Treasure on Pelican; Players', Dec 1952, Lady Macassar in Babes in the Wood and the Good Little Fairy-Birds!; at Hastings, Mar 1953, Bessie Field in The Sea Tower; at the Edinburgh Festival, 1953, played Sarah in A Match For the Devil; with Bognor Regis Repertory, May 1954, Flora in The Flying Sorceress; with the Irish Players at Wimbledon Theatre, July 1955, played Juno in Juno and the Paycock; Civic, Chesterfield, Mar 1957, played Bessie Field in The Sea Tower; Belgrade, Coventry, Feb 1960, played Mrs Gnobe in Never Had It So Good, subsequently appearing in the same part at the Theatre Royal, Stratford, E, Mar 1960; at the Birmingham Repertory Theatre, 1961–4, made the following guest appearances: Lady Wishfort in The Way of the World, Mrs Malaprop in The Rivals, Widow Lettwell in The Double Deceit, Madame Alexander in Colombe, and Lucy Fitton in All in Good Time; with Prospect Productions 1965–7, toured as Lady Woodvil and Foggy Nan in The Man of Mode, Juno in The Tempest, Queenie Mab in The Gamecock, and Lady Darling in The Constant Couple, playing the last part at the New, London, in June 1967; 1969, Colchester Repertory Theatre, the Nurse in Romeo and Juliet and Mrs Northrop in When We Are Married; joined the Royal Shakespeare Company in 1970, appearing at Stratford that season as the Duchess of York in Richard III, Mistress Overdone and Francisca in Measure for Measure (April), and as Queen Elinor in King John (June); toured, Sept 1972, as Sarah in Eden End; toured, Mar 1975, as Emmie in Murder Mistaken; has also broadcast and appeared on television.

Address: Muirton Dunsmore, Aylesbury, Bucks. *Tel:* 0296 623161.

BEL GEDDES, Barbara, actress

b New York City, USA, 31 Oct 1922; d of Norman Bel Geddes and his wife Helen Belle (Sneider); e Buxton Country School, Putney School, and Andrebrook; m (1) Carl Schreuer (mar dis); (2) Windsor Lewis (dec).

Made her first appearance on the stage at the Clinton Playhouse, Clinton, Conn, July 1940, walking on in The School for Scandal; made her first appearance in NY, at the Windsor Theatre, 10 Feb 1941, as Dottie Coburn in Out of the Frying Pan; in 1942, toured the Army Camps for USO, playing Judy in Junior Miss; Biltmore, Oct 1942, played Cynthia Brown in Little Darling; Longacre, Jan 1943, Alice in Nine Girls; Belasco, Mar 1944, Wilhelmina in Mrs January and Mr X; Fulton, Sept 1945, Genevra Langdon in Deep Are the Roots; Broadhurst, Oct 1950, Mordeen in Burning Bright; Henry Miller's, Mar 1951, Patty O'Neill in The Moon Is Blue; at the same theatre, Nov 1954, appeared as Rose Pemberton in The Living Room; Morosco, Mar 1955, played Margaret in Cat on a Hot Tin Roof; Coronet, Nov 1956, Mary in The Sleeping Prince; Morosco, Dec 1959, Katherine Johnson in Silent Night, Lonely Night; Helen Hayes, Mar 1961, Mary in Mary, Mary; Locust, Philadelphia, Oct 1965, Alice in The Porcelain Year; Booth, Feb 1966, took over from Anne Jackson the role of Ellen Manville in Luv; Plymouth, Nov 1967, Jenny in Everything in the Garden; Plymouth, Feb 1973, Katy Cooper in Finishing Touches; Ahmanson, Los Angeles, Nov 1973, again played Katy Cooper in Finishing Touches, and subsequently toured in this part; toured in 1975 in Ah, Wilderness!; has appeared frequently in stock, notably in Claudia, Lilian, Born Yesterday, The Voice of the Turtle, Wait Until Dark, Tobacco Road (Lake Forest, Ill, 1977), etc; entered films, 1947, in The Long Night, and has since appeared in many pictures, including Summertree, 1971; has appeared on television since 1954 in various dramatic roles, most recently in the series Dallas; designs greeting cards for George Caspari Inc.

Recreations: Painting and animals. *Address:* c/o APA, 120 West 57th Street, New York, NY 10019.

BELL, Ann, actress

b Wallasey, Cheshire, 29 Apr 1939; d of John Forrest Bell and his wife Marjorie (Byrom); e Birkenhead High School; m Robert Laing; trained for the stage at RADA; went to Nottingham Repertory.

Made her first professional appearance, Sept 1959, in Take the Fool Away!; after a season at Nottingham, joined the Old Vic Company, Sept 1960, where her parts included Nina in The Seagull, Olivia in Twelfth Night and Constance Neville in She Stoops to Conquer; Arts, May 1962, played Natasha in The Lower Depths; toured, 1963, for Prospect Productions, as Belinda in The Provok'd Wife, appearing in the same production at the Vaudeville, July 1963; Globe, Mar 1964, Miss Pringle in Mother's Boy; Arnaud, Guildford, 1964, appeared in The Devil's Disciple; made her New York debut at the Booth, Sept 1966, as Valerie Pitman in Help Stamp Out Marriage; returned to Nottingham, 1967, to play Desdemona in Othello and five parts in Beware of the Dog, transferring in the latter production to the St Martin's, June 1967; Criterion, Sept 1969, Jennifer in So What About Love; Royal Court, Mar 1972, Penelope D'Orsay in Veterans; ICA Theatre, Sept 1974, Anna in Away From It All; Royal Court, Aug 1978, played Tess in Eclipse; National Theatre 1979, took over as Grace Tranfield in The Philanderer; films include To Sir With Love; The Reckoning and The Statue; television credits, since 1959, include Jane Eyre, An Unofficial Rose, The Lost Boys and Best of Friends.

Recreations: Reading, music. *Address:* c/o Leading Artists, 60 St James's Street, London SW1.

BELL, John, actor and director

b Newcastle, NSW, 1 Nov 1940; s of Albert John Bell and his wife Joyce Agnes (Feeney); e Marist College, Maitland NSW, and Sydney University (BA Hons); m Anna Maria Dobrowolska (the actress Anna Volska); trained for the stage under Alice Crowther, 1960–63, and at the Bristol Old Vic Theatre School, 1964.

Made his first stage appearance at the Old Tote, Sydney, 1963, as Trofimov in The Cherry Orchard; here he also played Hamlet, 1963; at the Adelaide Festival, 1964, title role in Henry V; made his first London appearance at the Aldwych, 22 Dec 1965, as Rosencrantz in Hamlet; remained with the RSC and appeared at Stratford in their 1966 and 1967 seasons, playing parts such as Lennox in Macbeth and Paris in Romeo and Juliet, 1967; taught acting at the Bristol Old Vic theatre school, 1969, and at the National Institute of Dramatic Art, Sydney, 1970; at the Old Tote, Sydney, played such roles as the title part in Arturo Ui and Klestakov in The Government Inspector, 1971; title role in Uncle Vanya, 1972; Petruchio in The Taming of the Shrew, 1973; Berowne in Love's Labour's Lost, 1974; co-founder and a permanent Director of the Nimrod Theatre, Sydney, 1971, where he has played the title role in Richard III, 1975; Prince Hal in Henry IV (both parts), 1978; Hatch in The Sea, 1979; Volpone, 1980; has directed for the Old Tote and Nimrod, recently Romeo and Juliet, Travelling North, and The Venetian Twins, 1979, the last for Nimrod at Sydney Opera House; his Nimrod production of The Christian Brothers was seen in England at the Riverside Studios, Hammersmith, Oct 1979; The Club, Hampstead, Dec 1979, and Old Vic, Jan 1980, was also a Nimrod production; for Sydney Theatre Company, 1980, played the title role in Cyrano de Bergerac; awarded the OBE for services to the theatre, 1979.

Favourite parts: Hamlet, Arturo Ui. *Address:* Nimrod Theatre, 500 Elizabeth Street, Surry Hills, NSW 2010, Australia. *Tel:* 648 8475.

BENEDICTUS, David, director and dramatic author
b London, 16 Sept 1938; *s* of Henry Jules Benedictus and his wife Kathleen Constance (Ricardo); *e* Eton, Balliol College, Oxford and the State University of Iowa; *m* Yvonne Antrobus; has been a journalist and dramatic critic.

His play The Fourth of June was produced in 1964; directed his own first production in 1968 at the Traverse, Edinburgh, Angels (Over Your Grave) and Geese (Over Mine), which he also wrote; has since directed Tom Paine (Bristol), 1968; A Winter's Tale (Dartington), Dracula (Windsor) and Hump (Newcastle, also wrote), 1969; Icarus' Mother and Grant's Movie (Open Space), 1970; assistant director, Royal Shakespeare Company, season 1970–1; directed his musical compilation, What a Way to Run a Revolution (Cockpit) 1971; Fallen Angels and Fumed Oak (Brighton) 1972; Betjemania, 1976; has written and directed for television and broadcast frequently; wrote the television series House of Caradus, 1979; is the author of a number of novels including: The Fourth of June; You're a Big Boy Now; A World of Windows, and The Rabbi's Wife; Chairman, Censorship Committee, Writers Guild; antiques correspondent, London *Evening Standard..*

Clubs: Arts, PEN. *Address:* The Pelican, 20 Alexandra Road, East Twickenham, Middlesex.

BENJAMIN, Louis, impresario and theatre management
b London, 17 Oct 1922; *s* of Benjamin and his wife Harriet; *e* Highbury County Secondary School; *m* Vera Doreen Ketteman.

Joined Moss Empires Ltd in 1937; second asst manager, London Palladium, 1945; asst manager, Victoria Palace, 1948, later box office manager; general manager, Winter Gardens, Morecambe, 1953; sales controller, Pye Records, 1959; managing director, 1963; chairman, 1973– ; managing director, Moss Empires, 1970– ; is also deputy chairman and joint managing director of Stoll/Moss Theatres; appointed joint managing director, ATV Corporation, 1975–77; a deputy chairman of ATV Corporation (ACC), 1977– ; chairman, Bermans and Nathans, 1975; chairman, Brunskill and Kingman, 1974— ; member, executive board, Variety Club of Great Britain; vice-president, Entertainment Artistes' Benevolent Fund; companion, Grand Order of Water Rats; presents Royal Variety Performance, 1979– ; theatres controlled by Moss Empires under Mr Benjamin include London Palladium and Victoria Palace; he has presented numerous shows (pantomimes, Liberace, Bing Crosby, Shirley MacLaine, Ginger Rogers etc) at London Palladium and key provincial theatres.

Hobbies: Showbusiness, his family and antique collecting. *Address:* Moss Empires Ltd, Cranbourn Mansions, Cranbourn Street, London WC2. *Tel:* 01-437 2274 *and* 01-262 5502.

BENNETT, Alan, actor and dramatic writer
b Armley, Leeds, 9 May 1934; *s* of Walter Bennett and his wife Lilian Mary (Peel); *e* Leeds Modern School and Exeter College, Oxford.

Made his first stage appearance at the Edinburgh Festival, Aug 1959, in the Oxford Theatre Group's revue, Better Late; appeared again at Edinburgh, Aug 1960, in the revue Beyond the Fringe, of which he was part-author; subsequently made his first professional appearance in London at the Fortune, May 1961, in the same revue; Royal Court, July 1962, played the Archbishop of Canterbury in Blood of the Bambergs; in Oct 1962, he went to New York with the original Beyond the Fringe company to appear at the John Golden; returning to London, played the Rev Sloley-Jones in A Cuckoo in the Nest, Royal Court, Oct 1964; Apollo, Oct 1968, appeared as Tempest in his own play Forty Years On; has since written Getting On (1971); Habeas Corpus (1973); took over the part of Mrs Swabb in Habeas Corpus at the Lyric, Feb 1974; Habeas Corpus was performed in NY, 1975; wrote The Old Country, 1977; his appearances on television since 1961 include the series On the Margin, which he also wrote; author of the television plays including A Day Out, Sunset Across The Bay, A Visit from Miss Prothero and six plays for LWT, 1979.

Recreation: Writing. *Address:* c/o Chatto and Linnit, Globe Theatre, Shaftesbury Avenue, London W1. *Tel:* 01–439 4371.

BENNETT, Hywel, actor
b Garnant, South Wales, 8 Apr 1944; *s* of Gordon Bennett and his wife Sarah Gwen (Lewis); *e* Henry Thornton Grammar School, Clapham, London; trained for the stage at RADA; *m* Cathy McGowan (mar dis).

Made his first London appearance at the Queen's, June 1959, as Ophelia in the Youth Theatre's Hamlet; played in repertory at Salisbury and Leatherhead, 1965; toured, Sept 1965, as Wormwood in Dear Wormwood; Arts, Feb 1966, Lennie in A Smashing Day; Edinburgh Festival, Aug 1967, Puck in A Midsummer Night's Dream; Mermaid, Apr, 1970, Prince Hal in both parts of Henry IV; Young Vic, Aug 1972, played Antony in Julius Caesar; Shaw, Oct 1972, Bakke in Bakke's Night Of Fame; Gardner Centre, Brighton, Sept 1973, Stanley in The Birthday Party; toured S Africa, Feb 1974, in the title role of Hamlet; played Danny in Night Must Fall at the Sherman, Cardiff, May 1974 and again at the Shaw, Mar 1975; Belgrade, Coventry, 1974, Jimmy Porter in Look Back In Anger; toured, Sept 1974, as Konstantin in The Seagull, Birmingham Repertory, Dec 1975, title part in Toad of Toad Hall; Comedy, Jan 1977, took over as Simon in

Otherwise Engaged; Her Majesty's, Sept 1979, Andreas Capodistriou and Inspector Bowden in The Oily Levantine; has directed Gaslight, Lincoln 1971; The Promise, Sheffield; A Lily In Little India, Coventry, 1974; I have Been Here Before, Cardiff, Move Over Mrs Markham, Rosencrantz and Guildenstern are Dead (both Leatherhead), 1975; A Man for All Seasons, Birmingham, 1976; films, since 1966, include The Family Way, The Virgin Soldiers, Loot and Alice in Wonderland; television, since 1962, includes Romeo and Juliet, The Idiot. Death of a Teddy Bear, Tinker, Tailor, Soldier, Spy, and Shelley.

Recreations: Fishing, cooking. *Address:* 5 Rosehill Road, London SW 18.

BENNETT, Jill, actress
b Penang, Federated Malay States, 24 Dec 1931; *d* of James Randle Bennett and his wife Nora Adeline (Beckett); *e* Priors Field, Godalming; *m* (1) Willis Hall (mar dis); (2) John Osborne (mar dis); trained for the stage at the Royal Academy of Dramatic Art.

Began her career at the Shakespeare Memorial Theatre, Stratford-on-Avon, 1949 season; made her first appearance on the London Stage at the St James's, Aug 1950, as Anni in Captain Carvallo; at the same theatre, May 1951, played Iras in Antony and Cleopatra, and Iras in Caesar and Cleopatra, in Sir Laurence Olivier's season; at the New, Jan 1955, played Helen Eliot in The Night of the Ball; Saville, Aug 1956, Masha in The Seagull; Arts, Nov 1956, Mrs Martin in The Bald Prima Donna; Aldwych, Dec 1956, Sarah Stanham in The Touch of Fear; New, Dec 1957, Isabelle in Dinner with the Family; at the Lyric, Hammersmith, Nov 1959, played Penelope in Last Day in Dreamland, and Penelope Belford in A Glimpse of the Sea (double-bill); Arts, Apr 1961, Susan Roper in Breakfast for One; Mermaid, Oct 1961, played Feemy Evans in The Showing-Up of Blanco Posnet, and Lavinia in Androcles and the Lion (double-bill); Oxford Playhouse, Feb 1962, Estelle in In Camera (Huis Clos); Piccadilly, May 1962, Ophelia in Castle in Sweden; Royal Court, Dec 1962, played Hilary in The Sponge Room, and Elizabeth Mintey in Squat Betty (double-bill); New Arts, Oct 1964, played Isabelle in The Love Game; Royal Court, June 1965, Countess Sophia Delyanoff in A Patriot For Me; Hampstead Theatre Club, Nov 1965, Anna Bowers in A Lily in Little India; Old Vic in a National Theatre Season, Aug 1966, took over Imogen Parrott in Trelawney of the Wells, and Oct 1966, played Katerina in The Storm; Royal Court, May 1968, appeared as Pamela in Time Present, transferring to the Duke of York's, July 1968—for this performance she won the *Evening Standard* and Variety Club Awards for best actress; Royal Court, Jan 1970, played Anna Bowers in Three Months Gone, transferring to the Duchess, Mar 1970; Royal Court, Aug 1971, Frederica in West of Suez, in which she transferred to the Cambridge, Oct; Royal Court, June 1972, Hedda in Hedda Gabler; Queen's, June 1973, took over as Amanda in Private Lives; Palace, Watford, July 1973, Leslie Crosbie in The Letter; Greenwich, Jan 1975, Mrs Isobel Sands in The End of Me Old Cigar; Royal Court, June 1975, Fay in Loot; National Theatre (Old Vic, Feb, subsequently Lyttleton, Mar 1976), Sally Prosser in Watch It Come Down; Apollo, Jan 1977, Mrs Shankland and Miss Railton-Bell in Separate Tables; Chichester Festival, Mrs Tina in The Aspern Papers, 1978, The Queen in The Eagle Has Two Heads and Maggie Cutler in The Man Who Came to Dinner, 1979; films in which she has appeared recently, include: The Charge of the Light Brigade, Inadmissible Evidence, Julius Caesar, I Want What I Want, etc; television plays in which she has appeared include The Heiress, The Three Sisters,

Design for Living, The Parachute, Rembrandt, Almost a Vision, The Old Crowd, etc.
Recreations: Lying in the sun, riding, and skiing.

BENNETT, Joan, actress
b Palisades, New Jersey, 27 Feb 1910; *d* of Richard Bennett and his wife Adrienne (Morrison); *e* St Margaret's School, Waterbury, Conn; and L'Hermitage, Versailles, France; *m* (1) John Marion Fox (mar dis); (2) Gene Mackey (mar dis); (3) Walter Wanger (mar dis); (4) David Wilde.

First appeared on the stage with her father at the Longacre, New York, Sept 1928, as Daisy in Jarnegan; Biltmore, 1929, played Soledad in The Pirate; after seven years in Hollywood she re-appeared on the stage in 1937 in a US tour of Stage Door; toured 1948 and 1951, as Susan Trexel in Susan and God; US tour, 1952–3, as Gillian Holroyd in Bell, Book and Candle; US tour, 1953, as the film star in Best Foot Forward; US tour, 1956, as Alice Walters in Anniversary Waltz; US tour, Sept 1956–Mar 1957, as Jessica in Janus; Helen Hayes, NY, Apr 1958, Mother in Love Me Little; US tour, 1959, Dolly Fabian in Once More with Feeling; US tour, Sept 1960–Mar 1961, Katherine Dougherty in The Pleasure of His Company; Coconut Grove, Miami, Apr 1963, played Edith Lambert in Never Too Late; first appeared on the London stage at the Prince of Wales, Sept 1963, as Edith Lambert in Never Too Late; toured the US, 1965, in the same role; appeared with the Bucks County Playhouse, New Hope, Pa, 1972–3; Royal Poinciana Playhouse, Palm Beach, Fla, Jan 1975, Jessica in Janus; first entered films in 1929 opposite Ronald Colman in Bulldog Drummond and has since played in innumerable films, notably Disraeli, Little Women, Scarlet Street, The Macomber Affair, The Woman in the Window, etc; first appeared on television in 1949.
Address: 67 Chase Road, Scarsdale North, NY 10583

BENNETT, Michael, choreographer and director.
Choreographed his first Broadway musical at the Mark Hellinger, 15 Dec 1966, A Joyful Noise; since then has choreographed Henry, Sweet Henry, 1967; Promises, Promises, which he also directed, 1968; Coco, which he also directed, 1969; Company, also co-directed, 1970; Follies, also co-directed and for which he won the Antoinette Perry (Tony) Award in both categories 1971; directed the drama Twigs, 1971; at Her Majesty's, London, Jan 1972, choreographed Company; New York, choreographed and directed Seesaw, 1973, for which he received the Tony Award; directed God's Favorite, 1974; conceived, directed, and choreographed A Chorus Line, originally at the New York Shakespeare Festival Public Theater and then at the Shubert, 1975, receiving two Tony Awards and the Pulitzer Prize; directed A Chorus Line in London, 1976; Majestic, Dec 1978, presented Ballroom, which he also directed and choreographed, again receiving a Tony award.
Address: 890 Broadway, New York, NY 10003.

BENNETT, Peter, actor
b London, 17 Sept 1917; *s* of Major R H E Bennett, MC, and his wife Dorothy (Lowe); *e* Malvern College; *m* Sheila Bramwell-Jones; studied for the stage at the Royal Academy of Dramatic Art.

Made his first appearance on the stage at the Pleasure Gardens Theatre, Folkestone, 27 Jan 1936, as Ma Ta in Lady Precious Stream; first appeared in London, at the Arts Theatre, 9 May 1936, as Possum and Ed Sweet in Little Ol' Boy; subsequently appeared at the Mercury, Westminster, Ambassadors', and Open Air Theatres; at the New Theatre, Jan 1939, played Hui Ming in The Western Chamber; Em-

bassy, Feb 1939, Johann Breitstein in Counsellor-at-Law; Open Air Theatre, June–Sept 1939, played Pandar in Pericles, Fabian in Twelfth Night, etc; Kingsway, Dec 1939, General Wei in Lady Precious Stream; Palace, July 1940, Kasim Baba in Chu-Chin-Chow, and again in July 1941; Adelphi, Dec 1941, Starkey in Peter Pan; again appeared at Open Air Theatre, July 1942; Westminster, Sept–Dec 1942, played Gratiano in The Merchant of Venice, Vernon and Poins in King Henry IV (Part I), and Poins and Davy in Part II, and Quince in A Midsummer Night's Dream; Phoenix, Aug 1943, De Beausset in War and Peace; Cambridge, Dec 1943, again played Starkey in Peter Pan; Open Air, May 1944, the Clown in The Winter's Tale; Lyric, Hammersmith, Aug 1944, Third Witch and Porter in Macbeth; toured, Nov 1944, as Perkins in The Golden Fleece; King's, Hammersmith, Aug 1945, played Arthur Clough in The Spinster of South Street, and Face in The Alchemist; Embassy, Oct 1945, Ernie in Zoo in Silesia, and June 1946, Corporal Cramp in Love Goes to Press; Embassy, Aug 1946, John Dashwood in Sense and Sensibility; first appeared on New York stage at the Biltmore Theatre, 1 Jan 1947, as Corporal Cramp in Love Goes to Press; Embassy, May 1948, Henry in Symphony in Violence; Q, Nov 1948, Mr Calthorpe in For Better, For Worse; Gateway, Feb 1949, appeared as Gavin Bainbridge in Burn, Witch, Burn; Fortune, Nov 1949, Fag in The Rivals; during 1949–50, played a number of parts at the Playhouse, Amersham, and Theatre Royal, Stratford; Theatre Royal, Stratford, Dec 1950, played Scrooge in A Christmas Carol; Royal, Bristol, June 1951, played Dr Miseria in To Live in Peace; at the Festival of Britain Church, Aug 1951, appeared as Caiaphas in The Man Born To Be King; Players', Mar 1952, Motley in The Castle Spectre; Gateway, July 1952, directed Avalanche in Speculum; New Torch, June 1953, played Prosser in Portrait of a Gentleman; same theatre, Sept 1953, Mr Harrison Crockstead in A Marriage Has Been Arranged; Q, Jan 1954, Mr Hughes in Birds of Sadness; Richmond, Sept 1954, Mr Allnut in The Name Is Smith; Embassy, Oct 1954, Wedgewood in Wild Goose Chase; Royal Windsor, Nov 1954, Councillor Hedges in Let's Talk Turkey; joined the Guildford Theatre Company, May 1955, and played Lon Dennison in The Wooden Dish; Piccadilly, Nov 1955, played Carlos Gervanzoni in The Strong Are Lonely; New Lindsey, Feb 1957, Bernard Fell in A For Angel, B For Bed; Royal Court, June 1957, James Walton in The Waiting of Lester Abbs (in a Production without Décor for The English Stage Company); Scala, Dec 1962, played Mr Noah in Noddy in Toyland; New, Cardiff, Dec 1964, Scrooge in A Christmas Carol, again at the Arts, Cambridge, Dec 1966, and on tour, 1967; Mermaid, July 1971 and tour, played Mr Sole in The Old Boys; Act Inn, Oct 1972 (lunchtime), Hector in Humulus the Muted Lover; Theatre Upstairs, July 1975, Albert in Heroes; Chiltern Festival, 1977, Boswell in The Trial of Dr Johnson; Director, Festival of British Theatre Ltd, 1975; Council Member of British Actors' Equity 1970–80; appointed to the National Council for Drama Training, 1979; has appeared in over 200 films and TV productions as well as radio, recently in the film Tarka the Otter and the television play The Old Crowd.
Favourite parts: Scrooge, and Face in The Alchemist. *Recreations:* Collecting assorted objects and walking long distances. *Clubs:* Garrick and Green Room. *Address:* 39 Bedford Gardens, Campden Hill, W8 7EF. *Tel:* 01–727 4581.

BENSON, George, actor
b Cardiff, South Wales, 11 Jan 1911; *s* of Leslie Bernard Gilpin Benson and his wife Isita Lenora (Waddington); *e* Blundell's School (Keats Medallist, 1927 and 1928); *m* (1)

Jane Ann Sterndale Bennett (mar dis); (2) Pamela White; studied for the stage at the Royal Academy of Dramatic Art (Silver Medallist, 1930).

While still at the Academy, made his first appearance on the stage at the Malvern Festival Theatre, 24 Aug 1929, as a Roman Soldier in Caesar and Cleopatra; made his first appearance in London at the Cambridge Theatre, 4 Sept 1930, in various small parts in Charlot's Masquerade; Savoy, Dec 1930, played Willie in Wonder Bar; Jan–Mar 1932, appeared at the Festival Theatre, Cambridge; Comedy, London, Apr 1932, played George Pelham in Faces; Faculty of Arts, May 1932, Ben and Trapland in Love for Love; Embassy, Oct 1932, Sam Gerridge in Caste; toured in Egypt and Australia, 1932–3, with Nicholas Hannen and Athene Seyler's Company; next appeared at the Savoy, Nov 1933, in Please; Coliseum, Feb 1934, the Courtier in The Golden Toy; His Majesty's, Nov 1934, Snyde in Mary Read; Comedy, May 1935, played in Shall We Reverse?; Vaudeville, Sept 1935, in Stop— Go!, Dec 1935, King Hildebrand in What a Witch!, and Mar 1936, in The Town Talks; Gate, June 1936, Socrates in No More Peace; Ambassadors', Aug 1936, made a notable success as Edward Gill in The Two Bouquets; Open Air, Sept 1937, Dromio of Ephesus in The Comedy of Errors; Gate, Nov 1937, Vlas Fillipovich in Distant Point; Little, Jan 1938, appeared in the revue, Nine Sharp, which ran through the year; Wyndham's (for Stage Society), Dec 1938, Gus Michaels in Paradise Lost; Old Vic, Jan 1939, played Tony Lumpkin in She Stoops to Conquer; Little, Apr 1939, appeared in The Little Revue, and Apr 1940, Sir Jasper Fidget in The Country Wife; toured, June 1940, in Nine Sharp; Criterion, Sept 1940, directed In Town Again; Wyndham's, Oct 1940, appeared in and directed the revue, Diversion; served in HM Forces, in the Royal Artillery, 1940–6; re-appeared on the stage, Garrick, Apr 1946, in Better Late; Playhouse, Dec 1946, appeared in the revue, Between Ourselves; made his first appearance in the USA, at the Empire, New York, 29 Oct 1947, as Desmond Curry in The Winslow Boy, and toured in this in the United States and Canada, until 1948; after his return to England, joined the Old Vic Company at the New, for the season 1949–50, playing Costard in Love's Labour's Lost, Bolshintsov in A Month in the Country, Jacques in The Miser, Marcellus and 1st Gravedigger in Hamlet; His Majesty's, Nov 1950 appeared as Poupart in Music at Midnight; Lyric, Hammersmith, May 1951, played in The Lyric Revue, and appeared in this production at the Globe, Sept 1951; Globe, July 1952, appeared in The Globe Revue; Arts, May 1954, played Pasqualino in The Impresario from Smyrna; Arts, Sept 1954, Mr Pooter in The Diary of a Nobody; toured with the Old Vic Company in Australia, 1955, playing Launcelot Gobbo and the Prince of Arragon in The Merchant of Venice, Grumio in The Taming of the Shrew and Pompey in Measure for Measure; Victoria Palace, June 1956, played the Duke of Epping in Jubilee Girl; Edinburgh Festival, Lyceum, Sept 1956, Mr Gilbey in Fanny's First Play; Edinburgh Festival, Lyceum, Aug 1957, Sibilot in Nekrassov, subsequently appearing in the same production at the Royal Court, Sept 1957; at the same theatre, Dec 1957, played the Magistrate in Lysistrata; Piccadilly, May 1959, Wellington Potts in Caught Napping; Royal Court, Dec 1959, played Arthur Groomkirby in One Way Pendulum, transferring with the production to the Criterion, Feb 1960; Strand, May 1961, played Dr Crippen in Belle, or the Ballad of Dr Crippen; Edinburgh Festival, and subsequently Royal Court, Sept 1961, played Mr Bolt in August for the People; Oxford Playhouse, Oct 1961; Boss Mangan in Heartbreak House, subsequently appearing at Wyndham's, Nov 1961, in the same production;

Haymarket, Nov 1962, played Rupert Tilling in The Tulip Tree; Ashcroft, Croydon, Feb 1964, played Henry Carter in The Excursion; Theatre Royal, Stratford, E, May 1964, played Thring in The Man Who Let It Rain; Shaftesbury, Dec 1964, the Earl of Loam in the musical Our Man Crichton; Hampstead Theatre Club, Sept 1965, Count Bodo in The Marriage of Mr Mississippi; Yvonne Arnaud, Guildford, July 1966, and subsequent tour, Dudley in A Family and a Fortune; Yvonne Arnaud, June 1967, Lord Pilco in The Last of Mrs Cheyney, subsequently appearing in the same production at the Phoenix, July 1967; Yvonne Arnaud, Sept 1967, Simon, Fred and Reginald in The Adventures of Tom Random; Phoenix, Oct 1968 to Jan 1970, Steward, Carpenter and January in Canterbury Tales; at the Mermaid, played Justice Shallow in Henry IV Part 2, May 1970, June 1970, Gonzalo in The Tempest; Sept 1970, Inquisitor in St Joan; Secretary of the League of Nations in Geneva, 1971; Birmingham Rep, June 1972, Dean Judd in Dandy Dick; Gardner Centre, Brighton, Aug 1972, Rev Harold Davison in The Vicar of Soho; Arnaud, Guildford, Nov 1972, Christopher Glowrey in Nightmare Abbey; Mermaid, Dec 1972, Squire Trelawney in Treasure Island; toured, Feb 1973, with the Cambridge Theatre Co as The Waiter in You Never Can Tell; Theatre Royal, Windsor, Sept 1973, Polonius in Hamlet; Chairman, Society for Theatre Research, 1968–72; has appeared frequently in films, and in radio and television plays; suffered a stroke in 1974.
Address: 20 Makepeace Avenue, London, N6 6EJ.

BENTHAM, Frederick, theatre consultant, lighting designer and author
b 23 Oct 1911; *s* of Percy George Bentham and his wife Ellen Celia (Hobbs); *e* St Paul's School, Regent Street Polytechnic and the Central School of Arts and Crafts; *m* Ilse Ruhm; after a period at GEC under Basil Davis, theatre consultant, joined Strand Electric in 1932.

Here he introduced lanterns such as the Pageant and the Mirror Spot; pioneered remote control in Britain with the Light Console in 1935; in charge of research and development for Strand until 1965, he was in consequence responsible at that time for the lighting control systems in all the principal theatres and television studios in Britain and in a number overseas; director, Strand Electric, 1957–70; PR and Technical Liaison Manager to Rank Strand 1970–3; designed the DDM, first theatre lighting control to use standard minicomputer, 1972; Wyndham's, 1974, devised and gave solo Teach-In; editor of *Tabs* quarterly 1956–73; of *Sightline* 1973– ; author of Stage Lighting, 1950, The Art of Stage Lighting, 1968 (new edition 1976) and New Theatres in Britain, 1970; Fellow of the Chartered Institute of Building Services (formerly the Illuminating Engineering Society); Past Master of The Art Workers Guild; Chairman of ABTT, 1973–8.
Recreations: Canal cruising; colour music. *Address:* 24 Amherst Road, London, W13. *Tel:* 01–997 1375.

BENTLEY, Eric (Russell), BA (Oxon), LittB (Oxon), PhD (Yale), director, playwright, dramatic critic, author, editor
b England, 14 Sept 1916; *s* of Fred Bentley and his wife Laura (Evelyn); *e* Bolton's School; Oxford University; Yale University; Honorary Doctor of Fine Arts, Univ of Wisconsin, 1975; Hon DLitt, University of East Anglia, 1979; *m* Joanne Davis.

At the Schloss Leopoldskron, Salzburg, Austria, Apr 1949, led a theatre month for the Salzburg Seminar in American Studies, and directed Sweeney Agonistes; led another theatre month, June 1950, and presented ten productions from England, France, Germany, Ireland, and Italy, and directed Him with Kenneth Tynan in the leading part; at the Abbey, Dublin, 1950, directed The House of Bernarda Alba; Schauspielhaus, Zurich, 1950, co-directed the German language première of The Iceman Cometh; in 1951, directed the US tour of Purgatory, Riders to the Sea, and The Shadow of the Glen, for the Young Ireland Theatre Co; Phoenix, New York, Dec 1956, directed his own translation of The Good Woman of Setzuan; his play The Red, White, and Black produced at the LaMama ETC, Mar 1971, and directed it when it transferred to the Players on 30 Mar 1971; his play Are You Now Or Have You Ever Been? produced by the Yale Repertory Theater in Nov 1972; his play The Recantation of Galileo Galilei produced by Wayne State Univ, Nov 1973; and 1967–68; his play Expletive Deleted produced at the Theater of the Riverside Church, NY, 3 June 1974 in 1979 wrote Lord Alfred's Lover (Gainesville, Fla) and The Fall of the Amazons (Buffalo, NY); play adaptations and translations include: The Private Life of the Master Race, La Ronde, The Good Woman of Setzuan, A Man's a Man, Mother Courage and Her Children, Right You Are (If You Think You Are), Henry IV (Pirandello), The Underpants, The Emperor, Baal, Edward II, In the Swamp, The Exception and the Rule, The Caucasian Chalk Circle; Guggenheim Fellow, 1948–9 dramatic critic for *The New Republic*, 1952–6; since 1953, has been Brander Matthews Professor of Dramatic Literature at Columbia University; Charles Eliot Norton Professor of Poetry, Harvard University, 1960–1; Artist in Residence for the Ford Foundation in Berlin, 1964–5; received the George Jean Nathan Award for Dramatic Criticism, 1967; was the subject of the television program Creative Person in Apr 1967; CBS Playwriting Fellow, Yale Univ, 1976–7; Katharine Cornell Professor of Theatre, State University of New York (Buffalo), 1977–; elected Fellow of the American Academy of Arts and Sciences, 1969; author of the following books: A Century of Hero Worship (1944), The Playwright As Thinker (1946), Bernard Shaw (1947), In Search of Theatre (1953), The Dramatic Event (1954), What Is Theatre? (1956), The Life of the Drama (1964), Theatre of Commitment (1967), Theatre of War (1972); served as Editor for the following books: The Importance of Scrutiny (1948), From the Modern Repertory (a series issued between 1949–56), The Modern Theatre (a series issued between 1955–60); The Classic Theatre (1958–61), The Genius of the Italian Theatre (1964); Shaw on Music, Let's Get a Divorce, The Storm Over The Deputy, The Brecht-Eisler Songbook, The Great Playwright's, Thirty Years of Treason, etc; he has also made recordings of Bentley on Brecht, Brecht Before the Unamerican Committee, A Man's a Man, etc.
Address: West End Avenue, New York, NY 10025.

BERGHOF, Herbert, actor, director, teacher
b Vienna, Austria, 13 Sept 1909; *s* of Paul Berghof and his wife Regina; *e* Vienna; *m* (1) Alice Hermes (mar dis); (2) Uta Hagen; studied for the stage at the Royal Academy of Dramatic Art, Vienna, and with Alexander Moissi and Max Reinhardt.

Made his first appearance on the stage at the Duetsches Volkstheater, Vienna, Sept 1927, in Don Carlos; during the ensuing twelve years, appeared in more than 120 plays, in Vienna, Berlin, Zurich, Paris, and at the Salzburg Festivals, playing in all the Continental classics, in Shakespeare (Romeo, Orlando, Hamlet, etc.), and in numerous modern plays, including The Soldier in The Unknown Soldier, Marius in the play of that name, Marchbanks in Candida, Dubedat in The Doctor's Dilemma, Oswald in Ghosts, etc; came to New York, where he directed From Vienna, at the Music Box,

June 1939; made his first appearance in NY, at the Little, Feb 1940, when he co-directed with Ezra Stone and played in Reunion in New York; National, Washington, DC, Apr 1941, Captain Miller in Somewhere in France; New School for Social Research, 1941, the Fool in King Lear; same theatre, Dec 1941, Kummerer in The Criminals; at the Shubert Theatre, 3 Apr 1942, Nathan in Nathan the Wise; Studio Theatre, Nov 1942, played Tieck in Winter Soldiers; Guild, Dec 1942, Panin in The Russian People; Belasco, Nov 1943, Otto in The Innocent Voyage; St James, during 1944, for a time played Hakim in Oklahoma!, and at the Martin Beck, in the same year, Jacobowski in Jacobowski and the Colonel; Forrest, Nov 1944, Gustav Eberson in The Man Who Had All the Luck; Coronet, Oct 1945, Maurice in Beggars Are Coming to Town; toured Canada and US, Dec 1945–Mar 1946, as Jean in Dr Lazare's Pharmacy; Playhouse, Dec 1946, Captain Karel Palivec in Temper the Wind; Biltmore, May 1947, Dmitri Savalev in The Whole World Over; directed The Key and Rip Van Winkle, 1947; Cort, Feb 1948, Pastor Manders in Ghosts, and Judge Brack in Hedda Gabler; Imperial, July 1949, Bartholdi in Miss Liberty; Barbizon Plaza, Nov 1949, title-role of Torquato Tasso; Fulton, Aug 1950, Dr Wangel in The Lady from the Sea; Erlanger, Buffalo, Jan 1951, played The Critic in The Guardsman; New York City Center, May 1952, Prince Mikail Alexandrovitch Ouratieff in Tovarich; Morosco, Nov 1952, Mr Miller in The Deep Blue Sea; Golden, Apr 1956, directed Waiting for Godot, and Ethel Barrymore, Jan 1957, directed the same play with an all-Negro cast; Ambassador, Dec 1956, directed Protective Custody; Ann Arbor, Michigan Festival, 1957, directed and starred in The Affairs of Anatol; Phoenix, NY, Feb 1958, directed The Infernal Machine; Cambridge Drama Festival, Boston, July 1959, directed Twelfth Night; Bucks County Playhouse, New Hope, Pa, Aug 1959, directed The Queen and the Rebels; Henry Miller, Dec 1959, played Henry Wirz in The Andersonville Trial; Provincetown Playhouse, Jan 1960, played Krapp in Krapp's Last Tape; Vancouver, Aug 1961, directed Men, Women, and Angels, and Do You Know the Milky Way?; Billy Rose, Oct 1961, directed Do You Know the Milky Way?; Sheridan Square Playhouse, Feb 1962, directed This Side of Paradise; Vivian Beaumont, Mar 1969, Edward Teller in In the Matter of J Robert Oppenheimer, and repeated this role in the revival in June 1969; Peachtree Playhouse, Atlanta, Ga, Jan 1975, directed The Sponsor; Ethel Barrymore, Oct 1976, directed his translation of Poor Murder; has also played numerous parts in summer theatres; charter member of Actors Studio, 1947; has also taught acting for many years, at the following places in NY: The New School for Social Research, The American Theatre Wing, The Neighborhood Playhouse, Columbia University, and at the HB (Herbert Berghof) Studio; founded the HB Playwrights Foundation in 1964, and has directed for it Tomorrow by Horton Foote and William Faulkner, Seize the Day by Saul Bellow, Democracy and Esther, Kaspar, etc; has appeared in motion pictures since 1952, including: Five Fingers, Red Planet Mars, Cleopatra (1963), etc; has also played on television.
Favourite parts: Hamlet, Oedipus, Dubedat, Nathan, etc.
Address: 27 Washington Square North, or 120 Bank Street, New York City.

BERGMAN, Ingrid, actress

b Stockholm, Sweden, 29 August 1915; *d* of Justus Bergman and his wife Friedel (Adler); *e* Lyceum, Flickor; *m* (1) Dr Peter Lindstrom (mar dis); (2) Roberto Rossellini (mar dis); (3) Lars Schmidt; studied for the stage at the Royal Dramatic Theatre School, Stockholm.

Commenced her career in films 1936, and appeared in a number of productions before going to Hollywood, 1939, to appear in Intermezzo (Escape to Happiness); made her first appearance on the New York stage, 44th Street Theatre, 25 Mar 1940, as Julie in Liliom; at Santa Barbara, California, 1941, played Anna Christopherson in Anna Christie; Alvin Theatre, NY, Nov 1946, appeared as Mary Grey (Joan) in Joan of Lorraine; at the San Carlo Opera House, Naples, Dec 1953, appeared as Joan in Honegger's Joan of Arc at the Stake; made her first appearance on the London stage at the Stoll, 20 Oct 1954, in the same part; at the Opera House, Stockholm, Feb 1955, again appeared as Joan; Théâtre de Paris, Paris, Dec 1956, played Laura in Tea and Sympathy; Théâtre Gaston Baty-Montparnasse, Paris, Dec 1962, Hedda Gabler in the play by that name; appeared in the opening production at the Yvonne Arnaud Theatre, Guildford, Surrey, May 1965, as Natalia Petrovna in A Month in the Country, subsequently appearing in the same production at the Cambridge, London, Sept 1965; Broadhurst, NY, Oct 1967, played Deborah in the première production of Eugene O'Neill's More Stately Mansions; Cambridge, London, Feb 1971, Lady Cicely Wayneflete in Captain Brassbound's Conversion; Ethel Barrymore, NY, Apr 1972, repeated this last part after a tour of the US; Albery, London, Sept 1973, Constance Middleton in The Constant Wife; Shubert, NY, Apr 1975, repeated this last part after a tour of the US; Chichester Festival Theatre, 1977 season, played Helen Lancaster in Waters of the Moon; also Haymarket, Jan 1978; among the films in which she has appeared are Dr Jekyll and Mr Hyde, Casablanca, For Whom the Bell Tolls, Gaslight, Spellbound, The Bells of St Mary's, Joan of Arc, Stromboli, Anastasia, The Inn of the Sixth Happiness, Indiscreet, Murder on the Orient Express, Autumn Sonata, etc; received the Academy Award for her rôles in Gaslight and Anastasia; appeared in an all-star television production of Hedda Gabler, Dec 1963; received an Emmy Award for her performance in The Turn of the Screw (1960).

BERGNER, Elisabeth, actress

b Vienna, 22 Aug 1900; *d* of the late Emil Bergner and his wife Anna Rosa (Wagner); *e* Vienna; *m* Dr Paul Czinner (dec); studied for the stage at the Vienna Conservatory, 1915–19.

Made her first appearance on the stage at the City Theatre, Zurich, under the direction of Dr Alfred Reucker, in the autumn of 1919; after playing a number of small parts, appeared as Ophelia in Hamlet, with the late Alexander Moissi; during 1920, at Zurich, she played Rosalind in As You Like It; she then returned to Vienna, making her first appearance there at the Burgtheater, as Rosalind; subsequently she appeared in Munich, under Otto Falckenberg; she made her first appearance in Berlin in The Wicked Mr Chu, and subsequently, at the Deutches Volkstheater, under Max Reinhardt, played Katherine in The Taming of the Shrew, the Queen in Richard II and Rosalind in As You Like It; she also played Julie in Miss Julie, Hannele, Nora Helmer in A Doll's House, Magda, Viola in Twelfth Night, Juliet, etc; in 1924, she appeared as Joan in Saint Joan, which gained her an international reputation; she also played Marguerite in The Lady of the Camelias, and repeated her former success as Rosalind; in 1925, appeared in Der Kreidekreis (The Circle of Chalk) and He Wants to Have His Fun; at the Koeniggraetzer Theater, Berlin, 1926, she played Mrs Cheyney in The Last of Mrs Cheyney, under Barnovsky; made a further success at the same theatre, 1927, when she appeared as Tessa in The Constant Nymph, followed at the Staattheater, by her performance of Portia in The Merchant of

Venice; in 1928, commenced a tour through Holland, Denmark, Sweden, Germany and Austria, playing Hannele, Kaiser Karl's Geisel, Einsame Menschen, The Taming of the Shrew, Richard II, Queen Christina, The Circle, Miss Julie, Lanzelot and Sanderein, The Circle of Chalk, As You Like It and Saint Joan; in 1929, played Nina Leeds in Strange Interlude; in 1930–1, under Reinhardt, again played Juliet, with Francis Lederer as Romeo; in 1931, played Alkmena in Amphitryon 38; then spent two years in Paris, in films; made her first appearance on the English stage at the Opera House, Manchester, 21 Nov 1933, under C B Cochran, as Gemma Jones in Escape Me Never, making her first appearance in London, at the Apollo Theatre, 8 Dec 1933, in the same part, in which she achieved instantaneous success; made her first appearance in New York under the joint auspices of the Theatre Guild and C B Cochran, at the Shubert Theatre, 21 Jan 1935, when she again played Gemma in Escape Me Never, duplicating her London success; at His Majesty's, London, Dec 1936, played David in The Boy David, Sir James Barrie's last play, specially written for her; at Malvern, Aug 1938, played Joan in Saint Joan; subsequently went again to the United States; at the Booth Theatre, NY, Aug 1943, played Sally in The Two Mrs Carrolls, which ran for two seasons, and continued to tour in this, 1945; at the Booth, Feb 1945, she staged The Overtons; Barrymore, Oct 1946, played the Duchess in The Duchess of Malfi; Music Box, Apr 1948, appeared as Ellen Croy in The Cup of Trembling; at Washington, June 1949, played Alkmena in Amphitryon 38; toured in Australia, 1950, in The Two Mrs Carrolls; re-appeared on the English stage at the Opera House, Manchester, Nov 1950, as Toinette in The Gay Invalid, and played this part at the Garrick, Jan 1951; toured Germany and Austria, 1954, in The Deep Blue Sea; toured Germany and Austria, 1957, as Mary Tyrone in Long Day's Journey Into Night; Berlin Festival, Oct 1959, played Mrs Patrick Campbell in Dear Liar, subsequently touring Germany and Austria with the same production; Shubert, New Haven, Nov 1961, played Nina Kacew in First Love; Düsseldorf, Germany, Sept 1964, Countess Aurelia in The Madwoman of Chaillot, playing the same part in England, Nov 1967, at the Arnaud, Guildford, and the Oxford Playhouse; Greenwich, Oct 1973, Mrs Orban in Catsplay; received the Schiller Prize, 1963, being the first actress to receive the award; received the *Goldeneband* of the International Film Festival, Berlin, 1963 and 1965; first appeared in films, 1923, in Der Evangelimann (The Evangelist), and has since appeared in Ariane, Dreaming Lips, Catherine the Great, Stolen Life, etc.
Recreations: Walking and music. *Address:* 42 Eaton Square, London SW1.

BERKOFF, Steven, actor, director, and writer
b London, 3 Aug 1937; *s* of Alfred Berkoff and his wife Pauline (Hyman); *e* Raines Foundation, Stepney, and Hackney Downs Grammar School; *m* Shelley Lee; trained for the stage at the Ecole Jacques Le Coq, Paris, and the Webber-Douglas Academy, London.
His first professional appearance was at the Empire, Finsbury Park, Aug 1959, as Louis in A View from the Bridge; at the Lyric, Hammersmith, July 1961, played a bellboy in Oh Dad, Poor Dad, . . .; worked in various reps before forming the London Theatre Group, with whom he has since been seen in London on tour, in Europe, Israel and Australia in a number of works directed by him and usually also written or adapted by him; these include The Penal Colony, first produced 1968, an adaptation from Kafka, as were Metamorphosis, in which he played Gregor, 1969, The Trial, in which

he played Titorelli, 1971, and Knock at the Manor Gate, 1972; Miss Julie and The Zoo Story (double-bill); Agamemnon, playing the title role, Miss Julie versus Expressionism, 1973; The Fall of the House of Usher, playing Usher, 1974; his first original play, East, was first produced at the Edinburgh Festival, 1975; the company played a season at the Cottesloe, Aug 1977, consisting of Metamorphosis, Usher, and East, with East transferring to the New London in the same month; all three were again seen at the New London, Feb 1978; in 1979 directed and played the title role in Hamlet, Edinburgh Festival, and wrote and directed Greek, Croydon Warehouse; films include Barry Lyndon, A Clockwork Orange, and The Passenger; author of a collection of short stories, Gross Intrusion.
Favourite parts: Hamlet, Mike in East, Usher. *Address:* c/o Joanna Marston, 4 Hereford Square, London SW7.

BERLE, Milton (*né* Berlinger), actor
b New York City, 12 July 1908; *s* of Moses Berlinger and his wife Sarah (Glantz); *e* Professional Children's School, NY; *m* (1) Joyce Mathews (mar dis); (2) Joyce Mathews (mar dis again); (3) Ruth Cosgrove Rosenthal.
Made his earliest appearances in children's parts in various films for the Biograph Company; made his first appearance on the regular stage, at the Globe Theatre, Atlantic City, 29 Mar 1920, in a small part in Floradora, and first appeared in NY, at the Century Theatre, 5 Apr 1920, in the same play; subsequently appeared in vaudeville for many years, finally touring with his own company; Broadway, Sept 1932, appeared in Earl Carroll Vanities; Imperial, Aug 1934, played Windy Walker in Saluta; in 1935, he toured in Life Begins at 8.40; subsequently he appeared in The Ziegfeld Follies; Biltmore, Sept 1939, played Arthur Lee in See My Lawyer; Winter Garden, Apr 1943, appeared again in The Ziegfeld Follies; at the Ritz Theatre, Nov 1943, presented (with Clifford Hayman) I'll Take the High Road; toured, Oct 1945, as Walter Gribble, Jun, in Spring in Brazil; at the Broadhurst, June 1951, in association with Sammy Lambert and Bernie Foyer, presented Seventeen; toured, summer, 1963, as Jerry Biffle in Top Banana; Ethel Barrymore, Dec 1968, Max Silverman in The Goodbye People; toured, 1970, as Barney Cashman in Last of the Red Hot Lovers; State Fair Music Hall, Dallas Texas, Aug 1971, Noah in Two by Two; Westbury, Long Island, Music Fair, Oct 1971, in The Milton Berle Show; same theatre, June 1972, Barney Cashman in Last of the Red Hot Lovers; same theatre, Nov 1972, appeared in The Milton Berle Show; Westchester Country Playhouse, Aug 1973, Ben Chambers in Norman, Is That You?; toured, 1975, as Ben Chambers in Norman, Is That You?; Studebaker, Chicago, Sept 1975, played in The Best of Everybody; Arlington Park, Ill, 1976, in The Sunshine Boys; has appeared extensively in cabaret, notably in a revue at the Desert Inn, Las Vegas, Nevada, Mar 1964; Caesar's Palace, Las Vegas, Jan 1972; Desert Inn, Las Vegas, Oct 1972; Playboy Plaza, Miami Beach, Fla, Dec 1972; Frontier, Las Vegas, Mar 1974, and the Sands in June 1974; Hyatt Regency O'Hare, Chicago, Ill, June 1975; first appeared in Hollywood films, 1937, and recently in Lepke (1974); for many years was the leading comedian on American television, appearing in his own series and frequently as a guest on other programs; recent appearances include The Muppet Show; has also contributed, intermittently, a humorous column of chit-chat to *Variety*; has written the lyrics for many popular songs, including: Sam, You Made the Pants Too Long, I'm So Happy I Could Cry, Leave the Dishes in the Sink, Ma, etc; received the Humanitarian Award of the Yiddish Theatrical Alliance (1951); NATAS named him Man of the Year

(1959); wrote Laughingly Yours, 1939; published his reminiscences, 1945, under the title, Out of My Trunk; author of his autobiography Milton Berle, 1974.

Address: c/o Irwin H Roseberg, 430 Park Avenue, New York City, 10022.

BERLIN, Irving (*né* Baline), composer and lyricist
b Temun, Russia, 11 May 1888; *s* of Moses Baline and his wife Leah (Lipkin); *e* New York; *m* (1) Dorothy Goetz (dec); (2) Ellin Mackay; first went to the United States in 1893.

Commenced his career at the age of sixteen, singing and playing in restaurants in NY; his first published song was Marie from Sunny Italy, 1907, and he scored his first notable success when he published Alexander's Rag-Time Band, 1911; other popular songs have been My Wife's Gone to the Country, I Want to Go Back to Michigan, Everybody's Doin' It, Ragtime Violin, I Want to Be in Dixie, When the Midnight Choo-Choo Leaves for Alabam, Snooky-Ookums, Down in Chattanooga, The International Rag, When I Lost You, When I Leave the World Behind, White Christmas, Easter Parade, Always, Blue Skies, How Deep Is the Ocean?; at the Casino, NY, July 1910, appeared in Up and Down Broadway; contributed songs to The Ziegfeld Follies, 1911; composer and lyricist of the following revues and musical plays: Watch Your Step, 1914; Stop! Look! Listen! 1915, produced in London, at the Empire, 1916, as Follow the Crowd; The Century Girl (with Victor Herbert), 1916; The Cohan Revue, 1918 (with George M Cohan), 1917; The Ziegfeld Follies of 1918, The Canary, Yip Yip, Yaphank, 1918; The Ziegfeld Follies of 1919 and of 1920; author and composer of The Music Box Revue, each season 1921 to 1924, produced at The Music Box Theatre, NY; The Cocoanuts, 1925; The Ziegfeld Follies, 1927; Face the Music, 1932; As Thousands Cheer, 1933; Louisiana Purchase, 1940; This Is the Army (in which he also appeared, singing Oh, How I Hate to Get Up in the Morning), 1942; Annie Get Your Gun, 1946; Miss Liberty, 1949; Call Me Madam, 1950; Mr President, 1962; for the revival of Annie Get Your Gun, NY State, June 1966, contributed new music and lyrics; has also composed the music and written the lyrics for the films Top Hat, Follow the Fleet, On the Avenue, Alexander's Rag Time Band, Carefree, Second Fiddle, Holiday Inn, Blue Skies, Easter Parade, White Christmas (Academy Award for the title song), There's No Business Like Show Business, and various films of his stage musicals; has written and composed over 800 songs; honors include the Medal of Merit for This Is the Army, Legion of Honour of France, Congressional Gold Medal for his song God Bless America, and honorary degrees from Bucknell, Fordham and Temple Universities; at the Lewisohn Stadium, July 1963, was saluted in a special program commemorating his 75th birthday; Medal of Freedom, 1977.

Clubs: Mason, Elk, Lambs, and Friars; is the President of the music-publishing firm, Irving Berlin Inc. *Address:* 1290 Avenue of the Americas, New York City. *Tel:* Circle 7–4200.

BERLINGER, Warren, actor
b Brooklyn, New York, 31 Aug 1937; *s* of Elias Berlinger and his wife Frieda (Shapkin); *e* Columbia University; *m* Betty Lou Keim.

Made his first appearance on the stage at the Imperial Theatre, NY, May 1946, when he played the Little Boy in Annie Get Your Gun; at the Plymouth, 1951, took over the role of Bibi in The Happy Time, subsequently touring in two productions of the play; Playhouse, Oct 1952, played Dave Gibbs in Bernardine; Lyceum, Sept 1953, played Johnny Reynolds in Take a Giant Step; Broadhurst, Apr 1954,

played Okkie Walters in Anniversary Waltz; Playhouse, Oct 1955, Dick Hewitt in A Roomful of Roses; at the same theatre, Feb 1958, played Ernie Lacey in Blue Denim; Brooks Atkinson, Feb 1961, Buddy Baker in Come Blow Your Horn, subsequently touring, 1962–3, in the same play; made his first appearance in London at the Shaftesbury Theatre, Mar 1963, when he played J. Pierpont Finch in How to Succeed in Business Without Really Trying; Bucks County Playhouse, Pa, July 1965, played the title-role in the musical Tom Jones; Westbury Music Fair, Long Island, May 1967, played in The Rubaiyat of Howard Klein; Mark Taper Forum, Los Angeles, 1968, played in Who's Happy Now?; toured, 1977–8, as Marvin and Mort in California Suite; Lunt-Fontana, Dec 1978, Eddie Bell in A Broadway Musical; entered films, 1956, and notable productions in which he has appeared include Teenage Rebel, Blue Denim, All Hands on Deck, The Long Goodbye (1973), Lepke (1974), etc; has appeared regularly on television since 1947.

Favourite part: J. Pierpont Finch. *Recreation:* Theatre. *Address:* 10642 Arnel Place, Chatsworth, California.

BERMAN, ED., writer, director, producing manager, and head of the Father Christmas Trade Union
b 8 Mar 1941; *s* of Jack Berman and his wife Ida (Webber); *e* Harvard (BA 1962), Exeter College, Oxford (Rhodes Scholar).

Author, as ED.B., of the plays Freeze, 1966; Stamp, Super Santa, 1967; Sagittarius, Virgo, The Nudist Campers Grow and Grow, 1968; The Alien Singer, 1978; founded the Inter-Action Trust, 1968, and has since been Artistic Director of numerous associated ventures, including the Ambiance Lunch-Hour Theatre Club, the Almost Free Theatre, Prof Dogg's Troupe and BARC – the British American Repertory Company; productions for these companies include the premieres of work by John Arden, Wolf Mankowitz, James Saunders and Tom Stoppard; his production of the latter's Dirty Linen, and New-Found-Land, seen first at the Almost Free in April 1976, transferred in June 1976 to the Arts, where it was still running in April 1980; for BARC, 1979, directed Stoppard's Dogg's Hamlet, Cahoot's Macbeth; activist, community artist, educational film maker, author, publisher and performer, noted for his appearances as Prof R L Dogg, Otto Premiere Check, and Super Santa; awarded the MBE in 1979.

Recreations: Solitude, conversation, sensuality, and music. *Address:* Inter-Action Housing Co-operative, 75 Willes Road, London NW5. *Tel:* 01-485 0881.

BERNETTE, Sheila, actress
b London, 30 Mar; *e* Harris Private School and Clarks College; trained for the stage at the Italia Conti and Aida Foster schools.

Made her London debut in 1957 at the Wyndham's, when she joined the cast of The Boy Friend; first New York appearance, 1961, in Victorian Music Hall at the Strollers, 54th St; a constant performer in Victorian Music Hall at the Players, London, since 1964; has also appeared in pantomime, including So-Shy in Aladdin, Palladium, 1970; Royal Variety performance, Palladium, 1970; Ambassadors', June 1977, Miss Tweed in Something's Afoot; films include Sons and Lovers, and The Magnificent Seven Deadly Sins; frequent TV since her first appearance on the Arthur Askey Show in 1953.

Address: c/o CCA, The White House, 29 Dawes Road, London SW6.

BERNHARDT, Melvin, director
b Buffalo, New York, 26 Feb; *s* of Max Bernhard and his wife

Kate (Benatovich); *e* University of Buffalo (BA), Yale University (MFA).

Directed his first play in NY, Conerico Was Here to Stay, at the Cherry Lane, 3 Mar 1965; since then has directed the American premiere of Eh? at the Playhouse-in-the-Park, Cincinnati, Ohio, 1966; Father Uxbridge Wants to Marry, A View from the Bridge (Hartford Stage Company), 1967; Muzeeka, Who's Happy Now? (tour), The Loves of Don Perlimplin and Belissa (National Theater of the Deaf Repertory), Honor and Offer (world première, Cincinnati), 1968; The Homecoming (Hartford), Cop-Out, (B'way début) 1969; The Effect of Gamma Rays on Man-in-the-Moon Marigolds, Off-B'way, 1970 ("Obie" award); Early Morning, La Mama ETC, 1970; And Miss Reardon Drinks a Little, B'way, 1971, Tour, 1972; made his London directing début on 13 Nov 1972 at the Hampstead Theatre Club with The Effect of Gamma Rays on Man-in-the-Moon Marigolds; Echoes, NYC, 1973; Other Voices, Other Rooms, Buffalo Studio Arena Theatre, 1973; The Killdeer, Public Theatre, NYC, 1974; Children, Manhattan Theatre Club, 1976, ("Obie" award); The Middle Ages, Hartman Theatre, Stamford, Conn, 1978; Da, NYC 1978, Nat'l Tour, 1979 ("Tony" award, Drama Desk award, etc); Since 1974, director of the NBCTV serial, Another World.

Address: c/o Gilbert Parker, Curtis Brown Ltd, 575 Madison Avenue, New York, NY.

BERNSTEIN, Leonard, composer, conductor, pianist, and lecturer
b Lawrence, Massachusetts, 25 Aug 1918; *s* of Samuel J Bernstein and his wife Jennie (Resnick); *e* Boston Latin School and Harvard University; studied music at the Curtis Institute of Music; studied also with Walter Piston, Fritz Reiner, Randall Thompson, Serge Koussevitsky, *et al*; *m* Felicia Montealegre Cohn (dec).

In addition to various compositions for concert performance, and the one-act opera Trouble in Tahiti, 1955, he has composed the scores for the following: On the Town, 1944; Fancy Free (ballet by Jerome Robbins), 1944; Facsimile (ballet by Jerome Robbins), 1946; The Age of Anxiety (ballet by Jerome Robbins), 1949, is based on his Symphony No 2; Wonderful Town, 1953; Candide (NY Theatre Critics Award), 1956; West Side Story, 1957; Leonard Bernstein's Theatre Songs, 1965; composed the incidental music for Peter Pan, 1950; The Lark, 1955; incidental songs and music for The First-born, 1958; wrote the text and music for the Kaddish Symphony (Symphony No 3), which he conducted in Boston and NY, Apr 1964; Philharmonic Hall, Apr 1964, conducted and played a police clerk and a reporter in Marc Blitzstein's The Cradle Will Rock; Theatre Four, Nov 1964, served as a musical consultant for a revival of The Cradle Will Rock; On the Town revived at the Imperial, 31 Oct 1971; wrote the texts with Stephen Schwartz and the music for Mass, produced at the opening of the Kennedy Center, Washington, DC, 8 Sept 1971, and at the Metropolitan Opera on 26 June 1972 and subsequently in Vienna and elsewhere; wrote the music for the ballet Dybbuk, produced by the New York City Ballet, 16 May 1974; Candide revived with a new book and new orchestrations at the Broadway on 8 Mar 1974; By Bernstein, a musical revue, 1975; score for 1600 Pennsylvania Avenue, 1976; score for the film On the Waterfront, 1954; was Assistant Conductor of the New York Philharmonic, 1943, and made his début as a conductor in Nov of that year; appointed Music Director of the New York Philharmonic, 1953, and served in this post until May 1969, having by then conducted the orchestra in 939 concerts; given the

lifetime title of Laureate Conductor, 1969; 1957 to 1971 was Music Director and Conductor of the Philharmonic's Young People's Concerts, which have been televised in the USA and 29 other countries; made his operatic début at La Scala, Milan, Italy, when he conducted Cherubini's Medea, starring Maria Callas, and, later, La Sonnambula and La Boheme; Metropolitan Opera, NY, Mar–Apr 1964, conducted Falstaff; Vienna State Opera, 1966, Falstaff, 1968, Der Rosenkavalier, and 1970, Fidelio; Metropolitan Opera, 1970, conducted Cavalleria Rusticana; Metropolitan Opera, 1974, conducted Carmen; has conducted the major symphony orchestras of the world; toured extensively with the Philharmonic, including Japan in 1970; author of The Joy of Music, 1959, Leonard Bernstein's Young People's Concerts, 1962, The Infinite Variety of Music, 1966 and The Unanswered Question, 1976; has appeared frequently on television in other capacities, notably on Omnibus, 1955, and Leonard Bernstein and the New York Philharmonic at various times; has received numerous awards, including: Einstein Commemorative Award, Newspaper Guild of New York Page One Award and Citation, The Peabody, Sylvania, Emmy, Alice M Ditson Awards, etc; has been decorated by Chile, Finland, France, Austria, and Italy; has made well over 100 recordings of classical music; Norton Lecturer at Harvard Univ, 1973.

Address: 1414 Avenue of the Americas, New York, NY 10019.

BERRY, Eric, actor
b London, 9 Jan 1913; *s* of Frederick William Berry and his wife Anna Lovisa (Danielson); *e* City of London School; studied for the stage at the Royal Academy of Dramatic Art, where he gained a Silver Medal.

Made his first appearance on the stage at the Everyman Theatre, Hampstead, Apr 1931, in Spilt Milk; during 1932, appeared at the Embassy Theatre in several productions, subsequently playing at Edinburgh and Glasgow, with the St Martin's Players; made his first appearance in the West-end, at the New Theatre, 7 Dec 1932, as Falk Brandon in The Cathedral; Lyric, Aug 1933, played Fahnrich in The Ace; Daly's, Apr 1934, Hugh Bennett in Dark Horizon; was engaged with the Hull Repertory company, 1934–5; Embassy and Savoy, Mar 1937, played Scipio in The Road to Rome; Strand, June 1937, George Khitov in Judgment Day; during 1938, toured in Scandinavia, as John Worthing in The Importance of Being Earnest; Saville, June 1939, Guido von Allmen in Juggernaut; served in the Army during the War, 1940–6; during 1944 appeared in several plays in Egypt and the Western Desert, playing and directing; after demobilization, 1946, was engaged as leading man at the Playhouse, Liverpool, remaining until 1948; St James's, June 1948, appeared as Lopahin in The Cherry Orchard; Duchess, Aug 1948, Charles Appleby in Eden End; toured in Germany, 1949, as Claudius in Hamlet; Arts Theatre, Oct 1949, played Mamaev in The Diary of a Scoundrel, and Jan 1950, Sir George Crofts in Mrs Warren's Profession; Saville, Mar 1950, Arnold Littlejohn in The Platinum Set; Arts, June 1950, Banquo in Macbeth; Sept 1950, Ugo Praga in The Mask and the Face; Oct 1950, Lord Burleigh in Queen Elizabeth, and Dec 1950, the Lefthand Property Man in Lady Precious Stream; Arts, Jan 1951, George Tesman in Hedda Gabler; toured, 1951, in Frou-Frou; Watergate, Dec 1951, Dame Gladys Flagpole in Puss in Red Riding Breeches; same theatre, Feb 1952, appeared in the revue See You Again; Westminster, Feb 1952, played Mr Toobad in Nightmare Abbey; went to Bermuda, 1952, and played in The Magistrate; at the Edinburgh Festival, 1953, appeared in the revue See You Later; Lyric, Hammersmith, Dec 1953, played in

The Lyric Revue, and at the St Martin's, May 1954, appeared in the revised version of the same production, entitled Going to Town; made his first appearance on the New York stage at the Royale, 30 Sept 1954, as Percival Brown in The Boy Friend, which established a record run (over a year) for a British musical production; 1956–7, US coast-to-coast tour with The Boy Friend; Alexandra, Toronto, Canada, Feb 1958, played Thurio in Two Gentlemen of Verona and Major Clovell in The Broken Jug, with the Canadian Festival Company, subsequently appearing in the same productions at the Phoenix, NY, Mar 1958; Phoenix, NY, Oct 1958, played the Hon Charles Piper in The Family Reunion; Dec 1958, Tench in The Power and the Glory; Feb 1959, Squire Sullen in The Beaux' Stratagem; at the Coronet, NY, played the Client in The Great God Brown; Phoenix, Jan 1960, the Troll King in Peer Gynt; Mar 1960, Falstaff in Henry IV, Parts 1 and 2; Playhouse in the Park, Philadelphia, Aug 1961, played Charles Gringoire in Turn on the Night, and Drinkwater in Captain Brassbound's Conversion; Plymouth, NY, Nov 1961, played Shillem in Gideon; Stratford, Conn, June 1962, played Falstaff in Henry IV Part 1; Henry Miller's, Mar 1964, played a number of roles in The White House; Billy Rose, Dec 1964, the Cardinal in Tiny Alice; Circle-in-the-Square, 1965, appeared in The White Devil; 1966, toured as Inspector Hubbard in Dial M for Murder, which he also directed, and as Lord Porteous in The Circle; Meadow Brook Theatre, Rochester, Michigan, seasons 1966–9, parts include the title-roles in King Lear and John Gabriel Borkman, and James Tyrone in Long Day's Journey into Night; 1970, toured in The Canterbury Tales; Brooks Atkinson, NY, Stephen Spettigue in Charley's Aunt; Goodman, Chicago, Sir Toby Belch in Twelfth Night, 1970; Bijou, NY, May 1971, Max in The Homecoming; Ethel Barrymore, Apr 1972, Sir Howard Hallam in Captain Brassbound's Conversion; Imperial, Oct 1972, Charles in Pippin, and played this part for nearly six years, including a national tour.

Favourite parts: Toad in Toad of Toad Hall, the Captain in The Father, and Falstaff. *Recreations:* Travelling and swimming. *Club:* Green Room. *Address:* 36 Prentis Road, Streatham, London, SW16. *Tel:* 01–769 0978; c/o LK Strauss, 440 East 57th Street, New York, NY 10022. *Tel:* PL3 7651.

BERUH, Joseph, producer and director
b Pittsburgh, Pennsylvania, 27 Sept 1924; *s* of William I Beruh and his wife Clara (Parnes); *e* Carnegie Institute and Mellon University; *m* Kathleen Murray (dec).

Began his career in the theatre as an actor; made his New York début at the Theatre de Lys, 10 Mar 1954, as Crookfinger Jake in The Threepenny Opera; began his career as a producer at the Sheridan Square Playhouse, 25 May 1959, with a revival of the Jerome Kern musical Leave It to Jane; began his career as director with A Sound of Hunting, 1954, and has since directed The Seven at Dawn, 1961; has produced or co-produced the following plays: Kittiwake Island, 1960; Promenade, 1969; Instructions for the Running of Trains, etc on the Erie Railway to Go into Effect Jan 1, 1862, 1970; served as production associate for Look to the Lilies and The Engagement Baby, 1970; Waiting for Godot, Long Day's Journey into Night, Godspell, 1971; co-produced his first London play at the Wyndham's, 11 Nov 1971, with Godspell; Elizabeth I, Comedy, 1972; Nourish the Beast, Gypsy (London), The Enclave, 1973; The Magic Show, Gypsy (NY), 1974; Blasts and Bravos: An Evening with H L Mencken, The Night That Made America Famous, 1975; American Buffalo, 1977; entered film production in Nov 1974 with The Wild Party, and has since produced Godspell, Squirm, and Blue Sunshine.

Address: 1650 Broadway, New York, NY. *Tel:* 212–765–5910.

BETHENCOURT, Francis, actor
b London, 5 Sept 1926; *s* of Charles de Bethencourt and his wife Dorothy (Baker); *e* Xaverian College, Mayfield, Sussex; *m* (1) Judy Hall (mar dis); (2) Nancy Nugent (mar dis).

Made his professional debut at the Arts, 23 Nov 1943, as a servant in The Recruiting Officer; after repertory experience at Watford Palace, 1944–45, toured as Danny in Night Must Fall, Favell in Rebecca, etc; made his New York debut at the Shubert, 8 Dec 1948, as Henry Norris in Anne of the Thousand Days; toured the US in The Happy Time, 1951–52; Plymouth, Oct 1952, Capt Lesgate in Dial 'M' for Murder; Stratford, Conn, opening season, 1955, Benedick in Much Ado About Nothing; Phoenix, Dec 1955, Leading Man in Six Characters in Search of an Author; Booth, Feb 1957, played a Friend in Visit to a Small Planet; with the National Repertory Co, season 1964–65, toured as Brack in Hedda Gabler and Hastings in She Stoops to Conquer; Billy Rose, Oct 1965, Capt Foster in The Right Honourable Gentleman; Renata, Mar 1967, Capt O'Sullivan in Hamp; Lyceum, Mar 1970, Warder Whitbread in Borstal Boy; Queens Playhouse, Oct 1972, Col Pickering in Pygmalion; John Golden, Jan 1977, McTeazle in Dirty Linen; has played many classical and modern roles in regional theatre; first film, Royal Wedding, 1950; subsequent films include This Earth Is Mine; TV work includes plays and series; is the author of a number of teleplays.

Address: c/o Hesseltine-Baker Associates, 119 West 57th Street, New York, NY 10019.

BETTIS, Valerie, dancer, actress, director, and choreographer
b Houston, Texas; *d* of Royal Holt Bettis and his wife Valerie Elizabeth (McCarthy); *e* University of Texas; *m* (1) Bernardo Segall (mar dis); (2) Arthur A Schmidt; studied ballet with Hanya Holm, 1937–40.

First appeared on the stage in New York with the Hanya Holm Dance Company, 1937, and later toured until 1940; World's Fair, NY, 1939 and 1940, danced in Railroads on Parade; director of modern dance at the Perry-Mansfield School, Steamboat Springs, Colarado, and was dancer and choreographer at the Colorado Springs Dance Festival, 1942 and 1943; danced and toured in her own and others' ballets, 1942–4; Shubert, Philadelphia, Nov 1944, choreographed and danced in Glad to See You, her first musical comedy production; Adelphi, NY, May 1945, appeared for a season in her own ballets; again toured and appeared in NY in solo concerts in 1945 and 1946; dancer and choreographer at Jacob's Pillow Dance Festival, Lee, Mass, July 1946; toured South America in solo concerts of her work, summer, 1946; Broadway, Dec 1946, choreographed Beggar's Holiday; New York City Center, Mar 1947, danced in her Virginia Sampler with the Ballets Russes de Monte Carlo; toured with her own company, including appearances in NY and Jacob's Pillow, 1947–8; Museum of Modern Art, NY, Jan 1948, appeared in An Evening of American Dance; Century, Apr 1948, played Tiger Lily and principal dancer in the revue Inside the USA, and toured in this production in 1949; toured with her own dance company, 1949–50; Winter Garden, Mar 1950, played Kitty in Great to Be Alive!; Kaufman Auditorium, May 1950, danced with her own company; Cambridge Summer Theatre, Boston, Aug 1950, played in There Are Crimes and Crimes; Mark Hellinger, NY, Dec 1950, played in the revue Bless You All; choreographed Peer Gynt, at the ANTA, Jan 1951; toured, summer, 1953, in The Frogs of Spring; danced in her ballet A Streetcar Named Desire with the American Ballet Theatre, 1954; ANTA, May 1955, appeared with her own company in an American Dance Festival; Lydia Mendelssohn, Ann Arbor, Mich, June 1955, played Leona Samish in The Time of the Cuckoo; Kaufman Auditorium, Apr 1956, appeared with her company in Circa 56; same theatre, Nov 1956, appeared in the concert-reading of Children of the Ladybug; Carnegie Hall, 25 Nov 1956, appeared in the opera The Soldier; Forrest, Philadelphia, Feb 1957, played Calypso in Maiden Voyage; Ambassador, NY, Mar 1958, played the Serpent Fusima and Chloe in Back to Methuselah; Rooftop, June 1958, choreographed Ulysses in Nighttown; summer stock, 1958, played Ninotchka in Silk Stockings; Juilliard Concert Hall, May 1959, danced in a concert of her works; made her London début at the Arts, 21 May 1959, when she choreographed and played Mrs Thornton and Bella-Bella in Ulysses in Nighttown, and later toured in this production in Paris, Amsterdam, and The Hague; toured with her dance company in America, 1960–1, including appearances in New York and Jacob's Pillow; Playhouse-in-the-Park, Philadelphia, July 1961, played Camilia Jablonski in Invitation to the March; Stage 73, NY, May 1962, directed If Five Years Pass; Theatre de Lys, July 1962, took over various parts in Brecht on Brecht; toured as co-narrator of America Dances, Feb–Mar 1963; in 1963 founded her own dance studio in NY, where she continues to teach; founder, artistic director and president of The Dancers' Studio Foundation Inc; 46th Street, Nov 1966, choreographed Pousse-Café; Felt Forum, Mar 1968, choreographed Final Solutions; Artist in Residence of the University of California at Los Angeles, 1968–9, where she taught and choreographed Arena for One for the UCLA Dance Company; directed and choreographed On Ship for the New York University Dance Company and the UCLA Dance Company, 1970; Eden's Expressway, NY, Feb 1975, directed The Corner; Theatre at St Clement's, June 1976, choreographed and directed Echoes of Spoon River; Newman, 1978, choreographed, directed and danced Next Day; among her notable ballets are The Desperate Heart, As I Lay Dying, The Golden Round (based on Macbeth), Domino Furioso Columbine, And the Earth Shall Bear Again, etc; first choreographed for films in 1951 when her The Desperate Heart was filmed for An American Dance Trilogy, and has since arranged dances for An Affair in Trinidad, Salome, Athena, Let's Do It Again, etc; was choreographer and dancer for the television series *Valerie Bettis Dancers,* 1946, and has since appeared frequently as dancer, actress, and choreographer, notably on Holiday, The Stronger, Unguarded Moment, *Paul Whiteman Revue,* An Evening with Richard Rodgers, All Star Revue, 135th Street (opera by George Gershwin), The Women, The Sound and the Fury, etc.

Recreation: Painting. *Address:* 16 East 11th Street, New York, NY 10003. *Tel:* YU2 7414.

BEWES, Rodney, actor
b Bingley, Yorks, 27 Nov 1937; *s* of Horace Bewes and his wife Bessie; trained at the Royal Academy of Dramatic Art; *m* Daphne (Bewes).

First appeared on stage at the age of sixteen as Daventry in Escapade at the Royalty, Morecombe; spent three years in repertory; made his first London appearance at the Comedy, Oct 1961, as Seeley in A Night Out; Garrick, Feb 1966, played Ingham in Little Malcolm and his Struggle Against the Eunuchs; Arts, June 1968, Lemmy in The Foundations; toured, Spring 1974, as Henry in My Fat Friend; ICA, Sept 1974, played Mike in Away From It All; Thorndike, Leatherhead, Oct 1976, Douglas LeQuesne in The Happiest Tears in

Town; first television appearance 1960, since when he has appeared in many plays and the series The Likely Lads and Dear Mother . . . Love Albert, the latter co-written and co-produced by himself; also wrote the series Ted and Lucy; films include Billy Liar and Spring and Port Wine, Saint Jack, and The Spaceman and King Arthur.

Favourite parts: Will Mossop in Hobson's Choice and Billy in Billy Liar. *Address:* c/o ICM, 22 Grafton Street, London W1.

BICAT, Tony, writer, and director
b Reading, Berks, 11 Mar 1945; *m* Jennifer Gaskin.

Co-founder of Portable Theatre, for whom he directed six of their first twelve productions, 1968–72; author of the plays Devils Island, 1977; Zigomania, 1978; lyricist, with Nick Bicât, for One for the Road, 1971; Scott of the Antarctic, England's Ireland, 1972; Teeth 'n' Smiles, 1976; has written and directed for films and TV, most recently Electric in the City, BBC, 1979.

Address: c/o Margaret Ramsay, 14a Goodwin's Court, St Martin's Lane, London WC2.

BIKEL, Theodore, actor and singer
b Vienna, Austria, 2 May 1924; *s* of Josef Bikel and his wife Miriam (Riegler); *m* (1) Ofra Ichilov (mar dis); (2) Rita Weinberg; *e* Vienna, Tel Aviv and London; prepared for the stage at Royal Academy of Dramatic Art, London.

First appeared on the stage with the Habimah Theatre, in Israel, Nov 1943, as the Village Clerk in Tevye the Milkman; at the Chamber Theatre, Israel (which he helped form), 1945, played Charley in Charley's Aunt, and the Father in The Insect Play; first appeared on the London stage in 1948 in You Can't Take It with You; Aldwych, Oct 1949, played Pablo Gonzalez in A Streetcar Named Desire; toured, 1950, as Harold Mitchell in the last play; Wyndham's, May 1951, played the Russian Colonel in The Love of Four Colonels; New, 1954, took over Jan in Dear Charles; first appeared in New York at the Morosco, Feb 1955, as Inspector Massoubre in Tonight in Samarkand; Longacre, Nov 1955, played Robert de Baudricourt in The Lark; Cort, Nov 1957, Dr Jacobson in The Rope Dancers; Lunt-Fontanne, Nov 1959, Captain Georg von Trapp in The Sound of Music, which he played for more than two years; Theatre de Lys, Sept 1962, took over various roles in the concert reading Brecht on Brecht; Martin Beck, Apr 1964, played Samuel Cole in the musical version of Cafe Crown; 46th Street, Mar 1966, Prof George Ritter in Pousse-Café; Caesar's Palace, Las Vegas, Nevada, Dec 1967, Tevye in Fiddler on the Roof; toured with the national company as Tevye; in 1969, played Tevye in Honolulu, Hawaii; toured as Tevye in 1971; Westbury, Long Island, Music Fair, Mar 1971, appeared in concert; toured in 1971 and 1972 as Tevye in Fiddler on the Roof; toured in 1972 in Jacques Brel Is Alive and Well and Living in Paris; Westbury Music Fair, June 1972, played Meyer Rothschild in The Rothschilds; toured 1974, in Jacques Brel Is Alive and Well and Living in Paris; at Mister Kelly's, Chicago, Feb 1974, and the St Regis, NY, Apr 1974, appeared in cabaret; toured as Chekhov in The Good Doctor, 1975; toured in the title-rôle of Zorba, 1976; Hunter College Assembly Hall, 5 Apr 1975, appeared in concert; Circle-in-the-Square, Sept 1978, the Major in The Inspector General; toured as Tevye in Fiddler on the Roof, 1979; first appeared in films in 1950, and has since appeared in The Little Kidnappers, I Want to Live, The Defiant Ones, My Fair Lady, The Russians Are Coming, The Russians Are Coming, The Little Ark, etc; first appeared on television in 1955 and has appeared regularly in all the major shows; member of the Council of Actors Equity Association,

1961 (Vice-President, 1964), elected President of the Actors Equity Association in May 1973, 1976 and 1979; appointed to the National Council for the Arts, 1977.

Favourite part: Zorba. *Recreations:* Chess and photography. *Address:* William Morris Agency, 1350 Avenue of the Americas, New York, NY 10019. *Tel:* 586–5100.

BILLINGTON, Kevin, director

b 12 June 1934; *e* Bryanston and Queens' College, Cambridge; *m* Rachel Pakenham.

Directed his first stage play, Find Your Way Home, at the Open Space, 12 May 1970; has since directed, in London unless otherwise stated, Me (Glasgow), 1972; The Birthday Party, Bloody Neighbours, 1975; The Caretaker, Emigrés, 1976; The Homecoming, 1978; TV directing work, since *Tonight* in 1960, includes many documentaries and, recently, Echoes of the Sixties (NBC) and Henry VIII (BBC), 1979; The Jail Diary of Albic Sachs, 1980; films since Interlude, 1968, include The Rise and Rise of Michael Rimmer and Light at the Edge of the World.

Address: 30 Addison Avenue, London W11.

BILLINGTON, Michael, dramatic critic and author

b Leamington Spa, 16 Nov 1939; *s* of Alfred Billington and his wife Patricia (Bradshaw); *e* Warwick School and St Catherine's, Oxford.

Acted and directed with OUDS and the ETC at Oxford, 1958–61; trained as a journalist with the *Liverpool Daily Post and Echo,* 1961–2; Public Liaison Officer and subsequently director for Lincoln Theatre Company, 1962–4; deputy drama, film and television critic for *The Times* 1965–71; drama critic of the *Guardian,* 1971–; film critic of the Illustrated London News and the *Birmingham Post,* 1968–; author of The Modern Actor, 1974; How Tickled I Am, 1977; broadcasts regularly on *Critics' Forum, Kaleidoscope, etc;* received the IPC Critic of the Year award, 1975.

Recreations: Cricket and travel. *Address:* 15 Hearne Road, London W4.

BIRCH, Patricia, choreographer and director; *m* William Becker.

Began her theatre career as a dancer in the Martha Graham Dance Company; entered musical comedies, and appeared with the New York City Light Opera Company at the City Center, Sept 1957, in Carousel and, Mar 1958, in Oklahoma!; at the Lunt-Fontanne, Oct 1958, danced in Goldilocks; at the Winter Garden, 27 Apr 1960, made her dramatic début as Anybodys in a revival of West Side Story; Maidman Playhouse, 3 Jan 1962, Constance in Fortuna; Mar 1967, assistant director for You're a Good Man, Charlie Brown, and served in this capacity in the San Francisco production in May 1968; choreographed her first musical at the Jan Hus Playhouse, 27 Nov 1968, Up Eden; directed special sequences in Fireworks, 1969; choreographed The Me Nobody Knows, 1970; F Jasmine Addams, 1971; Grease, 1972; The Real Inspector Hound and After Magritte, 1972; A Little Night Music, 1973; New, London, 26 June 1973, Grease; Over Here!, Candide, 1974; Diamond Studs, 1975; Pacific Overtures, Music Is, 1976; Happy End (co-director), Hot Grog, 1977; Street Scene (NY City Opera), Really Rosie (director), Zoot Suit (LA), They're Playing Our Song, Gilda Radner—Live from New York, 1979; film work includes the choreography for Grease, Sgt Pepper's Lonely Hearts Club Band, and A Little Night Music; director of the film Angel, 1980; for TV, was resident choreographer for *The Electric Company,* 1971–74, and worked on *Saturday Night Live,* 1979.

Address: c/o Franklin Weisberg, 505 Park Avenue, New York, NY 10022.

BIRD, David, actor

b Dulwich, London, 4 Sept 1907; *s* of John Bird and his wife Anne (Robinson); *e* Alleyn's School, Dulwich, and St Edmund Hall, Oxford; *m* Joyce Wodeman; formerly a tutor.

Made his first appearance on the stage at the Croydon Repertory Theatre, Oct 1932, as Shaun in On the Spot; first appeared in London, at the Westminster Theatre, 5 Nov 1934, as Fitch in Youth at the Helm; was with the Birmingham Repertory Company at the Malvern Festival, 1935, as Castrone in Volpone, and in 1066 and All That; at the Gate, Apr 1937, played Smeedings in Lord Adrian; Arts, May 1937, Colonel Meade in Daughter of Ind and subsequently played numerous parts at this theatre, 1942–4, including Lawyer Cribbs in The Drunkard, Sir Anthony Absolute in The Rivals, Colonel Lukyn in The Magistrate, Tarleton in Misalliance, Bullock in The Recruiting Officer, Dr Paramore in The Philanderer, Sir Tunbelly Clumsy in A Trip to Scarborough, Juggins in Fanny's First Play; at the St Martin's, Nov 1944, again played Lukyn in The Magistrate; Piccadilly, June 1945, Brigadier Jouet and Senator Brisson in Jacobowsky and The Colonel; Theatre Royal, Brighton, Sept 1945, Sandoz in Thirteen to the Gallows; St James's, May 1946, Thomas Peacock and Captain Fleming in The Kingmaker; Lyric, Hammersmith, Dec 1947, played Sir John Friendly and Tug in The Relapse, appearing in these parts at the Phoenix, Jan 1948; Arts, Dec 1948, CSM Buff in Gog and MacGog; Arts, Jan 1949, Uncle Gregory in A Pair of Spectacles; Phoenix, May 1949, Boniface in The Beaux' Stratagem, which ran until Aug 1950; Arts, Dec 1950, appeared as Su and Mu in Lady Precious Stream; Arts, Feb 1951, Nicholai Kirsanov in Spring at Marino; Arts, Apr–June 1951, appeared in a Shaw Festival of one-act plays; same theatre, Jan 1952, Dupont-Dufort Senior, and The Town Crier, in Thieves' Carnival; Q, Mar 1952, Arrowsmith in Song of the Centipede; Arts, June 1952, Henry Horatio Hobson in Hobson's Choice, and Sept 1952, The Devil in Don Juan in Hell; Old Vic, June 1953, Archbishop of Canterbury, and Fluellen, in the Bristol Company's production of Henry V; joined the Bristol Old Vic Company for the 1953–4 season, and among other parts played Sir Sampson Legend in Love For Love, Don Jerome in The Duenna, Mario Castiglioni in The Castiglioni Brothers, Lopakhin in The Cherry Orchard, etc; Grand, Blackpool, Feb 1954, played Sir Wellington Hacker, MP, in Liberty Bill, and toured in this part; Westminster, July 1954, again played Don Jerome in The Duenna; Lyric, Hammersmith, May 1955, appeared as De Beaudricourt in The Lark; Arts, Mar 1956, played Angelo in a musical version of The Comedy of Errors; Saville, Aug 1956, played Ilya Shamrayev in The Seagull; Garrick, July 1957, Uncle Fritz in Oh! My Papa!; Aldephi, Sept 1958, played Mr Babcock in Auntie Mame; 1959–61, was a member of the BBC Drama Repertory Company; joined the Old Vic Company, to appear at the Edinburgh Festival, Aug 1961, as the Pope and Wrath in Doctor Faustus, and as the Earl of Pembroke in King John, subsequently appearing at the Old Vic, Sept, 1961, in both plays; between Oct 1961–May 1962, he played the following parts (in the same company): Sir Toby Belch in Twelfth Night, Ross in Macbeth, Lord Stanley in Richard III, Decius Brutus in Julius Caesar, and Stephano in The Tempest; Savoy, May 1963, played Arthur Brown MA in The Masters; Mermaid, Apr–July 1964, played Duncan and the Doctor in Macbeth, Calianax in The Maid's Tragedy, and Sir Hugh Lacy in The Shoemaker's Holiday; Westminster, Feb 1965, played Henry

Thornton in Mr Wilberforce MP; Mermaid, Dec 1965, Squire Trelawney in Treasure Island; Library, Manchester, Apr 1966, Dr Blomax in The Workhouse Donkey; Chichester Festival Season, 1966, Ross in Macbeth and Father Dominic in The Fighting Cock, re-opening at the Duke of York's, Oct 1966; Chichester, 1967, Dr Rundle in The Farmer's Wife, Boniface in The Beaux' Stratagem, Tardiveau in An Italian Straw Hat, Mazzini Dunn in Heartbreak House, re-opening at the Lyric, Nov 1967; Intimate, Palmers Green, June 1968, Harry in Out of Order; Nottingham, Jan 1969, Rice in The Entertainer; Saville, June, 1969, Actor in The Resistible Rise of Arturo Ui; Criterion, May 1970, the Bishop in Flint; Piccadilly, Oct 1970, Claud Nau in Vivat! Vivat Regina!; at the Phoenix, Leicester, Sept 1972–May 1973, his parts included Leonato in Much Ado About Nothing; Belgrade, Coventry, Mar 1974, Sir Richard Hawkey in Manoeuvres; Mermaid, May 1974, Sudbury in The Great Society; Oxford Festival, Sept 1974, Archbishop of Rheims in St Joan; Mermaid, Aug 1975, Duke of Domesday in On The Rocks.
Address: 69 Burlington Avenue, Kew, Surrey.

BIRD, John, actor and dramatic author
b Nottingham, 22 Nov 1936; *s* of Horace George Bird and his wife Dorothy May (Haubitz); *e* High Pavement GS, Nottingham, and King's, Cambridge; *m* Bridget Simpson.
After appearing in and directing plays and revue at Cambridge, joined the Royal Court, 1960, as assistant to George Devine and later Associate Artistic Director; founded the Establishment theatre club in 1961 with Peter Cook, where he wrote and performed satire for a year before touring the US with the Establishment company; in New York opened The New York Establishment, 1963, and a straight theatre, the New; returned to England, 1964; his adaptation of the play Council of Love (by Oscar Panizza) was performed at the Criterion, Aug 1970; toured, Apr 1971, as Harry Berlin in Luv; at the Arnaud, Guildford, Sept 1972, played Bernard White in Who's Who; made his West End début at the Lyric, 10 May 1973, as Sir Percy Shorter in Habeas Corpus; Open Space, May 1978, played Barry in The Ball Game; has appeared frequently on television, since 1962, including several series of his own and also series written and performed with Eleanor Bron and John Fortune; SFTA Light Entertainment Personality of the Year, 1966; films include: Take a Girl Like You, and The Seven Per Cent Solution.
Recreations: Music, photography, high-energy physics. *Address:* c/o Chatto and Linnit, The Globe Theatre, Shaftesbury Avenue, London W1.

BIRNEY, David, actor and director
b Washington, DC, 23 Apr; *s* of Edwin B Birney and his wife Jeanne (McGee); *e* Dartmouth College (AB), and UCLA (MA); *m* (1) Jean Concannon (mar dis); (2) Meredith Baxter.
Professional debut 6 July, 1965, at the Barter Theatre, Abingdon, Va, as Simon in Hay Fever; at the Barter, 1965–66, his parts included the Streetsinger in Threepenny Opera, Algernon in The Importance of Being Earnest, and Orsino in Twelfth Night; for the Hartford Stage Company, 1966–67, played parts including Fedotik in Three Sisters and Clov in Endgame; Delacorte, NY, for the New York Shakespeare Festival, season 1967, played Antipholus of Syracuse in The Comedy of Errors, the Dauphin in King John, and Chiron in Titus Andronicus; toured with the Strolling Players, Sept 1967, in an anthology of Brecht and Strindberg; at the Village Gate, Nov 1967, played Chorus and Egg of Head in MacBird; American Place, Jan 1968, Edmund in Ceremony of Innocence; Forum, Lincoln Center, Mar 1968,

Young Man in Summertree; Vivian Beaumont, May 1969, Cleanthes in The Miser; Triangle, July 1969, Andocides in The Long War; Astor Place, Sept 1969, Wilson in The Ruffian on the Stair and Kenny in The Erpingham Camp; as a guest artist at the state U of Pennsylvania, July 1970, played Hamlet; Vivian Beaumont, Nov 1970, Yang Sun in The Good Woman of Setzuan; same theatre, 1971, played Christy Mahon in The Playboy of the Western World, Jan, Hovstad in An Enemy of the People, Mar, and Haemon in Antigone, May; Mark Taper Forum, LA, Aug 1971, Adolphus Cusins in Major Barbara; Arena Stage, Buffalo, Mar 1972, Mercutio in Romeo and Juliet; Arlington Park, Chicago, Jan 1973, Valentine in You Never Can Tell; toured, May 1973, as Sky Masterson in Guys and Dolls; American Shakespeare Festival, Stratford, Conn, Jun 1974, Romeo in Romeo and Juliet; for the St Louis Municipal Opera, 1975, King Arthur in Camelot; Mark Taper, 1979, Kentridge in The Biko Inquest; toured, 1979, as Higgins in the St Louis production of My Fair Lady; has directed The Zoo Story (Barter, 1965), Yanks 3, Detroit 0, Top of the Seventh (Stratford, 1974), and A Life in the Theatre (Matrix, LA, 1980); films, since Caravan to Vaccares, 1974, include See You Monday, 1979; frequent TV appearances include leads in *Bridget Loves Bernie, The Adams Chronicles*, and Serpico.
Favourite parts: Mercutio, Christy Mahon, Hamlet, Higgins. *Club:* Players. *Address:* 14186 Alisal Lane, Santa Monica, CA 90402.

BISHOP, Kelly, actress
b Colorado Springs, Colo, 28 Feb 1944; *d* of Lawrence Boden Bishop and his wife Jane Lenore (Wahtola); *e* Denver Public Schools and Carlmont HS, Belmont, Calif; *m* (1) Peter Miller; (2) Lee Leonard; trained for the stage at the American Ballet Theatre School, Denver, and the San Jose Ballet School.
Made her first professional appearance 1 Nov 1962, as Carole Bishop, in the corps de ballet at the Radio City Music Hall; Broadway debut, 3 Sept 1967, in the chorus of Golden Rainbow; Shubert, Dec 1968, Company Nurse in Promises, Promises; Imperial, 1971, danced in On the Town; Broadhurst, Nov 1973, played a number of parts in Rachael Lily Rosenblum; at the Chateau de Ville, May 1974, Anita in West Side Story; toured, Dec 1974, with the National company of Irene, as Helen McFudd; at the Public, May 1975, created the part of Sheila in A Chorus Line, transferring with the production to the Shubert, July 1975; remained with the company until Aug 1976, and during the run changed her name from Carole to Kelly Bishop; Chicago, Sept 1977, took over as Mary in Vanities; Chelsea Westside, Jun 1978, Julie in Piano Bar; first film, 1977, An Umarried Woman; TV, since 1976, includes *Hawaii 5-0;* received a 'Tony' for her performance in A Chorus Line.
Favourite parts: Sheila, Anita. *Address:* c/o Lionel Larner, 850 Seventh Avenue, New York, NY 10019.

BLACK, David, producer and director
b New York City, 20 Nov 1931; *s* of Algernon D Black and his wife Elinor (Goldmark); *e* Harvard University (BA 1953); *m* Linda Cabot; formerly a violinist, tenor, and a mutual fund salesman.
Hudson Theatre, NY, Oct 1961, produced his first play, Look! We've Come Through; has since produced or co-produced the following plays: The Aspern Papers, 1962; The Ides of March, his first London production at the Haymarket, and Semi-Detached, NY, 1963; Cambridge Circus, The Knack, 1964; Ready When You Are, C B ! The Impossible Years, 1965; Until the Monkey Comes, The Bird, the Bear,

the Actress, Those That Play the Clowns, The Impossible Years (London), 1966; The Natural Look, To Clothe the Naked, 1967; George M! 1968; Fire! Jazz Requiem for Martin Luther King, Salvation, 1969; Paris Is Out! Salvation (Los Angeles), 1970; Earl of Ruston, 1971; A Funny Thing Happened on the Way to the Forum (revival), a musical version of Lysistrata, 1972; directed his first NY production, The Advertisement, at the Provincetown Playhouse, Oct 1974; directed Augusta, (Rosewood), 1975; Cabaret, One Flew Over the Cuckoo's Nest, 1976; Shay (London), 1977.

Recreations and hobbies: Horseback riding, tennis, conservation. *Address:* 251 East 51st Street, New York, NY 10022. *Tel:* 753–1188.

BLACK, Kitty (Dorothy), dramatic author
b Johannesburg, South Africa, 30 Apr 1914; *d* of Francis Black and his wife Elizabeth Johanna (Albertyn); *e* Roedean, Johannesburg, St Albans and Paris.

Formerly a secretary and a pianist; adapted The Prince of Bohemia (from Robert Louis Stevenson's story, The Suicide Club), 1941; Landslide (with David Peel), 1943; Men Without Shadows, and The Respectable Prostitute (from Jean-Paul Sartre), 1947; Crime Passionnel (from Sartre), 1948; Point of Departure (from Jean Anouilh), 1950; The Untamed (from Jean Anouilh), 1951; Lucifer and the Lord (from Jean-Paul Sartre), 1952; The Public Prosecutor (from Fritz Hochwälder), The Snow Was Black (from Simenon) 1953; Kean (from Jean-Paul Sartre), 1954; Three Sisters (with Miki Iveria), 1955; Donadieu (from Fritz Hochwalder), 1956; Wings of the Wind (from Alexandre Rivemale), 1957; The Innocent Man (from Fritz Hochwalder), 1958; Love from Italy (from Louis Ducreux), 1960; The Rehearsal (from Jean Anouilh, with Pamela Hansford Johnson), Bonne Soupe (from Felicien Marceau), 1961; The Singing Dolphin (original idea), 1963; Isabelle (from Jacques Deval), Maxibules (from Marcel Aymé), 1964; The Soldier's Tale (with Michael Flanders), 1970; Sword of Vengeance (from Fritz Hochwalder), 1975; Riding to Jerusalem (from Evelyn Coquet), 1978; producer and editor of simultaneous translations for World Theatre Seasons 1963–75 at the Aldwych Theatre; Secretary of The Apollo Society.

Recreations: Music, knitting, and golf. *Clubs:* Royal Mid Surrey Golf Club and Royal West Norfolk Golf Club. *Address:* 16 Brunswick Gardens, London, W8 4AJ. *Tel:* 01–229 0931.

BLACKMAN, Honor, actress
e Ealing High School; *m* Maurice Kaufmann; trained for the stage at the Guildhall School of Music and Drama.

Made her London debut at the Globe, Dec 1946, as Monica Cartwright in The Gleam; Apollo, Dec 1947, played Mary Dering in The Blind Goddess; Cambridge, Feb 1954, Lorraine McKay in The Fifth Season; more recently, at the Strand, July 1966, Susy Henderson in Wait Until Dark; Palace, Dec 1968, Doris, and Laura Jesson in Mr and Mrs; Theatre Royal, Windsor, Oct 1969, and Piccadilly, Apr 1970, Barbara Love in Who Killed Santa Claus?; toured, 1972–3 as Mrs Markham in Move Over Mrs Markham, visiting Australia and N America; Comedy, Apr 1975, played Margaret in The Exorcism; Arnaud, Guildford, June 1975, Mrs Millamant in The Way Of The World; same theatre, Feb 1976, Paula Cramer in Motive; toured, Aug 1977, as Hester in The Deep Blue Sea; Northcott, Exeter, 1979, again played Millamant, and Désirée in A Little Night Music, touring in the latter rôle; has appeared in numerous films, since 1946; television, since 1950, includes The Avengers, first series; is the author of Honor Blackman's Book of Self-Defence.

Recreations: Watching soccer, reading. *Address:* c/o London Management, 235 Regent Street, London W1A 2JT.

**BLAINE, Vivian (*née* Stapleton), actress
b Newark, NJ, 21 Nov 1921; *d* of Lionel P Stapleton and his wife Wilhelmina (Tepley); *e* Southside High School, Newark; *m* (1) Manuel George Frank (mar dis); (2) Milton Rackmil (mar dis); (3) Stuart Clark; studied for the stage at the American Academy of Dramatic Art.

First appeared on the stage as a child, in variety, at the Mosque Theatre, Newark; continued in this medium and first appeared in New York, 1939; subsequently toured in the musical play One Touch of Venus, also in Light Up the Sky and Born Yesterday; appeared in variety at the Casino Theatre, London, in June 1947; summer 1949, toured in Bloomer Girl; at the 46th Street Theatre, NY, 24 Nov 1950, appeared as Miss Adelaide in Guys and Dolls, in which she scored a great success; at the Coliseum, London, 28 May 1953, repeated her success in this part; Starlight, Dallas, Texas, summer 1955, played in Panama Hattie; Lyceum, NY, July 1956, took over the part of Celia Pope in A Hatful of Rain, subsequently touring in the play; ANTA, Apr 1958, played Irene Lovelle in Say, Darling; Henry Miller's, Mar 1963, Angela in Enter Laughing; summer tour, 1964, played Adelaide in Guys and Dolls and Nell Henderson in Mr President; New York City Center, June 1966, again played Miss Adelaide, and subsequently toured; toured US, 1968–9, as Marion Hollander in Don't Drink the Water; toured Sept 1970–May 1971 as Hortense in Zorba; toured, 1971, as Frances Black in Light Up the Sky; Alvin, Oct 1971, took over from Jane Russell as Jo Anne in Company; Westchester Country Playhouse, July 1973, Phyllis Rogers Stone in Follies, and subsequently toured in this part; also toured, 1973, in Twigs, playing all the female roles; Westbury, Long Island, Music Fair, Aug 1973, again played Jo Anne in Company; toured, 1974, as Dolly Gallagher Levi in Hello, Dolly!; toured, 1975, as Frances Black in Light Up the Sky; Brothers and Sisters, NY, May 1975, appeared in cabaret; Studebaker, Chicago, Sept 1975, played in The Best of Everybody; has also toured in Born Yesterday, Gypsy, Rain, Cactus Flower, I Do, I Do, and as Blanche du Bois in Streetcar Named Desire; first appeared in films, 1942, in Through Different Eyes, and has since played in numerous pictures, including: Something for the Boys, State Fair (1945), Guys and Dolls, Richard (1972), etc; is also a prominent performer on television.

Recreations: Golf, horseback riding, and tennis. *Address:* c/o Becker and London, 15 Columbus Circle, New York, NY.

BLAIR, Isla, actress
b Bangalore, South India, 29 Sept 1944; *d* of Ian Baxter Blair-Hill and his wife Violet Barbara (Skeoch); *e* West Preston Manor School; *m* Julian Glover; trained for the stage at RADA.

First appeared on the stage at the Strand Theatre, 3 Oct 1963, as Philia in A Funny Thing Happened on the Way to the Forum; subsequent roles in repertory include: Sorel Bliss in Hay Fever, Nora in A Doll's House, and Relatively Speaking, all at Leatherhead; for the Royal Shakespeare Company, 1971, played Emilia in The Man of Mode, Aldwych, Sept, and Aglaya in Subject to Fits, The Place, Oct; Globe, Aug 1972, Rhoda in the Cambridge Theatre Company's Popkiss; Thorndike, Leatherhead, Mar 1973, Lydia Languish in The Rivals, visiting Bucks County Playhouse, Pa, with the production; joined Prospect Theatre Company, June 1973, to play Viola in Twelfth Night and appear in The Grand Tour; toured the Middle East with these productions and appeared at the Round House, Sept 1973; with the Bristol Old Vic, Theatre Royal, 1974–5, her parts included: Desdemona in Othello, Mary in Vivat! Vivat Regina! Dottie in Jumpers, Maggie Hobson in Hobson's Choice, Varya in The Cherry Orchard, and Heloise in Abelard and Heloise; Birmingham Rep, Oct 1974, Maurille in Blues Whites and Reds; toured with Prospect, 1975, in the title role in Miss Julie; Thorndike, Leatherhead, Mar 1976, Amanda in Private Lives; again with Prospect, 1978, played Lydia Languish in The Rivals, Sept, and Regan in King Lear, Oct, both at the Old Vic, and toured Australia in Great English Eccentrics; Nottingham Playhouse, July 1979, Gilda in Design for Living; Sept–Oct 1979, returned to appear for the reformed Company at the Old Vic as Miss Biddy in Miss in Her Teens and Leonora in The Padlock (double bill), and Geraldine in What the Butler Saw; films, since A Flea in Her Ear, 1976, include: Battle of Britain and Taste the Blood of Dracula; TV since 1965, includes: Rookery Nook, Forgotten Love Songs, and An Englishman's Castle.

Favourite parts: Dotty in Jumpers, Maggie Hobson, Miss Julie. *Address:* 19 Ullswater Road, Barnes, London SW13.

BLAIR, Joyce, (*née* Ogus), actress and dancer
b London, 4 Nov 1932; *d* of Myer Ogus and his wife Deborah (Greene); *m* Henry Sheridan-Taylor.

Made her first appearances on the stage as a child, in Quality Street at the Embassy, Feb 1945 and in A Doll's House, Winter Garden, Jan 1946, playing Emmy; Drury Lane, Nov 1951, played Ensign Lisa Minelli in South Pacific; toured, 1952, as Lois Lane (Bianca) in Kiss Me Kate; St Martins, Apr 1953, played Pearl Harvey in The Teddy Bear; Coliseum, May 1953, Mimi in Guys and Dolls; Duke of York's, Sept 1955, appeared in The Punch Revue; Lyric, Hammersmith, Nov 1956 and Lyric, Dec 1956, Marcia Grey in Grab Me a Gondola, later taking over the part of Virginia Jones; Fortune, Oct, 1960, appeared in the revue And Another Thing; Comedy, May, 1962, Nancy Twinkle in Little Mary Sunshine; New, Bromley, 1963, Irma in Irma la Douce; Vaudeville, Apr 1963, appeared in the revue All Square; Duchess, Aug 1969, played Mona Kent in Dames at Sea; Duke of York's, Sept 1971, Serena Bradie in Romance; Westminster, Sept 1973, Miranda Frayle in Relative Values; Civic, Darlington, Feb 1974, Helen in Suddenly At Home; New, Hull, Aug 1975, Susan in The Little Hut; toured Mar 1976, in Pyjama Tops; Edinburgh Festival, Aug 1976, Gladys Bumps in the Oxford Playhouse production of Pal Joey; Arnaud, May 1977, appeared in Cole; Her Majesty's Oct 1978, Rita Green in Bar Mitzvah Boy; Comedy, Feb 1979, Myra in Forty Love; has appeared in several pantomimes; films include Yield to the Night and Mr Ten Per Cent; has appeared many times on television since her first appearance in 1955, in plays, series and variety; also a regular radio broadcaster.

Favourite part: Annie in Annie Get Your Gun, which she played at sixteen. *Recreations:* Painting and dressmaking. *Address:* c/o Barry Burnett Ltd, Suite 409, 190 Piccadilly, London W1.

BLAIR, Lionel (*né* Ogus), actor, dancer and choreographer
b Montreal, Canada, 12 Dec 1931; *s* of Myer Ogus and his wife Deborah (Greene); *m* Susan Davis; began his career as a child actor.

Making his first appearance on stage at the Grand, Croydon, Dec 1942, in The Wizard of Oz; first London appearance, 1943, in The Watch on the Rhine at the Aldwych; Lyric, Aug 1943, appeared in the revue Flying Colours;

played child parts in the 1944 season of the Memorial Theatre, Stratford; Phoenix, May 1945, Dexter Franklin in Kiss and Tell; Embassy, Oct 1945, Johnny in Zoo in Silesia; repertory in Belfast, 1946; Embassy, Oct 1946 and Princes, Mar 1947, Harry Palfrey in Peace Comes to Peckham; Saville, 1948, danced in Bob's Your Uncle; Coliseum, 1952, danced in Kiss Me, Kate; Vaudeville, Apr 1953, Ronnie in Red-Headed Blonde; Glasgow and Edinburgh, 1955–7, choreographed the Five Past Eight shows; Fortune, Oct 1960, appeared in the revue And Another Thing; Saville, July 1968, Dick Trevor in Lady Be Good; 1969, directed and choreographed a tour of No, No, Nanette; Palace, Apr 1970, choreography for At the Palace; Civic, Darlington, Feb 1974, appeared with his sister, Joyce Blair, in Suddenly At Home; has appeared in three Royal Command Performances; film appearances since 1951 include A Hard Day's Night and The Magic Christian; has made numerous television appearances since 1949, most recently in *Give Us A Clue*, and provided choreography for many shows.

Address: c/o Peter Charlesworth, 2nd Floor, 68 Old Brompton Road, London SW7 3LQ.

BLAKELY, Colin, actor
b Bangor, Co Down, Northern Ireland, 23 Sept 1930; *s* of Victor Charles Blakely and his wife Dorothy Margaret Ashmore (Rodgers); *e* Sedbergh School, Yorks; *m* Margaret Whiting.

Formerly employed as a merchant in his family's sports retail business; after some early experience as an amateur with the Bangor Operatic Society, he made his first professional appearance with the Ulster Group, Belfast, April 1958, as Dick McCardle in Master of the House; at the Lyceum, Edinburgh, Sept 1958, played Kevin McAlinden in The Bonfire; made his first appearance in London, at the Royal Court, Sept 1959, with the English Stage Company, as the Second Rough Fellow in Cock-a-Doodle-Dandy; subsequently appearing as A Pugnacious Collier in Serjeant Musgrave's Dance, Oct 1959, and as Thomas Noon (*alias* Kelly) in The Naming of Murderer's Rock, in a Production Without Décor, Nov 1959; Arts, Jan 1960, played Phil Hogan in A Moon For the Misbegotten; Royal Court, Mar 1960, again played Thomas Noon in The Naming of Murderer's Rock; Princes, May 1960, played Warren Baxter in Over the Bridge; Belgrade, Coventry, July 1960, Josh in Dreaming Bandsmen; joined the Royal Shakespeare Company, Stratford-on-Avon, Apr 1961, to play Lord Hastings in Richard III, Touchstone in As You Like It, and the Duke of Venice in Othello; Royal Court, Dec 1961, played Cox in Box and Cox, and Schmitz in The Fire-Raisers; at the same theatre, Jan 1962, played Bottom in A Midsummer Night's Dream; joined the National Theatre Company, Old Vic, Oct 1963, to appear as Fortinbras Captain in the inaugural production of Hamlet, subsequently appearing in the following parts: Kite in The Recruiting Officer, Dec 1963; Peider in Andorra, the title-part in Philoctetes, Pizarro in The Royal Hunt of the Sun (also Chichester Festival), John Proctor in The Crucible, Hobson in Hobson's Choice, Sergeant in Mother Courage, Ben in Love For Love, 1965; appeared with the National Theatre Company in Moscow and Berlin, Sept 1965; Captain Jack Boyle in Juno and the Paycock, Apr 1966; the title part in Volpone, Creon in Oedipus, 1968; at the Royal Court, Feb 1970, played Doctor Astrov in Uncle Vanya; rejoined the Royal Shakespeare Company to play Deeley in Old Times, June 1971; Titus Andronicus, Stratford, Oct 1972, and Aldwych, Aug 1973; Criterion, Feb 1973, played Torvald Helmer in A Doll's House; Soho Poly, Mar 1973, directed and played Blakey in The Illumination Of Mr Shannon; in the RSC's season at The Place, Oct 1973, played Casement in Cries From Casement, General Muster in Section Nine; Old Vic, Feb 1975, for National Theatre played Capt Shotover in Heartbreak House; ICA, July 1975 and Old Vic, Dec 1975, Vukhov in Judgement; Albery, Apr 1976; Marlin Dysart in Equus; Queen's, Apr 1977, Dennis in Just Between Ourselves; Lyric, Nov 1977, Domenico Soriano in Filumena; Kennedy Center, Washington DC, 1978, title rôle in Semmelweiss; films in which he has appeared include: Saturday Night and Sunday Morning, Murder On The Orient Express, Equus, Nijinsky, etc; made his first television appearance in 1960, and principal plays include: When Silver Drinks, Son of Man, Man Friday, Donkey's Years, etc.

Favourite parts: Phil Hogan, Schmitz, and John Proctor. *Recreations:* Golf, sailing, sketching, and the piano. *Address:* c/o Leading Artists, 60 St James's Street, London SW1.

BLAKEMORE, Michael, director and former actor
b Sydney, Australia, 18 June 1928; *s* of Conrad Howell Blakemore and his wife, Una Mary (Litchfield); *e* The King's School and Sydney University; *m* Shirley Blakemore; first job in the theatre was as press agent for Robert Morley during the Australian tour of Edward, My Son, 1949; trained for the stage at the Royal Academy of Dramatic Art, 1950–2.

He made his first professional appearance, 1952, at the Theatre Royal, Huddersfield, as the doctor in The Barretts of Wimpole Street; worked for several years in repertory at Birmingham, Bristol, Coventry, etc; first London appearance, Princes, Mar 1958, as Jack Poyntz in School; played small parts at Stratford in the Memorial Theatre's 1959 season; appeared in two seasons at the Open Air, Regent's Park, playing Sir Toby in Twelfth Night and Holofernes in Love's Labour's Lost, 1962; Dogberry in Much Ado About Nothing and Theseus in A Midsummer Night's Dream, 1963; Comedy, Dec 1963, Badger in Toad of Toad Hall; toured Australia, 1965, as Palmer Anderson in A Severed Head; joined the Citizens', Glasgow, 1966–7; here his parts included George in Who's Afraid of Virginia Woolf? and Maitland in Inadmissible Evidence; began directing during this period and plays directed, at the Citizens' or the Close, include: The Investigation, Little Malcolm, Stephen D, Nightmare Abbey, 1966; The Visions of Simone Machard, A Choice of Wars, Rosmersholm, 1967; then directed in London: A Day in the Death of Joe Egg, 1967 (also New York, 1968, as Joe Egg); The Strange Case of Martin Richter, 1968; The Resistible Rise of Arturo Ui, The National Health (National Theatre), 1969; Widowers' Houses, 1970; Forget-me-not Lane, 1971; Design for Living, 1973; Knuckle, 1974; Don's Party (Royal Court), 1975; associate director, The National Theatre, 1971–6; productions included Tyger (co-director), Long Day's Journey Into Night, 1971; The Front Page, Macbeth, 1972; The Cherry Orchard, 1973; Grand Manoeuvres, 1974; Engaged, 1975; Plunder, 1976; subsequent productions, in London unless otherwise stated, include Separate Tables, Privates On Parade (RSC), Candida, The White Devil (Guthrie, Minneapolis), Hay Fever (Denmark), 1977; Deathtrap, Players (NY), 1978; appeared as an actor in films and television; author of the novel, Next Season.

Address: 15 Gardnor Mansions, Church Row, London, NW3. *Tel:* 01–435 9951.

BLECKNER, Jeff, director.
b Brooklyn, NY; *s* Jack S. Bleckner and his wife Etta (Paluba); *e* Amherst College (BA), Yale Univ (MFA); *m* Jeanne Hepple.

First play directed was Little Malcolm and His Struggle Against the Eunuchs at the Yale Univ Experimental Theatre,

Nov 1967; a director at the Long Wharf, New Haven, Conn, 1967–8 season; taught and directed at Yale School of Drama, 1967–9; New York, 25 May 1968, made his directorial début with Coriolanus; at the Astor Place, 1 Apr 1970, directed the double-bill of Sam Shepard's The Unseen Hand and Forensic and the Navigators; Arena Stage, Washington, 1971, directed Twelfth Night; for the New York Shakespeare Festival directed The Basic Training of Pavlo Hummel and the off-Broadway and Broadway productions of Sticks and Bones, for which he received the Antoinette Perry (Tony) Award, 1971; The Secret Affairs of Mildred Wild, Old Times (Mark Taper Forum, Los Angeles), 1972; The Orphan, 1973; The Death and Life of Jesse James (Mark Taper Forum), 1974; The Father (Yale Repertory), 1975; FDR (Washington), 1977; The Goodbye People, 1979; directed the television production of Sticks and Bones, 1972, and has also directed episodes of *Another World, Doc, Guiding Light*, etc.

Address: Howard Rosenstone, William Morrow Agency, 1350 Avenue of the Americas, New York, NY. *Tel:* 586–5100.

BLISS, Helena (*née* Helena Louise Lipp), actress and singer
b St Louis, Mo, 31 Dec 1917; *d* of Albert Lipp and his wife Augusta (Clemens); *e* Hosmer Hall and Washington University; *m* John Tyers.

Her first professional engagements were in radio and television, singing scenes from grand opera; made her first appearance on the stage at the Alvin Theatre, New York, 17 Nov 1939, as Helen in Very Warm for May; at the 46th Street Theatre, Dec 1939, sang in the chorus of Du Barry Was a Lady; Imperial, Oct 1941, played Helen Marcy in Let's Face It; in Mar 1943, joined the Philadelphia Opera Company, and sang leading soprano roles, Mimi in La Bohème, Rosalinda in Die Fledermaus, Marguerite in Faust; was next engaged to sing leading roles in Los Angeles and San Francisco; re-appeared in NY, at the Imperial, Aug 1944, and made a great success when she played Nina Hagerup in Song of Norway, for eighteen months; appeared at Forest Park, St Louis, 1945, in the leading parts in Rose Marie, The Desert Song, Babes in Toyland, Chu-Chin-Chow; returned to Los Angeles and San Francisco, 1946, and appeared as Musetta in Gypsy Lady, also playing the same part at the Century, NY, Sept 1946; made her first appearance on the London stage, at His Majesty's Theatre, 7 Mar 1947, in the same part when the piece was re-named Romany Love; she again appeared in St Louis, 1948; at the New York City Center, Mar–Apr 1949, with the New York City Opera Company, as Claire in Troubled Island, Nedda in Pagliacci, etc; St Louis, 1949, appeared as the Marchioness of Shayne, Sarah and Sari in Bitter Sweet, and again played in this piece in Pittsburg, July 1951; St Louis, July 1951, appeared in Miss Liberty; Coliseum, London, Dec 1951, succeeded Patricia Morison as Lilli Vanessi and Katharine in Kiss Me Kate; Los Angeles, May 1952, again appeared in Song of Norway; New York City Center, May 1954, played Julie in a revival of Show Boat; played the same part at Jones Beach, NY, in the summers of 1956 and 1957; played in summer stock in Kiss Me Kate and Pal Joey, 1959; in 1961, 1962, and 1964 played in Sacramento, Calif, in Gypsy, Take Me Along, and Kiss Me, Kate; at the Starlight Theatre, Kansas City, 1964, played in Milk and Honey; in productions sponsored by the NY State Department, appeared with the Sacramento (Calif) Light Opera Association in Mexico City, Oct 1966, in Carousel and Show Boat; Dorothy Chandler Pavilion, Los Angeles, May 1974, Lady Thiang in The King and I; has also appeared in productions of The Merry Widow, The Great Waltz, The Firefly, The Chocolate Soldier, and other standard repertory operettas and operas; principal television appearance was in The Merry Widow.

Recreations: Horseback riding and gardening.

BLOOM, Claire, actress

b London, 15 Feb 1931; *d* of Edward Bloom and his wife Elizabeth (Grew); *e* Badminton School, Bristol, and Fern Hill Manor, New Milton; *m* (1) Rod Steiger (mar dis); (2) Hillard Elkins; gained a scholarship to the Guildhall Schools of Music and Drama; studied under Eileen Thorndike and then attended the Central School of Speech Training.

She made her first appearance on the stage at the Oxford Repertory Theatre, Oct 1946, as Private Jessie Killigrew in It Depends What You Mean; subsequently playing Helen in An Italian Straw Hat, and Jessie in Pink String and Sealing Wax; made her first appearance on the London stage, at the Duchess Theatre, 6 Mar 1947, walking-on in The White Devil, and at the same theatre, June 1947, played in He Who Gets Slapped; His Majesty's (for the Under Thirty Group), Sept 1947, Erinna in The Wanderer; Stratford-on-Avon Memorial Theatre, Apr–Sept 1948, appeared as Blanch in King John, Ophelia in Hamlet and Perdita in The Winter's Tale; Lyric, Hammersmith, Feb 1949, Daphne Randall in The Damask Cheek; Globe, May 1949, Alizon Eliot in The Lady's Not for Burning; Globe, Jan 1950, Isabelle in Ring Round the Moon; joined the Old Vic Company for the 1952–3 season, when she appeared as Juliet, and as Jessica in The Merchant of Venice; at the Edinburgh Festival, 1953, played Ophelia in Hamlet; remained with the Old Vic Company for the season 1953–4, when she again appeared as Ophelia, and played Helena in All's Well That Ends Well, Viola in Twelfth Night, Virgilia in Coriolanus, Miranda in The Tempest; at the Palace, July 1955, appeared as Cordelia in King Lear; Old Vic, June 1956, again played Juliet in Romeo and Juliet, prior to appearing with the same company on tour in Canada and the United States, Sept 1956–Mar 1957; made her first appearance in New York at the Winter Garden, Oct 1956, as Juliet in Romeo and Juliet, also playing the Queen in Richard II; Apollo, London, Apr 1958, played Lucile in Duel of Angels; Music Box, NY, Jan 1959, played the Wife in Rashomon; Royal Court, Apr 1961, played Johanna in Altona, transferring with the production to the Saville, June 1961; at the Spoleto Festival of Two Worlds, Italy, July 1963, played Andromache in The Trojan Women; Phoenix, Sept 1965, Sasha in Ivanov; Playhouse, NY, Jan 1971, Nora in A Doll's House and Hedda in Hedda Gabler; Broadhurst, NY, Jan 1972, Mary Queen of Scots in Vivat! Vivat Regina!; Criterion, London, Feb 1973, repeated the part of Nora; Piccadilly, Mar 1974, Blanche du Bois in A Streetcar Named Desire; Morosco, NY, Oct 1976, Miss Giddens in The Innocents; Haymarket, Oct 1977, Rebecca West in Rosmersholm; entered films, 1948, in The Blind Goddess, films include: Look Back in Anger, Richard III, The Spy Who Came In From The Cold; Limelight, etc; television appearances include Juliet in the Old Vic production of Romeo and Juliet (NY), 1957, and more recently Henry VIII, and Brideshead Revisited.

Favourite part: Blanche du Bois. *Recreations:* The ballet and reading. *Address:* c/o Michael Linnit, Globe Theatre, Shaftesbury Avenue, London W1.

BLOUNT, Helon, actress and singer

b Big Spring, Texas, 15 Jan 1929; *d* of Ralph Eugene Blount, Sr and his wife Alma Helon (Shipp); *e* University of Texas at Austin, where she trained for the stage in the Music and Drama Dept and achieved a Master's degree in music; *m* Keith Kaldenberg.

First appeared on the stage in 1951 at the State Fair Music Hall, Dallas, Texas; made her New York début at the Imperial, 3 May 1956, as a Neighbor and standby for the role of Cleo in The Most Happy Fella; US tour, Dec 1957–June 1958, played Cleo in The Most Happy Fella; Mayfair, NY, 5 Feb 1962, played Police Matron Jonsen in Fly Blackbird; Actor's Playhouse, Dec 1962, played Mrs Farrell in River-wind; 46th Street, 1963, took over as Miss Jones in How To Succeed in Business Without Really Trying, and stayed in the part until 1965; 46th Street, Mar 1965, Mrs Victoria Haslam in Do I Hear a Waltz?; Theatre Four, Oct 1966, Katie in My Wife and I; Bert Wheeler, Nov 1967, Sarah in Curley McDimple; Broadhurst, Jan 1969, Mother-in-Law in The Fig Leaves Are Falling; Winter Garden, Apr 1971, Deedee West in Follies; Shubert, Century City, Cal, July 1972, again played in Follies; Village Gate, Nov 1972, Attendant in A Quarter for the Ladies Room; Masters, May 1973, Mrs Farrell in Riverwind; Booth, Dec 1975, Standby for part of Mme Matroppo in Very Good Eddie; Manhattan Theatre Club, July 1977, performed a one-woman show on the life of Sophie Tucker, Last of the Red Hot Mamas; has also toured in stock as Nettie in Carousel, Rosalie in Carnival, the Mother Abbess in The Sound of Music, Housekeeper in Man of La Mancha (1979), etc; other stock rôles include Fraulein Schneider in Cabaret, Mother in Babes in Toyland, Meg in Damn Yankees, Rose in Destry, etc.

Address: 346 Littleworth Lane, Sea Cliff, Long Island, NY. *Tel:* 516–OR 6–1860.

BLUNDELL, Graeme, actor and director

b 8 July 1945; *s* of Jack Walter Blundell and his wife Jean Elsie; *e* Merrilands HS, Coburg HS, and Melbourne U; *m* (1) Kerry Dwyer (mar dis); (2) Margot Hilton, playwright.

Made his first professional appearance with the Melbourne Theatre Company, 1966, as Alan Hopgood in Private Yuk Objects; played in many productions for MTC, 1966–69, including A Flea in Her Ear, Incident at Vichy and Major Barbara; directed the first play produced at La Mama, Melbourne, Three Old Friends, 1968; other productions for La Mama included Dimboola, Norm and Ahmed, and The Front Room Boys, before the workshop company moved to the Pram Factory, Melbourne, 1969, becoming the Australian Performing Group; for them he directed a number of productions until 1973 including Marvellous Melbourne, Don's Party, and The Feet of Daniel Mannix; in 1976 played Sam Jenkins in How Does Your Garden Grow for MTC; toured Australia, 1967, as George in Same Time Next Year; founding director, 1976, Hoopla Productions, later Hoopla Theatre Foundation, 1977; has since been involved with the company as actor or director in many productions, including Golden Oldies (director), 1977; films include Alvin Purple, Don's Party, and Weekend of Shadows; regular TV appearances include the series *Alvin*.

Recreation: Carlton FC. *Address:* 974 Lygon Street, North Carlton, Victoria 3054.

BLYTHE, John, actor

b London, 13 Oct 1921; *s* of Bobby Blythe and his wife Dorothy (Monkman); *e* Bickley Hall and Felsted; *m* (1) Nan Wilden (dec); (2) Marie Helene.

His first stage appearance was as a child at Drury Lane, 29 Oct 1925; first adult appearance, Market Theatre, Aylesbury, 9 Oct 1939, as the Lord Chief Justice in Night Must Fall; London début, St Martin's, 18 May 1940, as John Anstruther in a House in the Square; 'Q', Jan 1944, played Fancourt Babberley in Charley's Aunt; Apollo, Oct 1944 Dick Lawrence in Daughter Janie; His Majesty's, Mar 1945,

Bob Harrison in Irene; Scala, Feb–Mar 1946, in a Bernard Miles season, played Humphrey Dane in A Century for George, Johnny Martin in Let Tyrants Tremble, and Jack Smith in Face of Coal; Hippodrome, Feb 1952, Charley Boy in Bet Your Life; at the Windmill, Nov 1953, appeared as principal comedian, subsequently touring the Tivoli circuit in Australia, 1955; returning to England, he toured the Moss circuit, Nov 1955, as feed to Bob Hope; Adelphi, 1960, took over as Fred in When in Rome; Place, 1964, took over as Max Detweiler in The Sound of Music; Drury Lane, 1966, took over as Horace Vandergelder in Hello Dolly; Prince of Wales, 1970, took over as Dobitch in Promises, Promises; Duke of York's, Sept 1971, Jim Wainwright in Romance; Leeds Playhouse, Nov 1971–Nov 1972, played leading roles including Toad in Toad of Toad Hall, Billy in The Entertainer, and Subtle in The Alchemist; Piccadilly, May 1973, Phil Weber in Gypsy; same theatre, Mar 1976, Steward and Al Dallas in Very Good Eddie; Adelphi, May 1977, took over the role of Madame Lucy in Irene, leaving the cast to play Ben in Dean, London Casino, Aug 1977; returned as Madame Lucy, Dec 1977; has made over 80 films since his first in 1939, including: This Happy Breed, The VIPs, and Love Among the Ruins; numerous TV appearances, since 1951, include a spell as host for *Sunday Night at the Palladium* and, more recently, Funny Man and The Good Companions.

Recreations: Writing and collecting humour. *Clubs:* Eccentric, Lord's Taverners. *Address:* 19 Belvedere Close, Teddington, Middx. *Tel:* 01–977 2793.

BOCK, Jerry, composer
b New Haven, Connecticut, 23 Nov 1928; *s* of George Joseph Bock and his wife Rebecca (Alpert); *e* University of Wisconsin; *m* Patricia Faggen.

The first musical for which he composed the music was My Dream, produced as the high school play at the Flushing High School Auditorium, Flushing, New York, May 1945; while at university wrote Big As Life, produced in 1948; first composed music for a Broadway play when he contributed songs to the revue Catch a Star, Plymouth, Sept 1955; since has composed Mr Wonderful, 1956; The Ziegfeld Follies, 1957; The Body Beautiful, 1958; Fiorello! 1959; She Loves Me, 1963; Fiddler on the Roof, 1964; The Apple Tree, 1966; The Rothschilds, 1970; composed weekly revues for Camp Tamiment, Pa, 1950, 1951, 1953; first composed for the films in 1955 with the background score of Wonders of Manhattan; has written music and sketches for the television series *The Admiral Broadway Revue* (1949–51), *The Show of Shows* (1949–51), *The Mel Torme Show* (1951–2), *The Kate Smith Hour* (1953–4), etc.

Recreations and hobbies: Gardening and tennis. *Address:* 555 Fifth Avenue, New York, NY 10017.

BOGDANOV, Michael, director and dramatic author
b London, 15 Dec 1938; *s* of Francis Benzoigne Bogdin and his wife Rhoda (Rees); *e* Lower School of John Lyon, Harrow, Trinity College, Dublin (MA), and in Munich and at the Sorbonne, Paris; *m* Patricia Ann Warwick.

In Dec 1968 directed his own musical adaptation of Le Bourgeois Gentilhomme, The Bootleg Gentleman, at the Oxford Playhouse; first London production, A Comedy of the Changing Years, Theatre Upstairs, 24 Feb 1969; assistant director, Rabelais, 1970; assistant director, Royal Shakespeare Company, 1970; associate director, Tyneside Theatre Company, 1971–73; associate director, Leicester Theatre Trust, 1973–77; director, Phoenix Theatre, Leicester, Jan 1974; here in Sept 1976 directed Richard III, Hamlet and The Tempest in repertory under the general title He That Plays

the King; other work at Leicester included the opening production of the Haymarket, The Recruiting Officer; for the National Theatre, 1977, directed his adaptation of Sir Gawain and the Green Knight, and The Hunchback of Notre Dame; for the RSC, 1978, directed The Taming of the Shrew; director, The Young Vic, 1978–80; his productions here have included Bartholomew Fair, The Canterbury Tales, 1978; Richard III, Hamlet and The Tempest (as the 'Action Man' trilogy), 1978 and 1979, and Faust!, 1979; directed Shadow of a Gunman (RSC), The Seagull (Tokyo), 1980; associate director, The National Theatre, 1980– ; TV work, as writer and director, includes scripts (with Terence Brady) for the series *Broad and Narrow*, as well as two years as a director with Telefis Eireann, 1967–69; writing apart from that already mentioned includes revues, children's shows, and books and lyrics for The Hypochondriac, an adaptation from Molière.

Address: 148 Erlanger Road, London SE14.

BOLAM, James, actor
b Sunderland, 16 June 1938; *s* of Robert Alfred Bolam and his wife Marion Alice (Drury); *e* Bede Grammar School, Sunderland and Bemrose School, Derby.

He made his first appearance on stage at the Royal Court, Sept 1959, as Michael in a production without décor of The Kitchen; at the same theatre in 1960 played Lord Mayor and Smith in The Happy Haven, Sept, and Vakov in Platonov, Oct; Mermaid, Apr 1961, appeared in the Wakefield Mystery Cycle; again at the Royal Court reappeared as Michael in The Kitchen, June 1961; as Starveling in A Midsummer Night's Dream, Jan 1961; as Tom in The Knack, Mar 1962; Saville, Dec 1962, Tom Midway in Semi- Detached; Mermaid, May 1965, Attendant in Oedipus the King; Mermaid, July 1965, Mercury in Four Thousand Brass Halfpennies; Strand, Sept 1965, Private Meek in Too True to Be Good, transferring to the Garrick; Hampstead, Apr 1966, Evans in Events While Guarding the Bofors Gun; made his first New York appearance at The Music Box, Oct 1966, as Frank More in How's the World Treating You?; Lyric, London, Feb 1968, played Frank in The White Liars and Brindsley Miller in Black Comedy; Royal Court, Apr 1969, Colin Shaw in In Celebration; toured, 1970, for Cambridge Theatre Company as Face in The Alchemist and Trepliov in The Seagull; Belgrade, Coventry, June 1971, Bamforth in The Long And The Short And The Tall; Gardner, Brighton, Sept 1971, Robespierre in The Silence of Saint-Just; Royal Court, Mar 1972, Trevor Hollingshead in Veterans; Gardner, Brighton, Aug 1972, appeared in The Vicar of Soho; toured, Mar 1973 in the title role of Butley; also as Leonard in Time and Time Again, Apr 1974; Young Vic, Jan 1975, played Macbeth; Royal Court, Feb 1976, Dave in Treats; Ambassadors, Oct 1978, John Terry in Who Killed Agathie Christie?; for Cambridge Theatre Co, 1980, toured in Arms and the Man; film appearances, since 1961, include A Kind of Loving, Half a Sixpence and Otley; first television appearance, 1963; subsequently in plays and series including *The Likely Lads, Only When I Laugh,* and *When the Boat Comes In.*

Recreation: Horses. *Address:* c/o Barry Burnett, Suite 409, Princes House, 119 Piccadilly, London, W1.

BOLGER, Ray, actor
b Dorchester, Mass, 10 Jan 1904; *s* of James Edward Bolger and his wife Anne (Wallace); *e* Dorchester High School; *m* Gwendolyn Rickard.

Had experience as an amateur before making his first appearance in Boston, 1922 with the Bob Ott Musical Com-

edy repertory company, where he remained for two years; subsequently appeared in vaudeville for several years; made his first appearance on the New York legitimate stage at the Imperial, 8 June 1926, in The Merry World; at the Casino de Paris, July 1926, played in A Night in Paris; subsequently toured in The Passing Show of 1926; Palace, 1926, played in Ritz-Carlton Nights, and toured in this play, 1927–8; at the Alvin, Nov 1929, played Georgie in Heads Up; Apollo, Sept 1931, appeared in George White's Scandals; Winter Garden, Aug 1934, in Life Begins at 8.40; Imperial, Apr 1936, played Phil Dolan III in On Your Toes; then went to Hollywood to appear in films, and remained there nearly four years; at the Broadhurst, NY, May 1940, appeared in Keep Off the Grass; Shubert, June 1942, played Sapiens in By Jupiter; subsequently appeared for nearly three years for the USO Camp Shows, in the USA and overseas; re-appeared in NY, at the Adelphi, Mar 1946, in Three to Make Ready; St James, Oct 1948, played Charley Wykeham in Where's Charley? (Charley's Aunt), which ran until 1950 and for which he received the Antoinette Perry (Tony) Award and the Donaldson Award; toured, 1951, in Where's Charley?; Winter Garden, Mar 1962, Professor Fodorski in All American; toured, summer 1965, in The Ray Bolger Show; at the Empire Room, Waldorf Astoria, NY, Feb 1967, and Mar 1968, appeared in cabaret; Lunt-Fontanne, Mar 1969, Phineas Sharp in Come Summer; Von Wenzel Hall, Sarasota, Fla, Jan 1980, appeared in concert; films include: The Wizard of Oz, The Harvey Girls, The Great Ziegfeld, Where's Charley?, The Runner Stumbles, etc; has appeared frequently on television, notably in his own series *Washington Square*, and *The Entertainer* (1976).
Address: c/o Actors Equity Association, 165 West 46th Street New York, NY 10036.

BOLT, Robert, dramatic author
b Sale, Manchester, 15 Aug 1924; *s* of Ralph Bolt and his wife Leah (Binnion); *e* Manchester Grammar School, and Manchester University; *m* (1) Celia Anne Roberts (mar dis); (2) Sarah Miles (mar dis).
Formerly a teacher; served in the Royal Air Force, and Army, 1943–6; author of the following plays, The Critic and the Heart (Oxford Playhouse), 1957; Flowering Cherry (Haymarket, London, where it ran for 435 performances), 1957, and (Lyceum, New York), 1959; The Tiger and the Horse, A Man For All Seasons, 1960 (ANTA, New York), 1961; Gentle Jack, 1963; The Thwarting of Baron Bolligrew, 1965; Brother and Sister, 1967; Vivat! Vivat Regina! (Chichester Festival and Piccadilly), 1970; State of Revolution (National Theatre), 1978; received the NY Drama Critics Award, 1962, for A Man For All Seasons as the Best Foreign Play of the year; author of the screen plays Lawrence of Arabia (Film Academy Award), 1962; Dr Zhivago; A Man For All Seasons, Ryan's Daughter, and Lady Caroline Lamb (which he also directed).
Address: c/o Margaret Ramsay, 14a Goodwin's Court, St Martin's Lane, London, WC2.

BOND, C G (Christopher Godfrey), playwright, director, and actor
b Sussex, 1945; *s* of the actor Godfrey Bond and his wife Mavis (Edwards); trained for the stage at the Central School of Speech and Drama, and at Drama Centre.
Acted as a child, including appearances at the Memorial Theatre, Stratford-upon-Avon; after drama school with the Victoria Theatre company, Stoke-on-Trent, 1968–70; resident dramatist, 1971–72; artistic director, 1976–79, Everyman Theatre, Liverpool; author of the plays Sweeney Todd,

the Demon Barber of Fleet Street, produced Stoke-on-Trent, 1970; Mutiny, 1970; Downright Hooligan, 1972; Tarzan's Last Stand, Judge Jeffreys, 1973; The Country Wife (adapted from Wycherley), 1974; Under New Management, The Cantril Tales (co-author), 1975; Scum: Death, Destruction and Dirty Washing, 1976; Sweeney Todd was adapted into a musical, 1979, by Hugh Wheeler; acted and directed with Contact Theatre, 1980; author of the book You Want Something Cold to Drink.
Address: c/o Blanche Marvin, 21 St John's Wood High Street, London NW8.

BOND, Edward, dramatist
b London, 18 July 1934; *m* Elisabeth Pablé.
Is the author of the following plays: The Pope's Wedding, 1962; Saved, 1965 (NY 1970); Narrow Road to the Deep North, 1968; Early Morning, 1968 (NY 1971); Black Mass, 1970; Passion, Lear, 1971; The Sea, Bingo: Scenes of Money and Death, 1973; The Fool: Scenes of Bread and Love, 1975; A-A-America, (Grandma Faust, and The Swing), Stone, 1976; The Woman, The Bundle, new Narrow Road to the Deep North, 1978; The Worlds, 1979 (also directed); directed The Woman for the National Theatre, 1978; has adapted The Three Sisters, 1967; Spring's Awakening, 1974; The White Devil, 1976; wrote librettos for the operas We Come to the River, 1976, and The English Cat, 1979; ballet Orpheus, 1978; screenplays include Blow-Up, 1967, and Laughter in the Dark, 1969; his Theatre Poems and Songs were published 1978; Hon D Litt, Yale University, 1977.
Address: c/o Margaret Ramsay, 14a Goodwin's Court, St Martin's Lane, London WC2.

BOND, Gary, actor
b Alton, Hampshire, 7 Feb 1940; *s* of James Ker Bond and his wife Violet Clara (Brett); *e* Churcher's College; trained for the stage at the Central School of Speech and Drama.
He made his first stage appearance in 1963 at the Connaught, Worthing in Not in the Book; at the same theatre, Apr 1963, played Simon Sparrow in Doctor in the House; made his first London appearance at the Royal Court that Aug as Pip in Chips With Everything, transferring with the production to the Plymouth, New York, in Oct; Hampstead, Apr 1965, played Frank in Mrs Warren's Profession; Saville, Apr 1966, Joe in On the Level; Arnaud, Guildford, Aug 1967, John Shand in What Every Woman Knows; Royal, Windsor, Nov 1967, Giles Cadwallader in The Man Most Likely To . . .; toured with the Prospect Company in 1968, playing Sebastian in Twelfth Night, Pte Swan in No Man's Land and Sergius in Arms and the Man; Open Air, Regent's Park, June 1970, played Benedick in Much Ado About Nothing and Byron in The Lord Byron Show; Nov 1970, at Hampstead, played Karl Sandys in We Were Dancing, George Pepper in Red Peppers and Jasper Featherways in Family Album, in the triple-bill Tonight at 8.00, transferring to the Fortune, Jan 1971; toured, Feb 1972, with the Cambridge Theatre Company as Oswald Alving in Ghosts; Young Vic, 1972, Antipholus in The Comedy or Errors; played Joseph in the Young Vic's Joseph and the Amazing Technicolour Dreamcoat at the Edinburgh Festival, Aug 1972 and subsequently at the Round House, Nov 1972 and the Albery, Feb 1973; Greenwich, Sept 1974, Simon in More Stately Mansions; with the Bristol Old Vic Company, Sept–Dec 1975, played Barnet in The National Health, Hurst in Serjeant Musgrave's Dance, Edward in Old Flames and Johny Hobnails in Afore Night Come; Arts, Feb 1976, again played Edward in Old Flames; Arts, Feb 1976, again played Edward in Old Flames; joined the RSC, 1976, to play Hevern in The

Zykovs, April, and Willie Oban in The Iceman Cometh, May; Comedy, Sept 1976, took over as Damien Foxworth in Getting Away With Murder; Alexandra, Toronto, Nov 1976, appeared in The Scenario; Chichester, May 1977, Brutus in Julius Caesar, also appearing in his one-man show on Lord Byron; Savoy, May 1978, Toby in Alice's Boys; Prince Edward, Nov 1978, took over as Che in Evita; first film, Zulu, 1963, since when his appearances include Anne of the Thousand Days and Outback; television appearances, since 1962, include Great Expectations, The Main Chance, The Duchess of Malfi, and Wings of Sons.

Recreations: Riding, driving. *Address:* c/o Larry Dalzell Associates, 3 Goodwin's Court, St Martin's Lane, London WC2.

BOND, Sudie, actress, singer, dancer
b Louisville, Kentucky, 13 July 1928; *d* of James Roy Bond and his wife Carrie (Showers); *e* Fassifern School, Hendersonville, North Carolina, Virginia Intermont College, Rollins College (BA 1953), and New York University; *m* Massen Cornelius Noland (mar dis); studied dance with Jose Limon, Martha Graham, and Merce Cunningham, and acting with Herbert Berghof and Uta Hagen.

Made her NY début at the Circle in the Square, 24 Apr 1952 as Mrs Winemiller in the revival of Summer and Smoke; City Center, May 1952, played Olga in Tovarich; Coronet, Jan 1957, Estelle in Waltz of the Toreadors; City Center, Aug 1958, Agnes Gooch in Auntie Mame; subsequently toured in this last part; toured, summer 1959, as Lily in A Piece of Blue Sky; York, Jan 1961, Grandma in The American Dream; Cort, Jan 1962, Justine in The Egg; Cherry Lane, Feb 1962, in a program entitled Theatre of the Absurd, played Grandma in The American Dream, Grandma in The Sandbox, Nell in Endgame and the title-role of Bertha, receiving the *Village Voice* Obie Award for these performances; Cort, Nov 1962, Miss Prose in Harold; Plymouth, Mar 1963, Mrs Lazar in My Mother, My Father, and Me; Cherry Lane, Mar 1964, again played Grandma in The American Dream; Provincetown Playhouse, May 1964, Vivienne in Home Movies and Nona in Softly, and Consider the Nearness; Bouwerie Lane, Feb 1965, Matron in The Great Western Union; The Playhouse, Oct 1965, Miss Hammer in The Impossible Years; Plymouth, Sept 1967, Betsy Jane in Keep It in the Family (Spring and Port Wine); Anspacher, Apr 1968, Hana in The Memorandum; Spoleto Festival, Italy, 1968, and Billy Rose, Sept 1968, Old Woman in Quotations from Chairman Mao-Tse Tung; Billy Rose, Oct 1968, Grandma in The American Dream; Actors Playhouse, Nov 1969, played various roles in Harold Pinter's Sketches in a program with the overall title The Local Stigmatic; Morosco, 1970, succeeded Polly Rowles as Mrs Margolin in Forty Carats; Helen Hayes, Nov 1970, Clara in Hay Fever; Broadhurst, June 1972, took over as Miss Lynch in Grease; Broadhurst, Apr 1974, Street Lady in Thieves; Bucks County Playhouse, New Hope, Pa, June 1974, played in The Mind with a Dirty Man; Shubert, Sept 1974, took over from Betty Henritze as Ma in Over Here; Roundabout, Apr 1976, Carlotta in The Cherry Orchard; Center Stage, Baltimore, 1978, appeared in The Shadow Box; Royale, 1979, took over as Miss Lynch in Grease; The Annex, Sept 1979, Roseanna in Dance for Me, Simeon; has appeared extensively in NY as a dancer; cofounded The Paper Bag Players, a children's theatre group that has toured frequently, including England; has appeared in films such as Andy, A Thousand Clowns, Samuel Beckett's Film, The Tiger Makes Out, Cold Turkey, They Might Be Giants, Tomorrow; for television has recreated several of her performances in absurdist plays, and has also played on many

dramatic series including The New Temperature's Rising, 1973–4, and in Maude, All in the Family, Mary Hartman, Mary Hartman, etc.

Recreation: Swimming. *Hobby:* Painting. *Address:* c/o Jeff Hunter, 119 West 57th Street, New York, NY 10019.

BONUS, Ben, producer, playwright, actor.
Specializes in Yiddish-language productions and has appeared in New York in Father and Son, Oct 1956; at the Brooks Atkinson, Nov 1966, played Yosl-Ber and produced Let's Sing Yiddish, and, May 1967, produced and appeared in the revue Sing, Israel, Sing; Belasco, Oct 1970, adapted the book and played Hershel of Ostropolis in Light, Lively and Yiddish; Mayfair, Mar 1972, played in the revue Song of Israel; Norman Thomas Auditorium, Oct 1979, appeared in Let There Be Joy.

BOOKE, Sorrell, actor
b Buffalo, New York, 4 Jan 1930; *e* Columbia and Yale Universities.

First appeared in NY at the Phoenix, 17 Mar 1955, as Doctor Julio in The White Devil; Phoenix, 25 Apr 1955, appeared in Moby Dick; Phoenix, Oct 1955, played a Soldier in The Carefree Tree; New York City Center, Jan 1956, the Duke of Albany in Orson Welles's production of King Lear; Phoenix, Apr 1956, played a Footman in A Month in the Country; Coronet, 1 Nov 1956, made his Broadway début as the Butler in The Sleeping Prince; Coronet, Oct 1957, Rip Voorhees in Nature's Way; Renata, Jan 1958, Abramovitch, Erbstein, Jimmy Jones, Corky, and Morrie in Winkelberg; Ford's, Baltimore, Mar 1959, Mayor Honorat in The Gay Felons; Billy Rose, Oct 1959, the Burglar in Heartbreak House; 54th Street, Feb 1960, Darling in Caligula; Maidman Playhouse, Mar 1960, The Father in Jeannette; New York City Center, Apr 1960, Senator Billboard Rawkins in Finian's Rainbow; Broadhurst, 1960, understudied Tom Bosley in the title-role of Fiorello!; Key, Apr 1961, played in Evenings with Chekhov; Cort, Sept 1961, Ol' Cap'n Cotchipee in Purlie Victorious; New York City Center, June 1962, Fiorello LaGuardia in Fiorello!; Henry Miller's, May 1964, Daniel Webster, Reverend Fuller, Stephen Douglas, Ulysses S Grant, Dr W W Keen, John Hay in The White House; American Place, Feb 1966, title-role in Jonah; Billy Rose, Jan 1967, Milton Rademacher in Come Live with Me; Henry Miller's, Nov 1968, Updike in Morning, Cecil in Noon, and Fibber Kidding in Night; Ahmanson, Los Angeles, Mar 1972, played in Richard II; appeared in the films The Take and The Bank Shot in 1974, and has played in several other films.

Address: c/o David Shapira and Associates, 9100 Wilshire Boulevard, Beverly Hills, Calif.

BOOTH, James, (*né* Geeves-Booth), actor
b Croydon, Surrey, 19 Dec 1933; *s* of Ernest Edward Geeves-Booth and his wife Lilian Alice (Edwardes); *e* Southend Grammar School; *m* Paula Delaney; studied for the stage at the Royal Academy of Dramatic Art.

He made his first appearance on the stage as a member of the Old Vic Company, 1956–7; at the Theatre Royal, Stratford, E, Feb 1958, played Sempronio in Celestina, subsequently appearing at the same theatre in the following productions: Commentator in Love and Lectures and Giuseppe in The Man of Destiny (double-bill); the IRA Officer in The Hostage; Bob Cratchit in The Christmas Carol, 1958; Tosher in Fings Ain't Wot They Used T' Be; Freewill in The Dutch Courtesan, 1959; Wyndham's, June 1959, made his first appearance in the West End, when he again played the IRA Officer in The Hostage; Theatre Royal, Stratford, E, Dec 1959, again played Tosher in Fings Ain't Wot They Used T' Be, prior to appearing in the same production at the Garrick, Feb 1960; following a run of more than a year, he appeared at the Oxford Playhouse, Sept 1961, as Stanley Castleton in Big Soft Nellie; at the Royal Court, Dec 1961, played Box in Box and Cox, and Eisenring in The Fire Raisers (double-bill); New Arts, Apr 1962, played AC/2 Neville Harrison in Nil Carborundum; Oxford Playhouse, 1962, played Mick in The Caretaker; joined the Royal Shakespeare Company, Stratford-on-Avon, Sept 1962, to play Dr. Pinch in The Comedy of Errors, and Edmund in King Lear, subsequently appearing in both productions at the Aldwych Theatre, Dec 1962; Gaiety, Dublin, Apr 1964, played Murray Burns in A Thousand Clowns, subsequently appearing in the same production at the Comedy, London, June 1964; Shaftesbury, Dec 1965, Robin Hood in Twang; Chichester Festival, Aug 1970, played Face in The Alchemist; for the Welsh Drama Company, Cardiff, autumn 1973, played Osip in The Government Inspector, Kite in The Recruiting Officer and Archie Rice in The Entertainer; Theatre Royal, Stratford E, Jan 1974, Chief-Supt Craddock in Gentlemen Prefer Anything; for the RSC at Stratford-on-Avon, played Pompey in Measure for Measure, Sept 1974 and appeared in Afore Night Come, Nov 1974; played Tristan Tzara in their New York production of Travesties, Ethel Barrymore, Oct 1975; repeated the part in Washington DC, Jan 1977; entered films, 1959, and principal pictures include: The Trials of Oscar Wilde, Sparrers Can't Sing, Robbery, The Bliss of Mrs Blossom, Macho Callaghan, etc; television appearances include: The Ruffians, The Great Gold Bullion Robbery, The Vessel of Wrath, etc.

Favourite parts: Those I can relax in. *Recreation:* Underwater fishing. *Address:* c/o William Morris Agency (UK) Ltd, 147 Wardour Street, London W1V 3TB.

BOOTH, Shirley (*née* Thelma Booth Ford), actress
b New York City, 30 Aug 1907; *d* of Albert James Ford and his wife Virginia (Wright); *e* NY; *m* (1) Edward F Gardner (mar dis); (2) William H Baker (dec).

Made her first appearance on the stage in Hartford, Conn, 1919, with the Poli Stock Company, in The Cat and the Canary; made her first appearance on the NY stage at Wallack's, 26 Jan 1925, as Nan Winchester in Hell's Bells; Wallack's, Nov 1925, played Peggy Bryant in Laff That Off; Princess, Oct 1926, Betty Hamilton in Buy, Buy, Baby; Wallack's, Oct 1927, Mary Marshall in High Gear; National, Sept 1928, Emily Rosen in The War Song; Longacre, Apr 1931, Marg in The School for Virtue; President, Oct 1931, Bobby Marchante in The Camels Are Coming; Provincetown, Nov 1931, Annie Duval in Coastwise; Guild, May 1933, Elisa Zanotti in The Mask and the Face; Bijou, Feb 1934, in After Such Pleasures; Barbizon-Plaza, Nov 1934, in Sunday Nights at Nine; Playhouse, Jan 1935, Mabel in Three Men on a Horse; Vanderbilt, Apr 1937, Mrs Loschavio in Excursion; Hudson, Nov 1937, Carrie Nolan in Too Many Heroes; at Shubert (for the Theatre Guild), Mar 1939, Elizabeth Imbrie in The Philadelphia Story, which ran over a year; Biltmore, Dec 1940, Ruth Sherwood in My Sister Eileen, which ran for two years; Ethel Barrymore, Apr 1943, Leona Richards in To-Morrow the World, which ran over a year; Alvin, May 1945, Louhedda Hopsons in Hollywood Pinafore; Playhouse, Dec 1946, Susan Pengilly in Land's End; Mansfield, Jan 1948, Maggie Welch in The Men We Marry; Morosco, Nov 1948, played Grace Woods in Goodbye, My Fancy (Antoinette Perry 'Tony' Award); 48th Street Theatre, Nov 1949, Abby Quinn in Love Me Long;

Booth, Feb 1950, Lola in Come Back, Little Sheba (Tony Award); Alvin, Apr 1951, Cissy in A Tree Grows in Brooklyn; Empire, Oct 1952, Leona Samish in The Time of the Cuckoo (Tony Award); Majestic, Apr 1954, Lottie Gibson in By the Beautiful Sea; Broadhurst, NY, Oct 1955, played Bunny Watson in Desk Set, subsequently touring in the play; Royale, NY, Dec 1957, played Mrs Ackroyd in Miss Isobel; Winter Garden, NY, Mar 1959, Juno Boyle in Juno; Playhouse, Ivoryton, NY, July 1959, played the title-role in Nina; Eugene O'Neill, Apr 1960, Fanny in A Second String; Valley Music Theatre, Woodland, California, 1956, again played Lola in Come Back, Little Sheba; Playhouse, Ogunquit, Maine, 1967, played in The Torchbearers; Lunt-Fontanne, Mar 1970, Mother Maria in the musical Look to the Lilies; Helen Hayes, Nov 1970, Judith Bliss in a revival of Hay Fever; Central City, Colorado, Opera House, Aug 1971, Veta Louise Simmons in Harvey, and subsequently toured in this part; toured 1972 as Mrs Gibson in Mourning in a Funny Hat; has appeared in several films, including: Come Back, Little Sheba (for which she received the Academy Award), and The Matchmaker; played Miss Duffy on radio's *Duffy's Tavern* for several years; 1961–8, played the title-role in the television series *Hazel*, receiving some 30 awards, including the Emmy.

Favourite part: Lola in Come Back, Little Sheba. *Address:* PO Box 103, Chatham, Ma 02633.

BOSCO, Philip, actor
b Jersey City, New Jersey, 26 Sept 1930; *s* of Philip Lupo Bosco and his wife Margaret Raymond (Thek); *e* Catholic University of America; *m* Nancy Ann Dunkle; formerly a carnival worker and truck driver; prepared for the stage with James Marr, Josephine Callan, and Leo Brady.

First appeared on the stage at St John's School, Jersey City, June 1944, as Machiavelli the Cat in The Fairy Cobbler; while at the Catholic University appeared in several Shakespearean productions, including the title-roles in Hamlet and Richard III and Malvolio in Twelfth Night; from 1957 to 1960 was a resident actor with the Arena Stage in Washington, DC, appearing in some twenty plays in repertory; from Apr 1958 to Feb 1959, toured the US as Brian O'Bannion in Auntie Mame, making his New York stage début in the same part at the City Center, Aug 1958; at the Belvedere Lake Amphitheatre, Central Park, July 1960, played Angelo in Measure for Measure; Martin Beck, Nov 1960, Heracles in The Rape of the Belt; 46th Street, May 1961, Will Danaher in Donnybrook; Mayfair, Dec 1961, Hawkshaw in The Ticket-of-Leave Man; at the Shakespeare Festival, Stratford, Conn, played Henry Bolingbroke in Richard II, and the title-role in Henry IV, Part 1, in 1962; Kent in King Lear, Rufio in Antony and Cleopatra, Pistol in Henry V, and Aegeon in Comedy of Errors, 1963; Benedick in Much Ado About Nothing and Claudius in Hamlet, 1964; title-role in Coriolanus, 1965; Delacorte, NY, Aug 1966, Duke of Buckingham in King Richard III; joined the Lincoln Center Repertory Theatre and first appeared with that company at the Vivian Beaumont, Oct 1966, as Lovewit in The Alchemist; Feb 1967, Jack in The East Wind; Apr 1967, Sagredo in Galileo; Jan 1968, Bastard of Orleans in Saint Joan; Feb 1968, Hector in Tiger at the Gates; Apr 1968, Comte de Guiche in Cyrano de Bergerac; Nov 1968, Kent in King Lear; Forum, for the same company, Dec 1968, Zelda and Mr Gray in An Evening for Merlin Finch; Vivian Beaumont, Mar 1969, Curtis Moffat, Jr, in In the Matter of J Robert Oppenheimer; May 1968, Anselme in The Miser; June 1969, again played Curtis Moffat, Jr in In the Matter of J Robert Oppenheimer; Nov 1969, Nick in The Time of Your Life; Jan

1970, Baron de Charlus in Camino Real; Mar 1970, Captain Bovine in Operation Sidewinder; Forum, May 1970, Jupiter in Amphitryon; Vivian Beaumont, Nov 1970, First God in The Good Woman of Setzuan; Jan 1971, Jimmy Farrell in The Playboy of the Western World; Mar 1971, Peter Stockman in An Enemy of the People; May 1971, Creon in Antigone; Nov 1971, Earl of Leicester in Mary Stuart; Jan 1972, Prime Minister in Narrow Road to the Deep North; Jan 1972, Antonio in Twelfth Night; Apr 1972, Reverend John Hale in The Crucible; Nov 1972, Mikhail Skrobotov in Enemies; Jan 1973, Corporal Stoddart in The Plough and the Stars; Mar 1973, Gratiano in The Merchant of Venice; Apr 1973, Harold Mitchell in A Streetcar Named Desire; Vivian Beaumont, Jan 1976, Crofts in Mrs Warren's Profession; Delacorte, Central Park, June 1976, Pistol in Henry V; Beaumont, Oct 1976, Mack the Knife Threepenny Opera; Mitzi E Newhouse, Mar 1977, Sgt Cokes in Streamers; Delacorte, summer 1977, again played Mack the Knife; Circle in the Square, Nov 1977, Warwick in Saint Joan; Belasco, Mar 1978, appeared in Stages; Theatre Four, May 1978, Goosen in The Biko Inquest; Circle in the Square, Dec 1978, Mendoza in Man and Superman; Trafalgar, Apr 1979, Dr Emerson in Whose Life Is It Anyway?; Roundabout Stage One, Nov 1979, Dr Spigelsky in A Monk in the Country; Circle in the Square, Feb 1980, Andrew Undershaft in Major Barbara; received the Shakespeare Society Award (1957) and the Drama Critics Award in 1960 for his performance in The Rape of the Belt; first appeared in films in 1961 in Requiem for a Heavyweight and has since played in A Lovely Way to Die, etc; first appeared on television in 1960 in The Prisoner of Zenda and has since appeared on various dramatic series, including: *The Nurses, O'Brien, Hawk, The NET Play of the Month,* etc.

Favourite parts: Richard III, Pistol, Thomas Mendip in The Lady's Not for Burning, Hamlet, Malvolio, Benedick, Cyrano de Bergerac. *Hobbies and recreations:* Horses and girls. *Address:* Actors Equity Association, 165 West 46th Street, New York, NY 10036.

BOSLEY, Tom, actor
b Chicago, Illinois, 1 Oct 1927; s of Benjamin Bosley and his wife Dora (Heyman); e Lakeview High School and De Paul University, Chicago; m Jean Eliot.

First appeared on the stage at the Fine Arts, Chicago, for the Canterbury Players as Simon Stimson in Our Town; at the 11th Street Theatre, Chicago, June 1947, played Papa Bonaparte in Golden Boy; appeared with the Woodstock, Illinois, Summer Playhouse, 1947-8; made his New York début at the Cherry Lane, 1 Feb 1955, as Dupont-Dufour in Thieves' Carnival; Cherry Lane, June 1955, Homer Bolton in Morning's at Seven; Fourth St, Oct 1956, Yakov in The Seagull; Phoenix, Dec 1956, various parts in The Power and the Glory; Phoenix, Feb 1959, Scrub in The Beaux' Stratagem; Broadhurst, Nov 1959, Fiorello H LaGuardia in the musical Fiorello! and continued in this part for two years, receiving the Antoinette Perry (Tony) Award, The ANTA Award, *Variety*'s NY Drama Critics Poll, Page One Award for this performance; Winter Garden, Nov 1962, Izzy Einstein in Nowhere to Go But Up; Booth, Jan 1963, Vince Brinkman in Natural Affection; Morosco, Mar 1964, Cabouche in A Murderer Is Among Us; Morosco, Mar 1965, Inspector Levine in Catch Me If You Can; toured, 1965-6, as Milt Manville in Luv; Alvin, Apr 1968, Hyman Kaplan in The Education of HYMAN KAPLAN; Ivanhoe, Chicago, 1970, played in A Shot in the Dark; first appeared in films in 1963 in Love with a Proper Stranger, and has since

played in The World of Henry Orient, Divorce American Style, Yours, Mine, Ours, The Secret War of Private Frigg, To Find a Man (1972); first appeared on television in 1952 and has since appeared in Arsenic and Old Lace, *Ben Casey, The FBI, Bonanza,* as a regular in the *Debbie Reynolds Show, The Dean Martin Show* and many others.

Address: Burton Moss Agency, 113 N San Vincente Boulevard, Beverly Hills, Cal 90211 *Tel:* 655 1156.

BOUCHIER, Chili (*née* Dorothy Bouchier); actress
b London, 12 Sept 1909; d of Frank Edwin Bouchier and his wife Alice Irene (Clack); e Fulham; m Harry Milton (mar dis); (2) Peter de Greeff (mar dis); (3) Bluey Hill.

Studied for the stage under Madam Cleaver Lee; was formerly engaged as a mannequin until 1927, when she first appeared in films; made her first appearance on the stage at the Piccadilly, 8 Sept 1930, as Phyllis in Open Your Eyes; subsequently toured in Lavender; at the Adelphi, Mar 1934, played Bella Weinberg in Magnolia Street; Palace, Manchester, Dec 1934, Puss in Boots; London Hippodrome, Dec 1936, Mother Goose; during 1939, toured with her own Film Repertory Company, playing The Dominant Sex, White Cargo, French Leave, The Man in Possession, The Chinese Bungalow, and French Without Tears; during 1941, toured in The Naughty Wife and almost a Honeymoon; 1942, toured in Jam Today; at the Q, Aug 1942, played Sanchia in Who Killed My sister; next toured as Maimie Scott in A Little Bit of Fluff, and appeared in the same part at the Ambassadors', Feb 1943; subsequently toured in the same part, for ENSA, in Egypt; during 1944, toured in Lady Be Careful; Grand, Croydon, Jan 1945, played Teresia O'Toole in The Man Who Wrote Murder; toured, Oct 1945, as Amelia Simpson in Lovely Lady; appeared in this part at the Q, Aug 1946; New Lindsey, Mar 1948, Charlotte in Paulette; Alexandra, Stoke Newington, Mar 1950, appeared as Iris Wilson in Loophole; Comedy, May 1952, played Jane Keith in the revue Rendezvous; Prince's, Aug 1953, Violet Bloom in Age of Consent; Roof Garden Theatre, Bognor Regis, Aug 1954, Elizabeth in Too Short a Date; toured, 1955, as Lady Angkatell in The Hollow; toured, 1956, as Olivia Brown in Love in Idleness; toured, 1957-8, as Denise in Dear Charles; after a period devoted to writing and the study of languages, returned to the stage at the Palace, Westcliff, 1966, playing Aunt Alicia in Gigi and appearing in The Pen is Mightier; toured, 1966, as Hattie in The Full Treatment; summer 1967, appeared at the Pier theatres, Llandudno and Bournemouth, as Bertha in Boeing-Boeing; Christmas 1967, played Mrs Fezziwig and Mrs Cratchit in A Christmas Carol, at the Winter Garden, Blackpool, and the Connaught, Eastbourne; toured, 1968, in Just the Ticket; summer season, Pier, Llandudno, 1968, Lady Chesapeake in Big Bad Mouse; again toured, autumn 1968, as Lady Charlotte Fayre in Perchance to Dream; toured, 1969, in Little Jack; Roar Like a Dove, tour, 1970; Christmas 1970, Ashcroft, Croydon, repeated the parts of Mrs Fezziwig and Mrs Cratchit; Ambassadors', 1971-2, and St Martin's, 1973-4, Mrs Boyle in The Mousetrap; Prince of Wales, Apr 1975, Betty Chumley in Harvey; Round House, July 1976, Margaret in I Can't Imagine Tomorrow; toured, 1977 and 1978, in Doctor in the House, including appearances in Rhodesia and Canada; New Brewhouse, Taunton, Dec 1978, Mrs Leverett in Rookery Nook; Her Majesty's, Nov 1979, Mrs Possett in the same play; has played in over sixty films since her first in 1927.

Recreations: Writing and languages. *Address:* c/o Vincent Shaw Associates, 75 Hammersmith Road, London W14.

BOVA, Joseph, actor
b Cleveland, Ohio, 25 May 1924; *s* of Anthony Bova and his wife Mary (Catalano); *e* Northwestern University; *m* Lee Lawson; formerly a program director for NBC; prepared for the stage with Alvina Krause and Lee Strasberg of the Actors Studio.

First appeared on the stage in Cleveland, 1936, as David in a Federal Theatre Project production of It Can't Happen Here; at the Cleveland Playhouse, 1953, played in Stalag 17; 1954, Francis X Dignan in King of Hearts; 1957, Sakini in Teahouse of the August Moon; first appeared in New York at the Carnegie Hall Playhouse, 15 Jan 1959, as Chip in On the Town; Phoenix, May 1959, played Prince Dauntless in Once upon a Mattress, which later transferred to the Alvin; Delacorte, Aug 1960, Tranio in The Taming of the Shrew; Martin Beck, Nov 1960, Theseus in The Rape of the Belt; Plymouth, Aug 1961, succeeded Clive Revill as Bob in Irma La Douce and subsequently toured in this part; Majestic, Apr 1964, Shim in Hot Spot; 46th Street, Oct 1963, substituted for Orson Bean as Charlie in Never Too Late; Theatre Four, Nov 1964, Junior Mister in The Cradle Will Rock; Delacorte, June 1965, Costard in Love's Labour's Lost; Aug 1965, Thersites in Troilus and Cressida; Aug 1966, title-role in King Richard III; June 1960, Antipholus of Ephesus in The Comedy of Errors; Aug 1968, Mercutio in Romeo and Juliet; Public, Mar 1969, M'sieur Pierre in Invitation to a Beheading; Ethel Barrymore, Mar 1970, Mr Lee in The Chinese; Colonial, Boston, Nov 1972, Coviello in Comedy; Joseph E Levine—Circle in the Square, Apr 1974, Jake Jackson in An American Millionaire; Delacorte, July 1974, Ford in The Merry Wives of Windsor; American Place, Nov 1974, played various roles in The Beauty Part; Papermill Playhouse, Millburn NJ, 1976, Milt in Luv; NY Shakespeare Festival, July 1976, Fluellen in Henry V; Goodman, Chicago, Sept 1977, Dunois in Saint Joan, playing the same part at the Circle in the Square, Nov; Stratford, Conn, July 1978, played in Twelfth Night; first appeared in films in The Young Doctors, 1962, and has since played in Pretty Poison and Serpico (1973); first appeared as writer-producer-actor on children's television programs, Cleveland, 1951, and continued in these capacities until 1954, and then in NY until 1958; has also appeared on television in Once upon a Mattress, The Tin Drum, *Kojak*, etc.
Recreations: Golf, tennis, bridge. *Address:* c/o Richard Astor Agency, 119 West 57th Street, New York, NY 10019.

BOVASSO, Julie, playwright, actress, director, producer
b Brooklyn, New York, 1 Aug 1930; *d* of Bernard Michael Bovasso and his wife Angela Ursula (Padovani); *e* City College of NY; *m* (1) George Ortman (mar dis); (2) Leonard Wayland (mar dis); prepared for the stage with Uta Hagen, Herbert Berghof, Mira Rostova, and Harold Clurman.

Made her début at age 13 with the Davenport Free Theatre, Aug 1943, as a Maid in The Bells; joined the Rolling Players and played Gwendolyn in The Importance of Being Earnest, Salome, and Hedda Gabler, 1947–9; Studio, May 1949, Belissa in Don Perlimplin; Globe Repertory, July 1949, Lona Hessel in Pillars of Society; Provincetown Playhouse, June 1950, Emma in Naked and Countess Geschwitz in Earth Spirit; Theatre Workshop, Oct 1950, Zinida in He Who Gets Slapped; Cherry Lane, May 1952, for the Living Theatre, the title-role of Faustina; San Francisco Repertory Theatre, Nov 1952, Anna Petrovna in Ivanov; returned to NY where she founded the Tempo Playhouse where she produced and directed avant garde plays, introducing to America the works of Jean Genet, Eugene Ionesco, and Michael de Ghelderode, among others; Tempo Playhouse, Aug 1953, played Margot in Jean Cocteau's The Typewriter; Oct 1954, Madeleine in

Amedee; May 1955, Claire in The Maids; May 1956, Solange in The Maids; Oct 1956, the Student in The Lesson in a double-bill with Escurial, which she produced and directed; John Golden, Oct 1957, Henriette in Monique; Cherry Lane, Dec 1959, Luella in Dinny and the Witches; Theatre de Lys, Jan 1960, the Wife in Victims of Duty; Gramercy Arts, Apr 1961, Lucy and Martha in Gallows Humor; American Shakespeare Festival, Stratford, Conn, June 1962, Mistress Quickly in Henry IV, Part 1; Playhouse in the Park, Cincinnati, Ohio, Apr 1964, Madame Rosepettle in Oh Dad, Poor Dad, Mama's Hung You in the Closet and I'm Feeling So Sad; Henry Miller's, Oct 1965, Mrs Prosser in Minor Miracle; Cincinnati Playhouse, 1966, Esmeralda in The Skin of Our Teeth; Center Stage, Baltimore, Feb 1967, Irma in The Balcony; Cincinnati, season 1968, appeared in The Madwoman of Chaillot and Crime on Goat Island; Ellen Stewart, Dec 1969, wrote and directed The Moondreamers; ANTA, Feb 1970, wrote, directed, and played Gloria B Gilbert in Gloria and Esperanza; her play Down by the River Where Water Lilies Are Disfigured Every Day produced by the Trinity Square Repertory Company, Providence, RI, Dec 1971, and by the Circle Repertory Company, NYC, Mar 1975; Brooklyn Academy of Music, Dec 1972, played the Mother in The Screens and received the NY Critics Poll Award for this performance; her short plays Shubert's Last Serenade, The Final Analysis, and Super Lover produced by LaMama ETC in 1975; for the same theatre wrote and directed The Nothing Kid and Standard Safety, also in 1975; has received five Obie Awards for best actress (The Maids), best experimental theatre, and for writing, directing, and acting in Gloria and Esperanza; film work includes Saturday Night Fever, 1977; on television has played in the serial *From These Roots*, 1958–60, and as Pearl in The Iceman Cometh, 1960, on the *US Steel Hour, The Defenders*, etc; has taught a professional acting workshop since 1966, and held teaching positions at such institutions as Sarah Lawrence College and the New School for Social Research.
Recreation: Painting. *Address:* Harvey and Hulto Associates, 110 West 57th Street, New York, NY 10019.

BOWDEN, Charles, producer and director
b Somerville, Mass; *s* of John J Bowden and his wife Elizabeth (Donahue); *e* Harvard University (class of 1935); *m* Paula Laurence.

Began his career as an actor of the Wharf Players, Provincetown, Mass, Summer 1929, as a Youth in The Drunkard; for the New London, New Hampshire, Players, 1930–2, played in Ah, Wilderness! Meet the Prince, Hedda Gabler, In Any Language, and Dr Knock; Ford Hall Forum, Boston, Mass, 1930–2, played in The Three Sisters, The Proposal, and There's Gold in Them Hills; made his New York début at the St James, 23 Oct 1936, as an Orderly in Ten Million Ghosts; Manhattan Opera House, Jan 1937, played various parts in the Max Reinhardt production of The Eternal Road; Mansfield, Nov 1937, Demetrius in Antony and Cleopatra; St James, Oct 1938, various roles in the Maurice Evans production of Hamlet; St James, Jan 1939, Shallow in Henry IV, Part 1; toured with Lunt and Fontanne, 1940, as Pantaloon and the Tailor in The Taming of the Shrew; turned to production and stage managed the tour of There Shall Be No Night, 1941; served in the US Army under General Patton, 1941–5, achieving the rank of Captain; on returning to civilian life was technical director for the Lunts' production of O Mistress Mine, at the Empire, Jan 1946; Shubert, Nov 1949, technical director and played Reilly in I Know My Love; Managing Director of the Westport, Conn, Country Playhouse, 1948–53; owned and operated the New Parsons

Theatre in Hartford, Conn, and the Bahama Playhouse in Nassau, The Bahamas, 1950–4; has produced or co-produced Seagulls over Sorrento, which he also directed, 1952; At Home with Ethel Waters, 1953; Ruth Draper in a solo program and Ruth Draper and Paul Draper in concert, 1954; All in One, which consisted of Trouble in Tahiti, Paul Draper in a dance recital, and Twenty-Seven Wagons Full of Cotton, 1955; Fallen Angels, which he also directed, Ruth Draper and Her Company of Characters, 1956; Hotel Paradiso, 1957; Auntie Mame in three separate touring productions, which he also directed, 1957–9; Romanoff and Juliet touring production starring Bert Lahr, which he also directed, Season of Choice, which he also directed, 1959; Caligula, 1960; The Night of the Iguana, 1961; Slapstick Tragedy, 1966; directed Song of the Grasshopper, 1967; produced the tour of A Streetcar Named Desire, 1969–70; co- produced The Changing Room, 1973; Don't Call Back, 1975; is the first Vice President of the Catholic Actors Guild, a life member of St Jude Apostolate, a member of the Harvard Alumni Association; member of the board of directors of The New Dramatists, 1976; Direct Theatre, 1977; a producer and director for Public Announcement Services of various nation-wide Telephone Companies, 1976: joined Phone Programs, a subsidiary of Air Time, Inc, NY, as Creative Director, 1978: has lectured widely on various aspects of the theatre.

Recreation: Gardening. *Address:* 263 West End Avenue, New York, NY 10022. *Tel:* (212) 371–5450.

BOWEN, John, dramatist
b Calcutta, India, 5 Nov 1924; *s* of Hugh Griffith Bowen and his wife Ethel May (Cook); *e* Queen Elizabeth's Grammar School, Crediton, Devon, Pembroke College, Oxford and St Anthony's College, Oxford.

Formerly a journalist and copywriter; his plays include I Love You, Mrs Patterson, 1964; After the Rain, 1966; Little Boxes, 1968; The Disorderly Women and Fall and Redemption, 1969; The Waiting Room (one-act) and The Corsican Brothers, 1970; Heil, Caesar and Robin Redbreast, 1974; Florence Nightingale, 1975; Which Way are You Facing? 1976; Singles, 1977; Bondage (one-act), Young Guy Seeks Part-time (one-act), The Inconstant Couple (translation, from Marivaux), 1978; also contributed to Mixed Doubles, 1969; has written many television plays since 1960; drama producer with Thames TV, 1978–9; novels include After the Rain, The Centre of the Green, The Birdcage and A World Elsewhere.

Address: Old Lodge Farm, Sugarswell Lane, Edgehill, nr Banbury, Oxon. *Tel:* Tysoe 401.

BOWERS, Lally (*née* Kathleen Bowers), actress
b Oldham, Lancs, 21 Jan 1917; *d* of Albert Ernest Bowers and his wife Kate (Richardson); *e* Hulme Grammar School, Oldham.

Formerly a secretary; trained for the stage with James Bernard; first engaged at the Shakespeare Memorial Theatre, Stratford-on-Avon, 1936, as an understudy, and walking-on in various productions; Manchester Repertory, 1936–8, and Sheffield, 1938–43; joined the Old Vic Company at the Playhouse, Liverpool, and during the 1943–4 season appeared as Nora in A Doll's House, Viola in Twelfth Night, Aunt Lily in Ah! Wilderness and Miss Havisham in Great Expectations; first appeared in London at the Phoenix, 7 June 1944, as Norrie in The Last of Summer; Lyric, Hammersmith, July 1946, played Baroness Aurore Dudevant (George Sand) in Summer At Nohant; appeared in repertory at Southport and Guildford 1946–7, and at the Birmingham Repertory Theatre, 1949–50; Ambassadors', Aug 1950,

played Lucinda in For Love or Money; Arts, Dec 1950, Madam Wang in Lady Precious Stream; Arts, Jan 1951, Miss Juliana Tesman in Hedda Gabler; Lyric, Hammersmith, June 1952, Maisie in The Pink Room; Arts, Oct 1953, Annie Twohig in Drama At Inish; at the Q, Mar 1955, played Mrs Laing in The Dashing White Sergeant, and Apr 1955, Mrs Gudgeon in The Breath of Fools; Royal, Birmingham, May 1955, appeared in Love and Kisses; Bristol Old Vic, Dec 1955, The Fairy in Dick Whittington; Arts, Mar 1956, the Abbess in The Comedy of Errors (musical version); Phoenix, Apr 1956, Lady Mulligan in Camino Real; Edinburgh and Berlin Festivals, Sept 1956, Mrs Gilbey in Fanny's First Play; Bristol Old Vic, Dec 1956, Fairy Snowflake in The Sleeping Beauty; Oxford Playhouse, Oct 1957, Madame de Montrachet in Dinner With the Family, subsequently appearing in the same production, New, London, Dec 1957 (won the Clarence Derwent Award, 1958, for this performance); Oxford Playhouse, July 1958, Princess Charlotte Borescu in The Honour of the Family; Westminster, Nov 1958, Mrs Lawrence in No Concern of Mine; Memorial Theatre, Stratford-on-Avon, Feb 1959, Naomi Ellis in In the Red; Bristol Old Vic, June 1959, Queen Elizabeth in No Bed For Bacon; Lyric, Hammersmith, Mar 1960, Evelyn Longtree in The Dancing Heiress; Wyndham's, June 1960, played Miss Elizabeth Cripley, Mildred Pilkington and Mrs Norton in Call It Love; Pembroke, Croydon, Nov 1960, A Clergyman's Wife in The Pleasure Garden; Lyric, Hammersmith, Dec 1961, played the White Queen in Alice Through the Looking Glass; Piccadilly, May 1962, Agatha in Castle in Sweden; Arts, July 1962, Anna in The Empire Builders; Garrick, Nov 1963, played Betty Brogan in Difference of Opinion; Duke of York's, June 1965, Mrs Mercy Croft in The Killing of Sister George, and at the Belasco, New York, Oct 1966; Haymarket, Dec 1967, Hilda Randolph in Dear Octopus; Hampstead Theatre Club, Oct 1968, appeared as the Registrar, Mrs Dart, Landlady, and Miss Fotheringill in Spitting Image, transferring to the Duke of York's, Oct 1968; Criterion, Aug 1970, played Mary in Council of Love; Mermaid, Dec 1970, Hortensia in The Watched Pot; Arnaud, Guildford, Nov 1973, Jennifer in My Son's Father; Gaiety, Dublin, Oct 1976, also Theatre Royal, Sydney, Nov, Lady Bogmore in Dead-Eyed Dicks; Alexandra, Birmingham, and Royal Alexandra, Toronto, May 1978, appeared in Picture of Innocence; films include Our Miss Fred and The Slipper and the Rose; TV includes Pygmalion, The Importance of Being Earnest and Going Straight.

Favourite parts: Candida, Lady Cicely Wayneflete in Captain Brassbound's Conversion, Mrs Millamant in The Way of the World, and Maggie Hobson in Hobson's Choice. *Recreations:* Reading, walking, and learning dialects. *Address:* c/o Larry Dalzell Associates, Ltd, 3 Goodwin's Court, St Martin's Lane, London, WC2.

BOWLES, Anthony, composer, and muscial director
b 18 Sept 1931; *s* of Herbert Bowles and his wife May (Archer); *e* Amersham GS and the Royal Academy of Music.

His first theatrical appearance was at the Royal Hippodrome, Eastbourne, in 1948, as a pit pianist for twice-nightly variety; his long career as musical director extends from Cranks, 1956 (London and Broadway), to Evita, London, 1978; has also composed the musicals Shut up and Sing, RADA, 1960; Excuse Me for Living, LAMDA, 1964; Mandrake, Criterion, 1970; Love in the Country, Guildhall School of Music, 1974; has orchestrated a number of other musicals, including Fire Angel, 1976; has worked as director on his own shows as well as at the Young Vic, Royal Exchange, Manchester, etc; musical director, LAMDA,

1963–73; taught at the Guildhall School of Music, 1972–78 (Fellow, 1974); composed incidental music for a number of plays at Nottingham, the National, Chichester, the Young Vic, etc; film music includes scores for Isadora and Leo the Last; TV work includes the musical No, No, 1969 (composer and musical director).

Recreations: Messing about in boats, food and wine, things French. *Address:* 15 Lonsdale Square, London N1.

BOWLES, Peter, actor
b London, 16 Oct 1936; *s* of Herbert Reginald Bowles and his wife Sarah Jane; *e* High Pavement GS, Nottingham; *m* Susan Alexandra Bennett; trained for the stage at RADA, 1953–55.

Made his first professional appearance at the Playhouse, Nottingham, 1953, as Young Cato and Trebonius in Julius Caesar; London debut, 12 June 1956, as Abraham in the Old Vic Company's Romeo and Juliet, in which he also made his New York debut at the Winter Garden, 24 Oct 1956; spent seasons in repertory at Oxford, Nottingham, Coventry and the Bristol Old Vic; Royal Court, Sept 1960, played Dr Copperthwaite in The Happy Haven; same theatre, Oct 1960, Kirill Glagoliev in Platonov; Phoenix, Mar 1961, First Messenger in JB; Comedy, Oct 1961, Roger in Bonne Soupe, transferring with the production to the Wyndham's, Feb 1962; New Arts, Aug 1963, Pringle in Afternoon Men; Aldwych, Feb 1964, Grand Inquisitor in The Rebel; Queen's, June 1969, Roland Oliver QC in The Stiffkey Scandals of 1932; Garrick, July 1975, Paul in Absent Friends; Arts, June 1976, Withenshaw in Dirty Linen; Royal Court, Aug 1978, Bennet in Eclipse; Theatre Royal, Haymarket, Oct 1978, Prince of Salestria in Look after Lulu; Bristol Old Vic, Aug 1979, Hedley in Born in the Gardens; Globe, Feb 1980, again played Hedley; films include Blow Up, The Charge of the Light Brigade, and A Day in the Death of Joe Egg; TV series since 1958 include *Rumpole of the Bailey*, *Pennies from Heaven*, and *To the Manor Born*.

Recreation: Modern British art. *Club:* Chelsea Arts. *Address:* c/o Leading Artists, 60 St James's Street, London SW1.

BOYLE, Billy, actor
b Dublin, Eire, 24 Feb 1945; *s* of William Boyle and his wife Kathleen (Noone); *e* O'Connell's School Dublin.

Trained for the stage at the Flanagan School, making his first appearance at the Theatre Royal, Dublin, in variety, Nov 1953; his first London appearance was at the Theatre Royal, Stratford E, Apr 1962, as Conn Geraghty in The Scatterin'; Adelphi, Sept 1964, Terry Collins in Maggie May; Drury Lane, June 1966, took over as Barnaby Tucker in Hello, Dolly!; Phoenix, Mar 1968, played the Clerk of Oxford, Absalom, and John in Canterbury Tales; Hampstead, May 1970, Matt in The Fantasticks and Jimmy in The Rainmaker, playing the same parts in Ibiza; Harrogate, Apr 1971, Christy Mahon in The Playboy of the Western World; Intimate, Johannesburg, SA, Nov 1971, Runnicles in No Sex Please, We're British; Soho Poly, Nov 1972, Lieut O'Connor in a lunchtime production of The Scheming Lieutenant; Greenwich, Dec 1972, Prince Bulbo in The Rose and the Ring; Thorndike, Leatherhead, Mar 1973, David in The Rivals, visiting Bucks County Playhouse, Pa, in the same production; Drury Lane, May 1974, Arthur Crabtree in Billy, playing the title role on several occasions on the indisposition of Michael Crawford; May Fair, May 1976, appeared in the revue What's a Nice Country Like US Doing in a State Like This?; films, since his first in 1969, include Groupie Girl, Barry Lyndon, and Side by Side; television includes Jackanory.

Recreations: Tennis, riding, football, guitar. *Club:* Green Room. *Address:* c/o International Artists Representation, Fourth Floor, 235 Regent Street, London W1R 8AX.

BOXER (Cyril) John, actor
b London, 25 Apr 1909; *s* of Arthur Michael Boxer and his wife Florence Mary (Cooke); *e* Grocers' Company School; *m* Constance Margaret Macalaster; formerly engaged in a stockbroker's office; studied for the stage at the Royal Academy of Dramatic Art (Bancroft Gold Medal).

He made his first appearance on the stage at the Savoy Theatre, 4 Nov 1928, in The Dark Path; Arts and Globe Theatres, Apr 1929, appeared as the APM in The Infinite Shoeblack; Comedy, Sept 1929, Robert Carlton and the Cattle Thief in Secrets; at the Embassy, Sept 1930–Apr 1931, played in more than twenty different productions; Playhouse, May 1931, Palmer in The Crime at Blossoms; St Martin's, Aug 1931, Claud Eccles in The Young Idea, Nov 1931, Jones in Britannia of Billingsgate, and Mar 1932, Sexton in Precious Bane; Embassy, Nov 1932, Radius in RUR; Royalty, Dec 1932, Tod Bartlett in A Cup of Happiness; Q, Feb 1933, Michael in Miss Black's Son; Little, May/June 1933, George Rous in Strife, and John Gilson in The Burgomaster of Stilemonde; Apollo, Dec 1933, the Ballet Master in Escape Me Never; St Martin's, Sept 1934, succeeded Ivan Brandt as John Williams in The Wind and the Rain; Arts, Dec 1934, Josh Blair in Glory Be . . .; first appeared on the New York stage, at the Shubert Theatre, 21 Jan 1935, as the Ballet Master in Escape Me Never; Lyric, Hammersmith, Sept–Nov 1935, Lorenzo in The Merchant of Venice, and Seyton and the Sergeant in Macbeth; Q, Apr and Duke of York's, June 1936, Seaton in Miss Smith; His Majesty's, Dec 1936, Abner in The Boy David; Strand (for Repertory Players), Jan 1937, and Wyndham's, Feb 1937, Claude in George and Margaret, which ran for two years; during this period appeared in a number of productions for the Repertory Players; at Richmond, May, and Saville, June 1939, played Ernst von Allmen in Juggernaut; Piccadilly, Nov 1939, again played Claude in George and Margaret; Streatham Hill, July 1940, Macfarlane in Women Aren't Angles; Torch, Sept 1948, appeared as Jan Spring in Ten Shilling Doll; Arts, Apr 1949, Mr Hardcastle in She Stoops to Conquer; Arts, Aug 1950, played Leicester Paton in Home and Beauty, and again appeared in this part at the St Martin's, Sept 1950; Strand (for Repertory Players), Sept 1950, David Warren in I Married Two Men; toured South Africa, 1951, as Petty Officer Herbert in Seagulls Over Sorrento; Arts, Feb 1952, played Freddie Allerton in a revival of To See Ourselves; Apollo, June 1952, took over the part of Petty Officer Herbert in Seagulls Over Sorrento; Globe, Mar, played PC Phillips in The White Carnation; in the Autumn of 1953, toured as Dan Archer in The Archers; during 1954, was engaged solely in films, television, and sound radio; Q, Jan 1955, played Sir Gregory Ramsden in The Evidence I Shall Give; Q, Apr 1955, played Sir William Garrick in Lucky Strike, and at the Apollo, Sept 1955, appeared in the same part; Theatre Royal, Windsor, Sept 1956, played Alderman Hardacre in Mr Kettle and Mrs Moon; at the Lyric (for the Repertory Players'), Sept 1957, and subsequently at the Westminster, Apr 1958, played Malcolm Turnbull in Any Other Business?; New Shakespeare Theatre, Liverpool, Oct 1958, Captain Cecil Lewis in The Iceman Cometh; Memorial Theatre, Stratford-on-Avon, Feb 1959, George Thorne in In the Red; Mermaid, Dec 1959, Captain Smollett in Treasure Island; Lyric, Hammersmith, Sept 1960, played Gollup in Mister Johnson; Hampstead Theatre Club, Oct 1966, Gordon Gray in In the Matter of J Robert Oppenheimer, and at the Fortune, Dec

1966; Arts, June 1968, Poulder in The Foundations; Theatre Royal, Brighton, 1974, Col Edmunds in The French Mistress; Haymarket, Mar 1975, Lord Justice Brayle in The Case in Question; joined BBC Drama Repertory Co, June 1963; entered films, 1935, and has since appeared in innumerable pictures and on television.

Recreations: Swimming, do-it-yourself and reading. *Address:* Representation Joyce Edwards, 8 Theed Street, London, SE11.

BRACKEN, Eddie, actor and director
b Astoria, New York, 7 Feb 1920; *s* of Joseph L Bracken and his wife Catherine; *e* the Professional School for Actors; *m* Connie Nickerson.

First appeared on the stage at age six in Astoria for the Knights of Columbus as the Purser in The Good Ship Leviathan; made his professional début at the Plymouth, 9 Sept 1931, as a Western Union Boy in The Man on Stilts; Bijou, Mar 1933, Hank Parkes in The Lady Refuses; American Music Hall, Mar 1934, a Boy in The Drunkard; Broadhurst, Sept 1935, Alfred in Life's Too Short; 46th Street, Sept 1936, Cadet Brown in So Proudly We Hail; Longacre, Oct 1936, a Plumber in Iron Men; Biltmore, June 1937, succeeded Frank Albertson as Billy Randolph in Brother Rat; Biltmore, Apr 1938, Hal in What a Life; toured as Henry Aldrich in What a Life and directed a summer stock production, 1939; Imperial, Oct 1939, Jo Jo Jordan in Too Many Girls; went to Hollywood to make films; during World War II toured service camps and hospitals in the South Pacific and USA; toured, 1953–4, as Richard Sherman in The Seven Year Itch, and played this part at the Fulton, NY, May 1955; Apr 1956, took over from Burgess Meredith as Sakini in the touring production of The Teahouse of the August Moon; toured as Richard Sherman in The Seven Year Itch, as Charlie Reader in The Tender Trap, and as George MacCauley in Will Success Spoil Rock Hunter? 1956; Broadway, Apr 1957, Archy in Shinbone Alley; Drury Lane, Sept 1957, Erwin Trowbridge in Three Men on a Horse; Music Theatre, Columbus, Ohio, June 1958, Charles Wykeham in Where's Charley?; Grist Mill Playhouse, Andover, New Jersey, July 1958, Kreton in Visit to a Small Planet; toured as Augie Poole in The Tunnel of Love, Aug–Dec 1958; toured in The Seven Year Itch and as Jack Jordan in Say Darling, 1959; Martin Beck, Feb 1960, co-produced and played Pistol in Beg, Borrow or Steal; 1960, toured as Fergie Howard in The Golden Fleecing, Leprechaun in Finian's Rainbow, and Ensign Pulver in Mr Roberts; Brooks Atkinson, Feb 1961, directed How to Make a Man; toured in The Teahouse of the August Moon and The Tender Trap, 1962; Shubert, Boston, Sept 1965, Howard Bevans in Hot September; Plymouth, 1966, took over as Felix Ungar in The Odd Couple; toured, 1967–8, as Richard Pawling, George, and Chuck in You Know I Can't Hear You When the Water's Running; toured, summer 1972, in The Girl in the Freudian Slip; Country Dinner Playhouse, Dallas, Texas, summer 1973, played Harry Lambert in Never Too Late; toured 1974 in Born Yesterday; in 1975 took over from Robert Alda in the tour of The Sunshine Boys; Country Dinner Playhouse, Dallas, Texas, Dec 1975, played in Hot Line to Heaven; toured, 1977–80, as Horace Vandergelder in Hello Dolly!, including engagements at the Lunt-Fontanne, NY, Mar 1978, Theatre Royal, Drury Lane, Sept 1979, and Shaftesbury, Feb 1980; entered films in the 1920's in the Our Gang series, as the Rich Boy, and subsequently appeared in the Kiddie Trouper series, also in the 1920's; returned to Hollywood for Too Many Girls, 1940, Life with Henry, 1941, The Miracle of Morgan's Creek, 1944, Hail, the Conquering Hero, 1944,

Summer Stock, 1950, A Slight Case of Larceny, 1953, Shinbone Alley, 1971, etc; was a radio gag writer for Bob Hope, 1934–6, and played Dizzy in the series *Henry Aldrich,* later appearing on his own programs in Hollywood and Bay Shore, Long Island (1963–5); first appeared on television in 1956 in Front Row Center, and since has appeared frequently on various dramatic programs and variety shows, including: Archy and Mehitabel; wrote a syndicated column for The Sunrise Press, 1963, called Crackin' with Bracken; co-owner of the Staircase Theatre, NY, 1970.

Address: Actors Equity Association, c/o Hartig-Josephson Agency, 527 Madison Avenue, New York, NY 10022.

BRADY, Terence, actor and dramatic author
b London, 13 Mar 1939; *s* of Frederick Arthur Noel Brady and his wife Elizabeth Mary (Moore); *e* Merchant Taylors' (Sandy Lodge) and Trinity College, Dublin; *m* Hon Charlotte Bingham.

He made his first stage appearance Nov 1957, Players', Dublin, as Fishkin in Jim Dandy; Theatre Royal, Stratford, E, Apr 1961, played Pat Frame and Patrick Mudley in Glory Be!; same theatre, Jan 1962, appeared in the revue Would Anyone Who Saw the Accident, which he also co-wrote; later in 1962 took over from Peter Cook in the revue Beyond the Fringe, at the Fortune, remaining with the production until 1964; Eblana, Dublin (Festival), Oct 1966, played Tel and other parts in A Quick One 'Ere . . ., which he also co-wrote; May Fair, May 1967, appeared in the revue In the Picture; Swan, Worcester, Nov 1967, Graham Slater in A Present from the Corporation, transferring to the Fortune in the same month; first film, Baby Love, 1968; television since 1961, includes numerous appearances in series; is a frequent broadcaster; apart from the revues mentioned above he also co-wrote Three to One On (tour, 1968); has written numerous television scripts with his wife, including the series *One of the Family, Yes, Honestly* and *Thomas and Sarah;* has also written novels and works for radio.

Favourite parts: Morgenhall in The Dock Brief; Bamforth in The Long and the Short and the Tall. *Recreations:* Oil painting, wild life conservation, music, horse-riding. *Address:* c/o A D Peters & Co, 10 Buckingham Street, London, WC1.

BRAHMS, Caryl, dramatic author and critic.
She is the author, with Ned Sherrin, of stage shows including No Bed for Bacon, 1959; Cindy-Ella, or I Gotta Shoe, 1962; The Spoils, 1968; Nicholas Nickleby, 1969; Sing A Rude Song, 1970; Fish Out of Water (adapted), 1971; Liberty Ranch, 1972; Nickleby and Me, 1975; Beecham, 1980; her television writing includes The Great Inimitable Mr Dickens (with Ned Sherrin); has published several works of ballet criticism and a number of novels, most of the latter with S J Simon; several of these have been filmed. *Address:* 3 Cambridge Gate, Regent's Park, London, NW1. *Tel:* 01–935 6439.

BRAMBELL, Wilfrid, actor
b Dublin, 22 Mar 1912; *s* of Henry Lytton Brambell and his wife Edith (Marks); *e* Kingstown Grammar School; originally a journalist; trained for the stage by his parents and at the Abbey Theatre, Dublin.

He made his first stage appearance as a child, entertaining the first wounded of the war in Nov 1914; his early experience was in the Irish theatre; subsequently in repertory at Swansea, Bristol (Old Vic), Bromley and Chesterfield; London appearances include small parts in The Shadow of the Glen and Riders to the Sea, Watergate, July 1950; Dominick

Mapother in Blind Man's Buff, St Martin's, Oct 1953; Lewis in Do Not Pass Go, Hampstead, June 1966; Bernard Laroque in The Deadly Game, Savoy, Apr 1967; Steward, Carpenter and January in Canterbury Tales, Phoenix, Mar 1968; toured, Dec 1970, as Scrooge in A Christmas Carol; in repertory at Leicester Phoenix, 1971; Crucible, Sheffield, 1972; London Casino, Dec 1974, Badger in Cinderella; Old Vic, Nov 1976, appeared in The Ghost Train; he is perhaps best known for his television and radio work in Steptoe and Son published his autobiography All Above Board, 1976.

Address: c/o Crouch Associates, 59 Frith Street, London W1.

BRENTON, Howard, dramatic author
b Portsmouth, Hants, 13 Dec 1942; *s* of Donald Henry Brenton and his wife Rose Lilian (Lewis); *e* Chichester HS and St Catherine's College, Cambridge; *m* Jane Margaret Brenton.

While at Cambridge wrote a play, Ladder of Fools, 1965; his one-act play, It's My Criminal, was performed at the Royal Court, London, 1966; joined Portable Theatre, 1969, for whom he wrote Christie in Love, 1969, Fruit, 1970; is also the author of Winter, Daddykins, 1966; Revenge (Royal Court Theatre Upstairs), Heads, Gum & Goo, The Education of Skinny Spew (triple bill), 1969; Wesley, 1970; Scott of the Antarctic, A Sky-blue Life, 1971; Hitler Dances, How Beautiful With Badges, Measure For Measure (adaptation), 1972; Brassneck (with David Hare); Mug, Magnificence, 1973; The Churchill Play, 1974; Weapons Of Happiness (National Theatre), 1976; Epsom Downs (for Joint Stock), 1977; Sore Throats (for RSC), 1979; collaborated in the multi-author Lay By, 1971, England's Ireland, 1972;, and Deeds, 1978; wrote the film Skinflicker, 1973; TV plays include: Lushly (1972), The Saliva Milkshake (1975) and The Paradise Run (1976); *Evening Standard* Best Play of the Year Award for Weapons of Happiness, 1976.

Recreation: Painting. *Address:* c/o Margaret Ramsay Ltd, 14a, Goodwin's Court, St Martin's Lane, London WC2. *Tel:* 01–240 0961.

BRETT, Jeremy (*né* Huggins), actor
b Berkswell, near Coventry, 3 Nov 1935; *s* of Colonel H W Huggins, DSO, MC, DL, and his wife Elizabeth Edith Cadbury (Butler); *e* Eton College; *m* Anna Massey (mar dis); studied for the stage at the Central School of Speech and Drama.

He began his career at the Library Theatre, Manchester, in 1954; made his first London appearance at the Old Vic, Apr 1956, as Patroclus in Troilus and Cressida, subsequently appearing as Malcolm in Macbeth, Paris in Romeo and Juliet, and the Duke of Aumerle in Richard II; made his first appearance in New York with the same company, at the Winter Garden, Oct 1956, as the Duke of Aumerle in Richard II, and again playing Paris, Malcolm, and subsequently Troilus in the modern-dress production of Troilus and Cressida; toured the US and Canada with the same productions, until Mar 1957; at the Aldwych, London, Aug 1957, played Roderick in Meet Me By Moonlight; Globe, May 1958, played Ron in Variations on a Theme; Piccadilly, Apr 1959, William MacFly in Mr Fox of Venice; Savoy, May 1959, Archie Forsyth in the musical Marigold; Saville, Oct 1959, Sebastian in The Edwardians; Princes, Apr 1960, the Rev Richard Highfield in Johnny the Priest; at the Strand, June 1961, played the title part in Hamlet; Royal Court, Aug 1961, played Peter in The Kitchen; at the Chichester Festival, June 1963, played Dunois in Saint Joan, and July 1963, Maurice Sweetman in The Workhouse Donkey; Brooks

Atkinson, NY, Feb 1964, played Father Riccardo Fontana in The Deputy; on returning to England, at the Birmingham Repertory, Feb 1965, Gilbert in A Measure of Cruelty; Cambridge, London, Sept 1965, Beliaev in A Month in the Country; Adeline Genee, East Grinstead, Feb 1967, Ronnie in Any Just Cause; joined the National Theatre Company, Old Vic, in the 1967 season, appearing as Orlando in As You Like It (Oct), Valère in Tartuffe (Nov), and has since played the following parts: Kent in Edward the Second, Berowne in Love's Labour's Lost, 1968; Che Guevara in Macrune's Guevara (also at the Jeannetta Cochrane), 1969; Bassanio in The Merchant of Venice and, at the Cambridge, George Tesman in Hedda Gabler, 1970; played the Son in A Voyage Round My Father, Haymarket, Aug 1971; Thorndike, Leatherhead, Sept 1972, Gaston in Traveller Without Luggage; Greenwich, May 1973, John Rosmer in Rosmersholm; Phoenix, Nov 1973, Otto in Design For Living; Stratford, Ontario, June 1976, Mirabell in The Way of the World; and Theseus/Oberon in A Midsummer Night's Dream; Arnaud, Guildford, Dec 1976, played Robert Browning in Robert and Elizabeth, Ahmanson, Los Angeles, 1978, title rôle in Dracula; since 1955, he has appeared in the following films: War and Peace, and My Fair Lady; first appeared on television in 1954, and principal performances include: Dorian Gray in The Picture of Dorian Gray, Jacques in Dinner With the Family, Danilo in The Merry Widow and Joseph Surface in School For Scandal.

Favourite parts: Hamlet, and Peter in The Kitchen. *Recreations:* Archery and riding. *Address:* c/o William Morris Agency (UK) Ltd, 147 Wardour Street, London W1V 3TB. *Tel:* 734 9361.

BREUER, Lee, writer, and director
b Philadelphia, 6 Feb 1937; *s* of Joseph B Breuer and his wife Sara (Leopold); *e* UCLA (BA 1958); *m* the actress/director Ruth Maleczech.

Directed for the San Francisco Actors' Workshop and for his own experimental company, 1963–65; in Europe 1965–70, he studied the work of the Berliner Ensemble and Grotowski, and directed Mother Courage, Paris; The Messingkauf Dialogues, Edinburgh Festival, 1968; Play, Paris, 1969; brought the company of Play to New York, 1970, as Mabou Mines, and was their artistic director until the group adopted a collaborative directorship in 1976; writer and director of the group's three Animations: Red Horse, 1970 revised 1972; B Beaver, 1974; Shaggy Dog, 1978; also directed them in Mabou Mines Performs Samuel Beckett, 1975, including his own adaptation of The Lost Ones; A Prelude to Death in Venice, 1980; for the American Dance Festival, summer 1976, choreographed and directed The Saint and the Football Players; for New York Shakespeare Festival, 1980, directed The Screens; has taught and lectured at NYU, Yale Drama School, most of the campuses of the University of California, and in many other colleges and art centres; has published poetry and criticism as well as the scripts of his Animations; artistic director of Re.Cher.Chez., a studio for the experimental performing arts.

Address: 92 St Marks Place, New York, NY 10009. *Tel:* 989 4953.

BRICUSSE, Leslie, composer, and lyricist
b 1931; *e* Cambridge U; *m* the actress Yvonne Romain.

Wrote and directed the 1954 Footlights Revue, Out of the Blue, which transferred to the Phoenix, London, July 7; Globe, Nov 1954, appeared in An Evening with Beatrice Lillie; co-wrote words and music for Lady at the Wheel, 1958; with Anthony Newley wrote book, music and lyrics for

Stop the World, I Want to Get Off, 1961, New York 1962; wrote lyrics for Pickwick, 1963, NY 1965; again with Anthony Newley wrote book, music and lyrics for The Roar of the Greasepaint – The Smell of the Crowd, NY 1965, and The Good Old Bad Old Days, London 1973; wrote book, music and lyrics for Kings and Clowns, co-wrote (with Newley) The Travelling Music Show, wrote lyrics for Over the Rainbow, all London, 1978; his film work includes screenplay and score for Charley Moon, 1956, and scores for Doctor Doolittle, Goodbye Mr Chips, Scrooge, etc; for television, with Anthony Newley, wrote a musical adaptation of Peter Pan, 1975.

Address: c/o Broadcast Music Inc, 320 West 57th Street, New York, NY 10019.

BRIDGE, Peter, producer
b Wimbledon, 5 May 1925; s of Stephen Henry Howard Bridge and his wife Ella Mary (Twine); e Tyttenhanger Lodge, Seaford, and Bryanston School, Dorset; m Roslyn Mary Foster.

He first entered management in 1948, when he presented a tour of Set To Partners, which was subsequently produced at the Embassy, London, Sept 1949, under the new title of Rain Before Seven; co-produced Party Manners, 1950; appointed Assistant Manager at the Arts Theatre Club, 1951; appointed Manager at the Winter Garden, 1952; Executive with Messrs Keith Prowse, and Theatre Tickets and Messengers, 1953–5; Manager of Sport for Associated-Rediffusion, 1955–7; returned to management at the Lyric, Hammersmith, Nov 1957, when he produced The Queen and the Welshman; he has since produced or co-produced the following: Any Other Business, 1958; Caught Napping, 1959; Inherit the Wind, 1960; The Landing Place (Repertory Players'), On the Brighter Side, Finian's Rainbow, Guilty Party, 1961; The Lizard on the Rock, Period of Adjustment, Breaking Point, Calculated Risk (New York), 1962; Stephen D, Six of One, Difference of Opinion, 1963; Spoon River, Past Imperfect, Mr Whatnot, Chaganog, Let's Make An Opera, 1964; Happy End, The Chaganog Revue, Too True to be Good (also Edinburgh Festival), An Ideal Husband, Say Who You Are, 1965; The Rose and the Ring, Julius Caesar Jones, Ad-Lib, Come Spy with Me, Strike a Light, Wait Until Dark, Help Stamp Out Marriage (USA), On Approval, 1966; The Promise, Volpone, The Diary of a Madman, Happy Family, Relatively Speaking, Getting Married, The Man in the Glass Booth, Black New World, The Others, A Midsummer Night's Dream, The Promise (NY), Number 10, Dear Octopus, Stephen D (NY), 1967; Justice, Hay Fever (also in Toronto), Zigger Zagger, The Man in the Glass Booth (NY), 1968; The Boys in the Band, Just a Show, The Night I Chased the Women with an Eel, As Dorothy Parker Once Said, Children's Day, Zoo Zoo Widdershins Zoo (Edinburgh Festival), On the Rocks, Birds on the Wing, 1969; How the Other Half Loves, When We Are Married, 1970; How The Other Half Loves (NY), 1971.

Recreations: Tennis, golf, collecting records and magazines. *Clubs:* Garrick, Arts (Life Member), Wig and Pen. *Address:* 15 Claremont Road, London N6. *Tel:* 348 8676.

BRIEN, Alan, dramatic critic
b Sunderland, Co Durham, 12 Mar 1925; s of Ernest Brien and his wife Isabella (Patterson); e Bede Grammar School, Sunderland, and Jesus College, Oxford; m (1) Pamela Jones; (2) Nancy Newbold Ryan; (3) Jill Tweedie.

He served as an air-gunner with the Royal Air Force, 1944–7; film critic of Truth, 1954–5; television critic, The Observer, 1955–6; film critic, Evening Standard, 1955–7; drama critic, The Spectator, 1958–61; drama critic of The

Sunday Telegraph, 1961–8; weekly essayist, New Statesman, 1967–72; diarist, Sunday Times, 1968–76; film critic, 1976–; regular contributor to Punch.

Recreations: Walking, talking, eating, sleeping, and writing autobiography. *Clubs:* Jack's, Garrick. *Address:* 14 Falkland Road, London NW5. *Tel:* 01–485 9074.

BRIERLEY, David, General Manager, Royal Shakespeare Company
b Marple, Cheshire, 26 July 1936; s of Ernest William Brierley and his wife Jessie (Stanway); e Stockport GS and Clare, Cambridge; m Ann Fosbrooke Potter.

At Cambridge handled business for a number of university societies, including the ADC, of which he was President 1958; joined the Royal Shakespeare at Stratford as an ASM, 1961; Stage Manager, 1962; General Stage Manager, Aldwych Theatre, 1963–5; Administrative Assistant to Peter Hall, 1965–8; General Manager, RSC, 1968–; is a trustee of the ADC, Cambridge, Governor of South Warwickshire College of Further Education, Director of West End Theatre Managers Ltd; member, Executive Committee, Society of West End Theatre.

Recreation: Reading. *Address:* c/o Royal Shakespeare Theatre, Stratford-upon-Avon. *Tel:* Stratford 3693.

BRIERS, Richard, actor
b Croydon, Surrey, 14 Jan 1934; s of Joseph Benjamin Briers and his wife Morna Phyllis (Richardson); e Wimbledon, and privately; m Ann Davies.

Formerly a clerk; trained for the stage at the Royal Academy of Dramatic Art, where he won the Silver Medal, and also a scholarship to the Liverpool Playhouse Repertory Company, where he appeared, 1956–7; toured Oct 1957, as Blisworth in Something About a Sailor; appeared in repertory at Leatherhead, and the Belgrade, Coventry, Jan–Oct 1958; toured, Nov 1958, as Joseph Field in Gilt and Gingerbread, subsequently making his first London appearance at the Duke of York's, Apr 1959, in the same part and play; St Martin's, Feb 1960, played Bill in Special Providence (in the double-bill Double Yoke); Duke of York's, May 1960, played Christian Martin in It's in the Bag; Arts, June 1960, played Bartholomeus II in The Shepherd's Chameleon, and Detective in Victims of Duty (double-bill); at the same theatre, Jan 1961, played James Whinby in The Form, and The Tramp in A Slight Ache, in the triple bill Three, subsequently appearing in the same production at the Criterion, Feb 1961; Criterion, Sept 1962, played David Madison in Miss Pell is Missing; Edinburgh Festival, Lyceum, Aug 1964, played Lieut William Hargreaves in Hamp; toured, Nov 1964, as Gerald Popkiss in Rookery Nook; Queen's, Apr 1965, played Roland Maule in Present Laughter; Vaudeville, Feb 1966, Mortimer Brewster in Arsenic and Old Lace, Duke of York's, Mar 1967, Greg in Relatively Speaking; St Martin's, Jan 1968, played William Falder in Justice; Criterion, June 1968, Moon in The Real Inspector Hound; Prince of Wales, Apr 1969, Bois d'Enghien in Cat Among the Pigeons; Garrick, July 1970, played five parts in The Two Of Us; Criterion, Feb 1972, took over the title part in Butley; toured, Autumn 1972, as Richard in Richard III; Criterion, July 1973, played Sidney Hopcroft in Absurd Person Singular; Garrick, July 1975, Colin in Absent Friends; Lyric, Oct 1979, Colin in Middle-Age-Spread; films in which he has appeared include A Matter of Who, Fathom and All the Way Up; first appeared on television, Apr 1956, and numerous performances include: Brothers in Law (TV and radio series), Marriage Lines (also radio), The Good Life and The Other One.

Favourite parts: Butley, Sidney Hopcroft. *Recreations:* Reading, gardening, cinema and theatre going. *Address:* International Creative Management Ltd, 22 Grafton Street, London, W1X 3LD. *Tel:* 01–629 8080.

BRIGHTON, Pam, director
b Yorkshire, 22 Oct 1946; *d* of Norman Brighton and his wife Marjorie; *e* London School of Economics (BSc [Econ], 1967); *m* Guy Sprung (mar dis).

Trainee director at the Royal Court theatre, where her first production was The Sport of My Mad Mother, May 1970; has since worked with the Young Vic, Hampstead and Half Moon in London; her production of Ashes at the Open Space, Jan 1974, won the Beaumont award; moved to Canada 1976, where she has directed in Montreal, Regina, Toronto, and Stratford, Ont, where she directed Barren/Yerma, season 1979; has directed for TV in Canada with CBC and BBC and appeared in BBC/TV's *Days of Hope*, 1975.

Address: 7 The Aberdeens, 100 Bain Avenue, Toronto M4K 1E8, Canada. *Tel:* 465 7673.

BRISBANE, Katharine, critic and publisher
b Singapore, 7 Jan 1932; *d* of David William Brisbane and his wife Myra Gladys; *e* Presbyterian Ladies College, Perth, and the University of Western Australia (BA); *m* Philip Edward Parsons, senior lecturer, School of Drama, University of New South Wales.

Theatre critic, *The West Australian*, 1959–61, 1962–65; national critic, *The Australian*, 1967–74; in 1971, with her husband, established The Currency Press, Australia's major dramatic publishing company; reviews Sydney productions for *The Australian* and for *Theatre Australia*; her publications include contributions on Australian drama and dramatists to The Literature of Australia (1976), World Drama (ed Nicoll, 1977), Contemporary Dramatists (1977) and New Currents in Australian Writing (1978), as well as critical and historical introductions to many Currency publications.

Address: Currency Press Pty Ltd, 87 Jersey Road, Woollahra, NSW 2025, Australia. *Tel:* Sydney 32 4481.

BRISSON, Frederick, producer
b Copenhagen, Denmark, 17 Mar 1913; *s* of Carl Brisson, the distinguished stage and film actor, and his wife Cleo; *e* Rossall College, England; *m* Rosalind Russell (dec).

Formerly an actor's agent with offices in London, Paris, and Hollywood; first stage production was at the Savoy, London, Dec 1930, when he co-produced Wonder Bar; at the Hippodrome, London, Sept 1932, co-produced The Merry Widow; Adelphi, London, Oct 1937, co-produced Transatlantic Rhythm; came to America and engaged in artists' representation and film production; first Broadway production was at the St James, May 1954, when he co-produced The Pajama Game; has since produced or co-produced Damn Yankees, 1955; New Girl in Town, 1957; The Pleasure of His Company, The Gazebo, 1958; Five Finger Exercise, 1959; Under the Yum-Yum Tree, 1960; The Caretaker, First Love, 1961; The Time of the Barracudas, 1963; Alfie, 1964; Generation, 1965; The Flip Side, 1968; Coco, 1969; Twigs, 1971; Jumpers, 1974; So Long, 174th Street, 1976; entered film production in England in 1937 with Two Hearts in Three-Quarters Time, and subsequently co-produced Prince of Arcadia and, 1938, produced Moonlight Sonata; entered Hollywood Film production in 1948 when he founded Independent Artists Pictures and produced The Velvet Touch; has subsequently produced Never Wave at a Wac, The Pajama Game, Damn Yankees, Five Finger Exercise, Under

the Yum-Yum Tree, Generation, Mrs Pollifax—Spy, etc; served in the Air Force as Lieutenant-Colonel during World War II and was awarded the US Legion of Merit and the King Christian X Medal of Denmark.

Recreations: Tennis, swimming, boating, golf, still photography. *Address:* 745 Fifth Avenue, New York, NY. *Tel:* PL 2–2220.

BRISTOW, Charles, lighting designer
b Liverpool, 7 Feb 1928; *s* of Charles Bristow and his wife Lily Mary (Bianchi); *e* Rathbone School and Enfield Technical Institute, Liverpool; *m* Angela Noakes.

Trained as a theatre electrician at the Royal Court, Liverpool, under his father; appointed chief electrician and lighting designer, Sadler's Wells, 1954, a post he held for twelve years; has designed lighting for over 500 productions of ballet, opera and plays in Britain, Europe and N America; has lectured extensively on theatre lighting; founder member, Society of British Theatre Designers; lighting consultant to the London Coliseum; Theatre Royal, Glasgow (Scottish Opera); Paris Lido (also designer); consultant designer to Madame Tussauds, London and Amsterdam.

Recreation: Photography. *Address:* 9 Talbot Road, London N6. *Tel:* 01–348 9855.

BRITTON, Tony, actor
b Birmingham, 9 June 1924; *s* of Edward Leslie Britton and his wife Doris Marguerite (Jones); *e* Edgbaston Collegiate School, Birmingham, and Thornbury Grammar School, Glos; *m* (1) Ruth Hawkins (mar dis); (2) Eva Birkefeldt.

He made his first professional appearance at the Knightstone Pavilion, Weston-Super-Mare, Oct 1942, in Quiet Weekend; after war service, followed by a period in rep, including Manchester, made his first London appearance at the Winter Garden, Jan 1952, as Ramases in The Firstborn; at the same theatre, Mar 1962, played Vizard in The Constant Couple; Edinburgh Festival, 1952, and tour, appeared in The Player King; appeared at the Memorial Theatre, Stratford-on-Avon, seasons 1953–4, where his parts included Bassanion in The Merchant of Venice, Lysander in A Midsummer Night's Dream, Mercutio in Romeo and Juliet, Thersites in Troilus and Cressida and Cassio in Othello; New, Jan 1955, played Julian Lovell in The Night of the Ball; same theatre, May 1956, Gaston Lachaille in Gigi; at the Old Vic, season 1960–1, played Trigorin in The Seagull and Henry Percy in Henry IV, Part I; St Martin's, Oct 1962, George Appleby in Kill Two Birds; toured, 1964–6, as Higgins in My Fair Lady; Lyric, Mar 1967, Julian in Cactus Flower; Vaudeville, Nov 1967, Lord Illingworth in A Woman of No Importance; Duchess, Sept 1968, Roger Lawrence in A Boston Story; Vaudeville, June 1970, Mr Paradine Fouldes in Lady Frederick, transferring with the production to the Duke of York's, Sept 1970; Vaudeville, Mar 1971, Philip Markham in Move Over Mrs Markham; Drury Lane, May 1973, Jimmy Smith in No, No, Nanette; Wyndham's, Oct 1974, Col Rudolph von Schmettau in The Dame of Sark; Globe, Mar 1976, David Pulman in The Chairman; Garrick, July 1977, Rev A K Bulstrode in The Bells of Hell; Comedy, Feb 1978, Palmer Forrester in Murder Among Friends; Haymarket, Leicester, Oct 1978, and national tour, 1979; Professor Higgins in My Fair Lady, subsequently at the Adelphi, Nov 1979; films, since his first in 1956, include Sunday, Bloody Sunday, There's A Girl In My Soup and The Day of the Jackal; numerous television appearances, since 1952, include The Dame of Sark and the series The Nearly Man and Robin's Nest.

Favourite parts: Col von Schmettau, Professor Higgins. *Recreations:* Golf, cricket, gardening, photography, wine. *Clubs:* Garrick, Surrey CCC, MCC, Lord's Taverners, Stage Golfing. *Address:* c/o International Creative Management Ltd, 22 Grafton Street, London, W1X 3LD. *Tel:* 01–629 8080.

BROAD, Jay, director and playwright
b Newcastle, Pa, 5 Aug 1930; *s* of Henry Broad and his wife Celia; *e* Westminster College, Penn State University.

Director of Theatre Atlanta, 1965–70; director, PAF Playhouse, Huntington Station, NY, 1975–80, where he initiated a policy of staging only new or unproduced plays; his own plays include Red, White and Maddox (written and directed with Don Tucker), Theatre Atlanta, 1968 and Cort, NY, 1969; The Great Big Coca-Cola Swamp in the Sky, 1971; Conflict of Interest, 1972; the Killdeer (Public, NY), 1974; To Kill a Mockingbird (adaptation), 1975; White Pelicans, 1976; Events from the Life of Ted Snyder (revision of The Killdeer), 1977; as well as the premieres of his own work he has directed numerous plays, including Are You Now or Have You Ever Been?, NY, 1973; visiting lecturer, 1978, Yale School of Drama.
Address: 100 Riverside Drive, New York, NY 10024.

BROCKETT, Oscar G, educator and arts administrator
b Hartsville, Tenn, 18 Mar 1923; *s* of Oscar Hill Brockett and his wife Minnie (Dee); *e* Peabody College (BA 1947), Stanford University (MA 1949, PhD 1952); *m* Lenyth Spenker (dec).

Assistant professor of drama, Stetson University, 1952–56; University of Iowa, 1956–63; professor and later distinguished professor of drama, Indiana U, 1963–78; Ashbel Smith professor of drama and dean, College of Fine Arts, U of Texas, 1978–present; has held visiting professorships at U of Southern California, U of Illinois and Bristol U; posts held include that of President, American Theatre Association, 1976; writings include History of the Theatre, 1968 revised 1977; Perspectives on Contemporary Theatre, 1971; Century of Innovation: a history of European and American theatre since 1870 (with Robert Findlay), 1973; The Essential Theatre, 1976 revised 1979.
Address: 6124 Wagon Bend Trail, Austin, TX 78744. *Tel:* 512-447 8780.

BRODZIAK, Kenn, OBE, producing manager
b Sydney, NSW, 31 May 1913; *s* of Leopold Stanley Brodziak and his wife Violet (Alexander); *e* Sydney Boys' HS; formerly an articled law clerk.

Assistant producer Tivoli Theatres, 1945–46; managing director Aztec Services Pty Ltd, 1946–79; managing director J C Williamson Productions Ltd, 1976–80; chairman 1976– ; has produced or co-produced over 150 concert and stage attractions in Australia and New Zealand, including Rusty Bugles, The White Sheep of the Family, Mourning Becomes Electra, Dark of the Moon, Bonaventure, Black Chiffon, To Dorothy A Son, The Little Foxes, See How They Run, 1947–58; Larger Than Life, People in Love, 1959; The Black and White Minstrel Show, 1962–68; Stop the World I Want to Get Off, 1964; The Windmill Revue, Instant Marriage, 1965; Robert and Elizabeth, 1966; There's a Girl in My Soup, 1967; Black Comedy, The Boys in the Band, 1968; Canterbury Tales, Hair, Not Now Darling, 1969; Forty Carats, Wise Child, 1970; Who Killed Santa Claus?, Charlie Girl, Godspell, 1971; No No Nanette, The Mating Season, 1972; Two Gentlemen of Verona, 1973; Pippin, 1974; The Magic Show, Why Not Stay for Breakfast, 1975; More Canterbury Tales, 1976;

A Chorus Line, Funny Peculiar, Boeing-Boeing, Big Boys, 1977; Othello, The Apple Cart (both Chichester Festival company), Dracula, The Human Voice, The Bear, Annie, 1978; Deathtrap, The Two Ronnies, 1979; Up in One, Find the Lady, Shut Your Eyes and Think of England, 1980; individual performers he has presented include Dave Brubeck, Cliff Richard, The Beatles, Bob Dylan, Rod McKuen and Bette Davis; is the author of a number of plays, including Desire Brings Welcome, Positions Vacant, and Completely Incomplete; awarded the OBE, 1978, for services to the theatre.
Recreations: Horse-racing, swimming, gourmet cooking. *Club:* Friars, NY. *Address:* 80 Collins Street (Level 5), Melbourne, Victoria, Australia. *Tel:* 03-654 3311.

BRON, Eleanor, actress
b Stanmore, Middlesex; *d* of Sydney Bron and his wife Fagah (Green); *e* North London Collegiate School and Newnham, Cambridge.

After appearing with various university groups including the Footlights, made her professional début in revue at the Establishment club, London, Jan 1962; went to the US with the Establishment company, 1963; Making her New York début there in revue; first West End appearance, Comedy, June 1966, as Jennifer Dubedat in The Doctor's Dilemma; Bristol Old Vic, 1967, played Jean Brodie in The Prime of Miss Jean Brodie; subsequent parts played at Bristol include the title role in Major Barbara, 1969; Hilda Wangel in The Master Builder, Sheila in A Day in the Death of Joe Egg, and Mme Dubonnet in The Boy Friend; at the Connaught, Worthing, played the title role in Hedda Gabler and Peggen Mike in The Playboy of the Western World; toured, Apr 1971, as Ellen in Luv; Greenwich, Sept 1971, Rose in The Sandboy; Arnaud, Guildford, Sept 1972, Joanna in Who's Who; Bristol, June 1973, and Queen's, July, Countess of Chell in The Card; toured, summer 1974, as Gittel in Two for the Seesaw; Arnaud, Guildford, Oct 1975, Portia in The Merchant of Venice; Greenwich, May 1976, Mrs Faber in The Prince of Darkness; Playhouse, Nottingham, July 1976, Amanda in Private Lives; with the Royal Exchange Company, Manchester, 1977–8, played Elena in Uncle Vanya, Monica in Private Lives, and Margaret Barrett in A Family; Riverside Studios, Jan 1978, Charlotta in The Cherry Orchard; Theatre Royal, Haymarket, July 1978, again played Margaret Barrett in A Family; Playhouse Upstairs, Liverpool, Nov 1979, presented her one-woman show, On Her Own; films, since Help, include: Alfie, Two for the Road, and Women in Love; TV, since 1964, include plays and a number of series, including some written with John Fortune; author of Life and Other Punctures, 1978.
Favourite parts: Hedda, Ellen, Jean Brodie. *Recreation:* Music. *Club:* Zoological Society. *Address:* c/o Fraser and Dunlop, 9 Regent Street, London W1. *Tel:* 734 7311.

BROOK, Faith, actress
b York, 16 Feb 1922; *d* of Clive Brook and his wife Mildred (Evelyn); *e* in California, USA, and in Switzerland and England; *m* (1) Dr Charles Moffett (mar dis); (2) Michael Horowitz (mar dis); studied for the stage under the late Kate Rorke, Dame May Whitty, and at the Royal Academy of Dramatic Art.

She made her first apearance on the stage at the Lobero Theatre, Santa Barbara, California, Aug 1941, as Rose in Lottie Dundass; first appeared in New York, at the Cort Theatre, 23 Dec 1941, as Marion Curwood in Letters to Lucerne; made her first appearance in London, at the Garrick Theatre, 11 Nov 1942, as Marie in Aren't Men

Beasts; served in the ATS during the War, from Mar 1943 to Nov 1945, and appeared with the Unit, Stars in Battledress, playing Patricia in Flare Path, Mabel Crum in While the Sun Shines, and other parts; after the War, Jan 1946, joined the Bristol Old Vic company, playing Dorinda in The Beaux' Stratagem, Pauline in Jenny Villiers, Lady Macduff in Macbeth, Olivia in Twelfth Night, Olga in Keep in a Cool Place; St James's, Mar 1947, played Louise Packard in Truant in Park Lane; Wyndham's, July 1947, Alice Langdon in Deep Are the Roots; Martin Beck Theatre, New York, Mar 1948, Gloria Clandon in You Never Can Tell; on returning to London, joined the Old Vic company and from Sept 1948 to May, 1949, played Olivia in Twelfth Night, Helen of Troy in Dr Faustus, Mrs Millamant in The Way of the World, Charlotte Ivanovna in The Cherry Orchard; went to NY, 1949, where she appeared in over 30 television plays; Henry Miller, Nov 1950, succeeded Margaret Phillips as Celia Coplestone in The Cocktail Party; in summer stock, 1951, appeared in The Devil's Disciple, The Tempest, Too True To Be Good, Don Juan in Hell; during 1952–3, played Sheila Wendice in Dial M For Murder, with the National Company in Chicago, and in NY; Apollo, London, Feb 1954, appeared as Mary Terriford in The Burning Glass; New Watergate, Feb 1955, Inez in Vicious Circle; Connaught, Worthing, May 1955, Anne Irving in The Leopard; Aldwych, Oct 1955, the Visitor in The Whole Truth; Arts, Jan 1957, played Helene Donaldo in No Laughing Matter; St Martin's, Mar 1958, Agnes Potter in The Kidders; Phoenix, Mar 1959, took over the part of Lady Dungavel in Roar Like a Dove; Adelphi, Nov 1960, played Frances Darling in Little Darlings; Pembroke, Croydon, Oct 1961, played Paula Tanqueray in The Second Mrs Tanqueray; Vaudeville, Mar 1963, Laura Foster in Licence To Murder; New Arts, Sept 1964, played Kathy and Angela Wallace in Games; Criterion, Oct 1964, took over the part of Antonia in A Severed Head; Yvonne Arnaud Theatre, Guildford, June 1965, played Dalila in Samson Agonistes; Savoy, July 1967, Patricia in Minor Murder; Vaudeville, Sept 1967, Woman in Fill the Stage With Happy Hours; Royal Court, Feb 1968, played Mrs Forbes in Backbone; Apollo, Dec 1969, Olivia in His, Hers and Theirs; toured with Prospect Theatre Company, 1971, as Gertrude in Hamlet and Lady Macsycophant in The Man of the World, appearing in the former part at the Cambridge Theatre, London, Aug 1971; Hampstead, Nov 1973, appeared in The Ride Across Lake Constance; Gardner Arts Centre, Brighton, and tour, 1976, the daughter in All Over; Queen's, Sept 1977, Veronica in The Old Country; TV includes War and Peace, Angels, and After Julius.

Recreations: Painting, cooking. *Address:* c/o Boyack and Conway Ltd, 8 Cavendish Place, London W1.

BROOK, Peter, CBE, director
b London, 21 Mar 1925; *s* of Simon Brook and his wife Ida (Jansen); *e* Gresham's School and Magdalen College, Oxford; *m* Natasha Parry.

Directed his first production in London at the Torch, 1943, with Dr Faustus, followed at the Chanticleer Theatre, 1945, by a revival of The Infernal Machine; has since directed Pygmalion, Man and Superman, King John, and The Lady from the Sea, 1945; Love's Labour's Lost, The Brothers Karamazov, The Vicious Circle, 1946; Men Without Shadows, The Respectable Prostitute, Romeo and Juliet, 1947; Boris Godunov, Covent Garden, 1948; Dark of the Moon, 1949; Ring Round the Moon, The Little Hut, Measure For Measure (Stratford-on-Avon), A Penny For a Song, The Winter's Tale, Colombe, 1951; Venice Preserv'd, The Little Hut (New York); Faust (NY), 1953; The Dark Is Light

Enough, Both Ends Meet, The House of Flowers (NY), 1954; The Lark, Titus Andronicus (Stratford-on-Avon), also designer and composer of the music for the last-named production, 1955; Nov 1955, under the auspices of the British Council, directed the Stratford Shakespeare Memorial Company in Hamlet, at the Moscow Art Theatre, and in London, 1956; The Power and the Glory (also composed the music), The Family Reunion (also designed the sets), A View From the Bridge, La Chatte sur un Toit Brûlant (Cat on a Hot Tin Roof) at the Théâtre Antoine in Paris, 1956; Titus Andronicus (London and European tour), The Tempest (also composed music and designed sets), Time and Again, 1957; Irma La Douce, The Visit, opening play at the Lunt-Fontanne Theatre, NY; Vu Du Pont (A View From the Bridge) (Paris), Eugen Onegin (Metropolitan, NY), 1958; The Fighting Cock (NY), 1959; Le Balcon (The Balcony) (Paris), The Visit (London), Irma La Douce (NY), 1960; King Lear (also designed—Stratford-on-Avon, London), 1962; The Physicists, The Tempest (co-directed in Stratford-on-Avon), The Perils of Scobie Prilt (tour), Serjeant Musgrave's Dance (Paris), 1963; The Marat/Sade, The Physicists (NY), 1964; The Investigation, The Marat/Sade (NY), 1965, for which production he won the NY Drama Critics Award for the Best Director 1965–6; US (London), 1966; Seneca's Oedipus (also designed), 1968; A Midsummer Night's Dream (Stratford, NY and London) 1970–1; founded the Centre International de Créations Théâtrales, Paris, 1971; activities with the Centre have included Orghast for the Shiraz Festival at Persepolis, Iran, Sept 1971; a tour of Central Africa, 1972, presenting mime plays; Timon of Athens (directed), Théâtre Bouffes du Nord, Paris, Oct 1974; The Ik, tour 1975–6 including the Round House, London; Ubu, 1977; Antony and Cleopatra (RSC), 1978; Conference of the Birds, 1979; directed opera at Covent Garden, 1949–50; directed the films of The Beggar's Opera, 1953, Moderato Cantabile, 1960, Lord of the Flies, 1964; Tell Me Lies (film of US), 1967; King Lear, 1969; Meetings with Remarkable Men, 1979; directed a television production of King Lear in NY, 1953; author of the television plays, The Birthday Present, and Box For One, 1955; author of The Empty Space, 1968; since June 1962, co-director of the Royal Shakespeare Theatre; received the honour of Commander of the British Empire, 1965.

Recreations: The theatre, cinema and painting. *Address:* c/o CIRT, 9 Rue du Cirque, Paris 75008, France.

BROOK, Sara, costume designer.

Designed her first New York production's costumes for A Whitman Portrait at the Gramercy Arts, 11 Oct 1966; since then has designed the costumes for Just for Love, Big Time Buck White, 1968; A Home Away From, The Front Page, and the tours of Hamlet and Rosencrantz and Guildenstern Are Dead, 1969; Child's Play, The Chinese and Dr Fish (double-bill), Nature of the Crime, The Candyapple, Inquest, 1970; WC (tour), Ari, And Miss Reardon Drinks a Little, The Philanthropist, A Gun Play, Twigs, 1971; Pygmalion, Captain Brassbound's Conversion, The Little Black Book, Hurry, Harry, Happy Days, Act Without Words I, Krapp's Last Tape, 1972; Echoes, Children of the Wind, 1973; My Fat Friend, 1974; The Hashish Club, 1975.

BROOKE, Harold, dramatist
b London, 14 Sept 1910; *s* of Thomas Todd and Constance Brooke; *e* Marlborough and Clare College, Cambridge; *m* Kay Bannerman.

He is the author, with Kay Bannerman, of the following plays: Fit for Heroes, 1945; The Nest Egg, 1952; All For Mary, 1954; The Call of the Dodo, 1955 (presented in

Worthing, 1957, as Love and Marriage, in Edinburgh, 1963, as There's A Yank Close Behind Me and in London, 1963, as Let's Be Frank); Once A Rake, 1957; Love At Law, 1958 (presented in London, 1959, as How Say You?); Handful of Tansy (Don't Tell Father), 1959; Death and All That Jazz, 1961; The Snowman, 1965; Let Sleeping Wives Lie, 1967; It Shouldn't Happen to a Dog, 1970, She Was Only an Admiral's Daughter, 1972; Take Zero, 1974; All For Mary was filmed in 1956; film scripts (with Kay Bannerman) also include The Iron Maiden and No, My Darling Daughter.

Recreation: Travel. *Club:* Green Room. *Address:* Babergh Hall, Great Waldingfield, Sudbury, Suffolk.

BROOKE, Paul, actor
b London, 24 Nov 1944; *s* of Henry James Sinclair Brooke and his wife Helen; *e* Marlborough and King's College, London (BA); *m* Diana Lawson.

Made his first professional appearance at the Arts, London, on 1 Aug 1968, as Pobedonostev in The Rasputin Show; at the Theatre Upstairs, played Matron in Blim at School, July 1969; Bung in Revenge, Sept 1969; Osteopath in Fruit and Alexander Pope in What Happened to Blake, Sept 1970; joined the Young Vic company and played parts including Hamm in Endgame, Hardcastle in She Stoops to Conquer, 1972; played God and Reuben in the company's production of Joseph and the Amazing Technicolor Dreamcoat, at the Edinburgh Festival, Sept 1972, Round House, Nov 1972, Albery, Feb 1973; played Biondello in The Taming of the Shrew and Geronte in Scapino, 1974, visiting the Brooklyn Academy of Music in these roles, Mar 1974, and making his Broadway debut as Geronte at the Circle in the Square, 18 May 1974; Leeds Playhouse, Oct 1974, Stephano in The Tempest, transferring with the production to the Wyndham's, Feb 1975; joined the RSC at Stratford, season 1976, in which he played a number of roles including Baloun in Schweik and William Coombe in Bingo; season 1977, his parts included Angelo in The Comedy of Errors and Epicure Mammon in The Alchemist; repeated these three roles in London, 1977–78; Stratford, 1978, played Baptista in The Taming of the Shrew, Antonio in The Tempest, Holofernes in Love's Labour's Lost, and Lepidus in Antony and Cleopatra; repeated these roles (except Antonio) at the Aldwych, season 1979, also playing Kammerling in Once in a Lifetime; first film, Straight on Till Morning, 1972, recently Agatha; TV includes The Last Train Through the Harecastle Tunnel, and The Comedy of Errors.

Favourite parts: Hamm, Epicure Mammon. *Recreations:* Travel, opera. *Address:* 2 Hebron Road, London W6 0PQ.

BROOKES, Jacqueline, actress
b Montclair, New Jersey, 24 July 1930; *d* of Frederick J Brookes and his wife Maria Victoire (Zur Haar); *e* Hunter College High School, New York, and State University of Iowa (BFA 1951); prepared for the stage at the Royal Academy of Dramatic Arts on a Fulbright Scholarship, 1953.

First appeared on the stage at the Metropolitan Opera House, NY, 1943, as an extra in La Boheme; made her professional stage début in a legitimate production at the Jan Hus Playhouse, 14 Oct 1953, as Emilia in Othello; Provincetown Playhouse, July 1954, played Phaedra in The Cretan Woman; in 1954 appeared with Katharine Cornell in The Dark Is Light Enough; Phoenix, Mar 1955, Vittoria Corombona in The White Devil; Théâtre Sarah Bernhardt, Paris, June 1955, in ANTA's Salute To France program played the Second Woman in Medea; Antioch Shakespeare Festival, Yellow Springs, Ohio, July 1955, Lady Macbeth, the Queen in Cymbeline, and the Jailer's Daughter in Two Noble

Kinsmen; Plymouth, NY, Oct 1955, a Woman and understudied Cassandra in Tiger at the Gates; American Shakespeare Festival, Stratford, Conn, June 1956, Blanche of Spain in King John, Juliet in Measure for Measure, and, later, succeeded Mildred Dunnock as Constance in King John; Theatre East, Nov 1956, Celimene in The Misanthrope; Phoenix, Mar 1957, title-role of The Duchess of Malfi; Stratford, Conn, June 1957, Desdemona in Othello and Ursula in Much Ado About Nothing; toured, 1957–8, as Ursula in Much Ado About Nothing; Cape Playhouse, Dennis, Mass, Aug 1958, Sheila in Dial M for Murder; Renata, NY, Oct 1958, Anna Petrovna in Ivanov; University of Michigan Drama Festival, May 1959, Lady Macbeth; Boston University, Oct 1959, the Mother in Kinderspiel; San Diego National Shakespeare Festival, Old Globe Theatre, summer, 1960, Portia in Julius Caesar, Rosalind in As You Like It, and Gertrude in Hamlet; joined the Association of Producing Artists (APA) and, in 1960, played Ilona in Anatol, Zerbinette in Scapin, Goneril in King Lear, Helena in A Midsummer Night's Dream and Ophelia in Hamlet; Old Globe, San Diego, summer, 1961, Viola in Twelfth Night, Portia in The Merchant of Venice, and Elizabeth in Richard III; for the APA, 1961–2, Mrs Molloy in The Matchmaker, the Stepdaughter in Six Characters in Search of an Author, Katherine in The Taming of the Shrew, Elizabeth Proctor in The Crucible, and Dona Lucia in Charley's Aunt; University of Kansas, 1963, Madame Ranevsky in The Cherry Orchard; Martinique, NY, Mar 1963, the Stepdaughter in Six Characters in Search of an Author; Old Globe, San Diego, Cal, summer 1963, Helena in A Midsummer Night's Dream, Hermione in The Winter's Tale, and Cleopatra; City Center, NY, Oct 1963, St Joan in the opera St Joan at the Stake; Stratford, Conn, June 1964, Elizabeth in Richard III and Beatrice in Much Ado About Nothing; Old Globe, San Diego, Cal, summer 1965, Mistress Page in The Merry Wives of Windsor, Queen Katherine in King Henry VIII, and Volumnia in Coriolanus; Theatre de Lys, Oct 1965, appeared in An Evening's Frost; Ypsilanti Greek, Ypsilanti, Michigan, summer, 1966, played in The Oresteia and The Birds; Theatre de Lys, Dec 1966, Lavinia in Come Slowly, Eden; Old Globe, San Diego, Cal, summer 1967, Maria in Twelfth Night, Emilia in Othello, and Helena in All's Well That Ends Well; Dublin Festival, Oct 1969, Gertrude Eastman Quevas in In the Summer House; Forum, NY, Dec 1969, Renata in The Increased Difficulty of Concentration; ANTA, Jan 1970, Diane in Watercolor; St George's Church, Apr 1970, Atossa in The Persians; American Place Theatre, Oct 1970, appeared in Sunday Dinner; Philharmonic Hall, 1970, played the title-role in the opera Herodiade for the Little Orchestra Society; Brooks Atkinson, Mar 1971, Abbess of Argenteuil in Abelard and Heloise; Actors Studio, May 1972, Carrie in The Silent Partner; Edison, Dec 1972, Mother in A Meeting by the River; Mercer-Shaw, May 1973, Marion in Owners; Central Arts, Nov 1973, Marion Akers in Hallelujah!; URGENT, Mar 1974, Kath in Entertaining Mr Sloane; Playhouse II, Jan 1975, Grace Dunning in Knuckle; Ensemble Studio, May 1975, appeared in Dream of a Blacklisted Actor; at the Cathedral of St John the Divine, played Jocasta in Oedipus, 1977; Agave in The Bacchae, 1978; De Lys, Dec 1978, Halie in Buried Child; Brooklyn Academy, May 1979, Dorothea Merz in On Mount Chimborazo; Phoenix, Oct 1979, Betsy Hunt in The Winter Dancers; Circle Repertory, Jan 1980, took over as Gertrude in Hamlet; has appeared in six seasons at the Eugene O'Neill Playwrights' Conference, Waterford, Conn, most recently 1979; appeared in the film The Werewolf of Washington, 1973, and recent films include The Last Embrace, Melvin and Howard, and The Killing;

first appeared on television in 1955 and has since been seen in plays and serials, most recently Guiding Light, and Hard Hats and Legs.

Recreation: Tennis. *Address:* c/o Kimble-Parseghian Inc, 250 West 57th Street, New York, NY 10019.

BROTHERSON, Eric, actor and vocalist
b Chicago, Ill, 10 May 1911; *s* of John Henry Brotherson and his wife Ella (Stankowitz); *e* Illinois Wesleyan University and University of Wisconsin (BA); *m* Helen Harsh (dec); formerly engaged as a schoolmaster, in insurance and as a puppeteer.

Made his first appearance on the stage at the Shubert Theatre, New Haven, Conn, 16 Oct 1937, as a guest in Between the Devil, and first appeared in New York, at the Imperial Theatre, 22 Dec 1937, in the same piece; at the Music Box, Jan 1939, was in the chorus of Set to Music; Alvin, Sept 1941, played Russell Paxton in Lady in the Dark, which he played until July 1943; 46th Street, Sept 1943, Byron Burns in My Dear Public; served in the US Navy, from 1944–6; while in the Navy in Hawaii played in Blithe Spirit with Mildred Natwick; Los Angeles Civic Opera, 1947, played Falke in Rosalinda; Broadhurst, Jan 1948, and toured 1949, in Make Mine Manhattan; Ziegfeld, Dec 1949, Henry Spofford in Gentlemen Prefer Blondes, touring in the part 1951–52; Playhouse, April 1953, Simon Jenkins in Room Service; Los Angeles Civic Opera, 1953, played in The Great Waltz; Cort, Sept 1954, Ferelli in The Fifth Season; toured United States and the Soviet Union, 1957–63, as Jamie, later Zottan Karpathy and Col Pickering, in My Fair Lady; New York State Theatre, July 1964, played Sir Edward Ramsey in a revival of The King and I; toured as Radbury in Pleasures and Palaces, 1965; Music Center, Los Angeles, July 1965, Hartkopf in The Great Waltz; toured US, 1967–8, as Horace Vandergelder in Hello, Dolly!; Theatre Royal, Drury Lane, London, Sept 1970, made his London début when he again played Hartkopf in The Great Waltz; Curran, San Francisco, Cal, May 1971, Van Cortlandt in Knickerbocker Holiday; appeared with the Goodman, Chicago, 1971–2 season; Los Angeles Civic Light Opera, 1972, played Max Detweiler in The Sound of Music; Cirque, Seattle, Wash, Feb 1975, Sam Nash, Jesse Kiplinger, and Roy Hubley in Plaza Suite; St James, Nov 1975, played in the revue A Musical Jubilee; same theatre, 1977, again played in My Fair Lady; Showboat, Tampa, Fla, 1978, played Colonel Pickering, completing a career total of over 3300 performances in My Fair Lady; appeared in the films Star, 1967, Bedknobs and Broomsticks, 1970, Blacula, 1972; first appeared on television in 1949, and has since appeared regularly.

Favourite parts: Russell Paxton in Lady in the Dark, and Spofford in Gentlemen Prefer Blondes. *Recreations:* Swimming and bridge. *Address:* Actors Equity Association, 165 West 46th Street, New York, NY 10036.

BROWN, Arvin, artistic director, Long Wharf Theatre, New Haven, Conn.
b Los Angeles, 1940; *e* Stanford University (BA), Harvard University (MA), Bristol University (Fulbright Scholar); *m* Joyce Ebert; trained for the stage at Yale School of Drama.

Supervisor of the apprentice program at Long Wharf in its first season, summer 1965, he directed his first play there, Long Day's Journey into Night, on 6 May 1966; appointed artistic director, 1967, and has held that post to the present; numerous major productions have been premiered at Long Wharf, and many have moved to Broadway, including the following directed by Mr Brown himself: Solitaire/Double Solitaire, 1971; The National Health, 1974; Ah! Wilderness!,

1975; Watch on the Rhine, 1980; recent Long Wharf productions he has directed include The Autumn Garden, 1976; Hobson's Choice, The Lunch Girls, 1977; Two Brothers, The Philadelphia Story, 1978; I Sent a Letter to My Love, Privates on Parade, 1979; Watch on the Rhine, Mary Barnes, 1980; on and off-Broadway, apart from the plays mentioned, he has directed A Whistle In the Dark, 1968; Hay Fever, 1970; Long Day's Journey into Night, 1971; 27 Wagons Full of Cotton/A Memory of Two Mondays, 1976; Strangers, 1979; he has also directed at the Mark Taper Forum and Ahmanson, LA, and the Kennedy Center, Washington DC; directed the film Cold Sweat, 1973; work for TV includes Amahl and the Night Visitors, and PBS productions of The Widowing of Mrs. Holroyd, Ah! Wilderness!, Forget-Me-Not Lane, and Blessings.

Address: Long Wharf Theatre, 222 Sargent Drive, New Haven, CT 06511.

BROWN, Georgia (*née* Klot), actress
b London, 21 Oct 1933; *d* of Mark Klot and his wife Anne (Kirshenbaum); *e* Central Foundation Grammar School, London; *m* Gareth Wigan.

Made her first appearance on the stage at the Royal Court, London, Feb 1956; as Lucy in The Threepenny Opera, subsequently transferring with the production to the Aldwych, Mar 1956; made her first appearance in the United States, at the Theatre-de-Lys, off Broadway, Sept 1957, when she took over the part of Lucy in The Threepenny Opera; on returning to England, at the Royal Court, Jan 1960, played Jeannie in The Lily White Boys; New, June 1960, played Nancy in Oliver!; left the London cast to appear in the same production in the United States, at the Philharmonic, Los Angeles, Aug 1962, also touring in the US, before making her first Broadway appearance at the Imperial, Dec 1962; Adelphi, London, Feb 1965, took over the part of Maggie in Maggie May; Royal Court, Mar 1971, Widow Begbick in Man is Man; Music Box, NY, Oct 1977, took over in Side by Side by Sondheim; first appeared on television in 1951, in variety, and has since appeared in Mother Courage, the *Ed. Sullivan Show*, etc; her films include The Seven Per Cent Solution; she has also appeared in cabaret worldwide, notably at the Blue Angel, New York.

Address: c/o William Morris Agency Ltd, 147–149 Wardour Street, London, W1V 3TB.

BROWN, John Russell, Professor of English, University of Sussex 1971–
b Bristol, 15 Sept 1923; *s* of Russell Alan Brown and his wife Olive Helen (Golding); *e* Monkton Combe School and Keble College, Oxford; *m* Hilary Sue Baker; first Professor and Head of Department of Drama and Theatre Arts, University of Birmingham 1964–71; appointed Associate Director, The National Theatre, 1973.

He has directed Macbeth, Liverpool, and Chin-Chin, Southampton, 1965; The White Devil, Liverpool, 1969; Secrets, London, 1974; Old Times, tour, 1977; Hamlet, tour, 1978; for the National Theatre he has directed Crossing Niagara, 1975, They Are Dying Out, 1976, Judgement, 1977, and Macbeth (co-directed), 1978; co-directed Twelfth Night for US television, 1967; is the author of several works on the theatre, notably Shakespeare's Plays in Performance, 1967; Effective Theatre, 1969; Theatre Language, 1971; Free Shakespeare, 1974; member, Arts Council Drama Advisory Panel, 1978–; Chairman of Review Committee, 1979; member of Advisory Committee, British Theatre Museum.

Address: The National Theatre, London, SE1.

BROWNE, Coral, actress

b Melbourne, Australia, 23 July 1913; *d* of Leslie Clarence Brown and his wife Victoria Elizabeth (Bennett); *e* Melbourne; *m* (1) Philip Westrope Pearman (dec); (2) Vincent Price; originally studied painting.

Made her first appearance on the stage at the Comedy Theatre, Melbourne, 2 May 1931, as Margaret Orme in Loyalties; remained in Australia until 1934, playing such varied parts as Wanda in The Calendar, Mimi in A Warm Corner, Myra in Hay Fever, Madge in Let Us Be Gay, Mrs Murdo Fraser in The First Mrs Fraser, Suzy in Topaze, Manuela in The Command to Love, Diane in The Quaker Girl, Orinthia in The Apple Cart, Fräulein von Bernberg in Children in Uniform, Hedda in Hedda Gabler, Mrs Dearth in Dear Brutus, etc; her first engagement in London was at the Vaudeville Theatre, Oct 1934, as understudy to Nora Swinburne as Helen Storer in Lover's Leap, in which part she made her first appearance on the London stage, during that month; at the Arts, Feb, 1935, played Concordia in Mated, and Apr 1935, Lady Amerdine in Basalik; Embassy, May 1935, Mary Penshott in This Desirable Residence, and Jan 1936, Victoria in The Golden Gander; St Martin's, June 1936, Connie Crawford in Heroes Don't Care; Royalty (for G Club), Dec 1936, Lydia Latimer in Death Asks a Verdict; New, Mar 1937, the Widow in The Taming of the Shrew; Strand (for Repertory Players), May 1937, Adah Isaacs Menken in The Great Romancer; New, June 1937, Ida Ferrier in the same play; Prince's, July 1937, Jacqueline in The Gusher; Strand (Repertory Players), Mar 1939, the Empress Poppæa in Emperor of the World; New, Jan 1940, Madeleine in Believe It or Not; Savoy, Dec 1941, Maggie Cutler in The Man Who Came to Dinner; Sept 1943, Ruth Sherwood in My Sister Eileen; June 1944, Mrs Cheyney in The Last of Mrs Cheyney; Savoy, Nov 1946, appeared as Lady Frederick Berolles in Lady Frederick; Garrick, Nov 1947, Elma Melton in Canaries Sometimes Sing; Aldwych, July 1948, Bathsheba in Jonathan; Adelphi, Dec 1949, played Boss Trent in Castle in the Air; Old Vic, Oct 1951, appeared as Emilia in Othello, and Mar 1952, as Regan in King Lear; Cambridge, Aug 1952, played Constance Russell in Affairs of State, which ran for eighteen months; Strand, Nov 1954, Laura Foster in Simon and Laura; Haymarket, July 1955, Nina Tessier in Nina; Winter Garden, New York, Jan 1956, played Zabina in Tamburlaine the Great; Old Vic, London, May 1956, Lady Macbeth in Macbeth; toured the USA with the Old Vic Company, Oct 1956, again playing Lady Macbeth, and Helen in Troilus and Cressida, appearing in the latter part at the Winter Garden, NY, Dec 1956; at the Old Vic, London, Sept 1957–Feb 1958, played the following parts, Gertrude in Hamlet, Helena in A Midsummer Night's Dream, and Goneril in King Lear; joined the Shakespeare Memorial Theatre Company for their visit to Moscow, Dec 1958, playing Gertrude in Hamlet; Haymarket, London, Apr 1959, played Katherine Dougherty in The Pleasure of His Company; Piccadilly, Nov 1960, played Albertine Prine in Toys in the Attic; at the Comedy, Oct 1961, played Marie Paule in Bonne Soupe, transferring with the production to Wyndham's, Feb 1962; Theatre Royal, Brighton, Aug 1963, played the Countess in The Rehearsal, prior to appearing in the same production at the Royale, NY, Sept 1963; Her Majesty's, London, May 1964, played Mrs Rossiter in The Right Honourable Gentleman; Billy Rose, NY, Oct 1965, again played Mrs Rossiter in The Right Honourable Gentleman; Phoenix, Oct 1966, Mrs Erlynne in Lady Windermere's Fan; Queen's, Mar 1969, Mrs Prentice in What the Butler Saw; Lyric, June 1970, Lady Warwick in My Darling Daisy; Old Vic, Dec 1970, for the National Theatre Company,

appeared as Mrs Warren in Mrs Warren's Profession; Royal Court, May 1973, Louise Rafi in The Sea; Haymarket, Feb 1974, Emily in The Waltz of the Toreadors; Queen's, June 1975, The Countess in Ardèle; Mark Taper Forum, Los Angeles, Dec 1976, Mrs Lenin in Travesties; also Lady Bracknell in The Importance of Being Earnest; recent films include The Ruling Class, Theatre of Blood and The Drowning Pool.

Hobby: Collecting art and needlepoint. *Address:* 16 Eaton Place, London, SW1.

BROWNE, E Martin, CBE, director and actor

b Zeals, Wilts, 29 Jan 1900; *s* of Colonel Percival John Browne and his wife Bernarda Gracia (Lees); *e* Eton and Christ Church, Oxford University; *m* (1) Henzie Raeburn (dec); (2) Audrey Rideout.

He was formerly engaged in adult education and as a director of religious drama; made his first appearance on the stage at the Regent Theatre (for the 300 Club), 22 May 1927, as the Elder in David; went to the Unites States in 1927, and played in various stock companies, 1927–30; appeared at the Mercury Theatre, London, Nov 1935, playing the Fourth Tempter and Knight in Murder in the Cathedral; at the Canterbury Festival, 1936, the Skeleton in Cranmer of Canterbury; again played in Murder in the Cathedral, at the Duchess, Oct 1936, at the Old Vic, June 1937, and the Ritz Theatre, New York, 16 Feb 1938, when he made his first appearance in NY; Garrick, London, June 1938, Professor Strassman and Rev Tyndal-Morgan in Trumpeter Play!; Arts, Sept 1938, Liam Poer in Blind Man's Buff; Westminster, Mar 1939, Hon Charles Piper in The Family Reunion; Director of the Pilgrim Players, associated with the Arts Council, 1939–48; assumed the direction of the Mercury Theatre, Sept 1945, for the production of poetical plays; directed Murder in the Cathedral, 1935; Mutiny, Cranmer of Canterbury, and Panic, 1936; In Theatre Street, The Virgin and the Clerk, and A Midsummer Night's Dream (Stratford-on-Avon), 1937; The Last Day, Sanctity, 1938; The Family Reunion, 1939; The Way of the Cross, 1940; The Dragon and the Dove, and A Change for the Worse, 1942; The Old Man of the Mountains, This Way to the Tomb, and The Shadow Factory, 1945; A Phoenix Too Frequent, 1946; directed Kate Kennedy, 1947; The Firstborn, A Change for the Worse (in which he appeared as St Eloi), and Coriolanus, Old Vic, 1948; at the Henry Miller, NY, Jan 1950, directed The Cocktail Party; subsequently directed this play in London, at the New, May 1950; directed the York Mystery Plays at York Festival, 1951, also in 1954, 1957 and 1966; Don Juan, at the Devon Festival, 1953; The Confidential Clerk, Edinburgh Festival, and Lyric, London, 1953; also directed The Confidential Clerk at the Morosco, NY, Feb 1954; directed The Flood, York Festival, 1954; Murder in the Cathedral (in which he played Becket), at Gloucester Cathedral, 1955; Lyceum, Edinburgh, Apr 1956, directed A Man Named Judas; Canterbury Festival, June 1958, directed Christ's Comet (also played the Angel of the Tree); Edinburgh Festival, Aug 1958, directed The Elder Statesman, subsequently at the Cambridge, Sept 1958; Westminster Abbey, June 1960, directed The Play of Daniel; Visiting Professor in Religious Drama at the Union Theological Seminary, NY, for six months of each year, 1956–62, and directed the following plays (for the first time in the USA), Christ in the Concrete City, The House By the Stable, Grab and Grace, The Mystery of the Finding of the Cross, Cranmer of Canterbury, Cry Dawn in Dark Babylon; for Omnibus television, NY, Jan 1959, he directed Prince Orestes; Danforth Visiting Lecturer in Drama to the Association of American

Colleges, 1962–5, touring extensively in the US with his wife, with recitals of Shakespeare, T S Eliot, and the Mediaeval Mystery Plays; Hon Drama Adviser to Coventry Cathedral, 1962–5, directing The Mysteries there in 1962 and 1964; at the Yvonne Arnaud, Guildford, directed Murder in the Cathedral, 1967; The Family Reunion and Our Town, 1968; Everyman and The Long Christmas Dinner, 1970; directed the first performance in Canterbury Cathedral of Murder in the Cathedral, Sept 1970; Director of the British Drama League, 1948–57; author of The Making of T S Eliot's Plays, 1969, and Two in One, 1980; received the honour of Commander of the British Empire in the New Year Honours, 1952; Fellow of the Royal Society of Literature since 1955; Hon DLitt (Lambeth), 1971.

(*Died Apr 1980*)

BROWNE, Roscoe Lee, actor
b Woodbury, New Jersey, 1925; *e* Lincoln University, Middlebury College, Columbia University; formerly a teacher at Lincoln University.

Made his New York début as a Soothsayer and Pindarus in the NY Shakespeare Festival production of Julius Caesar, 1956, and subsequently played with that company in The Taming of the Shrew, 1956; Aaron in Titus Andronicus, Balthazar in Romeo and Juliet, 1957; and understudied Othello, 1958; Theatre Marquee, June 1958, Cothurnus in Aria da Capo; St Mark's Playhouse, May 1961, Archibald in The Blacks; Theatre de Lys, Jan 1962, played in the revue Brecht on Brecht; Lyceum, Feb 1962, Corporal in General Seeger; Booth, Dec 1962, Deacon Sitter Morris in Tiger, Tiger, Burning Bright; Delacorte, Aug 1962, the Fool in King Lear; Arena, Washington, DC, May 1963, again played in Brecht on Brecht and the Street Singer in The Threepenny Opera; Sheridan Square Playhouse, July 1963, again played in Brecht on Brecht; Delacorte, Aug 1963, Autolycus in The Winter's Tale; Martin Beck, Oct 1963, the Narrator in The Ballad of the Sad Cafe; American Place, Nov 1964, Babu in Benito Cereno; Delacorte, Aug 1965, Ulysses in Troilus and Cressida; Vivian Beaumont, Oct 1965, St Just in Danton's Death; Longacre, Sept 1966, appeared in the revue A Hand Is on the Gate, which he also arranged from various sources and directed; Playhouse in the Park, Cincinnati, Ohio, 1966, Babu in Benito Cereno; Long Wharf, New Haven, Conn, Dec 1966, Sheridan Whiteside in The Man Who Came to Dinner; Mobile for the NY Shakespeare Festival, June 1967, Mosca in Volpone; New Theatre for Now, Los Angeles, 1969–70 played in several productions; Mark Taper Forum, Los Angeles, 1970, Makak in The Dream on Monkey Mountain; St Mark's Playhouse, Mar 1971, repeated this last role; New Theatre for Now, Los Angeles, 1971–2 season, played in A Rap on Race; Academy Festival, Chicago, June 1974, played Ephraim Cabot in Desire Under the Elms; American Place, Apr 1976, again played Babu in Benito Cereno; A Hand is on the Gate was revised at the Afro-American Studio, 1976, 1977; Other Stage (Public Theatre), May 1979, Albert Perez Jordan in Remembrance; first appeared in films in 1962 in The Connection, and has since played in Black Like Me, The Cool World, The World's Greatest Athlete, Superfly TNT (1973), etc; first appeared on television in Green Pastures, 1952, and has since played in various dramatic programs, including: Benito Cereno, *Espionage, The Defenders,* etc.

Address: Actors Equity Association, 165 West 46th Street, New York, NY 10036.

BROWNING, Susan, actress and singer
b Baldwin, Long Island, New York, 25 Feb 1941; *e* Pennsylvania State University.

Made her NY début at The Music Box, 18 Dec 1963, as Elizabeth Pringle in Love and Kisses; Orpheum, 12 Feb 1964, played Meg in the musical Jo; toured Oct 1964–May 1965 as Felice in After the Fall; appeared with The Theatre Group, Los Angeles, in the 1965–6 season; Cafe au Go Go, May 1968, played in the 11 one-act play production Collision Course; Alvin, Apr 1970, April in Company; John Golden, Feb 1973, Wednesday November in Shelter; Shubert, 11 Mar 1973, played in the revue Sondheim: A Musical Tribute; St Clement's, Apr 1973, Southern Comfort in Whiskey; Delacorte, June 1973, Phebe in As You Like It; Playhouse II, Jan 1974, Kate in The Removalists; Palace, Mar 1975, Agnes Sorel in Goodtime Charley; Stockbridge, Mass, July 1975, Tree in The Butterfingers Angel; has also appeared off-off-Broadway in Dime a Dozen, The Night Little Girl Blue Made Her Social Début, Seventeen, The Boys from Syracuse, 1965–7.

Address: Actors Equity Association, 165 West 46th Street, New York, NY 10036.

BRUCE, Brenda, actress
b Manchester; *d* of George Alexander Findlay Bruce and his wife Ellen Isabella (Vowles); *e* at the Convent of the Holy Family of Nazareth; *m* (1) Roy Rich (dec); (2) Clement McCallin (dec); studied ballet dancing under Margaret Saul.

Made her first appearance on the stage at the Theatre Royal, Exeter, 24 Dec 1934, in a ballet of The Babes in the Wood; first appeared in London, at the Strand Theatre, 25 Apr 1935, in the chorus of 1066 and All That; for three years, 1936–9, appeared with the Birmingham Repertory Company, also appearing at the Malvern Festivals with the company; among the parts she played Lydia Languish in The Rivals, Toni Rakonitz in The Matriarch, Anne in The Brontës of Haworth Parsonage, etc; in Oct 1939, toured as Carol Sands in Goodness, How Sad!; joined the repertory company at the Liverpool Playhouse, Nov 1939, and the Alexandra, Birmingham, Mar 1940, playing leads; toured for ENSA in revue, Jan 1941, and later, as Joanna in Yes and No and Sally in The Two Mrs Carrolls; in 1942, toured in More New Faces; at the Q, from Jan 1943, played Vivie in Mrs Warren's Profession, Mary in Michael and Mary, Kate Hardcastle in She Stoops to Conquer; at the Ambassadors', June 1943, appeared in Sweet and Low; Globe, Dec 1943, played Mabel Crum in While the Sun Shines, in which she continued, 1944–6; New Theatre (for Repertory Players), Mar 1946, Marcella Prince in No Footlights; Lyric, Hammersmith, Nov 1946, Polly Eccles in Caste; Fortune, Dec 1946, succeeded Glynis Johns as Pam in Fools Rush In; Lyric, Hammersmith, June 1947, Eliza Doolittle in Pygmalion; Wyndham's, Oct 1947, Dolly Clandon in You Never Can Tell; New, June 1948, Doris Mead in The Gioconda Smile; Arts, Apr 1949, Miss Hardcastle in She Stoops to Conquer; Lyric, Hammersmith, June 1949, played Susan Lawn in Love in Albania, and appeared in this part at the St James's, July 1949; Arts, Jan 1950, Vivie Warren in Mrs Warren's Profession; Playhouse, Apr 1950, Leonora Yale in The Green Bay Tree; Arts, Aug 1950, appeared as Victoria in Home and Beauty, and played this part at the St Martin's, Sept 1950; Arts, Apr–June 1951, appeared in the Shaw Festival of one-act plays; Aldwych, Oct 1951, played Anne-Marie in Figure of Fun; at the same theatre, Oct 1952, Francie Dosson in Letter From Paris; Scala, Dec 1952, played Peter Pan; made her first appearance on the New York stage at the Playhouse, 28 Oct 1953, as Freda Jefferies in Gently Does It; Apollo, June 1954, Margaret Ross in Both Ends Meet; Royal, Brighton, Oct 1955, Odette in The Captain's Lamp; Arts, Feb 1956, played Mlle de Sainte-

Euverte in The Waltz of the Toreadors, subsequently transferring with the production to the Criterion, Mar 1956; Edinburgh Festival, Sept 1956, played Z in Village Wooing, and Dora Delaney in Fanny's First Play, followed by a tour of Germany, Holland, and the English provinces, with the company; Arts, Jan 1957, played Adelina Barbier in No Laughing Matter; Lyric, Hammersmith, Apr 1958, played Lily Loudon in What Shall We Tell Caroline?, subsequently transferring with the production to the Garrick; Vaudeville, Oct 1960, played Louie in This Year, Next Year; Royal Court, Nov 1962, played Winnie in Happy Days; New, Bromley, Nov 1963, Amy Preston in Woman in a Dressing Gown, subsequently appearing at the Vaudeville, Feb 1964, in the same play; joined the Royal Shakespeare Company, Aug 1964, to play the following parts in repertory: Emilie Paumelle in Victor, Mrs Murray in Eh? and Mistress Page in The Merry Wives of Windsor; since then she has appeared for the Company at Stratford (unless otherwise stated) in the following parts: The Duchess in The Revenger's Tragedy, 1966 and 1967; Marjorie Newquist in Little Murders and Cuca in The Criminals (both Aldwych), 1967; Mistress Page in The Merry Wives of Windsor (also Aldwych), 1968 and 1969; Bawd and Dionyza in Pericles, Paulina in The Winter's Tale, Maria in Twelfth Night, 1969; Queen Gertrude in Hamlet, Queen Elizabeth in Richard III, 1970; Paulina in Enemies (Aldwych), 1971; Irma in The Balcony (Aldwych), 1971; Lady Capulet in Romeo and Juliet, 1973; Voice I in Sylvia Plath, Oct 1973, Mrs Hall in Comrades, Oct 1974, and Madame Poitier in The Beast, Nov 1974, all at The Place; appeared in Sylvia Plath at the Brooklyn Academy of Music, Jan 1974; toured, Jan 1975, in The Hollow Crown; played Mistress Page in The Merry Wives of Windsor, 1975, at Stratford, also playing Queen Margaret in Richard III at The Other Place, Oct; Aldwych, Mar 1976, again played Mistress Margaret Page; joined Prospect (later the Old Vic) Company, 1978, to play Margaret Devize in The Lady's Not for Burning, Babakina in Ivanov, and Gertrude in Hamlet, both on tour at the Old Vic; played the last rôle at Elsinore, Aug 1979, and on tour in China, Nov 1979; returned to the RSC, Stratford 1980, as the Nurse in Romeo and Juliet; first appeared in films, 1943, in Millions Like Us, and recent films include: Law and Disorder, Peeping Tom, Swallows and Amazons, etc; has also made numerous television appearances, including the series *Rich and Rich,* Girl in a Bird Cage, A Chance to Shine, Dr Finlay's Casebook, etc; recent TV work includes The Plantagenets; nominated the TV Actress of 1962; has also broadcast frequently on sound radio.
Favourite Parts: Vivie in Mrs Warren's Profession and The Woman in A Village Wooing. *Recreations:* Painting and writing. *Address:* c/o International Creative Management Ltd, 22 Grafton Street, London W1X 3LD.

BRUCE, Carol, actress and singer
b Great Neck, Long Island, New York, 15 Nov 1919; *d* of Harry Bruce and his wife Beatrice; *e* Jamaica, LI, and Erasmus High School; *m* Milton Nathanson (mar dis).
Made her first appearance in Montreal, as a singer, with Lloyd Huntley's dance band; first appeared on the NY stage at the Alvin Theatre, 28 Aug 1939, in George White's Scandals of 1939; after appearing in Nice Goin', appeared at the Imperial Theatre, May 1940, as Beatrice in Louisiana Purchase; 46th Street, Sept 1942, appeared in the revue New Priorities of 1943; she then went to Hollywood and appeared in films for three years; at the Ziegfeld Theatre, Jan 1946, played Julie in the revival of Show Boat; Starlight Operetta

Co, Dallas, Texas, July 1948, Evalina in Bloomer Girl; New York City Center, Sept 1948, again played Julie in Show Boat; Broadhurst, Jan 1949, appeared in the revue Along Fifth Avenue; in summer theatres, 1949, played Liza Elliott in Lady in the Dark; summer theatres, 1950, Annie Oakley in Annie Get Your Gun; Olney Summer Theatre, July 1952, appeared in One Touch of Venus; toured, 1953–4, as Vera Simpson in Pal Joey; made her first appearance in London at the Princes, 31 Mar 1954, as Vera Simpson in Pal Joey; following her return to the United States, appeared in summer stock, 1955, in Show Boat and The Shanghai Gesture and in 1956, as Alice Walters in Anniversary Waltz; toured in the summer of 1958 in Fallen Angels; City Center, May 1961, played Vera Simpson in Pal Joey; Billy Rose, Feb 1962, took over the role of Tilly Siegel in A Family Affair; 46th Street, Mar 1965, Signora Fioria in Do I Hear a Waltz?; St Regis Maisonette, Paris, Oct 1966, appeared in cabaret; Trinity Square, Providence, RI, Dec 1966, Verena Talbo in The Grass Harp; Palace, NY, Oct 1967, Mrs Boyd in Henry, Sweet Henry; Goodspeed Opera House, East Haddam, Conn, July 1971, Dolly Bloomer in Bloomer Girl; toured beginning Aug 1975 as Madame Serena in The Cooch Dancer; appeared in the film The Messenger, 1970; has also made frequent appearances on television, most recently in *WKRP;* holder of honorary degrees from University of Eastern New Mexico, Brandeis V, and St Edward's, Austin, Texas.
Address: c/o Actors Equity Association, 165 West 46th Street, New York, NY 10036.

BRUFORD, Rose Elizabeth, Hon RAM, former Principal of the Rose Bruford College of Speech and Drama
b London, 22 June 1904; *d* of Frank Bruford and his wife Elizabeth (Weston); *e* Brondesbury and Kilburn High School, and Bath High School; trained at the Central School for Speech and Drama, 1922–4.
Lecturer at the Royal Academy of Dramatic Art, 1941–4; Director of Drama at the Royal Academy of Music, 1940–50; Founder and former Principal of the Rose Bruford College of Speech and Drama, 1950; has acted as Lecturer, Examiner, and Adjudicator of Speech and Drama throughout Great Britain, and also in South Africa and Rhodesia; Poetry Reader for BBC Radio; Lecturer on Speech and Drama for the BBC Overseas Service; author of Speech and Drama, 1948; Teaching Mime, 1958; a member of The Drama Board; Coach of diction, principal singers, Sadler's Wells Opera Company; Hon Fellow of the Institute of Mime; made an Honorary Member of the Royal Academy of Music, 1944.
Recreations: Swimming, travel, reading. *Address:* 33 Pontoise Close, Sevenoaks, Kent. *Tel:* Sevenoaks 56113.

BRUSTEIN, Robert, actor, director, critic, educator, administrator
b Brooklyn, New York, 21 Apr 1927; *s* of Max Brustein and his wife Blanche (Haft); *e* High School of Music and Art, Columbia Grammar School, Merchant Marine Academy, Amherst College (BA 1948), Yale University School of Drama, Columbia University (MA 1950), University of Nottingham, England, on a Fulbright Scholarship, 1953–5, Columbia University (PhD 1957); *m* Norma Cates (dec).
Acted with various stock companies and on television, 1950–7; was drama critic for *The New Republic,* 1959–68; cultural critic for *The New York Review of Books,* 1964–5; instructor of English at Cornell University, 1955–6; instructor in drama at Vassar College, 1956–7; at Columbia University was lecturer in drama, 1957, assistant professor of dramatic literature, 1958–62, associate professor of dramatic litera-

ture, 1963–5, full professor 1965–6; Dean of the Yale Drama School, and professor of Drama and English Literature at Yale, 1965–79; Artistic Director of the Yale Repertory Theatre, which he founded, 1965–79; appointed Professor of English, Harvard University, 1979; Director of American Repertory Theatre and of Loeb Drama Center, Harvard, 1980; served as exchange drama critic for *The Observer*, London, 1972–3; author of The Theatre of Revolt, 1964, The Plays of Strindberg (editor), 1964, Seasons of Discontent, 1966, The Third Theatre, 1968, Revolution as Theatre, 1970, and numerous articles in reviews and journals in America and England, including *The New York Times*; received a Guggenheim Fellowship and a Ford Fellowship, 1960–1, and another Ford Fellowship, 1964–5; received the George Jean Nathan award for dramatic criticism, 1962 and the George Polk Award in Journalism, 1964.

Address: 57 Lakeview Avenue, Cambridge, Mass 02318.

BRYAN, Dora (*née* Broadbent), actress
b Southport, 7 Feb 1924; *d* of Albert Broadbent and his wife Georgina (Hill); *e* Oldham; *m* Bill Lawton.

Made her first appearance on the stage as a child, in pantomime at Manchester in 1935; at the Lyric, 22 July 1947, appeared as Phyllis Mere in Peace In Our Time; Criterion, June 1948, played Eva in Travellers Joy, which ran for over two years; Aldwych, Sept 1950, played Phyllis in Accolade; at the Lyric, Hammersmith, May 1951, appeared in The Lyric Revue, which transferred to the Globe, Sept 1951; Globe, July 1952, played in The Globe Revue; Lyric, Hammersmith, Dec 1953, played in the revue At the Lyric, and at the St Martin's, May 1954, appeared in a revised version of this production, Going To Town; Strand, Nov 1954, played Janet Honeyman in Simon and Laura; Winter Garden, Aug 1955, Lily Bell in The Water Gipsies; Adelphi, Apr 1957, played Julie Skidmore in The Lovebirds; Garrick, July 1958, appeared in the revue Living For Pleasure; Princes, Aug 1962, played Lorelei in Gentlemen Prefer Blondes; Adelphi, Sept 1963, appeared in the revue Six of One; at the Hippodrome, Brighton, Aug 1964, starred in Here's Dora; Edinburgh Festival, and Strand, London, Sept 1965, played Nurse Sweetie in Too True to be Good; Royal Court, Liverpool, Dec 1965, starred in The Dora Bryan Show; Drury Lane, May 1966, took over the title rôle in Hello Dolly!; Prince of Wales, Dec 1968, played nine parts in They Don't Grow on Trees; Chichester Festival, July 1970, Dol Common in The Alchemist; Arnaud, Guildford, Apr 1973, Alice Garth-Bander in George and Margaret; Palace, Westcliff, Nov 1973, appeared in An Evening with Dora Bryan and Friends; London Palladium, Christmas 1973, Sheila in Jack and the Beanstalk; Chichester Festival, May 1974, Clarissa in The Confederacy; toured, autumn 1974, as Sheila in Relatively Speaking; Her Majesty's, Nov 1979, Mrs Leverett in Rookery Nook; first appeared in films 1948, in Fallen Idol, and has since appeared in over forty productions, including A Taste of Honey.

Address: c/o Herbert de Leon, 13 Bruton Street, London, W1. *Tel:* 01–493 0343.

BRYAN, Robert, lighting designer
b Derby, 25 Aug 1934; *s* of Joseph William Bryan and his wife Gladys; *e* Hull University, 1952–56; *m* Ann Daly; formerly a science teacher.

Lit his first professional production, Seagulls over Sorrento, at the Opera House Harrogate, in 1960; first London lighting design, Mr Whatnot, Arts, 1963; went to Kenya, 1965–69, to teach; since his return has lit numerous productions, including The National Health, Jumpers and Undiscov-

ered Country at the National Theatre; Privates on Parade and Once in a Lifetime for the RSC; and Forget-Me-Not Lane, Butley, and Night and Day in the West End; made his New York lighting debut with this last play, 1979; has lit for the English and Welsh National Operas, the Royal Opera and the Royal Ballet, as well as at Glyndebourne, where he has been lighting director since 1972; has also lit for the Burgtheater in Vienna; television work includes a number of operas for Southern Television.

Recreations: Reading, squash, walking. *Address:* 19 Blatchington Hill, Seaford, East Sussex. *Tel:* 0323 892308.

BRYANT, Michael, actor
b London, 5 Apr 1928; *s* of William Frederick Bryant and his wife Ann Mary (Kerrigan); *e* Battersea Grammar School; *m* Josephine Martin; trained for the stage at the Webber-Douglas School.

Made his first appearance on the stage at the Palace Pier, Brighton, in the summer of 1951, as the Young Collector in A Streetcar Named Desire; Oxford Playhouse, Nov 1955, played Fred in The Narrow Corner; made his first appearance in London at the Arts Theatre, Nov 1956, as the Second Furniture Remover in The New Tenant; Arts, Jan 1958, played Willie Oban in The Iceman Cometh, subsequently transferring with the production to the Winter Garden, Mar 1958; Comedy, July 1958, played Walter Langer in Five Finger Exercise; following a run of one year, he made his first appearance in New York, Dec 1959, in the same part and play, subsequently touring with the production in the United States; at the Haymarket, London, Jan 1961, he took over the title part in Ross, which he played for more than a year; New Arts, Jan 1963, played Rudge in Next Time I'll Sing to You; Savoy, Mar 1963, played The Man in Trap For a Lonely Man; Queen's, Nov 1963, Jacko in Gentle Jack; joined the Royal Shakespeare Company at the Aldwych, Aug 1964, to play Victor Paumelli in Victor, and Oct 1964, Selim Calymath in The Jew of Malta, performing both plays in repertory; Aldwych, Feb 1965, appeared as Bernard Wideawake in The Wideawakes in the programme Expeditions 2; same theatre, May 1965, played the Dauphin in Henry V; June 1965, Teddy in The Homecoming; Duke of York's, Apr 1968, played Andre Laevsky in The Duel; Royal Court, Dec 1968, Johnson in This Story of Yours; Cambridge Theatre, Feb 1972, the Prime Minister in Siege; Aldwych, Dec 1975, Captain von Blixen in the RSC's production of The Return of A J Raffles; Criterion, June 1976, Toby Musgrave in The Family Dance; joined the National Theatre Company, 1977, playing Lenin in State of Revolution, May, General Petypon du Grêlé in The Lady from Maxim's, Oct; in 1978 played the title rôle in Brand, Apr, Sir Paul Plyant in The Double Dealer, Sept, David Roberts in Strife, Nov; Von Aigner in The Undiscovered Country, June, Jacques in As You Like It, Aug, Gregers Werle in The Wild Duck, Dec 1979; Iago in Othello, Mar 1980; films include Nicholas and Alexandra, and The Ruling Class; television performances include Talking to a Stranger, the series The Roads to Freedom, and The Duchess of Malfi.

Recreations: Music and ornithology. *Address:* Glebe Cottage, Longfield, Kent. *Tel:* Longfield 2160.

BRYCELAND, Yvonne, actress
b Cape Town, S Africa, 18 Nov; *d* of Adolphus Walter Heilbuth and his wife Clara Ethel (Sanderson); *e* St Mary's Convent, Cape Town; *m* (1) Daniel Bryceland (mar dis); (2) Brian Astbury; formerly a newspaper librarian.

Made her first stage appearance at Rondebosch, Cape Town, as a movie actress in Stage Door, in 1947; her acting career in South Africa includes seven years with the Cape Performing Arts Board, 1964–71, playing such parts as Mme Desmortes in Ring Round the Moon, 1964, Georgie in Winter Journey, 1966, Miss Madrigal in The Chalk Garden, 1968, Mme Ranevskaya in The Cherry Orchard, 1970; in 1969 she started working with Athol Fugard creating the roles of Millie in People Are Living There and Lena in Boesman and Lena, and Clytemnestra/Iris in Orestes, 1971; after leaving Capab toured South Africa with Fugard before, in March, 1972, founding The Space, Cape Town, with Brian Astbury; here she created Frieda in Fugard's Statements after an Arrest under the Immorality Act, 1972, as well as playing such parts as Mary Tyrone in Long Day's Journey into Night, 1973, Amanda Wingfield in The Glass Menagerie, 1974, Bananas in The House of Blue Leaves, Anne in Ashes, 1976, and the title roles in The Bitter Tears of Petra von Kant, 1976, Mother Courage, and Medea, 1977; her first London appearance was at the Theatre Upstairs, 19 July 1971, in Boesman and Lena; at the Royal Court, Jan 1974, in Statements, also touring Europe, and repeating the part at the Royal Court, Jan 1975; created Sophia in Dimetos for the Edinburgh Festival, 1975, Comedy, May, 1976; Hester in Hello and Goodbye, Riverside Studios, Feb 1978; joined the National Theatre Company, 1978, playing a Witch in Macbeth, June, Hecuba in The Woman, Aug; in 1979/80 played Queen Margaret in Richard III, Gina Ekdal in The Wild Duck, and Emilia in Othello; appeared in the film of Boesman and Lena, 1972; TV work includes People Are Living There and Hello and Goodbye.

Favourite parts: Millie, Lena, Hester, Clytemnestra/Iris.
Address: c/o Ronnie Waters, ICM, 22 Grafton Street, London W1.

BRYDEN, Bill (William Campbell Rough Bryden), director and dramatic author
b Greenock , Scotland, 12 Apr 1942; *s* of George Bryden and his wife Catherine (Rough); *e* Greenock HS; *m* the Hon Deborah Morris.

Directed his first professional production, Misalliance, at the Belgrade, Coventry, Oct 1965; assistant to William Gaskill at the Royal Court, 1966–8; directed his first London production, Journey of the Fifth Horse, at this theatre in Oct 1967; other productions for the Royal Court include: Backbone, 1968, Passion (at Alexandra Park), Corunna, The Baby Elephant, 1971; Associate Director, Royal Lyceum, Edinburgh, 1971–; productions here include his own plays Willie Rough (1972) and Benny Lynch (1974); The Bevellers, 1973; The Iceman Cometh, 1974; The Flouers of Edinburgh, 1975; at the Edinburgh Festival, directed The Thrie Estates, 1973, How Mad Tulloch Was Taken Away, 1975, and wrote the libretto for the opera Hermiston, also 1975; appointed an associate director of the National Theatre, 1975, where his productions have included: Spring Awakening, Romeo and Juliet (Mobile), 1974; The Playboy of the Western World, 1975; Watch It Come Down, Il Campiello, Counting the Ways, 1976; The Passion (co-director), Old Movies (also author), The Plough and the Stars, 1977; appointed Director of the National's Cottesloe Theatre, 1978, where he has directed Lark Rise (co-director), American Buffalo, The World Turned Upside Down (co-director), 1978; Dispatches (also adapted), Candleford (co-director), The Long Voyage Home, 1979; Hughie, The Iceman Cometh, 1980; Willie Rough and Benny Lynch have been seen on television; in 1979 appointed a director of Scottish Television.

Address: The National Theatre, South Bank, London SE1 9PX. *Tel:* 01–928 2033.

BRYDEN, Ronald, dramatic critic, dramaturge
b Port of Spain, Trinidad, 6 Dec 1927; *s* of William Francis Bryden and his wife Flossie (Samuel); *e* Ridley College, St Catherine's, Ont, University of Toronto and King's College Cambridge; *m* Patricia Leslie Bowen-Davies.

Theatre critic, *New Statesman,* 1964–6; *The Observer,* 1967–71; Play Adviser,, Royal Shakespeare Company, 1972–6; Professor, Graduate Centre for the Study of Drama, University of Toronto, 1977–; Governor, Stratford Shakespearian Festival Foundation, Ontario, 1978–.

BRYNNER, Yul, actor
b Sakhalin Island, 11 July 1915; *e* The Sorbonne, Paris.

Early experience as a singer in Parisian nightclubs at age thirteen was followed by five years in European circus as an acrobat, flying trapeze clown, etc; joined the Théâtre des Mathurins as a trainee director; later worked in England with Michael Chekhov; went to New York with the Chekhov Players, making his Broadway debut with them at the Little, 2 Dec 1941, as Fabian in Twelfth Night; he appeared in London plays too during this time; his first major Broadway role was that of Tsai-Yong in Lute Song, Plymouth, Feb 1946; St James, Mar 1951, played the King in The King and I, receiving a Tony and other awards for this performance and spending four years in the role; entered films until 1975, when he returned to the stage as Odysseus in Odyssey, which toured for a year before being seen at the Palace, NY, Jan 1976, under the title Home, Sweet Homer; Uris, May 1977, played the King in a successful revival of The King and I, and again at the London Palladium, Jun 1979, played the part for over a year; first film, 1949, Port of New York; his many subsequent films include The King and I (Oscar), Anastasia, The Brothers Karamazov, The Magnificent Seven, Invitation to a Gunfighter, The Double Man, Catlow, Westworld, etc; worked as a TV director with CBS, 1948; active for thirteen years with the UN High Commission for Refugees.

Address: c/o Screen Actors Guild, 7750 Sunset Blvd, Los Angeles, CA 90046.

BUCK, David, actor
b London, 17 Oct 1936; *s* of Joseph Buck and his wife Enid Marguerite (Webb); *e* Mill Hill School and Christ's College, Cambridge.

Made his first professional appearance at the Royal Court, Aug 1958, as the Orator in The Chairs; at the same theatre, Oct 1958, played Capt Dann in The Tent; Playhouse, Oxford, Jan 1959, Yoshikyo in Prince Genji; joined the Royal Shakespeare Company, Apr 1959, later becoming an Associate Artist; played minor roles in the 1959 season; parts in the 1960 season included Diomedes in Troilus and Cressida; season 1961, parts included Rosencrantz in Hamlet, Oliver in As You Like It, Tyrell in Richard III and Montano in Othello; for the RSC at the Aldwych, 1961–2, played Yasha in The Cherry Orchard, the Adjutant and other parts in The Caucasian Chalk Circle, Richard in Curtmantle and De Cerisay in The Devils; Open Air, Regent's Park, July 1967, played the title role in Cyrano de Bergerac; Belgrade, Coventry, Feb 1972, Abelard in Abelard and Heloise; toured Canada, Nov 1972, as Milo in Sleuth; Oct 1973, played Capt Plume in The Recruiting Officer, opening production of the Haymarket, Leicester; Theatre Royal, Bristol, Oct 1977, Polydor in The Sunset Touch; Palace, Watford, Oct 1978, Simon Hench in Otherwise Engaged; entered films, 1963; his frequent television performances, also since 1963, include Mystery and Imagination, Hornblower, and The Idiot; writing includes several plays for radio such as The Resurrectionists and The Image of God.

Favourite part: Cyrano. *Recreations:* Early theatre history, music, swimming. *Address:* c/o Trafalgar Perry Ltd, 4 Goodwin's Court, St Martin's Lane, London WC2.

BUFMAN, Zev, actor and producer
b Tel-Aviv, Israel, 11 Oct 1930; *s* of Mordekhai Bufman and his wife Hayah (Torban); *e* Balfour High School, Tel-Aviv, Los Angeles City College, Los Angeles State College (MA 1957); *m* (1) Leah Debora Habas (mar dis); (2) Vilma Greul Auld; formerly engaged in the import and export of steel and lumber.

Began his theatrical career as a cabaret entertainer in Tel-Aviv, 1950, in an act called The Israeli Danny Kaye; made his legitimate stage début at the Tustin (Calif) Playbox, July 1951, as a Quack Doctor in The Imaginary Invalid; played in stock the Russian Spy in See How They Run, 1951; Eddie in Lady in the Dark, Mr Lundie in Brigadoon, Theodatus in Caesar and Cleopatra, 1952; Huntington Hartford, Hollywood, Calif, Oct 1956, played Harry in Merton of the Movies; turned to production in Los Angeles in July 1958 with A Hole in the Head at the Civic Playhouse, Los Angeles, and has since produced or co-produced the following plays: Laffcapades of '59, Fair Game, Murder in the Red Barn, The Barber of Seville, Mendel the Beatnik, Our Town, Pajama Tops (all in Hollywood, 1959); Vintage '60 (Hollywood and New York), A Timid Evening with Don Rickles (Los Angeles), Carnival Island, and Only in America (both in Hollywood), 1960; Second City (Hollywood), The Fantasticks (Los Angeles and San Francisco), The Egg (Chicago), Elsa Lanchester Herself (Hollywood), 1961; The Egg (NY), Little Mary Sunshine, A Curious Evening with Gypsy Rose Lee, Under the Yum-Yum Tree (all Hollywood), Pajama Tops (West Coast tour), Write Me a Murder (Los Angeles), The Premise (Miama, Florida), 1962; The Tenth Man (Los Angeles and Miami), Sunday in New York (Los Angeles), Pajama Tops (NY), God Bless Our Bank (tour), Lord Pengo, A Calculated Risk, The Tender Trap, Come Blow Your Horn, Tchin-Tchin, King of Hearts, Madly in Love, A Shot in the Dark (all Miami), A Thousand Clowns, Mary, Mary, 1963; Fair Game for Lovers (Miami and NY), In One Bed . . . (And Out the Other) (tour), 1964; Minor Miracle (NY), 1965; Any Wednesday (tour), 1966; Marat/Sade and Spofford (NY), On a Clear Day You Can See Forever (US–Canada tour), 1967; Mike Downstairs, Soldiers, Your Own Thing Jimmy Shine, Big Time Buck White (all NY), The Star-Spangled Girl (tour), 1968; Spitting Image, Buck White (both NY), Your Own Thing (London and US tours), 1969; Story Theatre (NY), 1970; Ovid's Metamorphoses (NY), 1971; The American Revolution, Part I (Ford's, Washington, DC), 1973; The Trouble with People . . . (Miami), 1974; The Magnificent Yankee (Washington DC), 1976; Peter Pan, Oklahoma!, 1979; entered films as an actor in 1952 when he played Farrid in Bengal Rifles, and appeared in films for the next six years, including Flight to Tangiers, The Prodigal, The Ten Commandments, Buccaneer, etc; in 1964 received a citation from the mayor of Los Angeles for successfully operating on a year-round basis four theatres in Hollywood (Ivar, Grand Comedy, Music Box, and Las Palmas).
Address: Coconut Grove Playhouse, Miami Beach, Fla.

BULLINS, Ed, playwright, poet, and short story writer
b Philadelphia, Pa, 2 July 1935; *s* of Bertha Marie (Queen).
First productions on the stage were How Do You Do, The Rally, or Dialect Determinism, and Clara's Ole Man, presented at the Firehouse Repertory Theatre, San Franci-

sco, Cal, Aug 1965; first production in London was at the Ambiance Lunch Hour Theatre, Aug 1968, The Electronic Nigger; author of the following, among other, plays: The Electronic Nigger, A Son Come Home, In the Wine Time, 1968; The Gentleman Caller, A Black Quartet, 1969; The Pig Pen, Street Sounds, 1970; In New England Winter, The Fabulous Miss Marie, for which he received the Obie (off-Broadway) Award, 1971; Goin' a Buffalo, The Duplex, The Corner, Home Boy, 1972; House Party, 1973; The Taking of Miss Janie, 1975; The Mystery of Phyllis Wheatley, Jo Anne!!!, Home Boy (lyrics), The Devil Catcher, 1976; Daddy, 1977; Man-Woman: Michael, 1978; is working on a 20-play The Twentieth Century Cycle about the black experience in America, was writer-in-residence of the New Lafayette Theater; has also been playwright-in-residence at The American Place Theater; past editor of the magazine *Black Theater*; has taught at Fordham University, Columbia, University of Massachusetts, Bronx Community College; a collection of his short stories, *The Hungered One*, published in 1971; a novel, The Reluctant Rapist, 1973; lectures extensively in colleges and universities, including Dartmouth, University of California at Berkeley, Clark College, etc; his plays have been produced at Cafe LaMama, Public Theatre, Workshop of the Players Art, Lincoln Center, American Place, and other repertory theatres; has received the Vernon Rice—Drama Desk Award; Guggenheim Fellowship Grant, Creative Artists Program Service Grant, National Endowment for the Arts Grant, etc.
Address: 932 East 212th Street, New York, NY 10469. *Tel:* 547 1227.

BULLOCK, Christopher, theatre administrator
b Wilmslow, Cheshire, 8 June 1934; *e* All Saints College, Bloxham; *m* Jacqueline Wilson; trained for the stage under Sir Barry Jackson at the Birmingham Rep.
After National Service, returned to Birmingham 1954–58 as ASM, Stage Manager and finally Stage Director; 1958–60 Stage Manager, later Production Manager, Belgrade Theatre, Coventry; Production Manager, Oxford Playhouse, 1961; to Liverpool Playhouse as Production Manager, 1962–68; General Manager and Licensee, 1968–76; Administrative Director and Company Secretary, 1976– ; Chairman of CORT, 1976–77.
Address: 42 School Lane, Bidston, Merseyside L43 7RQ. *Tel:* 051-709 8478.

BULOFF, Joseph, actor
b Vilno, Lithuania; *s* of Benjamin Buloff and his wife Sarah (Rotlast); *m* Luba Kadison.
First appeared on the stage as a child in Vilno, in 1918; 1923–27, remained with a permanent company in Europe, the Vilna Troupe; went to the United States in 1928, to play at the Yiddish Art Theatre; joined the Chicago People's Institute as a director and teacher of acting, 1929; with his wife, Luba Kadison, has performed in Europe, South America, South Africa, Israel, and has produced, directed and acted in plays in Yiddish, Russian, Polish, and Rumanian; first played in English, at the Bayes, NY, Nov 1936, in Don't Look Now; Longacre, Feb 1937, Sidney Castle in Call Me Ziggy; Guild, Oct 1937, Zaniano in To Quito and Back; Broadhurst, May 1938, Istvan in The Man from Cairo; Longacre, Apr 1940, Aaron Greenspan in Morning Star; Henry Miller, Nov 1941, William Auchinschlon in Spring Again; at the St James, Mar 1943, appeared as Ali Hakim in Oklahoma! which he played for nearly four years; Biltmore, Mar 1947, Feodor Vorontsov in The Whole World Over; Martin Beck, Feb 1952, directed Mrs McThing; first ap-

peared in London at the Cambridge, 24 Feb 1954, as Max Pincas in The Fifth Season; at the Cort, NY, Sept 1954, played the same part, and subsequently toured in the same production; National, Dec 1958, succeeded Walter Matthau as Maxwell Archer in Once More with Feeling; Cort, Oct 1959, Detective Inspector Petrov in Moonbirds; Billy Rose, Oct 1960, Fishel Shpunt in The Wall; Gramercy Arts, Feb 1962, played in three Chekhov plays under the omnibus title A Chekhov Sketchbook; Playhouse, Philadelphia, June 1962, Felice in A Garden in the Sea; toured the US, 1964, as Paul Hirsch in Dear Me, the Sky Is Falling; Hayser, Chicago, Jan 1965, again played in A Chekhov Notebook, which he also directed; Playhouse in the Park, Philadelphia, June 1965, Glas in Slow Dance on a Killing Ground; Playhouse, Paramus, NJ, July 1965, played Friedrich Welt in Fidelio; toured US, Jan–Apr 1970, as Gregory Solomon in The Price; Folksbiene, NY, Nov 1970, directed and played Simkhe Meyer in The Brothers Ashkenazi; Folksbiene, Nov 1972, played the title-role and directed Yoshke Musikant; Eden, Oct 1973, co-adapted and played David Shapiro in Hard to Be a Jew; Eden, Oct 1975, directed and played Max Pincus in a Yiddish musical version of The Fifth Season; Harold Clurman, Apr 1979, Gregory Solomon in The Price, transferring to the Playhouse, June; first appeared in films in 1940, and has since played in Let's Make Music, Somebody Up There Likes Me, Silk Stockings, etc; is a frequent performer on television.
Address: Actors Equity Association, 165 West 46th Street, New York, NY 10036.

BUNDY, William, OBE, technical administrator, lighting designer, and theatre consultant
b Nottingham, 20 Sept 1924; *s* of Hector William Bundy and his wife May; *e* William Crane School, Nottingham, and the Royal Navy Electrical School, Portsmouth; *m* Rosemary Lindsay.
Began his career in the theatre as a touring electrician for HM Tennent, 1941–42; after service in the Navy, rejoined Tennent's 1946–48; Chief Electrician for the Old Vic tour of Australia and New Zealand, 1948–49; technical consultant, Icelandic National Theatre, 1949–50; with Strand Electric 1950–51; Chief Electrician, Royal Opera House, 1951; Ballet Stage Manager, 1957; Stage Director, 1958; Technical Director, 1970; Technical Administrator, 1974; left to join Theatre Projects Consultants, 1976, also retained as technical consultant to the ROH; joined the National Theatre as Technical Administrator, Dec 1977; as lighting designer has lit over 150 ballets and operas for major companies in London and abroad; awarded the OBE, 1970, for services to the theatre.
Hobbies: Industrial and theatre archaeology, model steam trains. *Address:* 3 Branstone Road, Kew Gardens, Surrey. *Tel:* 940 1576.

BUNNAGE, Avis, actress
b Manchester, Lancs; *d* of William Bunnage and his wife Evaline (Ward); *e* Chorlton Central School: *m* Derek Orchard; formerly a telephonist and nursery teacher.
Made her first professional appearance on the stage at the Chorlton Repertory Theatre, Manchester, 1947, when she played Tabitha in The Brontës; first appeared in London at the Embassy Theatre, May 1952, with the Theatre Workshop Company, in a number of parts in Uranium 235, transferring with the production to the Comedy, June 1952; with the same company, at the Theatre Royal, Stratford, E, played the following parts: Franceschina in The Dutch Courtesan, Petra in An Enemy of the People, Peasant Woman in The Good Soldier Schweik, 1954; Mari in The Midwife, Dolores in The

Legend of Pepito, Yvette in Mother Courage and Her Children (Devon Festival, Barnstaple), Pascula in The Sheep-Well, Baroness de Champigny in The Italian Straw Hat, 1955; at the Sarah Bernhardt, Paris, 1955, and at the Duke of York's, Mar 1956, played Baroness von Botzenheim and Madame Kati Wendler in The Good Soldier Schweik; returned to the Royal, Stratford, E, Apr 1956, to play the following parts: Queen Isabella in Edward II, Lady Cicely Waynflete in Captain Brassbound's Conversion, 1956; Georgette in The School for Wives, Widow Quinn in The Playboy of the Western World, First Witch and the Gentlewoman in Macbeth (also Zurich and Moscow), Sancha in And the Wind Blows, 1957; Rosaria and Grazia in Man, Beast, and Virtue, Lanie Ellis in Unto such Glory, Helen in A Taste of Honey, Meg Dillon in The Hostage, Mrs Fezziwig and Mrs Cratchit in A Christmas Carol, 1958; Wyndham's, Feb 1959, again played Helen in A Taste of Honey; Royal, Stratford, E, May 1960, Mrs Kelly and Mrs Fitzpatrick in Ned Kelly; made her first appearance in New York at the Cort, Sept 1960, as Meg Dillon in The Hostage; toured Canada in the same part; on returning to England, at the Royal, Stratford, E, June 1961, played Dr Mildred Watson in They Might Be Giants; Garrick, Oct 1961, took over the part of Lily in Fings Ain't Wot They Used T' Be; Sarah Bernhardt, Paris, subsequently Wyndham's, June 1963, appeared in various parts in Oh, What a Lovely War!; at the latter theatre, Dec 1963, the Duchess of Margate in Merry Roosters Panto; Assembly Hall, Edinburgh, Aug 1964, played Mistress Quickly in Henry IV; Theatre Royal, Stratford E, Feb 1966, Blanche in Sweet Fanny Adams, and Nov 1967, Marie in The Marie Lloyd Story; Her Majesty's, Feb 1968, took over as Golde in Fiddler on the Roof until Aug 1969, when she toured South Africa in the part, resuming it at Her Majesty's theatre in May 1970; Shaw, Oct 1971, Ivy Careless in Slip Road Wedding; toured, Apr 1972 in Stringer's Last Stand; at the Theatre Royal, Stratford E, played Mrs Brum in Costa Packet, Oct 1972; directed The Big Rock Candy Mountain, Dec 1972; played Minister of Health in Is Your Doctor Really Necessary?, Feb 1973, and Mrs Lovett in Sweeney Todd, May 1973; Theatre Royal, York, Oct 1973, Mrs Malaprop in The Rivals; Drury Lane, May 1974, Alice Fisher in Billy; New London, May 1977, Ma in Lionel; films in which she has appeared include: The L Shaped Room, The Loneliness of the Long Distance Runner, Sparrers Can't Sing, Tom Jones, Panic, etc; first appeared on television, 1959, in Probation Officer, and principal performances include: Love on the Dole, My Lords, Ladies, and Gentlemen and The Mayor of Casterbridge.
Favourite parts: All. *Recreation:* Gardening. *Address:* c/o Nems Enterprises Ltd, 29–31 King's Road, London SW3.

BURBRIDGE, Edward, scenic designer.
Designed his first NY production, Misalliance, at the Sheridan Square Playhouse, 25 Sept 1961; since then has designed the Marat/Sade, 1967; began his long association with the Negro Ensemble Company in 1968 with The Song of the Lusitanian Bogey, and also that year designed The Summer of the 17th Doll, Kongi's Harvest, Mike Downstairs, Daddy Goodness, Jimmy Shine, Big Time Buck White, God Is a (Guess What?) 1968; Does a Tiger Wear a Necktie? Spitting Image, Malcochon, Contribution, String, Man Better Man, The Reckoning, Our Town, Buck White, 1969; Five on the Black Hand Side, Steal the Old Man's Bundle, The Shepherd of Avenue B, Ododo, 1970; Perry's Mission, Rosalie Pritchett, The Dream on Monkey Mountain, Ride a Black Horse, The Sty of the Blind Pig, 1971; Ti-Jean and His Brothers, A Ballet Behind the Bridge, Frederick Douglas

. . . Through His Own Words, 1972; Status Quo Vadis, The Visit, Chemin de Fer, Holiday, 1973; What the Wine-Sellers Buy (costumes), Absurd Person Singular, 1974; The First Breeze of Summer, 1975 (television version, 1976); Absent Friends (tour), 1977; The Last Minstrel Show, 1978.

BURDEN, Hugh, actor and dramatic author

b Colombo, Ceylon, 3 Apr 1913; *s* of Harry Archibald Burden and his wife Caro Cecil (Jackson); *e* Beaumont College; *m* Joy Hodgkinson (mar dis); studied for the stage at the Central School of Dramatic Art and the Royal Academy of Dramatic Art.

Made his first appearance on the stage at the Grafton Theatre, 8 Oct 1933, as Evan in Singing Gold; then joined the Croydon Repertory Company, Nov 1933; Vaudeville, Mar 1934, played the Third Voice in Good Friday; May 1935, toured as Dr Dession in Mesmer; Aldwych, Nov 1935, Jack Ross in Legend of Yesterday; Prince's, Apr 1936, Ray Bennett in The Frog; Savoy, May 1936, Alfred Bridges in The Happy Medium; Strand (for Repertory Players), Nov 1937, Peter Smiley in The Seat of Mars; Arts, Apr 1938, Jack Grimmett in Murder Without Tears; Players, Apr 1938, Coleridge in Charles and Mary; Holborn Empire, May 1938, Fag in The Rivals; Arts and Haymarket, Oct 1938, Stephen Firbanks in A Party for Christmas; at the Barn Theatre, Shere, July 1939, appeared as Jasper Darke in The House in Dormer Forest; served in HM Forces, from Sept 1939, to Jan 1941, in Hampshire Regiment and Indian Army; Wyndham's, Feb 1942, succeeded Michael Wilding as Denys Royd in Quiet Week-end; St James's, Oct 1942, played Voulain in The Duke in Darkness; Q, Mar 1943, and Arts, Apr 1943, Mark in The Young and Lovely; Phoenix, June 1944, Martin in The Last of Summer; Wyndham's, Sept 1944, Guy Saunders in The Banbury Nose; Arts, Dec 1944, Puff in The Critic; Globe, Feb 1945, succeeded Michael Wilding as the Earl of Harpenden in While the Sun Shines; toured, Apr 1945, as Napoleon Buonaparte in Josephine; Wyndham's, July 1945, succeeded Ronald Ward as Richard Llewellyn in The Years Between; Embassy, Aug 1945, Gordon van Ketzler in Myself a Stranger, and Nov 1945, Alexei in The Gambler; at Wyndham's, Jan 1946, again played Llewellyn in The Years Between; Piccadilly, May 1947, Angel Clare in Tess of the D'Urbervilles; Arts, Sept 1947, John Bannister in Child's Play; Fortune, May 1948, the Unknown Man in The Paragon; toured in Germany, Apr 1949, playing Hamlet, and John Tanner in Man and Superman; Vaudeville, Aug 1949, succeeded Robert Flemyng as Alan Howard in French Without Tears; Arts, Aug 1950, William in Home and Beauty, and played the same part at the St Martin's, Sept 1950; Vaudeville, May 1951, appeared as James IV in The Thistle and the Rose; New Boltons, Feb 1952, Capt Clement Yule in The High Bid; Saville, July 1952, Geoff Ainsworth in Albert, RN; Q, Nov 1953, Gordon Anstey in The Painted Devil, in which he also toured; New Watergate, Feb 1955, played Garcin in Vicious Circle; Criterion, Sept 1955, played Vladimir in Waiting for Godot; Bristol Old Vic, Oct 1956, Alceste in The Slave of Truth; Oxford Playhouse, Nov 1958, Pasquale in Too Many Ghosts; Arts, June 1959, James Hyland in The Rope Dancers; Pembroke, Croydon, Mar 1962, played Col Hugo Flynn in Flynn's Last Drive; New Arts, July 1962, Leon Dupont in The Empire Builders; Theatre Royal, Windsor, Oct 1966, Harcourt-Reilly in The Cocktail Party; Ashcroft, Croydon, Feb 1973, Jonah in Nightfall; first appeared in films, 1941, in Ships with Wings; is the author of the following plays: Trouble for Two, 1937; The House in Dormer Forest, 1939; The Young and Lovely, 1943; Myself a Stranger (with his mother), 1945; No Footlights, 1946; To My Love (adapted

from Edgar Neville's Spanish comedy El Baile), 1956; has also written for television.

Recreation: The piano. *Clubs:* Garrick, Savage and Green Room. *Address:* c/o *Spotlight*, 42–43 Cranbourn Street, London, WC2 7AP.

BURGE, Stuart, CBE, director and former actor

b Brentwood, Essex, 15 Jan 1918; *s* of Henry Ormsby Burge and his wife Kathleen (Haig); *e* Eagle House School and Felsted School; *m* Josephine Parker; formerly a civil engineer.

Made his first appearance on the stage at the Old Vic, Dec 1936, as the Fourth Clown in The Witch of Edmonton, subsequently appearing as the Player Queen in Hamlet, and Boy in Henry V, 1937; stage manager for the Old Vic tours of European capitals, 1939 and 1947, between 1939–46, was a member of the company at the Bristol Old Vic, and the Oxford Playhouse; first appeared on Broadway at the New Century, Feb 1952, as Bates in Venus Observed; began his career as a director in 1948, with a travelling repertory company; directed his first London production (with Basil Coleman) at the Lyric, Hammersmith, Nov 1949, with Let's Make an Opera, and again at the same theatre, Dec 1950; appointed director of the Queen's Theatre, Hornchurch, 1952, where he directed over sixty productions; subsequent productions include: The Dock Brief, and What Shall We Tell Caroline? (double-bill), Hook, Line, and Sinker, 1958; Curtmantle, 1962; The Workhouse Donkey (Chichester Festival), 1963; Henry V (Bristol Old Vic and Old Vic), Richard II (Stratford, Ontario), Othello (Dubrovnik Festival), 1964; Henry IV (Parts I and II) (Stratford, Ontario), 1965; his production of Henry V, 1964, toured extensively overseas; in 1966 he directed Public and Confidential and Serjeant Musgrave's Dance (USA); 1967, The Judge, and The Two Gentlemen of Verona; in 1968 he became director of the Nottingham Playhouse, opening with King John; his productions have since included: The Ruling Class (later at the Piccadilly), Macbeth, The Alchemist (later at the National Theatre), The Demonstration, The Dandy Lion (children's play), 1969; The Daughter in Law, The Idiot, A Yard of Sun (also at the National Theatre) and Lulu (later at the Royal Court and the Apollo), 1970–1; The Rivals, A Close Shave, 1971; The Tempest, A Doll's House, See How They Run, 1972; The White Raven, The Devil is an Ass, 1973; left Nottingham Playhouse 1973; Edinburgh Festival 1976, and National Theatre, May 1977, co-directed the Birmingham Repertory Company's productions of Measure For Measure and The Devil is an Ass; Artistic Director of the Royal Court Theatre from Feb 1977, where his productions include Fair Slaughter (1977), Eclipse (1978), and The London Cuckolds (1979); directed his first film, 1959, with There Was a Crooked Man, and has since directed Othello (based on the National Theatre production), The Mikado and Julius Caesar; television productions include: The Power and the Glory, The Devil and John Brown (Writer's Award, 1964), his own adaptations of Under Western Eyes, Luther (USA), School for Scandal, and Bill Brand, and recently, Sons and Lovers; awarded the CBE in the New Year's Honours, 1974.

Address: c/o Chatto and Linnit Ltd, Globe Theatre, Shaftesbury Avenue, London W1.

BURKE, Alfred, actor

b New Cross, London, 28 Feb 1918; *s* of William Burke and his wife Sarah Ann O'Leary; *e* Leo Street Boys' School and Walworth Central School; *m* Barbara Bonelle.

Trained for the stage at RADA; made his first professional appearance at the Barn theatre, Shere, Surrey, July 1939, in

The Universal Legacy; worked for a number of years in repertory at theatres such as the Library, Manchester, Midland Theatre Company, Nottingham Playhouse, Birmingham Rep; with the latter he appeared at the Old Vic, July 1952, as George in Part III of Henry VI; same theatre, July 1953, repeated this part and in parts I and II played Henry Beaufort; made his West End début at the Duchess, Oct 1953, as second man in The MacRoary Whirl; Piccadilly, Jan 1964, the Pastor in The Father; Leeds Playhouse and Edinburgh Festival, Sept 1970, title-role in Pirandello's Henry IV; Leeds, Sept 1971, Strindberg in Pictures in a Bath of Acid; Worcester Cathedral, Oct 1971, Becket in Murder in the Cathedral; Royal Court, Mar 1972, Abel Murdoch in a production without décor, The Centaur; Oxford Playhouse, Oct 1973, title-role in Dr Knock; his films include: The Angry Silence, Children of the Damned, and One Day in the Life of Ivan Denisovich; TV, since his first appearance in 1950, includes plays such as The Birthday Party and his own series, *Public Eye.*

Recreations: Music, soccer. *Address:* c/o Joy Jameson, 7 West Eaton Place Mews, London SW1X 8LY.

BURKE, David, actor
b Liverpool, 25 May 1934; *s* of Patrick Burke and his wife Mary (Welsh); *e* St Francis Xavier's College, Liverpool and Corpus Christi, Oxford; *m* Anna Calder-Marshall.

Trained for the stage at RADA; made his first professional appearance at Sidmouth, summer season, July 1960, playing Sgt Cadwallader in The Unexpected Guest; his early experience was with the Bristol Old Vic Company, with whom he made his London début at the Old Vic, 14 June 1962, as Anatol Kuragin in War and Peace, transferring with the production to the Phoenix later that month; Royal Court, July 1968, Dan in The Hotel in Amsterdam; spent a number of years with the Royal Lyceum company, Edinburgh, where his parts included: Othello, Macbeth, Proctor in The Crucible, Astrov in Uncle Vanya, Flamineo in The White Devil, and O'Rourke in The Bofors Gun; Thorndike, Leatherhead, Mar 1971, Marvin Macy in Ballad of the Sad Café; Royal Court, Nov 1972, Con in A Pagan Place; toured, with Prospect Company, spring 1973, in The Country Wife; Criterion, July 1973, Geoffrey in Absurd Person Singular; Young Vic, Oct 1975, again played Othello; Edinburgh Festival 1976 and National Theatre 1977, played with the Birmingham Repertory Company as Angelo in Measure For Measure, and as Engine in The Devil is an Ass; Hampstead, Feb 1978, David in Bodies; Greenwich, Oct 1978, Hugo in An Audience called Edouard; Ambassadors, Apr 1979, again played David in Bodies; TV, since his first appearance in 1963, includes: The Guardians, The Woodlanders, and The Love School.

Favourite parts: Undershaft in Major Barbara, Proctor in The Crucible, and Flamineo in The White Devil. *Recreation:* Acting. *Address:* c/o Larry Dalzell Associates, 3 Goodwin's Court, St Martin's Lane, London WC2. *Tel:* 01–240 3086.

BURKE, Patricia, actress
b Milan, Italy, 23 Mar 1917; *d* of Tom Burke and his wife Marie (Alt); *e* England, Australia and the United States; *m* (1) Michael William Kimpton (mar dis); (2) Group-Captain Duncan C Macdonald (mar dis); studied for the stage under Warde Morgan.

Made her first appearance on the stage at the Gate Theatre, London, 28 Feb 1933, as Gretl in I Hate Men; she then appeared at the Open Air Theatre, Regent's Park, June 1933; at the Adelphi, Oct 1933, played the first Chorus Girl in Nymph Errant; Daly's, Apr 1934, Daphne Bennett in Dark

Horizon; New Theatre, Oxford, June 1934, Isla in The Case of the Frightened Lady; appeared at the Malvern Festival, July–Aug 1934; New, Sept 1934, played Rachel in A Man's House; Streatham Hill, Dec 1934, played Alice in the pantomime Dick Whittington; Aug 1935, toured as Belinda in Sweet Aloes, and Mar 1936, as Dee Halsey in The Old Maid; Savoy, June 1936, played Precious Stream in Lady Precious Stream; Duchess, July 1936, Jill Gaywood in Spring Tide; Empire, Sheffield, Dec 1936, the Prince in Cinderella; Phoenix, Apr 1937, Joan Baker in Climbing; Palace, Sept 1937, Ruth Marsden in Take It Easy; London Hippodrome, Oct 1937, Rene in Hide and Seek; Adelphi, May 1938, appeared in the revue, Happy Returns; then studied dancing with Buddy Bradley, Vera Volkova and de Voss; Covent Garden, Dec 1938, Prince Charming in Red Riding Hood; Duchess (for Sunday Theatre), June 1939, Sarah in The Jews of York; Princes, Aug 1939, Mary Pugh in Sitting Pretty; Coliseum, Dec 1939, the Prince in Cinderella; Saville, Apr 1940, appeared in the revue, Up and Doing, and again appeared in this, May 1941; His Majesty's, May 1942, appeared in Big Top; Coliseum, Dec 1942, played Colin in Mother Goose; London Hippodrome, June 1943, scored a great success as Gabrielle in The Lisbon Story, which ran over a year; during 1944–5, toured for a year, with ENSA, in Italy, Middle East, and Burma; at the Saville, Feb 1946, played Terry Randall in Stage Door; Wyndham's, Aug 1946, Deborah Pomfret in Clutterbuck; Edinburgh Festival, with the Old Vic Company, Aug 1947, Katherina in The Taming of the Shrew, and Doll Common in The Alchemist; New, Nov 1947, for the Old Vic Company, appeared as Katherina in The Taming of the Shrew; at the same theatre, Dec 1947, Duchess de la Tremouille in St Joan; at the Connaught, Worthing, 1948, Rosalind in As You Like It; Q, Sept 1948, played Martha Hansford in Sweethearts and Wives, and appeared in the same part at Wyndham's, Feb 1949; Q, June 1949, Maria Faber in Trifles Light as Air; Bedford, Camden Town, Apr 1950, played Trilby in the play of that name; at the Lyceum, Edinburgh, Aug 1950, during the Festival, appeared as Connie May in The Atom Doctor; Empire, Liverpool, Dec 1950, played Captain Valentine in Humpty Dumpty; Arts, Sept 1951, played Mrs Worthley in Mrs Dot; Lyric, Hammersmith, May 1952, Imogen Parrott in Trelawny of the Wells; Court, Aug 1952, Adriana in The Comedy of Errors; Ambassadors', Nov 1952, Charlotte Young in Murder Mistaken; King's Hammersmith, Apr 1953, Olalla Quintana in The Wandering Jew; New, Bromley, Oct 1953, the Queen of Ardenburg in Nun's Veiling; Saville, May 1954, appeared in the revue Cockles and Champagne; Piccadilly, Sept 1955, played Caroline in Romance in Candlelight; Streatham Hill, Dec 1955, Robin Hood in Babes in the Wood; Finsbury Park, Dec 1956, Principal Boy in Robin Hood; Royal Court, Dec 1957, Lampito in Lysistrata, subsequently transferring to the Duke of York's, Feb 1958; Savoy, July 1958, Mrs Edgar Rice in The Trial of Mary Dugan; High Wycombe, Sept 1958, the Queen in The Eagle has Two Heads; Cambridge, May 1959, Lady Whitehall in Let Them Eat Cake; Royal Court, Dec 1960, played Kit in The Lion in Love; King's, Southsea, Apr 1961, played Cora-Belle Elmore in Belle; Globe, Sept 1961, Betty Draycot in The Mimic (Repertory Players'); toured as Lady Fitzadam in The Amorous Prawn, 1963; Phoenix, Leicester, Oct 1963, Maisie in Life Worth Living; same theatre, Aug 1965, played Ruth in A Change of Face; toured as Denise in Dear Charles, 1966; Watford, 1967, played title rôle in The Killing of Sister George (also at Richmond); Bradford, 1967, Mrs Cheveley in An Ideal Husband; Adelphi, 1968, took over as Mrs Kay Conner in Charlie Girl; Wimbledon, Christmas 1971, Queen in Alice in Wonderland;

toured, Apr 1972, in Stringer's Last Stand; films include: The Lisbon Story, Trojan Brothers, The Happiness of Three Women, The Impersonator, and Soft Beds, Hard Battles; has appeared frequently on television and radio; Drama Adviser to Hope, Leresche and Steele.

Recreations: Living and loving. *Address:* c/o *Spotlight*, 42–43 Cranbourn Street, London, WC2.

BURLINGAME, Lloyd, scenic, costume, and lighting designer.

Designed the décor for his first New York production, Leave It to Jane, at the Sheridan Square Playhouse, 25 May 1959; has since designed Answered the Flute, 1960; Cockeyed Kite, 1961; Moon on a Rainbow Shawl, The School for Scandal, The Sea Gull, The Tavern, Half-Past Wednesday, The Collection (lighting), The Dumbwaiter (lighting), 1962; The Lady of the Camellias (lighting and associate designer), Caesar and Cleopatra (décor and costumes), The Blue Boy in Black (décor and lighting), 1963; Pimpernel! (décor and lighting), The Physicists (design supervision), The Secret Life of Walter Mitty (décor and lighting), The Tavern, The Alchemist (also costumes), That 5 AM Jazz, Alfie, 1964; The Great Western Union (also costumes), Boeing, Boeing, The Right Honourable Gentleman (lighting only), Marat/Sade (décor and lighting), Inadmissible Evidence (lighting), 1965; Philadelphia, Here I Come, First One Asleep, Whistle (décor and lighting), The Loves of Cass McGuire, Help Stamp Out Marriage (lighting only), 1966; The Astrakhan Coat (décor and costumes), Arms and the Man (décor and costumes), There's a Girl in My Soup (lighting only), Brief Lives (lighting), Keep It in the Family, 1967; Joe Egg (décor and lighting), Woman Is My Idea, The Flip Side (lighting), Rockefeller and the Red Indians (lighting), 1968; Love Is a Time of Day (décor, costumes, lighting), Hadrian VII (lighting), 1969; Opium (lighting), Not Now, Darling (décor and costumes), 1970; A Midsummer Night's Dream, The Philanthropist (both lighting only), The Ballad of Johnny Pot (décor and lighting), 1971; Vivat Vivat! Regina (lighting), The Shadow of a Gunman, Via Galactica (lighting), 1972; designed the London and Dublin productions of Philadelphia, Here I Come, in London at the Lyric, 20 Sept 1967; was resident designer for the Detroit Repertory Theatre, 1967.

BURNETT, Carol, actress and singer
b San Antonio, Texas, 26 Apr 1933; *d* of Joseph Thomas Burnett and his wife Louise (Creighton); *e* Hollywood High School, and University of California; *m* (1) Don Saroyan (mar dis); (2) Joe Hamilton; prepared for the stage at the Theatre Arts Department, University of California.

Following her first appearance on the stage in a University production, she made her first stage appearance in New York at the Phoenix, off-Broadway, May 1959, as Princess Winnifred in Once upon a Mattress, transferring with the production to the Alvin, Nov 1959, and running for 460 performances; Starlight, Kansas City, Mo, summer 1961, played title-role in the musical Calamity Jane; toured the USA, 1962, in An Evening with Carol Burnett; State Fair Music Hall, Dallas, Texas, summer 1963, again played Calamity Jane; Mark Hellinger, May 1964, played Hope Springfield in Fade Out—Fade In, withdrew from the cast because of illness, to reappear at the same theatre, Feb 1965, in a new version of the same musical; at the National Guard Armory, Washington, DC, Jan 18, 1965, played in the 1965 Inaugural Gala for President Lyndon B Johnson; Huntington Hartford, Los Angeles, May 1971, Karen Nash, Muriel Tate, and Norma Hubley in Plaza Suite; same theatre, June 1973, Agnes in I Do, I Do; Opera House, Sydney, Australia, Oct

1973, appeared in a variety show; State Fair Music Hall, Dallas, Texas, June 1974, Agnes in I Do, I Do, and subsequently toured; Huntington Hartford, LA, Apr 1977, Doris in Same Time Next Year; first appeared on television in 1955, and has since made regular guest appearances in *The Garry Moore Show,* subsequently appearing in Calamity Jane, Once upon a Mattress, Julie (Andrews) and Carol at Carnegie Hall, *The Carol Burnett Show, Carol Burnett and Friends,* etc; has received the Emmy Award, 1961 and 1963, and the Peabody Award, 1963, among others; had her own radio show in 1961; has played in night clubs, notably The Blue Angel, NY, 1957 and 1959; first appeared in films in 1963, in Who's Been Sleeping in My Bed.

Favourite parts: Adelaide in Guys and Dolls and Annie in Annie Get Your Gun. *Recreations:* Golfing and water-skiing. *Address:* c/o CB Distribution Co, 9911 West Pico Boulevard, Los Angeles, Calif 90035.

BURR, Robert, actor
b Jersey City, New Jersey; *e* Colgate University.

Made his Broadway début at the Mansfield, 26 Dec 1947, in the Chorus of The Cradle Will Rock; Alvin, 1948, played a Seaman in Mister Roberts, then toured as Reber in this play, 1949–50; Broadhurst, 10 Mar 1951, appeared as a Citizen in Romeo and Juliet; Broadhurst, 1954, took over as Chris Steelman in Anniversary Waltz; Shubert, New Haven, Conn, Nov 1955, played Gus in Top Man; New York City Center, 12 Jan 1956, Servant to Cornwall in Orson Welles's production of King Lear; Martin Beck, May 1956, Draco de la Crux in The Lovers; New York City Center, Mar 1957, Matt of the Mint in The Beggar's Opera; Martin Beck, Mar 1958, Evans in Who Was That Lady I Saw You With?; The Players, Jan 1959, Edgar in King Lear; Henry Miller's, Dec 1959, Lieutenant, the Court Clerk in The Andersonville Trial; Billy Rose, Oct 1960, German Sergeant in The Wall; St James, Sept 1963, Miltitz in Luther; Lunt-Fontanne, Apr 1964, Bernardo and understudied Richard Burton as Hamlet in Hamlet; Delacorte, June 1964, took over on the second performance from Alfred Ryder in the title-role of Hamlet and played it for the rest of the run; Shubert, Nov 1964, Lou MacNiall in Bajour; Delacorte, July 1965, title-role of Coriolanus; Circle in the Square, Dec 1965, Francisco de Medicis, Duke of Florence in The White Devil; ANTA, 1966, took over from Christopher Plummer as Francisco Pizarro in The Royal Hunt of the Sun; Alvin, Sept 1966, Dan Packard in Dinner at Eight; Delacorte, July 1967, Philip the Bastard in King John; US tour, 1969–70, The Player in Rosencrantz and Guildenstern Are Dead, and the title-role in Hamlet; Delacorte, July 1970, Lord Talbot in The Wars of the Roses; Lyceum, Dec 1971, Lionel Masters in Wild and Wonderful; ANTA, Feb 1972, Commanding General in The Love Suicide at Schofield Barracks; Ahmanson, Los Angeles, Nov 1973, played in Cyrano de Bergerac; Delacorte, June 1975, Ghost in Hamlet; Vivian Beaumont, Dec 1975, again played Ghost in Hamlet; appeared at the O'Neill Playwrights' Conference, Waterford, Conn, 1977; Milwaukee Rep, Nov 1977, appeared in Long Day's Journey into Night and Ah, Wilderness!; Center Stage, Baltimore, Md, 1978, appeared in Measure for Measure; has also appeared in films in Picnic, Remains to Be Seen, A Shot in the Dark, A Man for all Seasons, etc.

Address: c/o The Gage Group, 1650 Broadway, New York, NY 10019.

BURRELL, Sheila, actress
b Blackheath, London, 9 May 1922; *d* of John Burrell and his wife Mary Ethel (Hutchinson); *e* St John's School, Bexhill-on-Sea; *m* (1) Laurence Payne (mar dis); (2) David Sim;

studied for the stage at the Webber-Douglas School of Singing and Dramatic Art.

Made her first appearance on the stage, 1942, playing Patsy in The Patsy, entertaining troops; made her first appearance in London, at the Prince of Wales's Theatre, 20 Apr 1944, as Rose in The Rest is Silence; Chanticleer, June 1944, played Sonja in Happily Ever After?, and then appeared at Liverpool, as Katherine in The Taming of the Shrew; at the Arts, Oct 1944, Judy in The Bread-winner; Feb 1945, Rosetta in Leonce and Lena; Chanticleer, Mar 1945, Maia Rubeck in When We Dead Awaken; Arts, Apr 1945, Celestine in An Italian Straw Hat; Oct 1947, Mrs Rosenberg in Smith; at Dundee, 1947, played Bathsheba in Jonathan; during 1948, appeared at Croydon and at the Embassy, as Louka in Arms and the Man, Gilda in Design for Living, Judy in The Shining Hour; she also played a season at the Dublin Gate Theatre, appearing in Abdication, The Vigil, and The Mountains Look Different; Lyric, Hammersmith, Mar and Ambassadors', Apr 1949, played Barbara Allen in Dark of the Moon; Embassy, July 1949, Elizabeth in Fit for Heroes; toured, Feb 1950, as Ann Boleyn in The White Falcon; Duchess, Apr 1950, Clara, in The Man With the Umbrella; Watergate, Nov 1950, Margot in The Typewriter; Q, Feb 1951, Letticia in The Watchman; New Boltons, Apr 1951, played She in Happy and Glorious; joined the Bristol Old Vic Company for the 1951–2 season, when she appeared as Juliette in The Traveller Without Luggage, Curley's Wife in Of Mice and Men, Perpetua in Venus Observed, and Rosaline in Love's Labour's Lost; Vaudeville, May 1952, played Linda Cooper in Sweet Madness; Embassy, Mar 1953, Rosina in The Herald Angels; Strand (for Repertory Players), May 1954, Elizabeth Glossop in Lola; Q, Sept 1954, Aimée in Finishing School; Bristol Old Vic, Feb 1956, played Goneril in King Lear; Arts, Apr 1959, Sedra in Dark Halo; Connaught, Worthing, Oct 1960, played Joanne in The Warm Peninsula; Theatre Royal, Bristol, May 1963, Honor Klein in The Severed Head, subsequently appearing at the Criterion, London, July 1963, in the same production; made her first appearance in New York at the Royale, Oct 1964, in the same play; Arnaud, Guildford, Feb 1968, Shatov in Call Me Jacky; for the Royal Shakespeare Company in Stratford's 1970 season, she played Margaret in Richard III, Constance in King John and Lucetta in The Two Gentlemen of Verona, also appearing in the latter part at the Aldwych, Dec 1970; Palace, Watford, May 1971, Nora Colerne in The Superannuated Man; Royal Court, Aug 1971, Mrs James in West of Suez, transferring to the Cambridge; joined the National Theatre at the Old Vic, 1972, to play Duchess of Gloucester in Richard II, Mar; Lady Sneerwell in The School for Scandal, May; First Witch in Macbeth, Nov; for the Actors Company, 1974–75, she played Agave in The Bacchae, Madame Pernelle in Tartuffe, Madame Giry in The Phantom of the Opera, and Monica in The Last Romantic; Round House, Aug 1978, Dame Purecraft in Bartholomew Fair; Soho Poly, Apr 1979, Evelyn in Personal Effects; has also taken part in several broadcast and television plays, and appeared in films.

Favourite parts: Barbara in Dark of the Moon, Honor Klein, and Queen Margaret in Richard III. *Address:* c/o Richard Jackson Ltd, 59 Knightsbridge, London, SW1.

BURROWS, Abe, dramatic author and director
b New York City, 18 Dec 1910; *s* of Louis A Burrows and his wife Julia (Salzberg); *e* NY; *m* Carin Smith.

Formerly in accountancy and a commercial broker, and also a writer for radio and television, including: *This Is New York,* 1938, *Rudy Vallee Program,* 1940, *Duffy's Tavern,*

1940–5, *Abe Burrows' Show,* 1946–7, etc; author of Guys and Dolls (with Jo Swerling), 1950, which received the Drama Critics Circle and the Tony Awards; Three Wishes for Jamie (with Charles O'Neal), 1952; Can-Can, 1953; Silk Stockings (with George S Kaufman and Leueen McGrath), 1955; Say, Darling (with Richard and Marian Bissell), 1958; First Impressions, 1959; How to Succeed in Business Without Really Trying, 1961 (London, 1963), which received the Pulitzer Prize, the Drama Critics Circle, and the Tony Awards; Cactus Flower, 1965; Four on a Garden, 1971; Hellzapoppin, 1976; directed the productions of Two on the Aisle, 1952; Can-Can, 1953; Reclining Figure, 1954; Happy Hunting, 1956; Say Darling, 1958; First Impressions, Golden Fleecing, 1959; How to Succeed in Business Without Really Trying (also co-produced), 1961; What Makes Sammy Run? 1964; Cactus Flower, 1965 (London, 1967); Forty Carats, 1968; Four on a Garden, 1971; No Hard Feelings, tour of Good News, which he also adapted, 1973; his autobiography, Honest, Abe, published 1980; member of the Dramatists Guild, Society of Stage Directors and Choreographers, Directors Guild of America, AFTRA, ASCAP, and Screen Writers Guild.

Hobby: Painting. *Address:* c/o William Morris Agency, 1350 Avenue of the Americas, New York, NY 10019.

BURTON, Margaret, actress and singer
b Keighley, Yorks, 18 Mar 1924; *d* of Arthur Henry Burton and his wife Alice (Pickles); *e* Holycroft School, Keighley; *m* (1) David Nixon (mar dis); (2) Arnold Moseley (mar dis); (3) Michael Garvey; trained at the Royal Manchester College of Music.

First stage appearance in Calcutta, Sept 1945, in an ENSA revue; toured Britain, June 1946, in Twinkle; with the Fol-de-Rols, 1947–48; toured, 1949, as Margot Bonvalet in The Desert Song; 1950, as Mariana in The Lady of the Rose; Pavilion, Bournemouth, Aug 1951, Teresa in The Maid of the Mountains, touring in this role until Nov 1952; her first West End appearance was as Colin in Mother Goose at the Palladium, 22 Dec 1954; Players', May 1955, Kitty Hemming in Twenty Minutes South; Piccadilly, Sept 1955, Michele in Romance in Candlelight; Players', Oct 1956, Portia Browne in The Three Caskets; Floral Hall, Scarborough, Summer 1958, in Light Up the Town; Players', Mar 1961, again played Portia Browne; first NY appearance, The Strollers', Oct 1961, in Time Gentlemen Please!; Candie Gardens, Guernsey, Summer 1965, in One Enchanting Evening; Westminster, July 1967, Annie Jaeger in Annie; Criterion, Apr 1970, Sostrata in Mandrake; Her Majesty's, Melbourne, Oct 1976, Wife of Bath in More Canterbury Tales; Albery, Oct 1978, took over the part of Mrs Corney in Oliver!; has appeared frequently as principal boy in pantomime, and more recently in leading light opera roles at Sadler's Wells and the London Coliseum, including Helen in La Belle Hélène; first film, 1972, The Comedy Man; has appeared a number of times on TV and made many broadcasts as a singer.

Address: c/o Robert Mackintosh Personal Management, 56 Golden House, Great Pulteney Street, London W1.

BURTON, Richard, CBE, actor
b Pontrhydfen, South Wales, 10 Nov 1925; *e* Port Talbot Secondary School and Exeter College, Oxford University; *m* (1) Sybil Williams (mar dis); (2) Elizabeth Taylor (twice: both dis); (3) Susan Hunt.

Made his first appearance on the stage at the Royal Court Theatre, Liverpool, Nov 1943, as Glan in Druid's Rest; first appeared in London, at the St Martin's Theatre, 26 Jan 1944, in the same part, which he played for three months; he then went up to Oxford University, and for the OUDS, 1944, played Angelo in Measure for Measure; served with the Royal Air Force, 1944–7; reappeared on the stage at the Lyric Theatre, Hammersmith, Feb 1948, as Mr Hicks in Castle Anna; Globe, May 1949, played Richard in The Lady's Not For Burning; Lyric, Hammersmith, Jan 1950, Cuthman in The Boy With a Cart; at Brighton, Mar 1950, played Tegeus in A Phoenix Too Frequent; first appeared in New York, at the Royale Theatre, 8 Nov 1950, as Richard in The Lady's Not For Burning; at the Plymouth, Dec 1951, played the Musician in Legend of Lovers; appeared at the Lyric, Hammersmith, Apr 1952, as Capt Montserrat in Montserrat; at the Edinburgh Festival, 1953, with the Old Vic Company, appeared as Hamlet; remained with the Old Vic Company for the 1953–4 season, when he again played Hamlet, and also appeared as Philip the Bastard in King John, Sir Toby Belch in Twelfth Night, Caius Martius in Coriolanus and Caliban in The Tempest; again appeared at the Old Vic, Dec 1955, in the title-part of Henry V, and Feb 1956, when he alternated with John Neville as Othello and Iago in Othello; Morosco, NY, Nov 1957, played Prince Albert in Time Remembered; Majestic, NY, Dec 1960, played Arthur in Camelot; Lunt-Fontanne, NY, Apr 1964, played the title-rôle in Sir John Gielgud's production of Hamlet; received the NY Drama Critics Award, 1961, for the Best Performance in a Musical, in Camelot; Oxford Playhouse, Feb 1966, played the title-rôle in Dr Faustus for the OUDS; Plymouth, NY, Mar 1976, took over the part of Martin Dysart in Equus; first entered films, 1948, in The Last Days of Dolwyn; he has since appeared in the following films: My Cousin Rachel, The Desert Rats, The Robe, Look Back in Anger, Cleopatra, The VIP's, Becket, Hamlet (Broadway production), Who's Afraid of Virginia Woolf?, Where Eagles Dare, Anne of the Thousand Days, Under Milk Wood, Exorcist II, Equus, The Wild Geese, etc; received the CBE in the Birthday Honours, 1970; Fellow of St Peter's College, Oxford, 1975–.

Address: c/o Major Donald Neville-Willing, 85 Kinnerton Street, London SW1. *Tel:* 01–235 4640

BURY, John, designer

b Aberystwyth, Wales, 27 Jan 1925; *s* of Charles Rugely Bury and his wife Emily Francis Margaret (Adams); *e* Hereford Cathedral School, and University College, London; *m* (1) Margaret Greenwood (mar dis); (2) Elizabeth Duffield; formerly an Observer in the Fleet Air Arm of the Royal Navy.

Began his career as an actor with the Theatre Workshop Company at the Theatre Royal, Stratford, E, Mar 1954, when he played Major Planel in The Fire Eaters; for the same company, May, 1954, he played Captain Horster and designed the production for An Enemy of the People; subsequently designer for Theatre Workshop for the following productions: The Cruel Daughters, The Chimes, 1954; Richard II, Volpone, Mother Courage and Her Children (Devon Festival), 1955; Edward II, The Quare Fellow, 1956; You Won't Always Be On Top, 1957; Celestina, Love and Lectures, and The Man of Destiny (double-bill, also directed); Unto Such Glory, and The Respectable Prostitute (double-bill), A Taste of Honey, A Christmas Carol, 1958; Fings Ain't Wot They Used T' Be, The Dutch Courtesan, 1959; Sam, the Highest Jumper of Them All, Ned Kelly, Every Man in His Humour, Sparrers Can't Sing, Progress to the Park, 1960; Oh, What a Lovely War!, 1963 and (New York) 1964; has designed numerous plays for the Royal Shakespeare Company, of which he was appointed Head of Design in 1964; these include Afore Night Come, Measure

for Measure, Macbeth, 1962; The Physicists (also NY 1964), Julius Caesar, The Wars of the Roses, 1963; Andorra, Richard II, Henry IV, Henry V, Eh?, 1964; The Homecoming (also NY 1967), Hamlet, 1965; The Government Inspector, The Meteor, 1966; Coriolanus, Macbeth, The Criminals, 1967; Indians, 1968; A Delicate Balance, Dutch Uncle, Landscape and Silence, The Silver Tassie, Henry VIII, 1969; Old Times, 1971; All Over, 1972; Head of Design, National Theatre, 1973–; designs for the company include TVHE Tempest, The Freeway, Grand Manoeuvres, 1974; Happy Days, No Man's Land, Hamlet, 1975, all at the Old Vic; for the new National Theatre he has designed Tamburlaine, Counting the Ways, 1976; No Man's Land, Julius Caesar, Volpone, Judgement, Happy Day, The Country Wife, 1977; The Cherry Orchard, Macbeth, Betrayal, Strife, 1978; The Fruits of Enlightenment and Amadeus (also lighting), 1979; Othello, 1980; other productions he has designed include the York Mystery Cycle of 1963; The Blood Knot, 1964; Honour and Offer, The Lionel Touch, 1969; The Battle of Shrivings, The Rothschilds (NY), 1970; Hedda Gabler, A Doll's House (both NY), 1971; Via Galactica (NY), 1972; Sleuth, Phèdre (both Tokyo), 1973; his opera designs include Moses and Aaron, The Magic Flute, La Calisto, The Marriage of Figaro, and Tristan and Isolde; co-winner, Gold Medal for Scene Design, Prague Quadriennale, 1976.

Recreations: Sailing, gardening. *Address:* 14 Woodlands Road, London, SW13.

BUTLIN, Jan, director and dramatic author

b Wanstead, London, 16 Feb 1940; *d* of Ernest Gordon Butlin and his wife Ethel Charlotte (Gower); *e* Hillside School, Haslemere, and Petersfield County HS; *m* Martin King.

Trained for the stage at RADA and made her début as an actress at the Castle, Farnham, 1959, in Separate Tables; directed her first production, Where the Rainbow Ends, at the Intimate, Palmer's Green, 1970; here in the same year she directed her own history of the music hall, They've Knocked Down the Empires Now; she has since directed Alice in Wonderland (Stratford), 1972; Two and Two Make Sex, 1973; A Ghost on Tiptoe, There Goes the Bride, 1974; Miss Adams Will Be Waiting (Guildford), Rosencrantz and Guildenstern are Dead (Farnham), 1975; has also directed productions at Leicester, Windsor, Richmond, Johannesburg and elsewhere; directed her adaptation of Carry on, Jeeves, 1976; One of the Family, 1976; Perfect Pitch, 1977; Sleuth (tour) 1978; has written for TV, including the series Life Begins at Forty, and radio and is the author of Staging a Play, 1971.

Recreations: Music, cats and her herb garden. *Address:* c/o Richard Stone, 18/20 York Buildings, Adelphi, London WC2.

BUTTON, Jeanne, costume designer

b 8 May 1930; *d* of C C Button and his wife Marjorie (Ault); *e* Carnegie Institute of Technology (BS) and Yale School of Drama; *m* Stephen A Sbarge (mar dis).

Her first Broadway costume designs were for Tambourines to Glory, at the Little, Feb 1963; subsequent Broadway credits include The Watering Place, Henry V, 1969; The Robber Bridegroom, 1975; Wings, 1979; has costumed over 60 productions off-Broadway, notably MacBird, 1967; has worked with the Acting Company, American Shakespeare Festival, Yale Rep and other regional companies; opera designs include costumes for Satyricon, Amsterdam State Opera; for TV designed a year of *Search for Tomorrow* (CBS), etc; has taught at Yale School of Drama and currently at NYU School of the Arts; co-author of A History of Costume, 1978.

Address: 125 Riverside Drive, New York, NY 10024. *Tel:* 580 2356.

BUZO, Alexander, dramatic author
b Sydney, NSW, 23 July 1944; *s* of Zihni Josef Buzo and his wife Elaine Winifred Walker (Johnson); *e* The Armidale School and the University of New South Wales; *m* Merelyn Johnson; formerly a public servant.

His first play, Norm and Ahmed, was produced at the Old Tote Theatre, Sydney, 9 Apr 1968; he has since written Rooted, 1969 (produced Hampstead, 1973); The Front Room Boys, 1970 (Royal Court, London, 1971); The Roy Murphy Show, 1971; Macquarie, Tom, 1972; Coralie Lansdowne Says No, 1974; Martello Towers, 1976; Makassar Reef, 1978; Big River, 1980; scripted the film Rod, 1972; TV writing includes: King Arthur, and Legend of Robin Hood; resident playwright, Melbourne Theatre Company, 1972–3; member, Australian Writers' Guild; awarded the Gold Medal of the Australian Literature Society, 1972.

Recreations: Cricket, tennis, surfing, tourism. *Address:* 14 Rawson Avenue, Bondi Junction, Sydney, NSW 2022, Australia.

BYERLEY, Vivienne, theatre press representative
b London; *d* of Isaac Stanley Byerley and his wife Grace Constance (Inge); *e* privately; was formerly engaged in secretarial work.

Appointed Press representative to The Company of Four, Oct 1945; subsequently with the Young Vic, during 1946–7; appointed representative to H M Tennent, Ltd, Feb 1947.

Address: Apollo Theatre, Shaftesbury Avenue, London W1V 7HD. *Tel:* 01–437 3681.

BYRNE, John playwright, and painter
b Paisley, 6 Jan 1940; *s* of Patrick Byrne and his wife Alice (McShane); *e* St Mirin's Academy, Paisley, and Glasgow School of Art; *m* Alice Simpson; is a professional artist.

His first play to be performed was Writer's Cramp, Edinburgh Festival, Aug 1977; he has since written The Slab Boys, 1978; Normal Service, 1979; The Loveliest Night of the Year, 1979, retitled Threads for its Hampstead performance in 1980; writing for TV includes The Butterfly's Hoof, The Slab Boys.

Address: c/o Margaret Ramsay, 14a Goodwin's Court, St Martin's Lane, London WC2.

BYRNE, Patsy (Patricia), actress
b Ashford, Kent, 13 July 1933; *d* of Basil Reginald Byrne and his wife Edith (Morton); *e* Ashford County Grammar School; *m* Patrick John Seccombe; trained for the stage at the Rose Bruford College of Speech and Drama.

Appeared at the Queen's, Hornchurch, Nov 1955, as Susan Barwell in Mayor's Nest, and after four years in repertory, at Hornchurch, Guildford, and Coventry, she made her first appearance in London, with the Belgrade Theatre Company (Coventry), at the Royal Court Theatre, July 1958, as Bessie Blatt in Chicken Soup With Barley; at the same theatre, June 1959, played Jennie Beales in Roots, subsequently transferring with the production to the Duke of York's, July 1959; Royal Court, Oct 1959, played Annie in Serjeant Musgrave's Dance; at the same theatre, Dec 1959, played Aunt Mildred in One Way Pendulum, subsequently transferring to the Criterion, Feb 1960; Royal Court, June 1960, again played Jennie Beales in Roots, succeeding Joan Plowright as Beatie Bryant towards the end of the run; joined the Royal Shake-

speare Theatre Company, Dec 1960, on long-term contract, appearing in repertory at the Aldwych Theatre, Dec 1960, as Maria in Twelfth Night; Jan 1961, as the Kitchen Maid in Ondine; Feb 1961, as Sister Gabrielle in The Devils; at the Royal Shakespeare Theatre, Stratford-on-Avon, July 1961, played Audrey in As You Like It; and Oct 1961, Bianca in Othello; Aldwych, Dec 1961, Dunyasha in The Cherry Orchard; Aldwych, Jan 1962, again played Audrey in As You Like It; Mar 1962, played the leading part of Grusche in The Caucasian Chalk Circle; Aug 1962, played Blae in Curtmantle; at the Mermaid, Apr 1963, played Miss Hoyden in the musical Virtue in Danger, transferring with the production to the Strand, June 1963; Royal, Brighton, Feb 1964, Nerissa in The Merchant of Venice, and Hermia in A Midsummer Night's Dream, prior to a tour of Latin America and Europe; returned to the Royal Shakespeare, Aldwych, July 1964, to play Mother in Picnic on the Battlefield in the programme Expeditions One; July 1964, Nell in Endgame; Oct 1964, Betty Dorrick in Eh?; Dec 1964, Mistress Ford in The Merry Wives of Windsor; Royal Shakespeare, Apr 1965, Jacquenetta in Love's Labour's Lost, Bellamira in The Jew of Malta, and Nerissa in The Merchant of Venice; Aldwych, Jan 1966, played Maria Antonovna in The Government Inspector; Royal Shakespeare, Apr 1966, Doll Tearsheet in Henry IV Part Two and Maria in Twelfth Night; Chichester Festival, 1974, Flippanta in The Confederacy; Birmingham Repertory, 1975, played Dora Strang in Equus, Mar, and Miss Prism in The Importance of Being Earnest, May; Birmingham Rep, Feb 1976, Mrs Parker in When We are Married; Chichester, 1979 season, played Miss Prism in The Importance of Being Earnest and Mrs Stanley in The Man Who Came to Dinner; Chichester, May 1976, Mrs Noah in Noah; television appearances include The Cherry Orchard and As You Like It (Royal Shakespeare Company), Androcles and the Lion, The Cellar and the Almond Tree, etc.

Favourite parts: Grusche, Audrey, Miss Hoyden, and Jennie Beales. *Recreations:* Reading and travelling. *Address:* c/o Crouch Associates, 59 Frith Street, London W1.

BYRNE, Peter, actor
b London, 29 Jan 1928; *s* of James Byrne and his wife Elizabeth Emily (Massey); *e* Finchley Grammar School, London; trained for the stage at the Italia Conti School.

First stage appearance, Oct 1944, at the Knightstone Theatre, Weston-super-Mare, playing the third Elf in Where the Rainbow Ends; made his first London appearance at the Stoll, Aug 1945, playing Smart, a Will Hay schoolboy, in the revue For Crying Out Loud; Golders Green, May 1952 and Hippodrome, Nov 1952, PC Andy Crawford in The Blue Lamp; St Martin's, Feb 1956, Hon George D'Alroy in She Smiled at Me; Duchess, Aug 1966, took over the part of Robert Castin in Boeing-Boeing; Globe, Dec 1968, took over as Robert Danvers in There's a Girl in My Soup; transferred with the play to the Comedy, Aug 1969; O'Keefe Centre, Toronto, Mar 1973, Philip Markham in Move Over Mrs Markham; toured, Mar 1976, as Milo Tindle in Sleuth, June 1976, as David Ryder in Murder With Love; toured, 1977, as Tony Price in Double Edge, and, in 1978, as Michael Starwedder in The Unexpected Guest; Wyvern, Swindon, Dec 1979, directed Jack and the Beanstalk, also playing Baron Killjoy; has appeared in repertory at Farnham, Hornchurch, Nottingham, Windsor and Worthing; was director of productions at the Palace Court, Bournemouth, 1966; made his first television appearance in 1953 and has appeared subsequently in plays and series, including twenty years in *Dixon of Dock Green*.

Favourite parts: Robert Castin, Andy Crawford and Robert Danvers. *Recreations:* Cricket, tennis, astronomy. *Club:* Green Room. *Address:* c/o Renée Stepham Ltd, Panton House, 25 Haymarket, London, SW1. *Tel:* 01–930 4944.

C

CAESAR, Irving (*né* Isaac), lyricist, composer, librettist, performer
b New York City, 4 July 1895; *s* of Morris Caesar and his wife Sofia (Selinger); *e* Chappaqua Mountain Institute, College of the City of New York (1915); was a stenographer with the Ford Peace Expedition in 1915, and a press representative.

Toured in vaudeville; his first lyrics for the theatre were Swanee, with George Gershwin as composer, for Al Jolson in Sinbad, Winter Garden, 14 Feb 1918; has since written Kissing Time, Lady Kitty, Inc, Hitchy-Koo, 1920; Lola in Love, Greenwich Village Follies (with John Murray Anderson), Pins and Needles, 1922; Here's Howe, The Greenwich Village Follies (with Anderson), 1923; The Greenwich Village Follies (with Anderson and Cole Porter), Betty Lee (with Otto Harbach), 1924; No, No, Nanette, The Bamboula, Mercenary Mary, 1925; Sweetheart Time, No Foolin' (also playwright), Betsy (libretto with David Freedman), 1926; Yes, Yes, Yvette, Hit the Deck, Talk About Girls, 1927; Americana (with J P McEvoy), New Americana, 1928; Polly, Nice to See You, George White's Scandals, Nina Rosa, 1929; Ripples (with Graham John), 9:15 Revue, 1930; adapted (with Aben Kandel) and lyrics for The Wonder Bar, George White's Scandals, 1931; George White's Music Hall Varieties, 1932; Melody, Shady Lady (playwright), 1933; Thumbs Up, 1934; The White Horse Inn, Transatlantic Rhythm, 1936; Russian Bank, 1940; My Dear Public, a revue which he also co-authored with Chuno Gotterfeld and produced, 1943; wrote several screenplays in Hollywood, beginning in 1935; devised a revue called A Biography in Song in which he performs his own materials, and appeared in it at the Theatre de Lys, 6 Dec 1971, Town Hall, 24 Jan 1973, Town Hall, 28 Nov 1973, and elsewhere; No, No, Nanette revived in NY in 1971; responsible for the Irving Caesar Foundation; contributor of many articles to *Variety*.

Recreations: The theatre, reading, swimming. *Club:* Friars.
Address: 850 Seventh Avenue, New York, NY.

CAESAR, Sid, actor
b Yonkers, New York, 8 Sept 1922; *s* of Max Caesar and his wife Ida (Raffel); *e* Yonkers High School; *m* Florence Levy.

Formerly a saxophonist and clarinetist with the Charlie Spivak, Claude Thornhill, and Shep Fields dance bands; served in the US Coast Guard, 1942–4, and during this time played in the USCG orchestra and wrote sketches for the USCG revue Six on, Twelve off; made his NY theatre début at the Strand, 1944, in the revue Tars and Spars; at the Broadhurst, Jan 1948, played in the revue Make Mine Manhattan; reappeared in NY after many years in television at the Lunt-Fontanne, Nov 1962, playing several roles in Little Me; toured in Little Me, 1964; Broadhurst, Jan 1971, various roles in Four on a Garden; Westport Country Playhouse, Conn, June 1972, Barney Cashman in Last of the Red Hot Lovers; Caribe Hilton, San Juan, Puerto Rico, Feb 1973, returned to cabaret; Arlington Park, Chicago, Aug 1973, Mel Edison in The Prisoner of Second Avenue; Rainbow Grill, NY, Apr 1974, appeared in cabaret; Arlington Park, Ill, Oct 1974, played in Double Take; Crystal Palace, Dallas, Mar 1975, Barney Cashman in Last of the Red Hot Lovers; first appeared in films in 1946 in Tars and Spars, and since has

played in It's A Mad, Mad, Mad, Mad World, 1963, Ten from Your Show of Shows, 1973; first appeared on television in 1949 in *Broadway Revue* and continued in television as one of its favorite satirists and comedians on *Your Show of Shows* (1950–4), *Caesar's Hour* (1954–7), *Sid Caesar Invites You* (1958), *Sid Caesar Show* (BBC, 1958), *The Sid Caesar Show* (1963–4), and, later, in various specials and variety programs; has also appeared extensively in cabaret since 1947; received the Donaldson Award for Make Mine Manhattan, five Emmy Awards, and the Sylvania Award for his work in television.

Address: Actors' Equity Association, 165 West 46th Street, New York, NY 10036.

CAHN, Sammy, lyricist and performer
b New York City, 18 June 1913; *s* of Edward Joseph Cohen and his wife Myrtle Ellen (Perdue); *m* (1) Gloria Delson (mar dis); (2) Tita Basile Curtis.

Wrote lyrics for his first Broadway show High Button Shoes, produced at the Century, 9 Oct 1947; since then has written lyrics for Two's Company, 1952; Eddie Fisher at the Winter Garden, 1962; Les Poupees de Paris, 1964; Skyscraper, 1965; Walking Happy, 1966; Look to the Lilies, 1970; performed in the revue of his works called Words and Music at the Golden, 16 Apr, 1974; made his London stage début at the New London, Sept 1974, in his show Sammy Cahn's Songbook; Huntington Hartford, Los Angeles, Dec 1975, appeared in Words and Music; author of his autobiography I Should Care, 1974; is also a noted Hollywood lyricist, often teaming with Jimmy Van Heusen, and won the Academy Award four times for his lyrics; wrote lyrics for Tonight and Every Night, 1944, Anchors Aweigh, 1945, Wonder Man, 1945, April in Paris, 1954, The Court Jester, 1955, A Flea in Her Ear, 1969, Journey Back to Oz, 1974, etc.

Address: ASCAP, 1 Lincoln Plaza, New York, NY 10023.

CAIRNCROSS, James, actor
b Dunfermline, Fife, 21 Dec 1915; *s* of James Cairncross and his wife Mildred Lizzie McNab; *e* Dunfermline HS and Edinburgh University (1933–35); trained for the stage under Michel St Denis at the London Theatre Studio, 1936–38.

Made his first professional appearance at the Phoenix, 6 Oct 1938, as Fyodor in The White Guard; in repertory at Perth, 1939, and (after war service) at the Old Vic, Liverpool, 1945–46; Piccadilly, Dec 1946, Thyreus in Antony and Cleopatra; Her Majesty's, May 1947, Mr Waxman and Montague Burton in Edward My Son, transferring to the Lyric; appeared in The Thrie Estates at the Edinburgh Festival, 1949, and also in 1951, 1973; at the Arts, Salisbury, 1949–51; Citizens', Glasgow, 1951–52; Bristol Old Vic, 1952–53; Edinburgh Festival, 1952, 1953, in The Highland Fair; Vaudeville, Aug 1954, played three parts in Salad Days, staying with the production until 1958; Saville, Apr 1959, two parts in Candide; Bristol Old Vic, 1959–60; Vaudeville, Mar 1960, two parts in Follow That Girl; Royal Court, July 1961, Prior and Eck in Luther, playing the same parts at the Edinburgh Festival and afterwards at the Phoenix; in repertory at Nottingham Playhouse, 1963, and Oxford Playhouse,

1964–65; Phoenix, May 1965, Sir Edwin Challoner in A Heritage and Its History; Queen's, Oct 1967, Leonid Andreyich in The Cherry Orchard; Open Air, Regent's Park, season 1968, played Dr Caius in The Merry Wives of Windsor and Duke of Milan in Two Gentlemen of Verona; Piccadilly, Apr 1970, Jack Campbell Barnes in Who Killed Santa Claus?; for Prospect, 1971, played Polonius and First Gravedigger in Hamlet; Mermaid, Apr 1975, Dr Blenkinsop in The Doctor's Dilemma; member of the Royal Lyceum company, Edinburgh, 1975–79; for Bristol Old Vic, 1979, played Priam and Nestor in Troilus and Cressida, and Justice Balance in The Recruiting Officer, visiting the Edinburgh and Buxton Festivals; has toured in Africa and the Far East for the British Council; has played the part of Badger in Toad of Toad Hall on a number of occasions since 1970; TV, since 1952, includes Sutherland's Law, The Tempest, and Edna, the Inebriate Woman.

Recreations: Cooking, listening to music. *Address:* 16 Melbury Road, London W14 8LT.

CAIRNEY, John, actor, director and writer
b Glasgow, 16 Feb 1930; *s* of Thomas Cairney; *e* St Mungo's Academy, Glasgow School of Art and Glasgow University; *m* Sheila Parker; trained for the stage at the Royal Scottish Academy of Music and Drama.

In repertory with the Wilson Barret company, 1952–53; Citizens', Glasgow, 1953–54; Bristol Old Vic, 1954–56; 1960–74 played leads as a guest with many major Scottish and other repertory companies, including Hamlet, Citizens', Oct 1960; Archie Rice in The Entertainer, Dundee, Apr 1972; title role in Cyrano de Bergerac, Newcastle, Nov 1974; his solo performance as Robert Burns was seen at the Traverse, Edinburgh, Jan 1965, as There Was a Man, and he has since played Burns in Britain, Europe, the USA and Canada; since 1970, for his company Shanter productions, he has written, directed, presented and appeared in such solo programmes as A Mackintosh Experience, The Robert Burns Story, The William McGonagall Story, The Private Life of R L Stevenson, The Ivor Novello Story, The Scotland Story, The Robert Service Story, and An Evening with John Cairney; these productions have been seen in Britain, N America, the Far East, New Zealand and in Moscow; films, since Ill Met by Moonlight in 1956, include Victim, and Cleopatra; TV, since 1953, includes the series *This Man Craig* as well as plays and versions of his one-man shows, some of which have also been issued as recordings; founder of Theatre Consultants, Scotland, 1970, and the Robert Burns Festival, Ayr, 1975.

Address: 197 Onslow Drive, Denistoun, Glasgow.

CALDER-MARSHALL, Anna, actress
b Kensington, London, 11 Jan 1947; *d* of Arthur Calder-Marshall and his wife Nancy Violet (Sales); *e* Convent of the Immaculate Heart of Mary, Billingshurst; *m* David Burke; trained for the stage at LAMDA.

Made her first stage appearance in Sept 1967, in A Severed Head at the Repertory, Birmingham; remained with the company, 1967, playing parts including Saint Joan, Juliet in Romeo and Juliet and Solveig in Peer Gynt; Edinburgh Festival, Aug 1968, played Ophelia in the 69 Theatre Company's Hamlet; Lyceum, Edinburgh, Aug 1969, Hedwig in the Scottish Actors' Company production of The Wild Duck, again in the Festival; made her first London appearance at the Royal Court, Feb 1970, as Sonya in Uncle Vanya; Edinburgh Festival, Aug 1970, Beatrice in The Changeling at the Lyceum, also appearing in a late-night entertainment at the Traverse, Bedtime Through the Century; Hampstead, Jan 1971, Perdita in The Formation Dancers; Chichester

Festival, July 1971, Cleopatra in Caesar and Cleopatra; Theatre Royal, Bristol, Apr 1972, Cressida in the Bristol Old Vic's Troilus and Cressida; returned to Chichester, July 1972, to play Jennet Jourdemayne in The Lady's Not For Burning; Hampstead, Dec 1972, Mabel Crum in While the Sun Shines; for Prospect, toured as Margery Pinchwife in The Country Wife, Spring 1973; Criterion, July 1973, Eva in Absurd Person Singular; Lyceum, Edinburgh, Oct 1974, Viola in Twelfth Night; Royal Court, Jan 1975, Annie in Objections to Sex and Violence; Hampstead, May 1975, Janet in Dear Janet Rosenberg, Dear Mr Kooning; joined the RSC, Oct 1975, to play Miss Mopply in Too True To Be Good at the Aldwych; Edinburgh Festival, 1976, and National Theatre, May 1977, appeared in the Birmingham Repertory Company's production of The Devil is an Ass as Mrs Fitzdotterel, and as Isabella in their Measure For Measure; Theatre Upstairs, Apr 1977, in For All Those Who Get Despondent; Greenwich, Dec 1979, played Kate Hardcastle in She Stoops to Conquer; first television appearance 1967, since when she has appeared regularly in plays and drama series, recently Bloomers; Emmy award, 1970; first film Wuthering Heights, 1970.

Recreations: Painting, writing, gardening. *Address:* c/o Larry Dalzell Associates, 3 Goodwin's Court, St Martin's Lane, London, WC2.

CALDERISI, David, director and producer
b Montreal, Canada, 21 June 1940; *s* of Raffaele Calderisi and his wife Carolina (de Francesco); *e* McGill University; trained for the stage at the London Academy of Music and Dramatic Art and was initially an actor.

At the New Arts, July 1966 to Feb 1967, directed a series of sixteen lunch-hour plays, notably The Audition, Play, The Experiment and Will Somebody Please Say Something; he has since directed plays including The Fire Raisers (Vancouver), 1968; K D Dufford, 1969; and Theatre of Death, 1970; co-director, 1966, with David Halliwell, of Quipu Productions Ltd, a network of artistic interaction, whose work included the presentation of further seasons of lunchtime theatre; returned to Canada where he has since directed in Winnipeg, etc.

Recreations: Reading, chess, snooker.

CALDICOT, Richard, actor
b London, 7 Oct 1908; *s* of James Stuart Bull and his wife Edith Emily (Sutton); *e* Dulwich; *m* Judith Mary Gray; trained for the stage at RADA.

Made his first professional appearance at the Theatre Royal, Huddersfield, 1928, as Charles Lomax in Major Barbara; Lyric, Hammersmith, Oct 1928, played Mr Hopkins in the Critic; Savoy, Jan 1929, L/Cpl Broughton in Journey's End; Lyric, Hammersmith, 1930, played Hastings in She Stoops to Conquer, Apr, Lane in The Importance of Being Earnest, July, and Argaleon in Marriage à la Mode, Oct; Cambridge Theatre, 1931, various parts in La Chauve-souris; Arts, also 1931, Simon Balcairn in Vile Bodies; Embassy, 1931, Kester Woodseaves in Precious Bane; season at Birmingham Rep, 1931; Queen's, 1932, Ignatz Scheel in Caravan; appeared at the Malvern Festival, 1934; Royalty, 1934, the Atheist in Within the Gates; New, 1934, first soldier in A Man's House, Apollo, 1935, Mark Dowser in Duet in Floodlight; at the Gaiety, played Georges in Swing Along, Sept 1936, Pantages in Going Greek, Sept 1937, and Jose Regalo in Running Riot, Aug 1938; Lyric, Dec 1939, Staff Colonel in Somewhere in England; served 1940–45 with the Gordon Highlanders and the 7th Rajput Regiment, Indian Army; Saville, Feb 1946, Fred Powell in Stage Door; in variety with

Leslie Henson, Victoria Palace, 1946; Lyric, May 1947, Harry Soames in Edward, My Son; Lyric, Hammersmith, Oct 1949, and St James's, Nov 1949, Shamrayef in The Seagull; Saville, July 1952, Henry Dawson in Albert RN; Phoenix, June 1957, Altert Honeydew in Six Months' Grace; St Martin's, Mar 1958, Chase Allen in The Kidders; Duke of York's, July 1958, Al Baur in The Joshua Tree; Royal Court, Oct 1959, the Parson in Serjeant Musgrave's Dance. Duchess, Apr 1960, Capt Foster in A Shred of Evidence; Strand, June 1971, Mr Bromhead in No Sex Please, We're British, playing the part until Feb 1976; Arts, June 1977, took over as McTeazle in Dirty Linen; national tour, 1979, later Adelphi, Nov, Col Pickering in My Fair Lady; films, since The Card in 1951, include: The VIP's, The Spy Who Came in from the Cold, Firepower, etc; numerous TV appearances since 1947 include plays and series.

Favourite parts: Capt Foster in A Shred of Evidence, Harry Soames in Edward, My Son. *Clubs:* Green Room, Stage Golfing Society. *Address:* c/o Essanay Ltd, 75 Hammersmith Road, London W14.

CALDWELL, Zoe, OBE, actress, director
b Hawthorn, Victoria, 14 Sept 1933; *e* Methodist Ladies College, Melbourne; *m* Robert Whitehead, producer.

One of the original members of the Union Theatre Repertory Company, Melbourne, Australia, making her first professional appearance with them in 1953; with the Elizabethan Theatre Trust, 1954–7, her rôles included Bubba in Summer of the Seventeenth Doll; appeared for two seasons with the Shakespeare Memorial Theatre Company, Stratford-on-Avon, England, 1958–9, as the Daughter of Antiochus in Pericles, and Margaret in Much Ado About Nothing, subsequently touring Russia with the company in Hamlet, Twelfth Night, and Romeo and Juliet; Memorial Theatre, Stratford-on-Avon, Apr 1959, played Bianca in Othello, Helena in All's Well that Ends Well, a Fairy in A Midsummer Night's Dream, and Cordelia in King Lear; Royal Court, Nov 1960, played Ismène in Antigone, and the Whore in Cob and Leach, in the double-bill Trials by Logue; at the same theatre, Feb 1961, played Isabella in the revival of The Changeling; Mar 1961, played Jacqueline in Jacques; Stratford Shakespearean Festival, Stratford, Ontario, June 1961, played Rosaline in Love's Labour's Lost, and Aug 1961, Sonja Downfahl in The Canvas Barricade; Manitoba Theatre Centre, 1961, played Pegeen Mike in Playboy of the Western World; at the Adelaide Festival of the Arts, Australia, Mar 1962, played the title-part in Saint Joan, subsequently touring with the production; for the Elizabethan Theatre Trust, Sydney, July 1962, played in The Ham Funeral; Union, Melbourne, Oct 1962, played Nola Boyle in The Season at Sarsaparilla; in the opening season of the Minnesota Theatre Company, Tyrone Guthrie Theatre, Minneapolis, 1963, played Frosine in The Miser, and Natasha in The Three Sisters; Manitoba Theatre Center, 1964, played the title part in Mother Courage; Goodman Theatre, Chicago, 1964, the Countess Aurelia in The Mad Woman of Chaillot; Guthrie Theatre, Minneapolis, May 1965, played Millamant in The Way of the World, Grusha in The Caucasian Chalk Circle, and Frosine in a revival of The Miser; Broadway, New York, Dec 1965, took over the part of the Prioress in The Devils; Longacre, NY, Feb 1966, played Polly in The Gnädiges Fraulein in Slapstick Tragedy; Shaw Festival, Niagara-on-the-Lake, summer 1966, played Orinthia in The Apple Cart and Lena Szezepanowska in Misalliance; at the Stratford Festival, Ontario, July–Oct 1967, Cleopatra in Antony and Cleopatra, Lady Anne in Richard III and Mrs Page in The Merry Wives of Windsor; Helen Hayes, NY, Jan 1968, Jean

Brodie in The Prime of Miss Jean Brodie, winning a Tony Award as Best Dramatic Actress; Ellen Stewart, NY, May 1970, played the title role in Colette; Haymarket, London, Sept 1970, Emma Hamilton in A Bequest to the Nation; Shubert, NY, Nov 1972, Eve in The Creation of the World and Other Business; Kennedy Center, Washington, Sept 1973, appeared in Love and Master Will; Vivian Beaumont Theatre, Lincoln Center, NY, Apr 1974, Alice in The Dance of Death; Eisenhower, Washington DC, Dec 1975, and Brooklyn Academy, Jan 1976, Mary Tyrone in Long Day's Journey into Night; Belasco, Oct 1977, directed An Almost Perfect Person; Stratford, Ontario, June 1979, directed Richard II; television appearances include: The Apple Cart, Macbeth, and The Lady's Not for Burning; awarded the OBE in the New Year Honours, 1970.

CALLOW, Simon, actor
b London, 15 Jun 1949; *s* of Neil Francis Callow and his wife Yvonne Mary (Guise); *e* Oratory Grammar School, London, and Queen's University, Belfast; trained for the stage at Drama Centre.

Made his first professional appearance at the Assembly Hall, Edinburgh, July 1973, in The Thrie Estates; in repertory at Lincoln and Edinburgh, 1973–74, his parts included Crown Prince Maximilian in Schippel, Traverse, Aug 1974, in which role he made his London debut at the Open Space, 17 Oct 1974; Theatre Upstairs, Feb 1975, appeared in Mrs Grabowski's Academy; Mermaid, Apr 1975, Redpenny in The Doctor's Dilemma; Prince of Wales, Oct 1975, again played the Crown Prince in what was now called Plumber's Progress; Bush, Mar 1976, Pieter de Groot in Soul of the White Ant; at the same theatre appeared in Blood Sports, June, and Juvenalia, July 1976; with the Joint Stock company, 1977, his roles included Kutchevski in Devil's Island, Royal Court, Feb; Sayers in A Mad World, My Masters, Young Vic, May, and Sandy in Epsom Downs, Round House, Aug; Bristol Old Vic, Apr 1978, title role in Titus Andronicus; Royal Court, Jun 1978, Boyd in Flying Blind; Half Moon, 1978, played Ui in The Resistible Rise of Arturo Ui, Oct, and various roles in The Machine Wreckers, Nov; Birmingham Rep (Studio), Sept 1978, Eddie in Mary Barnes, transferring with the production to the Royal Court, Jan 1979; joined the National Theatre Company, 1979, to play Orlando in As You Like It, Aug, and Mozart in Amadeus, Nov, both at the Olivier; TV, since 1974, includes Wings of Song, The Dybbuk, and Instant Enlightenment including VAT.

Address: c/o Marina Martin, 7 Windmill Street, London W1.

CALLOWAY, Cab, singer, actor, orchestra leader
b Rochester, NY, 24 Dec 1907.

Appeared in vaudeville at the Palace, 12 Oct 1930 with his troupe; appeared at the Palace 14 June 1931; toured extensively with his orchestra; reappeared on the New York stage at the Ziegfeld, 10 Mar 1953, as Sportin' Life in Porgy and Bess, in the role originally intended for him by the composer George Gershwin, after touring the US in this part; toured US and Europe in this part, 1953–4; July 1957, appeared in The Cotton Club Revue of 1957; St James, 12 Nov 1967, took over as Horace Vandergelder in an all-Black production of Hello, Dolly!; toured as Horace Vandergelder in Hello, Dolly! in 1971; Rainbow Grill, NY, Feb 1973, appeared with his orchestra; Lunt-Fontanne, Dec 1973, played Hines in The Pajama Game; appeared with his orchestra at the Riverboat, NY, Jan 1976; appeared in St Louis, 1979, with the national touring company of Eubie!; has appeared frequently in films, notably in The Big Broadcast, 1932, International House, 1933, Stormy Weather, 1943, Sensations of 1945, St Louis Blues, 1958, A Man Called Adam, 1966, etc.

Address: 1040 Knollwood Road, White Plains, NY 10603.

CALVERT, Phyllis, actress
b London, 18 Feb 1915; *d* of Frederick Bickle and his wife Anne (Williams); *e* Margaret Morris School of Dancing and the Institut Français; *m* Peter Murray Hill (dec); studied for the stage under Margaret Morris.

Made her first appearance on the stage at the Lyric, Hammersmith, 19 Nov 1925, as Ann Wildersham in Crossings, when Ellen Terry made her last appearance on the stage; appeared with the Malvern Repertory Company, 1933–6; appeared with repertory company at Theatre Royal, Exeter, May 1935; Coventry Repertory Company, 1936–7, and York Repertory Company, 1937–8; at the Kingsway, Apr 1939, played Lilah Haydon in A Woman's Privilege; at the Q, and Embassy, June 1939, Judy Stevens in Punch Without Judy; Apollo, Aug 1942, Patricia Graham in Flare Path; at the Scala, Dec 1947, appeared as Peter Pan; St James's, Jan 1953, played Stella Hampden in Escapade; Strand, Aug 1954, succeeded Celia Johnson as Laura Hammond in It's Never Too Late; Phoenix, Sept 1956, played Mary Denney in A River Breeze; Royal Court, Feb 1958 (in a Production without Décor), Margaret in Love From Margaret; Globe, June 1959, Mary Rhodes in The Complaisant Lover; Globe, Apr 1961, played the Countess in The Rehearsal; Royal Court, Liverpool, Nov 1962, Freda in The Hot Tiara; Lyric, Mar 1963, Therese in Menage à Trois; Savoy, Oct 1963, Paula Barlow in Portrait of Murder; Duke of York's, Sept 1964, played Agnes in A Scent of Flowers; Queen's, Apr 1965, Liz Essendine in Present Laughter; Vaudeville, Nov 1967, played Mrs Arbuthnot in A Woman of No Importance; Arnaud, Guildford, June 1970, Ruth in Blithe Spirit, transferring in that part to the Globe in July; Oct 1971, toured with the Oxford Playhouse Company as Madame Ranevskaya in The Cherry Orchard; Theatre Royal, York, Aug 1973, played The Wife in All Over and Judith Bliss in Hay Fever; Haymarket, Oct 1973, took over the part of Queen Mary in Crown Matrimonial; toured, Spring 1975, as Judith Bliss; toured, Autumn 1975, as Sheila Broadbent in The Reluctant Debutante; Ambassadors, Oct 1976, Delia in Dear Daddy; Northcott, Exeter, Apr 1978, Lidya Vasilyevna in Old World; same theatre, Apr 1979, appeared in A Lonesome Thing; Queen's, Mar 1980, appeared in Before the Party; first appeared in films, 1939, and has appeared, notably, in Kipps, The Young Mr Pitt, The Man in Grey, Fanny by Gaslight, Madonna of the Seven Moons, Men of Two Worlds, They Were Sisters, Mr Denning Drives North, The Net, Mandy, Indiscreet, Oscar Wilde (with Robert Morley), etc.

Recreation: Swimming. *Hobby:* Collecting books on Costume. *Address:* c/o Nems Management Ltd, 29 King's Road, London SW3.

CAMPBELL, Douglas, actor and director
b Glasgow, 11 June 1922; *s* of Dugald Campbell and his wife Ethel (Sloan); *m* Ann Casson, actress.

First appeared on the stage with the Old Vic Company on tour, 1941–2, with Sir Lewis Casson and Dame Sybil Thorndike, in Medea, and in Jacob's Ladder; toured extensively and appeared in repertory at Bristol, Glasgow, etc, 1943–9; in the first Edinburgh Festival, 1948, played Wantonness in Tyrone Guthrie's production of The Thrie Estates, and also made further appearances in the Festival, 1949–50; re-joined the Old Vic Company in Jan 1951, to play the Duke of

Bourbon in Henry V, Captain Kearney and Cadi of Kintafi in Captain Brassbound's Conversion, and Page in The Merry Wives of Windsor, and subsequently toured Belgium and Holland in these plays; Old Vic season, 1951–2, played Theseus in A Midsummer Night's Dream, and Othello; toured in South Africa with the Old Vic Company, 1952, when he played Othello and Macbeth; during the Old Vic season, 1952–3, appeared as Chorus in Romeo and Juliet, Antonio in The Merchant of Venice, Julius Caesar and Octavius Caesar in Julius Caesar; at the Shakespeare Festival, Stratford, Ontario, July 1953, played Parolles in All's Well That Ends Well, and Hastings in Richard III; on returning from Canada, joined the Bristol Old Vic company, Oct 1953, when he appeared as Antony in Antony and Cleopatra, and Nov 1953, as Robert Bailey I in Old Bailey; returned to Canada, 1954, and at the annual Shakespeare Festival, Stratford, Ont, has since appeared in the following productions: Pompey in Measure for Measure, Baptista in The Taming of the Shrew, 1954; Casca in Julius Caesar, Œdipus in Œdipus Rex, and directed Stravinsky's A Soldier's Tale, 1955; Pistol in Henry V, Falstaff in The Merry Wives of Windsor, 1956; Claudius in Hamlet, Sir Toby Belch in Twelfth Night, 1957; Falstaff in Henry IV, part I, and directed The Winter's Tale, 1958; Touchstone in As You Like It, and the title-part in Othello, 1959; directed A Midsummer Night's Dream, and played The Boatswain in HMS Pinafore, 1960; the title-part in Henry VIII, Menenius Agrippa in Coriolanus, and arranged dances in The Pirates of Penzance, 1961; Don Alhambra del Bolero in The Gondoliers, 1962; Hotspur in Henry IV, part I, directed Julius Caesar, and Lopahin in The Cherry Orchard, 1965; founded the Canadian Players, 1954, and toured with the following productions: Saint Joan (directed and played Cauchon and De Baudricourt), 1954; Macbeth (directed and played Macbeth), 1955; Peer Gynt (directed), 1956; Othello (directed), Man and Superman (played John Tanner), 1957; The Devil's Disciple (played General Burgoyne), 1959; with the Stratford (Ontario) Festival Company, appeared at the Edinburgh Festival, Aug 1956, as Pistol in Henry V, and Œdipus in Œdipus Rex; at the Phoenix, NY, Oct 1957, played the Earl of Leicester in Schiller's Mary Stuart; at the same theatre, Mar 1958, appeared with the Stratford (Ont) Festival Company, as The Duke of Milan in The Two Gentlemen of Verona, and Apr 1958, as The Judge in The Broken Jug; Old Vic, Dec 1960, Bottom in A Midsummer Night's Dream, and Feb 1961, played Falstaff in Henry IV, part I; Plymouth, NY, Nov 1961, played the title-role in Gideon, subsequently taking over the part of the Angel in the same production, Apr 1962; Ethel Barrymore, NY, Nov 1962, directed Moby Dick; at the opening season of the Tyrone Guthrie Theatre, Minneapolis, May–July 1963, directed The Miser, and Death of a Salesman; Lyceum, NY, Nov 1963, directed and appeared in the anthology The Golden Age; Guthrie, Minneapolis, May–July 1964, directed and played Robert de Beaudricourt and English Soldier in Saint Joan, and played the title-role in Volpone; at the same theatre, May 1965, staged the battles in Richard III and directed The Way of the World, and Sept 1965, again directed The Miser; Stratford, Ontario, 1965, played Hotspur, in Henry IV, part I, and directed Julius Caesar; at the Tyrone Guthrie, Sept 1966, directed Doctor's Dilemma; Stratford, Ontario, June 1968, directed Romeo and Juliet and Cinderella; Billy Rose, NY, Dec 1968, played Clytemnestra and Athena in The House of Atreus; Mark Taper Forum, Los Angeles in the 1968–9 season, directed The Adventures of the Black Girl in Search of Her God; Goodman, Chicago, 1969, played Winston Churchill in Soldiers; same theatre, 1971, played in Marching Song; toured the USA, July–Nov 1971, as the Narrator, Dr Pangloss, and Martin in Candide; at the Crucible, Sheffield, 1971–2, his parts included Simon Eyre in The Shoemaker's Holiday (also directed), and Aslak and the Button Moulder in Peer Gynt; Walnut, Philadelphia, 1973, directed Juno and the Paycock; Avon Stage, Stratford, Ont, June 1974, Baron de Gondre-marck in La Vie Parisienne; Banff Festival, Canada, Aug 1975, directed Carnival; St George's, Islington, July 1976, directed Richard III; Plymouth, NY, Sept 1976, took over as Martin Dysart in Equus; played the part in Washington, Sept 1976; Walnut, Philadelphia, Dec 1976, directed Enter a Free Man; Theater Calgary, Jan 1978, appeared in The Con-demned of Altona; played the title-part in the film Œdipus Rex (directed by Tyrone Guthrie), 1956; wrote and directed three half-hour films on Macbeth, 1963; television appea-rances include: Hamlet, The Prince and the Pauper, The Crucible and the series Bill Brand; has also directed Peer Gynt on television; appointed Associate Artistic Director of the Tyrone Guthrie Theatre, Minneapolis, 1963, and Artistic Director, 1965; founder of Theatre North, 1973.

Recreations: Fencing, painting, argument, and shove-ha'penny.

CAMPBELL, Judy, actress
b Grantham, Lincs, 31 May 1916; *d* of John Arthur Gamble and his wife Mary (Fulton); *e* St Michael's Convent, East Grinstead, Sussex; *m* Lieut-Commander David Birkin, DSC, RNVR; both of her parents were on the stage, her father was also the author of several plays under his professional name of J A Campbell.

Made her first appearance on the stage at the Theatre Royal, Grantham, Easter, 1935, as a Guest in The Last of Mrs Cheyney, and appeared there in repertory throughout the season; played a season of repertory at the Opera House, Coventry, May 1935, followed by a further season at Theatre Royal, Brighton, 1936; made her first appearance in London, at the People's Palace, 5 Apr 1937, as Anna in Anthony and Anna; in July 1937, appeared there as Natasha Malakoff in Bulldog Drummond Hits Out, and played the same part at the Savoy Theatre, Dec 1937; played a season of Shakespeare and Shaw at the Festival Theatre, Cambridge, 1938; toured, July–Dec 1938, as Irene in Idiot's Delight, with Vic Oliver; joined the Liverpool Playhouse Company, 1939–40, playing leading parts; at the Comedy, Apr 1940, made a hit in the revue, New Faces, with the song A Nightingale Sang in Berkeley Square; again appeared in New Faces at the Apollo, Mar 1941; at His Majesty's, July 1941, played Lola Malo in Lady Behave; Apollo, Nov 1941, Phyllis Tree in Ducks and Drakes; Aldwych, Apr 1942, Marthe de Brancovis in The Watch on the Rhine; toured, Sept 1942–Mar 1943 with Noël Coward, creating the parts of Joanna in Present Laughter and Ethel in This Happy Breed, also playing Elvira in Blithe Spirit and appearing with Noël Coward in twice-weekly troop concerts; Haymarket, Apr 1943, appeared in Present Laughter and This Happy Breed on alternate nights under the general title Play Parade; at the Duchess, July 1943, Elvira in Blithe Spirit; Arts, Aug 1944, Mirandolina in Mine Hostess (La Locandiera); Phoenix, Dec 1944, Diana Flynn in Another Love Story; toured, 1946, as Lydia in Call Home the Heart; Embassy, Apr 1948, Joanna in Portrait of Hickory; toured, 1948, as Marda Shale in This is Where We Came In; Lyric, Hammersmith, Apr 1949, played Princess Louise in Royal Highness; Savoy, Nov 1951, Miranda Frayle in Rela-tive Values; Cambridge, Oct 1954, Joanna in Book of the Month; Cambridge, Apr 1956, followed Celia Johnson as Sheila Broadbent in The Reluctant Debutante; St Martin's, Feb 1960, played Helen in A Sparrow Falls (in the double-bill

entitled Double Yoke); Oxford Playhouse, Oct 1961, played Hesione Hushabye in Heartbreak House, subsequently ap-pearing in the same production at Wyndham's, Nov 1961; toured Feb 1963, as Lorette Heller in Domino; New Arts, Aug 1964, played Lady Slingsby-Craddock in Mr Whatnot; Haymarket, Jan 1966, Mrs Clandon in You Never Can Tell; Arts, June 1967, played Christine Mannon in Mourning Becomes Electra, and later at Baalbek and the Edinburgh Festival, 1968; Duke of York's, Sept 1967, took over the part of Sheila in Relatively Speaking; toured, May 1971, with the Cambridge Theatre Company in Hay Fever, playing Judith Bliss; toured, Autumn 1972, in Death On Demand; for the Bristol Old Vic, played Lady Touchwood in The Double Dealer at the Hong Kong Arts Festival, Feb 1973; toured, May 1974, as Jennifer in My Son's Father; Oxford Playhouse, Oct 1975, Linda Loman in Death of a Salesman; Bristol Old Vic, May 1976, Beth in Le Weekend; Theatre Royal, Wind-sor, Mar 1978, Bron in The Old Country; is author of the plays Sing Cuckoo, 1950; The Bright One, 1958; first ap-peared in films, 1940, in Saloon Bar; TV includes The Chinese Prime Minster, The Sea, and Love among the Artists.

Recreations: Reading, writing. *Address:* c/o Hutton Man-agement Ltd, 194 Old Brompton Road, London SW5.

CAMPBELL, Ken, actor, director, and dramatic author
b Ilford, Essex, 10 Dec 1941; *s* of Anthony Colin Campbell and his wife Elsie (Handley); trained for the stage at RADA.

Made his professional debut as an actor in 1962; directed his play, Jack Sheppard (Anything You Say Will Be Twisted), at the Octagon, Bolton, Apr 1969, and at the Mermaid, Jun; Royal Court, Dec 1969, directed Insideout; Leeds Playhouse, Dec 1970, played the title role in his pantomime-play Old King Cole; from 1971–74 toured with his own company, Ken Campbell's Roadshow, visiting ven-ues from public bars to the Theatre Upstairs in such shows as Bar Room Tales, An Evening with Sylveste McCoy, the Human Bomb, and Stonehenge Kit the Ancient Brit; his musical Bendigo (written with Dave Hill and Andy Andrews) was seen at Nottingham Playhouse, June 1974; at the Royal Court, Oct 1974, played Stu Lyons in his play The Great Caper; Theatre Upstairs, Dec 1974, directed Remember the Truth Dentist; at Nottingham, June 1976, played Jordan Knockem in Bartholomew Fair; co-founder and artistic direc-tor, 1976–80, of the Science Fiction Theatre of Liverpool, whose marathon production of his adaptation of Illuminatus was the opening show at the National Theatre's Cottesloe; other productions directed for this group include the ten-play cycle The Warp, and The Hitch-Hiker's Guide to the Galaxy, both seen in London, 1979; appointed artistic director, Everyman Theatre, Liverpool, May 1980; his other writings include the short plays Just Go Will You, Harry, 1969; Christopher Pea, You See the Thing Is This, 1970; Pilk's Madhouse, 1973; Skungpoomery, 1975; and the musical Walking Like Geoffrey, 1975; translated Waechter's Schools for Clowns, 1977.

Address: Studio 96, Haverstock Hill, London NW3.

CAMPBELL, Patton, designer
b Omaha, Nebraska, 10 Sept 1926; *s* of Ralph Campbell and his wife Frances (Patton); *e* Central High School, Omaha, Yale University (BA 1950), Yale University School of the Drama (MFA 1952).

Was assistant scenic designer for the Cape Playhouse, Dennis, Mass, 1948–50; scenic designer for the Barnstor-mers, Tamworth, New Hampshire, 1951; scenic designer at the Famous Artists Country Playhouse, Fayetteville, New

York, 1954; his first scenic designs for a Broadway production were at the Plymouth, 26 Jan 1955, for The Grand Prize; has since designed the costumes for Trouble in Tahiti, 27 Wagons Full of Cotton, 1955; Fallen Angels, 1956; A Hole in the Head, and The Makropoulos Secret, at Santa Fe, New Mexico, as resident scenic, costume, and lighting designer for the Santa Fe Opera Company, The Rake's Progress, Ariadne auf Naxos, 1957; Falstaff, Capriccio, Cinderella, La Boheme, 1958; Fledermaus, Anne Boleyn, The Abduction from the Seraglio, The Barber of Seville, returned to NY and for the New York City Opera designed Wuthering Heights and for the City Center designed costumes for The Mikado, 1959; The Inspector General for the New York City Opera, There Was a Little Girl, 1960; The Conquering Hero, HMS Pinafore, The Pirates of Penzance, and for the New York City Opera Wings of the Dove, 1961; All American, 1962; A Month in the Country, 1963; the touring production of Oliver! and After the Fall, Natalia Petrovna for the New York City Opera, Madam Butterfly and The Lady from Colorado for the Central City (Colorado) Opera, and Katya Kabanova, Gianni Schicchi, and Il Tabarro for the Juilliard Opera Theatre, 1964; Miss Julie, Capriccio, and Lizzie Borden for the New York City Opera, and Man of La Mancha, The Glass Menagerie, Great Scot! Agatha Sue, I Love You, On a Clear Day You Can See Forever (tour), Gone with the Wind at the New Imperial, Tokyo, Japan, and for the New York City Opera, La Traviata and The Ballad of Baby Doe, 1966; Come Live with Me, The Natural Look, 1967; executed his first designs for London for the production of Man of La Mancha at the Piccadilly, Loot, The Pirates of Penzance, The Mikado, HMS Pinafore, and, for the Santa Fe Opera, Der Rosenkavalier, 1968; Cosi Fan Tutte and La Tosca, both for the Santa Fe Opera, 1969; Scarlett at the Imperial Theatre, Tokyo, The Fisherman and His Wife for the Opera Company of Boston, The Makropoulos Affair for the New York City Opera, 1970; Susannah, New York City Opera, 1971; revival of Man of La Mancha, Gone with the Wind (Drury Lane, London), 1972; Gone with the Wind (Los Angeles), 1973; Captain Jinks of the Horse Marines, Kansas City Lyric, 1975; La Belle Helene, New York City Opera, 1976; Regina, Houston Opera, 1980; designed his first television production for Lizzie Borden, 1967, and has since designed The Fisherman and His Wife, 1970; Between Time and Timbuktu, 1972, The Ballad of Baby Doe, 1976; has taught design as instructor at Barnard College, 1955–7, instructor at NY University, 1962–7, and as Associate Professor at Columbia University, 1967–71, 1979–80, Associate Professor at the State University of New York, Purchase, NY, 1975–6.

Recreations: Reading and cooking. *Address:* 46 West 95th Street, New York, NY. *Tel:* 866–1757.

CAMPTON, David, playwright
b Leicester, 5 June 1924; *s* of David Campton and his wife Emily; *e* Wyggeston Grammar School; formerly a clerk with the Leicester Education Department and the East Midlands Gas Board.

From 1955–67 was closely associated with Stephen Joseph's Theatre in the Round, Scarborough, as writer, actor, director and occasionally manager; in addition to radio and TV scripts has written over forty one-act plays for the stage, sundry sketches, fifteen full-length plays and four adaptations; his work has been seen in provincial theatres in England, in Munich, Vienna and the USA, but (apart from contributions to revues) not yet in the West End; his principal plays include The Cactus Garden, 1953; The Lunatic View, 1957; Frankenstein, 1959; Four Minute Warning (consisting of Little Brother: Little Sister, Mutatis Mutandis and Soldier from the

Wars Returning), 1960; Usher, 1962; Comeback, 1963; Dead and Alive, 1964; Cock and Bull Story, 1965; Timesneeze, The Life and Death of Almost Everybody, 1970; Carmilla, 1972; Everybody's Friend, 1975; Ragerbo!, 1976; Zodiac, 1977; The Great Little Tilley, After Midnight, Before Dawn, 1978; with this last he won the British Theatre Association's original one-act play award in 1978, having won it in 1975 with Everybody's Friend.

Address: 35 Liberty Road, Leicester LE3 8JF. *Tel:* 0533-873951.

CANNAN, Denis, dramatic author and former actor
b Oxford, 14 May 1919; *s* of Captain H J Pullein-Thompson, MC and his wife Joanna (Cannan); *e* Eton; *m* (1) Joan Ross (mar dis); (2) Rose Evansky.

Made his first appearance on the stage at Henley-on-Thames, 1936, as Richard Hare in East Lynne; during 1937–9, played in various repertory companies; served in the Army, 1939–46; after demobilization, 1946, joined the company of the Citizens' Theatre, Glasgow, where he played a great variety of parts, including Hjalmar in The Wild Duck, Valentine in You Never Can Tell, Hsieh Ping Quei in Lady Precious Stream, etc; at the Malvern Festival, 1949, Sempronius in The Apple Cart, Kneller in In Good King Charles's Golden Days, the Widower in Buoyant Billions, etc; made his first appearance in London, at the Princes Theatre, 10 Oct 1949, in the last mentioned part; joined the company of the Bristol Old Vic, 1950, playing Oliver in As You Like It, Julius Caesar and Octavius in Julius Caesar; Haymarket, Mar 1951, played Samuel Breeze in A Penny For a Song; Duke of York's, Oct 1951, Harold Trewitt in All the Year Round; is the author of Max, People's Palace and Malvern Festival, 1949; Captain Carvallo, St James's, 1950; Colombe (translated from Anouilh), New, 1951; Misery Me, Duchess, 1955; You and Your Wife, Bristol Old Vic, 1955; The Power and the Glory (adaptation, with Pierre Bost), Phoenix, 1956, and Phoenix, New York, 1958; Who's Your Father? Cambridge, 1958; original text of US, Royal Shakespeare Company, Aldwych, 1966; adaptation of Ibsen's Ghosts for the same company, 1967; One at Night, Royal Court, 1971; The Ik (adaptation and collaboration), Paris 1975, London, 1976; Dear Daddy, 1976 (Play of the Year Award); has also written the screenplays of several feature films, including A High Wind in Jamaica; author of two radio plays, and TV plays including One Day at a Time, and Home Movies.

Recreation: Loitering. *Address:* 103 Clarence Gate Gardens, Glentworth Street, London NW1 6QP.

CANTOR, Arthur, producer
b Boston, Mass, 12 March 1920; *s* of Samuel S Cantor and his wife Lillian (Landsman); *e* Harvard (BA 1940); *m* Deborah Rosmarin Miller (dec).

Began his theatrical career as press representative for the Playwright's Company, 1945, and in addition to representing many American plays, handled the publicity for the Gate Theatre of Dublin and the Habimah of Tel-Aviv during their 1948 tours; entered independent publicity representation in 1952 and continues active in this field; entered production in Nov 1959, when he co-produced (with Saint-Subber) The Tenth Man at the Booth; since then has produced or co-produced the following plays; All the Way Home, 1960; Gideon, 1961; A Thousand Clowns, A Matter of Position (Philadelphia), 1962; Man in the Moon, Put It in Writing, The Golden Age, Three Cheers for the Tired Businessman (Chicago), Camelot (tour), 1963; The Passion of Josef D, The Committee, Oliver! (tour), 1964; The Trigon, which he also directed, La Grosse Valise, 1956; The World of Gunter

Grass, 1966; Of Love Remembered, People Is the Thing That the World Is Fullest of, By George, and directed a revival of The Tenth Man, 1967; The Theatre of Genoa in The Venetian Twins, The Concept, The Wizard of Oz, 1968; Tango, Winnie the Pooh, and a revival of The Concept, 1969; Golden Bat, 1970; in London, 1970–1, co-produced Vivat! Vivat! Regina, Blithe Spirit, A Bequest to the Nation, The Winslow Boy, Butterflies Are Free, Captain Brassbound's Conversion and The Patrick Pearse Motel; Montparnasse, Paris, 1971, co-produced Old Times; has since produced, in New York unless otherwise stated, Vivat! Vivat! Regina, Promenade, All!, Captain Brassbound's Conversion, The Little Black Book, 1972; tour of The Day After the Fair, 42 Seconds from Broadway, 1973; In Praise of Love, 1974; Souvenir (Los Angeles), Private Lives, The Constant Wife, 1975; Emlyn Williams as Charles Dickens, Dylan Thomas Growing Up, The Innocents, The Bed Before Yesterday (tour), 1976; A Party with Betty Comden and Adolph Green, Housewife, Superstar!, 1977; My Astonishing Self, The Biko Inquest, St Mark's Gospel, The Playboy of the Weekend World, 1978; On Golden Pond, 1979; managing director, H M Tennent Ltd, 1973–present.

Clubs: Harvard and the Players. *Address:* 234 West 44th Street, New York, NY 10036. *Tel:* 391–0450.

CAREY, Denis, director
b London, 3 Aug 1909; *s* of William Denis Carey and his wife May (Wilkinson); *e* St Paul's School, London, and Trinity College, Dublin; *m* Yvonne Coulette.

Formerly in an Income Tax Consultant's Office, before making his first appearance at the Royal Court, 26 Dec 1921, as Micky in The Great Big World; made several appearances at the Gate and Abbey Theatres, Dublin, 1929–34; appeared in London and New York, 1935–9; acted for the Pilgrim Players, 1940–3; Glasgow Citizens' Theatre Company, 1943–5, and the Midland Theatre, Coventry, 1945–6; Lyric, Hammersmith, Feb 1947, played Jack Manders in Galway Handicap; Lyric, Hammersmith, July 1947, played Clochet in Men Without Shadows; directed his first production Happy As Larry, at the Mercury, Sept 1947, transferring to the Criterion, Dec 1947; subsequently directed Georgia Story and The Playboy of the Western World, 1948; appointed Associate Director at the Arts Theatre, Salisbury, 1948; Director of the Bristol Old Vic Company 1949–54; during this time he directed more than thirty plays for the company, of which the following were also presented in London: Two Gentlemen of Verona (Old Vic); Henry V (Old Vic); Salad Days; during the same period he also directed An Italian Straw Hat (Old Vic), 1952; The Merchant of Venice (Stratford-on-Avon), 1953; Twelfth Night (Old Vic), 1954; has since directed Twelfth Night at the Théâtre Nationale de Belgique, in Brussels, Oct 1954; The Taming of the Shrew (Old Vic), Dec 1954; A Kind of Folly, Feb 1955; appointed first Director of the American Shakespeare Theatre, Stratford, Connecticut, and in July 1955, directed Julius Caesar and The Tempest; has since directed the following productions: A Girl Called Jo, 1955; Romanoff and Juliet, Much Ado About Nothing (Old Vic), 1956; Free As Air, Man of Distinction, Waiting For Godot (Bristol Old Vic), 1957; The Heart's a Wonder (musical version of The Playboy of the Western World), 1958; Mr Fox of Venice, The Cherry Orchard (Ottawa), The Taming of the Shrew (Ottawa), 1959; Follow That Girl, Othello (Théâtre Nationale de Belgique), The Truth About Billy Newton, Hooray For Daisy, 1960; Mam'zelle Nitouche, The Golden Years (tour), The Flanders Mare (Bristol Old Vic), 1961; Twelfth Night (Ludlow Castle, and Open Air, Regent's Park), 1962; appointed Artistic

Director of the Bristol Old Vic Company on a 14 week tour to Pakistan, India, and Ceylon, Jan 1963, when he directed Hamlet and A Man For All Seasons; on his return to England directed: The Life in My Hands (Nottingham Playhouse), Armstrong's Last Goodnight (Glasgow, Citizens'), The Golden Rivet, 1964; A Scent of Flowers (Bristol Old Vic), The Cherry Orchard (Nottingham Playhouse), Volpone (Nottingham Playhouse), Where the Saints Go Cycling In (Dublin Festival), The Happiest Days of Your Life (Bristol Old Vic), 1965; Juno and the Paycock (Gaiety, Dublin), 1966; directed the following plays for the Bristol Old Vic: Hedda Gabler, The Playboy of the Western World, I'll Get My Man, 1966; The Way of the World, DP, 1967; most recently The Cocktail Party, 1976; directed Hobson's Choice at the Alhambra, Bradford, 1968; Royal Court, Feb 1970, played Telyegin in Uncle Vanya; Mermaid, June 1971, Ocean in Prometheus Bound; toured the world, 1972–3, as Egeus/Quince in the RSC's production of A Midsummer Night's Dream; directed a touring production of The Pilgrim's Progress, Apr 1973; at the Globe, Feb 1974, played Gunga Din in Chez Nous; at Greenwich played Dr Lombardi in the Artful Widow, Apr 1976, and Feste in Twelfth Night, Mar 1977, Shaftesbury, Mar 1978, Jawan in Kismet; films include: The Day of the Jackal; frequent TV appearances include: *General Hospital* and *Sutherland's Law.*

Address: c/o Vernon Conway, 248–50 Lavender Hill, London SW11 1JW.

CAREY, Joyce, actress
b London, 30 Mar 1898; *d* of Gerald Lawrence and his wife Lilian (Braithwaite); *e* Westgate-on-Sea and London; studied for the stage under Miss Kate Rorke at the Florence Etlinger Dramatic School.

Made her first appearance on the stage at the Queen's Theatre, 30 June 1916, when she played the Princess Katherine in Henry V, in an all-woman cast; at the Strand Theatre, 14 Oct 1916, made her professional début as Hilda Gregory in a revival of Mr Wu; she was then engaged by Sir George Alexander for the St James's Theatre, and appeared there Jan 1917, as Jacqueline in The Aristocrat, and June 1917, as Miss Hooker in Sheila; appeared at the Kingsway, Oct 1917, as Miss Phelps in One Hour of Life; Royalty, July 1918, Hildegarde Culver in The Title; Savoy, Apr 1919, Gwendolyn Ralston in Nothing but the Truth; New, May 1919, Lucie in The Altar of Liberty; she appeared at Stratford-on-Avon, summer season, Aug 1919, as Anne Page in The Merry Wives of Windsor, Perdita in The Winter's Tale, Titania in A Midsummer Night's Dream, Miranda in The Tempest and as Juliet; at the New Theatre, Nov 1919, played Meg in Little Women; Prince of Wales, Feb 1920, appeared as Leonora in The Young Person in Pink; Duke of York's, Mar 1920, Jessica in The Merchant of Venice; at the Haymarket, Mar 1920, in her original part in The Young Person in Pink; Royalty, Sept 1920, played Rosario in The Romantic Young Lady; Aldwych, Feb 1921, played Miranda in The Tempest; Prince of Wales, Mar 1921, Elsie Challoner in The Charm School; at the Strand, Apr 1921, again played Princess Katharine in Henry V, with a cast entirely composed of women; subsequently toured in The Charm School; Wyndham's, May 1922, played Joanna Trout in Dear Brutus; Garrick, Feb 1923, Hattie Friedman in Partners Again; Adelphi, July 1923, again played Leonora in The Young Person in Pink; Drury Lane, Sept 1923, Lady Angela Vale in Good Luck; at the Lyric, Hammersmith (for the Fellowship of Players), Sept 1923, Perdita in The Winter's Tale; Kingsway, Nov 1923, Hermia in A Midsummer Night's Dream; Comedy, Mar 1924, Freda Fortnum in Far Above Rubies;

Regent, July 1924 (for the Fellowship of Players), Celia in As You Like It; at the Garrick, Dec 1924, Phyllis Burton in Six Cylinder Love; at the Empire, New York, Dec 1925, played Sarah Hurst in Easy Virtue, and played the same part at the Duke of York's, London, June 1926; appeared at the Playhouse, NY, Jan 1927, as Meta in The Road to Rome, and continued in this, 1927–8; at the Majestic, Nov 1928, played Vermilia in The Jealous Moon; Forrest, Apr 1929, Nita in Paolo and Francesca; Booth, Oct 1929, Nora Gerrish in Jenny; Maxime Elliott, Oct 1930, Olivia in Twelfth Night; Nov 1930, Sonia Tippet in Art and Mrs Bottle; Empire, Feb 1931, Arabel Moulton Barrett in The Barretts of Wimpole Street; Selwyn, Jan 1932, Chrysothemis in Electra of Sophocles; Belasco, Dec 1932, Emilia in Lucrece; in Aug 1933, toured as Mary Howard in When Ladies Meet; on returning to London, appeared at the Phoenix, Nov 1933, as Celia in As You Like It; Ambassadors', Jan 1934, Julia Melville in The Rivals; Wyndham's, Oct 1934, Lady Farrington in Sweet Aloes; again visited America, and at San Francisco, played in The Shining Hour, and at the Martin Beck Theatre, NY, Feb 1935, played Arabel in a revival of The Barretts of Wimpole Street; on returning to London, resumed her part in Sweet Aloes; Booth, NY, Mar 1936, played the same part; Phoenix, London, Apr 1936, appeared in To-Night at 8.30 and appeared in the same parts at the National Theatre, NY, Nov 1936; Ambassadors', London, May 1938, played June Furze in Spring Meeting; Globe, Jan 1939, the Hon Gwendolen Fairfax in The Importance of Being Earnest; toured, 1940, with John Gielgud, for ENSA; toured, 1941, in Fumed Oak, and Hands Across the Sea (To-Night at 8.30); toured, 1942, as Ruth in Blithe Spirit, Liz Essendine in Present Laughter, and Sylvia in This Happy Breed, and appeared at the Haymarket, Apr 1943, in the two last-mentioned parts; subsequently toured for ENSA, 1943, in Blithe Spirit; Duchess, June 1944, succeeded Irene Browne as Ruth in Blithe Spirit, and played this until Mar 1946; Haymarket, Apr 1947, Liz Essendine in Present Laughter; Q, Sept 1949, Rose Hardynge in Marriage Playground; Q, Feb 1951, Dora Middleton in The Watchman; Piccadilly, Oct 1951, Alice Winter in The White Sheep of the Family; Phoenix, Sept 1952, Lady Harriet Ripley in Quadrille; Westminster, July 1954, played the title-rôle in The Duenna; Lyric, Apr 1956, Cuckoo Honey in South Sea Bubble; Globe, Nov 1956, Isabel Sorodin in Nude with Violin; left the cast to appear in the NY production, Belasco, Nov 1957, alternating with a revival of Present Laughter, Jan 1958, in which she played her original part of Liz Essendine; St Martin's, London, June 1958, played Mrs Walworth in Speaking of Murder; Arts, Jan 1959, the Duchesse Dupont-Dufour in Traveller Without Luggage; Cambridge, Feb 1960, Mrs Lee in The Wrong Side of the Park; Globe, June 1961, played Joan Byrne in Dazzling Prospect; Arts, Nov 1961, Mrs Sparrow in The Cupboard; Queen's, Nov 1962, played Mrs Sedley in the musical Vanity Fair; toured, Apr 1965, as Caroline Channing-Frome in Heirs and Graces; Strand, Oct 1965, Valentine Besson in Maigret and the Lady; Garrick, Dec 1966, Lady Markby in An Ideal Husband; New, Feb 1967, played Aunt Juley in Howard's End; Haymarket, Dec 1967, Belle Schlesinger in Dear Octopus; Westminster, Nov 1969 played May Beringer in The Old Ladies, transferring in that part to the Duchess, Dec 1969; Sadler's Wells, June 1972, Miss Trafalgar Gower in Trelawney, transferring to the Prince of Wales, Aug 1972; Savoy, Apr 1974, Mrs Barnstable in A Ghost on Tiptoe; Vaudeville, Mar 1979, Miss Marple in A Murder Is Announced; has appeared in a number of television plays and series, among them *Father Dear Father, The Cedar Tree*, and Waste; appeared in the films, The Way to the Stars, Brief Encounter,

Cry the Beloved Country and A Nice Girl Like Me, etc; under the *pseudonym* of Jay Mallory, was the author of the play Sweet Aloes, 1934, which ran over a year, and of A Thing Apart, 1938.

Recreations: Reading and crossword puzzles. *Address:* c/o Essanay Ltd, 75 Hammersmith Road, London W14.

CARGILL, Patrick, actor and dramatic author
b London, 3 June 1918; *s of* Ronald Jasper Cargill and his wife Agnes Winifred (Birch); *e* Haileybury College, and Royal Military College, Sandhurst; formerly in the Indian Army.

Made his first appearance on the stage with the Forsyth Players at the De La Warr Pavilion, Bexhill, remaining as a member of the company for nearly a year; joined Anthony Hawtrey's Company, appearing at Buxton, Croydon, and the Embassy Theatre, London; appeared with the Royal, Windsor, over a period of seven years; made his first appearance in the West End at the London Hippodrome, May 1953, in the revue High Spirits; at the Duke of York's, July 1954, played Allan in Meet a Body; Phoenix, Sept 1956, played Mr Symington-Smythe in A River Breeze; Westminster, June 1957, played Wilkinson in Dear Delinquent, transferring with the production to the Aldwych, Dec 1957; Strand, Mar 1959, Andrew Spicer in Wolf's Clothing; Apollo, Feb 1962, played Bernard in Boeing-Boeing, taking over the leading part for three weeks in Mar 1964; Yvonne Arnaud, Guildford, Aug 1965, Stuart Wheeler in Say Who You Are, subsequently appearing in the same production at Her Majesty's Oct 1965; Strand, June 1968, directed Not Now Darling (also in Australia, 1969); St Martin's, Jan 1970, played Ramsey in his own production of Play on Love; Globe, July 1970, Charles in Blithe Spirit; Cambridge Theatre, Sept 1973, George in Two and Two Make Sex; repeated the parts in his own production of the play, touring Australia and Canada, 1974–5; Mermaid, June 1976, Celimare in Some of My Best Friends Are Husbands; Savoy, Mar 1978, Andrew Wyke in Sleuth; Richmond, Dec 1979, appeared in Dick Whittington; made his first appearance in films in 1952, and pictures include: Doctor in Love, Carry on Jack, Help!, Countess From Hong Kong, Every Home Should Have One, Inspector Clouseau, and The Picture Show Man; his many television appearances since 1951 include the series *Top Secret, Father, Dear Father, Ooh, La La!* (co- producer), and The Many Wives of Patrick; co-author of Ring For Catty (from which the film Carry On Nurse was made), 1956; Smith By Any Other Name, 1964.

Recreations: Tennis and motor racing. *Address:* c/o London Management, 235–241 Regent Street, London, W1Y 2JT.

CARIOU, Len (*né* Leonard), actor, singer, director, and administrator
b St Boniface, Manitoba, Canada, 30 Sept 1939; *s* of George Marius Cariou and his wife Mary Estelle (Moore); *e* Holy Cross School, St Paul's College, Winnipeg; previously employed as a sales clerk of farm machinery and men's clothing; trained for the stage at the Stratford, Ontario, and Tyrone Guthrie, Minneapolis, Minnesota, theatres, and with Kristin Linklater, Fran Bennett, and Judith Liebowitz.

First appeared on the stage at the Rainbow, Winnipeg, Manitoba, June 1959, in chorus of Damn Yankees; joined the Stratford Shakespearean Festival of Canada and, in 1962, played Walter Sugarsop in The Taming of the Shrew, and various parts in The Tempest, Macbeth, and Cyrano de Bergerac; in 1963 played Margarelon in Troilus and Cressida, Servilius in Timon of Athens, and various parts in Cyrano de Bergerac and The Comedy of Errors; made his début in

England at the Chichester Theatre, Apr 1964, as Longaville in Love's Labour's Lost; returned to Stratford, Ontario, and, in 1964, played Sir John Bushy in Richard II, Cleonte in Le Bourgeois Gentilhomme, and various parts in The Country Wife; at the Tyrone Guthrie, Minneapolis, Minnesota, for the Minnesota Theatre Company, 1966, played in The Skin of Our Teeth, S S Glencairn, and as Orlando in As You Like It; same company, 1968, played Orestes in The House of Atreus, Feste in Twelfth Night, and Musgrave in Serjeant Musgrave's Dance; made his New York début with this company at the Billy Rose, Dec 1968, when he again played Orestes in The House of Atreus; at the American Shakespeare Festival and Academy, Stratford, Conn, summer 1969, played in Much Ado About Nothing, The Three Sisters, and the title-role in Henry V; ANTA, NY, Nov 1969, again played the title-role of Henry V with this company; Palace, Mar 1970, Bill Sampson in the musical Applause, and continued in this part for more than a year; Tyrone Guthrie, 1971, Christian in Cyrano de Bergerac, and in The Taming of the Shrew; Morosco, Feb 1972, John Wheeler in Night Watch; became Associate Director of the Tyrone Guthrie in 1972 and directed Of Mice and Men and, in July, played Oberon in A Midsummer Night's Dream; Guthrie, Nov 1972, Œdipus in Œdipus the King; Shubert, Feb 1973, Frederick Egerman in A Little Night Music; Shubert, 11 Mar 1973, appeared in Sondheim: A Musical Tribute; St Clement's, Jan 1974, directed The Petrified Forest; Guthrie, July 1974, title-role of King Lear and, Aug, played in The Crucible; Helen Hayes, Mar 1975, directed Don't Call Back; appointed Artistic Director, Manitoba Theatre Centre, Winnipeg, season 1975, appearing in Equus and Cyrano de Bergerac, and directing Of Mice and Men; Marymount Manhattan, Jan 1977, and Guthrie, Minneapolis, Apr, appeared in the monologue A Sorrow Beyond Dreams; Lyceum, NY, Dec 1977, Richard Landau in Cold Storage; Uris, Mar 1979, title-role in Sweeney Todd (winning a 'Tony'); first appeared on television in Nov 1965, as Ragnar Brovik in The Master Builder, and has since played in Juno and the Paycock, and recently Who'll Save Our Children?; films include A Little Night Music and One Man.

Recreations: Baseball, golf, tennis, gymnastics. *Address:* c/o STE Representation, 888 Seventh Avenue, New York, NY 10019.

CARLISLE, Kitty, actress and singer
b New Orleans, La, 3 Sept 1914; *d* of Dr Joseph Conn and his wife Hortense (Holzman); *e* Château Mont-Choisi, Lausanne, Switzerland, and at private schools in London, Paris and Rome; *m* Moss Hart (dec); studied for the stage at the Royal Academy of Dramatic Art, London, and with Dullin at the Théâtre de l'Atelier in Paris.

Made her first appearance on the stage at the Capitol Theatre, New York, 1932, in the title-role of a tabloid version of Rio Rita; next appeared at the Morosco Theatre, 14 Oct 1933, as Prince Orlofsky in Champagne Sec; Center Theatre, Oct 1936, played Katarina in White Horse Inn; Majestic, Dec 1937, Marie Hiller, Charlotte and Franzi in Three Waltzes; made her first appearance in straight plays at the Ridgeway Theatre, White Plains, NY, July 1938, when she appeared as Diana Lake in French Without Tears, subsequently appearing in The Night of January 16th; in summer theatres, 1939, appeared in A Successful Calamity and Tonight or Never; Ethel Barrymore, NY, June 1940, played Pamela Gibson in Walk with Music; Boston Opera House, May 1943, Sonia in The Merry Widow; Cleveland, Ohio, July 1943, Gilda in Design for Living; Philadelphia, June 1944, Leonora in There's Always Juliet; summer theatres, 1946, appeared in

Tonight or Never; Ziegfeld, Dec 1948, Lucretia in Benjamin Britten's opera, The Rape of Lucretia; summer theatres, 1949, appeared in The Man Who Came to Dinner; Broadhurst, NY, Apr 1954, played Alice Walters in Anniversary Waltz; City Center, NY, May 1956, played Katherine in Kiss Me Kate; Elitch Gardens, Denver, Colorado, and tour, July 1965, Content Lowell in The Marriage-Go-Round; made her Metropolitan Opera début on New Year's Eve, 1966, when she played Prince Orlovsky in Fledermaus, repeated the role in the winter, 1967, season, and toured with the Company in spring, 1967; appeared in concert with the Philadelphia Orchestra at the Saratoga Performing Arts Center, 1967; toured, 1970–1, as Irene Livingston in Light Up the Sky; again toured, Aug–Dec 1971, as Irene Livingston in Light Up the Sky; toured, summer 1972, in this part; Boston Opera Company, 17 Feb 1973, Duchess of Krackenthorp in Daughter of the Regiment; Metropolitan Opera House, June 1973, Prince Orlovsky in Fledermaus; toured, summer 1973, in Don't Frighten the Horses; toured, summer 1975, in You Never Know; entered films 1934, and has appeared successfully in several pictures including: She Loves Me Not, Here Is My Heart, and with the Marx Brothers in A Night at the Opera; has appeared on television regularly on the long-running program To Tell the Truth; is active in administrative capacities, notably as Chairman of Governor Rockefeller's Conference on Woman, May 1966; as special consultant to the Governor on women's opportunities; is a member of the Visiting Committee of the Board of Overseers of Harvard University for the Music Dept; Visiting Committee on the Arts, MIT; elected Associate Fellow at Yale University; writes the column Kitty's Calendar for Women's Unit News; tours extensively as a lecturer with First Person Singular; currently chairman, NY State Council for the Arts; DHL, New Rochelle, Hartwick, Marymount Colleges.

Recreations: Swimming. *Address:* Keedick Lecture Bureau, 475 Fifth Avenue, New York, NY 10017.

CARMICHAEL, Ian, actor
b Hull, 18 June 1920; *s* of Arthur Denholm Carmichael and his wife Kate (Gillett); *e* Scarborough College and Bromsgrove School, Worcestershire; *m* Jean Pyman Maclean; studied for the stage at the Royal Academy of Dramatic Art.

Made his first appearance at the People's Palace, Mile End, 1939, as a Robot in RUR; at the Embassy, 29 Nov 1939, appeared as Claudius in Julius Caesar; toured, June–Aug 1940, in the revue Nine Sharp; Apollo, Feb 1947, played Teddy Dyeswood and Arthur in She Wanted A Cream Front Door; Mercury, July 1947, Jean in I Said To Myself; Arts, Oct 1947, Christopher Mackintosh in Cupid and Mars; Q, Dec 1947, Norman Reese in Out of the Frying Pan; Players, Nov 1948, appeared in the revue What Goes On?; Q, Dec 1948, played Edward Govan in I Walk Unseen; toured, 1949, as Norman in The Lilac Domino; Stoll, Feb 1950, played Otto Bergmann in a revival of Wild Violets; Lyric, Hammersmith, May 1951, appeared in The Lyric Revue, transferring to the Globe in this production, Sept 1951; Globe, July 1952, appeared in The Globe Revue; Hippodrome, May 1953, appeared in the revue High Spirits; Lyric, Hammersmith, Dec 1953, appeared in the revue At The Lyric, and at the St Martin's, May 1954, played in a revised version of this production, Going To Town; Strand, Nov 1954, played David Prentice in Simon and Laura; her Majesty's, Dec 1957, played Augie Poole in The Tunnel of Love; Piccadilly, Oct 1959, The Tramp in The Love Doctor; Savoy, Mar 1960, Elliott Nash in The Gazebo; Vaudeville, Dec 1961, played Parker Ballentyne in Critic's Choice; Strand, Mar 1963, Nicholas in Devil May Care; Ashcroft, Croydon, 1963, appeared in Sunday in New York; toured, Mar 1964, as Victor Hood in March Hares; made his first appearance in New York at the Cort, Feb 1965, as Robert in Boeing-Boeing; Yvonne Arnaud Theatre, Guildford, Aug 1965, David Lord in Say Who You Are, prior to appearing at Her Majesty's, Oct 1965, in the same play; Strand, Apr 1967, played St John Hotchkiss in Getting Married; Lyric, May 1968, Michael in I Do! I Do!; toured England and appeared in Canada as Charlie in Birds On The Wing; toured South Africa, summer 1972, in Darling, I'm Home; Oxford Festival, Aug 1974, played Mr Dewlip in Springtime for Henry; Vaudeville, Oct 1976, Graham in Out on a Limb; first appeared in films in 1947, and subsequently played numerous starring roles in such films as Lucky Jim, I'm All Right, Jack, School for Scoundrels, etc; most recent film, The Lady Vanishes, 1979; his numerous television appearances include the series The World of Wooster, Bachelor Father and a number of serials based on Dorothy Sayers' stories of Lord Peter Wimsey; also directed the series Mr Pastry's Progress, It's A Small World, and We Beg To Differ, as well as other light entertainment shows; published his autobiography, Will the Real Ian Carmichael, 1979.

Recreations: His home, cricket and reading. *Clubs:* MCC, Lord's Taverners (Chairman, 1970–71). *Address:* c/o London Management, 235–241 Regent Street, London, W1A 2JT.

CARMINES, Al, composer, lyricist, performer, director, producer
b Hampton, Va, 25 Jul 1936; *s* of Alvin Allison Carmines and his wife Katherine (Graham); *e* Swarthmore College and Union Theological Seminary.

Mr Carmines is pastor of the Judson Memorial Church, New York City, where many of his works were first produced; among the many operas, cantatas, musical comedies, and operettas for which he composed the score, and normally the lyrics and libretto, are Home Movies, Softly, And Consider the Nearness, 1964; Promenade (text and lyrics by Maria Irene Fornes) 1965; The Gorilla Queen, with text by Ronald Tavel, and In Circles, an opera based on Gertrude Stein's A Circular Play, and in which he performed the role of Dole at the Judson Memorial, 13 Oct 1967, and at the Cherry Lane, 4 Nov 1967; wrote the opera The Sayings of Mao-Tse-Tung, Jan 1968; at the Gramercy Arts, June 1968, again performed Dole in In Circles; Astor Place, Jan 1969, played the piano in his musical adaptation of Peace from Aristophanes; Promenade (extended version), 1969; lyrics and music for the tour of WC, and for Wanted, and Joan, 1971; appeared in cabaret Upstairs at the Downstairs, Feb 1972; A Look at the Fifties, Life of a Man, The Making of Americans to a text by Gertrude Stein, 1972; at the Truck and Warehouse, June 1973, wrote, lyrics, music, played Oscar Wilde in, and directed Faggot; music, lyrics and direction for Religion, Oct 1973; The Future, which he also directed, 1974; in cabaret at Reno Sweeney, Aug 1974; Brooklyn Academy of Music, Apr 1974, music and text of the opera The Duel; Judson Poet's, music and performed in Listen to Me, Oct 1974; book, lyrics, music, and directed Sacred and Profane Love, and Why I Love New York, 1975; music for A Manoir, 1977; In Praise of Death, 1978; his oratorio Christmas Rappings has been performed each year since 1969; received an Obie for sustained achievement Off-Broadway, 1979.

Address: Judson Poets' Theater, Judson Memorial Church, 55 Washington Square South, New York, NY 10012.

CARNEY, Art, actor
b Mount Vernon, New York, 4 Nov 1918; *s* of Edward M Carney and his wife Helen (Farrell); *e* A B Davis H S, Mount Vernon; *m* (1) Jean Meyers (mar dis); (2) Barbara Isaac.

Toured New England, 1956, as Richard Sherman in The Seven Year Itch; Ivoryton, Conn, Playhouse, 1956, played Elmer P Dowd in Harvey; made his NY début at the Cort, 20 Nov 1957, as James Hyland in The Rope Dancers; later transferring with the play to the Henry Miller's; Biltmore, Dec 1961, played Frank Michaelson in Take Her, She's Mine; Plymouth, Mar 1965, Felix Ungar in The Odd Couple; Vivian Beaumont, July 1968, Andy Tracey in Lovers; Music Box, Sept 1968, again played in Lovers; Eugene O'Neill, 5 June 1972, took over from Peter Falk as Mel Edison in The Prisoner of Second Avenue; Ahmanson, Los Angeles, Oct 1972, repeated this part; Arlington Park, Chicago, Feb 1974, Oscar Madison in The Odd Couple, thus having played both the male leads in this play; Westbury Music Fair, Long Island, Nov 1974, Mel Edison in The Prisoner of Second Avenue; has also appeared extensively in vaudeville and in cabaret; made his first film, Pot of Gold, in 1941, and has since appeared in The Yellow Rolls Royce, 1965; Harry and Tonto, 1974, for which he received the Academy Award, W W and the Dixie Dance Kings, 1975; made his television début on the *Morey Amsterdam Show* in 1948, and later made a great success as Ed Norton in *The Honeymooners,* 1950–9, and *The Jackie Gleason Show,* 1969–71; has also appeared in Uncle Harry, Burlesque, Panama Hattie, 1954, Charley's Aunt, Incredible Irishman, 1957, Harvey, Peter and the Wolf, 1958, Our Town, 1959, Call Me Back, 1960, Lanigan's Rabbi, 1976, and numerous other dramatic and variety programs; has received three Emmy Awards, 1953, 54, and 55, and three Sylvania Awards, 1954 and 1959 (twice).

Club: The Lambs. *Address:* Actors Equity Association, 165 West 46th Street, New York, NY 10036.

CARNOVSKY, Morris, actor, director, and teacher
b St Louis, Mo, 5 Sept 1897; *e* Washington University; *m* (1) Florence Lasersohn (mar dis); (2) Phoebe Brand.

Made his first appearance on the professional stage in Boston, Mass, with the Henry Jewitt players and subsequently appeared with E E Clive's company, spending three years with the two companies; made his first appearance on the New York stage at the Provincetown Theatre, 20 Dec 1922, as Reb Aaron in The God of Vengeance; from 1923 to 1930 was engaged with the Theatre Guild, and during that period at the Guild and Martin Beck Theatres, played the following among other parts: The Commissioner of Police in The Failures, La Hire in Saint Joan, Philip Speed in The Creaking Chair, Riva-Palacio in Juarez and Maximilian, The Second Federal Man in Ned McCobb's Daughter, Aliocha in The Brothers Karamazov, Centuri and Aggazi in Right You Are if You Think You Are, Dr Schutzmacher in The Doctor's Dilemma, Tedaldo and Kubla Khan in Marco Millions, The Judge in Volpone, Director Bezchyba in The Camel Through the Needle's Eye, Uncle Vanya in Uncle Vanya, Nicobar in The Apple Cart, Stephen Field in Hotel Universe, Bacon in Elizabeth the Queen; joined the Group Theatre in Sept 1931, and with the exception of two productions with the Theatre Guild remained with the company at various theatres to play the following parts: Sept 1931, Robert Connelly in The House of Connelly; Dec 1931, in the revue 1931; Mar 1932, Father Martinez in Night over Taos; Sept 1932, Rufus Sonnenberg in Success Story; (Guild) Mar 1933, Levering in Both Your Houses; Sept 1933, Dr Levine in Men in White; (Guild) Mar 1934, Dr Lewis Golden in Gentlewoman; Nov 1934, Will Parrot in Gold Eagle Guy;

Feb 1935, Jacob in Awake and Sing; Mar 1935, Fayette in Waiting for Lefty; Dec 1935, Leo Gordon in Paradise Lost; Mar 1936, The Speaker in The Case of Clyde Griffiths; Nov 1936, Chief of the Allied Command in Johnny Johnson; Nov 1937, Mr Bonaparte in Golden Boy; made his first appearance on the London stage at the St James's, 21 June 1938, in the last-mentioned part; on returning to NY, appeared with the Group, Nov 1938, as Ben Stark in Rocket to the Moon; Nov 1939, Captain Joshua in Thunder Rock; Feb 1940, Rosenberger in Night Music; he next appeared at the Morosco, Oct 1940, as John Adam Kent in Suzanna and the Elders; Biltmore, Dec 1940, played Mr Appopolous in My Sister Eileen; Cort, Jan 1942, David Cole in Café Crown; Windsor, Feb 1943, Kulkov in Counterattack; Plymouth, Mar 1948, Sam Blumenfeld in Joy to the World; Broadhurst, Dec 1950, played Peter Stockmann in An Enemy of the People; Playhouse, Wilmington, Delaware, Mar 1951, Sig Ratchett in Let Me Hear the Melody; associated with the Actors Laboratory in California, 1940–50, where he directed the production of Volpone, The Dragon, Monday's Heroes, and also appeared in The Banker's Daughter; Barbizon-Plaza, NY, May 1953, Aaron Katz in The High School and Presiding Angel in A Tale of Chelm in a double-bill entitled The World of Sholom Aleichem; 4th Street, Oct 1954, the Tzaddik in The Dybbuk; same theatre, Feb 1955, Andrey in The Three Sisters; Plymouth, Oct 1955, Priam in Tiger at the Gates; Martin Beck, NY, May 1956, Probus in The Lovers; since 1956 has appeared regularly with the American Shakespeare Festival Co of Stratford, Connecticut, in the following parts: the Earl of Salisbury in King John, the Provost in Measure for Measure, Gremio in The Taming of the Shrew, 1956, again appearing in the last two parts at the Phoenix, NY, in Jan and Feb 1957; Stratford, Conn, Shylock in The Merchant of Venice, and Antonio in Much Ado About Nothing, 1957; Belasco, NY, Nov 1957, played Jacob Friedland in Nude with Violin; Stratford, Conn, Claudius in Hamlet, and Peter Quince in A Midsummer Night's Dream, 1958; Morosco, NY, Dec 1958, Mr Sacher in The Cold Wind and the Warm; returned to Stratford, Conn, playing Capulet in Romeo and Juliet, and Dr Caius in The Merry Wives of Windsor, 1959; played Feste in Twelfth Night, Prospero in The Tempest, and Lepidus in Antony and Cleopatra, 1960; Longacre, Jan 1961, Logician in Rhinoceros; Globe, San Diego, California, June 1961, Shylock in The Merchant of Venice; Billy Rose, Jan 1962, Morris Siegel in A Family Affair; Goodman, Chicago, 1962, Azdak in The Caucasian Chalk Circle; US tour, Oct 1962–Feb 1963, Mr Baker in Come Blow Your Horn; Goodman, Chicago, 1963, again played Shylock in The Merchant of Venice; Stratford, Conn, 1963, title-role of King Lear; Goodman, Chicago, Apr 1964, and Schonberg Hall, Los Angeles, June 1964, again played King Lear; Coconut Grove Playhouse, Miami, Mar 1965, Dr Max Faessler in The Man with the Perfect Wife; Stratford, Conn, June 1965, again played King Lear; Stratford, Conn, June 1967, Creon in Jean Anouilh's Antigone and Shylock in The Merchant of Venice; Stratford, Conn, 1969, Polonius in Hamlet and in The Three Sisters; toured, 1969, as Galileo Galilei in Lamp at Midnight; appeared with the Long Wharf Theater, New Haven, Conn, 1970–1 season, and in 1971–2 played there in A Swan Song; Stratford, Conn, 1971, Prospero in The Tempest; Stratford, June 1975, again played King Lear; Lab, NY, Oct 1975, directed Volpone; McCarter, Princeton, Mar 1976, appeared in Awake and Sing; has appeared in films, in The Life of Emile Zola, Rhapsody in Blue, Cyrano de Bergerac, Tovarich, etc; has appeared on television in Medea, The World of Sholom Aleichem, and The Chicago Eight Conspiracy Trial.

Address: c/o Actors Equity Association, 165 West 46th Street, New York, NY 10036.

CARO, Warren, management executive
b Brooklyn, New York, 24 Feb 1907; *s* of Arthur B Caro and his wife Madeline (Davidsburg); *e* Boys High School, New York City, Cornel University (BA 1927, JD 1929); *m* Nancy Kelly; formerly a lawyer, during World War II served as Lieutenant Commander in the US Coast Guard and naval aide to the Governor of Alaska.

Was production associate for Summer of the 17th Doll at the Coronet, 22 Jan 1958; and for The Glass Menagerie, June 1961; at the New York City Center, 25 Jan 1950, played a British General in a revival of Arms and the Man; Cort, 1961, took over the role of a Senator in Advise and Consent; member of the League of New York Theaters and Producers and served on its Board of Governors since 1949; Council of the Living Theater, as Secretary and on the Board of Directors since 1950; on the Board of Directors of the Independent Booking Office, 1957; on the Advisory Board of the New Dramatists Committee; Chairman of the Board of Trustees of the American Academy of Dramatic Arts; a founder of the NY chapter of the National Academy of Television Arts and Sciences; a founder and first president of the American TV Society; a founder of the Shaw Society of America; Executive Director of the Theater Guild—American Theater Society since 1946; Vice President of Theater Guild Productions Inc; served State Dept as US delegation chairman to the first ITI conference in Prague, 1948, and Zurich, 1949; member of the advisory committee for the John F Kennedy Center for the Performing Arts, Washington, DC; received a special Antoinette Perry (Tony) Award for his activities with the Theater Guild—American Repertory Company, 1961; joined the Shubert Organization as Director of Theater Operations in 1967.
Recreation: Music. *Address:* The Shubert Organization Inc, 225 West 44th Street, New York, NY 10036. *Tel:* 221–7500.

CARPENTER, Carleton, actor
b Bennington, Vermont, 10 July 1926.
Made his Broadway début 2 Mar 1944 at the Playhouse as Tittman (Shakespeare) in Bright Boy; at the National, 23 May 1944, Rinn in Career Angel; Adelphi, Mar 1946, appeared in the revue Three to Make Ready; International, 3 Sept 1947, played Larry Masters in The Magic Touch; Lyric, Bridgeport, and Locust St, Philadelphia, Sept 1947, played a Sailor in The Big People; Imperial, Dec 1953, appeared in the revue John Murray Anderson's Almanac; made films in Hollywood for some years then returned to the stage at the Broadway Congregational Church, 17 Feb 1957, as Lee in A Box of Watercolors; Henry Miller's, 11 Apr 1957, Maxime in Hotel Paradiso; Cherry Lane, Jan 1962, David Greenfield in A Stage Affair; toured beginning Apr 1965 as Cornelius Hackl in Hello, Dolly!; St James, 1966, took over as Cornelius Hackl and subsequently toured again in this part; Coconut Playhouse, 1968, played in Lock Up Your Daughters; Theatre Four, 1969, took over as Michael in The Boys in the Band; McAlpin Rooftop, Mar 1970, played the title-role of Lyle, but did not open in this part; Washington Theater Club, Washington, DC, 1971, played in Curse You, Spread Eagle; Mercer-O'Casey, Feb 1972, Brinnin in Dylan; toured in Light up the Sky, 1972; St Clement's, NY, 1973, appeared in The Greatest Fairy Story Every Told; Village Gate, Oct 1974, in What Is Turning Gilda So Grey?; Cubiculo, Nov 1975, in A Good Old-Fashioned Revue; has appeared frequently in films, notably in Lost Boundaries, 1948, Two Weeks, With

Love, 1950, Summer Stock, 1951, Take the High Ground, 1954, Some of My Best Friends Are . . ., 1971, That's Entertainment, 1974, etc.

Address: Chardavoyne Road, Warwick, NY 10990.

CARPENTER, Constance, actress and vocalist
b Bath, 19 Apr 1906; *d* of Harold Carpenter and his wife Mabel Anne (Cottrell); *e* Harley Street Schools, Bath; *m* (1) Paul Ord Hamilton (mar dis); (2) Commander J H S Lucas-Scudamore, RN (mar dis); (3) Captain James Kennedy.

First appeared on the stage at the Little Theatre with Lila Fields, 1916; at the Lyceum, Feb 1917, sang as one of the choristers in Seven Days Leave; at the London Pavilion, Oct 1921, appeared in The Fun of the Fayre; went to America, and at the Times Square Theatre, Jan 1924, appeared in André Charlot's Revue of 1924; at the Selwyn Theatre, Nov 1925, played in The Charlot Revue of 1926; Imperial, Nov 1926, played Mae in Oh, Kay; Vanderbilt, Nov 1927, Alice Carter in A Connecticut Yankee, and continued in this for a year; George M Cohan, Mar 1929, played Connie Block in Hello, Daddy; she then returned to London and at Daly's, Oct 1929, played Alice Carter in A Yankee at the Court of King Arthur; London Pavilion, Apr 1930, succeeded Ada May in Cochran's 1930 Revue; Cambridge, Sept 1930, appeared in Charlot's Masquerade; Lyceum, Dec 1930, played Polly Perkins in Robinson Crusoe; returned to New York, and at the Music Box, June 1931, played in The Third Little Show; again returned to London, and at the Lyceum, Dec 1931, played Cinderella; Aldwych, Mar 1932, Evie Wynne in Dirty Work; Piccadilly, Oct 1932, Joy Armstrong in All for Joy; Majestic, NY, Dec 1934, Gioconda and Marella in Music Hath Charms; King's, Southsea, Dec 1935, Jack in Jack and the Beanstalk; Strand, Apr 1936, Lucille Phelps in Baby Austin; toured in the United States, from Sept 1936, as Precious Stream in Lady Precious Stream; Golder's Green, Dec 1937, Princess Elaine in Humpty Dumpty; Adelphi, May 1938, appeared in Happy Returns; Criterion, Sept 1938, Diana Lake in French Without Tears; Coliseum, July 1939, appeared during repertory season, as Ann Perryman in The Flying Squad, etc; toured, 1939, in Other People's Houses, and Almost a Honeymoon; toured, 1940, in Wild Violets; during the War, toured for ENSA in the Middle East, and during 1943, joined Alice Delysia's company at Cairo, and played Gabrielle in The French for Love; returned to England, 1944, and toured for the American Red Cross; again toured for ENSA, 1945, in Holland and Germany, and 1946, in India and Burma; resumed acting in England, 1950, when she toured as Mrs Dunne in Castle in the Air; St James, NY, Aug 1952, succeeded Gertrude Lawrence as Anna Leonowens in The King and I; Globe, London, Nov 1954, appeared in An Evening with Beatrice Lillie; in Summer Theatre, Corning, NY, July 1959, played Mame Dennis in Auntie Mame; York Playhouse, Oct 1960, Lady Parvula de Panzoust in Valmouth; Royale, Apr 1963, took over the role of Miss Swanson in Lord Pengo; Colonial, Boston, July 1963, Ethel Tubwell in Jennie; Mineola, Long Island, Apr 1966, played in Peter Pan; toured US, Dec 1969–Apr 1970, as the Wife of Bath in Canterbury Tales; Royale, Oct 1971, Mrs Elbourne in The Incomparable Max; toured, 1975, as Emmeline Marshall in Irene; commenced film career 1930, in Just for a Song.

Address: c/o Stephen Draper Agency, 37 West 57th Street, New York, NY 10019.

CARPENTER, Freddie, director
b Melbourne, Victoria, 15 Feb 1908; *s* of James Carpenter and his wife Jean (Dunstone); *e* Sydney Grammar School.

Made his first appearance on the stage at the Princess Theatre, Melbourne, 20 Dec 1924, in the chorus of The Rise of Rosie O'Reilly; during the next three years appeared as leading dancer in a number of musical comedies in Melbourne and Sydney; made his first stage appearance in New York, at the Erlanger Theatre, Apr 1928, as the Young King in Almanac; made his first London appearance at the Palladium, May 1929, dancing with Frances Mann; he appeared as feature dancer at the Winter Garden, Sept 1930, in Follow a Star; toured, 1931, in Lavender; London Hippodrome, Jan 1932, in Bow Bells; Daly's, Feb 1934, in Yours Sincerely; Aldwych, July 1934, in That Certain Something; Embassy, Mar 1935, and Shaftesbury, Apr 1935, in Let's Go Gay; Coliseum, Dec 1936, in Cinderella; Music Box, NY, Oct 1937, in I'd Rather Be Right; from 1935 directed the dances in a number of musical plays, including Tulip Time, Life Begins at Oxford Circus, 1935; The Town Talks, Mother Goose, 1936; And On We Go, 1937; Maritza, Bobby Get Your Gun, 1938; The Dancing Years, Funny Side Up, 1939; Up and Doing, Present Arms, 1940; Lady Behave, 1941; The Love Racket, 1943; The Lilac Domino, 1944; Irene, The Gaieties, Big Boy, 1945; returned to Australia, 1946, to stage Follow the Girls; 1950–65, directed all the Howard and Wyndham pantomimes; has directed a large number of shows, including The Dancing Years (revival), Love is My Reason, 1947; Limelight, Serenade, 1948; The Lilac Domino, The Sleeping Beauty, 1949; Belinda, Dear Miss Phoebe (musical numbers), Sally (revival), 1952; One Fair Daughter, 1953; The Merry Widow (tour), 1959; The Billy Barnes Revue, Rose Marie, A Wish for Jamie (also devised), 1960; Kind Sir (tour), 1961; A Love for Jamie, 1962; How to Succeed in Business Without Really Trying (Melbourne), A Touch of Tartan (tour), 1963; Never Too Late (Melbourne), A Funny Thing Happened on the Way to the Forum (Sydney), 1964; The World of Jamie, 1967; Let's Get Swinging, Queen Passionella, 1968; The Corbett Follies, The Tommy Cooper Show, 1969; Danny La Rue at the Palace, 1970; Cinderella (Manchester), 1970; Charlie Girl (Melbourne), Cinderella (Coventry), 1971; No, No, Nanette (Melbourne), 1972; The Danny La Rue Show, Cowardy Custard (S Africa), 1973; Irene (Sydney), Hans Andersen, 1974; The Ronnie Corbett Revue (Paignton), Queen Daniella, 1975; Irene, 1976; Something's Afoot (Hong Kong), The Danny La Rue Show (Scarborough) 1978; Danny La Rue Australian tour, 1979; has also arranged dances for several films, including Carnival, London Town, The Winslow Boy, etc; also dance numbers in several productions on television, including the tribute to Sir Winston Churchill, Ninety Years On, Nov 1964; the Noël Coward Revue (associate producer), and The Jimmy Tarbuck Show; served in the RAF, Mar 1941–Sept 1944.

Recreation: Swimming. *Address:* 8 Elm Row, Hampstead, London, NW3. *Tel:* 01–435 0679.

CARRADINE, John (*né* Richmond Reed), actor
b New York City, 5 Feb 1906; *s* of William Reed Carradine and his wife Genevieve Winifred (Richmond); *e* Episcopal Academy, Philadelphia, NY, and Graphic Art School, Philadelphia; *m* (1) Ardanelle McCool (mar dis); (2) Sonia Henius (mar dis); (3) Doris I Rich (mar dis); (4) Emily Cisneros.

Made his first appearance on the stage, at the St Charles Theatre, New Orleans, in Camille, 1925; Egan Theatre, LA, 1927, played in Window Panes; he then became a marine artist and portrait painter, and subsequently was engaged as a designer for C B de Mille in Hollywood; he entered films in 1928, and appeared in innumerable pictures; at Los Angeles and San Francisco, 1941, appeared as Louis XI in The Vagabond King; toured, 1943–4, with his own repertory company, playing Shylock, Othello, Iago and Hamlet; Brighton, Brooklyn, NY, July 1945, Allan Manville in My Dear Children; appeared at Bridgeport, Conn, Nov 1945, as Matthew in Murder Without Crime; reappeared on the NY stage, Town Hall, Aug 1946, as Jonathan Brewster in Arsenic and Old Lace; Ethel Barrymore, 15 Oct 1946, the Cardinal in The Duchess of Malfi; Toledo, Dec 1946, Rupert Cadell in Rope; Maxine Elliott, Dec 1947, the Inquisitor in Galileo; City Center, Jan–Feb 1948, Voltore in Volpone, and Nyunin in The Wedding; Music Box, Apr 1948, Walter Fowler in The Cup of Trembling; National, Oct 1948, Benjy in The Leading Lady; Belasco, Dec 1948, The Ragpicker in The Madwoman of Chaillot, and toured in this, 1949–50; appeared in summer theatres 1949, as Dr Austin Sloper in The Heiress; 1950, as Brutus in Julius Caesar, Sir Robert in the Winslow Boy, and in Shadow and Substance; 1951, played the leading part in Silver Whistle, Mephistopheles in Dr Faustus, and Jeeter Lester in Tobacco Road; at the New York City Center, Jan 1955, played Kit Carson in a revival of The Time of Your Life; US tour, Oct 1960–Apr 1961 Nickles in JB; Alvin, NY, May 1962, Lycus in A Funny Thing Happened on the Way to the Forum, and continued in this part for nearly two years; toured, 1966, as Fagin in Oliver!; Alhambra, Jacksonville, Florida, Sept 1970, Jeeter Lester in Tobacco Road; Arlington Park, Ill, 1973, played in The Fantasticks and You Never Can Tell; toured, 1974, in Arsenic and Old Lace; Episcopal Academy, Philadelphia, Dec 1974, directed and played Sir Thomas More in A Man for All Seasons; has appeared in many modern and classical plays on the Pacific Coast, and many summer stock seasons; first played in films under the name John Peter Richmond in Tol'able David (1930), The Invisible Man (1933), Cleopatra, The Black Cat (1934), etc; as John Carradine has played in Bride of Frankenstein, Les Miserables, The Crusades (1935), Winterset (1936), Jesse James (1939), Adventures of Mark Twain (1944), Cheyenne Autumn (1964), Hex (1973), The Shootist (1976), and many others.

Favourite parts: Jeeter Lester, Othello, Sir Thomas More, Sir Robert in The Winslow Boy, Shylock, and Dr Sloper in The Heiress. *Recreations:* Sculpture, tennis and sailing. *Club:* Players. *Address:* c/o Actors Equity Association, 165 West 46th Street, New York, NY 10036.

CARROLL, Vinnette, actress, director, administrator
b New York City, 11 Mar 1922; *d* of Edgar E Carroll and his wife Florence (Morris); *e* Long Island University (BA 1944), New York University (MA 1946), Columbia University Graduate School; studied for the stage with Erwin Piscator, Lee Strasberg, and Stella Adler; formerly engaged as a clinical and industrial psychologist.

First appeared on the stage at the New School for Social Research, 1948, as Clytemnestra in Agamemnon, and later appeared as the Nurse in Romeo and Juliet, the Duchess in Alice in Wonderland, and the River Elbe in Outside the Door, 1948–50; her first stock production was with the Southold Playhouse, Long Island, summer 1948, when she played Addie in The Little Foxes; for the same group, summer 1949, Bella in Deep Are the Roots; toured, 1950, as Ftatateeta in Caesar and Cleopatra; toured the US and the West Indies in a one-woman variety show, 1952–7; City Center, NY, Feb 1956, played a Negro Woman in A Streetcar Named Desire, with Tallulah Bankhead starred; summer stock, 1956, played Catherine in A Grass Harp; Ethel Barrymore, Jan 1957, Amelie in Small War on Murray Hill; Martinique, Mar 1958, Tituba in The Crucible; made her

London début at the Royal Court, 4 Dec 1958, as Sophia Adams in Moon on a Rainbow Shawl; Longacre, NY, Dec 1959, Dora in Jolly's Progress; Lenox Hill Playhouse, May 1960, directed Dark of the Moon for the Equity Library Theatre; Phoenix, Jan 1961, played Dido in The Octoroon; directed Ondine for the ELT, Apr 1961; 41st Street, Dec 1961, directed Black Nativity; directed The Disenchanted for the ELT, Jan 1962; East 11th Street, Jan 1962, played Sophia Adams in Moon on a Rainbow Shawl; Criterion, London, Aug 1962, directed and played the Narrator in Black Nativity; Festival of the Two Worlds, Spoleto, Italy, 1962, narrated and directed Black Nativity; Piccadilly, London, Feb 1963, again directed Black Nativity; Astor Place Playhouse, Dec 1963, made a musical adaptation of James Weldon Johnson's God's Trombone called Trumpets of the Lord; Vaudeville, London, Oct 1964, again directed Black Nativity; Greenwich Mews, NY, 1965, directed The Prodigal Son; Brooks Atkinson, Apr 1969, her adaptation Trumpets of the Lord was revived; New York City Center, Apr 1969, conceived and directed But Never Jam Today; Consultant to the Council and presently Artistic Director of the Urban Arts Corps, for which she conceived and directed Don't Bother Me: I Can't Cope, 1971; Urban Arts Corps, 1971, directed Bury the Dead and Croesus and the Witch; Playhouse, Apr 1972, directed Don't Bother Me, I Can't Cope, which became one of the longest running NY productions with 1065 performances; Mark Taper Forum, Los Angeles, Cal, June 1972, directed Don't Bother Me, I Can't Cope, 1971; Urban Arts Corps, Feb 1973, directed Step Lively, Boy; 1974–5, co-author and directed The Ups and Downs of Theophilus Maitland, conceived and directed the Power to Love, and directed Old Judge is Dead; Spoleto Festival, Italy, June 1975, co-author, directed, and played the Narrator for Your Arm's Too Short to Box with God; Ford's, Washington, DC, Nov 1975, and Lyceum, NY, Dec 1976, again directed this last play; Urban Arts Corps, 1976, directed Play Mas, conceived and directed I'm Laughin' But I Ain't Tickled and a new edition of But Never Jam Today; directed Alice (also wrote), The Gingham Dog, 1977; adapted and directed When Hell Freezes Over I'll Skate, Lincoln Center, 1979 (also for TV); again directed But Never Jam Today, Longacre, July 1979; has taught drama at the High School of the Performing Arts, NY, since 1955; was Director of Ghetto Arts Projects for the New York State Council on the Arts; first appeared in films in A Morning for Jimmy, 1960, and has since played in One Potato, Two Potato, 1963, Up the Down Staircase, 1969, Alice's Restaurant, 1970; played Bernice in A Member of the Wedding for Granada Television, London, 1960, and, in America, narrated and directed Black Nativity, 1962, and conceived, adapted, and supervised the production of Beyond the Blues and Jubilation, 1964; has also appeared on other dramatic and discussion programs, notably on NET in 1970 and in the special Sojourner, 1975; received the Obie Award for her role in Moon on a Rainbow Shawl, 1961; received the Ford Foundation Grant for Directors, 1960–1.

Recreations and hobbies: Sports cars, horseback riding, building furniture. *Address:* Urban Arts Corps, 227 West 17th Street, New York, NY 10011. *Tel:* 924–7820.

CARSON, Jeannie (*née* Jean Shuff), actress and singer
b Yorkshire, 28 May 1929; *d* of Frederick Shuff and his wife Netta (Hardy); *m* (1) William Redmond (mar dis); (2) Biff McGuire.

First appeared as a child, on tour, 1942; first appeared on the West End stage at the Hippodrome, 23 Oct 1947, in the revue Starlight Roof; subsequently appeared at the Palladium in the revue Here, There and Everywhere; Casino,

1949, appeared in the revue Latin Quarter; Cambridge, July 1950, played Baby Belgrave in Ace of Clubs; Casino, Mar 1951, appeared in the revue Latin Quarter of 1951; at the same theatre, Dec 1951, played Aladdin in pantomime; at the Saville, Sept 1952, appeared as Jerusha Abbott in Love from Judy, which ran for nearly eighteen months; made her first appearance in New York, at the City Center, Apr 1960, as Sharon McLonergan in Finian's Rainbow; Opera House, Blackpool, Mar 1961, again played Sharon McLonergan in Finian's Rainbow; Lunt-Fontanne, NY, July 1962, took over the part of Maria Rainer in The Sound of Music, subsequently appearing in the same part on tour, Sept 1962–3; US tour, Oct 1963–4, played Guenevere in Camelot; US tour, 1964–5, Lizzie Curry in 110 in the Shade; Piccadilly, London, July 1966, Sarah Chapman in Strike a Light; Goodspeed Opera House, East Haddam, Conn, Aug 1966, the title-role in Maggie; toured, 1967, in She Loves Me; toured, 1968–9, as Stephanie in Cactus Flower; John Golden, NY, Mar 1970, Queen Victoria, Bessie Bellwood, Florence Nightingale, and Alice Crabbe in Blood Red Roses; Theater Club, Washington, DC, Mar 1972, Catherine Sloper in Washington Square; Seattle, Washington, Repertory Company, Jan 1974, Justine Gaveston in A Family and a Fortune; toured, 1974, as Anne Miller in 6 Rms, Riv Vu; Seattle Repertory, Mother Day in Life with Father, Dec 1974; Nora in A Doll's House, Feb 1975; title-role in The Madwoman of Chaillot, Feb 1976; Katie Bradford in Eminent Domain, Apr 1978; first appeared in films in 1948; has appeared on television since 1955, notably in her own shows Hey, Jeannie and The Jeannie Carson Show, and in Best Foot Forward, The Rivals, Little Women, etc.

Hobby: Dog breeding. *Recreations:* Horse riding and cooking. *Address:* c/o Actors Equity Association, 165 West 46th Street, New York, NY 10036.

CARTERET, Anna (*née* Wilkinson), actress
b Bangalore, India, 11 Dec 1942; *d* of Peter John Wilkinson and his wife Patricia Carteret (Strahan); *e* Arts Educational Schools, Tring, Herts, where she was trained for the stage; *m* Christopher Morahan.

Made her first appearance as a Cloud and a Jumping Bean in Jack and the Beanstalk at the Palace, Watford, Dec 1957; Scala, Dec 1960, first London appearance, as Wendy in Peter Pan; worked in repertory, including Windsor and Lincoln, 1962–3; Bristol Old Vic, 1964–6; her performances here included Honey in Who's Afraid of Virginia Woolf?, Titania in A Midsummer Night's Dream, Gloria Clandon in You Never Can Tell, Mariana in Measure for Measure, Polly Peachum in The Beggar's Opera, Cyprienne in Let's Get a Divorce, Constance in She Stoops to Conquer, and Anitra and the Green Woman in Peer Gynt; Shaftesbury, Oct 1966, Fiona Jones in Big Bad Mouse; joined the National Theatre Company at the Old Vic, 1967, where her performances have included: Chorus in Oedipus, Elena in The Advertisement, 1968; Norma in Rites, Nurse Sweet in The National Health, Jacquenetta in Love's Labours Lost, Fusima in Back to Methuselah, Maria in The Travails of Sancho Panza, 1969; Nerissa in The Merchant of Venice, Giacinta in Scapino (Young Vic), Roxane in Cyrano (Cambridge), 1970; Virgilia in Coriolanus, Lucile in Danton's Death (New Theatre), 1971; Secretary in Jumpers, Queen Isabel in Richard II, Peggy Grant in The Front Page, Anabella in 'Tis Pity She's A Whore (mobile production), Maid in School for Scandal, Lady Macbeth's Gentlewoman in Macbeth, 1972; Anya in The Cherry Orchard, Olivia in Twelfth Night (mobile), Virginia in Saturday, Sunday, Monday, Susie Plaistow in The Party, 1973; Theatre Royal, Bristol, Sept 1974, played Eliza

in the Bristol Old Vic's Pygmalion; returned to the National, Jan 1975, to play Fanny Wilton in John Gabriel Borkman at the Old Vic; played the same part at the Lyttelton, Mar 1976; Greenwich, Mar 1977, Olivia in Twelfth Night; at the St George's, Islington, 1977 season, played Portia in The Merchant of Venice, Isabella in Measure for Measure, and Mistress Page in The Merry Wives of Windsor; Greenwich, Feb 1978, Mrs Cheveley in An Ideal Husband; Greenwich, Mar 1978, Dona Elvira in Don Juan; Hampstead, Jan 1979, Ann Troubridge in Daughters of Men; returned to the National Theatre Company to play various parts in Lark Rise, Adele Natter in Undiscovered Country, June; Phoebe in As You Like It (Aug), Queen Elizabeth in Richard III, Nov, 1979; film appearances, since 1959, include The Plank and Dateline Diamonds; has appeared on TV since 1959, originally as a dancer and later in plays and series, including *The Pallisers, The Glittering Prizes,* and *Send in the Girls.*

Recreations: Gardening, walking and dancing. *Address:* c/o Fraser and Dunlop, 91 Regent Street, London, W1.

CARY, Falkland L, MB, BA, dramatic author
b Kildare, Ireland, 2 Jan 1897; *s* of Henry John Litton Cary and his wife Katherine Frances (Boyd); *e* Aldenham School, and Trinity College, Dublin; formerly (and until Apr 1946), engaged as doctor of medicine.

Author of Burning Gold, 1943; Candied Peel, 1945; Murder Out of Tune, 1945; But Once a Year, 1948; Bed of Rose's, 1949; Madam Tic-Tac (with Philip Weathers), 1950; The Paper Chain (with Ivan Butler), 1953; Pitfall, The Owner of Redfields, 1954; Sailor, Beware! (with Philip King), 1955; The Hypnotist (with Philip Weathers), 1956; The Dream House (with Philip King), 1957; Danger Inside (with Ivan Butler), 1958; The Shadow Witness (with Philip Weathers), 1959; Watch It, Sailor! (with Philip King), 1960; The Proof of the Poison (with Philip Weathers), Rock-a-Bye Sailor, 1962; Big Bad Mouse (with Philip King), 1964; Meet Aunt Mildred (with Don Carrol); is the author of TV plays including Pitfall, The Hammer, and Gentlemen at Twilight, as well as works for radio.

Recreations: Greenhouse, model railways and amateur theatricals. *Address:* Hallands, Fleet, Hants. *Tel:* Fleet 4229.

CASH, Rosalind, actress
b Atlantic City, New Jersey, 31 Dec 1938; *d* of John Cash and his wife Martha (Curtis); *e* City College of New York; previously worked as a hospital aide, waitress, salesgirl, and nightclub singer; prepared for the stage with Edmund Cambridge and Vinnette Carroll and at the Negro Ensemble Company.

First appeared on the stage at the Harlem YMCA, NY, 1958, in Langston Hughes's Soul Gone Home; made her Broadway début at the 46th Street, 19 Jan 1966, as Mrs Hoyt in The Wayward Stork; Chelsea Theater Center, Feb 1967, Sonja in Junebug Graduates Tonight!; Bouwerie Lane, May 1967, Lita in To Bury a Cousin; New York City Center, 13 June 1962, played a singer in Fiorello!; joined the Negro Ensemble Company and at the St Mark's Playhouse, 2 Jan 1968, appeared in Song of the Lusitanian Bogey, Apr 1968, played Segi in Kongi's Harvest, and later took over the role of Ogbo Aberi in this production, June 1968, Fanny in Daddy Goodness, July 1968, appeared in a revival of Song of the Lusitanian Bogey, Dec 1968, Third Extraordinary Spook in God Is a (Guess What?), Feb 1969, Adele Eloise Parker in Ceremonies in Dark Old Men, Apr 1969, Conteur in Malcochon, in the triple-bill, An Evening of One Acts; made her London début with the Negro Ensemble Company at the Aldwych, 5 May 1969, as Third Extraordinary Spook in God

Is a (Guess What?) in the World Theatre Season; St Mark's Playhouse, July 1969, Inez Briscoe in Man Better Man, Jan 1970, Ayo in The Harangues, Mar 1970, Mary in Day of Absence; Eastside Playhouse, June 1971, Carla in Charlie Was Here and Now He's Gone; Philadelphia Drama Guild, 1973, Adele Eloise Parker in Ceremonies in Dark Old Men; Delacorte, 31 July 1973, Goneril in The New York Shakespeare Festival production of King Lear; appeared in Boesman and Lena, 1976; in Evolution of the Blues, 1978; entered films in 1969 in All American Boy, and has since played in The New Centurions, Uptown Saturday Night, The Monkey Hustle, The Class of Miss McMichael (1977), 1974, etc; on television has appeared in Ceremonies in Dark Old Men, Sister, Sister, etc.

Hobbies and recreations: Painting, sewing, guitar, poetry. *Favourite parts:* Those performed for the Negro Ensemble Company. *Address:* c/o John Sekura, 1133 N Vista, Hollywood Calif 90046.

CASS, Henry, actor and director
b London, 24 June 1902; *s* of Benjamin Cass and his wife Sarah Ann (Wood); *e* Davenant Foundation School, London; *m* (1) Nancy Hornsby (dec); (2) Joan Hopkins.

Was engaged in commerce from 1916–23, when he made his first appearance on the stage; for three months was director of the Huddersfield Repertory Company under Alfred Wareing; appeared at the Embassy Theatre, Hampstead, Sept 1931, as Ibn Nahal in The Nelson Touch, Dr Kolenaty in The Macropulos Secret, and Karl in Twelve Thousand; at the Lyceum, Oct 1931, played Maurice d'Alvarez in Sensation; St Martin's, Dec 1931, Ibn Nahal in The Nelson Touch; Prince of Wales's (for Stage Society), Feb 1932, Miguel Lopez in Juarez and Maximilian; St Martin's, Mar–Apr 1932, Sexton in Precious Bane and Alfredo in Cloudy With Showers; he was then appointed director to the Repertory Theatre, Croydon, Sept 1932, and directed several notable productions, including The Edwardians, John Gabriel Borkman, The Rising Sun, Anna Christie, The Brontës, Hamlet, Gallows Glorious, Emil and the Detectives, Wuthering Heights, etc; The Brontës, Gallows Glorious, and Emil and the Detectives were subsequently transferred to West End London theatres; director to the Old Vic, 1934–May, 1935, and staged six Shakespearean plays, also Saint Joan, Hippolytus (Euripides), Major Barbara; Sept–Dec 1935, directed a new version of Peer Gynt, Julius Caesar, The Three Sisters, Macbeth, The School for Scandal, Richard III, St Helena, The Taming of the Shrew and King Lear; Daly's, Muted Strings, 1936, and Night Alone, 1937; Covent Garden, 1936, the opera Julia; Queen's, Women of Property, 1937; To Love and to Cherish, 1938; Prison Without Bars, Jitta's Atonement, Alien Corn, Julius Caesar (in modern dress), 1939; Desire Under the Elms, Abraham Lincoln, Cornelius, 1940; Murder Without Crime, London, W1, 1942; The Young and Lovely, Acacia Avenue, 1943; The Philanderer, 1944; It Happened in New York, 1945; Green Laughter, The Other Side, 1946; directed the production of Carmen, at Covent Garden, 1946; Tell Tale Murder, 1952; Man on Trial, 1957; since 1963, has regularly directed plays at the Westminster, including Give A Dog a Bone, Mr Brown Comes Down the Hill, Annie, High Diplomacy, Blindsight, GB, and The Forgotten Factor; has also directed numerous films.

Address: Crowham Manor, Westfield, Hastings, E Sussex.

CASS, Peggy, actress
b Boston, Massachusetts, 21 May; *d* of Raymond James Cass and his wife Margaret (Loughlin); *e* Cambridge Latin School;

m Carl Fisher (mar dis); prepared for the stage with Uta Hagen, Mira Rostova, and Tamara Daykarhanova.

First appeared on the stage in Australia, 1945, in a tour of The Doughgirls; made her first appearance in New York at the Belasco, 1948, when she took over the role of Maisie in Burlesque; at the Broadhurst, Oct 1949, played in the revue Touch and Go; Shubert, New Haven, Conn, Apr 1950, played Emily Clayton in House on the Cliff; Playhouse, Aug 1950, Liz Fargo in The Live Wire; Ziegfeld, May 1951, played The Woman Scorned in a scene from Burlesque in ANTA Album; Playhouse, Oct 1952, Helen in Bernardine; US tour, 1954–5, Mildred Turner in Oh, Men! Oh, Women!; Phoenix, 1955, appeared in the revue Phoenix '55; City Center, Sept 1955, played Bianca in Othello and Mistress Quickly in Henry IV, Part 1; US tour, 1955–6 played Madame Zelda in The Amazing Adele; Broadhurst, Oct 1956, played Agnes Gooch in Auntie Mame, for nearly two years, for which she received the Antoinette Perry (Tony) Award; ANTA, Feb 1960, appeared in the revue A Thurber Carnival; Morosco, Apr 1963, played Vera von Stobel in Children from Their Games; Morosco, June 1967, succeeded Kay Medford as Marion Hollander in Don't Drink the Water; Ethel Barrymore, May 1969, Mollie Malloy in The Front Page; same theatre, Oct 1969, repeated her role in The Front Page; Plymouth, 1969, took over from Maureen Stapleton the three leading roles in Plaza Suite; Westbury Music Fair, June 1971, again played in Plaza Suite; same theatre, June 1972, played in Last of the Red Hot Lovers; toured, 1974, as Alix Carpenter in A Community of Two; McCarter, Princeton, Jan 1978, in The Torch-Bearers; Helen Hayes, Oct 1979, Mother Basil in Once a Catholic; has also played in other stock and touring companies; appeared in the Dallas (Texas) State Fair summer musicals, Do Re Mi, 1962, Bells Are Ringing, 1963; has appeared in the films The Marrying Kind, 1952, and Auntie Mame, 1956; television appearances include; *The Hathaways, The Garry Moore Show, To Tell the Truth, The Jack Paar Show,* etc.

Favourite part: Agnes Gooch. *Address:* 200 East 62nd Street, New York, NY.

CASS, Ronald, composer
b Llanelli, Wales, 21 Apr 1923; *s* of Saul Cass and his wife Rachel (Palto); *e* Llanelli Grammar School, and the University College of Wales, Aberystwyth; *m* Valerie Carton; formerly a school teacher.

First contributed music to the revue 10.15, at the Irving Theatre, Sept 1951; he has since contributed compositions to the following revues: The Irving Revue, Just Lately, Intimacy at Eight, 1952; High Spirits, 1953; Intimacy at 8.30, 1954; For Amusement Only, 1956; Harmony Close, 1957; For Adults Only, 1958; The Lord Chamberlain Regrets . . . (also devised), 1961; Enrico, 1963; book and music for Jack and the Beanstalk, Palladium, 1968; part author of Kingdom Coming, 1972; musical director and main contributor to Deja Revue, musical director Move Along Sideways, 1975; author of the play A Well Ordered Affair, 1976; musical director, The Thoughts of Chairman Alf, 1977; writer and co-deviser, Blondes and Bombshells (cabaret), 1979; first composed music for films in 1961, and principal films include: The Young Ones, Summer Holiday, Go to Blazes, French Dressing, Wonderful Life; The Virgin and the Gipsy (in part), Best House in London (in part); since 1950, has composed music for television productions including: The Gentle Flame, Sing a Song of Sixpence, Easter in Rome, This is Tom Jones (three series); author of the novels True Blue, and Fringe Benefits, and of a book of theatrical humour entitled A Funny Thing Happened or An Anthology of Pro's.

Recreations: Bridge and cricket. *Address:* 27A Elsworthy Road, London, NW3. *Tel:* 01–586 4670.

CASTLE, John, actor
b Croydon, Surrey, 14 Jan 1940; *s* of Frederick William Castle and his wife, Marie Irene (Herbert); *e* Brighton College and Trinity College, Dublin; *m* Maggie Castle; trained for the stage at RADA.

His first professional appearance was on 5 June 1964, at the Open Air, Regent's Park, as Westmoreland in Henry V; at the Royal Court, 1965–6, his parts included Hogg and Trelawney in Shelley, Oct; Len in Saved, Nov; Private Hurst in Serjeant Musgrave's Dance, Dec 1965; Touchwood Jr in A Chaste Maid in Cheapside, Jan; Edward Voysey in The Voysey Inheritance, Apr; Malcolm in Macbeth, Oct 1966; joined the RSC at the Aldwych, June 1967, to play Oswald in Ghosts; with the Bristol Old Vic company, 1968, his parts included the title role in Luther and an appearance in Under Milk Wood; Royal Court, July 1969, Maskwell in The Double Dealer; made his first Broadway appearance, Feb 1970, as Jos in Georgy, at the Winter Garden; returning to England, toured, June–Dec 1970, for Prospect Productions, playing Don John and Claudio in Much Ado About Nothing and Jaffeir in Venice Preserved; Liverpool Playhouse, 1971, played Hamlet; Arnaud, Guildford, Aug 1974, Laurent in Thérèse; ICA, Sept 1974, O'Riordan in The Iron Harp; King's Head, Islington, Hal in Confession Fever, Nov 1977, and Zastrozzi, 1978; Thorndike, Leatherhead, Mar 1980, Leontes in The Winter's Tale; first film, Blow Up, 1966; subsequent pictures include The Lion in Winter and Man of La Mancha; first television appearance, 1964, recently in I Claudius, and Lillie.

Favourite parts: Luther, Hamlet and O'Riordan. *Recreation:* Bird-watching. *Address:* c/o ICM, 22 Grafton Street, London W1.

CAZENOVE, Christopher, actor
b Winchester, 17 Dec 1945; *s* of Arnold de Lerisson Cazenove and his wife Elizabeth Laura (Gurney); *e* Dragon School, Oxford, and Eton; *m* the actress Angharad Rees; trained for the stage at the Bristol Old Vic Theatre School.

Began his stage career at the Phoenix, Leicester, 1967 in Man and Superman; two seasons at Pitlochry, playing parts including Hamlet; made his West End debut at the Lyric, 5 Nov 1969, as Courtenay in The Lionel Touch; same theatre, Jun 1970, played Guy Vivian in My Darling Daisy; New, Nov 1970, John Watherstone in The Winslow Boy; Chichester, season 1975, played Christian De Neuvillette in Cyrano de Bergerac and Cassio in Othello, visiting the Hong Kong Festival in these roles; Globe, Mar 1979, played Richard in Joking Apart; made his Broadway debut at the Ambassador, 10 Apr 1980, as James Sinclair in Goodbye Fidel; his films include The Girl in Blue Velvet, Royal Flash, and Zulu Dawn (1979); frequent TV appearances include the series *The Regiment, Jennie,* and *The Duchess of Duke Street.*

Address: c/o Chatto and Linnit, Globe Theatre, Shaftesbury Avenue, London W1.

CECIL, Jonathan, actor
b London, 22 Feb 1939; *s* of Lord David Cecil and his wife Rachel (MacCarthy); *e* The Dragon School, Oxford, Eton and New College (BA in French); *m* (1) Vivien Heilbron, actress (mar dis); (2) Anna Sharkey, actress; trained for the stage at the London Academy of Music and Dramatic Art.

While at Oxford appeared with OUDS, the ETC and the Oxford Theatre Group; first professional appearance, Arts, Cambridge, July 1962, as Parkins in The Wit to Woo; in

repertory, 1963–64, at Northampton, Dundee and Hornchurch; LAMDA theatre, Nov 1964, title role in Vasco, in a Sunday night production; made his West End debut at the Phoenix, 18 May 1965, as Ralph in A Heritage and Its History; at Salisbury Playhouse, 1966–67, his parts included the Dauphin in St Joan, and Algernon Moncrieff in The Importance of Being Earnest; Open Air, Regent's Park, season 1967, played Flute in A Midsummer Night's Dream and First Fop in Cyrano de Bergerac; Queen's, Nov 1967, Basil Utterwood in Halfway up the Tree; Piccadilly, Feb 1969, Dinsdale Gurney in The Ruling Class; Apollo, Feb 1971, took over the part of Alwa in Lulu; Windsor Festival, Aug 1971, Backbite in The School for Scandal; Shaw, May 1972, Sir Andrew Aguecheek in Twelfth Night; Mermaid, July 1972, appeared in Cowardy Custard; Greenwich, Mar 1974, Osric in Hamlet; Lyric, June 1976, took over as Aubrey in The Bed Before Yesterday; Round House, Aug 1978, John Littlewit in Bartholomew Fair; Oxford Festival, July 1979, played Cecil Graham in Lady Windermere's Fan and Phipps in An Ideal Husband, followed by national tour; first film, The Yellow Rolls Royce, 1964; subsequent films include Otley and Barry Lyndon; TV, since 1964, includes plays and comedy series including Romany Jones.

Favourite parts: Aguecheek, Alwa. *Recreations:* Collecting vaudeville and operatic records, reading. *Address:* c/o Kate Feast Management, 43a Princess Road, London NW1.

CHADBON, Tom, actor
b Luton, Beds, 27 Feb 1946; *s* of Thomas William Chadbon and his wife Josie Yvonne (Cook); *e* Victoria College, Jersey and Chichester HS; trained for the stage at the Webber-Douglas Academy and at RADA; *m* (1) Hon Deborah Leather (mar dis); (2) Jane Hennessy.

First professional appearance, Sept 1967, at the Phoenix, Leicester, as a philosopher in Galileo; first London appearance, Jan 1968, as Valentine in Twelfth Night at the Royal Court; at the same theatre he has since played a succession of parts including Oliver in The Houses by the Green, Oct 1968; Barry in Saved, Feb 1969; the Prince of Wales in Early Morning, March, 1969 (in repertory with Saved); Tommie White in Insideout, Nov 1969; Laurie in Cheek (Theatre Upstairs) Sept 1970; John Lennon in No One Was Saved (Upstairs), Dec 1970; Round House, July 1971, Saturninus in Titus Andronicus; New Vic, Bristol, Apr 1973, Said in The Screens; Playhouse, Liverpool, Nov 1975, Stanley Kowalski in A Streetcar Named Desire; Old Vic, July 1976, Gasparo in The White Devil; Farnham, June 1977, Petie in Moving House; Greenwich, June 1978, Alan Jeffcote in Hindle Wakes; Lyric, Nov 1979, Brian in Middle-Age-Spread; over 100 TV appearances since Sept 1968 include Hamlet, A Room with a View, and *The Liver Birds*; films, since 1969, include The Beast Must Die, and Tess; TV appearances, since Sept 1968, include The Creeper, and the series The Expert.

Favourite part: Alan in Hindle Wakes. *Address:* c/o Larry Dalzell Associates, 3 Goodwin's Court, St Martin's Lane, London WC2.

CHAGRIN, Julian, actor and mime
b London, 22 Feb 1940; *s* of Francis Chagrin; *m* Claude Chagrin; trained for the stage at LAMDA (briefly) and under Jacques Lecoq in Paris.

Appeared with the Fol-de-Rols, 1958; Prince Charles, Feb 1964, appeared in Fielding's Music Hall; Edinburgh Festival, Aug 1964, appeared in Chaganog, which he also co-devised; the production was also presented at the Vaudeville, Dec 1964, and St Martin's, Apr 1965; Hampstead, June 1965, appeared in Splits on the Infinitive; has toured extensively in his solo performance One Is One, including a season at the Arts, Feb 1970; films include Blow Up, The Bliss of Mrs Blossom and The Concert; TV includes On the Braden Beat and the Gold Diggers; director, Julian Chagrin Films Ltd.

Recreations: Painting, reading, keeping fit.

CHAIKIN, Joseph, actor, director, producer.
b Brooklyn, New York, 16 Sept 1935; *e* Drake University, Des Moines, Iowa, 1950–3.

Made his NY début at the Carnegie Hall Playhouse, 26 Feb 1958, as Mr Atkins in Dark of the Moon; joined The Living Theatre and appeared with that group in Jan 1959 in Many Loves; June 1959, played Ephron in The Cave at Machpelah; Nov 1959, Mangini in Tonight We Improvise; Gate, July 1960, played the title-role in Santa Claus, Lazarus in Calvary, and Folial in Escurial; Living Theatre, May 1961, again played in Many Loves; Living Theatre, 1961–2 season, played Leach in The Connection, C Maynes in In the Jungle of Cities, and his parts in Many Loves; Sept 1962, Galy Gay in Man Is Man; Writers' Stage, May 1964, Furniture Mover in The New Tenant and The Detective in Victims of Duty in a double-bill Two by Ionesco; Players, Mar 1965, The Clown in Sing to Me Through Open Windows; Greenwich Mews, May 1965, Coolie in The Exception and the Rule; founded The Open Theatre in 1964 and is its President to date, whose purpose is to perform experimental theatre and which has presented many collaborative efforts; the troupe has toured extensively in the US, Canada, Europe, and the Middle East, performing in theatres, churches, prisons, out of doors, etc; Pocket, NY, Nov 1966, directed Interview in the triple-bill America Hurrah; made his London début when he directed The Open Theatre of New York in Interview at the Royal Court, 2 Aug 1967; Washington Square Methodist Church, NY, May 1970, The Open Theatre performed Terminal, The Serpent, both of which he directed, and Endgame, in which he played Hamm; other plays devised and performed by The Open Theatre include Viet Rock and Mutation Show; St Clement's, Sept 1973, his troupe performed Nightwalk, Terminal, and The Mutation Show; May 1974, Public, and, later, St Clement's, produced Electra; Manhattan Theater Club, directed The Seagull, and Exchange, directed A Fable, 1975; Mark Taper Forum, LA, Jan 1976, directed Electra; Public, Mar 1976, title-role in Woyzeck, same theatre, Dec 1977, directed The Oybbuk; Magic Theater, San Francisco, Jun 1978, performed in Tongues, a piece produced in collaboration with Sam Shepard; Habimah, Tel Aviv, June 1979, again directed The Dybbuk; Eureka, San Francisco, Sept 1979, and Public, NY, Dec 1979, performed Tongues in repertory with a new Shepard collaboration, Savage Love; assisted Peter Brook in his productions of US and The Tempest, 1966; director, 1976– , of the Winter Project, an annual workshop with actors, musicians and writers; has received many honours, including the Drama Desk Award, 1973, the Brandeis Award for Distinguished Actors, 5 Obie (off-Broadway) Awards for both direction and acting, and the New England Theatre Conference Award, 1970; Guggenheim Fellow, 1969; honorary PhD, Drake University, 1972; has received grants from the Ford Foundation, the National Endowment for the Arts, and The New York Council on the Arts; has written several articles published in international journals and the book The Presence of the Actor, 1972.

Address: Artservices, 463 West Street, New York, NY 10014. *Tel:* 989–4953.

CHAMBERLAIN, (George) Richard actor
b Beverly Hills, Calif, 31 Mar 1935; *s* of Charles Chamber-

lain and his wife Elsa; *e* Pomona, Cal, College, and studied voice at the Los Angeles Conservatory of Music; prepared for the stage with Jeff Corey.

Appeared first in college dramas, including King Lear; made his New York stage début at the Majestic, Dec 1966, as Jeff Claypool in the musical Breakfast at Tiffany's in a production that never officially opened; made his début in England at the Birmingham Repertory Theater, 1969, in the title-role of Hamlet; Seattle Repertory, Washington, 1971, played Richard II, and played this part at the Ahmanson, Los Angeles, Mar 1972, and at the Eisenhower, Washington, DC, May 1972; Chichester Festival, 19 July 1972, Thomas Mendip in The Lady's Not for Burning; Arlington Park, Ill, 1973, appeared in The Fantasticks; Ahmanson, Los Angeles, Nov 1973, played the title-role in Cyrano de Bergerac; Ahmanson, Dec 1975, Reverend Shannon in The Night of the Iguana; again at the Circle in the Square, NY, Oct 1976; Public/Other Stage, Nov 1978, played Wild Bill Hickock in Fathers and Sons; made his film début in A Thunder of Drums, 1962, and has since appeared in Petulia. The Madwomen of Chaillot, Julius Caesar, The Three Musketeers, The Towering Inferno, The Last Wave (1974), etc; played Dr Kildare in the television series of that name 1961–5, and has since played Hamlet (1970), F Scott Fitzgerald and the Last of the Belles, The Count of Monte Cristo, Centennial, etc; has also sung on television and made recordings of popular music.

Address: c/o ICM, 22 Grafton Street, London W1, or the William Morris Agency, 1350 Avenue of the Americas, New York, NY 10019.

CHAMPION, Gower, choreographer, director, dancer
b Geneva, Illinois, 22 June 1920; *s* of John W Champion and his wife Beatrice (Carlisle); *m* Marjorie Belcher (mar dis).

Began his career in cabaret, as a dancer, in 1936; made his Broadway début at the Broadhurst, June 1939, as a dancer in Streets of Paris; 44th Street, Jan 1942, played Campbell in The Lady Comes Across; Ethel Barrymore, Oct 1942, appeared in Count Me In; Coronet, Sept 1948, choreographed Small Wonder; National, Dec 1948, directed and choreographed the revue Lend an Ear, for which he received the Antoinette Perry (Tony) Award; Winter Garden, Apr 1951, choreographed Make a Wish; Plymouth, Apr 1955, directed, choreographed, and danced with his wife in 3 for Tonight; Martin Beck, Apr 1960, directed and choreographed Bye Bye Birdie, for which he received two Antoinette Perry (Tony) Awards; Imperial, Apr 1961, directed and choreographed Carnival; Plymouth, Mar 1963, directed My Mother, My Father, and Me; St James, Jan 1964, directed and choreographed Hello, Dolly! for which he received two Antoinette Perry Awards; directed and choreographed the same musical at Drury Lane, London, 1965; Henry Miller's, Mar 1966, directed Three Bags Full; 46th Street, Nov 1966, directed I Do! I Do!; Broadway, Jan 1968, directed and choreographed The Happy Time, for which he received two Antoinette Perry (Tony) Awards; for the American Conservatory Theatre of San Francisco, 1968, directed A Flea in Her Ear; at the Lyric, London, May 1968, directed I Do! I Do!; Shubert, Boston, Feb 1971, directed and choreographed Prettybelle; NY, 1972, directed and choreographed Sugar; directed the revival of Irene, 1973; directed and choreographed Mack and Mabel, 1974; Dorothy Chandler Pavilion, Los Angeles, Cal, 27 July 1975, directed and choreographed Lyrics by Ira Gershwin: Who Could Ask for Anything More?; NY, 1976, directed and choreographed Rockabye Hamlet; Dorothy Chandler Pavilion, LA, June 1977, directed and choreographed his adaptation of Annie Get Your Gun; Majestic, Apr 1978, took over as Dan Connors in The Act; Lunt-Fontanne, Dec 1978, supervised the production of A Broadway Musical; has appeared extensively in cabaret with Jeanne Tyler, 1936–41, and with his ex-wife, 1946–55; directed the Academy Awards television show, 1968; films in which he has appeared include: Mr Music, Showboat, Lovely to Look At, Everything I Have Is Yours, Jupiter's Darling, and directed the film My Six Loves.

Address: 1160, 10889 Wilshire Boulevard, Los Angeles, Calif. 90024. (*Died, Aug 25, 1980*)

CHANNING, Carol, actress and singer
b Seattle, Washington, 31 Jan 1921; d of George Channing and his wife Adelaide (Glaser); e Bennington College; m (1) Theodore Nadish (mar dis); (2) Al Carson (mar dis); (3) Charles F Lowe.

Made her first appearance on the New York stage at the Center Theatre, Jan 1941, as a singer in No for an Answer; Imperial, Oct 1941, appeared in Let's Face It, and was understudy and played for Eve Arden in this piece; Morosco, Dec 1942, played Steve in Proof Through the Night; engaged in cabaret and night-clubs; at the National, Dec 1948, appeared in Lend an Ear (for which she received the New York Drama Critics Award); Ziegfeld, Dec 1949, played Lorelei Lee in the musical version of Gentlemen Prefer Blondes, subsequently appearing in the same part at the Palace, Chicago, Sept 1951 and toured for two years; toured, 1953, as Eliza Doolittle in Pygmalion; Winter Garden, NY, 1953, took over the part of Ruth in Wonderful Town, subsequently touring in the same part; Winter Garden, NY, Nov 1955, played Flora Weems in The Vamp; in 1957 opened her own night-club act at the Tropicana Hotel, Las Vegas, and then toured for two years; Curran, San Francisco, Oct 1959, appeared in Show Business, and then toured for a season; Eugene O'Neill, Jan 1961, starred in the revue Show Girl, and toured in it for one year; in 1962, co-starred in the George Burns–Carol Channing Musical Revue, touring for a season; in 1963 toured in the title-role of the Theatre Guild production of The Millionairess; St James, Jan 1964, played Dolly Gallagher Levi in Hello, Dolly! and received the New York Drama Critics and Tony Awards; National Guard Armory, Washington, DC, 18 Jan 1965, entertained President Johnson in 1965 Inaugural Gala; continued playing in Hello, Dolly! in NY until Sept 1965, and then toured in the part until Jan 1966; at the Shubert, Jan 1966, again played Dolly; at the Jones Hall, Houston, Texas, Oct 1966, rejoined the touring show and continued in it until June 1967, by which time she had played Dolly for 1273 performances; made her London début at the Drury Lane, Apr 1970, in the revue Carol Channing and Her Ten Stout-Hearted Men, receiving the London Critics Award; Broadhurst, NY, Jan 1971, played the four heroines in Four on a Garden; toured 1971, in the revue The Carol Channing Show; Palmer House, Chicago, Jan 1972, appeared in cabaret; Ford's, Washington, DC, 1972, appeared in Festival at Ford's; Princess, Melbourne, Australia, 17 May 1972, appeared in Carol Channing and Her Gentlemen Who Prefer Blondes, and also appeared in this revue at the Regent, Sydney, 25 June 1972; Nugget, Reno, Nevada, July, and Palmer House, Chicago, Dec 1972, appeared in variety; Palace, Jan 1974, Lorelei Lee in Lorelei or Gentlemen Still Prefer Blondes; appeared in variety and cabaret in San Juan, Puerto Rico, Jan, Reno, May, and Chicago, Oct 1975; toured, 1975, as Lorelei Lee in Lorelei; toured Florida, Oct 1976, as Alma in a try-out of The Bed Before Yesterday; took up her role of Dolly again in 1977, touring the US and appearing at the Lunt-Fontanne, NY,

Mar 1978; Drury Lane, Sept 1979; Shaftesbury, Feb 1980; her films include The First Traveling Saleslady (1956), Thoroughly Modern Millie (1967), Archie and Mehitabel, etc; has appeared as a guest on more than fifty television programs and in a number of her own specials.

Address: c/o Charles Lowe Productions, 8749 Sunset Boulevard, Hollywood, California.

CHANNING, Stockard (*née* Susan Stockard), actress and singer
b New York, 13 Feb 1944; d of Lester Napier Stockard and his wife Mary Alice (English); e Harvard U; m (1) Walter Channing Jr (mar dis); (2) Paul Schmidt (mar dis); (3) David Debin.

Made her professional debut with the Theatre Company of Boston, 1966, as Candy Coke in The Investigation; played the Female Player in the Boston Company of Adaptation, Sept 1969, and took over the role at the Greenwich Mews, Mar 1970; made her Broadway debut at the St James, 1 Dec 1971, in the chorus of Two Gentlemen of Verona; Theatre Company of Boston, Dec 1972, Alice in Play Strindberg; Martin Beck, Apr 1973, Joanna Wilkins in No Hard Feelings; Ahmanson, LA, 1973, took over the part of Julia in Two Gentlemen of Verona; Mark Taper Forum, LA, Nov 1976, Mary in Vanities; Ahmanson, Feb 1978, Jane in Absurd Person Singular; Long Beach, Calif, Aug 1979, Rosalind in As You Like It; Imperial, Mar 1980, took over the part of Sonia Walsk in They're Playing Our Song; her films include Hospital, The Fortune, The Cheap Detective, and Grease; TV includes her own series Just Friends, retitled The Stockard Channing Show, 1979, and Silent Victory: the story of Kitty O'Neil.

Address: c/o Michael Ovitz, Creative Artists Associates, 1888 Century Park East, Los Angeles, CA 90067.

CHAPIN, Louis Le Bourgeois, dramatic and arts critic
b Brooklyn, New York, 6 Feb 1918; s of Louis Le Bourgeois Chapin and his wife Julia Appleton (Tuckerman); e Milton Academy, Massachusetts, and The Principia College, Elsah, Illinois; m Mary Lee Smith.

Formerly a radio announcer and director and college teacher in the field of the arts; a staff director for Columbia Broadcasting System, 1944–5; in St Louis, Missouri, from 1958–60, was contributing critic in music and the arts to The Christian Science Monitor; Boston, 1960–3, staff critic for the Monitor, writing on music, theatre, films, and the arts; 1963–6 was the Monitor's NY drama critic, writing also on films and other arts and since 1970 has served as its art critic and later as occasional correspondent; drama critic for Christianity and Crisis, 1970 to date; has also contributed articles to National Observer, Music Journal, Christian Herald, Musical America, High Fidelity, Arts, etc; author of books on Charles M Russell, 1978, and Frederic Remington, 1979; since 1968 has been director of Earl Rowland Foundation, documenting on audio filmstrips the major museum collection; Tutor in Writing, Empire State College, 1973– ; Treasurer of the New York Drama Desk, until 1975.

Recreations: Music-making, poetry, and play reading. *Club:* New Drama Forum Association. *Address:* 7 Dandy Drive, Cos Cob, Conn 06807. *Tel:* 203–6614220.

CHAPMAN, Constance, actress
b Weston-super-Mare, 29 Mar 1912; d of Cecil Charles Chapman and his wife Elizabeth Ann (Coulsting); e Redland H.S., Bristol; m Travers Cousins (mar dis); trained as a broadcaster.

Made her first stage appearance in May, 1938, at the Knightstone Theatre, Weston-super-Mare, in Hay Fever; appeared in repertory at Nottingham and Bristol, remaining with the Rapier Players, Bristol, 1941–53; 1953–67, worked almost exclusively in radio and television, returning to the Bristol Old Vic, Jan 1967, as Lady Wishfort in The Way of the World; subsequent appearances with the company, 1967–8, included Lady Alconleigh in The Pursuit of Love, and Grace in A Day in the Death of Joe Egg; made her London debut, Apr 1969, at the Royal Court as Mrs Shaw in In Celebration; at the same theatre, Oct 1969, played Mrs Ewbank in The Contractor; Fortune, Apr 1970, also played Mrs Ewbank; at the Nottingham Playhouse, 1972, played Mrs Malaprop in The Rivals and Meg in The Birthday Party; Manchester, 1973 (69 Theatre Co), Ivy in The Family Reunion; Greenwich, Dec 1974, Phoebe in The Entertainer; toured the world, 1974–5, as Juliana Tesman in the RSC's Hedda Gabler, appearing at the Aldwych, July 1975; Greenwich, Jan 1976, Nan in Love's Old Sweet Song; Queen's, Apr 1977, Marjorie in Just Between Ourselves; Haymarket, Oct 1977, Mrs Helseth in Rosmersholm; Round House, Apr 1979, Ivy in The Family Reunion, transferring to the Vaudeville, May; films, since The Raging Moon, 1970, include A Day in the Death of Joe Egg, and Lady Oscar; first TV appearance, 1954; recently in Just Between Ourselves, and Born and Bred.

Recreations: Gardening, dressmaking. *Address:* Ferncliffe Cottage, North Road, Leigh Woods, Bristol. *Tel:* Bristol 35322.

CHAPMAN, David, scenic designer, art director and architect

b Atlanta, Georgia, 11 Nov 1938; *s* of R S Chapman and his wife Ellen Graham; *e* Georgia Institute of Technology (BS 1960, B Arch 1963); *m* (1) Dianne Finn (mar dis); (2) the costume designer Carol Oditz; formerly an officer in United States Navy and a practising architect.

Has designed scenery for the following Broadway productions: Red, White and Maddox, 1969; Soon, 1972; Nash at Nine, Promenade All, 1973; Music! Music!, The Magic Show, 1974; Le Bellybutton, 1975; over 20 off-Broadway productions since 1969 include Lulu, Leaves of Grass, Where Has Tommy Flowers Gone?, 1971; God Says There Is No Peter Ott, 1972; Alpha Beta, Creeps, 1973; Once I Saw a Boy Laughing, 1974; Finn Mackool, 1975; Fixed, 1977; White Pelicans, 1978; work for regional theatres, since 1965, includes productions at the Asolo Theatre, Theatre Atlanta, Folger Theatre, Pittsburgh Public Theatre, PAF Playhouse, Syracuse Stage, etc; art director for the films Somebody Killed Her Husband, The Wolfen (1979); productions designed include The Seduction of Joe Tynan; TV designs include *The Dick Cavett Show*, The Annie Christmas Show, etc; theatre consultancy work since 1965 includes the Westbeth Theatre Center, Folger Theatre, and Theatre Atlanta.

Address: c/o Alfred Geller, 122 East 42nd Street, New York, NY 10017.

CHAPMAN, John R, dramatic author and actor

b London, 27 May 1927; *s* of Albert Roy Chapman and his wife Barbara Joyce (Fletcher); *e* Magdalen College School, Glasgow Academy, and University College School, London; *m* Betty Impey; trained for the stage at the Royal Academy of Dramatic Art.

Made his first appearance on the stage at the Embassy Theatre, May 1946, when he played Disher in National Velvet; Whitehall, Sept 1950, played the Scots Soldier in Reluctant Heroes, at the same theatre, Aug 1954, played

Danby in his own play Dry Rot, which ran for three and a half years; Wyndham's, Sept 1964, played Barry Layton in his play Diplomatic Baggage; author of the following plays: Dry Rot, 1954; Simple Spymen (which ran for three and a half years), 1958; The Brides of March, 1960; This is My Wife, Mr Stanniforth, 1963; Diplomatic Baggage, 1964; Not Now Darling and My Giddy Aunt (both with Ray Cooney) and Oh, Clarence!, 1968; Move Over Mrs Markham (with Ray Cooney), 1971; There Goes The Bride (with Ray Cooney), 1974; It Happened in Harrods, and (with Anthony Marriott) Shut Your Eyes and Think of England, 1977; made his first film appearance in 1952, in Reluctant Heroes; subsequently appearing in Not Wanted on Voyage; films written include: Dry Rot, The Night We Dropped A Clanger, Nothing Barred; first appeared on television, Oct 1956, in Queen Elizabeth Slept Here, subsequently appearing in Reluctant Heroes, Flat Spin, Come Prancing, etc; author of the following television plays: What a Drag, Between the Balance Sheets, also comedy series, including: *Hugh and I, Blandings Castle* (adapted from P G Wodehouse), and Happy Ever After (with Eric Merriman).

Recreations: Travelling and reading. *Club:* Dramatists'. *Address:* 48 Wildwood Road, London, NW11. *Tel:* 01–455 0343.

CHAPPELL, William, dancer, designer, and director

b Wolverhampton, Staffs, 27 Sept 1908; *s* of Archibald Chappell and his wife Edith Eva Clara (Blair-Staples); *e* at Clapham and Chelsea School of Art; studied dancing under Marie Rambert.

Made his first appearance on the stage at the Duke of York's Theatre, 19 Sept 1929, as a dancer in Jew Süss; toured in Ida Rubinstein's company on European tour, 1929–30, working under Massine and Nijinski; Adelphi, London, Jan 1932, appeared in Helen! and also appeared in C B Cochran's cabaret at the Trocadero, for which he also designed costumes; at the Savoy Theatre, 1932, danced in several ballets in the Camargo season; Alhambra, Nov 1932, appeared in the ballet A Kiss in Spring; Saville, Dec 1933, appeared as the Stranger in Beau Brummell; appeared at the Mercury and Duke of York's, 1934, during the Marie Rambert ballet seasons; Sadler's Wells Ballet company, 1934; appeared in Paris with the Sadler's Wells company; at Covent Garden, Mar 1939, danced at the Royal Command performance; designed scenery and costumes for the Camargo season at Savoy, 1932; Ballyhoo, 1932; He Wanted Adventure, 1933, also for several ballets at Sadler's Wells, since 1934, notably for Les Rendezvous, Les Patineurs, Giselle, The Judgment of Paris, etc; several revues at the Gate and Ambassadors' Theatres; designed the costumes for The Merry Widow, His Majesty's, 1943; Castle Anna (décor), Lyric, Hammersmith, 1948; Four, Five, Six (décor and costumes), Duke of York's, 1948; A la Carte (décor and costumes), Savoy, 1948; Point of Departure (costumes), Lyric, Hammersmith, 1950; at the Lyric Theatre, Aug 1950, played the Second Stranger in The Little Hut; Lyric, Hammersmith, May 1951, directed The Lyric Revue, which transferred to the Globe, Sept 1951; Phoenix, June 1951, arranged the dances for The Winter's Tale; Duchess, Jan 1952, designed costumes for Summer and Smoke; Criterion, Apr 1952, designed costumes for the revival of The Vortex; Irving, May 1952, arranged the dances and ensembles for Swing Back the Gate; Globe, July 1952, directed The Globe Revue, for which he designed the costumes and arranged the dances; Mercury, Jan 1953, directed The Princess and the Swineherd; Hippodrome, May 1953, directed the revue High Spirits, for which he also arranged the dances; Sadler's Wells,

May 1953, directed The Immortal Hour; Lyric, Hammersmith, Dec 1953, directed the revue At the Lyric, for which he also designed the costumes and arranged the dances; a revised version of the last-named production was presented at the St Martin's, May 1954, under the title Going to Town; Globe, Nov 1954, assistant director for An Evening With Beatrice Lillie; Lyric, Hammersmith, Dec 1954, directed Time Remembered, transferred to the New, Apr 1955; Duke of York's, June 1955, associate director, with Orson Welles, for Moby Dick; Lyric, Hammersmith, Sept 1955, directed The Buccaneer; has since directed the following productions, Charley's Aunt, 1955; South Sea Bubble, Man Alive!, 1956; Restless Heart, Hotel Paradiso (tour), 1957; Where's Charley?, Expresso Bongo, Living For Pleasure, 1958; Farewell, Farewell, Eugene, 1959; Joie de Vivre, 1960; On the Avenue, 1961; Six of One, So Much to Remember (also designed), 1963; Fielding's Music Hall (also devised), English Eccentrics (City Temple Theatre), One Man Show (Central School of Arts and Crafts), 1964; Travelling Light, Passion Flower Hotel (also designed costumes), 1965; Julius Caesar Jones (Jeanetta Cochrane), The Violins of Saint Jacques (also libretto, Sadler's Wells), Love and a Bottle (Gate, Dublin), 1966; The Beaux' Stratagem (Chichester), I'll Get My Man (Alexandra, Birmingham), 1967; The Entertainer (Nottingham), 1968; The Chalk Garden, 1971; Oh, Kay, 1974; In Praise of Love (tour), 1974; Fallen Angels (Dublin), 1975; A Moon for the Misbegotten (Dublin), 1976; Memoir, 1978; Camden Festival, Mar 1968, produced and designed the operas The First Commandment and Il Sogno di Scipione; other opera work includes The Marriage of Figaro, 1976, and Gianni Schicchi, 1978, at Sadler's Wells; has choreographed Ring Round the Moon, 1968; Cockie, 1973; Travesties, Bloomsbury, 1974; TV choreography includes specials for Beryl Reid; has illustrated several books, and is author of Studies in Ballet, and Fonteyn.
Favourite part: The Faun in L'Après-midi d'un Faun. *Recreations:* Walking, reading and the cinema. *Address:* c/o Adza Vincent Ltd, 11a Ivor Place, London, NW1.

CHARLES, Maria (*née* Maria Zena Schneider), actress
b London 22 Sept 1929; *d* of David Schneider and his wife, Celia (Ashken); *e* London; *m* Robin Hunter (mar dis); studied for the stage at the Royal Academy of Dramatic Art.
Made her first appearance on the stage at the Connaught Theatre, Worthing, Dec 1945, as The Dormouse in Alice in Wonderland; made her debut in London at the Prince of Wales Theatre, July 23, 1946, as Ruby Lockwood in Pick-Up Girl; Vaudeville, Nov 1951, Rosie in Women of Twilight; Watergate, Feb 1952, appeared in the revue, See You Again; Irving, May 1952, in the revue, Swing Back the Gate; Royal Court, Nov 1952, Sorrell Connaught in A Kiss for Adele; Embassy, Sept 1953, Florrie Solomon in Spring Song; Wyndham's, Jan 1954, Dulcie in The Boy Friend, in which she appeared for four and a half years; Globe, Feb 1965, Dulcie Du Bois in Divorce Me, Darling!; Players', Dec 1965, Fairy Sorayah in Ali Baba and the Forty Thieves; St Martin's, Mar 1968, Florence in Enter a Free Man; Prince of Wales, Jan 6, 1969, took over as Jessie Macfarlane, Mrs Dawkins, Bridgid O'Cooney, Mrs van Boven, Dellarosa Paravici, Miss Minter, Mary Thornton, Mrs Campbell-Scully and Mrs Zuckmeyer in They Don't Grow on Trees; Royal Lyceum, Edinburgh, Oct 1969, Felice Kovacs in Partners; Phoenix, Dec 1972, Piglet in Winnie the Pooh; Players', Dec 1973, Fairy Cabbage Rose in Beauty and the Beast; same theatre, June 1974, Annie Chapman in Jack the Ripper; Her Majesty's, Aug 1978, Mrs Dolly Gallagher Levi in The Matchmaker; Riverside Studios, Hammersmith, May 1979, Mistress Overdone in Measure for

Measure; Victoria Palace, July 23, 1979, took over as Miss Hannigan in Annie; first appeared in films, 1952, in Folly to be Wise; appearances since then include Great Expectations, The Return of the Pink Panther, and Cuba; she has appeared in numerous television drama productions, the most recent being Secret Army, Barmitzvah Boy, and Agony (1979).
Address: c/o Barry Brown Management, 47 West Square, London S.E.11. *Tel:* 01-582 6622.

CHARLES, Pamela (*née* Foster), actress and singer
b Croydon, Surrey, 10 June 1932; *d* of Charles Foster and his wife Dorothy (Austen); *e* Wallington County School for Girls; trained for the stage at the Sylvia Bryant Stage School and later at LAMDA.
Made her first professional appearance at the Hippodrome, Margate, Dec 1948, as the Spirit of the Beanstalk in Jack and the Beanstalk; first London appearance, Palace, Oct 1951, in the chorus of Zip Goes a Million; subsequently toured, Feb 1953, as Sally Whittle in this production; spent the summer season, 1954, with the Fol-de-Rols at the Winter Garden, Eastbourne; Winter Garden, London, Aug 1955, played Jane Bell in The Water Gypsies; played her first straight roles at the Theatre Royal, Windsor, June 1956; in repertory at Worthing, 1957–8; returned to Windsor, Oct 1958, as Polly Peachum in The Beggar's Opera; made her first appearance in New York, Feb 1959, when she took over the part of Eliza Doolittle in My Fair Lady at the Mark Hellinger; toured in UK, Sept 1963, as Doreen in The Private Ear and Belinda in The Public Eye; repertory at the Phoenix, Leicester, 1964–5; Theatre Royal, Bristol, May 1966, appeared in Sixty Thousand Nights; in repertory at the Royal Lyceum, Edinburgh, 1967; Phoenix, London, Mar 1968, played the Prioress, Pertelote, Proserpina and the Queen in Canterbury Tales; Ambassadors', 1971–2, played Molly in The Mousetrap; in repertory at Colchester, 1974–5, where her parts included Connie in Habeas Corpus; Theatre Royal, Stratford E, Oct 1975, appeared in Cranford; returned to Colchester, 1978, to appear in The Rover, and Something's Afoot; Genée, E Grinstead, Spring 1979, in Cowardy Custard; has appeared frequently in pantomime; TV appearances, since 1953, include plays and light entertainment.
Favourite parts: Eliza Doolittle, Childie in The Killing of Sister George. *Recreations:* Dressmaking, embroidery, gardening. *Address:* c/o Keith Whitall Management, 304 Sandycombe Road, Kew, Richmond, Surrey.

CHARLESON, Ian, actor
b Edinburgh, 11 Aug 1949; *s* of John Charleson and his wife Jane; *e* Royal HS, Edinburgh, and Edinburgh University (MA 1970); trained for the stage at the London Academy of Music and Dramatic Art.
Made his professional debut at the Edinburgh Festival, 1972, as Gad in the Young Vic production of Joseph and the Amazing Technicolor Dreamcoat; with the Young Vic, 1972–74, his parts included Jimmy Porter in Look Back in Anger, and Guildenstern in Rosencrantz and Guildenstern Are Dead; made his New York debut with the company in their season at the Brooklyn Academy of Music, Mar 1974, playing Lucentio in The Taming of the Shrew, Ottavio in Scapino, and Brian Curtis in French Without Tears; for Cambridge Theatre Company, 1975, played the title part in Hamlet; Queen's, July 1975, Dave in Otherwise Engaged; joined the National Theatre company, 1977, playing Octavius in Julius Caesar, Mar, and Peregrine in Volpone, Apr, both Olivier; joined the RSC, 1978, and in the Stratford season played Ariel in The Tempest, Tranio in The Taming of the Shrew and Longaville in Love's Labour's Lost, also appear-

ing in Piaf at the Other Place; played Tranio and Longaville at the Aldwych, Apr 1979, also Lawrence Vail in Once in a Lifetime, Sept; at the Warehouse, 1979, played Joe Maguire in The Innocent, May, and again appeared in Piaf, June; remained with Piaf when it transferred to the Aldwych, and Wyndham's; films include Jubilee, 1978; TV includes Rock Follies, Churchill's People, The Paradise Run, and most recently Antony and Cleopatra.

Recreations: Collecting jigsaws, reading, painting. *Address:* c/o Jeremy Conway, 8 Cavendish Place, London W1M 9DJ.

CHARNIN, Martin, director, lyricist, producer, composer, author, and actor
b New York City, 24 Nov 1934; *s* of William Charnin and his wife Birdie (Blakeman); *e* High School of Music and Art, Cooper Union (BA 1955); *m* (1) Lynn Ross (mar dis); (2) Genii Prior.

First produced play to which he contributed lyrics was the revue Kaleidoscope, at the Provincetown Playhouse, 17 Sept 1957; made his professional stage début at the Winter Garden, 26 Sept 1957, when he played Big Deal in the musical West Side Story; Renata, May 1959, wrote lyrics and sketches for Fallout Revue; Upstairs at the Downstairs, Sept 1959, contributed lyrics to the revue Pieces of Eight; Alvin, Nov 1959, appeared in the revue The Boys Against the Girls; Winter Garden, Apr 1960, again played Big Deal in West Side Story; wrote lyrics for the tour of Little Revue, 1960; Majestic, Apr 1963, wrote lyrics for Hot Spot; wrote lyrics for Zenda, which toured Calif, 1963; Renata, Apr 1965, contributed material to the revue Wet Paint; wrote the lyrics for Mata Hari, produced in Washington, DC, Nov 1967; Theatre de Lys, Dec 1968, wrote lyrics for Ballad for a Firing Squad, which he also directed; Imperial, Nov 1970, lyrics for Two by Two; conceived and directed Nash at Nine, 1973; directed Music! Music!, 1974; lyrics for Annie, which he directed in 1977, winning Tony awards for best musical and best musical score; directed three US national touring companies of Annie, also London, 1978; directed Barmitzvah Boy, London, 1978; lyrics for I Remember Mana, NY, 1979; has also written material for various musical and cabaret artists; wrote the lyrics for the television production Feathertop, 1961, and later for the *Jackie Gleason Show*; in 1970 won the Emmy Award for conceiving and producing Annie, The Women in the Life of a Man; directed George M!; other television shows for which he was responsible are 'S Wonderful, 'S Marvelous, 'S Gershwin, which won six Emmy Awards and the Peabody Award, and Dames at Sea; author of The Giraffe Who Sounded Like Ol' Blue Eyes, 1976; Annie: a theatre memoir, 1977.

Recreations: Painting and travel. *Address:* c/o Beam One Ltd, 157 850 Seventh Avenue, New York, NY, 10019. *Tel:* 489–1012.

CHASE, Mary (*née* Coyle), playwright
b West Denver, Colorado, 25 Feb 1907; *d* of Frank Coyle and his wife Mary (McDonough); *e* University of Denver and University of Colorado; *m* Robert L Chase.

Formerly a reporter for the *Rocky Mountain News*; first play produced was Me Third, written for the Federal Theatre Project in Denver, Colorado, in 1936; Me Third was also her first Broadway production, produced at the Henry Miller's, 5 Mar 1937, as Now You've Done It; since then has written A Slip of a Girl, 1941; Harvey, for which she received the Pulitzer Prize, 1944; The Next Half Hour, 1945; Mrs Mc-Thing, Bernardine, 1952; Lolita, produced at the Barter Theatre, Abingdon, Virginia, 1954; Midgie Purvis, 1961;

Cocktails with Mimi, Barter Theatre, 1973; Harvey produced at the Prince of Wales', London, 5 Jan 1949, and on various occasions and places since, most notably at the ANTA, NY, Feb 1970, and The Prince of Wales', Jan 1975; Harvey filmed in 1951, and Bernadine in 1957; also author of the children's books Loretta Mason Potts, 1958, and The Wicked Pigeon Ladies in the Garden, 1968.

Address: 505 Circle Drive, Denver, Colo 8020.

CHASEN, Heather, actress
b Singapore, 20 July 1927; *d* of Frederick Nutter Chasen and his wife Agnes Hewitt (MacCullough); *e* Pensionat Notre Dame, Pahung, and Princess Helena College; *m* John Webster; trained for the stage at RADA (briefly) and later under Mary Duff.

Made her first professional appearance in 1945 at the Castle, Farnham, as Marcella in Donna Clarines; first London appearance, 3 Mar 1954, at the Arts, as Leonardo's wife in Blood Wedding; after further repertory experience at Oxford and Salisbury, toured, July 1957, as Marcelle in Hotel Paradiso; Lyric, Hammersmith, Mar 1958, Rita Allmers in Little Eyolf; Arts, June 1958, Anna Dasousa in Templeton; Ambassadors, Nov 1958, took over the part of Mollie Ralston in The Mousetrap; Open Air, Regent's Park, June 1962, Helena in A Midsummer Night's Dream; Duke of York's, Nov 1962, Lee Miller in Policy for Murder; Playhouse, Oxford, 1963, Solange in The Maids; Bristol Old Vic, May 1963, transferring to Criterion, June 1963, Antonia in A Severed Head; made her New York debut in the same part at the Royale, Oct 1964, returning to take up the same part again at the Criterion, 1965; Theatre Royal, Windsor, Mar 1966, Nancy Morrow in Love from Liz; Wimbledon, Aug 1966; Mrs Barnington in Jorrocks; toured, Jan 1967, for Prospect productions, as Lady Coniston in A Murder of No Importance; Newcastle, Apr 1967, played Martha in Who's Afraid of Virginia Woolf?; Hippodrome, Golders Green, July 1967, Gillian Howard in Thriller of the Year; again at the Playhouse, Oxford, 1967–8, played parts including the Countess in Ardele, Gina Ekdal in The Wild Duck and Jacqueline Du Bois in Call Me Jacky, touring in the last production; Apollo, Sept 1969, took over as Matron in Forty Years On; Theatre Royal, Windsor, 1969, Lady Susan in Lady S; Vaudeville, June 1970, Marchioness of Mereston in Lady Frederick, transferring to the Duke of York's, Sept 1970; Phoenix, Leicester, Jan 1971, Hester in Hello and Goodbye; Thorndike, Leatherhead, Mar 1971, Mrs Fitzadam in The Amorous Prawn; Playhouse, Nottingham, autumn 1971, played Queen Margaret in Richard III and Agatha in The Magistrate; Belgrade, Coventry, Sept 1972, Helena in Children of the Wolf; Soho Poly, May 1973, Mrs Taylor in Baby Love; toured Canada, Dec 1974, as Katherine Daugherty in The Pleasure of His Company; Swan, Worcester, Mar 1975, Judith Bliss in Hay Fever; Kenneth More, Ilford, June 1975, Mrs Baker in Butterflies Are Free; at the King's Head, Islington, Alison in Diaries, Apr, and Comtesse de Saint Fond in Madame de Sade, Aug 1975; Arnaud, Guildford, Feb 1977, played Beatrice Lacy in Rebecca, and Dec 1978, Olivia Waynward in Murder in a Bad Light; Chichester, 1979 season, appeared as Edith de Berg in The Eagle Has Two Heads and Miss Preen in The Man Who Came to Dinner; television appearances, since 1957, include The Newcomers, and Marked Personal; has broadcast since 1959 in The Navy Lark.

Club: Buckstone. *Recreations:* Pottering in the garden, junk collecting. *Address:* c/o Richard Jackson Personal Management, 59 Knightsbridge, London, SW1X 7RA.

CHATER, Geoffrey (*né* Robinson), actor
b Barnet, Herts, 23 March 1921; *s* of Lawrence Chater

Robinson and his wife Gwendoline (Gwynne); *e* Marlborough College; *m* Jennifer Hill; served in the Army from 1940 to 1946.

Made his first stage appearance in 1947 at the Theatre Royal, Windsor, in A Midsummer Night's Dream; first London appearance Dec 1951 at the Comedy as the Constable in Master Crook; joined the Old Vic company for their 1954–5 season, playing small parts in a number of plays; Phoenix, March 1961, played Bildad in JB; Arts, March 1962, Tom in Everything in the Garden, transferring later to the Duke of York's; Arts, July 1962, Duke of Florence in Women Beware Women; Lyric, Hammersmith, June 1963, Jacques Heller in Domino; Arts, Sept 1964, George in Game II; Cambridge, Sept 1965, Yslaev in A Month in the Country; Mercury, May 1967, Hubert in The Detour; Royal Court, July 1969, Lord Froth in The Double Dealer; toured with Prospect, spring 1971, as Lord Lumbercourt in The Man of the World; appeared at the Theatre Upstairs, July 1972, in Was He Anyone?; Royal Court, June 1973, Alice in Magnificence; Nottingham Playhouse, Oct 1975, Sir Mulberry in Jug; King's Head, Islington, Mar 1976, Dr Frobisher in The Browning Version; Lyttelton, Apr 1976, Dr Bradman in the National Theatre's Blithe Spirit; Aldwych, Sept 1978, for RSC, Henry in Cousin Vladimir; made his first film appearance in 1957; films since then include Sammy Going South, If . . ., 10 Rillington Place, and Barry Lyndon; has appeared frequently on television since 1950.

Recreations: Squash, cricket, shrimping. *Club:* MCC. *Address:* c/o Nems Management Ltd, 29–31 King's Road, London SW3.

CHAYEFSKY, Paddy, dramatic author

b New York City, 29 Jan 1923; *s* of Harry Chayefsky and his wife Gussie (Stuchevsky); *e* College of the City of New York; *m* Susan Sackler; formerly a printer.

Author of the following plays: Middle of the Night, 1956; The Tenth Man, 1959; Gideon, 1961; The Passion of Josef D (also directed), 1964; The Latent Heterosexual, produced in Dallas, Texas, and at the Aldwych, London, 1968, etc; author of the following television plays: Holiday Song, Marty, Bachelor Party, The Mother, Catered Affair, Printer's Measure, The Big Deal, The Sixth Year, etc; author of screen-plays for Marty, Bachelor Party, The Middle of the Night, The Goddess, The Americanization of Emily, The Hospital, and Network; received the Academy Award for Marty, 1955, Hospital, 1972, and Network, 1977.

Recreation: Travel. *Club:* Dramatists Guild. *Address:* 850 7th Avenue, New York, NY 10019. *Tel:* Circle 6–5663.

CHEESEMAN, Peter, Artistic Director, Victoria Theatre, Stoke-on-Trent

b Portsmouth, 27 Jan 1932; *s* of Eric Cheeseman and his wife Gladys (Hugill); *e* Sheffield University; *m* Joyce Cheeseman.

Directed his first professional productions at the Playhouse, Derby, 1959; director of the Victoria Theatre, Stoke-on-Trent, from its opening in 1962; he has directed over half the theatre's productions including many plays written for Stoke by Peter Terson, such as A Night to Make the Angels Weep and The Mighty Reservoy; also seven local documentaries; has directed for television, including Fight for Shelton Bar; is an Hon MA of Keele University.

Recreations: Gardening, canoeing, birdwatching. *Address:* Victoria Theatre, Hartshill Road, Stoke-on-Trent, ST4 6AE. *Tel:* Newcastle (Staffs) 613954.

CHELTON, Nick, lighting designer

b Paddington, London, 18 June 1946; *s* of Frederick Harold

Chelton and his wife Violet Maud (Ingram); *e* Quintin School.

Trained as lighting designer with Theatre Projects, 1964–5; freelance electrician 1967–71, rejoining Theatre Projects as lighting designer, 1971; lit his first London production, Hamlet (with Alan Bates), Cambridge, Jan 1971; has since lit numerous productions in the West End and provinces, at Sadler's Wells, The Royal Court, the Old Vic, the Palladium and elsewhere; left Theatre Projects 1975 and became freelance; lighting consultant to Kent Opera; recent theatre work includes the RSC productions of Love's Labours Lost, The Way of the World, and Antony and Cleopatra; in opera, for the English National, Welsh National, and Scottish Opera, and for Covent Garden.

Address: 76 Rodwell Road, London SE22. *Tel:* 01–693 6213.

CHERRELL, Gwen, actress

b Leicester, 12 Mar 1926; *d* of George Chambers and his wife Irene (Steadman); *e* Alderman Newton's School for Girls, Leicester; studied for the stage at the Royal Academy of Dramatic Art.

Made her first appearance on the stage, at the Little Theatre, Leicester, July 1940, as Sophie Smerdon in The Farmer's Wife; made her first appearance in London, at the Lyric Theatre, Nov 1944, as Jane Crawley in Scandal at Barchester; was a member of the Worthing Repertory Company, 1946–7; joined the Birmingham Repertory Company, July 1947, and remained there a year, playing numerous parts; appeared at the St James's Theatre, with the Birmingham company, June 1948, as Lydia Languish in The Rivals; Comedy, Nov 1948, appeared in the revue, Slings and Arrows; Phoenix, May 1949, made a great success when she played Cherry in The Beaux' Stratagem, and for her playing of the part, gained the Clarence Derwent award for the best performance in a supporting role, for 1948–9; Arts, Nov 1950, Josepha Quarendon in Preserving Mr Panmure; Fortune, Dec 1950, Poll in The Silver Curlew; Aldwych, Feb 1951, again played Josepha Quarendon in Preserving Mr Panmure; Wyndham's, May 1951, appeared as Donovan in The Love of Four Colonels; Arts, Sept 1952, played Doña Ana in Don Juan in Hell; same theatre, June 1953, Raina in Arms and the Man; joined the Old Vic Company for the 1953–4 season, appearing as Diana in All's Well That Ends Well, Blanche of Castile in King John, Olivia in Twelfth Night, Valeria in Coriolanus, Iris in The Tempest; with the Old Vic Company at the Edinburgh Festival, 1954, played Lady Macduff in Macbeth; remained with the company for the 1954–5 season, appearing as Bianca in The Taming of the Shrew, Celia in As You Like It, and Doll Tearsheet in Henry IV (Pt II); Saville, Mar 1956, took over the part of Lydia Languish in The Rivals; St James's, Sept 1956, played Audrey Strange in Towards Zero; Bristol Hippodrome, Dec 1957, played Aladdin; Lyric, Hammersmith, Dec 1958 appeared as Charming the First in King Charming; Strand, Oct 1959, played Edith Rollo in Rollo, subsequently transferring to the Duchess, Feb 1960; New Arts, Oct 1962, played Catherine in Doctors of Philosophy; Vaudeville, Apr 1964, Helen Ritchie in Amber For Anna; Belgrade, Coventry, July 1965, played Sybil Cross in The Big Breaker; Yvonne Arnaud, Guildford, Nov 1965, Helen Saville in The Vortex; Strand, Nov 1970, Annie Parker in When We Are Married; toured S Africa, 1972, in Darling I'm Home; Westminster, Sept 1973, Dora Moxton in Relative Values; Arnaud, Apr 1977, Mrs Baxley in Laburnum Grove; Theatre Royal, Windsor, Nov 1977 and tour, Ruth in Two and Two Make

Sex; has appeared for the Repertory Players and also made numerous film and television appearances, including the series *Leave it to Charlie*; author of the play Members Only, screenplay of the film Don't Talk to Strange Men, and several television and radio plays, including: The Madam, It's Called Happy Families, Interior, Man in the Dark, and Treasure.

Address: c/o John Cadell Ltd, 64 Highgate High Street, London, N6 5HX.

CHERRY, Wal, director, Professor of Theater, Temple University.
b Ballarat, Victoria, 10 May 1932; *s* of Walter Joseph Cherry and his wife Vera Gladys (White); *e* St Patrick's College, Ballarat, Geelong HS, and the University of Melbourne; *m* Marcelle Lynette Mathieson.

After directing undergraduate and graduate productions at Melbourne University, became guest director at the Union Theatre Repertory, later Melbourne Theatre Company, for Summer and Smoke, 1956; director, Union Theatre Repertory Company, 1956–9; guest director, Playhouse, Perth, 1959, for A View from the Bridge and His Excellency; founded the Theatre Workshop and Actors Studio and The Theatre 60 Company, Melbourne, 1960, directing Shadow of a Gunman, All that Fall, and La Ronde; also directed Look Back in Anger, Perth, 1960; Under Milk Wood, Perth, Rhinoceros, Melbourne Theatre Company, 1961; founded the Emerald Hill Theatre, 1962, and directed a number of plays there 1962–6; directed After the Fall, Melbourne Theatre Company, 1964; The Balcony, Adelaide, 1965; Brecht on Brecht, Adelaide Festival, 1966; appointed to the chair of Drama, Flinders University, 1967; here he directed frequently; Professor of Theater, Temple University, Philadelphia, 1979– ; other productions include: This Story of Yours, St Martin's, Melbourne, 1969; Kean, South Australian Theatre Company, Follow the Leader, tour of Adelaide, Canberra and Israel, 1971; Ordeal by Fire, Melbourne Theatre Company, 1972; Tartuffe, California Institute of the Arts, 1973; The Seven Deadly Sins, New Opera South Australia, 1974; Jacques Brel Is Alive and Well and Living in Paris, New Opera, Flinders University and Adelaide Festival Centre Trust, The Threepenny Opera, New Opera and Adelaide Trust, 1975; Never the Twain, New Opera, Lysistrata, Flinders U, 1976; Never the Twain, Sydney Opera House and Canberra Playhouse, 1977; The Emigrants, Playbox Melbourne and Adelaide Festival Centre, The Private Life of the Master Race, Flinders U, 1978; Hitler without Auschwitz, U of California, San Diego, 1979; his writing includes verse, radio and TV scripts, and newspaper and magazine articles.

Recreation: Pottering about. *Address:* Department of Theater, School of Communications and Theater, Temple University, Philadelphia, Pa 19122. *Tel:* 215–787 8421.

CHESKIN, Irving W, administrator
b New York City, 19 July 1915; *s* of Henry A Cheskin and his wife Bertha Levitan; *e* Brooklyn College (BA 1936), New School for Social Research (MSS 1938), and University of Pennsylvania; *m* Mildred Estrin.

Formerly a professor of economics at the University of the State of New York; served as executive director of the Film Producers Association; in 1960 became Executive Director of the League of New York Theaters, and still serves in this post in this organization, which has changed its name to The League of New York Theaters and Producers.

Address: 226 West 47th Street, New York, NY 10036. *Tel:* JU 2–4455.

CHETWYN, Robert (*né* Suckling), director and former actor
b Chelsea, London, 7 Sept 1933; *s* of Frederick Reuben

Suckling and his wife Eleanor Laviner (Boffee); *e* Rutlish School; trained for the stage at the Central School of Speech and Drama.

First appeared as an actor with the Dundee Rep, 1952, subsequently appearing in repertory at Hull and Birmingham; directed his first play, Five Finger Exercise, at the Playhouse, Salisbury, Sept 1960; director of productions, Opera House, Harrogate, until Jan 1962; director of productions, Ipswich, until Dec 1964; resident producer, Belgrade, Coventry, until Jan 1966; associate director Mermaid Theatre, 1966; he has since directed the following plays, in London unless otherwise indicated: The Beaver Coat, There's a Girl in My Soup, A Present for the Past (Edinburgh Festival), 1966; Trifles and Tomfooleries (Shaw triple-bill), There's a Girl in My Soup (Sydney and New York), The Flip Side, 1967; The Importance of Being Earnest, The Real Inspector Hound, 1968; What the Butler Saw, The Country Wife (Chichester), The Bandwagon, Cannibal Crackers, 1969; The Bandwagon (Sydney), When We Are Married, 1970; Hamlet (also Prospect European tour), 1971; The Sandboy (Greenwich), 1971; Parents' Day, 1972; Who's Who, At the End of the Day, Why Not Stay for Breakfast? (Brussels, Norwich), 1973; Chez Nous, Springtime for Henry (Oxford Festival), Robin Redbreast (Guildford), Who's Who (Brussels), 1974; The Doctor's Dilemma, Kidnapped at Christmas, 1975; Getting Away with Murder, Private Lives (Melbourne and Sydney), 1976; It's All Right If I Do It, A Murder Is Announced, 1977; Arms and the Man, Luv (Amsterdam), 1978; Brimstone and Treacle, Bent, Pygmalion (National Theatre of Belgium), 1979; has directed for TV since Beyond A Joke, 1972, including the series Making Faces.

Recreations: Tennis, gardening, travel. *Address:* 1 Wilton Court, Eccleston Square, London SW1V 1PH.

CHODOROV, Edward, dramatic author and director
b New York City, 17 Apr 1914; *s* of Harry Chodorov and his wife Lena (Simmons); *e* Brown University; *m* Rosemary Pettit.

Commenced his career in the theatre in 1928, as assistant stage-manager; is the author of the following plays, all of which, except the first, he has directed: Wonder Boy, 1932; Kind Lady, 1935; Cue for Passion, 1940; Those Endearing Young Charms, 1943; Decision, 1944; Common Ground, 1945; Signor Chicago, 1947; Oh Men! Oh Women! 1953; The Spa, 1956; Listen to the Mocking Bird, Monsieur Lautrec, 1959; has also written and produced many films, including Craig's Wife, Yellow Jack, Undercurrent, Roadhouse, The Hucksters, etc; wrote a series of twenty-six plays for television under the collective title *The Billy Rose Show*.

Address: c/o Dramatists Guild, 234 West 44th Street, New York, NY 10036.

CHODOROV, Jerome, dramatic author and director
b New York City, 10 Aug 1911; *s* of Harry Chodorov and his wife Lena (Simmons); *m* Rhea Grand; was formerly engaged as a journalist and was on the staff of the *New York World*.

Subsequently went to Hollywood, where he was engaged as a scenarist for some time and where he met his collaborator, Joseph Fields, with whom he has written Schoolhouse on the Lot, 1938; My Sister Eileen, 1940; Junior Miss, 1941; served as Captain in the US Air Force, 1942–5; French Touch, 1945; Pretty Penny, 1949; Wonderful Town, 1953; The Girl in Pink Tights, The Tunnel of Love (with Fields and Peter de Vries), 1954; Anniversary Waltz, 1954; The Ponder Heart, 1956; The Happiest Man Alive, 1962; I Had a Ball (book of the musical), 1964; revised the book for The Great Waltz, 1965; wrote Three Bags Full, Dumas and Son, and revised the book for The Student Prince, 1966; directed the NY productions of Make a Million and The Gazebo, 1958; directed Blood, Sweat, and Stanley Poole, 1961; author of A Community of Two and directed its tour, 1974; Dorothy Chandler Pavilion, Los Angeles, July 1975, directed Wonderful Town; same theatre, 1978, co-adaptor of Pal Joey '78; author of Culture Caper, based on John Updike's novel, Bech, a Book, which had its première at the Ogunquit, Maine, Playhouse, July 1975; has collaborated in the writing of many screenplays, including: Louisiana Purchase, Rich Man, Poor Girl, My Sister Eileen, and Happy Anniversary, with Joseph Fields in 1959.

Address: c/o Dramatists Guild, 234 West 44th Street, New York, NY 10036.

CHRISTIE, Audrey, actress

b Chicago, Ill, 27 June 1912; *d* of Charles Christie and his wife Florence (Ferguson); *e* Lake View High School, Chicago; *m* (1) Guy Robertson (mar dis); (2) Donald Briggs; studied for the stage under Bertha Iles and under Marie Veatch for dancing.

Made her first appearance on the stage, 1927, with Marie Veatch's Six Chicago Steppers, a dancing act, on the Keith-Orpheum Circuit, making her first appearance in New York, at the Palace Theatre, 1928, in the same act; during the same year at Chanin's 46th Street Theatre, she played Babe O'Day in Good News; at the same theatre, Jan 1929, played Olive in Follow Thru; 44th Street, Mar 1931, succeeded Dorothy Williams in Sweet and Low; Music Box, 1932, appeared in Of Thee I Sing; Shubert, July 1933, played Francine in Shady Lady; Lyceum, Sept 1933, made a great success when she appeared as Billie Stonewall Jackson in Sailor Beware; 48th Street, Sept 1934, played Jean Wales in Alley Cat; Longacre, Oct 1934, Nellie Quinn in Geraniums in My Window; in St Louis, June–Aug 1936, appeared in No, No, Nanette, A Connecticut Yankee, The Red Mill, etc; Ethel Barrymore, NY, Dec 1936, Miriam Aarons in The Women, which she played until Mar 1938; Shubert, May 1938, Anna Murphy in I Married an Angel; Golden, Nov 1940, Ruth Conway in Return Engagement; Harris, Chicago, Feb 1941, played Ruth in My Sister Eileen; Hollywood Theatre, NY, Dec 1941, Mabel in Banjo Eyes; St James (for the Guild), Nov 1942, Kitty Trimble in Without Love; Morosco, Dec 1943, Olive Lashbrooke in The Voice of the Turtle, which she played for two seasons; Adelphi, Feb 1946, Crystal and the Duchess of Alba in The Duchess Misbehaves; first appeared in London at the Piccadilly, 9 July 1947, as Olive Lashbrooke in The Voice of the Turtle; Royale, NY, Nov 1948, Frances Black in Light Up the Sky; Empire, Oct 1951, Liz Kendall in Buy Me Blue Ribbons; toured summer of 1955 as Ruth Sherwood in Wonderful Town; Broadhurst, NY, June 1956, took over the role of Bunny Watson in The Desk Set; Longacre, Feb 1957, Connie McDougall in Holiday for Lovers; Coronet, Oct 1957, Mrs Fawcett in Nature's Way; Playhouse, Palm Springs, California, Jan 1958, Lillian Anders in The Pink Burro; Music Box, Dec 1958, took over the part of Lottie Lacey in The Dark at the Top of the Stairs, in which she toured in 1959; toured, Dec 1960, as Emma Pasternack in Midgie Purvis; Curran, San Francisco, 1967, Parthy Anne in Show Boat; Winter Garden, NY, 1968, took over the role of Vera Charles in Mame; US tour, 1969–71, as Maud Hayes in Forty Carats; has appeared in the films Splendour in the Grass, The Unsinkable Molly Brown, Harlow, etc; played the role of Dorothy in the television series *Fair Exchange*, 1964.

Favourite parts: Babe in Good News and Stonewall Jackson in Sailor, Beware. *Address:* 1425 Queen's Road, Los Angeles, Calif 90052.

CHURCH, Tony (*né* James Anthony Church), actor and director

b London, 11 May 1930; *s* of Ronald Frederic Church and his wife Margaret Fanny (Hart); *e* Hurstpierpoint College and Clare College, Cambridge; *m* Margaret Ann Blakeney.

Appeared in numerous productions while at Cambridge and made his professional debut with a company of ex-Cambridge actors in Aug 1953, playing Tito Belcredi in Henry IV at the Arts, Cambridge and later at the Arts, London; founder member of the Elizabethan Theatre Company, for whom he toured as Shylock in The Merchant of Venice and Malvolio in Twelfth Night, 1953–4; appeared in a number of roles with the Oxford Playhouse company, Oct 1954 to Sept 1955; Apollo, Nov 1955, played the Postman in Summertime; same theatre, March 1956, Paul LaBarca in One Bright Day; 1956–7, played leading roles in repertory at Hornchurch, Worthing and Nottingham; Arts, Jan 1958, played Hugo in The Iceman Cometh, transferring to the Winter Garden, March 1958, and later taking over the part of Hickey; joined the Royal Shakespeare Company in 1960, remaining until Jan 1967; at Stratford his parts included Antigonus in The Winter's Tale and Hortensio in The Taming of the Shrew, 1960; First Player in Hamlet, 1961; Pisanio in Cymbeline, Quince in A Midsummer Night's Dream and Cornwall in King Lear, 1962; Holofernes in Love's Labour's Lost, Ferneze and Machiavel in The Jew of Malta, Flavius in Timon of Athens and Polonius in Hamlet, 1965; Henry IV in both parts of the play of that name, 1966; at the Aldwych he played Newton in The Physicists, Lockit in The Beggar's Opera and Count Fontana in The Representative, 1963; the Schoolmaster in Pedagogue and the Father in No Why (Expeditions One) and Ferneze in The Jew of Malta, 1964; the Judge in The Investigation and Polonius in Hamlet, 1965; in Jan 1967, he became the first director of the Northcott, Exeter, a post he held until the end of 1970; there he directed Hamlet, Twelfth Night and The Boy Friend, also played many leading roles; May 1968, made his first New York appearance at the Billy Rose as Bishop Bell in Soldiers; toured Europe, 1969, with the RSC as Pandarus in Troilus and Cressida; returned to Stratford, 1971, to play Antonio in The Merchant of Venice, Sir Toby Belch in Twelfth Night, Leonato in Much Ado About Nothing and to act as Director of Studio Projects; toured Japan with RSC, 1972, and at the Aldwych played Third Knight/Tempter in Murder in the Cathedral, Kostylyov in The Lower Depths, and Pictish Poet in The Island of the Mighty; at Stratford, 1973, Friar Laurence in Romeo and Juliet, John of Gaunt in Richard II, Don Armado in Love's Labours Lost and Duke Senior in As You Like It; played Gaunt at Brooklyn Academy, NY, Jan 1974; in the same year, King Lear in the version of Lear at The Other Place, Stratford and The Place, London, Belarius in Cymbeline at Stratford and the Aldwych, and several parts in The Beast, at The Place; 1975, repeated Don Armado at the Aldwych, and with Lear at Brooklyn; played Henry VII in Perkin Warbeck, Buckingham and Richmond in Richard III at The Other Place, summer 1975; Ulysses in Troilus and Cressida, 1976, Stratford and 1977 Aldwych; Gloucester in King Lear at Stratford and the Aldwych, Rorlund in Pillars of the Community at the Aldwych, 1977; Don Armado in Love's Labour's Lost (Aldwych), Old Gobbo and Tubal in The Merchant of Venice (Warehouse), 1979; Menalaus and Odysseus in The Greeks (Aldwych), 1980; co-director of Actors-in-Residence (joint project of RSC and University of

California), 1976– ; films include Darling and Work is a Four-Letter Word; has appeared frequently on television and has made numerous spoken word recordings; has been Visiting Professor of Theatre and English at the University of Denver, University of California, Santa Barbara, College of Santa Fe, etc; awarded honorary degree by Exeter University, 1971.

Recreations: Singing, listening to music, river-rafting. *Favourite parts:* Falstaff, Archie Rice, Lear. *Address:* 38 Mansfield Road, London NW3 2HP. *Tel:* 01–485 3366.

CHURCHILL, Caryl, playwright

b London, 3 Sept 1938; *e* Trafalgar School, Montreal, and Lady Margaret Hall, Oxford (BA 1960); *m* David Harter.

Author of the plays Downstairs, produced Oxford, 1958; Having a Wonderful Time, 1960; Easy Death, Schreber's Nervous Illness, Owners, 1972; Perfect Happiness, 1974; Moving Clocks Go Slow, Objections to Sex and Violence, 1975; Light Shining in Buckinghamshire, 1976; Traps, 1977; Cloud Nine, 1979; Three More Sleepless Nights, 1980; contributed sketches to Floorshow, 1977; has written regularly for radio since The Ants, 1962; for TV wrote The Judge's Wife, 1972.

Address: 12 Thornhill Square, London N1.

CHURCHILL, Sarah, actress

b London, 7 Oct 1914; *d* of the Rt Hon Sir Winston Spencer Churchill, OM, MP, PC, CH and his wife Clementine (Hozier), CBE; *e* Notting Hill High School and Broadstairs; *m* (1) Vic Oliver (mar dis); (2) Anthony Beauchamp (dec); (3) Lord Audley (dec); studied ballet for some time.

Made her first appearance on the stage at the Adelphi Theatre, 4 Feb 1936, in the chorus of Follow the Sun; at the Mercury, Dec 1939, played Lucrezia in Mandragola; Embassy, Jan 1940, Hypatia Tarleton in Misalliance; New, Aug 1940, Ann in Outward Bound; Q, July 1941, Mary Rose in the play of that name; played a repertory season at the London Coliseum; subsequently joined the WAAF, in which she served until the end of 1945; reappeared on the stage, at Henley, Dec 1945, in Squaring the Triangle; toured, 1946, as Mrs Manningham in Gaslight; Garrick, May 1948, played Henrietta Moulton-Barrett in The Barretts of Wimpole Street; Q, Apr 1949, Rowena Wetherby in House on the Sand; made her first appearance on the American stage at Princeton, NJ, 27 June 1949, as Tracy Lord in The Philadelphia Story, subsequently touring in the same part; Morosco, New York, Apr 1951, played Nancy Willard in Gramercy Ghost; Scala, Dec 1958, appeared in the title-part in Peter Pan; Lyric, Hammersmith, Feb 1960, played Lisa in Night Life of the Virile Potato; toured 1960, as Eliza in Pygmalion; Pembroke, Croydon, May 1961, played Rosalind in As You Like It; Ashcroft, Croydon, Apr 1963, the Woman in From this Hill; Ashcroft, Croydon, Apr 1964, played Mathilde in Fata Morgana; Arts, Sept 1966, co-starred in A Matter of Choice; appeared in a Grand Guignol season at The Place, May 1971; Hayloft Dinner Th, Manassas, Va, Feb 1976, appeared in a musical based on her short story The Boy Who Made Magic; entered films 1940, in He Found a Star; is the author of two books of verse.

Address: c/o Al Parker, Ltd, 50 Mount Street, London, W1.

CILENTO, Diane, actress

b Brisbane, Australia, 5 Oct 1933; *d* of Sir Raphael West Cilento and his wife Phyllis (McGlew); *m* (1) Andrea Volpe (mar dis); (2) Sean Connery (mar dis); trained for the stage at the American Academy of Dramatic Art and RADA.

At the Library, Manchester, June 1953, played Juliet in Romeo and Juliet; Arts, June 1953, Louka in Arms and the Man; Q, Oct 1953, Gina Hayworth in One Fair Daughter; Duke of York's, Jan 1954, Dixie Evans in The Big Knife; for the Pegasus Theatre Society, Wyndham's, May 1954, played Diaphanta in The Changeling; Apollo, June 1955, played Helen in Tiger At the Gates, and subsequently in the New York production, Plymouth, Oct 1955; at the Manchester Opera House, Mar 1957, appeared in the title-part in Zuleika; Arts, London, June 1957, played Mia in Less Than Kind; Royal Court, May 1959, played Carol Cutrere in Orpheus Descending; Billy Rose, NY, Oct 1959, played Ellie Dunn in a revival of Heartbreak House; Plymouth, NY, Mar 1960, Marie-Paule in The Good Soup; on her return to England, at the Lyric, Hammersmith, July 1960, played the title-part in Miss Julie; Oxford Playhouse, Nov 1960, played Ersilia Drei in Naked; at the same theatre, Feb 1961, played Dona Inez de Castro in Queen After Death; Royal Court, Apr 1961, played Leni in Altona, subsequently transferring to the Saville, June 1961; Comedy, Feb 1962, played Anne Fox in My Place; Piccadilly, May 1962, Eleonore in Castle in Sweden; at the Royal Court, Apr 1963, again played Ersilia Drei in Naked; Saville, Sept 1965, played Beatrice in The Four Seasons; Royal Court, Oct 1967, Ludmila in Marya; Fortune, Dec 1969, Sarah in I've Seen You Cut Lemons; Old Vic, July 1970, played Nastasya in The Idiot for the National Theatre Company; Duchess, July 1973, took over as Katherine Winter in Collaborators; Greenwich, Nov 1976, Rosaria in The Artful Widow; Theatre Upstairs, Sept 1977, directed tuff; Open Space, Nov 1979, Laura in The Father; Theatre Royal, Stratford E, Mar 1980, directed The Streets of London; among her film appearances are Tom Jones and The Agony and the Ecstasy, and films she has made include Turning.

Address: Crouch Associates, 59 Frith Street, London W1.

CLANCY, Deidre, designer

b Paddington, London, 31 Mar 1943; adopted *d* of Julie M Clancy; *e* Convent of the Sacred Heart, Tunbridge Wells, and Birmingham College of Art; *m* Mike Steer.

Her first stage designs were for the Christmas pantomime, 1965, at Lincoln Theatre Royal; Royal Court, 16, at Lincoln Theatre Royal; Royal Court, 16 Mar 1967, designed costumes for The Daughter-in-Law; at this theatre has since designed costumes for The Ruffian on the Stair and The Erpingham Camp (double-bill: also sets), 1967; A Collier's Friday Night, The Widowing of Mrs Holroyd, 1968; Marya, 1969; Trixie and Baba, Early Morning, Uncle Vanya (last two also sets), 1970; Sleeper's Den, Lear (Bond), 1971; Crete and Sergeant Pepper, Hedda Gabler (last two also sets), 1972; the Sea (also sets), 1973; Entertaining Mr Sloane, 1975; other productions for which she has designed costumes include: June Evening, Manchester, 1968; Landscape and Silence, Forum, Lincoln Center (US début), 1970; Hamlet, Nottingham and London, Hedda Gabler, Macbeth (both also sets), Stratford, Ont, Cato Street, Young Vic, 1971; Willie Rough, Edinburgh, Quetzalcoatl, Round House 1972; The Thrie Estates, The Bevellers, both Edinburgh, Spring Awakening, Old Vic (National), Twelfth Night (for RSC), Grand Manœuvres, Old Vic, 1974; Trinity Tales (also sets), Birmingham, The Voysey Inheritance, How Mad Tulloch Was Taken Away (both Edinburgh), The White Devil, As You Like It (both Nottingham), The Playboy of the Western World (Old Vic), 1975; The White Devil, 1976; costume designs for the National Theatre include Watch It Come Down, Il Campiello, 1976; Volpone, The Madras House, The Plough and the Stars, 1977; Plenty, Strife, 1978; opera designs include Il Seraglio (also sets), Kent Opera, 1978; Eugene Onegin, Scottish Opera, 1979; Cosi Fan Tutte, Metropolitan, NY, 1980; film designs include: The Virgin and the Gypsy, The Girl from Petrovka; TV work includes various plays and series.

Recreation: Music. *Address:* c/o Simpson Fox Associates, 57 Fylmer Road, London SW6.

CLANTON, Ralph, actor

b Fresno, California, 11 Sept 1914; *s* of Edward William Clanton and his wife Bernice Vivian (Gibbs); *e* Stanford University.

Made his first appearance on the stage at the Mohawk Drama Festival, Schenectady, New York, 1939, in Romance; first appeared in NYC at the National, 11 Nov 1941, as Malcolm in the Maurice Evans production of Macbeth; NY, Feb 1943, appeared in God Strikes Back; Forrest, Mar 1943, appeared in the George Coulouris production of Richard III; Mansfield, Oct 1943, played Lieutenant James Richardson in Victory Belles; Mansfield, June 1944, William Douglas in A Strange Play; Shubert, 1944, took over as Cassio in the Paul Robeson production of Othello and repeated this part in the revival at the New York City Center, May 1945; Plymouth, May 1946, the Geni and the Imperial Chamberlain in the musical Lute Song; Alvin, Oct 1946, Comte de Guiche in Cyrano de Bergerac; Martin Beck, Nov 1947, Octavius Caesar in Antony and Cleopatra; Mansfield, Jan 1950, Robin Flemming in Design for a Stained Glass Window; New York City Center, Apr 1951, Petruchio in The Taming of the Shrew; New York City Center, Nov 1953, Comte de Guiche in Cyrano de Bergerac; Longacre, Mar 1954, Lord Henry Strait in The Burning Glass; appeared principally in films and television for some years; reappeared on Broadway, 14 Dec 1967, at the American Place, as the Bishop in The Ceremony of Innocence; St Clement's, Apr 1968, Palfrey in Endecott and the Red Cross; Broadhurst, Jan 1972, Ralph Nau in Vivat! Vivat Regina!; ANTA, Dec 1972, Minian Edwards in The Last of Mrs Lincoln; A Solo State, Fla, Oct 1976, and tour, in The Patriots; Roundabout, Sept 1976, Joseph Cuthbertson in The Philanderer; Brooklyn Academy, 1977, for BAM Theater Company, played William Sudley in The New York Idea, Mar, and Ferapont in Three Sisters, Apr; Roundabout, Oct 1977, Mr Crampton in You Never Can Tell; first appeared in films in 1950; first appeared on television in 1938 and has since appeared regularly.

Favourite parts: Cassio and Octavius Caesar. *Hobby:* Painting. *Address:* Actors Equity Association, 165 West 46th Street, New York, NY 10036.

CLARIDGE, Norman, actor

b London, 29 Aug 1903; *s* of Frederick George Claridge and his wife Beatrice Michie (Blain); *e* Latymer Upper School; *m* Beatrice Mary Archdale.

Made his first appearance on the stage at Weymouth, Aug 1924, as Sir Benjamin Backbite in The School for Scandal; played with the Benson Shakespearean Company for three seasons; joined the Birmingham Repertory Theatre, 1928, and made his first London appearance with that company, at the Court, Apr 1928, as Rolf in Harold; Playhouse, Jan 1930, played Giles in The White Assegai; and subsequently, Gregory Sweet in Devonshire Cream; Duchess, Dec 1930, Rupert Sparrow in Jane's Legacy; Queens, Jan 1932, George Smerdon in The Farmer's Wife; Apr 1932, Lorenz Kling in Caravan; Shaftesbury, May 1933, Salmon Brown in Gallows Glorious; His Majesty's, Nov 1934, Noah Harwood in Mary Read; at the Phoenix, Jan 1935, followed Robert Donat as Edward Earle in the same play; Q, Mar 1935, Joseph Percival

in Misalliance; Arts, Apr 1935, Captain Vivian in Basilisk; at the Whitehall for a time, and also on tour, played Anthony in Anthony and Anna; Mercury, Feb 1937, Ian Shawcross in The Ascent of F6; Westminster, July 1937, Laertes in Hamlet; 1938–9, played leading parts with the Howard and Wyndham Repertory Company in Scotland; 1945–6, appeared in ENSA Festival Co in the Middle and Far East; joined the Bristol Old Vic Company, 1946–7; New Lindsey, Nov 1947, played Oswald Bishop in Gingerbread House; toured, 1949, as Lord Shayne in Bittersweet; toured, 1950, as Supt Wilson in PC 49; St James's, Oct 1950, played Mr Tyrrell in Top of the Ladder; St James's, Feb 1951, Baron in The Madwoman of Chaillot; Hippodrome, Feb 1952, Lord Bretherton in Bet Your Life; Lyric, Hammersmith, Feb 1957, played Obregon in The Master of Santiago, and Mar 1957, Porcellio in Malatesta; Strand, Feb 1958, Sir William Rolander in Verdict; Vaudeville, May 1965, took over the parts of the Archbishop of Canterbury and the Editor of *The Times* in Portrait of a Queen; Strand, Nov 1967, played Admiral Sir Guy Lawrence in Number Ten (also in Toronto); Grove, Belfast, May 1968, played Mr Ingram in The Loves of Cass Maguire, and March 1970, the Archbishop of Pimlico in Hadrian the Seventh; Mermaid, July 1971, Sir George Ponders in The Old Boys and, May 1974, Salisbury in The Great Society; joined the National Theatre Company, 1975–78, and appeared in a number of supporting roles in plays including Troilus and Cressida (Young Vic), in which he played Priam; Tamburlaine the Great, Volpone, Julius Caesar, The Cherry Orchard, Macbeth, and The Woman; has also broadcast as a member of the BBC Drama Repertory Company.

Clubs: Savage, MCC. *Address:* 6 Hallam Court, 77 Hallam Street, London, W1N 5LR. *Tel:* 01–580 5937.

CLARK, Brian, playwright

b 1932; *e* Redland Training College, Central School of Speech and Drama, and Nottingham University; formerly staff tutor in drama, Hull University.

Contributed to Lay By, 1971, and England's Ireland, 1972; his first full-length play to be professionally produced was Whose Life Is It, Anyway?, Mermaid, Mar 1978, transferring to the Savoy and running for over a year; subsequently produced NY, 1979, and all over the world; a revised version, with the leading role rewritten for an actress, was produced in New York, 1980; also author of Can You Hear Me at the Back?, 1979; his short plays include Post Mortem, and Campion's Interview; extensive writing for television includes over twenty plays and the serial Telford's Change; author of Group Theatre, 1972; publishes plays and general books on the theatre under his own imprint of Amber Lane Press.

Address: c/o Judy Daish Associates, Globe Theatre, Shaftesbury Avenue, London W1.

CLARK, Ernest, actor

b Maida Vale, London, 12 Feb 1912; *s* of Bertie Clark and his wife Martha Augusta Ethel (Pettersson); *e* St Marylebone Grammar School; *m* (1) Rosamond Burne (mar dis); (2) Avril Hillyer (*née* Catherine Daniel) (mar dis); (3) Julia Lockwood; formerly a journalist.

Made his first appearance on the stage at the Festival Theatre, Cambridge, Oct 1937, as Charles Winter in Family Album (Tonight At 8.30); remained in repertory at Cambridge, and subsequently at Brighton and Sheffield; first appeared in London at His Majesty's, 20 July 1939, as the Emperor Charles V in The Devil To Pay; served six years in the Army, and was awarded the Military Cross in Normandy in 1944; on his return to the stage he toured, 1946, as Richard

Llewellyn in The Years Between, and in 1947 as Sir Robert Morton in The Winslow Boy; Strand, Feb 1948, appeared as James in Family Portrait; Lyric, Hammersmith, June 1948, played Prince Paul in Crime Passionnel, and appeared in this part at the Garrick, Aug 1948; toured, 1949, as Arnold Holt in Edward My Son; at the Edinburgh Festival, 1949, appeared as Alexander MacColgie Gibbs in The Cocktail Party; made his first appearance on the New York stage at the Henry Miller, 21 Jan 1950, in the same part; after returning to London, took over the same part at the New Theatre, 1950; Fortune, June 1951, played Dr John Christow in The Hollow; at the Edinburgh Festival, 1952, appeared as Sir Robert Clifford and Pedro de Ayala in The Player King; St James's, Jan 1953, played Dr Skillingworth in Escapade (Clarence Derwent Award); Q, Sept 1954, Humphrey Westerdale in Witch Errant; at the Henry Miller, NY, Dec 1954, appeared as Mr Myers, QC, in Witness For The Prosecution; Aldwych, Oct 1955, played Lewis Paulton in The Whole Truth; Savoy, Nov 1956, Inspector Gordon in Double Image; Players', Mar 1958, Professor Abercrombie in Gentlemen's Pastime; Grand, Leeds, Sept 1958, played Clifford Kester in These People, Those Books, and also toured with the play; toured, Sept 1959, as Mr Christie in Landscape With Figures; Saville, Dec 1959, played The Prawn in The Amorous Prawn; for the Repertory Players at the Lyric, Oct 1961, played John Smith in The Pander Touch; Strand, Sept 1962, Lewis Eliot in The New Men; Bristol Hippodrome, Dec 1963, Kleber Carlier in Monsieur Blaise; Malvern Festival, July 1965, played Mr Dennis in The Living Room; Aug 1965, George Kettle in Mr Kettle and Mrs Moon; spring, 1966, toured South America with A Slight Ache and The Private Eye, playing the husband in each play; on his return to England, appeared at the Cambridge, Mar 1967, as Major Heather in The Judge; Vaudeville, Sept 1970, Sir Dymock Blackburn QC in The Jockey Club Stakes; Mermaid, Nov 1971, Sir Orpheus Midlander in Geneva; Billingham, Oct 1974, and tour, Sir Anthony Smith in The Grouse Moor Image; Comedy, July 1976, Waldo Cunningham in Getting Away with Murder; Churchill, Bromley, Sept 1977, Andrew Wyke in Sleuth; Arnaud, Guildford, July 1978, Warwick Deeping in Balmoral; Lyric, Hammersmith, Dec 1979, Emperor of China in Aladdin; first appeared in films, 1948; has also appeared frequently on television, lately in several series based on Richard Gordon's Doctor novels; President of British Actors' Equity, 1969–73.

Club: Green Room. *Address:* c/o Leading Artists, 60 St James's Street, London SW1.

CLARK, John Pepper, playwright, poet, and educator
b Kiagbodo, Nigeria, 6 Apr 1935; *s* of Clark Fuludu Bekederemo and his wife Poro Clark Bekederemo; *e* Warri Government College and the University of Ibadan (BA in English, 1960); Parvin Fellow, Princeton, 1962–63; *m* Ebunoluwa Odutola; was formerly a journalist.

Since 1964 member of English department and currently Professor of English, University of Lagos, Nigeria; Professor Clark's writings include poetry, criticism and a number of plays, including Song of a Goat, produced Ibadan 1961, London 1965; The Masquerade, 1965; The Raft, 1966; Ozidi, 1966.

Address: University of Lagos, Lagos, Nigeria.

CLARK, John Richard, Director, National Institute of Dramatic Art, Sydney, Australia
b Hobart, Tasmania, 30 Oct 1932; *s* of James Rowland Purcell Clark and his wife Linda Helen (Knight); *e* The Hutchins School, Hobart, University of Tasmania (BA Hons,

MA), UCLA (MA); *m* Henrietta Hartley. Formerly a schoolteacher in London and Hobart.

His first production was Death of a Salesman, for Hobart Repertory Theatre, Apr 1959; for the Jane Street Theatre directed The Rise and Fall of Boronia Avenue, 1969; King Edward, 1971; Don's Party, 1972; for the Old Tote Theatre Company has directed The Bald Prima Donna, The Fire Raisers, 1963; Who's Afraid of Virginia Woolf?, 1964; Entertaining Mr Sloane, The Representative, 1965; The Homecoming, 1967; Childermas, 1968; has directed over twenty productions for the National Institute of Dramatic Art since 1960, including: The Merchant of Venice, 1974, The Country Wife, 1975, A Midsummer Night's Dream, 1976; Major Barbara, 1978; Artistic Advisor, Sydney Theatre Company, 1979, and directed The Caucasian Chalk Circle; directed the film Lagged, The Story of a Convict, 1968; member, Producers and Directors Guild of Australia; Chairman, New South Wales Government Advisory Council on Cultural Grants, 1976– .

Address: 41 Regent Street, Paddington, NSW 2021, Australia. *Tel:* 02-312 090.

CLARK, Peggy, lighting, scenic and costume designer
b Baltimore, Maryland, 30 Sept 1915; *d* of Professor Eliot Round Clark and his wife Eleanor (Linton); *e* Smith College (AB 1935) and Yale University (MFA 1938); *m* Lloyd R Kelley (dec).

Scenic designer at Green Mansions, Warrentown, NY, season 1938, and the Paper Mill Playhouse, Millburn, NJ, 1939; designed costumes for nine Broadway productions from The Girl from Wyoming, 1938, to The High Ground, 1951; sets and lighting for Gabrielle, 1941, Curtain Going Up, 1952, etc; lighting for more than 150 Broadway productions, 1949–1980, most recently Musical Chairs, 1980; also many national touring companies; lit 26 revivals, principally musicals, for NY City Center, 1957–66; also regular assignments for Los Angeles Civic Light Opera, 1952–66; Jones Beach summer musicals annually from 1961–73; Light Opera of Manhattan, 1976–78; has also lit ballets (including American Ballet Theatre, 1950–52) and industrial shows; has taught lighting design since 1965 at Lester Polakov's Studio and Forum of Stage Design, NY; at Smith College, 1967, 1969, and at Yale Drama School, 1969–70; has published a number of articles on lighting design; Fellow, USITT, March 1978.

Recreations: Watercolour painting, raising French bulldogs, sailing. *Address:* 36 Cranberry Street, Brooklyn, NY 11201.

CLEMENTS, Sir John (*cr* 1968), CBE, actor manager, and director
b London, 25 Apr 1910; *s* of Herbert William Clements and his wife Mary Elizabeth (Stevens); *e* St Paul's Schools and St John's College, Cambridge; *m* (1) Inga Maria Lillemor Ahlgren; (2) Kay Hammond.

Made his first appearance on the stage at the Lyric Theatre, Hammersmith, 1 Apr 1930, as Lucas Carey in Out of the Blue, subsequently appearing there as Jeremy in She Stoops to Conquer; Royalty, Dec 1930, played Hounslow in The Beaux' Stratagem; Little, Dec 1930, appeared in the revue, Caviare, and Feb 1931, played Vettore Capello in The Venetian; Gate, May 1931, Jokaanan in Salome; subsequently toured with Ben Greet's company, playing juvenile leading parts in Shakespearean repertory; Palladium, Dec 1932, played Jukes in Peter Pan; Cambridge, Mar 1933, Stephano in The Lady of Belmont; Arts, Apr 1933, Laertes in Hamlet (from the first quarto); Savoy, Sept 1933, Tony Cleeves in If Only Father . . .; Westminster, Apr 1934,

Ragnar Brovik in The Master Builder; Embassy, Sept 1934, Lucien in Napoleon; Gate, Nov 1934, Fyodor in Nichevo; in Dec 1935, founded the Intimate Theatre, Palmer's Green, and in the following year directed forty-two plays there, appearing in thirty-six leading parts; Strand (for 1930 Players), Feb 1937, played Heathcliff in Wuthering Heights; Intimate, May, 1937, wrote, directed and played the part of Malcolm in Young Society; Aug 1937, directed Yes and No, which was transferred to the Ambassadors', Oct 1937; Intimate, Dec 1937, played Hamlet; Feb 1938, Marshall in Only Yesterday, and Apr 1938, Elliot Pearson in Quiet is Best; Wyndham's, July 1939, Julian Entwhistle in Alien Corn; The Intimate Theatre was the first London Theatre to re-open after the outbreak of the War in Sept 1939, with French Without Tears; directed Wasn't It Odd, at the Intimate, June 1940; 1940–2, directed Saloon Bar, and The Outsider for ENSA and organized a special revue company to entertain Troops; at the Duchess, Mar 1942, played Tony Kenyon in Skylark; Globe, Apr 1943, Joe Dinmore in They Came to a City; Apollo, Nov 1944, Elyot Chase in the revival of Private Lives, which he also directed; he also organized special Sunday performances for the Troops; also directed Yes and No, Hay Fever, The Barretts of Wimpole Street, etc for ENSA; St James's, May 1946, under his own management appeared as the Earl of Warwick in The Kingmaker; St James's, July 1946, played Palamede in Marriage à la Mode, which he also directed; New, Dec 1947, with the Old Vic Company, played Dunois in St Joan; Jan 1948, Petruchio in The Taming of the Shrew, and Mar 1948, Caius Martius in Coriolanus; Lyric, July 1948, succeeded Robert Morley as Arnold Holt in Edward, My Son, which he played for nine months; returned to management at the Phoenix, May 1949, and appeared as Francis Archer in The Beaux' Stratagem, which he also directed, and which had a record run of over 500 performances; New, Feb 1951, presented and directed Man and Superman, playing the part of John Tanner; at the Princes, from June 1951, this production was given in its entirety at one performance each week, when in association with Esmé Percy he directed the Don Juan in Hell scene, playing Don Juan Tenorio; Criterion, Oct 1951, directed And This Was Odd; Duke of York's, Aug 1952, presented (with Anthony Vivian) and directed The Happy Marriage, which he adapted from Le Complexe de Philémon, and in which he appeared as Henry Mansell-Smith; St James's, Nov 1953, presented and directed Pygmalion, appearing as Prof Henry Higgins; Aldwych, Dec 1954, presented and directed The Little Glass Clock, and played the part of Armand; Saville, July 1955, presented The Shadow of Doubt, in which he played Arthur; in May 1955, he was appointed Advisor on Drama to Associated Rediffusion, Ltd, and contracted to present a number of television plays for this company; in July 1955, he joined the Board of Directors of the Saville Theatre, the management coming under his personal control, and presented the following plays, The Wild Duck, 1955; The Rivals (in which he played Sir Anthony Absolute), The Seagull, The Doctor's Dilemma, The Way of the World (in which he played Mirabell, and also directed), 1956; at the Piccadilly, Dec 1957, he co-presented and directed The Rape of the Belt, and played the part of Heracles; toured, Nov 1958, as Charles Yeyder in Gilt and Gingerbread, which he also presented, and in which he subsequently appeared at the Duke of York's, Apr 1959; Piccadilly, Oct 1959, co-presented The Marriage-Go-Round, in which he played Paul Delville; Duke of York's, June 1960, directed Will You Walk a Little Faster?; Phoenix, Mar 1961, played Mr Zuss in JB; Strand, Sept 1961, Sir Lewis Eliot in The Affair; joined the Old Vic Company to make his first appearance in New York at The City Center, Feb 1961, in the title-part of Macbeth, and subsequently as the Earl of Warwick in Saint Joan; Haymarket, London, Nov 1962, played Colin Elliot in The Tulip Tree; Savoy, May 1963, co-presented, directed, and played Paul Jago MA, in The Masters; Lyric, Oct 1964, played Edward Moulton-Barrett in the musical Robert and Elizabeth; Dec 1965, appointed Director of Chichester Festival Theatre where he presented the yearly season of plays (until 1973); 1966 season: appeared as the General in The Fighting Cock and in the title-rôle in Macbeth; 1967: directed The Farmer's Wife and Heartbreak House, also playing Captain Shotover in the latter production; 1968; Prospero in The Tempest; 1969; played Colonel Lukyn in The Magistrate (also directed), and Antony in Antony and Cleopatra; 1970; directed Arms and the Man and The Proposal; 1971; Antoine in Dear Antoine, also directing The Rivals, in which he played Sir Anthony Absolute; 1972; directed and played Sir Ralph Bloomfield Bonnington in The Doctor's Dilemma; 1973, played Antonio di San Floura in The Director of the Opera, also directing Dandy Dick; Christmas 1973, played Long John Silver in his adaptation (with Peter Coe) of Treasure Island; the following productions re-opened in the West End after their Chichester season: Duke of York's, Oct 1966, The Fighting Cock; Lyric, Nov 1967, Heartbreak House; Cambridge, Sept 1969, The Magistrate (which he also co-presented); Piccadilly, Oct 1970, Vivat! Vivat Regina (co-presented); Piccadilly, Nov 1971, Dear Antoine; Garrick, Oct 1973, Dandy Dick; for the Oxford Festival, Sept 1974, directed Saint Joan; Haymarket, Mar 1975, directed and played R J Selby in The Case In Question; Arnaud, Guildford, Mar 1976, James Fraser in The First Mrs Fraser; Chichester, 1977 season, directed Waters of the Moon; Plymouth, NY, Nov 1977, Antonio Querini in The Merchant; Chichester, 1979, General Burgoyne in The Devil's Disciple and Canon Chasuble in The Importance of Being Earnest; entered films 1934, and has appeared in many notable films, including Things To Come, Knight Without Armour, The Divine Spark, South Riding, Four Feathers, Convoy, Ships With Wings, They Came to a City, The Silent Enemy, etc; Vice-President of British Actors Equity, 1950–9; received the CBE in 1956 Birthday Honours; knighted, 1968.

Club: Garrick. *Address:* 7 Royal Crescent, Brighton, Sussex.

CLURMAN, Harold, director, manager, author, critic, lecturer

b New York City, 18 Sept 1901; *s* of Samuel Michael Clurman and his wife Bertha (Saphir); *e* Columbia University, NY, and Sorbonne, Paris, as well as Théâtre du Vieux-Colombier, under Jacques Copeau; studied direction with Richard Boleslavsky; *m* (1) Stella Adler (mar dis); (2) Juleen Compton.

His first connection with the theatre was at the Greenwich Village Playhouse in 1924, where he worked with Kenneth McGowan, Robert Edmond Jones, and Eugene O'Neill; joined the Theatre Guild in 1925, as assistant stage-manager, and in 1926 he appeared in small parts in The Goat Song, The Chief Thing, Juarez and Maximilian, etc; from 1929–31, was engaged as play-reader to the Guild; in 1931, founded the Group Theatre, of which he was managing director; many notable plays were produced under his management, including Night over Taos, The House of Connelly, 1931, Success Story, Men in White, Awake and Sing, Johny Johnson, Golden Boy, Waiting for Lefty, Rocket to the Moon, etc; staged Beggars Are Coming to Town, 1945; with Elia Kazan, presented Truckline Cafe, 1946; co-produced All My Sons, 1947; directed The Whole World Over, 1947; The Young and Fair, 1948; Montserrat, Tel-Aviv, Israel, 1949; The Member

of the Wedding; The Bird Cage, 1950; The Autumn Garden, 1951; Desire Under the Elms, The Time of the Cuckoo, 1952; The Emperor's Clothes, The Ladies of the Corridor, 1953; Mademoiselle Colombe, 1954; Bus Stop, Pipe Dream, Tiger at the Gates (London), 1955; Waltz of the Toreadors, Orpheus Descending, 1957; The Day the Money Stopped, A Touch of the Poet, The Cold Wind and the Warm, 1958; Heartbreak House, Sweet Love Remember'd, 1959; Jeannette, 1960; A Shot in the Dark, 1961; Natural Affection (Phoenix, Arizona), Judith (London), 1962; A Shot in the Dark (London), 1963; Incident at Vichy, 1964; Where's Daddy?, 1966; Uncle Vanya, 1969, for the Mark Taper Forum, Los Angeles; in 1945 published The Fervent Years—The Story of the Group Theatre, Lies Like Truth: Theatre Essays and Reviews, 1958, On Directing, 1973, All People Are Famous, The Divine Pastime: Theatre Essays, 1974; Ibsen, 1977; is a noted critic for *The Nation, New Republic* (1949–53), *New York* (*New York World Journal Tribune* magazine supplement), guest critic for the London *Observer* (1959–63), etc; Visiting Professor in the Theatre, Graduate Division, Hunter College, NY, 1967; since 1954 has conducted classes for actors; Chevalier of the Legion of Honour, France, 1956; served as Executive Consultant for the Repertory Theater of Lincoln Center for the Performing Arts, 1963–4.
Address: 205 West 57th Street, New York, NY.

COATES, Carolyn, actress
b Oklahoma City, Okla, 29 Apr; *d* of Glenn Clinton Coates and his wife Jessica Amanda (Owen); *e* University of California at Los Angeles; *m* James Noble; prepared for the stage with Lee Strasberg and with Paul Curtis of the American Mime Theatre, of which she was also a member.
First appeared on the stage at the Children's Theatre, Santa Monica, Calif, spring 1939, as Cinderella in A Modern Cinderella; first appeared in New York at the Gramercy Arts, Apr 1959, as Miss Jessel in The Innocents; for the national tour of Sweet Bird of Youth, 1960, was stand-by for Geraldine Page; Circle in the Square, NY, June 1961, took over the part of Madame Irma in The Balcony; same theatre, 1964, took over from Mildred Dunnock as Hecuba in The Trojan Women, and played in this part for eighteen months; joined the Lincoln Center Repertory Theater and, at the Vivain Beaumont, Dec 1965, played Miss Alithea in The Country Wife; Feb 1966, Johanna in The Condemned of Altona; Mar 1966, various roles in The Caucasian Chalk Circle; at Williamstown, Mass, played in stock engagements as Madame Arkadina in The Seagull and Madame Ranevskaya in The Cherry Orchard, 1965–6; Gramercy Arts, NY, Oct 1966, played The Woman in A Whitman Portrait; Cherry Lane, May 1967, Helen Radamacher in The Party on Greenwich Avenue; Studio Arena, Buffalo, NY, 1967, Agnes in A Delicate Balance; Theatre de Lys, Dec 1967, Elmira Ruggles in The Club Bedroom; Studio Theatre, for the Theatre Company of Boston, Mass, Mar 1968, the title-role in Phaedra; Billy Rose, Oct 1968, the Second Nurse in The Death of Bessie Smith and Mrs Barker in The American Dream; Studio Arena, Buffalo, Nov 1968, Elinor in The Lion in Winter; Longacre, NY, Jan 1969, Lorna in Fire!; made her London début on 17 Apr 1969, at the Open Space, as The Woman in A Whitman Portrait; returned to NY and, at the Martinique, Oct 1969, played Agnes in A Scent of Flowers; Forum, Jan 1970, for the Lincoln Center Repertory, Ophelia Beans, Dirty Gertie, and Nicotine Flightpath in The Disintegration of James Cherry; Berkshire Theatre Festival, Stockbridge, Mass, June 1970, Marge in Other People; New, NY, 1971, took over as Beatrice in The Effect of Gamma Rays on

Man-in-the-Moon Marigolds; Cincinnati Playhouse, Ohio, 1973, played Agnes in A Delicate Balance, Mary Tyrone in Long Day's Journey into Night, and Kate in Old Times; St Clement's Church, NY, Mar 1974, Aimee Semple McPherson in Alive and Well in Argentina; Indianapolis, Indiana, Repertory Company, Nov 1974, Regina in The Little Foxes; Long Wharf, New Haven, Conn, May 1975, Queen Margaret in Richard III; Coconut Grove Playhouse, Fla, 1975 Hester in Equus; Arena Stage, Washington, DC, 1976, Hesione Hushabye in Heartbreak House; Long Wharf, Nov 1976, Constance in The Autumn Garden; Walnut, Philadelphia, 1977, played Louise in Five Finger Exercise, Jan, and Ruth in Blithe Spirit, Feb; Manhattan Theatre Club, May 1977, Mrs Eastman-Cuevas in In the Summerhouse; Playhouse in the Park, Philadelphia, 1977, Hester in Equus; McCarter, Princeton, Dec 1977, appeared in three plays by Thornton Wilder; Playmakers Repertory, N Carolina, 1978, Gertrude in Hamlet; Studio Arena, Buffalo, Mar 1978, appeared in Coward in Two Keys; Parker Playhouse, Ft Lauderdale, Fla, 1978, Myra in Deathtrap; has played in six seasons at the O'Neill Playwrights Conference, Waterford, Conn; first appeared in films in The Hustler, 1961, and has since appeared in the film of Gamma Rays, 1972; first appeared on television in 1957 as a mime, recent appearances include *Knotts Landing* and *Dallas.*
Favourite parts: Hecuba and Agnes in A Delicate Balance. *Recreations:* Bicycling and reading. *Address:* 928 6th Street, Santa Monica, Calif 90403.

COCA, Imogene, actress
b Philadelphia, Pa, 18 Nov; *d* of Joseph Coca and his wife Sadie (Brady); *m* (1) Robert Burton (dec); (2) King Donovan.
First appeared on the stage in vaudeville as a dancer at the age of nine; later became a dancer and made her Broadway legitimate début at the National, 5 Oct 1925, as a Chorus Girl in When You Smile; toured, including an engagement at Werba's Theatre, Brooklyn, 1926, as Jan in Bubbling Over; appeared in vaudeville in Snow and Columbus and at the Palace, New York, 1927; Guild, June 1930, appeared in the revue Garrick Gaieties, and Oct 1930, in another edition of Garrick Gaieties; George M Cohan, July 1931, appeared in Shoot the Works; Imperial, Sept 1932, appeared in the revue Flying Colors; toured in vaudeville again then returned to NY and at the Fulton, Mar 1934, appeared in the revue New Faces of 1934; Playhouse, Dec 1934, appeared in the revue Fools Rush In; Vanderbilt, May 1936, appeared in New Faces of 1936; played in stock in Calling All Men, Spring Dance, etc, 1936–9; Ambassador, Sept 1939, played in Straw Hat Revue; toured, 1940, in A Night at the Folies Bergere; Majestic, Dec 1940, appeared in the revue All in Fun; Ziegfeld, June 1945, in the revue Concert Varieties; stock tour, 1948, played Addie in Happy Birthday; State Fair Music Hall, Dallas, Texas, Aug 1954, played Ruth in Wonderful Town; Plymouth, June 1956, took over from Claudette Colbert as Jessica in Janus; toured, 1957, as Essie in The Great Sebastians; Belasco, Oct 1958, Mimsy in The Girls in 509; toured in this last part in 1959; stock, 1960, Agnes in The Fourposter; toured, 1960–1, as Princess Winnifred in Once upon a Mattress; toured, 1961–2, in the revue A Thurber Carnival; Pasadena Playhouse, Calif, Sept 1962, the Queen in Under the Sycamore Tree; stock tour, 1962, Ella Peterson in Bells Are Ringing; toured, 1967, as Ellen Manville in Luv; Repertory Theatre, St Louis, 1969, played in You Can't Take It with You; Philadelphia Drama Guild, 1972, Mrs Malaprop in The Rivals; Arlington Park, Chicago, Aug 1973, Edna Edison in The Prisoner of Second Avenue, then toured in this

part Oct 1973–Apr 1974; Arlington Park, Ill, Oct 1974, played in Double Take; cabaret tour with Sid Caesar, 1977; St James, Feb 1978, Letitia Primrose in On the Twentieth Century, following a tour; has played in dinner theatres, often with her husband, in Send Me No Flowers, The Fourposter, The Solid Gold Cadillac, etc; first appeared in films in Bashful Ballerina, 1937, and has since played in Under the Yum-Yum Tree, Ten from Your Show of Shows, 1973, etc; first appeared on television on the *Admiral Broadway Revue*, 1949, then as a regular on *Your Show of Shows*, 1950–4, *Grindl*, 1963–4, and many other variety and dramatic programs; has appeared frequently in cabaret since 1926.

Address: Actors Equity Association, 165 West 46th Street, New York, NY 10036.

COCO, James, actor

b New York City, 21 Mar 1929; *s* of Feliche Coco and his wife Ida (Detestes); *e* Evander Childs High School; formerly a toy salesman, night clerk, waiter, dishwasher, about 100 others; studied for the stage with Uta Hagen at the Berghof Studio.

First appeared on the stage as a child playing Old King Cole in a Clare Tree Majors Children's Theatre production; first appeared in NY at the Henry Miller's, 11 Apr 1957, when he played Tabu in Hotel Paradiso; toured US, 1957–8, as Dr Waldo and Mr Shurr in the Constance Bennett version of Auntie Mame; Madison Avenue Playhouse, NY, Oct 1960, appeared in the revue Darwin's Theories; East End, Feb 1961, Tausch in The Moon in the Yellow River; Longacre, Oct 1961, the Doctor in Everybody Loves Opal; Ambassador, Jan 1962, Mr Hammidullah in A Passage to India; toured, 1962–3, as Morestan in A Shot in the Dark; Lunt-Fontanne, Nov 1963, O'Casey in Arturo Ui; East End, Feb 1964, Leslie Edwards in The Sponge Room, and Stanley Mintey in Squat Betty; Astor Place Playhouse, Oct 1964, The First in That 5 AM Jazz; Cherry Lane, Mar 1965, Roger Varnum in Lovey; Broadway, Nov 1965, A Sewerman in The Devils; ANTA Washington Sq, 1966, took over the role of the Barber in Man of La Mancha; Helen Hayes, Jan 1967, Inspector Rogers in The Astrakhan Coat; Cherry Lane, Oct 1967, Leo in Basement and Max in Fragments in the double-bill called Fragments; Billy Rose, Mar 1968, Lee in Here's Where I Belong; Gramercy Arts, Nov 1968, Window Washer in Witness; Greenwich Mews, Feb 1969, Marion Cheever in Next; Mark Taper Forum, Los Angeles, Oct 1969, again played Marion Cheever in Next; Eugene O'Neill, Dec 1969, Barney Cashman in Last of the Red Hot Lovers, and continued in this part for 18 months; Astor Place, Mar 1977, title-rôle in The Transfiguration of Benno Blimpie (one-act); same theatre, Dec 1977, directed Joe Masiell Not at the Palace; first entered films in Ensign Pulver, 1963, and has since appeared in Generation, End of the Road, A New Leaf, The Strawberry Statement, Man of La Mancha, Such Good Friends, Murder by Death, Wholly Moses (1980), etc; has appeared more than 25 times on the *Johnny Carson Show* on television, as well as in the series *Calucci's Department*, 1974, and *The Dumplings*, 1976, etc.

Favourite parts: Marion Cheever and Barney Cashman
Address: c/o APA, 120 West 57th Street, New York, NY 10019. *Tel:* 582 1500.

CODRON, Michael, manager and producer

b London, 8 June 1930; *s* of Isaac Codron and his wife, Lily (Morgenstern); *e* St Paul's School and Worcester College, Oxford; has presented or co-presented the following productions: Ring for Catty, 1956; A Month of Sundays, Share My Lettuce, 1957; Breath of Spring, Little Eyolf, The Dock Brief and What Shall We Tell Caroline?, The Birthday Party,

Honour Bright, Valmouth, 1958; Fool's Paradise, How Say You?, Pieces of Eight, 1959; The Wrong Side of the Park, The Caretaker, The Golden Touch, 1960; Three (triple bill), Stop It, Whoever You Are, One Over the Eight, The Tenth Man, Under Milkwood, Ducks and Lovers, Big Soft Nellie, 1961; Two Stars for Comfort, Everything in the Garden, Infanticide in the House of Fred Ginger, Rattle of a Simple Man, Doctors of Philosophy, End of Day, A Cheap Bunch of Nice Flowers, Cindy Ella, or I Gotta Shoe, 3 At Nine, 1962; An Evening of British Rubbish, Next Time I'll Sing To You, Licence to Murder, Kelly's Eye, Private Lives, The Lover and The Dwarfs (double-bill), Out of the Crocodile, Cockade, Cider With Rosie, 1963; Poor Bitos, The Brontës (recital), The Cloud, Hedda Gabler, Hang Down Your Head and Die, The Formation Dancers, The Subtopians, Entertaining Mr Sloane, See How They Run, A Scent of Flowers, Busybody, 1964; Travelling Light, The Killing of Sister George, Ride a Cock Horse, Anyone for England?, Entertaining Mr Sloane (New York), 1965; A Lily in Little India, Little Malcolm and His Struggle Against the Eunuchs, The Anniversary, There's a Girl in My Soup, When Did You Last See My Mother?, Public and Confidential, A Present from the Past, Big Bad Mouse, Four Degrees Over, 1966; The Judge, The Flip Side, Country Dance, Fill the Stage with Happy Hours, Wise Child, There's a Girl in My Soup (NY), The Boy Friend, Fanghorn, Everything in the Garden (NY), 1967; Not Now, Darling, Mrs Mouse Are You Within?, The Real Inspector Hound and The Audition (double bill), They Don't Grow on Trees, The Servant of Two Masters, The Flip Side (NY), 1968; The Death and Resurrection of Mr Roche, There'll Be Some Changes Made, The Bandwagon, 1969; It's a Two Foot Six Inches Above the Ground World, Girlfriend, The Contractor, Slag, The Two of Us, The Philanthropist, Not Now, Darling (NY), 1970; A Game Called Arthur, The Philanthropist (NY), The Foursome, Butley, A Voyage Round My Father, Slag, The Changing Room, 1971; Siege, Veterans, Me Times Me, Time and Time Again, Crown Matrimonial, Owners, My Fat Friend, Butley (NY), 1972; Collaborators, Savages, Habeas Corpus, The Sea, Absurd Person Singular, Crown Matrimonial (NY), 1973; Knuckle, Flowers, My Fat Friend (NY), The Golden Pathway Annual, The Norman Conquests, John, Paul, George, Ringo . . . and Bert, Absurd Person Singular (NY), 1974; A Family and a Fortune, Alphabetical Order, A Far Better Husband (tour), Ashes, Absent Friends, Otherwise Engaged, The Norman Conquests (USA), Habeas Corpus (USA), Stripwell, 1975; Treats, Funny Peculiar, Donkey's Years, Confusions, Teeth 'n' Smiles, Yahoo, 1976; Otherwise Engaged, Dusa, Fish, Stas and Vi, Just Between Ourselves, Oh Mr Porter, The Bells of Hell, Breezeblock Park, The Old Country, 1977; The Rear Column, Ten Times Table, The Homecoming, Alice's Boys, The Unvarnished Truth, Night and Day, 1978; Joking Apart, Stage Struck, Tishoo, Night and Day (NY), 1979.

Address: 117 Regent Street, London, W1. *Tel:* 01–437 3577.

COE, Peter, director

b London, 18 Apr 1929; *s* of Leonard Coe and his wife Gladys (Frith); *e* Latymer Upper School, College of St Mark and St John, and the London Academy of Music and Dramatic Art; *m* (1) Maria Caday (mar dis); (2) Tsai Chin (mar dis); (3) Suzanne Fuller (mar dis); (4) Ingeborg.

First Resident Director of London's Mermaid Theatre opened in May 1959; has since directed the following: Lock Up Your Daughters, The World of Suzie Wong, Treasure Island, Twelfth Night (India), 1959; Oliver! 1960; The Mira-

cle Worker, Julius Caesar (Israel), Oliver! (Australia), 1961; Castle in Sweden, Macbeth (Canada), Oliver! (USA), 1962; The Love of Three Oranges (Opera), Pickwick, The Rehearsal (USA), Next Time I'll Sing To You (USA), 1963; Caligula, In White America, Golden Boy (USA), 1964; The Angel of Fire (Opera), Pickwick (USA), Oliver! (Israel), 1965; The King's Mare, In the Matter of J Robert Oppenheimer, The Silence of Lee Harvey Oswald, On A Clear Day You Can See Forever (USA), 1966; Ernani (Opera), World War 2½, The Four Musketeers, An Italian Straw Hat (Chichester), 1967; The Skin of Our Teeth (Chichester), 1968; The Caucasian Chalk Circle (Chichester), 1969; A Doll's House, Peer Gynt (Chichester), The Hero (Edinburgh), Kiss Me Kate (Sadler's Wells Opera), 1970; Six (USA), Fish Out Of Water, The Marquise, Woman of the Dunes (USA: also wrote), 1971; The Black Macbeth, Tom Brown's Schooldays, Hamlet, 1972; Games, Storytheatre (India: also wrote), Decameron '73, Treasure Island (Chichester: also co-adaptor), 1973; Tonight We Improvise (Chichester), Candida (Vienna), The Trials of Oscar Wilde (Oxford: also devised), Poets to the People, 1974; Kingdom of Earth (Vienna), Romeo and Jeannette (Guildford), The Exorcism, 1975; Artistic Director, Bubble Theatre, 1975, for which he wrote and directed Cages, Storytheatre, The Great Exhibition and The Trial of Marie Stopes; Lucy Crown (also wrote), Ride! Ride!, Richard III (Denmark), Macbeth (Arts Council Tour), 1976; Tonight We Improvise (India), Jericho, Romeo and Juliet (Arts Council Tour), 1977; appointed Artistic Director, Citadel Theatre, Edmonton, Alberta, 1978; directed Flowers for Algernon (Queen's), 1979; Mister Lincoln (Morosco), 1980; directed his first film, Lock Up Your Daughters, 1968.
Address: The Old Barn, East Clandon, Surrey.

COFFEY, Denise, actress, director and writer
b Aldershot, Hants, 12 Dec 1936; *d* of Denis Christopher Coffey and his wife Dorothy (Malcolm); trained for the stage at the Glasgow College of Drama.

Made her debut at the Opera House, Dunfermline, April 1954, as various apparitions in Macbeth; Gateway, Edinburgh, 1962, played Mrs Malaprop in The Rivals; first London appearance, Mermaid, Dec 1962, as a Secretary in Rockets in Ursa Major; Aldwych, July 1963, played Mrs Coaxer in the RSC production of The Beggar's Opera; played a number of roles in classical revivals at the Mermaid, April 1964 to Sept 1965, including Cicely Bumtrinket in The Shoemaker's Holiday and Deodata in Lazarus, 1964; Dina in Right You Are, Phaedra in Four Thousand Brass Halfpennies and Fanny in Fanny's First Play, 1965; Nov 1964, at the Savoy, Edith in High Spirits; Edinburgh Festival, Aug 1967, the Pupil in The Lesson, and Hermia in A Midsummer Night's Dream transferring in the latter part to the Saville, Sept 1967; Mavis Pawson in Children's Day, Mermaid, Sept 1969, and Aurora Botterill in The Bandwagon, Oct; Royal Court, Dec 1972, played the Girl in A Sense of Detachment; joined the Young Vic Company, 1970, and played a major part in the company: as actress, her parts included Winnie in Happy Days, Bianca in The Taming of the Shrew, 1971; Beatrice in Much Ado about Nothing, 1973; Doll Common in The Alchemist, 1975; Ivy in If You're Glad I'll be Frank, 1972; as author of The Incredible Vanishing!!!!!, 1973, an adaptation from John Lennon, All Walks of Leg, 1975, Dreampeople and Skystop; as assistant to Frank Dunlop on a number productions, and director of her own The Incredible Vanishing!!!!!, 1973, Crete and Sergeant Pepper, 1974, Charley's Aunt, 1975 and 1976, Romeo and Juliet and The Importance of Being Earnest, 1977; finally as Associate

Director of the Young Vic Theatre, 1976–78; she also toured Europe and North America with the Company; she directed for Avon Touring Theatre, Bristol and the Theatre Upstairs; and since becoming a freelance, has directed for the Scottish Youth Theatre and the Neptune Theatre, Halifax, Nova Scotia; films, since 1960, include Georgy Girl, Far from the Madding Crowd and Sir Henry at Rawlinson End; first TV appearance 1959, since when she has played in series including her own Hold the Front Page, End of Part One, and Love Among the Artists.
Favourite parts: Cicely Bumtrinket, Aurora Botterill. *Recreations:* The sea, gardening, travel. *Address:* c/o Beryl Seton Agency, Suite 5, 1 Cranbourn Alley, Cranbourn Street, London WC2.

COGHILL, Prof Nevill, director and dramatic author
b Castletownshend, Co Cork, 19 April 1899; *e* Haileybury and Exeter College, Oxford; *m* Elspeth Nora (mar dis); fellow of Exeter College, 1925–57; Merton Professor of English Literature in the University of Oxford, 1957–66.

First stage production Samson Agonistes, 1930, in the gardens of Exeter College; between 1934 and 1966, directed many Shakespeare plays for OUDS and other university drama groups in Britain and the US; first London production, Jan 1945, A Midsummer Night's Dream at the Haymarket; Covent Garden, 1951, directed the opera Pilgrim's Progress; Playhouse, Oxford, 1966, directed Dr Faustus, later joint director of the film; wrote book (part) and lyrics of Canterbury Tales, London, 1968 and New York, 1969; Governor, Royal Shakespeare Theatre, 1956–; his publications include modern translations of Canterbury Tales and Troilus and Criseyde, Geoffrey Chaucer and Shakespeare's Professional Skills.

Recreations: Reading, writing, theatre and music. *Club:* Travellers. *Address:* Savran House, Aylburton, near Lydney, Glos. *Tel:* Lydney 2240.

COHEN, Alexander H, producer
b New York, NY, 24 July 1920; *s* of Alexander H Cohen and his wife Laura (Tarantous); *e* NY and Columbia Universities; *m* (1) Jocelyn Newmark (mar dis); (2) Hildy Parks.

Began his career as producer at Daly's, NY, Sept 1941, with Ghost for Sale, and then (in association with Shepherd Traube) at the Golden, NY, Dec 1941, presented Angel Street; has since produced or co-produced the following: Of V We Sing, They Should Have Stood in Bed, 1942; Bright Lights of 1944, 1943; The Duke in Darkness, 1944; Jenny Kissed Me, 1948; King Lear, 1950; Make A Wish, Courtin' Time, 1951; Be Your Age, 1953; The Magic and the Loss, 1954; The First Gentleman, 1957; Love Me Little, 1958; At the Drop of a Hat, 1959; An Evening with Mike Nichols and Elaine May, 1960; Impulse (O'Keefe Center, Toronto, Canada), An Evening with Yves Montand, Lena Horne in Her Nine O'clock Revue (US and Canadian tour), 1961; Beyond the Fringe, 1962; The School for Scandal, An Evening with Maurice Chevalier, Lorenzo, Sir John Gielgud in Ages of Man, *Karmon Israeli Dancers,* Man and Boy, 1963; Rugantino, Richard Burton as Hamlet, Comedy in Music (Victor Borge), 1964; Baker Street, Maurice Chevalier at 77, The Devils, 1965; Ivanov (NY), A Time for Singing, At the Drop of Another Hat, 1966; The Homecoming (Antoinette Perry 'Tony' Award), White Lies, Black Comedy, Little Murders, The Unknown Soldier and His Wife, Marlene Dietrich, Halfway up the Tree, Hellzapoppin (Montreal for *Expo* 67), 1967; Marlene Dietrich, 1968; Dear World, Home, 1970; Fun City, 6 Rms Riv Vu, 1972; Good Evening, 1973; Ulysses in Nighttown, Words and Music, Who's Who in Hell,

1974; Comedians, Hellzapoppin, 1976; in London, The Doctor's Dilemma, Man and Boy, 1963; The Roses Are Real, Season of Goodwill, 1964; Ivanov, 1965; You Never Can Tell, The Importance of Being Oscar, The Rivals, 1966; Halfway Up The Tree, The Merchant of Venice, 1967; Plaza Suite, The Price, Mixed Doubles, His, Hers, Theirs, 1969; Come As You Are, The Happy Apple, Who Killed Santa Claus?, 1776, 1970; Applause, 1972; Harvey, 1975; Anna Christie, 1977; I Remember Mama, 1979; between 1953–6 produced a number of Theatre Tours; in 1959 founded the Nine O'Clock Theatre; received the Sam S. Shubert Award, 1962–3 season; since 1967 has produced the annual television coverage of the Tony Awards, presented live from a New York Theatre; other TV productions include A World of Love for UNICEF; CBS: On the Air (A Celebration of 50 Years); and the 1978 Emmy Awards; Vice-President and Member of Board of Governors, League of New York Theatres and Producers; Director, Independent Booking Office; Vice-President and Trustee, Actors' Fund of America; Member, Society of West End Theatre.

Clubs: Players, City Athletic, and Friars. *Address:* 225 West 44th Street, New York, NY 10036; and 8 Sloane Street, London SW1. *Tel:* 757–1200 (NY), 245–9683 (London).

COLBERT, Claudette (*née* Lily Chauchoin), actress
b Paris, France, 13 Sept 1905; *d* of Georges Chauchoin and his wife Jeanne (Loew); *m* (1) Norman Foster (mar dis); (2) Dr Joel J Pressman (dec).

Made her first appearance on the stage at the Frazee Theatre, New York, Dec 1923, as Sybil Blake in The Wild Westcotts; toured, 1924, in The Marionette Man, We've Got to Have Money, The Cat Came Back; during 1925, toured in the all-star cast of Leah Kleschna, and also in High Stakes; Ritz, NY, Aug 1925, played Ginette in A Kiss in the Taxi, for a year; Eltinge, Aug 1926, Peggy Murdock in The Ghost Train; Century, Nov 1926, played Pilgrim in The Pearl of Great Price; Biltmore, Jan 1927, Lou in The Barker; Republic, Oct 1927, Sylvia Bainbridge in The Mulberry Bush; Little, Feb 1928, Carlotta D'Astradente in La Gringa; Cosmopolitan, Mar 1928, Aggie Lynch in Within the Law; made her first appearance on the London stage at the Playhouse, May 1928, as Lou in The Barker; Ambassador, NY, Sept 1928, played Patricia Mason in Fast Life; Biltmore, Nov 1928, Jill O'Dare in Tin Pan Alley; Martin Beck, Feb 1929, Ada Fife in Dynamo; Vanderbilt, NY, Sept 1929, played Nanette Dodge Kosloff in See Naples and Die; following a long and successful career in films, she re-appeared on the stage at Westport Country Playhouse, summer 1951, in Island Fling; re-appeared on the NY stage at the Plymouth, Apr 1956, when she took over the part of Jessica in Janus, from Margaret Sullavan; at the same theatre, Oct 1958, played Content Lowell in Marriage-Go-Round; Booth, Jan 1961, played Julia Ryan in Jake, Julia, and Uncle Joe; Ethel Barrymore, Sept 1963, Hedda Rankin in The Irregular Verb to Love; Royal Ponciana Playhouse, Palm Beach, Feb 1965, played Linda Marshall in Diplomatic Relations; New Locust, Philadelphia, 1974, Alix Carpenter in A Community of Two, and subsequently toured; toured, 1975, in Marriage-Go-Round; Biltmore, NY, Dec 1978, Lady Townsend in The Kingfisher, touring in the same role, 1979; among her many notable films are The Hole in the Wall (1929), The Sign of the Cross (1932), It Happened One Night (Academy Award), Imitation of Life, Cleopatra (all 1934), Parrish (1961) etc; has appeared on television in The Royal Family, The Guardsman, Blithe Spirit, etc.

Address: Bellerive, St Peter, Barbados, West Indies.

COLE, George, actor
b London, 22 Apr 1925; *s* of George Cole and his wife

Florence (Smith); *e* at Morden Council School; *m* Penelope Morrell.

Made his first appearance on the stage at the Grand, Blackpool, Sept 1939, in White Horse Inn; Prince of Wales's, Birmingham, June 1940, Ronald in Cottage to Let; first appeared in London, at Wyndham's, 31 July 1940, in the same part, in which he subsequently toured, and again played at Wyndham's, May 1941; at the New, Feb 1942, played Percy King in Goodnight Children; toured, 1942, in Old Master; Apollo, Aug 1942, played Percy in Flare Path; Playhouse, Oct 1943, Cohen in Mr Bolfry; Phoenix, July 1947, Dr Johnson in Dr Angelus; Westminster, Nov 1948, appeared as Walter Anderson in The Anatomist; Garrick, Mar 1950, Tom Donnelly in Mr Gillie; Lyric, Hammersmith, Sept 1951, appeared as Tegeus–Chromis in A Phoenix Too Frequent, and Hoel in Thor, With Angels; Citizens' Theatre, Glasgow, Oct 1952, played Joe Mascara in The Blaikie Charivari; Duchess, Mar 1955, Adam in Misery Me; Aldwych, Aug 1956, Cohen in a revival of Mr Bolfry; Strand, Apr 1958, Phanocles in The Brass Butterfly; St Martin's, Jan 1961, co-presented and played Morgan in The Bargain; Royal Court, Dec 1962, Leslie Edwards in The Sponge Room, and Stanley Mintey in Squat Betty (double-bill); toured, Nov 1963, as Toby Pilgrim in The Yes-Yes-Yes Man; New Arts, Feb, 1964, George Tesman in Hedda Gabler, transferring with the production to the St Martin's, Mar 1964; St Martin's, May 1965, played Mark in A Public Mischief; Strand, Sept 1965, Sergeant Fielding in Too True to Be Good; New Arts, July 1966, played Toby Pilgrim in The Waiting Game; Royal Court, Apr 1967, Andrey in The Three Sisters; Hampstead Theatre Club, July 1968, Ballad in The Ghost and Butler in No Principals, in the double bill, Doubtful Haunts; toured, Apr 1969, as Dr Peter Estriss in The Passionate Husband; Thorndike, Leatherhead, Oct 1969, played Mr Mortymer and Mr Pollard in There Was An Old Woman; New, Bromley, 1970, Victor Cadwallader in The Man Most Likely To . . .; May Fair, Mar 1971, took over Philip in The Philanthropist, a role which he played for two years, including a tour; Hampstead, Oct 1973, Richard in Country Life; New London, Dec 1974, appeared in Déjà Revue; Arnaud, Guildford, and tour, Feb 1976, Andrew Creed in Motive; Savoy, July 1976, Willoughby Pink in Banana Ridge; Arnaud, Nov 1978, Andreas Capodistriou/Inspector Fathom in The Case of the Oily Levantine; Hong Kong, 1978, appeared in Something's Afoot; Open Space, Feb 1979, Mr Bates in Brimstone and Treacle; Greenwich, Jan 1980, Skinner in Liberty Hall; first appeared in films, 1941, in Cottage to Let; has since appeared in numerous films; his many TV appearances include the series A Man of Our Times and, recently, Don't Forget to Write, and Minder.

Address: 7 West Eaton Place Mews, London, SW1.

COLEMAN, Cy, composer
As a child appeared as a concert pianist; has composed the scores for Wildcat, 1960; Little Me, 1962; Sweet Charity, 1966; Seesaw, 1973; I Love My Wife, 1977; On The Twentieth Century, 1978; Barnum, 1980; his film scores include Spartacus, 1960, Father Goose, Sweet Charity etc; work for TV includes specials for Shirley Maclaine; awards include a Tony and three Emmys; President, Notable Music Company.

Address: c/o ASCAP, 1 Lincoln Plaza, New York, NY 10023.

COLERIDGE, Sylvia, actress
b Darjeeling, India, 10 Dec 1909; *d* of John Francis Stanhope Duke Coleridge, and his wife Marjorie Mary (Kemball-Cooke); *e* Runton Hill, West Runton, Norfolk; *m* Albert George Fiddes-Watt.

First appeared on the stage at the Grand Theatre, Leeds, 9 May 1932, as Peggy Hughes in Your Money or Your Wife; first appearance in London, at the Kingsway Theatre, 19 Oct 1932, in two small parts in Versailles; during 1933–4, in repertory at the Playhouse, Oxford, etc; Globe, June 1935, Judith Oldham in Grief Goes Over; Embassy, Sept 1935, Fiammetta in The House of Borgia; Gate, Oct 1935, Elsa in Anatol; Embassy, Nov 1935; Maisie Turnpit in Murder Gang; Westminster, Dec 1935, Lucrezia in The Impressario from Smyrna; Gate, Mar 1936, Calonice in Lysistrata; Strand, May 1936, Annie in Aren't Men Beasts!; Old Vic, Sept–Oct 1937, Clara Eynsford-Hill in Pygmalion, and Mariana in Measure for Measure; Vaudeville, Nov 1937, Regina in Ghosts; Old Vic, Mar 1938, Nurse Appleby in The King of Nowhere; Phoenix, May 1938, Mrs Devereux in Married Unanimously; Duke of York's, Nov 1938, Margaret Roper in Traitor's Gate; Winter Garden, May 1939, Lady Macduff in Macbeth; Open Air Theatre, June 1939, Ursula in Much Ado About Nothing and Thaïsa in Pericles; appeared at the Malvern Festival, Aug 1939; Torch, Dec 1939, played Bianca in The Venetian, and again at the St Martin's, Feb 1940; at the Malvern Festival, Aug 1949, appeared as Queen Jemima in The Apple Cart, Mrs Secondborn in Buoyant Billions, etc; Princes, Oct 1949, again played Mrs Secondborn in Buoyant Billions; toured, Aug 1950, as Mrs Penniman in The Heiress, and Isabel Brocken in The Foolish Gentlewoman; Lyric, Hammersmith, Mar 1952, and Criterion, Apr 1952, Clara Hibbert in The Vortex; Phoenix, Sept 1952, Octavia in Quadrille; Arts, Apr 1954, Armande Mangebois in The Enchanted; Playhouse, Oxford, Dec 1954, played Grandmother in Listen to the Wind; Duke of York's, May 1956, played Iris in The House by the Lake; Old Vic Company, Sept 1960–May 1962, played the following parts: Paulina in The Seagull, Lady Capulet in Romeo and Juliet, 1960; Mistress Quickly in Henry IV part I, Lady Falconbridge in King John, Covetousness in Dr Faustus, Minnie in Mourning Becomes Electra, Witch and Gentlewoman in Macbeth, Duchess of York in Richard III, and Ceres in The Tempest; Savoy, Apr 1964, played Mrs Rankling in The Schoolmistress; Oxford Playhouse, Sept 1964, Mrs Amlet in The Confederacy; Arts, Cambridge, Nov 1964, Miss Prism in The Importance of Being Earnest; Citizens, Glasgow, 1964, Meg in The Birthday Party, and Kitty in The Circle; Mermaid, Feb 1965, Arina Pantelaymonovna in The Marriage Brokers; Arts, Cambridge, July 1965, played Miss Avery in Howard's End; LAMDA, Sept 1965, Granny in The City; Arts, Cambridge, Nov 1965, Mrs George in Getting Married; Hampstead Theatre Club, Jan 1966, played Madame La Tour in The Birdwatcher; Royal Court, Sept 1966, Mrs Carnock in Three Men for Colverton; Mermaid, Aug 1967, Lady Charlotte in The Fight for Barbara; Hampstead, Feb 1968, appeared as Rose in The Coffee Lace, in the double bill Little Boxes, transferring to the Duchess, Apr 1968; Mermaid, July 1971, Mrs Jaraby in The Old Boys; at Greenwich, played Anfisa in Three Sisters, Jan, and Maria Josefa in The House of Bernarda Alba, Mar 1973; Edinburgh Festival, Sept 1973, Mrs Argent in a monologue of that name, also Soho Poly, London, Oct; toured with the Prospect company, autumn 1974, as Mistress Quickly in Henry IV and V, Queen of France in Henry V; Royal Court, Jan 1975, Miss Forbes in Objections to Sex and Violence; Greenwich, July 1975, Countess in All's Well That Ends Well; Theatre Royal, Stratford E, Mar 1976, Mme Aigreville in Out of Practice; Olivier, Jan 1977, Helene in Tales from the Vienna Woods; has also broadcast and appeared on television, in *The Lotus Eaters, Henry VIII, Rebecca,* etc; first appeared in films, 1937, in Where's Sally?; later films include The Human Factor.

Favourite parts: Eliza in Pygmalion, Lady Kitty in The Circle, Amanda Wingfield in The Glass Menagerie. *Recreation:* Reading. *Address:* 7 Rowallan Road, London, SW6.

COLLIER, Patience (Rene Ritcher), actress
b London, 19 Aug 1910; d of Paul Ritcher and his wife, Eva (Spitzel); e Spaldings, Queen's Gate, St Monica's, Tadworth, and Villa St Monique, Auteuil, Paris; m H O J Collier, BA, PhD, MI Biol; studied for the stage at the Royal Academy of Dramatic Art, 1930–2, where she won Lady Tree's Elocution Award.

Made her first appearance on the stage at the Kingsway, Oct 1932, when she played five small parts in Komisarjevsky's production of Versailles; Cambridge, Oct 1932, appeared as Mrs Blount in Well Gentlemen; Haymarket, 1934, played the Italian Peasant in Josephine; Duke of York's, 1935, played the American wife in Roulette; after some years of playing leading parts in Repertory Theatres at Cambridge and Altrincham, she returned to London, Watergate Theatre, July 1950, to play Madame Zaros in The Velvet Moss; Lyric, Hammersmith, May 1954, played Charlotta Ivanovna in Sir John Gielgud's production of The Cherry Orchard; Lyric, May 1955, played Madame Parole in My Three Angels; during the Paul Scofield–Peter Brook season, Phoenix, Apr 1956, appeared as Maria in The Power and the Glory and June 1956, as Violet in a revival of The Family Reunion; Globe, Nov 1956, played Anya Pavlikov in Nude With Violin; Garrick, July 1958, appeared in the revue Living For Pleasure; toured, Oct 1959, as Swart Petry in The Sea Shell; Cort, New York, Sept 1960, played Miss Gilchrist in The Hostage; at the Mermaid, Aug 1961, played Putana in 'Tis Pity She's a Whore; joined the Royal Shakespeare Company 1961, and has since played the following parts at the Aldwych Theatre, and at the Royal Shakespeare, Stratford-on-Avon; Charlotta in The Cherry Orchard, 1961; Natella Abashwili in The Caucasian Chalk Circle, the Queen in Cymbeline, Regan in King Lear, Aemilia in The Comedy of Errors, 1962; Frau Lina Rose in The Physicists, Regan in King Lear (at the Théâtre des Nations, Paris), Mrs Diana Traipes in The Beggar's Opera, 1963; the Duchess of York in Richard II, Mistress Quickly in Henry IV parts I and II; Hostess and Alice in Henry V, 1964; Lady Harriet Boscoe in The Governor's Lady (Expeditions Two programme); Hostess and Alice in Henry V, Emma Takinainen in Squire Puntila and His Servant Matti, 1965; Anna Andreyevna in The Government Inspector, Eugenia in Tango, Frau Nomsen in The Meteor, Gratiana in The Revenger's Tragedy, 1966; became an Associate Artist of the Company, 1967; Cambridge, March 1967, played Serena in The Judge; returned to the Aldwych for the RSC's 1969–70 season in which she played Edna in A Delicate Balance, Dame Purecraft in Bartholomew Fair, Mrs Heegan in The Silver Tassie and the Duchess in The Revenger's Tragedy; Hampstead, Sept 1971, Bessie Berger in Awake and Sing; Aldwych (RSC), Jan 1972, The Nurse in All Over; Stratford E15, May 1972, Miss Gilchrist in The Hostage; Royal Court, Aug 1972, Sarah in The Old Ones; Greenwich, Mar 1973, La Poncia in The House of Bernarda Alba; Chichester Festival, July 1974, Anna in A Month in the Country; at the Old Vic (National Theatre), played Nurse Guinness in Heartbreak House, Feb 1975; Aldwych, 1976, for RSC, played Mrs Dudgeon in The Devil's Disciple and Avdotya in Ivanov; Olivier, 1978, Mother in Brand, Feb, and Charlotta in The Cherry Orchard, Oct; has also made over 2,000 broadcasts; entered films, 1968 and appearances include Every Home Should Have One, Perfect Friday, and The Countess Dracula.

Favourite parts: Charlotta in The Cherry Orchard, Alice in Henry V, and Lady Harriet Boscoe. *Recreations:* Home, going to the theatre. *Address:* 23 Campden Hill Road, London, W8 7DX. *Tel:* 01-937 5629.

COLLINS, Barry, playwright
b Halifax, Yorks, 21 Sept 1941; *e* Heath School, Halifax, and Queen's College, Oxford; *m* Anne Collins; formerly a teacher and journalist.

His first play, And Was Jerusalem Builded Here, was produced at Leeds Playhouse, 1972; subsequent plays are Beauty and the Beast (also Leeds), 1973; Judgement, 1974, produced at the National Theatre, 1975, 1977; The Strongest Man in the World, Nottingham, 1978; Toads, also Nottingham, 1979; Judgement, a one-character play, has been broadcast, and translated into ten languages; writing for TV includes The Lonely Man's Lover, 1974; The Witches of Pendle, 1976; The Hills of Heaven (serial), 1978.

Address: 1 Stafford Place, Halifax, West Yorkshire. *Tel:* 0422-66600.

COLLINS, Pauline, actress
b Exmouth, Devon, 3 Sept 1940; *d* of William Henry Collins and his wife Mary Honora (Callanan); *e* Convent of the Sacred Heart, Hammersmith, London; *m* John Alderton; trained for the stage at the Central School of Speech and Drama.

Made her debut at the Theatre Royal, Windsor, Sept 1962, as Sabina in A Gazelle in Park Lane; first London appearance, Prince of Wales, Aug 1965, as Lady Janet Wigton in Passion Flower Hotel; Royal Court, June 1967, Lou in The Erpingham Camp; Hampstead, July 1967, Nancy in The Happy Apple; Haymarket, Feb 1968, Cecily in The Importance of Being Earnest; Comedy, July 1969, Brenda Cooper in The Night I Chased the Women with an Eel; New, Jan 1970, Rosemary and Claire in Come as You Are, leaving the cast to play Nancy Gray in The Happy Apple when it opened at the Apollo, Mar 1970; Comedy, Jan 1974, played Judy in Judies; for the National Theatre, Old Vic, Aug 1975, Minnie Symperson in Engaged; Apollo, May 1976, appeared in Confusions; Royal Court, Feb 1978, Yeliena Ivanovna in The Bear; TV appearances, since 1962, include plays and series such as Thomas and Sarah.

Favourite part: Nancy Gray. *Recreation:* Writing. *Address:* c/o Nems Management Ltd, 29–31 King's Road, London SW3.

COLLISON, David (John), sound designer and consultant
b Ipswich, Suffolk, 5 Aug 1937; *s* of Douglas Roland Collison and his wife Molly (Hedgcock); *e* Ipswich School; *m* Annie Dodd, actress; formerly a trainee animal feed salesman.

Started in the theatre as an ASM at the Arts Theatre Club, 1955, under Peter Hall; continued to work in stage management until in 1958 he became Britain's first independent theatre sound consultant, building a sound effects library which now holds over 5000 catalogued items; designed a mixing console operated from the auditorium for Blitz!, 1962; has since been responsible for numerous other innovations in theatre sound design and equipment; has created sound tracks for numerous plays, including work for the RSC, National Theatre and English Stage Company; sound designer for more than seventy musicals since Pickwick, 1963, including many of the major musicals seen in London, such as A Funny Thing Happened on the Way to the Forum, Fiddler on the Roof, Cabaret, Company, Mame, Sweet Charity, Jesus Christ, Superstar, Billy and A Little Night Music; has also been responsible for sound for celebrity concerts, exhibi-

tions, etc; has been associated since 1959 with Richard Pilbrow, becoming managing director, Theatre Projects Sound Ltd, 1963; director, Theatre Projects Consultants Ltd, 1968; deputy managing director, Theatre Projects Services Ltd, 1973– ; Director, Theatre Projects Ltd, 1980– ; in these positions has designed sound systems or advised on sound for many major theatres in Britain, Europe, Africa and the Middle East; author of Stage Sound, 1976; founder member ABTT, Society of Theatre Consultants; lectures on theatre sound at LAMDA, etc.

Address: Crowsnest, Rectory Lane, Kingston Bagpuize, Oxon; Theatre Projects Ltd, 10 Long Acre, London WC2E 9LN. *Tel:* 01-240 5411.

COLON, Miriam, actress, producer, and Executive Director of the Puerto Rican Traveling Theatre Company, Inc
b Ponce, Puerto Rico, 1945; *m* George Edgar; *e* University of Puerto Rico; trained for the stage at the Erwin Piscator Dramatic Workshop and Technical Institute and with Lee Strasberg at the Actors Studio; also studied with Marcos Colón, Leopoldo Lavandero, and Ludwig Schajowicz.

Made her Broadway début at the Playhouse, 29 Dec 1953, as Frederica in In the Summer House; John Golden, Feb 1956, played Esperanza in The Inkeepers; Greenwich Mews, Oct 1956, Adelita Gomez in Me, Candido!; Orpheum, Mar 1965, Maria Esposito, Madonna, in Matty and the Moron and Madonna; founded the Pureto Rican Traveling Theatre and at the Greenwich Mews, 19 Dec 1966, appeared in her first bilingual production, alternating between English and Spanish as Juanita in The Ox Cart (La Carreta); appeared in the same part touring NYC in Aug 1967; John Golden, Mar 1969, Dolores Gonzales in The Wrong Way Light Bulb; produced the NYC parks tour of Crossroads, Aug 1969, and Town Hall, 8 Nov 1969; in 1970 produced and directed the NYC parks tour of The Golden Streets and produced Federico Garcia Lorca's El Malefico de la Mariposa (The Evil Spell of the Butterfly); in Aug 1971 produced and adapted A Dramatized Anthology of Puerto Rican Short Stories for a tour of NYC parks; at the Cathedral Church, May 1972, produced and played the title-role in The Passion of Antigona Perez; toured in the latter play in Aug 1972 in NYC parks; in 1973 Noo Yall, Molière's El Medico a Palos (The Doctor in Spite of Himself); in June 1974 produced and adapted Scribbles and The Innocent and produced The Guest in a triple-bill; At the End of the Street, 1974; Arrabal's Ceremony for an Assassinated Black Man, The Two Executioners, 1975; The Oxcart, 1977; Public/Anspacher, Jan 1979; Calpurnia in Julius Caesar; Bilingual Foundation for the Arts, LA, 1979, appeared in Fanlights; other productions of the Puerto Rican Traveling Theatre include Winterset, La Farsa del Amor Compradito, Los Titeres de Cachiporra, Pipo Subway No Sabe Reir, Ceremonia por un Negro Asasinado, The Angels Are Exhausted; and (1978) The FM Safe; has appeared in films, notably in The Appaloosa, One-Eyed Jacks, The Possession of Joel Delaney, and Isabella Negra; has appeared frequently in the various dramatic series on television.

Address: Puerto Rican Traveling Theatre, Co, Inc, 141 West 94th Street, New York, NY 10025.

COLT, Alvin, designer
b Louisville, Kentucky, 5 July 1916; *e* Department of Drama, Yale University.

First professional designs were for costumes for the American Ballet Caravan (now New York City Ballet Co) in 1940, for the ballets Charade and Pastorela (for which he also designed the scenery); designed for the Ballet Russe de

Monte Carlo the costumes for Saratoga, 1941; designed costumes for the Ballet Theatre productions of On Stage, Graziana, Slavonika (also scenery), Waltz Academy; first Broadway designs were for costumes for On the Town, Adelphi, Dec 1944; since then has designed costumes for the following productions: Around the World in 80 Days, 1946; Barefoot Boy with Cheek, Music in My Heart (also scenery), 1947; Clutterbuck, 1949; Guys and Dolls, 1950; Top Banana, 1951; The Frogs of Spring, Madame, Will You Walk? Guys and Dolls (first London designs, at the Coliseum, May), 1953; Fanny, The Golden Apple, Coriolanus, The Sea Gull, Sing Me No Lullaby, 1954; Pipe Dream (Antoinette Perry 'Tony' Award), The Lark, Finian's Rainbow (revival), The Doctor's Dilemma, Phoenix '55, Six Characters in Search of an Author, The Master Builder, The Carefree Tree, 1955; Li'l Abner, The Sleeping Prince, The Littlest Review, A Month in the Country, Diary of a Scoundrel, Miss Julie, The Stronger, Kiss Me, Kate (revival), 1956; Rumple, Copper and Brass, Maiden Voyage, Mary Stuart, Livin' the Life, 1957; The Infernal Machine, Blue Denim, Say, Darling, Crazy October, Hamlet (for American Shakespeare Festival Theatre, Stratford, Connecticut), 1958; First Impressions, Destry Rides Again, 1959; Greenwillow, Christine, Wildcat, 13 Daughters, 1960; Elizabeth the Queen, Mary Stuart (for National Repertory Theatre), 1961; The Aspern Papers, The Beauty Part, The Turn of the Screw (opera), Anatol, 1962; Abe Lincoln in Illinois, Here's Love, The Seagull, The Crucible, Ring Round the Moon (the last three for the National Repertory Theatre), 1963; Yeomen of the Guard, Something More! Wonderworld (for the New York World's Fair), Liliom, She Stoops to Conquer, and Hedda Gabler, for the National Repertory Theatre, 1964; Anna Karenina, The Rivals, The Trojan Women, 1965; The Paisley Convertible, Henry, Sweet Henry, and, for the National Theatre Repertory, The Imaginary Invalid, Tonight at 8.30, A Touch of the Poet, John Brown's Body, She Stoops to Conquer, 1967; Golden Rainbow, The Goodbye People, A Mother's Kisses, 1968; The Ballad of Johnny Pot, 1970; Sugar, 1972; Lorelei, Sugar (LA), 1974; Hellzapoppin (tour), 1976; Annie Get Your Gun (LA), 1977; has also designed the costumes for the NBC Opera Guild's productions of Madame Butterfly and The Marriage of Figaro and many other television productions, including 13 episodes of *The Adams Chronicles*, 1976, and numerous industrial show presentations, such as Buick, Ford, Oldsmobile, Milliken; costume designer for eight Tony Award Shows, and the 1978 Emmy Award Show; designer of special events for Neiman-Marcus, Dallas, 1962–; for the New York City Ballet has designed costumes for The Miraculous Mandarin and Kaleidoscope; designed the costumes for the films of Top Banana, Stiletto and L'il Abner.
Address: 90 Riverside Drive, New York, NY. *Tel:* 212–799 538.

COMDEN, Betty (*née* Cohen), lyricist, dramatic author, and actress
b Brooklyn, New York, 3 May 1919; *d* of Leo Cohen and his wife Rebecca (Sadvoransky); *e* Brooklyn Ethical Culture School, Erasmus Hall High School, and NY University (BS); *m* Steven Kyle.
Began her career in a cabaret act called The Revuers, with Adolph Green and Judy Holliday, devised by Adolph Green and herself; Adelphi, Dec 1944, co-author of the book and lyrics, and played Claire in On the Town; in collaboration with Adolph Green, she has since written the book and lyrics for the following productions: Billion Dollar Baby, 1945; Bonanza Bound! 1947; Two on the Aisle, 1951; Wonderful Town (lyrics only), 1953; Peter Pan (additional lyrics only),

1954; Bells Are Ringing, 1956; Say Darling (lyrics only), 1958; A Party with Betty Comden and Adolph Green (in which she also appeared), Do Re Mi (lyrics only), 1960; Subways Are for Sleeping, 1961; On the Town (London), 1963; Fade Out—Fade In, 1964 (revised 1965); Leonard Bernstein's Theatre Songs (some lyrics), 1965; Hallelujah, Baby (lyrics), 1967; Applause (book), 1970, which received the Antoinette Perry 'Tony' Award as best musical; at the Kaufman Auditorium, Jan 1971, appeared with Mr Green in Lyrics and Lyricists; On the Town revived in NY in 1971; Juilliard School of Music, 18 Dec 1971, performed in An Evening with Betty Comden and Adolph Green; Applause presented in London, 1972; lyrics for Lorelei, 1974; book for By Bernstein, 1975; Morosco, Feb 1977, appeared in A Party with Betty Comden and Adolph Green, later touring; book and lyrics for On the Twentieth Century, 1978; Peter Pan revived, 1979, NY; also in collaboration with Adolph Green, has written many screen plays and lyrics for films, including; Singin' in the Rain, The Band Wagon, On the Town, Good News, The Berkleys of Broadway, It's Always Fair Weather, Bells Are Ringing, Take Me out to the Ball Game, Auntie Mame, and What a Way to Go; television productions include Wonderful Town and Peter Pan (adaptation); has received numerous awards, including the Antoinette Perry, Donaldson, Outer Circle, and the Screen Writers Guild, and was twice nominated for Film Academy Awards; member of the Council of the Dramatists Guild.
Address: The Dramatists Guild, 234 West 44th Street, New York, NY 10036.

CONNELL, Jane (*née* Jane Sperry Bennett), actress
b Oakland, Calif, 27 Oct 1925; *d* of Louis Wesley Bennett and his wife Mary (Sperry); *e* Anna Head School, Berkeley, and University of Calif at Berkeley; *m* William Gordon Connell.
First appeared on the stage with the Straw Hat Revue Company, Lafayette, Calif in 1947, and remained with this company until 1953, touring New England, Calif, and Honolulu, Hawaii; Music Circus, Sacramento, 1954, played in New Faces of 1952; made her New York stage début at the President, Apr 1955, when she took over the Beatrice Arthur parts in Shoestring Revue; Theatre de Lys, Sept 1955, played Mrs Peachum in Threepenny Opera; Ethel Barrymore, June 1956, lead comedienne in New Faces of 1956; in summer 1957, appeared in revues at Tamiment and in 1958 at Flint and Detroit musical tents; played Kate in Girl Crazy, Katisha in The Mikado, Aunt Eller in Oklahoma!, Maud in Happy Hunting, Lady Jane in Rose Marie, etc, 1958; Music Circus, Sacramento, 1959, played Adelaide in Guys and Dolls, Mammy Yokum in L'il Abner, Agnes Gooch in Auntie Mame, Lalume in Kismet, Sue in Bells Are Ringing; made her London début at the Adelphi, 20 Sept 1960, when she played Princess Winnifred in Once upon a Mattress; Martinique, NY, Feb 1961, Mrs Spencer in The Oldest Trick in the World; Maidman, Jan 1962, Christina in Fortuna; York, Feb 1962, Lovey Mars in The Golden Apple; Music Circus, Sacramento, 1962, Mae Peterson in Bye Bye Birdie, Mrs Spofford in Gentlemen Prefer Blondes, and Sue in Bells Are Ringing; Sheraton Plaza, San Francisco, July 1962, Mme Dubonnet in The Boy Friend; Theatre de Lys, May 1963, played in the revue Put It in Writing; Playhouse on the Mall, Paramus, New Jersey, May 1964, Miss Ramphere in The Peacock Season; Shubert, New Haven, Conn, Dec 1964, Queen Fredrika in Royal Flush; Martin Beck, Oct 1965, Matilda Van Guilder in Drat! The Cat!; Winter Garden, May 1966, Agnes Gooch in Mame; Curran, San Francisco, Dorothy Chandler Pavilion in Los Angeles, April–Aug 1968, again

played Agnes Gooch in Mame; Mark Hellinger, Feb 1969, Gabrielle in Dear World; 1970 stage appearances were in Mame at the Huntington Hartford, Los Angeles, and at Dallas Summer Musical theatre; Roundabout, Apr 1971, Mrs Hardcastle in She Stoops to Conquer; McAlpin Rooftop, Oct 1971, Widow Merryweather and General Arden Clobber in Drat!; Theatre Four, Apr 1972, Mother in After Magritte and Mrs Drudge in The Real Inspector Hound; Brooks Atkinson, Nov 1972, Gamma in Lysistrata; Ahmanson, Los Angeles, Nov 1973, played in Cyrano de Bergerac; Roundabout Stage One, NY, Jan 1975, Mrs Malaprop in The Rivals; Mark Taper Forum, LA, Jan 1977, Miss Prism in The Importance of Being Earnest; same theatre, 1977, appeared in A History of the American Film; Beverly Hills Playhouse, 1977, appeared in Peculiar Pastimes; toured 1978–79 as Miss Hannigan in the National and West Coast companies of Annie; her early professional activities were in radio at NBC, San Francisco, 1946–53, Standard School broadcasts; 1955–60 cabaret for Julius Monk, Upstairs at the Downstairs and in 1963 at Plaza 9; entire year 1954 at Purple Onion in San Francisco, in club act with husband Gordon Connell; 1956 at Hungry i in San Francisco; television appearances include many series, such as Bewitched, All in the Family, Maude, Mary Hartman Mary Hartman, etc; films include: Ladybug, Ladybug, 1963; Mame, 1973, and Rabbit Test, 1977.

Address: c/o Bruce Savan, 120 West 57th Street, New York, NY.

CONNELLY, Marc, dramatic author, director, actor, and manager
b McKeesport, Pa, 13 Dec 1890; *s* of Patrick Joseph Connelly and his wife Mabel Fowler (Cook); *e* Washington; *m* Madeline Hurlock (mar dis); was originally a reporter on the *Pittsburgh Sun.*

Wrote the lyrics for Amber Express, 1916; revised Erminie, 1921; in collaboration with G S Kaufman has written the following plays: Dulcy, 1921; To the Ladies, The 49-ers, Merton of the Movies, 1922; Helen of Troy, New York, The Deep-Tangled Wildwood, 1923; Beggars on Horseback, Be Yourself, 1924; is also the author of The Wisdom Tooth, 1926; The Wild Man of Borneo (with H J Mankiewicz), 1927; The Green Pastures, 1930, which gained the Pulitzer Prize of that year; The Farmer Takes a Wife (with Frank B Elser), 1934; Everywhere I Roam (with Arnold Sundgaard), 1938; directed The Green Pastures, 1930; The Farmer Takes a Wife, 1934; Till the Cows Come Home, at the St Martin's, London, 1936; directed Having a Wonderful Time, 1937, under his own management; directed and co-produced The Two Bouquets and Everywhere I Roam, 1938; staged The Happiest Days, 1939; staged his own play, The Flowers of Virtue, Royale, Feb 1942; at the City Center, NY, Jan 1944, appeared as the Stage Manager in a revival of Our Town; at the Fulton, Feb 1945 presented (with Jean Dalrymple), and staged Hope for the Best; appeared at the New Theatre, London, Apr 1946, as the Stage Manager in Our Town; staged his own play, A Story for Strangers, at the Royale, Sept 1948; directed a revival of his own play, The Green Pastures, at the Broadway, Mar 1951; directed his own play Hunter's Moon at the Winter Garden, London, Feb 1958; appeared as Professor Osman in Tall Story, at the Belasco, NY, Jan 1959; has written the screenplays for Cradle Song, 1933, Captain Courageous, 1934; I Married a Witch, 1946; and played in the film The Spirit of St Louis, 1957; author of the books A Souvenir from Qam, 1965, and his memoirs Voices Offstage, 1969; was a professor of playwriting at the Yale University School of Drama, 1946–50; has conducted many seminars and lectures at other colleges and universities.

Clubs: Players, New York, and Savage, London. *Address:* 25 Central Park West, New York, NY.

CONRIED, Hans, actor
b Baltimore, Md, 15 Apr 1917; *s* of Hans Conried Jr and his wife Edith; *e* Columbia U; *m* Margaret Grant.

First appeared in New York at the Shubert, 7 May 1953, as Boris Adzinidzinadze in Can-Can; Belasco, Jan 1959, Prof Leon Solomon in Tall Story; Huntington Hartford, Jan 1966, played Andrew Pilgrim in The Absence of a Cello; toured US, Jan–Apr 1967, as Jim Bolton in Generation; Coconut Grove Playhouse, Miami, Florida, 1967, Walter Hollander in Don't Drink the Water; toured US, Sept 1969–Mar 1970, in the title-role of Spofford; Broadhurst, Apr 1971, played in the musical 70, Girls, 70; toured, summer 1971, as Ben Chambers in Norman, Is That You?; Minskoff, 1 July 1974, took over from George S Irving the role of Madame Lucy in Irene, played this part until Sept 1974, and then toured in it; Morosco, 1 Jan 1977, played Samuel Jones in Something Old, Something New; has also toured or played in stock productions of How the Other Half Loves, My Fair Lady, The Pleasure of His Company, Not in the Book, Take Her, She's Mine, etc; began his career on radio, playing such parts as Professor Kropotkin in *My Friend Irma* and Mr Schultz in *Life with Luigi*; has made over 100 films, including: Dramatic School, 1937, Mrs Parkington, 1944, Bus Stop, 1956, The Patsy, 1964, The Brothers O'Toole, 1973, etc; appears regularly on television, including Uncle Toonoose on *The Danny Thomas Show*, and recent appearances in *Supertrain, Fantasy Island* and *The Love Boat.*

Hobbies and recreations: Book and stamp collecting, Japanese sword guards, and Oriental art objects. *Address:* Actors Equity Association, 165 West 46th Street, New York, NY 10036.

CONTI, Tom, actor and director
b 22 Nov 1941; *s* of Alfonso Conti and his wife Mary; *e* Hamilton Park School, Glasgow; *m* the actress Kara Wilson; trained for the stage at the RSAMD, Glasgow.

Made his first appearance at the Citizens', Glasgow, Jan 1959, in The Roving Boy; in repertory in Glasgow and Edinburgh; appeared at the Edinburgh Festival, 1972, as Harry Vine in The Black and White Minstrels; King's Head, Islington, Oct 1972, Ben in Let's Murder Vivaldi; Royal Court, Apr 1973, Carlos in Savages, making his West End debut in the part at the Comedy, 20 June 1973; Hampstead, 1974, again played Harry Vine in The Black and White Minstrels, Jan, Enrico Zamati in Other People, July; same theatre, May 1976, title role in Don Juan; Aldwych, July 1976, for RSC, played Dick Dudgeon in The Devil's Disciple; Mermaid, Mar 1978, scored a great success as Ken Harrison in Whose Life Is It, Anyway?, transferring with the production to the Savoy, June 1978, and making his Broadway debut in the part at the Trafalgar, 17 Apr 1979 (Tony award); directed Last Licks (Longacre, NY), Nov 1979; Before the Party (Oxford Playhouse and Queen's, London), Jan 1980; TV, since Mother of Men in 1959, includes The Glittering Prizes, Madame Bovary and The Norman Conquests; films, since Galileo in 1974, include Full Circle and The Duellists.

Recreation: Flamenco guitar. *Address:* c/o Chatto and Linnit, Globe Theatre, Shaftesbury Avenue, London W1.

CONVILLE, David, director and producer
b Kashmir, India, 4 June 1929; *s* of Lt Col Leopold Henry George Conville, CBE and his wife Katherine Mary (Gispert); *e* Marlborough College; *m* Philippa Gail.

Formerly an actor, he made his debut at Ipswich in 1952 and played with various repertory companies and the Stratford Memorial company, making his first London appearance with the latter at the Palace, July 1955, in a minor role in Much Ado About Nothing; formed David Conville Productions, 1959, at first presenting various tours; co-presented Toad of Toad Hall, London, 1960; sole presenter, 1962 and each subsequent year; has also presented or co-presented: The Lord Chamberlain Regrets, 1961; Naked, 1963; The Platinum Cat, 1965; Suzanna Andler, Treasure Island (Chichester), 1973; Salad Days, The Lady and the Tiger, 1976; took over the management of the Open Air Theatre, Regent's Park, 1962; in 1963 formed the New Shakespeare Company to present classical seasons at the Open Air and tours; since that date he has presented 47 major productions for the Company; has directed several productions in repertory, and eight productions of Toad of Toad Hall; for the Open Air has directed Much Ado About Nothing, 1970 and tour; Twelfth Night, 1972 and 1979; A Midsummer Night's Dream, 1974–5, including Middle East tour, 1978; Old Times, 1974, Indian tour; Love's Labours Lost, 1976–7, and in 1978 at the Gandersheimer Domfestspiele; Macbeth tour, 1978; Julius Caesar tour, 1979; President of the Society of West End Theatre, 1975–7.

Address: 17 Gwendolen Avenue, London, SW15. *Tel:* 01–789 8327.

CONVY, Bert, actor

b St Louis, Missouri, 23 July 1934; *s* of Bert Fleming Convy and his wife Monica (Whalen); *e* North Hollywood High School, University of California at Los Angeles (BA 1955); *m* Anne Anderson; formerly a professional baseball player; prepared for the stage with Jeff Corey in Hollywood.

Made his first appearance on the stage at the Player's Ring, Hollywood, 1957, as Barnaby in The Matchmaker, and later appeared there in A Tree Grows in Brooklyn and as Billy Bigelow in Liliom; first appeared in New York at the John Golden, 4 Aug 1959, in the Billy Barnes Revue; Winter Garden, Nov 1962, Tommy Dee in Nowhere to Go But Up; Plymouth, May 1963, played in the revue The Beast in Me; Sullivan Street Playhouse, 1963, took over as El Gallo in The Fantasticks; Phoenix, Oct 1963, Rome in Mornin' Sun; Music Box, Dec 1963, Freddy Winters in Love and Kisses; Imperial, Sept 1964, Perchik in Fiddler on the Roof; Playhouse, Oct 1965, Richard Merrick in The Impossible Years; Broadhurst, Nov 1966, Clifford Bradshaw in Cabaret; Provincetown Playhouse, Feb 1969, Peter in Shoot Anything with Hair That Moves; Ethel Barrymore, May 1969, Hildy Johnson in The Front Page, and repeated this part when the play was revived at the same theatre, Oct 1969; Promenade, Feb 1971, conceived and directed Do It Again!; first appeared in films in Gunman's Walk, 1958, and has since played in Susan Slade, Act One, etc; has appeared extensively on television in such dramatic programs as *Alfred Hitchcock Presents, Perry Mason, The Untouchables, The Nurses, East Side/West Side,* etc, and recently in his own show.

Address: Actors Equity Association, 165 West 46th Street, New York, NY 10036.

CONWAY, Kevin, actor

b 29 May 1942; *s* of James Conway and his wife Margaret (Sanders, O'Brien); *m* the actress Mila Quiros; trained for the stage at Dramatic Workshop, New York City and with Uta Hagen; formerly a sales analyst with IBM.

Made his first professional appearance at the Elitch Gardens, Denver, in July 1967, as Andy in a tour of The Impossible Years; at the Long Wharf, New Haven, 1967,

played Philly Cullen in The Playboy of the Western World and Leo Davis in Room Service; in 1968, at Stage West, Springfield, Mass, played Tom in The Knack, and at the Charles Playhouse, Boston, Cliff in Look Back in Anger and First Messenger in The Bacchae; Provincetown Playhouse, Apr 1968, made his New York debut as Number Two in Muzeeka; Brooks Atkinson, Oct 1969, Black Hawk in Indians; at the Chelsea Theater Center, Brooklyn, Oct 1970, and the Cherry Lane, Nov, Fred in Saved; Arena Stage, Washington DC, 1971, Mike in Moonchildren; La Mama, 1971, various parts in an evening of Julie Bovasso plays; Royale, Feb 1972, again played Mike in Moonchildren; Vivian Beaumont, Jan 1973, Covey in The Plough and the Stars; in the same year took over the part of McMurphy in One Flew Over the Cuckoo's Nest at the Mercer-Hansberry, later transferring to the Eastside Playhouse; Eastside Playhouse, Dec 1973, Teddy in When You Comin' Back, Red Rider? (Obie and Drama Desk awards); also played the role at the Berkshire Playhouse, summer 1974; Brooks Atkinson, Dec 1974, George in Of Mice and Men; in 1975 again played Teddy, at the Westwood Playhouse, LA; Manhattan Theatre Club, Dec 1975, Allott in Life Class; at the Kennedy Center, Washington DC, also Dec 1975, and Brooklyn Academy, Jan 1976, Jamie in Long Day's Journey into Night; St Peter's Church, Jan 1979, and Booth, Apr 1979, Frederick Treves in The Elephant Man; made his debut as a director with Mecca, at the Quaigh, 1980; films, since Slaughterhouse Five, 1971, include Portnoy's Complaint, FIST, Paradise Alley, and The Funhouse, 1980; TV appearances include Hogan's Goat, The Scarlet Letter, and recently The Lathe of Heaven.

Favourite parts: McMurphy, Teddy, George. *Club:* Players. *Address:* Critter Productions, 25 Central Park West, New York, NY 10023. *Tel:* 582 9235.

COOK, Barbara, actress and singer

b Atlanta, Ga, 25 Oct 1927; *d* of Charles Bunyan Cook and his wife Nell (Harwell); *m* David LeGrant (mar dis).

Made her Broadway début at the Broadhurst, May 1951, as Sandy in Flahooley; City Center, Aug 1953, played Ado Annie Carnes in Oklahoma! and toured in this part in 1954; Mark Hellinger, Jan 1955, Hilda Miller in Plain and Fancy; Martin Beck, Dec 1956, Cunégonde in Candide; City Center, Sept 1957, Julie Jordan in Carousel; Majestic, Dec 1957, Marian Paroo in The Music Man, for which she received the Antoinette Perry (Tony) Award; City Center, May 1960, Anna Leonowens in The King and I; Shubert, Nov 1961, Liesl Brandel in The Gay Life; Eugene O'Neill, Apr 1963, Amalia Balash in She Loves Me; US tour, 1964, Molly Brown in The Unsinkable Molly Brown; Eugene O'Neill, Nov 1964, Carol Deems in Something More!; Music Box, Feb 1965, took over the role of Ellen Gordon in Any Wednesday, which was her first appearance in a straight play; New York State, July 1966, Magnolia in Show Boat; Broadhurst, Apr 1967, Patsy Newquist in Little Murders; toured, 1967 as Fanny Brice in Funny Girl; Martin Beck, Nov 1971, Dolly Talbo in The Grass Harp; Vivian Beaumont, Nov 1972, Kleopatra in Enemies; toured, 1973, in The Gershwin Years; Brothers and Sisters, NY, July 1974, appeared in cabaret; Carnegie Hall, 27 Jan 1975, appeared in a solo concert; Maisonette, St Regis Hotel, Mar 1975, again appeared in cabaret; has appeared on television in Bloomer Girl, Yeoman of the Guard, Alfred Hitchcock's program, *US Steel Hour, The Perry Como Show,* etc.

Address: Actors Equity Association, 165 West 46th Street, New York, NY 10036.

COOK, Peter, actor and satirist

b Torquay, 17 Nov 1937; *s* of Alexander Cook and his wife

Margaret; *e* Radley and Pembroke College, Cambridge; *m* (1) Wendy Snowden (mar dis); (2) Judy Huxtable.

While still at Cambridge, where he was President of the Footlights, 1959, wrote the revues Pieces of Eight (produced at the Apollo, 23 Sept 1959) and One Over the Eight (Duke of York's, Apr 1961); at the Edinburgh Festival, Lyceum Theatre, Aug 1960, appeared in Beyond the Fringe, of which he was co-author, and in which he made his West End acting début at the Fortune, 10 May 1961; after a run of more than a year in London, made his New York début in the same show at the John Golden, Oct 1962; in 1962 he also opened the satirical nightclub The Establishment; toured Australia, 1972, with Dudley Moore in their two-man show Behind the Fridge, which was seen in London at the Cambridge, Nov 1972, and in NY at the Plymouth, Nov 1973, under the title Good Evening; subsequently toured the US; his films include: A Dandy in Aspic, and The Rise and Rise of Michael Rimmer; television includes a number of series of *Not only . . . But Also*; a director of the magazine *Private Eye*; author with Dudley Moore of Dud and Pete, and The Dagenham Dialogues.

Recreations: Gambling, gossip, golf. *Address:* c/o Wright and Webb, 10 Soho Square, London W1. *Tel:* 01–734 9641.

COONEY, Ray, dramatic author, actor, director and manager
b London, 30 May 1932; *s* of Gerard Cooney and his wife Olive (Clarke); *e* Alleyn's, Dulwich; *m* Linda Dixon.

First appeared on stage as a boy actor in Song of Norway, Palace, 1946; Calcutta in the Morning, Players', 1947; The Hidden Years, Fortune, Jan 1948; after National Service worked in various repertory companies, 1952–6, including Blackburn, Aldershot and Worthing; Whitehall, 1956, joined the cast of Dry Rot, remaining with Brian Rix's company to play Corporal Flight in Simple Spymen, Mar 1958, also appearing in his own play One for the Pot, 1961; Ambassadors', 1964, took over Sgt Trotter in The Mousetrap; Prince of Wales, Jan 1966, Simon Sparrow in Doctor at Sea; Whitehall, 1967, took over Prosser in Uproar in the House; Adelphi, 1968, briefly took over Wainwright in Charlie Girl; Ambassadors', 1975, took over Timothy Westerby in There Goes The Bride; Savoy, 1976, briefly took over Mr Pink in Banana Ridge; has directed the following plays; Thark, 1965; In at the Death, 1967; Press Cuttings, Not Now, Darling (New York), 1970; Move Over, Mrs Markham, 1971; The Mating Game, 1972; Why Not Stay for Breakfast? 1973; Birds of Paradise, 1974; has presented or co-presented the following plays: Thark, 1965; Doctor at Sea, 1966; In at the Death, 1967; My Giddy Aunt, 1968; Dandy Dick (tour), The Mating Game (tour), 1970; Move Over Mrs Markham, 1971; Lloyd George Knew My Father, The Mating Game, 1972; Two and Two Make Sex, Say Goodnight to Grandma, Why Not Stay for Breakfast, At the End of the Day, 1973; The Dame of Sark, The Little Hut, The Bedwinner, There Goes the Bride, Jack the Ripper, A Ghost on Tiptoe, The Sack Race, 1974; Hinge and Bracket, Murder at the Vicarage, Ipi Tombi, 1975; Banana Ridge, Fringe Benefits, Dear Daddy, 1976; Fire Angel, Elvis, 1977; Spinechiller, Lady Harry, Whose Life Is It Anyway?, Clouds, 1978; Chicago, Bodies, Whose Life Is It Anyway? (New York); Brasil Tropical, Hello Dolly, Ain't Misbehavin', Beatlemania, Irma La Douce, Not Now Darling, 1979; author of the following plays: One for the Pot, 1961 (with Tony Hilton), which ran for over 1,000 performances at the Whitehall; Chase Me, Comrade, over 1,000 performances, Whitehall, 1964; Charlie Girl (book, with Hugh and Margaret Williams), 1965, over 2,000 performances, Adelphi; Stand by your Bedouin (with

Tony Hilton), 1966; Not Now, Darling, 1967; My Giddy Aunt, 1968; Move Over, Mrs Markham, 1969 (the last three with John Chapman); Why Not Stay for Breakfast? (with Gene Stone), 1970; There Goes the Bride (with John Chapman), 1974; created leading roles in the original try-outs of several of these plays; has also appeared in films and television farces and written a number of screenplays; member of the Society of West End Theatre Managers; in 1976, with Laurie Marsh, created the Cooney–Marsh Group, a theatre property company owning the Astoria and Shaftesbury theatres, London, and the Trafalgar Theatre, New York.

Recreations: Tennis, swimming, golf. *Clubs:* Dramatists, Green Room. *Address:* 66 Trafalgar Square, London WC2. *Tel:* 01–839 4855.

COOTE, Robert, actor
b London, 4 Feb 1909; *s* of Bert Coote and his wife Ada (Russell); *e* Hurstpierpoint College, Sussex.

Made his first appearance on the stage at the Pavilion, Lyme Regis, July 1925, as John the Manservant, in The Private Secretary; during the next two years, he toured as a member of the Shakespeare companies of both Charles Doran and D Basil Gill; Rusholme Repertory Theatre, Manchester 1927–9; toured South Africa, 1929, in Just Married and 77 Park Lane, with Guy Newell; made his first appearance in London at the Victoria Palace, Dec 1931, as The King in The Windmill Man, directed by his father; Lyric, Hammersmith, June 1932, played Horace Bream in Sweet Lavender; between 1930–4, toured with Frederica, Private Lives, For the Love of Mike, Mother of Pearl; toured Australia, 1934, with Alice Delysia in the last play; remained in Australia for two years to appear in a number of musicals, including: Anything Goes, Yes, Madam, Waltzes From Vienna, etc; after four years in Hollywood, he enlisted in the RCAF and was discharged as Squadron Leader in 1946, returning to Hollywood, 1946; made his first appearance in New York, Shubert, Jan 1953, as Col Rinder Sparrow in The Love of Four Colonels; Globe Theatre, London, 1954, took over the part of John Nedlow in Someone Waiting; Morosco, NY, Jan 1954, played Sir Michael Anstruther in Dear Charles; Mark Hellinger, Mar 1956, played Col Pickering in My Fair Lady; after nearly two years, he left the American cast to play the same part in the English production at Drury Lane, Apr 1958; toured Russia in the part, 1960; Majestic, NY, Dec 1960, played Pellinore in Camelot; at the Cambridge, London, Sept 1969, played Colonel Lukyn in The Magistrate; Vaudeville, Sept 1970, then Duke of York's, Col Richardson in The Jockey Club Stakes; played the same part in NY, Jan 1973, at the Cort, and toured Australia, 1975–76; Garrick, June 1974, Major Farmer in Birds of Paradise; St James's, NY, Mar 1976, again played Pickering in a revival of My Fair Lady; toured Australia, 1977–78, in The Pleasure of His Company; Brooks Atkinson, NY, 1979, took over as Ernest in Bedroom Farce; entered films, 1931, in Sally in our Alley, since which time he has appeared in numerous pictures, including A Yank at Oxford, Prudence and the Pill, etc; first appeared on television Feb 1951, and principal performances include Sheppey and the series, The Rogues, Whitehall Worrier and Best of Enemies.

Favourite parts: Tom Pryor in Outward Bound, and Col Pickering in My Fair Lady. *Recreations:* Golf, swimming, tennis. *Clubs:* Green Room, Players (NY), Stage Golfing Society, RAC, Lord's Taverners, Garrick. *Address:* c/o Richard Stone, 18–20 York Buildings, London WC2.

COPELAND, Joan (*née* Joan Maxine Miller), actress and singer
b New York City, 1 June; *d* of Isidore Miller and his wife

Augusta (Barnett); sister of Arthur Miller, the playwright; *e* Brooklyn College; *m* George J Kupchik; specially trained for the stage at the American Academy of Dramatic Arts and Actors Studio.

First appeared on the stage at the Brooklyn Academy of Music, 1945, as Juliet in Romeo and Juliet; made her NY début at the Equity Library Theatre, May 1946, as Desdemona in Othello; Belasco, Sept 1948, played Nadine in Sundown Beach; Hudson, Mar 1949, Susan Carmichael in The Detective Story; Coronet, Feb 1951, Evangeline Orth in Not for Children; Downtown National, Feb 1955, Betty Shapiro in The Grass Is Always Greener, and, Mar 1955, Elise in The Miser; Barbizon-Plaza, Nov 1957, Melanie in Conversation Piece; Martin Beck, Oct 1958, Maria in Handful of Fire; Gramercy Arts, Sept 1960, Mrs Erlynne in Delightful Season; Winter Garden, Nov 1963, took over from Vivien Leigh as Tatiana in Tovarich; toured US, 1964, as Eliza Doolittle in My Fair Lady; Eugene O'Neill, Nov 1964, Marchesa Valentina Crespi in Something More!; Morosco, Feb 1968, stand-by for Kate Reid in The Price and later played the role of Esther Franz; Mark Hellinger, 1969–70, stand-by for Katharine Hepburn in the title-role of Coco; Imperial, Nov 1970, Esther in Two by Two; John Drew, Easthampton, June 1975, played in End of Summer; Circle in the Square, June 1976, Vera in Pal Joey; Longacre, Sept 1976, Florence Grayson in Checking Out; Roundabout, 1979, took over the title-role in Candida; stock appearances include Mame, 1979; first appeared in films in The Goddess, 1957, and since has played in Middle of the Night, 1958, Roseland, 1977; first appeared on television in 1946 and has played Andrea Whiting in the serial *Search for Tomorrow,* Cora in The Iceman Cometh, and in various other serials and dramatic programs, recently *One Life to Live.*

Favourite parts: Eliza Doolittle, Melanie, and Vera. *Recreations:* Piano playing, dressmaking. *Address:* 88 Central Park West, New York, NY. *Tel:* 799 7017.

COPLEY, Paul, actor and writer
b Denby Dale, 25 Nov 1944; *s* of Harold Copley and his wife Rene; *e* Northern Counties College of Education; *m* the actress Natasha Pyne.

After a year as a teacher of English and Drama joined the Theatre in Education company at the Leeds Playhouse, 1971, where he made his professional debut in the autumn as Hugenberg in Lulu; Little, autumn 1972, played the manager in Bleats from a Brighouse Pleasure Ground; Theatre Upstairs, Dec 1973, title role in Mike Leigh's Dick Whittington; Birmingham Rep, June 1974, Dave the Joiner in Trinity Tales; Mermaid, Autumn '76 gave an award-winning performance as Pvt Hamp in For King and Country; Bush, Jan 1977, Jack in German Skerries; Royal Exchange, Manchester, Sept 1978, Terry in Sisters; Lyric, Belfast, Apr 1979, Ken Harrison in Whose Life Is It Anyway?; his play Pillion was presented at the Bush, Oct 1977 and subsequently televised; also author of Viaduct (Bush, 1980); other writing includes the TV plays Emmets and Hitch, and short stories for children's TV; films since Alfie Darling, 1974, include A Bridge Too Far, and Zulu Dawn; has appeared frequently in TV plays.

Address: c/o Kate Feast Management, 43A Princess Road, London NW1.

COPLEY, Peter, actor
b Bushey, Herts, 20 May 1915; *s* of John Copley and his wife Ethel (Gabain); *m* (1) Pamela Brown (mar dis); (2) Ninka Dolega (mar dis); (3) Margaret Tabor; studied for the stage at the Old Vic School, under Harcourt Williams and Murray Macdonald.

Made his first appearance on the stage at the Old Vic, Feb 1932, as the Gaoler in The Winter's Tale; he remained a member of the company until 1934; first appeared in the West-end at the Whitehall, Feb 1935, as the Footman in Viceroy Sarah; Westminster, Nov 1935, played Lucius in Timon of Athens; toured in South America, 1936, with Edward Stirling; Arts, 1936, played Jan in The Soul of Nicholas Snyders; Globe, Feb 1937, Arthur in Love, and How to Cure it; played a season at the Gate Theatre, Dublin, Jan–May, 1939; His Majesty's, Dec 1939, Claudius and Metelus Cimber in Julius Caesar (in modern dress); served in the Royal Navy, 1940–1; was with the repertory company at Oxford Playhouse, Apr–Dec 1941; toured, 1942, as Eddie in Golden Boy; St James's, Jan 1943, played Edgar in King Lear, and later during 1943, toured for CEMA, as Orsino in Twelfth Night; Lyric, Hammersmith, June 1944, played Robert in Madeleine; from Jan–May 1945, was director for the Worthing Repertory company; joined the Old Vic company at the New Theatre, May 1945, and remained with the company until May 1950, playing prominent parts in sixteen productions, notably Sneer in The Critic, Edmund in King Lear, de Valvert in Cyrano de Bergerac, Ananias in The Alchemist, Tranio in The Taming of the Shrew, Mowbray in Richard II, Brother Martin in Saint Joan, Sicinius Brutus in Coriolanus, Sir Andrew in Twelfth Night, Fainall in The Way of the World and Laertes in Hamlet; at the Edinburgh Festival (King's Theatre), Sept 1950, played the Fencing Master in the opera, Ariadne auf Naxos; Embassy, Mar 1951, played Herbert Filch in The Happy Family, and appeared in this part at the Duchess, May 1951; Embassy, Jan 1952, directed The Golden Grain, and in Apr 1952, directed The Magnificent Moodies; Westminster, May 1952, appeared as Mr Jingle in The Trial of Mr Pickwick; Arts, Dec 1953, Capt Mannering and the 1st Policeman in A London Actress; Wimbledon, May 1954, and subsequently on tour, played Farringdon in The Soldier and the Lady; Lyceum, Edinburgh, Feb 1955, Grivet in The Lovers; Q, Feb 1955, the Prison Chaplain in The Crime of Canon Wayd; Winter Garden, May 1955, again appeared as Grivet in The Lovers; Aldwych, Mar 1957, played Lester Lewis in Olive Ogilvie; Criterion, Aug 1957, took over Dr Bonfant in The Waltz of the Toreadors; Criterion, Dec 1959, played Charles Reese in A Clean Kill; St Martin's, Jan 1961, played Alec Glanville in The Bargain; Strand, Sept 1961, Alec Nightingale in The Affair; at the same theatre, Sept 1962, played Sir Hector Rose in The New Men; Savoy, May 1963, Charles Chrystal in The Masters; Comedy, Apr 1964, Mr Tuke in The Claimant; Richmond, Mar 1965, Celimare in The Family Way; Duke of York's, Aug 1966, Duncan Doubleday in Public and Confidential; Northcott, Exeter, 1967, Antonio in The Merchant of Venice; Mermaid, July 1971, Mr Nox in The Old Boys; Piccadilly, Nov 1971, Cravatar in Dear Antoine; Mermaid, Feb 1974, Inspector Pleat in Stevenson's Burning; Belgrade Two, Coventry, Oct 1974, Sartorius in Widowers' Houses; Bush, Jan 1977, Jack Williams in German Skerries; Olivier, Nov 1978, Frederick Wilder in Strife and at the same theatre, Mar 1979, Fyodor in The Fruits of enlightenment; has also appeared frequently in films and on television; called to the Bar by the Middle Temple, June 1963.

Hobby: The Law. *Address:* St James's Management, 22 Groom Place, London SW1.

CORBETT, Gretchen, actress
b Portland, Oregon, 13 Aug 1947; *d* of Henry Ladd Corbett, Jr, and his wife Katherine Minahen (Coney); *e* Carnegie Institute of Technology.

Made her professional début with the Oregon Shakespeare Festival, Ashland, as Desdemona in Othello; joined the Repertory Theatre in New Orleans, 1967, and played Juliet in Romeo and Juliet, Amy in Charley's Aunt, and Julia in The Rivals; made her New York début at the Sheridan Square Playhouse, 29 Aug 1967, when she succeeded Jacqueline Coslow as Louka in Arms and the Man; John Golden, Oct 1967, played Sonya in After the Rain; Circle in the Square, 1968, took over as Iphigenia in Iphigenia in Aulis; Gramercy Arts, Mar 1968, Jessie in The Bench; Morosco, Dec 1968, Trina Stanley in Forty Carats; Playhouse in the Park, Philadelphia, Pa, 1969, Wife in The Unknown Soldier and His Wife; Delacorte, June 1970, Joan La Pucelle in the New York Shakespeare Festival Theatre production of Henry VI, Part I; for the American Theatre Company, 1970, played Shaw's Saint Joan; Anderson, Feb 1971, Joan in The Survival of St Joan, and repeated this role at the Studio Arena, Buffalo, NY, later in 1971; Theatre de Lys, June 1971, Françoise in The Justice Box; toured, 1972, as Ruth in The Effect of Gamma Rays on Man-in-the-Moon Marigolds; New Jersey Shakespeare Festival, 1973, Rosalind in As You Like It; Long Wharf, New Haven, Conn, Oct 1973, Hilda Wangel in The Master Builder; Mark Taper, LA, Mar 1978, appeared in At the End of Long Island; first appeared in films in 1967 in Out of It, and since has played in Let's Scare Jessica to Death, 1971, etc; first appeared on television in 1968 in *NYPD*, and has since played in *Ghost Story, Kojak, Ironside, Banacek, Gunsmoke, Colombo*, etc.

Address: c/o Richard H Bauman, 1650 Broadway, New York, NY 10019.

CORBETT, Harry H, actor
b Rangoon, Burma, 28 Feb 1925; *m* (1) Sheila Steafel (mar dis); (2) Maureen Corbett.

Made his first stage appearance in repertory at Chorlton; ten years with the Theatre Workshop company, appeared at the Theatre Royal, Stratford, E, Feb 1954, as Freewill in The Dutch Courtesan, subsequently playing the following parts at the same theatre with the Theatre Workshop company: Peter Stockman in An Enemy of the People, Dr Palaprat in The Flying Doctor, the title-part in Johnny Noble, Mosbie in Arden of Faversham, Christophe in The Cruel Daughters, A Teacher, Dr Grunstein, Baldheaded Gentleman, and Police Sergeant in The Good Soldier Schweik, Hugo in The Prince and the Pauper, 1954; the title-part in Richard II, The Other Hanau in The Other Animals, Sir Politic Would-Be in Volpone, The Priest in The Midwife, Pepé in The Legend of Pepito, Chaplain in Mother Courage and Her Children (Devon Festival), 1955; toured, Oct 1955, as the First Player in Hamlet, prior to appearing in the same production in Moscow, and also at the Phoenix, London, Dec 1955; at the same theatre, Apr 1956, played Lieut of Police in The Power and the Glory; and June 1956, Downing in a revival of The Family Reunion; Saville, Dec 1956, Waitwell in The Way of the World; Royal Court, Sept 1957, Jules Palotin in Nekrassov; same theatre, Feb 1959, Young Man in Progress to the Park; Princes, Nov 1959, Mervyn Dalziel in Kookaburra; Royal, Stratford, E, May 1960, the title-part in Ned Kelly; same theatre, Nov 1960, directed Progress to the Park; Bristol Old Vic, Sept–Nov 1961, played Ralph Bates in Period of Adjustment, Henry VIII in The Flanders Mare, and Fred Cooper in The Big Client; Royal, Stratford, E, Oct 1962, Mr Rowbotham, and Man in the Cinema in What a Crazy World; Haymarket, Apr 1963, Albert Cobb in Who'll Save the Plowboy?; Prince of Wales, Apr 1965, played Brian Miller in Travelling Light; Vaudeville, Sept 1967, Albert Harris in Fill the Stage with Happy Hours; Alhambra,

Bradford, Oct 1969, Harry Johnson in Little Jack; toured Australia, 1972, in Last of the Red Hot Lovers; Globe, Bankside, July 1973, Macbeth in Macbeth; Casino, Dec 1974, Ben in Cinderella; Arnaud, Guildford, Apr 1977, played Bernard Baxley in Laburnum Grove; Churchill, Bromley, Dec 1979, Widow Twankey in Aladdin; notable television appearances include Harold Steptoe in the series *Steptoe and Son.*

Address: c/o Fraser and Dunlop Ltd, 91 Regent Street, London, W1R 8RU.

CORNWELL, Judy, actress
b London, 22 Feb 1942; *d* of Darcy Nigel Barry Cornwell and his wife Irene (McCullen); *e* Gympie, Queensland and Lewes Girls' GS; *m* John Parry; trained in ballet and was initially a student dancing teacher.

First stage appearance at the age of fifteen, as Cinderella in pantomime at the Hippodrome, Brighton; made her London debut, June 1963, in Oh, What a Lovely War! at Wyndham's, having appeared with the company at the Sarah Bernhardt, Paris; Arts, Aug 1964, played Agnes in Mr Whatnot; Theatre Royal, Stratford E, Feb 1966, Ruby in Sweet Fanny Adams; Gardner Centre, Sussex, 1970, Louise Maske in Bloomers, Aug, and Sadie in Don't Let Summer Come, Oct; joined the Royal Shakespeare Company, 1972, Stratford season, to play Calpurnia in Julius Caesar, Adriana in The Comedy of Errors, and Octavia in Antony and Cleopatra; Fortune, June 1973, Helen Brown in Who's Who; New Vic, Bristol, Oct 1975, Diana in Old Flames; played the same part at the Arts, Feb 1976; Lyric, Jan 1977, took over Alma in The Bed Before Yesterday; Open Space, July 1977, Jill in Mecca; first appeared in films 1966; recent films include Every Home Should Have One, Country Dance and Wuthering Heights; TV appearances, since 1961, London Assurance and The Mill on The Floss.

Favourite part: Sadie. *Recreations:* Theology, community activity, music, cooking, family life, philosophy. *Address:* c/o Larry Dalzell Associates, 3 Goodwin's Court, St Martin's Lane, London, WC2.

CORSARO, Frank, director, actor, and dramatic author
b New York City, 22 Dec 1924; *s* of Joseph Corsaro and his wife Marie (Quarino); *m* Mary Cross Lueders; prepared for the stage at the Yale University Drama School and at the Actors Studio.

Directed his first production at the Cherry Lane Theatre, off-Broadway, June 1947, with No Exit; subsequently directing Family Reunion, 1947; The Creditors, 1949; Heartbreak House, 1951; Naked, 1952, The Scarecrow, 1953; The Honeys, A Hatful of Rain, 1955; Susannah (opera), 1956; The Making of Moo, The Night Circus, 1958; A Piece of Blue Sky (Westport, Conn), Angel of Fire (Spoleto Festival, opera), The Night of the Iguana (one-act) and The Tiny Closet (double-bill, Spoleto Festival), 1959; Oh Dad, Poor Dad, Mama's Hung You in the Closet and I'm Feelin' So Sad (London), The Night of the Iguana, A Short Happy Life (tour), 1961; Baby Want a Kiss, 1964; The Sweet Enemy, Katerina Ismailova (opera), The Flaming Angel (opera), 1965; Fitz and Biscuit, 1966; Of Mice and Men (Seattle Opera Company), Koanga (National Opera Company, Washington, DC), 1970; Houston Grand Opera, 1970 directed Hugh the Drover; St Paul, Minn, Opera, 1971, directed Summer and Smoke; Jacksonville, Fla 1972, directed The Flower, and Hawk; Washington Opera, 1972 directed L'Incoronazione di Poppea; Houston, 1973 directed L'Histoire du Soldat, 1973 Lulu, Rinaldo, 1975; Caramoor Music Festival, Katonah, NY, 1974 directed Impresario,

Prima la Musica; American, Washington, DC, Sept 1973, directed Cervantes; directed The Seagull for the Houston, Texas, Grand Opera, Mar 1974; directed L'Ormindo for the Caramoor, NY, Festival, 1975; Uris, Oct 1975, directed Treemonisha; directed Cold Storage, Lyceum, 1977; Whoopee! (ANTA), Knockout (Helen Hayes), 1979; since 1966 directed operas for the New York City Opera Company, including: La Traviata, 1966; Madame Butterfly, I Pagliacci, Cavalleria Rusticana, 1967; The Crucible, Faust, 1968; Carrie Nation, Prince Igor, Rigoletto, 1969; Don Giovanni, 1972; Medea, Pelleas et Melisande, The Makropolus Case, A Village Romeo and Juliet, 1973; Manon Lescaut, 1974; Die Tote Stadt, 1975; at the City Center, NY, Apr 1951, played the Tapster in The Taming of the Shrew; Martin Beck, Apr 1952, took over the role of Dirty Joe in Mrs McThing; City Center, Mar 1953, played Lancelot Gobbo in The Merchant of Venice; acted in the film Rachel, Rachel, 1969; author of the play A Piece of Blue Sky; a book of memoirs, Maverick, 1978; directed his first television production in 1960 with his own play A Piece of Blue Sky.

Recreations: Tennis, ice-skating, music. *Address:* 33 Riverside Drive, New York, NY 10023. *Tel:* 874 1058.

CORSON, Richard, writer, teacher, and make-up consultant
e DePauw University and Louisiana State University.

Has taught at Louisiana State U, U of North Carolina, Vassar College, California State U at Long Beach, and Southern Methodist U, as well as giving guest lectures at many other colleges; has performed a programme of one-man character sketches throughout N America and in Britain; author of Stage Makeup, 1960 (5th Edition 1975); Fashions in Hair, 1964 (3rd Edition 1980); Fashions in Eyeglasses, 1967 (2nd Edition 1980); Fashions in Makeup, 1973.

Address: 121 Lincoln Place, Brooklyn, NY 11217.

COSSINS, James, actor
b Beckenham, Kent, 4 Dec 1933; *s* of William James Cossins and his wife Lily Ethel (Whitney); *e* Dulwich College PS and the City of London School; trained for the stage at the Royal Academy of Dramatic Art.

First stage appearance, Bromley Rep, June 1952, as a native porter in Rain; after National Service worked in repertory at Farnham, Ipswich, Hull, Salisbury and Nottingham, 1954–61; made his West End debut at the Duchess, 7 June 1961, as Edgar in Celebration; Comedy, Oct 1961, Joseph in Bonne Soupe, transferring to the Wyndham's; Royal Court, July 1962, Wimple in Plays for England; toured Europe as Canterbury, McMorris and Burgundy in the Bristol Old Vic production of Henry V, 1974, including performances at the Edinburgh Festival, Aug, and Old Vic (London), Sept; Vaudeville, May 1965, Gladstone in Portrait of a Queen; Duke of York's, Apr 1966, Henry in The Anniversary; made his first appearance on Broadway at Henry Miller's, 28 Feb 1968, again playing Gladstone in Portrait of a Queen; Open Air, Regent's Park, Jun 1968, Falstaff in The Merry Wives of Windsor; Apollo, Sept 1968, Peachum in The Beggar's Opera; Garrick, May 1969, Hardcastle in She Stoops to Conquer; Apollo, Dec 1971, Sir Francis Chesney in Charley's Aunt; Hampstead, Mar 1975, Arnold in Alphabetical Order, transferring to the May Fair, Apr; Apollo, May 1976, played four parts in Confusions; Savoy, Aug 1977, Roebuck Ramsden in Man and Superman; Royal Court, Aug 1978, Askey in Eclipse; toured UK, also Toronto, 1978–79, as Francis Mallock in Half-Life; Greenwich, May 1979, Mansky in The Play's the Thing; Vaudeville, Mar 1980, took over as Widdecombe in Stage Struck; has appeared in over 30

films since his first, Darling, in 1964; hundreds of TV appearances since 1951.

Favourite parts: Peer Gynt, Shylock, Capt Shotover. *Recreations:* Gardening, good food and collecting antique spectacles. *Address:* c/o Leading Artists Ltd, 60 St James's Street, London SW1.

COTES, Peter, FRSA (*né* Sydney Boulting), actor, producer and director
b Maidenhead, 19 Mar 1912; *s* of Arthur Boulting and his wife Rose (Bennett); *e* privately, and at the Italia Conti Stage School, Monclare and Taplow; *m* (1) Myfanwy Jones (mar dis); (2) Joan Miller.

Made his first appearance on the stage at Drury Lane Theatre, 2 May 1916, as The Page in a scene from Henry V, at the Shakespeare Tercentenary performance; Victoria Palace, 27 Dec 1926, played Major-General Tabloid in The Windmill Man, subsequently touring, first as John and afterwards as Slightly in Peter Pan; he played boys' parts for some years; understudied John Mills in Cavalcade at Drury Lane, Oct 1931, and Nelson Keys in Bow Bells, London Hippodrome, Jan 1932; Queen's, Apr 1932, played Mario in Caravan; subsequently appeared in films, cabaret and music-hall; debut as stage producer, 1936, with the revue Everybody Cheer; at the Portfolio Theatre, 1937, played Harsh in The Hand of the Potter, and Adolf Savoir in Small Hotel; Vaudeville, May 1937, appeared in Charlot's Non-stop Revue; on the outbreak of War, joined the Queen's Westminster Rifles, subsequently invalided out; at the Little Theatre, Bristol, 1941, with the repertory company; toured, 1941, as Charleston in Thunder Rock, and 1942, as Joe Bonaparte in Golden Boy, also in Tomorrow's Sun, Susie, and Flying Colours; Winter Garden, Dec 1943, played Starkey in Peter Pan; during 1944, was director of repertory at Worthing and Tunbridge Wells; toured, 1944, as Matt in To-Morrow's Eden, and at the Phoenix, Sept 1944, played Svara in The Last Stone; directed tours for the Arts Council, 1945; assumed the management of the New Lindsey Theatre, Apr 1946, opening with The Long Mirror; in May, 1946, directed Pick-up Girl, which was subsequently transferred to the Prince of Wales Theatre; also staged several important revivals at the New Lindsey, Apr–June 1946; has since directed The Animal Kingdom, Mid-Channel, 1947; Rocket to the Moon, The Master Builder, 1948; The Rising Wind, Miss Julie, 1949; directed two tours for the Arts Council, through the Welsh coalfields, of An Inspector Calls, and Anna Christie; in Sept 1948, founded the Peter Cotes Players at the Library Theatre, Manchester, staging a number of notable productions, of which two, Miss Julie and The Rising Wind, transferred to London in 1949; during the spring of 1950, toured as Paul Tabor in Birdcage; assumed control of the Boltons Theatre, Oct 1950, when it was renamed the New Boltons, and reopened Nov 1950, with The Children's Hour; during the subsequent season he produced Hamlet, Candida, Loaves and Fishes, Happy and Glorious, A Pin to See the Peepshow, The Biggest Thief in Town, Mrs Basil Farringdon, The Importance of Wearing Clothes, The Christmas Tree; he also presented his production of The Biggest Thief in Town at the Duchess, Aug 1951; he has since directed the following productions: Come Back, Little Sheba, The Mousetrap, The Man (which he also presented) 1952; The Father (Arts), and A Pin to See the Peepshow (Playhouse, New York) 1953; Walk Into My Parlour (tour), Mountain Fire (tour), Finishing School, Book of the Month, Happy Holiday, 1954; The Cardinal (Arts, Cambridge), 1957; Hot Summer Night, 1958; The Rope Dancers 1959; Girl on the Highway (which he also presented), 1960; A Loss of Roses, 1961; Hidden Stranger

(NY), The Odd Ones (tour), What Goes Up (also devised), 1963; So Wise, So Young, 1964; Paint Myself Black, 1965; The Impossible Years, 1966; Staring at the Sun and Janie Jackson (also presenting both), 1968; The Old Ladies (also co-presented), 1969; Look, No Hands (also presented), 1971; The Magic Man (also presented), 1977; film direction includes The Right Person, The Young and the Guilty, and Waterfront (co-director); in 1961, visited Australia for six months, inaugurating the Drama Department for Melbourne's Channel Seven; he has also directed numerous productions for both the BBC and ITV many of which he adapted; was Senior Drama Producer for Associated Rediffusion; Executive Producer for Future Films, Ltd; author of No Star Nonsense, 1949; A Handbook for the Amateur Theatre, 1957, part-author of The Little Fellow, 1965; George Robey, 1972; Elvira Barney, 1976; Circus, 1977, JP, 1978.

Recreations: Criminology, letter writing, watching and listening. *Club:* Savage, London; Players and University, New York. *Address:* 70 York Mansions, Prince of Wales Drive, London, SW11. *Tel:* 01–622 8546.

COTTEN, Joseph, actor

b Petersburg, Virginia, 15 May 1905; *s* of Joseph Cheshire Cotten and his wife Sally (Wilson); *m* (1) Lenore Kipp (dec); (2) Patricia Medina; prepared for the stage at the Hickman School of Expression in Washington, DC.

Engaged by David Belasco as an understudy and assistant stage manager for his last two productions at the Belasco Theatre: Dancing Partner, Aug 1930, and Tonight or Never, Nov 1930; Vanderbilt, Oct 1932, played Larry in Absent Father; Ethel Barrymore, Dec 1933, played Dick Ashley in Jezebel; Plymouth, 1935, appeared in Accent on Youth; Vanderbilt, Feb 1935, played Ralph Mendes in Loose Moments; Lyceum, Feb 1936, played the Policeman in The Postman Always Rings Twice; joined Orson Welles's Federal Theatre Project in 1936, and appeared at the Maxine Elliott in Horse Eats Hat; same theatre, Jan 1937, a Scholar in Dr Faustus; at the Mercury, Nov 1937 (also with Orson Welles), played Publius in Julius Caesar; and Jan 1938, Rowland Lacy in The Shoemaker's Holiday; Maxine Elliott, Nov 1938, Barrere in Danton's Death; at the Shubert, Mar 1939, played C K Dexter Haven in The Philadelphia Story, and toured the USA with the production, 1940; appeared in stock for David O Selznick for a season in La Jolla, California, 1947; reappeared on the New York stage at the National, Nov 1953, as Linus Larrabee, Jr, in Sabrina Fair; National, Oct 1958, Victor Fabian in Once More, With Feeling; US tour, Jan–May 1962, played Dr Flemming in Prescription: Murder; Ambassador, Oct 1962, played Julian Armstone in Calculated Risk; US tour, Jan–Mar 1964, appeared with his wife in the anthology Seven Ways of Love; Country Dinner Playhouse, Dallas, Texas, Feb 1974, played in The Reluctant Debutante; has also appeared in summer stock in Boston, 1931–2, Richmond, Virginia, and Bar Harbour, Maine, 1932; first appeared in films, 1940, with Orson Welles in Citizen Kane; subsequent films include The Magnificent Ambersons, Since You Went Away, Shadow of a Doubt, and A Delicate Balance, 1973, etc; first appeared on television in 1954 in The High Green Wall, and narrated the series *Hollywood and the Stars*, 1963–4.

Clubs: Players, Racquet and Tennis, New York, and Bucks, London. *Address:* 6363 Wilshire Boulevard, Los Angeles, California.

COTTON, Oliver, actor

b London, 20 June 1944; *s* of Robert Norman Cotton and his wife Ester; *e* Larkhall Lane School and Chiswick Polytechnic; *m* Catherine Stevens (mar dis); trained for the stage at the Drama Centre (1962–65).

Made his first stage appearance at Stage 73, NY, Nov 1965, as Mark in The Dwarfs and Kedge in A Night Out, also appearing in The Beggars Opera at the same theatre; repeated the part of Mark at the Traverse, Edinburgh, 1966, also playing Graham in The Local Stigmatic; played Graham at the Royal Court, Mar 1966; toured with Piccolo Theatre, 1966, in Four Hundred Years of English Comedy; joined the National Theatre company at the Old Vic, July 1966, taking over roles in Love for Love, The Storm, and Diego in The Royal Hunt of the Sun; Royal Court, Aug 1966, Mike in It's My Criminal, also guitarist for A Provincial Life, Oct; continued at the Old Vic as Borachio in Much Ado, First Player in Rosencrantz and Guildenstern Are Dead, Apr 1967; Oliver Martext and Sylvius in As You Like It, Oct 1967; in 1968 played in Volpone, Jan; Oedipus, Mar; Brecht's Edward II, Apr; and In His Own Write, Jun; Royal Court, Oct 1968, Lauffer, the tutor in The Tutor; same theatre, 1969, appeared in Erogenous Zones, and The Enoch Show, to which he also contributed; also in 1969 played Mercutio in Romeo and Juliet at the Ludlow Festival, and leading roles for a season at Cheltenham Rep; Royal Court, 1970, Dean in The Sport of My Mad Mother; same theatre, 1971, played Ferdinand in The Duchess of Malfi, Jan; Polly Baker in Man Is Man, Mar; Carpenter in Bond's Lear, Sept; Young Vic, Nov 1971, several parts in Cato Street; Round House, Mar 1972, Cortes in Quetzalcoatl; played several parts at Watford Palace that year, including an appearance in pantomime; Royal Court, 1973, Fergy in Captain Oates' Left Sock; founder member of Joint Stock, 1973, touring as Axel Ney Hoch in The Speakers; Royal Court, Aug 1974, Son in Bingo; Aldwych, Sept 1975, for RSC, John Abud in The Marrying of Anne Leete; rejoined the National Theatre, Dec 1975, to play Rosencrantz in Hamlet at the Old Vic and later in the new National Theatre, where his parts included Techelles in Tamburlaine the Great, Oct 1976; Clown in Force of Habit, Nov; Von Hierlinger in Tales from the Vienna Woods, Jan 1977; Decius Brutus and Messala in Julius Caesar, Mar; Judas in The Passion, Apr; Maj Hippisley Thomas in The Madras House, Jun; Mike Clayton in Half-Life, Nov; also title part in The Man with a Flower in His Mouth; Garrick, May 1978, Teddy in The Homecoming; again with the National, played General Fairfax in The World Turned Upside Down, Nov 1978, and Orrin in Dispatches, Jun 1979; Greenwich, Feb 1980, Kochetov in Liberty Hall; first film, 1967, Here We Go Round the Mulberry Bush; recently in The Day That Christ Died; TV work includes plays and series, most recently The Borgias; author of a TV play, The Intruder, 1967; his play Scrabble performed in the National Theatre's Experimental Season at the Jeannetta Cochrane, 1969.

Favourite parts: Axel Ney Hoch, John Abud. *Recreations:* Guitar, running. *Address:* c/o Green and Underwood, 3 Gunnersbury Lane, Ealing.

COTTRELL, Richard, director, manager and dramatic author

b London, 15 Aug 1936; *s* of Jack Hutchison Cottrell and his wife Mary Elizabeth (Nugent); *e* Radley and Jesus College, Cambridge.

While at Cambridge appeared in many productions and directed others; trained for the stage in Paris under Jean Perimony; entered management, 1962, at the Oxford Playhouse; director and manager, Prospect Theatre Company,

1962–9; general manager, Hampstead Theatre Club, 1964–6; director, Cambridge Theatre Company 1970–5; Director, Bristol Old Vic 1975–80; directed his first professional production at Hampstead, Jan 1966, The Birdwatcher; for Prospect directed tours of Thieves' Carnival 1966, The Constant Couple (also London), The Cherry Orchard (also Edinburgh Festival and London), The Birthday Party, 1967; Staircase, Richard II (also Edinburgh Festival and London), 1969; also Blithe Spirit (Lincoln), 1967; The Promise (Leicester), 1968; for Cambridge Theatre Company directed tours of The Alchemist, Semi-Detached, The Seagull, The Recruiting Officer, Chips with Everything, 1970; Hay Fever, The Three Sisters, Trelawny of the Wells, 1971; You and Your Clouds, Popkiss (also London), Ruling the Roost (first production of the Actors' Company, revived London 1974), 1972; Twelfth Night, Aunt Sally or the Triumph of Death, Jack and the Beanstalk, 1973; French Without Tears, Hamlet, Six Characters in Search of an Author, 1974; Entertaining Mr Sloane, 1975; also Bloomsbury (London), 1974; A Far Better Husband (tour), 1975; for Bristol Old Vic The National Health, Hard Times, 1975; Macbeth, Evening Light, Le Weekend, The Duchess of Malifi, Aladdin, 1976; Love's Labours Lost, Hamlet, Hedda Gabler, 1977; The Provok'd Wife, Cabaret, The Seagull, As You Like It, The Man Who Came to Dinner, 1978; Destiny, Troilus and Cressida, 1979; also She Stoops to Conquer, 1977, and A Bee in Her Bonnet, 1979, for Manitoba Theatre Centre; Waiting for the Parade (Lyric, Hammersmith), 1979; is the author of the play Deutsches Haus, 1959; adapted, with Lance Sieveking, Howards End, 1967, A Room With A View, 1968; has translated The Birdwatcher and Ruling the Roost (Feydeau); You and Your Clouds (Westphal), Tomorrow From Any Window (Grumberg), Aunt Sally or The Triumph of Death (Ionesco), The Seagull, The Cherry Orchard, The Three Sisters (Chekov); is a director of the Prospect Theatre Company, the Cambridge Theatre Company, the Hampstead Theatre Club.

Recreations: Music and travel. *Address:* 17 Charlotte Street, London, W1. *Tel* 01–580 1406.

COULOURIS, George, actor
b Manchester, England, 1 Oct 1903; *s* of Nicholas Coulouris and his wife Abigail (Redfern); *e* Manchester Grammar School; *m* (1) Louise Franklin (dec); (2) Elizabeth Clarke; formerly in his father's business; studied for the stage at the Central School of Speech Training and Dramatic Art under Elsie Fogerty.

Made his first appearance on the stage at the Rusholme Repertory Theatre, Manchester, May 1926, as the Rev William Duke in Outward Bound; first appearance on the London stage, Old Vic, 18 Oct 1926, as Sir Thomas Grey in Henry V, and subsequently played other small parts there; Daly's, London, Nov 1927, played Giuseppe in Sirocco; in Oct 1928, joined the company of the Cambridge Festival Theatre, where he played Yank in The Hairy Ape, Mercutio, Jaques, etc; Arts, London, Apr 1929, played Petronius in The Theatre of Life; Globe, May 1929, Jacques Bonalie in The Black Ace; made his first appearance on the New York stage at the Assembly Theatre, 9 Dec 1929, as Friar Peter in The Novice and the Duke (Measure for Measure); at the Martin Beck (for Theatre Guild), Apr 1930, played Sempronius in The Apple Cart; from 1930–2, played in stock companies in Boston and elsewhere; at the Embassy, London, Feb 1932, Tybalt in Romeo and Juliet; Gate, May 1932, the Bank Manager in From Morn to Midnight; returned to NY, and at Henry Miller's Theatre, Oct 1932, played Tallant

in The Late Christopher Bean; Morosco, May 1933, Julian Mosca in Best Sellers; Alvin (for the Guild), Nov 1933, Lord Burleigh in Mary of Scotland; Guild, Dec 1934, Lieut Cutting in Valley Forge; Booth, Dec 1935, Dr Shelby in Blind Alley; Martin Beck, Mar 1936, John de Stogumber in Saint Joan; St James', Oct 1936, Zacharey in Ten Million Ghosts; Mercury, Nov 1937, Marc Antony in Julius Caesar (in modern dress); Jan 1938, The King in The Shoemaker's Holiday; Apr 1938, Boss Mangan in Heartbreak House; Cort, Oct 1938, Mirabeau in Madame Capet; Jan 1939, Father Shaughnessy in The White Steed; Royale, Dec 1940, John Elliott in Cue for Passion; Martin Beck, Apr 1941, Teck de Brancovis in Watch on the Rhine; continued in this in NY and on tour, until June 1942; Forrest, NY, Mar 1943, Glo'ster in Richard III, which he also produced and staged; toured, 1946–7, in Blind Alley; City Center, May 1948, played Subtle in The Alchemist, and the Donkey Man in The Moon of the Caribbees; at the same theatre, June 1948, the Vagrant in The Insect Comedy; returning to England, he joined the Bristol Old Vic Company, Jan 1950, and during the season played Jaques in As You Like It, Tartuffe in the play of that name, also appearing in The Admirable Crichton, Julius Caesar, The Provok'd Wife; at the Lyric, Hammersmith, June 1950, with the Bristol Old Vic Company, again played Tartuffe; St Martin's, Aug 1950, appeared as Ulric Brendel in Rosmersholm; he appeared at the Edinburgh Festival, 1950, in The Man in the Overcoat; at Glasgow Citizens' Theatre, 1952, played King Lear; Criterion (for Under Thirty Group), Jan 1953, played King James I in Fool's Mate; Q, Feb 1953, Clumber Holmes in The Full Treatment; Embassy, May 1953, played Malvolio in Twelfth Night and Claudius in Hamlet; toured, Autumn 1953, as Smiley Coy in The Big Knife, and played the same part at the Duke of York's, Jan 1954; toured, Spring 1954, as the General in The Soldier and the Lady; Arts, Feb 1955, Paul Finch in The Ghost Writers; Q, Oct 1955, Charles Touchdown in Moonshine; Arts, Cambridge, Dec 1956, Hawkshaw in The Ticket-of-Leave Man; Princes, Mar 1957, John Pope Senior in A Hatful of Rain, also appearing in the revival of the play at the same theatre, Aug 1958; Arts, Cambridge, Feb 1959, Dr Stockmann in An Enemy of the People (Arthur Miller version); Mermaid, Sept 1962, Peter Flynn in The Plough and the Stars; Morosco, NY, Oct 1964, played Sir Samuel Holt in Beekman Place; Beaumont, NY, Feb 1966, the Father in The Condemned of Altona; Mark Taper Forum, Los Angeles, June 1967, Voltaire in The Sorrows of Frederick; returning to England he appeared at the Arts, Mar 1968, as the Earl of Theign in The Outcry; New, Dec 1968, played Sikorski in Soldiers; Richmond, 1970, Big Daddy in Cat On a Hot Tin Roof; Gardner Centre, Brighton, Sept 1973, Shylock in The Merchant of Venice; Globe, LA, Mar 1977, title-role in King Lear; has also appeared on television and broadcast, notably the autobiographical series To Hollywood and Back; entered films, 1933, and has appeared in numerous pictures, including Papillon and Murder on the Orient Express.

Favourite parts: Othello, Macbeth, and King Lear. *Recreations:* Tennis and music. *Address:* c/o Nems Management, 31 King's Road, London SW3.

COUNSELL, John, OBE, director, manager
b Beckenham, Kent, 24 Apr 1905; *s* of Claude Christopher Counsell and his wife Evelyn (Flemming); *e* Sedbergh, and Exeter College, Oxford; *m* Mary Kerridge; was a member of the OUDS, 1923–6; was formerly engaged as a tutor.

Made his first appearance on the stage at the Playhouse, Oxford, 18 Jan 1928, as Brian Strange in Mr Pim Passes By, and subsequently played several juvenile parts, besides acting as assistant stage-manager; toured, 1928–9, in Canada as stage-director for Maurice Colbourne's company; during 1929–30, played leading juvenile parts with the Northampton and Folkestone repertory companies; his first London engagement was at the New Theatre, Sept 1930, as stage-manager for Baliol Holloway's production of Richard III; 1930–3, was stage-director, scenic artist and eventually director of the Oxford Repertory company; 1933–4, director and joint manager of the Windsor Repertory company; Vaudeville, London, Oct 1934, played Poynter in Lover's Leap; during 1935–6, was engaged in broadcasting and films; during 1936, toured as Tubbs in Sweet Aloes; toured, in South Africa, 1936–7, in The Frog; in 1938, re-formed the Windsor Repertory company, which he managed until 1940; called to the Colours, 1940, as Territorial reservist, and served 1942–5, in North Africa, France, and Germany; wrote General Eisenhower's personal dispatches of the Tunisian and Italian campaigns; as a member of the planning staff of SHAEF, prepared all the papers relative to the surrender of Germany; demobilized, Oct 1945, with the rank of Lieut-Colonel; resumed management of the Windsor Repertory company, Oct 1945; in addition, has since directed Birthmark, Embassy, Mar 1947 and Playhouse, Apr 1947; Little Holiday, Kilburn Empire, Mar 1948; Captain Brassbound's Conversion, Lyric, Hammersmith, Oct 1948; The Man with the Umbrella, Duchess, Apr 1950; Who Goes There!, Vaudeville, Apr 1951; His House In Order, New, July 1951; Waggonload O' Monkeys, Savoy, Oct 1951; For Better, For Worse . . ., Comedy, Dec 1952; Anastasia, St James's, Aug 1952; Starlight, Golders Green Hippodrome, Apr 1956; Grab Me a Gondola, Lyric, Dec 1956; Three-Way-Switch, Aldwych, July 1958; How Say You? (also co-presented), Aldwych, Apr 1959; at the Theatre Royal, Windsor, Feb 1962, presented his 1,000th production at that theatre with You Never Can Tell; co-presented Ring of Jackals, Queen's, Feb 1965; Horizontal Hold, Comedy, May 1967; Aren't We All?, Savoy, June 1967; has led two overseas visits by the Windsor Theatre Company, playing Chasuble in The Importance of being Earnest (Hong Kong, 1966), Rev Samuel Gardner in Mrs Warren's Profession and David Bliss in Hay Fever (US Tour, 1968); author of Counsell's Opinion (autobiography), 1963; Play Direction, 1973.

Hobbies: Gardening and photography. *Club:* Green Room. *Address:* 3 Queen's Terrace, Windsor, Berks. *Tel:* Windsor 65344.

COURTENAY, Margaret, actress
b Cardiff, 14 Nov 1923; *d* of William Courtenay-Short and his wife Kitty Gordon (Clatworthy); *e* Whitchurch Grammar School; *m* Ivan Pinfield (mar dis); trained for the stage at LAMDA.

Made her first stage appearance at Cardiff Little Theatre, 1930, aged seven, as Astyanax in The Trojan Women; in repertory at Bexhill, 1946; with the Memorial Theatre, Stratford-upon-Avon, 1947–49, her parts included Bawd in Pericles, Juno in The Tempest and Helen in Cymbeline; Globe, 1949, understudied and played in Ring Round the Moon; Old Vic, May 1953, played Patience in Henry VIII; Duke of York's, 1954, Thirteen for Dinner; Piccadilly, 1954, took over a part in A Question of Fact; toured the US and Canada, 1954, as Hippolyta in A Midsummer Night's Dream, making her New York debut at the Metropolitan Opera House in the part, 21 Sept 1954; season at Wolverhampton Rep, 1955; at the Old Vic for three seasons Nov 1955– May 1958, including two tours of the US and one of Europe, playing parts including Gertrude in Hamlet, Goneril in King Lear, Andromache in Troilus and Cressida, Lady Capulet in

Romeo and Juliet, and finally repeating Patience in Henry VIII, May 1958; during this time she also played the Fitter in Restless Heart, St James's, May 1957; Pembroke, Croydon, 1960, Gertrude in Hamlet; Glyndebourne, season 1961, appeared in Ariadne auf Naxos; Phoenix, Apr 1962, Madame Elizabeth in Look Homeward, Angel; toured Australia, 1962, with Vivien Leigh in La Dame aux Camellias and Duel of Angels; Mermaid, Jun 1963, and Duchess, July, Ruby in Alfie; Oxford Playhouse and tour, 1964, in The Maids; Open Air, Regent's Park, season 1964, Mistress Quickly and Isabel in Henry V; Bristol Old Vic, 1964, Martha in Who's Afraid of Virginia Woolf?; Morosco, NY, Dec 1964, again played Ruby in Alfie; Duke of York's, Jun 1965, Madame Xenia in The Killing of Sister George; Chichester, Season 1967, Louisa Windeatt in The Farmer's Wife and Lady Bountiful in The Beaux' Stratagem; Mermaid, Apr 1968, Mrs Crowe in Hadrian VII; Drury Lane, Feb 1969, Vera Charles in Mame; Chichester, 1970, Catherine Petkoff in Arms and the Man; Her Majesty's, Oct 1971, Amelia Newsome in Ambassador; with the Welsh Theatre Company, 1972, appeared in Pig in a Poke and Uncle Vanya; Greenwich, July 1972, Mrs Culpepper in Liberty Ranch; toured with the Cambridge Theatre Company, 1973, as Mrs Clandon in You Never Can Tell; Lyric, May 1973, Muriel Wicksteed in Habeas Corpus; Phoenix, Mar 1976, played in 13 Rue de l'Amour; Haymarket, 1976, in The Case in Question; Apollo, Jan 1977, Mrs Railton-Bell in Separate Tables; Comedy, Feb 1978, Gertrude Saidenberg in Murder Among Friends; Old Vic, Sept 1978, and tour, Mrs Malaprop in the Prospect production of The Rivals; films include Isadora, and Royal Flash; frequent TV work includes both plays and series.

Favourite parts: Martha, Muriel Wicksteed. *Recreations:* Gardening, music, talking. *Address:* c/o Peter Browne Management, 13 St Martin's Road, London SW9.

COURTENAY, Tom, actor
b Hull, Yorkshire, 25 Feb 1937; *s* of Thomas Henry Courtenay and his wife Annie (Quest); *e* Kingston High School, Hull, and University College, London; *m* Cheryl Kennedy; trained for the stage at the Royal Academy of Dramatic Art.

Made his first appearance on the stage at the Lyceum Theatre, Edinburgh, Aug 1960, with the Old Vic Company, as Konstantin Treplyef in The Seagull, subsequently appearing in the same production at the Old Vic, Sept 1960; Old Vic, Feb 1961, played Poins in Henry IV (Part I), and Apr 1961, played Feste in Twelfth Night; at the Cambridge, June 1961, took over the part of Billy Fisher in Billy Liar; at the Old Vic, Jan 1964, joined the National Theatre Company, to play Andri in Andorra; Chichester Festival, 1966, played Trofimov in The Cherry Orchard, July, and Malcolm in Macbeth, August; joined the 69 Theatre Company, Manchester, 1966, playing parts including Lord Fancourt Babberley in Charley's Aunt, 1966; Hamlet (Edinburgh Festival, August 1968) and Young Marlow in She Stoops to Conquer, transferring in the latter part to the Garrick, May 1969; returning to the University Theatre, Manchester, Dec 1970, played the name part in Peer Gynt; Lord Fancourt Babberley in Charley's Aunt, Aug 1971, also Apollo, Dec 1971; Comedy, Aug 1972, Leonard in Time and Time Again; Manchester, May 1973, Capt Bluntschli in Arms and the Man; Greenwich, May 1974, and Globe, Aug 1974, played Norman in Alan Ayckbourn's trilogy, The Norman Conquests; Royal Court, Nov 1975, John Clare in The Fool; Royal Exchange, Manchester, Sept 1976, title part in The Prince of Homburg and Faulkland in The Rivals; Plymouth, NY, Feb 1977, Simon in Otherwise Engaged; Royal Exchange, Apr 1978, Raskolnikov in Crime and Punishment; Duke of York's, Nov

1978, Owen in Clouds; Royal Exchange, Mar 1980, Norman in The Dresser; entered films, Sept 1962, making an immediate success with The Loneliness of the Long Distance Runner; other notable films include: Billy Liar, King and Country, Dr Zhivago, Otley, One Day in the Life of Ivan Denisovitch, etc; first appeared on television, Apr 1961, and principal performances include: Private Potter and Dobley in The Lads.

Recreation: Listening to music and playing golf. *Address:* c/o CMA Ltd, 22 Grafton Street, London, W1.

COURTNEIDGE, Dame Cicely, actress
b Sydney, NSW, 1 Apr 1893; *d* of Robert Courtneidge and his wife Rosaline May (Adams); *m* Jack Hulbert (dec).

Made her first appearance on the stage at the Princes Theatre, Manchester, 1901, as Peasblossom in A Midsummer Night's Dream; returned to Australia with her father, and reappeared on the English stage at the Princes, Manchester, 30 Mar 1907, as Rosie Lucas in Tom Jones, made her first appearance on the London stage, at the Apollo Theatre, 17 Apr 1907, in the same part; Shaftesbury, July 1909, she played Chrysea in The Arcadians, and in 1910 appeared as Eileen Cavanagh in the same musical; same theatre, Sept 1911, appeared as Miyo Ko San in The Mousmé; May 1912, as Princess Clementine in Princess Caprice; Sept 1913, as Lady Betty Biddulph in The Pearl Girl; June 1914, Phyllis in The Cinema Star; May 1915, Eileen Cavanagh in The Arcadians; at the Pavilion, Glasgow, July 1915, Mabel in A Lucky Escape; subsequently again toured in The Pearl Girl; at the Prince of Wales, Birmingham, Sept 1915, played Cynthia Petrie in The Light Blues, and played the same part at the Shaftesbury Theatre, Sept 1916; at the Lyceum, Edinburgh, Dec 1916, played Margaret Potts in Oh, Caesar!; she then appeared in variety theatres with great success; at the Theatre Royal, Manchester, Christmas, 1918, appeared as Cinderella; subsequently appeared in variety theatres in songs and scenas; at the Royalty, Sept 1921, appeared in Ring Up; then returned to variety theatres; at the Little Theatre, Oct 1923, appeared in Little Revue Starts at Nine o'Clock; in 1924 toured in By-the-Way, appearing in the same revue at the Apollo, Jan 1925; made her first appearance in New York, at the Gaiety Theatre, 28 Dec 1925, in the same revue; after returning to London, appeared at the Gaiety, Aug 1926, in a revival of By-the-Way, and Dec 1926, as Peggy Bassett in Lido Lady; after a short tour in 1927, appeared at the Adelphi, Dec 1927, in Clowns in Clover, which ran until 1929; for a short time reappeared in variety theatres; Sept 1929, toured in The House that Jack Built, appearing in the same piece at the Adelphi, Nov 1929; Piccadilly, Jan 1931, appeared in Folly to Be Wise; appeared at the Victoria Palace, Feb 1934, in a Military scene; reappeared on the regular stage at the London Hippodrome, Oct 1937, as Sally and Mabel in Hide and Seek; Palace, Nov 1938, played Kay Porter in Under Your Hat, which ran, with a slight interruption on the outbreak of War, until 1940; toured, 1941, in Hulbert Follies; Palace, Apr 1942, played Kay Porter in Full Swing; Sept 1943, Terry Potter in Something in the Air; Phoenix, Nov 1945, Jo Fox in Under the Counter; at the Shubert, New York, 1947, again played Jo in Under the Counter; toured in Australia 1948–9, appearing in Under the Counter, and also playing in variety; Hippodrome, London, June 1949, played Her Excellency, Lady Frances Maxwell, in Her Excellency; from Oct 1950, toured as Gay Daventry in Gay's the Word, and appeared in this part at the Saville, Feb 1951; Piccadilly, May 1953, appeared in the revue Over the Moon; Her Majesty's, Aberdeen, Mar 1955, played Marion in The Joy of Living, and appeared in the same part at

Streatham Hill, Sept 1955; King's, Glasgow, Feb 1956, played Susie Green in Star Maker; Lyceum, Edinburgh, Nov 1956, Isabel Kilpatrick in Bachelor Borne, which was retitled The Bride and the Bachelor, at the Duchess, Dec 1956; after a short tour, appeared at the Apollo, Apr 1959, as Jane Hayling in Fool's Paradise; Royal Court, Liverpool, Sept 1960, played Isabel Kilpatrick in The Bride Comes Back, subsequently appearing at the Vaudeville in the same play, Nov 1960; Wimbledon, Dec 1961, appeared in the title-part of Mother Goose; King's, Edinburgh, Sept 1963, played Addie Lovell in There's a Yank Close Behind Me, subsequently appearing in the same play at the Vaudeville, Nov 1963, re-named Let's Be Frank; Prince Charles, Mar 1964, appeared as the Fairy Queen in Fielding's Music Hall; Savoy, Nov 1964, played Madame Arcati in High Spirits; toured, 1965, in The Reluctant Peer; Haymarket, Dec 1967, played Dora Randolph in Dear Octopus; Duke of York's, Nov 1968, Denise Darvel in Dear Charles; toured S Africa, July, and UK, Nov 1970, in Oh, Clarence; Vaudeville, Mar 1971, Olive Smythe in Move Over Mrs Markham; toured, 1973, as Lady Angkatell in The Hollow; in 1974, as Dame Beatrice Appleby in Breath of Spring and in Don't Utter a Note; toured, 1976 in Once More with Music; received the CBE in the New Year Honours, 1951, and the DBE in the New Year Honours, 1972; published a volume of autobiography, Cicely, 1953; commenced film career 1929, and has broadcast frequently since 1931.

(*Died 26 Apr 1980.*)

COURTNEY, Richard, drama and theatre scholar and teacher
b Newmarket, England, 4 June 1927; *s* of Arthur John Courtney and his wife Celia Annie; *e* Culford School and Leeds University; *m* Rosemary Gale.

Directed and appeared in a number of productions at University and afterwards at the Arts Theatre, Leeds, and in Rep in Yorkshire; taught at schools in England 1952–59; Senior Lecturer in Drama, 1959–67, Trent Park College of Education; Associate Professor of Theatre, 1968–71, University of Victoria, British Columbia; Professor of Drama, 1971–74, University of Calgary; Professor, 1974–present, Ontario Institute for Studies in Education, and University of Toronto Graduate Centre for Drama; Visiting Fellow, Spring 1979, Melbourne State College, Victoria; has lectured extensively in Australia, Canada, the UK and US; President, 1970–73, Canadian Child and Youth Drama Association; President, 1973–76, Canadian Conference of the Arts; Chairman, 1975–79, National Inquiry into Arts and Education in Canada; publications include Drama for Youth, 1964, Teaching Drama, 1965, The School Play, 1966, The Drama Studio, 1967, Play, Drama and Thought, 1968; The Dramatic Curriculum, 1980; author of various reports and numerous journal articles; played various roles on BBC radio, 1956–60.

Recreation: Creative writing. *Address:* 288 Major Street, Toronto, Ontario, M5S 2L6 *and* Elephant Butte, NM 87935.

COVINGTON, Julie, actress and singer
e Cambridge University.

Appeared with the Footlights and other groups while at Cambridge, and toured the US in the Oxford and Cambridge Shakespeare Company's production of A Midsummer Night's Dream, 1968; made her professional stage debut at the Round House, 17 Nov 1971, in Godspell, transferring with the production to the Wyndham's; at The Place, Mar 1973, played Marea Garga in In the Jungle of Cities; Bankside Globe, Aug 1973, Charmian in Antony and Cleopatra; Theatre Upstairs, Dec 1973, Gale in The Pleasure Principle;

Old Vic, Mar 1974, Iris in the National Theatre production of The Tempest; also with the National, played Janice in Weapons of Happiness, Lyttelton, July 1976; Riverside Studios, Jan 1978, Varya in The Cherry Orchard; returning to the Lyttelton, Apr 1978, played Alice Park in Plenty; Coliseum, Aug 1978, Anna I in The Seven Deadly Sins of Ordinary People; Royal Court, Mar 1979, Edward and Betty in Joint Stock's production of Cloud Nine; Hampstead, June 1980, Shelly in Buried Child; first film, The Adventures of Barry McKenzie, 1972; TV includes Rock Follies, Censored Scenes from King Kong, and The Voysey Inheritance; has made a number of successful records, including the original Evita.

Address: c/o Kate Feast Management, 43A Princess Road, London NW1.

COX, Brian, actor

b Dundee, 1 June 1946; *s* of Charles McArdle Campbell Cox and his wife Mary Ann Gillerline (McCann); *e* St Michael's RCJS, Dundee; *m* Caroline Burt; trained for the stage at LAMDA.

His early stage experience was as an ASM at Dundee Repertory Theatre, 1961; after leaving LAMDA, 1965, joined the Lyceum company, Edinburgh, followed in 1966 by two years with the Birmingham Rep, where his parts included the title-role in Peer Gynt, 1967, and Orlando in As You Like It, in which he made his London début when the production was seen at the Vaudeville, 13 June 1967; Assembly Hall, Aug 1968, Ulfhejm in the 69 Theatre Company's Edinburgh Festival production of When We Dead Awaken; Royal Court, Apr 1969, Steven in In Celebration; again at the Edinburgh Festival, Sept 1969, Gregers Werlè in The Wild Duck; Royal Court, Jan 1970, Alan in The Big Romance; Garrick, Feb 1971, Norman in Don't Start Without Me; Gardner Centre, Brighton, Aug 1971, Knight of Riprafratta in Mirandolina; Queen's, Oct 1971, Brian Lowther in Getting On; Open Space, Mar 1972, appeared as Gustav in a late night production of Creditors; Royal Court, June 1972, Eilert Lovborg in Hedda Gabler; at the Playhouse, Nottingham, autumn 1972, played Berowne in Love's Labour's Lost, title-role in Brand, Sergeant Match in What the Butler Saw, and D'Artagnan in The Three Musketeers; Royal Court, Aug 1973, Proctor in Cromwell; Edinburgh Festival, Sept 1973, directed The Man with a Flower in His Mouth, and The Stronger; Royal Exchange, Manchester, 1973, Sergius in Arms and the Man; toured with Prospect Theatre Company, Mar 1974, as Christian in The Pilgrim's Progress; Exchange, Manchester, Nov 1975, Sir Henry Harcourt Reilly in The Cocktail Party; and toured in Rogues and Vagabonds; joined the National Theatre Company 1976 to appear in Emigrés, Young Vic, July and at the Oliver, Oct, as Theridamas in Tamburlaine the Great; Olivier, Mar 1977, Brutus in Julius Caesar; Riverside Studios, July 1978, De Flores in The Changeling; returned to the National in Dec 1978 to play title-role in Herod, and Ireton in The Putney Debates; Royal Court, Feb 1979, Mickey in On Top; films, since Nicholas and Alexandra, 1970 include: In Celebration; TV since 1965, includes: The Devil's Crown, Out, Bothwell and Thérèse Raquin.

Favourite parts: Brand, De Flores. *Recreations:* Gym-work, working with drama students. *Club:* Savile. *Address:* c/o Larry Dalzell Associates, 3 Goodwin's Court, St Martin's Lane, London WC2. *Tel:* 01–240 3086.

COX, Constance, dramatic author

b Sutton, Surrey, 25 Oct 1915; *d* of John William Shaw and his wife Anne Elizabeth (Vince); *e* Sutton and Wallington, Surrey; *m* Norman Cox (dec).

Author or adaptor of the following plays: The Romance of David Garrick, 1942; The Boy from Belfast, Remember Dick Sheridan, 1944; Sleeping Dogs, Madame Bovary, 1945; Vanity Fair, 1946; The Picture of Dorian Gray, Georgia Story, 1948; Northanger Abbey, The Count of Monte Cristo, 1949; The Hunchback of Notre Dame, Spring at Marino, Mansfield Park, 1950; The Enemy in the House, 1951; The Nine Days Wonder, Because of the Lockwoods, The Woman in White, Lord Arthur Savile's Crime, 1952; Trilby, 1954; Quo Vadis, 1955; Heathcliff, 1959; The Caliph's Minstrel, 1965; Two Cities (book), 1969; Nightmare, 1972; Wuthering Heights, 1974; The Murder Game, 1976; is also the author or adaptor of numerous television plays and serials, including Jane Eyre, Vanity Fair, Precious Bane, The History of Mr Polly, Pride and Prejudice, Katy, Bleak House, Oliver Twist, Lorna Doone, Martin Chuzzlewit, Rogue Herries, A Tale of Two Cities, The Forsyte Saga, Rebecca of Sunnybrook Farm and radio serials, including War and Peace, The Pickwick Papers and The Barchester Chronicles.

Recreations: Motoring, gardening and croquet. *Club:* Sussex Playwrights. *Address:* 2 Princes Avenue, Hove, Sussex.

CRACKNELL, Ruth, actress

b Maitland, NSW, 6 Jul 1925; *d* of Charles Cracknell and his wife Winifred Goddard (Watts); *e* The North Sydney Girls' HS and the Independent Drama School; *m* Eric Phillips.

Made her first stage appearance in 1947, playing Mrs de Winter in Rebecca; early roles at the St James Playhouse, Sydney, in Shakespeare, Strindberg; appeared in a number of revues at Phillip Street Theatre, Sydney 1957–68; 1960, led the chorus in Murder in the Cathedral at first Adelaide Festival of the Arts; 1968, Independent Theatre, Sydney, Agnes in A Delicate Balance; 1970, University of NSW, Jocasta in Tyrone Guthrie's production of King Oedipus, later presented at the 1971 Perth Festival; Nimrod, Sydney, 1973, Mme Arkadina in The Seagull; Drama Theatre, Opera House, Sydney, 1974, Irene in What If You Died Tomorrow?, making her London theatre debut in the same part when the production was transferred to the Comedy, 2 Sept 1974; Old Tote, Sydney, 1975, Home; Old Tote and Theatre Royal, Sydney, 1976, Connie in Habeas Corpus; at the Playhouse, Adelaide, for the State Company, 1977, Mme Ranevsky in The Cherry Orchard, Mrs Candour in School for Scandal, and in her own one-woman show; Theatre Royal, Sydney, 1978; Delia in Bedroom Farce, transferring to Her Majesty's; Nimrod, 1979, Mrs Rafi in The Sea; Theatre Royal, Sydney, 1979, Fonsia in The Gin Game; Drama Theatre, Opera House, for Sydney Theatre Company, 1980, Daisy in Close of Play; first film, Smiley Gets a Gun, 1958; recently seen in The Singer and the Dancer, The Chant of Jimmy Blacksmith and The Night the Prowler; many appearances on Australian TV include Seven Little Australians, Ben Hall, The Oracle and The Golden Soak; in radio, amongst other work, has written and presented features on the poets Judith Wright and Anna Akhmatova for the ABC and BBC; created a Member of the Order of Australia, 1980.

Favourite part: The last. *Recreations:* Reading and walking — especially around art galleries. *Address:* c/o International Casting Service, 147A King Street, Sydney, NSW.

CRAIG, Helen, actress

b San Antonio, Texas, 13 May 1912; *d* of Edward J Craig and his wife, Emily (Cauthorn); *e* in Mexico and Chile; *m* John Beal.

Made her first appearance on the stage at the Hedgerow Repertory Theatre, 1929, as a Maid in A Doll's House, and played there for five years; also fulfilled various engagements at Pasadena, San Francisco, Santa Barbara, and Hollywood, and in summer theatres at Montclair and Maplewood, NJ; first appeared in New York, at the Masque Theatre, 16 Jan 1936, as Manuelita in Russet Mantle, and subsequently succeeded Martha Sleeper as Kay Rowley in the same play; Vanderbilt Theatre, May 1936, appeared in New Faces; Mercury, Nov 1937, Calpurnia in Julius Caesar; Empire, Nov 1938, Ann Jenkins in Soliloquy; Morosco, June 1939, succeeded Margaret Webster as Mary Magdalen in Family Portrait; Biltmore, Feb 1940, played Kira Argounova in The Unconquered; Belasco, Sept 1940, Belinda McDonald in Johnny Belinda; Mansfield, Oct 1941, Rosalind in As You Like It; Plymouth, Feb 1946, Princess Nieou-Chi in Lute Song; Playhouse, Dec 1946, Ellen Pascoe in Land's End; Circle Theatre, Los Angeles, May 1949, the title-role in Anouilh's Antigone; in summer theatres, 1950, appeared as Mrs Dearth in Dear Brutus; ANTA Playhouse, NY, Jan 1951, Angustias in The House of Bernarda Alba; summer theatres, 1952, played Maria Marescaud in A Murder in the Family; Theatre de Lys, NY, June 1953, Bella in Maya; Heritage, Stonington, Connecticut, July 1957, appeared in a dramatic recital of John Brown's Body; same theatre, July 1955, Dona Anna in a dramatic recital of Shaw's Don Juan in Hell; Henry Miller's, Feb 1965, Mama in Diamond Orchid; Red Barn, Northport, LI, Aug 1965, The Beggar in Some Winter Games; Martinique, Dec 1965, The Nurse in Medea; Sheridan Square Playhouse, Apr 1967, Mrs Onoria in To Clothe the Naked; Broadhurst, Oct 1967, Nora Melody in More Stately Mansions; Roxy, Hollywood, Cal, Nov 1975, Emma Goldman in Womanspeak; has played numerous roles in stock and repertory companies, including: Candida, Christine in Mourning Becomes Electra, Clytemnestra in Tower Beyond Tragedy, Antigone, Julius Caesar, Countess Aurelia in The Madwoman of Chaillot, etc; has directed many plays and children's plays; has taught acting at the Lenox School, NY, the Country School in Madison, Connecticut, and privately; first appeared in films, 1948, in They Live by Night, other films include The Snake Pit and Rancho de Luxe; has also played frequently on television, recently in Rich Man, Poor Man, *The Waltons, Kojak*, etc.

Address: c/o Actors Equity Association, 165 West 46th Street, New York, NY 10036.

CRAIG, Michael (*né* Gregson), actor
b Poona, India, 27 Jan 1928; *s* of Donald Gregson and his wife Violet (Winter); *e* Upper Canada College, Toronto; *m* Babette Collier; formerly a merchant seaman.

His first professional appearance was in Dec 1949, at the Castle, Farnham, as Balthazar in The Merchant of Venice; subsequently in repertory in York, Windsor and Oxford; Theatre Royal, Stratford E, Sept 1961, played Michael in A Whistle in the Dark, making his West End debut in the part when the play transferred to the Apollo, Oct 1961; Memorial Theatre, Stratford-on-Avon, July 1963, for the Royal Shakespeare Company, played Suffolk in Henry VI, part of the trilogy The Wars of the Roses; played the same part at the Aldwych, Jan 1964, also Jack Cade in Edward IV; St Martin's, May 1964, Hal Patterson in I Love You, Mrs Patterson; Prince of Wales, Apr 1966, Nick Arnstein in Funny Girl; made his first New York appearance at the Music Box, 2 Jan 1967, as Teddy in The Homecoming; Arnaud, Guildford, July 1971, Freddie in The Deep Blue Sea; toured Australia, 1971, as Mr Markham in Move Over Mrs Markham; Opera House, Sydney, 1978, played Prospero in The Tempest; films, since 1953, include The Angry Silence, Star and Country Dance; frequent TV appearances since 1951 include Saint Joan, Spoiled and The Hotel in Amsterdam.

Club: Stage Golfing Society. *Recreations:* Sport of all kinds, reading, writing. *Address:* c/o ICM, 22 Grafton Street, London, W1.

CRAIG, Wendy, actress
b Sacriston, Co Durham, 20 June 1934; *d* of George Dixon Craig and his wife Anne (Lindsay); *e* Durham and Darlington High Schools, and Yarm Grammar School; *m* John Alexander Bentley; trained for the stage at the Central School of Speech Training and Dramatic Art.

After repertory at Ipswich, made her first London appearance at the Irving Theatre, June 1955, in the revue Soho So What; Duchess, Sept 1955, played Monica Twigg in Mr Kettle and Mrs Moon; Aldwych, June 1956, played Daphne Jameson in Man Alive!; joined the English Stage Company at the Royal Court, Dec 1957, to play Middie Paradock in A Resounding Tinkle; Feb 1958, played Josie Elliott in Epitaph For George Dillon; Feb 1958, played Greta in The Sport of My Mad Mother; Apr 1958, again played Middie Paradock in a revised version of A Resounding Tinkle; at the Comedy, May 1958, again played Josie in Epitaph For George Dillon, when the production transferred under the new title of George Dillon; made her first appearance in New York at the John Golden, Nov 1958, as Josie in Epitaph For George Dillon; on returning to London, at the Fortune, Sept 1959, played Marion Dangerfield in The Ginger Man; Cambridge, Feb 1960, played Barbara in The Wrong Side of the Park; Arts, Jan 1961, The Girl in Lunch Hour, and Miss Haviour in The Form, in a triple bill entitled Three, subsequently transferring with the production to the Criterion, Jan 1961; Arts, Cambridge, Apr 1964, played Brenda in Something From Collette; St Martin's, May 1964, played Brenda in the same play re-titled I Love You Mrs Patterson; Piccadilly, June 1965, played Fanny in Ride A Cock Horse; Hampstead, May 1966, Deborah Solstice in Happy Family; Scala, Dec 1968, played the title-rôle in Peter Pan; Forum, Billingham, Feb 1972, Nora in A Doll's House; Apollo, Sept 1973, Katy Cooper, in Finishing Touches; Arnaud, Guildford, Aug 1975, Maggie Hobson in Hobson's Choice; Mermaid, Sept 1977, played Betty in Breezeblock Park; Lyceum, Edinburgh, Jan 1980, Alma in The Bed Before Yesterday; films in which she has appeared include: The Mind Benders, The Servant, The Nanny, etc; has appeared on television in numerous plays and the series Not in Front of the Children, for which the Variety Club named her BBC TV Personality of the Year, 1970; she won the Club's award, 1974, for And Mother Makes Five (ITV); most recent series Butterflies.

Favourite part: Middie Paradock in A Resounding Tinkle. *Recreation:* Listening to music. *Address:* c/o William Morris (UK) Ltd, 147/9 Wardour Street, London W1V 3TB.

CRANE, Richard, dramatic author and actor
b York, 4 Dec 1944; *s* of Rev Robert Bartlett Crane and his wife Nowell Chamberlain Harbord (Twidle); *e* St John's, Leatherhead and Jesus College, Cambridge; *m* Faynia Williams.

Acted in plays and revue at Cambridge, where he co-wrote and took part in the Footlights revue, 1966; appeared in repertory at Frinton, Bournemouth, Nottingham, Worcester, and with Brighton Combination, Traverse and the Lindsay Kemp Troupe; his play Three Ugly Women was produced at the Little Theatre Club, Feb 1967; since then he has written plays including: Crippen, The Tenant, Tom Brown, 1971; Decent Things, The Blood Stream, Mutiny on the Bounty, Bleak Midwinter, 1972; David King of the Jews, Thunder, Secrets, The Pied Piper, 1973; The Quest, 1974; Humbug, Mean Time, Venus and Superkid, Clownmaker, Bloody Neighbours (produced by the National Theatre at the ICA), 1975; Gunslinger, Nero and the Golden House, 1976; Satan's Ball, 1977; four of these plays, Thunder, The Quest, and Clownmaker and Satan's Ball, won *Scotsman* Fringe First

Awards at the Edinburgh Festival; appeared at the Traverse in his one-man show Gogol, touring festivals in Britain and Sweden for the British Council, 1978–79, and playing at the Theatre Upstairs, Sept 1979; Fellow in Theatre, University of Bradford, 1972–4; Thames TV Resident Dramatist, National Theatre, 1974–5; Member, Board of Directors, Edinburgh Festival Fringe Society; Arts Council Fellow in Creative Writing, University of Leicester, 1976; Literary Manager, Royal Court Theatre, 1978–79; Arts Council Bursary, 1979; first play for television, Rottingdean, and radio production of Gogol, 1979.

Recreations: Carpentry, swimming. *Address:* c/o Margaret Ramsay Ltd, 14a Goodwin's Court, St Martin's Lane, London WC2N 4LL. *Tel:* 01–240 0691.

CRANHAM, Kenneth, actor
b Dunfermline, Scotland, 12 Dec 1944; *s* of Ronald Cranham and his wife Margaret M'Kay Ferguson; *e* Tulse Hill School; *m* Diana Quick (mar dis); trained for the stage at Royal Academy of Dramatic Art.

While at school was a member of the National Youth Theatre, making his first appearance in Henry V at Sadler's Wells, Aug 1962; after RADA, where he won the Bancroft gold medal, joined the English Stage Company at the Royal Court, playing in Ubu Roi, July 1966; Wilson in The Ruffian on the Stair, Aug 1966; Jeanetta Cochrane, Sept 1966, Hal in Loot, making his West End debut in the same part when the play transferred to the Criterion; also made his Broadway debut as Hal at the Biltmore, 18 Mar 1968; again at the Royal Court played Len in Saved and Kiro in Narrow Road to the Deep North, Feb 1969; Len in Early Morning, Mar 1969; at the Bristol Old Vic, Mar–May 1973 played Edmund in Long Day's Journey into Night, Myshkin in Subject to Fits, and Prince Arthur in Early Morning; Royal Court, played Jed in Magnificence, June 1973 and Galactic Jack in The Tooth of Crime, June 1974; Greenwich, Dec 1974, Frank in The Entertainer; Mermaid, Apr 1975, Louis Dubedat in The Doctor's Dilemma; Duke of York's, 1975, took over title role in Entertaining Mr Sloane; Wyndham's, Jan 1976, Gethin Price in Comedians; joined the RSC at the Aldwych, 1976, and played Don Parritt in The Iceman Cometh, May, and Lvov in Ivanov, Sept; for the National Theatre, 1977, Nick in Strawberry Fields, Peter in The Passion, both Cottesloe, Apr; Christopher West in Old Movies and Harcourt in The Country Wife, Olivier, both Nov; Cottesloe, Feb 1978, Prof Maurice Stapleton in Love Letters on Blue Paper; Royal Court, Feb 1979, Ramble in The London Cuckolds; films, since Oliver! (1968) include Brother Sun, Sister Moon and Joseph Andrews; TV includes *Danger UXB*, and recently Thérèse Raquin and 'Tis Pity She's a Whore.

Favourite parts: Len in Saved, Galactic Jack. *Address:* c/o Jeremy Conway, 8 Cavendish Place, London W1M 9DJ.

CRAVEN, Gemma, actress
b Dublin, 1 June 1950; *d* of Gabriel Bernard Craven and his wife Lillian Josephine (Byrne); *e* Loretto College, Dublin and St Bernard's Convent, Westcliff-on-Sea; trained for the stage at the Bush Davies School.

Made her first professional appearance in Oct 1968 at the Palace Theatre, Westcliff, as the maid in Let's Get Divorce; in 1970 made her West End début when she took over the role of Anya in Fiddler on the Roof at Her Majesty's; The Place, Feb 1971, title-role in Audrey; Belgrade, Coventry, Aug 1971, Jenny Bell in Saturnalia; Thorndike, Leatherhead, Mar 1972, Sabrina in Sabrina Fair; Sadler's Wells, June 1972, Rose Trelawny in Trelawny, transferring with the production to the Prince of Wales; Chichester Festival, 1973, played

Jasmin in R Loves J, July, and Sheba in Dandy Dick, Aug, again appearing in the latter role at the Garrick, Oct 1973; Chichester, 1974, Corinna in The Confederacy, May, and Katya in A Month in the Country, July; Billingham Forum, Nov 1974, Elizabeth Snowden in Underground; Theatre Royal, Bristol, Feb 1975, Polly Peachum in The Threepenny Opera; Shaw, July 1976, Carol Melchett in Black Comedy; Thorndike, Leatherhead, Oct 1976, Shelley Jones and Meatball Jones in The Happiest Tears in Town; Gaiety, Dublin, June 1977, in Side by Side by Sondheim; also Yvonne Arnaud, Guildford and tour, Aug 1978; Globe, July 1979, appeared in Songbook; recent TV appearances include Pennies from Heaven, Must Wear Tights and She Loves Me; film appearances since 1976 include Kingdom of Gifts and Why Not Stay for Breakfast?.

Recreation: Crochet. *Address:* c/o Stella Richards Personal Management, 5 Rima House, Callow St, London SW3. *Tel:* 01–352 2667.

CRAWFORD, Cheryl, director and producer
b Akron, Ohio, 24 Sept 1902; *d* of Robert K Crawford and his wife Luella Elizabeth (Parker); *e* Buchtel College and Smith College, New York; joined the Theatre Guild in a secretarial capacity.

Subsequently appeared in minor parts in several plays, and later assisted in several of the productions until 1932; was casting director from 1926–30; she was one of the founders of the Group Theatre, 1931, and remained with that organization for eight years, directing The House of Connelly, 1931; Big Night, 1933; Till the Day I Die, Weep for the Virgins, 1935; her first independent production was All the Living, at the Fulton Theatre, 1938; at the Morosco Theatre, Mar 1939, presented Family Portrait; National, Feb 1940, presented Another Sun; with John Wildbeg, founded the summer theatre at Maplewood, NJ, producing a number of original plays; in 1941, she revived Porgy and Bess at this theatre with great success, and took the production to the Majestic, NY, Mar 1942; since then has produced, or co-produced, The Flowers of Virtue, A Kiss for Cinderella, 1942; Porgy and Bess, One Touch of Venus, 1943; The Perfect Marriage, The Tempest, 1944; with Eva Le Gallienne and Margaret Webster founded the American Repertory Theatre and, as managing director, co-produced Henry VIII, What Every Woman Knows, John Gabriel Borkman, Androcles and the Lion, A Pound on Demand, 1946, and Alice in Wonderland and Through the Looking Glass, 1947; presented Brigadoon, Skipper Next to God, A Temporary Island, Love Life, 1948; Regina, The Closing Door, 1949; in 1950 appointed Joint-General Director of the ANTA play series, which commenced operations at the ANTA Playhouse, Nov 1950, with The Tower Beyond Tragedy; Peer Gynt, The Rose Tattoo, Flahooley, Paint Your Wagon, 1951; Camino Real, Oh, Men! Oh, Women!, 1953; The Honeys, 1955; Mister Johnson, Girls of Summer, 1956; Good as Gold, 1957; Comes a Day, The Shadow of a Gunman, 1958; The Rivalry, Sweet Bird of Youth, 1959; The Long Dream, Kukla, Burr, and Ollie, Period of Adjustment, 1960; Brecht on Brecht, 1961; Andorra, Mother Courage and Her Children, Jennie, 1963; Doubletalk, 1964; Chu Chem (Philadelphia), 1966; The Freaking out of Stephanie Blake, 1967; Celebration, 1969; Colette (two productions), 1970; The Love Suicide at Schofield Barracks, The Web and The Rock, 1972; Yentl, 1975; Do You Turn Somersaults, 1978; is one of the founders and the Director of the Actors Studio; Executive Producer of the Actors Studio Theatre; Doctor of Fine Arts, Smith College, 1962; in 1964 was awarded the Brandeis University Medal of Achievement for Distinguished Contribution to American

Theatre Arts; Lawrence Longner award, 1977, for lifetime achievement in the theatre; is one of the directors of the New American Repertory Theatre.

Address: 301 West 45th Street, New York, NY 10036. *Tel:* LT1 3810.

CRAWFORD, Michael, actor
b Salisbury, Wilts, 19 Jan 1942; *e* St Michael's College, Bexley and Oakfield School, Dulwich.

Began his career as a boy soprano, appearing in the the original productions of Noye's Fludde and Let's Make an Opera; after numerous films and broadcasts as a juvenile, made his West End début at the Prince of Wales, 8 Apr 1965, as Arnold Champion in Travelling Light; Duke of York's, Apr 1966, Tom in The Anniversary; New York début Feb 1967, at the Barrymore, as Tom in White Lies and Brindsley Miller in Black Comedy, in a double-bill; Strand, June 1971, Brian Runnicles in No Sex Please—We're British; Drury Lane, May 1974, Billy Fisher in Billy; Prince of Wales, Sept 1976, George in Same Time Next Year; Queen's, June 1979, Charlie Gordon in Flowers for Algernon; his film appearances include: The Knack, Hello Dolly, and The Games; TV includes: his own series *Some Mothers Do 'Ave 'Em, Chalk and Cheese,* and *Sorry.*

Address: c/o Michael Linnit, Globe Theatre, Shaftesbury Avenue, London W1.

CREGAN, David (Appleton Quartus), Dramatist
b Buxton, Derbys, 30 Sept 1931; *s* of James Grattan Cregan and his wife Gertrude Isabella Martha (Fraser); *e* The Leys, Cambridge, and Clare College, Cambridge; *m* Ailsa Wynne Willson; formerly a teacher and mouse-poison salesman.

Author of the following plays, the first six of which were presented at the Royal Court; Miniatures, 1965; The Dancers, Transcending, Three Men for Colverton, 1966; The Houses By the Green, 1968; A Comedy of the Changing Years (opening play of the Theatre Upstairs), Tipper, 1969; Liebestraum, 1970; How We Held the Square, 1971; The Land of Palms, George Reborn, 1972; Cast Off, 1973; The King, 1974; Tina, 1975; Poor Tom, 1976; Tigers, 1978; Young Sir, 1979; author of the television plays That Time of Life, and I Want to Marry Your Son; Miniatures has also been televised; plays for radio, since 1975, include The Latter Days of Lucy Trenchard, The Monument, Inventor's Corner and Hope; author of a novel, Ronald Rossiter, 1958.

Recreations: Gardening, camping. *Address:* 124 Briars Lane, Hatfield, Herts. *Tel:* Hatfield 64587.

CRIBBINS, Bernard, actor
b Oldham, Lancs, 29 Dec 1928; *s* of John Edward Cribbins and his wife Ethel (Clarkson); *e* St Anne's Elementary School, Oldham; *m* Gillian McBarnet.

First appeared on stage, 1942, at the Coliseum, Oldham, in the Oldham Rep production of Lavender Ladies; joined the company professionally, Jan 1943; subsequently with the Piccolo Players, Manchester, and the Queen's Players, Hornchurch; first London appearance, Arts, Mar 1956, playing both Dromios in a musical version of The Comedy of Errors; Vaudeville, 1956, joined the cast of Salad Days; New Lindsey, Jan 1957, the Chicken in The Chicken Play; Lyric, Hammersmith, Apr 1957, Tony Peters in Harmony Close; Players, July 1957, Boris (the Dog) in Antarctica; Lyric, Hammersmith, Jan 1958, Fernando Fernandez in Lady at the Wheel, transferring to the Westminster, Feb 1958; Duke of York's, May 1958, Deadly Mortimer in The Big Tickle; Piccadilly, Nov 1958, Kiki Reger in Hook, Line and Sinker; Lyric, Hammersmith, 1960, appeared in the revue New

Cranks; Fortune, Oct 1960, revue, And Another Thing; Comedy, May 1962, Cpl Billy Jester in Little Mary Sunshine; Mermaid, Sept 1966, reader in The Fire of London; Strand, June 1968, Arnold Crouch in Not Now, Darling; toured Australia, 1973, in The Love Game; Criterion, Oct 1974, Timothy Westerby in There Goes the Bride; Arnaud, Guildford, Oct 1978, Murray in Forty Love; Royalty, Dec 1979, Herr Von Cuckoo in The Gingerbread Man; has appeared regularly in films since 1957, including The Railway Children; TV appearances since 1956, include his own series, Cribbins.

Recreations: Fishing, fly tying, beach-combing. *Address:* c/o Crouch Associates, 59 Frith Street, London W1.

CRINKLEY, Richmond Dillard, executive and director of the Vivian Beaumont Theater at Lincoln Center and producer
b Blackstone, Virginia, 20 Jan 1940; *s* of James Epes Crinkley and his wife Sarah Elizabeth; *e* University of Virginia and Oxford University.

Member of the English faculty of the University of North Carolina, 1967–69; Director of Programs, Folger Shakespeare Library, and Producer, Folger Theatre Group, 1969–73, presenting Shakespeare, the classics, and modern works including Total Eclipse, Happy Days, and Subject to Fits; assistant to the chairman of the John F Kennedy Center for the Performing Arts, Washington DC, 1973–76, where he presented productions including the following which were seen on Broadway: Summer Brave, The Skin of Our Teeth, Sweet Bird of Youth, 1975; The Royal Family, 1976; these were all part of the Bicentennial Theatre Season; executive director, 1976–78, American National Theatre and Academy, for which he produced Out of Our Father's House, 1978; Ladyhouse Blues, The Elephant Man (Tony award), 1979; Tintypes, 1980; executive director, Vivian Beaumont Theater, 1979— , whose opening production was a revival of The Philadelphia Story, Nov 1980; productions for television include Diary of a Madman, and Out of Our Father's House; publications include Walter Pater: Humanist, 1971.

Address: Vivian Beaumont Theater, 140 West 65th Street, New York, NY 10023.

CRISTOFER, Michael (Michael Procaccino), actor and dramatic author
b Trenton, NJ, 28 Jan 1945; *e* Catholic University, Washington DC.

Author of plays including Americommedia (street theatre), Plot Counter Plot, 1972; The Mandala (Philadelphia); The Shadow Box, 1975 (Pulitzer Prize, Tony award, 1977); Ice, 1976; Black Angel, 1978; as an actor has appeared at ACT, Seattle, Arena Stage, Washington, Long Wharf, New Haven, Theatre of the Living Arts, Philadelphia, and more recently at the Mark Taper Forum, LA, where he appeared in The Tooth of Crime, Confessions of a Female Disorder, 1973; as Carlos in Savages, 1974; as Colin in Ashes, 1976; made his NY debut at the Beaumont, Feb 1977, as Trofimov in The Cherry Orchard; American Place, Mar 1978, Charlie in Conjuring an Event; films include An Enemy of the People; TV work includes The Last of Mrs Lincoln and The Andros Targets.

Address: Actors Equity Association, 6430 Sunset Boulevard, Los Angeles, Calif 90028.

CROFT, Michael, OBE, director, National Youth Theatre
b 8 Mar 1922; *e* Burnage Grammar School, Manchester, and Keble College, Oxford.

Formerly an actor and schoolteacher, he became known for his Shakespearean productions at Alleyn's School; from these productions developed the National Youth Theatre, which he founded in 1956; has directed many of the company's subsequent productions, including premières of Zigger Zagger, 1967, The Apprentices, 1968, Fuzz, 1969, The Trip to Florence, 1974; England My Own, 1978; Shaw, Mar 1977, played the title-role in his own production of Henry IV; has also directed in Holland for the Haagsche Comedie, in Belgium for the Belgian National Theatre and the Théâtre Royale du Parc, and in New York, Mar 1979, directed Good Lads at Heart at the Brooklyn Academy of Music; in 1971 became director of the Dolphin Theatre Company, a professional company based on the Shaw Theatre, now permanent home of the NYT; has since directed regularly for the company; books include a novel, Spare The Rod, and Red Carpet to China.

Club: Savile. *Address:* 74 Bartholomew Road, London, NW5.

CROFT, Paddy, actress
b Worthing, Sussex; *e* Avondale College.

Appeared in the repertory theatres of Coventry, Canterbury, Preston, and Amersham, and in Dublin with the Gate Theatre; in Canada has appeared with the Toronto Crest Theatre, National Theatre in Ottawa, and the Manitoba Theatre Centre in Winnipeg; made her New York début at the One Sheridan Square, 12 Dec 1961, as Meg Dillon in The Hostage; for the Phoenix Theatre, Dec 1964, alternated as Mrs Whitefield and Miss Ramsden in Man and Superman; Gate, Mar 1965, Alice Fisher in Billy Liar; Actors' Playhouse, 1965, took over as Mrs Jackson in Live Like Pigs; appeared with the Playhouse in the Park, Cincinnati, Ohio, in the 1965 season; Belasco, Oct 1966, was standby in The Killing of Sister George and occasionally played the title-role; Helen Hayes, fall 1968, took over as Miss McKay in The Prime of Miss Jean Brodie; Longacre, Apr 1970, understudied Celeste Holm in the title-role of Candida; Promenade, Apr 1971, Cathleen in Long Day's Journey into Night, and won the Vernon Rice Obie Award for this role; Sheridan Square Playhouse, Feb 1972, Mrs Henderson in The Shadow of a Gunman; Vivian Beaumont, Jan 1973, Woman in The Plough and the Stars; Hartford Stage Company, 1973, appeared in Juno and the Paycock; Helen Hayes, Sept 1973, Mary, the Princess Royal and Countess of Harewood in Crown Matrimonial; McCarter, Princeton, 1974, played in You Never Can Tell; Eisenhower, Washington, DC, May 1975, Miss Erikson in Present Laughter; Center Stage, Baltimore, June 1976, appeared in The Real Inspector Hound and Black Comedy; toured, 1976–77, as Shatov in A Matter of Gravity; again at Center Stage, appeared in The Rivals, Dec 1977, and Blithe Spirit, May 1978; Hartford Stage Co, Conn, 1978, in Catchpenny Twist; Circle in the Square, Feb 1980, Rummy Mitchens in Major Barbara; has appeared in the film Finnegans Wake; has appeared frequently on television in various dramatic shows.

Address: c/o APA, 120 West 57th Street, New York, NY 10019.

CROMWELL, John, actor, producer, and director
b Toledo, Ohio, 23 Dec 1887; *e* Howe School, Howe, Ind; *m* (1) Alice Indahl (dec); (2) Marie Goff (mar dis); (3) Kay Johnson (mar dis); (4) Ruth Nelson.

Made his first appearance on the stage with the RC Herz Stock Company, Cleveland, 1907; he then toured for three years; appeared at Daly's, Aug 1910, in Baby Mine; served as general stage manager for William A Brady, 1911; stage director for the same manager, 1912; at the Playhouse, New York, Oct 1912, appeared as John Brook in Little Women; directed The Painted Woman, The Family Cupboard, and

The Things That Count, 1913; at the Thirty-ninth Street, Feb 1914, as Frank Andrews in Too Many Cooks; Playhouse, NY, 1915–17, in Grace George's Repertory Theatre, played Archibald Coke in The Liars, William Sudley in The New York Idea, Joe Garfield in Sinners, Captain Hamlin Kearney in Captain Brassbound's Conversion, Roger Morrish in The Earth, Charles Lomax in Major Barbara, Jules in L'Elévation; for this company directed The Man Who Came Back, 1916, and L'Elévation, 1917; Hudson, Jan 1918, directed and played Paul Brooks in The Indestructible Wife; same theatre, June 1919, directed and played Police Captain in At 9.45; at the Vanderbilt, Sept 1919, directed and played Frank Goward in She Would and She Did; made his London début at the Oxford, 8 Apr 1920, when he directed The Man Who Came Back; at the Comedy, June 1920, directed The Ruined Lady; Forty-eighth Street, NY, Aug 1920, directed and played Mr Tackaberry in Immodest Violet; Playhouse, July 1921, directed and played Roddy Caswell in The Teaser; Forty-eighth Street, NY, Aug 1921, Simpson in Personality; Playhouse, Nov 1921, Maillard in Marie Antoinette; Booth, Feb 1922, directed and played Walter Homer in The Law Breaker; Jolson, Oct 1922, directed The World We Live In; Playhouse, Aug 1925, produced and played Julian Rhenal in Oh! Mama; Oct 1925, produced and played Sam McCarver in Lucky Sam McCarver; Guild, Feb 1926, Engineer Borgheim in Little Eyolf; Maxine Elliott, Mar 1926, directed and played Mathew Dibble in Devils; Princess, Chicago, Mar 1926, Babe Callahan in Ned McCobb's Daughter; Lyceum, NY, Sept 1926, Gyp Gradyear in Fanny; Ambassador, Nov 1927, Captain McQuigg in The Racket; Henry Miller, Aug 1928, Wick Snell in Gentlemen of the Press; re-appeared on the NY stage, after an absence of fourteen years, at the Longacre Theatre, Nov 1942, when he directed and played Bob Adams in Yankee Point; after another absence of nine years, reappeared on the NY stage at the Alvin, Dec 1951, when he played John Gray in Point of No Return, for which he received the Antoinette Perry (Tony) Award; Martin Beck, Nov 1952, the Rev Gerald Harmston in The Climate of Eden; National, Nov 1953, Linus Larrabee in Sabrina Fair; also in London at the Palace, Aug 1954, and also directed the production: New York City Center, Dec 1954, played Mr Venables in a revival of What Every Woman Knows; Helen Hayes, Mar 1961, played Oscar Nelson in Mary, Mary; joined the Minnesota Theatre Company in 1963, and at the Guthrie Theatre, Minneapolis, May–July, played Anselme in The Miser, Player King in Hamlet, and Ben in Death of a Salesman; same theatre, 1964, played Duke of Exeter in Henry V, De Courcelles in Saint Joan, and Avocatore in Volpone; in 1965 Sir Robert Brackenbury in Richard III and various parts in The Caucasian Chalk Circle; in 1966 played in The Doctor's Dilemma; for the Yale Repertory Theatre, New Haven, Conn, 1970, played in Don Juan; Long Wharf, New Haven, Conn, Mar 1971, Father in Solitaire and Mr Potter in Double Solitaire; repeated these parts at the John Golden, Sept 1971; Long Wharf, Nov 1971, Old Ewbank in The Contractor; author of the play The Mystery of Pericluse produced at the Foundation, NY, June 1975; has also presented many plays on his own account, including: The Young Visiters, 1920; Drifting, 1921; Manhattan (also directed), 1922; Tarnish (also directed), 1923; Bewitched (also directed), 1924; It All Depends, Harvest (also directed), 1925; Kitty's Kisses (also co-directed), 1926; Women Go on Forever, 1927; Your Obedient Husband (also directed), 1938; also directed Bought and Paid For, 1921; The Silver Cord, 1926; What the Doctor Ordered, 1927; The Queen's Husband, 1928; The Ghost of Yankee Doodle, 1937; The Moon Vine, 1943; The Aspern Papers (Cleveland

Playhouse), 1963; The Madwoman of Chaillot (Cleveland Playhouse), 1964; commenced film career, 1928, in The Dummy; then turned his attention to film-direction, and has been responsible for the production of many notable films including: Tom Sawyer, Of Human Bondage, Prisoner of Zenda, Abe Lincoln in Illinois, Anna and the King of Siam, The Goddess, etc.

Address: Actors' Equity Association, 165 West 46th Street, New York, NY 10036.

CRONYN, Hume, actor and director
b London, Ontario, 18 July 1911; *s* of Hume Blake Cronyn and his wife Frances Amelia (Labatt); *e* Ridley College and McGill University, 1930–1; *m* Jessica Tandy; studied for the stage at the American Academy of Dramatic Art, 1932–4, and at the Mozarteum, Salzburg, Austria, summers, 1932–3.

While a student, in 1930–1, appeared with Montreal Repertory Theatre and McGill Player's Club in The Adding Machine, Dr Faustus, From Morn to Midnight, The Road to Rome, Alice in Wonderland, etc; first appeared in the USA with the National Theatre Stock Company, Washington, DC, as the Paper Boy in Up Pops the Devil, in 1931; joined Robert Porterfield's Barter Theatre Company as director in 1934, and played Austin Lowe in The Second Man, Dr Haggett in The Late Christopher Bean, Jim Hipper in He Knew Dillinger, and Doke Odum in Mountain Ivy; made his first appearance in New York at the Maxine Elliott, 1934, as the Janitor in Hipper's Holiday; joined the Jitney Players in 1935 and toured as Sir Charles Marlowe in She Stoops to Conquer, and as Gideon Bloodgood in The Streets of New York; at the Plymouth, Boston, and Garrick, Philadelphia, 1935, played Erwin Trowbridge in Three Men on a Horse; in NY at the Cort, 1936, played Green in Boy Meets Girl; Cort, 1937, Leo Davis in Room Service; subsequently appeared as Elkus in High Tor 1937, and Steve in Escape This Night, 1938; Windsor, NY, Mar 1938, played Abe Sherman in There's Always a Breeze; Ethel Barrymore, Feb 1939, played Harry Quill in Off to Buffalo; Longacre, Oct 1939, Andrei in The Three Sisters; also appeared in summer stock at the Lakewood Theatre, Skowhegan, Maine, May–Sept 1939, and May–Sept 1940, playing Hutchens Stubbs in Susan and God, Toby Cartwright in Ways and Means, George Davies in We Were Dancing, Francis O'Connor in Shadow and Substance, Christy Dudgeon in The Devil's Disciple, Floyd Lloyd in Kiss the Boys Goodbye, Judas in Family Portrait, Stage Manager in Our Town, Denis Dillon in The White Steed, Karl Baumer in Margin for Error, and Joe Bonaparte in Golden Boy; in 1940, appeared at the Golden as Peter Mason in The Weak Link, and at the Belasco as Lee Tatnall in Retreat to Pleasure; Lyceum, 1941, played Harley L Miller in Mr Big; produced, directed, and appeared in revue for Canadian Active Service Canteen, May 1941, and for USO Camp Shows, 1942–3, produced Junior Miss and produced and appeared in the revue It's All Yours; toured US military installations as Tommy Tarner in The Male Animal and in Canada, in a vaudeville sketch for Loan for Victory, 1944; after the war appeared at the Plymouth, 1948, as Jodine Decker in The Survivors; for ANTA, on tour, 1949, played Hamlet; Broadhurst, Mar 1950, directed Now I Lay Me Down to Sleep; Coronet, Nov 1950, directed Hilda Crane; Brattle Theatre, Cambridge, Mass, 1950, appeared as Gandersheim in The Little Blue Light; Ethel Barrymore, Oct 1951, played Michael in The Fourposter; Phoenix, Dec 1953, played Dr Brightlee in Madame, Will You Walk, which he also directed; toured, 1954–5, in Face to Face; Longacre, Apr 1955, played Curtis and Bennett Honey in The Honeys; ANTA Playhouse, Sept 1955, played Julian Anson in A Day

by the Sea; Ethel Barrymore, Oct 1957, directed The Egghead; toured and Coronet, Oct 1958, Oliver Walling in The Man in the Dog Suit; Palm Beach Playhouse, Florida, Mar 1959, directed and played Mr Trule in I Spy, John J Mulligan in Bedtime Story, Professor Nyukhin in The Harmful Effects of Tobacco, and Jerry in A Pound on Demand, with the overall title Triple Play; Playhouse, NY, Apr 1959, again directed and played in Triple Play, but as the Doctor in Portrait of a Madonna, substituted for I Spy; ANTA, Mar 1961, Jimmie Luton in Big Fish, Little Fish, for which he won the Della Austria Medal from the NY Drama League; Duke of York's, London, Sept 1962, again played the last role; Tyrone Guthrie Theatre, Minneapolis, Minn, 1963, played Harpagon in The Miser, Dr Tchebutykin in The Three Sisters, and Willy in Death of a Salesman; Lunt-Fontanne, NY, Apr 1964, Polonius in Sir John Gielgud's Hamlet, for which he received the Antoinette Perry (Tony) Award and the Variety New York Drama Critics Award; Martin Beck, Oct 1964, played Herbert Georg Beutler in The Physicists; Plymouth, Nov 1964, produced Slow Dance on a Killing Ground; with his wife appeared at the White House, Washington, DC, Feb 1965, at the request of the President, in Hear America Speaking; Guthrie, Minneapolis, May–Sept 1965, played the Duke of Gloucester in Richard III, Yepihodov in The Cherry Orchard, and Harpagon in The Miser; Martin Beck, Sept 1966, Tobias in A Delicate Balance, and toured in this part in 1967; Mark Taper Forum, Los Angeles, 1968, again played Harpagon in The Miser; Stratford Festival Theatre, Canada, Aug 1969, played Fr Rolfe in Hadrian VII, and toured US in this part until May 1970; toured, summer 1971, as Grandfather and Willie in Promenade All!; Ahmanson, Los Angeles, Nov 1971, Lt Commander Queeg in The Caine Mutiny Court Martial; Alvin, Apr 1972, Grandfather and Willie in Promenade All!, also touring, Jan 1973; Forum, Nov 1972, Willie in Happy Days, The Player in Act Without Words I, and Krapp in Krapp's Last Tape; played this last part at the St Lawrence Theatre Centre, Toronto, Canada, Arena Stage, Washington, DC and tour, 1973; Ethel Barrymore, Feb 1974, Verner Conklin in Come into the Garden, Maude and Hugo Latymer in A Song at Twilight in the double-bill Noël Coward in Two Keys; subsequently toured in these parts; toured, 1974–5, in dramatic reading The Many Faces of Love; Stratford, Ontario, Festival, 1976, Shylock in The Merchant of Venice and Bottom in A Midsummer Night's Dream; first appeared in films, 1942, and has since played in many successful films, including: Shadow of a Doubt, Beginning of the End, Cleopatra, Polonius in Hamlet, 1964, Gaily, Gaily, 1969, Conrach, The Parallax View, 1973; toured US, 1975, as Verner Conklin and Hugo Latymer in Noel Coward in Two Keys; John Golden, NY, Oct 1977, played Weller Martin in The Gin Game, which he also co-produced; subsequently toured the US and Canada, and played at the Lyric, London, July 1979, followed by a tour of Russia; Stratford Festival, Ontario, 1980, appeared in Foxfire (also co-author); has appeared regularly on television, including: The Bridge of San Luis Rey, The Fourposter, The Moon and Sixpence, etc; produced and appeared with his wife in the radio and television series *The Marriage*; received the Barter Theatre Award in 1961, for outstanding contribution to the theatre; in Dec 1964, received the American Academy of Dramatic Arts Award for Achievement by Alumni; in 1967 received the Leland Power Honor Award; received the Los Angeles Drama Critics award for The Caine Mutiny Court Martial, 1972; Straw Hat Award for directing Promenade, All!; Obic Award for Krapp's Last Tape, 1973, etc; Hon LLD, University of Western Ontario, London, Canada, 1974; Brandeis U Creative Arts Award, 1978.

Hobby: Photography. *Recreations:* Skin diving and fishing. *Club:* Players. *Address:* Box 85A, RR 2, Pound Ridge, New York, 10576.

CROPPER, Anna, actress
b Manchester, 13 May 1938; *d* of Jack Cropper and his wife Margaret (Horne); *e* Queen Ethelburga's, Harrogate and the Sorbonne; *m* William Roache, actor (mar dis); trained for the stage at the Central School of Speech and Drama.

Made her first stage appearance at Nottingham, as Solveig in Peer Gynt, 19 ; New Arts, Jan 1966, Diedre in How's the World Treating You? making her West End debut in this role at Wyndham's, 31 Jan 1966; Hampstead, Feb 1968, and Duchess, Apr 1968, played Miss Peel in The Coffee Lace and Jane Kempton in Trevor, in the double-bill Little Boxes; Mermaid, May 1971, Nora Reilly in John Bull's Other Island; Comedy, Apr 1975, took over as Rachel in The Exorcism; Apollo, Jul 1977, took over as Miss Cooper in Separate Tables; films include All Neat in Black Stockings, and Cromwell; frequent TV appearances in plays and series include Old Times, Robin Redbreast, The Lost Boys, and Mary's Wife.

Address: c/o Kate Feast, 43A Princess Road, London NW1.

CROSS, Beverley, dramatic author
b London, 13 April 1931; *s* of George Cross and his wife Eileen (Williams); *e* Nautical College, Pangbourne, and Balliol College, Oxford; *m* (1) Elizabeth Clunies-Ross (mar dis); (2) Gayden Collins (mar dis); (3) Maggie Smith.

Formerly a merchant seaman and actor; after leaving the Norwegian Merchant Service, he went up to Oxford, and made his first appearance as an actor in June 1953, in the OUDS production of Troilus and Cressida, in which he played Agamemnon; joined the Shakespeare Memorial Theatre Company, Stratford-on-Avon, 1954 season, and made his first professional appearance, Mar 1954, as a soldier in Othello; made his first London appearance at the Princes, Dec 1954, as Mr Fox in Toad of Toad Hall; Palace, July 1955, played Balthazar in Much Ado About Nothing, and subsequently a Herald in King Lear; his first play One More River was produced at the New Shakespeare, Liverpool, May 1958, subsequently coming to London to the Duke of York's, Oct 1959; directed Boeing-Boeing in Australia, 1964; at Wyndham's, Nov 1965, directed The Platinum Cat; he is also the author of the following: The Singing Dolphin, 1959; Strip the Willow, The Three Cavaliers, 1960; Belle; or the Ballad of Dr Crippen, 1961; Boeing-Boeing (adapted from the French of Marc Camoletti), Wanted on Voyage (adapted), 1962; Half-a-Sixpence (book of musical), 1963; The Mines of Sulphur (libretto), 1965; Jorrocks (book of musical), 1966; Phil the Fluter (co-author), 1969; The Rising of the Moon (libretto), 1970; Victory (libretto), 1970; Spook, 1973; The Great Society, Hans Andersen (book), 1974; Happy Birthday (translated and adapted from Camoletti), 1979; A Capital Transfer (libretto), 1979; awarded an Arts Council Bursary in 1960, under their scheme for the encouragement of new dramatists; began writing for films, 1961; contributed to Lawrence of Arabia; other screenplays include Jason and the Argonauts, The Long Ships, Ghenghis Khan, Half-a-Sixpence and The Clash of the Titans; television plays include The Dark Pits of War, and Catherine Howard; author of the novels Mars in Capricorn, 1955; The Night-walkers, 1956.

Recreation: Fishing. *Address:* c/o Curtis Brown, Ltd, Craven Hill, London, W2.

CROWDEN, Graham, actor
b Edinburgh, 30 Nov 1922; *s* of Harry Graham Crowden and

his wife Anne Margaret (Paterson); *e* Edinburgh Academy; *m* Phyllida Hewat.

Began his professional career as a student ASM at the Memorial Theatre, Stratford, 1944, walking on in various plays; subsequently gained wide experience in repertory at Stratford E, Dundee, Nottingham Playhouse, Bristol Old Vic and the Citizens', Glasgow; Open Air, Regent's Park, small parts in the 1952 season; first London appearance, Old Vic, July 1956, as Charles Lomax in the Bristol production of Major Barbara; played various parts at the Royal Court from Dec 1957 to Apr 1965, including Prosecuting Counsel in One Way Pendulum, Dec 1959 and Criterion, Feb 1960; the Doctor in Exit the King, Sept 1963 (also Edinburgh Festival); Casca in Julius Caesar, Nov 1964; during this period he also appeared at the Arts, as Bernard in Quartet for Five, Aug 1959, and as Wing-Cdr Howard in Nil Carborundum, Apr 1962; joined the National Theatre Company at the Old Vic, 1965, where his performances included Augustus Colpoys in Trelawny of the Wells, Nov 1965; Col Melkett in Black Comedy, Mar, Berlebeyo in A Bond Honoured, June 1966; the Player in Rosencrantz and Guildenstern are Dead, Apr, Foresight in Love for Love and Augustin Feraillon in A Flea in Her Ear, Canadian tour Oct–Nov 1967; Sir Politick Would-Be in Volpone, Jan, Archbishop of Winchester and Lightborn in Edward the Second, Apr 1968; leaving the company, he played the Devil in The Soldier's Tale, Bath Festival, June 1968; Pantalone in The Servant of Two Masters, Queen's, Dec 1968; Mermaid Shakespeare season, Apr–Aug 1970, played King Henry in Henry IV, parts I and II, and Prospero in The Tempest; returned to the Old Vic, to play Archie in Jumpers, Feb 1972; James in The Freeway, Sept 1974; Hector Hushabye in Heartbreak House, Feb 1975; Dublin Festival and tour, 1976; in Dead-Eyed Dicks; Edinburgh Festival, 1976, appeared in a recital, Rogues and Vagabonds; joined RSC, Apr 1977, to play Duke of Gloucester in Henry VI, Pts I & II, Menenius Agrippa in Coriolanus and Le Beau in As You Like It, at Stratford, Newcastle and the Aldwych; also at Newcastle and the Warehouse, London, Apr 1978, Filippo Strozzi in The Lorenzaccio Story; Royal Exchange, Manchester, Sept 1978, Dr Wangel in The Lady from the Sea; rejoined RSC, Mar 1979, and played Menenius at the Aldwych, and on continental tour; Roundhouse, May 1979, repeated the role of Dr Wangel; films, since his first in 1958, include The Ruling Class, O Lucky Man and Jabberwocky; has appeared in TV plays and series since 1956.

Recreations: Music, walking, tennis. *Club:* Savile. *Address:* 7A West Castle Rd, Edinburgh EH10 5AT.

CROWLEY, Mart, playwright
b Vicksburg, Miss, 21 Aug 1935; *e* Catholic U, Washington DC, and UCLA.

Author of The Boys in the Band, produced at Theatre Four, New York, 14 Apr 1968, and at Wyndham's, London, 11 Feb 1969, as well as in many other cities throughout the world; Remote Asylum produced in Los Angeles, 1970; A Breeze from the Gulf, produced in NY in 1973; The Boys in the Band was filmed in 1970.

Address: c/o Paul H Wolfowitz, Suite 22, 59 East 54th Street, New York, NY 10022.

CROWTHER, Leslie, actor
b West Bridgeford, Nottingham, 6 Feb 1933; *s* of Leslie Frederick Crowther and his wife Ethel Maraquita (Goulder); *e* Nottingham HS and Thames Valley Grammar School; *m* Jean Elizabeth Stone; trained for the stage as a child at the Cone-Ripman School.

Made his first professional appearance at the Open Air, Regent's Park, 2 June 1949, as 4th Watch in Much Ado About Nothing, playing other small parts in the same season; again appeared with the Open Air company, season 1950; his first West End appearance was in the revue High Spirits, at the Hippodrome, May 1953; 1954–9, appeared in summer shows with the Fol-de-Rols; Victoria Palace, May 1962, principal comedian in The Black and White Minstrel Show, remaining with the production until 1965; Garrick, July 1967, Jason in Let Sleeping Wives Lie; Great Yarmouth, summer 1970, appeared in Crowther's Crowd; Palladium, Dec 1970, Wishee-Washee in Aladdin; Richmond, Nov 1971, Adam Dexter in It Shouldn't Happen to a Dog; toured, Aug 1972 as Adam in She Was Only An Admiral's Daughter; toured, Nov 1977, as Herbert in High Infidelity; has played yearly in pantomime since 1974; appeared in the Royal Variety Performances of 1962, 1970 and 1978; television, since 1960, includes *The Black and White Minstrel Show, My Good Woman* and *Leslie Crowther's Scrap Book.*

Recreations: Cricket, tennis, Victoriana. *Clubs:* Lord's Taverners, Water Rats. *Address:* Temple Court, Corston, Bath, Avon.

CRUICKSHANK, Andrew, actor
b Aberdeen, Scotland, 25 Dec 1907; s of Andrew Cruickshank and his wife Mary Evelyn Grace Burnett (Cadger); e Aberdeen Grammar School; m Curigwen Lewis; originally intended for the profession of civil engineer.

Made his first appearance on the stage in the provinces, and appeared with various repertory companies; made his first appearance in London at the Savoy Theatre, 19 May 1930, in a non-speaking part in Othello; subsequently toured for a year with the Arts League Travelling Theatre; made his first appearance on the New York stage at the Empire Theatre, 14 Feb 1934, as Maudelyn in Richard of Bordeaux; at the Gate, London, May 1935, Prince Ernest, General Grey and John Brown in Victoria Regina; Playhouse, Dec 1935, Lord Clinton in Mary Tudor; appeared at Gate, during 1936–7, playing the Spartan Herald in Lysistrata, Sir Edward Clarke in Oscar Wilde, Parnell in Mr Gladstone, etc; joined the company of the Old Vic, Sept 1937, playing Banquo in Macbeth, Theseus in A Midsummer Night's Dream, Ludovico and Cassio in Othello; at the New, Mar 1938, played Dr Forbes in The Painted Smile; rejoined the Old Vic company, Sept 1938, and played O'Dwyer in Trelawny of the Wells, Roebuck Ramsden in Man and Superman, King Claudius in Hamlet (in its entirety) and Sir Lucius O'Trigger in The Rivals; Jan–Apr 1939, toured on the Continent and Egypt, with the Old Vic company; Lyceum, June 1939, played Rosencrantz in Hamlet, which he subsequently played at Elsinore; appeared at the Buxton Festival, Aug 1939, with the Old Vic company, playing the Duke of Marlborough in Viceroy Sarah, Chorus, Escalus and the Apothecary in Romeo and Juliet, Titus in The Devil's Disciple, Sir William Honeywood in The Good Natured Man; and Warwick in Saint Joan; appeared in the four last-mentioned plays, at Streatham Hill, Oct 1939; Old Vic, Apr–May 1940, played Cornwall in King Lear, and Sebastian in The Tempest; served in the Army, with the Royal Welsh Fusiliers, 1940–5, retiring with the rank of Major; re-appeared on the stage at the Lyric, Hammersmith, Dec 1945, as Richard Burbage in Spring 1600; Granville, May 1946, played Mark in The Nineteenth Hole of Europe, and June 1946, Fortunato in the play of that name, and Archie in Cellar; Duchess, Mar 1947, Duke of Florence in The White Devil; Criterion, Feb 1948, Hugh Wigmore in The Indifferent Shepherd; at the Memorial Theatre, Stratford-on-Avon, during the 1950 season, played Julius Caesar,

Wolsey in King Henry VIII, Leonato in Much Ado About Nothing, the Earl of Kent in King Lear, and Angelo in Measure for Measure; New Boltons, Feb 1951, played the Rev James Mavor Morrell in Candida, and in the following month appeared as Claudius in Hamlet; Vaudeville, May 1951, Lord Angus in The Thistle and the Rose; made his second appearance on the NY stage at the Cort, 4 Oct 1951, as the Earl of Warwick in Saint Joan; Westminster, London, June 1952, played Chief-Insp Hubbard in Dial M For Murder; toured, 1954, as Lot Johnson in Mountain Fire; Arts, Mar 1955, played Agamemnon in Sacrifice to the Winds; Westminster, Aug 1955, Richard Farrow in Dead on Nine; Duke of York's, May 1956, played Maurice in The House By The Lake, which ran for nearly two years; Pembroke, Croydon, Feb 1960, Henry Drummond in Inherit the Wind, subsequently transferring with the production to the St Martin's, Mar 1960; Pembroke, Croydon, Oct 1960, played WO Gant in Look Homeward, Angel; Queen's, Mar 1961, Dr Wangel in The Lady From the Sea; Pembroke, Croydon, Sept 1961, played Tom Howard in his own play Unfinished Journey; Phoenix, Apr 1962, again played WO Gant in Look Homeward, Angel; Ashcroft, Croydon, Nov 1962, Halvard Solness in The Master Builder; Ashcroft, Croydon, Sept 1963, Cornelius Melody in A Touch of the Poet; Grand, Leeds, Aug 1964, Mr Justice Carstairs in Alibi for a Judge; Savoy, Aug 1965, again played Mr Justice Carstairs in Alibi for a Judge; St Martin's, Sept 1969, Henry Oldershaw in The Crunch; Duke of York's, Nov 1971, The Judge in The Douglas Cause; toured, Feb 1972, as Solness in The Master Builder; Arnaud, Guildford, Apr 1973, title part in Noah; Savoy, May 1973, took over as Sir William Boothroyd in Lloyd George Knew My Father; Haymarket, Leicester, Nov 1976, Rubek in When We Dead Awaken; joined the National Theatre Company, 1978, and played Nestor in The Woman, John Anthony, in Strife, the Leading Peasant in The Fruits of Enlightenment, 1978; Duke Senior in As You Like It; Derby in Richard III, Count Orsini-Rosenberg in Amadeus, 1979; took over as Old Ekdal in The Wild Duck, March 1980; his play, Games, was produced at the Edinburgh Festival, 1975; entered films, 1938, in Auld Lang Syne, and has made numerous television appearances, notably as John Jarndyce in the serial Bleak House, and since 1963 as Dr Cameron in *Dr Finlay's Casebook*; Hon DLitt, St Andrew's, 1977.

Address: c/o Essanay Ltd, 75 Hammersmith Road, London W14.

CRUTTWELL, Hugh, director and Principal of the Royal Academy of Dramatic Art
b Singapore, 31 Oct 1918; s of Clement Chadwick Cruttwell and his wife Grace Fanny (Robin); e King's School, Bruton, and Hertford College, Oxford; m Geraldine McEwan; formerly a teacher.

Began his career as director at the Theatre Royal, Windsor, 1949; directed his first London production, The MacRoary Whirl, at the Duchess, Oct 1953; appointed Principal of The Royal Academy of Dramatic Art, Jan 1965.

Address: 8 Ranelagh Avenue, Barnes, SW13. *Tel:* 01–878 0695.

CRYER, David, actor and singer
b Evanston, Illinois, 8 Mar 1936; e DePauw University, Boston University, Yale Divinity School; m Gretchen Kiger (mar dis).

Appeared in summer theatres before making his New York début at the Sullivan Street Playhouse, 1962, when he took over as The Narrator in The Fantasticks; Maidman Playhouse, 29 Oct 1963, played Mark Livingston in The Streets of

New York; Broadhurst, 1964, took over the part of Bill Starbuck in 110 in the Shade; Curran, San Francisco, Aug 1964 and subsequent tour, Phil Mackey in 110 in the Shade; Mark Hellinger, Feb 1965, sang in the chorus of Fade Out—Fade In; with the original ACT company in Pittsburgh, 1965; co-produced and played the Narrator in two separate tours of The Fantasticks, Sept–Dec 1966 and Jan–Apr 1967; Theatre de Lys, Sept 1967, Mike Butler in Now Is the Time for All Good Men; co-produced and again toured in two separate companies and played the Narrator in The Fantasticks, Dec 1967–Jan 1968 and Jan 1968–Mar 1968; Theatre de Lys, June 1968, co-produced Futz!; Lunt-Fontanne, Mar 1969, Jude Scribner in Come Summer; 46th Street, summer 1969, took over from Ken Howard as Thomas Jefferson in 1776; Theatre de Lys, June 1970, Narrator in Whispers on the Wind; Mark Hellinger, Jan 1971, Ari Ben Canaan in Ari; Sullivan Street Playhouse, 1972, took over once again as The Narrator in The Fantasticks; Metropolitan Opera House, June 1972, alternated with Alan Titus as the Celebrant in Leonard Bernstein's Mass; John F Kennedy Center for the Performing Arts, Washington, DC, July 1973, Red Shadow and Pierre Birabeau in Desert Song, and repeated this part at the Uris, NY, Sept 1973; Mark Taper Forum, Los Angeles, Nov 1973, played in Brecht Sacred and Profane; Dorothy Chandler Pavilion, Los Angeles, May 1974, Lun Tha in The King and I; Portfolio Studio, NY, Dec 1974, in Portfolio Revue.
Address: Actors' Equity Association, 165 West 46th Street, New York, NY 10036.

CRYER, Gretchen (*née* Gretchen Kiger), actress and dramatic author
b Dunreith, Indiana, 17 Oct 1935; *e* DePauw University, Indiana; *m* David Cryer, actor (mar dis).
With Nancy Ford as composer, wrote book and lyrics for the musicals Now Is the Time for All Good Men, 1967; The Last Sweet Days of Isaac (Obie award, etc), 1970; Shelter (first Broadway production), 1973; I'm Getting My Act Together and Taking It on the Road, 1978; began her Broadway career at the Lunt-Fontanne, Nov 1962, as Miss Kepplewhite in Little Me; at the Broadhurst, Oct 1963, was in the chorus of 110 in the Shade; played the leads in her own Now Is the Time . . ., De Lys, Oct 1967, and I'm Getting My Act Together . . ., Public/Anspacher, Jun 1978, transferring to the Circle in the Square Downtown, Dec 1978; appeared at Manhattan Theatre Club, Oct 1973, in A Circle of Sounds, and has also performed her songs with Nancy Ford at the Town Hall and the Cookery, NY.
Address: Actors Equity Association, 165 West 46th Street, New York, NY 10036.

CUKA, Frances, actress
b London, 21 Aug 1936; *d* of Joseph Cuka and his wife Letitia Alice Annie (Francis); *e* Tollington Preparatory School, and Brighton and Hove High School; studied for the stage at the Guildhall School of Music and Drama.
Made her first appearance on the stage in Warrington, July 1955, as Effie in Meet Mr Callahan; after gaining further experience in a number of repertory companies in the provinces, joined the Theatre Workshop Company and appeared with them at the Zürich Festival, June 1957, and at the Moscow Art Theatre, July 1957, as Third Witch and Young Macduff in Joan Littlewood's production of Macbeth; on her return to England, appeared at the Theatre Royal, Stratford, Sept 1957, in the same play; Theatre Royal, Stratford, May 1958, played Josephine in A Taste Of Honey; Royal Court, Sept 1958, played Daffodil in The English Stage Company's

production Live Like Pigs; Royal Court, Oct 1959, played Nell in End-Game; Wyndham's, Feb 1959, played her original part of Josephine in A Taste of Honey; joined the Shakespeare Memorial Theatre Company, Stratford-on-Avon, 1960, and played the following parts: Julia in The Two Gentlemen of Verona, Jessica in The Merchant of Venice, Maria in Twelfth Night, and Cassandra in Troilus and Cressida; Pembroke, Croydon, Feb 1961, played Anne in The Expatriate; made her first appearance in New York° at the Booth Theatre, Apr 1961, when she succeeded Joan Plowright as Josephine in A Taste of Honey; toured the US, with the production, Sept 1961–Apr 1962; Queen's, London, Nov 1962, played Becky Sharp in the musical Vanity Fair; Ashcroft, Croydon, Apr 1963, the Girl in From this Hill; Hampstead Theatre Club, Apr 1964, Anna in All Good Children; Royal Court, Oct 1965, played the Leading Lady, Mary Godwin, and Miss Ferney in Shelley; Dec 1965, played Annie in Serjeant Musgrave's Dance; Jan 1966, Mrs Allwit in A Chaste Maid in Cheapside and Mrs Farraclough in The Dancers; for the Royal Shakespeare Company at the Aldwych, June 1966, played Marcelle in Days in the Trees; Apollo, Sept 1968, and tour for Prospect Productions, Lucy Lockit in The Beggar's Opera; returning to the Aldwych, played Ellen in Silence, July 1969, and Mrs Foran in The Silver Tassie, Sept 1969; Royal Court, Apr 1971, Sylvia Farrell in One At Night; toured with Prospect as Elizabeth in Richard III, 1972, Lady Fidget in The Country Wife, 1973; Bankside Globe, July 1973, Lady Duncan in Macbett; Shaw, June 1974, played parts in Under Milk Wood including Polly Garter; Greenwich, Sept 1974, Sarah Harford in More Stately Mansions; Aldwych, May 1975, and Ethel Barrymore (NY), Oct 1975, Nadya in Travesties; Prince of Wales, Sept 1976, Doris in Same Time Next Year; Belgrade, Coventry, Nov 1977, Beryl in Going Bust; Haymarket, Jan 1978, Evelyn Daly in Waters of the Moon; Royal Alexandra, Toronto, Nov 1978, Helen in Half Life; Lyric, Hammersmith, Nov 1979, Janet in Waiting for the Parade; films include Scrooge; has appeared regularly in television plays and serials, and has been heard in numerous radio plays, including (recently), Henry IV, Part II.
Recreations: Cooking, reading, opera, concert and theatre-going. *Address:* c/o Miller Management, 82 Broom Park, Teddington TW11 9NY, Middlesex.

CULLUM, John, singer and actor
b Knoxville, Tenn, 2 Mar 1930; *e* University of Tennessee; *m* Emily Frankel.
Made his New York début at the Shakespearewrights, 23 Oct 1957, as a Citizen, a Cobbler, and a Servant in Julius Caesar; at The Players, Jan 1959, served as stage manager for King Lear; later in 1959, took over as Grimaldi in 'Tis Pity She's a Whore at the same theatre; Barbizon-Plaza, Mar 1960, played Mastax in The Jackass; joined the New York Shakespeare Festival Theatre and at the Belvedere Lake, June 1960, played Duke of Orleans in King Henry V; July 1960, a Gentleman in Measure for Measure; Aug 1960, a Lord in The Taming of the Shrew; Majestic, Dec 1960, Sir Dinadan in Camelot; Shubert, New Haven, Conn, Feb 1962, Johnny Sykes in We Take the Town; Music Box, Apr 1962, Cassius in Infidel Caesar; New York Shakespeare Festival, Aug 1963, King of France in King Lear; Writer's Stage, Apr 1963, Cyril Bellamy in The Saving Grace; Gramercy Arts, Nov 1963, Timothy in Thistle in My Bed; Lunt-Fontanne, Apr 1964, Laertes to Richard Burton's Hamlet in the Sir John Gielgud production; Pabst, Milwaukee, Nov 1964, played Hamlet; Mark Hellinger, Oct 1965, Dr Mark Bruckner in On a Clear Day You Can See Forever; ANTA,

Washington Square, 1966, took over from Richard Kiley as Don Quixote (Cervantes) in Man of La Mancha; Renata, Nov 1966, Father Jerome Fogarty in The Frying Pan, Tom Dorgan in Eternal Triangle, and Denis Sullivan in The Bridal Night in the triple-bill Three Hand Reel; 46th Street, 1969, took over as Edward Rutledge in 1776; Broadhurst, 1972, took over as Lord Bothwell in Vivat! Vivat Regina!; Jones Beach, summer 1972, The King in The King and I; Goodman, Chicago, 1973, Thomas Mendip in The Lady's Not for Burning; Jones Beach, summer 1973, Billy Bigelow in Carousel; Ford's, Washington, DC, Nov 1973, Don Medigua in El Capitan; Alvin, Jan 1975, Charlie Anderson in Shenandoah, for which he received the Antoinette Perry (Tony) Award; Longacre, Jan 1977, Bobby Horvath in The Trip Back Down; Eisenhower, Washington DC, Apr 1977, Sigmund in The Archbishop's Ceiling; Goodspeed Opera House, East Haddam, autumn 1977, directed The Red Blue Grass Western Flyer Show; Colonnades, NY, Nov 1977, directed Zinnia; St James, Feb 1978, Oscar Jaffe in On the Twentieth Century (Tony Award); Orpheum, May 1979, directed People in Show Business Make Long Goodbyes; Music Box, July 1979, took over as Sidney Bruhl in Deathtrap; played his role in the film of 1776 (1972), also appearing in such films as Hawaii and All the Way Home; TV work includes the Richard Rodgers musical Androcles and the Lion, and Man Without a Country.

Address: Actors Equity Association, 165 West 46th Street, New York, NY 10036.

CULVER, Roland, actor
b Highgate, London, 31 Aug 1900; *s* of Edward Culver and his wife Florence (Tullidge); *e* Highgate College; *m* (1) Daphne Rye (mar dis); (2) Nan Hopkins; joined the Royal Air Force, 1918, and served as Pilot 1918–19; studied for the stage at the Royal Academy of Dramatic Art.

Made his first appearance on the stage, 1925, at the Hull Repertory Theatre, as Paul in Peter and Paul; first appeared in London, 1925, at the Century Theatre, with the Greater London Players; Scala, May 1925, played Jeffs Weems in Forbidden Fluids; toured, 1926, in Sun Up and in All the King's Horses; at the St Martin's, Dec 1926, Jack Harding in Behind the Beyond; Arts, Dec 1927, Lord Byron in Nathaniel Bendersnap; Prince of Wales's, Apr 1928, Harry in Gentlemen Prefer Blondes; St Martin's, Aug 1928, the Man from Nolans in Knight Errant; St Martin's, Oct 1928, George Penguard in 77 Park Lane; Garrick, June 1929, Andrew in The Stranger Within; Lyric, Hammersmith, Oct 1929, Anthony Musgrave in Beau Austin; Duke of York's, Apr 1930, Corporal Brown in Suspense; Arts, July 1930, Denis in Dance With No Music; Little, Aug 1930, Clotaire in John O'Dreams; Arts, Jan 1931, Ma in The Circle of Chalk; Duke of York's, Feb 1931, Casmir in The Rocklitz; St Martin's, Apr 1931, Captain Hastings in Black Coffee; Lyric, Hammersmith, Sept 1931, Sharper in The Old Bachelor; Q, May 1932, Gilbert Lester in An Average Man; Fortune, Oct 1933, Carol Shaw in Vacant Possession; Royalty, Apr 1934, Franco Spina in The Mask and the Face; Embassy, Oct 1935, and St Martin's, Nov 1935, Eliot Vines in Distinguished Gathering; Criterion, Nov 1936, Lieut Commander Rogers in French Without Tears; which ran until 1939; New, Jan 1940, Ford in Believe It or Not; Westminster, Nov 1943, Viscount Goring in An Ideal Husband; Phoenix, Dec 1944, George Wayne in Another Love Story; entered films, 1931, and has appeared in numerous successful pictures; was the first English actor to go to Hollywood, after the end of the 1939–45 War; on returning to England, appeared at the Strand, Sept 1949, as Ronald Knight, MA, in Master of Arts; Criterion, Oct 1950,

played Oscar in Who is Sylvia?; Duchess, Mar 1952, William Collyer in The Deep Blue Sea; Haymarket, Aug 1953, directed the revival of Aren't We All?; made his first appearance on the New York stage at the Coronet, 7 Oct 1953, as Philip in The Little Hut; Strand, London, Nov 1954, played Simon Foster in Simon and Laura; Phoenix, Aug 1956, played Colonel George Ferring in his own play, A River Breeze; Comedy, July 1958, played Stanley Harrington in Five Finger Exercise; appeared in the same part on Broadway, Music Box, NY, Dec 1959, subsequently touring in the US with the production Sept 1960–Apr 1962; Grand, Blackpool, Oct 1963, played Sir Richard Conyngham in Sergeant Dower Must Die, subsequently appearing in the same play at the Vaudeville, Nov 1963, when it was re-titled Shout for Life; Haymarket, Sept 1964, Dr Parker in Carving a Statue; Yvonne Arnaud, Guildford, Aug 1965, played Pavel Lebedev in Ivanov, prior to appearing at the Phoenix, London, Sept 1965, in the same play, and afterwards, touring America, with a season at the Shubert, NY, May 1966; Strand, 1967, took over the part of the Bishop in Getting Married; Jan 1968, O'Keefe, Toronto, played David Bliss in Hay Fever, returning to the Duke of York's in that part in Feb; Apollo, Dec 1969, took over as Rupert Cardew in His, Hers, and Theirs; Lyric, June 1970, played Lord Stamfordham in My Darling Daisy; Prince of Wales, Oct 1972, took over as Sir William Gower in Trelawny; Royalty, Sept 1974, played Charles Plummer in The Bedwinner; joined the National Theatre Dec 1975, to play Polonius in Hamlet, at the Old Vic, and Agamemnon in Troilus and Cressida, Young Vic, June 1976; he has also appeared in numerous films including French Without Tears and To Each His Own; TV appearances include *The Pallisers* and, recently, Saint Joan.

Favourite parts: Lord Goring in An Ideal Husband, and Oscar in Who is Sylvia? *Recreations:* Golf, swimming, and bridge. *Clubs:* Garrick, Lord's Taverners, and MCC. *Address:* The Old School, Fawley Green, Henley-on-Thames, Oxon. *Tel:* Henley-on-Thames 3778.

CUMMINGS, Constance, CBE, actress
b Seattle, Washington, USA, 15 May 1910; *d* of Dallas Vernon Halverstadt and his wife Kate Logan (Cummings); *e* St Nicholas School, Seattle; *m* Benn W Levy (dec).

Made her first appearance on the stage with the Savoy Stock company, San Diego, 1926, as the prostitute in Seventh Heaven; made her first appearance in New York, at the Alvin Theatre, 8 Nov 1928, in the chorus of Treasure Girl; Music Box, Apr 1929, appeared in The Little Show; Ritz, Mar 1930, played Carrie in This Man's Town; later in 1930, toured in June Moon; left the stage for films, 1931–4; made her first appearance on the London stage at the Comedy Theatre (for Repertory Players), 22 July 1934, as Alice Overton in Sour Grapes, and played the same part at the Apollo, Aug 1934; returned to NY, and at the Plymouth, Dec 1934, played Linda Brown in Accent on Youth; Savoy, London, Nov 1936, Regina Conti in Young Madame Conti and played the same part at the Music Box, NY, Mar 1937; Broadhurst, NY, Nov 1937, Emma Bovary in Madame Bovary; Mansfield, Jan 1938, Nellie Blunt in If I Were You; Shaftesbury, London, Sept 1938, Katherine in Goodbye, Mr Chips; Lyric, Mar 1939, Kate Settle in The Jealous God; at the Buxton Festival, for the Old Vic, Aug 1939 and at Streatham Hill, Oct 1939, played Juliet in Romeo and Juliet, Miss Richland in The Good Natured Man, and Joan in Saint Joan; Duchess, Mar 1942, played Lydia Kenyon in Skylark; Globe, Dec 1942, Gabby Maple in The Petrified Forest; at the Ethel Barrymore Theatre, NY, Feb 1945, Racine Gardner in One-Man Show; toured, June 1946, as Jane Pugh in Clutterbuck, and played this part at Wyndham's, Aug 1946; St James's, Apr 1948, Anna Luise Klopps in Happy with Either; at the same theatre, Sept 1948, played Madeleine in Don't Listen, Ladies!; St Martin's, Oct 1949, Laura Whittingham in Before the Party; Duke of York's, Nov 1950, played Martha Cotton in Return to Tyassi; St James's, Oct 1952, succeeded Googie Withers as Georgie Elvin in Winter Journey; Prince's, Feb 1953, played Ann Downs in The Shrike; Vaudeville, Sept 1953, Andrea in Trial and Error; Oxford Playhouse, Mar 1957, title-rôle in Lysistrata; Piccadilly, Dec 1957, Antiope in The Rape of the Belt; subsequently appeared at the Martin Beck, NY, Nov 1960, in the same play; Phoenix, London, Mar 1961, played Sarah in JB; at the Oxford Playhouse, Feb 1962, Inez in In Camera (Huis Clos), and the Countess of Amersham in A Social Success (double-bill); at the same theatre, Apr 1962, Katy Maartens in The Genius and the Goddess, transferring to the Comedy, London, June 1962; Westport Country Playhouse, Conn, Nov 1963, played C (Catherine) Gurnee in The Strangers; Piccadilly, London, May 1964, took over Martha in Who's Afraid of Virginia Woolf?; Malvern Festival, July 1966, played Liza Foote in Public and Confidential, transferring to the Duke of York's, Aug 1966; Vaudeville, Nov 1966, Julia Stanford QC in Justice is a Woman, and Apr 1967, Jane Banbury in Fallen Angels; Round House, Apr 1969, subsequently Lunt-Fontanne, NY, May 1969, Gertrude in Hamlet; Citizens', Glasgow, Sept 1969, Mrs Goforth in The Milk Train Doesn't Stop Here Any More; Belgrade, Coventry, Oct 1970, Claire in The Visit; joined the National Theatre company, 1971, playing Volumnia in Coriolanus, May, Leda in Amphitryon 38, June, Mary Tyrone in Long Day's Journey Into Night, Dec, the last two at the New Theatre; in 1973 at the Old Vic played Mme Ranevsky in The Cherry Orchard, May, and Agave in The Bacchae, Aug; Mermaid, April 1974, Mother in Children; Arnaud, Guildford, Nov 1974, Lady Champion-Cheney in The Circle; Royal Court, Oct 1975, Dodie in Stripwell; 1976, toured as the Wife in All Over; Bristol Old Vic, Sept 1976, played Mrs Warren in Mrs Warren's Profession; Newman, NY, June 1978, Emily Stilson in Wings, transferring to The Lyceum, Jan 1979, receiving a Tony Award for her performance; played this part in London at The Cottesloe (NT), Aug 1979; during World War II appeared in six plays for HM Forces; entered films, 1932, in Movie Crazy, and has appeared in many pictures; has also appeared on television; performed in concert recitals of St Joan at the Stake, and Peter and the Wolf; received the CBE in the New Year Honours, 1974.

Recreations: Gardening, swimming, and reading. *Address:* 66 Old Church Street, SW3. *Tel:* 01–352 0437.

CURRAH, Brian Mason, designer
b Plymouth, Devon, 19 Aug 1929; *s* of Frederick Dunstan Currah and his wife Barbara (White); *e* Liskeard County Grammar School and Plymouth College of Art; formerly a teacher of art and drama.

Designed his first production for the stage at the Hippodrome, Stockton, 1951, with Worm's Eye View; designed for Caryl Jenner, 1952–7; designed his first London production, Quartet for Five, Arts, Sept 1959; subsequent London productions include The Caretaker, 1960; Big Soft Nellie, Stop It Whoever You Are, The Tenth Man, 1961; The Gentle Avalanche, Say Nothing, The Ginger Man, 1963; The Glass Menagerie, 1965; Suite In Three Keys, Big Bad Mouse, 1966; After the Rain, The Sacred Flame, 1967; Close the Coalhouse Door, 1968; Pyjama Tops, 1969; I Never Sang for My Father, 1970; Broadway productions he has designed include

The Caretaker, 1961, and After the Rain, 1967; he has also designed for the Dublin, Edinburgh and Pitlochry Festivals, and for repertory theatres all over Britain, including spells as Head of Design for the inaugural seasons of the Arnaud, Guildford, 1965, and Playhouse, Leeds, 1970; tutor in design, Croydon College of Art, 1970–4; course co-ordinator, Worthing College of Art, 1974–8; head of design, Theatre Clwd, 1978; associate professor of design in the Drama Department, University of Alberta, 1979–.

Recreations: Gardening, motor-cycling. *Address:* Orchard Studios, Brook Green, London, W6. *Tel:* 01–602 1417.

CURRY, Julian, actor
b Devon, 8 Dec 1937; *s* of William Burnlee Curry and Marjorie Graham (McIldowie); *e* Dartington Hall and King's College, Cambridge (BA); *m* Sheila Reid, actress (mar dis).

Appeared in student productions at Cambridge; joined the Old Vic company May 1961, making his first professional appearance when he took over the walk-on part of a hunchbacked limping Veronese in Romeo and Juliet; also appeared in The Merchant of Venice, and toured the UK, US and Europe with the company until summer 1962; during this time he made his New York debut at the City Center, Feb 1962, playing small roles in Macbeth, Romeo and Juliet and Saint Joan; Hampstead, Dec 1962, Sorin in The Seagull; in repertory at Coventry, Bristol Old Vic and Oxford Playhouse, 1963–65; Malvern Festival, season 1965, played Gerald Croft in An Inspector Calls, Boon in You Never Can Tell, and Krapp in Krapp's Last Tape; toured, autumn 1965, as Ross in Prospect's Macbeth; Royal Court, Sept 1966, Rev Cedric Swan in Three Men for Colverton; appeared in repertory at Hornchurch, Leicester, 1977; joined the RSC at Stratford, 1968 season, playing parts including King of France in King Lear, Evil Angel and the Old Man in Doctor Faustus and Friar Francis in Much Ado About Nothing, touring the US with the last two, spring 1969; returned to the Aldwych season 1969, again playing Friar Francis, as well as Staff Wallah in The Silver Tassie, and Scrivener and Val Cutting in Bartholomew Fair; Leatherhead, Feb 1970, Apollodorus in Caesar and Cleopatra; toured with the Cambridge Theatre Company, 1970, as Praed in Mrs Warren's Profession, Teddy in The Homecoming, Brazen in The Recruiting Officer, and Pilot Officer in Chips with Everything; toured as Horatio in the Prospect's Hamlet, 1971, followed by a season at the Cambridge; Edinburgh Festival, 1972, Cyril in The Black and White Minstrels; joined the National Theatre Company at the Old Vic, 1973, to play Tiresias in Wole Soyinka's version of The Bacchae, followed by Angelo in Measure for Measure; Playhouse, Nottingham, May 1974, Capt Thompson in The Churchill Play; Hampstead, Jul 1974, Geoff Brock in Other People; Crucible, Sheffield, Mar 1975, Sir David Lindsay in Armstrong's Last Goodnight; Greenwich, summer 1975, again played Angelo; toured India and the Far East, spring 1976, for the British Council, in RSC productions of The Hollow Crown and Pleasure and Repentance; Soho Poly, May 1976, title part in Campion's Interview; Globe, Jul 1976, Alan Quine in Donkey's Years; Nottingham, autumn 1977, alternated the roles of Jack Worthing and Algernon Moncrieff in The Importance of Being Earnest; Greenwich, May 1978, Bernard Shaw in The Achurch Letters; Hampstead, July 1979, Dennis Broadley in Outside Edge, transferring to the Queen's, Sept; first film, Smashing Time, 1967; most recently Les Brontës; TV, since 1964, includes plays and series, most recently *Rumpole of the Bailey.*

Favourite parts: Angelo, Brazen, and Cyril in The Black and White Minstrels. *Recreations:* Pottery, music, soccer. *Address:* 14 Hillfield Park, London N10.

CURTIS, Keene, actor
b Salt Lake City, Utah, 15 Feb 1923; *s* of Ira Charles Curtis and his wife Polley Francella (Holbrook); *e* University of Utah (MS 1947).

Made his New York début, 18 Jan 1949, as standby for Jay Robinson as Archie in The Shop at Sly Corner; became a stage manager for the tour of Martha Graham's dance company, 1949–50; stage managed various plays, 1950–60, including The Constant Wife, The Male Animal, Mrs Patterson, The Dark Is Light Enough, Medea, Four Winds, Nude with Violin, Present Laughter, The Firstborn, Look After Lulu, Silent Night Lonely Night, the European tour of Martha Graham, the world tour of Eleanor Steber (the soprano), etc; joined the Association of Producing Artists as an actor in Bermuda, 1960, and played Franz in Anatole, Medvedenko in The Seagull, and Straker in Man and Superman; for the APA, at the McCarter Theatre, Princeton, New Jersey, 1960, played Tyson in The Lady's Not for Burning, the title-role in Scapin, Stevens in The Tavern, Agazzi in Right You Are If You Think You Are, Lane in The Importance of Being Earnest; in 1961 played Bottom in A Midsummer Night's Dream, the Player King in Hamlet, Feste in Twelfth Night, Oswald in King Lear, Sir Oliver in The School for Scandal, the Sheriff in The Tavern, Dr Dorn in The Seagull, Colonel Howard in Fashion; toured Australia and the Far East as stage manager for the Alvin Ailey–Carmen DeLavallade American Dance Company; returned to the US and for the APA played Selincourt in Penny for a Song, and Sir Benjamin Backbite in The School for Scandal, 1962; the IRA Officer in The Hostage, Salerio in The Merchant of Venice, Bagot in Richard II, Conrade in Much Ado About Nothing, Bottom in A Midsummer Night's Dream, Scapin, Sirelli in Right You Are . . ., the Sheriff in The Tavern, the Tartar in Lower Depths, 1963; for the APA appeared at the Phoenix, NY, repeated the last four parts and also played Du Croisy in Impromptu at Versailles; at the Phoenix, Dec 1964–June 1965, played Henry Straker in Man and Superman, Napoleon Bonaparte in War and Peace, and Egon in Judith; for the APA, 1965, played the Guide in Herakles, Molvik in The Wild Duck, and Boris Kolenkhov in You Can't Take It with You, repeating this last part at the Lyceum, NY, Nov 1965; played Sir Oliver in The School for Scandal, Sirelli in Right You Are, Kolenkhov in You Can't Take It with You, Pierre in War and Peace, including an engagement at the Royal Alexandria in Toronto, Canada, as Sir Oliver and Sirelli, and a season at the Lyceum, NY, when he repeated the last two parts, Nov 1966; Lyceum, 1967, played Kolenkhov, Napoleon in War and Peace, then toured as the Anarchist in Pantagleize, and as Kolenkhov and Sirelli, including an engagement at the Theatre Maisonneuve, Montreal, Quebec, Canada, as representative of the USA at Expo 70, then at the Royal Alexandra, Toronto, and the Lyceum, NY, when he also played Yepihodov in The Cherry Orchard; played the Anarchist in Pantagleize, Alex in The Cocktail Party, Oronte in The Misanthrope, including engagements at the Royal Alexandra, Toronto, and the Lyceum, NY, 1968; the Sergeant in Cock-a-Doodle Dandy, and the Player King in Hamlet, at the Lyceum, 1969; left the APA and, at the Pavilion, Pennsylvania State University, July 1969, played various roles in Collision Course; Imperial, Oct 1969, Colonel Mischa Oblensky in A Patriot for Me; Brooks Atkinson, Dec 1969, took over as Ned Buntline in Indians; John Golden, Mar 1970, Napoleon III in Blood Red Roses; Ellen Stewart, May 1970, The Captain, Max, George Wague, and a Reporter in Colette; Lunt-Fontanne, Oct 1970, Prince William of Hesse, Joseph Fouche, Lord Herries, and Prince Metternich in The Rothschilds (Tony award); Forum, Jan

1972, Keene Curtis in A Ride Across Lake Constance; Morosco, Feb 1972, Curtis Appleby in Night Watch; Uris, Nov 1972, Dr Isaacs in Via Galactica; Ahmanson, Los Angeles, 1974, The Inquisitor in Saint Joan; Ahmanson, 1975, Joshua in Ring Round the Moon; Lake Forest, Ill, summer 1975, Johnson in Too Much Johnson; Elitch Gardens, Denver, Colo, July 1975, various parts in the James Thurber revue Life on a Limb; Dorothy Chandler Pavilion, Los Angeles, May 1976, The Marquis in The Baker's Wife; Mark Taper Forum (Lab), LA, Jan 1977, appeared in The Middle Ages; Dallas Music Hall, Aug 1977, the Old Actor in The Fantasticks; Mark Taper, Nov 1977, Bert Challenor in Comedians; played Daddy Warbucks in the West Coast company of Annie, Curran, San Francisco, June 1978, and Shubert, LA; first appeared in films as Lennox in Orson Welles's Macbeth, 1947, and subsequently in Blade, 1973, Heaven Can Wait, 1978, etc.
Recreations: Carpentry and photography. *Address:* 6363 Ivarene Avenue, Hollywood, Cal 90068.

CUSACK, Cyril, actor
b Durban, S Africa, 26 Nov 1910; *s* of James Walter Cusack and his wife Alice Violet (Cole); *e* Dominican College, Newbridge, Co Kildare, and University College, Dublin; *m* Maureen Kiely (dec).

Made his first appearance on the stage as a child of seven on a tour in Co Tipperary, as Willie Carlyle in East Lynne; served his apprenticeship with the late Brefni O'Rorke in Irish fitups; joined the company of the Abbey Theatre, Dublin, in 1932, appearing in over 65 of its productions; was director for the Gaelic Players, 1935–6; made his first appearance in London at the Westminster Theatre, 4 May, 1936, as Richard in Ah, Wilderness! and later in the month, played the same part at the Ambassadors'; Mercury, Jan 1939, appeared as Christy Mahon in The Playboy of the Western World, a part he had previously played for several years; Q, June 1939, played Covey in The Plough and the Stars; Gate, May 1940, Michel in Les Parents Terribles; St Martin's, Feb 1941, Streeter in Thunder Rock; Haymarket, Mar 1942, Louis Dubedat in The Doctor's Dilemma; Gate Theatre, Dublin, 1942, directed his own play Tareis an Aifrinn; undertook the management of the Gaiety Theatre, Dublin, 1945, co-presenting, and playing Romeo in Romeo and Juliet; later formed Cyril Cusack Productions, Ireland, and presented The Last Summer, at the same theatre; Shaw season 1947, playing The Doctor's Dilemma, Bluntschli in Arms and the Man, Dick Dudgeon in The Devil's Disciple; People's Palace, London, May 1950, played Nosey in Pommy; at the Sarah Bernhardt Theatre, Paris, June 1954, during the First International Drama Festival, presented his own company in The Playboy of the Western World; at the Gaiety, Dublin, Feb 1955, presented the first performance of Sean O'Casey's play, The Bishop's Bonfire; Gaiety, Dublin, July 1956 (Shaw Centenary), presented Androcles and the Lion, in which he played Androcles; Bijou, New York, May 1957, played Phil Hogan in A Moon For the Misbegotten; Gaiety, Dublin, 1957, presented and played Hamlet; at the same theatre, Mar 1958, presented and played Roger Casement; Olympia, Dublin, Mar 1959, played President O'Beirne (and co-produced) Goodwill Ambassador, subsequently appearing in the same play in Boston, and at the Shubert, New Haven, Conn, Mar 1960; at the *Théâtre des Nations* Festival, Paris, summer 1960, also in Holland and Belgium, presented and appeared in Arms and the Man, and Krapp's Last Tape securing the International Critics Award; Gaiety, Dublin, Sept 1960, presented and played Doolin in The Voices of Doolin, also touring with the play; Dublin

Theatre Festival, Olympia, Dublin, Sept 1961, presented and played Mr O in his own play, The Temptation of Mr O; joined the RSC, at the Aldwych, Jan 1963, to play Johann Wilhelm Stettler in The Physicists; and at the Royal Shakespeare, Apr 1963, played Cassius in Julius Caesar; Old Vic (National Theatre Company), Jan 1964, played Can in Andorra; Jan 1967, played Conn in the Abbey Theatre Company's production of The Shaughraun, and at the Aldwych, May 1968, in the World Theatre Season; at the Dublin Festival, Oct 1968, Gaev in The Cherry Orchard; Gaiety, Dublin, Nov 1968, Fox Melarkey in Crystal and Fox; Abbey Theatre and tour, 1969–70, title role in Hadrian VII; Nov 1970, John F Kennedy Theatre, Honolulu, Menenius in Coriolanus; with the National Theatre at the Old Vic, 1974, played Antonio in The Tempest, Mar, and Masked Man in Spring Awakening, May; Abbey, Dublin, 1974–5 season, title role in The Vicar of Wakefield; 1976, Fluther Good in The Plough and the Stars, playing this part at the National Theatre, London, Sept 1977; Abbey, Dublin, and Malvern Festival, 1978, appeared in You Never Can Tell; Old Vic, Feb 1980, Drumm in A Life; he first appeared in films, 1917, in Knocknagow; recent films include: The Spy Who Came in from the Cold, Fahrenheit 451, The Taming of the Shrew, Galileo, The Day of the Jackal, etc; has appeared in numerous television plays, including: The Big Toe, Moon in the Yellow River, Deirdre, The Golden Bowl, etc; appointed to the Board of the Irish National Theatre, 1965; received an LLD, *honoris causa*, from the National University of Ireland, 1977; author of two poetry collections: Timepieces, 1972, and Poems, 1976.

Favourite parts: The Covey, Christy Mahon, Romeo, and Shavian parts. *Recreation:* Riding. *Clubs:* United Arts, Dublin and National University of Ireland, London. *Address:* Cluain Chaoin, Br Sorrento, Deilginis, Co Dublin, Eire, and 2 Vincent Terrace, London, N1. *Tel:* Dublin 859527 and 01–837 4060.

CUSACK, Sinéad, actress
b 18 Feb 1948; *d* of Cyril James Cusack, actor, and his wife Maureen, actress; *e* Holy Child Convent, Killiney, and Dublin University; *m* Jeremy Irons, actor.

Made her stage debut aged twelve, at the Olympia, Dublin, 1960, as Phoebe, a deaf mute, in The Importance of Mr O; after university played juvenile leads at the Abbey, Dublin; Gardner Centre, Brighton, 1971, played Beatrice/Joanna in The Changeling, and appeared in Mirandolina and The Silence of St Just; Shaw, Feb 1972, Juliet in Romeo and Juliet; New, Jul 1972, took over as Grace Harkaway in London Assurance; Gardner Centre, Sept 1973, Laura Wingfield in The Glass Menagerie; Ludlow Festival, 1974, Desdemona in Othello; Oxford Festival, 1976, and tour, Raina Petkoff in Arms and the Man; Piccadilly, Apr 1977, Lady Amaranth in Wild Oats; played the same role for the RSC at the Aldwych, Jun 1979, also Lisa in Children of the Sun, Oct, and Isabella in Measure for Measure, Nov; Stratford, season 1980, Celia in As You Like It, and Evadne in The Maid's Tragedy; films include Alfred the Great, Hoffman, and The Last Remake of Beau Geste; numerous TV appearances include The Shadow of a Gunman, Trilby, and Twelfth Night.

Address: c/o Hutton Management, 194 Old Brompton Road, London SW5.

CUSHING, Peter, actor
b Kenley, Surrey, 26 May 1913; *s* of George Edward Cushing and his wife Nellie Maria (King); *e* Purley, Surrey; *m* Helen Beck (dec); studied voice-production under Cairns James at the Guildhall School of Music and Drama; was formerly engaged as a clerk in a surveyor's office.

Made his first appearance on the stage, at the Connaught Theatre, Worthing, 1935, as Captain Randall in The Middle Watch; made his first appearance in New York, at the Mansfield Theatre, 21 Nov 1941, as Percival in The Seventh Trumpet; made his first appearance in London, at the Phoenix Theatre, 6 Aug 1943, as Alexander I, and Captain Ramballe in War and Peace; Q, Jan 1944, played Valentine Christie in The Dark Potential, and May 1944, Kevin Ormond in The Crime of Margaret Foley; Cambridge, Oct 1944, Private Charles in Happy Few; Globe, during 1944–5, played Lieut Colbert in While the Sun Shines; Criterion, Sept 1945, Faulkland in The Rivals; Q, Nov 1946, Dr Robson in The Curious Dr Robson; toured in Australia and New Zealand, with the Old Vic company, 1948, playing Joseph Surface in The School for Scandal, Duke of Clarence in Richard III, and Ivan Lomov in The Proposal; on returning to England, appeared in the same parts at The New Theatre, Feb–June 1949; Garrick, Jan 1951, played Valentine in The Gay Invalid; St James's, May 1951, during Sir Laurence Olivier's season, appeared as Bel Affris and Brittanus in Caesar and Cleopatra, and as Alexas Diomedes in Antony and Cleopatra; in 1952, appeared in Robert Helpmann's production of The Wedding Ring; toured, 1954, as the Soldier in The Soldier and the Lady; Duchess, May 1956, played Oliver Erwenter in The Silver Whistle; Aldwych, Aug 1959, Charles Norbury in The Sound of Murder; Yvonne Arnaud Theatre, Guildford, July 1956, played Sir Hector Benbow in Thark, subsequently appearing at the Garrick, Aug 1965, in the same production; Haymarket, Basingstoke, Nov 1975, Dr Austin Sloper in The Heiress; since 1951 has appeared extensively in television plays; first appeared in films, in Hollywood, 1939, in Vigil in the Night, and in England, 1948, in Hamlet; has since played in several notable productions.

Recreations: Country walks. *Hobbies:* Collecting books, cigarette cards, and model soldiers. *Address:* c/o John Redway, 16 Berners Street, London W1P 3DD.

CUSHMAN, Robert, critic, director, and occasional performer
b London, 7 Nov 1943; *s* of Harry Cushman and his wife Diana (Sowman); *e* Latymer Upper School and Clare College, Cambridge (MA); *m* Arlene Gould.

With the BBC, 1966–70; Arts Council trainee director, Greenwich, 1971–72, directing his first professional production there, Caste, on 14 Sept 1972; directed on the Fringe and in repertory, 1972–73; 1967–73 contributed reviews and articles on theatre to Plays and Players, etc; joined the *Observer* as theatre critic, 1973–   ; has also written on London theatre for the *New York Times*; Olivier, Dec 1977, devised and appeared in Nashville, an anthology of Ogden Nash's verse; enlarged versions have since been seen at the King's Head (lunchtimes), Oct 1978, in festivals, summer 1979, and as a full evening entertainment at the King's Head, Nov 1979, now entitled Nashville, New York; continues to write and present for radio.

Recreations: Swimming, collecting records. *Address:* The Observer, 8 St Andrew's Hill, London EC4.

CUTHBERTSON, Allan, actor
b Perth, W Australia, 7 Apr 1920; *s* of Ernest Cuthbertson and his wife Isobel Ferguson (Darling); *e* Hale School, Perth; *m* Dr Gertrude Willner.

Appeared on stage and Australian radio from an early age; came to England 1947 and on 7 Aug made his debut as Romeo in Romeo and Juliet at the Boltons; Embassy, Sept 1947, Martin Welford in Point Valaine; toured, Jan 1948, as Maj Fell in Little Holiday; Bristol Old Vic, 1948, Yury in The Apple Orchards, and Laertes in Hamlet, playing the latter part at the St James's, Jul; rep at Windsor, 1948–49; Lyric, Aug 1949, took over as Aimwell in The Beaux' Stratagem; Embassy, Jan 1950, and tour, Tom in Party Manners; New, Feb 1951, and Princes, Jun, Octavius Robinson in Man and Superman, later touring; in a subsequent tour played John Tanner, 1952; Westminster, Jul 1953, Col Henniker in Carrington VC; toured, Apr 1958, as Warner in The Last Word; 1959–71, guest appearances in repertory; Arts, Cambridge and tour, Apr 1971, Richard Greatham in Hay Fever; Queen's, Jun 1975, Villardieu in Ardèle; Old Vic, Nov 1976, and Vaudeville, Jan 1977, John Sterling in The Ghost Train; toured, Jul 1977, as Arthur Phillips in Castle in the Air; toured, May 1978, as Theodore Crozier in Hush and Hide; Hong Kong, Sept 1978, Sir Frederick Goudhurst in Shut Your Eyes and Think of England; Adelphi, June 1979 and tour, Sir Francis Chesney in Charley's Aunt; first film, Carrington VC, 1954; over forty others including Room at the Top, Tunes of Glory, and The Guns of Navarone; frequent TV appearances include plays and series such as Morecambe and Wise, Ripping Yarns, *The Tommy Cooper Hour*, etc.

Recreations: Collecting books and drawings, bookbinding, rambling. *Address:* 15 Berrylands, Surbiton, Surrey.

CUTHBERTSON, Iain, actor and director
b Glasgow, 4 Jan 1930; *s* of Sir David Paton Cuthbertson, CBE, and his wife Jean Prentice (Telfer); *e* Glasgow Academy, Aberdeen GS and Aberdeen University; *m* Anne Kristen.

Began his professional career in radio; first stage appearance, Leven, 1955, as the twin brothers in The Man Upstairs; worked with the Citizens' Theatre company, Glasgow, 1958–60; his parts included Othello, Proctor in The Crucible and Big Daddy in Cat on a Hot Tin Roof; with the same company, made his first London appearance at the Royal Court, July 1958, as Archibald Gascoyne in Gay Landscape; Assembly Hall, Edinburgh Festival, Aug 1960, played the title role in The Wallace; Arts, London, Abelard in Abelard and Heloise, Oct 1960, and Fr Antony in This Way to the Tomb, Nov 1960; Pitlochry Festival, 1961, played various leading roles; general manager and director of productions, Citizens', Glasgow, 1962–5; at the Citizens', May 1964, created the part of Armstrong in Armstrong's Last Goodnight; associate director, Royal Court, 1965, where he played Musgrave in Serjeant Musgrave's Dance, Dec 1965; translated, adapted and directed Ubu Roi, July 1966; Perth, 1967–8, director of a pilot scheme in Scottish Theatre; 1977, toured in the title-role in Dr Angelus; 1977–78 played the Major Domo in Ariadne Auf Naxes for Scottish Opera; Lyceum Edinburgh, Jan 1978, Boswell in Boswell's Johnson; Rector of Aberdeen University, 1975–78, and received a DLitt *honoris causa* from that University in 1978; first film 1970, The Railway Children; TV appearances, since 1956, include the series *The Borderers, Sutherland's Law,* and, more recently, *Destiny, The Story of Darwin,* Charlie Endell, and *Casting the Runes*; has taken part, as actor and writer, in over 1,000 broadcasts; writer of documentary films.

Recreation: Sailing. *Address:* c/o John French, 26 Binney Street, London W1.

D

DA COSTA, Morton (*né* Tecosky), director and actor
b Philadelphia, Pa, 7 Mar 1914; *s* of Samuel Tecosky and his wife Elsie Rose (Hulnick); *e* Cook Junior High School and Temple University, Philadelphia; originally intended to become a teacher, but interest in the theatre developed while at the University.

He became President of Theta Alpha Phi, the national honorary dramatic society; co-founded the Civic Repertory Theatre, Dayton, Ohio, 1937, and produced nearly 60 plays for that company; served as actor, partner, and director for the Port Players Summer Theatre, Port Washington, Wisconsin, 1938–45; made his first appearance on Broadway, at the Plymouth Theatre, Nov 1942, when he played the Broadcast Official in The Skin of Our Teeth, and understudied Montgomery Clift; Shubert, Apr 1944, played Gen William F Smith in War President; Playhouse New York, Mar 1945, appeared as Mr Flynn in It's a Gift; Columbus Circle, NY, Dec 1945, appeared as Osric in Maurice Evans' production of Hamlet; at the City Center, NY, May 1949, played Henry Straker in Man and Superman; same theatre, Dec 1949, directed She Stoops to Conquer; he has subsequently directed Captain Brassbound's Conversion, 1950; Dream Girl, The Wild Duck, 1951; Dark Legend, The Grey-Eyed People, 1952; Plain and Fancy, No Time for Sergeants, 1955; Plain and Fancy (London), Auntie Mame, 1956; The Music Man, 1957; Saratoga, 1959; The Wall, 1960; Hot Spot, 1963; To Broadway with Love (Texas Pavilions, NY World's Fair), 1964; Diplomatic Relations (Palm Beach), Family Things Etc, 1965; The Coffee Lover, 1966; Maggie Flynn (also co-author), 1968; Show Me Where the Good Times Are, 1970; The Women, 1973; A Musical Jubilee, 1975; Weekend with Feathers (tour), 1976; author of Morton da Costa's Book of Needlepoint, 1975; was awarded a Doctor of Humane Letters degree by Temple University, 1958; he has also produced and directed the films of Auntie Mame, and The Music Man, and directed Island of Love.
Address: 20 Dorethy Road, West Redding, Ct 06896.

DAILEY, Irene, actress, teacher
b New York City, 12 Sept; *d* of Daniel Dailey and his wife Helen (Ryan); *e* Mother Cabrini High School, NY; prepared for the stage with Lee Strasberg at the Actors Studio and with Robert Lewis, Uta Hagen, Mira Rostova, Jane White, dance with Anna Sokolow, and others.

Made her stage début at the Red Barn, Locust Valley, NY, June 1941, in Out of the Frying Pan, and later appeared in Room Service; made her NY début at the Longacre, 13 Jan 1943, as Shotput in Nine Cards; toured, 1944, as Caroline in Laughing Water; Belasco, Feb 1946, played Angie in Truckline Cafe; New York City Center, May 1951, Shirley in Idiot's Delight; toured in Skylark, 1952; Phoenix, Dec 1956, Mrs Shin in Good Woman of Setzuan; Music Box, Oct 1957, Adele Farnum in Miss Lonely- hearts; Equity Library, Feb 1957, Irene in Idiot's Delight; HB Studio, Mar 1959, Eloise in Uncle Wiggly in Connecticut; made her London début at the Lyric, Hammersmith, 1 June 1960, as Jasmine Adair in Tomorrow—with Pictures, and later transferred with this production to the Duke of York's; Erlanger, Philadelphia,

Oct 1961, Valeria in Daughter of Silence; McCarter, Princeton, New Jersey, Oct 1961, Abbie in Desire Under the Elms; Playhouse in the Park, Philadelphia, July 1962, Clara in Winterskill; same theatre, July 1963, Hannah Jelkes in The Night of the Iguana, and Aug 1963, Pamela Pew-Pickett in Tchin-Tchin; Biltmore, Feb 1963, Senora in Andorra; Sombrero Playhouse, Phoenix, Arizona, Feb 1964, Pamela Pew-Pickett in Tchin-Tchin; Royale, May 1964, Nettie Cleary in The Subject Was Roses; Cherry Lane, Jan 1966, Miss Quincey in Better Luck Next Time and Mrs Henry in A Walk in Dark Places in a double-bill entitled Rooms, White Barn, Westport, Conn, Aug 1966, Beatrice in The Effect of Gamma Rays on Man-in-the-Moon Marigolds; Ambassador, 1968, took over from Eileen Heckart various roles in You Know I Can't Hear You When the Water's Running; Ivanhoe, Chicago, Mar 1971, Beatrice in The Effect of Gamma Rays on Man-in-the-Moon Marigolds, and received the Sarah Siddons' Award for this performance; Studio Arena, Buffalo, NY, 1971, played in Buying Out; Ivanhoe, Chicago, 1972, played in The House of Blue Leaves; McCarter, Princeton, Oct 1973, Mme Arkadina in The Seagull; Loeb Theatre, Purdue, Ind, also 1973, Mary Tyrone in Long Day's Journey into Night; WPA, June 1976, appeared in Lotsa Ladies; Playwrights Horizons, Nov 1976, in Rio Grande; Three Muses, Hotel Ansonia, NY, Dec 1979, Cass in The Loves of Cass Maguire; appeared in the films Five Easy Pieces, The Grissom Gang, and The Amityville Horror; first appeared on television in *Robert Montgomery Presents*, 1951, and has since played in various dramatic series, including: *The Defenders, Twilight Zone, Dr Kildare, Another World* (Emmy Award, 1979), etc; author of the play Waiting for Mickey and Ava, 1978; founded the School of the Actors Company, NY, 1961, served as its artistic director; member, Ensemble Studio Theatre.
Recreations: Reading, charcoal sketching, water color painting, sports. *Address:* 151 East 19th Street, New York, NY.

DALE, Grover (*né* Grover Aitken), director, choreographer and actor
b Harrisburg, Pennsylvania, 22 July 1935; *s* of Ronal Rittenhouse Aitken and his wife Emma Bertha (Ammon); *e* McKeesport High School; *m* the actress Anita Rose Morris; at the age of 15, operated a dancing school in McKeesport with 7 employees and 125 students.

Made his professional debut in Pittsburgh, 6 June 1953, dancing in the chorus of Li'l Abner; Winter Garden, Sept 1957, played Snowboy in West Side Story; Alvin, Mar 1960, Andrew in Greenwillow; Broadhurst, Oct 1961, Barnaby Slade in Sail Away, making his London debut in the same role at the Savoy, 21 June 1962; Phoenix, Jan 1964, Mr Mackintosh in Too Much Johnson; Broadhurst, Apr 1965, Pearce in Half-a-Sixpence.

At the Billy Rose, Mar 1969, made his choreographic debut with Billy; joint choreographer with Michael Bennett for Seesaw, 1973, sharing a Tony; directed The Magic Show, 1974; directed King of Schnorrers, 1979; has appeared in the films The Unsinkable Molly Brown, 1963, Les Demoiselles de Rochefort, Half-a-Sixpence, and The Landlord, 1968.

Address: c/o Eric Shepard, 40 West 57th Street, New York, NY 10019.

DALE, Jim (*né* Smith), actor
b Rothwell, Northants, 15 Aug 1935; *s* of William Henry Smith and his wife Miriam Jean (Wells); *e* Kettering and District GS; *m* Patricia Gardiner; six years of ballet training.

Made his debut, 1951, as a solo comedian at the Savoy, Kettering; Lyric, Hammersmith, Nov 1964, played William Dowton in The Wayward Way; Edinburgh Festival, Aug 1966, Autolycus in The Winter's Tale, transferring to the Cambridge, Sept; Vaudeville, Feb 1967, the Burglar in The Burglar; Edinburgh Festival, Aug 1967, Bottom in A Midsummer Night's Dream, transferring to the Saville, Sept; joined the National Theatre Company at the Old Vic, 1969, and played Barnet in The National Health, Oct; Nicholas in The Travails of Sancho Panza, Dec; took over Costard in Love's Labour's Lost, 1970; Launcelot Gobbo in The Merchant of Venice, Apr 1970; for the Young Vic, played Scapino in The Cheats of Scapino, Sept 1970; Petruchio in The Taming of the Shrew, Nov 1970; Old Vic, 1971, played The Architect in The Architect and the Emperor of Assyria, Feb; Mr Lofty in The Good-Natured Man, Mar; Kalle in The Captain of Köpenick, Dec; toured Europe with the Young Vic, 1972, as Petruchio; Queen's, July 1973, Denry Machin in The Card; to New York (Brooklyn Academy), Mar 1974, with the Young Vic productions of The Taming of the Shrew and Scapino, co-directing and writing the music for the latter production, which transferred to the Circle in the Square, May 1974 and subsequently the Ambassador; has also appeared in pantomime; Mark Taper Forum, Los Angeles, Nov 1977, Gethin Price in Comedians; Long Wharf, New Haven, 1979, Terri Dennis in Privates on Parade; films, since 1963, include a number in the Carry On series as well as Digby— The Biggest Dog in the World, and more recently, Joseph Andrews, Bloodshy and Comedians; has appeared in TV light entertainment since 1957, and broadcast regularly as a disc jockey; a successful songwriter, he has also contributed music to several of the productions in which he has appeared.
Favourite parts: Scapino, Petruchio. *Address:* c/o ICM, 22 Grafton Street, London W1.

DALRYMPLE, Jean, producer and director
b Morristown, NJ, 2 Sept 1910; *d* of George Hull Dalrymple and his wife Elizabeth Van Kirk (Collins); *e* privately; *m* (1) Ward Morehouse (mar dis); (2) Maj-Gen P De Witt Ginder.

Formerly an actress, on the vaudeville stage in a one-act play which she wrote, directed and produced, and subsequently personal representative with John Golden; formed her own publicity organization, 1940; commenced play production with Hope for the Best, 1945; subsequently produced Brighten the Corner, 1945; Burlesque, 1946; Red Gloves, 1948; in summer theatres, 1950, she presented Harvey, The Voice of the Turtle, and The Second Man; in 1951, public relations officer for the Berlin Arts Festival productions of Oklahoma! and Medea; during 1953, at the New York City Center, became the General Director of the City Center Light Opera Company and the City Center Drama Company and subsequently has produced Cyrano de Bergerac, The Shrike, Richard III and Charley's Aunt; presented What Every Woman Knows, 1954; The Four Poster, The Time of Your Life, The Wisteria Trees, The Teahouse of the August Moon (in Spanish, at Mexico City), Brattle Shakespeare Players in Othello and Henry IV, Part I, 1955; New York City Center, presented King Lear, The Teahouse of the August Moon, The Glass Menagerie, Marcel Marceau, Mister Roberts, 1956; The Beggar's Opera, Brigadoon, The

Merry Widow, South Pacific, The Pajama Game, Carousel, 1957; Marcel Marceau (mime), Annie Get Your Gun, Wonderful Town, Oklahoma!, 1958; author of The Quiet Room, produced at Wyndham's, London, Mar 1958, and subsequently in Austria and Australia; The Most Happy Fella, Say, Darling, Lute Song, 1959; Finian's Rainbow, The King and I, Marcel Marceau, The Piccolo Teatro de Milano, and the Grand Kabuki of Japan, 1960; Porgy and Bess, Show Boat, South Pacific, Pal Joey, 1961; Can-Can, Brigadoon, Fiorello! 1962; Marcel Marceau, Brigadoon, Wonderful Town, Oklahoma! Pal Joey, The King and I, 1963; West Side Story, Porgy and Bess, My Fair Lady, Greek Art Theatre, D'Oyly Carte Opera Co, Brigadoon, 1964; Polish Mime Co, Moscow Art Theatre, Guys and Dolls, Kiss Me Kate, South Pacific, The Music Man, Oklahoma, 1965; How to Succeed in Business Without Really Trying, The Most Happy Fella, Where's Charley?, Guys and Dolls, The Country Girl, The Rose Tattoo, Elizabeth the Queen, Carousel, 1966; Finian's Rainbow, The Sound of Music, Wonderful Town, Life with Father, The Tenth Man, Brigadoon, and for Theatre Four produced and directed Beyond Desire and, at the Theatre de Lys, directed Postcards, 1967; My Fair Lady, The King and I, Carnival, 1968; as Executive Director of the American National Theatre and Academy, presented at ANTA the American Conservatory Theatre of San Francisco in Tiny Alice, A Flea in Her Ear, and The Three Sisters, the American Shakespeare Festival Theatre of Stratford, Conn, in Henry V, The Plumstead Playhouse of Long Island in Our Town, and the New York Shakespeare Festival Public Theatre in No Place to Be Somebody, 1969; the National Theatre of the Deaf in Sganarelle and Songs from Milk Wood, The Playwrights Unit in Watercolor and CrissCrossing, the La Mama Experimental Theatre Club in Gloria and Esperanza, the Phoenix Theatre Company in Harvey, the John Fernald Company in The Cherry Orchard, and the Trinity Square Repertory Company of Providence, RI, in Wilson in the Promise Land, 1970; co-produced The Web and the Rock, 1972; co-produced Naomi Court, 1974; co-produced Agnes de Mille in Conversations About the Dance, 1975; produced The Origin of Species (Westport, Conn, and Shreveport, La), 1978; at the Brussels World Fair, 1958, she was Co-ordinator of Performing Arts for the US, and presented a varied program of opera, musical comedy, ballet and drama; for her services on behalf of the Fair she received the Order of the Crown of Belgium; at the Hudson Celebration, Theatre-in-the-Park, Central Park, NY, July 1959, presented André Eglevsky's Petit Ballet, An Operetta Evening, Guys and Dolls, Can-Can, etc; television productions include: The Cherry Orchard, Crime of Passion, The Consul, Reunion in Vienna, and Carol Channing in Show Girl; author of the play The Feathered Fauna; of autobiography September Child; of Careers and Opportunities in the Theatre; From the Last Row, Jean Dalrymple's Pinafore Farm Cookbook; Folklore and Facts of National Nutrition (co-author); The Complete Handbook for Community Theatres; is a member of the National Council on the Arts and Treasurer of the American National Theatre and Academy; awarded an Honorary Degree of Doctor of Fine Arts by Wheaton College.
Address: 150 West 55th Street, New York, NY 10019. *Tel:* 246–7820.

DAMON, Stuart, actor
b Brooklyn, New York, 5 Feb 1937; *s* of Marvin Leonard Zonis and his wife Eva (Sherer); *e* Brandeis University; *m* Deirdre Ottewill.

First professional appearance in the chorus of Plain and Fancy, Lambertville Music Circus, NY, July 1957; Broadway debut, Alvin, Mar 1959, in the chorus of First Impressions; Plymouth, Apr 1960, appeared in the revue From A to Z; same theatre, Sept 1960, Frangipane in Irma la Douce, playing Nestor in the Las Vegas production, Sept 1961; Actors Playhouse, Apr 1962, Curt in Entertain a Ghost; Theatre Four, Apr 1963, Antipholus of Syracuse in The Boys from Syracuse; Forty-Sixth Street, Feb 1965, appeared in Do I Hear a Waltz?; came to London, 1965, and played Jack Conner in Charlie Girl, Adelphi, Dec; Piccadilly, Nov 1966, Harry Houdini in Houdini—Man of Magic; Marlowe, Canterbury, 1970, Macbeth in Macbeth; Richmond, April 1970, King Charles in Nell; Thorndike, Leatherhead, Feb 1973, Eddie Payne in Cadenza; Piccadilly, May 1975, Ben Silverman in The Sunshine Boys; TV appearances, in NY and London, include the series The Champions.

Recreation: Breeding, riding and training horses. *Address:* 31 Shawfield Street, London, SW3. *Tel:* 01–352 1305.

DANA, F. Mitchell (*né* Frank Livingston Mitchell II), lighting designer

b 14 Nov 1942; *s* of John D Mitchell and his wife Elizabeth Francis (Woods); *e* Utah State University and Yale University School of Drama; *m* Wendy Karen Bensinger; formerly a stage manager, production manager etc and swimming coach.

Has lit more than 250 professional theatre productions, including nearly fifty productions, 1972-80 for ACT, San Francisco, also McCarter, Princeton, 1969-71; Stratford, Ontario, season 1972; Pittsburgh Civic Light Opera, 1973-74; Goodman, Chicago, 1973-78; Mark Taper Forum, 1976-77; has also lit many tours and personal appearances; work for Broadway includes The Freedom of the City, 1974; The Inspector General, Man and Superman, Once in a Lifetime, 1978; TV work includes Take 5 and Slim Goodbody.

Recreations: Swimming, classical music, snorkelling. *Address:* 221 West 82nd Street, New York, NY 10024.

DANA, Leora, actress

b New York City, 1 Apr 1923; *d* of William Shepherd Dana and his wife Alberta (Webster); *e* Barnard College (BA 1946); *m* Kurt Kasznar (mar dis); studied for the stage at the Royal Academy of Dramatic Art, London, receiving the silver medal for acting, 1948.

Made her stage début at the Vaudeville, London, 27 Aug 1947, as June Farrell in The Chiltern Hundreds; returned to America and at the Belasco, NY, Dec 1948, played Irma in The Madwoman of Chaillot; Plymouth, Jan 1950, played Maman in The Happy Time; Alvin, Dec 1951, Nancy Gray in Point of No Return; toured in the last part, 1952-3; National, 1954, took over from Margaret Sullavan as Sabrina in Sabrina Fair; American Shakespeare Theatre, Stratford, Conn, July 1955, Portia in Julius Caesar; Shubert, New Haven, Conn, July 1955, Frances Lucas in A Quiet Place; played in stock at the Elitch Gardens, Denver, Colorado, 1957; Morosco, NY, Mar 1960, Alice Russell in The Best Man; toured in this last part, 1961-2; Festival of the Two Worlds, Spoleto, Italy, summer, 1962, Blackie in The Milktrain Doesn't Stop Here Anymore; University of Utah, Mar 1963, Eliza Gant in Look Homeward, Angel, and, Oct 1963, Claire Zachanassian in The Visit; Little Fox, NY, 1964, Mrs Constable in In the Summer House; Morosco, Oct 1964, Emily Bach-Nielsen in Beekman Place; toured Nov 1965–Mar 1966, with the National Repertory Theatre of Eva Le Gallienne as Gabrielle in The Madwoman of Chaillot, Lucy in The Rivals, and Andromache in The Trojan Women; Cherry Lane, Sept 1966, Lucia in The Long Christmas Dinner; with the John Fernald Company, Meadow Brook Theatre, Rochester, Michigan, 1967, played in John Gabriel Borkman; Cafe au Go Go, NY, May 1968, played various parts in the 11-part play Collision Course; The American Place, Dec 1968, Ann Jillett

in The Bird of Dawning Singeth All Night Long; Forum, Dec 1969, Dr Anna Balcar in The Increased Difficulty of Concentration; Actors Theatre, Louisville, Kentucky, 1970, played in Tobacco Road and repeated this part at the Playhouse in the Park, Cincinnati, Ohio; Theatre de Lys, Jan 1972, Meg in A Place Without Mornings; ANTA, Dec 1972, Elizabeth Edwards in The Last of Mrs Lincoln, and received the Antoinette Perry (Tony) Award for this part; 46th Street, Apr 1973, Fitter, Miss Watts, A Woman in The Women; toured 1974 in Elizabethan Gardens; Lenox, Mass, Arts Center, July 1974, Mrs Moore in Mourning Pictures; Lyceum, Nov 1974, Maggie in Mourning Pictures; Arena Stage, Washington, DC, Oct 1975, Mary Tyrone in Long Day's Journey into Night; Public/Newman, June 1976, Mary E Law in Rebel Women; Arena Stage, Jan 1977, in The Autumn Garden; Theatre of the Open Eye, Feb 1978, Mrs Vanderbilt in The Tennis Game; Three Muses, Hotel Ansonia, Dec 1979, Trilbe Costello in The Loves of Cass Maguire; first appeared in films in 1957 in The 3.10 to Yuma, and has since played in Kings Go Forth, Some Came Running, A Gathering of Eagles, The Norman Vincent Peale Story, etc; has appeared frequently on television in such dramatic programs as *Alfred Hitchcock Presents, Philco Playhouse, Ben Casey,* The Barretts of Wimpole Street, Rip Van Winkle, etc; received the Derwent Award for The Madwoman of Chaillot and the Twelfth Night Award for The Happy Time.

Recreations: Dancing, painting. *Address:* 11 East 63rd Street, New York, NY 10021.

DANEMAN, Paul, actor

b London, 26 Oct 1925; *s* of Frederick Daneman and his wife Dorothy Margaret (Almenrader); *e* Haberdashers' Aske's School, London, Sir William Borlase's School, Marlow, and Reading University; *m* (1) Susan Courtney (mar dis); (2) Meredith Kinmont; served with the RAF during the war and subsequently studied for the stage at RADA.

First appeared on the stage at the New Theatre, Bromley, 26 Dec 1947, as the front legs of a horse in Alice in Wonderland; Lyric, Hammersmith, 13 Apr 1949, played the part of a soldier in Royal Highness; May 1949, spent some time in repertory, before again appearing at the Lyric, Hammersmith, Jan 1950, as a Mower in The Boy With a Cart; also at the same theatre with the Bristol Old Vic Company, June 1950, as Damis in Tartuffe; Birmingham Repertory Theatre, Aug 1950–Oct 1952; with this company, appeared at the Old Vic, July 1952, as Richard in King Henry VI, Part III; in Sir John Gielgud's season at the Lyric, Hammersmith, Dec 1952, played Mowbray and the Bishop of Carlisle in Richard II; Embassy, June–July 1953, played Laertes in Hamlet and Sir Toby Belch in Twelfth Night; at Bulawayo, Aug 1953, with Sir John Gielgud's company, again appeared as Mowbray and Carlisle in Richard II; joined the Old Vic Company, Oct 1953, remaining until July 1955, during which time he played, among other parts, Justice Shallow in Henry IV, Feste in Twelfth Night, Tullus Aufidius in Coriolanus, Malcolm in Macbeth, Lucentio in The Taming of the Shrew; at the Arts, July 1955, played Vladimir in Waiting for Godot; at the Duke of York's, Sept 1955, appeared in The Punch Revue; Saville, Feb 1956, played Faulkland in a revival of The Rivals; Saville, Oct 1956, played Louis Dubedat in a revival of The Doctor's Dilemma; Arts, Jan 1957, Jean-Louis Deshayes in No Laughing Matter; Old Vic Company, London, Oct 1957–July 1958, during which time he played King Henry in Henry VI (Parts I, II, III), Pompey in Measure For Measure, Quince in A Midsummer Night's Dream, Fool in King Lear, Sir Toby Belch in Twelfth Night, Lord Chamberlain in Henry VIII;

appeared with the same company in Paris and Brussels, July 1958; Royal Court, Aug 1958, played Adolphus Cusins in Major Barbara; Lyric, Hammersmith, Nov 1959, appeared in a double bill, as George Fentrill in Last Day in Dreamland, and Tony Belford in A Glimpse of the Sea; with the Old Vic Company, Edinburgh Festival and London, Aug 1961–Mar 1962, played the following parts: the title-part in Dr Faustus, the Bastard in King John, Malvolio in Twelfth Night, the title-part in Richard III; Strand, Sept 1962, played Martin Eliot in The New Men; Nottingham Playhouse Company, subsequently touring West Africa, Jan–Mar 1963, played Macduff in Macbeth, Sir Andrew Aguecheek in Twelfth Night, and Bluntschli in Arms and the Man; toured Australia, Nov 1963–Dec 1964, as King Arthur in Camelot; Drury Lane, Feb 1965, took over the same part in the London production; Scala, Dec 1967, played Captain Hook and Mr Darling in Peter Pan; toured, Feb 1969, as Tom Hillyer in They Ride on Broomsticks; Haymarket, Oct 1969, took over as Frederick William Rolfe in Hadrian the Seventh; at the Garrick, Feb 1971, Eric in Don't Start Without Me; Little, Bristol, Nov 1973, played Charles Condamine in their Golden Jubilee production of Blithe Spirit; toured, Jan 1974, as Tony Henderson in his own production of Bell, Book and Candle; toured Australia, Jan 1975, in his one-man show, Who Do They Think They Are?; toured June 1975 as Richard Sherman in The Seven Year Itch; Vaudeville, Nov 1975, Henry Monk in Double Edge; Arnaud, Guildford, Oct 1976, played the title-role in Macbeth; Arnaud, Feb 1977, Maxim de Winter in Rebecca; Duke of York's Jan 1978, Inspector Millard in Spine Chiller; Arnaud, Malvern Festival and tour, Henry Higgins in Pygmalion; Apollo, Oct 1978, took over as Arthur Pullen in Shut Your Eyes And Think of England; Arnaud, May 1979, Dr Palmer in circumstantial Evidence; television appearances include the series *An Age of Kings, Not in Front of the Children, Never a Cross Word* and *Spy Trap.*

Recreations: Painting, photography, and walking. *Address:* c/o London Management, 235 Regent Street, London, W1.

DANIELS, Ron (Ronald George Daniel), director and former actor
b Niterói, Brazil, 15 Oct 1942; s of Percy Daniel and his wife Nellie; e in Brazil; m Anjula Harman; trained for the stage at Fundação Brasileira de Teatro.

Made his first professional appearance, 1960, as Romeo in Blood on Sunday, a Brazilian version of Romeo and Juliet, while a student at the Fundação Brasileira de Teatro in Rio de Janeiro; founder member, 1960–64, of the Workshop Theatre (Teatro Oficina) of São Paulo; awarded British Council Bursary to the British Drama League in Acting and Stagecraft, subsequently appearing in repertory at the Byre Theatre, St Andrew's, 1964, where his roles included Jimmy Porter in Look Back in Anger and Donal Davoren in Shadow of a Gunman; in 1965 and 1966 played a number of major roles at the Victoria, Stoke-on-Trent, including Orlando in As You Like It, Hotspur in Henry IV Part I, Higgins in Pygmalion, Macbeth, Brutus in Julius Caesar, Orgon in Tartuffe, Malvolio in Twelfth Night; directed his first production Electra by Sophocles and Plautus' Pot of Gold at the same theatre in 1966 followed by She Stoops to Conquer in 1967; Richmond 1967 played Benvolio in Romeo and Juliet; joined the Royal Shakespeare Company, 1968, taking over as Marc Antony on provincial tour and making his London debut in a major role as John Grass in Indians, Aldwych, 1968; returned as Assistant Director to the Victoria, Stoke, 1969–71, where his productions included Who's Afraid of Virginia Woolf?, Sweeney Todd, Fighting Man, Hamlet,

Major Barbara, The Recruiting Officer, Coriolanus, Drums in the Night, The Samaritan; as a freelance he then directed The Samaritan and The Long, the Short and the Tall (Shaw, 1971); Bang (Open Space), The Children's Crusade (National Youth Theatre), Female Transport (Half Moon) in 1973; The Motor Show (Half Moon), By Common Consent (NYT), Afore Night Come (The Other Place, RSC) in 1974; Afore Night Come (Long Wharf, New Haven, USA), Ashes (at the Young Vic), Serjeant Musgrave's Dance (Bristol), Into the Mouth of Crabs (National Theatre at the ICA), 1975; Made in Britain (Oxford Playhouse), Destiny (TOP, RSC), 1976; Artistic Director, RSC's The Other Place, Stratford-upon-Avon, 1977– ; Associate Director RSC, 1979– ; his RSC productions (at The Other Place unless otherwise stated) have been: 'Tis Pity She's a Whore, The Lorenzaccio Story, The Sons of Light, 1977; The Women Pirates (Aldwych Theatre), Hippolytus, 1978; Pericles, The Suicide, 1979; Romeo and Juliet (RST), Timon of Athens and Hansel and Gretel, 1980; has also directed the following in the US: Bingo (Obie award), Ivanov (1976), Puntila and his Servant Matti (1977) and Man is Man (1978) all at the Yale Repertory Theatre and Romeo and Juliet (1979) at the Guthrie, Minneapolis.

Address: Royal Shakespeare Theatre, Stratford-upon-Avon.

DANNER, Blythe, actress
b Philadelphia, Pa, e Bard College; m Bruce Paltrow.

Made her New York début at the 81st Street Theatre, 14 Nov 1966, as the Girl in The Infantry; National, Washington, DC, Nov 1967, Michele in Mata Hari; Forum, Mar 1968, the Girl in Summertree; Vivian Beaumont, Apr 1968, Sister Martha in Cyrano de Bergerac; Jan Hus Playhouse, Nov 1968, Violet Bean in Up Eden; Pocket, Mar 1969, Connie Odum in Someone's Comin' Hungry; Vivian Beaumont, May 1969, Elsie in The Miser; Booth, Oct 1969, Jil Tanner in Butterflies Are Free; Mark Taper Forum, Los Angeles, Cal, Aug 1971, played the title-role of Major Barbara; Vivian Beaumont, Mar 1972, Viola in Twelfth Night; Brooklyn Academy, Mar 1977, Cynthia Karslake in The New York Idea; Trafalgar, Jan 1980, Emma in Betrayal; has appeared in six Williamstown Festivals, 1977–79, playing parts including Nina in The Seagull, 1974, Isabel in Ring Round the Moon, 1975, Lisa in Children of the Sun, 1979; appeared in the films Lovin' Molly, The Great Santini (1980), etc; TV includes plays, specials and series.

Address: Actors Equity Association, 165 West 46th Street, New York, NY 10036.

DARE, Daphne, designer
b Yeovil, Somerset; d of Wilfred John Dare and his wife Majorie (Bollen); e Yeovil HS, Bath Academy of Art, and London University; began her career as a scene painter at the Birmingham Repertory Theatre.

Designed her first production, Amphitryon 38, for the Bristol Old Vic, 24 June 1958; at Bristol until 1963, when she designed for the Citizens', Glasgow. Costume designer for the BBC TV, 1964–8; Head of Design, Northcott Theatre, Exeter, 1967–8; Head of Design, Stratford Festival, Ontario, Oct 1974– ; here she redesigned the stage and auditoria of the Avon Theatre and the Third Stage, 1974; designed Measure for Measure, Trumpets and Drums, 1975; Antony and Cleopatra, The Way of the World, Three Sisters, 1976; The Importance of Being Earnest, 1976; Richard III, Miss Julie, The Guardsman, Hay Fever (costumes), 1977; The Winter's Tale, The Devils, Uncle Vanya, Private Lives (co-designed), also basic sets for Ned and Jack, Medea, Stargazing and Four

Plays by Samuel Beckett, 1978; Love's Labours Lost, Richard II, Henry IV, Parts I and II (co-designed), King Lear, 1979; The Beggar's Opera, The Seagull, 1980; her other design work, in London unless otherwise stated, includes: The Ballad of the False Barman, 1966; Abelard and Heloise (also New York), Two Gentlemen of Verona (Stratford-upon-Avon), 1970; Dear Antoine (Chichester), A Voyage Round My Father, Miss Julie, 1971; Veterans, Notes on a Love Affair, The Beggar's Opera, The Lady's Not for Burning (both Chichester), The Effect of Gamma Rays on Man-in-the-Moon Marigolds, 1972; Three Sisters, The House of Bernarda Alba, Habeas Corpus, Rosmersholm, Born Yesterday, Catsplay, Not Drowning But Waving, Zorba, 1973 film work includes costumes for Kes, 1968, Family Life, and Gumshoe. TV includes: *Dr Who* and Fall of Eagles; member, Society of British Theatre Designers.

Recreations: Cinemagoing, collecting tin and tole ware. *Address:* Stratford Festival Theatre, Stratford, Ontario, Canada. *Tel:* 271 4040.

DA SILVA, Howard (*né* Silverblatt), actor and director
b Cleveland, Ohio, 4 May 1909; *s* of Benjamin Silverblatt and his wife Bertha (Sen); *e* Carnegie Institute of Technology; *m* (1) Marjorie Nelson; (2) Nancy Nutter; formerly engaged as a steel worker.

Made his first appearance on the stage at the Civic Repertory Theatre, New York, Sept 1929, as the Actor in Lower Depths, and remained with the company until 1934, playing the Slave in The Would-Be Gentleman, the Apothecary in Romeo and Juliet (1929), Scaevola in The Green Cockatoo, the Orderly in The Three Sisters, Schumann in Siegfried, Ostrich and Cookson in Peter Pan, Hodges in Alison's House, the Second Coastguardsman in The Good Hope (1930), Gucsh in Camille, Mufti in The Would-Be Gentleman, Senator Lewis in Inheritors, Station- master in The Cherry Orchard (1931), Wolf Biefeld in Liliom, Fergsert in The Three Sisters, Countryman in Cradle Song, Dr Samuel Johnson in Dear Jane, the Cook and the White Knight in Alice in Wonderland (1932); at the New Amsterdam, Mar 1933, again played the Station-master in The Cherry Orchard; toured 1933–4 as Thorvald in A Doll's House, Brack in Hedda Gabler, and Solness in The Master Builder; joined the Brattle Repertory Company in Cambridge, Mass, and appeared as Astrov in Uncle Vanya, the Artist in When We Dead Awaken, and Don Victorio in Fortunato (1933–4); at the Civic Repertory Theatre, for Theatre Union, Dec 1934, played Sepp Kriz in Sailors of Cattaso, and Mar 1935, Hansy McCulloch in Black Pit; for the Cleveland Playhouse, 1935, played in Rain from Heaven, Between Two Worlds, and The Master Builder, and for the People's Theatre, Cleveland, directed Waiting for Lefty and The Inheritors; St James, NY, Oct 1936, Foreman in Ten Million Ghosts; Belasco, Nov 1937, Lewis in Golden Boy; Maxine Elliott, 1937, appeared as Larry Foreman in the Mercury Theatre Company production of The Cradle Will Rock; Fulton, Feb 1938, Old Man in Casey Jones; Plymouth, Oct 1938, played Jack Armstrong in Abe Lincoln in Illinois; St James, Nov 1939, Speed in Summer Night; Broadhurst, 1940, played the Guide in Two on an Island; St James's, Mar 1943, played Jud in Oklahoma!; Mansfield, Dec 1947, directed The Cradle Will Rock; at the Actors Laboratory, Hollywood, 1948–9, played in Monday's Heroes and The Bankers' Daughter and directed Proud Accents; Broadhurst, Oct 1950, played Friend Ed in Burning Bright; for the Actors Concert Theatre, 1951–2, directed and played in concert readings from Mark Twain, Sholom Aleichem and Anton Chekhov; Barbizon Plaza, Mar 1953, played Mendele, directed and co-produced The World

of Sholom Aleichem; Phoenix, Nov 1954, directed Sandhog; Phoenix, Feb 1956, played the Fixer in a revival of The Adding Machine; Phoenix, Nov 1956, played Noel Fedoseitch Mamaev in a revival of Diary of a Scoundrel; Rooftop Theatre, NY, Jan 1957, played the title-part in Volpone; Carnegie Hall Playhouse, Sept 1957, directed Tevya and His Daughters; Ambassador, Oct 1957, played Prosecutor Horn in Compulsion; Broadhurst, Nov 1959, played Ben Marino in Fiorello!; City Center, Feb 1960, directed a revival of The Cradle Will Rock; Cort, Sept 1961, directed Purlie Victorious; Music Box, Jan 1962, played Ottaker in Romulus; Philadelphia, Aug 1962, played Calchas in La Belle; Biltmore, Dec 1962, played Max Hartman in In the Counting House; Music Box, Mar 1963, played Paul Hirsch in Dear Me, The Sky Is Falling; York Playhouse, June 1963, directed Cages; ANTA, Oct 1963, directed The Advocate; Gramercy Arts, Nov 1963, directed Thistle in My Bed; Delacorte, June 1964, played Claudius in Hamlet; Theatre Four, Nov 1964, directed The Cradle Will Rock; co-author of the play The Zulu and the Zayda, 1965; Longacre, Dec 1966, directed My Sweet Charlie; Vivian Beaumont, July 1967, Archbishop in The Unknown Soldier and His Wife; 46th Street, Mar 1969, Benjamin Franklyn in 1776, which he played by special invitation of President Nixon at the White House, and which he continued to play in NY for two years; Walnut, Philadelphia, Mar 1972, played in Volpone; toured, summers, 1972 and 1973, in 1776; Queensborough Community College, Jan 1975, played in The Caucasian Chalk Circle; Coconut Grove Playhouse, Miami Beach, Fla, 1976, played in The Most Dangerous Man in America, which he co-authored; has also directed and appeared with stock companies, notably at the Crystal Lake, NY, Theatre, in 1955, and the Bucks County Playhouse, in 1956; first entered films in 1936, and has appeared in numerous pictures, being twice honored with Academy Award nominations for his performances in The Lost Weekend, and Two Years Before the Mast; first appeared on television 1949, and principal performances include the title-part in the *Walter Fortune* series and Anthony Celese in *For the People*, 1964–5; also played in The Missiles of October 1975, and in Stop, Thief, 1976.

Favourite parts: Ben Marino in Fiorello! Mendele in The World of Sholom Aleichem, and the White Knight in Alice in Wonderland. *Recreations:* Photography and sailing. *Address:* Croton-on-Hudson, New York, USA. *Tel:* 941 0924.

DAUPHIN, Claude (*né* Legrand), actor and managing director
b Paris (Corbeil), 19 Aug 1903; *s* of Franc Legrand-Nohain and his wife Madeleine (Dauphin); *e* Lycée Condorcet, Paris; *m* (1) Rosine Dariun (mar dis); (2) Maria Mauban (mar dis); (3) Norma Eberhardt; formerly a set designer for the Comédie Française, 1923–31, and writer.

Made his first appearance on the stage at the Théâtre de l'Odéon, Paris, Apr 1930, in the play Chapeau Chinois; has appeared in more than fifty plays in Paris, playing at the Gymnase, Variétés, La Madeleine and Ambassadeurs Theatres; directed the Claude Dauphin Theatre Company in Paris, 1945–50, and appeared in its productions; made his first appearance in New York at the Biltmore Theatre, Nov 1946, as Garcin in No Exit; at the Plymouth, NY, Jan 1950, played Papa in The Happy Time; at the same theatre, Nov 1955, played Denny in Janus; at the Roof Top Theatre, NY, Nov 1957, played Comte Hector de Clérembard in Clérembard; Phoenix, NY, Feb 1958, played The Voice in The Infernal Machine; toured, July–Sept 1958, as General St Pé in Waltz of the Toreadors; made his first London appearance at the Strand Theatre, Sept 1959, as André de Gascogne in

From the French; Longacre, NY, Feb 1960, played Bernard Laroque in The Deadly Game; toured, 1960, in Le Moulin de la Galette; toured, July–Sept 1961, as Paul Dolville in The Marriage-Go-Round; Alvin, NY, Jan 1962, Frank Brissels in Giants, Sons of Giants; Sarah-Bernhardt, Paris, Apr 1962, appeared in Adorable Julia; Montparnasse, Paris, 1963, appeared in Hedda Gabler and 1964 in Mon Faust; Théâtre de France, Paris, 1967, Tobias in Edward Albee's A Delicate Balance; Barbizon-Plaza, NY, Apr 1971, appeared with Le Treteau de Paris as Pierre Lannes in L'Amante Anglaise; Théâtre Edouard VII, Paris, Feb 1973, Shylock in The Merchant of Venice; Théâtre de Ville, Paris, 1974, played in The Creation of the World and Other Business; Athénée-Louis Jouvet, Oct 1975, Inspecteur in L'Arrestation; first appeared in French films, 1931; American films include Little Boy Lost, Murder in the Rue Morgue, The Quiet American, The Visit, Lady L, Rosebud, etc; first appeared on television in 1948, and has since been seen in numerous productions in France and the US including a two year series with Louis Jourdan, entitled *Paris Precinct*; Officer of the Légion d'Honneur.

Address: 12 Rue Lalo, Paris, 16e, France.

DAVENPORT, Nigel, actor
b Shelford, Cambridge, 23 May 1928; *s* of Arthur Henry Davenport and his wife Katherine Lucy (Meiklejohn); *e* St Peter's, Seaford; Cheltenham College; and Trinity College, Oxford; *m* (1) Helena Margaret White (dec); (2) Maria Aitken.

For the OUDS appeared as Bottom in A Midsummer Night's Dream, and The Cardinal in The Duchess of Malfi; made his first appearance on the professional stage at the Savoy Theatre, London, June 1952, when he played the Hon Peter Ingleton, which part he had been understudying, in Relative Values; joined the Shakespeare Memorial Theatre Company, 1953, and remained for the season; as a member of the Chesterfield Civic Theatre Company, 1954–5, he played in approximately seventy-five plays; on returning to London, he appeared at the Theatre Royal, Stratford, E, June 1955, as Horner in The Country Wife; joined the English Stage Company for their first season at the Royal Court, Apr 1956, to play the following parts: Captain Walcott in The Mulberry Bush, Thomas Putnam in The Crucible, Sculptor and Alfredo in Don Juan, Anthony Lissenden in The Death of Satan, Jellicoe in Cards of Identity, Policeman in The Good Woman of Setzuan, Quack in The Country Wife, 1956; Bro Paradock in A Resounding Tinkle, in a Production without Décor, 1957; Barney Evans in Epitaph for George Dillon, Bro Paradock in A Resounding Tinkle, Mr Jackson in Live Like Pigs, 1958; Theatre Royal, Stratford, E, Jan 1959, played Peter in A Taste of Honey, transferring to Wyndham's, Feb 1959, and Criterion, June 1959, with the same production; Royal Court, Sept 1959, played Mr Marango in The Kitchen, in a Production without Décor; at the same theatre, Mar 1960, Charles, King of Frankland in One Leg Over the Wrong Wall, in a Production without Décor; made his first appearance in the United States at the Biltmore, Los Angeles, Aug 1960, when he again played Peter in A Taste of Honey, subsequently appearing at the Lyceum Theatre, New York, Oct 1960, in the same part; Edinburgh Festival, Aug 1961, played Pittakos in Sappho; Comedy, Oct 1961, played Odilon in Bonne Soupe, subsequently transferring to Wyndham's, May 1962; New, Oxford, June 1963, Charles in The Perils of Scobie Prilt; Phoenix, Jan 1966, played Monceau in Incident at Vichy; Gate, Dublin, Oct 1966, C J Shine in Breakdown; Globe, Mar 1972, Jim North in Notes On A Love Affair; Cambridge Theatre, June 1976, Verskinin in

Three Sisters; films since 1958 include Look Back in Anger, A Man For All Seasons, The Royal Hunt of the Sun, The Virgin Soldiers, Villain, Living Free and Mary Queen of Scots; first appeared on television, 1952, and appearances include *South Riding*, The Apple Cart, *Oil Strike North*, and *The Prince Regent*.

Favourite parts: Othello, Bro Paradock, Hotspur, and Rupert in Rope. *Recreation:* Pulling out weeds.

Address: c/o Leading Artists, 60 St James's Street, London SW1.

DAVIDSON, Gordon, producer and director
b Brooklyn, New York, 7 May 1933; *s* of Joseph H Davidson and his wife Alice (Gordon); *e* Cornell University (BA), Case Western Reserve University (MA); *m* Judith Swiller.

Formerly a stage manager for the Phoenix Theatre Company and the American Shakespeare Festival Theatre, 1958–60, Dallas Civic Opera, 1960–1, Martha Graham Dance Company, 1962; became Managing Director of The Theatre Group, University of California at Los Angeles, 1965, where he produced An Evening of Tennessee Williams, Harold Pinter, Murray Schisgal, Robert Frost: Promises to Keep, The Deputy, which he also directed and which toured the US, Yeats and Company, Oh What A Lovely War! 1965–6 season; Next Time I'll Sing to You, Candide, which he also directed, The Birthday Party, Poor Bitos, 1966; became Artistic Director of this Group when it became Center Theatre Group of the Mark Taper Forum at the Music Center, Los Angeles, 1967, and produced The Devils, which he also directed, The Sorrows of Mr Frederick, The Marriage of Mr Mississippi, Who's Happy Now? which he also directed, 1967; The Miser, In the Matter of J Robert Oppenheimer, 1968, and also directed the latter play for the Repertory Theatre of Lincoln Center, NY, Mar 1969 and again in June 1969, winning the New York Drama Desk Award for direction; produced Camino Real, The Golden Fleece, Muzeeka, 1968; The Minnesota Theatre Company in The House of Atreus and The Resistible Rise of Arturo Ui, The Adventures of the Black Girl in Her Search for God, Chemin de Fer, Uncle Vanya, 1969; Murderous Angels, which he also directed, Crystal and Fox, Story Theatre, The Dream on Monkey Mountain, Rosebloom, which he also directed, 1970; Metamorphoses, Othello, The Trial of the Catonsville Nine, 1971; directed the last play in the New Theatre for Now series, Los Angeles, 1970, and for the Phoenix Theatre, NY, 1971, winning an Obie Award for direction; founded New Theatre for Now at the Mark Taper Forum and in 1970 received the Margo Jones Award for outstanding contribution to American playwrights; directed Murderous Angels, 1971; Metropolitan Opera House, June 1972, directed with Alvin Ailey Leonard Bernstein's Mass; Mark Taper Forum, 1972, directed Henry IV, Part 1; 1973 directed Mass; 1974 directed Hamlet and Savages; 1975 produced Once in a Lifetime and directed The Shadow Box; directed And Where She Stops Nobody Knows, 1976; The Shadow Box (Long Wharf and NY, winning a 'Tony'), Savages (NY), 1977; Getting Out, Black Angel, 1978; Terra Nova, 1979; has directed opera, notably a concert version of Berlioz' Beatrice and Benedick, starring Vanessa Redgrave and Stacy Keach, for the Los Angeles Philharmonic, Carmen, La Boheme, Cosi Fan Tutte for the Corpus Christi (Texas) Symphony; is Vice President of ANTA, President of Theatre Communications Group, member of the Theatre Panel of the National Endowment for the Arts, the International Theatre Institute's Advisory Council, and the UCLA Advisory Committee on Arts Administration, and was formerly President of the League of Resident Theatres;

is Consultant for Repertory Theatre of the Denver, Colorado, Center for the Performing Arts.

Address: Center Theatre Group, 135 North Grand Avenue, Los Angeles, Calif 90012. *Tel:* 213–972 7388.

DAVIES, Robertson, novelist and playwright

b Thamesville, Ontario, 28 Aug 1913; *s* of William Rupert Davies and his wife Florence Sheppard (McKay); *e* Upper Canada College, Toronto, Queen's University, Kingston, Ont. and Balliol College, Oxford; *m* Brenda Mathews (former stage manager of the Old Vic, London).

After acting in the Oxford University Dramatic Society and experience in the English provincial theatre, he made his London debut at the Duke of York's, Nov 1938, as Thomas Howard in Traitor's Gate; joined the Old Vic Company under Tyrone Guthrie, seasons 1938–39, where his parts included Snout in A Midsummer Night's Dream, the Widow and others in The Taming of the Shrew and the Archbishop in St Joan; concurrently taught at the Old Vic Drama School and did literary work for the Director; returned to Canada as Literary Editor of *Saturday Night,* 1940–42; appointed Editor of the *Peterborough Examiner,* 1942; Publisher, 1958–68; Visiting Professor, Trinity College, University of Toronto, 1960–62; appointed first Master of Massey College (a college for post-graduate work) which opened in Sept 1963; his plays, performed in Canada, and some also in Norway, Switzerland, Australia and at the Edinburgh Festival, include the following: Overlaid, 1947; Fortune, My Foe, Hope Deferred, The Voice of the People, Eros at Breakfast, At the Gates of the Righteous, 1948; King Phoenix, At My Heart's Core, 1950; A Masque of Aesop, 1952; A Jig for the Gypsy, 1954; Hunting Stuart, 1955; Love and Libel (adapted from his novel, Leaven of Malice), 1960; A Masque of Mr Punch, 1962; Question Time, 1975; Pontiac and the Green Man; he is author of the television play Brothers in the Black Art, 1974: Fortune, My Foe was also adapted for television, and A Jig for the Gypsy, for radio; his works on stage history include: Shakespeare's Boy Actors, 1939; Record of the Stratford Shakespeare Festival in three volumes: Renown at Stratford, 1953, Twice Have the Trumpets Sounded, 1954, and Thrice the Brinded Cat Hath Mew'd, 1955 (all with Tyrone Guthrie); contributor to The Revels History of Drama in English (Volume 7), 1975; other writings include essays and literary criticism, and four novels as well as the trilogy, Fifth Business, The Manticore and World of Wonders; (The Manticore received the Governor General's Award for Fiction, 1973;) published his addresses, One Half of Robertson Davies, 1977; a Fellow of the Royal Society of Canada since 1967; appointed a Companion of the Order of Canada, 1972; Hon Member, American Academy and Institute of Arts and Letters, 1980; his Honorary Doctorates include the LLD from the universities of Alberta, Queen's, Manitoba; DCL (Bishop's University); DLitts from universities throughout Canada; awarded a DUniv, 1975, and Hon Prof of the University of Calgary, 1978.

Recreation: Music. *Address:* Master's Lodging, Massey College in the University of Toronto, Canada.

DAVIS, Allan, director and producer

b London, 30 Aug 1913; *s* of Leslie Davis and his wife Daisy Victoria (Davis); *e* Cranbrook School, Sydney, and Sydney University, NSW, Australia; originally intended for a commercial career.

Made his first appearance on the stage at the Theatre Royal, Aldershot, Mar 1935, as Basil in Mr Wu; first appeared in London, at the Comedy, 10 May 1935, in Shall We Reverse?; subsequently became stage-manager at various

theatres, 1938–9; joined the Army, 1939, serving in Italy, Greece and Austria; demobilized 1946; director for Bexhill Repertory company, 1946; appointed assistant-director for Bristol Old Vic, July 1947; Director of the company, from Feb 1949 to July 1950; his productions at Bristol included Hedda Gabler, Winterset, Julius Caesar, Captain Carvallo, The Wilderness of Monkeys, Tartuffe, etc; he also directed King of Friday's Men, at the Lyric, Hammersmith, 1949, and Tartuffe, at the same theatre, 1950; at the invitation of the Rockefeller Foundation, Sept 1950, made an extensive lecture tour of University theatres throughout the United States; in Boston, 1951, directed Tartuffe; went to Hollywood, 1952, where he directed a film and many television films; returned to England, 1953, continuing film direction in this country; at Her Majesty's, May 1954, at the gala matinée given to celebrate the golden jubilee of Dame Sybil Thorndike and the centenary of the birth of Sir Herbert Beerbohm Tree, he directed the screen scene from The School for Scandal; New Watergate, Dec 1954, directed Arabian Nightmare; Saville, July 1955, directed The Shadow of Doubt; John Golden, New York, Feb 1956, directed Someone Waiting; Cambridge, Mar 1958, directed and co-presented Breath of Spring; Duke of York's, July 1958, directed The Joshua Tree; Apollo, Apr 1959, directed and co-presented Fool's Paradise; Alexandra, Birmingham, Aug 1959, directed and co-presented French Polish; Duchess, April 1960, directed A Shred of Evidence; he has since directed the following plays: The Bird of Time (also co-presented), 1961; The Big Killing, The Apricot Season, 1962; Spring and Port Wine (Birmingham, also co- presented), Honey I'm Home, 1964; Did You Feel It Move? The Morning After (Coventry, also co-presented), Spring and Port Wine (also co-presented), 1965; The Sacred Flame (Guildford, also co-presented), June Evening (Birmingham, also co- presented), 1966; The Sacred Flame (co-presented), Keep It in the Family (NY), 1967; The Night I Chased the Women With an Eel, 1969; Come As You Are (also co-presented), 1970; No Sex Please—We're British, 1971; Friends, Romans and Lovers, Fiddlers Three (both Guildford), 1972; Cadenza (Leatherhead), Signs of the Times (also co-presented), Birds of Paradise (Birmingham), 1973; A Touch of Spring (also co-presented), 1975; In the Red (also presented), Rolls Hyphen Royce, 1977.

Recreation: Sight-seeing. *Address:* 23 Ennismore Gardens, London, SW7. *Tel:* 01–629 8080.

DAVIS, Bette (*née* Ruth Elizabeth), actress

b Lowell, Mass, 5 Apr 1908; *d* of Harlow Morell Davis and his wife Ruth Elizabeth (Favor); *e* High Schools in New York City and Newton, Mass, and the Cushing Academy; studied dance with Roshanara and Martha Graham, and prepared for the stage with Michael Mordkin, Robert Bell, George Currie, and attended the John Murray Anderson School of the Theatre; *m* (1) Harmon Nelson (mar dis), (2) Arthur Farnsworth (dec), (3) William Grant Sherry (mar dis), (4) Gary Merrill (mar dis).

Made her professional début in a stock production of Broadway at the Temple, Rochester, NY fall 1928, also playing in Excess Baggage, Yellow and The Squall; made her NY début at the Provincetown Playhouse, 5 Mar 1929, as Floy Jennings in The Earth Between; toured, 1929, as Hedwig in The Wild Duck; Ritz, NY, Nov 1929, Elaine Bumpstead in The Broken Dish; appeared at the Cape Dennis, Mass, Playhouse, spring 1930, as Dinah in Mr Pim; Lyceum, Oct 1930, Bam in Solid South; went to Hollywood where she made her first film, as Laura in Bad Sister, 1931, and had a long and highly successful film career before reappearing in NY at the Alvin, 15 Dec 1952, in the revue

Two's Company; toured, 1959, in The World of Carl Sandburg, and appeared in this at the Henry Miller, Sept 1960; Royale, Dec 1961, played Maxine Faulk in The Night of the Iguana; returned to films and then toured, Mar–Apr in Bette Davis in person and on film; Shubert, Philadelphia, Oct 1974, played Miss Moffat in the musical of that name. Sydney, Australia, Opera House, 23 Mar 1975, appeared in An Informal Evening with Bette Davis, and subsequently toured Australia; made her London début at the Palladium, 12 Oct 1975, in An Informal Evening with Bette Davis; among her many films may be mentioned The Man Who Played God (1932), Of Human Bondage (1934), Dangerous, for which she received the Academy Award (1935), The Petrified Forest (1936), Jezebel (1938), for which she also received the Academy Award, Dark Victory (1939), The Private Lives of Elizabeth Essex (1939), The Letter (1940), The Little Foxes (1941), The Man Who Came to Dinner (1941), Watch on the Rhine (1943), Mr Skeffington (1944), The Corn Is Green (1945), All About Eve (1950), Whatever Happened to Baby Jane? (1962), Bunny O'Hare (1971), etc; has also appeared on television in *General Electric Theatre, Wagon Train, Alfred Hitchcock Presents,* Madame Sin, etc.
Address: c/o Thomas Hammond, 40 West 55th Street, New York, NY 10019.

DAVIS, Carl, composer
b New York, NY, 28 Oct 1936; s of Isidore Davis and his wife Sara (Perlmutter); e Bard College, NY; m Jean Boht.
Wrote the music for the revue Diversions, Downtown Theatre, NY, 7 Nov 1958; music for Twists, Arts, London, 16 Feb 1962; composer for the musicals The Projector, 1971; Pilgrim, Cranford, 1975; incidental music for plays including: Forty Years on, 1969; The Merchant of Venice (National), The Tempest, Council of Love, 1970; Much Ado About Nothing (RSC), King Lear (Prospect), 1971 Pericles (Prospect), 1973; The Marriage of Figaro (National), Summerfolk (RSC), A Month in the Country (Chichester), 1974; The Zykovs, The Devil's Disciple, Ivanov (all RSC), 1976; Saint Joan (Prospect), 1977; Saratoga (RSC), 1978; Antonio (Nottingham), 1979; has also written music for films and TV, including scores for Hollywood (Thames, 1979).
Recreations: Cooking, gardening, collecting graphics. Address: 34 Ambleside Avenue, London SW16. *Tel:* 01–7679 2742.

DAVIS, Joe, lighting designer
b London, 18 Dec 1912; s of William Carlton Davis and his wife Ellen (Ghan); m Jacqueline James.
Formerly with Strand Electric; joined HM Tennent Ltd on its inception in 1936 as lighting director and has lit all their productions; has worked with most of Britain's leading directors on a total of 550 major productions, for Tennent's and as a freelance; these include A View from the Bridge, The Lady's Not for Burning, Ring Round the Moon, Oklahoma, West Side Story, The Most Happy Fella, Under Milk Wood, Ross, My Fair Lady, Suite in Three Keys, The Price, A Bequest to the Nation, Godspell, Gipsy, Waters of the Moon, Filumena, the Millionairess; and the operas Bomarzo, The Nose, and Julietta; personal lighting director to Marlene Dietrich for 22 years; work abroad includes the New York production of Irma la Douce, 1960; Peter Brook's Hamlet, Moscow, 1955; and several at the Theater an der Wien, Vienna; founder and chairman, now Life President, Society of British Theatre Lighting Designers; first chairman, Association of British Theatre Technicians; Honorary Life Member of the Society of British Theatre Designers; Lighting Director of Theatre Sound and Lighting Services Ltd.

Recreation: Fishing. *Club:* Green Room. *Address:* Green Room Club, 8–9 Adam Street, London, WC2.

DAVIS, Ossie, actor, playwright, director
b Cogdell, Georgia, 18 Dec 1917; e Howard University, 1935–9; m Ruby Dee; trained for the stage with Paul Mann and Lloyd Richards.
Made his stage début with the Rose McClendon Players, in Harlem, 1941, in Joy Exceeding Glory; joined the US Army, 1942, and while in the Army in Liberia, Africa, wrote and directed the revue Goldbrickers of 1944; made his Broadway début at the Martin Beck, 21 Feb 1946, as Jeb Turner in Jeb; toured, 1947, as Rudolph in Anna Lucasta; American Negro Theatre Playhouse, New York, Mar 1948, John Hay in The Washington Years; National, Oct 1948, Trem in The Leading Lady; Lyceum, Jan 1949, Stewart in The Smile of the World; Martin Beck, Mar 1950, Jacques in The Wisteria Trees; New York City Center, Jan 1951, Jo in The Royal Family; Broadway, Mar 1951, Gabriel in The Green Pastures; Morosco, Oct 1951, Al in Remains to Be Seen; Music Box, Feb 1953, Dr Joseph Clay in Touchstone; Barbizon-Plaza, May 1953, stage managed The World of Sholom Aleichem; City Center, Feb 1955, Jacques in The Wisteria Trees; Alvin, 1956, took over as the Lieutenant in No Time for Sergeants; Imperial, Oct 1957, Cicero in Jamaica; Ethel Barrymore, Aug 1959, took over from Sidney Poitier as Walter Lee Younger in A Raisin in the Sun; Cort, Sept 1961, wrote and played the title-role in Purlie Victorious; Henry Hudson, May 1963, wrote Curtain Call, Mr Aldridge, Sir; Mayfair, Oct 1963, co-produced and played Sir Radio in Ballad for Bimshire; toured, 1964, in A Treasury of Negro World Writing; Cort, Nov 1965, Johannes in The Zulu and the Zayda; Broadway, Mar 1970, wrote the original book of the musical Purlie; directed and appeared in Take it from the Top, 1979; author of plays Alice in Wonder and Last Dance for Sybil; first appeared in films in No Way Out, 1950, and has since played in Fourteen Hours, The Joe Louis Story, The Cardinal, The Hill, The Scalphunters, Purlie Victorious, Hot Stuff, etc; directed the films Cotton Comes to Harlem, Kongi's Harvest, Countdown at Kusini, etc; appeared on television as The Emperor Jones; in Seven Times Monday, and recently in Roots: the Next Generations; and wrote School Teacher for *East Side/West Side*, 1963; played on radio in The Ossie Davis and Ruby Dee Story Hour; received the Emmy award for his role in Teacher, Teacher, 1969; Master of Ceremonies for the march on Washington, 1963, and for the Solidarity Poor People's Campaign, 1968; has received the Frederick Douglas Award of the New York Urban League.
Address: PO Box 1318, New Rochelle, NY 10802.

DAVIS, Ray C, actor, singer and choreographer
b Hendon, Middlesex; s of Charles Davis and his wife Lilian; m the choreographer Domini Winter; trained for the stage at the Andrew Hardie School, South Kensington.
After working as a dancer in such films as Half-a-Sixpence and Chitty Chitty Bang Bang, made his first appearance on stage in London at the Adelphi, May 1962, as the Student in Blitz!; Globe, Mar 1966, played Daniel in The Matchgirls; Piccadilly, June 1969, Anselmo in Man of La Mancha; Cambridge, May 1972, Obadiah in Tom Brown's Schooldays; toured, 1973 in West Side Story; Phoenix, Apr 1973, played Proteus in the musical version of The Two Gentlemen of Verona; 1973 and 1974, toured England and Canada in Great Expectations; Arnaud, Guildford, appeared in Cole: also in Toronto, Canada; Her Majesty's, July 1974, Jerry Jerningham in The Good Companions; Phoenix, Mar 1978, Will

Somers in Kings and Clowns; Her Majesty's, Oct 1978, Harold in Barmitzvah Boy; Watford Palace, 1979, appeared in Side By Side By Sondheim; television includes Cleo Laine and Noel Coward Specials, *Rainbow, Play School*, and frequent appearances on *The Good Old Days*.

Favourite part: Will Somers. *Recreations:* Playing guitar, cooking, walking, swimming, reading, gardening and do-it-yourself. *Address:* c/o Sara Randell, Saraband Associates, 348a Upper Street, Islington, London, NI.

DAVIS, Sammy, Jr, actor, singer, dancer
b New York City, 8 Dec 1925; *s* of Sammy Davis and his wife Elvira (Sanchez); *e* in public schools; *m* (1) Sonay White (mar dis); (2) May Britt (mar dis); (3) Altovise Gore.

First appeared on the stage at the age of three with the Will Mastin Troupe in vaudeville, subsequently touring with them and his father for many years; made his NY stage début at the Broadway, Mar 1956, as Charley Welch in Mr Wonderful, which ran for 388 performances; first appeared in London in cabaret in 1960; at the Prince of Wales, London, Aug 1961, appeared in An Evening with Sammy Davis, Jr; Olympia, Paris, Mar 1964, starred in vaudeville; Majestic, NY, Oct 1964, played Joe Wellington in the musical version of Golden Boy; Forrest, Philadelphia, Mar 1966, appeared in the one-man show Sammy Davis . . . That's All; Forest Hills, NY, 9 July 1966, appeared in concert; toured in cabaret in 1966 and 1967; toured Europe in cabaret, 1967; Auditorium, Chicago, Apr 1968, played Joe Wellington in Golden Boy; toured South Vietnam Feb 1972 in variety; Westbury Music Fair, Long Island, Apr 1972, appeared in a variety show; Alice Tully Hall, 21 May 1972, in variety; Elmwood Casino, Windsor, Ontario, May, Harrah's, Lake Tahoe, Nev, June, and Sands, Las Vegas, July and Sept 1972, appeared in cabaret; the White House, Washington, DC, 3 Mar 1973, appeared in a variety show; Sands, Las Vegas, Mar 1973, in cabaret; Kennedy Center Concert Hall, Washington, DC, June 1973, appeared in concert; Uris, NY, Apr 1974, appeared in Sammy on Broadway!; opened The Front Row, Cleveland, Ohio, July 1974, in a concert; Grosvenor House, London, July 1974, appeared in cabaret; Latin Casino, Philadelphia, Apr 1975, and Caesar's Palace, Las Vegas, Sept 1975, appeared in cabaret; London Palladium, Sept 1976, appeared in Variety; has appeared in two Royal Variety Shows; first entered films in 1928 in Rufus Jones for President, and has since appeared in Anna Lucasta, Porgy and Bess, Threepenny Opera, Oceans 11, Save the Children, 1973, etc; first appeared on television, 1950, and has performed in the *Ed Sullivan Show, GE Theatre, The Sammy Davies, Jr, Show, Tom Jones Show, Ben Casey, Rifleman, Sammy Davis and Company*, etc; Co-chairman of Los Angeles Chapter of NAACP Membership Drive; appointed member of National Advisory Council on Economic Opportunity, 1 July 1971; author of Yes I Can (autobiography), 1965.

Favourite part: Joe Wellington. *Recreations:* Photography and golf. *Clubs:* Friars, Negro Actors. *Address:* 9000 Sunset Boulevard, Los Angeles, Calif 90069. *Tel:* 213-273-8554.

DAWSON, Anna, actress
Originally a dancer; at the Savoy, 1959, appeared in the chorus of Marigold, later taking over the title-part; Vaudeville, Aug 1961, Carol Arden in Wildest Dreams; Palladium, Dec 1963, Sally in The Man in the Moon; Carrick, Mar 1967, Farina in Stand by Your Bedouin; Apr 1967, Monica Johnson in Uproar in the House; July, Muriel Kitson in Let Sleeping Wives Lie, these three in a Brian Rix Theatre of Laughter season; Mermaid, Mar 1969, Hilaret in Lock up Your

Daughters; Garrick, Oct 1969, Mary Porter in She's Done It Again; at Greenwich, appeared in Jack and the Beanstalk, Dec 1971, and played Mme Feydeau and Miss Trill in The Feydeau Farce Festival of Nineteen Nine, Feb 1972; Marlowe, Canterbury, June 1972, title-role in Irma La Douce; Edinburgh Festival, Sept 1972, and Round House, Oct, Lady Arabella Harvey in Stand and Deliver; O'Keefe Centre, Toronto, Apr 1973, appeared in Move Over Mrs Markham; Chichester, July 1973, Marfa Zlotochienko in R Loves J; toured, Mar 1974, as Helga Philby in A Bedful of Foreigners; Arnaud, Guildford, May 1974, Anne Finch in The Sacking of Norman Banks, transferring to the Ambassadors', July, when the play was renamed The Sack Race; New London, Dec 1974, appeared in the revue Déjà Revue; Duke of York's, Oct 1975, Gloria in Roger's Last Stand; Thorndike, Leatherhead, Oct 1976, Eva in Absurd Person Singular; Arnaud, Nov 1977, appeared in Hats Off!; Thorndike, Jan 1979, played Jan in Bedroom Farce; TV work includes *Dixon of Dock Green, The Benny Hill Show,* and *Life Begins at Forty*.

Address: c/o Barry Burnett Ltd, Suite 409, Princes House, 190 Piccadilly, London W1.

DAY, Richard Digby, director
b Cardiff, 27 Dec 1940; *s* of Donald Day and his wife Doris Soule (George); *e* Solihull School, Warwicks; trained for the stage at RADA, 1961–3, where he was Leverhulme Exhibitioner.

His first production was Arms and the Man, Playhouse, Nottingham, Apr 1964; director of productions, Bournemouth Theatre Company, 1966–8; associate director, Theatre Toronto, 1968, later director; English director 1969–71 of the Welsh National Theatre Company, for which his productions included Candida, 1968; Hamlet, 1969; Happy Days, Don Juan in Hell, L'Amante Anglaise, On Approval, The Beard, 1970; artistic director, 1968–73, New Shakespeare Company, which he has directed at the Open Air, Regent's Park, in Cyrano de Bergerac, 1967; The Merry Wives of Windsor, Two Gentlemen of Verona, 1968; the latter again in 1969, with The Merchant of Venice; A Midsummer Night's Dream, The Lord Byron Show (also devised), 1970; Romeo and Juliet, A Midsummer Night's Dream, 1971; The Tempest, 1972; As You Like It, 1973; Sweet Mr Shakespeare (also devised), 1975; The Man of Destiny, 1978; O'Flaherty VC, 1979; Director, Theatre Royal, York, 1972–76, where his productions included: The Cherry Orchard, 1972; Love On the Dole, 1973; Getting Married, Hamlet, 1974; Dear Octopus, The Concert, 1975; In Good King Charles's Golden Days, 1976; Director Northcott Theatre, Exeter, since Jan 1978, where productions have included: Travesties, Elektra, 'Tis Pity She's a Whore, 1978; Motherdear, Saint Joan, A Little Night Music, 1979; has also directed at Watford, Worcester and Guildford, and in Canada.

Recreations: Reading biography, opera and ballet-going, obsessive sight-seeing. *Address:* 29 Shipston Road, Stratford-upon-Avon.

DEAN, Isabel, actress
b Aldridge, Staffs; *d* of Conway Loveridge Hodgkinson and his wife Dorothy (Norman); *e* Edgbaston High School, Birmingham and Wendover; *m* William Fairchild (mar dis); originally studied painting at Birmingham School of Art.

In 1937, joined the Cheltenham Repertory company as a scenic artist; while there, studied acting and occasionally played small parts; appeared in repertory, 1939, at Brighton and Norwich; first appeared in London at the Vaudeville Theatre, 1 May 1940, as Maggie Buckley in Peril at End House; same theatre, Oct 1940, played Mariana in All's Well

That Ends Well; Phoenix, Apr 1943, appeared as Jenny in
Love for Love, subsequently appearing as Miss Prue in the
same play; Open Air Theatre, Regent's Park, June 1944,
played Golden Stream in Lady Precious Stream and Rosalind
in As You Like It; joined the Gielgud Repertory at the
Haymarket, Oct 1944, when she again played Prue in Love
for Love, understudied Peggy Ashcroft as Ophelia in Hamlet,
playing the part on several occasions; Jan 1945, appeared as
Hermia in A Midsummer Night's Dream; subsequently
played a season at the Oxford Repertory Theatre, playing
leads including Sally in Love on the Dole; New Lindsey, May
1947, Anna Burfitt in Dark Emmanuel; at the Boltons,
July–Nov 1947, played various parts, including Juliet in
Romeo and Juliet, and the Lady Elizabeth of York in The
Patched Cloak; Duchess, Feb 1949, Jacqueline Brown in The
Foolish Gentlewoman; Boltons, Jan 1950, appeared as Caro-
lina Sophia in Captain Banner; appeared at the Q, Sept 1954,
as Caroline Westerdale in Witch Errant; Royal, Brighton,
Nov 1954, played Mrs Bradley in The Duchess and the
Smugs; Westminster, June 1956, played Mary Dallas in Night
of the Fourth; Fortune, Sept 1959, Miss Frost in The Ginger
Man; Garrick, Apr 1962, played Mrs Turner in Two Stars for
Comfort; Theatre Royal, Windsor, Sept 1963, Caroline Cuffe
in Queen B, subsequently touring in the play; Royal Court,
July 1968, played Margaret in The Hotel in Amsterdam,
transferring in that part to the New Theatre, Sept 1968, and
to the Duke of York's, Dec 1968; Arnaud, Guildford, July
1971, Hester in The Deep Blue Sea; Royal Court, Mar 1972,
Margaret Murdoch in The Centaur; Nottingham Playhouse,
Autumn 1972, again played Hester in The Deep Blue Sea,
and Mrs Prentice in What the Butler Saw; Arnaud, Guild-
ford, Oct 1974, Norah Palmer in Robin Redbreast; Open
Space, Jan 1975, Angie in Claw; Royal Court, Nov 1975, Mrs
Emmerson in The Fool; Ambassadors, Oct 1976, Mary in
Dear Daddy; Bristol Old Vic, March 1976, Ina Sergeyevna in
Evening Light; Cottesloe, Nov 1977, Barbara Burney in
Half-Life; Royal Exchange, Manchester, Mar 1980, Her
Ladyship in The Dresser; her films include: Light in the
Piazza, High Wind in Jamaica, Oh! What A Lovely War, and
Inadmissible Evidence; since 1949, has appeared in numerous
television plays, including I Claudius, The Old Crowd, The
Italian Taste, etc.
Favourite parts: Sally in Love on the Dole, Hester in The
Deep Blue Sea, Rosalind and Miss Frost. *Recreations:* The
piano. *Address:* c/o Kate Feast, 43A Princes Road, London
NW1.

DEE, Ruby (*née* Ruby Ann Wallace), actress
b Cleveland, Ohio, 27 Oct; d of Marshall Edward Wallace
and his wife Emma Benson; e Hunter College (BA); m Ossie
Davis.
Prepared for the stage at the American Negro Theatre,
1941–4, with Morris Carnovsky, 1958–60, at the Actors
Workshop, with Paul Mann, and with Lloyd Richards; made
her Broadway début at the Cort, 29 Dec 1943, as a Native in
the drama South Pacific; Library (for the American Negro
Theatre), Nov 1944, played Ruth in Walk Hard; Martin
Beck, Feb 1946, Libby George in Jeb; Mansfield, June 1946,
took over the title-role of Anna Lucasta, and later toured in
the part; Maxine Elliot, Feb 1948, played Marcy in A Long
Way from Home; American Negro Theatre Playhouse, Mar
1948, Mrs Ellen McClellan in The Washington Years; Ly-
ceum, Jan 1949, Evelyn in The Smile of the World; Barbizon-
Plaza, Mar 1959, Defending Angel in The World of Sholom
Aleichem; Ethel Barrymore, Mar 1959, Ruth Younger in A
Raisin in the Sun; Cort, Sept 1961, Luttiebelle Gussie Mae
Jenkins in Purlie Victorious; toured colleges, Feb–Mar 1964,

in poetry readings for ANTA; toured with her husband,
1964, in A Treasury of Negro World Writing; American
Shakespeare Festival, Stratford, Conn, 1965, Cordelia in
King Lear and Kate in The Taming of the Shrew; Ypsilanti,
Michigan, Greek Theatre, June 1966, played Cassandra in
The Oresteia; Lydia Mendelssohn, Ann Arbor, Michigan,
Dec 1966, Julia Augustine in Wedding Band; Circle in the
Square, June 1970, Lena in Boesman and Lena; Walnut St,
Philadelphia, Nov 1971, played in The Imaginary Invalid;
Newman, Oct 1972, Julia Augustine in Wedding Band;
Delacorte, June 1975, Gertrude in Hamlet; first appeared in
films in No Way Out and The Jackie Robinson Story, 1950,
and has since played in St Louis Blues, Take a Giant Step, A
Raisin in the Sun, The Balcony, Uptight (also co-author),
Buck and the Preacher, Black Girl, Countdown at Kusini
(1974), etc; has appeared on television in Actor's Choice,
1960, and Seven Times Monday, 1961, Go Down Moses,
1963, in her play Twin-Bit Gardens, 1975, and various
dramatic programs, recently I Know Why the Caged Bird
Sings and Roots II; columnist for the NY Amsterdam News;
associate editor, Freedomways magazine; author of a poetry
anthology, Glowchild, 1972; Twin-Bit Gardens, revised as
Take It from the Top, presented in Philadelphia, 1979.
Favourite parts: Luttiebelle in Purlie Victorious, Lena in
Boesman and Lena, and Cleopatra in Antony and Cleopatra.
Recreations: Painting, reading, needlework. *Address:* PO
Box 1318, New Rochelle, NY 10802.

DEERING, Olive, actress.
Made her New York début at the Booth, 30 Dec 1932, in
Girls in Uniform; Ambassador, Nov 1933, played in Growing
Pains; National, May 1934, in Picnic; 58th St, Feb 1936, in
Searching for the Sun; 44th Street, Oct 1936, in Daughters of
Atreus; Manhattan Opera House, Jan 1937, appeared in Max
Rheinhardt's The Eternal Road; St James, Feb 1937, Queen
to Richard in Maurice Evans's production of Richard II; New
Yorker, Apr 1940, played in Medicine Show; Mecca, Jan
1941, in No for an Answer; Shubert, Mar 1941, in They Walk
Alone; Belasco, Apr 1942, in Nathan the Wise; Royale, Nov
1942, Regina Gordon in Counsellor at Law; 44th St, Nov
1943, Ruth in Winged Victory; Apr 1944, played in Yellow
Jack; Belasco, Nov 1945, Francey in Skydrift; Royale, Sept
1946, Mollie Malloy in The Front Page; President, Mar 1952,
Rose Perozzi in Dark Legend; Mar 1957, played in The
Trojan Women; American Shakespeare Festival Theatre,
Stratford, Conn, June 1957, Bianca in Othello; Billy Rose,
Mar 1961, The Contessa in The Devil's Advocate; ANTA,
Dec 1963, Eve Adamanski in Marathon '33; Stratford, Conn,
June 1966, A Woman of Canterbury in Murder in the
Cathedral; appeared with the Theatre Company of Boston,
1966–7 season; Brandeis University Theatre Arts, Waltham,
Mass, Nov 1966, Madame Arkadina in The Seagull; Ameri-
can Place, Dec 1967, Emma in The Ceremony of Innocence;
Manitoba Theatre Center, Winnipeg, appeared in After the
Fall, Apr 1970; also played Charlotte Shade in The Sun and
the Noon, Feb 1972; Cubiculo, NY, Oct 1976, in Mr McMan-
nis, What Time Is It?; St James, May 1977, Mrs Wayne in
Vieux Carré; appeared in the film of The Ten Command-
ments, 1956.
Address: Actors Equity Association, 165 West 46th Street,
New York, NY 10036.

DELANEY, Shelagh, dramatic author
b Salford, Lancs, 1939; e Brighton Secondary School.
She is the author of the following plays: A Taste of Honey
(London, 1958; New York, 1960); The Lion in Love (London, 1960; NY, 1963); The House that Jack Built (NY, 1979);

she received the Foyle New Play Award, NY Drama Critics Award, and an Arts Council Bursary for her first play, A Taste of Honey; her screenplays include A Taste of Honey, 1961; (co-wrote Academy Award); Charlie Bubbles, The Raging Moon, etc; writing for television includes the series The House that Jack Built; author of the novel Sweetly Sings the Donkey, 1964.

Address: c/o Hope, Leresche, and Sayle, 11 Jubilee Place, London, SW3.

De La TOUR, Frances, actress
b Bovingdon, Herts, 30 July 1944; *d* of Charles de la Tour and his wife Moyre (Fessas); *e* Lycee Francais de Londres; *m* Tom Kempinski; trained for the stage at the Drama Centre, London.

Made her first professional appearance with the Royal Shakespeare Company at Stratford-upon-Avon, July 1965, as a beggar in Timon of Athens; her London début was at the Aldwych with the same company as the School Superintendent's Wife in The Government Inspector, Jan 1966; at Stratford, Aug 1966, Alice in Henry V; season 1967, the Widow and Nicholas in The Taming of the Shrew, Apr, and Audrey in As You Like It, June, playing the same parts at the Aldwych, on tour and in Los Angeles in the same year; Aldwych, Aug 1967 and 1968, Miss Hoyden in The Relapse; Mar 1969, Doris Hoyden in Dutch Uncle; Stratford, 1970, played Helen in Dr Faustus (Theatregoround), Player Queen in Hamlet, and Helena in Peter Brook's A Midsummer Night's Dream, touring America in the last part (New York début Billy Rose, Jan 1971) and returning to the Aldwych, June 1971; in the same Aldwych season played Belinda in The Man of Mode, Sept, and Rosine in The Balcony, Nov; leaving the RSC, played Milly in High Time, Hampstead, Apr 1972; same theatre, Jan 1973, Violet in Small Craft Warnings, transferring to the Comedy, Mar; Hampstead, May 1973, Ruth Jones in The Banana Box, again transferring to the Apollo, June; Oxford Playhouse, 1975, Charlotte in The Vegetable, Jan, and Rosalind in As You Like It, Apr; Old Vic, July 1976, Isabella in The White Devil; Greenwich, June 1977, played Sophie Baines in Singles; Royal Court, Jan 1978, Else Jost in Laughter!; Half Moon, May 1978, Antonia in We Can't Pay? We Won't Pay!; Royal Court, Dec 1978, Mum in Wheelchair Willie; Hampstead, Jan 1979, Kate Lister in Daughters of Men; Half Moon, May 1979, Eleanor Marx in Landscape of Exile; Oct 1979, at the new Half Moon, played the title-role in Hamlet; Bush, Feb 1980, appeared in Duet for One; films include Our Miss Fred, Wombling Free and To the Devil A Daughter; television includes All Good Men, Housewives Choice, and the series *Rising Damp* (now filmed) and *A Cottage to Let.*

Address: c/o John Cadell, 2 Southwood Lane, London N6 5EE. *Tel:* 01–348 1914.

DELFONT, Bernard (cr Life Peer, 1976; Kt, 1974), producing manager
b Tokmak, Russia, 5 Sept 1909; *s* of Isaac Winogradsky and his wife Olga; *m* Carole Lynne.

First entered theatrical management in this country, 1941, with a tour of Room for Two; presented his first production in London, at the St Martin's, 1942, with Jam To-day; has since presented, Other People's Houses (revival), 1942; Sleeping Out, Old Chelsea, The Fur Coat, The Admirable Crichton (revival), The Student Prince (revival), and The Wingless Victory, Where the Rainbow Ends, 1943; Something for the Boys, 1944; associated with the revivals of Rookery Nook, Rose-Marie, 1942; tours of The Duchess of Dantzic and The Count of Luxembourg, 1943; Leslie Hen-

son's Gaieties and (with Tom Arnold) Gay Rosalinda, 1945; Here Come the Boys (with Lee Ephraim), 1946; produced The Bird Seller, 1947; took over the management of the Saville Theatre, 1947; toured Hellzapoppin, 1948; toured Bless the Bride, and The Chocolate Soldier, 1949; produced Her Excellency, London Hippodrome, June 1949; The Folies Bergère Revue, London Hippodrome, Sept 1949; Touch and Go, Prince of Wales's, May 1950; revived Spring Song, The King of Schnorrers, and Awake and Sing, at the Saville, Aug–Oct 1950; subsequently presented or co-presented the following productions: Bless the Bride (revival), Encore des Folies, 1951; Paris to Piccadilly, 1952; Anna Lucasta (revival), Champagne on Ice, Pardon My French, 1953; Anna Lucasta (revival), 1954; Paris By Night, 1955; Star Maker (tour), 1956; Rocking the Town, 1956; Plaisirs de Paris, We're Having a Ball, 1957; Where's Charley?, Large As Life, 1958; Fine Fettle, Swinging Down the Lane, 1959; Stars in Your Eyes, 1960; *Victor Borge,* Stop the World—I Want to Get Off, 1961; Come Blow Your Horn, An Evening With Yves Montand, *Karmon Israeli Dancers,* Every Night at the Palladium, The Rag Trade, 1962; Who'll Save the Plowboy?, Swing Along, Pickwick, Never Too Late, *Sammy Davis, Jnr, Maurice Chevalier,* 1963; Caligula, A Thousand Clowns, Startime, Maggie May, Little Me, In White America, Our Man Crichton, 1964; The Night of the Iguana, The Solid Gold Cadillac, The Roar of the Grease Paint—the Smell of the Crowd (New York), Doddy's Here, The Circle, Ride a Cock Horse, Pickwick (NY), Twang, Barefoot in the Park, The Killing of Sister George, Babes in the Wood, 1965; The Owl and the Pussycat, The Matchgirls, London Laughs, Funny Girl, Joey Joey, Cinderella, The Odd Couple, Way Out In Piccadilly, 1966; Doddy's Here Again, *Martha Graham and Dance Company,* Queenie, Sweet Charity, Robinson Crusoe, The Four Musketeers, 1967; Golden Boy, You're A Good Man, Charlie Brown, Jack and the Beanstalk, Hotel In Amsterdam, Time Present, Look Back In Anger (revival), 1968; Mame, Your Own Thing, What the Butler Saw, The Giveaway, Cat Among the Pigeons, 1969; Carol Channing with Her Ten Stout-Hearted Men, Danny La Rue at the Palace, The Great Waltz, 1970; Kean, Rabelais, Children of the Wolf, Lulu, 1971; Applause, The Threepenny Opera, The Good Old Bad Old Days, The Unknown Soldier and His Wife, 1972; A Doll's House, The Val Doonican Show, Good Evening (NY), The Wolf, Gomes, The Danny La Rue Show, 1973; Brief Lives, Henry IV, A Streetcar Named Desire, The Good Companions, The Island (NY), Sizwe Bansi Is Dead (NY), Who's Who In Hell (NY), Cinderella, 1974; Harvey, Dad's Army, The Plumber's Progress, Queen Daniella, 1975; Mardi Gras, La Grande Eugene, The Tommy Steele Anniversary Show (tour), 1976; Val Doonican (tour), It's Alright If I Do It, Danny La Rue (tour), 1977; Beyond the Rainbow, 1978; Charley's Aunt (co-presented), 1979; during 1947–8, reintroduced variety to the West End, at the London Casino, presenting Laurel and Hardy, Sophie Tucker, Harry Richman, Lena Horne, Olsen and Johnson, Mistinguett, etc; at the Pigalle Restaurant, May 1956, presented Pink Champagne, which ran for a year, followed by Champagne Punch; has presented pantomimes at Manchester, Liverpool, Birmingham, Coventry, Nottingham, Leeds, Bristol, Sheffield, Oxford, Wimbledon, Bradford and the London Palladium, and summer shows at Blackpool, Yarmouth, Bournemouth, Torquay, Morecambe, Llandudno, Ramsgate and Brighton; assumed the management, for a number of years, of the following theatres: Wimbledon Theatre, from June 1942, Whitehall Theatre, from May 1943, St Martin's Theatre, from Aug 1943, Winter Garden (with Mala de la Marr), from Dec 1944, and Royalty

Theatre, from June 1960; assumed the management of the Saville Theatre, 1946, the Prince of Wales Theatre, 1958, the Comedy Theatre, 1964, and the Shaftesbury Theatre, 1964; opened New London Theatre, 1973; converted London Hippodrome into The Talk of the Town Theatre Restaurant, 1958, and presents entertainment at this venue; Chief Executive of the EMI Group; is also a director of more than 30 companies which, in addition to stage presentations and films, cover television, records and property; was 1969 Chief Barker (President) of the Variety Club of Great Britain; President of the Entertainment Artistes' Benevolent Fund, for which he has presented annual Royal Variety Performance; Companion of the Grand Order of Water Rats, and a member of the Saints and Sinners.

Address: EMI Ltd, 20 Manchester Square, London W1A 1ES. *Tel:* 01–486 4488.

DE LIAGRE, Alfred Jun, producer, director, and manager
b New York City, 6 Oct 1904; *s* of Alfred de Liagre and his wife Frida (Unger); *e* Riverdale School and Yale University; *m* Mary Howard.

Commenced his career at the Woodstock Playhouse, 1930; in 1931 was assistant stage-manager to Jane Cowl; in conjunction with Richard Aldrich produced and directed the following plays in NY: Three Cornered Moon, 1933; By Your Leave, Pure in Heart (co-produced only) 1934; Petticoat Fever, 1935; Fresh Fields, 1936; has since produced and directed Yes, My Darling Daughter (also London), 1937; I Am My Youth, 1938; No Code to Guide Her, 1939; Mr and Mrs North, The Walrus and the Carpenter, 1941; Ask My Friend Sandy, The Voice of the Turtle (produced only); has since produced The Mermaids Singing, 1945; The Druid Circle, The Voice of the Turtle (London), 1947; The Madwoman of Chaillot, 1948; Second Threshold, 1950; The Madwoman of Chaillot (London), 1951; The Deep Blue Sea, 1952; Escapade (also directed), 1953; The Golden Apple, 1954; The Caine Mutiny Court Martial (tour), Janus, 1955; Janus (London), Nature's Way, 1957; The Girls in 509, JB, 1958; The Tumbler (with Roger L Stevens), 1960; Kwamina, 1961; Photo Finish, 1963; The Irregular Verb to Love, 1964; at the Paper Mill Playhouse, Millburn, NJ, Jan 1965, directed a revival of Janus; Love in E Flat, 1967; as Executive Producer of ANTA, presented, Sept–Oct 1969, The American Conservatory Theatre in The Three Sisters, Tiny Alice, and A Flea in Her Ear; in Nov 1969, the American Shakespeare Festival Theatre in Henry V and the Plumstead Playhouse in Our Town; Dec 1969, the New York Shakespeare Festival Theatre in No Place to Be Somebody; Jan 1970, the National Theatre of the Deaf in Sganarelle and Songs from Milkwood, and The Playwrights Unit in Watercolor and Criss-Crossing; Feb 1970, the La Mama Experimental Theatre Club in Gloria and Esperanza, and the Phoenix Theatre in Harvey, for an extended run; May 1970, the John Fernald Company in The Cherry Orchard, and the Trinity Square Repertory Company of Providence, RI, in Wilson in the Promise Land; co-presented Deathtrap, NY, 1978; member of the Board of Directors of the Actors Fund of America, ANTA, League of New York Theatres, National Repertory Theatre, Shakespeare Festival and Academy, John F Kennedy Cultural Center, Committee of Theatrical Producers, Yale Drama School; President of the American Theatre Wing.

Recreations: Tennis and golf. *Clubs:* Yale, Century, River, Maidstone. *Address:* 322 East 57th Street, or 245 West 52nd Street, New York, NY. *Tel:* PL 7–4133.

DELL, Gabriel (*née* del Vecchio) actor
b Barbados, BWI, 7 Oct 1923; *s* of Marcello del Vecchio,

MD; *m* Allyson Daniell; prepared for the stage with Lee Strasberg, Etienne De Croux, Von Heussenstamm.

First appeared on the stage as a child at the Guild, New York, 17 Oct 1932, as Ring Foy in The Good Earth; Belasco, Oct 1935, played TB in Dead End; entered films in this part, 1937, and remained in Hollywood for some years as a member of the Dead End Kids, playing in such films as Angels with Dirty Faces, 1938, and others; reappeared in NY at the Coronet, 1950, when he took over various parts in the revue Tickets, Please; Mark Hellinger, Apr 1955, played Spud in the musical Ankles Aweigh; Theatre in the Park, Aug 1959, played Boris Adzinidzinadze in Can-Can; 41st Street, Nov 1961, Emanu in The Automobile Graveyard; Maidman, Jan 1962, title-role in Fortuna; Cricket, Apr 1962, Leon V Kaufenman in Man Out Loud, Girl Quiet and Martino Hacoen Median in The Spanish Armada; City Center, May 1962, again played Boris in Can-Can; City Center, Feb 1963, Chick Clark in Wonderful Town and Ali Hakim in Oklahoma!; ANTA, Dec 1963, Al Marciano in Marathon '33; Majestic, Apr 1964, Comptroller Schub in Anyone Can Whistle; Longacre, Oct 1964, title-role in The Sign in Sidney Brustein's Window; Booth, 1965, took over from Alan Arkin as Harry Berlin in Luv; Gramercy Arts, Apr 1967, Andrew Prale in Chocolates; Cort, Nov 1967, Phil Caponetti in Something Diff'rent; Greenwich Mews, Feb 1969, the Contestant in Adaptation; Mark Taper Forum, Los Angeles, Calif, Oct 1969, again played the Contestant in Adaptation; Berkshire Theater Festival, Stockbridge, Mass, July 1971, played in The Goodbye People; Morosco, Jan 1972, Paul Martino in Fun City; Eugene O'Neill, June 1973, took over from Hector Elizondo as Mel Edison in The Prisoner of Second Avenue; Estelle R Newman, Oct 1974, Remo Weinberger in Where Do We Go from Here?; Ogunquit, Maine, Playhouse, July 1975, Henry Bech in Culture Caper; Little, Oct 1975, Fred in Lamp-post Reunion; has appeared in more than 50 musicals on the road and in stock; appeared in film Earthquake, 1974; first appeared on television in *Broadway Open House*, 1952, and later in the Steve Allen Show.

Address: Actors Equity Association, 165 West 46th Street, New York, NY 10036.

DE MILLE, Agnes, choreographer and danseuse
b New York City, 1905; *d* of William C de Mille and his wife Anna (George); *e* University of California; *m* Walter Foy Prude; studied dancing in London, under Koslov, Marie Rambert, Antony Tudor, and Tamara Karsavina.

First appeared, as a dancer, in NY, 1927, in La Finta Giardiniera; made her concert début, at the Republic Theatre, 1928; danced in the US, England, France, Denmark, etc, 1928–41; in 1929 she arranged the choreography for the revival of The Black Crook at Hoboken, NJ; at the Adelphi Theatre, London, 1933, she arranged and staged the dances for C B Cochran's production of Nymph Errant; has since arranged the dances for Leslie Howard's revival of Hamlet, 1936; for the film Romeo and Juliet, and the revue Hooray for What, 1937; Swingin' the Dream (A Midsummer Night's Dream), 1939; joined the Ballet Theatre, in NY, 1939, and from 1939–42, choreographed Black Ritual, Three Virgins and a Devil, and Rodeo; has since arranged the dances for The American Legend, 1941; Oklahoma! One Touch of Venus, 1943; Bloomer Girl, 1944; Carousel, 1945; Brigadoon, Allegro, 1947; Fall River Legend (ballet), 1948; Gentlemen Prefer Blondes (also directed), 1949; staged the entire production of Out of This World, 1950; arranged dances for Paint Your Wagon, 1951; The Girl in Pink Tights, 1954; in

Aug 1956, she danced the Priggish Virgin in Three Virgins and the Devil as well as the Cowgirl in Rodeo, at the Royal Opera House, Covent Garden, London, her début in this theatre; choreography for Goldilocks, 1958; Juno, 1959; Bitter Weird (Royal Winnipeg Ballet Co), Kwamina (for which she received the Antoinette Perry Award for Best Choreographer), 1961; 110 in the Shade, 1963; The Wind in the Mountains and The Four Marys (ballets), Carousel, 1965; Hunter College, Oct 1965, danced with the Royal Winnipeg Ballet in her The Rehearsal; choreographed the touring production of Where's Charley? 1966; choreographed and directed Come Summer, 1971; Hunter College Playhouse, 3 Nov 1974, appeared in Conversations About the Dance; her Heritage Dance Theatre toured 1973–5; Oklahoma! revived at the Palace, NY, 1979; has choreographed numerous other classical ballets for leading ballet companies; served as narrator for the television programs of the Bolshoi Ballet, 1965; President of Society of Stage Directors and Choreographers, Inc; member of National Council of the Performing Arts, 1965; author of the autobiographies Dance to the Piper and And Promenade Home; author of To a Young Dancer, Book of the Dance, Russian Journals, and Speak to Me, Dance with Me (1973); has received many awards and degrees, including the Donaldson and Variety's New York Critics Poll, both on several occasions, DHL's from Smith, Western, Hood, and Goucher Colleges, DFA's from Northwestern and California Universities, Litt D from Clarke University, etc.

Address: c/o Harold Ober Associates, 40 East 49th Street, New York, NY 10017.

DENCH, Judi, OBE, actress

b York, 9 Dec 1934; d of Reginald Arthur Dench and his wife Eleanora Olave (Jones); e The Mount School, York; m Michael Williams; studied for the stage at the Central School of Speech Training and Dramatic Art.

Made her first appearance on the stage with the Old Vic Company, at the Royal Court, Liverpool, Sept 1957, as Ophelia in Hamlet; made her first appearance in London at the Old Vic, Sept 1957, in the same production, and remained a member of the company for four seasons, 1957–61, playing the following parts: Juliet in Measure for Measure, First Fairy in A Midsummer Night's Dream, 1957; Maria in Twelfth Night, Katherine in Henry V (also New York), 1958; Phebe in As You Like It, Cynthia in The Double Dealer, Cecily Cardew in The Importance of Being Earnest, Anne Page in The Merry Wives of Windsor, 1959; Katherine in Henry V, Juliet in Romeo and Juliet, Kate Hardcastle in She Stoops to Conquer, Hermia in A Midsummer Night's Dream, 1960; during this period, she toured the United States and Canada, and appeared in Yugoslavia and at the Edinburgh Festival; Aldwych, Dec 1961, played Anya in The Cherry Orchard with the Royal Shakespeare Company; Royal Shakespeare, Stratford-on-Avon, Apr 1962, Isabella in Measure for Measure, subsequently playing Titania in A Midsummer Night's Dream; Aldwych, Aug 1962, Dorcas Bellboys in A Penny for a Song; Nottingham Playhouse, Jan 1963, played Lady Macbeth in Macbeth, subsequently touring West Africa with the production for the British Council also playing Viola in Twelfth Night; Lyric, London, May 1963, Josefa Lautenay in A Shot in the Dark; joined the Oxford Playhouse Company, Apr 1964, to play the following parts: Irina in The Three Sisters, Anna in The Twelfth Hour, 1964; Dol Common in The Alchemist, Jeannette in Romeo and Jeannette, Jacqueline in The Firescreen, 1965; Nottingham Playhouse, Sept 1965, played Isabella in Measure for Measure; Oct 1965, Amanda in Private Lives, Feb 1966, Barbara in The Astrakhan Coat, and Mar 1966,

Joan in St Joan; Oxford Playhouse, Nov 1966, Lika in The Promise, and Dec, Sila in The Rules of the Game, re-opening in the former production at the Fortune, Jan 1967; Palace, Feb 1968, Sally Bowles in Cabaret; joined the Royal Shakespeare Company, and in 1969 Stratford season played Bianca in Women Beware Women, Hermione and Perdita in The Winter's Tale, and Viola in Twelfth Night; toured Australia, Jan 1970, in the latter production, returning to the Aldwych, season 1970–1, to play Viola, Hermione/Perdita, and also Grace Harkaway in London Assurance, and Barbara Undershaft in Major Barbara; at Stratford, season 1971, played Portia in The Merchant of Venice, Viola, and the title role in The Duchess of Malfi; also 1st Fieldmouse, A Brave Stoat and Mother Rabbit in the Stratford production of Toad of Toad Hall, Christmas 1971; toured Japan, Jan 1972, playing Viola; New Theatre, April 1972, again played Grace Harkaway; Theatre Royal, York, Apr 1973, appeared in Content to Whisper; Apollo, Oct 1973, Vilma in The Wolf, transferring with the production to the Queen's and later the New London; Her Majesty's, July 1974, Miss Trant in The Good Companions; Albery, June 1975, Sophie Fullgarney in The Gay Lord Quex; returned to the Aldwych, Oct 1975, to play the Nurse in the RSC production of Too True to Be Good, transferring to the Globe, Dec 1975; Stratford, season 1976, played Beatrice in Much Ado About Nothing, Lady Macbeth, Adriana in The Comedy of Errors, and Regan in King Lear; Aldwych, 1977–8, again played Adriana and Beatrice, also Lona Hessell in Pillars of the Community, Millament in The Way of the World, and Lady Macbeth (Warehouse), for which she gained the SWET Best Actress Award (1977); Stratford, season 1979, played Imogen in Cymbeline; her considerable work for television since 1959 includes major roles in Hilda Lessways, Talking to a Stranger (Television Actress of the Year), An Age of Kings, Village Wooing, and Love in a Cold Climate; received the OBE in the Birthday Honours, 1970; Honorary Doctor of Letters, Warwick University, 1978.

Recreations: Sewing, drawing, catching up with letters. *Address:* c/o Julian Belfrage, Leading Artists Ltd, 60 St James's Street, London SW1.

DENHAM, Maurice, actor

b Beckenham, Kent, 23 Dec 1909; s of Norman Denham and his wife Eleanor Winifred (Lillico); e Tonbridge School; m Margaret Dunn (dec); formerly an engineer.

Made his first appearance on the stage at the Little Theatre, Hull, 17 Aug 1934, as Hubert in The Marquise; he remained at Hull for two seasons in repertory, and in 1936, was with a repertory company at Brighton, and also at Croydon; first appeared in London, at the Arts Theatre, 14 June 1936, as George Furness in Rain Before Seven; at the Comedy, Dec 1936, played George in Busman's Honeymoon; Arts, Nov 1937, George Lumb in Flying Blind; Players', Feb 1938, Eddie Norman in Heaven and Charing Cross; Savoy (for Repertory Players), Oct 1938, Peter Mansky in A Room in Red, White and Blue; Gate, Nov 1938, Fletcher in The Heart Was Not Burned; in 1939, was associated with the well-known radio series ITMA, and after five years in the Army, joined another radio series, Much Binding in the Marsh; from 1946–9, was engaged acting in films; reappeared on the stage, at the Ambassadors', Nov 1949, as Henry Gow in Fumed Oak, and Willy Banbury in Fallen Angels; at the Arts, Apr–June 1951, appeared in the Shaw Festival of one-act plays; at the same theatre, Dec 1951, played Ilam Carve in The Great Adventure; Q, Nov 1952, Sam and George Titmarsh in The House at Bury Hill; Whitehall, June 1954, Stefan in Satellite Story; Wyndham's,

Dec 1956, played Sir Mark Evershed in Shadow of Fear, for The Repertory Players; Lyric, Hammersmith, Apr 1958, and Garrick, May 1958, played Fowle in The Dock Brief and Arthur Loudon in What Shall We Tell Caroline? (double bill); Cambridge, Dec 1958, Arthur Crabb in Who's Your Father?; Mermaid, June 1961, Henry Wirtz in The Andersonville Trial; joined the Old Vic Company, and appeared at the Edinburgh Festival, Aug 1961, in the title-part of King John, subsequently playing the same part at the Old Vic, Sept 1961; Dec 1961, played the title-part in Macbeth; Ashcroft, Croydon, Feb 1963, played Stone in The Sky is Green; Hampstead Theatre Club, Apr 1964, Dr Neuross in Do You Know the Milky Way?; Mermaid, Sept 1967, Nathan in Nathan the Wise; Mermaid, Mar 1970, Proteus in The Apple Cart; Royal Court, July 1971, Pierre Lannes in The Lovers of Viorne; Hampstead, Nov 1979, Serebryakov in Uncle Vanya; has appeared in numerous films; his many TV appearances include Talking to a Stranger.

Recreations: Painting and gardening. *Club:* Garrick. *Address:* c/o Derek Glynne, 17 Wilton Place, London SW1.

DENHAM, Reginald, actor, author and director
b London, 10 Jan 1894; *s* of Harry Barton Denham and his wife Emily Constance (Chapman); *e* City of London School; *m* (1) Moyna McGill (mar dis); (2) Lilian Oldland (mar dis); (3) Mary Orr; studied music and singing at the Guildhall School of Music.

Made his first appearance on the stage at His Majesty's Theatre, 2 Sept 1913, walking on in Joseph and His Brethren; remained at His Majesty's for two years, playing small parts, and then joined the Benson Shakespearean company, with which he also remained two years, playing over fifty character and juvenile parts; his first engagement after the war was at the Lyric, Hammersmith, Feb 1919, when he played Hawkins in Abraham Lincoln; at the Lyric, Apr 1919, played Paris in Romeo and Juliet; at The Queen's, July 1919, in The Cinderella Man; played for nine months under the management of J B Fagan, at the Court and Duke of York's, 1919–20; at the Garrick, Sept 1920, played Sidney in The Right to Strike; at the Apollo, Jan 1921, Lieutenant Graham in French Leave; at the Duke of York's, Nov 1921, Count Pietro Gamba in The Pilgrim of Eternity; at the Everyman Theatre, 1922, played a round of parts in plays by Bernard Shaw; since that date has been prominent as a director; among his productions may be noted If Four Walls Told, The Smiths of Surbiton, Biters Bitten, Coleman, 1922; Trespasses, The Man Who Ate the Popomack, 1923; was appointed director to the Oxford Players, by J B Fagan, Oct 1923, and during the next six months directed and played in eighteen plays; during 1924, he appeared at the Lyric, Hammersmith, for some time, playing Witwoud in The Way of the World; at the Ambassadors', Sept 1924, played Charley Blazy in Fata Morgana, which he also directed; directed No Man's Land, St Martin's, 1924, and Pollyanna, St James's, 1924; has since directed The Colonnade, The Czarina, Peer Gynt (OUDS), The Moon and Sixpence, 1925; For None Can Tell, A Man Unknown, Confession, After Dark, 1926; The Village, Wild-Cat Hetty, Compromising Daphne, The Tempest (OUDS), Sylvia, 1927; Lord Babs, The Man Who Changed His Name, For Better, For Worse, The House of Women, Such Men Are Dangerous (co-director), To What Red Hell (For None Can Tell), 1928; Rope, The Misdoings of Charley Peace, Jew Suss (with Matheson Lang), Tunnel Trench, Rope's End (New York), 1929; Joseph Suss (NY), Suspense, The Last Chapter, Topaze, An Object of Virtue, 1930; Cold Blood, 1932; Wellington, 1933; The Last Straw, 1937; Green Holly, Give Me Yesterday, Windfall, 1938; The

Distant Hand, Ladies in Retirement, 1939; First Night, 1940; subsequently went to America where he directed Jupiter Laughs, Ladies in Retirement, Suspect, 1940; Play with Fire, 1941; Guest in the House, Malice Domestic, Yesterday's Magic, 1942; The Two Mrs Carrolls, 1943; Dark Hammock, Wallflower, 1944; Round Trip, 1945; A Joy Forever, Obsession, Temper the Wind, 1946; Portrait in Black, Duet for Two Hands, 1947; The Man They Acquitted (London), 1949; The Devil Also Dreams, 1950; Gramercy Ghost, 1951; Dial M for Murder, 1952; Be Your Age, A Date with April, Sherlock Holmes, 1953; The Bad Seed, 1954; Janus, 1955; Hide and Seek, 1957; A Mighty Man Is He, 1960; returned to England and directed A Stranger in the Tea, 1960; Booth, NY, 1963, directed Once for the Asking; lectured and made television appearances in Australia and New Zealand, 1964; directed Hostile Witness (NY), 1965; Savoy, London, July 1967, directed Minor Murder, which he wrote with Mary Orr; directed You Never Can Tell at Washington University, Seattle, 1969; Stage 73, NY, Jan 1976, directed his wife's play Grass Widows; part-author, with Edward Percy, of The Last Straw, Suspect, 1937; Green Holly (Give Me Yesterday), 1938; The Distant Hand, Ladies in Retirement, 1939; author of First Night, 1940; Malice Domestic (with Percy), 1942; Wallflower (with Mary Orr), and Dark Hammock (with Mary Orr), 1944; Round Trip (with Mary Orr), 1945; Dogs Delight (with Percy), 1946; The Coral Snake (with Mary Orr), 1947; The Man They Aquitted (with Edward Percy), 1949; The Platinum Set (with Mary Orr), 1950; Sweet Peril (with Mary Orr), 1952; Be Your Age (with Mary Orr), 1953; A Dash of Bitters (with Conrad Sutton Smith), 1954; Stars in My Hair, 1958 (his autobiography) and, with Mary Orr, a book of reminiscences called Footlights and Feathers, 1966; translated from the Spanish plays by Alfonso Paso, Blue Heaven, Recipe for a Crime, and Oh Mama! No, Papa! 1963; author (with Mary Orr) The Wisdom of Eve, 1964, Minor Murder, 1966, and Double Honeymoon, 1979; also with Mary Orr wrote over 100 television scripts, 1947–50; is an Hon Member of the OUDS; was a member of the Committee of the Fellowship of Players and of the Repertory Players; joined the Executive Board of Paramount British Pictures, 1931; commenced directing films, 1932.

Club: Players, Coffee House. *Recreations:* Music and ornithology. *Address:* 100 West 57th Street, New York, NY 10019.

DENISON, Michael, actor
b Doncaster, Yorks, 1 Nov 1915; *s* of Gilbert Dixon Denison and his wife Marie Louise (Bain); *e* Harrow, and Magdalen College, Oxford; *m* Dulcie Gray; studied for the stage at the Webber-Douglas School.

Made his first appearance on the stage, at Frinton-on-Sea, Aug 1938, as Lord Fancourt Babberley in Charley's Aunt; first appeared in London, at the Westminster Theatre, 21 Sept 1938, as Paris in Troilus and Cressida; he played at that theatre, until Mar 1939, as Gordon Whitehouse in Dangerous Corner, Ghazan Khan in Marco Millions, Robert Devizes in The Will, Redpenny in The Doctor's Dilemma, Rev Alexander Mill in Candida; in May 1939, joined the A R Whatmore Players in Aberdeen; returned to the Westminster, London, Oct 1939, to play Peter Horlett in Music at Night and Stephen Undershaft in Major Barbara; in Mar 1940, joined the H M Tennent Players, appearing in repertory, in Edinburgh and Glasgow; served in the Army from June 1940 to Apr 1946; toured, Aug 1946, as Paul in Ever Since Paradise; Aldwych, Aug 1948, played Sir Nicholas Corbel in Rain on the Just; Strand, Nov 1949, Michael Fuller in Queen Elizabeth Slept Here; Ambassadors', Oct 1950, Michael in The Four Poster;

Winter Garden, May 1952, appeared as Stuart in Dragon's Mouth; St James's, Dec 1952, Clive Jevons in Sweet Peril; Criterion, June 1953, Brian in The Bad Samaritan; Prince's, Feb 1954, appeared as the White Knight, Tweedledee and Humpty Dumpty in Alice Through the Looking Glass; Westminster, June 1954, played Francis Oberon in We Must Kill Toni; toured South Africa with Dulcie Gray, Dec 1954–Feb 1955, in The Fourposter and Private Lives; joined the Shakespeare Memorial Theatre Company, Stratford-on-Avon, Apr 1955, and during the season appeared as Sir Andrew Aguecheek, as Bertram in All's Well That Ends Well, Dr Caius in The Merry Wives of Windsor, and Lucius in Titus Andronicus; Alexandra, Birmingham, Nov 1955, directed Dulcie Gray's first play, Love Affair; Chelsea Palace, Dec 1955, played the White Knight, Tweedledee, and Humpty Dumpty; in Alice Through the Looking Glass; Lyric, Hammersmith, June 1956, directed and played Philip Grant in Love Affair; Edinburgh Festival, Lyceum, Sept 1956, played A in A Village Wooing, and Lieut Duvallet in Fanny's First Play, also appearing in the same plays at the Berlin Festival, Oct 1956; Aldwych, Aug 1957, Charles Cuttinghame in Meet Me By Moonlight; Feb 1958, toured as Jeffrey Banning in Double Cross; Cambridge, May 1959, the Duke of Hampshire in Let Them Eat Cake; Piccadilly, June 1960, played the Rev James Morell in Candida, which subsequently transferred to Wyndham's, breaking the previous long-run record with a total of 160 performances; Wyndham's, Nov 1961, played Hector Hushabye in Heartbreak House; in Melbourne and Brisbane, Australia, Apr–July 1962, took over Henry Higgins in My Fair Lady; appeared at the opening of the City Centre Theatre, Hong Kong, Aug 1962, as A in A Village Wooing, and Harrison Crockstead in A Marriage Has Been Arranged; at the Berlin Drama Festival, Sept 1962, appeared with Dulcie Gray in a Shakespeare recital; at the opening of the Ashcroft Theatre, Croydon, Nov 1962, played Henry VIII in The Royal Gambit; New Arts, June 1963, and subsequently St Martin's, July 1963, Philip Herriton in Where Angels Fear to Tread; Apr–July 1964, toured England and the Continent with Dulcie Gray in a Shakespeare programme, Merely Players; Haymarket, Nov 1964, Simon Crawford in Hostile Witness; Strand, Dec 1965, played Sir Robert Chiltern in An Ideal Husband; St Martin's, Dec 1966, played the Duke of Bristol in On Approval, and Mar 1967, Mark in Happy Family; Strand, Nov 1967, Sebastian Fleming in Number Ten; Nottingham Playhouse, May–July 1968, played Charlie in Vacant Possession and Major Hissling in Confession at Night; St Martin's, Oct 1968, Andrew Pilgrim in Out of the Question; Fortune, Jan 1970, directed How He Lied to Her Husband, played A in Village Wooing and Balsquith in Press Cuttings, in Three, short plays by Bernard Shaw; Criterion, Nov 1970, Hjalmar Ekdal in The Wild Duck; toured, Apr 1971, as Lord Ogleby in The Clandestine Marriage; also in Sept 1971, in Village Wooing and Unexpectedly Vacant; Summer 1972, played Prospero in The Tempest and Malvolio in Twelfth Night, on tour and at the Open Air, Regent's Park; toured, Sept 1972, in The Dragon Variation, playing six parts; Ashcroft, Croydon, Dec 1972, played Tweedledee and White Knight in Alice Through the Looking Glass; Savoy, Oct 1973, Lew Trent in At the End of the Day; Ambassadors', July 1974, Norman Banks in The Sack Race; Coliseum, Dec 1974, Captain Hook and Mr Darling in Peter Pan; Cambridge Theatre, Apr 1975, Pooh-Bah in The Black Mikado; toured, Oct 1976, in The Earl and the Pussycat, and in the same year, as James Fraser in The First Mrs Fraser, and Edward Moulton Barrett in Robert and Elizabeth; 1977, toured as Sir Julian Twombley in his own adaptation of Pinero's The Cabinet Minister; 1978,

for Prospect at the Old Vic and on tour played: Malvolio in Twelfth Night, Hebble Tyson in The Lady's Not For Burning, and Lebedev in Ivanov; Prince of Wales, May 1979, for the National Theatre, took over the part of Ernest in Bedroom Farce; entered films, 1940, in Tilly of Bloomsbury, and has appeared in many productions, notably My Brother Jonathan, The Glass Mountain, Angels One Five, The Importance of Being Earnest; also made numerous television appearances, including over eighty as Boyd, QC between 1957–63; member of Council of British Actors' Equity Association, 1949–55, 1959–77; Vice-President 1952, 1961–3, 1974; director, New Shakespeare Company; member of the Drama Panel of the Arts Council, 1975–8; author of 'The Actor and His World' (with Dulcie Gray), 1964, and 'Overture and Beginners', 1973.

Recreations: Golf, gardening, painting, and motoring. *Address:* c/o Midland Bank Ltd, Buckingham Palace Road, SW1.

DENKER, Henry, dramatic author
b New York City, 25 Nov 1912; *s* of Max Denker and his wife Jennie; *e* Morris High School, New York City, New York University and New York Law School; *m* Edith Heckman; formerly an attorney and tax consultant.

Author of the following plays, produced on Broadway unless otherwise stated: Time Limit, 1956; A Far Country, 1960; A Case of Libel, 1964; Venus at Large, 1966; The Headhunters (Washington DC), 1974; The Girl Who Had Everything (Bucks County, Pa), 1975; Second Time Around (Sarasota), 1976; Something Old, Something New, 1976; Horowitz and Mrs Washington, 1980; author of the screenplays for Time Limit, 1960, Twilight of Honor, 1963; work for TV includes Give Us Barabbas, The Court Martial of Lieutenant Calley, Mother Seton (1980), etc; for radio spent ten years as producer, director, writer of The Greatest Story Ever Told; author of fourteen novels including The Experiment, The Starmaker, The Actress, Error of Judgement, etc; has taught playwriting at the American Theatre Wing and elsewhere.

Address: 241 Central Park West, New York, NY 10024.

DENNIS, Sandy, actress
b Hastings, Nebraska, 27 Apr 1937; *d* of Jack Dennis and his wife Yvonne; *m* Gerry Mulligan; prepared for the stage with Herbert Berghof at HB Studios.

First appeared on the stage at the Royal Poinciana Playhouse, Palm Beach, Florida, 1956, as Elma Duckworth in Bus Stop; at the Music Box, New York, Dec 1957, understudied the roles of Flirt Conroy and Reenie Flood in The Dark at the Top of the Stairs; toured, 1959, as Reenie Flood in this last play; Wilbur, Boston, Jan 1960, Nancy in Motel; made her NY stage début at the Eugene O'Neill, 20 Oct 1960, as Millicent Bishop in Face of a Hero; Ethel Barrymore, Nov 1961, Ann Howard in The Complaisant Lover; Eugene O'Neill, Apr 1962, Sandra Markowitz in A Thousand Clowns, for which she received the Antoinette Perry (Tony) Award and the *Variety* New York Critics Poll Award; Music Box, Feb 1964, Ellen Gordon in Any Wednesday for which she also received the Tony Award; Longacre, Oct 1967, Daphne in Daphne in Cottage D; Ivanhoe, Chicago, 1970, played Cherry in Bus Stop; Royale, Mar 1971, Teresa Phillips in How the Other Half Loves; toured, 1971 and 1972, as Anna Reardon in And Miss Reardon Drinks a Little; Biltmore, Jan 1973, Hannah Heywood in Let Me Hear You Smile; Ivanhoe, Chicago, July 1973, Blanche du Bois in A Streetcar Named Desire; Westport, Conn, Country Playhouse, July 1974, Billie Dawn in Born Yesterday, and subsequently toured in this part; Music Box, Oct 1974, Eva in

Absurd Person Singular; left the cast then rejoined it in 1975 at the same theatre; Playhouse in the Park, Philadelphia, July 1975, and tour, Maggie in Cat on a Hot Tin Roof; returned as Eva, Jan 1976; Brooks Atkinson, June 1976, took over as Doris in Same Time Next Year, playing the part for almost a year; entered films in 1961 in Splendor in the Grass, and has since played Honey in Who's Afraid of Virginia Woolf? for which she received the Academy Award, Up the Down Staircase, Sweet November, The Out of Towners, etc.

Address: Actors Equity Association, 165 West 46th Street, New York, NY 10036.

DE SHIELDS, Andre, actor, director and choreographer
b Baltimore, 12 Jan 1946; *s* of John Edward De Shields and his wife Mary Elizabeth (Gunther); *e* University of Wisconsin (BA 1970).

First stage appearance, Wilmington College, Ohio, 1965, as Walter Lee Younger in A Raisin in the Sun; choreographer for Bette Midler's Harlettes, 1973–77; first Broadway appearance, Ambassador, 14 Feb 1973, as Xander the Unconquerable in Warp; Truck and Warehouse, Feb 1974, The Old Movie in 2008½; Majestic, Jan 1975 title role in The Wiz; Manhattan Theatre Club, Feb 1978, appeared in Ain't Misbehavin', transferring to the Longacre, May, and making his London debut in the same show at Her Majesty's, 22 Mar 1979; has directed at La Mama and the Manhattan Theatre Club; in 1978 gave a one-man concert at Reno Sweeney, NY, entitled Midnight.
Favourite part: Xander the Unconquerable. *Address:* c/o Eisen Associates, 346 East 50th Street, New York, NY 10022.

DEWELL, Michael, producing manager
b Woodbridge, Conn, 1931; *s* of Mansfield Dewell and his wife Rolly (Dwy); *e* Yale (BA 1952) and Royal Acad of Dramatic Arts (Dipl 1954); *m* Nina Foch.

Made first stage appearance, 1954, touring with Margaret O'Brien in Kiss and Tell; numerous television roles, 1954–6, during service in US Army (1956–8) was Entertainment Director, US Chemical Corps (1956), Asst Exec Producer, TV Disivion of Dept of Defense (1957–8), founded National Phoenix Theater, 1959, and for it presented Sir Tyrone Guthrie's production of Mary Stuart (National Tour 1959–60); produced two National Tours of Once Upon a Mattress, 1961–2; created and produced The American Festival (Cambridge, Mass, 1961); Founder-Producer, National Repertory Theatre, 1961–present, for which he produced Elizabeth the Queen, 1961; Mary Stuart, 1962; Hedda Gabler, Liliom, 1963; The Crucible, The Seagull, 1964, Ring Round The Moon, She Stoops to Conquer, 1965, The Rivals, Madwoman of Chaillot, The Trojan Women, A Touch of the Poet, 1966; The Imaginary Invalid, 1967, for US Dept of Interior, supervised restoration of Ford's Theatre in Washington, DC as a legitimate stage, and re-opened it in 1968 with a repertory of John Brown's Body, She Stoops to Conquer, and The Comedy of Errors, founded Los Angeles Free Shakespeare Festival in 1963, and for it produced As You Like It, Macbeth, and The Comedy of Errors; founded National Play Award in 1976; Administrative Director and President, Academy of Stage and Cinema Arts, Los Angeles, 1975–present; productions for television include: Mary Stuart, 1962, Inaugural Night at Ford's 1968; many awards include: Antoinette Perry (Tony), 1950 for NRT repertory at Belasco, NY; Outer Circle Awards for best National Tour, 1960, 1965; served on Executive Committee, ANTA, 1962–7, Trustee, National Repertory Theatre Foundation, 1961–present, Acad of Stage and Cinema Arts, 1975–present,

Company Theatre Foundation 1968–70, Foundation for Multi-Media and The Arts, 1975–7, Bilingual Foundation of the Arts, 1977–present.

Address: National Repertory Theatre, PO Box 1884, Beverly Hills, Calif 90213.

DEWHURST, Colleen, actress
b Montreal, Canada, 3 June 1926; *e* Downer College for Young Ladies, Milwaukee, Wisconsin; *m* (1) James Vickery (mar dis); (2) George C Scott (mar dis); (3) George C Scott (mar dis); prepared for the stage at the American Academy of Dramatic Arts and with Harold Clurman and Joseph Anthony.

While a student appeared at the Carnegie Lyceum, Oct 1946, as Julia Cavendish in The Royal Family; made her professional New York début at the ANTA, Jan 1952, when she played one of the Neighbors in a revival of Desire Under the Elms; Winter Garden, Jan 1956, played a Memphis Virgin and a Turkish Concubine in Tamburlaine the Great; for the New York Shakespeare Festival, Aug 1956, Tamora in Titus Andronicus; Cherry Lane, Sept 1956, title-role in Camille; Emanuel Presbyterian Church, Nov 1956, Kate in The Taming of the Shrew; Actors Playhouse, Dec 1956, the Queen in The Eagle Has Two Heads; Forrest, Philadelphia, Feb 1957, Penelope in Maiden Voyage; New York Shakespeare Festival, Aug 1957, Lady Macbeth in Macbeth; Adelphi, NY, Nov 1957, Mrs Squeamish in The Country Wife; Circle-in-the-Square, Feb 1958, Laetitia in Children of Darkness; Festival of Two Worlds, Spoleto, Italy, summer 1958, Josie Hogan in A Moon for the Misbegotten; Heckscher, NY, Jan 1959, Cleopatra in Antony and Cleopatra; 54th Street, Feb 1960, Caesonia in Caligula; Belasco, Nov 1960, Mary Follet in All the Way Home, receiving the Antoinette Perry (Tony) Award for this role; Henry Miller's, Mar 1962, Phoebe Flaherty in Great Day in the Morning; Circle-in-the-Square, Jan 1963, Abbie Putnam in Desire Under the Elms; Delacorte, June 1963, Cleopatra in Antony and Cleopatra; Martin Beck, Oct 1963, Amelia Evans in The Ballad of the Sad Cafe; toured, summer 1965, as Martha in Who's Afraid of Virginia Woolf?; Studio Arena, Buffalo, Oct 1965, Josie Hogan in A Moon for the Misbegotten; Broadhurst, Oct 1967, Sara in More Stately Mansions; Sheridan Square Playhouse, Sept 1969, Hester in Hello and Goodbye; Vivian Beaumont, Nov 1970, Shen Teh in The Good Woman of Setzuan; Martin Beck, Mar 1971, The Mistress in All Over; Westport, Conn, Country Playhouse, Aug 1971, Nel Denton in The Big Coca-Cola Swamp in the Sky; Delacorte, June 1972, Gertrude in Hamlet; Circle in the Square—Joseph E Levine, Nov 1972, Christine Mannon in Mourning Becomes Electra; Morosco, Dec 1973, Josie Hogan in A Moon for the Misbegotten, receiving the Antoinette Perry (Tony) Award for this role; Circle in the Square, 29 Apr 1974, appeared in a Gala Benefit Show; Ahmanson, Los Angeles, Nov 1974, again played Josie Hogan in Moon for the Misbegotten; Long Wharf, New Haven, Conn, Oct 1975, Margaret in Artichoke; Music Box, Apr 1976, Martha in Who's Afraid of Virginia Woolf?; Belasco, Oct 1977, Irene Porter in An Almost Perfect Person; Promenade, Oct 1978, Lillian Hellman in Are You Now or Have Ever Been . . .?; Public/Newman, Feb 1979, Ruth Chandler in Taken in Marriage; Public, Oct 1979, appeared in O'Neill and Carlotta; appeared in the film The Nun's Story, 1959, Mc Q, 1974, etc; has appeared regularly on television since 1961, notably as Inez in No Exit, Cleopatra in Antony and Cleopatra, Medea, and in Focus.

Address: c/o STE Representation, 888 Seventh Avenue, New York, NY 10019.

DEWHURST, Keith, playwright
b Oldham, 24 Dec 1931; *s* of Joseph Frederick Dewhurst and his

wife Lily; *e* Rydal School and Peterhouse, Cambridge; *m* Eve Pearce; formerly a yarn-tester and journalist.

He is author of the following stage plays: Rafferty's Chant, 1967; Pirates, 1970; Brecht in '26, Corunna! 1971; Kidnapped (adaptation), 1972; The Miser (translation), 1973; The Magic Island, 1974; The Bomb in Brewery Street, 1975; One Short, 1976; Luggage (National Theatre), 1977; the adaptations Lark Rise, The World Turned Upside Down, and Candleford (NT), 1978–79; San Salvador, 1980; his work for television since Think of the Day, 1960, includes such plays as The Siege of Manchester, Last Bus (Japan Prize for Educational Television, 1968), Two Girls and A Millionaire, 1978; adaptations: Helen (Euripedes) and Just William; and episodes for several series; presenter of various series for BBC and Independent Television, including Extraordinary, YTV, 1978; Arts Columnist of *The Guardian*, 1968–72.

Address: c/o London Management, 235 Regent Street, London W1. *Tel:* 01 734 4192.

DEWS, Peter, director
b Wakefield, Yorkshire, 26 Sept 1929; *s* of John Dews and his wife Edna (Bloomfield); *e* QEGS, Wakefield and University College, Oxford; *m* Ann Rhodes; formerly a schoolmaster.

First production Crime Passionel at the Civic Playhouse, Bradford, July 1952; 1957, directed Henry V for OUDS; 1958, Picnic (Belgrade, Coventry); 1961, Macbeth (Playhouse, Nottingham); 1962, Henry IV (OUDS); 1963, Richard II (Ludlow Festival); 1964, Henry V, Twelfth Night, Hamlet (all in Chicago); 1965, Galileo (Edinburgh); Director of the Birmingham Repertory Theatre, 1966–72, where his numerous productions included As You Like It, which transferred to London in 1967, and Hadrian VII, which transferred to London in 1968 and which he also directed in New York in the same year; at the Chichester Festival Theatre he has directed Antony and Cleopatra, 1969; Vivat! Vivat Regina! (also London and NY), The Alchemist (in which he played Face), 1970; The Director of the Opera, 1973; Othello, 1975; his other productions, in London unless otherwise stated, include Crown Matrimonial (also NY, 1973), The Inferno (also played Prior Goldwell), 1972; As You Like It (Durban), Twelfth Night (Birmingham), 1973; The Waltz of the Toreadors, Hamlet (Durban; also played Claudius), King John (Stratford, Ont), Look Back In Anger (Coventry), 1974; Arms and the Man, Equus, Toad of Road Hall (all Birmingham), Equus also at Vancouver, Othello (Chichester), Coriolanus (Tel Aviv), 1975; 13 Rue de L'Amour, The Pleasure of this Company, The Circle, 1976; Man and Superman, Don Juan in Hell, When We Are Married (all Ottawa), Julius Caesar (Chichester), 1977; Othello (Australian tour), A Sleep of Prisoners (Chichester Cathedral), 1978; A Sleep of Prisoners, Julius Caesar (both Hong Kong Festival), The Devil's Disciple, The Importance of Being Earnest (both Chichester), 1979; Artistic Director, Chichester Festival Theatre, 1978–; Antoinette Perry Award, 1969, for best director with his NY production of Hadrian VII; his television productions, since 1956, have included such outstanding successes as the Shakespeare series An Age of Kings and The Spread of the Eagle; for the former he won the Guild of TV Producers Award for the best drama production, 1960.

Recreations: Acting and music. *Address:* c/o Larry Dalzell Associates Ltd, 3 Goodwins Court, St Martin's Lane, London WC2N 4LL. *Tel:* 01 240 3086.

DEXTER, John, director.
Began his career as director with the English Stage Company, June 1957, having previously worked as an actor on television and radio; he has directed the following productions: Yes—and

After (in a Production without Décor), 1957; Each in His Own Wilderness (in a Production without Décor), Chicken Soup With Barley, 1958; Roots, The Kitchen, Last Day in Dreamland, and A Glimpse of the Sea (double-bill), 1959; Chicken Soup With Barley, This Year, Next Year, I'm Talking About Jerusalem, Toys in the Attic, 1960; The Kitchen, South, The Keep, 1961; My Place, The Keep, England, Our England, Chips With Everything (co-directed), The Blood of the Bambergs, The Sponge Room, and Squat Betty (double-bill), 1962; Jackie the Jumper, Half-a-Sixpence, Saint Joan (Chichester and Edinburgh Festivals), Chips With Everything (New York), 1963; Associate Director of the National Theatre, 1963–6, 1971–5, for whom he directed the following productions: Saint Joan, 1963; Hobson's Choice, Othello, Royal Hunt of the Sun (also Chichester; co-directed), 1964; Armstrong's Last Goodnight (also Chichester; co-directed), Black Comedy (Chichester), 1965; Black Comedy, A Bond Honoured, The Storm, 1966; A Woman Killed with Kindness, Tyger (co-directed), The Good-Natured Man, 1971; The Misanthrope, Equus, 1973; The Party, 1973; The Misanthrope (NY), Phaedra Britannica, 1975; As You Like It, 1979; he also directed Do I Hear a Waltz? (NY), Royal Hunt of the Sun (NY), 1965; Black Comedy and White Lies (NY), The Unknown Soldier and His Wife (NY), Wise Child, 1967; The Old Ones, 1972; In Praise of Love, 1973; Equus (NY), Pygmalion, 1974; he directed his first film, The Virgin Soldiers, 1968; directed his first opera, Benevenuto Cellini, Covent Garden, 1966: subsequent productions in London, Paris or Hamburg include Boris Godunov, Billy Budd, La Forza Del Destino and Aida; now Director of Productions at The Metropolitan Opera, NY, where he has directed The Carmelites, Lulu and Don Pasquale.

Address: Metropolitan Opera House, Lincoln Center Plaza, New York, NY 10023.

DIAMOND, Margaret, actress
b London, 1916; *d* of Hugh Victor Diamond and his wife Gertrude Isobel (County); *e* London; studied for the stage at the Royal Academy of Dramatic Art.

Made her first appearance on the stage as a dancer, at the Théâtre des Champs-Elysées, Paris; subsequently appeared at the Plaza Cinema, London, as one of the Plaza Tiller Girls, also touring the Continent; from 1940–4, appeared in repertory at various towns; appeared with the Worthing Repertory Company, 1945–6; Lyric Theatre, Hammersmith, 4 Mar 1947, played Honor Rossiter in The Rossiters; Arts Theatre, Apr 1947, Elizabeth in Less Than Kind; Duchess, June 1947, Zinaida in He Who Gets Slapped; played repertory at Sheffield 1948, and Birmingham Repertory company, 1948; appeared in several plays at the Q Theatre, 1949; Embassy, July 1950, played Jane Armitage in Always Afternoon; St Martin's (for the Preview Theatre), Nov 1950, Auranthe in Otho, the Great; Arts, Cambridge, Feb 1952, played Sibyl Emerson in The Starcross Legend (subsequently re-titled After My Fashion); at the White Rock Pavilion, Hastings, Jan 1953, played the title-rôle in Lady Susan; Prince's, London, Feb 1953, Dr Barrow in The Shrike; Phoenix (for Repertory Players), Mar 1953, Stella in The Castle of Deception; Q, June 1953, Hester Guthrie in In Springtime; at the Playhouse, Liverpool, Aug 1954, appeared as Constance Warburton in Late Love, in Nov 1954, as Bid in Home Is the Hero, in Apr 1955, as Emma Blanket in The House of Benedicite, and in June 1955, as the Countess in Spring Quartet; Wyndham's (for Repertory Players), June 1956, Stella Waters in More Things in Heaven; Richmond, July 1956, Madame Zabaskin in The Lie Detector; Royal Court (in a Production without Décor, for the English Stage Company), Oct 1957, Barbara Baulkfast in The Waters of Babylon; Lyric (for Repertory Players), Jan 1958, Rachel Kerr in Tenebrae; Wyndham's (for Repertory Players), Apr 1959, Elsa Liebeck in Night Without Sleep; Lyric, Hammersmith, Oct 1959, Rebecca in Man on Trial; Globe (Repertory Players), Sept 1961, Catherine Costain in The Mimic; Northampton Repertory, Nov 1961, Lady Bracknell in The Importance of Being Earnest; at the Connaught, Worthing, Oct–Nov 1962, played the Dowager Lady Headleigh in The Claimant, and Mary Roberts in How Are You, Johnnie?; Connaught, Worthing, Sept 1964, Lettie Price in Twice Over Lightly; Theatre Royal, E, 15 May 1965, Hannah Trewin in Saint's Day; Pitlochry Festival, Apr–May 1967, played various parts in the repertoire, including: Mrs Candour in The School for Scandal, Mrs Gillie in Mrs Gillie and Lady Chavender in On the Rocks; in 1968, appeared in repertory at the Belgrade, Coventry; repertory at Colchester, 1974; with the National Theatre Company, 1975–6; toured, 1978, as the Archduchess Ferdinand in The Sleeping Prince; Belgrade Studio, Coventry, Nov 1978, played the Mother in Days in the Trees; her films include Esther Waters, and Victim.

Address: 7 Handel Street, London, WC1. *Tel:* 01–837 4767.

DIENER, Joan, actress, singer
b Cleveland, Ohio, 24 Feb; *e* Sarah Lawrence College; *m* Albert Marre.

Made her New York début at the Coronet, 15 Sept 1948, in the revue Small Wonder; Cort, Sept 1950, Deedy Barton in Season in the Sun; Music Circus, Sacremento, Calif, 1952, Kate in Kiss Me, Kate; Ziegfeld, Dec 1953, Lalume in Kismet; made her London début 20 Apr 1955, when she again played Lalume in Kismet; Shubert, Boston, Apr 1956, played in The Ziegfeld Follies; Philharmonic Auditorium, Los Angeles, July 1958, Isola Parelli in At the Grand, and repeated this part at the Curran, San Francisco, Sept 1958; Palladium, London, 1959, appeared in revue; in Italy and Germany, 1959–60, sang soprano roles in opera; Cambridge, Mass, Drama Festival, July 1960, sang in the opera La Belle Helene; summer stock, 1961, Frenchy in Destry Rides Again; toured, 1962, as Helen in La Belle, musical comedy version of La Belle Helene; Shubert, Philadelphia, Aug 1962, again played Helen in La Belle; ANTA, Washington Square, Nov 1965, Aldonza in Man of La Mancha; Ahmanson, Los Angeles, 1967 and Piccadilly, London, Apr 1968, again played Aldonza; Opera House, Brussels, and Champs-Elysées, Paris, 1968–9, Aldonza in a French version of Man of La Mancha; Broadhurst, Apr 1970, Kathleen Stanton in Cry for Us All; Vivian Beaumont, June 1972, again played Aldonza in a revival of Man of La Mancha; toured, Dec 1974–Jan 1976, as Penelope in Odyssey; Palace, Jan 1976, Penelope in Home Sweet Homer, retitled from Odyssey; at the Shaftesbury, London, Mar 1978, again played Lalume in the LA Civic Light Opera production of Kismet; has appeared frequently on television, notably in Androcles and the Lion, *Omnibus*, etc; has sung extensively on the operatic stage in the USA and Europe.

Address: c/o Floria Lasky, Fitelson and Mayers, 1212 Avenue of the Americas, New York, NY.

DIETRICH, Marlene (*née* Maria Magdalene von Losch), actress, singer, entertainer
b Schoenberg, Germany, 27 Dec 1900; *d* of Edward von Losch and his wife Josephine (Felsing); *e* Augusta Victoria School, Berlin Music Academy; *m* Rudolf Sieber; formerly a violinist; prepared for the stage with Max Reinhardt.

Commenced career in cabaret and on the stage in Berlin, appearing notably in the revue Es Liegt in die Luft, 1926; Berlin, 1926, appeared in Max Reinhardt's production of Broadway; at the Deutsche Theatre, Berlin, in 1928 appeared in Misalliance, also in the Max Reinhardt production; Berlin, 1929, appeared in the play Two Neckties; appeared in films from 1922 in Germany, including Manon Lescaut, A Modern DuBarry, Heads Up, Charley, all Germany 1926, the Imaginary Baron, His Greatest Bluff, and Cafe Electric, all Germany 1927, Princess Olala, 1928, The Woman One Longs For, The Ship of Lost Souls, Gefahren der Brautzeit, I Kiss Your Hand, Madame, and Der Blaue Engel (The Blue Angel), 1929; came to America to make films and remained in Hollywood for many years; during World War II toured extensively, entertaining Allied troops in Europe and at military bases throughout the world; commenced a career in cabaret in 1950, and has since concertized all over the world, including the Cafe de Paris, London, 1954, Rio de Janeiro, Paris, Berlin, Rome, Holland, Israel, Germany, South Africa, Australia, Russia, etc; made her London legitimate theatre début at the Queen's, 23 Nov 1964, in her show Marlene Dietrich; again toured, then made her New York début at the Lunt-Fontanne, 9 Oct 1967, in her one-woman show; Mark Hellinger, NY, Oct 1968, again appeared in her one-woman show; received a special Antoinette Perry (Tony) Award, 1968; since then has toured extensively, notably appearing in Viareggio, Italy, Apr 1972, on a tour of England and Wales, May–June 1973, including an appearance at the Queen's, London, 13 May 1972; appeared at the Espace Cardin, Paris, July 1973 and again in Sept 1973; toured America and Canada, appearing in Montreal, Toronto, Los Angeles, Washington, DC, etc, Nov–Dec 1973; July 1974, performed at the Candlewood, New Fairfield, Conn; Grosvenor House, London, Sept 1974, appeared in her one-woman show; Fairmont, Atlanta, Georgia, May 1975, appeared in her show; toured Australia for the third time in Sept 1975; among the many Hollywood films she has made are Morocco, 1930, Shanghai Express, 1932, The Scarlet Empress, 1934, Destry Rides Again, 1939, Kismet, 1944, Golden Earrings, 1947, A Foreign Affair, 1948, Witness for the Prosecution, 1957, Judgment at Nurenberg, 1962, etc; performed her one-woman show on television in the USA and in London in 1973; received the Medal of Freedom for her efforts in World War II; also Officer de la Legion d'Honneur of France; author of Marlene Dietrich's ABC's.

DIETZ, Howard, lyricist and playwright
b New York City, 8 Sept 1896; *s* of Herman Dietz and his wife Julia (Blumberg); *e* Columbia University; *m* (1) Elizabeth Hall; (2) Tanis Guinness Montagu; (3) Lucinda Goldsborough Ballard; formerly engaged in journalism and advertising; during World War I, served in US Navy.

Director of publicity for the Metro-Goldwyn-Mayer Picture Corporation, 1924–57; wrote lyrics for Dear Sir, 1924; Merry-Go-Round, 1927; author of The Little Show, lyrics of The Grand Street Follies of 1929, 1929; Here Comes the Bride (with Arthur Schwartz, London), lyrics of Garrick Gaieties, Second Little Show, Three's a Crowd, 1930; The Band Wagon (with George S Kaufman), 1931; Flying Colors (also produced and directed), 1932; Revenge with Music, 1934; At Home Abroad, 1935; Follow the Sun, lyrics for The Show Is On, 1936; Between the Devil (with Arthur Schwartz), 1937; lyrics for Keep Off the Grass, 1940; Dancing in the Streets (with John Cecil Holm and Matt Taylor), 1943; Jackpot, Tars and Spars (also produced), Sadie Thompson, 1944; Inside USA, 1948; the Metropolitan Opera version of Die Fledermaus in English (with Garson Kanin),

1950; a new English version of La Bohème, 1953; Ziegfeld Follies (in part), 1957; The Gay Life (with Arthur Schwartz), 1961; Jennie (with Arthur Schwartz), 1963; That's Entertainment, with Arthur Schwartz, 1972; at the Kaufman Auditorium, 3 Nov 1974, appeared in the series Lyrics and Lyricists; author of more than 1000 lyrics; author of his autobiography Dancing in the Dark, 1974; member of the Board of Directors, and Vice-President in Charge of Advertising and Publicity, of Loew's Inc, 1961; served on the Board of Directors of ASCAP, 1948–62.

Address: 180 East End Avenue, New York, NY 10028.

DIGNAM, Mark, actor

b Ealing, London, 20 Mar 1909; *s* of Edmund Grattan Dignam, OBE, and his wife Agnes Mary (Sheen); *e* King Edward VII School, Sheffield, Mount St Mary's College, and Neuchatel; *m* (1) Georgia MacKinnon (mar dis); (2) Helen Christie (mar dis); (3) Virginia Kirby; formerly engaged in journalism; studied for the stage as an amateur with the Sheffield Repertory Company.

Made his first appearance on the professional stage at the County Theatre, St Albans, 1930, in The Lonely House; in 1931, joined the Ben Greet Company, touring the English provinces; first appearance on the London stage, Kingsway Theatre, 18 Apr 1932, as the Bleeding Sergeant in Macbeth; Royalty, Dec 1932, played Adam Veryard in A Cup of Happiness, touring in the same part, 1933; at the Alhambra, London, Jan 1934, played Gloucester in Henry V; Playhouse, Apr 1934, George Hemsby in Libel!; Arts, Dec 1934, Donado in 'Tis Pity She's a Whore; and Mar 1935, Henry Armiger in Swords for Utopia; Ambassadors', Mar 1935, Strength in Everyman; Old Vic, Apr 1935, Bernardo in Hamlet; Jan–Sept 1936, with the Croydon Repertory Company; also appearing at the Royalty, Feb 1936, as Mantius in Catiline; and Arts, June 1936, as Nicholas Dalziel in Rain Before Seven; Westminster, Nov 1936–July 1937, played Relling in The Wild Duck, Justin O'Connell in Waste, Prof Weissmann in Crooked Cross, Serebryakov in Uncle Vanya, Boss Mangan in Heartbreak House, Johnny the Priest in Anna Christie, Schaaf in A Month in the Country, and the Ghost and First Player in Hamlet; at the Old Vic, Sept–Nov 1937, Colonel Pickering in Pygmalion, Provost in Measure for Measure and Buckingham in Richard III; Westminster, Nov 1937–June 1938, Ezra Mannon in Mourning Becomes Electra, Voltore in Volpone, Henry of York in The Zeal of Thy House, Bohun, QC, in You Never Can Tell and Zhevakin in Marriage; made his first appearance on the New York Stage, at the Fulton Theatre, 10 Oct 1938, as Mr E H Carson in Oscar Wilde; returning to England, appeared at the Westminster Theatre, Oct 1939–Apr 1940, as Charles Bendrex in Music at Night; Bill Walker in Major Barbara, and Ephraim Cabot in Desire Under the Elms; toured with the Old Vic Company in Wales, 1940–1, as Banquo in Macbeth, and McCarthy in The Time of Your Life; served in HM Forces, June 1941–Dec 1944, as a signaller in the Royal Artillery; was wounded at Anzio, and invalided out, Dec 1944; reappeared on the stage at the Arts Theatre, Mar 1945, as Pra in The Simpleton of the Unexpected Isles; at the Arts Theatre, Cambridge, June 1945, played Claudius in Hamlet; Arts Theatre Festival, London, from Sept 1945, played The Bishop in Getting Married, James Mortimore in The Thunderbolt, and Claudius in Hamlet; Arts, Mar 1946, Dr Wangel in The Lady from the Sea, and Apr 1946, Mr Robinson in Exercise Bowler; Piccadilly, Dec 1946, Agrippa in Antony and Cleopatra; Strand, June 1947, Harrison North in Angel; Edinburgh Festival, Aug 1947, played John of Gaunt in Richard II, and Baptista in The Taming of the Shrew; then

joined the Old Vic company, at the New Theatre, and from 1947 to 1950 played, among other parts, Baptista in The Taming of the Shrew, John of Gaunt in Richard II, Peter Cauchon in St Joan, Sicinius in Coriolanus, Malvolio in Twelfth Night, Petulant in The Way of the World, Lopahin in The Cherry Orchard, Holofernes in Love's Labour's Lost, Ignaty in A Month in the Country, Seigneur Anselm in The Miser, and Claudius in Hamlet, which he also played in Elsinore Castle; at the re-opening of the Old Vic, Nov 1950, appeared as the Sea Captain in Twelfth Night, and later in the season as Zeal-of-the-Land Busy in Bartholomew Fair, Exeter in Henry V, Sir Howard Hallam in Captain Brassbound's Conversion, and Sir Hugh Evans in The Merry Wives of Windsor; toured, Autumn, 1951, in His Excellency; Winter Garden, Jan 1952, played Seti the Second in The Firstborn; Arts, Sept 1952, Dean Harry Kennedy in Two Loves I Have . . .; Embassy, Nov 1952, Col Ritter von und zu Ruppertshausen in High Balcony; Arts, Dec 1952, William Corder in Maria Marten; Embassy, Feb 1953, played Izzy in Five Philadelphia Physicians; Westminster, July 1953, Major H Maunsell in Carrington, VC; Embassy, Jan 1955, The Presiding Angel and The Principal in The World of Sholom Aleichem; Apollo, Nov 1955, appeared as Consalvo in Summertime; joined the Shakespeare Memorial Theatre Company, Stratford-on-Avon, Apr 1956, and remained in that company for three seasons, playing the following parts: Ghost in Hamlet, Morocco in The Merchant of Venice, Duke of Venice in Othello, Provost in Measure For Measure, and Holofernes in Love's Labour's Lost, 1956; Christmas, 1956, played Badger in a revival of Toad of Toad Hall, also at the Memorial Theatre; Shakespeare Memorial Company, 1957, played Duke Frederick in As You Like It, Pandulph in King John, Casca in Julius Caesar, Pisanio in Cymbeline, and Antonio in The Tempest, also appearing with the company in the last production, Drury Lane, Dec 1957; Shakespeare Memorial Company, 1958, played Capulet in Romeo and Juliet, Malvolio in Twelfth Night, Claudius in Hamlet, and Simonides in Pericles; appeared with the Stratford company on their visit to Moscow and Leningrad, Nov and Dec 1958; Royal Court, London, Nov 1959, played Mr Kroll in Rosmersholm, transferring with the production to the Comedy, Jan 1960; Haymarket, May 1960, Auda Abu Tayi in Ross, which ran for over 700 performances; Ashcroft, Croydon, Feb 1963, played Humphrey Craik in The Poison Tree; toured, Sept 1963, as Mr James Formal in The Gentleman Dancing Master; Queen's, Mar 1964, Shamrayev in The Seagull; at the same theatre, June 1964, played Graham in Saint Joan of the Stockyards; Duke of York's, Sept 1964, Edgar in A Scent of Flowers; Lyceum, Edinburgh, Sept 1966, Alexander in A Present for the Past; Oxford Playhouse, Dec 1966, Mr Hardcastle in She Stoops to Conquer, and Feb 1967, the General in The Balcony; Queen's, Nov 1967, the Vicar in Halfway Up the Tree; Roundhouse, Mar 1969, and Lunt Fontanne, NY, May 1969, Polonius in Hamlet; Duchess, Feb 1970, Courcy, Croissy and Canavo in The Hallelujah Boy; Greenwich, Nov 1970, the Father in A Voyage Round My Father; Piccadilly, 1971, took over the part of Cecil in Vivat!, Vivat Regina!; joined the RSC, season 1972, to play Menenius in Coriolanus, Caesar in Julius Caesar and Marcus Andronicus in Titus Andronicus at Stratford, and again at the Aldwych, 1973; Aldwych, Feb 1974, Maurice Shanklin in Duck Song; May 1974, same theatre, Philip IV and Valladares in The Bewitched; for the National Theatre at the Old Vic, 1974, played Barry in The Freeway, Oct, and Gen Mercier in Grand Manoeuvres, Dec; Greenwich, July 1978, Nat in Hindle Wakes; Aldwych (RSC), Sept 1978, played Vladimir in Cousin Vladimir; Olivier, Dec 1979, for National

Theatre, Old Werk in The Wild Duck, and, Mar 1980, the Duke of Venice in Othello; has appeared in numerous radio plays, and recent television performances include The Sea, Hess, Disraeli, The XYY Man, and Suez; has also appeared in films, most notably in The Charge of the Light Brigade, Hamlet, Dead Cert, David, the Lion of Judah, etc.

Recreation: Swimming. *Address:* c/o London Management, 235–241 Regent Street, London, W1.

DISHY, Bob, actor.
b Brooklyn; *e* Syracuse University, NY.

Made his New York début when he joined the cast of Damn Yankees, 46th Street, 1956, as Rocky; appeared at the Orpheum, May 1959, in the revue Chic; Plymouth, Apr 1960, appeared in the revue From A to Z; toured, 1960–1, in the revue Medium Rare; Theatre Marquee, Feb 1961, played Charlie Paal in Molnar's There Is a Play Tonight; Happy Medium, Chicago, 1962, again played in Medium Rare; same theatre, June 1962, played in the revue Put It in Writing; Second City at Square East, New York, Sept 1963, appeared in the improvisational revue When the Owl Screams; Square East, Jan 1964, appeared in the improvisational revue Open Season at Second City; in Apr 1964 appeared in the improvisational revue The Wrecking Ball; Alvin, May 1965, played Harry Toukarian in Flora, The Red Menace; Theatre Four, Jan 1967, Sapiens in By Jupiter; Vivian Beaumont, July 1967, Inventor in The Unknown Soldier and His Wife; Cort, Nov 1967, Sheldon Bud Nemerov in Something Different; Ethel Barrymore, Dec 1968, Arthur Korman in The Goodbye People; ANTA, Jan 1969, took over from Elliott Gould as Alex Krieger in A Way of Life; Shubert, Nov 1972, Adam in The Creation of the World and Other Business; Circle in the Square, Apr 1974, Arnold Brody in An American Millionaire; Broadhurst, Dec 1976, Abner Truckle in Sly Fox; John Golden, May 1979, Paul Miller in Murder at the Howard Johnson's; films include Lovers and Other Strangers; TV since That Was the Week That Was includes Story Theater (also a director) and appearances in series such as Columbo, etc.

Address: 20 E 9th Street, New York, NY 10003.

DOBIE, Alan, actor
b Wombwell, 2 June 1932; *m* (1) Rachel Roberts (mar dis); (2) Maureen Scott.

Began his career at the Old Vic, Sept 1952, when he played Paris' Page in Romeo and Juliet, remaining as a member of the company to play Young Cato in Julius Caesar, First Priest in Murder in the Cathedral, and Sir Thomas Lovell in the Coronation production of Henry VIII, May 1953; joined the Bristol Old Vic Company, Sept 1953, where he played, among other parts: Firs in The Cherry Orchard, Ralph in The Shoemaker's Holiday, and The Tramp in the original production of Salad Days; returned to the Old Vic, Sept 1954, to play Seyton in Macbeth, Tranio in The Taming of the Shrew, Silvius in As You Like It, Henry Percy in Richard II, and Prince John in Henry VI; Bristol Old Vic season, 1955–6, played a number of leading parts including: King of the Ondines in Ondine, Mosca in Volpone, the Fool in King Lear, Robespierre in The Empty Chair, Captain Brazen in The Recruiting Officer, and Iago in Othello; toured, 1957, as Jimmy Porter in Look Back in Anger; at the Royal Court, Aug 1958, played Bill Walker in Major Barbara; at the same theatre, Sept 1958, played Col in Live Like Pigs; Westminster, Nov 1958, played Bernard Ross in No Concern of Mine; Lyric, Hammersmith, June 1959, played Capt Morgan in The Rough and the Ready Lot; Royal Court, Oct 1959, Private Hurst in Sergeant Musgrave's Dance; Comedy, Jan 1960,

took over the part of Ulric Brendel in Rosmersholm; Royal Court, Mar 1960, Halford in One Leg Over The Wrong Wall in a Production without Décor; Queen's, Aug 1970, played Louis Flax in The Tiger and the Horse; Royal Court, Dec 1960, appeared in a programme entitled Song in the Theatre; at the Ludlow Festival, June 1961, played the title part in Macbeth; Strand, Sept 1961, Donald Howard in The Affair; at the Edinburgh Festival, Aug 1962, played Becket in Curtmantle, subsequently appearing in repertory in the same production at the Aldwych, London, Oct 1962; at the same theatre, Oct 1962, played Prince Henry in The Devils, also in repertory; Royal Court, Aug 1963, played Corporal Hill in Chips With Everything, subsequently making his first appearance in New York at the Plymouth Theatre, Oct 1963, in the same production; Embassy, Aug 1965, in a Production without Décor, played Richard Blackwell in The World's Baby; Wyndham's, Oct 1965, took over Bill Maitland in Inadmissible Evidence; Oxford Playhouse, Sept 1966, played Mosca in Volpone; Hampstead Theatre Club, Nov 1966, Oswald in The Silence of Lee Harvey Oswald; Mermaid, Mar 1967, Captain Delano in Benito Cereno; Royal Court, Nov 1969, John Connor in Famine; Duchess, Feb 1970, Henri Perrin in The Hallelujah Boy; Royal Lyceum, Edinburgh, May 1970, played Tom in Mister; Mermaid, Dec 1970, Ludovic Bavvel in The Watched Pot; Greenwich, Feb 1971, played the title-role in Macbeth; Manitoba Theatre Centre, Winnipeg, Feb 1973, title-role in Hamlet; Belgrade, Coventry, Nov 1973, Professor Thorn in Assault with a Deadly Weapon; for the Bristol Old Vic Company at the Theatre Royal, 1974, he played George Moore in Jumpers, Higgins in Pygmalion, Martin Dysart in Equus, Frederick Walton in The Arrest; toured South Africa, 1975, as Martin Dysart; St George's, summer 1977, played Hamlet, Angelo in Measure for Measure, Falstaff in The Merry Wives of Windsor, Birmingham Rep and Edinburgh Festival, summer 1978, played Prospero in The Tempest and Bottom in A Midsummer Night's Dream; TV appearances include War and Peace, The Trial of Sinyavsky and Daniel, and as Sergeant Cribb; recent films include The White Bird.

Address: c/o Vernon Conway, 248 Lavender Hill, London SW11 1JW.

DODD, Ken, comedian
b Knotty Ash, Liverpool, 8 Nov 1929; *s* of Arthur Dodd and his wife Sarah (Gray); *e* Knotty Ash Village School, and Holt High School, Liverpool; formerly a travelling tinker.

Made his first appearance on the stage in variety at the Empire Theatre, Nottingham, Sept 1954; between 1956–64, appeared in summer variety shows in Blackpool, Great Yarmouth, Torquay, Bournemouth, etc; Coventry, Christmas, 1960, appeared in The Pied Piper of Hamelin; at the Opera House, Manchester, Christmas, 1961–2, and at the Royal Court, Liverpool, Christmas, 1963–4, starred in The Ken Dodd Show; made his first appearance in London at the Palladium, Apr 1965, in Doddy's Here; Liverpool Playhouse, Nov 1971, played Malvolio in their Diamond Jubliee production, Twelfth Night; has starred in pantomime in Birmingham, Blackpool and Manchester; he has appeared regularly on television and radio, both in variety and in his own series, such as Ken Dodd's World of Laughter.

Favourite part: The Pied Piper in The Pied Piper of Hamelin. *Recreations:* Script writing, racing, football. *Address:* 76 Thomas Lane, Knotty Ash, Liverpool.

DODIMEAD, David, actor
b Shepton Mallet, Som, 8 Apr 1919; *s* of Hedley Douglas Cox Dodimead and his wife Muriel (Weller); *e* Wells Cathedral School.

First professional appearance, Castle, Rochester, Nov 1937, as Marchbanks in Candida; after war service, spent two years with Donald Wolfit's company, 1946–8, touring Britain and North America and playing seasons at the Savoy, Apr 1947, and Westminster, May 1948; parts during this period included Don Pedro in Much Ado About Nothing, Albany in King Lear; played in repertory, 1948–51, at Coventry, Birmingham and Salisbury; Feb 1952, joined the company at the Memorial Theatre, Stratford, to play Ross in Macbeth and Oliver in As You Like It; Dec 1952, appeared in John Gielgud's season at the Lyric, Hammersmith, as Scroop in Richard II, and, May 1953, as Duke of Venice in Venice Preserved; 1953–5, repertory at Hornchurch; May 1955, toured Australia with the Old Vic, as Antonio in The Merchant of Venice and Vincentio in The Taming of the Shrew; Arts, Mar 1956, Aegeon in a musical version of The Comedy of Errors; Sept 1958, rejoined the Old Vic, where he played for two seasons; his parts included Antonio in The Merchant of Venice, Horatio in Hamlet, and Cranmer in Henry VIII; toured N America with the company, 1958, as Horatio and the King of France in Henry V; Mermaid, Livesey in Treasure Island, Dec 1959, and Exeter in Henry V, Feb 1960; toured extensively with the Old Vic, 1961–2; Arts, Mar 1963, Ademar de Gratignan in Divorce à la Carte; Savoy, May 1963, Lewis Eliot in The Masters; toured Europe with the Bristol Old Vic, 1964; Germany with the Birmingham Rep, 1965; 1965–7, played Bernard Shaw in Dear Liar, visiting over twenty countries; Mermaid, June 1967, Stan Brady in Rafferty's Chant; repertory at Edinburgh, Lyceum, 1968, followed by Nottingham Playhouse; played several leading parts here, including Sir Charles Gurney in The Ruling Class, which transferred to the Piccadilly, Feb 1969, Sir William Hamilton in The Hero Rises Up (also Edinburgh Festival, Sept 1969), Gloucester in King Lear and Subtle in The Alchemist; both the latter plays were presented at the Old Vic, Feb 1970; Manitoba Theatre Centre, Winnipeg, Nov 1970, James Tyrone in Long Day's Journey Into Night; toured, May 1971, as David Bliss in Hay Fever, with the Cambridge Theatre Company; Winnipeg, 1971, White Knight in Alice Through the Looking Glass; Mermaid, Oct 1971, took over as Mr Nox in The Old Boys; appearances in 1972 included Harpagon in The Miser, Neptune Theatre, Halifax, Nova Scotia, and Menelaus in Helen at the Phoenix, Leicester; Marlowe, Canterbury, 1973, played Osborne in Journey's End; Arnaud, Guildford, Aug 1973, Harry in The Collection; Chichester, Dec 1973, Dr Livesey in Treasure Island; Open Air, Regent's Park, 1974, played Theseus in A Midsummer Night's Dream, June and Theseus in The Two Noble Kinsmen, July; Greenwich, Sept 1974, Benjamin Tenard in More Stately Mansions; toured Asia in the same year as First Player and Grave Digger in Hamlet and The Player in Rosencrantz and Guildenstern are Dead; again played The Player at the Young Vic, Feb 1975, and repeated the part of Theseus in A Midsummer Night's Dream at the Open Air Theatre; toured South Africa, 1975, in the anthology Shakespeare's People, followed by tours of the Americas, Europe and New Zealand, 1976–8; has appeared in films including Julius Caesar (1970); has appeared on TV in Britain and N America, including the BBC serials The Black Tulip and Crime and Punishment.

Favourite parts: Subtle, Volpone and Toad. *Recreations:* Travelling, swimming, beachcombing. *Address:* 16 Melbury Road, London W14 8LT. *Tel:* 01–602 3313.

DONLAN, Yolande, actress
b Jersey City, NJ; *d* of James Donlan and his wife Theresa (Mollot); *e* Immaculate Heart Convent, Hollywood; *m* (1) Philip Truex (mar dis); (2) Val Guest.

Made her first appearance on the stage at the Los Angeles Philharmonic Auditorium, June 1938, as Julie in New Moon; and in the following month, appeared there in Roberta; at Los Angeles, Jan 1939, appeared in Earl Carroll Vanities; Blackstone Theatre, Chicago, June 1942, played in Goodnight Ladies, which ran for a year; made her first appearance in New York, at the Royale Theatre, 1 Aug 1944, as Julie Kent in School for Brides; at the Lakewood Theatre, Maine, July 1945, played in Kiss and Tell, Three's a Family, Over 21; at Boston, Mass, Sept 1946, played Billie Dawn in Born Yesterday; made her first appearance in London, at the Garrick Theatre, 23 Jan 1947, in the same part; St Martin's, Mar 1948, appeared as Cleo Singer in Rocket to the Moon; Strand, June 1948, played Lucrece in Cage Me a Peacock; Savoy, Nov 1950, Myrtle in To Dorothy, A Son; Vaudeville, Apr 1953, Surrey Smith in Red-Headed Blonde; Harrow Coliseum and Golders Green Hippodrome, Oct 1954, Joyce Carpenter in It's Different for Men; Aldwych, Mar 1957, the title part in Olive Ogilvie; Olympia, Dublin, May 1958, played Lizzie in The Rainmaker; Duke of York's, Nov 1959, Joy Lucas in And Suddenly It's Spring; toured, Sept 1965, as Slumtrimpet in Dear Wormwood; toured, May 1971 as Lotte in Chorus of Murder; Theatre Royal, Windsor, Mar 1972, played Mrs Shubert in Cut Throat; films include Expresso Bongo, The Adventurers, Seven Nights in Japan, etc; is the author of Sand in My Mink, 1955, Third Time Lucky, 1976, and Shake the Stars Down, 1977.

Recreations: Sketching, ballet, music, tennis. *Address:* c/o British Actors' Equity, 8 Harley Street, London W1.

DONLEAVY, J P, author and playwright
b New York, 23 Apr 1926; *s* of Patrick J. Donleavy and his wife Margaret (Walsh); *e* NY, and Trinity College, Dublin; *m* (1) Valerie Heron (mar dis); (2) Mary Wilson Price.

Author of the following: The Ginger Man (novel) 1955, (play) 1961; Fairytales of New York (play) 1960; A Singular Man (novel) 1963, (play) 1964; The Saddest Summer of Samuel S. (novella) 1966, (play) 1967; and of the novels: The Beastly Beatitudes of Balthazar B, 1968; The Onion Eaters, 1971; A Fairytale of New York, 1973; The Destinies of Darcy Darey, Gentleman, 1977; Schulz, 1980; The Ginger Man and Fairy Tales of New York have both been televised; received the *Evening Standard* Award for the Most Promising Playwright of 1960 for his play Fairy Tales of New York.

Address: Levington Park, Mullingar, Co Westmeath, Eire.

DONNELL, Patrick, theatre administrator
b Londonderry, Northern Ireland, 12 July 1916; *s* of William Edgar Marshall Donnell and his wife Florence (Gardiner); *e* Campbell College, Belfast; *m* (1) Mary Carolyn John (mar dis); (2) Floy Ellen Bell; from 1935–8, held a commission in the Royal Marines, but resigned, 1939, when he entered stage management.

For one year was engaged at the Gate and Gaiety Theatres, Dublin, and also at the Festival Theatre, Cambridge, where he occasionally played small parts; re-joined the Royal Marines as Lieutenant, 1940, subsequently being promoted to Lieut-Colonel, and commanded 47 (RM) Commando; awarded the DSO and also the Croix de Guerre; following demobilization, 1946, he joined the firm of H M Tennent, Ltd, as stage manager, subsequently Company Manager; joined the Shakespeare Memorial Theatre, Stratford-on-Avon, 1949; appointed General Manager, 1958; Administrator for the Barbican Theatre, 1967–71; Administrative Director, National Theatre, 1971–4; Associate Director, 1975–7; RSC Adviser for the Barbican Theatre.

Recreations: Theatre, canals, fishing. *Address:* 48 Carlisle Mansions, Carlisle Place, London, SW1.

DONNELLY, Donal, actor
b Bradford, Yorks, 6 July 1931; *s* of Dr James Donnelly and

his wife Nora (O'Connor); *e* Synge Street Christian Brothers School, Dublin; *m* Patsy Porter; trained for the stage at the Gate, Dublin.

Made his first professional appearance at the Gate, 1952, as Robin in Dr Faustus; made his first London appearance at the Royal Court, Oct 1959, as Sparky in Serjeant Musgrave's Dance; Piccadilly, Oct 1960, and St Martin's, Nov 1960, played Christy Mahon in The Playboy of the Western World; Theatre Royal, Stratford, April 1962, Jemmo Fitzgerald in The Scatterin'; Mermaid, Sept 1962, Ayamonn Breydon in Red Roses for Me; Helen Hayes, Feb 1966, made his New York début as Gareth O'Donnell (in private) in Philadelphia, Here I Come, repeating his performance at the Lyric, London, Sept 1967; Brooks Atkinson, NY, 1968, took over Bri in Joe Egg; Royale, NY, Dec 1969, directed The Mundy Scheme; St Martin's, London, Sept 1970, took over as Milo Tindle in Sleuth, also at the Music Box, NY, and Ahmanson, LA, 1972; repeated this performance in Britain (Malvern) and Europe, at the Astor Place, Jan 1978, and on tour in the US; toured the US, 1978, in The Last of Mrs Cheyney; Longacre, Apr 1979, Teddy in Faith Healer; Dublin Festival, 1976, appeared in a one-man show, My Astonishing Self; films include The Knack, The Mind of Mr Soames, and Waterloo; has appeared on television in plays including Juno and the Paycock, The Plough and the Stars and the series *Yes Honestly*.

Favourite parts: Christy Mahon, Gareth O'Donnell.
Recreations: Fulham FC, Dublin mountains and children.
Address: c/o Lionel Larner Ltd, 850 7th Avenue, New York, NY 10019.

DONNER, Clive, director
b London, 21 Jan 1926; *s* of Alex Donner and his wife Deborah (Taffel); *m* Jocelyn Rickards.

Directed his first production, The Formation Dancers, Arts Theatre, London, 18 Mar 1964; subsequent productions include: Twelfth Night, 1970, The Birthday Party, 1971 (both Nottingham); The Front Room Boys (Royal Court),1971; The Homecoming (Nottingham), 1972; Kennedy's Children, 1974; The Picture of Dorian Gray (Greenwich), Kennedy's Children (New York début, John Golden Theatre), 1975; started in films as an assistant film editor in 1942; films he has directed include: The Caretaker, Nothing But the Best, What's New Pussycat, and Alfred the Great; has directed television documentaries for BBC and ITV.
Address: c/o William Morris Agency, 147–149 Wardour Street, London W1. *Tel:* 01–286 7170.

DONOHUE, Jack, actor, director, dancer, choreographer
b New York City, 3 Nov 1908; *s* of John Donohue and his wife Helen (Ling); *e* Regis High School, NYC, and St Anne's Military Academy; *m* Tutta Rolf (mar dis); formerly a brokerage clerk and a riveter.

Made his NY stage début at the New Amsterdam, 16 Aug 1927, as a dancer in Ziegfeld Follies; Palm Gardens, 10 Sept 1927, appeared as a solo dancer in vaudeville; 46th St, 1928, danced in Good News; 46th St, Jan 1929, danced in Follow Through; Broadhurst, Jan 1931, in America's Sweetheart; George M Cohan, July 1931, in Shoot the Works; Manhattan, Sept 1931, in Free for All; choreographed Smiling Faces at the Shubert, Aug 1932; Alvin, Nov 1932, choreographed Music in the Air; Shubert, July 1933, appeared in and choreographed Shady Lady; made his London début at Drury Lane, 8 Sept 1933, as choreographer for Ball at the Savoy; Savoy, Nov 1933, choreographed Please!; Hippodrome, Feb 1934, choreographed Mr Whittington; made his London

stage début at the Saville, 22 Feb 1934, as Tim Regan in Here's How! which he also choreographed; Palace, London, Feb 1937, played Konstantine Morrosine in On Your Toes, and transferred with it to the Coliseum, Apr 1937; Strand, Nov 1937, played Steve in The Bowery Touch; Prince's, Apr 1938, Val in Wild Oats, and Aug 1939, Jimmy Gay in Sitting Pretty; Chat Noir, Oslo, Norway, 1940, appeared in revue; Folkan, Stockholm, Sweden, 1940, appeared in the revue Vita Plostrot; returned to USA and in St Louis, Missouri, 1940–1, at the Municipal Opera Company, directed and appeared in a dozen musicals, including: Denikov in Balalaika; Shubert, NY, 1940, appeared in Higher and Higher; 46th St, 1941, took over as Mike in Panama Hattie; Ziegfeld, Oct 1944, danced in and directed Seven Lively Arts; Century, Nov 1945, choreographed Are You with It?; Winter Garden, Nov 1951, directed Top Banana; Ziegfeld, May 1952, choreographed Of Thee I Sing; Curran, San Francisco, Aug 1952, directed Jollyana; Broadway, Mar 1956, directed Mr Wonderful; Alvin, Nov 1957, directed Rumple; Dorothy Chandler Pavilion, Los Angeles, Cal, May 1973, directed Oliver; has had a long career in films, as dance director for the Shirley Temple films, 1935–6, for George White's Scandals, Bathing Beauty, Music in the Air, all 1934, and Louisiana Purchase, 1941, Star-Spangled Rhythm, 1941, The Fleet's In, 1942, Girl Crazy, 1943, Anchors Aweigh, 1945, Calamity Jane, 1953, Babes in Toyland, 1961, directed Marriage on the Rocks, 1965, Assault on a Queen, 1966, etc; has directed numerous television productions, including the *Frank Sinatra Show*, the *Dean Martin Show*, the *Red Skelton Show*, and many specials.
Recreations: Horseback riding, boxing, sailing, water skiing. *Address:* 14155 Magnolia Boulevard, Van Nuys, Cal.

DORÉ, Alexander, director and actor
b Hampstead, London, 28 Aug 1923; *s* of Michael Doré and his wife Krikune (Luboff); *e* Kent College, Canterbury; *m* Edna Doré; formerly a schoolteacher.

Directed his first production, Murder Without Crime, at the Little, Aberystwyth, 1949; spent a period in rep, including five years as resident director at Leicester and two at Richmond; his first London production was Goodnight Mrs Puffin, July 1961; his first New York production was The Sunday Man, May 1964; he has since directed, in London unless otherwise stated, See How They Run, 1964; King Lear (Maynardville, South Africa) 1965; Big Bad Mouse, 1966; Dear Charles, 1968; Mixed Doubles, Pyjama Tops (also Australia and NZ), 1969; Caesar and Cleopatra (S Africa), 1970; Come When You Like, Bunny, 1972; Swap (tour), Pyjama Tops (tour), Robinson Crusoe (Cardiff), 1973; The Other Side of the Room, 1975; Lady Harry, 1978; has directed a number of productions in Holland; has appeared as an actor in the West End, as well as films and frequently on TV notably in the series Bright's Boffins; wrote the films The Wind of Change and Jungle Street.
Recreations: Will go anywhere to watch cricket or athletics.
Address: c/o Eric Glass Ltd, 28 Berkeley Square, London W1X 6HD. *Tel:* 01–629 7162.

DOSSOR, Alan, director
b Hull, 19 Sept 1941; *s* of Frederick Charles Dossor and his wife Anne (Lesley); *e* Bristol University; *m* Dinah Dossor (mar dis); trained for the stage at Bristol Old Vic Theatre School.

Started his stage career as an actor at Nottingham Playhouse, 1965–68, during this time directing his first productions, Mother Courage and Bread and Butter; worked for

two years at Newcastle, Sheffield, Edinburgh, Liverpool and Bolton, prior to becoming Artistic Director of the Everyman Theatre, Liverpool, 1970–75; there his productions included classics and plays by C G Bond, Henry Livings, John Mc-Grath, Adrian Mitchell, Brian Patten, Willy Russell, Mike Stott, C P Taylor, Ted Whitehead and Charles Wood; directed his first play in London at the Lyric, Aug, 1974, with John, Paul, George, Ringo . . . and Bert, and subsequent productions are as follows: Funny Peculiar (Garrick), 1976; Breezeblock Park (Whitehall), 1977; Flying Blind (Royal Court), Comings and Goings (Hampstead), 1978; Normal Service (Hampstead), Hotel Paradiso (tour), Bitter Apples (tour), 1979; Liberty Hall (Greenwich), Rose (re-opening of the Duke of York's), 1980; television direction includes the first series of *Don't Forget to Write* and *Pickersgill People.*
Address: 114 Lordship Road, London N16.

DOTRICE, Roy, actor
b Guernsey, Channel Islands, 26 May 1925; *s* of Louis Dotrice and his wife Neva (Wilton); *e* Dayton Academy; *m* Kay Newman; started acting while a prisoner-of-war in Stalagluft 3, Silesia, Germany in the Second World War.

Made his first appearance in the theatre, 1945, in a revue called Back Home, performed by ex-prisoners-of-war, in aid of the Red Cross; from 1945–55 played in a number of repertory theatres including: Liverpool, Manchester, Oldham, etc; in 1955, formed the Guernsey Repertory Theatre Company, where he directed and appeared in the permanent company until 1957; joined the Shakespeare Memorial Theatre Company, July 1958, becoming a long-term-contract player (re-named the Royal Shakespeare Company) in 1961; among the many parts he has played for the Royal Shakespeare Company are included: Egeus in A Midsummer Night's Dream, Duke of Burgundy in King Lear, 1959; Vincentio in The Taming of the Shrew, Antenor in Troilus and Cressida, 1960; Father Ambrose in The Devils, Firs in The Cherry Orchard, 1961; Simon Chachava in The Caucasian Chalk Circle, William Marshall in Curtmantle, Ajax in Troilus and Cressida, 1961; Caliban in The Tempest, the title-part in Julius Caesar, Duke of Bedford in Henry VI, Edward in Edward IV, and Edward IV in Richard III, in the triology of The Wars of the Roses, 1963; at the Aldwych Theatre, Jan 1964, again played the same parts in The Wars of the Roses; Royal Shakespeare, 1964 season, John of Gaunt in Richard II, Hotspur in Henry IV (Part I), and Shallow in Henry IV (Part II); repeating his performances in The Wars of the Roses; Aldwych, July 1965, played Jan Puntila in Squire Puntila and His Servant Matti; Aldwych, Oct 1965, appeared in a concert reading, The Investigation; Hampstead Theatre Club, Jan 1967, appeared as John Aubrey in the one-man production Brief Lives; New, Apr 1967, Man in World War 2½; first appearance on Broadway, at the John Golden, Dec 1967, again in Brief Lives; returned to the Royal Shakespeare Company at the Aldwych, Sept 1968, to play John Morley in The Latent Heterosexual and William Clark Brackman in God Bless; Criterion, Feb 1969, again appeared as Aubrey in Brief Lives, this time for a run of 213 performances, a world record for a one-man show; has since continued to give this performance world-wide; Chichester Festival, May 1970, Peer in Peer Gynt; Lyceum, Edinburgh, Oct 1970, Matthew Cragg in The Hero; Royal Court, Apr 1971, James Blanch in One At Night; Arts, Nov 1971, Adam in Mother Adam; Cambridge Theatre, May 1972, Dr Arnold in Tom Brown's Schooldays; toured Australia, autumn 1972, in Move Over Mrs Markham; Queen's, Nov 1973, played Gomes in the play of that name; toured, Oct 1976, as Oliver Crown in Lucy Crown; toured, Apr 1977, as Sir Anthony

Eden in Suez; Duke of York's, Oct 1977, Stranger in The Dragon Variation; Phoenix, Nov 77, Boanerges in The Apple Cart; toured Australia, 1978, as Iago in Chichester Festival Company's Othello; Queen's, Aug 1978, Professor van Helsing in The Passion of Dracula; Albery, Apr 1979, took over as Fagin in Oliver!; Capital Theatre, Edmonton, Alberta, 1979, one-man performance as Mister Lincoln, and at The Morosco, NY, Feb, 1980; television appearances include Dear Liar, The Caretaker (which won an Emmy Award when shown on US television), Brief Lives (for which he was voted Television Actor of the Year), and the serials Imperial Palace, and Dickens of London.
Favourite part: Aubrey in Brief Lives. *Recreations:* Baseball, fishing. *Club:* Garrick. *Address:* c/o Eric Glass Ltd, 28 Berkeley Square, London W1X 6HD.

DOUGLAS, Felicity (*née* Tomlin), dramatic author
b Camberley, Surrey; *d* of Maurice Hilliard Tomlin and his wife Caroline Douglas (Moore); *e* Francis Holland School, Westminster; *m* (1) David Robertson (mar dis); (2) Basil Dawson (dec).

After working as an actress and radio script-writer, she directed her first play, Home Is the Warrior (written with Basil Dawson), at Richmond in Aug 1946; in 1948 directed her play A Man Must Die at the Chepstow and subsequently at the St Martin's; wrote It's Never Too Late, 1952; adapted Alice Through the Looking Glass, 1952, and directed it at Chelsea Palace, 1955; adapted Rollo, 1959, from Marcel Achard's Patate; with Basil Dawson adapted Alibi for a Judge, 1965 and According to the Evidence, 1967, both from Henry Cecil's novels; again with Basil Dawson, wrote The Crunch, 1969; film writing, since 1956, includes My Teenage Daughter, It's Never Too Late and Rollo; has written extensively for TV and radio including episodes of Within These Walls and The Cedar Tree; also Armchair Theatre; is the author of several children's books, and a novel based on 'It's Never too Late'.
Recreations: Gardening, sailing, going to the theatre. *Address:* 111 Highlands Heath, London, SW15. *Tel:* –788 8718.

DOUGLAS, Melvyn (*né* Hesselberg), actor, producer, director
b Macon, Georgia, 5 Apr 1901; *s* of Edouard Hesselberg and his wife, Lena (Shackleford); *m* Helen Gahagan.

Made his first appearance on the stage in Chicago and subsequently played for two seasons with Jessie Bonstelle's stock company; made his first appearance on the New York stage at the Playhouse, 12 Jan 1928, as Ace Wilfong in A Free Soul; at the Klaw Theatre, Nov 1928, played Sergeant Terry O'Brien in Back Here; Forrest, Aug 1929, Boyd Butler in Now-a-Days; Eltinge, Jan 1930, Henry C Martin in Recapture; at the Shubert-Riviera, Mar 1930, and on tour, played Josef in Candle Light; Belasco, Nov 1930, the Unknown Gentleman in To-night or Never; Booth, Jan 1934, played Sheridan Warren in No More Ladies; Playhouse, Apr 1934, staged Moor Born; National, Oct 1934, staged Within the Gates; Cort, Dec 1934, played Carey Reed in Mother Lode, and also staged the production; Booth, Mar 1935, played Pat Dantry in De Luxe; Shubert, Dec 1935, Erik Nordgren in Tapestry in Gray; commenced film career 1931, and from 1936 appeared exclusively in films; during 1941–2, was engaged in civilian defence service, in Washington; in 1942, enlisted in the US Army as a private, transferred to special service with the rank of Captain; served overseas in India, China, and Burma, until 1945, when he was demobilized with the rank of Major; at the National, NY, Apr 1946, presented (with Herman Levin), Call Me Mister; from 1947–9, appeared only in pictures; reappeared on the regular stage at the Cort, Mar 1949, as Tommy Thurston in Two Blind Mice; Coronet, Feb 1950, Wally Williams in The Bird Cage; subsequently toured in Two Blind Mice; Playhouse, Wilmington, Mar 1951, Sayre Nolan in Let Me Hear the Melody; Lyceum, NY, Oct 1951, Steve Whitney in Glad Tidings, which he also staged; Lyceum, Nov 1952, Howard Carol in Time Out for Ginger; toured the United States in this part, 1953–5, and subsequently toured Australia; National, 1956, took over the part of Henry Drummond in Inherit the Wind, and also toured with the play; Forrest, Philadelphia, Feb 1957, Zeus in Maiden Voyage; Hinsdale, Illinois, June 1957, directed The Man in the Dog Suit; toured US and at the Coronet, March 1958, played General Saint-Pé in The Waltz of the Toreadors; Winter Garden, March 1959, Captain Jack Boyle in the musical Juno; Ambassador, Oct 1959, Griffith P Hastings in The Gang's All Here; Morosco, March, 1960, William Russell in The Best Man, for which he received the Tony Award, and subsequently toured in the play; Ambassador, Oct 1960, co-produced The 49th Cousin; ANTA, Dec 1967, played the title-role of Spofford; Carnegie Music Hall, Pittsburgh, Pa, Apr 1975, played in The Great American Fourth of July Parade; Cleveland, Ohio, Playhouse, Oct 1975, Justice Daniel Snow in First Monday in October; among his notable films are The Old Dark House (1932), Theodora Goes Wild (1936), Captains Courageous (1937), Ninotchka (1939), Billy Budd (1962), The Candidate (1972); received the Film Academy Award for his role in Hud, 1964; appeared on television in The Plot to Kill Stalin in 1958.

Address: William Morris Agency, 1350 Avenue of the Americas, New York, NY.

DOUGLAS, Torrington, MIPR, theatre press representative
b Muswell Hill, London; *s* of Alfred Robert Jean Douglas and his wife Florence (Barber); *e* Highgate School and in Paris; *m* Dorothea Hill; formerly engaged as an Art Editor, sports and feature writer; from 1939–44, served in the Admiralty Press Division, and was assistant Editor of Shipyard Spotlight, during that period.

First became a theatrical press representative, 1944; represents Emile Littler, Peter Saunders, Williamson Music, Ltd, Volcano Productions Ltd, etc; a founder member of the ALTPR; member of the Institute of Public Relations; member of the National Union of Journalists. *Address:* 23 Lodge Drive, Palmer's Green, London N13 5LA. *Tel:* 01–886 1572.

DOUGLAS, Wallace, director
b Winnipeg, Canada, 15 Aug 1911; *s* of Robert Barnett Finlayson and his wife Marcia Emily (Bird); *e* Bickley Hall, Kent; *m* (1) Peggy Bagot-Chester (mar dis); (2) Phillippa Durham-Matthews (mar dis); (3) Anne Crawford (dec); (4) Pamela Frost.

Formerly an actor, he trained at RADA, and made his first appearance on the stage at Theatre Royal, Windsor, Jan 1928, in The Best People; first appeared in London, at the Haymarket, 15 Dec 1928, as Mr Trundle in Mr Pickwick; Apollo, June 1929, Joe Reynolds in Coquette; 1929–30 toured Canada and the USA as Raleigh in Journey's End; Criterion, during 1931, played Ralph in After All, and Roger Page in Make Up Your Mind; Little, Oct 1932, Jack Barthwick in The Silver Box, and Ted Stanhope in Alison's House; Ambassadors', Dec 1932, Dan Puffy in The Streets of London; Savoy, Sept 1933, Derek in If Only Father . . .; Lyric, Oct 1934, Perry Stewart in Theatre Royal; Aldelphi, Feb 1936, appeared in Follow the Sun; Criterion, July 1936,

Vicente, in The Lady of La Paz; Savoy, Jan 1937, John in Night Sky; Wyndham's, Feb 1937, Richard Dobbs in Because We Must; Garrick, Nov 1937, Bill Stanton in It's A Wise Child; Phoenix, May 1938, Jack Glenby in Married Unanimously; Savoy, Jan 1938, Joey in Lot's Wife; commissioned KRRC and was a prisoner for five years during the war; since then he has directed Zoo in Silesia, 1945; Mr Bowling Buys a Newspaper, Love Goes to Press, Peace Comes to Peckham, 1946; My Friend Lester, 1947; Twice Upon a Time, Seagulls over Sorrento, 1949; Party Manners, The White Eagles, Music at Midnight, 1950; Collector's Item, Hobson's Choice, 1951; The Hungry God, 1952; Tomorrow is a Secret, The Gay Dog, Albert, RN, Dead Secret, Witness For the Prosecution, 1953; The Manor of Northstead, Dry Rot, Spider's Web, 1954; My Three Angels, Mrs Willie, 1955; One Bright Day, 1956; Lovebirds, A Month of Sundays, Ride a Cock Horse, The Happiest Millionaire, 1957; Simple Spymen, The Trial of Mary Dugan, 1958; Murder on Arrival, Let Them Eat Cake, Aunt Edwina, 1959; The Brides of March, It's in the Bag, 1960; A Gazelle in Park Lane (tour), The Magnificent Gourmet (tour), Ten Little Niggers, 1962; Chase Me, Comrade, The Diplomatic Baggage, 1964; Breakfast With Julia, Charlie Girl, 1965; Bang, Bang, Beirut (Guildford), Stand By Your Bedouin, Uproar in the House, Let Sleeping Wives Lie, 1967; My Giddy Aunt, 1968; Beat the Retreat, She's Done It Again, Phil the Fluter, 1969; Don't Just Lie There, Say Something!, 1971; She Was Only An Admiral's Daughter (tour), 1972; A Bit Between the Teeth, 1974; Don't Just Lie There, Say Something! (tour), 1975; Fringe Benefits, Reluctant Heroes, 1976; Mr Polly, High Infedelity (tour), 1977; Relatively Speaking, 1978; Find the Lady, 1979; 1973–74 directed in Australia and South Africa; has also produced and directed for TV, notably a number of Brian Rix productions.

Club: Garrick. *Address:* Oak Trees, Lewes Road, East Grinstead, Sussex.

DOUGLASS, Stephen (*né* Fitch), actor and singer
b Mount Vernon, Ohio, 27 Sept 1921; *s* of Arie D Fitch and his wife Nell Douglass (Dyer); *m* (1) Edith F Reis; (2) Christine Hilton Yates; studied for the stage with the American Theatre Wing and under Walter Hampden.

Made his first appearance on the stage at the Paper Mill Playhouse, Millburn, NJ, June 1942, in the chorus of Naughty Marietta; subsequently played in Mlle Modiste, Sweethearts, The Red Mill, etc; Oct 1946 to May 1947, was engaged as a singer at Billy Rose's Diamond Horseshoe; made his first appearance on Broadway, at the Majestic, New York, May 1947, taking over Billy Bigelow in Carousel and played the part until Mar 1949, and on tour; at Millburn, NJ, June 1949, played Johann Strauss in The Great Waltz, followed by Jeff Calhoun in Bloomer Girl, and Franz in Arms and the Girl on Broadway; made his first appearance on the London stage, at Drury Lane Theatre, 7 June 1950, as Billy Bigelow in Carousel; at the Winter Garden, NY, Apr 1951, played Paul Dumont in Make a Wish; Phoenix, Mar 1954, Ulysses in The Golden Apple; subsequently took over as Sid Sorokin in The Pajama Game; 46th Street, May 1955, played Joe Hardy in Damn Yankees; Alvin, Nov 1957, Nelson Crandel in Rumple; Jones Beach Music Theatre, NY, June 1958, Edward Grieg in a revival of Song of Norway; Oakdale Musical Theatre, Wallingford, Conn, Sept 1958, starred in a revival of Show Boat; Academy of Music, Philadelphia, Feb 1960, made début with New York City Opera Co as Rev Blitch in Susannah; US tour, 1960–1, Destry in Destry Rides Again; City Center, June 1961, Tommy Albright in Brigadoon; Broadhurst, Oct 1963, File in 110 in the Shade, subsequently touring in this role; NY State, July 1966, Gaylord Ravenal in Show Boat, and subsequently toured; Palace, London, Feb 1967, Bill Starbuck in 110 in the Shade; 46th Street, 1968, took over as Michael in I Do, I Do, and toured Australia in this part in 1969; Ford's Washington, DC, 1970, played El Gallo in The Fantasticks; has played and toured extensively in stock in The Chocolate Soldier, Roberta, Blossom Time, Fledermaus, Brigadoon, South Pacific, Kiss Me, Kate, etc, most recently in 110 in the Shade, 1978, and as Charlie Anderson in Shenandoah, 1979; has also performed on television since 1949.

Favourite parts: Billy Bigelow and Michael in I Do, I Do. *Recreation:* Sailing. *Hobby:* Color photography. *Address:* International Creative Management, 40 West 57th Street, New York, NY 10019.

DOWD, M'el, actress
b Chicago, Illinois, 2 Feb; *d* of John Dowd and his wife Catherine O'Conner; *e* Boone, Iowa, public school; *m* Henri Eudes; formerly a soda fountain attendant and switchboard operator; prepared for the stage at the Goodman Theatre, Chicago.

Made her New York début with the Shakespearewrights Company at the Jan Hus, 19 Oct 1955, as Lady Macbeth; for the same Company, Jan 1956, played Titania in A Midsummer Night's Dream, Feb 1956, Lady Capulet in Romeo and Juliet, and, Oct 1957, Portia in Julius Caesar; Ambassador, Mar 1958, Lilith in Back to Methuselah; toured in this last part, 1958; Sullivan Street Playhouse, Mar 1959, Katherine of Aragon in Royal Gambit; Martin Beck, Mar 1959, was standby for Geraldine Page in The Sweet Bird of Youth, and occasionally played the part, that of Princess Kosmonopolis; Majestic, Dec 1960, Morgan Le Fey in Camelot; Maidman, Apr 1963, Agrippina in The Emperor; Longacre, Oct 1963, Anita Corcoran in A Case of Libel; Billy Rose, Oct 1965, Mrs Emilia Pattison in The Right Honourable Gentleman; New York City Center, Apr 1967, Elsa Schraeder in The Sound of Music; Vivian Beaumont, July 1967, Woman in The Unknown Soldier and His Wife; Plymouth, Nov 1967, Louise in Everything in the Garden; Vivian Beaumont, Feb 1968, Andromache in Tiger at the Gates; Mark Hellinger, Feb 1969, was understudy to Angela Lansbury in the role of the Countess Aurelia in Dear World; St Clement's Church, for the American Place Theatre, Oct 1969, Great Aunt Amelia in Mercy Street; Brooks Atkinson, Oct 1970, Maude Bodley in Not Now Darling; Cherry Lane, Oct 1971, Norma in A Gun Play; Lunt-Fontanne, Nov 1972, Amelia Newsome in Ambassador; Manhattan Theatre Club, Mar 1979, Mary Cassett in Songs from the City Streets; Morosco, Jan 1980, Standby for Elizabeth (Irene Worth) in The Lady from Dubuque; first appeared in films in The Wrong Man, 1957, and has since played in This Could Be the Night, Man on Fire, The 300 Year Weekend, etc; has played Kate Farrow on the television serial *The Best of Everything, and in The Adams Chronicles,* 1975; *The Prince of Homburg,* 1977.

Favourite parts: Lady Macbeth and the Princess Kosmonopolis. *Recreation:* Painting. *Address:* Actors Equity Association, 165 West 46th Street, New York, NY 10036.

DOWN, Angela, actress
b London, 15 June 1943; *d* of Evelyn Henry Down and his wife Ann Winnifred; *e* Henrietta Barnett School; *m* the actor Tim Hardy; trained for the stage at the Central School of Speech and Drama.

She made her first stage appearance at Lincoln Repertory Theatre, 1963, in Billy Liar; further work in repertory included appearances at Manchester Library Theatre and

Bristol Old Vic; made her London debut at the Duke of York's, May 1968, as Emma in Mrs Mouse, Are You Within?; worked mainly in television for a period, returning to the stage as Irena in The Three Sisters, Cambridge Theatre, June 1976; Birmingham Rep, Oct 1978, played Portia Contarini in The Merchant; Ambassadors', Apr 1979, Helen in Bodies; television since 1965 includes Take Three Girls, War and Peace, Shoulder to Shoulder, The Glittering Prizes, King Lear, Scorpion Tales, and We, the Accused.

Address: c/o Larry Dalzell Associates, 3 Goodwin's Court, St Martin's Lane, London WC2.

DOWNS, Jane, actress
b Bromley, Kent, 22 Jan; *m* (1) Gerald Harper (mar dis); (2) Terence Alexander; studied for the stage at the Royal Academy of Dramatic Art (awarded Gold Medal).

Made her first London appearance at the Apollo Theatre, June 1954, when she played Clarissa Davenport in Both Ends Meet; toured Aug 1955, as Helen in Patience; Apollo, Sept 1955, played Catherine Stevens in Lucky Strike; at the Globe, Dec 1955, played Ela Delahay in a revival of Charley's Aunt; Phoenix, Sept 1956, played Sheila Campbell in A River Breeze; at the Cambridge, Mar 1957, played Mary Garvald in The Iron Duchess; Royal Court, Sept 1957, Veronique in Nekrassov; made her first appearance in New York with the Old Vic Company, at the Broadway Theatre, Dec 1958, when she played Olivia in Twelfth Night, followed by Alice in Henry V, subsequently touring with the company in the US; Edinburgh Festival, Sept 1961, played Blanch of Spain in King John, subsequently appearing in the same production at the Old Vic, Sept 1961, and remaining with the company to play Hazel Niles in Mourning Becomes Electra, Nov 1961; at the same theatre, for the Vic-Wells Association, Feb 1962, played Margery in The Shoemaker's Holiday; at the Apollo, Feb 1962, played Judith in Boeing-Boeing; after more than a year, she left the company to appear at the Queen's Theatre, Sept 1963, as Countess Antonescu in Man and Boy; Brooks Atkinson, NY, Nov 1963, again played Countess Antonescu in Man and Boy; Arnaud, Guildford, July 1966, Sharon in The Flip Side; Savoy, June 1967, the Hon Mrs Willie Tatham in Aren't We All?; Arnaud, Guildford, Sept 1967, Jane in The Adventures of Tom Random; Savoy, Oct 1968, Liz Walford in The Secretary Bird; toured, May 1971, in the Cambridge Theatre Company's Hay Fever, as Myra Arundel; Greenwich, Mar 1972, Anne in The Performing Husband; Richmond, Sept 1972, Clare in Two and Two Make Sex, playing the same part at the Cambridge Theatre, Aug 1973; Criterion, Oct 1974, Ursula Westerby in There Goes the Bride; Whitehall, Aug 1976, Isobel Hudson in Fringe Benefits; Shaftesbury, May 1977, Ethel Aubin in Rolls Hyphen Royce; for the Royal Shakespeare Company's Stratford season, 1979, she played: Mistress Page in The Merry Wives of Windsor, Maria in Twelfth Night, Calpurnia in Julius Caesar, and Emilie Mech in Baal (Other Place); Aldwych, Apr 1980, Maria in Twelfth Night, Mrs Nickleby in Nicholas Nickleby (June); her films include The League of Gentlemen, and Darling; TV appearances include plays and series.

Recreations: Cooking and gardening. *Address:* c/o Representation Joyce Edwards, 8 Theed Street, London SE1.

DRAKE, Alfred (*né* Capurro), actor, singer, director
b New York City, 7 Oct 1914; *s* of John M Capurro and his wife Elena Teresa (Maggiolo); *e* Brooklyn College (BA); *m* (1) Alma Rowena Tollefsen (mar dis); (2) Esther Harvey Brown.

Made his first appearance on the stage at the Adelphi Theatre, NY, 15 July 1935, in the chorus of The Mikado, during a season of Gilbert and Sullivan operas; he was next engaged at the Center Theatre, Oct 1936, in a small part in White Horse Inn; at the Shubert, Apr 1937, played Marshall Blackstone in Babes in Arms; Windsor, May 1938, Albert Porter in The Two Bouquets; Booth, Feb 1939, appeared in One for the Money; Ambassador, Sept 1939, appeared in The Straw Hat Revue; Booth, Feb 1940, in Two for the Show; Clinton, Conn, Aug 1940, appeared in After the Ball, Her Master's Voice, and Little Women; Windsor, Feb 1941, played Norman Reese in Out of the Frying Pan; Marblehead, Mass, July–Aug 1941, appeared in leading parts in Mr and Mrs North, The Gorilla, Dear Brutus, and The Yellow Jacket; Mansfield, Oct 1941, played Orlando in As You Like It; Wilmington, Del, and Baltimore, Nov 1941, appeared as Allen Connolly in The Admiral Had a Wife; at the Guild Theatre, Apr 1942, played Robert in Yesterday's Magic; St James, Mar 1943, Curly in Oklahoma!; International, Dec 1944, Barnaby Goodchild in Sing Out, Sweet Land; went to Hollywood, 1945, to appear in films; at the Broadway, NY, Dec 1946, appeared as Macheath in Beggar's Holiday; in summer theatres, 1947, played in The Promised Valley and Pursuit of Happiness; Mansfield, Dec 1947, Larry Foreman in The Cradle Will Rock; Plymouth, Mar 1948, Alexander Sorin in Joy to the World; New Century, Dec 1948, Fred Graham in Kiss Me, Kate; Westport, Conn, Aug 1952, Lamberto Laudisi in Pirandello's Right You Are; Lyceum, NY, Oct 1952, David Petri in The Gambler; St James, Mar 1953, succeeded Yul Brynner as the King in The King and I; Ziegfeld, Dec 1953, Hajj, the Public Poet, in Kismet, for which he received the New York Drama Critics Poll, Donaldson, and Antoinette Perry (Tony) Awards; made his first appearance on the London stage at the Stoll, 20 Apr 1955, when he again played Hajj in Kismet; American Shakespeare Festival, Stratford, Connecticut, summer 1957, Iago in Othello, and Benedick in Much Ado About Nothing, touring in the latter with Katharine Hepburn; toured in summer, 1958, as He in He Who Gets Slapped; Broadway, Nov 1961, Edmund Kean in Kean; California tour, Aug–Nov 1962, Hajj in Kismet; Plymouth, Feb 1963, played the title-role in Lorenzo; Curran, San Francisco, Aug 1963, Richard Rassendyl in Zenda; Mark Hellinger, Feb 1964, wrote the English subtitles for the Italian musical Rugantino; Lunt-Fontanne, Apr 1964, Claudius in Sir John Gielgud's production of Hamlet; New York State Theatre, June 1965, again played Hajj in Kismet, in which he subsequently toured; ANTA, Nov 1966, Soren Brandes in Those That Play the Clowns; Parker Playhouse, Fort Lauderdale, Fla, Feb 1967, Kip Roberts in The Name of the Game; ANTA, Sept 1967, Aristobulo in Song of the Grasshopper; Goodspeed Opera House, East Haddam, Conn, Summer 1968, Mr Hyde in After You, Mr Hyde, and the lead in On Time, of which he is co-author and in which he subsequently toured; Virginia Museum, Richmond, Mar 1973, directed The Royal Rape of Ruari Mascamunde; Uris, Nov 1973, Honore Lachalles in Gigi; Shea Center, Wayne, NJ, Mar 1975, Paul Sillary in Gambler's Paradise; Mark Hellinger, Sept 1975, Mr Antrobus in The Skin of Our Teeth; Hartman, Stamford, May 1976, Bart Starling in Stag at Bay; has directed the following productions: The Liar, Courtin' Time, Salt of the Earth, Millicent's Castle, The Man with a Load of Mischief, Love Me Little, Dr Willy-Nilly, Lock Up Your Daughters, The Advocate; is the author, with Edward Eager, of The Burglar's Opera and 76, and adaptations of La Belle Hélène, The Liar, Dr Willy-Nilly, The Gambler and Journeyman Angel; is Artistic Director of the National Lyric Arts Theatre Founda-

tion, Inc, 1968 to present; President of the Players Club since 31 Mar 1970; appeared in the film Tars and Spars, 1946; has appeared frequently on television in both the US and in England.
Recreations: Reading, bridge, and music. *Club:* Players. *Address:* c/o Elias A Jacobs, 4 West 56th Street, New York, NY 10019. *Tel:* 582–1222.

DREYFUSS, Richard, actor
b Brooklyn, NY, 1948.
Made his Broadway debut at Henry Miller's, 27 Feb 1969, as Stanley in But Seriously . . .; at the De Lys, Feb 1971, played Stephen in Line; McAlpin Rooftop, May 1971, appeared in And Whose Little Boy Are You?; Solari Ensemble, LA, Mar 1977, in The Tenth Man; Brooklyn Academy of Music, Apr 1978, Cassius in Julius Caesar; Delacorte, Aug 1979, Iago in The New York Shakespeare Festival production of Othello; films, since 1967, include The Graduate, Valley of the Dolls, Jaws, and The Goodbye Girl (Academy Award).
Address: c/o Actors Equity Association, 165 West 46th Street, New York, NY 10036.

DRIVAS, Robert (*né* Choromokos), actor and director
b Chicago, Illinois, 21 Nov 1938; *s* of James Peter Choromokos and his wife Hariklia (Cunningham-Wright); *e* Coral Gables, Florida, High School, University of Chicago; and University of Miami; trained with Sanford Meisner, Philip Burton, and at the Actors Studio.
Made his début as Danny in a stock production of Night Must Fall, Coral Gables, 1957; Actors Studio, Miami, Fla, 1957, played Tom, Jr in Sweet Bird of Youth; Coconut Grove Playhouse, Miami, 1957, Tom Lee in Tea and Sympathy; Highland Park Playhouse, Chicago, 1957, played in The Lady's Not for Burning; subsequently played in Death of a Salesman, Thieves' Ball, A View from the Bridge; made his New York début at the Coronet, 30 Apr 1958, as Rameses in The Firstborn; Ambassador, Mar 1960, Jacko in One More River; Billy Rose, Oct 1960, Stefan Mazur in The Wall; Mermaid, Oct 1961, Benny Rogers in Diff'rent; Cherry Lane, Oct 1962, Frankie in Mrs Dally Has a Lover; Plymouth, Feb 1963, Giorgio in Lorenzo; Ethel Barrymore, Sept 1963; Andrew Rankin in The Irregular Verb to Love; Royale, Apr 1965, Sigfrid in And Things That Go Bump in the Night; Gramercy Arts, Nov 1968, Young Man in Sweet Eros; Aug 1970, played in Fly Paper and Dracula in a bill called Cops and Horrors; Yale Repertory Theatre, New Haven, Conn, 1971, played the title-role in Where Has Tommy Flowers Gone?; Eastside Playhouse, Oct 1971, again played in Where Has Tommy Flowers Gone?; Bucks County Playhouse, New Hope, Pa, Jan 1973, Michael in A Breeze from the Gulf; Eastside Playhouse, Oct 1973, repeated this last part; Astor Place, Feb 1974, directed Bad Habits; Longacre, Jan 1975, directed The Ritz; Ethel Barrymore, May 1976, directed Legend; Yale Rep, Oct 1976, appeared in Julius Caesar; Astor Place, March 1977, directed Monsters, a double bill consisting of Side Show (in which he also played Arnold) and The Transfiguration of Benno Blimpie; Biltmore, Jan 1978, directed Cheaters; appeared in the film Road Movie, 1974; also directed Crazy American Girl and Whiskers, 1976; has appeared regularly on television dramatic shows since 1959.
Address: c/o APA, 120 West 57th Street, New York, NY 10019.

DRIVER, Donald, actor, director, playwright.
First appeared on Broadway at the Century, 14 Oct 1952, as Private Webster in Buttrio Square; New York City Center,

May 1954, played Frank in Show Boat; Mark Hellinger, Dec 1954, Jerry in Hit the Trail; New York City Center, May 1955, Og, The Leprechaun in Finian's Rainbow; Wilmington, Delaware, Feb 1959, Emile the Athlete in The Gay Felons; wrote and directed the US–Canada touring production From Paris with Love, Jan 1962; American Shakespeare Festival Theatre, Stratford, Conn, 1965, conceived the production of The Taming of the Shrew; directed the National Players Company in Marat/Sade, 1966, which performed at the Majestic, NY, Jan 1967; Orpheum, Jan 1968, wrote the book and directed Your Own Thing; has since directed Mike Downstairs, Jimmy Shine, 1968; Our Town, 1969; made his London début as writer and director of Your Own Thing at the Comedy, 6 Feb 1969; Ivanhoe, Chicago, 1971, wrote and directed Status Quo Vadis; Brooks Atkinson, Feb 1973, again directed his Status Quo Vadis; Wolf Trap Farm, Washington DC, Aug 1977, directed South Pacific.

Address: Society of Stage Directors and Choreographers, 1501 Broadway, New York, NY.

DROMGOOLE, Patrick, director

b Iqueque, Chile, 30 Aug 1930; *s* of Nicholas Arthur Humphrey Dromgoole and his wife Violet Alice Georgina (Brookes); *e* Dulwich College and University College, Oxford; *m* Jennifer Davies.

Directed a number of plays for societies at Oxford and in Aug 1954, directed the Oxford Theatre Group's Edinburgh Festival production of The Dog Beneath the Skin; his first London production, Watergate, Oct 1955, was Periphery, in which he also played the part of Urban; since then, plays he has directed, in London unless otherwise stated, include Cockade, 1963; Entertaining Mr Sloane, The Love Game, 1964; Little Malcolm and his Struggle Against the Eunuchs, The Anniversary, Othello (Habimah, Tel Aviv), 1966; A Flea in Her Ear (Habimah), 1967; Say Goodnight to Grandma, 1973; The Case of the Oily Levantine, 1979; has directed several films, since his first in 1965; among the more recent of his numerous TV productions are: Sky, Children of the Stones, Machine Gunner, and the series Kidnapped and Darkness and Danger; Assistant Managing Director and Director of Programmes, Harlech Television; Fellow of the Royal Television Society; author of Screen It, 1979.

Recreations: Farming and numismatics. *Club:* Savile. *Address:* Barrows Farm, Theale, Wedmore, Somerset. *Tel:* Wedmore 582.

DRURY, Alan, dramatist

b Hull, 22 May 1949; *s* of Harold Drury and his wife Patricia; *e* King Edward's School, Birmingham and Queens' College, Cambridge; formerly a local government clerk.

He is author of the following plays: Shoreline, Godot Has Come (translation), 1971; You Know Me, The Ancient Mariner (ballet), 1972; Fall, 1973; Other Views, The Hills (translation), Asides, 1974; The Man Himself (National Theatre), The Railway Game, Antonio, Spotty Hilda, 1975; Communion, Sparrowfall, Sense of Loss, Dick Turpin, Under the Skin, 1976; Margaret Clitheroe, A Change of Mind (NT), Diary of a Madman (translation), 1977; Simple Simon, Looking Back, 1978; An Empty Desk, 1979; An Honourable Man, 1980; he also wrote the book and lyrics for the musicals Silver, 1972; King David, 1975; Up and Away, 1976; has directed a number of plays including his own, and was responsible as writer-director for the improvised projects Soap Operas I, II, III (York and Billingham Theatre in Education, 1977–79), and The Training (ICA, 1978); Resi-

dent Dramatist, York Theatre Royal, 1976–78; Royal Court Theatre, 1979.

Hobbies: Conjuring and old railway timetables. *Address:* c/o John Rush, David Higham Associates, 5–8 Lower John Street, Golden Square, London W1.

DU BOIS, Raoul Pène, designer

b New York City, 29 Nov 1914; *s* of Raoul-Georges-Gontran Pène du Bois and his wife Bessie Hetherington.

Designed sets for several productions in Paris; his first designs in NY were costumes for Life Begins at 8.40, Winter Garden, Aug 1934; has since designed Jumbo, 1935; his first London design, Home and Beauty, 1937; The Two Bouquets, NY, Leave It to Me, The Ziegfeld Follies, 1938; Du Barry Was a Lady, Too Many Girls, One for the Money, Aquacade, 1939; Two for the Show, Panama Hattie, Hold on to Your Hats, 1940; Liberty Jones, 1941; Carmen Jones, 1943; The Firebrand of Florence, Are You with It? 1945; Heaven on Earth, Lend an Ear, 1948; Alive and Kicking, Call Me Madam, 1950; Make a Wish, 1951; New Faces of 1952, In Any Language, 1952; Wonderful Town, Maggie, Charley's Aunt, John Murray Anderson's Almanac, 1953; Mrs Patterson, 1954; Plain and Fancy, The Vamp, 1955; Ziegfeld Follies (sets and costumes for three different productions), Carmen Jones (costumes only), Bells Are Ringing, 1956; The Music Man (costumes only), 1957; Gypsy (costumes only), 1959; Maurice Chevalier (décor and lighting), The Student Gypsy, 1963; PS I Love You, Royal Flush, 1964; Darling of the Day, 1968; the double-bill Peter and the Wolf and Here and Now, Rondelay, 1969; No, No, Nanette, 1971; Rain, 1972; costumes and décor for Irene, 1973; costumes and décor for No, No, Nanette, London, and costumes for Gypsy, London, 1973; costumes for Gypsy, NY, 1974; costumes and décor for Doctor Jazz, 1975; Sugar Babies, 1979; has also designed for The Ballet Russe de Monte Carlo; received the Antoinette Perry (Tony) Award for Wonderful Town and No, No, Nanette; designed films, 1941–5, including Louisiana Purchase, Lady in the Dark, Dixie, etc.

Address: 9 West 75th Street, New York, NY 10023.

DUDLEY, William, designer

b London, 4 Mar 1947; *s* of William Stuart Dudley and his wife Dorothy Irene; *e* St Martin's School of Art, Slade School of Art.

Designed his first production, Hamlet, for Nottingham Playhouse, Oct 1970; has since designed the following productions: The Duchess of Malfi, Man is Man, Anarchist, Tyger (co-designed for National Theatre), Cato Street, The Good-Natured Man (National), 1974; Live Like Pigs, I Claudius, The Baker, the Baker's Wife and the Baker's Boy (Newcastle), 1972; Rooted, Magnificence, Sweet Talk, The Merry-Go-Round (Royal Court), 1973; Ashes, The Corn Is Green (Watford), Twelfth Night (Stratford), Harding's Luck, 1974; Fish in the Sea, As You Like It (Nottingham), The Fool (Royal Court), 1975; The Norman Conquests (Berlin), Small Change, As You Like It (opening of Riverside Studios, Hammersmith), Ivanov (RSC), 1976; The Cherry Orchard (Riverside), That Good Between Us (RSC), 1977; he has designed the following plays for the National Theatre: Lavender Blue, Touched, 1977; The World Turned Upside Down, Has Washington Legs?, 1978; Dispatches, Undiscovered Country, Lark Rise and Candleford, 1979; also designed Billy Budd at The Metropolitan Opera House, New York, 1978; member, Society of British Theatre Designers.

Recreations: Playing the concertina, browsing in bookshops, walking. *Address:* 58 Earlswood Road, London SE10. *Tel:* 01–858 8711.

DULLEA, Keir, actor
b Cleveland, Ohio, 30 May 1936; *e* San Francisco State College; prepared for the stage at the Neighborhood Playhouse.

Appeared with the John Drew Theatre, Totem Pole Playhouse, and Berkshire Playhouse in various stock productions; made his New York début at the Barbizon-Plaza, 13 Apr 1959, as Timmie Redwine in Season of Choice; Moore, Seattle, and Huntington Hartford, Los Angeles, Sept–Oct 1961, Nick in A Short Happy Life; appeared in films for some years, then reappeared in NY at the Belasco, Sept 1967, as Dr Jim Tennyson in Dr Cook's Garden; Booth, Oct 1969, Don Baker in Butterflies Are Free; American Shakespeare Festival, Stratford, Conn, July 1974, Brick in Cat on a Hot Tin Roof; ANTA, Sept 1974, again played Brick in Cat on a Hot Tin Roof; Golden, Apr 1975, Jimmy in PS Your Cat Is Dead!; has appeared in films such as The Hoodlum Priest, 1961, David and Lisa, 1962, Bunny Lake Is Missing, 1965, 2001: A Space Odyssey, 1967, Blood City, 1976, Full Circle, 1977, Leopard in the Snow, 1977, etc; TV includes Law and Order, 1976, Hostage Tower, Brave New Word, both 1979, etc.
Address: c/o M J Mitosky Esq, 150 Central Park South, New York, NY 10019.

DUNAWAY, Faye, actress
b Tallahassee, Florida, 14 Jan 1941; *e* University of Florida, Boston University; *m* Peter Wolf.

Made her New York début at the ANTA, Sept 1962, when she succeeded Olga Belin as Margaret More in A Man for All Seasons; ANTA, Washington Square, Jan 1964, played a Nurse in After the Fall; same theatre, Mar 1964, Faith Prosper in But for Whom Charlie; in 1965 took over the part of Elsie in After the Fall; Oct 1964, Maid to Beatrice in The Changeling; Jan 1965, understudied in Tartuffe; American Place, Nov 1965, Kathleen Stanton in Hogan's Goat; Mark Taper Forum, Los Angeles, 1972, played in Old Times; Ahmanson, Los Angeles, 1973, Blanche du Bois in A Streetcar Named Desire; has appeared in many films, notably as Bonnie Parker in Bonnie and Clyde, 1967, The Thomas Crown Affair, 1968, Little Big Man, 1970, Doc, 1971, Chinatown, 1974, The Voyage, 1975, Network, 1976, etc; TV work includes The Disappearance of Aimée, 1976.
Address: Screen Actors Guild, 7750 Sunset Boulevard, Los Angeles, Calif 90046.

DUNCAN, Ronald, dramatic author
b Salisbury, Rhodesia, 6 Aug 1914; *s* of Reginald John Duncan and his wife Ethel (Cannon); *e* Switzerland and Downing College, Cambridge; *m* Rose Marie Theresa Hansom; was editor of *The Townsman,* 1938–46.

Has written the following plays: This Way to the Tomb, 1945; The Eagle Has Two Heads (adaptation) 1946; The Rape of Lucretia (libretto) 1946; Stratton, 1949; The Typewriter (adaptation), 1950; Nothing Up My Sleeve, 1950; Don Juan, The Death of Satan, 1957; The Catalyst, Apollo de Bellac (adaptation), 1958; Christopher Sly (libretto), 1960; Abelard and Héloïse, 1961; Ménage à Trois, 1963; The Rabbit Race (adapted), 1963; The Seven Deadly Virtues, 1964; The Gift, 1968; Torquemada, 1969; The Trojan Women (adapted), Sloshed, 1974; author of many books, including Ben Jonson, Beauty and the Beast, The Solitudes, Saint Spiv, All Men Are Islands, How to Make Enemies (first two volumes of autobiography), Man (vols 1–5), The Tale of Tails, Unpopular Poems, For the Few.
Address: Mead Farm, Welcombe, near Bideford, Devonshire. *Tel:* Morwenstow 375.

DUNCAN, Sandy, actress
b Henderson, Texas, 20 Feb 1946; *d* of Mancil Ray Duncan and his wife Sylvia Wynne (Scott); *e* Lon Morris College; prepared for the stage with Wynn Handman, Utah Ground, and Toni Beck; *m* Thomas C Calcaterra, MD (mar dis).

Made her first appearance on the stage at the Dallas, Texas, State Fair Music Hall, Aug 1958, as a Child in The King and I; made her New York début at the New York City Center, 16 June 1965, as Zaneeta Shinn in The Music Man; same theatre, Dec 1966, played Louise in Carousel; Apr 1967, Susan Mahoney in Finian's Rainbow; Apr 1967, Liesl in The Sound of Music; Oct 1967, Mary Skinner in Life with Father; American Place, Dec 1967, Thulja in The Ceremony of Innocence; Orpheum, 1968, took over from Leland Palmer as Viola in Your Own Thing and subsequently toured USA and Canada in this part; Eugene O'Neill, Feb 1969, Alison, Molly, May, and the Sweetheart in Canterbury Tales; The Music Box, Dec 1969, April MacGregor in Love Is a Time of Day; Ambassador, Apr 1970, Maisie in The Boy Friend; Music Hall, Dallas, Texas, July 1975, title-role in Peter Pan; Mark Taper Forum, Nov 1976, Mary in Varities; Lunt-Fontanne, Sept 1979, again played Peter Pan; her tours and stock productions include Gipsy, The Music Man and Brigadoon; first appeared in films in Million Dollar Duck, 1970, and also played in Neil Simon's The Star-Spangled Girl, 1971; has appeared on television in the series *Funny Face,* and in *The Sandy Duncan Show,* 1973, as well as on many comedy and variety programs, including *Laugh-In,* and *The Muppet Show,* and recently in Roots.
Favourite parts: Louise in Carousel, Maisie in The Boy Friend. *Hobbies and recreations:* Needlepoint, plants and gardening, tennis. *Address:* 8243 Ashcroft Avenue, Los Angeles, Calif 90046. *Tel:* 213–659 5219.

DUNHAM, Joanna, actress
b Luton, Beds, 6 May 1936; *d* of Peter Dunham and his wife Constance (Young); *e* Bedales School and Slade School of Fine Art; *m* Harry Osbourne; trained for the stage at RADA.

Made her first professional appearance at the Royal Court, Liverpool, Aug 1958, as Sister Therese in The Deserters; Westminster, Feb 1960, made her London debut as Ellen in Visit to a Small Planet; Queen's, Mar 1961, played Hilda in The Lady from the Sea; joined the Old Vic company that summer, taking over the parts of Nerissa in A Merchant of Venice, June, and Juliet in Romeo and Juliet, July; made her New York debut in the latter production, Feb 1962, at the City Center; toured USA and Europe in the same part; New Arts, Mar and Globe, Apr 1964, Perdita in The Formation Dancers; Cambridge, Sept 1965, Vera in A Month in the Country; Jeanetta Cochrane, Aug 1966, the Woman in La Musica; New, Dec 1968, Helen in Soldiers; Oxford Playhouse, Sept 1970, Elena in Kean, followed by Desdemona in Othello, Oct; Hampstead, May 1974, Sarah in Bodywork; Hong Kong Theatre Festival, 1978, Rebecca West in Rosmersholm; first appeared in films as Mary Magdalen in The Greatest Story Ever Told and has since appeared in A Day at the Beach; TV appearances, since 1958, include Blithe Spirit, Dangerous Corner and the series Sanctuary and Van der Valk.
Favourite parts: Juliet, and Perdita in The Formation Dancers. *Recreations:* Gardening, cooking, Do-It-Yourself. *Address:* c/o Plunket Greene Ltd, 91 Regent Street, London W1.

DUNHAM, Katherine, dancer and choreographer
b Chicago, Ill, 22 June 1910; *d* of Albert Millard Dunham and

his wife Annette (Poindexter); *e* University of Chicago (PhB); *m* John Pratt; formerly engaged as librarian, writer and anthropologist; was trained for dancing in Chicago, under Mark Turbyfill, Ludmilla Speranzava and Ruth Page.

First public appearance, 1931, at the Chicago Beaux Arts Ball, in A Negro Rhapsody; appeared with the Chicago Opera Company, 1933–6; appeared in Chicago World's Fair, 1934–5; during 1937–8, devoted herself to research in dances in the West Indies; was dance director for the Labor Stage production of Pins and Needles, New York, 1937; first appeared on the NY stage, semi-professionally, at the Windsor Theatre, Jan 1938, in Tropics, and Le Jazz Hot; at the Martin Beck Theatre, Oct 1940, appeared as Georgia Brown in Cabin in the Sky, for which she also arranged the choreography; toured the West Coast, USA, and Canada, 1940–3; toured all over United States and Canada in Tropical Revue, 1943–5; Adelphi, NY, Sept 1945, was co-director of and danced in Carib Song; was producer, director and star of Bal Nègre, 1945–8, and in which she appeared at the Belasco, NY, Nov 1946; first appeared in London, at the Prince of Wales's, 3 June 1948, with her own company, in Caribbean Rhapsody, repeating her American success; Paris, Nov 1948–Jan 1949, appeared in Bal Nègre; Broadway, Apr 1950, choreographed, directed, and performed in Katherine Dunham and Her Company; choreographed opera productions for the Teatro Colón, Buenos Aires, Argentina, and the Santiago de Chile Opera, 1950; Broadway, Nov 1955, repeated her season of dances; 54th Street, Oct 1962, choreographed, directed, and performed in Bamboche; Metropolitan Opera House, Oct 1963, choreographed Aida; Wolf Trap Hilene Center, Vienna, Va, Aug 1972, directed and choreographed Scott Joplin's opera Treemonisha; has toured in nearly 60 foreign countries since 1947; first appeared in films, 1940, in Carnival of Rhythm; member of the Royal Society of Anthropology, London; founded the Katherine Dunham School of Cultural Arts, 1943, and served as its President for more than twenty years; Professor and Director of the Performing Arts Training Centre, Southern Illinois University, 1968– ; has contributed to magazines under the pseudonym of Kaye Dunn; author of Las Danzas de Haiti, Journey to Accompong, La Boule Blanche, L'Agya, A Touch of Innocence (autobiography, 1959), Kasamance, 1974; various television scripts produced in Europe and Mexico, etc.

Recreations: Reading and writing. *Address:* 338 West 88th Street, New York, NY 10024.

DUNLOP, Frank, director
b Leeds, 15 Feb 1927; *s* of Charles Norman Dunlop and his wife Mary (Aarons); *e* Kibworth Beauchamp Grammar School and University College, London; trained for the stage at the Old Vic school, London.

Director of his own young theatre company, The Piccolo Theatre, Manchester, 1954; directed The Enchanted, Bristol, 1955; resident director, Bristol Old Vic, 1956; wrote and directed for *Les Frères Jacques,* Adelphi, London, 1960; directed The Bishop's Bonfire, London 1961; Director, Nottingham Playhouse, 1961–4, including the inaugural season of the new Playhouse, 1963–4; has directed the following plays, in London unless otherwise stated: Schweik In the Second World War, 1963; Son of Oblomov, 1964; The Taming of the Shrew (Oklahoma), Any Wednesday, Too True to Be Good (also Edinburgh Festival), 1965; Saturday Night and Sunday Morning, The Winter's Tale (Edinburgh, Venice and London), The Trojan Women (Edinburgh Festival), 1966; these last two productions were for Pop Theatre, which he founded

and directed; The Burglar, Getting Married, Climb the Greased Pole, A Midsummer Night's Dream, The Tricks of Scapin, 1967; Zoo, Zoo, Widdershins Zoo, 1969 (the latter three plays, at Edinburgh Festival); Pantagleize, 1970, and Antony and Cleopatra, 1971, both Belgian National Theatre; Hullabaloo, A Sense of Detachment, Joseph and the Amazing Technicolour Dreamcoat, 1972; Pericles (Belgian National Theatre), 1973; Sherlock Holmes (RSC and New York), 1974; joined the National Theatre as Associate Director, 1967; Administrative Director, 1968–71; for the National he has directed Edward II (Brecht), Home and Beauty, 1968; Macrune's Guevara (co-directed), The White Devil, 1969; The Captain of Köpenick, 1971; founder director of the Young Vic, 1969; his productions for them include The Tricks of Scapino and The Taming of the Shrew, 1970; The Comedy of Errors, 1971; The Maids, Deathwatch, The Alchemist, Bible One (including Joseph), 1972; French Without Tears, Much Ado About Nothing, 1973; Scapino, 1974; Macbeth, 1975; author and director of Scapino in New York, Los Angeles, Australia and Norway, 1974–5; also directed Habeas Corpus (1975) and The Last of Mrs Cheyney (1978) in New York, where he founded BAM Theatre Company, 1976–78, directing The New York Idea, Three Sisters, The Devil's Disciple, The Play's the Thing and Julius Caesar; returned to England and directed Rookery Nook, Birmingham Rep, June 1979, and Haymarket, Nov 1979; Camelot (NY and tour), 1980; Antony and Cleopatra, 1976.

Address: c/o The Young Vic, The Cut, London, SE1.

DUNN, Geoffrey, actor and director
b London, 13 Dec 1903; *s* of Walter Thomas Dunn and his wife Minnie (Boot); *e* City of London School; was formerly employed as a copy-writer and artist with an advertising agency.

Made his first appearance on the stage at the Pump Room, Bath, Sept 1925 as Malvolio in Twelfth Night; first appeared in London, at the Little Theatre, 8 Dec 1925, as Queen Elizabeth's Usher in Gloriana; Kingsway, Mar 1927, appeared in Cosi Fan Tutte; during 1928–9, appeared at the Lyric, Hammersmith, in minor parts in The Beggar's Opera, Love in a Village, and La Vie Parisienne; from 1931–40, was director of opera at the Royal Academy of Music; toured on the Continent, 1933, 1934, and 1936, and in the United States and Canada, 1937–8; made his first appearance on the New York stage, at the Little Theatre, Jan 1938, in the title-rôle of Don Quixote; Kingsway, Oct 1938, played Ortensio in An Elephant in Arcady; 1939–45, was a teacher at Morley College Theatre School; 1940–2, was a teacher at the Old Vic School; at the Ambassadors', July 1942, appeared in Light and Shade; Orpheum, Golders Green, Dec 1942, played Gideon Bloodgood in The Streets of London; Arts, Feb 1943, Caesar in Androcles and the Lion; toured, 1943, with CEMA, as Sir Andrew Aguecheek in Twelfth Night; Scala, Dec 1943, played The White Knight in Alice Through the Looking Glass; Coliseum, May 1944, Prince Carlo in The Quaker Girl; St James's, Dec 1944, the Herald in The Glass Slipper; Arts, Apr 1945, Achille de Rosalba in An Italian Straw Hat, and May 1945, Ivan Hlestakov in The Government Inspector; Sadler's Wells, Oct 1945, Walter Phillips in The Forrigan Reel; St James's, Dec 1945, again played the Herald in The Glass Slipper; Lyric, Hammersmith, May 1946, Crito in The Thracian Horses; New Lindsey, Aug 1946, Mr Morgan in Tom Pike; Arts, Feb–Mar 1947, appeared as the Elderly Gentleman and the He-Ancient in Back to Methuselah; St James's, May 1947, Johann Dwornitschek in The Play's the Thing; Playhouse, Feb 1948, the Professor in Cockpit; Boltons, July 1948, Hapi in Corn in Egypt; Cam-

bridge, Nov 1948, Lerma in Home Is Tomorrow; Mercury, Jan 1949, Fra Timotheo in Mandragola; at the Q, May 1949, played Lewis Borden in Sleep on My Shoulder; Winter Garden, Apr 1950, Titorelli in The Trial; Duke of York's, Nov 1950, appeared as Christopher Green in Return to Tyassi; Duke of York's, Nov 1951, a Singer in Héloïse; Westminster, Feb 1952, the Hon Mr Listless in Nightmare Abbey; Players' Theatre, Dec 1952, Sir Rowland Macassar in Babes in the Wood and the Good Little Fairy-Birds!; Criterion, Jan 1953, Henry Howard in Fool's Mate (for the Under-Thirty Group); Haymarket, May 1953, played Pamphilius in The Apple Cart; Players', Dec 1953, Brunetta in Cinderella; Saville, Mar 1954, played Maximilian, Count von Endenstein, in The White Countess; Lyric, Hammersmith, Dec 1954, and at the New, Apr 1955, played Ferdinand in Time Remembered; at the Edinburgh Festival, 1955, appeared as Teiresias in A Life In the Sun; Aldwych, June 1956, played Mr Wembley in Man Alive!; Saville, Dec 1956, Petulant in a revival of The Way of the World; Globe, Sept 1957, took over Jacob Friedland in Nude With Violin; Lyric, Hammersmith, Oct 1958, played Cardinal Pirelli in Valmouth, transferring with the production to the Saville, Jan 1959; Royal Court, Apr 1960, played the Logician in Rhinoceros; Globe, July 1960, played the Ambassador in A Man For All Seasons; has read the simultaneous translation for Italian companies in nine Aldwych World Theatre seasons 1964–75; Glyndebourne Opera, Aug 1964, reader in simultaneous translation of La Bisbetica Domata; he is also the translator or author of many opera libretti including: Orpheus in the Underworld, 1960; La Belle Héléne, Xerxes, 1963; The Gypsy Baron, English Eccentrics (librettist), 1964; Bluebeard, 1965; Julius Caesar Jones (librettist), 1966; L'Ormindo, 1967; Don Giovanni, 1968; The Damnation of Faust, 1969; La Calisto, 1970; has also appeared in films and television.
Address: 19a Maunsel Street, London, SW1. *Tel:* 01–828 4645.

DUNNING, Ruth, actress
b Prestatyn, North Wales, 17 May 1911; *d* of John H Dunning and his wife Alice M S (Hunt-Jones); *e* Sale High School, Cheshire; *m* Jack Allen; formerly engaged in secretarial work.

Had ten years experience as an amateur, before she made her first appearance on the professional stage at the Garrick Theatre, 30 Jan 1935, walking on in Love on the Dole, and in July 1935, succeeded Wendy Hiller as Sally Hardcastle in that play; subsequently appearing as Sally at the Winter Garden and on provincial tour, 1935–6; People's Palace, June 1937, played Mary Williams in They Fly By Twilight; Vaudeville, Oct 1937, Phryne Ware in Punch and Judy; New, Sept 1938, Lady Ruth Cornwall in Can We Tell?; St James's, Nov 1938, Nella Saxby in Gentleman Unknown; Garrick, Jan 1939, Lady Eulalia in Hundreds and Thousands; Globe (for London International Theatre), Feb 1939, Violet Carney in The Courageous Sex; Kingsway, May 1939, Joyce Bennet in Uneasy Living; reappeared, at the Playhouse, June 1943, as Shura in The Russians; Q, Oct 1944, June in Lady Killer; played a season of repertory at Tunbridge Wells; Q, May 1945, played Sub Phayre in Temporary Ladies; Embassy, July 1945, Kate Grant in No Room at the Inn, and the same part at the Winter Garden, May 1946; St Martin's, Feb 1948, Mrs James in Gathering Storm; Q, Dec 1948, Madeline Grey in Madeline; New Lindsey, Mar 1950, Penelope Ellis in Murderer's Child; at the Aldwych, Sept 1950, appeared as Marion Tillyard in Accolade; Arts, Oct 1951, and Criterion, Jan 1952, played Pauline Callender in Third Person; Arts,

Mar 1974, played the Nurse and Beggar Woman in Blood Wedding; Apr 1958, toured as Beatrice in Much Ado About Nothing, and subsequently played the same part at the Open Air Theatre, Regent's Park, June 1958; Westminster, May 1959, played Lucy Morer in Beware of Angels; Pembroke, Croydon, May 1961, appeared as Vlasova in Mother; Hampstead Theatre Club, June 1964, played Mrs Melanie Humdinger in The Raft; Mermaid, Nov 1965, Daisy Crompton in Spring and Port Wine, transferring to the Apollo, Jan 1966; Open Air, Regents Park, May 1968, played Mistress Page in The Merry Wives of Windsor; Leeds Festival, Aug 1968, Helen in The Game; Shaw, Mar 1975, Mrs Bramson in Night Must Fall; has appeared in several productions at the Richmond and Q Theatres; entered films, 1938, in Save a Little Sunshine; recent appearances include The House in Nightmare Park; has also worked in radio and television, winning the Television Actress of the Year Award, 1961, and John Logie Baird Award, 1964; recent TV includes Sextet and An Unofficial Rose.
Recreations: Embroidery, gardening, swimming, and cooking. *Address:* c/o Plunket Greene Ltd, 91 Regent Street, London W1R 8RV.

DUNNOCK, Mildred, actress
b Baltimore, Md, 25 Jan 1900; *d* of Walter Dunnock and his wife Florence (Saynook); *e* Goucher University (BA) and Columbia University (MA); *m* Keith M Urmy; studied with Maria Ouspenskaya, Lee Strasberg, Robert Lewis, Elia Kazan, Tamara Daykarhanova; formerly a school-teacher.

Made her first appearance in New York, at the Selwyn Theatre, 28 Mar 1932, as Miss Pinty in Life Begins; Manhattan Opera House, Jan 1937, appeared in The Eternal Road; toured, 1938, with Katharine Cornell in Herod and Mariamne; National, NY, Nov 1940, played Miss Ronberry in The Corn Is Green; toured, 1941, with George M Cohan, in Madam, Will You Walk?; Martin Beck, June 1942, played Miss Giddon in The Cat Screams; subsequently toured in The Corn Is Green; Forrest Theatre, NY, Mar 1943, appeared as Queen Margaret in Richard III; Bijou, Apr 1944, played India Hamilton in Only the Heart; Martin Beck, Mar 1945, Rose in Foolish Notion; Plymouth, Feb 1946, Madame Tsai in Lute Song; Fulton, Nov 1946, Lavinia Hubbard in Another Part of the Forest; Booth, Mar 1948, Etta Hallam in The Hallams; National, Oct 1948, Williams in The Leading Lady; Morosco, Feb 1949, made a great success when she played Linda in Death of a Salesman; Biltmore, Nov 1950, Mrs Bayard Goodale in Pride's Crossing; City Center, Dec 1951, Gina in The Wild Duck; Westport Country Playhouse, Aug 1952, Signora Frola in Pirandello's Right You Are; Playhouse, Dec 1959, Mrs Constable in In the Summer House; Morosco, Mar 1955, Big Mama in Cat on a Hot Tin Roof; at the Shakespeare Festival, Stratford, Conn, June 1956, Constance in King John; Royale, NY, Nov 1956, Susan Shepherd in Child of Fortune; Forrest, Philadelphia, Feb 1957, Hera in Maiden Voyage; Orpheum, Montreal, Mar 1959, Mary Tyrone in Long Day's Journey into Night; Phoenix, NY, Dec 1959, appeared in the staged reading of Pictures in the Hallway; East 74th St Theatre, NY, Feb 1960, Mistress Phoebe Ricketts in The Crystal Heart; Helen Hayes, NY, Sept 1960, Gertrude Povis in Farewell, Farewell, Eugene; 41st Street, Jan 1962, Mrs Perpetua in The Cantilevered Terrace; at the Festival of Two Worlds, Spoleto, Italy, July 1962, Vera Ridgeway Condotti in The Milk Train Doesn't Stop Here Anymore; appeared in the same role at the Morosco, Jan 1963; Spoleto, Italy, July 1963, played in Just Wild About Harry and Hecuba in The Trojan Women; again played the last role at the Circle-in-the-Square, Dec 1963;

ANTA, Sept 1964, Madame Renaud in Traveller Without Luggage; Greenwich Mews, Feb 1966, The Nurse in Phèdre; Long Wharf, New Haven, Conn, May 1966, Mary Tyrone in Long Days Journey into Night; at the American Embassy, London, June 1966, played Oenone in Phèdre; Oakland National Repertory, Calif, Dec 1966, Amanda Wingfield in The Glass Menagerie; Theatre de Lys, NY, Feb 1967, The Mother in Willie Doesn't Live Here Anymore; appeared with the Long Wharf Theatre, New Haven, Conn, during the 1967–8 and 1968–9 seasons as Amanda Wingfield and in other parts; Ellen Stewart, NY, May 1970, Sido in Colette; appeared with the Yale Repertory Theatre during the 1969–70 season; Long Wharf, Nov 1970, Claire Lannes in A Place Without Doors, which she repeated at the Staircase, NY, Dec 1970; Manhattan Theater Club, May 1971, played in An Evening with Emily Dickinson and Robert Schumann; Goodman, Chicago, Sept 1971, Claire Lannes in A Place Without Doors; Manhattan Theater Club, Mar 1973, directed Luminosity Without Radiance: A Self-Portrait; toured, summer 1974, as Sido in Colette; Williamstown, Mass, July 1975, played in Ring Around the Moon; Circle in the Square, Sept 1976, the Mother in Days in the Trees; same theatre, Sept 1977, Mme Pernelle in Tartuffe; first appeared in films, 1945, in The Corn Is Green and has since played in Death of a Salesman, Kiss of Death, Baby Doll, Sweet Bird of Youth, The Spiral Staircase (1975), etc; has played various roles on television.

Address: c/o Actors Equity Association, 165 West 46th Street, New York, NY 10036.

DURANG, Christopher, playwright

b Montclair, New Jersey, 2 Jan 1949; *s* of Francis Ferdinand Durang and his wife Patricia; *e* Harvard College and Yale School of Drama.

In 1973 co-wrote and performed with Albert Innaurato a cabaret, I Don't Generally Like Poetry But Have You Read 'Trees'?, at the Manhattan Theatre Club; has since written Better Dead than Sorry, 1973; The Idiots Karamazov (with Innaurato), 1974; When Dinah Shore Ruled the Earth (with Wendy Wasserstein), The Nature and Purpose of the Universe, 1975; Titanic, Das Lusitania Songspiel (written and performed with Sigourney Weaver at the Van Dam, NY), The Marriage of Bette and Boo, 1976; A History of the American Film (book: seen on Broadway at ANTA, 1978), The Vietnamization of New Jersey, 1977; 'dentity Crisis, Sister Mary Ignatius Explains It All for You (one-act), 1979; with Sigourney Weaver performed a revised version of Das Lusitania Songspiel, Chelsea Westside, Dec 1979; Guggenheim fellowship in playwriting, 1979–80.

Address: c/o Helen Merrill, 337 West 22nd Street, New York, NY 10011.

DURAS, Marguerite, dramatic author

b Indo-China, 4 Apr 1914; *d* of Henri Donnadicu and his wife Marie (Legrand); *e* Sorbonne, Paris; mar dis.

Of her plays, the following have been performed in Britain and the US: The Square, La Musica, The Viaduct, Days in the Trees, L'Amante Anglaise (in US, A Place Without Doors; in UK, The Lovers of Viorne), Suzanna Andler, India Song, Eden Cinema; many of her novels have been filmed, including Moderato Cantabile, Une Aussi Longue Absence and The Sailor from Gibraltar; wrote screenplay for Hiroshima Mon Amour, and has written and directed films which include Nathalie Granger, India Song, and Le Camion.

Address: c/o MLR Ltd, 194 Old Brompton Road, London SW5.

DÜRRENMATT, Friedrich, dramatic author

b Konolfingen, Berne, Switzerland, 5 Jan 1921; *s* of Reinhold Duürrenmatt and his wife Hulda; *e* Universities of Zurich and Berne; *m* Lotte Geissler.

His first play to be produced was Es Steht Geschrieben, at the Schauspielhaus, Zurich, on 19 Apr 1947; he is also the author of the following plays: Der Blinde, 1948; Romulus Der Grosse (Romulus the Great), 1949; Die Ehe des Herrn Mississippi (The Marriage of Mr Mississippi), 1952; Ein Engel Kommt Nach Babylon (An Angel Comes To Babylon), 1953; Der Besuch Der Alten Dame (Time and Again subsequently re-titled The Visit), 1956; Frank Der Fünfte (Frank the Fifth), 1959; Die Physiker (The Physicists), 1962; Herkules und Der Stall des Augias (Hercules in the Augean Stables), an adaptation of his earlier radio play, 1963; The Meteor, 1966; Die Wiedertäufer, 1967; Play Strindberg, 1969; Portrait of a Planet, 1970; Der Mitmacher, 1973; Die Frist, 1977; his first play to be produced in London was The Marriage of Mr Mississippi at the Arts, Sept 1959; his first play to be produced in New York was The Visit at the opening of the Lunt-Fontanne Theatre, May 1958; also author of the Shakespearian adaptations, König Johann and Titus Andronicus, and of Urfaust, a version of Goethe's play; filmed versions of his own works include The Visit and The Marriage of Mr Mississippi, and he wrote the screenplay for Es Geschah am heiligen Tag; for radio, since his first play Herkules (1954)—see above—his works include: Abendstunde Im Spatherbst (Prix Italia, 1958), Die Panne, 1956, and Der Doppelgänger, 1960; he is also author of essays and collections including Theaterprobleme, 1955, Sätze aus Amerika, 1976, and Lesebuch, 1978; among his many novels since Pilatus, 1949, are Der Richter und sein Henker and Grieche Sucht Griechin (Mannheim Schillerpreis); other awards include the Grosser Schillerpreis, for Die Physiker, and a Grillparzer Preis for Besuch der alten Dame; he has received Honorary Doctorates from the Temple University, Philadelphia, and the Universities of Jerusalem and Nizza.

Address: Pertuis du Sault 36, CH 2005 Neuchâtel, Switzerland.

DU SAUTOY, Carmen, actress

b London, 26 Feb 1950; *d* of Arthur John Du Sautoy and his wife Viola (Stocker); *e* West Heath School, Sevenoaks; *m* Charles Savage, director.

Made her first stage appearance in a student production of The Lover at the University Theatre, Venice, 1968; following work in fringe theatre, 1971, including a time with the Portable Theatre Company, she appeared in repertory at Nottingham Playhouse and Leeds (1972), Crewe (1973–74), and Oxford Playhouse (1976), in parts including Lucy Lockit in the Beggar's Opera (which she also choreographed), Olivia in Twelfth Night, Rosie Probert in Under Milk Wood, Elsie in The Lunatic, the Secret Sportsman and the Woman Next Door, and Puss in Puss in Boots; English Theatre, Vienna, 1974, played Prossy in Candida; 1975 Bubble Theatre Company Season, parts included Marie in the The Trial of Marie Stopes, and Miss Macdonald in Cages; joined the Royal Shakespeare Company at Stratford, Feb 1977, to play Hippolyta in A Midsummer Night's Dream, and a Courtesan in The Comedy of Errors, repeating these parts in Newcastle, March–May, 1977, and also appearing as Cassandra in Troilus and Cressida; played the three parts again at the Aldwych during the 1977–78 season, also appearing as Mrs Lynge in Pillars of the Community and Mrs Fainall in The Way of the World; Stratford, season 1978–79, played Ceres in The Tempest, The Princess of France in Love's Labour's Lost, and at The Other Place, Lady Cummings in Captain Swing and Madeleine in Piaf, repeating all these roles excepting that of Ceres during the Newcastle season, Mar–May, 1979; Aldwych season 1979–80, again played the Princess of France, and also Miss Leighton in Once in a Lifetime and Elena in Children of the Sun; Warehouse, June 1979, repeated Madeleine in Piaf; repeated Miss Leighton at the Piccadilly, Feb 1980; films include Our Miss Fred and The Man with the Golden Gun; has appeared on British and German television.

Favourite parts: Mrs Fairall and Lucy Lockit. *Hobbies:* Science fiction, driving, jazz and belly dancing, skiing, tennis. *Address:* c/o Duncan Heath, Studio 1, 57 Redcliffe Road, London SW10. *Tel:* 01-351 4142.

DUSSAULT, Nancy, singer and actress
b Pensacola, Florida, 30 June 1936; *d* of Captain George Adrian Dussault and his wife Sarah Isabel (Seitz); *e* Northwestern University (BMus 1957, Phi Beta Kappa); *m* James D Travis; prepared for the stage with Alvina Kraus and studied singing with Lotte Lehmann.

Made her professional début at the Highland Park Music Theatre, Illinois, 1955, as a Nurse in South Pacific; same theatre, summers of 1955 and 1956, played in Guys and Dolls, Lady in the Dark, Kismet, The Golden Apple, Pal Joey; sang with the Chicago Symphony and received the Young Artist's Award of the Society of American Musicians; made her New York début at the Downtown, 7 Nov 1958, in the revue Diversions; New York City Center, Apr 1959, Jeanne in Street Scene; Barbizon Plaza, June 1959, Judy in Dr Willy Nilly; City Center, Oct 1959, Pitti-Sing in The Mikado; City Center, Feb 1960, Sister Mister in The Cradle Will Rock; Circle in the Square, Apr 1960, Bobbie in No for an Answer; Shubert, New Haven, Conn, Apr 1960, Hilaret in Lock Up Your Daughters; St James, Dec 1960, Tilda Mullen in Do Re Mi; Lunt-Fontanne, Sept 1962, took over as Maria in The Sound of Music; State Music Fair, Dallas, Texas, summer, 1963, Miss Agnes in Apollo and Miss Agnes; Washington, DC, Opera Company, June 1964, sang Beatrice in the American staged première of Beatrice and Benedict, by Hector Berlioz; Shubert, Nov 1964, Emily Kirsten in Bajour; New York City Center, Dec 1966, Carrie Pipperidge in Carousel; City Center, Apr 1967, Sharon McLonergan in Finian's Rainbow; toured, 1967, in Half a Sixpence; White House, Washington, DC, Feb 1968, played in a command performance of Fiorello!; toured, 1968, as Daisy Gamble in On a Clear Day You Can See Forever; Goodspeed Opera House, East Haddam, Conn, Dec 1968, the title-role in Peter Pan; Jones Beach, NY, July 1969, Ensign Nellie Forbush in South Pacific; Theatre de Lys, June 1970, appeared in Whispers on the Wind; The Other Stage, for the New York Shakespeare Festival, Feb 1970, Rose Trelawny in Trelawny of the 'Wells', Anspacher, Oct 1970, again played Rose Trelawny when the New York Shakespeare Festival revived Trelawny of the 'Wells'; Shubert, Philadelphia, Mar 1973, Mary McLeod in Detective Story; toured, summer 1973, in The Gershwin Years; Paper Mill Playhouse, Millburn, NJ, 1975, Irene in Irene; Town Hall, NY, 14 Jan 1976, appeared with Karen Morrow in the series Winter Interludes; Music Box, Sept 1977, took over from Millicent Martin in Side by Side by Sondheim; first appeared on television on 1 Jan 1961 on the *Ed Sullivan Show,* and has since appeared frequently on *The Gary Moore Show, Bell Telephone Hour,* The Beggar's Opera, Love Is, *The Dick Van Dyke Show* (1971), etc.

Favourite parts: Rose Trelawny, Peter Pan, Daisy Gamble. *Hobbies and recreations:* Needlework, cooking, reading, music. *Address:* c/o Heseltine-Baker Associates, 119 West 57th Street, New York, NY 10019.

DYALL, Valentine, actor
b London, 7 May 1908; *s* of Franklin Dyall and his wife Phyllis (Logan); *e* Harrow and Christ Church, Oxford; *m* (1) Marjorie Stonor (mar dis); (2) Bay Culme-Seymour (*née* Holder) (*dec*); (3) Kay Woodman.

While at Oxford was a member of the OUDS, and in 1930, played the title-role in Macbeth; made his first appearance on the stage at the Old Vic, 13 Sept 1930, as the Duke of Northumberland in Henry IV (Part I); at the re-opening of Sadler's Wells Theatre, Jan 1931, played the Priest in Twelfth Night; at the Queen's, later in the year, succeeded to the part of Surtees Cook in The Barretts of Wimpole Street; His Majesty's, Feb 1932, Strato in Julius Caesar; Kingsway, May 1932, Hastings in She Stoops to Conquer; Alhambra, Jan–Feb 1934, appeared in Henry V, Julius Caesar, etc; Lyric, Dec 1934, for a time, succeeded Laurence Olivier as Anthony Cavendish in Theatre Royal; Westminster, May 1935, played Julian Kerr in Disturbance; Lyric, Hammersmith, Nov 1935, Ross in Macbeth; Embassy, Apr 1936, Captain Adair and Lieut Campbell in England Expects . . .?; Playhouse, May 1936, Joe Gascoyne in My Son's My Son; Daly's, Aug 1936, Shaw in Chinese White; New, Feb 1937, Oliver in As You Like It; Coliseum, Mar 1937, Tristan L'Ermite in The Vagabond King; Apollo, Mar 1938, and again, at His Majesty's, Oct 1938, Mr Cherry in Idiot's Delight; from 1941–54 he was mainly engaged in films and broadcasting, although he appeared at the Comedy, Aug 1946, as Paul von Galen in The Other Side; Intimate, Mar 1954, appeared as Charles Stanton in Full Circle; Stoll, Oct 1954, played Brother Dominic in Joan of Arc at the Stake; toured, 1955, as Freddie in First Night; Court, Oct 1955, played Morton in The Sun of York; Palladium, Dec 1956, played Abanazar in The Wonderful Lamp; Victoria Palace, Nov 1958, Vladimir Previtch in Friends and Neighbours; Coventry, Aug 1960, appeared in the revue Here is the News; Pembroke, Croydon, Apr 1961, Mr James Formal in The Gentleman Dancing Master; Royal, Stratford, E, Dec 1961, played the Ogre in The Marvellous Story of Puss in Boots; Everyman, Cheltenham, Sept 1962, played Auda Abu Tayi in Ross; Mermaid, Jan 1963, Lord Fortnum of Alamein in The Bed-Sitting Room, transferring with the production to the Duke of York's, Mar 1963; Mermaid, Feb 1964, appeared in The Royal Commission Revue; Comedy, Dec 1964, Tarantyev in Son of Oblomov; Saville, May 1968, again played Lord Fortnum of Alamein in The Bed-Sitting Room; Royal Court, Dec 1969, Cardinal Richelieu in The Three Musketeers Ride Again; 1970, toured as Ezra in All in Good Time; toured, Summer 1974, in Who Goes Bare?; Royal Court, July 1975, Dr Rance in What the Butler Saw; narrator for the radio series The Man in Black; TV appearances include The Old Crowd, and the series *Secret Army.*

Recreations: Fishing, golf and playing the guitar. *Address:* c/o Essanay Ltd, 75 Hammersmith Road, London W14.

DYER, Charles Raymond, dramatic author, actor, novelist
b Shrewsbury, 1928; *s* of James S Dyer and his wife Florence (Stretton); *e* Queen Elizabeth's School, Barnet; *m* Fiona Thomson; served as a Flying Officer Navigator in the RAF, 1942–6.

Author of the following plays: Clubs Are Sometimes Trumps, 1948; Who On Earth!, 1951; Turtle in the Soup, 1953; The Jovial Parasite, 1954; Single Ticket Mars, 1955; Time, Murderer, Please, Poison in Jest, Wanted—One Body, 1956; Prelude to Fury, 1959; Rattle of a Simple Man, 1961; Gorillas Drink Milk, 1964; Staircase, 1965; Mother Adam, 1970; Hot Godly Wind, 1976; Loving Allelujah!, 1978; Roundabout, 1979; Rattle of a Simple Man ran for one year at the Garrick, London: both this play and Staircase have also been produced in NY and throughout the world; began his career as an actor at the New Theatre, Crewe, 1947, subsequently touring 1948–50, as Duke in Worm's Eye View; Prince of Wales, Mar 1955, played the Maître d'Hotel in Room for Two; Whitehall, Feb 1958, took over Flash Harry in Dry Rot, subsequently touring with the play; Yvonne Arnaud Theatre, Guildford, Feb 1966, starred in Wanted—One Body; directed the London productions of his play Mother Adam in 1971 and 1973; has appeared in the following films: Loneliness of a Long Distance Runner, Rattle of a Simple Man, and The Knack; appeared in the television series Hugh and I, 1965; author of the screenplays of Rattle of a Simple Man and Staircase, and also of the novels under the same titles.

Recreations: Amateur music and carpentry. *Address:* Old Wob, Austenwood, Gerards Cross, Bucks.

DYER, Christopher, stage designer
b 2 Feb 1947; *e* Ravensbourne College of Art and Design; *m* Jeannie Laird.

He designed his first production for the stage, Ghosts, at the Marlowe Theatre, Canterbury, 1968; after a time working in repertory, including the Bristol Old Vic, he joined the Royal Shakespeare Company, 1974, and has since designed the following plays for them: The Beast, 1974; Hamlet, Perkin Warbeck, Man is Man, 1975; Romeo and Juliet, The Iceman Cometh, Troilus and Cressida, Bingo, 1976; The Alchemist, 'Tis Pity She's a Whore, The Lorenzaccio Story, Days of the Commune, The Bundle, 1977; The Taming of the Shrew, The Jail Diary of Albie Sachs, Savage Amusement, The Women Pirates, The Hang of the Gaol, 1978; Pericles, The Innocent, Much Ado About Nothing, The Caucasian Chalk Circle, Children of the Sun, 1979; The Shadow of a Gunman, The Fool, Timon of Athens, Hansel and Gretel, 1980; joint winner of the Golden Troika award at the Prague International Stage Design Exhibition, 1979.

Address: 6 Windsor Terrace, Clifton, Bristol BS8 4LW. *Tel:* Bristol 24391.

DYSART, Richard A, actor
b Augusta, Me; *e* Emerson College, Boston.

First appeared on the New York stage at the Circle in the Square, 22 Nov 1958, as the Orderly in The Quare Fellow; Circle in the Square, Mar 1959, Howie Newsome in Our Town; Actors' Playhouse, Dec 1960, Barney Evans in Epitaph for George Dillon; same theatre, Apr 1961, Prison Guard in The Seven at Dawn; Martinique, Mar 1963, the Father in Six Characters in Search of an Author; toured USA, 1963–4, when he succeeded George Rose in the role of The Common Man in A Man for All Seasons; Royale, Feb 1965, Uncle Fred in All in Good Time; joined the American Conservatory Theatre and toured with Uncle Vanya, 1966, in Connecticut, Illinois, and California; Vivian Beaumont, Oct 1967, Horace Giddens in The Little Foxes; Ethel Barrymore, Dec 1967, repeated his role in The Little Foxes; Astor Place, Oct 1969, Mike in The Ruffian on the Stair and Erpingham in The Erpingham Camp in the double-bill Crimes of Passion; Long Wharf, New Haven, Conn, Nov 1970, Pierre Lannes in A Place Without Doors, and repeated this part at the Staircase, New York, Dec 1970; Newman, May 1972, Coach in That Championship Season, in the New York Shakespeare Festival production, and transferred with it to the Booth, 14 Sept 1972; Mark Taper Forum, LA, May 1978, Louis Puget in Black Angel; appeared in the films The Crazy World of Julius Vrooder, The Terminal Man, 1974.

Address: c/o Writers and Artists Agency, 162 West 56th Street, New York, NY 10019.

E

EASTON, Richard, actor
b Montreal, Canada, 22 Mar 1933; *s* of Leonard Idell Easton and his wife Mary Louisa (Withington); *e* Montreal; studied for the stage with Eleanor Stuart in Montreal, and at the Central School of Speech and Drama, London.

Made his first appearance on the stage in Knowlton, Canada, June 1947, as Wally in Our Town; member of the Canadian Repertory Theatre Company, 1951; joined the first Shakespearean Festival Company, Stratford, Ontario, June 1953, to play Sir Thomas Vaughan in Richard III; made his first appearance in London at the Apollo, June 1954, where he played Edward Kinnerton in Both Ends Meet; Palace, July 1955, played Claudio in Much Ado About Nothing, and Edgar in King Lear, with the Shakespeare Memorial Theatre Company, subsequently touring Europe and the English provinces; Stratford Shakespearean Festival, Ontario, June 1956, played Lord Scroop and Alexander Court in Henry V, and Slender in The Merry Wives of Windsor, subsequently appearing with the company at the Edinburgh Festival, Aug 1956, in Henry V; made his first New York appearance at the Phoenix, off-Broadway, Jan–Mar 1957, when he played Claudio in Measure for Measure, Lucentio in The Taming of the Shrew, and Delio in The Duchess of Malfi; Shakespeare Festival, Stratford, Conn, June–Aug 1957, played Roderigo in Othello, Claudio in Much Ado About Nothing, and Launcelot Gobbo in The Merchant of Venice; Adelphi, NY, Nov 1957, played Harcourt in The Country Wife; Ambassador, Mar 1958, Cain in Back to Methuselah; Stratford, Conn, June 1958, played Puck in A Midsummer Night's Dream, Osric in Hamlet and Florizel in The Winter's Tale; Barbizon Plaza, Nov 1958, played Timothy in Salad Days; Stratford, Conn, June 1959, Romeo in Romeo and Juliet, Puck in A Midsummer Night's Dream, Pistol in The Merry Wives of Windsor, and French Lord in All's Well That Ends Well; Wilbur, Boston, Jan 1960, played David in Motel; founder member Association of Producing Artists, NY, 1960; first season, May 1960, played Anatol in The Affairs Of Anatol, Constantine in The Seagull, Octavius in Man and Superman; Oct directed The Lady's Not For Burning, played Jack in The Importance of Being Earnest; Feb 1961, played Edgar in King Lear, title-role in Hamlet, Amiens in As You Like It, Orsino in Twelfth Night and Oberon in A Midsummer Night's Dream; Haymarket, London, Apr 1962, played Sir Harry Bumper in The School for Scandal, subsequently taking over the part of Joseph Surface, June 1962, and Charles Surface, Oct 1962; appeared in the same production in the last part at the Majestic, NY, Jan 1963; Piccadilly, London, Feb 1964, played Nick in Who's Afraid of Virginia Woolf?; Globe, Sept 1965, played Barry in Comfort Me With Apples; Opera House, Manchester, Nov 1965, played Fagin in Oliver and toured; Oxford Playhouse, Feb 1967 and subsequently touring, played Marlow in She Stoops to Conquer, The Bishop in The Balcony and the title-rôle in Richard II; returned to the US, 1967, where he appeared with the APA Repertory Company in NY and on tours, Berenger in Exit The King, Creep in Pantagleize and Trofimov in The Cherry Orchard, 1967; Alceste in The Misanthrope, Messenger in Cock-a-doodle-Dandy, and Claudius in Hamlet, 1969; San Diego Shakespeare Festival, summer, 1969, played Bru-

tus in Julius Caesar (also directed) and the title-rôle in Macbeth (also tour for APA); Los Angeles, Mark Taper Forum, 1970, played Bonham in Murderous Angels; Belgrade, Coventry, and tour, Sept 1971, Syd Sorokin in The Pyjama Game; Playhouse, NY, Dec 1971, again appeared in Murderous Angels; Thorndike, Leatherhead, June 1972, Walter Franz in The Price; Arnaud, Guildford, June 1972, Alexander in Friends, Romans and Lovers; Haymarket, Leicester, June 1975, Charles in Blithe Spirit; Harrogate, Aug 1975, Trigorin in The Seagull; 1977, toured in Caught on the Hop; Marlowe, Canterbury, Oct 1977, played Macbeth; Thorndike, Leatherhead, Jan 1978, Dysart in Equus; Crucible, Sheffield, Feb 1978, and tour, Aubrey Tanqueray in The Second Mrs Tanqueray; Edinburgh Festival, 1978, Theseus/Oberon in A Midsummer Night's Dream, and Caliban in The Tempest; Arnaud, Guildford, Feb 1979, and tour, Ernest Melton in Canaries Sometimes Sing; since 1952 has appeared on television in Canada, the US, and in England, notably in the BBC series *The Brothers* and recently in As You Like It.

Favourite parts: Hamlet, Nick in Who's Afraid of Virginia Woolf?, and Puck. *Recreations:* Music—singing of German Lieder. *Address:* 14 Earl's Terrace, London, W8.

EATON, Wallas, actor
b Leicester, 18 Feb 1917; *s* of John Walter Eaton and his wife Clara (Jarram); *e* Christ's College, Cambridge.

Made his first appearance on the stage, at Theatre Royal, Leicester, Aug 1936; first appeared in London, at the Old Vic, Aug 1939, as the Announcer in The Ascent of F6; Mercury, Mar–Apr 1940, played the 2nd Priest in Murder in the Cathedral, and Dromio of Ephesus in A New Comedy of Errors; Streatham Hill, July 1940, played Bauer in The Body Was Well Nourished; then joined the Army; was discharged with the rank of Major, 1944; at the Lyric, Hammersmith, Oct–Nov 1944, played Sergeant Fielding in Too True to be Good, and the Rev Alexander Mill in Candida; Arts, Jan–Feb 1945, appeared in The Letter, The Copy, and Leonce and Lena; Phoenix, May 1945, played the Convener in The Skin of Our Teeth; Lyric, Hammersmith, Mar 1946, Peter Grimsby in To-Morrow's Child; Playhouse, Dec 1946, appeared in Between Ourselves; Saville, Mar, 1947, in 1066 and All That; Comedy, Nov 1948, in Slings and Arrows; from that date to 1955, identified with the Radio show Take It From Here; Adelphi, Nov 1950, appeared in Take It From Us; Palace, Sept 1951, played Motty Whittle in Zip Goes a Million; Royal, Windsor, May 1953, Piotr Petrovsky in Anastasia; Royal, Brighton, Nov 1954, Bob Harvey in Chandelier for Charlie; Winter Garden, Aug 1955, Ernest in The Water Gipsies; Apollo, Jan 1958, followed Hugh Paddick in the revue For Amusement Only; Theatre Royal, Stratford, Dec 1959, played Horace Seaton, Percy Fortesque, and A Priest in Fings Ain't Wot They Used T' Be, transferring with the production to the Garrick, Feb 1960; where it ran for over two years; Piccadilly, Aug 1964, played Algernon Coker-Smith in Instant Marriage; Royal Court, Jan 1967, Sir Jolly Jumble in The Soldier's Fortune; since 1974 resident in Australia, where theatre includes The Bed Before Yesterday, Sydney, 1979; first appeared in films, 1940, in Caesar and

Cleopatra; since 1962, has appeared in numerous television productions in England and in Australia.

Recreation: Sailing. *Club:* Green Room. *Address:* c/o April Young Ltd, 16 Neal's Yard, Monmouth Street, London, WC2.

EBB, Fred, lyricist
b New York City, 8 Apr 1933; *s* of Harry Ebb and his wife Anna (Gritz); *e* New York University and Columbia University.

First show produced for which he supplied the lyrics was Flora, the Red Menace, at the Alvin, NY, May 1965; has since supplied the lyrics for Cabaret, 1967; The Happy Time, Zorba, 1968; Cabaret (London), 1969; book with Norman L Martin and lyrics for 70, Girls, 70, 1971; Zorba (London), 1973; book for Liza, 1974; adapted book with Bob Fosse and lyrics for Chicago, 1975; lyrics for The Act, 1978; wrote, directed and produced Liza in Concert at Carnegie Hall, Sept 1979; first production for television was in June 1970, with lyrics for Liza, a special starring Liza Minnelli; also Liza with a Z, 1972, Ole Blue Eyes Is Back (Frank Sinatra), 1974, Gypsy in My Soul (Shirley Maclaine), 1976, and Goldie and Liza Together, 1980; films include Funny Lady, Lucky Lady, Cabaret, A Matter of Time, New York, New York, French Postcards.

Hobby: Collecting musical show albums. *Address:* International Creative Management, 40 West 57th Street, New York, NY 10019.

EBERT, Joyce (*née* Joyce Anne Womack), actress
b Munhall, Pa, 26 June 1933; *d* of John Leib Womack and his wife Bertha Louise (Friedel); *e* Carnegie Institute of Technology (BA 1955); studied acting with Uta Hagen and the Actors Studio with Lee Strasberg; *m* (1) Michael Ebert; (2) Arvin Brown, director; trained for the stage with Uta Hagen and Lee Strasberg.

Made her début at the Pittsburgh Playhouse, Pa, Jan 1953, in White Sheep of the Family; at the Carnegie Institute in Pittsburgh appeared as Nina in The Seagull, Julia in The Rivals, and Miranda in The Tempest, 1953–5; Ashland, Oregon, for the Oregon Shakespeare Festival, 1953–4 seasons, played Ophelia in Hamlet, Portia in The Merchant of Venice, and Bianca in The Taming of the Shrew; made her New York début at the Lenox Hill playhouse, 8 Feb 1956, as Julie in Liliom; Renata, June 1957, Alithea Pinchwife in The Country Wife; Theatre 74, Mar 1958, Emmanuelle in Asmodee; same, May 1958, Flora in Sign of Winter; Group 20 Players, Wellesley, Mass, 1958, Maria in The School for Scandal, Clara Eynsford-Hill in Pygmalion, and Jessica in The Merchant of Venice; Players, NY, Jan 1959, Cordelia in King Lear; Royal Playhouse, Mar 1959, took over as Gertrude in Fashion; Old Globe, San Diego, Cal, for the Shakespeare Festival, 1959, Juliet in Romeo and Juliet, Princess of France in Love's Labour's Lost, and Lady Mortimer in Henry IV, Part 1; St Mark's Playhouse, NY, Nov 1959, Camille in No Trifling with Love; Arena Stage, Washington, DC, 1960, Margie in The Iceman Cometh and Isabella in Ring Round the Moon; American Shakespeare Festival Theater, Stratford, Conn, June 1960, Miranda in The Tempest; McCarter, Princeton, NJ, Sept 1960, Annie in Anatol; Phoenix, NY, Mar 1961, Ophelia in Hamlet; Williamstown, Mass, summer 1962, Gwendolyn in Becket, Annie Sullivan in The Miracle Worker, Nina in The Seagull, and Lady Larkin in Once upon a Mattress; Circle in the Square, NY, Dec 1962, played in Under Milk Wood and Twelve O'Clock in Pullman Car Hiawatha; Williamstown, Mass, 1963, Ann in Man and Superman, Elizabeth in A Far

Country, Miss Fellows in The Night of the Iguana, Varya in The Cherry Orchard, and Mrs Booth in Mr Booth; McCarter, Princeton, 1963, Pegeen Mike in The Playboy of the Western World; Martinique, Nov 1963, took over as the Stepdaughter in Six Characters in Search of an Author; Circle in the Square, Dec 1963, Andromache in The Trojan Women; ANTA, Washington Square, Jane 1965, Mariane in Tartuffe; Circle in the Square, 1966, took over as Vittoria Corombona in The White Devil; Mark Taper Forum, Los Angeles, Apr 1967, played in The Devils; joined the Long Wharf Theatre, New Haven, Conn, and played in Misalliance, Jan 1967; in the 1967–8 season played Laura Wingfield in The Glass Menagerie and also played in The Rehearsal; 1968–9 season played The Duchess of Malfi; 1969–70 season The Wife in Joe Egg; 1970–1 season Mrs Hardcastle in She Stoops to Conquer, and the Wife in Solitaire and Barbara in Double Solitaire in a double-bill; John Golden, NY, Sept 1971, repeated these last two parts; Long Wharf, 1971–2 season, Gertrude in Hamlet and Blanche du Bois in A Streetcar Named Desire; 1972–3 season, played in Forget-Me-Not Lane; 1973–4 played Matron in The National Health and Madame Arkadina in The Seagull; Circle in the Square, NY, Oct 1974, again played Matron in The National Health; Long Wharf, 1974–5, played in You're Too Tall, But Come Back in Two Weeks; 1975–6, Clara in The Show-Off, Maggie Wylie in What Every Woman Knows, Bertha Dorset in The House of Mirth, and Maisie Nadigan in Darlin' Juno; 1976–7, in The Autumn Garden, and The Shadow Box, playing Maggie in a production which transferred to the Morosco, Mar 1977; 1977–8, in Hobson's Choice and Macbeth; 1978–9, in I Sent a Letter to My Love, Rosmersholm and Summerfolk, playing Maria Lvovna in the last play; first appeared on television in Frontiers of Faith, 1956, and has since appeared on the major dramatic programs, including: *Suspense, Kraft Television Theatre,* etc.

Address: Actors Equity Association, 165 West 46th Street, New York, NY 10036.

ECCLES, Donald, actor
b Nafferton, Yorkshire, 26 Apr 1908; *s* of Dr Charles Henry Eccles and his wife Constance (Yarrow); *e* Highgate School; originally engaged in an insurance office.

First appeared on the stage at the Shubert Theatre, New York, 30 Oct 1930, as James Churchill in The Last Enemy; during 1932–3 toured Australia, New Zealand and Egypt with Sir Lewis Casson and Dame Sybil Thorndike; first appeared in London at the Piccadilly, 10 Apr 1934, as Johann Breitstein in Counsellor-at-Law; 1935–7 was with the Birmingham Repertory, also appearing at the Malvern Festival and the Shakespeare Memorial Theatre, Stratford-on-Avon; Saville, Nov 1938, played the Jew, in Geneva; served with the Royal Navy, 1939–45; Lyric, Hammersmith, July 1946, played Frédéric Chopin, in Summer at Nohant; Barrymore, NY, Oct 1946, appeared as Ferdinand in The Duchess of Malfi; Malvern Festival, 1949, played King Magnus in The Apple Cart; Prince's, Oct 1949, Junius's Father in Buoyant Billions; Adelphi, Nov 1951, the Foreign Minister in The Moment of Truth; Westminster, Feb 1952, Mr Hilary in Nightmare Abbey; Shakespeare Memorial Theatre Company, Stratford-on-Avon, 1953, played Gremio in The Taming of the Shrew, and appeared with this company at the Princes, Nov 1953, as Maecenas in Antony and Cleopatra; at the Q, Jan 1955, Dr Macdonald in The Visiting Moon; Stoll, Apr 1955, played Omar in Kismet; Shakespeare Memorial Theatre Company, Stratford-on-Avon, 1957–9, appeared in the following parts: Corin in As You Like It, Earl of Salisbury in King John, Caius Lucius in Cymbeline, Cicero and Titinius in Julius Caesar, 1957; Cousin Capulet in Romeo and Juliet, Gravedigger in Hamlet, Cleon in Pericles, Friar Francis in Much Ado About Nothing, 1958; Rinaldo in All's Well That Ends Well, Titus Lartius in Coriolanus, Starveling in A Midsummer Night's Dream, Gloucester's Tenant in King Lear, 1959; visited Moscow and Leningrad with the same company, Dec 1958; Belgrade, Coventry, July 1960, played the Bandmaster in Dreaming Bandsmen; Mermaid, Apr 1961, Lazarus in The Wakefield Mysteries; Oxford Playhouse, Oct 1961, played Mazzini Dunn in Heartbreak House, subsequently appearing in the same production at Wyndham's, Nov 1961; St Paul's Cathedral, July 1962, appeared as Lazarus in The Raising of Lazarus; Mermaid, Mar 1963, Leslie Piper in All in Good Time; Ipswich Arts, Sept 1964, played Baron von Wehrhahn in The Beaver Coat; Ashcroft, Croydon, Feb 1965, Nonno in The Night of the Iguana, transferring with the production to the Savoy, Mar 1965; Arnaud, Guildford, Feb 1967, played Fourth Tempter and Fourth Knight in Murder in the Cathedral, and Mar 1968, the Hon Charles Piper in The Family Reunion; Mermaid, Apr 1968, the Cardinal Archbishop of Pimlico in Hadrian the Seventh, transferring to the Haymarket, Mar 1969; toured, July 1970, for the Cambridge Theatre Company, Judge in The Chalk Garden; toured, Feb 1972, for the Cambridge Theatre Company, as Zombrovitch in You and Your Clouds; Apollo, Apr 1975, Oliver Seaton in A Family and a Fortune; Théâtre des Bouffes du Nord, Paris, 1976, Nonno in La Nuit de L'Iguane; 1977, toured in The Sorrows of Frederick; 1978, toured in She Stoops to Conquer and as Hawkins in The Kingfisher, in Toronto and Hong Kong; has broadcast since 1933, and appeared frequently on television since 1938.

Recreations: Golf and nature study. *Club:* Green Room. *Address:* c/o David White Assocs, Flat 4, 12 George Street, London W1R 9DF.

ECKART, Jean (*née* Jean Levy), designer and producer
b Glencoe, Ill, 18 Aug 1921; *d* of Herbert Levy and his wife Catharyn (Rubel); *e* Tulane University and Yale University; *m* William J Eckart.

In co-operation with her husband has designed settings for the following productions: Glad Tidings, To Dorothy, a Son, 1951; Gertie, 1952; Maya, The Scarecrow, The School for Scandal, The Little Clay Cart, Dear Pigeon, Oh Men! Oh Women!, 1953; The Golden Apple, Wedding Breakfast, Portrait of a Lady, 1954; Damn Yankees (also costumes), Reuben, Reuben, 1955; Mister Johnson (also costumes), L'il Abner, 1956; Damn Yankees (London), Livin' the Life, Copper and Brass, 1957; The Body Beautiful, 1958; Once upon a Mattress (also co-produced), Fiorello! (also costumes), 1959; Viva Madison Avenue!, Once upon a Mattress (London), 1960; The Happiest Girl in the World, Let It Ride, Take Her, She's Mine, 1961; Oh Dad, Poor Dad, Mama's Hung You in the Closet and I'm Feelin' So Sad, Never Too Late, 1962; She Loves Me, Never Too Late (London), Here's Love, 1963; Too Much Johnson, Anyone Can Whistle, She Loves Me (London), All About Elsie (for the New York World's Fair), Fade Out—Fade In, 1964; A Sign of Affection, Flora, the Red Menace, The Zulu and the Zayda, Oh Dad, Poor Dad, Mama's Hung You in the Closet and I'm Feeling So Sad (London), 1965; Mame, Where's Charley? (tour), Agatha Sue, I Love You, 1966; A Midsummer Night's Dream (Stratford, Conn), Hallelujah, Baby, 1967; The Education of Hyman Kaplan, Maggie Flynn, A Mother's Kisses, 1968; The Fig Leaves Are Falling, A Way of Life, Mame (London), 1969; Norman, Is That You?, Sensations, 1970; Of Mice and Men, 1974; designed costumes for the film of

Pajama Game, sets and costumes for Damn Yankees and The Night They Raided Minsky's (1969); has designed for television since 1950.

Address: 14 St Luke's Place, New York, NY 10014.

ECKART, William J, designer and producer
b New Iberia, Louisiana, 21 Oct 1920; *s* of William J Eckart and his wife Annette (Brown); *e* Tulane University and Yale University; *m* Jean Levy.

In co-operation with his wife has designed settings for the following productions: Glad Tidings, To Dorothy, a Son, 1951; Gertie, 1952; Maya, The Scarecrow, The School for Scandal, The Little Clay Cart, Dear Pigeon, Oh Men! Oh Women! 1953; The Golden Apple, Wedding Breakfast, Portrait of a Lady, 1954; Damn Yankees (also costumes), Reuben, Reuben, 1955; Mister Johnson (also costumes), L'il Abner, 1956; Damn Yankees (London), Livin' the Life, Copper and Brass, 1957; The Body Beautiful, 1958; Once upon a Mattress (also co-produced), Fiorello! (also costumes), 1959; Viva Madison Avenue! Once upon a Mattress (London), 1960; The Happiest Girl in the World, Let It Ride, Take Her, She's Mine, 1961; Oh Dad, Poor Dad, Mama's Hung You in the Closet and I'm Feelin' So Sad, Never Too Late, 1962; She Loves Me, Never Too Late (London), Here's Love, 1963; Too Much Johnson, Anyone Can Whistle, She Loves Me (London), All About Elsie (for the New York World Fair), Fade Out—Fade In, 1964; A Sign of Affection, Flora, the Red Menace, The Zulu and the Zayda, Oh Dad, Poor Dad, Mama's Hung You in the Closet and I'm Feeling So Sad (London), 1965; Mame, Where's Charley? (tour), Agatha Sue, I Love You, 1966; A Midsummer Night's Dream (Stratford, Conn), Hallelujah, Baby, 1967; The Education of Hyman Kaplan, Maggie Flynn, A Mother's Kisses, 1968; The Fig Leaves Are Falling, A Way of Life, Mame (London), 1969; Norman, Is That You? Sensations, 1970; Of Mice and Men, 1974; appointed Head of Theatre Design Studies of Southern Methodist University, Dallas, Texas, Sept 1971, for which he and his wife design productions; designed costumes for the film of Pajama Game, sets and costumes for Damn Yankees, and The Night They Raided Minsky's (1969); has designed for television since 1950.

Address: 14 St Luke's Place, New York, NY 10014.

EDA-YOUNG, Barbara, actress
b Detroit, Mich, 30 Jan 1945; *d* of Eddie Young and his wife Ann.

Made her professional debut Jun 1965 at Theatre Genesis, NY, as Velma Sparrow in Birdbath; at the Vivian Beaumont, Nov 1969, Babs in The Time of Your Life; Jan 1970, Olympe and Eva in Camino Real; Mar 1970, Honey in Operation Sidewinder, all these for the Repertory Theatre of Lincoln Center; also Forum, Nov 1971, The Girl and Doreen in Kool Aid; St James, Oct 1973, Stella Kowalski in A Streetcar Named Desire; at the Williamstown Festival, 1976, played Billie in Born Yesterday, Natasha in Three Sisters and Carol in Orpheus Descending; Manhattan Theatre Club, Mar 1977, Carmel in The Gathering; Williamstown, 1977, Maggie in After the Fall; Long Wharf, New Haven, 1978, Sylvia in Two Brothers, Mar, and Liz in The Philadelphia Story, Apr; Public, Nov 1978, Claudette in Drinks Before Dinner; her films include Serpico, 1974; TV includes *Another World*.

Address: c/o Coleman-Rosenberg, 667 Madison Avenue, New York, NY 10019.

EDDINGTON, Paul, actor
b London, 18 June 1927; *s* of Albert Clark Eddington and his

wife Frances Mary (Roberts); *e* The Friends School, Sibford Ferris, Oxon; *m* Patricia Scott.

Made his first appearance on the stage with ENSA, in the Garrison Theatre, Colchester, Oct 1944, in Jeannie; joined the Birmingham Repertory Company, 1945, remaining two seasons; Sheffield Repertory Company, 1947–52, training at the Royal Academy of Dramatic Art in 1951; Ipswich Repertory Company, 1953–5, after some years in television, he made his first appearance in London at the Comedy, Apr 1961, when he played the Rabbi in The Tenth Man; Belgrade, Coventry, June 1961, played Death in Thark, and Garry in Present Laughter; joined the Bristol Old Vic Company, Feb 1962, to play Andrei in War and Peace, subsequently appearing in the same production at the Old Vic, June 1962, and transferring to the Phoenix, later in the same month; returned to the Bristol Old Vic, Sept 1962–3, to play the title part in Brand, Henry II in Becket, Brutus in Julius Caesar, Parolles in All's Well That Ends Well, Albert Hesseltine in All Things Bright and Beautiful, Biedermann in The Fire Raisers, and Palmer Anderson in A Severed Head; he transferred with the last production to the Criterion, June 1963, leaving the cast after one year to make his first appearance in New York at the Royale, Oct 1964, in the same play; Bristol Old Vic, Feb 1965, played Benjamin Disraeli in Portrait of a Queen, transferring with the production to the Vaudeville, London, May 1965; New, Sept 1966, Captain Doleful in Jorrocks (Clarence Derwent award); Comedy, June 1967, Harry in Queenie; Apollo, Oct 1968, played Franklin in Forty Years On; with the Bristol Old Vic, Spring 1973, played James Tyrone in Long Day's Journey into Night, and Osborne in Journey's End; Criterion, April 1974, took over as Ronald in Absurd Person Singular, later transferring to the Vaudeville; and also directing at the Arnaud, Guildford, Feb 1976, a production of the play based on the original one; Globe, Apr 1977, took over Headingley in Donkey's Years; same theatre, Apr 1978, played Ray in Ten Times Table; Greenwich, Apr 1979, Sir Oliver Cockwood in She Would If She Could; Lyric, Oct 1979, Reg in Middle-Age-Spread; since 1955, he has appeared in numerous television plays and series, including: Quartet, *Frontier, Special Branch, The Good Life,* and *Yes, Minister*; member of Council of Equity, 1972–5; Governor, Bristol Old Vic Theatre Trust, 1975–.

Favourite parts: Brand, Elyot in Private Lives, Magnus in The Apple Cart, Sir Andrew Aguecheek, and Malvolio. *Recreations:* Reading and classical music. *Club:* Green Room. *Address:* c/o Michael Anderson, ICM Ltd, 22 Grafton Street, London W1.

EDDISON, Robert, actor

b Yokohama, Japan, 10 June 1908; *s* of Edwin Eddison and his wife Hilda Muriel (Leadam); *e* Charterhouse and Trinity College, Cambridge; read medicine at Cambridge; was President of the ADC at the University, 1929–30; joined the Festival Theatre company at Cambridge as a pupil.

Made his first professional appearance at that Theatre, 23 June 1930, as Robert Audley in Lady Audley's Secret; made his first appearance in London at the Arts Theatre, 10 Dec 1930, as the Elder Brother in Comus; Westminster Theatre, Oct 1931–July 1932, played Raby in The Anatomist, Dick in A Pair of Spectacles, the Leading Juvenile in Six Characters in Search of an Author, Sam in Tobias and the Angel, Vicente in The Kingdom of God and Sir Nathaniel in Love's Labour's Lost; Royalty, Apr 1933, played George Smith in The Brontës; Ambassadors', Aug 1934, played Nevil in Family Affairs; St James's, Oct 1935, Charles in Two Share a

Dwelling; Old Vic, Dec 1935, Siward in Macbeth; Westminster, Mar 1936, Publius Cornelius in Fulgens and Lucrece; Old Vic, Apr 1936, King of France in King Lear; Sadler's Wells, May 1936, Mr Cotton and Apis in Peer Gynt; Westminster, June 1936, Baron Heinrich in The Emperor of Make Believe; Duchess, July 1936, Peter in Spring Tide; His Majesty's Dec, 1936, Shammah in The Boy David; New, Feb 1937, Le Beau and William in As You Like It; Open Air, Aug–Sept 1937, Sebastian in Twelfth Night, Ferdinand in The Tempest, Antipholus of Ephesus in A Comedy of Errors; Ambassadors', Oct 1937, Rev John Bagshot in Yes and No; Whitehall, Apr 1938, Geoffrey Tracey in Ghost for Sale; Royalty, June 1938, in 8.45 and All That and July 1938, Eric Shaw in Little Stranger; Open Air, Aug, and St Martin's, Sept 1938, Raphael in Tobias and the Angel; Aldwych, Dec 1938, Henry Lester in Number Six; Players', June 1939, André in Luck of the Devil; Open Air Theatre, 1939 season, played Pericles, Oberon in A Midsummer Night's Dream, and Raphael in Tobias and the Angel; Queen's, Dec 1939, appeared in All Clear; Richmond, June 1940, played John Morton in The Good Young Man; Threshold, Nov 1940, Sir Peter Blakeney in The Scarlet Pimpernel; Q, Dec 1940, Allan in A Lass and a Lackey; during the War, served in the Navy, 1941–5; reappeared on the London stage, at the St James's, May 1946, as Edward IV in The Kingmaker; St James's, July 1946, Rhodophil in Marriage à la Mode; Haymarket, Apr 1947, appeared as Roland Maule in Present Laughter; Bristol Old Vic company, 1947–8 season, where he played Hamlet, Lord Goring in An Ideal Husband, Iago in Othello, Pip in Great Expectations, Cayley Drummle in The Second Mrs Tanqueray, Lovborg in Hedda Gabler, Valentine in You Never Can Tell, Emperor of China in Aladdin, etc; St James's, July 1948, with this company, again played Hamlet; joined the Old Vic company for the 1948–9 season, at the New, playing Feste in Twelfth Night, Mephistophilis in Dr Faustus, Witwould in The Way of the World, and Trofimov in The Cherry Orchard; Phoenix, May 1949, played Thomas Aimwell in The Beaux' Stratagem; at the re-opening of the Old Vic, Nov 1950, appeared as Sir Andrew Aguecheek in Twelfth Night, and subsequently, Bartholomew Cokes in Bartholomew Fair, Pistol in Henry V, Orestes in Electra and Slender in The Merry Wives of Windsor; Lichfield Cathedral, Sept 1951, Thomas Becket in Murder in the Cathedral; Embassy, Dec 1951, Cornelius Hackl in The Merchant of Yonkers; Q, Apr 1952, Peter in Night of Masquerade; Mercury, July 1952, Avalon in World Behind Your Back; Bristol Old Vic, Oct 1952, Angelo in Measure For Measure; Playhouse, Nottingham, Jan 1953, Prospero in The Tempest; Bristol Old Vic, Apr 1953, Hjalmar Ekdal in The Wild Duck; toured, July 1953, as Buckingham in the Old Vic production of Henry VIII; New Lindsey, Sept 1953, played Prince Nicki Altenburg in The Loyal Traitors; Royal, Windsor, Nov 1953, Charles Cartwright in The Sun and I; Playhouse, Nottingham, Jan 1954, played Edward II in Carnival King; Lyric, Hammersmith, May 1954, Epihodov in The Cherry Orchard; Playhouse, Manchester, Oct–Nov 1954, played Jacques Grand in The Angel of Montparnasse; St Thomas's Church, Regent Street, Apr 1955, appeared as Brother Sebastian in Our Lady's Tumbler; Open Air Theatre, June 1955, appeared as Prospero in The Tempest, Oberon in A Midsummer Night's Dream, and Straforel in The Romanticks; Arts, Nov 1956, played Mr Smith in The Bald Prima Donna, and the title-part in The New Tenant; Oxford Playhouse, Apr 1957, Newton Reeves in The Critic and the Heart; Dublin Festival, May 1957, John Worthing in The Importance of Being Earnest; Edinburgh Festival, Aug 1957, played Dom Sebastian and

The Stranger in The Hidden King; Arts, Dec 1957, Richard Jennings in A Stranger in the Tea; Lyric, Hammersmith, Mar 1958, Alfred Allmers in Little Eyolf; New Shakespeare, Liverpool, June 1958, James Callifer in The Potting Shed; Belgrade, Coventry, Sept 1959, directed Comedy of Love; at the same theatre, Oct 1959, played the title-role in Trog; Oxford Playhouse, Nov 1959, Lord Foppington in The Relapse; Leatherhead Repertory, May 1960, the Professor in The Professor's Love Story; York Festival, June 1960, God the Father in the York Cycle of Mystery Plays; Bromley, Nov 1960, played Jacob Bowers in All Good Children; Royalty, Jan 1961, Hendrik Jansen in Masterpiece; Bromley, Apr 1961, Mr Levert in Dead Letter; Arts, May 1961, General Villiers in Three Posts on the Square; Strand, June 1961, played Polonius in Hamlet; joined the Old Vic Company, and at the Edinburgh Festival, Aug 1961, played the King of France in King John, and Lucifer in Dr Faustus, subsequently appearing in both productions at the Old Vic, Sept 1961; Old Vic, Dec 1961, played Banquo in Macbeth, subsequently taking over the title part; Mar 1962, played the Duke of Clarence in Richard III; Apr 1962, Cassius in Julius Caesar; and May 1962, Trinculo in The Tempest; Ashcroft, Croydon, Feb 1963, played Fable in The Sky is Green; at the same theatre, May 1963, directed The Beaux' Stratagem; at the Library, Manchester, 1963–4, played Heracles in The Rape of the Belt, the Cardinal in The Prisoner, Shylock in The Merchant of Venice, Hodge in Beauty and the Beast, and Oberon in A Midsummer Night's Dream; toured, Sept 1964, as Gripe in The Confederacy; Scala, Dec 1964, played Captain Hook in Peter Pan (matinées only); Mermaid, Feb 1965, Ivan Podkolyossin in The Marriage Brokers, Hammon in The Shoemaker's Holiday; Mar 1965, Lamberto Laudisi in Right You Are (If You Think So); Apr 1965, John the Baptist in The Wakefield Mysteries; May 1965, High Priest in Oedipus the King; June 1965, Pandulph in Left Handed Liberty; Aug 1965, Rev Augustin Jedd in Dandy Dick; Sept 1965, Count O'Dowda in Fanny's First Play; Hampstead Theatre Club, Dec 1965, again played Hodge in Beauty and the Beast; Hampstead Theatre Club, Mar 1966, Mr Allingham in Adventures in the Skin Trade; Aldwych, May 1966, for Royal Shakespeare Company, played Eugene in Tango and Professor Schlatter in The Meteor (July); Hampstead, Oct 1966, Roger Robb in In the Matter of J Robert Oppenheimer, transferring to Fortune Theatre, Nov 1966; Lyceum, Edinburgh, Mar 1967, Shylock in The Merchant of Venice; Mercury, Apr 1967, Architruc in Architruc and The Man in Hypothesis; Haymarket, Feb 1968, Canon Chasuble in The Importance of Being Earnest; at the same theatre, Oct 1968, Joshua in Ring Round the Moon; Thorndike, Leatherhead, Feb 1969, Dr Sloper in The Heiress; Meadow Players (tour), Apr 1969, Vanya in Uncle Vanya; Edinburgh Festival, Aug 1969, Duke of York in Richard II, and Archbishop of Canterbury and Lightborn in Edward II; played the same parts Mermaid Theatre, Sept 1969, and on tour, re-opening at Piccadilly Theatre, Jan 1970; received the Clarence Derwent Award, 1970, for performance of Lightborn; Duke of York's, July 1970, Taverna in The Heretic; Arts, Cambridge, Nov 1970, for Prospect Productions, appeared in The World's A Stage; toured West Africa, Jan–Mar 1971, as Thomas More in A Man for All Seasons; Hampstead, July 1971, Cubbins in A Hearts and Minds Job; at Nottingham Playhouse, Oct 1971–Jan 1972, played Pocket in The Magistrate, The Player in Rosencrantz and Guildenstern Are Dead, and Lush in The Owl on the Battlements; founder member of the Actors' Company, 1972, for whom he has played Pinchard in Ruling the Roost, Bonaventura in 'Tis Pity She's a Whore, Father Akita in The Three Arrows, 1972; Serebryakov in The

Wood Demon, Billy in The Way of the World, appeared in Knots, 1973; title role in King Lear (playing this part, Serebryakov and Billy at the Brooklyn Academy of Music, Feb), Cleante in Tartuffe, Cadmus in The Bacchae, 1974; Colchester, Mar 1973, Father Perfect in The Prodigal Daughter; Royal Court, June 1973, Babs in Magnificence; joined the National Theatre Company, 1975, playing Philinte in The Misanthrope on its US tour, at the St James's, NY, and on its return to the Old Vic; Burleigh in Phaedra Britannica, Sept, Player King in Hamlet, Dec; Old Vic, Feb 1976, appeared in Tribute to A Lady; Young Vic (again for NT), June, played Pandarus in Troilus and Cressida, and Oct 1976, Prologue and Orcanes in Tamburlaine the Great, at the opening of the Olivier; joined Prospect, 1977, playing the following roles at the Old Vic and on tour: the Inquisitor in St Joan, Alexas in All for Love, 1977; Ghosts and First Player in Hamlet, Feste in Twelfth Night, the Chaplain in The Lady's Not for Burning, 1978; with the same Company (now the Old Vic Company), July 1979, Old Vic and world tour, played Polonius in Hamlet; he appeared regularly at the Players' Theatre, 1937–41; he broadcasts frequently, and has made many appearances on television.

Address: c/o *The Spotlight*, 43 Cranbourn Street, London, WC2.

EDGAR, David, playwright
b 26 Feb 1948; *s* of Barrie Edgar and his wife Joan; *e* Oundle School and Manchester University; *m* Eve Brook.

While a working journalist, wrote his first play Two Kinds of Angel, July 1970, which was performed at Bradford University; he has since written the following plays for the stage: Still Life, Man in Bed, 1971; Death Story, Excuses Excuses, Rent or Caught in the Act, England's Ireland, 1972; A Fart for Europe, Baby-Love, 1973; The Dunkirk Spirit, Dick Deterred, 1974; Fired, O Fair Jerusalem, The National Theatre, 1975; Events Following the Closure of a Motorcycle Factory, Blood Sports, Saigon Rose, Destiny, 1976 (RSC 1977); Wreckers, 1977; Our Own People, The Jail Diary of Albie Sachs (New York, 1979), Mary Barnes, 1978; Teendreams, 1979; Nicholas Nickleby (adaptation for RSC), 1980; he is also author of the television plays The Eagle has Landed and I Know What I Meant, and the radio play Ecclesiastes; Baby-Love and Destiny have also been televised; Fellow in Creative Writing, Leeds Polytechnic, 1972–74; Resident Playwright, Birmingham Repertory Theatre, 1974–75; Lecturer in Playwriting, University of Birmingham, 1975–78; UK/US Bicentennial Arts Fellow resident in the USA, 1978–79; a founder member of the Theatre Writers' Union, and Vice-Chairman of the Writers' Section of ACTT; regular contributor to theatre and political periodicals.

Address: c/o Dr Jan van Loewen, 81 Shaftesbury Avenue, London W1. *Tel:* 437 5546.

EDGEWORTH, Jane, MBE, FRSA, Director, Drama Department of The British Council
b London, 20 Nov 1922; *d* of William Henry Waight and his wife Gertrude (Edgeworth); *e* privately; *m* Richard Eastham; trained for the stage at the Guildhall School of Music and Drama, where she obtained her licentiate diploma (Elocution).

Began her career as an actress, during World War II, in ENSA, also serving as *Commère* for variety and musical shows, and eventually taking charge of the Military Concert Party Section; appeared in repertory at Leicester, Guildford, Leeds, Amersham, etc; a member of the administrative staff of Sadler's Wells Ballet, 1946–58, during which time she toured extensively in America and Europe; joined The

British Council's Drama Department, 1958, serving as Tours Manager; appointed Head of Drama Section, 1961; Representative of The British Council on the following committees: Drama and Dance Panels, Arts Council of Great Britain; Overseas Committee of the British Theatre Association; Executive Committee of the British Centre of the International Theatre Institute; Grand Council of the Royal Academy of Dancing; Imperial Society of Teachers of Dancing; received the MBE in the New Year Honours, 1965; became a Fellow of the Royal Society of Arts, 1969.

Recreations: Gardening, and animal welfare. *Address:* Sycamore House, County Oak, Nr Crawley, Sussex. *Tel:* Crawley 30596.

EDGLEY, Michael Christopher, MBE, producing manager
b Melbourne, 17 Dec 1943; *s* of Eric Edgley and his wife Edna; *e* Christian Brothers College, Perth, Australia; *m* Jennifer Gedge.

After a year as a trainee accountant, joined his father at His Majesty's Theatre, Perth, 1962, as office-boy/accountant, eventually becoming Manager of the theatre; toured, 1965, as his father's assistant with The Great Moscow Circus; on his father's death became head of the Company, and having bought His Majesty's Theatre, he sold and later re-leased it until 1975; as a producer he has been responsible for presenting entertainments throughout Australasia and Asia, in Australia notably four tours by The Great Moscow Circus from 1968; The Bolshoi Ballet, the Royal Winnipeg Ballet, the Nederlands Dans Theater, The Kirov Ballet, the Scottish Ballet, the London Festival Ballet and the Dance Theatre of Harlem; the Georgian State Dance Company, the Ballet Folklórico of Mexico, the Moiseyev Company and the Red Army Choir; Disney on Parade (twice), the Chichester Festival Theatre Company, the Vienna Boys' Choir, the D'Oyly Carte Opera Company; Dracula, Annie, A Chorus Line, and Evita; Nureyev, Fonteyn, Makarova and Baryshnikov; Shirley Bassey, Bette Davis, Shirley MacLaine, Rod McKuen, Marcel Marceau, Vincent Price, The Two Ronnies, Liv Ullman etc; in 1973 arranged the first Australian–Russian cultural exchange, and presented the first Chinese attraction in Australia; awarded an MBE for services to the performing arts, 1972; made a Citizen of Western Australia, 1975.

Address: PO Box 7072, Cloisters Square, Perth, Western Australia 6000. *Tel:* 321 2662.

EDWARDS, Ben (*né* George Benjamin Edwards), designer
b Union Springs, Alabama, 5 July 1916; *s* of William Thomas Edwards and his wife Sarah (McLaurine); *e* Feagin School of Dramatic Arts, Kane School of Art; *m* Jane Greenwood.

First professional designs were for setting and lighting for the Barter Theatre, Abingdon, Virginia, 1935, where he designed Mrs Moonlight, Pursuit of Happiness, Smiling Through, Beyond the Hills, The Silver Cord, etc, 1935–9; first design for New York was at the National, 23 Feb 1940, for Another Sun; served in the US Army, 1942–6, with the rank of Lieutenant; upon leaving the Army designed Medea, 1947; has since designed Sundown Beach, 1948; Diamond Lil with William De Forest, The Taming of the Shrew and Julius Caesar for Margaret Webster's Shakespeare Company, 1949; The Bird Cage, The Legend of Sarah, Captain Brassbound's Conversion, 1950; The Royal Family, King Richard II, The Taming of the Shrew, 1951; Desire Under the Elms, Sunday Breakfast, The Time of the Cuckoo, 1952; The Remarkable Mr Pennypacker, 1953; Lullaby, Sing Me No Lullaby, The Travelling Lady, Anastasia, 1954; Tonight in Samarkand, The Honeys, 1955; Someone Waiting, The Ponder Heart, 1956; The Waltz of the Toreadors, The Dark at the Top of

the Stairs, 1957; Jane Eyre, A Touch of the Poet, The Disenchanted, 1958; God and Kate Murphy, Heartbreak House, Ages of Man, 1959; Face of a Hero, 1960; Midgie Purvis, Big Fish, Little Fish (also co-produced), Purlie Victorious, A Shot in the Dark, 1961; The Aspern Papers, 1962; Harold (also co-produced), The Ballad of the Sad Cafe (also co-produced), 1963; Hamlet (Richard Burton in the John Gielgud production), The Changeling, 1964; The Family Way, A Race of Hairy Men (also co-produced), supervised with George Jenkins The Royal Hunt of the Sun, 1965; Nathan Weinstein, Mystic, Connecticut, Where's Daddy? How's the World Treating You? 1966; What Do You Really Know About Your Husband? More Stately Mansions, The Freaking Out of Stephanie Blake, 1967; designed for the Minnesota Theatre Company, 1968; The Mother Lover, 1969; designed for the Studio Arena Theatre, Buffalo, NY, 1970; Purlie, 1972; Look Away, Finishing Touches, The Prodigal Daughter (Washington, DC), A Moon for the Misbegotten, 1973; Figures in the Sand, A Moon for the Misbegotten (LA), 1974; Long Day's Journey into Night (Brooklyn), A Matter of Gravity, A Texas Trilogy (Washington and NY), 1976; Anna Christie, A Very Private Life (Buffalo), An Almost Perfect Person, A Touch of the Poet, 1977; designed the films Lovers and Other Strangers, Class of '44, Last of the Red Hot Lovers; first designed for television, 1952, for *The Ed Wynn Show,* and later for *Armstrong Circle Theatre,* etc.

Address: United Scenic Artists, 1540 Broadway, New York, NY 10036.

EDWARDS, Hilton, actor and director
b London, 2 Feb 1903; *s* of Thomas George Edwards and his wife Emily (Murphy); *e* Grammar School, East Finchley, and St Aloysius, Highgate.

Made his first appearance on the stage with the Charles Doran Shakespearean company, at the Theatre Royal, Windsor, 1920, as the First Player in Hamlet; made his first appearance on London stage, at the Old Vic, 6 Feb 1922, in a minor part in Othello, remained there until 1924, by which time he had appeared in all but two of Shakespeare's plays; he also sang baritone roles with the Old Vic Opera company; subsequently toured in South Africa, and on returning to London played in various productions; after appearing at the Royalty, Apr 1927, in two parts in The Dybbuk, went to Ireland, for a short tour with Anew McMaster, where he met his partner, Micheál Mac Liammóir, with whom he founded the Dublin Gate Theatre, 1928; has since directed over three hundred plays at that theatre and at the Gaiety Theatre, Dublin, and has played leading parts including—Peer Gynt, Cyrano de Bergerac, Macbeth, Shylock, Sheridan Whiteside, Uncle Harry, Mr Antrobus, etc; in 1934, played and directed in America, with Micheál Mac Liammóir and Orson Welles; at the Westminster, London, June 1935, directed Yahoo (also playing Jonathan Swift), The Old Lady Says No (playing Major Sirr), and Hamlet (playing Claudius), with the Dublin Gate Company; directed and played in Dublin and also in Cairo, Malta, Athens, Belgrade, Bucharest, etc, at invitation of British Council between 1936–9; Gate Theatre productions in Dublin include: Ghosts, Brand, The Infernal Machine, Mourning Becomes Electra, Antony and Cleopatra, The Skin of Our Teeth, and several new Irish plays by Denis Johnston, W B Yeats, Micheál Mac Liammóir, Brian Friel and others; at the Vaudeville, Feb 1947, for the Dublin Gate Theatre, directed Ill Met By Moonlight, playing the part of Prof Sebastian Prosper; Embassy, Nov–Dec 1947, played Tom Broadbent in John Bull's Other Island, which he directed, and also directed The Old Lady Says No and Where

Stars Walk; at the Mansfield Theatre, New York, Feb 1948, again played Tom Broadbent in his production of John Bull's Other Island, and directed The Old Lady Says No and Where Stars Walk; at the Gate, Dublin, Dec 1950, directed Home for Christmas, appearing as Sir Roderick Killjoy; at Elsinore, Denmark, 1953, produced Hamlet, and appeared in the part of Claudius; Gaiety, Dublin, Aug 1956, directed the revue Gateway to Gaiety; Gaiety, Dublin, Mar 1957, played Redmond O'Hanlon and directed Step-in-the-Hollow; Lyceum, Edinburgh, Apr 1958, and Lyric, Hammersmith, May 1958, directed The Key of the Door; Olympia, Dublin, Nov 1958, directed Micheál Mac Liammóir's adaptation of The Informer; Gaiety, Dublin, Mar 1960, presented with Micheál Mac Liammóir, and directed Orson Welles, in Chimes At Midnight; Dublin International Festival, Sept 1960, presented and directed Micheál Mac Liammóir in the solo entertainment The Importance of Being Oscar, the production transferring to the Apollo, London, Oct 1960, and subsequently to the Lyceum, NY, Mar 1961; this production also toured Australia, South America, etc; Aldwych, May 1963, presented and directed Mac Liammóir in I Must Be Talking to My Friends; Opera House, Belfast, June 1963, directed The Evangelist; Dublin Festival, Sept 1963, directed The Last PM, and Oct 1963, The Roses Are Real (also playing Karl Schultz); Vaudeville, London, Jan 1964, again played Karl Schultz and directed The Roses Are Real; Dublin Festival, Sept 1964, co-presented and directed Philadelphia Here I Come; Dublin Festival, June 1965, directed Mac Liammóir in Talking About Yeats; Gate, Dublin, Aug 1965, revived Philadelphia, Here I Come! prior to its transferring to the Helen Hayes, NY, Jan 1966, and a subsequent US tour; Ensemble, Amsterdam, Nov 1965, directed The Plough and the Stars; Helen Hayes, NY, Oct 1966, directed The Loves of Cass Maguire; Lyric, Sept 1967, directed London production of Philadelphia, Here I Come!; NY, Feb 1968, directed American production of Lovers; Gaiety, Dublin, Nov 1968, directed Crystal and Fox; Fortune, Aug 1969, directed London production of Lovers; Gate, Sept 1969, directed and played in Dublin Festival production of King Herod Explains; Mark Taper Forum, Los Angeles, Apr 1970, directed American production of Crystal and Fox; Abbey, Oct 1970, The Seagull; has also appeared in and directed films, and made television appearances, including Mr Micawber in David Copperfield; Head of Drama, Irish Television 1961–3; awarded the Freedom of the City of Dublin, 1973; LLD, National University of Ireland, and DLitt, TCD, 1974.

Recreations: Music and foreign travel. *Address:* Gate Theatre, 4 Harcourt Terrace, Dublin, Eire. *Tel:* Dublin 67609.

EDWARDS, Sherman, composer and lyricist
b New York City, 3 Apr; *s* of Nathan Harrison Edwards and his wife Rachel Lillian (Rosenblat); *e* New York University, Cornell University; *m* Ingrid Secretan.

Composed the music, wrote the lyrics, and conceived the entire production of 1776, presented at the 46th Street, 16 Mar 1969; first London production, 1776, presented at the New, 16 June 1970; first score, 1954, Kid Galahad, with Elvis Presley; subsequently Flaming Star, GI Blues, 1776 (1972), etc; TV scores, since 1950, include Club Embassy, Opera versus Jazz (series), Who's Afraid of Mother Goose? etc.

Recreations: Sailing, sports, and archaeology. *Address:* Boonton Manor, New Jersey. *Tel:* 201–334–8334.

EGAN, Peter, actor
b London, 28 Sept 1946; *s* of Michael Thomas Egan and his wife Doris (Pilk); *e* St George's Secondary School, Maida Vale; *m* actress Myra Frances; trained for the stage at

RADA, 1964–66; formerly a draughtsman, capstan operator and porter.

Made his first appearance on stage as the cream-faced loon in Macbeth at Chichester Festival Theatre, 1966 season, spending a second season there as understudy and as the Dandy in The Italian Straw Hat, 1967; played several parts at the Palace Court, Bournemouth, 1966, including Hamlet, and Clare in The Maids; Arnaud, Guildford, 1967, Millais in Ordeal By Marriage; Open Air, Regent's Park, summer 1968, played Proteus in The Two Gentlemen of Verona; Everyman, Cheltenham, 1969, Romeo in Romeo and Juliet; joined the Royal Shakespeare Company at Stratford-upon-Avon, Apr 1970, playing Valentine in The Two Gentlemen of Verona, Richmond and First Murderer in Richard III, and Osric in Hamlet, then making his first London appearance as Valentine at the Aldwych, Dec 1970; returned to Chichester, 1971, to appear as Jack Absolute in The Rivals, Apollodorus in Caesar and Cleopatra, and Alexander in Cher Antoine; Mermaid, May 1972, and Cambridge, July 1972, played Captain Stanhope in the 69 Theatre Company's production of Journey's End, for which he received a London Theatre Critic's Award, 1972; Albery, Nov 1974, John Shand in What Every Woman Knows; Old Vic (National Theatre), Aug 1975, Cheviot Hill in Engaged; Oxford Playhouse, 1976, and tour, Sergius in Arms and the Man; Shaftesbury, May 1977, Charles Rolls in Rolls Hyphen Royce; toured, 1977, in A Perfect Gentleman; Crucible, Sheffield, 1978, Henry Carr in Travesties; Lyric, Hammersmith, Oct 1979, Valentine in You Never Can Tell; Lyric Studio, Nov 1979, directed Landmarks; first appeared in films, 1969, in One Brief Summer, and subsequently in Hennessey, Callan and The Hireling; television since Cold Comfort Farm, 1968, includes many plays and series, most recently Lillie, The Prince Regent, and The Greeks.

Favourite parts: Hamlet, Stanhope and any good leading part. *Hobbies:* Good wine and food, poker, snooker, swimming, travel. *Address:* Airedale Avenue, Chiswick, London W4. *Tel:* 01 734 7311.

EIGSTI, Karl, designer
b Goshen, Indiana, 19 Sept 1938; *s* of Orie Jacob Eigsti and his wife Agnes (Weaver); *e* Indiana Univ, American Univ and Bristol Univ; *m* Mary Alice Sutherland.

Since 1969 has designed scenery for over 200 productions on and off Broadway and in most of the major US regional theatres, including 26 productions for Arena Stage, Washington DC; designed his first décor for a New York production with Bananas, produced at The Forum, 5 Dec 1968; since then has designed Inquest, Othello, Boesman and Lena, 1970; The House of Blue Leaves, 1971; Grease (lighting), The Passion of Antigona Perez (décor and lighting), 1972; The Karl Marx Play, Nourish the Beast, Baba Goya, 1973; Yentl, The Yeshiva Boy (Brooklyn), 1974; Wings, Yentl, Sweet Bird of Youth, 1975; Dandelion Wine, 1976; On the Lock In, Daddy, Joanne, 1977; Cold Storage, Once in a Lifetime, Eubie, Annie Get Your Gun (Jones Beach), 1978; The Diary of Anne Frank, Knockout, Murder at the Howard Johnson's, Losing Time, 100% Alive (LA), 1979; has
exhibited his designs in New York, Washington, Stratford, Conn, and in Europe, Member of the Board of Directors of Theatre Communications Group; lecturer at New York U, 1966–present; visiting associate professor of drama, SUNY at Purchase, 1979–80.

Address: 25 Fifth Avenue, New York, NY. *Studio:* 141 Fifth Avenue, New York, NY. *Tel:* 473–2279.

ELDER, Eldon, designer
b Atchison, Kansas, 17 Mar 1924; *s* of Clifford Phillips Elder

and his wife Signe (Larsen); *e* Denver University and Department of Drama, Yale University.

Designed scenery for The Father, at Provincetown Playhouse, 1949; designed for Westport Country Playhouse, 1950–1; has since designed settings for the following productions: The Long Days, Dream Girl, Idiot's Delight, Legend of Lovers, 1951; Venus Observed, Time Out for Ginger, The Grey-Eyed People, 1952; Take a Giant Step, and eleven productions for the St Louis Municipal Opera Company, 1953; The Girl in Pink Tights, and eleven productions for the St Louis Municipal Opera Company, 1954; Phoenix '55, All in One, The Young and Beautiful, Heavenly Twins, and three for St Louis, 1955; Fallen Angels, 1956; Shinbone Alley, 1957; Lulu, 1958; Drums Under the Window, 1960; Santa Fe opera productions of Der Rosenkavalier and The Ballad of Baby Doe, 1961; Rehearsal Call, for the Juilliard School of Music, Richard II, Henry IV (Part I) (both for American Shakespeare Festival Theatre, Stratford, Conn), The Fun Couple (also co-produced), The Affair, 1962; Morning Sun, 1963; Rugantino (scenic supervisor), I Knock at the Door, The Child Buyer, Pictures in the Hallway, 1964; Madame Mousse (Westport, Conn), The World of Ray Bradbury, Mating Dance, 1965; A Whitman Portrait, and designed the stage and décor for the Ypsilanti, Michigan, Greek Theatre productions of The Birds and The Oresteia, 1966; Of Love Remembered, Amazing Grace (Ann Arbor, Michigan), 1967; at the Open Space, London, 1970, designed The Drexler Plays; Pygmalion, 1972; Will Rogers USA, A Family and A Fortune, The Seagull, Hamlet, A Doll's House (last four Seattle Repertory), 1974; Cyrano de Bergerac (Seattle), Blasts and Bravos: An Evening with H L Mencken, 1975; Madwoman of Chaillot (Seattle Repertory), The Signalman's Apprentice (PAF Playhouse), Music Is, She Stoops to Conquer (Baltimore), 1976; Harry Outside (London), The Rivals (Baltimore), Love Letters on Blue Paper, End of the Beginning (both Syracuse), Give My Regards to Broadway (PAF), 1977; The National Health, The Master Builder (Seattle), 1978; Every Good Boy Deserves Favour, The Royal Family (Atlanta), Jitters (Long Wharf), Paris Was Yesterday, 1979; as art director and designer for the New York Shakespeare Festival since 1958, he has designed Othello, 1958; Twelfth Night, Julius Caesar, 1959; Henry V, Measure for Measure, The Taming of the Shrew, 1960, Richard II, Much Ado About Nothing, A Midsummer Night's Dream, 1961; designed for CBS Television, 1956; has designed the operas Giants in the Earth, Suor Angelica, My Heart's in the Highlands, and Prima Donna; has also designed Will Rogers's USA for television; visiting critic in Stage Design, Yale University, 1954; Professor of Stage Design, Brooklyn College, since 1956; received the Ford Foundation Grant for Theatre Design, 1960; author of Modern American Scene Design, and Will it Make a Theatre, 1979; has acted as designer/consultant for a number of theatre projects in the US; has held a number of lectureships and professorships at various colleges including Brooklyn (Professor, 1969) and Ohio State (Guest Professor, 1979).

Address: 27 West 67th Street, New York, NY 10023. *Tel:* 877 2858.

ELDER, Lonne III, playwright and actor
b Americus, Ga, 26 Dec 1931; *s* of Lonne Elder II and his wife; *e* Yale School of the Drama; *m* Judith Ann Johnson.

Made his New York début as an actor at the Ethel Barrymore, 11 Mar 1959, as Bobo in A Raisin in the Sun; toured in this part, 1960–1; St Mark's Playhouse, 15 Nov 1965, played Clem in Day of Absence; his play Ceremonies in

Dark Old Men, originally performed at Wagner College, Staten Island, NY, July 1965, was produced at the St Mark's Playhouse by the Negro Ensemble Company, 4 Feb 1969, and revived several times thereafter; this play received the Outer Critics Circle Award, the Vernon Rice-Drama Desk Award, the Stella Holt Memorial Playwrights Award, and the Los Angeles Drama Critics Award; also wrote Seven Comes Up—Seven Comes Down (one-act), 1977; wrote the films Sounder, 1971, Melinda, 1972; was staff writer for the *NYPD* television series, 1968, and for the *McCloud* series, 1970–1; received the John Hay Whitney Fellowship in Playwriting, the Stanley Drama Award in Playwriting, the America National Theatre Academy Award in Playwriting, the Joseph E Levine Fellowship in film-making at the Yale School of the Drama, and the John Golden Fellowship in Playwriting, also at Yale; is a member of the Writers Guild of America, West, The Black Academy of Arts and Letters, the Harlem Writers Guild, and the New Dramatists Committee.

Address: Bart/Levy Associates, 280 South Beverly Drive, Beverly Hills, Calif. *Tel:* 273–4152.

ELGAR, Avril (*née* Williams), actress
b Halifax, Yorkshire, 1 Apr 1932; *d* of Albert Leslie Elgar Williams and his wife Annie Rose; *e* various schools in India and England; *m* James Maxwell; trained for the stage at the Old Vic Theatre School, London.

Made her first professional appearance as Young Macduff and Second Witch in Macbeth, Oct 1952, on an Arts Council tour of Wales; London debut, Royal Court, Jan 1958, as Norah in Epitaph for George Dillon; at the same theatre, played Dodo in The Sport of My Mad Mother, Feb, and Mrs Ecto in The Hole, Apr; Comedy, May 1958, repeated the part of Norah in Epitaph for George Dillon, making her New York debut in the same part, John Golden, Sept; returning to England she played Lucille in Danton's Death at the Lyric, Hammersmith, Jan 1959; Garrick, June 1959, Peony in Farewell, Farewell, Eugene; again at the Royal Court, she played the Night Nurse in The Death of Bessie Smith and Grandma in The American Dream, in an Albee double-bill, Oct 1961; a woman in The Blood of the Bambergs, July 1962; Edinburgh Festival, Aug 1963, Asta in the 59 Theatre Company's Little Eyolf; Arts, Feb 1965, Miss Sympathy in Crawling Arnold; Royal Court, played three parts in Shelley, and Lilian Fawcett in The Cresta Run, Oct 1965; Lady Kix in A Chaste Maid in Cheapside, Jan 1966; Alice Maitland in The Voysey Inheritance, Apr 1966; Olga in The Three Sisters, Apr 1967; Joyce in The Ruffian on the Stair (one-act), June 1967; University Theatre, Manchester, Dec 1970, played Aase in the 69 Theatre Company's Peer Gynt; Greenwich, Sept 1971, Sheila in The Sandboy; Royal Court, Nov 1972, Miss Davitt and First Nun in A Pagan Place; Manchester, Oct 1972, Agatha in the 69 Theatre Company's The Family Reunion; Cottesloe (National Theatre), Nov 1977, Helen Mallock in Half Life, transferring to the Duke of York's, Mar 1978; Round House, Apr 1979, Agatha in the Royal Exchange Theatre Company's production of The Family Reunion, transferring to the Vaudeville, June 1979; films, since her first in 1958, include Spring and Port Wine; has appeared frequently on television, since 1955, recently in the series *Rosie* and *George and Mildred*.

Favourite parts: most of the above. *Recreations:* Gardening and the *Times* crossword. *Address:* c/o French's, 26–28 Binney Street, London W1. *Tel:* 01–629 4159.

ELIAS, Hector, actor
b Buenos Aires, Argentina, 24 Sept; *s* of Abraham Elias and his wife Concepcion (Ruffo); *e* Tres Arroyos High School and Bahia Blanca Technical College in Buenos Aires; formerly

occupied as an art director in Argentina and in an advertising studio in New York; trained for the stage with Uta Hagen and Herbert Berghof at the HB Studio, and with Stephen Strimpell, Robert Elston, and Milton Katselas.

Made his NY début at the Theatre West, 1967, as M'su Cahusac in Thornton Wilder's Queens of France; Astor Place, Nov 1968, Alberto in The Subscriber, Sister Apollonia Liguori in Susie Is a Good Girl and Patrick in The Grab Bag in a triple-bill with the overall title The Grab Bag; Downstage, played the Guard in Bars of Dawn; Theatre West, Judge Andrea in The License; Equity Library, played in Firebrand; Arena Repertory, played the Waiter in A Perfect Analysis; Theatre at Noon, Jerry in The Zoo Story; Drama Group, The Bellboy in No Exit, and Stage 15, Alyoshka in The Lower Depths, all between 1968–71; Puerto Rican Traveling Theater, Aug 1971, played Dr Max Medina in Dramatized Anthology of Puerto Rican Short Stories; Anspacher, Nov 1971, Sergeant Major in Sticks and Bones, and transferred with this production to the John Golden, Mar 1972; Puerto Rican Traveling Theater, Aug 1973, Leader in Noo Yall; first appeared in films in 1969 in Dealing, and has since played in Bang the Drum Slowly, The Master Gunfighter, Heroes, etc; has appeared on television in *All in the Family*, *Baretta*, *Police Woman*, *Soap*, and many other popular series, etc.

Favourite parts: Camus's Caligula, Jerry in The Zoo Story, God in Gideon. *Hobbies and recreations:* Drawing, photography, sports, gymnastics. *Address:* The Artists Group, 10100 Santa Monica Boulevard 310, Los Angeles, Calif 90067. *Tel:* 213–552 1100.

ELIZONDO, Hector, actor
b New York City, 22 Dec 1936; *s* of Martin Echevarria Elizondo and his wife Carmen Medina (Reyes); *e* Music, Arts and Commerce High School and the streets of NYC; *m* Carolee Campbell; prepared for the stage with Mario Siletti of the Stella Adler Studio, and with Frank Corsaro.

First appeared on the stage at the Equity Library Theatre, fall 1961, as Reber in Mr Roberts; Provincetown Playhouse, 20 Oct 1965, played Supervisor, Director, Soldier, and Attendant in Kill the One-Eyed Man!; Theatre Company of Boston, 1966–7 season, played in Marat/Sade, Archie in Armstrong's Last Goodnight, Oriental Manservant in Candaules, Commissioner, Vachel Lindsay in So Proudly We Hail, and the title-role of The Undertaker; Circle in the Square, May 1967, Carl Balicke in Drums in the Night; Alvin, Oct 1968, Blackface in The Great White Hope; Truck and Warehouse, June 1970, Attendant (God) in Steambath; New York Shakespeare Festival, summer 1972, Antony in Antony and Cleopatra; Eugene O'Neill, 2 Oct 1972, took over from Art Carney as Mel Edison in The Prisoner of Second Avenue; Vivian Beaumont, Apr 1974, Kurt in The Dance of Death; Broadhurst, Dec 1976, Simon Able in Sly Fox; first appeared in films in 1969 in Valdez Is Coming, and since has played in Born to Win, The Taking of Pelham 1, 2, 3, Report to the Commissioner, Cuba (1979), etc; first appeared on television on *The Wendy Barrie Show*, 1947, and has since played on *Kojak*, *The Doctors*, The Impatient Heart, *Colombo*, *Baretta*, and in his own series *Popi*, 1976, etc.

Favourite parts: God in Steambath, Mel in The Prisoner of Second Avenue, and the Manservant in Candaules, Commissioner. *Hobbies and recreations:* Kendo, Zen Buddhism, chess, backpacking, classical guitar playing, cooking various ethnic foods, and raising his son. *Club:* American Buddhist Academy. *Address:* 262 West 107th Street, New York, NY 10025. *Tel:* 575 1100.

ELKINS, Hillard, producer
b New York City, 18 Oct 1929; *s* of Max Elkins and his wife Rachel (Kaplan); *e* Brooklyn College and New York University; *m* (1) Claire Bloom (mar dis); (2) Judith Wilson; formerly engaged as a talent agent and manager.

Presented his first play at the Bucks County Playhouse, Pennsylvania, Aug 1958, when he produced Leonard Bernstein's musical version of Candide; presented his first play in NY, Come on Strong, at the Morosco, 4 Oct 1962; since then has produced or co-produced the following: Golden Boy in a musical version with Sammy Davis, Jr, 1964; made his London début as a producer at the Palladium, Oct 1967, when he again presented Golden Boy; Oh, Calcutta! 1969; The Rothschilds, 1970; A Doll's House and Hedda Gabler in repertory, starring Claire Bloom, 1971; An Evening with Richard Nixon and . . ., 1972; A Doll's House (London), 1973; A Streetcar Named Desire (London), The Island, Sizwe Banzi Is Dead, 1974; Carte Blanche (London), 1976; Kings and Clowns, The Travelling Music Show (both London), Stop the World I Want to Get Off, An Evening with Quentin Crisp, 1978; produced the films Alice's Restaurant, 1968, A New Leaf, 1971, A Doll's House, 1973; Sammy Stops the World, Richard Pryor Live in Concert, 1979; produced The Importance of Being Earnest on television, 1958.

Hobby: Photography. *Recreation:* Boating. *Address:* 19½ East 62nd Street, New York, NY. *Tel:* 838 3232.

ELLIOTT, Denholm, actor
b London, 31 May 1922, *s* of Myles Layman Farr Elliot and his wife Nina (Mitchell); *e* Malvern College; *m* (1) Virginia McKenna (mar dis); (2) Susan Robinson; studied for the stage at the Royal Academy of Dramatic Art; from 1940–5, served in the RAF (Bomber Command), and was a prisoner of War in Germany, 1942–5.

Made his first appearance on the stage at the Playhouse, Amersham, July 1945, as Arden Rencelaw in The Drunkard; first appeared in London, at the Criterion, 19 Feb 1946, as Grimmett in The Guinea Pig; St Martin's, Feb 1948, Jan-Erik in Frenzy; Lyric, Hammersmith, July 1948, Albin in The Green Cockatoo; St James's, Sept 1948, Pierre Blandinet in Don't Listen, Ladies!; Boltons, Apr 1949, Frank Shire in Horn of the Moon: Wyndham's, Sept 1949 (for the under 30 group), played John Keats in John Keats Lived Here; at the Malvern Festival, Aug 1949, appeared as Junius in Buoyant Billions, and played the same part at the Prince's Theatre, Oct 1949; St James's, Jan 1950, Edgar in Venus Observed, for which performance he gained the Clarence Derwent Award, for the best supporting performance of the year, 1950; first appeared in New York, at the Martin Beck Theatre, 23 Nov 1950, as Hugo and Frederic in Ring Round the Moon, for which performance he gained the Donaldson Award; at the John Golden, Feb 1951, played Julian in The Green Bay Tree; after returning to London appeared at St Thomas's Church, Regent Street, May 1951, as Pte Peter Able in A Sleep of Prisoners; Arts, Oct 1951, and Criterion, Jan 1952, played Kip Ames in Third Person; Royal, Brighton, Oct 1952, Giles Seabrook in A Fiddle at the Wedding; at the Edinburgh Festival, Aug 1953, and at the Lyric, London, in the following month, appeared as Colby Simpkins in The Confidential Clerk; Arts, Mar 1955, played Jan Wicziewsky in South; Opera House, Manchester, July 1955, Alan Bretherton in The Delegate; St James's, Aug 1956, played Alex Shanklin in The Long Echo; Fortune, Dec 1956, Stefan in Who Cares?; Phoenix, Apr 1957, Kilroy in Camino Real; John Golden, NY, Oct 1957, played Fernand in Monique; New Shakespeare, Liverpool, Aug 1958, Francis X Digman in King of Hearts; Arts, London, Jan 1959, played

Gaston in Traveller Without Luggage; Westminster, Sept 1959, Shem in The Ark; Shakespeare Memorial Theatre, Stratford-on-Avon, 1960 season, played Bassanio in The Merchant of Venice, Troilus in Troilus and Cressida; and Valentine in The Two Gentlemen of Verona; Lyric, Hammersmith, Apr 1961, again played Jan Wiciewsky in South; at the Belasco, NY, Oct 1961, played the Hon Clive Rodingham in Write Me a Murder; Royal, Brighton, Feb 1963, played the title part in Domino; toured with the National Repertory Theatre Company in the US, Oct 1963, as Trigorin in The Seagull, and the Rev John Hale in The Crucible, subsequently appearing at the Belasco, NY, Apr 1964 in both plays; New Arts, London, Apr 1965, played Chrystal in The Game as Played; ANTA, NY, May 1967, played Dr Diaforus in The Imaginary Invalid, Alec Harvey in Still Life, and Cornelius Melody in A Touch of the Poet; returned to the New Theatre, London, Jan 1970, where he appeared in Come As You Are, transferring to the Strand, June 1970; Royal Court, June 1972, Judge Brack in Hedda Gabler; Royal, Windsor, June 1973, Hughes Humphrey in Turn On; Hampstead, Aug 1973, James Ludlow in Mad Dog; Globe, Feb 1974, Dick in Chez Nous; joined the RSC at the Aldwych, Dec 1975, to play the title role in The Return of A J Raffles; Greenwich, June 1976, two parts in Heaven and Hell; Brooklyn Academy, NY, 1977, played Sir Wilfred Cates-Darby in The New York Idea, Mar, and Vershinin in Three Sisters, Apr; Open Space, Nov 1979, title role in The Father; first appeared in films, 1949, in Mr Prohack, and since in Nothing But the Best, King Rat, Alfie, The Apprenticeship of Duddy Kravitz, St Jacques, A Game for Vultures, Illusions, etc; TV includes Sextet, *Clayhanger*, and Donkey's Years.

Recreations: Piano playing, and swimming. *Address:* c/o The Garrick Club, Garrick Street, London WC2.

ELLIOTT, Michael, director
b London, 26 June 1931; *s* of Wallace Harold Elliott and his wife Edith Plaistow (Kilburn); *e* Radley College, and Keble College, Oxford; *m* Rosalind Knight.

Began his career with an amateur production of Christopher Fry's A Sleep of Prisoners, at the church of St Peter-in-the-East, Oxford, Dec 1952; after three years as a director with BBC Television, he directed his first London stage production at the Lyric, Hammersmith, Apr 1959, with Brand; he has since directed An Ideal Husband (Nottingham Playhouse); The Playboy of the Western World (Glasgow Citizens'), 1960; As You Like It (Royal Shakespeare and Aldwych), 1961–2; Two Stars For Comfort, 1962; an Associate Director of the Royal Shakespeare Company, 1961–2; appointed Artistic Director of the Old Vic for the last season, 1962, where he directed Peer Gynt, The Merchant of Venice, 1962; Measure for Measure, 1963; directed Little Eyolf (Edinburgh Festival), 1963; Miss Julie (Chichester Festival), 1965, and National Theatre, 1966; co-founder and artistic director of The 69 Theatre Company, for which he has directed: When We Dea Awaken, Edinburgh, 1968; Daniel Deronda and The Tempest, 1969; Catch My Soul and Peer Gynt, 1970, and became first resident Artistic Director of the Company at the Royal Exchange, Manchester, 1976; productions for the Company include: She Stoops to Conquer (also Garrick), 1969, The Family Reunion, 1973, The Cocktail Party, 1975; Uncle Vanya, 1977; Round House, Feb 1979, directed a season of Royal Exchange productions: The Ordeal of Gilbert Pinfold, Lady From the Sea, and The Family Reunion, which transferred to the Vaudeville, June 1979; The Dresser, 1980; appointed Chairman of the Arts Council Training Committee, 1969; Member of the Drama Panel,

1962–70; and of the planning committee of the ABTT until 1976; joined BBC Television, Mar 1956, and directed the following television productions: Brand, Women of Troy, Uncle Vanya, The Lower Depths, The Lady From the Sea, David and Broccoli, etc; produced The Glass Menagerie on American TV, 1964.

Club: Savile. *Address:* Savile Club, 69 Brook Street, London, W1.

ELLIOTT, Patricia, actress and singer
b Gunnison, Colorado, 21 July 1942; *d* of Clyde Porterfield Elliott and his wife Lavon Louise (Gibson); *e* University of Colorado and London Academy of Music and Dramatic Arts (1963–4); trained for the stage at LAMDA and with Wendy Hiller, Dame Sybil Thorndike, Sir Tyrone Guthrie, and prepared for singing with Phyllis Grandy.

First appeared on the stage at Quincy House, Harvard University, Jan 1962, as Maggie in Cat on a Hot Tin Roof; made her London début at the LAMDA Theatre Club, Jan 1964, as Irina in The Three Sisters; appeared with the Cleveland Playhouse, 1964 and 1965 seasons, playing the title-roles of Major Barbara and Antigone among others; for the Front Street, Memphis, Tennessee, Jan 1967; played Lady Macbeth; Minnesota Theatre Company, Minneapolis, 1967 and 1968 seasons, played Kate in She Stoops to Conquer, Chorus Leader in The House of Atreus, Thieves' Carnival, The Dance of Death, As You Like It, among others; appeared with the Long Island Festival Repertory, Mineola, NY, Apr–June 1968, As Irina in The Three Sisters; appeared at the Eugene O'Neill Foundation, Waterford, Connecticut, July 1968; made her NY début at the Vivian Beaumont, 7 Nov 1968 as Regan in King Lear; American Shakespeare Festival, Stratford, Conn, summer 1969, Beatrice in Much Ado About Nothing; ANTA, NY, Nov 1969, Alice in Henry V; St George's Church, for the Phoenix Theatre Co, Apr 1970, Young Woman of the Chorus in The Persians; The Olney Theatre, Maryland, summers 1970 and 1971, Gittel in Two for the Seesaw Patsy in Little Murders, Ruth in The Homecoming; The Cubiculo, NY, Oct 1970, The Girl in Waiting and Signora in The Academy in the triple-bill Infidelity Italian Style; 48th Street, Playhouse, Jan 1971, Mrs Kristine Linde in A Doll's House, and Feb 1971, played Mrs Elvsted and stood by for the title-role of Hedda Gabler when the two plays ran in repertory; Eisenhower Theater at the Kennedy Center, Washington, DC, in the first play to inaugurate that theatre, Oct 1971, played Mrs Kristine Linde in A Doll's House; Philadelphia Drama Guild, Jan 1972, Lydia Languish in The Rivals; Eastside Playhouse, NY, Mar 1972, Frances in In Case of Accident; Chelsea Theatre Center, May 1972, Alice, Duchess of Nevermore in The Water Hen; Shubert, Feb 1973, Countess Charlotte Malcolm in A Little Night Music, for which she received the Antoinette Perry (Tony) Award, the Theatre World Award, and the Drama Critics Award; Chelsea Theatre Center, April 1975, Jennie Diver in Polly; John Drew, Easthampton, LI, for the Phoenix Theatre Co, Countess in the Rehearsal and the Gertrude Lawrence parts in Tonight at 8.30, summer 1975; Chelsea Westside, NY, Nov 1975, played in the revue By Bernstein; same theatre, Nov 1976, Princess Natalia in the Prince of Homburg; McCarter, Dec 1976, Siri in The Night of the Tribades; Long Wharf, Jan 1977, and Morosco, Mar, Beverly in The Shadow Box; Circle in the Square, played Dorine in Tartuffe, Sept 1977, and Leontine in 13 Rue de l'Amour, Mar 1978; Manhattan Theatre Club, Feb 1979, Margaret Morley in Artichoke; Harold Clurman, June 1979, Ann in Wine Untouched; first appeared in films in Man Without a Country, 1973; first appeared on television for the

BBC, Apr 1964, in Shakespeare: Actors Discuss, and in USA, 1972, played Nora in A Doll's House; on radio, 1975, CBS *Mystery Theatre*, made regular appearances.

Favourite part: The one I am presently playing. *Recreations:* Swimming, yoga, living.

ELLIOTT, Paul, producing manager

b Bournemouth, 9 Dec 1941; *s* of Lewis Arthur Elliott and his wife Sybil Majorie (Wyatt); *m* Jenny Logan; formerly an actor and stage-manager.

His first production was a tour of Ring for Catty, 1965; with Duncan C Weldon presented over one hundred touring shows; formed Triumph Theatre Productions, presenting numerous tours at home and abroad, and West End productions including: When We Are Married, 1971; The Chalk Garden, 1971; Big Bad Mouse, 1972; Grease, 1973; The King and I, 1974; first New York production, Brief Lives, Oct 1974; The Dragon Variation, 1977; Forty Love, Hello Dolly, Beatlemania, Irma la Douce, 1979; overseas tours presented include several by the Royal Shakespeare Company, among them Hedda Gabler, Canada, USA, Australia, 1975; formed Paul Elliott Entertainments Ltd, Sept 1975; producer, Phoenix Theatre Season 1976, including: I Do, I Do, 13 Rue de l'Amour, Bus Stop, and The Pleasure of His Company; his first television production was Brief Lives, 1975, in Australia.

Recreations: Football, travelling, eating. *Club:* Green Room. *Address:* 323 Liverpool Road, London N1. *Tel:* 01–607 4107.

ELLIOTT, Stephen, actor

At the Alvin, 25 Jan 1945, played the Boatswain in Margaret Webster's production of The Tempest; Chanin Auditorium, Mar 1946, played Mickey in Walk Hard; Coronet, Dec 1946, Handler in Wonderful Journey; Fulton, Oct 1947, Colonel Edward Martin in Command Decision; Cort, Jan 1952, Dr Kramer in The Shrike; Shubert, Washington, DC, Nov 1952, Adam Banner in Rise by Sin; Cherry Lane, Dec 1956, Philip O'Dempsey in Purple Dust; Phoenix, Apr 1957, Muff Potter in Livin' the Life; Cort, Feb 1960, Admiral Trenton in Roman Candle; Shubert, Nov 1961, understudied the role of Anatol in The Gay Life; Brooks Atkinson, Feb 1963, understudied Peter Ustinov and Dennis King in Photo Finish; ANTA, Sept 1964, Georges Renaud in Traveller Without Luggage; Theatre de Lys, Nov 1964, played in I Knock at the Door; Theatre de Lys, Dec 1964, played in Pictures in the Hallway, the last two plays being staged readings of the autobiographies of Sean O'Casey; Majestic, Jan 1967, M Coulmier in Marat/Sade; Delacorte, June 1968, Owen Glendower in Henry IV, Part I and Lord Chief Justice in Henry IV, Part II; Vivian Beaumont, Nov 1968, Earl of Gloucester in King Lear; Sir Thomas in A Cry of Players; Mar 1969, John Lansdale in In the Matter of J Robert Oppenheimer, which he repeated in June 1969; May 1969, Magistrate in The Miser; Delacorte, Aug 1969, Sir Toby Belch in Twelfth Night; Mercury, Oct 1969, Michael Carney, Sr in A Whistle in the Dark; Winter Garden, Feb 1970, James Leamington in Georgy; Nov 1970, Shu Fu in The Good Woman of Setzuan; Vivian Beaumont, Jan 1971, Mr Mahon in The Playboy of the Western World; Mar 1971, Dr Stockman in An Enemy of the People; Nov 1971, Lord Burleigh in Mary Stuart; Forum, Jan 1972, Stephen Elliott in A Ride Across Lake Constance; Vivian Beaumont, Apr 1972, Deputy Governor Danforth in The Crucible; Shubert, Nov 1972, God in The Creation of the World and Other Business; Kennedy Center, Washington DC, 1973, appeared in The Prodigal Daughter; Matrix, LA, Jan 1980, in A Life in the Theatre; appeared in the films The Hospital, 1971, Death

Wish, 1974, Cutter and Bone, 1979, etc; TV appearances include *Beacon Hill*, *Executive Suite*, and numerous telefilms.

Address: c/o Merritt Blake, 409 N Camden, Beverly Hills, Calif.

ELLIS, Mary, actress and singer

b New York City, 15 June 1900; *e* NY; *m* (1) Edwin Knopf (mar dis); (2) Basil Sydney (mar dis); (3) J Muir Stewart Roberts (dec); was an art student for three years, and studied singing with Madame Ashforth.

Made her first appearance on the stage at the Metropolitan Opera House, NY, Dec 1918, in Sœur Angelica and appearing there, 1919–22 in roles including Mytil in The Blue Bird, Siebel in Faust and Gianetta in L'Elisir d'Amor; she then turned her attention to the dramatic stage, and at the Lyceum, NY, Dec 1922, appeared as Nerissa in The Merchant of Venice; at the Empire, Sept 1923, as the Dancer from Milan in Casanova; Henry Miller, Jan 1924, Brigid Shannahan and Ophelia O'Tandy in The Merry Wives of Gotham; at the Imperial, Sept 1924, was the original Rose-Marie in the musical play of that name; she was next seen at the Neighbourhood Theatre, Dec 1925, as Leah in The Dybbuk, and May 1926, as Rosario in The Romantic Young Lady; at Greenwich Village, Oct 1926, as Sonia in The Humble (Crime and Punishment); Forrest, Mar 1927, Anna in The Crown Prince; Garrick, Oct 1927, Katherine in The Taming of the Shrew (in modern dress); same theatre, Mar 1928, Baroness Spangenburg in 12,000; at the Lyceum, Feb 1929, Jennifer in Meet the Prince; at the Knickerbocker, June 1929, Becky Sharp in the all-star revival of the play of that name; at the Biltmore Theatre, Jan 1930, played Laetitia in Children of Darkness; made her first appearance on the London stage, at the Ambassadors' Theatre, 1 Oct 1930, as Laetitia in Knave and Quean; at the Lyric, Feb 1931, played Nina Leeds in Strange Interlude; on returning to America, appeared at the National, Washington, Sept 1931, in Cherries Are Ripe; at the Booth, NY, Jan 1932, played Teri in Jewel Robbery; again went to London, and at the Haymarket, May 1932, played Claire Furber in Queer Cattle; Haymarket, Jan 1933, Sybil Livingstone in Double Harness; His Majesty's, May 1933, Frieda Hatzfeld in Music in the Air; Sept 1934, Josephine in a play of that name; Drury Lane, May 1935, Militza Hajos in Glamorous Night; Lyric, Sept 1936, Tina Gerling in Farewell Performance; St James's, Jan 1938, Laurita Bingham in The Innocent Party; Drury Lane, Mar 1939, Maria Ziegler in The Dancing Years (which, like Glamorous Night, Ivor Novello wrote for her); from the outbreak of War, Sept 1939, was engaged in hospital welfare work and in giving concerts for the troops, and reappeared on the stage Nov 1943, at the Phoenix Theatre, as Marie Foret in Arc de Triomphe; at the Liverpool Playhouse, for the Old Vic, from Aug 1944, played Ella Rentheim in John Gabriel Borkman, Linda Valaine in Point Valaine, and Lady Teazle in The School for Scandal; Piccadilly, May 1945, Maria Fitzherbert in The Gay Pavilion; Q, Sept 1946, Miss Susie in The Rocking Horse, and Nov 1946, Mrs Dane in Mrs Dane's Defence; Embassy, Feb 1947, played Harriet Beecher Stowe in Hattie Stowe, and Sept 1947, Linda Valaine in Point Valaine; at the Phoenix, Sept 1948, appeared as Millie Crocker-Harris in The Browning Version, and Edna Selby in A Harlequinade; Lyric, Hammersmith, May 1950, Caroline Moore in If This Be Error, in which she subsequently toured; Embassy, Jan 1951, played the title-role in Celestina; with the Shakespeare Memorial Theatre Company, Stratford-on-Avon, during the 1952 season, played Volumnia in Coriolanus; Globe, June 1954, appeared as Mrs Erlynne in After the Ball; Arts, June 1955, played Christine Mannon in

Mourning Becomes Electra; Arts, Apr 1959, played Edie (Mother) Dennis in Dark Halo; Pembroke, Croydon, Oct 1960, played Eliza Gant in Look Homeward, Angel, subsequently appearing in the same part at the Phoenix, Apr 1962; Arnaud, Guildford, Nov 1968, Mrs Phelps in The Silver Chord; Feb 1970 played Mrs Warren in Mrs Warren's Profession at the same theatre; has also broadcast on radio; the many television plays in which she has appeared include The Distaff Side, Trespass, Great Catherine, Indifferent Shepherd, and The First Mrs Fraser; first appeared in films, 1935, in Bella Donna, and spent two years in Hollywood; notable films include: Paris Love Song, Fatal Lady, Glamorous Night, and Gulliver's Travels.

Address: c/o Chase Manhattan Bank, 1 Mount Street, London W1.

ELLIS, Vivian, composer and lyric writer
b Hampstead, 29 Oct; *s* of Harry Ellis and his wife, Maud (Isaacson); *e* Cheltenham College.

Commenced his career as a concert pianist, and was a pupil of Myra Hess; his first work for the theatre was the composition of additional numbers for The Curate's Egg, 1922; Mirrors, 1923; contributed numbers to The Little Revue and The Punch Bowl, 1924; composer of By-the-Way, 1924; subsequently, he contributed to Yoicks, Mercenary Mary, and Still Dancing, 1925; composer of Palladium Pleasures, and also contributed to Just a Kiss, Kid Boots, Cochran's Revue, My Son John, Merely Molly, 1926; Blue Skies, The Girl Friend, and Clowns in Clover, 1927; composer of Peg o' Mine, Will o' the Whispers, Vogues and Vanities, 1928; contributed to Charlot, 1928; in collaboration with Richard Myers, composed Mr Cinders, 1929; wrote additional numbers for A Yankee at the Court of King Arthur, and The House that Jack Built, 1929; part-composer of Cochran's 1930 Revue; composer of Follow a Star, Little Tommy Tucker, 1930; Folly to Be Wise, The Song of the Drum (with Herman Finck), Blue Roses, Stand Up and Sing (with Philip Charig), 1931; Out of the Bottle (with Oscar Levant), 1932; contributed to Please, 1933; composed Streamline, Jill Darling, 1934; since 1936, has written his own lyrics as well as composed the music for The Town Talks, Going Places, 1936; Hide and Seek, 1937; The Fleet's Lit Up, Running Riot, Under Your Hat, 1938; contributed to It's Foolish but it's Fun, 1943; Henson's Gaieties, and Fine Feathers, 1945; composed the music for Big Ben, 1946; Bless the Bride, 1947; Tough at the Top, 1949; lyrics and music for And So To Bed, 1951; Over The Moon, 1953; incidental music for The Sleeping Prince, 1953; lyrics and music for Listen to the Wind, 1954; music for The Water Gipsies, 1955; music for Half in Earnest (musical adaptation of Oscar Wilde's The Importance of Being Earnest), the opening production at the Belgrade Theatre, Coventry, 1958; contributed words and music to 4 to the Bar, 1961; part author of Six of One, 1963; composed the music for Mr Whatnot, 1964; contributed words and music, including the title song, for Chaganog, 1964; composer of many popular songs, including Spread a Little Happiness, She's My Lovely, I'm on a See-Saw, This is My Lovely Day, etc; also music for many films; is the author of several novels, Zelma, Faint Harmony, Day Out, Chicanery, Goodbye, Dollie; has published two volumes of autobiography, Ellis in Wonderland and I'm On a See-Saw, and the children's books, Hilary's Tune, Hilary's Holidays, The Magic Baton, 1961; How to Make Your Fortune on the Stock Exchange, 1962; How to Enjoy Your Operation, 1963; How to Bury Yourself in the Country, and How to be a Man-About-Town, 1965; contributor to The Rise and Fall of the Matinée Idol, 1974, and Top Hat and Tails, 1978; during the War, served from 1939–44, in the RNVR (Lieutenant-Commander, retired); Ivor Novello Award for outstanding services to British music, 1973; Deputy President of the Performing Right Society.

Recreation: Gardening, painting and operations. *Club:* Garrick. *Address:* c/o Performing Right Society, 29 Berners Street, London, W1.

ELSOM, John, theatre critic, author and dramatist
b Leigh-on-Sea, 31 Oct 1934; *s* of Leonard Ernest Elsom and his wife Marjorie Louise (Dines); *e* Brentwood School, Essex and Magdalene College, Cambridge; *m* the concert pianist, Sally Mays.

Wrote his first play Peacemaker, 1955, for the ADC, while at Cambridge: further plays being Well-Intentioned Builder, One More Bull, 1970; How I Coped, 1972; adult education lecturer in literature and drama, 1958–72; script and theatre correspondent Paramount Pictures, 1960–68; Theatre Correspondent, *The London Magazine*, 1963–68; Theatre Critic of *The Listener*, 1972– ; author of Theatre Outside London, 1971, Erotic Theatre, 1973, Post-War British Theatre, 1975, History of The National Theatre (with Nicholas Tomalin), 1978; member of the Critics Circle; a frequent broadcaster on Kaleidoscope and Critics Forum, and contributor to Contemporary Review; Liberal party candidate 1965–67, drafting their paper on The Arts, Change and Choice, 1978.

Hobbies: Cricket, music, games, reading. *Address:* 39 Elsham Road, Kensington, London W14 8HB.

EMMET, Alfred, OBE director
b Ealing, Middlesex, 29 Mar 1908; *s* of Edward Fletcher Emmet and his wife Mabel Ernestine (Eardley-Wilmot); *e* Rossall School; *m* (1) Mildred Hackett (mar dis); (2) Barbara Mary Hutchins.

Founder, 1933 of the Questors Theatre, Ealing, which under his direction, until 1969, became one of Britain's leading amateur companies; his productions there include the following premieres: The Dark River, 1943; Diary of a Scoundrel, 1946; Better a Dead Hero, 1954; Everybody Loves Celimare, 1958; A Quiet Clap of Thunder, 1961; The Other Palace, 1964; The Igloo, 1965; The Corruptible Crown, 1967; Director, International Theatre Weeks at the Questors; member of the British advisory group of the International Theatre Institute, the Committee of the International Amateur Theatre Association and the council of the British Theatre Institute; received the OBE in the New Year Honours, 1971.

Clubs: Arts. *Address:* 34 Culmington Road, Ealing, London, W13 9NH. *Tel:* 01–567 1478.

EMNEY, Fred, actor
b London, 12 Feb 1900; *s* of the late Fred Emney and his wife Blanche (Doris); *e* Cranleigh; *m* Hazel Wiles.

Made his first appearance on the stage at the Duke of York's Theatre, 6 Oct 1915, as the Page boy in Romance; appeared at Drury Lane Theatre, 26 Dec 1916, as the Squire in Puss in Boots; subsequently toured in musical comedy; went to the United States, 1920, to appear in vaudeville, and remained there until 1931; on his return appeared in English variety theatres; appeared at the London Hippodrome, 1 Feb 1934, as Lord Leatherhead in Mr Whittington; Alhambra, May 1935, played Bombi in The Flying Trapeze; Gaiety, Oct 1935, Ex-King Cyril in Seeing Stars; Sept 1936, Julien Breval in Swing Along; Sept 1937, Pollas Pollicapillos in Going Greek; Aug 1938, Charlie Col in Running Riot; Queen's, Dec 1939, appeared in All Clear; His Majesty's, May 1942, in Big Top; Winter Garden, July 1943, played Lord D'Arcy in

It's Time to Dance; Coliseum, Dec 1944, Lord Gorgeous in Goody Two Shoes; Saville, Sept 1945, Sir Frederick Bolsover in Big Boy, of which he was part-author; London Hippodrome, Oct 1947, appeared in the revue Starlight Roof; Saville, Feb 1950, played Rear-Admiral Archibald Ranklin in The Schoolmistress; His Majesty's, Nov 1950, Fred Piper in Blue for a Boy; Prince's, May 1953, Alexander The Great in Happy As a King, of which he was part-author; Royal Nottingham, June 1954, Alexander Warrington in Take Your Partners; Strand, Nov 1970, Henry Ormonroyd in When We Are Married; Forum, Billingham and Tour, Dec 1973, Erronius in A Funny Thing Happened on the Way to the Forum; recent films include The Magic Christian, The Italian Job, Lock Up Your Daughters, Oliver; has also broadcast and appeared on television, in Jokers Wild, The World of Beachcomber, World in Ferment, Old Boys' Network, etc.

Recreation: Golf. *Clubs:* Savage and Stage Golfing Society. *Address:* c/o Richard Stone, 18–20 York Bldgs, London WC2.

ENGAR, Keith M, educator, producer/director and actor
b Preston, Idaho, 2 Apr 1923; *s* of Charles J Engar and his wife Alveretta (Staples); *e* University of Utah, University of Minnesota and UCLA; *m* Amy K Lyman.

Originally a radio actor and announcer; director of radio-TV services, University of Utah, 1958–65; executive producer, 1964–present, Pioneer Memorial Theatre, University of Utah, where he has presented over 100 productions and directed more than a score of them; recently Funny Girl, 1979; as an actor he has played leading roles for the Utah Summer Festival, 1953–63, and at the Pioneer, recently as Popov in The Merry Widow, 1979; author of the plays Arthur and the Magic Sword, 1950; Montrose Crossing, 1954; All in Favour, 1958; book and lyrics for Rendezvous, 1958; The Bremen Town Musicians, 1970; Right Honourable Saint, 1976; Chairman, 1973–75, Utah Institute of Fine Arts; Chairman, 1977– , General Activities Committee, Church of the Latter Day Saints.

Address: Pioneer Memorial Theatre, University of Utah, Salt Lake City, UT 84112. *Tel:* 801-581 5819.

ENGEL, Susan, actress
b Vienna, Austria, 25 Mar 1935; *d* Fritz Engel and his wife Anni (Stefansky); *e* Sorbonne and Bristol University; *m* Sylvester Morand; trained for the stage at the Bristol Old Vic School.

Made her first appearance in 1959 at the Bristol Old Vic, in pantomime; first London appearance, Royal Court, Sept 1960 as Mrs Phineus in The Happy Haven; Mermaid, Apr 1961, played Mrs Noah in the Wakefield Mystery Cycle; Arts, Cambridge, 1962, Alice Arden in Arden of Faversham; from 1963 to 1966 was a member of the Royal Shakespeare Company, playing numerous parts at Stratford and at the Aldwych, including Calpurnia in Julius Caesar, 1963; Queen Elizabeth in The Wars of the Roses, 1963 and 1964; Doll Tearsheet in Henry IV, 1964; Adriana in The Comedy of Errors, 1965; Hampstead, Mar 1966, played Lucille Harris in Adventures in the Skin Trade; Royal Court, Oct 1966, Lady Macduff in Macbeth, later taking over the part of Lady Macbeth; Royal Court, July, and New, Sept 1968, Amy in The Hotel in Amsterdam; Round House, May 1970, Esther in The Friends; Thorndike, Leatherhead, Mar 1971, Amelia Evans in Ballad of the Sad Café; Alexandra Park Racecourse, Apr 1971, Old Woman in Passion; Royal Court, Aug 1972, Rosa in The Old Ones; Old Vic, for National Theatre, May 1974, Frau Gabor in Spring Awakening; Cambridge Theatre, June 1976, Olga in Three Sisters, Hampstead, June,

1977, Gulschan in The Ascent of Mount Fuji; Aldwych (RSC), Sept 1978, Katya in Cousin Vladimir; Open Space, Sept 1979, appeared in The Private Life of the Third Reich; Criterion, Nov 1979, Elaine Navazio in Last of the Red Hot Lovers; first appeared in films, 1967, in Charlie Bubbles and subsequently in King Lear, and Butley; television appearances, since 1966, include The Wars of the Roses, The Lotus Eaters, Exiles, and *Doctor Who.*

Address: 15 Compayne Gardens, London NW6.

EPSTEIN, Alvin, actor and director
b New York City, 14 May 1925; *s* of Harry Epstein and his wife Goldie (Rudnick); *e* Walden, DeWitt Clinton High Schools, High School of Music and Art, and Queen's College; studied dancing with Martha Graham in NY, and Olga Preobrajenska and Etienne Decroux (mime), in Paris, and acting with Sanford Meisner in NY.

First appeared on the stage with the Biarritz American University (US Army) touring European cities 1945–6, as Lord Rivers in Richard III; first appeared in NY with the Equity Library Theatre in the 1946–7 season as Wint Selby in Ah, Wilderness!; from 1947–51 was a member of the French Mime Theatre of Etienne Decroux, in Europe and the Middle East; toured 1951, as Sganarelle in The Doctor in Spite of Himself; from 1953–5 was a member of the Habima Theatre of Tel-Aviv, Israel, where he played Arthur Jarvis in Lost in the Stars, Victor Karenin in The Living Corpse, The Messiah in The Golem, Tony in The Mother, The Snake in Legend of 3 and 4, Willy Keith in The Caine Mutiny Court Martial, Count Carlo di Nolli in Pirandello's Henry IV, and The Fool in King Lear; joined Marcel Marceau's mime company, and at the Phoenix, NY, Sept 1955, appeared in the program Marcel Marceau and His Partners, transferring to the Ethel Barrymore in Oct 1955; City Center, Jan 1956, played The Fool in Orson Welles's production of King Lear; John Golden, Apr 1956, played Lucky in Waiting for Godot; Empire State Music Festival, Ellenville, NY, July 1956, Puck in A Midsummer Night's Dream; Cherry Lane, off-Broadway, Dec 1956, O'Killigan in Purple Dust; Kaufman Auditorium, May 1957, The Devil in L'Histoire du Soldat; Festival Theatre, Ravinia, Illinois, June 1957, Johnny Casside in Pictures in the Hallway; Boston Summer Theatre, Aug 1957, The Ragpicker in The Madwoman of Chaillot; Rooftop, NY, Nov 1957, Vicomte Octave de Clérambard in Clérambard; Cherry Lane, Jan 1958, Clov in Endgame; York Playhouse, Oct 1958, Claudius in The Golden Six; St George's Church, NY, Jan and Dec 1959, and Dec 1961, appeared as The Narrator in The Play of Daniel; Cambridge Drama Festival, Mass, July 1959, Feste in Twelfth Night; Plymouth, NY, Apr 1960, played in the revue From A to Z; studied under a Ford Foundation Grant, 1961–2; 54th Street, Mar 1962, Luc Delbert in No Strings; Actors Studio, Dec 1963, The Sergeant in Dynamite Tonite; Ethel Barrymore, Feb 1964, Constable Kentinov, Alexander Lomov, and Trotsky in The Passion of Josef D; Playhouse in the Park, Philadelphia, June 1964, appeared in the program Brecht on Brecht; Fred Miller, Milwaukee, Wisconsin, July 1964, played the title-role in Pirandello's Henry IV, appearing in the same part at the Harper, Chicago, Nov 1964; Loft, NY, Mar 1965, played in the dual-bill by Saul Bellow, A Wen and Orange Soufflé; Bucks County Playhouse, New Hope, Pa, May 1965, Bob McKelloway in Mary, Mary; Brooks Atkinson, NY, Nov 1965, various roles in Postmark Zero; Goodman, Chicago, Jan 1966, M Berenger in Pedestrian in the Air; co-founded the Berkshire Theatre Festival, Stockbridge, Mass, summer 1966, and played Mr Antrobus in The Skin of Our Teeth and Shylock in The Merchant of Venice; Yale

Repertory, New Haven, Conn, Dec 1966, The Sergeant in Dynamite Tonite; Martinique, NY, Mar 1967, again played in Dynamite Tonite, and received an Obie Award for the performance; Nassau Community College, Long Island, May 1967, Henry David Thoreau in At This Hour; Theatre de Lys, NY, June 1967, Theseus and Oberon in A Midsummer Night's Dream; Ravinia Festival, Chicago, Aug 1967, played in the revue The World of Kurt Weill; for the National Theatre of the Deaf, Mar 1968, directed On the Harmfulness of Tobacco; Huntington Hartford, Los Angeles, Calif, Apr 1968, Landau in The Latent Heterosexual; Ravinia Festival, Chicago, Aug 1968, again played in The World of Kurt Weill; in Sept 1968, joined the Yale Repertory Theatre as actor and director and as faculty member of the Yale Drama School, and played in God Bless, Grimm's Fairy Tales, and A Kurt Weill Cabaret; Yale, 1969, appeared as Dionysus in The Bacchae and the title-role of The Greatshot; The Bitter End, NY, June 1969, played in the revue Whores, Wars and Tin Pan Alley, and transferred in this production to the Sheridan Square Playhouse; Yale Repertory, Sept 1969, directed The Rivals and played in the Story Theatre version of Ovid's Metamorphoses; Yale, Spring 1970, played Maurice in Crimes and Crimes, Khlestakov in The Government Inspector, and the title-role in Molière's Don Juan; John Drew, Easthampton, Long Island, summer 1970, appeared with the Yale Repertory in Olympian Games and Three Stories by Philip Roth; Macloren Playhouse, Hollywood, Calif, Aug 1970, again played in Whores, Wars and Tin Pan Alley; Yale Repertory, Sept 1970, played in Olympian Games and Two Saints; Long Wharf, New Haven, Conn, Nov 1970, played The Questioner in A Place Without Doors, and repeated this role at the Staircase, NY, Dec 1970; Yale Repertory, 1971, title-role in Gimpel the Fool and, 1971–2 season, played in If I Married You for the Fun of It; Goodman, Chicago, Sept 1971, The Questioner in A Place Without Doors; Yale Repertory, 1971, directed The Seven Deadly Sins; Mar 1972, Husband in Life Is a Dream; May 1972, played in Happy End; appointed Associate Director, 1973, and in Apr 1973, directed the American première of Ionesco's Macbett and played the title-role; also Apr 1973, played Edward Bond's Lear; Oct 1973, co-directed and played Prospero in The Tempest; Dec 1973, directed In the Clap Shack; Feb 1974, directed The Rise and Fall of the City of Mahagonny; in 1974 played in the musical version of The Frogs; Oct 1974, Kirilov in The Possessed; May 1975, directed A Midsummer Night's Dream; Dec 1975, co-directed and played the Sergeant in Dynamite Tonite!; in 1976, Shakespeare in Bingo, Jan; directed Troilus and Cressida; Apr; directed Julius Caesar, Oct; played title-role in Ivanov, Nov; 1977, Grandfather in White Marriage, Apr; Artistic Director, Guthrie Theatre, Minneapolis, Sept 1977–July 1979, where he directed the Pretenders, The Rivals and The Beggars Opera; played Kochkariev in Marriage and performed his Kurt Weill Cabaret; during his tenure other Guthrie productions included the world premières of Teibele and Her Demon, Right of Way and a season of new plays at the Guthrie's second theatre; Bijou, NY, Nov 1979, again appeared in A Kurt Weill Cabaret; received the Brandeis University Creative Arts Award, 1965; received the Variety New York Drama Critics Award as the most promising actor of the year in 1956; first appeared on television in 1956 in *Studio One,* and has since played in Thérèse Raquin, Waiting for Godot, Prayers from the Ark, Terezin Requiem, Histoire du Soldat, Grimm's Fairy Tales, etc.

Favourite parts: Lucky and Pirandello's Henry IV. *Recreations:* Playing the harpsichord and the piano. *Address:* 344 West 84th Street, New York, NY 10024.

EPSTEIN, Pierre, actor and director
b Toulouse, France, 27 July 1930; *s* of Abraham Epstein and his wife Henriette (Castex); *e* University of Paris, Goddard College and Columbia University; *m* Dorée Lanouette (mar dis); trained for the stage at Ecole de l'Atelier, Paris and as a student of Harold Clurman.

Made his debut at St John's Church, NY, Dec 1955, in The Mountebanks; Booth, Oct 1961, made his first Broadway appearance as the Guard in A Shot in the Dark, later taking over the part of Morestan in this production; Henry Miller's, Mar 1963, Don Baxter in Enter Laughing; directed The Lesson, 1963, receiving an Obie; Ethel Barrymore, Feb 1967, Schuppanzigh in Black Comedy; Fortune, Oct 1968, Prosecutor in The People Versus Ranchman; Promenade, Jun 1969, Jailer in Promenade; Morosco, Jan 1972, Jose Rodriquez in Fun City; Broadhurst, Apr 1974, Harry in Thieves; Vivian Beaumont, May 1975, Henry Morlino in Little Black Sheep; for Phoenix, season 1975–76, his parts included Raymond in A Memory of Two Mondays; Washington DC, May 1976, Barnaby in The Baker's Wife; Manhattan Theatre Club, Jan 1979, Beethoven in Beethoven/Karl; Century, Apr 1979, Sam in Manny; Entermedia, Oct 1979, Kilgore Trout in God Bless You Mr Rosewater; St James, Feb 1980, Nocella in Filumena; has also appeared at the Arena Stage, Washington DC, PAF Playhouse, Huntington, etc; films include Popi, 1969, Diary of a Mad Housewife, 1970, Love and Death, 1974, Simon, 1980, etc; TV includes series and specials; has translated a number of plays from the French.

Address: c/o Dulcina Eisen, 346 East 50th Street, New York, NY 10022.

ESSEX, David, actor, singer and composer
b London, 23 July 1947; *s* of Albert Cook and his wife Doris; *e* Shipman Secondary School, London; *m* Maureen Neal; formerly an apprentice engineer.

After working as a singer and drummer, made his first appearance in repertory at the Festival Hall, Paignton, as Matt in a tour of The Fantasticks; toured, Feb 1968, as the Duke of Durham in Oh, Kay!; Arnaud, Guildford, Dec 1968, appeared in The Magic Carpet; London debut, May Fair Theatre, Jul 6, 1970, in the revue Ten Years' Hard; Round House, Nov 1971, played Jesus in Godspell, which transferred to the Wyndham's, Jan 1972, continuing there until Sept 1973; Palladium, Dec 1976, in variety; Prince Edward, Jun 1978, Che Guevara in Evita; has given concerts in twenty-one countries; films, since Assault, 1971, include That'll Be the Day, Stardust, and Silver Dream Racer (also music); first seen on television, 1966, in Five O'Clock Club, and has made innumerable TV appearances in his own shows or as a guest, in the UK, USA and throughout the world; received Variety Club Award for Most Promising Newcomer 1973, and Show-business Personality of the Year (joint award), 1978; many gold records; President of Roundabout and Act Clubs in the Save the Children Fund.

Hobbies: Theatregoing and horseriding. *Address:* c/o Derek Bowman, 1 Upper Brook Street, London W1.

ESSLIN, Martin, OBE, critic and radio producer
b Budapest, Hungary, 8 June 1918; *s* of Paul Pereszlenyi and his wife Charlotte (Schiffer); *e* Reinhardt Seminar of Dramatic Art and University of Vienna; *m* Renate Gerstenberg.

Joined the BBC 1940; Head of BBC Radio Drama Department 1963–1976, awarded the title of Professor by the President of Austria, 1967; Visiting Professor of Drama, Florida State University, 1969–77; Member, Arts Council of Great Britain, and Chairman of its Drama Panel, 1976–7; Professor of Drama, Stanford University, Calif, 1977– ; his books include: Brecht: A Choice of Evils, The Theatre of the Absurd, The Plays of Harold Pinter, Brief Chronicles, an Anatomy of Drama, and Artaud; contributor to *Drama, Plays and Players,* etc; awarded the OBE in 1972.

Hobby: Book collecting. *Club:* Garrick. *Address:* 24 Loudoun Road, London NW8. *Tel:* 01–722 4243.

EVANS, Dillon (David Evans), actor and director
b London, 2 Jan 1921; *s* of Corris W Evans and his wife Kathleen (Dillon), a dancer; *e* Leighton Park School, Reading; *m* (1) Hazel Terry (mar dis); (2) Karin Germershausen; trained for the stage at RADA.

Under the name of David Evans, made his first professional appearance at the Gate, 12 Oct 1938, as Melville in Private History; same theatre, Dec 1938, appeared in The Gate Revue, transferring with it to the Ambassadors', Mar 1939; Criterion, Jun 1947, played Wilkinson and a Medical Student in A Sleeping Clergyman; Haymarket, 1947, took over as Roland Maule in Present Laughter; Globe, May 1949, Nicholas Devize in The Lady's Not for Burning, making his Broadway debut in the same production at the Royale, 8 Nov 1950; Phoenix, London, Oct 1954, Nicholas Holroyd in Bell, Book and Candle; Lyric, Jul 1958, Jojo in Irma la Douce; Haymarket, Apr 1962, Trip in The School for Scandal, also playing this role and that of Snake at the Majestic, NY, Jan 1963, under the name of Dillon Evans; Lunt-Fontanne, Apr 1964, Osric and Reynaldo in Hamlet; Phoenix, London, Sept 1965, Kosich in Ivanov, in which he was also seen at the Shubert, NY, May 1966; Broadhurst, Jan 1972, de Quadra in Vivat! Vivat! Regina; Cort, Jan 1973, Charlie Wisden in The Jockey Club Stakes; Martin Beck, Oct 1977, Dr Seward in Dracula, playing the part until 1979; has also played touring roles in England, and appeared and directed for stock and regional companies in the US, as well as dinner theatre; over 40 film appearances from Goodbye Mr Chips, 1939, to Victim, 1962; TV work includes *Judd for the Defense.*

Favourite parts: Nicholas Holroyd, Nicholas Devize. *Address:* Webster Lock Road, Rosendale, NY 12472.

EVANS, Jessie, actress
b Mountain Ash, South Wales, 1 Aug 1918; *d* of James Thomas and his wife Ellen Beatrice (Eynon); *e* Swansea; *m* Donald Bain; was formerly a hospital nurse.

Made her first appearance on the stage, at the Grand Theatre, Blackpool, 22 Dec 1943, as Clog in Pen Don, by Emlyn Williams; toured in the Middle East from Feb 1944, with Emlyn Williams' company playing Madame Arcati in Blithe Spirit, Dora Parkoe in Night Must Fall, and Bessie Watty in The Corn is Green; was stage-manager at the St James's Theatre, Apr 1945, for The Wind of Heaven; first appeared in London, at the Phoenix Theatre, 19 Sept 1945, as Tina in A Bell for Adano; toured, 1946, as Mrs Wilkins in Dear Ruth, and Hilda in The Guest in the House; at the New Theatre, June 1946, played Nastasia in Crime and Punishment; went to America with John Gielgud, 1947, and first appeared in New York, at the Royale, 26 May 1947, as Miss Prue in Love for Love; Lyric, Hammersmith, Dec 1947, and Phoenix, Jan 1948, played Miss Hoyden in The Relapse; joined the company of the Bristol Old Vic, 1949, playing among other parts, Audrey in As You Like It, and Dorine in Tartuffe, and appeared at the Lyric, Hammersmith, June 1950, as Dorine in Tartuffe; at the Dolphin Theatre, Brighton, Apr 1950, played Doto in A Phoenix Too Frequent; Strand (for the Repertory Players), Sept 1950, played Sadie in I Married Two Men; Wyndham's, Oct 1950, Peggy Dobson in Home at Seven; Comedy (for Repertory Players), Mar 1951, Ruby in The China Ship; Lyric, Hammersmith,

Sept 1951, Doto in A Phoenix Too Frequent; Embassy, Dec 1951, Mrs Molloy in The Merchant of Yonkers; also Apr 1952, Maudie in The Magnificent Moodies; Aldwych, Oct 1952, Delia Dosson in Letter From Paris; Lyric, Hammersmith, Feb 1953, Foible in The Way of the World; toured on the Continent, Mar 1954, as Elvira in Blithe Spirit, appearing at Geneva, Berne and Montreux; Arts, London, May 1954, Togrina in The Impresario from Smyrna; Strand, Oct 1954, Moll Twiddle in The Adventures of Peregrine Pickle (for Repertory Players); at the Library Theatre, Manchester, Mar 1955, played the title-role in Saint Joan, and June 1955, Margery Pinchwife in The Country Wife; Bristol Old Vic, Sept 1955, played Mrs Levi in The Matchmaker; New, May 1956, played Sidonie in Gigi; Arts, Nov 1956, in the Eugene Ionesco double bill, played Mary in The Bald Prima Donna, and the Caretaker in The New Tenant; Royal Court, Aug 1960, Miriam Norton in The Keep; Barn Theatre, Smallhythe, Aug 1961, played the Mother in The Boy with a Cart; Royal Court, Nov 1961, and Feb 1962, again played Miriam Norton in The Keep, transferring with the last production to the Piccadilly, Mar 1962, receiving the *Clarence Derwent Award* for this performance, 1962; Barn Theatre, Smallhythe, Sept 1962, played Dynamene in A Phoenix Too Frequent; at the Saville, July 1963, played Mrs Bardell in Pickwick; for Welsh National Theatre, July 1964, played Mrs Malaprop in The Rivals; Marlowe, Canterbury, Sept 1965, Narrator in Under Milk Wood; Hampstead Theatre Club, Nov 1965, Mrs Hanker in A Lily in Little India, transferring to the St Martin's, Jan 1966; Playhouse, Newcastle, Oct 1967, played the title role in Mother Courage; Mermaid, Feb 1968, Third Reader in The Adventures of the Black Girl in Her Search for God, and Fifth Reader in Aerial Football: A New Game; Phoenix, Mar 1968, the Wife of Bath in The Canterbury Tales; Marlowe, Canterbury, Apr 1969, title role in The Killing of Sister George; Hampstead, June 1969, played the lead in Cannibal Crackers; returned to the Phoenix, Mar 1970, for a further three years as The Wife of Bath; for Bristol Old Vic Company, Mar 1974, Mrs Hardcastle in She Stoops to Conquer; Arnaud, Guildford, June 1975, Lady Wishfort in The Way of the World; Adelphi; June 1976, Mrs O'Dare in Irene; Shaftesbury, Apr 1979, again played Wife of Bath in Canterbury Tales; first appeared in films 1954, in Aunt Clara; has also appeared in television plays.

Favourite part: Mother Courage. *Recreations:* Wine tasting and watching ball games. *Address:* c/o Green & Underwood Ltd, 11 Garrick Street, London WC2E 9AR.

EVANS, Maurice, actor
b Dorchester, Dorset, 3 June 1901; *s* of Alfred Herbert Evans, JP and his wife Laura (Turner); *e* Grocers' Company School; was formerly engaged in music publishing.

Made his first appearances in public as a boy singer, and as an amateur, appeared in his father's adaptations of Thomas Hardy's novels, in Dorchester; made a great impression by his performances of St Francis of Assisi, at the Mary Ward Settlement, which led to his first appearance on the professional stage at the Festival Theatre, Cambridge, 26 Nov 1926, as Orestes in The Orestia of Æschylus; he remained at Cambridge for one season playing a variety of parts; made his first appearance in London, at Wyndham's, 25 Aug 1927, as PC Andrews in The One-Eyed Herring; Feb 1928, played Stephani in Listeners; Apr 1928, Sir Blayden Coote in The Stranger in the House; Ambassadors', June 1928, Jean in The Man They Buried; Wyndham's, July 1928, Hector Frome and Edward Clements in Justice; Aug 1928, Borring and Graviter in Loyalties; he was then seen at the Little Theatre, Sept 1928, as Wyn Hayward in Diversion; at the Apollo (for the

Stage Society), Dec 1928, and Savoy, Jan 1929, played 2nd Lieut Raleigh in Journey's End, in which he made a big success; at Streatham Hill, Apr 1930, played the Young Frenchman in The Man I Killed; Savoy (for the Repertory Players), Sept 1930, the Sailor in The Queen Bee; St James's, Oct 1930, succeeded Colin Clive as Professor Agi in The Swan; Ambassadors', Dec 1930, played Owen Llewellyn in To See Ourselves; New, June 1931, Marius in Sea Fever; Criterion, Aug 1931, Eric Masters in Those Naughty 'Nineties; subsequently toured as Ralph in After All; Arts, Jan 1932, appeared as Nigel Chelmsford in Avalanche; Lyric, Apr 1932, played Jean Jacques in The Heart Line; Globe, Sept 1932, Peter in Will You Love Me Always?; Royalty, Nov 1932, the Rev Peter Penlee in Playground; Arts, Mar 1933, Guy Daunt in Cecilia; Vaudeville, Apr 1933, Dick in The Soldier and the Gentlewoman; Wyndham's, July 1933, Arnold Waite in Other People's Lives; Drury Lane, Sept 1933, Aristide in Ball at the Savoy; Sadler's Wells and Shaftesbury, May 1934, Edward Voysey in The Voysey Inheritance; joined the Old Vic-Sadler's Wells Company, Sept 1934, and appeared during the season as Octavius Caesar in Antony and Cleopatra, King Richard II, Benedick in Much Ado About Nothing, the Dauphin in Saint Joan, Petruchio in The Taming of the Shrew, Iago in Othello, Hippolytus (of Euripides), Adolphus Cusins in Major Barbara, Silence in Henry IV (Part II), Hamlet, which he also played in its entirety; went to America in the autumn, and in Oct 1935, toured with Katharine Cornell, as Romeo in Romeo and Juliet; made his first appearance in New York, Martin Beck Theatre, 23 Dec 1935, as Romeo, with Katharine Cornell; at the same theatre, Mar 1936, played the Dauphin in Saint Joan; Lyceum, Oct 1936, Napoleon in St Helena; St James, Feb 1937, made a remarkable success when he appeared as Richard in Richard II, subsequently touring in the same part; Forrest, Philadelphia, Nov 1937, Sir John Falstaff in Henry IV (Part I); St James, NY, Oct 1938, made a further remarkable success when he appeared as Hamlet in its entirety, under his own management, followed at the same theatre, Jan 1939, by his appearance as Sir John Falstaff in Henry IV (Part I); 44th Street, Dec 1939, again played Hamlet; St James, Apr 1940, again played Richard II; St James (for the Theatre Guild), Nov 1940, played Malvolio in Twelfth Night, with Helen Hayes, and toured in this, 1940–1; at the National Theatre, Nov 1941, under his own management, appeared as Macbeth, and toured in this, 1942; was commissioned as Captain, AUS, Aug 1942; Major in 1944; from Dec 1942, to June 1945, was in charge of the Army Entertainment Section, Central Pacific theatre; reappeared in NY, at Columbus Circle Theatre, Dec 1945, in Hamlet for 131 performances in NY, touring until Apr 1947; Alvin, Oct 1947, John Tanner in his own production of Man and Superman, which ran for 293 performances; Music Box, Mar 1948, supervised the production of The Linden Tree; toured, 1948, in Man and Superman; City Center, May 1949, again played John Tanner in Man and Superman; Coronet, Oct 1949, appeared as Andrew Crocker-Harris in The Browning Version and Arthur Gosport in Harlequinade; City Center, Jan 1950, played Dick Dudgeon in The Devil's Disciple, and subsequently at the Royale, Feb 1950; later, toured in summer theatres in the same play; City Center, Jan 1951, appeared as Richard II; also Dec 1951, played Hjalmar Ekdal in The Wild Duck; Plymouth, Oct 1952, appeared as Tony Wendice in Dial M for Murder, until May 1954; Martin Beck, Oct 1953, presented (with Geo Schaefer), The Teahouse of the August Moon; Alvin, Oct 1955, presented (with Emmett Rogers) No Time for Sergeants, also presenting the English production (with Emmett Rogers) at Her Majesty's,

London, Aug 1956; Plymouth, NY, Oct 1956, played King Magnus in The Apple Cart, subsequently touring with the production, 1957; Billy Rose, NY, Oct 1959, played Captain Shotover and co-presented Heartbreak House; 46th Street, Oct 1960, played Rev Brock in Tenderloin; Playhouse, Feb 1962, HJ in The Aspern Papers; American Shakespeare Festival, Stratford, Conn, July 1962, appeared with Helen Hayes in Shakespeare Revisited: A Program for Two Players, and subsequently toured until Mar 1963; toured, 1965, in The Grass Is Greener; Kennedy Center for the Performing Arts, Washington, DC, Sept 1973, various parts including: Oberon, Othello, Romeo in Shakespeare and the Performing Arts; has also produced and appeared in television productions of Hamlet, Richard II, Macbeth, Twelfth Night, The Taming of the Shrew, The Devil's Disciple, The Tempest; films include: Kind Lady, Androcles and the Lion, Planet of the Apes, Rosemary's Baby, Gilbert and Sullivan, Jack of Diamonds, Thin Air, Planet of the Apes Revisited, and Macbeth for both cinema and television; was appointed Hon Artistic Supervisor of the New York City Center Theatre Company, 1949; became a citizen of the United States, Aug 1941.

Club: Players. *Address:* c/o Contemporary-Korman Artists, 132 South Lasky Drive, Beverly Hills, Calif 90212.

EVANS, Tenniel, actor
b Nairobi, Kenya, 17 May 1926; s of Geoffrey Charles Evans and his wife Alice Julia Tenniel (King); e Christ's Hospital and St Andrews University; m Evangeline Banks; trained for the stage at RADA.
Made his first stage appearance at St Michael's Abbey, York, June 1951, as the Archangel Michael in the York Mystery Plays; St Thomas' Church, Regent Street, London, 1952, played Arius in Christ's Emperor; his first West End appearance was at the Duchess, Aug 1958, as Sgt Cadwallader in The Unexpected Guest; Royal Court, Sept 1959, played Max in a production without décor of The Kitchen; Royal Court, Feb 1962, Russell Morton in The Keep, transferring to the Piccadilly; Savoy, Oct 1963, Tod Logan in Portrait of Murder; Hampstead, Apr 1965, Praed in Mrs Warren's Profession; Royal Court, July and Criterion, Sept 1967, Jeffrey Hanson in The Restoration of Arnold Middleton; Playhouse, Nottingham, played Casti-Piani in Lulu, Oct 1970, and Polonius in Hamlet, Nov 1970, transferring in the latter part to the Cambridge, Jan 1971; founder member of The Actors' Company, 1972, for whom he has played Vatelin in Ruling the Roost, Donado in 'Tis Pity She's a Whore, Tenjiku in The Three Arrows, 1972; Voynitsky in The Wood Demon, Waitwell in The Way of the World, Oswald in King Lear, also appearing in Knots, and Flow, 1974; Orgon in Tartuffe, Eric Lister in The Last Romantic, Mifroid in The Phantom of the Opera, 1975; Bristol Old Vic, Apr 1976, Sir Henry Harcourt-Reilly in The Cocktail Party and David in Le Weekend (May); Round House, Nov–Dec 1977, for The Actors Company, played the Inelegant Man in Do You Love Me?, and Lane and Merriman in The Importance of Being Earnest, which he also directed; Globe, Apr 1978, Lawrence in Ten Times Table, also, in 1979, directing a provincial tour of this play; 1979, directed far eastern tour of The Two of Us; films, since 1960, include Only Two Can Play and 10 Rillington Place; television, also since 1960, includes numerous plays and series, and most recently Constance Kent, Heydays Hotel, and Raven; sound radio, since 1958, includes 16 years on The Navy Lark, and many broadcast stories, among them his own Tales from the Rectory; also author of Dear Wormwood, which he directed at The Guildhall.
Favourite parts: Jeffrey Hanson, Voynitsky, Vatelin. *Recreations:* Gardening, writing. *Address:* Candlemas, Jordans, Nr Beaconsfield, Bucks. *Tel:* Chalfont St Giles 3165.

EVELING (Harry) Stanley, dramatist
b Newcastle Upon Tyne, 4 Aug 1925; *s* of Winifred Amy Louisa Eveling; *e* Rutherford College, Samuel King's School, King's College, Durham University and Lincoln College, Oxford; married; senior lecturer in philosophy, University of Edinburgh.

His plays include: The Balachites, 1963; Come and Be Killed, The Strange Case of Martin Richter, 1967; The Lunatic, the Secret Sportsman and the Woman Next Door, 1968; Dear Janet Rosenberg, Dear Mr Kooning, 1969; Mister, 1970; The Laughing Cavalier, Better Days, Better Nights, 1971; Caravaggio Buddy, 1972; Union Jack (and Bonzo), 1973; Shivvers, 1974; Dead of Night, 1975; Dear Janet Rosenberg, Dear Mr Kooning has also been televised, as has A Man Like That, 1966; currently TV critic for *The Scotsman*.

Recreations: Golf, logic. *Address:* 30 Comely Bank, Edinburgh.

EVERHART, Rex, actor
b Watseka, Illinois, 13 June 1920; *s* of Arthur M Everhart and his wife Jeanette (Dodson); *e* Western Military Academy, University of Missouri, Pasadena Playhouse School of the Theatre (BTA 1941), New York University (MA 1950); *m* (1) Jill Reardon (mar dis); (2) Mary Dell Roberts (mar dis); (3) Clair Richard; studied with Paul Mann, Martin Ritt, and Curt Conway.

Made his first appearance on the stage in May 1929, in Watseka, Illinois, playing an Indian Boy in the pageant History of Iroquois County; played various roles at the Santa Monica, California, Players, 1939–41; at the Pasadena, California, Playhouse, played George Bodell in Out of the Frying Pan and The Drunken Rowdy in One Sunday Afternoon, 1941, and Ten Pin in Knickerbocker Holiday and the Son in Because She Loved Him So, 1942; served in the US Navy with the rank of Lieutenant, 1942–7; acted in and directed plays at the New York University Theatre, 1947–50; resident actor at the Sarah Stamms Theatre, Newport, Rhode Island, 1950–2, and the Margo Jones Theatre, Dallas, Texas, 1952–3; American Shakespeare Festival, Stratford, Conn, July 1955, the Cobbler in Julius Caesar, Stephano in The Tempest, and Dogberry in Much Ado About Nothing; made his NY début at the Alvin, 20 Oct 1955, when he played a Colonel and Lt Abel in No Time for Sergeants; succeeded Myron McCormick as Sgt King in this play's touring edition, Jan 1957, and continued in this part until May 1958; Belasco, Jan 1959, Collins in A Tall Story; toured, 1959, as Schatzie in Say, Darling; Delacorte, for the New York Shakespeare Festival, Aug 1959, Casca in Julius Caesar; Cort, Oct 1959, Mr Perisson in Moonbirds; Phoenix, Nov 1959, the Drunk in Lysistrata; Phoenix, Dec 1959, played in the concert reading Pictures in the Hallway; same theatre, Jan 1960, Aslak and Herr Von Eberkopf in Peer Gynt, Mar 1960, Bardolph in Henry IV, Part I, and Apr 1960, Bardolph in Henry IV, Part II; toured, 1960, as Luther Billis in South Pacific; 46th Street, Oct 1960, Joe Kovac in Tenderloin; Stratford, Connecticut, June 1962, Bardolph in Henry IV, Part I; Walnut, Philadelphia, Sept 1962, the Policeman in A Matter of Position; Stratford, Connecticut, June 1963, Dromio in The Comedy of Errors, Michael Williams in Henry V, and the Sentinel in Caesar and Cleopatra; Belasco, Oct 1963, Lionel Davis in A Rainy Day in Newark; Stratford, Connecticut, June 1964, Dogberry in Much Ado About Nothing and First Gravedigger in Hamlet; Stratford, Connecticut, 1965, Junius Brutus in The Tragedy of Coriolanus, Grumio in The Taming of the Shrew; Lunt-Fontanne, Nov 1965, Stanley in Skyscraper; made his London début at the Queen's, Oct 1966, as Murray

in The Odd Couple; Lunt-Fontanne, Dec 1967, Bradbury in How Now, Dow Jones; Stratford, Connecticut, June 1968, Charles in As You Like It, the Editor in Androcles and the Lion, and Dull in Love's Labour's Lost; 46th Street, 1969, took over from Howard Da Silva during his illness as Benjamin Franklin in 1776, and toured in this part in 1970; Stratford, Conn, 1973, Pompey in Measure for Measure, Sir Jasper Fidget in The Country Wife, and Porter in Macbeth; Circle in the Square—Joseph E Levine, Dec 1973, Pat McGloin in The Iceman Cometh; in stock, summer 1975; 46th Street, 1976, took over as Amos Hart in Chicago; Goodman, Chicago, Dec 1977, appeared in Working, repeating his roles in the NY production at the 46th Street, May 1978; toured, July 1978, in Back Country; Feb 1979, in Home Again; and Oct 1979 in My Husband's Wild Desires Almost Drove Me Mad; appeared in the film The Seven Ups, 1973; recently in Matilda, 1977, and Friday the Thirteenth, 1979; first appeared on television in 1939, and has since played extensively in plays and series, including, recently, *The American Short Story* and *Beacon Hill*.

Address: Leaverton Associates, 1650 Broadway, New York, NY.

EWELL, Tom, actor
b Queensboro, Kentucky, 29 Apr 1909; *s* of Samuel William Tompkins and his wife Martine (Yewell); *e* University of Wisconsin; *m* (1) Judith Ann Abbott (mar dis); (2) Marjorie Gwynne Sanborn.

Made his first appearance on the stage at the Park Theatre, Madison, Wis, 18 Feb 1928, in The Spider; appeared in various stock companies, prior to making his first appearance in New York, at the Royale, 21 Feb 1934, as Red in They Shall Not Die; 46th Street, Oct 1934, appeared as a Novice in The First Legion; Longacre, Oct 1934, Denver in Geraniums in My Window; Booth, Mar 1935, in De Luxe; Broadhurst, Nov 1935, played Frank Martin in Let Freedom Ring; National, Jan 1936, Dennis Eady in Ethan Frome; Forrest, May 1936, Captain Tim in Tobacco Road; Music Box, Oct 1936, Larry Westcott in Stage Door, also toured, 1936, in Brother Rat; Guild, Dec 1938, Cornelius Hackl in The Merchant of Yonkers; Morosco, Mar 1939, Simon in Family Portrait; Morosco, Oct 1940, Brother Galusha in Suzanna and the Elders; Shubert (for the Theatre Guild), Feb 1941, Dick Brown in Liberty Jones; St James, Dec 1941, Daniel Marshall in Sunny River; during the War, served for four-and-a-half years as a Lieutenant in the USNR; after demobilization, starred on the Pacific Coast, 1946, in a revival of Roberta; Biltmore, NY, Feb 1946, played Glen Stover in Apple of His Eye; Booth, Feb 1947, Fred Taylor in John Loves Mary; Coronet, Sept 1948, starred in the revue, Small Wonder; in summer theatres, 1949, in The Male Animal; Westport Country Playhouse, Sept 1951, played the title-role in Kin Hunter; Fulton, NY, Nov 1952, appeared as Richard Sherman in the oustanding and long-running success, The Seven Year Itch, for which he received the Antoinette Perry (Tony) Award; Royale, NY, Feb 1957, Augie Poole in The Tunnel of Love; Henry Miller's, NY, Oct 1958, Leon Rollo in Patate; Central City, Col, Aug 1959, Elliott Nash in The Gazebo; ANTA, NY, Feb 1960, appeared in the revue A Thurber Carnival; made his London début at the Savoy, Apr 1962, in A Thurber Carnival; toured the US, 1962–3, as Frank Michaelson in Take Her, She's Mine; toured, summer 1964, in Thursday Is a Good Night; toured, summer 1965, as Harry Lambert in Never Too Late; Ethel Barrymore, Nov 1965, Edward T Wellspot in Xmas in Las Vegas; toured, 1966, as Mr Day in Life with Father; Palm Beach (Florida) Playhouse, Jan 1967, John O'Rourke in The Armored Dove, and subsequently toured; toured, 1967–8, as Dr Jack Kingsley in The Impossible Years; New, London, June 1968, Richard Pawling, George, Chuck, and Herbert in You Know I Can't Hear You When the Water's Running; toured US, 1968–9, in the three-part musical The Apple Tree, playing the Snake in The Diary of Adam and Eve, Balladeer in The Lady Or the Tiger? and the Narrator of Passionella; Actors Playhouse, July 1971, took over as Vladimir in Waiting for Godot; Walnut, Philadelphia, 1973, Captain Jack Boyle in Juno and the Paycock; toured, 1974, in What Did We Do Wrong?; first appeared in films, 1939, in Kansas Kid, and has since appeared in They Knew What They Wanted, Adam's Rib, The Seven Year Itch, State Fair, The Great Gatsby (1974), etc; played on radio in 1935 in The March of Time and Ellery Queen in 1936 and on The Ewells, 1966–8; has appeared on television, notably in his own series The Tom Ewell Show, in Baretta, etc.

Recreations: Golf and farming. *Address:* Actors Equity Association, 165 West 46th Street, New York, NY 10036.

EYEN, Tom, playwright and director
b Cambridge, Ohio, 14 Aug 1941; s of Abraham Eyen and his wife Julia (Farhat); e Ohio State; m Liza Giraudoux.

First wrote and directed a play at the age of eight, which he produced in his garage in Cambridge, Ohio, May 1950, and called (When) The Clock Strikes Thirteen; his New York début was at the La Mama Experimental Theatre Club, May 1964, when Ellen Stewart produced his play Frustrata, the Dirty Little Girl with the Red Paper Rose Stuck in Her Head, Is Demented!; since then has written many avant garde and experimental plays and musicals for Cafe La Mama, the Playwrights' Workshop, and the commercial theatre, most of which were performed by his troupe, The Theatre of the Eye, and directed by him: The White Whore and the Bit Player, My Next Husband Will Be a Beauty, 1964; Can You See a Prince? (a children's musical), The Demented World of Tom Eyen, Why Hanna's Skirt Won't Stay Down, Miss Nefertiti Regrets, 1965; Cinderella Revisited (a children's musical), Sinderella Revisited (adults' musical), Eyen on Eyen, Give My Regards to Off Off Broadway, 1966; Court, Sarah B Divine! (Part I), Grand Tenement and November 22, 1967; Why Johnny Comes Dancing Home, The Kama Sutra (An Organic Happening), Who Killed My Bald Sister Sophie? A Vanity Happening, Alice Through the Glass Lightly, 1968; The Four No Plays, Caution: A Love Story, Eye in New York, 1969; Areatha in the Ice Palace, What Is Making Gilda So Gray, Gertrude Stein and Other Great Men, The Dirtiest Show in Town, 1970; Theatre of the Eye made its London début at the Mercury, Mar 1970, in The White Whore and The Bit Player and Why Hanna's Skirt Won't Stay Down; made its West End début at the Duchess, May 1971, in The Dirtiest Show in Town; has since written 2008½: A Spaced Oddity, 1973; Sarah B Divine produced at the Jeannetta Cochrane, Mar 1973; Women Behind Bars, 1974; The Dirtiest Musical, 1975; Women Behind Bars (London), 1977; The Neon Woman, 1978; The White Whore and The Bit Player was filmed in 1969; TV work includes scripts for Mary Hartman, Mary Hartman, and The Bette Midler Special, 1977.

Recreations: Scuba diving and sky-diving. *Clubs:* Harvard, and Knights of Columbus. *Address:* c/o Bridget Aschenberg, International Creative Management, 40 West 57th Street, New York, NY 10019. *Tel:* 212–556 5720.

EYRE, Peter, actor
b New York City, 11 Mar 1942; s of Edward Joseph Eyre and His wife the Hon Dorothy Pelling (Acton); e Portsmouth Priory, Portsmouth, RI, and Downside.

Made his first appearance on the stage with the Old Vic Company at the Olympia, Dublin, Sept 1960, as a Thane in Macbeth, touring Russia and Poland with the same company, 1961; in repertory at Harrogate, Bradford and Glasgow, 1963–4; Hampstead, Feb 1964, played Tom Perry in The Tower; Lyric, Hammersmith, Oct 1964, Alexeyev in Oblomov, transferring with the production retitled Son of Oblomov, to the Comedy, Dec 1964; Mermaid, Mar 1967, title-role in Benito Cereno; Royal Court, Apr 1968, Prince Arthur in Early Morning; at Nottingham Playhouse, 1968–70, his parts included: Feste in Twelfth Night, Banquo in Macbeth, Konstantin in The Seagull, Dinsdale in The Ruling Class, Edgar in King Lear, and Prince Myshkin in The Idiot; Gardener Centre, Brighton, Sept 1971, St Just in The Silence of St Just; Liverpool, Feb 1972, Guildenstern in Rosencrantz and Guildenstern are Dead; Chichester Festival, 1973, played Konstantin in The Seagull, May and Major Tarver in Dandy Dick, July; Open Space, Nov 1973, played Ivan in Notes from the Underground; at Greenwich, 1974, Oswald in Ghosts, Jan, Konstantin in The Seagull, Jan, and Hamlet, Mar; for the RSC at the Place, 1974, played Axel in Comrades, Oct, Peters in The Beast, Nov; Open space, Dec 1974, Christian Maske in The Snob; toured Canada, the US and Australia with the RSC, 1975, as George Tesman in Hedda Gabler, playing the part at the Aldwych, July 1975; Cambridge Theatre, June 1976, Toozenbach in Three Sisters; Vaudeville, Mar 1977, the Friend in Stevie; Soho Poly, Sept 1977, played Philip in News, and, June 1978, directed Stoop; Haymarket, Leicester, Feb–Mar 1978, Raskolnikov in Crime and Punishment, Dolokhov in War and Peace, and Cain in Abel and Cain; Bristol Old Vic, Sept 1978, Jacques in As You Like It; Birmingham Rep, Apr 1979, Alceste in The Misanthrope and, May, the Cardinal in The Duchess of Maifi; Citizens, Glasgow, 1979, and Lyric, Hammersmith, Feb 1980, Ferdinando in Country Life; films include: Julius Caesar, Mahler, Hedda Gabler, and La Luna; TV work, since 1965, includes: The Death of Socrates, Platonov, A Misfortune, and The Birds Fall Down.

Recreations: Music, sleeping. *Address:* 12 South Terrace, London, SW7. *Tel:* 01–584 7418.

EYRE, Richard, director
b Barnstaple, Devon, 29 Mar 1943; s of Richard Hastings Eyre and his wife Minna Mary (Royds); e Sherborne and Peterhouse, Cambridge; m Sue Birtwistle.

Directed his first production, The Knack, at the Phoenix, Leicester, Dec 1965; Assistant Director, Phoenix Theatre, 1966; Associate Director, Royal Lyceum Theatre, Edinburgh, 1967; Director of Productions, 1970–2; his productions here included: Three Sisters, The Cherry Orchard, Trumpets and Drums, Schweyk in the Second World War, and The White Devil; for the Edinburgh Festival directed The Changeling, Random Happenings in the Hebrides, and Confessions of a Justified Sinner; won STV awards for the best production in Scotland, 1969, 1970, 1971; directed tours for the British Council to West Africa, 1971, and SE Asia, 1972; directed productions in 1972 for the 7:84 Company and the Everyman, Liverpool; Artistic Director, Nottingham playhouse, 1973–8; productions here included: Brassneck (co-directed), The Government Inspector, The Churchill Play, Bendigo, Comedians, Walking Like Geoffrey, Jug, The Plough and the Stars, Bartholomew Fair, Othello, The Cherry Orchard, The Alchemist, Deeds; in London he had directed his own adaptation of The Ha-Ha, 1968; The Giveaway, The Death and Resurrection of Mr Roche, 1970; The Great Exhibition, 1972; Jingo (for RSC), Comedians (Old Vic), 1975; White Suit Blues, Touched (Old Vic), 1977; for television he has directed: Waterloo Sunset, Comedians, The Imitation Game; produced BBC's Play for Today, 1978–9.

Recreation: Films. *Address:* 4 St Martin's Road, Stockwell, London SW9. *Tel:* 01–733 6207.

EYRE, Ronald, director and dramatic writer
b Mapplewell, Yorkshire, 13 Apr 1929; *s* of Christopher Eyre and his wife Mabel (Smith); *e* Queen Elizabeth Grammar School, Wakefield and University College, Oxford; taught for four years before becoming a television producer.

Directed his first stage production, Mar 1963, with Titus Andronicus at Birmingham Repertory; as well as further productions at Birmingham, he has since directed the following plays, in London unless otherwise stated: Widowers' Houses, 1965; Events While Guarding the Bofors Gun, 1966; Ghosts (Oxford), Bakke's Night of Fame, 1968; Enemy, 1969; Three Months Gone, London Assurance (Royal Shakespeare Company), Mrs Warren's Profession (National Theatre), 1970; Much Ado About Nothing (Royal Shakespeare Company), A Voyage Round My Father, 1971; Veterans, A Pagan Place, 1972; Habeas Corpus, 1973; Something's Burning (author and co-director), The Marquis of Keith (RSC: also adapted), London Assurance (New York), 1974; Saratoga (RSC), 1978; Othello (RSC), Tishoo, 1979; has broadcast frequently, and directed many television plays since 1957, among them most of the twelve he has written which include A Crack in the Ice, Bruno, and Are You There?; 1974–7 made the film series The Long Search for BBC.

Address: c/o Larry Dalzell, 3 Goodwin's Court, St Martin's Lane, London WC2. *Tel:* 01–240 3086.

EYSSELINCK, Walter, DFA, director and dramatic author
b Ghent, Belgium, 10 Nov 1931; *s* of Gaston Eysselinck and his wife Simonne (Defauw); *e* Ghent State University; *m* Janet Burroway (mar dis); trained for the stage at Ghent Royal Theatre School and Yale School of Drama.

After some years of teaching drama in the United States and Belgium, he directed both for stage and television in Belgium, 1963–7; Director of the Gardner Centre for the Arts, Sussex University, 1965–72; he has since directed the following productions at Brighton or the Gardner Centre: Le Piège de Méduse, 1967; Medea and Epitafios (double-bill, also Arts, London), The Fantasy Level and The Beauty Operators (also double-bill), 1968; Comrade Jacob (opening production of Gardner Centre Theatre), 1969; The Nuns, A Touch of the Poet; Don't Let Summer Come, 1970; The Protagonist, Mirandolina, The Silence of St Just, 1971; he is the author of a number of plays (including children's plays), translations and adaptations which have been performed in his native Belgium; his one-man adaptation of The Diary of a Madman was staged at the Duchess, Mar 1967; also adapted into English The Accusers (Neveux).

Recreations: New Orleans jazz, fishing.

F

FABER, Ron (*né* Ronald Anthony Faber), actor
b Milwaukee, Wisconsin, 16 Feb 1933; *s* of Clarence Ernst Faber and his wife Ethel (Backus); *e* Marquette University, Milwaukee; *m* (1) Elise Donahue (mar dis); (2) Paula Ann Price; formerly a salesman, social worker, foundry labourer, night porter, drama teacher, marionettist, factory worker, lighting assistant and television floor director.

Made his first stage appearance at the Marquette Players Theatre, 1954, as Richard Talbot in The Scarecrow; worked extensively with The Open Theatre, 1964–70, in productions including America Hurrah, The Serpent, Terminal, Ubu Cocu, Opera, and The Exception and the Rule; at the Mercer-O'Casey, Apr 1972, played Promos in And They Put Handcuffs on the Flowers (Obie and Drama Desk awards); same theatre, Nov 1972, the Patient in Dr Selavy's Magic Theatre; Circle in the Square, uptown, Jan 1973, Creon and the Tutor in Medea; Williamstown Summer Festival, 1973, Robert de Baudricourt and the English Soldier in Saint Joan; Mitzi E Newhouse, Dec 1973, Nestor and Priam in Troilus and Cressida; American Place, Nov 1974, several roles in The Beauty Part; Public, Mar 1976, the Captain in Woyzeck; Hartman, Stamford, Nov 1976, Edmund Scorn in The Reason We Eat; same theatre, Dec 1976, Dr Einstein in Arsenic and Old Lace; Yale Rep, season 1977, Matti in Puntila and His Chauffeur Malti; Encompass, Jun 1978, Pierpont Mauler in St Joan of the Stockyards; Guthrie, Minneapolis, 1978–79, Peachum in The Beggar's Opera; Majestic, Oct 1978, Blake in First Monday in October; American Place, May 1979, Carvalho in Tunnel Fever; Greenwich Mews Playhouse, 1979, Rosencrantz in Hamlet; Colonnades Theatre Lab, 1979, John Garga in In the Jungle of Cities; Yale Rep, season 1979–80, played Pa Ubu in Ubu Rex and Ellis in Curse of the Starving Class; films, since 1967, include The Exorcist and The Private Files of J Edgar Hoover (1980); regular TV appearances include specials and series.
Address: 155 Bank Street, New York, NY 10014.

FABRAY, Nanette (*née* Ruby Nanette Fabares), actress and singer
b San Diego, Calif, 27 Oct; *d* of Raoul B Fabares and his wife Lillian (McGovern); *e* Hollywood High School, and Los Angeles City College; *m* (1) David Tebet (mar dis); (2) Ranald MacDougall (dec); studied dancing under Bill Robinson, Ernest Belcher, George Danbury, and Danny Daniels, and music and voice at the Juilliard Conservatory of Music on a scholarship by Arthur Rodzinski.

Made her first appearance as Baby Nanette, in vaudeville, and also appeared in films; won two consecutive scholarships to the Max Reinhardt School of the Theatre, and appeared under his direction, 1939, as Sister Beatrice in The Miracle, the Daughter in Six Characters in Search of an Author, and Smeraldina in Servant with Two Masters; made her first appearance in New York, at the Mansfield Theatre, 25 Dec 1940, in the revue, Meet the People; Imperial, Oct 1941, played Jean Blanchard in Let's Face It; Shubert, Feb 1943, Antiope in By Jupiter; 46th Street, Sept 1943, Jean in My Dear Public; Alvin, Jan 1944, Sally Madison in Jackpot; Shubert Theatre, during 1945, Evelina in Bloomer Girl;

Shubert, Oct 1947, Sara Longstreet in High Button Shoes; 46th Street, Oct 1948, Susan Cooper in Love Life; 46th Street, Feb 1950, Jo Kirkland in Arms and the Girl; Winter Garden, Apr 1951, played Janette in Make a Wish; St James, Aug 1962, Nell Henderson in Mr President; Martin Beck, Apr 1973, Roberta Bartlett in No Hard Feelings; Cirque, Seattle, Washington, Feb 1975, played Karen Nash, Muriel Tate, and Norma Hubley in Plaza Suite; Dorothy Chandler Pavilion, Los Angeles, Cal, July 1975, Ruth in Wonderful Town; appears regularly in dinner theatre; has received three Emmy Awards, two Donaldson Awards, the Antoinette Perry Award, and the Eleanor Roosevelt Humanitarian Award; has received many other awards for her charitable works, including the 1963 Achievement Award of the Women's Division of Albert Einstein College, Woman of the Year in 1955, 1968, 1969, Human Relations Award of the Anti-Defamation League of B'nai B'rith, 1969, Cogswell Award of Gallaudet College, 1970, and the President's Distinguished Service Award, 1970; Doctor of Humane Letters, Gallaudet College, 1972; Doctor of Fine Arts, Western Maryland College, 1972; has also appeared on television, notably in the Sid Caesar series, *Caesar's Hour, The Carol Burnett Show, One Day at a Time*, etc; first appeared in films as a child, 1927, and subsequently in Elizabeth and Essex, 1938, A Child Is Born, 1939, The Band Wagon, 1952, The Happy Ending, 1970, Cockeyed Cowboys, 1972, Harper Valley PTA, 1978, etc.
Recreations: Rock collecting, fishing, and boating.
Address: 14360 Sunset Boulevard, Pacific Palisades, California.

FAIRBANKS, Douglas, Jr., KBE., actor
b New York City, 9 Dec 1909; *s* of Douglas Fairbanks, Sr, the film actor, and his wife Beth (Sully); *e* Pasadena Polytechnic School, Harvard Military Academy (Los Angeles), Collegiate Military School (NY); *m* (1) Joan Crawford (mar dis), (2) Mary Lee Epling Hartford; originally intended to be an artist, and studied painting and sculpture in London and Paris.

First appeared on the stage in Hollywood, Cal, 1929, in Young Woodley, and Saturday's Children; first appeared in England at the Opera House, Manchester, 7 May 1934, as Michael Robbins in The Winding Journey; made his London début at the Queen's, 19 Sept 1934, as Stephen in Moonlight Is Silver; in Aug 1934 appeared in Here Lies Truth; returned to America and, in the summer of 1940, toured Calif in Tonight at 8:30 in an all-star revival; toured US, 1968, as Professor Higgins in My Fair Lady; Chicago, Washington DC, Hollywood, 1970–2 played Biddeford Poole in The Pleasure of His Company; toured, 1973–4, in The Secretary Bird; Royal Alexandra, Toronto, Canada, Dec 1974, again played Biddeford Poole in The Pleasure of His Company, and toured; made his NY début at the Imperial, 9 Mar 1975, in A Gala Tribute to Joshua Logan; Eisenhower, May 1975, Garry Essendine in Present Laughter, and subsequently toured; Phoenix, London, July 1976, again played Biddeford Poole; first appeared in films in Stephen Steps Out, 1923; later films include: Little Caesar (1930), Catherine the Great (1934), The Prisoner of Zenda (1937), Gunga Din (1939),

Sinbad the Sailor (1947), and innumerable others; in 1935 started his own film-producing company with The Amateur Gentleman; in England formed his television-producing firm Douglas Fairbanks Presents and produced many short plays; in World War II served in the US Navy; has received the Silver Star Medal, the Legion of Merit, the Distinguished Service Cross, the Legion d'Honneur, and the Croix de Guerre; was appointed honorary KBE, Mar 1949, in recognition of his Anglo-American relationships; holder of many international honours, awards and degrees.

Address: The Beekman, 575 Park Avenue, New York, NY 10021.

FAIRWEATHER, David Carnegy, theatre press-representative
b London, 18 Oct 1899; *s* of David Fairweather, MD, JP, and his wife Jean (Miller); *e* Laleham; *m* Virginia Winter; began his career in a chartered accountant's office, and subsequently became a free-lance journalist.

Joined the staff of *Theatre World*, 1925; edited film section 1926–7; appointed editor Jan 1928, and acted in that capacity until 1940; in 1936, appointed editor of *Play Pictorial*; since 1940 acted as press-representative at various theatres, for Laurence Olivier, Henry Sherek, Linnit and Dunfee, John Clements, Murray Macdonald and John Stevens, and was responsible for press and public relations at the Chichester Festival Theatre, 1965–73; has contributed articles on theatre and films to several periodicals.

Recreation: Playgoing. *Address:* Flat 7, 98 Marylebone High Street, London, W1. *Tel:* 01–486 0681.

FAIRWEATHER, Virginia, theatre press-representative
b London, 25 Jan 1922; *d* of Cyril Winter and his wife Jessie (Thorpe); *e* privately and abroad; *m* (1) Leslie Julian Jones (mar dis); (2) David Fairweather.

Formerly an actress, beginning her career as a student at the Old Vic School, and making her first London appearance at the Criterion Theatre, June 1940, when she appeared in the revue Come Out of Your Shell; other revues in which she appeared include: Rise Above It, 1941; It's About Time, 1942; Garrick, Mar 1943, played Judy in Brighton Rock; appeared in the revue Better Late, 1946; has broadcast and appeared in more than 600 radio and television plays; left the stage in 1957, to join her husband in theatre publicity; represented the Chichester Festival 1962; press-representative for the National Theatre, 1962–7; author of the book, Cry God for Larry, 1969.

Recreations: Yorkshire terriers and junk shops. *Address:* Flat 7, 98 Marylebone High Street, London, W1. *Tel:* 01–486 0681.

FAITHFULL, Marianne, actress
b Hampstead, London, 29 Dec 1946; *d* of Robert Glynn Faithfull and his wife, Baroness Erisso; *e* St Joseph's Convent, Reading; *m* (1) John Dunbar; (2) Ben Brierly.

Made her first stage appearance at the Royal Court, Apr 1967, as Irina in Three Sisters; at the same theatre, Apr 1968, played Florence Nightingale in Early Morning; Round House, Mar 1969, Ophelia in Hamlet; toured, Sept 1970 as Desdemona in Catch My Soul; Hampstead, Aug 1973, Jane Ludlow in Mad Dog; Palace, Watford, Nov 1973, Countess Sophia in A Patriot for Me; Theatre Royal, Brighton, Christmas 1973, title role in Alice in Wonderland; St Martin's, Feb 1974, Miranda in The Collector; toured, Autumn 1975, as Lizzie Curry in The Rainmaker; films include I'll Never Forget Whatsisname, Girl on a Motor-cycle, and Ghost

Story; television includes Terrible Jim Fitch, and Lonesome Sally; has made many successful recordings as a pop singer.

Recreations: Reading, cooking, children. *Address:* Yew Tree Cottage, Aldworth, Berks.

FARENTINO, James, actor
b New York, 24 Feb 1938; *s* of Anthony Ferrantino and his wife Helen; *e* American Academy of Dramatic Arts; *m* the actress Michele Lee Dusick.

At the Royale, Dec 1961, played Pedro in The Night of the Iguana; Sheridan Square Playhouse, 1963, took over a part in The Days and Nights of BeeBee Fenstermaker; Little Fox, Mar 1964, Mr Solares in In the Summerhouse; appeared in One Flew Over the Cuckoo's Nest, Chicago, 1973; Vivian Beaumont, Apr 1973, Stanley Kowalski in A Streetcar Named Desire; Chicago, 1974, in The Best Man; Circle in the Square, Jun 1975, Biff in Death of a Salesman; Chicago, 1976, appeared in The Big Knife; toured, 1978, in California Suite; films, since Psychomania, 1962, include The Final Countdown, 1980; TV includes specials and series.

Address: c/o William Morris Agency, 151 El Camino, Beverly Hills, CA 90210.

FARLEIGH, Lynn, actress
b Bristol, 3 May 1942; *d* of Joseph Sydney Farleigh and his wife Marjorie Norah (Clark); *e* Redland High School, Bristol; *m* Michael Jayston (mar dis); trained for the stage at the Guildhall School of Music and Drama.

First professional appearance, Playhouse, Salisbury, May 1962, in Under Milk Wood; joined the Royal Shakespeare Company, 1966 and played Castiza in The Revenger's Tragedy at Stratford, Oct; played Ruth in the company's production of The Homecoming, Music Box, Apr 1967, making her New York début; first London appearance, Jan 1968, as Helena in the Royal Shakespeare Company's All's Well that Ends Well; also played Amanda in The Relapse, Aug and Portia in Julius Caesar, Nov 1968, all three parts at the Aldwych; Royal Court (Theatre Upstairs), July 1969, appeared in the double-bill Blim at School and Poet of the Anemones; Round House, Mar 1970, Simone in The Friends; Mermaid, Nov 1970, Beatrice Justice in Exiles; Aldwych, Mar 1973, Monique Combes in Suzanna Andler; Open Space, Jan 1974, Anne in Ashes; Mermaid, Apr 1975, Jennifer Dubedat in The Doctor's Dilemma; Theatre Upstairs, July 1975, Beryl in Sex and Kinship in a Savage Society; Albery, Nov 1975, appeared in a season with the Prospect Theatre Company, playing Charlotte in A Room With a View; St George's Islington, Apr 1976, Viola in Twelfth Night; St George's, July 1976, Lady Anne in Richard III; Hampstead, June 1977, Anwar in The Ascent of Mount Fuji; Almost Free, Dec 1977, Elizabeth in Sovereignty Under Elizabeth; Olivier, Apr 1978, Agnes in Brand; Warehouse (RSC), Mrs Forsythe in Shout Across the River and Dec 1978, Jane in The Hang of the Gaol; Lyttleton, May 1979, Margaret in Close of Play; first film, 1968, Three Into Two Won't Go; subsequent films include A Phoenix Too Frequent, Voices, The Word; television, since 1964, includes The Rivals, Eyeless in Gaza, Fall of Eagles and Brand.

Favourite parts: Ruth, Anne and Viola. *Recreations:* Gardening, cooking, canals. *Address:* c/o Boyack and Conway Ltd, 8 Cavendish Place, London W1M 9DJ.

FARQUHAR, Malcolm, director
b Swansea, 26 Oct 1924; *s* of Allan Farquhar and his wife Florence Mary (Rees); *e* Colston School, Bristol and Clevedon College.

Began his career as an actor, 1943, with the Rapier Players, Bristol; appeared with Birmingham Repertory, including his first London appearance, St James's, June 1948, as Capt Absolute in the Birmingham production of The Rivals; directed his first play, 1963, at the Connaught, Worthing; followed by seasons at the Alexandra, Birmingham and at Leatherhead; he has since directed the following plays in London: A Woman of No Importance, 1967; A Boston Story, 1968; Highly Confidential, 1969; Lady Frederick, Winnie the Pooh, 1970–1; artistic director, Everyman Theatre, Cheltenham, 1971– ; here he has directed the following world premières: This Stratford Business, The Law and Order Gang, 1971; As We Lie, 1973; The Daffodil Man, 1974; The Friendship of Mrs Eckley, 1975; Time to Kill, 1979; The Little Photographer, 1978; Don't Look at Me, 1979; directed a number of productions in S Africa, 1975–8.

Recreations: Collecting old gramophone records; gardening. *Address:* 6 Buckingham Road, Brighton BN1 3RA. *Tel:* 27451.

FARR, Derek, actor
b Chiswick, 7 Feb 1912; *s* of Gerald Farr and his wife Vera Eileen (Miers); *e* Cranbrook School, Kent; *m* (1) Carole Lynne (mar dis); (2) Muriel Pavlow; was formerly engaged as a schoolmaster.

Made his first appearance on the stage at the Barn Theatre, Oxted, Surrey, 1937, in a repertory company; first appeared on the London stage, at the Ambassadors', 9 Mar 1939, in The Gate Revue; St Martin's, Apr 1940, played John Anstruther in A House in the Square; during the War served in the Forces; after demobilization, appeared at the Fortune, Sept 1946, as Joe in Fools Rush In; mainly engaged in films, 1947–9; Savoy, July 1949, played Bruce Banning in Young Wives, Tale; Arts, Feb 1951, Eugene Bazarov in Spring at Marino; Royal, Brighton, Apr 1952, Stephen Binns in Adam's Apple; Strand, July 1952, Philip Langdon in The Step Forward; Ambassadors', Nov 1952, Edward Bare in Murder Mistaken; Vaudeville, Sept 1953, played Dudley in Trial and Error; Royal, Brighton, Oct 1955, Dr Alan Beresford in Dr Jo; Apollo, Mar 1956, played George Lawrence in One Bright Day; St Martin's, July 1957, George Maxwell in Odd Man In, Royal Court, Liverpool, Sept 1958, played Hannibal in A Fig For Glory; Strand, Mar 1959, played Julian Calvert in Wolf's Clothing; toured Australia and New Zealand, 1960; toured, Feb 1961, as Basil Martin in Milk and Honey; Cambridge, Feb 1962, Roy Collier in Signpost to Murder; again toured Australia, Sept 1963, in Mary, Mary; Phoenix, London, Nov 1964, played George in Every Other Evening; Arnaud, Guildford, Feb 1966, Mr Blundell in Wanted—One Body; Genée, East Grinstead, Feb 1967, Visitor in Any Just Cause; Garrick, Apr 1967, Sir Lindsay Cooper in Uproar in the House and July 1967, Henry B Wymark in Let Sleeping Wives Lie, playing the two parts in repertory for a time; Strand, June 1969, took over as Gilbert Bodley in Not Now Darling; first appeared in films, 1937, and has since played in many pictures; his many appearances on television since 1969 include: Dixon of Dock Green, Crossroads, Coronation Street, Nightingale Boys, The Avengers, The Duchess of Duke Street, Some Mothers Do 'Ave Em, Rumpole of the Bailey and, recently, Francis Durbridge Presents.

Recreation: Golf. *Address:* c/o Green & Underwood, 11 Garrick Street, London WC2.

FARRAH, Abd' Elkader, designer
b Boghari, Algeria, 28 Mar 1926; *s* of Brahim Farrah and his wife Fatima-Zohra Missoumi; *m* Simone Pieret; formerly a painter.

He designed his first production in 1953, the Opera Samson et Dalila for the Stadschouwberg, Amsterdam; since then he has designed more than 300 productions, some for the Royal Shakespeare Company, of which he is an associate artist; among the most notable, in London unless otherwise stated, are: The Cherry Orchard, 1961; The Tempest (Stratford), 1963; Puntila, 1965; The Burdies (Edinburgh Festival), 1966; The Three Sisters, 1967; Dr Faustus (Stratford), 1968; Tiny Alice, Richard III (Stratford), Oh! Calcutta! 1970; The Balcony, The Duchess of Malfi (Stratford), 1971; Murder in the Cathedral, 1972; Richard III (Comédie Française), Romeo and Juliet (Stratford), Henry IV (Pirandello: New York), The Taming of the Shrew (Stratford), A Lesson in Blood and Roses, 1973; Henry IV (Pirandello), The Bewitched, The Can Opener, 1974; Henry IV, Parts 1 and 2, Henry V (all Stratford), 1975, also London 1976; Mardi Gras, Carte Blanche, 1976; Henry VI, Parts 1, 2 and 3, Henry V, Coriolanus (these also Stratford), 1977–8; The Passion of Dracula, 1978; Head of theatrical design course, National Theatre School, Strasbourg, France, 1955–62; also National Theatre School of Canada, Montreal, Oct 1968–July 1969.

Address: c/o Royal Shakespeare Theatre, Stratford-on-Avon, Warwicks. *Tel:* 3693.

FARRAND, Jan, actress
b Denver, Colorado, 4 Feb 1925; *d* of William K Farrand and his wife Norma (Hadley); *e* University of Colorado, Boulder; *m* (1) Albert Marre (mar dis); (2) Colin MacLachlan.

Her early stage experience was as a founding member of the Brattle Theatre company, Cambridge, Mass, 1947–53; made her Broadway debut at the Morosco, 22 Nov 1950, as Miss Hoyden in The Relapse; for the NY City Center company, 1953, played Katherine in Love's Labour's Lost and Hypatia Tarleton in Misalliance, Feb, transferring in the latter role to the Ethel Barrymore, Mar; ANTA, Dec 1954, Henrietta Stackpole in Portrait of a Lady; Morosco, Feb 1955, Nericia in Tonight in Samarkand; City Center, Sept 1955, Desdemona in Othello and Lady Percy in Henry IV Part I; McAlpin Rooftop, May 1970, Mrs Prentice in What the Butler Saw; Roundabout, Jan 1977, Ella Rentheim in John Gabriel Borkman; Martin Beck, Apr 1977, Shirley Fuller in Ladies at the Alamo; has also appeared at most major regional theatres; first film, The Detective, 1963, and has since been seen in The Front, 1975; TV includes plays and series, recently *Kojak*.

Address: c/o Hesseltine Baker Associates, 119 West 57th Street, New York, NY 10019. (*Died, November 4, 1980*).

FARRELL, Charles, actor
b Dublin, Ireland, 6 Aug 1906; *s* of Samuel Farrell and his wife Mary; *e* Toronto, Canada; *m* Babbie McManus.

Made his first appearance on the stage, as a child, with a stock company at Detroit, Michigan, 1912; made his first appearance on the London stage at the Coliseum, 16 May 1921, as Sam Merton in The Crown Diamond; appeared at the St James's Theatre, Oct 1924, as Tim in The Nervous Wreck; Grand, Fulham, Mar 1925, played Snowey and Billy Plunkett in Derby Day; Adelphi, May 1926, Boano in Aloma; His Majesty's, Feb 1927, Pietro in The Wicked Earl; Globe, May 1929, Zeb Warner in The Black Ace; Adelphi, Sept 1929, Bill in Brothers; Q, Nov 1929, Murdock in The Devil's Pulpit; Ambassador's, Jan 1930, Yank in In the Zone; Fortune, Mar 1930, Rangi in Cape Forlorn; Comedy, Mar 1930, No 5 in Odd Numbers; Globe, Sept 1930, Vincent Jones in Street Scene; Wyndham's, Dec 1930, Connor in Smoky Cell; Comedy, Mar 1931, Bill Smith in Naughty

Cinderella; Arts, Oct 1931, Judge Skimp and Lord Mono-mark in Vile Bodies; Aldwych, Jan 1933, Supt Barker in A Bit of a Test; Embassy, Oct 1933, Aubrey McClintock in Son of Man; Comedy, Dec 1933, Charlie Shaw in Whistling in the Dark; Royalty, May 1934, Gat Charillo in The Quitter; His Majesty's, Nov 1934, Dick Corner in Mary Read; Piccadilly, July 1935, Spike O'Reilly in Public Saviour No 1; Haymarket, Aug 1936, 'Pal' Green in The Amazing Dr Clitterhouse; Strand, Nov 1937, Spider in The Bowery Touch; Drury Lane, June 1938, Joe Hooling in The Sun Never Sets; Feb 1939, toured in The Bowery Touch; Q, May 1940, played Spider in Wise Guys, which he also directed; London Hippodrome, Nov 1941, Borg in Get a Load of This, which he played for 20 months; Savoy, Sept 1943, The Wreck in My Sister Eileen; Embassy, Mar 1945, Timothy Battle in Father Malachy's Miracle; during 1946, was engaged as director at the Play-house Theatre, Buxton; Embassy, Oct 1946, played Daniel B Delane in Away from It All; at the same theatre, Oct 1947, Charlie Packer in Deliver My Darling; Palace, Mar 1948, Joe Erdman in Carissima, which ran over a year; New Lindsey, Jan 1950, Newt Hagar in New England Night; Princes, Mar 1950, Lieut Monoghan in Detective Story; in 1952, appeared for a short season at the Copenhagen Royal Theatre, and subsequently made a series of television films in Denmark; at Her Majesty's, London, Dec 1952, appeared as Patrolman Miller in Remains To Be Seen; Prince of Wales's, Sept 1963, played Mayor Crane in Never Too Late; same theatre, Apr 1975, S J Lofgren in Harvey; first appeared in films, 1912, with the old Vitagraph company, and has played in over two hundred and fifty, including Chimes at Midnight, and Coun-tess Dracula; has appeared frequently in radio and television plays; founder member British Actors' Equity Association, 1930, and Hon Treasurer 1949–75.

Address: c/o British Actors Equity, 8 Harley Street, Lon-don W1.

FARROW, Mia, actress
b California, 9 Feb 1946; *d* of John Villiers Farrow and his wife Maureen (O'Sullivan); *m* Andre Previn.

Made her first stage appearance at the Madison Avenue Playhouse, New York, in 1936, when she took over the part of Cecily Cardew in The Importance of Being Earnest; made her London début at the Shaw, July 1972, playing the title-role in Mary Rose; at Greenwich, played Irina in Three Sisters, Jan, and Adela in The House of Bernarda Albe, Mar 1973; joined the Royal Shakespeare Company at the Aldwych to play Ann Leete in The Marrying of Ann Leete, Sept 1975; Pavla Tselovanyeva in The Zykovs, Apr 1976; Sasha in Ivanov, Sept 1976; Barrymore, 8 Nov 1979, made her Broadway début as Phoebe Craddock in Romantic Com-edy; films include: Rosemary's Baby, John and Mary, and The Great Gatsby; TV, since 1964, includes: Peyton Place, John Belinda, and Peter Pan.

Recreations: Reading, riding, listening to music and certain people. *Address:* Reigate, Surrey.

FAYE, Joey (*né* Joseph Antony Palladino), actor, comedian
b New York City, 12 July 1910; *s* of Anthony Palladino and his wife Maria (Noto); *e* Textile High School, New York University; *m* Eileen Jenkins (mar dis); (2) Ginna Carr (dec); (3) Judy Carlin.

Made his professional début in vaudeville at Poli's Theatre, New Haven, Connecticut, 1931; made his NY début at Minsky's burlesque in the Republic Theatre, 1931; remained with Minsky's until 1938; toured, 1938, in Room Service, which was his first dramatic part; Music Box, NY, Sept 1938, played in the revue Sing Out the News; toured as Banjo in

The Man Who Came to Dinner, 1939–40; New York's World's Fair, summer, 1939, played in the revue Streets of Paris; National, Sept 1942, played himself in Strip for Action; Windsor, June 1943, Burleigh Sullivan in The Milky Way; Windsor, June 1943, Carlyle Benson in Boy Meets Girl; during the World War II toured for the USO and made his London début when he appeared with Marlene Dietrich and this troupe; Adelphi, NY, Apr 1944, Youssouf in Allah Be Praised; Adelphi, Feb 1946, Goya in The Duchess Misbe-haves; Shubert, New Haven, Connecticut, Apr 1946, Ruby in Windy City; Barbizon-Plaza, May 1946, played in the revue Tidbits of 1946; Shubert, New Haven, Apr 1947, Max in Three Indelicate Ladies; Shubert, NY, Dec 1947, Mr Pont-due in High Button Shoes; toured in the vaudeville show Meet the People, 1949–50; Winter Garden, Nov 1951, Pinky in Top Banana, and toured in this part, 1952–3; Longacre, 1955, Sol Schwartz in The Tender Trap; Shubert, Philadel-phia, Dec 1955, the Professor in The Amazing Adele; Shubert, New Haven, Mar 1956, Danny in Strip for Action; in Hollywood, Calif, 1959, played Gogo in Waiting for Godot; Lunt-Fontanne, Nov 1962, Bernie Buchsbaum in Little Me; New York City Center, Apr 1965, Benny South-street in Guys and Dolls; Coconut Grove Playhouse, Miami, Florida, 1967, directed, wrote, and played in Anatomy of Burlesque; Martin Beck, 1968, took over as Sancho Panza in Man of La Mancha, and continued in this part for one year; McAlpin Rooftop, Mar 1970, Hector in Lyle; Goodspeed Opera House, East Haddam, Conn, July 1974, appeared in DuBarry Was a Lady; toured, 1975, in That Wonderful World of Burlesque; toured, Nov 1976, in Hellzapoppin; first appeared in films in the 1930s in Warner Brothers short subjects, and has since played in Top Banana, The Tender Trap, Ten North Frederick, North to Alaska, The Grissom Gang (1971), The War Between Men and Women (1972), The Front (1976), etc; first appeared on experimental televi-sion in 1936 and since has played the Master of Ceremonies for *The Kraft Music Hall,* in his own series *The 54th Street Revue,* many times on the *Ed Sullivan Show,* and numerous others.

Favourite part: Gogo in Waiting for Godot. *Hobby:* Collecting comedy skits and sketches, of which he has gathered some 18,000. *Clubs:* Dutch Treat, Lambs. *Address:* 71 Winchester Avenue, Staten Island, NY 10312.

FAZAN, Eleanor, director, choreographer, actress
b Kenya, Africa, 29 May 1930; *d* of Herbert Fazan and his wife Sylvia (Hook); *e* Limulu Girls School, Kenya; trained as dancer at Sadler's Wells Ballet School, London; *m* Stanley Myers (mar dis).

Appeared as principal dancer in a number of musicals; at the London Hippodrome, May 1953, appeared in the revue High Spirits; Criterion, Apr 1954, appeared in the revue Intimacy at 8.30; for the next ten years was engaged in choreography and direction of plays; re-appeared on the stage at Wyndham's, Mar 1965, as Liz in Inadmissible Evidence; since 1956 she has directed or co-directed the following productions: Grab Me a Gondola, 1956; Zuleika, Share My Lettuce, Paddle Your Own Canoe, 1957; Chrysan-themum, 1958; One To Another, 1959; Aladdin, 1960; Beyond the Fringe, Bonne Soupe, 1961; Blitz!, The Rag Trade, 3 at Nine, 1962; Enrico, 1963; Nights at the Comedy, 1964; The Three Musketeers, 1966; Just a Show, The Three Musketeers Ride Again, 1969; Council of Love, 1970; Another Bride, Another Groom, 1975; The French Have a Song for It, 1979; she has choreographed numerous other productions, including: The Lily-White Boys, 1960; The Lord Chamberlain Regrets, 1961; The Chances (Chichester), The

Broken Heart, 1962; The Workhouse Donkey (Chichester), 1963; The Cherry Orchard (Chichester), 1966; An Italian Straw Hat (Chichester), 1967; Lulu, 1970; The Threepenny Opera, The Beggar's Opera, I Claudius, The Ruling Class, 1972; Habeas Corpus, Twelfth Night, Pericles, 1973; The Marriage of Figaro (National Theatre), Das Rheingold, Die Walküre (both Covent Garden), 1974; Tannhäuser, Peter Grimes, Siegfried, 1975; Götterdämmerung (Covent Garden), 1976; Privates on Parade (RSC), Lohengrin (Covent Garden), 1977; The Rake's Progress (Covent Garden), Peter Pan, 1979; has been responsible for the choreography of more than fifty television productions, including The One and Only Phyllis Dixey, 1978.

Address: c/o MLR, 194 Brompton Road, London SW5.

FEAST, Michael, actor
b Brighton, 25 Nov 1946; *s* of Edward Albert Feast and his wife May; *m* Kathleen Margaret Merrigan (the theatrical agent, Kate Feast); trained for the stage at the Central School of Speech and Drama.

Made his first stage appearance at the Phoenix, Leicester, 1968, as the Pope in Galileo; London debut at Shaftesbury, 27 Sept 1968, as Woof in the original cast of Hair; for '69 Theatre Company, Manchester played Ariel in The Tempest, 1969, and Nicely-Nicely Johnson in Guys and Dolls, 1972; 1973–74, appeared in My Sister and I, Skipper, Asides, The Carnation Gang (Bush); Heads, and The Education of Skinny Spew (Green Banana Room); Elizabeth I (Theatre Upstairs); Hampstead, Nov 1974, played Harold in Clever Soldiers; for the National Theatre (at the Old Vic, unless otherwise stated) played Ariel in The Tempest, Mar 1974, Foster in No Man's Land, Apr 1975, and also at the Wyndham's (July), The Man Himself (monologue), ICA and Young Vic Studio, Raymond in Watch it Come Down, Feb 1976; Shaw, Oct 1976, played Mercutio in Romeo and Juliet; returned to the '69 Theatre Company at the Royal Exchange, Manchester, 1976–77, and played Nick in What the Butler Saw, Henry in The Skin of Our Teeth, Teleyeghin in Uncle Vanya and Roland Maule in Present Laughter; Bush, and tour, Apr 1978, Dave in On the Out; Cottesloe (NT), June 1978, Bobby in American Buffalo; Queen's, Aug 1978, Renfield in The Passion of Dracula; Cottesloe, June 1979, Mayhew in Dispatches; films include I Start Counting, Brother Sun, Sister Moon, and McVicar; recent television appearances include The Lady from the Sea, Censored Scenes from King Kong, and The Chelsea Murders.

Address: c/o Kate Feast Management, 43A Princess Road, London NW1.

FEDER, A H (Abe), lighting and scenic designer
b Milwaukee, Wisconsin, 27 June 1909; *s* of Benjamin Feder and his wife Sane (Byfield); *e* Carnegie Institute of Technology, 1926–9; *m* Ciel Grossman.

Designed the lighting for his first New York production Trick for Trick, at Sam Harris Theatre, 18 Feb 1932; since then has designed and directed the lighting of One Sunday Afternoon, 1933; Four Saints in Three Acts, Calling All Stars, Gentlewoman, 1934; Ghosts, The Hook-Up, 1935; Conjurin' Man Dies, the Federal Theatre productions of Macbeth and Horse Eats Hat, New Faces of 1936, Walk Together Chillun, Triple-A Ploughed Under, Turpentine, Injunction Granted, Hedda Gabler, 1936; Became Head of Lighting for all Federal Theatre (WPA) projects including first presentations of 'Living Newspaper' (1935—41); The Tragical Historie of Dr Faustus, Native Ground, How Long, Brethren, Without Warning, I'd Rather Be Right, 1937; Diff'rent, Pygmalion, Coriolanus, Prologue to Glory, Big

Blow, Here Come the Clowns, The Cradle Will Rock, Immediate Comment (ballet), Androcles and the Lion, and the tour of The Ballet Caravan, 13 of a Nation, The Father, 1938; Sing for Your Supper, Speak of the Devil! 1939; A Passenger to Bali, Hold On to Your Hats, Johnny Belinda, 1940; co-ordinator of production and lighting designer for the first tour of the American Ballet Theatre, and designed 21 ballets including Giselle, The Great American Goof, Peter and the Wolf, as well as the play Angel Street, 1941; Autumn Hill, The Skin of Our Teeth, Magic, Hello Out There, The Walking Gentleman, 1942; designed the lighting and décor of The Gioconda Smile, and the lighting for The Tower Beyond Tragedy, Out of This World, 1950; Mary Rose, A Sleep of Prisoners, 1951; Three Wishes for Jamie, Dear Barbarians, The Sonja Henie Ice Revue (Santa Barbara, Cal), 1952; A Pin to See the Peep Show, 1953; The Immoralist, The Boy Friend (also décor), 1953; What Every Woman Knows, The Flowering Peach, 1954; The Wisteria Trees, Inherit the Wind, Seventh Heaven, The Skin of Our Teeth, (Paris), The Young and the Beautiful, 1955; My Fair Lady, 1956; A Clearing in the Woods, Visit to a Small Planet, Orpheus Descending, Time Remembered, 1957; Goldilocks, At the Grand (Los Angeles Light Opera), The Cold Wind and the Warm, 1958; Come Play With Me (also décor), Can-Can, A Loss of Roses, 1959; Greenwillow, Camelot, 1960; Tiger Tiger Burning Bright, 1962; Once for the Asking (also décor), 1963; Blues for Mr Charlie, The Three Sisters, 1964; On a Clear Day You Can See Forever, 1965; The Country Girl (also décor), Elizabeth the Queen (also décor), Carousel (also décor), 1966; Beyond Desire (also décor), Salute to the American Musical Theatre, White House, Wash, DC, 1967; The King and I, Carnival! My Fair Lady, 1968; Scratch, 1971; Goodtime Charley, Doctor Jazz, 1975; Carmelina, 1979; noted as a lighting innovator and lectures extensively in universities and to the profession; served as lighting designer andor consultant for the New York World's Fair, Expo '67 in Montreal, the San Francisco Civic Center, Rockefeller Plaza in NY, the Israel National Museum in Jerusalem, the Gallery of Modern Art in NY, Minskoff theatre, NY, etc; designed the lighting for all the theatres in the Kennedy Center for the Performing Arts, Washington, DC.

Address: Lighting by Feder, 15 West 38th Street, New York, NY 10018. *Tel:* 212–840 1471.

FEELY, Terence John, dramatist
b Liverpool, 20 July 1928; *s* of Edward Feely and his wife Mary (Glancy); *e* St Francis Xavier's School, Woolton, and Liverpool University; *m* Elizabeth Adams.

Formerly a political journalist and editor; author of the following plays: Shout for Life (originally produced as Sergeant Dower Must Die), 1963; Don't Let Summer Come, 1964; Adam's Apple, 1966; Who Killed Santa Claus?, Don't Let Summer Come (revised version), 1970; The Avengers (with Brian Clemens), 1971; Dear Hearts, 1974; Heute Kommt Der Weihnachtsmann (Germany), 1977; Mindbender, Qui a Tué Le Père (Brussels), 1979; has also written and produced numerous films and television plays, including Affairs of the Heart; also author of Rich Little Poor Girl.

Hobbies: Marksmanship, driving, antiques, gardening. *Club:* Carlton. *Address:* 21 Drayton Gardens, London SW10 9RY.

FEIFFER, Jules, playwright and satirist
b New York City, 26 Jan 1929; *s* of David Feiffer and his wife Rhoda (Davis); *m* Judith Sheftel.

He is a syndicated cartoonist whose work appears in *The Village Voice* and 105 newspapers in the US and abroad; his first play, The Explainers, adapted from his cartoons, was performed by The Playwrights at the Second City, Chicago, 1961; since then he has written the one-act play Crawling Arnold, 1961; had his cartoon Passionella adapted for Broadway as one act of the Broadway musical The Apple Tree, 1966; his first full-length play was Little Murders, produced in NY and by the Royal Shakespeare Company in London, 1967, voted best foreign play of the year by the London Drama critics, and awarded an Obie when revived Off-Broadway in 1969; God Bless was produced at the Yale Drama School and by the Royal Shakespeare Company in London, 1968; The White House Murder Case was produced in NY, 1970, and like Little Murders received the Outer Circle Critics Award; Yale Repertory Theatre, 1973–4 season, contributed sketches to The Watergate Classics; Knock Knock produced at the Circle Repertory, NY, Jan 1976 and the Biltmore, Feb and June 1976; Hold Me!, an entertainment based on his cartoons, produced at the American Place, NY, 1977; also contributed sketches to Collision Course and Oh, Calcutta; Little Murders was filmed, 1971, also Carnal Knowledge; has published 11 collections of cartoons, two novels, one cartoon-novel, and one screenplay; member of the Dramatists Guild Council.

Address: Field Newspaper Syndicate, 30 East 42nd Street, New York, NY 10017.

FEINGOLD, Michael, critic, translator and director
b Chicago, Illinois, 5 May 1945; *s* of Bernard C Feingold and his wife Elsie; *e* Columbia University, New York and Yale School of Drama (MFA, 1970).

Literary Manager, 1972–76, Yale Rep; Artistic Director, 1975–76, Theatre-at-Noon, NY; Literary Director, 1977–79, Guthrie Theater, Minneapolis; his many translations include plays by Brecht, including The Rise and Fall of the City of Mahagonny, 1974, and Happy End, 1972 (seen on Broadway, 1977); Ibsen, including When We Dead Awaken, 1971; Molière's The Bourgeois Gentleman, 1974; Diderot's Rameau's Nephew, 1976; Thomas Bernhard's Force of Habit, 1976; and operas by Offenbach and Donizetti; has directed off-off-Broadway, and at Yale and the Guthrie; recent productions he has directed include Two-Part Inventions, at Circle Rep, 1976, and the Goodman, Chicago, 1979; drama critic since 1970 for the *Village Voice.*

Address: 749 West End Avenue, New York, NY 10025.

FEIST, Gene, director and producer
b New York City, 16 Jan 1930; *s* of Henry Feist and his wife Harriet Fishbein; *e* Carnegie-Mellon University (BFA), New York University (MA); *m* Elizabeth Owens.

Directed his first play, The Matchmaker, at the New Theatre, Nashville, Tennessee, 15 Oct 1958; directed his first play in NY, Picnic on the Battlefield, at the Cherry Lane, 11 Feb 1962; in 1965 founded the Roundabout Theatre Co, Inc, in NY and has served as its Producing-Director since its inception; for the Roundabout has presented and, in most cases, directed the following: The Father, The Miser, Pelleas and Melisande, Pins and Needles, 1966–7; Waiting for Lefty, The Bond, King Lear, The Importance of Being Earnest, 1967–8; Journey's End, King Lear, Candida, Dance of Death, 1968–9; Trumpets and Drums (American première of the Brecht play), Macbeth, Oedipus, Lady from Maxim's (American première of the play by Feydeau) 1969–70; Hamlet in an all-male version, Tug of War, Uncle Vanya, Charles Abbott and Son, She Stoops to Conquer, 1970–1; also The Master Builder, An Evening of Russian Theatre, 1971; The Taming of the Shrew, Misalliance, John Whiting's Conditions of Agreement, Right You Are If You Think You Are, American Gothics, Anton Chekhov's Garden Party, Hamlet,

1972; The Play's the Thing, Ghosts, The Caretaker, Miss Julie, The Death of Lord Chatterley, The Father, 1973; The Seagull, The Circle, The Burnt Flowerbed, Rosmersholm, and for the opening of Roundabout Stage One, a much larger theater converted from a cinema house, All My Sons, 1974; The Rivals, James Joyce's Dubliners, What Every Woman Knows, Summer and Smoke, Dear Mr G, 1975; Clarence, The Cherry Orchard, The World of Sholom Aleichem, A Month in the Country, Love and Intrigue, The Merchant of Venice, The Philanderer, The Rehearsal, 1976; John Gabriel Borkman, Endgame, Dear Liar, You Never Can Tell, Naked, 1977; Othello, The Promise, The Showoff, Pins and Needles, 1978; Candida, Streetsongs, Little Eyolf, Awake and Sing, Family Business, Diversions and Delights, The Hotel in Amsterdam, A Month in the Country, 1979; Heartbreak House, The Bloodknot, The Dance of Death, She Stoops to Conquer, 1980; plays of his own which he has also directed include James Joyce's Dubliners, Jocasta and Oedipus, Wretched the Lionhearted, A Toy for the Clowns, Building Blocks, and most recently Sparta is Not the World, 1980; has also adapted many of the classics including Ibsen, Strindberg, and Chekhov.

Hobbies and recreations: Archaeology and horticulture.
Address: Roundabout Theatre, 333 West 23rd Street, New York, NY 10011. *Tel:* 924–7160.

FELDSHUH, Tovah, actress
b New York City, 27 Dec; *d* of Sidney Feldshuh and his wife Lillian (Kaplan); *e* Scarsdale High School, Sarah Lawrence College and University of Minnesota; *m* Andrew Harris Levy; trained for the stage with Uta Hagen and Jacques Lecoq.

Her professional debut was at the Guthrie, Minneapolis, July 1971, playing small parts in the play Cyrano de Bergerac; played more than twenty roles there over two seasons, and in Jan 1973 played the Foodseller and the Nun in the musical Cyrano, making her Broadway debut in these roles at the Palace, 13 May 1973; Ethel Barrymore, Oct 1974, Myriam in Dreyfus in Rehearsal; Brooklyn Academy, Dec 1974, title role in Yentl; Helen Hayes, May 1975, appeared in Rodgers and Hart; Eugene O'Neill, Oct 1975, again played Yentl; Stratford, Conn, season 1976, played Abigail Williams in The Crucible, and Celia in As You Like It; Brooklyn Academy, May 1977, Irina in the BAM Company's Three Sisters; McCarter, Princeton, Jan 1978, appeared in The Torchbearers; toured, Jun 1978, as Peter Pan; Broadway, Jan 1979, Dona Flor in Saravá; San Diego, Jun 1980, Juliet in Romeo and Juliet; first film, Nunzio, 1978; has since appeared in The Idolmaker, 1980, etc; TV includes The Amazing Howard Hughes, and Holocaust.

Favourite parts: Saint Joan, Viola, Rosalind, Juliet. *Address:* c/o Joel Dean, ICM, 8899 Beverly Boulevard, Los Angeles, CA 90048.

FERNALD, John, director
b California, USA, 21 Nov 1905; *s* of C B Fernald and his wife Josephine (Harker); *e* Marlborough College, and Trinity College, Oxford; *m* (1) Mary Cecil Kidd; (2) Jenny Laird; was formerly engaged as dramatic editor of the *Pall Mall Magazine.*

Produced extensively for amateurs, 1926–8; was stage-manager for Journey's End, Apollo, Dec 1928, and Savoy, Jan 1929; has since directed innumerable plays, notably The Duchess of Malfi, 1929; Mr Eno, 1930; She Passed Through Lorraine, 1931; Below the Surface, 1932; Wild Justice, The Mocking Bird, 1933; Sixteen, The Wise Woman, The Dominant Sex, 1934; Crime and Punishment, This Desirable

Residence, The House of Borgia, Distinguished Gathering, Murder Gang, 1935; Wisdom Teeth, Storm Song, The Composite Man, The Provoked Wife, 1936; during 1937, was associate producer for Associated British Pictures; returned to the theatre and directed Ghost for Sale, A Party for Christmas, Oscar Wilde, 1938; The Doctor's Dilemma, Only Yesterday, Major Barbara, 1939; joined the Navy, 1940; invalided with the rank of Lieutenant Commander RNVR, 1945, while in command of HM 18th LCT Flotilla; returned to the theatre, 1945, directing Letters to a Lady, The Crime of Margaret Foley, The Government Inspector, A Doll's House, Kiss and Tell; was Director of the Liverpool Playhouse, 1946–9, where he made over forty productions, including the first performances of Young Wives' Tale (as Wings to Fly With), The Human Touch, and The Silver Curlew; The Cherry Orchard, St James's, London, 1948; The Unquiet Spirit, Arts, Feb 1949; he then joined forces with Roy Rich at the Arts Theatre, opening in Aug 1949, with a revival of The Schoolmistress, Embassy, Sept 1949, directed Rain Before Seven; Arts, Dec 1949, The Silver Curlew; subsequently directed, at the same theatre, John Gabriel Borkman, Ivanov, Heartbreak House (his 200th production since 1926), The Mask and the Face, Preserving Mr Panmure, 1950; has since directed the following plays: Preserving Mr Panmure (Aldwych), Spring at Marino (Arts), The Thistle and the Rose (Vaudeville), The Love of Four Colonels (Wyndham's), The White Sheep of the Family (Piccadilly), The Moment of Truth (Adelphi), The Great Adventure (Arts), 1951; The Firstborn (Winter Garden), Nightmare Abbey (Westminster), Uncle Vanya and The Voysey Inheritance (Arts), Dial M For Murder (Westminster), In Chancery and The Holy Terrors (Arts), 1952; Escapade (St James's), The Seagull, and Second Best Bed (Arts), The Devil's General (Savoy), 1953; Crime and Punishment (Arts), The White Countess (Gaiety, Dublin), The Enchanted, and The Sun Room (Arts), Hannibal's Way (Arts, Cambridge), No Escape (Golders Green), Saint Joan (Arts), Peter Pan (Scala), 1954; The Rules of the Game (Arts), The Moon and the Chimney (Lyceum, Edinburgh), Saint Joan (St Martin's), The Midnight Family (Arts), The Remarkable Mr Pennypacker (New), Peter Pan (Scala), 1955; The House by the Lake (Duke of York's), Harmony Close (tour), 1956; Tea and Sympathy (Comedy), 1957; A Fig For Glory (Royal Court, Liverpool), Ghosts (Old Vic), 1958; The Coast of Coromandel (tour), Ghosts (Princes), 1959; A Lodging For a Bride (Westminster), The Seagull (Edinburgh Festival and Old Vic), 1960; The Enchanted (Liverpool Playhouse), 1961; Return to Mirredal (tour), The Affair (Henry Miller, New York), 1962; Close Quarters (tour), The Cherry Orchard (National, Johannesburg), Heartbreak House (Bristol Old Vic), 1963; Macbeth (Arizona), The Schoolmistress (Savoy), 1964; The Gift (Vanbrugh), Ivanov (Vanbrugh), 1965; Othello (National, Reykjavik), Private Lives (Bristol Old Vic), 1972; The Master Builder (Octagon, Bolton), Private Lives (Johannesburg), 1973; Coming of Age (Liverpool Cathedral), A Penny for a Song (Bolton), Who's Afraid of Virginia Woolf? (Leeds and tour), 1974; Time and Time Again (York), Jack in the Box, The Orchestra, Black Comedy, Raven (all Gardner Centre, Brighton), 1975; was Shute Lecturer in the Art of the Theatre, at Liverpool University, 1948; author of The Play Produced: an Introduction to the Technique of Producing Plays, 1933; Destroyer from America, 1942; part-author (with Jenny Laird) of And No Birds Sing, 1945; A Sense of Direction, 1968; Principal of the Royal Academy of Dramatic Art, 1955–65; artistic director, The John Fernald Company of the Meadow Brook Theatre, Michigan, USA, 1966–70; Futterer Lecturer and Professor of Drama, State University of NY, 1970–1.

Recreations: Yachting and travelling. *Club:* Garrick. *Address:* 2 Daleham Mews, Hampstead, London, NW3. *Tel:* 01–435 2992.

FERRER, José, actor, producer and director
b Santurce, Puerto Rico, 8 Jan 1912; *s* of Rafael Ferrer and his wife Maria (Cintron); *e* New York and Princeton University; *m* (1) Uta Hagen (mar dis); (2) Phyllis Hill (mar dis); (3) Rosemary Clooney (mar dis); originally studied architecture.

Made his first appearance on a show-boat on Long Island, 1934; he then appeared at the Summer Theatre, at Suffern, NY, 1935, with Joshua Logan's stock company; subsequently toured in A Slight Case of Murder, also acting as assistant stage-manager; first appeared on the NY stage at the 48th Street Theatre, 11 Sept 1935, as the Second Policeman in A Slight Case of Murder; in 1935, he also toured in Boy Meets Girl, and the following year, again appeared at Suffern, where he played in Caesar and Cleopatra; at the Empire, NY, Aug 1936, played The Lippincot in Spring Dance; Biltmore, Dec 1936, Dan Crawford in Brother Rat; Vanderbilt, Oct 1937, Frederick Parsons in In Clover; Martin Beck, Feb 1938, Vergez in How to Get Tough About It; Empire, Sept 1938, Billy Gashade in Missouri Legend; Jan 1939, Mr Wentworth in Mamba's Daughters; Ethel Barrymore, Nov 1939, Victor d'Alcala in Key Largo; Cort, Oct 1940, Lord Fancourt Babberley in Charley's Aunt; Plymouth, Sept 1942, George Roberts in Vickie, which he also staged; at the Imperial, Feb 1943, succeeded Danny Kaye as Jerry Walker in Let's Face It; Shubert, Oct 1943, played Iago in Othello, with Paul Robeson, in the record run of that play; toured in the same part, 1944–5; in Nov 1945, presented and staged Strange Fruit, at the Royale Theatre; toured 1946, as Sandor in The Play's the Thing, Cyrano de Bergerac, Richard III, and the Rajah of Rukh in The Green Goddess; Alvin, NY, Oct 1946, played Cyrano de Bergerac; in summer theatres, 1947, appeared in Design for Living, and Goodbye Again; became General Director of the New York City Theatre Company and appeared at the City Center, Jan–June 1948, as Volpone, Mr Manningham in Angel Street, Jeremy and Face in The Alchemist, Fat Joe in The Long Voyage Home, and the Yellow Commander in The Insect Comedy; Biltmore, Nov 1948, played Oliver Erwenter in The Silver Whistle; ANTA Playhouse, Dec 1950, appeared as Oscar Jaffe in Twentieth Century, which he also directed, and transferred to the Fulton, Jan 1951; 48th Street, May 1951, presented and directed Stalag 17, which ran for over a year; Ethel Barrymore, Oct 1951, directed The Fourposter, which ran for more than eighteen months; Cort, Jan 1952, directed The Shrike, in which he played Jim Downs; Playhouse, Apr 1952, presented and directed The Chase; Morosco, Mar 1953, directed My Three Angels; City Center, Nov 1953–Jan 1954, played the title-role in Cyrano de Bergerac, which he also directed, again appeared as Jim Downs in The Shrike (directed with Joseph Kramm), played Richard, Duke of Gloucester in Richard III, Lord Fancourt Babberley in Charley's Aunt, which he also directed, and directed a revival of The Fourposter; Alvin, Feb 1958, co-author of Oh, Captain! (which he also directed); 46th Street, NY, Nov 1958, played the title-role in Edwin Booth (also directed); Winter Garden, Mar 1959, directed Juno; Henry Miller's, Jan 1960, directed The Andersonville Trial; Santa Fé, New Mexico, summer 1960, directed and sang the title-role in Gianni Schichi; Broadway, Dec 1963, Grand Duke Charles in The Girl Who Came to Supper; Philharmonic Hall, NY, Apr 1964, appeared in Marc Blitzstein Memorial Concert; Royal Poinciana Playhouse, Palm Beach, Fla, Apr, 1965, Dr Coppelius in the ballet Coppelia; Mineola Playhouse, Long

Island, Apr 1965, played various roles in the musical Little Me; toured, 1965, in Around the World in 80 Days; Salt Lake City, Utah, Feb 1966, played the title-role of Oedipus Rex; ANTA, Washington Square, took over as Don Quixote and Cervantes in Man of La Mancha; toured, Sept 1966–Apr 1967, in these parts; ANTA, Washington Square, Apr 1967, again took over these parts; Coconut Grove Playhouse, Miami, 1968, played in You Know I Can't Hear You When the Water's Running, and directed this play at the New, London, in June 1968; Theatre de Lys, Mar 1972, directed The Web and the Rock; as Guest Director of the Cleveland Playhouse, Oct 1972, directed Christopher Fry's A Yard of Sun in its American première; toured, summer 1973, in A Song for Cyrano; Geary, San Francisco, May 1974, played in The Sunshine Boys; Imperial, NY, 9 Mar 1975, appeared in a Gala Tribute to Joshua Logan; Chichester Festival, May 1975, directed Cyrano de Bergerac; directed and played Doctor in Medal of Honour Rag, US tour, Sept 1976; Theatre de Lys, May 1978, took over from Ellis Rabb as Robert in A Life in the Theatre; same theatre, Oct 1978, Harry in White Pelicans (also co-presented); St James, Apr 1979, directed Carmelina; has also appeared in numerous films, notably in Cyrano de Bergerac, for which he received the Academy Award, 1950, Moulin Rouge, The Caine Mutiny, Cockleshell Heroes, Ship of Fools, Enter Laughing, I Accuse, The Shrike, Return to Peyton Place, Lawrence of Arabia, The Greatest Story Ever Told, etc.
Address: 2 Pennsylvania Plaza, New York, NY 10001.

FERRIER, Noel, actor
b Melbourne, Victoria, 20 Dec 1930; *s* of Sidney James Ferrier and his wife Madeline Alice; *e* Northcote High School, Melbourne; *m* Suzanne de Berenger.
While an accountant for MGM theatres (Australia), made his first stage appearance at the Arrow, Melbourne, 30 Mar 1951, as Charlie Norman in Heaven and Charing Cross; also appeared in Melbourne Theatre Company's world premiere of Summer of the Seventeenth Doll, as Roo, June 1955, and their Cat On a Hot Tin Roof as Big Daddy, 1957; for J C Williamson's played Bob Le Hotu in Irma La Douce, 1960–61, and Madame Lucy in Irene, 1974–75; has toured Australia in many shows including Tea and Sympathy, What the Butler Saw, Roar Like a Dove and Free as Air, and recently in Salad Days and Side by Side by Sondheim; in association with J C Williamson's has produced, promoted and appeared in several pantomime seasons; a director of his own company, *Tradeshow*, producing industrial shows; his work for television includes the Noel Ferrier Show, Noel Ferrier's Australia A-Z, and Blankety Blanks; films include Eliza Fraser, Alvin Purple, Demonstrator, and Avengers of the Reef, which he also produced.
Favourite parts: Big Daddy, Madame Lucy and Roo. *Clubs:* City Tatt's and Australian Journalist's. *Address:* 90 Wallis Street, Woollahra, 2025, NSW Australia. *Tel:* 0232 5235.

FERRIS, Barbara, actress
m John Quested.
Made her first professional appearance, Aug 1960, at the Theatre Royal, Stratford, East, as Nellie in Sparrers Can't Sing, making her West End debut in the same play at Wyndham's, Mar 1961; Wyndham's, Dec 1963, played Cinderella in Merry Roosters' Panto; Stratford, East, Mar 1964, Jess and Prunella Flack in A Kayf Up West; Royal Court, Nov 1965, Pam in Saved; Moll in A Chaste Maid in Cheapside, Jan 1966; Nancy in The Knack, Feb 1966; Girl in Transcending, Mar 1966; Globe, June 1966, Marion in There's A Girl in My Soup, making her New York debut in

the same part at the Music Box, Oct 1967; returned to the Apollo, London, Nov 1970, as Jil Tanner in Butterflies Are Free; Royal Court, May 1971, played Elise in Slag; Mermaid, Nov 1971, Begonia Brown in Geneva; Royal Court, June 1972, Mrs Elvsted in Hedda Gabler; Albery, Sept 1973, Marie-Louise Middleton in The Constant Wife; Hampstead, Mar 1975, Leslie in Alphabetical Order, transferring to the May Fair, Apr 1975; Hampstead, Aug 1976, Mara in Clouds; Lyttleton, May 1979, Ethel Bartlett in For Services Rendered; same theatre, Dec 1979, Annie Parker in When We Are Married; films, since 1964, include Interlude.
Address: c/o Crouch Associates, 59 Frith Street, London W1V 5TA.

FEUER, Cy, producer and director
b New York City, 15 Jan 1911; *s* of Herman Feuer and his wife Ann (Abrams); *e* Juilliard School of Music; *m* Posy Greenberg.
Formerly a musical director and composer for Republic Pictures, 1938–42, and 1945–7; served in the USAAF, 1942–5, with rank of Captain; in partnership with Ernest H Martin has produced the following plays: Where's Charley?, 1948; Guys and Dolls, 1950; Can-Can, 1953; The Boy Friend, 1954; Silk Stockings, 1955; Whoop-Up (also co-author), 1958; How to Succeed in Business Without Really Trying, which received the Pulitzer Prize for Drama, 1961; Little Me (also co-directed), 1962; Skyscraper (also directed), 1965; Walking Happy (also directed), 1966; The Goodbye People, 1968; The Act, 1977; co-managing director (with Ernest Martin) of the Los Angeles and San Francisco Light Opera Association, 1975– ; produced the films of Cabaret, 1972 and Piaf, 1974.
Address: 502 Park Avenue, New York, NY 10022. *Tel:* Plaza 9–4004.

FFRANGCON-DAVIES, Gwen, actress and singer
b London, 25 Jan 1896; *d* of David Ffrangcon-Davies and his wife Annie Frances (Raynor); *e* South Hampstead High School; studied for the stage under Mrs L Manning Hicks and Agnes Platt.
Made her first appearance on the stage at His Majesty's Theatre, 17 Apr 1911, walking on in A Midsummer Night's Dream; subsequently toured for some time playing Kiki in The Glad Eye, June in To-Night's the Night, Sombra in The Arcadians, etc; she also appeared at numerous concerts; during the war, 1917–18, was engaged at the Censor's Office; sang soprano lead at Glastonbury Festival, 1919–20; sang in The Immortal Hour, Bethlehem, and The Birth of Arthur, etc; appeared at the Old Vic, May 1920, as Etain in The Immortal Hour; joined the Birmingham Repertory Company, appearing in July 1921, as Etain in The Immortal Hour; in Sept 1921, played Phoebe Throssel in Quality Street, and numerous leading parts including Betty in The New Morality, Juliet, Lady Mary in The Admirable Crichton, etc; appeared at the Regent, Oct 1922, as Etain in The Immortal Hour; at Birmingham, May 1923, played Queen Mary in Mary Stuart, and subsequently Lucy in The Professor's Love Story; in Oct 1923, played Eve and the Newly Born in the first production of Back to Methuselah; at the Regent, Nov 1923, again played Etain in The Immortal Hour, and (for the Phoenix Society) Queen Isabella in Edward II; Dec 1923, played the Virgin Mary in Bethlehem; at the Court Theatre, Feb 1924, played Eve, Amaryllis and the Ghost of Eve in Back to Methuselah; at the Regent (for the Phoenix Society), Mar 1924, Cordelia in King Lear; May 1924, Juliet in Romeo and Juliet; returned to Birmingham, Oct 1924, opening as Hilda Wangel in The Master Builder; at Drury Lane Theatre, Dec

1924, played Titania in A Midsummer Night's Dream; at the Kingsway, Apr 1925, Cleopatra in Caesar and Cleopatra; June 1925, Betty Jones in The New Morality; Barnes, Sept 1925, Tess in Tess of the D'Urbervilles; Kingsway, Jan 1926, Etain in a revival of The Immortal Hour; Apr 1926, Marguerite in The Marvellous History of St Bernard; Shaftesbury (for the Venturers), June 1926, Zabette in Martinique; Everyman, Oct 1926, Olga Lessiter in Made in Heaven; Kingsway, Nov 1926, Mrs Dubedat in The Doctor's Dilemma; Ambassadors', Nov 1926, Elsie in Riceyman Steps; Kingsway, Jan 1927, Eliza Doolittle in Pygmalion; Feb 1927, Ann Whitefield in Man and Superman; Prince's (for the Venturers), May, 1927, Juliette in Might-Have-Beens; Savoy, July 1927, Ena in The Cage; Gate, Nov 1927, Bella in Maya; Court, Mar 1928, again appeared in Back to Methuselah; Apr 1928, Edith in Harold; Arts, June 1928, Myra Flint in Prejudice; Prince's, July 1928, Tommy in Contraband; Arts, Oct 1928, Eleanora in Easter; Arts and Garrick, Jan 1929, Elizabeth Herbert in The Lady with a Lamp; in the autumn toured as Florence Nightingale in the same piece; at Oxford, for the OUDS, Feb 1930, played Lady Macbeth; Arts, Mar 1930, and Criterion, Apr 1930, Nora Helmer in A Doll's House; Haymarket, Apr 1930, Ophelia in the all-star revival of Hamlet; New, May 1930, Magda in the play of that name; Queen's, Sept 1930, Elizabeth Moulton-Barrett in The Barretts of Wimpole Street; Feb 1932, Etain in a revival of The Immortal Hour; St Martin's, Mar 1932, Prue Sarn in Precious Bane; New, June 1932, Anne of Bohemia in Richard of Bordeaux; Wyndham's, Sept 1932, the Marquesa de Casa Reya in The Way of the Stars; New, Feb 1933, again played Anne of Bohemia in Richard of Bordeaux, which ran over a year; Cambridge, Mar 1933 (for Jewish Drama League), Portia in The Lady of Belmont; New, June 1934, Mary Stuart in Queen of Scots; Whitehall, Nov 1934, Naomi Jacklin in Flowers of the Forest; Piccadilly, Jan 1935, Elizabeth in a revival of The Barretts of Wimpole Street; Playhouse, Apr 1935, Ruth Honeywill in Justice; Arts, June 1935, Theophila Fraser in The Benefit of the Doubt; Savoy, Sept 1935, succeeded Flora Robson as Liesa in Close Quarters; Ambassadors', Feb 1936, Diana Huntley in Out of the Dark; Lyric, Oct 1936, Henrietta Maria in Charles the King; Queen's, May 1937, Miss Mason in He Was Born Gay, and Jan 1938, Olga in Three Sisters; Drury Lane, Sept 1938, Chorus in Henry V, Richmond, Dec 1938, and Apollo, Jan 1939, Mrs Manningham in Gas Light; Globe, Aug 1939, the Hon Gwendolen Fairfax in The Importance of Being Earnest; Piccadilly, July 1942, played Lady Macbeth to the Macbeth of John Gielgud; Phoenix, Oct 1942, again appeared in The Importance of Being Earnest; then went to South Africa, where, in association with Marda Vanne, she appeared from 1943–6, in the leading parts in Watch on the Rhine, Flare Path, What Every Woman Knows, Blithe Spirit, Milestones, The Wind of Heaven, A Month in the Country, etc; returned to England, 1946; St James's, Mar 1949, played the Queen Mother in Adventure Story; Memorial Theatre, Stratford-on-Avon, during the 1950 season, appeared as Queen Katharine in Henry VIII, Portia in Julius Caesar, Regan in King Lear, and succeeded Peggy Ashcroft as Beatrice in Much Ado About Nothing; in Nov 1950, visited Denmark, under the auspices of the British Council, giving readings from Shakespearean and other English plays, and talks on Shakespeare; appeared at the Old Vic, May 1953, as Queen Katharine in Henry VIII; New, Feb 1954, played Donna Lucia D'Alvadorez in Charley's Aunt; Lyric, Hammersmith, May 1954, played Mme Ranevsky in The Cherry Orchard; Apollo, Nov 1955, Aunt Cleofe in Summertime; Royal Court, Apr 1956, played Rose Padley in The English Stage Company's first

production The Mulberry Bush; Phoenix, June 1956, Agatha in The Family Reunion; Haymarket, Jan 1957, followed Peggy Ashcroft as Miss Madrigal in The Chalk Garden; Globe, Feb 1958, played Mrs Callifer in The Potting Shed; Edinburgh Festival, Lyceum, and subsequently at the Globe, Sept 1958, Mary Tyrone in Long Day's Journey Into Night; she received the *Evening Standard* Drama Award, 1959, for her performance in this play; joined the Royal Shakespeare Company at the Aldwych, Jan 1961, to play Queen Isolde in Ondine, and June 1961, the Queen Mother in Becket, appearing in both plays in repertory, and subsequently transferring with Becket to the Globe, Dec 1961, for a regular season; Aldwych, Aug 1962, played Hester Bellboys in A Penny for a Song, in repertory, for the Royal Shakespeare Company; Haymarket, Oct 1962, took over the part of Mrs Candour in The School for Scandal, prior to making her first appearance in New York at the Majestic, Jan 1963, in the same production; Queen's, London, Sept 1964, played Beatrice Portman in Season of Goodwill; Haymarket, Dec 1965, Amanda Wingfield in The Glass Menagerie; Lyceum, Edinburgh, Sept 1966, the Baroness in A Present for the Past; Royal Court, Feb 1970, Madame Voynitsky in Uncle Vanya; most recent film, Leo the Last; has also broadcast and appeared in numerous television plays in England and Canada, including Dear Octopus, The Hill (Canada and London), A Day by the Sea, The Old Man of Chelsea Reach, Finders Keepers, Liza, etc.

Recreations: Gardening. *Address:* c/o Larry Dalzell Associates, 3 Goodwin's Court, St Martin's Lane, London WC2.

FIANDER, Lewis, actor
b Melbourne, Victoria, 12 Jan 1938; *s* of Walter Lewis Fiander and his wife Mona Jane (King); *e* Trinity Grammar School, Melbourne; *m* Claire Loise Curzon-Price.

Made his first stage appearance at the National Theatre, Melbourne 1954, as Tom in Accolade, and played several parts for the National Company, 1954–56, including Launcelot Gobbo in The Merchant of Venice and Feste in Twelfth Night; 1959–60, appeared in ten productions for the Union Repertory Company, Melbourne, including Ishmael in Moby Dick-Rehearsed; Elizabethan Theatre Trust, Sydney, 1960–62, parts played included Leslie in The Hostage, Geoff in A Taste of Honey and Gobbo in The Merchant of Venice, with two performances as Shylock; made his London debut at the Theatre Royal, Stratford East, as Hughie in The One Day of the Year; Haymarket, 1963, took over First Gentleman in The School for Scandal; Mermaid, Apr 1963, Lory in Virtue in Danger, transferring to the Strand Theatre in June; for the National Theatre at the Old Vic, 1963–64, he understudied Hamlet, and parts played included de Courcelles in St Joan and Domingo in The Royal Hunt of the Sun; toured New Zealand, 1966, as Antipholus of Syracuse in the Royal Shakespeare Company's production of The Comedy of Errors; Citizen's Glasgow, 1966, title role in Stephen D; Duke of York's, Apr 1968, Deacon Pobyedov in The Duel; 1967–70, toured for the Oxford Playhouse Company in ten productions, playing parts including Truwit in The Silent Woman, Warwick in Saint Joan, and Peer Gynt; Bristol Old Vic, played Christian Talbot in The Pursuit of Love, 1967, and Mosca in Volpone, 1971; New Theatre (Albery), June 1970, played John Adams in 1776, and also in Australia, 1971, at Her Majesty's, Melbourne and Theatre Royal, Sydney; Piccadilly, Nov 1972, Lord Melbourne and Benjamin Disraeli in I and Albert; Chichester Festival Theatre, Christmas 1974, and Westminster, 1975, King Herod in Follow the Star; Her Majesty's, Melbourne, and Theatre Royal, Sydney,

1976, George in Same Time Next Year; Piccadilly, June 1977, took over Jack Rover in Wild Oats, for the Royal Shakespeare Company; Greenwich, Apr 1978, played Bluntschli in Arms and the Man; Criterion, May 1979, took over as Owen Shorter in Clouds; Chichester Festival, 1980, Littleton Coke in Old Heads and Young Hearts; has appeared in several films since The Password Is Courage, most recently in Sweeney 2; television includes Pride and Prejudice, Notorious Woman, and Smith.

Favourite parts: Leslie in The Hostage, Jack Rover and John Adams. *Address:* c/o Chatto and Linnit, Globe Theatre, Shaftesbury Avenue, London W1.

FICHANDLER, Zelda (*née* Diamond), producer and director *b* Boston, Massachusetts, 18 Sept 1924; *d* of Harry Diamond and his wife Ida (Epstein); *e* Cornell University (BA 1945), George Washington University (MA in dramatic arts, 1950), honorary Doctor of Humane Letters, Hood College, 1962; *m* Thomas C Fichandler; formerly employed as a research analyst in military intelligence, Russian division.

Founded, with Edward Magnum, the Arena Stage in Washington, DC, whose first production was She Stoops to Conquer, Aug 1950; since then has produced more than 250 plays, directed many of them: Arena Stage in the Hippodrome, 1950–1 season, Of Mice and Men, The Firebrand, The Delectable Judge, The Taming of the Shrew, Pygmalion, Alice in Wonderland, The Playboy of the Western World, Children of Darkness, The Adding Machine, The School for Wives, The Inspector General, Mr Arcularis, The Glass Menagerie, Twelfth Night, The Scarecrow, The Importance of Being Earnest; 1951–2 season, Julius Caesar, She Stoops to Conquer, Ladder to the Moon, Burning Bright, Twelfth Night, School for Scandal, Three Men on a Horse, Dark of the Moon, The Importance of Being Earnest, The Hasty Heart; 1952–3 season, Desire Under the Elms, Tonight at 8.30 (consisting of Fumed Oak, Ways and Means, Still Life), Lady Precious Stream, All Summer Long, The Country Wife, Our Town, Arms and the Man, The Country Girl, Boy Meets Girl, My Heart's in the Highlands; 1953–4 season, A Phoenix Too Frequent, The Happy Journey, The Bad Angel, Thieves' Carnival, Charley's Aunt, Ah, Wilderness!, Summer and Smoke, Blithe Spirit, The Cretan Woman, All My Sons, Room Service; 1954–5 season, The Crucible, Androcles and the Lion, Golden Boy, The Miser, The World of Sholom Aleichem (consisting of A Tale of Chelm, Bontche Schweig, and The High School), Rain, The Mousetrap; 1955–6 season was dark as Arena Stage closed to search for larger building; Arena Stage in The Old Vat; 1956–7 season, A View from the Bridge, Tartuffe, The Prisoner, The Girl on the Via Flaminia, Dream Girl, Three Plays (Bedtime Story, Portrait of a Madonna, and Man of Destiny), The Three Sisters, Witness for the Prosecution; 1957–8 season, The Doctor's Dilemma, Answered the Flute, Brother Rat, Juno and the Paycock, two plays Apollo and The Browning Version, Romeo and Juliet, Mademoiselle Colombe, Summer of the 17th Doll; 1958–9 season, The Front Page, three plays Once Around the Block, The Purification, and A Memory of Two Mondays, The Hollow, The Devil's Disciple, A Month in the Country, The Plough and the Stars, The Lady's Not for Burning, Epitaph for George Dillon; 1959–60 season, Major Barbara, Clandestine on the Morning Line, Three Men on a Horse, The Cherry Orchard, The Caine Mutiny Court-martial, The Iceman Cometh, Ring Around the Moon, The Disenchanted; 1960–1 season, The Gang's All Here, The Egg, The Rivals, Six Characters in Search of an Author, Silent Night, Lonely Night, Tiger at the Gates, three plays, Krapp's Last Tape, The End of the Beginning, and In the Zone, Man and

Superman; at Arena Stage, 6th and M Streets, SW, 1961–2 season, The Caucasian Chalk Circle, two plays, The American Dream, and What Shall We Tell Caroline, The Madwoman of Chaillot, The Moon in the Yellow River, Misalliance, The Burning of the Lepers, Uncle Vanya, The Time of Your Life; 1962–3 season, Once in a Lifetime, Under Milk Wood, Volpone, Twelve Angry Men, The Hostage, All the Way Home, Othello, The Threepenny Opera; 1963–4 season, The Devils, Battle Dream, Hotel Paradiso, The Wall, The Affair, Enrico IV, The Taming of the Shrew, Dark of the Moon; 1964–5 season, Galileo, The Rehearsal, Billy Budd, Heartbreak House, He Who Gets Slapped, Long Day's Journey Into Night, two plays, The Lonesome Train, and Hard Travelin'; 1965–6 season, Saint Joan, The Skin of Our Teeth, Project Immortality, The Three Sisters, Serjeant Musgrave's Dance, three plays, Mr Welk and Jersey Jim, The Lesson, and The Collection, Oh! What A Lovely War; 1966–7 season, Macbeth, The Magistrate, The Crucible, The Inspector General, Look Back in Anger, The Andersonville Trial; 1967–8 season, Major Barbara, Poor Bitos, The Great White Hope, The Blood Knot, The Tenth Man, Room Service, The Iceman Cometh; 1968–9 season, The Threepenny Opera, Six Characters in Search of an Author, King Lear, The Marat/Sade, Indians, Jacques Brel is Alive and Well and Living in Paris; 1969–70 season, Edith Stein, You Can't Take It With You, The Cherry Orchard, The Chemmy Circle, two plays, Enchanted Night, and The Police, Dance of Death, No Place to be Somebody; 1970–1 season, The Night Thoreau Spent in Jail, Mother Courage, The Ruling Class, Pueblo, Games, Awake and Sing, What the Butler Saw, and The Sign in Sidney Brustein's Window; 1971–2 season Pantagleize, Twelfth Night, The House of Blue Leaves, Status Quo Vadis, Tricks, Moonchildren, Uptight, A Conflict of Interest, The Dream Machine; 1972–3 season The Foursome, A Public Prosecutor Is Sick of It All, A Look at the Fifties, Raisin; 1973–4 Two by Samuel Beckett, Our Town, Inherit the Wind, Three Men on a Horse, The Resistible Rise of Arturo Ui, Relatively Speaking, Horatio, Tom, Leonce and Lena, The Madness of God, In Celebration; 1974–5 The Ascent of Mount Fuji, Death of a Salesman, Who's Afraid of Virginia Woolf?, Boccaccio, The Front Page, Julius Caesar, The Last Meeting of the Knights of the White Magnolia, The Dybbuk, The Ascent of Mount Fuji, Sizwe Banzi is Dead, and The Island; 1975–6 Long Day's Journey into Night, An Enemy of the People, Once in a Lifetime, Emlyn Williams as Charles Dickens, Cabrona, The Tot Family, Heartbreak House, What the Babe Said and Total Recall, Madmen, Waiting for Godot, Busy Dyin', Dandelion Wine, Death of a Salesman, The Front Page, Our Town; 1976–7 Forever Yours, Marie-Lou, Saint Joan, Emlyn Williams as Dylan Thomas, Growing Up, Saturday Sunday Monday, play, That Time, Footfalls, Streamers, Singers, Porch, Scooping, Exhibition, The Autumn Garden, Living at Home, Catsplay, The Lower Depths, A History of the American Film, 1977–8 Nightclub Cantata, The National Health, Starting Here Starting Now, The Caucasian Chalk Circle, Comedians, A Streetcar Named Desire, Hamlet, Gemini, Separations, Duck Hunting, The Desert Dwellers, Trappers; 1978–9 Tales from the Vienna Woods, The 1940s Radio Hour, The Past, Disability, Casualties, Ah Wilderness!, Curse of the Starving Class, Tintypes: A Ragtime Revue, Loose Ends, Don Juan, Nevis Mountain Dew, Idiot's Delight; received the Margo Jones Award for achievement in the theatre, 1971; toured the Soviet Union, 1973, where she directed Inherit the Wind; Doctor of Humane Letters conferred by Georgetown Univ, 1974; Doctor of Humanities conferred by George Washington Univ, 1975; Woman of the Year award, 1975; Presidents' Award for

Distinguished Civil Service from Catholic Univ, 1975; received a special Antoinette Perry (Tony) Award, 1976, the first such award for Theatrical work outside New York City.

Address: Arena Stage, 6th and M Streets, SW, Washington, DC 20024. *Tel:* 202–554 9066.

FIELD, Ron, choreographer and director
b Washington Heights, NY; *e* High School of the Performing Arts, NY; formerly an actor and dancer.

Choreographed his first New York musical, a revival of Anything Goes, at the Orpheum, 15 May 1962; has since choreographed Nowhere to Go But Up, 1962; Cafe Crown, 1964; Show Boat, Cabaret (also costume designs), 1966; Zorba, 1968; Applause, which he also directed and for which he won the Antoinette Perry (Tony) Awards in both capacities, 1970; On the Town, 1971; at Her Majesty's, London, 17 Nov 1972, choreographed and directed Applause; choreography and direction for Mack and Mabel (tour), 1976; King of Hearts, 1978; has choreographed nightclub acts for such performers as Liza Minelli and Ann-Margret; was responsible for the dances in the film New York, New York; choreography for TV includes Pinocchio, 1976; for NY City Opera choreographed Ashmedai, 1976.

Address: Society of Stage Directors and Choreographers, 1501 Broadway, New York, NY 10019.

FIELDING, Fenella, actress
b London, 17 Nov 1934; *e* North London Collegiate School; formerly a secretary.

Began her career as an understudy at the Saville Theatre, London, May 1954, in the revue Cockles and Champagne; at the Victoria Palace, June 1956, played Luba Tradjejka in Jubilee Girl; Lyric, Hammersmith, Oct 1958, played the Lady Parvula de Panzoust in Valmouth, subsequently transferring with the production to the Saville, Jan 1959; Apollo, Sept 1959, appeared in the revue Pieces of Eight, which ran for 429 performances; at the Pembroke, Croydon, 1961, played Phoebe in As You Like It and Lydia Languish in The Rivals; Belgrade, Coventry, Feb 1962, appeared in the revue Diversions for Five, or Twists, subsequently appearing in the same production at the Arts, London, Feb 1962, renamed Twists; her performance was named by *Variety* as Best in Revue in 1962; New Arts, Oct 1962, played Annie Wood in Doctors of Philosophy; at the same theatre Apr 1963, played Ellen in Luv; Vaudeville, Sept 1963, appeared in the revue So Much to Remember; Mermaid, June 1966, played Cyprienne in Let's Get a Divorce, transferring to the Comedy, July 1966; Chichester Festival, June 1967, played Mrs Sullen in The Beaux' Stratagem, and in August, Baroness de Champigny in An Italian Straw Hat; Mermaid, Oct 1967, Mrs Gracedew in The High Bid; Rupert J Jones Theatre, Oklahoma, USA, Oct 1968, appeared in the title-role in Lysistrata; returned, Nov 1968, to play Madame Arkadina in The Seagull at the Nottingham Playhouse; Phoenix, Leicester, Mar 1969, Hedda in Hedda Gabler; Gardner Centre, Brighton, Jan 1970, Nora in A Doll's House; first appeared in New York, at the Ellen Stewart Theatre, Oct 1970, when she took over the title-role in Colette; Greenwich, July 1971, Francine Chanal in Fish out of Water; toured, Nov 1971, in the Oxford Playhouse production of Colette; Traverse, Edinburgh, July 1972, Berinthia in The Relapse; Phoenix, Leicester, Dec 1972, title role in Helen; Open Space, also Dec 1972, Laverta in The Old Man's Comforts; Greenwich, June 1973, Lady Fancifull in The Provok'd Wife; toured, Sept 1973, as Yolande Chausson in Birds of Paradise; Criterion, Apr 1974, took over the part of Marion in Absurd Person Singular; Edinburgh Festival, 1976, appeared in Fielding Convertible;

Thorndike, Leatherhead, Mar 1977, Angie in A Marriage; Arnaud, Guildford, Nov 1977, Lady Tremurrain in The Case of the Oily Levantine; Chichester, July 1978, and Haymarket, Oct 1978, Claire in Look After Lulu; Lyric Studio, Hammersmith, Oct 1979, in Fenella on Broadway, W6; first appeared in films, 1959, and principal pictures include: Drop Dead, Darling, Doctor in Love, Doctor in Clover, etc; television appearances include The Ides of March, The Importance of Being Earnest, *That Was the Week That Was*, The Autograph, and *Ooh, La La!*.

Favourite parts: Lydia Languish, Lady Parvula, Mrs Gracedew, and Hedda Gabler. *Address:* c/o David White Associates, Fl 4, 12 St George's Street, London W1R 9DF.

FIELDING, Harold, producer
b Woking, Surrey; *s* of William Walter Weble Fielding and his wife Charlotte Agnes (Lewis); *e* privately; *m* Maisie Joyce Skivens.

Originally a concert violinist; from 1942 promoted concerts and tours for many world-famous artists and musicians; his Sunday Concert Series at the Opera House, Blackpool, commenced in 1945 and continues still; until 1963 operated a summer circuit of theatres in eight resorts; presented his first major London stage production, Rodgers and Hammerstein's Cinderella, at the Coliseum, Dec 1958; since then he has presented or co-presented the following productions, in London unless otherwise stated: Aladdin (Cole Porter), 1959; The Gazebo, The Billy Barnes Revue, 1960; The Music Man, Progress to the Park, The Bird of Time, Critic's Choice, 1961; A Thurber Carnival, Sail Away, Clap Hands, 1962; How Are You, Johnnie?, Half a Sixpence, Looking for the Action, Round Leicester Square, 1963; Fielding's Music Hall, 1964; Fielding's Music Hall (new edition), Half a Sixpence (New York), Charlie Girl, 1965 (a production which ran for 2,202 performances at the Adelphi); Man of Magic, 1966; Sweet Charity, 1967; You're A Good Man, Charlie Brown, 1968; Mame, Phil the Fluter, 1969; The Great Waltz, 1970; Show Boat, 1971; Gone with the Wind, Hullabaloo, 1972; Gone with the Wind (USA), Finishing Touches, 1973; Let My People Come, Hans Andersen, 1974; The Charles Pierce Show, 1975; Julie Andrews at the Palladium, Irene, Merry Widow (Australian Ballet), Petula at the Palladium, 1976; I Love My Wife, Hans Andersen (2nd Edition), 1977; The Two Ronnies Revue, Beyond the Rainbow, 1978; Charley's Aunt, The Two Ronnies Revue (Australia), My Fair Lady, 1979; on the Twentieth Century, 1980.

Address: 13 Bruton Street, London W1X 8JY. *Tel:* 01–629 3252.

FINLAY, Frank, actor
b Farnworth, Lancs, 6 Aug 1926; *s* of Josiah Finlay and his wife Margaret; *e* St Gregory the Great School, Farnworth, Lancs. *m* Doreen Shepherd; trained for the stage at RADA.

Appeared with the Guildford Repertory Theatre Company, Apr–May 1957, as Mr Matthews in Jessica, and as Mr Pinnock in The Telescope; Lyric, Hammersmith, Aug 1957, played the Gaoler in The Queen and the Welshman; at the Belgrade, Coventry, May 1958, Peter Cauchon in Saint Joan; and June, 1958, Harry Kahn in Chicken Soup With Barley, transferring with the last production to the Royal Court, London, July 1958; at the John Golden, New York, Nov 1958, played Percy Elliott in Epitaph for George Dillon; on returning to England, at the Royal Court, Apr 1959, played Eric Watts in Sugar in the Morning; Oct 1959, Private Attercliffe in Sergeant Musgrave's Dance; at the same theatre, June 1960, again played Harry Kahn in Chicken Soup

with Barley, Stan Man in Roots, and July 1960, Libby Dobson in I'm Talking About Jerusalem (the last three plays comprising The Wesker Trilogy); Sept 1960, Mr Crape Robinson in The Happy Haven; Oct 1960, Ivan Triletski in Platonov; at the same theatre, Apr 1962, played Corporal Hill in Chips With Everything, transferring with the production to the Vaudeville, June 1962; Chichester Festival, July 1963, played Chaplain de Stogumber in Saint Joan, and Alderman Butterthwaite in The Workhouse Donkey; at the Old Vic, Oct 1963, appeared as the First Gravedigger in the National Theatre Company's inaugural production of Hamlet; he has since played the following parts with the same company: Chaplain de Stogumber in Saint Joan, 1963; Willie Mossop in Hobson's Choice, Iago in Othello (also Chichester Festival), Cocledemoy in The Dutch Courtesan (also Chichester Festival), 1964; Giles Corey in The Crucible, Dogberry in Much Ado About Nothing, Cook in Mother Courage, 1965; appeared with the same company in Moscow and Berlin, Sept 1965, as Iago in Othello, and Willie Mossop in Hobson's Choice; Joxer Daly in Juno and the Paycock, Pavel Prokofyevich Dikoy in The Storm, 1966; Phoenix, Leicester, Oct, and Round House, Nov 1969, played Jesus in Son of Man; Aldwych, Feb 1970, Bernard in After Haggerty, repeating the part at the Criterion, Feb 1971; returned to the National Theatre Company to play Peppino in Saturday, Sunday, Monday, Oct, and Sloman in The Party, Dec 1973, Old Vic; again played Peppino at the Queen's, Oct 1974; Old Vic, Jan 1976, Freddy Malone in Plunder; Feb 1976, Ben Prosse in Watch it Come Down; played both these parts at the Lyttleton, Mar 1976; Josef Frank in Weapons of Happiness, July 1976; Old Vic, Feb 1976, appeared in Tribute to a Lady; Phoenix, Mar 1978, played Henry in Kings and Clowns; Lyric, 1978, took over as Domenico in Filumena, also playing the part at The St James's, NY, Feb 1980; films include: Othello, Cromwell, The Three Musketeers, The Ring of Darkness, The Wild Geese, Sherlock Holmes—Murder by Decree; television includes: Casanova, Don Quixote, Voltaire, *Bouquet of Barbed Wire*, Count Dracula, The Last Campaign.
Address: c/o Al Parker, 55 Park Lane, London W1. *Tel:* 01–499 4232.

FINNEY, Albert, actor
b Salford, Lancs, 9 May 1936; *s* of Albert Finney and his wife Alice (Hobson); *e* Salford Grammar School; *m* (1) Jane Wenham (mar dis); (2) Anouk Aimée (mar dis); studied at the Royal Academy of Dramatic Art.
Made his first appearance on the stage at the Birmingham Repertory Theatre, Apr 1956, when he played Decius Brutus in Julius Caesar; he remained a member of this company for nearly two years, playing, among other parts, Macbeth, Henry V, Francis Archer in The Beaux' Stratagem, Face in The Alchemist, and Malcolm in The Lizard on the Rock; made his first appearance in London, at the Old Vic, July 1956, when he played Belzanor in Caesar and Cleopatra, with the Birmingham Repertory Company; New, 28 May 1958, played Soya Marshall in The Party; joined the Shakespeare Memorial Theatre Company, Stratford-on-Avon, for the 100th Season, Apr 1959, and played Edgar in King Lear, Cassio in Othello, and Lysander in A Midsummer Night's Dream; Royal Court, Jan 1960, played Ted in The Lily-White Boys; at the Cambridge, Sept 1960, played the title-role in Billy Liar; after eight months, he left the cast to appear at the Paris International Festival of the *Théâtre des Nations*, July 1961, as Martin Luther in Luther; he subsequently appeared in the same play at the Holland Festival, prior to the London opening at the Royal Court, July 1961, for a limited run;

Edinburgh Festival, Aug 1961, and Phoenix, London, Sept 1961, again played the title-part in Luther; Royal Court, Feb 1962, played Feste in Twelfth Night, in a Production without Décor; Glasgow Citizens', Mar 1963, played the title-part in Pirandello's Henry IV; in the same season directed The Birthday Party, and School for Scandal; made his first appearance in New York at the St James's, Sept 1963, as Martin Luther in Luther; joined the National Theatre Company at the Old Vic, Feb 1965, to play Don Pedro in Much Ado About Nothing; Chichester Festival, July 1965, John Armstrong in Armstrong's Last Goodnight; Jean in Miss Julie, and Harold Gorringe in Black Comedy (double-bill); Old Vic, Oct 1965, again played Armstrong and re-directed Armstrong's Last Goodnight; at the same theatre, Feb 1966, appeared as Victor Chandebise and Poche in A Flea in Her Ear (*Evening Standard* Best Actor Award) and in Mar 1966, as Jean in Miss Julie, and Harold Gorringe in Black Comedy; Comedy, July 1967, co-presented A Day in the Death of Joe Egg: also in Feb 1968, at the Brooks Atkinson, NY, where he appeared as Bri; Royal Court, Jan 1972, Mr Elliot in Alpha Beta, transferring to the Apollo, Mar 1972; associate artistic director of the Royal Court, July 1972–5; at this theatre he played Krapp in Krapp's Last Tape, Jan 1973, directed The Freedom of the City, Feb 1973, played O'Halloran in Cromwell, Aug 1973, and directed Loot, June 1975; at the Globe, Feb 1974, played Phil in Chez Nous; rejoined the National Theatre, Dec 1975, to play Hamlet at the Old Vic and in the opening production at the Lyttleton, Mar 1976; title-role in Tamburlaine the Great, Olivier, Oct 1976; Mr Horner in The Country Wife, Nov 1977, Lopakhin in The Cherry Orchard, Feb 1978 and the title-role in Macbeth, June 1978, all at the Olivier, and John Bean in Has 'Washington' Legs?, at the Cottesloe, Nov 1978; in June 1965, he formed Memorial Enterprises Ltd, an independent production company for the presentation of television programs, films, and stage plays; principal films in which he has appeared include Saturday Night and Sunday Morning, Tom Jones, Charlie Bubbles, Alpha Beta, and Murder on the Orient Express; first appeared on television, Jan 1956, and has played in View Friendship and Marriage, The Claverdon Road Job, The Miser, Forget-Me-Not Lane, etc.
Address: c/o Memorial Films, 74 Campden Hill Court, Campden Hill Road, London W8.

FIRTH, David (David Firth Coleman), actor and singer
b Bedford, 15 Mar 1945; *s* of Ivor Firth Coleman and his wife Beatrice (Jenkins); *e* Bedford Modern School, Sussex University and the Guildhall School of Music; *m* Julia Elizabeth Gould.
Made his first stage appearance in London at the Garrick, Jan 1967, as Fyodor in an N.U.S. Drama Festival production of Notes from Underground; 1967–70, joined the Royal Shakespeare Company appearing in Stratford, London and touring the US and Europe in parts including Amiens in As You Like It, Balthasar in Much Ado About Nothing, Helenus in Troilus and Cressida and Sordido in The Revenger's Tragedy; New Theatre (Albery), June 1970, the Courier in 1776; Phoenix, Leicester, 1971, Orlando in As You Like It and Mercutio in Romeo and Juliet; 1972, toured as James in Me Times Me; Belgrade, Coventry, 1972, parts included Roger in After Haggerty and Jo Jo in Irma La Douce; returned to the Phoenix, Leicester, 1973 in Gawain and the Green Knight and Happy as a Sandbag, and also directed Purity there; joined the National Theatre, 1973 season, to play Donalbain in Macbeth, Yasha in The Cherry Orchard and Lucio in Measure for Measure (Old Vic); took over Attilio in Saturday, Sunday, Monday, also for the NT,

Queen's Theatre, 1974; Young Vic, 1975, Massingham in All Good Men; Greenwich, 1975, Parolles in All's Well That Ends Well and Lucio in Measure for Measure; Royal, Stratford East, Dec 1975, Nickleby in Nickleby and Me; Globe, Mar 1976, Richard Pershore in The Chairman; Wyndham's, Mar 1977, joined the cast of Side by Side by Sondheim; Greenwich, Apr 1979, Courtall in She Would and If She Could; Old Vic, Sept 1979, Captain Loveit in Miss in Her Teens and Leander in The Padlock; seen frequently on television since Search for the Nile, 1971: recent work includes Love for Lydia, Raffles, Nanny's Boy and Whodunnit.

Favourite parts: Lucio and Mercutio. *Address:* 1 Newry Road, St Margaret's, Twickenham, Middlesex. *Tel:* 01 892 1168.

FIRTH, Tazeena, designer
b Southampton, 1 Nov 1935; *d* of Dennis Gordon Firth and his wife Irene (Morris); *e* St Mary's, Wantage, and the Chatelard School.

Her first designs for the theatre were at the Theatre Royal, Windsor; subsequently at the Royal Court, A Resounding Tinkle; for RSC designed Two Gentlemen of Verona, 1969; Occupations, 1971; has worked as co-designer with Timothy O'Brien since 1961 (see his entry for details); joint winner (with Timothy O'Brien, Ralph Koltai and John Bury) of individual Gold Medal for set design, Prague Quadriennale, 1975.

Address: 33 Lansdowne Gardens, London SW8.

FISHER, Jules, lighting designer
b Norristown, Pa; 12 Nov 1937; *s* of Abraham Fisher and his wife Anne (Davidson); *e* Pennsylvania State University, Carnegie Institute of Technology (BFA 1960).

First lighting design was of a high school production of January Thaw, Mar 1954; worked as assistant stage manager and carpenter in the Valley Forge Music Fair, Devon, Pa, 1955; at the Shubert, Philadelphia, 1956, served as assistant electrician to The Most Happy Fella, The Ziegfeld Follies, and Mr Wonderful, and, at the Circle in the City, Philadelphia, 1956, designed the lighting for Death of a Salesman, The Girl on the Via Flaminia, and End As a Man; worked in stock and then made his New York début as lighting director at the 74th St, 15 Oct 1959, with All the King's Men; since then has designed Parade, Tobacco Road, the tour of West Side Story, Here Come the Clowns, Greenwich Village, USA, Marcus in the High Grass, 1960; The Eccentricities of Davy Crockett, Riding Hood Revisited, Willie the Weeper, the last three comprising Ballet Ballads, Donogoo, Cicero, The Tiger Rag, Go Show Me a Dragon, All in Love, Red Roses for Me, 1961; Moon on a Rainbow Shawl, The Banker's Daughter, The Creditors, Fly Blackbird, The Book of Job, The Golden Apple, This Side of Paradise, Nathan the Wise, Half-Past Wednesday, O Say Can You See! Riverwind, Porgy and Bess, and was lighting designer for the Casa Manana Theatre, Fort Worth, Texas, and the San Diego, Cal, Shakespeare Festival, 1962; The Love Nest, Six Characters in Search of an Author, Best Foot Forward, The Dragon, Spoon River Anthology, Telemachus Clay, The Ginger Man, The Trojan Women, The Establishment, An Evening with Maurice Chevalier, Enter Laughing, A Rainy Day in New York, Ole! Ole!, A Midsummer Night's Dream, Don Giovanni (opera), and tours of The Mikado and HMS Pinafore, 1963; Anyone Can Whistle, High Spirits, Wonder World, The White House, The Subject Was Roses, A Girl Could Get Lucky, The Tragical Historie of Doctor Faustus, I Had a Ball, Gogo Loves You, The Sign in Sidney Brustein's Win-

dow, PS I Love You, South Pacific (Toronto, Canada), 1964; Do I Hear a Waltz?, Pickwick, The Decline and Fall of the Entire World As Seen Through the Eyes of Cole Porter Revisited, Half a Sixpence, And Things That Go Bump in the Night, Square in the Eye, Leonard Bernstein's Theatre Songs, The Devils, The White Devil, The Yearling, Ben Bagley's New Cole Porter Revue, 1965; Suburban Tragedy, Make Like a Dog, Princess Rebecca Birnbaum, Young Marrieds Play Monopoly, Serjeant Musgrave's Dance, Hooray! It's a Glorious Day . . . and All That, The Kitchen, A Hand Is on the Gate, Eh?, The Threepenny Opera, Hail Scrawdyke! 1966; Black Comedy, White Lies, You're a Good Man, Charlie Brown, The Natural Look, You Know I Can't Hear You When the Water's Running, Little Murders, South Pacific, The Unknown Soldier and His Wife, A Minor Adjustment, Scuba Duba, The Trial of Lee Harvey Oswald, Iphigenia in Aulis, 1967; Before You Go, The Grand Music Hall of Israel, Here's Where I Belong, Canterbury Tales, Kongi's Harvest, Hair, The Only Game in Town, A Moon for the Misbegotten, The Happy Hypocrite, The Cuban Thing, The Man in the Glass Booth, 1968; But, Seriously . . ., The Watering Place, Someone's Comin' Hungry, Trumpets of the Lord, Promenade, Butterflies Are Free, 1969; Sheep on the Runway, Gantry, Minnie's Boys, Jakey Fat Boy, Dear Janet Rosenberg, Dear Mr Kooning, Inquest, The Engagement Baby, Home, 1970; Soon, Hamlet, No, No, Nanette, Lenny (also co-produced), Jesus Christ Superstar, 1971; Fun City, Pippin (Antoinette Perry (Tony) Award), Lysistrata, Mourning Becomes Electra, The Trials of Oz, 1972; Seesaw, Molly, Full Circle, The Iceman Cometh, Pippin (London), Uncle Vanya, 1973; Ulysses in Nighttown (Tony Award), Thieves, Liza at the Wintergarden, Billy (London), Sergeant Pepper's Lonely Hearts Club Band on the Road, 1974; Man on the Moon, Chicago, production supervision for Rolling Stones tour of USA, 1975; Rockabye Hamlet, 1976; American Buffalo, Beatlemania (also supervised production), Hair (revival), Golda, 1977; co-produced and lit Dancin', 1978, receiving a 'Tony' for his lighting of this and Beatlemania; lit the latter in London, 1979; has also lit the opera Natalia Petrovna, 1964, the ballets Jeux, 1966, Peter and the Wolf, 1969, the première season of the American Ballet, 1969–70, Laura Nyro concerts, 1969–70, the rock opera Tommy, 1973, the David Bowie concert tour, 1974, Hallelujah Hollywood, Las Vegas, Nevada, 1974, etc; serves as consultant to numerous theatres, notably Circle in the Square—Joseph E Levine, Westbury Music Fair, Deauville Star in Miami, the Rebekah Harkness, Studio Theatre of the Brooklyn Academy of Music, etc.

Recreations: Magic, invention, music, film-making. *Address:* 212 West 15th Street, New York, NY 10011.

FITZGERALD, Geraldine, actress
b Dublin, Eire, 24 Nov 1914; *d* of Edward Fitzgerald and his wife Edith; *e* Dublin Art School; *m* (1) Edward Lindsay Hogg (mar dis); (2) Stuart Scheftel.

First appeared on the stage at the Gate, Dublin, 1932; made her New York début at the Mercury, 29 Apr 1938, as Ellie Dunn in Heartbreak House; went to Hollywood to make films; Morosco, May 1943, played Rebecca in Sons and Soldiers; Shubert, New Haven, Dec 1945, Tanis Talbot in Portrait in Black; again went to Hollywood; Phoenix, Jan 1955, Jennifer Dubedat in The Doctor's Dilemma; New York City Center, Jan 1956, Goneril in King Lear; Ethel Barrymore, Apr 1957, Ann Richards in Hide and Seek; American Shakespeare Festival, Stratford, Connecticut, June 1958, Gertrude in Hamlet; Greenwich Mews, Oct 1961, The Queen in The Cave Dwellers; Cherry Lane, Mar 1965, Third

Woman in Pigeons; Ford's, Washington, DC, 1969, the Mother in Ah, Wilderness!; Promenade, NY, Apr 1971, Mary Tyrone in Long Day's Journey into Night; New York Society of Ethical Culture Auditorium, Oct 1971, co-author with Brother Jonathan OSF and played in Everyman and Roach; co-produced the Lincoln Center Community Street Festival, Aug–Sept 1972; WPA Theatre, Oct 1972, Jenny in The Threepenny Opera; Long Wharf, New Haven, Conn, Mar 1973, Juno Boyle in Juno and the Paycock, and Apr 1973, Amy in Forget-Me-Not Lane; co-produced the Lincoln Center Community Street Festival, Aug–Sept 1973, and adapted Mr Esteban, presented during the festival; Long Wharf, Oct 1973, Aline Solness in The Master Builder, and Nov 1973, Grandmother in the American première of D H Lawrence's The Widowing of Mrs Holroyd; New York Cultural Center, June 1974, appeared in Cabaret in the Sky; Long Wharf, Dec 1974, Essie Miller in Ah, Wilderness!; Walnut, Philadelphia, Apr 1975, Mary Tyrone in Long Day's Journey into Night; Stratford, Conn, June 1975, Mrs Webb in Our Town; Circle in the Square, Oct 1975, Essie Miller in Ah, Wilderness!; Walnut, Philadelphia, Dec 1975, Amanda Wingfield in The Glass Menagerie; Long Wharf, Jan 1977, and Morosco, Mar, Felicity in The Shadow Box; Helen Hayes, Dec 1977, Nora Melody in A Touch of the Poet; has appeared in New York and elsewhere since 1976 in her one-woman show Songs of the Streets; Public, Oct 1979, appeared in O'Neill and Carlotta; entered films in The Turn of the Tide, in England in 1934, and has since appeared in many films, including The Mill on the Floss, Wuthering Heights, Dark Victory, Watch on the Rhine, Wilson, Ten North Frederick, The Pawnbroker, Harry and Tonto (1974), etc; has appeared on television in The Moon and Sixpence, Dodsworth, and The Best of Everything.

Recreation: Painting. *Address:* Actors Equity Association, 165 West 46th Street, New York, NY 10036.

FITZGERALD, Neil, actor
b Tipperary, Ireland, 15 Jan 1893; *e* Trinity College, Dublin.

First appeared in New York, Aug 1937, in The Miles of Heaven; Longacre, 27 Feb 1940, played Martin Reardon in Leave Her to Heaven; Plymouth, Sept 1941, Walt Gibbs in The Wookey; Belasco, Feb 1942, Brigadier Husted in Plan M; Carnegie Hall, July 1942, Novakovich in The Merry Widow; St James, Nov 1942, Robert Emmett Riordan in Without Love; Broadhurst, June 1944, Rogers in Ten Little Indians; Booth, Sept 1945, Reverend Guilford Melton in You Touched Me!; The Playhouse, Jan 1948, Alcott in The Survivors; Mansfield, Jan 1950, Henry Maye in Design for a Stained Glass Window; 48th Street, Feb 1951, Melling in The High Ground; John Golden, Nov 1951, various parts in To Dorothy, A Son; Plymouth, Sept 1952, Mr Wardle in Mr Pickwick; Holiday, Nov 1954, Patrick Murphy in revival of Abie's Irish Rose; Henry Miller's, 1955, took over as Carter in Witness for the Prosecution; Theatre East, Mar 1957, A Priest in The Tinker's Wedding; 41st Street, Apr 1957, Solicitor-General in Oscar Wilde; John Golden, Oct 1957, Gouttez in Monique; off-Broadway, Apr 1959, Played in The Death of Cuchulain and On Baile's Strand; Longacre, Dec 1960, Father Curran in Little Moon of Alban; Martinique, May 1962, John Casey and Rector of Conglowes in James Joyce's A Portrait of the Artist as a Young Man and Maurice Desmond in The Barroom Monks; Booth, May 1964, MacIntosh in Roar Like a Dove; Renata, Nov 1966, Man in Eternal Triangle and Sean Donaghue in The Bridal Night in the triple-bill Three Hand Reel; Greenwich Mews, Mar 1967, appeared in the revue Carricknabauna; East 74th Street, Sept 1967, Mr Casey and The Confessor in Stephen D; Helen

Hayes, Jan 1969, Rector of St Andrew's College in Hadrian VII; Royale, Dec 1969, Charles Hogan in The Mundy Scheme; Martin Beck, Mar 1971, The Doctor in all Over; Playhouse, Dec 1971, Viscount Tamworth in Murderous Angels; Chelsea Manhattan, Oct 1973, Old Mr Ewbank in The Contractor; a successful Hollywood actor in the thirties, he also appeared in the film Savages (1972); has appeared frequently on television in various dramatic programs.

Address: Actors Equity Association, 165 West 46th Street, New York, NY 10036.

FLANNERY, Peter, playwright
b Jarrow, 12 Oct 1951; *s* of Andrew Flannery and his wife Anne; *e* St Joseph's Grammar-Technical School, Hebburn, and University of Manchester (BA Hons Drama).

Having gained a diploma in directing, Manchester University, 1974, wrote his first play Heartbreak Hotel, produced at Contact Theatre Manchester, 1975; he has since written Last Resort, 1976; Are You With Me?, 1977; Savage Amusement (Royal Shakespeare Company), The Boy's Own Story, 1978; The Adventures of Awful Knawful (co-author with Mick Ford, for RSC), Jungle Music, 1979; Resident Dramatist RSC, 1979–80.

Hobbies: Reading, walking, sport, music, running away from dogs. *Address:* 10 Main Road, Langley, Cheshire. *Tel:* Sutton 2115.

FLEETWOOD, Susan, actress
b St Andrews, Scotland, 21 Sept 1944; *d* of John Joseph Kells Fleetwood and his wife Bridget Maureen (Brereton); *e* at sixteen schools, latterly the Convent of the Nativity, Sittingbourne, Kent; trained for the stage at RADA (Gold Medal, 1964), touring Arizona in 1964 with a RADA company, for whom she played Rosalind in As You Like It, and Lady Macbeth.

Made her first professional appearance at the Everyman, Liverpool, 1964, as Lady Percy in Henry IV, part 1; in two years at this theatre played parts including: Gwendoline in The Importance of Being Earnest, Alison in Look Back in Anger, Sylvia in The Servant of Two Master, Lis in Fando and Lis, Beatrice in The Four Seasons and Margaret in The Great God Brown; joined the Royal Shakespeare Company, 1967, appearing first in a Theatregoround tour of The Hollow Crown; at the Aldwych, 1967, played Amanda in The Relapse, Aug, and Beba in The Criminals, Sept; appeared there in Under Milk Wood, Mar 1968; at Stratford, season 1968, played Regan in King Lear, Audrey in As You Like It, Cassandra in Troilus and Cressida, and Margaret in Much Ado About Nothing; Season 1969, Thaisa and Marina in Pericles, and Isabella in Women Beware Women; toured with the Cambridge Theatre Company, Oct 1970, as Nina in The Seagull and Sylvia in The Recruiting Officer; toured with Prospect, Mar–July 1971, as Lady Rodolpha in The Way of the World and Ophelia in Hamlet, visiting Europe, and appearing in the latter part at the Cambridge Theatre, London, Aug 1971; returning to the RSC, 1972, played Portia in The Merchant of Venice, June, Woman of Canterbury (chorus leader) in Murder in the Cathedral, Aug, and a Bondwoman in The Island of the Mighty, Dec, all at the Aldwych; Stratford, 1973, played the Princess of France in Love's Labours Lost, Aug, and Katherina in The Taming of the Shrew, Sept; in 1974 played Kaleria in Summerfolk, Aldwych, Aug, Bertha Alberg in Comrades, The Place, Oct, and Imogen in Cymbeline, Aldwych, Dec; same theatre, Apr 1975, Apr 1975, again played the Princess of France; joined the National Theatre Company to play Pegeen Mike in The Playboy of the Western World, Old Vic, Oct 1975, and

Ophelia in Hamlet, Dec 1975; repeated these roles at the new National Theatre, 1976, and played Jo in Watch it Come Down, Mar 1976; Zenocrate in Tamburlaine the Great, Oct; in 1977 she played Nora in The Plough and the Stars (Sept), Clair in Lavender Blue (Nov), and in 1978, Varya in The Cherry Orchard (Feb), appeared in Don John Comes Back from the War (Apr), and played Ismene in The Woman (Aug); returned to the RSC at Stratford for the 1980 season in which she played Rosalind in As You Like It; first appeared on television 1972, in The Watercress Girl; recent television includes Playboy of the Western World, Eustace and Hilda and Don't Be Silly; first film: Clash of the Titans.

Favourite parts: Nina in The Seagull, Marina/Thaisa in Pericles, and Imogen. *Address:* c/o Duncan Heath, Pembroke House, 61 Earls Court Road, London W8. *Tel:* 01–937 9898.

FLEMING, Lucy, actress
b Nettlebed, Oxon, 15 May 1947; *d* of Robert Peter Fleming and his wife Celia Elizabeth (Johnson); *e* Cranborne Chase School.

Began her career in repertory at the Castle, Farnham; made her first London appearance at the Royal Court, Aug 1965, in a Sunday-night production of A Collier's Friday Night, playing Maggie; subsequently played several parts at the Royal Court, including Helen Shelley in Shelley, Nov 1965; Gladys in The Performing Giant, Mar 1966; Ethel Voysey in The Voysey Inheritance, Apr 1966; Duke of York's, Feb 1968, Sorel Bliss in Hay Fever; St Martin's, Oct 1968, Joanna Pilgrim in Out of the Question; for Prospect Productions, toured as Lady Margaret in Edward the Second and Queen Isabel in Richard II, appearing at the Edinburgh Festival, Aug 1969, Mermaid, Sept 1969 and Piccadilly, Jan 1970, in these productions; Playhouse, Nottingham, Aug 1970, Grazia in A Yard of Sun, visiting the Old Vic with this production, Aug; Garrick, Feb 1971, Ruth in Don't Start Without Me; Crucible, Sheffield, June 1973, Viola in Twelfth Night; toured, Oct 1974, in Relatively Speaking; Palace, Watford, Feb 1980, Olivia in Night Must Fall; has also appeared in repertory at the University Theatre, Manchester, the Arnaud, Guildford and the Welsh National Theatre, Cardiff; television appearances, since 1967, include plays, serials, and the series *Survivors*.

Favourite parts: Comedy ones. *Address:* c/o Richard Stone, 18–20 York Buildings, London WC2.

FLEMING, Tom, actor, director, author and poet
b Edinburgh, Scotland, 29 June 1927; *s* of Peter Fleming and his wife Kate Ulla (Barker); *e* Daniel Stewart's College, Edinburgh.

Appeared in his first speaking part during a tour of India, Feb 1945, as Bruce McRae in The Late Christopher Bean; was the co-founder of the Edinburgh Gateway Theatre Company, 1953, and during the following nine years both directed and appeared in innumerable productions including John Shand in What Every Woman Knows, Gregers Werle in The Wild Duck, Shylock in The Merchant of Venice, Matthew in Follow Me; appeared regularly at the Edinburgh Festival, 1950–9, and played Divine Correction in The Thrie Estates, 1959 and 1973; joined the Royal Shakespeare Theatre Company, Stratford, 1962, to play the following parts: the Duke in Measure for Measure, the Porter in Macbeth, the title part in Cymbeline, and Kent in King Lear, transferring with the last production to the Aldwych, Dec 1962; at the Royal Shakespeare Theatre, Stratford-on-Avon, 1963, played Prospero in The Tempest, Brutus in Julius Caesar, and the Duke of Buckingham in Edward IV, and

Richard III (in the trilogy The Wars of the Roses); Aldwych, Feb 1964, again played the Earl of Kent in King Lear, prior to appearing in the same production on a British Council tour of the USSR, Europe, and the United States, Feb–June 1964; appointed first director of the Edinburgh Civic Theatre Trust, Mar 1965, and founded Royal Lyceum Theatre Company; directed his first production at the Lyceum, Edinburgh, Oct 1965, with The Servant of Two Masters; Nov 1965, played the title-part in Galileo; Citizens', Glasgow, Mar 1968, Knox in The Anatomist; Phoenix, Leicester, Nov 1970, played Van Gogh in Vincent; repeating this solo role at Hampstead, Apr 1971, Young Vic 1973, Adelaide Festival 1974, Perth Festival 1976; Perth, Oct 1971, played the title role in Henry of Navarre; Lyceum, Edinburgh, Oct 1975, directed The Apple Cart; at the same theatre, Nov 1976, played Knox in the Anatomist, and subsequently directed The Servant of Two Masters (Apr and Oct, 1977), appeared as Bernard Kevin in Revival (Apr, 1978), and took the title-role in Dr Angelus; his dramatic recitals have included Border and Ballad, Robert Fergusson, Carlyle and Jane, Edwin and Willa, William Soutar, and A Drunk Man Looks at the Thistle; he directed the Scottish Military Tattoo at Wolf Trap, Virginia, USA, in July 1976; films include King Lear, Mary Queen of Scots, and Meetings with Remarkable Men; first appeared on television, 1952, in The Black Eye by James Bridie; notable performances include: Jesus of Nazareth, and An Age of Kings; directed A World of His Own and wrote And Not For Glory, both TV films; radio performances include The Man Born To Be King; radio and TV commentator since 1952; author of So That Was Spring (poems), Miracle at Midnight, It's My Belief, 1954; A Festival of Edinburgh, 1960; Sax Roses for a Luve Frae Hame (poems), 1961.

Recreations: Hill-walking, motoring, music, and reading. *Address:* c/o Plunket Greene Ltd, 91 Regent Street, London W1R 8RU. *Tel:* 01–734 7311.

FLEMYNG, Robert, OBE, MC, actor and director
b Liverpool, 3 Jan 1912; *s* of George Gilbert Flemyng, MD, BA, and his wife Rowena Eleanor (Jacques); *e* Haileybury; *m* Carmen Martha Sugars; formerly a medical student.

Made his first appearance on the stage at the County, Truro, June 1931, as Kenneth Raglan in Rope; made his first appearance in London at the Westminster Theatre, 7 Oct 1931, walking on in The Anatomist; during 1932 toured with Violet Vanbrugh as Cyril Greenwood in After All; Lyric, May 1932, understudied in Dangerous Corner; joined the Liverpool Repertory Company at the Playhouse, Liverpool, 1932, and remained there three seasons, playing a variety of parts; at the St James's Theatre, Mar 1935, played Edward Brett in Worse Things Happen at Sea; Globe, Sept 1935, Dickie Reynolds in Accent on Youth; Daly's, Nov 1935, Tom Willetts in Tread Softly; Embassy and Savoy, Mar 1936, Bill Harvey in Wisdom Teeth; Arts, June 1936, Lord Lynates in When the Bough Breaks; Criterion, Nov 1936, Kit Neilan in French Without Tears, which he played for sixteen months; Strand, Apr 1938, Jones in Banana Ridge; made his first appearance on the New York stage at the Morosco Theatre, 8 Dec 1938, as Tony Fox-Collier in Spring Meeting; Ethel Barrymore, Apr 1939, Makepiece Lovell in No Time for Comedy; left the cast in Sept 1939, returned to England, and joined the RAMC, Sept 1939; was later commissioned, and was awarded the Military Cross, Eritrea, 1941; was mentioned in dispatches and awarded OBE (Military), Italy, 1944–5; reappeared on the stage, Oct 1945, at the Marigny, Paris, as the Earl of Harpenden in While the Sun Shines; Grand, Blackpool, Dec 1945, played Nigel Lorraine in The

Guinea Pig; appeared in the same part at the Criterion, London, Feb 1946, scoring a notable success; again visited the United States, appearing at the Royale, NY, Mar 1947, as Algernon Moncrieff in The Importance of Being Earnest; at the same theatre, May 1947, played Ben in Love for Love; after returning to England, appeared at Wyndham's, July 1948, as Rowlie Bateson in People Like Us; St James's, Mar 1949, Philotas in Adventure Story; Vaudeville, June 1949, played the Hon Alan Howard in a revival of French Without Tears; at the Lyceum, Edinburgh (Edinburgh Festival), Aug 1949, and at the Henry Miller, NY, Jan 1950, played Edward Chamberlayne in The Cocktail Party; Criterion, London, Oct 1950, Mark in Who Is Sylvia?; Criterion, Dec 1951, Sam Hartley in Indian Summer; Her Majesty's, Johannesburg, Mar 1952, played Philip in The Little Hut, and Toni Rigi in To Dorothy, A Son, subsequently touring in these parts throughout the Union of South Africa and Southern Rhodesia; Lyric, London, July 1952, succeeded Robert Morley as Philip in The Little Hut; again visited the United States, Oct 1952, and toured as leading man with Katharine Cornell in The Constant Wife; after returning to London appeared at the Duke of York's, July 1953, as David Slater in The Moon Is Blue; St Martin's, Apr 1954, played Rupert Forster in Marching Song; returned to the United States and appeared at the ANTA Playhouse, NY, Dec 1954, as Gilbert Osmond in Portrait of a Lady; Streatham Hill, Dec 1955, played Anthony Henderson in Bell, Book, and Candle, subsequently touring with the production; Bijou, NY, Jan 1957, played James Callifer in The Potting Shed; Apollo, Mar 1958, Powell in Beth; toured, June 1958, as David Warren in Dear Delinquent; Globe, Jan 1959, Kevin Carrell in Eighty in the Shade; St Martin's, Feb 1960, Colin in A Sparrow Falls (in the double bill Double Yoke); Phoenix, Sept 1960, played Hugo Cavanati in The Last Joke; Ashcroft, Croydon, Oct 1964, played Dr Sloper in The Heiress; toured Australia, 1965, as Anthony Wilcox in Difference of Opinion; Goodman, Chicago, Oct 1965, Harcourt-Reilly in The Cocktail Party; Theatre Royal, Newcastle, Mar 1966, and tour, played Garry Essendine in Present Laughter; St Martin's, Dec 1966, Richard Halton in On Approval, and Mar 1957, Gregory Butler in Happy Family; Lyric, Feb 1968, played Colonel Melkett in Black Comedy; Playhouse, Newcastle, Mar 1969, Shylock in The Merchant of Venice; Shaw Festival, Niagara-on-the-Lake, June 1969, Sir Colenso Ridgeon in The Doctor's Dilemma; Opera House, Manchester, Sept 1969, and tour, played Sir Broadfoot Basham in On the Rocks; Fortune, Jan 1970, Mr Bompas in How He Lied to Her Husband and General Michener in Press Cuttings, in the triple bill, Three; Lyric, June 1970, played Arthur du Cros MP in My Darling Daisy; Arnaud, Guildford, Nov 1970, Maitland in The Chalk Garden; New, Bromley, Mar 1971, Rev James Morrell in Candida; Empire, Liverpool, June 1971, appeared in a gala performance for HM the Queen; Haymarket, Jan 1972, played George Chudleigh in Harlequinade, in a midnight matinee for Sir Terence Rattigan; toured, Oct 1972, as Sir Max in Death on Demand (later The Pay-Off); Feb 1973, toured as Andrew Wyke in Sleuth; toured S Africa, Spring 1974, as Sebastian Crutwell in In Praise of Love, subsequently repeating the part at the Theatre Royal, Windsor, Feb 1975; toured, Apr 1975, as Philip in Relatively Speaking, also touring Canada with the production; Leeds Playhouse, Feb 1976, Gaev in The Cherry Orchard and title-role in Stripwell; Duke of York's, Aug 1976, Sorin in The Seagull; Hampstead, Oct 1977, Brother Joseph in The Dog Ran Away; toured, Aug 1978, as Sir Hugo Latymer in Just A Song at Twilight, in the double-bill Suite in Two Keys; Malvern Festival, May 1979, for the Birmingham

Repertory Company, played Lord Summerhays in Misalliance and Frederico Gomez in The Elder Statesman; Birmingham Rep, Aug 1979, Ernest in Bedroom Face; Gardner Centre, Brighton, Feb 1980 and tour, Sorin in The Seagull; has appeared in a number of Sunday night productions; directed the production of The Little Dry Thorn, Lyric, Hammersmith, 1947, French Without Tears, Vaudeville, 1949, and The Doll's House, Leatherhead, 1968; first appeared in films, 1936, in Head Over Heels and has since appeared in more than thirty films, including The Blue Lamp, The Man Who Never Was, and most recently, Young Winston, The Medusa Touch, The Four Feathers, and The Thirty Nine Steps; first seen on television in French Without Tears, 1949, and has since appeared in numerous series and plays including *Crown Court*, Loyalties, Rebecca, Edward and Mrs Simpson; has also appeared frequently on American TV; Council member, British Actors' Equity, 1959–63, 1969–72, 1974–5; Appeals Committee, 1979; Hon Treasurer, The Actors' Charitable Trust.

Recreations: Squash racquets, riding and walking. *Club:* Garrick. *Address:* London International, 11–12 Hanover Street, London, W1. *Tel:* 01–629 8080.

FLETCHER, Allen, director

b San Francisco, California, 19 July 1922; *s* of Allen Fletcher and his wife Jessica (Dinsmoor); *e* New Mexico Military Institute, Stanford University (BA 1947, MA 1950), Yale University School of Drama, 1951–2, Bristol Old Vic Theatre School, LAMDA, London, on a Fulbright Study Grant, 1957–8; *m* Anne Lawder.

Began his stage career as an actor at the Stanford (California) University Little Theatre, July 1946, playing Henry Gow in Fumed Oak; was on the faculty of Purdue University, 1948–50, teaching speech and directing various plays; Associate Professor at Carnegie Institute of Technology, 1952–9, teaching acting and directing; first directed professionally at the Oregon Shakespeare Festival, Ashland, Oregon, Aug 1948, with King John, followed by Othello, The Taming of the Shrew, 1949; Henry IV, Part I, 1950; Julius Caesar, 1952; Coriolanus, 1953; The Merry Wives of Windsor, 1954; Love's Labour's Lost, Richard III, 1956; for the Antioch Shakespeare Festival (Ohio), Aug 1957, directed Henry VIII; at the Old Globe Theatre, for the San Diego, California, Shakespeare Festival, directed Hamlet, 1955; King Lear, 1957; Much Ado About Nothing, 1958; Romeo and Juliet, Love's Labour's Lost, 1959; Hamlet, As You Like It, 1960; The Merchant of Venice, Richard III, 1961; Othello, 1962; Antony and Cleopatra, 1963; Two Gentlemen of Verona, 1966; for the Association of Producing Artists directed Man and Superman, The Importance of Being Earnest, 1960; As You Like It, Twelfth Night, 1961; at the Martinique, Dec 1960, directed the play Borak; joined the American Shakespeare Festival Theatre and Academy, Stratford, Connecticut, June 1962, and became Artistic Director and head of professional training program for the acting staff and directed Richard II, 1962; King Lear, 1963; Richard III, Much Ado About Nothing, 1964; Coriolanus, Romeo and Juliet, King Lear, 1965; in 1966 became Artistic Director of the Seattle Repertory Theatre, Washington, where he produced in repertory The Crucible, The Hostage, Blithe Spirit, Tartuffe, The Visit, The Night of the Iguana, 1966–7; Henry IV, Part I, The Rehearsal, You Can't Take It with You, The Rivals, The Father, The Threepenny Opera, 1967–8; Our Town, Juno and the Paycock, A Midsummer Night's Dream, Lysistrata, Serjeant Musgrave's Dance, A View from the Bridge, Mourning Becomes Electra, Three Cheers for What's-Its-

Name, Look Back in Anger, Big Nose Mary Is Dead and the Quickies, The Blacks, A Little Set-to, Short Sacred Rite of Search and Destruction, and, by invitation, visited the Bergen, Norway, International Festival with Who's Afraid of Virginia Woolf? 1968–9; Volpone, The Three Sisters, Once in a Lifetime, In the Matter of J Robert Oppenheimer, The Little Foxes, The Country Wife, Joe Egg, Summertree, The Initiation, 1969–70; in 1970 founded The Actors' Company and for them directed In the Matter of J Robert Oppenheimer, co-directed The Little Murders, and produced Summertree, at Ann Arbor, Michigan, for the University of Michigan Professional Theatre Program; for the American Conservatory Theatre has directed Death of a Salesman, 1965; Uncle Vanya, 1966; Arsenic and Old Lace, 1967; The Crucible, 1968; The Hostage, 1969; Hadrian VII, 1970; The Latent Heterosexual, An Enemy of the People, 1970–1; Paradise Lost, 1971–2; a Doll's House, That Championship Season, 1972–3; The Hotel Baltimore, The Miser, 1973–4; Pillars of the Community, The Ruling Class, 1974–5; Desire Under the Elms, This is—an Entertainment (world première of Tennessee Williams play), Peer Gynt, 1975–6; The Master Builder, Absurd Person Singular, 1977; Ah Wilderness!, Heartbreak House, 1978; in 1970 became Conservatory Director of the American Conservatory Theatre; for the New York City Center directed Rigoleto, 1960; HMS Pinafore, Aida, The Crucible, 1961; The Golem, The Turn of the Screw, The Passion of Jonathan Wade, 1962; Jeanne d'Arc au Bücher, 1963; The Yeomen of the Guard, 1965; The Pirates of Penzance, HMS Pinafore, The Yeoman of the Guard, 1968; has also directed Romeo and Juliette and Martha for the San Francisco Opera Company, 1961; Mr Gilbert, Mr Sullivan, and Mr Green for Playhouse in the Park, Philadelphia, 1961; The Matchmaker, 1961, and The Crucible, 1962, for Fred Miller's, Milwaukee, Wisconsin; for the Pacific Conservatory of the Performing Arts, The Mikado, 1974, Peer Gynt, 1975, Ah Wilderness!, Showboat, 1977, and Hamlet, 1979; taught classical and operatic acting at Circle in the Square Theatre School, 1961–2; taught directing at Brooklyn College, 1962; received a Ford Foundation Grant for study, 1959; has translated Ibsen's Wild Duck, An Enemy of the People, A Doll's House, Pillars of the Community, The Master Builder, Rosmersholm, and Peer Gynt; Chekhov's Uncle Vanya, and The Three Sisters.

Address: c/o The American Conservatory Theatre, 450 Geary Street, San Francisco, Calif 94102. *Tel:* 415–771 3880.

FLETCHER, Bramwell, actor

b Bradford, Yorks, 20 Feb 1904; *s* of Benjamin Fletcher and his wife Jean (Scott); *e* Crediton Grammar School; *m* (1) Helen Chandler (mar dis); (2) Diana Barrymore (mar dis); (3) Susan Robinson (mar dis); (4) Lael Wertenbaker; formerly with an insurance company in London.

Made his first appearance on the stage at Stratford-on-Avon, with the Memorial Company, May 1927; first appearance in London, at the Court Theatre, 4 Oct 1927, as Col Prince Yashvil in Paul I; Lyric, Jan 1928, played Oscar Nordholm in Sauce for the Gander; Arts, July 1928, and Kingsway, Aug 1928, Martin in Thunder on the Left; Duke of York's, Jan 1929, Harold Marquess in The Chinese Bungalow; Comedy, June 1929, Jimmie Chard in The Devil in the Cheese; made his first appearance on the New York stage, at the Sam H Harris Theatre, 27 Sept 1929, as Kent Heathcote in Scotland Yard; at the Cort, NY, Dec 1932, played Ray Fanshawe in Red Planet; Ethel Barrymore, Oct 1933, Colin Derwent in Ten Minute Alibi; Henry Miller, May 1934, Simon More in These Two; National, Oct 1934, the Dreamer

in Within the Gates; Cort, Apr 1935, Dick Shale in The Dominant Sex; Booth, Jan 1936, Hsieh Ping-Kuel in Lady Precious Stream; Shaftesbury, London, May 1936, Rodney Bevan in Boy Meets Girl; on returning to America, toured, 1937–8, in To-Night at 8.30, playing the Noël Coward parts; Playhouse, NY, Apr 1938, played Arnold Champion-Cheney in The Circle; Central City and Denver, Colorado, July 1938, Ruy Blas and Don Caesar in Ruy Blas; Playhouse, NY, Dec 1938, Mr Prior in Outward Bound; Plymouth, Nov 1939, Baron Max in Margin for Error; Henry Miller, Jan 1941, Jacob Wait in Eight O'clock, Tuesday; Shubert, Mar 1941, Louis Dubedat in The Doctor's Dilemma; Belasco, Jan 1944, Captain Sutton in Storm Operation; toured, 1944, and at the Ethel Barrymore, NY, Jan 1945, played Maxim de Winter in Rebecca; in Chicago, 1946–7, appeared in The Greatest of These; Dennis, Mass, 1947, played Richard Brinsley Sheridan in The Lady Maria; Booth, NY, Oct 1950, appeared as the Duke of Bristol in The Day After Tomorrow; also toured, 1950, as President Merrill in Goodbye My Fancy; ANTA Playhouse, NY, May 1951, played Collins in Getting Married; in summer theatres, 1951, played Matthew Store in Told to the Children; National, NY, Apr 1952, Mr Burgess in Candida; Westport Country Playhouse, July 1952, Mr Doolittle in Pygmalion; National, Feb 1953, Alick Wylie in Maggie; New York City Center, Feb 1953, and at the Ethel Barrymore, Mar 1953, played Lord Summerhays in Misalliance; also toured, 1953, in Pygmalion, again appearing as Doolittle; toured, 1954, as David Slater in The Moon Is Blue; also appeared at the Olney Theatre, Maryland, as Sir Henry Harcourt-Reilly in The Cocktail Party, and The Duke of Altair in Venus Observed; New York City Center, Feb 1955, played Gavin Leon Andree in The Wisteria Trees; John Golden, March 1956, Marechal François de Sevres in Little Glass Clock; Martin Beck, May 1956, Clement of Metz in The Lovers; summer stock, 1956, Aeneas Posket in Posket's Family Skeleton; between 1956 and 1961 played Henry Higgins in My Fair Lady at the Mark Hellinger, NY, over two hundred times; 4th Street, Apr 1962, played Ulric Brendel in Rosmersholm; Theatre Four, Nov 1962, played Leonid Andreyevich Gayef in The Cherry Orchard; ANTA, Dec 1962, played one performance of one-man show Parnassus, and subsequently toured USA for nearly two years; Goodman, Chicago, Oct 1963, Mephistopheles in Faust; Gate, Dublin, Dec 1964, author and appeared as Bernard Shaw in The Bernard Shaw Story; played this last role in its American première in Washington, DC, Feb 1965; Westport Country Playhouse, Conn, May 1965, played Andrew Undershaft in Major Barbara and Doolittle in Pygmalion, and again appeared in The Bernard Shaw Story; East 74th Street, NY, Nov 1965, again appeared in this one-man show and toured in it for three years under the auspices of Sol Hurok; Goodman, Chicago, Oct 1968, played Molière's The Miser; collaborated with Lael Wertenbaker on the Educational Theatre Project Operation Gadfly, a play for performance in colleges under the auspices of National Endowment for the Humanities, 1970; toured USA for National Humanities as lecturer and actor for three years; Loeb, Boston, Mass, Aug 1974, Lord Summerhays in Misalliance; Kansas City, Mo, Playhouse, Aug 1975, Speaker of the House in In the Well of the House; awarded Cockefair Grant by Univ of Missouri as Distinguished Theatre Artist of the year, 1975; Loeb, Boston, Feb 1976, again played Bernard Shaw in a revised version of his one-man show, and subsequently toured; entered films, 1928; has appeared in over two hundred leading roles in television plays.

Recreations: Walking and portrait painting. *Address:* RFD, Marlborough, New Hampshire. *Tel:* 603–827 3771.

FLETCHER, Robert (*né* Robert Fletcher Wyckoff), designer
b Cedar Rapids, Iowa, 29 Aug 1923; *s* of Harry Wyckoff, the actor known as Leon Ames, and his wife Mary Fletcher (Keahey); *e* Abraham Lincoln High School, Council Bluffs, Iowa, Harvard University, University of Iowa.

First production was at the Little Theatre, Council Bluffs, Iowa, 1938, when he directed and designed Night Must Fall; served as bombardier in the US Army Air Force, 1942–4; made his New York début as an actor at the National, 31 Oct 1944, as a Swiss Guard in Embezzled Heaven; Coronet, Dec 1945, Salarino in Dream Girl; Morosco, Nov 1950, Young Fashion in The Relapse; was a founding member of the Board of Directors of the Brattle Theatre, Cambridge, Massachusetts, 1947–52, and designed costumes for 87 productions for that company; designed sets for the New England Opera Company's productions of Carmen, La Boheme, and Pique Dame (The Queen of Spades); his first NY designs were for costumes for The Little Blue Light, produced at the ANTA, 29 Apr 1951; has since designed the costumes for La Gloire (ballet), 1952; Love's Labour's Lost, Misalliance, 1953; Walk Tall, and décor and costumes for Camp Tamiment, Pennsylvania, 1954; Othello, Henry IV, Part I, Julius Caesar, The Tempest, 1955; King Lear, The Abduction from the Seraglio (also sets, opera), Saint Joan, 1956; The Beggar's Opera, The Unicorn, the Gorgon, and the Manticore (ballet), Don Carlo (also sets, Chicago Lyric Opera), 1957; The Play of Daniel, Voyage to the Moon (Boston Opera Company), L'Assassinio nella Cathedrale (also sets, opera), The Firstborn, 1958; Taboo Revue (also sets and production), The Geranium Hat (sets only), Ole! (also sets), and sets and costumes for operas including The Rake's Progress, Cosi Fan Tutte, Thais, and La Gioconda, 1959; sets and costumes for The Tempest, Julius Caesar, Stratford, Connecticut, Helen of Troy, Cambridge Drama Festival, Massachusetts, Farewell, Farewell, Eugene, 1960; costumes for A Family Affair, The Happiest Girl in the World, How to Succeed in Business Without Really Trying, 1961; Dear Liar, A Pair of Pairs, Half Past Wednesday, The Moon Besieged, Nowhere to Go But Up, Little Me, 1962; Best Foot Forward (also sets), A Midsummer Night's Dream (also sets), Don Giovanni (also sets, New York City Opera), Palace (Robert Joffrey Ballet), 1963; Foxy, Icecapades, High Spirits (also sets and co-produced), 1964; co-produced The Queen and the Rebels, 1965; Walking Happy, 1966; A Midsummer Night's Dream (Stratford, Connecticut), L'Histoire du Soldat (Spoleto Festival, sets and costumes), 1967; Hadrian VII, NY, 1969; Borstal Boy, Cry for Us All, The Madwoman of Chaillot (sets only), Dear Love (décor, lighting), 1970; has worked from 1969 with the American Conservatory Theatre in San Francisco as actor and later as costume designer of productions including Oedipus Rex, Hamlet, Rosencrantz and Guildenstern are Dead, Hadrian VII, The Relapse, St Joan, The Tempest, and An Enemy of the People; Johnny Johnson (sets) and also co-produced, Cyrano de Bergerac, Private Lives, The Taming of the Shrew, Richard III, The Matchmaker (costumes only); designed sets and costumes for the San Francisco Ballet's production of Cinderella; How to Succeed in Business Without Really Trying (Los Angeles), 1975; costumes for Pal Joey '78 (LA), 1978; staff designer for NBCTV, 1954–60 and has since designed regularly for television.
Recreations: Painting, book collecting. *Address:* 1314 North Hayworth Avenue, Los Angeles, Calif 90046.

FLINT-SHIPMAN, Veronica, theatre and producing manager
b Walton-on-Thames, Surrey, 9 Mar 1931; *d* of Eustace William Flint and his wife Catherine Campbell (Insoll); *m* Gerald Flint-Shipman; trained as a dancer at the Legat School of Russian Ballet.

Owner and licensee of the Phoenix Theatre, London, which she took over in 1967; here she has presented a number of her productions, including: Winnie-the-Pooh, Dec 1974, which she also directed and choreographed; co-presented the Phoenix Theatre Season, 1976, including: I Do, I Do, 13 Rue de l'Amour, and Bus Stop; productions she has presented or co-presented elsewhere include: Night Must Fall (tour), 1968; Mother Adam (tour), 1970; Trelawny, 1972; Rock Nativity (tour), Edith Evans and Friends, Play Mas, 1974; is a director of her husband's film company, Impact Films Ltd; member, Society of West End Theatre.
Hobbies: Collecting glass, and first editions of children's books. *Address:* Phoenix Theatre, Charing Cross Road, London WC2. *Tel:* 01–836 7041.

FOCH, Nina, actress
b Leyden, Holland, 20 Apr 1924; *d* of Dirk Fock and his wife Consuelo (Flowerton); *e* Columbia University, and Parsons Art School; *m* (1) James Lipton (mar dis); (2) Dennis Brite (mar dis); (3) Michael Dewell; studied for the stage at the American Academy of Dramatic Arts.

Made her first appearance on the stage, 1941, touring with Charles Butterworth in Western Union, Please; made her first appearance on the New York stage, at the Booth Theatre, 4 Feb 1947, as Mary McKinley in John Loves Mary; toured, 1949, as Lizzie McKaye in The Respectful Prostitute; Empire, NY, Oct 1949, played Countess Olivia in Twelfth Night; Albany, NY, Mar 1950, appeared in Congressional Baby; Fulton, Apr 1950, played Dynamene in A Phoenix Too Frequent; in summer theatres, 1950, appeared in The Philadelphia Story, and Light Up the Sky; National, Dec 1950, played Cordelia in King Lear; American Shakespeare Festival Theatre, Stratford, Connecticut, June and July 1956, Isabella in Measure for Measure and Katharine in The Taming of the Shrew; appeared in the last two roles at the Phoenix, NY, in Jan and Feb 1957; Eugene O'Neill, Apr 1960, Jane in A Second String; has also played in summer stock; at the University of California in Los Angeles, 1960, played Masha in The Three Sisters, in 1961, appeared in the revue USA, in 1962, appeared in Brecht on Brecht, in 1965, played Freda Lawrence in I Rise in Flames Cried the Phoenix, Frances in Windows; directed the National Repertory Theatre production of Ways and Means from Tonight at 8.30, 1967; associate producer for the Inaugural Night reopening of Ford's Theatre in Washington, 1968; Seattle Repertory, Washington, 1972, The Wife in All Over; same company, 1974, Madame Arkadina in The Seagull; has taught extensively, serving on the faculty of Univ of Southern Cal as Adjunct Professor, 1965–6 Professor, 1966–7; Adjunct Professor, 1978–80; Artist in Residence, Univ of North Carolina, 1965–6 Univ of Ohio, 1966, California Institute of Technology, 1969; 1971 served on the faculty of the Centre of Advanced Film Studies of the American Film Institute 1971–4, and on the Senior Faculty, 1974–7; conducts the Nina Foch Studio in Hollywood; member of the Board of Governors of the Academy of Television Arts and Sciences since 1975; entered films 1944, appearing in some 50 films, including Executive Suite, The Ten Commandments, An American in Paris, Spartacus, Such Good Friends (1971), Mahagony (1976), etc; associate director of The Diary of Anne Frank (1959); has also, since 1947, appeared frequently on television.
Address: c/o Actors Equity Association, 165 West 46th Street, New York, NY 10036; and PO Box 1884, Beverly Hills, Calif 90213.

FONDA, Henry, actor
b Grand Island, Nebraska, 16 May 1905; *s* of William Brace

Fonda and his wife Herberta (Jaynes); *e* University of Minnesota; *m* (1) Margaret Sullavan (mar dis); (2) Frances Seymour Brokaw (dec); (3) Susan Blanchard (mar dis); (4) Afdera Franchetti (mar dis); (5) Shirlee Mae Adams.

Gained his early experience at the Omaha Community Playhouse, Omaha, Nebraska, where he made his first appearance, Sept 1925, as Ricky in You and I; played stock seasons with the University Players, West Falmouth, Cape Cod, 1928; made his first appearance on the New York stage at the Guild Theatre, 25 Nov 1929, walking on in The Game of Life and Death; subsequently played stock seasons at West Falmouth, Washington, Philadelphia and Baltimore; at the Harris Theatre, NY, Oct 1932, played Eustace in I Loved You Wednesday; Times Square, Mar 1933, the Gentleman in Forsaking All Others; Fulton, Mar 1934, appeared in New Faces; 46th Street, Oct 1934, made a great success when he played Dan Harrow in The Farmer Takes a Wife; 46th Street, Sept 1937, Hayden Chase in Blow Ye Winds; during World War II served in the US Navy in the South Pacific and was awarded a Bronze Star and a Presidential Citation; at the Alvin, Feb 1948, appeared as Lieut Roberts in Mister Roberts, which he played over two years; Alvin, Dec 1951, Charles Gray in Point of No Return; Plymouth, Jan 1954, Lieut Barney Greenwald in The Caine Mutiny Court Martial; Booth, Jan 1958, played Jerry Ryan in Two for the Seesaw; Morosco, Dec 1959, John in Silent Night, Lonely Night; Ethel Barrymore, Dec 1960, Parker Ballantyne in Critic's Choice; Ethel Barrymore, Feb 1962, Charles Wertenbaker in A Gift of Time; Morosco, Oct 1965, Jim Bolton in Generation; ANTA, Nov 1969, played the Stage Manager in Our Town; Mark Taper Forum, Los Angeles, Apr 1971, Abraham Lincoln in The Trial of A Lincoln, and subsequently toured; Ahmanson, Los Angeles, Nov 1971, directed The Caine Mutiny Court Martial; Eisenhower, Washington, DC, Jan 1972, Joe in The Time of Your Life, and subsequently toured; Helen Hayes, Mar 1974, title-role of Clarence Darrow; this run interrupted by his hospitalization, then toured; Minskoff, Mar 1975, again played Clarence Darrow and again toured; Imperial, 9 Mar 1975, appeared in a Gala Tribute to Joshua Logan; Royal Alexandra, Toronto, Canada, Apr 1975, played Clarence Darrow; made his London stage début at the Piccadilly, 17 July 1975, as Clarence Darrow; Eisenhower Theater, Washington DC, Dec 1977, Justice Daniel Snow in First Monday in October; repeated his performance at the Majestic, Oct 1978, and on tour, 1979; entered films, 1935, and has since appeared in innumerable pictures, including The Trail of the Lonesome Pine, Young Mr Lincoln, Grapes of Wrath, The Lady Eve, The Male Animal, Jezebel, The Oxbow Incident, My Darling Clementine, The Fugitive, Mister Roberts, The Wrong Man, Twelve Angry Men, Advise and Consent, Fail Safe, The Best Man, Cheyenne Social Club, There Was a Crooked Man, Sometimes a Great Notion, etc, most recently in Midway, 1976; has appeared on television as the marshal in his own series *The Deputy* and in *The Smith Family*, and also starred in several special programs, notably as Clarence Darrow, 1975; received a special 'Tony' Award, 1979.

Hobby: Photography. *Address:* c/o John Springer Associates, Inc, 667 Madison Avenue, New York City.

FONDA, Jane, actress
b New York City, 21 Dec 1937; *d* of Henry Fonda and his wife Frances Seymour (Brokaw); *e* Brentwood Town and Country School, Emma Willard's School, and Vassar College; *m* (1) Roger Vadim (mar dis); (2) Tom Hayden;

prepared for the stage with Lee Strasberg at the Actors Studio.

First appeared on the stage at the Omaha Playhouse, Omaha, Nebraska, 1954 as Nancy Stoddard in The Country Girl; played in stock as Patricia Stanley in The Male Animal, 1956, and Patty O'Neill in The Moon Is Blue, 1959; Westport Country Playhouse, Conn, July 1960, Jacky Durrant in No Concern of Mine; made her NY début at the Cort, Feb 1960, as Toni Newton in There Was a Little Girl; Music Box, Oct 1960, played Norma Brown in Invitation to a March; Lyceum, Oct 1962, Tish Stanford in The Fun Couple; Hudson, Mar 1963, Madeline Arnold in a revival of Strange Interlude; toured US Army bases and abroad in an anti-war revue FTA (Free the Army), 1970–1; first entered films, 1960, in Tall Story, and has since appeared in A Walk on the Wild Side, Period of Adjustment, Les Félins, La Ronde, Barbarella, They Shoot Horses, Don't They? Klute, for which she received the Academy Award, 1971, Julia, California Suite, Coming Home, The Electric Horseman, etc; first appeared on television in 1961 in A String of Beads.

Address: John Springer Associates, Inc, 667 Madison Avenue, New York, NY.

FOOTE, Horton, dramatic author
b Wharton, Texas, 14 Mar; *s* of Al H Foote and his wife Hallie (Brooks); *m* Lillian Vallish.

Formerly an actor; produced his first play, Texas Town, at the Weidman Studio, New York, 1941; author of the following plays: Out of My House, 1942; Only the Heart, 1944; Celebration (one-act), 1948; The Chase, 1952; The Trip to Bountiful, 1953; The Traveling Lady, 1954; John Turner Davis (one-act), The Midnight Caller (one-act), 1958; book for the musical Gone with the Wind, from the novel by Margaret Mitchell, produced at Drury Lane, London, May 1972, and the Dorothy Chandler Pavilion, Los Angeles, Aug 1973; since 1947 has written many plays for television, including The Trip to Bountiful, Young Lady of Property, Death of the Old Man, The Dancers, Flight, The Old Man, Tomorrow, The Night of the Storm, The Gambling Heart, etc; received the Academy Award and the Writers Guild of America Screen Award for his script To Kill a Mockingbird, 1962; wrote the film Tomorrow, 1972; member of the Texas Institute of Letters.

Address: The Dramatists Guild, 234 West 44th Street, New York, NY 10036.

FORBES, Brenda, actress
b London, 14 Jan 1909; *d* of E J Taylor and his wife Mary (Forbes); *m* (1) Frederic Voight (dec); (2) Merrill Shepard.

Made her first appearance on the stage at the Lyric Theatre, Hammersmith, with the Old Vic company, 12 Sept 1927, walking on in The Taming of the Shrew; at the Old Vic, Feb 1928, appeared in a number of productions; made her first appearance in New York, at the Empire, 9 Feb 1931, as Wilson in The Barretts of Wimpole Street, with Katharine Cornell; she remained in this company four years, and toured, 1932, in The Barretts of Wimpole Street; Belasco, Dec 1932, played Marina in Lucrece; toured 1933–4, as Lady Montague in Romeo and Juliet, Prossy Garnett in Candida, and appeared at the Martin Beck, NY, Dec 1934, as Lady Montague in Romeo and Juliet; Feb 1935, again played Wilson in The Barretts of Wimpole Street; Apr 1935, Beryl Hodgson in The Flowers of the Forest; Music Box, Nov 1935, Charlotte Lucas in Pride and Prejudice; Mansfield, Nov 1936, Jemima Barrett in Black Limelight; Guild, Mar 1937, Lisbet Skirving in Storm over Patsy; Broadhurst, Jan 1938, Mistress Binns in Y Obedient Husband; Martin Beck, Feb

1938, Elfrida von Zedlitz-Wetzel in Save Me the Waltz; Mercury, Apr 1938, Nurse Guinness in Heartbreak House; Booth, Feb 1939, appeared in One for the Money, and Feb 1940, in Two for the Show; Guild, Apr 1941, Mrs Banner in Yesterday's Magic; Shubert, May 1942, again played Prossy in Candida; Morosco, Sept 1942, Mrs Lane in Morning Star; Cort, Jan 1944, Miss Tinkham in Suds in Your Eye; Ethel Barrymore, Mar 1945, again appeared as Wilson in The Barretts of Wimpole Street; Adelphi, NY, Mar 1946, appeared in Three to Make Ready; Martin Beck, Nov 1950, played Isabella's Mother in Ring Round the Moon; toured, 1952, as Milly Tower in Jane (The Foreign Language); Coronet, NY, Nov 1954, played Lady Harriet Ripley in Quadrille; Henry Miller's, Oct 1956, Mabel Crosswaithe in The Reluctant Debutante; toured California, 1957, as Sheila Broadbent in The Reluctant Debutante; Drury Lane, Chicago, Jan 1963, Valerie Clayton in The Camel Bell; Goodman, Chicago, Apr 1963, Mrs Malaprop in The Rivals; Goodman, Chicago, Mar 1965, directed The Barretts of Wimpole Street; Helen Hayes, Oct 1966, played Trilbe Costello in The Loves of Cass McGuire; George Abbott, Jan 1968, Lady Vale in Darling of the Day; narrated Jeanne d'Arc au Bûcher for the Chicago Symphony Orchestra, 1968; Goodman, Chicago, 1970, played Lady Utterwood in Heartbreak House; Goodman, 1971, Mrs Bracknell in The Importance of Being Earnest; toured, Sept 1973–Jan 1974, as Letty Harnham in The Day After the Fair; Shubert, NY, Apr 1975, Mrs Culver in The Constant Wife; Arena, Houston, Texas, 1975, Lady Julia in The Cocktail Party; St James, NY, Mar 1976, Mrs Higgins in My Fair Lady; Goodman, Chicago, Nov 1977, played for a week in Side by Side by Sondheim; first appeared in films, 1940; has appeared on television, notably in Cocteau's La Voix Humaine, 1971.
Address: Rock Ridge, Alpine, New Jersey 07620.

FORBES, Meriel, actress
b London, 13 Sept 1913; *d* of Frank Forbes-Robertson and his wife Honoria (McDermot); *e* Eastbourne, Brussels, and Paris; *m* (Sir) Ralph Richardson.
Made her first appearance on the stage, in the provinces, in her father's company, as Mrs de Hooley in The Passing of the Third Floor Back, 1931; in 1931, joined the Dundee Repertory company; made her first appearance in London, at the Gate Theatre, 14 Sept 1931, as Simone D'Ostignac in Porcupine Point; Birmingham Repertory Theatre Company, 1931–2; toured in Musical Chairs, summer, 1932; Palace, London, 1933, understudied and played Kitty in Dinner at Eight; Q, Sept 1933, Joan Taylor in First Episode; Lyric, Oct 1933, Diana Mauteby in This Side Idolatry; Vaudeville, Dec 1933, Mary Wellman in Angel; Comedy, Jan 1934, Joan Taylor in First Episode; Shaftesbury, May 1934, Daisy Dowling in The Dark Tower; Duke of York's, Apr 1935, Dae Beldon in . . . And a Woman Passed By; Queen's, Mar 1936, Stella Hardcastle in Red Night; Drury Lane, May 1936, Princess Yraine in Rise and Shine; Haymarket, Aug 1936, Daisy in The Amazing Dr Clitterhouse; Whitehall, Dec 1937, Renée la Lune in I Killed the Count; Old Vic, Dec 1938, Julia in The Rivals; Strand, Apr 1940, Crystal Allen in The Women; during 1940–1, worked in VAD; joined Norman Marshall's company 1943, playing Milly Smith in A Soldier for Christmas, and Muriel Eden in The Gay Lord Quex; Wyndham's, Feb 1944, again played Milly in A Soldier for Christmas; Wyndham's, Apr 1948, Katerina Fantina in Royal Circle; Duchess, Dec 1949, Elizabeth Imbrie in The Philadelphia Story; Wyndham's, Mar 1950, Peggy Dobson in Home at Seven; New, June 1952, Patricia Smith in The Millionairess; Globe, Mar 1953, Lydia Truscott in The White

Carnation; with her husband toured Australia, 1955, in Separate Tables and The Sleeping Prince; Coronet, New York, Jan 1957, played Mlle de Sainte-Euverte in The Waltz of the Toreadors; St Martin's, London, Feb 1958, Mamie in Roseland; Haymarket, Oct 1958 followed Wendy Hiller as Isobel Cherry in Flowering Cherry, and subsequently toured with the play; Royal Court, 1959, played the Duchess of Clausonnes in Look After Lulu, transferring with the production to the New, Sept 1959; Haymarket, Apr 1962, played Lady Sneerwell in a revival of The School for Scandal, subsequently appearing in the same production at the Majestic, NY, Jan 1963; Royal, Brighton, Feb 1964, played Titania in A Midsummer Night's Dream, prior to touring South America, and also appearing in Lisbon, Madrid, Paris, and Athens, for The British Council, in the same production; toured Australia, 1973, and N America, 1974, as Lady Boothroyd in Lloyd George Knew My Father; entered films, 1934, her latest being Oh! What A Lovely War; played Lady Constance in the television series Blandings Castle.
Hobby: Serendipity. *Address:* 1 Chester Terrace, Regents Park, London, NW1. *Tel:* 01–486 5063.

FORD, Ruth, actress
b Hazelhurst, Mississippi, July 1920; *d* of Charles Lloyd Ford and his wife Gertrude (Cato); *e* University of Mississippi; *m* (1) Peter van Eyck (mar dis); (2) Zachary Scott (dec); formerly a photographer's model.
First appeared on the stage at the Ivoryton Playhouse, Conn, 1937, as Nanny in Ways and Means; joined Orson Welles's Mercury Theatre Company and first appeared in New York in Jan 1938, as Jane in The Shoemaker's Holiday; Mercury, Nov 1938, played Rosalie in Danton's Death; City Center, Nov 1939, Polly in Swingin' the Dream; Barbizon Plaza, Oct 1940, Irma Szabo in The Glass Slipper; US tour, 1946, appeared as Roxane in Cyrano de Bergerac; Biltmore, NY, Nov 1946, Estelle in No Exit; Ethel Barrymore, Nov 1947, played Yolan in This Time Tomorrow; at Krönborg Castle, Elsinore, Denmark, June 1949, played Ophelia in Hamlet; Biltmore, NY, Dec 1949, Deborah Pomfret in Clutterbuck; Brattle Theatre, Cambridge, Mass, 1950, again played Estelle in No Exit; ANTA, NY, Jan 1951, Martirio in The House of Bernarda Alba; Brattle Theatre, Cambridge, Mass, 1951, played leading roles in Macbeth, The Failures, A Phoenix Too Frequent, and Six Characters in Search of an Author; Fulton, Oct 1955, played Pia in Island of Goats; Boston Arts Festival, 1955, Sabina in The Skin of Our Teeth; Phoenix, off-Broadway, Feb 1956, played Mrs X in The Stronger, and Kristin in Miss Julie (double-bill); made her London début at the Royal Court, Nov 1957, as Mrs Gowan Stevens (Temple Drake) in Requiem for a Nun; John Golden, NY, Jan 1959, appeared in the same part and play; Festival of Two Worlds, Spoleto, Italy, summer 1962, played Mommie in The American Dream; Brooks Atkinson, Jan 1964, Witch of Capri in The Milk Train Doesn't Stop Here Anymore; Palm Beach, Feb 1965, Dorothy Cleves in Any Wednesday; Cherry Lane, off-Broadway, Mar 1965, appeared as Virginia Varnum in Lovely; Alvin, Sept 1966, Hattie Loomis in Dinner at Eight; Biltmore, Nov 1967, Judith Hastings in The Ninety-Day Mistress; Berkshire Festival, Stockbridge, Mass, 1969, played in Hunger and Thirst; Martin Beck, Nov 1971, Verena Talbo in The Grass Harp; Theatre de Lys, Oct 1972, Comtesse de Saint-Fond in Madame de Sade; Bucks County Playhouse, New Hope, Pa, Jan 1973, Lorraine in A Breeze from the Gulf, and repeated this part at the Eastside Playhouse, NY, Oct 1973; Mark Taper Forum, Los Angeles, Cal, May 1974, played Clarissa Halley-Yshott in The Charlatan; Barrymore, Oct 1976,

played a number of roles in Poor Murderer; Goodman, Chicago, Nov 1977, Mme Arkadina in The Seagull; McCarter, NJ, Nov 1978, Juliana Bordereau in The Aspern Papers; first appeared in films in 1941, and notable pictures include Wilson, Dragonwyck, Keys of the Kingdom, Act One, Play It As It Lays (1972), etc.

Favourite parts: Mrs Gowan Stevens (Temple Drake), Estelle, and Lorraine. *Recreations:* Collecting art, reading, talking, listening to music. *Address:* 1 West 72nd Street, New York, NY 10023. *Tel:* TR 3–5452.

FORSYTH, Bruce (*né* Bruce Forsyth Johnson), actor
b Edmonton, London, 22 Feb 1928; *s* of John Forsyth Johnson and his wife Florence Ada (Pocknell); *e* Latymer Grammar School, Edmonton; *m* (1) Olivia Calvert (mar dis); (2) Anthea Redfern; trained as a dancer by Dougie Ascott and Buddy Bradley.

He made his debut at the Theatre Royal, Bilston, Staffs, in 1942 as Boy Bruce in a variety act; has worked principally in variety, including a period as a comic at the Windmill, 1949–51; London Palladium, 1958, played Presto the Jester in the pantomime The Sleeping Beauty; at the Cambridge, Nov 1964, played seven leading parts in Little Me; Piccadilly, Oct 1969, Charlie in Birds on the Wing; New London, Oct 1975, appeared in his own one-man show, also touring; Her Majesty's, Mar 1978, Fred Limelight in The Travelling Music Show; first appearance in New York, Winter Garden, 12 June 1979, in his one-man show Bruce Forsyth on Broadway; appears regularly in summer shows and pantomime; first film, Star, 1967; subsequent appearances include Hieronymus Merkin and Bedknobs and Broomsticks; has made numerous television appearances, including a three-year spell compering *Sunday Night at the London Palladium*, and his own series, *The Generation Game* and *Play Your Cards Right*.

Recreation: Golf. *Address:* c/o London Management, 235–241 Regent Street, London W1A 2JT.

FORSYTHE, Henderson, actor and director
b Macon, Missouri, 11 Sept 1917; *s* of Cecil Proctor Forsythe and his wife Mary Katherine (Henderson); *e* Culver-Stockton College and State University of Iowa (MA 1940); *m* Dorothea M Carlson.

Made his professional stage début at the Erie Summer Theatre, Point Chautauqua, New York, Aug 1940, as Dickie Reynolds in Accent on Youth; same theatre, 1940, Geoffrey Cole in Vinegar Tree, and Prince Rudolph in Candlelight; Cleveland, Ohio, Playhouse, Sept 1940, played the Reporter in Margin for Error, and subsequently Spencer Grant in Here Today, Cupid Holliday in We Were Here First, and, in 1941, Tim Shields in Tony Draws a Horse, Paul Rambusch in Middletown Mural, and James in Family Portrait; served in the US Army, 1941–6, reaching the rank of Captain; Erie, Pennsylvania, Playhouse, 1946, played Rough in Angel Street, Harry Archer in Kiss and Tell, Benjamin Griggs in But Not Goodbye, and, in 1947, Ernest Friedman in Design for Living, Tommy Turner in The Male Animal, Norman in Out of the Frying Pan, Dr Shelby in Blind Alley, Horace Giddens in The Little Foxes, and various roles in My Sister Eileen; Cain Park, Cleveland Heights, Ohio, summer 1947, Reverend Jones in The Barber and the Cow, Grandpa Vanderhof in You Can't Take It with You, Mr Webb in Our Town, Clark Redfield in Dream Girl, and played in the revue Sing Out, Sweet Land; returned to Erie, Pennsylvania, Sept 1947, and played Albert Kummer in Dear Ruth, Kingsley in Stage Door, Uncle Harry in the play of that name, Dennis Curtin in Anything Can Happen, and, in 1948, Dr Ferguson

in Men in White, David Bellow in I Like It Here, Ned Farrar in Her Master's Voice, the title-role of The Late George Apley, and John in John Loves Mary; Cain Park, Cleveland Heights, 1948, Tchang in Lute Song, Prime Minister of China in The Reluctant Virgin, and Petruchio in The Taming of the Shrew, which also marked his directorial début; Erie Playhouse, Sept 1948, Grant Matthews in State of the Union, which he also directed, Dr Johnson in I Remember Mama, Professor Charles Burnett in Parlor Story, Kenneth Bixby in Goodbye Again, and, in 1949, Clark Redfield in Dream Girl, the Colonel in The Hasty Heart, Petruchio in The Taming of the Shrew, which he directed, the Doctor in Life with Father, Snowflake in Ruined by Drink, Bill Paige in The Voice of the Turtle; Erie Playhouse, 1949, Gen K C Davis in Command Decision, the Judge in Happy Birthday, Lance Corporal in See How They Run, Uncle Stanley in George Washington Slept Here, and, in 1950, Tommy Thurston in Two Blind Mice, directed The Cellar and the Well, Horatio Channing in Invitation to a Murder, Stephen Minch in Star Wagon, Father Moynihan in Jenny Kissed Me, the Colonel in Jacobowsky and the Colonel; made his New York acting and directing début at the ANTA, 10 Dec 1950, when he directed and played Mr Hubble in The Cellar and the Well; Erie Playhouse, 1951, Elwood P Dowd in Harvey, Matthew Cromwell in Strange Bedfellows, Clarke Storey in The Second Man, Jonah Goodman in The Gentle People, Macauley-Connor in The Philadelphia Story, Tom in The Glass Menagerie; Penn Playhouse, Meadville, Pennsylvania, 1951, Tommy Turner in The Male Animal, Elwood P Dowd in Harvey, and Nat in Ah, Wilderness!; Erie Playhouse, Oct 1951, Ed Devery in Born Yesterday, Curley in Green Grow the Lilacs, Bluntschli in Arms and the Man, and, in 1952, Mr Adams in Junior Miss, Jeff in The Curious Savage, directed The Women, Clarence Day in Life with Mother, Preston Mitchell in For Love or Money, Creon in Antigone, directed Charley's Aunt, Pappa Bonnard in The Happy Time, Stephen Wayne in First Lady, Henderson in Gramercy Ghost, Detective McLeod in Detective Story, Mr Brown in Let Us Be Gay, Derrick in Rip Van Winkle, and directed Montserrat; in 1953, Professor Pearson in The Velvet Glove, Clark Redfield in Dream Girl, Mister Roberts in the play of that name, Sam Stover in Apple of His Eye, Jason in Medea, Major Joppolo in A Bell for Adano, David Slater in The Moon Is Blue, Grandpa Vanderhof in You Can't Take It with You, Milo Alcott in Lo and Behold, and directed I Remember Mama; 1954, Sergeant Schultz in Stalag 17, the title-role in Father Malachy's Miracle, Walter Burns in Front Page, directed Be Your Age and As You Like It, Charles Colborn in Janie, Henderson in Bell, Book, and Candle, Malcolm Bryant in Point of No Return, Captain Ernest Caldwell in At War with the Army, and, in 1955, Howard Carol in Time Out for Ginger, O'Flingsley in Shadow and Substance, the Inspector in Dial M for Murder, Linus in Sabrina Fair, Professor Charles Burnett in Mother Was a Statesman, and He in The Fourposter; returned to NY, and at the Shakespearean Workshop, Jan 1956, played Friar Laurence in Romeo and Juliet; Circle in the Square, June 1956, took over from Conrad Bain as Larry in The Iceman Cometh; Music Box, Oct 1957, Ned Gates in Miss Lonelyhearts; Circle in the Square, Dec 1957, took over from Jason Robards, Jr, as Hickey in The Iceman Cometh; Actors Playhouse, Feb 1959, Peter Stockman in An Enemy of the People; Cambridge Drama Festival, Massachusetts, July 1959, Banquo in Macbeth; Provincetown Playhouse, May 1960, took over from Donald Davis as Krapp in Krapp's Last Tape; Gramercy Arts, June 1961, G Bernard Shaw in A Figleaf in Her Bonnet; Circle in the Square, May 1962, took over as Father

Francis in Someone from Assisi and the Father in Childhood; Cherry Lane, Nov 1962, Harry in The Collection; toured, 1962, as Chip Reegan in The Indoor Sport; Billy Rose, Jan 1964, took over from Arthur Hill as George in Who's Afraid of Virginia Woolf?; Actors Playhouse, May 1964, Bert in Dark Corners; Writers Stage, Dec 1964, Edward in A Slight Ache; Billy Rose, Oct 1965, Donald Crawford in The Right Honourable Gentleman; Shubert, Jan 1966, Cox, Miles, Doctor in Malcolm; Martin Beck, Sept 1966, Harry in A Delicate Balance; Booth, Oct 1967, Petey in The Birthday Party; Studio Arena, Buffalo, NY, 1967, Tobias in A Delicate Balance; ANTA, Feb 1970, William Chumley in Harvey; Helen Hayes, May 1970, Nelson Longhurst in The Engagement Baby; Public, Oct 1970, Dr Freytag in The Happiness Cage; Sheridan Square Playhouse, Feb 1971, Vladimir in Waiting for Godot; Eastside Playhouse, Mar 1972, Edward in In Case of Accident; Forum, Nov 1972, Austin in Not I; Playhouse II, Mar 1973, Norris Cummings in An Evening with the Poet-Senator; Alvin, Feb 1974, Priest in The Freedom of the City; Arena Stage, Washington, DC, Mar 1975, L D Alexander in The Last Meeting of the Knights of the White Magnolia; Kennedy Center, Apr 1976, repeated this last part and played Clarence Sickenger in The Oldest Living Graduate in a repertory of three plays called The Texas Trilogy; played these two parts at the Broadhurst, Sept 1976; Entermedia, Mar 1978, Sheriff Ed Earl Dodd in The Best Little Whorehouse in Texas, transferring with the show to the 46th Street, June 1978 and receiving a 'Tony' for his performance; appeared in the film Dead of Night, 1974; has appeared numerous times on television in various dramatic programs, including nineteen years on the serial *As the World Turns*.

Favourite parts: Larry, Hickey, Krapp, Harry in The Collection, George in Who's Afraid of Virginia Woolf? and Tobias in A Delicate Balance. *Recreations:* Wood carving, golf. *Address:* 204 Elm Street, Tenafly, New Jersey. *Tel:* 201–569 8737.

FORSYTHE, John (*né* John Lincoln Freund), actor
b Carney's Point, New Jersey, 29 Jan 1918; *s* of Samuel Jeremiah Freund and his wife Blanche Materson (Blohm); *e* University of North Carolina; *m* (1) Parker McCormick (mar dis); (2) Julie Warren; formerly a baseball commentator on the radio.

Made his first appearance on the stage at Clare Tree Major's Children's Theatre, Chappaqua, New York, Sept 1939, as the Captain in Dick Whittington and His Cat; first appeared in NY at the Plymouth, 22 Sept 1942, as Private Cootes in Vickie; Longacre, Nov 1942, played a Coast Guardsman in Yankee Point; 44th Street, Nov 1943, for the US Army Air Force, played in the revue Winged Victory; toured, 1944, as Bill Page in The Voice of the Turtle; 44th Street, 1945, played in Yellowjack; Belasco, 1946, played in Woman Bites Dog; Coronet, 1947, took over from Arthur Kennedy as Chris Keller in All My Sons; Biltmore, Feb 1947, Bill Renault, in It Takes Two; toured, 1949, in Mr Roberts, and took over in Oct 1950 from Henry Fonda in the title-role of this play at the Alvin, NY; Martin Beck, Oct 1953, Captain Fisby in The Teahouse of the August Moon; Westport Country Playhouse, Connecticut, June 1955, Detective McLeod in Detective Story; New York City Center, Dec 1956, directed Mister Roberts; Broadhurst, Mar 1968, Senator MacGruder in Weekend; Ahmanson, Los Angeles, Nov 1971, Lt Greenwald in The Caine Mutiny Court Martial; toured, summer 1972, in The Secretary Bird; first appeared in films, 1942, in Destination, Tokyo, and has since appeared in The Captive City, The Trouble with Harry, Madame X, In

Cold Blood, Topaz, And Justice for All (1979), etc; has appeared extensively on television in the series *Bachelor Father*, 1957 and subsequent years, Wuthering Heights, Teahouse of the August Moon, Miracle in the Rain, *To Rome with Love*, 1969–71; host-narrator of *World of Survival* since 1971, etc.

Favourite parts: Mr Roberts and Captain Fisby. *Recreations:* Sailing, sports, music, painting. *Address:* 11560 Bellagio Road, Los Angeles, Calif 90049.

FOSSE, Bob (*né* Robert Louis Fosse), director, choreographer, dancer, actor
b Chicago, Illinois, 23 June 1927; *s* of Cyril K Fosse and his wife Sarah (Stanton); *e* Amundsen High School, Chicago, and the American Theatre Wing (1947–8); *m* (1) Mary Ann Miles (mar dis); (2) Joan McCracken (mar dis); (3) Gwen Verdon (mar dis).

First appeared in vaudeville and cabaret at age 14; first legitimate part was in the chorus of the tour of Call Me Mister, 1948; toured, 1948–9, in the revue Make Mine Manhattan; made his New York début at the Royale, Jan 1950, in the revue Dance Me a Song; at the St James, May 1954, choreographed The Pajama Game; has since choreographed Damn Yankees, 1955; Bells Are Ringing, with Jerome Robbins, 1956; New Girl in Town, 1957; Redhead, which he also directed, 1959; City Center, May 1961, played Joey in a revival of Pal Joey; choreographed How to Succeed in Business Without Really Trying, 1961; Little Me, which he co-directed, 1962; City Center, May 1963, again played Joey in Pal Joey; made his London début Nov 1964, at the Cambridge when he choreographed Little Me; Palace, Jan 1966, directed and choreographed Sweet Charity; NY, 1972, directed and choreographed Pippin, for which he received two Antoinette Perry (Tony) Awards; Her Majesty's, London, 30 Oct 1973, directed and choreographed Pippin; NY, 1974, directed and choreographed Liza; 1975, adapted the book with Fred Ebb and directed and choreographed Chicago; 1977, directed and choreographed Dancin'; is Treasurer of the Society of Stage Directors and Choreographers; has received the Antoinette Perry (Tony) Award six other times: 1955, '56, '59, '63, '66, '78; first appeared in films in Give a Girl a Break, 1953, and has since played in The Affairs of Dobie Gillis, and Kiss Me, Kate; choreographed the films of The Pajama Game, Damn Yankees, and Sweet Charity; directed and choreographed the film Cabaret, 1972, for which he received the Academy Award; appeared as the Snake in the film The Little Prince, which he also choreographed, 1974; directed the film Lenny, 1974; directed and choreographed the television program Liza with a Z, for which he won the Emmy Award, 1973; has danced frequently on television as well as choreographed various musical and variety programs.

Address: Society of Stage Directors and Choreographers, 1501 Broadway, New York, NY 10019.

FOSTER, Barry, actor
b Beeston, Nottinghamshire; *s* of Charles Waterton Foster and his wife Dora (Dewey); *e* Southall County Grammar School; *m* Judith Shergold; formerly a plastics chemist; studied for the stage at the Central School of Speech and Drama.

Made his first appearance on the stage in Co Cork, Ireland, Aug 1952, when he played Lorenzo in The Merchant of Venice; first appeared in London at the New Theatre, Jan 1955, as The Electrician in The Night of the Ball; London Hippodrome, Apr 1955, played Hank Griffin in The Desperate Hours; Arts, Apr 1957, played Roger in The Balcony;

Comedy, Jan 1961, played Cornelius Christian in Fairy Tales of New York; at the same theatre, Feb 1962, played Paddy Kilmartin in My Place; Her Majesty's, June 1962, played the Guard-Angel in Judith; Royal Court, Sept 1962, appeared in the anthology Brecht on Brecht; New Arts, Jan 1963, played Dust in Next Time I'll Sing to You, subsequently transferring with the production to the Criterion, Feb 1963; Wimbledon, Sept 1963, played Ted in The Private Ear, and Julian in The Public Eye (double-bill), prior to making his first appearance in New York, at the Morosco, Oct 1963, in the same plays; Queen's, Dec 1964, played Ludovic in Maxibules; Mermaid, June 1966, Adhémar in Let's Get a Divorce, transferring to Comedy, July 1966; Nottingham Playhouse 1968–9 played King John and Macbeth among other parts; Duchess, Sept 1970, Stott in The Basement, and Willy in Tea Party; Criterion, May 1971, Bernard in After Haggerty; Comedy, July 1976, Damien Foxworth in Getting Away With Murder; Globe, Feb 1978, Barttelot in The Rear Column; toured with Cambridge Theatre Company, June 1979, in The Master Builder; Globe, Jan 1980, played Mo in Born in the Gardens; entered films, Nov 1955, and pictures include The Family Way, Twisted Nerve, Ryan's Daughter, The Wild Geese, etc; first appeared on television, 1956, and has since appeared in *Van der Valk,* Fall of Eagles, The Three Hostages, etc.

Favourite parts: Hamlet, Cornelius Christian, Oswald, and Deeley. *Recreations:* Music, riding, golf. *Address:* c/o Al Parker Ltd, 50 Mount Street, London, W1.

FOSTER, Frances, actress
b Yonkers, New York, 11 June 1924; *d* of George Henry Brown and his wife Helen Elizabeth; *e* High School, New York; *m* Robert S Foster (dec); trained for the stage at American Theatre Wing.

Made her professional debut at the City Center, NY, 2 Feb 1955, as Dolly May in The Wisteria Trees; Jan Hus, Sept 1956, Violet in Take a Giant Step; Martinique, 1958, took over the part of Tituba in The Crucible; Ethel Barrymore, Mar 1959, understudied and later played Ruth in A Raisin in the Sun; joined the Negro Ensemble Company, 1967, and has appeared in many of their productions since, notably in 1968 as Olive Leech in Summer of the Seventeenth Doll, Feb, Ogbo Aweri in Kongi's Harvest, Apr, and Lady in God is a (Guess What?), Dec; made her London debut in the last role at the Aldwych, May 1969, in the World Theatre Season; for NEC, 1970, played Luann Johnson in Brotherhood, Mar, and appeared in Akokawe, May; Vivian Beaumont, also May, Mrs Mi Tzu in The Good Woman of Setzuan; NEC, Jan 1971, title role in Rosalee Pritchett; De Lys, Mar 1971, Mrs Vanderkellan in Behold, Cometh the Vanderkellans; returning to NEC, played Alberta Warren in Sty of the Blind Pig, Nov, 1971; Mrs Drayton in A Ballet Behind the Bridge, Mar 1972; and Wilhelmina Brown in The River Niger, Dec 1972, transferring in this role to the Brooks Atkinson, Mar 1973; played Gremmar in First Breeze of Summer, May 1975, and transferred to the Palace, Jun; at the New Federal, 1978, appeared in Do, Lord, Remember Me, Mar, and as Aunt Duke and Potion Lady in Mahalia, Jun; again with NEC, Dec 1978, played Everelda Griffin in Nevis Mountain Dew, and Maumau in Daughters of the Mock; Jan, 1979, appeared in Everyman, and The Imprisonment of Obatala; films, since Take a Giant Step, 1958, include the Last Tenant and A Piece of the Action; TV work includes the mini-series King, and many other series including, recently, *All My Children*; has been artist-in-residence, CUNY; teaches acting at John Jay College Double Image Theatre.

Address: c/o Marge Fields, 250 West 57th Street, New York, NY 10019.

FOSTER, Gloria, actress
b Chicago, Ill, 15 Nov 1936; *e* Illinois State University; *m* Clarence Williams III.

Studied for the stage under Bella Itkin at the Goodman Theater, Chicago, where she played Medea, Oparre in Wingless Victory, and Sabina in The Skin of Our Teeth; also prepared at the University of Chicago Court Theater, where she played Jocasta in Oedipus Rex, Hecuba in The Trojan Women, and Volumnia in Coriolaus; Regent, Syracuse, New York, 1961, played Ruth in A Raisin in the Sun, and toured in this part, summer 1962; made her NY début at the Sheridan Square Playhouse, 31 Oct 1963, in In White America; Murray, Ravinia, Ill, 1965, played Andromache in The Trojan Women; Martinique, NY, Nov 1965, title-role in Medea; Longacre, Sept 1966, played in A Hand Is on the Gates; Vivian Beaumont, Dec 1966, title-role in Yerma; Goodman, Chicago, 1967, played in A Dream Play; Theatre de Lys, June 1967, Hippolyta and Titania in A Midsummer Night's Dream; Public Theater Annex, Feb 1972, Sister Son-Ji in a play by that name in a series of plays with the overall title Black Visions; Anspacher, Jan 1973, Madame Ranevskaya in The Cherry Orchard; Delacorte, Oct 1977, Clytemnestra in Agamemnon; Anspacher, Mar 1979, and Delacorte, June, Volumnia in Coriolanus; first appeared in films in The Cool World, 1963, and has since played in Nothing But a Man (1964), The Comedians (1967), Man and Boy (1972), etc; has appeared on television in Shakespeare's Women, and To All My Friends on Shore (1972), etc; received the Obie Award of the Village Voice for her performance in In White America, and also received the Vernon Rice Award from the Drama Desk for this part; received the Alpha Kappa Alpha Award, 1966, for outstanding contribution in the field of the arts.

Address: c/o Albert L Shedler, 225 West 34th St, New York, NY 10001. *Tel:* 212–564 6656.

FOSTER, Julia, actress
b Lewes, Sussex, 1942; *m* (1) Lionel Morton (mar dis); (2) Bruce Fogle.

Her early stage experience was with Brighton Repertory; London debut, Prince of Wales, Apr 1965, as Tricia Elliott in Travelling Light; Queen's, Mar 1969, played Geraldine Barclay in What the Butler Saw; Criterion, May 1970, Dixie in Flint; Playhouse, Nottingham, Oct 1970, the title part in Lulu, transferring to the Royal Court, Dec 1970, and the Apollo, Jan 1971; Globe, Mar 1972, Jenny Hogarth in Notes on a Love Affair; Lyric, Oct 1972, Anna in The Day After the Fair; New, Oxford, Sept 1974, title part in Saint Joan; King's Head, Mar 1977, Angie in Blind Date; New End, June 1978, Helen Dawes in The Singular Life of Albert Nobbs; Apollo, Apr 1979, Brigit 1 in Happy Birthday; Citizens, Glasgow, 1979, and Lyric, Hammersmith, Feb 1980, Giacinta in Country Life; Birmingham Rep, May 1980, appeared in After You With the Milk; films, since 1960, include Alfie and Half a Sixpence; television, since 1966, includes Crime and Punishment, and the series *Good Girl* and *Moll Flanders.*

Address: c/o ICM, 22 Grafton Street, London, W1.

FOSTER, Paul, dramatic author
b Penn's Grove, New Jersey, 1931; *e* Salem County Public Schools, Rutgers University and St John's University.

Is the author of the plays Hurrah for the Bridge, 1963; The Recluse, Balls, 1964; The Madonna in the Orchard, 1965; The Hessian Corporal, 1966; Tom Paine, 1967; Heimskringla or The Stoned Angels, 1969; Satyricon, 1970; Elizabeth I, 1971; Silver Queen Saloon, 1972; Marcus Brutus, 1974; co-founder and President since 1962 of La Mama Theater, where a number of his plays have had their first performance; his awards include the NY Drama Critics' Award, for Tom Paine, 1968.

Address: 236 East Fifth Street, New York, NY 10003.

FOX, William, actor
b Manila, Philippine Islands, 26 Jan 1911; *s* of Hubert Thornton-Fox and his wife Natividad (Perez-Rubio); *e* Haileybury College; *m* (1) Carol Rees (mar dis); (2) Patricia Hilliard; studied for the stage under Elsie Fogerty at the Central School of Dramatic Art, where he won the Gold Medal, 1930.

Made his first appearance on the stage at the Vaudeville Theatre, 30 Sept 1930, as Timothy Granger in The Bread-winner; Arts and New, Mar 1931, Lieut Banbury in OHMS; Ambassadors', June 1931, played John in A Knight Passed By; during 1931–2, toured with the London Comedy Actors and Greater London Players; Lyric, May 1932, played Gordon Whitehouse in Dangerous Corner; joined the Old Vic company for season 1932–3, playing among other parts, Orlando, Ferdinand, Florizel, etc; Queen's, Sept 1933, played Pietro in Night's Candles; Duke of York's, Nov 1933, Thomas Culpeper in The Rose Without A Thorn; Comedy, Jan 1934, Tony Wodehouse in First Episode; Savoy, June 1934, Charles Paton in Precipice; Vaudeville, Sept 1934, Walter Colt in Night Hawk; Duke of York's, Oct 1934, David Morley in Line Engaged; Queen's, Dec 1934, Adam Steele in Inside the Room; Comedy, Mar 1935, Feodor Ivanov in Delusion; New, May 1935, Bill Reid in Someone at the Door; Aldwych (for Repertory Players), Sept 1935, Eddie Royce in The World Waits; Lyric, Jan 1936, Richard in The Old and the Young; Comedy, Mar 1936, Gilbert Kent in Dusty Ermine; Savoy, Nov 1936, Arnold Zimmerman in Young Madame Conti, and made his first appearance on the New York Stage, at the Music Box Theatre, 31 Mar 1937, in the same part; on returning to London, appeared at the Royalty, Sept 1937, as Oliver Farrant in I Have Been Here Before; Playhouse, Dec 1938, played Det-Inspector Armitage in Under Suspicion; May 1939, toured as Count Endersdorf in Weep for the Spring; from Sept 1939 to Oct 1945, served in The London Irish Rifles, at home and abroad, reaching the rank of Major; associated in the foundation of the Reunion Theatre Association, for demobilized artists, 1946; reappeared on the stage at the Q, Jan 1946, as Richard Fletcher in Day After To-Morrow, and in Feb 1946, as Lord Dawlish in The Moonraker; Arts Theatre, Apr 1946, played Bill Laver in Exercise Bowler (also part-author); toured from Aug 1946, and then appeared at the St James's, Apr 1947, as Colin in Call Home the Heart; Nov 1947, Denzil in Private Enterprise; Feb 1948, Lester Ratcliffe in All This is Ended; Bath Festival, May 1948, Charles Surface in School for Scandal; Cambridge, Aug 1948, Capt Rex Fulljames, MP in Trouble in the House; Mercury, Jan 1949, appeared as Ligurio in Mandragola; Embassy, Sept 1949, John Masters in Rain Before Seven; Savoy, Jan 1950, Bruce Banning in Young Wives' Tale; joined the Shakespeare Memorial Theatre Company, Stratford-on-Avon, for the season of 1951; Lyric, Hamm, Apr 1961, played Edward Broderick in South; Pembroke, Croydon, Oct 1961, Cayley Drummle in The Second Mrs Tanqueray; Garrick, Apr 1962, played Colonel Cardew in Two Stars for Comfort; Belgrade, Coventry, Sept 1967, Caesar in Caesar and Cleopatra; Grand, Leeds, Aug 1968, Barron in The Genki Boys; Manchester, Oct 1973, Gerald in the 69 Theatre Company's production of The Family Reunion; played the same part in the Royal Exchange, 1979, revival of this production which went to the Roundhouse, Feb 1979, transferring to the Vaudeville, June 1979; BBC

Repertory Company, 1952–3, 1963–5, 1971–2; first film The Captive Heart, 1946, and most recent appearance in Les Routes des Exiles; first seen on television, 1938, in the Case of the Frightened Lady, and recently in When the Boat Comes in, and Crown Court.

Recreations: Pictures and prints, music, antiques. *Club:* Garrick. *Address:* Lower Woolwich, Rolvenden, Kent. *Tel:* Rolvenden 200.

FRANCIS, Alfred, OBE, theatre consultant
b Liverpool, 1909; *s* of Reginald Thomas Francis and his wife Ellen Sophia; *e* Liverpool College and Liverpool School of Architecture.

Early training in accountancy; 1932–9, song-writer and stage designer; 1939–45, Hon Organizing Sec, ENSA (Western Command); 1942, overture commissioned by Liverpool Philharmonic Society; 1943–50, reported Liverpool concerts for Daily Telegraph; Director of 1951 Liverpool Festival of Britain; 1952, Administrator of London Old Vic; 1958, Chairman of Old Vic Trust and Governors of the Royal Victoria Hall Foundation; 1958–66, Managing Director and later Vice-Chairman of Television Wales and the West (TWW); during that period on the Board of Donmar Productions and Piccadilly Theatre Ltd; also member (later chairman) of British Council Advisory Panel for Drama and Ballet and Board member of Commonwealth Festival; 1968–76, Executive Chairman, Welsh National Opera Company; 1966–7, member of Welsh Arts Council, Guild of Welsh Composers, Cardiff New Theatre Trust, etc. Various charitable appointments, including Chairman of the UK Committee for UNICEF; on Board of London Festival Ballet, D'Oyly Carte Trust, etc.

Address: Durley, Pensford Avenue, Kew, Richmond, Surrey. *Tel:* 01–876 1448.

FRANCIS, Arlene (*née* Arlene Kazanjian), actress
b Boston, Mass, 20 Oct; *e* Convent of Mount St Vincent Academy, Riverdale, New York, Finch Finishing School, and the Theatre Guild School, NYC; *m* Martin Gabel.

Made her first appearance on the stage in NY, at the Fulton Theatre, Feb 1936, as Anne in One Good Year; at the Maxine Elliott, Sept 1936, appeared in Horse Eats Hat; Ethel Barrymore, Dec 1936, played Princess Tamara in The Women; National, Oct 1937, Sylvia Jordan in Angel Island; Biltmore, Jan 1938, Eléna in All That Glitters; Mercury, Nov 1938, Marion in Danton; Golden, Dec 1938, Judy Morton in Michael Drops In; Maxine Elliott, Jan 1940, Catherine Daly in Young Couple Wanted; National, Oct 1940, Miriam in Journey to Jerusalem; Belasco, May 1942, Doris in The Walking Gentleman; Lyceum, Dec 1942, Natalia Chodorov in The Doughgirls, which she played for over a year; Booth, Feb 1945, Cora Overton in The Overtons; Cort, Dec 1945, Jacqueline Carlier in The French Touch; Music Box, Apr 1948, played Sheila Vane in The Cup of Trembling; Lyceum, Feb 1949, Madeleine Benoit-Benoit in My Name Is Aquilon; Dec 1949, Carolyn Hopewell in Metropole; National, Oct 1953, Constance Warburton in Late Love; National, Feb 1958, Dolly Fabian in Once More, With Feeling; toured US in same role, 1959; Ethel Barrymore, Mar 1963, took over from Margaret Leighton the role of Pamela Pew-Pickett in Tchin-Tchin; toured US 1963–4, as Jane Kimball in Kind Sir; Morosco, Oct 1964, Pamela Piper in Beekman Place; Westport Country Playhouse, Sept 1965, Evalyn in Mrs Dally; John Golden, Sept 1965, repeated this last part; Alvin, Sept 1966, Carlotta Vance in Dinner at Eight; toured 1967 in Old Acquaintance; toured, summer 1972, in Who Killed Santa Claus?; Uris, 1974, took over from Louise Kirtland as Aunt

Alicia in Gigi; toured, 1974, in Call Me Back; Helen Hayes, Mar 1975, Miriam Croyden in Don't Call Back; toured, summer 1975, in Sabrina Fair; has appeared in the films One Two Three and The Thrill of It All; played on television in *What's My Line?*, *The Arlene Francis Show*, etc.

Address: c/o Actors Equity Association, 165 West 46th Street, New York, NY 10036.

FRANCIS, Clive, actor
b London, 26 June 1946; *s* of the actor Raymond Francis and his wife Margaret (Towner); *e* Ratton Secondary Modern School, Eastbourne; *m* the actress Polly James; trained for the stage at RADA.

Made his first professional appearance in repertory at Bexhill-on-Sea, 1963, as Geoffrey Trent in The Bachelor Father, before going to RADA (Ronson and Tree Awards); after a tour in Prospect Productions' Getting Married and repertory at Worthing, Leicester and Derby, made his West-End debut at the Globe, 16 June 1966, as Jimmy in There's A Girl in My Soup; Queen's, Dec 1968, played Silvio in The Servant of Two Masters; Fortune, Jan 1970, appeared in three comedies by Bernard Shaw; Apollo, June 1972, Draycott Harriss in The Mating Game; Phoenix, July 1974, Ralph Partridge in Bloomsbury; for the Royal Shakespeare Company, Aldwych, Dec 1975, played Bunny in The Return of A J Raffles; Chichester Festival Theatre, June 1976, and Haymarket, Oct, Teddy Luton in The Circle, also playing Daniel in M Perrichon's Travels during the 1976 Chichester season; for Cambridge Theatre Company, 1977, played Freddy Page in The Deep Blue Sea, touring as Romeo in Romeo and Juliet in the same year; Globe, Feb 1978, Troup in The Rear Column; Chichester season, 1978, played Marcel Blanchard in Look After Lulu, and also at the Haymarket, Oct 1978; Royal Exchange, Manchester, Feb 1979, Vere Queckett in The Schoolmistress; Churchill, Bromley, 1979, played Norman in The Norman Conquests; has appeared in films and on television: recently in the TV production of The Rear Column, and Masada.

Hobbies: Antiquarian books, and collecting autograph letters of early twentieth-century literati. *Address:* 60 Thorne Street, Barnes, London SW13.

FRANKEL, Gene, director
b New York City, 23 Dec 1923; *s* of Barnet Frankel and his wife Anna (Tellerman); *e* New York University; *m* Pat Carter.

Directed his first production for the stage, Salem Story, New York City, 1946; since then has directed They Shall Not Die, 1947; 27 Wagons Full of Cotton, 1948; They Shall Not Die, 1949; Nat Turner, 1950; All My Sons, Stalag 17, My Heart's in the Highlands, Country Girl, A Streetcar Named Desire, at the Resident Theatre, Kansas City, 1951–3; Volpone, 1957; Richard II, Princeton, New Jersey, 1958; An Enemy of the People, again NY, 1959; Machinal, 1960; Once There Was a Russian, The Blacks, 1961; Brecht on Brecht, 1962; The Firebugs, 1963; The Blacks at the Akademie der Kunst, Berlin, Germany, and Teatro la Fenice, Venice, Italy, Enrico IV at the Harper, Chicago, 1964; Oh, Dad, Poor Dad, Mama's Hung You in the Closet and I'm Feeling So Sad, at the Atelje 212, Belgrade, Yugoslavia, 1965; Waiting for Godot, 1965 and A Cry of Players, 1966, Berkshire Theatre Festival; Niggerlovers, 1967; A Cry of Players for the Lincoln Center Repertory, Emperor Jones for a European tour, including an engagement at the Royal Lyceum, Edinburgh, Dream Play for Queen's College, 1968; To Be Young, Gifted, and Black, Indians, 1969; The Engagement Baby, 1970; Pueblo, at the Arena Stage, Washington, DC, A Gun

Play, 1971; Lost in the Stars, The Lincoln Mask, 1972; Othello (tour), 1973; Split Lip, 1974; The Mystery of Perricluse, The Night That Made America Famous, 1975; The Contessa of Mulberry Street, 1978; The Diary of Anne Frank (Hartman, Ct), 1979; received the Lola D'Annunzio Award and the Obie for his direction of Volpone; for Machinal received another Obie and the Vernon Rice Award of the Drama Desk; founder-director of the Berkshire Theatre Festival; has taught extensively, including a Visiting Associate Professorship at Boston University and Queens College, as Artist in Residence at the University of Wisconsin, at New York University, and at the American Theatre Wing; is Artistic Director of the Gene Frankel Theatre Workshop in NY; first directed a play for television, Volpone, in 1958, and since has directed To Be Young, Gifted, and Black, Moment of Fear, etc.

Recreation: Chess. *Addresses:* 4 Washington Square Village, New York, NY 10012, and Gene Frankel Theatre Workshop, 36 West 62nd Street, New York, NY 10023. *Tel:* 212–581 2775.

FRASER, Bill, actor
b Perth, Scotland, 5 June 1908; *s* of Alexander Fraser and his wife Betty (Scott); *e* Strathallan School; *m* Pamela Cundell; formerly engaged in a commercial career.

Made his first appearance on the stage at the Playhouse, Broadstairs, Aug 1931, as the Detective in The Fourth Wall; subsequently toured in India with R B Salisbury's company; during 1932, toured in The Outsider; formed Worthing Repertory Company, 1933, which he ran until 1939; made his first appearance in London, at the Comedy Theatre, 11 Apr 1940, in the revue, New Faces, and appeared in this again, at the Apollo, Mar 1941; then joined the RAF, and served as Signals Officer during the War; after demobilization, appeared at the Playhouse, Dec 1946, in the revue, Between Ourselves; Duke of York's, Mar 1948, in Four, Five, Six; Saville, Feb 1950, played John Mallory in The Schoolmistress; Prince of Wales's, May 1950, appeared in the revue, Touch and Go; Westminster, May 1956, played Palamède in Albertine By Moonlight; 1956–8, directed the summer revue Between Ourselves at coastal resorts; Mermaid, London, Aug 1963, played Bullinger in Schweyk in the Second World War; New Arts, Apr 1964, played Bert Mann in The Subtopians; Chichester Festival, June–Aug 1966, played Mr Sterling in The Clandestine Marriage, Pishchik in The Cherry Orchard and the Porter in Macbeth; during the following season, May–July 1967, at Chichester, he played Samuel Sweetland in The Farmer's Wife, Gibbet in The Beaux' Stratagem, the Corporal in An Italian Straw Hat and Boss Mangan in Heartbreak House, appearing in the latter production at the Lyric, Nov 1967; Haymarket, Oct 1968, played Messerschmann and Lieutenant Barrow in Ring Round the Moon; became a member of the Royal Shakespeare Company 1969, appearing at the Royal Shakespeare, Stratford, that season as Sir Toby Belch in Twelfth Night and Bishop Gardiner in King Henry the Eighth; for the National Theatre at the Old Vic, Dec 1970, played Sir George Crofts in Mrs Warren's Profession; with the same company, 1971, played Obermüller in The Captain of Köpenick, Mar, King George in Tyger (New Theatre), July, and Mr Croaker in The Good-Natured Man, Dec; Mermaid, Apr 1973, John Tarleton in Misalliance; same theatre, Feb 1974, Sgt Fender in Something's Burning; toured, May 1974, as Insp Goole in An Inspector Calls; Chichester Festival, May 1975, Morten Kiil in An Enemy of the People; Royal Court, Nov 1975, Admiral Lord Radstock in The Fool; Chichester, 1976, appeared in M Perrichon's travels, as Sir Toby Belch in Twelfth Night, and as Lord Porteous in The Circle, repeating the latter at the Haymarket, Oct 1976; first entered films, 1938, and films in which he has appeared include A Home of Your Own, Captain Nemo, and All the Way Up; television appearances include: *Bootsie and Snudge*, Rumpole of the Bailey, Comedians, and Flesh and Blood.

Recreations: Golf, swimming and writing. *Clubs:* Savage and Green Room. *Address:* c/o Crouch Associates, 59 Frith Street, London W1V 5FA. *Tel:* 01–734 2167.

FRASER, John, actor, and writer
b Glasgow, 18 Mar 1931; *s* of John Alexander Fraser and his wife Christina McCuish (Macdonald); *e* Glasgow HS.

Went on stage at age 16, playing Herodias' page in Salome at the Park, Glasgow, 1947; early experience includes a spell as ASM for the first Pitlochry season, 1951, and work at the Citizens', Glasgow; joined the Old Vic company and made his London debut with them as Octavius in Julius Caesar, Old Vic, 7 Sept 1955; other parts played here included Florizel in The Winter's Tale, Nov 1955; Claudio in Much Ado About Nothing, Oct, and Lorenzo in The Merchant of Venice, Dec 1956; Quintus in Titus Andronicus, Dromio in The Comedy of Errors (double-bill), Apr 1957; at the Lyric, Hammersmith, July 1958, played David Levy in The Hamlet of Stepney Green; Westminster, Nov 1958, Lee Durrant in No Concern of Mine; Royal Court, Apr 1959, Kendrick in Sugar in the Morning; work at the Traverse, Edinburgh, after this, included Bill Maitland in Inadmissible Evidence and Jimmy Porter in Look Back in Anger; St Martin's, Mar 1965, Peregrine in Stranger in My Bed; Apollo, Aug 1965, Cass in Any Wednesday; with the Stables Theatre Company, Manchester, in its first season, 1968–69, his parts included Flamineo in The White Devil, Dionysus in The Disorderly Women, and John Wilkes in The People's Jack; Piccadilly, July 1966, Tommy in Strike a Light; toured, 1968, as Horner in Prospect's The Country Wife; St Martin's, 1970, took over as Milo Tindle in Sleuth; Haymarket, 1973, took over as the Duke of Windsor in Crown Matrimonial; toured S Africa, 1976, as Martin Dysart in Equus; Savoy, Feb 1978, Harry Carmichael in Lady Harry; toured, 1979, as Lord Goring in An Ideal Husband, and Lord Darlington in Lady Windermere's Fan; for a number of years has toured Africa and Asia for the British Council with the London Shakespeare Group, presenting adaptations of Shakespeare for students etc; major roles in over 20 films include appearances in The Dam Busters, The Good Companions, Tunes of Glory, The Trials of Oscar Wilde, El Cid, and Isadora; TV, since Kidnapped in 1951, includes more recently A Legacy, The Arcata Promise, and Thundercloud; made a number of successful pop records in the '50s; author of the plays Cannibal Crackers, produced Hampstead, 1973, and Pure Filth, 1980; other writing includes a novel, Clap Hands If You Believe in Fairies (in the US, The Babysitter), and a book of travel, The Bard in the Bush.

Favourite part: Malvolio. *Address:* c/o Fraser and Dunlop, 91 Regent Street, London W1.

FRASER, Moyra, actress and dancer
b Sydney, Australia, 3 Dec 1923; *d* of John Newton Mappin Fraser and his wife Vera Eleanor (Beardshaw); *e* St Christopher's, Kingswood, and Eversfield, Sutton; *m* (1) Douglas Sutherland (mar dis); (2) Roger Lubbock; studied dancing at the Ripman School and the Sadler's Wells Ballet School.

Made her first appearance at Sadler's Wells, Dec 1937, when she danced in Casse-Noisette; remained with the Sadler's Wells Ballet Company until 1945, and the roles she danced included; Sabrina in Comus, Josephine in Wedding

Bouquet, Prelude in Sylphides, Queen of the Wilis in Giselle, the Lilac Fairy in The Sleeping Princess and the Hen in The Birds; at the Palace, Mar 1946, appeared as Adelina and The Spirit of Norway in Song of Norway; Covent Garden, 1949, appeared with the Covent Garden Opera Company, when she danced as Venus in The Olympians; Adelphi, June 1950, appeared as the Girl in the Window, and principal dancer in Golden City; St Martin's, June 1951, appeared in the revue Penny Plain; Casino, Dec 1952, played the Wicked Witch in Jack and Jill; Royal Court, Apr 1953, appeared in the revue Airs On A Shoestring; Comedy, Jan 1956, appeared in the revue Fresh Airs; Royal Court, Dec 1956, played Mrs Squeamish in The Country Wife, transferring with the production to the Adelphi, Feb 1957; Duke of York's, May 1958, played Poppy Fenton in The Big Tickle; Covent Garden, Dec 1958, danced, as an Ugly Sister, in the ballet Cinderella; joined the Old Vic Company, for the 1959–60 season, and played the following parts: Audrey in As You Like It, Lady Froth in The Double Dealer, and Mistress Page in The Merry Wives of Windsor; Lyric, Hammersmith, Dec 1961, played the Red Queen in Through the Looking Glass; Duchess, Mar 1963, appeared in the revue See You Inside; at the Mermaid, May 1964, appeared in the entertainment The Buxom Muse; Drury Lane, Aug 1964, played Morgan le Fey in Camelot; Whitehall, Aug 1967, Zoia Doudkina in Sign Here, Please; Haymarket, Oct 1968, Lady India in Ring Round the Moon; toured, Jan 1974, in Bell, Book and Candle; Phoenix, July 1974, played Lady Ottoline Morell in Bloomsbury; Casino, Dec 1975, in The Exciting Adventures of Queen Danniella; Civic, Johannesburg, July 1976, Maria Wislack in On Approval; Strand, Jan 1978, took over as Eleanor Hunter in No Sex Please, We're British; Thorndike, Leatherhead, June 1979, Sheila in Ask Me No Questions; ; she has also appeared in many films including The VIPs, Here We Go Round the Mulberry Bush and The Boy Friend; television appearances include: *The Good Life, Driveway, The Dora Bryan Show* and The Rescue.

Recreation: Cooking. *Address:* Weatherall Lodge, Well Road, London, NW3. *Tel:* 01–453 4047.

FRASER, Shelagh, actress
b Purley, Surrey; *d* of John Newton Mappin Fraser and his wife Vera Eleanor (Beardshaw); *e* St Christopher's School, Kingswood, Surrey; *m* Anthony Squire (mar dis); trained for the stage at the drama school attached to the Croydon Repertory Theatre.

Here she made her first appearance, walking on in Cranford; her early experience was in various repertory companies; London debut, Mar 1944, at the Comedy, as Effie in This Was a Woman; Globe, 1945, took over as Mabel Crum in While the Sun Shines, later touring Britain and Europe with the production; St James's, Apr 1947, played Hetty in Call Home the Heart; Mercury, Dec 1947, the title role in Kate Kennedy; New Lindsey, May 1949, Ta He in A Son of Heaven; Haymarket, Aug 1950, Lady Orreyd in The Second Mrs Tanqueray; Embassy, June 1951, Louka in Arms and the Man; Strand, Jan 1953, Patsy Fudunkel in Red Herring (Repertory Players); Arts, Oct 1953, Christine Lambert in Drama at Inish; Nottingham Playhouse, 1959, Flora in A Slight Ache; Bristol Old Vic Company, 1961, Fran Biedermann in The Fire Raisers; Edinburgh Festival, Sept 1965, Laura in Igloo; toured, 1967, as Martha in Who's Afraid of Virginia Woolf?; Open Space, Feb 1972, Mrs Shatlock in Sam; University, Newcastle, Feb 1973, Mrs Gynt in Peer Gynt; King's Head, Islington, Apr 1973, Frau Amel in Schellenbrack; Gardner Centre, Brighton, Sept 1973, Amanda Wingfield in The Glass Menagerie; Comedy, Mar

1974, Mrs Dunning in Knuckle; Lyceum, Edinburgh, Aug 1975 (Edinburgh Festival), Joanna in Games; Theatre Royal, Windsor, 1977, Agatha in A Delicate Balance; Liverpool Playhouse, 1978, Delia in Bedroom Farce; Theatre Royal, Windsor, 1979, Lady Hibury in A Friend Indeed; other stage appearances include various tours and repertory work at Bristol Old Vic, Nottingham, and Dublin; first appeared in films, 1943; recently in Star Wars; television work, since 1950, includes numerous appearances in plays and series, including A Family at War and, recently, The Professionals and Tycoon; has also appeared on American television; spent six months with the BBC drama repertory company, 1942, and has broadcast over 500 times altogether; is the author, with Dido Milroy, of the play Always Afternoon, produced at the Garrick, 1950; has also written five other plays and several children's books.

Favourite parts: Eliza in Pygmalion, Agatha in A Delicate Balance, and Flora in A Slight Ache. *Recreations:* Sailing, cooking. *Address:* 31 Cadogan Place, London, SW1. *Tel:* 01–235 1867.

FRAYN, Michael, dramatic writer
b London, 8 Sept 1933; *s* of Thomas Allen Frayn and his wife Violet Alice (Lawson); *e* Kingston GS and Emmanuel College, Cambridge; *m* Gillian Palmer; originally a journalist.

His collection of four short plays, The Two of Us, comprising Black and Silver, The New Quixote, Mr Foot, and Chinamen, was presented at the Garrick, 30 July 1970; he has since written The Sandboy, 1971; Alphabetical Order, 1975 (*Evening Standard* award for Best Comedy); Donkeys' Years, Clouds, 1976; Balmoral (Arnaud), 1978; revised as Liberty Hall, 1980; Make and Break, 1980; he translated The Cherry Orchard (1978), and The Fruits of Enlightenment (1979), for the National Theatre; TV writing includes Jamie and Birthday, and documentaries on Berlin, Vienna and the suburbs of London; a number of collections of his newspaper columns have been published, as well as novels including: The Tin Men, The Russian Interpreter, A Very Private Life, and Sweet Dreams; also a volume of philosophy: Constructions.

Address: c/o Elaine Greene Ltd, 31 Newington Green, London N16. *Tel:* 01–249 2971.

FREDRIK, Burry, producer and director
b 9 Aug 1925; *d* of Fredric Gerber and his wife Erna (Burry); *e* Sarah Lawrence College; *m* Gerard E Meunier (mar dis).

Began her professional career in 1949 as stage manager for King Lear at the Brattle Theatre, Cambridge, Mass, where she was later a set and lighting designer; production stage manager for The Relapse, Morosco, NY, 1950, and over 20 other Broadway shows; has co-produced the following plays on or off-Broadway: Thieves' Carnival (Tony award), 1955; Exiles, 1956; Too True to Be Good, 1963; Dear Love (Comedy, London), 1971; Look Away, 1973; Pretzels, 1974; Summer Brave, Travesties (Tony award), The Royal Family, 1975; The Night of the Tribades, An Almost Perfect Person, 1977; Buried Child, 1978; directed Kismet at the Princess, Melbourne, in 1955, and has since directed productions including The Decameron, NY, 1961; Milk and Honey (Papermill Playhouse, NJ), 1962; Finian's Rainbow (Melbourne), 1964; national tour of Dear Love (also produced), 1970; Wild and Wonderful, NY, 1971.

Address: 165 West 46th Street, New York, NY 10036. *Tel:* 212-575 1771.

FREEDMAN, Bill, producing manager
b Toronto, Canada, 13 Aug 1929; *s* of Benjamin Freedman and his wife Mary (Cohen); *e* University of Toronto; *m* Toby Robins; also a cinema operator.

His first production for the stage was Salad Days, presented in Toronto, Oct 1958 and subsequently in New York, Nov 1958, in association with Barry Morse; in Toronto he also presented Visit to a Small Planet, 1959 (with Barry Morse); Two for the Seesaw, 1960; Four Faces, 1963; in London, he has since presented or co-presented the following plays: The Love Game, 1964; Comfort Me With Apples, 1965; Staircase, 1966; Staircase (Broadway), Hadrian VII, 1968; Hadrian VII (Broadway), Anne of Green Gables, 1969; Who Killed Santa Claus?, 1970; Don't Start Without Me, Suddenly At Home, 1971; Who's Who (Guildford), 1973; The Gentle Hook, 1974; Candida, 1977; Flying Blind, 1978; producer of the film of Hadrian VII, 1971.

Recreations: Tennis, squash. *Clubs:* Garrick, RAC, Queens. *Address:* 3 Goodwin's Court, London WC2. *Tel:* 01–240 3086.

FREEDMAN, Gerald, director, producer, composer, playwright
b Lorain, Ohio, 25 June 1927; *s* of Dr Barnie B Freedman and his wife Fannie (Sepsenwol); *e* Northwestern University; formerly a musician and scenic designer; prepared for the stage under Alvina Krause.

At the Winter Garden, 26 Sept 1957, was directorial assistant for West Side Story; made his London Début as director of Bells Are Ringing at the Coliseum, 14 Nov 1957; Her Majesty's, Dec 1958, assistant to the director of West Side Story; served in the same capacity for the Paris and Israel productions of this show; was assistant to the director of Gypsy, May 1959; made his directorial début at the Carnegie Hall Playhouse, 15 Jan 1959, with a revival of On the Town; since then has directed The Taming of the Shrew, Rosemary, The Alligators, 1960, and composed the music for the last two in a double-bill, The Gay Life, 1961; The Tempest, 1962; As You Like It, Bil and Cora Baird's Marionette Theatre, 1963; West Side Story, Electra, 1964; The Day the Whores Came Out to Play Tennis, Sing to Me Through Open Windows, Love's Labour's Lost, 1965; A Time for Singing, for which he also wrote the book and lyrics with John Morris, Richard III, was associate artistic producer for the New York Shakespeare Festival production of All's Well That Ends Well, 1966; The Comedy of Errors, Hair, Hamlet, Titus Andronicus, 1967; Artistic Director of the New York Shakespeare Festival, 1967–71; directed Ergo, Henry IV, Part I, and Part II, King Lear (for the Repertory Theatre of Lincoln Center), and was Artistic Director for Romeo and Juliet and Hamlet, and wrote the lyrics for Take One Step, 1968; Cities in Bezique, Invitation to a Beheading, Peer Gynt, which he also adapted, Electra, Twelfth Night, Sambo, No Place to Be Somebody, 1969; Colette, 1970; Timon of Athens, The Incomparable Max, The Wedding of Iphigenia, Iphigenia in Concert, 1971; Hamlet, The School for Scandal (for the City Center Acting Company), The Creation of the World and Other Business, 1972; The Au Pair Man, 1973; The Robber Bridegroom, 1975; Mrs Warren's Profession, 1976; The Grand Tour, 1979; Artistic Director, 1978– , American Shakespeare Theatre, Stratford, Ct, for whom he has directed Twelfth Night, 1978 and 1979; The Tempest, Julius Caesar, 1979; has also directed operas such as Beatrix Cenci, L'Orfeo, The Barber of Seville, etc, in San Francisco, New York and Washington DC; most recent opera Otello, Arizona, 1979; also industrial shows; has directed extensively on television, since 1955, including Antigone, *Ford Theatre, Du Pont Show of the Week*, etc; has taught at Yale and the Juillard School, and lectured at Northwestern etc; received an Obie award for The Taming of the Shrew.

Address: 150 West 87th Street, New York, NY *Tel:* 724–0786.

FREEMAN, Al Jr, actor

b Antonio, Texas, 21 Mar 1934; *s* of Albert Cornelius Freeman and his wife Lottie Brisette (Coleman); *e* Los Angeles City College; *m* Sevara Clemon.

First appeared on the stage at the Ebony Showcase, Los Angeles, 1954, in Detective Story; first appeared in New York at the Ambassador, 17 Feb 1960, as Rex Tucker in The Long Dream; Arie Crown, Chicago, Oct 1961, played Silky Satin in Kicks and Co; Booth, NY, Dec 1962, Dan Morris in Tiger Tiger Burning Bright; Premise, June 1963, played in the improvisational revue The Living Premise; Astor Place Playhouse, Dec 1963, Reverend Ridgley Washington in Trumpets of the Lord; ANTA, Apr 1964, Richard Henry in Blues for Mister Charlie; made his London début at the Aldwych, 3 May 1965, as Richard Henry in Blues for Mister Charlie in a World Theatre Season presentation of the Actors Studio Theatre Company of NY production; Billy Rose, Nov 1964, John in Conversation at Midnight; St Mark's Playhouse, Dec 1964, Walker Vessels in The Slave; Warner Playhouse, Los Angeles, Cal, Mar 1965, Clay in Dutchman; Delacorte, Aug 1965, Diomedes in Troilus and Cressida; June 1966, Charles Dumaine in All's Well That Ends Well; July 1966, Lucio in Measure for Measure; Playhouse in the Park, Cincinnati, Ohio, July 1968, Kilroy in Camino Real; Booth, Mar 1969, Stanley Pollack in The Dozens; Lunt-Fontanne, Mar 1970, Homer Smith in the musical Look to the Lilies; Yale Repertory, New Haven, Conn, Nov 1972, Paul Robeson in Are You Now Or Have You Ever Been?; Circle in the Square—Joseph E Levine, Jan 1973, Jason in Medea; Westport Country Playhouse, Conn, Aug 1973, Willy Stepp in The Poison Tree; St Mark's Playhouse, Feb 1974, various parts in The Great Macdaddy; McCarter, Princeton, Nov 1979, appeared in 'Tis Pity She's a Whore; Hartford, Ct, Mar 1976, in Dream on Monkey Mountain; Marines', San Francisco, May 1976, took over a part in Kennedy's Children; for Phoenix, Jan 1978, played Bulldog in One Crack Out; first appeared in films in 1958 in Torpedo Run, and has since played in Dutchman, Finian's Rainbow, Sweet Charlie, A Fable, which he also directed, 1971, etc; has appeared frequently on television since 1955 when he played in a live drama, on GE Theatre, and has since played in My Sweet Charlie, *The FBI, Defenders, Judd for the Defense, Maude*, 1974, Hot l Baltimore, 1975, etc.

Favourite part: Richard Henry in Blues for Mister Charlie. *Recreations:* Golf, tennis, woodworking. *Address:* William Morris Agency, 1350 Avenue of the Americas, New York, NY 10019. *Tel:* 586–5100.

FREEMAN, Arny, actor

b Chicago, Illinois, 28 Aug 1908.

Made his New York début at the New York City Center, 23 May 1950, as Pablo Gonzales in A Streetcar Named Desire; same theatre, May 1951, played Luigi and a Mexican in Dream Girl; President, Mar 1952, Guglielmo Lorti in Dark Legend; New York City Center, May 1952, Martelleau in Tovarich; toured, summer 1952, in On Your Toes; New York City Center, Nov 1953, Sam Tager in The Shrike; Coronet, Jan 1956, Josef in The Great Sebastians; Shubert, Detroit, Mich, and subsequent tour, Oct 1956, again played the last part; Belasco, 1959, took over as Mike Giardineri in Tall Story; Cherry Lane, Apr 1960, Tonetti in Gay Divorce;

Majestic, Apr 1963, Nadir of D'hum in Hot Spot; 54th Street, Feb 1964, Sidney Fineman in What Makes Sammy Run?; Royale, Dec 1965, Señor Sanchez in Cactus Flower, and continued in this part for three seasons; Imperial, Mar 1970, Sam (Frenchie) Marx in Minnie's Boys; Cherry Lane, Oct 1971, Orlando in A Gun Play: Winter Garden, Nov 1972, Antonio in Much Ado About Nothing; toured, 1974–5, in The Sunshine Boys; Forty-Sixth Street, May 1978, appeared in Working; has appeared in films, including Popi, 1969; has appeared frequently on television, notably in Much Ado About Nothing, 1973.

Address: Actors Equity Association, 165 West 46th Street, New York, NY 10036.

FREEMAN, Morgan, actor

b Memphis, Tennessee, 1 June 1937; *s* of Grafton Curtis and his wife Mayme Edna; *e* Broad Street High School, Mississippi and Los Angeles City College; *m* Jeanette Adair Bradshaw (mar dis); formerly in the United States Air Force.

Made his first professional appearance at the Orpheum, NY, 1 Oct 1967, as Creampuff in the double-bill The Nigger-lovers; at the St James, Nov 1967, took over the part of Rudolph in Hello, Dolly!; summer season, 1969, played Foxtrot in Scubba Duba; ANTA, 1970–72, standby for the title role in Purlie, appearing a number of times in the part; Public/Annex, Apr 1972, Nate in Gettin' Together in a program entitled Black Visions; Martinique, Jul 1975, Sisyphus in Sisyphus and the Blue-Eyed Cyclops; Manhattan Theatre Club, May 1977, Zeke in The Last Street Play; American Place, Oct 1977, Sampson in Cockfight; repeated the role of Zeke at the Ambassador, Apr 1978, in what was now retitled The Mighty Gents; De Lys, Oct 1978, Winston in White Pelicans; Public, Mar 1979, and Delacorte, Jun 1979, title part in Coriolanus; first film, Brubaker, 1980; TV includes five years with *The Electric Company*, as well as films including Hollow Image, and Attica.

Address: c/o Jeff Hunter, 119 West 57th Street, New York, NY 10019.

FRENCH, Harold, actor and director

b London, 23 Apr 1900; *s* of William Joseph French and his wife Gertrude (Brady); *e* Edge Hill College, Wimbledon; *m* (1) Phyl Arnold (dec); (2) Mary Baker.

Made his first appearance on the stage at the Savoy Theatre, Oct 1912, when he succeeded Eric Rae as Mamillius in The Winter's Tale; he also appeared at the same theatre, Nov 1912, in Twelfth Night; at the Garrick, Dec 1913, played Crispian Carey in Where the Rainbow Ends, playing the same part in Dec 1914, and Dec 1915; was a member of the Liverpool Repertory Theatre Company and Gaiety, Manchester, 1912–13; at the Savoy, Feb 1914, appeared in A Midsummer Night's Dream; at the Haymarket, Apr 1916, played in The Mayor of Troy; Sept 1916, appeared there as Hafiz in Mr Jubilee Drax; was for nine months a member of the Birmingham Repertory Company; joined the Forces (RFC) 1917; on demobilization appeared at the Garrick Theatre, Mar 1919, as the Baron de Casterae and Athos in Cyrano de Bergerac; at the Prince of Wales's, Aug 1920, played Dick in The Blue Lagoon; at the St Martin's Theatre, Feb 1921, appeared as The Visitor in The Wonderful Visit; at the Garrick, Jan 1922, played Hoheno in The Bird of Paradise; at the Duke of York's, Feb 1923, Wilbur Jennings in Good Gracious, Annabelle!; at the Haymarket, Mar 1923, Stephen Audley in Isabel, Edward and Anne; at the Little Theatre, Oct 1923, appeared in Little Revue Starts at Nine o'Clock; in 1924 toured in By-the-Way, appearing at the Apollo, Jan 1925, in the same play; went to New York, and appeared at the Gaiety, Dec 1925, in the same play; on returning to London, appeared at the Gaiety, Dec 1926, as Spencer Weldon in Lido Lady; His Majesty's, Sept 1927, played Jimmy Winter in Oh, Kay!; Palace, Oct 1928, Lord Hampton in Virginia; during 1929 appeared in variety theatres; Gaiety, Jan 1930, played the Hon Robert Darrell in Darling, I Love You; Kingsway, Feb 1931, Henry in The Gay Princess; Prince of Wales's, Sept 1931, Maurice in Marriage à la Carte; Vaudeville, Jan 1932, George Lang in Whose Baby Are You?; Comedy, Apr 1932, Ted Stock in Faces; Duchess, June 1932, Michael Redvers in The Secret Woman; Strand, Aug 1932, Teddy Darling in Night of the Garter; Piccadilly (for Overture Players), Sept 1933, Greg Shaw in Among Friends; he has since directed Youth at the Helm, 1934; Three for Luck, 1934; Chase the Ace, The Inside Stand, 1935; Sauce for the Goose, French Without Tears, 1936; Ladies and Gentlemen, Blondie White, Plan for a Hostess, 1937; Design for Living, Sugar Plum, Second Helping, All Clear, 1939; Believe It or Not, Ladies into Action, 1940; No Time for Comedy, 1941; Another Love Story, 1944; The Philadelphia Story, 1949; Fortune Came Smiling, 1951; Tabitha, 1955; Odd Man In, Something About a Sailor (tour), 1957; Waltz of the Toreadors (tour), Gilt and Gingerbread, 1958; When in Rome . . ., 1959; The More the Merrier, The Bride Comes Back, 1960; The Affair, 1961; The New Men, Out of Bounds, 1962; Trap for a Lonely Man, 1963; The Claimant, 1964; A Public Mischief, 1965; A Share in the Sun, 1966; A Present From Harry (tour), 1970; Maynardville, Cape Town, S Africa, 1971, directed The Winter's Tale; in the same year directed The Merchant of Venice at Port Elizabeth, playing Shylock; has appeared in films since 1931, and has directed the productions of Jeannie, The Day Will Dawn, Mr Emmanuel, Dear Octopus, Secret Mission, Quiet Week-End, and episodes in the following Somerset Maugham films: Quartet, Trio, and Encore, etc.

Recreations: Golf, swimming and punting. *Clubs:* Green Room and Garrick. *Address:* c/o ICM, 22 Gratton Street, London W1.

FRENCH, Leslie, actor, singer and director
b Bromley, Kent, 23 Apr 1904; *s* of Robert Gilbert French and his wife Jetty Sands (Leahy); *e* London School of Choristers.

Made his first appearance on the stage at the Little Theatre, Christmas, 1914, at one of Jean Sterling Mackinlay's matinées; at 14, joined the Ben Greet company in 1918, and played a variety of parts; at the Comedy, Jan 1924, played Esmé in Alice Sit-by-the-Fire; Winter Garden, Sept 1924, the Artist in Primrose; appeared at the Everyman, 1926, in John Ferguson and The Pleasure Garden; Arts, Apr 1927, appeared in Picnic; Duke of York's, Sept 1927, played Asticot in the musical version of The Beloved Vagabond; June 1928, appeared in Many Happy Returns; at Glasgow, Christmas, 1928, played Dickie in Bluebell in Fairyland; at the London Hippodrome, 1929, understudied Bobby Howes in Mr Cinders; at the Old Vic, Dec 1929, played Puck in A Midsummer Night's Dream; during 1930, toured as Jim in Mr Cinders; joined the Old Vic Company, Sept 1930, appearing as Poins in Henry IV (Part I), Charles Oakley in The Jealous Wife, Ariel in The Tempest, Green and the Groom in Richard II, Eros in Antony and Cleopatra; at the re-opening of Sadler's Wells, Jan 1931, played Feste in Twelfth Night, and subsequently at the Old Vic and Sadler's Wells, played Balthazar and Verges in Much Ado About Nothing, Grumio in The Taming of the Shrew, and the Fool in King Lear; at the Phoenix (for the Stage Society), Dec 1931, played Hans, the Elder Brother, in The Children's Tragedy; Lyric, Hammer-

smith, Feb 1932, Bert Bones in Derby Day; at the Kingsway, Apr 1932, Feste in Twelfth Night; St Martin's, Sept 1932, Jimmie in Strange Orchestra; Open Air Theatre, June–Sept 1933, Feste in Twelfth Night, Amiens in As You Like It, Puck in A Midsummer Night's Dream, Ariel in The Tempest; Cambridge, Dec 1933, Hänsel in Hänsel and Gretel; at the Open Air Theatre, May–Sept 1934, appeared in his old parts, and as the Attendant Spirit in Comus, the Captain in Androcles and the Lion, and Mercutio in Romeo and Juliet; Winter Garden, Sept 1934, the Quack in Love is the Best Doctor; Embassy, Mar 1935, Dapper in The Alchemist; King's, Hammersmith, Apr 1935, Alf Summertop in The Magic Cupboard; Arts, May 1935, Algernon Swinburne in Rosetti; Open Air Theatre, June–Sept 1935, appeared as Feste, Sylvius in As You Like It, Zephyrus in Chloridia, the Attendant Spirit in Comus, Puck, Costard in Love's Labour's Lost; Adelphi, Dec 1935, Charles in Fritzi; Prince's, Manchester, Mar 1936, Prince Paul in How Do, Princess?; Open Air, July–Sept, 1936, Ariel, Puck, Costard, Feste, Touchstone in As You Like It; Ring, Blackfriars, Nov 1936, Chorus in Henry V; Adelphi, Feb 1937, Viscount Flower in Home and Beauty; Open Air, June–Sept 1937, Bottom in A Midsummer Night's Dream, Lucius in Julius Caesar, Spirit in Comus, Autolycus in The Winter's Tale, Feste and Ariel; People's Palace, Dec 1937, Dicky and the Sleepy King in Bluebell in Fairyland; went to New York where he made his first appearance, at the Windsor Theatre, 31 May 1938, as Edward Gill in The Two Bouquets; directed Much Ado About Nothing, for OUDS, 1938; Traitor's Gate, 1938; On a Summer's Day, 1939; The Tempest, for OUDS, 1939; Open Air Theatre, July–August 1939, again played Puck and Feste, and also appeared as Tobias in Tobias and the Angel; Whitehall, Dec 1939, appeared in Who's Taking Liberty? which he also directed; at Richmond, Dec 1941, appeared as the Widow Twankey in Aladdin; in 1943 Oswald in Ghosts, and at Perth, 1944, played Lord Babs in Charley's Aunt, and Danny in Night Must Fall; he has appeared in the ballet Everyman, at the Lyric, the Aldelphi, Princes, and His Majesty's and at the latter theatre also appeared as Feste in ballet of Twelfth Night; 1950, directed The Prodigal Father; Whitehall, June 1950, produced The Dish Ran Away; Open Air Theatre, Regent's Park, May 1951, played Puck in A Midsummer Night's Dream; New Boltons, May 1952, directed Up the Garden Path, and appeared as Tony Linnett; Open Air, Regent's Park, July 1952, played Pisanio in Cymbeline and the Attendant Spirit in Comus; at Westminster Abbey, June 1953, appeared as Dyrkin Townley in Out of the Whirlwind; Q, Apr 1954, directed The Sainted Sinners; Court, Oct 1955, directed The Sun of York, playing Richard, Duke of Gloucester; Open Air Theatre, Regent's Park, June 1958, presented (with Robert Atkins), directed, and played Grumio in The Taming of The Shrew, and July 1958, directed, and played Touchstone in As You Like It; more recently, has appeared in South Africa, as Shylock in The Merchant of Venice and Witwoud in The Way of the World; in England, at the Arnaud, Guildford, Mar 1968, played Dr Warburton in The Family Reunion; has directed several Shakespearean plays at various centres, including The Taming of the Shrew, As You Like It, The Winter's Tale, Othello, Twelfth Night, The Merry Wives of Windsor, The Tempest, Much Ado About Nothing and A Midsummer Night's Dream; in the Great Hall, Hampton Court Palace, June 1964, presented, directed and played Feste in Twelfth Night; at Chichester, July 1972, played the Chaplain in The Lady's Not for Burning; in conjunction with Cecilia Sonnenberg and René Ahrensen opened the Maynardville Open Air Theatre in Cape Town, late autumn 1955, and has since directed annual productions in Cape Town, including As You Like It, A Winter's Tale, A Midsummer Night's Dream, The Taming of the Shrew, Hamlet, etc; since 1965 has given a series of Shakespeare Recitals in London, South Africa and the USA, including The Young Vic, Sept 1975; Arnaud, July 1976, Dr Cornish in Caroline; has directed several panto-mimes in which he has also appeared, notably as Mother Goose, Buttons in Cinderella and Dame Trot in The Babes in the Wood; films in which he has appeared include La Strega, Death in Venice, More than a Miracle, etc; he has also made numerous television appearances, recently in Crown Court; has arranged the dances for several West End productions, and has frequently broadcast for the BBC; held his first exhibition of oil paintings at Parsons Galleries, 1954; presented with the Key to the City of Cape Town, Jan 1963, in recognition of his services to Art and Culture in South Africa; honorary life member of the Mark Twain Society of America, for his contribution to Shakespearian theatre.

Favourite parts: Ariel, Puck, Mr Cinders, Shylock, and the Spirit in Comus. *Recreations:* Dancing and skating. *Club:* Garrick. *Address:* Flat 2, 39 Lennox Gardens, London, SW1. *Tel:* 01–584 4797 *and* La Stalla, Dosso, Levanto, Italy.

FRENCH, Valerie (*née* Harrison), actress
b London, England, 11 Mar 1932; *d* of Frank Orvin Percy Harrison and his wife Muriel Clare (Smith); *e* Malvern Girls' College; *m* Thayer David (dec); studied dancing with David Lichine and Matt Mattox.

First appeared on the stage at the Theatre Royal, Windsor, 1951, in Treasure Hunt, and continued there in repertory; first appeared in London at the Saville, June 1954, in Cockles and Champagne, a revue; at the Duchess, Jan 1955, played Doreen in It's Different for Men; came to the USA to make films; toured the USA, 1962–3, as Dominique Beaurevers in A Shot in the Dark; made her New York début at the Belasco, 30 Nov 1965, as Liz in Inadmissible Evidence; Booth, Sept 1966, played Sarah Lord in Help Stamp Out Marriage; Eastside Playhouse, Oct 1968, Wendy in Tea Party; Booth, Feb 1969, Griselda in The Mother Lover; Anspacher, Oct 1970, Imogen Parrott in Trelawny of the 'Wells'; Ensemble Studio, Mar 1974, Cecily Hundson in Studs Edsel; Theatre de Lys, Sept 1975, Dark Marion in Finn McKool, The Grand Distraction; toured, 1975–6, as Madge Larrabee in Sherlock Holmes; Delacorte, June 1976, Alice in Henry V; Long Wharf, Aug 1976, Lucy in Alphabetical Order; Roundabout, Dec 1976, Fanny Wilton in John Ga-briel Borkman; Meadowbrook, Mich, season 1979, Ruth in Blithe Spirit; Public, May 1980, Sister Ubbidienza in Bici-cletta; first appeared in films in England, 1954, in The Constant Husband, and since has played in American films, notably Jubal, Shalako, The Garment Jungle, The Secret of Treasure Mountain, etc; first appeared on television in Cali-fornia, 1957, and since has played extensively on both UK and US television, notably in The Detour, The Prisoner, Ten Little Indians, Cinema Vérité, Arias and Arabesques, as a dancer, and on various dramatic series, such as *The Nurses, Schlitz Playhouse, Have Gun, Will Travel,* etc.

Hobbies: Chinoiserie and collecting snake jewellery. *Club:* Crockford's. *Address:* c/o C D Smith, Esq, 4 Church Close, Aldeburgh, Suffolk; Actors Equity Association, 165 West 46th Street, New York, NY 10036. *Tel:* 245 1925 (New York).

FREUDENBERGER, Daniel, director
b 17 Mar 1945; *s* of Joseph N Freudenberger and his wife Martha (Clapp); *e* Exeter, Harvard U and Pembroke Col-lege, Oxford.

Artistic Director, 1976–80, Phoenix Theatre, NY, for whom he directed Secret Service, Canadian Gothic/Ameri-can Modern, 1976; A Sorrow Beyond Dreams (also adapted), 1977; One Crack Out, City Sugar, 1978; Later, Big and Little, 1979; directed Curse of the Starving Class in Stuttgart, 1980; has directed frequently for National Public Radio, notably for the *Earplay* series.

Address: c/o Phoenix Theatre, 1540 Broadway, New York, NY 10036.

FREY, Leonard, actor
b New York City, 4 Sept 1938; *s* of Charles Frey and his wife Henrietta; *e* Art Schools, Brooklyn Museum and Cooper Union; trained for the stage at the Neighborhood Playhouse.

Made his first professional appearance in 1961 at the Players', NY, when he took over the role of Yellow Feather in Little Mary Sunshine; Imperial, Sept 1964, played Mendel, the Rabbi's son, and in Aug 1965 took over as Motel in Fiddler on the Roof, playing the part until 1967; Theatre Four, Apr 1968, Harold in The Boys in the Band, making his London debut in this part at the Wyndham's, 11 Feb 1969; Vivian Beaumont, Nov 1969, Harry the Hoofer in The Time of Your Life; same theatre, May 1970, Neil McRae in Beggar on Horseback; Forum, Nov 1971, Don in People Are Living There; Beaumont, Mar 1972, Sir Andrew Aguecheek in Twelfth Night; for Yale Rep, season 1972, appeared as M Jourdain in Le Bourgeois Gentilhomme, as Murray Zeller in A Break in the Skin, and as Lionel Stander in Are You Now Or Have You Ever Been?; Stratford, Ontario, Aug 1973, Podkolyossin in The Marriage Brokers; Mitzi E Newhouse, Nov 1973, Ulysses in Troilus and Cressida; Long Wharf, New Haven, transferring to the Circle in the Square, Oct 1974, Barnet in The National Health; appeared in Cincinnati, Jun 1975, in Oh! Coward; at the Kennedy Center, Washington DC, Aug 1975, in The Scarecrow; Biltmore, Jun 1976, as Wiseman and others in Knock, Knock; toured, Dec 1976, as Tony Cavendish in The Royal Family; for the Philadelphia Drama Guild, season 1978–79, appeared in Arms and the Man, and in the same season played in Two-Part Inventions at the Goodman, Chicago; his films include The Boys in the Band, The Magic Christian, and Where the Buffalo Roam (1979).

Address: 180 Waverly Place, New York, NY 10014.

FRIED, Martin, director
b New York City, 12 Oct 1937; *s* of Vladimer N Fried and his wife Natalia E (Frensky); *e* New York; *m* (1) Brenda Vaccaro (mar dis); (2) Lena Tabori; trained for the stage at American Theatre Wing, American Academy of Dramatic Arts and Columbia Theatre Department.

Boxed as a professional for three years; started in the theatre as an actor, 1952–60, also as a stage manager; his directing debut was for a national tour of The Best Man, Jan 1962; directed The Coop at the Actors Playhouse, Mar 1966; has since directed the following productions on or off-Broadway: The Country Girl, 1966; The Natural Look, Daphne in Cottage D, 1967; The Cannibals, This Bird of Dawning Singeth All Night Long, 1968; Papp, 1969; Duet for Solo Voice, 1970; Pinkville, Fingernails Blue as Flowers, 1971; The Silent Partner, Twelve Angry Men, 1972; Bread, 1974; Hughie/Duet, 1975; The Diary of Anne Frank, 1978; The Downstairs Boys, 1980; work with regional companies includes four seasons with Arena Stage, Washington DC, 1974–78, and productions for the Guthrie, Minneapolis, Stage West, Springfield Ill, Shaw Festival, Long Wharf, etc; has directed national tours and nearly fifty musicals for summer theatres etc; has directed regularly in Germany, recently Mother Courage, Munich and Bremen, 1979; has taught and directed at many colleges, and is a board member of the Actors Studio.

Address: 420 West End Avenue, New York, NY 10024.

FRIEDMAN, Bruce Jay, playwright and novelist
b The Bronx, 26 Apr 1930; *e* U of Missouri; *m* Ginger Howard (mar dis).

Author of the plays 23 Pat O'Brien Movies, 1966; Scuba Duba, A Mother's Kisses, The Car Lover, 1968; Steambath, 1970; First Offenders (With Jacques Levy: also co-directed), 1973; Foot in the Door, 1978; has published four novels and two collections of short stories.

Address: c/o The Lantz Office, 111 East 55th Street, New York, NY 10022.

FRIEL, Brian, dramatist
b Omagh, Northern Ireland, 9 Jan 1929; *s* of Patrick Friel and his wife Christina (MacLoone); *e* St Patrick's, Maynooth; *m* Anne Morrison; formerly a teacher.

His first play, The Francophile, was produced in Belfast in 1958; he has also written The Blind Mice (1961), The Enemy Within (1962), Philadelphia, Here I Come! (1966), The Loves of Cass McGuire (1967), Lovers (1968), Crystal and Fox (1969), The Mundy Scheme (1970), The Gentle Island (1972), The Freedom of the City (1974), Volunteers (1975), Living Quarters (1977), Faith Healer, Aristocrats (1979).

Address: Ardmore, Muff, Lifford, Co, Donegal, Ireland. *Tel:* Muff 30.

FRISBY, Terence, actor, director and dramatist
b New Cross, London, 28 Nov 1932; *s* of William Alfred Frisby and his wife Kathleen Campbell (Casely); *e* Dartford Grammar School; *m* Christine Vecchione (mar dis); trained for the stage at the Central School of Speech and Drama.

Made his first professional appearance, Aug 1957, at High Wycombe; acted and directed, 1957–66, under the name of Terence Holland, making his London debut, Mar 1958, at the Players', as Charlie Pepper in Gentlemen's Pastime; during this period most of his work was in repertory; Royal Court, Dec 1972, played First Man in A Sense of Detachment; Theatre Upstairs, Aug 1974, played the father in X; General Wax in Wax at Edinburgh Festival, 1976, and at Bush Theatre; Young Vic season, played Scrooge, Birdboot in The Real Inspector Hound, and Leslie in Seaside Postcard, 1977–8; Arts, Apr 1964, directed his own play, The Subtopians; is the author of the plays the Subtopians, 1962; There's a Girl in My Soup, 1966; The Bandwagon, 1969; It's All Right if *I* Do It, 1977; Seaside Postcard, 1978 (directed by himself at the Young Vic); has also written for television, including Take Care of Madam, Don't Forget the Basics, and Lucky Feller (series, London Weekend); There's a Girl in My Soup ran for more than six years in London, it was produced in New York, 1967, and filmed, 1970.

Recreations: Golf, chess. *Address:* c/o Harvey Unna Ltd, 14 Beaumont Mews, Marylebone High Street, London W1. *Tel:* 01–935 8589.

FRISCH, Max, dramatic author
b Zürich, Switzerland, 15 May 1911; *s* of Franz Frisch; *e* Technical High School and University, Zürich; formerly an architect.

Author of the following plays: Nun Singen Sie Wieder (Now They Are Singing Again), 1945; Santa Cruz, Die Chinesische Mauer (The Chinese Wall), 1946; Als Der Krieg Zuende War (When the War was Over), 1949; Graf Oederland (Count Oederland), 1951; Don Juan (Don Juan, or the

Love of Geometry), 1952; Biedermann (The Fire Raisers), 1958; Die grosse Wut des Philip Hotz (The Fury of Philip Hotz) (one-act), Andorra, 1961; Edge of Reason, 1964; Biografie, 1967; first television production, 1956; his plays have also appeared on English, German, and Italian television.

Clubs: PEN, and the Academy, Berlin. *Address:* Via Margutta 53, Rome, Italy.

FRY, Christopher, dramatic author
b Bristol, 18 Dec 1907; *s* of Charles John Harris and his wife Marguerite Hammond (Fry); *e* Bedford Modern School; *m* Phyllis Marjorie Hart.

Formerly a schoolmaster, actor and director; after six months as a schoolmaster, joined a repertory company, as an actor, at Bath; returned to his scholastic career for three years, in a preparatory school at Limpsfield; again returned to the stage, and was, for two years, director of a repertory company at Tunbridge Wells; toured, 1936, in Ivor Novello's Howdo, Princess?; subsequently toured all over the country as a lecturer; his play The Boy With a Cart, was produced 1938; wrote several plays for the BBC Children's Hour, 1939–40; was director at the Oxford Playhouse, 1940; served during the War, with the Pioneer Corps, 1940–4; returned to Oxford Playhouse, 1944, remaining as director, until 1946; meanwhile he had directed The Circle of Chalk, and The School for Scandal, at the Arts Theatre, London, Aug–Sept, 1945; directed his The Lady's Not For Burning, Guildford, 1971; author of the following plays: The Boy with a Cart, 1938; The Tower (Tewkesbury Festival), 1939; A Phoenix Too Frequent, 1946; The Lady's Not For Burning, Thor, with Angels (Canterbury Festival), The Firstborn (Edinburgh Festival), 1948; Venus Observed, Ring Round the Moon (from the French of Jean Anouilh) 1950; A Sleep of Prisoners, 1951; The Dark is Light Enough, 1954; Curtmantle, 1962; A Yard of Sun, 1970; is the translator of The Lark (Anouilh), Tiger at the Gates (Giraudoux), 1955; Duel of Angels (Giraudoux), 1958; Judith (Giraudoux), 1962; Peer Gynt (Ibsen), 1970; Cyrano de Bergerac (Rostand); films he has written include: The Beggar's Opera, A Queen is Crowned, 1952; Ben Hur, 1959; Barrabas, 1960; The Bible, 1964; television plays since 1974 include The Brontës of Haworth, The Best of Enemies and Sister Dora; wrote Can You Find Me: A Family History, 1978; awarded the Queen's Gold Medal for Poetry, 1962.

Address: c/o Actac Ltd, 16 Cadogan Lane, London, SW1.

FRYER, Robert, producer
b Washington, DC, 18 Nov 1920; *s* of Harold Fryer and his wife Ruth Reade; *e* Western Reserve University, Cleveland, Ohio (BA).

Produced his first play at the Alvin, New York, 1951, with A Tree Grows in Brooklyn (in association with George Abbott); has since produced or co-produced Wonderful Town, 1953; By the Beautiful Sea, 1954; The Desk Set, 1955; Shangri-La, Auntie Mame, 1956; Redhead, Saratoga, 1959; There Was a Little Girl, Advise and Consent, 1960; A Passage to India, 1962; Hot Spot, 1963; Roar Like a Dove, A Dream of Swallows, 1964; Sweet Charity, Mame, 1966; Chicago, The Norman Conquests, 1975; On the Twentieth Century, 1978; Sweeney Todd, 1979; became Managing Director of the Ahmanson Theater in the Center Theater Group, Los Angeles, 1971, and continues in this position as of 1980; has produced thirty-two productions there; produced the films The Boston Strangler, 1968; The Prime of Miss Jean Brodie, 1969; Travels with My Aunt, 1973; Mame and The Abdication, 1974; Great Expectations, 1975; Voyage of the

Damned, 1976; The Boys from Brazil, 1978; Vice-President of the Episcopal Actors Guild and member of the Board of Governors of the League of New York Theatres; produced for television, 1959, Rosalind Russell in Wonderful Town.

Recreations: Music and swimming. *Address:* c/o Marble Arch Productions, 4024 Radford Avenue, Studio City, Calif 91604. *Tel:* 213–760 2110.

FUGARD, Athol, dramatist, actor and director
b Cape Province, South Africa, 1932; *e* University of Cape Town; *m* Sheila Meiring.

Author of the plays No-Good Friday, 1959; Nongogo, 1960; Blood-Knot, 1961; People Are Living There, 1968; Hello and Goodbye, 1969; Boesman and Lena, 1970; Sizwe Bansi Is Dead (co-deviser), The Island (co-deviser), 1973; Statements After An Arrest Under The Immorality Act, 1974; Dimetos, 1975; A Lesson from Aloes, 1979; played Morris in the original production of Blood-Knot in South Africa, 1961; Hampstead, June 1966, again played Morris and directed; at the same theatre, also June 1966, directed The Trials of Brother Jero; at the Royal Court, Jan 1974, directed The Island, Sizwe Bansi and Statements; directed Dimetos at the Edinburgh Festival, Aug 1975, and at the Comedy, May 1976; directed Hello and Goodbye, Riverside, Feb 1978; has worked since 1964 with the Serpent Players, Port Elizabeth, with whom he originated Sizwe Bansi and The Island; work for television, in Britain, includes Blood-Knot (again playing Morris) and Mille Miglia.

Address: Box 5090, Walmer, Port Elizabeth, South Africa.

FULLER, Rosalinde, MBE, actress
b Portsmouth, Hants; *d* of Walter H Fuller and his wife Elizabeth G (White); *e* at home; the late Cecil Sharp was instrumental in discovering her.

On his advice she adopted singing as a profession; she went to America in 1914, and gave concerts of folk songs for four seasons; during 1918 appeared at the Folies Bergère, Paris, in the chorus of a revue; she gave entertainments to the American troops in France during 1919; made her first appearance on the regular stage at Maxine Elliott's Theatre, New York, 19 Mar 1920, when she appeared in Murray Anderson's revue What's in a Name? scoring an immediate success; she then appeared at the Longacre Theatre, Jan 1921, as Mary Burroughs in The Champion, her first straight part; at the Shubert Theatre, Aug 1921, appeared in The Greenwich Village Follies; at the Earl Carroll, June 1922, in Raymond Hitchcock's Pinwheel; she then appeared at the Sam H Harris Theatre, Nov 1922, as Ophelia to the Hamlet of John Barrymore and continued to play the part in NY, and on tour right through 1923; she then joined the Provincetown Players, and at the Provincetown Theatre, Apr 1924, appeared as the Bride in The Ancient Mariner and Angélique in George Dandin; at the Comedy, NY, Oct 1924, played Sibley Sweetland in The Farmer's Wife, and then at the Provincetown Playhouse, Dec 1924, appeared as Patience in Gilbert and Sullivan's opera; at Greenwich Village, Mar 1925, played Miss Prue in Love for Love; Comedy, Oct 1925, Irene in The Call of Life; Greenwich Village, Dec 1925, Beatrice de Cordova in The Fountain; Fifth Avenue Playhouse, Jan 1926, Constance Ussher in The House of Ussher; at the Klaw, Sept 1926, Mary Denvers in Scotch Mist; at the Lyceum, Dec 1926, Fiametta in What Never Dies, and Mansfield, Mar 1927, Margarita in Lost; on returning to England, made her first appearance on the London stage, at the Globe Theatre, 15 Nov 1927, as Nubi in The Squall; Arts Theatre, Feb 1928, as the Betrothed in The Unknown Warrior; at Wyndham's, Apr 1928, succeeded Sybil Thorndike as Rosamond Withers

in The Stranger in the House; at the Strand, July 1928, played Pauli Arendt in The Enemy; at the Lyric, Feb 1929, Felisi in Always Afternoon; at the Gate Theatre Studio, June 1929, Eleanor Owen in Welded; Fortune, Oct 1929, Irina in The Three Sisters; Court, Dec 1929–Mar 1930, Raina in Arms and the Man, Ann Whitefield in Man and Superman, Julia Craven in The Philanderer, Hypatia Tarleton in Misalliance; Streatham Hill, Sept 1930, Diana Field in The Cheat; Little, Nov 1930, again played the Betrothed in The Unknown Warrior; Apollo, Jan 1931, Renée Martinetti in Bed Rock; Court, Mar 1931, Vivie in Mrs Warren's Profession; Savoy, June 1931, Alda Cesarea in Death Takes a Holiday; Kingsway, May 1932, Elizabeth Ffoulkes in The Cheque-Mate; Duke of York's, June 1932, played in continuous Grand Guignol plays; Q, Apr 1933, Rose Giralda in a play of that name; Ambassadors', May 1933, Jeanne in Martine; Q, Sept 1933, Margot Gresham in First Episode; Embassy, Oct 1933, Julia in Son of Man; in Mar 1934, toured as Varsovina in Ballerina; Prince's, Sept 1934, Jill-all-alone in Merrie England; Westminster, Nov 1934, the Girl in The Unknown Warrior; Arts, Jan 1935, Julie in Miss Julie; Adelphi, Dec 1935, Fritzi in the musical play of that name; Royalty, May 1936, Ann in Marriage Settlement; Winter Garden, Sept 1936, Mary Sheldon and Helen Wainwright in Murder on Account; in the autumn of 1938, joined Donald Wolfit's Shakespearean Company playing Portia in The Merchant of Venice, Rosalind, Beatrice, Desdemona and Lady Macbeth; appeared in these parts at the People's Palace, London, Oct 1938; again toured in these parts, 1939, and at Dublin, in May 1939, also played Raina in Arms and the Man; appeared with Donald Wolfit's company at the Kingsway, Feb–Mar 1940, as Viola in Twelfth Night, Katherine in The Taming of the Shrew, Desdemona, Portia, and Beatrice; Palace, July 1940, Zahrat-Al-Kulub in Chu-Chin-Chow; Vaudeville, Dec 1940, Kate Pettigrew in Berkeley Square; Palace, July 1941, again played in Chu-Chin-Chow; toured, 1941, as Abbie in Desire Under the Elms; toured, 1943, as Leslie Crosbie in The Letter; 1944, as Jane Eyre, and as Olivia Russell in This Was a Woman; toured, 1945, as Madame Bovary in a play of that name, and appeared in this as Emma Bovary at the Q, Aug 1946; Alexandra, Stoke Newington, Mar 1947, played Anne Beaumont in Lady of the Night; in Aug 1947, went to California to play in summer theatres in Miss Julie; on her return, appeared at Dunfermline Abbey, Sept 1947, as Beauty in Everyman; toured, 1948, as Gisela in Dark Summer, and Laura in The Eleventh Hour, and 1949, as Janet Spence in The Gioconda Smile; Watergate, Jan 1950, played Fräulein Else in her own adaptation of the novel; toured, 1950, as Paula in Random Harvest; at the Watergate, June 1950, appeared in Masks and Faces, a programme of character impressions, her own adaptations from the works of Guy de Maupassant, Schnitzler, etc; has since developed and specialized in this form of entertainment, appearing in her Solo Theatre presentations all over this country, in NY, and in coast to coast tours of the US, with great success; Watergate, Nov 1950, played Solange in The Typewriter; New Boltons, Mar 1951, played Gertrude in Hamlet; toured, Apr 1951, as Delia in Women Are Murder; toured, July 1951, as Hattie in A Guardsman's Cup of Tea; Q, Mar 1952, and subsequently on tour, played Yvonne in Intimate Relations; New Boltons, May 1952, Mrs Violet Mason in Desire Shall Fail; Royal, Bath, June 1952, Abbie Streeter in The Streeter Case; toured, Sept 1952, as Sari Rilla in All Cats Are Grey; toured, Apr 1953, as Pamela Dark in Ladies in Waiting; at Darlington, July 1953, appeared as guest star in Jane Eyre and They Walk Alone; Sadler's Wells, July 1954, played Lady Isabel in East Lynne; New Lindsey, Sept 1954, Coral

Spenser in Fortune's Finger; during 1955 continued to appear in her Solo Theatre performances in England and the United States, and returned to the Arts, Oct 1956, with Hearts and Faces; Arts, Cambridge, Feb 1957, played Sister Teresa in The Cardinal; June 1957–60, appeared in Israel, the United States, Iraq, South Africa, and England, with her solo performances; return visit to South Africa and Uganda, 1961; June–Dec 1962, toured Australia, New Zealand, Fiji, Mauritius and Kenya; again toured Europe, 1963, with her solo performances; for the British Council, May–Dec 1964, toured Iran, Afghanistan, Malaysia, Australia, Trinidad, Jamaica, British Honduras, and the Bahamas, also touring South Africa, July–Oct 1965; Hampstead Theatre Club, Oct 1965, appeared solo in Subject To Love, then touring England, Holland, Sweden, Turkey and Poland; Arts Theatre Club, Jan 1968, solo performance, A Night With Guy de Maupassant, with which she toured from March to August in Australia, Tasmania, Manila, Hong Kong and Katmandu; Arts, Feb 1969, solo performance Anton Chekhov—Short Stories, followed by an English tour, and later (Mar–May 1970) a Swiss tour; Arts Theatre Club, 1970, solo performance, The Human Voice; Oct–Dec 1970, again toured England; further tours in England and overseas, 1971–5; premiered her new programme, The Snail Under the Leaf, based on the life and work of Katherine Mansfield, Durban, Sept 1975; entered films, 1929, and has appeared in numerous pictures; received the MBE in the New Year Honours, 1966.

Recreations: Reading, writing and walking. *Address:* 153 King Henry's Road, London, NW3. *Tel:* 01–722 6794.

FURTH, George, actor and playwright.

Made his New York début at The Playhouse, 19 Oct 1961, as Jordan in A Cook for Mr General; Majestic, Apr 1963, played Harley in the musical Hot Spot; New Theater for Now, Los Angeles, 1973, played in Tadpole; wrote his first Broadway play, the book for the musical Company, produced at the Alvin, 26 Apr 1970, and in London at Her Majesty's, Jan 1972; wrote Twigs, produced at the Broadhurst, Nov 1971; book for The Act, Majestic, Oct 1977; has appeared in films, notably Butch Cassidy and the Sundance Kid, 1969, Myra Breckenridge, 1970, Blazing Saddles, 1974, and many others; has also appeared on television in various dramatic programs.

Address: Actors Equity Association, 165 West 46th Street, New York, NY 10036.

G

GABEL, Martin, actor, producer, and director
b Philadelphia, Pa, 19 June 1912; *s* of Israel Gabel and his wife Ruth (Herzog); *e* Lehigh University, Pa; *m* Arlene Francis; studied for the stage at the American Academy of Dramatic Art.

Made his first appearance on the stage at the Lyceum Theatre, New York, 25 Apr 1933, as Emmett in Man Bites Dog; Fulton, Dec 1934, played Dumkopf in The Sky's the Limit; Chicago, Mar 1935, Frankie in Three Men on a Horse; Belasco, NY, Oct 1935, Hunk in Dead End; St James, Oct 1936, Peter in Ten Million Ghosts; Mercury, Nov 1937, Cassius in Julius Caesar (in modern dress); Nov 1938, Danton in Danton's Death; Maxine Elliott, Jan 1940, directed A Young Couple Wanted; New Yorker, Apr 1940, the Statistician in Medicine Show, of which he was also co-producer; Cort, Oct 1940, co-produced Charley's Aunt; Booth, Jan 1941, presented (with Carley Wharton), The Cream in the Well; Cort, Jan 1942, presented (with Carley Wharton), Café Crown; National, Oct 1945, staged The Assassin; at the Playhouse, Jan 1948, presented and staged The Survivors; National, Dec 1950, appeared as the Earl of Kent in King Lear; 48th Street, Apr 1953, presented (with Chandler Cowles) and staged Men of Distinction; Lyceum, Oct 1954, presented (with Henry Margolis) Reclining Figure, in which he appeared as Jonas Astorg; Belasco, Oct 1955, Irving Lasalle in Will Success Spoil Rock Hunter?; Playhouse, Jan 1957, co-produced The Hidden River; National, Oct 1958, co-produced Once More, With Feeling, which he also co-produced at the New, London, in July 1959; toured the US and at the Bijou, NY, Feb 1959, played Stephen A Douglas in The Rivalry; Shubert, New Haven, Dec 1959, co-produced Sweet Love Remember'd; ANTA, Mar 1961, played Basil Smythe in Big Fish, Little Fish, for which he received the Antoinette Perry (Tony) and *Variety* New York Drama Critics Awards; Morosco, Apr 1963, played Melvin Peabody in Children from Their Games; Broadway, Feb 1965, played Professor Moriarty in the musical Baker Street; John Golden, Sept 1965, produced Mrs Dally; Helen Hayes, Jan 1970, Joseph Mayflower in Sheep on the Runway; Morosco, Dec 1974, Mark Walters in In Praise of Love; played Dr Eggelhofer in the film of The Front Page, 1974; on television, 1964, Narrator for The Making of the President.
Address: Actors Equity Association, 165 West 46th Street, New York, NY 10036.

GAGLIANO, Frank (*né* Francis Joseph), playwright
b Brooklyn, New York, 18 Nov 1931; *s* of Francis Paul Gagliano and his wife Nancy (La-Barbera); *e* Queens College, University of Iowa, and Columbia University; *m* Sandra Gordon.

Formerly engaged as a copywriter; first play was The Library Raid, produced at the Alley Theatre, Houston, Texas, 12 Oct 1961; first play produced in NY was Conerico Was Here to Stay, at the Cherry Lane, 3 Mar 1965; is the author of the following plays: Night of the Dunce, 1966; Father Uxbridge Wants to Marry, The Hide-and-Seek Odyssey of Madeline Gimple (a children's play), 1967; The City Scene, 1969; The Prince of Peasantmania, produced by the Milwaukee Repertory Theatre Co, 1970; Quasimodo (musical), 1971; Anywhere the Wind Blows, 1972; In the Voodoo Parlor of Marie Leveau, The Commedia World of Lafcadio Beau, 1974; Congo Square, 1975 (with composer Claibe Richardson); The Resurrection of Jackie Cramer, 1976 (with composer Raymond Benson); The Total Immersion of Madeleine Favorini, 1979; author of the television play Big Sur, produced 20 Apr 1969; Father Uxbridge Wants to Marry produced on educational television; is a member of the Dramatists Guild, the New Dramatists Committee, the Eugene O'Neill Theatre Center, Actors Studio, the Writers Guild of America; taught at the Florida State University, 1969–73; University of Texas at Austin, 1973–5; Benedam Professor of Playwriting, West Virginia Univ, 1975–; awarded a Rockefeller Foundation grant, 1965–6; National Endowment for the Arts fellowship in playwriting, 1973; Guggenheim fellowship, 1974.
Recreations: Reading, listening to music. *Address:* c/o Gilbert Parker, 575 Madison Avenue, New York, NY 10022.

GALE, John, producer
b Chigwell, Essex, 2 Aug 1929; *s* of Frank Haith Gale and his wife Martha Edith (Evans); *e* Christ's Hospital; *m* Liselotte Ann Wratten.

Formerly an actor; presented his first production in association with Peter Bridge and Clement Scott Gilbert, at the St Martin's, Mar 1960, with Inherit the Wind; he has since produced or co-produced the following plays: Candida, 1960; On the Brighter Side, Caesar and Cleopatra, 1961; Boeing-Boeing, Big Fish, Little Fish, 1962; Devil May Care, Windfall, Where Angels Fear to Tread, The Wings of the Dove, 1963; Amber for Anna, The Easter Man, 1964; Boeing-Boeing (New York), Present Laughter, 1964; Maigret and the Lady, Dear Wormwood (tour), The Platinum Cat, 1965; The Sacred Flame, An Evening with GBS, 1966; Minor Murder, A Woman of No Importance, 1967; The Secretary Bird, Dear Charles, 1968; Highly Confidential, The Young Churchill, The Lionel Touch, 1969; Abelard and Heloise, 1970; No Sex Please, We're British, 1971; Lloyd George Knew My Father, The Mating Game, Parents' Day, 1972; At the End of the Day, Signs of the Times, 1973; Birds of Paradise, 1974; A Touch of Spring, Betzi, No Room for Sex (tour), 1975; Out on a Limb, 1976; Separate Tables, The Kingfisher, Sextet, Cause Célèbre, Shut Your Eyes and Think of England, 1977; Murder Among Friends, 1978; Under the Greenwood Tree, Can You Hear Me At the Back?, Happy Birthday, Middle Age Spread, 1979; The Secretary Bird and No Sex Please set records for the longest run at the Savoy and Strand theatres respectively; President, Society of West End Theatre Managers, 1972–5; Chairman of Theatres National Committee.
Recreations: Travel, rugby (Chairman, London Welsh RFC, 1978–9). *Clubs:* Garrick, Green Room. *Address:* Strand Theatre, Aldwych, London, WC2. *Tel:* 01–240 1656.

GALLACHER, Tom, playwright
b Alexandria, Dunbartonshire, 16 Feb 1934; *s* of Edward Gallacher and his wife Rose (Connolly); *e* thirteen primary schools in England and Scotland, two secondary schools in Scotland.

Author of the following full-length plays: Our Kindness to Five Persons, produced Glasgow, 1969; Mr Joyce Is Leaving Paris, 1971; Revival!, 1972; Schellenbrack, The Only Street, 1973; Personal Effects, 1974; A Laughing Matter, Hallowe'en, 1975; The Sea Change, 1976; The Evidence of Tiny Tim (with Joan Knight), 1977; Wha's Like Us – Fortunately, Stage Door Canteen (with John Scrimger), 1978; Jenny, 1979; has adapted A Presbyterian Wooing (from Pitcairne), 1976; Cyrano de Bergerac (Rostand), 1977; Deacon Brodie (Stevenson and Henley), 1978; An Enemy of the People (Ibsen), 1979; has also written one-acts and plays for radio, and the television plays The Trial of Thomas Muir, 1977, and If the Face Fits, 1978; writer-in-residence, Pitlochry Festival Theatre, 1975–78; Royal Lyceum Company, Edinburgh, 1978–present; member of drama committee, Scottish Arts Council, 1978–present.

Address: c/o Michael Imison, Dr Jan van Loewen Ltd, 81–83 Shaftesbury Avenue, London W1.

GALLAGHER, Helen, actress and singer
b Brooklyn, New York, 1926; *m* Frank Wise; studied at the American Ballet School.

Made her NY début at the Ziegfeld, 1945, when she took over a role in The Seven Lively Arts; Century, Sept 1945, appeared in Mr Strauss Goes to Boston; at the Alvin, Dec 1945, played various roles in Billion Dollar Baby; Ziegfeld, Mar 1947, in Brigadoon; Century, Oct 1947, played Nancy in High Button Shoes; Broadway, Oct 1949, appeared in the revue Touch and Go; made her London début in this revue at the Prince of Wales's, May 1950; Winter Garden, Apr 1951, Poupette in Make a Wish; Broadhurst, Jan 1952, Gladys Bumps in a revival of Pal Joey; Mark Hellinger, Feb 1953, played the title-role in Hazel Flagg; City Center, Apr 1955, Miss Adelaide in Guys and Dolls; City Center, May 1955, Sharon McLonergan in Finian's Rainbow; St James, May 1955, took over the role of Gladys in The Pajama Game; toured, 1956, as Chérie in Bus Stop; City Center, Mar 1957, Meg Brockie in Brigadoon; 54th Street, Feb 1958, Kitty in Portofino; City Center, Mar 1958, Ado Annie Carnes in Oklahoma! subsequently appearing in this role at the Municipal Opera, St Louis, Aug 1958; same theatre, also 1958, Miss Adelaide in Guys and Dolls; Palm Beach Playhouse, Florida, Mar 1959, Small Servant in Pound in Your Pocket; St Paul Civic Opera, St Paul, Minn, Jan 1964, appeared in The Pajama Game; at the reopening of the Palace, NY, Jan 1966, Nickie in Sweet Charity; Palace, July 1966, took over the role of Charity in this musical; toured, 1967–8, in the US and Canada as Nickie in Sweet Charity; Winter Garden, 1968, took over as Agnes Gooch in Mame; Broadhurst, Apr 1970, Bessie Legg in Cry for Us All; 46th Street, Jan 1971, Lucille Early in No, No, Nanette; toured, summer 1973, in the revue The Gershwin Years; toured, summer 1974, as Lucille Early in No, No, Nanette; Reno Sweeney, NY, Oct 1974, appeared in cabaret; Brooklyn Academy of Music, Oct 1974, Roz Duncan in Hot House; Theater Four, Apr 1976, appeared in Tickles by Tucholsky; Queen's Festival, June 1977, in The Gingerbread Lady; Public, Oct 1977, Arsinoe in The Misanthrope; has appeared in night clubs and on television.

Address: Actors Equity Association, 165 West 46th Street, New York, NY 10036.

GAMBON, Michael, actor
b Dublin, 19 Oct 1940; *s* of Edward Gambon and his wife Mary (Hoare); *e* St Aloysius School, London; *m* Anne Miller; formerly an engineer.

First appeared on the stage at the Gaiety, Dublin, 1962, as second Gentleman in Othello, followed by a European tour; joined the National Theatre Company at the Old Vic, 1963, where his parts included: Coster Pearmain in The Recruiting

Officer, Diego in The Royal Hunt of the Sun (also Chichester Festival), 1964; Herrick in The Crucible, Eilif in Mother Courage, Snap in Love for Love (also tour to Russia and Germany), 1965; Jerry Devine in Juno and the Paycock, 1966; with the Birmingham Repertory company, 1967–8, his parts included: Flynn in The Bofors Gun, Palmer Anderson in A Severed Head, Patrick Cullen in The Doctor's Dilemma, Cauchon in Saint Joan, the Button Moulder in Peer Gynt, Escalus in Romeo and Juliet, and the title-part in Othello; Forum, Billingham 1968, played Macbeth; Liverpool Playhouse, 1969, Andrew in In Celebration, and title-role in Coriolanus; joined the Royal Shakespeare Company at Aldwych, season 1970–1, to play Wiebe in The Plebeians Rehearse the Uprising, July, Charles Lomax in Major Barbara, Oct, and Surrey in Henry VIII, Dec, as well as Hotspur in When Thou Art King, Round House, Oct; Arnaud, Guildford, July 1972, Guy Holden in The Brass Hat; Greenwich, Sept 1973, Robin in Not Drowning But Waving; same theatre, May 1974, Tom in The Norman Conquests, transferring to the Globe, Aug 1975; Open Air, Regent's Park, July 1975, appeared as Gerry in a lunchtime production of The Zoo Story; Queen's, 1976, took over as Simon in Otherwise Engaged; Queen's, Apr 1977, Neil in Just Between Ourselves; Savoy, May 1978, Bertie in Alice's Boys; joined the National Theatre Company, 1978, playing Jerry in Betrayal, Nov, and Henry in Close of Play, May 1979; took over as Buckingham in Richard III, Feb 1980; Roderigo in Othello, Mar, 1980; TV, since 1964, includes: The Secret Agent, Tiptoe Through the Tulips, and The Seagull; films include: Othello, Nothing But the Night and The Beast Must Die.

Favourite part: Othello. *Recreations:* Flying, guitar, and collecting heavy industrial plant. *Address:* c/o Larry Dalzell Associates Ltd, 3 Goodwin's Court, St Martin's Lane, London WC2. *Tel:* 01–240 3086.

GARDE, Betty, actress
b Philadelphia, Pa, 19 Sept 1905; *d* of Charles Pierie Garde and his wife Katherine M (Cropper); *e* West Philadelphia High School; *m* Frank Lennon.

Made her first appearance on the stage at the Broadway, Philadelphia, May 1922, as the Maid in Nice People; remained in Philadelphia, 1922–4, with the Mae Desmond Players; toured, 1924, as Harriet Underwood in The Nervous Wreck; made her New York début at the Cohan, 26 Oct 1925, as Alma Borden in Easy Come, Easy Go; toured, 1926, as Julia Winters in The Poor Nut; from 1927–30, was leading lady with the Wright Players in Michigan; Fulton, NY, Nov 1931, Gloria Hall in The Social Register; Waldorf, Mar 1933, Millie in The Best People; spent six years on radio programs, principally on *Lux Radio Theatre* as Eddie Cantor's leading lady, 1935–7, and with Orson Welles's Mercury Players; reappeared on the stage at the Biltmore, Jan 1939, as Emma Wallace in The Primrose Path; Westport, Conn, summer 1941, played Madame Muscat in Liliom; St James, Mar 1943, Aunt Eller in Oklahoma!; in 1945 toured US Army installations overseas, playing, among other parts, Gertrude Lennox in Meet the Wife; Playhouse, Wilmington, Delaware, Feb 1952, Sarah Rock in A Little Evil; Downtown National, Mar 1955, Frosine in The Miser; New York City Center, Mar 1958, Aunt Eller in Oklahoma!; same theatre, Feb 1963, again played Aunt Eller in Oklahoma!; Henry Miller's, Dec 1966, Mrs Gordon in Agatha Sue, I Love You; East 74th Street, Sept 1967, Dante in Stephen D; Peachtree Playhouse, Atlanta, Ga, Jan 1975, Mrs Greenhouse in The Sponsor; entered films in 1929 in The Lady Lies, and subsequently appeared in Girl Habit, 1931, Call Northside 777, 1948,

Caged, 1950, The Wonderful World of the Brothers Grimm, 1962, etc; has appeared frequently on the major dramatic television programs, including *Hallmark Hall of Fame, Twilight Zone, One Step Beyond, The Real McCoys*, etc.

Hobbies: Cooking, animals and collecting classical phonograph records. *Recreations:* Piano playing and composing. *Address:* 3928 Carpenter Avenue, Studio City, Calif 91604. *Tel:* 213–760–0061.

GARDEN, Graeme, writer and actor
b Aberdeen, 18 Feb 1943; *s* of Robert Symon Garden and his wife Janet Ann; *e* Repton School, Emmanuel College, Cambridge and Kings College Hospital, London; *m* Liz Grice.

Appeared with the Footlights while at Cambridge; toured for Cambridge Theatre Company, and made his London debut at the Phoenix, Apr 1978, as Bert Hopkins in The Unvarnished Truth; toured, 1979, as Percy in Rattle of a Simple Man, and in Schooldays, 1980; Royal Court, Sept 1980, appeared in Cloud Nine; his play The Magicalympical Games was produced at Nottingham in 1976; TV, since *Twice a Fortnight*, 1967, includes several series of *The Goodies*, which he co-writes; member, Association of Illustrators.

Address: c/o Roger Hancock Ltd, 8 Waterloo Place, Pall Mall, London SW1.

GARDENIA, Vincent (*né* Scognamiglio), actor
b Naples, Italy, 7 Jan 1922; *s* of Gennaro Gardenia Scognamiglio and his wife Elisa (Ausiello); *e* in New York at PS 186 and the Shallow Junior High School; trained for the stage at the Italian Theater, NYC.

First appeared on the stage at the age of five at the 5th Avenue, Brooklyn, as the Shoe Shine Boy in Shoe Shine; first appeared professionally in NY at the Broadway Tabernacle Church, 13 Mar 1955, as Hugo, A Pirate in In April Once; Cherry Lane, May 1956, played Piggy in The Man with the Golden Arm; Rooftop, Jan 1957, Corvino in Volpone; Gate, Dec 1957, Fyodor in The Brothers Karamazov; Lunt-Fontanne, 5 May 1958, Blind Man in The Visit; Morosco, Dec 1958, Jim Nightingale in The Cold Wind and the Warm; Music Box, 1959, took over as the Deputy in Rashomon; York Playhouse, Sept 1959, Mittrich in The Power of Darkness; Cort, Nov 1959, Chairman in Only in America; Gate, Apr 1960, George H Jones in Machinal; Billy Rose, Oct 1960, Pavel Menkes in The Wall; Gramercy Arts, Apr 1961, Warden in Gallows Humor; Music Box, Nov 1961, Sergeant Manzoni in Daughter of Silence; Cherry Lane, Feb 1962, in a season called Theatre of the Absurd, played Hamm in Endgame and the Warden in Gallows Humor; Belasco, Oct 1962, Wilenski in Seidman and Son; Theatre de Lys, Nov 1962, Mr Jones and Workman in The Lunatic View in the ANTA Matinee Series; Charles Playhouse, Boston, 1967–8 season, Eddie Carbone in A View from the Bridge; Circle in the Square, Jan 1969, Carol Newquist in Little Murders; Sheridan Square Playhouse, Dec 1969, Charles Ferris in The Son Who Hunted Tigers in Jakarta and Nick Esposito in The Burial of Esposito in a production with the overall title Passing Through from Exotic Places; Ethel Barrymore, Mar 1970, Marty Mendelsohn in Dr Fish in the double-bill The Chinese and Dr Fish; American Place, Dec 1970, the Father in The Carpenters; Eugene O'Neill, Nov 1971, Harry Edison in The Prisoner of Second Avenue, for which he received the Antoinette Perry (Tony) Award; Eugene O'Neill, Dec 1974, Joe Benjamin in God's Favorite; Eugene O'Neill, June 1977, took over as Marvin and Mort in California Suite; Broadhurst, Jan 1978, took over as Foxwell J Sly in Sly Fox; Majestic, Dec 1978, Alfred Rossi in Ballroom; first appeared in films in Murder Inc, 1960, and has since played in Little

Murders, 1971, Bang the Drum Slowly, 1973, Deathwish, 1974, The Front Page, 1974, Heaven Can Wait, 1979, etc; first appeared on television in 1955 and has since played in *Studio One, The Untouchables, All in the Family, Maude,* 1974, and various other dramatic programmes.

Favourite parts: Willie Loman in Death of a Salesman, Eddie in A View from the Bridge, Carol Newquist in Little Murders. *Recreations:* Cooking, mountain climbing on 12th Avenue. *Address:* c/o Jay Julien, 9 East 41st Street, New York, NY 10017. *Tel:* OX 7–9680.

GARLAND, Patrick, director and dramatic author
s of Ewart Garland; *e* St Edmund Hall, Oxford.

Acted at Oxford, where he was president of OUDS, and for two years after coming down, 1959–61, with the Bristol Old Vic and other companies; has directed, in London unless otherwise stated, his adaptation of Brief Lives (also New York), 1967; Forty Years On, 1968; Brief Lives, The Stiffkey Scandals of 1932, 1969; Hair, Tel Aviv, and Cyrano (in his own adaptation for the National Theatre), A Doll's House, NY, 1970; Hedda Gabler, NY, 1971; Getting On, 1971; The Man Trap, Cheltenham, 1972; A Doll's House, Kilvert and his Diary, Mad Dog, 1973; Billy, 1974; Enemy of the People, Chichester, 1975; Signed and Sealed, M Perrichon's Travels, Chichester, 1976; The Apple Cart (also Australia), Murder in the Cathedral (Chichester Cathedral), Shut Your Eyes and Think of England, 1977; Waters of the Moon, Look After Lulu (Chichester), Under the Greenwood Tree (also adapted), 1978; Beecham, 1980; has produced and directed regularly for TV, notably the Famous Gossips series *On the Margin*, and The Snow Goose; also an interviewer; as well as the adaptations mentioned above, he has written poetry, short stories, television plays (including The Hard Case and Flow Gently, Sweet Afton) and a radio play, The Great Illusion; his dramatic anthology, The Rebel, was presented by the RSC at Stratford in 1964.

GARRETT, Betty, actress and singer
b St Joseph, Missouri, 23 May 1919; *d* of Curtis Garrett and his wife Elizabeth Octavia (Stone); *e* Tacoma, Washington; *m* Larry Parks (dec); studied for the stage at the School of the Theatre, and at the Neighborhood Playhouse, New York.

Made her first appearance on the stage at the Mercury Theatre, NY, Nov 1938, in Danton's Death; appeared as a leading dancer with the Martha Graham Company, 1938; appeared at the World's Fair, NY, 1939, in Railroads on Parade; Barbizon-Plaza, Apr 1940, played in You Can't Sleep Here; Pauline Edwards, Nov 1940, played in musical revue; Mail Studios, Dec 1940, played in A Piece of Our Mind; Majestic, 1941, took over roles in the revue All in Fun; toured, 1941, in Meet the People; Concert, Feb 1942, appeared in the revue Of V We Sing; Longacre, NY, Oct 1942, appeared in the revue Let Freedom Sing; Alvin, Jan 1943, played Mary Francis in Something for the Boys; Alvin, Jan 1944, played Sergeant Maguire in Jackpot; Winter Garden, Dec 1944, appeared in Laffin' Room Only; at the National, NY, Apr 1946, appeared in Call Me Mister; made her first London appearance at the Palladium, 29 May 1950, with her husband in a program of songs; toured Scotland and Canada, 1952, in vaudeville; toured the US, 1952–3, as Marion Maxwell in The Anonymous Lover; Shubert, NY, 1958, for two weeks took over the role of Ella Peterson in Bells Are Ringing; Martin Beck, Feb 1960, played Clara in Beg, Borrow, or Steal; Booth, Sept 1963, appeared in a staged reading of Spoon River Anthology; Cort, Sept 1964, played Penny Moore in A Girl Could Get Lucky; toured, 1965, as Gloria in The Tiger and Sylvia in The Typists; Mark Taper

Forum, Los Angeles, 1968, played in Who's Happy Now?; toured, 1968–70, as Karen Nash, Muriel Tate, and Norma Hubley in Plaza Suite; toured, 1972, as Catherine Reardon in And Miss Reardon Drinks a Little; Los Angeles, 1974–5, appeared in her show Betty Garrett and Other Songs; first entered films, 1948, in The Big City, and subsequently appeared in On the Town, My Sister Eileen, Words and Music, etc; has appeared on television in various dramatic roles.

Recreations: Painting and ceramics. *Address:* c/o Louis Mandel, 9454 Wilshire Boulevard, Beverly Hills, Calif 90212.

GASCOIGNE, Bamber, dramatic critic, author, and lyricist
b London, 24 Jan 1935; *s* of Ernest Frederick Orby Gascoigne and his wife Mary Louisa Hermione (O'Neill); *e* Eton College and Magdalene College, Cambridge; *m* Christina Ditchburn.

Began his career at the ADC Theatre, Cambridge, as author of the diversion Share My Lettuce, Feb 1957; this revue subsequently transferred to London, where it was given a professional production at the Lyric, Hammersmith, Aug 1957, at the Comedy, Sept 1957, and also at the Garrick, Jan 1958, running for over 300 performances; author of the plays Leda Had a Little Swan, 1968, The Feydeau Farce Festival of Nineteen Nine, 1972; he has appeared on television, since 1962, as Chairman of *University Challenge;* wrote and presented *The Christians,* 1977; dramatic critic of *The Spectator,* 1961–3; dramatic critic of *The Observer,* 1963–4; author of Twentieth Century Drama, 1962; World Theatre, 1968; Murgatreud's Empire, 1972; Fellow of the Royal Society of Literature, 1976.

Address: c/o Curtis Brown, 1 Craven Hill, London, W2.

GASCON, Jean, actor and director
b Montreal, Canada, 21 Dec 1921; *s* of Charles Auguste Gascon and his wife Rose (Dubuc); *e* Montreal; *m* Marie LaLonde; was for five years a medical student at the Université de Montreal, before joining a semi-professional theatre company in Montreal as a student, where he remained for four years; spent three years in France (studying for one year with Ludmilla Pitoeff in Paris).

During this time appeared in the title-role of L'Avare (Molière), also directing the play at the Centre Dramatique de l'Ouest, 1950; made his first appearance in New York at the Phoenix Theatre, Nov 1951, when he directed Molière's An Evening of Farces and The Imaginary Invalid; Théâtre du Nouveau Monde, Montreal, 1952, played Don Juan in Molière's Don Juan; he has since been associated with this theatre company, both as an actor and Artistic Director; during the summer of 1955, he directed the Théâtre du Nouveau Monde production of Molière's An Evening of Farces, at the Sarah Bernhardt Theatre during the Paris Festival; at the Gesu Theatre, Montreal, Jan 1956, directed and played the title-role in Nemo; Stratford Shakespeare Festival, Ontario, 1956, appeared as The Constable of France in Henry V; in 1958 he directed Théâtre du Nouveau Monde company when they visited NY, Paris, Brussels, Stratford (Ontario), and toured from coast to coast in Canada, with An Evening of French Farces (in which he also played Pancrace in Le Mariage Forcé and Béralde in Le Malade Imaginaire); Stratford Shakespeare Festival, Ontario, 1959, co-directed Othello; Phoenix, NY, 1959, directed Lysistrata; Stratford Festival, Ontario, June 1963, directed The Comedy of Errors; Chichester Festival, England, Apr 1964, directed the Stratford Ontario Company in Le Bourgeois Gentilhomme, the production subsequently included at the Stratford Festival, Ontario, June 1964; Avon, Stratford Festival, Ontario,

July 1965, directed The Rise and Fall of the City of Mahagonny, and The Marriage of Figaro; Old Vic, Sept 1965, directed and played Arnolphe in L'Ecole des Femmes, and directed Klondyke, with the Théâtre du Nouveau Monde Company; Stratford Festival, June 1966, co-directed Henry V; Avon, July 1966, directed and played Edgar in The Dance of Death; Stratford Festival, Ontario, July 1967, Dr Caius in The Merry Wives of Windsor; Artistic Director, Stratford Festival, 1968–74; in 1968, directed Tartuffe and The Seagull; 1969, directed Hadrian VII; 1970, directed The Merchant of Venice, Cymbeline, Tartuffe; 1971, directed The Duchess of Malfi, There's One in Every Marriage; 1972, directed Lorenzaccio, The Threepenny Opera; 1973, directed The Taming of the Shrew (also European tour), Pericles; 1974, directed The Imaginary Invalid (also Australian tour), Pericles, La Vie Parisienne; in 1975 directed The Miser (Lakewood, Ohio), and Cyrano de Bergerac (Winnipeg); Anatol (Montreal), 1976; Le Médecin Volant/Le Médecin Malgré Lui (double bill), Floralie (Ottawa), 1977; National Arts Centre Studio, May 1978, played the title-role in The Father; appeared in the film A Man Called Horse, 1970; made his first appearance on television, 1953, and has since played in numerous programmes including Œdipus Rex, and L'Annonce faite à Marie; holder of honorary degrees from six Canadian universities; Officer of the Order of Canada.

Recreations: Cooking, swimming, travelling. *Club:* Canadian Theater Center. *Address:* 956 Dunlop, Montreal, Canada. *Tel:* Reg 8–4346.

GASKILL, William, director
b Shipley, Yorks, 24 June 1930; *s* of Joseph Linnaeus Gaskill and his wife Maggie (Simpson); *e* Salt High School, Shipley, and Hertford College, Oxford; formerly a male nurse, factory worker, and a baker.

Directed his first production at Redcar, Yorks, Feb 1954, with The First Mrs Fraser; at the Theatre Royal, Stratford, E, June 1955, assisted the director of The Country Wife, also appearing as Quack in the production; Q Theatre, Nov 1955, directed The Hawthorn Tree; directed his first London production at the Royal Court, Dec 1957, with A Resounding Tinkle, in a Production without Décor, for the English Stage Company; he has since directed the following plays: Epitaph for George Dillon, the double-bill of A Resounding Tinkle (one-act version) and The Hole, Brixham Regatta, Epitaph for George Dillon (New York), 1958; Sugar in the Morning, One Way Pendulum, 1959; The Deadly Game (NY), The Happy Haven, 1960; Richard III (Stratford-on-Avon), That's Us, Arden of Faversham, 1961; The Caucasian Chalk Circle, Cymbeline (Stratford-on-Avon), Infanticide in the House of Fred Ginger, 1962; Baal, 1963; Associate Director of the National Theatre, 1963–5, for whom he directed the following productions: The Recruiting Officer, 1963; Philoctetes, The Dutch Courtesan (also at the Chichester Festival), 1964; Mother Courage, Armstrong's Last Goodnight (co-directed) (also Chichester Festival), 1965; Artistic Director of the English Stage Company, Sept 1965–July 1972; he directed the following plays for the Company, at the Royal Court (unless otherwise stated): Saved, 1965; A Chaste Maid in Cheapside, The Performing Giant (co-directed), Their Very Own and Golden City, Macbeth, 1966; The Three Sisters, Fill the Stage with Happy Hours (Vaudeville), 1967; Early Morning, 1968; Saved, Early Morning, The Double Dealer, 1969; Come and Go and Play (in the triple-bill Beckett 3 at the Theatre Upstairs), Cheek, 1970; Man is Man, 1971; Lear (Edward Bond), 1971; Big Wolf, 1972; The Sea, 1973; Director, since 1974, of Joint Stock Theatre Group for whom he has co-directed with Max Stafford-Clarke: The Speakers,

1974; Fanshen, 1975; Yesterday's News, 1976; A Mad World, My Masters, 1977; and directed The Ragged Trousered Philanthropists, 1978; An Optimistic Thrust, 1980; he has also directed the following, in London unless otherwise stated: Hadrian VII (Hamburg), 1969; The Beaux' Stratagem (National Theatre, and US tour), 1970; The Beaux' Stratagem (Hamburg), 1972; Measure for Measure (Exeter), 1972; Lear (Munich), Galileo (Hamburg), 1973; Snap, The Kitchen (Brussels), Love's Labours Lost (Sydney), 1974; The Government Inspector (Edinburgh), 1975; King Oedipus and Oedipus at Idonus (Dubrovnik), 1976; The Madras House (National Theatre), The Barber of Seville, La Bohème (both Wales), 1977; A Fair Quarrel (NT), The Gorky Brigade (Royal Court), 1979; directed his first television production, May 1956; principal productions include Zoo Time, etc.
Address: 124a Leighton Road, London, NW5.

GATES, Larry, actor
b St Paul, Minnesota, 24 Sept 1915; *s* of Lloyd Roland Gates and his wife Marion (Douglas Wheaton); *e* University of Minnesota; *m* (1) Tania Wilkof (dec); (2) Judith Seaton; originally trained in chemical engineering, and subsequently a field engineer and a school teacher.

Made his first appearance on the New York stage at the Nora Bayes, Oct 1939, as the Archangel Gabriel in Speak of the Devil; during the war, served in the Corps of Engineers; toured with the Abingdon Barter Theatre, 1946–7; toured with the Margaret Webster Shakespearean Company, 1948, as Casca in Julius Caesar and Christopher Sly in The Taming of the Shrew; at the Ethel Barrymore, Nov 1950, played Sidney Redlitch in Bell, Book and Candle; New York City Center, 1951, again played Christopher Sly in The Taming of the Shrew; Shubert, Jan 1953, played Colonel Wesley Breitenspiegel in The Love of Four Colonels; Martin Beck, Oct 1953, played Capt McLean in The Teahouse of the August Moon; Phoenix, 1954, played Clay Dixon in Sing Me No Lullaby; Phoenix, Oct 1955, Storyman in The Carefree Tree; Shubert, New Haven, Connecticut, Nov 1956, Logan Harvey in Build with One Hand; at the American Shakespeare Festival Theatre, Stratford, Connecticut, has played the following parts: Brabantio in Othello, Duke of Venice in The Merchant of Venice, Dogberry in Much Ado About Nothing, 1957; Montague in Romeo and Juliet, Snout in A Midsummer Night's Dream, Falstaff in The Merry Wives of Windsor, King of France in All's Well That Ends Well, 1959; Longacre, Nov 1959, John Devereaux in The Highest Tree; Playhouse-in-the-Park, Philadelphia, July 1962, played Maj-Gen Christopher Miller in Winterkill; toured, Feb 1963, in Mary, Mary; Longacre, Oct 1963, Boyd Bendix in A Case of Libel; Billy Rose, Nov 1964, Merton in Conversation at Midnight; Lincoln Center Repertory Theatre, Jan 1965, Orgon in Tartuffe; Westport Country Playhouse, Aug 1965, Tomaso in So Much of Earth, So Much of Heaven; for the Shaw Festival in Canada, 1967, played Undershaft in Major Barbara; Gramercy Arts, NY, Apr 1968, The Father in Carving a Statue; Center Stage, Baltimore, 1968, Max in The Homecoming; Center Stage, 1969, Shylock in The Merchant of Venice; Ivanhoe, Chicago, July 1969, Ben Hubbard in The Little Foxes; Ford's, Washington, DC, 1969, Nat Miller in Ah, Wilderness!; Ivanhoe, Chicago, 1971, Marcus Hubbard in Another Part of the Forest; Tyrone Guthrie, Minneapolis, Minn, Oct 1973, played in Waiting for Godot and Juno and the Paycock; University, Minneapolis, Feb 1974, played King Lear; Tyrone Guthrie, 1974, Organ in Tartuffe and Sir Oliver Surface in School for Scandal; Delacorte, NY, June 1975, Polonius and the First Gravedigger in Hamlet; Vivian Beaumont, Dec 1975, again played these parts in Hamlet; Ethel

Barrymore, Oct 1976, Prof Dzrembitsky in Poor Murderer; Meadow Brook, Mich, Sept 1977, Squire Hardcastle in She Stoops to Conquer; Eisenhower, Washington DC, Jan 1978, Chief Justice Crawford in First Monday in October, repeating this part at the Majestic, NY, Oct 1978, and on a subsequent tour, 1979; first appeared in films, 1951, and has since played in Cat on a Hot Tin Roof, The Remarkable Mr Pennypacker, Some Came Running, Airport, In the Heat of the Night, The Sand Pebbles, etc; has appeared regularly on television since 1951.
Recreation: Tree farming. *Clubs:* Players, Housatonic Valley Association. *Address:* Box 349, River Road, West Cornwall, Connecticut 06796. *Tel:* 203–672.

GAUNT, William, actor and director
b Leeds, 3 Apr 1937; *s* of William Ivor Gaunt and his wife Helen; *e* Giggleswick School and Waco University, Texas (BA in Drama); *m* the actress Carolyn Joan Lyster; trained for the stage at RADA.

Made his first stage appearance at the Royalty, Morecambe, 1955, in Worm's Eye View; his first London appearance was at the Apollo, 1967, when he took over as Julian in The Flip Side; Wyndham's, 1969, took over as Hank in The Boys in The Band; acted and directed with most major UK repertory theatres, 1965–75; has toured extensively for the British Council in Africa and the Far East; appointed Artistic Director, Liverpool Playhouse, 1979, where he appeared as Ken Harrison in Whose Life Is It, Anyway?, 1980; films include The Revolutionary and A Phoenix Too Frequent; TV work includes Sergeant Cork, The Foundation, etc.
Address: 31 Mount Street, Liverpool 1.

GAYNES, George (*né* Jongejans), actor and singer
b Helsinki, Finland, 3 May 1917; *s* of Gerrit Jongejans and his wife Iya Grigorievna Gay, Lady Abdy (father Dutch, mother Russian); *e* Summerfields, St Leonard's on Sea, College Classique in Lausanne, Switzerland, Scuola Musicale di Milano; *m* Allyn Ann McLerie; prepared for the stage with Lee Strasberg and John Daggett Howell.

First appeared on the stage in Lausanne, 1935, in an amateur production of Le Malade Imaginaire; first professional appearance was in May 1940 at the Teatro della Triennale, Milan, as Merlin in Luigi Dallapiccola's opera The Wizard; during World War II served in the Royal Netherlands Navy and the Royal British Navy; resumed his operatic career, appearing as bass with the Mulhouse, France, Opera, the Strasbourg Opera, and the New York City Opera, singing in Don Giovanni, Le Nozze di Figaro, Cenerentola, and various Gilbert and Sullivan operettas; made his New York theatrical début at the Ethel Barrymore, 15 Mar 1950, as Mr Kofner in the opera The Consul; New Century, Dec 1951, played Jupiter in Out of This World; adopted the professional name of George Gaynes in 1951, and at the University of Utah, Salt Lake, sang Danilo in The Merry Widow; Winter Garden, Feb 1953, Bob Baker in Wonderful Town; Artists, May 1956, King David in Absalom; New York City Center, Mar 1957, Mr Lockit in The Beggar's Opera; made his London début at the Coliseum, 14 Nov 1957, as Jeff Moss in Bells Are Ringing; York Playhouse, NY, Dec 1961, Erno Gero in Shadow of Heroes; Theatre de Lys, Nov 1961, appeared in the revue Brecht on Brecht; New York City Center, May 1962, Aristide Forestier in Can-Can; Winter Garden, Mar 1963, Buyer in The Lady of the Camellias; York Playhouse, Mar 1964, Prisoner in Dynamite Tonight; Washington, DC, Opera Co, 3 June 1964, sang Don Pedro in the American première of Berlioz's opera Béatrice et Bénédict; toured, summer 1964, as Henry Higgins in My Fair

Lady; New York City Center, Apr 1965, sang the title-role of The Mikado, and Sergeant Meryll in The Yeoman of the Guard; Music Box, 1965, took over from Don Porter as John Cleves in Any Wednesday; ANTA, Feb 1967, The Father in Of Love Remembered; Martinique, Mar 1967, Prisoner in Dynamite Tonite; St Clement's Church, May 1967, Mr Scott in Posterity for Sale; Inner City Repertory, Los Angeles, Cal, Sept 1967, Orgon in Tartuffe; Honolulu, Hawaii, Civic Light Opera, summer 1968, Henry Higgins in My Fair Lady; taught and acted at the Yale School of Drama Repertory Theatre, New Haven, Conn, 1968–9 season; Mark Taper Forum, Los Angeles, Apr 1971, Jupiter in Metamorphoses; Uris, NY, Nov 1973, Maitre du Frene in Gigi; Playhouse, Wilmington, Del, and subsequent tour, Jan 1974, Michael Jardine in Community of Two; Dorothy Chandler Pavilion, Los Angeles, July 1975, Robert Baker in Wonderful Town; entered films in 1962 in PT 109, and has since appeared in Doctors' Wives, Marooned, etc; has played on television since the early 1950s, notably in Le Bourgeois Gentilhomme, *Hawaii 5-O, Colombo, The Defenders,* etc.

Favourite parts: Henry Higgins, Leporello in Don Giovanni, Orgon, Hector, Prisoner in Dynamite Tonite. *Recreations:* Scuba diving, horseback riding, fencing. *Address:* Actors Equity Association, 6430 Sunset Boulevard, Hollywood, Calif 90028. *Tel:* 213–462–2334.

GAZZARA, Ben, actor
b New York City, 28 Aug 1930; s of Antonio Gazzara and his wife Angelina (Cusumano); e City College of NY; m (1) Louise Erickson (mar dis); (2) Janice Rule; prepared for the stage at Erwin Piscator's Dramatic Workshop and the Actors Studio.

First appeared on the stage at the Pocono Playhouse, Pennsylvania, July 1952, as Micah in Jezebel's Husband; toured in this play during summer of 1952; at Westport, 1953, appeared in Day of Grace; first appeared in NY at the Theatre de Lys, 15 Sept 1953, as Jocko De Paris, in End as a Man, and played the same part at the Vanderbilt, 14 Oct 1953, for which he received the New York Drama Critics Award as the most promising young actor of the season; at the Morosco, Mar 1955, appeared as Brick Pollitt in Cat on a Hot Tin Roof; Lyceum, Nov 1955, Johnny Pope in A Hatful of Rain; John Golden, Dec 1958, Joy in The Night Circus; Playhouse-in-the-Park, Philadelphia, July 1959, played in Epitaph for George Dillon; Hudson, Mar 1963, Edmund Darrell in a revival of Strange Interlude; ANTA, Sept 1964, Gaston in Traveller Without Luggage; First Chicago Center, Apr 1974, Erie Smith in Hughie; John Golden, Feb 1975, Erie Smith in Hughie and Leonard Pelican in Duet; Music Box, Apr 1976, George in Who's Afraid of Virginia Woolf?; entered films, 1957 in The Strange One, and has since played in Convicts Four, Anatomy of a Murder, Rage to Live, The Young Doctors, Husbands, QB VII, High Velocity, etc; appeared in the television series *Arrest and Trial,* and *Run for Your Life,* among others.

Recreation: Painting. *Address:* Actors Equity Association, 165 West 46th Street, New York, NY 10036.

GELBART, Larry, dramatic author
b Chicago, Ill, Feb 1923; s of Harry Gelbart and his wife Frieda; e John Marshall HS, Chicago, Fairfax HS, LA; m actress-singer Pat Marshall.

Wrote the book for The Conquering Hero, 1961; book (with Burt Shevelove) for A Funny Thing Happened on the Way to the Forum, 1962, winning a Tony award; author of the plays Jump, seen in London 1971; Sly Fox, 1976; film scripts include The Notorious Landlady, The Wrong Box and

Little Me; has worked in TV since 1952 in various capacities, notably as originator, writer and co-producer of the long-running series *M.A.S.H.*

Address: Ghent, NY 12075. *Tel:* 518-CH8 7014.

GELBER, Jack, playwright and director
b Chicago, Illinois, 12 Apr 1932; s of Harold Gelber and his wife Molly (Singer); e University of Illinois (BS 1953); m Carol Westenberg.

He wrote The Connection, which was produced by The Living Theatre, 15 July 1959; since then has written The Apple, also for The Living Theatre, 1961; Square in the Eye, 1965; Eighty-First Street Theatre, June 1966, directed Arnold Wesker's The Kitchen; wrote The Cuban Thing, which he also directed, 1968; at the Aldwych, London, for the Royal Shakespeare Company, 4 July 1968, directed Indians; Forum, Nov 1971, directed Kool Aid; Playwright in Residence at the American Place, New York, 1972, for which he wrote Sleep and directed The Chickencoop Chinaman, and The Kid, for which he received the Obie Award; Anspacher, Jan 1974, adapted and directed Barbary Shore, from the novel of Norman Mailer; in 1976 directed A Streetcar Named Desire (Lake Forest, Ill), and his own Jack Gelber's New Play: Rehearsal (American Place); directed Eulogy for a Small-Time Thief (Ensemble Studio), 1977; Seduced (American Place), 1979; wrote the screenplay for The Connection, 1962; received the Obie, Vernon Rice, and *Variety's* New York Drama Critics Poll Awards for The Connection, 1963–4, and 1966; received a Guggenheim Fellowship, 1963–4, and 1966; CBS Yale Univ Fellowships, 1974; NEA Fellowships, 1975.

Address: 697 West End Avenue, New York, NY 10025. *Tel:* AC 2–6076.

GELLNER, Julius, director and former actor
b Bohemia, 1899; s of Max Gellner and his wife Anna (Löbl); e Prague; m Maria Byk (mar dis).

Began his career as an actor in Germany in 1918; directed his first play, Spring's Awakening, in Munich, 1923; 1925, Associate Director and later Managing Director of the Munich Kammerspiele, until 1933; 1933–38 Associate Director of the German Theatre in Prague; came to London in 1939; first London production, New, July 1942, Othello for the Old Vic company; has since directed War and Peace, 1943; three plays in the Scala Trade Union Festival, 1946; The Trap, 1949; The Tempest, 1951; Associate Director, Mermaid Theatre, 1959–, where he has directed Henry V, John Gabriel Borkman, Emil and the Detectives, Red Roses for Me, Macbeth, The Possessed, The Marriage; The Imaginary Invalid and The Miser, 1966; Nathan the Wise, 1967; Othello (co-director), 1971; The Great Society (co-director), 1974; co-author of The Immortal Haydon, 1977; has also directed more than 20 plays in Israel since 1949, including a spell as Artistic Director of Habimah, the Hebrew National Theatre, 1962–5.

Recreations: Watching sport, reading. *Address:* 12 Grovewood, Sandycombe Road, Kew, Richmond, Surrey. *Tel:* 01–948 2352.

GEMMELL, Don (John Nisbet), director and manager
b Glasgow, Scotland, 26 Aug 1903; s of James John Gemmell and his wife Agnes L (Richardson); e Kelvinside Academy and Edinburgh Academy.

Began his career as an actor, appearing for three years at the Q Theatre, and subsequently making his first London appearance at the Royalty, Apr 1927, as a Hunchback in The Dybbuk; joined the English Players in Paris for a year, 1929; made his first appearance at the Players Theatre, July 1931, as a Filing Clerk and Reporter in The Life Machine, transferring with the production to the Garrick, Aug 1931; joined the Cambridge Festival Theatre Company for two years; Embassy, June 1936, played Dr Adler in Professor Bernnardi, transferring with the production to the Phoenix, July 1936; 1936–9, was engaged in films and television; re-appeared on the stage at the Players', June 1939, as Gaston le Brice in the musical Luck of the Devil; on the outbreak of war, he acted as chairman and producer at the Players', being appointed director of the theatre, Jan 1947; he has since supervised all the productions at the Players' Theatre, the following having transferred to the West End of London: The Boy Friend, 1954; Twenty Minutes South, 1955; King Charming, 1958; House of Cards, 1963; Divorce Me, Darling, 1965; he is also Chairman and co-director of Players Ventures, Ltd, a company formed to present additional West End productions; these have included: Commemoration Ball, 1956; The Buskers, The Crooked Mile, 1959; Johnny the Priest, 1960; films in which he has appeared include: The Ghost Goes West, Things to Come, Knight Without Armour, etc; first appeared on television in 1937, being seen as the Narrator in a series of plays by Stephen Leacock.

Recreation: The theatre. *Address:* Elms Farm, Sewards End, Saffron Walden, Essex.

GEMS, Pam, playwright
b Bransgore, Hampshire, 1 Aug 1925; *d* of Jim Price and his wife Elsie Mabel (Annetts); *e* Brockenhurst County Grammar School and University of Manchester; *m* Keith Gems.

Author of the following full-length plays: Betty's Wonderful Christmas, produced 1971; Go West, Young Woman, 1974; Dead Fish, 1976, later staged as Dusa, Fish, Stas and Vi; Queen Christina, 1977; Piaf, 1978; her short plays include My Warren, 1973; The Project, Guinevere, 1976; Franz into April, 1977; Ladybird, Ladybird, 1979; plays for TV include A Builder by Trade, 1962, and We Never Do What They Want (from The Project), 1978.

Address: 45 Walham Grove, London SW6.

GENET, Jean, dramatic author, poet and novelist
b 19 Dec 1910; *s* of Gabrielle Genet.

His first play Les Bonnes (The Maids), was produced at the Théâtre Athénée, Paris, in 1947; he is also the author of the following plays: Haute Surveillance (Deathwatch), 1949; Le Balcon (The Balcony), 1957; Les Nègres (The Blacks), 1959; Les Paravents (The Screens), 1961; Les Bonnes was first produced in London, at the Mercury Theatre, Oct 1952, in French, and subsequently at the New Lindsey, June 1956, in an English translation, in a double-bill; his plays have also been produced in Paris, New York, Vienna, Athens, Sweden, Denmark, Switzerland, Poland, and Berlin; his novels include Our Lady of the Flowers, 1940, The Thief's Journal, The Miracle of the Rose, Funeral Rites, and Querelle de Brest; also author of Letters to Roger Blin: Reflections on the Theatre, 1966 (English translation 1969) and the film Un Chant d'Amour (Love Song).

Address: c/o Rosica Colin Ltd, 4 Hereford Square, London SW7 4TU.

GEORGE, Colin, director and actor
b Pembroke Dock, Wales, 20 Sept 1929; *s* of Edward Thomas George and his wife Helen Mary (Sandercock); *e* Caterham School, Surrey and University College, Oxford; *m* Dorothy Vernon.

Co-founder, 1953, of the Elizabethan Theatre Company, for which he toured in Shakespeare; subsequently worked as an actor in repertory at Coventry and Birmingham; began

directing at Nottingham Playhouse, 1957, where he was for a time associate director; Duchess, June 1961, played Jack Lucas in Celebration; Old Vic, Mar 1962, directed his first London production, Richard III; artistic director, Ludlow Festival, 1964–6; director, Sheffield Playhouse, 1965–74; at Sheffield, as well as directing numerous productions, including several premières, he founded Theatre Vanguard, 1967, a touring company visiting schools, clubs, etc; advised on the building of the Crucible Theatre, Sheffield, opened in 1971 under his direction; member, Arts Council Young People's Theatre Panel, 1972–4; directed Mr Whatnot (Coventry), 1974; founder of Drama Department, University of New England, NSW, Australia, 1975, where he directed three Australian plays under the title Family Possessions; 1976–9, for the State Theatre Company of South Australia, directed revivals and new Australian work including Just Ruth, Too Early to Say; directed Oedipus, Adelaide Festival of the Arts, 1979; other productions include Peer Gynt, Hamlet, the Shaughraun, Mate!, and the Australian première of A Manual of Trench Warfare; and L'Elisir D'Amore for the State Opera Company; he has also directed in Dublin, Malta, Warsaw, Yugoslavia, and Canada, including world première of Vatzlav at Stratford, Ontario.

Address: Drama Department, University of New England, Armidale, NSW, Australia.

GERSTAD, John (*né* Gjerstad), actor, producer, director, playwright
b Boston, Massachusetts, 3 Sept 1924; *s* of Leif Gjerstad and his wife Adelaide (Johannesen); *e* Boston Latin School and Harvard University; *m* Annabel Lee Nugent.

Made his first appearance on the New York stage, at the Shubert Theatre, Oct 1943, when he played a Senator to Paul Robeson's Othello; 46th Street, Mar 1945, played Hank Gudger in Dark of the Moon; toured Italy for the USO, 1945, in Three's a Family; Lyric, Bridgeport, Conn, Jan 1946, played John Roberts in By Appointment Only; Plymouth, Mar 1948, appeared in Joy to the World; Coronet, Feb 1951, played Hitch Imborg in Not for Children; City Center, Apr 1952, played Michael Barnes in a revival of The Male Animal, and transferred with this production to the Music Box, May 1952; Fulton, NY, Nov 1952, directed The Seven Year Itch, which ran for nearly three years; Aldwych, London, May 1953, directed his first English production with the same play; Cort, NY, Feb 1955, directed The Wayward Saint; Holiday, NY, Feb 1956, directed Début; directed a touring production of The Male Animal, 1956; John Golden, Oct 1956, directed Double in Hearts; Ethel Barrymore, May 1957, presented, in association with Frederick Fox and Elliott Nugent, The Greatest Man Alive; 46th Street, Sept 1958, co-produced and directed Howie; Ford's, Baltimore, Oct 1959, presented, with Theatrical Interests Plan, Inc, and in association with Henry Sherek, Odd Man In; 1959, co-produced, for Theatrical Interests Plan, Inc, the National tour of Look Homeward, Angel; Bucks County Playhouse, New Hope, Pa, Sept 1961, played Van Lenner, Mr Krumgold, Rukeyser and Hanratty in The Beauty Part; Playhouse, Jan 1962, co-produced The Captains and the Kings; John Drew, Easthampton, NY, Aug 1964, directed The Glass Rooster; Paramus, New Jersey, July 1965, played Lee Manning in Abundantly Yours; Renata, NY, Oct 1965, directed Play That on Your Old Piano; ANTA, Nov 1967, Jesse Bellknap, George Robinson, Elbert Briggs, and Harrison Edwards in The Trial of Lee Harvey Oswald; Lunt-Fontanne, Mar 1969, Labe Pratt in Come Summer; New York State, June 1969, Cord Elam in Oklahoma!; Royale, Oct 1969, Reverend Sickles in The Penny Wars; Martin

Beck, Mar 1971, Newspaperman in All Over; Cort, Apr 1972, Joe Ryals in All the Girls Came Out to Play, which he also directed; directed his version of Thunder Rock at the Lyric, NY, and White Barn, Ct, 1979, also Actors Studio, 1980; author of the following plays: Sun at Midnight, 1940; The Monday Man (with James Lee) 1947; The French Have a Word for It (with James Lee), 1948; When the Bough Breaks (with Robert Scott), 1950, The Fig Leaf (with Norman Brooks), 1952; Jam, Thunder Rock (musical version), 1975; The High Bouncing Lover; book for Snap-Shot, 1980; adapted The Wild Duck, 1944, and Ghosts, 1945, for the Equity Library Theatre; dialogue director for the film Lost Boundaries, 1949, and has since played in No Way to Treat a Lady, Up the Down Staircase, A Lovely Way to Die, BS I Love You, Star, etc; has written, directed, played in and presented programs on all television networks; co-founder and director of Theatrical Interests Plan, Inc.

Recreation: Playing bridge. *Club:* The Players. *Address:* 345 East 57th Street, New York, NY 10022. *Tel:* MU 8–0490.

GERSTEN, Bernard, producer and director

b Newark, New Jersey, 30 Jan 1923; *s* of Jacob Israel Gersten and his wife Henrietta (Henig); *e* West Side High School, Newark, Rutgers University (1940–2); *m* Cora Cahan.

While in Army served as technical director of Maurice Evans's Special Services Unit in Hawaii for two years; made his New York début as Assistant Stage Manager for the Maurice Evans Production of GI Hamlet at the International, 13 Dec 1945, and subsequently on tour; producer at the Hunterdon Hills Playhouse, Jutland, NJ, 1947, and played Jake in Papa Is All; stage manager for Kathleen Mansfield, NY, Feb 1948; technical director of Actors Laboratory, Hollywood, Cal, 1948; production stage manager for New Stages, NY, Nov 1948–May 1949; since then has been stage manager for Anna Christie, All You Need Is One Good Break, The Guardsman (tour), 1950; produced a triple-bill of Sean O'Casey plays, Yugoslav Hall, NY, 1951; stage manager for Tovarich, 1952; A Certain Joy (tour), The World of Sholom Aleichem, 1953; Sand Hog, 1954; Guys and Dolls, South Pacific, Finian's Rainbow, 1955; Mr Wonderful, 1956; Brigadoon, 1957; Edwin Booth, 1958; The Legend of Lizzie, 1959; Roman Candle, Laurette (New Haven), Do Re Mi, 1960 and directed No for an Answer at the Circle in the Square; made his London début at the Prince of Wales's, 12 Oct 1961, as co-director of Do Re Mi; Executive Stage Manager for the American Shakespeare Festival, Stratford, Conn, with Othello, The Merchant of Venice, Much Ado About Nothing, 1957; Hamlet, A Midsummer Night's Dream, The Winter's Tale, 1958; Romeo and Juliet, The Merry Wives of Windsor, All's Well That Ends Well, a Midsummer Night's Dream, 1959; joined the New York Shakespeare Festival as Associate Producer in 1960, and served in this capacity for Henry V, Measure for Measure, The Taming of the Shrew, 1960; Much Ado About Nothing, A Midsummer Night's Dream, Richard II, 1961; King Lear, The Tempest, The Merchant of Venice, 1962; Antony and Cleopatra, As You Like It, The Winter's Tale, 1963; Hamlet, Othello, Electra, A Midsummer Night's Dream, 1964; Coriolanus, Troilus and Cressida, 1965; All's Well That Ends Well, 1966; The Comedy of Errors, Hair, 1967; The Memorandum, Henry IV, Part 1, Romeo and Juliet, Huui, Huui, 1968; Cities in Bezique, Invitation to a Beheading, No Place to Be Somebody, Peer Gynt, Twelfth Night, Sambo, 1969; Mod Donna, The Wars of the Roses, Parts 1 and 2, Richard III, Sambo, The Happiness Cage, Trelawny of The Wells, Jack MacGowran in the Works of Samuel Beckett, 1970; Subject to Fits, Slag, Here Are Ladies, Blood, Underground, The

Basic Training of Pavlo Hummel, Two Gentlemen of Verona, Dance wi' Me, Nigger Nightmare, Sticks and Bones, The Black Terror, The Wedding of Iphigenia and Iphigenia in Concert, Timon of Athens, The Tale of Cymbeline, 1971; Black Visions, That Championship Season, Older People, The Hunter, Much Ado About Nothing, Hamlet, Ti-Jean and His Brothers, the Corner, Wedding Band, The Children, 1972; Siamese Connections, The Orphan, As You Like It, King Lear, Two Gentlemen of Verona, Boom Boom Room, Troilus and Cressida, The Au Pair Man, Lotta, 1973; More Than You Deserve; Short Eyes, Les Femmes Noires, Barbary Shore, The Emperor of Late Night Radio, The Killdeer, The Tempest, What the Wine-Sellers Buy, The Dance of Death, Macbeth, Pericles, The Merry Wives of Windsor, Richard III, Mert & Phil, Where Do We Go From Here?, Sweet Talk, The Last Days of British Honduras, In the Boom Boom Room, 1974; Kid Champion, Fishing, Time Trial, A Chorus Line, Black Picture Show, A Midsummer Night's Dream, A Doll's House, The Taking of Miss Janie, Little Black Sheep, Hamlet, Trelawny of The Wells, The Leaf People, Jesse and the Bandit Queen, Hamlet (again), 1975; Rich and Famous, Apple Pie, So Nice They Named It Twice, Rebel Women, Threepenny Opera, Streamers, Henry V, Measure for Measure, For Colored Girls, etc, 1976; The Cherry Orchard, Threepenny Opera, Agamemnon, Miss Margarida's Way, 1977; The Water Engine/Mr Happiness, Runaways, Catsplay (Manhattan TC), All's Well That Ends Well, The Taming of the Shrew, 1978; left the NY Shakespeare Festival and co-produced Ballroom, 1978; Bosoms and Neglect, 1979; has also produced on television, notably as production supervisor for NBC-TV 1951 and associate producer for the New York Shakespeare Festival productions Sticks and Bones, Much Ado About Nothing, and Wedding Band; vice-president, operations and development, Omni Zoetrope (Francis Ford Coppola's motion picture company), 1979–; president, 1979, American Arts Alliance.

Address: Omni Zoetrope, 916 Kearny Street, San Francisco, Calif 94133.

GHOSTLEY, Alice, actress

b Eve, Missouri, 14 Aug 1926; *d* of Harry Francis Ghostley and his wife Edna Muriel (Rooney); *e* University of Oklahoma; *m* Felice Orlandi.

Formerly a cabaret entertainer; made her first appearance on the stage in New York at the Royale, May 1952, in the revue New Faces of 1952, in which she toured during 1953–4; Phoenix, Nov 1954, played Sheela Cavanaugh in Sandhog; Playhouse, Apr 1955, Dinah in Trouble in Tahiti; Winter Garden, June 1956, Miss Brinklow in the musical version of Shangri-La; Phoenix, Apr 1957, Aunt Polly in Livin' the Life; Playhouse, Jan 1958, Lois in Maybe Tuesday; ANTA, Feb 1960, appeared in the revue A Thurber Carnival; Music Box, Dec 1962, Octavia Weatherwax, Kitty Entrail, and Grace Fingerhead in The Beauty Part; City Center, Oct 1963, appeared in Gentlemen Be Seated; Longacre, Oct 1964, played Mavis Parodus Bugson in The Sign in Sidney Brustein's Window, receiving the Antoinette Perry Award and New York Drama Critics Award for the Best Actress in a supporting role, 1965, for this performance; toured in the last play, 1965; toured, 1965, in Love Is a Ball; toured, 1975, in Stop, Thief, Stop; Alvin, 1977, took over as Miss Hannigan in Annie; first appeared in films in 1954 in New Faces, and has since played in To Kill a Mockingbird, My Six Loves, etc; has appeared frequently on television.

Address: Actors Equity Association, 165 West 46th Street, New York, NY 10036.

GIBSON, William, dramatic author

b New York City, 13 Nov 1914; *s* of George Irving Gibson

and his wife Florence (Doré); *e* College of the City of New York; *m* Margaret Brenman.

Author of the following plays: I Lay in Zion, which was produced by the Topeka Civic Theatre, Topeka, Kansas, 1943, and in which he played a part; A Cry of Players, Topeka, 1948; Two for the Seesaw, 1958; The Miracle Worker, Dinny and the Witches, 1959; Golden Boy (book only), 1964; A Cry of Players produced by the Lincoln Center Repertory Theatre, 1968; American Primitive, 1969; his original play Two for the Seesaw turned into the musical Seesaw, 1973; The Butterfingers Angel, Mary and Joseph, Herod the Nut, and Twelve Carols in a Pear Tree, 1975, Golda, 1977; author of a book of poems, Winter Crook, 1947; author of the novel, The Cobweb, 1954; The Seesaw Log (a chronicle of the production of Two for the Seesaw), 1959; a family chronicle A Mass for the Dead, 1968; A Season in Heaven, 1975; Shakespeare's Game (criticism), 1978; films include: Two for the Seesaw, The Miracle Worker and The Cobweb; first television play The Miracle Worker, 1957.

Address: Stockbridge, Massachusetts.

GIELGUD, Sir John, CH 1977; Kt 1953; actor and director *b* London, 14 Apr 1904; *s* of Frank Gielgud and his wife Kate (Terry-Lewis); *e* Westminster School; studied for the stage at Lady Benson's school, and at the Royal Academy of Dramatic Art, gaining scholarships at both.

Made his first appearance on the stage, at the Old Vic, 7 Nov 1921, as the Herald in Henry the Fifth; subsequently appearing in King Lear, Wat Tyler, and Peer Gynt; during 1922 toured in The Wheel, understudying and acting as stage-manager; at the Regent, May 1923, played Felix in The Insect Play; June 1923, the Aide-de-Camp to General Lee in Robert E Lee; at the Comedy, Dec 1923, Charles Wykeham in Charley's Aunt; from Jan–Feb 1924, was with J B Fagan's repertory company at the Oxford Playhouse; at the Regent, May 1924, played Romeo in Barry Jackson's revival of Romeo and Juliet; in Oct 1924, again joined the repertory company at the Oxford Playhouse; at the Aldwych (for the Phoenix Society), May 1925, played Castalio in The Orphan; Little, May 1925, succeeded Noel Coward as Nicky Lancaster in The Vortex; Lyric, Hammersmith, May 1925, Peter Trophimoff in The Cherry Orchard; Little, Oct 1925, Konstantin Treplev in The Sea-Gull; Dec 1925, Sir John Harrington in Gloriana; Princes (for Play Actors), Dec 1925, Robert in L'Ecole des Cocottes; Savoy, Jan 1926, Ferdinand in The Tempest; Barnes, Feb–Mar 1926, Baron Nikolay in The Three Sisters and George Stibelev in Katerina; New, Oct 1926, succeeded Noel Coward as Lewis Dodd in The Constant Nymph; Strand (for Stage Society), June 1927, played Dion Anthony in The Great God Brown; in 1927 toured in The Constant Nymph; went to New York, and made his first appearance there, at the Majestic Theatre, 19 Jan 1928, as the Grand Duke Alexander in The Patriot; returned to London, Feb 1928; Wyndham's, Mar 1928, played Oswald in Ghosts; Globe, June 1928, Dr Gerald Marlowe in Holding Out the Apple; Shaftesbury, Aug 1928, Captain Allenby in The Skull; Court, Oct 1928, Felipe Rivas in The Lady from Alfaqueque and Alberto in Fortunato; Strand, Nov 1928, John Marstin in Out of the Sea; Little, Feb 1929, Fedor in Red Rust; Garrick, Apr 1929, succeeded Leslie Banks as Henry Tremayne in The Lady with a Lamp; Arts, June 1929, played Bronstein (Trotsky) in Red Sunday; joined the Old Vic company, Sept 1929, playing Romeo in Romeo and Juliet, Antonio in The Merchant of Venice, Cléante in The Imaginary Invalid, Richard II, Oberon, Mark Antony in

Julius Caesar, Orlando, The Emperor in Androcles and the Lion, Macbeth and Hamlet; at the Queen's, Apr 1930, repeated his performance of Hamlet; Lyric, Hammersmith, July 1930, played John Worthing in The Importance of Being Earnest; rejoined the Old Vic company, Sept 1930, and played Hotspur in Henry IV (Part I), Prospero, Lord Trinket in The Jealous Wife, Antony in Antony and Cleopatra; at the re-opening of Sadler's Wells Theatre, Jan 1931, played Malvolio in Twelfth Night; during the remainder of the season, played Sergius Saranoff in Arms and the Man, Benedick, and King Lear; he then went to His Majesty's, May 1931, and played Inigo Jollifant in The Good Companions; Arts, Nov 1931, and Criterion, Apr 1932, Joseph Schindler in Musical Chairs; New, June 1932, Richard II in Richard of Bordeaux, and made a very great success when the play was produced for a run at the same theatre, Feb 1933, when it ran over a year; he was also responsible for the direction of the play; St Martin's, Sept 1932, directed Strange Orchestra; at Wyndham's, Sept 1933, directed Sheppey; Shaftesbury, Jan 1934, with Richard Clowes, presented Spring 1600, and also directed the play; New, June 1934, directed Queen of Scots; Wyndham's, July 1934, played Roger Maitland in The Maitlands; New, Nov 1934, again played Hamlet, also directing the play, which then achieved the second longest run on record for this play; at the New, Apr 1935, directed The Old Ladies; New, July 1935, Noah in the play of that name; New, Oct 1935, Mercutio in Romeo and Juliet, which he also directed; in Nov 1935, played Romeo in the same production; the play was performed 186 times, the longest run on record for this play; New, May 1936, played Boris Trigorin in The Seagull; Empire, NY, Oct 1936, and subsequently at the St James, again played Hamlet; Queen's, London, May 1937, played Mason in He Was Born Gay, which he also directed (with Emlyn Williams); he then assumed the management of the Queen's Theatre for a season, and from Sept 1937, to May 1938, appeared there as King Richard in Richard II, Joseph Surface in The School for Scandal, Vershinin in The Three Sisters, and Shylock in The Merchant of Venice; was also responsible for the direction of Richard II and The Merchant of Venice; Ambassadors', May 1938, directed Spring Meeting; Queen's, Sept 1938, played Nicholas Randolph in Dear Octopus; Globe, Jan 1939, John Worthing in The Importance of Being Earnest, which he also directed; Globe, Apr 1939, directed Scandal in Assyria and May 1939, presented Rhondda Roundabout; Lyceum, June 1939, again played Hamlet in the final performances given at that theatre, prior to its demolition; subsequently went to Elsinore to play the same part at Kronborg Castle; Globe, Aug 1939, again played Worthing in The Importance of Being Earnest, subsequently touring in the same part, and played it again at the Globe, Dec 1939; directed The Beggar's Opera at the Haymarket, Mar 1940, and in Apr 1940, appeared as Captain Macheath, owing to the illness of Michael Redgrave; returned to the Old Vic, Apr 1940, and again played King Lear, and in May 1940, Prospero in The Tempest; at the Globe, 1940, in aid of the Actors' Orphanage, appeared in Fumed Oak, Hands Across the Sea, and Swan Song, subsequently touring in these for ENSA, in Army and RAF Garrison theatres; Globe, Jan 1941, played Will Dearth in Dear Brutus, which he also directed; Apollo, Nov 1941, directed Ducks and Drakes; Piccadilly, July 1942, appeared as Macbeth, which he directed; Phoenix, Oct 1942, again appeared in The Importance of Being Earnest; in Dec 1941, went to Malta and Gibraltar to entertain the troops; Haymarket, Jan 1943, played Louis in The Doctor's Dilemma; Phoenix, Apr 1943, played Valentine in Love for Love, which he also directed, and which ran for a year;

directed Landslide, at the Westminster, Oct 1943; The Cradle Song, Apollo, Jan 1944; Crisis in Heaven, Lyric, May 1944; The Last of Summer, Phoenix, June 1944; played a repertory season at the Haymarket, from Oct 1944 to May 1945, appearing as Arnold Champion-Cheney in The Circle, Valentine in Love for Love, Hamlet, Oberon in A Midsummer Night's Dream, and Ferdinand in The Duchess of Malfi; directed Lady Windermere's Fan at the Haymarket, Aug 1945; subsequently went to Burma, playing Hamlet and Charles Condamine in Blithe Spirit, for the forces of SEAC; returned to England, Mar 1946; toured, May 1946, as Raskolnikoff in Crime and Punishment, and played this at the New Theatre, June 1946; toured in Canada and the United States, Jan 1947, in The Importance of Being Earnest, and Love for Love Royale, NY, Mar 1947, appeared as John Worthing in The Importance of Being Earnest; May 1947, Valentine in Love for Love; National, Oct 1947, played Jason in Medea, which he also directed; Dec 1947, appeared as Raskolnikoff in Crime and Punishment; after returning to England, at the Haymarket, July 1948, directed The Glass Menagerie; Globe, Sept 1948, directed Medea; at the same theatre, Nov 1948, played Eustace Jackson in The Return of the Prodigal; Haymarket, Feb 1949, directed The Heiress; Globe, May 1949, played Thomas Mendip in The Lady's Not For Burning, which he directed in association with Esmé Percy; Stratford-on-Avon, June 1949, directed Much Ado About Nothing; Apollo, Sept 1949, directed Treasure Hunt; Lyric, Hammersmith, Jan 1950, directed Shall We Join the Ladies? and The Boy with a Cart; at the Memorial Theatre, Stratford-on-Avon during the 1950 season, played Angelo in Measure for Measure, Benedick in Much Ado About Nothing, Cassius in Julius Caesar, and King Lear; subsequently went to the United States and at the Royale, NY, Nov 1950, again played Thomas Mendip in The Lady's Not For Burning; after returning to England, appeared at the Phoenix, June 1951, as Leontes in The Winter's Tale; Criterion, Dec 1951, directed Indian Summer; Phoenix, Jan 1952, directed Much Ado About Nothing, in which he played Benedick; subsequently directed Macbeth, for the Shakespeare Memorial Theatre Company, Stratford-on-Avon; commenced a season at the Lyric, Hammersmith, Dec 1952, when he directed Richard II; this was followed in Feb 1953, by his production of The Way of the World, in which he appeared as Mirabell; in May 1953, he played Jaffier in Venice Preserv'd; he then took his company to Rhodesia, opening in Bulawayo, July 1953, when he appeared as Richard II; his next appearance in London was at the Haymarket, Nov 1953, as Julian Anson in A Day by the Sea, which he also directed; New, Feb 1954, directed Charley's Aunt; Lyric, Hammersmith, May 1954, directed his own adaptation of The Cherry Orchard; Shakespeare Memorial Theatre, Stratford-on-Avon, Apr 1955 directed Twelfth Night; for the Shakespeare Memorial Theatre Company, toured the Continent and the English provinces as Benedick in Much Ado About Nothing, which he directed, and as King Lear, appearing in both these parts at the Palace, London, July 1955; Haymarket, Apr 1956, directed The Chalk Garden; Globe, Nov 1956, played Sebastien in Nude With Violin, which he also directed; Covent Garden, June 1957, directed his first opera, The Trojans; Shakespeare Memorial Theatre, Stratford-on-Avon, Aug 1957, played Prospero in The Tempest, and appeared in the same production at Drury Lane, Dec 1957; Globe, Feb 1958, played James Callifer in The Potting Shed; at the same theatre, May 1958, directed Variations on a Theme; Old Vic, May 1958, played Cardinal Wolsey in Henry VIII, subsequently visiting Paris, Antwerp, and Brussels, with the same company; Comedy, July 1958, directed Five Finger Exercise; began a thirteen week tour of

Canada and the United States, Sept 1958, with Ages of Man (a solo Recital, selected from George Rylands' Shakespeare Anthology), concluding with a limited run at the 46th Street Theatre, NY, Dec 1958; Globe, London, June 1959, directed The Complaisant Lover; opened the Queen's Theatre, July 1959, with his Recital Ages of Man; Cambridge Drama Festival, Boston, Aug 1959, and Lunt-Fontanne, NY, Sept 1959, directed Much Ado About Nothing, in which he also played Benedick; Music Box, NY, Dec 1959, directed Five Finger Exercise; returned to London and appeared for a limited run at the Haymarket, Apr 1960, with his Recital Ages of Man; Phoenix, Sept 1960, played Prince Ferdinand Cavanati in The Last Joke; Covent Garden, Feb 1961, directed A Midsummer Night's Dream (Benjamin Britten's opera); ANTA, NY, Mar 1961, directed Big Fish, Little Fish; Globe, London, June 1961, directed Dazzling Prospect; Royal Shakespeare, Oct 1961, played the title part in Othello; Aldwych, Dec 1961, Gaev in his own version of The Cherry Orchard; Haymarket, Apr 1962, directed The School for Scandal; toured Haifa, Jerusalem, Tel Aviv, Aug 1962, with Ages of Man; Haymarket, Oct 1962, took over Joseph Surface in The School for Scandal, prior to appearing in the same production at the Majestic, NY, Jan 1963; Lyceum, NY, Apr 1963, appeared for a limited run in Ages of Man; Haymarket, Aug 1963, played Julius Caesar and co-directed The Ides of March; toured Australia and New Zealand 1963, with his Recital Ages of Man; Lunt-Fontanne, NY, recorded the Ghost and directed Hamlet; Philharmonic Hall, NY, Mar 1964, appeared in a Recital Homage to Shakespeare; toured Scandinavia, Finland, Poland, and the USSR, May 1964, with Ages of Man; Billy Rose, NY, Dec 1964, played Julian in Tiny Alice; Yvonne Arnaud Theatre, Guildford, Aug 1965, directed and played Nikolai Ivanov in Ivanov, prior to appearing at the Phoenix, Sept 1965, and the Shubert, NY, May 1966, in the same production; Nov–Dec 1966, toured South America and the US Universities for the British Council with his recital Men and Women of Shakespeare; Old Vic, Nov 1967, played Orgon in the National Theatre production of Tartuffe; Queen's, Nov 1967, directed Halfway Up the Tree; Old Vic, Mar 1968, played the title-role in Oedipus; Coliseum, Aug 1968, directed the opera Don Giovanni; Apollo, Oct 1968, played the Headmaster in Forty Years On; Lyric, Feb 1970, Gideon in The Battle of Shrivings; Royal Court, June, and Morosco, NY, Nov 1970, played Harry in Home, receiving the *Evening Standard* joint Best Actor Award for his performance; Chichester Festival, July 1971, played Julius Caesar in Caesar and Cleopatra; Royal Court, Mar 1972, Sir Geoffrey Kendle in Veterans; at the Queen's, Sept 1972, directed Private Lives; Albery, Sept 1973, directed The Constant Wife; for the National Theatre at the Old Vic, Mar 1974, played Prospero in The Tempest; Royal Court, Aug 1974, Shakespeare in Bingo; Royal, York, Nov 1974, Milton in Paradise Lost; also at the Old Vic, for the Apollo Society, Dec 1974; in Spring 1975 directed the US tours of Private Lives and The Constant Wife; Old Vic, Apr 1975 and Wyndham's, July 1975, played Spooner in the National Theatre production of No Man's Land, and did so again at the Lyttelton, Apr 1976 and Jan 1977, and the Longacre, NY, Nov 1976; Albery, June 1975, directed The Gay Lord Quex; at the Old Vic, Feb 1976, took part in Tribute to a Lady; Olivier, Mar 1977, title-role in Julius Caesar, and Apr 1977, Sir Politic Wouldbe in Volpone; Cottesloe, Nov 1977, Sir Noel Cunliffe in Half-Life, transferring to the Duke of York's, Mar 1978; Ages of Man, which was first performed for the Arts Council in 1956, has also been heard at the Edinburgh and Bath Festivals and in Holland, Germany, Italy, Switzerland, and Paris; after his performances in Paris, he was made a Chevalier of the Légion d'Honneur; has played Hamlet over 500 times to date; he also directed Romeo and Juliet, at the New Theatre, Oxford, for the OUDS, Feb 1932; and Richard II, also for the OUDS; he received the honorary degree of Doctor of Laws of St Andrews University, June 1950; Hon DLitt, Oxford University, June 1953; created Knight Bachelor in the Coronation and Birthday Honours, 1953; Companion of Honour, 1977; President of RADA, 1977; appeared in the films Insult, and The Good Companions, 1932; more recent films include: 11 Harrowhouse, Gold, Galileo, Murder on the Orient Express, and The Conductor; made his first television appearance in A Day by the Sea, London, Mar 1959; other appearances include: The Cherry Orchard, Ivanov, The Mayfly and the Frog, Deliver Us from Evil, *Edward VII* and Why Didn't They Ask Evans, 1980; author of Early Stages (autobiography), 1939; Stage Directions, 1963; Distinguished Company, 1972; An Actor and His Times, 1979.

Recreations: Stage designing and music. *Address:* c/o ICM, 22 Grafton Street, London W1.

GILBERT, Lou (*né* Gitlitz), actor
b Sycamore, Illinois, 1 Aug 1909; *s* of Morris Gitlitz and his wife Rose (Chosid); *e* Central High School, Cleveland, Ohio; *m* Martha Lou Hawkins.

Gained his early stage experience at the Cleveland Playhouse, where he first appeared on the professional stage as Lapo in The Jest, 1924; continued with that group and played Macbeth, White Wings, The Adding Machine, The Green Cockatoo, and Augustus Fogg in Fashion, 1928–9; joined the Jewish Peoples Institute, Cleveland, and stage managed the production of The Royal Family, 1929, and played Dobchinsky in The Inspector General, 1929; Blanquet in Bird in Hand, 1930; Tanchum in The Golem and played the Shoemaker in the Institute's production of The Tenth Man at the Palace, Chicago, May 1931; formed the Chicago Repertory Group, 1933, and played various parts in various theatres, including Fremont in Precedent, Apr 1933; Morry Norton in Fortune Heights, Mar 1935; Harry Fayett in Waiting for Lefty, May 1935; Kucher in The Young Go First, Apr 1936; the Chain Gang Captain in Hymn to the Rising Sun, June 1936; Pop in Black Pit, Nov 1936; Private Webster in Bury the Dead, Nov 1937; John L Lewis in One Third of a Nation, Feb 1938; Harry in The Cradle Will Rock, Oct 1939; Matt Mathews in A Time to Remember, Feb 1940; Jedediah Peck in The Man of Monticello, May 1941; disbanded the group; appeared as Inspector Slannery in Thunder Rock, Cedarhurst, LI, New York, Jan 1944; made his NYC début at the Henry Hudson Hotel, Apr 1944, as The Man in the Audience in That They May Win; Lyric, Allentown, Pa, July 1944, Burle Sullivan in The Milky Way, and Binion in Room Service; Fulton, NY, Apr 1945, Second Italian Soldier in Common Ground; Coronet, Oct 1945, Ziggie in Beggars Are Coming to Town; Belasco, Feb 1946, Man with a Pail in Truckline Cafe; Harris, Chicago, Aug 1946, Luigi in Dream Girl; New York City Center, Jan 1948, Notorio in Volpone; Maxine Elliott, Apr 1948, Charlie in Hope Is a Thing with Feathers; Hudson, Mar 1949, Joe Feinson in Detective Story; Broadhurst, Dec 1950, Town Drunkard in An Enemy of the People; Colonial, Boston, Mar 1952, Dr Maurice Ritz in The Grass Harp; President, May 1952, Dan Harkavy in The Victim; summer stock, 1952, Simon Cabot in Desire Under the Elms and E T Ganning in First Lady; President, Dec 1952, Sam in Whistler's Grandmother; 48th Street, Jan 1954, the Super in His and Hers; summer stock 1954, Mannheim in The Front Page, Mr Cracheton in The Apollo of Bellac, and played in The Shewing Up of Blanco Posnet; Fourth Street,

Oct 1954, Sender in The Dybbuk; Holiday, Nov 1954, Mr Cohen in Abie's Irish Rose; toured, 1955, as Felix Ducatel in My Three Angels; President, Nov 1955, Kugelman in Highway Robbery; New York City Center, Feb 1956, Pablo Gonzalez in A Streetcar Named Desire; Phoenix, Apr 1956, Mr Shaaf in A Month in the Country; Casino, Newport, RI, summer 1956, Dr Brubaker in The Seven Year Itch and Max Pincus in The Fifth Season; Belasco, Mar 1957, Pilsudski in Good As Gold; Arena, Apr 1957, Tchebutykin in The Three Sisters; Cort, May 1957, took over from Jack Gilford as Dr Dussel in The Diary of Anne Frank; toured in this last part, July 1957–June 1958; stock, 1958, played the Doctor in The Dragon Slayer, Dr Chumley in Harvey, and, 1959, Russian Commissar in Silk Stockings and the Woodcutter in Rashomon; York Playhouse, Dec 1959, Augusto in Time of Vengeance; Tapia Theatre, San Juan, Puerto Rico, Dec 1959, Dr Einstein in Arsenic and Old Lace, Feb 1960, Mackenzie in The Pleasure of His Company, and, Mar 1960, Eddie Brock in Born Yesterday; Cleveland Playhouse, Nov 1960, Ellis in Between Two Worlds; toured, 1960–1, as Doc in West Side Story; Cort, Jan 1962, Judge, Uncle, and Barbedart in The Egg; Delacorte, July 1962, Gonzalo in The Tempest; Delacorte, Aug 1962, French Doctor in King Lear; Biltmore, Dec 1962, Harry Stein in In the Counting House; Second City, Chicago, Feb 1963, Mac Davies in The Caretaker; Berkshire Playhouse, Stockbridge, Mass, 1964, The Spaniard in Journey to Bahia and Mr Baker in Come Blow Your Horn; York Playhouse, Mar 1964, Soldier in Dynamite Tonight; The Players, Mar 1965, Ottoman in Sing to Me Through Open Windows and Old Gayve in The Day the Whores Came Out to Play Tennis; Cherry Lane, May 1966, Benny Grossman in Big Man; Martinique, Mar 1967, Shell-Shocked Soldier in Dynamite Tonite; Nave, July 1967, Christopher Columbus in a play of that name, and, Aug 1967 Hardrader in The Happy Haven; Arena, Washington, 1967, Goldie in The Great White Hope, and appeared in The Tenth Man; Alvin, Oct 1968, again played Goldie in The Great White Hope; Vivian Beaumont, Nov 1970, Wang in The Good Woman of Setzuan; Eisenhower, Washington, DC, Jan 1972, Arab in The Time of Your Life; Delacorte, Aug 1972, Antonio in Much Ado About Nothing; Shubert, Nov 1972, Chemuel, Angel of Mercy in The Creation of the World and Other Business; American Place, May 1973, Old Man in Baba Goya; Delacorte, June 1973, Adam in As You Like It; Cherry Lane, Oct 1973, Old Man in Nourish the Beast; US tour, 1974, Mr Greenberg in A Community of Two; Cambridge, Mass, 1976, appeared in The Price; Penn State, 1977, in Awake and Sing; Chelsea Theater Center, Jan 1978, Joseph in Old Man Joseph and His Family; entered films as Pablo Gonzalez in Viva Zapata, 1952, and notable films since include: Middle of the Night, Across the River, Julietta of the Spirits (Fellini), Requiem for a Heavyweight, Petulia, The Great White Hope, Marathon Man, The Last Embrace, etc; first appeared on television in 1948 in What Makes Sammy Run, and has since played in *The Billy Rose Theatre, Naked City, Playhouse 90*, etc.

(*Died 6 Nov 1978.*)

GILBERT, Olive, actress and singer
b Carmarthen, Wales.

Spent the greater part of her early career with the Carl Rosa Opera Company, having made her first appearance with that company at Glasgow, and played the contralto roles in that company for many years, including Carmen, Delilah, Mignon, Amneris in Aida, Sujuki in Madame Butterfly, Fricka in Valkyrie, etc; with this company appeared at the Scala, 11 June 1924, as Mrs Tully in Bubbles; King's,

Hammersmith, Sept 1925, Volpino in The Apothecary; Lyceum, July 1929, Carmen in the opera of that name; has appeared in seasons of Grand Opera at Covent Garden, Lyceum, and Strand Theatres; at Drury Lane, May 1935, Cleo Wellington in Glamorous Night; Sept 1936, Madame Simonetti in Careless Rapture; Sept 1937, Queen Manuelita in Crest of the Wave; Mar 1939, Cäcilie Kurt in The Dancing Years; toured, Oct 1939, in Song Parade; toured, June 1940, as Mrs Fremantle in I Lived With You, and from Sept 1940 to Feb 1942, as Cäcilie in The Dancing Years, and appeared in the same part, at the Adelphi, from Mar 1942 to June 1944; Phoenix, Nov 1943, also appeared as Agnes Sorel in Arc de Triomphe; again toured, Oct 1944, in The Dancing Years; London Hippodrome, Apr 1945, played Ernestine Flavelle and Mrs Bridport in Perchance to Dream; Palace, Sept 1949, Countess Vera Lemainken in King's Rhapsody; toured South Africa, 1952, in King's Rhapsody; toured in The Dancing Years, 1953–5, and again 1959–60; Palace, May 1961, played Sister Margaretta in The Sound of Music, a part which she continued to play until Jan 1967, throughout the play's run of over 2,000 performances; Piccadilly, Apr 1968, the Housekeeper in Man of La Mancha, playing the same part when the play reopened, June 1969; toured, Jan 1971, as Phoebe in Glamorous Night; subsequently toured in Bless the Bride, Oct 1971; Perchance to Dream, Feb 1972, as Ernestine Flavell; King's Rhapsody, Aug 1972, as Countess Vera.
Address: 11 Aldwych, London, WC2. *Tel:* 01–836 3315.

GILDER, Rosamond, author and dramatic critic
b Marion, Mass, 17 July 1891; *d* of Richard Watson Gilder and his wife Helena (de Kay); *e* New York; her father was the poet, and editor of *The Century Magazine.*

Held the positions of drama critic, assistant editor and editor of *Theatre Arts Monthly*, 1924–48; Secretary of the American National Theatre and Academy, 1945–50; appointed Vice-President of ANTA, 1963; appointed Director of the US Center of the International Theatre Institute, 1948, subsequently being elected President of the ITI, 1963; President of the ITI of the USA, 1968 to present; Representative of ANTA on the National Commission for UNESCO, 1948–54; Editorial Secretary of the National Theatre Conference, 1932–6; Director of the Bureau of Research and Publication, Federal Theatre, 1934–5; appointed Honorary Member of the New York Drama Critics Circle, 1950; author of the following works: The Letters of Richard Watson Gilder, 1916; A Theatre Library, 1932; Theatre Collections in Libraries and Museums (with George Freedley), 1936; John Gielgud's Hamlet, 1937; Enter the Actress, the First Woman in the Theatre, 1960; translated and assisted in the writing of Emma Calvé's memoirs My Life, 1922; awarded the Médaille de Reconnaissance Française; Antoinette Perry Award, 1949; American Educational Theatre Award of Merit, 1961; Officier de L'Ordre des Arts et des Lettres, 1964; honorary LHD from the University of Denver, 1969; Benjamin Franklin Fellow of the Royal Society of Arts, London, 1970; has written numerous articles and essays on the theatre, and also lectured in Europe, the United States, India and Japan.
Club: Cosmopolitan. *Address:* 24 Gramercy Park, New York, NY 10003, and 1860 Broadway, New York, NY.

GILFORD, Jack (*né* Jacob Gellman), actor
b New York City, 25 July; *s* of Aaron Gellman and his wife Sophie (Jackness); *e* Commercial High School, Brooklyn; *m* Madeline Lee.

Began his theatrical career as a comedian at an amateur night at the Bronx Opera House, Mar 1934; toured Pa in Leavitt and Lockwood Revue, Apr 1934; toured as a comedian in vaudeville, 1934–5; toured in the Milton Berle Revue, 1935–8; toured US and Canada in the Ina Ray Hutton Revue, 1937–8; again toured in vaudeville and made his NY legitimate début at the Music Box, Jan 1939, when he played with Elsie Janis in revue; Hollywood Playhouse, Mar 1940, appeared in the revue Meet the People; Mansfield, Dec 1940, again played in Meet the People, and subsequently toured; toured in vaudeville with Paul Whiteman and Jimmy Dorsey's bands, etc, 1941; Mansfield, Feb 1942, played Barney Snediker in They Should Have Stood in Bed; Ethel Barrymore, Oct 1942, appeared in the revue Count Me In; Hollywood, July 1943, again played in Meet the People; toured with the USO in the Pacific in variety, 1945; toured in vaudeville and variety; Winter Garden, Jan 1950, played in the revue Alive and Kicking; Palace, Mar 1950, played in vaudeville; Playhouse, Aug 1950, Sol Margolies in The Live Wire; Metropolitan Opera House, Dec 1950, Frosch in Fledermaus, and has played this role in its various revivals in 1958–9, 1962–3, 1969–70; Barbizon Plaza, May 1953, Bontche Schweig in The World of Sholom Aleichem; Theatre de Lys, Jan 1955, Alexander Gross in The Passion of Gross; Barbizon Plaza, Mar 1955, in Once over Lightly; Cort, Oct 1955, Mr Dussel in The Diary of Anne Frank; Plymouth, Oct 1957, Second Soldier in Romanoff and Juliet; 54th Street, Oct 1958, Dr Ullman in Drink to Me Only; Henry Miller's, Mar 1959, Yacob von Putziboum in Look After Lulu; Phoenix, May 1959, King Sextimus in Once upon a Mattress; Booth, Nov 1959, Mr Zitorsky in The Tenth Man; played in stock productions of The Desert Song, Can-Can, and Cinderella, 1961; Bucks County Playhouse, Pa, Sept 1961, Goddard Quagmire in The Beauty Part; Phoenix, Dec 1961, The Sergeant in The Policeman; Alvin, May 1962, Hysterium in A Funny Thing Happened on the Way to the Forum; Broadhurst, Nov 1966, Herr Schultz in Cabaret; Lyceum, Oct 1969, Erwin Trowbridge in Three Men on a Horse; Studio Arena, Buffalo, NY, 1970, played in The Price; 46th Street, Jan 1971, Jimmy Smith in No, No, Nanette, toured, summer 1973, in Anything Goes; toured, summer 1974, in The Sunshine Boys; Royal Poinciana Playhouse, Palm Beach, Fla, Jan 1975, Richard Sherman in The Seven Year Itch; Broadhurst, Dec 1976, Jethro Crouch in Sly Fox; first appeared in films in Hey Rookie, 1944, and since has played in A Funny Thing Happened on the Way to the Forum, The Incident, Catch 22, They Might be Giants, Save the Tiger, etc; has appeared on television in The World of Sholom Aleichem, The Cowboy and the Tiger, Once upon a Mattress, and in major variety and dramatic series; has also appeared extensively in cabaret since 1936.
Address: Actors Equity Association, 165 West 46th Street, New York, NY 10036.

GILL, Brendan, critic, playwright, author
b Hartford, Conn, 4 Oct 1914; *s* of Michael Henry Gill and his wife Elizabeth (Duffy); *e* Kingswood School and Yale University (BA 1936); *m* Anne Barnard.

Co-author with Maxwell Anderson of the play The Day the Money Stopped, based on his novel and produced at the Belasco, New York, Feb 1958; wrote the book for the musical La Belle, produced at the Shubert, Philadelphia, Aug 1962; joined *The New Yorker* as a contributing editor in 1936; became its film critic in 1961; appointed its drama critic in 1967, in which position he still serves; author of the novel The Trouble of One House, which received a Special Citation from the National Book Award, 1951; author of Cole, a biography of Cole Porter, 1971; Tallulah, a biography of Tallulah Bankhead, 1972; Happy Times, with photographs by Jerome Zerbe, 1973; Here at The New Yorker, a history of the magazine, 1974; Lindergh Alone, 1977; and of many short stories and poems; President of the Municipal Art Society, and Deputy President of the Victorian Society in America; Vice-President, the Film Society of Lincoln Center.

Recreation: Architecture. *Clubs:* Century, The Coffee House, Grolier, Elizabeth. *Address: The New Yorker*, 25 West 43rd Street, New York, NY 10036. *Tel:* OX 5–1414.

GILL, Peter, director, dramatic author and former actor *b* Cardiff, 7 Sept 1939; *s* of George John Gill and his wife Margaret Mary (Browne); *e* St Illtyd's College, Cardiff.

An actor from 1957–65, he directed his first production, without décor, at the Royal Court in Aug 1965, A Collier's Friday Night; plays directed since then, at the Royal Court or its Theatre Upstairs unless otherwise stated include; The Ruffian on the Stair, O'Flaherty VC (Mermaid), A Provincial Life (in his own adaptation), 1966; The Soldier's Fortune, The Daughter-in-Law, Crimes of Passion, June Evening (tour), 1967; The Widowing of Mrs Holroyd (season, with his two previous Lawrence productions), Over Gardens Out (also wrote), 1968; Life Price, Much Ado About Nothing (Stratford, Conn), The Sleeper's Den (also wrote), 1969; Landscape and Silence (Lincoln Center), Hedda Gabler (Stratford, Ont), 1970; The Duchess of Malfi, Macbeth (Stratford, Ont), Cato Street (Young Vic), 1971; Crete and Sergeant Pepper, A Midsummer Night's Dream (Zurich), The Daughter-in-Law (Bochum), 1972; The Merry Go Round, Twelfth Night (Stratford, later Aldwych), 1974; As You Like It (Nottingham, Edinburgh Festival, and opening of Riverside Studios), The Fool, 1975; Small Change (also wrote), 1976; Director, since 1976, of Riverside Studios, Hammersmith, where his productions include The Cherry Orchard (own version), The Changeling, 1978; Measure for Measure, 1979; his play The Sleeper's Den was first performed in 1965; his production of The Daughter-in-Law won first prize at the Belgrade International Theatre Festival, 1968; associate artistic director, Royal Court Theatre, 1970–2.

Address: c/o Margaret Ramsay, 14a Goodwin's Court, St Martin's Lane, London WC2N 4LL. *Tel:* 01–240 0691,01–836 7403

GILLESPIE, Dana, actress, singer, and songwriter *b* London, 30 Mar 1949; *d* of Henry Gillespie and his wife Anne; *e* Arts Educational Trust.

Began her professional career as a singer at age 16; at the Marlowe, Canterbury, Aug 1968, appeared in the musical Liz; made her London debut at the Round House, 21 Dec 1970, as a lead singer in Catch My Soul, transferring with the production to the Prince of Wales, 1971; at the Palace, Dec 1972, played Mary in Jesus Christ, Superstar; joined the National Theatre Company at the Old Vic, Mar 1974, to play Juno in The Tempest; Prince of Wales, Mar 1976, Celandine in Mardi Gras; film appearances, since The Lost Continent, 1966, include Mahler, 1975, and Bad Timing, 1979; TV, since her first appearance on *Ready Steady Go* as a singer, 1965, includes *Little and Large* and *Hazell*; has written many of her own songs and made four LP's.

Recreations: Sports, especially riding and water sport (was British Water Ski Champion for four consecutive years). *Address:* c/o Richard Stone, 18–20 York Buildings, London WC2. *Tel:* 839 6421.

GILLESPIE, Robert, actor, director and intermittent writer *b* Lille, France, 9 Nov 1933; *s* of James William Gillespie and his wife, Madeleine Katalin (singer); *e* Sale County Grammar School; trained for the stage at RADA.

After leaving RADA joined the Old Vic company, making his first professional appearance at the Old Vic, 16 Sept 1953, as an old courtier in Hamlet; remained with the company for two years, playing minor roles including Adam in As You Like It, and Fleance in Macbeth; subsequently in repertory at Theatre Workshop, Glasgow Citizens', where he played Queeg in The Caine Mutiny Court Martial, Ipswich, the Royal Court, London, and the Belgrade, Coventry; various parts at the Mermaid, 1961–66, included two seasons as Israel Hands in Treasure Island, 1961 and 1963, Dodger in The Shoemaker's Holiday, 1964, Major Tarver in Dandy Dick and Juggins in Fanny's First Play, 1965, Motes in The Beaver Coat, 1966; Round House, 1968, appeared in The Hero Rises Up; more recently, appeared at the Theatre Upstairs, 1975, in Paradise; began his career as a director with Semi-Detached at Lincoln in 1963; has directed regularly since 1970, especially at the King's Head, Islington, where his productions include Mr Joyce is Leaving Paris (also Dublin Festival), Let's Murder Vivaldi, 1972; Revival!, Schellenbrack, 1973; Spokesong, 1976 (transferred to Vaudeville, 1977); Da, 1977; Period of Adjustment, 1978; Fearless Frank, 1979 (also NY debut production, 1980); has also directed for the Eblana, Gate, and Abbey, Dublin, Orange Tree, Richmond etc; directed a UK tour of Play It Again, Sam, 1979; author of material for That Was the Week That Was, 1962–63, and of the plays Napoleon, Session 2, 1973; Matthew, Mark, Luke and Charlie, 1979; has appeared in films since A Night to Remember, 1957, also in The National Health, The Prisoner of Zenda, etc; co-directed Mr Joyce Is Leaving Paris, 1972; frequent TV appearances since 1956, particularly in thrillers and comedy series, recently Mary's Wife and *Keep It in the Family*.

Recreations: Reading and the cinema. *Address:* 10 Irving Road, London W14.

GILLETTE, Anita (*née* Luebben), actress and singer *b* Baltimore, Maryland, 16 Aug 1936; *d* of John A Luebben and his wife Juanita; *m* Dr Ronald Gillette; formerly a secretary; studied at the Peabody Conservatory and with Lee Strasberg and Robert Lewis.

First appeared on the stage at the North Shore Music Theatre, in Beverly, Mass, summer 1958, as Sophie in Roberta; first appeared in New York at the Broadway in 1959, when she took over the role of Thelma in Gypsy; Maidman, Feb 1960, appeared in the revue Russell Patterson's Sketchbook; Imperial, Apr 1961, played Gypsy in Carnival! subsequently taking over the role of Lili in the same production; Winter Garden, Mar 1962, played Susan in All American; O'Keefe Center, Toronto, June 1962, Sarah Browne in Guys and Dolls; St James, Oct 1962, Leslie Henderson in Mr President; made her London début at the Lyric, Nov 1963, in the title-role of Pocohantas; toured the USA, 1964, as Leslie Henderson in Mr President; Broadhurst, Feb 1965, Angela Crane in Kelly; City Center, Apr 1965, Sarah Browne in Guys and Dolls; Municipal Opera, St Louis, May 1965, appeared in Meet Me in Saint Louis; Civic Light Opera, Los Angeles, June 1965, Resi in The Great Waltz; US Embassy, London, June 1966, appeared in revue sponsored by the Festival of American Arts and Humanities; toured US, summer 1966, as Eliza Doolittle in My Fair Lady; Morosco, Nov 1966, Susan Hollander in Don't Drink the Water; Broadhurst, 1968, took over as Sally Bowles in Cabaret; Winter Garden, Oct 1969, Betty Compton in Jimmy; Curran, San Francisco, Cal, May 1971, Tina Trenhoven in Knickerbocker Holiday; Public, NY, Jan 1976, played the female roles in Rich and Famous; in stock, 1976, in Bus Stop; Mark Taper Forum, LA, Jan 1977, in repertory in Travesties and The Importance of Being Earnest; Ahmanson, Oct 1977, and Imperial, Dec 1977, Jennie Malone in Chapter Two; first appeared on television in 1962, and has since been seen in *The Garry Moore Show, The Ed Sullivan Show, P M East,* and *Tonight.*

Address: c/o Susan Smith Agency, 850 Seventh Avenue, New York, NY 10019.

GILMORE, Peter, actor and singer
b Leipzig, 25 Aug 1931; *e* Friend's School, Great Ayton, Yorks; *m* (1) Una Stubbs (mar dis); (2) Jan Waters (mar dis); trained for the stage at RADA.

Made his first professional appearance, June 1952, as a stooge in variety; Lyric, Hammersmith, Oct 1958, played David Tooke in Valmouth, transferring to the Saville, Jan 1959 and making his West End debut in the same part; Piccadilly, Oct 1959, Leander in The Love Doctor; Vaudeville, Mar 1960, Tom in Follow That Girl; Apollo, Sept 1961, Matt in The Fantasticks; Mermaid, May 1962, transferring to Her Majesty's, Aug 1962, Ramble in Lock Up Your Daughters; May Fair, Mar 1964, Sir Lucius O'Trigger in All in Love; London Palladium, Dec 1966, Prince Charming in Cinderella; Edinburgh Festival, Aug 1967 and Saville, Sept 1967, Lysander in A Midsummer Night's Dream; Royal Court, Oct 1967, Rubin in The Journey of the Fifth Horse; toured for Prospect Productions, also appearing at the Apollo, Sept 1968, as Captain Macheath in The Beggar's Opera; Shaw, March 1974, played Murray Fearn in Only A Game; toured, autumn 1975, as Starbuck in The Rainmaker; has appeared in a number of films including the Carry On series and Oh! What a Lovely War!; TV appearances include Make Me an Offer, The Beggar's Opera and *The Onedin Line.*

Favourite parts: Ramble, Macheath. *Recreations:* Architecture, history. *Club:* Arts. *Address:* c/o William Morris Agency, 149 Wardour Street, London W1.

GILROY, Frank D, playwright
b New York City, 13 Oct 1925; *s* of Frank B Gilroy and his wife Bettina (Vasti); *e* Dartmouth College.

First produced play was The Middle World, performed at Dartmouth in 1949; first NY production was Who'll Save the Plowboy? which received the Obie award for best American play of 1962; since then has written The Subject Was Roses, which received the Pulitzer Prize, 1964; That Summer—That Fall, 1967; The Only Game in Town, 1968; four short plays under the title Present Tense, consisting of Come Next Tuesday, Twas Brilling, So Please Be Kind, and Present Tense, 1972; Last Licks, 1979; wrote his first film, The Fastest Gun Alive, in 1957, and since then has written, in addition to adaptations of his plays, the screenplay for Desperate Characters, which he also produced and directed, 1971; author of the novels Private, 1970, From Noon Till Three, 1973 (screenplay and direction, 1976); wrote, produced and directed the film Once In Paris, 1978; wrote his first play for television in 1952, and has since written for *Playhouse 90, Omnibus, Studio One, US Steel Hour, Kraft Theatre,* etc; President of the Dramatists Guild, 1969–71; council member, 1965–present.

Address: The Dramatists Guild, 234 West 44th Street, New York, NY 10036.

GINGOLD, Hermione, actress
b London, 9 Dec 1897; *d* of James Gingold and his wife Kate (Walter); *e* London; *m* (1) Michael Joseph (mar dis); (2) Eric Maschwitz (mar dis); studied for the stage under Rosina Filippi.

Made her first appearance on the stage at His Majesty's Theatre, 19 Dec 1908, as the Herald in Pinkie and the Fairies, and also appeared there, June 1909, as the Page in The Merry Wives of Windsor; Old Vic, Apr 1914, played Jessica in The Merchant of Venice; Ambassadors', May 1921, played Liza in If; Criterion, Aug 1922, the Old Woman in The Dippers; appeared at the Gate Theatre, 1931–3, in Little Lord Fauntleroy and as the Second Daughter in From Morn to Midnight, Lavinia in One More River, Lily Malone in Hotel Universe, and Vidette in I Hate Men; Q, Nov 1934, Camille in Mountebanks; Gate, Dec 1935, appeared in This World of Ours; Saville, Apr 1936, in Spread It Abroad; Arts, Sept 1936, played May in Laura Garrett; Mercury, Apr 1937, The Leading Lady in In Theatre Street; Gate, Dec 1938, and Ambassadors', Mar 1939, appeared in The Gate Revue; Ambassadors', May 1940, in Swinging the Gate; Comedy, June 1941, in Rise Above It, and Dec 1941, in a second edition; Phoenix, June 1942, in Sky High; Ambassadors', June 1943, in Sweet and Low; Feb 1944, in Sweeter and Lower, which ran over two years; May 1946, in Sweetest and Lowest; Comedy, Nov 1948, in Slings and Arrows, of which she was part-author; at the Ambassadors', Nov 1949, appeared as Mrs Rocket in Fumed Oak and Jane Banbury in Fallen Angels; made her first appearance on the American stage at the Brattle Theatre, Cambridge, Mass, Mar 1951, when she appeared in the revue It's About Time; next appeared at the Imperial, New York, Dec 1953, in the revue John Murray Anderson's Almanac; toured America in the summer of 1956 in the revue Sticks and Stones; Huntington Hartford, Los Angeles, Nov 1956, starred in The Sleeping Prince; toured America in the summers of 1957 and 1958 in Fallen Angels; Alvin, NY, March 1959, Mrs Bennet in First Impressions; Plymouth, Apr 1960, in the revue From A to Z; toured, July 1960, as Julia Maltby in Abracadabra; Martin Beck, NY, Sept 1962, took over the part of Clara Weiss in Milk and Honey; Phoenix, NY, Jan 1963, took over Madame Rosepettle in Oh Dad, Poor Dad, Mama's Hung You in the Closet, and I'm Feelin' So Sad, subsequently touring in the production, and reappearance on Broadway at the Morosco, Aug 1963, in the same play; Chandler Pavilion, Los Angeles, Aug 1967, Celeste in Dumas and Son; McCarter, Princeton, New Jersey, 1968, played in Charley's Aunt; Cambridge, June 1969, Agnes Derringdo in Highly Confidential; Shubert, NY, Feb 1973, Mme Armfeldt in A Little Night Music; played the same part at the Adelphi, London, Apr 1975; Huntington Hartford, LA, July 1978, appeared in Side by Side by Sondheim; has appeared in many films, including Gigi, Around the World in 80 Days, Bell, Book and Candle, The Naked Edge, The Music Man, Promise Her Anything, etc; has made numerous television appearances; received the Donaldson Award and the Hollywood Foreign Press Award; published the first instalment of her autobiography, The World Is Square, 1945; author of Sirens Should be Seen and Not Heard.

Hobbies: Interior decoration and collecting china. *Address:* 405 East 54th Street, New York City, NY 10022.

GINSBURY, Norman, dramatic author
b London, 8 Nov 1903; *s* of Jacob Ginsbury and his wife Rachel Cecily (Schulberg); *e* Grocers' Company School and London University; *m* Dorothy (Sarah) Jennings; was formerly an analytical chemist.

He is the author of the following plays: Viceroy Sarah, 1934; Walk in the Sun, 1939; also wrote new versions of Ibsen's Ghosts, 1937, and The Enemy of the People, 1939; in collaboration with the late Winifred Holtby was the author of

Take Back Your Freedom, 1939; made a new version of Peer Gynt, Old Vic, 1944, New York, 1960; author of The Firstcomers, 1944; The First Gentleman, 1945; adapted The Gambler, 1945; a new version of Ibsen's A Doll's House, 1946; The Happy Man, 1948; School for Rivals, 1949; Portrait by Lawrence (with Maurice Moisewitsch), 1950; Ladies For You, 1955; Rosmersholm (new version), 1960; The Pillars of Society (new version), John Gabriel Borkman (new version), The Old Lags' League (one-act), 1961; The Dance of Death (translation), 1966; The Shoemaker and the Devil, 1968; The Safety Match (from Chekhov), 1973; The Wisest Fool, 1974.

Address: 10 Bramber House, Michelgrove, Eastbourne, Sussex. *Tel:* Eastbourne 29603.

GISH, Lillian, actress
b Springfield, Ohio, 14 Oct 1893; *d* of James Lee Gish and his wife Mary (Robinson); *e* Dayton, Ohio, and Baltimore.

Made her first appearance on the stage in 1902, at Rising Sun, Ohio, in a melodrama, In Convict Stripes; subsequently danced in one of Sarah Bernhardt's productions; at the Republic Theatre, New York, 8 Jan 1913, played Marganie in A Good Little Devil, in which Mary Pickford played the leading part, under the management of David Belasco; entered films, then returned to the regular stage in 1930, and appeared at the Cort Theatre, NY, Apr 1930, as Helena in Uncle Vanya; in Central City, Colorado, July 1932, played Marguerite Gautier in Camille, appearing in the same part at the Morosco Theatre, NY, Nov 1932; Longacre, Apr 1933, played Effie Holden in Nine Pine Street; Belasco, Jan 1934, Christina Farley in The Joyous Season; National, Oct 1934, the Young Whore in Within the Gates; made her first appearance in Great Britain at the King's Theatre, Glasgow, Mar 1936, as Charlotte Lovell in The Old Maid; Empire, NY, Oct 1936, played Ophelia in Hamlet, with John Gielgud; Empire, Sept 1937, Martha Minch in The Star Wagon; Broadhurst, Jan 1939, Grace Fenning in Dear Octopus; appeared in Chicago, 1940, as Vinnie in Life with Father, and toured in this, 1941; at the Guild Theatre, NY, Nov 1942, played Jane Gwilt in Mr Sycamore; in summer theatres, 1947, played the Marquise Eloise in The Marquise, and Leonora in The Legend of Leonora; National, Dec 1947, Katerina Ivanova in Crime and Punishment; toured, 1950, as Miss Mabel, in the play of that name; Martin Beck, Oct 1950, played Ethel in The Curious Savage; again toured, 1951, as Miss Mabel; Henry Miller's, NY, Nov 1953, played Mrs Carrie Watts in The Trip to Bountiful; toured with her sister in The Chalk Garden, 1956; Congress Hall, Berlin, Germany, played in a dedicatory program of one-act plays, including Portrait of a Madonna and The Wreck of the 5.25; Phoenix, NY, Oct 1958, played Agatha in The Family Reunion; Belasco, Dec 1960, Catherine Lynch in All the Way Home; Chicago, 1962–3 season, Mrs Moore in A Passage to India; 54th Street, Mar 1963, Mrs Mopply in a revival of Too True to Be Good; Shakespeare Festival Theatre, Stratford, Conn, summer 1965, played Nurse in Romeo and Juliet; Ziegfeld, NY, Nov 1965, Dowager Empress in Anya; Longacre, Jan 1968, Margaret Garrison in I Never Sang for My Father; toured Moscow, Paris, London, Edinburgh, and the US, 1969–70, in a one-woman concert program Lillian Gish and the Movies— The Art of Film 1900–28; Circle in the Square—Joseph E Levine, June 1973, Marina in Uncle Vanya; St James, Nov 1975, appeared in the revue A Musical Jubilee; commenced film career 1912, and appeared in many of the early notable productions, including The Birth of a Nation, Intolerance, Souls Triumphant, Hearts of the World, The Great Love, Broken Blossoms, Way Down East, The Orphans of the

Storm, The White Sister, Romola, etc; more recent films include Duel in the Sun, The Cobweb, The Unforgiven, A Wedding (1978), etc; has appeared on television regularly since 1948, including roles in The Trip to Bountiful, Morning's at Seven, Ladies in Retirement, *The Defenders*, Breaking Point, as Hostess of the series *The Silent Years*, 1975, etc; Trustee of American Academy of Dramatic Arts, 1966–7; author of the autobiographical books, The Movies, Mr Griffith, and Me, 1969; Dorothy and Lilian Gish, 1973; holds a Doctor of Fine Arts degree from Rollins College, and a Doctorate of Performing Arts from Bowling Green State U.

Recreation: Travel. *Address:* 430 East 57th Street, New York, NY 10022.

GLASSCO, Bill, director and producer
b Quebec City, 30 Aug 1935; *s* of John Grant Glassco and his wife Willa; *e* Princeton University, Oxford University and University of Toronto; *m* Jane Glassco (mar dis); trained for the stage at School of the Arts, NYU.

His first stage activity, while at Princeton, was as a composer; directed his first professional production, Creeps, at the Factory Theatre Lab, Toronto, Feb 1971; later in 1971 founded Tarragon Theatre, Toronto, where as artistic director he has supervised a program of works by new Canadian playwrights, himself directing the premieres of works by David Freeman (revision of Creeps, 1971, Battering Ram, 1972, You're Gonna Be Alright, Jamie Boy, 1974), David French (Leaving Home, 1972, Of the Fields, Lately, 1973, One Crack Out, 1975, Jitters, 1979), etc; also the premieres in English of Le Temps d'Une Vie by Roland Lepage and the following plays by Michel Tremblay: Forever-Yours, Marie-Lou, 1972, Hosanna, 1974, Bonjour, là, Bonjour, 1975, Damnée Manon, Sacrée Sandra, 1979, and The Impromptu of Outremont, 1980; with John van Burek translated the first three of these; work outside Tarragon includes productions for the Stratford, Ontario, Shakespeare Festival, Vancouver Playhouse, Long Wharf, New Haven, and his Broadway debut, Bijou, 14 Oct 1974, directing Hosanna.

Address: 171 Robert Street, Toronto M5S 2K6. *Tel:* 416-923 1859.

GLEASON, John, lighting designer
b Brooklyn, New York, 10 Apr 1941; *s* of John Gleason and his wife Sue (Manzolillo); *e* Hunter College, NY.

First lighting design was for Tartuffe, 14 Jan 1965, produced by the Repertory Theater of Lincoln Center at ANTA Washington Square Theatre; since then has designed La Grosse Valise, The Porcelain Year, 1965; The Alchemist, 1966; Father Uxbridge Wants to Marry, Happiness, Walking to Waldheim, and the national tour of the National Theater of the Deaf productions, 1967; Saint Joan, Tiger at the Gates, Cyrano de Bergerac, King Lear, A Cry of Players, Summertree, Bananas, An Evening for Merlin Finch, Lovers and Other Strangers, The Great White Hope, We Bombed in New Haven, A Great Career, A Midsummer Night's Dream for Stratford, Ontario, 1968; Blueprints, A Tale of Kasane, Gianni Schichi, In the Matter of J Robert Oppenheimer, The Inner Journey, Home Fires, Cop-Out, Hamlet, The Miser, The Year Boston Won the Pennant, The Time of Your Life, The Increased Difficulty of Concentration, and Hamlet and The Alchemist, for Stratford, Ontario, 1969; Camino Real, Songs from Milk Wood, Sganarelle, Brighttower, The Disintegration of James Cherry, Operation Sidewinder, Silence, Landscape, Candida, Amphitryon, Othello, The Good Woman of Setzuan, Two by Two, and for the American Shakespeare Festival, Stratford, Conn, Hamlet, All's Well That Ends Well, Othello, The Devil's Disciple, 1970; The

Playboy of the Western World, An Enemy of the People, Antigone, Mary Stuart, The Birthday Party, Pictures in the Hallway, Play Strindberg, People Are Living Here, Frank Merriwell, and for Stratford, Conn, The Tempest, The Merry Wives of Windsor, Mourning Becomes Electra, 1971; Narrow Road to the Deep North, Twelfth Night, Enemies, The Ride Across Lake Constance, Duplex, Suggs, Happy Days, Act Without Words, Not I, Krapp's Last Tape, The Love Suicide at Schofield Barracks, Tough to Get Help, Small Craft Warnings, 1972; The Plough and the Stars, A Streetcar Named Desire, The Women, Veronica's Room, The Pajama Game, and for the Cincinnati Playhouse in the Park A Delicate Balance, A Streetcar Named Desire, Raisin in the Sun, Kiss Me, Kate, Old Times, 1973; Lorelei, Over Here, All Over Town, Perfect Pitch for the Kennedy Center for the Performing Arts, Washington, DC, Savages, for the Mark Taper Forum, Los Angeles, for which he received the Los Angeles Drama Critics Circle Award, and for the Cincinnati Playhouse in the Park Harvey, Tartuffe, Arsenic and Old Lace, Monkey, Monkey, Bottle of Beer! Travelers, Who's Who in Hell, 1974; Present Laughter, Scarecrow, The Royal Family (all Washington, DC), Don't Call Back, Hello, Dolly!, Truckload, and, for Cincinnati, Oh! Coward, Hot l Baltimore, That Championship Season, and, for the Manhattan School of Music, Le Nozze de Figaro, 1975; My Fair Lady, Monty Python Live, The Duchess of Malfi (Mark Taper Forum), The Royal Family, Herzl, An Evening with Diana Ross, 1976; Boris Godunov (Miami), Macbeth (Dallas Opera), Savages, 1977; The Dodge Boys, Getting Out (Mark Taper), Angel, Platinum, 1978; The Playboy of the Western World (Irish Ballet), 1979; has been resident designer for the Eugene O'Neill Center, Waterford, Conn, The National Theater of the Deaf, the Repertory Theater of Lincoln Center, the Cincinnati Playhouse in the Park, and is currently resident designer for the Dallas Civic Opera; has served as design consultant for a number of theater projects; received the Maharam Foundation Theatre Design Award for the 1972–3 season; teaches advanced lighting design at the New York University School of the Arts.

Hobbies and recreations: Painting, photography, reading, music. *Club:* Charter member of Thursday Night Gourmet Society. *Address:* 170 West 73rd Street, New York, NY 10023. *Tel:* 787–5957.

GLENVILLE, Peter, actor and director
b Hampstead, London, 28 Oct 1913; *s* of Shaun Glenville and his wife Dorothy (Ward); *e* Stonyhurst College, and Christ Church, Oxford University.

At Oxford was a member of the OUDS and President, 1934; while at Oxford, played the title-part in Edward II, Pandulph in King John, Puck in A Midsummer Night's Dream (directed by Max Reinhardt), Mephistopheles in Dr Faustus, Richard III, and Hamlet (Jubilee performance, 1935); appeared with the OUDS at the Open Air Theatre, Regent's Park, 26 June 1934, as Richard III; made his first appearance on the professional stage with the Manchester Repertory Company, 10 Sept 1934, as Dr Agi in The Swan; also played Toni Perelli in On the Spot, Jack Maitland in The Maitlands, and Eugene Marchbanks in Candida; Arts Theatre, London, May 1935, played Dante Gabriel Rossetti in Rossetti; Open Air, June 1935, Orsino in Twelfth Night; Cambridge, Aug 1935, Octavius Robinson in Man and Superman; Duke of York's, Oct 1935, appeared in The Hangman; Playhouse, Oxford, Dec 1935, Tony Cavendish in Theatre Royal; Memorial Theatre, Stratford-on-Avon, 1936 season, played Romeo, Petruchio, Mark Antony, etc; Theatre Royal, Margate, 1937, played a season as leading man; Old Vic, Mar

1939, Lucentio in The Taming of the Shrew; Shaftesbury, Jan 1940, Tony Howard in Behind the Schemes; Tavistock Little, Jan 1940, Charlie Stubbs in Down Our Street; Arts, Sept 1940, Œdipus in The Infernal Machine; Vaudeville, Oct 1940, Bertram in All's Well That Ends Well, and Prince Hal in King Henry IV (Part I); Globe, June 1941, Robert in The Light of Heart; Haymarket, Mar 1942, succeeded Cyril Cusack, as Louis Dubedat in The Doctor's Dilemma; appointed as director for the Old Vic company, at the Liverpool Playhouse, Aug 1944, where he staged John Gabriel Borkman, Point Valaine, The Second Mrs Tanqueray, etc; he also revived The Alchemist, playing Face, and in Feb 1945, directed and played Hamlet; Lyric, London, Sept 1945, succeeded John Mills as Stephen Cass in Duet for Two Hands; Lyric, Hammersmith, Feb 1946, directed The Time of Your Life, and Oct 1946, played John Wilkes Booth in The Assassin; also appeared in various productions at the Q, and for play-producing societies; since 1947, he has directed the following plays: Point Valaine, 1947; Major Barbara, The Gioconda Smile, Crime Passionnel, The Browning Version, A Harlequinade, The Return of the Prodigal, 1948; Adventure Story, The Power of Darkness, 1949; in NY staged The Browning Version, A Harlequinade, 1949; The Innocents, 1950; The Curious Savage (for the Theatre Guild), 1950; Romeo and Juliet, 1951; returned to London and directed Summer and Smoke, 1951; Under the Sycamore Tree, The Innocents, Letter from Paris, 1952; The Living Room, 1953; The Prisoner, Separate Tables, 1954; at the Fulton, NY, Oct 1955, he presented and staged Island of Goats; co-presented and directed his own translation of Hotel Paradiso (London), 1956; directed Separate Tables (NY), 1956; presented Hotel Paradiso (NY) 1957; directed Rashomon (NY), Take Me Along (NY), Silent Night, Lonely Night (NY), 1959; Becket (NY), 1960; Tchin-Tchin (NY), 1962; Tovarich (NY), 1963; Dylan (NY), 1964; Everything in the Garden (NY), 1967; A Patriot for Me (NY), 1969; A Bequest to the Nation (London), 1970; and Cut Cry (NY), 1973; also directed the films, The Prisoner, Term of Trial, Becket, Summer and Smoke, Hotel Paradiso, The Comedians, etc.

Recreations: Travel and history. *Address:* c/o Frosch, 450 Park Avenue, New York, NY 10022.

GLOVER, John, actor
b Kingston, New York, 7 Aug 1944; *s* of John S Glover and his wife Cade (Mullins); *e* Towson State College.

Made his first professional appearance at the Barter, Abingdon, Va, as Eugene Gant in Look Homeward, Angel, in 1963; at the Martinique, Oct 1969, played Godfrey in A Scent of Flowers; at the Public, 1971, took over the part of Prince Myshkin in Subject to Fits; Truck and Warehouse, also 1971, took over as Ronnie in House of Blue Leaves; his first Broadway appearance was at the Shubert, 22 Mar 1972, as Ward Nichols in The Selling of the President; for New Phoenix, at the Lyceum, Dec 1972, played William Brown in The Great God Brown and Pierrot in Don Juan, and at the Ethel Barrymore, 1973, played the Teacher in The Visit, Planteloup in Chemin de Fer, Nov, and Johnny Case in Holiday, Dec; Public/Newman, Jun 1976, Dr Samuel Sutler in Rebel Women; Circle in the Square, Jun 1977, Algernon Moncrieff in The Importance of Being Earnest; Hudson Guild, Oct 1977, Patrick in Treats; has appeared with many resident regional companies, including the American Shakespeare Festival, 1975; films include Julia, Annie Hall, The Last Embrace, and The Incredible Shrinking Woman.

Favourite part: Hamlet. *Address:* c/o Susan Smith and Associates, 9869 Santa Monica Boulevard, Beverly Hills, CA 90212.

GLOVER, Julian, actor

b St John's Wood, London, 27 March 1935; *s* of C Gordon Glover and his wife Honor (Wyatt); *e* St Paul's School, Hammersmith and Alleyn's, Dulwich; *m* (2) Isla Blair.

Made his first appearance on stage at the New Theatre, Bromley, 1953, in pantomime; trained at RADA; from 1957 to 1959 played small parts in three Stratford seasons, including Albany in King Lear, 1959; first appearance on the London stage, April 1961 as the SS Officer in Altona, at the Royal Court; transferred, June 1961, to the Saville; at the Royal Court, July 1961, and at the Phoenix, September 1961, played the Knight in Luther; again at the Royal Court, Feb 1962, Orsino in Twelfth Night; March 1962, Tolen in The Knack; New Arts, May 1962, The Baron in The Lower Depths; Royal Court, April 1963, Franco Laspiga in Naked; Haymarket, August 1963, Brutus in The Ides of March; toured South America and Europe, 1964, as Demetrius in A Midsummer Night's Dream and Morocco in The Merchant of Venice; Edinburgh Festival, Sept 1964, played Hotspur in Joan Littlewood's Henry IV; Hampstead, Feb 1966, M Robert in The Pastime of M Robert; toured, 1967, for Prospect Productions as Hector in Thieves' Carnival and Boswell in Boswell's Life of Johnson; New, June 1967, Standard in The Constant Couple; Arnaud, Guildford, 1968, Harry in The Family Reunion; at Bristol Old Vic, 1970, for Prospect again toured as Boswell, as Pierre in Venice Preserved, and as Benedick in Much Ado, having played Don John and Boswell at the Edinburgh Festival in Aug; with the Royal Shakespeare Company, 1971, played Mr Medley in The Man of Mode, Aldwych, Sept, and Rogozhin in Subject to Fits, The Place, Oct; Forum, Billingham, Mar 1973, Capt Starkey in We Bombed in New Haven; Bankside Globe, Aug 1973, Antony in Antony and Cleopatra; Arnaud, Guildford, June 1974, Mr Manningham in Gaslight; Open Space, July 1974, Sherlock Holmes in Sherlock's Last Case; Arnaud, Guildford, June 1975, Mirabell in The Way of the World; Queen's, July 1975, Jeff in Otherwise Engaged; Lyttelton, Oct 1976, Archie in the National Theatre's revival of Jumpers; for the Royal Shakespeare Company, Stratford, June 1977, played Warwick in Henry VI, parts 1, 2 and 3, and Oct 1977, Tullus Aufidius in Coriolanus; repeated Warwick in Henry VI at the Aldwych, Apr 1978, and played King Charles VI of France in Henry V; Old Vic, Mar 1978, took part in the triple bill Great English Eccentrics; Aldwych, Sept 1978, Gordon in Cousin Vladimir, and Oct 1978, Alonzo in the Changeling; Old Vic, Aug 1979, Claudius in Hamlet; first appeared in films, 1964, in Tom Jones; subsequent pictures include Nicholas and Alexandra, and Juggernaut; his numerous television appearances include An Age of Kings.
Favourite parts: Boswell and Benedick. *Recreations:* Carpentry, writing (for himself!). *Address:* c/o Boyack & Conway Ltd, 8 Cavendish Place, London W1. *Tel:* 01–636 3916.

GODDARD, Willoughby, actor

b Bicester, 4 July 1926; *m* Ann Phillips.

Made his first appearance on the stage at the Oxford Playhouse, 1943, as The Steward in Saint Joan; after a period in repertory, he first appeared in London at the Arts Theatre, Dec 1948, as Horngolloch in Gog and Magcog; Royal Court, Sept 1952, played Attwater in Ebb Tide; Q, Dec 1953, played Mr Holmes in No Other Verdict, transferring with the production to the Duchess, Jan 1954; Royal, Windsor, July 1954, played Regen in Tug of War; Arts, Sept 1954, Gowing in The Diary of a Nobody; Duchess, May 1955, again appeared in The Diary of a Nobody; Phoenix, Apr 1956, played the Governor's Cousin in The Power and the Glory;

Royal Court, Jan 1960, played The Chairman of the Committee and the Managing Director in The Lily-White Boys; Globe, July 1960, The Cardinal in A Man for All Seasons; made his first appearance in New York at the Imperial, Jan 1963, as Mr Bumble in Oliver!; toured in England, 1964, as Sir in The Roar of the Greasepaint, the Smell of the Crowd; New, Sept 1966, played Marmaduke Muleygrubs JP in Jorrocks; toured with Prospect Productions, 1968, as Sir Toby in Twelfth Night; Aldwych, Oct 1969, played Zeal-of-the-Land Busy in Bartholomew Fair; with Prospect Productions, Nov 1972–Apr 1974, he played Sir Toby in Twelfth Night, Pandar in Pericles, and Presumption and Giant Despair in The Pilgrim's Progress; Chichester Festival, July 1974, Bolshintsov in A Month in the Country and First Shepherd in Oidipus Tyrannus; Palladium, Dec 1974, Col Guldberg in Hans Andersen; Apollo, Nov 1977, Sir Frederick in Shut Your Eyes and Think of England; Stratford, season 1979/80, Sir Toby Belch in Twelfth Night, Duke of Venice in Othello; he has also appeared frequently in films and on television.
Recreations: Bibliomania. *Address:* 77 Gloucester Road, Hampton-on-Thames, TW12 2UQ. *Tel:* 01–941 0369.

GODFREY, Derek, actor

b London, 3 June 1924; *s* of Frederick William Godfrey; *e* Emmanuel School, London; *m* Diana Fairfax; studied for the stage with the Old Vic Theatre School.

Made his first appearance on the stage with the Young Vic Players at the Hippodrome, Stockport, Sept 1949, when he played Richard II in A Shakespeare Miscellany; first appeared in London at the Old Vic, Dec 1950, also with the Young Vic Company, as John Abbott in The Black Arrow; appeared as a member of the company at the Shakespeare Memorial Theatre, Stratford-on-Avon, during the 1952 season, and also toured Australia with the company, 1953; on returning to England, he appeared in repertory at the Nottingham Playhouse, and with the Bristol Old Vic, 1953–6, before appearing with the Bristol Old Vic Company, at the Old Vic, July 1956, when he played Adolphus Cusins in Major Barbara; joined the Old Vic Company, London, Sept 1956, and played the following parts: Poet in Timon of Athens, Iachimo in Cymbeline, Don John in Much Ado About Nothing, 1956; Duke of Milan in Two Gentlemen of Verona, Enobarbus in Antony and Cleopatra, the title-part in Titus Andronicus, Earl Rivers and Sir James Tyrrel in Richard III, Duke of Suffolk in Henry VI (Parts I and II), and Richard in Henry VI (Part III), Lucio in Measure for Measure, Oberon in A Midsummer Night's Dream, 1957; Edgar in King Lear, and Cardinal Campeius in Henry VIII, 1958; joined the Shakespeare Memorial Company, Stratford-on-Avon, 1960 season, to play Proteus in The Two Gentlemen of Verona, Orsino in Twelfth Night, Hector in Troilus and Cressida, and Time in The Winter's Tale; at the Aldwych, London, Nov 1960, he played Antonio in The Duchess of Malfi, and repeated his performance of Orsino in Twelfth Night, Dec 1960; became a long-term contract player with the Royal Shakespeare Company, Jan 1961, and appeared in repertory at the Aldwych in the following parts: the King of the Ondines in Ondine, Prince Henri du Conde and De la Rochepozay in The Devils, and Petruchio in The Taming of the Shrew, 1961; at the New Arts, Mar 1962, played Bernard in Everything in the Garden; Royal Shakespeare Theatre, Stratford-on-Avon, Apr 1962, Petruchio in The Taming of the Shrew; Edinburgh Festival, Aug 1962, Henry in Curtmantle, subsequently appearing at the Aldwych, Oct 1962, in the same part; at the same theatre, Oct 1962, played Hector in Troilus and Cressida; made his first appearance in the USA, at the Biltmore, Los Angeles,

Mar 1963, in the anthology The Hollow Crown; Aldwych, July 1963, Macheath in The Beggar's Opera; Oxford Playhouse, Jan 1964, Arnolph, The Marquis and Molière in the trilogy The School for Wives, Booth, New York, May 1964, played Lord Dungavel in Roar Like a Dove; Aldwych, Aug 1964, Charles Paumelle in Victor; Oct 1964, Machiavel in The Jew of Malta; Saville, Sept 1965, Herod in The Overdog; Mermaid, Jan 1966, played Leonard Charteris in The Philanderer; Belgrade, Coventry, Sept 1966, Cyrano in Cyrano de Bergerac; Comedy, May 1967, James Woodley in Horizontal Hold; Aldwych, July 1967, Alfred Chamberlain in Little Murders; Playhouse, Nottingham, Sept 1968, played the Earl of Gurney in The Ruling Class, transferring in that part to the Piccadilly, Feb 1969; Old Vic, National Theatre Season, 1969–70, took over Mirabell in The Way of the World, appeared as Bracchiano in The White Devil and Don Quixote in The Travails of Sancho Panza; Arts, Cambridge, July 1970, played Trigorin in The Seagull; with the RSC at Stratford, season 1971, played Prince of Arragon in The Merchant of Venice, Malvolio in Twelfth Night and Benedick in Much Ado About Nothing; Lyceum, Edinburgh, Sept 1972, and Round House, Oct, Jonathan Wild in Stand and Deliver!; Playhouse, Nottingham, May 1973 and Bankside Globe, June, Malveole in The Malcontent; Arnaud, Guildford, Feb 1974, Grey in The Guessing Game; Old Vic, July 1974, for National Theatre, played Count Almaviva in The Marriage of Figaro; Mermaid, Apr 1975, Sir Colenso Ridgeon in The Doctor's Dilemma; Open Space, Feb 1976, title-role in Anatol; Lyttleton, May 1977, Meercraft in The Devil is an Ass; Haymarket, Jan 1978, Julius Winterhalter in Waters of the Moon; Shaftesbury, Sept 1978, Abraham von Helsing in Dracula; Arnaud, Guildford, Nov 1978, Quentin Hereford in Murder in a Bad Light; Nottingham Playhouse, Sept 1979, played Balurdo in Antonio, and, Oct, doubled as Claudius and the Ghost in Hamlet; received the Clarence Derwent Award, 1957, for his performance as Iachimo in Cymbeline; first entered films, 1962, in Act of Mercy; first appeared on television, 1957, as Iachimo in Cymbeline, subsequently appearing in Mary Rose, Henry IV (Pirandello), The Empty Chair, etc.
Favourite parts: Toad in Toad of Toad Hall, Lopakhin in The Cherry Orchard, Giovanni in 'Tis Pity She's a Whore, and Petruchio in The Taming of the Shrew. *Address:* c/o Fraser & Dunlop, 91 Regent Street, London W1.

GOETZ, Ruth Goodman, dramatist
b Philadelphia, 11 Jan 1912; *d* of Philip Goodman and his wife Lily (Cartun); *e* Miss Marshall's School, New York and in Paris; *m* Augustus Goetz (dec).
Formerly a story editor and in costume design; collaborated with her husband in the following plays: Franklin Street, 1940; One Man Show, 1945; The Heiress adapted from Henry James's novel Washington Square, 1947; The Immoralist, adapted from the novel by André Gide, 1954; The Hidden River, adapted from Storm Jameson's book, 1957; author of Sweet Love Remember'd, 1959; revised The Immoralist for a NY revival, 1963; adapted Madly in Love from the French of André Roussin, 1963; with Bart Howard adapted Play on Love from the French of Françoise Dorin, produced at St Martin's, London, Jan 1970; collaborated with her husband in the following films: The Heiress, 1949, for which she received an Academy Award Oscar; Sister Carrie, 1950; Rhapsody, Trapeze, Struck Struck, etc.
Address: The Dramatists Guild, 234 West 44th Street, New York, NY 10036.

GOLDEN, Michael, actor
b Bray, Ireland, 15 Aug 1913; *s* of Thomas Golden and his wife Bridget (Mulligan); *e* St Edna's School; *m* Jean Ann Cockayne.

Made his first appearance on the stage at the Abbey Theatre, Dublin, Apr 1932, as the Sergeant in Rose of Battle; in 1939, toured with H V Neilson's Shakespearean company; Gate Theatre, Dublin, Aug 1939 to May 1940; toured in Shaw repertory, Jan–June 1941; appeared at the Playhouse, Oxford, Jan 1942, to Mar 1943; made his first appearance in London, at the Arts Theatre, 17 Mar 1943, as Timmy in The Well of the Saints, subsequently playing The Devil in Don Juan in Hell; same theatre, May 1943, Peter Sheeran in The Old Foolishness; Playhouse, June 1943, Safonov in The Russians; Whitehall, Oct 1943, Alan Crocker in The Dark River; toured, Jan 1944, as Laurent in Guilty (Thérèse Raquin), appearing in the same part at the Lyric, Hammersmith, Apr 1944; Arts, June 1944, played André Merin in The Sulky Fire; Lyric, Hammersmith, Oct–Dec 1944, The Burglar in Too True to be Good, Morell in Candida, A in A Village Wooing and Higgins in Pygmalion; toured, 1945, as Heathcliff in Wuthering Heights; Citizen's Theatre, Glasgow, Oct–Nov 1945, Lancelot in a play of that name, Robert in Glory Hole, and Father O'Shaughnessy in The White Steed; Stratford-on-Avon, Shakespeare Memorial Theatre, season 1947, played Chorus in Dr Faustus, the Duke in Measure for Measure, Bolingbroke, Montague and Orsino; His Majesty's, Oct 1947, appeared as Bolingbroke in King Richard II, Montague in Romeo and Juliet, Orsino in Twelfth Night; in 1948, at Canterbury Festival, played Cyman in Thor With Angels; Embassy, Mar 1949, Robert Stanforth in They Walk Alone; at the Bedford, Camden Town, 1949, appeared in a Shaw repertory season; Q, May 1950, Capt René Legrand in The Bridge of Estaban; Arts, Aug 1950, played Shinto in The Gentle Gunman, and Oct 1950, Leicester in Queen Elizabeth; Irving, Nov 1951, played Marcus Andronicus in Andronicus; Embassy, Dec 1951, appeared in the same part, and also played The Man in Something More Important; Court, July 1952, appeared as A in A Village Wooing, and Sept 1952, as Capt Davis in Ebb Tide; Princess, Feb 1956, played Feeney in Summer Song; Royal Court, July 1956, played the Rev Samuel Gardner in Mrs Warren's Profession, in the Shaw Centenary; Strand, May 1958, Det Inspector Ogden in Verdict; Duchess, Aug 1958, Inspector Thomas in The Unexpected Guest; toured, Mar 1960, as Higgins in Pygmalion; Lyric, Hammersmith, Oct 1960, played Mike Glavin in Sive; New Arts, Nov 1963, played Charles in Poor Bitos, transferring with the production to the Duke of York's, Jan 1964; toured as Inspector Lord in Spider's Web, 1965–6, taking the same part in 1969 at the Theatre Royal, Windsor, where he also played Squeezum in Lock Up Your Daughters, 1967, Murray in The Odd Couple, 1968, and Edward in Pink String and Sealing Wax, 1970; Library, Manchester, 1971, Mr Link in After Haggerty; Belgrade, Coventry, 1972, Mr Link; Theatre Royal, Windsor, Sept 1973, Gravedigger and Player King in Hamlet; same theatre, 1974, Cuthbertson in The Philanderer; first appeared in films, 1944, in The Canterbury Tale, and has since appeared in numerous pictures.
Favourite parts: Macbeth, and Brand in Ibsen's play. *Recreations:* Reading, music, and conversation. *Address:* Flat 3, 2 Dane Road, St Leonards-on-Sea, East Sussex.

GOLDIE, Hugh, director and former actor
b Tywardreath, Cornwall, 5 Dec 1919; *s* of Dr Arthur Evelyn Goldie and his wife Ruby Lena (Parnell); *e* Exeter Chorister's School and King's, Taunton; *m* Eva Johanna Urbach.
Began his career in 1938 as an ASM with the Sheffield Repertory Company; after service with the RAF, 1940–6 (DFC and bar) returned to the theatre; studied design, 1947, at the Old Vic Theatre Centre; directed his first professional production, Hobson's Choice, at the Sheffield Playhouse, July 1949;

Stage director, Liverpool Playhouse, 1949–50; associate director, Oxford Playhouse, 1950–1; designed A Sleep of Prisoners, London and New York, 1951, and was assistant director; made his London debut as an actor, Oct 1952, playing the Doctor in The Square Ring at the Lyric, Hammersmith; June 1953, directed his first London production, Love's Labour's Lost, at the Open Air, Regent's Park; a director of the Elizabethan Theatre Company, 1953; director of productions, Oxford Playhouse, 1954; resident director, Theatre Royal, Windsor, 1954–7; artistic director, Alexander, Johannesburg, 1959–61; associate producer, Theatre Royal, Windsor, 1974–; productions he has directed, in London unless otherwise stated, include: Mrs Gibbons' Boys, 1956; The Last Word (tour), 1958; Signpost to Murder, The Wind Might Change (tour), Policy for Murder, 1962; The Yes-Yes-Yes Man (tour), 1963; Busybody, 1964; Spin of the Wheel (tour), Alibi for a Judge, 1965; Countercrime (tour), The Waiting Game, 1966; According to the Evidence, 1967; The Queen's Highland Servant, Lady be Good, 1968; A Woman Named Anne, How the Other Half Loves (tour), 1970; Make No Mistake (Guildford), 1971; The Owl and the Pussy Cat and An Inspector Calls (both tours), 1972; All My Sons (Bolton), Through the Looking Glass (S Africa), 1973; The Hasty Heart (tour), The Tilted Scales (Bristol), 1974; Murder with Love (tour), 1976; Arsenic and Old Lace, Laburnum Grove, 1977; Sleuth, 1978; has also directed frequently in repertory as well as staging pageants at the Royal Festival Hall and the Albert Hall.

Recreations: Cricket, skiing, interior design. *Clubs:* Eccentrics, Lord's Taverners, Middlesex CCC. *Address:* 50 Waldegrave Park, Twickenham, Middlesex.

GOLDMAN, James, dramatic author
b Chicago, Ill, 30 June 1927; *s* of Clarence Goldman and his wife Marion; *e* Chicago University and Columbia University; *m* the producer Barbara Deren.

His first play to be produced was They Might Be Giants, seen at the Theatre Royal, Stratford E, Jun 1961; in October of the same year, his play Blood, Sweat and Stanley Poole (written with his brother William) was produced at the Morosco, NY; has also written book and lyrics for Family Affair, 1962; the play The Lion in Winter, 1966; book for Follies, 1971; screenplays include They Might be Giants, Nicholas and Alexandra, The Lion in Winter, and Robin and Marian; author of a TV musical, Evening Primrose; his novels include Waldorf, The Man from Greek and Roman, and Myself As Witness.

Address: c/o Sam Cohn, ICM, 40 West 57th Street, New York, NY 10019.

GOOCH, Steve, playwright, critic and translator
b Surrey, 22 Jul 1945; *e* Emanuel School, Wandsworth and Trinity College, Cambridge.

His first full-length work to be produced was an adaptation of Great Expectations, Liverpool Playhouse, Dec 1970; author of the plays Will Wat, If Not, What Will?, produced 1972; Nick, 1972; Female Transport, Dick (Christmas play), 1973; The Motor Show (with Paul Thompson), 1974; Strike '26 (with Frank McDermott), 1975; Made in Britain (with Thompson), Our Land, Our Lives, 1976; Back Street Romeo, 1977; The Women Pirates Ann Bonney and Mary Read (for RSC), 1978; translated and adapted Man Is Man, 1971; Big Wolf, Candide (as It's All for the Best), The Mother, 1972; Cock Artist, 1974; Rosie, 1977; publications, other than dramatic work, include a translation of Wolf Biermann's Poems and Ballads; assistant editor, *Plays and*

Players, 1972–73; resident dramatist, Half Moon Theatre, 1973–74, and Greenwich Theatre, 1974–75.
Address: 18 Vauxhall Grove, London SW8.

GOODMAN, Dody, actress
b Columbus, Ohio, 28 Oct; *d* of Dexter Goodman and his wife Leona; *e* North High School, Columbus.

Formerly a dancer, and studied dancing at the Jorg Fasting School, Columbus, the School of the American Ballet, and the Metropolitan Opera Ballet School, 1939–43; made her New York début as a dancer in the corps de ballet of Radio City Music Hall, 1940; made her Broadway début as a dancer at the Century, 9 Oct 1947, in the chorus of High Button Shoes; Imperial, July 1949, danced in the chorus of Miss Liberty; Imperial, Oct 1950, in the chorus of Call Me Madam; Winter Garden, Feb 1953, played Violet in Wonderful Town; President, Feb 1955, appeared in Shoestring Revue; Barbizon-Plaza, Nov 1956, appeared in Shoestring '57; Players, Jan 1960, appeared in the revue Parade; toured, Sept 1960–May 1961, as Winnifred in Once upon a Mattress; New York City Center, June 1962, Dora in Fiorello!; Belasco, Oct 1963, Elizabeth Lamb in A Rainy Day in Newark; Square East, Dec 1965, appeared in New Cole Porter Revue; Booth, May 1969, Sally Ellis in My Daughter, Your Son; Ethel Barrymore, Oct 1969, Jenny in The Front Page; toured, summer 1971, as Sally Ellis in My Daughter, Your Son; Mummers, May 1972, Dolly Gallagher Levi in The Matchmaker; her play Mourning in a Funny Hat produced at the Ogunquit, Maine, Playhouse in July 1972; Palace, Jan 1974, Mrs Ella Spofford in Lorelei or Gentlemen Still Prefer Blondes; Shubert, Philadelphia, Oct 1974, Miss Ronberry in Miss Moffat; Mark Taper Forum, Los Angeles, July 1975, Miss Leighton in Once in a Lifetime; in stock, summer 1976, in George Washington Slept Here; Charles Playhouse, Boston, 1978, appeared in Side by Side by Sondheim; first appeared in films in Bedtime Story, 1964; recent films include Silent Movie, and Grease; has appeared on television in *The Sid Caesar Show, Martha Raye Show, Sergeant Bilko,* and as a regular on *The Jack Paar Show,* 1957–64, as the Mother in *Mary Hartmann, Mary Hartmann,* 1976, etc.

Address: Actors Equity Association, 165 West 46th Street, New York, NY 10036.

GOODWIN, John, Head of publicity and publications for the National Theatre
b London, 4 May 1921; *s* of Albert Edwin Goodwin and his wife Jessie Helen (Lonnen); *e* Christ's Hospital, Horsham; *m* Suzanne Ebel; during the War, served in the Forces, as a Lieutenant RNVR, 1940–5.

After demobilization, was associated as press representative with David Fairweather, 1946–7, for the Old Vic company, at the New Theatre, 1946; Ambassadors', 1946; Garrick, 1947; New, 1947; represented Basil Dean's British Theatre Group at the St James's, 1948; represented the Shakespeare Memorial Theatre, 1948–56, rejoining the company in 1958; Head of publicity and publications for the Royal Shakespeare Company, Stratford and London,1960–74, before being appointed to the same post at the National Theatre from its opening on the South Bank; author of short stories, articles and A Short Guide to Shakespeare's Plays, 1979.

Address: 52a Digby Mansions, Lower Mall, London, W6.

GOOLDEN, Richard, OBE, actor
b London, 23 Feb 1895; *s* of Percy Pugh Goolden Goolden and his wife Margarida (da Costa Ricci); *e* Charterhouse and New College, Oxford (BA); was Secretary of OUDS in 1923; played a number of parts while at the University.

Made his first appearance on the professional stage with J B Fagan's Oxford Players, at the Oxford Playhouse, 22 Oct 1923, as Mazzini Dunn in Heartbreak House; he remained with this company for seven seasons, playing nearly fifty character parts; made his first appearance London at the Ambassadors' Theatre, 30 Mar 1925, as Owain Flatfish in A Comedy of Good and Evil; appeared at the Memorial Theatre, Stratford-on-Avon, 1925; Royalty, Sept 1925, played Firs in The Cherry Orchard; Lyric, Hammersmith, Apr 1926, appeared in Riverside Nights; Nov 1926, played the Professor in The Would-Be Gentleman; Everyman, Mar 1927, The Singer and the Works Manager in The White Château; Lyric, Hammersmith, June 1927, Master P Crummles in When Crummles Played and Frederick in George Barnwell; Strand, Oct 1927, Gabriel in The Kingdom of God; Royalty, 1928, for a time played Mr Blanquet in Bird in Hand; Little, Sept 1928, Peel in The New Sin; Kingsway, Oct 1928, Ben Brooke in Thunder on the Left; Arts and Garrick, Jan 1929, William Nightingale and Corporal Jones in The Lady With a Lamp; Kingsway, Oct–Nov 1929, Sand in The Rising Sun and Moses in The School for Scandal; Garrick, Mar 1930, Saint-Gaudens in The Lady of the Camellias; Kingsway, Mar 1930, Papa Cottin in The Artist and the Shadow; Haymarket, Apr 1930, the Second Gravedigger in the all-star revival of Hamlet; Duke of York's, Oct 1930, Shadrick Tuggle in All that Glitters; Lyric, Dec 1930, Mole in Toad of Toad Hall, which he played annually to 1934; in May, 1931, played a repertory season at the Opera House, Malta, with Sybil Arundale; Fortune, Aug 1931, Rooper in The Silver Box; Little, Sept 1931, Pooley in Off the Map; Arts, Nov 1931, and Prince of Wales's, Dec 1931, Pierre in She Passed Through Lorraine; during 1932, appeared at the Festival Theatre, Cambridge, and with the Masque Theatre at Edinburgh and Glasgow; Westminster, July 1932, played Costard in Love's Labour's Lost; subsequently toured in Canada, with Barry Jones and Maurice Colbourne in Too True to be Good; Little, Feb 1933, played Henry Briggs in Cock Robin; Piccadilly, May, 1933, Gamaliel in Caesar's Friend; Lyric, Hammersmith, June 1933; Pasquinot in The Fantasticks; Old Vic, Sept 1933, Sir Andrew Aguecheek in Twelfth Night; Sadler's Wells, Nov 1933, Lord Sands and Cranmer in Henry VIII; Royalty, Apr 1934, Pier Zanotti in The Mask and the Face! Embassy, Oct–Nov 1934, Aslaksen in An Enemy of the People, Lob in Dear Brutus, and Uncle in Ding and Co; Mar 1935; Abel Drugger in The Alchemist, and in Let's Go Gay; Criterion, Apr 1935, Mr Dibble in All Rights Reserved; Aldwych, Aug 1935, appeared as Joe Clayton in The Dominant Sex; Lyric, May 1936, played Fletherington in Bees on the Boatdeck; Old Vic, Oct 1936, Jasper Fidget in The Country Wife; Westminster, Mar 1937, Mazzini Dunn in Heartbreak House; Daly's, Apr 1937, Prince Paul in The Grand Duchess; Embassy, Dec 1937, Henry Blake in The Worm that Turned, and Syd Fish in Painted Sparrows; Mar 1938, toured as Henry Penny in Mr Penny's Tuppence, which he also directed; Open Air Theatre, June 1938, played Quince in A Midsummer Night's Dream; Arts, Sept 1938, Theobald Thin in Blind Man's Buff; Haymarket, Dec 1938, Lord Fancourt Babberley in Charley's Aunt; Criterion, May 1939, Professor Cunningham in Grouse in June; during 1942, toured as Ebenezer in The Old Town Hall, and played in this at the Winter Garden, Oct 1942; St James's, Jan 1943, played the Fool in King Lear; Arts, Aug 1943, Ludovic in The Watched Pot; Scala, from Feb 1944, appeared in a variety of parts in Shakespearean repertory with Donald Wolfit, including Launcelot in The Merchant of Venice, William in As You Like It, Roderigo in Othello, Polonius in Hamlet, and Corbaccio in Jonson's Volpone; Lyric, Hammersmith,

Oct–Dec 1944, The Monster in Too True to be Good, and Doolittle in Pygmalion; Winter Garden, Mar 1945, again played with Wolfit's company; Granville, Walham Green, May 1945, appeared in a season of Grand Guignol; Arts, Aug 1945, played Chu-Chu in The Circle of Chalk; Duke of York's, Dec 1945, the Odd Man in The Land of the Christmas Stocking; Comedy, Feb 1946, Rev Arthur Humphreys in See How They Run; Garrick, Nov 1946, Rev Septimus Bodkin in Treble Trouble; Boltons, Apr 1947, Mr Chimney in Neighbours; Savoy, Apr 1947, appeared as the Fool in King Lear; Q, July 1948, Mr Roll in Gaily I Go; Globe, Nov 1948, Dr Glaisher in The Return of the Prodigal; Embassy, Apr 1949, played the Author in On Monday Next . . . and appeared in the same part at the Comedy, June 1949; New Theatre, Bromley, May 1949, Mr Pim in Mr Pim Passes By; St James's, Aug 1950, Caspar Darde in Captain Carvallo; St James's, May 1951, appeared as Theodotus in Caesar and Cleopatra, and Lepidus in Antony and Cleopatra; Arts, Oct 1952, Mr Podgers in Lord Arthur Savile's Crime; Dolphin, Brighton, Dec 1952, Mole in Toad of Toad Hall; King's, Hammersmith, Feb 1953, The Fool in King Lear; Playhouse, Oxford, May 1953, William in You Never Can Tell; Duchess, London, Oct 1953, Leonard Bence in The MacRoary Whirl; Richmond, Nov 1953, Hodge in Beauty and the Beast; Westminster, June 1954, Harris in We Must Kill Toni; Lyric, Hammersmith, Dec 1954, Lord Hector in Time Remembered, also appearing in this part at the New, Apr 1955; New Lindsey, Feb 1956, Gaffer Chickwidden in Trevallion; New Lindsey, Jan 1957, Uncle in The Chicken Play; Lyric, Hammersmith, Mar 1957, Platina in Malatesta; Royal Court, Oct 1958, Nagg in End Game; Royal Court, July 1959, the Mayor in Look After Lulu, subsequently transferring with the production to the New, Sept 1959; Winter Garden, Dec 1959, the White Rabbit in Alice in Wonderland; Coventry, Aug 1960, appeared in the revue Here is the News; Arts, New 1961, played Mr Jones in The Cupboard; Mermaid, May 1962, Politic in Lock Up Your Daughters, transferring with the production to Her Majesty's, Aug 1962; Queen's, Mar 1965, for the Repertory Players', Don Gonzalo in A Juan By Degrees; Lamda, Sept 1966, Paul-Albert Renoir in Never Say Die; Playhouse, Derby, Aug 1967, Crabtree and Moses in The School for Scandal; Open Air, Regent's Park, played Shallow in The Merry Wives of Windsor, June 1968; Old Gobbo in The Merchant of Venice, July 1969; and Verges in Much Ado About Nothing, July 1970; Oxford Playhouse, July 1973, Old Gobbo in The Merchant of Venice and Lob in Dear Brutus; Round House, June 1975, The Pedant in The Taming of the Shrew; Arts, June 1976, Bernard in New-found-land; Open Air, Regent's Park, July 1976, Sir Nathaniel in Love's Labours Lost, repeating the role in May 1977, and also playing King Charles VI in Henry V in June 1977; Oxford Festival, 1978, Broomy in A Conception of Love; since 1960, he has appeared each year (except 1962) as the Mole in the Christmas production of Toad of Toad Hall, which in 1963 he co-directed; during 1936–7, broadcast a weekly programme as Mr Penny; subsequently toured in variety theatres in this character; in 1941–2, broadcast The Old Town Hall; in earlier years played for every Sunday-producing society of note, and has appeared in various films; received the Variety Club of Great Britain's Special Award, 1976.

Recreations: Household repairs, walking, arguing, and Edwardian Music Hall songs. *Club:* United Oxford and Cambridge University. *Address:* 15 Oakley Street, SW3. *Tel:* 01–352 7123.

GORDON, Hayes, OBE, actor, director and producing manager

b Boston, USA, 25 Feb 1920; *s* of Sam Gordon and his wife

Bertha (Paket); *e* Massachussetts College of Pharmacy; *m* Helen Terry; studied for the stage under Lee Strasberg, Sandy Meisner etc.

His early acting career in the US included parts such as Sam in Oklahoma!, St James, New York, Mar 1943; Gordon Williams in Winged Victory, 44th Street, Nov 1943; Barker in Show Boat, Ziegfeld, Jan 1946; Sandy Dean in Brigadoon, Ziegfeld, Mar 1947; Van Brunt in Sleepy Hollow, St James, June 1948; appeared in the revues Small Wonder, Coronet, Sept 1948, and Along Fifth Avenue, Broadway, 1949; toured the US and Canada, 1950, as Tommy in Brigadoon; went to Australia, 1952, and starred in Kiss Me Kate, Melbourne, 1952; Annie Get Your Gun, 1953; Kismet, 1956; Fiddler on the Roof, 1967, Daddy Warbucks in Annie, 1978, etc, all of which toured Australia; has played stock seasons at the Peabody Playhouse, Boston, Papermill Playhouse, New Jersey, St Louis Municipal Opera and Pittsburgh Light Opera; has also appeared in concerts and cabaret, and toured US Service Clubs in Japan; films, since 1943, include: Stage Door Canteen and Winged Victory; has made frequent broadcasts and TV appearances in the US and Australia, also produced; Principal of the Ensemble Studios, Sydney, which he founded in 1954; Governing Director of Ensemble Productions and the Ensemble Theatre, Sydney, which he founded in 1958 and where he has directed over fifty plays; has directed ten musicals for the Menzies Theatre Restaurant; produced and/or directed two Royal Pageants in Sydney, and staged the opening of the first Festival of the South Pacific, Fiji; directed Who Killed Santa Claus, Australian tour, 1971; directed The Royal Hunt of the Sun for the first Christchurch Festival of Arts, New Zealand, 1973; co-produced Long Day's Journey into Night, Sydney, 1979; awarded the OBE in the New Year Honours, 1979.

Recreations: Sailing, Archery and Goldbricking. *Address:* Ensemble Theatre, Milson's Point, 2061, New South Wales, Australia. *Tel:* 929 8877.

GORDON, Ruth, actress and dramatic author
b Wollaston, near Boston, Mass, 30 Oct 1896; *d* of Clinton Jones and his wife Annie (Ziegler); *e* Quincy High School, Mass; *m* (1) Gregory Kelly (dec); (2) Garson Kanin; studied for the stage at the American Academy of Dramatic Arts.

Made her first appearance on the stage at the Empire Theatre, New York, 21 Dec 1915, as Nibs in Peter Pan, with Maude Adams; at the Eltinge, 1916, played Blanny in Fair and Warmer; on tour, Jan 1918, played Lola Pratt in Seventeen; 1919–20, played in Piccadilly Jim; in Chicago, 1920, played Cora Wheeler in Clarence; English's Opera House, Indianapolis, 1921, appeared in stock; in 1922, with Gregory Kelly, established a stock company at Indianapolis; Little, NY, 1922, played Grace in The First Year, subsequently touring in the play; Frazee, Aug 1923, Winsora in Tweedles; Belmont, Jan 1925, Katherine Everett in Mrs Partridge Presents; Booth, Aug 1925, Eva Hutton in The Fall of Eve; same theatre, Jan 1927, Bobby in Saturday's Children, Morosco, Jan 1929, Serena Blandish in the play of that name; Martin Beck (for the Theatre Guild), Apr 1930, Lily Malone in Hotel Universe; Henry Miller, Sept 1930, Ilona Stobri in The Violet; Plymouth, Apr 1931, Trixie Ingram in The Wiser They Are; Playhouse, Oct 1931, Susie Sachs in A Church Mouse; Ethel Barrymore Theatre, Sept 1932, Mary Hilliard in Here To-day; Cort, Mar 1933, Elizabeth Rimplegar in Three Cornered Moon; Royale (for Theatre Guild), Feb 1934, Lucy Wells in They Shall Not Die; Guild Theatre, Oct 1934, Harriet Marshall, Wilhelmina and Hope Cameron in A Sleeping Clergyman; Westport, Conn, July 1935, Mrs Pinchwife in The Country Wife; Berkshire Playhouse, Stockbridge,

Mass, 1935, Epiphania in The Millionairess; White Plains, NY, 1935, appeared in Captain Brassbound's Conversion; National, NY, Jan 1936, Mattie Silver in Ethan Frome; made her first appearance on the London stage, at the Old Vic, 6 Oct 1936, as Mrs Pinchwife in The Country Wife, and returned to NY, to appear at the Henry Miller Theatre, Dec 1936, in the same part; Morosco, Dec 1937, Nora Helmer in A Doll's House; Princeton, NJ, Jan 1939, Linda Marsh in The Birds Stop Singing; Stockbridge, Mass, July 1939, appeared in Here To-day; Majestic, Boston, Dec 1941, Sheila Wyatt Munson in Portrait of a Lady; Royale, May 1942, Iris Ryan in The Strings, My Lord, Are False; Ethel Barrymore, Dec 1942, Natasha in The Three Sisters; Music Box, Jan 1944, Paula Wharton in Over Twenty-One, of which she was the author; Hudson, Sept 1947, co-produced How I Wonder; National, Oct 1948, Gay in her own play The Leading Lady; Lyceum, Jan 1949, Sara Boulting in The Smile of the World; in summer theatres, 1949, appeared as Natalia in A Month in the Country; Westport Country Playhouse (for the Theatre Guild), 1950, Adele in The Amazing Adele; re-visited England and appeared at the Royal, Newcastle, Aug 1954, as Mrs Levi in The Matchmaker, subsequently appearing in the same part at the Haymarket, Nov 1954; played this part in Edinburgh and Berlin, 1955; returned to NY, and at the Royale, Dec 1955, appeared once more in the same part for over a year; Plymouth, Mar 1960, Marie-Paule I in The Good Soup; Piccadilly, London, Apr 1962, Countess Mamie Haugabrook in A Time to Laugh; Plymouth, NY, Mar 1963, Rona Halpern in My Mother, My Father, and Me; Belasco, Sept 1965, Mrs Lord in her adaptation of a French play called A Very Rich Woman; Helen Hayes, Oct 1966, Cass in The Loves of Cass McGuire; Ethel Barrymore, Oct 1974, Zina in Dreyfus in Rehearsal; in addition to the plays mentioned, she is the author of Years Ago, 1946; first appeared in films, 1939, in Abe Lincoln in Illinois, subsequent films include Dr Ehrlich's Magic Bullet, Two-Faced Woman, Edge of Darkness, The Loved One, Inside Daisy Clover, Rosemary's Baby (for which she received the Academy Award), What Ever Happened to Aunt Alice?, Where's Poppa?, Harold and Maude, Boardwalk, My Bodyguard, etc; author, with Garson Kanin, of the screenplays Man and Wife, Adam's Rib, A Double Life, The Marrying Kind, and Pat and Mike, and of the TV film Hardhat and Legs, 1980; author of the autobiographical Myself Among Others, 1971, My Side, 1976, and An Open Book, 1979; appeared on television as Mommy in The American Dream, 1963.

Address: 200 West 57th Street, New York, NY 10019.

GORDONE, Charles Edward, Playwright and director
b Cleveland, Ohio, 12 Oct 1927; *s* of William Lee Gordone and his wife Camille (Morgan); *e* Los Angeles City and State College, New York University, Columbia University; previously occupied in various aspects of show business.

Author of No Place to Be Somebody, produced at The Other Stage, 4 May 1969, and which received the Pulitzer Prize, The Drama Desk Award, and the Critics' Circle Award as the best play of the year; Morosco, 9 Sept 1971, directed a revival of No Place to Be Somebody; at the Wilshire Ebell, Los Angeles, 26 July 1974, his play Baba Chops was first produced; author of The Last Chord, which he directed off-Broadway, 1976; in the Ensemble Studio's festival Marathon '78 directed Leaving Home; his play A Qualification for Anabiosis was also produced in this festival; New Federal, Nov 1979, played Bob in Crazy Horse; AMDA Studio, Dec 1979, Ficsur in Liliom; played one of the voices in the animated film Heavy Traffic, 1973; is a member of the Actors Studio.

Recreation: Horses. *Address:* William Morris Agency, 1350 Avenue of the Americas, New York, NY 10019.

GORELIK, Mordecai, designer, director and educator
b Shchedrin, Russia, 25 Aug 1899; *s* of Morris Gorelik and his wife Bertha (Dirskin); *e* Boys High School, Brooklyn, New York, and the Pratt Institute, 1920; *m* (1) Frances Strauss (dec); (2) Loraine Kabler; studied design with Robert Edmond Jones, Norman Bel Geddes, and Serge Soudeikin.

Was an instructor-designer at the School of the Theatre, NY, 1921–2; and at the American Academy of Dramatic Arts, NY; painted scenery and served backstage at the Provincetown Playhouse, 1921; designed King Hunger, Players Club, Philadelphia, Dec 1924; since then has designed over 40 professional productions, including: Processional for the Theatre Guild, 1925; Nivarna, 1926; Loudspeaker, 1927; The Final Balance, God, Man, and the Devil, 1928; 1931, 1931; Success Story, 1932; Little Ol' Boy, Men in White, All Good Americans, 1933; Gentlewoman, Sailors of Cattaro, 1934; Mother, The Young Go First, 1935; Golden Boy, 1937; Tortilla Flat, Casey Jones, Thunder Rock, 1938; designed his first show in London, at the St James, 21 June 1938, for the production of Golden Boy; Night Music, 1940; Volpone, Los Angeles, 1944; in Biarritz, France, for the Biarritz American University, 1945, designed and directed Doctor Knock and The Front Page and designed Volpone, All My Sons, NY, Paul Thompson Forever, Los Angeles which he also wrote and directed, 1947; Desire Under the Elms, NY, Danger, Men Working, Los Angeles, which he also directed, 1952; St Joan, The Flowering Peach, 1954; A Hatful of Rain, 1955; supervised the design of the Comédie Française and the Old Vic Company for their American visits; directed and designed Born Yesterday, Toledo, Ohio, 1956; The Sin of Pat Muldoon, NY, 1957; Guests of the Nation, NY, 1958; A Distant Bell, NY, 1960; The Dybbuk, Brigham Young University, Provo, Utah, which he also directed, 1961; The Firebugs, which he adapted and co-directed, 1963; translated The Firebugs, presented at the Bouwerie Lane, NY, Mar 1975; was on the faculty of the American Academy of Dramatic Arts, 1926–32, The Drama Workshop of the New School of Social Research, 1940–1, the Biarritz American University, Biarritz, France, 1945–6, University of Toledo, Ohio, 1956, University of Hawaii, New York University, 1956, Bard College, 1959, Brigham Young University, 1961; since 1960 has been research professor in theatre at Southern Illinois University, where he has directed and designed The Annotated Hamlet, 1961, The House of Bernarda Alba, Marseilles, 1962, The Good Woman of Setzuan, 1964, The Firebugs, etc; has also taught at and designed and directed The Dybbuk at San Jose (Calif) State College and Southern Illinois University; is the author of the plays Rainbow Terrace and Megan's Son and the book New Theatres for Old, 1940, as well as articles for the Encyclopaedia Britannica and other encyclopaedias and periodicals; was expert consultant in theatre for the US Military Government in Germany, 1949; received a Guggenheim Fellowship, 1936–37, a Rockefeller Foundation Grant, 1949–51, for study of European theatre, and a Fulbright Scholarship, 1967, for study of Australian theatre; first design for films was Days of Glory, 1944, and has since designed None But the Lonely Heart, Salt to the Devil, Our Street, L'Ennemi publique No 1, 1954; member of American Educational Theatre Association, Speech Communication Association, American Theatre Research Association, etc.
Address: 19532 Sandcastle Lane, Huntington Beach, Calif 92647.

GORING, Marius, actor
b Newport, Isle of Wight, 23 May 1912; *s* of Dr Charles Buckman Goring, MD, BSc (Hon Fellow University College), and his wife Kate Winifred (Macdonald); *e* Perse School, Cambridge, and at the Universities of Frankfurt, Munich, Vienna, and Paris; *m* (1) Mary Westwood Steel (mar dis); (2) Lucie Mannheim (dec); (3) Prudence Fitzgerald; studied for the stage under Harcourt Williams and at the Old Vic dramatic school.

Made his first appearance on the stage, at Cambridge, 1925, in Crossings; first appeared on the London stage at the Rudolph Steiner Hall, Dec 1927, as Harlequin at one of Jean Sterling Mackinlay's matinées; also appeared with her during her seasons, 1928–9; at the Old Vic, Dec 1929, appeared as a fairy in A Midsummer Night's Dream; in May 1931, toured in France and Germany with the English Classical Players; played two seasons at the Old Vic and Sadler's Wells, Sept 1932–May 1934, appearing as the Persian in Caesar and Cleopatra, and subsequently during the first season as Trip in The School for Scandal, Malcolm and (for a time) Macbeth in Macbeth, and Romeo; during 1933–4, at Old Vic, played Sebastian in Twelfth Night, Epihodov in The Cherry Orchard, Campeius in Henry VIII, Friar Peter and Abhorson in Measure for Measure, Alonzo in The Tempest, Buckram in Love for Love, Malcolm in Macbeth, and Hugh Voysey in The Voysey Inheritance; first appeared in the West-End at the Shaftesbury, May 1934, in the last mentioned part; in the autumn of 1934 to spring of 1935, toured France, Belgium, and Holland with the Compagnie des Quinze, acting in French, as Hamlet, Tarquin in Viol de Lucrèce, and Barclay in Riders to the Sea; Old Vic, Apr 1935, played Fortinbras, and subsequently Hamlet in Hamlet; New, July 1935, Japhet in Noah; Duke of York's, Oct 1935, Gallows Lasse and the Blind Man in The Hangman; Westminster, Oct 1935, Aubert in Sowers of the Hills; Playhouse, Dec 1935, Philip of Spain in Mary Tudor; His Majesty's, Apr 1936, Amor in The Happy Hypocrite; in July 1936, toured as Vincent in Ante Room; New, Sept 1936, Max in Girl Unknown; Westminster, Nov 1936, Gregers Werle in The Wild Duck; Old Vic, Dec 1936–Apr 1937, Frank Thorney in The Witch of Edmonton, First Player and Fortinbras in Hamlet, Feste in Twelfth Night, and Chorus in Henry V; Shaftesbury, June 1937, Peter de Meyer in Satyr; Comedy, Sept 1937, Wolfe Guildeford in The Last Straw; Ambassadors', Feb 1938, Arthur Primmer in Surprise Item; Phoenix, Oct 1938, Leonid Schervinsky in The White Guard; Duke of York's, Feb 1939, directed Nora (A Doll's House); Mar 1939, played Lord Bantock in Lady Fanny, which he also directed, and Apr 1939, Schimmelmann in Nina; Lyceum, June 1939, appeared as the First Player and Osric in Hamlet, subsequently playing the same parts at Elsinore; Rudolf Steiner Hall, Dec 1939, played the Storyteller and Pip in Great Expectations; Old Vic, May 1940, Ariel in The Tempest, which he also partly directed; joined the Army, June 1940; in Nov 1941, was appointed supervisor of productions of BBC, broadcasting to Germany; toured, 1947, in Germany, playing Monsieur Lamberthier, in English and German; during a season at the Arts Theatre, July 1948, appeared as John Rosmer in Rosmersholm, and later in the same month, as the Burglar in Too True to Be Good; Sept 1948, Trophimof in The Cherry Orchard; Oct 1948, played Smirnov in The Bear, and Podkolyossin in Marriage; Nov 1948, Maurice in The Third Man; during 1949, played Ernest in Daphne Laureola, in German, in Berlin; appeared in musical comedy in Berlin, 1950, playing in Berlin dialect; at the St James's, London, Feb 1951, played the Ragpicker in The Madwoman of Chaillot; joined the Shakespeare Memorial Theatre Company, Stratford-on-Avon, 1953, and during the season appeared as Richard III, Octavius Caesar in Antony and Cleopatra, Petruchio in The

Taming of the Shrew, and the Fool in King Lear; appeared with this company at the Princes, London, Nov 1953, as Octavius Caesar in Antony and Cleopatra; at Wuppertal, Germany, 1954–5, appeared in Gogol's Marriage and Tchekov's Dangers of Tobacco, playing in German; in 1957, founded a company of Shakespeare Comedians, performing scenes from Shakespeare, and appearing in Paris, 1957, Holland, Finland, and India, 1958–9; joined the Royal Shakespeare Company, Stratford-on-Avon, Apr 1962, to play Angelo in Measure for Measure, subsequently appearing at the Aldwych, Aug 1962, as Sir Timothy Bellboys in A Penny for a Song, for the same company; Lyric, Mar 1963, played Charles in Ménage à Trois; Dublin Festival, Sept 1963, played Teddy in The Poker Session, subsequently appearing at the Globe, London, Feb 1964, in the same play; toured, June 1965, as Magnus in The Apple Cart; toured, Sept 1965, as General Burgoyne in The Devil's Disciple; Vaudeville, Jan 1968, directed his own adaptation of The Bells, in which he played Mathias, and Lend Me Five Shillings, in which he played Mr Golightly; Nottingham Playhouse, Nov 1969, played Bright in The Demonstration; St Martin's, Aug 1971, took over as Andrew Wyke in Sleuth; Arnaud, Guildford, Aug 1974, played James I in The Wisest Fool; Theatre Royal, York, Mar 1975, Gustav Heideg in The Concert; Bankside Globe, Aug 1975, took part in poetry reading, This Wooden O; Liverpool Rep, Sept 1975, Arthur Wicksteed in Habeas Corpus, and at the same theatre, July 1976, repeated the part of Andrew Wyke in Sleuth; Theatre Royal, Windsor, Feb 1977, and subsequent tour in Jubilee Gaieties; Northcott, Exeter, Apr 1980, played the Emperor Franz Josef in Woe to the Sparrows; one of the founders of the London Theatre Studio, Jan 1936; entered films, 1936, and has appeared in a number of notable pictures; has also broadcast frequently on radio and television, notably in *The Expert*.

Recreations: Walking and travelling. *Address:* c/o Film Rights Ltd, 113–117 Wardour Street, London, W1. *Tel:* 01–437 7151.

GORMAN, Cliff, actor

b New York City, 13 Oct; *e* University of California at Los Angeles, University of New Mexico, and New York University; *m* Gayle Stevens.

First appeared on the stage at the American Place, NY, 11 Nov 1965, as Petey Boyle in Hogan's Goat; Anspacher, Mar 1968, played Arnulf in Ergo; Theatre Four, Apr 1968, Emory in Boys in the Band; Huntington Hartford, Mar 1969, again played this last part, and subsequently toured; Brooks Atkinson, May 1971, Lenny Bruce in Lenny, and received the Antoinette Perry (Tony) Award for this performance; Ahmanson, LA, Oct 1977, and Imperial, NY, Dec 1977, Leo Schneider in Chapter Two; first appeared in films in Justine, 1969, and has since played in Boys in the Band, Cops and Robbers, Rosebud, An Unmarried Woman, Night of the Juggler, etc; has also played on television in *Police Story*, *Paradise Lost*, *Class of '63*, etc.

Address: c/o William Morris Agency, 1350 Avenue of the Americas, New York, NY 10019.

GOTTFRIED, Martin, drama critic

b New York, 9 Oct 1933; *s* of Isidore Gottfried and his wife Rachel (Weitz); *e* Columbia College and Columbia Law School; *m* (1) Judith Houchins (mar dis); (2) Jane Lahr; formerly in United States Army Military Intelligence.

Classical music critic, *The Village Voice*, 1961–63; drama critic, *Women's Wear Daily*, 1963–74; *New York Post*, 1974–77; *Saturday Review*, 1977– ; *Cue New York*, 1977–79;

author of a play, The Director, produced 1972; books include A Theater Divided, 1968, Opening Nights, 1970, and Broadway Musicals, 1979.

Address: 17 East 96th Street, New York, NY.

GOTTLIEB, Morton, producer and manager

b Brooklyn, New York, 2 May 1921; *s* of Joseph W Gottlieb and his wife Hilda (Newman); *e* Erasmus High School, Brooklyn, and Yale University (BA, 1941).

Began his theatrical career at the age of seven at the Brooklyn Academy of Music, as a singer in Go Home and Tell Your Mother; made his professional stage début at the Shubert, New Haven, Conn, Jan 1941, in Liberty Jones; turned to press representation, for Theatre Inc, and represented Pygmalion, 1945 and the Old Vic in NY, 1946; was assistant business manager for Dream Girl, and Joan of Lorraine, 1946; general manager and press representative of the Cape Playhouse, Dennis, Mass, 1947–8; company manager for the NY production of Eastward in Eden, Nov 1947; business manager for Lamp at Midnight, Dec 1947, The Respectful Prostitute, Feb 1948, and To Tell the Truth, Apr 1948; general manager for Edward, My Son, Sept 1948, and for the Australian tour of this production, 1949; general manager for An Enemy of the People, 1950; became general manager for the Henry Miller's Theatre, 1951, and also for other Gilbert Miller productions, including Gigi, Caesar and Cleopatra, Antony and Cleopatra, 1951, and Horses in Midstream, 1953; produced his first show, a tour of Arms and the Man, in 1953; since then has produced or co-produced the following plays: His and Hers, and, with Laurence Olivier at the St James, Waiting for Gillian, his first London production, as well as the pre-Broadway tryouts of The Stronger Sex, The Last Tycoon, and The Facts of Life, 1954; the stock tours of A Palm Tree in a Rose Garden, The Better Mousetrap, The Amazing Adele, 1956; A Adventure, 1959; the tour of The Best Man, 1962; Enter Laughing, Chips with Everything, 1963; The White House, PS, I Love You, 1964; The Killing of Sister George, 1966; The Promise, 1967; Lovers, We Bombed in New Haven, 1968; The Mundy Scheme, 1969; Sleuth, which won the Antoinette Perry (Tony) Award as the best play of the year, 1970; Veronica's Room, 1973; Same Time Next Year, 1975; Tribute, 1978; Faith Healer, Romantic Comedy, 1979; has also served as the general manager of the American Shakespeare Festival, Stratford, Conn, 1956–7, the Cambridge, Mass, Drama Festival, 1959, and for the NY productions of Sail Away, 1961, The Affair, 1962, and The Hollow Crown, 1963; was company manager of The Travelling Lady, Tea and Sympathy, 1954; The Sleeping Prince 1956; The Rope Dancers, 1957; The Gazebo, A Handful of Fire, 1958, Look After Lulu, Cheri, Five Finger Exercise, 1959; Duel of Angels (tour), Under the Yum-Yum Tree, 1960; The Best Man, 1961; produced the films Sleuth, 1972; Same Time Next Year, 1977.

Recreations: Watching old movies. *Address:* 165 West 46th Street, New York, NY 10036, and 26 West 9th Street, New York, NY 10011. *Tel:* 575 7960 and AL 4 4717.

GOUGH, Michael, actor

b Malaya, 23 Nov 1917; *s* of F B Gough and his wife Frances Atkins (*née* Bailie); *e* Rose Hill School, Tunbridge Wells, Durham School, and Wye Agricultural College; *m* (1) Diana Graves (mar dis); (2) Anne Leon (mar dis); (3) Anneke Wills (mar dis); a student at the Old Vic School, 1936.

Made his first appearance on the stage at the Old Vic, in that year, and played small parts during the 1936–7 season; made his first appearance on the New York stage, at the John Golden Theatre, 13 Dec 1937, as Philip Vesey in Love of

Women; at the Westminster, London, Mar 1938, played Hilary and Simon in The Zeal of Thy House; New, Nov 1938, Gregory Rose in The Story of an African Farm; toured, 1939, in Idiot's Delight; Torch Theatre, Mar 1940, played Marchese Carlo di Nollo in This Man was Henry; Westminster, Apr 1940, Simon Cameron and William Scott in Abraham Lincoln; Q, June 1940, Karl Rolf in The Comic Artist; Globe, Sept 1940, Briggs in Thunder Rock; after the War, appeared with the Liverpool Old Vic company and at the Oxford Playhouse, and at the Piccadilly, June 1945, played the Dice Player in Jacobowsky and the Colonel; Criterion, Sept 1945, Fag in The Rivals; toured, 1946, in Craven House; St James's, Sept 1946, played Gerard in But for the Grace of God; Arts, Mar 1948, Nicholas Devize in The Lady's Not For Burning; Lyric, Hammersmith, June, and Garrick, Aug 1948, Hugo in Crime Passionnel; Aldwych, Dec 1948, Evan in September Tide; Duchess, Aug 1949, Hugh Joyce in Fading Mansion; Phoenix, Mar 1950, Gerard in The Way Things Go; New, May 1951, appeared as Laertes in Hamlet; at the same theatre, Dec 1951, played Julien in Colombe; Criterion, Apr 1952, Nicky Lancaster in a revival of The Vortex; Apollo, Feb 1954, Tony Lack in The Burning Glass; Arts, Nov 1954, Michel in The Immoralist; Court, Mar 1955, Peter Manson in The Burning Boat; Q, May 1955, Jani in An Act of Madness; Saville, Dec 1955, played Gregers Werle in The Wild Duck; Drury Lane, Nov 1956, the Admiral in Fanny; St Martin's, Feb 1958, Joe Leonard in Roseland; at the same theatre, Apr 1958, played Howard Holt in Something to Hide; Lyric, Hammersmith, Mar 1959, Gustav in Creditors; Strand, June 1960, took over Duddard in Rhinoceros; Vaudeville, Oct 1960, played Joe in This Year, Next Year; Her Majesty's, June 1962, played Joachim in Judith; at the Royal Court, Oct 1962, took over in the anthology Brecht on Brecht; at the same theatre, Feb 1963, played Mr Luxton in Jackie the Jumper; Arts, Cambridge, May 1963, Theseus in Phèdre; toured, June 1963, as Plinio Ceccho in Who? Where? What? Why?; Mayfair, Aug 1963, took over the part of the Stage Manager in Six Characters in Search of an Author; Comedy, Nov 1963, directed Offer of a Dream for the Repertory Players; toured the US, Nov 1963, in the anthology The Hollow Crown; Strand, Oct 1965, Theo Besson in Maigret and the Lady; Wyndham's, Feb 1967, took over as Teddy Lloyd in The Prime of Miss Jean Brodie; Royal Court, July 1969, played Dr Parks in Captain Oates' Left Sock; toured South America, 1969, for the British Council, in A Slight Ache, The Lover, The Public Eye, and Village Wooing; Arts, Cambridge, Feb 1972, Pastor Manders in Ghosts; Crucible, Sheffield, Nov 1973, Edward Carpenter in Free for All; Belgrade, Coventry, Nov 1974, title part in King Lear; same theatre, Jan 1975, and later at the ICA, London, appeared in Events in an Upper Room; Sept 1975, for the National Theatre at the Old Vic, played Sir Richard Metcalfe in Phaedra Britannica; Feb 1976, Glen in Watch it Come Down, also appearing in this part at the Lyttelton, Mar 1976; at the Olivier, Oct 1976, played the Soldan of Egypt in Tamburlaine the Great, The Count in Il Campiello and Dec 1976, He in Counting the Ways; Lyttelton, Mar 1977, Ernest in Bedroom Farce; Cottesloe, Apr 1977, John the Baptist in The Passion; Cottesloe, Feb 1978, Victor Marsden in Love Letters on Blue Paper, and Mar 1978 played several parts in Lark Rise; repeated the part of Ernest in Bedroom Farce at Brooks Atkinson, NY, Mar 1979, for which he won a Tony Award; Queen's, Mar 1980, Aubrey Skinner in Before the Party; has also appeared in films such as The Go-Between, Savage Messiah and The Legend of the Hill House, and in numerous television plays, most recently, Suez.

Favourite parts: King Lear, and He in Counting the Ways.
Address: c/o Plunket Greene Ltd, 91 Regent Street, London W1R 8RU.

GOULD, Elliott (*né* Goldstein); actor
b Brooklyn, New York, 29 Aug 1938; *s* of Bernard Goldstein and his wife Lucille (Raver); *e* Professional Children's School and Columbia University, 1955–6; *m* Barbra Streisand (mar dis); studied acting with Vladimir Protevitch, voice with Jerome Swinford, and dance with Sonya Box and Bill Quinn.

Made his NY début at the Alvin, Nov 1957, in the chorus of Rumple; ANTA, Apr 1958, played Earl Jorgenson in Say Darling; New York City Center, Feb 1959, again played this last part; Plymouth, Sept 1960, played an Usher, Priest, and Warder in Irma La Douce, subsequently taking over the part of Polyte-le-Mou; Shubert, Mar 1962, played Harry Bogen in I Can Get It for You Wholesale; made his London début at the Prince of Wales, 26 May 1963, as Ozzie in On the Town; Martin Beck, Oct 1965, Bob Purefoy in Drat! The Cat!; Broadhurst, Apr 1967, Alfred Chamberlain in Little Murders; ANTA, Jan 1969, Alex Krieger in A Way of Life; films include The Night They Raided Minsky's, MASH, Little Murders, I Love My Wife, The Touch, The Long Goodbye, California Split, Nashville, Harry and Walter Go to New York (1976), etc; has appeared on television in Once upon a Mattress, 1964.
Address: Actors Equity Association, 165 West 46th Street, New York, NY 10036.

GOULD, John, composer and performer
b Newquay, Cornwall, 1 July 1940; *s* of Arthur Jack Gould and his wife Jeanette Rose (Paton); *e* Clifton College, and St Edmund Hall, Oxford; formerly an accountant.

Wrote and appeared in undergraduate revues and musicals at Oxford, including Hang Down Your Head and Die, which transferred to the Comedy Theatre, March 1964 and in which he played the piano; made his London début at the Mermaid, 31 July 1966, in the revue Four Degrees Over, which he also co-wrote; transferred to the Fortune, Sept 1966; has since contributed to and appeared in the revues Three to One On, 1968; Postscripts, 1969; Down Upper Street, 1971; Just the Ticket, 1973; Think of a Number, 1975; Apollo, 1969, musical director of Forty Years On; his one-man show was first seen at the Jeanetta Cochrane, Jan 1971, subsequently throughout Britain, and in Johannesburg, 1973; returned to the Mayfair, 1974; The Luck of the Bodkins (co-adapted), 1978; he is the composer of the musicals Sweet Fanny, 1965; A Present from the Corporation, 1967; Who Was That Lady, 1970; On the Boil, 1972; Betjemania, 1976; appeared in the stage version of his own radio show, Bars of Gould, 1977; Director of WSG Productions Ltd and Whirligig (Children's Theatre).
Address: 98 Nelson Road, London SW19. *Tel:* 01–540 1915.

GOULET, Robert, actor and singer
b Lawrence, Mass, 26 Nov 1933; *s* of Joseph Goulet and his wife Jeanette (Gauthier); *e* Edmonton, Alberta, Canada, High School and the Royal Conservatory of Music, Toronto; studied singing with Joseph Furst and Ernesto Vinci; *m* (1) Louise Longmore (mar dis), (2) Carol Lawrence.

Made his concert début in Edmonton, 1951, in Handel's Messiah; at the Crest, Toronto, played in Thunder Rock and Visit to a Small Planet; Shakespeare Festival, Stratford, Ontario, summer 1958, played Captain MacHeath in The Beggar's Opera; Theatre-under-the-Stars, Vancouver, BC, Canada, played in South Pacific, Finian's Rainbow, and Gentlemen Prefer Blondes; came to the US and at the Packard Music Hall, Warren, Ohio, summer 1959, played Sid Sorokin in The Pajama Game and Jeff in Bells Are Ringing; made his New York début at the Majestic, 3 Dec 1960, as

Lancelot in Camelot, and was a great success; Broadway, Jan 1968, Jacques Bonnard in The Happy Time, for which he received the Antoinette Perry (Tony) Award; Dorothy Chandler Pavilion, Los Angeles, Sept 1975, Lancelot in Camelot; produced the US tour of Gene Kelly's Salute to Broadway, 1975; Westbury and Valley Forge, July 1979, Bill in Carousel; entered films in His and Hers, 1964, and has since played in Honeymoon Hotel, Underground, etc; has appeared extensively in cabaret with his wife Carol Lawrence; on television has appeared with major musical programs, as star of his own series, and in The World of Lerner and Loewe, The Judy Garland Show, Brigadoon, Carousel, Kiss Me, Kate, and for Granada in England; has also recorded extensively.

Address: American Guild of Musical Artists, 1841 Broadway, New York, NY.

GOW, Ronald, dramatic author

b Heaton Moor, near Manchester, 1 Nov 1897; *s* of Anthony Gow and his wife Clara (Ashworth); *e* Altrincham Grammar School, and Manchester University (BSc); *m* Wendy Hiller; was formerly engaged as research chemist and as a schoolmaster.

Author of Gallows Glorious, 1933; My Lady Wears a White Cockade, 1934; Love on the Dole (adapted), 1935; author of Ma's Bit o' Brass, 1938; Jenny Jones (musical) (adapted), 1944; Tess of the D'Urbervilles (adapted), 1946; Jassy (adapted), 1947; Ann Veronica (adapted), 1949; The Edwardians (adapted), 1959; author of Mr Rhodes, 1961; Watch and Ward (adapted), 1964, re-titled A Boston Story, 1968; The Friendship of Mrs Eckley, 1975.

Club: Dramatists'. *Address:* Spindles, Stratton Road, Beaconsfield, Bucks. *Tel:* Beaconsfield 3788.

GRACE, Nickolas, actor and director

b West Kirby, Cheshire, 21 Nov 1949; *s* of Leslie Halliwell Grace and his wife Jean (Cave-Mathieson); *e* King's, Chester and Forest, Essex; trained for the stage at the Central School of Speech and Drama.

Made his first stage appearance at the Royalty, Chester, aged 11, as second Watch in Much Ado About Nothing; in 1965 and 1968 directed the British entry for the Interdrama Festival, Berlin; after drama school had a season at Frinton, 1969; movement director for The Contractor, Royal Court, Oct 1969; in rep at Manchester Library, 1969; made his West End debut 7 Apr 1970, as Ernie in Erb, Strand; Theatre Upstairs, Jun 1970, Steve in The Sport of My Mad Mother; Old Vic, Aug 1970, Alfio in the Nottingham Playhouse production of A Yard of Sun; toured with Cambridge Theatre Co, Oct 1970, as Dickie in Chips with Everything; for Prospect, Feb 1971, toured as Player Queen and Second Gravedigger in Hamlet; Open Space, Sept 1971, Ward in My Foot, My Tutor; joined the RSC in Mar 1972, playing Alyoshka in The Lower Depths, Second Priest in Murder in The Cathedral, Aumerle in Richard II, and Biondello in The Taming of the Shrew, and visiting the US with the company to play Aumerle at the Brooklyn Academy, Jan 1974; artistic director, summer 1974, Frinton Theatre Co; autumn 1974, Waltham Forest Theatre; toured, Jun 1975, as Kyle in The Gentle Hook; at the opening of the Derby Playhouse, Sept 1975, played Hamlet; rejoined the RSC, Jan 1976, and in seasons at Stratford and in London his parts included Hitler in Schweyk, Florizel in The Winter's Tale, Aenaes in Troilus and Cressida, Dromio of Ephesus in The Comedy of Errors, Abel Drugger in The Alchemist, Coco in The Days of the Commune, and Witwoud in The Way of the World; for Bristol Old Vic, May 1978, MC in Cabaret; Shaftesbury, Aug

1978, Renfield in Dracula; for the Old Vic Company, autumn 1979, played Fribble in Miss in Her Teens and Mungo in The Padlock (double-bill), and Nicholas Beckett in What the Butler Saw; Greenwich, Apr 1980, Rudge in Next Time I'll Sing to You; Bristol Old Vic, June and Old Vic, July, 1980, Puck in A Midsummer Night's Dream; member of the editorial board of *Drama* since 1968; has taught movement and directed at Central School, LAMDA etc; films include City of the Dead, 1975, and Europe after the Rain, 1978; TV work includes The Love School, The Professionals, The Serpent Son, and Brideshead Revisited, 1980.

Recreations: Sunshine, swimming, singing. *Address:* c/o Sara Randall, Saraband Associates, 348A Upper Street, London N1.

GRADE, Lew (Lord Grade: cr Baron, 1976; Kt, 1969), theatre owner and producer

b 25 Dec 1906; *s* of Isaac Winogradsky and his wife Olga; *e* Rochelle Street School; *m* Kathleen Sheila Moody.

Chairman and Chief Executive, Associated Communications Corporation Ltd; President, ATV Network Ltd; joint managing director, Lew and Leslie Grade Ltd, agents, until 1955; Chairman, Stoll Moss Theatres Ltd, 1973–present.

Address: ACC House, 17 Great Cumberland Place, London W1A 1AG.

GRAHAM, Ronny, actor, director, lyricist, composer

b Philadelphia, Pa, 26 Aug 1919; *s* of Steve Graham and his wife Florence (Sweeney); *e* Germantown High School, Philadelphia; *m* (1) Jean Spitzbarth (mar dis); (2) Ellen Hanley (mar dis).

Made his legitimate début at the Brattle Theatre, Cambridge, Mass, 21 Mar 1951, in the revue It's About Time; made his New York début at the Royale, 16 May 1952, in the revue New Faces of 1952, to which he contributed music, lyrics, and sketches; Longacre, Oct 1954, played Charlie Reader in The Tender Trap; Golden, Sept 1957, wrote music, lyrics, and other material for the revue Mask and Gown; Upstairs at the Downstairs, Oct 1957, played in the revue Take Five, which he also wrote and composed; summer tour, 1960, played Mr Applegate in Damn Yankees; Broadhurst, May 1962, wrote the lyrics for Bravo, Giovanni!; Upstairs at the Downstairs, Feb 1963, played in Graham Crackers, which he also wrote and composed; same theatre, July 1963, directed Money; Louisiana Pavilion, New York State Fair, May 1964, played in America, Be Seated, which he also directed; Eugene O'Neill, Nov 1964, played Monte Checkovitch in Something More!; Renata, Apr 1965, contributed material to the revue Wet Paint; Eugene O'Neill, Nov 1965, directed Mating Dance; Booth, May 1968, contributed lyrics, music, and sketches to New Faces of 1968; Upstairs at the Downstairs, Mar 1969, directed Free Fall; directed the tour of Jeremy Troy, 1969; Belasco, Mar 1970, directed Grin and Bare It! and Postcards; Ethel Barrymore, Apr 1970, directed A Place for Polly; St Louis Repertory, Mo, 1971, appeared in Room Service; Seattle, Washington, Repertory, 1973–4 season, appeared in That Championship Season; Brothers and Sisters, NY, Oct 1975, appeared in cabaret; has performed frequently in cabaret since 1950; first appeared in films in New Faces, 1954, for which he also wrote the screenplay; appeared in Dirty Little Billy (1972); on television has performed in Highlights of the New Faces, *Omnibus,* *The Johnny Carson Show, Toast of the Town* and other variety programs.

Recreations: Chess and collecting rare libretti and scores. *Address:* Actors Equity Association, 165 West 46th Street, New York, NY 10036.

GRAINER, Ron, composer

b Atherton, Australia, 11 Aug 1922; *s* of Ronald Albert Grainer and his wife Margaret (Clark); *e* St Joseph's College, Nudgee, Brisbane; *m* Jennifer Marilyn Dodd (mar dis); received his musical training at the Sydney Conservatorium.

He has provided incidental music for productions including Andorra (National Theatre), 1964; Come As You Are, 1970; music for the musicals Robert and Elizabeth, 1964; On the Level, 1966; Sing a Rude Song, 1970; Nickleby and Me, 1975; is also the composer of film and TV scores, and of several well known signature tunes, such as those for the BBC series Maigret, Steptoe and Son and Dr Who.

Interests: Ecology, electronics in music and new age ideas. *Address:* c/o RK Records, 34 Windmill Street, London W1.

GRAINGER, Gawn, actor

b Glasgow, Scotland, 12 Oct 1937; *s* of Charles Neil Grainger and his wife Elizabeth (Gall); *e* Westminster City School; *m* Janet Key; trained for the stage at the Italia Conti School.

Made his first London appearance as a boy in 1950, when he played the Boy King in King's Rhapsody, at the Palace; in repertory at Dundee, 1961; Ipswich, 1962–4; Bristol (Old Vic), 1964–6; his parts at Bristol included the title-role in Kean, Christy Mahon in The Playboy of the Western World, Romeo, Laertes in Hamlet, and Claudio in Measure for Measure; toured the world in the last three parts, making his New York début as Romeo at the City Center, Feb 1967; at the Music Box, NY, Oct 1967, played Jimmy in There's a Girl in My Soup; returning to London, played Cyril Bishop in The Giveaway, Garrick, Apr 1969; James Boswell in The Douglas Cause, Duke of York's, Nov 1971; joined the National Theatre at the Old Vic, 1972; his parts for the company have included: McCue in The Front Page, July, Macduff in Macbeth, Nov 1972; Oronte in The Misanthrope, Feb, Officer in The Bacchae, Aug, Roberto in Saturday, Sunday, Monday, Oct, Jeremy Haynes in The Party, Dec 1973; Stephen Lloyd in Next of Kin, May, Figaro in The Marriage of Figaro, July 1974, toured the US as Oronte in the National production of The Misanthrope, 1975, appearing at the St James, NY, Mar; Osric in Hamlet, Old Vic, Dec 1975, and at the Lyttelton, Mar 1976; Old Vic, Feb 1976, took part in Tribute to a Lady; Usumcasane in Tamburlaine the Great, Olivier, Oct; and repeated at the National, May 1977; for the National, played the following parts: Juggler in Force of Habit, Nov 1976; Casca in Julius Caesar, Mar 1977; Soldier in the Passion, Apr 1977; June 1977, in To Those Born Later; Corporal Stoddard in The Plough and the Stars, Sept 1977; Mr Dorilant in The Country Wife, Nov 1977; Schoolmaster in Brand, Apr 1978; Ajax in The Woman, Aug 1978; Charles I in The World Turned Upside Down, Nov 1978, and the same month, Wesley in Has "Washington" Legs?; Jack/Nick in The Long Voyage Home, Feb 1979; George/General Heller in Dispatches, June 1979; Doctor/Squire/Landlord/Rector in Lark Rise and Sir Timothy in Candleford, Oct and Nov, 1979; author of the plays Four to One, 1976; Vamp Till Ready, 1978; Lies in Plastic Smiles, 1979; Paradise Lost, 1980; films, since his first appearance in 1958, include: Mastermind; TV includes: Son of Man, and panel appearances in the NY edition of What's My Line.

Favourite parts: Figaro, Serjeant Musgrave, Richard III. *Recreations:* Pool, poker, tennis, and Arsenal FC. *Address:* c/o David White Associates, Fl 4, 12 St George Street, London W1R 9DF. *Tel:* 01–499 8317.

GRANT, Bob, actor and playwright

b Hammersmith, London, 14 Apr 1932; *s* of Albert George Grant and his wife Florence (Burston); *e* Aldenham School; *m* Kim Benwell; trained for the stage at PARADA.

Made his first appearance, 1952, as Sydney in Worm's Eye View at the Court Royal, Horsham; London debut, Mar 1956, in the Theatre Workshop production of The Good Soldier Schweik at the Duke of York's; with the same company appeared at the Theatre Royal, Stratford, and the Théâtre des Nations festival, Paris (best actor award) as Kitely in Everyman in his Humour, July 1960; Fred Jugg in Sparrers Can't Sing, Aug 1960, transferring with the latter production to Wyndham's, Mar 1961; Mr Twigg in Big Soft Nellie, Nov 1961; Adelphi, May 1962, Mr Locke in Blitz!; Piccadilly, Aug 1964, Eastwood in Instant Marriage, for which he wrote book and lyrics; Shaftesbury, Dec 1965, Sheriff of Nottingham in Twang; returning to Theatre Workshop at Stratford, he played the title part in Macbird, Apr 1967, Constant in Intrigues and Amours, May, and George Brown in Mrs Wilson's Diary, Sept; transferred in the last part, Oct 1967, to the Criterion; Royal Court, Oct 1968, played Mervyn Molyneux in The Houses by the Green; Whitehall, Sept 1969, Leonard Jolly in Pyjama Tops; Theatre Royal, Stratford, Apr 1972, Sid in The Londoners; toured Australia, Oct 1973, as Brian Runnicles in No Sex Please, We're British; Eastbourne, Nov 1974, played Jack in his own play, Package Honeymoon; toured, Feb 1975, as Rev Mark Thompson in Darling Mr London (also co-author); toured, Aug 1975, as Charlie Barnet in One for the Pot; toured as Christopher Sly in The Taming of the Shrew, Feb 1977; Birmingham Rep, Dec 1977, Scrooge in A Christmas Carol; Brian Runnicles in No Sex Please, We're British, in Perth, W Australia, 1978; Ashcroft, Croydon, Dec 1979, Dame Trot in Jack and the Beanstalk; is also the author, with Anthony Marriott, of No Room for Sex, and I Want to Be a Father, Madam; film appearances, since 1962, include Help!, Till Death Do Us Part, and three films based on his successful TV series, *On the Buses.*

Favourite parts: Fancourt Babberley in Charley's Aunt, Scrooge in A Christmas Carol. *Recreation:* Sailing. *Address:* c/o Richard Stone, 18–20 York Buildings, London, WC2. *Tel:* 01–839 6421.

GRANT, Joyce, actress

b Bloemfontein, South Africa, 23 Jan 1924; *d* of James Hugh Grant and Magdaline (Kleinhans); *e* Eunice Girls High, Bloemfontein and University of Cape Town; trained for the stage at the Central School, London.

Made her first stage appearance at the Little Theatre, Cape Town, 1949, as the Yellow Ant in The Insect Play; came to England and played parts at the Questors, Ealing, 1950; in rep at High Wycombe, 1952, Dundee and Guildford, 1953; returned to South Africa, 1954–60, where she toured in parts such as Mrs Candour in School for Scandal, Lola in Come Back, Little Sheba, and Emma Hornett in Sailor Beware; returned to the UK 1960; Princes, Dec 1961, played Mrs Dawes and Asphynxia in Salad Days; Comedy, Jan 1963, appeared in An Evening of British Rubbish; Prince Charles, Feb 1964, in Fielding's Music Hall; New Arts, Oct 1964, in Four and a Tanner; Apollo, May 1965, in Nymphs and Satires; made her New York debut at the Ethel Barrymore, Oct 1968, as Mrs Rockefeller in Rockefeller and the Red Indians; Apollo, London, Mar 1970, Miss Wheeler in The Happy Apple; Hampstead, Dec 1970, played three parts in Tonight at Eight, transferring to the Fortune in this production, Jan 1971; Duke of York's, appeared in Once upon a Time, Dec 1972; Oxford Playhouse, Oct 1973, Mme Remy in Doctor Knock; Casino, Dec 1974, Fairy Godmother in Cinderella; Greenwich, Oct 1975, Clara Hibbert in The Vortex; Arnaud, Guildford, Mar 1977, title-role in The Duenna; Ambassadors', Jun 1977, Lady Manley-Prowe in

Something's Afoot; Regent, May 1978, Algy in The Club; Garrick, Oct 1978, Helga ten Dorp in Deathtrap; other appearances include tours and guest appearances with regional companies such as Nottingham Playhouse, 1964; TV work includes plays and series, recently The Dancing Years, 1979.

Favourite parts: Helga ten Dorp, Amanda Wingfield in The Glass Menagerie, and Mrs Candour. *Recreations:* Gardening and motoring. *Address:* c/o Boyack and Conway, 8 Cavendish Place, London W1.

GRANT, Micki (*née* M Louise Perkins) composer, lyricist, actress and singer
b Chicago; *d* of Oscar William Perkins and his wife Gussie (Odessa); *e* University of Illinois, Roosevelt University and dePaul University; *m* (1) Milton Grant (mar dis); (2) Charles R McCutcheon (mar dis); formerly a typist, insurance claims clerk and bus girl.

Made her New York debut at the Mayfair, Feb 1962, as Camille in Fly Blackbird; Sheridan Square Playhouse, Jul 1963, appeared in Brecht on Brecht; at the Little, Nov 1963, Marietta in Tambourines to Glory; Greenwich Mews, Jan 1964, Annabelle in Jerico-Jim Crow; Theatre Four, Aug 1964, Ella Hammer in The Cradle Will Rock; De Lys, Jun 1965, appeared in Leonard Bernstein's Theatre Songs; Cherry Lane, Jan 1969, in To Be Young, Gifted, and Black; has also appeared with many regional companies; since 1970 has worked extensively as a composer-lyricist with Vinnette Carroll at the Urban Arts Corps, NY, for whom she wrote music for Moon on a Rainbow Shawl, 1970; Croesus and the Witch (Aha!), Bury the Dead, 1971; book, music and lyrics for Don't Bother Me, I Can't Cope, 1971, in which she appeared on Broadway, 1972, at the Playhouse and later the Edison; music and lyrics for Step Lively, Boy, 1973; The Ups and Downs of Theophilus Maitland, 1974; I'm Laughing but I Ain't Tickled, 1976; co-wrote Your Arms Too Short to Box with God, also seen on Broadway, 1976 and 1980; music and lyrics for Alice, 1977; in addition has written music and lyrics for The Prodigal Sister, 1974; some songs for Working, 1978; additional lyrics for Eubie, 1979; and a musical, It's So Nice to Be Civilized, 1979 (Broadway, 1980); work for TV includes writing for The Infinity Factory (NET), and appearances in series and serials.

Favourite parts: Marietta in Tambourines to Glory, Gloria in The Gingham Dog. *Address:* c/o Bertha Case, 42 West 53rd Street, New York, NY 10019.

GRANT, Pauline, director, choreographer and dancer
b Moseley, Birmingham; *d* of Percy Frank Grant and his wife Elizabeth Mary (Webb); *e* St Paul's Convent, Edgbaston, Birmingham; *m* (1) Wing-Commander Brenus Gwynne Morris (mar dis); (2) S H Newsome; studied dancing at the Ginner-Mawer School of Dance and Drama, and classical ballet with Antony Tudor, Igor Schwezoff, and Vera Volkova.

Made her first appearance on the stage at the People's Theatre, St Pancras, as Columbine in Make Believe; became director of Ballet, at the Neighbourhood Theatre, Kensington; gave a season of Lunch Hour Ballet, at the Little, Feb; Cambridge Theatre, 1942, was solo dancer in the New Russian Ballet; toured, 1942–4, for ENSA, with French Ballet, dancing principal roles and being responsible for the choreography; Cambridge Theatre, Apr 1944, appeared with her own company in A Night in Venice, as Columbina; Aug 1944, gave a programme of one-hour ballet, subsequently rejoining A Night in Venice; Prince's, Sept 1945, arranged the Masque and ballets for Merrie England; Adelphi, May 1946, appeared with the Pauline Grant Ballet in Can-Can, for

which she also devised the choreography; devised the ballets and dances for Piccadilly Hayride, Prince of Wales's, 1946; The Bird Seller, Palace, 1947; King's Rhapsody (also soloist), Palace, 1949; Wild Violets, Stoll, 1950; Zip Goes a Million, Palace, 1951; Love from Judy, Saville, 1952; choreographed all the Palladium pantomimes, 1950–6; at the Cambridge, Oct 1954, directed her first straight play with Book of the Month; between 1954–5, directed the following productions on ice at the Empress Hall, Earl's Court: White Horse Inn on Ice, Cinderella on Ice, and Wildfire; at Coventry Theatre directed and scripted pantomimes with S H Newsome from 1956–68, including three originals: The Pied Piper, The Frog Prince and Beauty and the Beast; was choreographer for the opening season at the Arnaud Theatre, Guildford, June 1965; for this theatre wrote, directed and choreographed The Pied Piper, 1973; choreographer for the Royal Shakespeare Company at Stratford and later at the Aldwych, London, 1950–69; choreographed her first play in New York, Lunt-Fontanne, Sept 1959, with the RSC's As You Like It; has been choreographer for productions at Covent Garden, Glyndebourne (where she was director of ballet for the Festival Opera), and Sadler's Wells (Director of the English National Opera Movement Group at the Coliseum from 1969–); 1978–9, choreographed at Santa Fe Opera, New Mexico; 1979, choreographer for the Opera Theatre, St Louis, Missouri; director of the Peter Pan touring company; a director, since 1972, of MUDRA, the Brussels-based School for Perfection of Theatre Arts, founded by Maurice Béjart; lectures and demonstrates in England and America on modern genres in dance, mime and movement; films include: Happy Go Lovely, The Duke Wore Jeans, and Moll Flanders; directed the *Julie Andrews Show* for television.

Recreations: Gardening and fast cars. *Address:* 4 Halkin Mews, Belgrave Square, London, SW1X 8JZ.

GRAVES, Peter, actor and singer
b London, 21 Oct 1911; *s* of Henry Algernon Claud (7th Baron) Graves and his wife Vera Blanche Neville (Snepp); *e* Harrow; *m* Vanessa Lee; was formerly engaged in estate agents' and insurance business.

Made his first appearance on the stage at the Opera House, Manchester, 1 Sept 1934, in the revue Streamline; first appeared in London, at the Palace, 28 Sept 1934, in the same production; Drury Lane, May 1935, played Nico in Glamorous Night; Haymarket, Dec 1935, succeeded Robert Andrews as John in Full House; His Majesty's, Apr 1936, Captain Tarleton in The Happy Hypocrite; Drury Lane, Sept 1936, Jimmy Torrence in Careless Rapture, understudied Ivor Novello and occasionally played his part of Michael; Arts, Mar 1937, played Donald Thrale in The Heavenly Passion; at Daly's, May 1937, played the Hon Charles Glenn in African Dawn; Drury Lane, Sept 1937, Lord William Gantry in The Crest of the Wave; Sept 1938, the Dauphin in Henry V; Mar 1939, Franzel in The Dancing Years; Streatham Hill, Dec 1939, M Deladier in Second Helping, and at the Lyric, Apr 1940, the same part, when the play was renamed Ladies into Action; joined the Windsor repertory company, Apr 1941, playing a variety of parts; toured, Oct 1941, as Peter von Hohenburg in Blossom Time; Adelphi, Mar 1942, again played Franzel in the revival of The Dancing Years; Phoenix, Nov 1943, appeared as Pierre Bachelet in Arc de Triomphe; Palace, Mar 1945, Prince Orlofsky in Gay Rosalinda, and played the same part in a revival of this production at the Prince's, Aug 1946; Q, Dec 1946, Max Perry in Divorce on Tuesday; Duke of York's, May 1947, Bill Whittaker in We Proudly Present; toured, from June 1948, as Sir Graham Rodney in Perchance to Dream; toured, from

Apr 1949, as Elyot Chase in Private Lives; toured in the United States, from Aug 1949, as Evan in September Tide, with Gertrude Lawrence; returned to London, and at the Phoenix, Oct 1950, appeared as Valentine Brown in Dear Miss Phoebe; Stoll, Apr 1952, Prince Danilo in The Merry Widow; Palace, Feb 1953, John Beaumont in The Glorious Days; Globe, June 1954, Lord Windermere in After the Ball; Winter Garden, Aug 1955, played Mr Bryan in The Water Gipsies; toured, June 1956, as Charles in The Gay Deceiver; King's, Glasgow, Dec 1958, played Lord Ranelagh in Old Chelsea, and toured with the production; toured, Sept 1959, playing the part of Count Danilo in The Merry Widow; Connaught, Worthing, Nov 1960, played Philip Clair in Kind Sir; Hippodrome, Bristol, Dec 1960, The Emperor in Aladdin; toured Australia, Oct 1961–3, as Captain von Trapp in The Sound of Music; toured in England, Mar 1964, as Elyot Chase in Private Lives; Duchess, Jan 1965, took over the part of the Earl of Lister in The Reluctant Peer; Phoenix, July 1967, played Charles in The Last of Mrs Cheyney; Duke of York's, Nov 1968, Dominique in Dear Charles; toured South Africa, June 1969, as the Earl of Caversham in An Ideal Husband; March 1970, toured as Hubert in A Boston Story and Sept, as Rupert in His, Hers and Theirs; Drury Lane, Feb 1971, took over as Hartkopf in The Great Waltz; toured, Sept 1972, as Moore in Who Killed Santa Claus?; Strand, Jan 1977 to date (1980), played Leslie Bromhead in No Sex Please, We're British; recent television includes The Duchess of Duke Street, Quiller and Father Brown; first appeared in films, 1940, in Kipps; recent films include The Slipper and the Rose.

Favourite parts: Pierre in Arc de Triomphe, Danilo in The Merry Widow, Elyot Chase and Captain Von Trapo. *Recreation:* Lawn tennis (played at Wimbledon Tennis Championships, 1932–3). *Address:* c/o *The Spotlight*, 42 Cranbourn Street, London, WC2. *Tel:* 01–437 3002.

GRAY, Charles (*né* Donald Marshall Gray), actor
b Bournemouth, 29 Aug 1928; *s* of Donald Gray and his wife Maud Elizabeth (Marshall); formerly worked in an estate agent's office.

Made his first stage appearance at the Open Air, Regent's Park, May 1952, as Charles the Wrestler in As You Like It, remaining for the season to play other small parts; after a season of walk-ons at the Memorial Theatre, Stratford, 1953, joined the Old Vic company, Oct 1954, playing small parts; these increased in size until, in the 1956 season, he played Macduff in Macbeth, Escalus in Romeo and Juliet, Lodovico in Othello, Achilles in Troilus and Cressida, and Bolingbroke in Richard II; toured Canada and the USA with the company, autumn 1956, making his first appearance in New York, Sept 1956, at the Winter Garden, as Bolingbroke; other parts played on the tour were Escalus, Lennox in Macbeth, and Achilles; Saville, Apr 1958, Captain Mavors in Expresso Bongo; Broadway, NY, Nov 1961, Prince of Wales in Kean, playing under the name of Oliver Gray; returning to England, May 1962, played Bernard Acton in Everything in the Garden at the Duke of York's; Old Vic, Nov 1962, Sir Epicure Mammon in The Alchemist; Arts, Nov 1963, Maxime in Poor Bitos, later Duke of York's, Jan 1964, and Cort, NY, Nov 1964, receiving the Clarence Derwent award for his performance; Billy Rose, Oct 1965, Sir Charles Dilke in The Right Honourable Gentleman; Royal Court, Aug 1970 and May Fair, Sept 1970, Braham in The Philanthropist; Queen's, June 1975, General St Pé in Ardèle; Chichester, 1979 season, Sheridan Whiteside in The Man Who Came to Dinner; first appeared in films, 1958; recent film work includes The 7% Solution, The House on Garibaldi Street and The Legacy;

TV, since 1957, includes The Cherry Orchard, Julius Caesar and Richard III.
Address: c/o London Management Ltd, 235–241 Regent Street, London, W1.

GRAY, Dolores, actress and singer
b Chicago, Ill, 7 June 1924; *d* of Harry and Barbara Marguerite Gray; *e* privately, in Los Angeles; *m* Andrew Crevolin; studied singing and acting under her mother.

Commenced her career as a singer in cabaret at restaurants and supper clubs in San Francisco; in 1940, she appeared as a new discovery with Rudy Vallee in his radio program, also with Milton Berle and others; she appeared in cabaret, June 1944, at the Copacabana Supper Club, New York, followed by her first appearance on the regular stage at the Ziegfeld Theatre, NY, 7 Dec 1944, in Seven Lively Arts; she was then featured in her own radio program, 1945; Century Theatre, Nov 1945, played Bunny La Fleur in Are You with It?; at the Shubert, New Haven, Conn, Oct 1946, played Diana Janeway in Sweet Bye and Bye; made her first appearance in London, at the Coliseum, 7 June 1947, as Annie Oakley in Annie Get Your Gun, scoring an instantaneous success; the play ran until May 1950; during 1948, she studied at the Royal Academy of Dramatic Art, and at Drury Lane Theatre, Oct 1948, she appeared as Nell Gwynne in an excerpt from Good King Charles's Golden Days, at a performance given in aid of the fund to rebuild the RADA Theatre; after returning to the United States, appeared at the Mark Hellinger, NY, July 1951, in the revue Two on the Aisle; in summer theatres, 1952, played Eliza Doolittle in Pygmalion; New Century, NY, Sept 1953, Cornelia in Carnival in Flanders, for which she received the Antoinette Perry (Tony) Award; played in summer theatre in Can-Can, 1957, Silk Stockings, 1958–9, and Lady in the Dark, 1959; appeared at the London Palladium, 1958, and toured the Continent; Imperial, April 1959, Frenchie in Destry Rides Again for eighteen months; returned to London and appeared in cabaret at *The Talk of the Town,* Feb 1963; toured, 1966, as Annie Oakley in Annie Get Your Gun; Alvin, Mar 1967, Louraine Sheldon in Sherry!; Piccadilly, London, Dec 1973, took over from Angela Lansbury as Rose in Gypsy; Brothers and Sisters, NY, Feb–Mar 1975, appeared in cabaret; Imperial, 9 Mar 1975, appeared in Gala Tribute to Joshua Logan; has also played in summer theatre productions of Wildcat, The Unsinkable Molly Brown, The Pajama Game, Gypsy (1978), etc; appeared in the films Kismet, The Opposite Sex, Designing Woman, etc, has appeared frequently on English and American television.
Address: Actors Equity Association, 165 West 46th Street, New York, NY 10036.

GRAY, Dulcie, actress and author
b Kuala Lumpur, Federated Malay States, 20 Nov 1919; *d* of Arnold Savage Bailey and his wife Kate Edith Clulow (Gray); *e* Wallingford, Wokingham, and Swanage; *m* Michael Denison; studied for the stage at the Webber-Douglas School of Dramatic Art.

Made her first appearance on the stage at His Majesty's Theatre, Aberdeen, 8 May 1939, as Sorel Bliss in Hay Fever; subsequently appeared in repertory with the HM Tennent company at Edinburgh and Glasgow, 1940, and with the Harrogate Repertory Company, 1940–1; first appeared in London, at the Open Air Theatre, 16 July 1942, as Maria in Twelfth Night, and subsequently appeared as Hermia in A Midsummer Night's Dream and Bianca in The Taming of the Shrew; Piccadilly, Oct 1942, played Alexandra Giddens in The Little Foxes; Westminster, Dec 1942, again played Hermia; Garrick, Mar 1943, Rose Wilson in Brighton Rock;

Westminster, Oct 1943, Vivien in Landslide; Playhouse, Apr 1945, Greta in Lady from Edinburgh; St James's, Feb 1946, Ruth Wilkins in Dear Ruth; Apollo, May 1946, appeared as Jean Ritchie in The Wind is Ninety; toured, June 1946, in Fools Rush In; Aldwych, Aug 1948, Nurse Ransome in Rain on the Just; Strand, Nov 1949, Norah Fuller in Queen Elizabeth Slept Here; Ambassadors', Oct 1950, played Agnes in The Four Poster; Watergate, Oct 1951, appeared in the revue See You Later; Winter Garden, May 1952, played Nina in Dragon's Mouth; St James's, Dec 1952, Robina Jevons in Sweet Peril; toured, 1953, as Anna Lutcar in The Distant Hill; Westminster, June 1954, Toni Oberon in We Must Kill Toni; Arts, Sept 1954, Mrs Pooter in The Diary of a Nobody; toured South Africa, Dec 1954–Mar 1955, as Agnes in The Four Poster; Chelsea Palace, Dec 1955, played the White Queen in Alice Through the Looking Glass; Lyric, Hammersmith, June 1956, Marion Field in Love Affair; toured South Africa and Australia, July 1956–May 1957, as Lady Shotter in South Sea Bubble, and Laura Reynolds in Tea and Sympathy; Duchess, July 1958, played Sarah Banning in Double Cross; Playhouse, Oxford, Dec 1958, the title part in Candida; Cambridge, May 1959, the Duchess of Hampshire in Let Them Eat Cake; Bath Festival, May 1960, again played Candida, and appeared in the same production at the Piccadilly, June 1960, subsequently transferring to Wyndham's, Aug 1960, breaking the previous long run record with a total of 160 performances; Oxford Playhouse, Apr 1961, played Mary in The Bald Prima Donna, and the Old Woman in The Chairs (double-bill); Oxford Playhouse, Oct 1961, played Lady Utterword in Heartbreak House, transferring with the production to Wyndham's, Nov 1961; at the opening of the Hong Kong City Centre Theatre, Aug 1962, appeared as Z in A Village Wooing, and Lady Aline in A Marriage has been Arranged; Berlin Drama Festival, Sept 1962, appeared with Michael Denison in a Shakespeare Recital; at the opening of the Ashcroft Theatre, Croydon, Nov 1962, played Katerina of Arragon in Royal Gambit; New Arts, June 1963, played Caroline Abbott in Where Angels Fear to Tread, transferring to the St Martin's, July 1963; Apr–July 1964, toured with Michael Denison in a Shakespeare programme Merely Players; Birmingham Repertory, Oct 1964, played Madame Arkadina in The Seagull; Strand, Dec 1965, Lady Chiltern in An Ideal Husband; St Martin's, Dec 1966, played Maria Wislack in On Approval and again in March 1967, in repertory with Susan in Happy Family; Strand, Nov 1967, Julia Pyrton in Number Ten; Playhouse, Nottingham, May–July 1968, played May in Vacant Possession and Yulya Glebova in Confession at Night; St Martin's, Oct 1968, Celia Pilgrim in Out of the Question; Fortune, Jan 1970, played Z in Village Wooing and Mrs Banger in Press Cuttings; Criterion, Nov 1970, Gina Ekdal in The Wild Duck; toured, Apr 1971, as Mrs Heidelberg in The Clandestine Marriage; toured, Sept 1971, in Village Wooing; Royal, Windsor, Feb 1972, Ellen Blake in The Dragon Variation; Ashcroft, Croydon, Dec 1972, appeared in Through the Looking Glass; Savoy, Oct 1973, Mabel Jackson in At the End of the Day; Ambassadors', July 1974, Grace Bishop in The Sack Race; Comedy, Nov 1974, Olivia Cameron in The Pay-Off; toured, Aug 1976, as Ellen Creed in Ladies in Retirement; toured, May 1977, as Lady Twombley in The Cabinet Minister; Vaudeville, Sept 1977, Miss Marple in A Murder is Announced; Prince of Wales, Jan 1979, Delia in Bedroom Farce; toured, Apr 1980, as Evelyn in The Kingfisher; has appeared in numerous television plays; author of Love Affair (play), and numerous detective novels (many of them adapted for radio); her book Butterflies on My Mind won the *Times Educational Supplement*'s senior award, 1978; co-author (with Michael

Denison) of The Actor and His World; has appeared in numerous films, including: My Brother Jonathan, The Glass Mountain, The Franchise Affair, etc.

Favourite parts: Rose in Brighton Rock, and the Duchess of Hampshire in Let Them Eat Cake. *Recreations:* Swimming and butterflies. *Address:* c/o Midland Bank, 89 Buckingham Palace Road, London, SW1.

GRAY, Elspet, actress

b Inverness, Scotland, 12 Apr 1929; d of James MacGregor Gray and his wife Elspet Eleanor (Morrison); e St Margaret's, Hastings and Presentation Convent, Srinagar, India; m Brian Rix; trained for the stage at RADA.

Made her first professional appearance, Apr 1947, at the Grand, Leeds, as Phyllis in Edward, My Son, making her London debut in the same part at His Majesty's, May 1947; Whitehall, Sept 1950, played Gloria Dennis in Reluctant Heroes; Strand, Mar 1959, Janet Spicer in Wolf's Clothing; Wyndham's Sept 1964, Pamela Layton in The Diplomatic Baggage; Garrick, 1967, played in her husband's farce season as Melanie Sinclair in Uproar in the House, Apr and Liz in Let Sleeping Wives Lie, July; toured, Spring 1971, in four plays by Vernon Sylvaine; O'Keefe, Toronto, Apr 1973, appeared in Move over Mrs Markham; Palace, Westcliff, June 1973, Ursula Westerby in Come Back to My Place; Duke of York's, Oct 1975, Lucinda in Roger's Last Stand; Thorndike, Leatherhead, May 1977, Sarah in The Norman Conquests, and repeated the role at the Arnaud, Guildford, Sept 1979; Theatre Royal, Stratford E, Mar 1980, appeared in The Streets of London; films, since her first in 1949, include Reluctant Heroes and Goodbye, Mr Chips; has appeared on television since 1950, in numerous Brian Rix farce presentations and recently in *Fawlty Towers*.

Address: York House, Roedean Crescent, Roehampton, London, SW15.

GRAY, Linda, actress and singer

b Harrogate, Yorks, 10 July 1910; d of William Baxter and his wife Lily (Gray); e High School for Girls, Beverley, Yorks; formerly engaged on the concert platform.

Made her first appearance on the stage, at the Theatre Royal, Brighton, Aug 1929, in the chorus of the D'Oyly Carte Opera Company; first appeared in London, at the Savoy Theatre, 21 Oct 1929, in the chorus of The Gondoliers; remained with the D'Oyly Carte Company for six years; among the parts she played were Lady Saphir in Patience, Leila in Patience, Kate in The Pirates of Penzance, Giulia in The Gondoliers, etc; she also toured with the company in Canada and the United States; made her first appearance in New York, at the Martin Beck Theatre, Sept 1934, as Kate in The Pirates of Penzance; on returning to England, appeared at the Adelphi, Feb 1936, in Follow the Sun; Covent Garden, Nov 1936, appeared as Kate in Julia; toured, Aug 1937, as Laura in Two Bouquets; His Majesty's, Mar 1938, played Violet Travers in Operette; Kingsway, Oct 1938, Anastasia in An Elephant in Arcady; Globe, Apr 1939, Vashti in Scandal in Assyria; Haymarket, Mar 1940, appeared as Lucy Lockit in The Beggar's Opera; Prince's, Aug 1941, in Fun and Games; Prince's, Aug 1942, Lilian Russell in Wild Rose; Saville, Mar 1943, Grace Graves in Junior Miss; Prince's, Sept 1945, played Queen Elizabeth in Merrie England, and toured in this until Aug 1947; Strand, June 1948, played Cassandra in Cage Me a Peacock; Salisbury Arts Theatre, Christmas, 1949, played Aladdin in the pantomime; Prince's, May 1950, Lady Kirkham in His Excellency; Saville, Sept 1952, Mrs Grace Pritchard in Love From Judy; at the same theatre, Dec 1954, Countess Gisèle D'Eguzon in Accounting

For Love; Hippodrome, Derby, Apr 1955, Portia in The Gay Venetians, subsequently touring in this part; St Martin's, Feb 1956, played the Marquise de St Maur in She Smiled at Me; Drury Lane, Apr 1958, Mrs Eynsford-Hill in My Fair Lady; Strand, Oct 1963, played Domina in A Funny Thing Happened on the Way to the Forum; Prince of Wales, Nov 1966, appeared in the revue Way Out in Piccadilly; Arnaud, Guildford, July 1969, played Mrs Wadsworth D Harcourt in Anything Goes, transferring to the Saville, Nov 1969; Arnaud, Mar 1970, played Aunt March in Little Women; and Dec, the Queen of Hearts in Alice in Wonderland; Piccadilly, Feb 1973, first reader in Mistress of Novices; has also appeared on television, and in many films.

Favourite parts: Lucy Lockit in The Beggar's Opera, and Queen Elizabeth. *Recreation:* Looking for antiques. *Address:* 3 Hunter Street, Brunswick Square, London, WC1.

GRAY, Nicholas Stuart, dramatic author, actor, and director
b Scotland, 23 Oct 1919; *s* of William Stuart Gray and his wife Lenore May (Johnston); *e* private schools.

Author of the following plays: The Tinder-Box, The Haunted, 1948; Beauty and the Beast, 1949; The Princess and the Swineherd, 1952; The Hunters and the Henwife, The Marvellous Story of Puss in Boots, 1954; New Clothes for the Emperor, The Imperial Nightingale, The Seventh Swan, 1958; The Other Cinderella, 1960; The Wrong Side of the Moon, 1966; Lights Up (script and lyrics), 1967; New Lamps For Old, 1968, and Gawain and the Green Knight; he has also appeared in a number of his own plays as follows: at the Torch Theatre, Aug 1948, played Francis Cornwall in The Haunted; at the Mercury, Jan 1953, played Prince Etienne in The Princess and the Swineherd; at the Fortune, Apr 1955, and also Dec 1955, played Puss in The Marvellous Story of Puss in Boots; at the Arts, Dec 1958, played Piers in New Clothes for the Emperor; at the Gateway, Edinburgh, Aug 1966, played Tomlyn in The Wrong Side of the Moon, and at the Jeannetta Cochrane, Dec 1968; at the Arnaud, Guildford, Apr 1970, Jinnee of the Lamp in New Lamps for Old, which he also directed; he has also directed and played at repertory theatres in Brighton, Cambridge, Eastbourne, Frinton, and Windsor; first appeared on television in 1947, and performances include Prince Etienne in The Princess and the Swineherd and Francis Cornwall in The Haunted; he has also written a number of novels including The Edge of Evening, and Killer's Cookbook, 1976.

Recreations: Painting, gardening, and cats. *Address:* c/o Laurence Fitch, 113 Wardour Street, London W1.

GRAY, Simon, dramatist
b Hayling Island, Hants, 21 Oct 1936; *s* of James Davidson Gray and his wife Barbara Cecelia Mary (Holliday); *e* Westminster, Dalhousie University and Trinity College, Cambridge; *m* Beryl Mary Kevern; Lecturer in English Literature, Queen Mary College, London.

Author of the plays Wise Child, 1967; Dutch Uncle, 1968; The Idiot (adaptation), 1970; Spoiled, Butley, 1971; Otherwise Engaged, 1975; Molly, 1976; Dog Days, 1977; The Rear Column, 1978; Close of Play, Stage Struck, 1979; first play to be performed in New York was Wise Child (1972); has written numerous plays for television since 1966, including Death of a Teddy Bear (Writers Guild Award), Plaintiffs and Defendants, and Two Sundays; has also published four novels.

Recreations: Watching football and cricket. *Address:* c/o Clive Goodwin Associates, 12 Upper Addison Gardens, London W14. *Tel:* 01–602 6381.

GREEN, Adolph, author, lyricist, and entertainer
b Bronx, New York, 2 Dec; *s* of Daniel and Helen Green; *e* De Witt Clinton High School, NY; *m* Phyllis Newman.

Began his career in the cabaret act The Revuers, devised by himself and Betty Comden, in which they both appeared with Judy Holliday; at the Adelphi, NY, Dec 1944, co-author (with Betty Comden) of the book and lyrics, and played Ozzie in On the Town; in collaboration with Betty Comden he has since written the book and lyrics of the following musical productions: Billion Dollar Baby, 1945; Bonanza Bound! (also played Leonardo da Vinci), 1947; Two on the Aisle, 1951; Wonderful Town, 1953; Peter Pan (additional lyrics), 1954; Bells Are Ringing, 1956; Say, Darling!, 1958; A Party with Betty Comden and Adolph Green (in which he also appeared), 1958–9; Do-Re-Mi (lyrics only), 1960; Subways Are for Sleeping, 1961; On the Town (London), 1963; at the Philharmonic Hall, NY, 19 Apr 1964, performed in a revival of The Cradle Will Rock; Fade Out—Fade In, 1964 (revised, 1965); Leonard Bernstein's Theatre Song (some lyrics), 1965; Hallelujah, Baby, 1967; book with Betty Comden for Applause, 1970; appeared with Betty Comden at the Kaufman Auditorium, Jan 1971, in the program Lyrics and Lyricists; On the Town revived at the Imperial, 31 Oct 1971; Juilliard School of Music, 18 Dec 1971, performed in An Evening with Betty Comden and Adolph Green; Applause produced at Her Majesty's, Nov 1972; lyrics with Betty Comden for Lorelei or Gentlemen Still Prefer Blondes, 1974; book with Betty Comden for By Bernstein, 1975; appeared at the Morosco, Feb 1977, in A Party with Betty Comden and Adolph Green; with Betty Comden wrote the book for On The Twentieth Century, 1978; in collaboration with Betty Comden he has also written the screenplays and lyrics for Good News, Singin' in the Rain, The Barkleys of Broadway, It's Always Fair Weather, Bells Are Ringing, Take Me Out to the Ball Game, Auntie Mame, What a Way to Go; television productions include Wonderful Town and Peter Pan; has received numerous awards, including the Antoinette Perry (Tony), Donaldson, and the Screenwriters Guild Award.

Address: John Springer Associates, Inc, 667 Madison Avenue, New York, NY.

GREEN, Paul, playwright and author
b Lillington, North Carolina, 17 Mar 1894; *s* of William Archibald Green and his wife Betty Lorine (Byrd); *e* Buie's Creek Academy, 1914, University of North Carolina (AB, 1921), Cornell University, 1922–3; *m* Elizabeth Lay.

First play produced in New York was No 'Count Boy, at the Belasco, 6 May 1925; since then has written many one-act plays, including the following listed by date of publication: The Last of the Lowries, The Lord's Will, 1922; Tixin's, 1924; In Aunt Mahaly's Cabin, 1925; Supper for the Dead, 1926; The Man Who Died at 12 O'Clock, 1925; White Dresses, 1926; Unto Such Glory, 1927; Quare Medicine, 1928; Hymn to the Rising Sun, 1936; The Southern Cross, 1938; The Critical Year, Franklin and the King, 1939; The No 'Count Boy (white version), 1953; This Declaration, Chair Endowed, 1954; The Sheltering Plaid, 1965; has written the following full-length plays, also listed by date of publication: The Field God and In Abraham's Bosom, which won the Pulitzer Prize, 1927; Tread the Green Grass, 1929; The House of Connelly, 1931; Roll, Sweet Chariot, Shroud My Body Down, 1935; The Lost Colony, Johnny Johnson (which was revived in NY, Apr 1971), 1937; The Enchanted Maze, 1939; Native Son (which he adapted with Richard Wright from Mr Wright's novel), The Highland Call, 1941; The Common Glory, 1948; Faith of Our Fathers, 1950; an American version of Peer Gynt, 1951; Wilderness Road, 1956; The Founders, 1957; The Confederacy, 1959; The Stephen Foster Story, 1960; Cross and Sword, 1966; Texas, 1967; Trumpet in the Land, The Honeycomb, 1972; adapted into English the libretto of the opera Carmen, 1954; since 1937 has concentrated on the writing of symphonic dramas in amphitheatres built specially for them, notably, The Lost Colony, 1937 to present, at Roanoke Island, North Carolina; The Common Glory, 1947–76, Williamsburg, Virginia; Faith of Our Fathers, Washington, DC, 1950–1; The Seventeenth Star, Columbus, Ohio, 1953; The Wilderness Road, 1955–6–7, 1973 to present, Berea, Kentucky; The Founders, 1957–8–64, Williamsburg, Virginia; The Confederacy, 1958–9, Virginia Beach, Virginia; The Stephen Foster Story, 1959 to present, Bardstown, Kentucky; Cross and Sword, 1965 to present, St Augustine, Florida; Texas, 1966 to present, Canyon, Texas; Trumpet in the Land, 1970 to present, New Philadelphia, Ohio; Drumbeats in Georgia, 1972–3, Jekyll Island; Louisiana Cavalier, 1976, Natchitoches, La; We the People, Columbia, Md, 1976; The Lone Star, 1977 to present, Galveston, Texas; Palo Duro, 1978 to present, Palo Duro Canyon, Texas; has published the following collections of plays: The Lord's Will and Other Carolina Plays, 1925; Lonesome Road; Six Plays for the Negro Theatre, 1926; In the Valley and Other Carolina Plays, 1928; Out of the South: The Life of a People in Dramatic Form, 1939; Five Plays of the South, 1963; has written the following novels and short story collections: Wide Fields, 1928; The Laughing Pioneer, 1932; This Body the Earth, 1935; Salvation on a String, 1946; Dog on the Sun, 1949; Words and Ways, 1968; Home to My Valley, 1970; Land of Nod and Other Stories, 1976; published these collections of essays: The Hawthorn Tree, 1943; Forever Growing, 1945; Dramatic Heritage, 1953; Drama and the Weather, 1958; Plough and Furrow, 1963; has compiled a number of songbooks; wrote the scripts to the motion pictures Cabin in the Cotton, State Fair, 1932; Dr Bull, Voltaire, 1933; David Harum, 1934; Black Like Me, 1963; and many others; his radio plays are collected in The Free Company Presents, 1941, and Wings for to Fly: Three Plays of Negro Life, 1959; at the University of North Carolina, Chapel Hill, was Instructor and Associate Professor of Philosophy, 1923–39, Professor of Dramatic Art, 1939–44, and Professor of Radio, Television, and Motion Pictures, 1962–3; was President, American Folk Festival, 1934–5; President, National Theatre Conference, 1940–2; member of the Executive Commission of the US National Committee for UNESCO, 1950–2, and was its delegate to the Paris conference, 1951; Rockefeller Foundation Lecturer, 1951, in Asia, on American theatre; Director of ANTA, 1959–61; member of National Institute of Arts and Letters, Southeastern Theatre Conference, etc; was Guggenheim Fellow for study of European Theatre, 1928–30; Honorary LittD from Western Reserve University 1941, Davidson College, 1948; University of North Carolina, 1956, Berea College, 1957, University of Louisville, 1957; Campbell College, 1959; North Carolina School of the Arts, 1976; Moravian College, 1976; received the Theta Alpha Phi Medallion of Honor, 1965, North Carolina Achievement Award, 1965, Susanne M Davis Award, 1966, and the Morrison Award, 1968; National Theatre Conference Citation, 1975; North Carolina Distinguished Citizen Award, 1976; American Theatre Association Award for Distinguished Service to the Theatre, 1978..

Hobby: Music, several volumes of which he has compiled and published. *Recreation:* Gardening. *Address:* Old Lystra Road, Chapel Hill, North Carolina. *Tel:* 919–933 8581.

GREENE, Graham, CH, dramatic author and novelist
b Berkhamsted, 2 Oct 1904; *s* of Charles Henry Greene and his wife Marion (Raymond); *e* Berkhamsted school and Balliol College, Oxford; *m* Vivien Dayrell-Browning; an established author of many novels.

He has written the following plays: The Heart of the Matter (adapted with Basil Dean, from the novel of the same name), 1950; The Living Room, 1953; The Potting Shed, 1957; The Complaisant Lover, 1959; Carving a Statue, 1964; The Return of A J Raffles, 1975; For Whom the Bell Chimes, 1980; his novel, The Power and the Glory, was adapted for the stage by Denis Cannan and Pierre Bost, and has been performed in London, Paris, and New York; films written include: Brighton Rock, The Fallen Idol, The Third Man, Our Man in Havana, and The Comedians; novels include: Stamboul Train, 1932; Brighton Rock, 1939; The Power and the Glory, 1940; The Ministry of Fear, 1943; The Heart of the Matter, 1948; The Third Man, 1950; The End of the Affair, 1951; The Quiet American, 1955; Our Man in Havana, 1958; The Comedians, 1966; Travels With My Aunt, 1969; The Honorary Consul, 1973; The Human Factor, 1978; Companion of Honour in the New Year Honours, 1966; Hon DLitt, Cambridge, 1962; Hon Fellow, Balliol College, Oxford, 1963; Hon DLitt, Edinburgh, 1967; Hon DLitt, Oxford, 1979.

Address: c/o The Bodley Head, 9 Bow Street, London, WC2.

GREENWOOD, Jane, designer
b England, 30 Apr 1934; *d* of John Richard Greenwood and his wife Florence Sarah Mary (Humphries); *e* Merchant Taylor's Girls School, Liverpool, and Central School of Arts and Crafts; *m* Ben Edwards.

First designs for the stage were for costumes for the Oxford Repertory production of Pirandello's Henry IV, at the Playhouse, 1958; first designs for London were the costumes for The Hamlet of Stepney Green, at the Lyric, Hammersmith, 15 July 1958; first designs for New York were in association with Ray Diffen, at the Madison Avenue Playhouse, 25 Feb 1963, for The Importance of Being Earnest; since then has designed the costumes for The Ballad of the Sad Cafe, 1963; Hamlet (Richard Burton in Sir John Gielgud's production), Incident at Vichy, 1964; Tartuffe, Half a Sixpence, A Race of Hairy Men!, 1965; Nathan Weinstein, Mystic, Connecticut, Where's Daddy?, The Killing of Sister George (supervision), 1966; What Do You Really Know About Your Husband? (tour), More Stately Mansions, The Prime of Miss Jean Brodie, The Comedy of Errors (National Repertory Theatre), 1967; The Seven Descents of Myrtle, I'm Solomon, 1968; The Wrong Way Light Bulb, The Penny Wars, Crimes of Passion, Angela, 1969; Hay Fever, Les Blancs, Sheep on the Runway, Gandhi, 1970; Seventy, Girls, Seventy, The House of Blue Leaves, Antigone, 1971; Wise Child, That's Entertainment, 1972; A Moon for the Misbegotten, Look Away, Finishing Touches, The Prodigal Daughter (Washington, DC), 1973; Figures in the Sand, Cat on a Hot Tin Roof, 1974; Same Time Next Year, Finn McKool, The Grand Distraction, 1975; California Suite, A Texas Trilogy, 1976; Otherwise Engaged, Caesar and Cleopatra, Anna Christie, Vieux Carré, The Night of the Tribades, An Almost Perfect Person, 1977; Cheaters, The Prince of Grand Street (pre-Broadway), The Kingfisher, 1978; The Umbrellas of Cherbourg, Faith Healer, Knockout, Happy Days, Father's Day, Romantic Comedy, A Month in the Country, 1979; designed 23 productions for the American Shakespeare Festival, Stratford, Conn, 1966–76; has also designed for the Metropolitan Opera, the City Center Opera Company, the Guthrie Theatre in Minneapolis, Studio Arena, Buffalo,

McCarter, Princeton, and the Ahmanson, Los Angeles; TV designs include A Touch of the Poet; film work includes Last Embrace, and Can't Stop the Music, 1980; teaches a course in design at the Lester Polakov Design Studio, NY, and lectures at the Juilliard School Department of Drama, NY, and at Yale.

Address: 321 West 19th Street, New York, NY 10011. *Tel:* WA 9–2931.

GREENWOOD, Joan, actress

b Chelsea, London, 4 Mar 1921; *d* of Sydney Earnshaw Greenwood and his wife Ida (Waller); *e* St Catherine's, Bramley, Surrey; *m* André Morell (dec); studied for the stage at the Royal Academy of Dramatic Arts.

Made her first appearance on the stage, at the Apollo Theatre, 15 Nov 1938, as Louisa in The Robust Invalid; Strand, Feb 1939, played Timpson in Little Ladyship; Lyric, Apr 1939, Little Mary in The Women, and played the same part when the play was revived at the Strand, Apr 1940; Richmond, May 1940, played Pamela Brent in Dr Brent's Household; Q, Jan 1941, appeared in the revue, Rise Above It; Adelphi, Dec 1941, played Wendy in Peter Pan, and toured in the same part, 1942; Q, Jan 1943, Netta in Striplings; Whitehall, May 1943, Henriette in Damaged Goods; Cambridge, Aug 1943, succeeded Deborah Kerr as Ellie Dunn in Heartbreak House, subsequently touring for ENSA; during 1944, played a season with the Worthing Repertory company, and toured with Donald Wolfit's Company, playing Ophelia in Hamlet, and Celia in Volpone; at the Oxford Playhouse, from Feb 1945, played Lady Teazle, Cleopatra, Nora Helmer in A Doll's House, etc; toured from Dec 1945, in It Happened in New York; at the St Martin's, Apr 1948, played Bertha in Frenzy; Savoy, July 1949, Sabina Pennant in Young Wives' Tale; Scala, Dec 1951, played Peter Pan; St James's, May 1953, Noel Thorne in The Uninvited Guest; made her first appearance on the NY stage at the Morosco, 11 Feb 1954, as Lucasta Angel in The Confidential Clerk; at the Lyceum, Edinburgh, Jan 1955, played A Visitor in The Moon and the Chimney; Phoenix, London, Sept 1955, succeeded Lilli Palmer as Gillian Holroyd in Bell, Book and Candle; Royal Court, June 1956, played Mrs Mallett in Cards of Identity; at the same theatre, Dec 1957, the title part in Lysistrata, transferring with the production to the Duke of York's, Feb 1958; St Martin's, Dec 1958, played Hattie in The Grass is Greener; Oxford Playhouse, Feb 1960, played the title part in Hedda Gabler; Criterion, Apr 1961, played Hedda Rankin in The Irregular Verb to Love; Chichester Festival, July 1962, played Calantha in The Broken Heart, and Elena in Uncle Vanya; New Arts, Feb 1964, again played Hedda in Hedda Gabler, transferring with the production to the St Martin's, Mar 1964; New Lyric, Hammersmith, Oct 1964, played Olga in Oblomov, transferring to the Comedy, Dec 1964, when the play was re-titled Son of Oblomov; ANTA, NY, Nov 1966, Valentina Ponti in Those that Play the Clowns; Vaudeville, Apr 1967, Julia Sterroll in Fallen Angels; Richmond, 1968, Candida in Candida; Duchess, Apr 1969, Mrs Rogers in The Au Pair Man; New, Bromley, 1970, Lady Kitty in The Circle; Arnaud, Guildford, Nov 1970, Miss Madrigal in The Chalk Garden; toured, Sept 1972 as Stella in Eden End; Duchess, Sept 1973, played The Diva in Before Dawn, and Lydia Crutwell in After Lydia, in the programme In Praise of Love; Leeds Playhouse, Feb 1976, Madame Ranevsky in The Cherry Orchard; first appeared in films, 1941, in My Wife's Family; her many subsequent pictures include The Hound of the Baskervilles and The Water Babies.

Hobby: Circuses. *Recreations:* Ballet dancing, sleeping, reading and talking. *Address:* c/o The Spotlight, 42 Cranbourn Street, London, WC2.

GREGG, Hubert, actor, author, lyric writer and composer

b London, 19 July 1916; *s* of Robert Gregg and his wife Alice (Bessant); *e* St Dunstan's; *m* (1) Zoë Gail (mar dis); (2) Pat Kirkwood (mar dis).

Studied for the stage at the Webber-Douglas School of Singing and Dramatic Art, appearing there as Julien in Martine, which was transferred to the Ambassadors' Theatre, 23 May 1933, when he made his first appearance on the professional stage, in the part of Julien; in the autumn of 1933, joined the Birmingham Repertory Company for the eight months season, playing a variety of juvenile parts; appeared at the Open Air Theatre, Regent's Park, May–Sept 1934, as Silvius in As You Like It, later playing the part of Orlando; Ferdinand in The Tempest, Younger Brother in Comus, the Black Prince in the first production of The Six of Calais, and Benvolio in Romeo and Juliet; Westminster, Feb 1935, played Pip in The Convict; Embassy, Mar 1935, and subsequently at the Prince's, played Kastril in The Alchemist; Old Vic, Apr 1935, Rosencrantz in Hamlet; Open Air, June–Sept 1935, Sebastian in Twelfth Night, Le Beau in As You Like It, Demetrius in A Midsummer Night's Dream, and Longaville in Love's Labour's Lost; Gate, Oct 1935, Robert in National 6; Fortune (for Stage Society), Nov 1935, Digby Walsh in Not for Children; Croydon Repertory, Apr–May 1936; Open Air, July–Sept 1936, played Ferdinand in The Tempest, Silvius in As You Like It, Longaville in Love's Labour's Lost; Sebastian in Twelfth Night, and the Elder Brother in Comus; Nov 1936, toured with the Chantecler Co, as the Gardener in the opera The Marriage of Figaro; Ring, Blackfriars, Nov 1936, King Henry in Henry V and Jan 1937, Claudio in Much Ado About Nothing; Duke of York's, Mar 1937, Frederick Hackett in Great Possessions; made his first appearance on the New York stage, at the Henry Miller Theatre, 28 Sept 1937, as Kit Neilan in French Without Tears, and returned to London, at the Criterion, Feb 1938, to play the same part to the end of the run at the Piccadilly; played the part nearly 650 times; St James's, June 1939, played Peter Scott-Fowler in After the Dance; joined the Army, Oct 1939; served in the ranks in the Lincolnshire Regiment, and as a commissioned officer in the 60th Rifles (KRRC); Vaudeville, Sept 1942, played Polly in Men and Shadow; left 1943, to take up a post in Intelligence; invalided out, July 1943; Vaudeville, Oct 1943, played Michael Carraway in Acacia Avenue; Globe, July 1945, succeeded Michael Wilding, as the Earl of Harpenden in While the Sun Shines; Apollo, June 1947, played Tom D'Arcy, MP, in Off the Record; Q, June 1949, and Piccadilly, Sept 1949, Gabriel Hathaway in Western Wind; at the Devonshire Park, Eastbourne, and Hippodrome, Margate, Aug 1950, Peter Scott-Fowler in After the Dance, and Sept 1950, Father in Life With Father, and Rodney in Young Wives' Tale; Oct 1950, played Hamlet at the same theatres; also, 1950, directed the touring production of The Ex-Mrs Y; Arts, Cambridge, Feb 1951, produced The Hollow, and appeared in the part of Dr John Christow; directed the same play at the Fortune, London, June 1951, but on that occasion did not appear in the production; toured, 1952, as Toni Rigi in To Dorothy, A Son, which he also directed; Winter Garden, Nov 1954, temporarily took over from D A Clarke-Smith as Mr Myers in Witness For the Prosecution; at the Royal, Nottingham, Oct 1957, directed The Call of the Dodo; St Martin's, June 1958, directed Speaking of Murder; Duchess, Aug 1958, directed The Unexpected Guest; Prince of Wales,

Nov 1958, played John Blessington-Briggs in Chrysanthemum; Strand, Sept 1959, directed his comedy, From the French; Duchess, Mar 1960, directed Go Back For Murder; Royal, Windsor, July 1960, played Sir Geoffrey Randell-Hunter in his own comedy, Villa Sleep Four; Phoenix, Feb 1961, the Rev Lionel Toop in Pools Paradise; Duchess, Dec 1962, directed Rule of Three; New, Bromley, Jan 1965, played Bertie Wilcox in Who's Been Sleeping . . .?; toured, Mar 1965, in Villa Sleep Four; Royal, Windsor, Jan 1966, played André in From the French; Everyman, Cheltenham, Dec 1966, Squeezum in Lock Up Your Daughters; toured, Oct 1967, as Roger in his own play, The Rumpus; Chichester Festival, May–July 1968, played Alexander MacColgie Gibbs in The Cocktail Party, Antonio in The Tempest and the Announcer in The Skin of Our Teeth; University, Newcastle, Dec 1970, David Bliss in Hay Fever; Chichester Festival, May–July 1971, played Sir Lucius O'Trigger in The Rivals, Marcellin in Dear Antoine and Britannus in Caesar and Cleopatra; Savoy, July 1971, re-staged The Secretary Bird; Piccadilly, Nov 1971, again played Marcellin in Dear Antoine; toured, 1972–3, as Hugh Walford in The Secretary Bird, which he also directed; May 1975, played Patrick Delafield in Knuckle, at the Haymarket, Leicester; Redgrave, Farnham, Feb 1976, directed French Without Tears; Royal, Windsor, June 1976 and tour, directed While the Sun Shines, playing the Duke of Ayr and Stirling; Haymarket, Leicester, 1978, played Lord Summerhayes in Misalliance and Duncan in Macbeth; since 1975 has toured in solo performances, notably his Words by Elgar, Music by Shaw, which has been seen at the Malvern and Edinburgh Festivals; has acted and directed at various theatres, for the Repertory Players; wrote lyrics and music for Strike a New Note, 1943; The Love Racket, and Sweet and Low, 1944; Strike It Again, 1945; Leslie Henson's Gaieties, 1945; Better Late, 1946; Together Again, 1947; Sauce Tartare, 1949; is the author of the plays We Have Company, Cheque Mate, Villa Sleep Four, Who's Been Sleeping . . .? From the French (under the pseudonym Jean-Paul Marotte), and The Rumpus; has appeared in numerous films, including Robin Hood, The Maggie, Svengali, Doctor at Sea, Simon and Laura, and also, in association with Vernon Harris, wrote the screenplay of Three Men In a Boat, also After the Ball (adapted from his television play The Great Little Tilley); has frequently broadcast for the BBC in series (radio and television) in drama, variety, readings and record programmes; broadcast his series of 40 one-hour programmes on the history of the London theatre in 1975; has produced over 300 programmes for commercial radio; has written more than a hundred songs, several achieving great success, notably I'm Going to Get Lit Up When the Lights Go Up in London and Maybe It's Because I'm a Londoner; is the author of two novels, April Gentleman and A Day's Loving.
Recreations: Writing, composing and cinematography. *Club:* Garrick. *Address:* c/o BBC, Broadcasting House, London, W1A 1AA.

GREGORY, Andre, producer and director
At the Gate, 14 Oct 1959, co-produced Deirdre of the Sorrows; co-produced The Blacks, 1961; directed his first New York play, PS 193, at The Writer's Stage, 30 Oct 1962, and has since directed Firebugs, 1963; Tartuffe, 1967; The Bacchae, 1969; Alice in Wonderland, 1970; Endgame, 1974; Sea Gull, Our Late Night, 1975; Jinxs Bridge, 1976; is the artistic director of The Manhattan Project, which has toured extensively in Alice In Wonderland, including the Edinburgh Festival.
Address: The Manhattan Project, c/o The Bunch, 115 Central Park West, New York, NY 10023.

GREY, Joel, actor
b Cleveland, Ohio, 11 Apr 1932; *s* of Mickey Katz, the comedian; prepared for the stage at the Cleveland Playhouse and the Neighborhood Playhouse, New York.
Made his stage début at the Cleveland Playhouse, 1941, as Pud in On Borrowed Time; made his NY début at the Phoenix, 22 May 1956, in The Littlest Revue; Brooks Atkinson, 1961, took over from Warren Berlinger as Buddy Baker in Come Blow Your Horn; toured, 1963–4, as Littlechap in Stop the World—I Want to Get Off; Broadhurst, 1965, took over as Arthur Kipps in Half a Sixpence; Broadhurst, Nov 1966, Master of Ceremonies in Cabaret, for which he received the Antoinette Perry (Tony) Award and the New York Critics Poll; Palace, Apr 1968, George M Cohan in George M!; Curran, San Francisco, May 1969, again played in George M!; Maddox Hall, Atlanta, Ga, July 1972, appeared in 1776; Fairmont Hotel, San Francisco, Cal, Nov 1972, appeared in cabaret; Riviera, Las Vegas, Dec 1972, appeared in cabaret with Liza Minnelli; Caribe Hilton, San Juan, Puerto Rico, Jan 1973, and Empire Room, Waldorf Astoria, NY, Feb 1973, played in cabaret; Music Hall, Cleveland, Ohio, Oct 1973, appeared in concert; Westbury Music Fair, Long Island, May 1974, appeared in a variety show, and subsequently toured; Palace, Mar 1975, Charley in Goodtime Charley; Nanuet, NY, Star, June 1975, appeared in The Joel Grey Show; Public, Jan 1977, Stony McBride in Marco Polo Sings a Solo; Williamstown Theatre Festival, Aug 1977, title-role in Platonov; Palace, NY, Jan 1979, S L Jacobowsky in The Grand Tour; for New York City Opera, Mar 1980, Olim in Silverlake; appeared in the film of Cabaret, for which he received the Academy Award, 1973; other films include Man on a Swing, Buffalo Bill and the Indians, and The Seven Per Cent Solution; has appeared on television in George M!, and as host of the public TV series Live from Wolf Trap.
Address: Actors Equity Association, 165 West 46th Street, New York, NY 10036.

GRIFFIN, Hayden, designer
b Pietermaritzburg, S Africa, 23 Jan 1943; *s* Robert John Warder Griffin and his wife Doreen (Tuck); *e* Maritzburg College, SA; *m* Carol Anne Lawrence; trained as a designer at Sadler's Wells.
Designed his first production, Caesar and Cleopatra, for the Belgrade, Coventry, Sept 1976; first London production Trixie and Baba, Royal Court, Aug 1968; first New York production, Rockefeller and the Red Indians, Barrymore, Oct 1968; has since designed London productions including: Narrow Road to the Deep North, 1968; The Farm, 1973; Duck Song, Runaway, Bingo, Comrades, Crete and Sergeant Pepper, 1974; The End of Me Old Cigar, Lenny, 1975; has designed the following plays for The National Theatre, unless otherwise stated: Watch It Come Down, Weapons of Happiness, Yesterday's News (Theatre Upstairs), Il Campiello, 1976; Devil's Island (Royal Court), A Mad World, My Masters (Joint Stock), The Madras House, 1977; Plenty, The Woman, Cousin Vladimir (RSC), 1978; A Fair Quarrel, The Long Voyage Home, As You Like It, The Case of the Oily Levantine (Her Majesty's), 1979; The Iceman Cometh, 1980; Head of Design, Northcott, Exeter, 1970–2; has also designed for Nottingham Playhouse, Royal Lyceum, Edinburgh, Bristol Old Vic and in Aarhus and Vienna; designer for the York Mystery Cycle, York, 1976; associate lecturer for the English National Opera Design School.
Recreations: Walking, surfing, watching football. *Address:* 22 Drake Road, Newport, Isle of Wight. *Tel:* 098–381 6172.

GRIFFITH, Hugh, actor
b Marian Glâs, Anglesey, North Wales, 30 May 1912; *s* of

William Griffith and his wife Mary (Williams); *e* Llangefni Grammar School; *m* Adelgunde Margaret Beatrice Dechend; formerly a bank clerk; studied for the stage at the Royal Academy of Dramatic Art, where he received the Bancroft Gold Medal, 1939.

One of his first professional appearances was at the Mercury Theatre, Jan 1939, as Jimmy Farrell in The Playboy of the Western World; Globe, May 1939, played the Rev Dan Price in Rhondda Roundabout; Mercury, and Duchess, Oct 1939, Shawn Keogh in The Playboy of the Western World; Embassy, Nov and His Majesty's, Dec 1939, Marullus, Popilius Lena and Lepidus in Julius Caesar (in modern dress); St Martin's, Feb 1940, played Concini in The Venetian; appeared at the Q, and Embassy, in some revivals, and toured in The Millionairess; during the War, served from Sept 1940–Mar 1946, in India; joined the Shakespeare Memorial Theatre company, Stratford-on-Avon, for the 1946 season, playing Trinculo in The Tempest, Holofernes in Love's Labour's Lost, King of France in Henry V, Touchstone in As You Like It, and Mephistopheles in Dr Faustus; Arts Theatre, Dec 1946, played Old Wilmot in Fatal Curiosity; Duchess, Mar 1947, Cardinal Monticelso in The White Devil; Lyric, Hammersmith, July 1947, the Senator in The Respectable Prostitute; Arts, Feb 1948, Rev John Williams in A Comedy of Good and Evil; Mercury, Apr 1948, Christopher Mahon in The Playboy of the Western World, and Jan 1949, Nicia in Mandragola; Grand, Swansea, Oct 1949, played King Lear; toured, 1950, as Cranmer in The White Falcon, and Ulric Brendel in Rosmersholm; Lyric, Hammersmith, Nov and Duke of York's, Dec 1950, the Father in Point of Departure; at Stratford-on-Avon, season 1951, played Gaunt in Richard II and Caliban in The Tempest; made his first appearance on the New York stage at the Plymouth, 26 Dec 1951, appearing in the last-named part, when the play was re-entitled Legend of Lovers; St James's, London, Jan 1953, played Andrew Deeson in Escapade; Lyceum, Edinburgh, Feb 1954, and at the Aldwych, Apr 1954, appeared as Bellman in The Dark Is Light Enough; Arts, Feb 1956, and Criterion, Mar 1956, played General St Pé in The Waltz of the Toreadors; after more than a year, he left the company, and appeared at the Ethel Barrymore, NY, Nov 1957, as W O Gant in Look Homeward, Angel; Old Vic, London, May 1959, played Count Cenci in The Cenci; Aldwych, Mar 1962, played Azdak in The Caucasian Chalk Circle; Biltmore, NY, Feb 1963, the Teacher in Andorra; Royal Shakespeare, Stratford-on-Avon, Apr 1964, played Falstaff in Henry IV (Parts I and II), in the Quatercentenary Festival season; Nottingham Playhouse, Mar 1972, Prospero in The Tempest, also touring Europe with the production; first entered films, 1939, subsequent films include: Ben Hur (Academy Oscar Award), Tom Jones, How to Steal A Million, Start the Revolution Without Me, etc; notable television appearances include: Long John Silver in Treasure Island (NY), and Luther Flannery in The Walrus and the Carpenter series (London), 1965.

Favourite part: King Lear. *Recreation:* Golf. *Club:* Garrick. *Address:* c/o ICM Ltd, 22 Grafton Street, London, W1.

GRIFFITHS, Derek, actor and musician
b Woking, Surrey, July 1946; *s* of Donald Griffiths and his wife Estelle Barbara; *e* Tufnell Park, London; formerly a teacher.

Made his first stage appearance at the Edinburgh Festival, Aug 1969, as Sir Andrew Aguecheek in a performance of Twelfth Night; at Greenwich, Oct 1969 appeared as a musician in Martin Luther King; Feb 1970, played four parts in

Sing a Rude Song, making his West End début in the same production at the Garrick, 26 May 1970; again at Greenwich, Oct 1970; Mickey in Down the Arches; same theatre, July 1972, played Tommy Hawk in Liberty Ranch, and King Rat in Dick Whittington, Dec 1972; Phoenix, Apr 1973, Thurio in the musical Two Gentlemen of Verona; Cambridge Apr 1975, Ko-Ko in The Black Mikado, which he played for over a year; Norwich, Aug 1976, El Gallo in The Fantasticks; Young Vic, Oct 1977, played Scapino; Royal Exchange, Manchester, Dec 1977, directed his own version of Dick Whittington, for which he also wrote music and lyrics; same theatre, June 1979, co-adapted The Three Musketeers (also music and lyrics); TV, since 1970, includes children's programmes (as presenter), Her Majesty's Pleasure, and music for Bod, Ditch Baby, and the series Heads and Tails; films, since 1971 include: Up Pompeii.

Favourite parts: Ko-Ko, Azdak in the Caucasian Chalk Circle, and Sir Andrew Aguecheek. *Recreation:* Flying. *Address:* 652 Finchley Road, London NW3H 7NT. *Tel:* 01–458 7288.

GRIFFITHS, Trevor, dramatic author
b Manchester, 4 Apr 1935; *s* of Ernest Griffiths and his wife Ann (Connor); *e* St Bede's College, Manchester and Manchester University; *m* Janice Elaine Stansfield.

His first play to be produced was The Wages of Thin (one-act), at the Stables, Manchester, Nov 1969; has subsequently written Occupations, performed 1970; Apricots, Thermidor, 1971; Sam, Sam, 1972; The Party, 1973; The Party (revised), 1974; Comedians, All Good Men, 1975; contributed to the group work Lay By, 1971; Comedians produced in New York, 1976; co-wrote Deeds, 1978; his writing for television includes: Absolute Beginners, Through the Night, and Bill Brand; member, Institute for Workers Control.

Recreations: Soccer, chess, music. *Address:* c/o Goodwin Associates, 12 Upper Addison Gardens, London W14. *Tel:* 01–602 6381.

GRIMALDI, Marion, actress and singer
b London, 20 Aug 1926; *d* of George Henry Grimaldi and his wife Gladys (Winter); *e* privately; trained for the stage at RADA; first professional appearance, Boltons, June 1948, as Manette in Les Cloches de Corneville.

Made her West End debut, May 1951, in a small part in Hassan, at the Cambridge; worked in repertory until June 1954, when she played Mrs Hurst-Green in After the Ball, at the Globe; Royal Court, Mar 1955, Jane Manson in The Burning Boat; Piccadilly, Dec 1955, Meg in A Girl Called Jo; New, 1956, took over as Polly Garter in Under Milk Wood; Players', July 1957, the Snow Queen in Antarctica; Palace, Feb 1958, Donna Lucia in Where's Charley?; Bristol Old Vic, 1959, Viola in No Bed for Bacon; Vaudeville, Mar 1960, Cora Miskin in Follow That Girl; Pembroke, Croydon, Dec 1960, Belle in A Christmas Carol; Globe, June 1961, appeared in the revue On the Avenue; Piccadilly, Oct 1962, Thea in Fiorello!; Leatherhead, Sept 1963, Mrs Erlynne in Lady Windermere's Fan; same theatre, Jan 1964, Maggie in Hobson's Choice; Players', Dec 1965, Ardinelle in Ali Baba; at the opening of the Arnaud, Guildford, June 1965, played Diana in Lionel and Clarissa; Globe, Mar 1966, Annie Besant in The Match Girls; Sadler's Wells, 1966, sang Queen Clementine in Bluebeard; at Bromley and Canterbury, 1966 and 1967, played Maria in The Dancing Years; Belgrade, Coventry, 1967, Lady Godiva in Godiva Was a Lady; Comedy, Nov 1967, Mme Dubonnet in The Boy Friend; Leatherhead, 1969, Mrs Linden in A Doll's House; Playhouse,

Oxford, and tour, 1969, Frosina in The Miser; Playhouse, Derby, 1970, Lady Bracknell in The Importance of Being Earnest; appeared in Under Milk Wood at the Arts, May 1971 and subsequently at the Edinburgh Festival and Sadler's Wells; Phoenix, Mar 1972, The Prioress, Serpolette and Proserpina in The Canterbury Tales; Richmond, 1973, Mrs Niven in Darling, You Were Wonderful; toured, June 1973, as Henrietta in The Hollow; Coliseum, Dec 1974, Mrs Darling in Peter Pan; Thorndike, Leatherhead, Feb 1975, Martha in The Constant Wife; Princess, Torquay, 1975–6, Queen Evilina in Snow White; Theatre Royal, Brighton, June 1976, Florrie Crump in One of the Family; New Theatre, Hull, 1977, again played Queen Evilina; appeared in the Royal Command Performances, 1953 and 1958; has also played pantomime; TV work, since 1956, has included musicals and straight plays; also a regular concert and recording artist, and radio includes a broadcast honouring The Centenary of the Clown, Joseph Grimaldi, 1978.

Favourite parts: Polly Garter, Queen Evilina, and all larger-than-life characters. *Recreations:* Tennis, riding, watching cricket, and gambling. *Clubs:* Surrey CCC, Players' Theatre. *Address:* c/o Tim Wilson, 4 Church Road, Richmond, Surrey.

GRIMES, Tammy, actress and singer

b Lynn, Mass, 30 Jan 1934; *d* of Luther Nichols Grimes and his wife Eola Willard (Niles); *e* Beaver Country Day School, Chestnut Hill, Mass, and Stephen College, Columbia, Missouri; studied also at the Neighborhood Playhouse School of the Theatre; *m* Christopher Plummer (mar dis).

Made her New York début as a replacement for Kim Stanley as Chérie in Bus Stop, at the Music Box, in 1955; US tour, 1955–6, appeared as Adele in The Amazing Adele; Phoenix, NY, May 1956, appeared in The Littlest Revue; US tour, 1956, played Agnes Sorel in The Lark; Rooftop, NY, Nov 1957, played the Flounder in Clérembard; Shakespeare Festival Theatre, Stratford, Ontario, Canada, 1958, played Mistress Quickly in Henry IV, Part I, and Mopsa in The Winter's Tale; Henry Miller's, NY, Mar 1959, Lulu D'Arville in Look After Lulu; Winter Garden, Nov 1960, played Molly Tobin in The Unsinkable Molly Brown, and toured in this part, 1962; Booth, Apr 1963, played Cyrenne in Rattle of a Simple Man; Alvin, Apr 1964, Elvira in High Spirits; toured California, 1965, in Rattle of a Simple Man; Burlingame, California, summer 1965, appeared in Finian's Rainbow; toured, 1965, in The Private Ear and The Public Eye (double-bill); Huntington Hartford, Los Angeles, Apr 1967, played in the revue The Decline and Fall of the Whole World as Seen Through the Eyes of Cole Porter; Broadhurst, May 1968, Fran Walker in The Only Game in Town; Billy Rose, Dec 1969, Amanda Prynne in Private Lives; toured, summer 1971, in The Warm Peninsula; Walnut St, Philadelphia, Nov 1971, played in The Imaginary Invalid; toured, 1973, as Molly Tobin in The Unsinkable Molly Brown; Walnut St, Philadelphia, Jan 1974, Kate in The Taming of the Shrew; toured, spring 1974, as Amanda Prynne in Private Lives; Eisenhower, Washington, DC, June 1974, Pamela Fox in Perfect Pitch; Academy Festival, Lake Forest, Ill, Aug 1974, played in The Play's the Thing; Studio Arena, Buffalo, Dec 1974, title-role in Gabrielle; Royal Poinciana Playhouse, Palm Beach, Fla, Mar 1975, Vicky in My Fat Friend; Westport, Conn, Country Playhouse, Aug 1975, Lydia Cruttwell in In Praise of Love; St James, NY, Nov 1975, appeared in the revue A Musical Jubilee; Ahmanson, LA, Apr 1976, and O'Neill, NY, Oct 1976, played Hannah Warren, Diana Nichols, and Gert Franklin in California Suite; Hudson Guild, Jan 1978, title-role in Molly; Circle in the Square,

June 1978, Elmire in Tartuffe; Playhouse, Feb 1979, Paula Cramer in Trick; American Place, June 1979, Marian in Father's Day; Roundabout Stage One, Dec 1979, Natalya in A Month in The Country; received the Antoinette Perry (Tony) Award and New York Drama Critics Award for her performance as Molly in The Unsinkable Molly Brown, 1961, and the Tony and Critics Award for Private Lives, 1970; her films include Three Bites of the Apple, Play It As It Lays, The Runner Stumbles, Somebody Killed Her Husband, and Can't Stop the Music (1980); has appeared regularly on the dramatic and variety television programs.

Recreations: Walking, acting and travelling. *Address:* c/o John Trainer, 345 Park Ave, New York, NY. *Tel:* 759 7755.

GRIZZARD, George, actor

b Roanoke Rapids, North Carolina, 1 Apr 1928; *s* of George Cooper Grizzard and his wife Mary Winifred (Albritton); *e* University of North Carolina; formerly employed in advertising; prepared for the stage with Sanford Meisner and Alan Schneider.

Made his first appearance on the stage at the Crossroads Theatre, Bailey's Crossroads, Va, 1945, as a Miner in The Corn Is Green and subsequently as Raymond Pringle in Kiss and Tell; played with the Arena Stage, Washington, DC, Oct 1950, as Sam Bean in The Delectable Judge, Biondello in The Taming of the Shrew, White Rabbit in Alice in Wonderland, and returned to the same company, Jan 1952, to play Rowley in School for Scandal, Harvey in Three Men on a Horse, Witch Boy in Dark of the Moon, Yank in Hasty Heart, Eben in Desire Under the Elms, Don in All Summer Long; first appeared on Broadway at the Ethel Barrymore Theatre, Feb 1955, as Hank Griffin in The Desperate Hours; Lyceum, New York, Nov 1956, Angier Duke in The Happiest Millionaire; Coronet, Dec 1958, Shep Stearns in The Disenchanted; Eugene O'Neill, Oct 1960, Harold Rutland, Jnr, in Face of a Hero; ANTA, Mar 1961, Ronnie Johnson in Big Fish, Little Fish; Folksbiene Playhouse, Mar–Apr 1962, Joseph Surface in The School for Scandal and the Vagabond in The Tavern; Billy Rose, Oct 1962, Nick in Who's Afraid of Virginia Woolf? leaving the production to join the first company to appear at the Guthrie Theatre, Minneapolis, Minnesota, May–Sept 1963, where he played the title-role in Hamlet, Clerk in The Miser, and Captain Solyony in The Three Sisters; Guthrie Theatre, Minneapolis, May 1964, the title-role in Henry V, Mosca in Volpone and the Dauphin in Saint Joan; Brooks Atkinson, NY, May 1965, Tom in The Glass Menagerie; University of Chicago, Feb 1966, Alceste in The Misanthrope; Westport Country Playhouse, Conn, July 1966, Simon in The Thinking Man; Olney, Maryland, Aug 1966, the title-role in Stephen D; Studio Arena, Buffalo, Oct 1966, the title-role of Cyrano de Bergerac; Ambassador, Mar 1967, Jack Barnstable, Salesman, and Herbert in You Know I Can't Hear You When the Water's Running; Ethel Barrymore, Sept 1968, played in the revue Noel Coward's Sweet Potato, and again played in this revue when it was revived at the Booth, Nov 1968; John Golden, Apr 1969, Vincent in The Gingham Dog; Music Box, Apr 1970, Julius Rosenberg in Inquest; Bucks County Theater Co, New Hope, Pa, 1971–2 season, played in The Headhunters; Billy Rose, Mar 1972, Bernie Dodd in The Country Girl; Shubert, Nov 1972, Lucifer in The Creation of the World and Other Business; Helen Hayes, Oct 1973, King Edward VIII in Crown Matrimonial; Carnegie Music Hall, Pittsburgh, Pa, Apr 1975, played in The Great American Fourth of July Parade; Brooklyn Academy of Music, 17 Dec 1975, Tony Cavendish in The Royal Family, and transferred with this production to the Helen Hayes 30 Dec 1975; Eugene O'Neill,

June 1976, played Billy, Sidney, and Stu in California Suite; Hartford Stage, Conn, Dec 1977, Ralph Michaelson in Past Tense; Circle in the Square, Dec 1978, John Tanner in Man and Superman; toured, July–Aug 1979, as Sidney Bruhl in Deathtrap; received the Variety Drama Critics Poll Award for his role in The Desperate Hours; entered films, 1960, and notable pictures include Advise and Consent, From the Terrace, Happy Birthday, Wanda June, etc; first appeared on television, 1951, and principal performances include My Three Angels, Notorious and *The Adams Chronicles* (1976).
Address: New Preston, Conn 06777.

GRODIN, Charles, actor and director
b Pittsburgh, Pa, 21 April 1935; *e* University of Miami, Fla; prepared for the stage at the Pittsburgh Playhouse; also studied with Uta Hagen and Lee Strasberg.

Made his New York début at the Plymouth, 25 Oct 1962, as Robert Pickett in Tchin-Tchin; Ambassador, Sept 1964, played Perry Littlewood in Absence of a Cello; with Maurice Teitelbaum wrote the book and lyrics for Hooray! It's a Glorious Day . . . And all That, which he also directed at the Theatre Four, Mar 1966; Brooks Atkinson, Sept 1968, directed Lovers and Other Strangers; Truck and Warehouse, May 1970, played Tandy in Steambath during previews; Broadhurst, Apr 1974, directed Thieves; Brooks Atkinson, Mar 1975, played George in Same Time, Next Year, and subsequently toured; Little, March 1977, produced and directed Unexpected Guests; played in the film The Heartbreak Kid, 1972, and has since played in 11 Harrowhouse, 1974, etc.
Address: Actors Equity Association, 165 West 46th Street, New York, NY 10036.

GROSBARD, Ulu, director
b Antwerp, Belgium, 9 Jan 1929; *s* of Morris Grosbard and his wife Rose (Tennenbaum); *e* University of Chicago (BA 1950), Yale Drama School, 1952–3; *m* Rose Gregorio; formerly a diamond cutter.

Directed his first play, A View from the Bridge, at the Gateway Playhouse, Belleport, Long Island, July 1957; directed his first play in New York, The Days and Nights of Beebee Fenstermaker, at the Sheridan Square Playhouse, Sept 1962; since then has directed The Subject Was Roses, 1964; A View from the Bridge, 1965; The Investigation, 1966; That Summer—That Fall, 1967; The Price, 1968; American Buffalo, 1977; The Woods, 1979; began in films in 1961 as assistant director of Splendor in the Grass, and since has served as assistant director of West Side Story, The Hustler, The Miracle Worker, and as unit manager for The Pawnbroker; directed the film The Subject Was Roses, 1968, and has since produced and directed Who Is Harry Kellerman and Why Is He Saying Those Terrible Things About Me?, Straight Time, and True Confessions (1980); was production manager for the television series *Deadline*, 1959–60, and directed The Investigation, 1967.
Recreations: Chess and swimming. *Address:* 29 West 10th Street, New York, NY 10011.

GROSS, Shelly, producer
b Philadelphia, Pa, 20 May 1921; *s* of Samuel Gross and his wife Anna; *e* University of Pennsylvania (AB 1942), Northwestern University (MSJ 1947); *m* Joan Seidel; served in the US Navy as Lieutenant, 1942–6; formerly a radio and TV announcer.

With Lee Guber is officer and director of Music Fair Enterprises, Inc, which owns and operates six summer musical theatres; Valley Forge Music Fair, Devon, Pa Westbury,

Long Island, Music Fair, Camden County Music Fair, Haddonfield, NJ, Shady Grove Music Fair, Gaithersburg, Md, Painters Mill Music Fair, Owings Mills, Md, and Storrowtown Music Fair, West Springfield, Mass, founding them at various times since 1955; operator of the John B Kelly Playhouse in the Park, Philadelphia, Pa; has co-produced national tours of Li'l Abner, 1958, The Pleasure of His Company, The Andersonville Trial, 1960, Thurber Carnival, 1961, Carnival! 1962, etc; produced his first New York show, Catch Me If You Can, at the Morosco, 9 Mar 1965, also in association with Messrs Guber and Ford; since then has co-produced Sherry! 1967; The Grand Music Hall of Israel, 1968; Inquest, 1970; Lorelei (tour), 1973 (New York), 1974; Charles Aznavour on Broadway, Tony Bennett and Lena Horne Sing, 1974; The King and I, 1977; Annie Get Your Gun (Jones Beach), 1978; Murder at the Howard Johnson's, 1979; author of a number of novels including Havana X, 1978.
Address: Music Fair Enterprises, Inc, 32 East 57th Street, New York, NY. *Tel:* 759 2810.

GROUT, James, actor and director
b London, 22 Oct 1927; *s* of William Grout and his wife Beatrice Anne; *e* Trinity GS; *m* Noreen Jean Grout; trained for the stage at RADA.

Made his first professional appearance at the Old Vic, Nov 1950, as Valentine in Twelfth Night, remaining with the company, 1951, to play roles including Warwick and Jamy in Henry V; spent three seasons, 1953–5, at the Memorial Theatre, Stratford, where his parts included Christopher Sly in The Taming of the Shrew, Ajax in Troilus and Cressida and Lennox in Macbeth; Royal Court, Dec 1957, later transferring to the Duke of York's, the Athenian General in Lysistrata; Ambassadors', 1958, took over the part of Giles Ralston in The Mousetrap; Royal Court, Jan 1960, played four upright citizens in The Lilywhite Boys; Haymarket, May 1960, Franks in Ross; Cambridge, Mar 1963, Harry Chitterlow in Half a Sixpence, making his Broadway debut in the same part at the Broadhurst, Apr 1965; Garrick, Jan 1967, Corbaccio in Volpone; Mermaid, June 1967, Rafferty in Rafferty's Chant; Fortune, June 1969, Norman Budgett in Sometime, Never; Criterion, May 1970, Inspector Hounslow in Flint; Phoenix, Leicester, May 1971, played George in Straight Up; Queen's, June 1971, directed The Patrick Pearse Motel; Savoy, July 1972, Hubert Boothroyd MP in Lloyd George Knew My Father; Aug 1972, directed On the Road for the Soho Theatre; Greenwich, June 1973, Sir John Brute in The Provok'd Wife; 1974–5, toured North America, Korea and Japan with the Royal Shakespeare Company's production, The Hollow Crown; *Phoenix, Mar 1976, Duchotel in 13 Rue de l'Amour*; Mermaid, July 1976, directed Some of My Best Friends are Husbands; Vaudeville, Sept 1976, directed Out on a Limb; Vaudeville, Sept 1977, played Inspector Craddock in A Murder is Announced; TV appearances, since 1949, include *The First Lady, Born and Bred, All Creatures Great and Small*, and *Turtle's Progress*; he has also directed for the repertory companies at Coventry, Hornchurch, Leatherhead, Leeds and Oxford; is an Associate Member of the Royal Academy of Dramatic Art.
Favourite part: Chitterlow. *Recreations:* Cricket, music. *Address:* c/o Crouch Associates Ltd, 59 Frith Street, London W1. *Tel:* 01–734 2167.

GROUT, Philip, director
b Sheffield, Yorks, 13 June 1930; *s* of John Lewis Anderton Grout and his wife Mary Elizabeth (Harris); *e* Abbotsholme School, Derbys.

Directed his first production, The Affair, at Guildford Repertory Theatre, 1962; first London production, How's the World Treating You?, New Arts, and subsequently Wyndham's (also co-presented) Jan 1966; has since directed the following productions, in London unless otherwise stated; Mrs Warren's Profession, The Pastime of M Robert, Happy Family, How's the World Treating You? (Broadway), 1966; Little Boxes, Doubtful Haunts, 1968; The Hallelujah Boy, 1970; The Licentious Fly, Geneva, The Tender Trap (tour), 1971; A Touch of Purple, Abelard and Heloise (S Africa), 1972; Lover, The Caretaker (Young Vic), A Touch of Spring (S Africa), 1973; Who Saw Him Die?, Crown Matrimonial (S Africa), 1974; The Last Romantic (Actors Company), 1975; Artistic Director, the Ludlow Festival, since 1974, for which he has directed Othello, 1974, Twelfth Night, 1975, Hamlet, 1976; subsequent productions include: Widowers' Houses (Wimbledon), The Wild Duck (Welsh National), Butley (Vienna), Ghosts (Cambridge), Otherwise Engaged, Twelfth Night, Merchant of Venice (all S Africa), Hess (Young Vic, 1978; also New York, 1979); has also directed frequently in repertory at theatres including the Arnaud, Guildford, Thorndike, Leatherhead, Royal Lyceum, Edinburgh, Belgrade, Coventry, Theatre Royal, Windsor, Churchill Bromley and Palace, Watford.

Recreation: Music. *Address:* 5 Dickenson Road, London, N8. *Tel:* 01–340 7722.

GUARE, John, playwright
b New York City, 5 Feb 1938; *s* of John Edward Guare and his wife Helen (Grady); *e* Georgetown University and the Yale School of Drama (MFA).

First play produced was Universe, at the Oswego Garage, Atlantic Beach, NY, July 1949; since then has written To Wally Pantoni, We Leave a Credenza, 1964, produced by the Barr-Wilder-Albee Workshop, 1965; Day for Surprises, 1965; Loveliest Afternoon of the Year, 1966; Muzeeka, 1967, which was also his first play produced in London, at the Open Space, 25 Feb 1969; Cop Out, 1968; Home Fires, 1969; The House of Blue Leaves, 1970; adapted and wrote the lyrics for Two Gentlemen of Verona, 1971, for which he received the Antoinette Perry (Tony) Award; Un Pape à New York, produced at the Gaieté-Montparnasse, Paris, 1972; Marco Polo Sings a Solo, 1973; Rich and Famous, 1974, produced at the Public, NY, 1976; Landscape of the Body, 1977; Bosoms and Neglect, 1979; co-author with Milos Forman of the screenplay of Taking Off, 1970; member of the Dramatists Guild Board of Directors and of the Authors League; adjunct professor of playwriting, Yale School of Drama, 1979–80.

Address: c/o R Andrew Boose, Konecky Barovic, 1 Dag Hammarskjold Plaza, New York, NY 10017. *Tel:* 940 8343.

GUBER, Lee (*né* Leon M), producer
b Philadelphia, Pa; 20 Nov 1920; *s* of Jack Guber and his wife Elizabeth (Goldberg); *e* Temple University (BS 1942, MA 1949), University of Michigan, University of Pennsylvania (1952–5); studied directing at the American Theater Wing, 1957, and film production at the New School for Social Research, 1962; served as Lieutenant in the US Army, World War II.

With Shelly Gross and Frank Ford owns, operates, and produces musicals at six summer theatres; Valley Forge Music Fair, Devon, Pa, Westbury, Long Island, Music Fair, Camden County Music Fair, Haddonfield, New Jersey, Sandy Grove Music Fair, Gaithersburg, Md, Painters Mill Music Fair, Owings Mills, Md, and Storrowtown Music Fair, West Springfield, Mass, founding them at various times since 1955; operator of the John B Kelly Playhouse in the Park,

Philadelphia, Pa, since 1964; produced national tours of Li'l Abner, 1958; The Pleasure of His Company, The Andersonville Trial, 1960; A Thurber Carnival, 1961; Carnival! 1962; produced his first musical in New York, The Happiest Girl in the World, at the Martin Beck, 3 Apr 1961; since then has co-produced Catch Me If You Can, 1965; Sherry! 1967; The Grand Music Hall of Israel, 1968; Inquest, 1970; Lorelei (tour), 1973 and New York, 1974;. Charles Aznavour on Broadway, Tony Bennett and Lena Horne Sing, 1974; The King and I, 1977; Annie Get Your Gun (Jones Beach), 1978; Murder at the Howard Johnson's, 1979; member, New York State Council on the Arts.

Address: Music Fair Enterprises, Inc, 32 East 57th Street, New York, NY 10022. *Tel:* 759 2810.

GUINNESS, Sir Alec (*cr* 1959); CBE, actor
b London, 2 Apr 1914; *e* Pembroke Lodge, Southbourne, and Roborough, Eastbourne, *m* Merula Salaman; formerly a copy-writer in an advertising agency for eighteen months; studied for the stage at the Fay Compton Studio of Dramatic Art.

Made his first appearance on the stage at the Playhouse, 2 Apr 1934, walking-on in Libel!; then appeared at the Cambridge Theatre, Sept 1934, in a minor part in Queer Cargo; New, Nov 1934, played Osric and the Third Player in Hamlet; July 1935, the Wolf in Noah; Oct 1935, Sampson and the Apothecary in Romeo and Juliet; May 1936, The Workman and, later, Yakov in The Seagull; joined the Old Vic company, and Sept 1936–Apr 1937, appeared as Boyet in Love's Labour's Lost, Le Beau and William in As You Like It, Old Thorney in The Witch of Edmonton, Reynaldo and Osric in Hamlet, Aguecheek in Twelfth Night, and Exeter in Henry V; in June 1937, at Elsinore, with the Old Vic company, played Osric, Reynaldo and the Player Queen in Hamlet; joined John Gielgud's company at Queen's Theatre, Sept 1937, and during the season played Aumerle and the Groom in Richard II, Snake in The School for Scandal, Feodotik in The Three Sisters, and Lorenzo in The Merchant of Venice; Richmond, June 1938, played Louis Dubedat in The Doctor's Dilemma; rejoined the Old Vic company, Sept–Dec 1938, and played Arthur Gower in Trelawny of the 'Wells', Hamlet (in its entirety and in modern dress) and Bob Acres in The Rivals; Jan–Apr 1939, toured with the Old Vic company on the Continent and in Egypt, playing Hamlet, Chorus in Henry V, Bob Acres in The Rivals, and Emile Flordon in Libel; at the Old Vic, June 1939, played Michael Ransom in The Ascent of F6; in July 1939, played Romeo at Perth, in Scottish Theatre Festival; Rudolf Steiner Hall, Dec 1939, Herbert Pockett in Great Expectations, which he also adapted; Globe, Mar 1940, Richard Meilhac in Cousin Muriel; Old Vic, May 1940, Ferdinand in The Tempest; toured, 1940, as Charleston in Thunder Rock; joined the Royal Navy, 1941, as an ordinary seaman; commissioned, Apr 1942; in Dec 1942, was released for a month to appear at the Henry Miller Theatre, New York, as Flight-Lieut Graham in Flare Path; re-appeared on the London stage, Lyric, Hammersmith, June 1946, as Mitya in The Brothers Karamazov, which he also adapted; Arts, July 1946, Garcin in Vicious Circle; joined the Old Vic company at the New, and from Sept 1946, to May 1948, appeared as the Fool in King Lear, Eric Birling in An Inspector Calls, Comte de Guiche in Cyrano de Bergerac, Abel Drugger in The Alchemist, Richard II, the Dauphin in St Joan, Hlestakov in The Government Inspector, Menenius Agrippa in Coriolanus; at the New, Sept 1948, for the Old Vic company, produced Twelfth Night; Savoy, Feb 1949, played Dr James Y Simpson in The Human Touch; Lyceum, Edinburgh, Aug 1949, and Henry

Miller Theatre, NY, Jan 1950, appeared as the Unidentified Guest in The Cocktail Party; New, London, May 1951, appeared as Hamlet, also directing the play; Aldwych, Apr 1952, played the Scientist in Under the Sycamore Tree; at the Stratford Shakespearean Festival, Ontario, July 1953, played Richard III, and the King in All's Well That Ends Well; Globe, London, Apr 1954, played the title-role in The Prisoner; Winter Garden, May 1956, Boniface in Hotel Paradiso; Haymarket, May 1960, the title-role in Ross, receiving the *Evening Standard* Award, 1961, for this performance; Edinburgh Festival, and the Royal Court, London, Sept 1963, played Berenger the First in Exit the King; Plymouth, NY, Jan 1964, played Dylan Thomas in Dylan, receiving a Tony Award; Phoenix, London, Jan 1966, Von Berg in Incident at Vichy; Royal Court, Oct 1966, played Macbeth; Wyndham's, Oct 1967, Mrs Artminster in Wise Child; Chichester Festival, May 1968, played Harcourt-Reilly in his own production of The Cocktail Party and subsequently at Wyndham's (Nov 1968) and Haymarket (Feb 1969); Arnaud, Guildford, July 1970, John in Time Out of Mind; Haymarket, Aug 1971, the Father in A Voyage Round My Father; Lyric, May 1973, Dr Wicksteed in Habeas Corpus; Apollo, April 1975, Dudley in A Family and a Fortune; Queen's, Oct 1976, co-devised and played Jonathan Swift in Yahoo; Queen's, Sept 1977, Hilary in The Old Country; entered films, 1947, in Great Expectations, subsequently in Oliver Twist, Kind Hearts and Coronets, The Man in the White Suit, The Lavender Hill Mob, The Bridge on the River Kwai (British Film Academy and Academy Oscar Awards), The Horse's Mouth, Tunes of Glory, Lawrence of Arabia, Dr Zhivago, Cromwell, Murder by Death, Star Wars, etc; television appearances include The Wicked Scheme of Jebel Jacks (USA), Conversation at Night, Caesar and Cleopatra; and recently, Tinker, Tailor, Soldier, Spy; created CBE in the Birthday Honours, 1955; Knight Bachelor, New Year Honours, 1959; Hon DLitt, Oxford, 1978.

Address: c/o London Management, 235–241 Regent Street, London W1.

GUNN, Moses, actor and director

b St Louis, Mo, 2 Oct 1929; *e* Tennessee AIU and University of Kansas; *m* Gwendolyn Landis.

St Mark's Playhouse, 1962, Took over as the Governor in The Blacks; Sheridan Square Playhouse, Oct 1963, appeared in the revue In White America; Antioch Shakespeare Festival, summer 1964, played parts including Banquo in Macbeth, Prospero in The Tempest, and Jaques in As You Like It; toured, 1965, in In White America; St Mark's Playhouse, Nov 1965, First Citizen, Industrialist, Pious, and Rastus in Day of Absence; Stage 73, Apr 1966, Able and Coke in Bohikee Creek; Delacorte, July 1966, Provost in Measure for Measure; Longacre, Sept 1966, played in the revue A Hand Is on the Gates; Chelsea Theater Center, Feb 1967, Muslim in Junebug Graduates Tonight!; Delacorte, Aug 1967, Aaron in Titus Andronicus; joined the Negro Ensemble Company and, at the St Mark's Playhouse, Jan 1968, played various parts in Song of the Lusitanian Bogey; Feb 1968, Roo Webber in Summer of the Seventeenth Doll; Apr 1968, Kongi in Kongi's Harvest; June 1968, Daddy Goodness in the play of that name; July 1968, again played in Song of the Lusitanian Bogey; Delacorte, Aug 1968, Capulet in Romeo and Juliet; Public, Jan 1969, Goddam Passmore, Dead White Father and Reverend Passmore in The Owl Answers, and Man Beast in A Beast's Story in the double-bill Cities in Bezique; Tambellini's Gate, Mar 1969, Nick in The Perfect Party; Cherry Lane, 1969, took over various parts in To Be Young, Gifted, and Black; Tambellini's Gate, Mar 1970,

directed Contributions; American Shakespeare Festival, Stratford, Conn, summer 1970, title-role in Othello; ANTA, Sept 1970, again played Othello; St Mark's Playhouse, Nov 1971, Blind Jordan in The Sty of the Blind Pig; Vivian Beaumont, Mar 1972, Orsino in Twelfth Night; Westport, Conn, Country Playhouse, Aug 1973, Benjamin Hurspool in The Poison Tree; St Mark's Playhouse, Mar 1975, Milton Edward in The First Breeze of Summer; Playhouse in the Park, Philadelphia, 1975, repeated the role of Blind Jordan; Ambassador, Jan 1976, Benjamin Hurspool in The Poison Tree; same theatre, Nov 1976, took over from Billy Dee Williams as Martin Luther King in I Have a Dream; Dartmouth, NH, 1977, Joshua Tain in Our Lan'; Yale Repertory, season 1979, Jacques in As You Like It; has appeared in films since 1970 including: The Great White Hope, Shaft, The Iceman Cometh, Amazing Grace, Rollerball, Remember My Name, etc; has appeared frequently on television in Of Mice and Men, The Borgia Stick, Mr Carter's Army, *Kung Fu*, Roots, etc.

Address: Actors Equity Association, 165 West 46th Street, New York, NY 10036.

GUNTER, John, designer

b Billericay, Essex, 31 Oct 1938; *s* of Herbert Carl Gunter and his wife Charlotte Rose (Reid); *e* Bryanston School and the Central School of Art and Design; *m* Micheline McKnight.

Resident designer at the Royal Court, 1965–6, when he designed six productions including Saved, 1965, and The Knack, 1966; for the same theatre has since designed The Soldier's Fortune, Marya, 1967; the D H Lawrence trilogy, 1968; The Double Dealer, The Contractor, Insideout, 1969; AC/DC, The Philanthropist (also Broadway), 1970; West of Suez, 1971; Entertaining Mr Sloane, 1975; Flying Blind, Inadmissible Evidence, 1978; work outside London includes productions for Nottingham Playhouse, notably Comedians, 1975, and Chichester Festival; a number of his Royal Court productions transferred to the West End, where he has also been responsible for God Bless, Julius Caesar (both RSC), 1968; Comedians (also Broadway), Jingo (RSC), 1975; The White Devil, 1976; Stevie, The Old Country, 1977; Tishoo, Death of a Salesman (National), Born in the Gardens, 1979; Rose, 1980; resident designer, Zurich Schauspielhaus, 1972–4, and has also worked extensively in Germany as well as in Vienna and Buenos Aires; Head of Theatre Design Department, Central School of Art and Design, 1974–present; member, Arts Council Training Committee.

Recreations: Travelling, fishing. *Address:* 25 Hillfield Park, Muswell Hill, London N10.

GURNEY, A R Jr (Albert Ramsdell Gurney Jr), dramatic author

b Buffalo, NY, 1 Nov 1930; *s* of Albert Ramsdell Gurney and his wife Marion (Spaulding); *e* Williams College and Yale School of Drama (MFA); *m* Mary Goodyear.

Author of plays including The Golden Fleece, 1968; Scenes from American Life, 1971; Children, 1974; Who Killed Richard Cory?, 1975; The Wayside Motor Inn, 1977; The Middle Ages, 1978; The Golden Age, 1980; for television adapted O Youth and Beauty, 1979; author of the novels The Gospel According to Joe, 1974, and Entertaining Strangers, 1977; currently a professor in the department of humanities, Massachusetts Institute of Technology.

Address: 20 Sylvan Avenue, West Newton, MA 02165.

GURNEY, Rachel, actress

b Eton; *d* of Samuel Gurney Lubbock and his wife, Irene

(Scharrer); *e* Challoner School, London; *m* Denys Rhodes (mar dis).

Made her first appearance in London at the Criterion, as Lynne Hartley in The Guinea-Pig, which ran for more than a year; Criterion, June 1947, Lady Katherine in a revival of The Sleeping Clergyman; Westminster, May 1949, Thea in Black Chiffon; Bristol Old Vic, Feb 1949, appeared in Rain on the Just; in repertory at Bristol Old Vic, 1950; Arts, April–June 1951, appeared in a season of one act plays by Bernard Shaw; Duke of York's, Feb 1952, Mabel in First Person Singular; Arts, May 1952, Alice in The Voysey Inheritance; Duke of York's, July 1952, Mrs Pless in The Trap; Embassy, Oct 1952, Mrs George Lamb in Caro William; Westminster, July 1953, Valerie Carrington in Carrington VC; Westminster, May 1954, Avice Brunton in The Bombshell; Haymarket, Apr 1956, played Olivia in The Chalk Garden for more than eighteen months; in 1958 she toured India and Ceylon for The British Council in a Shakespearean programme; St Martin's, July 1959, she took over the part of Hilary in The Grass is Greener; Piccadilly, Aug 1966, played Lady Chiltern in An Ideal Husband; Dublin Festival and English tour, Sept 1969, as Lady Chavender in On the Rocks; Arnaud, Guildford and tour, Nov 1974, Freda Caplan in Dangerous Corner; Palladium, Dec 1975, Mrs Darling in Peter Pan; O'Keefe Centre, Toronto, Oct 1976, Lady Chiltern in An Ideal Husband; first appearance in New York, Roundabout Theatre, Oct 1977, as Mrs Clandon in You Never Can Tell; Academy Festival, Lake Forest, Illinois, played Mrs Prentice in What the Butler Saw; McCarter, Princeton, Mar 1979, Hesione Hushabye in Heartbreak House; Circle in the Square, NY, Feb 1980, Lady Britomart in Major Barbara; numerous parts in television productions including Lady Marjorie Bellamy in *Upstairs, Downstairs*.

Address: c/o London Management, 235 Regent Street, London W1.

GUSSOW, Mel, drama critic and author
b New York City, 19 Dec 1933; *s* of Don and Betty Gussow; *e* Middlebury College, Vermont and Columbia University Graduate School of Journalism; *m* Ann Beebe.

Since 1969 a drama critic on the *New York Times;* drama critic for WQXR, the radio station of the *New York Times*; previously an associate editor, *Newsweek* magazine; adjunct assistant professor of Cinema Studies, New York University School of Continuing Education; author of Don't Say Yes until I Finish Talking: a biography of Darryl F Zanuck, 1971; Guggenheim Fellow, 1979.

Address: New York Times, 229 West 43rd Street, New York, NY 10036.

GWILYM, Mike, actor
b Neath, Glamorgan, 5 Mar 1949; *s* of Arthur Aubrey Remmington Gwilym and his wife Renée Mathilde (Dupont); *e* Wycliffe College, Gloucester, Davidson College, N Carolina, and Lincoln College, Oxford.

Made his first professional appearance at the Playhouse, Sheffield, 1969, as Prince Hal in Henry IV, part 1; at the Citizens', Glasgow, 1970–3, where his parts included: Robespierre in Danton's Death, Estragon in Waiting for Godot, Maurice in AC/DC, and the title-role in Tartuffe; at the Edinburgh Festival, 1972, played the title-role in Tamburlaine and Malvolio in Twelfth Night; Arnaud, Guildford, Sept 1973, Angelo in Measure for Measure; joined the Royal Shakespeare Company and played Peter of Pomfret and Death, the Presenter in King John, Memorial Theatre, Mar, and Edgar in Lear at The Other Place, Stratford, and at the Place, London, Oct 1974; at the Aldwych, made his first London appearance in Summerfolk, 27 Aug 1974, as Vlass; has subsequently played Costard in Love's Labour's Lost, George Leete in The Marrying of Anne Leete, 1975; at Bristol Old Vic, Feb 1976, played Macbeth; at the Aldwych, Apr 1976, Mykhail Zykov in The Zykovs; Stratford, 1976, Troilus in Troilus and Cressida and Antipholus of Ephesus in Comedy of Errors; at The Other Place, Stratford, May 1977, Surly in The Alchemist; Aldwych, season 1977, repeated the parts of Troilus and Antipholus, also playing Johann Tonnesen in Pillars of the Community, Nov, Francois in The Days of the Commune, Dec, Wang in the Bundle (Warehouse), Dec; Hampstead, May 1979, John Baildon in Then and Now; Aldwych, Jan 1980, Achilles and Orestes in The Greeks; television includes How Green Was My Valley, and *The Racing Game.*

Favourite parts: Robespierre, Vlass. *Address:* c/o Ken McReddie, 48 Crawford Street, London W1. Tel: 01–724 0555.

GWYNNE, Fred, actor
b New York City, 10 July 1926; *e* Harvard University; *m* Jean Reynard.

First appeared in New York at the Martin Beck, 20 Feb 1952, as Stinker in Mrs McThing; New York City Center, Feb 1953, Dull in Love's Labour's Lost; Broadhurst, Oct 1953, Luther Raubel in The Frogs of Spring; Plymouth, Sept 1960, Polyte-le-Mou in Irma la Douce; Shubert, Oct 1963, Marvin Shellhammer in Here's Love; Plymouth, Oct 1972, Abraham Lincoln in The Lincoln Mask; Estelle R Newman, Jan 1974, Major Michael Dillon in More Than You Deserve; American Shakespeare Festival, Stratford, Conn, July 1974, Big Daddy in Cat on a Hot Tin Roof; ANTA, Sept 1974, repeated this last part; Stratford, Conn, June 1975, Stage Manager in Our Town, and July 1975, Autolycus in The Winter's Tale; Broadhurst, Sept 1976, Col J C Kincaid in A Texas Trilogy; Minskoff, May 1978, W O Gant in Angel; Lyceum, Sept 1978, Jock Riley in Players; Manhattan Theatre Club, Jan 1979, Otto Marvuglia in Grand Magic; played Herman Munster in the television series *The Munsters,* from 1964 for several seasons.

Address: Actors Equity Association, 165 West 46th Street, New York, NY 10036.

H

HACK, Keith, director
b Göttingen, Germany, 1948; *e* Monash (Melbourne), Erlangen and Cambridge Universities.

Worked for a year with Helene Weigel at the Berliner Ensemble, and afterwards at the Théâtre de la Cité, Lyon, before joining the Citizens', Glasgow, as assistant director, 1969; resident director, 1970–71; at the Round House, 1971, directed Titus Andronicus; productions he has since directed, in London unless otherwise stated, include In the Jungle of the Cities, 1973; Measure for Measure (RSC, Stratford), 1974; The Sons of Light (Newcastle), Scribes, 1976; Barbarians, Scribes (NY), The Good Woman of Setzuan, The Father, 1977; Vieux Carré, 1978; The Duchess of Malfi (Birmingham), A Lovely Sunday for Crève Coeur, The Winter Dancers (both NY), 1979; author of plays and adaptations including Candide 1970, and Nana.
Address: c/o British Actors Equity, 8 Harley Street, London W1.

HADDRICK, Ron, MBE, actor
b Adelaide, South Australia, 9 Apr 1929; *s* of Alexander Norman Haddrick and his wife Olive May (Gibson); *e* Adelaide High School; *m* Margaret Lorraine Quigley; formerly a (Dental) Prosthetic technician; studied voice production at Adelaide University.

Made his first appearance on the stage at the Tivoli Theatre, Adelaide, 1948, when he played Stanislaus in The Eagle Has Two Heads; joined the Shakespeare Memorial Theatre Company, Stratford-on-Avon, 1954, and remained for five seasons, playing roles which included: Hubert in King John, Tybalt in Romeo and Juliet, Antonio in Twelfth Night and Horatio in Hamlet; made his first appearance in London, Princes, Dec 1954, when he played Alfred in Toad of Toad Hall; appeared for the Elizabethan Theatre Trust, Sydney, Australia, as John Tanner in Man and Superman, Jamie Tyrone in Long Day's Journey Into Night, and Brutus in Julius Caesar, 1959; Heracles in The Rape of the Belt, James Mavor Morell in Candida, Monsewer in The Hostage, Fourth Tempter and Fourth Knight in Murder in the Cathedral, also appearing at the Adelaide Festival of Arts in the last play, 1960; Palace, Sydney, 1961, played Alf Cook in The One Day of the Year, subsequently playing the same part at the Theatre Royal, Stratford, London, E, Oct 1961; at the Union Theatre, Sydney, Jan 1962, played Jacko in Naked Island; Adelaide Festival of the Arts, Mar 1962, played Dunois in Saint Joan, subsequently touring in the play; since 1963 has appeared in many productions for Sydney's Old Tote Theatre Company, including: Jamie Tyrone in Moon for the Misbegotten, Azdak in The Caucasian Chalk Circle, Pinchwife in The Country Wife, the name part in Othello, Claudius in Hamlet, and Oedipus in Sir Tyrone Guthrie's production of King Oedipus (1970); played Nandor in The Guardsman at Perth Festival, Feb 1971 and Parade Theatre, Sydney, Mar 1971; Foster in National Health, Parade Theatre, Sydney, Aug 1971, followed by the Mayor in The Government Inspector, Sept 1971; Oct 1971, Ormund in I've Been Here Before, Community Theatre, Sydney; Baptista in The Taming of the Shrew, Parade Theatre, Feb 1972; Gov Lachlan Macquarie in Macquarie for MTC at Russell St Theatre, Melbourne, May 1972; The Father in Forget-Me-Not Lane, Parade Theatre, Aug 1972; Brigadello in How Could You Believe Me When I Said I'd be Your Valet When You Know I've Been a Liar All My Life, Parade Theatre, Nov 1972; Friar in 'Tis Pity She's a Whore, Octagon Theatre, Perth Festival, Jan 1973, and Parade Theatre, Sydney, Feb 1973; Magistrate in Lysistrata, Parade Theatre, July 1973; led The Old Tote Theatre Company in the opening season of the Drama Theatre at the Sydney Opera House playing York in Richard II and Ken Collins in What If You Died Tomorrow, in repertoire, the latter transferring to The Elizabethan Theatre, Sydney, Feb 1974 and Comedy Theatre, Melbourne, Apr 1974; subsequently this production played a season at the Comedy Theatre, London, Sept 1974; in June 1974, played Macbeth in Old Tote's production in the Opera Theatre at the Sydney Opera House; in the Drama Theatre, Feb 1975, the Button Moulder in Peer Gynt; Alan West in Savages, Theatre Royal, Hobart and Princess Theatre, Launceston, Apr 1975; Harry in Home, Parade Theatre, Sydney, Aug 1975; Drama Theatre, Sydney Opera House, played Ezra Mannon in Mourning Becomes Electra (Mar 1976), Horace Vandergelder in The Matchmaker (June), and Uncle Peter in The Plough and the Stars (Mar 1977); Parade, Sydney, May 1977, Logan and Posh Jim in Unspeakable Acts; Queensland Theatre Company, Aug 1977, Major General Anderson-Green in The Brass Hat; Nimrod, Sydney, Dec 1977, played Jock in The Club, transferring to the Theatre Royal, Jan 1978, and touring Mar–Aug, 1978; Theatre Royal, Sydney, Oct 1978, Ernest in Bedroom Farce; Neutral Bay Music Hall, Sydney, Feb 1979, Jardine Leachman in Lost to the Devil; returned to London to play Jock in The Club, Hampstead, Jan 1980, and Old Vic, Mar; first appeared on television, Dec 1954, and notable parts he has played include: Dave Ruben in Reunion Day (London), David King in A Sleep of Prisoners, Petruchio in The Taming of the Shrew, Dr Redfern in The Outcasts and title-roles in Tartuffe and The Stranger (Australia); received the MBE in the New Year Honours, 1974.
Favourite parts: John Tanner, Azdak, Alf Cook, Jamie Tyrone, and Oedipus. *Recreation:* Cricket (played for South Australia, 1952). *Address:* 17 Kessell Avenue, Homebush West, New South Wales, Australia.

HAGEN, Uta, actress
b Göttingen, Germany, 12 June 1919; *d* of Dr Oskar Frank Leonard Hagen and his wife Thyra Amalie (Leisner); *e* Germany, and University of Wisconsin (semester); *m* (1) José Ferrer (mar dis); (2) Herbert Berghof; studied for one term at the Royal Academy of Dramatic Art, London.

Made her first appearance on the stage, Aug 1937, at Dennis, Mass, with Eva Le Gallienne's Civic Repertory Company, playing Ophelia in Hamlet; first appeared in New York, at the Shubert Theatre (for the Theatre Guild), 28 Mar 1938, as Nina in The Seagull, in which she subsequently toured; at the Vanderbilt, Apr 1939, played Edith in The Happiest Days; Ethel Barrymore, Dec 1939, Alegre d'Alcala in Key Largo; toured in the leading role of The Admiral Had a Wife, 1941; during the summer of 1942, appeared at

Cambridge, Mass, and Princeton, as Desdemona in Othello, with Paul Robeson; Plymouth Theatre, Sept 1942, played Vickie Roberts in Vickie; Shubert, Oct 1943, again played Desdemona in Othello, with Robeson; toured in the same part, 1944–5, and repeated it at the New York City Center, May 1945; Biltmore, Mar 1947, Olga Vorontsov in The Whole World Over; in summer theatres, 1947, played Natasha in Dark Eyes; at the Barbizon Plaza, Dec 1947, appeared as Margaret in Faust, in German, and also in German, in Jan 1948, Hilda in The Master Builder; toured, 1947, and appeared at the City Center, Jan 1948, as Mrs Manningham in Angel Street; Ethel Barrymore, June 1948, succeeded Jessica Tandy as Blanche in A Streetcar Named Desire; toured in this part, 1948–9, again played it in NY, June–Dec 1949; again toured in the same part, 1949–50, and played it again at the City Center, NY, May 1950; Lyceum, Nov 1950, appeared as Georgie Elgin in The Country Girl, for which she received the Donaldson Award, the Antionette Perry (Tony) Award, and the NY Drama Critics Award; Cort, Oct 1951, played the title-role in Shaw's Saint Joan, for the Theatre Guild; City Center, May 1952, appeared as the Grand Duchess Tatiana Petrovna in Tovarich, and later toured summer theatres in this part; Cort, Oct 1952, played Hannah King in In Any Language; toured summer theatres, 1953, as Georgie Elgin in The Country Girl; Booth, Apr 1954, played Grace Wilson in The Magic and the Loss; toured summer theatres, 1954, in The Lady's Not for Burning and The Deep Blue Sea, and 1955, in Cyprienne; Ann Arbor Drama Festival, May 1955, played in The Affairs of Anatol, and subsequently toured; Fulton, Oct 1955, appeared as Agata in Island of Goats; Phoenix, Apr 1956, Natalia Petrovna in A Month in the Country; Phoenix, Dec 1956, Shen Te in The Good Woman of Setzuan; toured summer theatres in 1957 as all the women in The Affairs of Anatol; Bucks County Playhouse, New Hope, Pennsylvania, Aug 1959, Argia in The Queen and the Rebels; Grace Church, NY, Apr 1960, Angélique in Port Royal; Vancouver Festival, Aug 1961, Leah in Men, Women and Angels; Billy Rose, NY, Oct 1962, Martha in Who's Afraid of Virginia Woolf? for which she received the Tony Award; left the cast to make her first London appearance at the Piccadilly, Feb 1964, in the same play, for which she received the London Drama Critics Award; Lyceum, Mar 1968, Madame Ranevskaya in The Cherry Orchard; Belasco, Feb 1980, Charlotte von Stein in Charlotte; made her film debut in The Other, 1972; The Boys from Brazil; has also appeared in television work includes Macbeth, Out of Dust, and A Month in the Country; since 1947, has also taught acting at the Herbert Berghof Studio; author of Respect for Acting, 1973; Love of Cooking, 1976; Hon DFA, Smith College, 1978.

Recreations: Cooking, piano, handicrafts. *Address:* 27 Washington Square North, New York City, NY, 10011.

HAGUE, Albert, composer

b Berlin, Germany, 13 Oct 1920; *s* of Dr Harry Marcuse and his wife Mimi (Heller), adopted son of Dr Eliott B Hague; *e* Royal Conservatory, Rome (St Cecilia), and College of Music of the University of Cincinnati (B Mus 1942); *m* Renee Orin.

Wrote his first stage score for Reluctant Lady, produced at the Cain Park Theatre, Cleveland, Ohio, 27 July 1948; wrote, in part, the incidental music for The Madwoman of Chaillot, his first score for a New York production, when it was presented at the Belasco, 27 Dec 1948; since then has contributed songs to the revue Dance Me a Song, 1950; written the incidental music to All Summer Long, 1954; composed the score for the musical Plain and Fancy, 1955;

composed the score for the musical Redhead, 1959; Cafe Crown, 1964; The Fig Leaves Are Falling, 1969; Miss Moffat (Philadelphia), 1974; Surprise! Surprise!, 1979; composed the scores for the films Coney Island USA, 1951, and The Funniest Man in the World, 1969; appeared in the film Fame; composed his first score for a television production, The Mercer Girls, 1953, and since has composed the score for How the Grinch Stole Christmas, 1966, etc; received the Antoinette Perry (Tony) Award for Redhead.

Recreations: Table tennis, bridge, poker. *Clubs:* Lambs, Dutch Treat, Players. *Address:* c/o ASCAP, 1 Lincoln Plaza, New York, NY 10023.

HAIGH, Kenneth, actor

b Yorkshire, 25 March 1931; *s* of William Haigh and his wife Margaret (Glyn); *e* Gunnersbury Grammar School, London; studied for the stage at the Central School of Speech Training and Dramatic Art; *m* Myrna Stephens.

Made his first appearance on the stage at Drogheda, Eire, 1952, when he played Cassio in Othello; made his first appearance in London, at the New Lindsey, Sept 1954, when he played Geoffrey Baines in Dear Little Liz; subsequently appeared during the Shakespearean Season, at the Open Air Theatre, Regent's Park; joined the English Stage Company for their first season at the Royal Court Theatre, 1956–7, when he played the following parts, Peter Lord in The Mulberry Bush, the Rev John Hale in The Crucible, Jimmy Porter in Look Back in Anger, and Beaufort in Cards of Identity; made his first appearance in New York at the Lyceum Theatre, Oct 1957, again playing Jimmy Porter in Look Back in Anger, subsequently touring with the production; at the 54th Street Theatre, NY, Feb 1960, played the title-role in Caligula; Arts, London, Aug 1960, played Jerry in The Zoo Story; Royal Court, Apr 1961, played Franz von Gerlach in Altona, transferring with the production to the Saville, June 1961; joined the Royal Shakespeare Company at the Aldwych, June 1962, to play The Friend in Playing With Fire, and James in The Collection (double-bill); Royal Shakespeare, Stratford-on-Avon, Apr 1963, played Mark Antony in Julius Caesar; Phoenix, Apr 1964, again played the title-role in Caligula; Adelphi, Sept 1964, played Patrick Casey in Maggie May; Edinburgh Festival, and Strand, London, Sept 1965, played The Burglar in Too True to be Good; Yale University, US, May 1967, played Prometheus in Prometheus Bound, the title role in Enrico IV, and directed 'Tis Pity She's a Whore; St Clement's Church, NY, Apr 1968, played Governor Endecott in Endecott and the Red Cross; Duke of York's, London, Jan 1969, took over as Laurie in The Hotel in Amsterdam; Mermaid, June 1971, title role in Prometheus Bound; Greenwich, Oct 1974, Rupert Forster in Marching Song; Haymarket, Leicester, 1975, title role in The Father; Manchester Cathedral, Jan 1976, Benedict in 69 Theatre Company's Much Ado About Nothing; Citadel, Edmonton, Alberta, 1977, played Dysart in Equus and Higgins in Pygmalion; O'Neill, New York, Feb 1977, took over as Sidney in California Suite; Chichester Festival, 1978, Henry Jarvis in The Aspern Papers and The Prince of Salestria in Look After Lulu; American Shakespeare Festival, Stratford, Conn, 1979, played Malvolio in Twelfth Night, Brutus in Julius Caesar and Prospero in The Tempest; Cort, Mar 1980, F Scott Fitzgerald in Clothes for a Summer Hotel; entered films, 1955, and has since appeared in Cleopatra, Eagle in a Cage, The Bitch, etc; first appeared on television, 1954, and productions in which he has played include the series *Man at the Top* and *Search for the Nile*, Moll Flanders and, recently, Hazlitt in Love; Hon Professor, Yale Drama School.

Recreations: Cricket, literature, and wine. *Address:* c/o Savile Club, 69 Brook Street, London, W1.

HAILEY, Oliver, playwright
b Pampa, Texas, 7 July 1932; *s* of Oliver D Hailey, Sr and his wife Hallie May (Thomas); *e* University of Texas (BFA) and Yale University (MFA); *m* Elizabeth Forsythe; formerly a newspaper reporter.

His first play, Hey You, Light Man! was produced at the University of Kansas, 9 May 1961, and in New York, 1 Mar 1963, at the Mayfair; has since written First One Asleep, Whistle, 1966; Who's Happy Now? 1969; Continental Divide, produced in Washington, DC, 1970; Father's Day, 1971; For the Use of the Hall, produced by the Trinity Square Repertory, Providence, Rhode Island, 1974; And Where She Stops Nobody Knows, produced at the Mark Taper Forum, Los Angeles, 1976; Red Rover, Red Rover, produced Minneapolis, 1977; Tryptych, Los Angeles, 1979; I Won't Dance, Buffalo, 1980; Hey You, Light Man! was his first play produced in England, at the New, Bromley, 8 Mar 1971; received the Drama Desk—Vernon Rice Award for this play, 1963; various of his plays have been produced on television.
Address: 11747 Canton Place, Studio City, Calif 91604. *Tel:* 763–7827.

HAIRE, Wilson John, playwright
b Belfast, 6 Apr 1932; *s* of Wilson Haire and his wife Annie (Boyce); *e* Clontonacally Primary School, County Down; *m* Rita Lenson (mar dis); (2) Sheila Baron (mar dis); (3) Karen Elizabeth Mendelsohn; originally a carpenter.

An actor with Unity Theatre, 1962–67, he was co-director of Camden Group Theatre, 1967–71; his first play was The Clockin Hen, 1968; has since written The Diamond Bone and Hammer, Along the Shoughs of Ulster, 1969; Within Two Shadows, 1972; Bloom of the Diamond Stone, 1973; Echoes from a Concrete Canyon, 1975; Letter from a Soldier, 1976; Lost Worlds, comprising Newsflash, Wedding Breakfast, and Roost (National Theatre), 1978; joint resident dramatist, Royal Court Theatre, 1974; resident dramatist, Lyric, Belfast, 1976; author of the TV plays Letter from a Soldier, The Dandelion Clock, 1975, The Pact, 1976.
Address: c/o Marc Berlin, London Management, 235–241 Regent Street, London W1.

HALE, Georgina, actress
b Essex, 4 Aug 1943; *d* of George Robert Hale and his wife Dot (Fordham); *m* John Forgeham, actor (mar dis); originally a hairdresser; trained for the stage at RADA.

Made her professional debut at Stratford as a walk-on; subsequently in rep at Canterbury, Windsor, Ipswich, etc, and the Liverpool Playhouse, 1967, where her parts included the title role in Gigi, and Juliet in Romeo and Juliet; Thorndike, Leatherhead, Oct 1975, played Liza Doolittle in Pygmalion; at the Derby Playhouse, July 1976, Nina in The Seagull, making her London debut in the production when it transferred to the Duke of York's, Aug; Hampstead, May 1978, Marie Caroline David in The Tribades; Open Space, July 1978, Melanie in Boo Hoo; Royal Exchange, Manchester, Apr 1979, Bobbi Michele in Last of the Red Hot Lovers, transferring to the Criterion, Nov; films, since Eagle in a Cage, 1970, include The Devils, The Boyfriend, Mahler, McVicar, The Watcher in the Woods, and The World Is Full of Married Men; frequent TV appearances include the series *Budgie* and *Upstairs, Downstairs*, and plays such as Electra, Plaintiffs and Defendants, The Seagull, etc.
Favourite parts: All. *Address:* 74A St John's Wood High Street, London NW8.

HALE, John, playwright and director
b Woolwich, 5 Feb 1926; *e* Borden GS, Sittingbourne, and Royal Naval College, Greenwich; *m* Valerie June Bryan.

Spent ten years in the Royal Navy before entering the theatre as a stage hand; founder and artistic director, Lincoln Theatre, 1955–58; artistic director, Arts, Ipswich, 1958–59; Bristol Old Vic, 1959–61; governor, 1963–71 and associate artistic director, 1968–71, Greenwich; resident playwright and again associate artistic director, 1975–76; author of the following plays, which he directed on their first production: It's All in the Mind, Hampstead, 1968; The Black Swan Winter, Hampstead, 1969; Spithead, Greenwich, 1969; Lorna and Ted, Greenwich, 1970; In Memory of . . . Carmen Miranda (one-act), Greenwich, 1975; Love's Old Sweet Song, Greenwich, 1976; author of Who Needs Enemies?, RSC (Warehouse), 1978, and Library, Manchester, 1980, revised as The Case of David Anderson, QC; also wrote the one-acts Decibels, 1969, Here Is the News, 1970; directed well over a hundred productions while at Lincoln, Ipswich, Bristol etc; for television directed a number of plays for H M Tennent, 1961–64; has written regularly for TV since 1965; presenter of the radio programme A Good Read; author or co-author of screenplays including Anne of the Thousand Days, 1969, and Mary Queen of Scots, 1971; author of seven novels including The Grudge Fight, 1964, and Lovers and Heretics, 1976.
Address: 46 Upper Dane Road, Margate, Kent CT9 26X.

HALES, Jonathan, dramatic author and director
b London, 10 May 1937; *s* of James Alfred Hales and his wife Dorothy May (Broadbent); *e* Owen's School, EC1, Christ's College, Cambridge (Open Scholar) and University of Texas (Fulbright Scholar); *m* (1) Mary Jane Cherry (mar dis); (2) Gillian Diamond; in Texas he studied with Ben Iden Payne and acted at the Ashland, Oregon, Festival, 1961 and the Banff, Canada, Festival, 1963.

On his return from America he joined the Royal Shakespeare Company as a walk-on in the 1964 Histories season and stayed with the RSC for two and a half years; during this time he also directed in the Stratford Studio; after Stratford he freelanced as writer and director; first professional production The Knight of the Burning Pestle, Marlowe Theatre, Canterbury, 1966; 1967–68 Director of Productions, Phoenix Theatre, Leicester, where his production included Danton's Death, Galileo and Planchon's The Three Musketeers, for which he wrote the adaptation; 1968–69 he freelanced as director and writer and in 1970 joined the Royal Court Theatre as director and Literary Manager; here his productions included The Foursome, which transferred from the Theatre Upstairs to the Fortune Theatre, 1971, The Lovers of Viorne, 1971; his own plays The Centaur (Production without Decor) and Brussels, 1972; the latter transferred to the Greenwich Theatre, 1972; The Sea Anchor, 1974, and Mrs Grabowski's Academy, 1975; left the Royal Court in 1974 and his productions since then have included Judies (Comedy Theatre), 1975, The Entertainer (Sherman, Cardiff), 1975, Epitaph for George Dillon (Young Vic), 1975, Old Flames, Bristol, 1975, which transferred to the Arts, London, 1976; The Sanctuary Lamp, Abbey, Dublin, 1976, The Family Dance, Criterion, 1976; Mecca, Open Space, 1977; as an Associate Director of the Abbey, Dublin, he has also directed The Morning After Optimism, 1977, and Wild Oats, 1978; co-author of Alice's Boys, Savoy, 1978; he has written many plays for television, including The Comic, Places Where They Sing, Diane and The Chelsea Murders; wrote the screenplays for the films The Mirror Crack'd . . ., High Road to China and The Shipkiller.

Recreations: Reading, music, the opera and being with his two sons. *Address:* 117 Canfield Gardens, London NW6. *Tel:* 01–624 5249.

HALL, Adrian, director
b Van, Texas, 3 Dec 1927; *s* of Lennie and Mattie Hall; *e* East Texas University; served 2 years in US Army; stage training from pioneers in repertory system, Margo Jones, Dallas, Texas, Gilmore Brown, Pasadena, California and Stella Holt, Greenwich Muse Theatre, New York City; Honorary degrees include Brown University DFA, 1972 and Rhode Island College DFA, 1977.

Directed extensively off-Broadway 1955–64, including Orpheus Descending, The Mousetrap, Red Roses For Me, The Trip to Bountiful, Journey with Strangers and Riverwind; national tour Toys in the Attic; directed at major repertory theatres in the United States including Guthrie Theatre, Yale Rep, Barter Theatre, Milwaukee Rep; founder and artistic director of Trinity Square Repertory Company, Providence, Rhode Island since 1964, a two-theatre complex operating year round with permanent acting company; extensive touring, Boston, Philadelphia, Washington, Phoenix and New York City, Edinburgh Festival in 1968; for television directed with Trinity Square Repertory Company, Brother to Dragons; directed and co-authored with Richard Cumming Feasting with Panthers 1974, Life Among the Lowly 1976, House of Mirth 1979 and Edith Wharton Biography 1980.

Address: 201 Washington Street, Providence, RI 02903. *Tel:* 401-521 1100.

HALL, Grayson, (*née* Shirley Grossman), actress
b Philadelphia; *e* Temple U, Cornell U; *m* Sam Hall.

First appeared, as Shirley Grayson, playing Ann Whitefield in Man and Superman at the Equity Library Theatre, 20 Feb 1953; at the Circle in the Square, June 1955, played the Actress in La Ronde; as Grayson Hall, at the Circle in the Square, Mar 1960, played the Penitent in The Balcony; Cricket, Oct 1961, Agata in The Buskers; St James, Dec 1961, Myra Blake in Subways Are for Sleeping; Writers Stage, Jan 1963, Crystal Seekfest in The Love Nest; Renata, Oct 1964, Connie Cerelli in Shout from the Rooftops; ANTA, Nov 1966, Fran Gerdes and the Queen in Those That Play the Clowns; Circle in the Square, June 1971, Madge in The Last Analysis; Provincetown Playhouse, Oct 1971, Melba in Friends, and Stephanie de Milo in Relations, in a double bill; Brooklyn Academy of Music, Dec 1971, Wanda in The Screens; Theatre at St Clement's, Oct 1973, Mrs Fugleman in Secrets of the Citizens Correction Committee; Manhattan Theatre Club, Mar 1975, Louise Rafi in The Sea; Roundabout Stage One, June 1975, Comtesse de la Briere in What Every Woman Knows; Booth, Oct 1975, First Interpreter in The Leaf People; American Place, Sept 1976, Arlene in Jack Gelber's New Play: Rehearsal; Chelsea Theater Center, Mar 1977, and Martin Beck, May 1977, The Fly in Happy End; Manhattan Theatre Club, May 1978, appeared in Rib Cage; first appeared in films in The Night of the Iguana, 1964, and subsequently played in That Darn Cat, Adam at 6 a.m., etc; has appeared frequently on television, notably in the long-run series *Dark Shadows*.

Address: Actors Equity Association, 165 West 46th Street, New York, NY 10036.

HALL, Sir Peter (*cr* 1977), CBE, Director of the National Theatre Company
b Bury St Edmunds, Suffolk, 22 Nov 1930; *s* of Reginald Edward Arthur Hall and his wife, Grace (Pamment); *e* Perse School, Cambridge, and St Catharine's College, Cambridge

(MA Hons, Hon Fellow, 1964); Hon Doctor, University of York, 1966; Chevalier des Ordres des Arts et des Lettres, 1965; Assoc Professor of Drama, University of Warwick, 1966; Hon Doctorates, University of Reading 1973, University of Liverpool, 1974, University of Leicester, 1977; *m* (1) Leslie Caron (mar dis); (2) Jacqueline Taylor.

Directed more than 20 productions for the Cambridge ADC, Marlowe Society, and University Actors; first professional production, Theatre Royal, Windsor, 1953; directed a number of plays at repertory theatres, before being appointed Assistant Director of the Arts Theatre, London, Jan 1954, where he directed Blood Wedding, and The Immoralist, 1954; appointed Director of the theatre, Jan 1955, and between 1955–6 directed the following plays: The Lesson, South, Mourning Becomes Electra, Waiting For Godot, The Burnt Flower-Bed, Listen To the Wind, 1955; The Waltz of the Toreadors, Gigi (New), Love's Labour's Lost (Stratford-on-Avon), The Gates of Summer (tour), 1956; he resigned his post at the Arts, July 1956, and in 1957, he formed his own producing company, The International Playwrights' Theatre, and at the Phoenix, Apr 1957, directed their first production, Camino Real; at Sadler's Wells, May 1957, directed his first opera The Moon and Sixpence (which was also the first opera to be commissioned by The Sadler's Wells Trust); at the Shakespeare Memorial Theatre, July 1957, directed Cymbeline; staged his first production on Broadway at the Cort, Nov 1957, with The Rope Dancers; on returning to England, Jan 1958, he directed the following plays: Cat On a Hot Tin Roof, Twelfth Night (Stratford-on-Avon), Brouhaha, Shadow of Heroes, 1958; Madame De . . ., and A Traveller Without Luggage, A Midsummer Night's Dream (Stratford-on-Avon), Coriolanus (also Stratford), 1959; The Wrong Side of the Park, The Two Gentlemen of Verona, Twelfth Night, Troilus and Cressida (with John Barton), (the last three productions at Stratford-on-Avon), 1960; as Managing Director, 1960–8 (subsequently on the Board of Directors), created the Royal Shakespeare Company to act as a permanent ensemble, playing at the Aldwych as well as Stratford-on-Avon, in modern plays as well as Shakespeare; during that period he directed the following plays for the RSC, unless otherwise stated: Ondine, Becket, Romeo and Juliet, 1961; A Midsummer Night's Dream, The Collection (one-act, co-directed), Troilus and Cressida, 1961; The Wars of the Roses (adaptation with John Barton of Henry VI (Parts I, II, and III), and Richard III, renamed Henry VI, Edward IV, and Richard III), A Midsummer Night's Dream, 1963; Richard II, Henry IV (Parts I and II), Henry V, The Wars of the Roses, Eh?, 1964; The Homecoming, Hamlet, 1965; The Government Inspector, Staircase, 1966; The Homecoming (New York), Macbeth (also touring Finland and Russia with the production), 1967; A Delicate Balance, Dutch Uncle, Landscape and Silence (double-bill), 1969; The Battle of Shrivings (Lyric), 1970; Old Times (also NY), 1971; All Over, Alte Zeiten (Vienna), Via Galactica (NY), 1972; co-director of National Theatre, Apr 1973; director Nov 1973–; for the National Theatre he has directed The Tempest, 1973; John Gabriel Borkman, Happy Days, 1974; No Man's Land, Hamlet, Judgement, 1975; Tamburlaine the Great, 1976; these last were the opening productions of the Lyttelton and the Olivier theatres, respectively; Bedroom Farce (co-directed), Volpone, The Country Wife, 1977; The Cherry Orchard, Macbeth (co-directed), Betrayal, 1978; Amadeus, Betrayal (NY), 1979; Othello, 1980; his opera productions include the following at Covent Garden: Moses and Aaron, 1965; The Magic Flute, 1966; The Knot Garden, 1970; Eugene Onegin, Tristan and Isolde, 1971; at Glyndebourne he has directed La Calisto, 1970; Il Ritorno d'Ulisse, 1972; The Marriage of Figaro, 1973; Don Giovanni, 1977; Cosi Fan Tutte, 1978; Fidelio, 1979; directed his first film, Work is a Four Letter Word, in 1966, and has since directed A Midsummer Night's Dream, Three into Two Won't Go, Perfect Friday, The Homecoming, and Akenfield; he also directed the television production of The Wars of the Roses, 1965; awarded the CBE, Birthday Honours, 1963; London Critics' Best Director, 1963; NY Tony Award Best Director, 1966; Hamburg University Shakespeare Prize, 1967; Member of the Arts Council, 1969; co-director Royal Opera, 1971.

Recreation: Music. *Address:* The Wall House, Mongewell Park, Wallingford, Berks.

HALL, Willis, dramatic author
b Leeds, Yorkshire, 6 Apr 1929; *e* Cockburn High School, Leeds; *m* (1) Jill Bennett (mar dis); (2) Dorothy Kingsmill-Lunn (mar dis); (3) Valerie Shute.

Author of the following plays: The Royal Astrologers, 1958; The Long and the Short and the Tall, 1959; Last Day in Dreamland (one-act) and A Glimpse of the Sea (one-act), 1959; since then he has written, with Keith Waterhouse unless otherwise stated, the following: Billy Liar, Chin-Chin (adapted from the French), 1960; Celebration, 1961; England, Our England, Azouk (adapted with Robin Maugham), All Things Bright and Beautiful, The Sponge Room (one-act), Squat Betty (one-act), 1962; Come Laughing Home, The Gentle Knight (own one-act), The Love Game (own adaptation), 1964; Say Who You Are, 1967; Whoops-a-Daisy, 1969; Children's Day and Who's Who, 1970; The Card (book), Saturday, Sunday, Monday (adaptation), All Things Bright and Beautiful, 1973; since then his own plays include: Walk on, Walk on, Kidnapped at Christmas, 1975; Christmas Crackers, Stag Night, 1976; Filumena (adaptation), A Right Christmas Caper, 1977; the following plays have been produced in New York: The Long and the Short and the Tall, 1962; Billy Liar, 1963; Squat Betty, The Sponge Room, 1964; Help Stamp Out Marriage (American title for Say Who You Are), 1966; Saturday, Sunday, Monday, 1974; films he has written (with Keith Waterhouse) include: Whistle Down the Wind, A Kind of Loving, Billy Liar, Man in the Middle, and Torn Curtain; television includes Song at Twilight and the series Budgie, and Worzel Gummidge (both written with Keith Waterhouse).

Address: c/o London Management, 235–241 Regent Street, London, W1.

HALLIWELL, David, dramatist, director, actor and producer
b Brighouse, Yorks, 31 July 1936; *s* of Herbert Halliwell and his wife Ethel (Spencer); *e* Victoria Secondary Modern School, Rastrick, Hipperholme GS, and Huddersfield College of Art.

Author of the plays Concerning Out and In, 1958; Little Malcolm and his Struggle Against the Eunuchs, 1964; A Who's Who of Flapland, 1965; K D Dufford, 1968; Muck From Three Angles, 1970; A Last Belch for the Great Auk, Bleats from a Brighouse Pleasureground, 1971; Janitress Thrilled by Prehensile Penis, 1972; devised and directed the improvised plays: The Freckled Bum, Minyip, 1975; Progs, and A Process of Elimination, 1975; Prejudice (John Whiting Award), 1977, also directed, 1978; A Rite Kwik Metal Tata, 1978; Persons in the Act of Mooting, The House (for Joint Stock), 1979; has directed a number of plays, several at the Little Theatre, London; directed The Only Way Out, 1976; Lovers, 1978; Little Malcolm was produced in New York, 1966, under the title Hail Scrawdyke!, and has been filmed;

works for television include Cock, Hen and Courting Pit, Triple Exposure, Steps Back, Daft Mam Blues, Meriel the Ghost Girl and two episodes of *Crown Court*; Flapland was originally written for radio in 1965 and broadcast in 1967 and 'Was It Her?' was written in 1979; co-founder in 1966, with David Calderisi, of Quipu, a production company which presented principally lunchtime theatre; co-founder, 1979, of Wridirectors, a Company for Writer–directors; Resident Dramatist, Royal Court Theatre, 1976–7; Resident Dramatist, Hampstead Theatre, 1978–9.

Recreations: Animal parapsychology, it says on the form, and indoor golf. *Address:* 28 Chepstow Court, Chepstow Crescent, London, W11 3ED. *Tel:* 01–727 1091.

HAMBLETON, T Edward, producer and director
b Maryland, 12 Feb 1911; *s* of T Edward Hambleton and his wife Adelaide (McAlphin); *e* Gilman County School, St Paul's School, and Yale University; *m* (1) Caroline Hoysradt (dec); (2) Merrell Hopkins; studied at the Yale Drama School.

Manager of the summer theatre, Matunuck, Rhode Island, 1935–7; before serving as Lt-Cmdr, USNR, in World War II, produced in New York Robin Landing, I Know What I Like, and The First Crocus; on returning to civilian life, he produced the following plays in NY, for The Experimental Theatre, a company sponsored by the ANTA for the presentation of new plays: The Great Campaign, 1946; Galileo, which had previously been produced by him on the West Coast, 1947; Temporary Island, Ballet Ballads, 1948; Biltmore, NY, Nov 1950, produced Pride's Crossing; in 1953, with Norris Houghton, founded the 1100 seat Phoenix Theatre, off-Broadway, where they produced the following plays: Madam Will You Walk?; Coriolanus, The Golden Apple (transferred to the Alvin, NY, Apr 1954); The Sea Gull, 1953–4; Sing Me No Lullaby, Sandhog, The Doctor's Dilemma, The Master Builder, The White Devil, Phoenix '55, Moby Dick, 1954–5; The Carefree Tree, The Terrible Swift Sword, Six Characters in Search of an Author, The Adding Machine, a double-bill of Miss Julie and The Stronger, Queen After Death, A Month in the Country, The Mother of Us All, Four Premières (Ballet Theatre), The Littlest Revue, Marcel Marceau in his American première, Anna Christie, Venice Preserv'd, Characters and Chicanery, and Bil and Cora Baird's Marionette Theatre, 1955–6; The Duchess of Malfi (in association with John Houseman), Saint Joan, Diary of a Scoundrel, The Good Woman of Setzuan, Livin' the Life, The American Shakespeare Festival Company in Measure for Measure and The Taming of the Shrew, An Evening of Lyric Theatre by the After Dinner Opera Company, *Ballet Theatre,* Bil and Cora Baird's Marionette Theatre, The Merry-Go-Rounders, 1956–7; Mary Stuart, The Makropoulos Secret, a double-bill of The Chairs and The Lesson, The Infernal Machine, the Stratford Festival Company of Canada in The Two Gentlemen of Verona and The Broken Jug, *Le Théâtre du Nouveau Monde* in Le Malade Imaginaire and An Evening of Three Farces, Tobias and the Angel, A Sleep of Prisoners, Everyman Today, *Ballet Theatre, The Marionette Theatre of Braunschweig, The World of Cilli Wang,* For Humans Only, The Transposed Heads, 1957–8; The Family Reunion, *Théâtre du Vieux-Colombier de Paris* in Britannicus, The Power and the Glory, The Beaux' Stratagem, *Angna Enters,* Once upon a Mattress (in association with Norris Houghton and William and Jean Eckart), 1958–9; Coronet, NY, Oct 1959, produced as manager of Phoenix Theatre, The Great God Brown; Phoenix, produced Lysistrata, Pictures in the Hallway, Peer Gynt, Henry IV, Part I, Henry IV, Part II, *Angna Enters, Merce*

Cunningham Dance Company, and *Le Théâtre du Vieux-Colombier* in Le Misanthrope and L'Otage, 1959–60; The Stratford Festival production of HMS Pinafore, She Stoops to Conquer, The Plough and the Stars, The Octoroon, Hamlet, *Yuriko Dance Company, Tamiris-Nagrin Dance Company,* 1960–1; The Stratford Festival production of The Pirates of Penzance, Androcles and the Lion, The Policemen, The Dark Lady of the Sonnets, Who'll Save the Plowboy? Oh, Dad, Poor Dad, Mama's Hung You in the Closet and I'm Feelin' So Sad, But It Is Nothing, The Littlest Circus, 1961–2; Abe Lincoln in Illinois, The Taming of the Shrew, The Dragon, Persephone, Nancy Cole's Theatre of the Little Hand, 1962–3; Morning Sun, Next Time I'll Sing to You, Too Much Johnson, Margaret Webster in The Brontes, and The APA (Association of Producing Artists) at the Phoenix in Right You Are, The Tavern, Scapin, The Impromptu at Versailles, and The Lower Depths, 1963–4; Doctor Faustus, and APA at the Phoenix in Man and Superman, War and Peace, and Judith, 1964–5; Lyceum, NY, APA-Phoenix, produced You Can't Take It with You, 1965–6; The School for Scandal, You Can't Take It with You, Right You Are, We, Comrades Three, the Wild Duck, War and Peace, 1966–7; The Show-Off, Pantagleize, Exit the King, The Cherry Orchard, 1967–8; The Show-Off, Pantagleize, Cock-a-Doodle Dandy, The Misanthrope, The Cocktail Party, Hamlet, 1968–9; Phoenix presented Harvey at ANTA, The Criminals at the Sheridan Square Playhouse, and The Persians at St George's Episcopal Church, 1969–70; a tour of Harvey, and for the Phoenix, The Trial of the Catonsville Nine, The School for Wives, Murderous Angels, 1971; for the New Phoenix Repertory Company, The Great God Brown, Don Juan, A Meeting by the River, 1972; Strike Heaven on the Face, Games, After Liverpool, The Government Inspector, The Visit, Chemin de Fer, Holiday, 1973; The Removalists, In the Voodoo Parlor of Marie Leveau, Love for Love, Pretzels, The Rules of the Game, 1974; The Member of the Wedding, Knuckle, Dandelion Wine, Meeting Place, 1975; Twenty-seven Wagons Full of Cotton, A Memory of Two Mondays, They Knew What They Wanted, Ladyhouse Blues, Canadian Gothic/American Modern (one-acts), Marco Polo, 1976; A Sorrow Beyond Dreams, G R Point, Scribes, Hot Grog, Uncommon Women and Others, The Elusive Angel, 1977; One Crack Out, City Sugar, Getting Out, 1978; Later, Says I, Says He, Big and Little, Chinchilla, 1979; 1962–3, for Lumadrama, Inc, produced sound and light spectacle The American Bell at Independence Hall in Philadelphia; member of the Council of Living Theatre; The Golden Apple received the New York Drama Critics Award, 1954; president of the board of the Hampden–Booth Theatre Collection and Library; vice-president, Center Stage.

Club: Players and The Century Association. *Address:* Timonium, Maryland.

HAMILTON, Margaret, actress
b Cleveland, Ohio, 12 Sept 1902; *d* of Walter J Hamilton and his wife Jennie Adams; *e* Hathaway-Brown High School, Cleveland, and Wheelock Kindergarten Training School, Boston, Mass; previously a kindergarten and nursery school teacher; *m* Paul Boynton Meserve (mar dis).

Studied for the stage, by doing and observing, at the Cleveland Playhouse, where she first appeared on the stage in 1923 in The Man Who Ate the Popomack; made her New York début at the Booth, Apr 1932, when she played Helen Hallam in Another Language; Morosco, Nov 1933, Hattie in Dark Tower; 46th Street, Oct 1934, Lucy Gurget in Farmer Takes a Wife; engaged in films in Hollywood for nine years; at the 48th Street, NY, Nov 1943, played Gertrude in

Outrageous Fortune; Patio, Los Angeles, Calif, 1946, played the Aunt in On Borrowed Time; Mansfield, Jan 1948, Gwennie in The Men We Marry; El Capitan, Hollywood, Sept 1950, Aunt Addie in Little Boy Blue; Berkshire Playhouse, Stockbridge, Mass, summer 1951, Mrs Hammer in The Silver Whistle and Mrs Fisher in The Show-Off; Royale, NY, Jan 1952, Lucy Bascombe in Fancy Meeting You Again; Phoenix, Feb 1956, Mrs Zero in The Adding Machine, and, Nov 1956, Mme Kleopatra Mamaeva in Diary of a Scoundrel; City Center, Apr 1958, played Dolly Tate in Annie Get Your Gun; toured, summer 1958, as Mrs Dudgeon in The Devil's Disciple; Lunt-Fontanne, Oct 1958, Bessie in Goldilocks; Civic, Los Angeles, Apr 1962, Grandma in The American Dream; Pocket, NY, May 1963, Clara in Save Me a Place at Forest Lawn; Westport Country Playhouse, Conn, Nov 1963, Louise in The Strangers; Bucks County Playhouse, July 1965, Mrs Western in Tom Jones; Helen Hayes, NY, Jan 1966, Connie Tufford in UTBU; NY State, July 1966, Parthy Ann Hawks in Show Boat; Seattle Repertory, Dec 1966, Madame Arcati in Blithe Spirit, and 1967–8 season, Mrs Malaprop in The Rivals; Lunt-Fontanne, Mar 1969, Dorinda Pratt in Come Summer; NY State, June 1969, Aunt Eller in Oklahoma!; ANTA, Nov 1969, Mrs Soames in Our Town; American Shakespeare Festival, Stratford, Conn, 1970, Mrs Dudgeon in The Devil's Disciple; Alley, Houston, Texas, 1970, Madame Arcati in Blithe Spirit; Studio Arena, Buffalo, NY, 1971, played in The Nephew; Seattle, Washington, Repertory, Oct 1971, Madame Desmortes in Ring Round the Moon; took over from Ruth McDevitt as Stella Livingston in the tour of Light Up the Sky, 1972; became Vice President of the AMAS Repertory Theater, NY, and at the Beaumont Hall, 1973, presented An Evening with the Bourgeosie, Othello, The Three Sisters, and House Party: A Musical Memory; Forrest, Philadelphia, Feb 1974, Madame Armfeldt in A little Night Music, and subsequently toured; with the BAM Theatre Company, Brooklyn, spring 1977, played Miss Heneage in The New York Idea and Anfisa in Three Sisters; Ahmanson, LA, Dec 1977, and BAM, Feb 1978, Mrs Dudgeon in The Devil's Disciple; appeared with the Cleveland Playhouse Company, season 1978–9; has also played frequently in stock in such plays as On the Town, Bells Are Ringing, A Tree Grows in Brooklyn, Bloomer Girl, The Wizard of Oz, etc; entered films, 1933, in Another Language, and notable films include The Wizard of Oz, State of the Union, The Farmer Takes a Wife, My Little Chickadee, The Anderson Tapes (1971), Journey Back to Oz (1974); Member of the Council of Actors Equity Association; first appeared on television in 1950 and since has played regularly on all the networks.

Favourite parts: Helen Hallam in Another Language, Grandma in The American Dream, Margaret in The Father, and Hattie in Dark Tower. *Address:* c/o Michael Thomas Agency, 22 East 60th Street, New York, NY.

HAMLETT, Dilys, actress and singer
b Tidworth, Hants, 12 Mar 1928; *d* of Sidney Hamlett, MBE, TD, and his wife Mary Jane (Evans); *m* Casper Wrede (mar dis); formerly a secretary, she trained for the stage at the Old Vic School, 1950–2.

Her first London appearance was at His Majesty's, Sept 1952, walking on as the Lady Ghost in The Innocents; at the Edinburgh Festival, Aug 1953, played the title role in Miss Julie; after repertory appearances in 1954, joined the Shakespeare Memorial Theatre Company, season 1955, to play first witch in Macbeth and understudy Vivien Leigh; at Stratford, season 1956, her parts included Ophelia in Hamlet and Mariana in Measure for Measure; Lyric, Hammersmith, Jan

1959, Julie in Danton's Death; same theatre, Apr 1959, Agnes in Brand; Oxford Playhouse, Dec 1959, Miss Quested in A Passage to India, subsequently playing the same part at the Comedy, Apr 1960; Royalty, Mar 1961, Kate Keller in The Miracle Worker; at the Old Vic, Season 1952–3, played Solveig in Peer Gynt, Sept 1962, Isabella in Measure for Measure, Apr 1963, and took over the part of Desdemona in Othello; Edinburgh Festival, Aug 1963, Rita in Little Eyolf; toured, Jan 1964, as Eva Hood in March Hares; with Century Theatre, Manchester, 1966–8, her roles included Mary Tyrone in Long Day's Journey into Night, Marie Louise in The Ortolan, Portia in The Merchant of Venice, Amanda in Private Lives, and Widow Quinn in The Playboy of the Western World; for the 69 Theatre Company, played Gertrude in Hamlet, Edinburgh Festival, Aug 1968; appeared in The Trial of St Joan, Apr 1969; played the wife in Country Matters, Sept 1969; Apollo, Dec 1971, Donna Lucia in the 69 Theatre Company's Charley's Aunt; Theatre Royal, York, 1972, Alice in Tiny Alice; York Minster, May 1973, title role in The Trial of Joan of Arc; Open Air, Regent's Park, July 1973, Rosalind in As You Like It; at the Northcott, Exeter, 1974, her parts included Catherine Petkoff in Arms and the Man, and Vera in Pal Joey; Her Majesty's, Oct 1975, Eleanor in Thomas and the King; Toulouse, 1976, Kate in Old Times; Northcott, Exeter, Oct 1976, and tour, Cleopatra in Antony and Cleopatra; Exeter University, 1976, played the title-role in Honegger's St Joan; Theatre Royal, Watford, 1977, Mrs Warren in Mrs Warren's Profession; York, 1977, Martha in Who's Afraid of Virginia Woolf; Royal Exchange, Manchester, Sept 1977, Norwegian Lady in The Ordeal of Gilbert Pinfold; Ambassador's, Oct 1977, took over as Mary in Dear Daddy, and played Delia in the South African tour of the same play, 1977–8; Sept–Oct 1978, toured Europe as Paulina in the Royal Exchange's production of The Winter's Tale and played the part in Manchester, Nov; Northcott, Exeter, Apr 1979, Alix in Motherdear; Royal Exchange, May 1979, Countess in The Deep Man and, Nov, Mme Ranevskaya in The Cherry Orchard; she has devised and toured in her one-woman show, Needs and Notions, in Finland and throughout England; has also directed The Creditors and A Man for All Seasons; first appeared in films 1962, recently in What Changed Charlie Farthing?; TV appearances, since her first in 1956, include Pavlova, Uncle Vanya, Twelfth Night and Brand.
Recreations: Reading, travelling, riding. *Address:* c/o Peter Brown Management, 13 St Martin's Road, London SW9.

HAMLISCH, Marvin, composer
b New York, NY, 2 Jun 1944; *e* Queens College, NY (BA 1964); graduate of the preparatory division, Juilliard School of Music.
Wrote the music for A Chorus Line, 1975, for which he received a Tony award and the Pulitzer Prize; music for They're Playing Our Song, 1979; work in films includes scores for The Way We Were, including the song Evergreen, and The Spy Who Loved Me, including the title song Nobody Does It Better; also musical adaptation for The Sting; winner of three Academy Awards, 1974.
Address: c/o ASCAP, 1 Lincoln Plaza, New York, NY 10023.

HAMMERSTEIN, James, director and producer
b New York City, 23 Mar 1931; *s* of Oscar Hammerstein II, the librettist and lyricist, and his wife Dorothy Blanchard; *e* George School, Newton, Pa, University of North Carolina; *m* (1) Barbara Regis (mar dis), (2) Millette Alexander.

First engaged in the theater as a replacement extra at the Alvin, NY, Sept 1950, during the run of Mister Roberts; served as a stage manager for Music in the Air, The Fourposter, 1951; Maggie, Me and Juliet, 1953; On Your Toes, 1954; Damn Yankees, 1955; directed his first London production, Damn Yankees, at the Coliseum, 28 Mar 1957; directed a number of touring production and stock companies, such as Show Boat, Carmen Jones, Flower Drum Song, Harvey, The Tender Trap, The King of Hearts, South Pacific, etc, 1958–63; at the Playhouse, 27 Feb 1958, co-produced Blue Denim; at the St James, Dec 1958, served as stage manager for Flower Drum Song; directed his first play in New York, Absence of a Cello, at the Ambassador, 21 Sept 1964; since then has directed a revival of South Pacific, 1965; The Paisley Convertible, 1967; It's Called the Sugar Plum, The Indian Wants the Bronx, The Basement, Tea Party, 1968; the tour of Canterbury Tales, 1969; Acrobats, Line, 1971; Wise Child, Butley, 1972; The Beauty Part, 1974; Tuscaloosa's Calling Me . . . But I'm Not Going, 1975; Getting Through the Night, Goodbye and Keep Cold, 1976; The Rear Column, 1978; UK tour of Oklahoma!, 1980; was a resident director for the Eugene O'Neill Playwrights' Conference 1975.
Recreations: Piano, tennis, skin-diving, chess. *Address:* Tweed Boulevard, Piermont, New York. *Tel:* 914–EL9 3342.

HAMPSHIRE, Susan, actress
b London, 12 May 1942; *m* Pierre Granier-Deferre (mar dis).
Following an early training in ballet, made her first appearance on the stage at the Roof Top Theatre, Bognor Regis, Apr 1957, as Dora in Night Must Fall; first appeared in the West End, at the Saville Theatre, Apr 1958, as Cynthia in Expresso Bongo; at the Vaudeville, Mar 1960, played Victoria in Follow That Girl; Pembroke, Croydon, Dec 1960, appeared as Elaine Musk, Miss Kelly, Gertrude Gentle, and Charlotte Groves in Fairy Tales of New York, subsequently playing the same parts when the play was produced at the Comedy, Jan 1961; Ashcroft, Croydon, Nov 1963, played Marion Dangerfield in The Ginger Man, transferring with the production to the Royal Court, Nov 1963; St Martin's, June 1964, Miss Jones in Past Imperfect; Ashcroft, Croydon, Feb 1966, played Kate Hardcastle in She Stoops to Conquer; Arnaud, Guildford, Aug 1966, Helen Hayle in On Approval; St Martin's, May 1968, Mary in The Sleeping Prince; Greenwich, Nov 1972, Nora in A Doll's House; Shaw, Oct 1974, Katherina in The Taming of the Shrew; Coliseum, Christmas 1974, title role in Peter Pan; Arnaud, Guildford, Feb 1975, Jeannette in Romeo and Jeannette; Shaw, May 1975, Rosalind in As You Like It; Greenwich, Apr 1976, played the title-role in Miss Julie; Chichester, 1976, Elizabeth Champion-Cheney in The Circle, transferring to the Haymarket, Oct 1976; Thorndike, Leatherhead, Jan 1977, and Hong Kong Festival, Raina in Arms and the Man; Malvern Festival, May 1977, Ann Whitefield in the Royal Shakespeare Company's production of Man and Superman, playing the part at the Savoy, Aug 1977–Feb 1978; Hampstead, May 1978, Siri von Essen-Strindberg in The Tribades; Greenwich, Oct 1978, Victorine in An Audience Called Edouard; Haymarket, Mar 1979, Irene St Claire in The Crucifer of Blood; Phoenix, Sept 1979, took over as Ruth Carsan in Night and Day; films in which she has appeared include: Night Must Fall, Rogan, A Room in Paris, Living Free, Neither the Sea Nor the Sand, Dr Jekyll and Mr Hyde, and Roses and Green Peppers; principal television performances include: An Ideal Husband, and the series *The First Churchills*, *The Pallisers*, and *Forsyte Saga*.
Favourite parts: Fairy Tales of New York. *Recreations:* The study of English period design, writing, music, drawing. *Address:* c/o Chatto and Linnit, Globe Theatre, Shaftesbury Avenue, London W1. *Tel:* 01–439 4371.

HAMPTON, Christopher, dramatic author

b Fayal, Azores, 26 Jan 1946; *s* of Bernard Patrick Hampton and his wife Dorothy Patience (Herrington); *e* Lancing and New College, Oxford.

Wrote his first play, When Did You Last See My Mother?, in 1964; it was performed at the Royal Court, June 1966, in a production without décor, later transferring to the Comedy; produced at the Sheridan Square Playhouse, New York, Jan 1967; resident dramatist, Royal Court, 1968–70, where he wrote Total Eclipse, 1968 and The Philanthropist, 1970; has since written Savages, 1973; Treats, Signed and Sealed (adaptation), 1976; is responsible for the following translations: Marya (Babel), 1967; Uncle Vanya, Hedda Gabler, A Doll's House, 1970; Don Juan, 1972; Tales from the Vienna Woods, 1977; Don Juan Comes Back from the War, Ghosts, 1978; The Wild Duck, 1979; first play for television, Able's Will, 1977; Total Eclipse, The Philanthropist, Savages, Treats and Marya have all been televised; A Doll's House and Tales from the Vienna Woods have been filmed; Plays and Players London Critics Award for Best Play for The Philanthropist (1970), and Savages (joint winner, 1973), also *The Evening Standard* Best Comedy Award, for the former.

Recreations: Travel, cinema. *Club:* Dramatist's. *Address:* c/o Margaret Ramsay Ltd, 14A Goodwin's Court, St Martin's Lane, London, WC2.

HANCOCK, Christopher, actor

b Bishop Auckland, 5 June 1928; *s* of Maurice Arthur Hancock and his wife Alicia Margaret (Hodgson); *e* Durham Cathedral Choir School and Bootham School, York; *m* Ann Walford; trained for the stage at the Old Vic Theatre School, London.

His first stage appearance was as a child at the Little, Middlesbrough, 1934, playing 3 am in Tomorrow; his early experience was in repertory, including walk-ons at the Old Vic, 1951; Lyric, Hammersmith, July 1958, Mr Green in The Hamlet of Stepney Green; Comedy, Apr 1960, made his West End debut as Mr Das in A Passage to India; Mermaid, May, and Her Majesty's, Aug 1962, Quill in Lock Up Your Daughters; 1963–8, repertory at the Nottingham Playhouse, where he played many leading roles; joined the Bristol Old Vic company, Aug 1969; Wyndham's, Jan 1970, played Fr Yeo in the Bristol production of It's a 2 ft 6 in Above the Ground World; Criterion, Oct 1970, Old Ekdal in The Wild Duck; Mermaid, Nov 1971, played The Bishop, and Mr Battler, in Geneva; same theatre, May 1972, Captain Hardy in Journey's End; at Hampstead played Sir Thomas Clissold in Mad Dog, Aug, and Ernest, first Philip and second Philip in Country Life, Oct 1973; Drury Lane, May 1974, Mr Shadrack in Billy; Bath and Cheltenham Festivals, June–July 1977, played The Narrator in The Soldiers Tale; Theatre Upstairs, Jan 1978, Jigger Hannafin in Ses I, Ses He; July–Oct 1978, Royal Shakespeare Company small-scale tour, played Feste in Twelfth Night and Rhode in Three Sisters; Royal Court, Feb 1979, Roger in The London Cuckolds; Arnaud, Guildford, June 1979, Dudley Robinson in Circumstantial Evidence; first appeared on TV, 1959; recent appearances include Love for Lydia, The Devil's Crown, and A Case of Spirits.

Hobbies: Tailoring and photography. *Address:* 108 Thorkhill Road, Thames Ditton, Surrey.

HANCOCK, Sheila, OBE, actress

b Blackgang, Isle of Wight, 22 Feb 1933; *d* of Enrico Cameron Hancock and his wife Ivy Louisa (Woodward); *e* Dartford County Grammar School; *m* (1) Alec Ross (dec);

(2) John Thaw; studied for the stage at the Royal Academy of Dramatic Art.

Made her first appearance on the stage while still at school, at the Scala, Dartford, Apr 1950, as Beth in Little Women; after appearing in a number of repertory companies, including York, Guildford, and Bromley, she made her first appearance in London, at the Duke of York's, Sept 1958, when she took over the part of Lily Thompson in Breath of Spring; Lyric, Hammersmith, July 1959, appeared in the revue One to Another, subsequently transferring to the Apollo, Aug 1959; Theatre Royal, Stratford, E, Oct 1959, played Gwen in Make Me an Offer, transferring with the production to the New, Dec 1959; Duke of York's, Apr 1961, appeared in the revue One Over the Eight; Garrick, Sept 1962, played Cyrenne in Rattle of a Simple Man, which ran for a year; New, Bromley, Mar 1964, directed The Taming of the Shrew; Oxford Playhouse, May 1965, played Praxagora and An Even Older Woman in The Parliament of Women; made her first appearance in New York at the Lyceum, Oct 1965, when she played Kath in Entertaining Mr Sloane; Duke of York's, London, Apr 1966, played Karen in The Anniversary; Royal Court, Jan 1967, Lady Dance in The Soldier's Fortune; Vaudeville, Sept 1967, Maggie Harris in Fill the Stage with Happy Hours; Aldwych, Jan 1969 played Julia in A Delicate Balance; Criterion, Sept 1969, Maggie in So What About Love; Aldwych, Jan 1972, the Daughter in All Over; Hampstead, Nov 1972, Beatrice in The Effect of Gamma Rays on Man-in-the-Moon Marigolds; Criterion, July 1973, Marion in Absurd Person Singular; New London, Dec 1974, appeared in the revue Déjà Révue; Lyric, Aug 1976, took over the part of Alma in The Bed Before Yesterday; Arts, Cambridge, 1977, played Hester in The Deep Blue Sea; Victoria Palace, May 1978–9, Miss Hannigan in Annie; for Cambridge Theatre Co, directed The Constant Wife (1979) and In Praise of Love (1980); Drury Lane, July 1980, Mrs Lovett in Sweeney Todd; made her first appearance in films, 1960, in Girl in a Boat and recently in The Anniversary; first appeared on television, 1959, and has since appeared in the series The Rag Trade, *Mr Digby Darling, Now Take My Wife* and *But Seriously, It's Sheila Hancock*; received the OBE in 1974.

Recreations: Music and reading. *Address:* c/o John Redway, 16 Berners Street, London W1P 3DD.

HANDL, Irene, actress

b London, 27 Dec 1901; *d* of Frederick Handl and his wife Marie (Schuepp); *e* London; studied for the stage for twelve months at the Embassy School of Acting.

Made her first appearance on the stage at the Embassy, 2 Feb 1937, as the Stout Woman in Night Alone; at Wyndham's, Feb 1937, made an immediate success when she played Beer, the Maid, in George and Margaret, which ran for nearly two years; during this period she appeared for the Repertory Players at the Strand, Feb 1938, as Mrs Bartle in Full Flavour; May 1938, Frau Schneckenroth in Rovina; Savoy, Nov 1938, Lucia in Never Goodbye; Arts, May 1938, played Rose in A Star Comes Home; during the War, appeared in a variety of character parts at the Garrison Theatre, Salisbury, and elsewhere; Playhouse, Mar 1945, played Mrs Beale in Great Day; Phoenix, Nov 1945, Eva in Under the Counter; Embassy, Feb 1946, Alice in Mr Bowling Buys a Newspaper; Fortune, Aug 1946, Miss Patch in Day After Tomorrow; Q, Dec 1946, played Edie in Divorce on Tuesday; Duke of York's, May 1947, Franzi Mahler in We Proudly Present; Comedy, Mar 1949, Effie in Summer in December; Q, Sept 1949, Laura Baker in Marriage Playground; Vaudeville, Apr 1950, Mrs Thripp in Cry Liberty;

King's, Glasgow, June 1951, Millicent Browne-Ffolliat in Will I Do?; Embassy, Nov 1951, Mrs Poyser in Magnolia Street Story; Royal, Brighton, Dec 1951, Nanny in Bold Lover; Duke of York's, London, Feb 1952, played Miss Oakley in First Person Singular; Opera House, Manchester, Aug 1952, Mrs Laura Baker in The Wedding Ring; Richmond, Mar 1953, Mrs Jannaway in Goodnight, Sweet Prince; New Lindsey, May 1955, Mrs Piper in Strange Request; Garrick, July 1955, Elsie Knowles in Home and Away; Victoria Palace, June 1956, played Mrs Pullar in Jubilee Girl; Strand, July 1961, played Amelia Puffin in Goodnight, Mrs Puffin, which ran for nearly two years; toured Australia, June 1963–Dec 1963, in the same part; toured England, spring, 1964, as Hilde in Everything Happens on Friday; Duke of York's, Dec 1964, played Lily Piper in Busybody; toured Australia and New Zealand, 1966, in the same part; Richmond, Nov 1966, Helena Hope in Dear Miss Hope; Chichester Festival, May 1967, Thirza Tapper in The Farmer's Wife; Sept 1967, toured in Dear Miss Hope; Savoy, June 1968, and tour Lady Eppingham and Beatrice Horrocks in My Giddy Aunt; Sept 1970 toured as Lydia in His, Hers & Theirs; Arnaud, Guildford, April 1972, Bessie Trimble in Chorus of Murder; Devonshire Park, Eastbourne, Oct 1972, Mrs Puffin in Goodnight Mrs Puffin; June 1973 toured as Madame Arcati in Blithe Spirit; St Martin's, Jan 1974, Lily Piper in Dead Easy; National Theatre, July 1974, May in The Freeway; Greenwich, Jan 1975, Lady Bracknell in The Importance of Being Earnest; May 1975 toured as Mrs Bramson in Night Must Fall; Oct 1975 toured as Mrs Swabb in Habeas Corpus; Shaftesbury, Dec 1976, Madame Purvis in Emu in Pantoland; Haymarket, June 1978, Emma Kilner in A Family; toured, 1979, as Audrey in Ten Times Table; entered films, 1937 and has appeared successfully in numerous pictures including The Italian Job, I'm All Right Jack and Two Way Stretch; since 1953 has regularly broadcast and appeared on television including A Legacy and For The Love of Ada; author of The Sioux and The Gold Tip Pfitzer.

Address: c/o London Management, 235–241 Regent Street, London W1.

HANDMAN, Wynn, director, producer, teacher
b 19 May 1922; *s* of Nathan Handman and his wife Anna; *e* City College of New York (BA), Columbia University (MA), Neighborhood Playhouse School of the Theatre (1948).

Taught acting and directed productions at the Neighborhood Playhouse School of the Theatre, 1950–5; founded the Wynn Handman Studio, 1955, where he has taught acting till the present; directed The Power of Darkness, produced at the York, Sept 1959; co-founder and Artistic Director of The American Place Theatre since its inception, 1963, an organization devoted to further the development of American playwrights; has been responsible for the productions there of The Old Glory, a double-bill consisting of My Kinsman, Major Molineux, and Benito Cereno, by Robert Lowell, 1964; Harry, Noon, and Night by Ronald Ribman, Hogan's Goat, by William Alfred, 1965; Jonah, by Paul Goodman, The Journey of the Fifth Horse, by Ronald Ribman, Who's Got His Own, by Ronald Milner, The Displaced Person, by Cecil Dawkins, 1966; La Turista, by Sam Shepard, Posterity for Sale, by Niccolo Tucci, Father Uxbridge Wants to Marry, by Frank Gagliano, The Ceremony of Innocence, by Ronald Ribman, 1967; The Electronic Nigger and Others, three short plays by Ed Bullins called a Son, Come Home, The Electronic Nigger, and Clara's Ole Man, Endecott and the Red Cross, by Robert Lowell, The Cannibals, by George Tabori, Trainer, Dean, Liepolt & Company, three short plays called The Acquisition, by David Trainer, This Bird of Dawning

Singeth All Night Long, by Phillip Dean, and The Young Master Dante, by Werner Liepolt, 1968; Boy on the Straight-Back Chair, by Ronald Tavel, Papp, by Kenneth Cameron, Mercy Street, by Anne Sexton, 1969; Five on the Black Hand Side, by Charlie D Russell, Two Times Two, consisting of The Last Straw, by Charles Dizenzo and Duet for Solo Voice, by David Scott Milton, The Pig Pen, by Ed Bullins, Sunday Dinner, by Joyce Carol Oates, The Carpenters, by Steve Tesich, 1970; Pinkville, by George Tabori, Black Bog Beast Bait, by Sam Shepard, Fingernails Blue as Flowers, by Ronald Ribman, Lake of the Woods, by Steve Tesich, 1971; The Chickencoop Chinaman, by Frank Chin, The Kid, by Robert Coover, The Little Theater of the Deaf, 1972; Freeman, by Phillip Dean, The Karl Marx Play, by Rochelle Owens, Baba Goya, by Steve Tesich, 1973; Bread, by David Scott Milton, a Festival of Short Plays, including Shearwater, by William Hauptman, Cream Cheese, by Lonnie Carter, Dr Kheal, by Maria Irene Fornes, and Love Scene, by Robert Coover, The Year of the Dragon, by Frank Chin, The Beauty Part, by S J Perelman, At Sea with Benchley, Kalmar, and Ruby, 1974; Jean Shepherd Plays Jean Shepherd, Killer's Head and Action, a double-bill by Sam Shepard, Rubbers and Yanks 3 Detroit 0 Top of the Seventh, a double-bill by Jonathan Reynolds, Gorky, by Steve Tesich, 1975; Every Night When the Sun Goes Down, The Old Glory (revival), Jack Gilber's New Play: Rehearsal, Comanche Cafe/Domino Courts (one-acts), 1976; Isadora Duncan Sleeps with the Russian Navy, Jules Feiffer's Hold Me!, Cold Storage, Cockfight, Passing Game, 1977; Fefu and Her Friends, Conjuring an Event, Touching Bottom, 1978; Seduced, Tunnel Fever, 1979.

Address: The American Place Theatre, 111 West 46th Street, New York, NY 10019.

HANDS, Terry, director
b Aldershot, Hants, 9 Jan 1941; *s* of Joseph Ronald Hands and his wife Luise Bertha (Köhler); *e* Woking Grammar School and Birmingham University; trained for the stage at RADA, 1962–4.

Founder-director, Everyman Theatre, Liverpool, 1964–6, where his productions included The Importance of Being Earnest, Look Back in Anger, Richard III, and Fando and Lis; joined the Royal Shakespeare Company, 1966, as artistic director of Theatregoround, presenting touring productions; for them he directed The Proposal, The Second Shepherds' Play, 1966; The Dumb Waiter, Pleasure and Repentance (anthology), Under Milk Wood, 1967; associate director, RSC, 1967–77; Co-Artistic Director, 1978; for them he has directed The Criminals (Aldwych), 1967; The Merry Wives of Windsor (Stratford and Aldwych), The Latent Heterosexual (Aldwych), 1968; Pericles, The Merry Wives, Women Beware Women (all Stratford), Bartholomew Fair (Aldwych), 1969; The Merry Wives (Japan, tour), Richard III (Stratford), 1970; The Merchant of Venice (Stratford), The Man of Mode, The Balcony (both Aldwych: co-translated the latter), 1971; The Merchant of Venice (Aldwych and tour), Murder in the Cathedral (Aldwych), 1972; Romeo and Juliet (Stratford), Cries from Casement (The Place), 1973; Bewitched (Aldwych), The Actor (Australian tour: also devised), 1974; Stratford Centenary Season, 1975, comprising Henry V, Henry IV (both parts) and The Merry Wives of Windsor; the same productions were seen at the Aldwych, 1976; also at the Aldwych, 1976, directed Old World; Henry VI, Parts 1, 2, 3, and Coriolanus (Stratford 1977 and Aldwych 1978); The Changeling (Aldwych 1978); Twelfth Night (Stratford 1979 and Aldwych 1980); Children of the Sun (Aldwych 1979); As You Like It, Richard II,

Richard III (Stratford 1980); for the Comédie Française, he has directed Richard III (also Avignon Festival), 1972; Pericles, 1974; Twelfth Night, 1976; Le Cid (1977); Murder in the Cathedral (1978); his production of Richard III was given the French Critics' award, 1972, as Meilleur Spectacle de l'Année; Chevalier des Ordres des Arts et des Lettres, 1975; in the same year he was appointed consultant-director of the Comédie Française; he has also directed Troilus and Cressida (1978) and As You Like It (1979) at The Burgtheater, Vienna; and the operas Otello (Paris 1976), and Parsifal (Covent Garden, 1979).

Address: c/o Royal Shakespeare Theatre, Stratford-on-Avon, Warwicks. *Tel:* Stratford 296655.

HANLEY, William, playwright
b Lorain, Ohio, 22 Oct 1931; *s* of William Gerald Hanley and his wife Anne (Rodgers); *e* Cornell University (1950–1), American Academy of Dramatic Arts (1954–5); *m* Pat Stanley.

First produced plays were two one-acters, Whisper into My Good Ear and Mrs Dally Has a Lover, presented at the Cherry Lane, 10 Oct 1962, and for these plays received the Vernon Rice Award; wrote Conversations in the Dark, produced at the Walnut Street, Philadelphia, Dec 1963; Slow Dance on the Killing Ground, 1964; Today Is Independence Day, produced with Mrs Dally Has a Lover under the title Mrs Dally, 1965; Flesh and Blood, 1968; The Gypsy Moths (screenplay), 1969; Blue Dreams (novel), 1971; Mixed Feelings (novel), 1972; Leaving Mount Venus (novel), 1976.

Address: 190 Lounsbury Road, Ridgefield, Conn, 06877. *Tel:* 438 5326.

HANSON, John (*né* Watts), singer and actor
b Oshawa, Ont, 31 Aug 1922; *s* of Arthur Leonard Charles Watts and his wife Ethel (Hanson); *e* Dumfries Academy, Scotland; *m* Brenda Stokes; formerly a production engineer.

Began his professional career as a singer, making his first appearance, Oct 1946, in a concert at the Town Hall, Birmingham; in 1957 he began appearing in touring productions of musicals from the past, playing the Red Shadow in The Desert Song; this was followed by Karl Franz in The Student Prince, 1959, Francois Villon in The Vagabond King, 1960, Baron von Schober in Lilac Time, 1963, Baldasare in Maid of the Mountains, 1964; toured, 1965, in the leading role in The World of Ivor Novello; 1966, played John Carteret in the tour of When You're Young, for which he wrote the book, music and lyrics; Palace, May 1967, again played the Red Shadow in The Desert Song, making his West End debut; the production transferred, Feb 1968, to the Cambridge, where it was succeeded, June 1968, by The Student Prince, in which he again played Karl Franz; the London productions of The Student Prince and The Desert Song were presented at Blackpool in summer seasons 1969 and 1970 respectively; toured, 1971, in A Waltz Dream; Prince of Wales, July 1972 (also tour), played John Carteret in his own musical adaptation of Smilin' Through; since then he has toured in Lilac Time, and Desert Song, 1973–4; Rose Marie, 1974; Dancing Years and Glamorous Night, 1975, playing Anthony Allen, New London, Nov; 1976–7, produced and directed farewell tour of his Student Prince; continues touring in romantic musicals; 1976–80 appeared in Bournemouth Sunday Concerts; other concert performances include appearances at the Royal Festival and Albert Halls, and numerous summer seasons; has appeared many times in pantomime, usually as Robin Hood; has made over 350 TV appearances, notably in his series *John Hanson Sings;* has

also broadcast more than 1250 times and made twenty-one LP records (golden disc, 1977).

Recreations: Gardening, songwriting, badminton. *Address:* Deva House, Silverdale Avenue, Walton-on-Thames, Surrey. *Tel:* 27053.

HARBOTTLE, G Laurence, solicitor
b Newcastle upon Tyne, 11 Apr 1924; *s* of George Harbottle and his wife Winifred Ellen Benson; *e* The Leys School and Emmanuel College, Cambridge; formerly a Captain and Adjutant in the Royal Artillery, 1942–47.

Chairman of Theatre Centre Ltd, 1959–present; also of Prospect Productions Ltd, 1955 and 1966–77; 69 Theatre Company Ltd 1968–72 and Royal Exchange Theatre Company Ltd, 1973–present; Cambridge Theatre Company Ltd, 1969–present; deputy chairman, Central School of Speech and Drama, 1977–present; a director or former director of other theatre companies including The Watermill, Newbury, 1970–75, and The Bush (Alternative Theatre Company Ltd), 1975–77; member of the Arts Council, 1976–78; Drama Panel, 1974–78; Training Committee, 1977–78; chairman, Housing the Arts, 1977–78; President, 1979–81, TMA/CORT/ATPM (unified as the Theatrical Management Association); council member, Institute of Contemporary Arts; senior partner since 1956 of Harbottle and Lewis, solicitors.

Club: Savile. *Address:* 34 South Molton Street, London W1.

HARBURG, Edgar Y (known as E Y or Yip), lyricist and playwright
b New York City, 8 Apr 1898; *s* of Lewis Harburg and his wife Mary (Ricing); *e* College of the City of New York (BS 1918); *m* (1) Alice Richmond (mar dis); (2) Edelaine Roden.

Formerly a journalist and writer of light verse for periodicals and newspapers; contributed his first lyrics to a Broadway production for Earl Carroll's Sketchbook, July 1929; since then has written lyrics for The Garrick Gaieties, Earl Carroll's Vanities, 1930; Shoot the Works, 1931; Ballyhoo of 1932, Americana, Walk a Little Faster, 1932; Ziegfeld Follies, Life Begins at 8.40, 1934; Hooray for What! 1937; Hold On to Your Hats, 1940; Bloomer Girl, 1944; Finian's Rainbow, of which he was also co-author with Fred Saidy, 1947; Flahooley (also co-author), 1951; Jamaica (also co-author), 1957; The Happiest Girl in the World, of which he was also co-author, 1961; Darling of the Day, The Wizard of Oz, an adaptation for puppets of the film, 1968; appeared at the Kauffmann Auditorium of the YMHA, NY, 1971, in the series Lyrics and Lyricists, and appeared again in Jan 1972; lyrics for the pantomime version of The Wizard of Oz, produced at the Victoria Palace, London, 26 Dec 1972; book and lyrics for I Got a Song, produced at the Studio Arena, Buffalo, NY, Sept 1974; wrote his first lyrics for films, 1930, for The Sap from Syracuse, and since has written the lyrics for Queen High, 1930; Moonlight and Pretzels, Leave It to Lester, 1933; the Count of Monte Cristo, Take a Chance, 1934; The Singing Kid, The Gold Diggers of 1937, 1936; Andy Hardy Gets Spring Fever, 1937; The Wizard of Oz (Academy Award for lyrics), A Day at the Circus, 1939; Babes on Broadway, 1941; Ship Ahoy, Cairo, Rio Rita, 1942; Cabin in the Sky, Song of Russia, 1943; Meet the People, Hollywood Canteen, Can't Help Singing, Kismet, 1944; Centennial Summer, Stage Struck, California, 1946; Gay Purr-ee, 1962; Finian's Rainbow, 1969; also received a citation for his song Seems Like Happiness Is Just a Thing Called Joe from Cabin in the Sky, 1943; TV includes talk shows as well as specials devoted to his songs; author of Rhymes for the Irreverent, 1965, and At This Point in Rhyme, 1976;

received a DLitt, *honoris causa,* from the University of Vermont, May 1971; James K Hachett Award from City College, NY, 1972; elected to the Song Writer's Hall of Fame, 1973; Hon DFA, Columbia College, Chicago, 1978.

Recreation: Golf. *Club:* Mink Meadows Golf Club, Martha's Vineyard. *Address:* 262 Central Park West, New York, NY 10024. *Tel:* SU 7–6996.

HARDIMAN, Terrence, actor

b Forest Gate, London, 6 Apr 1937; *s* of Edward John Hardiman and his wife Rose (Breeden); *e* Buckhurst Hill County HS, Essex and Fitzwilliam House, Cambridge; *m* Rowena Cooper.

While at Cambridge played leading parts for the Marlowe Society and the ADC, of which he was President; made his professional debut at the Old Vic, Oct 1961, walking on in Dr Faustus; remained with the company until July 1962, playing small parts; 1962–5, repertory with the Bristol Old Vic, where his parts included Roderigo in Othello and Boyet in Love's Labour's Lost, Dauphin in Henry V; joined the Royal Shakespeare Company at Stratford, 1966; his appearances there included Ambitioso in The Revenger's Tragedy, 1966; Gremio in The Taming of the Shrew, Corin in As You Like It, 1967; Albany in King Lear, Mefistofilis in Dr Faustus, Don John in Much Ado About Nothing, 1968; John Littlewit in Bartholomew Fair (Aldwych), 1969; Lucio in Measure for Measure, Clarence in Richard III, Starveling in A Midsummer Night's Dream, 1970; at the Jeanneta Cochrane, Apr 1972, played Guppy in Lying Figures; Thorndike, Leatherhead, Oct 1973, Benedick in Much Ado About Nothing; same theatre May 1974, Bernard Link in After Haggerty; Oxford Playhouse, 1976, played Horner in The Country Wife; Greenwich, Oct 1976, Hunt in Scribes; Haymarket, Oct 1977, Mortensgaard in Rosmersholm; Hampstead, Jan 1979, David Lister in Daughters of Men; Old Vic, Nov 1979, appeared in The Undisputed Monarch of the English Stage; has lectured and performed at American universities as a member of the Actors in Residence project; first appeared on television, 1964; recent appearances include *Secret Army*; films include Pope Joan.

Recreations: Writing, drawing, listening to music. *Address:* 20 Elgin Mansions, Elgin Avenue, London, W9 1JG. *Tel:* 01–286 3927.

HARDING, John, actor and dramatic author

b Uxbridge, Middx, 20 June 1948; *s* of Kenneth William Harding and his wife Hilary (Thomson); *e* Pinner G S and Manchester University (BA Hons in Drama); *m* Gillian Heaps.

Made his first stage appearance as the rear half of Buttercup, the Cow, in Jack and the Beanstalk, New Theatre, Bromley, Dec 1969; at Greenwich, Nov 1970, played Whitaker in The Long and the Short and the Tall; spent a period with Theatre Centre, 1971, touring schools and directing; made his West End debut as James in My Fat Friend, Globe, 6 Dec 1972; Hornchurch, 1973, appeared as Antipholus in The Comedy of Errors; Crucible, Sheffield, 1974, Sir Andrew Aguecheek in Twelfth Night; Globe, July 1976, Taylor in Donkey's Years; Actors' Company tour and Round House, Nov 1977–8, John Worthing in the Importance of Being Earnest, and Elegant Man in Do You Love Me; Chichester Festival Theatre tour, 1978, Arnold in The Circle; for the National Theatre at the Olivier, 1978–9, he played the following parts: Mellifont in The Double Dealer, Edgar Anthony in Strife, Vasily in The Fruits of Enlightenment, Kreindl in Undiscovered Country and Richmond in Richard III; co-wrote (with John Burrows) and also appeared in For

Sylvia, 1972, The Golden Pathway Annual, 1973, Loud Reports (also with Peter Skellern), 1975; The Manly Bit, 1976; co-author of the musical Dirty Giant, 1975; has appeared in For Sylvia on television, and in Do You Dig It?, which he wrote with John Burrows.

Recreations: Squash, Rock'n'roll. *Address:* c/o Larry Dalzell Associates, 3 Goodwin's Court, St Martin's Lane, London WC2.

HARDWICK, Paul, actor

b Bridlington, Yorks, 15 Nov 1918; *s* of George Hardwick and his wife Edith Anne (Malton); *e* Bridlington School, and University of Birmingham (BA).

Made his first appearance on the stage at the Piccadilly Theatre, Dec 1946, when he played Scarus in Antony and Cleopatra; Aldwych, Dec 1947, played Old Siward in Macbeth; joined the Shakespeare Memorial Company, Stratford, 1948, and remained a member for three seasons; at the Phoenix, London, June 1951, played Cleomenes in The Winter's Tale, and Jan 1952, Conrade in Much Ado About Nothing; Lyric, Hammersmith, Dec 1952–May 1953, was a member of John Gielgud's Company and played in Richard II, The Way of the World, and in Venice Preserv'd; Phoenix, Nov 1953, played the Major-Domo in The Sleeping Prince; Palace, Aug 1954, played Monsieur D'Argenson in Sabrina Fair; toured Europe as a member of the Shakespeare Memorial Company in Titus Andronicus, June 1957, subsequently appearing at the Stoll, July 1957; Shakespeare Memorial Company, Stratford-on-Avon, 1958, during which time he played a variety of parts including Camillo in The Winter's Tale, Morocco in The Merchant of Venice, and Antiochus in Pericles; toured the USSR, 1958–9, in Hamlet and Romeo and Juliet; became a long-term contract player when the Shakespeare Memorial Theatre was re-named the Royal Shakespeare, Jan 1961, and has since played the following parts: Roderigo in Othello, Pischik in The Cherry Orchard, 1961; the Duke in As You Like It, Provost in Measure for Measure, Bottom in A Midsummer Night's Dream, Baptista in The Taming of the Shrew, Sergeant in Macbeth, Belarius in Cymbeline, 1962; made his first appearance in New York, with the same company, at the Henry Miller Theatre, Jan 1963, in The Hollow Crown; on returning to England played Bottom in A Midsummer Night's Dream, The Cardinal in The Representative, 1963; Buckingham in Edward IV and Richard III (The Wars of the Roses trilogy), Edmund Langley in Richard II, Pistol in Henry IV (Part II), Ancient Pistol in Henry V, Duke of Gloucester in Henry VI (The Wars of the Roses trilogy), 1964; Ancient Pistol in Henry V, 1965; The Charity Commissioner in The Government Inspector, 1966; Mercury, July 1966, for the International Theatre Club, played Philip Hassinger in Jenusia; Mermaid, Feb 1968, Second Reader in The Adventures of the Black Girl in Her Search for God, and Third Reader in Aerial Football: A New Game; for Prospect Productions at the Edinburgh Festival, Aug 1969, he played John of Gaunt in Richard the Second and the Earl of Warwick and Sir John Maltravers in Edward the Second, playing the same parts at the Mermaid (Sept), and the Piccadilly (Jan 1970); Criterion, Nov 1970, Dr Relling in The Wild Duck; at The Place, Oct 1971, General Ivoglin in the RSC's Subject to Fits; Edinburgh Festival, Sept, and Round House, Oct 1972, Lord Harvey in Stand and Deliver; several overseas tours, 1972–5, for RSC in The Hollow Crown, and Pleasure and Repentance; toured with Prospect, 1974, as Falstaff in both parts of Henry IV, including performances at the Round House, Sept; Comedy, June 1976, the Mayor in Signed and Sealed; for the Chichester Festival Theatre season, 1977, he appeared as Casca in

Julius Caesar, Boanerges in The Apple Cart and Robert Lancaster in Waters of the Moon, subsequently playing Boanerges at the Phoenix (Nov 1977), and Robert Lancaster at the Haymarket (Jan 1978); again at the Haymarket, Oct 1978, he played General Koschnadieff in Look after Lulu; Greenwich, Dec 1979, Mr Hardcastle in She Stoops to Conquer; since 1945, has appeared in a number of films, including: Dead Secret, Zeffirelli's Romeo and Juliet, Julius Caesar, etc; television productions in which he has appeared include many classics, notably, The Wars of the Roses, Sword of Honour (Waugh), The Possessed, What Maisie Knew, The Tempest, the series *Man at the Top*, and Churchill and the Generals.

Favourite parts: Bottom, and all the good ones. *Address:* c/o Plunket-Greene, 110 Jermyn Street, London, SW1. *Tel:* 01–930 0811.

HARDWICKE, Edward, actor
b London, 7 Aug 1932; s of Cedric Hardwicke and his wife Helena (Pickard); e Stowe School; m Anne Iddon; trained for the stage at RADA.

First appeared on the London stage in June 1954 at the Arts, walking on in The Impresario of Smyrna; from Sept 1954–7 appeared with the Bristol Old Vic Company in repertory, followed by seasons at the Old Vic, 1957–8; Oxford Playhouse, 1959–60; Vaudeville, Aug 1961, played Mr Muffle in Wildest Dreams; Saville, Apr 1962, Sam Young in Photo Finish; Vaudeville, 24 July 1963, Tailor and Justice in The Provoked Wife; joined the National Theatre company, 1964, playing parts including Montano in Othello, 1964; Camille Chandebise in A Flea in Her Ear and Ben in Love for Love, 1966; toured Canada in these two parts, 1967; took over the part of Rosencrantz, in Rosencrantz and Guildenstern are Dead, 1968; Anthony Witwoud in The Way of the World, Jacques in The White Devil, 1969; Lebedev in The Idiot, Praed in Mrs Warren's Profession, 1970; Guido Veranzi in The Rules of the Game, 1971; at the Palace, Watford, July 1973, played Howard Joyce in The Letter; at the Bristol Old Vic, Autumn 1973, his parts included Astrov in Uncle Vanya; Haymarket, Dec 1975, Richard Halton in On Approval; Arnaud, Guildford, Nov 1976, Sir Robert Chiltern in An Ideal Husband; Lyttelton (National Theatre Company), Oct 1977, played Dr Mongicourt in The Lady from Maxim's; Piccadilly, May 1979, Jack Hartnoll in Can You Hear Me at the Back?; his first film was Hell Below Zero, 1953; TV, since 1959, includes Son of Man, *Colditz*, and The Withered Arm.

Address: c/o ICM, 22 Grafton Street, London W1.

HARDY, Joseph, director and actor
b Carlsbad, New Mexico, 8 Mar 1929; s of Joseph A Hardy, Jr and his wife Edith Clare (Clement); e New Mexico Highland University (BA, MA, DFA), Yale University School of the Drama (MFA).

Directed his first play at the New Mexico Highlands University, Las Vegas, New Mexico, May 1951, when he staged Hands Across the Sea and The Shoemaker's Prodigious Wife; directed his first play in New York, The Streets of New York, at the Maidman Playhouse, Oct 1963; since then has directed Dark Corners, Mr Grossman, Thieves' Carnival, 1964; Berlin's Mine, Night of the Dunce, 1966; You're a Good Man, Charlie Brown, Johnny No-Trump, House of Flowers, 1967; directed his first play in London, You're a Good Man, Charlie Brown, at the Fortune, 1 Feb 1968; Play It Again, Sam (also London), 1969; Child's Play, for which he received the Antoinette Perry (Tony) Award, What the Butler Saw, Bob and Ray, The Two and Only, 1970; You're a

Good Man, Charlie Brown (revival), Child's Play (Queen's, London), 1971; Children! Children!, The Real Inspector Hound, After Magritte, 1972; Gigi, and at the Ahmanson, Los Angeles, Cyrano de Bergerac, The Crucible, 1973; Dorothy Chandler Pavilion, Los Angeles, The King and I, and at the Ahmanson, The Time of the Cuckoo, 1974; Ahmanson, Ring Round the Moon, The Night of the Iguana, 1975; The Baker's Wife (Dorothy Chandler), The Night of the Iguana (NY), 1976; Diversions and Delights (San Francisco and NY), 1978; Romantic Comedy (NY), 1979; has also directed productions of You're a Good Man, Charlie Brown in San Francisco, Los Angeles, Boston, Toronto, and Chicago; entered films as a producer, 1967, with Dr Glas; has produced on television the serials *Love of Life, A Time for Us, Ben Jerrod, Love Is a Many Splendored Thing,* commencing in 1959; has directed many plays for PBS; directed Great Expectations for ITV/NBC..

Address: Creative Artists Agency, 9300 Wilshire Boulevard, Beverly Hills, Ca 90210.

HARDY, Robert, actor
b 29 Oct 1925; s of Maj Henry Harrison Hardy and his wife Jocelyn (Dugdale); e Rugby and Magdalen College, Oxford; m (1) Elizabeth Fox (mar dis); (2) Sally Pearson.

Began his career as a member of the Shakespeare Memorial Theatre Company, 1949, subsequently visiting Australia with the company, Oct 1949, when he played among other parts Banquo in Macbeth; on returning to England, appeared with the Memorial Theatre Company, Stratford-on-Avon, 1950–1; made his first London appearance at the Phoenix, Jan 1952, as Claudio in Much Ado About Nothing; Lyric, Hammersmith, Sept 1952, played Dick Frewer in The River Line, transferring with the production to the Strand, Oct 1952; joined the Old Vic Company, May 1953, to play the Lord Chamberlain in the Coronation production of Henry VIII, rejoining the company at the Old Vic, Sept 1953, to play the following parts: Laertes in Hamlet, Sebastian in Twelfth Night, Titus Lartius in Coriolanus, Ariel in The Tempest, Duncan in Macbeth, Dumaine in Love's Labour's Lost, Hortensio in The Taming of the Shrew, 1954; Thomas Mowbray and the Bishop of Carlisle in Richard II, Prince Henry in Henry IV (Parts I and II), 1955; at the Edinburgh Festival, Aug 1955, played Admetus in A Life in the Sun; toured, autumn, 1955, as Pierre in The Captain's Lamp; made his first appearance on Broadway at the John Golden Theatre, Feb 1956, as Martin in Someone Waiting; on returning to London at the Hippodrome, June 1956, played Lieut Willis Seward Keith in The Caine Mutiny Court Martial; Phoenix, Apr 1957, played Byron in Camino Real; Cort, New York, Sept 1957, played Jeremy Paget in Four Winds; rejoined the Shakespeare Memorial Theatre Company, Stratford-on-Avon, for the season, 1959, to play the following parts: King of France in All's Well That Ends Well, Oberon in A Midsummer Night's Dream, Sicinius Velutus in Coriolanus, and Edmund in King Lear; Comedy, Feb 1960, took over the part of Rosmer in Rosmersholm; Bristol Old Vic, Mar 1961, played The Count in The Rehearsal, subsequently transferring with the production to the Globe, Apr 1961; at the Bristol Old Vic, May 1963, played Martin Lynch-Gibbon in A Severed Head, transferring with the production to the Criterion, July 1963; left the cast to appear at The Ravinia Festival, Illinois, Aug 1964, to play the title parts in Henry V and Hamlet; New, June 1967, for Prospect Productions, played Sir Harry Wildair in The Constant Couple; Fortune, Dec 1969, Robert in I've Seen You Cut Lemons; Lyric, Feb 1974, took over as Dr Wicksteed in Habeas Corpus; he has appeared in numerous television productions, including the series *An Age of Kings, Elizabeth, Edward VII*, Twelfth Night, and *All Creatures Great and Small*; films include Ten Rillington Place, Young Winston, and Yellow Dog; author of the documentary films The Picardy Affair, The Longbow, and Horses in Our Blood, and of the book, Longbow.

Address: c/o Chatto and Linnit, Globe Theatre, Shaftesbury Avenue, London W1.

HARE, David, dramatic author
b Sussex, 5 June 1947; *s* of Clifford Theodore Rippon and his wife Agnes (Gillmour); *e* Lancing and Jesus College, Cambridge; *m* Margaret Matheson.

Co-founder of Portable Theatre, a travelling experimental group, 1968–71; literary manager, Royal Court Theatre, 1969–70; Resident Dramatist 1970–1; Resident Dramatist, Nottingham Playhouse, 1973; co-founder Joint Stock Theatre group, 1974; he has written the following plays: How Brophy Made Good, 1969; Slag (Hampstead), What Happened to Blake, 1970; The Rules of the Game, adapted (National Theatre), Layby, collaboration (Traverse), 1971; The Great Exhibition (Hampstead), England's Ireland, collaboration (Round House), 1972; Brassneck (with Howard Brenton, Nottingham), 1973; Knuckle (Comedy), 1974; Fanshen (Joint Stock), Teeth 'n' Smiles (Royal Court), 1975; Plenty (National Theatre), 1978; Slag received the *Evening Standard* Award, 1970, and Knuckle the John Llewellyn Rhys Award, 1974; plays he has directed include Christie in Love (Portable Theatre), 1969; Brassneck, The Pleasure Principle (Theatre Upstairs), 1973; The Party (National Theatre tour), 1974; Teeth 'n' Smiles, 1975; Weapons of Happiness (National Theatre), 1976; Devil's Island (Royal Court), 1977; Plenty, 1978; his most recent plays for television, Licking Hitler (BAFTA best TV play, 1978), and Dreams of Leaving, which he also directed himself.

Recreation: Golf. *Address:* c/o Margaret Ramsay Ltd, 14a Goodwin's Court, St Martin's Lane, London WC2. *Tel:* 01–240 0691.

HARE, Doris, MBE, actress and singer
b Bargoed, Mon, 1 Mar 1905; *d* of Herbert Edwin Hare and his wife Kate (Tansley); *m* Dr J Fraser Roberts.

Has been on the stage since early childhood, having made her first appearance at the age of three, at the Alexander Portable Theatre, Bargoed, when she appeared in Current Cash; appeared in fit-ups, music-halls and choruses; made her first appearance in London, at the Palace, Walthamstow, 1916, as Sally in The Scarlet Clue; has toured in revue all over Great Britain and Ireland, in Australia, South Africa, etc; in 1930, toured in Gracie Fields' part in The Show's the Thing; at the Adelphi, Sept 1932, appeared in Words and Music; at the Comedy, 1933, in How d'you do?; Comedy, Oct 1934, Hi-Diddle-Diddle; Coliseum, Apr 1935, played Kathie in Dancing City; Prince of Wales's, Sept 1935, appeared in Voilà! Les Dames; made her first appearance in New York, at the Ethel Barrymore Theatre, 28 Sept 1936, as Mrs Terence in Night Must Fall; Saville, London, Nov 1937, appeared in It's In the Bag, and May 1938, in Pélissier's Follies of 1938; Apollo, Nov 1938, Toinette in The Robust Invalid; Savoy, Feb 1940, appeared in Lights Up; Holborn Empire, Aug 1940, in Apple Sauce; Adelphi, June 1945, played Sans-Gêne in Sweet Yesterday; Saville, Apr 1947, appeared in 1066 and All That; Trocadero, Elephant and Castle, Dec 1947, played Colin in Mother Goose; Duke of York's, Aug 1948, appeared in Four, Five, Six!; New Lindsey, Nov 1950, played Amalie in Symphonie Pastorale; St Martin's, July 1952, Nellie in Lion's Corner; Winter Garden,

Sept 1953, Mrs Southern in Lucky Boy; New Watergate, Nov 1953, appeared in the revue The Pleasure of Your Company; at Eastbourne, July 1954, appeared as the Duchess of Wistburgh in A Horse! A Horse!; Winter Garden, Aug 1955, played Mrs Higgins in The Water Gipsies; Adelphi, Nov 1956, appeared with the Lady Ratlings in The Lady Ratlings on Parade; Lyric, Hammersmith, Oct 1958, played Grannie Tooke in Valmouth, subsequently transferring with the production to the Saville, Jan 1959; Lyric, Hammersmith, Sept 1959, appeared as Sheena Mulvaney, Dame Enid Stillwell, Hesta Cropper, and Wilma Wurtz in The Quiz Kid; Royal Court, Dec 1961, played Babette Biedermann in The Fire Raisers, and Mrs Bouncer in Box and Cox (double-bill); Pembroke, Croydon, Mar 1962, Mrs Mundy in The Prince of Portobello; Arts, July 1962, played the Mother of Leantio in Women, Beware Women; joined the Royal Shakespeare Company, 1963, as a long-term contract artist, and played the following parts: Aldwych, Jan 1963, Matron Marta Bell in The Physicists; June 1963, Fairy Matron in A Midsummer Night's Dream; July 1963, Mrs Peachum in The Beggar's Opera; June 1964, Meg in The Birthday Party, Mrs Trevis in Afore Night Come; Oct 1964, Katherine in The Jew of Malta; Dec 1964, Mistress Quickly in The Merry Wives of Windsor; Chichester Festival, for the National Theatre Company, July 1965, played Mrs Mossop in Trelawny of the 'Wells', and Miss Furnival in Black Comedy; Old Vic, Nov 1965, again played Mrs Mossop in Trelawny of the 'Wells', and Mar 1966, again played Miss Furnival; Piccadilly, Nov 1966, Momma in Man of Magic; Chichester Festival, May–July 1967, played Mary Hearn in The Farmer's Wife and Nurse Guinness in Heartbreak House, transferring in the latter part to the Lyric, Nov 1967; toured, autumn 1972, as Sally Blunt in Fiddlers Three; toured, autumn 1973, as Gertrude in Birds of Paradise, Strand, 1974, took over the part of Eleanor Hunter in No Sex Please, We're British; Oct 1977, toured as the Nurse in Romeo and Juliet; Haymarket, Jan 1978, played Mrs Ashworth in Waters of the Moon; toured South America and Israel as Mrs Swabb in Habeas Corpus, 1978; during the 1939–45 War, broadcast regularly as Commère to *Shipmates Ashore*, and was awarded the MBE for services to the Merchant Navy; TV appearances include *She'll Have to Go*, and Why Didn't They Ask Evans? (1980).

Recreation: Gardening. *Address:* 7 Cavendish Street, Chichester, Sussex. *Tel:* 0243–785880.

HARE, Ernest Dudley, actor
b Highgate, London, 5 Dec 1900; *s* of George Dudley Hare and his wife Ellen Annie (Rickard); *e* Highgate; *m* Gladys Muriel Newbury-Thomas; was formerly engaged as a reporter.

Made his first appearance on the stage at the London Hippodrome, 14 June 1920, in the chorus of Jig Saw; Holborn Empire, Dec 1923, played the Genie of the Carpet in Where the Rainbow Ends; during 1924, played repertory at Stratford-on-Avon Memorial Theatre; in 1925, played a season at the Théâtre Albert 1, Paris; appeared at Stratford, 1926–32; then played with the Hull Repertory company; subsequently toured in the United States and Canada; Holborn Empire, Dec 1932, again played the Genie of the Carpet in Where the Rainbow Ends; Phoenix, May 1933, Joe in High Temperature; joined the company of the Old Vic-Sadler's Wells, Sept 1933, playing Antonio in Twelfth Night, Abergavenny and Suffolk in Henry VIII, Sebastian in The Tempest, Trapland in Love for Love, Duncan and Siward in Macbeth, and Denis Tregoning in The Voysey Inheritance, also playing the last-mentioned part at the Shaftesbury, May 1934; Royalty, June 1934, played Hindley Earnshaw in

Wuthering Heights; Old Vic, Sept 1934, Agrippa in Antony and Cleopatra; His Majesty's, Nov 1934, Ockles and Feather-stone in Mary Read; Playhouse, Dec 1935, Pembroke and Norfolk in Mary Tudor; Arts, Apr 1936, Major Ogilvy in Indian Summer; Gate, May 1936, Parnell in the play of that name; Queen's, Sept 1936, the Inspector in Follow Your Saint; Old Vic, Nov 1936–Apr 1937; The Duke in As You Like It, Carter in The Witch of Edmonton, Marcellus in Hamlet, Antonio in Twelfth Night, Cambridge and Williams in Henry V; June 1937, appeared at Elsinore Castle, with Old Vic company as Marcellus in Hamlet; Queen's, Sept 1937, played Ross, Salisbury, and the Gaoler in Richard II; Nov 1937, Trip in The School for Scandal; Apr 1938, Tubal in The Merchant of Venice; Ambassadors', July 1938, appeared in Spring Meeting; Old Vic, Sept 1938, Mr Ablett in Trelawny of the 'Wells'; Oct 1938, Marcellus in Hamlet (in its entirety and modern dress); Jan–Apr 1939, toured with Old Vic company on the Continent and in Egypt; Old Vic, June 1939, played Dr Williams in The Ascent of F6; Queen's, Sept 1939, William Tabb in Rebecca; rejoined the Old Vic company, Sept 1939, at Buxton, playing Godolphin in Viceroy Sarah, and in Oct 1939, at Streatham Hill, played in Romeo and Juliet, The Devil's Disciple, The Good-Natured Man, and Stogumber in Saint Joan; Queen's, Apr 1940, Mr Fortescue in Rebecca; toured with the Old Vic company, 1941–2, in the industrial centres, in Shakespearean repertory; at the New Theatre, July 1941, played Hubert in King John, and Creon in Medea, and July 1942, Montano in Othello, and Page in The Merry Wives of Windsor; appeared with the company, at the Liverpool Playhouse, from Dec 1942, played the Father in Six Characters in Search of an Author, Ferrovius in Androcles and the Lion, and Seward in Abraham Lincoln; Arts Theatre, Feb 1944, Master Joannes in The Witch; joined the Haymarket repertory company, with John Gielgud, Oct 1944, and during the season, played Voltimand, the Captain, and Francisco in Hamlet, Snug in A Midsummer Night's Dream, and the Marquis of Pescara in The Duchess of Malfi; toured, Oct 1945, in India and Burma, with John Gielgud, as Claudius in Hamlet; New, June 1946, played the Ex-Soldier in Crime and Punishment; Aldwych, Jan 1947, played Wilson in Jane; toured, during Mar 1947, as Lord Augustus Lorton in Lady Windermere's Fan; with the Bristol Old Vic, Dec 1947, played Madgwick in Great Expectations; Prince of Wales's, Jan 1949, William R Chumley, MD, in Harvey, subsequently touring in the same part, 1950; joined the Old Vic Company for the 1951–2 season, appearing as Ortygius in Tamburlaine the Great, Mr Sterling in The Clandestine Marriage, the Duke of Albany in King Lear and the First Senator in Timon of Athens; at the Zurich Festival, 1952, appeared with the Old Vic Company in Timon of Athens; joined Donald Wolfit's Company at the King's, Hammersmith, for the season Feb–Apr 1953, and played Creon in Œdipus, the Earl of Kent in King Lear, Sir Toby Belch, the Duke in The Merchant of Venice, Duncan and Siward in Macbeth, Andrea Michelotti in The Wandering Jew, and Vincentio in The Taming of the Shrew; remained with the company for a second season, Aug–Nov 1953, playing a further wide range of parts; at the Arts, Sept 1954, appeared as Mr Perkup in The Diary of a Nobody; toured Australia with the Old Vic Company, 1955, as Baptista in The Taming of the Shrew, the Duke in The Merchant of Venice, and the Provost in Measure for Measure; Haymarket, Jan 1956, José Bustillos in The Strong Are Lonely; joined the Old Vic Company, May 1956, and played the following parts: Ross in Macbeth, Capulet in Romeo and Juliet, Northumberland in Richard II, prior to appearing with the same company at the Winter Garden, NY, Oct 1956, in the same productions; also

in addition, Dec 1956, played Ajax in Tyrone Guthrie's production of Troilus and Cressida; Richmond, Surrey, Oct 1957, played Sir John Laverton in Fact and Friction; toured, Sept 1958, as the Farmer in The Broken Jug; Savoy, May 1968, played Lord Derby in The Queen's Highland Servant, and later at the Leeds Festival; Phoenix, July 1974, the General in Bloomsbury; films include All the Way Up, Percy, and International Velvet; television appearances include Special Duties and, recently, Waxwork.

Recreation: Golf. *Address:* Stonehill Cottage, St Leonard's, Nr Tring, Herts. *Tel:* Cholesbury 315.

HARE, Will, actor
b Elkins, West Virginia, 30 Mar 1919; *s* of George Thomas Hare and his wife Frances Laetitia (Satterfield); *e* grammar school in Richmond, Virginia, high school in Baltimore, Md; prepared for the stage at the American Actors' Theatre.

First appeared in New York at the Manhattan Opera House, 1937, in The Eternal Road; at the Martin Beck, Apr 1942, played in The Moon Is Down; Cort, 12 Jan 1944, played Danny Feeley in Suds in Your Eyes; Bijou, Apr 1944, played Albert Price in Only the Heart; Henry Miller's Oct 1944, Joe Willard in The Visitor; Theatre de Lys, June 1953, Maitreya in The Little Clay Cart; Henry Miller's, Nov 1953, Houston Ticket Man in The Trip to Bountiful; Henry Miller's, 1955, took over as the Court Stenographer in Witness for the Prosecution; East End, Mar 1962, directed The French Way; ANTA, Dec 1963, played in Marathon '33; Actors Playhouse, Jun 1965, Mr Jackson in Live Like Pigs; Theatre de Lys, Jan 1967, Old Man in The Viewing; Greenwich Mews, Mar 1968, Frank Elgin in Winter Journey; Mercer-O'Casey, Feb 1972, Dylan Thomas in Dylan; Anspacher/Public, May 1972, played in Older People; Actors Studio, Jan 1973, Perry Wilson in I want to Go to Vietnam; McAlpin Rooftop, Apr 1973, Fox Malarkey in Crystal and Fox; Vivian Beaumont, Dec 1973, took over as the Harold in Boom Boom Room; Actors Studio, Dec 1973, James Tyrone in Long Day's Journey into Night; Manhattan Theatre Club, Aug 1974, Davies in The Caretaker; Actors Studio, Oct 1974, Deeley in Old Times; Theatre de Lys, Jan 1975, played in The Long Valley; has also played Estragon in Waiting for Godot at the Charles Street, Boston, 1970, and He in He Who Gets Slapped, Deeley in Old Times, etc; first appeared in films in Alfred Hitchcock's The Wrong Man, 1956, and has since played in The Effect of Gamma Rays on Man-in-the-Moon Marigolds, etc; has appeared regularly on television for the past 20 years, most recently as Albert Cluveau in The Autobiography of Miss Jane Pitman (1975), The Rimers of Eldritch, etc.

Favourite parts: Dylan Thomas, He, and Deeley in Old Times. *Address:* 233 Hillspoint Road, Westport, Conn., 06880. *Tel:* 203–227 7208.

HARPER, Gerald, actor
b London, 15 Feb 1929; *s* of Ernest George Harper and his wife Mary Elizabeth (Thomas); *e* Haileybury; *m* (1) Jane Downs (mar dis); (2) Carla; formerly a medical student; trained for the stage at RADA 1949–51.

First appeared on the London stage Apr 1951, at the Arts, as He in How He Lied to Her Husband and in two other parts; at this theatre he played in three further Shaw programmes, May–June 1951; Knobby in Right Side Up, 1951; Freddie Perkins in Mrs Dot, Sept 1951; Dupont-Dufort Jr in Thieves' Carnival, Jan 1952; joined the Liverpool repertory company, 1952–3; returned to the Arts, Feb 1953, as Nöjd in The Father; Cambridge, Sept 1954, Ernest Very in No News From Father; Embassy, June 1955, Lionel Proudfeet in The

Lion in the Lighthouse; Globe, Dec 1955, Jack Chesney in Charley's Aunt; Savoy, June 1957, Jack Amersham in Free as Air; Theatre-in-the-Round, London, Nov 1957, Theramenes in Phèdre; made his New York debut at the Broadway, Sept 1958, as Sebastian in Twelfth Night, in an Old Vic Season; Haymarket, May 1960, A/c Dickinson in Ross; returned to NY, Feb 1965, to play Bernard in Boeing-Boeing at the Cort; Globe, Sept 1965, Roy in Comfort Me With Apples; Greenwich, Mar 1970, Chateau-Renaud in The Corsican Brothers; Round House, Mar 1971, Orator and Ponocrates in Rabelais; Greenwich, July 1971, Jacques Offenbacque in Fish Out of Water; Fortune, Sept 1971, Glenn Howard in Suddenly at Home; Arnaud, Guildford, Nov 1973, James Pettit in My Son's Father; Bristol Old Vic, Mar 1974, Iago in Othello; Duke of York's, Oct 1974, Henry in the Oxford Festival production of The Little Hut; Vaudeville, May 1976, played Michael in Baggage; Whitehall, Mar 1977, David Clifton in In the Red; Arnaud, Guildford, Jan 1978, the Prince Regent in The Sleeping Prince, also tour; Haymarket, 1979, took over the part of Sherlock Holmes in The Crucifer of Blood; films, since 1955, include The Dambusters, The Shoes of the Fisherman, Tunes of Glory, and The Lady Vanishes; he has his own radio programme, and has appeared frequently on television since 1956, notably in the series *Adam Adamant* and *Hadleigh*, playing the title part in each.

Recreations: Eating, riding, reading other people's letters. *Address:* c/o Larry Dalzell, 14 Clifford Street, London, W1. *Tel:* 01-499 3811.

HARRIS, Barbara (*née* Markowitz) actress
b Evanston, Illinois, 1937; *d* of Oscar Harris and his wife Natalie (Densmoor); prepared for the stage with Paul Sills.

Made her stage début in 1959 with the Playwrights Theatre Club, Chicago; joined the Second City, an improvisational theatre group, in Chicago, 1960; made her New York début at the Royale, 26 Sept 1961, in From the Second City; Phoenix, May 1962, played Rosalie in Oh Dad, Poor Dad, Mama's Hung You in the Closet and I'm Feelin' So Sad, and received the Obie Award for this performance; rejoined the Second City group and at the Square East, May 1962, appeared in Seacoast of Bohemia and Alarums and Excursions; Martin Beck, Mar 1963, played Yvette Pottier in Mother Courage and Her Children; Second City at Square East, Sept 1963, played in When the Owl Screams; Square East, Jan 1964, played in Open Season at Second City; York, Mar 1964, Tlimpattia in Dynamite Tonight; Mark Hellinger, Oct 1965, Daisy Gamble in On a Clear Day You Can See Forever; Shubert, Oct 1966, Eve, Passionella, Ella, and Princess Barbara in The Apple Tree and won the Antoinette Perry (Tony) Award for this performance; Royale, Oct 1969, directed the Penny Wars; Anderson, Apr 1970, Jenny in Mahagonny; appeared in the film A Thousand Clowns, 1965, and later in Oh, Dad, Poor Dad, Mixed Company, Nashville, etc.

Address: Actors Equity Association, 165 West 46th Street, New York, NY 10036.

HARRIS, Julie, actress
b Grosse Pointe Park, Michigan, 2 Dec 1925; *d* of William Pickett Harris and his wife Elsie (Smith); *e* Grosse Pointe Country Day School; *m* (1) Jay I Julien (mar dis); (2) Manning Gurian (mar dis); (3) Walter E Carroll; trained for the stage with Charlotte Perry at the Perry–Mansfield Theatre Workshop, Steamboat Springs, Colorado; attended Yale University School of the Drama, 1944–5.

Made her first appearance in New York at the Playhouse, Mar 1945, as Atlanta in It's a Gift; Century, NY, Mar 1946, appeared as a member of the Old Vic Company, in Henry IV,

Part II, and also in Œdipus; Booth, Oct 1946, played Nelly in a revival of The Playboy of the Western World; International, NY, Apr 1947, played the White Rabbit in Alice in Wonderland, transferring with this production to the Majestic, May 1947; National, Mar 1948, appeared as a Weird Sister in Michael Redgrave's Macbeth; Belasco, Sept 1948, played Ida Mae in Sundown Beach; Fulton, Nov 1948, played Nancy Gear in The Young and the Fair; Mansfield, Apr 1949, Angel Tuttle in Magnolia Alley; Fulton, Oct 1949, Delisa in Montserrat; Empire, Jan 1950, Frankie Adams in The Member of the Wedding, which ran for more than a year; Empire, Nov 1951, played Sally Bowles in I Am a Camera, and toured with this play; Longacre, Jan 1954, played Colombe in Mlle Colombe; Longacre, Nov 1955, played Jeanne d'Arc in Anouilh's The Lark, and also toured with the production; Adelphi, Nov 1957, played Margery Pinchwife in The Country Wife; Helen Hayes, Oct 1959, played Ruth Arnold in The Warm Peninsula; at the Stratford Shakespearean Festival, Ontario, June 1960, played Juliet in Romeo and Juliet, and Blanche in King John; Longacre, Dec 1960, Brigid Mary Morgan in Little Moon of Alban; Booth, Oct 1961, Josefa Lantenay in A Shot in the Dark; ANTA, Dec 1963, June (Havoc) in Marathon '33; Delacorte, June 1964, Ophelia in Hamlet; Brooks Atkinson, Dec 1964, Annie in Ready When You Are, CB!; Lunt-Fontanne, Nov 1965, Georgina in the musical Skyscraper; Tappen Zee Playhouse, Nyack, NY, June 1967, Blanche du Bois in A Streetcar Named Desire; Morosco, Dec 1968, Ann Stanley in Forty Carats, for which she received the Antoinette Perry (Tony) Award; Repertory, New Orleans, 1970, played in The Women; Morosco, Mar 1971, Anna Reardon in And Miss Reardon Drinks a Little; toured, 1971–2, in this last part; Ethel Barrymore, Apr 1972, Claire in Voices; ANTA, Dec 1972, Mary Lincoln in The Last of Mrs Lincoln, and received the Tony for this part; Vivian Beaumont, Dec 1973, Mrs Rogers in The Au Pair Man; Morosco, Dec 1974, Lydia Cruttwell in In Praise of Love; Longacre, Apr 1976, gave a solo performance as Emily Dickinson in The Belle of Amherst, subsequently touring in the part, including a season at the Phoenix, London, Sept 1977; Palace, NY, Apr 1979, Gertie Kessel in Break a Leg; Ahmanson, LA, Feb 1980, Ethel Thayer in On Golden Pond; first entered films in 1952, playing her original parts in The Member of the Wedding and I Am a Camera, and has since appeared in East of Eden, Reflections in a Golden Eye, The People Next Door, Requiem for a Heavyweight, The Hiding Place, Voyage of the Damned, etc; television appearances include: The Lark, Little Moon of Alban, Johnny Belinda, A Doll's House, Anastasia, Pygmalion, The Holy Terror, The Heiress, The Power and the Glory, He Who Gets Slapped, and Victoria Regina.

Address: c/o Actors Equity Association, 165 West 46th Street, New York, NY 10036.

HARRIS, Margaret F, designer
b Shortlands, Kent, 28 May 1904; *d* of William Birkbeck Harris and his wife Kathleen (Carey); *e* Downe House, Kent.
See under Motley.
Recreation: Sailing. *Address:* 40 Smith Square, London SW1P 3HL.

HARRIS, Robert, actor
b 28 Mar 1900; *s* of A Herschell Harris and his wife Sarah (Anstie); *e* at Sherborne School and New College, Oxford; studied for the stage at the Royal Academy of Dramatic Art, and received the Reandean scholarship at the Critics' Circle Schools of Acting Competition, July 1923.

Made his first appearance on the professional stage at the St Martin's Theatre, 15 Aug 1923, as Sennett in The Will; at the Lyric, Hammersmith (for the Fellowship of Players), Sept 1923, played Florizel in The Winter's Tale; at the St Martin's, Nov 1923, played Max in Fledglings; at the Queen's, Nov 1923, understudied Owen Nares in The Little Minister; Jan 1924, played Nicholas Draicott in A Magdalen's Husband; at the Ambassadors', Jan 1924, Phoenix in the play of that name; Feb 1924, Martin Farren in The Way Things Happen; at the Regent (for the Fellowship of Players), July 1924, Silvius in As You Like It; in Aug 1924, went on tour, playing the Rev Gavin Dishart in The Little Minister; at Drury Lane, Dec 1924, appeared as Oberon in A Midsummer Night's Dream; Regent (for the Fellowship of Players), Feb 1925, Prince Henry in King Henry IV (Part II); Everyman, Mar 1925, Timothy Carstairs in The Painted Swan; New Oxford, Apr 1925, The Caliph in Kismet; with the Birmingham Repertory Company, May 1925, played St Bernard in The Marvellous History of St Bernard; St Martin's, July 1925, Lieut Oswald in The Show; Court (for 300 Club), July 1925, and Playhouse, Aug 1925, Second-Lieut Grayle in Prisoners of War; then went to New York, and appeared at the Empire, Dec 1925, as John Whittaker in Easy Virtue; Kingsway, Apr 1926, again played The Marvellous History of St Bernard; Everyman, Oct 1926, played Keld Maxwell in The Rat Trap; Criterion, Feb 1927, Jacques Rijar in The Marquise; Regent (for the 300 Club), May 1927, David in a play of that name; Globe, May 1928, Archie Pretty in Mud and Treacle; Arts, July 1928, Basil Tripp in Down Wind; again went to NY, and at the Henry Miller, Nov 1928, played Maurice Tabret in The Sacred Flame; on returning to London, appeared at the Little, June 1929, as George in Water; Apollo, Sept 1929, Tony Quinton in Yesterday's Harvest; Ambassadors', Oct 1929, Philip Gore in A Girl's Best Friend; Royalty, Dec 1929, Con Delaney in The Amorists; Comedy, Apr 1930, Anthony Howard in The Silent Witness; Arts, May 1931, Arthur Kingsley in The Mantle; joined the Old Vic-Sadler's Wells Company, Sept 1931, and played the Dauphin in King John, Lucentio in The Taming of the Shrew, Oberon, Chorus in Henry V, Mark Antony in Julius Caesar, the Chronicler in Abraham Lincoln, Cassio, Feste, and Hamlet; New, June 1932, the Earl of Oxford in Richard of Bordeaux; St Martin's, Sept 1932, Val in Strange Orchestra; St Martin's, May 1933 (for RADA Players), Frank in Love for Sale; Shaftesbury, July 1933 (for Overture Players), Louis Constantine in Laying the Devil; St Martin's, Oct 1933, Charles Tritton in The Wind and the Rain, which ran for over two years; Shaftesbury, Feb 1936, Thierry Keller in Promise; Garrick, Nov 1936, succeeded Roger Livesey as Frank Burdon in Storm in a Teacup; Lyceum, NY, Dec 1936, John Keats in Aged 26; Empire, NY, Mar 1937, Eugene Marchbanks in Candida; Westminster, London, Nov 1937, Orin Mannon in Mourning Becomes Electra; Westminster, Sept 1938, to Mar 1939, with the London Mask Theatre, Troilus in Troilus and Cressida (in modern dress), Robert Caplan in Dangerous Corner, Kublai, the Great Khan, in Marco Millions, Anatol in A Farewell Supper, Mr Devizes, senr, in The Will, and Downing in The Family Reunion; Globe, Mar 1939, Nigel in We at the Crossroads; St James's, June 1939, David Scott-Fowler in After the Dance; Westminster, Oct 1939, David Sheil in Music at Night, and Dec 1939, Adolphus Cusins in Major Barbara; Old Vic, Apr 1940, Edgar in King Lear; went overseas, Feb 1944, to play for ENSA, as Denys Royd in Quiet Week-End, and played the same part at Wyndham's, Apr 1944; Aldwych, Aug 1944, appeared as Michael Frame in To-Morrow the World, which ran for a year; Lyric, Hammersmith, Jan 1946, played Witts in Death of a Rat;

went to Stratford-on-Avon Memorial Theatre, Apr 1946, to play leading parts; remained there for the 1947 season, playing Prospero, Escalus, Richard II, Faustus in Doctor Faustus; His Majesty's, Oct 1947, played Escalus in Romeo and Juliet, and Richard II; Arts, Apr 1948, Robert in Break-Up; St Martin's, Nov 1948, Gregers Werle in The Wild Duck; Piccadilly, May 1949, Mr Capes in Ann Veronica; St Martin's, Aug 1950, John Rosmer in Rosmersholm; at the Booth, NY, Nov 1950, appeared as Gregory Black in Edwina Black; Arts, London, July 1951, Edward Mission Walker in Poor Judas; Embassy, Oct 1952, William Lamb in Caro William; at Westminster Abbey, June 1953, appeared as Dr Fountaine in Out of the Whirlwind; Gaiety, Dublin, Feb 1954, played Maximilian, Count von Erdenstein, in The White Countess; at the Saville, London, Mar 1954, appeared as Hugo Klaren in the same play; New, Jan 1955, Sir Richard Alleyn in The Night of the Ball; Royal, Nottingham, Sept 1955, Don Pedro di Miura in The Strong Are Lonely and appeared in this part at the Piccadilly, Nov 1955, and Haymarket, Jan 1956; joined the Shakespeare Memorial Theatre Company, Stratford-on-Avon, for the 1957 season, and played the title-part in King John, Jaques in As You Like It, the title-part in Cymbeline, and Alonso in The Tempest, appearing with the company in the last production at Drury Lane, Dec 1957; Old Vic Company, 1959–61, played John of Gaunt in Richard II, Peter Cauchon in St Joan, Lord Burleigh in Mary Stuart, Peter Quince in A Midsummer Night's Dream, the title-part in Henry IV part I, and Shylock in The Merchant of Venice; toured the USA, 1963–4 as Sir Thomas More in A Man For All Seasons; Brooks Atkinson, NY, Aug 1964, took over Pope Pius XII in The Deputy; Hampstead Theatre Club, Oct 1966, played the name part in In The Matter of J Robert Oppenheimer, transferring to the Fortune, Nov 1966; Edinburgh Festival, Sept 1968, General Manning Mannon in Mourning Becomes Electra; Court House Theatre, Niagara-on-the-Lake, Ontario, summer season, 1970, played the Headmaster in Forty Years On; Lyceum, Edinburgh, Oct 1970, the Prime Minister in The Hero; Arnaud, Guildford, 1971, the Judge in Make No Mistake; recent films include: Ransom, and Love Among the Ruins; recent TV includes Henry V, and Edward and Mrs Simpson.

Clubs: Garrick, Chelsea Arts. *Address:* c/o Green and Underwood, 3 The Broadway, Gunnersbury Lane, London W3 8AP.

HARRIS, Rosemary, actress
b Ashby, Suffolk, 19 Sept; d of Stafford Berkley Harris and his wife Enid Maude Frances (Campion); m (1) Ellis Rabb (mar dis); (2) John Ehle.

First appeared on the stage at the Roof Garden Theatre, Bognor Regis, 1948, in Winter Sunshine; spent over two years in repertory, and then became a student at the Royal Academy of Dramatic Art for a year; made her first appearance in New York at the Martin Beck, Nov 1952, as Mabel in The Climate of Eden; first appeared in London at the Aldwych, 14 May 1953, as The Girl in The Seven Year Itch; toured, 1954, as Lucasta Angel in The Confidential Clerk; with the Bristol Old Vic Company, Oct 1954–Apr 1955, appeared as Beatrice in Much Ado About Nothing, Elizabeth Proctor in The Crucible, Françoise Piquetot in Image in the Sun, Portia in The Merchant of Venice, Isabel in The Enchanted, Mrs Golightly in The Golden Cuckoo and Hermione in The Winter's Tale; at the Old Vic, Sept 1955, played Calpurnia in Julius Caesar, and, later in the season, Dorcas in The Winter's Tale, Desdemona in Othello, and Cressida in a modern dress production of Troilus and Cressida; appeared in the same production, and with the same company, at the Winter Garden, NY, Dec 1956; ANTA, Feb 1958, played Hilde in Interlock; Coronet, Dec 1958, played Jere Halliday in The Disenchanted; joined the Group 20 Players in Wellesley, Mass, 1958–9 season, and played Eliza Doolittle in Pygmalion, Beatrice in Much Ado About Nothing, Ann Whitefield in Man and Superman, and Peter Pan; Helen Hayes, Feb 1960, played Lennie in The Tumbler; joined the Association of Producing Artists repertory company, directed by Ellis Rabb, and between 1960–2, toured the US in the following parts: Lady Teazle in The School for Scandal, Bianca in The Taming of the Shrew, Cecily in The Importance of Being Earnest, Gabrielle in Anatole, Phoebe in As You Like It, Ann Whitefield in Man and Superman, Nina and Madame Arkadina in The Seagull, Viola in Twelfth Night, Titania in A Midsummer Night's Dream, and Virginia in The Tavern; at the Chichester Festival, England, July 1962, played Constantia in The Chances, and Penthea in The Broken Heart; with the APA, at the University of Michigan, Ann Arbor, Aug 1962–Mar 1963, played Regina in Ghosts, Lady Teazle in School for Scandal, Virginia in The Tavern, The Girl in We Comrades Three, Duchess of Gloucester in Richard III, and Portia in The Merchant of Venice; Chichester Festival, July 1963, played Ilyena in Uncle Vanya; Old Vic, Oct 1963, played Ophelia in the National Theatre Company's inaugural production of Hamlet, subsequently appearing as Ileyna in Uncle Vanya, and as the First Woman in Play, Apr 1964; with the APA at the University of Michigan, Sept 1964, played the title-part in Judith, Natasha in War and Peace, and Violet in Man and Superman, subsequently appearing at the Phoenix, NY, with the same company Dec 1964; Ann Arbor, Michigan, Oct 1965, played Megara in Herakles; Lyceum, NY, Nov 1965, Alice in You Can't Take It with You; Ambassador, Mar 1966, Eleanor in The Lion in Winter, for which she received the Antoinette Perry (Tony) Award; Lyceum, for the APA-Phoenix 1966–7 season, played Gina in The Wild Duck, Signora Ponza in Right You Are, Natasha Rostora in War and Peace, Lady Teazle in School for Scandal, and again played Alice in You Can't Take It with You; Lyric, London, Feb 1969, Karen Nash, Muriel Tate and Norma Hubley in Plaza Suite, for which she received the *Evening Standard* best actress award; Ahmanson, Los Angeles, Mar 1970, Irene in Idiot's Delight; Billy Rose, Nov 1971, Anna in Old Times; Vivian Beaumont, Mar 1973, Portia in The Merchant of Venice, and Apr 1973, Blanche Du Bois in A Streetcar Named Desire; Brooklyn Academy of Music, 17 Dec 1975, Julie Cavendish in The Royal Family; transferred with this production to the Helen Hayes, 30 Dec 1975; for the BAM Theater Company, 1977, played Vida Phillimore in The New York Idea, Mar, and Olga in Three Sisters, Apr; Williamstown Theatre Festival, 1978, Natalia Petrovna in A Month in the Country; Kennedy Center, Washington DC, 1979, appeared in Home and Beauty; has appeared in the films Beau Brummell, The Shiralee, A Flea in Her Ear, The Boys from Brazil, etc; first appeared on television in England in Cradle of Willow, 1951, and has since played there and in US in Othello, The Prince and the Pauper, Twelfth Night, Wuthering Heights, Notorious Woman, Holocaust, and *The Chisholms*.

Address: c/o Milton Goldman, ICM, 40 West 57th Street, New York, NY 10019, *and* c/o Lawrence Evans, ICM, 22 Grafton Street, London W1.

HARRISON, John, director
b London, 7 June 1924; *s* of George Henry John Harrison and his wife Florence Emily (Cockram); *e* Sir Walter St John's School, London; *m* (1) Daphne Slater (mar dis); (2) Linda

Gardner; trained for the stage at the Birmingham Repertory Theatre, where he made his acting debut in 1944.

Member of Birmingham repertory company 1944–5; with Stratford Memorial Theatre Company 1946–7, playing parts including Benvolio and Chorus in Romeo and Juliet (also London debut, His Majesty's, 6 Oct 1947), Longaville in Love's Labour's Lost, Ferdinand in The Tempest, and the Dauphin in Henry V; toured Australia with Anew McMaster, 1949, as Cassio in Othello, Ghost in Hamlet; director of productions, David Garrick theatre, Lichfield, 1949; Nottingham Playhouse, 1952–7; Artistic Director, Birmingham Repertory Theatre, 1962–6; Director, Leeds Playhouse, 1972–; has also directed at Bristol, Zagreb, Chicago, and in London, where his productions include Pericles, 1950; Hamlet, 1951; The Easter Man, 1964; The Tempest (from Leeds), 1975; Bergen International Festival, 1979, and UK tour, directed his Leeds production of Every Good Boy Deserves Favour; is the author of the plays Gone to Ground, 1968; Unaccompanied Cello, 1970; Knight in Four Acts, 1973, and of many TV scripts; has also directed and produced for television.

Recreation: Music, reading, doing nothing. *Address:* c/o Leeds Playhouse, Calverley Street, Leeds. *Tel:* 42141.

HARRISON, Kathleen, actress
b Blackburn, Lancs, 23 Feb 1898; *d* of Arthur Harrison and his wife Alice Maud (Parker); *e* Clapham High School; *m* J H Back; studied for the stage at the Royal Academy of Dramatic Art, 1915–16; she then married and went to live abroad for eight years.

On her return she appeared at the Pier Theatre, Eastbourne, 28 June 1926, as Mrs Judd in The Constant Flirt; made her first appearance in London, at the Savoy, 22 July 1927, as Winnie in The Cage; at the Court, Aug 1928, played Florrie in Aren't Women Wonderful?; Jan 1929, went on tour playing Albertina Keggs in A Damsel in Distress; Garrick, Oct 1929, Selina in Happy Families; Prince of Wales's, June 1930, Mary in Badger's Green; Nov 1930, Helen in The Man Who Kissed His Wife; Piccadilly (for the Repertory Players), Dec 1930, Florrie Smallwood in The Merchant and Venus; Duchess, Dec 1930, Daisy Ford in Jane's Legacy; Prince of Wales's, June 1931, Burton in Lovers' Meeting; Haymarket, Dec 1931, Graves in Can the Leopard . . .?; Arts, Nov 1932, the Girl in Other People's Lives; Dec 1932, Jenny Simons in Silver Wedding; at the Westminster, Feb 1934, Edith in Private Room; Q, July 1934 and Duke of York, Oct. 1934, Minnie in Line Engaged; Duchess, May 1935, Mrs Terence in Night Must Fall; St James's, Dec 1936, Mrs Quill in O Mistress Mine; Q, Oct 1937, Julia in Square Pegs; Whitehall, Dec 1937, Polly in I Killed the Count; Haymarket, June 1938, Winkie in Comedienne; Duchess, Sept 1938, Mrs Watty in The Corn is Green; Apollo, Nov 1941, Judy in Ducks and Drakes; Apollo, Aug 1942, Mrs Miller in Flare Path, which ran until 1944; toured in the Middle East, 1944, with Emlyn Williams, in Flare Path, Blithe Spirit, Night Must Fall; Lyric, May 1946, Violet in The Winslow Boy; Vaudeville, Mar 1949, played Mrs Tennyson in A Woman's Place; Duchess, Feb 1950, Mrs Holmes in Flowers for the Living; Lyric, Hammersmith, Jan 1951, Mrs Jones in The Silver Box; Haymarket, Apr 1951, appeared as Mrs Ashworth in Waters of the Moon; toured, 1953, as Mabel Fuller in The Gentle Rain; Duke of York's, Sept 1954, played Nannie Cartwright in All For Mary; Globe, Nov 1956, played Cherry-May Waterton in Nude with Violin; Aldwych, Apr 1959, played Gladys Pudney in How Say You?; Aldwych, Feb 1960, Emma Hornett in Watch It Sailor!; Chichester Festival, July 1962, played the

Landlady in The Chances; Duchess, May 1963, Dora in Norman; toured, June 1964, as Rose in Smith by any Other Name; Hampstead Theatre Club, Oct 1964, played Mrs Watty in The Corn is Green; Yvonne Arnaud Theatre, Guildford, July 1965, Mrs Frush in Thark, transferring with the production to the Garrick, Aug 1965; toured in All for Mary and Goodnight Mrs Puffin, 1970; Harvey, 1971; Young Vic, Feb 1972, played Mrs Hardcastle in She Stoops to Conquer; has appeared in numerous films since 1931; television appearances include Mrs Thursday, Shades of Greene, Our Mututal Friend, and Danger UXB.

Address: c/o Plunket Green Ltd, 91 Regent Street, London W1R 8RU. *Tel:* 01–437 5191.

HARRISON, Rex, actor
b Huyton, Lancs, 5 Mar 1908; *s* of William Reginald Harrison and his wife Edith (Carey); *e* Liverpool College; *m* (1) Noel Marjorie Collette Thomas (mar dis); (2) Lilli Palmer (mar dis); (3) Kay Kendall (dec); (4) Rachel Roberts (mar dis); (5) Elizabeth Harris (mar dis); (6) Mercia Tinker.

Made his first appearance on the stage at the Liverpool Repertory Theatre, Sept 1924, as the Husband in Thirty Minutes in a Street, and remained with the company until 1927; subsequently toured in Charley's Aunt, Potiphar's Wife, Alibi, The Chinese Bungalow, A Cup of Kindness; made his first appearance in London at the Everyman Theatre, 26 Nov 1930, as the Hon Fred Thrippleton in Getting George Married; Prince of Wales's, Feb 1931, played Rankin in The Ninth Man; during 1931, played repertory at Cardiff, and toured as Ralph in After All; toured 1932, in Other Men's Wives and For the Love of Mike; Lyric, London, 1933, appeared in Another Language; during 1933–4, toured in Road House and Mother of Pearl; Whitehall, London, May 1934, played Peter Featherstone in No Way Back; Piccadilly (for Repertory Players), Nov 1934, John Murdoch in Our Mutual Father; Fulham, Nov 1934, Anthony Fair in Anthony and Anna; St Martin's, Feb 1935, Paul Galloway in Man of Yesterday; Queen's, Nov 1935, Mark Kurt in Short Story; Aldwych (for Repertory Players), Jan 1936, Rodney Walters in Charity Begins . . .; made his first appearance on the New York stage, at the Booth Theatre, 2 Mar 1936, as Tubbs Barrow in Sweet Aloes; returned to London and appeared at the St Martin's, June 1936, as Tom Gregory in Heroes Don't Care; Criterion, Nov 1936, played the Hon Alan Howard in French Without Tears, in which he played for over a year; Haymarket, London, Jan 1939, played Leo in Design for Living; Haymarket, Mar 1941, Gaylord Easterbrook in No Time for Comedy, which ran a year; joined the RAFVR, 1942; released 1944, and appeared in the films Blithe Spirit, I Live in Grosvenor Square, and The Rake's Progress; went to Hollywood, 1945, where he made half-a-dozen pictures; Shubert, NY, Dec 1948, played Henry VIII in Anne of a Thousand Days; New Theatre, London, May 1950, appeared as the unidentified Guest in The Cocktail Party; Ethel Barrymore, NY, Nov 1950, played Shepherd Henderson in Bell, Book and Candle; New Century, Feb 1952, played Hereward in Venus Observed; Shubert, Jan 1953, appeared as The Man in The Love of Four Colonels, and directed the production; Phoenix, London, Oct 1954, directed Bell, Book and Candle, and appeared as Anthony Henderson, the play running for over a year; Haymarket, July 1955, directed Nina; Mark Hellinger, NY, Mar 1956, played Henry Higgins in the world première of My Fair Lady; after two years with the company, he left to appear in the London production at Drury Lane, Apr 1958; Winter Garden, Dec 1958, directed The Bright One; returned to NY, ANTA, Dec 1959, and played the General in Jean Anouilh's The Fighting Cock;

Royal Court, London, Oct 1960, played the title-part in Platonov, receiving the *Evening Standard* Award, 1961, for this performance; Edinburgh Festival, and Royal Court, London, Sept 1961, played Sir Augustus Thwaites in August for the People; Lyric, Nov 1969, Lionel Fairleigh in The Lionel Touch; toured North America, 1973, including NY, in the title role of Pirandello's Henry IV; played the same part at Her Majesty's, London, Feb 1974; Morosco, NY, Dec 1974, played Sebastian Crutwell in In Praise of Love; Chichester, 1976, M Perichon in M Perichon's Travels; Palace, NY, Feb 1977, Caesar in Caesar and Cleopatra; Biltmore, Dec 1978, Cecil in The Kingfisher; first entered films, 1929, and has appeared in innumerable pictures; recent films include: My Fair Lady (Academy Award for Best Film Actor, 1964), Dr Doolittle, Staircase, The Agony and the Ecstasy, and A Flea in Her Ear; awarded the Order of Merit (Italy), 1966.

Favourite parts: Higgins, Caesar. *Clubs:* Green Room, Garrick, and Beefsteak, London; Players, New York; Travellers', Paris. *Address:* c/o ICM Ltd, 22 Grafton Street, London, W1.

HART, Diane, actress
b Bedford, 20 July 1926; *d* of James George Hart and his wife Eleanor (O'Rourke); *e* Abbot's Hill School, King's Langley; *m* Kenneth Macleod; trained for the stage at RADA in 1941, leaving after two terms.

First appeared on the stage in 1943 at Finsbury Park Empire as a Feed in a Comedy Sketch with Pat Aza; made her first London appearance in Oct 1944 at the Apollo as Paula Rainey in Daughter Janie; Embassy, June 1947, played Betty in Miranda; Vaudeville, Aug 1947, Bessie in The Chiltern Hundreds making her first New York appearance in the same part at the Booth, Oct 1949; Criterion, Oct 1950, Daphne, Nora and Doris in Who is Sylvia; Lyric, Oct 1952, took over Susan in The Little Hut; Arts, Mar 1953, played Cyprienne des Prunelles in her adaptation of Divorce à la Carte; Ambassadors, Nov 1953, took over for six months as Mollie Ralston in The Mousetrap; Phoenix, Nov 1964, played Suzanne Leroy in Every Other Evening; Vaudeville, Nov 1967, Mrs Allonby and Lady Stutfield in A Woman of No Importance; Vaudeville, July 1968, Joan Cadwallader in The Man Most Likely To; Royal Court (Upstairs), Sept 1970, Mother in Cheek; same theatre, Jan 1971, Mrs Er . . . Um in Morality; Vaudeville, 1972, took over as Joanna Markham in Move Over, Mrs Markham; Everyman, Cheltenham, Apr 1974, played the title role in Mrs Dot; Genée, East Grinstead, July 1974, Susan Clifton in The Bank Manager; Arnaud, Guildford, Mar 1975, Mavis in Miss Adams Will Be Waiting; first film, 1946; more recent appearances include Enter Inspector Duval and Games Lovers Play; TV, also since 1946, includes plays and series.

Recreations: Politics and annoying critics. *Address:* 5 Ordnance Hill, St John's Wood, London, NW8. *Tel:* 01–722 3579

HARVEY, Frank, actor, dramatic author and director
b Manchester, 11 Aug 1912; *s* of Frank Harvey and his wife Grace (Akerman); *e* Wellington (Som), and St Catharine's College, Cambridge; *m* Margaret Inchbold.

Made his first appearance on the stage, June 1934, at the Festival Theatre, Cambridge, in The Young Idea; is the author of Murder To-Morrow? 1938; Saloon Bar, 1939; Brighton Rock (adaptation), 1943; The Poltergeist, 1946; Elizabeth of Ladymead, 1948; The Non-Resident, 1950; The Chertsey Apprentice, 1952; Norman, 1963; The Station Master's Daughter, 1967; The Day After the Fair, 1972· The

Prospect Behind Us, 1973; has also written many screenplays.
Recreations: Beer and skittles. *Clubs:* Savage and Dramatists'. *Address:* East Hill, Ottery St Mary, Devon. *Tel:* Ottery 2709.

HARVEY, Peter, designer
b Quirigua, Guatemala, 2 Jan 1933; *s* of Francis William Harvey and his wife Zena Erica (Henriquez); *e* Ridley College, St Catherine's, Ontario, Bolles School, Jacksonville, Florida, and the University of Miami, Coral Gables, Florida.

First designs for the stage were at the Dade County Auditorium, 24 Apr 1954, for the ballet Pantomime for Lovers (décor and costumes); first designs for New York were at the Theatre Marquee, 28 Sept 1959, for The Confederates; since then has designed the décor for Noontide, The Thracian Horses, One Way Pendulum, 1961; Plays for Bleecker Street, PS 193, 1962; Put It in Writing, The Immoralist (also costumes), 1963; Baby Want a Kiss (also costumes), Noye's Fludde (also costumes) (opera), 1964; All Women Are One (costumes), The Sweet Enemy (also costumes), All in Good Time (costumes only), Good Day, The Exhaustion of Our Son's Love (also costumes), 1965; The Mad Show, Hooray! It's a Glorious Day . . . And All That (also costumes), Concerning Oracles (also costumes), ballet, Brahms-Schoenberg Quartet, ballet, The Butter and Egg Man (also costumes), 1966; The Death of the Well-Loved Boy, Walking to Waldheim, Happiness, The Jewels, ballet, 1967; The Boys in the Band, Red Cross, Muzeeka, Sweet Eros, Witness, Dames at Sea (also costumes), 1968; designed his first London production for The Boys in the Band, Wyndham's, Feb 1969, and, Aug 1969, designed Dames at Sea at the Duchess; returned to America and designed the sets and costumes for Watercolor, Criss-Crossing, Transfers, Park, and designed the décor for Exchange, One Night Stands of a Noisy Passenger, The Nuns, and The Survival of St Joan (sets and costumes), 1970; décor and costumes for The Survival of St Joan, décor for Johnny Johnson, Dramatized Anthology of Puerto Rican Short Stories, 1971; Keep Off the Grass (tour), 1972; Welcome to Andromeda, Variety Obit, The Children's Mass (also costumes), 1973; Sextet, Kaboom, 1974; Black Picture Show, A Letter for Queen Victoria, Straws in the Wind, The Government Inspector, (Hartman, Stamford, Conn), 1975; The Sorrows of Frederick (also costumes), 1976; Unsung Cole, 1977; The Effect of Gamma Rays on Man-in-the-Moon Marigolds (also costumes), A Midsummer Night's Dream (ballet, Zürich), 1978; TV work includes décor for four ballets in WNET's Dance in America series; has taught scenic and costume design at the Pratt Institute since 1970.
Address: 121 Prince Street, New York, NY. *Tel:* 473 8136

HARWOOD, Ronald, (*né* Horwitz), playwright
b Cape Town, South Africa, 9 Nov 1934; *s* of Isaac Horwitz and his wife Isobel (Pepper); *e* Sea Point Boys' High School, Cape Town; *m* Natasha Riehle; trained for the stage at RADA.

An actor from 1952–59, including tours with Sir Donald Wolfit's company, and a season with the 59 Theatre Company, Lyric Hammersmith, 1959; author of the plays Country Matters, produced Manchester, 1969; The Ordeal of Gilbert Pinfold (from Evelyn Waugh's novel), 1977; A Family, 1978; The Dresser, 1980; librettist for The Good Companions, 1974; writing for television includes The Barber of Stamford Hill, Private Potter (with Casper Wrede), and a documentary about Waugh, A Sense of Loss; presenter, 1978–79, of the programme Read All About It; author of a biography of Wolfit, 1971, and a number of novels including The Girl in Melanie Klein and Articles of Faith (Winifred Holtby Prize);

member of the Literature Panel of the Arts Council; chairman, Writers Guild.
Club: Garrick. *Address:* Berrygrove House, West Liss, Hampshire.

HASSO, Signe (*née* Signe Larssen), actress
b Stockholm, Sweden, 15 Aug 1918; *d* of Kefas Larsson and his wife Helfrid (Lindström); *m* Harry Hasso (mar dis).

Made her first appearance on the stage, 1928, in The Imaginary Invalid, at the Royal Dramatic Theatre, Stockholm; gained a scholarship to the Royal Dramatic Academy, Stockholm; played Manuela in Maids in Uniform, 1934 as leading lady at the Blanche Theatre, Stockholm; returned to the Royal Dramatic Theatre and has appeared in classical plays in Scandinavia, Austria, etc, in parts including Norah in The Doll's House, Hilda in The Master Builder, and also in works by Strindberg, Eugene O'Neill, Maxwell Anderson, and other dramatists, in addition to numerous Shakespeare productions; made her first appearance on the New York stage, at the Cort Theatre, 8 Dec 1941, as Judith in Golden Wings; first appeared on the London stage at the St Martin's Theatre, 22 Aug 1950, as Rebecca West in Rosmersholm; Booth Theatre, NY, Nov 1950, played Elizabeth Graham in Edwina Black; Lyceum, Oct 1951, played Maud Abbott in Glad Tidings; in summer theatres, 1952, appeared in Love from a Stranger; 4th Street, NY, Jan 1956, played Elena Andreevna in Uncle Vanya; Plymouth, Oct 1956, Orinthia in The Apple Cart; US tour as Miss Madrigal in The Chalk Garden, 1957; Edinburgh, and Lyric, Hammersmith, London, May 1958, Stella in The Key of the Door; toured America in The Frenzy of Peace and Quiet, summer 1958; Lilla, Stockholm, Jan 1959, appeared in The Final Moment, marking her return to the Swedish theatre after a twenty-year absence; toured America in the title-role of Mary Stuart, 1959–60; in Stockholm, 1960–1, again played in The Final Moment; Paramus, NJ, Aug 1961, starred in Five Finger Exercise; Upsala and Stockholm, 1963, played in Pirandello's The Mountain Giants; Curran, San Francisco, Sept 1963, Rina Gives in The Tender Heel; US tour with the National Repertory Theatre in Liliom and Hedda Gabler, 1964–5; Circle, Kansas City, Mo, Apr 1967, Miss Alice in Tiny Alice; Broadhurst, NY, 1967, took over from Lotte Lenya the role of Fraülein Schneider in Cabaret, and toured in this part in 1968–9; Palm Beach, Fla, 1973, title-role in Colette; toured, 1975, as Mrs Jolly in Come and Be Killed; Folkan Theatre, Stockholm, Oct 1978, played Madame Armfeldt in A Little Night Music; has received many awards, including the Angers de Wahl Award for Maids in Uniform, 1934; the Swedish Film Academy Award for Career, 1937, the first Scandinavian award ever given to an actor or actress in the theatre, 1939; was knighted by the King of Sweden, 1972, with the Royal Order of Vasa; received the Grand Prix d'Edison, 1965, for her lyrics to Scandinavian Folk Songs, etc; her many notable films include The House on 92nd Street, Seventh Cross, Heaven Can Wait, A Double Life, etc, also numerous Swedish and Australian films; has appeared regularly on television in Europe and America in such plays as Reunion in Vienna, The Two Mrs Carrolls, Camille, Mary Stuart, Colette, etc; writes her own songs and short stories, and is the author of the novels Momo, 1977, and Kom Stott, 1978, as well as a book of poems, Hoppa Hage (Verbal Lace), 1979.
Favourite part: Miss Alice in Tiny Alice. *Interests:* Medicine, philosophy. *Address:* 215 West 90th Street, New York, NY 10024.

HASTINGS, Hugh, actor, pianist and dramatist
b Sydney, NSW, 31 Jan 1917; *s* of Hugh James Williamson

and his wife Margaret (Du Veen); *e* Fort Street High School, Sydney; formerly a cow-hand, a schoolteacher, assistant film director, etc.

Made his first appearance on the stage in Sydney, 1935, as Kit in Cat's Cradle; after coming to England, was engaged with the Dundee Repertory company, 1939, and St Andrews Repertory company, 1939–40; during the War, served in the Royal Navy, for five-and-a-half years; made his first appearance in London, at the Ambassadors', 1946, in Sweetest and Lowest; during 1947, toured in Murder Without Crime, and as Duke in Worm's Eye View, and with the Arts Council, as Algy in The Importance of Being Earnest; during 1948, was engaged as director for H J Barlow's Repertory company, at the Wednesbury Hippodrome; subsequently toured in Fly Away Peter; toured, 1948–9, in House on the Sand; New Lindsey, Nov 1952, played Rolf in his own play, Touch of the Sun; Irving, May 1954, appeared in the revue Do Look In; New Arts, Sept 1966, contributed some original material to and appeared in A Matter of Choice, also touring with the production; 1970, partnered Bill Pertwee in cabaret; Royal Court, Dec 1972, played Father in A Sense of Detachment; joined the Young Vic company, 1974, with whom he toured in America and Australia; during five years with the Company, his parts included the Headwaiter in Scapino; Brabantio/Gratiano in Othello; Brassett in Charley's Aunt, Maingot in French Without Tears, Willie in Happy Days, Araminta Ditch in All Walks of Leg, Baptista in The Taming of the Shrew, Merriman in The Importance of Being Earnest, Lord Coote in If You're Glad, I'll Be Frank, etc; is the author of Seagulls Over Sorrento, 1949; Red Dragon, 1950; Inner Circle, Touch of the Sun, 1952; Pink Elephants, 1955; Blood Orange, 1958; Scapa! (also composed the music), 1962; Purple Patch, 1963; The Tattoo Parlour, 1965; Green Carnation, The Boy, 1973.

Recreations: The theatre, and watching cricket. *Address:* c/o Eric Glass Ltd, 28 Berkeley Square, London, W1.

HASTINGS, Michael, playwright
b Brixton, 2 Sept 1938; *s* of Max Emmanuel Gerald Hastings and his wife Marie Catherine; *e* in Brixton; *m* Victoria Hardie; conscripted by George Devine to work at the Royal Court Theatre as trainee actor and writer; formerly an apprentice in bespoke tailoring.

His first play to be produced was Don't Destroy Me, seen at the New Lindsey, 25 Jul 1956; has since written Yes and After, produced 1957; The World's Baby, 1963; The Silence of Lee Harvey Oswald, 1966 (published as Lee Harvey Oswald: A Far Mean Streak of Indepence Brought on by Negleck, 1966); The Silence of Saint-Just, 1971; For the West (Uganda), 1977; Gloo Joo, 1978; Full Frontal, 1979; Carnival War a Go Hot, 1979; Midnight at the Starlight, 1980; and another unperformed autobiographical play, The Cutting of the Cloth, 1973; writing for TV includes For the West (Congo), 1965, Blue as His Eyes the Tin Helmet He Wore, and Murder Rap, 1980; author of five novels including The Game, 1957, Tussy Is Me, 1968, and And in the Forest the Indians, 1975, as well as a book of short stories, biographies of Rupert Brooke and Sir Richard Burton, and a collection of poems.

Address: 2 Helix Gardens, Brixton Hill, London SW2.

HAUSER, Frank, CBE, director
b Cardiff, 1 Aug 1922; *s* of Abraham Hauser and his wife Sarah (Corne); *e* Cardiff High School, and Christ Church, Oxford.

Began his career, 1948, as a Drama Producer with the BBC, where he remained until 1951; first theatre engagement, New, London, May 1951, co-directed Hamlet (with Alex Guinness); Arts, Salisbury, resident director, 1952–3; St James's, May 1953, directed The Uninvited Guest; appointed Artistic Director of the Midland Theatre Company, 1954–5, and his production of The Queen and the Rebels at Coventry, was transferred to the Haymarket, Oct 1955, with substantially the same cast; Director of the Meadow Players at the Oxford Playhouse, 1956–74; the following Oxford productions transferred to London: Dinner With The Family, 1957; The Hamlet of Stepney Green, 1958; Rollo, 1959; A Passage To India, Candida, 1960; Hamlet, Heartbreak House, 1961; The Genius and the Goddess, 1962; Misalliance, Divorce à la Carte, 1963; A Heritage and its History, 1965; Volpone, 1966; The Promise (also New York), 1967; Kean (which he also translated), 1971; The Wolf, 1973; he also directed the Oxford Playhouse Company for the following tours: Holland, Switzerland, and Italy, 1958; Portugal, Copenhagen, Switzerland, Italy, 1959; and a tour to India, Pakistan, and Ceylon (under the auspices of the British Council), 1959; directed Hamlet at the Roman Theatre, Verona, Italy, 1963, and Twelfth Night (Stratford, Conn), 1966; directed La Traviata (Sadler's Wells), 1960; Iolanthe (Sadler's Wells), 1962; Orfeo (Sadler's Wells), 1965; Il Matrimonio Segreto (Glyndebourne), 1965; Cinderella (London Casino: also wrote), 1974; Twelfth Night, (St George's, Islington), 1976; All for Love (Old Vic), 1977; The Beaux' Stratagem (Melbourne), 1978; Canaries Sometimes Sing (tour), The Alchemist (Melbourne), 1979.

Recreation: Piano. *Club:* Savile. *Address:* 5 Stirling Mansions, Canfield Gardens, London NW6.

HAVERGAL, Giles, Director, Citizens' Theatre, Glasgow
b Edinburgh, 9 June 1938; *s* of Dr Henry MacLeod Havergal, and his wife Margaret Graham Hyacinth (Chitty); *e* Harrow, and Christ Church, Oxford.

Directed his first professional production in Apr 1963, at Oldham Repertory Theatre Club, with How Are You Johnny?; artistic director, Palace, Watford, 1966–8, directing plays including The Silk Room, Sweet Bird of Youth and The Spoils; appointed director, Citizens', Glasgow, 1969; his productions there include The Milk Train Doesn't Stop Here Any More, Nicholas Nickleby, Hamlet, The Taming of the Shrew, and, since 1970, a series of John Gould/Myles Rudge pantomimes; appointed Regent's Lecturer in Drama, University of California, Santa Barbara, 1978–.

Recreations: Reading, music. *Address:* Citizens' Theatre, Glasgow, C5. *Tel:* 041–429 5561.

HAVOC, June (*née* Hovick), actress, playwright and director
b Seattle, Washington, 8 Nov 1916; *d* of John Olav Hovick and his wife Rose; *m* William Spier; sister of the late Gypsy Rose Lee.

Has been on the stage since she was a child, having appeared first in pictures, and later in vaudeville on the Orpheum Circuit; subsequently appeared in vaudeville and also with the Municipal Opera company, St Louis; first appeared in musical comedy at the New Amsterdam Theatre, 2 Nov 1936, as Rozsa in Forbidden Melody; subsequently appeared in Chicago, in The Women; at the Ethel Barrymore, Dec 1940, played Gladys in Pal Joey; in films in Hollywood, 1941–3; Winter Garden, Jan 1944, Montana in Mexican Hayride; Alvin, Nov 1944, Sadie in Sadie Thompson; Plymouth, Oct 1945, Venetia Ryan in The Ryan Girl; Golden (for the Theatre Guild), Dec 1945, Ferne Rainier in Dunnigan's Daughter; in Cambridge, Mass, Aug 1946,

played Amy in They Knew What They Wanted; Coronet, 1946, took over Georgina Allerton in Dream Girl; at the Circle, Los Angeles, 1948, played Sadie Thompson in Rain, and Anna in Anna Christie; Music Box, New York, June 1951, succeeded Celeste Holm as Irene Elliott in Affairs of State; in summer theatres, 1952, appeared in Private Lives, and again played Sadie Thompson in Rain; Locust, Philadelphia, Nov 1957, played Rose Stone in One Foot in the Door; Phoenix, NY, Feb 1958, Queen Jocasta in The Infernal Machine; Shakespeare Festival, Stratford, Conn, June 1958, played Titania in A Midsummer Night's Dream; Phoenix, NY, Feb 1959, played Mrs Sullen in The Beaux' Stratagem; Helen Hayes, NY, Oct 1959, played Joanne de Lynn in The Warm Peninsula; toured European capitals and Israel for US State Department, appearing at the Théâtre des Nations, Paris, etc, spring 1961, as Sabina in The Skin of Our Teeth and as Kate Keller in The Miracle Worker; also toured South America for the State Department; ANTA, Dec 1963, directed Marathon '33 (adapted from her autobiography Early Havoc); Alvin, Sept 1966, Millicent Jordon in Dinner at Eight; toured, summer 1967, as Agnes in A Delicate Balance; Royal Poinciana Playhouse, Palm Beach, Florida, Feb 1968, Clea in Black Comedy; appointed Artistic Director of Repertory Theatre, New Orleans, La, 1969, and since has directed Luv, The Women, The Threepenny Opera (also played Jenny), A Streetcar Named Desire, The Fantasticks, The Skin of Our Teeth (also played Sabina), As You Like It, Love Regatta, for which she wrote the scenario and which she choreographed, Angel Street, The Elinor Glyn Liquid Memorial Love Regatta (in which she also played), The Burd, Androcles and the Lion, The Stolen Prince, Pinocchio, 1971; toured, 1972, as Beatrice in The Effect of Gamma Rays on Man-in-the-Moon Marigolds; Tyrone Guthrie, Sept 1973, Fanny Brads in her own play I, Said the Fly; Actors Studio, May 1974, directed her musical play A Glorious Tintinnabulation; toured, July 1975, as Phebe Moore and Florence Brown in Come and Be Killed; Martin Beck, Nov 1975, Mrs Swabb in Habeas Corpus; first appeared in films in 1918 and played in Hal Roach comedies 1918–24; later films include My Sister Eileen, Iron Curtain, Gentlemen's Agreement, Red Hot and Blue, A Lady Possessed, Story of Molly X, Can't Stop the Music (1980), etc; performed on more than 300 radio programs; made her television début in 1949 and has played dramatic roles since, including: Anna Christie, The Bear, Cakes and Ale, etc; in America, during the 1964–5 season, appeared in the color television series More Havoc; published a second volume of autobiography under this title, 1980; since 1978 has been engaged in the restoration of the historic village of Cannon Crossing in Connecticut.
Address: Cannon Crossing, Wilton, Ct 06897.

HAWK, Jeremy, actor
b Johannesburg, South Africa, 20 May 1918; s of Douglas Lange and his wife June (Langley); e Harrow; m Joan Heal (mar dis); formerly in the wool trade; trained for the stage at RADA.

Made his first appearance at the Theatre Royal, Huddersfield in 1936 as Travers in Housemaster; first London appearance Apr 1940, in the revue New Faces at the Comedy; St Martin's, Aug 1941, played Albert in Ladies in Retirement; Aldwych, Jan 1947, appeared in Jane; Whitehall, July 1947, played Capt Bracken, MC, in Whirlpool; Prince of Wales, Jan 1949, Dr Sanderson in Harvey; Lyric, Hammersmith, May 1951 and Globe, Sept 1951, appeared in The Lyric Revue; Comedy, Nov 1967, played Percival Browne in The Boy Friend; Apollo, Mar 1970, Mr Bassington in The Happy Apple; Savoy, Sept 1970, took over the part of Hugh Walford

in The Secretary Bird; St Martin's, Mar 1973, Greg Miles in Lover; toured, Autumn 1973, as Henry Lodge in Move Over Mrs Markham; Duke of York's, Apr 1974, took over as Victor Cadwallader in The Man Most Likely To . . ., subsequently touring in the same part; at the Arnaud, Guildford, played Clive Champion-Cheney in The Circle, Nov 1974, Uncle Ben in Death of a Salesman, Jan 1975, and Philip Logan in The First Mrs Fraser, Mar 1976; toured S Africa, 1975, in The Pay Off; 1976, toured as Philip Logan in The First Mrs Fraser; Her Majesty's, July 1977, John Davenport in Cause Célèbre; first appeared in films 1940; subsequent appearances include In Which We Serve, Who Done It? and Lucky Jim; has made many television appearances as compere and straight man for comedians such as Arthur Askey, Benny Hill and Norman Wisdom; compered Criss Cross Quiz for five years.
Recreations: Golf, bridge, skiing. *Club:* Green Room. *Address:* c/o Richard Stone, 18–20 York Buildings, London WC2.

HAWTHORNE, Nigel, actor
b Coventry, 5 Apr 1929; s of Dr Charles Barnard Hawthorne and his wife Agnes Rosemary (Rice); e Christian Brothers' College and the University of Cape Town.

Made his first professional appearance at the Hofmeyr Theatre, Cape Town, 5 Apr 1950, as Archie Fellowes in The Shop At Sly Corner; first London appearance Nov 1951 as Donald in You Can't Take It With You at the Embassy (Swiss Cottage); first West End appearance, after returning, 1957, to South Africa, as Fancy Dan in Talking To You at the Duke of York's, 4 Oct 1962; Apollo, May 1965, appeared in the revue Nymphs And Satires; toured, 1965, in Oh! What A Lovely War; Phoenix, Apr 1967, played the Angry Neighbour in In At The Death; Theatre Royal, Stratford, E, Nov 1967, Sir Oswald Stoll in The Marie Lloyd Story; Criterion, Dec 1967, joined the cast of Mrs Wilson's Diary as Roy Jenkins; Royal Court, Sunday, 31 Mar 1968, played Prince Albert in Early Morning; Sept 1968, same theatre, played various parts in Total Eclipse; also Count Wermuth in The Tutor; Royal Court, 1969, played the Commodore in Narrow Road To The Deep North, Feb; Prince Albert in Early Morning, Mar; Lord Touchwood in The Double Dealer, July; Commander Pemberton in Insideout, Dec; at Sheffield Playhouse, season 1970, his parts included Falstaff and Macbeth; 1970, Niall in Curtains at the Traverse Theatre for the Edinburgh Festival, also at the Open Space, Jan 1971; Feb 1971, for Cambridge Theatre Company, The Player in Rosencrantz and Guildenstern Are Dead; Royal Court, Aug 1971, Christopher in West of Suez, transferring to the Cambridge, Oct 1971; Soho Poly, Mar 1972, the Judge in The Trial of St George; April 1972, season at the Young Vic, where his parts included Face in The Alchemist, Baptista in The Taming of the Shrew, and Brutus in Julius Caesar; Royal Court, Dec 1972, the Chairman in A Sense of Detachment; May Fair, Mar 1973, took over as Philip in The Philanthropist; Hampstead, Nov 1973, and May Fair, Dec 1973, appeared in The Ride Across Lake Constance; Theatre Upstairs, Apr 1974, the Colonel in Bird Child; toured N America, June 1974, as Touchstone in the National Theatre production (all-male) of As You Like It, appearing at the Mark Hellinger, New York; Mermaid, Apr 1975, Cutler Walpole in The Doctor's Dilemma; Queen's, July 1975, Stephen in Otherwise Engaged; Opening of Riverside Studios, May 1976, Touchstone in As You Like It; Hampstead, Aug 1976, Owen in Clouds; Aldwych (RSC), Feb 1977, Major Giles Flack in Privates on Parade (Clarence Derwent Award, 1977, and SWET Best Supporting Actor

Award); King's Head, Mar 1977, Brian in Blind Date; Mermaid, Oct 1977, Abbé de Pradts in The Fire that Consumes; Haymarket, Dec 1978, Julius Sagamore in The Millionairess; Hampstead, Nov 1979, played the title-role in Uncle Vanya; author of a stage play, Sitting Ducks, 1976; first seen on television 1956: most recent appearances in Marie Curie, Edward and Mrs Simpson, The Tempest, and *Yes, Minister*.

Favourite part: Falstaff. *Recreations:* Drawing, swimming, cycling, gardening and collecting works by Gordon Craig. *Address:* 66 Ockenden Road, London N1.

HAYDEN, Terese, actress, producer, director
b Nashville, Tennessee, 25 Feb 1921; *e* Vanderbilt University (1940), American Academy of Dramatic Arts (1940–1), member of Actors Studio; *m* William Clow (mar dis).

Made her professional début as an actress with the Roadside Theatre, Washington, DC, 1941; toured, 1942, in US and Canada, in Angel Street; 1943–4, organized productions for military hospitals and canteens; founder and first editor of Player's Guide, 1944; co-founded the Equity Library Theatre, 1944, and has functioned with it as actress, producer, and director, including Isabella in Measure for Measure, 1944; One Man Show, Live Life Again, Jason, 1945; Margaret in Fanny's First Play, 1947; Epifania in The Millionairess, 1948; and the title-role of Candida, 1963; at the Royale, Nov 1945, was production assistant to José Ferrer for Strange Fruit; resident director of the Crest Theatre, Long Beach, New York, summer 1946; made her Broadway début as an actress at the Alvin, 1947, when she took over the role of Aurore in Joan of Lorraine; toured as an understudy and was assistant stage manager for A Streetcar Named Desire, 1949; on Broadway co-produced with Sam Wanamaker Parisienne, Lady from the Sea, Borned in Texas, Crimes and Crimes (Boston), 1950; resident director of the Ivy Tower Playhouse, Spring Lake, New Jersey, summer 1951; directed and produced Dinosaur Wharf, Broadway, 1951; at the Theatre de Lys, 1953, produced Maya, The Scarecrow, The School for Scandal, which she also directed, and The Little Clay Cart; was associated with Herman Shumlin, 1953–63, and, among other activities, was assistant director of Inherit the Wind, 1955, and Bicycle Ride to Nevada; resident director of the Ivy Tower Playhouse, summer 1956, and co-director of the University Theatre, Princeton, New Jersey, 1956; co-produced and directed The Secret Concubine, off-Broadway, 1960; resident director of the Cherry Lane Theatre, in Pennsylvania, 1962, directing Our Town and Charley's Aunt; produced and directed Five Evenings, off-Broadway, 1963; formed the Young People's Repertory Theatre, 1967, and at the Sheridan Square Playhouse, Jan 1967, produced When Did You Last See My Mother? and Antigone (also directed); produced and directed Owners, 1973; directed Mame Sang the Blues (Ensemble Studio), and Penelope (American Place), 1978; has also directed productions of Othello, Hamlet, and The Plebeians Rehearse the Uprising at the Actors Studio; artist-in-residence, University of North Carolina, 1975; technique director, Circle-in-the-Square Professional Workshop and NYU, 1974–present; produced and directed the films This Property Is Condemned and Hello Out There; entered television in 1950 as an actress in *Philco Playhouse, Hollywood Screen Test*, etc; has also been production assistant director for *Vanity Fair*, 1952, *Aldrich Family*, 1953, etc.

Address: Actors Equity Association, 165 West 46th Street, New York, NY 10036.

HAYES, Helen, actress
b Washington, DC, 10 Oct 1900; *d* of Francis van Arnum Brown and his wife Catherine Estelle (Hayes); *e* Sacred Heart Convent, Washington; *m* Charles MacArthur (dec).

Made her first appearance on the stage at the Belasco Theatre, Washington, 22 Jan 1909, impersonating the Gibson Girl and the Nell Brinkley Girl in a matinée of Jack the Giant Killer; Columbia, Washington, May 1909, played Prince Charles in A Royal Family; subsequently appeared in The Prince Chap, and A Poor Relation for the same company, the Columbia Players, 1909, and in The Barrier and Little Lord Fauntleroy (title role), 1911; The Seven Sisters, 1912, etc; made her first appearance on the New York stage at the Herald Square Theatre, 22 Nov 1909, as Little Mimi, in Old Dutch; at the Broadway Theatre, June 1910, played Psyche Finnigan in The Summer Widowers; at the Broadway, Oct 1911, appeared as Fannie Hicks in The Never Homes; toured, 1912, in The June Bride; appeared regularly at the Empire, NY, Sept 1914, as Little Simone in The Prodigal Husband; 1915–17, appeared with the Poli Players, Washington; during 1917–18 toured as Pollyanna Whittier in Pollyanna; at the Globe Theatre, NY, Sept 1918, played Margaret Schofield in Penrod; at the Empire, NY, Dec 1918, appeared as Margaret in Dear Brutus; at Washington, June 1919, played Dorothy Fessenden in On the Hiring Line; at the Hudson, Sept 1919, played Cora Wheeler in Clarence; at the Park Theatre, Oct 1920, Bab in a play of that name; at the Gaiety, NY, Oct 1921, Seeby Olds in The Wren; Nov 1921, Mary Anne in Golden Days; at the Liberty, Feb 1922, played Elsie Beebe in To the Ladies, in which she played for two years; at the Gaiety, NY, Mar 1924, Mary Sundale in We Moderns; at the Empire, NY, June 1924, Constance Neville in She Stoops to Conquer; at the Booth Theatre, Aug 1924, Catherine Westcourt in Dancing Mothers; at the Henry Miller, Dec 1924, Dinah Partlett in Quarantine; at the Guild Theatre, Apr 1925, Cleopatra in Caesar and Cleopatra; Ritz, Nov 1925, Georgia Bissell in Young Blood; Bijou, Apr 1926, Maggie Wylie in What Every Woman Knows; Maxine Elliott, Nov 1927, Norma Besant in Coquette; continued in this in NY, and on tour, 1928–9; Broadhurst, Sept 1930, played Nellie Fitzpatrick in Mr Gilhooley; Empire, Dec 1930, Peggy Chalfont in Petticoat Influence; Henry Miller Theatre, Nov 1931, Lu in The Good Fairy; Alvin, NY (for the Theatre Guild), Nov 1933, Mary Stuart in Mary of Scotland; in Sept 1934, toured in the same part; County, Suffern, NY, Aug 1935, appeared in Caesar and Cleopatra; Broadhurst, Dec 1935, appeared as Queen Victoria in Victoria Regina, and in which she toured from coast to coast, 1937–8; her performance in this play gained her the Drama League of NY medal for the most distinguished performance of the year, 1936; in Chicago, Jan 1938, played Portia in The Merchant of Venice; County, Suffern, NY, Sept 1938, Maggie Wylie in What Every Woman Knows; Martin Beck, NY, Oct 1938, again played in Victoria Regina; at the Martin Beck, Oct 1939, played Miss Scott in Ladies and Gentlemen; St James (for the Guild), Nov 1940, Viola in Twelfth Night; Shubert (for the Guild), Oct 1941, Madeleine Guest in Candle in the Wind; Henry Miller, Mar 1943, Harriet Beecher Stowe in Harriet, which she played in NY and on tour until 1945; Bucks County Playhouse, July 1946, and on tour, played Mrs Grey in Alice Sit-by-the-Fire; Broadhurst, NY, Oct 1946, Addie in Happy Birthday; made her first appearance in London at the Haymarket, 28 July 1948, as Amanda Wingfield in The Glass Menagerie; in summer theatres, 1949, played in Good Housekeeping; Martin Beck, Mar 1950, Lucy Andree Ransdell in The Wisteria Trees; ANTA Playhouse, Mar 1951, presented a revival of Mary Rose; Feb 1952, appeared as Mrs Howard V Larue II in Mrs McThing; City Center, Dec 1954, again played Maggie Wylie in What Every Woman Knows, and Feb 1955, Lucy André Ransdell in a revival of The Wisteria Trees; Sarah Bernhardt, Paris, June

1955, and ANTA Playhouse, Aug 1955, Mrs Antrobus in The Skin of Our Teeth; Théâtre-de-Lys, NY, Oct 1956, appeared as Mistress of Ceremonies in Lovers, Villains, and Fools; at the City Center, NY, Nov 1956, again played Amanda Wingfield in The Glass Menagerie; Morosco, Nov 1957, played the Duchess in Time Remembered; made her first appearance at the Helen Hayes Theatre, NY, Oct 1958, when she played Nora Melody in A Touch of the Poet; Tappan Zee, Nyack, NY, July 1959, played Lulu Spencer in A Adventure; National, Washington, DC, Feb 1961, Mrs Antrobus in The Skin of Our Teeth and Amanda Wingfield in The Glass Menagerie, subsequently touring in these roles in 13 European capitals and Israel for the US State Department; also toured South America for the State Department; American Shakespeare Festival Theatre, Stratford, Conn, summer 1962, appeared with Maurice Evans in the recital Shakespeare Revisited: A Program for Two Players; US tour, Oct 1962–Mar 1963, in the same recital; Henry Miller, May 1964, played the following Presidents' wives: Abigail Adams, Dolly Madison, Mrs Lincoln, Mrs Cleveland, and Mrs Wilson, in The White House; formed the Helen Hayes Repertory Company, 1964, to sponsor tours of Shakespeare readings in universities; toured the Far East, Nov 1965–Jan 1966, with Romney Brent, for the US State Department Division of Americans Abroad, and, while in Japan, played Amanda Wingfield in The Glass Menagerie on television; toured the US, Apr–May 1966, with the Helen Hayes Repertory Co; joined the APA-Phoenix, and at the Lyceum, NY, Nov 1966, played Mrs Candour in The School for Scandal and Signora Frola in Right You Are; Dec 1966, in We, Comrades Three; Dec 1967, Mrs Fisher in The Show-Off which she repeated in Sept 1968, then played in Boston at the Shubert, and subsequently toured; Ethel Barrymore, Oct 1969, Mrs Grant in The Front Page, the role which was originally written about her own mother; ANTA, Feb 1970, Veta Louise Simmons in Harvey, also for the Phoenix Theatre; Catholic University, Washington, DC, May 1971, Mary Tyrone in Long Day's Journey into Night; published her autobiography, A Gift of Joy, 1965; co-author with Anita Loos of Twice over Lightly, 1972; received honorary Doctor of Fine Arts from Princeton University, 1956, and other honorary degrees from Hamilton College, Smith College, Columbia, Brown, Denver, Brandeis, New York Universities, Carnegie Institute, etc; has been awarded the Medal of the City of New York and the Medal of Arts, Finland; nominated Woman of the Year by the United Service Organization (USO), 1974; President of American National Theatre Academy, 1951–3; commenced film career 1931, and has appeared in numerous pictures, including The Sin of Madeline Claudet, for which she won the Academy Award, 1931, Arrowsmith, A Farewell to Arms, Anastasia, Airport, for which she received the Academy Award, Herbie Rides Again (1974), Helen Hayes: Portrait of an American Actress (1974), One of Our Dinosaurs is Missing (1975), etc; has appeared on many radio shows, including *The Helen Hayes Theatre*, 1940–1; has appeared on television in various dramatic and discussion programs, including: The Twelve Pound Look, Mary of Scotland, The Skin of Our Teeth, etc.
Address: c/o Lucy Kroll, 390 West End Avenue, New York, NY 10024. *Tel:* TR7—0627.

HAYMAN, Lillian, actress and singer
b Baltimore, Md, 17 July 1922; *d* of Otha J Hayman and his wife Leila (Polk); *e* Virginia Union, Edward Waters College in Fla, and Wilberforce University, Ohio; previously occupied as a school teacher.
Made her first appearance on the stage in 1947, in Greenwich Village, NY, as Momma in Dream About Tomorrow; toured the US commencing Dec 1953 as a singer in Porgy and Bess,

later taking over the role of Maria from Georgia Burke; Broadway, NY, 13 Apr 1957, made her Broadway debut as Mother in Shinbone Alley; New York City Center, May 1961, again played in Porgy and Bess; 54th Street, Oct 1961, Mammy Trader in Kwamina; New York City Center, May 1964, Pearl in Porgy and Bess; Mermaid, May 1963, Mrs Franklin in Along Came a Spider; Martin Beck. Apr 1967, Momma in Hallelujah, Baby!; Broadhurst, Apr 1971, played in 70 Girls, 70; Royale, May 1972, Beulah Jackson in Tough to Get Help; 46th Street, Oct 1972, took over as Pauline in No, No, Nanette; Winter Garden, Mar 1975, Georgia Sheridan in Doctor Jazz; has also played in stock and touring companies as Queenie in Show Boat, Hattie in Kiss Me, Kate, in Free and Easy, The Amen Corner, etc; appeared in the film The Night They Raided Minsky's, 1968; first appeared on television on 3 May 1968 and has since played in the soap opera *One Life to Live,* on *Mod Squad,* the Leslie Uggams Show, in Barefoot in the Park, *The Alan King Show,* etc.
Favourite parts: The Mother roles. *Recreations:* Fishing and boating. *Address:* 190–09 111th Road, Hollis, Long Island, New York, 11412. *Tel:* 454–2939.

HAYMAN, Ronald, writer and director
b Bournemouth, 4 May 1932; *s* of John Hayman and his wife Sadie (Morris); *e* St Paul's and Trinity Hall, Cambridge; *m* Monica Lorimer (sep); trained for the stage at Guildhall (part-time).
Made his acting debut at the Pavilion, Rhyl, 1957, as juvenile lead in Sleeping Partnership; his first play, The End of an Uncle, was produced at the Wimbledon Theatre, 1959; at the Arts, 1961, directed Deathwatch, and The Splits; has since directed productions including Jungle of the Cities (also translated), 1962; The Igloo, 1965; The Servant, An Evening with GBS, 1966; My Foot, My Tutor, Home Front, 1971; Bremen Coffee, 1974; Troilus and Cressida, 1977; author of many books on theatre topics, including critical studies of a number of individual playwrights, and Techniques of Acting, 1969; John Gielgud, 1971; Playback, 1973; The Set-Up, 1974; How to Read a Play, 1976; Artaud and After, 1977; Theatre and Anti-Theatre, British Drama since 1955, 1979; lectures for the Extra-Mural Department of London University.
Recreations: Music, travel, food. *Address:* 25 Church Row, London NW3 6UP. *Tel:* 435 1977.

HAYNES, Tiger, actor and musician
b 13 Dec 1914; *s* of William Haynes and his wife Susanna; *e* public schools; *m* the actress Joy Hatton.
First appeared on Broadway in New Faces of 1956, at the Ethel Barrymore, 14 June 1956; in the sixties appeared in City Center productions of Finian's Rainbow and Kiss Me Kate; Mark Hellinger, May 1964, appeared as Bojangles in Fade Out – Fade In; toured, Sept 1969, as Tick in The Great White Hope; St James, 1972, took over as the Duke of Milan in Two Gentlemen of Verona, the musical; Lunt-Fontanne, Dec 1973, Charlie in The Pajama Game; Majestic, Jan 1975, Tinman in The Wiz; Lunt-Fontanne, Dec 1978, Sylvester Lee in A Broadway Musical; Winter Garden, Dec 1979, Marley in Comin' Uptown; films include All That Jazz; numerous TV and radio appearances, including his own show with his group, The Three Flames, with whom he recorded his song Open the Door, Richard; recent TV includes On the Five Forty-Eight.
Favourite parts: George Washington in New Faces, Tick in The Great White Hope, Bojangles in Fade-Out – Fade In, and Tinman. *Address:* 313 West 14th Street, New York, NY 10014.

HAYS, Bill, director

b Wingate, Co Durham, 15 Mar 1938; *s* of William Hays and his wife Eleanor Allison (Hamilton); *e* Edward VII Grammar School, Nuneaton and Birmingham College of Art; *m* Eileen Jill Brooks.

Directed his first stage production in 1961 for the Living Theatre, Leicester; directed his first London production in 1968 at the Fortune, Close the Coalhouse Door; in 1969, directed The Hero Rises Up (Nottingham) and As Dorothy Parker Once Said (London); artistic director of the new Leeds Playhouse, 1970–1, where he directed plays including: Simon Says, Henry IV (also Edinburgh Festival) and Love for Love, 1970; Tight at the Back, and Pictures in a Bath of Acid, 1971; directed The Ghost Train, Old Vic, 1976; has directed numerous television plays since 1962, including The Caucasian Chalk Circle, and Looking for Clancy.

Address: The Old Bakery, Tilmastone, Nr Deal, Kent.

HAYS, David, designer

b New York City, 2 June 1930; *s* of Mortimer Hays and his wife Sarah (Reich); *e* Woodmere Academy, Harvard College (AB 1952), Fulbright Scholarship to study at the Old Vic (1952–3), Yale University School of the Drama (1953–4), Boston University (MFA 1955); *m* Leonore Landau.

Apprentice designer at the Brattle Theatre, Cambridge, Massachusetts, 1949–52; student at the Old Vic, London, 1952–3; designer at Green Mansion (summer) Theatre, 1954; designed at the opera department of the Tanglewood Festival, 1955; first NY design was for sets and lighting of The Cradle Song, 1 Dec 1955; since then has designed the following productions: The Innkeepers, The Iceman Cometh, Long Day's Journey into Night, 1956; The Masquers and Pastorale, ballets, Career, 1957; Stars and Stripes, ballet, Endgame, Children of Darkness, Hamlet, A Midsummer Night's Dream, Salad Days, The Quare Fellow, The Night Circus, 1958; The Rivalry, Wozzeck (opera, co-designed), Triple Play, The Triumph of St Joan, opera, Gagaku (Japanese dancers), The Tenth Man, Romeo and Juliet, Macbeth, Our Town, and the ballets Native Dancers and Episodes, 1959; Roman Candle, The Cradle Will Rock, The Balcony, All the Way Home, Love and Libel, and the ballets, Theme and Variations, Panamerica, Donizetti Variations, Liebeslieder Waltzes, Creation of the World, Ebony Concerto, Les Biches, and Ragtime, 1960; also in 1960 served as technical supervisor to the Kabuki Theatre, Tokyo, for the visit of the New York City Ballet; Smiling the Boy Fell Dead, Look, We've Come Through, Gideon, 1961; A Family Affair, No Strings, A Matter of Position (Philadelphia), In the Counting House, 1962; Lorenzo, Desire Under the Elms, Strange Interlude, Next Time I'll Sing to You, and the ballets Bugaku, Arcade, The Chase, Fantasia (lighting only), 1963; Marco Millions, A Murderer Among Us, Baby Want a Kiss (lighting only), The Last Analysis, Hughie, The Changeling, and the ballets Quatuor, Clarinade, 1964; Peterpat, Diamond Orchid, Tartuffe, Matty and the Morons and Madonna, Mrs Dally, Drat! The Cat! 1965; UTBU, Dinner at Eight, We Have Always Lived in the Castle, Yerma, 1966; Dr Cook's Garden, The Tenth Man, 1967; Saint Joan, Tiger at the Gates, Cyrano de Bergerac, The Goodbye People, A Cry of Players, 1968; The Miser, 1969; Songs from Under Milkwood, The Gingerbread Lady, Two by Two, Gone with the Wind (Imperial, Tokyo), 1970; décor for Gone with the Wind, Drury Lane, London, May 1972, and Dorothy Chandler Pavilion, Los Angeles, Aug 1973; Platinum, 1978; instructor in stage design at New York University, 1961–2, Boston University, 1963, Columbia Univ., 1965–66, National Theatre Institute, 1970; Associate Professor at Connecticut College; is Vice President, O'Neill Theatre Center; founder, 1967, and General Director of the Center's National Theatre of the Deaf; Advisor to Performing Arts, Harvard College; with John Johansen, was architect and designer of the Mummers Theatre, Oklahoma City, 1963; received a Ford Foundation Grant for the project Eight Theatres: Ideal Concepts; received Obie Awards for The Quare Fellow and The Balcony and received the *Variety* New York Drama Critics Poll for No Strings; received Outer Circle Award, 1967, honorary DHL from Gallaudet College, 1975.

Recreation: Sailing, holding the passage record in a small boat from Africa to New York, and the Feller Trophy, 1979. *Address:* 118 East 64th Street, New York, NY 10021. *Tel:* PL 3-7893.

HAYTER, James, actor

b Lonuvla, India, 23 Apr 1907; *s* of Owen Chilton Goodenough Hayter and his wife Violet Mary (Wakefield); *e* Dollar Academy, Scotland; *m* (1) Marjorie Lane (mar dis); (2) Mary Elizabeth Rose Shaw; studied for the stage at the Royal Academy of Dramatic Art.

Made his first appearance on the professional stage in the provinces, Dec 1925, in The Sport of Kings; Nov 1926, toured as Joe Purdie in the same play, and in 1927, as Harvey in The Unfair Sex; appeared with repertory companies, 1927–33, at Northampton, Shrewsbury, Dundee, Perth, etc; from Nov 1933–June 1934, appeared with the Birmingham Repertory Theatre company; ran his own repertory company at Perth, July–Dec 1934, also directing and playing leading parts; Coventry Repertory Company, Jan–July 1935; Birmingham Repertory Theatre company, July 1935–May 1936; made his first appearance on the London stage at Daly's, 8 Sept 1936, as Andrew Young in The Composite Man; Streatham Hill, Mar 1937, and Savoy, Apr 1937, appeared in the revue And On We Go; Criterion, Sept 1937, Brian Curtis in French Without Tears, Strand (for Repertory Players), Oct 1937, Stanley Melland in Trouble for Two; Royalty, June 1938, appeared in 8.45 and All That; Savoy, Feb 1940, appeared in Lights Up; Strand, July 1940, Macfarlane in Women Aren't Angels; joined the Royal Armoured Corps, Nov 1940, and was demobilized, Nov 1945; re-appeared in London, at the Arts Theatre, June 1946, as Earl Godwin in The Dove and the Carpenter; Boltons, Oct 1947, Rev Charles Dowson in The Hidden Years, playing the same part at the Fortune, Jan 1948; Arts, Dec 1948, played Dr MacKessock in Gog and MacGog; Playhouse, May 1949, Joseph Lawson in Shooting Star; made his first appearance on the New York stage at the Broadhurst, 10 Mar 1951, as Friar Laurence in Romeo and Juliet; toured in England, 1953, as George Fuller in The Gentle Rain; at the Haymarket, July 1955, played Adolphe Tessier in Nina; Princes, Nov 1957, played the Emperor, the President, and the Dictator in Royal Suite; Strand, May 1959, Armand Brazier in Change of Tune; Drury Lane, Oct 1959, followed Stanley Holloway as Alfred Doolittle in My Fair Lady; toured with the London Company of My Fair Lady, 1964–5; Derby Playhouse, Sept 1966, again played Doolittle, and, Dec, the Baron in Cinderella; Vaudeville, Nov 1967, Archdeacon Daubeny in A Woman of No Importance; Duke of York's, Apr 1968, Samoylenko in The Duel; Lyric, Aug 1968, Beach in Oh, Clarence!; Palace, Manchester, Oct 1969, Crummles in Back into the Limelight; toured, June 1972, as Charles in Forget-Me-Not Lane; entered films, 1936, and has appeared in numerous pictures since that date; he has also appeared frequently on television.

Favourite parts: The Rev Charles Dowson, Adolphe Tessier, Mr Pickwick and Friar Tuck. *Recreations:* Music and travel. *Club:* Arts Theatre. *Address:* Eric L'Epine Smith Ltd, 14 Clifford Street, London, W1X 2LT. *Tel:* 01–493 3824/5.

HAYTHORNE, Joan, actress

b Ealing, 12 Apr 1915; *d* of Arnold Thompson Haythornthwaite and his wife Dora (Spedding); *e* Queenswood, Eastbourne; Les Fougères, Lausanne, and Lausanne University; *m* Lindsay Shankland (dec).

Made her first appearance on the stage on the Continent; then studied at the Royal Academy of Dramatic Art; made her first appearance on the British stage, at the Victoria Theatre, Dundee, 1932, in My Wife's Family; appeared with the Manchester Repertory company, Rusholme, 1934–8; York repertory company, 1940; repertory at the Alexandra, Birmingham, and at Wolverhampton, 1941–3; made her first appearance in London, at the Q Theatre, 2 Nov 1943, as Miss Jones in Three Wives Called Roland; Westminster Theatre, Nov 1943, played one of the guests in An Ideal Husband; Arts, Apr 1944, Julia in The Philanderer, and May 1944, Berinthia in A Trip to Scarborough; subsequently, at the Garrison Theatre, Salisbury, played Julia Melville in The Rivals; Playhouse, Mar 1945, Miss Fisher in Great Day; made a notable success at the Winter Garden Theatre, Sept 1945, when she played Mary Haddon in Young Mrs Barrington; New (for Repertory Players), Mar 1946, Susan Fosgate in No Footlights; Lyric, Hammersmith, Aug 1946, Sister Hoyle and Elinor Rich in Fear No More; Arts, Feb–Mar 1947, appeared in Back to Methuselah; Embassy, June 1947, played Isabel in Miranda; Apollo, Dec 1947, Lady Dering in The Blind Goddess; Ambassadors', Apr 1948, Essie in Little Lambs Eat Ivy; Savoy, July 1949, played Mary Banning in Young Wives' Tale; toured, Feb 1950, as Catherine of Aragon in The White Falcon; Ambassadors', May 1951, Carol Verity in Taking Things Quietly; New, July 1951, Geraldine Ridgeley in His House In Order; made her first appearance on the New York stage at the New Century, for the Theatre Guild, 13 Feb 1952, as Rosabel Fleming in Venus Observed; Aldwych, London, Nov 1952, played Iris Ingle in Wild Horses; Arts, Dec 1953, Hilda Langley in A London Actress; Embassy, Oct 1954, Lady Elrood in Wild Goose Chase; Q, Jan 1955, Olivia Curtis in The Visiting Moon; Citizens' Theatre, Glasgow, Feb 1955, Adelaide Avalon in The Isle of Women; Westminster, June 1957, played Lady Warren in Dear Delinquent, and transferred with the production to the Aldwych, Dec 1957; Cambridge, Dec 1958, Clara Crabb in Who's Your Father?; Bristol Old Vic, Feb–Mar 1960, Helen in A Taste of Honey, and Queen Elizabeth in Mary Stuart; Royal, Windsor, Sept 1960, played Nancy Liddell in The Big Noise; toured, May 1961, as Margaret Munson in Kind Sir; Royal, Stratford, E, Aug 1962, played Winifred in Say Nothing; Ashcroft, Croydon, Feb 1964, Mary Sellars in The Excursion; at the same theatre, Apr 1964, Mrs Sarrett in The Judge's Story; Arts, June 1966, Lady Catherine de Bourgh in Pride and Prejudice; Haymarket, Oct 1972, Mabell, Countess of Airlie in Crown Matrimonial; first appeared in films, 1946, in Top Secret, and subsequently in Svengali, The Feminine Touch, Three Men in a Boat, Star, Decline and Fall, etc; since 1953 has also appeared frequently on television, recently in *The Duchess of Duke Street*, Home and Beauty, and Flesh and Blood.

Favourite part: Essie in Little Lambs Eat Ivy. *Address:* c/o Dodo Watts in association with Julia MacDermot, 14 Leamore Street, London, W6.

HEAL, Joan, actress and singer

b Vobster, Somerset, 17 Oct 1922; *d* of Edgar Charles Heal and his wife Ada (Willcox); *e* Bath High School; *m* (1) Jeremy Hawk (mar dis); (2) David Conyers (mar dis); studied for the stage at the Old Vic School and London Mask Theatre School, and at the Buddy Bradley School of Dancing.

First appeared at the Garden Theatre, Bideford, 1940, as Mrs Terence in Night Must Fall; at the Saville, 11 Apr 1946, appeared in the chorus of the revue, Here Come the Boys; at the Cambridge, May 1948, appeared as a soubrette in the revue Maid to Measure; at the Hippodrome, Dec 1948, played Nancy in High Button Shoes; appeared at the Cambridge, in 1949, in the revue, Sauce Tartare; Cambridge, Apr 1950, appeared in the revue, Sauce Piquante; His Majesty's, Nov 1950, played Cecile in Music at Midnight; Lyric, Hammersmith, May 1951, and Globe, Sept 1951, appeared in The Lyric Revue; Globe, July 1952, in The Globe Revue; Criterion, Apr 1954, appeared in the revue, Intimacy at 8.30; Piccadilly, Dec 1955, played Jo in A Girl Called Jo; Lyric, Hammersmith, Nov 1956, Virginia Jones in Grab Me a Gondola, subsequently transferring with the production to the Lyric, W1, Dec 1956, where the musical ran for 673 performances; Bristol Old Vic, Sept 1958, played Lady Cicely in Captain Brassbound's Conversion; Bristol Old Vic, Mar 1959, played Katharine in The Taming of the Shrew; Queen's, July 1960, played Chi-chi in Joie de Vivre; Adelphi, Dec 1960, played the Fairy Godmother in Cinderella; Globe, June 1961, appeared in the revue On the Avenue; Nottingham Playhouse, Oct 1961–Jan 1962, played the following parts: Penelope in A Slight Accident, Mrs Pringle in Alas, Poor Fred, and Katharine in The Taming of the Shrew; Ashcroft, Croydon, May 1963, played Mrs Sullen in The Beaux' Stratagem; Mermaid, Aug 1963, Mrs Kopecka in Schweyk in the Second World War; at the Nottingham Playhouse, Mar 1964, played Chispa in The Mayor of Zalamea; Apr 1964, Brenda in Saturday Night and Sunday Morning; May 1964, Granny Barnacle in Memento Mori; Globe, London, Feb 1965, played Madame K in Divorce Me, Darling; Bristol Old Vic, Aug 1965, Mrs Squeezum in Lock Up Your Daughters!; Prince of Wales, Feb 1966, Brenda in Saturday Night and Sunday Morning; Criterion, Aug 1966, appeared in the revue The Decline and Fall of the Entire World as Seen Through the Eyes of Cole Porter; Mayfair, May 1967, directed In the Picture; Royal Court, July 1967, Woman in Ogodiveleftthegason; Intimate, Palmer's Green, Feb 1969, Miss Drillard in Collapse of Stout Party; Hampstead Theatre Club, Nov 1970, Agave in The Disorderly Women; toured S Africa, 1971, as Julia in Fallen Angels; Arnaud, Guildford, Oct 1971, Mrs Sedley and Miss Crawley in Vanity Fair; joined the Young Vic company, 1972, playing Leah and Potiphar's wife in Joseph and the Amazing Technicolour Dreamcoat, including its run at the Albery, Feb 1973; with the company visited Brooklyn Academy, Mar 1974, playing Curtis in The Taming of the Shrew; Ambassadors', Mar 1975, Mrs Burslow Sr in the Young Vic's Grandson of Oblomov; Oxford Playhouse, and tour, May 1975, Salvation Army Major in Happy End; Theatre Royal, York, Sept 1975, played Belle in Dear Octopus; Young Vic, Sept 1976, Lady More in A Man For All Seasons; same theatre, Nov 1976, Beryl Bligh in If You're Glad I'll be Frank, and Mrs Drudge in The Real Inspector Hound (double bill); has also appeared in films since 1950.

Favourite parts: Jo in A Girl Called Jo and Belle in Dear Octopus. *Recreations:* Cooking, walking, reading, and travel. *Club:* Sunningdale Ladies' Golf Club. *Address:* 26 Brunswick Court, Regency Street, London, SW1.

HEAP, Douglas, designer

b London, 7 Aug 1934; *s* of the miniature theatre entertainer Clifford Vernon Heap and his wife Alexandra Jessica (Richmond); *e* Claysmore School and Byam Shaw School of Drawing and Painting; *m* the painter and prop maker Jennifer Pennell.

Head of Design at the Royal Academy of Dramatic Art since 1969; his first designs were for Bid Time Return, 1958, at the Academy's Vanbrugh Theatre; designed Boesman and Lena for the Theatre Upstairs, 1971, and has since designed all Athol Fugard's productions in Britain; other designs, in London unless otherwise stated, include AC/DC, Within Two Shadows, 1971; Crete and Sergeant Pepper, The Old Ones, 1972; The Freedom of the City, 1973; X, Play Mas, 1974; Loot, 1975; Pygmalion (Nottingham), 1976; Shirt Sleeves in Summer, The Father (Old Tote, Sydney), The Ascent of Mount Fuji, 1977; A and R, Piaf (Stratford), 1978; Piaf, The Turn of the Screw (Kent Opera), 1979; his first designs for New York were those for Size Banzi Is Dead/ The Island, at the Edison, 1974.

Recreations: Cricket, crosswords. *Address:* 702 High Road, Buckhurst Hill, Essex. *Tel:* 989 8043.

HECKART, Eileen, actress

b Columbus, Ohio, 29 Mar 1919; *d* of Leo Herbert Heckart and his wife Esther (Stark); *e* Ohio State University; *m* John Harrison Yankee Jnr; studied for the stage at the American Theatre Wing.

First appeared in New York at the Blackfriars Guild, 1943, in Tinker's Dam; toured, 1944, in Janie, and 1945, in Windy Hill; in 1948, appeared in The Stars Weep; 48th Street, May 1949, took over Eva McKeon in The Traitor; Coronet, Jan 1950, played Nell Bromley in Hilda Crane; Cort, Oct 1952, played Valerie McGuire in In Any Language; Music Box, Feb 1953, appeared as Rosemary Sidney in Picnic, gaining the Outer Circle Award and the Daniel Blum Citation for this performance; 46th Street, Dec 1954, played Mrs Daigle in The Bad Seed, for which she received the Donaldson Award; Coronet, Sept 1955, appeared in two plays by Arthur Miller, as Beatrice in A View from the Bridge, and Agnes in A Memory of Two Mondays; at the Music Box, Dec 1957, Lottie Lacey in The Dark at the Top of the Stairs, receiving the New York Drama Critics Award, 1958; played at the Congress Hall, Berlin, Germany, 1958, in Before Breakfast; Music Box, Oct 1960, Deedee Grogan in Invitation to a March; City Center, May 1961, Melba Snyder in Pal Joey; Longacre, Oct 1961, Opal in Everybody Loves Opal; Billy Rose, Jan 1962, Tilly Siegel in A Family Affair; 54th Street, Mar 1963, Nurse (Sweetie) in a revival of Too True to Be Good; Stadium, Columbus, Ohio, July 1964, Regina Giddens in The Little Foxes; summer tour, 1964, as Leora Samish in The Time of the Cuckoo; Royale, Apr 1965, Ruby in And Things That Go Bump in the Night; Biltmore, Sept 1965, took over the role of Mrs Banks in Barefoot in the Park; Ambassador, Mar 1967, Harriet, Edith, and Muriel in You Know I Can't Hear You When the Water's Running; Booth, Feb 1969, Mrs Haber in The Mother Lover; Booth, Oct 1969, Mrs Baker in Butterflies Are Free; made her London début at the Apollo, Nov 1970, in this last part; toured, 1971, as Beatrice in The Effect of Gamma Rays on Man-in-the-Moon Marigolds; Westport, Conn, Country Playhouse, Aug 1972, Martha in Remember Me; Music Box, Oct 1973, The Woman in Veronica's Room; McCarter, Princeton, NJ, Feb 1975, title-role in Mother Courage and Her Children; Stratford, Conn, June 1975, Mrs Gibbs in Our Town; toured, 1976, as Eleanor Roosevelt in a one-woman show, Eleanor; Martin Beck, Apr 1977, Bella Gardner in Ladies at the Alamo; first appeared in films 1955, in Miracle in the Rain, and subsequently in The Bad Seed, Bus Stop, Hot Spell, Heller in Pink Tights, Butterflies Are Free, for which she received the Academy Award in 1973, The Hiding Place, etc; has also appeared on television, winning the Sylvania Award as the Character Actress of the Year, 1954, and an Emmy in 1967

for her performance in Save Me a Place at Forest Lawn, and has played the Aunt on *The Mary Tyler Moore Show*, 1976; Honorary Doctorate of Laws, Sacred Heart University, 1973.

Address: 135 Comstock Hill Road, New Canaan, Connecticut. *Tel:* WO 6–3860.

HEDLEY, Philip, theatre and television director

b Manchester, 10 Apr 1938; *s* of Leonard Hedley and his wife Lois (Gould); *e* University of Sydney; trained for the stage at East Fifteen Acting School, London.

Began his professional career as an actor/ASM at Liverpool Playhouse, 1963–64; taught at the E15 Acting School, later becoming assistant principal, 1964–66; taught at LAMDA, 1966–67, before becoming a director; his first production was The Rivals for the Theatre Royal, Lincoln, 1967, and in the same year he directed Live Like Pigs at the Royal Court; artistic director, 1968–70, Lincoln Theatre Royal, where his many productions included the premieres of There Is a Happy Land, The Finest Family in the Land, and an adaptation of Alice Through the Looking Glass; artistic director, 1970–72, Midlands Arts Theatre Company, Birmingham, where his productions included premieres of works by Henry Livings and David Cregan; in 1971 also directed The National Health for the Old Tote, Sydney; assistant director to Joan Littlewood at the Theatre Royal, Stratford E, 1972–74; as a freelance director since 1974 has worked in English regional theatre, also Canada and the Sudan; West End work includes Happy as a Sandbag, 1975; Leave Him to Heaven, 1976; in Sept 1979 resigned as Chairman of the Board of the Theatre Royal, Stratford E, to become its Artistic Director; has served on the Arts Council's Drama Panel and various other committees; has taught and directed at a number of drama schools as well as those already mentioned, in Britain and abroad; for TV has directed Happy as a Sandbag, Leave Him to Heaven, and Mother Nature's Bloomers, 1978.

Address: 69 Paramount Court, University Street, London WC1.

HEELEY, Desmond, designer

Began his career with Birmingham repertory company; his first success as a designer was with costumes for Toad of Toad Hall at the Memorial Theatre, Stratford-on-Avon, Dec 1948; the production played several seasons at Stratford, and was presented in London, Dec 1954; he has since designed in London, Stratford, Ontario (nineteen productions 1957–78, most recently Titus Andronicus), Minneapolis (Guthrie Theatre, seven productions, 1974–79) and elsewhere; his work at Stratford-on-Avon includes costumes for Titus Andronicus, 1955; Hamlet, 1956; The Merchant of Venice (décor), 1960; Much Ado About Nothing (also décor), Romeo and Juliet, 1961; his other work, in London unless otherwise stated, includes designs for The Lark (costumes only), 1955; Titus Andronicus (co-designer), 1957; Twelfth Night, Macbeth (both Old Vic), 1958; Farewell, Farewell Eugene (costumes only), The Double Dealer (Old Vic), 1959; Toad of Toad Hall, 1960; The Devils (costumes only), Oh, Dad, Poor Dad, 1961; Misalliance, Divorce à la Carte, Gentle Jack, Hamlet (Old Vic), 1963; Carving a Statue, 1964; La Contessa (tour), 1965; Rosencrantz and Guildenstern Are Dead (Old Vic and New York), 1967; for the latter production he received a Tony as best designer of 1967; The Way of the World (Old Vic), 1969; In Praise of Love, Cyrano (NY), 1973; Teibele and Her Demon (NY), 1979; he has also designed many operas and ballets in England and abroad, recently Faust (Covent Garden), The Merry Widow (Australian Ballet), and Don Pasquale (Metropolitan Opera).

HEFFERNAN, John, actor
b New York City, 30 May 1934; *e* City College of New York, Columbia University, Boston University (BFA).

Co-founded the Charles Street Playhouse, Boston, where he played various roles, notably Judge Cool in The Grass Harp, Eddie Carbone in A View from the Bridge, and in Blood Wedding, The Iceman Cometh, Hotel Paradiso, Shadow of a Gunman, The Crucible, etc; made his NY début at the Masque, 13 May 1958, as Arthur Olden in The Judge; New York Shakespeare Festival, Aug 1959, played Lepidus in Julius Caesar; Coronet, Oct 1959, Older Draftsman in The Great God Brown; Phoenix, Nov 1959, Lykon in Lysistrata; Jan 1960, Aase's Father in Peer Gynt; Mar 1960, various parts in Henry IV, Part I; Apr 1960, Robert Shallow and a Drawer in Henry IV, Part II; New York Shakespeare Festival, Aug 1960, Tailor and Pedant in The Taming of the Shrew; Phoenix, Nov 1960, Tony Lumpkin in She Stoops to Conquer; Dec 1960, Young Covey in The Plough and the Stars; Jan 1961, Jacob McCloskey in The Octoroon; Mar 1961, Polonius in Hamlet; Nov 1961, Androcles in Androcles and the Lion; Masque, Sept 1962, Galy Gay in A Man's a Man; New York Shakespeare Festival, Aug 1963, Old Shepherd in The Winter's Tale and Touchstone in As You Like It; St James, Sept 1963, Weinard in Luther, and, Jan 1964, succeeded Albert Finney in the title-role and subsequently toured in this last part; Gate, Sept 1964, Subtle in The Alchemist; Billy Rose, Dec 1964, Butler in Tiny Alice; Brooks Atkinson, Nov 1965, played in the episodic Postmark Zero; Shubert, Jan 1966, Kermit in Malcolm; Sheridan Square Playhouse, June 1967, Captain Bluntschli in Arms and the Man; Vivian Beaumont, Jan 1968, the Inquisitor in Saint Joan; Felt Forum, Mar 1968, Chorus Leader in Final Solutions; Anspacher, Apr 1968, Jan Ballas in The Memorandum; Belasco, Sept 1968, John Rocky Park in Woman Is My Ideal; Henry Miller's, Nov 1968, Tillich in Morning, Kerry in Noon, and Robin Breast Western in Night; Public, Mar 1969, Cincinnatus the Prisoner in Invitation to a Beheading; Delacorte, July 1969, Solveig's Father, Priest, Button Moulder in Peer Gynt; Broadway, Mar 1970, Old Captain in Purlie; Sheridan Square Playhouse, Feb 1972, co-produced and played Seumas Shields in The Shadow of a Gunman; Syracuse, NY, Repertory, 1973, Bernard Shaw In Dear Liar; Booth, May 1974, took over from Paul Benedict as Jason Pepper, MD, in Ravenswood and Hugh Gumbo in Dunelawn in the production Bad Habits; Manhattan Theatre Club, Mar 1975, Hatch in The Sea; Circle in the Square, Mar 1976, Professor Arnholm in The Lady from the Sea; Biltmore, June 1976, Abe in Knock Knock; Broadhurst, Dec 1976, Lawyer Craven in Sly Fox; has appeared in the films, The Time of the Heathen and The Sting (1973).
Address: Actors Equity Association, 165 West 46th Street, New York, NY 10036.

HELLMAN, Lillian, dramatic author
b New Orleans, La, 20 June 1905; *d* of Max Bernard Hellman and his wife Julia (Newhouse); *e* New York and Columbia Universities; *m* Arthur Kober (mar dis).

Formerly engaged as a reader and press-representative, prior to becoming play-reader to Herman Shumlin, who was responsible for the presentation of her early plays; author of The Children's Hour, 1934 (which ran for 691 performances); Days to Come, 1936; The Little Foxes, 1939; Watch on the Rhine, 1941 (New York Drama Critics Circle Award); The Searching Wind, 1944; Another Part of the Forest, 1946, which she also staged; Montserrat (adaptation), 1949, which she also staged; The Autumn Garden, 1951; The Lark (adaptation), 1955; Candide (adaptation), 1956; Toys in the

Attic, 1960 (Drama Critics Circle Award); My Mother, My Father, and Me (based on the novel How Much? by Burt Blechman), 1963; author of some lyrics in Leonard Bernstein's Theatre Songs, 1965; films include The Little Foxes, Dead End, The North Star, These Three, etc; published autobiographies An Unfinished Woman, 1969, Pentimento, 1973, and Scoundrel Time, 1976; taught at Harvard University, 1961 and 1967, and Yale University, 1966, in seminars on literature and writing; is a member of the National Academy of Arts and Letters, and of the American Academy of Arts and Sciences; in May 1964, received the Gold Medal for Drama of the National Institute of Arts and Letters.
Address: 630 Park Avenue, New York, NY 10021.

HELPMANN, Sir Robert (*cr* 1968) actor and dancer
b Mount Gambier, Australia, 9 Apr 1909; *s* of James Murray Helpmann and his wife Mary (Gardiner); *e* Prince Alfred's College, Adelaide.

First appeared on the stage at the Theatre Royal, Adelaide, 1922, as a solo dancer in The Ugly Duckling; began his professional career as a dancer, appearing at His Majesty's, Sydney, Apr 1927, as the Principal Dancer in Frasquita, subsequently touring Australia and New Zealand; he also appeared in Australia as Principal Dancer in Tip-Toes and Queen High, 1927; This Year of Grace, 1929; The New Moon, The Merry Widow, and Katinka, 1930; Criterion, Sydney, Apr 1932, appeared as Septimus Barrett in The Barretts of Wimpole Street; made his first appearance in London as an actor at the Gate Theatre, 28 Feb 1933, in a small part in I Hate Men; next appeared with the Vic-Wells Ballet, Mar 1933; at the Lyric, Hammersmith, June 1933, danced in the ballet in The Fantasticks; in Sept 1933, danced as Satan in Job; principal dancer of Sadler's Wells Ballet from that date until 1950; Lyric, Hammersmith, June 1933, and later at the Open Air Theatre, Regent's Park, acted and danced in The Fantasticks; Open Air, June 1934, principal dancer in various programmes of ballet; also at the Savoy, June 1934, played Duval in Precipice; Adelphi, Feb 1935, appeared as leading dancer in the revue, Stop Press; Old Vic, Dec 1937, Oberon in A Midsummer Night's Dream; Playhouse, Apr 1938, Felix, Mr Cricket, and Chief of Yellow Ants in The Insect Play; Mercury, Nov 1938, danced as guest artist with Ballet Rambert; Old Vic, Dec 1938, again played Oberon; Mar 1939, Gremio, the Tailor, and Nicholas in The Taming of the Shrew; Ambassadors', May 1940, appeared in the revue Swinging the Gate; New Theatre, Feb 1944, appeared as Hamlet; Covent Garden, Dec 1946, appeared as Oberon in the masque, The Fairy Queen; in 1947, in association with Michael Benthall, undertook the artistic direction of the Duchess Theatre, and commenced operations there Mar 1947, with the revival of The White Devil, in which he played Flamineo, and June 1947, when he played Prince in He Who Gets Slapped; joined the Shakespeare Memorial Theatre Company, Stratford-on-Avon, for the 1948 season, and appeared as King John, Hamlet and Shylock; appeared with Sadler's Wells Ballet at the Florence Festival, 1949; danced as guest artist at Royal Theatre, Copenhagen, July 1949; Covent Garden, Sept 1949, played Mercury in the opera The Olympians; with the Sadler's Wells Ballet, toured USA and Canada, 1949, and USA again in 1950; Covent Garden, Jan 1950, directed Madame Butterfly; in the same month appeared as guest artist at the New Theatre, Oslo; in Apr 1950, appeared as guest artist at La Scala, Milan; Adelphi, June 1950, in association with Michael Benthall, directed Golden City; toured, June–July 1950, with Margot Fonteyn; Sadler's Wells, Feb 1951, appeared as guest artist with the Theatre Ballet in The Prospect Before Us; St

James's, May 1951, played Apollodorus in Caesar and Cleopatra and Octavius Caesar in Antony and Cleopatra; appeared in these two parts at the Ziegfeld, New York, Dec 1951; New, London, June 1952, played the Doctor in The Millionairess; Opera House, Manchester, Aug 1952, directed The Wedding Ring; Shubert, NY, Oct 1952, again appeared as the Doctor in The Millionairess; Old Vic, London, Mar 1953, directed Murder In the Cathedral; Covent Garden, June 1953, appeared on Coronation Night as guest artist, dancing Prince Siegfried in Swan Lake; Jan 1954, directed the opera Le Coq d'Or; Old Vic, Apr 1954, directed The Tempest; Globe, June 1954, directed After the Ball; at the Edinburgh Festival, 1954, played Oberon in A Midsummer Night's Dream, and devised the choreography; also acted and danced as the Devil in The Soldier's Tale, again devising the choreography; from Sept 1954, toured the United States and Canada with the Old Vic Company as Oberon in A Midsummer Night's Dream; Old Vic, Mar 1955, directed As You Like It; toured Australia from May 1955, with the Old Vic Company, appearing as Shylock, Petruchio in The Taming of the Shrew and Angelo in Measure for Measure; Covent Garden, Feb 1956, directed Le Coq d'Or; Old Vic, June 1956, directed Romeo and Juliet, the production subsequently appearing at the Winter Garden, NY, Oct 1956; joined the Old Vic Company, London, Dec 1956–May 1957, and played the following parts: Shylock, Launce in The Two Gentlemen of Verona, Saturnius in Titus Andronicus, Dr Pinch in The Comedy of Errors, and the Duke of Gloucester in Richard III, he also directed Antony and Cleopatra; Edinburgh Festival, Aug 1957, played Georges de Valera in Nekrassov, subsequently appearing in the same production, Royal Court, Sept 1957; Globe, Nov 1957, took over the part of Sebastien in Nude With Violin; danced with the Royal Ballet, 1958, in The Rake's Progress, Hamlet, Coppelia, Miracle in the Gorbals, Petrushka; toured Australia, 1958–9, in Nude with Violin, also with the Royal Ballet; directed Aladdin, Marriage-Go-Round, London, 1959; Duel of Angels, NY, 1960; Finian's Rainbow (tour), Twelfth Night, Duel of Angels, The Lady of the Camelias (last three productions for the Old Vic World Tour), 1961; Covent Garden, 1963, devised and directed a new production of Swan Lake; directed Dame Margot Fonteyn's World Tour, 1963; directed Camelot, 1964; La Contessa (tour), 1965; Metropolitan Opera, NY, May 1965, narrated A Wedding Bouquet (Gertrude Stein ballet), with the Royal Ballet Co; Covent Garden, Nov 1969, again narrated A Wedding Bouquet; Royal, Sydney, July 1971, directed Conduct Unbecoming; Coliseum, Dec 1971, directed Peter Pan; this production has been restaged several times; choreographer for the following ballets, Comus, Hamlet, The Birds, Miracle in the Gorbals, Adam Zero, Elektra, etc; created the Ballets The Display, Yugen, Sun Music, and appeared as Don Quixote and Dr Coppelius (1969–70) for the Australian Ballet Company; Sydney Opera House, 1973, directed The Sleeping Beauty; devised and directed The Merry Widow for the Australian Ballet Company, 1975; co-produced the Australian tour of Stars of World Ballet in Gala Performance, 1978–9; has also appeared in such films as Henry V, The Red Shoes, The Tales of Hoffman, Chitty Chitty Bang Bang, Don Quixote, The Mango Tree, and Patrick (1979); played the Devil and arranged the choreography for the film The Soldier's Tale, 1963; has broadcast and appeared on television, including solo performances in Australia; received the Honour of Commander of the British Empire in the Birthday Honours, 1964; Knight of the British Empire, New Year Honours, 1968; received the Scroll of Honour (Norway), 1950; Order of the Knight of the Northern Star (Sweden);

director of Australian Ballet Company, 1975; director of Adelaide Festival of Arts, 1970.

Recreations: Swimming, riding and tennis. *Address:* c/o Midland Bank Ltd, 70 St Martin's Lane, London WC2.

HENDERSON, Dickie, OBE, actor and music-hall comedian
b London, 30 Oct 1922; s of Dick Henderson and his wife Winifred May (Dunn); e St Joseph's College, Beulah Hill; m (1) Dixie Ross (dec); (2) Gwyneth Wycherley.

Made his first appearance on the stage at the Empire, Middlesborough, 1938, as a dancer in variety; Savoy, Aug 1948, appeared in the revue À la Carte; Hippodrome, Sept 1949, appeared in Folies Bergère Revue; Her Majesty's, Dec 1952, played Waldo Walton in Remains To Be Seen; Prince's, May 1953, Paul in Happy As a King; Casino, Oct 1953, played Dickie Fletcher in Wish You Were Here; Her Majesty's, Jan 1955, succeeded Eli Wallach as Sakini in The Teahouse of the August Moon; Prince of Wales's, Feb 1957, appeared in variety; and at the same theatre, Apr 1957, in the revue Plaisirs de Paris; Adelphi, Dec 1959, Andy Persichetti in the musical When In Rome . . .; Prince of Wales, Feb 1965, followed Max Bygraves as star in Round About Piccadilly; Arnaud, Guildford, May 1966, and tour, Davey Dunn in Bang, Bang Beirut; Royal, Windsor, May 1968, Chuck Clark in Come Live With Me; Intimate, Palmers Green, Apr 1969, Angus Neil in Forever April; played Fred Florence in Stand By Your Bedouin at Torquay, Summer 1969, Weston-super-Mare, 1970, and Southend, 1971; Wolverhampton, Apr 1970, appeared in The Bride Makes Three and toured; has made numerous appearances at the London Palladium in variety, and taken part in seven Royal Command Performances, once as compere; has appeared in cabaret worldwide, including London, Hong Kong and Monte Carlo; his numerous television appearances include 126 performances of *The Dickie Henderson Show, Sunday Night at the London Palladium* (as compere), I'm Dickie—That's Showbusiness, Face the Music, and in the US, the Jack Paar and Ed Sullivan Shows; also guest appearances in Holland and Germany; he is a past Chairman and Vice-President of the Variety Club of Great Britain; received the OBE in the Jubilee Honours, 1977, for his services to charity.

Recreation: Golf (past captain of Vaudeville Golfing Society). *Clubs:* Lord's Taverners, Sparks, Green Room, Saints and Sinners. *Address:* c/o London Management, 235–241 Regent Street, London, W1.

HENDERSON, Florence, actress and singer
b Dale, Indiana, 14 Feb 1934; d of Joseph Henderson and his wife Elizabeth (Elder); e St Francis Academy, Owensboro, Kentucky; m Ira Bernstein; studied acting with Christine Johnson and at the American Academy of Dramatic Arts.

Made her stage début at the Imperial, New York, June 1952, as the New Girl in Wish You Were Here; toured, Aug 1952–May 1953, as Laurey in Oklahoma!; New York City Center, Aug 1953, again played Laurey in Oklahoma! subsequently touring again in this part; Los Angeles Civic Light Opera Association, summer 1953, played Resi in The Great Waltz, and appeared in this production at the Curran, San Francisco; Majestic, Nov 1954, played the title-role in Fanny; appeared in industrial shows for Oldsmobile, 1958–61; toured, 1961, as Maria Rainer in The Sound of Music, receiving the Sarah Siddons Award for her performance of this part in Chicago; Broadway, Dec 1963, played Mary Morgan in The Girl Who Came to Supper; NY State, June 1967, Ensign Nellie Forbush in a revival of South Pacific; toured, 1974, as Annie Oakley in Annie Get Your Gun; for Los Angeles and San Francisco Civic Light Opera, appeared in The Sound of Music, 1978, and Bells Are Ringing, 1979; frequent cabaret appearances include Las Vegas and Lake Tahoe; has appeared on television in *The Brady Bunch*, as well as many specials.

Address: c/o Katz–Gallin–Morey, 9255 Sunset Boulevard, Los Angeles, Calif 90069.

HENDERSON, Robert, director and actor
b Ann Arbor, Mich, USA, 19 Dec 1904; *s* of William D Henderson and his wife Mary (Barton); *e* Universities of Michigan, Harvard and Princeton, BA, MA, PhD; *m* Estelle Winwood; studied for the stage under Louis Jouvet at the Théâtre des Champs-Elysées, Paris.

Made his first production, at the Rockford Theatre, Rockford, Ill, when he staged The Firebrand, 1926; in New York, he directed the productions of the Electra of Sophocles, 1932; Ghosts, 1935; When We Are Married, and The Importance of Being Earnest, 1939; First Stop to Heaven, and The Beautiful People, 1941; toured To-Night at 8.30, all over America; was founder and director of the Ann Arbor Festival; director of the Bonstelle Theatre, Detroit, and also directed seasons at the Royal Alexandra Theatre, Toronto; in London, he has directed the productions of Caviar to the General, The Beautiful People, SS Glencairn, I Said to Myself, The Shelley Story, Tobacco Road, 1947; Beyond the Horizon, Jason, 1948; The Compelled People, The Monkey Puzzle, The Return of Peter Grimm, 1949; The School for Scoundrels, Murder's Child, Forsaking All Others, Lovely, Lovely Money, Don't Lose Your Head, 1950; The Foolish Gentlewoman (with Peter Dearing), 1951; Age of Consent, 1953; appeared at the Stoll, Sept 1951, as Colonel Page in Rainbow Square; Coliseum, Mar 1952, played the Secretary of State in Call Me Madam; toured, 1954, as Captain Brackett in South Pacific; Comedy, July 1956, played the Prison Governor in The Quare Fellow; Coliseum, Mar 1957, Welch in Damn Yankees; at the same theatre, Nov 1957, Larry Hastings in Bells Are Ringing; Savoy, July 1958, Judge Nash in the revival of The Trial of Mary Dugan; New Shakespeare, Liverpool, Sept 1958, Dr Lyman in Bus Stop; Theatre Royal, Stratford, Apr 1960, Mr Horniman in Sam, the Highest Jumper of Them All, and May 1960, Superintendent Nicholson in Ned Kelly at the same theatre; at the Pembroke, Croydon, Sept 1960, played Horn in Compulsion, and Oct 1960, Will Pentland in Look Homeward, Angel; Mermaid, June 1961, Major Hosmer in The Andersonville Trial; Duke of York's, Oct 1962, played R J Pinkerton in Across the Board on Tomorrow Morning (in the double-bill Two Plays); Edinburgh Festival, Aug 1964, played the Rev Jimmy Dexter in Happy End; joined The Play House Company, Cleveland, Ohio, season 1964–5; artistic director, 1968–, of Studio '68 of Theatre Arts, London; directed The Mad Woman of Chaillot, London and NY, 1969–70; Duke of York's, May 1970, played Dr Mayberry in I Never Sang for My Father; Arnaud, Guildford, June 1972, McComber in Ah Wilderness!; Round House, June 1977, Judge Collister in The Red Devil Battery Sign; his many film appearances include, Cat and Mouse, The Great Gatsby, Phase Four, Valentino, Superman, and Julia.

Address: c/o Pamela Simons, 9–15 Neal Street, London, WC2. *Tel:* 01–240 0228.

HENEKER, David, MBE, composer and lyricist
b Southsea, 31 Mar 1906; *s* of General Sir William Heneker, KCB, KCMG, DSO and his wife Clara (Jones); *e* Wellington College and Royal Military College, Sandhurst; *m* (1) Ellen Hope (mar dis); (2) Gwenol Satow; formerly Regular Army Officer 1925–48.

Has written music and lyrics for the following productions: Expresso Bongo (jointly), Irma la Douce (joint adaptation and lyrics only), 1958; Make Me an Offer (jointly), The Art of Living (jointly), 1960; Half a Sixpence, 1963; Charlie Girl (jointly), 1965; Jorrocks, 1968; Phil the Fluter (jointly), 1969; Popkiss (jointly), 1972; Half a Sixpence was also filmed; has collaborated on music and lyrics for The Two Faces of Dr Jekyll and I've Gotta Horse; Irma ran for 1512 performances at The Lyric, and 524 in New York (1960), and Charlie Girl for 2202 performances at The Adelphi; Make Me An Offer received the *Evening Standard* Award for Best Musical, 1960, and Jorrocks, The Plays and Players Award for Best Musical, 1968; has also received three Ivor Novello Awards; Chairman, 1968–73 of the Songwriters Guild of Great Britain; President, 1973–.

Recreations: Walking and cooking. *Address:* c/o Curtis Brown Ltd, 1 Craven Hill, London W2.

HENRITZE, Bette, actress
b Betsy Layne, Ky, 23 May; *e* University of Tennessee; trained for the stage at the American Academy of Dramatic Arts.

Made her Broadway debut, 23 Dec 1948, at the Hudson as Mary Delaney in Jenny Kissed Me, under the name of Bette Howe; toured Virginia with the Barter Theatre Company, 1950; appeared at the Mamasquan Theatre, NJ, 1951; at the Cherry Lane, 27 Dec 1956, as Cloyne in Purple Dust; Phoenix, Dec 1958, played a Peasant Woman in The Power and the Glory; Nov 1959, Nirodike in Lysistrata; Jan 1960, appeared in Peer Gynt, Nov 1960, Pimple in She Stoops to Conquer; Dec 1960, Bessie Burgess in The Plough and the Stars; Jan 1961, Mrs Peyton in The Octoroon; Alvin, Jan 1962, Mrs Gensup in Giants, Sons of Giants; New York Shakespeare Festival, July 1961, Margaret in Much Ado About Nothing; Aug 1961, Duchess of York in King Richard II; Jun 1962, Nerissa in The Merchant of Venice; Aug 1962, Goneril in King Lear; Anderson, Jan 1963, Mary Todd in Abe Lincoln in Illinois; One Sheridan Square, Apr 1963, Cross-Lane Nora in The Lion in Love; Delacorte, June 1963, Charmian in Antony and Cleopatra; Aug 1963, Paulina in The Winter's Tale; Martin Beck, Oct 1963, Mrs Hasty Malone in The Ballad of the Sad Cafe; Henry Miller's, May 1964, various roles in The White House; Delacorte, July 1964, took over from Sada Thompson as Emilia in Othello; Martinique, May 1965, Louise, Maja, Landlady, and Young Lady in Baal; Delacorte, June 1966, Mariana in All's Well That Ends Well; July 1966, Mariana in Measure for Measure; Cherry Lane, Sept 1966, Ermengarde in The Long Christmas Dinner, and Mlle Pointevin in Queens of France in a production with the overall title Thornton Wilder's Triple Bill; St Clement's Church, Dec 1966, Mrs Shortley in The Displaced Person; Cherry Lane, Feb 1967, Mary Windrod in The Rimers of Eldritch; Belasco, Sept 1967, Bea Schmidt in Dr Cook's Garden; Billy Rose, Mar 1968, Mrs Bacon in Here's Where I Belong; American Place, Dec 1968, Edna in The Acquisition; Astor Place, Oct 1969, Jessie Mason in The Erpingham Camp; Delacorte, June 1970, Margaret Jourdain in Henry IV, Part 1; Duchess of York in Henry IV, Part II; and Dutchess of York in Richard III; Estelle Newman, Oct 1970, Anna Ames in The Happiness Cage; Anspacher, May 1972, played in Older People; Delacorte, Aug 1972, Ursula in Much Ado About Nothing, and repeated this part at the Winter Garden, Nov 1972; Anspacher, Nov 1973, Trixie in Lotta; Shubert, Mar 1974, Mother in Over Here!; Mitzi E. Newhouse, Oct 1974, Margaret in Richard III; American Shakespeare Festival, Stratford, Conn, Jun 1975, Mrs Soames in Our Town; Jul 1975, Paulina in The Winter's Tale;

Lyceum, Dec 1975, Elizabeth in Angel Street; McCarter, Princeton, Mar 1976, and Stratford, Conn, June 1976, again played Paulina, also playing Mrs Putnam in The Crucible at Stratford; Long Wharf, New Haven, Dec 1976, Nora in Home; McCarter, Princeton, and Annenberg, Philadelphia, 1978, Anna in A Month in the Country and Jenny in The Torch Bearers; Manhattan Theatre Club, Apr 1978, Mrs Mihaly Almasi in Catsplay, transferring with the production to the Promenade; Circle in the Square, Dec 1978, Susan Ramsden in Man and Superman; McCarter, 1979, Nurse Guinness in Heartbreak House; toured, summer 1979, as Helga Ten Dorp in Deathtrap; Roundabout Stage One, Dec 1979, Anna in A Month in the Country; films include The Hospital, and All That Jazz; TV work includes Ryan's Hope, Another World, etc.

Address: Actors Equity Association, 165 West 46th Street, New York, NY 10036.

HENSON, Nicky, actor
b London, 12 May 1945; *s* of Leslie Lincoln Henson and his wife Harriet Martha (Collins); *e* St Bede's, Eastbourne and Charterhouse; *m* Una Stubbs (mar dis); trained as a stage manager at RADA.

Made his first stage appearance as a guitarist in 1961; first London appearance, Vaudeville, Apr 1963, in the revue All Square; Drury Lane, Aug 1964, played Mordred in Camelot; Prince of Wales, Aug 1965, Ellis in Passion Flower Hotel; Palladium, May 1966, appeared in the revue London Laughs; Edinburgh Festival, Sept 1967, played the Soldier in The Soldier's Tale; Mermaid, Nov 1967, Niko in Climb the Greased Pole; Phoenix, Mar 1968, played Squire, Nicholas and Damon in Canterbury Tales; toured, Sept 1969, as Bill in Zoo, Zoo, Widdershins Zoo; Strand, Dec 1969, Toad in Toad of Toad Hall; joined the Young Vic company to play parts including Ottavio in The Cheats of Scapin, the Soldier in The Soldier's Tale, Pozzo in Waiting for Godot, Grumio in The Taming of the Shrew, Herod in the Wakefield Nativity Plays and Messenger in Oedipus (also wrote music), 1970; Young Marlow in She Stoops to Conquer, Lucio in Measure for Measure, Mercutio in Romeo and Juliet, 1971; Solange in The Maids, Greeneyes in Deathwatch, Jack Sheppard in Stand and Deliver (Edinburgh Festival and Round House), Jimmy Porter in Look Back in Anger, 1972; Rosencrantz in Rosencrantz and Guildenstern are Dead, 1973; Hampstead, Nov 1973 and May Fair, Dec appeared in The Ride Across Lake Constance; Shaw, Jan 1974, The Bus Driver in Mind Your Head; Greenwich, Mar 1974, Laertes in Hamlet; Open Air, Regent's Park, May 1974, Bottom in A Midsummer Night's Dream; Shaw, Oct 1974, Petruchio in The Taming of the Shrew; Casino, Dec 1974, Buttons in Cinderella; Prince of Wales, Mar 1976, Lorne in Mardi Gras; Arnaud, Guildford, Oct 1976, Leonardo da Vinci in Later Leonardo; Young Vic, Dec 1976, Lord Fancourt Babberley in Charley's Aunt; Thorndike, Leatherhead, Jan 1977, and Hong Kong Festival, Captain Bluntschli in Arms and the Man; Malvern Festival, May 1977, and Savoy, Aug, played Henry Straker in Man and Superman; King's Head, Aug 1977, Oedipus in Oedipus at the Crossroads; joined the National Theatre, 1978, and played the following parts at the Olivier: Yepikhodov in The Cherry Orchard (Feb), Malcolm in Macbeth (May), Heros in The Woman (Aug), Mr Brisk in The Double Dealer (Oct), Captain Ager in A Fair Quarrel (Mar 1979); Birmingham Rep, June 1979, and Her Majesty's, Nov 1979, played Gerald Popkiss in Rookery Nook; returned to the National, May 1980, to appear in the double-bill, The Browning Version and Harlequinade; films, since 1963, include Witchfinder General, There's A Girl in My Soup, The Bawdy Adventures of

Tom Jones, and Number 1 of the Secret Service; occasional television since 1962 includes the series Prometheus.

Favourite part: Pozzo. *Club:* Gerry's. *Recreations:* Songwriting, reading, motorcycling. *Address:* c/o Richard Stone, 18–20 York Buildings, London, WC2.

HEPBURN, Katharine, actress
b Hartford, Conn, 9 Nov 1909; *d* of Dr Thomas N Hepburn and his wife Katharine (Houghton); *e* Hartford School for Girls and Bryn Mawr College; *m* Ludlow Ogden Smith (mar dis).

Appeared in amateur productions at College, before making her first appearance on the professional stage in Baltimore, 1928, under the management of Edwin Knopf, in The Czarina; at Great Neck, Long Island, 1928, appeared in The Big Pond; made her first appearance on the New York stage at the Martin Beck Theatre, 12 Sept 1928, as one of the hostesses in Night Hostess, under the name of Katherine Burns; at the Cort Theatre, Nov 1928, played Veronica Sims in These Days; at the Plymouth, Nov 1928, understudied Hope Williams in Holiday, but did not play; in 1929, toured for five weeks as Grazia in Death Takes a Holiday; at the Guild Theatre, Apr 1930, played Katia in A Month in the Country; Maxine Elliott, Nov 1930, Judy Bottle in Art and Mrs Bottle; in 1931, played a summer stock season at Ivoryton, Conn; Morosco, NY, Mar 1932, made a success when she played Antiope in The Warrior's Husband; Martin Beck, Dec 1933, played Stella Surrege in The Lake; New Haven, Conn, Dec 1936, and on tour, 1937, played Jane Eyre in the play of that name; Shubert, NY, Mar 1939, Tracy Lord in The Philadelphia Story; St James (for the Guild), Nov 1942, Jamie Coe Rowan in Without Love; Cort, Jan 1950, appeared as Rosalind in As You Like It, and later, made an extensive tour in the same part; made her first appearance on the London stage at the New, 27 June 1952, as The Lady in The Millionairess; played the same part at the Shubert, NY, Oct 1952; toured Australia with the Old Vic Company, 1955, as Portia in The Merchant of Venice, Katharine in The Taming of the Shrew, and Isabella in Measure for Measure; at the Shakespeare Festival, Stratford, Conn, July 1957, played Portia in The Merchant of Venice, and Beatrice in Much Ado About Nothing; toured, Jan 1958, in the latter play; Stratford, Conn, June 1960, played Viola in Twelfth Night, and Cleopatra in Antony and Cleopatra; Mark Hellinger, Dec 1969, played Coco Chanel in the musical Coco, and toured in this part in 1971; Dorothy Chandler Pavilion, Los Angeles, Apr 1971, again played in Coco, then resumed the tour; Broadhurst, Feb 1976, Mrs Basil in A Matter of Gravity, subsequently touring in the role; entered films, Oct 1932, in A Bill of Divorcement, subsequent films include Morning Glory (Academy Award), Little Women, The Little Minister, Mary of Scotland, Quality Street, Stage Door, The African Queen, Summertime, The Rainmaker, Desk Set, Long Day's Journey into Night (Cannes Film Festival Award), Guess Who's Coming to Dinner? (Academy Award), A Lion in Winter (Academy Award), A Delicate Balance, Rooster Cogburn (1975), etc.

Recreations: Tennis, swimming, riding, and golf. *Address:* 201 Bloomfield Avenue, West Hartford, Connecticut.

HEPPLE, Jeanne, actress
b London, 2 Aug 1936; *d* of Arthur Hepple and his wife Irene Jeannette (Cutts); *e* Nonsuch Grammar School, Cheam, Surrey, and Ewell Technical College, Surrey; *m* (1) G Brian Phelen (mar dis); (2) Jeff Bleckner; formerly a Laboratory assistant in Research Antibiotics; studied for the stage at the Guildhall School of Music and Drama.

Made her first appearance in London at the Royal Court, Sept 1959, as Julia in Cock-a-Doodle-Dandy; Everyman, Cheltenham, Oct 1960, played Terry Jamieson in You in Your Small Corner; Little, Bromley, Feb 1961, played Hilde Wangel in The Masterbuilder; Arts, Mar 1961, again played Terry Jamieson in You in Your Small Corner; joined the Royal Shakespeare Company, and at the Aldwych, July 1961, played the Saxon Girl in Becket; subsequently appearing as Phebe in As You Like It; Zuleika in The Caucasian Chalk Circle; Judith in The Dance of Death; New Arts, July 1962, played Bianca in Women, Beware Women; Chichester Festival, June–Sept 1963, played a Waitress in The Workhouse Donkey, and understudied and occasionally played the title-part in Saint Joan, and Sonia in Uncle Vanya; joined the National Theatre Company, and at the Old Vic, Oct 1963, appeared as a Court Lady in the inaugural production of Hamlet; subsequently playing the following parts: Lucy in The Recruiting Officer, Dec 1963; Vicky Hobson in Hobson's Choice, Kaia in The Masterbuilder, 1964; Mary Warren in The Crucible (Clarence Derwent Award for best supporting performance, 1965), Hilde Wangel in The Masterbuilder (also tour), Alice Hobson in Hobson's Choice, 1965; made her first appearance in New York, at the Belasco, Nov 1965, as Shirley in Inadmissible Evidence; Theatre de Lys, Mar 1966, Annie in Serjeant Musgrave's Dance; ANTA, May 1967, played the following parts: Beline in The Imaginary Invalid, Olive Lloyd Ransome in Ways and Means, Myrtle Bagot in Still Life and Sara Melody in A Touch of the Poet; member of Yale University's acting company and taught acting at Yale, 1967–8; member of Playhouse in the Park Company, Cincinnati, 1968, playing St Joan; for Seattle Repertory Company, season 1969, played Olga in Three Sisters; Delacorte, NY, June 1970, Lady Grey (Queen Elizabeth) in The Wars of the Roses (Parts 2 and 3); Royale, Mar 1971, Mary Detweiler in How the Other Half Loves; Morosco, Feb 1972, Helga in Nightwatch; 1971–4, various appearances with the Public Theater, NY, including Margaret in Much Ado About Nothing; films in which she has appeared include The Kitchen, and Lunch Hour; first appeared on television, 1960, and principal performances include Serjeant Musgrave's Dance, The De Maupassant Story, The Search, etc; taught acting at Yale, 1967–8; Brooklyn College, NY, 1974; Actors and Directors Lab, Beverly Hills, 1979–.

Recreations: Gardening, cooking, and crafts. *Address:* c/o Susan Smith, 9869 Santa Monica Boulevard, Beverly Hills, Calif.

HEPPLE, Peter, editor, *The Stage*
b Wood Green, London, 2 Jan 1927; *s* of William Hepple and his wife Marjory (Mayes); *e* City of London School; *m* Josephine Barnett.

Trained as a surveyor, but after National Service with the Royal Engineers entered publishing; editor for the Institute of Petroleum, 1965–72; first wrote for *The Stage* 1950, initially as variety reviewer, later as drama critic and night life columnist for ten years; appointed editor, 1972; has also contributed to a number of British and overseas newspapers and magazines on theatre, cinema, music etc; drama critic and theatre columnist of *Where to Go in London,* 1966–77.

Recreations: Football, and music of all types. *Address:* 12 Minchenden Crescent, Southgate, London N14. *Tel:* 01–886 4223.

HEPTON, Bernard, actor and director
b Bradford, 19 Oct 1925; *s* of Bernard Austin Heptonstall and his wife Hilda (Berrington); *e* St Bede's Grammar School, Bradford; *m* (1) the actress Nancie Oldfield Jackson (dec); (2)

Hilary Liddell, actress and teacher; trained for the stage at the Northern Theatre School and studied under Esmé Church and Rudolph Laban; formerly an aeronautical engineering apprentice.

Made his first stage appearance at Bradford Civic Playhouse, 1942, as a Soldier in The Virgin Goddess; after repertory experience at York, Manchester, Bromley, etc, joined the Birmingham Repertory Company as an actor, 1951, later becoming Director of Productions, 1957–60; during this time arranged fights for Stratford, the Old Vic, etc; director of productions, Liverpool Playhouse, 1961–62; from 1962–66 a drama producer/director for BBCTV; returned to acting, 1967; with the Bristol Old Vic Company, 1970–71, his parts included Jaques in As You Like It, Vershinin in The Three Sisters, the Headmaster in Forty Years On, Tesman in Hedda Gabler and Gremio in The Taming of the Shrew; played the last two roles on the company's tour of South America, 1971; Mermaid, July 1971, Swingler in The Old Boys; Arnaud, Guildford, Oct 1975, Shylock in The Merchant of Venice; toured, 1978, in Game of Kings; St George's Islington, season 1979, played the title roles in Julius Caesar and Richard II, and Jaques in As You Like It; films since 1948 include Get Carter, The Six Wives of Henry VIII, and Voyage of the Damned; numerous TV appearances since 1957 include plays, the series *Colditz, Squirrels, Secret Army,* and Tinker, Tailor, Soldier, Spy.

Favourite parts: Richard II, Sir Thomas More in A Man for All Seasons. *Recreations:* Gardening, cricket, music and mountains. *Address:* c/o Bryan Drew, 81 Shaftesbury Avenue, London W1.

HERBERT, Jocelyn, designer
b London, 22 Feb 1917; *d* of Alan Patrick Herbert and his wife Gwendolen Harriet (Macnalty); *e* St Paul's Girl's School, London; *m* Anthony B Lousada (mar dis).

Designed her first production for the English Stage Company at the Royal Court Theatre, May 1957, with The Chairs; she has since designed the following productions, at the Royal Court unless otherwise stated: The Sport of My Mad Mother, The Lesson, Endgame, 1958; Roots, Sergeant Musgrave's Dance, 1959; Chicken Soup With Barley, I'm Talking About Jerusalem, Trials By Logue, 1960; The Changeling, Richard III (Stratford-on-Avon), The Kitchen, Luther, 1961; A Midsummer Night's Dream, Chips With Everything, Happy Days, 1962; Baal, Skyvers, Exit the King, 1963; The Seagull, Othello (National Theatre), St Joan of the Stockyards, Inadmissible Evidence, Julius Caesar, 1964; Mother Courage (National Theatre), A Patriot For Me, Inadmissible Evidence (New York), 1965; The Lion and the Jewel, Ghosts (Aldwych), Orpheus and Euridice (Sadler's Wells), 1966; Life Price, Hamlet (Round House and NY), 1969; Beckett 3 (Theatre Upstairs), Three Months Gone, Home (also NY), 1970; A Woman Killed with Kindness, Tyger (both National Theatre), The Changing Room, 1971; Not I, Krapp's Last Tape, Savages, Cromwell, 1973; Life Class, Pygmalion (Albery), 1974; The Force of Destiny (Paris Opera), What the Butler Saw, Teeth 'n' Smiles, 1975; Footfalls, That Time, 1976; The Merchant (NY), Lulu (Metropolitan Opera, NY), 1977; Saratoga (Aldwych), 1978; Happy Days, Il Seraglio and The Rise and Fall of the City of Mahoganny (both Metropolitan Opera), 1979; Early Days (National), 1980; appointed Colour Consultant for the film Tom Jones, and was Production Designer for the following films: Isadora, If..., Hamlet, Ned Kelly, and O Lucky Man.

Address: 45 Pottery Lane, London W11.

HERLIE, Eileen, actress
b Glasgow, Scotland, 8 Mar 1920; *d* of Patrick Herlihy and his

wife Isobel (Cowden); *e* Shawland's Academy, Glasgow; *m* (1) Philip Barrett (mar dis); (2) Witold Kuncewicz (mar dis).

Made her first appearance on the stage at the Lyric, Glasgow, 1938, with the Scottish National Players in Sweet Aloes; in 1939, appeared with the Rutherglen Repertory Company; toured, 1942, as Mrs de Winter in Rebecca, and made her first appearance in London, in this part, at the Ambassadors' Theatre, 26 Dec 1942; at the Scala Theatre, Apr 1943, again played Mrs de Winter in Rebecca, and May 1943, Peg in Peg O'My Heart; toured, 1944, as Regina in The Little Foxes; joined the Old Vic company at the Playhouse, Liverpool, and during 1944–5, appeared there as Mrs Fanny Wilton in John Gabriel Borkman, Varvara in Lisa, Paula in The Second Mrs Tanqueray, Lady Sneerwell in The School for Scandal, Anna Christopherson in Anna Christie, the Queen in Hamlet, Dol Common in The Alchemist, and Stella de Gex in His Excellency the Governor; Lyric, Hammersmith, Nov 1945, played Andromache in The Trojan Women; Feb 1946, Mary L in The Time of Your Life; May 1946, Alcestis in The Thracian Horses, and Sept 1946, the Queen in The Eagle Has Two Heads, appearing in the same part at the Haymarket, Feb 1947; Edinburgh Festival, Aug and Globe Theatre, Sept 1948, Medea in the play of that name; Haymarket, Aug 1950, played Paula in The Second Mrs Tanqueray; Lyric, Hammersmith, Feb 1953, played Mrs Marwood in The Way of the World, and May 1953, Belvidera in Venice Preserv'd; King's, Glasgow, Nov 1953, Irene Carey in A Sense of Guilt; Haymarket, London, Nov 1954, Mrs Molloy in The Matchmaker; made her first appearance on Broadway, at the Royale, Dec 1955, in the same part, when the play ran for 488 performances; Phoenix, New York, Dec 1957, played Emilia Marty in The Makropoulos Secret; Stratford Shakespeare Festival, Ontario, June 1958, Paulina in The Winter's Tale, and Beatrice in Much Ado About Nothing; John Golden, NY, Nov 1958, Ruth Gray in Epitaph for George Dillon, and also when the play was revived at Henry Miller's, Jan 1959; Shubert, Oct 1959, appeared as Lily in Take Me Along; Winter Garden, Mar 1962, Elizabeth Hawkes-Bullock in the musical All American; Brooks Atkinson, Feb 1963, Stella in Photo Finish; Lunt-Fontanne, Apr 1964, Gertrude in Sir John Gielgud's production of Hamlet; Brooks Atkinson, Nov 1967, Lady Fitzbuttress in Halfway up the Tree; Ivanhoe, Chicago, 1971, Martha in Who's Afraid of Virginia Woolf? and Clare in Out Cry; Ethel Barrymore, Mar 1973, Countess Matilda Spina in Emperor Henry IV; Helen Hayes, Oct 1973, Queen Mary in Crown Matrimonial; Westport, Conn, Country Playhouse, July 1974, again played Mary in Crown Matrimonial, and subsequently toured; Ivanhoe, Chicago, Oct 1974, Essie Sebastian in The Great Sebastians; entered films, 1947, in Hungry Hill, also appearing in Hamlet, and Freud.

Recreations: Music and reading. *Address:* c/o Milton Goldman, ICM, 40 West 57th Street, New York, NY 10019.

HERMAN, Jerry, (*né* Gerald), composer and lyricist
b New York City, 10 July 1933; *s* of Harry Herman and his wife Ruth (Sachs); *e* Parson's School of Design, University of Miami (AB 1961); served in the US Army, 1954–55.

Wrote the music and lyrics for his first musical play, I Feel Wonderful, produced at the Theatre de Lys, 18 Oct 1954; since then has composed and written Nightcap, 1958; Parade, 1960; the song Best Gold in the revue From A to Z, 1960; Milk and Honey, Madame Aphrodite, 1961; Hello, Dolly!, for which he received the Antoinette Perry ("Tony") Award, 1964; Mame, 1966; Dear World, 1969; Mack and Mabel, 1974; The Grand Tour, 1978; on 24 Nov 1974, appeared at

the Kaufmann Concert Hall, NY, in An Evening with Jerry Herman; Hello, Dolly! produced at the Drury Lane, London, 2 Dec 1965, marking his London debut; Mame produced at the Drury Lane Feb 1969; both these last musicals were made into films.

Recreations: Architecture and design. *Address:* Dramatists Guild, 234 West 44th Street, New York, NY, USA 10036.

HERON, Joyce, actress
b Port Said, Egypt, 6 Nov 1916; *d* of Colonel Sir George Wykeham Heron, CMG, CBE, DSO, etc, and his wife Elsa (Burch); *e* Ancaster House, Bexhill-on-Sea; *m* Ralph Michael; studied for the stage at the Embassy Theatre School.

Made her first appearance on the stage at the Embassy, 16 Feb 1937, as the Young Lady in Tavern in the Town; subsequently toured as Carol Newton in Mr Penny's Tuppence; appeared at the Q, May–June 1938, in Youth and Mrs Meredith and The Last Day; Comedy, Aug 1938, played Iris Robinson in Give Me Yesterday; Sept 1938, Mary in Room for Two; Oct 1940, Lucia Galen in High Temperature, and July 1942, Grena in Murder Without Crime; Arts, Apr 1943, appeared as Cherry in The Young and Lovely; Garrick, Oct 1943, as Benita in She Follows Me About; St Martin's, Apr 1945, Joan Deal in The Shop at Sly Corner; Embassy, June 1946, Jane Mason in Love Goes to Press, and played the same part at the Duchess, July 1946; made her first appearance in New York, at the Biltmore, 1 Jan 1947, as Jane in Love Goes to Press; Arts, July 1948, the Patient in Too True to Be Good; Aug 1948, Emira in Tartuffe; Oct 1948, Agafya in Marriage; St Martin's, Apr 1949, played Harriet in Twice Upon a Time; Embassy, Sept 1949, Julia Cleaver in Rain Before Seven; Opera House, Leicester, Apr 1951, Evie Dawn in Waggonload O' Monkeys; Aldwych, London, Oct 1951, Regine in Figure of Fun; St James's, Nov 1952, Diana Sackville in Dead Secret; at the Playhouse, NY, Oct 1953, appeared as Charlotte Young in Gently Does It; Lyric, Hammersmith, May 1958, played Lilian Marne in The Key of the Door; toured, May 1960, as Anna in A Piece of Silver; Phoenix, Dec 1960, played Delia Moss in The Geese Are Getting Fat; Pembroke, Croydon, May 1962, played Mary in The Summer People, subsequently touring with the production; Vaudeville, Nov 1966, Coral Harper in Justice is a Woman; New, July 1967, took over as Daisy Crompton in Spring and Port Wine; Ashcroft, Croydon, Mar 1970, Mrs Dale in At Home With the Dales; Westminster, Mar 1970, Hermione Hurst in Blindsight, and July 1970, Mrs Wilson in The Forgotten Factor; Connaught, Worthing, Feb 1971, the Mother in Women Around; toured Apr 1972 as Aline Solness in The Master Builder; Whitehall, May 1977, Martha Brewster in Arsenic and Old Lace; first appeared in films, 1942, in Women Aren't Angels.

Recreation: Dress designing. *Address:* c/o Essanay Ltd, 75 Hammersmith Road, London, W14.

(*Died Apr 1980.*)

HERSEY, David, lighting designer
b Rochester, NY, 30 Nov 1939; *s* of C Kenneth Hersey and his wife Ella (Morgan); *e* Oberlin College, Ohio.

After six years, 1961–7 in the US as actor, stage manager and lighting designer, during which he was involved in some 75 productions (including his NY acting debut at the Martinique, 1962, as the Stage Manager in Six Characters in Search of an Author), moved to England 1968, to join Theatre Projects Ltd; founded David Hersey Associates Ltd 1971; Lighting Supervisor, National Theatre, 1974–; since lighting his first London production, She Stoops to Conquer, at the Garrick, May 1969, he has lit over 100 productions for most of England's major theatre, opera and ballet companies, including the National Theatre, the Royal Shakespeare Company, Royal Opera, Royal Ballet, Scottish Ballet, Ballet Rambert, London Contemporary Dance, English National Opera; recent West End credits include Elvis, Evita, The Crucifer of Blood, The King and I; he lit the ballet sequences for the film Nijinsky in 1979; work overseas includes Austria, France, Germany, Canada and Iran; member executive committee, Society of British Theatre Designers.

Recreations: Jewellery making, boating. *Address:* 20 Gainsborough Court, Nether Street, London N12. *Tel:* 01–446 3337.

HESTON, Charlton (*né* Carter), actor
b Evanston, Illinois, 6 Oct 1922; *s* of Russell Whitford Carter and his wife Lilla (Charlton); *e* Northwestern University; *m* Lydia Clarke; studied for the stage at the Northwestern University School of Speech.

At the Thomas Wolfe Memorial Theatre, Asheville, NC, 1947, which he co-directed with his wife, played in State of the Union and The Glass Menagerie; made his first appearance on Broadway at the Martin Beck Theatre, Nov 1947, as Proculeius in Antony and Cleopatra, with Katharine Cornell; at the Cort, New York, Jan 1949, played Glenn Campbell in Leaf and Bough; Lenox Hill Playhouse, Feb 1949, A2 in Cock-a-Doodle-Doo; Mansfield, NY, Jan 1950, played John Clitherow in Design for a Stained Glass Window; in summer theatres, 1952, appeared in The Traitor; City Center, NY, Dec 1956, played Lieut Roberts in a revival of Mister Roberts; Helen Hayes, NY, Feb 1960, played Kell in The Tumbler; Mill Run Playhouse, Skokie, Ill, June 1965, played Sir Thomas More in A Man for All Seasons; Ahmanson, Los Angeles, Dec 1972, John Proctor in The Crucible; Ahmanson, Jan 1975, played Macbeth; appeared at the same theatre, Feb 1977, in Long Day's Journey into Night, and in Feb 1979 as More in A Man for All Seasons; first entered films, 1950, in Dark City, and has appeared in numerous pictures including: The Greatest Show on Earth, The Ten Commandments, The Buccaneers, The Big Country, Ben Hur (Academy Award), The Agony and the Ecstasy, Planet of the Apes, Will Penny, Airport 1975, Earthquake, Battle of Midway, Crossed Swords, etc; first television appearance, 1949, in Julius Caesar, and since has played Macbeth, The Taming of the Shrew, Jane Eyre, Wuthering Heights, Of Human Bondage, etc; author of the book An Actor's Life; President of the Screen Actors Guild, 1966–9; Chairman, American Film Institute, and Center Theatre Group, LA.

Favourite part: Macbeth. *Recreations:* Tennis and horseback riding. *Address:* c/o George Thomas, 1334 Lincoln 130, Santa Monica, Calif 90401.

HEWES, Henry, dramatic critic
b Boston, Massachusetts, 9 Apr 1917; *s* of Dr Henry Fox Hewes and his wife Margaret (Warman); *e* Harvard University and Columbia University (BS); *m* Jane Fowle; served as a technical sergeant in the US Air Force, 1945.

Began as a copy boy for *The New York Times*, 1949, later becoming a staff writer; associate dramatic critic, *Saturday Review*, 1951; dramatic critic, 1954–77; executive director, Greater New York Chapter of ANTA, 1953–8; executive secretary, The Board of Standards and Planning for the Living Theatre, 1956–66, and of the American Theatre Planning Board, 1966 and currently; editor of the Off-Broadway section of The Best Plays, 1958–9, 1959–60, appointed editor, 1961–2, also edited 1962–3, 1963–4; editor of Famous American Plays of the 1940's, 1960; International Theatre Yearbook, 1977–; adapted Accounting for Love

(from the French play La Belle Aventure, by Robert de Flers, G A Caillvet, and M Etienne Rey), which was produced in London (Saville), Dec 1954; adaptor and director of Tennessee Williams's Three Players of a Summer Game, Westport, Conn, 1955; Theatre de Lys, New York, Jan 1957, directed an experimental version of Hamlet, with title-part played Siobhan McKenna; director of Our Very Own Hole in the Ground, NY, 1972; Great Lakes Shakespeare Festival, Cleveland, Ohio, 1974, adapted and directed a Watergate Version of Measure for Measure; moderator of TV seminars on theatre under the auspices of the American Theatre Wing, 1976–; Vice President of the New York Drama Critics Circle, 1969, and President 1972–3; President of the Drama Desk, 1965–74; Chairman of the Margo Jones Award Committee, 1967; lecturer Sarah Lawrence College, 1955–6; Columbia University, 1956–7; Salzburg Seminar in American Studies, 1970; New School for Social Research, 1972–; Chairman of the Joseph Maharam Award Committee; 1965–; Board of Directors, American Theatre Wing, 1972–; Secretary, American Theatre Critics' Association, 1974–.

Address: 1326 Madison Avenue, New York City. *Tel:* Atwater 9–5679.

HEWETT, Christopher, actor and director
b Worthing, 5 Apr; *s* of Christopher Fitzsimon Hewett and his wife Eleanor Joyce (Watts); *e* Beaumont College.

Began his career with the Oxford Playhouse Company, 1940–2; first appeared on the West End stage at His Majesty's, 4 Mar 1943, as Khadja in The Merry Widow; Prince of Wales, Apr 1944, appeared as Prosecuting Counsel in The Rest Is Silence; at the Q, May 1944, played the Hotel Manager in The Millionairess; later in the same year, at the Ambassadors', took over from Bonar Colleano in the revue Sweeter and Lower; Ambassadors', May 1946, appeared in the revue Sweetest and Lowest; Comedy, Nov 1948, in the revue Slings and Arrows; next appeared at the Comedy when he took over the part of Norwood Beverly in On Monday Next; toured, 1952, as Fred Graham in Kiss Me, Kate; Casino, Oct 1953, played Pinky Harris, in Wish You Were Here; Saville, May 1954, acted as assistant director of the revue Cockles and Champagne; at the Longacre, New York, June 1955, directed sketches in the revue Almost Crazy; Mark Hellinger, NY, Mar 1956, played Bystander and Zoltan Karpathy in My Fair Lady; Apr 1956, directed sketches for The Ziegfeld Follies tour; at the Broadway Congregational Church, NY, Oct 1957, the Archangel Raphael in Tobias and the Angel; County Playhouse, Westport, Conn, July 1960, Uncle Edward in Roar Like a Dove; Plymouth, Apr 1960, directed A to Z; toured, Sept 1960, as Roberts in The Unsinkable Molly Brown; Broadway, Nov 1961 Barnaby in Kean; Henry Miller, Sept 1962, Tom Orbell in The Affair; Theatre Four, Apr 1963, directed The Boys from Syracuse; Drury Lane, London, Nov 1963, again directed The Boys from Syracuse; City Center, NY, May 1966, directed Where's Charley?; Theatre Four, Off-Broadway, Jan 1967, directed and co-presented By Jupiter; Royal Poinciana, Palm Beach Fla, Mar 1967, directed The 5.07; Music Fair, Westbury, Aug 1967, directed Peg; Helen Hayes, NY, Jan 1969, played Father St Albans in Hadrian the Seventh; Jones Beach, July 1970, Max Detweiler in The Sound of Music; Ritz, Feb 1973, directed No Sex, Please, We're British; Roundabout, Mar 1974, Lord Porteous in The Circle; same theatre, Dec 1974, Sir Anthony Absolute in The Rivals; Vivian Beaumont, Oct 1975, O'Dwyer in Trelawney of the 'Wells'; St James, Dec 1976, Malvolio in Music Is; Jones Beach, June 1977, Finian in Finian's Rainbow; Queens Festival, Nov 1977, Scrooge in A Christmas Carol; Shaftesbury, London, Mar 1978, the Wazir in Kismet; Public/Other Stage, Feb 1979, Sir Rodney Blessington in New Jerusalem; has also directed and played in several late-night revues at the Watergate Theatre Club, and appeared in cabaret at Ciro's, Café de Paris, etc; broadcast as Welbeck Doom in the radio series Home At Eight (London), and in numerous radio programmes in the US; has appeared in films since 1941, including The Lavender Hill Mob and The Producers; television appearances include: *Alfred Hitchcock Presents,* The Defenders, Perry Mason, Dr Kildare, etc.

Hobby: Collecting Staffordshire China. *Recreation:* Swimming. *Address:* c/o Hesseltine–Baker Associates, 119 West 57th Street, New York, NY 10019.

HEWETT, Dorothy, playwright
b Perth, Australia, 21 May 1923; *d* of Arthur Thomas Hewett and his wife Doris Irene; *e* University of Western Australia; *m* (1) Lester Lloyd Davies (mar dis); (2) the writer Mervyn John Lilley; formerly a university tutor, journalist, advertising copywriter, nurse's aid and spinning mill operator.

Her first play, This Old Man Comes Rolling Home, had its premiere at the New Fortune Theatre, Perth, in 1966; has since written Mrs Porter and the Angel, 1969; The Chapel Perilous, 1971; Bon-Bons and Roses for Dolly, 1972; Catspaw (rock opera), The Tatty Hollow Story, 1974; Joan (musical), 1975; The Golden Oldies, 1976 (performed at the King's Head, Islington, 1978); Pandora's Cross, 1978; The Man from Mukinupin, 1979; Zimmer (with Robert Adamson), 1980; author of a novel, Bobbin Up, 1959, and of several collections of poetry, as well as theatre and literary criticism.

Address: 195 Bourke Street, Darlinghurst, NSW 2025. *Tel:* Sydney 3585689.

HICKMAN, Charles, actor and director
b Snaresbrook, Essex, 18 Jan; *s* of Charles Richard William Hickman and his wife Rita (Raison); *e* Chigwell School; studied for the stage at the Royal Academy of Dramatic Art.

Made his first appearance on the stage at the Globe Theatre, 10 Apr 1923, as Arthur Wells in Aren't We All?; in 1925, toured as Algy Fairfax in Diplomacy, and 1926–7, in Lavender Ladies, Hay Fever, The Love Game, and Cat's Cradle; at Q, June 1927, played Toby Sinclair in The Price; at Everyman, June–Sept 1927, appeared in revivals of Windows, Hindle Wakes, and A Family Man; Strand, Dec 1927, played Denis Cobtree in Dr Syn; Everyman, Jan 1928, Harold in The Eldest Son; Arts, Oct 1928, Benjamin in Easter; Nov 1928, Truman in The Clandestine Marriage; Royalty, 1929, Gerald in Bird in Hand, subsequently going to New York, and appearing at the Booth Theatre, 4 Apr 1929, in the same part; during 1930, toured in the United States, in the same part; on returning to London, 1930, at the Comedy, succeeded Robert Harris as Anthony Howard in The Silent Witness; Apollo, Jan 1931, played Norman Chase in Bed Rock; Victoria Palace, Mar 1931, appeared in Chelsea Follies; Haymarket, June 1931, played Geoffrey Barrowdale in Marry at Leisure; Duchess, Jan 1932, Johnny March in Windows; St Martin's (for the Sunday Players), May 1932, John Marvin in his own play, Half-Holiday; joined the Old Vic-Sadler's Wells company, Sept 1932; Q, May 1933, Reggie Cawston in The Methods of Margot; Embassy, Dec 1933, Widow Twankey in Aladdin; Shaftesbury, Nov 1934, Giotto in For Ever; Westminster (for the Charta Theatre), Dec 1934, Jean in The Fisher of Shadows; Whitehall, Feb 1935, Captain Vanbrugh in Viceroy Sarah; Garrick, Nov 1938, Rudolf in Elizabeth of Austria; King's, Hammersmith, May 1939, Frederick in The Return of Peter Grimm; His Majesty's, May 1942, appeared in Big Top; New, Oct 1944, played Osric in Hamlet; was director for the Wilson Barrett

company at the King's, Hammersmith, and in Scotland, 1939; has since directed The Peaceful Inn, 1940; Sweet and Low, 1943; Sweeter and Lower, Keep Going, Daughter Janie, 1944; Lady from Edinburgh, Young Mrs Barrington, The Vicar of Wakefield, 1945; Song of Norway, Sweetest and Lowest, Mother Goose, 1946; Call Home the Heart, Annie Get Your Gun, The Red Mill, Outrageous Fortune, The Blind Goddess, 1947; Cage Me a Peacock, Little Lambs Eat Ivy, Slings and Arrows (of which he was also part-author), 1948; Breach of Marriage, A Woman's Place, Black Chiffon, Bonaventure, 1949; The Schoolmistress; His Excellency, Dear Miss Phoebe, 1950; Count Your Blessings, Taking Things Quietly, Zip Goes a Million, 1951; Sunset in Knightsbridge, The Young Elizabeth, And If I Laugh, Love From Judy, Wild Horses, 1952; The Man Upstairs, Red-Headed Blonde, Drama at Inish, A London Actress, 1953; Wedding In Paris, The Party Spirit, 1954; The Tender Trap, The Water Gipsies, 1955; Summer Song, The Bride and the Bachelor, 1956; Silver Wedding, 1957; The Merry Widow, Verdict, The Big Tickle, A Day in the Life Of . . ., Matilda Shouted Fire, 1958; And Suddenly It's Spring, 1959; Land of Smiles, The Merry Widow (Australia), 1960; Sound of Music (Australia), Memory of Another Summer, 1961; The King and I (Australia), 1962; All Square, 1963; The Reluctant Peer, Everything Happens on Friday, Is Australia Really Necessary? (Australia), 1964; The Circle, 1965; The Last of Mrs Cheyney, 1966; Robert and Elizabeth (Australia), 1967; Night Must Fall (tour), Oh! Clarence, 1968; Androcles and the Lion, Present Laughter (South Africa), On a Foggy Day, 1969; Divorce in Chancery, 1970; Mistress of Novices, Relative Values, 1973; The Sack Race, The Dame of Sark, 1974; The First Mrs Fraser (tour), Ladies in Retirement, 1976; Quadrille, 1977; A Murder is Announced, 1979.

Address: c/o Eric Glass Ltd, 28 Berkeley Square, London, W1.

HICKSON, Joan, actress
b Kingsthorpe, Northampton, 5 Aug 1906; *d* of Alfred Harold Squire Hickson and his wife Edith Mary (Bogle); *e* Oldfield, Swanage, Dorset; *m* Dr Eric N Butler; studied for the stage at the Royal Academy of Dramatic Art.

Made her first appearance on the stage on a provincial tour, 1927, as Lady Shoreham in His Wife's Children; made her first appearance in London at the Arts Theatre, 1 July 1928, as the Maidservant in The Tragic Muse; next appeared at the New Theatre, Aug 1928, as Miss Mould in A Damsel in Distress; New, Apr 1929, played Mrs Pottle in Baa, Baa, Black Sheep; Shaftesbury, Aug 1929, Nancy Hewitt in The Middle Watch; Sept 1930, Gladys Rumbelow in Leave It To Psmith; Embassy, Apr 1931, Mrs Carrington in The Crime at Blossoms; from 1931–3, played three seasons at the Playhouse, Oxford; Shaftesbury, Apr 1933, Susan in Crime on the Hill; Embassy, Jan 1935, and Vaudeville, Feb 1935, Edith Clane in Summer's Lease; Embassy, Oct 1935, and St Martin's, Nov 1935, Dorinda Caswell in Distinguished Gathering; Embassy, Nov 1935, Madame Henry in Murder Gang; Apr 1937, Aunt Prudence in Festival Time; St Martin's, May 1937, Edna in A Ship Comes Home; Prince's, July 1937, Mrs Myrtle Gunn in The Gusher; Garrick, Nov 1937, Bertha in It's a Wise Child; Aldwych, Jan 1940, Miss Fowler in As You Are; Arts, Aug 1942, Natalya in The Proposal; Open Air, June 1944, Silver Stream in Lady Precious Stream; Q, Dec 1944, Ida in See How They Run; Piccadilly, Mar 1945, Miss Pryce in Appointment with Death; Criterion, Feb 1946, Mrs Read in The Guinea Pig; New Lindsey, Mar 1949, played Kate Mitchell in Foxhole in the Parlor; Q, May 1949, Gladys in Sleep on My Shoulder; Embassy, Sept 1949, Emma

Hamilton in Rain Before Seven; Piccadilly, June 1952, played Mrs James in The Gay Dog; Q, Sept 1953, Milly Hodbury in Two In the Bush; Aldwych, June 1956, played Oakshott in Man Alive!; Comedy, July 1967, Grace in A Day in the Death of Joe Egg, appearing at the Brooks Atkinson, New York, in the same part, Feb 1968; Theatre Upstairs, Jan 1971, Evelyn Pargeter in Morality; Greenwich, Apr 1971, and Apollo, May 1971, Amy in Forget-Me-Not Lane; Queen's, July 1973, Mrs Machin in The Card; Old Vic, Oct 1974, for National Theatre Company, Evelyn in The Freeway; Lyttelton, June 1976, Mrs Bradman in Blithe Spirit; same theatre, March 1977, Delia in Bedroom Farce, appearing at the Brooks Atkinson, New York, March 1979, in the same part, for which she received a 'Tony' Award as best actress in a supporting role; entered films, 1934, in Widow's Might; has appeared in numerous television productions, including Sinister Street, Bachelor Father, and Why Didn't They Ask Evans?

Address: c/o Plunket Greene Ltd, 110 Jermyn Street, London, SW1.

HIKEN, Gerald, actor and director
b Milwaukee, Wisconsin, 23 May 1927; *s* of Nathan Hiken and his wife Marian (Shapiro); *e* University of Wisconsin; *m* Barbara Lerner.

At the Linden Circle, Milwaukee, June 1949, produced, directed, and played Richard in Hay Fever; subsequently assistant director of the Little Theatre, Houston, Texas, and appeared in Twelfth Night, and The Physician in Spite of Himself, 1949–50; Rice Institute, Houston, 1951, directed Earnest and Beautiful People; appeared at the Erie, Pa, Playhouse, 1951–3, Brattle Theatre, Cambridge, Mass, 1952, and the Arena Stage, Washington, DC, 1953–5, among other professional troupes; first appeared on the New York stage at the Fourth Street, off-Broadway, Oct 1955, as Trofimoff in The Cherry Orchard; at the same theatre, Jan 1956, played Telegin in Uncle Vanya; Martin Beck, May 1956, played Blaise in The Lovers; Fourth Street, Oct 1956, Semyon Medvedenko in The Seagull; Phoenix, Dec 1956, Wong in The Good Woman of Setzuan; Theatre East, 1957, took over the role of Alceste in The Misanthrope; Circle-in-the-Square, 1957, took over the role of Dan Parritt in The Iceman Cometh; Bijou, Oct 1957, played The Father in The Cave Dwellers; Cherry Lane, Feb 1958, took over Clov in Endgame; Renata, Apr 1958, The Supervisor in The Enchanted; Actors, Playhouse, Feb 1959, Hovstad in An Enemy of the People; Henry Miller's, May 1959, Max the Millionaire in The Nervous Set; Fourth Street, Sept 1959, Andrei Prozoroff in The Three Sisters; ANTA, Dec 1959, played Michepain in The Fighting Cock; Ambassador, Oct 1960, Moishe in The 49th Cousin; Gramercy Arts, Apr 1961, Condemned Man and Hangman in Gallows Humor; East 74th Street, Sept 1961, Arthur Groomkirby in One Way Pendulum; Plymouth, Apr 1962, took over the role of Gideon in Gideon; Theatre de Lys, Oct 1962, joined cast of Brecht on Brecht; Martin Beck, Mar 1963, was assistant director of Mother Courage and Her Children; Ziegfeld, Feb 1964, played Shortcut in Foxy; Morosco, June 1964, Andrei in The Three Sisters; made his first appearance in London at the Aldwych, May 1965, when he again played Andrei in The Three Sisters with the Actors Studio Company of NY, in the World Theatre Season; UCLA Theater Group, July 1966, Stanley in The Birthday Party; received the Clarence Derwent Award for the 1955–6 season, and the Obie Award in 1956; resident lecturer in acting at Stanford University, 1965, and appointed Artistic Director of Stanford Repertory Theatre, 1966, where he remained until June 1968; during this time he played the

title-role in Scapin, 1965; Lafeu in All's Well That Ends Well, Wong in The Good Woman of Setzuan, Caesar in Antony and Cleopatra, 1966; Gaev in The Cherry Orchard, Bill Maitland in Inadmissible Evidence, the Playwright in Once in a Lifetime, the Author in The Cavern, 1967; Mathern in Cock-a-Doodle Dandy, Ossip in The Inspector General, and Sydney in The Sign in Sydney Brustein's Window; with Paul E Richards performed, 1968–77, as The New Theatre, a two-man touring repertory theatre featuring original works; Morosco, Nov 1977, Morris Meyerson in Golda; Hartford Stage, Conn, Mar 1978, Ed Lemon in Mackerel; Eisenhower, Washington DC, May 1978, Steve Miller in Gracious Living; Ahmanson, LA, Feb 1979, played The Common Man in A Man for All Seasons; Chelsea Westside, May 1979, title-role in Strider, transferring with the production to the Helen Hayes, Nov 1979; Member of The National Humanities Faculty, 1970–2; first entered films in Uncle Vanya, in 1956, and has since appeared in The Goddess, Invitation to a Gunfighter, and Funnyman; first appeared on television in July 1956 in *Camera Three*, and has since appeared in *Play of the Week, Omnibus, Hallmark Hall of Fame, Mission Impossible, Judd for the Defense*, etc.

Favourite parts: All the Chekhov roles. *Address:* 910 Moreno Avenue, Palo Alto, Calif 94303.

HILARY, Jennifer (Mary), actress
b Frimley, Surrey, 14 December 1942; *d* of Richard Mounteney Hilary and his wife Rosemary Lillian (Reynolds); *e* Elmhurst Ballet School, Camberley, Surrey; trained for the stage at the Royal Academy of Dramatic Art, where she was awarded the Bancroft Gold Medal, 1961.

Joined the Liverpool Playhouse Company and made her first appearance on the stage at the Liverpool Playhouse, Apr 1961, as Nina in The Seagull, subsequently playing Isabel in The Enchanted, Lady Teazle in The School for Scandal, Cilla Curtis in Amateur Means Lover, and Cecily in The Importance of Being Earnest; joined the Birmingham Repertory Theatre Company, Feb 1962, to play Miranda in The Tempest, Lydia Languish in The Rivals, Lucile in Duel of Angels, Sarah Rigg in Walker, London, Alison in Look Back in Anger, the Cheshire Cat in Alice in Wonderland, and Cressida in Troilus and Cressida; made her first appearance on Broadway at the Royale, Sept 1963, as Lucile in The Rehearsal; on her return to London, at the Haymarket, May 1964, succeeded Susannah York as Milly Theale in The Wings of the Dove; Duke of York's, Sept 1964, played Zoe in A Scent of Flowers; at the opening of the Yvonne Arnaud Theatre, Guildford, June 1965, played Vera in A Month in the Country; Shubert, New York, May 1966, Sasha in Ivanov; Duke of York's, London, Mar 1967, Virginia in Relatively Speaking; Booth, NY, Jan 1968, Alison Ames in Avanti!; toured, autumn 1971, as Jennet Jourdemayne in The Lady's Not for Burning; Phoenix, Leicester, Aug 1972, played Milly in Bodywork; toured S Africa, Nov 1972, as Alison Ames in Avanti (retitled A Touch of Spring); Greenwich, Oct 1975, Helen Saville in The Vortex; Ambassadors, Oct 1976, Gillian in Dear Daddy; Bristol Old Vic, Feb 1977, Lady Brute in The Provok'd Wife; Royal Exchange, Manchester, Sept 1978, Adrienne in Sisters; Toronto, 1978–9, appeared in Half Life; appeared in the film Becket, June 1963, and has since been seen in The Heroes of Telemark, The Idol, and One Brief Summer; made her first appearance on television, July 1961, as The Girl in The Tenpenny Scandal and has subsequently played in a variety of productions, including The Woman in White, the trilogy, Exiles, and recently, Charades, Alphabetical Order, Speed King, and *Sam*.

Favourite parts: Nina, Lucile, Zoe, Jennet, Lucy in Alphabetical Order, and Cressida. *Address:* c/o London Management Ltd, 235–241 Regent Street, London, W1. *Tel:* 01–734 4192.

HILL, Arthur, actor
b Melfort, Saskatchewan, Canada, 1 Aug 1922; *s* of Olin Drake Hill, QC, and his wife Edith Georgina (Spence); *e* Melfort Schools, King Edward High School Vancouver, ad the University of British Columbia; *m* Peggy Hassard.

Began his career as a boy actor in Canada; made his first appearance on the professional stage in England, at Wimbledon Theatre, London, Nov 1948, when he played Finch in Home of the Brave, transferring to the Westminster, Jan 1949, when the play was re-titled The Way Back; Arts, May 1949, played Tommy Turner in The Male Animal, transferring with the production to the New, June 1949; at the same theatre, Feb 1951, played Hector Malone in the revival of Man and Superman, transferring to the Princes, June 1951, where he appeared in the full version of the play; St James's, Apr 1952, played Paul Unger in Winter Journey; Haymarket, Nov 1954, played Cornelius Hackl in The Matchmaker, making his first appearance on Broadway, at the Royale, Dec 1955, in the same part and play; subsequently toured the US with the production; Ethel Barrymore, New York, Nov 1957, played Ben Grant in Look Homeward, Angel, which ran for over 500 performances; Ambassador, Oct 1959, played Bruce Bellingham in The Gang's All Here; Belasco, Nov 1960, played Jay Follet in All the Way Home; at the Billy Rose, Oct 1962, played George in Who's Afraid of Virginia Woolf? receiving the Drama Critics Award and the Antoinette Perry Award as the Best Actor of the Season, 1963; after leaving the NY cast, he appeared in the London production of Who's Afraid of Virginia Woolf? at the Piccadilly, Feb 1964, in his original part; Eugene O'Neill, NY, Nov 1964, played Bill Deems in Something More!; Locust, Philadelphia, Oct 1965, Harold Potter in The Porcelain Year; Broadhurst, Oct 1967, Simon Harford in More Stately Mansions; Yale Repertory, Nov 1977, Scott in Tarra Nova; films in which he has appeared include The Deep Blue Sea, The Ugly American, Moment to Moment, Harper (The Moving Target), The Chairman, Te Andromeda Strain, Rabbit Run, Killer Elite, Future World, A Bridge Too Far, The Champ, A Little Romance, etc; since 1958 he has made numerous television appearances, both in England and the United States, including: The Million Pound Note, Born Yesterday, Ethan Frome, The First Freedom (BBC), *Owen Marshall, Counsellor at Law,* 1971–4, etc.
Favourite parts: Tommy Turner, Cornelius Hackl, and George in Who's Afraid of Virginia Woolf? *Recreations:* Reading, sailing. *Address:* 1515 Club View Drive, Los Angeles, Calif. *Tel:* 277–2866.

HILL, George Roy, director and author
b Minneapolis, Minnesota, 20 Dec 1922; *s* of George Roy Hill and his wife Helen Frances (Owens); *e* Yale University and Trinity College, Dublin; *m* Louisa Horton.

Directed his first production Biography at the Gate, Dublin, Eire, in May 1948; has since directed the following plays in New York: Look Homeward, Angel, 1957; The Gang's All Here, 1959; Greenwillow, Period of Adjustment, 1960; Moon on a Rainbow Shawl, 1962; Henry, Sweet Henry, 1967; directed his first film, 1962, and has since directed Period of Adjustment, Toys in the Attic, The World of Henry Orient, Hawaii, Thoroughly Modern Millie, Butch Cassidy and the Sundance Kid, The Sting, for which he received the Academy Award, 1973, The Great Waldo Pepper, 1975,

Slaughterhouse-Five, Slap Shot, 1976, A Little Romance, 1979, etc; first television production 1954, and subsequent productions include: A Night to Remember, Helen Morgan, Child of Our Time, Judgment at Nuremberg, etc.
Address: 259 East 78th Street, New York, NY 10021. *Tel:* LE 5–8987.

HILL, Ken, writer and director
b Birmingham, 28 Jan 1937; *s* of Ernest Hill and his wife Hilda Beryl (James); *e* King Edward's Grammar School, Birmingham; formerly a local government officer, basket weaver, driver, insurance salesman, wages clerk, light engineering firm production manager, etc.

His first play, Night Season, was produced at the Alexandra, Birmingham, in 1963; has since written Forward — Up Your End, in which he made his debut as an actor at the Theatre Royal, Stratford E, 1972; played a number of parts here with the Theatre Workshop Company, 1973, and was appointed artistic director, 1974; wrote and directed the plays Is Your Doctor Really Necessary?, The Count of Monte Cristo (also lyrics), Land of the Dinosaurs (also lyrics), Dracula, 1974; Bloody Mary (also lyrics), 1975; left Theatre Workshop, 1975, and has since written the following plays and musical plays: Phantom of the Opera, The Curse of the Werewolf, Mafeking, 1976; The Hunchback of Notre Dame, 1977; The Mummy's Tomb, The Three Musketeers, 1978; The Living Dead, 1979; for the Musical Theatre Company, 1978–79, directed Joseph and the Amazing Technicolor Dreamcoat, The Mikado, and Fiddler on the Roof; has appeared on television as presenter of ATV Today; wrote and directed a TV musical, All the Fun of the Fair, 1979.
Recreations: Cricket, military history, science fiction. *Address:* 17 Arlington Court, Arlington Road, Twickenham, Middlesex.

HILL, Lucienne (*née* Palmer), dramatic author
b London; *d* of Arthur Palmer and his wife Louise (Moutarde); *e* Hendon County School and Somerville College, Oxford; *m* Andrew Broughton.

Began her career in the theatre as an actress at Birmingham Rep, 1950–2; she has adapted and translated the following plays: Ardèle (Anouilh), Thieves' Carnival (Anouilh), 1952; The Waltz of the Toreadors (Anouilh), 1956; No Laughing Matter (Salacrou), Paddle Your Own Canoe (Max Regnier), Restless Heart (Anouilh), 1957; Becket (Anouilh), 1961; Castle in Sweden (Françoise Sagan), 1962; Trap For a Lonely Man, Poor Bitos (Anouilh), 1963; Victor (Roger Vitrac), Traveller Without Luggage (Anouilh, New York), 1964; The Cavern (Anouilh), 1965; The Fighting Cock (Anouilh), 1966; Monsieur Barnett, 1967; Dear Antoine (Anouilh), 1971; The Baker, the Baker's Wife and the Baker's Boy (Anouilh), 1972; The Director of the Opera (Anouilh), 1973; You Were So Sweet When You Were Little (Anouilh), The Arrest (Anouilh), 1974; Ardèle (revised), The Scenario, Dear Birdies, The Britches (all Anouilh), 1975; she is author of the play The Second Sting (New York), 1965; has written one radio play, Storm at Brewer's End and her radio adaptations include Camus' Les Justes, and Anouilh's La Foire D'Empoigne.
Recreations: Gardening and the opera. *Address:* Peri, Loddon Drive, Wargrave, Berkshire.

HILL, Ronnie (Ronald Sidney Hill), composer, lyric writer and journalist
b London, 21 Mar 1911; *s* of Thomas Sidney Hill and his wife Edith Emily (Albury); *e* Leys School, and Christ's College, Cambridge.

Contributed music and lyrics to This Year, Next Year (Gate), 1934; This World of Ours (Gate), 1935; Surprise Item (Ambassadors'), 1938; The Gate Revue (Ambassadors'), 1939; Black and Blue (Hippodrome), 1939; Sky High (Phoenix), 1943; Players, Please (Players'), 1947; What Goes On (Players'), 1948; Latin Quarter (Casino), 1951; Excitement (Casino), 1952; Set to Music (New Watergate), 1953; New Watergate Revue (4 Editions), 1954; also composed incidental music to Beauty and the Beast (Westminster), 1950; Puss in Boots (Fortune), 1955; contributed music and lyrics to The World's the Limit (Windsor), including Royal Performance, 1955; composed the score of a musical version of Caste (Windsor), 1955; music and lyrics for Sleeping Beauty (Windsor), 1974; has composed music for and appeared in television programmes; has also appeared as a singer in variety and in many broadcasts, and directed radio series including On Stage, Everybody; regular contributor to *Theatre World*, 1961–5.

Recreations: Reading and watching lawn tennis. *Club:* RNVR. *Address:* 76 Dorset House, Gloucester Place, London, NW1. *Tel:* 01-935 1886.

HILL, Rose, actress and singer
b London, 5 June 1914; d of Henry Hill and his wife Rose (Lynch); m John St Leger Davis; studied for the stage under various tutors and won a scholarship to the Guildhall School of Music; formerly a shorthand typist.

First appeared at the Q, Dec 1939, as a member of the chorus in The Two Bouquets; joined Sadler's Wells Opera in 1941, remaining with this company as a principal soprano until 1948; with the English Opera Group, 1948, appeared as Lucy Lockit in The Beggar's Opera; Lyric, Hammersmith, Nov 1948, and Globe, Jan 1949, appeared in the revue, Oranges and Lemons; later in the same year appeared in revue at the Boltons Theatre; St Martin's, June 1951, appeared in revue, Penny Plain; St Martin's, May 1953, played Mrs Gill in a revival of The Two Bouquets; Arts, Sept 1954, Daisy Mutlar in The Diary of a Nobody; Royal Court, Oct 1954, joined the cast in the revue, Airs On a Shoestring, which ran for 772 performances; Comedy, Jan 1956, appeared in the revue Fresh Airs; toured, Sept 1956, as Dolly Gander in Harmony Close, subsequently appearing in the same part at the Lyric, Hammersmith, Apr 1957; Players', Oct 1958, appeared in the revue Child's Play; Palace, Aug 1959, appeared in the revue Fine Fettle; Mermaid, Apr 1961, spoke The Landlady's Tale in Take a Life; Strand, May 1961, played Belle in Belle, or the Ballad of Dr Crippen; Arts, Dec 1961, and subsequently Criterion, Feb 1962, appeared in the revue 4 To The Bar; New, Bromley, Oct 1962, Mother in A Slow Roll of Drums; Whitehal, May 1966, Momma Fink in Come Spy with Me, which ran for fifteen months; Arnaud, Guildford, Sept 1967, appeared as Aunt Elsie, Aunt Ethel and Aunt Gloria in The Adventures of Tom Random; Apr 1968, played the Minister of Transport in The Station Master's Daughter at the same theatre; Fortune, May 1968, Ruth Rosenfeld in Cindy; Arnaud, Dec 1969, the Witch in The Wizard of Oz; Richmond Theatre, Feb 1971, the Doctor's wife in Harvey; toured with the Cambridge Theatre Company, May 1971, as Clara in Hay Fever, and again in Oct 1971 as Mrs Mossop in Trelawny of the 'Wells'; Arnaud, Guildford, July 1971, Mrs Elton in The Deep Blue Sea; same theatre, Feb 1972, Mrs Frencham in Not Now, Darling; Sadler's Wells, Mar 1972, Lady Julia Merton in Lord Arthur Savile's Crime; Royal Court, Aug 1972, Millie in The Old Ones; toured, 1973, as Miss Smythe in Move Over, Mrs Markham, repeating the part at Windsor, 1974; toured, July 1974, as Nanette Parry in Breath of Spring; Royal Court, Jan

1975, Madge in Objections to Sex and Violence; Theatre Upstairs, June 1975, Mrs Provis in Moving Clocks Go Slow; Royal Court, May 1976, Nell in Endgame and Mother's Voice in Footfalls, in a Beckett season; Apollo, Jan 1977, Miss Meacham in Separate Tables; Royal Exchange, Manchester, 1978, Florence Goodman in The Gentle People; toured for the Royal Shakespeare Company, 1978, as Anfisa in The Three Sisters, playing the part at The Other Place, Stratford, Oct 1979.

Favourite parts: Millie in The Old Ones, and Miss Meacham in Separate Tables; and in opera, Lucy Lockit in The Beggar's Opera and Susanna in The Marriage of Figaro. *Hobbies:* Gardening and cooking. *Address:* c/o Richard Stone, 18–20 York Buildings, London, WC2.

HILLER, Dame Wendy, DBE, actress
b Bramhall, Cheshire, 15 Aug 1912; d of Frank Watkin Hiller and his wife Marie Elizabeth (Stone); e Winceby House School, Bexhill; m Ronald Gow; commenced her career as a student at the Manchester Repertory Theatre, Sept 1930, making her first appearance on the stage there, Sept 1930, as the Maid in The Ware Case; she played several small parts and understudied during the next year and became assistant stage-manager in 1931; in 1932, toured in Evensong; from May to Nov 1934, toured as Sally Hardcastle in Love on the Dole; made her first appearance in London, at the Garrick, 30 June 1935, as Sally in Love On the Dole, scoring an instantaneous success; made her first appearance on the New York stage, at the Shubert Theatre, Feb 1936, in the same part and repeated her success; Malvern Festival, July 1936, played Joan in Saint Joan and Eliza Doolittle in Pygmalion; toured, from Aug 1943, for CEMA, in factory centres, as Viola in Twelfth Night; Apollo, Jan 1944, played Sister Joanna in a revival of The Cradle Song; New, July 1945, Princess Charlotte in The First Gentleman; joined the Bristol Old Vic Company for the 1946 season, playing Tess in Tess of the D'Urbervilles, Portia in The Merchant of Venice, and Pegeen Mike in The Playboy of the Western World; New, Nov 1946,Tess in Tess of the D'Urervilles; again appeared in the last named part at the Piccadilly, May 1947; at the Biltmore, NY, Spt, 1947, appeared as Catherine Sloper in The Heiress; Piccadilly, London, May 1949, played Ann Veronica Stanley in Ann Veronica; at the Haymarket, Jan 1950, succeeded Peggy Ashcroft as Catherine in The Heiress; at the same theatre, Apr 1951, appeared as Evelyn Daly in Waters of the Moon, which ran for two years; New, Jan 1955, played Margaret Tollemache in Night of the Ball; joined the Old Vic Company for the 1955–6 season, when she played Portia in Julius Caesar, Mistress Page in The Merry Wives of Windsor, Hermione in The Winter's Tale, Emilia in Othello, and Helen in the modern dress production of Troilus and Cressida; Bijou, NY, May 1957, played Josie Hogan in A Moon For the Misbegotten; Haymarket, London, June 1958, followed Celia Johnson as Isobel Cherry in Flowering Cherry; Gaiety, Dublin, June 1959, played Marie Marescaud in All in the Family; Lyceum, NY, Oct 1959, played Isobel Cherry in Flowering Cherry; Piccadilly, Nov 1960, played Carrie Berniers in Toys in the Attic; Royal Windsor, Oct 1961, played Mary Kingsley in Mr Rhodes; Playhouse, NY, Feb 1962, Miss Tina in The Aspern Papers; Lyric, Dec 1963, Susan Shepherd in The Wings of the Dove; Birmingham Repertory, Feb 1965, Elizabeth in A Measure of Cruelty; Edinburgh Festival, Sept 1966, Martha in A Present For the Past; Duke of York's, Feb 1967, Nurse Wayland in The Sacred Flame; Edinburgh Festival, Aug 1968, Irene in When We Dead Awaken; Lyric, Feb 1970, Enid in The Battle of Shrivings; Arts, Cambridge, Feb 1972, Mrs Alving in Ghosts;

Haymarket, Oct 1972, Queen Mary in Crown Matrimonial; Old Vic, Jan 1975, for National Theatre, Gunhild Borkman in John Gabriel Borkman; Albery, Oct 1975, Edith Grove in Lies; Lyttelton, Mar 1976, again played Gunhild Borkman; Chichester, May 1977, and Haymarket, Jan 1978, Mrs Whyte in Waters of the Moon; commenced film career, 1937, and has appeared in Pygmalion, Major Barbara, Separate Tables (Academy Award, 1959); Sons and Lovers, A Man for all Seasons, Murder on the Orient Express, etc; recent TV work includes Richard II; awarded the OBE, 1971; created Dame, 1975.

Recreation: Gardening. *Address:* Stratton Road, Beaconsfield, Bucks. *Tel:* Beaconsfield 3788.

HINES, Patrick, actor
b Burkeville, Texas, 17 Mar 1930; *s* of Ruben Mainer Hines and his wife Edice (Miller); *e* University of Texas (BFA in 1952); formerly a school teacher; served in the US Army, 1954–6; prepared for the stage by Ben Iden Payne.

First appeared on the stage at the Oregon Shakespeare Festival, Ashland, Oregon, Aug 1952, as Alonzo in The Tempest; 1953, as Menenius Agrippa in Coriolanus, Gremio in The Taming of the Shrew, Tubal in The Merchant of Venice, and Regnier in Henry VI, Part I, Leonato in Much Ado About Nothing, Flavius in Julius Caesar, and Capt Gower in Henry V; American Shakespeare Festival Theatre, Stratford, Connecticut, summer, 1956, played Lord Bigot (later Earl of Pembroke) in King John, Friar Peter in Measure for Measure, and Baptista in The Taming of the Shrew; made his New York début at the Phoenix Theatre, Jan 1957, repeating his roles in Measure for Measure and The Taming of the Shrew; same theatre, Mar 1957, played Pescara in The Duchess of Malfi; Antioch Shakespeare Festival, summer 1957, played the title-roles in Henry VIII and Julius Caesar as well as Bottom in A Midsummer Night's Dream and Sir Toby Belch in Twelfth Night; on tour, 1957, Friar Francis in Much Ado About Nothing and later, Leonato in the same play; Stratford, summer 1958, Rosencrantz in Hamlet, Egeus in A Midsummer Night's Dream, and Antigonus in The Winter's Tale; Orpheum, NY, Mar 1959, Lord Mayor in The Geranium Hat; Stratford, summer 1959, Old Capulet in Romeo and Juliet, Egeus in A Midsummer Night's Dream, Page in The Merry Wives of Windsor, and the Duke of Florence in All's Well That Ends Well; Coronet Theatre, NY, Oct 1959, played Mr Brown in The Great God Brown; Phoenix, NY, Nov 1959, the Magistrate in Lysistrata; Jan 1960, Ingrid's Father, Mr Cotten, and Begriffenfeldt in Peer Gynt; Mar 1960, Thomas Percy (Worcester) in Henry IV, Part I; Stratford, summer 1960, Gonzalo in The Tempest, Mardian in Antony and Cleopatra, and the Priest in Twelfth Night, also serving as assistant to the director for the last two plays; US tour, Sept 1960–Feb 1961, as Quince in A Midsummer Night's Dream also served as assistant director; Stratford, spring 1961, co-directed Twelfth Night; Stratford, summer 1961, Ross in Macbeth, Agamemnon in Troilus and Cressida, and Frederick in As You Like It, again serving as assistant director for the season; Ambassador, NY, Jan 1962, Dr Callendar in A Passage to India; Stratford, summer 1962, Duke of York in Richard II and Earl of Worcester in Henry IV, Part I; Fred Miller Theatre, Milwaukee, autumn and winter 1962–3, Hucklebee in The Fantasticks; Stratford, summer 1963, Gloucester in King Lear, Pothinus in Caesar and Cleopatra, Solinus in The Comedy of Errors, Charles VI in Henry V; Miller Theatre, Milwaukee, autumn 1963, directed The Madwoman of Chaillot; Stratford, summer 1964, Polonius in Hamlet, Buckingham in Richard III, and Leonato in Much Ado About Nothing; Stratford, summer

1965, Earl of Gloucester in King Lear, Menenius Agrippa in Coriolanus, and Friar Laurence in Romeo and Juliet; Broadway Theatre, Nov 1965, Father Mignon in The Devils; Stratford, summer, 1966, Casca in Julius Caesar, Toby Belch in Twelfth Night, and Justice Silence in Henry IV, Part II; for the Seattle, Washington, Repertory Theatre, 1966–7, Pat in The Hostage, Danforth in The Crucible, the Burgermeister in The Visit, Capt Ahab in Moby Dick, and Falstaff in The Merry Wives of Windsor; and, 1967–8, Mr Kirby in You Can't Take It with You, Falstaff in Henry IV, Part I, Sir Lucius O'Trigger in The Rivals, and Peachum in The Three Penny Opera, also directing Krapp's Last Tape and Infancy and Childhood (double bill); for the Oregon Shakespeare Festival, 1968, directed Hamlet and played the title-role in Henry VIII; Seattle Repertory, 1968–9, Bottom in A Midsummer Night's Dream and Capt Boyle in Juno and the Paycock; Trinity Square Theatre, Providence, Rhode Island, Jan–Mar 1969, played Max in The Homecoming; Oregon Shakespeare Festival, 1969, Prospero in The Tempest and Friar Laurence in Romeo and Juliet which he also directed; Mendelssohn Theatre, Ann Arbor, Michigan, autumn 1969, played Simon Laquedeem in The Chronicles of Hell; toured, Dec 1969–Apr 1970, as the Miller in Canterbury Tales; Delacorte Theatre, NY, for the New York Shakespeare Festival, July–Aug 1970, Cardinal Beaufort in The Wars of the Roses; on tour, Sept 1970–Sept 1971, John Dickinson in 1776; Ahmanson, Los Angeles, Mar 1972, Earl of Northumberland in Richard II; Eisenhower, Washington, DC, May 1972, again played this last part; Palace, NY, May 1973, Montfleury in the musical Cyrano; Circle in the Square, Joseph E Levine, Dec 1973, Ed Mosher in The Iceman Cometh; Mitzi E Newhouse, Oct 1974, Edward IV and Lord Mayor in Richard III; McCarter, Princeton, NJ, Feb 1975, Swedish Commander in Mother Courage; Arena Stage, Washington, DC, Mar 1975, Red Grover in The Last Meeting of the Knights of the White Magnolia; Fulton Opera House, Lancaster Pa, summer 1975, played Benjamin Franklin in 1776, Sheridan Whiteside in The Man Who Came to Dinner, and directed The Tavern; Eisenhower, Washington DC, Apr 1976, and Broadhurst, NY Sept, Red Grover in A Texas Trilogy; Palace, NY, Feb 1977, Pothenius in Caesar and Cleopatra; for Phoenix, Oct 1977, Charles Eden in Hot Grog; Goodman, Chicago, Feb 1978, Dogberry in Much Ado About Nothing; directed this play at the Margo Jones, Dallas, 1978; Ahmanson, LA, Feb 1979, Wolsey in A Man for All Seasons; Mark Taper, LA, Apr 1979, Gonzalo in The Tempest; University of Texas, 1979, played Col Kincaid in The Oldest Living Graduate, El Paso, Oct, and Estragon in Waiting for Godot, Austin, Nov; film début, 1972, Samuel Chase in 1776, and later in WW and the Dixie Dance Kings, The Brink's Job, etc; first appeared on television in 1957 and has since played on *Camera Three, Eye on New York, Repertory, USA, A World Apart, The Adams Chronicles*, etc.

Favourite parts: Menenius Agrippa in Coriolanus, Henry VIII, Bottom, York in Richard II, Falstaff, Capt Boyle, Dickinson in 1776, Gloucester in King Lear, and Red Grover in Texas Trilogy. *Recreations:* Travel, the study of history, and cooking. *Address:* 46 West 95th Street, New York, NY 10025. *Tel:* UN 5–3518.

HINGLE, Pat, actor
b Denver, Colorado, 19 July 1923; *s* of Clarence Martin Hingle and his wife Marvin Louise (Patterson); *e* University of Texas; *m* Alyce Dorsey (mar dis); formerly employed as a labourer, waiter, and construction worker; studied for the stage at the Theatre Wing, Berghof Studio, and Actors Studio.

Made his first appearance on the stage at the Centre Playhouse, Rockville Centre, New York, June 1950, when he played Lachie in Johnny Belinda; first appeared in NY, at the Theatre de Lys, Sept 1953, as Harold Koble in End As a Man; Longacre, Jan 1955, played Joe Foster in Festival; Morosco, Mar 1955, played Gooper in Cat on a Hot Tin Roof; Longacre, Nov 1956, Jules Taggart in Girls of Summer; Music Box, Dec 1957, Rubin Flood in Dark at the Top of the Stairs; ANTA, Dec 1958, played the title-role in JB but had to leave the cast after six weeks, following an accident; Longacre, Feb 1960, played Howard Trapp in The Deadly Game; at the American Shakespeare Festival, Stratford, Conn, June 1961, played the title-role in Macbeth, and Hector in Troilus and Cressida; Hudson, Mar 1963, Sam Evans in a revival of Strange Interlude; ANTA, Apr 1964, Parnell in Blues for Mr Charlie; Cort, Sept 1964, Andy Willard in A Girl Could Get Lucky; Brooks Atkinson, May 1965, Gentleman Caller in a revival of The Glass Menagerie; Plymouth, Feb 1966, took over as Oscar Madison in The Odd Couple; Cort, Oct 1967, Harry Armstrong in Johnny No-Trump; Morosco, Feb 1968, Victor Franz in The Price; Royale, Feb 1970, Joseph Dobbs in Child's Play; Shubert, Mar 1972, Senator George Mason in The Selling of the President; Booth, June 1973, took over from Richard Dysart as the Coach in That Championship Season; McCarter, Princeton, NJ, Oct 1975, Hermann Starr in A Grave Undertaking; Circle in the Square, Mar 1976, Dr Wangel in The Lady from the Sea; Arena Theatre, Buffalo, Nov 1976, Willy Loman in Death of a Salesman; toured, Sept 1978, in his one-man show Thomas Edison: Reflections of a Genius; films in which he has appeared include: The Strange One, Splendor in the Grass, The Ugly American, All the Way Home, No Down Payment, The Super Cops, Deadly Honeymoon (1974), etc; first appeared on television, 1951.

Favourite parts: Rubin Flood and JB. *Recreation:* The Guitar. *Address:* 11860 Chandler Boulevard, N Hollywood, Calif 91607.

HIRD, Thora, actress
b Morecambe, Lancs, 28 May 1913; *d* of James Henry Hird and his wife Mary Jane (Mayor); *e* Morecambe; *m* James Scott; has been on the stage since early childhood.

Began her career at the Royalty Theatre, Morecambe, 1931; made her first appearance in London, at the Vaudeville Theatre, 4 Oct 1944, as Mrs Gaye in No Medals; New Lindsey, Jan 1948, played Mrs Holmes in Flowers for the Living; Embassy, Sept 1948, and Duke of York's, Mar 1949, Emmie Slee in The Queen Came By; Embassy, and Playhouse, Aug 1949, Ada Lester in Tobacco Road; Wimbledon, Jan 1951, played Mrs Lurgan in Dangerous Woman; Embassy, Mar 1951, Lilian Lord in The Happy Family, playing the same part at the Duchess, May 1951; Lyric, Hammersmith, Jan 1952, and Duke of York's, Mar 1952, played Momma Brodsky in The Same Sky; Strand, Sept 1952, Mattie Gerrity in The Troublemakers; Palace, Nov 1953, Sal Brown in The Love Match; Garrick, Sept 1957, played Ada Thorpe in Saturday Night At the Crown; Lyceum, Sheffield, Mar 1958, Aggie Thompson in Come Rain, Come Shine; Oldham Repertory Theatre, Nov 1958, Maggie McTaggart in Happy Days; St Martin's, June 1961, played Rosie Stafford in You Prove It; toured, June 1963, as Victoria Pugh in The Best Laid Schemes; toured, 1964, as Thora Piper in Camp Beds; Grand, Blackpool, summer 1965, appeared in My Perfect Wife; Palladium, May 1966, co-starred in London Laughs; Playhouse, Perth, Feb 1972, appeared in Saturday Night at the Crown; Drury Lane, May 1973, played Pauline in No, No, Nanette; entered films, 1940, in Next of Kin, and has

since appeared in numerous pictures; television appearances include the series Ours is A Nice House, Meet the Wife, In Loving Memory, and Flesh and Blood, as well as plays such as When We Are Married.

Favourite parts: Mrs Holmes in Flowers for the Living, and Emmie in The Queen Came By. *Recreation:* Reading. *Hobbies:* Being a housewife, collecting old brass and gardening. *Address:* c/o Felix de Wolfe, 1 Robert Street, London WC2N 6BH.

HIRSCH, John Stephan, director
b Siofok, Hungary, 1 May 1930; *s* of Joseph Hirsch and his wife Ilona (Horvath); *e* Israel Gymnasium in Budapest and the University of Manitoba, Canada.

Directed his first play, The Time of Your Life, at the Little Theatre, Winnipeg, Manitoba, Canada, 1951; joined the Stratford Shakespearean Festival, Ontario, 1965, as director of The Cherry Orchard, and has since directed Henry VI, 1966; Richard III, Colors in the Dark, 1967; A Midsummer Night's Dream, The Three Musketeers, 1968; Satyricon, 1969; The Three Sisters, 1976; directed his first play in New York at the Vivian Beaumont, for the Repertory Theater of Lincoln Center, Dec 1966, Federico Garcia Lorca's Yerma, and has since directed for this company Galileo, 1967; St Joan, 1968; The Time of Your Life, 1969; Beggar on Horseback, 1970; Playboy of the Western World, Antigone, 1971; directed the Broadway production of We Bombed in New Haven, 1968; directed AC/DC for the Chelsea Theater Center of Brooklyn, 1970; for the Theatre du Nouveau Monde, Montreal, directed Mère Courage, 1964; for the Habimah, Tel Aviv, Israel, directed The Seagull, 1970; was Associate Artistic Director of the Stratford, Ontario, Shakespearean Festival, 1967–9; is the founder of the Theatre 77, Manitoba Theatre Centre; for the St Lawrence Arts Centre, Toronto, Sept 1974, adapted and directed The Dybbuk; again at the Mark Taper Forum, Los Angeles, 1975; Stratford, Ont, Sept 1976, directed Three Sisters; directed The Tempest (Mark Taper) and Saint Joan (Seattle), 1979; has written plays for children as well as poetry; has broadcast on theatrical subjects; awarded the Service Medal, Order of Canada; Molson Prize, 1976; holds an honorary DLitt from the University of Manitoba, and an honorary Doctor of Laws degree from the University of Toronto; is an honorary fellow of the University College, University of Manitoba; has lectured at the National Theatre School of Canada, at Columbia University, New York University, etc; received the Outer Circle Critics Award for directing St Joan and the Obie Award for AC/DC; entered film production in Canada with In The Shadow of the City, 1955; first directed on television in 1954, and has since directed 15 Miles of Broken Glass and The Three Musketeers; Head of TV Drama, Canadian Broadcasting Corporation, 1974–7; consultant, 1978–.

Address: 187 Hudson Drive, Toronto, Ontario M4T 2K7. *Tel:* 488 1051.

HIRSCH, Judd, actor and director
b New York City, 15 Mar 1935; trained for the stage at AADA.

Made his Broadway debut at the Biltmore in 1966 when he took over a part in Barefoot in the Park; at the New, Oct 1967, played the Thief in Scuba Duba; with the Theatre of Living Arts, Philadelphia, season 1969–70; Cherry Lane, Jan 1973, Senator in Mystery Play; Circle in the Square, Mar 1973, began a long association with the Circle Repertory company, playing Bill in Hot 1 Baltimore; appeared with them in Prodigal, Dec 1973; directed Not Enough Rope for them in Jun, 1974; Circle Rep, Jan 1976, transferring to the

Biltmore, Feb, Wiseman in Knock, Knock; Imperial, Dec 1977, George Schneider in Chapter Two; Circle Rep, May 1979, and Brooks Atkinson, Feb 1980, Matt Friedman in Talley's Folly; films include King of the Gypsies and Ordinary People, 1980; TV work includes leads in *The Law, Delvecchio,* and *Taxi.*

Address: c/o Hesseltine Baker Associates, 119 West 57th Street, New York, NY 10019.

HIRSCHHORN, Clive, drama critic
b Johannesburg, 20 Feb 1940; *s* of Colin Kalman Hirschhorn and his wife Pearl (Rabinowitz); *e* The University of the Witwatersrand, Johannesburg (BA 1960).

Theatre critic since 1966, *Sunday Express;* also film critic 1966–69; author of a play, A State of Innocence, produced at the Library Theatre, Johannesburg, in 1958, and of books including Gene Kelly: a Biography, The Films of James Mason, and The Warner Brothers Story.

Recreations: All aspects of the cinema, music. *Address:* 42D South Audley Street, London W1.

HOBBS, William, fight arranger
b Hampstead, London, 29 Jan 1939; *s* of Kenneth Beresford Hobbs and his wife Joan Frances (Lindsay); *e* UCS, Hampstead, and St Andrew's Cathedral Choir School, Sydney, Australia; *m* Janet Milner Riley; trained as an actor at the Central School of Speech and Drama; formerly a member of Australian Olympic Fencing Training Squad (1955).

After repertory work at Colchester, Worthing and Bristol Old Vic, joined the Old Vic Company in London, 1960, as actor and fight director; arranged fights for Zeffirelli's Romeo and Juliet, Old Vic, Oct 1960; Chichester, 1962, fights for The Chances; fight director, National Theatre, 1963–72; RSC, Stratford, season 1972; Chichester Festival, 1975; has arranged fights for many notable stage productions in England and Germany, including the opera Tom Jones (Aldeburgh Festival, 1977), Zastrossi (King's Head, 1978), Pericles (Stratford, 1979), A Fair Quarrel (National, 1979); devised and directed Royal Tumble, 1971; tutor in stage fight, Central School of Speech and Drama, London, and Odense Theater, Denmark; author of the book Techniques of the Stage Fight, 1967, republished as Stage Combat–Action to the Word, 1979; joint founder, Society of British Fight Directors; has designed fights for films since 1961, including, recently, The Duellists and Flash Gordon; his more recent work for television includes Robin Hood, Romeo and Juliet, and Julius Caesar.

Recreations: Writing, chess, music, fencing. *Address:* c/o Meg Poole, Richard Stone, 18–20 York Buildings, London WC2N 6JU. *Tel:* 01–839 6421–8.

HOBSON, Sir Harold, (*cr* 1977), CBE, dramatic critic
b Thorpe Hesley, near Rotherham, Yorks, 4 Aug 1904; *s* of Jacob Hobson and his wife Minnie (McKegg); *e* Sheffield Grammar School and Oriel College, Oxford (BA 1928; MA, 1935); *m* Gladys Bessie (Elizabeth) Johns (dec).

His first appointment as dramatic critic was with the *Christian Science Monitor,* to which he contributed from 1932–72; assistant-literary editor *Sunday Times,* 1944; assistant dramatic critic, *The Sunday Times,* 1944–7; television critic, the *Listener,* 1947; dramatic critic, *The Sunday Times,* 1947–76, and continues as a special writer; dramatic critic of *Drama,* 1976–; author of a novel, The Devil in Woodford Wells, many essays in the *Saturday Book* series, and two volumes of his collected dramatic criticisms, Theatre, 1948, and Theatre II, 1950; is the author of Verdict at Midnight, 1952; The Theatre Now, 1953; The French Theatre of

To-day, 1953; Indirect Journey (autobiography), 1978; editor of The International Theatre Annual; is a Councillor of The Critics' Circle, and was President, 1955; Chevalier of the Legion of Honour, 1960; returned this decoration, 1968; CBE, 1971; knighthood (Jubilee Honours List), first to be awarded for services to drama criticism; Hon Fellow, Oriel College, Oxford, 1974; Hon DLitt, Sheffield University, 1977.

Recreations: Bridge, motoring and going to the theatre. *Clubs:* Beefsteak, MCC. *Address:* 905 and 906 Nelson House, Dolphin Square, London, SW1. *Tel:* 01–834 3800.

HOBGOOD, Burnet M, educator and director
b Lotumbe, Zaire, 23 Jun 1922; *s* of Henry Clay Hobgood and his wife Tabitha (Alderson); *e* Transylvania College (BA 1947), Western Reserve University (MFA 1950), and Cornell University (PhD 1964); *m* Jane Bishop.

Chairman, drama and speech department, Catawba College, 1950–61; Professor of drama and theatre, Chairman of theatre department, Southern Methodist University, 1964–75; Professor of theatre and Head, department of theatre, College of Fine and Applied Arts, University of Illinois at Urbana-Champaign, 1975–present; first professional experience as a director was a production of Uncle Harry, Lexington, Ky, Nov 1947; has since directed many summer productions professionally as well as directing at the various schools in which he has taught, specialising in new plays, Shakespeare and Greek tragedy; posts held with the American Theatre Association include that of president, 1970; writings include play adaptations, journal articles, and the book Discovering the Theatre, 1980.

Address: 3 Illini Circle, Urbana IL 61801. *Tel:* 217-333 2371.

HOCHHUTH, Rolf, dramatic author
b Eschwege/Werra, Germany, 1 Apr 1931; *s* of Walter Hochhuth and his wife Ilse (Holzapfel); *e* Realgymnasium, Eschwege; *m* Marianne Heinemann; formerly a reader and editor in a publishing house.

His first play to be produced was Der Stellvertreter at the Theatre Kurfurstendam, Berlin, 20 Feb 1963; the same play was also produced at the Aldwych, London, Sept 1963, under the title of The Representative, and at the Brooks Atkinson, New York, Feb 1964, under the title of The Deputy; he is also the author of Soldiers, 1967; Guerillas, 1970; Die Hebamme, 1972; Tod eines Jägers, 1976; Jurists, 1980.

Address: c/o Rowohlt Theater-Verlag, Hamburger Strasse 17, 2057 Reinbek, Hamburg, Germany.

HODGEMAN, Edwin, actor
b Adelaide, 26 June 1935; *s* of William Alfred Hodgeman and Flora Isabel (Watt); *e* Lefevre Boys Technical; trained for the stage at the National Institute of Dramatic Art, Sydney; formerly a clerk with the South Australian Gas Company.

Made his first professional appearances on a tour of NSW country towns in 1962, playing Duncan in Macbeth, Shylock in The Merchant of Venice, and Cassius in Julius Caesar; appeared with the Stratford, Ontario, festival company, seasons 1963–64, making his English debut with the company at Chichester, Apr 1964, as a dancer in Le Bourgeois Gentilhomme and Ventidius in Timon of Athens; Old Tote, Sydney, 1967, played Ahmed in Norm and Ahmed; at theatres in Adelaide, 1969–72, played major roles including Berenger in Exit the King, Davies in The Caretaker, 1969; title roles in Hadrian VII, Kean and The Master Builder, 1971; Face in The Alchemist, 1972; Russell Street, Melbourne, Oct 1974, Martin Dysart in Equus; same theatre,

1975, Gower in Pericles; Playhouse, Adelaide, Aug 1975, Iago in Othello; same theatre, 1976, Simon Hench in Otherwise Engaged and Methuselah in Last of the Knucklemen; also title role in Macbeth, 1977; Athenaeum, Melbourne, 1978, Christy Mahon in Playboy of the Western World, and Ui in The Resistible Rise of Arturo Ui; Playhouse, Adelaide, 1979, played Tiresias in Oedipus Rex, Claudius in Hamlet, and Donny in American Buffalo; films include The Fourth Wish, The Money-Movers, Labrynths, and Survivor; TV since O'Flaherty VC, 1966, includes plays and series.

Recreation: Collecting engravings and etchings. *Address:* 4 Swift Avenue, Dulwich, South Australia. *Tel:* 332 8026.

HOFFMAN, Dustin, actor and director
b Los Angeles, California, 8 Aug 1937; *s* of Harry Hoffman and his wife Lillian (Gold); *e* Santa Monica City College; *m* Anne Byrne; prepared for the stage at the Pasadena Playhouse and with Barney Brown, Lonny Chapman, and Lee Strasberg.

First appeared on the stage as a child at the John Burroughs Junior High School, Los Angeles, when he played Tiny Tim in A Christmas Carol; first played in New York at the Sarah Lawrence College, 1960, as the Young Man in Gertrude Stein's Yes Is for a Very Young Man; Playhouse, Oct 1961, played Ridzinski in A Cook for Mr General; joined the Theatre Company of Boston in Jan 1964, and during that year played Clov in Endgame, Dunlavin in The Quare Fellow, C Couch, called Babboon, in In the Jungle of Cities, Nicholas Triletski in A Country Scandal, Ben in The Dumbwaiter, Bert Hudd in The Room, Pozzo in Waiting for Godot, Zapo in Picnic on the Battlefield, Hugo in Dirty Hands, and Peter in The Cocktail Party; McCarter, Princeton, New Jersey, Oct 1964, played Frankie in Three Men on a Horse; American Place, NY, Mar 1965, Immanuel in Harry, Noon and Night; American Place, Apr 1966, Zoditch in The Journey of the Fifth Horse; Berkshire Theatre Festival, Massachusetts, Aug 1966, played The Old Jew in a play of that name, Max in Reverberations, and Jax in Fragments in a production with the overall title Fragments; Circle in the Square, Oct 1966, Valentine Brose in Eh?; Brooks Atkinson, Dec 1968, title-role in Jimmy Shine; Booth, Dec 1974, directed All Over Town; first appeared in films in 1968, in The Tiger Makes Out, and has since played in The Graduate, Midnight Cowboy, John and Mary, Little Big Man, Straw Dogs, Papillon (1973), Lenny (1974), All the President's Men (1976), Kramer vs Kramer (1980), etc; first appeared on television in June 1961, in *Naked City*, and since has played in The Star Wagon, The Trap of Solid Gold, and The Journey of the Fifth Horse.

Hobbies and recreations: Tennis, jazz piano playing, photography. *Address:* 315 East 65th Street, New York, NY. *Tel:* 472-3738.

HOFFMAN, Jane, actress
b Seattle, Washington, 24 July; *d* of Samuel Lewis Hoffman and his wife Marguerite (Kirschbaum); *e* University of California (BA); *m* (1) James W McGlone, Jr (mar dis); (2) William Friedberg (mar dis); (3) Richard McMurray (mar dis); prepared for the stage with Maria Ouspenskaya, Tamara Daykarhanova, and at the Actors Studio, of which she is a charter member.

First appeared on the stage in a school production of Charley's Aunt, 1923; made her professional début with the Henry Duffy Stock Company, Seattle, 1926, as the Kid in The Poor Nut; toured, July 1936, as the Secretary in Personal Appearance; made her New York début at the Maxine Elliott, 26 Oct 1940, in the revue 'Tis of Thee; 44th Street,

Apr 1941, appeared in Crazy with the Heat, and subsequently toured in this revue; toured in Pal Joey, 1942; Paper Mill Playhouse, Millburn, New Jersey, Aug 1942, played in The Desert Song and The New Moon; Imperial, NY, Oct 1943, Rose in One Touch of Venus; National, Mar 1945, Lotus in Calico Wedding; Empire, Nov 1945, Mrs James in Mermaids Singing; stock, 1946, played the Sister in The Constant Wife, and, 1947, Dagmar in The Trial of Mary Dugan and Marion Froude in Biography; Maxine Elliott, Mar 1948, Miss Evans in A Temporary Island; Playhouse, Olney, Maryland, July 1948, played in Chicken Every Sunday and Twentieth Century; Royale, Sept 1948, Mrs Whiting in A Story for Strangers; Cort, Mar 1949, Miss Johnson in Two Blind Mice; McCarter, Princeton, New Jersey, June 1949, Liz in The Philadelphia Story; same theatre, July 1949, Stella in Anna Lucasta, and subsequently toured in this part; Martin Beck, Feb 1951, Flora in The Rose Tattoo; Westport, Connecticut, Country Playhouse, Sept 1952, Ada Ryan in Tin Wedding; Martin Beck, Jan 1953, Mrs Putnam in The Crucible; Phoenix, Dec 1956, Mrs Yang in The Good Woman of Setzuan; Ambassador, Dec 1958, Amy Underhill in The Third Best Sport; Jazz Gallery, May 1960, Mommy in The Sand Box; Longacre, Jan 1961, the Housewife in Rhinoceros; York Playhouse, Jan 1961, Mommy in The American Dream; Cherry Lane, Feb 1962, Mommy in The Sand Box, Mommy in The American Dream, the Mother in Picnic on a Battlefield, and Mrs Peep in The Killer, in a repertory season called Theatre of the Absurd; stock, 1962, appeared in the revue The World of Jules Feiffer; Martin Beck, Mar 1963, Old Woman and Peasant Woman in Mother Courage and Her Children; Cherry Lane, May 1963, Mommy in The American Dream; Cort, Feb 1964, Mrs Bennington in Fair Game for Lovers; Morosco, Mar 1964, Mlle Suisson in A Murderer Among Us; Cherry Lane, Apr 1964, again played Mommy in The American Dream; Library of Congress, Washington, DC, May 1964, the Nurse in Medea; Garrick, Dec 1964, Charity Perrin in The Child Buyer; played for two seasons of repertory, 1956–7, with the Stanford Repertory Theatre, California; toured, 1967, as Agnes in A Delicate Balance; played with the Long Island Festival Repertory, 1968; Gramercy Arts, NY, Feb 1969, Grandma in A Corner of the Bed; Pocket, Mar 1969, Mrs Gershon in Someone's Comin' Hungry; New, Sept 1969, played in the revue The American Hamburger League; New Theatre Workshop, Nov 1969, Duchess of York in Richard III; Forum, Lincoln Center, Dec 1969, Vlasta Huml in The Increased Difficulty of Concentration; Theatre de Lys, Nov 1970, the Mother in Slow Memories; Circle in the Square, June 1971, Tante Frumkah in The Last Analysis; Playhouse, Nov 1972, Lady Mount-Temple in Dear Oscar; Biltmore, Dec 1975, Gertrude Saidenberg in Murder Among Friends; Lyceum, NY, 1978–9, standby for Constance Cummings in Wings; Public/Newman, Dec 1979, Hannah Galt in The Art of Dining, also playing the part at the Eisenhower, Washington, 1980; charter member of Ensemble Studio Theater, where she directs, acts and teaches; first appeared in films in A Hatful of Rain, 1957, and has since played in Ladybug, Ladybug, Up the Sandbox, Black Harvest, Day of the Locust, The Gift, etc; first appeared on television in 1946, and since has played in Waltz of the Toreadors, The Sand Box, and in the dramatic series *East Side/West Side*, *Love of Life* (1971–75), *Popi*, *Kojak*, etc.

Favourite parts: Mommy in The American Dream, Agnes in A Delicate Balance, and Vlasta Huml in The Increased Difficulty of Concentration. *Recreations:* Gardening, tennis. *Address:* 16 St Luke's Place, New York, NY.

HOFSISS, Jack, director
b New York, 28 Sept 1950; *s* of Christian Leo Hofsiss and his wife Cecilia Kathleen; *e* Georgetown University, George Washington University and Catholic University.

Directed Rebel Women for the NY Shakespeare Festival at the Public, Jun 1976; has since directed Out of Our Father's House, 1977; The Elephant Man, 1979; also workshop productions for the Public, 1978; received the Tony for The Elephant Man; work for TV includes Another World, The Best of Families, The Sorrows of Gin (PBS), etc.

Address: c/o ICM, 40 West 57th Street, New York, NY 10019.

HOGG, Ian, actor
b Newcastle upon Tyne, 1 Aug 1937; *s* of Walter Alexander Hogg and his wife Ena Mary (Robinson); *e* Durham School, and St John's College, Durham University; *m* Dorothea Margaret Hogg; trained for the stage at the Drama Centre, London, 1961–4.

First appeared on the London stage, Sept 1964 at the Aldwych as Turkish Bassoe in The Jew of Malta, with the Royal Shakespeare Company; since that time appeared regularly with the company, of which he was an associate artist; his parts have included the Military Representative in The Marat/Sade, Aldwych, Nov 1965 and Martin Beck, New York (first appearance), Dec 1965; Major Friedli in The Meteor, member of company in US, Aldwych, 1966; Lavache in All's Well that Ends Well, Tybalt in Romeo and Juliet, Seyton in Macbeth, Stratford, 1967; member of Peter Brook's company for The Tempest project, Paris and Round House, London, Apr–June 1968; Lester Freitag in The Latent Heterosexual, James in God Bless, Aldwych, 1968; at the Royal Court, May 1970, played Perowne in AC/DC; Stratford, Ontario, June 1971, title role in Macbeth; Stratford-on-Avon, season 1972, played the title role in Coriolanus, Menas in Antony and Cleopatra, and Lucius in Titus Andronicus; Birmingham Repertory, season 1973–4, played De Flores in The Changeling, Willie Mossop in Hobson's Choice, and the title role in Henry V, visiting the Hong Kong Festival in the last part; Newcastle, Mar 1976, John in The Sons of Light; Hampstead, Jan 1977, L D Alexander in The Last Meeting of the Knights of the White Magnolia; Globe, Mar 1977, took over Shell in Donkey's Years; National Theatre, Jan 1979, Howard Bartlett in For Services Rendered; first film, King Lear, 1971; others include: The Hireling, Hennessy, and The Legacy; television since 1968 includes: Total Eclipse, Savages, *The Devil's Crown*, Ibsen and The Living Grave.

Favourite parts: Perowne in AC/DC, Coriolanus, and L D Alexander. *Recreations:* Riding, goatkeeping, reading. *Address:* 40 Cedars Road, Hampton Wick, Kingston-Upon-Thames, Surrey. *Tel:* 01–977 2067.

HOLBROOK, Hal (*né* Harold Rowe Holbrook), actor
b Cleveland, Ohio, 17 Feb 1925; *s* of Harold Rowe Holbrook, Sr, and his wife Aileen (Davenport); *e* Culver Military Academy and Denison University; *m* (1) Ruby Elaine Johnston (mar dis); (2) Carol Rossen; specially prepared for the stage with Edward A Wright at Denison University and with Uta Hagen at the HB Studio.

First appeared on the stage at the Cain Park Theatre, Cleveland, July 1942, as Richard in The Man Who Came to Dinner, and, later, played in The Vagabond King and In Time to Come; spent four seasons in stock in Granville, Ohio, at Denison University, in such plays as The Male Animal, Three Men on a Horse, Our Town, George Washington Slept Here, The Guardsman, The Constant Wife, and directed The Winslow Boy, 1947–50; toured with Ruby Elaine Johnston in scenes from the classics, 1948–53; first appeared in New York at the Purple Onion (night club) Feb 1955, in his original one-man show Mark Twain Tonight! and

repeated this performance at the Upstairs at the Duplex, Oct 1955; Westport, Connecticut, Country Playhouse, summer, 1958, played in a musicalized The Doctor in Spite of Himself; made his Broadway début at the 41st Street, 6 Apr 1959, in Mark Twain Tonight!; toured the US, Europe, and Saudi Arabia, 1959–60–1, and toured the US, 1963, in this one-man show; Billy Rose, Oct 1961, played The Young Man in Do You Know the Milky Way?; American Shakespeare Festival, Stratford, Connecticut, summer 1962, played John of Gaunt in Richard II and Hotspur in Henry IV, Part I; Anderson, Jan 1963, the title-role in the Phoenix Theatre production of Abe Lincoln in Illinois; toured, 1963, as Andrew Mackerel in The Mackerel Plaza; joined the Lincoln Center Repertory Theatre and at the ANTA Washington Square, Jan 1964, played Harley Barnes and alternated with Jason Robards as Quentin in After the Fall; Feb 1964, Marco Polo in Marco Millions; Dec 1964, A Major in Incident at Vichy; Jan 1965, Prologue and M Loyal in Tartuffe; Brooks Atkinson, Aug 1965, took over the Gentleman Caller in The Glass Menagerie; Longacre, Mar 1966, again played in his one-man show Mark Twain Tonight!; and subsequently toured; Shubert, Mar 1967, took over from Alan Alda as Adam, Captain Sanjur, Flip, and Prince Charming in The Apple Tree; Longacre, Jan 1968, Gene Garrison in I Never Sang for My Father; Martin Beck, July 1968, took over as Cervantes and Don Quixote in Man of La Mancha; Belasco, Feb 1969, Mr Winters in Does a Tiger Wear a Necktie?; American Place, Dec 1971, Winnebago in Lake of the Woods; Ford's, Washington, DC, 1972, played in Mark Twain Tonight!; toured, 1975–7, in Mark Twain Tonight!, and performed the show at the Imperial, Mar 1977; first appeared in films in 1966 as Gus Leroy in The Group and has since played in Wild in the Streets, The People Next Door, The Great White Hope, Magnum Force (1973), The Girl from Petrovka (1974), etc; first appeared on television in 1953 in *Hollywood Screen Test*, and played in the serial *The Brighter Day*, 1954–9, in Mark Twain Tonight!, A Clear and Present Danger, The Glass Menagerie, *The Senator* (1970) for which he received the Emmy Award, That Certain Summer (1973); etc.

Favourite parts: Mark Twain, Hotspur, Quentin in After the Fall, Don Quixote in Man of La Mancha. *Recreations:* Riding and sailing. *Club:* The Players. *Address:* Actors Equity Association, 165 West 46th Street, New York, NY 10036.

HOLDEN, Jan (*née* Wilkinson), actress
b Southport, Lancs, 9 May 1931; *d* of John Broadley Wilkinson and his wife Alice (Holden); *e* Lowther College, Abergele, N Wales; *m* Edwin Richfield; trained for the stage at the Old Vic Theatre School.

First appeared on the stage 1950 at the Theatre Royal, Windsor, in various small parts in 1066 and All That; first appeared on the London stage in June 1958 at the St Martin's, as Connie Barnes Ashton in Speaking of Murder; Apollo, Dec 1958, took over the part of Isolde in The Tunnel of Love; Her Majesty's, Oct 1965, played Sarah Lord in Say Who You Are; Lyric, Jan 1971, took over Fiona Foster in How The Other Half Loves; Savoy, July 1976, Eleanor Pound in Banana Ridge; Apollo, June 1978, Valerie Holbrook in Shut Your Eyes and Think of England; films include I Am A Camera and The Best House in London; television, since 1953, includes plays and series, most recently, *Agony*.

Recreations: Interior decorating, gardening. *Address:* c/o Richard Stone, 18–20 York Bldgs, London WC2 6JU. *Tel:* 01–839 6421–8.

HOLDER, Geoffrey, actor, dancer, choreographer
b Port of Spain, Trinidad, West Indies, 1 Aug 1930; *s* of

b Port-of-Spain, Trinidad, West Indies, 1 Aug 1930; *s* of Arthur Holder and his wife Louise (De Frense); *e* Queens Royal College, Port-of-Spain; *m* Carmen de Lavallade, the dancer.

First appeared on stage as a member of his brother Boscoe's dance company, Trinidad, 1942; formed his own dance troupe, 1950; toured with it in Puerto Rico and the Carribean, 1953; made his US debut with his company in Castle Hill, Mass, 1953, subsequently appearing at the White Barn, Westport, Conn, and the Jacob's Pillow Dance Festival, Lee, Mass; made his New York debut at the Alvin, 30 Dec 1954, as The Champion and Baron Samedi in House of Flowers; engaged as a solo dancer by the Metropolitan Opera for Aida and La Perichole, 1956–57 season; Marines, Jones Beach, summer 1957, solo dancer in Showboat; appeared as a solo dancer twice yearly at the Kaufmann Auditorium, NY, 1956–60; made his dramatic debut at the Ethel Barrymore, 21 Jan 1957, as Lucky in Waiting for Godot; appeared at Theatre Under the Stars, June 1957, and Radio City Music Hall, Nov 1957; danced at the Festival of Two Worlds, Spoleto, Italy, 1958; designed costumes and danced with the John Butler Dance Theatre, appearing in NY, 1958; choreographed Brouhaha at the Folkesbiene Playhouse, Apr 1960; Cambridge Drama Festival, Mass, appeared in Twelfth Night, Jul 1959; danced in the Vancouver, Canada, Festival, Aug 1960; at the International Festival, Lagos, Nigeria, 1962; and with his own troupe at the Harkness Dance Festival, Delacorte, NY, Sept 1963; for the Actors Studio choreographed Mhil Daiim, Mar 1964; Brooks Atkinson, Feb 1964, appeared in the *revue* Josephine Baker and Her Company, and again when the *revue* played Henry Miller's, Mar 1964; continued touring extensively; Actors Studio, Dec 1973, Good Dragon in The Masque of St George and the Dragon; Studio Arena, Buffalo, NY, Sept 1974, choreographed I Got a Song; Majestic, Jan 1975, designed the costumes and directed The Wiz, receiving the Antoinette Perry ("Tony") Award in each category; Mark Hellinger, Mar 1978, costumes, choreography and direction for Timbuktu; first appeared in films in England in All Night Long, 1961, and subsequently played in Everything You've Ever Wanted to Know About Sex But Were Afraid to Ask, and as Baron Samedi in Live and Let Die (1973), etc; has appeared regularly on television since 1953, with his dance troupe and in The Bottle Imp (1958), Aladdin, and as choreographer in New York and Boston, etc; is a noted painter and has exhibited extensively in the US and Puerto Rico; has toured in cabaret, including The Village Gate, NY, 1959–60, etc; author of Black Gods, Green Islands, 1957, and of numerous articles.

Address: 215 West 92nd Street, New York, NY. *Tel:* 873-9474.

HOLDER, Owen, actor
b London, 18 Mar 1921; *s* of Henry George Holder and his wife Emily Maud (Ramsey); *e* Reedham Orphanage, Purley, Surrey; *m* Joyce Cummings; formerly an office boy, a commercial artist, and a dermatologist's assistant.

Made his first appearance on the stage at the Theatre Royal, Bristol, 1938, in pantomime; at the Boltons, Feb 1947, played 4288 Smith in Now Barabbas . . ., and subsequently appeared in this part at the Vaudeville, 7 Mar 1947; first appeared on the New York stage at the Empire, 29 Oct 1947, as Dickie Winslow in The Winslow Boy, subsequently touring the United States in this part; Westminster, May 1949, played Roy in Black Chiffon; Haymarket, Apr 1951, John Daly in Waters of the Moon; Saville, Mar 1954, played Frederick, Count von Mellingen in The White Countess; Duchess, Feb

1955, appeared as Eustace in his own play, A Kind of Folly; Aldwych, Aug 1956, played Cully in the revival of Mr Bolfry; Lyric, Jan 1958, directed Tenebrae (for the Repertory Players); Oxford Playhouse, July 1958, played (in a double bill), Jacques Rendel in Hardly Respectable, and Dr Guido Werning in The Festival of Bacchus; Salisbury Playhouse, Nov 1961, directed The Walled Garden; Victoria Palace, Dec 1961, directed Billy Bunter Shipwrecked; Lyric, Dec 1963, and Haymarket, played Lord Mark in The Wings of the Dove; toured as Dr Rank in A Doll's House, 1969; Harrogate, 1972, played the Bishop-who-never-was in Mr Sydney Smith Coming Upstairs; toured as Edward VIII in Crown Matrimonial in South Africa, 1973, and the UK, 1974; directed In Praise of Love (S Africa and Windsor), 1974; toured, 1975, in a one-man show, The Duke Over the Water; toured, 1977, in Ten Little Indians; 1979, toured as Edward VIII in For the Woman I Love; he is the author of the plays: The Art of Living, 1952, Facts of the Heart, 1953, O'Flanagan's Circus, 1957, Milly and Scotch, 1958; Signs of Life, Samuel Johnson (one-man show), 1979; besides many films and television plays.

Recreations: Reading, walking and talking. *Address:* Dormer Cottage, Lynchmere, nr Haslemere, Surrey. *Tel:* Liphook 723818.

HOLE, John, theatre director
b 23 Aug 1939; *s* of George Vincer Hole and his wife Gertraut Johanna Anna (von Broeske Koppe); *e* Westminster School, Balliol College, Oxford; *m* Ginnie Withers; trained for the stage at the Mermaid Theatre, on a Leverhulme Bursary in theatre management, 1962–63.

House manager, Mermaid Theatre, 1964–66; theatre manager, Yvonne Arnaud, Guildford, 1966–67; director, Swan Theatre, Worcester, 1967–74, where he began a long association with David Wood (see entry) as producer of his musicals for children; director, Queen's, Hornchurch, 1974–80; here he directed a number of productions, including Tommy, which he also co-devised and which transferred to the West End in Feb 1979; former member of Arts Council Touring Committee; Chairman, Bubble Theatre; director, 1980– , Vagabond Productions.

Recreations: Rock climbing, rock music, cricket, squash. *Address:* 12 Maidenstone Hill, Greenwich, London SE10.

HOLGATE, Ron, actor and singer
b Aberdeen, South Dakota, 26 May 1937; *s* of C H Holgate and his wife Helen (Fishbeck); *e* Northwestern University, New England Conservatory and Music Academy of the West; studied for the stage with Alvina Krause, Boris Goldovsky and Lotte Lehmann.

First professional appearance was at the Wilbur, Boston, Sept 1958, as Germont in La Traviata; his New York debut was at the Martin Beck, 10 Oct 1961, as a Policeman in Milk and Honey; at the Broadway, Mar 1962, sang for the Martha Graham Company; Alvin, May 1962, Miles Gloriosus in A Funny Thing Happened on the Way to the Forum; Palace, 1966, took over as Vittorio Vidal in Sweet Charity; 46th Street, Mar 1969, Richard Henry Lee in 1776 (Tony award); Shubert, Mar 1973, appeared in Sondheim, a Musical Tribute; Martin Beck, Nov 1974, Ianiello in Saturday, Sunday, Monday; Palace, Jan 1979, the Colonel in The Grand Tour; Rialto, May 1980, Joe Preston in Musical Chairs; has toured in South Pacific, Do I Hear a Waltz?, etc; summer and stock work includes A Little Night Music and The Sound of Music; films include 1776; first TV appearance 1961.

Address: 235 West 75th Street, New York, NY 10023.

HOLLAND, Anthony, designer
b Macclesfield, 3 June 1912; *s* of William Holland and his wife Annie (Thorneycroft); *e* Macclesfield Grammar School; studied at the Manchester School of Art.

Designed his first production at the Liverpool Playhouse, 1933, with The Road to Rome; designer at the Manchester Repertory, 1934–6; designed his first London production, at the Little, Nov 1936, with The King and Mistress Shore; designer at the Oxford Playhouse, 1936–40; served as a navigator in the Royal Air Force, 1941–6; has since designed the following productions: The Eagle Has Two Heads, Lady Frederick, 1946; Edward My Son, The Sleeping Clergyman, Life With Father, You Never Can Tell, 1947; The Indifferent Shepherd, Traveller's Joy, Jonathan, People Like Us, Rain on the Just, Edward My Son (New York), One Wild Oat, 1948; The Human Touch, Champagne For Delilah, The Man in the Raincoat (Edinburgh Festival), The Player King (Edinburgh Festival), The Philadelphia Story, 1949; The Non-Resident, The Cocktail Party, The Hat Trick, The Four Poster, Music At Midnight, Return to Tyassi, Blue for a Boy, 1950; The Seventh Veil, The Three Sisters, Zip Goes a Million, 1951; Winter Journey, The Trap, 1952; The Glorious Days (Act 3), The Redheaded Blonde, 1953; Hippo Dancing, 1954; The Tender Trap, Kismet (Australia), 1955; The Devil's Disciple, 1956; Six Months Grace, Silver Wedding, Meet Me by Moonlight, Roar Like a Dove, The Happiest Millionaire (costumes only), 1957; The Stepmother, The Pied Piper, 1958; How Say You?, The Merry Widow (tour), The Amorous Prawn, 1959; A Visit to a Small Planet, It's in the Bag, Roger the Sixth, Settled Out of Court, 1960; You Prove it, The Affair, 1961; Miss Pell is Missing, 1962; Ménage à Trois, Black Chiffon (tour), 1963; The Reluctant Peer, The Sound of Music (Carré, Amsterdam), The Schoolmistress, Hostile Witness, 1964; Return Ticket, An Ideal Husband, 1965; Arsenic and Old Lace, Wait Until Dark, Justice is a Woman, An Ideal Husband, 1966; Sign Here Please, Let's All Go Down the Strand, Mr Pim Passes By, 1967; Justice, Oh, Clarence! 1968; They Ride on Broomsticks, Never Say Die, 1969; Lady Frederick (costumes only), A Present from Harry, The Jockey Club Stakes, 1970; Spoiled, Look, No Hands, Peter Pan (Coliseum), The Secretary Bird, Promises, Promises (these two Amsterdam), 1971; Dial M for Murder, Darling I'm Home, A Touch of Spring (all S Africa), Lloyd George Knew My Father, Fiddlers Three, 1972; Lover, Relative Values (costumes), 1973; A Ghost on Tiptoe, Birds of Paradise, The Dame of Sark, 1974; Double Edge, 1975; On Approval, A Murder is Announced, 1977; Picture of Innocence, Suite in Two Keys, Plaza Suite (Amsterdam), 1978; The Man Who Came to Dinner (Chichester), 1979; has designed the following operas: Le Convenienze Teatrali, 1972; Robinson Crusoe, 1973, Torquato Tasso, 1974; L'Etoile du Nord, 1975 (all for Camden Festival); Florimel (Opera da Camera), 1973; Maria Golovin, The School for Fathers, Il Castello Di Kenilworth, Rigoletto (Belfast), 1977; since 1954 has designed the following pantomimes: Goldilocks, 1954; Cinderella, 1955; Mother Goose, 1957; Sinbad the Sailor, 1958; Beauty and the Beast, 1959; The Pied Piper, 1960; The Frog Prince, 1961; Tom Thumb, 1965; Jack and the Beanstalk, 1975; he has also designed twenty-eight ice shows, and the Nederlanse Revue, at the Carré Theatre, Amsterdam, 1959–69.
Address: c/o Ronnie Waters, ICM, 22 Grafton Street, London W1 *and* 3 Albert Studios, Albert Bridge Road, London, SW11. *Tel:* 01–228 7944.

HOLLIS, Stephen, director
b Oxford, 26 Jan 1941; *s* of Frederick Hollis and his wife Olive; *e* Haberdashers' Aske's School, Elstree and University of Grenoble.

Began work in the theatre as an ASM at the Royal Court, 1967; assistant director, Watford Palace, 1968–69, directing his first production, Little Malcolm and His Struggle against the Eunuchs, and five other plays including The Homecoming; resident director, 1969–70, Citizens', Glasgow, where his productions included premieres of Sam Foster Comes Home, and Spoiled, which he also directed at the Haymarket, Feb 1971; in the same year directed Mr Kilt and The Great I Am, Hampstead, and productions at Cambridge and Leeds; artistic director since 1972 of Watford Palace, where notable productions include Don Juan, Orpheus Descending, 1972; Dutch Uncle, The Milk Train Doesn't Stop Here Any More, A Patriot for Me, 1973; Three Sisters, 1974; Out on the Lawn, 1975; Rain, 1978; in the West End his productions include Molly, 1978, Stage Struck, 1979; directed a British Council tour to the Far East of Pygmalion and The Merchant of Venice, 1976; in the same year went to New York on a Bicentennial Fellowship and there made his US directing debut with The Philander, followed by In the Summerhouse, and Molly.
Address: 37 Arundel Gardens, London W11.

HOLLOWAY, Julian, actor, producer, director and writer
b Watlington, Oxford, 24 June 1944; *s* of the actor Stanley Augustus Holloway and his wife the actress Violet Marion (Lane); *e* Harrow School; *m* the actress Zena Walker (mar dis); trained for the stage at RADA.

Made his professional debut at the Vaudeville, 25 Apr 1963, in the revue All Square; Royal Court, June 1966, played Jimmy in When Did You Last See My Mother?, transferring with the production to the Comedy, Jul; Hampstead, Sep 1968, Tom in Spitting Image, again transferring with the play to the Duke of York's, Oct; Globe, Jul 1975, later Apollo, Dec, took over as Tom in The Norman Conquests; toured, 1976, in the Cambridge Theatre Company's Pygmalion, as Professor Higgins; Westminster, May 1977, Mortimer Brewster in Arsenic and Old Lace; has directed at The Crucible, Sheffield and The Thorndike, Leatherhead; first film Nothing But the Best, 1963, most recently Rough Cut, 1979; producer and co-author of two short films, The Spy's Wife and The Chairman's Wife; associate producer for the film The Brute and co-producer on Loophole; has appeared frequently on television since Our Man at St Mark's, 1963, recently in The Sweeney, Rebecca, etc.
Club: MCC. *Address:* c/o NEMS Management, 29–31 King's Road, London, SW3.

HOLLOWAY, Stanley, OBE, actor and singer
b London, 1 Oct 1890; *m* (2) Violet Marion Lane; was originally a seaside concert artist.

Made his first appearance in London at the Winter Garden Theatre, 20 May 1919, as Captain Wentworth in Kissing Time, and appeared at the same theatre, Sept 1920, as René in A Night Out; he was an original member of The Co-Optimists, at the Royalty, 27 June 1921, and remained with them until the company was disbanded in 1927; he then appeared at the London Hippodrome, Nov 1927, as Bill Smith in Hit the Deck; at His Majesty's, Sept 1928, as Lieut Richard Manners in Song of the Sea; at the Vaudeville, Apr 1929, appeared in Cooee; July 1929, again appeared with the revived Co-Optimists; London Hippodrome, Apr 1930, appeared with The Co-Optimists of 1930; Savoy, July 1932, played in Savoy Follies; Lyceum, Oct 1932, in Here We Are Again; Drury Lane, Apr 1934, Eustace Titherley in Three Sisters; at the Prince of Wales's, Birmingham, Dec 1934, made his first appearance in pantomime, as Abanazar in Aladdin, and played the same part, each succeeding Christmas, at Leeds, Golder's Green, Edinburgh, and Manchester respectively; Duke of York's, Nov 1936, appeared in All Wave; London Palladium, Apr 1938, in London Rhapsody; toured, June 1938, in All the Best; at the Saville Theatre, Apr 1940, and again in May 1941, appeared in Up and Doing, and Apr 1942, in Fine and Dandy; Casino, Dec 1946, played Squire Skinflint in Mother Goose; New, May 1951, played the First Gravedigger in Hamlet; appeared with the Old Vic Company at the Edinburgh Festival, 1954, as Bottom in A Midsummer Night's Dream; then toured the United States and Canada in this production, making his first appearance in New York at the Metropolitan Opera House, Sept 1954; Mark Hellinger, NY, Mar 1956, played Alfred P Doolittle in My Fair Lady, leaving the cast to return to England to play the same part in the Drury Lane production, Apr 1958; Ethel Barrymore, NY, Oct 1960, appeared in a one-man entertainment Laughs and Other Events; Forrest, Philadelphia, Apr 1964, played Lester Linstrom, Irving, Policeman, and Lester Lenz in Cool Off; Canadian Shaw Festival, played Burgess in Candida 1970, and William in You Never Can Tell, 1973; toured Australia and Hong Kong, 1977, in The Pleasure of His Company; entered films 1921, in The Rotters, and has appeared in numerous pictures, including his original part of Alfred P Doolittle in My Fair Lady, 1964, and recently in Desperate Journey; television appearances include the series *Our Man Higgins* (US), 1962–3; has also appeared at many of the leading variety theatres throughout the United Kingdom.

Clubs: Garrick and Green Room. *Address:* Pyefleet, Tamarisk Way, East Preston, Sussex.

HOLM, Celeste, actress

b New York City, 29 Apr; *d* of Theodor Holm and his wife Jean (Parke); *e* in Holland, France, and Chicago; *m* (1) Ralph Nelson (mar dis); (2) Francis E H Davies (mar dis); (3) A Schuyler Dunning (mar dis); (4) Wesley Addy; studied dancing, singing, and acting under Adolph Bolm, C H Mundy, and Benno Schneider.

Made her first appearance on the stage in a summer stock company at Orwigsburg, Deer Lake, Pa, 1936; toured 1937, understudying Ophelia in Hamlet, subsequently playing Cyrstal in The Woman; made her first appearance in NY, at the Little Theatre, 25 Nov 1938, as Lady Mary in Gloriana; at the Booth Theatre, Oct 1939, played Mary L in The Time of Your Life; National, Feb 1940, Maria in Another Sun, and May 1940, the Daughter in The Return of the Vagabond; Henry Miller, Jan 1941, Marcia Godden in Eight O'Clock Tuesday; Hudson, Mar 1941, Lady Keith-Odlyn in My Fair Ladies; Guild, Jan 1942, Emma in Papa Is All; Longacre, May 1942, Fifi Oritanski in All the Comforts of Home; Playhouse, Oct 1942, Calla Longstreth in The Damask Cheek; St James's, Mar 1943, Ado Annie Carnes in Oklahoma!; Shubert, Oct 1944, Evelina in Bloomer Girl; New York City Center, Dec 1949, Kate Hardcastle in She Stoops to Conquer; Royale, Sept 1950, Irene Elliott in Affairs of State, written specially for her by Louis Verneuil; City Center, Jan 1952, Anna Christopherson in Anna Christie; St James's, July 1952, for a time replaced Gertrude Lawrence as Anna in The King and I; 48th Street, Jan 1954, Maggie Palmer in His and Hers; Melody Circus, Detroit, Aug 1956, starred in Sudden Spring; toured, 1957, as Eve and Lilith in Back to Methuselah; ANTA, NY, Feb 1958, Mrs Price in Interlock; Ambassador, Dec 1958, Helen Sayre in Third Best Sport; Spa, Saratoga Springs, NY, July 1959, appeared in the revue What a Day; in summer theatres, June 1960, Kate Sedgwick in Royal Enclosure; Music Box, Oct 1960, Camilla Jablonski in Invitation to a March, and subsequently toured in this part; Maidman, May 1963, Natalya Petrovna in A

Month in the Country; toured the US, 1963–4 in a programme Theatre-in-Concert, and continued to tour for this programme in the US and abroad; Playhouse-in-the-Park, Philadelphia, Aug 1963, Angela Burgeon in Madly in Love; toured, summer 1965, in The Grass Is Greener; Pasadena (Calif) Playhouse, Apr 1967, Irene Elliott in Affairs of State; Shubert, Chicago, 1967, Mame Dennis in Mame, and took over in this part at the Winter Garden, NY, in 1967, and toured; Longacre, Apr 1970, Candida Morell in Candida; Studio Arena, Buffalo, NY, Jan 1972, title-role in Mama; summer tour, 1972, as Mrs Baker in Butterflies Are Free; Studio Arena, 1973, Mrs Baker in Butterflies Are Free; toured, summer 1973, as Hedda Rankin in The Irregular Verb to Love; toured, 1975, in Light Up the Sky; Woodstock, NY, Playhouse, Aug 1975, Samantha Greenberg in And Nothing But; Martin Beck, Nov 1975, Lady Rumpers in Habeas Corpus; Studio Arena, Buffalo, May 1977, Myra Matthews in A Very Private Life; Mark Hellinger, May 1979, Julia Fayle in The Utter Glory of Morrissey Hall; Williamstown Festival, Mass, July 1979, Judith Bliss in Hay Fever; Harold Clurman, Dec 1979, appearing as Janet Flanner in her one-woman show, Paris Was Yesterday; went to Hollywood, 1945, and first appeared in films in Three Little Girls in Blue; gained Academy Award for her performance in Gentleman's Agreement; and was nominated for the award for her performances in Come to the Stable and All About Eve; played Aunt Polly in Tom Sawyer, 1973; appeared on television first in 1949 and has since appeared in numerous dramatic and variety programs, including an appearance in 1965 as the Fairy Godmother in a musical version of Cinderella; recently in Backstairs at the White House; knighted, May 1979, by King Olav of Norway.

Address: c/o Actors Equity Association, 165 West 46th Street, New York, NY 10036.

HOLM, Hanya (*née* Johanna Eckert), choreographer, director

b Worms-am-Rhein, Germany; *d* of Valentin Eckert and his wife Marie (Moerschel); *e* Englische Fraulein Convent, Mainz; Hoch Conservatory, Frankfurt, 1913–15; Dalcroze Institute, 1916; Wigman School of the Dance, Dresden, 1921; *m* Reinhold Martin Kuntze (mar dis).

Appeared in Max Reinhardt's The Miracle before joining the Dalcroze Institute; after joining the Wigman School of Dance became Co-director until 1931; member of the original Mary Wigman dance company, 1923, and toured with it until 1928; at Ommen, Holland, 1927–8, directed productions of plays during the summer; State Playhouse, Dresden, 1927, danced in Stravinsky's L'Histoire du Soldat; Munich, 1930, associate director to Mary Wigman of Totenmal, in which she also danced; founder, 1931, of the New York Wigman School of Dance, which in 1936 became the Hanya Holm School of Dance; made her American début dancing with her company in Denver, Colorado, 1936; toured with this company, appearing annually in New York, 1936–44; made her NY début as a musical comedy choreographer at the Maxine Elliott, 9 May 1948, with The Eccentricities of Davey Crockett, last of three Ballet Ballads; since then has choreographed The Insect Comedy, $E = MC^2$, Kiss Me, Kate, 1948; Blood Wedding, 1949; The Liar, Out of This World, 1950; made her London début as choreographer at the Coliseum, 8 Mar 1951, with Kiss Me, Kate; My Darlin' Aida, NY, 1952; The Golden Apple, 1954; Reuben, Reuben, (Boston), 1955; My Fair Lady, for which she received the Antoinette Perry (Tony) Award, The Ballad of Baby Doe, an opera which she also directed at the Central City Opera House, Colorado, 1956; Where's Charley? and My Fair Lady in London, 1958;

Orpheus and Eurydice, an opera which she also directed at the Queen Elizabeth, Vancouver, BC, 1959; Christine, Camelot, NY, 1960; Orpheus and Eurydice, O'Keefe Center, Toronto, Ontario, 1962; My Fair Lady (Habimah, Tel Aviv), 1964; Anya, 1965; first appeared on television with her dance company in 1939 in the satire, Metropolitan Daily, the first modern dance production on US TV, and since has appeared frequently on talk and variety shows and has choreographed Pinocchio, 1957, Dinner with the President, 1963, etc; choreographed the film The Vagabond King, 1956; was Director of the dance department of the Musical and Dramatic Theatre Academy, NY; instructor at Colorado College, 1961 to date; for the Colorado Festival directed Il Cavaliere Errante, 1971, and directed and choreographed L'Heure Espagnole, L'Enfant et les Sortilèges, 1972; The Italian Girl in Algiers, 1973; Iolanthe, 1974; The Abduction from the Seraglio, 1975; Gianni Schicchi, 1976; member of the Dance Advisory Panel, ANTA, 1962 to date; is a Fellow of the International Institute of Arts and Letters, Kreuzlingen, Switzerland, 1961 to date; director of Colorado College Summer Dance Session, 1941 to date; staff member of Juillard School, NY, 1975 to present; Honorary DFA, Colorado College, 1960; DFA, Adelphi University, Garden City, NY, 1969.

Address: c/o Selma Tamber, 46 West 54th Street, New York, NY 10019. *Tel:* 246–9776.

HOLM, Ian (*né* Ian Holm Cuthbert), actor
b Goodmayes, Ilford, Essex, 12 Sept 1931; *s* of Dr James Harvey Cuthbert and his wife Jean Wilson (Holm); *e* Chigwell Grammar School; *m* Lynn Mary Shaw (mar dis); studied for the stage at the Royal Academy of Dramatic Art.

Made his first appearance on the stage at the Shakespeare Memorial Theatre, Stratford-on-Avon, Mar 1954, as a Spear Carrier in Othello; remained as a member of the company for two seasons, playing, among other parts, Donalbain in Macbeth, and Mutius in Titus Andronicus, 1955; appeared at the Worthing Repertory Theatre for six months during 1956; made his first London appearance at the Lyric, Hammersmith, June 1956, as Rupert Bliss in Love Affair; toured Europe, June 1957, with Sir Laurence Olivier, playing Mutius in Titus Andronicus, subsequently appearing in the same production at the Stoll Theatre, July 1957; at the Shakespeare Memorial Theatre, Stratford-on-Avon, appeared for three seasons in the following parts: Peter in Romeo and Juliet, Sebastian in Twelfth Night, Verges in Much Ado About Nothing, 1958; Puck in A Midsummer Night's Dream, the Fool in King Lear, 1959; Lorenzo in The Merchant of Venice, Gremio in The Taming of the Shrew, 1960; became a long-term contract artist when the company was re-named the Royal Shakespeare Company, Jan 1961, and has since appeared in London and Stratford-on-Avon in the following parts: at the Aldwych, First Judge in Ondine, Mannoury in The Devils, Little Monk in Becket, Gremio in The Taming of the Shrew, and Trofimov in The Cherry Orchard, 1961; Royal Shakespeare, Stratford, Apr 1962, played Claudio in Measure for Measure, Puck, and Gremio; Aldwych, Oct 1962, played Troilus in Troilus and Cressida; Royal Shakespeare, 1963, Ariel in The Tempest, Richard in Edward IV, and the title part in Richard III (the last two plays forming part of the trilogy The Wars of the Roses); Aldwych, Jan 1964, again played Richard in Edward IV, and Richard III; Royal Shakespeare, Apr 1964, played Henry, Prince of Wales, in Henry IV (Parts I and II), the title-part in Henry V (*Evening Standard* Award, 1965, for Best Actor), and again appeared in Edward IV, and Richard III; Aldwych, June 1965, played Lenny in The Homecoming; Aldwych, Oct

1965, appeared in a reading of The Investigator; Royal Shakespeare, Apr–Aug 1966, again played Henry, Prince of Wales in Henry IV (I and II) and the title part in Henry V, also appearing as Malvolio in Twelfth Night; Music Box, Jan 1967, made his first New York appearance as Lenny in The Homecoming, winning a Tony Award for the Best Supporting Actor in a Drama, 1967; returned to the Royal Shakespeare, Sept 1967, as Romeo in Romeo and Juliet; Round House, May 1970, Manfred in The Friends; Haymarket, Sept 1970, Nelson in A Bequest to the Nation; Traverse, Edinburgh, Aug 1972, Buddy in Caravaggio Buddy; Royal Court, May 1973, Hatch in The Sea; Hampstead, July 1974, Dave in Other People; Hampstead, Nov 1979, played Voinitsky in Uncle Vanya; his films include: A Midsummer Night's Dream, The Fixer, Events Whilst Guarding the Bofors Gun (Academy Award for Best Supporting Actor), The Homecoming, Juggernaut, and Shout at the Devil; made his first appearance on television, 1956, and recently, in *The Sweeney*, and The Lost Boys.

Favourite parts: Richard III, Puck and Gremio in The Taming of the Shrew. *Recreations:* Tennis, and walking with a dog. *Address:* c/o Leading Artists, 60 St James's Street, London SW1.

HOLM, John Cecil, actor and dramatic author
b Philadelphia, Pa, 4 Nov 1904; *s* of Charles Hedley Holm and his wife Lucinda (Bair); *e* Public Grade School, Philadelphia, West Philadelphia High School, and University of Pennsylvania; *m* (1) Fae Pittenger Brown (dec); (2) Dolores Leids Boland.

Had amateur experience with the Mask and Wig Club at University before making his first appearance on the stage at the Colonial Theatre, Pittsfield, Mass, 3 Oct 1925, as Dempsey in The Devil Within; subsequently was stage manager and actor with the Lillian Desmond Players, 1926, and the Plateau Players, 1927; toured as Roy Lane in Broadway, 1927; at Times Square, NY, 1928, understudied Lee Tracy, as Hildy Johnson in The Front Page, and made his first appearance on the New York stage in this part in Jan 1929; in the autumn toured as Wilson in the same play; Biltmore, Dec 1929, played Charles Black in Whirlpool; Apr 1930, Thomas Mason in Penal Law 2010; Oct 1930, Doggie in The Up and Up; Alvin, Oct 1931, Mac in Wonder Boy; Times Square, Mar 1932, James Knox in Bloodstream; Empire, Oct 1932, Gordon Whitehouse in Dangerous Corner; Alvin (for the Theatre Guild), Nov 1933, Jamie in Mary of Scotland; part-author (with George Abbott) of Three Men on a Horse, 1935 produced in London, 1936, where he also directed it, revived in NY, 1942, where he also directed it, and revived again in 1969; author of Four Cents a Word, 1938; Best Foot Forward, 1941; Dancing in the Streets (part-author), 1943; Brighten the Corner, 1945; revised book of Sweethearts, 1947; Gramercy Ghost, 1951; Golden Harvest, 1953; The South-west Corner, 1955; co-author of Banjo Eyes and Let It Ride (musical based on Three Men on a Horse), 1941 and 1961; revised Best Foot Forward, 1963; returned to the stage as an actor at the Cort, Jan 1960, playing Dr Holden in A Mighty Man Is He; Martin Beck, Feb 1961, Luther Plunkett in Midgie Purvis; St James, Oct 1962, played Chester Kincaid in Mr President; ANTA, Oct 1963, played Arthur Burns in The Advocate; 41st Street, Dec 1963, Mr Twilling in Her Master's Voice; Helen Hayes, Feb 1966, Ben Burton in Philadelphia, Here I Come; Jones Beach, June 1968, Capt George Brackett in South Pacific; Morosco, Dec 1968, Mr Latham in Forty Carats, and continued in this part through 1969 and 1970; has also played frequently in stock, notably in Never Too Late in 1965, and as Pickering in three different touring productions of My Fair Lady; in 1958, appeared in the film It Happened to Jane; has also played frequently on television; published his autobiography, Sunday Best, 1942; is author of the book McGarrity and the Pigeons, 1947.

Recreations: Fishing, antique collecting, and writing. *Club:* The Players. *Address:* Tanglewylde Avenue, Bronxville, NY. *Tel:* 914 SW 3–6338.

HOLME, Thea, actress and author

b London, 27 Dec 1907; *d* of Philip Mainwaring Johnston and his wife Florence Anna (Wynne); *e* Dulwich; *m* Stanford Holme; formerly an art student; studied for the stage at the Central School for Speech Training and Dramatic Art.

Made her first appearance on the stage at the Richmond Theatre, Sept 1924, as Hippolyta in A Midsummer Night's Dream, with the Ben Greet Players; appeared with that company, at the Théâtre Albert Iᵉʳ, Paris, Jan 1925; July 1925, appeared with the English Players at the International Exhibition, Paris, as Dolly in You Never Can Tell, and Cecily Cardew in The Importance of Being Earnest; in 1927, toured as Rhoda Marley in Rookery Nook, and 1928, as Kitty Stratton in Thark; made her first appearance in New York, at the Columbia University Theatre, Oct 1929, as Beatrice in Much Ado About Nothing; made her first appearance in London, at Golder's Green, 15 Sept 1930, as Cynthia Mc-Todd in Leave It to Psmith, playing the same part at the Shaftesbury Theatre; at the Oxford Playhouse, 1931, played lead in repertory, also appearing for the OUDS, Feb 1931, as Yasmin in Hassan; at the Criterion, Aug 1931, played Doris Wilder in Those Naughty Nineties; appeared at the Arts, Nov 1931, and Prince of Wales's, Dec 1931, as Joan in She Passed Through Lorraine; at the Q, Feb 1932, played Ophelia in Hamlet; Prince of Wales, Mar 1932, Ada in I Lived With You, in which she subsequently toured; Embassy, Oct 1932, played Esther Eccles in Caste, Nov 1932, Helena Glory and Helena in RUR, Joan Brandon in The Cathedral; appeared at the New Theatre, Dec 1932, in the last-mentioned part; Playhouse, Jan 1933, Clare Mitchell in Flies in the Sun; Apollo, May 1933, Anne Brontë in Wild Decembers; Embassy, July 1933, Ethel Smedley in Beauty and the Barge; Q, Oct 1933, the Princess in The Shadow Princess; Saville, Dec 1933, Lady Ella in Beau Brummell; Westminster, Feb 1934, Lilla in Private Room; at the Arts Theatre, Apr 1934, played Ophelia in the production of the first quarto Hamlet; appeared at Canterbury, with the Old Stagers, Aug 1934, as Lady Teazle in The School for Scandal, and Joan Greenleaf in Bird in Hand; Little, Oct 1934, the Duchess of Portsmouth in Royal Baggage; Shaftesbury, Nov 1934, Gemma Donati in For Ever; Westminster, Feb 1935, Estella in The Convict; Savoy, Mar 1935, Lady Victoria Alton in The Aunt of England; Oxford Festival Theatre, July 1935, played Lady Precious Stream in the play of that name, Viola in Twelfth Night, etc; Little, Nov 1935, played Lady Precious Stream, transferring to the Savoy, 1936; Gate, Apr 1937, Bessie Branson in Lord Adrian; toured, 1937, as Viera in Tuberin 5; Q, Dec 1937, played Lady Olivia in Sweet Nell of Old Drury; Apollo, Feb 1938, Mary Summers in Black Swans; Tewkesbury Festival, July 1938, Sara in Tobias and the Angel; Open Air, Regent's Park, Aug 1938, Phebe in As You Like It; reopened at the New Playhouse, Oxford, Oct 1938, and in Feb 1939, appeared there as Joan in Saint Joan, and June 1939, as Ilse in Reunion in Vienna; at the outbreak of War, 1939, joined the original BBC repertory company; Stratford-on-Avon, 1940 season, played leads at the Memorial Theatre; Piccadilly Theatre, July 1942, appeared as Lady Macduff in Macbeth; toured with CEMA, 1942–4, playing Kate Hardcastle in She Stoops to Conquer, and Precious

Stream in Lady Precious Stream; appeared at the Mercury, Feb 1943, in She Stoops to Conquer, and at the Open Air Theatre, July 1943, and June 1944, directed and played Lady Precious Stream; Open Air, July 1944, directed, and played Viola in Twelfth Night; toured, Aug 1950, as Catherine Sloper in The Heiress; author of Roman Holiday, produced 1937; Mansfield Park (with Joan Riley, from Jane Austen's novel), 1951; has appeared on television in the serial, Nicholas, Nickleby, 1969; she is also the author of the following television adaptations: The Enchanted April, and Mr Skeffington; radio serials include versions of Northanger Abbey and Mansfield Park, The Girl Who Would have been Queen and six of the series Married to a Genius; her books include: The Carlyles at Home, 1965; Chelsea, 1971; Prinny's Daughter, 1976; Caroline, 1979, appointed a Fellow of the Royal Society of Literature, 1971.

Address: Denville Hall, Northwood, Middlesex.

HOLT, Thelma, actress and manager

b 4 Jan 1933; *d* of David Holt and his wife Ellen Finnagh (Doyle); *e* St Anns Girls School; *m* (1) Patrick Graucob (mar dis); (2) David Pressman (mar dis); trained for the stage at the Royal Academy of Dramatic Art.

Made her first professional appearance at the Globe, 11 June 1953, as a servant in The Private Life of Helen, later taking over the part of Hermione; subsequent experience in rep and the West End; in 1968, with Charles Marowitz, founded the Open Space theatre, where she appeared in a number of productions including Marowitz's various Shakespeare collages; played Portia in the opening production of the new Open Space, 1977; joined the Round House Trust, Jul 1977, as its Director, and has since presented a varied programme in the Round House's two theatres, including visits by major regional and overseas companies.

Recreation: Talking to God. *Address:* The Round House, Chalk Farm Road, London NW1. *Tel:* 267 2541.

HOLT, Will, dramatic author and lyricist

b Portland, Maine, 30 Apr 1929; *s* of Dr William Holt and his wife Marjorie (Scribner); *e* Phillips Academy, Exeter, Williams College, Mass and Richard Dyer-Bennett School of Minstrelsy, Aspen, Colo; *m* the actress Dolly Jonah.

Originally a folk-singer, he made his professional debut singing at the Village Vanguard, NY, Dec 1947; debut as an actor at the Coconut Grove, Palm Beach, Fla, 1957, as Ted Snow in Say Darling; wrote the book and lyrics for Come Summer, seen at the Lunt-Fontanne, Mar 1969; lyrics for The Me Nobody Knows, 1970; book for Over Here!, 1974; book and concept for Me and Bessie, 1974; lyrics for Music Is, 1976; book and concept for Platinum, 1978; author of the novels Savage Snow, and Sabine, both 1980.

Address: 45 East 66th Street, New York, NY 10021.

HOLZER, Adela, producer.

Produced her first play in New York, Where Has Tommy Flowers Gone?, at the Eastside Playhouse, 7 Oct 1971; since then has produced or co-produced the following: Voices, Dude, 1972; Brainchild (Philadelphia), Bad Habits, Sherlock Holmes, All Over Town, 1974; The Ritz, Treemonisha (opera), 1975; Me Jack, You Jill, 1976; Something Old, Something New, Monsters (Side Show and The Transfiguration of Benno Blimpie), 1977.

Address: 17 East 35th Street, New York, NY 10001. *Tel:* 697 8115.

HOME, William Douglas, dramatic author

b Edinburgh, Scotland, 3 June 1912; *s* of 13th Earl of Home and his wife Lilian (Lambton), daughter of the 4th Earl of Durham; *e* Eton and New College, Oxford, BA Hist; *m* Rachel Brand; served in World War II, 1940–4.

Formerly an actor, having studied at the Royal Academy of Dramatic Art, and made his first appearance with the Brighton Repertory Theatre, 1937; first appeared in London, at the New Theatre, 8 Sept 1937, as Brian Morellian in Bonnet Over the Windmill; St Martin's, 10 Mar 1938, played Johnny Greystroke in Plan for a Hostess; Vaudeville, July 1948, for a time, played Lord Pym in The Chiltern Hundreds; took over the part of Jimmy Broadbent in The Reluctant Debutante, for some performances, Oct 1955; Theatre Royal, Brighton, Feb 1960, played Colonel Ryan in Aunt Edwina; is the author of the following plays: Great Possessions, 1937; Passing By, 1940; Now Barabbas, The Chiltern Hundreds, 1947; Ambassador Extraordinary, 1948; Master of Arts, The Thistle and the Rose, 1949; Caro William, 1952; The Bad Samaritan, 1953; The Manor of Northstead, 1954; The Reluctant Debutante, 1955; The Iron Duchess, 1957; Aunt Edwina, 1959; Up a Gum Tree, 1960; The Bad Soldier Smith, 1961; The Cigarette Girl, 1962; The Drawing Room Tragedy, 1963; The Reluctant Peer, Two Accounts Rendered (double-bill), 1964; Betzi, A Friend in Need, 1965; A Friend Indeed, 1966; The Queen's Highland Servant, The Grouse Moor Image, The Secretary Bird, 1968; The Jockey Club Stakes, 1970; The Douglas Cause, 1971; Lloyd George Knew My Father, At the End of the Day, 1972; The Dame of Sark, The Lord's Lieutenant, 1974; Betzi (new version), 1975; In the Red, The Kingfisher, Rolls Hyphen Royce, 1977; The Editor Regrets, 1978; first play in New York, The Chiltern Hundreds, produced as Yes M'Lord (1949); author of the film adaptations: Now Barrabas, The Chiltern Hundreds, The Colditz Story, The Reluctant Debutante; published his autobiography, Half-Term Report, 1954; also Mr Home Pronounced Hume, 1979.

Recreations: Playwriting, politics, bridge and golf. *Club:* Travellers'. *Address:* Drayton House, East Meon, Hants.

HOOD, Morag, actress
b Glasgow, 12 Dec 1942; *d* of Thomas Hood and his wife Helen Dallas (Kelso); *e* Bellahouston Academy, Glasgow and Glasgow University.

Made her first professional appearance at the Metropole, Glasgow, 1964, in Wedding Fever; gained early experience in Rep in Scotland, including Pitlochry, season 1965; at Liverpool Playhouse, season 1966; at Bristol Old Vic, 1968, played Alison in The Lady's Not for Burning; made her West End debut at the Queen's, 18 Dec 1968, as Clarice in The Servant of Two Masters; Greenwich, Mar 1973, Martirio in The House of Bernarda Alba; in the same year played Elise in The Miser at the Lyceum, Edinburgh, and Juliet in Romeo and Juliet at the Liverpool Playhouse; at the Piccadilly, Mar 1974, Stella Kowalski in A Streetcar Named Desire; Edinburgh, 1975, Kate in The Flo'ers of Edinburgh; Greenwich, Mar 1976, Annette in The Bells; toured, 1976, as Kay in Time and the Conways; joined the National Theatre company, 1976, to play parts including Gasparina in Il Campiello, Celia in Volpone, The Shrimp in The Lady from Maxim's, and Esmeralda in The Hunchback of Notre Dame; Chichester Festival, 1978, The Marquise in The Inconstant Couple; Hampstead, May 1979, Isabel in Then and Now; returned to the National, 1979, and at the Cottesloe appeared in Lark Rise, Candleford, and as Cora in The Iceman Cometh, Mar 1980; first film, Wuthering Heights, 1970; also in Diversions, 1979; TV includes Persuasion, War and Peace, The Camerons, and Breeze Anstey.

Favourite parts: Stella Kowalski, Gasparina, Isabel. *Address:* c/o Larry Dalzell Associates, 3 Goodwin's Court, St Martin's Lane, London WC2.

HOOKS, Robert, actor, director, producer, co-founder of the Negro Ensemble Company
b Washington, DC, 18 Apr 1937; *s* of Edward Hooks and his wife Bertha (Ward); *e* Temple University.

As Bobbie Dean Hooks made his debut 12 Sept 1960 at the Wilbur, Boston, Mass, as George Murchison in A Raisin in the Sun, and subsequently toured for nearly a year; toured, Sept 1961–Apr 1962, as The Boy in A Taste of Honey; made his New York debut at the Booth 22 Dec 1962, as Dewey Chipley in Tiger Tiger Burning Bright; Mayfair, Oct 1963, played Dennis Thornton in Ballad for Bimshire; St Mark's Playhouse, 1963, took over as Deodatus Village in The Blacks; Lunt-Fontanne, Nov 1963, Played in Arturo Ui; Brooks Atkinson, Jan 1964, played a Stage Assistant in the revised version of Tennessee Williams's The Milk Train Doesn't Stop Here Anymore; as Robert Hooks appeared at the Cherry Lane, 24 Mar 1964, as Clay in Dutchman; Delacorte Mobile, June 1965, title role in King Henry V; St Mark's Playhouse, Nov 1965, Junie in Happy Ending and John in Day of Absence, which he also produced; Billy Rose, Mar 1966, Razz in Where's Daddy?; Martin Beck, Apr 1967, Clem in Hallelujah, Baby!; with Gerald S Krone under a Ford Foundation Grant organized the Negro Ensemble Company and, as Executive Director, at the St Mark's Playhouse, which has been its home ever since, produced Song of the Lusitanian Bogey, Jan 1968; has since produced Summer of the Seventeenth Doll, Kongi's Harvest, in which he also played Daoudu, Apr, Daddy Goodness, God Is a (Guess What?), 1968; made his London debut at the World Theatre Season, Aldwych, May 1969, when he presented his troupe in Song of the Lusitanian Bogey and God Is a (Guess What?); in NY presented Ceremonies in Dark Old Men, which won the Pulitzer Prize as best play of the year, An Evening of One Acts, Man Better Man, The Reckoning, 1969; The Harangues, in which he also appeared in Jan, Ododo, Brotherhood, Day of Absence, also directed the last two, 1970; Perry's Mission, Rosalee Pritchett, The Dream on Monkey Mountain, Ride a Dark Horse, The Sty of the Blind Pig, 1971; A Ballet Behind the Bridge, Frederick Douglass . . . Through His Own Words, The River Niger, 1972 (also on Broadway, May 1973); The Great Macdaddy, Black Sunlight, Nowhere to Run, Nowhere to Hide, Terraces, Heaven and Hell's Agreement, In the Deepest Part of Sleep, 1974; The First Breeze of Summer (also on Broadway), Liberty Call, Orrin, Sugar-Mouth Sam Don't Dance No More, The Moonlight Arms, The Dark Tower, Waiting for Mongo, Welcome to Black River, 1975; Eden, Livin' Fat, The Brownsville Raid, 1976; The Great Macdaddy, The Offering, 1977; Black Body Blues, The Twilight Dinner, Nevis Mountain Dew, The Daughters of the Mock, 1978; Plays from Africa, A Season to Unravel, Old Phantoms, Home, The Michigan, 1979; founded the DC Black Repertory Company, Washington, DC, 1973–7, and at the Eisenhower, May 1973, directed and played Village in The Blacks; directed Day of Absence, 1975; has appeared in films in Hurry, Sundown, The Last of the Mobile Hotshots, Trouble Man (1972), etc; has also appeared on television, in NYPD, etc.

Address: St Mark's Playhouse, 133 Second Avenue, New York, NY 10003. *Tel:* 674–3530.

HOOPER, Ewan, actor, director and manager
b Dundee, 23 Oct 1935; *s* of Brian Eynon Hooper, and his wife Margaret Jean (Stewart); *e* Dundee High School; *m* Marion Fiddick.

First appeared on the stage in May 1957, at the Sarah Bernhardt, Paris, walking on in Titus Andronicus; first appearance on the London stage July 1957, at the Stoll, in the same production; Lyric, Hammersmith, Nov 1957, played Henry Beaufort in The Queen and the Welshman; in repertory at the Citizens', Glasgow, 1958–9 and at the Bristol Old Vic, 1959–62; Old Vic, London, June 1962, played Napoleon in the Bristol production of War and Peace; Dublin Festival, Sept 1962, and Venice Festival, appeared in A Touch of the Poet; Theatre Royal, Stratford, E, Oct–Nov 1964, appeared as Narrator and Shepherd in Electra, Talthybius in The Trojan Women, and Pylades in Iphigeneia; there also, in Feb 1965, he played the title role in Georges Dandin; Hampstead, Oct 1968, Jack Elliott in It's All in the Mind; Royal Court, Aug 1974, William Combe in Bingo; Hornchurch, 1979, title-role in Uncle Vanya; founded Greenwich Young People's Theatre, 1966, and The Tramshed, Woolwich, 1974; founder, in 1962, of the Greenwich Theatre, which was rebuilt and opened under his direction, Oct 1969; remained as Director there until 1978, and regular appearances included Valentine Joyce in Spithead, Nov 1969; Creon in Medea, Apr 1970; Pat in The Hostage, June 1970; Orgon in Tartuffe, 1976; Creon in The Sons of Oedipus, First God in The Good Person of Szechwan, 1977; Peter in Don Juan, 1978; directed What a Mouth, May 1970; Down the Arches (also wrote), Oct 1970; The Little Giant, Apr 1972; Marching Song, Oct 1974; appeared in the monodrama In Memory of . . . Carmen Miranda, Dec 1975; is also the author of Martin Luther King, 1969 and A Man Dies (with Ernest Marvin); films include How I Won the War and Julius Caesar; television, since 1963, includes Hunter's Walk and King Lear.

Favourite parts: Orgon in Tartuffe, and Uncle Vanya. *Club:* Arts. *Address:* c/o Sara Randall, 348A Upper Street, London N1.

HOPKINS, Anthony, actor
b Port Talbot, S Wales, 31 Dec 1937; *s* of Richard Arthur Hopkins, and his wife Muriel Annie (Yeats); *e* Cowbridge Grammar School, Glamorgan; *m* Jennifer Lynton; trained for the stage at RADA, 1961–3, and Cardiff College of Drama.

First appeared on the stage in 1960 at the Library Theatre, Manchester, as Mickser in The Quare Fellow; after repertory experience at Leicester, Liverpool and Hornchurch, first appeared on the London stage, Nov 1964, at the Royal Court, as Metellus Cimber in Julius Caesar; joined the National Theatre company, 1966, where his parts have included an Irregular Mobiliser in Juno and the Paycock, Etienne Plucheux in A Flea in Her Ear, 1966; in Oct, of that year, played Blagovo in A Provincial Life in a Sunday-night production at the Royal Court; took over Edgar in The Dance of Death, also played Andrei Prosorov in The Three Sisters, and Audrey in an all-male As You Like It, 1967; the Emperor in The Architect and the Emperor of Assyria, John Frankford in A Woman Killed with Kindness, Coriolanus in Coriolanus, 1971; title role in Macbeth, 1972; Chichester Festival, July 1972, Petruchio in The Taming of the Shrew; Plymouth, New York, Oct 1974, Martin Dysart in Equus; played the same part at the Huntington Hartford, LA, Aug 1977; Mark Taper, Apr 1979, Prospero in The Tempest; films, since The Lion in Winter in 1967, include The Looking Glass War, All Creatures Great and Small, and Dark Victory; television, also since 1967, includes Charles Dickens, Danton, War and Peace, QB VII, etc.

Recreations: Astronomy, the piano. *Address:* c/o ICM, 22 Grafton Street, London W1.

HOPKINS, John, dramatic author
b London, 27 Jan 1931; *e* Raynes Park CGS, and St Catharine's College, Cambridge; *m* (1) Prudence Balchin (mar dis); (2) the actress Shirley Knight.

Author of the plays This Story of Yours, produced at the Royal Court, 1968; Find Your Way Home, Open Space, 1970, NY, 1974; Economic Necessity, Leicester, 1973; Next of Kin, National Theatre, 1974; Losing Time, Manhattan Theatre Club, 1979; screenplays include Thunderball, 1965, The Virgin Soldiers, and The Offence; extensive writing for TV includes over 50 episodes of *Z Cars*, adaptations, and plays including the quartet Talking to a Stranger and the sextet Fathers and Families, 1977; author of the novels The Attempt, 1967, and Tangier Buzzless Flies, 1972.

Address: 24 Malmains Way, Beckenham, Kent.

HORDERN, Michael (Murray), CBE, actor
b Berkhampsted, 3 Oct 1911, *s* of Edward Joseph Calverley Horden, CIE, RIN, and his wife Margaret Emily (Murray); *e* Brighton College; *m* Grace Eveline (Eve) Mortimer; formerly in business.

Appeared for several seasons at the St Pancras People's Theatre, as an amateur; made his first appearance on the professional stage at the People's Palace, Mar 1937, as Lodovico in Othello; subsequently toured in Scandinavia and Baltic capitals, with Westminster Productions, as Sergius in Arms and the Man, and Henry in Outward Bound; from 1937–9, appeared in repertory at the Little Theatre, Bristol; Whitehall, Apr 1940, played PC James Hawkins in Without the Prince, subsequently playing the Stranger in the same play; during the War, served in the Navy, 1940–5; returned to the stage, at the Intimate Theatre, Palmer's Green, Jan 1946, as Torvald Helmer in A Doll's House; Aldwych, July 1946, played Richard Fenton in Dear Murderer; Covent Garden, Dec 1946, Bottom in The Fairy Queen; Saville, June 1947, Captain Hoyle in Noose; Stratford-on-Avon Memorial Theatre, Dec 1948, Mr Toad in Toad of Toad Hall; Embassy, Apr 1949, Pascal in A Woman in Love; toured, Oct 1949, as Rev John Courtenay in Stratton; Shakespeare Memorial Theatre, Stratford-on-Avon, Dec 1949, again played Mr Toad in Toad of Toad Hall; Arts Theatre, Apr 1950, played Nikolai Ivanov in Ivanov, and June 1950, Macduff in Macbeth; Princes, Oct 1950, Christopher in Party Manners; Arts, Sept 1951, Paul Southman in Saint's Day; joined the Shakespeare Memorial Theatre Company, Stratford-on-Avon, for the 1952 season, and played Menenius in Coriolanus, Caliban, Jaques in As You Like It, and Sir Politick Would-Be in Volpone; appeared at the Edinburgh Festival, 1953, as Polonius in Hamlet; joined the Old Vic Company for the 1953–4 season, when he again appeared as Polonius, and as Parolles in All's Well That Ends Well, King John, Malvolio in Twelfth Night and Prospero in The Tempest; at the Haymarket, July 1955, played Georges de Fourville in Nina; Saville, Oct 1955, played Sir Ralph Bloomfield Bonington in The Doctor's Dilemma; Lyric, Hammersmith, Apr 1958, appeared in a double bill as Tony Peters in What Shall We Tell Caroline? and as Morgenhall in The Dock Brief, transferring the plays to the Garrick, May 1958; rejoined the Old Vic Company, Oct 1958, to play Cassius in Julius Caesar, Pastor Manders in Ghosts, the title-part in Macbeth, and Mr Posket in The Magistrate; made his first appearance in New York at the Cort, Oct 1959, when he played Alexander Chabert in Moonbirds; Sadler's Wells, Apr 1960, the Narrator in Stravinsky's Œdipus Rex; for the Royal Shakespeare Company, at the Aldwych, played the following parts: June 1962, The Father in Playing With Fire and Harry in The Collection (double-bill); Oct 1962, Ulysses in Troilus and Cressida; Jan 1963, Herbert Georg Beutler in The Physicists; Royal, E15,

May 1965, Paul Southman in Saint's Day; Duke of York's, Mar 1967, Philip in Relatively Speaking; St Martin's, Mar 1968, George Riley in Enter a Free Man; returned to the Royal Shakespeare Company at the Aldwych, Jan 1969, to play Tobias in A Delicate Balance; Nottingham Playhouse, Oct 1969, played the title-role in King Lear, visiting the Old Vic, Feb 1970; Criterion, May 1970, title-role in Flint; joined the National Theatre at the Old Vic to play George Moore in Jumpers, Jan 1972; John of Gaunt in Richard II, Mar 1972; Gayev in The Cherry Orchard, May 1973; at the Royal Court, Oct 1975, played Graham Stripwell in Stripwell; Bristol Old Vic, Apr 1976, Fedya in Once Upon A Time; for the RSC at Stratford-upon-Avon, 1978 season, he played Prospero in The Tempest, and Don Adriano de Armado in Love's Labour's Lost; Roundhouse, Feb 1979, Gilbert Pinfold in The Ordeal of Gilbert Pinfold in the Royal Exchange Manchester production, having formerly played the part in Manchester, Sept 1977; first appeared in films, 1939; numerous TV appearances include King Lear, 1975; awarded the CBE in the New Year Honours, 1972.

Recreation: Fishing. *Clubs:* Garrick and Flyfishers. *Address:* c/o ICM Ltd, 22 Grafton Street, London, W1.

HORNER, Richard, producer, manager
b Portland, Oregon, 29 June 1920; *s* of Godfrey Richard Hoerner and his wife Ruby (Weller); *e* Oregon State University, University of Washington (BA 1942); *m* Lynne Stuart; served in the US Navy 1942–46, reaching the rank of Lieutenant.

Made his stage debut in a walk-on role at the Oberammergau Passion Play's production in Corvallis, Ore, 1934; played in stock in Conn and Pa 1946–47; business manager for the Windham, NH, Playhouse, 1948; made his New York debut as stage manager for The Curious Savage at the Martin Beck, 24 Oct 1950; since then has been stage manager, general manager, and company manager for Captain Carvallo (tour), 1950; The Constant Wife, 1951; Paris '90, 1952; I've Got Sixpence, Martha Graham Dance Company, Twin Beds (tour), Agnes De Mille Dance Theatre, 1953; The Pajama Game, On Your Toes, 1954; The Dark Is Light Enough, Damn Yankees, 1955; co-produced his first New York play, Debut, at the Holiday, 5 May 1955; general manager for Cranks, 1956; New Girl in Town, West Side Story, Copper and Brass, Clerambard, 1957; co-produced a tour of Damn Yankees, general manager for Blue Denim, The Next President, Goldilocks, Make a Million, 1958; Redhead, The Geranium Hat, Destry Rides Again, The Nervous Set, Chic, Take Me Along, Little Mary Sunshine, Fiorello! 1959; became general manager of the Eugene O'Neill, 1959, for Russell Paterson's Sketchbook, The Crystal Heart, The Cool World, The Jackass, Farewell Farewell Eugene, Greenwich Village USA, Face of a Hero, Love and Libel, The Rules of the Game, 1960, when he became a general manager of the 46th Street; Rhinoceros, Show Girl, The Tattooed Countess, Moby Dick, Young Abe Lincoln, A Call on Kuprin, The Thracian Horses, Sing Muse, 1961; New Faces of 1962, The Aspern Papers, Isle of Children, and became general manager of the Alvin, 1962; The Boys from Syracuse, 1963; co-produced High Spirits, 1964; co-produced The Queen and the Rebels, 1965; Hadrian VII, 1969; general manager for Norman, Is That You?, Borstal Boy, 1970; formed Lester Osterman productions with Lester Osterman and produced Butley, 1972; Crown Matrimonial, A Moon for the Misbegotten, 1973; Will Rogers' USA, Sizwe Bansi is Dead, The Island, 1974; Rodgers and Hart, 1975; produced Ragged Ann and Andy (film), 1976; general manager for Da, The Irish National Ballet, 1977; co-produced The Crucifer of Blood,

Blues in the Night, 1978; produced The Music Man (Jones Beach), 1979.

Club: New York Athletic Club. *Address:* 575 Lexington Avenue, New York, NY 10022.

HOROVITCH, David, actor
b London, 11 Aug 1945; *s* of Morris Horovitch and his wife Alice Mary; *e* St Christopher School, Letchworth; *m* Jane Elizabeth Gwynn Roberts; trained for the stage at the Central School of Speech and Drama.

Made his professional debut at the Everyman, Cheltenham, Sept 1966, as Brother Martin in Saint Joan; his London debut was at the Globe, Nov 1968, where he took over the part of Jimmy in There's a Girl in My Soup, later transferring to the Comedy; Mermaid, Jun 1971, Hermes in Prometheus Bound; Apollo, Dec 1971, Jack Chesney in Charley's Aunt; Bucks County Playhouse, Pa, 1973, played Faulkland in the Thorndike company's visiting production of The Rivals; Mermaid, Aug 1973, Gerald Croft in An Inspector Calls; Greenwich, Apr 1975, Jack Worthing in The Importance of Being Earnest; Greenwich, Mar 1976, Christian in The Bells; Mermaid, Sept 1976, Capt Midgley in For King and Country; St George's, Islington, season 1977, played Bassanio in The Merchant of Venice, Claudio in Measure for Measure, Laertes in Hamlet, and Slender in The Merry Wives of Windsor; Greenwich, Apr 1979, and tour, Mr Freeman in She Would if She Could; Haymarket, Sept 1979, took over as Dr Watson in The Crucifer of Blood; Riverside Studios, May 1980, Casca in Julius Caesar; has also played leading parts with a number of regional companies including Nottingham, Leicester, and the 69 Theatre Company, Manchester; regular TV work includes roles in various series, recently The Prince Regent, The Sandbaggers, Bognor, etc.

Favourite parts: Jack Tanner in Man and Superman, and Bernard in Everything in the Garden. *Recreations:* Cricket, reading, walking. *Address:* c/o John French, 26–28 Binney Street, London W1.

HOROVITZ, Israel, playwright
b Wakefield, Massachusetts, 31 Mar 1939; *s* of Julius Charles Horovitz and his wife Hazel Rose (Solberg); *e* Royal Academy of Dramatic Art, City University of New York; *m* Doris Keefe (mar dis).

Wrote his first play, The Comeback, in 1957, which was also his first produced play, at the Suffolk and Ermerson Theatres, Boston, 1960; since then has written the following plays, listed in the order of their production: This Play Is About Me, 1961; The Hanging of Emanuel, 1962; The Death of Bernard the Believer, 1963; The Simon Street Harvest, Hop, Skip and Jump, 1964; It's Called the Sugar Plum, 1965; The Indian Wants the Bronx, 1966; Line, which was also his first play to be produced in NY, at the Cafe La Mama, 1967; Rats, Chiaroscuro, 1968; Leader, The Honest-to-God Schnozzola, Morning, 1969; The World's Greatest Play, Acrobats, Shooting Gallery, 1970; Hero, The Wakefield Plays: Part One, 1971; Dr Hero, Part Two, Alfred the Great, Our Father's Failing, Part Three, Alfred Dies, 1973–76, and a comic triptych, consisting of The First, The Last, The Middle, 1974; Spared, Uncle Snake, 1975; The Primary English Class, Stage Directions, The Reason We Eat, 1976; Mackerel, 1978; presently completing The Quannapowit Quartet, consisting of Hopscotch, and (to date) The 75th; his plays have been produced in Paris, Rome, London, Budapest, Bonn, Berlin, Montreal, Sydney, Frankfurt, Marseilles, Amsterdam, Tokyo, and other cities and have been translated into nearly twenty languages; has received various awards, including the Vernon Rice-Drama Desk, The Obie, the Jersey City *Journal* Award, literature award of National Academy of Arts and Letters, and the Prix de Jury for his film play of The Strawberry Statement; was a Fellow of the RADA, London, 1961–3, the Playwright-in-Residence, Royal Shakespeare Company, 1965, a Rockefeller Foundation Fellow in Playwriting, 1967–8–9–70, Professor of English and Playwright-in-Residence, College of the City of New York, 1968; Fanny Hurst Visiting Playwright, Brandeis University, 1974–6; has also written the screenplays for Speed Is of the Essence, Camerian Climbing, The Sad-Eyed Girls in the Park, 1971; first play produced on television was in 1969, and since has written Play for Trees, Funny Books, Happy, etc; author of the books First Season Capella, 1971 (produced as a play, written with David Boorshin, 1978); Nobody Loves Me, 1975; Spider Poems and Other Writings, 1976.

Hobbies and recreations: Teaching, poker, Descartes, chess, guitar, and his children and their friends. *Club:* The Players. *Address:* c/o Gloria Safier, 667 Madison Avenue, New York, NY; and c/o Margaret Ramsay, 14a Goodwins Court, London, WC2. *Tel:* TE 8–4868 (New York).

HOSKINS, Bob, actor
b Bury St Edmunds, Suffolk, 26 Oct 1942; *s* of Robert Hoskins and his wife Elsie (Hopkins); *e* Stroud Green School, Finsbury Park; *m* Jane Livesey.

Made his first appearance at the Victoria, Stoke-on-Trent, 1969, as Peter in Romeo and Juliet; other parts at Stoke included Christopher Pig; with Century Theatre, 1970, his parts included Pinchwife in The Country Wife; at the Theatre Upstairs, Feb 1971, appeared in The Baby Elephant; Royal Court, Mar 1971, Uriah Shelley in Man is Man; in the same year played Lenny in The Homecoming and the title role in Richard III, at Hull Arts Centre, and Azdak in The Caucasian Chalk Circle, at the Northcott, Exeter; Royal Court, Sept 1971, various soldiers in Edward Bond's Lear; Young Vic, Nov 1971, Butcher Brunt in Cato Street; Royal Court, Mar 1972, Bernie the Volt in Veterans; Dartington Hall, 1973, title role in Bond's Lear; Bankside Globe, Aug 1973, Sextus Pompeius in Antony and Cleopatra; Royal Court, 1974, appeared in Geography of a Horse Dreamer; Albery, May 1974, Doolittle in Pygmalion; for Oxford Playhouse, summer 1975, played Touchstone in As You Like It, and Bill Cracker in Happy End, transferring to the Lyric in the latter part, Aug 1975; Aldwych, season 1976, for RSC, Rocky in The Iceman Cometh, Borkin in Ivanov, and Sergeant in The Devil's Disciple; Jeannetta Cochrane, Aug 1977, Jake in England, England; Cottesloe (NT), Nov 1978, appeared in The World Turned Upside Down, and played Joe Veriatio in Has Washington Legs?; films include The National Health and Royal Flash; TV, since 1972, includes Her Majesty's Pleasure and Thick as Thieves.

Favourite parts: Bernie the Volt, Richard III, and Lear. *Recreations:* Writing, listening to music, his children. *Address:* c/o Hope and Lyne, 5 Milner Place, London N1.

HOUGHTON, Norris, director, producer, and designer
b Indianapolis, Indiana, 26 Dec 1909; *s* of Charles D M Houghton and his wife Grace (Norris); *e* Princeton University.

Interest in the theatre began in 1931, when working as stage manager and designer with a non-professional company at West Falmouth, Mass; designed his first production in New York, at the Biltmore, 1932, for the play Carry Nation; subsequently designed Spring in Autumn, 1933; In Clover, 1937; Stop-Over, How to Get Tough About It, Dame Nature, Waltz in Goosestep, Good Hunting, Whiteoaks, 1938; was Art Director for the St Louis Municipal Opera,

1939–40, where he designed 18 musical productions; was Lecturer in Drama, Princeton University, 1941–2; served in the United States Naval Reserve, 1942–5, as Lieutenant; directed his first play in London at the Aldwych, Dec 1947, with Macbeth (Michael Redgrave); National, NY, Mar 1948, again directed Macbeth (Michael Redgrave); Lecturer in Drama, Columbia University, 1948–53; director of Elitch's Gardens Theatre, Denver, 1949–50; Biltmore, Dec 1949, directed Clutterbuck; Biltmore, Feb 1951, directed and co-presented Billy Budd; with T Edward Hambleton, 1953, became managing-director of the Phoenix Theatre, NY, and presented the following plays: Madam Will You Walk, 1953; Coriolanus, The Golden Apple, The Seagull (also directed), Sing Me No Lullaby, Sandhog, 1954; The Doctor's Dilemma, The Masterbuilder, The White Devil, Phoenix 55, The Carefree Tree, The Terrible Swift Sword, Six Characters in Search of an Author, 1955; The Adding Machine, a double-bill of Miss Julie, and The Stronger, Queen After Death, A Month in the Country, The Mother of Us All, Four Premières (ballet programme), The Littlest Revue, Saint Joan, Diary of a Scoundrel, The Good Woman of Setzuan, 1956; Coronet, Nov 1956, designed the sets for The Sleeping Prince; presented at the Phoenix, The Duchess of Malfi (with John Houseman), Livin' the Life, Mary Stuart, The Makropoulos Secret (also designed settings), The Infernal Machine, 1957; a double-bill of The Chairs and The Lesson, The Two Gentlemen of Verona and The Broken Jug (The Stratford Festival Company, Canada), Le Théâtre du Nouveau Monde, The Family Reunion (also designed settings), Théâtre du Vieux Colombier de Paris, The Power and the Glory, 1958; The Beaux' Stratagem, Once upon a Mattress (co-produced with William and Jean Eckart), 1959; resigned his directorship of the Phoenix at the end of the 1958–9 season; remained vice-president and member of the board of directors of Theatre Incorporated (the parent organization), as well as Trustee of the National Repertory Theatre; Adjunct Professor of Drama, Barnard College, 1953–8; Adjunct Professor of Drama, Vassar College, 1959–60; Hon DFA, Denison College, 1959; returned as co-managing director of the Phoenix in 1961, and has since presented Androcles and the Lion, The Policeman, The Dark Lady of the Sonnets, 1961; Who'll Save the Plowboy? (also designed decor), Oh Dad, Poor Dad, Mama's Hung You in the Closet and I'm Feelin' So Sad, 1962; Abe Lincoln in Illinois, The Taming of the Shrew, The Dragon, Next Time I'll Sing to You, The Brontës, 1963; Too Much Johnson, The Tragical Historie of Doctor Faustus, and the APA (Association of Producing Artists) in Right You Are, The Tavern, The Lower Depths, Scapin, Impromptu at Versailles, 1964; the APA in Man and Superman, War and Peace, Judith, and supervised the production of You Can't Take It with You; Chairman, Department of Drama, Vassar College, 1962–7; Dean of Theatre Arts, State University of New York, College at Purchase, 1967–75, Professor of Theatre Arts, 1975 to present; Berg Professor of English, NYU, 1975; Bingham Professor of Humanities, University of Louisville, 1979; received Guggenheim Fellowships in 1934, 1935, and 1960; President, National Theatre Conference, 1969–71; Associate Editor of *Theatre Arts* magazine, 1945–8; author of Moscow Rehearsals, 1936; Advance from Broadway, 1941; But Not Forgotten, 1952; Return Engagement, 1962; The Exploding Stage, 1972; producer-director of CBS Television Workshop, 1951–2; lecturer on educational television programs 1958–9; President, American Council for the Arts in Education, 1973–5; Fellow of the American Academy of Arts and Sciences.

Clubs: Bucks (London), Century, Coffee House (NY). *Address:* Division of Theatre Arts, State University of New York, College at Purchase, Purchase, New York 10577, and 11 East 9th Street, New York, NY 10003.

HOUSE, Eric, actor

A member of the Shakespeare Festival Theatre, Stratford, Ontario, from its inception in 1953, when he played Sir Christopher Urswick, Scrivener, etc, in Richard III and Morgan in All's Well That Ends Well; in subsequent Stratford Festivals, to 1964, he played Justice in Measure for Measure, Gremio and the Tailor in The Taming of the Shrew, and the Priest in King Œdipus, 1954; Prince of Arragon in The Merchant of Venice and Metellus Cimber and Claudius in Julius Caesar, 1955; Winter Garden, New York, Jan 1956, played Mycetes, Capolin, etc, in Tamburlaine the Great; Stratford, Ontario, 1956, played Fluellen in Henry V and Sir Hugh Evans in The Merry Wives of Windsor; Edinburgh Festival, Scotland, 1956, again played Fluellen in Henry V and Old Shepherd and Priest in King Œdipus; Westminster, London, Dec 1956, played Lester MacMichaels in Mrs Gibbons' Boys; Arts, London, Apr 1957, the Judge in The Balcony; Phoenix, NY, Dec 1957, played Hauck-Sendorf and Allendorf in The Makropoulos Secret; Phoenix, Mar 1958, Valentine in Two Gentlemen of Verona; Crest, Toronto, 1959, played Archie Rice in The Entertainer, and Fool in King Lear; Stratford, Ontario, 1960, Sir Joseph Porter in HMS Pinafore, in which he also appeared at the Phoenix, NY, Sept 1960; Stratford, Ontario, 1961, Major-General Stanley in The Pirates of Penzance, appearing in the same production at the Phoenix, NY, Sept 1961; Her Majesty's, London, Feb 1962, played Sir Joseph Porter in HMS Pinafore, and Major-General Stanley in The Pirates of Penzance; Lyric, Hammersmith, Nov 1962, appeared in the revue Clap Hands, which transferred to the Prince Charles, Dec 1962; Stratford, Ontario, 1963, played Koko in The Mikado; at the Chichester Festival, England, Apr 1964, played Boyet in Love's Labour's Lost, the Dancing Master in Le Bourgeois Gentilhomme, and a Merchant and Baths Attendant in Timon of Athens; at Stratford, Ontario, played the Duke of York in Richard II, Sir Jasper Fidget in The Country Wife, and the Dancing Master in Le Bourgeois Gentilhomme, 1964; trans-Canada tour, 1964–5, appeared in the historical revue All About Us; Confederation Memorial Centre, Charlottetown, Prince Edward Island, July 1966, the Mayor in The Ottawa Man; Charles Playhouse, Boston, Mass, Oct 1966, played in Love for Love; Manitoba Theatre Centre, Winnipeg, Jan 1967, played in A Funny Thing Happened on the Way to the Forum; Charles Playhouse, Boston, Mar 1967, directed Oh, What a Lovely War, Apr, played Bill Maitland in Inadmissible Evidence, and again played in Love for Love; Billy Rose, NY, May 1968, played General Sikorski in Soldiers; appeared with the Tyrone Guthrie Theater Company, Minneapolis, Minn, 1970–1 season; Playhouse in the Park, Cincinnati, Feb 1976, appeared in What the Butler Saw; Alley, Houston, Jan 1978, in Root of the Mandrake; same theatre, season 1978–9, appeared in The Happy Time.

HOUSEMAN, John, director, producer, and actor

b Bucharest, Rumania, 22 Sept 1902; *s* of George Haussmann and his wife May (Davies); *e* Clifton College, England; *m* Joan Courtney.

Directed his first professional production with the Gertrude Stein-Virgil Thomson opera Four Saints in Three Acts, at the Wadsworth Athenaeum, Hartford, Connecticut, which transferred to the 44th Street Theatre, New York, Feb 1934; directed Valley Forge (Theatre Guild), The Lady from the Sea, and produced Archibald MacLeish's first play Panic, 1935; for the Federal Theatre's Negro Theatre Project, produced a Haitian Macbeth, and for the Federal Theatre's Project 891, produced Doctor Faustus, The Cradle Will Rock, Horse Eats Hat, all of which were directed by Orson Welles, 1935; directed Leslie Howard in Hamlet, 1936; with Orson Welles founded the Mercury Theatre, 1937, and produced the modern dress Julius Caesar, The Shoemaker's Holiday, Heartbreak House, Danton's Death, 1937–8; directed Liberty Jones, Anna Christie (with Ingrid Bergman), Hello, Out There, and co-produced (with Orson Welles) Native Son, 1941; in Dec 1941, joined the Office of War Information as Chief of the Overseas Radio Program Bureau; went to Hollywood, 1944, where he produced several motion pictures; returned to NY, Feb 1946, where he directed Lute Song; co-produced Joy to the World, 1948; directed King Lear with Louis Calhern, 1950; directed Coriolanus with Robert Ryan, 1954; between these productions he returned many times to Hollywood; from 1956–9 he was Artistic Director of the American Shakespeare Festival at Stratford, Connecticut, where, among others, he directed or co-directed the following: King John, Measure for Measure, 1956; Othello, Much Ado About Nothing, 1957, in which year he also co-produced The Duchess of Malfi at the Phoenix, NY; Hamlet, A Winter's Tale, 1958; The Merry Wives of Windsor, All's Well That Ends Well, 1959; at the City Center, NY, 1959, directed The Devil and Daniel Webster; Artistic Director of the UCLA Professional Theatre Group, 1959–64, and directed The Three Sisters, Six Characters in Search of an Author, Measure for Measure, The Iceman Cometh, and King Lear, and produced The Child Buyer and The Egg; Stratford, Conn, 1966, directed Murder in the Cathedral; Stratford, Conn, 1967, directed Macbeth; Producing Director of APA Phoenix, 1967–8, and directed The Chronicles of Hell and co-directed with Ellis Rabb Pantagleize; Producing Director with this group 1969–70, and co-produced, The Criminals, 1970; directed The Country Girl, 1972; became Artistic Director of the City Center Acting Company, and in that capacity presented at the Good Shepherd—Faith Church, Sept 1972, The School for Scandal, USA, The Hostage, Women Beware Women, Next Time I'll Sing to You, Lower Depths; directed Don Juan in Hell, and for the City Center Acting Company presented at the Billy Rose, Dec 1973, The Three Sisters, The Beggar's Opera, Measure for Measure (which he also directed), Scapin, Next Time I'll Sing to You; directed Henry Fonda as Clarence Darrow, 1974; Carnegie Music Hall, Pittsburgh, 19 Apr 1975, directed and played in The Great American Fourth of July Parade; for the City Center Acting Company at the Rebekah Harkness, 1975, presented The Robber Bridegroom, Edward II, The Time of Your Life, The Three Sisters; among operas directed are The Devil and Daniel Webster, 1940, Othello (1962) and La Tosca (1964) for the Dallas Civic Opera, The Mines of Sulphur (1968), Antigone (1969), and The Losers (1971), for the Juilliard Opera Theatre; films which he has produced include The Blue Dahlia, Letter to an Unknown Woman, The Bad and the Beautiful, Julius Caesar, Executive Suite, All Fall Down, Lust for Life, etc; for the US Government produced the films Tuesday in November, 1944, and Voyage to America, 1964; won the Academy Award for his performance in the film The Paper Chase, 1974; played in Rollerball, Three Days of the Condor, The Cheap Detective, Gideon's Trumpet, etc; for radio edited The Mercury Theatre on the Air, 1938–9; for television produced the series *The Seven Lively Arts,* 1957, the series *Playhouse 90,* 1958–9, The Dancer's World and Three by Martha Graham, 1969; played in Truman at Potsdam, Six Characters in Search of an Author, *The Paper Chase,* etc; President of the National Theatre Conference, 1970; received the National Arts Club Gold Medal Drama Award, Feb 1973; author of his autobiography Run-Through, 1972; Director of the Drama Division of the Juilliard School of the Performing Arts, 1968–76; Visiting Professor of Performing Arts, USC, 1977–9.

Address: 20178 Rockport Way, Malibu, Calif 90265.

HOUSTON, Donald, actor

b Tonypandy, South Wales, 6 Nov 1923; *s* of Alexander Houston and his wife Elsie May (Jones); *m* Brenda Hogan.

Made his first appearance on the stage, with the Pilgrim Players, Aug 1940, at Penzance, as Saul in Terror of Light; remained with this company for two years, playing Tobias in Tobias and the Angel, subsequently appearing as the Angel in the same play; joined the Oxford Repertory company, Feb 1943, playing a variety of parts, including Morgan Evans in The Corn is Green, Tybalt in Romeo and Juliet, Hector Malone in Man and Superman, etc; joined the RAF, Dec 1943, until 1946; returned to the Oxford Repertory company, 1946; made his first appearance in London, at the Arts Theatre, 1 Jan 1947, as Ragnar Brovik in The Master Builder; toured, Apr 1947, in Doctor Jekyll and Mr Hyde; Mercury, July 1947, appeared in I Said to Myself; engaged in films from Nov 1947, to Aug 1949; at the Edinburgh Festival, Aug 1949, played Peter Quilpe in The Cocktail Party, and at the New Theatre, London, May 1950, appeared in the same part; Winter Garden, Dec 1951, appeared as St George of England in Where the Rainbow Ends; at the Edinburgh Festival, Aug 1956, appeared as the Narrator in Under Milk Wood, subsequently playing in the same production at the New, Sept 1956; made his first appearance in New York at the Henry Miller Theatre, Oct 1957, in the same part and play; joined the Old Vic Company, 1959–60 season, and played the following parts: Jaques in As You Like It, Maskwell in The Double Dealer, Dunois in Saint Joan, John Shand in What Every Woman Knows, and the title-role in Henry V; Strand, Sept 1967, appeared as Robert Williams in The Others; Chichester Festival, May 1975, Morten Kiil in An Enemy of the People; entered films, 1947, in The Blue Lagoon.

Favourite parts: Oswald in Ghosts, and George in The Black Eye. *Hobbies:* Collecting gramophone records and pottering. *Recreation:* Watching cricket and football. *Clubs:* Arts Theatre, and Lords Taverners. *Address:* c/o Boyack & Conway, 8 Cavendish Place, London W1.

HOUSTON, Renée, actress

b Johnstone, Renfrewshire, Scotland, 24 July 1902; *d* of James Gribbin and his wife Elizabeth (Houston); both her parents were variety artists; *m* Donald Stewart (dec).

Made her first appearance on the stage 1916, while still at school; subsequently appearing in concerts; appeared with her sister, Billie, as the Houston Sisters; in variety theatres all over Great Britain, from 1920–35, they appeared at the Royal Variety Performance, May 1926, and in 1931, toured in France and Switzerland; wrote and produced the revue, More Dam Things, for Tom Arnold; dissolved partnership with her sister, owing to the latter's illness, 1935; made her first appearance in musical comedy at the London Hippodrome, 27 June 1935, as Jenny McGregor in Love Laughs . . .!; London Hippodrome, Sept 1936, played Kirstie Cameron in Certainly Sir!; returned to variety theatres in partnership with her husband, and in 1938 again appeared at the Royal Variety Performance; toured in South Africa, 1939; has appeared successfully in numerous provincial pantomimes; at the Cambridge Theatre, May 1949, made a great success when she appeared in the revue, Sauce Tartare; subsequently returned to variety theatres; reappeared with her sister, for one night, at the Victoria Palace, 5 Mar 1950; at the Saville, May 1954, appeared in the revue Cockles and Champagne; Garrick,

Southport, Nov 1956, played Lottie in Rock 'n' Roll Murder; New, Aug 1958, took over Elsie Sharp in The Party; Phoenix, 1959, took over the part of Muriel Chadwick in Roar Like a Dove; Phoenix, Oct 1962, played Emma Hornett in Rock-a-bye, Sailor; Mermaid, Feb 1965, played Fyokia Ivanovna in The Marriage Brokers; at the Metropole, Glasgow, Mar 1965, played Martha McTaggart in Beneath the Wee Red Lums; Apr 1968, toured as Leonora Fiske in Ladies in Retirement; Metropole, Glasgow, Mar 1970, played Emma Hornett in Sailor Beware; June 1970, toured as Muriel Chadwick in Roar Like A Dove; Duke of York's, Jan 1971, Mrs McLachlan in Meeting At Night; toured, 1976, in Little Women; first appeared in films, 1941, in A Girl Must Live, and films include The Horse's Mouth, and the Carry On series; was a member of the panel in the *Petticoat Line* radio series, and appeared frequently on television; has published an autobiography, Don't Fence Me In.

(*Died 9 Feb 1980.*)

HOWARD, Alan, actor

b London, 5 Aug 1937; *s* of Arthur John Howard and his wife Jean Compton (Mackenzie); *e* Ardingly; *m* Stephanie (Howard).

Made his first stage appearance at the Belgrade, Coventry, Apr 1958, as a footman in Half in Earnest; remained with the company, 1958–60, playing parts including Frankie Bryant in Roots, June 1959, and transferring to the Royal Court in this production, also June; then transferred to the Duke of York's, July 1959; Belgrade, Apr 1960, Dave Simmonds in I'm Talking About Jerusalem; Royal Court, June–July 1960, played Monty Blatt in Chicken Soup with Barley, Frankie Bryant in Roots and 1st removal man in I'm Talking About Jerusalem; Pembroke, Croydon, Jan 1961, Kenny Baird in A Loss of Roses; Royal Court, Feb 1961, de Piraquo in The Changeling; Chichester Festival, July 1962, played the Duke of Ferrara in The Chances and Nearchus in The Broken Heart; Mermaid, Apr 1963, Loveless in Virtue in Danger, transferring to the Strand, June 1963; Arts, Aug 1963, Fotheringham in Afternoon Men; toured South America and Europe, 1964, for Tennent Productions, as Bassanio in The Merchant of Venice and Lysander in A Midsummer Night's Dream; Phoenix, May 1965, Simon in A Heritage and Its History; at the Playhouse, Nottingham, 1965, played Angelo in Measure for Measure and Bolingbroke in Richard II; joined the Royal Shakespeare Company, 1966, for which he has since played, at Stratford unless otherwise stated, Orsino in Twelfth Night, Burgundy in Henry V and Lussurioso in The Revenger's Tragedy, 1966; Jaques in As You Like It (also Los Angeles, 1968), Young Fashion in The Relapse (Aldwych), 1967; Edgar in King Lear, Achilles in Troilus and Cressida and Benedick in Much Ado About Nothing, 1968 (these three parts also in revivals at the Aldwych); Bartholomew Cokes in Bartholomew Fair, Lussurioso in The Revenger's Tragedy (both Aldwych), 1969; also Benedick in Los Angeles; Mephistophilis in Doctor Faustus, Hamlet in Hamlet, Theseus/Oberon in A Midsummer Night's Dream and Ceres in The Tempest, 1970; made his New York debut at the Billy Rose, Jan 1971, in the Stratford production of A Midsummer Night's Dream; at the Aldwych, season 1971–2, played Theseus/Oberon, Nikolai in Enemies, Dorimant in The Man of Mode, and The Envoy in The Balcony; Traverse, Edinburgh, July 1972, Cyril Jackson in The Black and White Minstrels; Aug 1972–Aug 1973, again toured as Theseus/Oberon, visiting East and West Europe, the USA, Japan and Australia; Hampstead, Nov 1973, Erich von Stroheim in The Ride Across Lake Constance, transferring to the May Fair, Dec; Hampstead, Jan 1974, again played Cyril in The Black and White Minstrels; returning to the RSC he played Carlos II in The Bewitched, Aldwych, May 1974; title role in Henry V, and Prince Hal in the two parts of Henry IV, Stratford, season 1975 and Aldwych, Jan 1976; Rover in Wild Oats, Aldwych, Dec 1976; Stratford, 1977 season, again played the title-role in Henry V, and also the title-roles in the three parts of Henry VI and Coriolanus, playing all these roles at the Aldwych, summer 1978; Stratford, Oct 1978, and Aldwych, July 1979, Mark Antony in Antony and Cleopatra; Aldwych, Oct 1979, Chepurnoy in Children of the Sun; films, since 1960, include Victim and Work is a Four-Letter Word; television, since 1961, includes Philoctetes, The Way of the World, and Comets Among the Stars.

Recreations: Reading, writing, music. *Address:* c/o Derek Glynne Ltd, 17 Wilton Place, London SW1.

HOWARD, Ken, actor
b El Centro, California, 28 Mar 1944; *s* of Kenneth Joseph Howard, Sr and his wife Martha Carey (McDonald); *e* Amherst College (AB 1966), Yale Drama School, 1968.

First appeared on the stage at the Congregational Church, Manhasset, Long Island, Mar 1960, as Buffalo Bill in Annie Get Your Gun; made his New York début at the Shubert, Dec 1968, as Karl Kubelik in Promises, Promises; 46th Street, Mar 1969, played Thomas Jefferson in 1776; Royale, Feb 1970, played Paul Reese in Child's Play, for which he received the Antoinette Perry (Tony) Award; for the Philadelphia Drama Guild, 1972, played in Volpone; Uris, Mar 1973, Jerry Ryan in the musical Seesaw; Vivian Beaumont, May 1975, Jack Hassler in Little Black Sheep; Theatre of the Stars, Atlanta, Ga, July 1975, Jerry Ryan in Seesaw; Morosco, Dec 1975, Tom in the three-play series The Norman Conquests; Mark Hellinger, May 1976, The President in 1600 Pennsylvania Avenue; first appeared in films in Tell Me That You Love Me, Junie Moon, 1969, and has since appeared in The Strange Vengeance of Rosalie (1972) and 1776 (1972).

Favourite parts: Billy Bigelow in Carousel and Chance Wayne in Sweet Bird of Youth. *Recreation:* Sleeping in the afternoon. *Address:* 42 West 36th Street, New York, NY.

HOWARD, Pamela, theatre designer
b Birmingham, 5 Jan 1939; *d* of Joseph Howard (formerly Hoffman) and his wife Ann (Gatoff); *e* Kings Norton Grammar School for Girls, Birmingham College of Art, Slade School of Fine Art, University College London; *m* Michael Rudolph Mills.

Her early designs included work for the Belgrade, Coventry, Ipswich Arts, and Birmingham Rep; senior lecturer, 1964–67, Birmingham College of Art; visiting lecturer, 1964–67, Croydon College of Art; first year tutor in Theatre Design, 1972–present, Central School of Art and Design; later designs include work for Birmingham Rep (Blues, Whites and Reds, 1974), Nottingham Playhouse (The White Devil, 1975, Bartholomew Fair, 1976, White Suit Blues, 1977, The Alchemist, 1978), and Riverside Studios (The Cherry Orchard, Treetops, 1978, Masaccio Festival, 1979); decor for Prospect's War Music, 1977; for the National Theatre designed costumes for The Philanderer, Has Washington Legs?, 1978; for RSC's Othello, 1979; Terra Nova (Chichester), The Beggar's Opera, 1980; since 1966 has designed over 20 productions for Unicorn, of which she was a director; author of numerous journal articles on theatre design.

Recreations: Music, travel, languages. *Address:* 73 Medfield Street, Roehampton Village, London SW15 4JY.

HOWARD, Roger, playwright
b 19 June 1938; *e* Dulwich College, University of Bristol and University of Essex; *m* Anne Mary Zemaitis; trained for the stage at RADA.

Taught English at Nankai University, Tientsin, China, 1965–67; lecturer, Peking University, 1972–74; playwright in residence, Mercury Theatre, Colchester, 1976; fellow in creative writing, University of York, 1976–78; Henfield writing fellow, University of East Anglia, 1979; lecturer, University of Essex, 1979– , where he founded Theatre Underground; since 1966 has written a very large number of plays, of which may be mentioned The Meaning of the Statue, and Writing on Stone, for Ambiance, 1971–72; The Auction of Virtues, for Portable, 1972; three plays for Essex University Theatre, 1976; History of the Tenth Struggle (The Tragedy of Mao in the Lin Piao Period), ICA, 1976; A Feast During Famine, for Wakefield Tricycle, 1977; Women's Army, for Omoro, and Margery Kempe, for MK productions, 1978; Queen, Alsager College, The Society of Poets, U of East Anglia, A Break in Berlin, U of Essex, 1979; has published critical and review articles in literary and theatre periodicals, as well as poems and stories; an editor of the theatre magazine Platform since 1979; his books include Mao Tse-Tung and the Chinese People, 1977, and Contemporary Chinese Theatre, 1979.

Address: Church Road, Little Waldingfield, Sudbury, Suffolk CO10 0SN.

HOWARD, Trevor, actor
b Cliftonville, Margate, Kent, 29 Sept 1916; *s* of Arthur John Howard and his wife Mabel Grey (Wallace); *e* Clifton College; *m* Helen Cherry; studied for the stage at the Royal Academy of Dramatic Art, where he received a production Scholarship, 1933; won BBC prize, 1934.

While still training at the RADA, made his first appearance, at the Gate Theatre, 1934, in Revolt in a Reformatory; at the Embassy, Apr 1934, played Schwenck in The Drums Begin; Winter Garden, Sept 1934, in Androcles and the Lion; Westminster, Dec 1934, Sagisaka in The Faithful and Harry Conway in Alien Corn; Q, Feb 1935, played Jack Absolute in The Rivals; Embassy, Feb 1935, Dmitri in Crime and Punishment; Court, Mar 1935, Hon Willie Tatham in Aren't We All?; Playhouse, Apr–May 1935, Walter How in Justice, Charles Hornblower in The Skin Game, and The Journalist in A Family Man; Westminster, Oct 1935, William O'Farrell in Lady Patricia; Aldwych, Nov 1935, Fred Johnson in Legend of Yesterday; Westminster, Nov 1935, Lucullus in Timon of Athens; appeared at the Memorial Theatre, Stratford-on-Avon, during the 1936 season; at the Criterion, Nov 1936, played Kenneth Lake in French Without Tears, for two years, during which time he appeared at the Arts, Oct 1937, as Bryan Elliott in Waters of Jordan, and May 1938, as Ronnie Dent in A Star Comes Home; again played at Stratford-on-Avon, during the season of 1939; subsequently appeared in seasons of repertory at Colchester and Harrogate; served in the Armed Forces, 1940–3; reappeared on the stage at the Arts Theatre, Nov 1943, as Captain Plume in The Recruiting Officer, and in Dec 1943, appeared there as Joachim Bris in On Life's Sunny Side; Wyndham's, Feb 1944, played Ronald Vines in A Soldier for Christmas; Arts, Nov 1944, Mat Burke in Anna Christie; New, Nov 1947, with the Old Vic Company, played Petruchio in The Taming of the Shrew; Savoy, Sept 1953, General Harras in The Devil's General; Lyric, Hammersmith, May 1954, played Lopahin in The Cherry Orchard; Garrick, Apr 1962, played Sam Turner in Two Stars For Comfort; Piccadilly, Jan 1964, played the Captain in The Father; Haymarket, Feb 1974, General St-Pé in The Waltz of the Toreadors;

Toronto, 1977, appeared in Scenario; first appeared in films, 1944, in The Way Ahead, and has appeared in numerous pictures, including: Brief Encounter, The Third Man, The Heart of the Matter, Sons and Lovers, Mutiny on the Bounty, The Charge of the Light Brigade, Ryan's Daughter, A Doll's House and, more recently, The Count of Monte Cristo, Slavers, and Night Flight; received the British Film Academy's Award, 1959, for his performance in The Key; appeared as Lovberg in an all star television production of Hedda Gabler, 1962; other TV includes Catholics and The Shillingbury Blowers.

Address: Rowley Green, Arkley, Herts.

HOWARTH, Donald, dramatist and director

b 5 Nov 1931; *s* of Arthur Howarth and his wife Phoebe Rose Bertha (Worsdell); formerly an actor, he trained for the stage at the Esme Church Theatre School.

His first play, Lady On the Barometer (later called Sugar in the Morning), was produced at the Royal Court, Sept 1958, co-directed by the author; the following of his plays have since been performed: All Good Children, 1961, performed under his direction 1964; A Lily in Little India, 1965 (also directed); Ogodiveleftthegason, 1967 (also directed); Three Months Gone, 1970; Othello Sleges Blankes, Scarborough (both Cape Town), 1972; The Greatest Fairy Story Ever Told (New York), 1973; The Illumination of Mr Shannon (Dublin), 1974; The Front Room (Leeds), 1975; directed Play Mas, 1974; Parcel Post, 1976; Rum an Coca Cola, London 1976, NY 1977; Literary Manager, Royal Court Theatre, 1975–6; several of his plays have been performed on television.

Recreations: Salerooms, mending things. *Address:* c/o Margaret Ramsay Ltd, 14a Goodwins Court, St Martin's Lane, London, WC2. *Tel:* 01–240 0691.

HOWE, George, actor

b Valparaiso, Chile, South America, 19 Apr 1900; *s* of Edgar Winchester Howe and his wife Beatrice (Macqueen); *e* Harrow, Royal Military College, Sandhurst, and Christ Church College, Oxford (BA); studied for the stage at the Royal Academy of Dramatic Art.

Made his first appearance on the stage at the Regent Theatre, 1 Aug 1923, as Captain Udall in Robert E Lee; at the Lyric, Hammersmith, Sept 1923, played Clown in The Winter's Tale; Kingsway, Nov 1923, Puck in A Midsummer Night's Dream; during 1924, played with the Stratford-on-Avon Festival company, and 1924–5, was with the Birmingham Repertory company; Kingsway, Nov 1925, played Athelstane Lilley in The Old Adam; Wyndham's, Feb 1926, Polverino in The Firebrand; Kingsway, Apr 1926, Miolans in The Marvellous History of St Bernard; Sept 1926, Alfred Robinson in Rosmersholm; Ambassadors', June 1927, Michael in The Spot on the Sun; Q, and Little, Oct 1927, Rev Thomas Howard in The Red Umbrella; Globe, Nov 1927, Finito in The Squall; Court, Apr 1928, Edward the Confessor in Harold; Vaudeville, Aug 1928, appeared in Charlot 1928; Arts, Nov–Dec 1928, played Canton in The Clandestine Marriage, and Gregory in The Lion Tamer; His Majesty's, Jan 1929, Augustus and Vogue in Beau Geste; Lyric, Oct 1929, Etienne in He's Mine; Arts, Jan 1930, St Nicholas in The Humours of the Court; joined the Old Vic company, Sept 1930, and appeared there and at Sadler's Wells, as Worcester in King Henry IV (Part I), Trinculo in The Tempest, Oakley in The Jealous Wife, Sir Andrew in Twelfth Night, Petkoff in Arms and the Man, Leonato in Much Ado About Nothing, Gloucester in King Lear; at the Cambridge, Sept 1931, Mariana in Elizabeth of England; Globe, Feb

1932, Second Examiner in Punchinello; New, June 1932, John Maudelyn in Richard of Bordeaux; Embassy, Sept 1932, Cardinal Dupin in Miracle of Verdun; Palladium, Dec 1932, Starkey in Peter Pan; New, Feb 1933, Sir Simon Burley and Hobb in Richard of Bordeaux; June 1934, Rizzio and Taylor in Queen of Scots; Nov 1934, Polonius in Hamlet; Oct 1935, Friar Laurence in Romeo and Juliet; Criterion, July 1936, appeared as Alcalde in The Lady of La Paz; Old Vic, Jan 1937, Polonius in Hamlet (in entirety); New, Mar 1937, Baptista in The Taming of the Shrew; appeared at Kronborg Castle, Elsinore, with the Old Vic company, June 1937, as Polonius in Hamlet; Queen's, Sept 1937 to June 1938, played Duke of York in Richard II, Crabtree in The School for Scandal, Spiridonitch in Three Sisters, and Arragon and the Duke in The Merchant of Venice; Kingsway, Oct 1938, Massuccio in An Elephant in Arcady; Westminster, Dec 1938, Chu-Yin in Marco Millions; Criterion, Mar 1939, Mr Puttick in Sugar Plum; Lyceum, June 1939, again played Polonius; subsequently again went to Elsinore to play the same part; Globe, Aug 1939, played Canon Chasuble in The Importance of Being Earnest, subsequently touring in the same part; Chanticleer, Mar 1940, Henry Munden in Belle View; toured, July–Sept 1940, for ENSA, in Plays and Music; Globe, Jan 1941, played Lob in Dear Brutus; toured, Jan–June 1942, in RAF camps in South Wales, as director; Vaudeville, July 1942, played Edouard Laroche in Salt of the Earth; Wimbledon, Aug 1942, Mr A B Raham in Home and Beauty; from Jan–July 1943, was director at the Repertory Theatre, Birmingham; toured, Sept 1943, with the Travelling Repertory Theatre, in The Moon is Down; Q, Feb 1944, played Professor Mallory in Zero Hour; Cambridge Theatre, May 1944, Delaqua in A Night in Venice; continued in this until Sept 1945; at the Arts, Apr 1945, directed The Italian Straw Hat; from Oct 1945, to Feb 1946, toured with John Gielgud in India and the Far East, as Polonius in Hamlet, and Dr Bradman in Blithe Spirit; at Opera House, Cairo, played Crabtree and Moses in The School for Scandal; toured in Germany, for the BAOR, July 1946, in The Apple Cart; Piccadilly, Dec 1946, played Lepidus and Diomedes in Antony and Cleopatra; Palace, May 1947, Ottokar Katzenhammer in The Bird Seller; Strand, July 1947, the Ven Augustus Paradine, DD, LLD, in My Wives and I; Lyric, Hammersmith, Nov 1947, Scribe in The Little Dry Thorn; Apollo, Mar 1948, Godfrey Pond in The Happiest Days of Your Life, which he played over 600 times; Boltons, Feb 1950, Dean Lesley in Lady Patricia; Lyric, Hammersmith, Aug 1950, Professor Gadsby in View Over the Park; Royale, New York, Nov 1950, Hebble Tyson in The Lady's Not For Burning; Phoenix, London, June 1951, played the Old Shepherd in The Winter's Tale; Phoenix, Jan 1952, the Friar in Much Ado About Nothing; at the Plymouth, NY, Sept 1952, played the title-role in Mr Pickwick; Haymarket, London, Aug 1953, appeared as the Rev Ernest Lynton in Aren't We All?; Lyric, Hammersmith, May 1954, Semyonov-Pistchik in The Cherry Orchard; Arts, Nov 1954, Bocage in The Immoralist; Stoll, Dec 1954, Mr Pinkwhistle in Noddy in Toyland; toured, Feb 1955, as Sir George Treherne in Both Ends Meet; joined the Memorial Theatre Company, Stratford-on-Avon, Apr 1956, and played the following parts: Polonius in Hamlet, Old Gobbo and the Duke of Venice in The Merchant of Venice, Boyet in Love's Labour's Lost, and Escalus in Measure for Measure; Arts, Mar 1957, played Dr Willy in The Wit to Woo; toured June 1958, as Father Callifer in The Potting Shed; Old Vic, May 1961, played Tubal in The Merchant of Venice; with the same company appeared at the City Center, NY, Feb 1962, in the following parts: 2nd Witch in Macbeth, the Inquisitor in Saint

Joan, and Chorus and the Apothecary in Romeo and Juliet, subsequently touring the US with the productions; during the last season of the Old Vic Company, London, Oct 1962–Apr 1963, appeared in the following parts: Old Gobbo in The Merchant of Venice, Gratiano in Othello, Escalus in Measure for Measure; Theatre Royal, Brighton, Feb 1964, played Salarino in The Merchant of Venice, and Egeus in A Midsummer Night's Dream, prior to touring Europe and South America for the British Council in both productions; Ashcroft, Croydon, Feb 1966, played Mr Hardcastle in She Stoops to Conquer; Royal Court, Apr 1966, Mr Booth in The Voysey Inheritance; same theatre, May 1966, John Casper and Alfie Harrington in Their Very Own and Golden City; Savoy, June 1967, again played Rev Ernest Lynton in Aren't We All; Royal Court, July 1969, Sir Paul Plyant in The Double Dealer; University Theatre, Manchester, for the '69 Theatre Company, Gonzalo in The Tempest; Greenwich, Mar 1970, played the General in The Corsican Brothers; Royal Court, Sept 1971, Old Councillor in Lear; same theatre, Nov 1973, the Vicar in The Merry-Go-Round; Greenwich, 1974, played Sorin in The Seagull, Jan, and Gravedigger in Hamlet, Mar; Queen's, Oct 1974, Catiello in Saturday, Sunday, Monday; Riverside Studios, Jan 1978, Firs in The Cherry Orchard; Theatre Royal, Windsor, Mar 1978, Lob in Dear Brutus; Chichester Festival season, 1978, appeared as Sir John Pontefract in A Woman of No Importance and Gigot in Look After Lulu, repeating the latter part at the Haymarket, Oct 1978; has also appeared for the 300 Club, Renaissance Society, etc in special performances, and in films, radio, and television plays.
Favourite parts: Polonius and Mr Pickwick. *Recreations:* Swimming and sun-bathing. *Address:* c/o Peter Eade Ltd, 9 Cork Street, London W1.

HOWELL, Jane, director
e Bristol University; trained for the stage at Bristol Old Vic Theatre School.

Gained her early experience at the Belgrade, Coventry, latterly as assistant director; director of productions, Queen's, Hornchurch, for two years; joined the English Stage Company at the Royal Court, 1965, as associate director, with special responsibility for the Royal Court's Schools scheme; her productions at that theatre included Serjeant Musgrave's Dance, 1965; The Dancers and Transcending (double-bill), The Voysey Inheritance, 1966; Roots, The Dragon, 1967; Twelfth Night, Trixie and Baba, The Houses by the Green, 1968; Narrow Road to the Deep North, Revolution, 1969; Old Vic, Bristol, 1970, directed the Winter's Tale; director, Northcott Theatre, Exeter, 1971–3; her productions here included Bingo, which she also directed at the Royal Court, 1974; has since directed The York Mystery Cycle, York Minster, 1976; Cousin Vladimir, Aldwych, 1978; member of the Arts Council Drama Panel, 1973–; direction for television recently includes St Joan and The Dybbuk.
Address: c/o BBC Television Centre, Wood Lane, London W12.

HOWELLS, Ursula, actress
b London, 17 Sept 1922; *d* of Herbert Norman Howells and his wife Dorothy Eveline (Goozee); *e* St Paul's Girls School; *m* (1) James Davy Dodd (mar dis); (2) Anthony Pélissier; studied for the stage with Anthony Hawtrey at the Dundee Repertory Theatre.

Made her first appearance on the stage at the Dundee Repertory Theatre, Sept 1939, as Joan Greenleaf in Bird in Hand, and remained there until 1942, at first playing small parts, with stage-management, subsequently playing leading parts for a year; joined the Oxford Repertory company in 1942, where she remained until 1944; made her first appearance in London, at the Embassy, 6 Feb 1945, as Henrietta Turnbull in Quality Street; subsequently playing Peggy McNab in Father Malachy's Miracle, and Judith Drave in No Room at the Inn; Whitehall, Dec 1945, played the Hon Elizabeth Wimpole in Fit for Heroes; Westminster, May 1946, Judy Dawson in Frieda; Embassy, Oct 1946, Gloria Palfrey in Peace Comes to Peckham, and Shirley Marsh in Away from it All; Aldwych, Jan 1947, Anne Tower in Jane; Saville, Nov 1947, Nancy Tennant in Honour and Obey; Q, Oct 1948, Kay Llewellyn in Humoresque; Strand, Sept 1949, Fiona Spender in Master of Arts; Winter Garden, May 1950, Marguerite in Madam Tic-Tac; made her first appearance on the New York stage at the Golden, 14 Mar 1951, as Miss Smith in Springtime For Henry; Embassy, London, Nov 1952, played Leopoldine von Schellendorffer in High Balcony; King's, Edinburgh, Apr 1953, Mary Dallas in Night of the Fourth; Princes, Feb 1962, played Mary Ashbury in The Big Killing; Gaiety, Dublin, May 1962, and subsequently Criterion, July 1962, Katie Newton in The Gimmick; New Arts, Oct 1962, Leonora in Doctors of Philosophy; toured, Oct 1963, as Margaret Conyngham in Sergeant Dower Must Die, subsequently appearing at the Vaudeville, Nov 1963, in the same play, under the title Shout For Life; Duchess, Mar 1965, played Leila in Return Ticket; Haymarket, Dec 1967, Cynthia Randolph in Dear Octopus; Thorndike, Leatherhead, Sept 1969, played Eleanor in The Lion in Winter, the theatre's opening production; Globe, Oct 1970, took over as Ruth in Blithe Spirit; Cambridge Theatre, July 1974, took over as Clare in Two and Two Make Sex.
Favourite parts: Celia in The Cocktail Party, Candida, and Eleanor in The Lion in Winter, Nina in The Seagull. *Recreations:* Reading, gardening and dressmaking. *Address:* c/o ICM Ltd, 22 Grafton Street, London, W1.

HOWERD, Frankie, OBE, (*né* Francis Howard), actor
b York, 6 Mar 1921; *e* Eltham, and Shooter's Hill Grammar School, London; formerly an insurance clerk; served in the Royal Artillery during World War II, subsequently producing and appearing in his own show for Forces Entertainment.

Began his stage career in London at the Stage Door Canteen, Piccadilly, Apr 1946; made his first professional appearance on the stage at the London Palladium, Oct 1950, in Out of This World; at the same theatre, Dec 1952, played Idle Jack in the pantomime Dick Whittington; at the Prince of Wales's, Sept 1953, appeared in the revue Pardon My French, which ran for 759 performances; Globe, Dec 1955, played Lord Fancourt Babberley in Charley's Aunt; Old Vic, Dec 1957, played Bottom in A Midsummer Night's Dream; toured, July 1958, as Boniface in Hotel Paradiso; Prince of Wales's, Oct 1958, played Alister in Mister Venus; at the Plaza, Jersey, CI, Aug 1963, starred in Glamorama of 1963; Strand, Oct 1963, played Prologus and Pseudolus in A Funny Thing Happened on the Way to the Forum; Prince of Wales, Nov 1966, starred in Way Out in Piccadilly; first appeared on Broadway at the Ethel Barrymore, Oct 1968, as John Emery Rockefeller in Rockefeller and the Red Indians; London Palladium, Dec 1973, appeared in Jack and the Beanstalk; Alexandra, Birmingham, Dec 1979, Billy Crusoe in Robinson Crusoe; entered films, 1954, appearing in The Runaway Bus, Carry on Doctor, Carry on Up the Jungle, Up the Chastity Belt, Sgt Pepper's Lonely Hearts Club Band, etc; first appeared on television, 1952, and has since starred in *The Frankie Howerd Show, That Was the Week That Was, Up Pompeii,* etc; received the Variety Club of Great Britain award as Show Business Personality of the Year in 1967 and 1972; awarded the Order of the British Empire in 1977.

Recreations: Reading, walking, music and tennis. *Address:* 67 Brook Street, London, W1. *Tel:* 01–629 9121.

HOWES, Sally Ann, actress and singer
b St John's Wood, London, 20 July; *d* of Bobby Howes and his wife Patricia (Malone Clark); *e* Queenswood College, Herts; *m* (1) Maxwell Coker (mar dis); (2) Richard Adler (mar dis); (3) Andrew Maree.

First appeared on the stage at the Alhambra, Glasgow, 1951, in Caprice; in the same year made her first appearance on the West End stage at the Prince of Wales in the revue Fancy Free; also toured the Moss Empire theatres in variety, 1951, and appeared in the Royal Variety Performance of that year; at the London Hippodrome, 18 Feb 1952, played Jane in Bet Your Life; Her Majesty's, Feb 1953, played Jennifer Rumson in Paint Your Wagon; Golder's Green Hippodrome, Dec 1954, appeared as Robin Hood in the pantomime Babes in the Wood; Piccadilly, Sept 1955, played Margaret in Romance in Candlelight; Princes, Feb 1956, played Karolka in Summer Song; Pigalle, Liverpool, Feb 1957, Celia Pope in A Hatful of Rain, appearing in the same part at the Princes, Mar 1957; made her first appearance on Broadway at the Mark Hellinger, Feb 1958, when she took over the part of Eliza in My Fair Lady; 54th Street, New York, Oct 1961, played Eve in Kwamina; City Center, NY, May 1962, Fiona MacLaren in Brigadoon, appearing at the same theatre, Jan 1963, in the same part; 54th Street, NY, Feb 1964, played Kit Sargent in What Makes Sammy Run?; Chandler Pavilion, Los Angeles, 1972, Maria Rainer in The Sound of Music; St Martin's, Mar 1973, Suzy Martin in Lover; Adelphi, Oct 1973, and Chandler Pavilion, Los Angeles, 1974, Anna Leonowens in The King and I; Arnaud, Guildford, Aug 1975, Ann Whitefield in Man and Superman; same theatre, Dec 1976, Elizabeth Barrett in Robert and Elizabeth; London Palladium, Dec 1977, Jenny Lind in Hans Anderson; first appeared in films, 1942, in Thursday's Child; more recently in The Admirable Crichton, and Chitty Chitty Bang Bang; TV, since 1958, includes Brigadoon, *Marcus Welby MD, The Man from Shiloh,* etc.

Recreations: Reading, travel, decorating, cooking. *Addresses:* International Creative Management, 9255 Sunset Boulevard, Los Angeles, Calif 90669, *and* Fraser and Dunlop Ltd, 91 Regent Street, London W1R 8RU.

HOWLETT, Noel, actor
b Maidstone, Kent, 22 Dec 1901; *s* of Francis Robert Howlett and Mary Milles (Whitehead); *e* King's School, Canterbury, and Leeds University; also studied at Mirfield Theological College.

Made his first appearance on the stage at the Pleasure Gardens Theatre, Folkestone, July 1925, as Morse in The Second Mrs Tanqueray; subsequently became a schoolmaster, 1926–8; spent the next five years in repertory and on tour; in 1935 was director at the Hull Repertory Theatre and subsequently at Watford and Margate; made his first appearance in London at the Embassy Theatre, 13 Apr 1936, as Sir William Hamilton in England Expects . . .; Embassy, June, and Phoenix, July 1936, played Professor Filitz in Professor Bernhardi; Embassy, Sept 1936, Paul Deronlède in The Tiger; Lyric, Oct 1936, Colonel John Downes and Nye in Charles the King; Strand (for Repertory Players), Jan 1937, and Wyndham's, Feb 1937, Malcolm in George and Margaret, the production running for nearly two years; Mar 1939, toured as Dr Fenwick in Drawing Room; Wyndham's, July 1939, played Stockton in Alien Corn; Duchess, Jan 1940, Mr

Pennywise in The Golden Cuckoo; Embassy, Jan 1940, Lord Summerhays in Misalliance; Richmond, Apr 1940, Henry Portal in Blue Goose; Q, Apr 1940, Rev Arthur Thorne in Passing-By, which he also directed; Neighbourhood, Sept 1940, Captain Hagberd in To-Morrow; during the War, served in RASC (Military Section of ENSA executive), 1941–5; demobilized as Major i/c Production, ENSA, ME, Dec 1945; toured in Italy, 1946, for ENSA, directing three plays; returned to London, at the Arts, Sept 1946, where, in association with Leonard Brett, he directed The Constant Wife; Aldwych, Oct 1946, played Friar Francis in Much Ado About Nothing; Arts, Jan 1947, Knut Brovik in The Master Builder; New Lindsey, Feb 1948, Mr Thomas in Golden Rain; New, June 1948, Dr Libbard in The Gioconda Smile; toured in Germany, 1949, playing Polonius in Hamlet; Q, Feb 1950, Sir Walter Rendell in Sauce for the Goose; Ambassadors', Mar 1950, succeeded Maurice Denham as Willy Banbury in Fallen Angels, and Henry in Fumed Oak; at the Q, Apr 1951, played Harris in We Must Kill Toni; also Oct 1951, Col Willingham in Cry For the Moon and Edward Forrest in Night Call; New Lindsey, Jan 1952, Mr Johnson in In Search of Yesterday; Duke of York's, July 1952, Mrs Pless's Brother in The Trap; St Martin's, July 1952, directed Lion's Corner; Royal Court, Liverpool, Aug 1952, appeared as Henry VII in The Player King; New, London, Dec 1952, Edward in Dear Charles; joined the Shakespeare Memorial Theatre, Stratford-on-Avon, for the season of 1953, when he appeared as Old Gobbo in The Merchant of Venice, King Edward IV in Richard III, Baptista in The Taming of the Shrew, and the Earl of Gloucester in King Lear; St James's, London, Apr 1954, played Dr Barry in Waiting for Gillian; toured, Oct 1954, as the Very Rev Dr Cedric Hogarth in It's Different for Men; Court, Mar 1955, Arnold Hamble, QC, in Uncertain Joy; toured Australia, 1956–8, as the Prosecuting Counsel in Witness for the Prosecution, Henry in Hippo Dancing, and Uncle Ernest in Double Image; Garrick, London, Apr 1962, played Mr Joyce in Two Stars For Comfort; Queen's, Dec 1963, the Reverend Treadgold in Gentle Jack; Lyric, Hammersmith, Mar 1966, Pedro in Santa Cruz; Criterion, May 1970, Dr Colley in Flint; Shaw Festival, Niagara-on-the-Lake, Canada, 1972, played Lord Summerhays in Misalliance and the Bishop in Getting Married; Chichester, July 1974, Chorus Leader in Oidipus Tyrannus; Canterbury, Jan 1975, and Harrogate, Apr 1975, General Boothroyd in Lloyd George Knew My Father; Shaw, May 1975, Adam in As You Like It; Harrogate, Aug 1975, Sorin in The Seagull; Arts, 1976, took over as Bernard in New-Found-Land; Mermaid, Dec 1977, played the King in The Point; his films, since A Yank at Oxford, 1938, include Serious Charge, Lawrence of Arabia, and The Selkie; numerous TV appearances include: *The Forsyte Saga,* Vanity Fair and, more recently, *The Good Life,* Happy Ever After and A Moment in Time.

Address: c/o Jimmy Garrod Management, 66 Alleyn Road, West Dulwich SE21 8AH.

HUDD, Roy, comedian
b Croydon, 16 May 1936; *s* of Harold Charles Hudd and his wife Evelyn Bahram; *m* Ann Vera Lambert; formerly a commercial artist, window dresser, flyman, sugar shoveller and messenger.

Started stage work in variety at the Metropolitan Music Hall, Edgeware Road, London, in 1958; at the Garrick, 1969, played Jim Busby in The Giveaway; appeared with Danny La Rue at the Palace, Apr 1970; at the Young Vic, season 1973, played Rosencrantz in Rosencrantz and Guildenstern Are Dead, and Dogberry in Much Ado About Nothing; at the same theatre in Nov 1976 played Frank in If You're Glad I'll be Frank, and Birdboot in The Real Inspector Hound, in a double-bill; Albery, Dec 1977, Fagin in Oliver!; has appeared in music hall, pantomime, and in his own one-man show based on music hall favourites, recently at the Haymarket, Leicester, 1980; films, since 1968, include Up Pompeii and two sequels; has appeared frequently on television, including a number of his own series; author of a book on Music Hall.

Address: c/o Morris Aza, 652 Finchley Road, London NW11 7NT. *Tel:* 458 7288.

HUDSON, Verity, manager
b Lahore, 17 May 1923; *d* of George James Samms-Hudson and his wife Gladys Florence (Cope); *e* privately; *m* Kenneth Fraser (dec).

Started her stage career as ASM at the Theatre Royal, Windsor, in 1946; deputy SM and acted at Aldershot 1947, followed by an Arts Council season in the West Riding where she became Company Manager; Toured Austria and Italy with the Combined Services Entertainment 1947 and was ASM and U/S in Present Laughter at the Haymarket; in 1948 joined Peter Saunders as Company Manager for The Perfect Woman; subsequently became Stage Manager and General Manager for the Peter Saunders group of companies; since 1969 an executive director of the group; in Nov 1969 became a member of the Society of West End Theatre and in 1975 was the first woman to be elected a member of the Executive Council.

Recreations: Gardening (gently) and going to the theatre.
Address: Peter Saunders Ltd, Vaudeville Theatre Offices, 10 Maiden Lane, London WC2E 7NA.

HUGHES, Barnard, actor
b Bedford Hills, NY, 16 Jul 1915; *s* of Owen Hughes and his wife Madge (Kiernan); *m* Helen Stenborg.

First appeared on the stage with the Shakespeare Fellowship Company, New York, Oct 1934, as the Haberdasher in The Taming of the Shrew; first appeared on Broadway at the Belmont, 16 Mar 1936, as the Son in Please, Mrs Garibaldi; Lyceum, Apr 1949, played Martin in The Ivy Green; National, Nov 1951, Clancy in Dinosaur Wharf; toured, 1954–56, as Captain McLean in the Teahouse of the August Moon; New York City Center, Nov 1956, repeated this last part; Theatre East, Dec 1957, Lanty in The Will and the Way; Erlanger, Philadelphia, Nov 1958, Doctor Genoni in Enrico IV (Pirandello); Sam S Shubert, Feb 1959, Captain Norcross in A Majority of One; Cort, Nov 1960, August in Advise and Consent; Fourth Street, Apr 1962, Peter Mortensagaard in Rosmersholm; Theatre Four, Feb 1963, Nils Krogstad in A Doll's House; ANTA, Oct 1963, The Governor in The Advocate; Lyceum, Dec 1963, Bert Howell in Nobody Loves an Albatross; Lunt-Fontanne, Apr 1964, Marcellus, Priest in John Gielgud's production of Hamlet; Lyceum, Nov 1964, Father Frank Feeley in I Was Dancing; American Place, Nov 1965, Father Stanislas Coyne in Hogan's Goat; US tour, 1966, took over from Robert Young as Jim Bolton in Generation; Lunt-Fontanne, Dec 1967, Senator McFetridge in How Now, Dow Jones; John Golden, Mar 1969, Judge Belknap in The Wrong Way Light Bulb; Helen Hayes, Jan 1970, General Fitzhugh in Sheep on the Runway; Theatre de Lys, Feb 1971, Arnall in Line; Brooks Atkinson, Mar 1971, Fulbert in Abelard and Heloise; Anspacher, May 1972, played in Older People; Delacorte, June 1972, Polonius in Hamlet, and Aug 1972, Dogberry in Much Ado About Nothing, and repeated this last part at the Winter Garden, Nov 1972; Circle in the Square—Joseph E Levine, June 1973, Alexander Serebryakov in Uncle Vanya; Eugene

O'Neill, Nov 1973, various parts in The Good Doctor; Delacorte, Jun 1974, Gower in Pericles, and Jul 1974, Sir John Falstaff in The Merry Wives of Windsor; Booth, Dec 1974, Dr Lionel Morris in All Over Town; Morosco, May 1978, title-role in Da, for which he received a 'Tony' and several other awards; subsequently toured in the role; first appeared in films in 1969 in Midnight Cowboy, and has since played in Hospital, Rage, Cold Turkey, Where's Papa?, etc; first appeared on television in 1946 as Bob Cratchit in A Christmas Carol, and has since played in Pueblo, Much Ado About Nothing, Look Homeward, Angel, *Doc* (1975–76), The Judge (Emmy Award), etc.

Favourite parts: Dogberry, Polonius, Serebryakov, Da. *Club:* Players, NY. *Address:* International Creative Management, 40 West 57th Street, New York, NY 10019.

HUGHES, Dusty (Richard Holland Hughes), director and playwright
b 16 Sept 1947; *s* of Harold Henry Hughes and his wife Winifred Elsie (Holland); *e* Queen Elizabeth's Grammar School, Wakefield and Trinity Hall, Cambridge (BA 1968); *m* the performance artist Natasha Morgan; trained with Thames Television (Regional Theatre Trainee Director Scheme).

Theatre editor and critic, *Time Out* magazine, 1973–76; since 1976 artistic director, the Bush Theatre, London W12, which has presented a number of premieres and given a London platform to many of the alternative theatre's touring companies; among the many plays he has directed at the Bush are The Soul of the White Ant, 1976; Vampire, Happy Birthday Wanda June, 1977; In at the Death (also devised), 1978; his own play Commitments received its first production here in June 1980; member, Drama Panel and New Writing Committee, Arts Council.

Address: 5 Armiger Road, London W12.

HUGHES, Mick, lighting designer
b London, 10 May 1938; *s* of George Samuel Hughes and his wife Mildred May (Lovelock); *e* Harvey Grammar School, Folkestone and Chiswick County Grammar School; formerly a television cameraman with the BBC, fairground barker at Battersea, and barman at the Mermaid Theatre.

Began his professional career as an electrician with the Margate Stage Company, 1961, and in that year designed the lighting for his first production, Gaslight, at the Theatre Royal, Margate; later worked at Birmingham Rep and the Arnaud, Guildford; from 1966–70 and 1974–79, lighting designer for the Chichester Festival; his first West End lighting design was for the Chichester production of The Fighting Cocks, Duke of York's, 1966; he has since lit a large number of London productions including Time and Time Again, 1972; Absurd Person Singular, 1973; The Homecoming, 1978; Stage Struck, 1979, etc; work for the National Theatre includes Mrs Warren's Profession, 1969, Death of a Salesman, 1979; lighting designer for the Hong Kong Arts Festival, 1976–80; has also lit for the Akademie Theater, Vienna; from 1967–72 directed about forty productions at the Swan, Worcester; directed Seven Keys to Doomsday, Adelphi, Christmas 1974; teaches stage lighting at Birmingham Polytechnic.

Recreation: Sailing. *Address:* Farm Cottage, School Lane, Bosham, Sussex. *Tel:* 0243-573767.

HUMPHREY, Cavada, actress
b New Jersey; *e* Ashley Hall, Charleston, South Carolina, and Smith College; *m* Jerome Kilty.

First appeared on the stage at the age of four in a solo ballet at the Philadelphia Academy of Music; first appeared in New York at the Blackfriars Theatre, 2 Apr 1943, as Esther in A Man's House; made her Broadway début at the Fulton, Mar 1944, as Naomi Fisher in The House in Paris; Belasco, Mar 1946, played Madame Sajou in The Song of Bernadette; at the International, in the American Repertory Theatre Season, 1946–7, played a variety of parts; Winter Garden, Nov 1948, played Miss Swenson in As the Girls Go; City Center, Jan 1950, a Parent in The Corn Is Green and Mrs Williams in The Devil's Disciple; Royale, Feb 1950, again appeared in The Devil's Disciple; City Center, Jan 1951, played the Duchess of Gloucester in Richard II; May 1951, Widow in The Taming of the Shrew and, Feb 1953, Maria in Love's Labour's Lost; Theatre de Lys, Oct 1953, Madame Zoe in Moon in Capricorn; City Center, Sept 1955, Emilia in Othello, and Lady Mortimer in Henry IV, Part I; Phyllis Anderson, Nov 1957, Wowkle in The Girl of the Golden West; US tour, Dec 1958–Jan 1959, appeared as Mrs Trellington in Listen to the Mocking Bird; made her London début at the Criterion, 14 June 1960, as Mrs Patrick Campbell in Dear Liar, subsequently toured South Africa with her husband in the same play; Marquee, NY, Mar 1962, again played Mrs Patrick Campbell in Dear Liar; toured South Africa 1962, again played Mrs Patrick Campbell in Dear Liar; toured South Africa, 1962–3, and again in 1964, as Martha in Who's Afraid of Virginia Woolf?; Astor Place Playhouse, NY, Mar 1964, played Stella in Life Is a Dream; Garrick, Feb 1965, Mother-in-Law in Colombe; Lyceum, 1966, Grand Duchess Olga in You Can't Take It with You; Delacorte, July 1967, Queen Elinor in King John; Cort, Mar 1968, Lady Fitch, the Doctor, and Aunt Mildred in Leda Had a Little Swan; Comedy Club, 1969, Eleanor of Aquitane in The Lion in Winter; Longacre, Apr 1970, Prosperine Garnett in Candida; toured, 1970, as Madame Arcati in Blithe Spirit; has played many parts in stock productions, including a season with Margaret Webster's Company at Woodstock, NY, 1951; at the Brattle Theatre, Cambridge, Mass, 1951–6, played Goneril in King Lear, the Mother in Six Characters in Search of an Author, Olga in Three Sisters, Anna Ivanovna in Ivanov, Lady Sneerwell in School for Scandal, Genevieve in The Long Christmas Dinner, Lady Mortimer in Henry IV, Part I, Margaret in Much Ado About Nothing, Emilia in Othello, and Cassandra in Troilus and Cressida; Chicago, 1954, appeared in the title-role of The Madwoman of Chaillot, and, at the Studebaker, 1957, as The Actress in The Guardsman; at Wellesley, Mass, 1960, appeared as Mme Desmortes in Ring Round the Moon, Violet in Man and Superman, Mrs Higgins in Pygmalion, Blanche in A Streetcar Named Desire; at the Boston Festival, 1958, played the Gypsy Fortune Teller in The Skin of Our Teeth, and 1964, Madrecita in Camino Real, and Clodia Pulcher in the US première of her husband's play The Ides of March; at the University of Michigan, Ann Arbor, 1962, appeared with the APA as Lady Sneerwell, Hester in Penny for a Song, and The Mother in We Comrades Three; Theatre de Lys, Oct 1972, Baroness de Simiane in Madame de Sade; Stage 73, Feb 1973, Queen Elizabeth I in the one-character play Henry's Daughter; Aelesund, Norway, Dec 1973, again played in this part; Queen's Playhouse, 1976, Judith Bliss in Hay Fever; Van Dam, 1976, Elizabeth I in Henry's Daughter; has toured with this piece since 1975 in the USA and Britain, including appearances at the Tower of London and many historic houses; recently at the Walnut Street, Philadelphia, 1979; first appeared in films, 1948, in Naked City, and has since appeared in Thoroughly Modern Millie, 1966; first appeared on television, 1946, and has since played many parts, includ-

ing Dear Liar, 1965, Dark Shadows, 1968, The Prodigal, 1969, The Adams Chronicles, 1975, etc.

Recreations: Studying the Elizabethan age, dress and fashion history, modern *haute couture. Address:* c/o Bryan Drew, 81 Shaftesbury Avenue, London W1.

HUMPHRIES, Barry, comedian and author
b Melbourne, 17 Feb 1934; *e* Melbourne Grammar School and Melbourne University; *m* (2) Diane Millstead.

Came to England in 1959 and made his first London appearance at the Lyric, Hammersmith, 10 Dec, as Jonas Fogg in The Demon Barber; at the New, Jun 1960, played Mr Sowerberry in the original production of Oliver!, making his New York debut in the same part at the Imperial, 6 Jan 1963; subsequently played Fagin in New York and in London at the Piccadilly, 1968; since 1961 has delighted the civilised and much of the uncivilised world with his one-person entertainments featuring Dame Edna Everage and Sir Leslie Patterson; these have been A Nice Night's Entertainment, 1962; Excuse I!, 1964; Just a Show, 1968, seen at the Fortune, Mar 1969; A Load of Olde Stuffe, 1971; At Least You Can Say You've Seen It, 1974; Housewife! Superstar!, seen at the Apollo, Mar 1976, and at Theatre Four, NY, Oct 1977; Isn't It Pathetic at His Age, in Australia 1978; A Night with Dame Edna, Piccadilly, Dec 1978; films include Bedazzled, 1964, and Arise Sir Les, 1980; frequent TV appearances including his own shows; his books include Tid, 1962, Bizarre, 1964, The Wonderful World of Barry McKenzie (with Nicolas Garland), 1968, Dame Edna's Coffee Table Book, 1977, Les Patterson's Australia, 1978, The Life and Times of Sandy Stone, and The Treasury of Australian Kitsch, 1980; Hon Member, British Gladiolus Society.

Recreation: Painting. *Clubs:* Athenaeum, Oxford and Cambridge, Garrick. *Address:* c/o Kenneth Thomson, 26 Evelyn Mansions, Carlisle Place, London SW1P 1NH.

HUNT, Hugh, CBE, MA, Emeritus Professor (Drama), Manchester University; director
b Camberley, Surrey, 25 Sept 1911; *s* of Captain Cecil Edwin Hunt, MC, and his wife Ethel Helen (Crookshank); *e* Marlborough College, and Magdalen College, Oxford; *m* Janet Mary Gordon.

While at Oxford, was a member of the OUDS, President, 1933–4, when he directed King John at the New Theatre, 1933; director at the Maddermarket Theatre, Norwich, 1934; at Croydon Repertory Theatre, 1934–5, directed Everyman, The Rivals, King Lear, Candida, Touch Wood, etc; at the Westminster, 1934–5, directed King Lear, Rose and Glove, Children in Uniform, Othello, etc; director to the Abbey Theatre, Dublin, 1935–8, directing over thirty original Irish plays, including Shadow and Substance, Blind Man's Buff, Katie Roche, etc; directed The White Steed at the Cort Theatre, New York, Jan 1939; served in HM Forces, 1939–45, during which period he directed The Golden Cuckoo, Duchess, 1940; Shadow and Substance, Duke of York's, 1943; appointed director for the Old Vic Company at the Theatre Royal, Bristol, Dec 1945, and remained until 1948, directing The Beaux' Stratagem, Tess, The Playboy of the Western World, Weep for the Cyclops, Rain on the Just, The Rivals, etc; during this period he also directed Tess of the D'Urbervilles, at the New, 1946, and at the Piccadilly, 1947; King Lear, Much Ado About Nothing, Embassy, 1947; Hamlet, St James's, 1948; for the Old Vic Company, at the New Theatre, he directed The Cherry Orchard, 1948; he was appointed Director of the Old Vic, 1949–53, and directed Love's Labour's Lost, 1949; Hamlet, 1950 (also at Elsinore); at the reopening of the Old Vic Theatre, Nov 1950, directed

Twelfth Night; subsequently at the Old Vic, directed Captain Brassbound's Conversion, The Merry Wives of Windsor, 1951; King Lear, Romeo and Juliet, 1952; The Merchant of Venice, Julius Caesar, 1953; at the Saville, Mar 1954, directed The White Countess; in Feb 1955, he was appointed Director of the Elizabethan Theatre Trust, Sydney, Australia; while in Australia, directed Medea with Judith Anderson, Hamlet, with Paul Rogers, Murder in the Cathedral, with Robert Speaight, also Julius Caesar, and Twelfth Night; resigned from Elizabethan Theatre Trust and returned to England, 1960; for the Arts Council, Oct 1960, directed an English tour of Five Finger Exercise; directed The Shaughraun during the World Theatre Season at the Aldwych, 1968; appointed Artistic Director of the Abbey, Dublin, Dec 1969, and has since directed The Hostage, 1969; the double-bill Well of the Saints and The Dandy Dolls, 1970; The Wicklow Wedding, 1972; Peer Gynt (Sydney), 1974; The Plough and the Stars (Sydney), 1977, etc; first Professor of Drama at the University of Manchester, 1961–73; appointed member of the Independent Television Authority, July 1964–9; member of the Drama Panel of the Arts Council 1965–8; director of Sadler's Wells Opera Trust, 1965–8; member of the Drama Panels of The Welsh Arts Council and The North Welsh Arts Association; council member of Contact Theatre, Manchester; author of the plays, The Invincibles, 1937; Moses' Rock, 1938; In the Train (with Frank O'Connor), 1954; author of the books The Director in the Theatre, Old Vic Prefaces: Shakespeare and the Producer, 1954; The Making of Australian Theatre, The Live Theatre, 1962; The Abbey, Ireland's National Theatre, 1979.

Club: Garrick. *Address:* Cae Terfyn, Criccieth, Gwynedd LL52 O5A.

HUNT, Peter, director and lighting designer
b Pasadena, California, 16 Dec 1938; *s* of George S Hunt and his wife Gertrude (Ophuls); *e* The Hotchkiss School, Yale University (BA, MFA); *m* (1) Virginia Osborn (mar dis); (2) Barbette Tweed.

Began his career as an actor at Hotchkiss, where he also designed the lighting for his first play, Merry Mount; designed his first professional New York play, The Sap of Life, at the One Sheridan Square Theatre, 2 Oct 1961; designed the lighting for Cracks, 1963; Tambourines to Glory, Color of Darkness, 1964; Dynamite Tonight, The Wayward Stork, 1966; Have I Got One for You, Noel Coward's Sweet Potato, The Firebugs, 1968; for five years was lighting designer for Richard Rodgers at Lincoln Center, and New York State Theatre, where he designed the lighting for Kismet, Carousel, Annie Get Your Gun, West Side Story, and the tours of Oliver, Sound of Music, and Camelot, 1964–8; since 1957 has been associated with the Williamstown Theatre, where he is presently Associate Director, and where he directed his first play, The Fantasticks; he has lit and directed extensively in the regional repertory theatres; directed his first play in NY at Lincoln Center, Booth, 1968; followed by 1776, 1969; Georgy, 1970; Scratch, 1971; made his London début as director at the New Theatre, 1970, with 1776; at Williamstown, July 1972, directed Arturo Ui; directed Goodtime Charley, Give 'em Hell, Harry, and (for Williamstown) Savages, 1975; The Magnificent Yankee (Washington DC), 1976; Bully (NY), 1977; S Miles is Me (San Francisco), 1978; directed the film of 1776 (1971); directed the film Gold (1974).

Recreations: Flying his own plane. *Address:* 249 East 48th Street, New York, NY.

HUNTER, Kim (*née* Janet Cole), actress
b Detroit, Mich, 12 Nov 1922; *d* of Donald Cole and his wife Grace (Lind); *e* Miami Beach High School; *m* (1) William A Baldwin (mar dis); (2) Robert Emmett; studied at the Actors Studio.

Made her first appearance on the stage with a little theatre group, Miami, Nov 1939, as Penny in Penny Wise; first appeared in New York at the Ethel Barrymore, 3 Dec 1947, as Stella Kowalski in A Streetcar Named Desire; toured, 1950, in Two Blind Mice; Alvin, Jan 1951, played Luba in Darkness at Noon; Playhouse, Apr 1952, Ruby Hawes in The Chase; toured, summer of 1952, in They Knew What They Wanted; Coronet, Dec 1952, appeared as Karen Wright in The Children's Hour; Longacre, Oct 1954, played Sylvia Crews in The Tender Trap; McCarter, Princeton, New Jersey, Jan 1958, Kate Adams in This Is Goggle; Shakespeare Festival Theatre, Stratford, Conn, 1961, played Rosalind in As You Like It, Witch in Macbeth, and Helen in Troilus and Cressida; Belasco, Oct 1961, Julie Sturrock in Write Me a Murder; Bucks County Playhouse, New Hope, Pa, May 1964, Paula Maugham in Linda Stone Is Brutal; Otterbein College, Ohio, Feb 1965, Dowager Empress in Anastasia; White Barn, Westport, Conn, July 1966, Emily Dickinson in Come Slowly, Eden, which she repeated at the Library of Congress in Washington, DC, and the Theatre de Lys, Nov 1966; Broadhurst, Mar 1968, Miss Wilson in Weekend; Long Island Repertory Festival, Mineola, NY, 1968, Alma Winemiller in Eccentricities of a Nightingale and Masha in The Three Sisters; Theatre de Lys, Nov 1968, Hester in Hello and Goodbye; toured, summer 1969, as Jean Brodie in The Prime of Miss Jean Brodie; Royale, Oct 1969, Carrie Bishop in The Penny Wars; US tour, beginning Sept 1971, as Catherine Reardon in And Miss Reardon Drinks a Little; 46th Street, Apr 1973, Mary Haines in The Women; toured, summer 1975, as Lydia in In Praise of Love; Roundabout, Mar 1976, Mme Ranevskaya in the Cherry Orchard; Bucks County Playhouse, New Hope, Pa, Nov 1976, Miss Madrigal in The Chalk Garden; Studio Arena, Buffalo, Apr 1977, Elizabeth in Elizabeth the Queen; Greenwood, SC, Sept 1977, Romaine in Witness for the Prosecution; Buffalo, Nov 1977, Julia in Semmelweiss; NJ Theatre Forum, Apr 1978, Emily Dickinson in The Belle of Amherst; has acted in stock since 1940 in such plays as The Importance of Being Earnest, Claudia, Wuthering Heights, A Hatful of Rain, The Dark at the Top of the Stairs, Summer and Smoke, Born Yesterday, Major Barbara, etc; first appeared in films 1943, in The Seventh Victim, and has since played in a number of productions, including A Streetcar Named Desire (Academy Award), and Zira in the *Planet of the Apes* series; television appearances since 1948 include Give Us Barrabas, and series including: *Cannon, Ironside, Columbo, Edge of Night,* Backstairs at the White House (1979), and numerous other dramatic and variety programmes; author of Autobiographical cookbook Loose in the Kitchen, 1975.

Recreations: Cooking, music, books, and dancing. *Address:* 42 Commerce Street, New York, NY 10014.

HUNTER, Victor William, theatre manager
b Clapham, London, 6 Apr 1910; *s* of Victor Cyril Hunter, and his wife Dorothea Suzanne (Bridgett); *m* Isobel Mitchell Leggat Byfield.

Commenced in the theatre as box office assistant at the Alhambra Theatre, London, 1925; joined Wyndham's Theatre, Jan 1933; served with the Indian Army, 1939–45; manager New Theatre, 1945–53; general manager The Wyndham Theatres Ltd, 1953–69; Director, 1972–5; consultant member of the Society of West End Theatre, 1976–.

Recreations: Cricket, rugby. *Clubs:* Arts Theatre, MCC. *Address:* 7 Paxton Terrace, London, SW1. *Tel:* 01–834 4949.

HUNTLEY, Raymond, actor
b Birmingham, 23 Apr 1904; *s* of Alfred Huntley and his wife Fannie (Walsh); *e* King Edward's School, Birmingham; *m* June Bell (mar dis).

Made his first appearance on the stage at the Birmingham Repertory Theatre, 1 Apr 1922, in A Woman Killed With Kindness; remained at Birmingham until 1924; made his first appearance in London at the Court Theatre, 22 Feb 1924, as Acis in As Far As Thought Can Reach (Part V, Back to Methuselah); Mar 1924, appeared there as Rev Septimus Tudor in The Farmer's Wife; during 1925–6, toured as Churdles Ash in the same play; 1926–7, toured in repertory with Hamilton Deane; Little Theatre, London, Feb 1927, played Count Dracula in Dracula; 1927–8, toured as Philip Voaze in Interference; from 1928–30, toured in Dracula in the United States; made his first appearance on the New York Stage at the Vanderbilt Theatre, 23 Feb 1931, as Angelo Querini in The Venetian Glass Nephew; returned to England, 1931, and played leads in the Alexandra stock company, Birmingham; Queen's, Jan 1932, again played Tudor in The Farmer's Wife; subsequently played leads at Edinburgh and Glasgow with the Reando company; during 1932–3, toured as the Count Dubarry in The Dubarry; Garrick, June 1933, played Pettingwaite in Clear All Wires; Fortune, Sept 1933, Cookson in What Happened Then?; Wyndham's, Jan 1934, Major Kilpatrick and Stringer, and subsequently Chatham, in Clive of India; Ambassadors', Mar 1934, Alexei Turbin in The White Guard; Duchess, Mar 1935, the ex-Officer and Fletcher in Cornelius; Old Vic, Jan 1936, Hastings in Richard III; Feb 1936, Sir George Cockburn in St Helena, playing the same part at Daly's, Mar 1936; Lyric, May 1936, Slivers in Bees on the Boat Deck; Queen's, Sept 1936, Chapman in Follow Your Saint; Savoy, Nov 1936, Dr Reuchlin in Young Madame Conti, and played the same part at the Music Box, NY, Mar 1937; Daly's, July 1937, Rev John Fulton in The First Legion; Duchess, Aug 1937, Alan in Time and the Conways; Duke of York's (for London International Theatre), Oct 1937, Kashdak in Susannah and the Elders; Duchess, May 1938, Professor Hans Skaedia in Glorious Morning; St Martin's, Oct 1938, Councillor Albert Parker in When We Are Married; Globe, May 1939, Captain Guy Felton in Rhondda Roundabout; Queen's, Apr 1940, Frank Crawley in Rebecca; toured in the same part, 1941, and again played it at the Strand, May 1942; Globe, Apr 1943, Malcolm Stritton in They Came to a City; Apollo, Nov 1944, Victor Prynne in Private Lives; toured, Apr 1945, as Count Barras in Ah! Josephine; Lyric, Hammersmith, Aug 1946, Mr Arcularis in Fear No More; Embassy, Nov 1946, Col Sanderson, DSO, in The Day of Glory; Duke of York's, Mar 1947, Clive in The Anonymous Lover; Ambassadors', July 1949, Henry Martin in The Late Edwina Black; 48th Street Theatre, NY, Sept 1950, appeared as Robert Christie in Black Chiffon; after Criterion, Oct 1951, as Frank Kemp in And This Was Odd; Vaudeville, Apr 1952, Theodore Brumfit in Lords of Creation; Savoy, Dec 1953, Sir Mohammed D'Urt in No Sign of the Dove; Westminster, May 1954, James Rice in The Bombshell; Saville, July 1955, Manning in The Shadow of Doubt; Savoy, Nov 1956, Ernest Fanshaw in Double Image; Westminster, Apr 1958, Sir Norman Tullis in Any Other Business?; Westminster, Jan 1959, Det Superintendent Coates in The Woman on the Stair; Piccadilly, May 1959, Dr Rodd in Caught Napping; Phoenix (Repertory Players), Apr 1961, played Sir Nicholas Ennor in The Landing Place; Garrick, Nov 1963, John Freyling in Difference of

Opinion; Arnaud, Guildford, July 1966, and tour, Edgar in A Family and A Fortune; Garrick, Dec 1966, Earl of Caversham in An Ideal Husband; Strand, Apr 1967, Collins in Getting Married; New, Dec 1968, Paymaster General in Soldiers; Apollo, Jan 1977, Mr Fowler in Separate Tables; entered films, 1934, and has appeared in numerous pictures, and also on television, recently in Upstairs, Downstairs.

Recreation: Reading. *Club:* Garrick. *Address:* c/o Leading Artists, 60 St James's Street, London SW1.

HURNDALL, Richard, actor
b Darlington, Co Durham, 3 Nov 1910; *s* of Henry Atkinson Hurndall, and his wife Mary Jane (Gibbon); *e* Scarborough College; *m* (1) Mona Berridge (mar dis); (2) Ivy Carlton (dec); (3) Margaret Ward; trained for the stage at RADA.

First appeared on the London stage 29 Dec 1930, at the Fortune, as the Footman in A Pantomime Rehearsal; appeared with various repertory companies, 1931–6; toured, 1937, as Lord Fancourt Babberley in Charley's Aunt; also toured in Three Men on a Horse and Viceroy Sarah, playing Harley in the latter; further repertory experience culminated in two and a half years with the Coventry repertory company, 1938–40; Memorial Theatre, Stratford-on-Avon, 1940 season, played Orlando in As You Like It, Bassanio in The Merchant of Venice, Laertes in Hamlet and Young Marlow in She Stoops to Conquer; after army service 1940–5, took over in Private Lives, 1946, at the Apollo and later the Fortune; toured, 1947, in The Gleam; Embassy, Jan 1948, played Bruno in As You Desire Me and Adrian in Yes and No; after a period largely devoted to radio and television, played Dawson-Hill in The Affair, Strand, Sept 1961; Captain Smith in The New Men at the same theatre, Sept 1962; Vernon Royce in The Masters, Savoy, May 1963 and later at the Piccadilly; Haymarket, Nov 1964, Sir Peter Crossman in Hostile Witness; Vaudeville, Nov 1966, Hugh Campbell, QC, in Justice is A Woman; Cambridge, June 1969, Clive in Highly Confidential; first appeared in films, 1945, and his appearances include Joanna, Zeppelin and Royal Flash; has appeared frequently on television since his first appearance in 1946, recently in Philby, Burgess and Maclean, and Enemy at the Door; his radio work includes a spell with the BBC drama repertory company, 1949–52.

Recreations: Genealogy, bridge. *Address:* c/o Essanay Ltd, 75 Hammersmith Road, London, W14. *Tel:* 01–602 4161.

HURRAN, Dick, director
b Ipswich, 7 Dec 1911; *s* of Alfred James Hurran and his wife Florence Miriam (Bell); *e* Ipswich Grammar School; *m* Pamela Arliss.

Began his career in concert-parties, 1929, subsequently appearing in touring revues, and acting as assistant stage manager, etc; appeared at the Windmill from 1937 until 1939; was then appointed Entertainments Director at the Coconut Grove night club, writing, directing and appearing in all productions there until July 1940; served in the RAF, 1940–5; joined the Moss Empires organization, 1945, as writer and composer, and contributed music and lyrics to the Palladium revues High Time, 1946, and Here, There and Everywhere, 1947; also wrote the music and lyrics for the revue Piccadilly Hayride, Prince of Wales, 1946; in 1948, joined Bernard Delfont Ltd, as Chief of Productions, for whom he has directed: Folies Bergère Revue, 1949; Touch and Go, 1950; Encore des Folies, 1951; Paris to Piccadilly, 1952; Pardon My French, 1953; Paris By Night, Painting the Town, 1955; Round About Piccadilly, 1964; in addition, he has directed Folies Bergère revues in Australia and South Africa; in 1957, joined Granada Television as Executive-Director for the

Chelsea At Nine series; joined Howard and Wyndham Ltd as Executive-Director, 1958, and has since directed all the Five Past Eight series of revues at the Alhambra, Glasgow, in addition to productions at the Opera House, Manchester, and the Royal Court, Liverpool; staged the Royal Variety Performances at the Alhambra, Glasgow, July 1958, and July 1963; resigned from the Board of Howard and Wyndham, and re-joined the Delfont Organization, Sept 1970; appointed to the board of directors, Blackpool Tower Company, 1971, and has since been responsible for staging large scale summer revues at the Opera House and ABC Theatre there; directed The Max Bygraves Revue, Victoria Palace, 1972; The Cilla Black Show, London Palladium, 1973; in May 1975 staged his first Circus Spectacular, Tower Circus, Blackpool.

Recreations: Gardening and watching football. *Club:* International Variety. *Address:* Stocks, Bishop's Walk, Addington, Surrey. *Tel:* 01–654 4502.

HURT, John, actor

b Chesterfield, Derbys, 22 Jan 1940; *s* of the Rev Arnould Herbert Hurt, and his wife Phyllis (Massey); *e* The Lincoln School, Lincoln; formerly a painter; trained for the stage at RADA.

Made his stage debut in Aug 1962, at the Arts, London, as Knocker White in Infanticide in the House of Fred Ginger; later that year he joined the cast of Chips With Everything at the Vaudeville; Arts, Sept 1963, played Len in The Dwarfs; Edinburgh Festival, Aug 1964, played the title role in Hamp; Wyndham's, Mar 1965, Jones in Inadmissible Evidence; Garrick, Feb 1966, Malcolm Scrawdyke in Little Malcolm and his Struggle Against the Eunuchs; Aldwych, Nov 1966, for the Royal Shakespeare Company, played Victor in Belcher's Luck; Gaiety, Dublin, 1969, Octavius in Man and Superman; Hampstead, Jan 1972, Peter in Ride a Cock-Horse; Mermaid, Mar 1972, Mick in The Caretaker; Dublin Festival, Eblana Theatre, Oct 1973, Martin in The Only Street, subsequently at the King's Head, Islington; Soho Poly, Dec 1973, played the Ruffian in The Ruffian on the Stair, and Ben in The Dumb Waiter; Aldwych, for RSC, June 1974, Tristan Tzara in Travesties; Bristol Old Vic, Nov 1974, The Young Man in The Arrest; films since 1962 include A Man for All Seasons, 10 Rillington Place and, recently, Midnight Express, Alien and Heaven's Gate; television since 1960 includes The Playboy of the Western World, The Naked Civil Servant, I, Claudius, and Crime and Punishment.

Address: c/o Leading Artists, 60 St James's Street, London W1.

HURT, Mary Beth (*née* Supinger), actress

b 26 Sept, Marshalltown, Iowa; *d* of Forrest Clayton Supinger and his wife Delores Lenore (Andre); *e* University of Iowa; *m* Bill Hurt (mar dis); trained for the stage at New York University School of the Arts.

For the NY Shakespeare Festival played Celia in As You Like It, at the Delacorte, Jun 1973; Nurse and Uncle Remus in More than You Deserve, Jan 1974, at the Public, and Marina in Pericles, Delacorte, Jun 1974; for the New Phoenix, at the Helen Hayes, played Miss Prue in Love for Love, Nov 1974, and Frankie Addams in The Member of the Wedding, Jan 1975; Vivian Beaumont, Oct 1975, Rose Trelawny in Trelawny of the 'Wells'; for Phoenix, Apr 1976, Caroline Mitford in Secret Service and Susie in Boy Meets Girl; Vivian Beaumont, Feb and Jun 1977, Anya in The Cherry Orchard; Mark Taper Forum, LA, 1978, Vi in Dusa, Fish, Stas and Vi; American Place, Jun 1979, Estelle in Father's Day; first film, Interiors, 1978; has since appeared in

Head over Heels, 1979, Change of Seasons, 1980; TV appearances include The 5:48, for PBS, 1979.

Favourite part: Susie in Boy Meets Girl. *Address:* c/o Bill Treusch, 853 Seventh Avenue, New York, NY 10036.

HUSMANN, Ron, actor, singer

b Rockford, Ill, 30 Jun 1937; *s* of B J Husmann and his wife Emma (Ohlhues); *e* Northwestern University (BS 1959); *m* Patsy Peterson.

Made his stage debut as a member of the chorus of the Highland, Ill, Music Theater, summer, 1956; made his New York debut at the Theatre-in-the-Park, 21 July 1959, as Joey Biltmore in Guys and Dolls; Broadhurst, 23 Nov 1959, played a Card Player in Fiorello!; 46th Street, Oct 1960, played Tommy in Tenderloin; State Fair Music Hall, Dallas, Texas, summer 1961, Tommy in Brigadoon; Winter Garden, Mar 1962, Edwin Bricker in All American; toured, 1963, as Nestor in Irma la Douce; Majestic, Dec 1970, Captain Fisby in Lovely Ladies, Kind Gentlemen; Theatre Four, Mar 1971, Hector in Look Where I'm At!; Imperial, Oct 1971, Gabey in revival of On the Town; Minskoff, 1973, took over from Monte Markham as Donald Marshall in Irene; toured in this last part, Sept 1974–May 1975; first appeared on television on the Bell Telephone Hour, June, 1964, and subsequently became a regular on the Steve Allen Show, etc; recent appearances include Ziegfeld: A Man and His Women; National Chairman, Good Shepherd Lutheran Homes for the Retarded.

Recreation: Gardening. *Address:* Actors Equity Association, 165 West 46th Street, New York, NY 10036.

HUTT, William, actor and director

b Toronto, Canada, 2 May 1920; *s* of Edward De Witt Hutt and his wife Caroline Frances Havergal (Wood); *e* Vaughan Road Collegiate, North Toronto Collegiate, and Trinity College (University of Toronto); was a member of Trinity College Dramatic Society, 1946–8; and a student at the Hart House Theatre, University of Toronto, 1947–9.

Made his first professional appearance with the Bracebridge Summer Stock Company, Ontario, 1948; during the next five years toured Canada with various companies, and also played leading parts with summer stock companies; Stratford (Ontario) Shakespeare Festival, July 1953, played Sir Robert Brackenbury in Tyrone Guthrie's opening production of Richard III with Alec Guinness, subsequently appearing at the same theatre in the following parts: Froth in Measure for Measure, Chorus Leader in King Œdipus, Hortensio in The Taming of the Shrew, 1954; Old Gobbo in The Merchant of Venice, Ligarius in Julius Caesar, 1955; Ford in The Merry Wives of Windsor, Archbishop of Canterbury in Henry V, 1956; Polonius in Hamlet, 1957; Don Pedro in Much Ado About Nothing, 1958; Jacques in As You Like It, and Lodovico in Othello, 1959; Prospero in The Tempest, Banquo in Macbeth, and Carbon in Cyrano de Bergerac, 1962; Pandarus in Troilus and Cressida, Carbon in Cyrano de Bergerac, Alcibiades in Timon of Athens, 1963; the title-role in Richard II, Dorante in Le Bourgeois Gentilhomme, 1964; Shallow in Henry IV (Part II), Marcus Brutus in Julius Caesar, Gaev in The Cherry Orchard, 1965; Grand Duke Michael in Last of the Tsars, Chorus in Henry V, and Earl of Warwick in Henry VI, 1966; George in Richard II, Khlestakov in The Government Inspector, in which he also toured Canada and played at the Expo '67 in Montreal, and Enobarbus in Antony and Cleopatra, 1967; Tartuffe, Trigorin in The Seagull, and directed Waiting for Godot, 1968; again played Tartuffe, Sir Epicure Mammon in The Alchemist, and the Duke in Measure for Measure, 1969; appointed Associate

Director of the Stratford National Company, and again played Tartuffe on a Canadian tour, 1970; directed Much Ado About Nothing and played Volpone, 1971; directed As You Like It and played King Lear, 1972; toured Europe in the latter rôle, 1972–3; directed A Month in the Country and The Marriage Brokers, 1973; toured Australia as Argan in The Imaginary Invalid, 1973–4, repeating the role at Stratford, 1974, also playing Don Adriano in Love's Labours Lost; appointed director, Festival Stage, 1974; season 1975, directed Saint Joan, and Oscar Remembered, and played the Duke of Vienna in Measure for Measure, Capt Brazen in Trumpets and Drums and Lady Bracknell in The Importance of Being Earnest; 1976, co-directed Hamlet and The Tempest, played Prospero, The Duke in Measure for Measure, Chebutykin in the Three Sisters and repeated Lady Bracknell; in 1977 his parts were King of France in All's Well That Ends Well, Pastor Manders in Ghosts, and David Bliss in Hay Fever; in 1978 played Falstaff in The Merry Wives of Windsor, and the title-roles in Uncle Vanya and Titus Andronicus; 1979, Nestor in The Woman and Fool in King Lear, also repeating his performance as Lady Bracknell; following the Stratford Festival seasons, 1954–6, he toured Canada and the United States with the Canadian Players, playing the title parts in Hamlet and Macbeth, the Button Moulder in Peer Gynt, and the Earl of Warwick in St Joan; made his first appearance in New York at the Winter Garden, Jan 1956, as Teschelles in Tamburlaine the Great; Assembly Hall, Edinburgh Festival, Aug 1956, appeared with the Stratford (Ontario) Festival Company as the Chorus Leader in King Œdipus, and as the Archbishop of Canterbury in Henry V; Phoenix, NY, Nov 1957, played the Earl of Shrewsbury in Mary Stuart, and Dec 1957, Dr Kolonaty in The Makropoulos Secret; Bristol Old Vic, Mar 1959, appeared as James Tyrone in Long Day's Journey into Night; Salisbury Playhouse, Jan 1960, William Newton in The Truth About Billy Newton; Duke of York's, Sept 1960, played Alan Bennet in Waiting in the Wings; toured the US, Aug 1961, as Lawford Craig in Sail Away; with the Canadian Players toured Canada and USA as King Lear, and Thomas Mendip in The Lady's Not for Burning, 1961–2; toured Canada, with the same company, 1962–3, in a staged reading, Masterpieces of Comedy; toured Canada, 1963–4, as Elyot Chase in Private Lives; at the Chichester Festival Theatre, England, Apr 1964, appeared with the Stratford (Ontario) Company as Don Adriano in Love's Labour's Lost, Dorante in Le Bourgeois Gentilhomme, and Alcibiades in Timon of Athens; Billy Rose, NY, Dec 1964, played the Lawyer in Tiny Alice; Manitoba Theatre Centre, Winnipeg, Dec 1965, played in Andorra, and Mar 1966, Czar Nicholas II in Nicholas Romanov; toured Canada as Feste in Twelfth Night, 1967; Vivian Beaumont, NY, for Lincoln Center Repertory, Jan 1968, Earl of Warwick in Saint Joan; Theatre Toronto, Jan 1969, played Edward II in Marlowe's play of that name; Leatherhead, England, 1970, Caesar in Caesar and Cleopatra; Chichester Festival, 1970, played in Peer Gynt, Claude Nau in Vivat! Vivat Regina! and Epicure Mammon in The Alchemist; Artistic Director, Theatre London, Ont, where recent productions (1979) include Little Mary Sunshine (directed) and John A—Himself (title-role); his production of Oscar Remembered was seen at the Round House, London, Mar 1979; made his first film with Leonid Kipnis, as the Prologue and Chorus Leader in Œdipus Rex, 1956, and since has played Tsar Nicholas II in The Fixer, 1967; has appeared frequently on television in Canada, and also in England; first winner of the Tyrone Guthrie Award (1954) for acting and directing; received Doctorate of Fine Arts from University of Ottawa, 1969; Hon D Litt, Guelph University, 1974; made

companion of the Order of Canada, which is Canada's highest honour, in Dec 1969.

Favourite parts: Hamlet, James Tyrone in Long Day's Journey into Night. *Recreations:* Golf, swimming, fishing, and music. *Club:* Celebrity, Toronto. *Address:* 4 Waterloo Street N, Stratford, Ontario N5A 5H4, Canada

HUTTON, Geoffrey, drama critic
b Southampton, 18 Oct 1909; *s* of Thomas John Hutton and his wife Lavinia Annette; *e* King Edward's School, Southampton, Scotch College, Melbourne, Ormond College, Melbourne University; *m* (1) Necia Noel Bednall (dec); (2) Nancy Estelle Charlholmes.

Drama and ballet critic of the Argus, Melbourne, 1934–54; The Age, 1954–74; The Australian, 1975–present; his writings include Adam Lindsay Gordon, the Man and the Myth, It Won't Last a Week, Melba, and C J Dennis.

Recreations: Music, gardens. *Address:* 14 Stirling Street, Kew, Victoria 3101.

HYDE-WHITE, Wilfrid, actor
b Bourton-on-the-Water, Glos, 12 May 1903; *s* of William Edward White and his wife Ethel Adelaide (Drought); *e* Marlborough; *m* (1) Blanche Hope Aitken (Blanche Glynne) (dec); (2) Ethel Drew; studied for the stage at the Royal Academy of Dramatic Art.

Made his first appearance on the stage, at Ryde, Isle of Wight, Aug 1922, as Maitland in Tons of Money; made his first appearance in London, at the Queen's, 7 May 1925, as the Juror in Beggar on Horseback; Wyndham's, Feb 1926, played Courtier in The Firebrand; Prince of Wales, Feb 1927, Alphonse in The Rat; toured, 1928, in The Terror; St James's, Dec 1928, played the Avocat-Général in No Other Tiger; Queen's, Mar 1929, the Police Sergeant in The Man at Six; Ambassadors', Oct 1930, Salterthwaite in The Grain of Mustard Seed; Playhouse, May 1931, Mr Carrington in The Crime at Blossoms; toured, 1932, in South Africa; at the Aldwych, Jan 1933, played PC Peck in A Bit of a Test; Lyceum, Nov 1933, Marks in The Terror; Savoy, Mar 1935, the Marquess of Alresford in The Aunt of England; St Martin's, Jan 1936, General Gratz in Sauce for the Goose; Ambassadors', Mar 1936, The Man in Her Last Adventure; appeared in films only, from 1936–40; reappeared, at the Q, Apr 1940, as Captain Batty-Jones in A Lady Reflects; Embassy, May, and Criterion, June 1940, appeared in Come Out of Your Shell; Criterion, Sept 1940, in In Town Again; Comedy, June 1941–2, in two editions of Rise Above It; Comedy, June 1942, in It's About Time; Westminster, Oct 1944, played George Prout in It Depends What You Mean; toured, Apr 1946, as Kenneth Doble in Elusive Lady; Strand, July 1947, Charles Brunel in My Wives and I; made his first appearance in New York at the Shubert, 3 Oct 1947, as Sir Alec Dunne in Under the Counter; St James's, London, Apr 1948, Christopher Benson in Happy with Either; Duchess, Dec 1949, William Tracey in The Philadelphia Story; St James's, May 1951, appeared with Sir Laurence Olivier's company as Brittanus in Caesar and Cleopatra, and Lemprius Euphronius in Antony and Cleopatra; appeared with the same company in these productions at the Ziegfeld, NY, Dec 1951; next appeared in London at the Cambridge Theatre, Aug 1952, as Philip Russell in Affairs of State; Lyric, Apr 1954, played Henry in Hippo Dancing; Duchess, Feb 1955, appeared as William in A Kind of Folly; Cambridge Theatre, May 1955, played Jimmy Broadbent in The Reluctant Debutante; after more than a year in the London production, he left the cast to play the same part on Broadway, Henry Miller, NY, Oct 1956; Pavilion, Bournemouth, Sept 1957, played Anthony J Drexel Biddle in The Happiest Millionaire; Criterion, Mar 1958, Andrew Bennett in Not in the Book; Criterion, Sept 1962, Richard Pell in Miss Pell is Missing; Haymarket, May 1963, Sir Ralph Bloomfield-Bonington in The Doctor's Dilemma; Phoenix, Oct 1966, Lord Augustus Lorton in Lady Windermere's Fan; Duke of York's, Jan 1971, George Triple in Meeting At Night; Duke of York's, 1972, took over as the Marquis of Candover in The Jockey Club Stakes, playing the role at the Cort, NY, Jan 1973; Eisenhower Washington DC, Nov 1973, Father Perfect in The Prodigal Daughter, also touring the UK, May 1974, in this part; toured England, July 1975, as Andrew Bennett in Not in the Book; Phoenix, July 1976, Mackenzie Savage in The Pleasure of His Company; Arnaud, Guildford, Nov 1976, played the Earl of Caversham in An Ideal Husband; Shaftesbury, May 1977, Claude Johnson in Rolls Hyphen Royce; toured, Oct 1977, as Lord Chesterfield in A Perfect Gentleman; Arnaud, Sept 1978, again played Lord Augustus in Lady Windermere's Fan; made his first appearance in films, 1934, in Rembrandt, and has appeared in numerous pictures, recent films include: The Browning Version, The Million Pound Note, Betrayed, Quentin Durward, The March Hare, North West Frontier, Two Way Stretch, Let's Make Love, Ada, The Castaways, Crooks Anonymous, On the Fiddle, My Fair Lady, etc.

Recreations: Racing and cricket. *Clubs:* Green Room, and Buck's. *Address:* 30 South Audley Street, London, W1, and Palm Springs, Calif.

HYLAND, Frances, actress
b Saskatchewan, Canada, 25 Apr 1927; *d* of Thomas Hyland and his wife Jesse (Worden); *e* University of Saskatchewan; *m* George McCowan; studied for the stage at the Royal Academy of Dramatic Art.

Made her first appearance at the Aldwych, London, June 1950, when she took over as Stella Kowalski in A Streetcar Named Desire; at the Lyric, Hammersmith, Jan 1952, played Esther Brodsky in The Same Sky, and appeared in this part at the Duke of York's, Mar 1952; Strand, July 1952, played Mary Silver in The Step Forward; Savoy, Feb 1953, Hester Worsley in A Woman of No Importance; Q, Nov 1953, Gertie in Little Idiot; at the Lyceum, Edinburgh, Feb 1954, played Gelda in The Dark Is Light Enough; returned to Canada, Stratford Festival, Ontario, June 1954, to play Isabella in Measure for Measure, and Bianca in The Taming of the Shrew; at the same Festival, 1955, played Portia in The Merchant of Venice; toured with the Canadian Players, 1956–7, as Desdemona in Othello, and Ophelia in Hamlet; Stratford Festival, Ont, July 1957, again played Ophelia, and also Olivia in Twelfth Night; made her first appearance on Broadway, at the Ethel Barrymore Theatre, Nov 1957, when she played Laura James in Look Homeward, Angel; Stratford Festival, Ont, June 1959, played Desdemona in Othello, and Phebe in As You Like It; Piccadilly, London, Apr 1962, played Fleur-Therese Haugabrook in A Time to Laugh; Ethel Barrymore, New York, Nov 1962, Young Actress in Moby Dick; Chichester Festival Theatre, England, Apr 1964, appeared with the Stratford (Ontario) Company, as the Princess of France in Love's Labour's Lost, and Lucile in Le Bourgeois Gentilhomme; Stratford, June 1964, again played Lucile in Le Bourgeois Gentilhomme, and Goneril in King Lear; Stratford Festival, June 1965, Doll Tearsheet in Henry IV (Part II), Calpurnia in Julius Caesar, and Varya in The Cherry Orchard; Stratford Festival, 1967, Margaret in Richard III and Mistress Ford in The Merry Wives of Windsor; for the Shaw Festival at Niagara on the Lake, Ontario, 1968, played Lady Utterwood in Heartbreak House,

and Francine in Feydeau's The Chemmy Circle; Niagara on the Lake, 1971, the title-role of Candida; Washington, DC, Theater Club, May 1973, played in The Ecstasy of Rita Joe; Goodman Theater Center, Chicago, Oct 1973, appeared in The Freedom of the City; directed Private Lives for Manitoba Theatre Centre, Winnipeg, Apr 1976; Goodman, Chicago, Nov 1976, Mary Tyrone in Long Day's Journey into Night; Theater Calgary, Feb 1978, directed The Playboy of the Western World; appeared at the Shaw Festival, Niagara-on-the-Lake, season 1978; directed Othello for the Stratford Festival, 1979; has also appeared in leading parts at the Crest Theatre, Toronto, and made frequent appearances on television, including the series *The Great Detective* for CBC; films include The Changeling; Officer of the Order of Canada.

Recreations: Reading and walking. *Address:* PO Box 520, Stratford, Ontario N5A 6V2.

HYMAN, Earle, actor
b Rocky Mount, North Carolina, 11 Oct 1926; *s* of Zachariah Hyman and his wife Maria Lilly (Plummer); *e* Public School 26, and Franklin K Lane High School, Brooklyn, New York; studied with Eva Le Gallienne at the American Theatre Wing, with Robert Lewis, and at the Actors Studio, of which he has been a member since 1956.

First appeared on the NY stage at the American Negro Theatre, 1943, as the Diaperman in Three's a Family; Hudson, 1943, played in Run, Little Chillun; Mansfield, Aug 1944, Rudolf in Anna Lucasta; made his first appearance in London at His Majesty's, Oct 1947, in the same play and part; US tour, 1947, Everett du Shane in A Lady Passing Fair; Lenox Hill Playhouse, Apr 1949, Turner Thomas in Sister Oakes; Martin Beck, Nov 1952, Logan in The Climate of Eden; City Center, Mar 1953, played Prince of Morocco in The Merchant of Venice; Jan Hus Auditorium, Oct 1953, played the title-role in Othello, and Feb 1955, Prince of Morocco in The Merchant of Venice; American Shakespeare Festival, Stratford, Conn, 1955, Pindarus and Soothsayer in Julius Caesar and Boatswain in The Tempest; Alvin, Oct 1955, played a Lieutenant in No Time for Sergeants; Martin Beck, Mar 1956, the title-role in Mister Johnson; Stratford, Conn, June 1956, Melun in King John; Phoenix, Sept 1956, played Dunois in Saint Joan; Theatre de Lys, Jan 1957, Voice of the Player King in Hamlet; Ethel Barrymore, Jan 1957, played Vladimir in Waiting for Godot; Phoenix, Mar 1957, Antonio in The Duchess of Malfi; Stratford, Conn, June 1957, the Prince of Morocco in The Merchant of Venice and the title-role in Othello; Phoenix, Feb 1958, played Ghost of Laius in The Infernal Machine; Stratford, Conn, summer 1958, Horatio in Hamlet, Philostrate in A Midsummer Night's Dream, and Autolycus in The Winter's Tale; Royal Court, London, Dec 1958, Ephraim in Moon on a Rainbow Shawl; Adelphi, London, Aug 1959, Walter Lee in A Raisin in the Sun; Stratford, Conn, summer 1960, Caliban in The Tempest and Alexas in Antony and Cleopatra; Equity Library Theatre, NY, 1963, played in Mister Roberts; Bergen, Norway, 1963, played the title-role of Othello in Norwegian; US tour and Carnegie Recital Hall, Dec 1963, appeared in the concert reading The Worlds of Shakespeare; Stage 73, NY, Mar 1964, appeared in the Shakespeare anthology, The White Rose and the Red; toured Scandinavia, 1964, for the Norwegian State Travelling Theatre, appearing in Othello, The Emperor Jones, and scenes from Shakespeare in Norwegian; St Clement's Church, NY, Feb 1966, The Angel in Jonah; Vivian Beaumont, Jan 1968, Captain La Hire in Saint Joan; Repertory Theatre, St Louis, 1970, again played Othello; Longacre, Nov 1970, Abioseh Matoseh in Les Blancs; Theatre de Lys, Dec 1970, the title-role in The Life and Times of J Walter Smintheus; Center Stage, Baltimore, Md, played in The Seagull; Theatre de Lys, Jan 1973, directed and played Alex in Orrin; Anspacher, Jan 1973, Leonid Gayev in The Cherry Orchard; American Place, Oct 1973, various roles in House Party; Cincinnati, Ohio, Playhouse, 1974, played in Waiting for Godot; Richmond, Va, Feb 1976, again played The Emperor Jones; Hartman, Conn, Mar 1977, Dr Winston Gerrard in As to the Meaning of Words; Delacorte, NY, Aug 1977, Chorus Leader in Agamemnon; Roundabout, Jan 1978, title-role in Othello; Public/Anspacher, Jan 1979, Cicero in Julius Caesar; Public/Anspacher, Mar 1979, and Delacorte, June, Cominius in Coriolanus; Public/Other Stage, May 1979, Ezra Pilgrim in Remembrance; received a Norwegian Award as the Best Actor of the Year for his performance as The Emperor Jones; first appeared in films in 1954 in The Bamboo Prison, and has since played in The Possession of Joel Delaney (1972), etc; first appeared on television in 1953 and has played Adam Hezdrel in The Green Pastures, Jim in Huckleberry Finn, the Shepherd in Emmanuel, etc.

Favourite parts: Othello and Mister Johnson. *Recreations:* Languages, especially Norwegian and the study of Henrik Ibsen. *Address:* 109 Bank Street, New York, NY 10014. *Tel:* OR 5-2683.

I

IDE, Patrick, theatre manager
b Loughton, Essex, 21 Mar 1916; *s* of William Ide and his wife Sarah Eleanor (French); *e* Aldenham School.

Formerly an actor, commenced his career at the Castle Theatre, Rochester, 1931; in 1935, was appointed a director of Westminster Productions, Ltd; designed and painted for The Emperor of Make Believe, at the Westminster, 1936, and The New Comedy of Errors, Grafton, 1936; same year, organised the first season of plays at the People's Palace, Mile End; 1937–8, managed tours in Scandinavia and adjoining countries for Westminster Productions; co-presented his first West End play, Poison Pen, Shaftesbury, 9 Apr 1938; director of Piffard and Robinson Productions, lessees of the Duke of York's Theatre, 1943–50; with the late Hilda G Scott, formed the producing company of Scott and Ide, Ltd; served with the RAF, 1941–5; Publicity Manager for the Old Vic, 1950–61; licensee of the Saville Theatre 1953–5; appointed to the Council of Management of the Century Travelling Theatre, 1962; administrator of the Mermaid Theatre, 1962–4; consultant to the design of the new Sheffield Theatre, 1968, the new Lancaster Theatre and proposed St George's Theatre, Islington, 1969; originator (with James Verner) of The Black Mikado, 1975; appointed a governor of the Old Vic, 1978; consultant for the renovation of the Duke of York's Theatre, 1979; Managing Director, Theatre Investment Fund; Deputy Chairman, Actors' Charitable Trust.

Recreation: Swimming. *Clubs:* Green Room, Garrick. *Address:* Kidd's Hill Farm, Coleman's Hatch, Hartfield, Sussex. *Tel:* Forest Row 2421.

INGHAM, Barrie, actor
b Halifax, Yorkshire, 10 Feb; *s* of Harold Ellis Stead Ingham, and his wife Irene (Bolton); *e* Heath Grammar School, Halifax, Yorkshire; *m* Tarne Phillips; formerly an Officer in the Royal Artillery.

First appeared on the stage 2 Apr 1956, at the Pier Pavilion, Llandudno in Beggar My Neighbour, followed by a year at the Library Theatre, Manchester; first London appearance Sept 1957, at the Old Vic as Fortinbras in Hamlet; for the Old Vic company he subsequently played various parts in London and at the Sarah Bernhardt, Paris, including Lennox in Macbeth, 1958; Lelie in Sganarelle, Damis in Tartuffe, and Cecil Farringdon in The Magistrate, 1959; for the same company also played at the Edinburgh Festival in Julius Caesar and Mary Stuart; made his New York debut in Sept of that year as Claudio in Much Ado About Nothing, at the Lunt-Fontanne; returning to London, played Alan Howard in Joie de Vivre, Queen's, Feb 1960; Royal Court, Sept 1960, Henry Golightly in The Happy Haven; toured, Oct 1960, as Richard Adam in Strip the Willow; Gaiety, Dublin, June 1961, Percy French in The Golden Years followed by a season in the revue Pottering About at the Theatre Royal; Prince's, May 1962, appeared in the revue England, Our England; Mermaid, Apr 1963, Young Fashion in Virtue in Danger, transferring with the production to the Strand, June 1963; returned to the Mermaid to play Nicholas Stavrogin in The Possessed, Oct 1963, and Dionysus in The Bacchae, Feb 1964; Saville, 1964, took over as Jingle in Pickwick; at the same theatre, Apr 1966, played Clancy Pettinger in On the

Level; joined the Royal Shakespeare Company, Sept 1967, to play Lalo in Criminals; he has since appeared with the company at Stratford and at the Aldwych in roles including Buffalo Bill in Indians, Lord Foppington in The Relapse, Brutus in Julius Caesar, 1968; Leontes in The Winter's Tale (also touring Japan and Australia), Aguecheek in Twelfth Night, 1969; Dazzle in London Assurance, 1970; appeared in the RSC's Pleasure and Repentance, Edinburgh Festival, Aug 1970; April 1971 toured Australia in his one-man show, Love, Love, Love; Mermaid, Jan 1972, Love, Love, Love; Piccadilly, June 1973, Herbie in Gypsy; Vaudeville, March 1974, Ben in Snap; Sept 1974, played the Duke in Measure for Measure at Stratford; Feb 1975, toured Australia and multi-racial audiences in S Africa (July), in one-man show The Actor; His Majesty's, Melbourne, May 1975, directed Gypsy; Vaudeville, Nov 1975, Tony Price in Double Edge; Comedy, Melbourne, Sept 1976, Elyot Chase in Private Lives; Neighborhood Playhouse, New York, Oct 1978, appeared in The Actor, followed by American tours in 1978 and 1979; awarded Associate Artist Membership of Royal Shakespeare Company, 1974; Australian Theatre Most Distinguished Actor, 1975; UK Consultant to the International Theatre Arts Forum, 1976; Visiting Professor of Drama at the University of Texas at Austin, Texas, 1979; Drama Consultant to Baylor University, 1980; appeared frequently on television, in USA, on Masterpiece Theatre, and in Britain through six series—Hine, The Power Game, The Caesars, Beyond a Joke, The Victorians, and Funny Man (1980); favourite film roles, since 1961, include Robin in Challenge for Robin Hood, and St Clair in Day of the Jackal.

Recreations: Songwriting, riding. *Addresses:* c/o Milton Goldman, ICM, 40 West 57th Street, New York, NY 10019 *or* c/o Dennis Sellinger, ICM, 22 Grafton Street, London W1.

INNAURATO, Albert, playwright
b Philadelphia, Pa, 1948; *e* Yale School of Drama (MFA 1974).

Early works include Summit and Lytton Strachey Lucubrates de Rerum Sexualium; for Yale Cabaret, 1972, with Christopher Durang, wrote I Don't Generally Like Poetry but Have You Read 'Trees'?; has since written The Transfiguration of Benno Blimpie, produced Yale 1973, NY, 1976, London 1978; Gemini, 1976 (first Broadway production); Earthworms, Ulysses in Traction, 1977; has served as resident playwright with Circle Rep and the Public Theatre, NY.

Address: 244 Waverly Place, New York, NY 10014.

INNOCENT, Harold, actor
b Coventry, 18 Apr 1935; *s* of Harry Collins Harrison and his wife Jennie (Henry); *e* Broad Street Secondary School and Churchfield High School, Coventry; trained for the stage at the Birmingham School of Speech Training and Dramatic Art.

His first professional appearance, while still a student, was as a walk-on in Iphigenia in Aulis, Birmingham Rep, 195 ; after early rep experience in Felixstowe, Nottingham and Oldham, joined the Old Vic company in 1956 and remained with them until 1959, touring Europe and the US; went to Los Angeles, 1959, working there until 1962 and playing parts including Burgoyne in The Devil's Disciple at the Horseshoe Stage, and Shylock in The Merchant of Venice at the Rancho Playhouse; returned to England, 1962, and at the Mermaid, Apr 1963, played Bull in Virtue in Danger, transferring to the Strand, Jun; Mermaid, Aug 1963, Baloun in Schweyk in the Second World War; seasons followed with the Bristol Old Vic, with parts including the Dean in Dandy Dick, Stanley in The Birthday Party, Dame Chat in Gammer Gurton's Needle, etc; Nottingham Playhouse, playing the title role in Julius Caesar, Judge Brack in Hedda Gabler, Mephistopheles in Dr Faustus, etc; Edinburgh Festival, 1968, Giri in The Resistible Rise of Arturo Ui; Chichester, season 1969, Kazbeki in The Caucasian Chalk Circle, and Wycke in The Magistrate, transferring in the latter role to the Cambridge, Sept 1969; toured, 1970, with the New Shakespeare Company as Dogberry in Much Ado About Nothing; Young Vic, Feb 1971, God in The Wakefield Nativity Play and Hamm in Endgame; Chichester, season 1971, played Pothinus in Caesar and Cleopatra, General Hoetzler in Reunion in Vienna, and the Lawyer in Dear Antoine, transferring in the last role to the Piccadilly, Nov 1971; again at Chichester in 1972 to play Peachum in The Beggar's Opera, Grumio in The Taming of the Shrew, and Tappercoom in The Lady's Not for Burning; played the title role in Toad of Toad Hall at Chichester, Dec 1972; toured with Prospect, 1973–74, playing Malvolio in Twelfth Night, the Bawd in Pericles, Valverde in The Royal Hunt of the Sun, and Mr Worldly Wiseman in Pilgrim, and visiting Europe, Russia and the Middle East with the company, as well as a season at the Round House, Aug 1973, and a run of Pericles at Her Majesty's, May 1974; Young Vic, Nov 1974, Leonato in Much Ado About Nothing and the Major in Crete and Sergeant Pepper; University, Newcastle, 1976, Nebewohl in Sons of Light; Globe, Jul 1976, Rev R D Sainsbury in Donkey's Years; Hampstead, Jun 1977, Mambet in The Ascent of Mount Fuji; with Prospect at the Old Vic, Jun 1978, in the series Great English Eccentrics; joined the National Theatre, 1979, to play Sydney Ardsley in For Services Rendered, May, and Herbert Soppitt in When We Are Married, Dec; other recent appearances include regular seasons at the Bristol Old Vic, including Sheridan Whiteside in The Man Who Came to Dinner, 1978; TV work, since his first appearance in Hollywood, 1959, includes recently The Further Adventures of Oliver Twist, A Tale of Two Cities, etc.

Favourite parts: Sheridan Whiteside, Sydney Ardsley, General Burgoyne. *Recreations:* Music, history. *Address:* c/o Susan Angel Associates Ltd, 10 Greek Street, London W1V 5LE. *Tel:* 439 3086.

IONESCO, Eugène, dramatic author
b Slatina, Rumania, 26 Nov 1912; *s* of Eugène Ionesco and his wife Thérèse (Icard); *m* Rodica Burileanu; having lived from 1913–25 in Paris, he returned to Rumania to become a student of the Literature Faculty in Bucharest; formerly a teacher of French, and also a literary critic; in 1938, he received a Government Grant, and returned to Paris, becoming a French citizen.

His first play La Cantatrice Chauve (The Bald Prima Donna) was produced at the Théâtre des Noctambules, Paris, May 1950; he is the author of the following plays: La Cantatrice Chauve (The Bald Prima Donna), 1949; La Leçon (The Lesson), Jacques, ou la Soumission (Jacques, or Obedience), 1950; Les Chaises (The Chairs), L'Avenir est dans les Oeufs (The Future is in Eggs), 1951; Victimes du Devoir (Victims of Duty), 1952; Le Nouveau Locataire (The New

Tenant), 1953; Amédée, ou Comment s'en Débarrasser (Amédée, or How to Get Rid of It), 1954; L'Impromptu de L'Alma (Improvisation, or the Shepherd's Chameleon), Le Tableau (not published), 1955; Tueur sans Gages (The Killer), 1957; Rhinocéros, 1958; Scène à Quatre, 1959; Apprendre à Marcher (a pantomime-ballet), 1960; Le Piéton de l'Air (Pedestrian in the Air), Le Roi se Meurt (Exit the King), 1962; Bedlam Galore for Two or More (one-act), 1964; La Soif et La Faim (Hunger and Thirst), 1966; Jeux de Massacre, 1969; Macbett, 1972; Ce Formidable Bordel, 1974; The Man with the Suitcase, 1975; Entre la Vie et le Rêve (with Claude Bonnefoy), Antidotes, 1977; has written several sketches, including La Jeune Fille à Marier (Maid to Marry), 1960; the following are the short stories from which some of the plays were adapted: Oriflamme (Amédée, ou Comment s'en Débarasser), Une Victime du Devoir (Victimes du Devoir), La Photo du Colonel (Tueur sans Gages), and Rhinocéros; author of the narration for the Polish film Monsieur Tête which received the Prix de la Critique, Tours Festival, 1959; author of the episode Anger in the film Seven Capital Sins; Chevalier des Arts et Lettres, 1961; elected to Académie Française, 1970; Chevalier de la Légion d'Honneur, 1970.

Address: c/o C and B (Theatre) Ltd, 18 Brewer Street, London, W1.

IRELAND, Dr Kenneth, OBE, Festival Director and Secretary of Pitlochry Festival Theatre, Scotland
b Edinburgh, Scotland, 17 June 1920; *s* of Richard Morison Ireland, WS, and his wife Erna (Herrmann); *e* Edinburgh Academy and Edinburgh University (Bachelor of Law); *m* Moira Lamb; served as a L-Bdr in the Royal Artillery, 1941–2, and as a WO II in the Intelligence Corps, 1942–6, in World War II.

General Manager of the Park Theatre, Glasgow, 1946–9; studied for a summer session at the Pasadena Playhouse, California, 1947; General Manager of Pitlochry Festival Theatre, 1951–3; appointed General Manager and Secretary, 1953–7; appointed Festival Director and Secretary on the death of the Founder John Stewart, 1957; Pitlochry Festival Companies have toured to Northern Ireland, Coventry, Glasgow and Edinburgh, and (since 1967) regularly throughout Scotland; Chairman, Tourist Association of Scotland, 1967–9; Vice-Chairman, Scottish Tourist Consultative Committee, 1977–; elected Founder Fellow, Tourism Society (Scotland), 1978, Chairman, 1979–; Secretary, Federation of Scottish Theatres, 1966–9; Chairman, 1974–; Chairman, ABTT (Scotland), 1972–; has broadcast and lectured extensively at home and abroad; received the OBE in the New Year Honours, 1966, the E-SU in Scotland's William Thyne Award, 1970, and the honorary degree of DUniv from Stirling University, 1972.

Recreations: Music, travel and going to the theatre and art galleries. *Address:* Knockendarroch House, Pitlochry, Perthshire PH16 5DR, Scotland. *Tel:* 0796 2555.

IRVING, George S (*né* George Irving Shelasky), actor and singer
b Springfield, Massachusetts, 1 Nov 1922; *s* of Abraham Shelasky and his wife Rebecca (Sack); *e* Classical High School, Springfield, and Leland Powers School, Boston; *m* Maria Karnilova; prepared for the singing stage with Cora Claiborne, Henry Jacobi, Max Rudolph, William Tarrasch, Elena Gerhardt in London, and others.

First appearance on the stage was in Apr 1940, as the suitor in a school production of The Marriage Proposal; made his professional début in stock, at the Casino, Sandwich, Massachusetts, June 1941, in Dark Victory; continued in stock and in a touring production of The Student Prince, 1941; for the St Louis Municipal Opera Company, June 1942, played in Glamorous Night, Sally, Song of the Flame, Girl Crazy, Show Boat, and The New Moon; Paper Mill Playhouse, Millburn, New Jersey, Sept 1942, played in The Vagabond King, Babes in Toyland, and Robin Hood; made his Broadway début at the St James, 31 Mar 1943, in the chorus of Oklahoma!; appeared in the chorus of Lady in the Dark, 1943; joined the US Army and served until 1946; National, Apr 1946, appeared in the revue Call Me Mister; made his London début at the Aldwych, May 1948, singing Ben in the opera The Telephone and Mr Gobineau in the opera The Medium, repeating these roles at the Théâtre de La Renaissance, Paris, June 1948; Broadhurst, Jan 1949, appeared in the revue Along Fifth Avenue; Shubert, Philadelphia, Sept 1949, played the Senator in That's the Ticket; Ziegfeld, Dec 1949, played Mr Gage in Gentlemen Prefer Blondes; State Fair Music Hall, Dallas, Texas, summer 1952, Harry in A Tree Grows in Brooklyn, Dr Engel in The Student Prince, and Jigger in Carousel; Alvin, Dec 1952, played in the revue Two's Company; Majestic, May 1953, Dario in Me and Juliet; Her Majesty's, Montreal, Quebec, 1953, sang Varlaam in the opera Boris Godunov; Shubert, July 1954, took over from Hans Conried as Boris in Can-Can and subsequently toured in this part; Shubert, Nov 1956, Larry Hastings in Bells Are Ringing; New York City Center, Mar 1957, Mr Peachum in The Beggar's Opera; Broadway, Apr 1957, Big Bill in Shinbone Alley; Plymouth, Mar 1960, played various parts in The Good Soup; Shubert, New Haven, Connecticut, Apr 1960, Setmore in Lock Up Your Daughters; East 74th Street, May 1960, took over as McGee in Oh Kay; Plymouth, Oct 1960, the Inspector in Irma la Douce; Music Box, Jan 1962, Metallus in Romulus; Broadhurst, May 1962, Signor Bellardi in Bravo, Giovanni; Belasco, Oct 1962, Rosenzweig in Seidman and Son; Broadway, Mar 1963, Charles Davis in Tovarich; Morosco, Mar 1964, Marolles in A Murderer Among Us; Morosco, Dec 1964, Mr Smith in Alfie!; Ziegfeld, Nov 1965, Chernov in Anya; Vivian Beaumont, Apr 1967, Ballad Singer in Galileo; Broadway, Jan 1968, Phillippe Bonnard in The Happy Time; Jan Hus Playhouse, Nov 1968, Hannibal Beam in Up Eden; Promenade, June 1969, the Mayor in Promenade; Broadhurst, Jan 1971, TV Repairman, Real Estate Agent in Four on a Garden; Shubert, Apr 1972, Richard M Nixon in An Evening with Richard Nixon and . . .; Colonial, Boston, Nov 1972, Capitano Cockalorum in Comedy; Minskoff, Mar 1973, Madame Lucy in Irene, and received the Antoinette Perry (Tony) Award for this performance; Lunt-Fontanne, Dec 1974, Elbert C Harland in Who's Who in Hell; Hartman, Stamford, Conn, Nov 1975, The Mayor in The Government Inspector; Harkness, Apr 1976, played three parts in So Long, 174th Street; toured, Apr–Sept 1977, as Bob in the LA Civic Light Opera's Irma La Douce; PAF Playhouse, Huntington, Jan 1978, Chairman in Down at the Old Bull and Bush; Circle in the Square, June 1978, Herman Glogamer in Once in a Lifetime; Majestic, June 1979, Uncle Chris in I Remember Mama; has also appeared frequently in summer stock productions of musicals and plays, including South Pacific, The Remarkable Mr Pennypacker, Annie Get Your Gun, The Soft Touch, Silk Stockings, Fledermaus, The Boy Friend, Li'l Abner, Oh Captain! etc; has sung on television in *Barry Wood's Variety Show*, 1948, and since then in the operas Chicken Little, The Mighty Casey, The Sleeping Beauty, on *Omnibus*, etc.

Address: Actors Equity Association, 165 West 46th Street, New York, NY 10036.

IRVING, Jules (*né* Jules Israel), director and producer
b Bronx, New York, 13 Apr 1925; *s* of Jacob Israel and his wife Ida Siegel (Emanuel); *e* NY and Stanford Universities; *m* Priscilla Pointer; from 1949 to 1962 was Professor at San Francisco State College, teaching theatre history, acting, and directing.

Author of various children's theatre plays; began his professional career as an actor at the Center Stage, NY, 21 Jan 1939, in the play The American Way; played in other productions in NY and in stock; co-founded and was co-producing director with Herbert Blau, of The San Francisco Actor's Workshop, 1952, serving as actor, too, during the early days; directed his first play for the Workshop, Hotel Universe, on 28 Feb 1952, and since then directed I Am a Camera, Hedda Gabler, Blood Wedding, The Miser, Lysistrata, Death of a Salesman, Girl on the Via Flaminia, The Ticklish Acrobat, The Entertainer, The Plaster Bambino, The Rocks Cried Out, Krapp's Last Tape, The Zoo Story, Misalliance, Friedman and Son, Henry IV, The Glass Menagerie, Telegraph Hill, The Caretaker, The Wall, and co-produced more than 100 other plays; the Workshop toured regularly in the West, played six weeks in NY in 1958, and subsequently at the Brussels World's Fair, played at theatre festivals in Paris, Dublin, Berlin, Edinburgh, and Amsterdam; appointed Co-Director, with Herbert Blau, of The Repertory Theater of Lincoln Center on 25 Jan 1965; upon Mr Blau's resignation on 12 Jan 1967, became Director, in which position he functioned until 1973; for Lincoln Center has directed the productions of The Caucasian Chalk Circle, The Alchemist, An Enemy of the People, and, on the smaller stage The Forum, The Inner, Journey, The Birthday Party, Landscape, and Silence; directed the touring production of In the Matter of J Robert Oppenheimer; has produced, at the Vivian Beaumont, the Forum, and for Theater-in-the-Schools, a touring arm of the Lincoln Center, the following plays: Danton's Death, The Country Wife, 1965; The Condemned of Altona, The Caucasian Chalk Circle, The Alchemist, Yerma, 1966; The East Wind, Galileo, The Little Foxes in an invitational production by Saint-Subber, In White America, Walking to Waldheim, Happiness, 1967; Saint Joan, Tiger at the Gates, Cyrano de Bergerac, Summertree, King Lear, A Cry of Players, Bananas, An Evening for Merlin Finch, 1968; In the Matter of J Robert Oppenheimer, The Miser, The Inner Journey, The Year Boston Won the Pennant, The Time of Your Life, Camino Real, The Increased Difficulty of Concentration, 1969; Operation Sidewinder, Landscape, Silence, Beggar on Horseback revived as a musical, Amphitryon, The Good Woman of Setzuan, 1970; The Playboy of the Western World, The Birthday Party (also directed), Silence, Landscape (directed both), Antigone, An Enemy of the People (also directed), Mary Stuart (also directed), Play Strindberg, Kool Aid, People Are Living There, Delicate Champions, 1971; Narrow Road to the Deep North, The Ride Across Lake Constance, Anna Sokolow's Players Project, The Duplex, Twelfth Night, The Crucible, Suggs, Natural, Enemies, Happy Days, Act Without Words I, Krapp's Last Tape, 1972; The Plough and the Stars, The Merchant of Venice, A Streetcar Named Desire, 1973; also presented and directed the Broadway production of A Streetcar Named Desire at the St James, Oct 1973; was Founding Secretary and Former President of the Regional Theater Council of ANTA; former member of the Drama Advisory Panel of the Regional Arts Council of the San Francisco Bay Area; member of the board of directors of the Theatre Communications Group, and a member of its Executive Committee; former member of the Executive Board of the Society of Stage Directors and Choreographers; President,

Organization of Legitimate Theatres; member of the American Educational Theatres Association and of the Speech Association of America.

Club: Family (San Francisco).

IVES, Burl, actor, singer, author
b Hunt City Township, Illinois, 14 June 1909; *s* of Frank Ives and his wife Cordella; *e* Eastern Illinois State Teachers College, Juilliard School of Music; *m* Helen Peck Ehrlich.

During the Depression was a vagabond, working at odd jobs such as professional football, travelling with a tent show, singing with an evangelist's troupe, and collected folk music; made his New York début at the Shubert, May 1938, in I Married an Angel; Alvin, Nov 1938, played the Tailor's Apprentice in The Boys from Syracuse; National, Apr 1940, played in Heavenly Express; while serving in the US Army, at the Broadway, July 1942, played himself in This Is the Army, and subsequently toured; International, Dec 1944, played in the revue Sing Out, Sweet Land; New York City Center, Dec 1949, played Squire Hardcastle in She Stoops to Conquer; toured, 1952–3, as Ben Rumson in Paint Your Wagon, playing this part at the Blackstone, Chicago; New York City Center, May 1954, Captain Andy in Show Boat; Morosco, Mar 1955, Big Daddy in Cat on a Hot Tin Roof; Dallas Theatre Center, Dallas, Texas, Dec 1961, Joshua Beene in Joshua Beene and God; Belasco, Sept 1967, Dr Leonard Cook in Dr Cook's Garden; Nugget, Sparks, Reno, Nevada, July 1974, appeared in cabaret; entered films in 1946 in Smoky, and has since played in numerous films, including East of Eden, Cat on a Hot Tin Roof, The Big Country, for which he received the Academy Award in 1958, Our Man in Havana, Rocket to the Moon, The McMasters (1970), etc; was known as The Wayfaring Stranger, a singer of folk ballads, in a radio program of that name; has appeared frequently on television variety and musical programs and in the series OK Crackerby and The Bold Ones; has published several books of folk songs, including Burl Ives Song Book, Burl Ives Sea Songs, Burl Ives Book of Irish Songs, America's Musical Heritage—Song in America, Wayfarer's Note Book, his autobiography The Wayfaring Stranger, and others.

Address: Fitelson and Mayers, 1212 Avenue of the Americas, New York, NY 10036.

IZENOUR, George C, theatre consultant, inventor, and educator
b New Brighton, Pennsylvania, 24 July 1912; *s* of Charles Stevens Izenour and his wife Wilhelmina (Fresman); *e* Wittenberg College; *m* Hildegard Hilt.

Director of drama at Wittenburg College, 1934–36; director of lighting for WPA theatre projects in Los Angeles and San Francisco, 1936–39; founder, 1939, Yale research laboratory in technical theatre; professor of Theatre Design, Yale School of Drama, 1961–77; has served as theatre consultant to numerous projects in the US and abroad; inventor of various improvements in theatre lighting and technology; author of Theatre Design, 1977.

Address: 10 Alston Avenue, New Haven, Conn 06515. *Tel:* 387 7751.

J

JACKER, Corinne (*née* Corinne Litvin), writer
b Chicago, 27 June 1933; *d* of Thomas Henry Litvin and his wife Theresa; *e* Stanford University and Northwestern University; *m* Richard Edward Jacker (mar dis).

Her first play to be performed was The Scientific Method, at the American Shakespeare Festival, Stratford, Conn, 1970; subsequent plays include Seditious Acts, 1970; Travellers, 1973; Breakfast, Lunch and Dinner, Bits and Pieces, 1975; Harry Outside, Night Thoughts and Termina, Other People's Tables, 1976; My Life, 1977; After the Season, 1978; Later, 1979; Domestic Issues, 1980; writing for TV includes series episodes, and recently The Jilting of Granny Weatherall, 1980; author of various works of non-fiction, and poems; has taught playwriting at NYU, 1976–78, and Yale, 1979.

Address: 110 West 86th Street, New York, NY 10024. *Tel:* 787 4835.

JACKSON, Anne, actress
b Allegheney, Pa, 3 Sept 1926; *d* of John Ivan Jackson and his wife Stella Germaine (Murray); *e* Brooklyn, New York; *m* Eli Wallach.

Gained early experience at the Neighborhood Playhouse, NY, and studied for the stage under Sanford Meisner, Herbert Berghof, and Lee Strasberg at the Actors Studio; made her first appearance on the stage at Wilmington, Del, Dec 1944, as Anya in The Cherry Orchard; made her first appearance in NY at the City Center, 1 Jan 1945, as one of the guests in the same play; Forrest Theatre, Feb 1945, played Alice Stewart in Signature; subsequently toured, 1945, as Zelda Rainier in Dunnigan's Daughter; was engaged with the American Repertory Company, at the International Theatre, Nov 1946–Feb 1947, appearing in minor parts in What Every Woman Knows, Henry VIII, Androcles and the Lion, as Frida Foldal in John Gabriel Borkman, and Miss Blake in Yellow Jack; toured, 1947, as Bella in The Barretts of Wimpole Street; Belasco, Jan 1948, played Judith in The Last Dance; Music Box, Oct 1948, Nellie Ewell in Summer and Smoke; Mansfield, Apr 1949, Nita in Magnolia Alley; 48th Street, Nov 1949, Margaret Anderson in Love Me Long; Fulton, Aug 1950, Hilda in The Lady from the Sea; Arena (Hotel Edison), Oct 1950, Louka in Arms and the Man; Booth, Nov 1951, played Coralie Jones in Never Say Never; Henry Miller, Dec 1953, Mildred Turner in Oh, Men! Oh, Women!; ANTA, Feb 1956, the Daughter in The Middle of the Night; Martin Beck, 1957, followed Glynis Johns as Major Barbara in the play of the same name; Longacre, Jan 1961, Daisy in Rhinoceros; Theatre de Lys, Jan 1962, appeared in the concert reading Brecht on Brecht; Orpheum, Feb 1963, appeared with her husband in the double-bill The Tiger and The Typists; made her London stage début at the Globe, May 1964, in the last two plays; Booth, NY, Nov 1964, Ellen Manville in Luv; toured, 1966, in The Tiger and The Typists; John Golden, Apr 1968, The Actress in The Exercise; Music Box, Apr 1970, Ethel Rosenberg in Inquest; toured, summer 1971, as Mother H, Grandmother H, Doris, and Joan J in Promenade, All!; Alvin, Apr 1972, again played her parts in Promenade, All!; Eisenhower, Washington, DC, July 1973, Madame St Pé in The Waltz of the Toreadors; Joseph E Levine—Circle in the Square, Sept

1973, again played in this last part, and subsequently toured; Hartford, Conn, Stage Company, Dec 1974, Madame Ranevskaya in The Cherry Orchard; Public, NY, Jan 1977, Mrs McBride in Marco Polo Sings a Solo; Long Wharf, New-haven, Apr 1977, Diana in Absent Friends; toured with this production, summer 1977; Theatre Four, Dec 1978, Mrs Frank in The Diary of Anne Frank; has also played stock seasons in Bucks County, Clinton, NJ, etc, and with Equity Library and Actors Studio; entered films, 1950, in So Young, So Bad, and since has played in Zig Zag, Lovers and Other Strangers, The Secret Life of an American Wife, Dirty Dingus Magee, etc.

Favourite parts: Hilde in The Master Builder, and Anya in The Cherry Orchard. *Recreation:* Dancing. *Address:* c/o William Morris Agency, 1350 Avenue of the Americas, New York, NY 10019.

JACKSON, Freda, actress
b Nottingham, 29 Dec 1909; *d* of John Edward Jackson and his wife Mary (Stones); *e* High Pavement School and University College, Nottingham; *m* Henry Bird, ARCA.

She first appeared on the professional stage, with the Northampton Repertory company, 1 Jan 1934, as Ruth Rolt in Sweet Lavender, remaining with the company for two years, eventually playing leads; made her first appearance in London at the Q Theatre, 13 July 1936, as Nurse Wayland in The Sacred Flame; subsequently toured with Emlyn Williams as Nurse Libby in Night Must Fall; Old Vic, Oct–Dec 1936, played Lucy in The Country Wife and Audrey in As You Like It, again playing Audrey at the New Theatre, Feb 1937; Embassy, May, and Strand, June 1937, Mme Giulia Grevelli in Judgment Day; St James's, Nov 1937, Carlotta in The Silent Knight; King's, Hammersmith, Jan 1938, Kathie in Gaily We Set Out; Old Vic, Sept–Dec 1938, Avonia Bunn in Trelawny of the 'Wells', Player Queen in Hamlet (in its entirety and in modern dress) and Lucy in The Rivals; toured with the Old Vic company, Jan–Apr 1939, on the Continent and in Egypt, playing the same parts, and Abigail in Viceroy Sarah; Phoenix, Nov 1939, played Mme Crevelli in Judgment Day; in 1940–1, at the Stratford-on-Avon Memorial Theatre, played Katherine in The Taming of the Shrew, Mrs Malaprop in The Rivals, Nurse in Romeo and Juliet, Maria in Twelfth Night, and Mrs Quickly in The Merry Wives of Windsor; also toured for ENSA; New Theatre (with the Old Vic company), July–Aug 1942, played Emilia in Othello, and Mistress Ford in The Merry Wives of Windsor, and at the Playhouse Liverpool, with the same company, 1943, appeared as Clarissa in The Confederacy, and Irina in The Seagull; Playhouse, June 1943, Valya in The Russians; toured, Mar 1944, as Sally Furness in To-Morrow's Eden, and subsequently, for CEMA, as Stella in Eden End; Embassy, July 1945, scored a big success as Mrs Voray in No Room at the Inn; Aug 1945, again played Sally in To-Morrow's Eden; Winter Garden, May 1946, repeated her success in No Room at the Inn; at the Embassy, between 1947 and 1949, played Lydia in Deliver My Darling, Laura in The Father, and Claustrophobia in Cinderella or No Room in the Shoe; appeared at the Duchess, Jan 1949, as Laura in The Father; Embassy, Mar 1949, Emmy Baudine in They Walk Alone;

Playhouse, June 1949, Kate McShane in This Walking Shadow; toured, 1949, as Norah in The Righteous Are Bold, and 1950, as Janet in Deadlock; Q, Sept 1950, Anna in Anna Christie; toured, 1950, as Violet in Desire Shall Fail; Old Vic, Feb 1952, played Goneril in King Lear, and subsequently toured Northern Europe and Scandinavia in this part for the British Council; Victoria Palace, June 1952, played Helen Allistair in Women of Twilight; Q, Dec 1952, Jane Mannion in Tell Tale Murder; Embassy, Apr 1953, Sister Barton in Starched Aprons; also Aug 1953, Agatha Payne in The Old Ladies; Gaiety, Dublin, 1953, again appeared as Anna in Anna Christie; during 1954 made guest appearances at Windsor, Richmond, Northampton, etc, in Women of Twilight; at Northampton Repertory Theatre, July 1955, played Marguerite Gautier in a new translation of The Lady of the Camellias; toured, 1956, as the Mother in Intimate Relations; Phoenix, Apr 1957, played Gypsy in Camino Real; Apollo, Apr 1958, Barbette in Duel of Angels; Royal Court, Oct 1959, Mrs Hitchcock in Sergeant Musgrave's Dance; Mermaid, Feb 1961, played Gunhild Borkman in John Gabriel Borkman; Bristol Old Vic, Nov 1961, played the title-part in Mother Courage; Royal Court, Apr 1963, Onoria in Naked; New Lyric, Hammersmith, June 1964, played Alice Molland in The Man on the Stairs; toured, July 1964, as Grandma in Error of Judgement; toured, Sept 1965, as Mrs Dudgeon in The Devil's Disciple; toured, Mar 1967, in Arsenic and Old Lace; Belgrade, Coventry, Sept 1967, title role in Mother Courage; toured, 1969, as Grannie Whiteoaks in Whiteoaks; Strand, Nov 1970, Maria Helliwell in When We Are Married; Queen's, July 1972, played Livia in I, Claudius; toured, Aug 1973, as Phoebe Rice in The Entertainer; toured, Sept 1974, as Aunt March in Little Women; toured, Sept 1975, in Pride and Prejudice; Northampton Rep, Golden Jubilee, 1977, Lady Bracknell in The Importance of Being Earnest; has appeared in films, including Henry V, Great Expectations, No Room at the Inn, Women of Twilight, Bhowani Junction, Boy With a Flute, Tom Jones, House at the End of the World, etc; has also broadcast, and recent television appearances include She Fell Among Thieves and The Kilvert Diaries.

Favourite part: Mother Courage. *Recreations:* Reading, needlework and music. *Address:* c/o London Management, 235–241 Regent Street, London, W1.

JACKSON, Glenda, CBE (1978), actress
b Birkenhead, Cheshire, 9 May 1936; *d* of Harry Jackson, and his wife Joan; *e* West Kirby County Grammar School for Girls; *m* Roy Hodges (mar dis); trained for the stage at RADA.

First appeared on the stage in Feb 1957, at Worthing as a student in Separate Tables; first appearance on the London stage, Sept 1957, at the Arts, as Ruby in All Kinds of Men; Lyric, Hammersmith, Mar 1962, Alexandra in The Idiot; Mermaid, June 1963, played Siddie in Alfie, transferring with the production to the Duchess, July 1963; joined the Royal Shakespeare Company and appeared in the experimental Theatre of Cruelty season, LAMDA, Jan 1964; in the 1965 Stratford season, played the Princess of France in Love's Labour's Lost, Apr; Ophelia in Hamlet, Aug; at the Aldwych, played Eva in Puntila, July 1965; reader in The Investigation, Oct 1965; Charlotte Corday in the Marat/Sade, Nov 1965, repeating this performance in her New York début at the Martin Beck, Dec 1965 and receiving the *Variety* award as the most promising actress; Aldwych, Oct 1966, took part in US; Royal Court, Apr 1967, Masha in Three Sisters; Fortune, Nov 1967, Tamara Fanghorn in Fanghorn; Duchess, Apr 1973, Katherine Winter in Collaborators; Greenwich,

Feb 1974, Solange in The Maids; toured Britain, USA and Australia, 1975, as Hedda Gabler in a Royal Shakespeare Company production, which was also seen at the Aldwych, July 1975, Old Vic, July 1976, Vittoria Corombona in The White Devil; Vaudeville, Mar 1977, played the title-role in Stevie; for the RSC at Stratford, Oct 1978, Cleopatra in Antony and Cleopatra, and at the Aldwych, July 1979; Duke of York's, Mar 1980, title-role in Rose; films since 1968, include Women in Love (Oscar), Sunday Bloody Sunday, The Music Lovers, A Touch of Class (Oscar), Sarah, House Calls, Lost and Found; Hedda Gabler and Stevie have also been filmed; television since 1960 includes the series *Elizabeth R.*; received an Hon DLitt, Liverpool University, 1978.

Recreations: Reading, driving and travel. *Address:* c/o Crouch Associates, 59 Frith Street, London W1.

JACKSON, Gordon, OBE, actor
b Glasgow, 19 Dec 1923; *s* of Thomas Jackson and his wife Margaret (Fletcher); *e* Hillhead High School, Glasgow; *m* Rona Anderson; formerly a draughtsman.

Made his first stage appearance in 1943 at the MSU Theatre, Rutherglen, Scotland, as Dudley in George and Margaret; after repertory experience in Glasgow, Worthing and Perth, made his London début at the Apollo, Jan 1951, when he took over as Able Seaman McIntosh in Seagulls Over Sorrento; Duke of York's, July 1955, played the Young Actor (Ishmael) in Moby Dick; Sadler's Wells, July 1958, narrated The Soldier's Tale; Royal Court, Oct 1966, Banquo in Macbeth; Edinburgh Festival, Sept 1967, again narrated The Soldier's Tale; Garrick, Oct 1967, Mr Booker in Wise Child; Royal Court, Dec 1968, Baxter in This Story of Yours; Round House, Feb 1969, Horatio in Hamlet, receiving the Clarence Derwent Award for his performance: made his New York début in the same production at the Lunt-Fontanne, May 1969; Playhouse, Oxford, Oct 1969, played Alfred in The Signalman's Apprentice; Stratford, Ontario, June 1970, Tesman in Hedda Gabler; with the Young Vic, Sept 1970, played Creon in Oedipus and again narrated The Soldier's Tale; Royal Court, July 1971, Interrogator in The Lovers of Viorne; same theatre, March 1972, Rodney in Veterans; toured, March 1973, as David in What Every Woman Knows; Aldwych, March 1975 (for RSC), Banquo in Macbeth; Chichester Festival, May 1976, title-role in Noah, and Malvolio in Twelfth Night; film appearances, since his first in 1941, include Tunes of Glory, The Great Escape, and The Prime of Miss Jean Brodie; television, since 1955, includes *Upstairs, Downstairs,* for which he received the Royal Television Society Award, 1975 and, in 1976, an Emmy; and, most recently, The Professionals.

Recreations: Music and gardening. *Address:* c/o ICM Ltd, 22 Grafton Street, London W1X 3LD.

JACOBI, Derek, actor
b London, 22 Oct 1938; *s* of Alfred George Jacobi, and his wife Daisy Gertrude (Masters); *e* Leyton County High School and St John's College, Cambridge.

After appearances in leading roles with the National Youth Theatre, and with the ADC and Marlowe Society at Cambridge, joined the Birmingham Repertory Theatre, making his first professional appearance on 20 Sept 1960, as Stanley Honeybone in One Way Pendulum; at the Chichester Festival, 1963, played Brother Martin in Saint Joan, June, and PC Liversedge in The Workhouse Donkey, July; joined the National Theatre Company, making his London début at the Old Vic, Oct 1963, as Laertes in Hamlet, and until 1971 appeared regularly in the company's repertoire, playing numerous parts including Felipillo in The Royal Hunt of the Sun, Cassio in Othello (both also Chichester), Simon Bliss in Hay Fever, 1964; Don John in Much Ado About Nothing, Brindsley Miller in Black Comedy (Chichester), 1965; the latter part also at the Old Vic and Queen's, 1966; Tusenbach in Three Sisters, Touchstone in As You Like It, 1967; King of Navarre in Love's Labour's Lost, 1968; Edward Hotel in Macrune's Guevara, Adam in Back to Methuselah, 1969; Myshkin in The Idiot, Lodovico in The White Devil, 1970; Sir Charles Mountford in A Woman Killed with Kindness, 1971; Greenwich, Oct 1971, Orestes in Electra; for Birmingham Rep, May 1972, played the title role in Oedipus Rex and Mr Puff in The Critic, in a double bill; for Prospect Theatre Company played Ivanov, Nov 1972; Buckingham in Richard III, 1972; Sir Andrew Aguecheek in Twelfth Night and the title role in Pericles, 1973 (including European and Middle East tour); played Pericles at Her Majesty's, London, June 1974; Chichester Festival, July 1974, Rakitin in A Month in the Country; toured, Jan 1975, in The Hollow Crown and Pleasure and Repentance; Arnaud, Guildford, Aug 1975, played Will Mossop in Hobson's Choice; with Prospect, Nov 1975, played Rakitin in A Month in the Country, and Cecil Vyse in A Room with a View, at the Albery; for the same company, at the Old Vic, appeared as Hamlet and as Octavius Caesar in Antony and Cleopatra, 1977 season; played Thomas Mendip in The Lady's Not For Burning and the title-role in Ivanov, 1978 season, also appearing that year at the same theatre in The Lunatic, The Lover and The Poet, and The Grand Tour (in the triple-bill, Great English Eccentrics); July 1979, played Hamlet for Prospect for a second season at the Old Vic, subsequently touring with that production in Scandinavia (including Elsinore), Australia, Japan and China (first Western theatre tour of China); first film, 1965, Othello; subsequently appeared in The Day of the Jackal, The Odessa File, and The Human Factor; has appeared on television, notably in *The Pallisers, I, Claudius,* Man of Straw, Philby, Burgess and Maclean, and Richard II.

Recreations: Music and reading. *Address:* c/o ICM Ltd, 22 Grafton Street, London W1.

JACOBI, Lou, actor
b Toronto, Ontario, Canada, 28 Dec 1913; s of Joseph Jacobi and his wife Fay; e Jarvis Collegiate School; m Ruth Ludwin.

Made his stage début at the Princess, Toronto, 1924, as the Young Hero in The Rabbi and the Priest; made his professional début at the Museum, Toronto, 1949, in the revue Spring Thaw; made his London début at Her Majesty's, 16 Dec 1952, as Morris Rosenberg in Remains to Be Seen; Prince's, Mar 1954, Ludlow Lowell in Pal Joey; Embassy, Jan 1955, Father Abraham in Bontche Schweig, Rabbi David in A Tale of Chelm, and the Russian Tutor in The High School in the production with the overall title The World of Sholom Aleichem; Streatham Hill, May 1955, played Miller in Into Thin Air; made his New York début at the Cort, 5 Oct 1955, as Mr Van Daan in The Diary of Anne Frank; toured in this last part, 1957–8; Booth, Nov 1959, Schlissel in The Tenth Man; Brooks Atkinson, Feb 1961, Mr Baker in Come Blow Your Horn; Mark Hellinger, May 1964, Lionel Z Governor in Fade Out—Fade In; Mark Hellinger, Feb 1965, again played Lionel Z Governor in Fade Out—Fade In; Morosco, Nov 1966, Walter Hollander in Don't Drink the Water; ANTA, Jan 1969, Max Krieger in A Way of Life; Lyceum, Feb 1970, Ben Chambers in Norman, Is That You?; Plymouth, Oct 1971, Epstein in Epstein and Tzuref in Eli, the Fanatic, in the triple-bill Unlikely Heroes; Waldorf-Astoria, May 1972, appeared in the Milliken Breakfast Show; summer 1974, took over as Al Lewis in The Sunshine Boys on tour

and continued touring; Biltmore, Jan 1978, Howard in Cheaters; entered films in England, 1956, in A Kid for Two Farthings, and has since appeared in The Diary of Anne Frank, Song Without End, Irma la Douce, Everything You've Ever Wanted to Know About Sex But Were Afraid to Ask, etc; first appeared on television in London, 1954, on *The Rheingold Theatre,* and in the USA has played on *The Milton Berle Show, The Defenders, Alfred Hitchcock Presents, The Dean Martin Show,* and various other dramatic and variety programs.

Address: Actors Equity Association, 165 West 46th Street, New York, NY 10036.

JACOBS, Sally (*née* Rich), designer
b London, 5 Nov 1932; d of Bernard Maxwell Rich and his wife Esther (Bart); e St Martin's School of Art and Central School of Arts and Crafts, London; m Alexander Jacobs.

Formerly a film continuity girl; designed her first production, Five Plus One, for the Edinburgh Festival, Aug 1961; her first London production was Twists, Arts, Feb 1962; she has since designed the following productions, largely for the Royal Shakespeare Company: Women Beware Women, The Empire Builders, London, 1962; Theatre of Cruelty, The Screens, The Formation Dancers, The Marat/Sade, London, 1964; Love's Labour's Lost, Stratford, The Marat/Sade, New York, 1965; Twelfth Night, Stratford, US, London, 1966; Muzeeka, Los Angeles, 1968; A Midsummer Night's Dream, Stratford, 1970 and NY, 1971; Brecht: Sacred and Profane, for the Mark Taper Forum, Los Angeles, and Ajax, for the Forum's Laboratory, 1973–4 season; Savages, LA, 1974; directed Oedipus at Colonus, Forum Laboratory, Oct 1975; has regularly designed productions at the Mark Taper Forum, including The Three Sisters, Ashes, Cross Country, 1975–6; Gethsemane Springs, 1977; décor for Ice, NY, 1979; film work includes costumes for Nothing But the Best and Catch Us If You Can, designs for the film of Marat/Sade; lecturer in theatre design, California Institute of the Arts, Los Angeles, 1970–.

Address: Mark Taper Forum, 135 North Grand Avenue, Los Angeles, Calif 90012.

JACQUES, Hattie (*née* Josephine Edwina Jacques), actress
b Kent, 7 Feb 1924; d of Robin Rochester Jacques and his wife Mary Adelaide (Thorn); e Godolphin and Latymer School; m John Le Mesurier (mar dis).

Made her first appearance on the stage Player's Theatre, Aug 1944, and subsequently played at the same theatre in pantomimes, plays and revues; toured with the Young Vic Company, 1947–8, as Smeraldina in The King Stag; Players', Dec 1948, played the Fairy Queen in The Sleeping Beauty in the Wood; Players', Dec 1949, played Marygolda in Beauty and the Beast, Players', Dec 1950, played Cogia Baba, adapted and contributed lyrics (with Joan Sterndale Bennett) to Ali Baba; Players', Dec 1951, played the Fairy Queen, and adapted (with Joan Sterndale Bennett), Riquet With The Tuft; St Martin's, Aug 1952, appeared in the revue The Bells of St Martin's; Players', Dec 1953, played Fairy Fragrant, and adapted Cinderella, a Victorian pantomime; Players', Apr 1954, directed The Players' Minstrels; Players', Dec 1954, played Fairy Antidota in The Sleeping Beauty in the Wood; Players', May 1955, directed Twenty Minutes South, transferring to the St Martin's, July 1955; Westminster, May 1956, played Madame Leonie Urwig in Albertine by Moonlight; Players', Dec 1956, adapted (with Joan Sterndale Bennett), Ali Baba; Palladium, May 1958, appeared in the revue Large as Life; Players', Dec 1960, adapted (with Joan Sterndale Bennett) Riquet With The Tuft; toured, May 1979, in Hatful of Sykes; made her first appearance in films in 1946, and has since appeared in numerous pictures including Nicholas Nickleby, The Magic Christian, and the Carry On series; television appearances include No, No, Nanette and several series, in particular with Tony Hancock and Eric Sykes; directed television Minstrel Show; radio performances include Itma, 1948–9, Educating Archie, 1950–4.

Favourite part: Fairy Queen, Victorian pantomime. *Recreations:* Collecting records, old theatre postcards. *Address:* c/o Felix De Wolfe, Robert Street, Adelphi, London, WC2.

(*Died Oct 1980.*)

JAFFE, Sam, actor
b New York City, 8 Mar 1893; s of Bernard Jaffe and his wife Ada (Steinberg); e New York City College (BSc) and Columbia University; m (1) Lillian Taiz (dec); (2) Bettye Ackerman.

Made his first appearance on the stage with the Washington Players, at the Bandbox Theatre, NY, 1915, in The Clod; toured with that organization for some time and then toured in repertory with the Kearn's-Sommes Shakespeare Company; Comedy, Feb 1918, The Minister in Youth; Comedy, Mar 1918, Rev Samuel Gardner in Mrs Warren's Profession; Greenwich Village, Nov 1920, played Kristensen in Samson and Delilah; Plymouth, Dec 1921. Leibush in The Idle Inn; Provincetown, Dec 1922, Reb Ali in The God of Vengeance; Klaw, Mar 1924, Izzy Goldstein in The Main Line; Broadhurst, Sept 1924, Eli Iskovitch in Izzy; Provincetown, Apr 1925, Lum Crowder in Ruint; Fulton, Sept 1925, Yudelson in The Jazz Singer, which he played for three years; National, Nov 1930, Kringelein in Grand Hotel; Henry Miller Theatre, Sept 1934, Herchkowitz in The Bride of Torozko; Manhattan Opera House, Jan 1937, the Adversary in The Eternal Road; Morosco, Dec 1937, Nils Krogstad in A Doll's House; Penn State University, 1938, Shylock in The Merchant of Venice; Belasco (for the Group Theatre), Jan 1939, Jonah Goodman in The Gentle People; toured, 1941, as Rosenbaum in The King's Maid; New School, 1941, played King Lear; at the Cort, Jan 1942, played Hymie in Café Crown; Mansfield, Mar 1944, played Svoboda in Thank You, Svoboda; in Chicago, 1946–7, appeared in The Greatest of These; Barrymore, NY, Nov 1947, played Wouterson in This Time Tomorrow; Brattle, Cambridge, Mass, 1950, played Tartuffe, and repeated this role at the Ivor, Hollywood, 1952; in summer theatres, 1952, appeared as Paul Virag in Blue Danube, which he adapted: Longacre, NY, Jan 1954, played Gourette in Mademoiselle Colombe; Phoenix, May 1954, Peter Sorin in The Seagull; toured, Sept–Nov 1954, as the Inquisitor in Saint Joan; Kauffman Auditorium, 1956, played the title-role of Tartuffe; toured, 1956, as Cauchon in The Lark; Phoenix, Feb 1956, Zero in The Adding Machine; Ahmanson, Los Angeles, Mar 1970, Dr Waldersee in Idiot's Delight; Dickinson State College, ND, 1971, Shylock in the Merchant of Venice; Off-Broadway Theatre, San Diego, Cal, 1972, Shaddick in Storm in Summer; Palace, NY, Mar 1979, Tarun Maharaj in A Meeting by the River; with George Freedley founded the Equity Library Theatre in 1944; entered films, 1934, in The Scarlet Empress, and has since played in many films, including Lost Horizon, Gunga Din, 13 Rue Madeleine, Gentlemen's Agreement, Asphalt Jungle for which he received the Venice International Award in 1950, Ben Hur, Les Espions in French, QB VII (1975), etc; on television played Dr Zorba in *Ben Casey*, 1961–5 and has appeared in many other series and dramatic programs; received the Paul Robeson Award, 1978.

Address: 302 North Alpine Drive, Beverly Hills, Calif 90210.

JAGO, Raphael Bryan, principal and administrator of the Webber Douglas Academy of Dramatic Art
b Falmouth, 7 Aug 1931; s of Cecil George Jago and his wife Cora Ethel; e Falmouth Grammar School; m Penelope Jane Garton (mar dis); trained for the stage at the Guildhall School of Music and Drama; formerly an assistant piano buyer and international telephone operator.

Directed the opening production at the Middlesborough Little Theatre, Caesar and Cleopatra, 1957; directed seasons at the Theatre Royal, York, and Opera House, Harrogate, 1958; assistant to Joan Littlewood at the Theatre Royal, Stratford E, 1959; principal and administrator of the Webber Douglas Academy of Dramatic Art, London; chairman, 1978–80, Conference of Drama Schools; chairman, British Theatre Institute; hon secretary, Drama and Theatre Education Council.

Address: Webber Douglas Academy, 30–36 Clareville Street, London SW7. *Tel:* 370 4154.

JAMES, Brian, actor
b Maryborough, Victoria, 5 Jul 1920; s of Melville Charles James (formerly Bishop of St Arnaud, Victoria) and his wife Cecile Edith Kingston (Vickery); e Ballarat Church of England Grammar School and Associated Teachers' Training Institute, Melbourne; trained for the stage at the Central School, London; formerly a schoolmaster.

Made his first stage appearance in the part of Fred in Present Laughter, Princess, Melbourne, 1948; after training at the Central School, understudied the part of P/O Herbert in Seagulls over Sorrento, at the Apollo, 1951, and returned to Australia, 1952, to play the part on tour; 1952–55 toured in this part and subsequently in Reluctant Heroes, Charley's Aunt, and Worm's Eye View; in 1960–61 toured as Bernie Dodd in Winter Journey, and Bernard Kersal in The Constant Wife; Adelaide Festival, 1961, and tour, The Inquisitor in Saint Joan; with the Melbourne Theatre Company, 1963–66, numerous roles included Anderson in The Devil's Disciple, Rev Wakeman in A Cheery Soul, Claudius in Hamlet, George in Who's Afraid of Virginia Woolf?, the Cardinal in The Representative, the Old Prince in War and Peace, and Tobias in A Delicate Balance; with the Independent Theatre, Sydney, 1967–68, played Harry in Staircase, Wacka in The One Day of the Year, and the Bishop of Chelsea in Getting Married; appearances with the Old Tote Company, Sydney, 1963–75, include Biedermann in The Fire Raisers, Undershaft in Major Barbara, Sir William Gower in Trelawny of the 'Wells', and Jack in Home; 1969–73, for Melbourne Theatre Company, played many parts including Bishop Bell in Soldiers, Walter Franz in The Price, King of France in Tyrone Guthrie's All's Well That Ends Well, Gloucester in King Lear, Kite in The Recruiting Officer, and Archie in Jumpers; with the South Australian Theatre Company, Adelaide, 1973–78, his parts included James Tyrone in Long Day's Journey into Night, Menenius in Coriolanus, Mr Hardcastle in She Stoops to Conquer, Gayev in The Cherry Orchard, Joe Keller in All My Sons, Brighella in The Servant of Two Masters, and the title role in Cymbeline; Her Majesty's, Melbourne, 1976, played Chaucer in More Canterbury Tales; for Queensland Theatre Co, Brisbane, 1979, William in You Never Can Tell; films include On the Beach, 1959, Between the Wars, and The Fourth Wish, 1975; frequent appearances on Australian TV in plays and series, recently Skyways, 1979.

Favourite parts: Harry in Staircase, the Cardinal in The Representative, and Gloucester in King Lear. *Recreations:* Visiting islands, writing. *Address:* 12 William Street, South Yarra, Victoria 3141. *Tel:* 241 6200.

JAMES, Emrys, actor

b Machynlleth, Montgomeryshire, 1 Sept 1930; *s* of James Harold James, and his wife Elen (Roberts); *e* Machynlleth Grammar School and University of Wales; *m* Sian Davis; trained for the stage at RADA.

First appeared on the stage Sept 1954, at the Playhouse, Liverpool, as Dudley in The Young Elizabeth; at Stratford, 1956, played Guildenstern in Hamlet and Claudio in Measure for Measure; joined the Bristol Old Vic, 1958–9, where his parts included Touchstone in As You Like It and the Narrator in Under Milk Wood; first appeared on the London stage Sept 1959, at the New, as Private Evans in The Long and the Short and the Tall; at the Old Vic, 1960–2, he played Feste in Twelfth Night, Malcolm in Macbeth, and Richmond in Richard III; Sunderland Empire, Feb 1963, played the title part in the North East Theatre Festival production of Hamlet; Lyric, 1964, took over Juror no 9 in Twelve Angry Men; at the Ludlow Festival, June 1965, again played Hamlet; joined the Royal Shakespeare Company, 1968, playing the following parts, at the Aldwych unless otherwise stated: Sir Hugh Evans in The Merry Wives of Windsor (also Stratford) Sitting Bull in Indians, Worthy in The Relapse, 1968; Gower in Pericles (Stratford), 1969; the Boss in The Plebeians Rehearse the Uprising, Feste in Twelfth Night, Cranmer in Henry VIII (these two also Stratford 1969), 1970; Cardinal in The Duchess of Malfi, Shylock in The Merchant of Venice, Iago in Othello (all three at Stratford), 1971; Iago, Merlin in The Island of the Mighty, 1972; Mephistophilis in Dr Faustus, 1974; title role in King John (previously Stratford), 1975; Stratford, season 1975, played Chorus in Henry V, the title role in both parts of Henry IV, and Sir Hugh Evans in The Merry Wives of Windsor, repeating Chorus and Henry IV at the Aldwych, Jan 1976; Old Vic, May 1977, Cauchon in Saint Joan; Stratford, June 1977, and Aldwych, Apr 1978, played York in all three parts of Henry VI; Stratford, Sept 1977, and Aldwych, Sept 1978, Jacques in As You Like It; The Other Place, Jan 1978, and Warehouse, Apr 1978, Edgar in The Dance of Death; Aldwych, Oct 1978, De Flores in The Changeling; is a Royal Shakespeare Company associate artist; films since 1963 include Darling, The Man in the Iron Mask, and In Search of Eden; has appeared regularly on television since 1957, most recently in Testament of Youth.

Recreations: Cats, art, books, music, France, acoustic gramophone. *Address:* c/o John Cadell Ltd, 2 Southwood Lane, London N6. *Tel:* 01–348 1914.

JAMES, Gerald, actor

b Brecon, South Wales, 26 Nov 1917; *e* Brecon Boys' Grammar School; *m* Joan James; formerly a County Youth Employment Officer; trained for the stage at RADA.

Made his first London appearance Sept 1958 at the Old Vic, as Davison in Mary Stuart; played a number of parts with the Old Vic Company, 1958–62, including Gonzalo in The Tempest, Sir Hugh Evans in The Merry Wives of Windsor, Fluellen in Henry V, Friar Laurence in Romeo and Juliet, Glendower in Henry IV etc; made his New York début with the company at the City Center, Feb 1962, repeating the part of Friar Laurence; Saville, July 1963, played Tupman in Pickwick, remaining with the cast until 1965, when he joined the National Theatre Company at the Old Vic; his parts 1965–71 included Leonato in Much Ado About Nothing, Telfer in Trelawny of the 'Wells', Corin in As You Like It, M

Loyal in Tartuffe, 1967; Dull in Love's Labour's Lost, 1968; Capt Jones-Parry in H, Rees in The National Health, 1969; Boniface in The Beaux' Stratagem, Ragueneau in Cyrano, 1970; Policeman, Governor and Porter in The Captain of Köpenick, 2nd Lictor in Coriolanus, William Blake in Tyger (New Theatre), Butler in The Good-Natured Man, 1971; joined the RSC at Stratford, season 1972, to play Junius Brutus in Coriolanus, Casca in Julius Caesar, Angelo in The Comedy of Errors and Sextus Pompeius in Antony and Cleopatra; Royal Court, Apr 1974, and Duke of York's, June 1974, Philips in Life Class; Comedy, June 1976, Brigot in Signed and Sealed; recent television includes Sally Ann, and Sapphire and Steel.

Recreations: Cricket. *Clubs:* MCC and Glamorgan. *Address:* 8 The Green, Aston Rowant, Oxford. *Tel:* 0844 52673.

JAMES, Peter, director

b Enfield, Middx, 27 July 1940; *s* of Arthur Leonard James and his wife Gladys (King); *e* Enfield G S, Birmingham University and Bristol University.

Co-founder and Associate Director, Everyman Theatre, Liverpool, 1964–7, where he directed his first professional production, The Caretaker, in Autumn 1964; Artistic Director 1967–70; directed over thirty productions for the Everyman, also visiting the US twice; Associate Director, Young Vic, 1970–2, for whom his productions included The Wakefield Mystery Plays, Little Malcolm, Happy Days and Endgame (double bill), Romeo and Juliet, Julius Caesar, The Dwarfs, The Shadow of a Gunman, The Painters, and The Comedy of Errors (Edinburgh Festival); Artistic Director, Shaw Theatre, Jan–June 1974, directing Mind Your Head, The Importance of Being Earnest, and The King; Artistic Director, Crucible Theatre, Sheffield, 1974–, where his productions to date include No Good Friday, Nongogo, Charley's Aunt, Waiting for Godot, Dracula, As You Like It, Cabaret, Travesties, The Second Mrs Tanqueray, Much Ado About Nothing, and Chicago (which transferred to the Cambridge Theatre, London, in Apr 1979); other productions he has directed include Oh What a Lovely War (Sheffield), Bakke's Night of Fame (Shaw), Twelfth Night (National Theatre Mobile Production), 1972; Jumpers, Old Times (both Melbourne), A Slight Ache (RSC), As You Like It (Cameri, Tel Aviv: own musical version), Macbeth (Shaw), 1973; Tartuffe (Actors Company, Edinburgh Festival), 1974; The Comedy of Errors (own musical version), Landscape and A Slight Ache (all Cameri), Twelfth Night (Sevriomennik, Moscow—first British director in post-revolutionary Russia), 1975; Equus, Three Sisters (both Cameri), 1976; member, Arts Council Drama Panel, 1968–75; member, the Drama Board; President, New Theatre Committee, International Theatre Institute, 1974–7.

Address: Crucible Theatre, 55 Norfolk Street, Sheffield, S1 1DA. *Tel:* 0742–760621.

JAMES, Polly, actress

b Blackburn, Lancs, 8 July 1941; *d* of James Gerard Devaney and his wife Alice (Howson); *e* Notre Dame Convent, Blackburn and the Yorkshire College of Housecraft; *m* Clive Francis; formerly a teacher of domestic science, she trained for the stage at RADA.

Her first professional experience was with the Arthur Brough Players at the Lees Pavilion, Folkestone, 1963, playing various parts; first London appearance 22 Oct 1964, at the Royal Court, as Gladys in A Cuckoo in The Nest; New York debut at the Broadhurst, Apr 1965, as Anne Pornick in Half a Sixpence; at the Piccadilly, 1966, took over as Corrie in Barefoot in the Park; at the Northcott, Exeter, 1967–8, her parts included Polly Peachum in The Beggar's Opera and Lika in The Promise; New, Apr 1969, title part in Anne of Green Gables, for which she won several awards including the *Variety* critics' award for best performance of 1969; with the Royal Shakespeare Company at Stratford, 1971, played Nerissa in The Merchant of Venice, Mar, Margaret in Much Ado About Nothing, May, and Katharine in a Theatregoround production of Henry V; again played Margaret at the Aldwych, Dec 1971; Piccadilly, Nov 1972, Queen Victoria in I and Albert; Manchester, Oct 1975, Celia Coplestone in The Cocktail Party; toured, Sept 1976, as Cicely Courtneidge in Once More With Music; King's, Edinburgh, Dec 1977, appeared as Aladdin; Oxford Playhouse, 1978, Maggie in Hobson's Choice; Aldwych (RSC), Dec 1978, Effie in Saratoga; Pavilion, Bournemouth, Dec 1979, played one of the Babes in the Wood; Birmingham Rep, Apr 1980, Princess Victoria in Motherdear; TV appearances, since her first in 1968, include the series *The Liver Birds*, Our Mutual Friend, the trilogy A Divorce, and Sweepstake's Game.

Recreations: Handicrafts, sewing. *Address:* c/o James Sharkey, Fraser and Dunlop Ltd, 91 Regent Street, London W1R 8RU.

JAMESON, Pauline, actress

b Heacham, Norfolk, 5 June 1920; *d* of Eric Storrs Jameson and his wife Flora Isobel (Reed); *m* Leslie Lewington; studied for the stage at the Royal Academy of Dramatic Art.

Made her first appearance on the stage, Sept 1938, with the Colwyn Bay Repertory Company; first appeared in London, at the Q Theatre, 1 Sept 1942, as Beatrice in London, W1; Criterion, Sept 1945, played Lucy in The Rivals; Arts, Feb 1947, Catherine in The Wise Have Not Spoken; New Lindsey, Feb 1948, Biddie in Golden Rain; then joined the Old Vic company, at the New Theatre, and Mar 1948, appeared as Valeria in Coriolanus; Apr 1948, played Bianca in The Taming of the Shrew; appeared there from Sept 1948–Jan 1949, as Maria in Twelfth Night, Covetousness in Dr Faustus, Mrs Marwood in The Way of the World, and Dunyasha in The Cherry Orchard; Haymarket, Feb 1949, Maria in The Heiress, and in Aug 1949, for one month, succeeded Peggy Ashcroft as Catherine Sloper in the same play; at the re-opening of the Old Vic, Nov 1950, again played Maria in Twelfth Night, and later in the season appeared as Grace Wellborn in Bartholomew Fair, Alice in Henry V, Chrysothemis in Electra; Arts, June 1952, played Maggie Hobson in Hobson's Choice; in the autumn of 1952, joined the Bristol Old Vic Company, and during the season appeared as Lady India in Ring Round the Moon, Mariana in Measure for Measure, Kate Hardcastle in She Stoops to Conquer, Moussia Karlene in The Bridge, and Doll Common in The Alchemist; Lyric, Hammersmith, Feb 1953, played Mrs Fainall in The Way of the World; Arts, Sept 1953, played the title-role in a revival of Penelope; Lyric, Hammersmith, May 1954, played Varya in The Cherry Orchard; toured, 1955, as Thérèse in Hippo Dancing; Shakespeare Festival Theatre, Stratford, Ontario, 1956, Mistress Page in The Merry Wives of Windsor; Assembly Hall, Edinburgh, Aug 1957, Donna D'Ossuna in The Hidden King; Apollo, Apr 1958, Eugénie in Duel of Angels; Old Vic, Feb–Mar 1959, played the Wife in Sganarelle, Elmire in Tartuffe, and Agatha Posket in The Magistrate; Queen's, Aug 1959, Mrs Prest in The Aspern Papers; New Arts, July 1962, played Livia in the Royal Shakespeare Company's production of Women, Beware Women; Wyndham's, Nov 1962, Miss Vaughan in Out of Bounds; joined the Royal Shakespeare Company to appear at the Aldwych, Jan 1964, as the Abbess in The Comedy of

Errors, and Feb 1964, as Regan in King Lear, prior to touring with both productions for the British Council, in Europe, the USSR and the US Feb–June 1964; during this period she made her first appearance in New York, at the State Theatre, May 1964, in both plays; Hampstead Theatre Club, Oct 1964, played Miss Moffat in a revival of The Corn is Green; Aldwych, May 1966, played Eleonora in the RSC's Tango; Wyndham's, Sept 1967, took over the name part in The Prime of Miss Jean Brodie; Vaudeville, Nov 1967, Mrs Allonby in A Woman of No Importance; Chichester Festival, 1968, played Lavinia in The Cocktail Party (May) and Mrs Antrobus in The Skin of Our Teeth (July), repeating the former role at Wyndham's (Nov) and the Haymarket; Traverse, Edinburgh, 1971, appeared in Speak Now; Coliseum, Dec 1972, Mrs Darling in Peter Pan; Albery, Sept 1973, Martha Culver in The Constant Wife; again at the Albery, Nov 1975, for Prospect Productions, played Anna Semyonevna in A Month in the Country, and Mrs Honeychurch in A Room with a View; Arnaud, Guildford, Feb 1977, Mrs Danvers in Rebecca; Round House, in a Royal Exchange, Manchester, Season, Feb 1979, Mrs Scarfield and Mother in The Ordeal of Gilbert Pinfold, and Lady Monchensey in The Family Reunion, which transferred to the Vaudeville, June 1979; first appeared in films, 1948, in Esther Waters, subsequent films include: The Queen of Spades, The Millionairess, Crooks Anonymous, etc; recent TV includes: The Barretts of Wimpole Street and Lillie.

Addresses: 7 Warrington Gardens, London, W9. *Tel:* 01–286 6470 *and* Crockham Farmhouse, Hernhill, Faversham, Kent.

JAMPOLIS, Neil Peter, stage designer

b 14 Mar 1943; *s* of Samuel A Jampolis and his wife Beatrice R (Swenken); *e* Arizona State University, University of Chicago and Goodman Theatre-Art Institute of Chicago; *m* the lighting designer Jane Reisman.

Has designed scenery, costumes, and especially lighting for numerous productions in New York and outside; his first Broadway engagement was as set supervisor and lighting designer for Borstal Boy, at the Lyceum, 1969; other notable NY work includes design for One Flew Over the Cuckoo's Nest, 1971; lighting for Sherlock Holmes, 1974 (Tony award); designs for Pilobolus Dance Theatre, 1978; responsible for scenery, costumes or lighting for over 80 operatic productions in North and South America and Europe since 1968, including two world and three American premieres.

Address: 142 West 44th Street, New York, NY 10036. *Tel:* 921 0425.

JANIS, Conrad, actor and musician

b New York City, 11 Feb 1928; *s* of Sidney Janis, and his wife Harriet; *e* progressive school in NY; *m* (1) Vicki Quarles (mar dis); (2) Ronda Copland.

First appeared on the stage at the Lyceum, NY, 2 Sept 1942, as Barlow Adams in Junior Miss, and toured in this play almost immediately thereafter; 46th Street, Mar 1945, played Floyd Allen in Dark of the Moon; Empire, Oct 1945, Barney Brennen in The Next Half Hour; formed a jazz band called The Tailgaters with which he toured extensively in cabaret, theatres, concert halls, etc; reappeared on the stage at the Lyceum, Apr 1952, as Charlie in The Brass Ring; Lyceum, Nov 1952, Eddie Davis in Time Out for Ginger; Phoenix, Nov 1955, Cantrell in The Terrible Swift Sword; Huntington Hartford, Los Angeles, played in sketches and led his jazz band in the revue Joy Ride; Booth, Feb 1957, Conrad in Visit to a Small Planet; made his London début at the Duchess, 11 June 1958, as Timothy Bertram in The

Velvet Shotgun; Playhouse, NY, Johnny King in Make a Million; 48th Street, Nov 1961, Adam in Sunday in New York; ANTA, Dec 1963, Rudy in Marathon '33, for which he also provided the music and led his jazz band, the Tail Gate Five; Ethel Barrymore, May 1969, Kruger in The Front Page; same theatre, Oct 1969, again played Kruger in The Front Page; Martin Beck, Apr 1973, Jimmy Skouras in No Hard Feelings; Brooks Atkinson, 20 Oct 1975, took over as George in Same Time Next Year, and subsequently toured; is a co-director of the Janis Gallery, dealers in avant garde and other contemporary art; entered films in Snafu, 1945, and has since played in Margie, The Brasher Doubloon, Beyond Glory, Airport 1975, The Duchess and the Dirtwater Fox, Roseland, The Buddy Holly Story (1978), etc; has appeared frequently on television since 1950 in *Suspense, Barnaby Jones, Maude, Mork and Mindy,* and some 300 others.

Address: 6 West 57th Street, New York, NY. *Tel:* 586 0110.

JARVIS, Martin, actor

b Cheltenham, 4 Aug 1941; s of Denys Harry Jarvis and his wife Margot Lillian; e Whitgift School; m (2) the actress Rosalind Ayres; trained for the stage at RADA (Vanbrugh award, 1962).

While at RADA, played Henry V for the National Youth Theatre; began his professional career at the Library Theatre, Manchester, Oct 1962, as Sebastian in Twelfth Night; at the New Arts, Oct 1963, played Drummer in one of the three plays in Cockade; same theatre, Nov 1973, Franz Delanoue in Poor Bitos, making his West End debut in the role when the production transferred to the Duke of York's, 6 Jan 1964; New Arts, Nov 1965, and Vaudeville, Jan 1966, Octavius Robinson in Man and Superman; May Fair, Sept 1969, Owen Gereth in The Spoils of Poynton; Mermaid, Oct 1969, Piers Cramp in The Bandwagon; in Apr 1972 played Jack Absolute in the Thorndike, Leatherhead, production of The Rivals, which was also seen at the University Theatre, New York; Theatre Royal, Windsor, Sept 1973, played the title role in Hamlet; toured, 1974, as Father Michael in The Prodigal Daughter; in 1975 played Adam in recitals of Paradise Lost at Chichester, the Old Vic etc; Chichester Festival, Jul 1976, and Haymarket, Oct, Arnold Champion-Cheney in The Circle; Churchill, Bromley, 1978, Edward VIII in The Woman I Love; appeared in Canada, 1978, and at the Hong Kong Arts Festival, as Young Marlow in She Stoops to Conquer; appeared in the film The Last Escape, 1969, and subsequent films include Ike; TV includes The Forsyte Saga, Nicholas Nickleby, the series *Rings on Their Fingers*, and Breakaway; over a thousand radio appearances; has written many short stories for BBC radio, and a play, Bright Boy, which has also been broadcast; council member, National Youth Theatre.

Favourite part: Arnold in The Circle. *Recreations:* Music, cooking. *Address:* 64 Grafton Road, London W3.

JAYSTON, Michael (né James), actor

b Nottingham, 29 Oct 1936; s of Vincent James, and his wife Myfanwy (Llewelyn); e Becket Grammar School, Nottingham and Nottingham University; m (1) Lynn Farleigh (mar dis); (2) Heather Mary Sneddon (mar dis); (3) Elizabeth Smithson; formerly a trainee accountant; trained for the stage at the Guildhall School of Music and Drama.

First appeared on the stage 21 July 1962, at the Salisbury Playhouse, as Corporal Green in The Amorous Prawn; from the Salisbury Repertory Company, he joined the Bristol Old Vic; Bristol, Apr 1964, played various parts in Beyond the Fringe; joined the Royal Shakespeare Company, 1965, to

play parts including Exeter in Henry V, Aldwych, May; Storyteller in The Thwarting of Baron Bolligrew, Aldwych, Dec; Laertes in Hamlet, Stratford, Apr 1966; Lenny in The Homecoming, Music Box, New York, July 1967; Oswald in Ghosts, Bertram in All's Well That Ends Well, reader in The Hollow Crown, Custer in Indians, and Young Fashion in The Relapse, Aldwych, 1968; Arnaud, Guildford, Mar 1972, played Henry II in Becket; joined the National Theatre at the Old Vic, 1974, to take over the part of Martin Dysart in Equus and to play Charles Appleby in Eden End; toured as Martin Dysart in Equus, 1976, and took over the part again at the Albery, Sept; Greenwich, Mar 1980, Elyot Chase in Private Lives; transferring to the Duchess, Apr 1980; films, since 1968, include Nicholas and Alexandra, A Bequest to the Nation, The Homecoming and Zulu Dawn; has appeared in numerous television productions since 1963, including *The Power Game,* Beethoven, Jane Eyre and, recently, The Last Romantic, Gossip From the Forest and Tinker, Tailor, Soldier, Spy.

Recreations: Cricket, darts, riding, TV sport, gardening, rolling up people's trouser legs, and gambling. *Clubs:* MCC, Lord's Taverners, Eccentrics, S.P.A.R.K.S. *Address:* Leading Artists, 60 St James's Street, London SW1.

JEANS, Isabel, actress

b London, 16 Sept 1891; d of Frederick George Jeans and his wife Esther (Matlock); e London; m (1) Claude Rains (mar dis); (2) Gilbert Edward Wakefield (dec).

Made her first appearance on the stage at His Majesty's Theatre, 16 Dec 1909, as Daffodil in Pinkie and the Fairies; she remained at His Majesty's some time, playing various small parts; her first speaking part in London was at the Garrick, Mar 1913, when she played Peggy Bannister in The Greatest Wish; in May 1913, played Mdlle Villette in Croesus; at His Majesty's, Jan 1914, played Nu in The Darling of the Gods; during 1915–16, toured in the United States with Granville Barker's company, playing Titania in A Midsummer Night's Dream, Fanny in Fanny's First Play, Mdlle de la Garandière in The Man Who Married a Dumb Wife; on her return to London, appeared at the Haymarket, Apr 1916, as Phoebe Pound in The Mayor of Troy; then went to His Majesty's, Aug 1916, walking on in Chu-Chin-Chow, in which she remained until 1918; at the Ambassadors', Mar 1917, played her old part in The Man Who Married a Dumb Wife; at the Kingsway, Jan 1919, played Jane Packard in Oh, Joy; at the Winter Garden, May 1919, Lady Mercia Merivale in Kissing Time; Lyric, Hammersmith (for the Phoenix Society), Jan 1921, Celia in Volpone, and in Nov 1921 (for the Phoenix), Aspatia in The Maid's Tragedy; at the Shaftesbury, Jan 1922 (for the Phoenix), played the First Constantia in The Chances; from Feb to Apr 1922, was engaged at the Everyman, playing Fanny in Fanny's First Play, Raina in Arms and the Man, Hypatia in Misalliance, and Olivia in Twelfth Night; at the Duke of York's, May 1922, played Claire Vervier in Nuts in May; at Daly's, Nov 1922 (for the Phoenix), Abigail in The Jew of Malta; in Mar 1923, went to Amsterdam, to play Laura Pasquale in At Mrs Beam's; at the Shaftesbury, June 1923 (for the Phoenix), played Cloe in The Faithful Shepherdess; at the Regent, June 1923 (for the same), Celia in Volpone; at the Strand, Sept 1923, succeeded Cathleen Nesbitt as Hilda Norbury in The Eye of Siva, and at His Majesty's, Nov 1923, succeeded her as Yasmin in Hassan; at the Regent, Feb 1924 (for the Phoenix), played Margery Pinchwife in The Country Wife; at the Shaftesbury, Apr 1924, Mrs Armitage in A Perfect Fit; at the RADA Theatre, May 1924 (for the Three Hundred Club), Lady Flutter in The Discovery; at the Regent, June 1924 (for the

Phoenix), Laetitia Fondlewife in The Old Bachelor; at the Prince of Wales's, June 1924, Zélie de Chaumet in The Rat; at the Scala, Nov 1924 (for the Play Actors), Mrs Berridge in Dear Father; Aldwych (for the Stage Society), Feb 1925, Susan Maddox in The Bright Island; Lyric, Hammersmith, Mar 1925, Lydia Languish in The Rivals; Garrick, Aug 1925, Elsie in Cobra; Haymarket, Nov 1925, succeeded Fay Compton as the Lady in The Man with a Load of Mischief; Coliseum, Jan 1926, played in The Honeymoon; Everyman, Feb 1926, Nell Gwynn in Mr Pepys; Queen's, Apr 1926, Lady Dare Bellingham in Conflict; July 1926, Sibyl Risley in The Way You Look At It; Everyman, Dec 1926, Margery Pinchwife in The Country Wife; Q, Jan 1927, Leo Garey in The Yorick Hotel Case; Prince of Wales's, Feb 1927, again played Zelie in The Rat; Arts, Dec 1927, Irène in La Prisonnière; Strand, May 1928, Amytis in The Road to Rome; Court, Apr 1929, Leo in The Garey Divorce Case; Strand, July 1929, Estelle Duparc in Beauty; Royalty, Dec 1929, Diana in The Amorists; Ambassadors', Jan 1930, Crystal Wetherby in The Man in Possession; went to New York, and appeared at the Booth Theatre, Nov 1930, in the same part; returned to London, and at the Strand, Aug 1931, played Leslie in Counsel's Opinion; Apollo, Nov 1932, Mrs Jelliwell in Springtime for Henry; Strand, Apr 1933, Mrs Wislack in On Approval; Shaftesbury, Jan 1934, Lady Coperario in Spring 1600; Criterion, Mar 1935, Lucy Lockit in The Beggar's Opera; Haymarket, Aug 1935, Lola Leadenhall in Full House; His Majesty's, Apr 1936, La Gambogi in The Happy Hypocrite; Wyndham's, Sept 1936, Alice Galvoisier in Mademoiselle; Strand, May 1937, Lady Georgina in Ladies and Gentlemen; Lyric, Apr 1940, Susanna Venables in Ladies Into Action; Playhouse, Nov 1942, Victoria in Home and Beauty; Cambridge, Mar 1943, Lady Utterwood in Heartbreak House; Haymarket, Aug 1945, Mrs Erlynne in Lady Windermere's Fan, which she played until Jan 1947, and subsequently toured in the same part; Cort, NY, Dec 1948, appeared as Mrs Emmeline Lucas in Make Way for Lucia; reappeared in London at the Lyric, Hammersmith, Oct 1949, as Mme Arkadina in The Seagull, and played the same part at the St James's, Nov 1949; Vaudeville, Aug 1951, played the Countess in Ardèle; Lyric, Hammersmith, Mar 1952, played Florence Lancaster in The Vortex, and appeared in this part at the Criterion, Apr 1952; Savoy, Feb 1953, played Mrs Allonby in a revised version of A Woman of No Importance; at the Edinburgh Festival, 1953, appeared as Lady Elizabeth Mulhammer in The Confidential Clerk, and played this part at the Lyric Theatre, London, Sept 1953; again appeared as Lady Elizabeth in The Confidential Clerk at the Paris Festival of Dramatic Art, 1954; Piccadilly, Apr 1956, played Madame Caroline de Charenton in Commemoration Ball; New, Oxford, Sept 1956, played Sophie Faramond in The Gates of Summer; Phoenix, Oct 1966, Duchess of Berwick in Lady Windermere's Fan; Haymarket, June 1967, took over Mrs Malaprop in The Rivals; at the same theatre, Feb 1968, played Lady Bracknell in The Importance of Being Earnest, and Oct 1968, Madame Desmortes in Ring Round the Moon; Piccadilly, Nov 1971, Carlotta in Dear Antoine; made her first appearance on television in The Confidential Clerk, July 1955; has also appeared in numerous films; her performances include Aunt Alicia in Gigi, 1957.

Favourite parts: Margery Pinchwife in The Country Wife, Mrs Erlynne and Lady Bracknell. *Address:* c/o IFA Ltd, 11–12 Hanover Street, London, W1.

JEFFORD, Barbara (Mary), OBE, actress
b Plymstock, near Plymouth, Devon, 26 July 1930; *d* of Percival Francis Jefford and his wife Elizabeth Mary Ellen (Laity); *e* Taunton, Somerset; *m* (1) Terence Longdon (mar

dis); (2) John Turner; studied for the stage at The Hartly-Hodder Studio, Bristol, and the Royal Academy of Dramatic Art, where she gained the Bancroft Gold Medal.

Made her first appearance on the stage at the Dolphin Theatre, Brighton, Apr 1949, walking-on in Our Town; made her first appearance in London, at the Q Theatre, 28 June 1949, as Bertha in Frenzy; Dundee Repertory Company, Oct 1949–Jan 1950, where she played Lydia Languish in The Rivals, Janet Spence in The Gioconda Smile, among other parts; she was then engaged for the Shakespeare Memorial Theatre, Stratford-on-Avon, and Apr 1950, played Isabella in Measure for Measure, with John Gielgud; during the season she also played Anne Bullen in Henry VIII, Calpurnia in Julius Caesar, and Hero in Much Ado About Nothing; toured Germany with the company, 1950, in the last-named part; remained at Stratford-on-Avon for the 1951 season, when she appeared as Lady Percy in Henry IV (Parts I and II), the Queen of France in Henry V, and Juno in The Tempest; Lyric, Hammersmith, May 1952, played Rose Trelawny in Trelawny of the 'Wells'; toured Australia and New Zealand, 1953, with the Shakespeare Memorial Theatre Company, when she appeared as Desdemona in Othello, Rosalind in As You Like It, and Lady Percy in Henry IV; remained with the company for the 1954 season at Stratford-on-Avon, again playing Desdemona, and also appearing as Helena in A Midsummer Night's Dream, Katherine in The Taming of the Shrew, and Helen in Troilus and Cressida; toured New Zealand, 1954–5, with the New Zealand Players Company, as Jennett Jourdemayne in The Lady's Not For Burning; after her return to England, appeared at the Apollo, London, June 1955, as Andromache in Tiger at the Gates; made her first appearance on the New York stage at the Plymouth, 4 Oct 1955, in the same play; returned to London and joined the Old Vic Company, Sept 1956, to play the following parts: Imogen in Cymbeline, Beatrice in Much Ado About Nothing, Portia in The Merchant of Venice, 1956; Julia in The Two Gentlemen of Verona, Tamora in Titus Andronicus and the Courtesan in The Comedy of Errors, Lady Anne in Richard III; Baalbek, Lebanon, played Portia in The Merchant of Venice, with the Old Vic Co; at the Old Vic, played Queen Margaret in Henry VI, Parts 1, 2 and 3; Isabella in Measure for Measure, 1957; Regan in King Lear, Viola in Twelfth Night, 1958; from Sept 1958 to Feb 1959, toured America with the Old Vic Co, as Ophelia in Hamlet and Viola in Twelfth Night; returned to the Old Vic, London where, in Apr 1959, she played Beatrice in The Cenci; during 1959–60, played Rosalind in As You Like It; Gwendolen Fairfax in The Importance of Being Earnest, and the title-role in Saint Joan; toured Great Britain, Sept–Dec 1960, as Lady Macbeth in Macbeth, Saint Joan, and Gwendolen in The Importance of Being Earnest; toured the USSR, and Poland, Jan 1961, in the same plays; Old Vic, Apr 1961, again played Viola in Twelfth Night; Paris Festival, June 1961, appeared in her recital Heroines of Shakespeare, subsequently touring Finland and West Germany, Aug–Sept 1961; Old Vic, Nov 1961, Lavinia in Mourning Becomes Electra; City Center, NY, Feb 1962, played Lady Macbeth and the title-part in Saint Joan, subsequently touring the US with both plays; Old Vic European tour, June–Aug 1962, appeared in Saint Joan; Oxford Playhouse, Oct 1962, Lina Szczepanowska in Misalliance, and Nov 1962, Dora in The Just; Royal Court, Jan 1963, again played Lina in Misalliance, transferring with the production to the Criterion, Jan 1963; at the new Mayfair Theatre, June 1963, played the Step-Daughter in Six Characters in Search of An Author; Royal, Brighton, Feb 1964, played Portia in The Merchant of Venice, and Helena in A Midsummer Night's

Dream, prior to touring South America with both plays, Mar–Apr 1964, and also appearing with the same company at the Paris Festival, June 1964; Piccadilly, June 1965, played Nan in Ride a Cock Horse; Oxford Playhouse, Sept 1965–Jan 1966, Cleopatra in Antony and Cleopatra, and Lady Cicely in Captain Brassbound's Conversion, and the title-part in Phèdre; Nottingham Playhouse, Oct 1966, Cleopatra in Antony and Cleopatra, and Nov 1966, Maggie Harris in Fill the Stage With Happy Hours; Oxford Playhouse, Feb 1967, Irma in The Balcony; Aldwych, July 1967, for the Royal Shakespeare Company, Patsy Newquist in Little Murders; Arnaud, Guildford, 1968, The Woman in As You Desire Me; toured Canada, West Africa and the Middle East, with a recital, The Labours of Love, devised with John Turner, in which they also toured South America in early 1969 and the Far East, Oct 1969–Feb 1970; Arts, Cambridge, Nov 1970, appeared in The World's a Stage for Prospect Productions; toured S America, spring 1971, as Katharina in The Taming of the Shrew and as Hedda Gabler in the Bristol Old Vic productions; Traverse, Edinburgh, Sept 1971 (Edinburgh Festival), played the Wife in The Novelist; toured Australia, spring 1972, in The Labours of Love; Piccadilly, Feb 1973, Mother Vauzou in Mistress of Novices; Oxford Playhouse, 1973, played Portia in The Merchant of Venice, July, and Alice Dearth in Dear Brutus, Aug; toured, May 1974, as Clementine in A Man and His Wife; Arnaud, Guildford, Nov 1974, Olwen Peel in Dangerous Corner; Chichester Festival, 1975, played Roxane in Cyrano de Bergerac, and Katharine Stockmann in An Enemy of the People; Harrogate, 1975, Irina Arkadina in The Seagull; Bristol Old Vic, Oct 1975, Hesione Hushabye in Heartbreak House; King's Head, Islington, Jan 1976, Mrs Crocker-Harris in The Browning Version; joined the National Theatre company, May 1976, to take over Gertrude in Hamlet, at the Lyttelton; Olivier, Oct, Zabina in Tamburlaine; Jan–Feb 1977, toured the Middle East and Greece in The Labours of Love; Mar 1977–Apr 1978, joined the Prospect Company to play Gertrude in Hamlet, Thetis in War Music, Cleopatra in All for Love and Antony and Cleopatra, playing seasons at the Old Vic and Edinburgh Festival, visiting Europe and the Middle East, and returning to tour the provinces; Comedy, Aug 1978, played Margaret Beaufort in The Dark Horse; Lyric, Jan 1979, took over the title-role in Filumena; Brighton Festival, May 1979, Miss Amelia in The Ballad of the Sad Café; June 1979, joined the Old Vic Company to play the Nurse in Romeo and Juliet, and Anna Andreyevna in The Government Inspector; films include Ulysses, A Midsummer Night's Dream and Shoes of the Fisherman; has also appeared in numerous television plays, including Edna, The Inebriated Woman, The Visitors, and Skin Game; she has also broadcast in many radio plays and serials; received the Order of the British Empire in the New Year Honours, 1965 and the Jubilee Medal, 1977.

Favourite parts: Cleopatra and Joan. *Address:* c/o Fraser & Dunlop Ltd, 91 Regent Street, London, W1.

JEFFREY, Peter, actor
b Bristol, 18 Apr 1929; *s* of Arthur Winfred Gilbert Jeffrey and his wife Florence Alice (Weight); *e* Harrow and Pembroke College, Cambridge; *m* Yvonne Bonnamy.

His first professional appearance was with the Chorlton-cum-Hardy repertory company, Manchester, in 1951, in the play Never Get Out; toured for two years 1953–5 with the Elizabethan Theatre Company in Shakespeare, making his London debut with this company at the Westminster, 29 June 1953, as Julius Caesar and Dardanius in Julius Caesar; other parts with the company included Exeter in Henry V, Escalus in Romeo and Juliet, Horatio in Hamlet and Carlisle in

Richard II; with the Bristol Old Vic, seasons 1957–9, his roles included Estragon in Waiting for Godot, de Guiche in Cyrano de Bergerac, Billy Rice in The Entertainer, Laertes in Hamlet, and David Bliss in Hay Fever, joined the Royal Shakespeare Company, 1960, and at Stratford that year played Lucentio in The Taming of the Shrew, Agamemnon in Troilus and Cressida, and Paulina's Steward in The Winter's Tale; at the Aldwych, Dec 1960, Delio in The Duchess of Malfi; Feb 1961, de Cerisay in The Devils, later taking over the part of de Laubardemont; Stratford, 1962, Banquo in Macbeth, Escalus in Measure for Measure, and Albany in King Lear, also playing the last part at the Aldwych, Dec 1962; again at the Aldwych, May 1966, Stomil in Tango; toured, 1966, for Prospect Productions in the title role in Macbeth; Shaw, May 1972, Malvolio in Twelfth Night; rejoined the RSC, Aug 1975, to play Percy in Jingo at the Aldwych; Globe, July 1976, Buckle in Donkey's Years; Lyttelton, May 1979, Wilfred Cedar in For Services Rendered; same theatre, Dec 1979, Henry Ormonroyd in When We Are Married; films, since Becket in 1963, include If . . ., The Fixer and O Lucky Man; TV includes *The Plane Makers, Elizabeth R.* and The Common.

Favourite parts: Macbeth, Percy. *Recreations:* Golf and squash. *Address:* c/o London Management, 235–241 Regent Street, London W1. *Tel:* 01-734 4192.

JEFFREYS, Anne (*née* Carmichael), actress and singer
b Goldsboro, NC, 26 Jan 1923; *d* of Mack Curtis Carmichael and his wife Kate Hurt (Jeffreys); *e* Anderson College; *m* Robert Sterling.

Began her career with the New York City Opera Co, 1940–1, singing Mimi in La Boheme and Cio-Cio San in Madame Butterfly; Hollywood Playhouse, Calif, 1941, appeared in the revue Fun for the Money; Greek, Los Angeles, June 1946, Sara in Bittersweet; appeared at the Academy of Music, Brooklyn, 22 Oct 1946, when she sang the title-role in La Tosca; first appeared on Broadway, at the Adelphi Theatre, 9 Jan 1947, as Rose Maurrant in the musical version of Street Scene; Greek Theatre, Los Angeles, June 1947, appeared in Bittersweet, playing the same part in July 1948, at the same theatre as well as at the San Francisco Opera; Greek Theatre, Los Angeles, July 1947, Sonia Ladoye in The Merry Widow; toured, Feb 1948, as Rita Cavallini in My Romance, and appeared in this part at the Shubert Theatre, NY, Oct 1948; sang La Tosca with the Los Angeles Philharmonic in May 1949; Shubert Theatre, Chicago, July 1949, played Kate in Kiss Me, Kate, in the National Company, and remained with the company until May 1950; at the Century, NY, June 1950, appeared in the same part, succeeding Patricia Morison; at the Opera House, San Francisco, July 1951, again appeared in Bittersweet; Mark Hellinger, NY, Mar 1952, played Maeve Harrigan in Three Wishes for Jamie; toured California, July 1957, as Alice in Anniversary Waltz; toured California in June 1959, as Ella Peterson in Bells Are Ringing; toured, Dec 1960, as Frenchy in Destry Rides Again; toured California, Aug–Nov 1962, as Lalume in Kismet; California, 1963, Rosabella in The Most Happy Fella and Julie in Carousel; again played Ella Peterson in Bells Are Ringing and Alice in Anniversary Waltz, California, 1964; toured US, 1964, as Guinevere in Camelot; New York State Theatre, June 1965, Lalume in Kismet, and subsequently toured; toured 1966 in Ninotchka and Bells Are Ringing; toured 1967 in Do I Hear a Waltz?; Packer Playhouse, Fort Lauderdale, Fla, Feb 1967, Alice Roberts in The Name of the Game; toured 1968 in Light Up the Sky and Desert Song; 1969 in Pal Joey and Song of Norway; 1970 in Marriage-Go-Round and The King and I; 1975 in Take Me

Along; 1976, in Children, Memphis, and Camelot, Sacramento; in Follies, Milwaukee, 1977; High Button Shoes, Milwaukee and Seattle, and The Sound of Music, Tucson, 1978; The Sound of Music, Seattle, 1979; The King and I, Seattle, 1980; entered films, 1942, in I Married an Angel, and since has appeared in Step Lively, Zombies on Broadway, Boy's Night Out, etc; first appeared on television on Milton Berle's program in 1948, and since has appeared in the series *Topper* and *Love That Jill*, The Merry Widow, Dearest Enemy, and numerous dramatic and variety programs.

Address: c/o Actors Equity Association, 165 West 46th Street, New York, NY 10036.

JELLICOE, Ann, dramatic author and director
b Middlesborough, Yorks, 15 July 1927; *d* of John Andrea Jellicoe; *e* Polam Hall School, Darlington, Co Durham, and Queen Margaret's School, Castle Howard, York; *m* Roger Mayne; trained for the stage at the Central School of Speech and Drama (Elsie Fogerty Prize, 1947).

Began her career in the theatre as an actress and stage manager in repertory, also directing a number of plays; in 1953, returned to the Central School as a teacher of acting; author of the following plays: The Sport of My Mad Mother, 1956; The Knack, 1961; Shelley, 1965; The Giveaway, 1969; The Rising Generation (a pageant), 1960; for children: You'll Never Guess! 1973; Clever Elsie, 1974; A Good Thing or a Bad Thing, 1974; translated Rosmersholm, 1959; The Lady from the Sea, 1961; The Seagull, 1964; directed (with George Devine) her own play The Sport of My Mad Mother, 1958; she has since directed the following plays: For Children, 1958; The Knack (with Keith Johnstone), 1962; Skyvers, 1963; Shelley, 1965; Six of the Best (co-director), A Worthy Guest, 1974; Flora and the Bandits, 1976; The Reckoning (a community play for Lyme Regis) 1979; founded the Cockpit Theatre Club to Experiment with the Open Stage, 1951, and directed the following plays for them: The Confederacy, The Frogs, Miss Julie, Saint's Day, The Comedy of Errors, and Olympia; Literary Manager, Royal Court Theatre, 1973–4; founded the Colway Theatre Trust to produce community plays, 1980.

Recreation: Reading theatrical biography. *Address:* c/o Margaret Ramsay Ltd, 14a Goodwin's Court, St Martin's London, WC2.

JENKINS, David, stage designer and art director
b Hampton, Virginia, 30 Jul 1937; *s* of F Raymond Jenkins and his wife Cecelia (Chandler); *e* Earlham College and Yale University (MFA); *m* the stage designer Leigh Rand.

His first Broadway designs were for The Changing Room, at the Morosco, 6 Mar 1973; productions he has since designed for the New York stage include The Freedom of the City, 1974; Rodgers and Hart, Gorky, 1975; Checking Out, 1976; Saint Joan, 1977; The Elephant Man, Says I Says He, Strangers, The Art of Dining, 1979; I Ought to Be in Pictures, The Student Prince, 1980; has also designed for many major regional theatres including the Arena Stage, Goodman, Long Wharf, McCarter, Mark Taper Forum, Trinity Square, etc; art direction for films and television includes plays by Chekhov, O'Neill, and Neil Simon.

Address: 285 Riverside Drive, New York, NY 10025.

JENKINS, George, designer
b Baltimore, Maryland; *s* of Benjamin W Jenkins and his wife Jane (Clarke); *e* University of Pennsylvania, 1929–31; *m* Phyllis Adams.

Formerly an interior designer and architect; was assistant to Jo Mielziner, 1937–41; first designs for the stage were the sets and lighting for Early to Bed, produced at the Broadhurst, 17 June 1943; has since designed Mexican Hayride, I Remember Mama, 1944; Dark of the Moon, Common Ground, Strange Fruit, Are You with It? 1945; Lost in the Stars, 1949; Bell, Book, and Candle, 1950; The Trial (London), 1951; Three Wishes for Jamie, 1952; Gently Does It, 1953; The Immoralist, The Bad Seed, 1954; Ankles Aweigh, The Desk Set, 1955; Too Late the Phalarope, The Happiest Millionaire, 1956; The Merry Widow, Rumple, 1957; Two for the Seesaw, 1958; Tall Story, The Miracle Worker, 1959; One More River, Critic's Choice, 1960; A Thousand Clowns, 1962; Jennie, 1963; Everybody Out, The Castle Is Sinking, 1964; Catch Me If You Can, Generation, 1965; Wait Until Dark (also London), The Student Prince (San Francisco), 1966; The Only Game in Town, 1968; Night Watch, 1972; Sly Fox, 1976; has also designed for the Jones Beach Marine Theatre summer productions of Song of Norway, 1958, Hit the Deck, 1960, Paradise Island, 1961; Around the World in 80 Days, 1963; Mardi Gras, 1966; for the San Francisco Opera has designed La Boheme, Cosi Fan Tutte, and Ariadne auf Naxos; designed the décor for films including The Best Years of Our Lives, 1946, The Secret Life of Walter Mitty, 1947, A Song Is Born, The Miracle Worker, Klute, 1776, The Paper Chase, Funny Lady, All the President's Men (Oscar 1977), The China Syndrome, The Postman Always Rings Twice (1980), etc; designed the television productions of Out of the Dark, The Royal Family, Annie Get Your Gun, An Evening with Mary Martin, An Afternoon with Mary Martin, etc; was theatre consultant for the Hopkins Center of Dartmouth University, 1962, the Marine Stadium in Miami, Florida, 1963, and The Annenberg Theatre Complex, University of Pennsylvania.

Addresses: 124 East 72nd Street, New York, NY 10021. *Tel:* 535–4234 *and* 740 Kingman Avenue, Santa Monica, Calif 90402. *Tel:* 459 2739.

JENKINS, Hugh, director, Theatres Trust
b London, 27 Jul 1908; *s* of Joseph Walter Jenkins and his wife Emily Florence (Gater); *e* Enfield Grammar School; *m* Ethel Marie Crosbie.

Assistant General Secretary, British Actors Equity, 1950–64; Labour MP for Putney, 1964–79; Minister for the Arts, 1974–76; Director, Theatres Trust; member of board, National Theatre; former chairman, Theatres Advisory Council; writings include The Culture Gap, 1979.

Address: 75 Kenilworth Court, Lower Richmond Road, London SW15. *Tel:* 788 0371 *and* 10 St Martin's Court, London W1. *Tel:* 836 8591.

JENKINS, Megs, actress
b Cheshire, 21 Apr 1917; *d* of Reginald William Jenkins and his wife Nellie Susanna (Ray); *e* Claughton College, Cheshire; *m* G A Routledge; studied for the stage at the School of Dancing and Dramatic Art, Liverpool.

Had amateur experience before making her first appearance on the professional stage at the Playhouse, Liverpool, 21 Sept 1933, as the German Hausfrau in The Lift that Failed; remained at Liverpool, with the Repertory Company, until 1937; first appeared in London, at the Players' Theatre, Dec 1937, in the first edition of Late Joys; appeared at the same theatre, Feb 1938, as Fanny Norman in Heaven and Charing Cross; at the New Theatre, Sept 1938, played Maggie Bywoods in Can We Tell?; Players', Oct 1938, Bianca in What Next, Baby?; New, Nov 1938, Trana in Story of an African Farm; Q, Jan 1939, Lorelei Winkel in Walk in the Sun; St Martin's, Mar 1939, again played Fanny Norman in Heaven and Charing Cross; Players', June 1939, Claudine in Luck of the Devil; Apollo, Feb 1940, made a great success when she played Fan in The Light of Heart; Ambassadors', July 1942, appeared in Light and Shade; Arts, Dec 1942, played Mary Wilson in The Drunkard; Duke of York's, May 1943, Thomasina in Shadow and Substance; Vaudeville, Oct 1943, Shirley in Acacia Avenue; St James's, Dec 1944, Arethusa in The Glass Slipper, and Apr 1945, played Bet in The Wind of Heaven; Arts, Apr 1949, Mrs Hardcastle in She Stoops to Conquer; Garrick, Mar 1950, Mrs Gillie in Mr Gillie; Embassy, Feb 1951, played Gwenny in a revival of The Late Christopher Bean; Lyric, Hammersmith, Nov 1951, played Mrs Winemiller in Summer and Smoke, and appeared in the same part at the Duchess, Jan 1952; Piccadilly, June 1952, Maggie Gay in The Gay Dog; Haymarket, Nov 1953, Miss Mathieson in A Day by the Sea; made her first appearance on the New York stage at the ANTA Playhouse, 26 Sept 1955, when she again played Miss Mathieson in A Day by the Sea; Comedy, London, Oct 1956, played Beatrice in A View From The Bridge (for which she received the Clarence Derwent Award for the Best Supporting Performance 1956-7); Piccadilly, May 1957, played Margaret Dyson in A Dead Secret; Mayfair, June 1963, played the Mother in Six Characters in Search of An Author; Savoy, Apr 1964, Miss Dyott in The Schoolmistress; Duchess, Mar 1965, Margaret Goodson in Return Ticket; St Martin's, Mar 1968, Persephone in Enter A Free Man; Aldwych, Mar 1969, for the Royal Shakespeare Company, May Godboy in Dutch Uncle; Open Space, Sept 1969, Margaret Moon in Hallowe'en; New, Nov 1970, Grace Winslow in The Winslow Boy; Globe, July 1972, Janet Storace in Parents' Day; toured, July 1975, as Sylvia Bennett in Not in the Book; Theatre Royal, Windsor, 1978, played Miss Holroyd in Bell, Book and Candle; first appeared in films, 1939, in The Silent Battle and subsequently in over a hundred others, including The Innocents, and Oliver!; recent TV includes *Oh No! It's Selwyn Froggit*, *Worzel Gummidge*, and *Young At Heart*.

Favourite parts: Fan in The Light of Heart and Bet in The Wind of Heaven. *Address:* c/o Joseph & Wagg, 78 New Bond Street, London, W1.

JENKINS, Warren, director and actor
b Chelsea, London; *s* of Thomas Jenkins and his wife Sarah Margaretta (Christopher); *e* London; *m* Jennifer Maddox; studied for the stage at the Royal Academy of Dramatic Art, Royal College of Music, and privately under Komisarjevsky, and Stuckgold (New York Studio).

Made his first appearance on the stage at the Repertory Theatre, Hull, 6 Sept 1926, as Captain Holt in To Have the Honour; made his first appearance in London, at the Court Theatre, 4 Oct 1927, as Kirilov and Lieut Bibikov in Paul I; Strand, Oct 1927, played Felipe in The Kingdom of God; at the Court, with the Birmingham Repertory Company, Feb–Apr 1928, played Fleance in Macbeth (in modern dress), Wulfnoth in Harold, and Biondello in The Taming of the Shrew (in modern dress); Apollo, Oct 1928, the Public Prosecutor in The Brass Paper Weight; Gate, Jan 1929, and Kingsway, Feb 1929, Snobson in Fashion; Strand, July 1929, Adolphe in Beauty; Adelphi, Dec 1930, appeared in Ever Green; Gate, Nov 1931, the Rover in The Red Rover; Adelphi, Jan 1932, Philocomus and Ajax I in Helen!; Gate, Oct 1932, Bridegroom, Troll King and Eberkoff in Peer Gynt; Ambassadors', Nov 1932, Paul in Philomel; Mar 1933, toured in Words and Music; Gate, Dec 1933, Uncle Tom in Uncle Tom's Cabin; Royalty, Apr 1934, Luigi Bunghi in The Mask and the Face; Shaftesbury, Nov 1934, Troubadour in

For Ever; Royalty, Dec 1934, the Red Rover in The Red Rover's Revenge; Strand, Apr 1935, appeared in 1066 and All That; Fortune (for Stage Society), Nov 1935, directed Not for Children; Gate, June 1936, Mr Noah in No More Peace; Ambassadors', Aug 1936, Albert Porter in The Two Bouquets; Gate, Nov 1937, Gennadi in Distant Point; Whitehall, Apr 1938, Mr Blow in Ghost for Sale; Phoenix, Dec 1938, Feste in Twelfth Night; toured, Jan 1939, as Mac in I Can Take It; Whitehall, Dec 1939, played Blackshirt and Neutralus in Who's Taking Liberty?; served in the Far East with the Friends' Ambulance Unit, China Convoy, 1940–4; undertook a lecture tour of India, Australia, New Zealand, and the United States, 1945; was Chief of Field Operations, Far East Division, at HQ, UNRRA, Washington, DC, 1946–7; after his return to England he directed All My Sons, at the Lyric, Hammersmith, May 1948, transferred to the Globe, June 1948; director for the Ipswich Repertory Theatre, 1948–51; since 1950 has directed both new and classic plays at the Manchester Library Theatre, and for the Arena Theatre; directed Ipswich Pageant (Festival of Britain), 1951; a musical version of She Stoops to Conquer (King's Lynn Festival), 1951; The Square Ring, 1952; Down Came a Blackbird, St Chad of the Seven Wells (Lichfield Cathedral Festival), 1953; The Lovers, No News From Father, The Crucible (Bristol Old Vic), 1954; Uncertain Joy, The Gay Venetians (tour), The Beggar's Opera (Canterbury Festival), 1955; The Queen and the Rebels, and The Sleeping Beauty (Bristol Old Vic), 1956; Oh! My Papa! (Bristol Old Vic), 1957; the latter production was subsequently transferred to the Garrick, London, July 1957; A Man for All Seasons (Bristol Old Vic), Mother Courage (Bristol Old Vic), Three (Nottingham Playhouse), 1961–2; The Eagle Dreams (Cairo), 1962; appointed Director of the Welsh National Theatre Company, Apr 1962, for whom he directed A Man for All Seasons, The Rough and the Ready Lot, The Miser, Treasure Island, 1962; War and Peace, Antigone, 1963; Macbeth, Jackie the Jumper, etc; he has also directed Ménage à Trois, Pinocchio, 1963; Mr Whatnot, 1964; Director of the Belgrade Theatre, Coventry, 1966–74, where his productions included: Cyrano de Bergerac, Oh, My Papa!, 1966; Never Say Die, 1969, in which year he also toured Eastern Europe for the British Council; The Doctor and the Devils, 1970; Confrontation, The Price, 1971; Bunny, After Haggerty, 1972; The Front Page, The Beaux' Stratagem, 1973; Manoeuvres, 1974; toured the Middle East for the British Council, 1974; he has also directed for the Arts Council, Cambridge Arts Theatre, and directed productions at the Royal Festival Hall, Royal Albert Hall, etc; 1957–62, directed television and film productions, and has adapted and written original television and film scripts.

JENN, Myvanwy, actress
b Aberystwyth, 12 Nov 1928; *d* of Stanley Jenkins and his wife Helen; trained for the stage at the Guildhall School of Music and Drama and the Royal Academy of Music.

First appeared on stage in 1956 as one of The Terry Sisters, a close harmony duo; first London appearance, as Vanne Terry, playing a number of parts in Wildest Dreams, Vaudeville, 3 Aug 1961; Princes, Aug 1962, appeared in Gentlemen Prefer Blondes; worked extensively with Joan Littlewood's Theatre Workshop, with whom she played a Nurse and Lady French in Oh, What a Lovely War, Stratford E, Mar 1963, and Wyndham's, Jun 1963; Lady Percy in Henry IV, Edinburgh Festival, Aug 1964; Broadway debut, Broadhurst, Sept 1964, in Oh, What a Lovely War; at Stratford E, April 1967, played Lynda MacBird in MacBird, and in Sept 1967, title role in Mrs Wilson's Diary, in which she transferred to the

Criterion, Oct; at Hampstead, Dec 1971, played Fern in His Monkey Wife; Chichester Festival, May 1972, Dolly Trull in The Beggar's Opera; returned to Stratford E, to play Viola in So You Want to Be in Pictures, Nov 1973, and Double O in Gentlemen Prefer Anything, Jan 1974; at the Majestic, NY, May 1979, played Dame Sybil Fitzgibbons in I Remember Mama; work for British TV includes A Family at War, Tom's Midnight Garden and Servants and Masters.

Favourite parts: Nurse, Mrs Wilson, Dame Sybil. *Address:* Star Route, Spencertown, NY 12165, *and* c/o Harbour and Coffey, 9 Blenheim Street, London W1.

JENS, Salome, actress
b Milwaukee, Wisconsin, 8 May 1935; *d* of Arnold John Jens and his wife Salomea (Szujeuska); *e* University of Wisconsin, 1953–4, Northwestern University, 1954–5; *m* (1) Ralph Meeker (mar dis); (2) Lee Leonard; prepared for the stage with Herbert Berghof and at the Actors Studio; formerly engaged as a secretary.

Made her New York stage début at the Longacre, 8 Oct 1956, as Miss Ferguson in Sixth Finger in a Five Finger Glove; Sullivan Street Playhouse, June 1958, Mary in The Bald Soprano and Roberta in Jack; Coronet, Dec 1958, Georgette in The Disenchanted; Gate, Oct 1959, Deirdre in Deirdre of the Sorrows; in stock played Abbie Putnam in Desire Under the Elms, and in Will Success Spoil Rock Hunter? 1959; Martinique, Oct 1959, played in the revue USA; Circle in the Square, Mar 1960, The Girl in The Balcony; Music Box, Apr 1961, Martha Bernays Freud in A Far Country; Pittsburgh Playhouse, 1962, Lady Macbeth in Macbeth; Brooks Atkinson, Oct 1962, Anna in Night Life; Circle in the Square, 1963, took over from Colleen Dewhurst as Abbie Putnam in Desire Under the Elms; Delacorte, Aug 1963, for the New York Shakespeare Festival, Hermione in The Winter's Tale; ANTA-Washington Square, for The Repertory Theater of Lincoln Center, Jan 1964, Louise in After the Fall; Mar 1964, Gilian Prosper in But for Whom, Charlie; Jan 1965, Elmire in Tartuffe; Belasco, Feb 1966, Elaine in First One Asleep, Whistle; Melodyland, Berkeley, California, July 1966, Amanda Prynne in Private Lives; toured, 1966, as Doris W in The Owl and the Pussycat; Theatre de Lys, NY, Dec 1967, Nancy in The Meeting; Mark Hellinger, Apr 1968, Makedah in I'm Solomon; Circle in the Square, June 1968, Josie Hogan in A Moon for the Misbegotten; Imperial, Oct 1969, Countess Sophia Delyanoff in A Patriot for Me; Mark Taper Forum, Los Angeles, 1970, played in Crystal and Fox; Circle in the Square at Ford's, Washington, DC, 1971, Abigail in John and Abigail; Vivian Beaumont, Nov 1971, title-role in Mary Stuart; Forum, Jan 1972, Salome Jens in The Ride Across Lake Constance; American Shakespeare Festival, Stratford, Conn, summer 1972, Cleopatra in Antony and Cleopatra; Actors Studio, May 1973, Julie Holliman in A Break in the Skin; Mark Taper Forum, Los Angeles, Mar 1974, Queen Gertrude in Hamlet; Huntington Hartford, LA, Nov 1974, appeared in One Flew Over the Cuckoo's Nest; entered films, 1961, in Angel Baby, and has since played in The Fool Killer, 1963 (released 1966), Me, Natalie, Seconds, etc; has appeared frequently on television in various dramatic series, including *US Steel Hour, Naked City, The Defenders, Gunsmoke,* etc.

Address: c/o Coleman–Rosenberg, 667 Madison Avenue, New York, NY 10021.

JESSEL, George, actor, producer, and author
b New York City, 3 Apr 1898; *s* of Joseph A Jessel and his wife Charlotte (Schwartz); *e* public schools; *m* (1) Florence Courtney (mar dis); (2) Florence Courtney (mar dis); (3) Florence Courtney (mar dis); (4) Norma Talmadge (mar dis); (5) Lois Andrews (mar dis); (6) Paula Jacobson.

Made his first appearance, in vaudeville, in 1909, with Jack Weiner and Walter Winchell as The Imperial Trio; subsequently joined Gus Edwards' Boys and Girls and toured with Gus Edwards' vaudeville troupe, 1910–14; came to England in 1914, and appeared in variety theatres; made his first appearance in London at the Victoria Palace, and toured until 1917; toured US, 1917–19; on returning to NY appeared in Gaieties, 1919; at the Winter Garden wrote, produced, and appeared in The Troubles of 1920, at the Alhambra, Sept 1920; Palace, Aug 1921, The Troubles of 1921; Fifth Avenue, Jan 1922, appeared in a solo act; wrote, produced, and appeared in George Jessel's Troubles, and later toured, 1922; with Rufus Lemaire, produced Helen of Troy, NY, at the Selwyn, NY, June 1923; Palace, May 1924, played in George Jessel and Company; at the Fulton Theatre, NY, 14 Sept 1925, played Jack Robin in The Jazz Singer, in which he made a remarkable success, and has since played the part over a thousand times; appeared in vaudeville, Chicago, Mar 1928; at the National Theatre, Sept 1928, played Eddie Rosen in The War-Song, of which he was also part-author; Liberty, Feb 1930, Joseph in a play of that name; Ritz, Mar 1930, produced This Man's Town; 46th Street, Nov 1930, played in Sweet and Low; Brighton Beach, July 1931, appeared in Box of Tricks, for which he wrote the lyrics, music, and sketches, and designed the sets and costumes; Palace, Nov 1931, appeared in The Canton-Jessel Show; Casino de Paree, 1934, appeared in Bizarrities; produced tour of Glory for All, 1937; produced Little Old New York at the World's Fair, 1939–40; Broadhurst, Oct 1941, presented High Kickers, of which he was part-author, and in which he played George M Krause, Sen; toured in this last part, June–Aug 1942; presented Show Time, 1942, in which he also appeared; retired from the stage, 1943, in order to direct films; reappeared at the Paramount, Los Angeles, Oct 1950, in Red, White and Blue; toured, July 1957, in the revue Showtime; toured in cabaret with Sophie Tucker and Ted Lewis, in 1965; has toured Vietnam, entertaining troops at the war front at various times in the 1960's; Apr 1972 marked the 150th troop tour since World War I; Carnegie Hall, Apr 1972, appeared in a solo performance; toured England and Germany's Army bases, Dec 1972–Jan 1973; toured, 1975, in That Wonderful World of Vaudeville; entered films, in 1911 with Eddie Cantor in Widow at the Races, and re-entered films in 1926, in Private Izzy Murphy, and has appeared in many pictures; has produced many films, including The Dolly Sisters, Nightmare Alley, Dancing in the Dark, When My Baby Smiles at Me, Tonight We Sing, etc, 1945–53; appeared on radio in 1934 and often since, notably in *Jessel's Jamboree,* 1938–9, *George Jessel's Celebrity Program,* 1940, and *The George Jessel Show,* 1958; has appeared regularly on television since 1953 as guest and host on various comedy and talk shows; called The Toast Master General of the United States in recognition of his dinner speeches, which he has delivered since 1925 in support of various political, humanitarian, and social causes, such as James J Walker's Mayoral campaign, Bonds for Israel, City of Hope Medical Center, and at the White House for several Presidents, the Lambs Club roastings, etc; is the author of many songs and sketches; published his autobiography, So Help Me, 1943, and has since written Hello Momma, 1946, This Way, Miss, 1955, You, Too, Can Make a Speech, 1956, Jessel, Anyone? 1960; Elegy in Manhattan, 1961, Talking to Mother, Halo over Hollywood, 1964, Between the Giants and I, 1966, The World I Live In, 1975; voted Man of the Year by the Beverly Hills B'nai B'rith, 1952; honorary member of the United States Air Force.

Recreation: Book collecting. *Clubs:* Hillcrest, and Writers'. *Address:* 10000 Pico Boulevard, Los Angeles, Calif.

JEWEL, Jimmy (James Arthur Thomas Jewel), comedian and actor

b Sheffield, 4 Dec 1912; *s* of Jimmy Jewel and his wife Gertrude; *m* Belle Bluett.

Made his first stage appearance at the age of 10 in the pantomime Robinson Crusoe, at the Alhambra, Barnsley; left school at 14 to work with his father, making and painting their own scenery and props and appearing in revues and sketches; was for thirty years partner in the variety act Jewel and Warriss, with his cousin Ben Warriss; topped the bill at the London Palladium in this act, 1946, on his first London appearance; later in his career turned to straight acting, and played Willie Clarke in The Sunshine Boys at the Piccadilly, May 1975; Eddie Waters in Comedians, Nottingham Playhouse, 1975, repeating the role with great success at the National theatre at the Old Vic, Nov 1975, and Wyndham's, Jan 1976; again at Nottingham, May 1977, played Willy Loman in Death of a Salesman; films include Starlight Serenade, 1942, What a Carry On, and Let's Have a Murder; has appeared on TV in variety programmes since 1942, and more recently in plays such as Spanner in the Works, Lucky for Some, and the series *Funny Man*; active in several production companies promoting TV and stage plays.

Favourite parts: Willie Clarke, Eddie Waters, Willy Loman. *Address:* c/o Jill Foster Ltd, 35 Brompton Road, London SW3. *Tel:* 581 0084.

JOHNS, Glynis, actress

b Pretoria, South Africa, 5 Oct 1923; *d* of Mervyn Johns and his wife Alys Maude (Steel-Payne); *e* Clifton High School and Hampstead High School; *m* (1) Anthony Forwood (mar dis); (2) David Ramsey Foster (mar dis); (3) C P L Henderson (mar dis); (4) Elliot Arnold.

Made her first appearance on the stage at the Garrick Theatre, 26 Dec 1935, as Ursula in Buckie's Bears; Old Vic, Feb 1936, and Daly's, Mar 1936, played Hortense in St Helena; Gate, Nov 1936, appeared in The Children's Hour; Embassy, Dec 1936, the Elf and the Child in The Melody That Got Lost; Embassy, May, and Strand, June 1937, Sonia Kuman in Judgment Day; Phoenix, Dec 1937, Cinderella in A Kiss for Cinderella; Richmond, Apr and Wyndham's, Oct 1938, Miranda in Quiet Wedding; Phoenix, Nov 1939, again played Sonia in Judgment Day; Wyndham's, July 1941, Miranda Bute in Quiet Week-End; Cambridge Theatre, Dec 1943, Peter in Peter Pan; toured, Oct 1944, as Corinne in I'll See You Again; Fortune, Sept 1946, Pam in Fools Rush In; Phoenix, Mar 1950, Mary Flemin in The Way Things Go; made her first appearance on the New York stage at the Plymouth, 30 Jan 1952, in the title-role in Gertie; Martin Beck, NY, Oct 1956, played the title-role in Major Barbara; at the Coconut Grove, Florida, Mar 1958, played Jennifer Wren in Plaintiff in a Pretty Hat; 54th Street, NY, Mar 1963, Miss Mopply in Too True to Be Good; Garrick, July 1966, Anne of Cleves in The King's Mare; New, Jan 1970, appeared in Come As You Are, transferring in this production to the Strand, June 1970; toured S Africa, 1971, as Ann Stanley in Forty Carats; toured UK, USA and Australia, 1971–2, as The Marquise; Shubert, NY, Feb 1973, played Desirée Armfeldt in A Little Night Music; Ahmanson, Los Angeles, 1975, Madame Desmortes in Ring Round the Moon; Phoenix, London, Mar 1976, Leontine in 13 Rue de l'Amour; Her Majesty's, July 1977, Alma Rattenbury in Cause Célèbre; entered films, 1937, and has appeared in South Riding, Frieda, An Ideal Husband, Miranda, State

Secret, No Highway, Encore, The Card, Personal Affair, Rob Roy, The Beachcomber, Mad About Men, The Court Jester, Loser Takes All, The Sundowners (Oscar Award nomination), The Chapman Report, Mary Poppins, Under Milk Wood, etc.

Address: c/o ICM Ltd, 22 Grafton Street, London, W1.

JOHNS, Mervyn, actor

b Pembroke, South Wales, 18 Feb 1899; *s* of William Johns and his wife Margaret (Samuel); *e* Llandovery; *m* (1) Alys Maude Steele-Payne; (2) Diana Churchill; was formerly a medical student at the London Hospital; studied for the stage at the Royal Academy of Dramatic Art, where he received the gold medal and other awards.

Made his first appearance on the stage at the Comedy Theatre, 28 Aug 1923, as a Sailor in The Elopement; Comedy, Mar 1924, played Richards in Far Above Rubies, and June 1924, Trant in Dead Man's Pool; Feb 1925, toured in and stage-managed Pollyanna, and Jan 1926, in The Last Waltz; from Sept 1926 to June 1934, played comedy leads at the Little Theatre, Bristol, and was for some time producer there; in 1928, toured for ten months in South Africa; Apollo Theatre, London, Oct 1934, played in Hyde Park Corner; Embassy, Oct 1936, Sir John Brute in The Provoked Wife; Vaudeville, Dec 1936, King Hildebrand in The Sleeping Beauty; Ring, Feb 1937, Sir Hugh Evans in The Merry Wives of Windsor, which he again played at the Open Air Theatre, June 1937; Open Air, June 1937, played Snug in A Midsummer Night's Dream; Duchess, Aug 1937, Ernest Beevors in Time and the Conways; Haymarket, June 1938, Ted Jones in Comedienne; New, Sept 1938, Smithson in Can We Tell?; Whitehall, Mar 1939, Sir Patrick Cullen in The Doctor's Dilemma; Globe, June 1939, Shoni Lloyd in Rhondda Roundabout; Wyndham's, Nov 1939, Wickers in Saloon Bar; St James's, Dec 1942, succeeded Michael Redgrave as Gribaud in The Duke in Darkness; Cambridge Theatre, Apr 1943, played Captain Shotover in Heartbreak House; New Theatre, Hull, Nov 1944, played in The Golden Fleece; Lyric, Hammersmith, June 1947, Doolittle in Pygmalion; Ambassadors', Mar 1949, Michael Norbury in Love's a Funny Thing; Embassy, Aug 1949, appeared as Jeeter Lester in Tobacco Road, and later in the same month played this part at the Playhouse; Westminster, Apr 1951, played Harold Martin in The Martin's Nest; Duke of York's, Nov 1951, Fulbert in Héloïse; at the same theatre, Apr 1952, appeared as Shurie in The Mortimer Touch; Royal Court, Nov 1961, and Feb 1962, played Ben Morton in The Keep, transferring with the production to the Piccadilly, Mar 1962; Hampstead Theatre Club, Apr 1964, Jacob in All Good Children; New, Cardiff, Apr 1965, Mr Withers in Heirs and Graces; Sadler's Wells, Mar 1972, Baines in Lord Arthur Savile's Crime; entered films, 1934, and has appeared in numerous pictures, most recently The National Health, and The Confessional; recent television includes *The New Avengers, Kilvert's Diaries* and *Shoestring*.

Recreations: Motoring and golf. *Address:* c/o Stella Richards Personal Management, 5 Rima House, Callow Street, London SW3.

JOHNSON, Celia, CBE, actress

b Richmond, Surrey, 18 Dec 1908; *d* of John Robert Johnson, MRCS, LRCP and his wife Ethel (Griffiths); *e* St Paul's Girls' School and abroad; *m* Peter Fleming (dec); studied for the stage at the Royal Academy of Dramatic Art.

Made her first appearance on the stage at the Theatre Royal, Huddersfield, Aug 1928, as Sarah in Major Barbara; made her first appearance in London at the Lyric, Hammersmith, Jan 1929, when she succeeded Angela Baddeley as Currita in A Hundred Years Old; in Aug 1929, toured as Thérèse Meunier in Typhoon, with the Dennis Neilson Terry company; Kingsway, Mar 1930, played Suzette in The Artist and the Shadow; and at the Lyric, Apr 1930, Loveday Trevelyan in Debonair; May 1930, Juliet in the balcony scene from Romeo and Juliet; Playhouse, June 1930, Doris Lea in Cynara; Arts, Sept 1930, Elle in L'Occasion (in French); Vaudeville, Mar 1931, Elizabeth in The Circle; Savoy, June 1931, Grezia in Death Takes a Holiday; Criterion, July 1931, succeeded Madeleine Carroll as Phyl in After All; then went to America, and made her first appearance in New York, at the Broadhurst Theatre, 5 Nov 1931, as Ophelia in Hamlet; on returning to London, appeared at the Globe, Feb 1932, as Judy in Punchinello; Apollo, Mar 1932, played Elsa in The Man I Killed; St James's, June 1932, Leone Merrick in The Vinegar Tree; Arts, June 1932, Anne Hargreaves in As It Was In The Beginning; Haymarket, Aug 1932, the Hon Cynthia Lynne in To-Morrow will be Friday; Embassy, Jan 1933, Betty Findon in Ten Minute Alibi; Lyric, Jan 1933, succeeded Edna Best as Stella Hallam in Another Language; Arts, Feb 1933, Celia Desmond in These Two; Haymarket, Feb 1933, again played Betty Findon in Ten Minute Alibi; Embassy, May 1933, Sheila Grey in Sometimes Even Now; St Martin's, Sept 1933, Janet Carr in The Key; Oct 1933, Anne Hargraves in The Wind and the Rain, which she played for two years; St James's, Feb 1936, Elizabeth Bennet in Pride and Prejudice; Aug 1937, Judith in Old Music, and May 1939, Jacqueline Hochepot in Sixth Floor; Queen's, Apr 1940, played Mrs de Winter in Rebecca; Haymarket, Sept 1942, succeeded Vivien Leigh as Jennifer in The Doctor's Dilemma; after an absence of five years from the stage, reappeared at the New, Dec 1947, with the Old Vic Company, in the title-role of St Joan; in 1950, toured in Italy, with the Old Vic Company, playing Viola in Twelfth Night; Aldwych, May 1951, appeared as Olga in Three Sisters; Westminster, June 1954, played Laura Hammond in It's Never Too Late; Cambridge, May 1955, Sheila Broadbent in The Reluctant Debutante; Haymarket, Nov 1957, played Isobel Cherry in Flowering Cherry; St Martin's, Dec 1958, Hilary in The Grass is Greener; at the same theatre, Feb 1960, directed Special Providence (in the double bill Double Yolk); Wyndham's, Nov 1960, played Pamela Puffy-Picq in Chin-Chin; Haymarket, Nov 1962, played Clare Elliot in The Tulip Tree; Phoenix, Oct 1963, Helen Hampster in Out of the Crocodile; joined the National Theatre Company at the Old Vic, June 1964, to play Mrs Solness in The Master Builder; Mar 1965, took over the part of Judith Bliss in Hay Fever; Chichester Festival, July 1966, played Madame Ranyevsky in The Cherry Orchard; Duke of York's, Mar 1967, Sheila in Relatively Speaking; O'Keefe, Toronto, Jan 1968, again played Judith Bliss in Hay Fever, returning to play the part at the Duke of York's, Feb 1968; Nottingham Playhouse, Nov 1970, Gertrude in Hamlet, and also at the Cambridge, Jan 1971; Savoy, Oct 1972, took over the part of Lady Boothroyd in Lloyd George Knew My Father; Oxford Festival, Sept 1974, and Wyndham's, Oct 1974, Sybil Hathaway in The Dame of Sark; Lyric, May 1977, Evelyn in The Kingfisher; has appeared in films, notably in In Which We Serve, Dear Octopus, This Happy Breed, Brief Encounter, A Kid for Two Farthings, The Good Companions, The Prime of Miss Jean Brodie, etc; received the honour of Commander of the British Empire in the Birthday Honours, 1958.

Address: Merrimoles House, Nettlebed, Oxon.

JOHNSON, Richard, actor

b Upminster, Essex, 30 July 1927; *s* of Keith Holcombe Johnson and his wife Frances Louisa Olive (Tweed); *e* Parkfield School and Felsted; *m* (1) Sheila Sweet (mar dis); (2) Kim Novak (mar

dis); studied for the stage at the Royal Academy of Dramatic Art.

First appeared at the Opera House, Manchester, July 1944, in a small part in Hamlet, and played in the same production during Sir John Gielgud's repertory season which opened at the Haymarket, Sept 1944; during this season also played small parts in Love For Love, The Circle, and The Duchess of Malfi; played in repertory at Perth, 1945; served in the Royal Navy, 1945–8; returned to repertory at Perth, 1948–9; toured, 1949, in The Happiest Days of Your Life and The Paragon; Bedford, Camden Town, Jan–Apr 1950, appeared in a season of old melodrama; Embassy, May 1950, played Marius Tertius in The First Victoria; St James's, Feb 1951, played Pierre in The Madwoman of Chaillot; Open Air Theatre, May 1951, Demetrius in A Midsummer Night's Dream; Ambassadors', May 1952, George Phillips in After My Fashion; joined the Bristol Old Vic Company for the 1953 season; was engaged solely in broadcasting and television during 1954; at the Lyric, Hammersmith, May 1955, appeared as Beauchamp, Earl of Warwick, in The Lark; visited Moscow with Peter Brook's production of Hamlet, playing Laertes, Nov 1955 (the first British company to visit Russia since the revolution); repeated his performance at the Phoenix, London, Dec 1955; Saville, Feb 1956, Jack Absolute in The Rivals; Duchess, Oct 1956, Lord Plynlimmon in Plaintiff in a Pretty Hat, which later transferred to the St Martin's; at the Shakespeare Memorial Theatre, Stratford-on-Avon, played the following parts: Orlando in As You Like It, Mark Antony in Julius Caesar, Leonatus in Cymbeline, and Ferdinand in The Tempest, 1957; Drury Lane, Dec 1957, again played in The Tempest; Shakespeare Memorial Theatre, 1958, Romeo in Romeo and Juliet, Sir Andrew Aguecheek in Twelfth Night, the title-role in Pericles, and Don John in Much Ado About Nothing; in Nov–Dec 1958, played in Moscow and Leningrad in Romeo and Juliet and Twelfth Night; Cambridge, London, Feb 1960, Henry Lee in The Wrong Side of the Park, which later transferred to the St Martin's; Aldwych, Dec 1960, again played Sir Andrew Aguecheek in Twelfth Night, when the Shakespeare Memorial Company (re-named Royal Shakespeare Company), began their first repertory season in their new London home; he subsequently appeared for them as Hans in Ondine, Jan 1961, and Urbain Grandier in The Devils, Feb 1961, and in the anthology The Hollow Crown, June 1961; made his first appearance in New York at the Ethel Barrymore, Nov 1961, as Clive Root in The Complaisant Lover; on returning to London he again appeared at the Aldwych, Oct 1962, as Grandier in The Devils; Lyceum, NY, Nov 1963, devised The Golden Age; he also appeared in The Hollow Crown at the Geneva, Holland, and Paris Festivals; formed Pageant Entertainments Ltd, in 1969; Criterion, Feb 1969, produced Brief Lives; returned to the RSC to play Mark Antony in Julius Caesar and in Antony and Cleopatra, Stratford, 1972 season, and Aldwych, July 1973; Her Majesty's, Oct 1975, played Thomas in Thomas and the King; Lyttelton, June 1976, Charles in Blithe Spirit; also for the National Theatre played Pontius Pilate in The Passion, Pinchwife in The Country Wife, 1977; Nandor in The Guardsman, 1978; TV performances include A Marriage, and Murder in Your Mind; first appeared in films, 1950, in Captain Horatio Hornblower; other films include The Pumpkin Eater, The Amorous Adventures of Moll Flanders, and The Beloved (also co-produced).

Favourite part: Warwick in The Lark. *Recreations:* Country pursuits, music, and travel. *Address:* c/o Leading Artists, 60 St James's Street, London SW1.

JOHNSON, Van, actor and singer, formerly a dancer

b Newport, Rhode Island, 25 Aug 1916; *s* of Charles Johnson and his wife Loretta (Snyder); *e* Newport High School; *m* Eve Abbott Wynn (mar dis).

Made his first appearance in New York at the Vanderbilt, 19 May 1936, in the chorus of New Faces of 1936; toured as a singer in vaudeville, 1936; Rainbow Room, NYC, 1936, played in Eight Men in Manhattan; Imperial, Oct 1939, played the Student in Too Many Girls; Ethel Barrymore, Dec 1940, understudied Gene Kelly as Joey Evans, played Victor, and danced in Pal Joey; entered films for a number of years, returning to the stage in his London debut at the Adelphi, 9 Mar 1961, as Professor Harold Hill in The Music Man; Morosco, NY, Oct 1962, played Herbert H Lundquist in Come on Strong; Eugene O'Neill, Nov 1965, Bruce Barrett in Mating Dance; toured, Sep—Oct 1966, as Dr Mark Bruckner in On a Clear Day You Can See Forever; Coconut Grove Playhouse, Miami, Fla, 1968, Robert Danvers in There's a Girl in My Soup; State Fair Music Hall, Dallas, Texas, summer 1968, Jeff Moss in Bells Are Ringing; Morosco, Jan 1970, took over as Billy Boylan in Forty Carats; toured, summer 1971, as Robert Danvers in There's a Girl in My Soup; toured, 1972, in Help Stamp Out Marriage; Studio Arena, Buffalo, NY, Feb 1974, again played in There's a Girl in My Soup; Country Dinner Playhouse, Dallas, Texas, Apr 1974, in Help Stamp Out Marriage; Drury Lane, Chicago, June 1974, Paul Friedman in 6 Rms, Riv Vu; toured, 1975, as Robert in Boeing-Boeing; made his film debut in his original part in Too Many Girls, 1940, and has since played in The Human Comedy, Madame Curie, Till the Clouds Roll By, Battleground, The Caine Mutiny, Brigadoon, Eagle over London (1973). and many others; first played on television in The Pied Piper of Hamelin, 26 Nov 1957.

Address: Alan Foshko Associates, 305 West 52nd Street, New York, NY 10019. *Tel:* JU2–2417.

JOHNSTON, Denis (William), OBE, dramatic author
b Dublin, Eire, 18 June 1901; *s* of the Hon William John Johnston, Judge of the Supreme Court, and his wife Kathleen (King); *e* St Andrews College, Dublin, Merchiston Castle, Edinburgh, Christ's College, Cambridge (MA), and Harvard University, USA; Barrister-at-law (Inner Temple and King's Inns, and Northern Ireland); *m* (1) Shelah Richards (mar dis); (2) Betty Chancellor.

Author of the following plays: The Old Lady Says 'No'!, 1929; The Moon in the Yellow River, 1931; A Bride for the Unicorn, 1933; Storm Song, 1934; Blind Man's Buff (adapted from Ernst Toller), 1936; The Golden Cuckoo, 1938; The Dreaming Dust, 1940, revived in 1946, as Weep for the Cyclops; A Fourth for Bridge, 1948; Strange Occurrence on Ireland's Eye (re-written from Blind Man's Buff), 1956; The Scythe and the Sunset, 1958; Director of the Dublin Gate Theatre, 1931–36; appeared at the Westminster, London, Apr 1936, as An-Lu-Shan in Armlet of Jade; co-directed Ah, Wilderness, at the Westminster, May 1936; joined the BBC, 1936, becoming a television producer at Alexandra Palace, in 1938; served as a BBC War Correspondent, 1942–45; appointed Programme Director, BBC Television Service, 1946–47; Director of the Provincetown Playhouse, New York, 1952; Professor of English at Mount Holyoke College, Mass, 1950–60; Head of Theatre Department, Smith College, Northampton, Mass, USA, 1960–66; has held visiting Professorships at the U of Iowa, U of California at Davis, NYU, and Whitman College, Washington; author of the autobiography Nine Rivers from Jordan, 1953; In Search of Swift (biography), 1959; Hon D Litt, U of Ulster, 1979.

Recreation: Sailing. *Clubs:* Garrick, Royal Irish Yacht Club. *Address:* 8 Sorrento Terrace, Dalkey, Co Dublin, Eire.

JOHNSTON, Margaret, actress
b Sydney, NSW, 10 Aug 1918; *d* of James Johnston and his wife Emily; *e* Sydney University; *m* Al Parker (dec).

Made her first appearance on the stage at Sydney, 1936; on coming to England, studied under Dr Stefan Hock, and at the Royal Academy of Dramatic Art; made her first appearance in London, at Wyndham's, Nov 1939, as the Waitress and Jean in Saloon Bar; played repertory seasons at Worthing, Coventry, etc; at Wyndham's, 1940, understudied Elizabeth Allan, as Janet Royd in Quiet Wedding; during 1941–2, appeared in several plays at the Q Theatre, including To Fit the Crime, which was transferred to the Comedy, July 1942, as Murder Without Crime, in which she played the part of Jan, for twelve months; at the Phoenix, June 1944, appeared as Angele Kernahan in The Last of Summer; Lyric, Hammersmith, Oct 1945, Susanna Willard in The Shouting Dies, and Feb 1946, Kitty Duval in The Time of Your Life; Garrick, May 1948, played Elizabeth Barrett in The Barretts of Wimpole Street; Embassy, and subsequently at the Garrick, July 1950, played Laurie Phillipson in Always Afternoon; toured, Oct 1950, as Rita in Chuckeyhead Story; Lyric, Hammersmith, Nov 1951, played Alma Winemiller in Summer and Smoke, and appeared in this part at the Duchess, Jan 1952; Vaudeville, Sept 1952, played Miranda Bolton in Second Threshold; Aldwych, Apr 1954, Gelda in The Dark Is Light Enough; at the Shakespeare Memorial Theatre, Stratford-on-Avon, 1956 season, played Portia in The Merchant of Venice, Desdemona in Othello, and Isabella in Measure for Measure; Royal Court, Apr 1959, played Mrs Gabrielle Broadbent in Sugar in the Morning; Savoy, July 1959, Emma Gore in The Ring of Truth; Royalty, Jan 1961, played Marie van Maasdijk in Masterpiece; Chichester Festival, Aug 1966, Lady Macbeth in Macbeth; has also appeared in films, notably in Portrait of Clare, Touch and Go, Life at the Top, etc.

Address: 50 Mount Street, London W1.

JONES, David, director
b Poole, Dorset, 19 Feb 1934; *s* of John David Jones, and his wife Gwendolen Agnes Langworthy (Ricketts); *e* Taunton School and Christ's College, Cambridge; *m* Sheila Allen.

Formerly a television director; his first production on the London stage, 1961, at the Mermaid, was the triple bill Sweeney Agonistes, Purgatory, and Krapp's Last Tape; he has since directed the following plays, largely for the Royal Shakespeare Company, of which he is an associate artist: The Empire Builders, 1962; Saint's Day (Stratford, E), The Governor's Lady (one-act), The Investigation (with Peter Brook), 1965; Belcher's Luck, 1966; As You Like It (Stratford and London), 1947; Diary of a Scoundrel (Liverpool), The Tempest (Chichester), 1968; in the same year his production of As You Like It visited Los Angeles and was revived at Stratford; The Silver Tassie, 1969; After Haggerty, The Plebeians Rehearse the Uprising, 1970; Enemies, 1971; The Lower Depths and The Island of the Mighty, 1972; Love's Labour's Lost, 1973; Duck Song and Summerfolk, 1974; The Marrying of Ann Leete, The Return of A J Raffles and Twelfth Night (Stratford, Ontario), 1975; in 1975 his production of Summerfolk visited New York where it won an Obie award, accompanied by a revival of his Love's Labour's Lost, which returned to play in London; The Zykovs, Ivanov, 1976; All's Well That Ends Well (Stratford, Ontario), 1977; Cymbeline, Baal, 1979; company director for the London seasons 1969–72; Artistic Director (Aldwych), 1975–7; appointed Artistic Director, Brooklyn Academy of Music Theatre Company, 1979; first television production, 1958, for

Monitor, on which he worked until 1964; more recently, he has produced Ice Age, The Beaux' Stratagem, Langrishe Go Down, and Play of the Month, 1977–9; introduced *The Present Stage* series, 1965, the arts magazine *Review*, 1971–2, and The Case of Eliza Armstrong, 1974.

Recreations: Chess, reading modern poetry and escaping to mountains and/or islands. *Address:* Brooklyn Academy of Music, 30 Lafayette Avenue, Brooklyn, NY 11217.

JONES, Disley, designer

b Burton-on-Trent, 15 Jan 1926; *s* of Harold Jones and his wife Marie Beatrice (Day); *e* Avondale School, Sutton Cold-field, Warwickshire; formerly a window dresser, engineering draughtsman, nurseryman, florist, and farm hand.

Designed his first production for the Midland Theatre Company at the College Theatre, Coventry, 1946, with Twelfth Night; subsequently designed productions for the following repertory theatres: Manchester Intimate, 1947; Dundee Repertory, 1949; High Wycombe, Worthing, Wolverhampton, Oxford Playhouse, Bristol Old Vic, 1950–6; designed his first London production at the Arts Theatre, Apr 1953, with The Seagull; he has since designed the following productions: Arms and the Man, The Bespoke Overcoat, Penelope, 1953; The Impresario From Smyrna, 1954; Listen to the Wind, 1955; Gigi, Who Cares?, *Jose Greco Ballet*, 1956; Subway in the Sky, Malatesta, The Mirror, *Ballet Rambert*, Share My Lettuce, 1957; The Dock Brief, and What Shall We Tell Caroline?, Chrysanthemum, Edward II (Cambridge Marlowe Society), 1958; One to Another, The Demon Barber, 1959; Tomorrow With Pictures, The Proposal, and Miss Julie, Out of this World, 1960; Rhinoceros (Icelandic National Theatre), South, Bonne Soupe, Out of My Mind, 1961; The Rag Trade, The Blue Bird, 3 At Nine, 1962; The Rivals, Romeo and Juliet (Aarhus Theatre, Denmark), Hamlet (Icelandic National Theatre), 1963; The Mikado (D'Oyly Carte), Nights at the Comedy, Instant Marriage, 1964; The Solid Gold Cadillac, Nymphs and Satires, Something Nasty in the Woodshed, 1965; Come Spy With Me, Strike A Light and Jorrocks, 1966; The Good Old Days, 1972; designed his first television production, Mar 1960, with All Summer Long; other productions include: The Rehearsal, Summer's Pride, The Teachers, The Funambulists; first film as production designer Mikado, 1965, followed by The Long Day's Dying, The Italian Job, The Revolutionary and Murphy's War.

Recreations: Gardening, travelling, going to the cinema, and collecting picture post cards. *Address:* 7 Lansdowne House, Lansdowne Road, London, W1. *Tel:* 01–727 9354 and Snape (Suffolk) 417.

JONES, Dudley (Gilbert), actor

b Watford, Herts, 26 Dec 1914; *s* of Harold William Jones and his wife Annie (Toms); *e* Watford Grammar School; *m* (1) Carol Hill (dec); (2) Julia Wootten; formerly a laboratory assistant, and clerk; trained for the stage at the Royal Academy of Dramatic Art, where he received the Lever-hulme Scholarship.

Made his first appearance on the stage at the Barn Theatre, Oxted, Surrey, 1936, when he played Tony Lumpkin in She Stoops to Conquer; Birmingham Rep, Dec 1936, Puck in A Midsummer Night's Dream; Stratford, 1937, appeared in Shakespeare Season; made his first appearance on the London stage at the Embassy, Nov 1937, as the Singer in Cymbeline; Westminster, Jan 1938, played Nano in Volpone; Savoy, Oct 1938, played Emilio in An Elephant in Arcady; Open Air, Regent's Park, 1938 season, parts included Snug in A Midsummer Night's Dream, and, 1939, Feste in Twelfth

Night; served in the Royal Air Force, 1940–6; Shakespeare Memorial Company, Stratford-on-Avon, 1946–7, playing among other parts: Gower (Pericles), Costard, Pompey, Fluellen, Feste, and Lancelot Gobbo; at the Playhouse, Feb 1948, played Bauer in Cockpit; Mercury, Jan 1949, Siro in Mandragola; Arts, Apr 1949, played Tony Lumpkin in She Stoops to Conquer; at the same theatre, Dec 1949, Abe in The Silver Curlew; made his first appearance in America, when he toured the United States, 1950–1, as Touchstone in As You Like It, with Katharine Hepburn; Strand, London, Oct 1951, played Pelham Humphrey in the musical And So To Bed; Arts, May 1953, played the Beadle in Second Best Bed; at the same theatre, Jan 1955, Dr Spiga in The Rules of the Game; joined the Old Vic Company, 1955–7, to play a variety of parts including: Sir Hugh Evans in The Merry Wives of Windsor, Nestor in Troilus and Cressida, and Dogberry in Much Ado About Nothing; toured the United States with the Old Vic Company, 1958–9, playing the First Gravedigger in Hamlet, Fluellen in Henry V, and Feste in Twelfth Night; toured England, 1961, as Davis in The Caretaker; Royal Court, Nov 1961, played Alvin Morton in The Keep; Garrick, Apr 1962, Mr Bream in Two Stars for Comfort; toured, 1962, as Wyn in Loud Organs; Royal Court, Feb 1963, played the Rev Richie Rees in Jackie the Jumper; Ashcroft, Croydon, May 1963, Gibbet in The Beaux' Stratagem; Mermaid, Aug 1963, played Hitler and Little Fat Man in Schweyk in the Second World War; Bristol Old Vic, Feb 1964–May 1966, played Cardinal of Macao in The Successor, Eric Fawcett in They Called the Bastard Stephen, Major Petkoff in Arms and the Man, Bitos in Poor Bitos, Bottom in A Midsummer Night's Dream, Firs in The Cherry Orchard, De Stogumber in Saint Joan, and George Daubeny in Sixty Thousand Nights; Malvern Festival, July–Aug 1966, played M Remy in False Confessions, Leth-ington in The Castaway, Napoleon in The Man of Destiny and Androcles in Androcles and the Lion; St Martin's, June 1967, Potapov and others in Beware of the Dog; Scala, Dec 1967, Smee in Peter Pan; Bristol Old Vic, May 1968, Sorin in The Seagull, the Chaplain and Matthew Skips in The Lady's Not for Burning; Piccadilly, Feb 1969, Daniel Tucker in The Ruling Class; Bristol Old Vic, Aug–Dec 1970, Petkoff in Arms and the Man and Canon Chasuble in The Importance of Being Earnest; Bristol Old Vic, Spring 1971, played Mr Shaw in In Celebration, Basho in Narrow Road to the Deep North, and Mr Prosser in The Investiture; toured, Sept 1971, as Tapper-coom in The Lady's Not for Burning; Globe, Aug 1972, Harold Twine in Popkiss; Bristol, Spring 1973, Baptista in The Taming of the Shrew, Sir Paul Pliant in The Double Dealer, and Max Harkaway in London Assurance, returning in Feb 1974 to play Henry Ormondroyd in When We Are Married; Her Majesty's, July 1974, Truby, Tarvin and Ridvers in The Good Companions; Windsor, May 1975, Sir Percy Shorter in Habeas Corpus; Bristol Old Vic, Mar 1976, played Augustin Feraillon in A Flea in Her Ear; Mermaid, July 1976, Bocadon in Some of My Best Friends are Husbands; Redgrave, Farnham, June 1977, Rev Gardner in Mrs Warren's Profession, and Hugo Birch in Spider's Web; Connaught, Worthing, Sept 1977, Grayton Faucit in The Stamp Collectors; Arnaud, Guildford, Nov 1977, Silas Bazeby in The Case of the Oily Levantine; Ludlow Festival, 1978, Christopher Sly and The Pedant in The Taming of the Shrew; Edinburgh Festival, Aug 1978 and tour, Price in Shifts; Arnaud, Guildford, Jan 1979 and tour, Mayhew in Witness for the Prosecution; has appeared in a number of films and on television, recently in Rosie, and I Didn't Know You Cared.

Favourite part: Fluellen. *Recreations:* Gardening and odd-jobbery. *Address:* c/o Bryan Drew Ltd, 81 Shaftesbury Avenue, London, W1.

JONES, Gemma, actress

b London, 4 Dec 1942; *d* of Griffith Jones, and his wife Irene (Isaac); *e* Francis Holland School, London; trained for the stage at RADA 1960–2, receiving the Bancroft Gold Medal.

First professional appearance, Jan 1963, at the Ashcroft Theatre, Croydon, as Cherry in The Beaux' Stratagem; first appeared on the London stage Feb 1963 at the Phoenix, as Johanna in Baal; Mermaid, June, and Duchess, July 1963, played Gilda in Alfie; at the Playhouse, Nottingham, 1964–5, played parts including Portia in The Merchant of Venice and Adele in The Cavern, transferring to the Strand, Nov 1965, in the latter production, and receiving the Clarence Derwent award for her performance; Hampstead, Feb 1966, Eugenie in The Pastime of M Robert; Thorndike, Leatherhead, Apr 1966, Victoria in Portrait of A Queen; Wimbledon, July 1966 the title role in Saint Joan; New, Feb 1967, Helen Schlegel in Howard's End; Open Air, Regent's Park, July 1968, Julia in Two Gentlemen of Verona; Repertory, Birmingham, Mar 1969, Ophelia in Hamlet; Fortune, Sept 1969, Valerie Jordan in There'll Be Some Changes Made; Thorndike, Nov 1969, Nina in The Seagull; Theatre Royal, Bath (for Bristol Old Vic), May 1971, Christina of Sweden in The Abdication; Queen's, Oct 1971, Polly Oliver in Getting On; toured the world, 1972–3, as Hippolyta/Titania in the RSC's production of A Midsummer Night's Dream; joined the National Theatre at the Old Vic to play Susan Lloyd in Next of Kin, May 1974, and the Countess in The Marriage of Figaro, July 1974; Nottingham Playhouse, Nov 1975, Blanche DuBois in A Streetcar Named Desire; Garrick, May 1978, Ruth in The Homecoming; Queen's, July 1979, Helen in And a Nightingale Sang; first film, The Devils, 1971; television, since 1962, includes: The Lie, The Way of the World, and *The Duchess of Duke Street.*

Favourite parts: Katherina in The Taming of the Shrew, Ida in See How They Run. *Recreation:* Reading. *Address:* c/o Larry Dalzell Associates Ltd, 3 Goodwin's Court, St Martin's Lane, London, WC2. *Tel:* 01–240 3086.

JONES, Griffith, actor

b London, 19 Nov 1910; *s* of William Thomas Jones and his wife Eleanor (Doughty); *e* Polytechnic Secondary School, and University College, London; *m* Irene Isaac; studied for the stage at the Royal Academy of Dramatic Art, where he was gold medallist in 1932.

While still at the Academy, made his first appearance on the stage at the Embassy Theatre, 24 Dec 1930, as Achmed in Carpet Slippers; Q, Jan 1931, played Nuitane in Aloma, and Embassy, Feb 1931, Leiba in Lady in Waiting; Vaudeville, Apr 1932, the Commentator in Vile Bodies; Globe, May 1932, Michael O'Dea in Ourselves Alone; New (for Arts Theatre), June 1932, Sir John Montague in Richard of Bordeaux; Ambassadors', Nov 1932, Arnold Rowe in Philomel; Playhouse, Apr 1933, Weyland in The Rats of Norway; Lyric, Aug 1933, Lieut Hensch in The Ace; Apollo, Dec 1933, Caryl Sanger in Escape Me Never; Open Air, Aug 1934, Romeo; made his first appearance in New York, at the Shubert Theatre, 21 Jan 1935, as Caryl in Escape Me Never; Arts, Feb and Criterion, Apr 1936, Clive Monkhams in After October; Lyric, Sept 1936, Captain Michael Torday in Farewell Performance; Queen's, July 1937, Arne in Women of Property; St Martin's, Aug 1937, Will Heatley in Gertie Maude; His Majesty's, Mar 1938, Nigel in Operette; Westminster, Dec 1938, Marco Polo in Marco Millions; Shaftesbury, May 1939, Eric Carrington in Behold the Bride; New, Jan 1940, Dick Lawson in Believe It or Not; subsequently, during 1940, played Eben in Desire Under the Elms, and Albert Feather in Ladies in Retirement; he then joined the

Army, and was demobilized in 1945; reappeared on the London stage, at the Haymarket, Aug 1945, when he played Lord Darlington in Lady Windermere's Fan, and played in this until 1947; during 1947–8, appeared in films; toured, 1948, as Jan in The Farm of Three Echoes; Prince's, May 1949, played Clive Riordan in A Man About a Dog; Embassy, Oct 1950, the Nobleman in The Man With a Load of Mischief; St Martin's, Apr 1951, appeared in Shavings, a programme of one-act comedies by Bernard Shaw, when he played A in Village Wooing, and Shakespeare in The Dark Lady of the Sonnets; at the Irving, Nov 1951, and Embassy, Dec 1951, appeared in seasons of Grand Guignol, playing in The Mask, Andronicus, and Dalgarni (of which he was the author); Saville, May 1952, played the Earl of Dawlish in The Moonraker; Phoenix, Sept 1952, the Marquess of Heronden in Quadrille; toured, 1953–4, as Tweedledum and the Red Knight in Alice Through the Looking Glass, and played these parts at the Prince's, Feb 1954; late in 1954, toured as Hilton Denver in The Love Machine; Westminster, Aug 1955, played Robert Leigh in Dead on Nine; at the Irving, Oct 1955, appeared in the revue Blueprint; toured, 1958, as Archie Rice in The Entertainer; toured, 1959, in Expresso Bongo; Lyric, Hammersmith, June 1960, played Lincoln Brooks in Innocent as Hell; Richmond, Feb 1962, played James Murray in Someone to Kill; Flora Robson Theatre, Newcastle, Dec 1962, played Long John Silver in Treasure Island; toured, 1963–4, as Gustav Bergmann in Close Quarters, with Flora Robson; Comedy, Sept 1964, played the title part in The Home Secretary, and Charles in Lady JP 2, in the double-bill entitled Two Accounts Rendered; Strand, Nov 1965, The Count in The Cavern; Arnaud, Guildford, Apr 1966, played Sir Colenso Ridgeon in The Doctor's Dilemma, repeating the part at the Comedy, June 1966; Duke of York's, June 1971, took over as Sir Dymock Blackburn in The Jockey Club Stakes; at Nottingham Playhouse, Sept 1973, played James Avon in Brassneck, and Baptista in The Taming of the Shrew; Crucible, Sheffield, Apr 1974, Sir Peter Teazle in The School for Scandal; Stratford, season 1975, played Ghost in Hamlet, Stanley in Perkin Warbeck, and Stanley in Richard III, all at The Other Place, and Glendower in Henry IV, part 1, Lord Chief Justice in Henry IV, part 2, at the Memorial Theatre; repeated Ghost at the Round House, Jan 1976, and Glendower and Lord Chief Justice at the Aldwych, Jan 1976; Stratford, 1976 season, Escalus in Romeo and Juliet, Antigonus in The Winter's Tale, and Duncan in Macbeth, playing the latter role at the Other Place (Aug), the Memorial Theatre (Apr 1977), and Warehouse, London, Sept 1977; Aldwych season, 1977, Aegeon in A Comedy of Errors, Egeus in A Midsummer Night's Dream, Escalus, and Vigeland in Pillars of the Community; RSC tour, summer 1978, appeared in Twelfth Night and Three Sisters; Stratford, 1979 season, played the Soothsayer and Jupiter in Cymbeline, Gower in Pericles (Other Place), and Chebutkin in Three Sisters; has appeared extensively in films and television plays.

Recreations: Piano, and walking. *Address:* c/o Rolf Kruger Management, 54 Eardley Crescent, London, SW5.

JONES, James Earl, actor

b Arkabutla, Mississippi, 17 Jan 1931; *s* of Robert Earl Jones and his wife Ruth (Williams); *e* University of Michigan (BA 1953); prepared for the stage with the American Theatre Wing, receiving his diploma in 1957; also studied with Lee Strasberg and Tad Danielewsky.

Made his stage début at the University of Michigan, 1949, as Brett in Deep Are the Roots, subsequently playing Verges in Much Ado About Nothing, the King in The Birds, and

David King in A Sleep of Prisoners; joined the Manistee, Michigan, Summer Theatre, and, 1955–9, played in Stalag 17, The Caine Mutiny, Velvet Gloves, The Tender Trap, Arsenic and Old Lace, The Desperate Hours, and the title-role of Othello, etc; first New York assignment was as understudy to the role of Perry Richards at the Ethel Barrymore, 9 Oct 1957, in The Egghead; first appeared on the stage in NY at the Graystone Hotel, 1957, as Sergeant Blunt in Wedding in Japan; Cort, Jan 1958, Edward in Sunrise at Campobello; Eugene O'Neill, Feb 1960, Harrison Thurston in The Cool World; Belvedere Lake, for the New York Shakespeare Festival, June 1960, Williams in Henry V and July 1960, Abhorson in Measure for Measure; St Marks Playhouse, May 1961, Deodatus Village in The Blacks; Woolman Memorial, for the New York Shakespeare Festival, July 1961, Oberon in A Midsummer Night's Dream, and, Aug 1961, Lord Marshall in Richard II; Actors Playhouse, Oct 1961, Roger Clark in Clandestine on the Morning Line; The Living Theatre, Dec 1961, played in The Apple; East 11th Street, Jan 1962, Ephraim in Moon on a Rainbow Shawl; Music Box, Apr 1962, Cinna in Infidel Caesar; Shakespeare, July 1962, Caliban in The Tempest and Prince of Morocco in The Merchant of Venice; Writer's Stage, Oct 1962, Mario Saccone in PS 193; Writer's Stage, Jan 1963, George Gulp in The Love Nest; Delacorte, for the New York Shakespeare Festival, June 1963, Camillo in The Winter's Tale; Equity Library, Oct 1963, title-role in Mister Johnson; Phoenix, Nov 1963, Rudge in Next Time I'll Sing to You; Cricket, Mar 1964, Zachariah Pieterson in The Blood Knot; Delacorte, July 1964, title-role in Othello, and repeated this part at the Martinique; Martinique, Apr 1965, Ekart in Baal; Delacorte, June 1965, Junius Brutus in Coriolanus, and, Aug 1965, Ajax in Troilus and Cressida; Vivian Beaumont, Oct 1965, Philippeau in Danton's Death; New York Sheakespeare Festival, summer 1966, played Macbeth; Longacre, Sept 1966, played in the revue A Hand Is on the Gates; toured Europe, summer 1967, in the title-role of The Emperor Jones; Arena Stage, Washington, DC, Dec 1967, Jack Jefferson in The Great White Hope; Purdue University Theatre, Lafayette, Indiana, 1968, Lennie in Of Mice and Men; Alvin, Oct 1968, again played Jack Jefferson in The Great White Hope, and received the Antoinette Perry (Tony) Award for this performance, which he played for more than a year; Circle in the Square, June 1970, Boesman in Boesman and Lena; Longacre, Nov 1970, Tshembe Matoseh in Les Blancs; Mark Taper Forum, Los Angeles, Apr 1971, played Othello; Delacorte, June 1972, Claudius in Hamlet; Anspacher, Jan 1973, Lopahin in The Cherry Orchard; Delacorte, July 1973, played King Lear; Joseph E Levine—Circle in the Square, Dec 1973, Theodore Hickman (Hicky) in The Iceman Cometh; same theatre, 29 Apr 1974, played in a Gala Benefit Show; Brooks Atkinson, Dec 1974, Lennie in Of Mice and Men; toured, 1977, in a one-man play, Paul Robeson, in which he appeared at the Lunt-Fontanne, Jan 1978, Booth, Mar 1978, and Her Majesty's, London, July 1978; has received the Obie Award on several occasions; entered films in Dr Strangelove, 1963, and has since played in The Comedians, 1967, The End of the Road, 1968, The Great White Hope, 1970, Claudine, 1974, The River Niger, 1975, The Last Remake of Beau Geste, 1976, A Piece of the Action, 1977, etc; has appeared on television regularly in dramatic series, *Camera Three, East Side/West Side,* Jesus of Nazareth, Roots II, etc.
Recreation: Chess. *Address:* Lucy Kroll Agency, 390 West End Avenue, New York, NY 10024.

JONES, Mary, actress
b Rhayader, Radnorshire, Wales; d of Captain Alban Jones, RNR, DSO, and his wife Annie Elizabeth (Roberts); e Woodriding School, Hatch End, and Royal Naval School,

Twickenham; studied for the stage at the Central School for Speech Training and Dramatic Art.
Made her first appearance on the stage with the Greater London Players, 27 Nov 1934, as the Stenographer in The Trial of Mary Dugan; at the Globe, June 1935, Mary Lou Maling in Grief Goes Over; Q, Jan 1936, played Betty Finley in Ten Minute Alibi; from Sept–Dec 1936, played juvenile leads at the Prince of Wales's, Cardiff, in repertory season; Arts, Feb 1937, Evelyn Fairfield in Come Out To Play; toured on the Continent, Feb–Apr 1937, in Shakespearean and Shaw repertory; Théâtre Michel, July 1937, played Frankie in George and Margaret; made her first appearance on the New York stage at the Ritz Theatre, 3 Jan 1938, as Carol in Time and the Conways, and on returning to England, toured in the same part; New, Sept 1938, played Sally Hollick in Can We Tell?; Kingsway, Feb 1939, Prudence Fairley in To Love and To Cherish; New, Feb 1943, Nerissa in The Merchant of Venice; Q, Jan 1944, Louise Heller in The Family Upstairs; toured, 1944, as Fenella in This Was a Woman; Arts, Oct 1947, Cynthia Cooksey in Cupid and Mars; Feb 1948, Mari Jones in A Comedy of Good and Evil; Grand, Swansea, for the Arts Council, May 1949, appeared as Cordelia in King Lear; Gateway, Jan 1950, Sally Gough in Palm of My Hand; Embassy, Sept 1950, played Nancy in Soldier Boy; Nov 1950, Blodwen in Hands Around the Wall; appeared at the Bath Festival, 1951, as Lydia Languish in The Rivals; Irving, Oct 1952, played Louisa in Condemned to Live; visited Turkey, Dec 1954, where she appeared at the Kücük Sahne Theatre, Istanbul, in the title-role in Candida; at the Opera House, Harrogate, July 1955, played Cornelia in Misery Me and Jill Manning in Waiting for Gillian; Central Hall, Edinburgh, Sept 1959, Scarabesca in Blood Will Out; Royal Court, Mar 1960, Mrs Dora Jenkins in The Naming of Murderer's Rock; Royal Court, Dec 1961, played Mrs Golovin in The Scarecrow in a Production without Décor; Comedy, Feb 1962, Betty Bassett in My Place; Westminster, Mar 1969, played Margaret Krohn in Hide-Out, May 1970, Louisa in Blindsight, July 1970, Mrs Rankin in The Forgotten Factor; toured, Sept 1972, as Queen Elena in King's Rhapsody; Bush, Feb 1979, played Margaret in Independence; entered films, 1938, and has appeared in numerous pictures; has also taken part in frequent radio and television productions, including the original broadcast of Under Milk Wood; recent TV includes *Crossroads, The Perils of Pendragon,* and *General Hospital.*
Hobbies: Antiques, sea shells and painting. *Address:* 23 Priory Terrace, London, NW8. *Tel:* 01–624 6101.

JONES, Paul (*né* Pond), actor
b Portsmouth, Hampshire, 24 Feb 1942; s of Norman Henry Pond and his wife Amelia Josephine (Hadfield); e Edinburgh Academy and Jesus College, Oxford; m Sheila MacLeod; formerly a singer.
First appeared on the stage, Feb 1969, at the Open Space, as John Argue in Muzeeka; first West End appearance, Queen's, May 1969, as 2nd Lieut Arthur Drake in Conduct Unbecoming, a part which he repeated on his New York début, Oct 1970, at the Ethel Barrymore; Hampstead, May 1973, and Apollo, June 1973, Noel Parker in The Banana Box; Her Majesty's, Oct 1973, title-role in Pippin; Theatre at New End, Apr 1974, Orestes in You Were So Sweet When You Were Little; Belgrade, Coventry, Oct 1974, played Edmund in King Lear and Trench in Widowers' Houses; with Prospect Theatre Company, 1975, played Christian in Pilgrim at the Edinburgh Festival, Aug and the Round House, Oct; Ludlow Festival, 1976, title-role in Hamlet; Playhouse, Nottingham, Oct 1976, Cassio in Othello; Chichester Festival,

1977, leading roles in In Order of Appearance; Oct 1977, toured as Romeo in the Young Vic's Romeo and Juliet; Shaftesbury, Dec 1977, Francis Drake in Drake's Dream; Westminster, 1978 and 1979, played Joseph in Joseph and the Amazing Technicolour Dreamcoat; Riverside, May 1979, Claudio in Measure For Measure; first film, Privilege, 1966; subsequently, The Committee, and Demons of the Mind; first television appearance, 1963, as a singer; performs frequently, vocals and on harmonica with the Blues Band, and on disc; records include Evita.

Hobbies: Collecting Blues Records, Victorian and Edwardian theatre postcards, Avoiding Musicals. *Address:* c/o Michael Linnit, Globe Theatre, Shaftesbury Avenue, London W1.

JONES, Peter, actor and dramatic author
b Wem, Shropshire, 12 June 1920; *s* of William Jones and his wife Sarah Lillian (Francis); *e* Wem Grammar School and Ellesmere College; *m* Jeri Sauvinet.

Made his first appearance on the stage at the Grand, Wolverhampton, 1936, as The Times Reporter in The Composite Man; first appeared on the West End stage at the Haymarket, 6 Apr 1942, when he took over the part of the Newspaper Man in a revival of The Doctor's Dilemma; Westminster, June 1943, played Thomas in The Imaginary Invalid; at the Arts, July 1943, appeared in a festival of English comedy, playing Fag in The Rivals, Clincher, Jnr, in The Constant Couple, Gunner in Misalliance, Trevor Bavvel in The Watched Pot, and Isadore in The Magistrate; Prince of Wales, Apr 1944, played Duncan in The Rest Is Silence; Apollo, Sept 1944, took over the part of Cpl Packett in a revival of How Are They At Home?; Arts, Mar 1945, appeared as The Simpleton in The Simpleton of the Unexpected Isles; Apr 1945, Fadinard in An Italian Straw Hat; New, June 1946, Zamietov in Crime and Punishment; Lyric, Hammersmith, June 1949, and St James's, July 1949, played Will Ramillies in Love In Albania; Lyric, Hammersmith, Mar 1952, and Criterion, Apr 1952, Bruce Fairlight in a revival of The Vortex; Vaudeville, Sept 1952, took over the part of Valentine Crisp in his own play, Sweet Madness; Lyric, Sept 1953, appeared as B Kaghan in The Confidential Clerk; Comedy, Dec 1955, played Homer Bolton in Morning's At Seven, subsequently transferring to the Westminster, Feb 1956; Arts, May 1956, contributed sketches, co-directed, and played various parts in the revue Late Interlude; Strand, Feb 1958, Syd McCaffey in Touch It Light; Memorial Theatre, Stratford-on-Avon, Feb 1959, Jack in In the Red; Saville, Sept 1959, Pop Larkin in The Darling Buds of May; Bromley, May 1961, played Easter in Doctor at Sea; Piccadilly, Dec 1962, Mr Fenner in The Rag Trade; toured Australia and New Zealand, Feb 1964–May 1965, as Robert in Boeing-Boeing; Arnaud, Guildford, Sept 1966, played Ernie in his production of his own play Angie and Ernie; King's, Edinburgh, Apr 1970, Harry in It's Underneath that Counts; Arnaud, Guildford, Feb 1971, Henry Jackson in The Night of the Blue Demands; Hampstead, Jan 1973, Monk in Small Craft Warnings, transferring to the Comedy, Mar 1973; Ludlow Festival, 1976, Polonius in Hamlet; Palace, Plymouth, Dec 1979, Baron Hardup in Cinderella; is also the author of the plays The Party Spirit (with John Jowett), 1954 and The Rescue, 1973; first appeared in films, 1943, in Fanny By Gaslight; has also broadcast in the BBC series In All Directions, of which he was part-author with Peter Ustinov; appears frequently on television, notably in the series *The Rag Trade, Mr Digby Darling,* in his own scripts for *Comedy Playhouse,* and recently in Mr Big (which he co-authored), Oneupmanship and M'Lords, Ladies and Gentlemen; recent

radio includes The Hitch-Hiker's Guide to the Galaxy; has also scripted films and made cabaret and lecture appearances.

Recreations: Painting, camping, cooking. *Address:* 32 Acacia Road, London, NW8. *Tel:* 01–722 0082.

JONES, Tom, playwright and lyricist
b Littlefield, Texas, 17 Feb 1928; *s* of W T Jones and his wife Jessie (Bellomy); *e* University of Texas (BFA 1949, MFA 1951); *m* Elinor Wright.

Contributed lyrics to Shoestring '57, at the Barbizon-Plaza, Nov 1956, and to Kaleidoscope, 1957; wrote book and lyrics for The Fantasticks, which has occupied the Sullivan Street Playhouse, NY, since May 3, 1960, as the world's longest-running musical; has also written lyrics for 110 in the Shade, 1963; book and lyrics for I Do! I Do! (Tony award), 1966; Celebration, 1969; lyrics for Colette, 1970; book and lyrics for Philemon, 1974; director of the film A Texas Romance, 1909 (1965); television writing includes book and lyrics for A New York Scrapbook, 1961; The Fantasticks and Philemon have also been televised.

Address: West Cornwall, CT 06796.

JORY, Victor, actor
b Dawson City, Alaska, 23 Nov 1902; *s* of Edwin Jory and his wife Joanna (Snyder); *e* Dawson City and in Vancouver, Pasadena, and University of Canada; *m* Jean Innes.

Made his first appearance on the stage in Vancouver, 1929, and appeared in various stock companies in Cincinnati, Columbus and Dayton, Ohio, Denver, etc, for several years; mainly appeared in films, in Hollywood, 1933–43, occasionally appearing in the regular theatre at Pasadena and Los Angeles, acting and producing; in Chicago, 1942, played Mr Manningham in Angel Street, during its run there; appeared at the Booth Theatre, New York, 3 Aug 1943, as Geoffrey in The Two Mrs Carrolls; Ethel Barrymore, Oct 1944, played Dale Williams in The Perfect Marriage; toured, Feb–Mar 1945, as Lt-Cmdr William Marshall in Bill Comes Back; toured 1945, as Laurent in Thérèse, and appeared in the same part at the Biltmore Theatre, Oct 1945; at the International, NY, for the American Repertory Theatre, Nov 1946, to Mar 1947, played King Henry in Henry VIII, John Gabriel Borkman, Ferrovius in Androcles and the Lion, James Carroll in Yellow Jack; toured, 1947, as Jack Rance in The Girl of the Golden West; he then spent a further three years in Hollywood; reappeared in NY at the City Center, Jan 1950, as Anthony Anderson in The Devil's Disciple, and played the same part at the Royale, Feb 1950; toured, 1950, in The Spider; at Ford's Theatre, Baltimore, Jan 1951, appeared in Mr Barry's Etchings; Booth, NY, June 1951, took over the part of George Crane in Season in the Sun, and toured in this play, 1952; in summer theatres, 1952, appeared as Elyot Chase in Private Lives; toured, 1953, in Bell, Book and Candle; toured, 1954, in My Three Angels; toured, Oct 1957–8, as Big Daddy in Cat on a Hot Tin Roof; starred in the tour of The Happiest Millionaire, and toured summer 1964, in The Best Man; Actors Theatre, Louisville, Kentucky, 1970, Jeeter Lester in Tobacco Road; same theatre, 1970, Narrator in Our Town, 1972, Willy Loman in Death of a Salesman; Sept 1973, James Tyrone in Long Day's Journey into Night; Mar 1976, in The Last Meeting of the Knights of the White Magnolia; Oct 1976, in The Best Man; in The Front Page, Jan 1978, etc; has played in nearly 130 films, including: Tom Sawyer, Gone with the Wind, State Fair, The Fugitive Kind, The Miracle Worker, Papillon (1973), etc; since 1950 has played leading parts in more than 200 television productions; has specialized in making children's record albums, including Peter and the Wolf, Tubby the Tuba, Peter Pan, etc.

Address: Actors Equity Association, 165 West 46th Street, New York, NY 10036.

JOYCE, Stephen, actor

b New York City, 7 Mar 1931; *s* of Stephen Joyce, Sr and his wife Ruth (Reilly); *e* Fordham University; *m* Billie J Jones.

First appeared on the stage in Okinawa, 1953, when he played Sakini in Teahouse of the August Moon; made his NY début with the New York Shakespeare Festival, summer 1956, as Romeo in Romeo and Juliet; Theatre East, Mar 1957, played Michael Byrne in The Tinker's Wedding and Bartley in Riders to the Sea in a production with the title Three Plays by John Millington Synge; 54th Street, Feb 1959, played Henry Appleton in The Legend of Lizzie; American Shakespeare Festival, Stratford, Conn, June 1965, played the title-role of Coriolanus and Edgar in King Lear; Old Globe, San Diego, Calif, 1965, Leontes in The Winter's Tale; Seattle Repertory Theatre, 1966, Biff in Death of a Salesman and the title-role of Hamlet; American Shakespeare Festival, summer 1966, played Archbishop of York in Falstaff, First Tempter in Murder in the Cathedral, and Marcus Antonius in Julius Caesar; ANTA, Nov 1966, The Prince in Those That Play the Clowns; Renata, Dec 1966, took over as Father Jerome Fogarty in The Frying Pan, Tom Dorgan in Eternal Triangle, and Denis Sullivan in The Bridal Night in a production with the overall title Three Hand Reel; Shubert, New Haven, Feb 1967, played various roles in The Hemingway Hero; East 74th Street, Sept 1967, Stephen Dedalus in Stephan D; Vivian Beaumont, Jan 1968, Brother Martin Ladvenu in Saint Joan; John Golden, Apr 1968, The Actor in The Exercise; Theatre de Lys, Feb 1969, played in the revue An Evening with James Agee; Village South, June 1969, Ben Bran in The Report, The Coach in Football, and Old Local in Fireworks for a Hot Fourth in a production with the overall title Fireworks; joined the Yale Repertory, New Haven, Conn, and in Mar 1972, played Segismund in Life Is a Dream; May 1972, played in Happy End; Oct 1972, Paul Holliman in A Break in the Skin; Nov 1972, Larry Parks in Are You Now Or Have You Ever Been?; Apr 1973, Banco and Macol in Ionesco's Macbett; also Apr 1973, played in Edward Bond's Lear; Oct 1973, Caliban in The Tempest; Olney, Maryland, Playhouse, Aug 1973, Charlie Now in Da; Ivanhoe, Chicago, 1974, again played in Da; Olney, Md, Playhouse, Aug 1974, Richard Halvey in Summer; again at Olney, summer 1975, in The Glass Menagerie; Hartman, Conn, transferring to the Little, NY, May 1976, Father Rivard in The Runner Stumbles; Hudson Guild, Feb 1977, in Savages; for Phoenix, May 1977, Hunt in Scribes; Hartman, 1978, in The Auction Tomorrow; has also played with various other stock and repertory companies; first appeared on television in 1956 and has played on *Matinee Theatre, Play of the Week, Omnibus, Ben Casey, Rawhide,* and approximately 200 other programs.

Favourite parts: Stanley Kowalski in A Streetcar Named Desire and Bri in Joe Egg. *Hobbies and recreations:* Painting, physical exercise, horseback riding, farming. *Address:* 145 Platt Lane, Milford, Connecticut 06460. *Tel:* 203–874 6059.

JULIA, Raul, actor

b San Juan, Puerto Rico, 9 Mar 1940; *s* of Raul Julia and his wife Olga (Arcelay); *e* University of Puerto Rico; *m* Merel Poloway; trained for the stage with Wynn Handman.

First appeared in New York at the Astor Place Playhouse, 17 Mar 1964, as Astolfo in La Vida Es Sueñõ, acting in Spanish; appeared in The Marriage Proposal, June 1966;

Mobile, for the New York Shakespeare Festival, Aug 1966, Macduff in Macbeth, marking the beginning of a long association with that company; Greenwich Mews, Dec 1966, Luis in The Ox Cart; Delacorte, Aug 1967, Demetrius in Titus Andronicus; Bouwerie Lane, Oct 1967, Cradeau in No Exit; Anspacher, Apr 1968, A Clerk in The Memorandum; Orpheum, 1968, took over as Orson in Your Own Thing; Henry Miller's, Sept 1968, Chan in The Cuban Thing; Fortune, Mar 1969, A Workman in Paradise Gardens East and Jesus in Conerico Was Here to Stay in the double bill Frank Gagliano's City Scene; Arena Stage, Washington, DC, May 1969, Grand Duke Alexis and Uncas in Indians; Brooks Atkinson, Oct 1969, again played these last parts in Indians; St George's Church, Apr 1970, Persian Elder in The Persians; Stairway, Nov 1970, Paco Montoya in The Castro Complex; St Clement's Church, Mar 1971, Consequently Joe in Pinkville; Delacorte, July 1971, Proteus in a musical version of Two Gentlemen of Verona; St James, Dec 1971, again played Proteus in Two Gentlemen of Verona; Delacorte, June 1972, Osric in Hamlet; Uris, Nov 1972, Gabriel Finn in Via Galactica; Delacorte, June 1973, Orlando in As You Like It, and, July 1973, Edmund in King Lear; Other Stage, Mar 1974, Commissioner in The Emperor of Late Night Radio; St Clement's Church, Nov 1974, Jaimie Lockhart in The Robber Bridegroom; Circle in the Square, Dec 1974, Charley Wykeham in Where's Charley?; Vivian Beaumont, May 1976, Mack the Knife, in Threepenny Opera; same theatre, Feb 1977, Lopatkin in The Cherry Orchard; returned with the production, June 1977; Baltimore, May 1978, title-role in Dracula, taking over this role at the Martin Beck, 1979; Delacorte, Aug 1978, Petruchio in The Taming of the Shrew; same theatre, Aug 1979, title-role in Othello.

Address: 119 West 57th Street, New York, NY 10019.

JUSTIN, John, actor

b London, 24 Nov 1917; *e* Bryanston, Dorset; *m* (1) Barbara Murray (mar dis); (2) Alison McMurdo.

Gained early experience with the Plymouth Repertory Company, with whom he made his first appearance, Aug 1933; was subsequently with the Liverpool Repertory Company; studied at the Royal Academy of Dramatic Art, 1937; made his first appearance on the London stage, at the Queen's Theatre, 1937, in John Gielgud's repertory company; Arts, Jan 1938, played Jim Harris-Carr in But for the Grace; Queen's, Sept 1938, Hugh Randolph in Dear Octopus; Globe, Jan 1939, the Footman in The Importance of Being Earnest; during the War, served as a Pilot in the RAF, 1940–5; reappeared on the stage, at the Torch Theatre, Sept 1945, as Richard Rowan in Exiles; appeared at the Richmond Theatre, 1945–6, as Robert Browning in The Barretts of Wimpole Street, and Jimmy Dugan in The Trial of Mary Dugan; Lyric, Hammersmith, May 1946, played Admetus in The Thracian Horses, and toured in this; Shakespeare Memorial Theatre, Stratford-on-Avon, 1948 season, played the Dauphin in King John, Lorenzo in The Merchant of Venice, Horatio in Hamlet, Florizel in The Winter's Tale, Paris in Troilus and Cressida, and Cassio in Othello; at the Bedford, Camden Town, Oct 1949, played Robin, Guy and Paul in The Wind on the Heath; Scala, Dec 1949, Mr Darling and Captain Hook in Peter Pan, subsequently touring in this, 1950; Bedford, May 1950, played Wilfred Denver in The Silver King; Q, Aug 1950, Richard Dahl in Give Me Yesterday; Duke of York's, Nov 1950, Francis Hubbard in Return to Tyassi; Q, Apr 1951, played Francis Oberon in We Must Kill Toni; at the Ipswich Arts Theatre, May 1951, appeared in Gunpowder, Treason and Plot, and played the title-role in

Captain Carvallo; Arts, London, Mar 1952, Dr Mikhail Lvovich Astrov in Uncle Vanya; Q, June 1952, Philip Langdon in The Step Forward; Court, July 1952, played Norman Huntley in Miss Hargreaves; Duchess, July 1956, Horace Wigsley Pearson in Someone To Talk To; Aldwych, Mar 1957, Alec Grimes in Olive Ogilvie; New, Dec 1957, Georges in Dinner with the Family; Scala, Dec 1958, and subsequent tour, Captain Hook and Mr Darling in Peter Pan; joined the Old Vic Company, Sept 1959, and played the following parts, Mellefont in The Double Dealer; Orlando in As You Like It; John Worthing in The Importance of Being Earnest; and King Richard in Richard II; made his first appearance in the US at the Forrest, Philadelphia, Oct 1960, as Lieut Kenneth Boyd in Little Moon of Alban, subsequently appearing at the Longacre, New York, Dec 1960, in the same production; Playhouse, Oxford, Dec 1962, played Des Prunelles in Divorce à la Carte, in which he also toured, appearing at the New Arts, Mar 1963, in the same play; Open Air, Regent's Park, June 1963, played Don Pedro in Much Ado About Nothing; Ambassador's, Nov 1963–4, took over the part of Giles Ralston in The Mousetrap; Queen's, Dec 1964, Badger in Toad of Toad's Hall; Open Air, Regent's Park, June 1965, the Banished Duke in As You Like It; Northampton Repertory, Sept 1965, Willy Loman in Death of a Salesman; Comedy, Dec 1965, Badger in Toad of Toad Hall; Royal Court, Dec 1970, played Prince Escerny and Puntschu in Lulu, transferring to the Apollo, Jan 1971; toured S Africa, 1971, in Who Killed Santa Claus?; Open Air, Regent's Park, June 1972, Sir Andrew Aguecheek in Twelfth Night; King's Head, Islington, Mar 1974, appeared in Old Fruit; toured, May 1974, as Lord Glenalan in A Man and His Wife; toured, Sept, as Mr Laurence in Little Women; went to W Germany, spring 1975, to give recitals of Blake and Shakespeare for the British Council; Westminster, March 1977, played Bruce in Fire; Edinburgh Festival, 1978, appeared in Pallor Game; has acted in thirty films since 1939, including Lisztomania and Valentino; first television appearance, 1949, in Antigone; first entered films 1937.

Recreations: Riding and swimming. *Address:* c/o The Spotlight, 42–43 Cranbourn Street, London, WC2.

K

KAHN, Michael, director

b New York City; *s* of Frederick Joseph Kahn and his wife Adele (Gaberman); *e* Columbia College, and Columbia University.

Was executive producer of PS 193, presented at The Writers' Stage, NY, 30 Oct 1962; directed his first play in NY at the same theatre, 25 Jan 1963, The Love Nest; since then has directed Funnyhouse of a Negro, The New Tenant, Victims of Duty, That 5 AM Jazz, Helen, America Hurrah (Cafe La Mama première production), The Owl Answers, 1964; Thornton Wilder's triple-bill, a program consisting of The Long Christmas Dinner, Queens of France, and The Happy Journey to Trenton and Camden, Measure for Measure, 1966; The Rimers of Eldritch, The Cavern, The Freaking Out of Stephanie Blake, and, for the American Shakespeare Festival Theatre in Stratford, Connecticut, The Merchant of Venice, 1967; Here's Where I Belong, Camino Real (Cincinnati), The Death of Bessie Smith, and, at Stratford, Richard II and Love's Labour's Lost, 1968; Crimes of Passion, and, having been appointed Artistic Director of the American Shakespeare Festival Theatre, Stratford, Connecticut, Henry V and The Three Sisters, 1969; Othello, All's Well That Ends Well, 1970; The Merry Wives of Windsor, Mourning Becomes Electra, and, for the Harold Prince, Philadelphia, Hough in Blazes, 1971; Julius Caesar, Antony and Cleopatra (both for Stratford, Conn), Women Beware Women (for the City Center Acting Company), Tartuffe (for the Philadelphia Drama Guild), 1972; Macbeth, Measure for Measure (both for Stratford), Shakespeare and the Performing Arts (Kennedy Center, Washington, DC), The Epic of Buster Friend (NY), 1973; The Tooth of Crime (Goodman, Chicago), Romeo and Juliet (Stratford), Cat on a Hot Tin Roof (Stratford and NY), Beyond the Horizon (for McCarter, Princeton, NJ), 1974; 'Tis Pity She's a Whore (Goodman, Chicago), Our Town, The Winter's Tale (both Stratford), Mother Courage, A Grave Undertaking, Section Nine (all for McCarter, Princeton), 1975; The Heiress, The Winter's Tale, A Streetcar Named Desire (all McCarter), Eleanor (Ford's, Washington DC), The Crucible, The Winter's Tale, As You Like It (all Stratford), 1976; Angel City, A Wilder Triple Bill (both McCarter), The Night of the Tribades (NY), 1977; The Torch-Bearers, Put Them All Together (McCarter), 1978; Grand Magic (NY), A Month in the Country (McCarter and NY), 1979; is also Head of the Interpretation Department of the Drama Division of the Juilliard School; became Artistic Director of the McCarter Theater, Princeton, NJ, 1974; co-artistic director, The Acting Company, 1978– .

Address: c/o McCarter Theatre, Box 526, Princeton, NJ 08540.

KALFIN, Robert, director and producer

b New York City, 22 Apr 1933; *s* of Alfred A Kalfin and his wife Hilda (Shulman); *e* H S of Music and Art, NY, Alfred University (BA 1954), Yale School of Drama (MA 1957).

Director and producer of The Golem, St Mark's Playhouse, Feb 1959; adapted and directed The Good Soldier Schweik, Actors Playhouse, summer 1961; directed a number of productions at the Tanglewood Barn Theatre, Clemmons, NC, season 1964; in 1965 founded the Chelsea Theater Center and has since been its artistic director; the company has presented over 100 productions and since 1967 these have been given in the Brooklyn Academy and more recently at the Chelsea Theater Center in Manhattan; at the Circle in the Square produced and directed Tarot, 1971; Kaddish, 1972; productions which have transferred to Broadway include Candide, 1974; Yentl, 1975; Happy End, 1977; and Strider, 1979, the last three directed by Mr Kalfin; he has also directed for US and Canadian regional theatres; for TV directed his Chelsea production of The Prince of Homburg, 1976.

Address: 312 West 20th Street, New York, NY 10011.

KANDER, John, composer and musician

b Kansas City, Missouri, 18 Mar 1927; *s* of Harold Kander and his wife Berenice (Aaron); *e* Oberlin College (BA 1951), Columbia University (MA 1954).

While at Oberlin composed his first scores for the theatre, Second Square and Opus Two, 1950, and Requiem for Georgie, 1951; was choral director and conductor for the Warwick Musical Theatre, Rhode Island, summers, 1955–7; was pianist for The Amazing Adele, 1956, and for the Florida production of An Evening with Bea Lillie, 1956; conducted the orchestra for the New York revival of Conversation Piece, 1957; arranged the dance music for Gypsy, 1959, and Irma la Douce, 1960; composed his first Broadway score for A Family Affair, produced at the Billy Rose, 27 Jan 1962; since then has composed the music for Never Too Late, 1962; Flora, The Red Menace, 1965; Cabaret, 1966; The Happy Time, Zorba, 1968; 70, Girls, 70, 1971; Zorba produced in London at Greenwich, Nov 1973; Chicago, 1975; The Act, 1977; TV work includes music for Liza with a Z, 1974 (Emmy Award); film scores include Something for Everyone, Funny Lady, Lucky Lady, and the film of Cabaret; received the Antoinette Perry (Tony) Award for his score for Cabaret.

Address: The Dramatists Guild, 234 West 44th Street, New York, NY 10036.

KANE, Richard, actor

b Birmingham, 17 Sept 1938; *s* of Charles Edward Wright and his wife Kathleen Mary (Wallhead); *e* City School, Lincoln and Leeds University; *m* (1) Jean Hastings (mar dis); (2) Jennifer Lee; after acting in various productions at university, trained for the stage at RADA.

Made his first professional appearance at the Summer Theatre, Frinton-on-Sea, Aug 1962, in Simple Spymen; first London appearance, 15 July 1964, at the Open Air Theatre, Regent's Park, as Tranio in The Taming of the Shrew, subsequently touring the Far East in this part, and as Aumerle in Richard II and Sebastian in The Tempest; Citizens', Glasgow, Nov 1965, Estragon in Waiting for Godot; other parts here 1966–7 included Malcolm Scrawdike in Little Malcolm, Fancourt Babberley in Charley's Aunt, Jean in Miss Julie and the title role in O'Flaherty VC (double bill), and Givola in Arturo Ui; Chichester, July 1968, Ariel in The Tempest; Oxford Playhouse, 1968, Bluntschli in Arms and the Man, Sept, and the Intendant in Pippa Passes, Oct; at Bristol Old Vic, Gerald Popkiss in Rookery Nook, Dec 1968, and John Shand in What Every Woman Knows, Feb 1969; again at Chichester, season 1969, Shauva in The Caucasian Chalk Circle, Isidore in The Magistrate, Quack in The

Country Wife, and Dolabella in Antony and Cleopatra; at the Stables, Manchester, 1970, Ted in Ellen, Apr and Gramsci in Occupations, Oct; Chichester, 1970, Lomov in The Proposal, Nicola in Arms and the Man, and Abel Drugger in The Alchemist; Open Space, Apr 1971, The Man in Tira; Edinburgh Festival, Aug 1971, for Royal Lyceum Theatre Company, Robert Wringham in Confessions of a Justified Sinner; at the Young Vic, 1972, his parts included Madame in The Maids and Lefranc in Deathwatch (double bill), Biondello in The Taming of the Shrew, Dapper in The Alchemist, Antipholus in The Comedy of Errors, and the title role in Epitaph for George Dillon; Royal Court, Mar 1973, Simon in a Sunday night production, The Fourth World; Hampstead, Nov 1973, Wilson in President Wilson in Paris; Open Space, Feb 1974, Bob in The Collected Works; Phoenix, July 1974, Mark Gertler in Bloomsbury; Theatre Royal, Lincoln, Sept 1974, title role in Macbeth; Mercury, Colchester, Nov 1974, Hamm in Endgame; Arnaud, Guildford and tour, Feb 1975, Lucien in Romeo and Jeannette; Open Space, May 1975, Jupp in Prisoner and Escort; Leeds Playhouse, Sept 1975, Yossarian in Catch 22; Playhouse, Leeds, Feb 1976, Lopakhin in The Cherry Orchard; Playhouse, Nottingham, May 1976, Capt Brazen in Trumpets and Drums; Greenwich, Sept 1976, Arnold in Scribes, and Nov 1976, Monsieur Lebleu in The Artful Widow; Piccadilly, Aug 1978, Nightingale in Vieux Carre; Bush, Apr 1979, Leslie Whiting in The Tax Exile; Hampstead, July 1979, Roger in Outside Edge, transferring to the Queen's, July 1979; appeared in the film, A Bridge Too Far, 1976; TV, since 1965, includes Joseph and the Amazing Technicolour Dreamcoat, *Devenish*, and Who's Who.

Favourite parts: Ariel, Gramsci. *Recreations:* Gardening, football, reading. *Address:* c/o William Morris, 147–149 Wardour Street, London W1V 3TB.

KANIN, Garson, director and dramatic author, former actor
b Rochester, New York, 24 Nov 1912; *s* of David Kanin and his wife Sadie (Levine); *e* James Madison High School, NY; *m* Ruth Gordon.

Originally intended to be a professional musician and at an early age was a proficient instrumentalist on the saxophone and clarinet; his first engagement was in an orchestra, and subsequently he appeared in vaudeville; he then studied for the stage at the American Academy of Dramatic Art; made his first appearance on the stage at the Playhouse, NY, 24 Apr 1933, as Tommy Deal in Little Ol' Boy; Morosco, Oct 1934, played the Young Man in Spring Song; Ethel Barrymore, Nov 1934, Red in Ladies' Money; was then engaged by George Abbott, as actor and also as assistant director for Three Men on a Horse, Boy Meets Girl, and Room Service; at the Playhouse, Jan 1935, played Al in Three Men on a Horse; Plymouth, Oct 1935, Izzy Cohen in The Body Beautiful; Cort, Nov 1935, Green in Boy Meets Girl; Golden, Mar 1936, Vincent in Star Spangled; directed Too Many Heroes, Hitch Your Wagon, 1937; went to Hollywood in 1937, as a director of films, and directed A Man to Remember, Bachelor Mother, They Knew What they Wanted, Next Time I Marry, The Great Man Votes, My Favorite Wife, Tom, Dick and Harry, etc; served from 1941 in the US Army (Training Film Section), at Fort Monmouth, NJ, and in Europe in the OSS, where, with Carol Reed, he directed The True Glory, which received the Academy Award as best documentary, 1945; author of the play Born Yesterday, which he directed and produced at the Lyceum, NY, Feb 1946; since 1945 has directed the following plays in NY: The Rugged Path, 1945; Years Ago, 1946; How I Wonder (also co-produced), 1947; The Leading Lady, 1948; The Smile of the World (of which

he was the author), 1949; The Rat Race (author), 1949; The Live Wire (author), 1950; Fledermaus (for which he also wrote the new English libretto for the Metropolitan Opera House), 1950; The Diary of Anne Frank, 1955; at the Globe Theatre, London, May 1955, directed Into Thin Air; directed Small War on Murray Hill, NY, 1957; A Hole in the Head, 1957; The Good Soup (which he also adapted), 1960; Do-Re-Mi (also author), 1960 (and London, 1961); Sunday in New York, 1961; A Gift of Time (also adapted from a novel), 1962; Come on Strong (also author), 1962; Funny Girl, 1964; I Was Dancing, 1964; A Very Rich Woman (also produced), 1965; We Have Always Lived in the Castle, 1966; Remembering Mr Maugham, in which he also appeared, having adapted the play from his book, New Theatre for Now, Los Angeles, July 1969; Idiot's Delight, Los Angeles, 1970; Dreyfus in Rehearsal, which he also adapted, 1974; author of the screenplay It Should Happen to You, and co-author (with his wife Ruth Gordon) of A Double Life, Adam's Rib, Pat and Mike, The Marrying Kind and many others, most recently Hardhat and Legs; wrote and directed the films Some Kind of Nut and Where It's At, 1969; directed a number of others; author of many short stories, of which The Right Hand Man and The Damndest Thing (re-named Six People, No Music) and Something to Sing About have been performed on television; wrote and directed the television version of Born Yesterday, 1956; writer of other TV material including Scandal, 1980; author of the novel Blow Up a Storm, 1959; Tracy and Hepburn; An Intimate Memoir, 1971; A Thousand Summers, 1973; Hollywood, 1974; it Takes a Long Time to Become Young, One Hell of an Actor, 1977; Moviola, 1979; received Achievement Award (American Academy of Dramatic Arts), 1958.

Clubs: Players, Lambs, The Friars, The Coffee House, *Address:* 200 West 57th Street, New York, NY 10019.

KANNER, Alexis, actor
b Bagnères du Luchon, France, 2 May 1942; *s* of Joseph Kanner and his wife Doris (Fishler); *e* in Montreal, Canada.

In a Birmingham Repertory Theatre season, 1961, among other roles played Caliban in The Tempest; Gate, Dublin, also 1961, Hotspur in Henry IV; Royal Court, Oct 1961, played the young man in The American Dream; made his West End début at the Duke of York's, Oct 1962, as Harry Mallory in Across the Board on Tomorrow Morning; worked with Peter Brook's Royal Shakespeare Company experimental group, 1964–5, where his parts included Sa'id in The Screens, and Hamlet in the Peter Brook/Charles Marowitz Theatre of Cruelty production, 1965–6; Arts, Oct 1966, played the title part in a lunchtime production of Sammy; Open Space, May 1970, Julian Weston in Find Your Way Home; first starred in films, 1968; other appearances include Goodbye Gemini and Connecting Rooms; has appeared frequently on television since 1963, including the series, Softly, Softly.

Recreations: Squash, amateur photography, riding. *Address:* c/o ICM, 22 Grafton Street, London, W1.

KARLIN, Miriam, actress
b Hampstead, 23 June 1925; *d* of Harry Samuels and his wife Céline (Aronowitz); *e* South Hampstead High School; studied for the stage at the Royal Academy of Dramatic Art.

First appeared on tour with ENSA, 1943, as Miss Callaghan in The Family Upstairs; first appeared in London at the Lyric, Hammersmith, 14 Feb 1946, as Lorene in The Time of Your Life; Strand, Aug 1947, played Miss Sharp in Separate Rooms; Cambridge, May 1948, appeared in the revue, Maid to Measure; Embassy, Oct 1951, and Vaudeville, Nov 1951,

played Olga in Women of Twilight; first appeared in New York, at the Plymouth, 3 Mar 1952, in the last-named part; Victoria Palace, June 1952, again played Olga in Women of Twilight; Embassy, Feb 1953, appeared as Sadie Thompson in Rain; Sept 1953, Mrs Solomons in Spring Song; Jan 1954, Sadie in The Boychik; Saville, May 1954, appeared in the revue, Cockles and Champagne; toured, July–Sept 1954, as Miss Myers in No Escape; Embassy, Jan 1955, played The Angel Rochele in A Tale of Chelm, the First Angel in Bentche Schweig, and Hannah in The High School, three plays presented as The World of Sholom Aleichem; Aldwych, Apr 1955, appeared as Mrs Daigle in The Bad Seed; Arts, Dec 1955, played Miranda in Listen to the Wind; Lyric, Hammersmith, Feb 1956, Lina Szczepanowska in a revival of Misalliance; Phoenix, Nov 1956, Mrs Van Daan in The Diary of Anne Frank; Arts, Sept 1957, Annie Angel in All Kinds of Men, Saville, Oct 1957, Rose in The Egg; Strand, June 1958, appeared in the revue For Adults Only; Theatre Royal, Stratford, Dec 1959, played Lilly Smith in Fings Ain't Wot They Used T'Be, subsequently transferring with the production to the Garrick, Feb 1960; Royal, Stratford, E, Mar 1962, played Marian Alexander in The Secret of the World; Piccadilly, Dec 1962, Paddy in The Rag Trade; toured Australia, 1964–5, in Is Australia Really Necessary?; Jeanetta Cochrane, May 1966, played Flora Molar in Out From Under, Hilda in Orange Souffle and Marcella Vankuchen in The Wen in the triple-bill The Bellow Plays, transferring with the production to the Fortune, June 1966; Her Majesty's, Feb 1967, Golde in Fiddler on the Roof; King's, Edinburgh, Apr 1970, Hilda in It's the Underneath that Counts; Playbox, Melbourne, Feb 1971, Mrs Baker in Butterflies Are Free; Hampstead, Apr 1972, Vera in High Time; Open Space, Sept 1972, Nora Scrubbs in Alpha Alpha; Watford Palace, Nov 1972, title role in Mother Courage; Greenwich, Nov 1973, Madame Hortense in Zorba; toured, Sept 1974, as Martha in Who's Afraid of Virginia Woolf?; Chichester Festival, May 1974, the Mother in Tonight We Improvise; Phoenix, May 1975, gave a solo performance as Liselotte in Diary of a Madame; same theatre, May 1976, Grace Hoyland in Bus Stop; Vienna, Aug 1975, and Edinburgh Festival again gave solo show as Liselotte; Haymarket, Leicester, played Jocasta in Oedipus Rex, Madame Dubonnet in The Seagull, 1975; Arkadina in The Seagull, Judith Bliss in Hay Fever, and Liselotte (Studio), 1976; Palace, Watford, Dec 1977, the Fairy Godmother in Cinderella; returned to Leicester, 1978, as Alma in The Bed Before Yesterday; Gardner Centre, Brighton, 1978, appeared in We Can't Pay, We Won't Pay; Bromley, Feb 1979, Sheila in Relatively Speaking; Hong Kong Festival, Apr 1979, Alma in The Bed Before Yesterday; Scottish Opera Company, June 1979, Golde in Fiddler on the Roof; Greenwich, Aug 1979 and tour, Ernestine Wilton in The Undertaking, appearing at The Fortune, Oct 1979; has made many appearances in cabaret and on television, and has broadcast frequently.
Favourite parts: Flora, Hilda and Marcella in The Bellow Plays, and Golde. *Hobby:* The collection and study of amusing characters, conversations and accents. *Recreations:* Cooking and gardening. *Address:* c/o ICM Ltd, 22 Grafton Street, London, W1.

KARNILOVA, Maria, ballerina, actress
b Hartford, Connecticut, 3 Aug 1920; *d* of Phillip Dovgolenko and his wife Stephanida (Karnilovich); studied ballet with Margaret Curtis, Michael Mordkin, and Michel Fokine at the Metropolitan Opera School, 1927–34; *m* George S Irving.
First appeared on the stage of the Metropolitan Opera in 1927, dancing in the Children's Corps de Ballet; danced with the Dandria Opera Company, Caracas, Venezuela, 1935;

soloist with the Ballet Theatre, 1939–48, 1955–6, and 1959; ballerina with the Metropolitan Opera Company, 1952–3; repertory includes: Helen of Troy, Giselle, Bluebeard, Judgment of Paris, Fledermaus, Billy the Kid, La Boutique Fantasque, Jardin aux Lilas, Gala Performance, etc; made her musical comedy début at the Majestic, 9 Feb 1938, when she danced in the chorus of Stars in Your Eyes; Alvin, May 1945, danced in Hollywood Pinafore; National, Apr 1946, danced in Call Me Mister; toured, 1948, in High Button Shoes; Alvin, Dec 1952, was principal dancer in Two's Company; St Louis Municipal Opera, 1953, danced in Cyrano de Bergerac; State Fair Music Hall, Dallas, Texas, 1953, danced in New Moon, and Paint Your Wagon; made her dramatic début at the Kansas City Starlight Theatre, 1953, when she played Vera Barova in On Your Toes; Cambridge Drama Festival, Massachusetts, 1956, played Dolly Trull in The Beggar's Opera; New York City Center, Mar 1957, again played Dolly Trull; Provincetown Playhouse, June 1957, appeared in the revue Kaleidoscope; Alvin, Sept 1958, appeared in Jerome Robbins' Ballet: USA; Broadway, May 1959, played Tessie Tura in Gypsy; Broadhurst, May 1962, Signora Pandolfi in Bravo, Giovanni; Fred Miller's, Milwaukee, Wisconsin, Dec 1962, Dolly Gallagher Levi in The Matchmaker; State Fair Music Hall, Dallas, Texas, 1963, Therese Kolodney in Apollo and Miss Agnes; Imperial, NY, Sept 1964, Golde in Fiddler on the Roof and continued in this part for more than three years, receiving a 'Tony' for her performance; Imperial, Nov 1968, Hortense in Zorba; Uris, Nov 1973, Inez Alvarez in Gigi; Eugene O'Neill, Dec 1974, Rose Benjamin in God's Favorite; PAF Playhouse, Huntington, Dec 1977, Fanny Darby in Down at the Old Bull and Bush; made her film début in The Unsinkable Molly Brown, 1964; has appeared frequently on television.
Address: Actors Equity Association, 165 West 46th Street, New York, NY 10036.

KASHA, Lawrence, N, producer, playwright and director
b Brooklyn, New York, 3 Dec 1933; *s* of Irving Kasha and his wife Rose (Katz); *e* Fagin International School, New York University (BA 1954, MA 1955); also studied at the American Theatre Wing, 1957, and acting with Harold Clurman and Robert Lewis (1956–7).
He was production assistant for Silk Stockings, at the Imperial, NY, 24 Feb 1955; stage manager for the tour of Silk Stockings and the NY production of Li'l Abner, 1956; directed the touring version of Li'l Abner, 1958; directed musical comedies at the Colonie Summer Theatre, Latham, NY, 1959; produced his first NY show, Parade, at the Players, 20 Jan 1960; directed summer tours of Silk Stockings, High Button Shoes, The Male Animal, South Pacific, Desert Song, 1960; stage manager for the NY production of How to Succeed in Business Without Really Trying, 1961; produced and directed the Hollywood, Calif, presentation of Parade, 1961; produced Future Perfect at the Cape Playhouse, Dennis, Massachusetts, and directed a summer tour of Gentlemen Prefer Blondes, 1961; at the O'Keefe Center, Toronto, Ontario, directed Guys and Dolls and The Most Happy Fella, 1962; produced and directed The Con Edison Show, NY, directed Anything Goes, NY, and directed Plain and Fancy, Westchester, 1963; co-produced She Loves Me, NY, directed musicals at the State Fair Music Hall, Dallas, Texas and directed A More Perfect Union at the La Jolla, California, Playhouse, 1963; associate director of Funny Girl, NY, directed The Sound of Music, San Bernardino, California, directed Bajour, NY, and the tour of Camelot, 1964; made his London début at the Prince of Wales, 13 Apr 1966, when he directed Funny Girl; directed Show Boat, NY, 1966;

directed the tour of Cactus Flower, and tour of Star Spangled Girl, co-produced A Mother's Kisses, New Haven, Connecticut, 1968; co-produced Applause, NY, 1970, directed Lovely Ladies, Kind Gentlemen, NY, 1970; co-produced Father's Day, Inner City, NY, 1971; co-produced Seesaw, No Hard Feelings, NY, 1973; in 1978 produced and directed Heaven Sent, which he co-wrote with David S Landay, New Las Palmas Theater, LA; also produced, co-wrote and directed Seven Brides for Seven Brothers (tour); author with Hayden Griffin of The Pirate, 1968; with Lionel Wilson of Where Have You Been, Billy Boy?, 1969; TV productions include specials such as Applause, 1973, Komedy Tonite, 1978, and the series Busting Loose, 1977.

Address: 2229 Gloaming Way, Beverly Hills, Calif 90210.

KASZNAR, Kurt S, (*né* Serwischer), actor
b Vienna, Austria, 13 Aug 1913; *s* of Nathan Serwischer and his wife Leopoldine (Schweiger); *e* Gymnasium, Vienna, and Minerva University, Zurich; *m* (1) Cornelia Whooly (dec); (2) Leora Dana (mar dis); prepared for the stage by Max Reinhardt in the Reinhardt Seminars in Vienna.

First appeared on the stage in the Cathedral Square in Salzburg, 1931, as Prologue in Jedermann; first appeared in New York with the Reinhardt Company at the Manhattan Opera House, 1937, playing seven parts in The Eternal Road; at the 44th Street, NY, Jan 1941, produced Crazy with the Heat; 46th Street, June 1943, played the Commander in First Cousins, a one-act play which he also wrote, and which, with four others, won a service contest and was produced under the omnibus title The Army Play-by-Play; Plymouth, Mar 1948, played Dmitri Oumansky in Joy to the World; Cort, Dec 1948, Signor Cortese in Make Way for Lucia; Lenox Hill Playhouse, Mar 1949, Punchus in The 19th Hole of Europe, Fulton, Oct 1949, a Monk in Montserrat; Plymouth, Jan 1950, Uncle Louis in The Happy Time, which ran for more than sixteen months; ANTA, May 1955, played Boule in Seventh Heaven; Phoenix, off-Broadway, Dec 1955, played the Director in Six Characters in Search of an Author; John Golden, Apr 1956, Pozzo in Waiting for Godot; Henry Miller, Mar 1959, Prince of Salestria in Look After Lulu; Lunt-Fontanne, Nov 1959, Max Detweiler in The Sound of Music, in which he appeared for over two years; Biltmore, Oct 1963, Victor Velasco in Barefoot in the Park; City Center, Mar 1965, Mackie in Die Dreigroschen Oper; Piccadilly, London, Nov 1965, Victor Velasco in Barefoot in the Park; New Theater for Now, Los Angeles, 1972, played in In a Fine Castle; Pittsburgh, Pa, Playhouse, Sept 1972, Tevye in Fiddler on the Roof; Philadelphia Drama Guild, Nov 1972, Orgon in Tartuffe; Ahmanson, Los Angeles, Nov 1973, played in Cyrano de Bergerac; Yale Repertory, New Haven, Conn, Jan 1974, Sheldon Farenthold in The Tubs, Feb 1974, Trinity Moses in The Rise and Fall of the City of Mahagonny, Mar 1974, Doctor in Geography of a Horse Dreamer, and Apr 1974, Chief Councilman in Shlemiel the First; Meadowbrook, Cedar Grove, NJ, May 1974, again played Tevye in Fiddler on the Roof; toured, Dec 1974, in Don Juan in Hell; Ahmanson, LA, Apr 1975, appeared in Ring Round the Moon; Arlington Park, Ill, 1976–7, in the Mousetrap; Brooklyn Academy, Feb 1978, Nansky in The Play's the Thing; appeared in stock productions of My Three Angels, Once More, with Feeling, The Happy Time, The Little Hut, Arms and the Man, etc; first appeared in films in 1926 when he played in two silent pictures in Vienna with Max Linder, and since appeared in innumerable films including Lili, The Happy Time, A Farewell to Arms, My Sister Eileen, 55 Days at Peking, and Casino Royale; appeared regularly on television.

(*Died 6 Aug 1979.*)

KATSELAS, Milton, director
b Pittsburgh, Pennsylvania, 22 Feb 1933; *s* of George Katse-

las and his wife Dena (Katsoyannis); *e* Carnegie Institute of Technology; *m* Patricia Letts.

Directed his first production, The Time of the Cuckoo, at the Saranac Lake, New York, Theatre, in 1957; since then has directed, also at Saranac Lake, Our Town and Cat on a Hot Tin Roof; directed his first NYC production, The Zoo Story, at the Provincetown Playhouse, 14 Jan 1960; in NY has directed Call Me by My Rightful Name, The Garden of Sweets, 1961; On an Open Roof (also co-produced), 1963; a revival of The Rose Tattoo, 1966; Butterflies Are Free, 1969; Camino Real, 1970; made his London début, Nov 1970, at the Apollo, when he again directed Butterflies Are Free; has also directed various national company and touring production as well as repertory theatre productions, notably Who's Afraid of Virginia Woolf? Coriolanus (San Diego Shakespeare Festival), 1965; The Crucible (Arena Stage, Washington), Othello (San Diego), On a Clear Day You Can See Forever, 1967; The Lion in Winter, 1968; The Trial of A Lincoln, 1971; Promenade, Apr 1977, directed Jockeys, which he also wrote with Frank Spiering; has also directed stock and touring productions of Macbeth for the Pittsburgh Playhouse, The Price, Camino Real for the Mark Taper Forum of Los Angeles, The Glass Menagerie, Incident at Vichy, After the Fall, A View from the Bridge, The Country Girl, The Visit, Dark at the Top of the Stairs, The Great White Hope, Streamers (1977), etc; directed the film of Butterflies Are Free, his début, in 1971.

Address: 600 West End Avenue, New York, NY *Tel:* SU 7–5299.

KAY, Charles (*né* Piff), actor
b Coventry, 31 Aug 1930; *s* of Charles Herbert Beckingham Piff, and his wife Frances (Petty); *e* Warwick School and Birmingham University; trained originally to be a dental surgeon; then trained for the stage at RADA, where he was awarded the Bancroft Gold Medal in 1958.

First appeared on the stage in Oct 1958, at the Belgrade Theatre, Coventry, as Sadi in Uncle Dunda; first appeared on the London stage in June 1959, at the Royal Court, as Jimmy Beales in Roots; transferred with the production to the Duke of York's, July 1959; Arts, Sept 1960, played Magpie in The Naked Island; Royal Court, Feb 1961, Franciscus in The Changeling; same theatre, July 1961, and Phoenix, Sept 1961, Pope Leo in Luther; Royal Court, Feb 1962, Sir Andrew Aguecheck in a production without décor of Twelfth Night; Strand, Sept 1962, Eric Sawbridge in The New Men; joined the Royal Shakespeare Company, Apr 1963, for whom his parts included Octavius in Julius Caesar, and Clarence in The Wars of the Roses, Stratford, 1963; Archbishop of Canterbury and Dauphin in Henry V, Stratford, 1964; Ferdinand of Navarre in Love's Labour's Lost, Lancelot Gobbo in The Merchant of Venice, Antipholus of Ephesus in The Comedy of Errors, Player Queen and Osric in Hamlet, Stratford, 1965; Dobchinsky in The Government Inspector, Jochen in The Meteor, and Moloch in The Thwarting of Baron Bolligrew, Aldwych, 1966; New, June 1967, Beau Clincher in The Constant Couple; with the National Theatre Company, 1967–71, for whom he appeared in parts including: Verges in Much Ado About Nothing, Celia in an all-male As You Like It, 1967; Gaveston in Edward II, Sir Nathaniel in Love's Labour's Lost, 1968; Hamlet in Rosencrantz and Guildenstern Are Dead, Loach in The National Health, 1969; Arragon in The Merchant of Venice, Soloni in The Three Sisters (Los Angeles), and de Guiche in Cyrano, 1970; Superintendent and General in The Captain of Köpenick, Sicinius Veletus in Coriolanus, Robespierre in Danton's

Death (New), 1971; Arts, Cambridge, May 1972, Harold Twine in Popkiss; Mercury, Colchester, Mar 1973, Fr Vernon in The Prodigal Daughter; joined the Actors Company, 1974, and played Tartuffe at the Edinburgh Festival, Aug, and 2nd Messenger in The Bacchae; later redirected Tartuffe and played James in The Last Romantic, Comte de Chagny in The Phantom of the Opera, at Wimbledon, June 1975; Playhouse, Leeds, Nov 1975, Shylock in The Merchant of Venice; toured India, Far East, Australia and New Zealand with The Hollow Crown, 1976; Old Vic, May 1977, the Dauphin in St Joan; Chichester Festival, 1977, played Cassius in Julius Caesar; Garrick, May 1978, Sam in The Homecoming; Haymarket, Dec 1978, Doctor in The Millionairess; Birmingham Rep, May 1979, Daniel de Bosola in The Duchess of Malfi; first film, Bachelor of Hearts, 1958; recent appearances include: Nijinsky; television, also since 1958, includes: The Duchess of Malfi, Fall of Eagles, and Loyalties.

Favourite parts: Fancourt Babberley in Charley's Aunt, Richard III. *Recreations:* Reading, music, bridge. *Address:* 18 Epple Road, London, SW6. *Tel:* 01–736 5762.

KAY, Richard, actor
b Newcastle upon Tyne, 16 Mar 1937; *s* of Arthur William Kay, and his wife Alison Beatrice (Fraser); *e* Leighton Park School, and Emmanuel College, Cambridge; *m* Venetia Maxwell; formerly a teacher of English.

After appearances with various university societies at Cambridge, including the Marlowe (president 1961), made his first professional appearance in the autumn of 1962 at the Derby Playhouse, as a dervish in Gordon of Khartoum; in repertory, 1963, at the Playhouse, Liverpool; first London appearance, Jan 1964, as Berwick in The Fourth of June; Arts, July 1964, played the title part in Edward II; toured, 1966, for the Arts Council as Prince Hal in Henry IV, Part I; joined the National Theatre, 1967, and appeared in parts including Phoebe in an all-male As You Like It, Damis in Tartuffe, 1967; Dumaine in Love's Labour's Lost, 1968; Strephon in Back to Methuselah, 1969; Salerio in The Merchant of Venice, Prince Shulovsky in The Idiot, 1970; Willy Wormser and Stutz in The Captain of Köpenick, Mercury in Amphitryon 38, 1971; for the Young Vic, played Leandro in The Cheats of Scapino, second messenger in Oedipus, and Tranio in The Taming of the Shrew, 1970; Tom Moore in Byron, The Naked Peacock, 1971; Romeo in Romeo and Juliet, 1972; left the National Theatre, 1972; Sadler's Wells, 1972, played Chris Keller in All My Sons, Apr, and Faulkland in The Rivals, May; Theatre Upstairs, July 1972, Mr Putney in Was He Anyone?; Shaw, Mar 1974, John Worthing in The Importance of Being Earnest; Leeds Playhouse, 1975, played The Dauphin in Saint Joan and Mr David in Meanwhile Backstage in the Old Front Room; first film, 1970, the National Theatre's Three Sisters; Playhouse, Leeds, Sept 1976, Chaplain in Catch 22; Casson Studio, Leatherhead, Nov 1976, Errol Philander in Statements After an Arrest Under the Immorality Act; Young Vic, July 1977, John in Gross Prophet, and The Bishop in The Actress and the Bishop; New End, Sept 1977, Harry Harrison in Harry Outside; St George's, 1979, Cassius in Julius Caesar (Apr), Duke of Aumerle in Richard II (May), and Amiens in As You Like It (June); Arts, 1980, took over as Arthur in New-Found-Land; television, since 1964, includes: Wuthering Heights, *Edward and Mrs Simpson,* and *Lillie.*

Favourite parts: Edward II, Prince Hal. *Recreations:* Reading, writing, gardening. *Address:* c/o Green & Underwood, 3 Broadway, Gunnersbury, Lane, London W3 8HR. *Tel:* 01–993 6183.

KAYE, Danny (*né* Daniel Kominski), actor
b Brooklyn, New York, 18 Jan 1913; *s* of Jacob Kominski and his wife Clara (Memorovsky); *e* Thomas Jefferson High School, Brooklyn; *m* Sylvia Fine; originally intended to enter the medical profession.

Commenced his career in vaudeville, travelling all over the United States and Asia in the revue La Vie Paris; subsequently toured with Abe Lyman's band and, in 1938, appeared at the Dorchester Hotel, London, in cabaret; first appeared on the regular stage at the Keynote, NY, Mar 1939, in Left of Broadway; Ambassador Theatre, NY, 29 Sept 1939, in The Straw Hat Revue; at the Alvin Theatre, Jan 1941, played Russell Paxton in Lady in the Dark; Palace, 1941, appeared in vaudeville; Imperial, Oct 1941, Jerry Walker in Let's Face It; reappeared in London, at the Palladium, 2 Feb 1948, in variety; he also appeared in the Royal Variety performances at the Palladium, 1948–52; performed at the Canadian National Exhibition, 1950; Curran, San Francisco, Sept 1952, appeared in variety; appeared in NY at the Palace Theatre, Jan 1953, in variety; Shubert, Detroit, 1955, Greek, Los Angeles, 1958, Curran, San Francisco, 1959, Sydney and Melbourne, Australia, 1959, Framingham, Mass, 1961, also played in variety programs; Ziegfeld, Apr 1963, appeared in a variety program; Philharmonic Hall, 29 Mar 1965, conducted New York Philharmonic in a benefit concert for the pension fund; toured Vietnam warfronts, 1966, for the USO; reappeared on the musical stage at the Imperial, Nov 1970, as Noah in Two by Two; Metropolitan Opera House, 4 Jan 1973, devised and hosted Opera Laugh-In, which he repeated several times thereafter and also televised; Festival Hall, London, Sept 1975, conducted the London Symphony Orchestra in a charity concert; first entered films, 1944, in Up in Arms, and has since appeared in Wonder Man, Kid from Brooklyn, The Secret Life of Walter Mitty, That's Life, The Inspector-General, Hans Christian Andersen, Knock on Wood, The Court Jester, Merry Andrew, Me and the Colonel, On the Double, The Man from the Diner's Club, The Madwoman of Chaillot; received a special Academy Award in 1954; star of his own television program for several seasons beginning in 1963.

Club: Lambs. *Address:* Box 750, Beverly Hills, Calif.

KAYE, Stubby, actor and singer
b New York City, 11 Nov 1918; *e* DeWitt Clinton High School, Bronx; *m* Angela Bracewell.

Won a contest on the Major Bowes Amateur Hour on radio, 1939; appeared as a singer at the Loew's Boulevard Theatre, Bronx, New York, 1939; toured as a comedian in vaudeville, 1939–42; made his London debut during World War II in USO productions; made his New York legitimate debut at the 46th Street, 24 Nov 1950, as Nicely-Nicely Johnson in Guys and Dolls; St James, Nov 1956, Played Marryin' Sam in Li'l Abner; Longacre, Oct 1961, Solomon in Everybody Loves Opal; Colonial, Boston, Dec 1973, Pooch Kearney in Good News, and subsequently toured in this part for one year before appearing in it at the St James, Dec 1974; Longacre, Nov 1975, took over from Jack Weston as Gaetano Proclo in The Ritz; was emcee for the dance bands of Charlie Barnett and Freddy Martin and has appeared widely in clubs and cabaret as a singer and comedian; repeated his roles in the films of Guys and Dolls, 1955, and Li'l Abner, 1959, and has also played in The Dirtiest Girl I Ever Met, 1973, etc; has also played on television.

Address: Actors Equity Association, 165 West 46th Street, New York, NY 10036.

KEACH, Stacy, actor and director
b Savannah, Georgia, 2 June 1941; *s* of Stacy Keach, Sr and his wife Mary Cain Peckham; *e* University of California at Berkeley; attended the Yale School of Drama, and on a

Fulbright Scholarship, attended the London Academy of Music and Dramatic Art.

First appeared on the stage while in elementary school in a production of Rip Van Winkle; while at the University of California, 1959–63, acted in many productions, including The Antifarce of John and Leporello, To Learn to Love, Galileo (Brecht), Purple Dust, The Changeling, Bartholomew Fair, Escurial, A Touch of the Poet, and Don Juan, directed The American Dream and C'est La Vie, and directed and wrote The 1960 Axe Revue; at the Tufts Arena, 1961, played Armand in Camille; Oregon Shakespeare Festival, Ashland, 1962, played Westmoreland in Henry IV, Part II, and, 1963, leading roles in The Comedy of Errors, Romeo and Juliet, Love's Labour's Lost, and the title-role of Henry V; at the Yale Drama School, 1963, played in The Voyage; made his London début as director in 1964 when he directed Pullman Car Hiawatha, The Stronger, and The Maids at the Academy of Music and Dramatic Art; Delacorte, June 1964, made his New York début playing Marcellus and the First Player in the New York Shakespeare Festival production of Hamlet; London Academy, 1965, played in Julius Caesar and Hughie; toured England, 1965, in Playing with Fire; returned to NY and joined the Repertory Theater of Lincoln Center and, at the Vivian Beaumont, played Cutler and Turnkey in Danton's Death; Dec 1965, Mr Horner in The Country Wife; Mar 1966, various roles in The Caucasian Chalk Circle; at the Williamstown, Massachusetts, Summer Theatre, 1966, played in Annie Get Your Gun, You Can't Take It with You, Lion in Winter, and Marat/Sade; at the Long Wharf, New Haven, Connecticut, 1966, played in The Three Sisters and Oh, What a Lovely War; Village Gate, NY, Feb 1967, played the title-role in MacBird!; for the Yale Repertory, 1967, played in We Bombed in New Haven, Orpheum, NY, Oct 1967, August in The Demonstration and The Man in Man and Dog in the production The Niggerlovers; Yale Repertory, 1968 played in Henry IV, The Three Sisters, and Coriolanus; Delacorte, June 1968, Sir John Falstaff in Henry IV, Parts I and II; Vivian Beaumont, Nov 1968, Edmund in King Lear; Arena Stage, Washington, DC, spring 1969, Buffalo Bill in Indians; Delacorte, July 1969, title-role of Peer Gynt; Brooks Atkinson, Oct 1969, again played Buffalo Bill in Indians; Los Angeles Music Center, 1970, Benedict in Beatrice and Benedict, the opera of Berlioz based on Much Ado About Nothing; Promenade Theatre, NY, May 1971, Jamie in Long Day's Journey into Night; Long Wharf, New Haven, Conn, 1971, played Hamlet; Delacorte, NY, June 1972, played Hamlet; Mark Taper Forum, Los Angeles, Mar 1974, again played Hamlet; Long Beach Theatre Festival, Sept 1978, title-role in Cyrano de Bergerac; Music Box, 1979, took over the part of Sydney Bruhl in Deathtrap; Cottesloe, Jan 1980, appeared in the National Theatre production of Hughie, as Eric Smith; received the Obie and the Vernon Rice Drama Desk Awards for both MacBird! and Long Day's Journey into Night; entered films in The Heart Is a Lonely Hunter, 1968, and has since played in End of the Road, The Traveling Executioner, Brewster McCloud, Doc, Fat City, The New Centurions, Luther, Conduct Unbecoming, Jesus of Nazareth, Up in Smoke, The Ninth Configuration, 1978, The Long Riders, 1979, etc; has been seen on television in Macbeth, Twelfth Night, The Winter's Tale, Wright Brothers, and his own film The Repeater; recently seen in a number of TV films and the series Caribe; formed his own production company, Positron Productions Ltd.

Recreations: Tennis, riding, skiing, roller skating. *Address:* Global Business Management, 9601 Wilshire Boulevard, Suite 300, Beverly Hills, Calif 90210.

KEAN, Marie, actress
b Rush, Co Dublin, Ireland, 27 June 1922; *d* of John Kean and his wife Margaret (Foley); *e* Loreto College, Dublin; *m* William L Mulvey; trained for the stage at the Gaiety School of Acting, Dublin by Ria Mooney.

First appeared on the stage June 1947 at the Gaiety Theatre, Dublin, as Naomi in Noah; member of the Abbey Theatre company, Dublin 1949–61, for whom she has since reappeared regularly; first London appearance, Theatre Royal, Stratford E, July 1962, as Anna Livia Plurabelle in The Voice of Shem; Mermaid, Sept 1962, played Mrs Cogan in The Plough and The Stars; Arts, Nov 1962, Charlotte Russe in A Cheap Bunch of Nice Flowers; Phoenix, Feb 1963, Landlady and Maja in Baal; Winnie in Happy Days, Stratford East, 1964; worked with Peter Brook's experimental group, 1964, playing the Mother in The Screens, Donmar Rehearsal Theatre, May; Globe, Apr 1965, Daisy Connolly in The Paper Hat; Mermaid, Sept 1966, Mrs O'Flaherty in O'Flaherty VC; Gardner Centre, Brighton, Aug 1970, Nora Melody in A Touch of the Poet; Dublin, 1973, again played Winnie in Happy Days; Bristol Old Vic, Oct 1973, played Marina in Uncle Vanya, and Mrs Hewlett in Plunderl; joined the Royal Shakespeare Company and played in Stratford Season 1976, as the Nurse in Romeo and Juliet, Aemilia in A Comedy of Errors, A Weird Sister in Macbeth (Other Place, and also Memorial Theatre, Apr 1977, and Warehouse, Sept 1977); also played the first two roles at the Aldwych, June–July 1977, Mrs Rummel in Pillars of the Community (Aug); and Madame Cabet in Days of the Commune (Nov); films, since 1957, include: Great Catherine, Ryan's Daughter and Barry Lyndon; television, since 1961, includes: The Plough and the Stars and Jane Eyre.

Favourite parts: Anna Livia Plurabelle, Winnie in Happy Days. *Club:* Arts, Dublin. *Recreations:* Cooking, gardening. *Address:* 98 Heath Street, Hampstead, London, NW3.

KEAN, Norman, producer, theatre owner, and general manager
b Colorado Springs, Colo, 14 Oct 1934; *s* of Barney B Kean and his wife Flora (Bienstock); *e* University of Denver (1952–54); *m* Gwyda DonHowe.

First appeared on the stage in a high school production of A Date with Judy, Feb 1946; made his professional debut at the Bar Harbour, Maine, Playhouse, summer 1953, as Wint Selby in Ah, Wilderness!, which he also designed; continued acting, managing, and designing in stock; made his NY debut as stage manager for Johnny Johnson, at the Carnegie Hall Playhouse, 21 Oct 1956; since then has managed or stage-managed Orpheus Descending, 1957; Waltz of the Toreadors, A Touch of the Poet, 1958; Shakespeare Festival Players tour, 1959; Camino Real, Laurette (New Haven), The Pleasure of His Company (tour), 1960; directed stock productions of The Importance of Being Earnest, Gigi and Charley's Aunt, general manager for the Bayanihan Philippine Dance Co, 1961; General Seeger, Half Past Wednesday, Royal Dramatic Theater of Sweden (Seattle and NY), The Matchmaker (tour), Tiger, Tiger, Burning Bright, 1962; Cages, co-produced The Worlds of Shakespeare, and became general manager of the Phoenix Theater, 1963–70; general manager for 24 productions of the APA-Phoenix Repertory Company; produced A Woman and the Blues, 1966; general manager, Oh! Calcutta!, Pantagleize, The Show Off, 1967; The Cocktail Party, The Misanthrope, 1968; Hamlet, 1969; presented Opium, general manager, Orlando Furioso, 1970; co-produced Happy Birthday, Wanda June, general manager, The Ballad of Johnny Pot, 1971; co-produced with John Heffernan The Shadow of a Gunman, general manager, Don't Bother Me, I Can't Cope, 1972; Fame, and produced Hosanna, Sizwe Banzi is Dead, The Island, 1974; Boccaccio,

Me and Bessie, 1975; Oh! Calcutta!, 1976; A Broadway Musical, By Strouse, 1978; designed and built the Edison Theatre, NY, 1970, which he operates as President of Edison Enterprises Inc; Lectures at New York University, School of Continuing Education; Member Board of Governors, League of New York Theatres and Producers, 1970–present; Board of Trustees, American Academy of Dramatic Arts, 1977–present.

Club: Friars. *Address:* Edison Theatre Building, 240 West 47th Street, New York, NY 10036. *Tel:* 586-7870.

KEANE, John B, playwright

b Listowel, Co Kerry, 21 Jul 1928; *s* of William Brendan Keane and his wife Hannah (Purtill); *e* St Michael's College, Listowel; *m* Mary Teresa O'Connor; formerly a chemist's assistant, furnace operator, barman and fowl-buyer.

His first play to be produced was Sive, Listowel, 1959, and London, 1961; has since written the following plays, all of which received their first production in Ireland, and many of which have been seen in the United States: Sharon's Grave, 1960; The Highest House on the Mountain, Many Young Men of Twenty, 1961; No More in Dust, 1962; Hut 42, The Man from Clare, 1963; The Year of the Hiker, 1964; The Field, 1965; The Roses of Tralee, 1966; The Rain at the End of the Summer, 1967; Big Maggie, 1969; The Change in Mame Fadden, Moll, 1971; The One-Way Ticket, 1972; Values (Consisting of The Springing of John O'Dorey, Backwater, and The Pure of Heart), The Crazy Wall, 1973; Matchmaker, 1975; The Good Thing, 1976; The Buds of Ballybunion, 1978; The Chastitute, 1980; has also published short stories, verse, and collections of prose; writes weekly columns for the *Dublin Evening Herald* and the *Limerick Leader*; President, Irish PEN Consultative Assembly; Hon D Litt, Trinity College, Dublin, 1977.

Address: 37 William Street, Listowel, Co Kerry, Eire. *Tel:* 068-21127.

KEATING, Charles, actor

b London, 22 Oct 1941; *s* of Charles James Keating and his wife Margaret (Shevlin); *e* England and Canada; *m* Mary Ellen Chobody.

First stage appearance, Buffalo Studio Theatre, NY, 1959; seasons with several companies on both sides of the Atlantic, beginning with the Cleveland Play House in 1960 and the Provincetown Playhouse on Cape Cod before being drafted into the US Army; involved in Special Services as a performer and director, mounting productions of Shakespeare, contemporary plays, musicals; in 1966 joined the Charles Playhouse in Boston, playing Valentine in Love for Love, Laertes in Hamlet, Eilif in Mother Courage; 1967, appeared for a season as a night club entertainer at The Moors on Cape Cod before joining the Tyrone Guthrie Theatre in Minneapolis, 1968–70; his parts here included Antony in Julius Caesar, Caliban in The Tempest, Hurst in Sergeant Musgrave's Dance, title-role in Baal, Giri in Arturo Ui, Pylades in The House of Atreus; appeared on Broadway in the two latter productions, making his début at the Billy Rose Theatre on 17 Dec 1968 as Pylades; while a member of the Guthrie Theatre, he toured the Midwest under the auspices of the Minnesota State Arts Council as a solo performer in When I Was A Boy with Never a Crack in My Heart, and What is Past, Passing or to Come; before returning to England in 1971, he directed several productions: The Madness of Lady Bright for the Guthrie, Macbeth at the Crawford Livingston Theatre in St Paul, and an award-winning production of The

Scarecrow for the American College Theatre Festival, 1971; for the opening season of the Crucible Theatre, Sheffield, was an actor/director; with this company in July 1972 appeared as Ralph in The Shoemaker's Holiday, and Cromwell in A Man for All Seasons at the Bankside Globe Playhouse; joined the Royal Shakespeare Company, 1973, and at Stratford that season played Ross in Richard II, Oliver in As You Like It, and the nameless Lord in The Taming of the Shrew; also at The Other Place in Stratford he was seen as the King in De Ghelderode's Escurial; Brooklyn Academy of Music, Jan 1974, again played Ross; Stratford, 1974, gave Cloten in Cymbeline at the Memorial Theatre, Edmund in Lear at The Other Place; again played Edmund at The Place in London, Oct 1974, and at Brooklyn, Feb 1975; at the Aldwych, Nov 1975, Consul Casimir in The Marquis of Keith, and repeated the part of Cloten in December; in Jan 1976, returned again to the US with a group of five RSC actors to initiate a programme called AIR (Actors In Residence) at several American Universities, appearing in the following recitals: The Hollow Crown, Shall I Compare Thee, and Groupings; after this tour he returned to the Chichester Festival, 1976, to play Orsino in Twelfth Night, and Ham in Noah; in 1977, played Macbeth for the Cleveland Playhouse in Ohio, returning again to Chichester for Julius Caesar (Mark Antony), The Applecart (American Ambassador), Jerry in The Zoo Story, and Murder in the Cathedral, which he co-directed in Chichester Cathedral; television work includes Richard II, Dream of Living, The Professionals, and Edward and Mrs Simpson; films include Charlie Muffin and Brideshead Revisited.

Address: c/o Dodo Watts Agency, 4 Broom Close, Teddington, Middlesex.

KEATS, Viola, actress

b Doune, Perthshire, 27 Mar 1911; *d* of William Sanderson Smart and his wife Shirley (Keats); *e* Convent of Notre Dame de Zion, Worthing; *m* (1) Harold Peterson (dec); (2) William Kellner; studied for the stage at the Royal Academy of Dramatic Art, where she received the Bancroft Gold Medal in 1933.

Made her first appearance on the stage at the Playhouse, Liverpool, with the Liverpool Repertory Company, 21 Apr 1930, as Sarah Hurst in Easy Virtue; she remained with that company until the end of the 1931–2 season, playing a variety of parts; made her first appearance on the London stage at the Apollo Theatre, 5 Sept 1933, as Alex Millward in The Distaff Side; at Fulham, Jan–Feb 1934, played Rosemary Grey in Busy Body and Corinna Deane in Play; Shaftesbury, Apr 1934, Lucille Drayton in There's Always To-Morrow; Comedy, May 1934, Sally in All's Over Then; Q, July 1934, Eva Whiston in Line Engaged; made her first appearance in New York at the Booth Theatre, 25 Sept 1934, as Alex in The Distaff Side; Vaudeville, London, Sept 1936, Patricia Sommers in Gentle Rain; Henry Miller, NY, Feb 1938, Liz Pleydell in Once is Enough; appeared at the Q, London, Aug 1939, as Margaret Heal in The Fanatics; at the National, NY, Nov 1941, played Lady Macduff in Macbeth; Cort, Aug 1943, Jan in Murder Without Crime; Golden, June 1944, succeeded Judith Evelyn, as Mrs Manningham in Angel Street, and toured in the same part, 1945–6; Music Box, Mar 1948, Jean Linden in The Linden Tree; Shubert, Feb 1950, played Elizabeth Boleyn in Anne of a Thousand Days; toured in Australia, Feb 1950, as Blanche in A Streetcar Named Desire; at the Q, London, Sept 1953, played Diana Hartland in Down Came a Blackbird, and appeared in this part at the Savoy, Dec 1953; Strand, May 1958, played Anja Hendryk in Verdict; Edinburgh Festival, Aug 1958, played Mother Josephine in Bernadette; Royal, Stratford, E, Jan 1962, played Dame Eloise in On a Clear Day You Can See Canterbury; Ashcroft, Croydon, Nov 1962, played Aline Solness in The Masterbuilder, transferring with the production to the Arts, Dec 1962; Haymarket, Aug 1964, took over the part of Susan Shepherd in The Wings of the Dove; Ashcroft, Croydon, Oct 1964, played Lavinia in The Heiress; at the same theatre, Mar 1965, Leonora Fiske in Ladies in Retirement; Georgian Theatre, Richmond, Yorks, Sept 1965, Lady Townley in The Man of Mode; Ashcroft, Croydon, Feb 1966, Mrs Hardcastle in She Stoops to Conquer; Arts, Oct 1966, Madame Severin in The Swallows; Savoy, June 1967, Lady Frinton in Aren't We All?; Arnaud, Guildford, Oct 1967, Mrs Winemiller in The Eccentricities of A Nightingale; Arnaud, Guildford, Nov 1971, Miss Bourne in The Ghost Train; Wyndham's, June 1972, took over as the Abbess in Abelard and Heloise; later toured in the same role; Arnaud, Sept 1972, Mother in Six Characters in Search of an Author; Old Vic, May 1974, for National Theatre, Margaret Lloyd in Next of Kin; Thorndike, Leatherhead, Feb 1975, Mrs Culver in The Constant Wife; has also appeared in numerous films, and television productions in England and the United States.

Recreation: Reading. *Address:* c/o Herbert De Leon Ltd, 13 Bruton Street, London, W1.

KEEL, Howard (*né* Harold), actor and singer
b Gillespie, Illinois, 13 Apr 1919; *e* Fallbrook, California, High School; formerly an aircraft sales representative; *m* Helen Anderson.

Made his stage début under the name Harold Keel at the Majestic, 1946, when he succeeded John Raitt as Billy Bigelow in Carousel; St James, 1946, took over the role of Curly in Oklahoma!; made his London début at the Drury Lane, Apr 1947, as Curly in Oklahoma!; entered films, 1948; reappeared on the stage at the New York City Center, Sept 1957, as Billy Bigelow in Carousel; Winter Garden, Dec 1959, Clint Maroon in Saratoga; Broadhurst, 1963, took over from Richard Kiley as David Jordan in No Strings, and subsequently toured in this part until Jan 1964; toured summer, 1964, as Lancelot in Camelot; Mineola, Long Island, Playhouse, Mar 1965, again played in Camelot; toured, 1965, as Emile de Becque in South Pacific; toured, 1966, as Billy Bigelow in Carousel; toured US and Canada, 1967–8, as Dr Mark Bruckner in On a Clear Day You Can See Forever; toured, 1969, in Plaza Suite; Her Majesty's, London, Oct 1971, Lewis Lambert Strether in Ambassador; Fremont, Las Vegas, Nevada, Mar 1972, appeared in variety with Kathryn Grayson; toured, summer 1972, in Dark of the Moon; Westbury, NY, Music Fair, Sept 1972, Cervantes and Don Quixote in Man of La Mancha; Lunt-Fontanne, Nov 1972, Lewis Lambert Strether in Ambassador; Westbury Music Fair, 1973, played in The Unsinkable Molly Brown, and subsequently toured; toured 1974 as Michael in I Do, I Do; Palladium, London, June 1974, appeared in variety; toured Australia, July–Aug 1975, in cabaret; toured US, Sept 1975, in Gene Kelly's Salute to Broadway; toured, May 1976, in A Musical Jubilee; has also appeared in summer stock productions of Kismet, Mr Roberts, Sunrise at Campobello, Kiss Me, Kate, The Rainmaker, South Pacific (1977), etc; entered films in England, 1948, in The Small Voice, and in the US has since played in Annie Get Your Gun, Show Boat, Kiss Me, Kate, Rose Marie, Seven Brides for Seven Brothers, Jupiter's Darling, The War Wagon, The Bushwackers, etc; appears on television in Tomorrow.

Address: Actors Equity Association, 165 West 46th Street, New York, NY 10036.

KEELER, Ruby, actress and dancer
b Halifax, Nova Scotia, 25 Aug 1909; *e* Professional Chil-

dren's School, New York; *m* (1) Al Jolson (mar dis); (2) John Lowe (dec).

Made her first professional appearance in cabaret as a buck-dancer in partnership with Patsy Kelly; made her legitimate theatre début at the Liberty, NY, 23 Dec 1923, in the chorus of The Rise of Rosie O'Reilly; remained in chorus work for some years; Ritz, Jan 1927, played Ruby in Bye, Bye Bonnie; New Amsterdam, Mar 1927, Mazie Maxwell in Lucky; Knickerbocker, Oct 1927, Mamie and Ruby in Sidewalks of New York; New Amsterdam, Dec 1928, appeared in Whoopee; Ziegfeld, July 1929, appeared in the revue Show Girl; entered films, and reappeared on the stage at the Grand Opera House, Chicago, Illinois, 15 July 1940, as Shirley in Hold onto Your Hats; retired from the theatre for thirty years; reappeared on the stage at the 46th Street, Jan 1971, as Sue Smith in No, No, Nanette, which was a great success; Westbury, Long Island, Music Fair, Aug 1974, again played Sue Smith in No, No, Nanette; entered films in 42nd Street, 1933, and since has played in Gold Diggers of 1933, Footlight Parade, 1933; Dames, Flirtation Walk, 1934; Go into Your Dance, Shipmates Forever, 1935; Colleen, 1936; Ready, Willing and Able, 1937; Mother Carey's Chickens, 1938; Sweethearts of the Campus, 1941; her films have enjoyed several retrospective revivals, notably in London and in New York, 1971.

Recreation: Golf. *Address:* Actors Equity Association, 165 West 46th Street, New York, NY 10036.

KEEN, Geoffrey, actor
b London, 21 Aug 1916; *s* of Malcolm Keen; *e* Bristol Grammar School, where in 1935 he gained the Leverhulme Scholarship to study at the Royal Academy of Dramatic Art; studied for the stage at the RADA, where he gained the Bancroft Gold Medal, 1936; *m* (1) Hazel Terry (mar dis); (2) Madeleine Howell (mar dis); (3) Doris Groves.

Made his first appearance on the stage at Bristol, 9 May 1932, as Trip in The School for Scandal; made his first appearance in London at the Old Vic, 17 Mar 1936, as Florizel in The Winter's Tale; and the following month played Edgar in King Lear; Queen's, Sept 1936, played David French in Follow Your Saint; Cambridge, Oct 1936, Dan in Night Must Fall; Royalty, Feb 1937, Will Hopcyn in The Ripening Wheat; Duke of York's, Mar 1937, the Hon Gerald Sinclair in Great Possessions; St James's, Aug 1937, Brian Decker in Old Music; Saville, Feb 1938, Bije Warner in Welcome Stranger; in the autumn of 1938, toured with Donald Wolfit's Shakespearean company; Savoy, Dec 1938, Israel Hands in Treasure Island; joined the Stratford-on-Avon Shakespearean company, Apr 1939, and played Lucentio in The Taming of the Shrew, Orlando in As You Like It, Clarence in Richard III, Cassio in Othello, Sebastian in Twelfth Night, Cominius in Coriolanus; joined the Army, 1940; for four years served in Stars in Battle Dress, playing many leading parts in Men in Shadow, While the Sun Shines, etc, both at home and overseas; reappeared on the London stage at Arts Theatre, Mar 1946, playing Lyngstrand in The Lady from the Sea, and Apr 1946, Geoffrey Stewart in Exercise Bowler; toured on the Continent for the British Council, 1946–7, in Hamlet, Othello, and Candida; Piccadilly, Mar 1947, played Cassio in Othello and Eugene Marchbanks in Candida; Aldwych, Aug 1948, Justin Corbel in Rain on the Just; joined the Shakespeare Memorial Theatre Company, Stratford-on-Avon, May 1957, to play Cassius in Julius Caesar, and Iachimo in Cymbeline; Arts, Jan 1959, played Georges in Traveller Without Luggage, and the Ambassador in Madame De . . . (double bill); Haymarket, May 1960, played the Turkish Military Governor in Ross; left the cast to make his first appearance in New York at the Eugene O'Neill, Dec 1961, in the same play; Queen's, London, Sept 1963, played Sven Ericson in Man and Boy; Brooks Atkinson, NY, Nov 1963, again played Sven Ericson in Man and Boy; Piccadilly, Feb 1973, Bishop of Nevers in Mistress of Novices; Savoy, May 1978, Mr Pym in Alice's Boys; since 1947 has appeared in many films, including Odd Man Out, The Third Man, Doctor in the House, Genevieve, Carrington, VC, Doctor at Sea, The Angry Silence, Sink the Bismark, Live Now, Pay Later, Dr Zhivago, Born Free, etc; has made numerous television appearances, including five series of *The Troubleshooters*, Mr Rolls and Mr Royce, Churchill and the Generals, and *Crown Court*.

Favourite parts: Florizel, and Dan in Night Must Fall. *Address:* c/o London Management, 235–41 Regent Street, London W1A 2JT.

KEITH, Brian, (*né* Robert A Keith), actor
b Bayonne, NJ, 14 Nov 1921; *s* of the actor Robert Lee Keith and his wife the actress Helena (Shipman); *e* East Rockaway High School, New York; *m* the actress Victoria Young; served in the United States Marine Corps, 1941–45.

First appeared on stage at the Shubert, New Haven, 1946, in Heyday; first Broadway appearance, Alvin, 18 Feb 1948, as Mannion in Mister Roberts; at the Alvin, Jan 1951, played Ilyich in Darkness at Noon; Ethel Barrymore, Sept 1951, Lash in Out West of Eighth; played in the Chicago production of the Moon Is Blue, 1951; Boston, 1952; Jezebel's Husband in The Emperor of Babylon; returned to the stage, 1979, when he took over the title role in Da, at the Morosco; has appeared in more than 60 films since his first, The Pied Piper of Malone, 1925; has since appeared in Boomerang, 1946; recently in Wind River, 1979; TV since 1951 includes series and specials, recently The Seekers, 1979.

Favourite part: Da. *Address:* c/o Guild Management, 9911 West Pico Boulevard, Los Angeles, CA 90035.

KEITH, Penelope (*nee* Hatfield), actress
b Sutton, Surrey; *d* of Frederick Arthur Walter Hatfield and his wife Constance Mary (Nutting); *e* Annecy Convent, Seaford, Sussex, and at Bayeux; *m* Rodney Timson; trained for the stage at the Webber-Douglas School.

Made her first professional appearance at the Civic Theatre, Chesterfield, 21 Sept 1959, as Alice Pepper in The Tunnel of Love; after repertory experience here and at a number of theatres, joined the Royal Shakespeare Company, 1963, to play Simcox's wife and Lord Mayor's wife in the trilogy The Wars of the Roses, July; played the same parts on her London debut at the Aldwych, 11 Jan 1964; Hampstead, Dec 1966, Big Molly in Ballad of the False Barman; same theatre, Jun 1970, Tiny Cruise-Orb in Mr Kilt and the Great I Am; Fortune, Sept 1971, Maggie Howard in Suddenly at Home; Greenwich, Mar 1973, Magdalena in The House of Bernarda Alba, and Oct 1973, Ilona in Catsplay; Palace, Watford, Feb 1974, Julia in Fallen Angels; again at Greenwich, May 1974, Sarah in the trilogy The Norman Conquests, transferring to the Globe, Aug 1974; Open Air, Regent's Park, Sept 1975, reader in Sweet Mr Shakespeare; Globe, July 1976, Lady Driver in Donkey's Years, receiving the Variety Club and SWETM awards; Chichester, 1977 season, appeared as Orinthia in The Apple Cart, repeating the part at the Phoenix, Nov 1977; Haymarket, Dec 1978, Epifania in The Millionairess; TV since 1961, includes the series Kate, *The Good Life, To The Manor Born*, and also Private Lives, The Norman Conquests and Donkey's Years; films, since Every Home Should Have One, 1970, include Penny Gold and Take a Girl Like You.

Recreations: Gardening, bridge, theatregoing. *Address:* c/o

Howes and Prior, 66 Berkeley House, Hay Hill, London W1. *Tel:* 01-493 7570.

KELLIN, Mike, actor
b Hartford, 26 Apr 1922; *s* of Samuel Kellin and his wife Sophie (Botuck); *e* Bates College, Boston University, Trinity College and Yale University School of Drama; *m* (1) Nina Carserman (dec); (2) Sally Moffet; trained for the stage at The Randall School, Hartford.

Made his professional debut as the Elevator Boy in Junior Miss, at the Clinton Playhouse, Conn, summer 1946; first Broadway appearance, Booth, 8 Mar 1949, as Sgt MacVay in At War with the Army; also toured in this role; Coronet, Feb 1950, Frank in The Bird Cage; City Center, Jan 1955, Krupp in The Time of Your Life; Mark Hellinger, Apr 1955, Joe Mancinni in Ankles Aweigh; Shubert, Nov 1955, Hazel in Pipe Dream; Stratford, Conn, Aug 1956, and Phoenix, Feb 1957, Christopher Sly in The Taming of the Shrew; Renata, Jan 1958, title role in Winkelberg; 54th Street, Feb 1959, Sean Murphy in God and Kate Murphy; Longacre, Jan 1961, Dribble in Rhinoceros; Martin Beck, Mar 1963, the Cook in Mother Courage and Her Children; Plymouth, Oct 1966, took over as Oscar Madison in The Odd Couple; toured as Tevye in Fiddler on the Roof, 1971; Longacre, Jul 1975, took over as Carmine in The Ritz; St Clement's, Jan 1976, Walter Cole in American Buffalo; Cherry Lane, Jun 1976, Emil Varec in Duck Variations; has directed several plays off and off-off Broadway, and in 1979 wrote the book, music and lyrics for The Riffraff Revue; first film, At War with the Army, 1944; recently in Midnight Express; TV includes *The Wackiest Ship in the Army* (1965) and many other shows.

Favourite parts: Oscar Madison, Tevye, and Kulyigin in Three Sisters. *Address:* 23 Clinton Avenue, Nyack, NY 10960. *Tel:* 914-358 2506.

KELLY, Nancy, actress
b Lowell, Mass, 25 Mar 1921; *d* of John A Kelly and his wife Ann Mary (Walsh); *e* Immaculate Conception Academy, New York City, St Lawrence Academy, and Bentley School for Girls; *m* (1) Edmond O'Brien (mar dis); (2) Fred Jackman, Jr (mar dis); (3) Warren Caro; was a model as a child.

Made her Broadway début at the Charles Hopkins Theatre, Mar 1931, as Buteuse Maiden in Give Me Yesterday; Plymouth, Oct 1937, played Blossom Trexel in Susan and God; toured, 1942, as Evelyn Heath in Guest in the House; Henry Miller, Dec 1942, Patricia Graham in Flare Path; after an absence in Hollywood where she made a number of films, she re-appeared at the National, NY, Feb 1949, as Marion Castle in The Big Knife; Cort, Sept 1950, played Emily Crane in Season in the Sun, subsequently touring in the same play, 1951; Fulton, Sept 1951, played Kate Scott in Twilight Walk; toured, 1953, as Georgie Elgin in The Country Girl; 46th Street, Dec 1954, played Christine Penmark in The Bad Seed, subsequently touring in the play, 1955–6; Henry Miller's, NY, Dec 1957, played Katy Maartens in The Genius and the Goddess; Bijou, Feb 1959, Adele Douglas in The Rivalry; Cort, Jan 1960, played Barbara Smith in A Mighty Man Is He; New Hope, Pa, Aug 1961, played Jane McLeod in A Whiff of Melancholy; Alvin, NY, Jan 1962, Myra Brisset in Giants, Sons of Giants; Royal Alexandra, Toronto, Sept 1962, played Ellen Hurlbird in Step on a Crack; Billy Rose, NY, July 1963, played Martha for some performances in Who's Afraid of Virginia Woolf?, subsequently touring the US in the same play, 1963–4; Billy Rose, Sept 1968, The Long-Winded Lady in Quotations from Chairman Mao Tse-Tung; Ahmanson, Los Angeles, 1971, Irene in Remote Asylum; toured, Oct 1971–May 1972, as Evy Meara in The Gingerbread Lady; Long Wharf, New Haven, Conn, May

1975, Mistress Shore in Richard III; has twice received the Sarah Siddons Award in Chicago as Actress of the Year, 1956 and 1964; received the Antoinette Perry (Tony) Award for The Bad Seed; made film début in 1926 in The Untamed Lady, followed by The Great Gatsby, etc; in sound films has played in Stanley and Livingston, Jesse James, Friendly Enemies, The Bad Seed, etc; performed on radio's *The March of Time*, 1933–7, *The Shadow*, 1936–7, and others; played on television in The Pilot for *Studio One*, 1956, for which she received an Emmy, and on *Climax, Alfred Hitchcock Presents*, etc.

Address: Actors Equity Association, 165 West 46th Street, New York, NY 10036.

KELLY, Patsy, actress and singer
b Brooklyn, NY, 21 Jan 1910.

Toured in vaudeville with Ruby Keller in a dance act; made her NY legitimate debut at the Shubert, 28 Nov 1927, in the revue Harry Delmar's Revels; Globe, 15 Oct 1928, played Bobbie Bird in Three Cheers; Earl Carroll's, July 1929, appeared in the revue Sketch Book; New Amsterdam, July 1930, appeared in the revue Earl Carroll's Vanities; Nora Bayes, Mar 1931, played in the musical Wonder Bar; Palace, Apr 1932, played in vanderville; Imperial, Sept 1932, appeared in the revue Flying Colors; went to Hollywood where she appeared as a leading comedienne in films for many years; 46th Street, 19 Jan 1971, Pauline in No, No, Nanette, and received the Antoinette Perry ("Tony") Award for this part; Minskoff, Mar 1973, Mrs O'Dare in Irene; toured, Sept 1974–May 1975; as Mrs O'Dare in Irene; made her film debut in Going Hollywood, 1933, and has since played in The Girl from Missouri, Pigskin Parade, Ever Since Eve, The Cowboy and the Lady, Please Don't Eat the Daisies, Rosemary's Baby (1968), and numerous others; has also appeared on television and in cabaret.

Address: Actors Equity Association, 165 West 46th Street, New York, NY 10036.

KEMP, Jeremy (*né* Walker), actor
b near Chesterfield, Derbys, 3 Feb 1935; *s* of Edmund Reginald Walker, and his wife Elsa May (Kemp); *e* Abbotsholme School, Staffs; trained for the stage at the Central School of Speech and Drama, 1955–8.

First appeared on the stage, Summer 1957, at the Arts Theatre, Felixstowe, Suffolk, as the Landlord in Misery Me; first appeared on the London stage June 1958, at the Royal Court, as the Orator in The Chairs; later that year, joined the Old Vic, remaining with the company for two seasons in which he played small parts, including Malcolm in Macbeth, 1958; Sgt Lugg in The Magistrate, Oliver in As You Like It, 1959; joined the Nottingham Playhouse Company, 1960, appearing in various roles, including Frank Broadbent in Celebration, which transferred to the Duchess, June 1961; Arts, Aug 1963, played Hector Barlow in Afternoon Men; Phoenix, Jan 1966, the Major in Incident at Vichy; Haymarket, Feb 1971, Richard Howarth in Spoiled; Mermaid, Mar 1972, Aston in The Caretaker; Olivier, Oct 1979, Buckingham in Richard III; first film, 1961; recent appearances include The Blue Max, Darling Lili, and The Belstone Fox; television, since 1960, includes the series *Z Cars, Colditz*, and various plays.

Recreations: Bad ski-ing, other sport, pure idleness. *Clubs:* Lord's Taverners, Stage Golfing Society. *Address:* c/o Leading Artists, 60 St James's Street, London SW1.

KEMPSON, Rachel, actress
b Dartmouth, Devon, 28 May 1910; *d* of Eric William Edward Kempson, headmaster (retired), RN College, Dartmouth, and his wife Beatrice Hamilton (Ashwell); *e* St Agnes

School, East Grinstead, and Oaklea, Buckhurst Hill; *m* (Sir) Michael Redgrave; studied for the stage at the Royal Academy of Dramatic Art.

Made her first appearance on the stage at the Memorial Theatre, Stratford-on-Avon, 17 Apr 1933, as Hero in Much Ado About Nothing, subsequently playing Juliet and Ophelia; made her first appearance in London, at the Westminster Theatre, 8 Nov 1933, as Blanca in The Lady from Alfaqueque; at Stratford-on-Avon, 1934, played Ariel, Olivia in Twelfth Night, Princess in Love's Labour's Lost, Titania, Hero and Juliet; Savoy, Oct 1934, played Christina in Two Kingdoms; in Feb 1935, appeared at the Playhouse, Oxford, as Anne in The Witch and Stella in The Sacred Flame; appeared with Liverpool Repertory Company at Playhouse, Liverpool, Mar 1935, and played Naomi in Flowers of the Forest; during the 1935–6 season, appeared as Yvonne in Youth at the Helm; Eulalia in A Hundred Years Old, Anne of Bohemia in Richard of Bordeaux, Anne in The Wind and the Rain, Viola in Twelfth Night, Agnes Boyd in Boyd's Shop, Victoria in A Storm in a Teacup, etc; Old Vic, Sept 1936, played the Princess of France in Love's Labour's Lost; Westminster, Jan 1937, Celia in Volpone; Oxford, for the OUDS, June 1937, Viola in Twelfth Night; Queen's, Nov 1937, Maria in The School for Scandal; Playhouse, Nov 1938, Jane in The Shoemaker's Holiday; Richmond, Mar 1940, played Jean Howard in Under One Roof; toured, June 1940, as Naomi in Family Portrait, Sept 1941, as Naomi in Noah, and Feb 1942, as Mrs Bradman in Blithe Spirit; Phoenix, Sept 1943, played Faith Ingalls in The Wingless Victory; Garrick, Mar 1944, Lucy Forrest in Uncle Harry; Piccadilly, June 1945, Marianne in Jacobowsky and the Colonel; Arts, Dec 1946, played Charlotte in Fatal Curiosity; Q, Jan 1947, Chris Forbes in Happy as Kings; Oct 1947, Councillor Dr Rosamond Long in The Sparks Fly Upwards; Fortune, May 1948, Joan in The Paragon; Globe, Nov 1948, Violet Jackson in The Return of the Prodigal; Playhouse, Oxford, May 1949, appeared as Candida in the play of that name; Dunfermline Abbey, Aug 1949, Queen Margaret in The Saxon Saint; St James's, Jan 1950, appeared as Hilda Taylor-Snell in Venus Observed; at the same theatre, Oct 1950, Katie in Top of the Ladder; St James's, Jan 1952, played Maman in The Happy Time; joined the Shakespeare Memorial Theatre Company, 1953, and during the season appeared as Queen Elizabeth in Richard III, Octavia in Antony and Cleopatra, and Regan in King Lear; appeared with this company at the Princes, London, Nov 1953, again playing Octavia and subsequently touring Holland, Brussels and Paris in the part; Lyric, Hammersmith, Sept 1954, played Mrs Thea Elvsted in Hedda Gabler, and appeared in this part at the Westminster, Nov 1954; toured Holland, Denmark and Norway, 1955, in the same production; at Belfast, Apr 1955, appeared with the Dublin Gate Theatre Company, as Theodora in Not for Children; joined the English Stage Company at the Royal Court, Apr 1956, and played the following parts: Cora Fellowes in The Mulberry Bush, Mrs Ann Putnam in The Crucible, Evelyn in The Death of Satan, Miss Black Panorbis in Cards of Identity, and Mrs Mi Tzu in The Good Woman of Setzuan; Shakespeare Memorial Theatre Company, Stratford-on-Avon, 1958 season, played, Lady Capulet in Romeo and Juliet, Dionyza in Pericles, and Ursula in Much Ado About Nothing, subsequently appearing as Lady Capulet when the company visited Moscow and Leningrad, Dec 1958; Dublin Festival, Sept 1961, and subsequently the Vaudeville, London, Oct 1961, played Mary in Teresa of Avila; Queen's, Mar 1964, played Polina Andreyevna in The Seagull; at the same theatre, June 1964, Martha in Saint Joan of the Stockyards; Yvonne Arnaud Theatre, Guildford, June 1965,

Chorus in Samson Agonistes, and Lady Mary in Lionel and Clarissa; Royal Court, Dec 1972, Older Lady in A Sense of Detachment; Queen's, Nov 1973, Lady Childress in Gomes; Old Vic, July 1974, for National Theatre, Nancy in The Freeway; Apollo, Apr 1975, Blanche in A Family and a Fortune; Queen's, Sept 1977, played Bron in The Old Country; has also appeared on television; recent performances include: Love for Lydia, Sweet Wine of Youth, and Kate the Good Neighbour; entered films, 1945, in The Captive Heart; other films include: Georgy Girl, The Jokers, Charge of the Light Brigade, The Virgin Soldiers, and Jane Eyre.

Address: 42 Ebury Mews, London SW1.

KEMP-WELCH, Joan, actress and director
b Wimbledon; *d* of Vincent Green and his wife Helen (Kemp-Welch); *e* Roedean; *m* (1) Ben H Wright; (2) Peter Moffatt.

First appearance on the stage, 1927, in Maya, Gate Theatre: played here till 1928; 1929, Wyndham's, Ghosts and Arts, John Gabriel Borkman; 1930, Comedy, Silent Witness, and Lyceum, Traffic; 1931 toured in Baa Baa Black Sheep, Cynara, Admirals All; Phoenix, Feb 1932, Miss Macadam in Lovely Lady; 1932–3 repertory at Q Theatre; Savoy, Mar 1934, Clara in Finished Abroad, and repertory at Northampton; parts included Tondeleyo in White Cargo, Portia in The Merchant of Venice, Maria in Twelfth Night, etc; Phoenix, 1935, Bessie in Glory Be; Criterion, 1935, Charlotte in Nina; 1936 toured in the title-role in Nina, also touring S Africa with Late Night Final, and Boy Meets Girl; 1937, with Baxter Somerville Company at Royal, Brighton; Phoenix, Jan 1938, The Melody That Got Lost; Duke of York's, Feb 1939, Ellen in Nora (A Doll's House), and Mar 1939, Diana in Lady Fanny; St James's, Dec 1939, Lucy Gillham in Ladies in Retirement, same part St Martin's, Aug 1941; St James's, Dec 1942, Mrs Thompson in It Happened in September; Whitehall, May 1943, Damaged Goods; 1944, Director at the Buxton Repertory Theatre; 1945–8, Director at Colchester Repertory, touring India with Pink String and Sealing Wax, in 1945; 1948–51, Director of Wilson Barrett Company in Scotland, directing over 250 plays including Hedda Gabler, The Cherry Orchard, Winterset, A Street Car Named Desire, Desire Under the Elms, An Ideal Husband, Coward comedies, revues, pantomime at Blackpool and Aberdeen; Court, 1952, Miss Hargreaves; 1953–4, New Theatre, Bromley, among other plays: The Young Elizabeth; 1955, New Watergate, directed Vicious Circle, and (Q Theatre) Desire Under the Elms; Westminster, 1956, Dead on Nine, and Albertine by Moonlight; 1968–9, Pitlochry Festival, You Can't Take it With You, Our Town, How's the World Treating You?; has since directed The Price, Leatherhead, 1972; The Anniversary (Coventry), A Man and His Wife (Pitlochry), Dangerous Corner (Guildford), 1974; French Without Tears (Leatherhead), Wait Until Dark (Guildford), 1975; Cranford, musical (Theatre Royal, Stratford), The Other Side of the Swamp, 1976; It Happened in Harrods (Arnaud), 1977; from 1977–9 her many productions in South Africa include: The Deep Blue Sea, Cause Célèbre, Home, and The Elocution of Benjamin Franklin; for the Cambridge Theatre Company she directed I Am Who I Am (1978), and Winter Journey (1979); King's Head, Oct 1979, directed Shades of Brown; first film, 1938; subsequent films include They Flew Alone, The Citadel, Mr Chips, etc; television director since 1954—awards include TV Oscar for Light Entertainment for Cool for Cats, 1958; Silver Dove UNNRA for Ballet, Laudes Evangeli, 1962; and Prix Italia for The Lover, 1963; Desmond Davis Award for her services to

television, 1963; Wilkie Baird award for creative work on TV; productions include The Birthday Party, A View From the Bridge, A Midsummer Night's Dream, the Greek Electra and, recently, Laudes Evangeli, Lady Windermere's Fan, Romeo and Juliet.

Hobbies: Gardening and travel. *Address:* 11 Chilworth Mews, London, W2. *Tel:* 01–262 0547.

KENDAL, Felicity, actress
b Olton, Warwickshire, 25 Sept 1946; *d* of Geoffrey Kendal, and his wife Laura (Liddell); *e* at six convents in India; *m* Drewe Henley (mar dis).

First appeared on the stage in 1947, at the age of nine months, when she was carried on as the Changeling Boy in A Midsummer Night's Dream; grew up touring India and the Far East with her parents' theatre company, playing page-boys at age eight and graduating through Puck, at nine, to parts such as Viola in Twelfth Night, Jessica in The Merchant of Venice and Ophelia in Hamlet; returned to England, 1965; made her London début at the Savoy, July 1967, as Carla in Minor Murder; at the Phoenix, Leicester, 1968, played parts including Katherine in Henry V and Lika in The Promise; for the National Theatre, at the Old Vic, Aug 1969, played Amaryllis in part II of Back to Methuselah; Open Air, Regent's Park, summer 1970, played Hermia in A Midsummer Night's Dream and Hero in Much Ado About Nothing; and appeared in The Lord Byron Show; Playhouse, Oxford, Sept 1970, played Anne Danby in Kean, repeating the part at the Globe, Jan 1971; Oxford Playhouse, Feb 1972, Juliet in Romeo and Juliet; for Actors Company, Sept 1972, played Annabella in 'Tis Pity She's a Whore, at the Edinburgh Festival and on tour; Greenwich, May 1974, Annie in the trilogy The Norman Conquests, transferring to the Globe, Aug 1974; Little, Bristol, Mar 1976, Vitoshka in Once Upon a Time; Greenwich, Apr 1978, Raina in Arms and the Man; Duke of York's, Nov 1978, played Mara in Clouds, receiving the Variety Club Best Actress of 1979 Award, for her performance; for National Theatre, Nov 1979, Constanze in Amadeus, and Mar 1980, Desdemona in Othello (both Olivier); first film, Shakespeare Wallah, 1964; television, since 1966, includes: *Edward VII,* and *The Good Life.*

Recreations: Holidays in France. *Address:* c/o Chatto and Linnit Ltd, Globe Theatre, Shaftesbury Avenue, London W1.

KENNEDY, Arthur, actor
b Worcester, Mass, 17 Feb 1914; *s* of Dr J T Kennedy and his wife Helen (Thompson); *e* Worcester Academy, Carnegie Institute of Technology; *m* Mary Cheffey.

Made his first appearance in New York at the St James, Sept 1937, when he played Bushy in King Richard II; same theatre, Jan 1939, Sir Richard Vernon in Henry IV (Part I); Maxine Elliott, May 1939, Jerry Dorgan in Life and Death of an American; Ethel Barrymore, Apr 1940, Smithers in International Incident; appeared with the Group Theatre in summer productions; at the Coronet, NY, Jan 1947, played Chris Keller in All My Sons; Morosco, Feb 1949, Biff in Death of a Salesman, which he played until May 1950, and for which he received the Antoinette Perry (Tony) Award; Cort, Dec 1952, Dave Ricks in See the Jaguar; Martin Beck, Jan 1953, John Proctor in The Crucible; Booth, Jan 1956, Lt-Colonel William Edwards in Time Limit; Ambassador, Oct 1956, Patrick Flannigan in The Loud Red Patrick; in Mar 1961, took over the title-role in the US tour of Becket; Hudson, May 1961, again played Becket; Morosco, Feb 1968, Walter Franz in The Price; Music Box, Oct 1973, the Man in Veronica's Room; entered films, 1940, in City for

Conquest and since has played in High Sierra, Air Force, Boomerang, The Glass Menagerie, Champion, The Desperate Hours, Trial, Elmer Gantry, Lawrence of Arabia, Fantastic Voyage, My Old Man's Place, 1971, etc; has also played on television.

Address: c/o Actors Equity Association, 165 West 46th Street, New York, NY 10036.

KENNEDY, Cheryl, actress and singer

b Enfield, Middlesex, 29 Apr 1947; *d* of Richard Wilson Kennedy and his wife Margaret Rose (Hickson); *e* Holy Family Convent, Enfield; *m* (1) David Murphy (mar dis); (2) Tom Courtenay; trained for the stage at the Corona Stage School.

First professional appearance, Theatre Royal, Stratford, Oct 1962, as Marylin in What a Crazy World; first West End appearance, March 1963, as Victoria in Half a Sixpence at the Cambridge; has since appeared in a number of other musicals; Vaudeville, Jan 1965, Agnes in The Wayward Way; Globe, March 1966, Winnie in The Matchgirls; New, Sept 1966, Belinda in Jorrocks; Comedy, June 1957, Polly in Queenie; returned to the same theatre, Nov 1967, as Polly Browne in The Boy Friend; Arnaud, Guildford, March 1970, played Jo in Little Women; New, June 1970, Martha Jefferson in 1776; Birmingham Rep, Oct 1971, Elizabeth Bennet in First Impressions; Comedy, Aug 1972, Joan in Time and Time Again; Oxford Festival, Aug 1974, Miss Smith in Springtime for Henry; Garrick, July 1975, Evelyn in Absent Friends; Bristol Old Vic, Apr 1978, Kay in Time and the Conways; Queen's, June 1979, Alice Kinnian in Flowers for Algernon; first film Doctor in Clover, 1965; has appeared in numerous programmes on television since 1964, including recently The Sweeney, Couples, What Every Woman Knows, Schalcken and Rings on Their Fingers.

Recreations: Motor racing, swimming and stamp collecting. *Address:* c/o Larry Dalzell Associates, 3 Goodwin's Court, St Martin's Lane, London, WC2.

KENNEDY, Harold J, actor, director and playwright

e Dartmouth College and Yale Drama School.

Made his theatrical debut, Mar 1941, as producer of Treat Her Gently; made his New York debut as an actor at the Mansfield, 28 Dec 1941, as Terry in In Time to Come; The Playhouse, 23 Jan 1945, played Tony in his own play A Goose for the Gander; reappeared in New York at the Ethel Barrymore, May 1969, as Ben-singer in The Front Page, which he also directed; same theatre, Oct 1969, again directed and played in The Front Page; toured, 1970–71, as Carleton Fitzgerald in Light Up the Sky, which he also directed; Shubert, Mar 1973, played Endicott Sims in Dectective Story, which he also directed; toured, 1973, in his own play Don't Frighten the Horses; directed the tour, 1974, of Tonight at 8.30; toured, 1975, in Sabrina Fair, which he also directed; Ford's, Washington, DC, 1975, played Carleton Fitzgerald in Light Up the Sky, which he also directed and in which he subsequently toured; John Golden, Mar 1976, directed Me Jack, You Jill; Century, Apr 1979, directed Manny; is also the author of The Inkwell and of Goodbye Ghost, both of which were produced for tours; has appeared in films in The Captive City, Run for Cover, Macao, Rhubarb, It Could Happen to You, etc; appeared as a regular on the television series *Mama,* 1949–57, and wrote some of the scripts; has appeared also in The Front Page, *Suspense, Dragnet, Studio One,* etc; is a noted lecturer on the theater, and has appeared at the Town Hall, NY, four times in this capacity.

Address: Society of Stage Directors and Choreographers, 1501 Broadway, New York, NY 10019.

KENNEDY, Patrica, actress

b Queenscliff, Victoria, 17 Mar 1917; *d* of Walter Stewart Kennedy and his wife Julia Lucy (Barnes); *e* Presentation Convent and Mercy Teachers' Training College, Melbourne; trained for the stage at the Modern School of Drama.

Made her first professional appearance at the Garrick Theatre, Melbourne, 1935, as Agnes in Richard of Bordeaux; Princess, Melbourne, 1947, Portia in The Merchant of Venice; National, Melbourne, 1949, title role in Antigone; same theatre, 1955, title role in Candida; Comedy, Melbourne, 1956, Miss Madrigal in The Chalk Garden; subsequently toured Australasia in this part, for which she won the Erik Kuttner award; National, 1960, Lady Macbeth in Macbeth; with the Melbourne Theatre Company, her appearances have included Emilia Pattison in The Right Honourable Gentleman, 1967; Goody Nurse in The Crucible, Headmistress in The Prime of Miss Jean Brodie, Anfisa in Three Sisters, and Lady Britomart in Major Barbara, 1969; St Martin's, Melbourne, 1969, Mrs Alving in Ghosts; at the Citizen's, Glasgow, 1969, played Agnes in A Delicate Balance, repeating this part at the Bristol Old Vic, where she also played Lady Sneerwell in School for Scandal; Princess, Melbourne, and tour, 1970, Countess in All's Well That Ends Well; Theatre Royal, Hobart, 1971, Mrs Alving in Ghosts and Mrs Candour in School for Scandal; Princess, 1971, and tour, Sarah Benson in The Man Who Shot the Albatross; South Australian Theatre Company, Adelaide, 1973, Mary Tyrone in Long Day's Journey Into Night; Adelaide Festival, 1974, Abbess in The Comedy of Errors, and Mrs Hardcastle in She Stoops to Conquer; Nimrod, Sydney, 1976, played the Wife in All Over; The Playhouse, Adelaide (State Theatre Company), Kate in All My Sons (1977), and Amanda in The Glass Menagerie (1978); Drama Theatre, Sydney Opera House, 1978, Judith Bliss in Hay Fever; Athenaeum (Melbourne Theatre Company), appeared as Martha in Arsenic and Old Lace; films include The Getting of Wisdom, and My Brilliant Career; she has been a frequent broadcaster in plays and serials since 1938; TV work includes Black Chiffon, The Physicists, and The Rivals.

Recreations: Reading, walking, theatregoing. *Address:* c/o June Cann Management, 283 Alfred Street North, North Sydney, Australia 2060. *Tel:* 02–922 3066.

KENT, Barry (*né* Sautereau), actor

b London, 19 Feb 1932; *s* of René Sautereau and his wife Caroline (Hedges); formerly an aircraft engineering apprentice; trained privately for the stage under Mabel Corran (singing) and Mary Phillips (drama).

Made his first professional appearance in Mar 1957 at the Theatre Royal, Brighton, as Sam in Harmony Close, and his first London appearance at the Lyric, Hammersmith, Apr 1957, in the same part; Players', June 1957, played a Ship's Captain in Antarctica; Coliseum, Aug 1957, joined the chorus of Damn Yankees; Palace, Feb 1958, Reggie in Where's Charley?; Scarborough, June 1959, played Count Danilo in The Merry Widow; Strand, May 1961, Augustus in Belle; Drury Lane, Aug 1964, Lancelot in Camelot; same theatre, Feb 1969, Beauregard in Mame; Alhambra, Durban, and SA tour, Jan 1980, appeared in Christian; has appeared on television since 1956 in musical programmes.

Favourite part: Lancelot. *Recreation:* Charity work. *Club:* Water Rats. *Address:* c/o Sydney Levington, 53 Flag Court, Courtenay Terrace, Hove, Sussex.

KENT, Jean (*née* Field), actress
b London, 29 June 1921; *d* of Norman Carpenter Field and his wife Georgina (Noakes); *e* St Mary's Convent, Peckham Rye, and Bedford College, Dulwich; *m* Jusuf Hurst; was trained by her parents for the stage.

First appeared as a child dancer, July 1932, at the Theatre Royal, Bath; was in the chorus, and appeared as a soubrette, at the Windmill, 1934–6; for a time was professionally known as Jean Carr, and under this name at the King's, Hammersmith, Dec 1938, appeared as Felix, in The Sleeping Beauty; Ambassadors', 1939, appeared in The Gate Revue; Criterion, June 1940, in the revue, Come Out Of Your Shell; Holborn Empire, Aug 1940, in the revue, Apple Sauce; Streatham Hill, Dec 1940, played Colin in Mother Goose; Palladium, Mar 1941, appeared in a revival of the revue, Apple Sauce; New Lindsey, Jan 1951, played Gilberte in Frou-Frou; Saville, May 1952, Anne Beaumont in The Moonraker; at the Q, Mar 1953, played the Queen, in a revival of The Eagle Has Two Heads; Sept 1953, Barbara Leigh in Uncertain Joy; Jan 1954, Jennet Jourdemayne in The Lady's Not For Burning; during 1954, toured South Africa in The Deep Blue Sea; Duchess, Feb 1955, played Sarah Bellaire in A Kind of Folly; Duke of York's, May 1955, succeeded Betty Paul as Mary Millar, in All For Mary; St Martin's, Feb 1956, played Esther Eccles in She Smiled at Me; King's, Glasgow, Feb 1956, Jane Mortimer in The Gay Deceiver; toured, Sept 1958, as Mary Lester in A Touch of the Sun; Savoy, May 1959, Madame Marly in the musical Marigold; Duchess, Apr 1960, played Laura in A Shred of Evidence; Leatherhead, Oct 1962, played Mrs Moreen in The Parents; toured, June 1963, as Jennifer Grayhame in The Hanging Man; Connaught, Worthing, Jan 1964, played Liza in Winter in Ischia; toured, Apr 1964, as Portia in The Merchant of Venice; Connaught, Worthing, 1965, played the name part in Caroline (Jan), Mrs Malaprop in The Rivals (Mar), and Jan 1966, appeared in The Spider's Web; Mar 1966, toured in The Wrong Side of the Park; Lyceum, Edinburgh, Apr 1966, played Mrs Squeezum in Lock Up Your Daughters; Phoenix, Apr 1967, Jennifer in In At the Death; 1969, toured South Africa as Mrs Cheveley in An Ideal Husband; toured, 1971–2, as Maxine Charlesworth in Home on the Pig's Back; Strand, Mar 1973, took over the part of Eleanor Hunter in No Sex Please—We're British; Seven Arts Theatre, Salisbury, Rhodesia, 1975, played Queen Mary in Crown Matrimonial; 1977, toured South Africa as Alma in The Bed Before Yesterday; Arnaud, Jan 1978, played the Grand Duchess Charles in The Sleeping Prince, subsequently touring Great Britain in the role; Vaudeville, Mar 1979, Letitia Blacklock in A Murder is Announced; first appeared in films 1934, and since 1943 has appeared in numerous productions, notably Trottie True, The Woman in Question, and The Browning Version; recent television includes *Tycoon*.

Favourite parts: Cecily Cardew in The Importance of Being Earnest, and Millicent in Seventeen. *Hobbies:* Oil painting and cooking. *Address:* c/o Herbert de Leon, 13 Bruton Street, London, W1.

KENTON, Godfrey, actor
b London, 13 Apr 1902; *e* Edward VI Grammar School, and St Paul's Theological College, Burgh, Lincs; *m* (1) Vivienne Bennett (mar dis); (2) Mary Isabella Whitfield (mar dis); (3) Sheila Ann Margaret Broadhurst (mar dis); studied at the Royal Academy of Dramatic Art; was originally intended for the Church.

Made his first appearance on the stage at the Theatre Royal, Brighton, 15 May 1922, as James Dixon Plimpit in Mr Garrick; made his first appearance in London at the Duke of York's, Dec 1922, as the Poplar Tree in The Blue Bird; played leading juvenile parts with Lena Ashwell's Players, 1925–7, including Orlando, Raffles, Ariel, Robin Hood, etc; at Stratford-on-Avon, 1925–6, played second juvenile parts; played at the Northampton Repertory Theatre, 1928; appeared at the Old Vic, 1928–9, as Malcolm in Macbeth, Fenton in The Merry Wives of Windsor, Thorolf in The Vikings, etc; returned to Northampton, to play leads, 1929–30; at the re-opening of Sadler's Wells Theatre, Jan 1931, played Orsino in Twelfth Night; Everyman, June 1931, played Hon Jimmy Treherne in Episode; New, May 1932, Sebastian in Twelfth Night; Gate, Sept 1932, Horace Tiptree in One More River; appeared at the Birmingham Repertory Theatre, 1933; appeared at the Malvern Festival, July–Aug 1934; Westminster, Sept 1934, played Tausch in The Moon in the Yellow River; Feb 1935, William Budge in They Do These Things in France; His Majesty's, Feb 1935, Poins in Henry IV (Part I); Westminster, May 1935, Cassio in Othello; Malvern Festival, July–Aug 1935, played Hugh Hyering in The Simpleton of the Unexpected Isles, Tom Wrench in Trelawny of the Wells, 1066 and All That, etc; Grafton, Sept 1935, played Antipholus of Syracuse in In Such a World; Lyric, Hammersmith, Jan 1936, played Faust; Arts, Feb 1936, Armand in After October; His Majesty's, Apr 1936, Count Karaloff in The Happy Hypocrite; Westminster, July 1936, John in A Bride for the Unicorn; Aldwych, Aug 1936, Clive in After October; Stratford-on-Avon, 1937 season, Oberon in A Midsummer Night's Dream, Edgar in King Lear, Leonatus Posthumous in Cymbeline and Laertes in Hamlet; Ritz, New York, Jan 1938, Alan in Time and the Conways; Comedy, London, Aug 1938, Arthur Every in Give Me Yesterday; Shaftesbury, Sept 1938, Upton and Ralston in Goodbye, Mr Chips; at Northampton, 1939, played Romeo; Embassy, Nov 1939, Marcus Brutus in Julius Caesar (in modern dress), and His Majesty's, Dec 1939, Julius Caesar; Richmond, Jan 1940, Hilary Strahan in First Night; Westminster, Apr 1940, the Chronicler in Abraham Lincoln; Bournemouth, June 1940, Judas in Family Portrait; appeared at Stratford-on-Avon Memorial Theatre, 1940–1, as Romeo, Mark Antony, Jack Absolute, Orsino, etc; from Oct 1941–June 1944, was with the BBC; joined Donald Wolfit's company, Aug 1944, touring all over Great Britain, also playing in Paris, Brussels, and Egypt, appearing as Malcolm in Macbeth, Bassanio in The Merchant of Venice, Edmund in King Lear, Don Pedro in Much Ado About Nothing, etc, and played these parts at the Winter Garden, Mar–Apr 1946; at the Arts, Feb–Mar 1947, appeared in Back to Methuselah; Martin Beck, NY, Sept 1948, played Ellerby Burton in Edward, My Son; Phoenix, London, Jan 1950, Dr Schrader in The Non-Resident; New Lindsey, Dec 1950, Nicholas Renoux in Poor Old Gaston; New Boltons, Feb 1952, played Felix in Still Waters; New, Apr 1952, appeared as William Cecil in The Young Elizabeth; was engaged with the BBC Repertory Company, Oct 1953–Oct 1955; Northampton Repertory, Aug 1956, played Hugo in Make Believe; BBC Repertory Company, 1957–9; Strand, June 1960 (for the Repertory Players), played George in Chance a Cockney; Apollo, Sept 1960 (for the Repertory Players), Edward Bromley in Refer to Drawer; Westminster, Feb 1967, Josiah Swinyard in Happy Deathday; Haymarket, Sept 1967, Solanio in The Merchant of Venice; has appeared in Son et Lumière at Winchester Cathedral, York Minster, and St Paul's; television appearances include: Out of the Unknown, David Copperfield, and *Dixon of Dock Green*; BBC Drama Repertory Company, 1960–2, 1968–70, 1973–4, 1976, 1979–80; BBC Schools Company, 1964–6.

Recreations: Music and books. *Address:* c/o Richard Stone, 18–20 York Buildings, London WC2N 6JU.

KENWRIGHT, Bill, director and producing manager
b Liverpool, 4 Sept 1945; *s* of Albert Kenwright and his wife Hope (Jones); *e* Liverpool Institute High School; *m* the actress Anouska Hempel (mar dis).

Originally an actor, he made his earliest stage appearance at Liverpool Playhouse, Christmas 1957, in Toad of Toad Hall; his first London appearance was at the Prince of Wales, 24 Aug 1965, as Craddock in Passion Flower Hotel; Open Air, Regent's Park, season 1966, played Flute in A Midsummer Night's Dream; other acting experience includes tours, 1970, in the title roles of Alfie, and Billy Liar, and a tour in 1974 as Don in Butterflies Are Free, which he also directed; in recent years has concentrated on management, and his company, David Gordon Productions, has been responsible for more than two hundred shows since 1970, both tours worldwide and West End productions, the latter including, recently, Who Killed 'Agatha' Christie? and The Undertaking, 1979; has directed a number of these himself, notably West Side Story, 1973 and 1974; Big Sin City, 1978; Joseph and the Amazing Technicolor Dreamcoat, 1980; has made many pop records, several of them appearing in the hit parade.
Recreation: Everton FC. *Address:* 405 Strand, London WC2. *Tel:* 836 2613.

KERNAN, David, actor
b London, 23 June 1939; *s* of Joseph Kernan, and his wife Lily May (Russel); *e* Porchester College, Bournemouth; formerly a trainee catering manager.

First appeared on the stage in 1945 at the YWCA, Oxford, as a child walk-on in Quality Street; first appeared on the London stage in 1958 in Where's Charley? at the Palace; appeared, Apr 1961, at the Phoenix, in the revue On the Brighter Side; Shaftesbury, Dec 1964, played the Hon Ernest Woolley in Our Man Crichton; New, June 1970, Edward Rutledge in 1776; Greenwich, July 1972, Charles H Marlow II in Liberty Ranch; Adelphi, April 1975, Count Carl-Magnus Malcolm in A Little Night Music; Mermaid, May 1976, appeared in Side by Side by Sondheim, transferring to Wyndham's; made his NY début in this show at the Music Box, 18 Apr 1977; films, since Gaolbreak in 1964, include Zulu and The Day of the Jackal; has appeared many times on television since 1959.
Recreations: Swimming, squash, travel. *Address:* c/o London Management, 235–241 Regent Street, London, W1.

KERR, Bill, actor
After appearances as a child in vaudeville in Australia, and later as an actor, came to England in 1947; made his first appearance on the London stage, 8 May 1950, at the People's Palace, as Bluey in Pommy; at the Coliseum, Mar 1957, Applegate in Damn Yankees; Adelphi, Sept 1960, Wizard in Once Upon a Mattress; Duke of York's, 1963, took over a number of parts in The Bed Sitting Room; Comedy, 1964, appeared in Son of Oblomov; Globe, Sept 1969, Bogart in Play It Again, Sam; Sadler's Wells, Mar 1972, Herr Winkelkopf in Lord Arthur Savile's Crime; Greenwich, July 1972, Col Culpepper in Liberty Ranch; Prince of Wales, Dec 1972, Simon in The Good Old, Bad Old Days; toured, Dec 1973, as Senex in A Funny Thing Happened on the Way to the Forum; Mermaid, July 1974, appeared in Cole; Ambassador's, 1975, took over the part of Charles Badcock in There Goes the Bride; Arnaud, Guildford, Nov 1975, Wilfred Potts in Don't Just Lie There, Say Something; Duke of York's, Apr 1976, various parts, including the Tramp, in Salad Days; has appeared in a number of films; extensive radio and TV work includes *Hancock's Half Hour*.

Address: c/o Richard Stone, 18–20 York Buildings, London WC2.

KERR, Deborah, actress
b Helensburgh, Scotland, 30 Sept 1921; *d* of Arthur Charles Kerr-Trimmer and his wife Kathleen Rose (Smale); *e* Northumberland House, Bristol; *m* (1) Anthony Charles Bartley (mar dis), (2) Peter Viertel; prepared for the stage under her aunt, Phyllis Smale, at her school of dramatic art, Bristol.

First appeared on the stage at the Knightstone Pavilion, Weston-Super-Mare, 1937, as Harlequin in the mime play Harlequin and Columbine; first appeared in London at Sadler's Wells, 1938, in the corps de ballet of Prometheus; at the Open Air, Regent's Park, 1939, walked on in various Shakespeare productions; joined the repertory company at the Playhouse, Oxford, May 1940, and first appeared as Margaret in Dear Brutus and later as Patty Moss in The Two Bouquets; Cambridge, London, Mar 1943, Ellie Dunn in Heartbreak House; toured in England and Scotland in this last part, 1943; toured Holland, France, Belgium for ENSA as Mrs Manningham in Angel Street, 1945; made her New York debut at the Ethel Barrymore, 30 Sept 1953, as Laura Reynolds in Tea and Sympathy; toured, Nov 1954, in the US in this last part; reappeared in London at the Lyric, Oct 1972, as Edith Harnham in The Day After the Fair; Shubert, Los Angeles, Sept 1973, again played this last part, and toured in it until Jan 1974; Shubert, NY, Jan 1975, Nancy in Seascape; repeated this part at the Shubert, Los Angeles, Apr 1975; Shubert, Los Angeles, Oct 1975, Julie Stevens in Souvenir; Ahmanson, LA, Feb 1977, Mary Tyrone in Long Day's Journey into Night; Albery, London, Jun 1977, title-role in Candida; Eisenhower, Washington DC, Aug 1978, and tour, Mrs Cheyney in The Last of Mrs Cheyney; has had a long film career, first appearing in England in Contraband, 1939, and subsequently in Major Barbara, Black Narcissus, Edward, My Son, King Solomon's Mines, Quo Vadis, The King and I, Separate Tables, The Night of the Iguana, Casino Royale, and numerous others; first appeared on television in England, 1961, in Three Roads to Rome.
Recreations: Tennis, walking, piano. *Club:* English Speaking Union. *Address:* Klosters, 7250 Grisons, Switzerland.

KERR, Jean, dramatic author
b Scranton, Pa, 10 July 1923; *d* of Thomas J Collins and his wife Kitty (O'Neill); *e* Marywood College, Scranton, Pa, and Catholic University, Washington, DC; *m* Walter Kerr, the drama critic.

Her first play, Jenny Kissed Me, was produced at the Hudson, New York, 1948; has since written Touch and Go (with her husband), 1949; two sketches for John Murray Anderson's Almanac, 1953; King of Hearts (with Eleanor Brooke), 1954; Goldilocks (with her husband), 1958; Mary Mary, 1961; Poor Richard, 1964; Finishing Touches (produced in NY and London), 1973; author of the books Please Don't Eat the Daisies and The Snake Has All the Lines, which were adapted for a television series, 1965; wrote Penny Candy, 1970; How I Got to be Perfect, 1978; in 1955 adapted The Good Fairy for a television production; received an LHD degree, *honoris causa*, from Northwestern University in 1960.
Address: 1 Beach Avenue, Larchmont, New York.

KERR, Walter, drama critic, author, and director
b Evanston, Illinois, 8 July 1913; *s* of Walter S Kerr and his wife Esther M (Daugherty); *e* Northwestern University; *m* Jean Collins; formerly an Associate Professor at the Catholic University, Washington, DC.

Was drama critic for the *Commonweal Magazine* before being appointed drama critic of *The New York Herald Tribune* in 1951; joined *The New York Times* as Sunday drama critic in 1966; daily critic, 1979–; co-author of the revue Count Me In, 1942; wrote and directed Sing, Out, Sweet Land, 1945; Touch and Go (in collaboration with his wife), 1949; King of Hearts (written by his wife, Jean Kerr, in collaboration with Eleanor Brooks), 1954; Goldilocks (author of book with Jean Kerr, and of lyrics with Jean Kerr and Joan Ford), 1958; author of books of drama criticism, including How Not to Write a Play, 1955, Criticism and Censorship, 1957, Pieces of Eight, 1958, The Decline of Pleasure, 1962, The Theatre in Spite of Itself, 1963, which won the George Jean Nathan Prize, Tragedy and Comedy, 1967, Thirty Plays Hath November, 1969, God on the Gymnasium Floor, 1971, The Silent Clowns, 1975, Journey to the Center of the Theater, 1979; served as host for the 1965 television series Esso Repertory Theatre; won the Pulitzer Prize for drama criticism, 1978.
Address: 1 Beach Avenue, Larchmont, New York.

KERRIDGE, Mary, actress and writer of pantomimes
b London, 3 Apr 1914; *d* of Ernest Kerridge and his wife Antoinette Elizabeth (Ficke); *e* Highbury, Wimbledon and University College, London; *m* John Counsell; formerly a secretary, a model and a receptionist.
Made her first appearance on the stage at the King's, Southsea, 1934, as Ada in The Late Christopher Bean; subsequently in repertory at Margate and Bath; toured in No Exit, 1936; first appeared in London, at the Strand Theatre, 12 Mar 1937, as the first Female Guest in The Squeaker; was engaged in her husband's repertory at the Theatre Royal, Windsor, 1938–47; toured, 1941, in Peril at End House; 1943, toured with Donald Wolfit's company; Alexandra, Stoke Newington, Feb 1947, played Smitty in Cry Havoc; Embassy, Mar and Playhouse, Apr 1947, Wanda in Birthmark; toured, 1948, as Irga in Little Holiday; Embassy, Oct 1948, played Anne Sargent in Lend Me Robin; Vaudeville, Dec 1949, Sarat Carn in Bonaventure; St James's, Oct 1950, Kath in Top of the Ladder; New, July 1951, played Nina in a revival of His House in Order; at the Open Air Theatre, Regent's Park, May 1952, played Rosalind in As You Like It, and July 1952, Imogen in Cymbeline; St James's, Aug 1953, played Anna Brown in Anastasia; Royal, Windsor, Oct 1954, directed Kind Cousin; also at Windsor, July 1955, appeared as Clare Duncan in The One and Only; Westminster, Dec 1956, played Myra Hood in Mrs Gibbons' Boys; St Martin's, Apr 1958, Karen Holt in Something to Hide; Arts, Nov 1959, Mrs Clarissa Hengen in A Man's Job; Royal, Windsor, Feb 1962, played Liz Forester in Orange Island; joined the Old Vic Company, Mar 1962, to play Queen Elizabeth in Richard III, and Apr 1962, Portia in Julius Caesar; St Martin's, May 1963, played Freda in The Hot Tiara; Gaiety, Dublin, Oct 1963, and subsequently the Vaudeville, London, Jan 1964, played Hilde Schultz in The Roses Are Real; Comedy, Sept 1964, Mrs Grey in The Home Secretary and Violet in Lady JP 2, in a double-bill, entitled Two Accounts Rendered; Royal, Windsor, June 1965, played Mrs Malaprop in The Rivals; 1968, toured North America with Windsor Royal Theatre Company, appearing as Mrs Cheveley in An Ideal Husband, Mrs Warren in Mrs Warren's Profession, and Judith Bliss in Hay Fever; Fortune, May 1976, Madame Alvarez in Gigi; first appeared in films, 1935, in Paradise for Two, and since 1950 has played in Anna Karenina, The Blue Peter, Richard III, The Duke Wore Jeans, The Gaunt Woman, and No Longer Alone; has appeared frequently in television plays from 1937—Waterloo to 1970—The Misfits; is a Director of

the Theatre Royal Windsor; she has written the scripts for twenty-five pantomimes.
Favourite parts: Phoebe in The Entertainer, and Judith Bliss. *Recreations:* Painting and cooking. *Address:* Theatre Royal, Windsor, Berks.

KERT, Larry (*né* Frederick Lawrence Kert), actor and singer
b Los Angeles, California, 5 Dec 1930; *s* of Harry Kert and his wife Lillian (Pearson); *e* Los Angeles City College; studied acting with Sanford Meisner at the Neighborhood Playhouse, and singing with Keith Davis.
Made his professional début as a member of the group called Bill Norvas and the Upstarts, playing in cabaret and variety shows, including an engagement at the Roxy in New York, 1950; made his musical comedy début at the Coronet, NY, Apr 1950, in the chorus of the revue Tickets, Please; Players Ring, Hollywood, California, 1952, appeared in Look Ma, I'm Dancin'; Imperial, NY, Dec 1953, played in the chorus of the revue John Murray Anderson's Almanac, appearing from time to time in the material originally performed by Harry Belafonte; Shubert, Boston, Apr 1956, appeared in the revue The Ziegfeld Follies; Broadway, Nov 1956, took over as the stage manager in Mr Wonderful; Winter Garden, Sept 1957, played Tony in West Side Story, and was a great success; toured in this part, 1959–60; Winter Garden, Apr 1960, again played Tony in West Side Story; Palm Springs, California, Mar 1961, sang in the operas The Medium and The Telephone; summer tours, 1961, played in West Side Story, Pal Joey, and The Merry Widow; Billy Rose, Jan, 1962, Gerry Siegal in Family Affair; Shubert, June 1962, took over from Elliott Gould as Harry Bogen in I Can Get It for You Wholesale; toured the US and Canada in this part, 1962–3; Majestic, Dec 1966, Carlos in Breakfast at Tiffany's; Broadway, 1968, took over as Clifford Bradshaw in Cabaret; Lunt-Fontanne, Dec 1969, Mario, the Fool in La Strada; Alvin, May 1970, took over from Dean Jones as Robert in the first weeks of Company and played the part for more than a year; made his London début at Her Majesty's, 18 Jan 1972, as Robert in Company; Shubert, 11 Mar 1973, appeared in Sondheim: A Musical Tribute; toured Canada and the US, Jan–Oct 1973, as Proteus in Two Gentlemen of Verona in a musical version; City Center, Apr 1974, appeared in the revue Music! Music!; Los Angeles, Sept 1974, Joe in Sugar; St James, Nov 1975, appeared in the revue A Musical Jubilee, subsequently touring; Music Box, NY, Aug 1971, joined the cast of Side by Side by Sondheim, also appearing in this show at the Huntington Hartford, LA, Apr 1978; first appeared on television in the chorus of the *Ed Sullivan Show,* 5 May 1950.
Favourite parts: Tony, Mario, and Robert. *Recreations:* Raising Ibizan hounds and jumping horses. *Address:* 29 Bethune Street, New York, NY 10014. *Tel:* 924–1379.

KESTELMAN, Sara, actress
b London, 12 May 1944; *d* of Morris Kestelman and his wife Dorothy; *e* Camden School for Girls; 13 years ballet training with Laura Wilson; trained for the stage at the Central School of Speech and Drama.
Made her first professional appearance at the Open Air, Regent's Park, 1960, as a nymph in The Tempest; after experience at the Liverpool Playhouse and the Library Theatre, Manchester, where her parts included Abigail in The Crucible and Cecily in The Importance of Being Earnest, joined the Royal Shakespeare Company at Stratford, season 1968, playing minor roles including Lechery in Dr Faustus; at the Aldwych, made her London debut, 19 Jun 1969, as Cassandra in Troilus and Cressida, also playing Margaret in

Much Ado About Nothing, July, and Jessie Taite in The Silver Tassie, Sept; Stratford, 1970, Jane Shore in Richard III, Apr, and Hippolyta/Titania in A Midsummer Night's Dream, Aug, making her Broadway debut in the latter role at the Billy Rose, Jan 20 1971, and returning to the Aldwych with the production, June 1971; also played Kleopatra in Enemies, July 1971; and Natasha in Subject to Fits, the latter part at The Place, Oct 1971; Queen's, July 1972, Messalina in I Claudius; Birmingham Rep, Sept 1972, Lady Macbeth in Macbeth, also playing Ruth in The Homecoming; Bristol Old Vic, autumn 1973, Yelena in Uncle Vanya and Prudence in Plunder; Aldwych, Nov 1974, Countess Werdenfels in The Marquis of Keith; toured for the RSC in The Hollow Crown, and Pleasure and Repentance, to the US, 1974, and Japan, 1975; for the Cambridge Theatre Company, 1976, appeared as Sally Bowles in I Am A Camera; National Theatre, 1977–8 season, played Alexandra Kollontai in State of Revolution, Madame Petypon in The Lady from Maxim's and took over as Susannah in Bedroom Farce; Greenwich, May 1978, Janet Achurch in The Achurch Letters; returned to the National (Olivier), Sept 1978, to play Lady Touchwood in The Double Dealer, and Enid Underwood in Strife, and has appeared at the same theatre in 1979, as the Lady With A Monocle in The Fruits of Enlightenment, Mrs Wahl in Undiscovered Country, and Rosalind in As You Like It; her platform performances during this period include Dorothy Parker and Brecht's Songs and Poems; films, since Zardoz in 1973, include Lisztomania, Break of Day, and The Life of Nobel; TV work, since 1965, includes The Caucasian Chalk Circle, Peer Gynt, Under Western Eyes, Kean, *Crown Court*, and *The New Avengers*.

Favourite parts: Prudence in Plunder, the Countess in The Marquis of Keith. *Recreations:* Singing, photography, indoor plants. *Address:* c/o Saraband Associates, 59 Frith Street, London W1.

KIDD, Michael (*né* Milton Greenwald), dancer, choreographer and director
b New York City, 12 Aug 1919; *s* of Abraham Greenwald and his wife Lillian; *e* College of the City of New York and School of the American Ballet, 1937–9; *m* (1) Mary Heater (mar dis); (2) Shelah Hackett; formerly a copy boy for the *New York Daily Mirror* and a photographer.

Made his début as an understudy to the role of the Adversary's Follower in The Eternal Road, at the Manhattan Opera House, 7 Jan 1937; began a distinguished career as a dancer at the Chicago Opera House, 16 Oct 1938, in the Ballet Caravan's première of Billy the Kid; performed with Eugene Loring's Dance Players, 1941–2; solo dancer with Ballet Theatre, 1942–7, appearing in such ballets as Pillar of Fire, Dim Lustre, Fancy Free, Undertow, Romeo and Juliet, Giselle, Coppelia, etc; appeared as a dancer in the ballet Interplay in Concert Varieties, at the Ziegfeld, June 1945; was scenarist and choreographer of On Stage, in which he also danced The Handyman at the Boston Opera House, Oct 1945; he has since choreographed Finian's Rainbow, 1947; Hold It and Love Life, 1948; Arms and the Girl and Guys and Dolls, 1950; Can-Can, 1953; Here's Love, 1963; Skyscraper, 1965; has choreographed and directed L'il Abner, 1956 (also co-produced); Destry Rides Again, 1959; Wildcat (also co-produced), 1960; Subways Are for Sleeping, 1961; Ben Franklin in Paris, 1964; The Rothschilds, 1970; Cyrano, 1973; Good News, 1974; directed Pal Joey '78, Ahmanson, LA, 1978; received the Antoinette Perry (Tony) Award for Finian's Rainbow, Guys and Dolls, Can-Can, L'il Abner, Destry Rides Again; choreographed the films Where's Charley? 1952, The Band Wagon, 1953, Knock on Wood, Seven Brides

for Seven Brothers, 1954, Guys and Dolls, 1955; directed Merry Andrew, 1958, Star, 1969, Hello, Dolly!, 1970; appeared in the film It's Always Fair Weather, 1955; played the Choreographer in the film Smile, 1975.

Address: Society of Stage Directors and Choreographers, 1501 Broadway, New York, NY 10019.

KIDD, Robert, director
b Bo'ness, Scotland, 23 Feb 1943; *s* of Robert Buchanan Kidd and his wife Barbara Scott (Simpson); *e* Boroughmuir Secondary School, Edinburgh and Royal Scottish Academy of Music, Glasgow.

His first professional production was When Did You Last See My Mother, which he directed in a Sunday-night performance at the Royal Court, 4 July 1966; the production transferred to the Comedy; plays he has since directed, in London unless otherwise stated, include: The Man of Destiny (also Vancouver), 1966; The Restoration of Arnold Middleton, Marya, 1967; Summer, Total Eclipse, 1968; The Entertainer, Cages (both Edinburgh), 1969; The Philanthropist, Nicholas Nickleby (Nottingham), 1970; Macbeth (Virginia), The Philanthropist (New York–Broadway début), 1971; Siege, Butley (Melbourne), Eye Winker, Tom Tinker, 1972; Savages, Twelfth Night and A Doll's House (both Edinburgh), 1973; 1974–5, Associate Director of the Royal Lyceum Company, Edinburgh, where he also directed Major Barbara, The Voysey Inheritance and The Sash; 1975–7, Joint Artistic Director, Royal Court Theatre, where he produced Treats and Mother's Day (1976); has since directed An Ideal Husband, Hindle Wakes (both Greenwich), Everything in the Garden (Toneelgrouep, Arnhem), 1978; Grease (co-directed), Middle-Age Spread, 1979; has appeared on Television as a reporter/interviewer, and directed Swallows for BBC TV, 1974.

KILEY, Richard, actor and singer
b Chicago, Illinois, 31 Mar 1922; *s* of Leo Joseph Kiley and his wife Leonore (McKenna); *e* Loyola University, Chicago; *m* (1) Mary Bell Wood (mar dis); (2) Patricia Ferrier; prepared for the stage at the Barnum Dramatic School, Chicago.

First appeared on the stage at the Mt Carmel High School, Chicago, 1938, in the title-role of The Mikado; first appeared in New York, 1947, with the Equity Library Theatre as Poseidon in The Trojan Women; New Stages, off-Broadway, Mar 1949, played Jacob in The Sun and I; US tour, 1950, Stanley Kowalski in A Streetcar Named Desire; Shubert, Boston, Dec 1951, Joe Rose in A Month of Sundays; City Center, Feb 1953, Percival in Misalliance, transferring with the production to the Ethel Barrymore, Mar 1953; Ziegfeld, Dec 1953, The Caliph in Kismet; Phoenix, off-Broadway, Oct 1954, Ben Collinger in Sing Me No Lullaby; Booth, Jan 1956, Major Harry Cargill in Time Limit!; Spoleto Festival, Italy, June 1958, James Tyrone in A Moon for the Misbegotten; 46th Street, NY, Feb 1959, Tom Baxter in Redhead, for which he received the Antoinette Perry Award; Cort, Nov 1960, Brig Anderson in Advise and Consent; 54th Street, Mar 1962, David Jordan in No Strings; Shubert, May 1964, took over the leading role in Here's Love; Martin Beck, Dec 1964, Stan the Shpieler in I Had a Ball; Goodspeed Opera House, East Haddam, Conn, June 1965, played in a musical version of Purple Dust and Cervantes and Don Quixote in Man of La Mancha; ANTA, Washington Square, NY, Nov 1965, again played Cervantes and Don Quixote in Man of La Mancha, for which he received the Antoinette Perry Award; toured California in this play, 1967–8; Lunt-Fontanne, Oct 1968, Caesar in Her First Roman; Piccadilly, London, June

1969, made his London début as Cervantes and Don Quixote in Man of La Mancha; Concert Theatre, Honolulu, Hawaii, June 1970, again played in Man of La Mancha; Royale, Oct 1971, Enoch Somes and A V Laider in The Incomparable Max; Ethel Barrymore, Apr 1972, Robert in Voices; Vivian Beaumont, June 1972, Cervantes and Don Quixote in a revival of Man of La Mancha; Walnut, Philadelphia, Dec 1972, title-role in Tartuffe; American, Washington, DC, Sept 1973, Cervantes and Don Quixote in the straight play Cervantes; Music Box, Oct 1974, Ronald in Absurd Person Singular; toured, 1975, in Ah, Wilderness!; Kennedy Center, Washington, DC, Feb 1976, Mr Sloper in The Heiress; repeated this last part at the Broadhurst, NY, Apr 1976; Eisenhower, Washington DC, Jun 1977, appeared in The Master Builder; Man of La Mancha revived at the Palace, NY, Sept 1977, and toured 1978 and 1979; Edinburgh Festival, 1979, took part in a poetry recital with HSH Princess Grace of Monaco; first appeared in films in 1950 and has since played in The Blackboard Jungle, Pickup on South Street, The Mob, The Little Prince, Looking for Mr Goodbar, 1979, etc; first appeared on television in 1946, and has since played in Patterns, Arrowsmith, POW, *Medical Center*, The Andros Targets, etc.

Favourite part: Man of La Mancha. *Recreations:* Writing and carpentry. *Club:* Players. *Address:* c/o Stephen Draper, 37 West 57th Street, New York, NY 10019.

KILLEEN, Sheelagh, costume designer
b Dublin, 30 Sept 1940; *d* of Ronald Killeen and his wife Margot (Davenport-Scotten); *e* Tiffins Grammar School for Girls; trained at Kingston School of Art, Wimbledon College of Art and Slade School of Fine Art.

After early experience in the costume departments of Covent Garden, Sadler's Wells, the National Theatre, etc, joined the Mermaid Theatre as assistant to Adrian Vaux, 1966, where her first costumes for the stage were those for Let's Get a Divorce, Jun 1966; at the same theatre until 1969, other costume designs included those for The Man of Destiny and O'Flaherty VC, and Shadow of a Gunman (also sets); recent designs in London include A Seventh Man, 1976; design adviser since 1974 to Foco Novo; has worked as costume designer for a number of TV companies, latterly ATV; costume designer for the film Sweet William, 1978.

Address: 16 Kings Grove, London SE15.

KILTY, Jerome, actor, director, dramatic author
b Pala Indian Reservation, California, 24 June 1922; *s* of Harold Kilty and his wife Irene (Zellinger); *e* Guildhall School of Drama, London, 1945–6, Harvard University, BA, 1949; *m* Cavada Humphrey.

Made his first appearance on the stage in California, 1937, as a schoolboy, walking-on in Max Reinhardt's production of Faust; co-founded the Brattle Theatre, Cambridge, Mass, where he served as director, producer, and actor, 1948–52; first appeared on Broadway, at the Morosco, Oct 1950, as Coupler in The Relapse; City Center, NY, Feb 1953, played the King of Navarre in Love's Labour's Lost, with the New York City Drama Company; at the same theatre, Mar 1953, played Gunner in Misalliance; Playhouse, Sept 1953, played Mr Ringwood in A Pin to See the Peep Show; Broadhurst, Oct 1953, played Asa McK Gelwicks in The Frogs of Spring; Coronet, Nov 1954, played the Rev Edgar Spevin in Quadrille; artistic director, director, and actor with the Group 20 Players, Wellesley, Mass, 1955–60, and with this troupe, at the City Center, Sept 1955, played Iago in Othello; at the same theatre, Oct 1955, played Sir John Falstaff in Henry IV (Part I); toured, 1955–6, as Harry Kaye in Will Success Spoil

Rock Hunter?; Studebaker, Chicago, Jan 1957, Benedick in Much Ado About Nothing, and, Mar 1957, directed and played the Actor in The Guardsman; at the Phyllis Anderson Theatre, off-Broadway, Nov 1957, directed The Girl of the Golden West; Renaissance Theatre, Berlin, adapted and directed Dear Liar; Billy Rose, NY, Mar 1959, directed Dear Liar; made his first appearance in London, at the Criterion Theatre, June 1960, as Bernard Shaw in Dear Liar; Athénée, Paris, Oct, 1961, directed Dear Liar; Piccadilly, London, Feb 1962, directed Marie Bell in Les Violons Parfois; Theatre Marquee, NY, Mar 1962, again appeared in Dear Liar; Renaissance Theatre, Berlin, Nov 1962, directed Die Iden des Maerz (The Ides of March), which he adapted from the novel by Thornton Wilder; Quirino, Rome, Italy, Dec 1962, directed Dear Liar; Gymnase, Paris, Jan 1963, directed Les Violons Parfois; Barbizon-Plaza, NY, May 1963, adapted and directed a German-language version of Dear Liar; toured South Africa, 1963, as George in Who's Afraid of Virginia Woolf?; Haymarket, London, Aug 1963, author and co-director with John Gielgud of The Ides of March; Piccadilly, London, Feb 1964, George in Who's Afraid of Virginia Woolf?; Boston Arts Festival, 1964, directed Saint Joan, Man and Superman, and The Ides of March; Quirino, Rome, Oct 1964, directed the Italian version of Oh, What a Lovely War! and, Feb 1965, directed The Ides of March; Apollo, London, May 1965, co-author of the revue Nymphs and Satires; author of Don't Shoot Mabel It's Your Husband, 1965, produced in San Francisco in 1967 and in NY in 1968; American Shakespeare Festival, Stratford, Conn, 1966, played the title-role in Falstaff; Geary, San Francisco, Dec 1966, staged Dear Liar, and, in Nov 1967, played Bernard Shaw in this play; Huntington Hartford, Los Angeles, June 1967, directed Dear Liar; Stratford, Conn, June 1967, directed Anouilh's Antigone; associate director of The American Conservatory Theatre, San Francisco, 1966–8, and, in Feb 1968, directed his play Long Live Life; during the seasons 1967–9 was visiting actor and director at the Goodman Theatre, Chicago, the Yale Repertory Theatre, and the Alley Theatre, Houston, Texas; at the Player Theatre, NY, Dec 1968, directed Possibilities; Teatro Nuovo, Milan, Italy, Mar 1969, directed Lascio Alle Mie Donne; adapted from the works of Robert and Elizabeth Barrett Browning the play Dear Love, and played Robert Browning in its première at the Alley Theatre, Houston, Texas, Sept 1970, and subsequently toured with Myrna Loy; Helen Hayes, Apr 1972, translated The Little Black Book; his play Look Away produced at the Playhouse, Jan 1973; his play Dear Love produced at the Comedy, London, May 1973; author of The Laffing Man, 1974; directed a French version of Dear Liar, Paris, 1974; directed an Italian version of Dear Liar, Rome, Dec 1975; directed Mrs Warren's Profession, Rome, 1976; appeared in Dear Liar at the Roundabout, NY, Apr 1977; Goodman, Chicago, 1978, played Walt Whitman in Two-Part Inventions; Costa Nesa, Calif, 1979, Trissotin in Les Femmes Savantes; Old Globe, San Diego, 1979, directed and played title-role in Julius Caesar; Roundabout, Dec 1979, Arkady Islayev in A Month in the Country; author of book for What the Devil, musical, 1977; play, Hey Marie!, 1978; book for Barnum, 1980; his play Dear Liar received Berlin Festival Critics Award, 1961, Vienna Critics Award, 1962, the Baton du Brigadier of France, 1961–2, Paume d'Or of Italy, 1962–3, and the Stanislavsky Centenary Medal, Moscow, 1963; Kitty Cane Award for Theatrical merit, established at Univ of Kansas, 1962; Visiting Professor of Drama, Univ of Oklahoma, 1971, Texas, 1972, Kansas, 1973; holder of O'Conner Chair of Literature, Colgate Univ, 1974; first appeared on television, 1951, and has since played in over a hundred programs; author of numerous television plays.

Favourite parts: GBS in Dear Liar, Falstaff, Tartuffe. *Recreations:* Gardening, reading, horse racing. *Club:* Players, New York. *Address:* PO Box 1074, Weston, Conn 06880.

KING, John Michael, actor
b New York, 13 May 1926; *s* of the actor Dennis John King and his wife Edith (Wright); *e* Hill School; *m* Beverly S Sorg; trained for the stage at the American Academy of Dramatic Arts.

Made his Broadway debut in Inside USA, at the Century, Apr 1948; appeared in minor roles and chorus parts in a number of musicals including Courtin' Time, 1951, Buttrio Square, 1952, Me and Juliet, 1953, Hit the Trail, 1954, Ankles Aweigh, 1956; his first major Broadway role was as Freddie Eynsford-Hill in the original My Fair Lady, Mark Hellinger, Mar 1956; recent performances include Sir Edward Ramsay in The King and I, Uris, May 1977; Carlton Smith in Carmelina, St James, Apr 1979; has also toured and appeared in stock; frequent TV appearances include *All My Children* and *As the World Turns.*
Address: c/o Gloria Dolan Management, 850 Seventh Avenue, New York, NY 10019.

KING, Woodie Jr, producer and director
b Alabama, 27 Jul 1937; *s* of Woodie King and his wife Ruby (Jones); *e* Wayne State University; *m* the casting agent Willie Mae Washington; trained for the stage at Will-O-Way School of Theatre.

Drama critic, 1959–62, the *Detroit Tribune;* cultural arts director, 1965–70, for Mobilization of Youth, NYC; since 1970 artistic director and later overall director of the Henry Street Settlement's Arts for Living Center, in whose New Federal and Pilgrim theatres he has presented a number of important new plays and revivals, particularly of work by black playwrights; at Lincoln Center co-produced The Taking of Miss Janie, 1975; on Broadway has co-produced The First Breeze of Summer, 1975; For Colored Girls . . ., 1976; his career as a director includes What the Wine Sellers Buy, 1974, a national tour of Sizwe Bansi Is Dead, 1975, Daddy, 1977 etc; as an actor made his Broadway debut at the Alvin, 3 Oct 1968, as the Young Negro in The Great White Hope; off-Broadway he appeared in Lost in the Stars, Who's Got His Own, and Day of Absence; producer of several films including The Long Night, 1976; his own film appearances include Serpico; TV includes documentary production and roles in NYPD, *As the World Turns,* etc; author of a number of articles and short stories.
Address: New Federal Theatre, 466 Grand Street, New York, NY 10002. *Tel:* 766 9295.

KINGSLEY, Ben, actor
b Snaiton, Yorkshire, 31 Dec 1943; *s* of Rahimtulla Harji Bhanji and his wife Anna Lyna Mary; *e* Manchester Grammar School; *m* Gillian Alison Macaulay Sutcliffe, theatre director; formerly a laboratory research assistant.

Began his professional career on a schools tour for Theatre Centre, 1964; in rep at Stoke-on-Trent, 1965, where his parts included Doolittle in Pygmalion; Arts, Feb 1966, narrated and wrote music for A Smashing Day; Chichester, season 1966, played First Murderer in Macbeth and a Party Guest in The Cherry Orchard; joined the Royal Shakespeare Company and at Stratford, season 1967, played small parts including Amiens in As You Like It; made his London debut with the company at the Aldwych, Aug 1967, as the wigmaker in The Relapse; Stratford, season 1968, played Oswald in King Lear, Aeneas in Troilus and Cressida, and Conrade

in Much Ado About Nothing, repeating the two last at the Aldwych, season 1969, and playing The Croucher in The Silver Tassie and Winwife in Bartholomew Fair; at Stratford, 1970, Ratcliff in Richard III, Claudio in Measure for Measure and Demetrius in Peter Brook's Midsummer Night's Dream; also Ariel in The Tempest; played Demetrius on tour in the US, and at the Aldwych, Jun 1971; followed by Sinsov in Enemies, Jul; at The Place, Oct 1971, played Gramsci in Occupations and Ippolit in Subject to Fits; Newcastle, 1972, Puck in The Faery Queen; Kings Head, later The Place, Oct 1973, Johnnie in Hello and Goodbye; followed by Fritz in A Lesson in Blood and Roses, The Place, Nov; Royal Court, Jan 1974, Errol Philander in Statements, touring Europe with this production and returning to the Royal Court, Jan 1975; again with the RSC, Stratford 1975, played Slender in The Merry Wives of Windsor, Bonze Wang in Man Is Man, and Hamlet in Buzz Goodbody's Other Place production of Hamlet, appearing in the last two at the Round House, Feb 1976; Nottingham Playhouse, followed by Comedy, May 1976, Danilo in Dimetos; for the National Theatre, 1977, played Mosca in Volpone, Vukhov in the monodrama Judgement, and Trofimov in The Cherry Orchard; rejoined the RSC, Stratford season 1979, to play Frank Ford in The Merry Wives of Windsor, Iachimo in Cymbeline, Brutus in Julius Caesar, and (at The Other Place) the title role in Baal; RSC London season 1980, played Baal at the Warehouse, repeated Ford and played Squeers in Nicholas Nickleby at the Aldwych; first film, Fear Is the Key, 1972; TV includes The Love School and Every Good Boy Deserves Favour.
Favourite parts: Ariel, Hamlet, Ford, Mosca. *Address:* New Pebworth House, Pebworth, Stratford-upon-Avon, Warwickshire.

KINGSLEY, Sidney, dramatic author and director
b New York City, 22 Oct 1906; *e* Townsend Harris Hall, and Cornell University; *m* Madge Evans.

While at the University, was a member of the Dramatic Club, for which he wrote several one-act plays; subsequently he appeared with the Tremont stock company, Bronx, NY; his first play to be produced professionally was Men in White, Broadhurst Theatre, NY, 26 Sept 1933, which achieved universal success; he directed it at the Lyric, London, 1934, and it was produced in all the major European capitals; the play gained the Pulitzer prize for the best American play of the year; his second play Dead End, which he also directed, at the Belasco, NY, Oct 1935, was also an immediate success and was awarded the Theater Club Medal, Apr 1936, and was produced throughout Europe; directed his next play, Ten Million Ghosts, 1936; has since written The World We Make (also directed), 1939; The Patriots, 1943, which gained the New York Drama Critics Circle Award, 1942–3; Detective Story, 1949; Darkness at Noon (from a novel), 1951, which won several awards, including the New York Drama Critics Circle; Lunatics and Lovers, 1954; Night Life, which he also produced, 1962; The World We Make and Detective Story have also been produced in many European countries; Darkness at Noon was subsequently adapted into French (with Leo Lapary) as Le Zéro et l'Infini for Théâtre Antoine, Paris, Jan 1960; The Patriots produced on television, 1976; President of The Dramatists Guild, Inc.
Address: The Dramatists Guild, Inc, 234 West 44th Street, New York, NY 10036.

KINGSTON, Mark, actor
b Greenwich, 18 Apr 1934; *s* of Harold William Kingston and his wife Lilian Maria (Smith); *e* Greenwich Secondary School; *m* Marigold Angela Sharman; trained for the stage at the London Academy of Music and Dramatic Art.

First stage appearance was at the Boscombe Hippodrome, Dec 1954, as the Emperor of China in Aladdin; subsequently in rep with various companies including Birmingham, with whom he made his London debut at the Old Vic, 30 Jul 1956, as a Porter in Caesar and Cleopatra; toured the world with the Old Vic company, 1961–62, in parts including Feste in Twelfth Night; on his return took over as Sgt Trotter in The Mousetrap, Ambassadors', 1962; New Arts, Apr 1964, Tom Mann in The Subtopians; Queen's, Jul 1964, Juror no 5 in Twelve Angry Men; with the Chichester Festival company, 1968, his parts included Sebastian in The Tempest and Sergeant in The Unknown Soldier and His Wife; Wyndham's, Nov 1968, Peter Quilpe in the Chichester production of The Cocktail Party; Haymarket, Aug 1971, played several parts in A Voyage Round My Father; Royal Court, Mar 1972, Henry Conrad in a workshop production of The Centaur; New London, Jan 1973, again played the Sergeant in The Unknown Soldier and His Wife; Greenwich, May 1974, and Globe, Aug, Reg in The Norman Conquests; toured, 1975, with the Oxford Playhouse company, as Willie Loman in Death of a Salesman; Queen's, Oct 1976, Narrator in Yahoo; Duke of York's, Nov 1978, Ed in Clouds; Warehouse, Jun 1980, for RSC, Frank in Educating Rita; has directed a number of plays for the Thorndike, Leatherhead, including Romanoff and Juliet, The Odd Couple, and Who's Afraid of Virginia Woolf?, and the musical Nell, Richmond, 1970; films, since Wonderful Things, 1957, include Saint Jack and Lady Oscar, both 1978; TV, since 1955, includes *Beryl's Lot* and *Time of My Life*.

Clubs: Green Room, Stage Golfing Society. *Address:* 27 Sydney Road, Richmond, Surrey.

KINNEAR, Roy (Mitchell), actor
b Wigan, Lancs, 8 Jan 1934; *s* of Roy Muir Kinnear and his wife Annie Smith (Durie); *e* George Heriots School, Edinburgh; *m* Carmel Cryan (actress); studied for the stage at the Royal Academy of Dramatic Art.

Made his first appearance on the stage at the Newquay Theatre, Newquay, June 1955, as Albert in The Young in Heart; first appeared in London at the Theatre Royal, Stratford, E, Oct 1959, as Fred in Make Me an Offer, subsequently transferring with the production to the New, Dec 1959, in the same part; Theatre Royal, Stratford, E, June 1960, played Master Mathew in Every Man in His Humour; at the same theatre, Aug 1960, played the RO Man and Sid in Sparrers Can't Sing; Nov 1960, Charlie Modryb in Progress to the Park; Wyndham's, Mar 1961, again played in Sparrers' Can't Sing; Theatre Royal, Stratford, E, June 1961, played Blevins Playfair in They Might Be Giants; at the same theatre, Nov 1961, played Mr Marris in Big Soft Nellie; and Jan 1962, Father Matthew in On a Clear Day You Can See Canterbury; Princes, May 1962, appeared in the revue England, Our England; Oxford Playhouse, Feb 1963, played Sid Hotson in The Affliction; Comedy, June 1964, Leo Herman in A Thousand Clowns; Royal Court, May 1965, John P Jones in Meals on Wheels; Palladium, Dec 1965, Nicholas in Babes in the Wood; joined the Royal Shakespeare Company, Dec 1966, to play the Baron in The Thwarting of Baron Bolligrew at the Aldwych, subsequently appearing there and at Stratford-on-Avon in the 1967 season, as Baptista in The Taming of the Shrew and Touchstone in As You Like It, and as Bull in The Relapse (Aldwych only); Ahmanson, Los Angeles, Jan 1968, again played Touchstone and Baptista; Old Vic, Dec 1969, Sancho in the National Theatre production of The Travails of Sancho Panza; Criterion, Apr 1970, Ligurio in Mandrake; St Martin's, Jan 1974, Supt Baxter in

Dead Easy; The Place, Oct 1974, for RSC, Ben in The Can Opener; Casino, Dec 1974, Valeria in Cinderella; Duke of York's, Oct 1975, Fred in Roger's Last Stand; Arnaud, Dec 1977, Gepetto in Pinocchio; Adelphi, Nov 1978, Mayor Enrico in Beyond the Rainbow; first entered films, Oct 1961, and has appeared in Three Musketeers, Four Musketeers, Juggernaut, The Last Remake of Beau Geste, etc; since Jan 1956, he has appeared in such television productions as *That Was the Week That Was*, A Slight Case of . . ., his own series, *Inside George Webley*, and *Shades of Greene*.

Addresses: c/o Richard Stone, 18–20 York Buildings, London WC2. *Tel:* 01–839 6421 *and* UK Management Inc, 1052 North Carol Drive, Los Angeles, Calif 90069. *Tel:* 213–275 9599.

KIPNESS, Joseph, producer
Presented his first New York production, Bright Lights of 1944, at the Forrest, 16 Sept 1943; since then has produced or co-produced the following plays; The Duke in Darkness, 1944; Star Spangled Family, 1945; High Button Shoes, 1947; All You Need Is One Good Break, 1950; Women of Twilight, Conscience, 1952; Be Your Age, 1953; La Plume de Ma Tante, 1958; Have I Got A Girl for You!, 1963; I Had a Ball, 1964; La Grosse Valise, 1965; But, Seriously . . ., 1969; Applause, 1970; Father's Day, Inner City, 1971; Seesaw, No Hard Feelings, 1973; Rockabye Hamlet, The Primary English Class, 1976; I Love My Wife, Jockeys, 1977; King of Hearts, 1978; The Goodbye People, Teibele and Her Demon, 1979; co-produced the tours of Shootin' Star, 1946, and That's the Ticket, 1948; is also a restaurateur in New York.

Address: 144 West 52nd Street, New York, NY 10020.

KIPPAX, H G (Harold Gemmell), journalist and drama critic
b Sydney, 6 Oct 1920; *s* of Arthur Craigie Kippax and his wife Marion Emily Gibson; *e* Knox Grammar School and Sydney University; *m* Susan Carolyn James (mar dis).

Joined the *Sydney Morning Herald* as a cadet journalist in 1938 and has served the newspaper in many capacities since, including London Editor 1949–50, Literary Editor 1965–68, foreign correspondent etc; dramatic critic 1966–74, 1977–present; theatre critic, under the name 'Brek', for the *Nation* magazine, 1958–66; founding member, Metropolitan Theatre, Sydney, 1945–46; writings other than journalism include essays and prefaces to plays.

Recreations: Conversation, music, wine, cricket. *Address:* 4 View Street, Woollahra, Sydney, NSW. *Tel:* 387 2502.

KIPPHARDT, Heinar, dramatic author
b Heidersdorf/Schlesien, Germany, 8 Mar 1922; *e* Universities of Bonn, Königsberg, Breslau, and Düsseldorf; formerly a Doctor of Medicine, literary adviser, and director.

His first play to be produced was Shakespeare dringend gesucht, at the Deutsches Theater, Berlin, June 1953; he was resident dramatist at this theatre, 1951–9, and at the Munich Kammerspiele, 1969–71; he is also the author of the following plays: Der Aufstieg des Alois Piontek, 1956; Die Stühle des Herrn Szmil, 1960; Der Hund des Generals, 1962; In der Sache J Robert Oppenheimer (The Oppenheimer Affair), 1964; Joel Brand, die Geschichte eines Geschäfts, 1965; Die Nacht in der der Chef geschlachtet wurde, 1967; Die Soldaten (adapted from J M R Lenz), 1968; Sedanfeier, 1970; television plays include: Bartleby, 1962; Der Hund des Generals, In der Sache J Robert Oppenheimer, Die Geschichte von Joel Brand, 1964, Leben des schizophrenen Dichters Alexander März, 1975, Die Soldaten, 1977; his awards include Deutscher Nationalpreis, 1953; Schiller

Gedächtnispreis, 1962; Gerhard Hauptmann-Preis, 1964; Prix Italia, 1976.

Address: 8059 Angelsbruck, Post Fraunberg, W Germany. *Tel:* 08762 1829.

KIRK, Lisa, actress, singer, dancer

b Brownsville, Pa, 25 Feb; *e* Charleroi High School; *m* Robert Wells; prepared for the stage at the Pittsburgh Playhouse.

Majestic, NY, Oct 1947, played Emily in Allegro; New Century, Dec 1948, Lois Lane and Bianca in Kiss Me, Kate; Shubert, 1964, took over from Janis Paige as Doris Walker in Here's Love, and subsequently toured in this part; sustained an injury that prevented her dancing for several years; Pittsburgh, Pa, 1973, Margo Channing in Applause; re-appeared in New York at the Majestic, 6 Oct 1974, as Lottie Ames in Mack and Mabel; Kaufmann Concert Hall, 24 Nov 1974, appeared in An Evening with Jerry Herman; John Golden, Mar 1976, Bibi in Me Jack, You Jill, marking her first non-singing part; has also toured in Showboat, Say, Darling, and Panama Hattie; has toured in cabaret in Europe and the USA; has appeared on television in various musical programs, including A Toast to Jerome Kern, The Man in the Moon, Shubert Alley, The Tony Awards, and in The Taming of the Shrew.

Address: Actors Equity Association, 165 West 46th Street, New York, NY 10036.

KIRKLAND, Sally, actress

b New York City, 31 Oct 1944; *m* Michael Jarrett; prepared for the stage at the Actors Studio.

Made her New York debut at the Ethel Barrymore, 17 Oct 1962, as an understudy in Step on a Crack; Writers' Stage, 25 Jan 1963, Cindy Sweetspent in The Love Nest; Circle in the Square, May 1966, played in the title role in Fitz; Stage 73, Mar 1968, played various parts in Tom Paine; Theatre de Lys, June 1968, Narrator in Futz!; Gramercy Arts, Nov 1968, The Girl in Sweet Eros and Miss Presson in Witness; Actors Playhouse, Dec 1970, Young Girl in The Noisy Passenger in a production with the overall title One Night Stands of a Noisy Passenger; Theatre de Lys, June 1971, Delphine in The Justice Box; Forum, Dec 1971, Avis Honor in Delicate Champion; Actors Studio, Feb 1972, Marcia in Felix; American Place, May 1972, Lee in The Chickencoop Chinaman; Eastside Playhouse, Oct 1971, took over as Nedda Lemon in Where Has Tommy Flowers Gone?; Mark Taper Forum Lab, Los Angeles, Cal, 1974, played in Canadian Gothic; San Francisco, May 1976, took over as Rona in Kennedy's Children; has appeared in the films Going Home (1971), The Way We Were (1973), Cinderella Liberty (1973), Big Bad Mama (1974), etc; has also appeared on television.

Address: Actors Equity Association, 165 West 46th Street, New York, NY 10036.

KIRKWOOD, James, author and actor

b Los Angeles, Calif, 22 Aug 1930; *s* of the actor and director James Kirkwood, Sr and his wife the actress Lila (Lee); trained for the stage with Sanford Meisner, Neighborhood Playhouse.

Began his acting career in 1947 as Jean d'Arc in a tour of Joan of Lorraine; Broadway debut, Coronet, 1949, when he joined the revue Small Wonder; has also appeared on various other tours; frequent appearances on TV have included four years in Valiant Lady (CBS); his first play to be produced was an adaptation of his novel There Must Be a Pony, which toured in 1962; has since written UTBU (Unhealthy to Be Unpleasant), 1965; P S Your Cat Is Dead (from his novel),

1975, revised 1978; co-author of the book for A Chorus Line, 1975 (Tony award, Pulitzer prize); his other novels include Good Times/Bad Times, 1968; Some Kind of Hero, 1975; Hit Me with a Rainbow, 1980.

Recreation: Tennis. *Address:* 58 Oyster Shores Road, East Hampton, NY 11937.

KIRKWOOD, Pat, actress and singer

b Pendleton, 24 Feb 1921; *d* of William Kirkwood and his wife Norah (Carr); *e* Levenshulme High School, Manchester; *m* (1) John William Atkinson Lister (mar dis); (2) Spiro de Spero Gabriele (dec); (3) Hubert Gregg (mar dis).

Made her first appearance on the stage at the Salford Royal Hippodrome, 1936, in a variety act, The Schoolgirl Songstress; after subsequent performances in variety, appeared at the New, Cardiff, Dec 1936, as Princess Dorothy in Jack and the Beanstalk; made her first appearance in London, at the Princes Theatre, 24 Dec 1937, as Dandini in Cinderella; Hippodrome, Sept 1939, played in Black Velvet; Palladium, Sept 1940, in The Top of the World; Theatre Royal, Nottingham, Dec 1940, appeared as the Princess in Aladdin; His Majesty's, July 1941, played Bonnie Drew in Lady Behave; Hippodrome, Nov 1942, Winnie Potter in Let's Face It; at Blackpool, July 1943, appeared in Happidrome; at the Coliseum, Dec 1943, played Prince Rupert in Humpty Dumpty, and Dec 1944, Robin Goodfellow in Goody Two Shoes; London Hippodrome, Oct 1947, appeared in the revue Starlight Roof; Casino, Dec 1948, Prince Rupert in Humpty Dumpty; Saville, Aug 1949, Angelina in Roundabout; Casino, Dec 1949, Little Tommy Tucker in Little Miss Muffet; Cambridge, July 1950, Pinkie Leroy in Ace of Clubs; Prince of Wales's, May 1951, appeared in the revue Fancy Free; Scala, Dec 1953, appeared as Peter Pan, also touring; Desert Inn, Las Vegas, 1954, made her American cabaret début; Princes, Feb 1955, played Ruth in Wonderful Town and later that year appeared in the Royal Variety Performance at the Victoria Palace; Hippodrome, Brighton, Dec 1957, Jack in Jack and the Beanstalk; Prince of Wales's, Nov 1958, played Chrysanthemum Brown in Chrysanthemum, transferring to the Apollo, Feb 1959; Phoenix, Feb 1961, played Penelope Troop in Pools Paradise; Royal, Windsor, Oct 1961, Elsie in Villa Sleep Four; New, Oxford, Dec 1961, played Robin in Robin Hood; Everyman, Cheltenham, Dec 1966, Mrs Squeezum in Lock Up Your Daughters; toured, Feb 1967, as Constance in The Constant Wife; toured Oct 1967, as Melanie in The Rumpus; University, Newcastle, Dec 1970, Judith Bliss in Hay Fever; toured, 1971, in the title role of Lady Frederick; His Majesty's, Aberdeen, Dec 1971, played Robin Hood in Babes in the Wood; toured, Apr 1972, as Lottie Landers in A Chorus of Murder; Aberdeen, Dec, played Dick Whittington; toured, July 1973, as Mrs Markham in Move Over Mrs Markham; Theatre Royal, Newcastle, Dec 1973, Aladdin; Edinburgh Festival, Sept 1976, Vera in Pal Joey; toured, 1977, as Mrs Gay Lustre in The Cabinet Minister; first appeared in films, 1937, in Save a Little Sunshine, and films include: Me and My Pal, Band Waggon, Stars in Your Eyes, No Leave, No Love, After the Ball, etc; throughout her career, has appeared on the variety stage, and also in cabaret; co-starred with her husband in the television series From Me to You, 1957, and also in the radio series *My Patricia*, 1956; has also starred in the television productions The Pat Kirkwood Show, Our Marie, Pygmalion and The Great Little Tilley.

Recreations: Walking, swimming and reading. *Address:* c/o British Actors' Equity, 8 Harley Street, London, W1.

KIRTLAND, Louise, actress

b Lynn, Mass, 4 Aug 1910; *d* of Thos Edgar Jelly and his wife

Hannah Isabelle (Dukeson); *e* English High School, Lynn; *m* A L Alexander; studied singing under Lilian Weeks.

Made her first appearance on the stage at school in Lynn, 1925, as Miss Curtis in The Charm School; subsequently toured and appeared in stock; made her first appearance in New York, at Daly's, 4 Nov 1927, as Gladys Blake in The Wicked Age; in 1928, toured in My Maryland; Martin Beck, Sept 1928, played Peggy in Night Hostess; Little, Feb 1929, took over as Tavie Ferguson in That Ferguson Family; Biltmore, Aug 1929, Dorothy Ruth in Getting Even; Waldorf, Nov 1930, Katie Zimmer in Light Wines and Beer; Playhouse, Oct 1931, Olly Frey in A Church Mouse; Cort, Oct 1932, Ethel in Tell Her the Truth; Casino, Feb 1933, Ninon Revelle in Melody; Shubert, July 1933, Peggy Stetson in Shady Lady; Oct 1933, Lola Valette in Her Man of Wax; Majestic, Jan 1934, succeeded Olga Baclanova as Sonya Sonya in Murder at the Vanities; 44th Street, May 1934, Jane McMurray in The Only Girl; subsequently toured with Lenore Ulric; 58th Street, Sept 1935, Sister Pauline in Few Are Chosen; toured, 1936, in To Be Continued; Ritz, NY, Dec 1937, Elaine Carley in Love in My Fashion; Salem, Mass, Mar 1938, Anne Browne in American Wing; subsequently appeared in cabaret in Boston; toured, 1941, in No, No, Nanette; Detroit, Oct 1942, Grace Harrington in Life of the Party, and Oct 1943, Betty in Little Women; in Boston, 1943, played in Stage Door; toured, 1944, as Fifi in Rosalinda, and in 1945, in The Student Prince, and Let Us Be Gay; from 1938–50, for twelve seasons played leading parts in stock companies, at Portland, Me, and Worcester, Fitchbury, and Holyoke, Mass, Louisville, Ky, St Louis Municipal Opera, etc; in summer theatre, 1947, played in Anything Goes; Broadhurst, NY, Jan 1949, appeared in the revue Along Fifth Avenue; Winter Garden, Jan 1950, in Alive and Kicking; Fulton, May 1952, took over as Andrée in Gigi; toured, 1954, as Lilly Sears in Tea and Sympathy; Coronet, Jan 1957, Madame Dupont-Fredaine in Waltz of the Toreadors; Royale, June 1957, took over as Alice Pepper in The Tunnel of Love; Renata, Jan 1958, Birdie in Winkelberg; Broadway, Mar 1963, Grace Davis in a musical version of Tovarich; Paper Mill Playhouse, Milburn, New Jersey, Nov 1966, Lily in Take Me Along; toured, 1967–8, as Mrs Upson and the Dance Teacher in Mame; toured, 1971, as Maud in Forty Carats, with Lana Turner; Meadow Brook, Rochester, Mich, 1972, played in The Torch-Bearers; Uris, NY, 1974, took over from Agnes Moorehead as Aunt Alicia in Gigi; has also toured in Death of a Salesman, Look Homeward, Angel, An Evening with Tennessee Williams, Black Chiffon, Susan and God, Blithe Spirit, The Marriage-Go-Round, The Unsinkable Molly Brown, Take Me Along, The Boy Friend, Bells Are Ringing, Damn Yankees, No, No, Nanette, Oklahoma!, Carousel, The Music Man, Dracula (1978), etc; most recent film, Roseland; has also appeared frequently on television.
Recreations: Study of philosophy. *Address:* Ansonia Hotel, 2109 Broadway, New York, NY 10023.

KITCHIN, Laurence, critic and former actor
b Bradford, Yorks, 1913; *e* Bootham School, York, and King's College, London; *m* Hilary Owen.
Originally an actor, he studied under Elsie Fogerty and appeared in over 600 performances of Housemaster, which opened at the Apollo, Nov 1936, as Old Crump; correspondent and critic on theatre topics, *The Times*, 1956–62; Lecturer in Drama, Bristol University, 1966–70; Visiting Professor of Drama, Stanford University, 1970–2; Visiting Professor, later Professor, Brooklyn College, City University

of New York, 1972–6; Visiting Professor in Shakespeare Studies, Simon Fraser University, 1976–7; his film appearances included Pimpernel Smith and The Poison Pen; his books include Mid-Century Drama, and Drama in the Sixties; has made over 300 broadcasts, and has recently made a series of verse translations from the Italian, French and Spanish, for the BBC.
Club: Athenaeum. *Address:* c/o National Westminster Bank, 33 St James's Square, London W1.

KITT, Eartha, singer and actress
b North, South Carolina, 26 Jan 1930; *d* of William Kitt and his wife Mamie (Reily); *e* New York School of the Performing Arts; *m* William McDonald.
Made her NY stage début at the Belasco, 21 May 1945, as a member of Katherine Dunham's dance troupe in the revue Blue Holiday; Belasco, Nov 1946, again danced with Miss Dunham's troupe in Bal Nègre, and subsequently toured Europe in this production; in France, Germany, and Belgium, 1951, played Helen of Troy in Orson Welles's production of Faust; Royale, NY, May 1952, appeared in the revue New Faces of 1952; National, Dec 1954, Teddy Hicks in Mrs Patterson; Broadway, Apr 1957, Mehitabel in Shinbone Alley; Longacre, Dec 1959, Jolly in Jolly's Progress; toured, 1965–6, as Doris W in The Owl and the Pussycat; Arnaud, Guildford, Oct 1970 and Criterion, London, Dec 1970, Mrs Gracedew in The High Bid; Belgrade, Coventry, Sept 1972, and Criterion, Dec 1972, Bunny Novak in Bunny; toured US, May 1976, in A Musical Jubilee; Mark Hellinger, Mar 1978, Sahleem-La-Lume in Timbuktu!, subsequently touring with the production, 1979–80; has appeared regularly in cabaret; first appeared in films in New Faces, 1954, and since has played in St Louis Blues, the title role in Anna Lucasta, The Saint of Devil's Island, Synanon, etc; has appeared on television regularly since 1953 in variety programmes and in Salome, Wingless Victory, etc, and received the Golden Rose of Montreux for Kaskade, a Swedish television production, 1962; wrote her autobiography Thursday's Child, 1956, and a second volume, Alone with Me, 1976.
Address: Actors Equity Association, 165 West 46th Street, New York, NY 10036.

KLEIN, Robert, comedian, and actor
b The Bronx, 8 Feb 1942; *e* Alfred University, New York and Yale School of Drama; *m* the opera singer Brenda Boozer.
Early work with the Second City company in Chicago led to his New York debut with the company at Square East, 21 Apr 1966, in 20,000 Frozen Grenadiers; Shubert, Oct 1966, played two parts in The Apple Tree; Booth, May 1968, appeared in New Faces of 1968; Henry Miller, Nov 1968, Junior in Morning, Asher in Noon, and the Man in Night in the triple-bill Morning, Noon and Night; Imperial, Feb 1979, Vernon Gersch in They're Playing Our Song; gained his first experience as a writer/comedian at the Improvisation club, 1966–69, and has since made a number of very successful comedy albums, as well as appearing in a series of Annual Robert Klein Reunions at Carnegie Hall; films include The Landlord, Hooper, and The Bell Jar, 1980; TV includes talk shows and several of his own specials for Home Box Office.
Address: c/o Rollins and Joffe, 130 West 57th Street, New York, NY 10019.

KLINE, Kevin, actor
b St Louis, 24 Oct 1947; *s* of Robert Joseph Kline and his wife Peggy (Kirk); *e* St Louis Priory and Indiana University; trained for the stage at Juilliard Drama Center and studied with Harold Guskin.

Appeared with the New York Shakespeare Festival company at the Delacorte, season 1970, in minor roles in the first two parts of Henry VI, and in Richard III; a founding member of The Acting Company, he appeared in their first season at the Good Shepherd — Faith Church, Sept 1972, playing Charles Surface in The School for Scandal, Vaska Pepel in The Lower Depths, the IRA Officer in The Hostage, and Guardiano in Women Beware Women; made his Broadway debut with the company in their Billy Rose season, 19 Dec 1973, as Vershinin in Three Sisters, also playing Macheath in The Beggar's Opera, Friar Peter in Measure for Measure, and Leandre in Scapin; on tour with the company he played Tony Lumpkin in She Stoops to Conquer, Mirabell in The Way of the World, and Tom in The Knack; at the Harkness, Oct 1975, Jaimie Lockhart in The Robber Bridegroom and McCarthy in The Time of Your Life; Hudson Guild, Apr 1977, Clym Yeobright in Dance on a Country Grave; at the St James, Feb 1978, played Bruce Granit in On the Twentieth Century (Tony award); Circle in the Square, Jun 1979, Paul in Loose Ends; Delacorte, for the New York Shakespeare Festival, July 1980, Pirate King in The Pirates of Penzance; TV includes The Time of Your Life for PBS.

Recreations: Musical composition, travel, sports. *Address:* 313 West 90th Street, New York, NY.

KLOTZ, Florence, designer

b New York City; *d* of Philip Klotz and his wife Hannah (Kraus); attended the Parsons School of Design.

Her first design for the stage was the costumes for A Call on Kuprin, produced at the Broadhurst, May 1961; has since designed the costumes for Take Her, She's Mine, 1961; Never Too Late, 1962; On an Open Roof, Nobody Loves an Albatross, 1963; Everybody Out, The Castle Is Sinking, One by One, The Owl and the Pussycat, 1964; The Mating Dance, 1965; Best Laid Plans, This Winter's Hobby, Its a Bird . . . It's a Plane . . . It's Superman, 1966; Golden Boy (coordinator for the tour), 1968; Norman, Is That You?, Paris Is Out, 1970; Follies, 1971, for which she received the Antoinette Perry (Tony) Award; A Little Night Music (Tony Award), Sondheim: A Musical Tribute, 1973; Dreyfus in Rehearsal, 1974; Pacific Overtures (Tony Award), Legend, 1976; Side by Side by Sondheim, 1977; On the Twentieth Century, Broadway, Broadway (tour), 1978; Harold and Maude, 1980; first designed for films in Germany in 1969, and designed the American film Something for Everyone, 1970; A Little Night Music, 1977.

Address: 1050 Park Avenue, New York, NY. *Tel:* 876–4546.

KLUGMAN, Jack, actor

b Philadelphia, Pa, 27 Apr 1922; *s* of Max Klugman and his wife Rose; *e* Carnegie Institute of Technology; studied at the American Theatre Wing; *m* Brett Somers.

Made his New York début in the Equity Library Theatre production of Stevedore, 18 Feb 1949, subsequently playing in Saint Joan, Nov 1949, and Bury the Dead, Jan 1950; toured as Dowdy in Mister Roberts, 1950–1; made his Broadway début at the ANTA, 12 Mar 1952, as Frank Bonaparte in Golden Boy; Phoenix, Jan 1954, played a Citizen and a Volscian Servant in Coriolanus; Playhouse, Nov 1956, Carmen in A Very Special Baby; Broadway, May 1959, Herbie in the musical Gypsy; Plymouth, Apr 1963, took over from Anthony Quinn as Caesario Grimaldi in Tchin-Tchin; Plymouth, 1966, took over from Walter Matthau as Oscar Madison in The Odd Couple; made his London début at the Queen's, Oct 1966, when he again played Oscar Madison in The Odd Couple; Belasco, Dec 1968, the title-role in The Sudden and Accidental Re-education of Horse Johnson; Maddox Hall, Atlanta, Ga, Aug 1972, Oscar Madi-

son in The Odd Couple; played in this part in Miami, Fla, and Houston, Texas, July 1973; toured the US in this part, 1974; toured the US and Canada in this part, 1975; entered films in Time Table, 1956, and played in 12 Angry Men, Cry Terror, Days of Wine and Roses, Goodbye Columbus, etc; has appeared regularly on television in *Suspicion, Studio One*, Kiss Me, Kate, The Time of Your Life, the series *Harris Against the World, The Odd Couple*, 1970–5, *Quincy*, etc, receiving an Emmy Award for his performance in Blacklist, 1964, and as best actor in a series for *The Odd Couple*, 1971 and 1973.

Address: Actors Equity Association, 165 West 46th Street, New York, NY 10036.

KNEALE, Patricia, actress

b Torquay, Devon, 17 Oct 1925; *d* of William Lawrence Kneale and his wife Isabel Mary (Dodds); *e* Eastbourne and privately; *m* (1) Jeremy Geidt (mar dis); (2) Neil J Osborne; was formerly engaged as a shorthand-typist; gained the Meggie Albanesi scholarship to the Royal Academy of Dramatic Art, where she was awarded the Kendal prize and the Bancroft Gold Medal.

Made her first appearance on the stage at the Open Air Theatre, Regent's Park, 22 May 1947, as Olivia in Twelfth Night, subsequently playing Golden Stream in Lady Precious Stream, and Titania in A Midsummer Night's Dream; Lyric, Hammersmith, Nov 1947, played Hagar in The Little Dry Thorn; Q, Feb 1948, Gwan in Trespass; Open Air Theatre, 1948 season, Celia in As You Like It, Blanch of Spain in King John, and Hermia in A Midsummer Night's Dream; subsequently toured all over England, for the Arts Council; Open Air Theatre, 1949 season, Hero in Much Ado About Nothing, Luciana in The Comedy of Errors, Silvia in The Two Gentlemen of Verona, Ariel in The Tempest, and Elizabeth and Care in Faust; Q, Sept 1949, Anna in By Adoption; toured Apr–July 1950, with Ralph Lynn in The Ex-Mrs Y; subsequently appeared in repertory at Leatherhead and Halifax; toured, Aug 1951, in the leading part in Black Coffee; Nottingham Playhouse, Jan 1951–June 1952, played leading parts in repertory; Open Air Theatre, Regent's Park, June 1953, played Rosaline in Love's Labour's Lost; at the Edinburgh Festival, Aug 1954, played Isabella in Marlowe's Edward II; toured for the Arts Council, Jan 1955, as Gertrude in Hamlet; Cambridge Arts Theatre, May 1955, played Lady Coniston in Lord Arthur Savile's Crime, and Aug 1955, Arkadina in The Seagull; Open Air Theatre, June 1956, took over the part of Rosalind in As You Like It; at the same theatre, Aug 1956, Viola in Twelfth Night; with the same company, visited Lebanon, Sept 1956, also playing Gertrude in Hamlet; Ipswich Repertory, Jan–May 1957; Oxford Playhouse, Dec 1957, played Pia, in the first performance in England of Ugo Betti's Crime on Goat Island; May 1958, toured as Doll Tearsheet in Henry IV, Part 2, and Lady Percy in Henry IV, Part I; Arts, Oct 1959, played Olympia in The Marriage of Mr Mississippi; Gateway, Edinburgh, Aug 1960, played the title-part in Mary Stuart (Björnsen); Edinburgh Festival, 1966, appeared in the PopTheatre productions of The Trojan Women and The Winter's Tale; Bournemouth, 1966 and 1967, played various parts, including Martha in Who's Afraid of Virginia Woolf?; Phoenix, Leicester, Jan–Mar 1968, Phoebe in The Entertainer and the Nurse in Loot; Playhouse, Newcastle, Sept 1968, Beatrice in A View From the Bridge; Welsh National Theatre, 1969–70, played the following roles: Gertrude in Hamlet; Winnie in Happy Days and Dona Ana in Don Juan in Hell; Open Air, Regent's Park, summer, 1970, appeared as Hippolyta in A Midsummer Night's Dream, Margaret in Much Ado About

Nothing and in The Lord Byron Show; Open Air, Regent's Park, season 1971, played Lady Capulet in Romeo and Juliet, and Hippolyta in A Midsummer Night's Dream; York Minster, Oct 1972, Leader of the Chorus in Murder in the Cathedral; Theatre Royal, York, Nov 1972, Barren Woman in Three Women; Bush, London, Nov 1973, Mrs Smith in The Bald Prima Donna; at Harrogate, she played Sheila Broadbent in The Reluctant Debutante (1975), Mrs Warren in Mrs Warren's Profession (1977), and Dora Strang in Equus (1978); toured, Sept 1978–June 1979, as Dora Bunner in A Murder is Announced; has also appeared frequently on television.

Recreations: Music and cooking. *Address:* c/o Peter Eade Ltd, 9 Cork Street, London, W1X 1PD.

KNIGHT, David (*né* Mintz), actor
b Niagara Falls, New York, 16 Jan 1927; *s* of Rev Eugene Grafton Mintz and his wife Mary Letitia (Knight); *e* Syracuse University and Whittier College; formerly a teacher at Putney School, Vermont, where he remained for three years; *m* Wendy McClure.

Made his first appearance on the stage at the Putney (Vermont) Summer Theatre, 1949, when he played Sergius Saranoff in Arms and the Man; on his arrival in England, studied for the stage at the Royal Academy of Dramatic Art; made his first appearance in London, at the Hippodrome, June 1956, when he played Barney Greenwald in The Caine Mutiny Court Martial; Savoy, July 1958, played Jimmy Dugan in a revival of The Trial of Mary Dugan; at the New Shakespeare, Liverpool, Oct 1958, played Theodore Hickman in The Iceman Cometh; Oxford Playhouse, Feb 1960, played Eilert Lovborg in Hedda Gabler; Comedy, Apr 1961, Arthur Landeau in The Tenth Man; Oxford Playhouse, Feb 1962, played Garcin in In Camera; Mermaid, Mar 1962, played Sergius in a revival of Arms and the Man; Shaftesbury, Mar 1963, played Bud Frump in How to Succeed in Business Without Really Trying; toured, Apr 1965, as Mario Garani in La Contessa; Lyceum, Edinburgh, Sept 1966, played Charles in A Present For the Past; Saville, June 1968, Rudi Klebe in The Dancing Years; St Martin's, Oct 1968, Otis Clifton in Out of the Question; Arnaud, Guildford, Sept 1969, played Philip Ross in The Will, and Toby Cartwright in Ways and Means; Apollo, Sept 1973, Jeff Cooper in Finishing Touches; 1975–6, acting Head of Drama, University of Winnipeg; 1977–date Professor of Theatre and Head of Acting, University of Illinois, where at Krannert Centre for the Performing Arts he played Thomas More in A Man for All Seasons (July, 1977), Martin Dysart in Equus (July 1979), and directed The Canterbury Tales (1979), and The Runner Stumbles (1980); entered films, 1954, and has since appeared in numerous pictures; first appeared on television, 1957, as Abe Lincoln in Abe Lincoln in Illinois, and principal television appearances include: Strange Interlude, Berkeley Square, Kate, etc.

Favourite parts: Barney Greenwald and Martin Dysart. *Recreations:* Travel, music, and reading. *Club:* Savage. *Addresses:* 409 Brookens Drive, Urbana, Illinois 61801 *and* c/o London Management, 235–241 Regent Street, London, W1.

KNIGHT, Esmond, actor and singer
b East Sheen, Surrey, 4 May 1906; *s* of Francis Charles Knight and his wife Bertha Clara (Davis); *e* Westminster School; *m* (1) Frances Clare (mar dis); (2) Nora Swinburne.

Made his first appearance professionally, at the Old Vic, 12 Sept 1925, as Balthasar in The Merchant of Venice; while at the Vic, he also appeared in the chorus of various operas, and danced in ballets; in 1926, he toured with Russell Thorndike as Denis in Doctor Syn, and then returned to the Old Vic, 1926–7, to play juveniles; at the St James's, May 1927, played Valentine in Twelfth Night; Everyman, May 1927, Philips in The Return; he then toured for a year as Arthur Varwell in Yellow Sands, with the Birmingham Repertory company; at the Princes, July 1928, played Hobart in Contraband; Kingsway, Sept 1928, Mr Richmond in Thunder on the Left; Wyndham's, Oct 1928, Michael Allen in To What Red Hell? at the Gate, Jan 1929, and Kingsway, Feb 1929, Colonel Howard in Fashion; during 1929, played for six months in Paris, appearing in Maya, etc; at the Arts, Oct 1929, played Louis in Improper People; Criterion, Nov 1929, Michael in Art and Mrs Bottle; at Streatham, Apr 1930, Erik in The Man I Killed; Queen's, May 1930, Rosencrantz in Hamlet; at the Cambridge, Oct 1930, played for Henry Kendall in Charlot's Masquerade; Arts, Oct 1930, played Lionel Eno in Mr Eno, His Birth, Death, and Life; Gate, May 1931, The Young Syrian in Salome; Alhambra, Aug 1931, Johann Strauss Jun, in Waltzes from Vienna; Garrick, Jan 1932, The Singer in Volpone; Faculty of Arts, May 1932, Valentine in Love for Love; in Aug 1932, toured in Waltzes from Vienna; Drury Lane, Oct 1932, played Otto Bergmann in Wild Violets; Drury Lane, Apr 1934, Gypsy Hood in Three Sisters; Palace, Sept 1934, appeared in Streamline; Little, June 1936, played the Parasite and Chief Engineer in The Insect Play; Cambridge, July 1936, Danny in Night Must Fall; Little, Nov 1936, Richard, Duke of Gloucester in The King and Mistress Shore; Lyric, Feb 1937, Peter Marsh in Wise Tomorrow; Daly's, May 1937, de Waal in African Dawn; Arts, Sept 1937, Vincent Van Gogh in Van Gogh; Phoenix, Jan 1938, Johnson in The Melody that Got Lost; Playhouse, Apr 1938, again in The Insect Play; toured, 1938, as the Duke of Cheviot and Otto Fresch in Crest of the Wave; Phoenix, Dec 1938, Orsino in Twelfth Night; in Jan 1939, in conjunction with Wilson Barrett, opened at the King's, Hammersmith, in a season of repertory; at this theatre, Apr 1940, played Calvin Driscoll in Through the Night, and Alan Harper in The Peaceful Inn, and appeared in the last-mentioned part at the Duke of York's, May 1940; Open Air, July 1940, played Lysander in A Midsummer Night's Dream; joined the Navy in 1940, and while serving in HMS *Prince of Wales*, 1941, was blinded in the action against the *Bismarck;* partially regained his sight and was able to appear in the film The Silver Fleet, 1943; reappeared on the stage, at the Lyric, May 1944, when he played the English Soldier in Crisis in Heaven; Princes, Mar 1945, played Richard in Three Waltzes; King's Hammersmith, Mar–June 1946, with the Travelling Repertory Theatre company, appeared in Romeo and Juliet, Saint Joan, Man and Superman, In Time to Come, and Electra; Lyric, Hammersmith, Dec 1947, appeared as Worthy in The Relapse, and played the same part at the Phoenix, Jan 1948; joined the Shakespeare Memorial Theatre Company, at Stratford-on-Avon, for the 1948 season, appearing as Leontes, Gratiano, Christopher Sly, and the Ghost in Hamlet; Arts, Mar 1949, Dr Cornish in Caroline; Criterion, Oct 1950, played Williams in Who Is Sylvia?; during Sir Laurence Olivier's season at the St James's, May 1951, played Belzanor in Caesar and Cleopatra, and Menas in Antony and Cleopatra; appeared with his own company in Bermuda, Sept 1951; Duke of York's, Nov 1951, played Hugo in Héloise; Lyric, Hammersmith, Apr 1952, appeared as Salcedo in Montserrat; made his first appearance on the New York stage at the Ethel Barrymore, Feb 1953, as the Baron in The Emperor's Clothes; Prince's, London, Aug 1953, played Fred Nutting in Age of Consent; Phoenix, Jan 1955, succeeded Wilfrid Lawson as Sydney Redlitch in Bell,

Book and Candle; Hippodrome, June 1956, Captain Randolph Southard in The Caine Mutiny Court Martial; Queen's, Hornchurch, Jan 1957, Bernard Dulac in Head of the Family; Adelphi, Mar 1957, Mr Pinchwife in The Country Wife; Lyric, Hammersmith, Sept 1958, Serge Petugin in The Russian; May 1960, toured as Martin Keller in A Piece of Silver; Queen's, Mar 1961, played Ballested in The Lady From the Sea; joined the Royal Shakespeare Company at the Aldwych, Oct 1961, to take over the part of King Louis of France in Becket, and Nov 1961, the part of Baptista in The Taming of the Shrew; Garrick, Apr 1962, played Drake in Two Stars for Comfort; joined the Old Vic Company for its last season at the Old Vic, Sept 1962, to play the following parts: the Troll King, Herr von Eberkopf, and the Farmer of Heggstad in Peer Gynt, Antonio in The Merchant of Venice, Lovewit in The Alchemist, 1962; Pompey in Measure for Measure, 1963; Mermaid, Apr–May 1965, appeared in The Wakefield Mystery Plays, followed by Creon in Oedipus The King and Oedipus at Colonus, William Marshall in Left-Handed Liberty, Amphitryon in Four Thousand Brass Half-pennies, and Sir Tristam Mardon in Dandy Dick; Edinburgh Festival, Aug 1966, Camillo in The Winter's Tale, and at the Cambridge, Sept 1966; Strand, Apr 1967, General Bridgenorth in Getting Married; Hampstead Theatre Club, Apr 1969, Sam Pitt in The Black Swan Winter; Greenwich, Oct 1969, the Interlocutor in Martin Luther King, and Nov 1969, Admiral Lord Howe in Spithead; Royal Lyceum, Edinburgh, May 1970, Daddy in Mister; Greenwich, Sept 1970, Hans Joseph in The Servants and the Snow; Duchess, Feb 1971, again played Daddy in Mister; Manchester Royal Exchange, Oct 1973, Warburton in the 69 Theatre Company's production of The Family Reunion; also gave his one-man show, Agincourt—The Archer's Tale; Manchester Cathedral, Sept 1975, Alexander Gibbs in The Cocktail Party; Greenwich, Jan 1976, Tom in Love's Old Sweet Song; Cambridge, Aug 1976, took over Chebutykin in The Three Sisters; Open Air, Regent's Park, 1976 season, again performed Agincourt—The Archer's Tale, and played Chorus in Henry V; 69 Theatre Company, Manchester and also City of Munster Festival, May 1978, Marmelador in Crime and Punishment; for the same company, Feb 1979, appeared as Dr Warburton in The Family Reunion at Manchester, and also at the Round House in April, transferring to the Vaudeville in June, 1979; first appeared in films, 1931, and played recently in Anne of the Thousand Days, The Yellow Dog, Robin and Marian, etc; has also made numerous television appearances, including Man of Straw, Ballet Shoes, and Quiller.

Address: c/o Peter Eade Ltd, 9 Cork Street, London, W1.

KNIGHT, Joan, director
b 27 Sept 1924; *d* of Henry Knight and his wife Mary Agnes; *e* Larkhill Convent, Preston; trained for the stage at Bristol Old Vic Theatre School.

Worked with the Midland Theatre Company and Perth Theatre Company, 1952–57, beginning her career as a director while at Perth; director and administrator, Castle, Farnham, 1959–65; director, Ludlow Festival, 1967–69; artistic director, Perth Theatre, 1968–present, also director of productions, Pitlochry Festival Theatre, 1976–77; has directed at most of the major UK repertory theatres, including Bristol (Old Vic), Edinburgh (Royal Lyceum), Guildford (Arnaud), Leicester (Phoenix) and Nottingham (Playhouse); in London has directed six recastings of The Mousetrap, as well as The Gentle Avalanche, 1963, The Striplings, 1964, and Return Ticket, 1965; adaptations for the stage include Wuthering Heights, Jane Eyre, The Hound of the Baskervilles, and Great Expectations.

Address: Inchbank House, Main Street, Bridgend, Perth, Scotland.

KNIGHT, Shirley, actress
b Goessel, Kan, 5 July 1936; *d* of Noel Johnson Knight and his wife Virginia (Webster); *e* Phillips and Wichita Universities; *m* (1) Gene Persson (mar dis); (2) John Hopkins; trained for the stage with Erwin Piscator and Lee Strasberg.

First appeared on the stage in 1958 playing Alison in Look Back in Anger at the Pasadena Playhouse; made her NY début at the Theatre de Lys, 11 Nov 1963, playing Katherine in Journey to the Day; Morosco, June 1964, Irina in The Three Sisters; Warner Playhouse, Los Angeles, Mar 1965, Lulu in Dutchman; Cherry Lane, Jan 1966, Jenny Zubitsky in Better Luck Next Time and Helen Windsor in A Walk in Dark Places in a double bill called Rooms; Ethel Barrymore, Oct 1966, Constance in We Have Always Lived in the Castle; Bristol Old Vic, Oct 1967, Jean in And People All Around; Music Box, Mar 1969, Janet in The Watering Place; Gardner Centre, Brighton, 1970, Sara Melody in A Touch of the Poet; Nottingham Playhouse, July 1971, title-role in Antigone; Haymarket, Leicester, Oct 1973, in Economic Necessity; John Golden, Nov 1975, Carla in Kennedy's Children, for which she won a 'Tony' Award; McCarter Theater, Princeton, Oct 1976, Blanche in A Streetcar Named Desire; Chelsea Theater Center, Mar 1977, played Lt Lillian Holiday in Happy End; Drake Theater, Chicago, July 1977, Betty in Landscape of the Body, and at the Public, NY, Sept 1977; Dock St, Charleston, June 1978, Dorothea in A Lovely Sunday for Creve Coeur, and also Jan 1979 at the Hudson Guild, NY; Manhattan Theater Club, Sept 1979, Ruth in Losing Time; Studio Arena Theater, Buffalo, 1980, Lil in I Won't Dance; made her film début in 1959 in Five Gates to Hell, and has since appeared in Dark at the Top of the Stairs, Sweet Bird of Youth, The Group, Petulia, Dutchman, The Rain People, etc; has appeared on television in over two hundred plays, including a number by her husband, John Hopkins.

Favourite parts: Lulu in Dutchman and the lead in Economic Necessity. *Recreations:* Music, philosophy. *Address:* Actors Equity Association, 165 West 46th Street, New York, NY 10036.

KNOX, Alexander, actor
b Strathroy, Ontario, Canada, 16 Jan 1907; *s* of William John Knox and his wife Jean (Crozier); *e* University of Western Ontario; *m* Doris Nolan.

Made his first appearance on the stage at the Peabody Playhouse, Boston, Mass, USA, 12 Feb 1929, as John Purdie in Dear Brutus, and remained there until Nov 1930; made his first appearance in London at Wyndham's, 16 Dec 1930, as Ferdinand Steinberg in Smoky Cell; Embassy, Sept 1936, played Dillon in The Tiger; Westminster, Apr 1937, Larry in Anna Christie; Old Vic, Nov 1937–Apr 1938, Catesby in Richard III, Old Man and the Scotch Doctor in Macbeth, Snout in A Midsummer Night's Dream, Brabantio in Othello and Dr McGilp in The King of Nowhere, in which he scored a great success; Embassy, June 1938, Robert Gillet in Babes in the Wood; Saville, Nov 1938, The Judge in Geneva; Lyric, Feb 1939, Jim Settle in The Jealous God; appeared at the Malvern Festival, Aug 1939, in Good King Charles's Golden Days, and Old Master; then returned to America; at the 51st Street, Theatre, New York, May 1940, played Friar Laurence in Romeo and Juliet; Biltmore, Sept 1940, Dr Paul Venner in Jupiter Laughs; Hudson, Jan 1942, Jason Otis in Jason; Ethel Barrymore, Dec 1942, Baron Tuzenbach in The Three Sisters; Empire, Dec 1949, played Vail Trahern in The Closing Door, of which he was the author; returned to London and appeared at the Duke of York's, Nov 1950, as Gilbert Cotton in Return to Tyassi; at the King's, Edinburgh, Mar 1952, played Prof Thompson in Cupid and Psyche; St James's, Oct 1952, succeeded Michael Redgrave as Frank Elgin in Winter Journey; at the Old Vic, May 1953, appeared as Cardinal Wolsey in Henry VIII; Arts, Sept 1955, played John in The Burnt Flower Bed; Assembly Hall, Edinburgh, Aug 1968, Arnold Rubek in When We Dead Awaken; first entered films, 1938; went to Hollywood, 1943, and has appeared in numerous films, most notably as President Wilson in Wilson and in Accident, Khartoum, Nicholas and Alexandra, Puppet on a Chain, etc; television appearances include Meeting at Potsdam, 1976; is the author of the novels, Bride of Quietness, Night of the White Bear (1970), several detective novels, and of the plays Old Master, 1939; Red on White, 1963; The Closing Door, 1964.

Address: Actors Equity Association, 165 West 46th Street, New York, NY 10036.

KOBART, Ruth (*née* Ruth Maxine Kohn), actress, singer
b Des Moines, Iowa, 24 Apr 1924; *d* of Morris L Kohn and his wife Sadie (Finkelstein); *e* American Conservatory of Music, Chicago (B Mus, 1945), Hunter College (MA 1959).

Made her first appearance on the stage at the Jewish Community Center, Des Moines, 1934, in a dance recital; made her professional singing début with the Lemonade Opera Company, Greenwich Mews Playhouse, 27 June 1947, as the Witch, Rosina Daintymouth, in Hansel and Gretel; at the same theatre and with the same Opera Company, sang the title-role in The Duenna, June 1948, Clarissa in The Man in the Moon, June 1949, The Mother in The Stranger, Aug 1949, and Manuela in Don Pedro, June 1953; made her Broadway début at the Shubert, 30 Nov 1955, in the chorus and as understudy to Helen Traubel in Pipe Dream, playing this part some twenty times; toured with the NBC Opera Company, 1956–7; was a member of the New York City Opera Company from 1958–66, appearing in such roles as Augusta Tabor in The Ballad of Baby Doe, Miss Todd in The Old Maid and the Thief, Nettie in Carousel, Mrs Ott in Susannah, Emma Jones in Street Scene, Katisha in The Mikado, the Mayor's Wife in The Inspector General, and roles in Die Schweigsame Frau, The Rape of Lucretia, etc; American Pavilion, Brussels World's Fair, summer 1958, played Agatha in the opera Maria Golovin; Martin Beck, Nov 1958, repeated this last part in the American première; Greenwich Mews, Mar 1959, Manuela in the Lemonade Opera production of Olé; with the Little Orchestra Society has appeared in performances of Babar the Elephant, 1953; Hansel and Gretel, 1954, The Thirteen Clocks, 1958, and The Apothecary, 1960; 46th Street, Oct 1961, played Miss Jones in How to Succeed in Business Without Really Trying; Alvin, May 1962, Domina in A Funny Thing Happened on the Way to the Forum; New York City Center, Dec 1965, Aunt Eller in Oklahoma!; joined the American Conservatory Theatre in 1967, and at the Geary, San Francisco, has played Madame Pernelle in Tartuffe, Jan 1967; Madame Pampinelli in The Torchbearers, Feb 1967; Lady Hurf in Thieves' Carnival, Aug 1968, Mommy in The American Dream, Dec 1968; ANTA, Oct 1969, with ACT, played Olivia in A Flea in Her Ear and Anfisa in The Three Sisters; toured, 1970, as Mrs Margolin in Forty Carats, as the Maid in Boeing, Boeing, and in Last of the Red Hot Lovers; Curran, San Francisco, May 1971, Mistress Schermerhorn in Knickerbocker Holiday; Geary, San Francisco, Jan 1975, appeared in Street Scene; Dorothy Chandler Pavilion, Los Angeles, May 1975, Miss Jones in How to Succeed in Business Without Really Trying; Geary, Feb 1978, appeared in Hotel Paradiso; toured, 1979, as Miss Hannigan in Annie; first appeared in films, 1966, in How to Succeed in Business Without Really Trying; first

appeared on television in 1952 in the NBC Television Opera production Gianni Schicchi, and since has sung in The Marriage of Figaro, Macbeth, Maria Golovin, The Consul, etc.

Favourite parts: Domina, and Augusta Tabor. *Address:* c/o Fifi Oscard Associates, 19 West 44th Street, New York, NY 10036.

KOHLER, Estelle, actress
b South Africa, 28 Mar; *d* of Charles William Henry Kohler, and his wife, *née* Sussens; *e* Cape Town University, South Africa; trained for the stage at RADA.

First appeared on the stage in 1961 at the Hofmeyer Theatre, Cape Town, South Africa as Evelyn Foreman in The Tenth Man; other parts played in South Africa include Anya in The Cherry Orchard; joined the Royal Shakespeare Company at Stratford, 1966, to play Ophelia in Hamlet, Apr and Olivia in Twelfth Night, June 1966; Helena in All's Well That Ends Well, June and Juliet in Romeo and Juliet, Sept 1967; returning to the company, 1970, played Isabella in Measure for Measure, Apr, Silvia in The Two Gentlemen of Verona, July, and Miranda in The Tempest, Oct; made her London début at the Aldwych, Dec 1970, when she repeated her performance of Silvia; Aldwych, Oct 1971, Beatrice Justice in Exiles; The Place, also Oct 1971, Angelica in Occupations; Aldwych, Nov 1971, Carmen in The Balcony; Aldwych, Dec 1972, Gwenhwyvar in The Island of the Mighty; Stratford, season 1973, played Juliet in Romeo and Juliet, Mar and Rosaline in Love's Labour's Lost, Aug; The Place, Oct 1973, Voice 2 in Sylvia Plath; Aldwych, Aug 1974, Varvara in Summerfolk; Aldwych, 1975, again played Rosaline, Apr and played Sarah, Lady Cottesham in The Marrying of Anne Leete, Sept; 1976, Judith in the Devil's Disciple, Anna in Ivanov; Crucible, Sheffield, 1977, played Hedda in Hedda Gabler; Roundhouse, June 1977, Woman Downtown in The Red Devil Battery Sign, transferring to the Phoenix in July; Open Space, July 1978, Sally in Boo Hoo; New End, Hampstead, April 1979, She in La Musica; co-devisor of a National Theatre platform performance based on the biblical *Song of Songs*, also performing it at the Jerusalem Spring Festival; she is an Associate Artist of the Royal Shakespeare Company; first television appearance, 1968, New York in The Admirable Crichton; recent appearances include The Beaux' Stratagem.

Favourite parts: Juliet and Ophelia. *Recreation:* Cooking. *Address:* c/o Duncan Heath, 57 Redcliffe Road, London SW10.

KOLTAI, Ralph, designer
b Berlin, 31 July 1924; *s* of Dr Alfred Koltai and his wife Charlotte (Weinstein); *e* Berlin and Central School of Arts and Crafts, Holborn, London.

Designed his first production, the opera Angelique, at the Fortune, Feb 1950; has since designed over 130 operas, plays and ballets in Argentina, Australia, Austria, Bulgaria, Canada, Denmark, France, Germany, Italy, Norway, the United Kingdom, and the United States; he is an Associate of the Royal Shakespeare Company; productions include: The Caucasian Chalk Circle, 1962, The Representative, 1963, The Birthday Party, Endgame, The Jew of Malta, 1964, The Merchant of Venice, Timon of Athens, 1965, Little Murders, 1967, Major Barbara, 1970, Too True to be Good, 1975, Old World, Wild Oats, 1976, Love's Labour's Lost, 1978; at The Other Place: The Mouthorgan (devised), 1975, Sons of Light, 1978, Hippolytus, 1979, Baal, 1979; Romeo and Juliet 1980; for The National Theatre: As You Like It, 1967, Back to Methuselah, 1968, State of Revolution, 1977, The Guardsman, Brand, 1978, Richard III, The Wild Duck, 1979; Chichester: The Tempest, 1968, Oedipus Tyrannus, 1974; West End includes: Billy (Drury Lane, 1974), Rosmersholm (Haymarket, 1978); Opera includes: for The Royal Opera House: Taverner, 1972, The Icebreak, 1979; for The English National Opera (previously Sadler's Wells): Carmen, 1961, Murder in the Cathedral, 1962, The Rise and Fall of the City of Mahagonny, 1963, Duke Bluebeard's Castle, 1972; The Ring Cycle, from 1970; The Seven Deadly Sins, 1978; for Scottish Opera: Don Giovanni, 1964, Boris Godunov, 1965, The Rake's Progress, 1967, Elegy for Young Lovers, 1970, Otello, 1964 and 1975; Head of Theatre Department, Central School of Art and Design, 1965–73; received the London Drama Critics Award for As You Like It and Little Murders, 1967; co-winner of the Individual Gold Medal for Stage Design—Prague Quadriennale, 1975; co-winner of 'Golden Troika' National Award, Prague, 1979; received Designer of the Year Award, Society of West End Theatres in 1978, for Brand.

Address: c/o PL Representation, 194 Old Brompton Road, London SW5 0AS. *Tel:* 01–373 1161.

KOPIT, Arthur, playwright
b New York City, 10 May 1937; *s* of George Kopit and his wife Maxine (Dubin); *e* Harvard University (BA 1959); *m* Leslie Ann Garis.

Author of the following plays, the early ones produced at Harvard University: The Questioning of Nick, 1957, which he adapted and directed for television, 1959; Gemini, and with Wally Lawrence Don Juan in Texas, On the Runway of Life You Never Know What's Coming Off Next, 1957; Across the River and into the Jungle, 1958; Sing to Me Through Open Windows, To Dwell in a Palace of Strangers, 1959; Oh Dad, Poor Dad, Mama's Hung You in the Closet and I'm Feelin' So Sad, 1960, London, 1961, NY, 1962, and Paris, in a production he directed at the Théâtre des Bouffes-Parisiens, Oct 1963; The Day the Whores Came Out to Play Tennis, Mhil'daim, 1963; What the Gentlemen Are Up To, And As for the Ladies, 1964; Sing to Me Through Open Windows produced in NY, 1965; The Conquest of Everest, produced on television, 1966; Indians, produced by the Royal Shakespeare Company, Aldwych, 4 July 1968, Arena Stage, Washington, DC, and HY, 1969; Secrets of the Rich, 1976; Wings, 1978; received the Outer Circle and the Vernon Rice Awards for Oh Dad, Poor Dad, Mama's Hung You in the Closet and I'm Feelin' So Sad; adjunct professor of playwriting, Yale School of Drama, 1979– .

Clubs: Hasty Pudding, Harvard. *Address:* The Dramatists Guild, 234 West 44th Street, New York, NY 10036.

KOPS, Bernard, playwright
b Stepney, London, 28 Nov 1926; *s* of Joel Kops, and his wife Jenny Zetter; *e* Stepney Jewish School; *m* Erica Gordon; formerly a bookseller.

Is the author of the following plays: The Hamlet of Stepney Green, Goodbye World, Change for the Angel, The Dream of Peter Mann, Stray Cats and Empty Bottles, Enter Solly Gold, and David It Is Getting Dark; is the author of the radio play Home Sweet Honeycomb and television plays including: Just One Kid, It's a Lovely Day Tomorrow, and Moss; has also published novels and poems as well as an autobiography, The World is a Wedding; resident dramatist, Bristol Old Vic, 1958.

Recreation: Cooking. *Club:* Arts. *Address:* Flat 1, 35 Canfield Gardens, London, NW6. *Tel:* 01–437 7888.

KOSSOFF, David, actor
b London, 24 Nov 1919; *s* of Louis Kossoff and his wife Anne Rebecca (Shaklovitz); *e* Elementary, art and architecture schools; *m* Jennie Jenkins; formerly an interior designer and aircraft draftsman; studied for the stage privately.

Made his first appearance at the Unity Theatre, Nov 1942, as Juan Rojo in Spanish Village; remained at the Unity until 1945, during which time he wrote and directed many shelter and troop shows; joined the BBC Repertory Company, Aug 1945, remaining until Oct 1951; Wyndham's, June 1952, took over the part of Colonel Alexander Ikonenko in The Love of Four Colonels; Princes, Feb 1953, played Sam Tager in The Shrike; Arts, June 1953, Morry in The Bespoke Overcoat; Arts, July 1953, Tobit in Tobias and the Angel; Savoy, Dec 1953, Prof Lodegger in No Sign of the Dove; Embassy, Jan 1954, played Nathan in The Boychik, and again appeared as Morry in The Bespoke Overcoat; Embassy, Jan 1955, played Mendele in The World of Sholom Aleichem; New, Oxford, Sept 1956, played Prince Basilios in Gates of Summer; Johannesburg, 1957, appeared in his original part in The World of Sholom Aleichem; Arts, London, May 1957, appeared as *raconteur* in a solo programme, With One Eyebrow Slightly Up; Lyric, Hammersmith, Oct 1959, played Elias in Man on Trial; at the Palladium, June 1960, appeared in the revue Stars in Your Eyes; Comedy, Apr 1961, played Schlissel in The Tenth Man; Prince of Wales, Feb 1962, Mr Baker in Come Blow Your Horn; Prince Charles, Oct 1963, appeared in his own one-man show Kossoff at the Prince Charles; Liverpool Playhouse, Aug 1965, Morris Seidman in Seidman and Son; Australia, Mar 1966, appeared in his one-man-show at The Arts, Adelaide; Wilbur, Boston, USA, Dec 1966, played Cohen in Two Weeks Somewhere Else; Theatre de Lys, off-Broadway, New York, Jan 1967, oneman-show A Funny Kind of Evening with David Kossoff; Arnaud, Guildford, Oct 1969, played Jacob Mann in his own play On Such a Night; Mermaid, Jan 1970, Morry Swartz in Enter Solly Gold; Palladium, Dec 1971, Baron Hardup in Cinderella; Belgrade, Coventry, Sept 1972, and Criterion, Dec 1972, Aaron Bromberg in Bunny; since 1973 has appeared frequently in his second one-man show, As According to Kossoff; films include A Kid for Two Farthings, A Woman for Joe, and House of Secrets; has appeared in numerous television programmes, including Mr Larkin in The Larkins, Little Big Business, and Storytime (telling his own Bible stories).

Favourite parts: Big ones. *Hobbies:* Writing bestsellers. *Recreation:* The theatre. *Address:* 45 Roe Green Close, Hatfield, Herts.

KRASNA, Norman, dramatic author
b Corona, Long Island, New York, 7 Nov 1909; *e* NY and Columbia Universities, and Law School of St John's University, Brooklyn.

Film critic of *New York World*, 1928; drama editor of *New York Evening Graphic*, 1929; is the author of Louder Please, 1931; Small Miracle, 1934; The Man with Blond Hair (also directed), 1941; Dear Ruth, 1944; John Loves Mary, 1947; Time for Elizabeth (with Groucho Marx; also directed), 1948; Kind Sir, 1953; Who Was That Lady I Saw You With? 1958; Sunday in New York, 1961; Watch the Birdie, 1964; Love in E Flat, 1967; Kein Problem (Berlin), 1969; Bunny (London), 1972; We Interrupt This Program . . ., 1975; Lady Harry (London), 1978; has also written original stories and screenplays for more than twenty-five films, including: Fury, Bachelor Mother, The Devil and Miss Jones, Indiscreet, Princess O'Rourke (for which he received the Academy Award, 1943), White Christmas, Sunday in New York, etc; received Screen Writers Guild Laurel Award, 1959; has served as producer of several films, 1952 to present.

Address: 1807 Blonay, Switzerland.

KRETZMER, Herbert, critic and dramatic author
b Kroonstad, Orange Free State, South Africa, 5 Oct 1925; *e* Rhodes University, Grahamstown; *m* Elisabeth Margaret Wilson.

Entered journalism, 1946; drama critic, *Daily Express,* London, 1962–78; television critic, *Daily Mail,* London; wrote book and lyrics of Our Man Crichton, presented at the Shaftesbury, Dec 1964; lyrics for The Four Musketeers, Drury Lane, Dec 1967; lyric writing in other fields includes the film Hieronymus Merkin, regular contributions to That Was The Week That Was and other television shows, and several hit songs.

Address: 55 Lincoln House, Basil Street, London, SW3. *Tel:* 01–589 2541.

KRUPSKA, Danya, dancer and choreographer
b Fall River, Massachusetts, 23 Aug 1923; *d* of Bronislaw Krupski and his wife Anna (Niementowska); *e* Lankenau School for Girls, Philadelphia, and dance with Ethel Phillips Dance Studio, Catherine Littlefield Ballet Studio, Mordkin Studio, Philadelphia and New York, Aubrey Hitchins Studio, with Egorova in Paris, Syvilla Fort; studied acting with Robert Lewis, 1952–3; *m* (1) Richard La Marr (mar dis); (2) Ted Thurston.

Has danced since the age of six in concerts in Philadelphia and in Europe, touring under the name of Dania Darling in Poland, Rumania, Austria, Hungary, Palestine, etc, until 1937; toured Europe with the Catherine Littlefield Ballet, 1937, and danced with that company in Chicago, 1938; joined George Balanchine's American Ballet Company, 1938; was a soloist with the Radio City Music Hall Ballet, 1939–40; made her dramatic début when she took over the title-role of Johnny Belinda from Helen Craig in the touring production; Royale, Aug 1943, danced in the revue Chauve Souris; toured as the Dream Laurey in Oklahoma! 1943–5, and played this part in the NY production at the St James, Sept 1945–June 1946; became assistant to Agnes de Mille and served in that capacity for the choreography of Allegro, 1947, the Ballet Theatre production of Fall River Legend, in which she danced the role of Lizzie Borden, Metropolitan Opera House, Apr 1948, The Rape of Lucretia, 1948, and Gentlemen Prefer Blondes, 1949; choreographed Seventeen, 1951; assistant to Agnes de Mille for the choreography of Paint Your Wagon, 1951; Shubert, May 1953, played Mimi and assistant choreographer to Michael Kidd for Can-Can; Mark Hellinger, Mar 1954, Hattie Hopkins and standby for Renée Jeanmaire as Lisette Gervais in The Girl in Pink Tights, playing the last role a number of times; choreographed Shoestring Revue, 1955; The Most Happy Fella, 1956; Annie Get Your Gun, Rose Marie, Guys and Dolls, Gentlemen Prefer Blondes, Oklahoma!, The King and I, The Most Happy Fella at the State Fair Music Hall, Dallas, Texas, 1957–8; The Carefree Heart (tour), 1957; The Most Happy Fella (NY), 1958; The Gypsy Baron for the Metropolitan Opera, 1959; Oh, Kay! 1960; the ballet Pointes on Jazz for the American Ballet Theatre, The Happiest Girl in the World, Show Boat, 1961; Fiorello! 1962; Rugantino (Rome), Apollo and Miss Agnes (Dallas), 1963; Rugantino (NY), That Hat (also directed), 1964; Her First Roman, 1968; Zorba at the National, Reykjavik, Iceland, 1970; Company, and The Fantasticks, at the Storan, Gothenburg, Sweden, 1971; Oklahoma! (also directed), National Theatre, Reykjavik, 1972; No, No, Nanette, Porgy and Bess (also directed), both Malmo, 1973; Joseph and the Amazing Technicolor Dreamcoat (also directed), Philadelphia, Gabrielle, Buffalo, NY, 1974; A Report to the Stockholders, Rex, 1975; Showboat, Malmo, 1976; Chicago (also directed), Copen-hagen, 1977; Cabaret, Helsingborg, Guys and Dolls (also directed), Arrhus, 1978; Once Upon a Mattress (also directed), Reykjavik, 1979; has also directed and choreographed for the North Shore Music Circus, etc; has choreographed the television production of The Ballad of Tom Sawyer, 1956, Burlesque, 1957, HMS Pinafore, 1959, Salute to the Peace Corps, 1966, and for *The Buick Hour, The Colgate Comedy Hour,* etc.

Address: 564 West 52nd Street, New York, NY 10019. *Tel:* CI 7–2945.

KULUKUNDIS, Eddie, producing manager
b London, 20 Apr 1932; *s* of George Elias Kulukundis, and his wife Eugenie (Diacakis); *e* Collegiate School, New York, Salisbury School, Connecticut, and Yale University.

Has presented or co-presented the following productions in London, unless otherwise stated: Enemy 1969; The Happy Apple, Poor Horace, The Friends, How the Other Half Loves, Tea Party and The Basement (double bill), The Wild Duck, The Disorderly Women, 1970; After Haggerty, Hamlet, Skyvers, Charley's Aunt, The Owl and the Pussycat Went to See, The Plotters of Cabbage Patch Corner, Straight Up, How the Other Half Loves (Broadway), 1971; London Assurance, Journey's End, The Old Ones, A Pagan Place, The Plotters of Cabbage Patch Corner, Between the Bars, 1972; Small Craft Warnings, A Private Matter, Cromwell, The Farm, Dandy Dick, 1973; The Maids, The Waltz of the Toreadors, Life Class, Children, Pygmalion, The Great Society, Play Mas, The Gentle Hook, Sherlock Holmes (Broadway), London Assurance (Broadway), 1974; Don's Party, A Little Night Music, Entertaining Mr Sloane, Loot, The Gay Lord Quex, What the Butler Saw, Travesties, Lies, The Sea Gull, A Month in the Country, A Room with a View, Too True to be Good, Travesties (Broadway), The Bed Before Yesterday, 1975; Banana Ridge, Dimetos, Old Flames, Wild Oats, 1976; Candida, Man and Superman, Once A Catholic, 1977; Privates On Parade, Flying Blind, Gloo Joo, 1978; Bent, Once a Catholic (Broadway), Last of the Red Hot Lovers, 1979; Born in the Gardens, Beecham, 1980.

Club: Garrick. *Address:* c/o Knightsbridge Theatrical Productions Ltd, 2 Goodwin's Court, St Martin's Lane, London, WC2. *Tel:* 01–240 2196.

KUSTOW, Michael, director and writer
b London, 18 Nov 1939; *s* of Marcus Kustow and his wife Sarah (Cohen); *e* Haberdasher's Aske's, Wadham College, Oxford and Bristol University; *m* (1) Elisabeth Leigh (mar dis); (2) Orna Spector.

With the Théâtre Nationale Populaire, 1960–61, played Duc de Buckingham in Les Trois Mousquetaires, appeared in Edward II, and assisted Roger Planchon in his direction of Schweyk in World War II; co-wrote (with Adrian Mitchell) and directed the street pageant Punch and Judas, Trafalgar Square, 1962; with the RSC from 1963–67, he founded Theatregoround, the mobile theatre unit, and worked as assistant to Peter Brook on productions including US, to which he contributed material; at the ICA, 1968–71, work included the direction of I Wonder, which he co-wrote with Adrian Henri; associate director, 1973–present, National Theatre, with a special responsibility for the NT's Platform Performances; for these has directed work by Brecht, Ted Hughes, Philip Larkin, Robert Lowell, Groucho Marx, Pinter, Frederick Raphael, etc, plays by Woody Allen, Vaclav Havel, Peter Handke, and Iris Murdoch, and all of Shakespeare's Sonnets; adapted Anatol, 1979; The Soldier's Tale, 1980.

Address: 84 Etheldene Avenue, London N10.

KYLE, Barry, director

b London, 25 Mar 1947; *s* of Albert Ernest Kyle and his wife Edith Ivy (Gaskin); *e* Beal Grammar School and Birmingham University (BA, 1968; MA, 1969); *m* the actress Chrissy Iddon.

Chairman, Birmingham University Theatre Group, 1967–68; after early work with Ed Berman, began his professional career on a Thames TV bursary as associate director of the Liverpool Playhouse, 1969–71, where he directed 21 productions including his first, Saved, 1969; Oh, What a Lovely War, 1970; Prometheus Bound, 1971; The Odd Couple, 1972; directed at York, 1972; in 1973 joined The RSC, for which he directed his dramatic portrait, Sylvia Plath, at the Place, 20 Oct; for the RSC in London and Stratford he has since directed Comrades, 1974; co-directed King John, Cymbeline, 1974; directed Richard III, 1975, and co-directed Perkin Warbeck, Cymbeline; directed Dingo, 1976, co-directed Romeo and Juliet, Troilus and Cressida, King Lear; directed That Good Between Us, Frozen Assets, Dingo, 1977; Measure for Measure, The Churchill Play, 1978; The Churchill Play, The White Guard, Sore Throats, Julius Caesar, Measure for Measure, 1979; The Maid's Tragedy, 1980; directed The Merchant of Venice for the Cameri, Tel Aviv, 1980.

Recreations: Politics, sport, music, owls. *Address:* Royal Shakespeare Company, Aldwych Theatre, London WC2.

L

LACK, Simon (*né* Macalpine), actor
b Cleland, Scotland, 19 Dec 1917; *s* of Alexander Macalpine and his wife Euphemia (Ritchie); *e* Eastbank Academy, Glasgow.

First appeared on the stage at the Lyceum, Edinburgh, 3 June 1935, in a small part in The Letter; remained with the Brandon-Thomas repertory companies at Edinburgh and Glasgow, 1935–7; first appeared on the West End stage at the Duke of York's, 13 Sept 1938, as Tom Buchlyvie in The Last Trump; played a number of parts at the Q, King's Hammersmith, and Richmond Theatres, 1938; Westminster, Nov 1939, played Rupert Amesbury in Music at Night; served with the Lancashire Fusiliers and The Buffs, 1940–6, being mentioned in despatches; reappeared on the stage at the Arts, May 1946, as David Cedar in You Won't Need the Halo; Lyric, Hammersmith, Oct 1946, David Herold in The Assassin; Aldwych, Jan 1947, played Gilbert Frobisher in Jane; Strand, June 1948, Sextus Tarquinius in Cage Me A Peacock; Criterion, July 1949, took over the part of Tom Wright in Travellers' Joy; Savoy, Nov 1951, played the Hon Peter Ingleton in Relative Values; New, Feb 1954, Jack Chesney in Charley's Aunt; Globe, May 1965, Tarver in The Chinese Prime Minister; Duke of York's, Nov 1971, Colonel Stewart in The Douglas Cause; has also appeared in films and on television, recently in *Enemy at the Door* and Telford's Change.
Favourite parts: Richard in Ah! Wilderness, and Dan in Night Must Fall. *Recreations:* Tennis, swimming and reading. *Address:* 9 Cork Street, London, W1. *Tel:* 01–734 3433.

LACY-THOMPSON, Charles Robert, solicitor
b 13 June 1922; *s* of Thomas Alexander Lacy-Thompson and his wife Vera Florence; *e* Charterhouse, Trinity College, Cambridge and University of Virginia.

After war service, 1942–46, became an articled clerk to McKenna & Co, solicitors, 1947–49; information officer, 1951–55, for British Information Services in Washington DC and San Francisco; senior contracts officer, Rediffusion Television Ltd, 1955–66; since 1966 secretary and legal adviser to the Society of West End Theatre, Theatrical Management Association, and Theatres National Committee; joint secretary, London and Provincial Theatre Councils.
Recreation: Lawn tennis. *Address:* Bedford Chambers, The Piazza, Covent Garden, London WC2E 8HQ. *Tel:* 836 0971.

LAFFAN, Kevin Barry, dramatist
b Reading, Berks, 24 May 1922; *s* of Patrick Laffan and his wife Amelia (Old); *m* Jeanne Thompson.

Formerly an actor and director; wrote his first play, First Innocent, 1957, under the name of Kevin Barry; this was presented at the Everyman, Reading, which he ran for seven years; plays he has since written include: The Superannuated Man, 1967 (Irish Life Drama Award, Dublin Festival); Zoo, Zoo, Widdershins, Zoo, 1969 (NUS Drama Festival best play award); It's A Two Foot Six Inches Above the Ground World, 1970 (London début); There Are Humans at the Bottom of My Garden, 1972; Never So Good, 1977; The Wandering Jew, 1979; writing for television, since 1961,

includes Lucky for Some, You Can Only Buy Once; creator of the series *Beryl's Lot* and *Emmerdale Farm*.
Recreations: Reading, walking. *Address:* c/o ACTAC, 16 Cadogan Lane, London, W1. *Tel:* 01–235 2797.

LAHR, John, critic and author
b Los Angeles, Cal, 12 July 1941; *s* of Bert Lahr, the actor and his wife Mildred (Schroeder); *e* Riverdale Country Day School, Yale University, and Worcester College, Oxford University; *m* Anthea Mander.

Is a drama critic for the Village Voice, NY; has also written Notes on a Cowardly Lion a biography of his father, 1969; Up Against the Fourth Wall, 1970; a Casebook on Harold Pinter's The Homecoming (with his wife), Showcase I, as editor, 1971; Astonish Me, The Autograph Hound (novel), Life-Show, 1973; Prick Up Your Ears, a biography of Joe Orton, 1978; with John Hancock wrote the script of the film Sticky My Fingers, Fleet My Feet; is a member of PEN, the Drama Desk, Drama Critics Circle, and is on the Board of Directors of Choreoconcerts.
Recreations: Fishing, squash, softball. *Address:* 418 East 88th Street, New York, NY 10028. *Tel:* 289–3533.

LAIRD, Jenny, actress
b Manchester, 13 Feb 1917; *d* of Edward Laird and his wife Phyllis Taylor; *e* Maidstone High School and London University; *m* John Fernald; was formerly a copy-writer in an advertising agency; studied for the stage under Kate Rorke and Elsie Fogerty.

Made her first appearance on the stage at the Brixton Theatre, with the repertory company, 1936, as Sydney Fairfield in A Bill of Divorcement; at Richmond, Nov 1937, played Jill Silverton in Spangled Hemp; first appeared in London, at the Garrick Theatre, 6 Jan 1938, as Daphne in This Money Business; Haymarket, June 1938, played Inga Angers in Comedienne; Arts and Haymarket, Oct 1938, Caroline Firbanks in A Party for Christmas; Vaudeville, 1939, Carol in Goodness, How Sad!; Westminster, Oct 1939, Anne Winter in Music at Night; Dec 1939, Jenny Hill in Major Barbara; Kingsway, Apr 1940, Bubbles Thompson in While Parents Sleep; Torch, May 1940, Roberta in Portrait of Helen; Richmond, June 1940, Ginette in Between Five and Seven; Westminster, Aug 1940, Judy Evison in Cornelius; Arts, June 1943, Mary in The Judgment of Doctor Johnson; Westminster, Aug 1943, Morag in Mr Bolfry; Arts, Nov 1943, Rose in The Recruiting Officer, and July 1945, Nora Helmer in A Doll's House; Scala, Mar 1946, Marion in A Century for George, and Sally Edwards in The Face of Coal; New Lindsey, Apr 1947, appeared as Jeannie in The 49th State; Mercury, Aug 1947, Jane Claire Clairmont in The Shelley Story; Embassy, Oct 1947, Doreen Benner in Deliver My Darling; Arts, Feb 1949, Ida in The Unquiet Spirit; Embassy, Apr 1949, Catherine Villiers in A Woman in Love; Arts, June 1949, Miss Roberts in The Mollusc; Phoenix, Jan 1950, Fan in The Non-Resident; Embassy, June 1950, appeared as Olwen Arvon in The White Eagles; Arts, July 1950, Ellie Dunn in Heartbreak House; Arts, Feb 1951, Thenichka in Spring at Marino; also Dec 1951, Janet Cannot in The Great Adventure; Westminster, Jan 1952, played

Charmian in Sunset in Knightsbridge; New Boltons, Feb 1952, Emma in Still Waters and Cora Prodmore in The High Bid; Arts, Mar 1952, Sophia Alexandrovna in Uncle Vanya, and Apr 1953, Masha in The Seagull; Westminster, July 1953, appeared as Capt A Graham, WRAC, in Carrington VC; Arts, Apr 1954, played Pauline Lambert in The Sun Room; Duke of York's, May 1956, Stella in The House by the Lake; Lyceum, Edinburgh, Feb 1962, played Christine Fletcher in Return to Mirredal; toured, Sept 1965, as Mike's Mother in Dear Wormwood; New Arts, Feb 1966, Mum in A Smashing Day; Edinburgh Festival, Aug 1966, Mother Gothel in The Wrong Side of the Moon; at Meadowbrook Theatre, Detroit, US, appeared in the following parts: Mrs Clandon in You Never Can Tell, Ella Rentheim in John Gabriel Borkmann, 1967; Arkadina in The Seagull, Queen Jemima in The Applecart, 1968; Queen Leda in Amphitryon '38, 1969; at the same theatre and the Institute of Arts, Detroit, played Julia in The Cocktail Party, Mary Tyrone in Long Day's Journey into Night, 1969; Madame Ranevsky in The Cherry Orchard, 1970, also making her New York début in the role at the ANTA theatre, May 1970; Octagon, Bolton, 1971, the Nurse in The Father, and Mrs Goforth in The Milk Train Doesn't Stop Here Any More; Newcastle, 1971, for Tyneside Theatre Company, Madame Ranevsky in The Cherry Orchard; Shaw, 1972, appeared in After Magritte, and The Real Inspector Hound (double bill); toured, June 1975, as Monica Bare in Murder Mistaken; film appearances include: Painted Boats, Wanted for Murder, and Black Narcissus; TV includes The Forsyte Saga and *The Onedin Line*, Lillie, and Henry IV, Part 2; author (with John Fernald) of And No Birds Sing, 1945; Hannibal's Way (adaptation), 1954; A Fig for Glory (adaptation), 1958.

Recreation: Gardening. *Hobby:* Cats. *Address:* 2 Daleham Mews, London, NW3. *Tel:* 01–435 2992.

LAMBERT, J W, CBE, DSC, dramatic critic
b London, 21 Apr 1917; *s* of Walter Henry Lambert and his wife Ethel Mary (Mutton); *e* Tonbridge School; *m* Catherine Margaret Read, Hon ARCM.

Associate Editor and Chief Reviewer of *The Sunday Times*, Literary and Arts Editor, 1960–76; London critic of *Drama* since 1951; deputy theatre critic of *The Sunday Times*; regular broadcaster on the theatre in Critics Circle, Choosing a Library and other BBC programmes; member of National Council, British Theatre Association; member of British Council Drama Advisory Committee; Chairman, 1967–8; Member of Arts Council Drama Panel 1966–8; Chairman, 1968–76; Member of Arts Council Theatre Enquiry, 1968–70; Vice-Chairman, Arts Council New Activities Committee, 1969–70; author of Drama in Britain 1964–73; Member of Council of RADA, 1972– ; Chairman, Old Vic Trust, 1977–8; Director Theatres Investment Fund, 1972– ; Chairman, Opera 80, 1979– ; awarded the Distinguished Service Cross, 1944; received the CBE, in 1970 Birthday Honours; Officier de L'Ordre des Arts et des Lettres, 1975.

Recreation: Singing. *Clubs:* Garrick and Beefsteak. *Address:* 30 Belsize Grove, London, NW3. *Tel:* 01–722 1668.

LAN, David, playwright
b Cape Town, 1 June 1952; *s* of Chaim Joseph Lan and Lois Carklin; *e* University of Cape Town and London School of Economics; also a social anthropologist.

His first play, Painting a Wall, was produced at the Almost Free Theatre, 1974; has since written Bird Child, produced 1974; Paradise, Homage to Been Soup, 1975; Not in Norwich, The Winter Dancers, 1977; Red Earth, 1978; Sergeant Ola and His Followers, 1979; The Winter Dancers produced

by Phoenix in NY, 1979; the same play won the John Whiting Award, 1977.

Address: c/o Margaret Ramsay Ltd, 14A Goodwin's Court, St Martin's Lane, London WC2.

LAND, David, producing manager
b London, 22 May 1920; *s* of Solomon Land and his wife Sarah; *e* Davenant Foundation Grammar School, London; *m* Alexandra Zara Levinson.

After war service with the RASC, formed David Land (Agency) Limited, specializing in open air international attractions; in this role introduced the Harlem Globetrotters to Europe; secretary and administrator since 1948 of the Dagenham Girl Pipers; in May 1969 became personal manager to Tim Rice and Andrew Lloyd Webber; deputy chairman since 1979, Robert Stigwood Group; has co-produced Jesus Christ Superstar, New York 1971, London 1972; Joseph and the Amazing Technicolor Dreamcoat, London 1973; Jeeves, London 1975; Evita, London 1978, Broadway 1979 (Tony award).

Recreations: Sport, Churchilliana, poker and bridge. *Address:* 118–120 Wardour Street, London W1 *and* Nevill House, Nevill Road, Rottingdean, Sussex. *Tel:* 01-437 3224.

LANDEN, Dinsdale, actor
b Margate, Kent, 4 Sept 1932; *s* of Edward James Landen, and his wife Winifred Alice; *e* King's School, Rochester; *m* Jennifer Daniel; trained for the stage at the Florence Moore Theatre Studios, Hove, Sussex.

First appeared on the stage Nov 1948, at the Dolphin Theatre, Brighton, as Bimbo in Housemaster; toured Australia with the Old Vic, 1955; first appeared on the London stage in May 1957, at the Piccadilly, as Archie Gooch in A Dead Secret; Saville, Jan 1958, played John Lester in A Touch of the Sun; Arts, Oct 1959, Ben Birt in My Friend Judas; at the Memorial Theatre, Stratford, summer season 1960, his parts included Launcelot Gobbo in The Merchant of Venice, Fabian in Twelfth Night, Biondello in The Taming of the Shrew; Open Air, Regent's Park, July 1964, Henry V in the play of that name and Petruchio in The Taming of the Shrew; Hampstead, Oct 1967, Jack in Honeymoon; toured, 1968, for Prospect Productions as Aguecheek in Twelfth Night, Lt Bannen in No Man's Land, and Bluntschli in Arms and the Man; Hampstead, Apr 1969, Stanley in Before You Go; St Martin's, Jan 1970, Francis in Play on Love; Royal Court, Aug 1970, Donald in The Philanthropist, transferring to the May Fair, Sept 1970; Nottingham Playhouse, Dec 1971, Captain Winkle in The Owl on the Battlements; New, Apr 1972, Dazzle in London Assurance; Aldwych, Mar 1973, Michel Cagre in Suzanna Andler; Theatre Upstairs, Dec 1973, Robert in The Pleasure Principle; toured, Jan 1974, as Edmund Cornhill in Odd Girl Out; Hampstead, Mar 1975, John in Alphabetical Order, transferring to the May Fair, Apr 1975; Old Vic, Jan 1976, for National Theatre, D'Arcy Tuck in Plunder; also transferred to the Lyttelton, Mar 1976; Hampstead, Feb 1978, Mervyn in Bodies; returned to the Lyttelton, May 1978, to play D'Arcy Tuck, and Leonard Charteris in The Philanderer; Ambassadors', Apr 1979, again played Mervyn in Bodies; first film, The Valiant, 1961, subsequent films include: Every Home Should Have One; television, since 1959, includes The Glittering Prizes, Fathers and Families, *Devenish*, and *Pig in the Middle*.

Favourite parts: Petruchio and Iago. *Recreations:* Swimming, thinking about boating. *Club:* Stage Golfing Society. *Address:* c/o ICM, 22 Grafton Street, London W1.

LANE, Burton (*né* Burton Levy), composer
b New York City, 2 Feb 1912; *s* of Lazarus Levy and his wife Frances; *e* High School of Commerce; *m* (1) Marion Seaman (mar dis); (2) Lynn Daroff Kaye.

First produced show for which he composed two songs was Three's a Crowd, at the Selwyn, 15 Oct 1930; soon afterwards was represented on Broadway in this and three other shows simultaneously, contributing music for two songs to Singin' the Blues, one to The Third Little Show, and the complete score for the ninth edition of Earl Carroll's Vanities; contributed a song to Americana, 1932; went to Hollywood, 1933; returned to Broadway for Hold on to Your Hats, 1940; Laffing Room Only, for which he was also co-librettist, 1944; Finian's Rainbow, 1947; On a Clear Day You Can See Forever, 1965; Carmelina, 1979; president of AGAC, 1957–66; first score for films was Dancing Lady, 1933, and since then Babes on Broadway, 1941, Royal Wedding, 1951, Give a Girl a Break, 1953, etc; composed the scores for the television productions of Junior Miss, 1958, Heidi's Song, 1980.

Recreations: Chess and golf. *Address:* ASCAP, 1 Lincoln Plaza, New York, NY 10023.

LANG, Harold, dancer, actor, singer
b Daly City, California, 21 Dec; *s* of Alois Nicholas Lang and his wife Adela Rosa (Martinez); *e* Vista Grande Grammar School and Jefferson Union High School.

First appeared on the stage in 1939 at the San Francisco Opera House in a production of Der Rosenkavalier; toured with the *Ballet Russes de Monte Carlo*, and the *American Ballet Theatre*; first appeared in New York at the Century, Sept 1945, as a solo dancer in Mr Strauss Goes to Boston; Adelphi, Mar 1946, appeared in the revue Three to Make Ready; Adelphi, Jan 1948, played Eddie Winkler in Look Ma, I'm Dancin'; New Century, Dec 1948, Bill Calhoun and Lucentio in Kiss Me, Kate; made his London début at the Royal Opera House, Covent Garden, Mar 1950, as a guest artist with George Balanchine's *New York City Ballet*; Winter Garden, NY, Apr 1951, appeared as Ricky in Make a Wish; Ziegfeld, May 1951, played scenes from Make a Wish in ANTA Album; Broadhurst, Jan 1952, appeared as Joey in the long-running revival of Pal Joey; Princes, London, May 1954, again played Joey in Pal Joey; City Center, Jan 1955, played Harry in The Time of Your Life; Winter Garden, June 1956, Robert Henderson in Shangri-La; toured as a guest artist with the *American Ballet Theatre*, Aug–Dec 1956; Winter Garden, Mar 1957, appeared in the revue Ziegfeld Follies; Carnegie Hall Playhouse, Jan 1959, Gabey in a revival of On the Town; US tour, Sept 1960–Mar 1961, appeared as the Jester in Once upon a Mattress; Shubert, Mar 1962, Teddy Asch in I Can Get It for You Wholesale; Swan, Milwaukee, Wisconsin, Dec 1963, Joey in Pal Joey; Square East, NY, Mar 1965, appeared in the revue The Decline and Fall of the Entire World as Seen Through the Eyes of Cole Porter Revisited; toured, 1973, in The Gershwin Years; has also appeared in cabaret in Hollywood and Las Vegas; Professor of Dance at Univ of California, Chico, Calif, since 1972

Address: #39, 555 Vallombrosa, Chico, Calif 95926.

LANG, Robert, actor and director
b Bristol, 24 Sept 1934; *s* of Richard Lionel Lang and his wife Lily Violet (Ballard); *e* Fairfield Grammar School and St Simons Church School; *m* Ann Bell, actress; formerly a meteorologist; trained for the stage at the Bristol Old Vic Theatre School.

Made his first professional appearance for the Bristol Old Vic company at the Theatre Royal, Bristol, Mar 1956, as the doctor in King Lear; remained with the company until June 1957, playing parts including Uncle Ernest in Oh! My Papa,

transferring with this production to the Garrick, July 1957; toured as Tony Lumpkin in an Arts Council production of She Stoops to Conquer, 1957, subsequently returning to the Bristol Old Vic until June 1958; with the Nottingham repertory company, Aug 1958–May 1959, his parts included Platonov in the play of that name; Bristol, June 1959, played Polonius in No Bed for Bacon; returning to Nottingham, Aug 1959, played parts including Charles in Blithe Spirit, Archie Rice in The Entertainer, the title-role in Richard III and Sgt-Major Tommy Lodge in Celebration, transferring in the latter part to the Duchess, June 1961; Canterbury, Sept 1961, played the title part in Othello; Royal Court, Jan 1962, Theseus in A Midsummer Night's Dream; Aldwych, 1962, for the Royal Shakespeare Company, took over Louis of France in Becket, and played the Actor in The Lower Depths for the same company at the Arts; Chichester Festival, July 1962, Petruchio in The Chances; Bristol, also 1962, played the title role in Becket; Chichester Festival, June 1963, Cauchon in Saint Joan and Sgt Lumber in The Workhouse Donkey; Saint Joan was also produced at the Edinburgh Festival, Aug 1963; joined the National Theatre company, Oct 1963, and subsequently played roles including Cauchon, First Player in Hamlet, Yefim in Uncle Vanya, Capt Brazen in The Recruiting Officer, 1963; Anyone in Andorra, Odysseus in Philoctetes, Roderigo in Othello, Martin Ruiz in The Royal Hunt of the Sun, Richard Greatham in Hay Fever, 1964; Rev Hale in The Crucible, Scandal in Love for Love, 1965; visited Moscow and Berlin as Roderigo and Scandal, 1965; Etienne Plucheux in A Flea In Her Ear, later taking over as Chandebise/Poche, 1966; Kurt in The Dance of Death, 1967; toured Canada, also 1967, as Scandal, Chandebise/Poche and Kurt; Corvino in Volpone, Mortimer in Edward II (Brecht), William Cardew in Home and Beauty, 1968; in the same year directed The Covent Garden Tragedy as part of a National Theatre triple bill; played Gen Havelock in H, Mirabell in The Way of the World, Franklyn Barnabas in Back to Methuselah, and Ash in The National Health, 1969; took over Shylock in The Merchant of Venice, 1970; Apollo, Feb 1972, John Colombo in The Beheading; toured, Oct 1972, as Sir Toby Belch in the New Shakespeare Company's Twelfth Night; appointed to the board of directors, New Shakespeare Company, 1972; Artistic Director, Cambridge Theatre Company, 1975–6; he directed this company in Fears and Miseries of the Third Reich, and School for Scandal, 1974; The Importance of Being Earnest, 1975; other productions he has directed include Home and Beauty (Leatherhead), 1971; Twelfth Night (Regent's Park), 1973; Thark (Exeter), 1975; his films include: Interlude, A Walk with Love and Death, Night Watch, and The First Great Train Robbery; TV, since 1958, includes An Age of Kings, That Was the Week That Was, and recently, two series of *1990*, Waste, Mathilda's England, and Donkey's Years.

Favourite parts: Scandal, Platonov, Richard III. *Recreations:* Pisciculture, photography. *Address:* c/o Leading Artists, 60 St James's Street, London W1. *Tel:* 01–491 4400.

LANGELLA, Frank, actor
b Bayonne, NJ, 1 Jan 1940; *s* of Frank Langella and his wife; *e* Syracuse University, NY; trained for the stage with Seymour Falk.

Made his New York debut at the Bouwerie Lane, 7 Nov 1963, as Michel in The Immoralist; American Place, Nov 1964, played the title role in Benito Cereno; Cherry Lane, Oct 1965, The Young Man in Good Day; Circle in the Square, Dec 1965, Flamineo in The White Devil; Long Wharf, May 1966, Jamie in Long Day's Journey into Night; Vivian Beaumont, Dec 1966, Juan in Yerma; Mark Taper

Forum, Los Angeles, Apr 1967, Urbain Grandier in The Devils; Circle in the Square, Nov 1967, Achilles in Iphigenia at Aulis; appeared with the Long Island Festival Repertory, Mineola, NY, Apr–Jun 1968; Vivian Beaumont, Nov 1968, Will (Shakespeare) in A Cry of Players; Williamstown Festival, summer 1971, title-role in Cyrano de Bergerac; appeared with Yale Repertory, 1971–72 season; McCarter, Princeton, NJ, 1972, played the lead in The Tooth of Crime; Guthrie Theater Company, Minneapolis, Minn, 1972–73 season, played Oberon in A Midsummer Night's Dream and Loveless in The Relapse; Studio Arena, Buffalo, Mar 1973, Petruchio in The Taming of the Shrew; appeared in The Seagull, Williamstown, 1974 season; Shubert, Jan 1975, Leslie in Seascape, for which he received the Antoinette Perry Award; Shubert, Los Angeles, Apr 1975, again played in Seascape; Williamstown, July 1975, played in Ring Around the Moon; Chelsea Theater Center, Oct 1976, title-role in The Prince of Hamburg; Martin Beck, Oct 1977, scored a great success in the title-role of Dracula; films include The Deadly Trap, The Wrath of God, recently Dracula, 1979.

Address: Actors Equity Association, 165 West 46th Street, New York, NY 10036.

LANGHAM, Michael, director

b Bridgwater, Somerset, 22 Aug 1919; *s* of Seymour Langham and his wife Muriel Andrews (Speed); *e* Radley College, and the University of London; *m* Helen Burns; studied for the law until Sept 1939; served with the Gordon Highlanders, 1939–45.

His first production was for the Arts Council Midland Theatre Company, Coventry, May 1946, when he directed Twelfth Night, and where he remained as Director of Productions for two years; Director of Productions at the Birmingham Repertory Theatre, 1948–50; Memorial Theatre, Stratford-on-Avon, May 1950, directed Julius Caesar; directed his first London production at the Garrick, Jan 1951, in The Gay Invalid (Molière's Le Malade Imaginaire); Embassy, Jan 1951, directed Pygmalion; Théâtre des Galeries, Brussels, May 1951, directed André Obey's French adaptation of Richard III; Berlin Festival, Aug 1951, directed Othello with the Old Vic Company, the production subsequently appearing at the Old Vic, London, Oct 1951; at the Haagsche Comedie, The Hague, Jan 1952, directed The Merry Wives of Windsor (in Dutch); Old Vic, Mar 1952, directed The Other Heart; appointed Director of Productions at the Citizens Theatre, Glasgow, 1953–4; Q Theatre, Sept 1954, directed Witch Errant; Festival Theatre, Stratford, Ontario, July 1955, directed Julius Caesar; Artistic Director of the Stratford Shakespearean Festival, Ontario, Sept 1955, and appointed General Manager in addition to Artistic Director in Aug 1957, and there directed the following productions: Henry V (also at the Edinburgh Festival); The Merry Wives of Windsor, 1956; Hamlet, 1957; Henry IV, Part I, Much Ado About Nothing, 1958; Romeo and Juliet, 1960; Coriolanus, Love's Labour's Lost, 1961; Two Programmes of Shakespearean Comedy, The Taming of the Shrew, Cyrano de Bergerac, 1962; Troilus and Cressida, Timon of Athens, 1963; Love's Labour's Lost, and Timon of Athens (Chichester Festival, England, in The Shakespeare Quatercentenary Programme), King Lear, The Country Wife, 1964; Henry V (co-directed), The Last of the Tsars, 1966; Antony and Cleopatra, 1967; The School for Scandal, 1970; in addition he has directed The Beggar's Opera (Sadler's Wells), 1954; The Diary of a Scoundrel, Meeting at Night, When We Were Married (last three productions at Crest, Toronto), 1955; Hamlet (Stratford-on-Avon), 1956; The Two Gentlemen of Verona (Old Vic), 1957; The Broken Jug (Phoenix, New York), The Two Gentlemen of Verona (Phoenix, NY), 1958; The Merchant of Venice (Stratford-on-Avon), A Midsummer Night's Dream (Old Vic), 1960; Much Ado About Nothing (Stratford-on-Avon), 1961; Andorra (Biltmore, NY), 1963; The Prime of Miss Jean Brodie (Helen Hayes, NY), 1968; The Way of the World (National Theatre, London), 1969; A Play by Aleksandr Solzhenitsyn at The Guthrie Theater, Minneapolis, Minnesota, 1970; Artistic Director of The Guthrie Theater, 1971–7, where he directed the following productions: Cyrano de Bergerac, The Taming of the Shrew, and The Diary of a Scoundrel, 1971; The Relapse, Oedipus the King, 1972; Oedipus the King (revival), The Merchant of Venice, 1973; King Lear, Love's Labour's Lost, and The School for Scandal, 1974; Private Lives, 1965; Measure for Measure, The Winter's Tale, The Matchmaker, 1976; The National Health (co-directed), She Stoops to Conquer, Design for Living, 1977; for the New York Shakespeare Festival at the Anspacher, 1979, directed Julius Caesar, Jan, and Coriolanus, Mar; for The British Council, 1952, gave a lecture tour in Australia, and in Jan 1953, directed Richard III on an open stage for the University of Western Australia; television productions include his own script of The Affliction of Love (NY), 1963; adapted Cyrano de Bergerac, July 1962; adapted Two Programmes of Shakespearean Comedy, 1962; HonDLitt McMaster University, Ontario, 1962; appointed Artistic Consultant to La Jolla Theatre Project, California, 1965.

Address: Society of Stage Directors and Choreographers, 1501 Broadway, New York, NY 10036.

LANGNER, Philip, producer

b New York City, 24 Aug 1926; *s* of Lawrence Langner and his wife Armina (Marshall), the producers; *e* The Hotchkiss School, Lakeville, Conn, 1943, Yale University (BS 1948); *m* Marilyn Clark.

Member of the board of the American Shakespeare Festival and Academy; produced Seagulls over Sorrento at the John Golden, 11 Sept 1952; joined the Theater Guild, 1956, as associate producer, and became co-director in 1961; productions in New York include The Tunnel of Love, 1957; The Summer of the Seventeenth Doll, Sunrise at Campobello, Back to Methuselah, Third Best Sport, 1958; Requiem for a Nun, A Majority of One, Triple Play, The Highest Tree, Jolly's Progress, 1959; The 49th Cousin, Invitation to a March, The Unsinkable Molly Brown, Love and Libel, 1960; The Captains and the Kings, Something about a Soldier, A Passage to India, Seidman and Son, 1962; Dear Me, The Sky is Falling, 1963; The Child Buyer, 1964; All Women Are One, The Royal Hunt of the Sun, 1965; Help Stamp Out Marriage, 1966; The Homecoming, 1967; Darling of the Day, 1968; Absurd Person Singular, 1974; A Musical Jubilee, 1975; Golda, 1977; co-owner of the Westport, Conn, Country Playhouse; served there as managing director 1948–54; producer at the Bahama Playhouse, Nassau, BWI, 1951–52; managing director of the New Parsons, Hartford, Conn, 1952–54; producer, Mechanic Theatre, Baltimore, Md, 1978–79; entered film production with Judgment at Nuremburg, 1961, and since has co-produced A Child Is Waiting, The Pawnbroker, Slaves, Born to Win (1971), etc.

Address: 135 Central Park West, New York, NY 10023. *Tel:* 265–6170.

LANSBURY, Angela, actress

b London, 16 Oct 1925; *d* of Edgar Isaac Lansbury and his wife Moyna (Macgill); *e* South Hampstead High School for Girls, 1934–9; Webber-Douglas School of Dramatic Arts,

1939–40; Feagin School of Drama, New York, 1942; *m* Peter Pullen Shaw.

Made her NY début at the Henry Miller's, 11 Apr 1957, as Marcelle in Hotel Paradiso; Lyceum, Oct 1960, Helen in A Taste of Honey; Majestic, Mar 1964, Cora Hoover Hooper in Anyone Can Whistle; Winter Garden, May 1966, Mame Dennis in Mame, for which she received the Antoinette Perry (Tony) Award; Curran, San Francisco, Apr 1968, and subsequent tour, again played in Mame; Mark Hellinger, Feb 1969, Countess Aurelia, the Madwoman of Chaillot in Dear World, for which she again received the Tony Award; Shubert, Boston, Feb 1971, Prettybelle Sweet in Prettybelle; made her London début at the Aldwych 31 Jan 1972 as The Mistress in the Royal Shakespeare Company production of All Over; Westbury, Long Island, Music Fair, July 1972, again played Mame Dennis in Mame; Shubert, 11 Mar 1973, appeared in Sondheim: A Musical Tribute; Piccadilly, London, May 1973, Rose in Gypsy; Shubert, Los Angeles, Apr 1974, Rose in Gypsy, and subsequently toured; Winter Garden, Sept 1974, again played Rose and received the Tony Award for this part; Old Vic, London, Dec 1975, Gertrude in Hamlet, for the National Theatre, in which part she also appeared at the opening of the Lyttelton, Mar 1976; Uris, Mar 1979, Mrs Lovett in Sweeney Todd, for which she received the 'Tony' Award; received the Sarah Siddons Award in Chicago, 1974, for her role in Gypsy; entered films in Gaslight, 1944, and has since played in many others, including National Velvet, The Picture of Dorian Gray, The Harvey Girls, Bel Ami, Till the Clouds Roll By, The Reluctant Debutante, The Manchurian Candidate, The Summer of the 17th Doll, The Dark at the Top of the Stairs, Something for Everyone, Bedknobs and Broomsticks, Death on the Nile, The Lady Vanishes, etc.

Address: Actors Equity Association, 165 West 46th Street, New York, NY 10036.

LANSBURY, Edgar, producer, designer
b London, 12 Jan 1930; *s* of Edgar Isaac Lansbury and his wife Charlotte Lilian (McIldowie); *e* UCLA, 1947–50, and Otis Art Institute, Los Angeles; *m* Rose Anthony Kean.

Began his theatrical career as a scenic designer and art director, being apprenticed at Windham Playhouse, Windham, New Hampshire, 1947; designed for this theatre, 1953–4; first designs in New York were for The Wise Have Not Spoken, produced at the Cherry Lane, 10 Feb 1954; designed A Sound of Hunting, The Master Builder, Young Woodley, 1954; Misalliance, 1955; designed Jackhammer, which he also co-produced at the Marquee, 5 Feb 1962; designed Five Evenings, 1963; produced and designed The Subject Was Roses, 1964; since then has been primarily a producer, presenting on his own or in partnership with others the following plays: The Alchemist, 1964; First One Asleep, Whistle, 1966; That Summer—That Fall, Arms and the Man, Fragments, 1967; The Only Game in Town, 1968; A Way of Life, To Be Young, Gifted, and Black, The Millionairess, Promenade, 1969; Look to the Lilies, The Engagement Baby, 1970; Waiting for Godot, Long Day's Journey into Night, Godspell, 1971; Elizabeth I, 1972; Gypsy (London), Nourish the Beast, The Enclave, 1973; The Magic Show, Gypsy, 1974; Blasts and Bravos: An Evening with H L Mencken, The Night That Made America Famous, 1975; was art director for the film War Hunt, 1962, and produced the films The Subject Was Roses, 1967, Godspell, 1973, The Wild Party, 1976, Squirm, 1977, Blue Sunshine, 1978, etc; art director for ABC television, 1955, and for *The Red Skelton Show,* 1956–60, *Playhouse 90,* 1957–9, *Studio One,* 1959, *The Defenders,* 1963, the series *Coronet Blue,* various special programs; produced Star Witness, 1961, etc.

Recreations: Cello, painting, tennis, ski-ing. *Club:* Players. *Address:* 1650 Broadway, New York, NY 10036. *Tel:* 765–5910.

LAPOTAIRE, Jane, actress
b Ipswich, Suffolk, 26 Dec 1944; stepdaughter of Yves Lapotaire and his wife Louise Elise (Burgess); *e* Northgate Grammar School, Ipswich; *m* Roland Joffé; trained for the stage at the Bristol Old Vic Theatre School.

Made her first professional appearance, Bristol Old Vic, Sept 1965, as Ruby Birtle in When We Are Married; subsequent parts at Bristol, 1965–7, included Vivie in Mrs Warren's Profession, Natasha in War and Peace, and Ruth in The Homecoming; with the National Theatre at the Old Vic, 1967–71, her parts included Judith in The Dance of Death, Antoinette in A Flea in Her Ear, 1967; Mincing, and later Mrs Fainall in The Way of the World, Tania in Macrune's Guevara, Zanche in The White Devil, Don Quixote's niece in The Travails of Sancho Panza, 1969; Jessica in The Merchant of Venice, 1970; Lieschen in The Captain of Köpenick, 1971; with the Young Vic, 1970–1, her parts included Zerbinetta in Scapino, Katherina in The Taming of the Shrew, Jocasta in Oedipus, and Isabella in Measure for Measure; joined the Royal Shakespeare Company and played Viola in Twelfth Night, Stratford Aug 1974 (also Aldwych Feb 1975); Lady Macduff in Macbeth, Oct, and Sonya in Uncle Vanya, the last part at The Other Place, Dec; Nottingham Playhouse, Aug 1975, and Edinburgh Festival, Rosalind in As You Like It; toured with the Prospect Theatre Company, Oct 1975, and appeared with the company at the Albery, Nov 1975, as Vera in A Month in the Country and as Lucy Honeychurch in A Room with a View; Riverside Studios, May 1976, Rosalind in As You Like It; Bristol Old Vic, Nov 1976, title-role in The Duchess of Malfi; Stratford, Aug 1978, Rosaline in Love's Labours Lost, repeating the part at the Aldwych, Apr 1979; The Other Place, Oct 1978, and Warehouse, June 1979, title role in Piaf, transferring with the production to the Aldwych, Dec 1979, Wyndham's, Jan 1980, and Piccadilly, Feb 1980; received Best Stage Actress, 1979, and other awards for this performance; films include Antony and Cleopatra in 1971; TV, since 1967, includes Stocker's Copper, The Other Woman, Marie Curie, and The Devil's Crown.

Favourite parts: Sonya, Isabella, Viola. *Recreations:* Home and family, cooking, gardening. *Address:* c/o Boyack and Conway, 8 Cavendish Place, London W1. *Tel:* 01–636 3916.

LARKIN, Peter, designer
b Boston, Mass, 26 Aug 1926; *s* of Oliver W Larkin and his wife Ruth (McIntyre); *e* Deerfield (Mass) Academy and Yale University School of Drama; studied design with his father; *m* Mary Ann Reeve.

He has designed the following productions: The Wild Duck, 1951; First Lady, Dial M for Murder, A Streetcar Named Desire (Canada, ballet), 1952; The Teahouse of the August Moon, 1953; Ondine, Peter Pan, 1954; Inherit the Wind, No Time for Sergeants, 1955; Shangri-La, New Faces of 1956, Protective Custody, 1956; Good as Gold, Compulsion, Miss Isobel, 1957; Blue Denim, Goldilocks, The Shadow of a Gunman, 1958; First Impressions, Only in America, 1959; Greenwillow, Wildcat, Laurette, 1960; Giants, Sons of Giants, We Take the Town, Nowhere to Go But Up, 1962; Marathon '33, The Seagull, The Crucible, Ring Round the Moon, 1963; Rich Little Rich Girl, Liliom, She Stoops to Conquer, 1964; The Porcelain Year, 1965; The Great Indoors, Happily Never After, Anna Christie (Los Angeles), Hail Scrawdyke! 1966; Scuba Duba, 1967; Les Blancs, Sheep on the Runway, 1970; Twigs, WC (tour), 1971; Wise Child, 1972; Let Me Hear You Smile, 1973; Thieves, 1974; Cracks, 1976; Ladies at the Alamo, 1977; Dancin', 1978; G R Point, Break a Leg, 1979; has also designed for the O'Neill Playwrights' Conference, Waterford, Conn; has received the Antoinette Perry (Tony) Award for Teahouse of the August Moon, Ondine, Inherit the Wind, and No Time for Sergeants.

LaRUSSO, Louis II, playwright

b Hoboken, New Jersey, 13 Oct 1935; *s* of Louis LaRusso and his wife Mary (Turso); *e* Demarest High School, New Jersey; *m* Maureen O'Rourke (mar dis).

His first play to be performed was The Honeymoon, seen at the Eastside Playhouse, 4 May 1975; author of Lamppost Reunion, produced 1975; Wheelbarrow Closers, 1976; Sunset, 1977; Momma's Little Angels, 1978; Knockout, 1979; Marlon Brando Sat Right Here, 1980.

Address: 111 Willow Terrace, Hoboken, NJ 07030.

LATIMER, Hugh, actor

b Haslemere, Surrey, 12 May 1913; *s* of Hugh Latimer and his wife Vera (Eden); *e* Oundle and Caius College, Cambridge; *m* Sheila Murray Gairns; studied for the stage at the Central School of Dramatic Art.

Made his first appearance on the stage, at the Brixton Theatre, Nov 1936, as Worthing in White Cargo; first appeared in the West-end, at the St James's, Feb 1937, as Mr Bingley in Pride and Prejudice, subsequently touring in this; Shaftesbury, Nov 1937, played the Officer of the Guard in Thank You, Mr Pepys; appeared at the Embassy, 1939, in Rope, Julius Caesar, etc; His Majesty's, Dec 1939, played in Julius Caesar (in modern dress); Embassy, May, and Criterion, June 1940, appeared as the Compère in Come Out of Your Shell; served in the Army, 1940–6; Embassy, Aug 1947, played Basil Gilbert in Jane Steps Out; New, Sept 1947, Franklin Blake in The Moonstone; Q, Oct 1947, Councillor Philip Marvin in The Sparks Fly Upward, and Jan 1948, Bernard Farrell in Poisoned Chalice; Granville, Mar 1948, Colin Nesbitt in No Party Manners; Garrick, July 1948, Owen Russell in Written for a Lady; Embassy, Nov 1948, and St Martin's, Jan 1950, Detective-Sergeant Bullock in A Lady Mislaid; His Majesty's (for Repertory Players), May 1950, Rev Brian Turner in Unexpected Island; Whitehall (for the Under 30 Theatre), Dec 1950, Sir Roland de Bois in Sing Cuckoo; Royal, Windsor, Jan 1951, played Prince Michael Barianevsky in Rough Shooting; Q, June 1951, Peter Carrington in Lacking a Title; Royal, Brighton, July 1951, Lord Phillpot in The Gainsborough Girls; Q, Oct 1951, Dudley in . . . And All Things Nice, and Feb 1952, Rodney Allen in Not Proven; Wimbledon, Feb 1952, Charles Drummond in The Enemy of Time; Saville, July 1952, Schoolie Brown in Albert, RN; at the Q, Oct–Nov 1952, Nigel Dean in Joking Apart, and Stephen Hodgson in It's Never Too Late; Strand, Jan 1953, for the Repertory Players, appeared as Keith in Red Herring; Q, Feb 1953, Alec Bestwood in Birthday Honours, and May 1953, Peter Hubbard in Half-Seas Over; Criterion, Oct 1953, again played Alec Bestwood in Birthday Honours; Q, May 1955, the Strange Man in Identity Unknown; toured, Aug 1955, as Peter Hubbard in Double Crossing; Palace, Westcliffe, Oct 1955, played Gilbert Peko in Portrait by Peko; toured, and Fortune, June 1956, Julian in To My Love (formerly entitled El Baile); Lyric, Hammersmith, Dec 1956, the King in The Marvellous Story of Puss in Boots; toured, 1958, as Tony St Clare in Love or Money and as Ogelby in Touch It Light; Strand, May 1959, Marquis de Castellane in Change of Tune; Criterion, Dec 1959, Mr

Schofield in A Clean Kill; Edinburgh Festival, and Royal Court, Sept 1961, played Dr Swinburne in August for the People; Lyric, July 1963, played Hubert Palling in Windfall; Jan 1967, toured for Prospect Players, as Lord Uxbridge in A Murder of No Importance; Savoy, May–June 1967, took over the part of Hugh Walford in The Secretary Bird; Lyric, Dec 1967–Jan 1968, took over as Lionel Fairleigh in The Lionel Touch; first appeared in films, 1946, in Corridor of Mirrors; has also appeared on television.

Recreations: Shooting, sailing, photography, and silversmithing. *Clubs:* Green Room, Lord's Taverners, and MCC. *Address:* c/o John Cadell, 2 Southwood Lane, London N6.

LAUCHLAN, Agnes, actress

b Putney, London, 10 Feb 1905; *d* of Henry David Lauchlan and his wife Minnie Agnes Haliburton (Reekie); *e* The Study, Wimbledon; studied for the stage at the Royal Academy of Dramatic Art.

Made her first appearance on the stage at the New Theatre, 26 Mar 1924, walking-on in the production of Saint Joan; joined the Lena Ashwell players 1926, and played the Princess Elinor in Robin Hood, and Destiny and the Queen in Tristan and Isolt, at the Century Theatre; at the Everyman, 1928, played Mabel in The Eldest Son, Mrs Starck in Comrades and Constanza in Ginevra; in 1929, toured with Leon M Lion, as Margaret in Loyalties; New, Dec 1929, played Madame Molnar in Madame Plays Nap; Globe, Sept 1930, Alice Simpson in Street Scene; Royalty, Feb 1931, Diana in Money, Money!; Kingsway, June 1931, Madeleine in The Heir; at the Embassy, Jan–Nov 1932, played Daisy in Rough to Moderate, Lady Capulet in Romeo and Juliet, Pepita in Madame Pepita, Hannah in The Twelfth Hour, Eustasia in The Dover Road, Ellen Stiles in The Cathedral; New, Dec 1932, again played Ellen in The Cathedral; Open Air Theatre, July–Sept 1933, Helena in A Midsummer Night's Dream, and Iris in The Tempest; Embassy, Jan 1934, Geraldine in Genius at Home; Ambassadors', Mar 1934, Lady Fidget in The Country Wife; Sept 1935, Olga Ranelagh in As Bad as I Am; Ambassadors', Nov 1935, Emma Peacock in Our Own Lives; Westminster, Mar 1937, Lady Utterword in Heartbreak House; Garrick, May 1937, Marianne Bell-Mason in Sarah Simple; Old Vic, Dec 1937, Helena in A Midsummer Night's Dream; Whitehall, Apr 1938, Lady Tracey in Ghost for Sale; Garrick, June 1938, Mrs Fortescue in Trumpeter, Play!; Royalty, July 1938, Charlotte Shaw in Little Stranger; Apollo, Dec 1938, Bonnie Hallam in Windfall; Criterion, Mar 1939, Mrs Puttick in Sugar Plum; Little, Apr 1940, Lady Fidget in The Country Wife; Adelphi, July 1940, Hilda Randolph in Dear Octopus; Q, Dec 1940, Lillian in A Lass and a Lackey; Duchess, 1942–3, Madame Arcati in Blithe Spirit; Playhouse, Liverpool (for the Old Vic), Sept 1944, Maria Kalitine in Lisa, and Mrs Cortelyou in The Second Mrs Tanqueray; King's, Hammersmith, Mar 1946, the Nurse in Romeo and Juliet; St Martin's, June 1948, Lady Sarah Belloc in Point to Point; Vaudeville, Mar 1949, played Lady Deeming in A Woman's Place; Piccadilly, May 1949, Lady Palsworthy in Ann Veronica; Embassy, June 1950, the Duchess of Mull in Shepherd's Warning; Oct 1950, Lady Charles Lamprey in A Surfeit of Lampreys; Mercury, Dec 1950, the Queen in A Glass of Water; Theatre Royal, Windsor, 1952, Mme Desmortes in Ring Round the Moon; Oxford Playhouse, 1953, Mme Ranevsky in The Cherry Orchard; at the Q, Oct 1953, appeared as Mrs Heyworth in One Fair Daughter; Pitlochry Festival Theatre, May 1955, played Christabel in The Lady from Edinburgh, Georgiana Tidman in Dandy Dick, Doña Filomena in A Hundred Years Old, etc; Royal Court, Apr 1956, Geraldine Loughton-

Moore in The Mulberry Bush; at the same theatre, Apr 1956, Rebecca Nurse in The Crucible; same theatre, May 1956, the Abbess in Don Juan; same theatre, June 1956, Mrs Paradise in Cards of Identity; New, Oxford, Sept 1956, Mrs Boris Honey in Your Young Wife; Apollo, Apr 1959, Brigette Blair in Fool's Paradise; Belgrade, Coventry, Sept 1964, played Lady Bracknell in The Importance of Being Earnest; Phoenix, July 1967, Lady Frinton in The Last of Mrs Cheyney; Vaudeville, Nov 1967, Lady Hunstanton in A Woman of No Importance; Lyric, Aug 1968, Lady Constance Keeble in Oh, Clarence!; appeared at the Arnaud, Guildford, Aug 1971, as Mrs Otery in Mary Rose, and in Apr 1973, as Mrs Noah in Noah; Garrick, June 1974, Gertrude in Birds of Paradise; television appearances include: Dr Finlay's Casebook, and Kate.

Recreations: Music and reading. *Address:* White Gates, Ramsden Road, Godalming, Surrey. *Tel:* Godalming 213.

LAURENCE, Paula (*née* de Lugo), actress
b Brooklyn, New York, 25 Jan; *d* of Benjamin de Lugo and his wife Lily (D'Alba); *m* Charles Bowden.

Made her first appearance on the stage at the Maxine Elliott Theatre, Jan 1937, with the Federal Theatre Project, in Horse Eats Hat, and subsequently played Helen of Troy in Doctor Faustus: was then engaged for some time in cabaret; Adelphi, Apr 1939, played in the revue Sing for Your Supper; at the Lyceum, Nov 1941, played Hilda in Junior Miss; Alvin, Jan 1943, Chiquita Hart in Something for the Boys; Imperial, Oct 1943, Molly Grant in One Touch of Venus; Adelphi, Feb 1946, Miss Kiester and The Queen of Spain in The Duchess Misbehaves; Alvin, Oct 1946, The Duenna in Cyrano de Bergerac; toured, 1947, in Dark Eyes; City Center, Jan–Feb 1948, Lady Politic Wouldbe in Volpone, and Anna in The Wedding, and June 1948, the Female Beetle in The Insect Comedy; Majestic, 1948, deputized for Beatrice Lillie in Inside USA; Broadhurst, May 1950 Colombina in The Liar; Cort, Sept 1950, Molly Burden in Season in the Sun; Gayety, Washington, May 1952, and in the same month at the New York City Center, played Fernande Dupont in Tovarich; Country Playhouse, Westport, Conn, Aug 1952, Amalia in Right You Are; New York City Center, Nov 1953, Roxane's Duenna in Cyrano de Bergerac; Phoenix, Jan 1954, Valeria in Coriolanus; City Center, Jan 1955, Society Lady in The Time of Your Life; summer, 1955, toured as Mme Arcati in Blithe Spirit; City Center, Sept 1956, Miss P Opinion in Orpheus in the Underworld; City Center, Mar 1957, Mrs Coaxer in The Beggar's Opera; Henry Miller, June 1957, took over the part of Mme, Boniface in Hotel Paradiso; John Drew, Easthampton, NY, Sally Brass in A Pound in Your Pocket, and later played this part at the Royal Poinciana Playhouse, Palm Beach, Fla, in Mar 1959; again played the Society Lady in The Time of Your Life for the United States Performing Arts Program at the Brussels International Exhibition in Oct 1958; Blackstone, Chicago, Dec 1961, and Royale, NY, Jan 1962, deputized for Bette Davis as Maxine Faulk in The Night of the Iguana, playing the role in both cities; Music Circus, Lambertville, NJ, Aug 1962, Mae Peterson in Bye Bye Birdie; Music Box, Dec 1963, Sally Jordan in Have I Got a Girl for You!; Winter Garden, June 1964, took over the role of Mrs Strakosh in Funny Girl; toured, summer 1965, as Mae Peterson in Bye Bye Birdie; Shubert, May 1966, Zinaida Savishna in Sir John Gielgud's production of Ivanov; Ethel Barrymore, Nov 1967, took over as Miss Furnival in Black Comedy; Circle in the Square, Dec 1969, Varda Shimansky in Seven Days of Mourning; Roundabout, Jan 1974, Ilva Andreyevna in The Seagull; has also played in stock productions of such plays as No, No, Nanette,

A Connecticut Yankee, The Women, On Approval, The Shewing Up of Blanco Posnet, Three Men on a Horse, A Little Night Music, Once upon a Mattress, etc; her articles are regular features of *Playbill*, and she has also published in *Vogue,* Mademoiselle, Cue, etc; author of Setting the Scene for 25 Years of Tony Awards, 1971; her work in caricature has been exhibited in many galleries in the US; recent films include The Eyes of Laura Mars and Firepower.

Address: c/o Actors Equity Association, 165 West 46th Street, New York, NY 10036.

LAURENTS, Arthur, dramatic author and director
b New York, 14 July 1918; *s* of Irving Laurents and his wife Ada (Robbins); *e* Cornell University.

Author of the following: Home of the Brave, 1945; Heart-song, 1947; The Bird Cage, 1950; The Time of the Cuckoo, 1952; A Clearing in the Woods, 1956; West Side Story (musical), 1957; Gypsy (musical), 1959; Invitiation to a March (also directed), 1960; Anyone Can Whistle (musical), (also directed), 1964; Do I Hear a Waltz? (musical based on The Time of the Cuckoo), 1965; Hallelujah, Baby (musical), 1967; directed the musical I Can Get It For You Wholesale, 1962; at the Washington, DC, Theatre Club, Feb 1973, directed his play The Enclave, which he also directed at Theatre Four, NY, Nov 1973; Piccadilly, London, 29 May 1973, directed Gypsy; Winter Garden, NY, Sept 1974, again directed Gypsy; directed his play Scream, at the Alley, Houston, 1978; directed and co-wrote The Madwoman of Central Park West, Twenty-Two Steps, NY, 1979; is also the author of radio scripts and screenplays, among which may be mentioned Rope, The Snake Pit, Caught, Bonjour Tristesse, Anastasia, The Way We Were, The Turning Point, and of the novels The Way We Were, 1972, The Turning Point, 1977; longtime council member of the Dramatists' Guild.

Recreations: Skiing, both water and snow, tennis. *Address:* Dune Road, Quogue, New York.

LAURIE, John, actor
b Dumfries, Scotland, 25 Mar 1897; *s* of the late William Laurie and his wife Jessie Anne (Brown); *e* Dumfries Academy; *m* (1) Florence Saunders (dec); (2) Oonah V Todd-Naylor; served with the Hon Artillery Company in the War, 1916–18; originally intended to become an architect; studied for the stage at the Central School of Speech Training, Royal Albert Hall.

Made his first appearance on the stage at the Lyceum Theatre, Dumfries, Mar 1921, as John Shand in What Every Woman Knows; made his first appearance in London, at the Old Vic, 16 Aug 1922, as Pistol in The Merry Wives of Windsor; remained at that theatre until Mar 1925, playing a great variety of parts; from Apr–Sept 1925, appeared with the Stratford-on-Avon Festival Company, playing such parts as Hubert in King John, Autolycus in The Winter's Tale, Costard in Love's Labour's Lost, etc; at the New Theatre, Dec 1925, played Cyrus P Hunsaker in Quinney's; Feb 1926, Conrade in Much Ado About Nothing; Mar 1926, Armand in Prince Fazil; at the Prince's, Dec 1926, played Lennox in Macbeth; Century, Feb 1927, Tristan in Tristan and Isolt; returned to Stratford-on-Avon, Apr–Sept 1927, during which period he appeared as Hamlet; appeared at the Q, Dec 1927, in Enchantment, Anti-Christ, and The Simoun; Lyric, Hammersmith, Jan 1928, Pistol in King Henry V; Strand, Feb 1928, Joel in Judith of Israel; returned to the Old Vic, Sept 1928, as leading man, playing Armado in Love's Labour's Lost, Sigurd in The Vikings at Helgeland, Touchstone, Feste, Macbeth, Hamlet, Buckingham, Adam in Adam's Opera, etc; at the Court, Feb 1930, played Claudius in

Hamlet; New, Sept 1930, Lord Hastings in Richard III; Arts, Oct 1930, Paul of Tarsus in The Passing of the Essenes; Globe, Jan 1931, Rev Adam Macadam in The Improper Duchess; Nov 1931, Pelling in And So to Bed; New, Apr 1932, Prince Lucien and Colonel Campbell in Napoleon; May 1932, Feste in Twelfth Night; Little, Oct 1932, Richard Knowles in Alison's House; Arts, Nov 1932, Parolles in All's Well that Ends Well; Shaftesbury, Apr 1933, Inspector Groves in Crime on the Hill; Open Air Theatre, June–Sept 1933, Orsino in Twelfth Night, Oliver in As You Like It, Lysander in A Midsummer Night's Dream; Embassy, Oct 1933, Herr Huebertz in Son of Man, and Sir Thomas Seymour in The Tudor Wench, playing the last-mentioned part also at the Alhambra, Nov 1933; Apollo, Nov 1933, John Philip Kemble in Mrs Siddons; Ambassadors', Jan 1934, Faulkland in The Rivals; Mar 1934, Sparkish in The Country Wife; Open Air Theatre, Aug 1934, Alonzo in The Tempest; Sept 1934, Lysander in A Midsummer Night's Dream; Winter Garden, Sept 1934, Clitandre in Love is the Best Doctor; Embassy, Jan 1935, Ferdinand in The Duchess of Malfi; His Majesty's, Feb 1935, Douglas in Henry IV (Part I); St Martin's (for Phoenix Society), Mar 1935, Flamineo in The White Devil; Open Air Theatre, June–Sept 1935, Sir Andrew Aguecheek in Twelfth Night, Oliver in As You Like It, Comus, Flute in A Midsummer Night's Dream; Criterion, Mar 1936, Rosmer in Rosmersholm and Lovborg in Hedda Gabler; Lyric, May 1936, Gaster in Bees on the Boatdeck; toured in South Africa, Aug–Nov 1937, playing lead in Late Night Final, Boy Meets Girl, The Case of the Frightened Lady; Ambassadors', Feb 1938, McKay in Surprise Item; Fortune, June 1938, MacDonald in White Secrets; Stratford-on-Avon, season of 1939, played Othello, Richard III, Malvolio, Jaques, and Sicinius Velutus in Coriolanus; Mercury, Dec 1939, Nicia in Mandragola; Duke of York's, May 1940, Hatlock in The Peaceful Inn; Cambridge, May 1943, Captain Shotover in Heartbreak House; at the Perth Festival, Aug 1945, directed Hamlet in its entirety, and played the title-role; Embassy, Aug 1946, played Col Brandon in Sense and Sensibility; Glasgow Citizen's Theatre, Sept 1947, played John Knox in the play of that name; Savoy, Feb 1949, Professor Syme in The Human Touch; Q, Feb 1950, MacAdam in MacAdam and Eve, in which he subsequently appeared at the Lyceum, Edinburgh, Jan 1951, and Aldwych, London, Mar 1951; Arts, Jan 1952, played Peterbono in Thieves' Carnival; Gateway, Edinburgh, Feb 1955, appeared in the title-role of The Laird o' Grippy; Apollo, London, July 1955, played Demokos in Tiger at the Gates; made his first appearance on the New York stage at the Plymouth, 4 Oct 1955, in the last-mentioned part; in Jan 1958, began a nine-week tour of India and Ceylon for the British Council in excerpts from Shakespeare and other English classics; July–Dec 1959, toured Australia with J C Williamson's Shakespearean Co, playing Lear, Shylock, Bottom, and Autolycus; Phoenix, London, May 1962, played Arthur Cameron in The Lizard on the Rock; joined the Royal Shakespeare Company to appear at the Aldwych, Feb 1964, as Gloucester in King Lear, prior to touring for the British Council with the production, in Europe, and the USSR, followed by eight weeks in the United States, 1964; Chichester Festival, July–Sept 1966, played Firs in The Cherry Orchard and Duncan in Macbeth; Perth, Jan 1968, appeared as William McGonagall in The Hero of a Hundred Fights; is a founder member of the Apollo Society, for whom he has read poetry on many occasions; has also appeared for the Fellowship of Players, Greek Play Society, Stage Society, etc; entered films, 1930, in Juno and the Paycock, and has appeared in over a hundred films since that date; has ap-

peared frequently on television, including eight years in *Dad's Army*.

Recreations: Poetry and gardening. *Club:* Garrick. *Address:* Southfield, Chalfont St Peter, Bucks. *Tel:* Gerrard's Cross 83309.

LAVIN, Linda, actress
b Portland, Maine, 15 Oct 1937; *d* of David J Lavin and his wife Lucille (Potter); *e* College of William and Mary; *m* Ron Leibman.

First appeared on the stage at the Wayneflete School, Portland, Maine, 1942, as the White Rabbit in Alice in Wonderland; made her New York début at the East 74th Street, 16 Apr 1960, as Izzy in the revival of Oh, Kay!; Billy Rose, Jan 1962, played Wilma, Crying Daughter, Fifi of Paris, Quiet Girl in A Family Affair; Cort, Mar 1963, Barbara in The Riot Act; Actors Playhouse, 1965, took over as Evelyn in Kiss Mama; Renata, Apr 1965, played in the revue Wet Paint; East 74th Street, Oct 1965, Victoire in Hotel Passionato; The New, Jan 1966, played in the revue The Mad Show; Alvin, Mar 1966, Sydney in It's a Bird . . . It's a Plane . . . It's Superman; toured, 1966, as Daisy Gamble in On a Clear Day You Can See Forever; Cort, Nov 1967, Beth Nemerov in Something Different; Circle in the Square, Jan 1969, Patsy Newquist in Little Murders; Cort, Apr 1969, played all the women's roles in Cop-Out; Eugene O'Neill, Dec 1969, Elaine Navazio in Last of the Red Hot Lovers; John Drew, Easthampton, Long Island, June 1971, played in In the Beginning Moon, and A Servant of Two Masters; Bijou, Jan 1973, Leah in The Enemy Is Dead; Delacorte, summer 1975, Courtesan in The Comedy of Errors; Yale Repertory, New Haven, Conn, Dec 1975, Tlimpattia in Dynamite Tonite!; San Diego, 1979, Sonya in Uncle Vanya; received the Drama Desk Award, 1968–9, and the Outer Circle Award, 1968–9; first appeared on television in 1962 and since has played in The Beggar's Opera, Damn Yankees, *CBS Playhouse, Rhoda, Barney Miller, Harry O*, and her own series *Alice*, 1976.

Favourite parts: Elaine Navazio, Patsy Newquist, the Girl in Cop-Out. *Recreations:* Cooking, tennis. *Address:* Actors Equity Association, 165 West 46th Street, New York, NY 10036.

LAWRENCE, Carol (*née* Laraia), singer and actress
b Melrose Park, Ill, 5 Sept 1935; *m* Robert Goulet.

Made her New York debut at the Royale, 16 May 1952, in the revue New Faces of 1952; City Center, May 1955, played Liat in South Pacific; Winter Garden, June 1956, Arana in Shangri-La; Mar 1957, appeared in the revue The Ziegfeld Follies; Sept 1957, Maria in West Side Story; Dec 1959, Clio Dulaine in Saratoga; Apr 1960, Maria in a revival of West Side Story; St James, Dec 1961, Angela McKay in Subways Are for Sleeping; Brooks Atkinson, Oct 1962, Gia in Night Life; Flamingo, Las Vegas, Nev, Dec 1963, appeared in cabaret; toured, summer 1967, as Fanny Brice in Funny Girl; 46th Street, Dec 1967, took over from Mary Martin as Agnes in I Do! I Do!; toured, summer 1971, as Maria Rainer in The Sound of Music; Persian Room, NY, Oct 1971, appeared in cabaret; Dorothy Chandler Pavilion, Los Angeles, Sept 1975, Guinevere in Camelot.

Address: Actors Equity Association, 165 West 46th Street, New York, NY 10036.

LAWRENCE, Jerome, dramatic author, director
b Cleveland, Ohio, 14 July 1915; *s* of Samuel Lawrence and his wife Sarah (Rogen); *e* Ohio State University.

Began his career as a director and writer for radio, and also as a short story writer for the *Saturday Evening Post*; author of the following plays (with Robert E Lee): Look, Ma, I'm Dancin'! (book), 1948; The Laugh Maker, 1952 (rewritten as Turn on the Night, 1961, and The Crocodile Smile, 1970); Inherit the Wind, 1955; Auntie Mame, Shangri-La (based on James Hilton's novel, Lost Horizon: book and lyrics, with Lee and Hilton), 1956; The Gang's All Here, Only in America, 1959; A Call on Kuprin, 1961; Diamond Orchid, 1965 (rewritten as Sparks Fly Upwards, 1967); Mame, 1966; Dear World (based on The Madwoman of Chaillot), The Incomparable Max, 1969; The Night Thoreau Spent in Jail, 1971; The Incomparable Max produced in New York, 1971; directed the Dublin production of The Night Thoreau Spent in Jail, 1972; sole author of Live Spelled Backwards (A Moral Immorality Play), 1972; Jabberwock (with Robert E Lee), produced at the Dallas Texas, Theatre Center, 1972–3; First Monday in October, also directed at the Cleveland, Ohio, Playhouse, 1975; Inherit the Wind, and Auntie Mame have been translated into more than thirty languages each, and have been produced in many world capitals, also filmed; screenplays include: Joyous Season, The Night Thoreau Spent in Jail, and First Monday in October; author of Actor; The Life and Times of Paul Muni, 1974; one of the founders of Armed Forces Radio Service; wrote and directed the official Army-Navy programs for D Day, VE Day, and VJ Day; member, Drama Panel, US State Department Cultural Exchange; member of the Board of Standards and Planning for the Living Theatre; Vice President and member of the Board of Directors of ANTA; member of the Board of Directors of the American Conservatory Theatre, National Repertory Theatre, and of the Eugene O'Neill Foundation; Council Member, co-founder and President of the American Playwrights Theatre; co-founder and Judge of the annual Margo Jones Award; also member of ASCAP, Academy of Motion Picture Arts and Sciences, Council Member of The Dramatists Guild and of the Authors League of America, National President of the Radio Writer's Guild, Council Member, Writers' Guild of America, Academy of Television Arts and Sciences, Journalism Advisory Council; received an Honorary Doctor of Humane Letters Degree from Ohio State University, 1963; appointed Master Playwright of New York University, Institute of Performing Arts, 1967; Doctor of Literature, Fairleigh Dickinson Univ, 1968; Doctor of Fine Arts, Villanova Univ, 1969; Visiting Professor, Salzburg, Austria, Institute of American Studies, Ohio State Univ, Banff, Canada, School of Fine Arts, Baylor University, Texas; has received many awards and prizes in the theatre, including the Donaldson Award, Ohioana Award, Variety Critics Poll, both in NY and London; three times the winner of the Peabody Award for radio programmes; has contributed material to an extensive Lawrence and Lee collection at the Library and Museum of the Performing Arts, NY.
Club: Players. *Address:* 21056 Las Flores Mesa Drive, Malibu, Calif USA 90265.

LAWTON, Leslie, director and actor
b Dundee, 7 Feb 1942; *s* of Charles Lawton and his wife Margaret (Scott); *e* Sale Grammar School; *m* the actress Jenny Oulton; formerly an advertising copywriter.
Began his professional career as a boy actor in films and TV; after two years in advertising went into rep at the Liverpool Playhouse, making his debut there in Sept 1962 as Suliote in An Elegance of Rebels; further rep experience at York, Birmingham, Watford, Harrogate and Worthing; began directing at Folkestone Rep, as director of productions, 1968; artistic director, Watermill, Newbury, 1969;

Westcliff Palace, 1972–75; Liverpool Playhouse, 1975–79; Royal Lyceum, Edinburgh, 1979–present; directed and appeared in numerous productions at these theatres, including the premiere of Walk On, Walk On, which he directed at Liverpool in 1975; other directing work includes The Young Generation, 1972, Streamers 1978, both in London, and engagements in Canada and S Africa; author of the revue As Dorothy Parker Once Said, 1969; Women's Libby (also directed), 1971; Dilys with a Touch of Class, 1976; adapted The Dance of Death, 1975; first film, Hell Is a City, 1958; subsequently in Billy Liar, Battle of Britain, etc; TV since 1956 includes, recently, Strangers (Granada, 1979).
Favourite parts: Butley, Stanhope in Journey's End, Jack Absolute. *Address:* c/o Elspeth Cochrane Agency, 1 The Pavement, London SW4.

LAYE, Dilys (*née* Lay), actress
b London, 11 Mar 1934; *d* of Edward Charles Lay, and his wife Margot Catherine (Hewitt); *e* St Dominic's Convent, Harrow-on-the-Hill; *m* Alan Downer; trained for the stage at the Aida Foster School.
First appeared on the stage as a child, in Apr 1948, at the New Lindsey Theatre, as Moritz Scharf in The Burning Bush; first appeared on the London stage in Oct 1951, at the New, as Lettice in And So To Bed; Hippodrome, May 1953, appeared in the revue High Spirits; Criterion, Apr 1954, Intimacy at 8.30; made her New York début at the Royale, Sept 1954, as Dulcie in The Boy Friend; Apollo, June 1956, For Amusement Only; Her Majesty's, Dec 1957, Estell Novick in The Tunnel of Love; Theatre Royal, Stratford E, Oct 1959 and New, Dec 1959, the Redhead in Make Me an Offer; Her Majesty's, Oct 1965, Valerie Pitman in Say Who You Are; Playhouse, Oxford, 1958, Mrs Shin in The Good Woman of Setzuan; Mermaid, Sept 1969, Polly Butler in Children's Day; toured, 1970, as Miriam in The Keep; New, Bromley, 1971, Joan in The Man Most Likely To . . .; toured, 1971, as Hattie in The Grass is Greener; Aldwych, May 1974, Theresa Diego in the RSC production, The Bewitched; Hong Kong Festival, 1976, Brenda in A Bedfull of Foreigners; Old Vic, Oct 1976, and Criterion, Feb 1977, played Julie in The Purging and Helen in The Singer, in the double-bill, The Frontiers of Farce; 1978, toured in George and Mildred; 1979, toured in Murders in A Bad Light; films include Doctor at Large and several in the Carry On series; television appearances include the comedy series The Bed-Sit Girl and plays.
Recreations: Driving, crochet, knitting. *Address:* c/o London Management, 235–241 Regent Street, London, W1.

LAYE, Evelyn, CBE, actress and singer
b London, 10 July 1900; *d* of Gilbert Laye and his wife Evelyn (Froud); *e* Folkestone and Brighton; *m* (1) Sonnie Hale (mar dis); (2) Frank Lawton.
Made her first appearance on the stage, at the Theatre Royal, Brighton, Aug 1915, when she played the part of Nag-Ping in Mr Wu; made her first appearance in London, at the East Ham Palace, 24 Apr 1916, in the revue, Honi Soit, in which she subsequently toured; at the Lyceum, Edinburgh, Dec 1916, played Pyrrha in Oh, Caesar! and toured in this piece for some time; at Christmas, 1917, appeared at the Theatre Royal, Portsmouth, as Goody Two Shoes in the pantomime of that name; at the Gaiety Theatre, 14 Feb 1918, she succeeded Moya Mannering as Leonie Bramble in The Beauty Spot; at the same theatre, May 1918, played Madeline Manners in Going-Up; Oct 1919, Dollis Pym in The Kiss Call; Mar 1920, Bessie Brent in The Shop Girl; at the Queen's Theatre, Mar 1921, Mollie Moffat in Nighty Night;

Apr 1921, Mary Howells in Mary; Oxford, Aug 1921, appeared in The League of Notions; at the London Pavilion, Oct 1921, in Fun of the Fayre; Aug 1922, appeared as Prologue and Helen in Phi-Phi; she was then engaged for Daly's Theatre, and appeared May 1923, as Sonia in a revival of The Merry Widow; in Dec 1923, she played the title-role in Madame Pompadour; King's, Glasgow, Dec 1924, played Alice in The Dollar Princess, and played the same part at Daly's, Feb 1925; Daly's, June 1925, played Cleopatra in the piece of that name; Adelphi, Nov 1925, Betty in Betty in Mayfair; Sept 1926, Molly Shine in Merely Molly; Palace, Mar 1927, succeeded Winnie Melville as Princess Elaine in Princess Charming; Daly's, Dec 1927, played Lili in Lilac Time, Piccadilly, Apr 1928, George Ann Bellamy in Blue Eyes; Daly's, Dec 1928 again played Lili in Lilac Time; Drury Lane, Apr 1929, Marianne in The New Moon; made her first appearance in New York at the Ziegfeld Theatre, 5 Nov 1929, as the Marchioness of Shayne, Sarah Millick, and Sari Linden in Bitter Sweet; His Majesty's, London, Nov 1930, in the same parts; at the Lyceum, Apr 1931, again played in Bitter Sweet; July 1931, toured in Madame Pompadour; and Oct 1931, in Bitter Sweet; at the Adelphi, Jan 1932, played the title-role in Helen!; London Hippodrome, June 1933, Peggy in Give Me a Ring; at the Shrine Auditorium, Los Angeles, Oct 1935, again appeared in Bitter Sweet; Booth Theatre, NY, Mar 1936, played Belinda Warren in Sweet Aloes; Lyceum, London, May 1937, Princess Anna in Paganini; Majestic, NY, Dec 1937, Natalie Rives in Between the Devil; on returning to England, appeared in variety theatres; made her first appearance on the variety stage in London, Palladium, June 1938; Theatre Royal, Birmingham, Dec 1938, played Prince Florizel in the pantomime, The Sleeping Beauty; Savoy, Feb 1940, appeared in Lights Up; Coliseum, Sept 1942, played Violet Gray in The Belle of New York; Piccadilly, Aug 1943, Marie Sauvinet in Sunny River; His Majesty's, Dec 1943, the Prince in Cinderella; Prince's, Mar 1945, Katherine in Three Waltzes, subsequently touring in the same play; toured, from Apr 1946, as Laura Kent in Elusive Lady, and played this part at Wimbledon, July 1946; toured, 1948, as Lady Teazle in The School for Scandal; Palladium, Dec 1948, appeared as Prince Charming in Cinderella; Lyric, May 1949, Marina Verani in Two Dozen Red Roses; toured, from Sept 1950, as Stella in September Tide; Wimbledon, Dec 1950, played Joscelyn in Queen of Hearts; Wimbledon, July 1953, appeared in The Domino Revue; Scala, Dec 1953, Mrs Darling in Peter Pan; Hippodrome, Apr 1954, Marcelle Thibault in Wedding in Paris; Cambridge, July 1957, played Lady Marlowe in Silver Wedding; toured, Feb 1959, in the title-role of The Marquise; Saville, Dec 1959, played Lady Fitzadam in The Amorous Prawn, which ran for over two years; Prince of Wales, Jan 1964, succeeded Joan Bennett as Edith Lambert in Never Too Late; Ashcroft, Croydon, Apr 1965, played Lady Catherine in The Circle, subsequently appearing at the Savoy, June 1965, in the same production; Alhambra, Glasgow, Apr 1966, Annie Besant in Strike a Light, and at the Piccadilly, July 1966; Phoenix, Oct 1967, Muriel Willoughby in Let's All Go Down the Strand; Adelphi, Mar 1969, took over the part of Lady Hadwell in Charlie Girl during the absence of Anna Neagle; Palace, Nov 1969, Mrs Fitzmaurice in Phil the Fluter; toured, Sept 1970, in The Amorous Prawn; Strand, June 1971, Eleanor Hunter in No Sex Please—We're British; toured, Aug 1976, as Leonora Fiske in Ladies in Retirement; Northcott, Exeter, July 1979, and tour, Madame Armfeldt in A Little Night Music; has also appeared in many films, most recently Say Hello to Yesterday; also on radio and TV; is the author of Boo To My Friends, 1958; received the CBE in the Birthday Honours, 1973.

Address: c/o Film Rights Ltd, 113–117 Wardour Street, London, W1.

LAYTON, Joe (*né* Lichtman), choreographer and director
b Brooklyn, New York, 3 May 1931; *s* of Irving J Lichtman and his wife Sally (Fischer); *e* Brooklyn Public School, and the High School of Music and Art; studied with Joseph Levinoff, 1943–8; *m* Evelyn Russell; served US Army, 1952–4.

Formerly a dancer, appearing in Oklahoma!, High Button Shoes, Gentlemen Prefer Blondes, Wonderful Town, etc; while in the Army directed The Moon Is Blue, and directed and choreographed Brigadoon, On the Town, The Telephone, and The Medium, choreographed ballets for the Ballet Ho de Georges Reich, and danced with that company in Paris and Cannes, 1954–5; at the Provincetown Playhouse, NY, June 1957, assistant choreographer for Kaleidoscope; at the Tamiment Playhouse, Camp Tamiment, Penn, 1958, choreographer for The Princess and the Pea; has since been choreographer for the following productions: On the Town (revival), Once upon a Mattress, The Fashion Industry Show for the American Exhibition in Moscow, The Sound of Music, 1959; Greenwillow, Once upon a Mattress (London), Tenderloin, 1960; The Sound of Music (London), Sail Away! 1961; No Strings (also directed), Sail Away! (London), 1962; On the Town (London), The Girl Who Came to Supper (also directed), 1963; South Pacific (Toronto), Peter Pat (also directed), 1964; Drat the Cat (also directed), 1965; Waterside Theatre, Manteo, North Carolina, 1964–70, directed the historical pageant The Lost Colony; Sherry!, South Pacific, 1967; George M! 1968; Dear World, 1969; Carol Channing and Her Ten Stout-Hearted Men (London), Scarlett! (a Japanese language musical based on Gone with the Wind, Tokyo), Two by Two, 1970; The Grand Tour, a ballet for the Royal Ballet, 1971; OW, for the Royal Ballet, and Double Exposure for the Robert Joffrey Ballet, 1972; directed and choreographed Gone with the Wind at the Drury Lane, May 1972; Dorothy Chandler Pavilion, Los Angeles, Aug 1973, directed, choreographed, and co-produced Gone with the Wind; directed and choreographed Bette Midler's Clams on the Half Shell Revue, 1975; directed the world tours of Raquel Welch, Diana Ross, and The Carpenters, 1976; direction and choreography for Platinum, 1978; Barnum, 1980; received the Antoinette Perry Award for No Strings and George M!; first directed choreography for television in 1959, with Mary Martin and has since been choreographer for The Gershwin Years, Once upon a Mattress, My Name Is Barbra (Streisand), Color Me Barbra, both of which he also devised and directed; recently producer for a number of specials for such artists as Cher, Melissa Manchester, Dolly Parton and Carol Burnett, etc.

Recreation: Painting. *Address:* c/o Roy Gerber Associates, 9200 Sunset Boulevard, Los Angeles, Calif 90069. *Tel:* 213–550 0100.

LEE, Bernard, actor
b London, 10 Jan 1908; *s* of Edmund James Lee and his wife Nellie (Smith); *e* Liverpool Collegiate School; *m* Gladys Merredew; studied for the stage at the Royal Academy of Dramatic Art.

Made his first appearance on the stage at the Oxford Music Hall, London, 1914, as a small child, in a sketch, The Double Event, in which his father was acting; subsequently employed as fruit salesman at Southampton; after leaving the Academy, toured 1926 as Longford in White Cargo; in the same year was engaged with the Rusholme Repertory Company, Manchester; in 1928, was at the Repertory Theatre,

Cardiff, and from 1928–30, with the Regent Repertory Company, King's Cross; during 1930, toured as Captain Stanhope in Journey's End; during the summers of 1930–2, engaged with the Sunshine concert party, at the Summer Theatre, Shanklin; Fortune, Dec 1932, played Fred Kellard in Appearances; May 1933, Peter and Geoffrey Trail in Heritage; St Martin's, May 1933, Pip in Love for Sale; Embassy, Oct 1933, Sir John Harrington in The Tudor Wench; Lyceum, Nov 1933, Ferdinand Fane in The Terror; Kingsway, Feb 1934, Sir Thomas Seymour in The Queen Who Kept Her Head; Duke of York's, Mar 1934, Saunders in Without Witness; Phoenix, May 1934, Colin Derwent in Ten Minute Alibi; Kingsway, Jan 1935, Jimmy O'Bryan in Murder in Motley; Piccadilly, Apr 1935, Johnny Clayton in The Shadow Man; Arts, Sept 1935, Antoine Duval in The Philanthropist; Embassy, Oct 1935, Felix Montague in Distinguished Gathering; Nov 1935, Walter Grainger in Murder Gang; Queen's, Mar 1936, Private Whitman in Red Knight; Ambassadors', Apr 1936, Anthony Pittman and Ben Manassey in The Future that Was; Embassy, Oct 1936, Heartfree in The Provoked Wife; Savoy, Nov 1936, Stephen Horka in Young Madame Conti and Jan 1937, Ray Dawson in Night Sky; New, May 1937, Det-Inspector Kinneir in And the Music Stopped; Prince's, July 1937, Clarence, the Dodger, in The Gusher; Mansfield, New York, Jan 1938, Arthur Blunt in If I Were You; New, London, May 1938, Henry Hayes in People of Our Class; Arts, Sept 1938, Dr Frank Chavasse in Blind Man's Buff; Aldwych, Dec 1938, Tray Bong Smith in Number Six; Richmond, June 1939, Hayland Marlow in Without Motive?; at Oxford, Mar 1940, appeared in The Long Mirror; Richmond, June 1940, played Gordon in Penny Wise; served in the Army 1940–5; reappeared on the stage, at the Saville, Feb 1946, when he played David Kingsley in Stage Door; toured, June 1946, in Fools Rush In, and appeared as Paul in this play at the Fortune, Sept 1946; Lyric, July 1947, Fred Shattock in Peace In Our Time; Apollo, June 1950, played Able Seaman Turner in Seagulls Over Sorrento; Hippodrome, Apr 1955, appeared as Dan Hilliard in The Desperate Hours; toured, Oct 1962, as Detective-Superintendent in Act of Violence; Duchess, May 1963, played Charlie in Norman; Richmond Theatre, June 1971, played the General in Waltz of the Toreadors; Royal Court, Sept 1973, Mr Slattery in The Farm, transferring to the Mayfair, Nov 1973; Aldwych, Aug 1975, for RSC, Bernard in Jingo; has also appeared in numerous films, recently as M in the James Bond series, and on television in Talking to a Stranger, etc.

Recreations: Cricket, soccer, and golf. *Club:* Savage.
Address: Savage Club, Fitzmaurice Place, London, W1.

LEE, Eugene, set designer
b 9 Mar 1939; *s* of Eugene Lee and his wife Betty; *e* Carnegie-Mellon University and Yale University; *m* Franne Newman.

At the Martinique, NY, Mar 1969, designed sets for World War 2½; other designs for off-Broadway include Slaveship, and Saved, 1970, and from 1970 a number of productions of Alice in Wonderland; costumes for Alice were designed by his wife Franne, with whom he has since worked on most of his assignments; on Broadway these include Dude, 1972; Candide, 1974 (also Chelsea Theater Center, 1973); The Skin of Our Teeth, 1975; Some of My Best Friends, 1977; Sweeney Todd, Gilda Radner Live from New York, 1979; the Lees' designs for both Candide and Sweeney Todd won Tony awards; Mr Lee has designed for the Trinity Square company, RI, since 1968, and the Lees have also worked in other major regional theatres including Arena Stage, Washington DC, Center Stage, Baltimore, and Studio Arena, Buffalo;

opera design includes The Girl of the Golden West; TV work includes several seasons of *Saturday Night Live*.
Address: 31 Union Square West, New York, NY 10003.

LEE, Franne, costume designer
b 30 Dec 1941; *d* of Martin Newman and his wife Ann (Elton); *e* University of Wisconsin (MFA); *m* Eugene Lee.

Has been responsible for costume designs for productions on and off-Broadway and in American regional theatre, usually in conjunction with her husband, the set designer Eugene Lee; see entry for details.
Address: 31 Union Square West, New York, NY 10003.

LEE, Ming Cho, designer
b Shanghai, China, 3 Oct 1930; *s* of Tsufa F Lee and his wife Ing (Tang); *e* Shanghai, Hong Kong, Occidental College in Los Angeles (BA), University of California at Los Angeles; *m* Elizabeth Rapport; studied art with the water-colorist Kuo-Nyen Chang; apprentice and assistant designer to Jo Mielziner for five years.

First designs for the theatre were the sets of The Infernal Machine, produced at the Phoenix, New York, 3 Feb 1958; since then has designed the following Broadway and off-Broadway productions: The Crucible, Triad, 1958; The Moon Besieged, 1962; Walk in Darkness, Mother Courage, Conversations in the Dark, 1963; Othello, 1964; Slapstick Tragedy, A Time for Singing, 1966; Little Murders, 1967; Here's Where I Belong, King Lear, 1968; Billy, La Strada, 1969; Gandhi, 1970; All God's Children Got Wings, The Glass Menagerie, 1975; Romeo and Juliet, Caesar and Cleopatra, The Shadow Box, 1977; Mother Courage, Angel, 1978; The Grand Tour, 1979; has been principal designer for the New York Shakespeare Festival since 1962, designing the following productions for its various theatres and touring groups: The Merchant of Venice, The Tempest, King Lear, Macbeth, 1962; Antony and Cleopatra, As You Like It, A Winter's Tale, Twelfth Night, 1963; Hamlet, Othello, Electra, A Midsummer Night's Dream, 1964; Love's Labour's Lost, Coriolanus, Troilus and Cressida, The Taming of the Shrew, Henry V, 1965; All's Well That Ends Well, Measure for Measure, Richard III, 1966; The Comedy of Errors, Titus Andronicus, Hair, 1967; Henry IV, Parts I and II, Romeo and Juliet, Ergo, 1968; Peer Gynt, Electra, Cities in Bezique, Invitation to a Beheading, 1969; The Wars of the Roses (Henry VI, Parts I, II, and III, and Richard III), Sambo, Jack MacGowran in the Works of Samuel Beckett, 1970; Timon of Athens, Two Gentlemen of Verona, The Tale of Cymbeline, 1971; Older People, Hamlet, Much Ado About Nothing, Wedding Band, 1972; The Sea Gull, 1975; Colored Girls, 1976; designed Lolita, My Love in Philadelphia, and Remote Asylum in Los Angeles, 1971; Henry IV, Part I, in Los Angeles, 1972; designed the London production of Two Gentlemen of Verona, 1973; Lear (New Haven), 1973; for the Arena Stage in Washington, DC, designed The Crucible, 1967; The Tenth Man, Room Service, The Iceman Cometh, 1968; The Night Thoreau Spent in Jail, 1970; Our Town, 1972; Julius Caesar, 1975; Waiting for Godot, 1976; Don Juan, 1978; for the ballet troupes of Jose Limon, Martha Graham, Gerald Arpino, and Alvin Ailey has designed Missa Brevis, 1958; Three Short Dances, 1959; A Look at Lightning, 1962; Sea Shadow, 1963; Ariadne, The Witch of Endor, 1965; Olympics, Night Wings, 1966; Elegy, 1967; The Lady of the House of Sleep, Secret Places, A Light Fantastic, 1968; Animus, The Poppet, 1969: has designed extensively for opera companies, including the Peabody Arts Theatre of the Peabody Institute, Baltimore, for which he was designer, 1959–63, creating the décor for The Turk in Italy, The Old

Maid and the Thief, The Fall of the City, La Boheme, Amahl and the Night Visitors, The Pearl Fishers, Werther, and Hamlet; was Art Director and Designer in Residence of the San Francisco Opera, Fall Season, 1961; for the Empire State Music Festival designed Katya Kabanova, Peter Ibbetson, 1960, and The Pearl Fishers, 1961; for the Baltimore Civic Opera designed Tristan and Isolde, 1962; for the Opera Company of Boston designed Madama Butterfly, 1962; for the Metropolitan Opera National Company Madama Butterfly, 1965, and The Marriage of Figaro, 1966; for the Opera Society of Washington, DC Bombarzo, 1967; for the New York City Opera has designed Don Rodrigo, Julius Caesar, 1966; Le Coq d'Or, 1967; Bombarzo, Faust, 1968; Roberto Devereux, 1970; for the Hamburgische Staatsoper, Hamburg, Germany, Julius Caesar, 1969, and Lucia di Lammermoor, 1971; has been principal designer for the Juilliard Opera Theatre and the American Opera Center of the Juilliard School of Music since 1964, designing Katya Kabanova, Il Tabarro, Gianni Schicchi, 1964; Fidelio, The Magic Flute, 1965; The Trial of Lucullus, 1965; The Rape of Lucrezia, 1967; L'Ormindo, 1968; The Rake's Progress, Il Giuramento, 1970; has taught set design at the Yale Drama School and the New York University Washington Square College; has had several one-man shows of his water colors and designs, notably in Los Angeles and NY; for the New York Shakespeare Festival designed the Mobile Unit, the Florence Sutro Anspacher Theatre, and the Estelle R Newman Theatre, the last two for the complex known as the Public Theatre; designed the Garage Theatre for the Harlem School of the Arts; consultant for the Performing Arts, Center of the State University of New York at Purchase, NY, for the Cincinnati Music Hall's acoustical shell and proscenium arch, and for the Patricia Corbett Pavilion of the University of Cincinnati School of Music; member of the Theatre Projects Committee of the New York City Planning Commission; member of the American Theatre Planning Board; Vice-President of the United Scenic Artists Local Union 829, 1969–71; member of the California Water Color Society.

Address: 12 East 87th Street, New York, NY 10028. *Tel:* AT 9–0316.

LEE, Robert E, dramatic author
b Elyria, Ohio, 15 Oct 1918; *s* of C Melvin Lee and his wife Elvira (Taft); *e* Elyria High School, Northwestern University, and Ohio Wesleyan University; *m* Janet Waldo, actress.

Formerly an advertising executive; co-founder of Armed Forces Radio Service, American Playwrights Theatre, and the Margo Jones Award; author of the following plays (with Jerome Lawrence): Look, Ma, I'm Dancin'! (book), 1948; The Laugh Maker, 1952 (rewritten as Turn on the Night, 1961, and again as The Crocodile Smile, 1970); Inherit the Wind, 1955; Auntie Mame, Shangri-La (based on James Hilton's novel), 1956; The Gang's All Here, Only in America, 1959; A Call on Kuprin, 1961; Diamond Orchid, 1965 (rewritten as Sparks Fly Upward, 1967); Mame, 1966; Dear World (based on The Madwoman of Chaillot), The Incomparable Max, 1969; The Night Thoreau Spent in Jail, 1971; The Incomparable Max produced in New York, 1971; Jabberwock, produced at the Dallas Theater Center, 1972–3 season; sole author of Ten Days That Shook the World, which he directed at UCLA, 1973; co-author with Lawrence of First Monday in October, produced at the Cleveland, Ohio, Playhouse, 1975; sole author of Sounding Brass, NY, 1975; Inherit the Wind and Auntie Mame have been translated into more than thirty languages each, and have been performed all over the world, also filmed; joint author of

screenplays including Joyous Season, The Night Thoreau Spent in Jail, and First Monday in October; author, with Jerome Lawrence, of scripts for the radio series *The Railroad Hour*, 1948–54, and also of more than 500 radio and television scripts in the *Favorite Story* series, 1946–54; with Lawrence wrote book and lyrics for the TV musical Actor, 1977; received an honorary doctor of literature degree from Ohio Wesleyan University, 1962; Doctor of Humanities, Ohio State University, 1979; has contributed material to an extensive Lawrence and Lee Collection in the Library and Museum of the Performing Arts.

Address: 15725 Royal Oak Road, Encino, Calif 91316.

LEE, Vanessa, actress and singer
b Streatham, London, 18 June 1920; *d* of Alfred Moule and his wife Ellen (Gorringe); *e* Church of England School, Streatham; *m* (1) Warde Morgan; (2) Peter, 8th Baron Graves (actor Peter Graves); studied voice production and dancing at the Warde Morgan studio.

Made her first appearance on the stage, 1932, as the child, Lenschen in Autumn Crocus, appearing at various suburban halls; made her first appearance in London, at the Alhambra, 14 Aug 1935, as Ruby in Tulip Time; which ran for a year; subsequently sang in BBC programmes, and was heard in Band Waggon, etc; also sang at many concerts; toured, 1943, as Marjanah in Chu Chin Chow and Violet in The Belle of New York, and at Christmas 1943, appeared as principal boy in pantomime at the Alexandra Theatre, Birmingham; Winter Garden, Feb 1944, played the Countess of Stafford in Old Chelsea; from 1944–6, was engaged with Jack Taylor's revues, appearing each Christmas in pantomime; toured, 1946, as Maria Ziegler in The Dancing Years; Finsbury Park Empire, Christmas, 1946, played Dick in Dick Whittington; at the Casino, Mar 1947, was understudy for the part of Maria Ziegler in the revival of The Dancing Years; toured South Africa, 1947, to play Lydia, Veronica and Iris in Perchance to Dream, and on her return to England, she toured in the same play; at the Palace, Sept 1949, appeared as the Princess Christiane in King's Rhapsody; Palladium, Dec 1952, played Dick Whittington in pantomime; Globe, June 1954, appeared as Lady Windermere in After the Ball; toured, 1958, as Nancy Gibbs in Old Chelsea; toured, 1959, as Anna in The Merry Widow; Hippodrome, Bristol, Dec 1960, played the Princess in Cole Porter's Aladdin; toured, Apr 1961, as Jane Kimball in Kind Sir; went to Australia with her husband, where she took over the part of Maria in The Sound of Music in the Australian production, June 1962; on her return to England, toured spring, 1964, as Amanda in Private Lives; Scala, Dec 1965, Mrs Darling in Peter Pan; Phoenix, July 1967, Mrs Cheyney in The Last of Mrs Cheyney; 1969, toured South Africa as Lady Chiltern in An Ideal Husband; 1970, toured as Isobel in A Boston Story and Olivia in His, Hers and Theirs, playing the latter part on her return, Richmond, Nov 1970; toured, Sept 1972, as Barbara in Who Killed Santa Claus?; films include The Adventurers; numerous appearances on television, since 1937, including the series *Those Wonderful Shows*, King's Rhapsody, and as guest soloist with Vic Oliver, Mantovani, etc.

Favourite parts: Maria in The Dancing Years, and Christiane in King's Rhapsody. *Recreations:* Reading, crossword puzzles and tapestry work. *Address:* c/o ICM Ltd, 22 Grafton Street, London, W1.

LEECH, Richard (*né* Richard Leeper McClelland), actor
b Dublin, 24 Nov 1922; *s* of Herbert Saunderson McClelland and his wife Isabella Frances (Leeper); *e* Baymount Preparatory School, Haileybury College, and Trinity College, Dublin

(BA); *m* (1) Helen Hyslop Uttley (dec); (2) Diane Pearson; intended to be a doctor, and was in practice for one year, having obtained the medical degrees, MB, BCh, BAO.

Was a student at the Dublin Gate Theatre while studying medicine, and acted semi-professionally, at that theatre from 1942–5, having first appeared, 17 Mar 1942, as a Slave in The Vineyard; practised medicine, 1945–6; made his first appearance in London, at the Granville Theatre, Walham Green, 19 Aug 1946, playing small parts in Marrowbone Lane, and subsequently, in The White-headed Boy, and Drama at Inish; from Jan–Dec 1947, was engaged in repertory, at the County Theatre, Hereford, playing leading parts in The Corn is Green, The Hasty Heart, The Importance of Being Earnest, etc; Lyric, Hammersmith, Feb 1948, Nicholas Bell in Castle Anna, and May 1948, Chris Keller in All My Sons, playing the same part at the Globe, June 1948; Lyric, Hammersmith, Oct 1948, Captain Brassbound in Captain Brassbound's Conversion, and Feb 1949, Neil Harding in The Damask Cheek; Globe, May 1949, Humphrey Devize in The Lady's Not For Burning; Duke of York's, May 1950, Cyril Agthorne in The Hat Trick; made his first appearance on the New York stage, at the Royale, 8 Nov 1950, as Humphrey Devize in The Lady's Not For Burning; after returning to England appeared at the Arts, Ipswich, May 1951, as Robert Catesby in Gunpowder, Treason and Plot; Savoy, London, Nov 1951, played Crestwell in Relative Values, and continued in this part for over eighteen months; at the Q, May 1952, with Peter Dearing produced Bless You!; Royal, Brighton, Aug 1953, played Leicester in Queen Elizabeth; Q, Dec 1953, and Duchess, Jan 1954, played Paul Barclay in No Other Verdict; Court, Mar 1955, Giovanni Dawson in Uncertain Joy; Strand, Jan 1956, Baxter in Subway in the Sky; at the Globe, June 1960, played Henry VIII in A Man for All Seasons; Olympia, Dublin, Apr 1961, played Michael Byrne in Dazzling Prospect, subsequently playing the same part at the Globe, London, June 1961; at the King's Lynn Festival, July 1963, played the Narrator (Laurie Lee) in Cider with Rosie; Her Majesty's, May 1964, Donald Crawford in The Right Honourable Gentleman, taking over the part of Sir Charles Dilke in the same production, Aug 1965; Comedy, May 1967, played Charles Muspratt in Horizontal Hold; Wyndham's, Nov 1968, Alexander MacColgie Gibbs in The Cocktail Party, transferring to the Haymarket theatre; Belgrade, Coventry, Oct 1971, Walter Franz in The Price; same theatre, Feb 1972, Sir Anthony Absolute in The Rivals; Haymarket, Leicester, June 1976, Andrew Wyke in Sleuth; Shaftesbury, May 1977, Dr Campbell Thompson in Rolls Hyphen Royce; Mermaid, Mar 1978, Dr Emerson in Whose Life Is It, Anyway?, transferring to the Savoy, June 1978–Sept 1979; TV appearances include Dickens of London, Edward VII, Occupations and Brassneck; films include: The Dam Busters, The Young Churchill, A Night to Remember, etc; has broadcast many novels and given prose and poetry recitals; since Jan 1968, author of a column, Doctor in the Wings, in *World Medicine*.
Club: Garrick. *Hobbies:* Gardening and bricklaying. *Addresses:* 27 Claylands Road, London SW8 1NX *and* Wood End Cottage, Little Horwood, Bucks. *Tel:* Winslow 2301.

LE GALLIENNE, Eva, actress, director, and author
b London, 11 Jan 1899; *d* of Richard Le Gallienne and his wife Julie (Norregaard); *e* London and Paris; studied for the stage at the Royal Academy of Dramatic Art.
Made her first appearance on the stage at the Queen's Theatre, 21 July 1914, as a Page in Monna Vanna; next appeared at the Prince of Wales's Theatre, 29 May 1915, when she played Elizabeth in The Laughter of Fools; at His Majesty's, July 1915, played Victorine in Peter Ibbetson; she then went to America, making her first appearance in New York, at the Comedy Theatre, 26 Oct 1915, as Rose in Mrs Boltay's Daughters; at the Hudson, Jan 1916, played Jennie in Bunny; at the Fulton, Feb 1916, Mary Powers in The Melody of Youth; at the Shubert, Sept 1916, Patricia Molloy in Mr Lazarus; during the autumn 1916–17 toured in Rio Grande; at the Bijou, Oct 1917, played Dot Carrington in Saturday to Monday; at the Broadhurst, Dec 1917, appeared as Ottiline Mallinson in Lord and Lady Algy; at the Empire, NY, Feb 1918, the Duchess of Burchester in The Off-Chance; May 1918, Delia in Belinda; Henry Miller, Sept 1919, Eithne in Lusmore; at the George M Cohan Theatre, Dec 1919, played in Elsie Janis and Her Gang; at the Booth Theatre, May 1920, Elsie Dover in Not So Long Ago; at the Garrick, NY, Apr 1921, played Julie in Liliom; at the Provincetown Theatre, Mar 1923, played Simonetta Vespucci in Sandro Botticelli; at the Forty-eighth Street Theatre May 1923, Julia in The Rivals; at the Cort Theatre, Oct 1923, Alexandra in The Swan; Feb 1924, Hannele in Hauptmann's play of that name; at the Gaiety, NY, Mar 1924, Diane de Charence in La Vierge Folle; in June 1924, played Hilda Wangel in The Master Builder; at the Empire, NY, Aug 1924, again played Alexandra in The Swan, subsequently touring in the same part; Comedy, NY, Oct 1925, played Marie in The Call of Life; Maxine Elliott, Nov 1925, Hilda Wangel in The Master Builder; Booth, Jan 1926, Ella Rentheim in John Gabriel Borkman; opened the Civic Repertory Theatre on 25 Oct 1926, with the production of Saturday Night, adapted from the Spanish of Jacinto Benevente, in which she appeared as Imperia, and also staged the play; since that date appeared there as Masha in The Three Sisters, Hilda Wangel in The Master Builder, Ella Rentheim in John Gabriel Borkman, Mirandoline in La Locandiera, Viola in Twelfth Night, Sister Joanna in The Cradle Song, Aunt Isabel in Inheritors, Jo in The Good Hope, Sara Peri in The First Stone, Princess Orloff in Improvisations in June, Hedda Tesman in Hedda Gabler, Marie Louise in L'Invitation au Voyage, Varya in The Cherry Orchard, Peter in Peter Pan, Masha in The Seagull, Anna Karenina in The Living Corpse, Juanita in The Women Have Their Way, Lady Torminster in The Open Door, Juliet, Genevieve in Siegfried, Elsa in Alison's House, Marguerite in Camille, Julie in Liliom, Cassandra Austin in Dear Jane, the White Chess Queen in Alice in Wonderland; disbanded the Civic Repertory Company, in 1933; she then toured in Alice in Wonderland, A Doll's House, The Master Builder, Romeo and Juliet and Hedda Gabler; at the Broadhurst, NY, Nov 1934, appeared as the Duke of Reichstadt in L'Aiglon, which she also directed; subsequently revived Hedda Gabler and The Cradle Song; during 1935, toured in repertory; Shubert, NY, Dec 1935, again appeared in Rosmersholm, Camille, The Women Have Their Way, and also played Donna Laura in A Sunny Morning; Westport, Conn, June 1936, Angelica in Love for Love; Guild, NY, Nov 1936, Mathilda Wesendonck in Prelude to Exile; Mount Kisco, NY, June 1937, Mirandolina in The Mistress of the Inn; Cape Playhouse, Dennis, Mass, Aug 1937, appeared as Hamlet; Cort, NY, Oct 1938, Marie Antoinette in Madame Capet; 44th Street, Mar 1939, appeared in Frank Fay's Music-Hall, as Juliet in the balcony scene; in summer theatres, 1939, played Amanda in Private Lives; Guild Theatre, NY, Oct 1941, directed Ah, Wilderness!; St Louis, Mo, Dec 1941, played Mrs Malaprop in The Rivals, which she also directed for the Guild on tour, and at the Guild Theatre, Jan 1942; Broadhurst, May 1942, played Lettie in Uncle Harry; National, Jan 1944, Lyubov Andreyevna in The Cherry Orchard, which she also directed; Bilt-

more, Oct 1945, played Thérèse Raquin in Thérèse; in 1946, with Cheryl Crawford and Margaret Webster, founded the American Repertory Theatre, and appeared at the International, NY, Nov 1946, as Queen Katherine in Henry VIII, Comtesse de la Bière in What Every Woman Knows, and Ella Rentheim in John Gabriel Borkman; Apr 1947, the White Queen in Alice Through the Looking Glass; Cort, Feb 1948, Mrs Alving in Ghosts, and Hedda Tesman in Hedda Gabler; she toured, 1949–50, as Miss Moffat in The Corn Is Green; at Woodstock, NY, July 1950, played Signora Amaranta in Fortunato; at the Royale, NY, Jan 1954, played Lady Starcross in The Starcross Story; at the Holiday, Feb 1955, played Marcia Elder in The Southwest Corner; at the Theatre de Lys, NY, Jan 1957, gave a solo reading entitled An Afternoon with Oscar Wilde; Phoenix, NY, Oct 1957, played Queen Elizabeth in Schiller's Mary Stuart; toured, Dec 1958, as Lavinia Prendergast in Listen to the Mocking Bird; toured the US and Canada, 1959–60, as Queen Elizabeth in Mary Stuart; toured with the National Repertory Theatre, 1961–2, as Queen Elizabeth in Mary Stuart and Elizabeth the Queen; toured with the National Repertory Theatre, 1963–4, as Madame Arkadina in The Sea Gull and Madame Desmermortes in Ring Round the Moon, and also played these roles at the Belasco, Apr 1964; for the National Repertory tour of 1964–5 directed Liliom and Hedda Gabler; White Barn Theatre, Westport, Conn, Aug 1965, co-presented The Bernard Shaw Story; toured with the National Repertory, 1965–6, as the Countess Aurelia in The Madwoman of Chaillot and Hecuba in The Trojan Women; at the White Barn, July 1966, co-produced Come Slowly, Eden, Seven Ages of Bernard Shaw, Israeli Mime Theatre, and The Effect of Gamma Rays on Man-in-the-Moon Marigolds; at the Lyceum, with the APA Repertory Theatre, Jan 1968, played Queen Margaret in Exit the King and Mar 1968, directed her translation of The Cherry Orchard; American Shakespeare Festival, Stratford, Conn, 1970, the Countess in All's Well That Ends Well; Seattle, Washington, Repertory, Feb 1975, directed A Doll's House; White Barn, Westport, Conn, Aug 1975, Mrs Orpha Woodfin in The Dream Watcher; Brooklyn Academy of Music, 17 Dec 1975, Fanny Cavendish in The Royal Family, and transferred in this part to the Helen Hayes, 30 Dec 1975; toured in this role, 1976; Seattle Repertory, Nov 1977, Mrs Orpha Woodfin in The Dream Watcher; has received many honorary degrees, including: MA, Tufts College, 1927; DHL, Smith College, 1930; LittD, Russell Sage College, 1930; LittD, Brown University, 1933; LittD, Mt Holyoke College, 1937; DHL, Ohio Wesleyan University, 1953; LittD, Goucher College, 1961; DHL, University of North Carolina, 1964; has received many honors for her work in the theatre, including the Pictorial Review Award, 1926; The Society of Arts and Sciences Gold Medal; the Gold Medal for Speech of the American Academy of Arts and Letters; the Women's National Press Club Outstanding Woman of the Year Award, 1947; the Norwegian Grand Cross of the Royal Order of St Olav, 1961; an ANTA Special Award, 1964; and a Special Tony Award of the American Theatre Wing, 1964; published an autobiography, At 33, 1934; published a second volume of autobiography, With a Quiet Heart, 1953; part-author of the version of Alice in Wonderland, Dec 1932; adapted The Strong Are Lonely, 1953; she wrote a children's book Flossie and Bossie, 1949, translated Seven Tales of Hans Christian Andersen, 1959, Six Plays of Henrik Ibsen, 1957, The Wild Duck and Other Plays, 1961, The Nightingale, 1965; wrote The Mystic in the Theatre, a study of Eleonora Duse, 1966.
Address: Weston, Connecticut.

LEGGATT, Alison (Joy), actress
b Kensington, 7 Feb; *d* of W C F Leggatt and his wife Alice (Thompson); *e* St Winifred's, Eastbourne; *m* Lieut-Commander Shene Clarke, RN (mar dis); studied for the stage at the Central School of Dramatic Art, Royal Albert Hall, where she gained the Gold Medal, 1924.

Made her first appearance on the regular stage at the Scala Theatre (for the Repertory Players), Nov 1924, as the Girl of Jerusalem in Judas Iscariot; at the Haymarket, Dec 1924, appeared as a Court Gentleman in A Kiss for Cinderella; Feb 1925, walked on in Hamlet, and also understudied Fay Compton as Ophelia; appeared with the Stratford-on-Avon Festival Company, Apr–Sept 1925, in a number of small parts; at the Royalty (for the Play Actors), Oct 1925, played Crawford in This Woman Business; Comedy, Dec 1925, Mary Doane in 9.45; in 1926 was understudying Athene Seyler and Faith Celli in Caroline, at the Playhouse; at the Strand (for the Repertory Players), Oct 1926, played the Nurse in the unnamed play (subsequently entitled Many Waters), and Dec 1926, Ena Simmons in Aspidistras; at the Ambassadors', Mar 1927, Gwen Freeman in The Fanatics; Strand, Nov 1927, Margaret Mathews in Fear; Ambassadors', Dec 1927, Janet Rodney in March Hares; Shaftesbury, Aug 1928, Dorothy Merrill in The Skull; Arts, Sept 1928, Muriel Hayward in Diversion; Kingsway, Dec 1928, Jane Moonlight in Mrs Moonlight; Wyndham's, Jan 1929, Barbara Belting in Living Together; Apr 1929, Joan Shepperley in Mariners; Royalty, Dec 1929, Stella Norton in The Amorists; Arts, Jan 1930, Laura in The Humours of the Court; Arts and Apollo, Jan 1930, Freda in Nine Till Six; Drury Lane, Oct 1931, Edith Harris in Cavalcade; Duke of York's, Nov 1933, Katherine Tilney in The Rose Without a Thorn; Playhouse, Feb 1934, Kate Alcock in The Big House; Duchess, Sept 1934, Lilian Kirby in Eden End; in Oct 1935, toured with Noel Coward and Gertrude Lawrence in To-Night at 7.30, appearing in the six one-act plays which made up two programmes; the plays were presented at the Phoenix, Jan 1936, when the programme was re-named To-night at 8.30, and she played in Family Album, The Astonished Heart, Red Peppers, Hands Across the Sea, Fumed Oak and Shadow Play; Saville, Nov 1938, played Begonia Brown in Geneva; Savoy, June 1945, Mrs Lynch in Chicken Every Sunday; Lyric, Aug 1945, succeeded Elspeth March as Aunt Herda in Duet for Two Hands; Lyric, Hammersmith, Nov 1947, Milcah in The Little Dry Thorn; Wyndham's, July 1948, Mrs Underwood in People Like Us; Jan 1949, succeeded Mary Merrall as Nurse Braddock in The Gioconda Smile; Arts, Mar 1949, Maude Fulton in Caroline; Wimbledon, Oct 1949, Enid Wayne in The Man They Acquitted; New, May 1950, Lavinia Chamberlayne in The Cocktail Party; St James's, Oct 1950, played Bertie's Mother in Top of the Ladder; at the Old Vic, Apr 1952, played Emilia in Othello; at the Edinburgh Festival, 1953, played Mrs Guzzard in The Confidential Clerk, and appeared in this part at the Lyric, London, Sept 1953; toured, Aug 1954, in the same part; Royal Court, Feb 1958, played Mrs Elliott in The Epitaph for George Dillon, transferring with the production to the Comedy (re-titled George Dillon), May 1958; appeared in the same part at the John Golden, New York, Nov 1958, under the original title of the play, and after a short break, reopened in the play at the Henry Miller, NY, Jan 1959; Royal Court, London, Dec 1959, played Mabel Groomkirby in One Way Pendulum and appeared in the same production, Criterion, Feb 1960; Arts, Jan 1961, played the Manageress in Lunch Hour, Miss Ongew in The Form, and Flora in A Slight Ache, in the triple-bill Three, transferring with the production to the Criterion, Feb 1961; Princes, May 1962, appeared in the revue England, Our England; Oxford Playhouse, Oct–Nov 1962, played Mrs Tarleton in Misalliance, and the Grand

Duchess in The Just; Royal Court, Jan 1963, again played Mrs Tarleton in Misalliance, transferring with the production to the Criterion, Jan 1963; Chichester Festival, July 1963, Lady Sweetman in The Workhouse Donkey; Royal Court, July 1969, played Lady Plyant in The Double Dealer; recent films include: Far from the Madding Crowd and Goodbye, Mr Chips; she has also appeared in many television plays and serials, including The Old Wives' Tale, A Tale of Two Cities, *Edward VII*, etc.

Address: 64 St Mary Abbots Court, London, W14. *Tel:* 01–603 7463.

LEHMANN, Beatrix, actress

b Bourne End, Bucks, 1 July 1903; *d* of Rudolph Chambers Lehmann, JP, and his wife Alice Marie (Davis); *e* at home; studied for the stage at the Royal Academy of Dramatic Art, and with the late Rosina Filippi.

Made her first appearance on the stage at the Lyric Theatre, Hammersmith, May 1924, when she succeeded Elsa Lanchester as Peggy in The Way of the World; at the Adelphi, Sept 1925, played the Lady's Maid in The Green Hat, and understudied Tallulah Bankhead; St Martin's, Jan 1926, played Betty in Scotch Mist; St Martin's, May 1926, understudied Tallulah Bankhead as Amy in They Knew What They Wanted; Apollo (for the Venturers), June 1927, played Bella Griffiths in An American Tragedy; Court, Jan 1928, Judy O'Grady in The Adding Machine; Arts, July 1928, Joyce Clyde in Thunder on the Left; Lyric, Jan 1929, Lady Caroline Lamb in Byron; at the Gate, Jan–Sept 1929, Blazes in Twenty Below, Eva Berg in Hoppla, Bertha in The Race With the Shadow, Ella Downey in All God's Chillun Got Wings, Nju in Nju, Martha Hinley in The End of the Trail, etc; Apollo, Oct 1929, Susie Monican in The Silver Tassie; Savoy, Apr 1930, Myology in Brain; Player's, Nov 1930, Hazel Woodus in Gone to Earth; Feb 1931, toured as Maria Pouliski in On the Spot; Phoenix, June 1931, played Luella Carmody in Late Night Final; Festival Theatre, Cambridge, Nov 1931, Salome in the play of that name; Little, Apr 1933, The Cockney in Overture; Apollo, May 1933, Emily Brontë in Wild Decembers; Prince's, Aug 1933, Olalla Quintana in The Wandering Jew; Embassy, Oct 1933, and Alhambra, Nov 1933, Elizabeth in The Tudor Wench; Cambridge, Feb 1934, Sarah Glassman in Success Story; Embassy, Apr 1934, played Hilda Wangel in The Master Builder; Duchess, Sept 1934, Stella Kirby in Eden End; Gate, Feb 1936, Beatrice in Various Heavens; Q, Oct 1936, Charlotte Corday in a play of that name; Old Vic, Dec 1936, Winifred in The Witch of Edmonton; Arts, Feb 1937, Judith in First Night; Embassy, July 1937, Catherine in Up the Garden Path; Westminster, Nov 1937, Lavinia in Mourning Becomes Electra and July 1938, played the monologue The Human Voice; Shaftesbury, Jan 1939, Emmy Baudine in They Walk Alone; Westminster, Jan 1940, Abbie in Desire Under the Elms, in which she subsequently toured; Apollo, July 1941, Liesa Bergmann in Close Quarters; St Martin's, Feb 1942, Ilona Benson in Jam To-day; Duke of York's, June 1943, Mrs Alving in Ghosts; Garrick, Mar 1944, Lettie Quincey in Uncle Harry; in May 1946, was appointed director-producer of the Arts Council Midland Theatre company, Coventry; at the Arts, July 1946, played Ines in Vicious Circle; joined the Shakespeare Memorial Theatre Company, Stratford-on-Avon, for the 1947 season, and played Portia in The Merchant of Venice, Isabella in Measure for Measure, the Nurse in Romeo and Juliet, Viola in Twelfth Night, Duchess of Gloucester in Richard II; appeared in the last three parts at His Majesty's, Oct 1947; St James's, July 1948, played Jess Gold in No Trees in the Street; Rudolph Steiner Hall, July 1950, the Bawd in Peri-

cles; Embassy, Mar 1951, played Miss Kirby in a revival of Thunder Rock, and June 1951, Mrs Alving in Ghosts; Duke of York's, Dec 1951, Evelyn Vining in The Day's Mischief; Arts, Feb 1953, played Laura in The Father; Savoy, Dec 1953, Niobe D'Urt in No Sign of the Dove; Arts, Mar 1954, played the Mother in Blood Wedding; toured, 1955, as Sylvia Knight in First Night; Arts, Feb 1956, played Madame St Pé in The Waltz of the Toreadors, subsequently transferring with the production to the Criterion, Mar 1956; at the Lyric, Hammersmith, May 1958, appeared as Meg in The Birthday Party; Arts, Sept 1958, played Grace Lancaster in Something Unspoken, and Mrs Venable in Suddenly Last Summer (a double-bill entitled Garden District); Old Vic, Dec 1958, played Lady Macbeth in Macbeth; Queen's, Aug 1959, Miss Bordereau in The Aspern Papers; Royal Court, Oct 1964, played Mrs Spoker in A Cuckoo in the Nest; Edinburgh Festival, Sept 1965, Helen in Igloo; Old Vic, Oct 1966, played Maria Ignatyevna Kabanova in the National Theatre Production of The Storm; Mermaid, May 1967, played the title part in Hecuba, in the four-play sequence The Trojan Wars; Comedy, July 1969, Sarah Cooper in The Night I Chased the Women With An Eel; Chichester Festival, May 1970, Aase in Peer Gynt; Chichester, July 1971, Frau Lucher in Reunion in Vienna; Arts, Nov 1971, Mammles in Mother Adam; Piccadilly, Feb 1972, again played Frau Lucher; joined the RSC to play Morgan in The Island of the Mighty, Aldwych, Dec 1972, Nurse in Romeo and Juliet, and Duchess of York in Richard II, Stratford, season 1973; Royal Exchange, Manchester, Mar 1979, Dowager Lady Monchensey in The Family Reunion; President of British Actors' Equity Association, May 1945; entered films 1935, recently appearing in The Spy Who Came in from the Cold and Staircase; performed frequently on television, notably in Coriolanus and most recently in Crime and Punishment; also wrote two novels.

Favourite parts: Ella in All God's Chillun, and Blazes in Twenty Below.

(*Died 31 July 1979.*)

LEIBMAN, Ron, actor

b New York City, 11 Oct 1937; *s* of Murray Leibman and his wife Grace (Marks); *e* Ohio Wesleyan University; *m* Linda Lavin; prepared for the stage at the Actors Studio.

Made his NY début at the 41st Street, 27 Oct 1959, as Orpheus in Legend of Lovers; The Music Box, Mar 1963, played Peter Nemo in Dear Me, The Sky Is Falling; Cort, Sept 1963, played Rip Calabria in Bicycle Ride to Nevada; Brooks Atkinson, Feb 1964, Captain Salzer in The Deputy; for the Theatre of Living Arts, Philadelphia, Pa, 1965–7, played Clov in Endgame, Astrov in Uncle Vanya, Alceste in The Misanthrope, and Mr Puff in The Critic; Martinique, Sept 1967, Teddy in The Poker Session; for the Yale Repertory Theatre, New Haven, Conn, 1967–8, played Hermes in Prometheus Bound, Solyony in The Three Sisters, Mosca in Volpone, and Sergeant Henderson in We Bombed in New Haven; Ambassador, Oct 1968, again played Sergeant Henderson in We Bombed in New Haven; Cort, Apr 1969, played the male roles in Cop-Out; Village South, Jan 1970, Stan in Transfers, Bob in The Rooming House, and the title-role in Dr Galley in a bill with the overall title Transfers; Edison, May 1970, Gordon Miller in Room Service; Estelle R Newman, Feb 1976, various parts in Rich and Famous; Eugene O'Neill, Apr 1980, Herb in I Ought to Be in Pictures; received the Obie and the Drama Desk Awards for Transfers and the Drama Desk Award for We Bombed in New Haven; entered films in Where's Poppa? 1970, and has since played in Your Three Minutes Are Up, 1973, The Super Cops, 1974,

Won Ton Ton, 1976, Norma Rae, 1979, etc; television includes the series *Kaz*, for which he received an Emmy Award.

Address: 27 West 87th Street, New York, NY.

LEIGH, Mike, dramatic author and director
b Salford, Lancs, 20 Feb 1943, *s* of Alfred Abraham Leigh and his wife Phyllis Pauline (*née* Cousin); *e* Salford Grammar School; trained as an actor at the Royal Academy of Dramatic Art (1960–62), and at the Camberwell and Central Art Schools, and the London School of Film Technique; *m* Alison Steadman.

Directed and designed the original production of David Halliwell's Little Malcolm and His Struggle Against the Eunuchs, in which the author played the lead (Unity Theatre, 1965); Associate Director at the Midlands Arts Centre, 1965–66; Assistant Director, Royal Shakespeare Company, 1967–68; actor, Victoria Theatre, Stoke-on-Trent, 1966; directed The Knack for RSC Theatregoround, 1967, and The Life of Galileo for the Bermuda Arts Festival of 1970; his first original piece for the stage was The Box Play, produced at the Midlands Arts Centre, 1966; his subsequent works, all of them directed by him, and all evolved from scratch through improvisation, and scripted, are: My Parents Have Gone to Carlisle, and The Last Crusade of the Five Little Nuns (Midlands Arts Centre, 1966); Nenaa (RSC Studio, Stratford, 1967); Individual Fruit Pies (East-15 Acting School, 1968); Down Here and Up There (Theatre Upstairs, 1968); Big Basil (Manchester Youth Theatre, 1968); Epilogue (Sedgley Park/De La Salle Colleges, Manchester, 1969); Glum Victoria and the Lad with Specs (Manchester Youth Theatre, 1969); Bleak Moments (Open Space Theatre, 1970; A Rancid Pong (Basement Theatre, Soho, 1971); Wholesome Glory (Theatre Upstairs, 1973); The Jaws of Death (Traverse Theatre, 1973); Dick Whittington (Theatre Upstairs, 1973); Babies Grow Old (RSC, 1974); The Silent Majority (Bush Theatre, 1974); Abigail's Party (Hampstead, 1977); Ecstasy (Hampstead, 1979); his first film was Bleak Moments, 1971; subsequent films, all for BBC Television, are: Hard Labour (1973); Nuts in May (1976); The Kiss of Death (1977); Who's Who (1978); Grown-ups (1980); his BBC Studio plays are: The Permissive Society (1975); Knock For Knock (1976); Abigail's Party (1977).

Address: c/o A D Peters & Co Ltd, 10 Buckingham Street, London WC2 6BU.

LEIGH-HUNT, Barbara, actress
b Bath, 14 Dec 1935; *d* of Chandos Austin Leigh-Hunt and his wife Elizabeth (Jones); *e* Kensington High School, Bath; *m* the actor Richard Pasco; trained for the stage at Bristol Old Vic Theatre School.

Made her first professional appearance while still a student, in The Merry Gentleman, Bristol Old Vic, Dec 1953; joined the Old Vic Company, London, 1954, to tour as a walk-on in A Midsummer Night's Dream, visiting the Edinburgh Festival, 1954, and making her New York debut at the Metropolitan Opera House, 21 Sept 1954; rep at Lowestoft and Colwyn Bay, 1955–56; rejoined the Old Vic Company, season 1957–58, and toured Europe and N America in minor roles; at Guildford Rep, 1959; again with the Old Vic, season 1959–60, her parts included Maria in Twelfth Night, Helena in A Midsummer Night's Dream, and Portia in The Merchant of Venice; at Nottingham Playhouse, 1962, playing parts including Viola in Twelfth Night, then from 1963–69 with the Bristol Old Vic Company, playing a series of major roles and transferring to the West End in the company's productions of A Severed Head, Criterion, Jun 1963, as Rosemary, and Mrs

Mouse Are You Within?, Duke of York's, May 1968, as Anita Hill; during this time toured with the company in Europe and Israel, 1964, as Rosaline in Love's Labour's Lost; played Kate Hardcastle in She Stoops to Conquer, Bath Festival, 1965; toured UK as Saint Joan, also 1965, and as Victoria in Portrait of a Queen, 1966; toured N America and Europe as Isabella in Tyrone Guthrie's production of Measure for Measure, and as Ophelia in Hamlet, 1967; toured for Prospect, 1970, as Belvidera in Venice Preserv'd, at Hampstead, Jan 1971, played Maggie in The Formation Dancers; Bristol, 1973, Amanda in Private Lives; Edinburgh Festival, 1973, appeared in Prospect's Don Juan in Love; joined the RSC, 1973 to play Madge Larrabee in Sherlock Holmes, Jan 1974, and Krupskaya in Travesties, Jun, both at the Aldwych; played Madge Larrabee at the Broadhurst, NY, Nov 1974; Brighton Festival, 1975, appeared with Prospect in The Grand Tour; for RSC, 1975–77, played Mistress Ford in The Merry Wives of Windsor at Stratford, 1975, Aldwych, 1976; Queen Elizabeth in Richard III, The Other Place, 1975; Paulina in The Winter's Tale, Helen in Troilus and Cressida, Stratford, 1976; Goneril in King Lear, Helena, Aldwych, 1977; Orbison in That Good Between Us, Warehouse, 1977, and Teacher in Every Good Boy Deserves Favour, Royal Festival Hall, 1977; Bristol, 1978, Arkadina in The Seagull; Arnaud, Guildford, Feb 1979, and tour, Ann in Canaries Sometimes Sing; at Stratford, 1980 season, played Gertrude in Hamlet and Queen Margaret in Richard III; films, since Frenzy, 1971, include Henry VIII and His Six Wives, and A Bequest to the Nation; frequent TV since 1964 includes recently Mary's Wife, One Chance in Four, Every Good Boy Deserves Favour, and Cold Feet.

Favourite part: The next one. *Address:* c/o MLR Ltd, 194 Old Brompton Road, London SW5 OA5.

LE MASSENA, William, actor
b Glen Ridge, New Jersey, 23 May 1916; *s* of William Henry Le Massena and his wife Margery (Lockwood); *e* New York University (BFA 1939); studied with William Hansen at the American Theatre Wing and with Mira Rostova and Theodore Komisarjevsky.

Made his stage début while at University in As You Like It, 1935, and subsequently in Twelfth Night; first professional Broadway performance was at the Alvin, 5 Feb 1940, as the Pedant in The Taming of the Shrew; Alvin, Apr 1940, played Frank Olmstead in There Shall Be No Night; toured in this last part; Chanin, 1941, played a Gold Shirt in Mexican Mural; toured, 1942, as the Hermit in The Pirate; in the US Army, 1942–6; Columbus Circle, Mar 1946, took over as the Player King in Hamlet; toured in this last part; 1946; toured in Call Me Mister, 1946–7; New York City Center, Feb 1948, played a Guest in The Wedding; Century, Apr 1948, played in the revue Inside USA; Shubert, Nov 1949, William in I Know My Love and took over from Geoffrey Kerr as Frederic Chandler in this play in Jan 1950; New York City Center, May 1951, various roles in Dream Girl; Ziegfeld, July 1951, took over as Mr Esmond, Sr in Gentlemen Prefer Blondes; Royale, Dec 1951, M Redon-La-Mur in Nina; Lenox Hill Playhouse, Feb 1952, Vaughan in Fanny's First Play; State Fair Music Hall, Dallas, Texas, summer 1952, Pemberton Maxwell in Call Me Madam; toured, 1952–3, as Roger Blakesley in Point of No Return; 46th Street, Feb 1954, Lord and Judge in Ondine; toured, 1954, as Mr Jones in The Vegetable; Cherry Lane, Feb 1955, Peterbono in Thieves' Carnival; Playhouse, Jan 1956, William Danbury in Fallen Angels; New York City Center, Feb 1958, Pawnee Bill in Annie Get Your Gun; Cricket, Apr 1958, General St Pé in

Ardèle; 46th Street, Feb 1959, Howard Cavanaugh in Redhead; Broadway Chapel, Oct 1959, Bel-Kabbittu in Susannah and the Elders; toured, 1960, as Howard Cavanaugh in Redhead; ANTA, Jan 1961, Judge Callan in The Conquering Hero; Music Box, Jan 1962, Tullius in Romulus; Music Box, Dec 1962, various roles in The Beauty Part; Johannesburg, SA, 1964, played Senex in A Funny Thing Happened on the Way to the Forum; Actors Playhouse, Mar 1966, Sylvester in The Coop; toured, 1966–7, as Chitterlow in Half a Sixpence; New York City Center, Oct 1967, Reverend Dr Lloyd in Life with Father, and, Dec 1967, Mr Lundi in Brigadoon; Lunt-Fontanne, Mar 1969, Francis Faucett in Come Summer; Belasco, Mar 1970, Prof Persius Smith in Grin and Bare It!; Meadow Brook, Rochester, Mich, 1971, played in The Rainmaker; Circle in the Square, Oct 1971, Mr Addams in F Jasmine Addams; Meadow Brook, 1972, Oscar Madison in The Odd Couple, and 1972–3, played in A Doctor in Spite of Himself and The Front Page; toured, summer 1972, as Stephen Hopkins in 1776; toured, Jan–Apr 1974, as Father Ambrose in Waltz of the Toreadors; Booth, 1974, Colonel Hopkins in All Over Town; Walnut, Phila, Oct 1975, Gilbert Marshall in The Royal Family; Meadow Brook, Dec 1975, Horace Giddens in The Little Foxes; Kennedy Center, Washington, DC, May 1976 and Broadhurst, NY, Sept, Major Ketchum in A Texas Trilogy; Walnut, spring 1977, Polonius in Hamlet; Hudson Guild, Nov 1977, Bill in The Dodge Boys; Meadow Brook, Feb 1978, appeared in The Runner Stumbles; Music Box, 1978, took over as Porter Milgrim in Deathtrap; 18 Seasons with the Dallas, Texas, Summer Musicals, most recently as Max in The Sound of Music, 1977; has appeared in the films Carousel, The Wrong Man, The World of Henry Orient, Where's Poppa?, All That Jazz (1979), etc: first appeared on television in 1948 and has played regularly since in the major dramatic series.

Club: Players. *Recreations:* Motorcycling, photography, and travel. *Address:* 132 West 11th Street, New York, NY 10011. *Tel:* OR 5-2566.

LE NOIRE, Rosetta (*née* Burton), actress and singer
b New York City, 8 Aug 1911; *d* of Harold Charles Burton and his wife Marie (Jacques); *e* public schools, High School of Commerce, and Hunter College; *m* (1) William Le Noire (mar dis); (2) Egbert F Brown (dec); formerly a secretary and a playground instructress; prepared for the stage at the American Theatre Wing.

First appeared on the stage with the Federal Theatre Project at the Lafayette, NY, Apr 1936, as First Witch in Macbeth, subsequently appearing as the Bassa Moona Girl in Bassa Moona; at the Broadhurst, NY, 1939, played Peep-Bo in The Hot Mikado, and appeared in this part at the New York World's Fair in the Michael Todd production; toured in this production, 1941–2; toured US Army bases, 1943, as Emma in You Can't Take It with You, in the USO production; toured as the Maid in Janie, 1943–4; appeared on the NYC Subway Circuit in Decision and Three's a Family, June–July 1944; Mansfield, NY, Aug 1944, played Stella in Anna Lucasta, which ran for 957 performances; played this same part in a revival at the National, Sept 1947; 48th Street, Jan 1951, Rose Bolton in Four Twelves Are 48; Corning, NY, 1951, appeared in Show Boat, Three's a Family, Here Today, Anything Goes, Happy Birthday, and A Streetcar Named Desire; Lenox Hill Playhouse, Mar 1952, played in O Distant Land; Theatre de Lys, July 1954, Vonie in Supper for the Dead; Phoenix, Mar 1955, Zanche in The White Devil; City Center, May 1955, Third Sharecropper in a revival of Finian's Rainbow; Martin Beck, Mar 1956, Matumbi in Mister Johnson; ANTA, June 1956, Slave Girl in Ceremonies of In-

nocence; Jan Hus Auditorium, Sept 1956, Christine in a revival of Take a Giant Step; New York City Center, Apr 1958, the Mother in Lost in the Stars; Imperial, Apr 1959, Clara in Destry Rides Again; Broadway Congregational Church, Feb 1960, Grandmother in The Bible Salesman; Martinique, Feb 1961, again played in The Bible Salesman, and also played Madame Scarlatina in The Oldest Trick in the World in the double-bill Double Entry; City Center, Apr 1961, Bloody Mary in a revival of South Pacific; Actors Playhouse, Oct 1961, Clara in Clandestine on the Morning Line; Winter Garden, Apr 1963, Mollie in Sophie; Little, Nov 1963, Essie Belle Johnson in Tambourines to Glory; Greenwich Mews, Jan 1964, Petunia in a revival of Cabin in the Sky; ANTA, Apr 1964, Mother Henry in Blues for Mister Charlie; Martin Beck, Dec 1964, Ma Malooney in I Had a Ball; Eugene O'Neill, Feb 1966, Hattie Gaines in The Great Indoors; New York State, July 1966, Queenie in Show Boat, and subsequently toured Canada in this role; Parker Playhouse, Fort Lauderdale, Fla, Feb 1967, Bertha in The Name of the Game; Vivian Beaumont, Nov 1968, Meg in A Cry of Players; Imperial, Apr 1972, Grace Kumalo in Lost in the Stars; Chelsea Theater Center, Brooklyn, NY, Oct 1972, Mother Horn and Mom in Lady Day; became President and Artistic Director of AMAS Repertory Theatre and produced An Evening with the Bourgeoisie, Othello, The Three Sisters, and conceived and produced House Party: A Musical Memory, 1973; Vivian Beaumont, Apr 1973, A Woman in A Streetcar Named Desire, and repeated this part at the St James, Oct 1973; Eugene O'Neill, Dec 1974, Mady in God's Favorite; AMAS repertory, Feb 1975, conceived the idea of Bubbling Brown Sugar, which toured then opened at the ANTA; Brooklyn Academy of Music, 17 Dec 1975, Della in The Royal Family, and transferred in this part to the Helen Hayes, 30 Dec 1975; Bojangles originally produced at AMAS, 1979; lectured on film techniques for Lincoln Center Film Society, 1968–9; President of the AMAS Repertory Theatre, NY; played Stella in the film version of Anna Lucasta, and has also appeared in various Army films; played the Nurse in the film of The Sunshine Boys, 1975; recently in Broadway; first appeared on television in 1954 and has since appeared in such programs as *The Nurses, Studio One, Kraft Theatre, Lamp Unto My Feet,* and, in 1970–1, in the serials *A World Apart, The Guiding Light, Another World,* etc.

Favourite parts: Stella, Mollie, Sister Essie, and Mother Henry. *Recreations:* Word Games, designing and making hats, and weaving. *Address:* 1037 East 232nd Street, Bronx, New York. *Tel:* 881–4084.

LENYA, Lotte (*née* Karoline Blamauer), singer and actress
b Vienna, Austria, 18 Oct 1900; *d* of Franz Blamauer and his wife Johanna (Teuschl); *e* Zurich, where she studied ballet and drama, 1914–20; *m* (1) Kurt Weill (dec); (2) George Davis (dec); (3) Russell Detwiler.

Played in productions of Shakespeare in Berlin, 1920 and several years thereafter; at the Baden-Baden Chamber Music Festival, 1927, played Jenny in Kurt Weill's opera Little Mahagonny; Theater-am-Schiffbauerdamm, Berlin, Aug 1928, alternated as Lucy and Jenny in Die Dreigroschenoper; Stadttheater, Berlin, 1929, played Jocasta in Oedipus; Volksbuehne, Berlin, 1930, played in Danton's Death and The Awakening of Spring; Theater-am-Schiffbauerdamm, 1930, played in Pioniere in Ingolstadt; Theater-am-Kurfurstendamm, Berlin, 1931, played Jenny in Aufstieg und Fall der Stadt Mahagonny (Rise and Fall of Mahagonny); Volksbuehne, 1932, played in Song of Hoboken; left Germany and settled in Paris where, at the Théâtre des Champs-Elysées, 1933, she sang Anna I in The Seven Deadly Sins; concerts in

London and Paris, 1933–7; came to the US and, at the Manhattan Opera House, 7 Jan 1937, made her New York début as Miriam in Max Reinhardt's production of The Eternal Road; Shubert, Oct 1941, Cissie in Candle in the Wind; Alvin, Mar 1945, Duchess in The Firebrand of Florence; Martin Beck, Oct 1951, Xantippe in Barefoot in Athens; Theatre de Lys, Mar 1954, Jenny in The Threepenny Opera; same theatre, Sept 1955, again played Jenny in The Threepenny Opera; New York City Center, Dec 1958, Anna I in The Seven Deadly Sins; Theatre de Lys, Jan 1962, played in the revue Brecht on Brecht, and subsequently toured; Royal Court, London, Sept 1962, again played in Brecht on Brecht; Carnegie Hall, 8 Jan 1965, sang in a Kurt Weill Evening, including a German-language concert version of The Threepenny Opera; Broadhurst, Nov 1966, Fraülein Schneider in Cabaret; Holland Festival, Amsterdam, June 1971, appeared in revue; Los Angeles, 1973, Mother Courage in Mother Courage and Her Children; has given many concerts, notably at Town Hall, NY, 1951, Carnegie Hall, 1959 and 1960, Lewisohn Stadium, NY, 1958, and in Munich and Berlin, 1960; has recorded extensively, notably the works of Kurt Weill and Bertolt Brecht; entered films in Germany, 1930, in Die Dreigroschenoper, and in the US has played in The Roman Spring of Mrs Stone, 1961, and From Russia with Love, 1964; has appeared on television in the US and Germany.

Address: Actors Equity Association, 165 West 46th Street, New York, NY 10036.

LEONARD, Hugh (*né* John Keyes Byrne), dramatic author
b Dublin, Ireland, 9 Nov 1926; *s* of Nicholas Keyes Byrne and his wife Margaret (Doyle); *e* Presentation College, Dun Laoghaire; *m* Paule Jacquet; formerly a civil servant.

His first play, The Big Birthday, was produced at the Abbey Theatre, Dublin, 25 Jan 1956; he has since written the following plays: A Leap in the Dark, 1957; Madigan's Lock, 1958; A Walk on the Water, 1960; The Passion of Peter Ginty, 1961; Stephen D, 1962; Dublin One, 1963; The Poker Session, The Family Way, 1964; When the Saints Go Cycling In, 1965; Mick and Nick, 1966; The Quick and the Dead (double-bill), 1967; The Au Pair Man, 1968; The Barracks, 1969; The Patrick Pearse Motel, 1971; Da, 1973; Summer 1974; Irishmen (retitled A Suburb of Babylon), 1975; Some of My Best Friends are Husbands (from Labiche), 1976; Time Was, 1977; A Life, 1979; his first play to be produced in London was Stephen D at the St Martin's, Feb 1963; Tony Award for Da, 1978; wrote his autobiography, Home Before Night, 1979; since 1962, he has written for many television productions including: *Father Brown*, Strumpet City, and The Little World of Don Camillo; he has also scripted the films Interlude, Great Catherine and Percy.

Recreations: Travel, conversation, and driving. *Clubs:* Dramatists', The Players. *Address:* Theros, Coliemore Road, Dalkey, Co Dublin, Eire. *Tel:* Dublin 806187

LEONTOVICH, Eugénie, actress, director, playwright, drama coach
b Moscow, Russia, 21 Mar 1900; *d* of Konstantin Leontovich and his wife Ann (Joukovsky); *m* (1) Paul A Sokolov (mar dis); (2) Gregory Ratoff (mar dis); studied at the Imperial School of Dramatic Art, Moscow, and with Meyerhold, Vakhtangov, Komisarjevsky.

Made her first appearance on the stage in Faust, and later played in The Taming of the Shrew; was a member of the company of the Moscow Art Theatre; before the Russian revolution, appeared at the State Theatre, Moscow; after the revolution went to Paris and other continental cities; went to America in 1922, and made her first appearance on the New York stage at the Booth Theatre, 5 Oct 1922, in Revue Russe, which was imported by the Shuberts from Paris; played in Topics of 1923 and Artists and Models as a showgirl; subsequently toured in Blossom Time for several seasons, meanwhile studying the English language; appeared in Chicago, 1929, as Mrs Pepys in And So to Bed, also as Sarah Bernhardt in Fires of Spring, and subsequently as Marie in Candle Light, in which she also toured, and appeared at the Shubert-Riviera Theatre, NY, Mar 1930, in the last-mentioned part; at the National Theatre, Nov 1930, played Grusinskaia in Grand Hotel; toured in the same part, 1931–2; Broadhurst, NY, Dec 1932, Lilly Garland in Twentieth Century; during 1933–4, toured as Cavallini in Romance; Milwaukee, May 1934, played Madame Lisa Della Robbia in Enter Madame; Lyceum, NY, Feb 1935, played Novia in Bitter Oleander (Blood Wedding); made her first apearance on the London stage, at the Lyric Theatre, 24 Apr 1935, when she played the Archduchess Tatiana in Tovarich; New, Oct 1936, played Cleopatra in Antony and Cleopatra; toured in the United States, 1937–8, as the Archduchess in Tovarich; Belasco, NY, Jan 1943, played Natasha in Dark Eyes; Royal Alexandra, Toronto, Aug 1945, again played Mrs Pepys in And So to Bed; toured, 1946, in Obsession, and appeared as Nadya in this play at the Plymouth, NY, Oct 1946; again visited England, and at the New Lindsey, Jan 1947, played Gen Tanya in Caviar to the General, subsequently appearing in the same part at the Whitehall, Mar 1947; in Hollywood, June 1950, appeared as Madame Ranevsky in and directed her version of The Cherry Orchard; at Las Palmas, Hollywood, Oct 1952, appeared as Mrs Esther Jock in The Web and the Rock, and staged the production; Lyceum, NY, Dec 1954, played the Dowager Empress in Anastasia, and received the Antoinette Perry (Tony) Award for this performance; toured Australia in this role in 1956; Studebaker, Chicago, Nov 1956, directed Geraldine Page in A Month in the Country; Bijou, NY, Oct 1957, played the Queen in The Cave Dwellers; also directed the last play and played the Queen in Chicago and Texas, 1959–60; Broadhurst, May 1961, Madame Kuprin in A Call on Kuprin; Goodman, Chicago, Nov 1963, directed The Three Sisters; Goodman, May 1964, Mother Courage in Mother Courage and Her Children; at the Goodman has also starred in Enter Madame, and played the Fortune Teller in The Skin of Our Teeth; Actors Playhouse, May 1972, wrote, directed, and played in Anna K, adapted from Tolstoi's Anna Karenina; Little, Oct 1974, adapted and directed Medea and Jason; Stage 73, Nov 1975, directed And So to Bed; from 1948–52 had her own theatre, The Stage, in Los Angeles, where she directed and played in many productions; founded, in 1953, the Leontovich Theatre in Los Angeles; joined the faculty of the Goodman School of Drama, Chicago, in 1964, where she has directed Anna Karenina, The Three Sisters, The Cave Dwellers, Blood Wedding, And So to Bed, The Seagull, Lope de Vega's The Dog in the Manger, etc; has also directed productions at the Alley, Houston, Texas; directed The Sea Gull for Smith College, Northampton, Mass, where she was artist in residence and taught master's classes in acting; has also taught improvisation at Columbia College in Chicago; directed her revised version of Anna Karenina at Studio 68, London; in 1929, adapted Café de Danse from the French; author of The Laughing Woman, 1934; Dark Eyes (with Elena Miramova), 1943; Caviar to the General (with George S George), 1945; Good Virtue (from Richardson's Pamela); has appeared in several films, including: Anything Can Happen, Four Sons, The Man in Her Arms, etc; has also played on television in such shows as *Climax, Naked City, Playhouse 90, Studio One, US Steel Hour*, etc.

Address: 2140 Lincoln Park West, Chicago, Illinois 60614.

LERNER, Alan Jay, dramatic author and lyricist
b New York City, 31 Aug 1918; *s* of Joseph J Lerner and his wife Edith (Adelson); *e* at Bedales, in England, and at Choate and Harvard University; *m* (1) Ruth Boyd, (2) Marion Bell, (3) Nancy Olsen, (4) Micheline Musellin Posso di Bergo, (5) Karen Gundersson, (6) Sandra Payne, (7) Nina Bushkin.

His first production on the stage was in Detroit, 1942, when he wrote the book and lyrics for The Life of the Party; has since written the book and lyrics for the following musical productions: What's Up?, 1943, The Day Before Spring, 1945, Brigadoon, 1947, Love Life, 1948, Paint Your Wagon, 1951, My Fair Lady, 1956, Camelot, 1960, On a Clear Day You Can See Forever (also co-presented) 1965, Coco, 1969; Lolita, 1971; YMHA, New York, 12 Dec 1971, performed in the series Lyrics and Lyricists; book and lyrics for Gigi, 1973, for which he received the Tony Award; book for the revue Music! Music!, 1974; wrote the continuity for the tour of Gene Kelly's Salute to Broadway, 1975; book and lyrics for 1600 Pennsylvania Avenue, 1976; Carmelina, 1979; in addition to the films of his stage plays, he is also the author of the films An American in Paris, 1951, Gigi (also lyrics), 1958, and wrote the lyrics for the film A Royal Wedding, 1951; screenplay and lyrics for the film The Little Prince, 1974; received the New York Critics Circle Award for Brigadoon, 1947, the Academy Award for story and screenplay of An American in Paris, 1951, the New York Drama Critics Circle, Donaldson, and Antoinette Perry (Tony) Awards for My Fair Lady, 1956, Academy Awards for screenplay and song for Gigi, 1958, the Grammy Award for On a Clear Day You Can See Forever, 1965; received the Choate Alumni Seal; appointed by John F Kennedy to the President's Committee for the Cultural Center in Washington DC, 1962; President of the Dramatists Guild, 1958–63; elected to the Songwriters Hall of Fame, 1971.
Recreations: Tennis and boating. *Clubs:* Players, Lambs, Shaw Society. *Address:* 424 Madison Avenue, New York, NY 10017. *Tel:* 679–2211.

LETTS, Pauline, actress
b Loughborough, Leicestershire, 1 May 1917; *d* of Harry Letts and his wife Elise (Catlow); *e* Collegiate School for Girls, Leicester; *m* Geoffrey Staines; studied for the stage at the Royal Academy of Dramatic Art.

Made her first appearance on the stage with the Coventry Repertory Company, July 1935, as Sally in The Two Mrs Carrolls, and remained there, playing leading parts, 1935–6; appeared with the Festival Theatre Company, Stratford-on-Avon, during the 1938 season, as Miranda in The Tempest, Maria in Twelfth Night, Hermia in A Midsummer Night's Dream, Luciana in Comedy of Errors; joined the York Repertory Company 1939, and remained there playing innumerable leading parts until 1943; made her first appearance in London, at the Mercury Theatre, 30 Sept 1943, as Nan Hardwick in The Tragedy of Nan; at Wyndham's, Feb 1944, played Phoebe Ferguson in A Soldier for Christmas; Gateway, Nov 1945, Valerie Camber in The Long Mirror; Saville, Feb 1946, Kaye Hamilton in Stage Door; Lyric, Hammersmith, Feb 1948, Teresa Castlevance in Castle Anna; Lyric, London, Mar 1948, Evelyn Holt in Edward, My Son; Arts, Cambridge, May 1958, Rachel Verney in The Offshore Island; joined the Old Vic Company and played Portia in Julius Caesar, Oct 1958, Lady Macduff in Macbeth, Dec 1958, and Charlotte Verinder in The Magistrate, Mar

1959; joined the Royal Shakespeare Company, Stratford-on-Avon, Sept 1962, to play the Abbess in The Comedy of Errors; Northampton Repertory, May 1964, appeared as a Guest Artist to play Constance in King John; Northampton, May 1965, played the title-part in Candida and, June 1966, Martha in Who's Afraid of Virginia Woolf?; Traverse, Edinburgh, June 1967, appeared as Maggie in Grounds for Marriage; Harrogate Festival, Aug 1967, Netty Cleary in The Subject Was Roses; she has also performed in films, on radio, and television since 1946 includes The Generations and Tinker, Tailor, Soldier, Spy.
Favourite parts: Evelyn Holt in Edward, My Son and Rachel in The Offshore Island. *Recreations:* Work, theatre-going and Cordon Bleu cookery. *Address:* 28 Bonser Road, Twickenham, Middlesex.

LEVENE, Sam, actor
b New York City, 28 Aug 1905; *s* of Harry Levine and his wife Bethsheba (Weiner); *e* Stuyvesant High School; *m* Constance Hoffman; studied for the stage at the American Academy of Dramatic Art; was originally intended for medicine.

Made his first appearance on the stage at the Hudson Theatre, NY, 20 Apr 1927, as William Thompson in Wall Street; Longacre, Sept 1928, played in Jarnegan; Biltmore, Nov 1928, played the Troublecatcher in Tin Pan Alley; Waldorf, Mar 1929, the Gunman in Solitaire; Playhouse, May 1929, appeared in Street Scene; Forrest, Dec 1929, played Isadore Lipwitz in Headquarters; Ritz, Mar 1930, Rosso in This Man's Town; Biltmore, Oct 1930, took over as Solly in The Up and Up; Avon, Aug 1931, Copper in Three Times the Hour; Alvin, Oct 1931, Schwartz in Wonder Boy; Music Box, Oct 1932, Max Kane in Dinner at Eight; Martin Beck, Mar 1934, Busch in Yellow Jack; Cort, May 1934, took over as Gabby Sloan in The Milky Way; Morosco, Oct 1934, Milton in Spring Song; Playhouse, Jan 1935, Patsy in Three Men on a Horse, which ran for two years; Cort, May 1937, Gordon Miller in Room Service; Plymouth, Nov 1939, played Officer Finkelstein in Margin for Error; Belasco, Los Angeles, June 1943, appeared in Grand Guignol plays; Lyceum, NY, Nov 1945, played Private Dino Collucci in A Sound of Hunting; Royale, Nov 1948, played Sidney Black in Light Up the Sky, and toured in the same part, 1950; 46th Street Theatre, NY, Nov 1950, Nathan Detroit in Guys and Dolls; made his first appearance in London in the last-mentioned part, at the Coliseum, 28 May 1953; at the Haymarket, Nov 1954, played Horace Vandergelder in The Matchmaker; John Golden, NY, Jan 1956, played Fred Stanley in The Hot Corner (which he also directed); Longacre, Oct 1957, played Lou Winkler in Fair Game; in summer theatres, July 1958, starred in Middle of the Night; Billy Rose, NY, Oct 1959, played Boss Mangan in Heartbreak House; Plymouth, Mar 1960, Odilon in The Good Soup; toured, June 1960, in Make a Million; Billy Rose, Mar 1961, Dr Aldo Meyer in Devil's Advocate; Eugene O'Neill, Oct 1961, Patsy in Let It Ride; Belasco, Oct 1962, Morris Seidman in Seidman and Son, and toured in this part, Oct 1963–Feb 1964, in a production which he directed; Martin Beck, Apr 1964, Hymie in a musical revival of Café Crown; Belasco, Oct 1964, Philip Bummidge in The Last Analysis; Playhouse, Paramus, NJ, July 1965, Felix Krebs in Fidelio; Brooks Atkinson, Feb 1966, the title-role in Nathan Weinstein, Mystic, Connecticut; Playhouse, Aug 1966, took over as Dr Jack Kingsley in The Impossible Years, and toured in this part in 1967–8; toured, 1968–9, as Jack Hollender in Don't Drink the Water; Lyceum, Oct 1969, Patsy in Three Men on a Horse; Brooks Atkinson, Jan 1970, Daniel Brand in Paris Is Out!; toured, summer 1970, as Sidney Black in Light Up the Sky; Promenade, Nov 1970, Aaron in A Dream out of Time; toured, 1971 and 1972, as Sidney Black in Light Up the Sky; toured, 1971, as Daniel Brand in Paris Is Out!; Broadhurst, Dec 1972, Al Lewis in The Sunshine Boys; Hanna, Cleveland, Nov 1973, Al Lewis in The Sunshine Boys and subsequently toured; during the tour in 1974, took over from Jack Albertson as Willie Clark in this play; Ethel Barrymore, Oct 1974, Arnold in Dreyfus in Rehearsal; toured, 1975, as Sidney Black in Light Up the Sky; toured, 1975, in Sabrina Fair; Brooklyn Academy of Music, 17 Dec 1975, Oscar Wolfe in The Royal Family, and transferred in this part to the Helen Hayes, 30 Dec 1975; toured with this production, 1976; toured, 1978, as Itzak Goldfarb in The Prince of Grand Street; PAF Playhouse, Huntington, season 1978–9, appeared in Goodnight Grandpa; O'Neill, Apr 1980, Samuel Horowitz in Horowitz and Mrs Washington; entered films, 1936, in Three Men on a Horse, and has since appeared in After the Thin Man, Yellow Jack, Action in the North Atlantic, Boomerang, Brute Force, The Sweet Smell of Success, and numerous others; has appeared on television in *Omnibus, US Steel Hour,* The World of Sholom Aleichem, *The Untouchables,* etc.

Address: c/o Jeff Hunter, 119 West 57th Street, New York, NY 10019.

LEVENTON, Annabel, actress, singer and director
b 20 Apr 1942; *d* of Gerald Leventon and his wife Avril (Wright); *e* Watford Girls' Grammar School, and St Anne's College, Oxford; *m* John Adams; trained for the stage at London Academy of Music and Dramatic Art and Cafe La Mama, New York.

Made her first stage appearance at the Oxford Playhouse, Jun 1962, as Vera Alexandrovna, in a student production of A Month in the Country; after seasons in Bournemouth and with the Traverse, Edinburgh, went to New York, and worked at La Mama; her London debut was at the Shaftesbury, 26 Sept 1968, as Sheila in Hair, a part she also played at the Porte St Martin, Paris, Sept 1969; Open Air, Regent's Park, Jun 1970, played Helena in A Midsummer Night's Dream; for the Young Vic, autumn 1970, played Jocasta in Oedipus, Bianca in The Taming of the Shrew, and Mary in The Wakefield Nativity; May Fair, Apr 1971, took over as Celia in The Philanthropist; for Bristol Old Vic, Mar 1976, played Lucienne in A Flea in Her Ear and Lika in The Promise; King's Head, Sept 1976, Daisy Bell in Spokesong, transferring to the Vaudeville, Feb 1977; Hampstead, Jan 1979, Daphne Kershaw in Daughters of Men; Open Air, Jun 1980, Beatrice in Much Ado About Nothing; her directing experience includes Morecambe, seen at the Edinburgh Festival, 1975, and Hampstead, Dec 1975; Flux, London and NY, 1976; Elvis (assistant), 1977; films include Every Home Should Have One, 1969, and La Mur de L'Atlantique, 1971; TV, since 1969, includes *The New Avengers, Penmarric,* etc; member of the pop group Rock Bottom.

Favourite parts: Cherie in Bus Stop, Lika in The Promise.
Address: c/o Susan Angel Associates, 10 Greek Street, London W1.

LEVIN, Herman, producing manager
b Philadelphia, Pa, USA, 1 Dec 1907; *s* of Abraham Levin and his wife Jennie (Goldfin); *e* Universities of Pennsylvania and Missouri, St John's University Law School, Brooklyn; *m* (1) Evelyne Kraft (mar dis); (2) Dawn McInerney (mar dis); (3) Victoria Steiner (mar dis); was admitted to the New York Bar, 1935, and practised until 1946.

Presented the following productions: Call Me Mister (with Melvyn Douglas), 1946; No Exit (with Oliver Smith), Bonanza Bound, (with Smith), 1947; Richard III, 1949; Gentlemen Prefer Blondes (with Smith), 1949; Bless You All (with Smith), 1950; My Fair Lady, NY, 1956, and London, 1958; The Girl Who Came to Supper, 1963; The Great White Hope, 1968; Lovely Ladies, Kind Gentlemen, 1970; Tricks, 1973; My Fair Lady, 1976; elected president of the League of New York Theatres, management organization, 1955–7, 1962–3.

Address: 424 Madison Avenue, New York, NY 10017.

LEVIN, Ira, playwright and novelist
b New York, 27 Aug 1929; *s* of Charles Levin and his wife Beatrice (Schlansky); *e* Horace Mann School, NYC, Drake University, and NYU (AB 1950); *m* (1) Gabrielle Aronsohn (mar dis); (2) Phyllis Finkel.

His first play was an adaptation of No Time for Sergeants, seen at the Alvin, Oct 1955, and Her Majesty's, London, Aug 1956; subsequently author of the plays Interlock, produced 1958; Critic's Choice, 1960; General Seeger, 1962; Drat! The Cat! (book and lyrics), 1965; Dr Cook's Garden, 1967; Veronica's Room, 1973; Deathtrap, 1978; Break a Leg, 1979; his novels include A Kiss Before Dying, Rosemary's Baby, The Stepford Wives, and The Boys from Brazil, all of which have been successfully filmed; writing for TV includes his first script, The Old Woman, 1950.

Address: c/o Howard Rosenstone & Co, 1500 Broadway, New York, NY 10036.

LEVITON, Stewart, lighting designer
b Chingford, Essex, 8 Dec 1939; *s* of Simon Leviton and his wife Ivy Winifred (Hunt); *e* Sir Joseph Barret Secondary Modern School, Walthamstow; *m* Betty Bridger.

Designed his first production, The Circle, at the Savoy, 1963; Chief Lighting Engineer for the Royal Shakespeare Company at the Aldwych, where productions he has lit include Much Ado About Nothing, Bartholomew Fair, Tiny Alice, 1969; The Plebeians Rehearse the Uprising, Major Barbara, After Haggerty, London Assurance, 1970; Enemies, The Balcony, The Man of Mode, 1971; The Merchant of Venice, The Lower Depths, Murder in the Cathedral, The Island of the Mighty, 1972; Sherlock Holmes, Duck Song, The Bewitched, Summerfolk, 1974; Love's Labour's Lost, Henry IV, parts 1 and 2, Henry V, (Stratford 1975, Aldwych 1976), The Return of A J Raffles, 1975; Ivanov, Old World, Devil's Disciples, 1976; As You Like Like It, 1978; has also lit for the RSC in New York at the Brooklyn Academy, and in Europe.

Recreations: Photography, swimming. *Address:* 14 Wide Way, Mitcham, Surrey. *Tel:* 01–764 0423.

LEVY, Jacques, director and writer
b New York City, 29 July 1935; *s* of Milton Levy and his wife Jean (Brandler); *e* City College of New York (BA), Michigan State University (MA, PhD); formerly a clinical psychologist.

Directed his first play at the Summer Theatre, Topeka, Kansas, 1962, while on the staff of The Menninger Foundation Clinic; directed his first play in NY, off-off-Broadway, at the Judson Poets Theater, 1965; continued directing off-off-Broadway, at LaMama, the New Dramatists, and at the Judson, 1966; directed his first play off-Broadway, America Hurrah, 1966; directed America Hurrah in London at the Royal Court Theatre, 1967; has since directed in NY La Turista, at the American Place Theater, Scuba Duba, 1967; Red Cross, 1968; Oh! Calcutta! which he also conceived, 1969; Where Has Tommy Flowers Gone? at the Berkshire Theater Festival and in NY, 1971; Sleep, at the American Place, 1972; Mystery Play, The Foursome, 1973; Geography of a Horse Dreamer, 1975; Bob Dylan's Rolling Thunder

Revue, 1975–6; received the Obie Award, 1965–6 season, for distinguished direction off-off-Broadway; his play Berchtesgaden presented at Theater for the New City, 1976; wrote book and lyrics for Back Country, 1978; author of lyrics for songs recorded by The Byrds, Bob Dylan, etc; was a member of the Open Theater, 1965–8; has taught at Yale University, 1967, and New York University, 1968; is a member of the Society of Stage Directors and Choreographers.

Address: c/o Marian Searchinger, 888 Seventh Avenue, New York, NY 10019. *Tel:* 212–541 8582.

LEWENSTEIN, Oscar, manager

b London, 18 Jan 1917; *s* of Arthur Solomon Lewenstein and his wife Mary (Convisser); *e* Dunhurst and Ryde School; *m* Eileen Edith Mawson; was formerly an organizer for a Refugee Committee.

General Manager of the Glasgow Unity Theatre, 1947–9; associated with Anthony Hawtrey at the Embassy Theatre, 1950–2; General Manager of the Royal Court Theatre, 1952–4; since 1954, he has presented or been associated with the following productions: The World of Sholom Aleichem, The Punch Revue, Moby Dick, 1955; The Threepenny Opera, 1956; The Member of the Wedding, Nekrassov, 1957; Expresso Bongo, The Party, 1958; A Taste of Honey, The Long and the Short and the Tall, The Hostage, Make Me An Offer, 1959; The Lily-White Boys, Rhinoceros, The Art of Living, Billy Liar, 1960; Breakfast for One, Jacques, Altona, The Blacks, Celebration, Luther, 1961; My Place, Twists (revue), Play with a Tiger, The Secret of the World, The Scatterin, Fiorello, The Keep, End of Day, Semi-Detached, The Sponge Room, and Squat Betty (double-bill), All Things Bright and Beautiful, 1962; Baal, Luv, Three at Nine, 1963; The Brig, The Seagull, St Joan of the Stockyards, 1964; Meals on Wheels, 1965; Loot, 1966; Philadelphia, Here I Come! Fill the Stage with Happy Hours, Dingo, 1967; Time Present, The Hotel in Amsterdam, Spitting Image, Look Back in Anger, 1968; Your Own Thing, What the Butler Saw, The Giveaway, the Living Theatre season, Lovers, 1969; Lulu, 1970; Dimetos, 1976; Once a Catholic, 1977; Gloo Joo, 1978; director of Woodfall Film Productions, 1961–7; has produced the following films: Tom Jones (Associate Producer), 1963; Girl with Green Eyes, 1964; One Way Pendulum, The Knack, 1965; Mademoiselle, Sailor from Gibraltar, 1967; The Bride Wore Black, 1968; The Bed-Sitting Room (Co-Producer), 1969; 1789, 1971; a founder member of the English Stage Company Ltd, Chairman 1970–2; Artistic Director 1972–5.

Address: 5 Goodwin's Court, St Martin's Lane, London, WC2. *Tel:* 01–836 4792.

LEWIS, Arthur, producer, director and writer

b New York City, 15 Sept 1916; *s* of Albert Lewis and his wife Laura (Furst); *e* Beverly Hills High School, the University of Southern California, and Yale University; *m* Evelyn Eisner.

Formerly a film writer and producer; began his stage career as a stage manager at the Martin Beck Theatre, NY, Oct 1940, in Cabin in the Sky; at the Mark Hellinger, NY, Mar 1952, co-produced with his father Three Wishes for Jamie; directed his first London production at the Coliseum, May 1953, with Guys and Dolls; returned to Broadway as Associate Producer of Can-Can at the Shubert Theatre in 1953, The Boy Friend at the Royale in 1954, and Silk Stockings at the Imperial in 1955; in 1963 returned to London, and took over the operation of the Shaftesbury Theatre; he has produced or jointly presented the following productions in London: How to Succeed in Business without Really Trying, 1963; A Thousand Clowns, The Brig, Little Me (also directed), Our

Man Crichton, 1964; The Solid Gold Cadillac (also directed), Barefoot in the Park, 1965; The Owl and the Pussycat, Funny Girl, The Odd Couple, Joey, Joey (also directed), 1966; Queenie (also directed), 1967; Golden Boy, 1968; in 1968 he co-presented on Broadway Rockefeller and the Red Indians, 1969; started film career 1941 as a writer; films include: Oh, You Beautiful Doll, Golden Girl and Conquest of Cochise; he produced the film Loot; his productions for US television include the series Brenner, The Asphalt Jungle and The Nurses.

Recreations: Music and sports.

LEWIS, Robert, director, producer and actor

b New York City, 16 Mar 1909; *s* of Benjamin Lewis and his wife Sadie (Boss); *e* PS 144, Boys High School (Brooklyn), City College, NY, Juilliard School of Music.

Made his first appearance on the stage in NY, in repertory, at the Civic Repertory Theatre, 1929–30; worked in various capacities for the Group Theatre Acting Company, 1931–41, in some 25 plays, being appointed Director of the Group Theatre Studio, 1938; made his first appearance in London, St James's, June 1938, as Roxy Gottlieb in Golden Boy; has directed the following plays: Golden Boy (US touring company), 1938; My Heart's in the Highlands, 1939; Heavenly Express, 1940; Five Alarm Waltz, 1941; Mexican Mural (also produced), 1942; Noah (Actors Lab Production), 1945; Land's End, 1946; Brigadoon, 1947 (also in London, 1949); Regina (opera), 1949; The Happy Time, An Enemy of the People (with Fredric March), 1950; The Grass Harp, Regina (in concert form), 1952; Teahouse of the August Moon (Broadway, 1953, and London, 1954); Witness for the Prosecution, 1954; tour of Reuben Reuben, 1955; Mister Johnson (also co-produced), 1956; The Hidden River, Jamaica, 1957; Handful of Fire, 1958; Candide (London); Chéri (also co-produced), Juniper and the Pagans (US tour), 1959; Kwamina, 1961; Foxy, Traveller Without Luggage, 1964; On a Clear Day You Can See Forever, 1965; directed Crimes and Crimes at the Yale Repertory, New Haven, Conn, 1969–70 season; Long Day's Journey Into Night, Sydney Opera House, 1979; Harold and Maude, NY, 1980; entered films as an actor, 1942, in Tonight We Raid Calais, and has appeared in numerous pictures, including Monsieur Verdoux, Dragon Seed, Son of Lassie, etc, and directed Anything Goes, 1955; Professor at the Sarah Lawrence College, 1937; Professor of Yale University School of Drama, 1942, 1948, and 1967; Rockefeller Foundation Senior Research Associate, 1969; Yale Drama School Professor of Acting, 1973–4, and Chairman of Acting and Directing Departments, 1974–6; founded the Actors Studio (with Elia Kazan and Cheryl Crawford), 1947; Director of the Robert Lewis Theatre Workshop; author of Methods—or Madness? (based on a lecture series), 1958, translated into Portuguese in 1962; foreword to Stanislavsky's Creating a Role, 1961.

Recreation: Music. *Address:* Matthiessen Park, Irvington-on-Hudson, NY 10533.

LIBIN, Paul, producer and director

b Chicago, Ill, 12 Dec 1930; *s* of Ely Libin; *e* University of Illinois, Columbia University (BFA 1955); *m* Florence Rowe.

Produced his first play in New York, a revival of The Crucible, at the Martinique, Mar 1958; since then has produced or co-produced the following, principally at the Martinique: The Time of Vengeance, 1959; Between Two Thieves, 1960; Shadow of Heroes, 1961; The Bankers's Daughter, The Barroom Monks, A Portrait of the Artist as Young Man, 1962; Othello, 1964; Baal, In White America, Medea, 1965; Six from LaMama, 1966; Dynamite Tonight, A

Midsummer Night's Dream, 1967; The White House Murder Case, Chicago 70, Boesman and Lena, 1970; has directed Iphigenia in Aulis, 1967; A Moon for the Misbegotten, Morning, Noon, and Night, 1968; Trumpets of the Lord, Ah, Wilderness!, 1969; Arsenic and Old Lace, 1970; has served as general manager for Theodore Mann's Productions since 1963, including Six Characters in Search of an Author, And Things That Go Bump in the Night, The Royal Hunt of the Sun, The Zulu and the Zayda; became Managing Director of Circle in the Square, 1967, with Drums in the Night, and has since served in that capacity for many of the above-mentioned plays, plus Seven Days of Mourning, 1969, The Last Analysis, 1971, Mourning Becomes Electra, Medea, Here Are Ladies, Uncle Vanya, 1972–3; Waltz of the Toreadors, The Iceman Cometh, An American Millionaire, Scapino, 1973–4; The National Health, Where's Charley?, All God's Chillun Got Wings, Death of a Salesman, 1974–5; Ah, Wilderness!, The Glass Menagerie, The Lady from the Sea, Pal Joey, 1975–6; Days in the Trees, The Night of the Iguana, Romeo and Juliet, The Importance of Being Earnest, 1976–7; Tartuffe, Sain Joan, 13 Rue de L'Amour, Once in a Lifetime, 1977–8; Inspector General, Man and Superman, Spokesong, Loose Ends, 1978–9, etc.

Address: Circle in the Square, 1633 Broadway, New York, NY 10019. *Tel:* 581–3270.

LINDEN, Hal (*né* Harold Lipshitz), actor and singer
b New York City, 20 Mar 1931; *s* of Charles Lipshitz and his wife Frances (Rosen); *e* High School of Music and Art, Queens College, City College of New York (BBA 1952); *m* Frances Martin; studied voice with Lou McCollogh and John Mace, acting with Paul Mann, Lloyd Richards, and at the American Theatre Wing.

Formerly a musician; made his stage début at the Cape Cod Melody Tent, Hyannis, Massachusetts, June 1955, in the chorus of Mr Wonderful; Shubert, New Haven, Mar 1956, Chuck in Strip for Action; made his NY début at the Shubert, 29 Nov 1956, as understudy to Sydney Chaplin in the role of Jeff Moss in Bells Are Ringing, and took over this role, July 1958, subsequently touring in it, Mar–July 1959; Playhouse-in-the-Park, Philadelphia, Pennsylvania, July 1960, played in Angel in the Pawnshop; Alvin, Dec 1960, Matt in Wildcat; summer stock 1961, Pinky Harris in Wish You Were Here and Jeff Moss in Bells Are Ringing; Orpheum, May 1962, Billy Crocker in Anything Goes; stock, 1963, Sid Sorokin in The Pajama Game; Eugene O'Neill, Nov 1964, Dick in Something More!; Mark Hellinger, Apr 1967, No Face in Illya Darling; Shubert, Oct 1967, took over as the Devil in The Apple Tree; Alvin, Apr 1968, Yissel Fishbein in The Education of H*Y*M*A*N K*A*P*L*A*N; Ahmanson, Los Angeles, Nov 1968, Ernest in The Love Match; Lyceum, Oct 1969, Charlie in Three Men on a Horse; Lunt-Fontanne, Oct 1970, Mayer Rothschild in The Rothschilds, for which he received the Antoinette Perry (Tony) Award; Longacre, Jan 1972, Sidney Brustein in the musical version of The Sign in Sidney Brustein's Window; toured, 1972, in The Rothschilds; Washington, DC, Theater Club, Feb 1973, Ben in The Enclave; Lunt-Fontanne, Dec 1973, Sid Sorokin in The Pajama Game; first appeared in films in Bells Are Ringing, 1959; TV includes the series *Barney Miller*.

Address: c/o Paul Tush, 119 West 57th Street, New York, NY. *Tel:* 757–8414.

LINDFORS, Viveca, actress
b Uppsala, Sweden, 29 Dec 1920; *d* of Torsten Lindfors and his wife Karin (Dymling); *e* Stockholm, Royal Dramatic Theatre School, 1937–40; *m* (1) Folke Rogard (mar dis); (2)

Donald Siegel (mar dis); (3) George Tabori (mar dis); member of the Actors Studio since 1958.

Made her stage début at the Lyceum School for Girls, Stockholm, 1937, in Ann Sophie Hedvig; at the Royal Dramatic Theatre, Stockholm, appeared in French Without Tears, 1940, as the Bride in Blood Wedding, 1943, and Olivia in Twelfth Night, 1945; made her Broadway début at the Ethel Barrymore, 2 Dec 1952, as Inez Cabral in I've Got Sixpence; toured in An Evening with Will Shakespeare, 1952–3; toured in Bell, Book and Candle, 1953; made her London début at the Saville, 24 Mar 1954, as Sophia in The White Countess; Lyceum, New York, Dec 1954, Anna in Anastasia and subsequently toured in this part; New York City Center, Jan 1956, Cordelia in King Lear; Phoenix, Feb 1956, Miss Julie in the play of that name and Missy in The Stronger; stock, summer 1956, Anna in The Rose Tatto; Playhouse, Oct 1958, Livia in The Golden Six; Theatre de Lys, Apr 1959, Frieda in I Rise in Flames, Cried the Phoenix; 175 East Broadway Playhouse, Apr 1960, Sultana in Brouhaha; toured USA and South America, 1961, as Catherine in Suddenly, Last Summer, Princess del Lago in Sweet Bird of Youth, Natalia in I Am a Camera, and Miss Julie; Theatre de Lys, Jan 1962, played in the revue Brecht on Brecht; toured, 1962–3, as Elizabeth von Ritter in A Far Country; New York City Center, May 1963, Vera Simpson in Pal Joey; returned to Sweden, and in Stockholm, 1963, played in Brecht on Brecht; Brooks Atkinson, Nov 1965, played various roles in Postmark Zero; formed, with George Tabori, a five-member company called The Strolling Players, 1966; Gateway, St Louis, Missouri, 1966, again played in Brecht on Brecht; Berkshire, Massachusetts, Theatre Festival, July 1966, Portia in The Merchant of Venice; Orpheum, Oct 1967, Angela in The Demonstration and The Dog in Man and Dog in a double-bill with the overall title The Nigger-lovers; Theatre de Lys, Dec 1968, Cuba in Cuba Si and Teresa Carrar in The Guns of Carrar; Arena Stage, Washington, 1970, played Mother Courage in Mother Courage and Her Children; Arena Stage, fall, 1970, Alice in Dance of Death; Ritz, Apr 1971, again played Alice in Dance of Death; toured, 1972, in her play I Am a Woman; Theater in Space, Jan 1974, and again in Apr 1974, performed in I Am a Woman; Alley, Houston, 1978, appeared in Scream; repeated I Am a Woman at various theatres, recently the PAF Playhouse, Huntington; entered films in Sweden in 1941 in The Crazy Family, and first appeared in American films in To the Victor, 1948, since when she has made numerous films, including Four in a Jeep, I Accuse, King of Kings, Sylvia, No Exit, The Way We Were, 1973, etc; has performed frequently on television, notably as Mata Hari on *You Are There*, in scenes from Anastasia, The Last Tycoon, The Bridge of San Luis Rey, etc.

Address: 172 East 95th Street, New York, NY.

LINK, Peter, composer
b St Louis, Missouri, 19 June 1944; *s* of Lyman Link and his wife Virginia (Anderson); *e* Principia College and the University of Virginia; *m* Marta Heflin.

First production for the stage was at the Village Gate, New York, 12 Mar 1969, when he wrote the music and lyrics for Salvation, which he also directed; since then has composed incidental music for Earl of Ruston, The Wedding of Iphigenia, Iphigenia in Concert, 1971; Older People, The Hunter, Much Ado About Nothing, Lysistrata, 1972; The Orphan, The Good Doctor, 1973; Ulysses in Nighttown, 1974; Trelawny of the "Wells", The Comedy of Errors, 1975; The Nightly Gents, 1978; music for the musical King of Hearts, 1978; co-author of Island, produced Milwaukee, 1978; composed the music for the film Nightmare, 1974; composed the music for the television production of Much Ado About Nothing, 1972 and Vegetable Soup, 1975.

Hobby: Photography. *Address:* 285 Central Park West, New York, NY 10024. *Tel:* 787–7774.

LINNEY, Romulus, playwright
b Philadelphia, 21 Sept 1930; *s* of Romulus Zachariah Linney and his wife Maitland Thompson (Clabaugh); *e* Oberlin College and Yale University School of Drama (MFA); *m* Margaret Andrews.

First play to be produced was The Sorrows of Frederick, seen at the Mark Taper Forum, LA, Jun 1967; has since written The Love Suicide at Schofield Barracks, produced NY 1972; Democracy and Esther, 1973; Holy Ghosts, 1976; Old Man Joseph and His Family, 1977; Childe Byron, 1978; Tennessee (one-act), 1979 (Obie award); originally an actor in stock, he was stage manager at the Actors Studio, NY, 1960; he has held visiting professorships at a number of universities, including Columbia University, NY; author of the novels Heathen Valley, 1962, Slowly, By Thy Hand Unfurled, 1965; Of Jesus Tales, 1980, and various writings in literary periodicals.

Address: 235 West 76th Street, New York, NY 10023. *Tel:* 362 9183.

LIPMAN, Maureen, actress
b Hull, 10 May 1946; *d* of Maurice Lipman and his wife Zelma; *e* Newland High School, Hull; *m* the playwright Jack Rosenthal; trained for the stage at LAMDA.

First appeared on the stage at Watford, 1967, as Nancy in The Knack; with the Stables Theatre Company, Manchester, 1968–70, her parts included Lucy in Dracula, Zanche in The White Devil and appearances in a number of premieres; at the Theatre Upstairs, Nov 1970, played Eleanor Rigby in No One Was Saved; joined the National Theatre Company, 1971 and played the Second Randy Woman in Tyger at the New, Jul; Miss Richland in The Good-Natured Man, Dec 1971; Hospital Visitor in The National Health, Jan 1972, Maid in The School for Scandal, May, Molly Malloy in The Front Page, Jul, Third Witch in Macbeth, Nov, all at the Old Vic; in 1973 played the maid in Long Day's Journey into Night; for the RSC at Stratford, Jun 1973, Celia in As You Like It; Albery, Jun 1977, Proserpine Garnett in Candida; Open Space, May 1978, Janis in The Ball Game; Hampstead, Jul 1979, transferring to the Queen's, Sept, Maggie in Outside Edge; first film, Up the Junction, 1969; recently in The Knowledge, Dangerous Davies, St Trinian's; TV includes plays and series, recently her own series *Agony* and *Dissident*.

Favourite parts: Molly Malloy and Maggie in Outside Edge.
Address: c/o Sara Randall, 348A Upper Street, London N1.

LISTER, Laurier, actor, author, manager and director
b Sanderstead, Surrey, 22 Apr 1907; *s* of George Daniel Lister and his wife Susie May (Kooy); *e* Dulwich College; studied for the stage at the Royal Academy of Dramatic Art.

Made his first appearance on the stage at the Globe Theatre, 20 Feb 1925, as a dancer in the night-club scene in The Grand Duchess; Duke of York's, June 1926, appeared in Easy Virtue; he then played for six months at the Little Theatre, Bristol, 1926; during 1927, appeared at the Stratford-on-Avon Memorial Theatre and, autumn 1927, toured in Egypt with Robert Atkins' Shakespearean company; 1928–9, again at Stratford-on-Avon; in 1930, toured in South Africa with Olga Lindo's company; on his return, appeared at the Savoy, June 1931, as Eric Fenton in Death Takes a Holiday; Embassy, Nov 1931, played Tony Farraday in Stepdaughters of War; during 1932, played in repertory at

Croydon and Oxford; Arts and Westminster, Mar 1933, Dennis Gourlay in The Lake; Open Air, June 1933, Sebastian in Twelfth Night; subsequently toured in Finland with Sir Nigel Playfair; Royalty, June 1934, Edgar Linton in Wuthering Heights; Comedy, Feb 1935, Dick Elton in Mrs Nobby Clark; His Majesty's, May 1935, Arthur Stone in Hervey House; Criterion, July 1935, Christopher in This Desirable Residence; Playhouse, Sept 1935, Rylands in Immortal Garden; Gate, Apr, and New, Nov 1936, Montagu Harrison in Parnell; Lyric, Sept 1936, Peter in Farewell Performance; Embassy and Savoy, Mar 1937, Varius in The Road to Rome; Phoenix, Dec 1937, Lord Times in A Kiss for Cinderella; New, May 1938, Ernest Oddie in People of Our Class; Lyric, Sept 1938, Lieut-Commander Richard Sanford in The Flashing Stream, and played the same part at the Biltmore Theatre, New York, Apr 1939; Old Vic, June 1939, played Ian Shawcross in The Ascent of F6; Phoenix, Nov 1939, Marek in Judgment Day, subsequently playing Conrad Noli in the same play; Little, Apr 1940, Mr Dorilant in The Country Wife; toured, June 1940, as Simon in Family Portrait; joined RAF, 1940; demobilized 1945; reappeared on the London stage at the Lyric, Hammersmith, June 1946, as Father Paissy in The Brothers Karamazov; has written the following plays: The Soldier and the Gentlewoman (with Dorothy Massingham), 1933; When the Bough Breaks (with Henrietta Leslie), 1936; The Tree (with Henrietta Leslie), 1937; Against Our Hearts (with Max Adrian), 1937; She, Too, Was Young (with Hilda Vaughan), 1938; Tuppence Coloured (revue), which he devised and directed, 1947; Oranges and Lemons (revue), which he devised and directed, 1948; Forsaking All Other (with Hilda Vaughan), 1950; entered into management, 1951, presenting the revue Penny Plain at the St. Martin's, June 1951, which he devised and directed; at the St Martin's, Jan 1953, presented and directed The Gift; Court, Apr 1953, devised, presented and directed the revue Airs On a Shoestring, which ran for nearly two years; in Feb 1954, presented and directed All Night Sitting (tour); Fortune, June 1954, presented and directed Joyce Grenfell Requests the Pleasure; Saville, Dec 1954, presented, devised, and directed Pay the Piper (revue); Court, Mar 1955, The Burning Boat; Court, June 1955, devised and directed From Here and There (revue); Duke of York's, July 1955, presented Wild Thyme; Bijou, New York, Oct 1955, presented Joyce Grenfell Requests the Pleasure; Comedy, London, Jan 1956, devised and directed the revue Fresh Airs; St James's, Aug 1956, presented The Long Echo; Lyric, Hammersmith, Oct 1957, presented Joyce Grenfell: A Miscellany; spent some time in USA and Canada in 1957–8; returned to London, July 1959, as Artistic Director of LOP, Ltd, Sir Laurence Olivier's play producing company; Criterion, June 1960, presented Dear Liar; at the same theatre, Aug 1960, devised and directed The Art of Living (revue); Phoenix, Mar 1961, co-presented and directed JB; Royal, Stratford, E, Oct 1961, co-presented The One Day of the Year; Arts, Feb 1962, co-presented Twists (revue); Haymarket, Mar 1962, co-presented Joyce Grenfell; Queen's, Dec 1964, co-presented Maxibules; Queen's and St Martin's, Dec–Jan 1964–5, presented The Importance of Being Oscar, and I Must Be Talking to My Friends; Queen's, Mar 1965, co-presented Joyce Grenfell; appointed Assistant to Sir Laurence Olivier, Chichester Festivals, 1962–3; Director and Administrator of the Yvonne Arnaud Theatre, Guildford, Mar 1964–June 1975, where he directed the following plays: Lionel and Clarissa, Torpe's Hotel, A Midsummer Night's Dream, 1965; The Doctor's Dilemma (later at the Comedy), The Door, Night is For Delight, 1966; The Viaduct, One in the Eye (later at the Arts), The Adventures of Tom Random,

1967; The Station Master's Daughter, 1968; The Cardinal of Spain, Gilbert and Sullivan (Max Adrian), 1969; When We Are Married (later at the Strand), The Chalk Garden (later at the Haymarket), 1970; The Tilted Scales, 1971; Now and Then, The Circle (later at the Hong Kong Festival), 1974; The Way of the World, 1975; Arnaud, Guildford, Dec 1977, devised and directed the revue Hats Off!—to Michael Flanders and Donald Swann; Consultant Director, Arnaud Theatre, 1975– .

Recreations: Gardening and reading. *Address:* c/o National Westminster Bank, Ltd, 57 Aldwych, London, WC2.

LISTER, Moira, actress
b Cape Town, South Africa, 6 Aug 1923; *d* of Major James Martin Lister and his wife Margaret Winifred (Hogan); *e* Parktown Convent, Johannesburg; studied for the stage under Dr Hulbert and Amy Coleridge; *m* Vicomte d'Orthez.

Made her first appearance on the stage, 1929, as a child of six, with the University Players, Johannesburg, as the Prince in The Vikings of Helgeland; during 1936, appeared in Johannesburg, with Sir Seymour Hicks, in Vintage Wine; made her first appearance in London, at Golders Green Hippodrome, 12 Apr 1937, as Jeeby Cashler in Post Road, and appeared at the Queens a week later in the same part; returned to South Africa, and appeared in The Women, The Russians, Pawns in the Game, etc; after returning to England, appeared at the Playhouse, Apr 1944, as Diana in Six Pairs of Shoes; Q, June 1944, played Margaret Heiss in The Shop in Sly Street (The Shop at Sly Corner); St James's, Sept 1944, Laurel Somerset in Felicity Jasmine; Stratford-on-Avon, Shakespeare Memorial Theatre, 1945 season, Juliet, Desdemona, Olivia in Twelfth Night, Anne Bullen in King Henry VIII, Charmian in Antony and Cleopatra, and Kate Hardcastle in She Stoops to Conquer; St James's, May 1946, Isabel Neville in The Kingmaker, and July 1946, Palmyra in Marriage a la Mode; Haymarket, Apr 1947, Joanna Lyppiatt in Present Laughter; first appeared in New York, at the Booth Theatre, Dec 1948, as Madeleine in Don't Listen, Ladies!; Vaudeville, London, June 1949, played Diana Lake in French Without Tears; Cambridge, Apr 1950, appeared in the revue, Sauce Piquante; at Wyndham's, May 1951, appeared as the Princess in The Love of Four Colonels; Criterion, Oct 1953, Monica Bestwood in Birthday Honours; with the Shakespeare Memorial Theatre Company, 1955, toured the Continent and the English provinces, and with the company appeared at the Palace, London, July 1955, as Margaret in Much Ado About Nothing, and Regan in King Lear; St James's, Aug 1956, Kate Waterhouse in The Long Echo; Criterion, Dec 1957, Irene in Paddle Your Own Canoe; toured Africa and Australia in a one-woman show entitled People in Love, 1958–9; Savoy, London, March 1960, Nell Nash in The Gazebo, which ran for over a year; Strand, Mar 1963, played Virginia in Devil May Care; Richmond, May 1964, Sylvia in The Uncertain Heroine; Savoy, July 1964, Sylvia Barr in The First Fish; toured South Africa, Dec 1964–Mar 1965, in Bedtime Story; on returning to London, appeared at the Apollo, Aug 1965, as Dorothy in Any Wednesday; Strand, Apr 1967, Lesbia Grantham in Getting Married; Lyceum, Edinburgh, Summer 1969, played Connie in The Snow Angel, and Woman in Epiphany (double-bill) and Anne Preston in A Woman Named Anne, repeating the role at the Duke of York's, Feb 1970; Vaudeville, Feb 1971, Joanna Markham in Move Over Mrs Markham, for which she won the Variety Club of Great Britain's Silver Heart Award for The Best Stage Actress of 1971, following the West End run with a tour of Australia in the same role; Feb 1973, toured in Twigs, playing four parts;

November 1973, South African tour in Cowardy Custard; June 1974, Garrick, Birds of Paradise, playing Yolande; March 1975, Kay Brent in tour of Miss Adams Will Be Waiting; Arnaud, Guildford, Dec 1975, Miss Havisham in Great Expectations; Salisbury, Rhodesia, 1976, Mrs Hardcastle in She Stoops to Conquer; Hong Kong Festival, 1977, title role in Move Over Mrs Markham; Comedy, Feb 1978, and in South Africa, played Angela Forrester in Murder Among Friends; 1978–9, toured England, Ireland and Canada as Mrs Erlynne in Lady Windermere's Fan; first appeared in films in 1943, in The Shipbuilders, and has appeared in numerous pictures including The Deep Blue Sea, The Yellow Rolls-Royce and The Double Man; her work for television includes: Major Barbara, Simon and Laura and various series, among them *The Very Merry Widow*; she was the subject of a *This Is Your Life* programme in Feb 1971; her autobiography The Very Merry Moira was published in 1969.

Favourite parts: Juliet, Desdemona, and Joanna in Present Laughter. *Recreations:* Languages and sport. *Address:* c/o Richard Stone, 18–20 York Buildings, Adelphi, London, WC2.

LITTLE, Cleavon, actor
b Chickasha, Oklahoma, 1 June 1939; *e* San Diego State University; prepared for the stage at the American Academy of Dramatic Arts.

Made his New York debut at the Mobile Theater, 28 June 1966, as a member of the troupe in Macbeth; Village Gate, 22 Feb 1967, played the Muslim Witch and A Conspirator in MacBird!; The New, Oct 1967, Foxtrot in Scuba Duba; Mobile, June 1968, played Hamlet; Brooks Atkinson, Dec 1968, Lee Haines in Jimmy Shine; Pocket, Mar 1969, Paul Odum in Someone's Comin' Hungry; Stage 73, Sept 1969, Rufus in The Ofay Watcher; The Other Stage, Nov 1969, Father Xavier in Kumaliza; Broadway, Mar 1970, played the title role in the musical Purlie; Vivian Beaumont, Jan 1972, Shogo in Narrow Road to the Deep North; Mark Taper Forum, Los Angeles, May 1974, played in The Charlatan; Booth, Dec 1974, Lewis in All Over Town; Ambassador, Jan 1976, Willy Stepp in The Poison Tree; Brooklyn Academy, 1976, Narrator in Joseph and the Amazing Technicolor Dreamcoat; LA Shakespeare Festival, 1978, Oberon in A Midsummer Night's Dream; San Diego, Mar 1978, Simon Able in Sly Fox; appeared in the films Vanishing Point (1971), Blazing Saddles (1974), FM (1978), Greased Lightning (1978), and others; recent television includes *Loveboat*, 1980.

Address: c/o William Norris Agency, 151 El Camino Drive, Beverly Hills, Calif 90212.

LITTLER, Sir Emile (*cr* 1974), manager and producer
b Ramsgate, Kent, 9 Sept 1903; *s* of F R Littler and his wife Agnes; *e* Stratford-on-Avon; *m* Cora Goffin.

Commenced his career as assistant-manager at the Ambassador Theatre, Southend-on-Sea, 1922; business manager at the Court Theatre, London, 1923; subsequently engaged as general manager of several provincial touring companies, and stage-managed several plays and pantomimes; in 1925, was assistant stage-manager at the Birmingham Repertory Theatre; stage-manager for Yellow Sands, in United States, 1927, and was engaged in a similar capacity with Messrs Shubert Bros for The Silent House, for over two years; stage-manager for the production of Michael and Mary, Charles Hopkins Theatre, New York, 1929; St James's, London, Feb 1930, produced Michael and Mary; during 1930–1, engaged as assistant-producer in NY; in Sept 1931, became manager and licensee of the Birmingham Repertory

Theatre for Sir Barry Jackson, where he installed the first broadcasting studio in a theatre; started in management on his own account, Sept 1934; toured Jane Eyre; Godfrey Tearle in The Amazing Dr Clitterhouse, 1066 and All That, Call It a Day, Little Ladyship, The Corn is Green, Alice in Wonderland, Aloma of the South Seas, Victoria Regina, and Miss Hook of Holland, etc; his London productions include revivals at the Coliseum of the Maid of the Mountains, 1942; The Belle of New York, 1942; The Quaker Girl, 1944; original productions in London include: Claudia, 1942; Flying Colours, 1943; Shadow and Substance, 1943; Sunny River, 1943; Something in the Air (with Lee Ephraim and Tom Arnold), 1943; Panama Hattie (with Ephraim and Arnold), 1943; The Night and the Music, 1945; The Song of Norway, 1945; Annie Get Your Gun, 1947; Charley's Aunt (each Christmas, 1947–50); Lilac Time, 1949; Latin Quarter, Casino, 1948–53; Dear Miss Phoebe, 1950; Blue for a Boy, 1950; Zip Goes a Million, 1951; Third Person, 1951; Excitement (with Tom Arnold), 1952; Affairs of State, 1952; Love from Judy, 1952; Bruno and Sidney, 1953; Sabrina Fair (with Peter Daubeny), 1954; Book of the Month, 1954; Happy Holiday, 1954; Romance in Candlelight, 1955; Victor Borge, 1957; The Lovebirds, 1957; The Happiest Millionaire, 1957; The Iceman Cometh, 1958; Hot Summer Night, 1958; Let Them Eat Cake, 1959; Fine Fettle (with Bernard Delfont), 1959; Signpost to Murder, Kill Two Birds, 1962; The Right Honourable Gentleman, 1964; A Month in the Country (with Michael Redgrave Productions and FES (Plays) Ltd, 1965); The Impossible Years, Antonio and his Spanish Dance Company, 1966; 110 in the Shade, 1967; The Student Prince, 1968; At the Palace, 1970; Palace, April 1972, directed and presented The Maid of the Mountains; also written, presented, and directed, 15 pantomimes in London, at the Coliseum, Cambridge, Stoll, Palace, and Casino Theatres, and over 200 pantomimes in the British Isles; Chairman of London Entertainments Ltd, Ember Entertainments Ltd; Honorary Administrator of Plays and Players Ltd, Governor of the Royal Shakespeare Theatre, Stratford-on-Avon; founder of the Emile Littler Foundation; he is a Freeman of the City of London; also a member of Lloyds of London, Performing Rights Society, Royal Society of Arts; part author of Cabbages and Kings, Too Young to Marry, All in Marriage, Love Isn't Everything; knighted in the New Year Honours, 1974.

Recreations: Horse racing, swimming, tennis. *Clubs:* City Livery, RAC, Saints and Sinners Club of London, The Clermont Club. *Addresses:* Palace Theatre, Shaftesbury Avenue, London, W1. *Tel:* 01–734 9691; and 'The Trees', Ditchling, Sussex.

LITTLEWOOD, Joan, director.

Founded Theatre of Action, Manchester, 1933; Theatre Union, Manchester, 1934; directed for Theatre Workshop on tour in British Isles, Scandinavia, Germany and Czechoslovakia, 1945–53; directed her first London production at the Rudolf Steiner Hall, Oct 1947, with Operation Olive Branch (Aristophanes' play Lysistrata); Embassy Theatre, May 1952, directed Uranium 235, subsequently appearing as the Witch in the same production at the Comedy, June 1952; for Theatre Workshop, at the Theatre Royal, Stratford, London, she has directed the following plays: The Dutch Courtesan, The Fire Eaters, The Flying Doctor (also played Marinette), Johnny Noble, The Cruel Daughters (also adapted), The Chimes (also adapted), The Good Soldier Schweik (also Embassy Theatre), The Prince and the Pauper (also adapted), 1954; Richard II (also played Duchess of Gloucester), The Other Animals, Volpone, The Midwife (also played

Mrs Kepes), The Legend of Pepito, The Sheep Well, The Italian Straw Hat, 1955; The Good Soldier Schweik, Edward II; The Quare Fellow, 1956; You Won't Always Be On Top, And The Wind Blew, Macbeth, 1957; Celestina, Unto Such Glory, The Respectable Prostitute, A Taste of Honey, The Hostage, A Christmas Carol (which she also adapted), 1958; Fings Ain't Wot They Used T'Be, The Dutch Courtesan, Make Me An Offer, 1959; Ned Kelly, Every Man In His Humour, Sparrers Can't Sing, 1960; We're Just Not Practical, They Might Be Giants, 1961; Oh, What a Lovely War!, 1963; A Kayf Up West, 1964; Macbird, Intrigues and Amours, Mrs Wilson's Diary, The Marie Lloyd Story, 1967; Forward, Up Your End, The Projector, 1970; The Londoners, The Hostage, Costa Packet, 1972; So You Want to Be in Pictures, 1973; of these productions, The Good Soldier Schweik, The Quare Fellow, A Taste of Honey, The Hostage, Make Me An Offer, Fings Ain't Wot They Used T'Be, Sparrers Can't Sing, Oh, What a Lovely War!, Mrs Wilson's Diary transferred to the West End; directed her first production on Broadway, at the Cort, Sept 1960, with The Hostage; Broadhurst, New York, Sept 1964, directed Oh, What a Lovely War!; at the Devon Festival, Barnstaple, June 1955, she directed and played the title-part in Mother Courage and Her Children; Maxim Gorki, Berlin, 1960, directed Unternehmen ölzweig; at the Edinburgh Festival, Aug 1964, directed Henry IV; 1965–6, Centre Culturel Internationale, Tunisia; worked on the creation of children's environments around the Theatre Royal, 1968–75; left England to work in France, 1975; Hon Doctorate, Open University, 1977; directed the film Sparrers Can't Sing, 1963; awarded Medal for Outstanding Direction, Berlin; Olympic Award for Theatre, Taormina; Challenge Trophy of the Théâtre des Nations, Paris.

Address: Theatre Royal, Stratford, London, E15.

LIVINGS, Henry, dramatic author and actor

b Prestwich, Lancs, 20 Sept 1929; *s* of George Livings and his wife Dorothy (Buckley); *e* Prestwich, Stand Grammar School, and Liverpool University; *m* Fanny Carter.

Began his career in the theatre as an actor, appearing with the Century Mobile Theatre, Hinckley, Leics, Feb 1954, as Curio and Sebastian in Twelfth Night; made his first London appearance at the Theatre Royal, Stratford, E, May 1956, as Prisoner C in The Quare Fellow; Comedy, July 1956, again played the same part in the same play; his first play Stop It, Whoever You Are, was produced at the Arts, Feb 1961; author of the following plays: Thacred Nit (subsequently re-named Big Soft Nellie), 1961; Nil Carborundum, 1962; Kelly's Eye, 1963 (Britannica Award for Playwrights, 1965); Eh?, 1964; The Day Dumbfounded Got His Pylon (one-act), 1965; The Little Mrs Foster Show, 1966; Good Grief! 1967; Honour and Offer, 1969; The Finest Family in the Land, Six Pongo Plays, Grup, 1970; This Jockey Drives Late Nights, 1971; Cinderella, 1972; Glorious Miles, Jonah, 1973; Jack and the Beanstalk, and Six More Pongo Plays (including two for children), 1974; Jug, 1975; his first television play, Arson Squad, was produced in Apr 1961; he is also the author of the following television plays: Jack's Horrible Luck, A Right Crusader, There's No Room For You Here For a Start, Brainscrew, Don't Touch Him He Might Resent it, etc; radio plays include: The Weavers (adaptation), After the Last Lamp, The Day Dumbfounded Got His Pylon, A Public Menace (adaptation of Ibsen's Folkefiende), The Government Inspector (adaptation), etc; television appearances include: Get the Drift, based on the radio series Northern Drift, and Mother Nature's Bloomers.

Recreations: Beer. *Club:* Dobcross Band Club. *Address:* 33 Woods Lane, Dobcross, nr Oldham, Lancs. *Tel:* Saddleworth 2965.

LLOYD WEBBER, Andrew, composer

b London, 22 Mar 1948; *s* of William Southcombe Lloyd Webber and his wife Jean Hermione (Johnstone); *e* Westminster; *m* Sarah Jane Tudor Hugill.

Has written the music for Joseph and the Amazing Technicolour Dreamcoat, 1968, which was presented in London at the Albery, 1973; Jesus Christ Superstar, New York 1971, London 1972; Jeeves, London 1975; Evita, London, 1978 (recorded, 1976); first solo album, Variations, released 1977; composer of the album Tell Me on a Sunday, 1979; film scores include Gumshoe, and The Odessa File.

Hobby: Architecture. *Club:* Savile. *Address:* Savile Club, 67 Brook Street, London W1.

LOCKE, Philip, actor

b 29 Mar 1928; *s* of James Locke and his wife Frances; *e* St Marylebone Central School; trained for the stage at RADA.

Made his professional debut with Oldham Rep, 1954, as Feste in Twelfth Night; toured with the Old Vic Company, 1954, as Flute in A Midsummer Night's Dream (NY debut); at the Royal Court, 1958, played Geoffrey Colwyn-Stuart in Epitaph for George Dillon, Fak in The Sport of My Mad Mother, Carebo in The Hole, and Charles Lomax in Major Barbara; Royal Court, Mar 1962, Colin in The Knack; Queen's, Mar 1964, Medvedev in The Seagull; with the National Theatre company at the Old Vic, 1968–69, his parts included Boyet in Love's Labour's Lost, Jaques in As You Like It, etc; with the RSC, 1971, played Zakhar Bardin in Enemies, Libertini in Occupations, and the General in The Balcony; played Egeus/Quince in Peter Brooks's A Midsummer Night's Dream, Stratford, 1970, Aldwych, and world tour 1971–73; Aldwych, season 1973, played Lepidus in Antony and Cleopatra, Casca in Julius Caesar, and Junius Brutus in Coriolanus; Aldwych, 1974, Moriarty in Sherlock Holmes, Jan, and Cardinal Pontocarrero in The Bewitched, May; played Moriarty at the Broadhurst, NY, Nov 1974; Criterion, London, Aug 1975, Player in Rosencrantz and Guildenstern Are Dead; returned to the NT to play Horatio in Hamlet, Old Vic, 1975; Mycetes in Tamburlaine the Great, Olivier, Oct 1976; Caribaldi in Force of Habit, Lyttelton, Nov 1976; for RSC, Royal Festival Hall, Jul 1977, the Colonel in Every Good Boy Deserves Favour; Riverside Studios, Jan 1978, Gaev in The Cherry Orchard; Olivier, Nov 1979, Greybig in the NT's Amadeus; films include Thunderball, Escape to Athena, and Porridge; has appeared frequently on TV.

Favourite part: Gaev. *Address:* c/o MLR, 194 Old Brompton Road, London SW5.

LOCKWOOD, Margaret, actress

b Karachi, India, 15 Sept 1916; *e* Norwood, Sydenham Girls' High School, and Kensington; *m* Rupert W Leon (mar dis); studied for the stage under Italia Conti.

Made her first appearance on the stage at the Holborn Empire, 1928, as a fairy in A Midsummer Night's Dream; Scala, Dec 1929, appeared in the pantomime, The Babes in the Wood; Drury Lane, 1932, walked on in Cavalcade; she then studied at the Royal Academy of Dramatic Art; at the Q Theatre, June 1934, played Myrtle in House on Fire; Ambassadors', Aug 1934, Margaret Hamilton in Family Affairs; Arts, Jan 1936, Helene Ferber in Repayment; Duke of York's, July 1936, Trixie Drew in Miss Smith; Q, July 1937, Ann Harlow in Ann's Lapse; entered films, 1934, in Lorna Doone, and from 1937 devoted herself chiefly to that medium; returned to the stage, Apr 1949, when she toured as Amanda in Private Lives; at the Scala, Dec 1949, appeared as Peter Pan, which she again played, Dec 1950; at the Edinburgh Festival, 1951, played Eliza Doolittle in Pygmalion;

Savoy, London, Dec 1954, appeared as Clarissa Hailsham-Browne in Spider's Web, which ran for over a year; Savoy, Feb 1957, Dinah Holland in Subway in the Sky; Scala, Dec 1957, once again played Peter Pan; toured, 1958–9, as Jane Palmer in Murder on Arrival; Duke of York's, Nov 1959, Sally Seymour in And Suddenly It's Spring; toured, Feb 1961, as Barbara Martin in Milk and Honey; Cambridge, Feb 1962, played Sally Thomas in Signpost to Murder; Phoenix, Nov 1964, played Caroline in Every Other Evening; Strand, Dec 1965, and Garrick, Dec 1966; Mrs Cheveley in An Ideal Husband; Strand, Sept 1967, Claire Williams in The Others; St Martin's, July 1969, Diane in On a Foggy Day; Vaudeville, June 1970, played Lady Frederick Berelles in Lady Frederick; toured, Apr 1972, as Lady Felicity in Relative Values, also playing the part at the Westminster, Sept 1973; Vaudeville, Nov 1975, Helen Galt in Double Edge; 1977, toured in Quadrille; 1978, toured in A Suite in Three Keys; Birmingham Rep, Apr 1980, played Queen Alexandra in Motherdear; notable films include: The Wicked Lady, The Lady Vanishes, The Man in Grey, and recently The Slipper and the Rose; recent television includes three series of *Justice* and An Ideal Husband; *Daily Mirror* Television Award, 1961; Best Actress Awards from *TV Times*, 1971, and *The Sun*, 1973.

Recreations: Music, swimming, crossword puzzles, and reading. *Address:* c/o Herbert de Leon, Fielding House, 13 Bruton Street, London, W1.

LOEWE, Frederick, composer

b Vienna, Austria, 10 June 1901; *s* of Edmund Loewe, a singer, and his wife Rose, an actress; *e* Berlin, Germany, Military Academy, and Stern's Conservatory, Berlin; studied piano with Ferruccio Busoni and Eugene d'Albert and composition with Nicholas von Reznicek; *m* Ernestine Zwerline (mar dis); made his debut as a concert pianist in Berlin, 1914, at the age of 13; made his New York debut at Carnegie Hall, 1942.

Composed the music for his first play, Petticoat Fever, to which he contributed a song, at the Ritz, New York, 4 Mar 1935; since then has composed The Illustrators' Show, 1936; Salute to Spring, 1937; Great Lady, 1938; The Lamb's Club Gambols, 1938–42; Life of the Party (produced in Detroit, Mich), 1942; What's Up, 1943; with Alan Jay Lerner as lyricist composed The Day Before Spring, 1945; Brigadoon, 1947, which also was his first musical produced in London, at His Majesty's, 14 Apr 1949; paint Your Wagon, 1951; My Fair Lady, 1956; Camelot, which he also co-produced, 1960; Gigi, 1973, for which he received the Antoinette Perry ("Tony") award, 1973; wrote the score for the film Award, and for the films of various of his stage musicals; wrote the music for the television productions Salute to Lerner and Loewe, 1961, The Lerner and Loewe Songbook, 1962; received the Hollander Medal, Berlin, 1923, for his piano concerts; Doctor of Music, Redlands University, 1962.

Address: ASCAP, 575 Madison Avenue, New York, NY.

LOGAN, Joshua, director, producer, and dramatic author

b Texarkana, Texas, 5 Oct 1908; *s* of Joshua Lockwood Logan and his wife Susan (Nabors); *e* Culver Military Academy and Princeton University; *m* (1) Barbara O'Neill (mar dis); (2) Nedda Harrigan; was one of the founders of the University Players, at Falmouth, Mass; gained a scholarship to the Moscow Art Theatre, under Constantin Stanislavsky.

Made his first appearance on the stage at the Biltmore Theatre, New York, 29 Oct 1932, as Mart Strong in Carrie Nation; subsequently went to England, and directed The Day I Forgot, at the Globe, London, May 1933; on returning to the United States, directed Camille, in Boston, with Jane

Cowl, 1933; was, subsequently, assistant stage-manager for She Loves Me Not, 1933; It's You I Want, 1935; with J H Del Bondio, presented To See Ourselves, at the Ethel Barrymore, 1935; staged Hell Freezes Over, Ritz, 1935; was with the Summer Stock Theatre Company, at Suffern, NY, 1935; 46th Street, Jan 1936, played Robert Humphreys in A Room in Red and White; he then went to Hollywood where he directed films; returning to NY, he has since then staged On Borrowed Time, I Married an Angel, and Knickerbocker Holiday, 1938; Morning's at Seven, and Stars in Your Eyes, 1939; Two for the Show, Higher and Higher (also co-author), Charley's Aunt, 1940; By Jupiter, This Is the Army, 1942; he then joined the US Air Force Combat Intelligence, serving overseas; after demobilization, directed Annie Get Your Gun, and Happy Birthday, 1946; produced and staged John Loves Mary, 1947; staged Mister Roberts, of which he was part-author, 1948; South Pacific, of which he was also part-author, 1949; The Wisteria Trees, of which he was author, 1950; staged the production of Mister Roberts, at the London Coliseum, 1950; staged the production of South Pacific, Drury Lane, 1951; with Leland Hayward, presented in NY Wish You Were Here, which he wrote and directed, 1951; with the Theatre Guild, presented Picnic, which he directed, 1953; also presented and directed production of Kind Sir, 1953; with David Merrick presented Fanny, which he directed, and of which he was part-author with S N Behrman; presented and directed Middle of the Night, 1956; directed Blue Denim, 1958; directed The World of Suzie Wong, 1958; presented (with David Merrick) Epitaph for George Dillon, 1958; directed There Was a Little Girl, 1960; directed All American, Mr President, and Tiger, Tiger, Burning Bright, 1962; directed Ready When You Are, CB!, 1964; directed Hot September, 1965; directed Look to the Lilies, 1970; co-produced, wrote the book with Emlyn Williams, and directed Miss Moffat, Philadelphia, 1975; Imperial, NY, 9 Mar 1975, was saluted by A Gala Tribute to Joshua Logan, in which he also performed; presented Trick, 1979; directed Horowitz and Mrs Washington, 1980; among the films he has directed since 1955, are Picnic, Bus Stop, South Pacific, Sayonara, Tall Story, and Fanny.

Recreations: Photography and sculpture. *Clubs:* Players and River Club, New York. *Address:* Players Club, 16 Gramercy Park, New York, NY.

LONG, Avon, singer, actor, dancer
b Baltimore, Maryland, 18 June 1910; *s* of Charles Long and his wife Bertha; *e* Douglas High School. Baltimore; *m* Gretchen Cotton; prepared for the stage at the New England Conservatory, Allied Art Center, and the Sonya Koretna School of the Dance, all in Boston, Mass.

Made his New York debut at the Cotton Club, 1931, as the Brown Boy in Cotton Club Revue; toured in vaudeville on the Keith Circuit in Connie's Hot Chocolates, 1934; St Louis, Mo, Opera House, 1938, played in Gentleman Unafraid; made his Broadway debut at the Comedy, 19 Dec 1936, as Rhythm in the musical Black Rhythm; played Sportin' Life in Porgy and Bess at the Los Angeles Philharmonic Auditorium, 1938; Westport, Conn, Country Playhouse, 1939, Orestes in La Belle Helene; repeated this part in July 1941; Majestic, NY, Jan 1942, Sportin' Life in Porgy and Bess, which he repeated at the 44th Street, Sept 1943, and in two productions at the New York City Center, Feb 1944; Broadway, May 1945, Windy in Memphis Bound; Adelphi, Sept 1945, Fisherman in Carib Song; Broadway, Dec 1946, Careless Love in Beggar's Holiday; Broadway, Mar 1951, Ham, Magician, Angel in The Green Pastures; Broadway, May 1952, Lt Jim Crocker in Shuffle Along; National Dec 1954,

Mr D in Mrs Patterson; Greenwich Mews, Nov 1959, Magician in The Ballad of Jazz Street; Mayfair, Feb 1962, William Piper in Fly Blackbird; Westport Country Playhouse, Nov 1963, Narrator in The Threepenny Opera; toured as Sportin' Life in Porgy and Bess, 1965; Ethel Barrymore, May 1972, David in Don't Play Us Cheap; Studio Arena, Buffalo, NY, Oct 1973, played in Other Voices, Other Rooms; Shubert, Philadelphia, Pa, Oct 1974, Ole Mr Pete in Miss Moffat; AMAS Repertory, Feb 1975, John Sage and Dusty in Bubbling Brown Sugar; Imperial, 9 Mar 1975, ANTA, Feb 1976, again played John Sage in Bubbling Brown Sugar; has also played in Bloomer Girl, Carman Jones, Very Warm for May, Kiss Me, Kate, etc; in various touring productions; first appeared in films in Manhattan Merry-Go-Round, 1937, and has since played in Finian's Rainbow, Ziegfeld Follies, Harry and Tonto, The Sting, etc; has appeared regularly on television since 1949 in such shows as *Garroway-at Large, Us Steel Hour,* The Big Story, The Green Pastures, etc; is also a song writer.

Recreations and hobbies: Roller-skating, hooking rugs, crossword puzzles, oil painting. *Address:* 790 Riverside Drive, New York, NY.

LONGDON, Terence, actor
b Newark-on-Trent, Notts, 14 May 1922; *s* of Joseph Longdon and his wife Florence Violet (Tully); *e* Minster Grammar School, Southwell; *m* Barbara Jefford (mar dis); trained for the stage at RADA 1946–8.

First appeared on the stage in May 1948, at the Lyceum, Sheffield, as Robin in The French for Love; first appeared on the London stage in Sept 1948, at the Globe, as a Soldier in Medea; St James's, May 1949, played a Greek Soldier in Adventure Story; Apollo, Sept 1949, Philip Ryall in Treasure Hunt; Aldwych, May 1951, second officer in The Three Sisters; Garrick, Feb 1952, Tim in Red Letter Day; appearances at Stratford, 1951–4 include Prince Hal in Henry IV, Part I, Oliver in As You Like It, and Cassio in Othello; toured Australasia with the Stratford company, 1953; made his New York début with the Old Vic Company at the Metropolitan Opera House, Sept 1954, as Lysander in A Midsummer Night's Dream; Aldwych, Aug 1959, played Peter Marriott in The Sound of Murder; Arts, June 1966, Darcy in Pride and Prejudice; Duke of York's, Feb 1967, Colin in The Sacred Flame; Savoy, July 1967, Claude in Minor Murder; Savoy, Oct 1968, John Brownlow in The Secretary Bird, playing the part for over 1000 performances; Fortune, Sept 1971, Sam Blaine in Suddenly at Home; Ambassadors', July 1974, Charles Straker in The Sack Race; Arnaud, Guildford, Mar 1975, A Visitor in Miss Adams Will Be Waiting; Theatre Royal, York, Nov 1977, Sir Robert Morton in The Winslow Boy; Her Majesty's, Jan 1978, took over Mr Davenport in Cause Célèbre; Sheringham Little Theatre, July 1978, Dr Wangel in The Lady from the Sea; Crucible, Sheffield, Nov 1978, Ernest in Bedroom Farce, playing the same part at Watford Palace, Apr 1979, and in Vienna, May 1979, at the English Theatre; Belgrade Coventry, Apr 1980, appeared in Battery; first film, Angels One Five, 1951; subsequent film appearances include several Carry On films, and recently, Martian Chronicles, Wild Geese, and Sea Wolves; television, since 1947, includes the title-role in the series Garry Halliday, The New Avengers, The Cedar Tree, and The Sandbaggers.

Favourite part: Prince Hal. *Recreation:* Golf. *Address:* 10 Embankment Gardens, London, SW3. *Tel:* 01–352 5859.

LOOS, Anita, dramatic author and novelist
b Sisson, California, 26 Apr 1893; *d* of Richard B Loos and his

wife Minnie Ella (Smith); *e* High School, San Diego; *m* (1) Frank Pallma (mar dis); (2) John Emerson; contributed fiction to newspaper press at an early age.

Appeared on the stage in San Diego in Little Lord Fauntleroy, East Lynne, On the Yukon, The Prince Chap, The Jewess, Mary Jane's Pa, etc; author of the following plays: The Whole Town's Talking, 1923; The Fall of Eve (with John Emerson), 1925; Gentlemen Prefer Blondes (with Emerson), 1926; Pair o' Fools (with Emerson), 1926; The Social Register (with Emerson, and which she also directed), 1931; Happy Birthday, 1946; Gentlemen Prefer Blondes (musical version, with Joseph Fields), 1949; Gigi, 1951; The Amazing Adele, 1955; Chéri, 1959; Gogo Loves You, 1964; The King's Mare (adapted from the French and produced in London), 1966; original book of Lorelei or Gentlemen Still Prefer Blondes, 1974; is the author of the books Gentlemen Prefer Blondes, 1926; and But Gentlemen Marry Brunettes, 1928; A Mouse Is Born, 1951; No Mother to Guide Her, 1962; A Girl Like I, 1972; co-author with Helen Hayes of Twice over Lightly, 1972; author of Kiss Hollywood Goodbye, 1973; has written innumerable film scenarios, and, with John Emerson, wrote the books Breaking into the Movies, 1919, and How to Write Photoplays, 1921; at the Gramercy Arts, NY, May 1963, appeared with Carol Channing in An Evening of Theatrical Reminiscences.

LOQUASTO, Santo, designer.

e King's College, Wilkes Barre, Pa, and Yale Drama School

Began his career designing productions for repertory companies, including the Hartford Stage Company and the Long Wharf Theatre, New Haven, Conn, 1967–68 seasons; and the Yale School of Drama Repertory Theater, for which he translated The Bacchae and designed both the decor and costumes, Mar 1969; designed Narrow Road to the Deep North, Dec 1969; made his New York debut as designer at the Astor Place, 1 Apr 1970, with the decor for the double bill The Unseen Hand and Forensic and the Navigators; designed Sticks and Bones both on-Broadway and off-Broadway, 1971; That Championship Season, again for both on-and off-Broadway, The Secret Affairs of Mildred Wild, 1972; Siamese Connections, The Orphan, As You Like It, King Lear, A Public Prosecutor Is Sick of It All (Arena Stage, Washington, DC), 1973; The Tempest, The Dance of Death, Pericles, The Merry Wives of Windsor, Richard III, Mert and Phil, Cherry Orchard (Hartford Stage Company), and his first London designs for That Championship Season at the Garrick, 6 May, 1974; A Midsummer Night's Dream, A Doll's House, Hamlet, The Comedy of Errors, Awake and Sing (Hartford), Kennedy's Children, 1975; Murder Among Friends, Heartbreak House (Arena Stage), Legend, Measure for Measure, The Glass Menagerie (Hartford), 1976; The Lower Depths (Arena Stage), The Cherry Orchard, Agamemnon (costumes only), Miss Margarida's Way, Landscape of the Body, Golda, 1977; Curse of the Starving Class, The Play's the Thing, The Mighty Gents, Stop the World—I Want to Get Off, King of Hearts, 1978; Sarava, The Goodbye People, Bent, 1979; principal designer, Twyla Tharp Dance Foundation; other ballet design includes Don Quixote for the American Ballet Theatre, 1978.

Address: United Scenic Artists, 1540 Broadway, New York, NY.

LORD, Basil, actor

b Bexleyheath, 20 Mar 1913; *s* of Ralph Sidney Lord and his wife Margaret (Blythe); *e* Central School, Bexleyheath; originally engaged as a foreign exchange cashier; trained for the stage at the Gordon Douglas Studio Theatre.

First appeared at the Palace, Watford, 1934, in The Case of the Frightened Lady; in repertory, 1935–40; Whitehall,

1947–8, understudied and played for Ronald Shiner as Porter in Worm's Eye View; toured, 1949, in House on the Sand; Comedy, Oct 1949, for the Repertory Players, played Able Seaman Badger in Seagulls Over Sorrento; in 1950, succeeded Ronald Shiner as Porter in Worm's Eye View; St James's, Oct 1951, played Roderigo in the Orson Welles production of Othello; Piccadilly, June 1952, Spud Ryan in The Gay Dog; Apollo 1953, took over the part of Able Seaman Badger in Seagulls Over Sorrento; Whitehall, Aug 1954, played Flash Harry in Dry Rot; Globe, June 1955, for the Repertory Players, appeared as Herbert Hayhoe in As Black as She's Painted; toured, 1958, as Shorty Brown in Love or Money; Piccadilly, May 1959, Archie D'Arcy in Caught Napping; Pembroke, Croydon, Sept 1960, played Mr Bull in Lady Barker's Last Appearance, subsequently touring with the production; at the Whitehall, took over the part of Percy Pringle in Simple Spymen; at the same theatre, Aug 1961, played Charlie Barnet in One For the Pot, which ran for nearly three years; at the same theatre, July 1964–7, Constable Pulford in Chase Me, Comrade; Palace, Nov 1969, played Policeman O'Hara in Phil the Fluter; May 1970 toured as Mr Blore in Dandy Dick; toured, Apr 1971, as Canton in The Clandestine Marriage; in S Africa, 1972, played Col Sir Robert Richardson in The Jockey Club Stakes; Shaw, Mar 1973, Arnold Fearn in Only a Game; Gardner Centre, Brighton, Oct 1973, Old Gobbo in The Merchant of Venice; Northcott, Exeter, 1974, played Billy Rice in The Entertainer, and Sorin in The Seagull; Shaw, Jan 1975, Petey in The Birthday Party; returned to the Northcott to play Admiral Benbow in Thark, and Harry in Home, 1975, and two parts in The Italian Straw Hat, 1976; for the Actors' Company, Mar 1977, played Youatt in The Amazons and Billy Rice in The Entertainer; toured, Jan 1979, as Ernest in Bedroom Farce; has also appeared in pantomime as the Ugly Sister in Cinderella; directed his first production Some Like It Frozen in 1969, and Forever April in the same year; has made frequent appearances on television.

Favourite part: Badger in Seagulls Over Sorrento.
Recreations: Writing, gardening.
(*Died 3 Apr 1979.*)

LORTEL, Lucille, producer

b New York City; *d* of Harry Lortel and his wife Anna (Mayo); *e* Adelphi College, 1920, American Academy of Dramatic Arts, 1920–1; prepared for the stage with Arnold Korf and Max Reinhardt in Berlin; *m* Louis Schweitzer (dec).

Formerly an actress; began her career as an actress in stock in Albany, NY, 1924; toured with the Merkle Harder Repertory Company, 1924; played stock in Lewiston, Maine, 1924; made her NY début at the Selwyn, 23 Feb 1925, as the ingenue in Two by Two; Guild, Apr 1925, played a Handmaiden in the Theatre Guild production of Caesar and Cleopatra; took over the role of Iras in the same production; Empire, Aug 1925, Inez in The Dove; 48th Street, May 1926, Clara Rathbone in One Man's Woman; Princess, Jan 1927, took over as Elsa in The Virgin Man; toured as Poppy in The Shanghai Gesture, 1927; toured in stock and vaudeville, 1927–9, appearing at the Palace in The Man Who Laughed Last; Broadhurst, Sept 1932, French Maid in The Man Who Reclaimed His Head; retired from the theatre for some years; founded and became Artistic Director of The White Barn Theatre in Westport, Connecticut, 1947, where she has presented many plays, operas, concerts, and ballets, among which may be noted the American première of Red Roses for Me, William Saroyan's Jim Dandy, Alive and Kicking, 1948; Don Perlimplin and Belisa in the Garden, the première of the

Mendelssohn opera The Stranger, 1949; Murder in the Cathedral, 1950; the première of Maugham's Loaves and Fishes, 1951; Gertrude Stein's Brewsie and Willie, The Lottery, 1952; Geoffrey Holder and his company of dancers première, USA, 1953; Juno and the Paycock, 1954; the première of Tennessee Williams's Three Players of a Summer Game, Joan Littlewood's Père Goriot, 1955; American première of Garcia Lorca's Dona Rosita, Ghosts, I Knock at the Door, 1956; Baty's Dulcinea, American première of Ionesco's The Chairs, of John Whiting's Saint's Day, 1957; American première of Betti's Irene Innocente, Williams's Talk to Me Like the Rain, Maurois's Triple Cross, Giraudoux's Song of Songs, Blood Wedding, 1958; Langston Hughes's Shakespeare in Harlem, 1959; Yukio Mishima's Noh plays, Albee's Fam and Yam, Beckett's Embers, 1960; Schisgal's The Typists, Obaldia's The Deceased and The Grand Vizir, 1961; Brecht on Brecht, The World of Kurt Weill in Song, 1963; Fugard's The Blood Knot, The After Dinner Opera Company, 1964; The Long Valley, The Dream Watcher, 1975; also owner and operator of the Theatre de Lys in NY, 1955–75, where she has co-produced or produced The Threepenny Opera, 1955, which ran for seven years; Siobhan McKenna's Hamlet, 1955, inaugurating the ANTA Matinee Series which continues to the present time; The Mary Anthony Dance Theatre, Ethel Colt in Curtains Up, 1958; Two Philoctetes, I Rise in Flames, Cried the Phoenix, Sweet Confession, Electra, Harlequinade, 1959; Figuro in the Night, The Moon Shines on Kylenamoe, The Lunatic View, 1962; The Crown, The Ring, and the Roses, 1963; I Knock at the Door, Pictures in the Hallway, 1964; Square in the Eye, The Old Glory, Leonard Bernstein's Theatre Songs, 1965; Serjeant Musgrave's Dance, The Israel Mime Theatre, Margaret Webster in The Seven Ages of Bernard Shaw, Come Slowly, Eden, The Deadly Art, 1966; The Viewing, Conditioned Reflex, Willie Doesn't Live Here Anymore, A Funny Kind of Evening with David Kossoff, The Deer Park, Postcards, The Club Bedroom, Limb of Snow, The Meeting, 1967; Our Man in Madras, On Vacation, A Madrigal of Shakespeare, Mr and Mrs Lyman, Hello and Goodbye, Cuba Si, The Guns of Carrar, 1968; The Projection Room, Neighbors, An Evening with James Agee, A Round with Ring, Oh, Pioneers, 1969; Dream of a Blacklisted Actor, Cruising Speed 600 mph, Mrs Snow, 1970; Heritage, A Biography in Song (Irving Caesar's), Sally, George, and Martha, 1971; Madame de Sade, Wilde!, 1972; Love Gotta Come by Saturday Night, Orrin, Three on Broadway, The Interview, The Epic of Buster Friend, 1973; Scott and Zelda, Fire and Ice, The Prodigal Sister, Drums at Yale, 1974; Medal of Honor Rag, 1976; Getting Out, 1979; at other theatres in NY has also produced or co-produced A Sleep of Prisoners, 1951; The River Line, I Knock at the Door, 1957; Cock-a-Doodle Dandy, 1958; The Balcony, 1960; Happy as Larry, 1961; Put It in Writing, 1963; The Blood Knot, 1964; A Streetcar Named Desire, 1973; entered films in The Man Who Laughed Last, 1930; has received numerous awards, including the Obie, Margo Jones Award, both the NY and National ANTA Chapters Awards, for her work fostering new playwrights and directors and actors.
Address: 60 West 57th Street, New York, NY. *Tel:* PL 7-8359.

LOUDON, Dorothy, actress
b Boston, Massachusetts, 17 Sept 1933; *d* of James E Loudon, Jr and his wife Dorothy Helen (Shaw); *e* Syracuse University, Emerson College, American Academy of Dramatic Arts; *m* Norman Paris; prepared for the stage with Sawyer Falk, Lola Allbee, and Gertrude Binley Kay.

Formerly in cabaret, performing at such clubs as the Blue Angel, Ruban Bleu, Persian Room of the Plaza, etc; made her stage début at Camp Tamiment, Philadelphia, 1957, in revue; made her New York début at the Winter Garden, 10 Nov 1962, playing Wilma Risque in Nowhere to Go But Up; toured, Sept 1965–May 1966, as Ellen Manville in Luv; Ethel Barrymore, Sept 1968, played in the revue Noel Coward's Sweet Potato; Broadhurst, Jan 1969, played Lillian Stone in The Fig Leaves Are Falling; Lyceum, Oct 1969, Mabel in Three Men on a Horse; Shubert, Philadelphia, Feb 1971, Charlotte Haze in Lolita, My Love; toured, summer 1971, as Karen Nash, Muriel Tate, and Norma Hubley in Plaza Suite; toured, Oct–Dec 1971, as Beatrice in The Effect of Gamma Rays on Man-in-the-Moon Marigolds, and repeated this part at the Marine's, San Francisco, Jan 1972, for the ACT; 46th Street, Apr 1973, Edith Potter in The Women; Coconut Grove Playhouse, Miami Beach, Fla, Feb 1974, played in the Neil Simon revue The Trouble with People . . . And Other Things; toured, summer 1974, in Winning Is Better; Alvin, Apr 1977, Miss Hannigan in Annie, receiving a 'Tony' Award for this performance; Majestic, Dec 1978, Bea Aster in Ballroom; Uris, 1980, took over as Mrs Lovett in Sweeney Todd; has appeared frequently on television variety programs such as *The Kraft Music Hall, The Dean Martin Show, DuPont Project 20*, and with Perry Como, Jonathan Winters, Gary Moore, etc; most recently (1979) in her own mini-series Dorothy.
Recreations: Writing, painting, sewing, and playing the piano. *Address:* Lionel Larner, Ltd, 850 Seventh Avenue, New York, NY 10019. *Tel:* 246-3105.

LOVE, Bessie (*née* Horton), actress
b Midland, Texas, USA; *d* of John Cross Horton and his wife, Emma Jane (Savage); *e* Los Angeles, California; *m* William Ballinger Hawks (mar dis).

Left school to enter films with D W Griffith, and won immediate success, playing in all major film studios; made her first appearance on the stage in Santa Barbara, California, 1928, as Bonnie in Burlesque; toured as a top billing star in variety, before making her first appearance in New York at the Palace, 1931; came to live in England, 1935, and appeared in films and worked on radio; during the war worked with the American Red Cross; made her first appearance on the London stage at the Granville, Walham Green, Oct 1945, in a Grand Guignol season, as Julie in Say It with Flowers, and as the Actress in Zenobia; Lyric, June 1945, took over the part of Miss Dell in Love in Idleness, and at the end of the London run, toured with Lynn Fontanne and Alfred Lunt in Paris and Germany, playing to the troops, in the same play; Garrick, Jan 1947, played Mrs Hedges in Born Yesterday; Arts, May 1949, played Myrtle Keller in The Male Animal, transferring with this to the New, June 1949; Phoenix, July 1949, played the Laughing Woman in Death of a Salesman; appeared at the Gaiety, Dublin, 1951, as Amanda Wingfield in The Glass Menagerie; Phoenix, July 1954, played Bessie Bockser in The Wooden Dish; Arts, Mar 1955, Mrs Priolleau in South; Piccadilly, Dec 1955, Mrs Kirke in A Girl Called Jo; Arts, Sept 1956, Mrs Lily Mortar in The Children's Hour; Perth Repertory, Apr 1958, played Babe in the *première* of her own play, The Homecoming; Royal Court, May 1959, the Nurse in Orpheus Descending; Westminster, Feb 1960, played Reba Spelding in Visit to a Small Planet; Lyric, Hammersmith, Apr 1961, again played Mrs Priolleau in South; Princes, Aug 1962, and Strand, Nov 1962, played Mrs Ella Spofford in Gentlemen Prefer Blondes; Prince of Wales, Sept 1963, Grace Kimborough in Never Too Late; Queen's, June 1964, played A Worker in Saint Joan of the Stockyards;

New Arts, Nov 1964, the White Woman in In White America; Palace, Watford, July 1966, Amanda in The Glass Menagerie; Hampstead Theatre Club, Nov 1966, Marguerite Oswald in The Silence of Lee Harvey Oswald; Palace, Watford, Nov 1968, Aunt Nonnie in Sweet Bird of Youth; toured, Feb 1971, as Lavinia in The Heiress; Royal, Court, Aug 1971, Mrs Dekker in West of Suez, transferring to the Cambridge Theatre, Oct 1971; Drury Lane, May 1972, Aunt Pittypat in Gone with the Wind; first appearance in films, 1915, in The Flying Torpedo; other silent pictures include: Intolerance, The Aryan, Reggie Mixes In, The Lost World, Lovely Mary, Human Wreckage; appeared in MGM's first musical, Broadway Melody, also Hollywood Revue, Chasing Rainbows, etc; films made in England include: The Wild One, Isadora, Sunday Bloody Sunday, and Catlow; first appearance on television, 1946, and has since played in numerous productions, including You Can't Take It with You, Our Town, South, A Kiss for the Dying, etc; her autobiography, From Hollywood with Love, was published in 1977.

Recreations: Sewing, writing, knitting, embroidering, dancing. *Address:* c/o Jonathan Altaras, London Management, 235–241 Regent Street, London, W1.

LOVEJOY, Robin, OBE, director

b Labasa, Fiji, 17 Dec 1923; *s* of Casper Ebenezer Lovejoy and his wife Viti (Clark); *e* Boy's G S, Suva, Fiji; *m* Patricia Lucy Hughes; originally an actor.

Director, Metropolitan Theatre, Sydney, 1950–2, where he directed his first professional production, You Never Can Tell, 1950; Director, 1952, Arrow Theatre, Melbourne; Executive Producer, 1955, New South Wales National Opera; Resident Director of Drama and Opera, Australian Elizabethan Theatre Trust, 1955–8; productions for the Elizabethan Theatre include The Rivals, 1956, and Long Day's Journey into Night, 1959; Founder and Artistic Director, The Trust Players, Sydney, 1959–61; directed The One Day of the Year, Sydney, 1961; Harkness Fellow, 1961–3, spending two years' travel and research in the USA; Sadler's Wells, London, Jan 1962, directed La Bohème; guest director and artist in residence, Dallas Theatre Centre, Texas, 1962, where he directed The Rivals; Director, Old Tote Theatre Company, Sydney, 1965–74; productions in Sydney during this period included Rosencrantz and Guildenstern are dead, 1969; The Taming of the Shrew, Tartuffe, 1972; subsequently a freelance director and designer; directed What if You Died Tomorrow? (also London), 1974; appointed Artistic Adviser to the Victoria State Opera, Melbourne, 1977, and has directed the following operas for the Company: Maria Shiarda, 1975; L'Orfeo, Peleas et Melisande, 1977; The Barber of Seville, Idomeneo, 1978; for Australian Opera, Sydney, directed La Fanciulla del West and Idomeneo (1979); appointed Chairman of the Board of Studies, National Institute of Dramatic Arts, 1978; directed the film series Adventure Unlimited, 1963; for TV has directed King Lear, 1970, and The Taming of the Shrew, 1972; awarded the OBE in 1974, for sevices to Australian Theatre.

Recreations: Gardening, painting, restoring antique furniture. *Address:* 37 Bardwell Road, Mosman, NSW 2088, Australia.

LOWE, Arthur, actor

b Hayfield, Derbyshire, 22 Sept 1915; *s* of Arthur Lowe and his wife Mary (Ford); *m* Joan Cooper; formerly in the Army.

Made his first stage appearance at the Hippodrome, Hulme in Nov 1945 as Dickson in Bedtime Story; first London appearance, Duke of York's, April 1950, as Wilson in Larger Than Life; Cambridge, May 1951, played the Calligraphist in Hassan; Coliseum, March 1952, Senator Brockbank in Call Me Madam; Princes, March 1954, Mike in Pal Joey; Coliseum, Oct 1955, the Salesman in The Pajama Game; Piccadilly, May 1957, Bert Vokes in A Dead Secret; Savoy, July 1959, Mr Filby in The Ring of Truth; Arts, Feb 1961, Ald Oglethorpe in Stop It, Whoever You Are; Royal Court, Sept 1964, Hudson in Inadmissible Evidence; at the same theatre in January, 1967, played Sir Davey Dunce in A Soldier's Fortune; Old Vic, Nov 1968, A B Raham in the National Theatre production of Home and Beauty; Cambridge, April 1969, Mr Ramage in Ann Veronica; Old Vic, Mar 1974, Stephano in The Tempest; Royal Court, Aug 1974, Ben Jonson in Bingo; Shaftesbury, Oct 1975, played Capt Mainwaring in a stage adaptation of Dad's Army; Duke of York's, Oct 1977, George Redfern in Laburnum Grove; first appeared in films 1947, in London Belongs to Me and has since appeared in Sweet William, The Lady Vanishes, The Plank, etc; television appearances, since 1951, include the award-winning *Dad's Army*, *Potter*, and *Bless Me Father*.

Address: Flat C, 2 Maida Avenue, Little Venice, London, W2 1TF. *Tel:* 01–262 1782.

LUCE, Claire, actress

b Syracuse, New York, *d* of Frederick Luce and his wife Maud (Hinds); *e* Vermont and Rochester; *m* Clifford Warren-Smith (dec); studied dancing at the Denishawn School in NY, with Michel Fokine and Florence Colebrook Powers.

Made her first appearance in public in the ballet of the opera, Snow Maiden, managed by Sol Hurok, 1921; first appeared on the regular stage at the Longacre Theatre, 15 Aug 1923, in Little Jessie James; appeared at the Times Square Theatre, NY, Sept 1924, as Clair in Dear Sir; at the Music Box, Dec 1924, appeared in The Music Box Revue; for a time a dancer with Texas Guinan's troupe; during 1925 appeared at the Casino de Paris, in revue; at Palm Beach, 1926, appeared in Ziegfeld's Palm Beach Nights; at the Globe, NY, June 1926, appeared in No Foolin' (Ziegfeld's revue); at the New Amsterdam, Aug 1927, in The Ziegfeld Follies of 1927; made her first appearance in London, at Golder's Green, 26 Nov 1928, as Bonny in Burlesque, appearing in the same part at the Queen's, Dec 1928; after her return to America, appeared in Atlantic City, Aug 1929, as Nora Mason, in Scarlet Pages, and appeared in the same part at the Morosco, NY, Sept 1929; Booth, Dec 1931, played Judy Gelett in Society Girl; Ethel Barrymore, Nov 1932, Mimi in Gay Divorce; and played the same part at the Palace, London, Nov 1933; at Daly's, May 1934, played Nina Popinot in Vintage Wine; Mar 1935, Susette in Love and Let Love; Gaiety, May 1935, Maricousa in Gay Deceivers; Adelphi, Feb 1936, appeared in Follow the Sun; Daly's, June 1937, Nadja von Eckner in No Sleep for the Wicked; Music Box, NY, Nov 1937, Curley's Wife in Of Mice and Men, which she also played at the Gate, London, Apr 1939, and subsequently at the Apollo, May 1939; at the Open Air Theatre, Southwark Park, July 1941, and at Regent's Park, Aug 1941, played Katherine in The Taming of the Shrew, and subsequently Princess Katherine in King Henry V; she then toured for ENSA, for eight months, playing Katherine in The Taming of the Shrew, Anna Christie, Nora in A Doll's House, and Sadie Thompson in Rain; subsequently toured as Elvira in Blithe Spirit, for the USO; at the Stratford-on-Avon Memorial Theatre, Apr–Sept 1945, appeared as Viola in Twelfth Night, Beatrice in Much Ado About Nothing, Mistress Ford in The Merry Wives of Windsor, and Cleopatra in Antony and Cleopatra; at the Westminster Theatre, Jan 1946, played Mary Stuart, Queen of Scots, in Golden Eagle;

Q, May, 1946, and subsequently on tour played Becky Sharp in Vanity Fair, and played this part at the Comedy, Oct 1946; returned to America, and next appeared at the Booth, NY, as Tanis Talbot in Portrait in Black; Lyceum, Apr 1950, Rose Raymond in With a Silk Thread; in Somerset, Mass, July 1950, played Effie in The Devil Also Dreams; New York City Center, Apr 1951, played Katherine in The Taming of the Shrew; Music Box, May 1952, appeared as Beatrice in Much Ado About Nothing; toured from 1956–9 in a one-woman show called Fashions in Love; Theatre '58, Dallas, Jan 1958, Lucy Greer in And So, Farewell; Maidman, NY, Apr 1960, in a one-woman show called These Are My Loves; East 74th Street, Mar 1961, played Constance Wilde in Feast of Panthers; Easthampton, NY, July 1962, Miss Taylor in In the Time of My Life; John Drew, Easthampton, NY, Aug 1962, Mrs Eddy in Go from Me; toured, 1964, in a one-woman show, Woman; Auditorium of the Library and Museum of the Performing Arts, Apr 1966, Mother in The Wedding and The Funeral; Barter, Abingdon, Virginia, and Studio, Miami, 1966, Flora Goforth in The Milktrain Doesn't Stop Here Anymore; toured universities in Tennessee Williams and Friends; Highlands, North Carolina, Aug 1970, the Queen in The Cave Dwellers; at the Globe, Odessa, Tex, appeared as Mrs Patrick Campbell in Dear Liar, 1972, and directed Twelfth Night, 1974; in 1964–5 was a member of the faculty of the New York University Drama department and held an acting class; her book Letters from Patrick published in 1964; has made many recordings of works by Shakespeare, Wilde, Williams, George Jean Nathan, Heine, Colette, etc; has made numerous summer stock appearances; first appeared in films, 1930, in Up the River; has also made numerous television appearances, including Peer Gynt, Becky Sharp, etc.

Recreation: Painting (has had three one-woman exhibitions, between 1951–9). *Address:* 26 Gramercy Park South, New York, NY 10003.

LUCKHAM, Cyril, actor
b Salisbury, 25 July 1907; *s* of Charles Minty Luckham and his wife Mary Emmeline (Browne); *e* Royal Naval Colleges, Osborne and Dartmouth; *m* Violet Sylvia Lamb; originally in the Royal Navy, but invalided out, 1931, as a Lieutenant; studied for the stage with the Arthur Brough Players and the Folkestone Dramatic School.

First appeared at the Leas Pavilion, Folkestone, 1935, as a footman in The Admirable Crichton; appeared in repertory, 1935–44, at Folkestone, Manchester, Bristol, Coventry, Southport, etc; first appeared in London at the Arts, 11 July 1945, as Torvald Helmer in A Doll's House; played leading parts in repertory, at the Liverpool Playhouse, and with the Old Vic Company, 1945–51; at the St James's, June 1948, appeared as Leonid Gayev in The Cherry Orchard; Adelphi, Nov 1951, played The Victor in The Moment of Truth; Winter Garden, Jan 1952, Aaron in The Firstborn; Arts, Mar 1952, Voinitsky in Uncle Vanya; Wyndham's, Aug 1952, took over the part of Colonel Desmond De S Rinder-Sparrow in The Love of Four Colonels; Arts, June 1953, played Major Petkoff in Arms and the Man; Savoy, Sept 1953, played Oderbruch in The Devil's General; Aldwych, Mar 1954, The Vicar in I Capture the Castle; Arts, May 1954, Ali in a revival of The Impresario From Smyrna; Palace, Aug 1954, Fairchild in Sabrina Fair; Lyric, May 1955, Felix Dulay in My Three Angels; Phoenix, June 1956, Hon Gerald Piper in The Family Reunion; joined the Shakespeare Memorial Theatre in Stratford-on-Avon in 1957, and played the following parts: the Banished Duke in As You Like It, King of France in King John, Julius Caesar, Belarius in Cymbeline, and Gonzalo in

The Tempest, 1957; Friar Laurence in Romeo and Juliet, Feste in Twelfth Night, Polonius in Hamlet, Helicanus in Pericles, and Leonato in Much Ado About Nothing, 1958; Parolles in All's Well That Ends Well, Quince in A Midsummer Night's Dream, and Gloucester in King Lear, 1959; Old Vic, Sept 1960, played Sorin in The Seagull; toured, Oct 1960, as Francis Morgan in Strip the Willow; Saville, Aug 1962, took over the part of Reginald Kinsale in Photo Finish; at the same theatre, May 1963, played Dr Wolfgang Himmelmann in Night Conspirators; Yvonne Arnaud, Guildford, Nov 1965, David Lancaster in The Vortex; Haymarket, Jan 1966, M'Comas in You Never Can Tell; has also broadcast and appeared in many notable television productions, including, recently, Murder at the Wedding, The Omega Factor, and Donkey's Years; films include Providence.

Favourite parts: Feste, Col Rinder-Sparrow in The Love of Four Colonels, and Reginald Kinsale in Photo Finish. *Recreations:* Cricket, music, ornithology. *Address:* 70 Hampstead Way, London, NW11. *Tel:* 01–455 8612.

LUCKINBILL, Laurence George, actor
b Fort Smith, Arkansas, 21 Nov 1934; *s* of Laurence Benedict Luckinbill and his wife Agnes (Nulph); *e* University of Arkansas (BA 1955), Catholic University of America (MFA 1957); *m* (1) Robin Strasser (mar dis); (2) Lucie Arnaz, the actress; formerly a cannery worker, stage carpenter, and a US Information specialist; trained for the stage with Uta Hagen at the HB Studio, New York, and by George Kernodle at the University of Arkansas.

Made his first appearance on the stage at St Boniface Parish Hall, Fort Smith, Arkansas, Dec 1939, as China in a Pageant of All Nations; made his first appearance in New York at the Carnegie Playhouse, 29 Apr 1959, as the Old Shepherd in Oedipus Rex; Theatre Marquee, Feb 1961, played George Fabry in There Is a Play Tonight; Great Lakes Shakespeare Festival, Cleveland, Ohio, summer, 1962, Iago in Othello, Hotspur in Henry IV Part 1, and Justice Shallow in Henry IV, Part 2; ANTA, NY, 1963, took over as William Roper in A Man for All Seasons; toured US, July 1963–May 1964, in this last part; Morosco, Oct 1964, Simon Holt in Beekman Place; ANTA Washington Square, Jan 1965, Damis in Tartuffe; McCarter, Princeton, winter 1965, the title roles in Caligula and Bertolt Brecht's Galileo; June, 1965, played in Arms and the Man; Playhouse in the Park, Cincinnati, Ohio, 1966–67 season, played in Sodom and Gomorrah; American Conservatory Theatre, San Francisco, 1966, Biff Loman in Death of a Salesman and Edmund in King Lear; for the APA Repertory, 1966, played Orestes in The Flies; Theatre Four, NY, Apr 1968, Hank in The Boys in the Band; Fortune, Jan 1969, Sensuality in Horseman, Pass By; made his London debut at Wyndham's, 11 Feb 1969, as Hank in The Boys in the Band; Tambellini's Gate, NY, Jan 1970, Ted in The Electric Map in a double bill called The Memory Bank; McAlpin Rooftop, May 1970, Dr Prentice in What the Butler Saw; New Theater for Now, Los Angeles, Cal 1972, played Patrick in the premiere of Christopher Isherwood's A Meeting by the River; Edison, NY, Dec 1972, repeated this last part; New Theater for Now, 1973, played in Tadpole; Eastside Playhouse, NY, May 1973, Frank Elliot in Alpha Beta; Mark Taper Forum, Los Angeles, Oct 1975, Brian in The Shadow Box; Ethel Barrymore, Oct 1976, Hamlet in Poor Murderer; Morosco, Mar 1977, again played Brian in The Shadow Box; Public/Anspacher, Dec 1977, Simon in Prayer for My Daughter; Havemeyer Hall, Columbia U, title-role in Galileo, presented by the New York Actors' Theater, of which he is joint Artistic Director; Imperial, 1979, took over as George Schneider in Chapter Two; Circle in the Square, 1980, appeared in Past Tense; first appeared in films in The Boys in the Band, 1970, and has since played in Such Good Friends, The Delphi Bureau, The Money, etc; first appeared on television in 1964 as Pabundren in As I Lay Dying by William Faulkner, and has since played in the soap opera The Secret Storm, in The Boston Massacre, The Senator, The Delphi Bureau, etc.

Favourite part: Galileo. *Hobby:* Writing articles about the theater and films. *Address:* c/o Richard M Rosenthal, 445 Park Avenue, New York, NY 10022. *Tel:* 758–0809.

LUDLAM, Charles, actor, playwright, director, producer
b Floral Park, New York, 12 Apr 1943; s of Joseph William Ludlam and his wife Majorie (Braun); e Hofstra University.

Has appeared on the stage since childhood; when 17 founded his own theater in Northport, Long Island, where he produced O'Neill and Strindberg, among others; first appeared on the stage in New York at the 17th Street Studio, 1967, as Peeping Tom in The Life of Lady Godiva; in 1967 co-founded The Ridiculous Theatrical Company and, at the 17th Street Studio, produced and directed his play Big Hotel, in which he also played; since then has written Conquest of the Universe/When Queens Collide, 1967; with Bill Vehr, Turds in Hell, 1968; The Grand Tarot, 1969; Bluebeard, 1970; Eunuchs of the Forbidden City, 1971; also directed and played in all of them; Corn, a musical, in which he played Paw Hatfield at the 13th Street Theater, Nov 1972; Camille, A Tearjerker, in which he played Marguerite Gautier at the 13th Street, May 1973; Hot Ice, in which he played Buck Armstrong at the Evergreen, Feb 1974; played Marguerite Gautier in Camille, at the Evergreen, May 1974; produced and directed his puppet play Professor Bedlam's Punch and Judy, Evergreen, Oct 1974; wrote, produced, and directed Stage Blood in which he played Carleton Stone, Jr, at the Evergreen, Dec 1974; Evergreen, Apr 1975, played Baron Khanazar von Bluebeard in his play Bluebeard; Princetown Playhouse, Apr 1976, wrote, directed and appeared in Caprice; Truck and Warehouse, Apr 1977, book and direction for Der Ring Gott Farblonjet; opened One Sheridan Square as a permanent home for the Ridiculous Theatrical Company, where he has since presented, written and directed revivals such as Stage Blood and Camille, 1978, and new productions including The Ventriloquist's Wife, 1978; The Enchanted Pig, A Christmas Carol (playing Scrooge), 1979; toured Europe in 1971, making his London debut at the Open Space, as Baron Khanazar von Bluebeard; again toured Europe in 1973, playing Camille and Bluebeard in repertory; received an Obie Award in 1969 for his founding of the Ridiculous Theatrical Company; received a Guggenheim Fellowship in Playwriting, 1970; received the Obie Award again in 1973 for his roles in Corn and Camille.

Favourite parts: Bluebeard, Camille in his plays of those titles. *Hobbies and recreations:* Puppetry and horticulture. *Address:* 55 Morton Street, New York, NY 10014. *Tel:* 929–4914.

LUDLOW, Patrick, actor
b London, 24 Mar 1903; s of Henry Sutton Ludlow and his wife Laura Mary (Hawkins); e Eastbourne and University College School; m (1) Hylda Mary Blake Taylor (Paulette Ludlow) (mar dis); (2) Maja Garner.

Made his first appearance on the stage at the New Theatre, 27 Dec 1915, as John in a revival of Peter Pan; at the Ambassadors', Dec 1917, played Epimethus in Pandora, and The Wonder Tales; subsequently appeared as Hughie Cavanagh in The Boy; at the Queen's, Aug 1918, played Midshipman Wing Eden in The Luck of the Navy; in 1919 went to America, and appeared in the same part at the Manhattan Theatre, New York, Oct 1919; he also appeared in the United States as Alec in General Post and Charlie Harrison in Brewster's Millions; at the St James's, Aug 1920, played Tom Trainor in His Lady Friends; in 1922, toured in South Africa, as Billy in The Edge of Beyond, and Clay in Polly with a Past; during 1924, again toured in South Africa, with Thurston Hall, as Philip Marvin in The Broken Wing, etc; after returning to London, appeared at the St Martin's Theatre, 1925, in Spring Cleaning; subsequently toured as Fordyce in No 17; at the Globe, 1926, in Ask Beccles; Shaftesbury, 1927, in The High Road; Savoy, Dec 1927, Tim Hollander in The Cave Man; during 1928, toured as George in Compromising Daphne; Adelphi, July 1929, played Oliver Peploe in One Little Kiss; at the Ziegfeld Theatre, NY, Nov 1929, Lord Henry in Bitter Sweet; St Martin's, London, 1933, George in Strange Orchestra; King's, Hammersmith, Feb 1934, James Slade in The Happy Hostage, of which he was part-author and director; Victoria Palace, Sept 1934, Councillor Scoutmaster Ravenscroft in Young England; Arts, Oct 1934, Hon Billie Barnet in No Greater Crime; Phoenix, Dec 1935, Paul Tegle in The Limping Man; Richmond, Nov 1938, Tommy Weston in Chain Male; toured in Canada, 1939, with Maurice Colbourne and Barry Jones, as Lord Holland in Charles, the King; Henry Miller, NY, Jan 1940, played the Betrothed in Geneva; Vaudeville, London, Oct 1940, Dumain in All's Well that Ends Well, and Sir Richard Vernon and Godshill in King Henry IV (Part I); subsequently toured various camps, entertaining troops, as Steve in It's a Wise Child; New, Feb 1942, played Fairfax Haycraft in Goodnight Children; Q, Sept 1942, Commander Jeremy Moore in London, W1; Wimbledon, Oct 1942, Oscar Garanty in Lottie Dundass; Arts, Jan and Mercury, Feb 1943, Young Marlow in She Stoops to Conquer; formed his own company, 1943, and toured as Michael in Michael and Mary; 1944, as Dwight Houston in There's Always Juliet, and Bastien in By Candle Light; 1945, as Raymond in The Man in Possession; at the Rudolf Steiner Hall, Feb–Mar 1946, playing in By Candle Light, and Mr Manningham in Gaslight; subsequently produced and toured as Armand in Strictly Personal which he adapted from the French play Moumou, 1948; toured as Johnnie in The Anonymous Lover, and toured twice in Germany, in By Candle Light, and When We Are Married; during 1949, was directing and producing at Ventnor, IOW, and 1950, at the Palace Theatre, Maidstone; New Lindsey, June 1951, played Clive Farnley in Hand in Glove; also in 1951 presented, produced and appeared in The Respectable Prostitute; was engaged as General Manager of the Norwegian Ballet during its English tour of 1951; under his own management presented Here's To Us, 1952; at the Pilochry Festival, 1955, played the Dean in Dandy Dick, Professor Daunty in The Lady from Edinburgh, Petkoff in Arms and the Man and Don Everisto in A Hundred Years Old; Arts, 1957, Envoy in The Balcony; Richmond, 1963, George Dunlop in Upside Downing Street; Folkestone, 1965, Henry in This Thing Called Love and Pop in Hot and Cold in All Rooms; also toured Scotland, as David in Hay Fever; 1966, toured in Dear Charles as Michael, and appeared at Caux Festival playing Doctor Hippocrat in The Dictator's Slippers; Leatherhead, 1967, played the Admiral in The Luck of the Navy having played the Midshipman in the 1918 production; Palmer's Green, 1968, Harker in The Upper Crust; since 1927 has acted in more than eighty films (England and Hollywood) and has broadcast frequently; his television appearances include Cassius (favourite part) in Julius Caesar (NY), Kenilworth, and Grand Hotel; part-author of Faces, 1932, which was also filmed; Member of Theatrical Managers Association.

Recreations: Dancing, swimming and collecting Delft. *Address:* 14 Montpelier Walk, London, SW7. *Tel:* 01–589 1554.

LUDWIG, Salem, actor, director, teacher
b Brooklyn, New York, 31 July 1915; *s* of Isidore Ludwig and his wife Esna (Baronchuk); *e* John Adams High School, Brooklyn College; *m* Eulalie Noble; is a member of the Actors Studio.

First appeared on the stage in Long Beach, NY, July 1938, as the Bartender in The Drunkard; made his NY début at The Playhouse, 25 Apr 1947, as Ambrose in Miracle in the Mountains; Equity Library Theatre, Oct 1948, directed Man of Destiny; New Stages, Mar 1949, played an Ishmaelite Slave Trader in The Sun and I; Mansfield, Feb 1950, Harry in All You Need Is One Good Break; President, May 1952, Saul Schlossberg in The Victim; National, Mar 1953, Nursie in Camino Real; Theatre de Lys, June 1953, Quartermaster in Maya; Henry Miller's, Nov 1953, Traveler in The Trip to Bountiful; Greenwich Mews, Nov 1954, directed In Splendid Error; President, Dec 1954, Detective Sergeant Bender in The Troublemakers; National, Apr 1955, Mr Goodfellow in Inherit the Wind; left this production, then, in 1957, rejoined it in his former part; Carnegie Hall Playhouse, Sept 1957, Lazar Wolf in Tevya and His Daughters; Gate, Dec 1957, Fyodor in The Brothers Karamazov; Gate, June 1958, directed Mrs Warren's Profession; Coronet, Dec 1958, Professor Connelly in The Disenchanted; Longacre, Sept 1961, Dribble in Rhinoceros; Madison Avenue Playhouse, Apr 1962, Mayor Caphards in Witches' Sabbath; toured, 1962, as Dribble in Rhinoceros; Morosco, June 1964, Ferapont in the Actors Studio production of The Three Sisters; made his London début at the Aldwych, May 1965, in this last part when the Actors Studio played in The World Theatre Season; Cort, Nov 1965, Mourner in The Zulu and the Zayde; Cherry Lane, Dec 1966, Max Kupreef in Night of the Dunce; Gramercy Arts, Feb 1969, Grandpa in A Corner of the Bed; Gramercy Arts, Apr 1969, Johnny in The Honest-to-God Schnozzola and Leader in The Leader; Bijou, May 1970, Myron Berger in Awake and Sing; Avon, Stratford, Ontario, July 1970, Macey in The Friends; Royale, Las Vegas, Nevada, Oct 1970, Herb Miller in Shock of Recognition; Berkshire Playhouse, Stockbridge, Massachusetts, July 1971, directed Are You Now or Have You Ever Been Blue?; Royale, Feb 1972, Uncle Murry in Moonchildren; Astor Place, Mar 1973, directed Brother Gorski, and Nov 1973, co-produced The Foursome; Circle Repertory, Dec 1973, Bernie Nathan in Prodigal; Theatre de Lys, 1974, took over as Uncle Murry in Moonchildren; Roundabout, July 1974, Nicole in The Burnt Flowerbed; began his film career as a dancer in the musical Sweet Surrender, 1936, and has since played in I Love You, Alice B Toklas, America! America!, Never Love a Stranger, etc; first appeared on television in 1949, and has played many roles since, notably Sam Friskin in Malice in Wonderland, by S J Perelman, on *Omnibus*, as Assistant District Attorney Horace Kane in the series *The Defenders,* Harry on *Road to Reality*, etc; co-founded Solar Theatre, Inc, June 1971, a producing firm composed of actors; teaches acting techniques in NY.
Address: Archer King, Ltd, 777 Seventh Avenue, New York, NY 10019. *Tel:* 581–8513.

LUKE, Peter, playwright
b England, 12 Aug 1919; *s* of Sir Harry Luke, KCMG, DLitt and his wife Joyce (Fremlin); *e* Eton, Byam Shaw School of Art and Atelier André Lhote, Paris; *m* the actress June

Tobin; served in the Rifle Brigade 1940–46; formerly in the wine trade.

Worked in television 1958–67; his first play to be produced was his adaptation of Hadrian VII, Birmingham Rep, 1967, followed by Mermaid, 1968, and Helen Hayes, NY, 1969; has since written Bloomsbury, produced London, 1974; Proxopera (from a novel by Benedict Kiely), Dublin 1978; translated Rings for a Spanish Lady, 1974, and directed it at the Gaiety, Dublin, 1977; a director of the Gate Theatre, Dublin, 1977–80; plays and films for TV include Small Fish Are Sweet, 1958, Devil a Monk Would Be, and Black Sound — Deep Song, 1968; books include the autobiographical Sisyphus and Reilly, 1972; Enter Certain Players (editor), 1978, and a children's book, Paquito and the Wolf, 1980.
Recreations: Horses, tauromachia. *Address:* c/o Harvey Unna and Stephen Durbridge, 14 Beaumont Mews, Marylebone High Street, London W1N 4HE.

LUND, Art, actor and singer
b Salt Lake City, Utah, 1 Apr 1920; *s* of Arthur Earl Lund, and his wife Lillie Alma Sophia (Götberg); *e* Westminster Junior College, Salt Lake City, and Eastern Kentucky State College, Richmond; *m* Kathleen Bolanz; formerly a high school athletic coach, and a cabaret singer.

First appeared on the stage at the Music Circus, Lambertville, New York, June 1955, as The Wreck in Wonderful Town; made his NY stage début at the Imperial, 3 May 1956, as Joe in The Most Happy Fella, which ran for 676 performances; toured USA 1957–8, in the same role; at the Starlight Theatre, Kansas City, July 1958, again played Joe, and also played Bigelow in Carousel; Provincetown Playhouse, NY, Dec 1958, played Lennie in the musical version of Of Mice and Men; City Center, Feb 1959, again played Joe in The Most Happy Fella; Imperial, summer 1959, took over the role of Kent in Destry Rides Again; made his London début at the Coliseum, 21 Apr 1960, as Joe in The Most Happy Fella; 46th Street, NY, May 1961, John Enright in Donnybrook; City Center, June 1962, Ben in Fiorello!; Winter Garden, Apr 1963, Frank Westphal in Sophie; Her Majesty's, London, Dec 1963, David Jordan in No Strings; Casa Manana, Fort Worth, Texas, June 1964, Stephen Henderson in Mr President; St Louis Municipal Opera, July 1965, Starbuck in 110 in the Shade; 46th Street, Jan 1966, Roy Bailey in The Wayward Stork; City Center, May 1966, Joe in The Most Happy Fella; Majestic, Dec 1966, Doc Golightly in Breakfast at Tiffany's; Salt Lake City, Utah, 1966, played Harold Hill in The Music Man and, 1970, Michael in I Do, I Do; Dorothy Chandler Pavilion, LA, June 1977, appeared in Annie Get Your Gun; has appeared in the films Molly Maguires, 1968, and Ten Days Till Tomorrow and Decisions, Decisions, 1970; first appeared on television in 1951, and has since appeared in *Gunsmoke, Wagon Train, The Ed Sullivan Show* and with Carol Burnett in Calamity Jane, and many others.
Favourite parts: Bigelow, Joe, Frank Butler, Harold Hill, and David Jordan. *Recreations:* Sports and cars. *Club:* Lambs. *Address:* 15216 Sutton Street, Sherman Oaks, Calif. *Tel:* 788–2563.

LUNDEL, Kert Fritjof, designer
b Malmo, Sweden, 17 June 1936; *s* of Dennis Lundell and his wife Irma (Holmberg); *e* Yale Drama School, New Haven, Conn; prepared for the stage at the Goodman Memorial Theater, Chicago, Ill; *m* Margaretta Hover.
Designed his first show in New York, Gogo Loves You, at the Theatre de Lys, 9 Oct 1964; since then has designed the decor for Hogan's Goat (also lighting and costumes), 1965;

The Journey of the Fifth Horse, Who's Got His Own, Under the Weather (also in Spoleto, Italy), The Displaced Person (all also costumes), 1966; La Turista, Posterity for Sale, Skin of Our Teeth (Stockholm, Sweden), Not a Way of Life, The Basement, Fragments, The Ceremony of Innocence, 1967; Carry Me Back to Morningside Heights, The People vs. Ranchman, Walk Together Children, Julius Caesar (Providence, RI), 1968; The Perfect Party, Papp, Indians, Calling in Crazy, A Whistle in the Dark, 1969; We Bombed in New Haven, Generations (both in Maastricht, Holland), Duet for Solo Voice, The Last Straw, Sunday Dinner, The Castro Complex, The Carpenters, 1970; Coriolanus (Utrecht, Holland), Solitaire/Double Solitaire (also New Haven, Conn, and Edinburgh, Scotland), Soon, Aint Supposed to Die a Natural Death, Fingernails Blue as Flowers, Lake of the Woods (also costumes), 1971; Sleep, The Duplex, Don't Play Us Cheap, National Black Theater, A Revival, The Lincoln Mask, The Kid, The Sunshine Boys; 1972; The Enemy is Dead, Whiskey, A Break in the Skin, House Party, 1973; Bread, Brainchild (Philadelphia), Joan of Lorraine, 1974; The Dog Ran Away, Hughie, Duet, The Night That Made America Famous, The Taking of Miss Janie, Love Death Plays of William Inge, Section Nine (Princeton, NJ), Love Two, The Soft Touch (tour), 1975; Every Night When the Sun Goes Down, Rockabye Hamlet, 1600 Pennsylvania Avenue, 1976; Cold Storage, Passing Game, 1977; The November People, 1978; received the International Theatre Institute design competition award, 1965, and exhibited at the Musée d'Art Moderne, Paris; received a design grant from Germany, 1969; guest lecturer at the Smith College, Northampton, Mass, 1969, where he designed The Crucible; consultant in design to the American Place Theater in the construction of their new theater, 1971; designed his first film, Black Like Me, 1964; has designed for television commercials since 1961, and also for Peter Weiss's play The Investigation, 1967.

Club: National Arts, NY. *Address:* 955 Lexington Avenue, New York, NY 10021. *Tel:* 988–7248.

LuPONE, Patti, actress
b Northport, NY, 21 Apr 1949; trained for the stage at the Juilliard School.

Visited Europe, 1970, in a student company, appearing at the Young Vic in the title role of a musical, Iphigenia; made her NY professional debut with the Acting Company in their first season at the Good Shepherd-Faith Church, Oct 1972, playing Lady Teazle in The School for Scandal, Kathleen in The Hostage and Natasha in The Lower Depths; in their second season, at the Billy Rose, Dec 1973, played Irina in The Three Sisters, Lucy Lockit in The Beggar's Opera, Lizzie in Next Time I'll Sing to You, etc; at the Harkness, Oct 1975, played Rosamund in The Robber Bridegroom, Prince Edward in Edward II, Kitty Duval in The Time of Your Life and again played Irina; Kennedy Center, Washington DC, May 1976, Genevieve in The Baker's Wife; St Nicholas, Chicago, Nov 1977, Ruth in The Woods; Plymouth, May 1978, Rita and Lily La Pon in The Water Engine; 46th Street, May 1978, the Call Girl in Working; Hartford Stage, Conn, 1979, Monagh in Catchpenny Twist; Broadway, Sept 1979, played the title role in Evita, for which she received a Tony award; her films include King of the Gypsies, and 1941.

Address: c/o Jeff Hunter, 119 West 57th Street, New York, NY 10019.

LYNN, Jonathan, director, writer and actor
b Bath, 3 Apr 1943; *s* of Robin Lynn and his wife Ruth Helen (Eban); *e* Pembroke College, Cambridge; *m* Rita Eleanora Merkelis; studied with Mira Rostova in New York.

Commenced acting while at Cambridge and made his first professional appearance with the Footlights company at the Plymouth, NY, 1954, in Cambridge Circus on Broadway; first London appearance, New Arts, 2 Sept 1965, as Bob Lacey in The Traverse production of Green Julia; Her Majesty's, Feb 1967, Motel the Tailor in Fiddler on the Roof; Open Space, 1968, Angus and Bill in Blue Comedy; Theatre Upstairs, Feb 1969, Hitler in A Comedy of the Changing Years; Strand, Nov 1970, Gerald Forbes in When We Are Married; commenced directing in the same year with Four Degrees Over at the Northcott, Exeter; directed John Gould's one-man show, 1970–71; The Plotters of Cabbage Patch Corner, 1971; artistic director, Cambridge Theatre Company, 1976–present, for which he has directed a number of successful productions, including the following which transferred to London: The Glass Menagerie, 1977; The Gingerbread Man, 1977 (also 1978, 1979); The Unvarnished Truth, The Matchmaker, 1978; Songbook, 1979; for RSC directed Anna Christie, Stratford 1979, London 1980; in television has worked as an actor in several series and in plays such as Barmitzvah Boy and The Knowledge; co-writer of more than sixty TV comedy shows including the *Doctor* series, *My Brother's Keeper* (with George Layton), and *Yes Minister* (with Antony Jay); writing for films includes The Internecine Project, and training films for Video Arts; author of a novel, A Proper Man, 1976.

Recreations: Reading, cinema, music. *Address:* c/o Barry Burnett Organisation, Suite 409, Princes House, 190 Piccadilly, London W1.

LYNNE, Gillian, director and choreographer
b Bromley, Kent; *d* of Leslie Pyrke and his wife Barbara (Hart); *e* Arts Educational School; *m* Patrick St John Back, QC (mar dis).

Originally a dancer, she made her stage debut with the Sadler's Wells Ballet, 1944, remaining with the company for seven years, during which time she danced leading roles such as the Queen of the Wilis in Giselle, and the Lilac Fairy in Sleeping Beauty; leading dancer, London Palladium, 1951–2; in repertory at Hythe Windsor and the Devon Festival, 1953; Coliseum, Oct 1954, Claudine in Can Can; narrated Peter and the Wolf with the London Philharmonic Orchestra, 1958, miming all the characters; played Becky Sharp at Windsor, 1959; Lyric, Hammersmith, 1960 appeared in New Cranks; choreographed her first ballet, Owl and the Pussycat, Western Theatre Ballet, 1961; the revue, England Our England, 1962; Palladium Dec 1962, played the Queen of Catland; directed and choreographed Round Leicester Square, and Collages (Edinburgh Festival), 1963; has also directed The Matchgirls, 1966; Bluebeard (Sadler's Wells Opera), 1969; Love On the Dole (musical, Nottingham), 1970; Tonight at Eight, Lilywhite Lies (Nottingham), 1971; Once Upon a Time, Liberty Ranch, 1972; The Papertown Paperchase, 1973; Home is Best (Amsterdam), 1978; her work as a choreographer includes The Roar of the Greasepaint, Pickwick (both NY), 1965; Ambassador, 1971; The Card, 1973; Hans Andersen, 1974; My Fair Lady, Songbook, 1979; for the Royal Shakespeare Company has also staged A Comedy of Errors (musical), 1976; As You Like It (musical), 1977; The Way of the World, 1978; Once in a Lifetime, 1979; for the same Company, co-directed A Midsummer Night's Dream, 1977, and The Greeks, 1980; has also choreographed opera, including The Trojans, 1977, and Parsifal, 1979 (both Covent Garden), and in 1978, The Yeomen of the Guard, at the Tower of London; and also films such as Half a Sixpence, Man of La Mancha, and Quilp, and for a number of television shows.

Recreations: Rehearsing, cooking. *Address:* 25 The Avenue, Bedford Park, Chiswick, London W4. *Tel:* 01–995 6092.

M

McANALLY, Ray (Raymond), actor

b Buncrana, Donegal, Ireland, 30 Mar 1926; *s.* of James William Anthony McAnally and his wife Winifred (Ward); *e* National School, Moville, Donegal; St Eunan's College, Letterkenny, Donegal; and St Patrick's College, Maynooth, Kildare, Ireland; *m* Ronnie Masterton.

Made his first professional appearance on the stage at the Town Hall, Malin Town, Donegal, in 1942, as a member of Richard and Lilian Carrickford's Company in Strange House; studied for the stage at the Abbey Theatre, Dublin, becoming a member of the company in 1947; between 1947–63 appeared in over 150 plays with the Abbey Theatre Company in which he played, among others, the following parts: Michael Gillane in Cathleen Ni Houlihan, 1948; Leonardo in Blood Wedding, O'Flingsley in Shadow and Substance, 1949; Denis in The Whiteheaded Boy, Hugh O'Cahan in Professor Tim, 1950; Blanco in The Shewing Up of Blanco Posnet, Davoran in The Shadow of a Gunman, 1951; Fred Byrne in Grogan and the Ferret, 1952; Darrell Blake in The Moon in the Yellow River, 1953; Colm in Knockavain, 1954; Sgt Tinley in The Plough and the Stars (Sarah Bernhardt Theatre, Paris Festival, with Abbey Company), Dacey Adam in Twilight of a Warrior, 1955; Superintendent Brownrigg in Strange Occurrence on Ireland's Eye, MacDara in Winter Wedding, 1956; Christy in The Playboy of the Western World, Bartholomew Mulchrone in The Wanton Tide, 1957; Sgt Garside in A Right Rose Tree, 1958; Eddie in The Country Boy (for which he received the *Evening Herald* Actor of the Year Award), 1959; George John Lee in The Shaws of Synge Street, 1960; Justice McHenry in The Evidence I Shall Give, Gaffur in The Post Office, 1961; Becket in the Dublin Theatre Festival Production of Murder in the Cathedral (St Patrick's Cathedral), 1962; made his first London appearance at the New Arts Theatre, Nov 1962, as Bud Connor in A Cheap Bunch of Nice Flowers; at the Paris International Festival, 1962, played the First Merchant in The Countess Cathleen; Belfast Opera House, June 1963, played Pastor John Earls in The Evangelist; Olympia, Dublin, Sept 1963, Phil Kerrigan in the musical Carrie (Dublin Theatre Festival); toured the English provinces, Mar 1964, as Grantley Lewis in A Little Winter Love; at the Piccadilly, London, May 1964, took over the part of George in Who's Afraid of Virginia Woolf?; Olympia, Dublin, Nov 1965, 'The Bul' McCabe in The Field; Chichester Festival, July 1966, Lopakhin in The Cherry Orchard, and Aug, Macduff in Macbeth; Gaiety, Dublin, Oct 1966, John Kerr in Cemented with Love; Jeannetta Cochrane, June 1967, Dron in The Mighty Reservoy; Dublin Festival, Oct 1968, Quentin in After the Fall; Aldwych, Jan 1970, for the Royal Shakespeare Company, Lawyer in Tiny Alice; Greenwich, Sept 1970, Ted in Lorna and Ted; Shaw, July 1971, Rev Anderson in The Devil's Disciple; Abbey, Dublin, Sept 1971, title role in Macbeth; Olympia, Dublin, title role in the Dublin Festival production, Da; Eblana, Dublin, Aug 1974, directed The Gingerbread Lady; directed Out of Town (Cork), Kennedy's Children (Dublin), 1975; Gaiety, Dublin, Oct 1976, appeared in the Festival production, The Devil's Own People; Peacock, Dublin, Apr 1980, directed Of Mice and Men; entered films, 1957, and has since appeared in such films as She Didn't Say No!, Shake Hands With the Devil, The Naked Edge, Billy Budd, etc; first appeared on television, 1959, in Leap in the Dark, subsequent appearances include the series *The Little Father, Court Martial*, etc; has broadcast in over 500 programmes.

Favourite parts: George in Who's Afraid of Virginia Woolf? and Dacey Adam in Twilight of a Warrior. *Recreations:* Reading and golf. *Address:* c/o Fraser and Dunlop Ltd, 91 Regent Street, London, W1.

McCALLIN, Clement, actor

b London, 6 Mar 1913; *s* of Sidney Granger McCallin and his wife Helena (Robins); *e* Stanmore Park preparatory school and Stowe; *m* Philippa Anne Gurney; studied for the stage at the Royal Academy of Dramatic Art.

Made his first appearance on the stage at the Grafton Theatre, 8 July 1931, as Sammy in Hollywood; in the autumn of 1931, toured in the chorus of The Millionaire Kid; at the Q Theatre, Jan 1932, played Young Woodley, Rosencrantz in Hamlet and Jack Brunton in Square Rigged, subsequently played repertory at the Festival Theatre, Cambridge and Lyceum, Edinburgh; New, Feb 1933, played the Earl of Rutland in Richard of Bordeaux, subsequently playing Maudelyn and De Vere in the same play; Apr 1935, toured with the Arts League of Service Travelling Theatre; Old Vic, 1935–6, Trumpeterstrale in Peer Gynt, Marullus, Trebonius and Titinius in Julius Caesar, Malcolm in Macbeth, Brackenbury and King Henry in Richard III and General Gourgaud in St Helena; Daly's, Mar 1936, again played in St Helena; Criterion, July 1936, Clay van Rennen in The Lady of La Paz; Westminster, Jan 1937, Moritz in The Crooked Cross; Stratford-on-Avon Memorial Theatre, Apr–Oct 1937, played Henry V, Cymbeline, King of France in King Lear, Theseus in A Midsummer Night's Dream and Polixenes in The Winter's Tale; Oct 1937, toured with Donald Wolfit's company as Orsino in Twelfth Night, Bassanio in The Merchant of Venice, Tranio in The Taming of the Shrew and Malcolm in Macbeth; joined the Birmingham Repertory company, Feb 1938, playing the leading parts in Tobias and the Angel, The Boy David, Pride and Prejudice, etc, and returned for the 1938–9 season; St James's, Feb 1939, succeeded Alexander Knox as the Judge in Geneva; Strand, July 1939, Harold Goff in The Gentle People; Open Air, Aug 1939, succeeded Robert Eddison as Raphael in Tobias and the Angel, and appeared as Orsino in Twelfth Night; during the War, served in the Army, July 1940–5; reappeared on London stage, at the Arts, June 1946, as Barashkov in The Dove and the Carpenter; Lyric, Hammersmith, Nov 1946, played the Hon George d'Alroy in Caste; Embassy, May 1947, Edmund in King Lear; June 1947, Benedick in Much Ado About Nothing; Torch, Sept 1947, Challiss in The Long Shadow; Aldwych, Dec 1947, Macduff in Macbeth; Embassy, Apr 1948, Andrew Bellamy in Portrait of Hickory; Memorial Theatre, Stratford-on-Avon, 1949–50, Banquo in Macbeth and Don John in Much Ado About Nothing, followed by an Australian tour with the company; Lyric, Hammersmith, May 1950, Nick Grant in If This Be Error; Embassy, Sept 1950, Norman Langford in Soldier Boy; Oct 1950, the Nobleman's Man in The Man With a Load of Mischief; again

at the Embassy, Jan 1951, he appeared in the part of Calisto in Celestina; directed the fight scenes of Caesar and Cleopatra and Antony and Cleopatra, in Sir Laurence Olivier's productions at the St James's, May 1951, and the Ziegfeld, New York, Dec 1951; Court, London, July 1952, played John Everett Millais in The Bride of Denmark Hill, and William Shakespeare in Bernard Shaw in Heaven; Comedy, Aug 1952, again appeared as Millais in The Bride of Denmark Hill; Criterion, Dec 1953, for the Under Thirty Group, played Norman in Facts of the Heart; Duke of York's, Dec 1953, played Frederic in Thirteen for Dinner; went to Australia, 1954, where he appeared as Jan in Dear Charles; at the Elizabethan Theatre, Sydney, May 1957, appeared as the Ghost, First Player, and Fortinbras in Hamlet, subsequently appearing as Loveless in The Relapse, and Malvolio in Twelfth Night; Comedy, Melbourne, Dec 1960, and toured Australia, as Frank Elgin in Winter Journey; Comedy, Melbourne, Jan 1961, played in The Constant Wife; on returning to England, appeared at the Prince of Wales, London, Sept 1963, as Dr James Kimborough in Never Too Late; Shaftesbury, Dec 1963, Mr Quelch in Billy Bunter Meets Magic; toured, Aug 1964, as Mr Hunt in Alibi For a Judge; Mermaid, Jan 1966, Cuthbertson in The Philanderer; Pitlochry Festival, Apr–May 1966, played the following parts: Philip Logan in The First Mrs Frazer, Jan Letzaresco in Dear Charles, Jacob in Jeppe of the Mountain and Gayev in The Cherry Orchard; Arnaud, Guildford, Nov 1966, again played Letzaresco in Dear Charles; Westminster, Feb 1967, Professor Esteban Zoltan in Happy Deathday; Strand, Nov 1967, Ward Cooper in Number Ten; Westminster, Sept 1968, Rev Harcourt in Bishop's Move, and Dec 1968, Rat King in Give a Dog a Bone; for the Royal Shakespeare Company at Stratford, and the Aldwych, 1970, he played the following parts: Valdis and others in Doctor Faustus, Leader of the Players and others in Hamlet, Duke of Milan in The Two Gentlemen of Verona, Sebastian in The Tempest; in 1971 played Police Inspector in Enemies, and the Judge in The Balcony, at the Aldwych, and Terrini in Occupations, at the Place; Stratford, 1972, Cominius in Coriolanus, Marullus and Messala in Julius Caesar, Solinus in The Comedy of Errors, and Agrippa in Antony and Cleopatra; again at Stratford, season 1973, played Escalus in Romeo and Juliet, Northumberland in Richard II, and Duke Frederick in As You Like It; repeated the part of Northumberland at Brooklyn Academy, Jan 1974, and also at Stratford and the Aldwych, 1974; played Philip of France in King John, Stratford 1974, Aldwych 1975; Lucifer in Dr Faustus (Aldwych), Dr Ostermark in Comrades (The Place), 1974; Stratford, season 1975, Charles of France in Henry V, Northumberland in Henry IV, parts 1 and 2, and Frion in Perkin Warbeck, the last at The Other Place; repeated these parts in London, Jan 1976; Stratford, season 1977, Salisbury and Edmund Mortimer in Henry VI entered films 1938, in Stolen Life; has made many appearances on television, notably as Henry V, and as Cassius in Julius Caesar, he has also appeared in a number of television series including: Dr Finlay's Casebook, Compact, The Plane-makers, Front Page Story, etc; was Principal Tutor at the National Institute of Dramatic Art, Sydney, Australia.
(*Died August 1977.*)

McCALLUM, John, CBE, actor, manager and director
b Brisbane, 14 Mar 1918, *s* of John Neil McCallum and his wife Lilian Elsie (Dyson); *e* Oatlands, Harrogate, Knox College, Sydney and Church of England Grammar School, Brisbane; *m* Googie Withers; studied for the stage at the Royal Academy of Dramatic Art.
    First appeared at the Cremorne Theatre, Brisbane, 16 Aug 1934, in Henry VIII; Scala, Brisbane, 1935, appeared in Hamlet and Richard II; in England, appeared in repertory at the

People's Palace, Mile End, and at Tonbridge, Memorial Theatre, Stratford-on-Avon, 1939, Old Vic, 1949, playing Francisco in The Tempest and the Herald in King Lear; at the Westminster, Aug 1940, appeared as the Ex-officer in Corne-lius; served with 2/5 Field Regiment, Australian Imperial Forces, during the war; at the Theatre Royal, Sydney, 1945, played Baldasarre in The Maid of the Mountains, General Esteban in Rio Rita, and directed The Wind and the Rain; at the Q, June 1949, appeared as Tony Macrae in Western Wind, and played this part at the Piccadilly, Sept 1949; Lyric, Hammersmith, Aug 1950, played Sir Philip Hayes, KBE, in View Over the Park; St James's, Apr 1954, played James Manning in Waiting for Gillian; toured Australia and New Zealand, 1955, as Simon Foster in Simon and Laura, and Freddie Page in The Deep Blue Sea, directing both plays; Scala, Dec 1956, appeared as Mr Darling and Captain Hook in Peter Pan; Aldwych, Apr 1957, played Gil in Janus; Phoenix, Sept 1957, played Lord Dungavel in Roar Like a Dove; after nearly a year's run, he left the cast, July 1958, to take up appointment of Assistant Managing Director, J C Williamson's Theatres, Ltd, in Australia; Comedy, Mel-bourne, Mar 1959, again played Lord Dungavel in Roar Like a Dove (which he also directed); Comedy, Melbourne, Sept 1959, directed The Piccadilly Bushman; Her Majesty's, Mel-bourne, 1960, directed a second company in My Fair Lady; 1968, toured Australia with his own production of Relatively Speaking; Theatre Royal, Sydney, Sept 1969, directed and designed Plaza Suite; Her Majesty's, Melbourne, Apr 1970, directed My Fair Lady; Albery, London, Sept 1973, played John Middleton in The Constant Wife; Comedy, Melbourne, Oct 1974, played Campbell Sinclair in his own play, As It's Played Today, which he also directed; Chichester, 1976, Clive Champion-Cheney in The Circle, transferring to the Haymarket, Oct; Comedy, Melbourne, Nov 1978, and tour, Cecil in The Kingfisher; has played in 26 films including It Always Rains on Sunday, The Loves of Joanna Godden, Valley of Eagles etc; directed the film Nickel Queen, 1969; has appeared in many TV plays and produced series including *Skippy the Bush Kangaroo, Boney, Barrier Reef, Bailey's Bird,* and *Shannon's Mob;* Joint Managing Director of J. C Williamson's Theatres, Ltd, 1960–7; Chairman and Execu-tive Producer Fauna Productions, 1967; President, Produc-ers' and Directors' Guild of Australia, 1969–71; founder president, the Australian Film Council, 1970–1; received the CBE in the New Year Honours, 1971.
    Recreations: Cricket, golf, and gardening. *Clubs:* Garrick, Melbourne, and Australian, Sydney. *Address:* c/o 1740 Pitt-water Road, Bayview, NSW, Australia.

McCARTHY, Kevin, actor
b Seattle, Washington, 15 Feb 1914; *s* of Roy Winfield McCarthy and his wife Martha Thérèse (Preston); *e* School of Foreign Service, Georgetown University, Washington, DC, and University of Minnesota; *m* Augusta Dabney (mar dis).
    Made his first appearance on the New York stage, at the Plymouth Theatre, 15 Oct 1938, as Jasp in Abe Lincoln in Illinois; Guild Theatre, Dec 1940, played Richard Banning in Flight to the West; during the War, served with the US Air Force, and while serving, appeared at the 44th Street Thea-tre, Nov 1943, as Ronny Meade in Winged Victory, and subsequently toured in this part; Belasco, Feb 1946, played Maurice in Truckline Café; Alvin, Nov 1946, Dunois in Joan of Lorraine; Playhouse, Jan 1948, Morgan Decker in The Survivors; Lyceum, Nov 1948, Kurt Heger in Bravo!; made his first appearance in London, at the Phoenix Theatre, 28 July 1949, as Biff in Death of a Salesman; at the New York City Center, Jan 1952, played Matt Burke in Anna Christie,

and in Feb 1953, Berowne in Love's Labour's Lost; Morosco, Mar 1953, took over the role of Freddie Page in The Deep Blue Sea, and subsequently toured in this part; at the Phoenix, May 1954, Boris Trigorin in The Seagull; Booth, Dec 1955, Ayamonn Breydon in Red Roses for Me; Belasco, Feb 1958, Richard Morrow in The Day the Money Stopped; Booth, Mar 1959, for one week took over the part of Jerry Ryan in Two for the Seesaw; Gate, Dec 1959, Rupert Forster in Marching Song; toured, June 1960, as Jerry Ryan in Two for the Seesaw; Cort, Nov 1960, Van Ackerman in Advise and Consent; Ambassador, Jan 1962, Captain Dodd in Something About a Soldier; UCLA Theatre Group, Los Angeles, California, Oct 1963, appeared in Brecht on Brecht, in which he also appeared occasionally at Theatre de Lys in NY; Louisville, Kentucky, Festival, Feb 1964, Reverend Shannon in Night of the Iguana; Morosco, June 1964, Vershinin in The Three Sisters; toured, 1965–6, as Jerry Ryan in Two for the Seesaw; Cort, Apr 1967, Homer in A Warm Body; Royale, May 1967, took over from Barry Nelson as Julian in Cactus Flower; Theatre de Lys, Oct 1970, Harold Ryan in Happy Birthday, Wanda June, which closed during Equity's off-Broadway strike and re-opened at the Edison, Dec 1970; The Other Stage, Dec 1972, Dan in The Children; Williamstown, Mass, July 1974, Trigorin in The Seagull; Circle Repertory, May 1975, Harry Harrison in Harry Outside; Ethel Barrymore, Oct 1976, played several parts in Poor Murderer; recent summer stock appearances include The Lion in Winter, 1976; Equus, 1978; member of Actors Studio since its foundation in 1947; since 1950 has appeared in the films Death of a Salesman, Drive a Crooked Road, Gambler from Natchez, Stranger on Horseback, Annapolis Story, Nightmare, The Best Man, The Prize, Mirage, Invasion of the Body Snatchers, Hotel, An Affair of the Skin, Kansas City Bomber (1972), etc; has also appeared frequently on television.
Address: c/o William Morris Agency, 1350 Sixth Avenue, New York, NY 10019.

McCARTY, Mary, actress and singer
b Kansas, 1923.
Made her New York début at the St James, June 1948, as Eva in Sleepy Hollow; Coronet, Sept 1948, played in the revue Small Wonder; Imperial, July 1949, Maisie Dell in Miss Liberty; Mark Hellinger, Dec 1950, played in the revue Bless You All; retired from the stage for some years, then reappeared in Sept 1961, as Rose in the tour of Gypsy, and continued touring in this role until Jan 1962; Belasco, Oct 1963, played Brewster in A Rainy Day in Newark; again retired from the stage and reappeared at the Winter Garden, Mar 1971, as Stella Deems in Follies; Shubert, Century City, Cal, July 1972, again played Stella Deems in Follies; Shubert, 11 Mar 1973, appeared in Sondheim: A Musical Tribute; Waldorf-Astoria, June 1973, appeared in the revue Milliken Breakfast Show; Minskoff, Aug 1973, took over from Patsy Kelly as Mrs O'Dare in Irene; Brothers and Sisters, NY, Feb 1975, appeared in cabaret; 46th Street, June 1975, Matron in Chicago; Imperial, Apr 1977, Marthy Owen in Anna Christie; has appeared extensively in cabaret, notably at the Plaza, Waldorf-Astoria, and Copacabana; owned and operated her own club in NY called Mary-Mary; has appeared in films since she was a child including French Line, Babes in Toyland, Pillow Talk, My Six Loves, etc.
(*Died 3 April, 1980.*)

McCLANAHAN, Rue, actress
b Healdton, Oklahoma, 21 Feb; *d* of William Edwin McClanahan and his wife Dreda Rheua-Nell (Medaris); *e* University of Tulsa; prepared for the stage with Uta Hagen and Perry-Mansfield.

First appeared on the stage at the Erie Playhouse, Erie, Pa, Oct 1957, as Rachel in Inherit the Wind; first appeared in New York at the Players, 26 Oct 1964, as Hazel in the musical The Secret Life of Walter Mitty; Brooks Atkinson, Mar 1966, understudied the female leads in The Best Laid Plans; Village Gate, Feb 1967, Lady MacBird in MacBird!; Hartford, Conn, Stage Company, 1967–68 season, played in The Hostage and The Threepenny Opera; Brooks Atkinson, Dec 1968, Sally Weber in Jimmy Shine; Actors Playhouse, June 1969, Betty in The Golden Fleece in a double bill called Tonight in Living Color; Village South, Nov 1969, Faye Precious in Who's Happy Now?; Mercer–O'Casey, Feb 1972, Caitlin Thomas in Dylan; McAlpin Rooftop, Apr 1972, Avis in God Says There is No Peter Ott; John Golden, 1972, took over from Elizabeth Wilson as Harriet in Sticks and Bones; McAlpin Rooftop, Apr 1973, Crystal in Crystal and Fox; Eugene O'Neill, Apr 1977, took over as Hannah, Diana and Gert in California Suite; has also played extensively in stock in such plays as After the Fall, Who's Afraid of Virginia Woolf?, Death of a Salesman, Critics Choice (1979), etc; first appeared in films in They Might Be Giants, 1970, and has since played in The People Next Door; first appeared on television in Malibu Run, 1960, and has since appeared in Hogan's Goat, The Rimers of Eldritch, *All in the Family,* and as Vivian in the long-running series *Maude;* recently in Topper, 1979.
Hobbies and recreations: Hiking, reading, sewing, beachcombing, writing. *Address:* AFTRA, 1350 Avenue of the Americas, New York, NY.

McCLELLAND, Allan, actor
b Dunmurry, Northern Ireland, 31 Dec 1917; *s* of William M'Clelland and his wife Nell (Worland); *e* Ireland; *m* Charlotte French Cox; originally in practice as a speech therapist.
Made his first appearance on the stage at the Playhouse, Belfast, in 1936, as Raleigh in Journey's End; first appeared in London at the Arts, 5 Sept 1945, at St John Hotchkiss in Getting Married, produced during a festival season at this theatre; during this season he also played Clincher in The Constant Couple, Laertes in Hamlet, and succeeded Alec Clunes as Charles Surface in The School for Scandal; New Lindsey, Nov 1949, appeared as Denzil in his own play, Call it Madness; Vaudeville, May 1950, played Josef Lausman in The Ivory Tower; Lyric, Hammersmith, Apr 1951, Craig in Danger, Men Working; Ambassadors', July 1951, Peter in The Passing Day; at the same theatre, Nov 1952, he created the part of Christopher Wren in Agatha Christie's play The Mousetrap; Arts, May 1959, appeared as the Narrator in Ulysses in Nighttown; Lyric, Hammersmith, Mar 1966, Captain's Secretary in Santa Cruz; King's Head, Islington, Sept 1973, devised and performed a one-man show, George Moore's Celibate Lives; New End, June 1978, George Moore in The Singular Life of Albert Nobbs; has broadcast and appeared in numerous television plays, and is also the author of plays and short stories broadcast by the BBC.
Recreations: Cycling, golf, swimming and writing. *Address:* c/o IAR, Fourth Floor, 235 Regent Street, W1R 8AX. *Tel:* 01–439 8401/5.

McCOWEN, Alec (Alexander Duncan McCowen), **OBE,** actor
b Tunbridge Wells, 26 May 1925; *s* of Duncan McCowen and his wife Mary (Walkden); *e* Skinner's School, Tunbridge Wells; studied for the stage at the Royal Academy of Dramatic Art.

Made his first appearance at the Repertory Theatre, Macclesfield, Aug 1942, as Micky in Paddy The Next Best Thing; appeared in repertory 1943–5; toured India and Burma for ENSA, 1945, in Love In A Mist; continued in repertory, 1946–9, during which time he played one season at St Johns, Newfoundland; first appeared in London at the Arts, 20 Apr 1950, as Maxim in Ivanov; at the same theatre, Sept 1950, played Georges Almaire in The Mask and the Face, and Nov 1950, Kitts in Preserving Mr Panmure; Lyric, Hammersmith, Jan 1951, appeared in The Silver Box; Westminster, Apr 1951, played Brian in The Martin's Nest; made his first appearance on the New York stage at the Ziegfeld, 20 Dec 1951, as The Messenger in Antony and Cleopatra; Arts, May 1952, played Hugh Voysey in The Voysey Inheritance, and in Nov 1952, The Announcer in The Holy Terrors; at the St James's, Jan 1953, appeared as Daventry in Escapade, which ran for over a year; for the Repertory Players at the Adelphi, Nov 1953, played Larry Thompson in Serious Charge, and at Wyndham's, Feb 1954, Julian Heath in Shadow of the Vine; New, Bromley, June 1954, played Henri de Toulouse-Lautrec in Moulin Rouge; Haymarket, Nov 1954, appeared as Barnaby Tucker in The Matchmaker; Garrick, Sept 1955, played Vicomte Octave de Clérambard in The Count of Clérambard; Hippodrome, June 1956, played Dr Bird in The Caine Mutiny Court Martial; Arts, Jan 1957, Lancelot Berenson in No Laughing Matter; Edinburgh Festival, Aug 1958, played Michael Claverton-Ferry in The Elder Statesman, subsequently appearing in the same part at the Cambridge, Sept 1958; joined the Old Vic Company for the season 1959–60, and played the following parts: Mr Brisk in The Double Dealer, Touchstone in As You Like It, Algernon Moncrieff in The Importance of Being Earnest, Ford in The Merry Wives of Windsor, the Dauphin in Saint Joan, and subsequently took over the title part in Richard II; Old Vic, 1960–1, played Mercutio in Romeo and Juliet, Oberon in A Midsummer Night's Dream, and Malvolio in Twelfth Night; Garrick, Feb 1962, appeared in the revue Not To Worry; Piccadilly, May 1962, played Sebastian in Castle in Sweden; joined the Royal Shakespeare Company, and appeared at Stratford-on-Avon, Sept 1962, as Antipholus of Syracuse in The Comedy of Errors, and Oct 1962, as the Fool in King Lear, subsequently appearing at the Aldwych, Dec 1962, in both plays; at the same theatre, Sept 1963, played Father Riccardo Fontana in The Representative, in repertory; Aldwych, Dec 1963, again played Antipholus of Syracuse in The Comedy of Errors, and Feb 1964, the Fool in King Lear, prior to a British Council tour of both plays to the USSR, Europe, and the US, Feb–June 1964; Yvonne Arnaud Theatre, Guildford, July 1965, played Ronald Gamble in Thark, subsequently appearing at the Garrick, Aug 1965, in the same production; Strand, Nov 1965, played The Author in The Cavern; Hampstead Theatre Club, Sept 1966, played Arthur Henderson in After the Rain, subsequently appearing in the same production at the Duchess, Jan 1967, and the Golden, NY, Sept 1967; Repertory, Birmingham, May 1967, played Fr William Rolfe in Hadrian the Seventh, and then at the Mermaid, Apr 1968 (*Evening Standard* Award for Best Actor, 1968), and the Helen Hayes, NY, Jan 1969; Repertory, Birmingham, Jan 1970, appeared in the title part in Hamlet; Royal Court, Aug 1970, Philip in The Philanthropist, transferring to the May Fair, Sept 1970 (Variety Club Award, 1970); repeated the part at the Ethel Barrymore, NY, Mar 1971; Criterion, Aug 1972, took over the title-role in Butley; Hampstead, Dec 1972, directed While the Sun Shines; for the National Theatre, played Alceste in The Misanthrope, Feb 1973 (*Evening Standard* Award, 1973), Martin Dysart in Equus, July 1973, both at the Old Vic;

Albery, May 1974, Professor Higgins in Pygmalion; again played Alceste at the St James's, NY, Mar 1975, and the Old Vic, July 1975; Criterion, June 1976, Ben Musgrave in The Family Dance; Helen Hayes, NY, Feb 1977, repeated the role of Martin Dysart in Equus; Edinburgh Festival, 1977, played Antony in the Prospect Theatre Company's Antony and Cleopatra, and subsequently at the Old Vic (Nov); in 1978 he devised and directed his own solo performance of St Mark's Gospel at the Riverside Studios, the Mermaid and the Comedy, later taking the production to New York, where he appeared at the Marymount Manhattan and Playhouse Theaters; Wyndham's, Oct 1979, Frank in Tishoo!; National Theatre, May 1980, appeared in the Rattigan double-bill, The Browning Version and Harlequinade; published his autobiography, Young Gemini, in 1979; first appeared in films, 1952, in The Cruel Sea, and has since appeared in many pictures including Frenzy, and Travels with My Aunt, as well as televison plays.

Favourite part: Astrov in Uncle Vanya. *Recreations:* The piano and writing. *Club:* The Buckstone. *Address:* c/o Larry Dalzell, 3 Goodwin's Court, St Martin's Lane, London, WC2.

MacDERMOT, Galt, composer

Composed the music for his first New York musical, Hair, presented by the New York Shakespeare Festival Public Theatre at the Anspacher, 17 Oct 1967; this was great success and was reproduced at the Biltmore, 29 Apr 1968, and ran for, 1,742 performances; since then has composed music for Hamlet, 1967; Hair, produced at the Shaftesbury, London, 27 Sept 1968; Twelfth Night, 1969; Isabel's a Jezebel, 1970; Two Gentlemen of Verona, for which he recieved the Antoinette Perry ("Tony") Award, The Tale of Cymbeline, A Gun Play, Sticks and Bones, 1971; Dude, Via Galactica, 1972; The Karl Marx Play, Billy Hill (Coconut Grove Playhouse, Palm Beach, Fla), 1973; Two Gentlemen of Verona produced in London, 1973; The Charlatan, produced at the Mark Taper Forum, Los Angeles, Cal, 1974; Take This Bread, an oratorio, Straws in the Wind (in part), 1975; A Drink at the Well, 1976; Vieux Carré, I Took Panama, 1977; The Sun Always Shines for the Cool, 1979; Hair was filmed in 1979.

Address: ASCAP, 1 Lincoln Plaza, New York, NY 10020.

MacDONALD, Murray (né Walter MacDonald Honeyman), director and manager

b Glasgow, Scotland, 4 Aug 1899; s of Tom Honeyman and his wife Elsie (Smith); e Glasgow.

Formerly an actor with the Scottish National Players, 1919, under Andrew P Wilson, afterwards touring with various companies; played a repertory season at Bristol; toured in South Africa, 1930, with Olga Lindo's company in Her Past, The Stranger Within, The Patsy, The Constant Nymph, Peg O' My Heart, etc; appeared at the Ambassadors', London, July 1931, as Stephen Gill in Mrs Fischer's War, and at the Arts, Oct 1931, in various parts in Vile Bodies; engaged at the Old Vic for the season 1933–4; his first production in London was Viceroy Sarah, in conjunction with Tyrone Guthrie, Whitehall, Feb 1935; afterwards directed Farm of Three Echoes, 1935; Love From A Stranger, Miss Smith, When The Bough Breaks, 1936; Tavern in the Town, The Road to Rome, The Bat, The New School for Scandal, Judgment Day, Bonnet Over The Windmill (with Dodie Smith), Robert's Wife, A Kiss for Cinderella, 1937; People of Our Class, Comedienne, She, Too, Was Young, Good-bye Mr Chips, 1938; We at the Crossroads, Romeo and Juliet (for Old Vic), Judgment Day, 1939; White Elephants, Full

House, 1940; is part-author of The Lake (with Dorothy Massingham), 1933, Mrs Nobby Clark (with Major Gilbert Lennox), 1935; during the War, 1940–5, served in the Army; after demobilization, directed The Hasty Heart, The Shouting Dies, 1945; Stage Door, The Thracian Horses, The Eagle Has Two Heads, Lady Frederick, 1946; Life With Father, 1947; Frenzy, People Like Us, Rain on the Just, 1948; Daphne Laureola, Champagne for Delilah, King's Rhapsody, 1949; Home at Seven, The Second Mrs Tanqueray, 1950; The Guilty Party, 1951; Red Letter Day, Dear Charles, 1952; The Bad Samaritan, 1953; entered into management (Murray Macdonald and John Stevens, Ltd), to present and direct I Capture the Castle, 1954, and has since directed Simon and Laura, 1954; The Burning Boat, The Count of Clérambard, Small Hotel, The Wild Duck, 1955; Towards Zero, Double Image, The Long Echo, 1956; Subway in the Sky, Roar Like a Dove (also presented), 1957; presented The Stepmother, These People, Those Books (tour), 1958; Marigold (also directed), The Amorous Prawn (also directed), 1959; Nobody Here But Us Chickens (directed), The Birds and the Bees (tour) (also directed), The Geese Are Getting Fat, 1960; Time and Yellow Roses (also directed), Teresa of Avila, Death and All That Jazz (directed), 1961; Miss Pell is Missing (also directed), 1962; Norman (also directed), Queen B, 1963; The Golden Rivet, 1964; The Paper Hat (also directed), 1965; since 1965 he has directed the following plays: Arsenic and Old Lace, On Approval, 1966; The Sacred Flame, Let's All Go Down the Strand (also co-presented), 1967; Hay Fever, 1968; They Ride on Broomsticks (co-presented tour), His, Hers, and Theirs (also co-presented), 1969; The Jockey Club Stakes, 1970.

Address: 5 Paultons House, Paultons Square, London, SW3.

McDOUGALL, Gordon, director

b Inverness, Scotland, 4 May 1941; *s* of Donald James McDougall and his wife Sheila (McDonald); *e* Latymer Upper School and King's College, Cambridge.

After early experience at Cambridge, in repertory at Barrow-in-Furness, and as an assistant director at the Royal Court, 1965, became Artistic Director of the Traverse, Edinburgh, 1966–8, where his productions included a number of premieres such as The Restoration of Arnold Middleton, 1966, The Daughter-in-Law, 1967, Aberfan, Would You Look at Them Smashing All the Lovely Windows, 1968; his Traverse production of Mourning Becomes Electra was seen at the Arts, London, 1967, and the Baalbek and Edinburgh Festivals, 1968; founded the Stables Theatre Company, Manchester, 1969, where his productions until 1971 included Tom Paine, Romeo and Juliet, 1969; Occupations, 1970; Serjeant Musgrave's Dance, 1971; Artist in Residence, University of York, 1971; Artistic Director, Gardener Arts Centre, Brighton, 1972, where he directed The Vicar of Soho, The Dark River, and Twelfth Night; the latter production was restaged for the Bankside Globe Playhouse, 1973, in which year he also directed The Country Wife for Prospect Theatre Company; Professor of Drama, University of Waterloo, Ontario, 1973–4; since his return to England, he has been Artistic Director of the Oxford Playhouse Company (Anvil Productions Ltd) which he founded in 1974, and his productions have included: The Government Inspector (own translation), As You Like It, Happy End (also London), Uncle Vanya, Fitting for Ladies and For Heaven's Sake Don't Walk Around With Nothing On (own translation), The Country Wife, The Tempest, Dog Days, The Threepenny Opera, Brand, The Magicalympical Games, All's Well (also Hong Kong Arts Centre), Heartbreak House (also tour of Latin

America), The Country Holiday (own translation), King Lear, Touch and Go (also tours to Hong Kong and Latin America); founder and Artistic Director of Oxford Music Theatre, 1978–; author of a book, The Theatrical Metaphor, and translations including Tartuffe, as well as those mentioned above; TV work includes World in Action; also produced the nineteen Stables Theatre productions for television, directing two of them.

Recreations: Music, squash, travel. *Address:* 27 Gloucester Place, London W1.

MacDOUGALL, Roger, dramatic author

b Bearsden, Dumbartonshire, Scotland, 2 Aug 1910; *s* of Thomas MacDougall and his wife Margaret (Doig); *e* Bearsden Academy and Glasgow University; *m* Renée Dunlop.

Formerly a screenwriter; crippled by multiple sclerosis from 1955; has written the following plays: MacAdam and Eve, 1950; The Gentle Gunman, 1950; To Dorothy, a Son, 1950; Escapade, 1952; The Facts of Life, 1954; The Man In the White Suit, 1954; The Delegate, 1955; Double Image (with Ted Allan), 1956; Hide and Seek (with Stanley Mann), 1957; Trouble With Father, 1964; Jack in the Box, 1971.

Recreation: Music. *Clubs:* Screenwriters' and Arts Theatre. *Address:* 8 Willow Road, Hampstead, NW3. *Tel:* 01–794 6917.

McDOWALL, Roddy (Roderick Andrew), actor

b London, 17 Sept 1928; *s* of Thomas Andrew McDowall and his wife Winifred (Corcoran); *e* St Joseph's College, London, and Twentieth Century Fox Schoolroom, Hollywood, California; studied for the stage with Mira Rostova.

Made his first appearance on the stage at the Westport Country Playhouse, 1946, as Roger Woodley in Young Woodley; Salt Lake City Centennial, 1947, played Malcolm in Orson Welles's production of Macbeth; La Jolla Playhouse, Calif, 1948, Ninian in The First Mrs Fraser; toured Calif and Arizona, 1949–50, as Lachie in The Hasty Heart, and 1950–1 in O Mistress Mine; toured, 1951–2, as Richard in The Youngest; Alcazar, San Francisco, 1952, Walton in Remains to Be Seen; first appeared in New York, at the City Center Theatre, Mar 1953, as Bentley Summerhayes in Misalliance; 48th Street Theatre, Nov 1953, appeared as Daventry in Escapade; Phoenix, NY, Jan 1955, played Louis Dubedat in a revival of The Doctor's Dilemma; Stratford Festival, Conn, July 1955, played Ariel in The Tempest and Octavius in Julius Caesar; Alvin, NY, Oct 1955, played Ben Witledge in No time for Sergeants; Phoenix, NY, Nov 1956, played Yegor Gloumov in The Diary of a Scoundrel; Belasco, Mar 1957, played Benjamin in Good as Gold; Ambassador, Oct 1957, appeared as Artie Strauss in Compulsion; Martin Beck, Oct 1958, played Pepe in A Handfull of Fire; Henry Miller, Mar 1959, played Marcel Blanchard in Look After Lulu; ANTA, Dec 1959, played Tarquin in The Fighting Cock; Majestic, Dec 1960, played Mordred in Camelot; Helen Hayes, Jan 1967, Claud in The Astrakhan Coat; toured, 1976, in Charley's Aunt; his book of photographs Double Exposure was published in 1966; first entered films, 1938, and has since appeared in numerous pictures, including: Lassie Come Home, How Green Was My Valley, My Friend Flicka, The Pied Piper, Cleopatra, the Planet of the Apes series, Dirty Mary Crazy Larry (1974), etc; directed the film The Ballad of Tam Lin in 1969; made his first appearance on television in 1948, and principal performances include Ah Wilderness, Heart of Darkness, and The Tempest as well as the series *Planet of the Apes* (1975), and guest appearances in various dramatic shows.

Favourite parts: Artie Strauss in Compulsion, and Ariel in The Tempest. *Hobby:* Photography. *Address:* 300 Central Park West, New York, NY 10024.

McENERY, Peter, actor
b Walsall, Staffs, 21 Feb 1940; *s* of Charles McEnery and his wife Mary Ada (Brinson); *e* Walsall and Hove schools; studied for the stage with Iris Warren.

Made his first appearance on the stage at the Palace Pier Theatre, Brighton, May 1956, as Stanley Chadwick in Bed, Board and Romance; first appeared in London at the Haymarket, Jan 1958, when he played Tom (the part he was understudying) for some weeks, in Flowering Cherry; toured, Mar 1960, as Clive Harrington in Five Finger Exercise; Pembroke, Croydon, Oct 1960, played Eugene Gant in Look Homeward, Angel; joined the Royal Shakespeare Theatre Company for the 1961 season, to play: Laertes in Hamlet, Clarence in Richard III, Silvius in As You Like It, and Tybalt in Romeo and Juliet; Phoenix, Apr 1962, again played Eugene Gant in Look Homeward, Angel; New Arts, June 1962, played Johnny Hobnails in Afore Night Come; Aldwych, Oct 1962, again played with the Royal Shakespeare Company in repertory in the following plays: Philip of France in Curtmantle, Patroclus in Troilus and Cressida, and De Laubardemont in The Devils; Criterion, Feb 1963, played Rudge in Next Time I'll Sing to You; Queen's, Mar 1964, played Konstantin in The Seagull; Aldwych, June 1964, again played Johnny Hobnails in Afore Night Come; Royal Shakespeare Company, Stratford-on-Avon, Apr 1965, played the following parts: Ithamore in The Jew of Malta, and Bassanio in The Merchant of Venice; Phoenix, Leicester, Nov 1970, played Hamlet in Hamlet and also in Rosencrantz and Guildenstern Are Dead; Hampstead, May 1971, Mike in Disabled; Nottingham Playhouse, Sept 1971, directed Richard III; Nottingham, Nov 1971, Guildenstern in Rosencrantz and Guildenstern are Dead; at the Young Vic, 1972, played Donal Davoren in The Shadow of a Gunman, July, and Cassius in Julius Caesar, Aug; Duchess, July 1973, took over as Henry Winter in Collaborators; Open Space, Jan 1974, Colin in Ashes; Lyric, Oct 1975, Trigorin in The Seagull; St George's, Islington, June 1976, Romeo and Juliet; returned to the Royal Shakespeare Company for the 1977–78 season, playing the following parts in Stratford and/or London: Duke of Suffolk in Henry VI, Parts I and II, Orlando in As You Like It, Lorenzo in The Lorenzacchio Story, Yescanalo in Sons of Light, Albie Sachs in The Jail Diary of Albie Sachs; 1979–80 season: title-role in Pericles, Jerry Hyland in Once In Lifetime; since 1960, he has appeared in such films as: Tunes of Glory, Negatives, Entertaining Mr Sloane, La Curée, etc; television appearances include: Candida, Progress to the Park and *Clayhanger.*

Favourite part: Albie Sachs. *Recreations:* Skiing, squash, military history. *Address:* c/o Fraser and Dunlop Ltd, 91 Regent Street, London, W1R 8RU.

McEWAN, Geraldine (*née* McKeown), actress
b Old Windsor, 9 May 1932; *d* of Donald McKeown and his wife Nora (Burns); *e* Windsor County School; *m* Hugh Cruttwell.

Made her first appearance on the stage at the Theatre Royal, Windsor, Oct 1946, as an attendant of Hippolyta, in A Midsummer Night's Dream; played numerous parts with the Windsor Repertory Company, Mar 1949–Mar 1951; made her first appearance on the West End stage at the Vaudeville, 4 Apr 1951, as Christina Deed in Who Goes There! in which she made a marked success; at the same theatre, May 1952, played Janet Andrews in Sweet Madness; Q, Sept 1952, Janet Blake in For Love or Money; at the Comedy, Dec 1952, played Anne Purves, in For Better, For Worse . . ., which ran for eighteen months; Saville, May 1955, appeared as Julie Gillis, in The Tender Trap; Royal, Brighton and Streatham Hill, July–Aug 1955, played the title-role in Patience; Apollo, Nov 1955, played Francesca in Summertime; at the Shakespeare Memorial Theatre, Stratford-on-Avon, July 1956, played the Princess of France in Love's Labour's Lost; Royal Court, Feb 1957, played Frankie Adams in The Member of the Wedding; Palace, Dec 1957, Jean Rice in The Entertainer; Shakespeare Memorial Theatre Company, 1958 season, played Olivia in Twelfth Night, Marina in Pericles, and Hero in Much Ado About Nothing; she subsequently appeared with the same company in Moscow and Leningrad, Dec 1958; Strand, May 1959, played Marie Renaud in Change of Tune; Aldwych, Dec 1960, again played Olivia in Twelfth Night; Royal Shakespeare, Stratford-on-Avon, 1961 season, played Beatrice in Much Ado About Nothing, and Ophelia in Hamlet; Arts, Mar 1962, played Jenny Acton in Everything in the Garden, transferring with the production to the Duke of York's, May 1962; at the Haymarket, Oct 1962, took over the part of Lady Teazle in The School for Scandal, prior to making her first appearance in New York, at the Majestic, Jan 1963, in the same production; Wimbledon, London, Sept 1963, played Doreen in The Private Ear, and Belinda in The Public Eye (double-bill), prior to appearing in the same production at the Morosco, NY, Oct 1963, and subsequently touring in the US; on returning to England, toured Feb 1965, as Fay in Loot; Chichester Festival, July 1965, played A Lady in Armstrong's Last Goodnight, with the National Theatre Company, subsequently visiting Moscow and Berlin, Sept 1965, with the company, appearing as Angelica in Love For Love; Old Vic, Oct 1965, again played The Lady in Armstrong's Last Goodnight, and Angelica in Love For Love; she has subsequently appeared in the following roles for the National Theatre Company at the Old Vic; Raymonde Chandebise in A Flea in Her Ear (also at the Queen's), Angelica in Love for Love, 1966; Alice in The Dance of Death, 1967; toured Canada (including Expo 67) Oct–Nov 1967, again playing the parts of Alice, Angelica and Raymonde; Queen Anne in Brecht's Edward the Second, Victoria in Home and Beauty, 1968; appeared in An Evasion of Women (Jeannetta Cochrane), Millamant in The Way of the World, Ada in Rites, Vittoria Corombona in The White Devil, 1969; with the National at the New, Jul 1971, Alkmena in Amphitryon 38; Comedy, May 1973, played Elizabeth Barrett in Dear Love; Greenwich, Dec 1973, Zoë in Not Drowning But Waving; Globe, Feb 1974, Diana in Chez Nous; Duke of York's, Oct 1974, Susan in The Little Hut; Criterion, June 1975, appeared in Oh Coward; Haymarket, Dec 1975, Maria Wislack in On Approval; 1978 Chichester Festival Season, played Lulu in Look After Lulu, appearing in the same production at the Haymarket, Oct 1978; National Theatre, May 1980, appeared in The Rattigan double-bill, The Browning Version and Harlequinade; has appeared in many television productions, including Hopcraft into Europe, Dear Love, and The Statue and the Rose, and more recently, The Prime of Miss Jean Brodie.

Address: c/o Larry Dalzell Associates, 3 Goodwin's Court, St Martin's Lane, London WC2.

McGRATH, John, dramatist and director
b Birkenhead, Cheshire, 1 June 1935; *s* of John Francis McGrath, and his wife Margaret (McCann); *e* Alun Grammar School, Mold; *m* Elizabeth MacLennan.

Author of the following plays: A Man Has Two Fathers, The Tent, 1958; Why the Chicken, 1959; The Seagull (adapted), 1961; Events While Guarding the Bofors Gun,

1966; Bakke's Night of Fame, 1968; Comrade Jacob, 1969; Random Happenings in the Hebrides, 1970; Unruly Elements, Plugged Into History, Trees in the Wind, Soft or a Girl, 1971; Out of Sight, Underneath, Fish in the Sea, 1972; The Cheviot, the Stag, and the Black Black Oil, 1973; The Game's a Bogey, Boom, 1974; My Pal and Me, Lay Off, Little Red Hen, Yobbo Nowt, 1975; Out of Our Heads, Rat Trap, Orange and Lemons, 1976; Trembling Giant, Joe of England, 1977; Big Square Fields, Joe's Drum, Bitter Apples (musical), 1979; has directed many stage plays, including his own, several of which were written for the 7:84 Theatre Companies, founded by him in England, 1971, and Scotland, 1973; film scripts include: Billion Dollar Brain, The Bofors Gun (from his own play), and The Reckoning; has written for television since 1962, and directed many television plays.

Address: c/o Margaret Ramsay, 14a Goodwin's Court, London WC2. *Tel:* 01–240 0691.

MacGRATH, Leueen, actress
b London, 3 July 1914; *d* of Walter Michael Anthony MacGrath, DSO, MC, Croix de Guerre, and his wife Jean (Martin); *e* Sacréçäur, Lausanne, Farnborough Convent College, and Les Tourelles, Brussels; *m* (1) Christopher Burn; (2) Desmond Davis; (3) George S Kaufman (dec); studied for the stage at the Royal Academy of Dramatic Art.

Made her first appearance on the stage at the Garrick Theatre, 17 Apr 1933, as Miss Cathcart in Beggars in Hell; Playhouse, Nov 1933, played Benson in The Night Club Queen; New, Apr 1934, Hazel Graham in The Laughing Woman; Lyric, Apr 1935, Hélène Dupont in Tovarich; Phoenix, June 1935, Jacqueline Vesey in Love of Women; Embassy, Jan 1936, Laura in No Exit; St James's, Feb 1936, Lydia Bennet in Pride and Prejudice, which ran throughout the year; Arts, June 1936, Lucretia Borgia in Lucretia; Criterion, Jan 1937, succeeded Jessica Tandy in French Without Tears, in which she continued until 1939; Wyndham's, Nov 1939, played Queenie in Saloon Bar; Arts, Sept 1940, The Sphinx in The Infernal Machine; Theatre Royal, Glasgow, Oct 1941, Veronica Preston in Deep Is the River; Lyric, Mar 1942, Vicki in Blossom Time; Vaudeville, July 1942, Louise in Salt of the Earth; Apollo, autumn 1942, succeeded Phyllis Calvert as Patricia Graham in Flare Path, which she played throughout 1943; toured, May 1945, as Young Mrs Barrington in the play of that name, and appeared in the same part at the Winter Garden Theatre, Sept 1945; Embassy, July 1946, played Gwennie in Grim Fairy Tale; Q, Oct 1946, Maria Dean in Bold Lover; Mar 1947, Joan Chandler in The Tightrope Walkers; His Majesty's, May 1947, Eileen Perry in Edward, My Son; made her first appearance on the New York Stage at the Martin Beck, 30 Sept 1948, when she again played Eileen in Edward, My Son; Lyceum, Jan 1950, Isabel in The Enchanted; 48th Street, Feb 1951, played Sarah Cairn in The High Ground; Royale, Jan 1952, Amanda Phipps in Fancy Meeting You Again; Shubert, Jan 1953, played Donovan in The Love of Four Colonels; reappeared on the English stage at the Opera House, Manchester, Apr 1955, as Cassandra in Tiger at the Gates, subsequently playing the same part at the Apollo, London, June 1955, and at the Plymouth, NY, Oct 1955; Bijou, NY, Jan 1957, Sara Callifer in The Potting Shed; Orpheum, Jan 1959, Lucy in Maidens and Mistresses at Home and at the Zoo; City Center, Mar 1959, the Princess in a revival of Lute Song; John Drew, Easthampton, NY, Aug 1959, Louise Yeyder in Gilt and Gingerbread; Helen Hayes, NY, Sept 1960, played Peony Povis in Farewell, Farewell, Eugene; 4th Street, Sept 1961, Mrs Alving in Ghosts; Writers' Stage, Jan 1963, Belle Worthmore in The Love Nest; Tyrone Guthrie,

Minneapolis, Minn, Feb 1964, Ruby in And Things That Go Bump in the Night; Westport Country Playhouse, Aug 1965, Luisa in So Much of Earth, So Much of Heaven; Opera House, Manchester, Oct 1969, the lady in On the Rocks; Haymarket, Sept 1970, Lady Nelson in A Bequest to the Nation; Haymarket, Aug 1971, Mother in A Voyage Round My Father; Manhattan Theatre Club, NY, Jan 1975, Irina Arkadina in The Seagull; Circle Repertory Company, Oct 1976, title-role in A Tribute to Lili Lamont; she has also appeared on many occasions for the Repertory Players; collaborated with George S Kaufman as Author of The Small Hours, 1951; Fancy Meeting You Again, 1952; Silk Stockings (Musical), 1955; first appeared in films, 1938, in Pygmalion, and subsequently in Edward, My Son and Three Cases of Murder.

Recreations: Reading, arguing, and listening to music. *Address:* c/o Chatto and Linnit Ltd, Globe Theatre, Shaftesbury Avenue, London W1. *Tel:* 01–439 4371.

McGUIRE, Biff (*né* William J McGuire), actor
b New Haven, Conn, 25 Oct 1926; *s* of William Joseph Henry McGuire and his wife Mildred Elizabeth (Dwyer); *e* New Haven and Massachusetts State College and Shrivenham University in England, 1944; *m* (1) Gigi Gilpin (mar dis); (2) Jeannie Carson.

Made his first appearance on the stage at the Lyric, Hammersmith, in England, 14 Feb 1946, as a Sailor in The Time of Your Life; first appeared on the New York stage at the Broadhurst, 15 Jan 1948, in the revue Make Mine Manhattan; subsequently toured in Miss Liberty, and appeared in musical stock in One Touch of Venus, Roberta, Good News, etc; appeared on Broadway at the Majestic, Apr 1949, as Bob McCaffrey in South Pacific; Henry Miller, Mar 1953, took over from Barry Nelson as Donald Gresham in The Moon Is Blue, after playing in this piece in Chicago; returned to England to make his first appearance on the West End stage at the Duke of York's, 7 July 1953, as Donald Gresham in The Moon Is Blue; New York City Center, Jan 1955, Dudley in The Time of Your Life; Coronet, NY, Sept 1955, played Kenneth in A Memory of Two Mondays, part of a double-bill presented under the title of A View from the Bridge; Ethel Barrymore, May 1957, Steve Boyle in The Greatest Man Alive!; same theatre, Oct 1957, Martin Donahue in The Egghead; Colonial, Boston, Dec 1958, Martin McKenrick in Listen to the Mocking Bird; Palm Beach Playhouse, Mar 1959, Daniel Halibut in Bedtime Story, and Sammy in A Pound on Demand in a bill of one act plays with the overall title Triple Play; Playhouse, NY, Apr 1959, again played in Triple Play, to which was added Portrait of a Madonna, in which he played the Elevator Boy; 54th Street, Oct 1959, Craig Richards in Happy Town; Martin Beck, Feb 1960, Junior in Beg, Borrow or Steal; City Center, May 1960, Woody in Finian's Rainbow; US tour, 1962–3, Bob McKellaway in Mary, Mary; Helen Hayes, July 1963, again appeared in the last role; US tour, Oct 1963–May 1964, Arthur in Camelot; US tour, summer 1964, appeared in No Bed of Roses; US tour, 1964–5, Bill Starbuck in 110 in the Shade; Goodspeed Opera House, East Haddam, Conn, Aug 1966, played in Maggie; toured, 1967, in She Loves Me; toured 1968–9, as Julian in The Cactus Flower; Vivian Beaumont, Nov 1969, Tom in The Time of Your Life, and, May 1970, Dr Albert Rice in Beggar on Horseback; John Golden, Mar 1971, Tom in Father's Day; Lyceum, June 1971, Philip Berrigan in The Trial of the Catonsville Nine; Washington, DC, Mar 1972, Morris Townsend in Washington Square; Sheridan Square Playhouse, July 1972, various parts in Present Tense; Theater Club, Seattle, Washington, Repertory, Mar 1973, various parts in Promenade All; St James, Oct 1973, Harold Mitchell in A Streetcar Named Desire; toured, 1974, as Paul Friedman in 6 Rms, Riv Vu; Seattle Repertory, Jan 1974, Dudley Gaveston in A Family and a Fortune; Dec 1974, Father Day in Life with Father; and, Dec 1974, played in That Championship Season; Seattle Repertory, Apr 1978, Holmes Bradford in Eminent Domain; first appeared in films, 1950 and has since made several films, including Serpico (1973); first appeared on television in 1949, and has since played in more than a hundred productions; author of the play Off Center, 1963.

Recreations: Writing and painting. *Address:* 25 Sutton Place South, New York, NY. *Tel:* Templeton 8–4868.

McGUIRE, Dorothy, actress
b Omaha, Nebraska, 14 June 1918; *d* of Thomas Johnson McGuire and his wife Isabelle (Flaherty); *e* in a convent in Indianapolis, Indiana, Junior College, Omaha, and Pine Manor, Wellesley, Mass; *m* John Swope.

First appeared on the stage at the Community Theatre, Omaha, 1930, in A Kiss for Cinderella; played in stock in Deertrees, Maine; had her first engagement in New York at the Lyceum, 11 Jan 1938, as understudy in Stop-Over; next understudied Martha Scott as Emily in Our Town at the Morosco, and took over that part in July 1938; played a season in stock, then toured as Portia in My Dear Children, with John Barrymore, 1939; Center, NY, Nov 1939, played Helena in Swingin' the Dream; New Yorker, Apr 1940, Dora in Medicine Show; toured as Kitty in the Time of Your Life, 1940; Playhouse, Sept 1940, Ada in Kind Lady; Booth, Feb 1941, Claudia Naughton in Claudia, and received the New York Drama Critics Circle Award for this part; toured in a USO production of Dear Ruth, 1945; toured, 1947, in Tonight at 8.30; toured, 1950, as Alma Winemiller in Summer and Smoke; Plymouth, Dec 1951, The Actress in Legend of Lovers; National, Feb 1958, Elizabeth Willard in Winesburg, Ohio; reappeared on the stage at the Ahmanson, Los Angeles, Dec 1975, as Hannah Jelkes in The Night of the Iguana; repeated this part at the Circle-in-the-Square, NY, Oct 1976; Ahmanson, 1979, appeared in Cause Célèbre; first appeared in films in Claudia, 1943, and has since played in A Tree Grows in Brooklyn, The Enchanted Cottage, Wings of a Dove, Gentlemen's Agreement, Friendly Persuasion, for which she was named best actress by the National Board of Review, The Remarkable Mr Pennypacker, The Dark at the Top of the Stairs, and numerous others; on radio played Sue in the Serial *Big Sister,* 1937, and also played Ophelia in Hamlet, 1951; TV includes Rich Man Poor Man, 1976.

Recreations: Writing, swimming. *Address:* Actors Equity Association, 165 West 46th Street, New York, NY 10036.

McHALE, Rosemary, actress
b 17 Feb 1944; *d* of John William McHale and his wife Muriel Agnes (Evans); *e* Sutton H S; *m* Trevor Bowen; trained for the stage at Central School and at Drama Centre.

Made her first professional appearance at the Royal Court, 8 Aug 1965, as Nellie Lambert in A Collier's Friday Night; in repertory at the Everyman, Liverpool, 1965–6, her parts included Louka in Arms and the Man; at the Traverse, Edinburgh, Nov 1966, Maureen in The Restoration of Arnold Middleton; at the same theatre played Minnie in The Daughter-in-Law; Lyceum, Edinburgh, 1967–8, played parts such as Helena in The Ha-Ha, Julia in The Rivals, and Bianca in Othello; Hampstead, June 1968, again played Helena in The Ha-Ha; same theatre, Apr 1970, Joanne in Slag; toured, June 1970, with Cambridge Theatre Company, as Masha in The Seagull; won the Clarence Derwent award for these two

supporting roles; Royal Court, Sept 1971, Fontanelle in Bond's Lear; joined the Royal Shakespeare Company for Stratford season, 1972, playing Virgilia in Coriolanus, Apr, Luciana in The Comedy of Errors, June, and Charmian in Antony and Cleopatra, Aug; played Charmian at the Aldwych, July 1973; also appeared in Cries from Casement, Oct, and played Mme Voiture in A Lesson in Blood and Roses, Nov, both of these at The Place; Aldwych, May 1974, Queen Ana in The Bewitched; The Place, Oct 1974, Abel in Comrades, and Laria in The Beast, Nov 1974; Royal Court, Jan 1975, Jule in Objections to Sex and Violence; Duke of York's, June 1977, Mrs Elvsted in Hedda Gabler; Birmingham Rep, 1977, Eliza in Pygmalion and Ellida in The Lady from the Sea; Garrick, Oct 1978, Myra Bruhl in Deathtrap; TV, since 1968, includes The Brontës, The Way of the World, and, more recently, When the Actors Come, Just Between Ourselves, and Memories; Council Member, Drama Centre, London.

Recreations: Birds, bridge, children's tea parties, sewing. *Address:* c/o Patrick Freeman Management, 4 Cromwell Grove, London W6. *Tel:* 01–602 4035.

MACKAY, Fulton, actor
b Paisley, Renfrewshire, 12 Aug 1922; *s* of William McKay, and his wife Agnes (McDermid); *e* Clydebank HS; *m* Sheila Manahan; formerly a quantity surveyor; trained for the stage at RADA.

First appeared on stage in May 1947, on tour in Liverpool and Leeds, as a walk-on in Angel in which he made his first London appearance at the Strand, June 1947; in repertory at the Citizens', Glasgow, 1949–51 and 1953–8; Edinburgh Festival, Aug 1950, played King Humanitie in The Thrie Estates at the Assembly Hall; at the Arts, Sept 1960, played Oscar in Naked Island; same theatre, May 1962, Kleshch in The Lower Depths; joined the Old Vic company for season 1962–3, where his parts included the Preacher and Solveig's Father in Peer Gynt, Salerio in The Merchant of Venice, and Dapper in The Alchemist; Vaudeville, Nov 1966, Mr Miller in Justice Is A Woman; Royal Court, Apr 1969, Reardon in In Celebration; University Theatre, Manchester, Dec 1970, for the 69 Theatre Company, played Solveig's Father, Begriffenfeldt and the Button Moulder in Peer Gynt; a director of the Scottish Actors Company, for whom he directed The Wild Duck, at the Lyceum, Edinburgh Festival, Aug 1969; Greenwich, Apr 1971, Dr Wangel in The Lady From the Sea; Duke of York's, Nov 1971, Duke of Hamilton and Andrew Stuart in The Douglas Cause; Lyceum, Edinburgh, Feb 1972, Hughie in Willie Rough, repeating the part at the Shaw, Jan 1973; appeared at the Edinburgh Festival, 1973, as John the Commonweal in The Thrie Estates, and in The Man with a Flower in His Mouth; Shaw, Mar 1976, Davies in The Caretaker; National Theatre, June 1977, played Bill Ford in Old Movies, and, Apr 1978, St Peter and the Blind Man in The Passion; Arnaud, June 1978, McNab in Balmoral; for the Royal Shakespeare Company at the Warehouse, Dec 1978, Jardine in The Hang of the Gaol, and at the Other Place, Sept 1979, Chris Christopherson in Anna Christie; films, since his first appearance in 1951, include Gumshoe and Porridge; television, since 1949, includes the series *Special Branch, Porridge,* and *The Foundation;* he has also written several TV plays including Diamond's Progress, Girl with Flowers in Her Hair, and Dalhousie's Luck.

Recreation: Painting. *Address:* c/o NEMS Management, 31 King's Road SW3.

McKAY, Scott (*né* Carl Chester Gose), actor
b Pleasantville, Iowa, 28 May 1915; *s* of Chester Loring Gose

and his wife Edith Edna (Shawver); *e* North Denver, Colorado, High School, University of Colorado (1937); *m* (1) Margaret Spickers (mar dis), (2) Joan Morgan (dec); (3) Ann Sheridan (dec); (4) Anna-Marie McKay.

Made his first professional debut in Boston, Mass, 1937–38 season, in the Federal Theatre (WPA) productions of Arms and the Man, See Naples and Die, The Farmer Takes a Wife, and Fly Away Home; made his New York debut at the Hudson, 11 Nov 1938, as a walk-on in Good Hunting; Center, Jan 1939, played in The American Way; Surrey, Maine, summer 1939, played in Arms and the Man, The Grass Is Always Greener, and Art and Mrs Bottle; Longacre, Oct 1939, Fedotik in The Three Sisters; toured as Sandy in The Man Who Came to Dinner, 1940–41; Morosco, Apr 1941, The Sophomore in The Night Before Christmas; Cort, Dec 1941, Hans in Letters to Lucerne; Martin Beck, Apr 1942, Lt Prackle in The Moon Is Down; Cort, Oct 1942, Neil West in Eve of St Mark; Belasco, Jan 1943, Larry in Dark Eyes; Playhouse, Dec 1943, Lt Don Mallory in Pillar to Post; all the above roles were played under the name of Carl Gose; changed his name to Scott McKay and appeared at the Booth, May 1946, as Eric in Swan Song; Fulton, Nov 1946, Oscar Hubbard in Another Part of the Forest; Lyceum, 1946, took over as Paul Verral in Born Yesterday; 48th Street, Jan 1950, Tom Crosby in Mr Barry's Etchings; Playhouse, Aug 1950, Leo Mack in The Live Wire, subsequently touring in it; Ethel Barrymore, Nov 1950, Nicky Holroyd in Bell, Book, and Candle; made his London debut at the Aldwych, 10 Oct 1952, as George Flack in Letter from Paris; New York City Center, May 1952, Senator Keane in First Lady; toured in Josephine, 1953; National, Nov 1953, David in Sabrina Fair; Martin Beck, 1954, took over from John Forsyth as Captain Fisby in The Teahouse of the August Moon; toured in his last part, 1954–55; New York City Center, Mar 1957, Jeff Douglas in Brigadoon; Coronet, Oct 1957, Voles in Nature's Way; John Golden, Jan 1959, Gowan Stevens in Requiem for a Nun; toured, 1959–60, as Mervyn in Odd Man In; Helen Hayes, 1962, took over from Tom Poston as Bob McKellaway in Mary, Mary; Booth, Nov 1963, Ashley Robbins in Once for the Asking; New York City Center, Dec 1964, Jeff Douglas in Brigadoon; toured, 1966, as Milt Manville in Luv; Ethel Barrymore, Dec 1967, Oscar Hubbard in The Little Foxes; toured, 1969–71, as Billy Boylan in Forty Carats; Eastside Playhouse, Oct 1973, Teddy in A Breeze from the Gulf; toured 1975, in Ah, Wilderness!; Music Box, May 1975, took over as Ronald in Absurd Person Singular; South Street, Nov 1978, Jim Brady in The Tennis Game; toured, Jan 1979, in The Little Foxes; first appeared in films in 30 Seconds over Tokyo, 1944, and has since played in Guest in the House, Kiss and Tell, The Front, The Bell Jar, Santa Claus, etc.

Recreation: Writing. *Address:* Actors Equity Association, 165 West 46th Street, New York, NY 10036.

McKECHNIE, Donna, actress, dancer, singer
b Detroit, Mich, Nov 1940.

Made her New York debut at the 46th Street, 14 Oct 1961, as a dancer in How to Succeed in Business Without Really Trying; toured, 1963–64, as Philia in A Funny Thing Happened on the Way to the Forum; Alvin, 4 Apr 1968, played Kathy McKenna in The Education of H*Y*M*A*N K*A*P-*L*A*N; Shubert, Dec 1968, Vivien Della Hoya in Promises, Promises; Alvin, Apr 1970, Kathy in Company; Ahmanson, Los Angeles, May 1971, again played Kathy in Company; Imperial, Oct 1971, Ivy Smith in On the Town; made her London debut at Her Majesty's, 18 Jan 1972, as Kathy in Company; Shubert, 11 Mar 1973, choreographed and performed in Sondheim; A Musical Tribute; New York City Center, Apr 1974, appeared in the revue Music! Music!; Estelle R Newman, May 1975, Cassie in A Chorus Line, and repeated this part at the Shubert, July 1975, for which she received the Antoinette Perry (Tony) Award; repeated this role in San Francisco, May 1976, and again in New York, Sept 1976; Harold Clurman, June 1979, Lillian in Wine Untouched; appeared in the film The Little Prince, 1974.

Address: Actors Equity Association, 165 West 46th Street, New York, NY 10036.

McKELLEN, Ian, CBE, actor and director
b Burnley, Lancs, 25 May 1939; *s* of Denis Murray McKellen, and his wife Margery (Sutcliffe); *e* Wigan Grammar School, Bolton School and St Catharine's College, Cambridge (BA 1961).

After considerable success as an undergraduate actor, joined the company at the Belgrade, Coventry in 1961, where his first part was Roper in A Man For All Seasons; this was followed by repertory seasons at Ipswich, 1962–3, where he played, among others, the title-roles in Henry V and Luther, and Nottingham, 1963–4; at Nottingham Playhouse his parts included Aufidius in Coriolanus, Dec 1963; Arthur Seaton in Saturday Night and Sunday Morning, Apr 1964; the title-role in Sir Thomas More, June 1964; London début, Duke of York's, Sept 1964, as Godfrey in A Scent of Flowers; for the National Theatre Company, 1965, played Claudio in Much Ado About Nothing, Feb; the Protestant Evangelist in Armstrong's Last Goodnight and Capt de Foenix in Trelawny of the Wells (both Chichester Festival), July; Hampstead, Nov 1965, Alvin in A Lily in Little India, transferring to the St Martin's, Jan 1966; Royal Court, May 1966, Andrew Cobham in Their Very Own and Golden City; Mermaid, Sept 1966, the title part in O'Flaherty, VC and Bonaparte in The Man of Destiny, in a double-bill; Oxford Playhouse, Nov 1966, and Fortune, Jan 1967, Leonidik in The Promise, later making his Broadway début in the part at the Henry Miller, Nov 1967; returning to London, Feb 1968, played Tom in The White Liars and Harold Gorringe in Black Comedy at the Lyric; toured, Nov 1968, for Prospect Theatre Company, as Richard II; Liverpool Playhouse, May 1969, played Pentheus in The Bacchae and directed his first production, The Prime of Miss Jean Brodie; Edinburgh Festival, Aug 1969, again played Richard II for Prospect; also the title-role in Edward the Second; toured in both these parts, including appearances at the Mermaid, Sept 1969, and the Piccadilly, Jan 1970; Theatre Upstairs, July 1970, Darkly in Billy's Last Stand; Oct 1970, toured for Cambridge Theatre Company, as Capt Plume in The Recruiting Officer and Cpl Hill in Chips With Everything; toured with Prospect Theatre Company, Mar–July 1971, as Hamlet, transferring in August to the Cambridge Theatre; Crucible, Sheffield, Nov 1971, played Svetlovidov in the theatre's inaugural production, Swan Song; Palace, Watford, Mar 1972, directed The Erpingham Camp; founder-member of the Actors' Company, Edinburgh Festival, 1972, and touring as Giovanni in 'Tis Pity She's A Whore, Page-Boy in Ruling the Roost, and Prince Yoremitsu in The Three Arrows (Arts, Cambridge); Vaudeville, Feb 1973, directed A Private Matter; again with the Actors' Company, for 1973 Edinburgh Festival and tour as Michael, The Wood Demon in the play of that name, and footman in The Way of the World, later appearing in Knots (Shaw Theatre) and in King Lear as Edgar (Brooklyn Academy); appeared in these four plays, and as Giovanni, at Wimbledon, Mar–May 1974; made his debut with the Royal Shakespeare Company, Edinburgh Festival, 1974, as Dr Faustus, transferring to the Aldwych, Sept 1974; at this theatre he also played the title role in The Marquis of Keith, Nov 1974; Philip the Bastard in King John, Jan 1975; Savoy, Apr 1975, directed The Clandestine Marriage; Young Vic, June 1975, played Colin in Ashes; returned to RSC as Aubrey Bagot in Too True to Be Good, Oct 1975, Aldwych, and Dec 1975, Globe; Stratford, season 1976, played Romeo in Romeo and Juliet, Leontes in The Winter's Tale and the title-role in Macbeth (The Other Place); also appeared at the Edinburgh Festival in his solo show Words, Words, Words; Stratford, 1977, again played Macbeth (Royal Shakespeare Theatre), and Face in The Alchemist (The Other Place); Festival Hall, July 1977, Alex in Every Good Boy Deserves Favour; Edinburgh Festival, 1977, solo show Acting Shakespeare; 1977–8, Aldwych season, played Romeo, Karsten Bernick in Pillars of the Community, Face in The Alchemist and Langevin in Days of the Commune; appeared again for the RSC as Macbeth, at the Warehouse (Sept 1977), and the Young Vic (Apr 1978); 1978, directed RSC small-scale tour, playing Sir Toby in Twelfth Night and Andrei in Three Sisters; Royal Court, May 1979, transferring to the Criterion in July, Max in Bent; films, since 1969, include Alfred the Great, The Promise, and A Touch of Love; television, since 1965, includes David Copperfield, Ross, Hedda Gabler, Macbeth, Every Good Boy Deserves Favour; among his many awards he has received The Clarence Derwent Award 1964, *Plays and Players* Awards for most promising actor, 1976, Actor of the year (Macbeth), 1976; and Society of West End Theatre Awards for his performances as Bernicle (1977), Face (1978), and Max in Bent (1979); council member, British Actors' Equity, 1970–1.

Favourite parts: O'Flaherty, Edward II. *Address:* c/o Fraser & Dunlop, 91 Regent Street, London, W1. *Tel:* 01–734 7311.

McKENNA, Siobhan, actress
b Belfast, N Ireland, 24 May 1923; *d* of Owen McKenna and his wife Margaret (O'Reilly); *e* St Louis Convent, Louisville, Monaghan, and National University of Ireland; *m* Denis O'Dea.

Made her first appearance on the professional stage at the An Taibhdhearc Theatre, Galway, 1940, in Tons of Money, where subsequently she played Lady Macbeth, playing in Gaelic; during 1941, appeared in Shadow of a Gunman, The Plough and the Stars, The White Scourge, Winterset, Gaslight, Saint Joan, etc, and in 1942, in Mary Rose; all these plays were performed in Gaelic; from 1943–6, appeared at the Abbey Theatre, Dublin, playing in English, in The Countess Cathleen, The End House, Marks and Mabel, etc; she also played at the Abbey, in a number of Gaelic plays; made her first appearance on the London stage, at the Embassy Theatre, 3 Mar 1947, as Nora Fintry in The White Steed, playing the same part at the Whitehall, later in the same month; Q, 1949, played Helen Pettigrew in Berkeley Square; Duchess, Aug 1949, Maura Joyce in Fading Mansion; Embassy, June 1951, played Regina in Ghosts; at the Edinburgh Festival, 1951, appeared in The Whiteheaded Boy and as Pegeen Mike in The Playboy of the Western World; at the Duke of York's, Nov 1951, played the title-role in Héloise; played at the Memorial Theatre, Stratford-on-Avon, for nine months in 1952; Royal Glasgow, Apr 1953, Avril in Purple Dust; at the Arts, Sept 1954, she played Joan of Arc in Bernard Shaw's Saint Joan, transferring to the St Martin's, Feb 1955, and receiving the *Evening Standard* Award, for her performance; first appeared on the New York stage at the Ethel Barrymore, 26 Oct 1955, as Miss Madrigal in The Chalk Garden; at the Sanders Theatre, Cambridge, Mass, Aug 1956, played the title-role in Saint Joan, subse-

quently appearing in the same part at the Phoenix, NY, Sept 1956; Theatre-de-Lys, NY, Jan 1957, appeared in the title-role of an experimental version of Hamlet; at the Stratford Shakespearean Festival, Ont, July 1957, played Viola in Twelfth Night; Cort, NY, Nov 1957, played Margaret Hyland in The Rope Dancers; at the Cambridge Drama Festival, Mass, July 1959, again played Viola in Twelfth Night, and also Lady Macbeth in Macbeth; Wilbur, Boston, Jan 1960, played Isobel in Motel; at the Dublin Festival, Sept 1960, played Pegeen Mike in The Playboy of the Western World, subsequently touring Europe with the production before appearing in the same part at the Piccadilly, London, Oct, and St Martin's, Nov 1960; Dublin Festival, Sept 1961, played Joan Dark in Saint Joan of the Stockyards; Comedy, Mar 1962, played Anna Freeman in Play With a Tiger; Dublin Festival, Sept 1962, appeared in An Evening With Irish Writers; Queen's, London, June 1964, again played Joan Dark in Saint Joan of the Stockyards; Strand, Nov 1965, played Marie-Jeanne in The Cavern; Gaiety, Dublin, Aug 1966, Juno in Juno and the Paycock; Dublin Festival, Sept 1967, Cass in The Loves of Cass Maguire and, Oct 1968, Mme Ranevsky in The Cherry Orchard; St Martin's, July 1969, Pearl in On a Foggy Day; Strand, Feb 1970, Josie Connaught in Best of Friends; Playhouse, Oxford, Apr 1970, she gave a solo performance in Here Are Ladies, repeated at the Criterion, July 1970; Mermaid, July 1973, Juno Boyle in Juno and the Paycock, taking over the direction of this production on the death of Sean Kenny; Olympia, Dublin, Sept 1974, appeared in the Festival production, The Morgan Yard; Gate, Dublin, 1975, again appeared in Here Are Ladies; same theatre, June 1975, Julia Sterroll in Fallen Angels and, June 1976, Josie in A Moon for the Misbegotten; Abbey, Dublin, Aug 1976 and New York, Dec 1976, Bessie Burgess in The Plough and the Stars; Greenwich Festival, Feb 1977, Jocasta in Sons of Oedipus; Guelph Festival, Canada, and Olympia, Dublin, 1977, Sarah Bernhardt in Memoir, playing the same part at the Ambassadors; Jan 1978; Palace, NY, Mar 1979, Margaret in Meeting by the River; Abbey, Dublin, Feb 1980, Juno in Juno and the Paycock; since 1943 when she directed St Joan in Gaelic at An Taibhdear, Galway, she has directed these plays: Daughter from over the Water, and I'm Getting out of this Kip, Dublin, 1968; Tinker's Wedding, Shadow of the Glen, Riders to the Sea, Arts Festival, Toronto, 1973; Juno and the Paycock, 1973; Playboy of the Western World, also playing Widow Quinn in this production in the U.S. and subsequently touring England and visiting Hong Kong, 1977; five one-act plays in a bill entitled The Golden Cradle, including Riders to the Sea in which she also played the part of Maurya, Greenwich Festival, London, 1978; first appeared in films, 1946, in Hungry Hill, and has recently been seen in Playboy of the Western World, Philadelphia, Here I Come, Of Human Bondage and Here Are Ladies, excerpts from which have also been shown on R.T.E.; further recent television appearances include Cuckoo Spit, A Cheap Bunch of Nice Flowers, The Landlady and Lady Gregory (R.T.E.); she has translated Mary Rose, and Saint Joan into Gaelic.

Recreations: Reading, swimming and theatre-going. *Address:* (1) c/o Milton Goldman, ICM, 40 W 57th Street, New York 10019, USA. *Tel:* 212 556 5600; (2) c/o Nick Legh Heppel, Transcreative, 7A Sydney Place, London SW7 3NL. *Tel:* 01 581 0121.

McKENNA, T P (Thomas Patrick), actor
b Mullagh, Co Cavan, Ireland, 7 Sept 1929; *s* of Raphael P McKenna and his wife Mary (O'Reily); *e* Mullagh School and St Patrick's College, Cavan; *m* May White; formerly a bank

official; trained for the stage at the Abbey Theatre School of Acting.

First appeared on the stage 3 Oct 1953, at the Pyke Theatre, Dublin, as John Buchanan in Summer and Smoke; Gaiety, Dublin, Sept–Oct 1954, played in a Shakespeare season with the Anew McMaster company; joined the Abbey company, Jan 1955 and remained with them for eight years, playing over one hundred roles; first appeared on the London stage 12 Feb 1963 at St Martin's, as Cranly in Stephen D; Ashcroft, Croydon, Nov 1963, O'Keeffe in The Ginger Man; Royal Court, Nov 1964, Cassius in Julius Caesar; Garrick, Oct 1965, took over the part of the Burglar in Too True to Be Good; returned to the Abbey, July 1966, to appear in the new Abbey's opening production, Recall the Years; Gate, Dublin, Oct 1966, Ned Holloway in Breakdown (Dublin *Evening Herald* Best Actor award); joined the Nottingham Playhouse company, Aug 1968, to play roles including the Bastard in King John, Joseph Surface in The School for Scandal, Trigorin in The Seagull and Macduff in Macbeth; made his début as a director there, 1969, with The Playboy of the Western World; Royal Court, Oct 1969, Fitzpatrick in The Contractor, repeating the part at the Fortune, Apr 1970; joined the RSC to play Robert Hand in Exiles, and Bishop in The Balcony, Aldwych season 1971–2; Olympia, Dublin, Feb 1973, Andrew Wyke in Sleuth; Palace, Watford, Oct 1975, Ashley Dennis in Out on the Lawn; Aldwych, July 1976, Rev Anderson in The Devil's Disciple; Olympia, Dublin, Nov 1977, and also Hong Kong Festival, played Captain Boyle in Juno and the Paycock; Greenwich, July 1978, appeared in four roles in the five-play bill The Golden Cradle, from the Abbey Theatre, Dublin; Comedy, Oct 1978, Teddy in Molly; Arnaud, Guildford, Mar 1979, Gregers Werle in The Wild Duck; over thirty film appearances include Ulysses, The Charge of the Light Brigade, and Portrait of the Artist as a Young Man; TV, since 1963, includes The Rivals, The Duchess of Malfi, The Changeling, Fathers and Families, and Holocaust; hon life member, Abbey Theatre.

Favourite parts: Jamie in The Long Day's Journey Into Night, Cranly, Fitzpatrick. *Recreations:* Music, reading, sport. *Club:* Buckstone. *Address:* c/o Leading Artists, 60 St James's Street, London SW1. *Tel:* 01–491 4400.

McKENNA, Virginia, actress
b London, 7 June 1931; *d* of Terence Morell McKenna and his wife Anne Marie (Dennis); *e* Horsham, Sussex, and Herschel, Cape Town; *m* (1) Denholm Elliott (mar dis); (2) Bill Travers; studied for the stage at the Central School of Speech Training and Dramatic Art.

Her first appearance was at Dundee, Aug 1950, when she played Louise in Black Chiffon; first appeared on the West End stage at the Haymarket, 1 Mar 1951, as Dorcas Bellboys in A Penny For a Song; Phoenix, June 1951, played Perdita in The Winter's Tale; Lyric, Hammersmith, Sept 1952, appeared as Valerie Barton in The River Line, and played this part at the Strand, Oct 1952; Criterion, June 1953, Veronica in The Bad Samaritan; Aldwych, Mar 1954, Cassandra Mortmain in I Capture the Castle; joined the Old Vic Company, for the 1954–5 season, when she played Rosaline in Love's Labour's Lost, Queen to King Richard in Richard II, Rosalind in As You Like It, and Lady Mortimer in King Henry IV (Part I); joined the Royal Shakespeare Company at the Aldwych, May 1961, to take over the part of Sister Jeanne in The Devils, appearing in the repertory; Aldwych, July 1963, with the same company, played Lucy Lockit in The Beggar's Opera; toured with Cambridge Theatre Company, Oct 1971, as Masha in Three Sisters; Apollo, Feb 1972, Catherine Columbo in The Beheading; Hampstead, Oct 1973, Diana in

Country Life; Adelphi, Jan 1976, took over the part of Desirée Armfeldt in A Little Night Music; Hilton Theatre, Hong Kong, 1978, appeared in Something's Afoot; Palladium, June 1979, Mrs Anna Leonowens in The King and I; first appeared in films 1952 and received the *Evening Standard* Award for the Best Film Actress, 1967, for her part in Born Free; has also appeared on television; is the author of Some of My Friends have Tails, and co-author of On Playing with Lions; made her first LP in 1975, when two of her songs were published.

Favourite parts: Valerie in The River Line, and Capt Janine Mayhew in Shout Aloud Salvation (television). *Recreations:* Listening to music, walking, and reading. *Address:* c/o Leading Artists, 60 St James's Street, London SW1.

McKENZIE, James B, producer, actor, manager
b Appleton, Wisconsin, 1 May 1926; *s* of Basil F McKenzie and his wife Helen (Sherman); *e* Champion Military School Prairie du Chien, Wis, University of Wisconsin, University of Iowa (BA 1950), Columbia University (MA 1952); *m* Jeanne Bolan (dec); served in the US Navy, 1944–46.

Made his debut in a grade school production of Hamlet, playing the title role, and also produced, Appleton, Wis, 1936; was apprenticed at the Port Players, Milwaukee, Wis, 1942, where he also acted; acted in various stock groups, and also served as technical assistant and stage manager, publicist, etc, before making his New York debut as stage manager at the Shirtsleeve, 1950; continued in stock production, publicity, direction, and management, including Showcase Theatre, Chicago, Fred Miller's, Milwaukee, Wis, Westport, Conn, Country Playhouse, Paper Mill Playhouse, Millburn, NJ, Mineola, Long Island, Playhouse, Brown Theatre, Louisville, Kentucky, etc; was stage hand at the Metropolitan Opera House, 1956; general manager for Ballet Ballads, East 74th St, NY, Jan 1961; produced Major Barbara, May 1965; Booth, NY, 18 May 1967, co-produced The Girl in the Freudian Slip; co-founder of The Producing Managers Company, and presented the tour of The Impossible Years, 1967; tour of Cactus Flower, 1968; stage manager of Canterbury Tales, 1969; Executive Producer of the American Conservatory Theater, San Francisco, 1969–77, co-produced tour of Rosenkrantz and Guildenstern Are Dead, 1969; co-produced And Miss Reardon Drinks a Little, NY and tour, 1971; The Secret Affairs of Mildred Wild, NY 1972.

Recreation: Sailing. *Address:* 234 West 44th Street, New York, NY 10036. *Tel:* 391–1890.

McKERN, Leo (Reginald McKern), actor and director
b Sydney, New South Wales, 16 Mar 1920; *s* of Norman Walton McKern and his wife Vera (Martin); *e* Sydney Technical School; *m* Jane Holland; formerly an artist.

Made his first appearance on the stage at the Theatre Royal, Sydney, 1944, as the Chemist in Uncle Harry; arrived in England, Sept 1946; toured with the CSEU in Germany, and with the Arts Council, 1947; after playing in various repertory companies, he made his first appearance in London with the Old Vic Company, New Theatre, Oct 1949, when he played Forester in Love's Labour's Lost; remained with the company to play Jeremy in She Stoops to Conquer, 1949; Guildenstern in Hamlet, Simon in The Miser, Feste in Twelfth Night, Nightingale in Bartholomew Fair, 1950; Nym and Sir Thomas Erpingham in Henry V, Nym in The Merry Wives of Windsor, the Messenger in Electra and the Confectioner in Tchekov's The Wedding, 1951; the Fool in King Lear, and Apemantus in Timon of Athens, 1952; joined the Shakespeare Memorial Theatre Company tour to Australia,

1953, where he appeared as Iago in Othello, Touchstone in As You Like It, and Glendower and Northumberland in Henry IV Part I; on returning to England, he remained with the company at Stratford-on-Avon, 1954, to play Ulysses in Troilus and Cressida, Grumio in The Taming of the Shrew, Quince in A Midsummer Night's Dream, and Friar Lawrence in Romeo and Juliet; Princes, Dec 1954, played Toad in Toad of Toad Hall; Haymarket, Oct 1955, played the Traveller in The Queen and the Rebels; Lyric, Hammersmith, Apr 1956, Claggart in The Good Sailor; Comedy, Jan 1958, Big Daddy in Cat on a Hot Tin Roof; Aldwych, Aug 1958, Tyepkin in Brouhaha; Duke of York's, Sept 1959, directed The Shifting Heart; Strand, Oct 1959, played the title part in Rollo; Globe, July 1960, played The Common Man in A Man For all Seasons; Oxford Playhouse, Feb 1961, Ferrante in Queen After Death; made his first appearance in New York at the ANTA, Nov 1961, as Thomas Cromwell in A Man For All Seasons; on returning to England, joined the Old Vic Company for their last season, Sept 1962–3, to play the following parts: the title-part in Peer Gynt, Subtle in The Alchemist, 1962; Iago in Othello, 1963; appeared in the two opening productions at the new Nottingham Playhouse, Dec 1963, to play Menenius in Coriolanus, and Jan 1964, played the Governor in The Life in My Hands; Aldwych, Dec 1965, Baron Bolligrew in The Thwarting of Baron Bolligrew; Oxford Playhouse, Sept 1966, played the title-role in Volpone, and also at the Garrick, Jan 1967; went to Australia, 1970, and in Melbourne, 1971, played Governor Bligh in The Man Who Shot the Albatross, and Rollo in Patate; Oxford Playhouse, summer 1973, played Shylock in The Merchant of Venice, and Kelemen in The Wolf, transferring in the latter production to the Apollo, Oct 1973, and subsequently to the Queen's and the New London; since his return to England has appeared in Royal Exchange Company, Manchester, productions including Uncle Vanya and Crime and Punishment (1978); also Rollo, in which he again played the title-role, Mar 1980; first appeared in films, 1951 and has been seen in A Man For All Seasons and Ryan's Daughter; makes regular television appearances.

Favourite parts: Iago, The Common Man, and Peer Gynt. *Recreations:* Sailing, photography, swimming. *Address:* c/o ICM, 22 Grafton Street, London, W1.

MacLEISH, Archibald, poet and dramatic author
b Glencoe, Illinois, 7 May 1892; *s* of Andrew MacLeish and his wife Martha (Hillard); *e* Hotchkiss School, and Yale and Harvard Universities; *m* Ada Hitchcock.

Author of the following verse plays: Nobodaddy, 1925; Panic, 1935; JB, 1958; the last play ran for 364 performances at the ANTA Playhouse, NY, 1958–9, and has also been performed in West Germany, Holland, Brussels, Scandinavia, Italy, Israel, Greece, England (1961), Egypt and Mexico; Herakles, 1965; Scratch, a prose play, 1971; The Great American Fourth of July Parade, a verse play performed at the Carnegie Music Hall, Pittsburgh, Pa, Apr 1975; he is also the author of the following verse plays for radio: The Fall of the City, 1937; Air Raid, 1938; The Son of Man (prose), 1947; The Trojan Horse, 1952; This Music Crept by Me upon the Waters, 1953; in addition to his plays, he is the author of Union Pacific—A Ballet, 1934, poems, essays, and other prose works; Rede lecturer at Cambridge University, England, 1942; Boylston Professor, Harvard, 1949–63; Librarian of Congress, 1939–44; director of US Office of Facts and Figures, 1941–2; assistant director OWI, 1942–3; Assistant Secretary of State, 1944–5; American delegate to the Conference of Allied Ministers of Education in London, 1944; chairman of the American delegation, London UN Confer-

ence, to draw up constitution for UNESCO, 1945; chairman of the American delegation, first General Conference, UNESCO, Paris, 1946, and first American member of the executive council; served in the US Army, 1917–18; Commander of the Legion d'Honneur; Encomisado Order el Sol del Peru; twice received the Pulitzer Prize in Poetry, 1932 and 1953, and once in Drama, 1959; received the Bollingen Prize in Poetry, 1953; received the National Book Award in poetry, 1953; JB also received the Antoinette Perry Award, 1959; Presidential Medal of Freedom, 1977; National Medal for Literature, 1978; Gold Medal for Poetry, American Academy of Arts and Letters, 1979; former President of the American Academy of Arts and Letters; holds the degree of Hon MA, Tufts College, 1932; Hon LittD at the following universities: Harvard, Wesleyan, Pennsylvania, Illinois, Washington, Columbia, Princeton, and Yale; Hon LHD, Dartmouth, Amherst, Johns Hopkins, and the universities of California, Queen's, Ont, and Carlton College; Hon DCL, Union College; Hon DHL, Williams College.

Clubs: Century (NY), Tavern (Boston). *Address:* Conway, Massachusetts.

McLERIE, Allyn Ann, actress, vocalist, dancer
b Grand'Mère, Québec, Canada, 1 Dec 1926; *d* of Allan Gordon McLerie and his wife Vera Alma MacTaggart (Stewart); *e* Fort Hamilton High School, Brooklyn, New York; *m* (1) Adolph Green (mar dis); (2) George Gaynes; studied ballet with Martha Graham, Agnes De Mille, Hanya Holm, and others, and prepared for the stage with Tamara Daykarhanova, and with Lee Strasberg at the Actors Studio.

First appeared on the stage at the Imperial, Oct 1943, as a dancer in One Touch of Venus; Adelphi, Dec 1944, played the Second Ballet Girl and a Doll Girl in On the Town; Martin Beck, Dec 1945, took over the role of Ivy Smith in On the Town; Shubert (Philadelphia), Dec 1947, Eustasia in Bonanza Bound!; 46th Street, Jan 1948, took over Susan in Finian's Rainbow; toured in cabaret in a dance team with John Butler, 1947–8; St James, Oct 1948, Amy Spettigue in Where's Charley?; Imperial, July 1949, Monique duPont in Miss Liberty; Ziegfeld, 29 Jan 1950, played in a scene from Floradora in ANTA Album; toured Europe as a guest artist with the Ballet Theatre, 1950, dancing in Rodeo and Fancy Free; Broadway, Jan 1951, Amy Spettigue in Where's Charley?; made her London stage début at the Garrick in Nov 1951, when she took over the role of Myrtle in To Dorothy a Son; Booth, Jan 1956, WAC Corporal Jean Evans in Time Limit!; Coliseum (London), Nov 1957, Gwynne in Bells Are Ringing; Winter Garden, Apr 1960, Anita in West Side Story; City Center, Apr 1961, Ensign Nellie Forbush in South Pacific; Plymouth, May 1963, appeared in the revue The Beast in Me; toured, 1964, as Eliza Doolittle in My Fair Lady; New York State, July 1966, Ellie in Show Boat; Martinique, Mar 1967, Tlimpattia in Dynamite Tonite; for Inner City Repertory, Los Angeles, 1967, played Elmire in Tartuffe and Clytemnestra in The Flies; New Theater for Now, Los Angeles, 1970, played in LA Under Siege; Mark Taper Forum, Los Angeles, Mar 1973, Alma Stone in The Mind with the Dirty Man; Ahmanson, Los Angeles, Dec 1975, Judith Fellowes in The Night of the Iguana; Long Beach, 1978, appeared in Our Town; Manhattan Theatre Club, Jan 1979, appeared in Dancing in the Dark; Matrix, LA, 1979, Calpurnia in Julius Caesar; has also appeared in summer theatres in You Never Can Tell, King of Hearts, Ring Round the Moon, as Lola in Damn Yankees, Ninotchka in Silk Stockings, Gladys in The Pajama Game, Claudine in Can-Can, in Good News (Pittsburgh, 197), etc; first appeared in films in 1948 in Words and Music, and has since played in

Where's Charley? Desert Song, Battle Cry, The Reivers (1969), They Shoot Horses, Don't They? (1969), Cowboys (1971), The Way We Were (1973), All the President's Men (1978), etc; has appeared frequently on television in such programs as *Music for a Summer Night, American Musical Theatre, Lou Grant,* Beulah Land, etc.

Address: Actors Equity Association, 6430 Sunset Boulevard, Los Angeles, Calif 90028.

MacMAHON, Aline, actress
b McKeesport, Pa, 3 May 1899; *e* Barnard College, New York City; *m* Clarence S Stein.

Made her first appearance on the stage at the Neighborhood Playhouse, 29 Oct 1921, as Laura Huxtable in The Madras House, and Apr 1922, appeared there as Matilda in The Green Ring; Bijou, NY, June 1922, Anne in The Dover Road; Times Square, Sept 1922, Miss Files in The Exciters; 49th Street, Sept 1923, Molly Latimer in Connie Goes Home; at the Neighborhood, Oct 1923–May 1924, Decima in The Player Queen, Mag Maggot in This Fine-Pretty World, Babsy in The Shewing-Up of Blanco Posnet, Riemke van Eyden in Time Is a Dream, and in The Grand Street Follies; Winter Garden, June 1925, in Artists and Models; Mansfield, Nov 1926, Ruth Atkins in Beyond the Horizon; Martin Beck, Apr 1927, Rosalie Kent in Spread Eagle; Bayes, Aug 1927, Hildegarde Maxon in Her First Affair; Comedy, Feb 1928, Bella in Maya; Provincetown, Nov 1929, Tony Ambler in Winter Bound; San Francisco, 1930, and Plymouth, NY, July, 1931, May Daniels in Once in a Lifetime; Booth, Nov 1931, Margaret Brice in If Love Were All; at Stockbridge, Mass, June 1937, played Candida; at Ann Arbor, Mich, May 1938, appeared in The Ghost of Yankee Doodle; at Carmel, NY, June 1938, in Away from It All; Maxine Elliott, NY, Dec 1939, Mary in Kindred; National, Apr 1940, Betsy Graham in Heavenly Express; Cort, Oct 1942, Nell West in The Eve of St Mark; Kronberg Castle, Elsinore, Denmark, June 1949, Queen Gertrude in Hamlet, and subsequently toured Germany; Ivar, Los Angeles, Mar 1951, Countess Aurelia in The Madwoman of Chaillot; Morosco, Feb 1954, appeared as Mrs Guzzard in The Confidential Clerk; ANTA Playhouse, Sept 1955, Laura Anson in A Day by the Sea; at the Kauffman Concert Hall, NY, May 1956, took part in a staged reading of Pictures in the Hallway; Belasco, Sept 1957, took part in a staged reading of I Knock at the Door; Shubert, Washington, DC, Jan 1959, Mama Caparuta in The Poker Game; at the Stratford Shakespeare Festival, Conn, June 1959, the Nurse in Romeo and Juliet, and the Countess of Rossillion in All's Well That Ends Well; Belasco, NY, Nov 1960, Aunt Hannah Lynch in All The Way Home; Washington, DC, Dec 1961, Countess Aurelia in The Madwoman of Chaillot; American Shakespeare Festival Theatre, Stratford, Conn, summer 1965, Volumnia in Coriolanus; joined the Lincoln Center Repertory Theatre in 1966 and, at the Vivian Beaumont, Oct 1966, played Tribulation Wholesome in The Alchemist; Dec 1966, Alegria in Yerma; Feb 1967, Mrs Humphreys in The East Wind; Apr 1967, the Housekeeper in Galileo; at The Forum, Nov 1967, Mina in Walking to Waldheim; Vivian Beaumont Feb 1968, Hecuba in Tiger at the Gates; Apr 1968, Mother Marguerite in Cyrano de Bergerac; The Forum, Mar 1969, Mrs Peeles in The Inner Journey; Forum, Apr 1971, Mrs Casside in Pictures in the Hallway; Vivian Beaumont, Nov 1971, Mary's Nurse in Mary Stuart; Apr 1972, Rebecca Nurse in The Crucible; Oct 1975, Trafalgar Gower in Trelawny of the "Wells"; commenced film career 1931, in Five Star Final, and since has appeared in Life Begins, Once in a Lifetime, The Gold Diggers of 1933; Babbitt, Ah, Wilderness!, Kind Lady, The Search, All the

Way Home, and many others; television appearances include the Nurse in Medea, 1959, and many dramatic series and programs.

Address: 1 West 64th Street, New York, NY.

McMARTIN, John, actor
b Warsaw, Indiana; *e* Columbia University.

Made his New York debut at the Orpheum, 18 Nov 1959, as Corporal Billy Jester in Little Mary Sunshine; ANTA, Jan 1961, played Forrest Noble in The Conquering Hero; Morosco, Oct 1961, Captain Mal Malcolm in Blood, Sweat, and Stanley Poole; Walnut, Philadelphia, Sept 1962, Mr Dupar in A Matter of Position; Morosco, Apr 1963, Sidney Balzer in Children from Their Games; Belasco, Oct 1963, Edward Voorhees in A Rainy Day in Newark; Fisher, Detroit, Mich, Mar 1965, John Paul Jones in Pleasures and Palaces; Palace, Jan 1966, Oscar in Sweet Charity; Winter Garden, Apr 1971, Benjamin Stone in Follies; Shubert, Century City, Cal, July 1972, repeated this last part; Lyceum, for the New Phoenix Repertory, Dec 1972, Dion Anthony in The Great God Brown; also Dec 1972, Sganarelle in Don Juan; Shubert, 11 Mar 1973, appeared in Sondheim: A Musical Tribute; Mark Taper Forum, Los Angeles, Apr 1973, played in Forget-Me-Not Lane; Ethel Barrymore, for the New Phoenix Repertory, Anton Schill in The Visit and Fedot in Chemin de Fer; Helen Hayes, also for the New Phoenix, Nov 1974, Foresight in Love for Love and, Dec 1974, Leone Gala in The Rules of the Game; ANTA West, Los Angeles, 1975, appeared in Continental Divide; Long Wharf, Newhaven, Nov 1976, in The Autumn Garden; Public/Anspacher, Nov 1977, Alceste in The Misanthrope; Ahmanson, LA, Feb 1978, appeared in Absurd Person Singular; Long Wharf, 1978, in Journey's End; appeared in the film What's So Bad About Feeling Good, 1968, and also in Sweet Charity, All the President's Men, and Thieves (1975) etc.

Address: c/o Leaverton Associates, 1650 Broadway, New York, NY 10019.

McNALLY, Terrence, playwright
b St Petersburg, Florida, 3 Nov 1939; *s* of Hubert Arthur McNally and his wife Dorothy Katharine (Rapp); *e* Columbia University; formerly a newspaper reporter, tutor for the children of John Steinbeck, and stage manager at the Actors Studio.

First play produced was And Things That Go Bump in the Night, at the Tyrone Guthrie Theatre, Minneapolis, Minnesota, 4 Feb 1964; this was also his first play produced in New York, at the Royale, 26 Apr 1965; is the author of the following plays: Sweet Eros, Witness, Tour, Noon, Cuba Si, all produced in NY, 1968; Next, 1969; Where Has Tommy Flowers Gone? (Yale Repertory Theatre and New York), Bad Habits (John Drew, Easthampton), 1971; Botticelli, produced at the Old Post Office, Easthampton, NY, June 1971; Bringing It All Back Home, produced at the Provincetown Playhouse, July 1971; Whiskey, at the St Clement's Church, Apr 1973; The Tubs, at the Yale Repertory, Jan 1974; Bad Habits, being a double-bill of Ravenswood and Dunelawn, produced both off-Broadway and on Broadway, 1974; The Ritz, a revised version of The Tubs, produced on Broadway, 1975; Broadway, Broadway (John Drew, and Shubert, Philadelphia), 1979; is the author of the television plays Apple Pie and Last Gasps, 1966; adapted The Five Forty-Eight, PBS, 1979; author of the radio play The Lisbon Traviata, 1979; first plays produced in London were Sweet Eros and Next in a double-bill at the Open Space, 13 July 1971.

Address: 218 West 10th Street, New York, NY 10014. *Tel:* JU 6–5100.

McNAMARA, Brooks, professor, director and author
b 1 Feb 1937; *s* of Elmer Jenkins McNamara and his wife Margaret (Barry); *e* Knox College, Illinois, University of Iowa and Tulane University of Louisiana; *m* Maryann Jansen.

Professor of Drama, School of the Arts, New York University; director of the Shubert Archive; former director, American Society for Theatre Research, and of the Theatre Library Association (president, 1979); has designed stage settings for La Mama, The Performance Group, etc; author of The American Playhouse in the Eighteenth Century, Step Right Up, and (with Richard Schechner and Jerry Rojo) Theatres, Spaces, Environments; also numerous articles; contributing editor, *The Drama Review, Theatre Design and Technology, Popular Entertainment*; has lectured at a number of universities in the US and abroad.
Address: 4 Washington Square Village, New York, NY 10012.

MacNAUGHTAN, Alan, actor
b Bearsden, Dumbartonshire, 4 Mar 1920; *s* of Alan George MacNaughtan and his wife Mary Henrietta (Jebb); *e* Glasgow Academy; studied for the stage at the Royal Academy of Dramatic Art, where he gained the Bancroft Gold Medal, 1940.

Made his first appearance on the stage at the Old Vic, 15 Apr 1940, as the King of France in King Lear; engaged with the Birmingham Repertory Company, 1946–8, during which period he appeared with the company at the St James's, June 1948, as Bob Acres in The Rivals; in repertory at the Dolphin, Brighton, during the Tennent's 1948–9 season, and with the Sheffield Repertory Company, 1949–50; Arts, Nov 1950, played Hugh Loring in Preserving Mr Panmure; Dec 1950, played Hsieh Ping-Kuei in a revival of Lady Precious Stream; Aldwych, Feb 1951, again played Hugh Loring in Preserving Mr Panmure; Arts, Apr 1951, appeared in various parts in the Shaw Festival programme of one-act plays; Westminster, Feb 1952, played Scythrop Glowry in Nightmare Abbey; at the same theatre, June 1952, appeared as Max Halliday in Dial M For Murder, which ran for nearly a year; Gaiety, Dublin, Feb 1953, Hugo Klaren, in The White Countess; Arts, Apr 1953, played Boris Trigorin in The Seagull; St Martin's, Oct 1953, Seamus Ua Caoilte, in Blind Man's Buff; Arts, Dec 1953, Clive Crawford, in A London Actress; Westminster, June 1954, Douglas Oberon in We Must Kill Toni; Arts, Sept 1954, appeared as Burwin-Fosselton in The Diary of a Nobody, and played the same part at the Duchess, May 1955; Royal, Brighton, July 1955, played Lionel in Patience, and appeared in the same part at Streatham Hill, Aug 1955; Duke of York's, May 1956, played Mr Howard in The House by the Lake; Oxford Playhouse, Oct 1957, played Delmonte in Dinner With the Family, subsequently appearing in the same production at the New, Dec 1957; Cambridge, Apr 1959, played Daniel Monnerie in The Hidden River; made his first appearance on Broadway at the ANTA Theatre, Dec 1959, when he played the Baron in The Fighting Cock; Helen Hayes, New York, Apr 1960, played Mr Justice Blanchard in Duel of Angels, subsequently touring the US with the production; Pembroke, Croydon, Apr 1961, played Mr Gerrard in The Gentleman Dancing Master; Mermaid, Oct 1961, played Elder Daniels in The Shewing-Up of Blanco Posnet, and Spintho in Androcles and the Lion (double-bill); Nottingham Playhouse, Apr 1962, The Mayor in The Enemy of the People; Oxford Playhouse,

Oct 1962, played Lord Summerhayes in Misalliance, and Nov 1962, Skurattov in The Just; Royal Court, and Criterion, Jan 1963, again played Lord Summerhayes in Misalliance; Ashcroft, Croydon, Apr 1963, played Bernard Laroque in The Deadly Game; toured South America and Europe for the British Council, Mar–May 1964, as Antonio in The Merchant of Venice, and as Theseus in A Midsummer Night's Dream; Oxford Playhouse, Jan 1965, played Subtle in The Alchemist; toured, June 1965, as Proteus in The Apple Cart; Hampstead Theatre Club, Sept 1966, played the Rev Harold Banner in After the Rain; transferred to the Duchess, Jan 1967, and played the same part on Broadway at the Golden Theatre, Oct 1967; Mermaid, Apr 1968, Bishop of Caerleon in Hadrian the Seventh; Hampstead Theatre Club, Sept 1969, played the title-role in Papp; Apollo, Feb 1970, George Mason in Girlfriend; Watermill, Newbury, July 1970, the Captain in Dance of Death; Hampstead Theatre Club, Dec 1970, Hubert Charteris in We Were Dancing, Bert Bentley in Red Peppers, and Burrows in Family Album in the triple-bill, Tonight At Eight, transferring to the Fortune, Jan 1971; for Cambridge Theatre, Company, Oct 1971, toured as Vershinin in Three Sisters, and Telfer in Trelawny of the "Wells"; joined the National Theatre company, Mar 1972, where his parts include: Bishop of Carlisle and subsequently John of Gaunt in Richard II, Sir Oliver Surface in School for Scandal, Walter Burns in The Front Page, Duncan in Macbeth, 1972; Philinte in The Misanthrope, Archie in Jumpers, Frank Strang in Equus, 1973; Gayev in The Cherry Orchard, The Duke in Measure for Measure (mobile production), 1973; Dreyfus in Grand Manoeuvres, also tour of Australia in The Front Page, 1974; Mazzini Dunn in Heartbreak House, 1975; Arts. June 1977, appeared in Dirty Linen; Oxford Playhouse, Oct 1979, played the title-role in King Lear; recent television appearances include The Sandbaggers.
Favourite part: Walter Burns in The Front Page. *Recreations:* Tennis, walking, and sailing. *Address:* 19 Arundel Court, Arundel Gardens, London, W11. *Tel:* 01–727 6216.

McNEIL, Claudia, actress
b Baltimore, Maryland, 13 Aug 1917; *d* of Marvin Spencer McNeil and his wife Annie Mae (Anderson); formerly a licensed librarian; prepared for the stage with Maria Ouspenskaya.

For twenty-five years sang in night clubs, in vaudeville theatres, and on the radio; toured South America and Europe as a singer with the Katherine Dunham Dance Company; made her legitimate New York stage début at the Martin Beck Theatre, 1953, when she took over the role of Tituba in The Crucible; 85th Street Playhouse, May 1957, played Mamie in Simply Heavenly, appearing in the same role at the Playhouse, Aug 1957; National, Feb 1958, Mary in Winesburg, Ohio; Ethel Barrymore, Mar 1959, Lena Younger in A Raisin in the Sun, touring the US with the production 1960–1; Booth, Dec 1962, Mama in Tiger, Tiger, Burning Bright; toured, 1964, as Berenice in The Member of the Wedding; at the Théâtre des Nations, Paris, July 1965, played Sister Margaret in The Amen Corner, subsequently appearing in the same play at the Habimah, Israel, and at the Edinburgh Festival, Aug 1965; made her London début at the Saville, Oct 1965, in the same production and received the London Critics Poll Award as best actress for this performance; Cort, Nov 1967, played Sarah Goldfine in Something Different; Lunt-Fontanne, Oct 1968, Ftatateeta in Her First Roman; John Golden, Mar 1969, Mrs Devereaux in The Wrong Way Light Bulb; Tambellini's Gate, Mar 1970, Martha in Plantation and Mrs Grace Love in Contribution in a production with the overall title Contributions; Hartford, Conn, Stage Company, Jan 1975, Lena Younger in A Raisin in the Sun; Center Stage, Baltimore, Mar 1977, appeared in The First Breeze of Summer; first appeared in films, 1959, in The Last Angry Man, and has since played in the film version of A Raisin in the Sun and in There Was a Crooked Man, 1970; first appeared on television, 1952, in *The Molly Goldberg Show*, and has since appeared in *The Nurses*, The Member of the Wedding, etc.

Favourite parts: Lena Younger in A Raisin in the Sun, and the Mother in the film The Last Angry Man. *Hobbies:* Collecting glass and old English tureens. *Address:* 400 Central Park West, New York, NY 10025. *Tel:* MO 3-2955.

MacOWAN, Michael, CBE, director
b London, 18 Apr 1906; *s* of Norman MacOwan and his wife Violet (Stephenson); *e* Haileybury; *m* Alexis France; studied for the stage at the Royal Academy of Dramatic Art.

Formerly an actor and made his first appearance on the stage, 1925, touring in Charles Macdona's repertory company of Bernard Shaw's plays; made his first appearance in London at the Fortune Theatre, 6 Oct 1926, as Matviei in A Month in the Country; in the spring of 1927, toured as Little Billee in Trilby; Gate, London, Nov 1927, played the Painter in Maya; Savoy, Mar 1928, understudied in Young Woodley, subsequently playing Ainger in that play, for three months; Apollo, Oct 1928, played Alyosha in The Brass Paper Weight; toured in Australia and New Zealand, 1929, in Young Woodley; Criterion, Jan 1930, played Richard Sibley in Milestones; subsequently returned to the Gate Theatre, where he played several parts until the end of 1931; he then abandoned acting for directing; his first production was The Judgment of Dr Johnson, Arts, Jan 1932; joined the Eastbourne Repertory company, 1932; director, Hull Repertory company, 1933–4; directed several plays at the Croydon Repertory Theatre, 1934–5; was assistant-director and director of the Dramatic School at the Old Vic, 1935–6, also directing The Two Shepherds, The School for Scandal and The Winter's Tale; appointed director at the Westminster Theatre, Sept 1936, successfully directing there: A Month in the Country, The Wild Duck, Waste (With Granville Barker), The Crooked Cross, 1936; Uncle Vanya, Heartbreak House, Anna Christie, Hamlet, Mourning Becomes Electra, 1937; Volpone, You Never Can Tell, Troilus and Cressida, Dangerous Corner, Marco Millions, 1938; Miss Julie, Candida, Bridge Head, 1939; directed After the Dance, St James's, 1939; Music at Night, Westminster, 1939; Desert Highway, Playhouse, 1944; served in the Army, 1939–45; in 1945, was appointed Drama Director of the Arts Council of Great Britain; resigned from this position, Dec 1946; has since directed Tess of the D'Urbervilles, Headlights on A5, The Linden Tree, 1947; Cockpit, Eden End, Home is Tomorrow, 1948; The Foolish Gentlewoman, Marriage Story, Young Wives' Tale, Summer Day's Dream, 1949; The Ivory Tower, Rosmersholm, 1950; A Sleep of Prisoners (London and New York), A Phoenix Too Frequent, Thor, With Angels, 1951; The Vortex, The Winter's Tale (Ohel Theatre, Tel Aviv), The River Line, 1952; The Apple Cart, The Return, 1953; The Burning Glass, Waiting for Gillian, 1954; The Seagull, 1956; The Potting Shed, 1958; Horses in Midstream, 1960; also directed The Salt Land on television, 1955; Principal of the London Academy of Music and Dramatic Art 1954–66; Artistic director, 1972–73; received the CBE in the Birthday Honours, 1976.

Address: 3 Blake Gardens, London SW6. *Tel:* 01–736 3520.

McQUEEN, Butterfly, actress
b Tampa, Florida, 7 Jan 1911; *e* New York City College,

University of California at Los Angeles, Queens College; received a Bachelor of Arts degree from the City College of NY, 1975; formerly a children's nurse and a factory worker.

Made her stage début at the Biltmore, NY, 16 Dec 1936, in Brother Rat; Biltmore, Dec 1937, played Butterfly in Brown Sugar; Biltmore, Apr 1938, played in What a Life; Center, Nov 1939, played in Swingin' the Dream; entered films; toured extensively in a one-woman show, including an engagement at Carnegie Recital Hall in 1953; Jan Hus, Jan 1964, played Ora in The Athenian Touch; Bert Wheeler, May 1968, Hattie in Curley McDimple, a role that was specially written for her after the play had been running some months; Bert Wheeler, Aug 1969, played in the revue Butterfly McQueen and Friends; Lyceum, Oct 1969, Dora Lee in Three Men on a Horse; Ethel Barrymore, Jan 1970, took over as Jenny in The Front Page; Alice Tully Hall, 11 Aug 1973, appeared in a concert called Soul at the Center; Town Hall, 4 Feb 1976, appeared in a one-woman show in a series called Interludes; appeared as Prissy in the film Gone with the Wind, 1939 and played in Amazing Grace, 1974; has appeared on the television series *Oriole* in the title-role, and has also appeared as a guest on various other programs; is actively engaged in community betterment efforts in Harlem, NY.

Recreations: Music, sewing, reading. *Address:* 29 Mount Morris Park West, New York, NY 10027.

McSHANE, Ian, actor
b Blackburn, Lancs, 29 Sept 1942; *s* of Harry McShane and his wife Irene (Cowley); *e* Stretford Grammar School, Lancs; *m* (1) Suzan Farmer (mar dis); (2) Ruth Post; trained for the stage at RADA.

Made his first professional appearance at the Arts, London, Aug 1962, as Charley in Infanticide in the House of Fred Ginger; Vaudeville, Feb 1963, played Johnnie Leigh in How Are You, Johnnie?; Globe, June 1964, Ralph in The Easter Man; toured, Feb 1965, as Hal in the original production of Loot; Haymarket, Dec 1965, played Tom in The Glass Menagerie; Playhouse, Oxford, Nov 1966, Marat in The Promise, repeating the part in London at the Fortune, Jan 1967, and on his New York début at the Henry Miller, Nov 1967; Hampstead, Mar 1971, played John Sutcliffe in Ellen; Long Beach Theater Festival, Calif., Aug 1979, Jacques in As You Like It; films since The Wild and the Willing in 1962, include Villain and Yesterday's Hero; television, also since 1962, includes A Sound from the Sea, and recently, High Tide.

Favourite part: Tom in The Glass Menagerie. *Recreations:* Football, snooker, photography. *Address:* c/o Gerry Hall, The Swiss Centre, 10 Wardour Street, London W1. *Tel:* 01–724 2336.

McWHINNIE, Donald, director
b Rotherham, Yorks, 16 Oct 1920; *s* of Herbert McWhinnie and his wife Margaret Elizabeth (Holland); *e* Rotherham Grammar School, and Caius College, Cambridge.

Formerly with the British Broadcasting Corporation, where he was subsequently appointed Assistant Head of Sound Drama; directed his first London theatre production at the Royal Court, Oct 1958, with Krapp's Last Tape, for the English Stage Company; he has since directed the following plays: The Caretaker, The Duchess of Malfi, 1960; Three (triple-bill), The Tenth Man, The Caretaker (New York), 1961; A Passage to India (NY), Everything in the Garden, Macbeth (Stratford-on-Avon), Rattle of a Simple Man, Doctors of Philosophy, End of Day, Entertainment from Works of Samuel Beckett (Dublin Festival), 1962; Rattle of a Simple Man (NY), The Doctor's Dilemma, Alfie, Out of the Crocodile, 1963; The Fourth of June, Endgame, The Creeper (Nottingham Playhouse), 1964; All in Good Time (NY), The Creeper, The Cavern, 1965; Scrooge (Nottingham Playhouse), This Winter's Hobby (US tour), 1966; The Astrakhan Coat (NY), Happy Family, 1967; Tinker's Curse, and Vacant Possession (Nottingham Playhouse), 1968; Hamlet, The Interview and No Quarter (double-bill), There'll Be Some Changes Made, 1969; The Apple Cart, 1970; Meeting At Night, A Hearts and Minds Job, 1971; Endgame, Play and That Time (one-acts), 1976; principal television productions include Sword of Honour, Howard's End, and, recently, Love in a Cold Climate.

Recreation: Music. *Address:* 16 Chepstow Place, London W2. *Tel:* 01–229 2120.

MADDEN, Ciaran, actress
b 27 Dec 1945; *d* of Dr James George Madden and his wife Maria Elizabetti (Dawson); *e* New Hall Convent, nr Chelmsford, Essex, and Ruskin School of Art, Oxford; trained for the stage at RADA.

Made her professional début in Apr 1968, as Shirley Hughes in The Man Most Likely To . . ., which opened at the Alexandra, Birmingham, prior to its London opening at the Vaudeville, July 1968; Manchester, Apr 1969, for 69 Theatre Company, played Constance Neville in She Stoops to Conquer, transferring with the production to the Garrick, May 1969; Wyndham's, Dec 1970, took over the part of Heloise in Abelard and Heloise; Chichester Festival, May 1973, Angela in The Director of the Opera; Arnaud, Guildford, Sept 1973, Isabella in Measure for Measure; Arnaud, Nov 1974, Elizabeth in The Circle; visited Hong Kong with this production, 1975; Arnaud, Jan 1975, Miss Forsythe in Death of a Salesman; Open Space, May 1975, Isabella in an adaptation of Measure for Measure, by Charles Marowitz; Wimbledon, Mar 1976, Blanche in Widowers' Houses; Thorndike, Leatherhead, Oct 1979, title-role in Saint Joan; Lyric, Hammersmith, Feb 1980, played Vittoria in Country Life; television, since 1969, includes the serial Sense and Sensibility, Hamlet, Jennie, and Gawaine and the Green Knight.

Recreations: The piano, drawing, eating. *Address:* Glebe House, Tollesbury, nr Maldon, Essex.

MADDEN, Donald, actor
b New York City, 5 Nov 1933; *s* of Owen Madden and his wife Jane (Halloran); *e* College of the City of New York; Brandeis University.

In the summer 1955, played Edmund Kean in the US première of Jean-Paul Sartre's Kean; first appeared on the stage in NY at the Golden, June 1958, when he took over the role of Jimmy Porter in Look Back in Anger; Alvin, Mar 1959, played Charles Bingley in First Impressions; Belvedere Lake, Aug 1959, Mark Antony in Julius Caesar; at the Phoenix, off-Broadway, Nov 1959–Mar 1961, played the following parts: Kinesias in Lysistrata, a concert reading of Pictures in the Hallway, Hotspur in Henry IV (Part I), Young Marlow in She Stoops to Conquer, Lieutenant Langon in The Plough and the Stars, the title-role in Hamlet, Mar 1961; Ethel Barrymore, Oct 1962, played Mark Hurlbird in Step on a Crack; toured, June 1963, as Lewis Eliot in Time of Hope; Royal Court, London, Nov 1963, Chris in The Milktrain Doesn't Stop Here Anymore; Belasco, Dec 1964, played Jason Sample in One by One; toured, Mar 1966, as Henry VIII in A Man for All Seasons; toured, June 1966, as Elyot Chase in Private Lives; toured, July 1966, as George Gregory

in Jack Be Nimble; Ethel Barrymore, Feb 1967, Frank in White Lies and Harold Gorringe in Black Comedy; American Place, Dec 1967, King Ethelred in The Ceremony of Innocence; American Shakespeare Festival, Stratford, Conn, Apr 1968, title-role of Richard II; Eastside Playhouse, Mar 1969, Mark Conley in In a Bar of a Tokyo Hotel; toured, Aug 1969, as Richard Ford in Poor Richard; Delacorte, June 1970, the title-role of Richard III; Playhouse, Jan 1971, Torvald Helmer in A Doll's House, and Feb 1971, Eilert Lovborg in Hedda Gabler, and then alternated these roles in repertory; Ivanhoe, Chicago, July 1971, Felice in Out Cry; Williamstown, Mass, July 1972, title-role in Arturo Ui, and toured in this part; Goodman, Chicago, Deeley in Old Times; American Shakespeare Festival, Stratford, Conn, July 1975, Leontes in The Winter's Tale; Nat Home, June 1976, appeared in Tatiana Golikova is Dead; Roundabout Stage One, NY, Sept 1976, title role in The Philanderer; McCarter, Princeton, Dec 1976, August Strindberg in The Night of the Tribades; for Phoenix, NY, May 1977, Charlie in Scribes; Playhouse, Feb 1979, Wallace Barrows in Trick; made his film début as Dickinson in 1776 (1971); has appeared frequently on television, notably in Burning Bright, The Old Lady Shows Her Medals, *US Steel Hour,* Roots of Freedom, Kilroy in Camino Real (Granada), etc.

Address: c/o Jeff Hunter, 119 West 57th Street, New York, NY 10019. *Tel:* 757–4995.

MAGEE, Patrick, actor
b Armagh, N. Ireland.

His early experience was in Ireland with Anew McMaster's company; at the Arts, Jan 1958, and Winter Garden, Mar 1958, played Larry Slade in The Iceman Cometh; Royal Court, Oct 1958, title-role in Krapp's Last Tape; Arts, Mar 1959, Max in The Buskers; Royal Court, Sept 1959, Father Domineer in Cock-A-Doodle-Dandy; Theatre Royal, Stratford E, Sept 1961, Michael Carney in A Whistle in the Dark, transferring to the Apollo, Oct 1961; in Paris, 1963, played Hamm in Endgame; joined the Royal Shakespeare Company at the Aldwych, 1964, to play McCann in The Birthday Party, Roche in Afore Night Come, June; Hamm in Endgame, July; de Sade in The Marat/Sade, Aug; Matti in Puntila, July 1965; Ghost in Hamlet, Aug 1965 (Stratford); Aldwych, Nov 1965, again played de Sade, repeating his performance at the Martin Beck, New York, Dec 1965, and winning a Tony award; returning to the Aldwych, July 1966, played Wolfgang Schwitter in The Meteor; Harry Leeds in Staircase, Dec; Plymouth, NY, Sept 1967, Frank Brady in Keep It in the Family; again at the Aldwych, Mar 1969, Inspector Hawkins in Dutch Uncle; Lyric, Feb 1970, Mark in The Battle of Shrivings; Gardner Centre, Brighton, Aug 1970, Cornelius Melody in A Touch of the Poet; Roundhouse, July 1973, read the epic poem The Rough Field; Thorndike, Leatherhead, Oct 1974, Halvard Solness in The Master Builder; Royal Court, May 1976, Hamm in Endgame, and Face and Voice in That Time; Old Vic, July 1976, Monticelso in The White Devil; Lyric Studio, Hammersmith, Feb 1980, Mephistopheles in Dr Faustus, transferring to the Fortune, Mar; films include The Birthday Party, Hard Contract, Barry Lyndon, The Criminal, and A Clockwork Orange; has appeared frequently on television and in broadcast readings from Beckett.

Address: c/o NEMS Management, 29–31 King's Road, London SW3.

MALINA, Judith, director, producer, actress
b Kiel, Germany, 4 June 1926; *d* of Max Malina and his wife Rosel (Zamora); *e* Dramatic Workshop of the New School for Social Research; *m* Julian Beck.

Made her acting début in Aug 1945, at the Cherry Lane, New York, in By Any Other Name; President, Apr 1947, played the First Fury in The Flies; Cherry Lane, July 1947, Mildred Luce and Nineveh Girl in The Dog Beneath the Skin; Cherry Lane, July 1947, Zenobia Frome in Ethan Frome; with her husband founded The Living Theatre in 1947, which has flourished since in NY and Europe, the early productions being staged in various places, chiefly in their own home; among the early productions were Childish Jokes, He Who Says Yes and He Who Says No, Gertrude Stein's Ladies Voices, Dialogue of the Young Man and the Manikin; Cherry Lane, Mar 1951, played Statira in The Thirteenth God, which she also directed, marking her directing début; since has produced for The Living Theatre Doctor Faustus Lights the Lights, which she directed, Beyond the Mountains, in which she played Phaedra, Iphigenia, and Berenike, 1951; An Evening of Bohemian Theatre, a triple-bill of Ladies Voices, in which she played Gertrude, Pablo Picasso's Desire Trapped by the Tail, and T S Eliot's Sweeny Agonistes, all of which she directed, Faustina, Ubu Roi, and The Heroes, 1952; The Age of Anxiety, which she directed and played the Narrator, The Spook Sonata (directed), Orpheus (directed and played Death), The Idiot King (played the Nun), 1954; Tonight We Improvise (played Mommina), Phaedra (translated and played title-role), The Young Disciple (played the Old Crone), 1955; Voices for a Mirror, The Curious Fern, 1957; Many Loves (played Alise, Seraphina, Breen, and Clara), The Cave at Machpelah (played Sarah and Rebekah), The Connection (directed), Tonight We Improvise (played Mommina), Madrigal of War, All That Fall, Embers, Act Without Words I and III, Bertha, Theory of Comedy, Love's Labors, 1959; The Devil's Mother (directed), Faust Foutu, The Marrying Maiden (directed), The Women of Trachis (played Daysair), The Herne's Egg, Purgatory, A Full Moon in March, The Election (played a Stagehand), In the Jungle of Cities (directed), 1960; The Mountain Giants (played Countess Ilse), The Apple (directed), and, in Apr, took over the role of Mary Garga in In the Jungle of Cities, 1961; Man Is Man (played Leokadja Begbick), 1962; The Brig (directed), 1963; first took The Living Theatre to Europe in 1961, playing in Rome, Turin, Paris, Milan, Berlin, Frankfurt, in The Connection, Many Loves, In the Jungle of Cities; returned to Europe and toured in Switzerland, France, The Netherlands, Germany, and Belgium in The Connection, In the Jungle of Cities, and The Apple; made her London début with The Living Theatre at the Mermaid, Sept 1964, when she directed The Brig; remained in Europe with the Troupe, playing at the Academy of Liberal Arts, West Berlin, 1964; moved to Brussels, Mar 1965, and, at the Theatre 140, presented Mysteries; Brussels, Nov 1966, was co-author with Julian Beck and co-produced with him Frankenstein; Teatro Parioli, Rome, May 1967, produced a repertory season of Antigone, The Maids, Mysteries; toured Europe again before returning to America and, at the Brooklyn Academy of Music, Oct 1968, presented and acted in Frankenstein, Antigone (played title-role), Mysteries and Smaller Pieces, Paradise Now; toured in this repertory in 1969; toured in Brazil, 1971; The Legacy of Cain, consisting of 100 or more short plays to be performed in a village over a two-week period at various public sites, 1971; Rituals, Rites, and Transformation, performed first in Rio Clara and Umbu, Brazil, 1971; Washington Square Methodist Church, NY, Apr 1974, Seven Meditations on Political Sado-Masochism; settled with her troupe in Bordeaux, France, Nov 1975; appeared with them at the Round House, July 1979, in Prometheus; The Living Theatre has had profound effects on world avant garde acting, writing, and production, and has received numerous

awards, including, in Paris, 1961, for the Théâtre des Nations season the Grand Prix, the Medal for the Best Acting Company, and the Prix de l'Université; in the US has won the Lola D'Annunzio Award (1959), the Obie (Off-Broadway) Award for the best production (1960), the Brandeis University Creative Arts Award (1961), and the New England Theatre Conference Award (1962); first television production in June 1954, with Gertrude Berg's The Goldbergs; The Brig has been televised and filmed.

MALTBY, Richard Jr, director, writer and lyricist
b 6 Oct 1937; *s* of Richard E Maltby, Sr and his wife Virginia; *e* Phillips Exeter Academy and Yale University (BA 1959); married the script consultant Barbara Sudler.

At the Walnut Street, Philadelphia, Dec 1975, directed The Glass Menagerie; same theatre, May 1976, directed Long Day's Journey into Night; both these productions starred Geraldine Fitzgerald, whom he directed, 1975–79, on tours of her program Street Songs; adaptor and co-lyricist for Daarlin' Juno, Long Wharf, May 1976; directed and wrote lyrics for Starting Here, Starting Now, for Manhattan Theatre Club, 1977; conceived and directed Ain't Misbehavin' at the same theatre, 1978, transferring to the Longacre and winning a Tony award as best director of a musical; his songs, written with composer Richard Shire, have been extensively recorded; contributor of crosswords to *Harpers* magazine.
Address: c/o Flora Roberts Inc, 65 East 55th Street, New York, NY 10024.

MAMET, David, playwright and director
b Chicago, Illinois, 30 Nov 1947; *s* of Bernard Morris Mamet and his wife Lenore June (Silver); *e* Goddard College, Vermont and Neighborhood Playhouse School of the Theatre; *m* the actress Lindsay Crouse.

His early plays were one-acts, including Lakeboat, produced Marlboro, Vt, 1970; Squirrels, Sexual Perversity in Chicago, and Duck Variations, all produced Chicago, 1974; the last two were seen in a double-bill at St Clement's, NY, May 1975; the full-length American Buffalo, produced Chicago, 1975, marked his Broadway debut in 1977 and was also seen in London at the Cottesloe, 1978; recent plays produced include A Life in the Theater (one-act), The Water-Engine, Mr Happiness (one-act), Reunion and Dark Pony (one-acts), The Woods, all first seen 1977; Lone Canoe (musical: wrote book), 1979; author of a children's play, Revenge of the Space Pandas, also produced 1977; artistic director of the St Nicholas Theatre Company, Chicago, 1973–76, where several of his plays were premiered; associate artistic director and playwright in residence, Goodman Theatre, Chicago, 1978–present; has taught drama at Yale, the University of Chicago, etc; wrote screenplay for The Postman Always Rings Twice, 1980.
Address: c/o Howard Rosenstone & Co, 1500 Broadway, New York, NY 10019.

MANDER, Raymond Josiah Gale, actor, theatrical historian, joint founder and director of the Raymond Mander and Joe Mitchenson Theatre Collection
b London, 15 July; *s* of Albert Edwin Mander and his wife Edith Christina (Gale); *e* Battersea Grammar School.

Appeared as a semi-professional entertainer before and after leaving school in 1930; professional debut, Bedford, 1934, with the London Repertory Players as Herbert in Eliza Comes to Stay, remaining for a season and playing many parts; appeared at Wimbledon, Oct 1935, as a junior counsel in For the Defence, and in pantomime at the same theatre, Dec, and up to 1939; at the Arts and other little theatres,

1936; in rep at Darlington, 1937, and Brixton, 1938; Drury Lane, Sept 1938, appeared in Henry V; parts at the Dockland Settlement Theatre, 1938–39, included Page in The Merry Wives of Windsor; played twelve parts in a nine-play repertoire for the H V Nielson (formerly Benson) company, spring 1939; appearances 1939–42 include Northampton Rep, 1941, Players' Theatre, 1942; Garrick, 1941, played the Dustman in Room V; Globe, 1942, Ruby in The Petrified Forest; played the Dragon King in Where the Rainbow Ends, Mar 1942, and repeated this role on numerous occasions, including appearances at the Stoll and the Winter Garden, from 1942–45; at the Oxford Playhouse, 1942; stage director and actor in various tours etc until Aug 1944, when he directed and acted in a season at the Gateway, Notting Hill Gate; entered management at the Grand, Croydon, Jan–Jun 1945, presenting and directing plays including Charley's Aunt and The Ghost Train; toured in Europe for ENSA, 1945–46, in Pygmalion; made his last appearance as an actor at the Theatre Royal, Rochester, 1948, in a programme of one-act plays; in 1939 he and Joe Mitchenson founded their Theatre Collection, developing it over the years into a full-time occupation, with authorship and consultancy; in 1977 the Collection was formed into a trust, and the London Borough of Lewisham offered Beckenham Place as a permanent home for it; 'The Boys' are archivists to Sadler's Wells and the Old Vic Company; have arranged many exhibitions, including Fifty Years of British Stage Design, for the British Council, in the USSR, 1979; and have written numerous works on the theatre, including Hamlet Through the Ages, 1952; Theatrical Companions to Shaw, 1954, Maugham, 1955, Coward, 1957; A Picture History of British Theatre, 1957; The Theatres of London, 1961 revised 1975; 'stories in pictures' of British Music Hall, 1965 revised 1974, Musical Comedy, 1969, Revue, 1971, and Pantomime, 1973; Victorian and Edwardian Entertainment from Old Photographs, 1978; Guide to the Somerset Maugham Theatrical Paintings at the National Theatre, 1980; they have appeared frequently on television, talking on theatrical topics, and during the War presented many theatre record programmes.

Favourite part: Adolphus Cusins in Major Barbara. *Recreations:* Theatregoing, gardening. *Address:* 5 Venner Road, Sydenham SE26 5EQ. *Tel:* 778 6730.

MANKOWITZ, Wolf, dramatic author and producer
b 7 Nov 1924; *e* East Ham Grammar School, and Downing College, Cambridge; *m* Ann Margaret Seligman.

Author of the following plays: The Bespoke Overcoat, 1953; The Boychik, 1954; Expresso Bongo, 1958; Make Me An Offer, 1959; Belle, or The Ballad of Dr Crippen (book), 1961; The Mighty Hunter (one-act), It Should Happen to a Dog (one-act), 1962; Pickwick (book), 1963; Passion Flower Hotel (book), 1965; Stand and Deliver (book), 1972; The Hebrew Lesson (also directed), 1978; in association with Oscar Lewenstein he has presented: The World of Sholom Aleichem, Moby Dick, The Punch Revue, 1955; Expresso Bongo, The Party, The Deserters (tour), 1958; A Taste of Honey, The Hostage, and Make Me An Offer (all co-produced), 1959; The Lily-White Boys (co-produced), The Art of Living (co-produced), 1960; his association in management with Oscar Lewenstein was dissolved in July 1960, and he has since presented independently, The Lion in Love, This Year, Next Year, 1960; Belle, or The Ballad of Dr Crippen, 1961; re-entered theatrical management, 1970, in partnership with Laurence Harvey, presenting Siobhan McKenna in Here are Ladies; author of the film version of The Bespoke Overcoat, Expresso Bongo, Make Me An Offer, and A Kid For Two Farthings, other film scripts include: The Assassination Bureau, Black Beauty, Bloomfield (also co-produced), The Hireling; he is also the author of many television plays and series including *Dickens of London.*

Address: The Bridge House, Ahakista, Co. Cork, Eire. *Tel:* Kilcrohane 11.

MANN, Theodore (*né* Goldman), producer and director
b Brooklyn, New York, 13 May 1924; *s* of Martin Goldman and his wife Gwen (Artson); *e* Columbia and NY Universities and the Brooklyn Law School; *m* Patricia Brooks; formerly engaged as a lawyer.

Made his theatrical début at the Maverick Players, Woodstock, NY, summer 1950, when he produced Alice in Wonderland; co-founded Circle in the Square, 1951, where he has since functioned as Producer, and has presented and frequently directed as well the following plays: Dark of the Moon, Amata, Anouilh's Antigone, The Enchanted, 1951; Bonds of Interest, Yerma, Burning Bright, Summer and Smoke, 1952; The Grass Harp, American Gothic, 1953; The Girl on the Via Flaminia, 1954; The King and the Duke, La Ronde, Cradle Song, 1955; The Iceman Cometh, 1956; Children of Darkness, The Quare Fellow, 1958; Our Town, 1959; The Balcony, 1960; Under Milkwood, 1961; Plays for Bleecker Street, Under Milkwood, Pullman Car Hiawatha, 1962; Desire Under the Elms, The Trojan Women, 1963; The White Devil, 1965; Eh? 1966; Drums in the Night, Iphigenia in Aulis, 1967; A Moon for the Misbegotten, 1968; Little Murders, Seven Days in Mourning, 1969; The White House Murder Case, Boesman and Lena, 1970; The Last Analysis, F Jasmine Addams (and also wrote the book with G Wood from the novel of Carson MacCullers), 1971; Mourning Becomes Electra (directed: first production at the new uptown Circle in the Square), 1972; Medea, The Iceman Cometh, Here Are Ladies, Uncle Vanya, The Waltz of the Toreadors, Hot l Baltimore, 1973; An American Millionaire, Scapino, Where's Charley?, 1974; All God's Chillun Got Wings, Death of a Salesman, Ah, Wilderness!, The Glass Menagerie (directed), 1975; The Lady from the Sea, Pal Joey (directed), Days in the Trees, The Night of the Iguana, The Club, 1976; Romeo and Juliet (directed), The Importance of Being Earnest, Tartuffe, Saint Joan, 1977; 13 Rue de L'Amour, Once in a Lifetime, The Inspector General, Man and Superman, 1978; Spokesong, Loose Ends, 1979; Past Tense (directed), 1980; has also produced and directed in other theatres and for other managements the following plays: Long Day's Journey into Night, The Innkeepers, 1956; Camino Real, 1959; Smiling the Boy Fell Dead, 1961; General Seeger, Great Day in the Morning, 1962; Strange Interlude, Six Characters in Search of an Author, Trumpets of the Lord, 1963; Othello, Hughie, 1964; And Things That Go Bump in the Night, The Royal Hunt of the Sun, The Zulu and the Zayda, Baal, Live Like Pigs, 1965; Six from La Mama, 1966; A Midsummer Night's Dream, 1967; Morning, Noon, and Night, 1968; Trumpets of the Lord, 1969; at Ford's, Washington, DC, has produced A Moon for the Misbegotten, Trumpets of the Lord, Ah, Wilderness! Iphigenia in Aulis, 1969; Arsenic and Old Lace, 1970; John and Abigail, 1971; made his London début as producer at the Globe, May 1958, with Long Day's Journey into Night; first production for television was The Trojan Women, 1964, and since has produced Six Characters in Search of an Author, Trumpets of the Lord, etc.

Recreations: Basketball, tennis, farming, *Address:* Circle in the Square, 1633 Broadway, New York, NY 10019. *Tel:* 586 9424.

MANNING, Hugh Gardner, actor
b Birmingham, 19 Aug 1920; *s* of George Gardner Manning

and his wife Gertrude Julia (Wilkes); *e* Moseley Grammar School, Birmingham; formerly a municipal accountant; trained for the stage at the Birmingham School of Speech Training and Dramatic Art.

Made his first professional appearance in 1940 for Birmingham Repertory Theatre in an open-air production of Bird In Hand, playing Sir Robert Arnwood; touring and repertory experience, 1945–52, including Birmingham, 1945; two seasons at the Open Air, Regent's Park, 1946–7, taking over Bottom in A Midsummer Night's Dream, 1946, and playing Antonio in Twelfth Night, Ajax in Troilus and Cressida, and General Wei in Lady Precious Stream; Oxford Playhouse, 1948 and 1951–, where his rôles included Thomas Mendip in The Lady's Not for Burning, Dr Sloper in The Heiress and Sir Francis Chesney in Charley's Aunt; at Bristol Old Vic, 1950–1; Bristol Old Vic, 195–1, played Backbite in The School for Scandal, Tappercoom in The Lady's Not for Burning and doubled as de Beaudricourt and the Inquisitor in Saint Joan; Haymarket, May 1953, played Balbus in The Apple Cart; St Martin's, Oct 1953, Henry Harrican in Blind Man's Buff; Lyric, May 1955, Gaston Lemare in My Three Angels; toured, 1956, as Vitulesco in Mrs Willie; Old Vic, May 1961, Morocco in The Merchant of Venice; also played the Prince in Romeo and Juliet; toured the USA, Europe and the Middle East with the company, 1961–2, playing Ross in Macbeth (first New York appearance in this part at the City Center, Feb 1962), Archbishop in Saint Joan and Capulet in Romeo and Juliet; toured India, Pakistan and Ceylon, 1962–3, with Bristol Old Vic company, playing Ghost in Hamlet, Norfolk in A Man for All Seasons, and Major Petkoff in Arms and the Man; Arts, London, Nov 1963, played Vulterne (Mirabeau) in Poor Bitos, transferring to the Duke of York's, Jan 1964; Playhouse, Nottingham, May 1965, played the title-part in Volpone; toured, 1968, as Humpy in All For Mary; Duke of York's, Feb 1970, Coventry in A Woman Named Anne; Arnaud, Guildford, Oct 1970, and Criterion, Dec 1970, played Mr Prodmore in The High Bid; Little, Jan 1971, Martin Ripley in a lunchtime production, The Thompson Report; toured, Mar 1972, for Welsh Theatre Company in the title-role of Uncle Vanya, and as Pacarel in A Pig in a Poke; Open Air, July 1972, Sir Toby Belch in Twelfth Night; toured with the New Shakespeare Company, Oct 1973, as Jacques in As You Like It; Mercury, Colchester, Sept 1975, Jack in Home; Haymarket, Leicester, Oct 1975 played Mr Amish in Speak Now; for the Cambridge Theatre Company, May–Dec 1976, toured as Colonel Pickering in Pygmalion and Jack in Home; Theatre Royal, Windsor, Mar 1979, Duff in The Old Country; films include: The Dam Busters, Our Man in Havana, The Honey Pot and The Mackintosh Man; television, since 1947, includes The Cherry Orchard, The Venturers, and *Emmerdale Farm*; member of BBC drama repertory company 1948–50 and 1957–9; Vice-President, British Actors Equity, 1969–73; President, 1975, 1976.

Favourite parts: Bottom, Uncle Vanya. *Recreations:* Reading, gardening, tennis, bridge. *Address:* 29 Parliament Hill, London, NW3.

MARASCO, Robert, playwright
b New York, 22 Sept 1936; *s* of Anthony Marasco and his wife Lena (Carre); *e* Regis High School, and Fordham College; formerly a school teacher.

Wrote his first play, Child's Play, which was produced at the Royale, NY, 17 Feb 1970, and at the Queens, London, 16 Mar 1971; author of the novel, Burnt Offerings, 1974.

Address: William Morris Agency, 1350 Avenue of the Americas, New York, NY 10019. *Tel:* 568 5100.

MARCH, Elspeth, actress
b London; *d* of the late Colonel Harry Malcolm Mackenzie, MB, ChB, CIE and his wife Elfreda (Hudson); *e* Sherborne School for Girls, Dorset, and Ivy House, Wimbledon; *m* Stewart Granger (mar dis); studied for the stage at the Central School of Speech Training and Dramatic Art, under Elsie Fogerty.

Made her first appearance on the stage at the Westminster Theatre, 12 Dec 1932, as the Woman Passenger in Jonah and the Whale; at the Royalty, Apr 1933, understudied in The Brontës, and played Emily in this play, on occasions; Royalty, July 1933, played Emily in The Writing on the Wall; Q, June 1934, Olga Rachinova in The Flame, and Veronica in Triumph; from 1934–7, was engaged at the Birmingham Repertory Theatre where her many parts included the title-part in St Joan, and Elizabeth in The Barretts of Wimpole Street; also appeared at the Malvern Festivals, 1935–7, where she played Vashti in The Simpleton of the Unexpected Isles, Margaret Knox in Fanny's First Play, Miss Trafalgar Gower in Trelawny of the "Wells", Hypatia in Misalliance, 1066 and All That, Miss Brollikins in On the Rocks, Miss Sterling in The Clandestine Marriage, Mrs Higgins in Pygmalion, The Princess in Lady Precious Stream, Epifania in The Millionairess, Orinthia in The Apple Cart, Lady Teazle in The School for Scandal; St Martin's, Oct 1937, played Jane Gunning in Autumn; 1938–9, played repertory seasons at His Majesty's, Aberdeen, and Theatre Royal, Windsor; Mercury, Sept, and Duchess, Oct 1939, played Widow Quin in The Playboy of the Western World; Kingsway, Dec 1939, the Princess of the Western Regions in Lady Precious Stream; left the stage 1940–4, and served as a driver for the American Red Cross; reappeared in London, at the Lyric, July 1945, as Herda Sarclet in Duet for Two Hands; Arts, Oct 1946, the Governess in The Turn of the Screw; Globe, Dec 1946, Mrs Ruth Cartwright in The Gleam; Lyric, July 1947, Janet Braid in Peace in Our Time; Mercury, Mar 1948, Widow Quin in The Playboy of the Western World; Globe, Sept 1948, Chorus in Medea; Lyric, Hammersmith, Aug 1949, Maura Pender in The King of Friday's Men; Saville, Mar 1950, Marcia Wain in The Platinum Set; Embassy, May 1950, Queen Boadicea in The First Victoria; St James's, May 1951, appeared as Ftatateeta in Caesar and Cleopatra; Lyric, Hammersmith, Apr 1952, played Mathilde in Montserrat; 1953–4, played various leading parts at Windsor and Bromley Repertory theatres; Connaught, Worthing, Aug 1956, played the Countess of Avalon in Family Tree; during the run of Morning's At Seven at the Comedy, 1956, at short notice, took over the part of Ida, and played it for one week; Theatre, East, New York, Mar 1957, appeared with the Irish Players, as Maurya in Riders to the Sea, and as Mary Byrne in The Tinker's Wedding; Tara Theatre, NY, May 1958, also with the Irish Players, played Widow Quin in The Playboy of the Western World; Saville, London, Sept 1959, Ma Larkin in The Darling Buds of May; Mermaid, Mar 1962, played Catherine Petkoff in Arms and the Man; Prince of Wales, May 1963, Madam Dilly in On the Town; Lyric, Dec 1963, and Haymarket, 1964, played Maud Lowder in The Wings of the Dove; St Martin's, May 1965, Mrs Porter in A Public Mischief; Arnaud, Guildford, July 1966, Maria in A Family and A Fortune; at the same theatre, Oct 1967, Mrs Buchanan in The Eccentricities of a Nightingale; Duke of York's, Apr 1968, Marya Konstantine in The Duel; Wyndham's, May 1970, Abbess of Argenteuil in Abelard and Heloise; Globe, July 1972, played Mrs Muriel Daintry in Parents' Day; Gardner Centre, Brighton, Sept 1972, Ella Merriman in The Dark River; toured, July 1973, as Olivia Cameron in Death on Demand; Vaudeville, Mar 1974, Maude in Snap; Cambridge, Sept 1976, Dowager Empress in Anastasia; National Theatre, June 1977, played Mrs Huxtable in The Madras House, and, April 1978, Grandmother in Don Juan Comes Home from the War; first appeared in films, 1944, in Mr Emmanuel, other films include: Quo Vadis, The Miracle, The Rise and Rise of Michael Rimmer, Goodbye Mr Chips and The Magician of Lublin; she has also appeared in numerous television programmes including, recently, Rebecca, The Good Companions, Charlie Muffin and An Ideal Husband.

Recreations: The study and collection of antiques, and reading. *Address:* c/o ICM Ltd, 22 Grafton Street, London, W1.

MARCHAND, Nancy, actress

b Buffalo, New York, 19 June 1928; *d* of Raymond L Marchand and his wife Marjorie (Freeman); *e* Carnegie Institute of Technology; *m* Paul Sparer.

First appeared on the stage in 1946 at Ogunquit, Maine, in The Late George Apley; made her first appearance in NY at the City Center, Apr 1951, as the Hostess of the Tavern in The Taming of the Shrew; Brattle, Cambridge, Mass, 1950–2, played Princess of France in Love's Labour's Lost, Mrs Dudgeon in The Devils' Disciple, Tibueina in The Critic, Regan in King Lear, etc; City Center, Feb 1953, again played the Princess of France in Love's Labour's Lost; City Center, Mar 1953, Nerissa in The Merchant of Venice; Antioch, Ohio, Shakespeare Festival, 1954, Kate in The Taming of the Shrew, Nurse in Romeo and Juliet, and Amelia in Othello; Theatre de Lys, Apr 1955, Mrs Grant in Teach Me How to Cry; Phoenix, Dec 1956, Mrs Mi Tzu in The Good Woman of Setzuan; Royale, Dec 1957, Miriam Ackroyd in Miss Isobel; Stratford Shakespeare Festival, Conn, July 1958, played Paulina in The Winter's Tale; Stratford, Conn, July 1959, played Lady Capulet in Romeo and Juliet and Mistress Page in The Merry Wives of Windsor; Lunt-Fontanne, Sept 1959, played Ursula in Much Ado About Nothing; Circle-in-the-Square, Mar 1960, Madame Irma in The Balcony; Shubert, New Haven, Conn, Sept 1960, Jane Peyton in Laurette; for the Association of Producing Artists at the Folksbiene Playhouse, Mar 1962, played Lady Sneerwell in The School for Scandal, and Madame Arkadina in The Seagull; for the same troupe, in Ann Arbor, Michigan, 1963, Beatrice in Much Ado About Nothing, Amalia in Right You Are, Vaisilissa Karpovna in The Lower Depths; Phoenix, Mar 1964, appeared in repertory in the last two roles and as the Woman in The Tavern; Phoenix, Mar 1965, played the Prostitute in Judith, and Ann Whitefield in Man and Superman; Cherry Lane, Oct 1965, The Old Lady in Good Day; Henry Miller's, Mar 1966, Genevieve in 3 Bags Full; American Shakespeare Festival, Stratford, Conn, June 1966, a Woman of Canterbury in Murder in the Cathedral; Vivian Beaumont, for the Lincoln Center Repertory Theatre, Oct 1966, Dol Common in The Alchemist and, Dec 1966, Dolores in Yerma; Mark Taper Forum, Los Angeles, June 1967, played in The Sorrows of Frederick; John Golden, Oct 1967, Getrude Forbes-Cooper in After the Rain; Vivian Beaumont, Apr 1968, Duenna (Sister Claire) in Cyrano de Bergerac; Morosco, Dec 1968, Mrs Latham in Forty Carats; Morosco, Feb 1971, Ceil Adams in And Miss Reardon Drinks a Little; Vivian Beaumont, Nov 1971, Queen Elizabeth in Mary Stuart; Nov 1972, Tatiana in Enemies; and Jan 1973, Mrs Gogan in The Plough and the Stars; Long Wharf, New Haven, Conn, May 1973, Myra Power in Patrick's Day; Goodman, Chicago, 1973, Vera Simpson in Pal Joey; Goodman, Oct 1974, Madame Ranevskaya in The Cherry Orchard; Public/Newman, 1979, took over as Ruth Chandler in

Taken in Marriage; Lyceum, Apr 1980, Ida Bolton in Morning's at Seven; first appeared in films in 1957 in Bachelor Party and has since played in Me, Natalie, and Tell Me That You Love Me, Junie Moon; first appeared on television in 1950 and has played in Marty, Queen Elizabeth, Of Famous Memory, *Beacon Hill*, *Lou Grant*, etc.

Recreations: Needlework, reading. *Address:* 205 West 89th Street, New York, NY. *Tel:* Tr 3–7889.

MARCUS, Frank, dramatic author and theatre critic

b Breslau, Germany, 30 June 1928; *s* of Frederick James Marcus and his wife Gertie (Markuse); *e* Bunce Court School, Kent, and St Martin's School of Art; *m* Jacqueline Sylvester.

Normerly an actor, director, and antique dealer; his first play Minuet for Stuffed Birds was directed by himself at the Torch Theatre, London, May 1950; he is also the author of the following plays: The Man Who Bought a Battlefield, 1963; The Formation Dancers, 1964; The Killing of Sister George (*Evening Standard* best play of the year award), Cleo, 1965; Studies of the Nude, 1967; Mrs Mouse, Are You Within?, 1968; The Window (one-act), The Guardsman (adaptation), 1969; Notes on a Love Affair, Blank Pages (one-act), Christmas Carol (one-act), 1972; Beauty and the Beast, 1975; Anatol (translation), 1976; Blind Date (one-act), 1977; The Ballad of Wilfred II (one-act), 1978; The Weavers (translation), 1980; author of the following television plays: The Window, A Temporary Typist, 1966; The Glove Puppet, 1968; Blank Pages, 1969; Carol's Story, 1974; 1966–8 theatre critic for *The London Magazine* and *Plays and Players*; from 1968–78 theatre critic for *The Sunday Telegraph*.

Address: 42 Cumberland Mansions, Nutford Place, London, W1. *Tel:* 01–262 9824.

MARKHAM, David (*né* Peter Basil Harrison), actor

b Wick, near Pershore, Worcestershire, 3 Apr 1913; *s* of Herbert Basil Harrison and his wife Gethyn Bertha (Hayward); *e* Malvern College; *m* Olive-Marie Dehn; studied for the stage at the Royal Academy of Dramatic Art.

Made his first appearance on the stage at the Rusholme Repertory Theatre, Manchester, July 1934, in The Swan, and played juvenile parts there during the season; made his first appearance in London, at the King's Hammersmith, 25 Feb 1935, as Mark Saltmarsh in All Rights Reserved, which he also played at the Criterion, Apr 1935; Queen's, Mar 1936, played Private Charles Morton in Red Night; Duke of York's, Dec 1936, Peter Hunter in The Astonished Ostrich; Little, Jan 1937, Hareton Earnshaw in Wuthering Heights; Globe, Nov 1937, Bob Carson in Robert's Wife, which ran until 1939; Savoy (for the Stage Society), Mar 1939, the Bridegroom in Marriage of Blood; Playhouse, May 1939, Robin Villiers in Only Yesterday; Q, Aug 1939, John in The Fanatics; His Majesty's, Dec 1939, Octavius in Julius Caesar (in modern dress); Embassy, Jan 1940, Bentley Summerhays in Misalliance, and in the spring, 1940, played leading parts in repertory at Glasgow and Edinburgh; toured, May 1940, as Judah in Family Portrait, subsequently touring with the Old Vic Company (for CEMA), 1940–1, and 1941–2, as Trofimov in The Cherry Orchard; at the Playhouse, Liverpool (for Old Vic), from Aug 1943–4, played Bluntschli in Arms and the Man, Richard in Ah, Wilderness! Dr Rank in A Doll's House, Mercutio, etc; at the Playhouse, Oxford, May 1944, played Hamlet, and in July, George in Of Mice and Men; toured, 1945, with Wilson Barrett's company; Torch, Aug 1945, played John Rosmer in Rosmersholm; returned to the Playhouse, Liverpool, Sept 1945; Prince of Wales's, July

1946, played Peter Marti in Pick Up Girl; Lyric, Hammersmith, July 1947, appeared as Jean in Men Without Shadows, and as Fred in The Respectable Prostitute; toured, 1947, with the Old Vic Company, as Angel Clare in Tess of the D'Urbervilles; New Lindsey, Nov 1947, Terence Sullivan in Gingerbread House; Strand, Feb 1948, played Judah in Family Portrait; subsequently, at Wyndham's and Criterion, 1948, played Valentine in You Never Can Tell; Arts, Jan 1949, played Dick in A Pair of Spectacles, and Dr Harry Trench in Widowers' Houses; Feb 1949, Robert in The Unquiet Spirit; Chepstow, Apr 1949, George Ashton in Dear Heart!; Q, Mar 1950, Dr Waldon in Fire-Weed; May 1950, Richard Rowan in Exiles; Lyric, Hammersmith, Aug 1950, Dr Gavin Pethick in View Over the Park; New, Boltons, Nov 1950, Dr Joseph Cardin in The Children's Hour; New, Boltons, Jan 1951, Weaver in The Christmas Tree; also Mar 1951, appeared as Hamlet, and Oct 1951, as Basil Farrington in Mrs Basil Farrington, and Harry Marshall in A Call on the Widow; Court, Sept 1952, Herrick in Ebb Tide; Arts, Oct 1952, Lord Arthur Savile in Lord Arthur Savile's Crime; Lyric, Hammersmith, May 1954, Trofimoff in The Cherry Orchard; New, Bromley, Nov 1954, played Richard Festal in Three Steps to Eternity; at the Q, Oct 1955, played Mr Tarraway in Moonshine; Arts, Cambridge, Feb 1957, played Monsignor in The Cardinal; Arts, London, Oct 1957, Judge Montane in The Public Prosecutor; Gateway, Edinburgh, Feb 1962, played Dr Robert Masters in The Sleepless One; St Martin's, Jan 1964, Mr Manningham in The Fourth of June; at Perth Repertory, Mar 1965, directed The Enchanted; same theatre, Mar 1967, Hjalmar in The Wild Duck; Mermaid, Feb 1968, Fourth Reader in The Adventures of the Black Girl in Her Search for God, and Second Reader in Aerial Football; Gené, East Grinstead, Oct 1968, appeared in The Hollow Crown; Dec 1969, joined Stables Theatre, Manchester, where his parts included Sullivan in Twenty-six Efforts at Pornography; Aldwych, Jan 1972, for RSC, played the Doctor in All Over; Old Vic, Mar 1974, Gonzalo in the National Theatre production of The Tempest; New End, Nov 1977, the Doctor in Medal of Honour Rag; recent film appearances include: Meetings with Remarkable Men, Tess of the D'Urbervilles, and LVA Nuit Americaine; television, since The Doctor's Dilemma, 1945, includes leading parts in plays and serials, among them Edward II, The Voysey Inheritance, North and South, and, more recently, Loyalties and Telford's Change; he has also appeared on French television.

Recreations: Kremlinology, violin-playing, and pig-breeding. *Address:* Lear Cottage, Coleman's Hatch, Sussex. *Tel:* Forest Row 2302.

MARKS, Alfred, OBE, actor

b Holborn, London, 28 Jan 1921; *s* of Max Marks and his wife Gabrielle (Solomon); *e* Bell Lane School, London; *m* Paddie O'Neil; formerly an engineer and auctioneer.

First appeared on the stage as an amateur, at the age of nine, in a Boys' Brigade concert party; made his first professional appearance at the Kilburn Empire, 1946, in variety; at Manchester, 1950, appeared in High Button Shoes; Stoll, Sept 1951, played Leo in Rainbow Square; appeared at the Palladium, 1953, in variety; Coliseum, Oct 1954, played Boris Adzinidzinadze in Can-Can; at the Royal Festival Hall, Dec 1955, played Joseph Flint in Where the Rainbow Ends; Savoy, Oct 1958, played John Mallorie in A Day in the Life Of . . .; Palladium, Dec 1959, the King of Hearts in Humpty Dumpty; Royal Court, Dec 1961, played Gottlieb Biedermann in The Fire Raisers; toured, Mar 1962, as Van Houten in The Magnificent Gourmet; Palace, Manchester, Dec 1962, appeared in the title-part of King Cole; Edinburgh Festival,

Aug 1963, played Charlie Lewis in The Unshaven Cheek; made his first appearance in the United States at the Fisher, Detroit, Mar 1965, as Potemkin in Pleasures and Palaces; Mermaid, London, Nov 1965, played Rafe Crompton in Spring and Port Wine, transferring to the Apollo, Jan 1966 and touring Australia in the production, 1967–8; Piccadilly, Dec 1968, Mr Ashford and Mr Salteena in The Young Visiters; Whitehall, Mar 1969, Det Chief Inspector Newton in Dead Silence; London Palladium, Dec 1970, Abanazar in Aladdin; Garrick, Sept 1971, Sir William Mainwearing-Brown in Don't Just Lie There, Say Something; Palace, Westcliffe, May 1973, and tour, Archie Rice in The Entertainer; Bankside Globe, July 1973, Sir Toby Belch in Twelfth Night; Greenwich, Nov 1973, title-role in Zorba; Chichester Festival, 1974, played the Father in Tonight We Improvise, May, and Kreon in Oidipus Tyrannus; Hippodrome, Birmingham, Dec 1974, Abanazar in Aladdin; Piccadilly, May 1975, Al Lewis in The Sunshine Boys; Phoenix, May 1976, Gerald Lyman in Bus Stop; Shaftesbury, May 1977, Henry Royce in Rolls Hyphen Royce; toured, Sept 1978, as Frank Foster in How the Other Half Loves, subsequently playing this role in Hong Kong; Bromley, 1978, played the Baron and Sebastian Crutwell in the double-bill In Praise of Love, later touring with the production in Australia; Palladium, Dec 1978, Abanazar in Aladdin; Jerusalem Festival, Apr 1979, Sir Percy in Habeas Corpus; Jan 1980, toured as Tevye in Fiddler on the Roof; first appeared in films, 1953; awarded the OBE in the New Year Honours, 1976.

Hobbies: Engineering, carpentry and model building, still and ciné-photography. *Recreation:* Horse riding. *Club:* Albemarle. *Address:* Barry Burnett Organization Ltd, Suite 409, Princes House, 190 Piccadilly, London W1.

MARLOWE, Hugh (*né* Hugh Herbert Hipple), actor

b Philadelphia, Pennsylvania, 20 Jan 1911; *s* of George W Hipple and his wife Mildred (Schroeder); *e* Chicago; *m* (1) Edith Atwater (mar dis); (2) K T Stevens (mar dis); (3) Rosemary Tory.

Made his stage début at the Pasadena Playhouse, Calif; first appeared on the New York stage at the National, 18 Sept 1936, as Donald Drake in Arrest That Woman; Henry Miller's, Sept 1938, played Top Rumson in Kiss the Boys Good-Bye; Maxine Elliott's, Jan 1940, Jed Jones in Young Couple Wanted; Guild, Dec 1940, Charles Nathan in Flight to the West; Music Box, Oct 1941, Wayne Kincaid in The Land Is Bright; Broadway, Feb 1943, Charley Johnson in Lady in the Dark; in Chicago, 1944, played Bill Page in The Voice of the Turtle; Biltmore, Feb 1947, Todd Frazier in It Takes Two; Cort, June 1947, Mark McPherson in Laura; Booth, Oct 1947, Stephen Cass in Duet for Two Hands; retired from the stage and made films for nearly ten years; reappeared on the stage at the Alcazar, San Francisco, Apr 1956, as Bud Walters in Anniversary Waltz; Pasadena Playhouse, Nov 1957, Gil in Janus; Central City Opera House, Colorado, Aug 1958, played in And Perhaps Happiness; Moore, Seattle, Washington, 1961, Tucker Grogan in Invitation to the March; same theatre, Dec 1965, Dr John Neilson in The Rabbit Habit; Theatre de Lys, Jan 1967, Charles Francis Eitel in The Deer Park; Theatre de Lys, Dec 1967, Leonard in Postcards; Belasco, Sept 1968, Brigham Young in Woman Is My Idea; Roundabout Stage One, Oct 1974, Joe Keller in All My Sons; first appeared in films in 1937 in Married Before Breakfast, and since has played in many others, notably in Meet Me in St Louis, 12 O'clock High, All About Eve, Mr Belvedere Rings the Bell, Elmer Gantry, Thirteen Frightened Girls, etc; played Ellery Queen in both the radio and television productions of that name, and has appeared frequently on television in other dramatic parts, notably in the series *Another World*.

Address: Actors Equity Association, 165 West 46th Street, New York, NY 10036.

MAROWITZ, Charles, director and dramatic author
b New York City, 26 Jan 1934; *s* of Harry Julius Marowitz and his wife Tillie (Rosencranz); *m* Julia Crosthwait.

His first production was Doctor Faustus in 1948 at the Labor Temple Theatre, NYC; his first London production was in 1958 at the Unity, Marriage; co-director with Peter Brook in the experimental Theatre of Cruelty season, 1964; plays he has since directed (in London unless otherwise stated) include: The Trigon, 1964; The Bellow Plays, Loot, 1966; Fanghorn, 1967; Fortune and Men's Eyes, 1968; Jump, 1971; Macbett, Section Nine, 1973; Laughter!, 1978; founded the Open Space theatre, 1968; plays since presented there which he has directed include: Blue Comedy, Muzeeka and The Fun War (double-bill), 1969; Chicago/Conspiracy, Palach, 1970; The Critic as Artist, 1971; Sweet Eros, and Next (double-bill), 1971; The Four Little Girls, Sam Sam, The Tooth of Crime (co-directed), The Old Man's Comforts, 1972; Woyzeck (also adapted), The Houseboy, And They Put Handcuffs on the Flowers (also translated), 1973; Sherlock's Last Case, 1974; Artaud a Rodez (also wrote), 1975; Anatol, Hanratty in Hell, 1976; Boo Hoo, 1978; The Father (also adapted), 1979; directed Ubu, 1980; has directed a number of his own reworked adaptations from Shakespeare, the most recent at the Open Space and in various parts of the world; Hamlet, 1966, Macbeth, 1969; Othello, 1972; The Taming of the Shrew, 1973; Measure for Measure, 1975; Variations on the Merchant of Venice, 1976; he has directed his own adaptations of Ibsen in Norway: Hedda Gabler (Bergen) and Enemy of the People (National Theatre, Oslo); has directed programmes on theatrical subjects for television; is a regular contributor to the *New York Times,* the *Village Voice* and various theatre journals; a collection of his writings was published under the title Confessions of a Counterfeit Critic; collections since published have been The Act of Being (theories of acting), and The Marowitz Shakespeare (adaptations).

Address: 123 Tottenham Court Road, London, W1. *Tel:* 387 5175.

MARRE, Albert, director and producer
b New York City, 20 Sept 1925; *e* Townsend Harris High School, NY, Oberlin College (BA 1943), Harvard (MA 1948); *m* Joan Diener.

Director of the Allied Repertory Theatre, Berlin, Germany, 1946; became Managing Director of the Brattle Theatre Company, Cambridge, Massachusetts, producing 68 plays, of which he directed 45 between 1948 and 1952; directed his first NY production, The Little Blue Light, at the ANTA, 29 Apr 1951; Artistic Director for the New York City Center Drama Company, 1952–3, and directed the productions of Love's Labour's Lost, Misalliance, The Merchant of Venice, 1953; directed Kismet in NY 1953, and made his London début as director when he staged Kismet at the Stoll, 20 Apr 1955; directed Festival, The Chalk Garden, 1955; Shangri-La, Fledermaus, Saint Joan, 1956; Good as Gold, South Pacific (Los Angeles and San Francisco), Time Remembered, 1957; At the Grand, for the Los Angeles Civic Opera Company, 1958; produced the play The Love Doctor at the Piccadilly, London, Oct 1959; directed La Belle Helene (Boston), Rape of the Belt, 1960; Milk and Honey, 1961; Too True to Be Good, 1962; A Rainy Day in Newark, 1963; Never Live over a Pretzel Factory, Laurette for the Inter-

national Theatre Festival, Olympia, Dublin, 1964; Man of La Mancha, 1965; Chu Chem, Philadelphia, 1966; Cry for Us All, of which he was co-author, 1970; Curran, San Francisco, May 1971, directed Knickerbocker Holiday; a revival of Man of La Mancha, NY, and Hallowe'en at the Bucks County Playhouse, New Hope, Pa, 1972; directed and wrote the book with Roland Kibbee for Home Sweet Homer, 1975; NY revival of Man of La Mancha, 1977; tour, 1979; A Meeting by the River, 1979; has also directed for television, notably Androcles and the Lion and Craig's Wife.

Address: Society of Stage Directors and Choreographers, 1501 Broadway, New York, NY 10019.

MARRIOTT, Raymond Bowler, dramatic critic
b Brooklands, Cheshire, 8 Nov 1911; *s* of Herbert de Warren Marriott and his wife Mary Louisa (Macdonald); *e* Loretto Convent, Bowden and Worthington Road School, Sale.

Left school at fourteen and became a messenger boy on the *Daily Express,* Manchester; later a reporter in Liverpool and London; dramatic critic and feature writer for *The Era,* 1931–9; joined *The Stage* 1950; assistant editor 1952–76; dramatic critic 1954–; contributor to numerous periodicals and newspapers, including *Adam* and the *Guardian*; author of a series of Theatre Cards (obtainable at the British Theatre Museum), and also of a novel, The Blazing Tower.

Recreations: Reading biography, criminology. *Address:* The Stage, 47 Bermondsey Street, London EC1 3XT.

MARSDEN, Betty, actress
b Liverpool, 24 Feb 1919; *m* Dr James Wilson Muggoch.

First appeared on the stage at the Bath Pavilion, 1930, as the 1st Fairy in A Midsummer Night's Dream; made her first appearance in London at the Victoria Palace, 26 Dec 1931, as the Prince in The Windmill Man; subsequently gained a scholarship for six years at the Italia Conti Stage School; at the Royalty, Sept 1935, played Pamela in Closing At Sunrise; St Martin's, Oct 1937, played Doris in Autumn; Haymarket, June 1938, appeared as Vivian Morris in Comedienne; at the Saville, Mar 1939, played Freda Johnson in the revival of Johnson Over Jordan; at the Malvern Festival, 1939, appeared in Old Master; during the war toured for ENSA, in Old Master, Gaslight, and In Good King Charles's Golden Days; also at the Saville, Mar 1943, played Ellen Curtis in Junior Miss; Phoenix, July 1947, Mrs Corcoran in Dr Angelus; St James's, Sept 1948, Valentine in Don't Listen, Ladies!; appeared in revues at the Irving Theatre Club, 1950–1; at the Edinburgh Festival, 1951, appeared in the revue After The Show; Royal Court, Apr 1953, played in the revue Airs On A Shoestring, which ran for nearly two years; at the same theatre, June 1955, appeared in the revue From Here and There; Apollo, Feb 1958, played Lady ffoyte-Bowen in Keep Your Hair On; Lyric, Hammersmith, June 1958, Clare Carter in Honour Bright; Coliseum, Dec 1958, Fairy Godmother in Cinderella; Phoenix, Apr 1961, appeared in the revue On the Brighter Side; Savoy, Apr 1962, appeared in the revue A Thurber Carnival; Vaudeville, Apr 1964, played Opal in Everybody Loves Opal; Leatherhead, Nov 1964, played Winnie in Honey, I'm Home; Saville, Sept 1965, Salome and Cleopatra in The Overdog; Malvern Festival, July–Aug 1966, Madame Yvonne in The Laundry and Elizabeth in The Castaways; Richmond, Oct 1970, Lady Audley in Lady Audley's Secret; Shaw, Mar 1974, Lady Bracknell in The Importance of Being Earnest; Royal Court, July 1975, Mrs Prentice in What the Butler Saw, transferring to the Whitehall; Royal Court, Sept 1976, Mrs Johnson in Mothers Day; Strand, Jan 1977, took over Eleanor Hunter in No Sex Please—We're British; Oxford Festival, June 1979, played Lady Markby in An Ideal Husband, and the Duchess of Berwick in Lady Windermere's Fan; first appeared in films 1941, in Ships With Wings, and has since appeared in The Lovers, Let's Get Married, The Big Day, etc; television appearances include: *On the Bright Side*; she broadcast for eleven years in the series *Beyond Our Ken* and *Round the Horne*.

Address: c/o Fraser & Dunlop, 91 Regent Street, London, W1.

MARSHALL, Armina, producer, actress, playwright
b Alfalfa County, Oklahoma, 1900; *d* of Chalmers Marshall and his wife Elizabeth (Armina); *e* Anaheim, Cal, High School, University of Cal at Los Angeles; *m* Lawrence Langner, the producer (dec); mother of Philip Langner, with whom she is co-director of the Theater Guild; prepared for the stage at the American Academy of Dramatic Arts.

First appeared in New York at the Garrick, 25 Dec 1922, as a Nun in The Tidings Brought to Mary; same theater, Feb 1923, Kari in Peer Gynt; Jan 1924, Maid in The Race with the Shadow; Mar 1924, Mrs Blazy in Fata Morgana, Feb 1925, Mary in Ariadne; Guild, Oct 1925, Kati in The Glass Slipper; same theater, Dec 1925, Germaine Bachelet in Merchants of Glory; Feb 1927, Signora Ponza in Right Your Are If You Think You Are; Garrick, Apr 1927, Anne in Mr Pim Passes By; Biltmore, Apr 1929, Emily Bender in Man's Estate; Golden, Feb 1930, May Williston in Those We Love; 48th Street, Oct 1931, Lona Hessel in The Pillars of Society; Fulton, Dec 1931, Dorine in The Bride the Sun Shines On; Jul 1933, appeared in a tour of The Noble Prize; Music Box, Sept 1935, Mrs Gordon in If This Be Treason; retired from acting and, with her husband, wrote the plays The Pursuit of Happiness, produced at the Avon, NY 9 Oct 1933, On to Fortune, produced at the Fulton in Feb 1935, Suzanna and the Elders, Morosco, Oct 1940; also (with her husband) adapted Doctor Knock, 1936; for the Theatre Guild produced The Millionairess, Aug 1938; co-directed the Stage Door Canteen in Washington, DC, during World War II; supervised the production of Foolish Notion at the Martin Beck, Mar 1945; also The Iceman Cometh at the Martin Beck, Mar 1946; Theater Guild productions she has co-presented include Absurd Person Singular, 1974; Golda, 1977; director and trustee of the American Shakespeare Festival Theater and Academy at Stratford, Conn, founded by her husband; Chairman of the Board of the American Theater Society since 1958; Trustee of the American Academy of Dramatic Arts; as co-director of the Theater Guild headed its department of radio and TV 1948–62, overseeing many of its dramatic broadcasts; The Pursuit of Happiness was adapted into the musical Arms and the Girl in 1950.

Address: Theater Guild, 226 West 47th Street, New York, NY 10036. *Tel:* 265–1670.

MARSHALL, E G, actor
b Owatonna, Minn, 18 June; *e* Carlton College and University of Minnesota.

Made his stage debut with the touring repertory company The Oxford players in 1933; made his New York debut with the Federal Theater Project, Ritz, 19 Sept 1938, as Henry Onstott in Prologue to Glory; same troupe, Oct 1938, played in The Big Blow; Hudson, Jan 1942, Humphrey Crocker in Jason; Plymouth, Nov 1942, Mr Fitzpatrick in The Skin of Our Teeth; New Amsterdam Roof, Nov 1943, Gramp Maple in The Petrified Forest; Martin Beck, Mar 1944, Brigadier in Jacobowsku and the Colonel; Coronet, Oct 1945, Dave in Beggars Are Coming to Town; Belasco, Apr 1946, Sims in

Woman Bites Dog; Martin Beck, Oct 1946, Willie Oban in The Iceman Cometh; Ogunquit, Maine, Playhouse, Aug 1947, Judas in Dear Judas; Playhouse, Jan 1948, Finlay Decker in The Survivors; Maxine Elliot's, Apr 1948, Doc in Hope Is the Thing with Feathers; toured as Emmet in The Silver Whistle, Aug 1948; Lyceum, Oct 1952, Ernest Bruni in The Gambler; Martin Beck, Jan 1953, Reverend John Hale in The Crucible, and subsequently took over from Arthur Kennedy as John Proctor in the same production; Booth, Dec 1955, Brennan in Red Roses for Me; Phoenix, Mar 1956, Ferrante in Queen After Death; John Golden, Apr 1956, Vladimir in Waiting for Godot; Studebaker, Chicago, Ill, Nov 1956, Ephraim Cabot in Desire Under the Elms; Ambassador, Oct 1959, Walter Rafferty in The Gang's All Here; Vivian Beaumont, Oct 1967, Oscar Hubbard in The Little Foxes; Ethel Barrymore, Dec 1967, Benjamin Hubbard in The Little Foxes; Plymouth, 1969, took over as Sam Nash, Jesse Kiplinger, and Roy Hubley in Plaza Suite; Walnut Street, Philadelphia, Nov 1971, played in The Imaginary Invalid; Virginia Museum, Richmond, Feb 1973, played Macbeth; Helen Hayes, May 1973, appeared in the revue Nash at Nine; Long Wharf, New Haven, Conn, Oct 1973, Halvard Solness in The Master Builder; Peachtree Playhouse, Atlanta, Ga, Jan 1975, Phillip Hammer in The Sponsor; Cottesloe, June 1977, Walter F Bickmore in the National Theatre production of Old Movies; John Golden, 1978, took over as Walter Martin in The Gin Game; made his film debut in The House on 92nd Street, 1945, and has since played in 13 Rue Madeleine, Call Northside 777, The Caine Mutiny, Twelve Angry Men, Compulsion, The Pursuit of Happiness, Interiors, Superman, etc; has appeared regularly on television since 1947 in various dramatic programs, notably The Little Foxes, Clash by Night, The Plot to Kill Stalin, The Shrike (London, 1960) in the series *The Defenders,* for which he received the Emmy Award (1963), the series *The Bold Ones,* etc.

Recreations: Writing, cycling. *Address:* Actors Equity Association, 165 West 46th Street, New York, NY 10036.

MARSHALL, Norman, CBE, director
b Rawalpindi, India, 16 Nov 1901; *s* of Lt-Col Daniel Grove Marshall, IMS, and his wife Elizabeth (Mackie); *e* Edinburgh Academy and Worcester College, Oxford.

Formerly a journalist; after some experience as an actor on tour, joined the Cambridge Festival Theatre, 1926, as stage director; was later appointed one of the resident directors to the theatre, his first production being The Rumour, Feb 1927; subsequently directed The Insect Play, Emperor Jones, Beggar on Horseback, The Knight of the Burning Pestle, The Shoemaker's Holiday, etc; during 1928–9, was also guest-director to the Leeds Civic Playhouse; his first London production was Paul Among the Jews, at the Prince of Wales (for the Stage Society), June 1928; at the London Opera Festival, 1929, directed Handel's Julius Caesar; took over the direction of the Cambridge Festival Theatre, 1932, directing Marco Millions, Bastos the Bold, Love for Love, etc; Alhambra, 1932, produced A Kiss in Spring; assumed the direction of the Gate Theatre, London, 1934, and directed most of the plays presented there, including: Miracle in America, 1934; Victoria Regina, 1935; Lysistrata, Parnell, Oscar Wilde, The Children's Hour, 1936; Tobacco Road, Mr Gladstone, Elizabeth, la Femme sans Homme, 1937; The Masque of Kings, 1938; Asmodée, Of Mice and Men, 1939; also directed several of the plays of Jean Jacques Bernard and the annual Gate revues; went into management in the West End, in Nov 1936, when he presented Parnell at the New Theatre; June 1937, presented Victoria Regina at the Lyric, in association with Gilbert Miller; went into management in New York, Oct 1938, presenting Oscar Wilde at the Fulton Theatre; presented The Gate Revue at the Ambassadors', London, Mar 1939, and Of Mice and Men at the Apollo, May 1939; in addition to plays presented under his own management directed Because We Must, 1937; Elizabeth, 1938; The Intruder, 1939; Cousin Muriel, The Jersey Lily, Les Parents Terribles, Boys in Brown, 1940; presented and directed Swinging the Gate, at the Ambassadors', May 1940; served in the Army, 1940–2; returned to the theatre, at end of 1942, and directed The Petrified Forest, Globe, Dec 1942; then formed his own company, in association with the Arts Theatre, Cambridge, and CEMA; during the next eighteen months, directed at Cambridge and on tour, an extensive repertory of plays; also directed in various London Theatres, Uncle Vanya, 1943; A Soldier for Christmas, Madeleine, The Banbury Nose, 1944; The First Gentleman, 1945; To-Morrow's Child, 1946; Less Than Kind, Boys in Brown, Maya, Child's Play, 1947; Canaries Sometimes Sing, The Indifferent Shepherd, The Paragon, A La Carte, Miss Mabel, 1948; toured, 1949, in the British, French and American zones of Germany, with his productions of Hamlet, and Man and Superman; toured, 1950, in France, for the British Council with a Shakespearean repertoire, followed by a production of Twelfth Night at the Florence Festival, and subsequent tour of Italy; on his return directed Background, View Over the Park, 1950; toured in India and Pakistan, for the British Council, from Nov 1950, with abridged versions of nearly a dozen Shakespearean plays; returned to England, and directed The Day's Mischief, 1951; directed The Starcross Legend, The Player King (Edinburgh Festival), Sweet Peril, 1952; also in 1952, visited Israel and at the Kamerny Theatre, directed Volpone; directed The Pet Shop, His Eminence of England, The Crooked Finger, The Snow Was Black, Oddly Enough, 1953; We Must Kill Toni, Hail Caledonia! (Edinburgh Festival), 1954; Love Is News, 1955; All in the Family, 1959; Johnny the Priest, 1960; Nothing is For Free, Teresa of Avila, 1961; Fit to Print, 1962; Romeo and Juliet, Hamlet (last two plays in South Africa), 1964; The Fighting Cock (Chichester Festival), 1966; The Duel, 1968; The Cathedral (Canterbury Festival), 1969; Enemies (Durban), 1972; Head of Drama for Associated Rediffusion Ltd, 1955–9; author of The Other Theatre, The Producer and the Play; editor of the Chiltern edition of The Comedies of Congreve; part-author of The Essentials of Stage Planning; Chairman of The British Council's Drama Committee, 1961–8; Chairman of the Association of British Theatre Technicians, 1961–73; Chairman of the British Theatre Association; Vice-chairman of Theatres' Advisory Council, 1963–74; joint-chairman (with Sir Laurence Olivier) of the National Theatre Building Committee; a Governor of the Old Vic; in 1954, was Shute Lecturer on the Drama at the University of Liverpool; has also lectured on the theatre throughout the world; received the CBE in the Birthday Honours, 1975.

Club: Garrick. Address: 9 Arundel Court, Jubilee Place, London, SW3. *Tel:* 01–352 0456.

MARTELL, Gillian, actress
b Dunstable, Beds, 15 Mar 1936; *d* of Harry Martell, and his wife Mary (Garner); *e* Convent of the Holy Ghost, Bedford; *m* David Cockshott; trained for the stage at RADA winning the Bancroft Gold Medal.

First appeared on the stage in Aug 1956 at the Colchester Repertory Theatre, as Claudia in Claudia; her repertory experience included a period at the Nottingham Playhouse and her London début, June 1961, at the Duchess, was in the part of Alice Fuller in Celebration, which she had played at Nottingham; again at Nottingham, May 1965, played Marie Jeanne in The Cavern; Royal Court, Dec 1965, Mrs Hitchcock in Serjeant Musgrave's Dance, later taking over the part of Annie; at the same theatre, she has since played Mrs Touchwood in A Chaste Maid in Cheapside and Miss Partlip in The Dancers, Jan 1966; Honor Voysey in The Voysey Inheritance, Apr 1966; Jessie Sutherland in Their Very Own and Golden City, May 1966; Gentlewoman in Macbeth and Madame Azhogina in A Provincial Life, Oct 1966; Peg Levin in Backbone, Feb 1968; Trixie in Trixie and Baba, Aug 1968; Isabelle Rimbaud in Total Eclipse, Sept 1968; Georgina in Narrow Road to the Deep North, Feb 1969; Lady Froth in The Double Dealer, July 1969; Vi in Come and Go and Woman 2 in Play, Apr 1970; Stratford, Ontario, Summer, 1970, played Mrs Elvsted in Hedda Gabler; Hampstead, Nov 1971, played the novelist's wife in The Novelist; Royal Court, May 1973, Jessica Tilehouse in The Sea; same theatre, Aug 1974, Judith Shakespeare in Bingo; also Mary Lamb in The Fool, Nov 1975; Royal Court, Oct 1977, Mrs Shin in The Good Woman of Setzuan; Duke of York's, Feb 1980, Malpass in Rose; television, since 1956, includes This Happy Breed, The Winslow Boy, *Two's Company* and *Chalk and Cheese*.

Favourite parts: Trixie, Georgina. *Club:* Buckstone. *Address:* c/o Crouch Associates, 59 Frith Street, London W1. *Tel:* 01–734 2167.

MARTIN, Christopher (John Christopher Martin), actor, director, and designer
b New York City, 7 Dec 1942; *s* of the actor and writer Ian Martin and his wife, actress Inge (Adams); *e* New York University (BS, MA 1967).

Early experience as a rock musician with his band The Ramblers, and others; directed plays while at NYU, starting with The Caretaker, 1963, and formed his own repertory company there; in Dec 1967 founded CSC Repertory (the Classic Stage Company) and has since presented, directed and designed over 60 productions for the company; many of these were his own adaptations, including Moby Dick, Woyzeck, Rashomon, The Hound of the Baskervilles, Tartuffe, Hedda Gabler, Rosmersholm, The Marquis of Keith, and Don Juan; among the many leading roles he has played with the company are Tanner and Don Juan in Man and Superman, Astrov in Uncle Vanya, Creon in Antigone, Thomas Mendip in The Lady's Not for Burning, Max in The Homecoming, Ben Jonson in Bingo, and title roles in Hamlet, Richard II, and Serjeant Musgrave's Dance; has taught at NYU and Fordham, etc; founding president of the Off-Off Broadway Alliance, 1972–75.

Favourite parts: Max in The Homecoming, Ben Jonson in Bingo, Falstaff. *Address:* 564 Hudson Street, New York, NY 10014. *Tel:* 677 4210.

MARTIN, Elliot, producer
b Denver, Colorado, 25 Feb 1924; *s* of Will H Martin and his wife Elma A (Harvey); *e* University of Denver, 1943–46; *m* Majorie E Cuesta.

Made his debut in London at Drury Lane, 30 Apr 1947, as Fred in Oklahoma!; returned to the US and toured as an understudy in Allegro, 1948; made his New York debut at the Mark Hellinger, 25 Nov 1949, as a Prospector and a Neighbor in Texas, Li'l Darlin', for which he was also assistant stage manager; became executive assistant of the Westport, Conn, Country Playhouse, 1951; manager-director for a season of stock at the Bahama Playhouse, Nassau, BWI, and stage manager for the Westport Country Playhouse, 1952; production stage manager in New York for at Home with Ethel Waters, In the Summer House, 1953; The Girl on the Via Flaminia, Home is the Hero, Portrait of a Lady, 1954; Phoenix '55, The Heavenly Twins, 1955; The Innkeepers, Little Glass Clock, Long Day's Journey into Night, 1956; tour of The Matchmaker, 1957; tours of Inherit the Wind and The remarkable Mr Pennypacker, 1958; A Majority of One, 1959; The Unsinkable Molly Brown, 1960; co-produced his first play in New York, The Painted Days, at the Theatre Marquee, 6 Apr 1961; co-produced The Captains and the Kings, Seidman and Son, Never Too Late, 1962; co-produced Never Too Late in London at the Prince of Wales, 24 Sept 1963; co-produced Nobody Loves an Albatross, NY, 1963; Mating Dance, 1965; Dinner at Eight, 1966; More Stately Mansions, 1967; The Wrong Way Light Bulb, 1969; Abelard and Heloise, 1971; Emperor Henry IV, 1973; A Moon for the Misbegotten (which received a special Antoinette Perry 'Tony' Award), When You Comin' Back, Red Rider?, 1974; Of Mice and Men, Conversations with an Irish Rascal, 1975; tour of Morning's at Seven, 1976; Dirty Linen and New Found Land, Caesar and Cleopatra, A Touch of the Poet, 1977; The Kingfisher, 1978; Daisy Mayme (tour), 1979; Clothes for a Summer Hotel, 1980; Director of the Center Theater Group, Los Angeles, 1966–71, where he was responsible for sixteen world premieres and presented both the National Theatre Company of Great Britain and the Royal Shakespeare Company.

Recreation: Theatre. *Address:* 152 West 58th Street, New York, NY. *Tel:* 245 4176.

MARTIN, Ernest H, manager and producer

b Pittsburgh, Pa, 28 Aug 1919; *s* of Samuel Markowitz and his wife Cecilia (Sklar); *e* University of California in Los Angeles; *m* Nancy Guild.

His first production on Broadway, in association with Cy Feuer, was at the St James, 11 Oct 1948, when he presented Where's Charley?; has since presented, all in association with Cy Feuer, Guys and Dolls, 1950; Can-Can, 1953; The Boy Friend, 1954; Silk Stockings, 1955; Whoop-Up, 1958; How to Succeed in Business Without Really Trying, 1961; Little Me, 1962; Skyscraper, 1965; Walking Happy, 1966; The Goodbye People, 1968; The Act, 1977; with Mr Feuer co-managing director of the Los Angeles and San Francisco Civic Light Opera Association, 1975–; 1960–5, with Mr Feuer, operated the Lunt-Fontanne Theatre; with Mr Feuer produced the films Cabaret, 1972 and Piaf, 1974.

Address: 505 Park Avenue, New York, NY. *Tel:* Plaza 9–4004.

MARTIN, Mary, actress and singer

b Weatherford, Texas, 1 Dec 1913; *d* of Preston Martin and his wife Junita (Pressly); *e* Ward Belmont School, Nashville, Tenn, and University of Texas; *m* (1) Benjamin Hagman (mar dis); (2) Richard Halliday (dec); after leaving school, she studied and taught dancing.

Made her first appearance in public at the Trocadero Night Club, Hollywood, as a vocalist; made her first appearance on the regular stage at the Imperial Theatre, 9 Nov 1938, as Dolly Winslow in Leave It to Me; she then went to Hollywood, and made her first appearance in films, 1939, in The Great Victor Herbert, and remained in Hollywood until 1943, appearing in Rhythym on the River, Love Thy Neighbor, Kiss the Boys Good-Bye, New York Town, The Birth of the Blues, Star-Spangled Rhythm, Happy-Go-Lucky; at the Shubert, Boston, Mar 1943, appeared in Dancing in the Streets; reappeared in New York, at the Imperial, Oct 1943, Venus in One Touch of Venus, which ran until Feb 1945, and

toured in the same part until June 1945; toured, Dec 1945, and at the Plymouth, Feb 1946, played Tchao-Ou-Niang in Lute Song; again appeared in films, 1945, in Night and Day; made her first appearance on the London stage at Drury Lane, 19 Dec 1946, as Elena Salvador in Pacific 1860; toured all over the United States, 1947–8, as Annie Oakley in Annie Get Your Gun; Majestic, Apr 1949–June, 1951, Ensign Nellie Forbush in South Pacific; appeared in the same part in London at Drury Lane, Nov 1951; Alvin, NY, Nov 1953, Jane Kimball in Kind Sir; Curran, San Francisco, July 1954, appeared as Peter Pan; played the same part at the Philharmonic Auditorium, Los Angeles, Aug 1954, and at the Winter Garden, NY, Oct 1954; Sarah Bernhardt Theatre, Paris, June 1955, Sabina in The Skin of Our Teeth; toured in the same part July–Aug 1955 and at the ANTA Playhouse, NY, Aug–Sept 1955; Curran, San Francisco, June 1957, Nellie Forbush in a revival of South Pacific; same theatre, Aug 1957, Annie Oakley in a revival of Annie Get Your Gun; toured America in 1958 in a one-woman show Music with Mary Martin; Lunt-Fontanne, NY, Nov 1959, Maria von Trapp in The Sound of Music, for which she received the Theatre Wing's Tony Award, and also the New York Drama Critics' Award, 1959–60; Majestic, Oct 1963, Jennie Malone in Jennie; toured US and Vietnam, Tokyo, 1965, as Dolly Gallagher Levi in Hello, Dolly! subsequently appearing in the same role at Drury Lane, London, Dec 1965; 46th Street, NY, Nov 1966, Agnes in I Do! I Do!-and toured in this part for a year, beginning in Apr 1968; Imperial, 26 Mar 1972, appeared in A Celebration of Richard Rodgers; Forty-Sixth Street, Jan 1978, Lidya Vasilyevna in Do You Turn Somersaults?; has made several television appearances, including America Applauds, 1951, Ford's 50th Anniversary Show, 1953, the musical Peter Pan, 1955 and 1956, Annie Get Your Gun, 1957, the double appearance Mar 1959, in Magic with Mary Martin for children and Music with Mary Martin for adults, Together with Friends (with Noel Coward), Valentine, 1979, etc; her book Needlepoint published in 1969; wrote her autobiography My Heart Belongs, 1976.

Recreation: Needlepoint. *Address:* Actors Equity Association, 165 West 46th Street, New York, NY 10036

MARTIN, Millicent, actress

b Romford, Essex, 8 June 1934; *d* of William Andrew Martin and his wife Violet Eileen (Bedford); *e* St Mary's Convent School, Romford; *m* (1) Ronnie Carroll (mar dis); (2) Norman Eshley (mar dis); (3) Marc Alexander; studied for the stage at the Italia Conti Stage School.

Made her first appearance on the stage at the Royal Opera House, Covent Garden, 1948, in the children's chorus of The Magic Flute; Winter Garden, Oct 1948, appeared as a Handmaiden in The Lute Song; made her first appearance in New York at the Royale, Sept 1954, as Nancy in The Boy Friend; appeared at the Bucks County Playhouse, NY, Sept 1957, as Dejanira in Mistress of the Inn; Coconut Grove, Miami, Oct 1957, played Polly Brown in The Boy Friend; on returning to England, appeared at the Saville, Apr 1958, as Maisie in Expresso Bongo; Cambridge, Sept 1959 played Cora in The Crooked Mile, and made an instant success; Lyric, Hammersmith, Mar 1960, played Marion Laverne in The Dancing Heiress; Saville, Aug 1961, appeared in the revue The Lord Chamberlain Regrets; Pembroke, Croydon, May 1962, played Judy in State of Emergency; Shaftesbury, Dec 1964, played Tweenie in the musical Our Man Crichton; she also appeared in the Royal Variety Performance, Nov 1964; Scala, Dec 1967, Peter in Peter Pan; Chichester Festival, July 1968, Sabina in The Skin of Our Teeth; Hampstead Theatre Club, Dec 1970, and Fortune, Jan 1971, played three parts in the collection Tonight At Eight; Chichester Festival, May 1972, Polly Peachum in The Beggars' Opera; Queen's, July 1973; Ruth Earp in The Card; Vaudeville, Jan 1975, took over the part of Marion in Absurd Person Singular; Mermaid, May 1976, appeared in Side by Side by Sondheim, and transferred to Wyndham's, subsequently playing in the show on Broadway at the Music Box (May 1977) and the Huntington Hartford, Los Angeles; Minskoff, NY, Nov 1978, Madeleine in King of Hearts; first entered films, 1960 and has been seen in Alfie and Nothing But the Best, etc; made her first appearance on television 1958, and has since appeared in *That Was The Week That Was*, etc, she has also appeared in her own television series *Mainly Millicent*, and, more recently, in Song by Song; her television Awards include: the TV Society Award, Spanish Ondus Television Award (1963), Light Entertainment Award (1964).

Favourite parts: Polly Peachum, and parts in Side By Side By Sondheim. *Recreations:* Swimming, diving, music, cooking. *Address:* c/o London Management, 235–241 Regent Street, London, W1.

MARTIN, Vivienne, actress
b Kartaia, New Zealand, 28 Dec 1936; *d* of Douglas Martin and his wife Nadia (Billcliffe); *e* Wellington College, NZ; trained for the stage at RADA.

First appeared on the stage 15 Dec 1954, at the Playhouse, Oxford, as Moonbeam in Listen to the Wind; first appeared on the London stage in Feb 1956 at the Winter Garden, taking over Lily Bell in The Water Gipsies; at the Palace, Aug 1959, appeared in The Benny Hill Show; New, 1963, took over the part of Nancy in Oliver!; Morosco, May 1964, made her New York début in The Sunday Man; St Martin's, Apr 1965, appeared in Chaganog; Globe, Mar 1966, Kate in The Matchgirls; Saville, Oct 1966, Mary Grimaldi in Joey, Joey; Comedy, June 1967, Queenie in Queenie; played various parts in repertory at Nottingham Playhouse, including Grace Shelley in The Ruling Class, Nov 1968, repeating the part at the Piccadilly, Feb 1969; Palladium, 1968, took over Lorna Moon in Golden Boy; toured, 1970, as Golde in Fiddler On the Roof; toured Australia with Prospect Productions, May 1972, playing several parts and returning with the company to the Aldwych to play Regan in King Lear, June 1972; Belgrade, Coventry, Aug 1972, Dru Brown in Saturnalia; Playhouse, Weston-super-Mare, Mar 1973, appeared in The Starving Rich; Salisbury, July 1973, Olive in Summer of the Seventeenth Doll; Thorndike, Leatherhead, Oct 1974, Anna in Time and Time Again; Savoy, July 1976, Sue Long in Banana Ridge; Her Majesty's, Oct 1978, Sylvia in Bar Mitzvah Boy; films include: The Belles of St Trinian's; has appeared frequently on television.

Favourite part: Nancy. *Recreations:* Reading, travelling. *Address:* c/o Green & Underwood Ltd, 11 Garrick Street, London WC2E 9AR. *Tel:* 01–836 0411.

MASON, Beryl, actress
b Chatham, Kent, 30 Apr 1921; *d* of Sydney Charles Mason and his wife Lydia Agnes (McBride); *e* St Joseph's Convent, Sidcup; *m* David Wiggins; studied for the stage under Italia Conti.

Made her first appearance on the stage at the Holborn Empire, 15 Dec 1934, in Where the Rainbow Ends; Savoy, Oct 1936, appeared in Going Places, and at the Vaudeville, Dec 1936, in The Sleeping Beauty; London Hippodrome, Oct 1937, understudied Patricia Burke as Rene in Hide and Seek, and in Apr 1938, went on tour, playing this part; Palace, Nov 1938, understudied Leonora Corbett and, on occasions, played Carol Markoff in Under Your Hat, which ran until

1940; Prince of Wales's, Birmingham, Dec 1940, played Prince Pekoe in Aladdin; toured, Apr 1941, with George Formby, for ENSA; toured, Sept 1941, as Josephine in Lady Be Good; Comedy, June 1942, appeared in It's About Time; toured, Oct 1942, as Nina in Vintage Wine, and played the same part at the Comedy, May 1943; Comedy, June 1943, appeared as Irene Tomkin in The Fur Coat, and Nov 1943, as Gabrielle in This Time It's Love; toured, June 1944, in That Moon Again; Q, Sept 1944, played Phyllis Hapgood in Fly Away Peter . . .; same theatre, Dec 1944, and Comedy, Jan 1945, played Penelope Toop in See How They Run, which ran throughout the year; Comedy, Dec 1946, Katie Jones in The Man from the Ministry; toured, Sept 1948, in Cloudburst; Embassy, Apr 1949, played Daphne Wray in On Monday Next . . ., and appeared in the same part at the Comedy, June 1949, where the play ran until July 1950; toured, 1951, as Susan Dyer in Who On Earth!; toured, 1952, as Judy Sullivan in Love's A Nuisance; New, Bromley, Nov 1953, played Kate in Tea For Three; Hippodrome, Dec 1956, played Mrs Kirrin in The Famous Five; 1966–70, Bournemouth, Blackpool, Torquay and Great Yarmouth, has appeared in Wedding Fever for the Summer Season, except for 1969, when she appeared at Blackpool in His Favourite Family; Sept 1970, toured South Africa in Wedding Fever and Don't Tell the Wife; summer season, Torquay, 1971, Mrs Jameson in The Mating Game; Cliftonville, summer 1972, Edna in Don't Tell the Wife; toured New Zealand, 1973, in The Mating Game; has also appeared on television, notably in the series *Not in Front of the Children*, and *Crossroads*; first appeared in films, 1936, in Accused.

Favourite part: Nina in Vintage Wine. *Recreations:* Tennis and crossword puzzles. *Address:* 52 Coniston Court, Holland Road, Hove BN3 1JU. *Tel:* Brighton 779797.

MASON, Brewster, actor
b Kidsgrove, Staffordshire, 30 Aug 1922; *s.* of Jesse Mason and his wife Constance May (Kemp); *m* (1) Lorna Whittaker (mar dis); (2) Kate Meredith; studied for the stage at the Royal Academy of Dramatic Art (Bancroft Gold Medal).

Made his first appearance on the stage, while still a student at RADA, at the Finsbury Park Open Air Theatre, Aug 1947, as Dick Dudgeon in The Devil's Disciple; first appeared as a professional actor at the Lyric, Hammersmith, Sept 1948, as Flt/Sgt John Nabb in An English Summer; appeared as a member of the Brighton Repertory Company, 1948–9; Lyric, Hammersmith, Aug 1949, played Caesar French in The King of Friday's Men; Phoenix, June 1951, played Polixenes in The Winter's Tale, and Jan 1952, Borachio in Much Ado About Nothing; Lyric, Hammersmith, Dec 1952, played the Earl of Northumberland in Richard II, Feb 1953, Sir Wilful Witwoud in The Way of the World, and May 1953, Bedemar in Venice Preserved; at the Rhodes Centenary, Bulawayo, July 1953, with the same company again played Northumberland in Richard II; at the Haymarket, 1954, during the run of A Day by the Sea, appeared as Dr Farley; Princes, Dec 1954, played Mr Badger in Toad of Toad Hall; Haymarket, Nov 1957, played David Bowman in Flowering Cherry; Comedy, Mar 1960, played Victor Hodges, QC, in Look on Tempests; Haymarket, Aug 1960, took over the part of General Allenby in Ross; made his first appearance in New York, at the Henry Miller Theatre, Sept 1962, as Sir Lewis Eliot in The Affair; joined the Royal Shakespeare Company at the Aldwych, London, Feb 1963, to play Kent in King Lear, subsequently appearing at the Royal Shakespeare, Stratford, July 1963, as the Earl of Warwick in the trilogy The Wars of the Roses; at the Aldwych, Jan 1964, again appeared in The Wars of the

Roses; Aldwych, June 1964, played Goldberg in The Birthday Party; Royal Shakespeare, Stratford, July 1964, again played The Earl of Warwick in The Wars of the Roses; 1965 season, played Antonio in The Merchant of Venice, Boyet in Love's Labour's Lost, Alcibiades in Timon of Athens, and Claudius and Ghost in Hamlet; since then he has played the following parts, at Stratford, unless otherwise indicated: The Judge in The Government Inspector, Claudius and the Ghost in Hamlet, Sir Toby Belch in Twelfth Night, Menenius in Coriolanus, Lafeu in All's Well That Ends Well, Banquo in Macbeth, 1967; toured Finland and Russia in the latter two productions, Nov 1967, and Jan 1968, appeared in them at the Aldwych; the name part in Julius Caesar and Falstaff in The Merry Wives of Windsor (also Aldwych), Sir Tunbelly Clumsy in The Relapse (Aldwych), 1968; the Duke of Florence in Women Beware Women, Wolsey in King Henry the Eighth, Falstaff in The Merry Wives of Windsor, 1969; Andrew Undershaft in Major Barbara (Aldwych), Wolsey in King Henry the Eighth (Aldwych), 1970; Othello 1971, and Aldwych, July 1972; also toured Japan in this part; season 1975, Falstaff in both parts of Henry IV, and also in the Merry Wives of Windsor, repeating these parts at the Aldwych, Jan–Mar 1976; 1976–9 directed three plays at the Monomoy Theatre, Cape Cod, Mass.; has lectured regularly on drama since 1970 at the University of California at Irvine; teaches regularly at the Guildhall School of Music and Drama, of which he was elected a Fellow in 1976; films in which he has appeared include: The Dam Busters, Private Potter, etc; first appeared on television, 1953, subsequent appearances include: *Edward VII* and *The Pallisers*.

Favourite parts: Lopakhin, General Allenby, Othello and Falstaff. *Recreations:* Golf, reading and painting. *Clubs:* Naval, Garrick, Stage Golfing, Players' (NY). *Address:* c/o ICM Ltd, 22 Grafton Street, London W1.

MASON, James, actor
b Huddersfield, Yorks, 15 May 1909; *s* of John Mason and his wife Mabel Hattersley (Gaunt); *e* Marlborough College and Peterhouse College, Cambridge; *m* (1) Pamela Kellino (mar dis); (2) Clarissa Kaye; was intended to follow the profession of an architect.

Made his first appearance on the stage at the Theatre Royal, Aldershot, 23 Nov 1931, as Prince Ivan in The Rascal; made his first appearance in London at the Arts Theatre, 30 Apr 1933, as Oliver Brown in Gallows Glorious, playing the same part at the Shaftesbury, May 1933; joined the company of the Old Vic-Sadler's Wells, Sept 1933, and during the season played Valentine in Twelfth Night, Yasha in The Cherry Orchard, Cromwell in Henry VIII, Claudio in Measure for Measure, Jeremy in Love for Love, etc; New Theatre, June 1934, played the Earl of Arran and Paris in Queen of Scots; played with the Dublin Gate Theatre company 1934–37; Gate, London, Apr 1936, Captain O'Shea in Parnell; Embassy and Savoy, Mar 1937, Hannibal in The Road to Rome; Q, June 1937, Antoine in A Man Who Has Nothing; New, Sept 1937, Christopher Carson in Bonnet Over the Windmill; Gate, Nov 1938, Byron in The Heart Was Not Burned; St James's, May 1939, Henri Jouval in Sixth Floor; toured, Sept 1940, as John Garside in Divorce for Chrystabel; New Theatre, Oct 1941, played Paul Venner in Jupiter Laughs; first appeared on the New York stage at the Ethel Barrymore, 26 Mar 1947, as David in Bathsheba; at the Shakespearean Festival, Stratford, Ontario, 1954, appeared as Angelo in Measure for Measure, and Œdipus in Œdipus Rex; Playhouse, La Jolla, California, July 1957, Constantine Chase in Paul and Constantine; Playhouse, Ivoryton, Connecticut, Jul 1958, starred in Mid-Summer; Longacre, NY,

Apr 1979, played Frank in Faith Healer; author, with his first wife, of a book The Cats in Our Lives, for which he also supplied the drawings, 1949, and Favourite Cat Stories of James and Pamela Mason, 1957; entered films, 1935, in Late Extra, and the many notable films in which he has appeared include: Fanny By Gaslight, The Seventh Veil, The Wicked Lady, Odd Man Out, Rommel—The Desert Fox, Julius Caesar, The Trials of Oscar Wilde, The Pumpkin Eater, Lord Jim, Georgy Girl, Jesus of Nazareth, Heaven Can Wait, and The Boys from Brazil.

Address: c/o Al Parker Ltd, 50 Mount Street, Park Lane, London W1.

MASON, Marshall W, director
b Amarillo, Texas, 24 Feb 1940; *s* of Marvin Marshall Mason and his wife Lorine Chrisman (Hornsby); *e* Northwestern University (BS 1961); *m* Zita Litvinas (dec); trained for the stage at the Actors Studio.

Began directing at college, with Cat on a Hot Tin Roof, 1959; his first off-Broadway play was Little Eyolf, at the Actors' Playhouse, 1964; in 1965 began a long association with Lanford Wilson when he directed his Home Free; made his London directing debut with this play and The Madness of Lady Bright, Mercury, 1968; in Jul 1969 became the first Artistic Director of the Circle Repertory Company, which has been responsible for numerous world premiere productions as well as presenting the classics; his own notable productions here include The Hot 1 Baltimore, 1973; Battle of Angels, The Sea Horse, 1974; Harry Outside, The Mound Builders, 1975; Knock, Knock, Serenading Louie, 1976; Ulysses in Traction, 1977; The Fifth of July, 1978; Talley's Folly, Hamlet, Mary Stuart, 1979; on Broadway he made his directing debut with Knock, Knock, 1976; co-directed Gemini, 1977, and has since directed Murder at the Howard Johnson's, 1979; Talley's Folly, 1980; outside New York his work has been seen at the Mark Taper Forum, LA, PAF Playhouse, Huntington, Academy Festival Theater, Lakewood Ill, etc; for PBS TV directed The Mound Builders, 1975.

Recreations: Archaeology, travel. *Address:* 165 Christopher Street, New York, NY 10014. *Tel:* 691 3210.

MASSEY, Anna, actress
b Thakeham, Sussex, 11 Aug 1937; *d* of Raymond (Hart) Massey and his wife Adrianne (Allen); *e* London, New York, Switzerland, France, Italy; *m* Jeremy Brett (mar dis).

Made her first appearance on the stage at the Theatre Royal, Brighton, May 1955, as Jane in The Reluctant Debutante; subsequently making her first appearance in London at the Cambridge, May 1955, in the same play; left the cast in London to appear for the first time in New York, Henry Miller's, Oct 1956, to repeat her performance in The Reluctant Debutante; returned to England, and appeared at the Westminster, June 1957, as Penelope Shawn in Dear Delinquent; at the Edinburgh Festival, Lyceum, Aug 1958, played Monica Claverton-Ferry in The Elder Statesman, and appeared in this part at the Cambridge, London, Sept 1958; St Martin's, Feb 1960, played Jane in Special Providence (in a double-bill Double Yolk); Phoenix, Sept 1960, played Rose in The Last Joke; Royalty, Mar 1961, played Annie Sullivan in The Miracle Worker; Haymarket, Apr 1962, Lady Teazle in The School for Scandal; at the same theatre, May 1963, played Jennifer Dubedat in The Doctor's Dilemma; Her Majesty's, May 1964, Virginia Crawford in The Right Honourable Gentleman; Yvonne Arnaud Theatre, Guildford, Oct 1965, Laura Wingfield in The Glass Menagerie, subsequently appearing at the Haymarket, Dec 1965, in the same production; Wyndham's, Nov 1966, took over as Jean Brodie in The Prime of Miss Jean Brodie; Arnaud, Guildford, May 1967, Julia in First Day of a New Season; Apollo, Aug 1967, Candida in The Flip Side; Hampstead Theatre Club, Oct 1969, Rowena Highbury in This Space is Mine; Repertory, Birmingham, Jan 1970, Ophelia in Hamlet; Haymarket, Feb 1971, Joanna in Spoiled; Royal Court, May 1971, Ann in Slag; Old Vic, Feb 1975, for National Theatre, Ariadne Utterword in Heartbreak House; Aldwych, Aug 1975, for RSC, Gwendoline in Jingo; Royal Court, May 1976, First Woman in Play; Globe, Apr 1977, took over Lady Driver in Donkey's Years; National Theatre, May 1979, Marianne in Close of Play; made her first appearance on television, Oct 1955, as Jacqueline in Green of the Year, recent appearances include: The Mayor of Casterbridge, Rebecca and You're Not Watching Me, Mummy; first appearance in films as Sally in Gideon's Day, 1957; other films include: The Looking Glass War, Frenzy, Sweet William and Peeping Tom.

Recreation: Crossword puzzles. *Address:* c/o Boyack and Conway, 8 Cavendish Place, London W1.

MASSEY, Daniel (Raymond), actor
b London, 10 Oct 1933; *s* of Raymond (Hart) Massey and his wife Adrianne (Allen); *e* Eton and King's College, Cambridge; *m* (1) Adrienne Corri (mar dis); (2) Penelope Wilton.

Made his first appearance on the stage as a member of the Cambridge University Footlights Club, in Anything May, June 1956; first professional appearance Connaught, Worthing, July 1956, when he played Terry in Peril At End House; made his first appearance in New York, Ethel Barrymore Theatre, Jan 1957, as Lord Frederick Beckenham in Small War on Murray Hill; on his return to England, he made his first appearance in London at the Cambridge Theatre, Nov 1957, as Angier Duke in The Happiest Millionaire; Garrick, July 1958, appeared as a leading member of the company in the revue Living For Pleasure; Belgrade, Coventry, June 1959, played Johnnie Jackson in Dispersal; Theatre Royal, Stratford, Oct 1959, played Charlie in Make Me An Offer, subsequently appearing in the same production at the New, Dec 1959; Haymarket, Apr 1962, played Charles Surface in The School For Scandal; Nottingham Playhouse, Oct 1962, Athos in The Three Musketeers, and Nov 1962, George Jacob Holyoake in A Subject of Scandal and Concern; Eugene O'Neill, NY, Mar 1963, played Georg Nowack in the musical She Loves Me; Royal Court, London, Apr 1964, Mark Antony in Julius Caesar; Yvonne Arnaud Theatre, Guildford, May 1965, played Beliaev in A Month in the Country, and, June 1965, the Messenger in Samson Agonistes; Piccadilly, Nov 1965, Paul Bratter in Barefoot in the Park; Haymarket, Oct 1966, played Captain Absolute in The Rivals, and, Feb 1968, John Worthing in The Importance of Being Earnest; Close Theatre Club, Glasgow, Howarth in Spoiled; Wyndham's, Dec 1970, took over the part of Abelard in Abelard and Heloise; toured, Oct 1971, for Cambridge Theatre Company, as Tusenbach in Three Sisters and Tom Wrench in Trelawny of the Wells; Arnaud, Guildford, Mar 1972, played the title-role in Becket; Globe, Aug 1972, Gerald Popkiss in Popkiss; Uris, NY, Nov 1973, Gaston in Gigi; Phoenix, London, July 1974, Lytton Strachey in Bloomsbury; Albery, June 1975, Marquess of Quex in The Gay Lord Quex; Bristol Old Vic, Mar 1976, Laventry in Evening Light; Nottingham Playhouse, Oct 1976, title-rôle in Othello; Haymarket, Oct 1977, John Rosmer in Rosmersholm; for the National Theatre, Apr 1978, played Don Juan in Don Juan Comes Back from the War; June, Macduff in Macbeth; Nov, Robert in Betrayal; and in May 1979, took over the part of Charteris in the Philanderer; May Fair, Feb

1980, Henry James in Appearances; appeared in his first film, 1957, in Girls At Sea, subsequent films include: The Entertainer, and Star; has made numerous television appearances, including: The Roads to Freedom, and The Golden Bowl, Wings of Song, Able's Will and Heartbreak House.

Favourite parts: Rosmer, Lytton Strachey, Charteris. *Recreations:* Golf, gardening, classical music. *Address:* c/o Leading Artists Ltd, 60 St James's Street, London W1.

MASSEY, Raymond, actor and director
b Toronto, Canada, 30 Aug 1896; *s* of Chester Massey and his wife Anna (Vincent); *e* Appleby School, Ontario, Toronto University, and Balliol College, Oxford; *m* (1) Margery, *d* of Admiral Sir Sydney Fremantle (mar dis); (2) Adrianne Allen (mar dis); (3) Dorothy Ludington Whitney; served in the War, 1915–19, as Lieutenant in the Canadian Field Artillery, in France, 1916, where he was wounded, and in Siberia, 1918; instructor in gunnery and trench warfare at Yale and Princeton Universities, 1917–18.

Made his first appearance on the professional stage at the Everyman Theatre, July 1922, as Jack in In the Zone; at the Apollo, Oct 1922, played Roberts in Glamour; at the Everyman, Feb 1923, and Royalty, Apr 1923, James Bebb in At Mrs Beam's; Wyndham's, Dec 1923, Jones in The Rose and the Ring; Criterion, Feb 1924, Stanley Pitt in The Audacious Mr Squire; New, Mar 1924, Captain La Hire and Canon d'Estivet in Saint Joan; at the Prince's (for the Repertory Players), Mar 1925, played Lieut Gaythorne in Tunnel Trench, which he also directed; Wyndham's, May 1925, Jonty Drennan in The Round Table; at the Court (for the 300 Club), July 1925, and at the Playhouse, Aug 1925, played Captain Rickman in Prisoners of War; in Jan 1926, in conjunction with Allan Wade and George Carr, entered on the management of the Everyman Theatre, directing a number of plays, and gaining much experience in a variety of parts, notably Robert Mayo in Beyond the Horizon, Rufe Pryor in Hell-Bent for Heaven, Edmund Crowe in The Rat Trap, Mr Man in Brer Rabbit, Tommy Luttrell in The White Chateau, etc; at the Ambassadors', Apr 1927, made a notable hit when he played the Khan Aghaba in The Transit of Venus; Apollo (for the Venturers), June 1927, played the Rev MacMillan in An American Tragedy; Globe, Sept 1927, Reuben Manassa in The Golden Calf; Playhouse, Jan 1928, Austin Lowe in The Second Man; St Martin's, May 1928, Alister Ballantyne in Four People; New, June 1928, Joe Cobb in Spread Eagle; Garrick, Sept 1928, Lewis Dodd in The Constant Nymph; Globe, May 1929, Randolph Calthorpe in The Black Ace; Ambassadors', Jan 1930, Smitty in In the Zone, and Raymond Dabney in The Man in Possession; New, Oct 1930, Topaze in a play of that name; Phoenix, June 1931, Randall in Late Night Final; went to NY, and made his first appearance there, at the Broadhurst Theatre, 5 Nov 1931, as Hamlet; after returning to London, appeared at the Phoenix, Oct 1932, as Smith in Never Come Back; Adelphi, Nov 1932 (for King George's Pension Fund), Hiram Travers in Bulldog Drummond; Globe, Jan 1933, Dr Maclean in Doctor's Orders; at the Playhouse, Apr 1933, in conjunction with Gladys Cooper, directed The Rats of Norway, and played Hugh Sebastian; Lyric, Aug 1933, played Kurt von Hagen in The Ace; Nov 1933, Cleon in Acropolis; went to Canada, 1934, and co-produced and appeared at the Royal Alexandra, Toronto, Feb 1934, as David Linden in The Shining Hour, playing the same part at the Booth, NY, Feb 1934, and at the St James's, London, Sept 1934, also directing the play; National, NY, Jan 1936, played Ethan Frome in the play of that name; Apollo, London, Mar 1938, Harry Van in Idiot's Delight, which he also directed; Plymouth, NY, Oct 1938, Abraham Lincoln in Abe Lincoln in Illinois, which he played until 1940; Shubert, Mar 1941, Sir Colenso Ridgeon in The Doctor's Dilemma; Shubert, Apr 1942, James Havor Morell in Candida; joined the Canadian Army, 1942, and served as Major on Adjutant-General's Staff; invalided out, 1943; Plymouth Theatre, Nov 1943, played Rodney Boswell in Lovers and Friends; toured Europe, 1945, as the Stage Manager in the USO production of Our Town; Ethel Barrymore, Dec 1945, Henry Higgins in Pygmalion; Hudson, Sept 1947, played Prof Lemuel Stevenson in How in Wonder; in summer theatres, 1949, appeared in The Winslow Boy; Cort, Nov 1949, played the Captain in The Father, which he also directed; in summer theatres, 1950, appeared in Our Town; at the Civic Auditorium, Pasadena, Nov 1952, gave dramatic readings of the epic poem John Brown's Body; New Century, NY, Feb 1953, again gave dramatic readings of John Brown's Body and subsequently toured for nine months; at the opening of the American Shakespeare Festival Theatre, Stratford, Connecticut, July 1955, played Brutus in Julius Caesar and Prospero in The Tempest; Orpheum, Seattle, Sept 1957, Abraham Lincoln in The Rivalry; ANTA, NY, Dec 1958, Mr Zuss in JB; US tour, 1960, Abraham Lincoln in The Rivalry; reappeared on the London stage for the first time since 1938, at the Duke of York's, May 1970, as Tom Garrison in I Never Sang for My Father; Ahmanson, Los Angeles, Dec 1975, Nonno in The Night of the Iguana; he has also directed The White Château, An American Tragedy, The Wolves, The Crooked Billet, The Squall, 1927; Blackmail, Spread Eagle, 1928; The Sacred Flame, The Stag, The Silver Tassie, Symphony in Two Flats, 1929; The Man in Possession, Dishonoured Lady, 1930; Lean Harvest, Late Night Final, Grand Hotel, Full Circle, 1931; Ringmaster, Worse Things Happen at Sea, 1935; Heart's Content, 1936; The Orchard Walls, 1937; played over forty parts for the Stage Society, Phoenix Society, Repertory Players, Venturers, 300 Club, etc; is author of the play Hanging Judge (based on Bruce Hamilton's novel), 1952; commenced film career, 1930, and has appeared in over seventy pictures, including: The Scarlet Pimpernel, Hurricane, Abe Lincoln in Illinois, East of Eden, etc; appeared in his first television as the Stage Manager in Our Town, 1948, and recent appearances include: Dr Gillespie in the long-run series Dr Kildare; became a naturalized American citizen, 1944; holds the following honorary degrees: DLitt, Lafayette University, 1939; LLD, Queen's University, Kingston, Canada, 1949; DLitt, Hobart College, Geneva, NY, 1953; Doctor of Fine Arts, Northwestern University, 1959; DLitt, American International College of Massachusetts, 1960; DLitt, College of Wooster, 1966; author of autobiography, When I was Young, 1976.

Recreations: Golf and swimming. *Clubs:* Garrick, London; Century, New York. *Address:* 913 North Beverly Drive, Beverly Hills, Calif 90021.

MASSI, Bernice, actress
b Camden, New Jersey, 23 Aug; *d* of Vincent Massi and his wife Margaret (Scogna); *e* Camden Catholic High School; *m* Yuri Krasnapolsky, the symphonic orchestra conductor.

Made her professional début in Mar 1952, when she took over the role of Ensign Janet MacGregor in the tour of South Pacific; made her first appearance in New York at the Majestic, 8 Apr 1954, in the chorus of By the Beautiful Sea; Shubert, Apr 1955, took over as Gabrielle in Can-Can; Winter Garden, Nov 1955, sang in the chorus of The Vamp; in stock, 1955, played Lulu in Hit the Deck and Sara Brown in Guys and Dolls, and, 1956, Teddy Stern in Wish You Were Here and played in High Button Shoes; Booth, Jan 1958,

understudied Anne Bancroft as Gittel Mosca in Two for the Seesaw; Martin Beck, Feb 1960, Ethel in Beg, Borrow, or Steal; for the Kenley Players, Ohio, 1961, played Frenchy in Destry Rides Again and Gittel Mosca in Two for the Seesaw; 54th Street, Mar 1962, Comfort O'Connell in No Strings; 54th Street, Feb 1964, Laurette Harrington in What Makes Sammy Run?; ANTA Washington Square, July 1967, took over as Aldonza in Man of La Mancha and continued in this part for almost two years; Royale, Mar 1971, Fiona Foster in How the Other Half Loves; Bottom Line, May 1974, Goneril in Kaboom!; toured, 1975, in Cole Porter's You Never Know; toured, Mar 1978, as Yetta Feinstein in The Prince of Grand Street; first appeared on television in 1960 and has played on *The Ed Sullivan Show, The Tonight Show, The Mike Douglas Show, The Merv Griffin Show,* etc.

Recreation: Theatre. *Favourite parts:* Gittel Mosca, Comfort O'Connell, Aldonza. *Address:* Actors Equity Association, 165 West 46th Street, New York, NY 10036.

MATALON, Vivian, director
b Manchester, 11 Oct 1929; *s* of Moses Matalon and his wife Rose (Tawil); *e* Munro College, Jamaica; prepared for the stage at the Neighborhood Playhouse, New York.

Formerly an actor; at the Hippodrome, London, 1956, played Signalman Urban in The Caine Mutiny Court Martial; Princes, 1957, played Apples in A Hatful of Rain; Arts, June 1958, played Don Parritt in The Iceman Cometh; joined the staff of LAMDA in 1959; directed his first professional production in London at the Arts, Mar 1960, with The Admiration of Life; he has since directed the following plays, in London, unless otherwise stated: Season of Goodwill, 1964; The Chinese Prime Minister, The Glass Menagerie, 1965; Suite in Three Keys, After the Rain, 1966; First Day of a New Season, After the Rain (NY), 1967; Papp, Two Cities, The Signalman's Apprentice, 1969; Girl Friend, I Never Sang for My Father, 1970; Noel Coward in Two Keys (NY), The Gingerbread Lady, 1974; PS Your Cat Is Dead (NY), 1975; Eve (Stratford Ontario), Bus Stop, 1976; Heartbreak House (Princeton), 1979; Morning's at Seven (NY), 1980; Artistic director of the Hampstead Theatre Club, May 1970–Apr 1973; his productions there included: The Formation Dancers, Disabled, Awake and Sing, 1971; High Time, and The Garden, 1972; Small Craft Warnings, 1973; 1977–8 Visiting Professor of drama at Brandeis University; 1979, appointed Artistic Director of Academy Festival Theatre, Lake Forest, Illinois, and has directed Morning's At Seven and The Interview There; since Sept 1960, he has directed television productions, including Hearty Crafty, Willy, and A Man of Morality.

Address: 112 Christopher Street, New York, NY 10014. *Tel:* 212 929 3927.

MATHEWS, Carmen, actress
b Philadelphia, Pa, 8 May 1914; *d* of Albert Barnes Mathews and his wife Matilde (Keller); *e* Mary Lyon School, Bennett Junior College, Milbrook, New York; studied for the stage at the Royal Academy of Dramatic Art, London.

Made her first appearance on the stage, 1936, at the Shakespeare Memorial Theatre, Stratford-on-Avon; first appeared in NY, at the St James Theatre, 12 Oct 1938, walking-on in Hamlet, and subsequently, 1939–40, appeared there as Lady Mortimer in Henry IV (Part I), Ophelia in Hamlet, and the Queen in Richard II; Mansfield, NY, Nov 1941, played Lady Madeleine in The Seventh Trumpet; during 1942, toured in The Moon Is Down; Henry Miller, Mar 1943, Mary Beecher Perkins in Harriet; City Center, Jan 1945, Varya in The Cherry Orchard; National, Oct 1945, Ida

Stern in The Assassin; Henry Miller, Oct 1946, Elsa Meredith in Made in Heaven; Alvin, Oct 1947, Violet Robinson in Man and Superman; Lyceum, Apr 1949, Georgina Hogarth in The Ivy Green; next toured as Mrs Sullen in The Beaux' Stratagem; City Center, Dec 1949, Miss Neville in She Stoops to Conquer, and Jan 1950, Miss Ronberry in The Corn Is Green; at the Arena, NY, May 1950; Clara Hyland in The Show-Off; National, June 1951, played Theresa Tapper in Courtin' Time; in summer theatres, 1952, played Jezebel in Jezebel's Husband; Morosco, NY, Mar 1953, appeared as Emilie Ducotel in My Three Angels; at the Longacre, NY, Feb 1957, played Mary Dean in Holiday for Lovers; Coronet, Oct 1958, Eileen Stoddard in The Man in the Dog Suit;Billy Rose, Oct 1959, Lady Utterwood in Heartbreak House; Corning, NY, Summer Theatre, July 1961, Queen Aggravaine in Once upon a Mattress; Brooks Atkinson, Oct 1962, Ceil in Night Life; Plymouth, Feb 1963, Maria in Lorenzo; Curran, San Francisco, California, Aug 1963, Queen Mother in Zenda; American Shakespeare Festival Theatre, Stratford, Conn, summer 1964, Gertrude in Hamlet; Alvin, New York, Dec 1965, Mrs Hutto in The Yearling; Martin Beck, Sept 1966, Edna in A Delicate Balance; Florida State University, Tallahassee, Feb 1967, played in My Mother, My Father, and Me; Mark Hellinger, Apr 1968, Bathsheba in I'm Solomon; Mark Hellinger, Feb 1969, Constance in Dear World; Washington, DC, Theater Club, 1971, The Wife in All Over; Martin Beck, Apr 1972, Mrs Hanlon in Ring Round the Bathtub; Lunt-Fontanne, Nov 1972, Gloriana in Ambassador; appeared with the Long Wharf, New Haven, Conn, 1973–4 season; in Pygmalion at the same theatre, Jan 1975; Richmond, Va, Jan 1976, Mother in Children; has also appeared in touring productions, as Candida, and as Lady Utterwood in Heartbreak House, 1959–60; has played leading parts in many television plays.

Address: 400 East 52nd Street, New York, NY 10022, and West Redding, Conn.

MATTHAU, Walter (*né* Matthow), actor
b New York City, 1 Oct 1920; *s* of Milton Matthow and his wife Rose (Berolsky); *e* Oxford; *m* (1) Grace Johnson (mar dis); (2) Carol Grace Marcus; studied for the stage with Raiken Ben-Ari.
Made his first appearance on the stage at the Erie County Playhouse, July 1946, in Ten Nights in a Bar Room; first appeared on the NY stage at the President, 1946, as Sadovsky in The Aristocrats; President, May 1947, First Soldier in The Flies; Shubert, 1948, appeared in Anne of the 1000 Days; Broadhurst, NY, May 1950, played a Venetian Guard in The Liar; Cort, 1951, took over the role of John Colgate in Season in the Sun; Fulton, Sept 1951, played Sam Dundee in Twilight Walk; Royale, Jan 1952, played Sinclair Heybore in Fancy Meeting You Again; at the same theatre, Mar 1952, played George Lawrence in One Bright Day; US tour, summer 1952, in The Glass Menagerie; Cort, NY, Oct 1952, played Charlie Hill in In Any Language; Martin Beck, Dec 1952, played John Hart in The Grey-Eyed People; toured, Feb 1953, as Andrew Lamb in A Certain Joy; Longacre, NY, Oct 1953, Paul Osgood in The Ladies of the Corridor; at the same theatre, Mar 1954, played Tony Lack in The Burning Glass; at the City Center, Feb 1955, played Yancy in The Wisteria Trees, followed in Apr 1955, as Nathan Detroit in a revival of Guys and Dolls; Belasco, Oct 1955, played Michael Freeman in Will Success Spoil Rock Hunter? which ran for 450 performances; Forrest, Philadelphia, Feb 1957, played Odysseus in Maiden Voyage; National, NY, Oct 1958, played Maxwell Archer in Once More with Feeling, receiving the New York Drama Critics Award for this performance; Music

Box, Feb 1961, Potemkin in Once There Was a Russian; Booth, Oct 1961, played Benjamin Beaurevers in A Shot in the Dark, receiving the Antoinette Perry Award for this performance, 1961; Plymouth, Mar 1963, Herman Halpern in My Mother, My Father, and Me; Plymouth, Mar 1965, played Oscar Madison in The Odd Couple, receiving the New York Critics and the Antoinette Perry Awards for this performance, 1965; Mark Taper Forum, Los Angeles, Nov 1974, Captain Jack Boyle in Juno and the Paycock; entered films, 1954, and has appeared in pictures, including: A Face in the Crowd, Lonely Are the Brave, Charade, The Fortune Cookie (for which he received the Academy Award, 1967), The Odd Couple, Cactus Flower, Hello Dolly!, Plaza Suite, The Laughing Policeman, The Taking of Pelham 123, The Front Page, The Sunshine Boys, California Suite, etc; since 1948, has appeared on television, playing in Juno and the Paycock, The Rope Dancers, Two by Saroyan, etc.
Address: c/o Actors Equity Association, 165 West 46th Street, New York, NY 10036.

MATTHEWS, Jessie, OBE; actress
b Soho, London, 11 Mar 1907; *d* of George Ernest Matthews and his wife Jane (Townshend); *e* Pulteney Street (LCC) School for Girls, Soho; *m* (1) Henry Lytton jun (mar dis); (2) Sonnie Hale (mar dis); (3) Brian Lewis (mar dis); studied classical ballet with Madame Elise Clerc and Miss Freedman of Terry's Juveniles.
Made her first London appearance at the Metropolitan, Edgware Road, 29 Dec 1919, as a child dancer in Bluebell in Fairyland; first appeared for C B Cochran at the Palace Theatre, London, 15 May 1923, in The Music Box Revue; at the Duke of York's, Sept 1923, appeared in the chorus of London Calling!; made her first New York appearance at the Times Square Theatre, 9 Jan 1924, in André Charlot's Revue of 1924, which re-opened, Selwyn, Apr 1924, as Andrew Charleton's Revue of 1924; while appearing in this production at the Princess Theatre, Toronto, Feb 1925, she took over the lead from Gertrude Lawrence; returned to London and at the Prince of Wales, Oct 1925, appeared in Charlot's Revue; Prince of Wales, Oct 1926, played the lead in The Charlot Show of 1926; at the Earl Carroll Theatre, NY, Jan 1927, appeared in Earl Carroll's Vanities; she was then put under contract by C B Cochran, and at the London Pavilion, May 1927, appeared in One Dam Thing After Another; Strand, Jan 1928, played Melanie Page in Jordan; London Pavilion, Mar 1928, appeared in leading parts in This Year of Grace, and Mar 1929, in Wake Up and Dream; Selwyn Theatre, NY, Dec 1929, again appeared in Wake Up and Dream; returned to London and at the Adelphi, Dec 1930, played Harriet Green in Ever Green; Gaiety, Dec 1931, Paula Bond in Hold My Hand; Strand, May 1933, Sally in Sally Who?; appeared in the 6th Royal Command Variety Performance, 1935; after six years in films, reappeared on the regular stage, Jan 1939, when she toured as Sue Merrick and Gloria Grosvenor in I Can Take It; at the Phoenix, Mar 1940, appeared in the revue, Come Out to Play; Prince of Wales, Birmingham, Dec 1940, played the title-role in Aladdin; Shubert Theatre, New Haven, and Shubert Theatre, Boston, Mass, Dec 1941, played Jill Charters in The Lady Comes Across; returned to London and at the Princes Theatre, Aug 1942, played Sally in Wild Rose; Aug 1944, appeared for ENSA in Normandy; May 1946, commenced variety tour; Cambridge, London, May 1948, appeared in the revue, Maid to Measure; Wyndham's, Feb 1949, played Harriet Stirling in Sweethearts and Wives; Q, Apr 1949, played Madeleine in Don't Listen Ladies; King's, Hammersmith, May 1949, appeared in Playbill as Millie Crocker-Harris in The Browning

Version and as Edna Selby in A Harlequinade; Cambridge Theatre, Aug 1949, succeeded Zoë Gail in the revue, Sauce Tartare; at the New, Hull, Apr 1950, played Eliza Doolittle in Pygmalion; toured, 1950, as Boss Trent in Castle in the Air; Princess, Melbourne, June 1952, played Julia Lambert in Larger Than Life; Hippodrome, Preston, Dec 1953, Olivia Brown in Love in Idleness; toured, 1954, as Amanda Prynne in Private Lives; toured, 1955, as Denise Darvel in Dear Charles; Alexander Theatre, Johannesburg, 16 Dec 1955, played Julia Lambert in Larger Than Life; Theatre Royal, Sydney, Dec 1956, Jessica in Janus; Royal Court, Liverpool, July 1957, Gloria Faraday in Nest of Robins; visited Australia and America, Feb 1958–June 1960, for television commitments; Unity, Oct 1960, and Arts Council tour, Louise Harrington in Five Finger Exercise; Bristol Old Vic, Dec 1960, played Fairy Snowflake in Dick Whittington; Royal, Northampton, Feb 1961, Nurse Wayland in The Sacred Flame; toured, May–Aug 1961, as Alicia Storm in Port in a Storm; Pavilion, Torquay, June 1962, played Maggie Millward in What a Racket!; two seasons of cabaret at the Society, Mayfair, Apr and Dec 1964; at the Huntington Hartford Museum, NY, Oct 1965, appeared in A Tribute to Jessie Matthews; Cambridge, London, Aug 1966, played Violet Deakin in A Share in the Sun; Theatre Royal, Norwich, July 1969, appeared in Cockles and Champagne; Congress, Eastbourne, Dec 1969, played The Duchess of Monte Polo in Puss in Boots; Palace Court, Bournemouth, June–Sept 1970, Judith Bliss in Hay Fever and Mrs Bramson in Night Must Fall; Casson, Cardiff, Jan 1971 (for the Welsh Theatre Company), June Buckridge in The Killing of Sister George; Theatre Royal, York, Oct 1972, Lady Catherine Champion-Cheney in The Circle; Royalty, London, July 1973, Mrs Doasyouwouldbedoneby in The Water Babies; Shaftesbury, 3 Oct 1976, appeared in The Jessie Matthews show and subsequently toured; Arnaud, Guildford, Sept 1978 and tour, The Duchess of Berwick in Lady Windermere's Fan; Mayfair Music Hall, Santa Monica, Calif, appeared in Jessie Matthews in Concert; has made numerous broadcasts, including six years of *The Dales*, and television appearances; commenced film career 1923, in the silent production, The Beloved Vagabond, and has since appeared in 23 films, including: Evergreen, Head Over Heels, Victory Wedding (as director), and The Hound of the Baskervilles; recent television appearances include *Angels*, Edward and Mrs Simpson, and The Winter Ladies; is the author of an autobiography, Over My Shoulder, 1974; received the OBE in 1970.

Recreations: Drawing, gardening, motoring. *Address:* c/o CCA Personal Management Ltd, 29 Dawes Road, London SW6 7DT. *Tel:* 01-381 3551.

MATURA, Mustapha (*né* Mathura), dramatic author
b Port of Spain, Trinidad, 17 Dec 1939; s of Chandra Bhan Mathura and his wife Violet Ashbrook (Rivers); e Belmont Boys Intermediate R C School, Trinidad; m Mary Walsh; formerly a stockroom assistant.

His first plays to be performed were the Three Black Pieces, ICA, London, Aug 1970; has since written As Time Goes By, 1971; Nice, The Bakerloo Line, 1972; Play Mas, Black Slaves, White Chains, 1974; Rum and Coca Cola, Bread (National Theatre Summer season), 1976; More, More and Another Tuesday (double-bill), 1978; Independence (tour), The Factory, Welcome Home Jacko, 1979; The Bakerloo Line was televised in 1973; Play Mas was performed in New York, 1976; founded the Black Theatre Co-operative, 1978; his awards include the John Whiting and George Devine Awards.

Recreations: House plants, films, playing drums. *Address:* 5 Mayberry Place, Surbiton, Surrey. *Tel:* 01-390 1635.

MAUDE-ROXBY, Roddy, actor
b London, 2 Apr 1930; s of the Rev Howard Maude-Roxby, and his wife Joyce (McConnell); e Eton, and Royal College of Art; m Jane Lyle; formerly a painter.

First appeared on the stage 30 May 1951, at Southwark Cathedral, London, as an Angel in Your Trumpets, Angels!; Lyric, Hammersmith, July 1959, appeared in the revue One to Another; Royal Court, Dec 1959 and Criterion, Feb 1960, Kirby Groomkirby in One-Way Pendulum; toured, Aug 1960, in the revue Here is the News; Phoenix, Mar 1961, played Eliphaz in JB; Worthing, May 1971, Roland Maule in Present Laughter; Princes, Dec 1961, played several parts in a revival of Salad Days; toured, Aug 1962, in The Wit to Woo; Arts, Dec 1962, appeared in the revue Three at Nine; New, Oxford, June 1963, Roddy in The Perils of Scobie Prilt; later that year appeared with the Establishment company at The Establishment, making his New York début with the same company at the Strollers Theatre Club, Oct 1963; New, NY, May 1964, played Colin in The Knack; returning to England, played Raymond Knall in Miniatures, Apr 1965, Big Nose in Clowning, Dec 1965, Simon in Transcending, and Sylvester in The Performing Giant, Mar 1966, all at the Royal Court; returned to the US, 1966, to appear in revues and direct The Knack, also playing Tom, Canoe Place Inn, NY, July; played David Lord in Help Stamp Out Marriage, Booth, Sept; also appeared in cabaret at the Plaza, 9 Oct; again at the Royal Court, he played Tusenbach in The Three Sisters, Apr 1967; Riley in The Erpingham Camp, June 1967; Hampstead, Mar 1969, Norman Haggard in Have You Any Dirty Washing, Mother Dear?; since 1970 has appeared with the Theatre Machine, of which he is a founder member, in London, Berlin, Montreal, Vienna: Nov 1977 at the Theatre Upstairs in Playpen, in the Royal Court Young People's Theatre Scheme; Thorndike, Leatherhead, May 1970, Winsford in The Silent House; Royal Court, May 1971, Mr Wang in Man is Man; Alexandra Park Racecourse, Apr 1971, The Magician in Passion; Lyceum, Edinburgh, Oct 1971, Acaste in The Misanthrope; Lyric, May 1973, Canon Throbbing in Habeas Corpus; first film, 1960; subsequent pictures include: The Bliss of Mrs Blossom and The Aristocrats; television, since 1959, includes plays and comedy programmes.

Favourite part: Basil Prorgle. *Address:* c/o Aza Artistes, 01-458 7288 *and* Theatre Machine 01-748 4336 *and* 032-875 387.

MAULE, Annabel, MBE, actress
b London, 8 Sept 1922; d of Donovan Maule and his wife Mollie (Shiells); e Paris and at the Lycée Français de Londres in London; m Douglas Dickson (mar dis).

Made her first appearance on the stage at the Winter Garden Theatre, 20 Sept 1934, as Cupid in Love is the Best Doctor; Imperial Institute, Jan 1935, played Lina in Liebelei; Gate, Nov 1936, Lois Fisher in The Children's Hour; Kingsway, Dec 1936, Buckie in Buckie's Bears; Gate, Feb 1937, Gerard (her brother's part) in Invitation to a Voyage; St Martin's, Aug 1937, Sheila in Gertie Maude; Intimate, May 1938, Adèle Varens in Jane Eyre; Q, Jan 1939, Ann, in Call It a Day, and Mar 1939, Nonny in Touch Wood; King's, Hammersmith, May 1939, Brett in First Stop North; Q, 1939, Miranda Bute in Quiet Wedding; served in the WRNS throughout the War; reappeared on the stage, at the Gateway Theatre, June 1946, as Kitty Brown in As Good as a Feast; toured, June 1946, as Frieda in the play of that name; Q, Jan 1947, played Jill Spencer in Happy as Kings; Arts,

Apr 1947, Marianne in Less Than Kind; Lyric, Hammersmith, Oct 1947, played Judy Van Haan in Dark Summer, and appeared in the same part at the St Martin's, Dec 1947; Grand Theatre, Croydon, June 1948, appeared as Raina in Arms and the Man, Ruby in When We Are Married, and as Mary Rose; Richmond, Mar 1949, Dilys Griffiths in A Welsh Tale; Q, July 1949, Jarmila Daubek in The Ivory Tower; Duchess, Aug 1949, Sheila Joyce in Fading Mansion; Bedford, Camden Town, Oct 1949, Pamela Sternroyd in The Wind on the Heath; Coliseum, Harrow, Dec 1949, Anne Buscote in The Day After Tomorrow; Bedford, Camden Town, Feb 1950, Primrose Mallet in Primrose and the Peanuts; Prince's, May 1950, Peggy Harrison in His Excellency; at the Q, Sept 1951, played Celia Arnold in The Silent Inn; visited Kenya, and at the Studio Theatre, Nairobi, Nov 1952, appeared as Gillian Holroyd in Bell, Book and Candle; St James's, May 1957, played Jeannette in Restless Heart; Apollo, Feb 1960, appeared for The Repertory Players' as Anna in Skyrocket; at the Donovan Maule Theatre, Nairobi, 1962–4, played a variety of leading parts including: Lady Teazle in The School for Scandal, Portia in The Merchant of Venice, Lulu in Look After Lulu, and Maggie Hobson in Hobson's Choice; during this period, in her parents' absence, she also took over the management of the theatre; Marlowe, Canterbury, Oct 1965, Frances Beauchamp in Face to Face; Dec 1968, returned to Kenya and was appointed Artistic Director to the Donovan Maule Theatre, becoming Managing Director, Jan 1971, Chairman 1973; recent appearances at the theatre include Lydia in In Praise of Love, 1974, and Queen Mary in Crown Matrimonial, 1975; with the BBC Repertory Company, Apr 1954–Oct 1955; has also made numerous television appearances; translated and adapted Jezebel (Jean Anouilh), 1958; awarded the MBE in the Birthday Honours, 1975.
Address: PO Box 42333, Nairobi, Kenya, East Africa.

MAY, Elaine (*née* Elaine Berlin), actress, playwright, director
b Philadelphia, Pa, 21 Apr 1932; prepared for the stage with Maria Ouspenskaya; *m* (1) Marvin May (mar dis); (2) Sheldon Harnick (mar dis).
Technical assistant for Bruno and Sidney, produced at the New Stages, May 1949; went to Chicago and played in revue and cabaret at The Second City, perfecting an improvisatory style and devising sketches and other material; toured in cabaret with Mike Nichols, performing material of their own composition; made her New York stage début at the John Golden, 8 Oct 1960, in the revue An Evening with Mike Nichols and Elaine May; wrote the play A Matter of Position, produced at the Walnut Street, Philadelphia, Pennsylvania, Sept 1962; wrote Not Enough Rope, produced at the Maidman, NY, Feb 1962; directed The Third Ear, produced at the Premise, May 1964; Henry Miller's, Apr 1966, played Shirley in The Office; Greenwich Mews, Feb 1969, wrote Adaptation, which she also directed, and directed Next, in a double-bill; directed three separate touring productions of Adaptation and Next, 1969–70; Berkshire Theater Festival, Stockbridge, Mass, July 1971, directed The Goodbye People; Long Wharf, New Haven, Apr 1980, Martha in Who's Afraid of Virginia Woolf?; has performed extensively in cabaret, notably at the Compass, Chicago, 1954–7, the Village Vanguard, NY, and the Blue Angel, NY, 1957; appeared at Town Hall, May 1959; made her television début on *The Jack Paar Show,* 1957, and has since played on *Omnibus, Laugh Line, The Fabulous Fifties, Laugh-In,* etc; played in the film A New Leaf, which she also wrote and directed, 1971, wrote the screenplay for Such

Good Friends, 1971; directed the film The Heartbreak Kid, 1972.
Address: Actors Equity Association, 165 West 46th Street, New York, NY 10036.

MAY, Jack, actor
b Henley-on Thames, Oxon, 23 Apr 1922; *s* of Robert Arthur May and his wife Ruth Agnes (Wynne); *e* Forest School and Merton College, Oxford; *m* Margaret Petra Davies.
Made his first professional appearance at Colchester Repertory Theatre, Oct 1950, playing Titinius and other parts in Julius Ceasar; at the Birmingham Rep, 1950–5, he played many leading parts including Richard II, Uncle Vanya, and Dobell in Moon on the Yellow River; made his London debut with the Birmingham company at the Old Vic, 21 July 1972, playing Henry VI in part 3 of Shakespeare's play; played Henry in all three parts at Birmingham and at the Old Vic, July 1953; Haymarket, Aug 1971, the Headmaster in A Voyage Round My Father, touring Canada in the same part, 1972; Savoy, Sept 1973, Martin Knight in At the End of the Day; Albery, May 1974, Col Pickering in Pygmalion; films, since his first in 1957, include Goodbye Mr Chips, The Man Who Would Be King, and The Seven per cent Solution; has made over a thousand TV and radio appearances since his first in 1955: recent TV includes Poldark, A Horseman Riding By, and Noah's Castle.
Favourite parts: Henry VI, Richard II, Vanya. *Recreations:* Antiques, sport. *Address:* 24 Glenlyon Road, Eltham, London SE9 1AJ. *Tel:* 01–850 5155.

MAY, Val (Valentine), CBE, director
b Bath, Somerset, 1 July 1927; *s* of Claude Jocelyn Delabere May, and his wife Olive (Gilbert); *e* Cranleigh School, and Peterhouse College, Cambridge; *m* Penelope Sutton; trained at the Old Vic Theatre School.
At the Watergate, London, Nov 1950, directed The Typewriter, and Jan 1951, co-directed Medusa's Raft; assistant to the director at the Dundee Repertory Theatre, June 1951; associate director at the Salisbury Arts Theatre, Sept–Dec 1951; associate director at the Ipswich Repertory Theatre, Sept 1952–Apr 1953; director of the Ipswich Repertory Theatre, Aug 1953–7; director of the Nottingham Playhouse, Aug 1957–61; at the Old Vic, Nov 1959, directed Richard II; Strand, May 1961, directed the musical Belle, or the Ballad of Dr Crippen; Nottingham Playhouse, Mar 1961, and Duchess, London 1961, directed Celebration; appointed director of the Bristol Old Vic Company, Aug 1961; Old Vic, London, Nov 1961, directed Mourning Becomes Electra; Bristol Old Vic, Feb 1962, and Old Vic, London, June 1962, directed War and Peace, which transferred to the Phoenix later in the same month; Bristol Old Vic, Sept 1962, and Piccadilly, Oct 1962, directed Fiorello!; Bristol Old Vic, Oct 1962, and Phoenix, London, Dec 1962, directed All Things Bright and Beautiful; Bristol Old Vic, May 1963, and Criterion, London, July 1963, directed A Severed Head; Little (Bristol Old Vic), Oct 1963, directed The Pavilion of Masks; Bristol Old Vic, Apr 1964, and Old Vic, London, Sept 1964, directed Love's Labour's Lost (also British Council European tour); directed his first Broadway production at the Royale, Oct 1964, with A Severed Head; Bristol Old Vic, Feb 1965, and Vaudeville, London, May 1965, directed Portrait of a Queen; Bristol Old Vic, Apr 1965, and Duke of York's, London, June 1965, directed The Killing of Sister George; Bath Festival, June 1965, directed the Bristol Old Vic Company in She Stoops to Conquer; Little, Bristol, Nov 1965, directed Cleo; May 1966, devised and directed Sixty Thousand Nights, to mark Bicentenary of Theatre Royal, Bristol; New, Sept

1966, directed Jorrocks; Belasco, New York, Sept 1966, directed The Killing of Sister George; Bristol, Oct 1966, and City Centre, NY, Jan 1967, directed Romeo and Juliet, and Hamlet, followed by tour of USA, Berlin and Israel; Bristol, Apr 1967, directed Message from the Grassroots; Bristol, May 1967, directed The Pursuit of Love; Bristol, Nov 1967, and Wyndham's Feb 1968, directed The Italian Girl; Henry Miller's, NY, Feb 1968, directed Portrait of a Queen; Bristol, Apr 1968, and Duke of York's, May 1968, directed Mrs Mouse, Are You Within?, Bristol, May 1968, directed Brother and Sister; Prince of Wales, Nov 1968, directed They Don't Grow on Trees; Bristol, Apr 1969, and Ethel Barrymore, NY, Oct 1970, directed Conduct Unbecoming; Bristol, Nov 1969, and Wyndham's, Jan 1970, directed It's a Two-Foot-Six-Inches Above the Ground World; Bristol, Feb 1970, and Lyric, May 1970, directed Poor Horace; Theatre Royal, Bath, Mar 1971, directed The Taming of the Shrew, which then toured Latin America; Bristol, Jan 1972, and Prince of Wales, Aug 1972, directed Trelawny; Bristol, Feb 1973, directed The Taming of the Shrew, which then inaugurated Hong Kong Arts Festival; Bristol, June 1973, and Queen's, July 1973, directed The Card; Piccadilly, Oct 1974, directed Male of the Species and subsequently in Australia and New Zealand; Bristol, Nov 1974, directed The Arrest; Bristol, Feb 1975, directed The Threepenny Opera; edited and produced the National Theatre's final gala performance at the Old Vic, Tribute to the Lady, 28 Feb 1976; since then he has directed the following plays in London, unless otherwise stated: Murder Among Friends (New York), Baggage, Banana Ridge, 1976; An Ideal Husband (Toronto), 1977; The Dark Horse, Lady Windermere's Fan (Ottawa), 1978; Forty Love, The Wild Duck (tour), 1979; in June 1975, he was appointed Director of the Yvonne Arnaud Theatre, Guildford where his many productions have included: Man and Superman, Hobson's Choice (1975), An Ideal Husband (1976), The Case of the Oily Levantine (1977), The Sleeping Prince (1978), and The Grass is Greener (1979); co-directed his first television production Last Day in Dreamland, 1959; awarded the CBE in 1969 Birthday Honours.

Recreations; Reading, architecture, music, and astronomy. *Address:* Yvonne Arnaud Theatre, Guildford, Surrey, GU1 3UX.

MAYNE, Ferdy (*né* Mayer-Boerckel), actor
b Mayence, 11 Mar 1920; *s* of Carl Gottlieb Mayer, and his wife Paula (Wolf-Boerckel); *e* Frensham Heights School; *m* Deirdre de Peyer (mar dis); trained for the stage at RADA and Old Vic School.

First appeared on the stage in 1936 with the West Croydon Repertory Company, as The White Knight in Alice Through the Looking Glass; first London appearance, Aldwych, 1943, as Kurt Müller in The Watch On the Rhine; Embassy, Nov 1945, Eugene de Grieux in The Gambler; New, June 1946, Street Vendor's Assistant in Crime and Punishment; Lyric, Hammersmith, Nov 1947, Lot in The Little Dry Thorn; Prince of Wales, May 1948, Wealthy Lawyer in The Vigil; St James's, Sept 1948, played Michel Aubrion in Don't Listen, Ladies; Saville, Mar 1949, Duc de Frisac in Belinda Fair; Piccadilly, Feb 1950, Dr Costa in The Purple Fig Tree; Duchess, Apr 1950, Pierre in The Man with the Umbrella; Cambridge, May 1951, Captain of the Military in Hassan; Saville, July 1952, Hauptmann Schultz in Albert RN; Duke of York's, Sept 1954, Victor Montenay in All For Mary; Strand, Oct 1959, Noel Carradine in Rollo; St Martin's, July 1960, Haroun el Babin in The Brides of March; Lyric, Hammersmith, July 1961, Commodore Roseabove in Oh Dad, Poor Dad, Momma's Hung You etc; Her Majesty's,

Dec 1963, Louis de Pourtal in No Strings; Palace, 1965, took over Max Detweiler in The Sound of Music; Royal Court, June 1965, Judge Advocate Kunz in A Patriot for Me; Piccadilly, 1966, took over Victor Velasco in Barefoot in the Park; Gardner Centre, Brighton, Aug 1970, Frank Scarron in Bloomers; toured, Feb 1974, as the Editor in Signs of the Times; toured as Dracula in Dracula, 1975; his films, since his first in 1943, include: Where Eagles Dare, Dance of the Vampires, When Eight Bells Toll, Vengeance of the Pink Panther and Fedora; has appeared frequently on television.

Favourite part: Trigorin in The Seagull. *Recreations:* Tennis, ski-ing, swimming. *Club:* Hurlingham. *Address:* 124 Coleherne Court, Old Brompton Road, London, SW5. *Tel:* 01–373 1650.

MEACHAM, Anne, actress
b Chicago, Illinois, 21 July 1925; *d* of F David Meacham and his wife Virginia (Foster); *e* University of Rochester, Yale Drama School, Neighborhood Playhouse.

Made professional début in Bridgeton, Maine, summer 1946, as Mrs Brown in Claudia; toured US 1947, as Penny in The Fatal Weakness; toured, 1948, as Elsie Fraser in The First Mrs Fraser; made her New York début at the Lyceum, Mar 1952, as Ensign Jane Hilton in The Long Watch, for which she received the Clarence Derwent Award; US tour, Dec 1952–Apr 1953, as Laura Bateman in Masquerade; 46th Street, Feb 1954, played Violante in Ondine; Arena Stage, Washington, DC, Nov 1954, Lorna in Golden Boy; Theatre de Lys, Feb 1955, Aurora in The Immortal Husband; Ambassadors, Jan 1957, Gertrude Wentworth in Eugenia; Arena Stage, Washington, DC, May 1957, Romaine in Witness for the Prosecution; York Playhouse, NY, Jan 1958, Catherine Holly in Suddenly Last Summer, for which she won the Obie Award; 54th Street, Feb 1959, Lizzie Borden in Legend of Lizzie; Cort, Oct 1959, Elisa in Moonbirds; Arena Stage, Washington, DC, May 1960, Jere Halliday in The Disenchanted; Fourth Street, NY, Nov 1960, Hedda in Hedda Gabler, for which she received the Obie Award; Ambassadors', Jan 1962, played Adela Quested in A Passage to India; University of Michigan, Ann Arbor, for the Association of Producing Artists, summer and fall 1962, Maria in A School for Scandal, Violet in The Tavern, and Dorcas in A Penny for a Song; Miller, Milwaukee, Wisconsin, Jan 1963, Elma in As You Desire Me, and Feb 1963, Monica Claverton-Ferry in The Elder Statesman; US tour with Eva Le Gallienne's National Repertory Theatre, 1963–4, as Lady India in Ring Round the Moon, Nina in The Seagull, and Elizabeth Procter in The Crucible, appearing in the last two roles at the Belasco, NY, Apr 1964; Stage 73, May 1965, Dienaeira in The Wives; White Barn, Westport, Conn, July 1966, Vinnie Dickinson in Come Slowly, Eden; City Center, Nov 1966, Penelope Gray in Elizabeth the Queen; Alvin, Oct 1967, Gertrude in Rosencrantz and Guildenstern Are Dead; Playhouse in the Park, Cincinnati, and elsewhere, 1968, Countess Aurelia in The Madwoman of Chaillot; played a season with the Artists Theatre, Southampton, appearing in Knights of the Round Table and Little Eyolf; for the Hartford Stage Company, Conn, 1968, played Madame Arcadina in The Seagull; Eastside Playhouse, May 1969, Miriam in In the Bar of a Tokyo Hotel; Arena Stage, Washington DC, Nov 1969, Baronin in Edith Stein; Washington Theatre Club, 1971, Louise in Father's Day; Goodman, Chicago, season 1971–2, Gwendolyn Fairfax in The Importance of Being Earnest and Julie in The Royal Family; Central Arts, May 1974, title-role in The Latter Days of a Celebrated Soubrette; appeared in the films Lilith, 1964, Dear Dead Delilah, 1971, and Seizure, 1974, television performances include: Cathy in Wuthering Heights, Thérèse Raquin, *Another World,* etc.

Address: 59 West 12th Street, New York, NY 10011.

MEADOW, Lynne, director

b 12 Nov 1946; *d* of Franklin Raymond Meadow and his wife Virginia (Ribakoff); *e* Bryn Mawr College and Yale School of Drama.

Artistic director since 1972 of the Manhattan Theatre Club, NY, for whom she has directed productions including The Wager, Bits and Pieces, 1974; Golden Boy, 1975; The Pokey, Ashes, 1976; Chez Nous, 1977; Catsplay, 1978; Artichoke, The Jail Diary of Albie Sachs, 1979; other successful productions first presented at MTC include Starting Here, Starting Now, 1977, and Ain't Misbehavin', 1978; has also directed for the Eugene O'Neill Playwrights' Conference, and for Phoenix, with Marco Polo, 1976.

Address: Manhattan Theatre Club, 321 East 73rd Street, New York, NY 10021. *Tel:* 288 2500.

MEDFORD, Kay (*née* Regan), actress

b New York City, 14 Sept 1920; *d* of James Regan and his wife Mary (Kelly); *e* public and Catholic schools; formerly a waitress in a night club.

First appeared on the stage in NY at the Shubert, Nov 1951, when she played Cherry in Paint Your Wagon; Theatre de Lys, June 1953, played Celeste in Maya, and in July 1953, Charudatta's Wife in The Little Clay Cart; Imperial, Dec 1953, appeared in the revue John Murray Anderson's Almanac; Lyceum, Feb 1954, played Eadie in Lullaby; Playhouse, Dec 1954, Dr Zelda Barry in Black-Eyed Susan; Longacre, June 1955, appeared in the revue Almost Crazy; Ethel Barrymore, May 1956, played Martha in Wake Up, Darling; Broadway, 1956, took over the part of Lil Campbell in Mr Wonderful; Plymouth, Feb 1957, Sophie in A Hole in the Head; City Center, Sept 1957, Mrs Mullin in Carousel; Martin Beck, Oct 1958, Sylvi in Handful of Fire; toured, 1959, as Susie in The Poker Game; Martin Beck, Apr 1960, Mae Peterson in Bye Bye Birdie, and toured in this part in 1961–2; Biltmore, NY, Dec 1962, Mary Buckley in In the Counting House; Lyceum, Feb 1963, Sylvia Barr in The Heroine; City Center, May 1963, Melba Snyder in Pal Joey; Winter Garden, Mar 1964, Mrs Brice in Funny Girl; made her London stage début at the Prince of Wales, Apr 1966, in this last part; Morosco, Nov 1966, Mrs Hollander in Don't Drink the Water; toured, 1974, as Mrs Banks in Barefoot in the Park; toured, 1975, in Light up the Sky; Interart, Jan 1978, appeared in Where Memories Are Magic and Dreams Invented; received the New York Drama Critics Award for her performance in Bye Bye Birdie; first appearance in films in 1942 and has since played in Adventure, Rat Race, A Face in the Crowd, Butterfield 8, Lola, Windows (1980), etc; first appeared on television in 1947, and has appeared on *Omnibus, US Steel Hour, Suspense, Studio One*, as a regular on *The Dean Martin Show*, 1970–1, *Starsky and Hutch*, etc; appeared in London, in cabaret, in 1950.

(*Died 10 April 1980.*)

MEDOFF, Mark, playwright

b Mount Carmel, Ill, 18 Mar 1940; *s* of Lawrence R Medoff and his wife Thelma (Butt); *e* U of Miami (BA 1962) and Stanford U (MA 1966); *m* Stephanie Thorne.

Has taught at New Mexico U, Las Cruces, since 1966; currently dramatist in residence and chairman, drama department; his first play, The Kramer, was first produced in 1972 and seen at the Mark Taper Forum, LA, in 1973; has since written The Wager, also 1972; When You Comin' Back, Red Rider?, 1973; The Odyssey of Jeremy Jack (with Carleene Johnson), 1974; The Conversion of Aaron Weiss, 1977; Firekeeper, The Hallowe'en Bandit, 1978; Children of a Lesser God, 1979; made his Broadway debut with this play,

Mar 1980, winning a Tony; as an actor he has played the part of Teddy in When You Comin' Back, Red Rider? in Chicago, 1975, and New York.

Address: c/o English Department, Box 3E, New Mexico State University, Las Cruces, NM 88003.

MEEKER, Ralph (*né* Rathgeber), actor

b Minneapolis, Minnesota, 21 Nov 1920; *s* of Ralph Rathgeber and his wife Magnhild Senovia (Haavig); *e* Northwestern University, Evanston, Ill; *m* (1) Salome Jens (mar dis); (2) Colleen Rose Neary; studied for the stage with Alvina Krauss.

Made his first appearance at the Selwyn, Chicago, July 1943, as Bellboy in Dough-girls; first appeared in New York at the Royale, 29 Nov 1945, as Chuck in Strange Fruit; Alvin, Feb 1947, Mannion in Mr Roberts; Ethel Barrymore, June 1949, appeared as Stanley Kowalski in A Streetcar Named Desire, subsequently touring in the same part; Music Box, Feb 1953, played Hal Carter in Picnic, in which he appeared for over a year, before touring in the same part; Shubert, New Haven, Nov 1955, played Frank Copley in Top Man; John Golden, NY, Feb 1958, played Newton Reece in Cloud 7; Ambassadors, Jan 1962, Toat in Something About a Soldier; Sombrero Playhouse, Phoenix, Arizona, Feb 1962, Bernie Slovenk in Natural Affection; ANTA, Washington Square, Jan 1964, played Micky in After the Fall, and Mar 1964, Charles Taney in But for Whom Charlie; toured, summer 1965 in Mrs Dally Has a Lover, prior to appearing at the Golden, NY, Sept 1965, as Sam when the play was re-named Mrs Dally; Truck and Warehouse, July 1971, took over from Harold Gould as Artie Shaughnessy in House of Blue Leaves; Westwood Playhouse, Dec 1977, and Cannery, San Francisco, appeared in Streamers; first appeared in films, 1950; films include Run of the Arrow, Paths of Glory, Something Wild, The Dirty Dozen, The Happiness Cage, The Food of the Gods, etc; has appeared on television in The Lost Flight, etc.

Recreation: Music. *Address:* Actors Equity Association, 165 West 46th Street, New York, NY 10036.

MEISER, Edith, actress

b Detroit, Mich, 9 May 1898; *e* Liggett School, Detroit, Mich, Kox Schule, Dresden, Germany, Ecole de la Cour de St Pierre, Geneva, and Vassar College (1921); *m* Tom McKnight (mar dis).

Made her first debut in Jessie Bonstelle's stock company in Detroit, June 1921; toured in All Alone Susie, 1923; made her New York debut at the Longacre, 4 Dec 1923, as Matilda Mayhew in The New Way; Garrick, Mar 1924, played Katharine in Fata Morgana; same theatre, Oct 1924, Liesl in The Guardsman; same theatre, June 1925, played in Garrick Gaieties, a revue; Guild, Mar 1926, The Lady with the Dog in The Chief Thing; Garrick, May 1926, played in Garric Gaieties; Vanderbilt, Dec 1926, Dolores Barnes in Peggy-Ann; played in Vaudeville at the Palace, July 1927, and toured until 1928; Grove Street, Feb 1929, Martha Turner in Airways, Inc; Guild, June 1930, appeared in Garrick Gaieties; Liberty, Mar 1931, Glen Cornish in Greater Love; Guild, Sept 1931, Miss Scoville in He; Golden, Nov 1936, directed Double Dummy; National, Oct 1938, Josephine Lerner in A Woman's a Fool—To Be Clever; Lyceum, May 1940, Lydia Vaughn in The Strangler Fig, which she also adapted; Biltmore, Sept 1940, Fanny Leeming in Jupiter Laughs; Imperial, Oct 1941, Cornelia Abigail Pigeon in Let's Face it; Winter Garden, Jan 1944, Eadie Johnson in Mexican Hayride; Biltmore, May 1945, Jane Daniels in Round Trip; Golden, Nov 1945, Carrie in The Rich Full Life; Ford's,

Baltimore, Mar 1946, Senora Gonzalez in Twilight Bar; Erlanger, Buffalo, Sept 1946, Melissa Morgan in The Magnificent Heel; Wilbur, Boston, Sept 1947, Lyndia in The Stars Weep; Cort, Sept 1947, Mrs Clark in I Gotta Get Out; ANTA, May 1951, Lesbia Grantham in getting Married; National, 1954, took over from Luella Gear as Julia Ward McKinlock in Sabrina Fair; Booth, Apr 1954, Anita Harmon in The Magic and the Loss; Phoenix, Oct 1955, Widow Yang in The Carefree Heart; American Shakespeare Festival, Stratford, Conn, June 1956, Queen Elinor in King John and Francisca in Measure for Measure; toured, Sept 1956–Mar 1957, as Miss Addy in Janus; Majestic, in 1957, took over a role in Happy Hunting; Winter Garden, Nov 1960, Mrs McGlove in The Unsinkable Molly Brown; Stratford, Conn, June 1966, a Woman of Canterbury in Murder in the Cathedral; toured with the National Repertory Theatre, Feb 1968, in The Comedy of Errors; appeared with the Studio Arena, Buffalo, NY, 1968–69 season as Madame Arcati in Blithe Spirit, Queens Playhouse, Oct 1972, Mrs Higgins in Pygmalion; Philadelphia Drama Guild, Nov 1972, Mme Pernelle in Tartuffe; toured in Warm Perinsula, Hobsons Choice, 1972; The Unsinkable Molly Brown, 1973; A Little Night Music, as Madame Armfeldt, 1976; wrote the play The Wooden O, produced at the Barter, Abingdon Va, during its 30th anniversary; has produced extensively in radio, notably *The Hall of Fame,* Twenty Thousand Years in Sing-Sing, *The Will Rogers Show,* Irving Berlin series, etc; wrote scripts for several series; author of the novel Death Catches Up with Mr Kluck, which was filmed as Death on the Air (1937); first appeared in films in Glamour Boy, 1941, and has since played in Go West, Young Lady, Queen for a Day, Middle of the Night, etc; member of the Board of Governors of the Actors Equity Association, 1954 to present.
Address: 171 East 62nd Street, New York, NY. *Tel:* 838–3297.

MELFI, Leonard, playwright
b Binghamton, New York, 21 Feb 1935; s of Leonard John Melfi and his wife Louise Marie (Gennarelli); e Binghamton Central High School and St Bonaventure University; formerly engaged in numerous positions as waiter and in various carpenter jobs.
His first play to be produced was Lazy Baby Susan, presented at the Cafe La Mama in NY, 25 Oct 1962; author of the following plays, principally produced by various avant garde theatres in NY and Great Britain, etc; Birdbath, Sunglasses, Ferryboat, Pussies and Rookies, all produced at Theatre Genesis, NY, 1965; Times Square, produced with Birdbath at the Edinburgh Festival, and Niagara Falls, at the Cafe La Mama, 1966; The Shirt, produced by the Cafe La Mama and the Eugene O'Neill Foundation, and Hallowe'en, by the Playwrights Unit, NY, 1967; Jack and Jill and Stimulation at the Cafe La Mama and Stars and Stripes, a short play produced at the Cafe au GoGo, NY, in a bill with the overall title Collision Course, The Breech Baby, at the Loft Theatre, NY, Night, which was produced at the Henry Miller's in a bill with the overall title Morning, Noon, and Night, 1968; Having Fun in the Bathroom, Cafe La Mama, The Raven Rock for the New York Poets Festival Theatre, NY, Wet and Dry and Alive for the Loft Theatre, and The Jones Man for Act IV, Provincetown, Mass, 1969; his plays Birdbath and Hallowe'en were produced at the Open Space, London, in Sept 1969; Cinque, produced at the Royal Court, London, May 1970, by the Cafe La Mama; Ah! Wine!, produced by Drifting Traffic, 1971; Beautiful! (1972) and Sweet Suite (1973) at Theatre for the New City; Horse Opera (La Mama etc), 1974; Fantasies at the Frick (Open Space in Soho),

Porno Stars at Home (Courtyard Playhouse), 1977; Rusty and Rico and Lena and Louie (IRT), Taxi Tales (Century: Broadway début), 1978; his play Jack and Jill is one of the sketches included in Oh! Calcutta! first produced at the Eden, NY, June 1969; wrote the Italian film Mortadella (Lady Liberty), 1971; wrote the screenplays for Steppenwolf and Lady Liberty, 1972; wrote the television plays Puck! Puck! Puck!, What a Life!, 1969–71.
Hobbies and recreations: Abstract painting, sailing ships, writing songs, and being an Italian chef. *Address:* c/o Helen Harvey, 410 West 24th Street, New York, NY 10011. *Tel:* 212–675 7445.

MELFORD, Jill, actress
b London, 23 Nov 1934; d of Jack Kenneth Gambier Melford-Melford, and his wife Rene Mallory (Corbett); e Gardner School, New York; m John Standing; trained for the stage at the Ballet Arts School, NY.
First appeared on the stage in 1949 at the Westport Playhouse, as Tessa in Devil Take the Whittler; made her NY début in the same year as a dancer in Oklahoma at the St James; first London appearance, Aldwych, May 1953, as Miss Morris in The Seven Year Itch; Arts, Feb 1955, Marge Lovell in The Ghost Writers; Globe, May 1955, Jane Penny in Into Thin Air; Adelphi, Sept 1958, Pegeen Ryan in Auntie Mame; Arts, May 1959, played four parts in Ulysses in Nighttown; Saville, Sept 1959, Angela Snow in The Darling Buds of May; Lyric, Hammersmith, Nov 1960, Lorna in The Life of the Party; Her Majesty's, May 1964, Helen in The Right Honourable Gentleman; Globe, June 1966, Clare in There's A Girl in My Soup; Strand, June 1968, Janie McMichael in Not Now Darling; Strand, Feb 1970, Kate Connaught in Best of Friends; toured, Apr 1971, as Serena Churnside in Make No Mistake; Comedy, May 1975, Diana Claiborne in A Touch of Spring; Globe, Mar 1976, played Eve in The Chairman; toured, Sept 1978, as Fiona Foster in How the Other Half Loves, subsequently playing the part in Hong Kong; films include: The Servant, and Father Dear Father; television, since 1953, includes: Ring Round the Moon, *The Organization,* and *Crossroads.*
Address: 33 Flood Street, London SW3. *Tel:* 01–353 3322.

MELIA, Joe, actor
b London; e Cambridge University, where he appeared with the Cambridge Footlights.
Made his first London appearance 1960, when he took over the role of Bob le Hotu in Irma la Douce; Fortune, 1963, took over from Jonathan Miller in Beyond the Fringe; Royal Court, Mar 1965, Sam Wurlitzer in Happy End; Comedy, July 1967, Bri in A Day in the Death of Joe Egg; Royal Court, Aug 1968, Baba in Trixie and Baba; Mermaid, Jan 1970, Solly Gold in Enter Solly Gold; Gardner Centre, Brighton, Oct 1970, George in Don't Let Summer Come; Round House, Mar 1971, Panurge in Rabelais; Greenwich, Sept 1971, Phil in The Sandboy; Prince of Wales, Feb 1972, Macheath in The Threepenny Opera, transferring to the Piccadilly, Apr 1972; Fortune, June 1973, Timothy Black in Who's Who; Aldwych, Jan 1974, for RSC, Ubell Untermeyer in Section Nine; for the same company he played Fr Froylan in The Bewitched, Aldwych, May 1974 Bill in The Can Opener, The Place, Oct 1974, and Sgt Fielding in Too True to Be Good, Aldwych, Oct 1975, transferring in the latter role to the Globe, Dec 1975; Aldwych, Dec 1976, John Dory in Wild Oats; Aldwych, Feb 1977, and Piccadilly, Corporal Bonny in Privates on Parade; Lyric, Hammersmith, Dec 1979, (Widow) Twang Kee in Aladdin; RSC Stratford season 1980, Touchstone in As You Like It; numerous TV appear-

ances include the series *Foreign Affairs*, the panel game *Call My Bluff* and *Donkey's Years*; films include *Four in the Morning* and *Modesty Blaise*.

Recreations: Reading, football. *Address:* c/o The Spotlight, 42–43 Cranbourne Street, London WC2H 7AP. *Tel:* 01–586 0705.

MELLY, Andrée, actress
b Liverpool, 15 Sept 1932; *d* of Francis Heywood Melly and his wife Edith Maud (Isaac); *e* Brighthelmston, Birkdale, Belvedere High School, Liverpool, and Mon Fertile, Switzerland; *m* Oscar Quitak; her tutors for the stage included the late Iris Warren and Yat Malmgren.

Made her first appearance on the stage at the Little Theatre, Southport, Dec 1941, as Thomas in Quality Street; following four years in repertory theatres, she made her first appearance on the London stage at the Royal Court, July 1952, as Molly in Miss Hargreaves; was a member of the Old Vic Company, 1952–3; Vaudeville, Mar 1954, played Patty O'Neill in a revival of The Moon is Blue; Arts, Feb 1955, played Julie Bedford in The Ghost Writers; toured, Oct 1955, as Rose Lovell in Call of the Dodo; Duchess, Oct 1956, played Jennifer Wren in Plaintiff in a Pretty Hat; New Shakespeare, Liverpool, July 1958, played Cass Edgerton in Reclining Figure, subsequently touring with the play; New, Nov 1958, played Kathie Palmer in Hot Summer Night; toured, Oct 1960, as Ruth Arnold in Warm Peninsula; Apollo, Feb 1962, Jacqueline in Boeing-Boeing; left the cast to appear at the Duchess, May 1963, as Elizabeth Mayle in The Shot in Question; Comedy, June 1964, Sandra Markowitz in A Thousand Clowns; St Martin's July 1966, took over as Alice in The Killing of Sister George; Birmingham Repertory Theatre, Apr 1967, Rosalind in As You Like It; Hampstead Theatre Club, Feb, 1969, played four parts in the collection We Who Are About To . . . which transferred to the Comedy, Apr 1969, under the title Mixed Doubles; Thorndike, Leatherhead, Nov 1971, played the Girl in Lunch Hour, and Clea in Black Comedy, in a double-bill; Capitol, Horsham, Sept 1973, appeared in Mixed Blessings; first entered films, Apr 1951, and principal films she has appeared in include: The Belles of St Trinians, The Secret Tent, Brides of Dracula, etc; co-author (with Oscar Quitak) of a musical, Viva Francesco; first appeared on television, 1950, in Just William, subsequent appearances include: Woman in a Dressing-gown, Hot Summer Night, The Navigators, etc; she has also broadcast in numerous radio programmes.

Favourite parts: Jennifer Wren, Juliet, and Sally Bowles in I Am a Camera. *Recreations:* Travel, ski-ing, theatre and film-going, and being with friends. *Address:* c/o Richard Eastham Ltd, 110 Jermyn Street, London, SW1.

MELVILLE, Alan, lyric writer and dramatic author
b Berwick-on-Tweed 9 Apr 1910; *s* of William Alan Caverhill and his wife Janet (King); *e* Edinburgh Academy; formerly employed in his father's timber firm.

From 1936–40, was engaged with the BBC broadcasting feature programmes and producing; served with the RAF, 1941; demobilized 1946; author of sketches and lyrics for the following revues: Rise Above It, 1940; Scoop, 1942; Sky High, 1942; Sweet and Low, 1943; Sweeter and Lower, 1944; Sweetest and Lowest (entire book), 1946; part-author of the revue Between Ourselves, 1946; author of the revue A La Carte, 1948; wrote the lyrics for Gay's the Word, 1951, and Bet Your Life, 1952; part-author of the revue At The Lyric (and revised version, Going to Town); wrote the book and lyrics for Marigold, 1959; part-author of And Another Thing, 1960; wrote the book and lyrics for All Square, 1963;

part-author of Six of One, 1963; wrote book and lyrics for Congress Dances (also continental and TV versions), 1977; is author of the following plays: Jonathan, 1948; Top Secret, Castle in the Air, 1950; Devil May Care, Dear Charles (adaptation), 1952; Ambassador's Folly, 1953; The Bargain, Simon and Laura, 1954; Mrs Willie, 1955; Change of Tune, 1959; Everything Happens On Friday, 1964; Top Priority, 1969; Content to Whisper (adaptation), 1970; Demandez Vicky (Paris), 1971; Oops, 1973; Castle in the Air (revision), 1978; has also written novels, and two autobiographies, Myself when Young, 1955 and Merely Melville, 1971; wrote and appeared in many television programmes, notably A–Z, *Merely Melville*, etc; author of the television series: *Misleading Cases, The Very Merry Widow*, etc; author of a number of radio plays including: Pursuit of Love, Balance of Power, The Sun God, Madame de Pompadour, The Knocker and an adaptation of The Girl Who Came to Supper.

Recreations: Tennis, swimming, and going to the theatre. *Address:* 28 Victoria Street, Brighton, BN1 3FQ. *Tel:* Brighton 26682.

MELVIN, Murray, actor
b London; *s* of Hugh Victor Melvin and his wife Maisie Winifred (Driscoll).

Made his first appearance on the stage at the Theatre Royal, Stratford, E, Sept 1957, in Joan Littlewood's production of Macbeth; remained at the same theatre, to play the following parts: Belli in Man, Beast, and Virtue, Calisto in Celestina, Jodie Maynard in Unto Such Glory, Geoffrey in A Taste of Honey, Leslie in The Hostage, and Scrooge's Nephew in A Christmas Carol, 1958; made his first appearance in the West End of London, at Wyndham's, Feb 1959, when he played his original part of Geoffrey in A Taste of Honey; Theatre Royal, Stratford, Apr 1960, played Sam in Sam, The Highest Jumper of Them All; at the Paris Festival, Sarah Bernhardt Theatre, June 1960, played Brainworm in Every Man in His Humour; Theatre Royal, Stratford, E, Aug 1960, played Knocker in Sparrers Can't Sing; Princes, May 1962, appeared in the revue England, Our England; Theatre Royal, Stratford, Mar 1963, appeared in the musical Oh What a Lovely War! transferring with the production to Wyndham's, June 1963; Edinburgh Festival, Aug 1964, played Gadshill, Mortimer, Sir Richard Vernon, and Shadow in Joan Littlewood's production of Henry IV; made his first appearance in New York at the Broadhurst, Sept 1964, in Oh What a Lovely War! also playing the Devil in The Soldier's Tale; Piccadilly, Oct 1965, Jonathan in Oh Dad, Poor Dad, Mama's Hung You in the Closet and I'm Feelin' So Sad; Mermaid, Jan 1967, played the Orderly in Press Cuttings, and Adolphus in Passion, Poison and Petrifaction, in the triple-bill, Trifles and Tomfooleries; Prince of Wales, Apr 1969, Bouzin in Cat Among the Pigeons; New, Cardiff, Nov 1971, Dr Fausset in A Pig in a Poke; played the Devil in The Soldier's Tale at a Promenade Concert, London, 1975; Queen Elizabeth Hall, Oct 1975, the Speaker in Façade; Shaw, Dec 1975, Convict Gilbert in Kidnapped at Christmas; same theatre, Nov 1976, Convict Gilbert in Christmas Crackers; Comedy, Aug 1978, Marquis of Dorset in The Dark Horse; Round House, March 1979, W. B. Bunkhaus in Hoagy, Bix and Wolfgang Beethoven Bunkhaus; Thorndike, Leatherhead, Oct 1979, The Dauphin in Saint Joan; in 1971 played the Speaker in Peter Maxwell Davies' Super Missa L'Homme Armée, and has since directed his works, Miss Donnithorne's Maggot (1974), and The Martyrdom of St Magnus; and also Henze's The Raft of the Medusa (1977); first entered films, 1959, and has appeared in A Taste of Honey, Sparrers Can't Sing, The Devils, Tom Jones, Barry

Lyndon, etc; since 1959, has appeared on television in the following series: Probation Officer, Paradise Walk, Angel Pavement and in The Diary of a Nobody, Isadora Duncan and St Joan.

Favourite part: Leslie in The Hostage. *Address:* c/o Joy Jameson Ltd, 7 West Eaton Place Mews, London, SW1.

MERCER, David, dramatist
b Wakefield, Yorks, 27 June 1928; *s* of Edward Mercer and his wife Helen (Steadman); *e* King's College, Newcastle upon Tyne; *m* Dafna Hamdi; formerly a teacher.

Author of the following plays: The Buried Man, performed at the Manchester Library Theatre in 1962; The Governor's Lady (One-Act), Ride A Cock Horse, 1965; Belcher's Luck, 1966; After Haggerty, Flint, 1970; Duck Song, 1974; Cousin Vladimir, 1978; Then and Now, 1979; author of films Morgan (1965), Family Life, and Providence; his many television plays include: Where the Difference Begins, Let's Murder Vivaldi, Find Me, Shooting the Chandelier, The Ragazza and A Rod of Iron; received the *Evening Standard* Award for most promising playwright, 1965.

Recreation: Political studies. *Club:* Dramatists'. *Address:* c/o Margaret Ramsay Ltd, 14a Goodwin's Court, London, WC2. *Tel:* 01–240 0691.

MERCER, Marian, actress and singer
b Akron, Ohio, 26 Nov 1935; *d* of Samuel Mercer and his wife Nelle; *e* University of Michigan (BMus 1957); prepared vocally with Frances Greer.

Made her stage début, June 1953, as Annie Oakley in a high school production of Annie Get Your Gun; at the Ann Arbor (Michigan) Dramatic Festival, May 1954, appeared in Gentlemen, The Queens; made her professional début in stock at the Palmtree Playhouse, Sarasota, Florida, Oct 1957, in The Happiest Millionaire, followed by appearances in Holiday for Lovers and A Hole in the Head in 1958; at the Cleveland, Ohio, Musicarnival, summer 1958, performed in The Ballad of Baby Doe, Show Boat, The Most Happy Fella; Rickaway, Newark, New Jersey, Oct 1958, played in The Waltz of the Toreadors; Palm Beach, Florida, Musicarnival, 1958–9, played in Guys and Dolls, The Pajama Game, The Student Prince; toured in Bells Are Ringing, June-Aug 1959; made her New York début at the Lenox Hill Playhouse, Sept 1959, as Marcelle in the Equity Library Theatre production of Hotel Paradiso; Alvin, Mar 1960, sang in the chorus and was an understudy in Greenwillow; Broadhurst, Sept 1960, took over a role in Fiorello!; Orpheum, 1960, took over from Eileen Brennan in the title-role of Little Mary Sunshine; Alvin, Feb 1962, played in the revue New Faces of 1962; toured in stock productions of Bye Bye Birdie, Gypsy, Little Mary Sunshine, 1962–3; Shakespeare Summer Festival, Washington, DC, June 1963, played Beatrice in Much Ado About Nothing; East 74th Street, Oct 1965, Marcelle Paillardin in Hotel Passionato; joined the Repertory Theatre of St Louis, Missouri, during its première season, 1966–7, and, during 1967–8, played in The Hostage and Blanche Du Bois in A Streetcar Named Desire; Orpheum, Jan 1968, played Olivia in Your Own Thing; Sam S Shubert, Dec 1968, played Marge MacDougall in Promises, Promises, for which she received the Antoinette Perry (Tony) Award; Ethel Barrymore, Apr 1970, Polly in A Place for Polly; Repertory, St Louis, 1970, Desdemona in Othello; Helen Hayes, Nov 1970, Myra Arundell in Hay Fever; Orpheum, May 1971, appeared in a series of short plays called The Wanderers; Trinity Square Repertory, Providence, Rhode Island, 1970–1, played in The Taming of the Shrew and The Good and Bad Times of Cady Francis McCullum and Friends; Mark Taper Forum,

Los Angeles, 1972, played in Volpone; Seattle, Washington, Repertory, 1972, played in And Miss Reardon Drinks a Little; New Theater for Now, Los Angeles, 1973, played in Tadpole; toured, 1973, in Lovers and Other Strangers; Williamstown, Mass, July 1973, Gwendolen Fairfax in Nobody's Earnest; and, July 1974, Masha in The Seagull; appeared with the Seattle Repertory, Jan 1975, in The Waltz of the Toreadors; toured, 1978, including NY State Theater, Aug, as female lead in Stop the World—I Want to Get Off; Longacre, May 1979, Deirdre in Bosoms and Neglect; has appeared frequently on television since 1961, in TV films such as The Cracker Factory, and in a number of series.

Address: 1 West 72nd Street, New York, NY 10023.

MERCHANT, Vivien (*née* Thomson), actress
b Manchester, 22 July 1929; *d* of William Thomson and his wife Margaret (Macnaughton); *e* Bury Convent, Manchester; *m* Harold Pinter.

Made her first appearance on the stage as a child at the Peterborough Repertory Theatre, 1943, when she played Adèle in Jane Eyre; first appeared on the London stage at the Piccadilly Theatre, Aug 1945, as a dancer in Sigh No More; joined Donald Wolfit's Company and appeared at the Savoy, Apr 1947, as Phebe in As You Like It; Nottingham, 1947–9, appeared in the Harry Hanson Repertory Company; Cambridge, London, July 1950, played Mimi Joshua in Ace of Spades; at the King's, Hammersmith, Feb–Apr 1953, appeared with the Donald Wolfit Company in the following parts: Phebe in As You Like It, Jessica in The Merchant of Venice, Second Witch in Macbeth, Joanne de Beaudricourt in The Wandering Jew; New Torch, Mar 1954, played Anne Bronte in Welcome, Proud Lady; appeared in several plays at the Intimate, Palmer's Green, 1954–5; Richmond, Oct 1955, played Yasmi in Weekend at Woodcote; Coliseum, Harrow, Dec 1955, Diana Edmunds in Motive for Murder; Palace Court, Bournemouth, 1955–6, appeared in the Barry O'Brien Repertory Company; toured, 1957–8, playing leading parts with the J. Grant Anderson Repertory Company; Hampstead Theatre Club, Jan 1960, played Rose Hudd in The Room, transferring with the production to the Royal Court, Mar 1960; Her Majesty's, June 1962, played Susannah in Judith; New Arts, Sept 1963, played Sarah in The Lover; Aldwych, June 1965, played Ruth in The Homecoming, and made her first appearance on Broadway at the Music Box, Jan 1967, in the same part; Royal Shakespeare, Stratford, Aug 1967, Lady Macbeth in Macbeth, touring Finland and Russia in that production Nov–Dec, and returning to play in it at the Aldwych, Jan 1968; Hampstead Theatre Club, Feb 1969, appeared in the collection of plays We Who Are About To . . . transferring to the Comedy, Apr 1969, under the new overall title Mixed Doubles; Palace, Watford, Nov 1968, played Princess Kosmonopolis in Sweet Bird of Youth; Criterion, May 1970, Victoria in Flint; Edinburgh Festival, Aug 1970, appeared as Mary in Mary Stuart, Queen of Scots; Duchess, Sept 1970, Wendy in Tea Party; Mermaid, Nov 1970, Bertha in Exiles; joined the Royal Shakespeare Company at the Aldwych, 1971, to play Anna in Old Times, June, Mrs Lovett in The Man of Mode, Sept, and to repeat the part of Bertha in Exiles, Oct; Greenwich, Feb 1974, Madame in The Maids; Arnaud, Guildford, June 1974, Mrs Manningham in Gaslight; same theatre, Jan 1975, Linda in Death of a Salesman; Greenwich, Oct 1975, Florence Lancaster in The Vortex; same theatre, Jan 1976, Ethel in Love's Old Sweet Song; Gardner Centre, Brighton, Oct 1976, and tour, played The Mistress in All Over; Greenwich, Nov 1977, Laura in The Father; she has also appeared in repertory companies in Bradford, Chester, Westcliff, and at the Alexandra, Birmingham; films in which she has appeared include: The Way Ahead, Alfie, Accident, and The Homecoming; is seen frequently in television plays, among them The Collection, Weather in the Streets, The Lover, A Month in the Country and Don Juan in Hell.

Recreations: Table tennis, jazz, reading. *Club:* Ronnie Scott's. *Address:* c/o ICM Ltd, 22 Grafton Street, London W1.

MEREDITH, Burgess, actor and director

b Cleveland, Ohio, 16 Nov 1908; *s* of Dr William George Meredith and his wife Ida Beth (Burgess); *e* Amherst College (MA), Cathedral Choir School, New York, and Hoosac School; *m* (1) Helen Berrien (mar dis); (2) Margaret Perry (mar dis); (3) Paulette Goddard (mar dis); (4) Kaja Sunsten; formerly in commerce and, also, served as an ordinary seaman.

Made his first appearance on the stage walking on in productions of the Civic Repertory Theatre Company, New York, Dec 1929; his first speaking part was that of Peter in Romeo and Juliet, Apr 1930; he remained with the company until 1933, playing numerous parts in the varied repertory; he also appeared at the Comedy, Sept 1931, as Wick Martin in People on the Hill, and at 48th Street, Mar 1932, as Peon in Night over Taos; Empire, Apr 1933, Crooked Finger Jack in The 3-Penny Opera; Playhouse, Apr 1933, Red Barry in Little Ol' Boy, in which he made a very notable success; 46th Street, Nov 1933, made a further success when he played Buzz Jones in She Loves Me Not; Maxine Elliott, Oct 1934, Jim Hipper in Hipper's Holiday; Lyceum, Jan 1935, Seaman Jones in Battleship Gertie; Martin Beck, Feb 1935, Octavius Barrett in The Barretts of Wimpole Street; Apr 1935, Leonard Dobie in The Flowers of the Forest; Sept 1935, Mio in Winterset, which was written for him by Maxwell Anderson, and which was another great success; Jan 1937, played Van Van Dorn in High Tor; Empire, Sept 1937, Stephen Minch in The Star Wagon; at Boston, Feb 1939, Prince Hal and King Henry V in Five Kings; 44th Street, NY, Mar 1940, Liliom in the play of that name; Shubert, Apr 1942, Eugene Marchbanks in Candida; subsequently served with the United States Army; while in England, July 1943, appeared at the Royal Albert Hall, as the Speaker in Lincoln Portrait; Booth, NY, Oct 1946, played Christopher Mahon in The Playboy of the Western World; appeared at the Gaiety Theatre, Dublin, Aug 1947, as Mio in Winterset; Coronet, NY, Jan 1950, played Larry in Happy as Larry, which he also staged; toured, summer 1950, as Elwood P Dowd in Harvey; Cort, Sept 1950, staged Season in the Sun; at Wilmington, Mar 1951, staged Let Me Hear the Melody; in summer theatres, 1951, appeared in The Silver Whistle; at the Booth, NY, Dec 1951, directed the production of Lo and Behold!; Ethel Barrymore, June 1952, succeeded Hume Cronyn as Michael in The Fourposter; Broadhurst, Oct 1953, played Pa Pennypacker in The Remarkable Mr Pennypacker; in Bermuda, 1954, directed a production of Macbeth; on Broadway and on tour, 1955, appeared in Teahouse of the August Moon; Martin Beck, Oct 1956, Adolphus Cusins in Major Barbara; Royale, Dec 1956, co-produced Speaking of Murder (which he also co-produced at the St Martin's, London, June 1958); Edgewater Beach Playhouse, Chicago, July 1957, Dr Lao in The Circus of Dr Lao; Rooftop, NY, June 1958, conceived and directed Ulysses in Nighttown (which he also directed at the Arts, London, May 1959, and which was then presented at the Sarah Bernhardt, Paris, July 1959); Edgewater Beach Playhouse, Chicago, June 1958, Mr Pennypacker in The Remarkable Mr Pennypacker; Erlanger, Philadelphia, Nov 1958, the title-role in Enrico; 54th Street, NY, Feb 1959,

directed God and Kate Murphy; State Fair, Dallas, June 1959, played in The Vagabond King; Marine's, San Francisco, Sept 1959, Arnold St Clair in The Plaster Bambino; ANTA, NY, Feb 1960, conceived and directed A Thurber Carnival; toured, 1960, in An Evening with Burgess Meredith; Martin Beck, Feb 1961, directed Midgie Purvis; Bucks County Playhouse, New Hope, Pa, Aug 1961, directed A Whiff of Melancholy; Arie Crown, Chicago, Oct 1961, Mr Kicks in Kicks and Company; toured England, May 1963, as Erie Smith in the premiere of Eugene O'Neill's Hughie, subsequently playing this role at the Duchess, London, June 1963; ANTA, NY, Apr 1964, directed Blues for Mr Charlie; Lyceum, Nov 1964, played Daniel Considine in I Was Dancing; Aldwych, London, May 1965, again directed Blues for Mr Charlie for the Actors Studio Company; ANTA, Feb 1967, directed Of Love Remembered; Kalita Humphreys, Dallas, Texas, Mar 1968, directed The Latent Heterosexual; Winter Garden, Mar 1974, directed Ulysses in Nighttown; Westwood Playhouse, Ca, 1976, appeared in The Little Foxes; at various times, at summer theatres, has played Marchbanks in Candida, with Pauline Lord, Peggy Wood, Edith Barrett, etc, in the name part; was one of the founders of the New Stage Society; in Dec 1937, was elected Vice-President of Actors Equity and acting President; in 1938, elected third Vice-President; entered films, 1936, as Mio in Winterset, and has appeared in numerous pictures, including Of Mice and Men (1939), The Man (1972), The Day of the Locust (1975), Rocky (1976), and Rocky II (1979); has appeared frequently on television in Ah, Wilderness!, Waiting for Godot, Batman, etc.

Favourite part: Mio in Winterset. *Recreations:* Farming and writing. *Address:* Pomona, Rockland County, NY.

MERMAN, Ethel, actress and singer

b Astoria, Long Island, New York, 16 Jan 1909; *d* of Edward Zimmermann and his wife Agnes; *e* public schools and Bryant High School, Long Island; *m* (1) William B Smith (mar dis); (2) Robert D Levitt (mar dis); (3) Robert F Six (mar dis); (4) Ernest Borgnine (mar dis); formerly a typist and secretary.

Made her first appearance, 1928, in cabaret; in 1929, was engaged in vaudeville with Clayton, Jackson and Durante, and appeared with them at the Palace Theatre, NY; made a number of short films before appearing for the first time on the regular stage at the Alvin Theatre, NY, 14 Oct 1930, as Kate Fothergill in Girl Crazy; at the Apollo, NY, Sept 1931, appeared in George White's Scandals; Apollo, Nov 1932, played Wanda Brill in Take a Chance; Alvin, Nov 1934, Reno Sweeney in Anything Goes; Alvin, Oct 1936, Nails Duquesne in Red, Hot and Blue!; Majestic, Feb 1939, Jeannette Adair in Stars in Your Eyes; 46th Street Theatre, Dec 1939, May Daly and the Du Barry in Du Barry Was a Lady; and Oct 1940, Hattie Maloney in Panama Hattie; Alvin, Jan 1943, Blossom Hart in Something for the Boys; Imperial, May 1946, Annie Oakley in Annie Get Your Gun, which ran for three years; Imperial, Oct 1950, played Sally Adams in Call Me Madam; Majestic, Dec 1956, Liz Livingstone in Happy Hunting; Broadway, May 1959, Rose in Gypsy (for which performance she received the New York Drama Critics Award for the Best Female Lead in a Musical, 1959); toured the US Mar–Dec 1961, in the production; at the Flamingo, Las Vegas Nevada, Oct 1962, appeared in cabaret; made her London début in cabaret at *The Talk of the Town*, Mar 1964; Valley Music Theatre, Los Angeles, California, July 1965, played Sally Adams in a revival of Call Me Madam; NY State, May 1966, Annie Oakley in a slightly revised Annie Get Your Gun; Broadway, Sept 1966, repeated this part and subsequently toured in the production; Coconut Grove Playhouse, Miami, Fla, 1968, again played Sally Adams in Call Me Madam; St James's, 31 Mar 1970, took over as Dolly Gallagher Levi in a slightly revised version of Hello Dolly!; toured, summer 1974, in a variety show with Carroll O'Connor; Music Center Pavilion, Hollywood, Oct 1974, appeared in concert; Imperial, 9 Mar 1975, appeared in A Gala Tribute to Joshua Logan; received a Special Antoinette Perry (Tony) Award, 1972; films include: Kid Millions, 1934; Anything Goes, 1936; Stage Door Canteen, 1943; Call Me Madam, 1953; It's a Mad, Mad, Mad, Mad World, 1963; Won Ton Ton, 1976; has also appeared frequently on television, including Merv Griffin's Salute to Irving Berlin, May 1976.

Address: c/o Actors Equity Association, 165 West 46th Street, New York, NY 10036.

MERRICK, David, producing manager
b St Louis, Mo, 27 Nov 1912; *m* (2) Jeanne Gibson (mar dis).

Presented on his own account, or in association with others, the following plays: Bright Boy, 1944; Fanny 1954; the Matchmaker, 1955; Look Back in Anger, Romanoff and Juliet, Jamaica, 1957; The Entertainer, The World of Suzie Wong, Epitaph for George Dillon, Maria Golovin (musical drama), La Plume de Ma Tante, 1958; Destry Rides Again, Gypsy, Take Me Along, 1959; The Good Soup, Vintage 60, A Taste of Honey, Becket, Irma La Douce, Do Re Mi, 1960; Carnival, Sunday in New York, Ross, Subways Are for Sleeping, 1961; I Can Get It for You Wholesale, Stop the World—I Want to Get Off, Tchin-Tchin, 1962; Oliver!, Rattle of a Simple Man, The Rehearsal, Luther, 110 in the Shade, Arturo Ui, One Flew over the Cuckoo's Nest, 1963; Hello, Dolly!, Foxy, The Milk Train Doesn't Stop Here Anymore, Oh What a Lovely War!, A Severed Head, I Was Dancing, 1964; The Roar of the Greasepaint—The Smell of the Crowd, Pickwick, Hello, Dolly (London), Hot September, Inadmissible Evidence, The Cactus Flower, The MaratSade, 1965; Philadelphia, Here I Come, We Have Always Lived in the Castle, The Loves of Cass McGuire, Don't Drink the Water, I Do! I Do! 1966; The Astrakhan Coat, 110 in the Shade (London), Cactus Flower (London), Keep It in the Family, Rosencrantz and Guildenstern Are Dead, How Now, Dow Jones, Mata Hari (Washington, DC), 1967; The Happy Time, The Seven Descents of Myrtle, Rockefeller and the Red Indians, Promises, Promises, Forty Carats, 1968; Play It Again, Sam (also London), A Patriot for Me, The Penny Wars, Private Lives, Promises, Promises (London), 1969; Play on Love (London), The Battle of Shrivings (London), Child's Play, 1970; Four on a Garden, A Midsummer Night's Dream in the Royal Shakespeare production by Peter Brook, Child's Play (London), The Philanthropist, 1971; the Stratford Memorial Theatre of Canada in There's One in Every Marriage, Vivat! Vivat! Regina!, Moonchildren, Sugar, 1972; Out Cry, the tour of One-Night Stand, 1973; Mack and Mabel, The Misanthrope, Dreyfus in Rehearsal, Travesties, The Red Devil Battery Sign (Boston), Very Good Eddie, 1975; The Baker's Wife (Washington), 1976; produced the film The Great Gatsby, 1974.

Address: 246 West 44th Street, New York, NY 10036.

MERRILL, Bob, composer and lyricist
b Atlantic City, New Jersey, 17 May 1920; *e* Temple University.

Originally engaged as a night club singer and comedian, and also toured in vaudeville, 1935–41; wrote the lyrics and music for his first New York show, New Girl in Town, produced at the 46th Street, 14 May 1957; has since written

music and lyrics for Take Me Along, 1959; Carnival! 1961; lyrics only for Funny Girl, 1964; music and lyrics for Henry, Sweet Henry, 1967; book and lyrics for Prettybelle (Boston), 1971; lyrics for Sugar, 1972; book, music and lyrics for The Prince of Grand Street, 1978; received the Anglo-American Award, 1966; received the Drama Critics Circle Award for New Girl in Town and for Carnival; has been dialogue director for more than 20 films, and wrote the music and lyrics for The Wonderful World of the Brothers Grimm, 1962; screenplays include Mahogany, and WC Fields and Me; for television has been supervisor of network writers for NBC, 1943–4, director for CBS, 1950–1, production consultant for the television division of an advertising agency, 1949–56, and wrote the music and lyrics for Mr Magoo's Christmas Carol, 1963; his numerous hit songs include How Much Is That Doggie in the Window?

Address: ASCAP, 1 Lincoln Plaza, New York, NY 10023.

MICHAEL, Kathleen, actress
b London, 25 June 1917; *d* of Jack Smith and his wife Louise (Driscoll); *e* London; *m* Peter Hardy Woodham; formerly a shorthand-typist; gained an LCC two years scholarship to the Royal Academy of Dramatic Art, 1937.

Made her first appearance on the stage with the Sheffield Repertory Company, at Southport, Lancs, Sept 1939; she remained with that company, until 1943, when she toured for ENSA; during 1944, appeared with the Perth Repertory company; during 1945–6, toured for the Arts Council, in The Corn is Green, and The School for Scandal, and subsequently, with the Midland Theatre Company, under Beatrix Lehmann; made her first appearance in London, at the Torch Theatre, 1 Sept 1947, as Marikke in The Witches Ride; Lyric, Hammersmith, Jan 1948, played Ailsa Fergus in Bred in the Bone; Boltons, Apr 1948, the First Narrator in Lucrece; Wyndham's, July 1948, Ethel in People Like Us; Shakespeare Memorial Theatre, Stratford-on-Avon, 1949 season, played Imogen in Cymbeline, Titania in A Midsummer Night's Dream, Lady Macduff in Macbeth, and Anne Boleyn in King Henry VIII; Winter Garden, Apr 1950, Fräulein Bürstner in The Trial; Q, May 1950, Gay in Forsaking All Others, and Bertha in Exiles; Royal, Brighton, Sept 1952, played Kathie Starkie in The Gladiators; New, May 1956, played Andrée in Gigi; Arts, Cambridge, June 1957, Madeleine in Amédée; Royal Court, June 1960, Sarah Kahn in the first play in Arnold Wesker's trilogy Chicken Soup With Barley; at the same theatre, July 1960, again played Sarah Kahn, in the third play of the same trilogy, I'm Talking About Jerusalem; Piccadilly, June 1962, played Sarah in The Glad and the Sorry Season; Vanbrugh Theatre Club, Jan 1965, Edna Bickley in The Gift; Vaudeville, Jan 1968, played Catherine in The Bells, and the Hon Salina Shernought in Lend Me Five Shillings; Playhouse, Nottingham, Dec 1968, Iris Wormald in Whoops-A-Daisy; Playhouse, Nottingham, 1969, and Saville, June 1969, Woman in The Resistible Rise of Arturo Ui; Nottingham, Aug 1969, and Edinburgh Festival, Sept 1969, Lady Nelson in The Hero Rises Up; also at Nottingham, 1969, played Phoebe Rice in The Entertainer; in the first season of the Leeds Playhouse, Sept–Dec 1970, her appearances included Donna Matilde in Henry IV (also Edinburgh Festival), Simon Says (revue), Mistress Page in The Merry Wives of Windsor, Mrs Frail in Love for Love, and Amelia in Oh Glorious Jubilee; Forum, Billingham, 1971, Alice Blake in Never Say Die.

Address: c/o Bernard Gillman, 28 Elmdene, Tolworth, Surrey.

MICHAEL, Ralph (*né* Ralph Champion Shotter), actor
b London, 26 Sept 1907; *s* of Hamilton Godfrey Shotter and

his wife Bessie Hannah (Champion-Jones); *e* Bembridge School, Isle of Wight; *m* (1) Fay Compton (mar dis); (2) Joyce Heron (mar dis); (3) Jain Cameron; originally studied architecture.

Made his first appearance on the stage at the Chelsea Palace, 6 Aug 1930, as Christian in The Bells, with Henry Baynton, and toured with Baynton's company until Apr 1931, playing in extensive Shakespearean repertory; His Majesty's, Apr 1931, appeared as Gilles de Rais in Saint Joan, and later, at the Haymarket, played Brother Martin Ladvenu in the same play; Arts, May 1931, appeared as Jean Tiphaine in The Trial of Jeanne D'Arc; joined the Old Vic company, Sept 1931, remaining throughout the season, playing a variety of parts; appeared with the Denville stock company at Watford, June–Dec 1932, and with the Malvern repertory company, 1932–4; at the Haymarket, Feb 1935, played Sam Burridge in Barnet's Folly; was again with the Malvern company, 1935–6; Haymarket, Aug 1936, played the Constable in The Amazing Doctor Clitterhouse; Arts, June 1937, Bardolph in The Man Who Meant Well; toured, 1938, as Tommy Wishart in A Thing Apart; Haymarket, June 1938, played Owen Sands in Comedienne, and Dec 1938, Jack Chesney in Charley's Aunt; Playhouse, Feb 1939, John of Gishala in Jerusalem; Streatham Hill, May 1939, Bill in Drawing Room; served in the RAF, as rear-gunner, Sept 1939 to 1942; Vaudeville, Sept 1942, played Mordan in Men in Shadow; Apollo, June 1945, succeeded Raymond Huntley as Victor Prynne in Private Lives; Q, Mar 1946, Booze Anger in Ill Wind; Embassy, June 1946, Major Philip Brooke-Jervaux in Love Goes to Press, and played the same part at the Duchess, July 1946; made his first appearance on the New York stage at the Biltmore, 1 Jan 1947, in this part; returning to England, appeared at the Lyric, July 1947, as Albrecht Richter in Peace in our Time; Globe, Sept 1948, played Jason in Medea; New, June 1949, Mark Eldridge in Champagne for Delilah; Haymarket, Oct 1949, succeeded James Donald as Maurice Townsend in The Heiress; at the Shubert Theatre, Boston, Oct 1950, appeared as Gerard in The Day After Tomorrow; Princes, London, Mar 1951, appeared as Max Layton in The Seventh Veil; Arts, Sept 1951, Christian Melrose in Saint's Day; Savoy, Nov 1951, the Earl of Marshwood in Relative Values; toured, Feb 1953, as Michael Dennis in The Living Room; Embassy, Feb 1954, played the Father in a revival of The Mother; Arts, June 1954, the Father in Six Characters in Search of an Author, and appeared in this part at the St James's, July 1954; joined the Shakespeare Memorial Theatre, Stratford-on-Avon, 1955, and during the season played Lafeu in All's Well That Ends Well, Banquo in Macbeth, Bassianus in Titus Andronicus, and Master Page in The Merry Wives of Windsor; Arts, May 1956, played Colonel Rimini in Off the Mainland; following a European tour, June 1957, playing in Paris, Venice, Belgrade, Zagreb, Vienna, and Warsaw, he appeared at the Stoll, July 1957, as Bassianus in Titus Andronicus; Westminster, Apr 1958, Julian Armstrong in Any Other Business?; toured, Nov 1958, as Mortimer Wilmot in Gilt and Gingerbread; Cambridge, Apr 1959, played Adam Hartley in The Hidden River; Duchess, Apr 1960, John Cartwright in A Shred of Evidence; Old Vic, Sept 1960, Doctor Dorn in The Seagull; St Martin's, Aug 1961, played Theodore Henderson in Guilty Party; Saville, May 1963, General Otto von Schlitz in Night Conspirators; Royal Court, Feb 1970, Serebryakov in Uncle Vanya; Intimate, Johannesburg, July 1970, and South African tour, including eight black African townships, Andrew Wyke in Sleuth; Thorndike, Leatherhead, Feb 1972, Max Weiner in Touch of Purple; Royal Court, Dec 1972, Grandfather in A Sense of Detachment; Chichester Festival,

1973, played Dorn in The Seagull, May, and Sir Tristram Mardon in Dandy Dick, transferring in the latter part to the Garrick, Oct 1973; with the Actors Company, 1975, toured and played a season at the Wimbledon Theatre, June–July, as Gantry in The Last Romantic, Cadmus in The Bacchae and Pierrot in Jack and the Beanstalk (double-bill), and Debienne in The Phantom of the Opera; Nottingham Playhouse, Feb 1976, Colonel Pickering in Pygmalion; Royal Alexandra, Toronto, 1976, Mackenzie Savage in The Pleasure of His Company; Arts, Cambridge and Oxford Playhouse, 1977, played Prospero in The Tempest; Churchill, Bromley, 1977, Stanley Baldwin in The Woman I Love; joined Prospect Theatre Company to play Gloucester in King Lear at the Old Vic, Oct 1978, and on tour; and for the re-named Old Vic Company, in London and touring, played Montague in Romeo and Juliet (Aug 1979); the Charity Commissioner in The Government Inspector, Sept; Colonel Deacon in The 88, Nov; Lyric, Hammersmith, Feb 1980, Filippo in Country Life; first appeared in films, 1937, in John Halifax, Gentleman; other films include The Hasty Heart, Heroes of Telemark, Khartoum, and The Count of Monte Cristo; TV appearances since the earliest days of BBC television include: The Cocktail Party, and series including: *Sapper* and *Somerset Maugham;* is a Fellow of the Zoological Society.

Favourite part: Father in Six Characters in Search of An Author. *Recreations:* Swimming and drawing. *Club:* Stage Golfing Society. *Address:* 112 Tamworth Street, London SW6 1LE.

MICHELL, Keith, actor
b Adelaide, Australia, 1 Dec 1928; *s* of Joseph Michell and his wife Alice Maud (Aslat); *e* Pt Pirie High School, Adelaide Teachers' College, School of Arts and Crafts, and Adelaide University; *m* Jeannette Sterke; formerly an Art teacher.

Made his first appearance on the stage at the Playbox Theatre, Adelaide, 1947, as Roger in Lover's Leap; on coming to England trained for the stage at the Old Vic Theatre School; joined the Young Vic Theatre Company, to play Bassanio in The Merchant of Venice, 1950–1; first appearance in London, New, Oct 1951, as Charles II in the musical of And So To Bed; joined the Shakespeare Memorial Theatre Company for their Australian tour, 1952–3, to play Orlando in As You Like It and Hotspur in Henry IV, Part I; returned to Stratford-on-Avon for the season, 1954, where he appeared in The Taming of the Shrew, A Midsummer Night's Dream, Troilus and Cressida, and Romeo and Juliet; New Zealand tour, 1954–5, played Thomas in The Lady's Not For Burning; returned to the Shakespeare Memorial Theatre, 1955, to play Macduff in Macbeth, Master Ford in The Merry Wives of Windsor, and Orsino in Twelfth Night, and Parolles in All's Well That Ends Well; Royal Court, May 1956, played the title-part in Don Juan; joined the Old Vic Company, Oct 1956, to play Benedick in Much Ado About Nothing, Proteus in The Two Gentlemen of Verona, Antony in Antony and Cleopatra, and Aaron in Titus Andronicus; Lyric, July 1958, played Nestor/Oscar in Irma La Douce; made his first appearance in the United States at the National, Washington, DC, Sept 1960, in the same part and play, prior to appearing in the same production on Broadway, Plymouth Theatre, Sept 1960–June 1961; on returning to England, he appeared at the Aldwych, Mar 1962, as Vicomte de Valmont in The Art of Seduction; at the opening Chichester Festival, July 1962, played Don John in The Chances, and Ithocles in The Broken Heart; Royale, New York, Sept 1963, played the Count in The Rehearsal; visited Australia, to appear with

Googie Withers at the Comedy, Melbourne, Apr 1964, in The First Four Hundred Years, in celebration of the Shakespeare Quatercentenary; subsequently toured Australia and New Zealand with the same programme; Lyric, London, Oct 1964, played Robert Browning in the musical Robert and Elizabeth; Yvonne Arnaud, Guildford, Jan 1966, co-presented and played Kain Sutherland in Kain; Garrick, July 1966, Henry VIII in The King's Mare; Mermaid, Sept 1966, appeared in the anthology The Fire of London; Piccadilly, Apr 1968, Don Quixote (Cervantes) in Man of La Mancha, taking over the part at the Martin Beck, NY, Dec 1969; Wyndham's, May 1970, Peter Abelard in Abelard and Heloise; repeating the part in Los Angeles, and at the Brooks Atkinson, NY, Mar 1971; Bankside Globe, Aug 1972, played the title-part in Hamlet; Comedy, May 1973, Robert Browning in Dear Love; Artistic Director, Chichester Festival, 1974–; here he has played the Director in Tonight We Improvise, May 1974; Oidipus in Oidipus Tyrannus; appeared in his one-man show, Keith Michell in Concert, 1974; title-role in Cyrano de Bergerac, and Iago in Othello, 1975, appearing in both productions at the Hong Kong Arts Festival, 1976; directed and designed Twelfth Night and played Major Mathieu in M. Perrichon's Travels, 1976; devised, directed and designed In Order of Appearance, played Magnus in The Apple Cart, and Becket in Murder in the Cathedral (Chichester Cathedral), 1977; played Magnus in Luxembourg, Brussels, and at the Phoenix, Nov 1977; toured Australia with the Chichester Company, playing Othello and Magnus, 1978; Haymarket, Mar 1979, Sherlock Holmes in The Crucifer of Blood; Her Majesty's, Mar 1980, Oscar Jaffee in On The Twentieth Century; M Perrichon's Travels, 1976; since 1956 has appeared in a number of films, including: Hell Fire Club, Prudence and the Pill, Henry VIII and His Six Wives, and Moments; principal television performances include: Pygmalion, The Mayerling Affair, Traveller Without Luggage, Tiger at the Gates, Antony and Cleopatra, Ring Round the Moon, The Six Wives of Henry VIII, An Ideal Husband, Dear Love, and several of his own shows; also the dual role in The Great Impersonation, The Story of the Marlboroughs, and The Day Christ Died (American television); his LPs include The Sonnets and The Prophets and Captain Beaky: also the title of a book of poems he illustrated, 1975; exhibitions of his paintings include "New York", "Outback Australia", "Don Quixote" (1970), "Abelard and Heloise" and "Hamlet", 1972.

Recreations: Painting, photography, swimming, and riding. *Address.* c/o Chatto & Linnit Ltd, Globe Theatre, Shaftesbury Avenue, London W1.

MIDDLETON, Ray, actor and singer
b Chicago, Ill, 8 Feb 1907; *s* of Almor Middleton and his wife Lela (Owens); *e* University of Illinois, gaining a degree in music; also studied music at the Juilliard School of Music, New York.

Made his first professional appearance at the Detroit Civic Opera House; first appeared in New York, at the 44th Street Theatre, 21 Dec 1931, as the Giant in Jack and the Beanstalk; New Amsterdam, Nov 1933, played John Kent in Roberta; subsequently, in 1936, sang leading roles with the Chicago Opera Company; Ethel Barrymore Theatre, Oct 1938, played Washington Irving in Knickerbocker Holiday; Alvin Theatre, Aug 1939, appeared in George White's Scandals; went to Hollywood, 1940, where he appeared in several films, during the next three years; served in the US Air Force, 1943–6; at the Imperial Theatre, May 1946, played Frank Butler in Annie Get Your Gun; 46th Street Theatre, Oct 1948, Sam in Love Life; Majestic, May 1950, succeeded Ezio

Pinza as Emil de Becque in South Pacific; in San Francisco, Aug 1951, appeared in Annie Get Your Gun; toured, 1957 and 1963, in America in Song and Story; 54th Street, NY, Mar 1963, Sergeant Fielding in a revival of Too True to Be Good; Goodspeed Opera House, East Haddam, Conn, June 1965, Governor in Man of La Mancha and July 1965, played in Purple Dust; City Center, June 1965, Emile de Becque in South Pacific; ANTA, Washington Square, Nov 1965, played the Innkeeper in Man of La Mancha, and played in this part continuously until the play's closing in June 1971; appeared in the film Songs of Chicago, 1940, and since played in I Dream of Jeannie and Road to Denver, 1776, etc.

Address: c/o Actors Equity Association, 165 West 46th Street, New York, NY 10036.

MIDGLEY, Robin, director
b Torquay, Devon, 10 Nov 1934; *s* of Dr Roy Lee Midgley and his wife Margaret (Elles); *e* Blundell's and King's College, Cambridge; *m* Liane Aukin.

Directed his first professional production, The Seagull, at the Arts, Cambridge, 1956; first London production, Kill Two Birds, St Martin's, 1961; first New York production, Those That Play Clowns, ANTA, 1967; plays he has directed in London include Victor, Picnic on the Battlefield, The Pedagogue (all RSC), 1964; Oedipus the King, Oedipus at Colonus, Right You Are If You Think So, The Professor, 1965; Let's Get a Divorce, 1966; Rafferty's Chant, 1967; The Young Churchill, Son of Man, 1969; How the Other Half Loves, 1970 (also Australia and Greece); Vincent, 1971; Lloyd George Knew My Father, 1972 (also Australia and USA); Sextet, Cause Célèbre, Oliver (co-director), 1977; My Fair Lady (tour and Adelphi), 1979; Director of Productions, Phoenix Theatre, Leicester, 1968–73, and subsequently Artistic Director, Haymarket and Phoenix Theatres, 1973–; he has directed more than 70 productions at Leicester, many of which have toured nationally, or gone to the West End; first TV production 1961; was also a drama producer for BBC radio, 1956, and producer for Jamaica Broadcasting Corporation, 1960.

Address: 42 Avenue Road, Leicester. *Tel:* 0533–704765.

MIDLER, Bette, actress and singer
b Honolulu, Hawaii

Made her New York stage debut in the chorus of Fiddler on the Roof at the Imperial, 1966; took over the part of Tzeitel when the show moved to the Majestic, Feb 1967, and remained in the role for three years; at the Palace, Dec 1973, appeared in her own show, followed by a season at the Minskoff, Apr 1975, in Bette Midler's Clams on the Half-Shell Revue; Majestic, Dec 1979, appeared in Bette! Divine Madness; has toured extensively in Europe, Africa and the US; her first film appearance was as an extra in Hawaii; recently in The Rose, 1979; TV work includes her own award-winning specials and the *Tonight Show*.

Address: c/o Actors Equity Association, 165 West 46th Street, New York, NY 10036.

MILES, Sir Bernard (cr. Kt, 1969; Baron, 1979), CBE 1953, actor and director
b Uxbridge, 27 Sept 1907; *s* of Edwin James Miles and his wife Barbara (Fletcher); *e* Uxbridge County School and Pembroke College, Oxford; *m* Josephine Wilson; formerly a schoolmaster.

Made his first appearance on the stage at the New Theatre, 1 Sept 1930, as the Second Messenger in Richard III; subsequently property-master and scene-painter at People's Theatre, 1931; His Majesty's, Apr 1931, appeared in Saint

Joan, subsequently touring in the same play; Westminster, Dec 1934, the Workman in The Fisher of Shadows; spent five years as designer, stage-manager, stage-carpenter, property-master, character-actor, and scenic artist in repertory companies at Sheffield, Windsor, York, Brighton, Birmingham, Bournemouth, etc; at the New Theatre, Sept 1938, played Moore in Can We Tell?; appeared at the Players' Theatre, 1938–9, in Late Joys; Little, Apr 1939, in The Little Revue; Globe, July 1940, played Briggs in Thunder Rock; Wyndham's, 1940–1, played in Diversion and Diversion No 2; toured, 1941, with the Old Vic company, as Iago in Othello, and appeared with the company, at the New Theatre, July 1942, in the same part; Vaudeville, Sept 1942, with John Mills, produced Men in Shadow, and in Dec 1942, took over the leading part of Lew Messenger in that play; Scala, Mar 1946, played George Watkins in A Century for George, and Abel Honeyman in Let Tyrants Tremble, of which he was author; joined the Old Vic Company, at the New Theatre, for the 1947–8 season, appearing as Christopher Sly in The Taming of the Shrew, the Bishop of Carlisle in Richard II, Robert de Baudricourt and the Inquisitor in Saint Joan, Antonovitch in The Government Inspector, and on tour, Face in The Alchemist; in July 1950, went on the music-hall stage, appearing at London Palladium, etc; founder, with his wife, of The Mermaid Theatre, an Elizabethan-style playhouse; during the first season, Sept 1951, he produced Purcell's Dido and Aeneas (with Kirsten Flagstad, Edith Coates and Maggie Teyte), and The Tempest, in which he appeared as Caliban; during his second season, Sept–Oct 1952, in addition to the previous productions he presented A Trick to Catch the Old One, and Macbeth, in which he played the title-role; the Mermaid stage and tiring-house were reconstructed at the Royal Exchange, May 1953, and during a three-month season he presented As You Like It, Eastward Ho! Macbeth and Dido and Aeneas; in June 1957, his scheme for a new theatre in the City of London began with the building of the Mermaid Theatre at Puddle Dock; the theatre was opened in May 1959, with the musical play Lock Up Your Daughters (which he also adapted from Henry Fielding's Rape Upon Rape); this was followed, Dec 1959, with his adaptation of Treasure Island, in which he played Long John Silver; at the same theatre, Feb 1960, adapted (with Julius Gellner) a modern dress version of Henry V; and June 1960, directed and played the title-part in Bertolt Brecht's Life of Galileo; made his first appearance in Canada at the O'Keefe Centre, Toronto, Dec 1960, when he played Long John Silver in Treasure Island; Mermaid, London, Feb 1961, played the title-part in John Gabriel Borkman, June 1961, directed The Andersonville Trial; Nov 1961, directed The Long Sunset; Feb 1962, directed The Bed Bug; May 1962, played Squeezum in a revival of Lock Up Your Daughters, transferring with the production to Her Majesty's, Aug 1962; on returning to the Mermaid, Nov 1962, directed The Witch of Edmonton; Mar 1963, played Ezra Fitton in All in Good Time, transferring to the Phoenix, Apr 1963; Mermaid, July 1963, directed The Life of Galileo; Aug 1963, played Schweyk in Schweyk in the Second World War; Sept 1963, appeared in the anthology The Buxom Muse; Feb 1964, directed The Bacchae; June 1964, directed The Maid's Tragedy; Oct 1964, directed Don't Let Summer Come; Dec 1964, played Long John Silver in Treasure Island; May 1965, played Œdipus in Œdipus the King and Œdipus at Colonus; June 1965, Archbishop in Left-Handed Liberty; Aug 1965, directed and subsequently took over Noah Topping in Dandy Dick; Jan 1966, appeared in the one-man show On the Wagon; Apr 1966, played Argan in The Imaginary Invalid; Dec 1966, Long John Silver in Treasure Island; May 1967, directed Iphigenia in Aulis and

Hecuba in repertory with Electra and Orestes, in the play series The Trojan Wars; Nov 1967, played Charlie Pappalardo in Climb the Greased Pole; Mar 1969, directed a revival of his adaptation Lock Up Your Daughters; Aug 1969, edited and directed The Other House; Apr–May 1970, played Falstaff in both parts of Henry IV, performed in repertory; Sept 1970, directed St Joan; toured, Dec 1970, as Long John Silver in Treasure Island; presented his one-man show, Back to Square One, Apr 1971; played Iago in Othello, Sept 1971; directed The Price of Justice, Jan 1972; directed An Inspector Calls, Aug 1973; Long John Silver in Treasure Island, Dec 1973; co-directed The Great Society, May 1974, also playing John Ball; Long John Silver, Dec 1974; directed On the Rocks, Aug 1975, also playing Mr Hipney; Long John Silver (New London Theatre), Dec 1975; co-directed For King and Country, Sept 1976; adapted and played the King in The Point, Dec 1976; adapted and directed The Fire That Consumes, Oct 1977; Riverside, Jan 1980, appeared in his own one-man show, The Hindsight Saga; first appeared in films, 1937, in Channel Crossing, and subsequently played in Pastor Hall, Quiet Wedding, In Which We Serve, Moby Dick, The Man Who Knew Too Much, etc; was co-author (with Jeffrey Dell) of the film of Thunder Rock, and was co-author (with Charles Saunders) and co-director of Tawny Pipit, in which he also played lead; in collaboration, wrote the screen-play of The Guinea Pig, in which he also appeared, 1948; adapted Four Thousand Brass Halfpennies, 1965; author of The British Theatre, 1948; he received the honour of CBE, 1953, was knighted in the Birthday Honours, 1969, and created Baron Miles (Life Peer), 1979.

Hobby; Carpentry. *Club:* City Livery. *Address:* Mermaid Theatre, Puddle Dock, Blackfriars, London EC1.

MILES, Sarah, actress
m Robert Bolt (mar dis); trained for the stage at RADA.

Early experience in repertory at the Connaught, Worthing; Royal Court, June 1963, Anna Brierly in Kelly's Eye; joined the National Theatre Company at the Old Vic, 1964, to play in The Recruiting Officer; Jan 1965, also Old Vic, Abigail Williams in The Crucible; Hampstead, Nov 1966, Marina Oswald in The Silence of Lee Harvey Oswald; New, Apr 1967, Woman in World War 2½; Chichester Festival, May 1970, Mary Queen of Scots in Vivat! Vivat Regina!; Piccadilly, Oct 1970, again played Mary; Ahmanson, Los Angeles, Jan 1974, title-role in Saint Joan; at the same theatre played Sabina in The Skin of Our Teeth; American Conservatory Theater, Feb 1978, wrote and performed in her solo musical, S. Miles Is Me; films include: The Servant, Ryan's Daughter, Lady Caroline Lamb, The Hireling, The Sailor Who Fell from Grace with the Sea (1976), etc; TV films include Dynasty and Great Expectations.

Address: c/o Chatto & Linnit Ltd, Globe Theatre, Shaftesbury Avenue, London W1. *Tel:* 01–439 4371.

MILLAR, Mary (*née* Wetton), actress and singer
b Doncaster, 26 July; *d* of Horace Wetton and his wife Irene (Mellor); *e* Shirecliffe, Sheffield; *m* Rafael, theatrical photographer.

First appeared on the stage in Aug 1950, at the Empire Theatre, Sheffield, singing operatic arias in variety; played in variety, pantomime and summer shows; toured, Feb 1957, as Margot in The Desert Song; toured, Dec 1958, as Mary Fenton in Old Chelsea; again toured as Margot, May 1959; Dec 1960, Majestic, New York, appeared on Broadway, as standby for Julie Andrews as Guinevere in Camelot; Wimbledon, Nov 1961, Liz in Billy Liar, and appeared in Salad Days; May 1962, made her London début as Cloris in Lock

Up Your Daughters, transferring to Her Majesty's, Aug 1962; Duchess, Mar 1963, appeared in the revue, See You Inside; May Fair, Mar 1964, Lydia Languish in All In Love; Dublin Festival, Sept 1965, at the Olympia, played Lucy Westerna in Dearest Dracula; Richmond, Mar 1968, Lucy in Bless the Bride; Belgrade, Coventry, Feb 1969, played Hetty Widgett in Ann Veronica, later taking over the name part, in which she transferred to the Cambridge, Apr 1969; Arnaud, Guildford, June 1969, Julia in The Mating Game; Richmond, Oct 1971, again played Lucy in Bless the Bride, afterwards touring: Globe, Aug 1972, Poppy Dickie in the Cambridge Theatre Company's Popkiss; Queen's, Hornchurch, Feb 1973, Gwendolen in The Importance of Being Earnest; toured, Apr 1974, in Family Circle and in Nov, as Gwenda in Dial-In for Diolin; Apr 1975, appeared in the revue Small and Brassy at the King's Head, Islington, transferring to the Wyndham's (late-night), July 1975; Nice, Oct 1978, Mrs Falberg in Hermes Imagination; appears frequently in repertory at the Queens, Hornchurch; television, since 1953, includes: Titipu, Iolanthe and Rookery Nook.

Favourite part: Berinthia in Virtue in Danger, and Gwendoline in The Importance of Being Earnest. *Recreation:* Reproducing fashion plates and horse-riding. *Address:* Suite 16, 26 Charing Cross Road, London, WC2. *Tel:* 01–836 7672.

MILLAR, Ronald, actor and dramatic author
b Reading, 12 Nov 1919; *s* of Ronald Hugh Millar and his wife Dorothy Ethel (Dacre-Hill); *e* Charterhouse and King's College, Cambridge.

Made his first appearance on the stage at the Ambassadors' Theatre, 22 May 1940, in Swinging the Gate; Phoenix, Aug 1943, played Prince Kuragin in War and Peace; Playhouse, Oct 1943, Cully in Mr Bolfry; Lyric, Mar 1944, David Marsden in Murder for a Valentine, and June 1944, Flight-Lieut Chris Keppel in his own play, Zero Hour; Hippodrome, Oct 1944, Penry in Jenny Jones; St Martin's, Nov 1945, Colin Tabret in The Sacred Flame; Ambassadors', Mar 1946, Smith in Murder on the Nile; is the author of the following plays: Murder from Memory, 1942; Zero Hour, 1944; Frieda, 1946; The Other Side, 1946; Champagne for Delilah, 1949; Waiting for Gillian, 1954; The Bride and the Bachelor, 1956; The Big Tickle, 1958; The More the Merrier, The Bride Comes Back, 1960; The Affair, 1961; The New Men, 1962; The Masters, 1963; Robert and Elizabeth (book and lyrics), 1964; On the Level (book and lyrics) 1966; Number Ten, 1967; They Don't Grow on Trees, 1968; Abelard and Heloise, 1970; Parents' Day (co-author), 1972; Odd Girl Out, 1974; The Case in Question, 1975; Once More with Music (musical), 1976; is also the author of film scripts, including Frieda, The Miniver Story, Train of Events, Scaramouche, Rose-Marie, Never Let Me Go, etc; deputy chairman, Theatre Royal, Haymarket, 1977–.

Recreations: Music, tennis, and swimming. *Address:* 7 Sheffield Terrace, London W8. *Tel:* 01–727 8361.

MILLER, ann, (*née* Lucy Ann Collier), actress, dancer, singer
b Houston, Texas, 12 Apr 1919; *d* of John Collier and his wife Clara (Birdwell); *e* Albert Sidney Johnson High School, Houston, and Lawler Professional School, Hollywood; trained for dancing as a child; *m* (1) Reese Milner (mar dis), (2) William Moss (mar dis), (3) Arthur Cameron (mar dis).

Alvin, Aug 1939, appeared in George White's Scandals; first appeared in films in The New Faces of 1937 and continued in films for thirty years; reappeared in New York at the Winter Garden, 19 June 1969, when she took over the title role in the musical Mame; toured, 1974, as Reno

Sweeney in Anything Goes; also in 1976; toured, 1978–9, in Cactus Flower; Mark Hellinger, Oct 1979, Ann in Sugar Babies; has also played in Can Can, Hello Dolly, Panama Hattie, Blithe Spirit etc; among her numerous pictures may be mentioned Stage Door, Room Service, You Can't Take It with You, Having a Wonderful Time, Too Many Girls, Easter Parade, On the Town, Kiss Me, Kate!, Hit the Deck, That's Entertainment; has appeared frequently on television in talk shows, and in Dames at Sea; author of an autobiography, Miller's High Life.

Address: Actors Equity Association, 165 West 46th Street, New York, NY 10036.

MILLER, Arthur, dramatic author
b New York City, 17 Oct 1915; *s* of Isadore Miller and his wife Augusta (Barnett); *e* NY and University of Michigan (BA); *m* (1) Mary Grace Slattery (mar dis); (2) Marilyn Monroe (mar dis); (3) Ingeborg Morath.

Formerly a journalist on the *Michigan Daily*; gained the Hopwood Award for playwriting at the University of Michigan, 1936, and the Theatre Guild National Award, 1938; in 1938, joined the Federal Theatre Project; is the author of the following plays: The Man Who Had All the Luck, 1944; All My Sons, 1947, which gained the New York Drama Critics Circle Award, 1946–7; Death of a Salesman, 1948, which received the same award and the Pulitzer Prize, 1948–9; The Crucible, received the Antoinette Perry Award, 1953; A View from the Bridge, A Memory of Two Mondays, 1955; After the Fall, Incident at Vichy, 1964; expanded his one-act play A View from the Bridge into a full-length play, 1965; The Price, 1968; directed The Price at the Duke of York's, London, Feb 1969; The Creation of the World and Other Business, 1972; at the University of Michigan, Apr 1974, directed, performed the Narrator in, and wrote the musical play Up for Paradise; author of The Archbishop's Ceiling, 1977; The American Clock, 1980; adapted An Enemy of the People, 1950; author of the screenplay The Misfits, 1961; author of Situation Normal, 1944, and a novel Focus, 1946; a collection of short stories I Don't Need You Anymore, 1967; has contributed stories, essays, and articles to various magazines, including *Harpers, Saturday Evening Post, The New York Times Magazine,* etc; received a DHL (Hon) from the University of Michigan, 1956; Gold Medal for Drama from National Institute of Arts and Letters, 1959.

Address: c/o Katharine Brown, International Creative Management, 40 West 57th Street, New York, NY 10019.

MILLER, Harry M, producing manager
b Auckland, New Zealand, 6 Jan 1934; *s* of James Miller and his wife Sadie (Crown); *e* Rongatai College, Wellington, and Mt Albert G S, Auckland; *m* Wendy Paul.

Presented his first production, The Johnny O'Keefe Show, at Her Majesty's Theatre, Auckland, in 1957; productions in Australia include Present Laughter, Private Lives, Virginia Woolf, Porgy and Bess, 1966; The Boy Friend, The Boys in the Band, You Know I Can't Hear You When the Water's Running, 1967; Hair, Dames at Sea, The Secretary Bird, 1968; You're A Good Man Charlie Brown, Sleuth, A Load of Old Stuffe, 1969; Butterflies Are Free, Conduct Unbecoming, 1970; Winnie-the-Pooh, 1971; Jesus Christ Superstar, The Removalists, Butley, Grease, 1972; Don't Just Lie There, Say Something, No Sex Please, We're British, 1973; The Rocky Horror Show, 1974; Jesus Christ Superstar (New Production) 1975; co-presented The Removalists, London, 1973; TV productions include Entertaining With Kerr, 1965; Seekers, 1976; Chairman, Harry M Miller Attractions Pty Ltd; commercial and promotional consultant to Australian

Elizabethan Theatre Trust, 1968–70; Australian Opera, 1967–70; Australian Ballet Company, 1968–70; Melbourne Theatre Company, 1969–70; board member, National Institute of Dramatic Art, 1974–5; consultant, Canberra Arts and Science Festival, 1975; Australian Government Advisory Committee on US Bicentennial Celebrations, 1975 and, 1978; special advisor on Australian Bi-Centennial (1988); Chairman of Queen Elizabeth Silver Jubilee Celebrations in Australia, 1978.

Recreations: Horse riding, skiing, tennis, *Club:* The Auckland Club, NZ. *Address:* PO Box 41, Kings Cross, NSW 2011, Australia. *Tel:* 357 3077.

MILLER, Jason, playwright and actor
b Long Island City, NY, 22 Apr 1939; *e* University of Scranton and Catholic University.

Made his New York debut as an actor at the Mercury, 29 June 1969, as Pip in Pequod; Estelle Newman, Oct 1970, played The Assistant in The Happiness Cage; Public, Feb 1971, Paryfon Rogozhin in Subject to Fits; author of Nobody Hears a Broken Drum, produced at the Fortune, 19 Mar 1970 and which he rewrote in 1973; That Championship Season, off-Broadway and Broadway productions, 1972, which won the Antoinette Perry (Tony) Award and the Pulitzer Prize as best play of the year; It's a Sin to Tell a Lie; Circus Lady; Lou Gehrig Did Not Die of Cancer; That Championship Season produced in London at the Garrick, 6 May 1974; appeared in the film The Exorcist, 1973, and in The Nickel Ride; TV appearances include F Scott Fitzgerald in Hollywood; author of the screenplay of That Championship Season.

Address: c/o Earl Graham, 317 West 45th Street, New York, NY 10036.

MILLER, Joan, actress
b Nelson, British Columbia, Canada, 1910; *d* of Richard Wallace Miller and his wife Rhoda (Tingle); *e* King Edward High School, Vancouver, BC; *m* (1) John Godfrey (dec); (2) Peter Cotes.

Made her first appearance on the stage, at the Empress Theatre, Vancouver, 1930, in When Knights Were Bold; was awarded the Bessborough Trophy as best actress, at the Dominion Drama Festival, 1934; introduced to London by the late J T Grein; made her West End debut at His Majesty's, 25 Sept 1934, walking-on in Josephine, and Jan 1935, in Henry IV (Part I), also understudying Lady Tree and playing Mistress Quickly; Whitehall, May 1935, played May Stokes in Golden Arrow; this was followed by a season at the Open Air Theatre; Ambassadors', Oct 1935, the Maid in The Soldier's Fortune; Embassy, Sept 1936, Louise Michel in The Tiger; from 1936–9 mainly engaged in television, though she appeared at the Vaudeville, Feb 1938, for the Stage Society, as Hennie Berger in Awake and Sing; during 1942, appeared as Eliza Doolittle in Pygmalion, and during 1942–3, appeared at the Alexandra Theatre, Birmingham; Torch, Aug 1945, played Rebecca in Rosmersholm; New Lindsey, Apr–June 1946, Branwen Elder in The Long Mirror, Eva in For Services Rendered, and Mrs Collins in Pick-up Girl, which was subsequently transferred to the Prince of Wales and Casino Theatres; Lyric, Hammersmith, Oct 1947, Gisela Waldstein in Dark Summer, subsequently transferred to the St Martin's; during 1948, appeared at Manchester, as Ella Rentheim in John Gabriel Borkman, and also played Candida; Embassy, May 1949, played Frances Shelley in The Rising Wind; Lyric, Hammersmith, Aug 1949, Miss Julie in the play of that name; People's Palace, May 1950, Helen Winthrop in Birdcage; New Boltons, Nov 1950, Karen

Wright in The Children's Hour; New Boltons, Feb 1951, again played Candida; at the same theatre, Mar–Dec 1951, appeared as Mrs Fitzgerald in Loaves and Fishes, Julia Almond in A Pin to See the Peepshow, Helen in Mrs Basil Farrington, and Godiva in The Importance of Wearing Clothes; toured, 1952, as Lola in Come Back, Little Sheba; Her Majesty's, Dec 1952, appeared as Mrs Gillis in The Man, and played the same part in a revival at the St Martin's, Feb 1953; made her first appearance on the New York stage at the Playhouse, 17 Sept 1953, when she again played Julia Almond in A Pin to See the Peepshow; in London, at the Phoenix, July 1954, played Clara Dennison in The Wooden Dish; Playhouse, Oxford, Jan 1957, played the title-part in Medea; joined the Shakespeare Memorial Theatre Co, Stratford-on-Avon, Apr 1957, and played the following parts: Constance in King John, Portia in Julius Caesar, the Queen in Cymbeline, and Juno in The Tempest; New, Nov 1958, played Nell Palmer in Hot Summer Night; Arts, July 1959, Margaret Hyland in The Rope Dancers; Princes, Feb 1960, Hannah Kingsley, QC, in Girl on the Highway; Pembroke, Croydon, Jan 1962, played Helen Baird in A Loss of Roses; Longacre, NY, Jan 1963, played Contessa Catherine Minadoli in Hidden Stranger; at the Theatre Royal, Bristol, Apr 1963, appeared in A Woman Alone, solo-performance; toured, May 1963, as Margaret Pardee in The Odd Ones; Ashcroft, Croydon, Sept 1963, played Nora Melody in A Touch of the Poet; toured, Oct 1964, as Mrs Laurentz in So Wise, So Young; Phoenix, Leicester, Nov 1965, played Marya in Uncle's Dream; Vaudeville, Mar 1968, Sally in Staring at the Sun; Arnaud, Guildford, Sept 1969, Lucy Amorest in The Old Ladies, playing the same part at the Westminster, Nov 1969, and transferring to the Duchess, Jan 1970; Arnaud, Guildford, Aug 1971, Mrs Morland in Mary Rose; guest appearances at the Theatre Royal, York, as Mrs Warren in Mrs Warren's Profession, Feb 1972, and Mrs George in Getting Married, May 1974; Arnaud, Aug 1974, Madame Raquin in Therese; toured, Oct 1975, as Lavinia Penniman in The Heiress; 1976–78, guest appearances include The Dame of Sark, Theatre Royal, York; Madame d'Alvarez in Gigi, Swan, Worcester; Judith Bliss in Hay Fever, Watermill, Newbury; Amanda Wingfield in The Glass Menagerie, Liverpool Playhouse; she has appeared in numerous films and frequent television appearances since 1955 include such title-roles as Jane Clegg, Woman in a Dressing Gown, and, on Australian television, Candida and other classics; has also appeared in and written numerous radio scripts; author of Television in the Making, 1956; The Woman Poet, 1977.

Favourite parts: Queen Elizabeth in Elizabeth the Queen, and Rebecca West in Rosmersholm. *Club:* Lansdowne. *Recreations:* Reading and interior decoration. *Address:* 70 York Mansions, Prince of Wales Drive, London SW11. *Tel:* 01–622 8546.

MILLER, Jonathan, actor, author, and director
b London, 21 July 1934; *s* of Emanuel Miller and his wife Betty Bergson (Spiro); *e* St Paul's School, London, and St John's College, Cambridge; graduated as a doctor of medicine from University College Medical School; *m* Helen Rachel Collet.

Made his first appearance on the stage at the Phoenix, London, 6 July 1954, in the Cambridge Footlights Club revue Out of the Blue; at the Edinburgh Festival, Lyceum Theatre, Aug 1960, appeared in the revue Beyond the Fringe, of which he was also co-author; Arts, Cambridge, Apr 1961, again appeared in Beyond the Fringe, making his first professional appearance in London at the Fortune Theatre, May 1961, in the same revue; after more than a year's run in London, he made his first appearance in New York at the John Golden Theatre, Oct 1962, with the original company in Beyond the Fringe; directed his first London production, Under Plain Cover at the Royal Court, July 1962; American Place Theatre, NY, Nov 1964, directed The Old Glory; plays he has since directed include: Come Live With Me (New Haven, USA), 1966; Benito Cereno, Prometheus Bound (Yale University), 1967; The School for Scandal (Nottingham), 1968; King Lear (Nottingham and the Old Vic), 1969; The Merchant of Venice (National Theatre), The Tempest, 1970; Prometheus Bound, Danton's Death (National), 1971; The School for Scandal (National), The Taming of the Shrew (Chichester), 1972; The Malcontent (Nottingham), The Seagull (Chichester), 1973; Associate Director, National Theatre, 1973–5; at Greenwich, 1974, directed Ghosts, The Seagull, and Hamlet; at the Old Vic, 1974, directed The Marriage of Figaro and The Freeway; Greenwich, 1975, The Importance of Being Earnest; directed Three Sisters, 1976; Greenwich, Apr 1979, She Would if She Could; operas directed include: Arden Must Die, 1973; The Cunning Little Vixen, Glyndebourne, 1975; Flying Dutchman, Frankfurt, Marriage of Figaro, Coliseum, 1979; for Kent Opera, 1974–7, directed Cosi Fan Tutte, Rigoletto, Orfeo and Eugene Onegin; he is an Associate Director of English National Opera; directed his first feature film Take a Girl Like You, 1970; appeared in the first issue of the television programme *Tonight*, 1957; directed the television revue What's Going On Now? (NY) and has since directed the following on English television: films of Plato's Dialogues, and Alice in Wonderland, a biography of Chekhov and the TV film Whistle and I'll Come to You; author of Anne Hutchinson in the television series *Profiles in Courage* (NY); film and television critic of *The New Yorker*, 1963; Editor of the English television programme *Monitor*, 1964; wrote and presented the series *The Body in Question*, 1978; made his début as a film actor as Kirby Groomkirby in One Way Pendulum, 1964.

Recreation: Writing. *Address:* 63 Gloucester Crescent, London, NW1. *Tel:* 01–485 6973.

MILLIGAN, Spike Ahmaddnagar (Terence Alan), actor, director, and author
b India, 16 Apr 1918; *s* of Leo Alphonso Milligan and his wife Florence Mary Winifred (Kettleband); *e* Poona, St Paul's High School, Rangoon, and Brownhill Boys School, Catford; *m* (1) June (mar dis); (2) Patricia Ridgway (dec).

Made his first appearance on the stage at the age of eight in a nativity play at the Convent of Jesus St Mary, Poona; at the Mermaid Theatre, London, Dec 1961, played Ben Gunn in Treasure Island; at the same theatre, Jan 1963, co-director and also played the part of Mate in The Bedsitting Room, transferring with the production to the Duke of York's, Mar 1963; New Lyric, Hammersmith, Oct 1964, played the title-part in Oblomov, subsequently appearing at the Comedy, Dec 1964, in the same part under the new title of Son of Oblomov; Mermaid, Oct 1966, directed and played Mate in his new version The Bedsitting Room, transferring to the Saville, May 1967; Mermaid, Dec 1967, Ben Gunn in Treasure Island; repeated this part in 1973 and 1974, and at the New London, Dec 1975; Adelphi, June 1974 appeared in his one-man show For One Week Only, also touring; Young Vic, Mar 1980, adapted Ubu; films include: The Magic Christian, Alice's Adventures in Wonderland, The Three Musketeers, and The Life of Brian; has appeared frequently on television, notably in his own series The Best of Beachcomber, Q5–Q9, Curry and Chips, The Best of British, and on radio in *The Goon Show*; co-author of the play, The Bedsitting Room; has

written numerous television and radio scripts, as well as books of nonsense, verse, novels including Puckoon, Adolf Hitler—My Part in His Downfall, Rommel: Gunner Who? and children's books including: The Bald Twit Lion.

Recreation: Sleeping. *Address:* c/o Spike Milligan Productions, 9 Orme Court, London, W2.

MILLINGTON, Rodney, consultant to *The Spotlight*
b London, 15 Aug 1905; *s* of Walter S Millington and his wife Adelaide (Hall); *e* Malvern, and Lincoln College, Oxford; while at the University appeared with the OUDS.

Made his first appearance on the professional stage, Sept 1926, at the Cambridge Festival Theatre, as Morris in Magic; in 1927, appeared as Mr Zero in The Adding Machine; made his first appearance in London at the Everyman, 9 May 1928, as Bernard Ravenscroft in The World's End; at the Globe Theatre, June 1928, played Bobby Cotton in Holding Out the Apple; in 1928, appeared with the Hull Repertory company, and 1929, Northampton Repertory Company; Ambassadors', Sept 1929, played Willie Ward in The Misdoings of Charley Peace; Duke of York's, Apr 1930, the Young Soldier in Suspense; Arts, Oct 1930, the Journalist in Mr Eno, his Birth, Death and Life; Embassy, Jan 1931, Warwick Entwhistle in The Rising Generation; New, June 1931, the Mechanic in Sea Fever; Wyndham's, Nov 1931, Sulieman Ali in Port Said; Embassy, July 1933, in Vessel's Departing; Lyric, June 1934, Dr Chrisp in Men in White; became a director of *The Spotlight Casting Directory*, July 1931, and on the death of the late W Keith Moss, 1935, became managing director until 1971; senior partner 1971–7, when he became consultant to the publication.

Address: The Spotlight, Ancaster House, 42 Cranbourn Street, WC2. *Tel:* 01–437 7631.

MILLS, Hayley, actress
b London, 18 Apr 1946; *d* of John Mills and his wife Mary Hayley (Bell); *e* Elmhurst Ballet School, Camberley, Surrey; *m* Roy Boulting (mar dis).

Made her first stage appearance at the New Victoria, 19 Dec 1969, in the title role of Peter Pan; Criterion, Nov 1970, played Hedwig in The Wild Duck; Prince of Wales, Aug 1972, Rose Trelawny in Trelawny; Comedy, May 1975, Alison Ames in A Touch of Spring; Arnaud, Guildford, Feb 1977, Mrs de Winter in Rebecca; Chichester Festival, July 1979, Hon Gwendolen Fairfax in The Importance of Being Earnest; extensive film work, since her debut in Tiger Bay, 1958, includes The Family Way, and Take a Girl Like You; TV appearances include *The Danny Kaye Show*.

Recreations: Swimming, tennis, riding, skiing. *Address:* c/o ICM, 22 Grafton Street, London W1. *Tel:* 01–629 8080.

MILLS, Sir John, CBE, actor
b Suffolk, 22 Feb 1908; *s* of Lewis Mills and his wife Edith (Baker); *e* Norwich; *m* (1) Aileen Raymond (mar dis); (2) Mary Hayley Bell; formerly engaged in clerical work.

Made his first appearance on the stage at the London Hippodrome, 21 Mar 1929, in the chorus of The Five o'Clock Girl; played his first part, 1929, when he went to India and the Far East, to tour as Lieut Raleigh in Journey's End; subsequently appeared there in Young Woodley, Mr Cinders and in Hamlet; on returning to London, appeared at the New Theatre, Dec 1930, as Lord Fancourt Babberley in Charley's Aunt; London Pavilion, Mar 1931, appeared in Cochran's 1931 Revue; Duke of York's, May 1931, played Birkinshaw in London Wall; Drury Lane, Oct 1931, Joe Marryot in

Cavalcade; Adelphi, Sept 1932, appeared in Words and Music; London Hippodrome, 1933, Cliff Read in Give Me a Ring; Saville, Dec 1934, played Bobby Jones in Jill, Darling; Queen's, Mar 1936, Private Syd Summers in Red Night; Strand, May 1936, Roger Holly in Aren't Men Beasts!; Saville, June 1937, appeared in Floodlight; Piccadilly, Dec 1937, Roger Miller in Talk of the Devil; Saville, May 1938, appeared in Pélissier's Follies of 1938; Old Vic, Dec–Feb 1939, Puck in A Midsummer Night's Dream, and Young Marlow in She Stoops to Conquer; Globe, Mar 1939, Tommy in We at the Crossroads; Gate, Apr and Apollo, May 1939, George in Of Mice and Men; Vaudeville, Sept 1942, Lew in Men in Shadow; Lyric, June 1945, Stephen Cass in Duet for Two Hands; both these two last plays were written by his wife; Strand, June 1947, directed Angel; reappeared on the stage at the St James's, Oct 1950, as Bertie in Top of the Ladder; Aldwych, Oct 1951, played Freddie in Figure of Fun; St James's, May 1953, Candy in The Uninvited Guest; New, Feb 1954, Lord Fancourt Babberley in Charley's Aunt; made his first appearance in New York at the Eugene O'Neill Theatre, Dec 1961, when he played the title-part in Ross; Garrick, London, Sept 1963, played Otto Moll and co-directed Power of Persuasion; Royal Court, Mar 1972, played Laurence D'Orsay in Veterans; Savoy, Oct 1973, Henry Jackson in At the End of the Day; Her Majesty's, July 1974, Jess Oakroyd in The Good Companions; Arnaud, Guildford, Dec 1975, and tour, Joe Gargery in Great Expectations; toured as Mr Malcolm and Major Pollock in Separate Tables, 1976, playing these roles at The Apollo, Jan 1977; commenced film career, 1932, and has appeared in almost a hundred films, including: Dunkirk, Tiger Bay, Tunes of Glory (Venice International Film Award, 1960), Sky West and Crooked (directed), Ryan's Daughter (Oscar, 1971), Young Winston, The Human Factor, Trial by Combat, The Devil's Advocate, and The 39 Steps; he has also appeared on television, in the series *The Zoo Gang*, Dr Strange, Quatermass (1978), and Young at Heart (1980); member of the Board of Governors, London Independent Television Producers, Ltd 1963; Chairman of the Stars Organization for Spastics, 1975–8; received the CBE in the New Year's Honours, 1960: Knighted in the Prime Minister's Honours, 1976; Fellow of Boston University, 1977.

Recreations: Golf, tennis, riding, and swimming. *Clubs:* Garrick and Green Room. *Address:* c/o ICM Ltd, 22 Grafton Street, London W1.

MILLS, Juliet, actress
b London, 21 Nov 1941; *d* of John Mills and his wife Mary Hayley (Bell); *e* Elmhurst Ballet School, Camberley, Surrey; *m* Russell Alquist.

Made her first appearance on the stage at the Chelsea Palace Theatre, London, Dec 1955, when she played Alice in Alice Through the Looking Glass; Comedy, July 1958, played Pamela Harrington in Five Finger Exercise; following a year's run in London, she made her first appearance in New York at the Music Box, Nov 1959, in the same production, subsequently touring in the US; on her return to London, she appeared at the Scala, Dec 1960, as Wendy in Peter Pan; Piccadilly, July 1962, played Kitty in The Glad and Sorry Season; Aldwych, June 1963, played Titania in A Midsummer Night's Dream for the Royal Shakespeare Company; Morosco, NY, Dec 1964, played Gilda in Alfie; Phoenix, Oct 1966, Lady Windermere in Lady Windermere's Fan; Garrick, May 1969, Kate Hardcastle in She Stoops to Conquer; toured US, 1976, in The Mousetrap; Royal Poinsiana Playhouse, Palm Beach, Fla, Feb 1980, played Mrs Kemble in The Elephant Man; Nottingham Playhouse, Apr 1980, Catherine

Slopes in The Heiress; made her first appearance in films, 1941, at the age of eleven weeks, in In Which We Serve; subsequent films include: No, My Darling Daughter, Twice Around the Daffodils, Carry On Sailor, and The Rare Breed (Hollywood); first appeared on television in the United States, 1960.

Recreations: Cooking, skating, riding, tennis. *Address:* Crouch Associates, 59 Frith Street, London W1. *Tel:* 01–734 2167.

MINER, Jan (*née* Janice), actress
b Boston, Mass, 15 Oct 1917; *d* of Walter Curtis Miner and his wife Ethel Lindsey (Chase); *e* Beaver County Day School, Chestnut, Mass, and the Vesper George School of the Arts, Boston; *m* Richard Merrell; prepared for the stage with Lee Strasberg, David Craig, Ira Cirker, and Don Richardson.

Made her stage debut at the Copley Theater, Boston, Mass, 1945, in Street Scene; spent three years at this theatre; Playhouse, Cincinnati, Ohio, summer 1958, Frances Black in Light Up the Sky; made her New York debut at the Theatre Marquee, 18 Feb 1958, in Obbligato; Longacre, Apr 1960, played Peggy in Viva Maddison Avenue!; Cape Playhouse, Dennis, Mass, July 1960, Lottie Lacey in The Dark at the Top of the Stairs; 74th Street, Apr 1961, Pampina in The Decameron; Cricket, Feb 1962, Alice Lambkin in Dumbbell People in a Barbell World; Mineola, Long Island, Playhouse, Aug 1962, Reporter in There Must Be a Pony; Mermaid, Nov 1962, Yvonne in Intimate Relations; Morosco, Jan 1963, stand-by and appeared for Hermione Baddeley in The Milk Train Doesn't Stop Here Anymore; Winter Garden, Mar 1963, Prudence in The Lady of the Camellias; Palace Vaudeville, 1963, in Long Distance; Stage 73, May 1965, Third Woman in The Wives; Eugene O'Neil, Oct 1967, Nancy Reed in The Freaking Out of Stephanie Blake; American Shakespeare Festival, Stratford, Conn, June 1966, Hostess Quickly in Henry IV and a Woman of Canterbury in Murder in the Cathedral; Stratford, Conn, June 1968, Megaera in Androcles and the Lion; Jan Hus Playhouse, Dec 1968, Mabel in Lemonade and Lila in The Autograph Hound; Stratford, Conn, summer 1970, played in All's Well That Ends Well and Emilia in Othello; ANTA, Sept 1970, again played Emilia in Othello; Stratford, Conn, summer 1971, played in The Merry Wives of Windsor; Booth, 1971, took over as Mrs Baker in Butterflies Are Free; Stratford, Conn, summer 1972, played in Major Barbara; 46th Street, Apr 1973, Countess de Lage in The Woman; Martin Beck, Nov 1974, Aunt Meme in Saturday Sunday Monday; Olney, Md, Playhouse, Aug 1975, Amanda Wingfield in The Glass Menagerie and Mrs Fisher in The Show Off; Long Wharf, New Haven, Conn, Nov 1975, Mrs Fisher in The Show-Off; Broadhurst, NY, Apr 1976, Lavinia in The Heiress; Circle in the Square, Mar 1977, Nurse in Romeo and Juliet; Darien Dinner Theatre, 1977, Mme Arcati in High Spirits; Long Wharf, Apr 1978, Margaret Lord in The Philadelphia Story; Sports Festival, USA, 1978, Bodey in A Lovely Sunday for Crève Coeur; Long Wharf, 1979, transferring to the John Golden, Jan, 1980, Fanny Farrelly in Watch on the Rhine; appeared in the films Lenny, 1974, Willie and Phil, 1980; has appeared frequently on television since 1954, recently in Out of Our Father's House, 1978.

Address: c/o Lester Lewis Agency, 156 East 52nd Street, New York, NY. *Tel:* PL 3–5082.

MINNELLI, Liza May, actress, singer, dancer
b Los Angeles, Cal, 12 Mar 1946; *d* of Vincente Minnelli, the designer and stage and film director, and his wife Judy Garland (Frances Gumm), the singer and actress;

e Scarsdale, NY, High School, University of Paris de la Sorbonne, 1962–63; *m* (1) Peter Allen (mar dis), (2) Jack Haley, Jr; prepared for the stage at the HB Studio with Uta Hagen and Herbert Berghof.

Made her stage debut at the Cape Cod Melody Top, Hyannis, Mass, July 1962, in Take Me Along, and later performed in The Flower Drum Song; also in July 1962 played in a stock production of The Diary of Anne Frank; made her New York debut at the Stage 73, 2 Apr 1963, as Ethel Hofflinger in Best Foot Forward; Mineola, Long Island, Playhouse, Jan 1964, played Lili in Carnival, and subsequently toured; appeared in revue, Nov 1964; Alvin, May 1965, played Flora in Flora, The Red Menace, and received the Antoinette Perry ("Tony") Award for this performance; made her London debut at the Palladium, 1964, in concert with her mother; Olympia, Paris, Dec 1971, appeared in variety; Palladium, London, 11 May 1973, appeared in variety, and at the Royal Festival Hall, 12 May, and the Rainbow, 13 May; Winter Garden, NY, Jan 1974, appeared in the revue Liza, for which she received the "Tony" Award; toured Europe, including engagements in Paris, Vienna, Berlin, Hamburg, Copenhagen, Frankfurt, Gothenburg, Madrid, Jan 1975; 46th Street, 8 Aug 1975, stood in for Gwen Verdon as Roxie Hart in Chicago, and continued in this part until 13 Sept; Metropolitan Opera House, 9 May 1976, played in A Star-Spangled Gala; Majestic, Oct 1977, Michelle Craig in The Act; Promenade, Jan 1979, played three weeks as Lillian Hellman in Are You Now or Have You Ever Been?; Carnegie Hall, Sept 1979, appeared in concert; has toured extensively in cabaret, notably at the Riviera, Las Vegas, Harrah's, Lake Tahoe, Nevada, Torre del Duque, Nueva Andalucia, Spain, etc; was named the Female Star of the Year in the Las Vegas Entertainment Awards, 1972 and 1974; made her first film as a child, In the Good Old Summer Time, 1949, and has since appeared in Charlie Bubbles, The Sterile Cuckoo, Tell Me That You Love Me, June Moon, Cabaret (for which she received the Academy Award), That's Entertainment, Lucky Lady (1976); has appeared regularly on television in variety shows such as the *Ed Sullivan Show*, the *Judy Garland Show*, her own special Liza with a Z, for which she received the Emmy Award, Liza and Goldie, etc.

Address: Creative Management Associates, Ltd, 40 West 57th Street, New York, NY.

MIRREN, Helen, actress
b 1946.

Gained her first experience with the National Youth Theatre, culminating in her appearance as Cleopatra in Antony and Cleopatra, Old Vic, Sept 1965; Manchester, 1967, played Kitty in Charley's Aunt and Nerissa in The Merchant of Venice; joined the Royal Shakespeare Company at Stratford, season 1967, to play Castiza in The Revenger's Tragedy, May, and Diana in All's Well that Ends Well, June; Cressida in Troilus and Cressida, Aug 1968; Hero in Much Ado About Nothing, Oct 1968; at the Aldwych, 1969, she played Cressida, June; Hero, July; Susie Monican in The Silver Tassie, Sept; Win-the-Fight Littlewit in Bartholomew Fair, Oct; Castiza, Nov; returning to Stratford, 1970, played Lady Anne in Richard III, Apr; Ophelia in Hamlet, June; Julia in The Two Gentlemen of Verona, July, repeating the last part at the Aldwych, Dec; Aldwych, 1971, played Tatyana in Enemies, July; Harriet in The Man of Mode, Sept, title-role in Miss Julie (The Place), Oct; Elyane in The Balcony, Nov; worked with Peter Brook's Centre Internationale de Recherches Theatrales in Africa and US, 1972–3; returned to the RSC to play Lady Macbeth, Stratford, Oct 1974, and

Aldwych Mar 1975; Royal Court, Sept 1975, Maggie in Teeth 'n' Smiles; Lyric, for Lyric Theatre Company, played Nina in The Seagull, and Ella in The Bed Before Yesterday, in repertory from Nov 1975; Wyndham's, May 1976, again played Maggie in Teeth 'n' Smiles; for the RSC, Stratford, June 1977, played Queen Margaret in Henry VI, Parts 1, 2 and 3, and also at the Aldwych, April 1978; Riverside Studios, May 1979, Isabella in Measure for Measure; films, since Age of Consent, 1969, include: Savage Messiah, and O Lucky Man; television includes: Miss Julie, The Apple Cart, and The Little Minister.

Address: c/o Al Parker Ltd, 50 Mount Street, London W1.

MITCHELL, David, designer
b Honesdale, Pennsylvania, 12 May 1932; *s* of Amos D. Mitchell and his wife Ruth (Cole); *e* Pennsylvania State College (1950–4), Boston University (1957–9); served in US Army (1955–7); *m* Emily J. Fouts.

His first design for New York was the New York Shakespeare Festival production of Henry V, directed by Joseph Papp, 1965; the same year designed Medea at the Martinique; designed New York Shakespeare Festival's productions, Macbeth, 1966; Volpone, Naked Hamlet, 1967; touring production of Naked Hamlet, Berkshire Theater Festival's A Cry of Players, 1968; The Increased Difficulty of Concentration for Repertory Theater of Lincoln Center (sets and costumes), 1969; Steambath, Colette, Trelawny of the "Wells", 1970; How the Other Half Loves, The Basic Training of Pavlo Hummel, The Incomparable Max, 1971; New York Shakespeare Festival productions of The Cherry Orchard, 1972 and Barbary Shore, 1973; Short Eyes at the Public and later at the Vivian Beaumont, The Cherry Orchard at the Goodman (Chicago), The Wager, In the Boom Boom Room (revival), Enter a Free Man, 1974; Little Black Sheep and Trelawny of the "Wells" at the Vivian Beaumont, Shoe Shine Parlor, 1975; Apple Pie, Mrs Warren's Profession, Henry V, Mondongo, A Photograph, 1976; Annie, I Love My Wife, The Marriage Proposal (for the Family), The Gin Game (Long Wharf and New York), I Love My Wife (London), 1977; Working, Annie (London), End of the War, 1978; I Remember Mama, The Price, The Gin Game (London), 1979; designed the operas Madame Butterfly and Lord Byron for the Juilliard School, Aida and Falstaff for the Teatro Municipal, Santiago, Chile, Pelleas et Melisande for New England Conservatory, Manon for San Francisco Opera, Macbeth for Washington Opera and Houston Grand Opera, Boris Godunov for Cincinnati Opera and Canadian Opera, The Italian Straw Hat (American première) for Santa Fe Opera, Mephistophele for New York City Opera, Aida for Deutsche Oper Berlin, Il Trovatore for Paris Opera; designed Journeys for John Butler and the Pennsylvania Ballet, was scenic supervisor for the New York City Ballet's Ravel Festival and designed sets and costumes for George Balanchine's The Steadfast Tin Soldier for the repertory and for PBS's Dance in America television series; designed the film Rich Kids, 1979; received the Antoinette Perry (Tony) award for Annie as well as the Outer Critics Circle award and the Los Angeles Drama Critics Circle Award.

Address: 153 West 88th Street, New York, NY 10024.

MITCHELL, Ruth (*née* Kornfeld), producer, director
b Newark, New Jersey, 24 Sept 1919; *d* of Arthur Kornfeld and his wife Miriam (Mitchell); *e* West Side High School, Newark.

Made her stage debut as a dancer and an actress at the Mohawk Drama Festival, Schenectady, NY, 1936; toured with the Clare Tree Major children's theatre production of

Pinocchio, 1937; toured in Rio Rita, 1938; began her career as a stage manager with the touring productions of The Second Mrs Tanqueray and Her Carboard Lover, 1942–43; made her New York debut as stage manager for Memphis Bound, Broadway, 24 May 1945; assistant to the director of Annie Get Your Gun at the Imperial, 16 May 1946; since then has been stage manager or production stage manager for Happy Birthday, 1946; Mister Roberts, 1948; The King and I (also its tour), 1951–54; Pipe Dream, 1955; Bells Are Ringing, 1956; West Side Story, 1957; made her London debut as stage manager of West Side Story at Her Majesty's, 12 Dec 1958; Gypsy, Fiorello!, 1959; Tenderloin, 1960; O'Keefe Center, Toronto, Ontario, Canada, 10 July 1961, directed West Side Story; Take Her, She's Mine, 1961; A Funny Thing Happened on the Way to the Forum, 1962 (London, 1963); She Loves Me, 1963 (London, 1964); Poor Bitos, Fiddler on the Roof, 1964; redirected Fiddler on the Roof, 1976; assistant director, On the Twentieth Century, 1978; Sweeney Todd, 1979; in association with Harold Prince has co-produced It's a Bird . . . It's a Plane . . . It's Superman, cabaret, 1966; Zorba, 1968; Company, 1970; Follies, 1971; Company (London), 1972; A Little Night Music, 1973; Candide, 1974; A Little Night Music, (London) 1975; Pacific Overtures, 1976; Side by Side by Sondheim, 1977; executive producer, West Side Story, 1980; assistant director for the film of A Little Night Music.

Recreations: Needlepoint, water ski-ing, cooking. *Address:* 1270 Avenue of the Americas, New York, NY 10020. *Tel:* 399 0960.

MITCHELL, Stephen, TD, manager
b Aberdeen, 31 Aug 1907; *s* of Alexander Mitchell and his wife Marion Louisa (Stephen); *e* Edinburgh Academy and Aberdeen University; *m* Phyllis Grace Allan (dec); originally intended for the legal profession, and is a Bachelor of Law.

Entered theatrical management when he presented (with Ronald Adam) Judgment Day, at the Strand Theatre, June 1937; has since presented The Corn is Green, Duchess, 1938; Little Ladyship, Strand, 1939; The Light of Heart, Apollo, 1940, and The Morning Star, Globe, 1941, both in association with H M Tennent Ltd; Clutterbuck, Wyndham's, 1946; Ever Since Paradise, New, 1947; Gathering Storm, St Martin's, 1948; Royal Circle, Wyndham's, 1948; Playbill, Phoenix, 1948; The Power of Darkness, Lyric, 1949; The Way Things Go, Phoenix, 1950; Golden City, Adelphi, 1950; Snow White and the Seven Dwarfs (for Teneb Productions), St James's, 1951; First Person Singular (which he also directed), Duke of York's, 1952; The Innocents, Her Majesty's, 1952; High Spirits, Hippodrome, 1953; Separate Tables, St James's, 1954; The Night of the Ball, New, 1955; Tiger at the Gates, Apollo, 1955; A Day By the Sea, ANTA Playhouse, New York, 1955; Harmony Close, King's, Glasgow; Separate Tables, Music Box, NY, 1956; Olive Ogilvie, Aldwych; Restless Heart, St James's, 1957; Beth, Apollo; Something to Hide, St Martin's, 1958; Marigold, Savoy, 1959; The Brides of March, 1960; Masterpiece (with Richard Friedman), Royalty The Angry Deep (tour, with Kenneth More), 1961; Pocahontas, Lyric; John Gabriel Borkman (with David Ross), Duchess, 1963; The Creeper, St Martin's, 1965; The Duel, Duke of York's, 1968; was lessee of the Phoenix Theatre, 1938–9; President of Society of West End Theatre Managers, 1956–8; during the war, served from Sept 1939, as Captain in the Gordon Highlanders; demobilized, as Major, 1945, and awarded the Territorial Decoration, having served in France, 1940, and in France and Germany, 1944–45.

Recreations: Golf, bridge. *Club:* Garrick. *Address:* London Pavilion Chambers, Great Windmill Street, London W1.

MITCHELL, Warren, actor
b London, 1926; *m* Constance Wake; trained for the stage at RADA.

First professional appearance, Finsbury Park Open Air Theatre, 1950; Coliseum, Oct 1954, Theophile in Can-Can; Royal Court, Feb 1956 and Aldwych, Mar 1956, played Crookfinger Jake in The Threepenny Opera; Aldwych, Mar 1969, for RSC, Mr Godboy in Dutch Uncle; Criterion, Aug 1970, Satan in Council of Love; Queen's, Sept 1971, Herbert in Jump; Royal Court, Oct 1974, Ion Will in The Great Caper; Stratford E, Oct 1976, appeared in The Thoughts of Chairman Alf; has repeated this performance since in a number of theatres in Britain and Australia; Sydney, Australia, Oct 1978, played the title-rôle in King Lear; Playhouse, Perth, Mar 1979, Willy Loman in Death of a Salesman; returned to play the same part for the National Theatre Company, Lyttleton, Sept 1979, receiving the SWET award as Best Actor for this performance; films, since 1956, include: Moon Zero Two, All the Way Up, and Meetings with Remarkable Men; television includes: *Till Death Us Do Part,* and Moss.

Address: c/o Plunket Greene Ltd, 110 Jermyn Street, London, SW1.

MITCHENSON, Joe (Francis Joseph Blackett Mitchenson), actor, theatrical historian, joint founder and director of the Raymond Mander and Joe Mitchenson Theatre Collection
b London, 4 Oct; *s* of Francis Mitchenson and his wife Sarah (Roddam); *e* privately; trained as a child dancer and then at the Fay Compton Studio of Dramatic Art.

Made his first stage appearance at the King's, Hammersmith, 28 Mar 1934, as a junior counsel in Libel!, transferring with the production to the Playhouse, Apr 1934; played small parts in London and elsewhere, 1934–37, including a season of rep at Cheltenham, 1936; in autumn 1937 joined the Portfolio Playhouse, Fay Compton's private theatre, as stage manager, acting in many productions before leaving in Oct 1938; appearances 1938–39 include Fenton in The Merry Wives of Windsor, Dockland Settlement Theatre, Feb 1939; joined the Royal Horse Artillery, Jan 1941; invalided out, Mar 1943; returned to the theatre as stage director and actor, including a season at the Gateway, Notting Hill Gate, 1944; entered management at the Grand, Croydon, Jan–Jun 1945, directing and acting in plays including Charley's Aunt and The Ghost Train; toured in Europe for ENSA, 1945–46, as Freddie in Pygmalion; made his last stage appearance as an actor at the Theatre Royal, Rochester, 1948, in a programme of one-act plays; in 1939 he and Raymond Mander founded their Theatre Collection, developing it over the years into a full-time occupation, with authorship and consultancy; in 1977 the Collection was formed into a trust, and the London Borough of Lewisham offered Beckenham Place as a permanent home for it; 'The Boys' are archivists to Sadler's Wells and the Old Vic Company; have arranged many exhibitions, including Fifty Years of British Stage Design, for the British Council, USSR, 1979; and have written numerous works on the theatre, including Hamlet Through the Ages, 1952, Theatrical Companions to Shaw, 1954, Maugham, 1955, Coward, 1957; A Picture History of British Theatre, 1957; The Theatres of London, 1961 revised 1975; 'stories in pictures' of British Music Hall, 1965 revised 1974, Musical Comedy, 1969, Revue, 1971, and Pantomime, 1973; Victorian and Edwardian Entertainment from Old Photographs, 1978; Guide to the Somerset Maugham Theatrical Paintings at the National Theatre, 1980; they have appeared frequently on television, talking on theatrical topics, and during the War presented many theatre record programmes.

Favourite part: Mrs Priskin's Other Guest in Goodness How Sad. *Recreations:* Collecting anything and everything theatrical, sunbathing. *Address:* 5 Venner Road, Sydenham SE26 5EQ. *Tel:* 778 6730.

MOFFAT, Donald, actor, director
b Plymouth, England, 26 Dec 1930; *s* of Walter George Moffat and his wife Kathleen Mary (Smith); *e* King Edward VI School, Totnes, and Dartington Hall, Devon, 1951–2; *m* (1) Anne Murray; (2) Gwen Arner; prepared for the stage at the Royal Academy of Dramatic Art, 1952–4.

First appeared on the stage in 1947 as the Earl of Loam in a school production of The Admirable Crichton; at the Edinburgh Festival, Aug 1954, played the First Murderer in Macbeth, and made his London début in this part at the Old Vic, 9 Sept 1954; Vaudeville, Aug 1954, was stage manager for Salad Days; Old Vic, Jan 1955, Sir Stephen Scroop in Richard II; Apr 1955, Earl of Douglas in Henry IV, Part I; Apr 1955, Earl of Warwick in Henry IV, Part II; Piccadilly, May 1956, was stage manager for Romanoff and Juliet; came to America and, for the University Players, Princeton, New Jersey, 1957, played the role of Stage Manager in The Skin of Our Teeth; made his New York début at the Henry Miller's, 15 Oct 1957, as Mr Ogmore and Nogood Boyo in Under Milkwood; Sullivan Street Playhouse, 1958, played Mr Martin in The Bald Soprano and Grandfather Jack in Jack; Colonial, Boston, Dec 1958, Detective Inspector Bruton in Listen to the Mockingbird; Renata, Jan 1959, took over as Shabyelsky in Ivanov; Lunt-Fontanne, Sept 1959, Verges in Much Ado About Nothing; Helen Hayes, Feb 1960, George in The Tumbler; same theatre, Apr 1960, Clerk of the Court in Duel of Angels; Akron, Ohio, Shakespeare Festival, 1960, played the title-role of Richard II, Earl of Worcester in Henry IV, Part I, Justice Shallow in Henry IV, Part II, and Chorus in Henry V; toured Canada and the US, 1961, as Pat in The Hostage; joined the Association of Producing Artists, and, for the season at the McCarter, Princeton, New Jersey, 1961, played Laudisi in Right You Are . . . If You Think You Are, Geronte in Scapin, Dr Dorn in The Seagull, and Reverend Canon Chasuble in The Importance of Being Earnest; Akron Shakespeare Festival, 1961, played Macbeth, Malvolio in Twelfth Night, Gremio in The Taming of the Shrew, and directed A Midsummer Night's Dream; Sheridan Square Playhouse, Sept 1961, Mr Tarlton in Misalliance; Ambassador, Jan 1962, Sam McBryde in A Passage to India; Great Lakes Shakespeare Festival, Cleveland, Ohio, 1962, played Richard II, Touchstone in As You Like It; Henry Miller's, Sept 1962, Julian Skeffington in The Affair; Playhouse-in-the-Park, Cincinnati, Ohio, 1963, Dick Dudgeon in The Devil's Disciple, A and B in Act Without Words, and Henry IV in The Emperor; Phoenix, Mar 1963, Gremio in The Taming of the Shrew; Great Lakes Shakespeare Festival, 1963, played Henry V, Duke Vincentio in Measure for Measure, and directed Julius Caesar and The Merry Wives of Windsor; Players, Jan 1964, Aston in The Caretaker; Phoenix, Dec 1964, alternated as Octavius Robinson and Jack Tanner in Man and Superman; Jan 1965; Andrei in War and Peace; Lyceum, Nov 1965, Martin Vanderhof in You Can't Take It with You; McCarter, Princeton, New Jersey, 1966, directed Miss Julie; Lyceum, Nov 1966, Lamberto Laudisi in Right You Are . . .; Jan 1967, Hjalmar Ekdal in The Wild Duck; Feb 1967, Martin Vanderhof in You Can't Take It with You; Mar 1967, Andrei in War and Peace; Mar 1968, Lopahin in The Cherry Orchard; summer 1968, directed New York . . . and Who to Blame It On, a street theatre play for the APA/Phoenix; Jan 1969, co-directed and played Sailor Jack Mohan in Cock-a-Doodle Dandy; Mar 1969, Horatio in

Hamlet; Mark Taper Forum, Los Angeles, 1969, played Chanal in Chemin de Fer; New Theater for Now, Los Angeles, 1970, Richard in Father's Day; repeated this part at the John Golden, Mar 1971, and also directed the production; Bucks County Playhouse, New Hope, Pa, 1970–1 season, title-roles in Hadrian VII and The Magistrate; Mark Taper Forum, Los Angeles, June 1971, played in The Trial of the Catonsville Nine; Seattle, Washington, Repertory, 1971, played in Hotel Paradiso; Ahmanson, Los Angeles, Dec 1972, played in The Crucible; Mark Taper Forum, Apr 1973, played in Forget-Me-Not Lane; Seattle Repertory, 1973, played in The Tavern; Studio Arena, Buffalo, 1973, played in Child's Play, and Mar 1974, Harpagon in The Miser; Studio Arena, Mar 1975, directed and played Moricet in 13 Rue de l'Amour; Los Angeles Actors Theatre, Apr 1975, played in The Kitchen, and Sept 1975, directed and played in Cock-a-Doodle Dandy; Westwood Playhouse, Los Angeles, Apr 1976, Captain Shotover in Heartbreak House; Academy Festival Theatre, Chicago, Aug 1976, John Tarleton in Misalliance; LA Actors Theatre, Jan 1977, Estragon in Waiting for Godot; same theatre, Oct 1977, played Krapp's Last Tape, and directed the Wakefield Mystery Plays, Dec 1977; Mark Taper Forum, LA, Jan 1979, Scott in Terra Nova; appeared in the film Pursuit of the Graf Spee, 1957, and has since played in Rachel, Rachel, Great Northfield, Minnesota, Raid, The Terminal Man, Earthquake, On the Nickel (1979), etc; has played on television in Ad Astra, 1958, and on such dramatic programs as *Armstrong Circle Theatre, DuPont Show of the Month, Bonanza, High Chaparral, Camera Three,* in the series *The New Land* and *Logan's Run,* and plays such as Forget-Me-Not Lane, Tartuffe (1979), etc.

Favourite parts: Hjalmar Ekdal, Estragon and Lamberto Laudisi. *Recreation:* Photography. *Address:* 223 33rd Street, Hermosa Beach, Calif 90254. *Tel:* 376–3875.

MOFFATT, John, actor
b London, 24 Sept 1922; *s* of Ernest George Moffatt and his wife Letitia (Hickman); *e* East Sheen County School.

He made his first appearance on the stage in Liverpool, Oct 1944, as Carl, the Raven, in The Snow Queen; 1945–50, was a member of various repertory companies, including: Perth, Oxford, Windsor, and the Bristol Old Vic; made his first London appearance at the Lyric, Hammersmith, June 1950, as Loyale in Tartuffe; at the same theatre, Nov 1950, played the Hotel Waiter in Point of Departure, subsequently transferring with the production to the Duke of York's, Dec 1950; Watergate, Mar 1951, appeared in the late night revue Late Night Extra; Phoenix, June 1951, played 2nd Lord and Paulina's Steward in The Winter's Tale; at the same theatre, Jan 1952, played Verges in Much Ado About Nothing; Lyric, Hammersmith, Oct 1952, played Frank Ford in The Square Ring; Haymarket, May 1953, Nicobar in The Apple Cart; Aldwych, Apr 1954, Jacob in The Dark is Light Enough; Duchess, Sept 1955, Dr Grenock in Mr Kettle and Mrs Moon; at the Royal Court, June 1956–Aug 1957, appeared in the following parts: Dr Bitterling in Cards of Identity, 2nd God in The Good Woman of Setzuan, Mr Sparkish in The Country Wife (transferring to the Adelphi, Feb 1957, for a limited run), Secretary in The Apollo de Bellac, Mr Fairbrother in The Making of Moo, Edwin Goosebell in How Can We Save Father?; made his first appearance in New York at the Adelphi, NY, Nov 1957, as Mr Sparkish in The Country Wife; on his return to England, toured, Sept 1958, as Mr Saxmann in The Holiday; joined the Old Vic Company, Sept 1959, to play the Le Beau in As You Like It, Bishop of Carlisle in Richard II, Chaplain de Stogumber in

Saint Joan, Dr Caius in The Merry Wives of Windsor, Mr Venables in What Every Woman Knows, and the Dauphin and Duke of Burgundy in Henry V; toured with the same company, Sept 1960, as Algernon in The Importance of Being Earnest, 2nd Witch in Macbeth, and De Stogumber in Saint Joan, also visiting Russia and Poland; Royal Court, Mar 1961, appeared as Jacques's Father in Jacques; at the same theatre, July 1961, Cardinal Cajetan in Luther, subsequently transferring to the Phoenix, Sept 1961 (receiving the Clarence Derwent Award for the best supporting performance of 1961); Mermaid, Apr 1963, Lord Foppington in Virtue in Danger, transferring to the Strand with the production, June 1963; St James's, NY, Sept 1963, again played Cardinal Cajetan in Luther; Oxford Playhouse, Apr 1964, played Kulygin in The Three Sisters, and at the same theatre, May 1964, played Orestes Petrovykh in The Twelfth Hour; Mermaid, Feb 1965, Ilya Fomitsh Katsharyov in The Marriage Brokers; Hampstead Theatre Club, May 1965, directed and appeared in Victorian Music Hall; Mermaid, Mar 1966, Von Wehrhahn in The Beaver Coat; Arnaud, Guildford, June 1966, devised, directed and appeared in Victorian Music Hall, and toured with this production; Royal, Bury St Edmunds, Feb 1967, Lord Fancourt Babberley in Charley's Aunt; Genée, East Grinstead, Aug 1967, Henry in The Fantasticks; Arnaud, Guildford, Dec 1967, Dame Trot in Jack and the Beanstalk; Royal, Bury St Edmunds, Apr 1968, Victorian Music Hall; Duke of York's, Nov 1968, Jan Letzaresco in Dear Charles; Feb 1969, joined the National Theatre Company and appeared as Fainall in The Way of the World, De Histingua in A Flea in Her Ear, Cardinal Monticelso in The White Devil, Judge Brack in Hedda Gabler, and Leicester Paton in Home and Beauty; Young Vic, Sept 1970, Geronte in Scapino; for the National Theatre, 1971, he played Von Schlettow, Krakauer, and the Chief of Police in The Captain of Köpenick, May, Menenius Agrippa in Coriolanus, May, and Sir Joshua Rat in Tyger (New Theatre), July; Apollo, Feb 1972, Monsignor Silva in The Beheading; Mermaid, July 1972, appeared in Cowardy Custard; Arts, Cambridge, Dec 1973, Dame Trot in Jack and the Beanstalk; Theatre Royal, York, Dec 1974, Widow Twankey in Aladdin; Palace, Watford, Sept 1975, Bob le Hotu in Irma la Douce; Lyric, played Sorin in The Sea Gull, Oct 1975, and Victor Keene in The Bed Before Yesterday, Dec 1975, in repertory for the Lyric Theatre Company; Chichester Festival Theatre, May 1977, played Ethelred the Unready and others in In Order of Appearance; same theatre, Dec 1977, Olly in Follow the Star; Apr 1978, Bangkok, Hong Kong and English tour of Oh, Coward!; Theatre Royal, York, Nov 1978, Garry Essendine in Present Laughter; Theatre Royal, Bristol, Dec 1978, Dame Trot; Greenwich, May 1979, Sandor Turai in The Play's the Thing; has written five pantomimes and played frequently in them as Dame; has appeared extensively on television since his first appearance in 1953; entered films 1955.

Favourite parts: Garry Essendine, Lord Foppington and Dame in pantomime. *Address:* c/o Plunket Greene Ltd, 91 Regent Street, London W1.

MOHYEDDIN, Zia, actor

b Lyallpur, Pakistan, 20 June 1933; *s* of Khadim Mohyeddin, and his wife Mumtaz (Jehan); *e* Punjab University; *m* Sheri Zamani Khan; trained for the stage at RADA.

Played leading roles in the principal theatres of Pakistan, 1956–7; first appeared on the London stage in Apr 1960, at the Comedy, as Dr Aziz in A Passage to India; repeated the part on his New York début, Jan 1962, at the Ambassador; toured, 1964, as Surly in The Alchemist; Garrick, Jan 1967,

Mosca in Volpone; Hudson, NY, Mar 1968, Raju in The Guide; Birmingham Repertory, Sept 1968, Shylock in The Merchant of Venice; toured, 1969, as Sir Jaffna in On the Rocks; 1972–6, Director Arts Academy, and subsequently, Director General, National Ensemble of Pakistan; first film, 1961, Lawrence of Arabia; subsequent pictures include: Sammy Going South, Bombay Talkie, and Ashanti!; he has appeared on television since 1955, and has written, directed and produced shows in England and Pakistan, where he starred in his own show, 1971–2; most recent TV, Death of a Princess, 1980.

Favourite parts: Cassius in Julius Caesar, Angelo in Measure for Measure. *Recreations:* Bridge, reading. *Club:* Savile. *Address:* c/o Plunket Greene Ltd, 91 Regent Street, London W1.

MOISEIWITSCH, Tanya, CBE, designer

b London, 3 Dec 1914; *d* of Benno Moiseiwitsch and his wife Daisy (Kennedy); *e* at various schools in England; *m* Felix Krish (dec).

Designed her first production at the Westminster, London, Dec 1934, with The Faithful; at the Abbey Theatre, Dublin, Sept 1935, designed Deuce of Jacks; she designed over fifty productions for this theatre, from 1935–9; her first West-end production was The Golden Cuckoo, at the Duchess, 1940; at the Oxford Playhouse, 1941–4, designed for a weekly repertory, which included plays by Shakespeare, Shaw, Tchekhov, Bridie, etc; designed for the Old Vic company, at the Playhouse, Liverpool, 1944–5, including productions of Dr Faustus, John Gabriel Borkman, The School for Scandal, Point Valaine, etc; designed for the Theatre Royal, Bristol, 1945–6, and at the New Theatre, London, 1945–6, Uncle Vanya, The Critic, and Cyrano de Bergerac; subsequently designed the following productions: The Time of Your Life, 1946; Bless the Bride, 1947; The Beggar's Opera (Sadler's Wells), The Cherry Orchard (Old Vic), 1948; A Month in the Country (Old Vic), Henry VIII (Stratford-on-Avon), Treasure Hunt, 1949; Home at Seven, The Holly and the Ivy, Captain Carvallo, 1950; in 1951, assisted by Alix Stone, she designed Richard II, Henry IV, Parts I and II, and Henry V for the Shakespeare Memorial Theatre; she subsequently designed The Passing Day, Figure of Fun, and A Midsummer Night's Dream (Old Vic), 1951; in 1952, designed the Shakespeare Memorial Theatre production of Othello, which toured Australia and New Zealand; designed The Deep Blue Sea, 1952; Julius Caesar (sets), and Henry VIII (sets and costumes) (Old Vic), 1953; with Tyrone Guthrie, designed the Festival Tent at Stratford, Ontario, 1953, and has designed over 20 productions for the annual festivals, most recently Cymbeline, 1970, The Imaginary Invalid, 1974 (also Australian tour); Associate Director, Stratford Festival Stage, 1974–; designed The Match-maker; Edinburgh Festival, 1954, A Life In the Sun, Edinburgh Festival, 1955; Piccolo Teatro, Milan, 1955, designs for The Cherry Orchard; designed Measure For Measure (Stratford-on-Avon), 1956; The Two Gentlemen of Verona (Old Vic), 1957; The Two Gentlemen of Verona, The Broken Jug (Stratford, Ontario, touring company), The Bright One, Much Ado About Nothing (Stratford-on-Avon), 1958; The Merchant of Venice (Habimah Theatre, Tel-Aviv), All's Well That Ends Well (Stratford-on-Avon), 1959; The Wrong Side of the Park, 1960; Ondine, 1961; The Alchemist (Old Vic), 1962; Volpone (National Theatre at the Old Vic), 1968; The Persians (Crucible, Sheffield), 1972; The Misanthrope (National Theatre: Old Vic, 1973, NY 1975); Phaedra Britannica (Old Vic), 1975; The Voyage of Edgar Allan Poe (world première, Minnesota Opera), 1976; Rigoletto (Metropolitan Opera),

New York début, 1977; All's Well That Ends Well, Stratford, Ontario, 1977; The Double Dealer (N.T.), 1978; designed the following productions at the Tyrone Guthrie Theatre, Minneapolis: Hamlet, The Miser, The Three Sisters, 1963; Saint Joan, 1964; The Way of the World, The Cherry Orchard, The Miser, 1965; received the CBE in the Birthday Honours, 1976; Diplome D'Honneur, Canadian Conference of the Arts; Hon DLitt, Birmingham University, 1964; Hon Fellow, Ontario College of Art, 1979.

Recreation: c/o National Westminster Bank, 185 Sloane Street, London SW1X 9QS.

MOLLISON, Clifford, actor

b London, 1897; *s* of the late William Mollison and his wife Evelyn (McNay); *e* in Scotland and at Thanet College; *m* (1) Muriel Pope; (2) Avril Wheatley.

Made his first appearance on the stage at the Criterion Theatre, 16 Jan 1913, as Bertie Bradley in Billy's Fortune; at the Prince of Wales's, Sept 1913, played the Messenger Boy in Girls; after being invalided from the Army, appeared at the Kingsway, Apr 1919, as the Soldier in Judith, and June 1919, as the Rev Cecil McKinley in St George and the Dragons; subsequently toured as Robert Bennett in Nothing but the Truth, and with Gertrude Elliott in Eyes of Youth, and Come Out of the Kitchen; at the Strand, Jan 1921, played Stephen Vereker in A Safety Match; at the St Martin's, Mar 1922, Robert and Edward Graviter in Loyalties; Apr 1923, Jacob Berman in RUR; at the Ambassadors', June 1923, Bryan Ropes in The Lilies of the Field; at the St Martin's, Aug 1923, Robert Devizes in The Will; Jan 1924, Roger in A Magdalen's Husband; Jan 1924, succeeded Leslie Banks as Alfred Cope in The Likes of Her; at the Queen's, Mar 1924, played Pepito in Conchita at the St Martin's Mar 1924, succeeded Nicholas Hannen as Tregay in The Forest; at Drury Lane, June 1924, played Scaife in London Life; at the Queen's, Aug 1924, Benton in Pansy's Arabian Night; Sept 1924, Steadman in The Claimant; at Drury Lane, Dec 1924, Flute in A Midsummer Night's Dream; Everyman, Mar–Apr 1925, played Mr Molyneux in The Painted Swan, and Mr Charon, Jun, in Overture; St James's, June 1925, William in The River; St Martin's, July 1925, the Reporter in The Show; Savoy, Sept 1925, Harvey Fane in The Unfair Sex; Regent (for Play Actors), Mar 1926, Auberon Quin in The Napoleon of Notting Hill; Haymarket, Apr 1926, Honey in This Woman Business; Savoy, Oct 1926, Donald Warden in Love's a Terrible Thing; Daly's, Feb 1927, Adolar Von Sprintz in The Blue Mazurka; Palace, Sept 1927, Richard Dennison in The Girl Friend; Shaftesbury, Nov 1928, King Stephan in Lucky Girl; New, July 1929, Earl of Cavender in Bees and Honey; Piccadilly, Feb 1930, Frederick Tile in Here Comes the Bride; Prince Edward, Oct 1930, Bob Dering in Nippy; Coliseum, Apr 1931, Leopold in White Horse Inn; London Hippodrome, June 1932, Peter Partridge in Out of the Bottle; Haymarket, Dec 1932, Paul Frohner in Business With America; Phoenix, May 1933, Tony Hamilton in High Temperature; Gaiety, May 1935, Pat Russell in Gay Deceivers; Coliseum, Nov 1935, Timothy in Twenty to One; London Hippodrome, July 1936, Billy Early in No, No, Nanette; Adelphi, Dec 1936, Nicki in Balalaika, which ran until Apr 1938, and subsequently he toured in the same part; Aldwych, June 1939, played Jessop Crawley in To Kill a Cat; Savoy, Feb 1940, appeared in Lights Up; Duke of York's, July 1940, played Tony Hamilton in High Temperature; Adelphi, May 1946, Paul Latour in Can-Can; Comedy, Dec 1946, played Sergt Henry Brown in The Man from the Ministry; Wimbledon, Aug and St Martin's, Sept 1947, Tim in The Girl Who Couldn't Quite; Garrick, July 1948, Ben in Written for a

Lady; toured in Australia, 1950, in Is Your Honeymoon Really Necessary?; at the Q, July 1951, played Percy Ulrick Brown in Post Haste; Wyndham's, Mar 1953, succeeded Peter Ustinov as Carabosse in The Love of Four Colonels; New, Bromley, July 1953, Lord Rupert Swain in Lady in Evidence; Golders Green Hippodrome, July 1956, played Algernon Addington-Shaw in Talk of the Town Hall; Chelsea Palace, Dec 1956, Dodo and the Mad Hatter in Alice in Wonderland; Westminster, Oct 1959, played Syd Berg, and also directed The Kensington Squares; Globe, June 1955, for Repertory Players, directed As Black as She's Painted; Hippodrome, Brighton, Jun 1963, played Inspector Findlay in Bogey 7; toured Australia, 1964, as Hysterium in A Funny Thing Happened on the Way to the Forum; Northcott, Exeter, and Cardiff, Sept 1974, Dr Dorn in The Seagull; Northcott, Exeter, Aug–Sept, 1976, Moonface Martin in Anything Goes, and Pocock in Now, Here's A Funny Thing; Johannesburg, S.A., 1979, starred in On Golden Pond; has also starred in numerous films including Almost a Honeymoon, 1930; first appeared on television 1932, and, more recently, has been seen in *Potter*, *The Expert*, 1990, and many others.

Recreations: Cricket, flying and tennis. *Clubs:* MCC, Garrick, Green Room (President since 1965), and Stage Golfing Society. *Address:* c/o Eric Glass Ltd, 28 Berkeley Square, London W1X 6HD.

MONTAGUE, Lee, actor

b Bow, London, 16 Oct 1927; *e* Coopers' Company School; *m* Ruth Goring; trained for the stage at the Old Vic School, 1948–50.

Made his first professional appearance at the re-opened Old Vic, Oct 1950, walking on in Twelfth Night; at the Old Vic, season 1951–2, played Usumcasane in Tamburlaine the Great, Edmund in King Lear and Flaminius in Timon of Athens; made his New York début, Nov 1952, at the Martin Beck, as Gregory Hawke in The Climate of Eden; appeared with the Bristol Old Vic Company, season 1953, in parts including: Ben in Love for Love and the Dauphin in Henry V; in the latter production toured Switzerland and appeared at the Old Vic, London; Westminster, Oct 1956, played Francis X Gibbons in Mrs Gibbons' Boys; Stoll, July 1957, Demetrius in Titus Andronicus; Arts, Jan 1958 and Winter Garden, Mar 1958, Rocky Pioggi in The Iceman Cometh; Old Vic, season 1962–3, played Shylock in The Merchant of Venice, Oct 1962; Face in The Alchemist, Nov 1962; Angelo in Measure for Measure, Apr 1963; Royal Court, May 1965, Charles Smith in Meals on Wheels; Lyceum, New York, Oct 1965, Ed in Entertaining Mr Sloane; Aldwych, Sept 1968, Irving Spaatz in The Latent Heterosexual; Playhouse, Oxford, and tour, Sept 1970, Iago in Othello; Oxford Playhouse, Oct 1971, and tour, Lopakhin in The Cherry Orchard; Bristol Old Vic, Mar 1972, played the title-role in Volpone, and Grigory Charnota in Flight; toured as Jack Rawlings in Who Killed Jack Robin? 1972; playing the same role when the play was performed at the Haymarket, May 1974, under the title Who Saw Him Die?; Stratford E, July 1976, title-role in The Father; Royal Exchange, Manchester, 1977, played Dr Prentice in What the Butler Saw and Mr Antrobus in The Skin of Our Teeth; Her Majesty's, 1977–8, took over O'Connor in Cause Célèbre; Criterion, Nov 1979, played Barney Cashman in The Royal Exchange Company's production of Last of the Red Hot Lovers; films, since Moulin Rouge in 1952, include recently, Mahler, Jesus of Nazareth, A London Affair, and Silver Dream Racer; his numerous television appearances, since 1956, include: Eleanor Marx, Darwin's Dream, Holocaust, Comrades, and the series *Feet First*.

Favourite parts: Iago in Othello, Face, Irving Spaatz and Barney Cashman. *Recreations:* Squash, bridge, music, tennis and travel. *Address:* c/o Representation Joyce Edwards, 8 Theed Street, London, SE1.

MONTGOMERY, Earl, actor
b Memphis, Tennessee, 17 Apr 1921; *s* of Earl Montgomery and his wife Augusta (McColour); *e* Harvard College (BA 1943).

First appeared on the stage in Memphis, Tennessee, 1929, as Prince Charming in a school production of The Sleeping Beauty; made his professional debut at the Gretna Playhouse, Gretna, Pennsylvania, summer 1947, as Simon Jenkins in Room Service; first appeared in New York at the Maxine Elliott, 7 Dec 1947, as the Mathematician in Galileo; Music Box, Oct 1948, Roger Doremus in Summer and Smoke; Morosco, Nov 1952, Dr Bull in The Relapse; Plymouth, Sept 1952, Tupman in Mr Pickwick, New York City Center, Feb 1953, Boyet in Love's Labour's Lost; Mar 1953, Salario in The Merchant of Venice; Broadhurst, Sept 1953, Liebermann in The Strong Are Lonely; Booth, Nov 1955, the Inspector in Heavenly Twins; Martin Beck, May 1956, the Abbot in The Lovers; Phoenix, Sept 1956, de Stogumber in Saint Joan; Booth, Feb 1957, Cameraman in Visit to a Small Planet; took over the role of Roger Spelding in this play, July 1957, and subsequently toured in this part; Actors Playhouse, June 1959, took over as Peter Stockman in An Enemy of the People; Henry Miller's, Mar 1959, Oudatte in Look After Lulu; Hamilton, Bermuda, May 1960, Ramsden in the APA production of Man and Superman; St James, Oct 1960, Bishop of London in Becket; Music Box, Jan 1962, Zeno in Romulus; Festival of the Two Worlds, Spoleto, Italy, 1962, performed in Atti Unici; Winter Garden, Mar 1963, Ribaud in The Lady of the Camellias; Broadway, Apr 1963, took over as M Chauffourier-Dubieff in Tovarich; Royale, Sept 1963, Damiens in The Rehearsal; joined the Repertory Theatre of Lincoln Center, and, at the Vivian Beaumont, Mar 1966, played various roles in The Caucasian Chalk Circle; Oct 1966, Ananias in The Alchemist; Feb 1967, Mr Crockett in The East Wind; Apr 1967, Informer and Mathematician in Galileo; Jan 1968, D'Estivet in Saint Joan; Feb 1968, Priest in Tiger at the Gates; Apr 1968, Citizen in Cyrano de Bergerac; Lunt-Fontanne, Oct 1968, Pothinus in Her First Roman; Circle in the Square—Joseph E Levine, Sept 1973, Father Ambrose in Waltz of the Toreadors; entered films in 1963 as Alexander Woollcott in Act One; first appeared on television in *Love of Life*, 1952, and has since played frequently in various dramatic programmes, such as *Omnibus, Robert Montgomery Presents, The Jackie Gleason Show,* etc.

Address: c/o Actors Equity Association, 165 West 46th Street, New York, NY 10036.

MONTGOMERY, Elizabeth, designer
b Kidlington, Oxford, 15 Feb 1902; *d* of William Montgomery and his wife Marta (Corbett); *e* London; *m* Patrick Wilmot (dec); *vide post* Motley.

Recreation: Sailing. *Address:* 27 Grumann Hill Road, Wilton, Connecticut.

MOODY, Ron (*né* Ronald Moodnick), actor
b London, 8 Jan 1924; *s* of Bernard Moodnick and his wife Kate (Ogus); *e* London School of Economics, London University (BSc (Econ)); formerly a Research Graduate in Sociology.

Made his first appearance on the stage at the New Lindsey Theatre, London, Dec 1952, in the revue Intimacy at Eight; Dec 1953, appeared in the sequel More Intimacy at Eight; Criterion, Apr 1954, appeared in Intimacy at 8.30; after a run of more than 500 performances, he appeared at the Apollo, June 1956, in another revue For Amusement Only, which ran for nearly 700 performances; Strand, June 1958, appeared in the revue For Adults Only; Saville, Apr 1959, played the Governor of Buenos Aires in Candide; New, June 1960, played Fagin in the musical Oliver; Bristol Old Vic, Dec 1962, wrote the book, lyrics, and music, and played the title-part in Joey; Saville, Oct 1966, wrote book, lyrics and music and played title-role in Joey, Joey; Scala, Dec 1966, appeared as Mr Darling and Captain Hook in Peter Pan; Marlowe, Canterbury, Aug 1968, Aristophanes in Liz; Palladium, 1968, appeared in Royal Command Performance; Belgrade, Coventry, Aug 1971, directed his musical, Saturnalia, for which he wrote the story and music; Bankside Globe, Aug 1972, played Polonius and First Gravedigger in Hamlet; Coliseum, Dec 1972, again played Captain Hook in Peter Pan; went to Los Angeles and San Francisco, Mar 1973, to direct and play Fagin in a revival of Oliver!; Savoy, Apr 1975, played Mr Sterling in The Clandestine Marriage; Palladium, Dec 1975, Capt Hook in Peter Pan; Theatre Royal, Stratford East, Oct 1976, wrote book, lyrics and music and played title-role in The Showman; London Casino, Dec 1977, Mr Darling and Captain Hook in Peter Pan; Canada, 1978, played the title-role in Richard III; made his first appearance in films, July 1953, in Davy; subsequent films include: Murder Most Foul, Oliver! (receiving for his performance as Fagin, the Hollywood Golden Globe, Moscow Film Festival, and Variety Club of Great Britain Awards for the Best Film Actor, 1969), and recently, Dominique, and The Spaceman and King Arthur; first appeared on television 1953, and recent television performances include: Is That Your Body, Boy?, Taste, Baden Powell, and, in the US, The Word and Nobody's Perfect; he has also appeared in cabaret, and has performed his one-man show, Move Along Sideways, in Britain and the US; author of a novel, The Devil You Don't, 1979.

Favourite parts: Vagabond Student in For Amusement Only, Pierrot (mime) in For Adults Only, Governor in Candide, and Fagin in Oliver! *Recreations:* Writing, music, painting, theatre-history and archaeology. *Address:* Ingleside, 41 The Green, London N14. *Tel:* 01–886 9677.

MOORE, Dudley, actor and composer
b London, 19 Apr 1935; *s* of John Moore and his wife Ada Francis (Hughes); *e* Dagenham County High School, Guildhall School of Music and Magdalen College, Oxford; *m* (1) Suzy Kendall (mar dis); (2) Tuesday Weld (mar dis).

Made his first professional appearance at the Lyceum, Edinburgh, Sept 1960, in the Festival production of Beyond the Fringe, to which he also contributed music; made his London début in the same production, Fortune, May 1961, and his New York début also, at the John Golden in Oct 1962; Globe, Sept 1969, played Allan Felix in Play It Again, Sam; has also composed music for a number of productions, including: Serjeant Musgrave's Dance, Royal Court, 1959; The Caucasian Chalk Circle, Aldwych, Mar 1962 (RSC); England, Our England (revue), Princes, May 1962; toured Australia and New Zealand with Peter Cook, 1971, in their revue Behind the Fridge, which then played for a year at the Cambridge Theatre, London, Nov 1972, and subsequently for over a year at the Plymouth, NY, Nov 1973, under the title, Good Evening; toured USA, 1975; films include: Bedazzled and Thirty Is a Dangerous Age, Cynthia, The Hound of the Baskervilles, and 10; television appearances since 1959 include three series of his own *Not Only . . . But Also*.

Recreation: Music. *Address:* c/o Mary Walker, 21 Hasker Street, London SW3.

MOORE, Robert, actor and director
b Detroit, Michigan, 7 Aug 1927; s of Samuel W Moore and his wife Forrest L (Rash); e Catholic University of America, Washington, DC.

First appeared on the stage under the name Brennan Moore at the Hudson, New York, 23 Dec 1948, as Owen Parkside in Jenny Kissed Me; next appeared on the stage at the Jan Hus, 30 Dec 1959, as Ron Bronson in Alley of the Sunset; Cherry Lane, Feb 1961, Lewis Cadman in The Tiger Rag; directed his first NY production, The Ticket-of-Leave Man, at the Midway, 22 Dec 1961; ANTA, Nov 1964, understudied the role of F Sherman in The Owl and the Pussycat; Royale, Dec 1965, played Harvey in Cactus Flower and remained in this part for two years; Plymouth, Nov 1967, Jack in Everything in the Garden; at the Theatre Four, 14 Apr 1968, directed The Boys in the Band; directed Promises, Promises, 1968; made his London debut as director with The Boys in the Band, at Wyndham's, 11 Feb 1969; in NY directed Last of the Red Hot Lovers, 1969; The Gingerbread Lady, 1970; Lorelei or Gentlemen Still Prefer Blondes, My Fat Friend, 1974; Deathtrap, 1978; They're Playing Our Song, 1979; made his film début as an actor in Tell That You Love Me, Junie Moon, 1970; director of the films Murder by Death, 1976; The Cheap Detective, 1978; Chapter Two, 1980.

Address: c/o Stark Hesseltine, 119 West 57th Street, New York, NY 10019.

MOORE, Stephen, actor
b Brixton, London, 11 Dec 1937; s of Stanley Moore, and his wife Mary Elisabeth (Anderson); e Archbishop Tenison's Grammar School; trained for the stage at the Central School of Speech and Drama 1956–9 (Laurence Olivier prize winner).

First appeared on the stage July 1959, at the Theatre Royal, Windsor, as 1st Immigration Officer in A View From the Bridge; first appeared on the London stage Sept 1959, at the Old Vic, as William in As You Like It; with the Old Vic Company, 1959–61, he played parts including: Slender in The Merry Wives of Windsor, Dec 1959; Flute in A Midsummer Night's Dream, Dec 1960; Aguecheek in Twelfth Night, Apr 1961; Orin Mannon in Mourning Becomes Electra, Nov 1961; Mermaid, Oct 1962, played Quicksilver in Eastward Ho; Duchess, June 1963, Jack in Hughie; again at the Mermaid, played Ivan Shatov in The Possessed, Oct 1963; Messenger in The Bacchae, Feb 1964; Arts, Feb 1967, Webster in Will Somebody Please Say Something; Mermaid, May 1967, Achilles and Polymestor in The Trojan Wars; same theatre, Aug 1967, Jimmy Wesson in The Fight for Barbara; in repertory, 1968–9, at Windsor, Colchester and the Bristol Old Vic; toured United States with the Windsor company, Sept 1968, as Lord Goring in An Ideal Husband; at Bristol, Nov 1969, played Mick Goonahan in It's A Two Foot Six Inches Above the Ground World, transferring with the production to Wyndham's, Jan 1970; Ambiance, Apr 1970, Harris in a lunchtime production of After Magritte; joined the Bristol Old Vic Company, spring 1971, to appear in The Iceman Cometh, Hedda Gabler and The Taming of the Shrew, touring S America in the last as Hortensio; played Petruchio in the same production at Bristol, Mar 1973, and at the Hong Kong Festival, same year; The Place, Oct 1973, for RSC, played Fenwick in Section Nine, transferring to the

Aldwych, Jan 1974; Birmingham Repertory, 1974, Azdak in The Caucasian Chalk Circle; Theatre Upstairs, Sept 1974, Jeep in Action; Royal Court, Jan 1975, Phil in Objections to Sex and Violence; same theatre, Feb 1976, Patrick in Treats, transferring to the Mayfair, Mar; Almost Free, April 1976, Arthur in a lunchtime production of Dirty Linen and Newfound Land, which transferred as an evening production to the Arts, June; Mar 1977, joined National Theatre Company to play Trevor in Bedroom Farce, transferring to the Prince of Wales, Nov 1978, and making his Broadway debut in the part; Brooke Atkinson, Mar 1979: achieved a total of almost 600 performances in this role; also played the following parts for the N.T.: Lunacharsky in State of Revolution, May 1977; Dr Pettypon in The Lady From Maxim's, Oct 1977; Raymond Brock in Plenty, April 1978; Hjalmar Ekdal in The Wild Duck, Dec 1979; Cassio in Othello, Mar 1980; television, since 1961, includes: *Rock Follies*, Just Between Ourselves, Soldiers Talking Cleanly, and Keep Smiling; films include A Bridge Too Far, The White Bus, and Diversion.

Favourite parts: Aguecheek, Orin Mannon, Raymond Brock and Azdak. *Recreation:* Watching Chelsea FC. *Address:* c/o Ken McReddie, 48 Crawford Street, London W1. *Tel:* 01–724 1518.

MORAHAN, Christopher, director and producing manager
b London, 9 July 1929; s of Thomas Hugo Morahan and his wife Nancy Charlotte (Barker); e Highgate School; m (1) Joan Murray (dec); (2) Anna Carteret; trained for the stage at the Old Vic Theatre School with Michel St. Denis, and worked with Margaret Harris and George Devine.

Initially an actor, and subsequently a television director from 1957, his first stage production was Little Murders in July 1967 at the Aldwych for the Royal Shakespeare Company; he has since directed the following plays: This Story of Yours, 1968; Flint, 1970; The Caretaker, 1972; joined the National Theatre, 1977, to direct State of Revolution, Sir is Winning, The Lady From Maxim's, 1977; Brand, The Philanderer, Strife, 1978; The Fruits of Enlightenment, Richard III, The Wild Duck, 1979; he is Deputy Director of the National Theatre and Co-director of the Olivier; from 1972–6 he was Head of Plays, BBC TV, responsible for productions including The Glittering Prizes, Just Another Saturday (Italia Prize), 84 Charing Cross Road, and The Chester Mystery Cycle; since Emergency Ward 10, 1957, he has directed over 150 television programmes, notably Talking to a Stranger, Uncle Vanya, Old Times, Fathers and Families; also directed the films Diamonds for Breakfast and All Neat in Black Stockings; Chairman, Society of Film and Television Arts, 1966; received that Society's TV Drama Award, 1969; one-time director of Shield Productions with David Mercer and Harold Pinter.

Recreations: Walking, photography, gardening, theatre, travel and his family. *Address:* c/o National Theatre, Upper Ground, London SE1. *Tel:* 01–928 2033.

MORE, Kenneth, CBE, actor
b Gerrards Cross, Bucks, 20 Sept 1914; s of Charles Gilbert More and his wife Edith Winifred (Watkins); e Victoria College, Jersey; m (1) Beryl Johnstone (mar dis); (2) Mabel Edith Barkby (mar dis); (3) Angela Douglas.

Made his first appearance on the stage at the Windmill Theatre, Aug 1935, in a revue sketch; during the war, 1939–45, served as a Lieutenant in the RNVR; on returning to the stage appeared at the Aldwych, Nov 1946, as the Rev Arthur Platt in the revival of And No Birds Sing; New Lindsey, Feb 1947, played Eddie in Power Without Glory, and appeared in this part at the Fortune, Apr 1947; Lyric,

July 1948, played George Bourne in Peace In Our Time; Phoenix, Mar 1950, John in The Way Things Go; Duchess, Mar 1952, played Freddie Page in The Deep Blue Sea; Theatre Royal, Brighton, Jan 1961, co-presented and directed The Angry Deep; Phoenix, Oct 1963, played Peter Pounce in Out of the Crocodile; Shaftesbury, Dec 1964, played Crichton in the musical Our Man Crichton; Savoy, Oct 1968, Hugh Walford in The Secretary Bird; New, Nov 1970 played Sir Robert Morton in The Winslow Boy; Queen's, Oct 1971, George Oliver in Getting On; Vaudeville, June 1973, Andrew Perry in Signs of the Times; Vaudeville, June 1977, Duke of Bristol in On Approval; first appeared in films 1948, in Scott of the Antarctic, and has since played in Genevieve, Doctor In the House (British Film Academy Award as the best actor, 1954), The Deep Blue Sea (Venice Volpi Cup, best actor, 1955); The Admirable Crichton, Sink the Bismarck, Reach for the Sky, The Greengage Summer, The Mercenaries, Battle of Britain, Scrooge, The Slipper and the Rose, etc; recent television appearances include: *The Forsyte Saga* and *Father Brown*, author of the books: Happy Go Lucky, 1959; Kindly Leave the Stage, 1965; More or Less (autobiography), 1978; awarded the CBE in 1970 New Year Honours.

Favourite part: Freddie Page in The Deep Blue Sea.
Recreation: Golf. *Clubs:* Garrick, Stage Golfing Society, Green Room. *Address:* 27 Rumbold Road, London SW6.

MORENO, Rita (*née* Rosa Dolores Alverio), actress and dancer
b Humacao, Puerto Rico, 11 Dec 1931; *m* Leonard Gordon.

Made her New York debut, aged 13, at the Belasco, 13 Nov 1945, as Angelina in Skydrift; made her London debut at the Lyric, 29 Apr 1964, as Ilona Ritter in She Loves Me; Longacre, Oct 1964, Iris Parodus Brustein in The Sign in Sidney Brustein's Window; George Abbott, Feb 1970, Sharon Falconer in Gantry; Eugene O'Neill, 1970, took over from Linda Lavin as Elaine Navazio in Last of the Red Hot Lovers; Shubert, Philadelphia, Mar 1973, Shoplifter in Detective Story; Long Wharf, New Haven, Conn, 1973–74 season, Staff Nurse Norton in The National Health; Circle in the Square, Oct 1974, repeated this last part; Longacre, Jan 1975, Googie Gomez in The Ritz, for which she received the Antoinette Perry (Tony) Award; Long Wharf, May 1977, Serafina in The Rose Tattoo; entered films in 1950 in So Young, So Bad, and has since appeared in many others, including Singin' in the Rain, The King and I, Summer and Smoke, West Side Story (for which she received the Academy Award), Carnal Knowledge, The Ritz, Happy Birthday Gemini, The Four Seasons (1980), etc; appears regularly in cabaret; TV work includes *The Electric Company*.
Address: c/o William Morris Agency, 151 El Camino, Beverly Hills, Calif 90212.

MORGAN, Diana, dramatic author and actress
b Cardiff, 29 May 1910; *d* of Charles Morgan and his wife Diana Jane (Gwynne-Thomas); *e* Howells School, Llandaff; *m* Robert MacDermot-Barbour (dec); studied for the stage at the Central School of Speech Training and Dramatic Art.

Made her first appearance on the stage at the Arts in a matinee of her own play Cindelectra which was subsequently performed at Croydon Repertory Theatre; Drury Lane, Oct 1931, appeared in Cavalcade; in May 1932, joined Newcastle Repertory where she remained for six months; subsequently toured in The Cage; played Mari in A Comedy of Good and Evil at the Arts; Vaudeville, Apr 1933, appeared as Annie in The Soldier and the Gentlewoman; Aug 1933, toured in

Howell of Gwent; at the Festival Theatre, Cambridge, 1933–4, her parts included: Alice in Alice in Wonderland, Minnie in A Comedy of Good and Evil, Louka in Arms and the Man, etc; May 1934, Ambassadors, took over as Mrs Dainty-Fidgit in The Country Wife; Old Vic, 1935, Aphrodite in Hippolytus; Gate, Apr 1935, Minnie in A Comedy of Good and Evil, Old Woman in Lysistrata and Phyllis in Parnell; Wyndham's, 1938, Betto in She, Too Was Young; Arts, Feb 1948, again played Minnie in A Comedy of Good and Evil; Embassy, June 1950, played Cassandra Vaughan-Jones in her own play The White Eagles; Ambassadors, May 1952, Chloe Gwynne in her own play After My Fashion; May 1970, for the Welsh National Theatre, Mrs Pritchard in her own play, The Little Evenings; author with her husband of This World of Ours, 1935; Your Number's Up!, 1936; Bats in the Belfry, 1937; The Gate Revue, 1938; Let's Face It, 1939; Swinging the Gate, 1940; Swing Back the Gate, 1952; Love Is News (from the French), 1955; contributed to By Degrees, 1933; Let's Go Gay, 1935; This Year—Next Year, and Spread it Abroad, 1936; Members Only, 1937; Black and Blue, 1938; Don't Spare the Horses, All Clear, 1940; The New Ambassador's Revue, 1941; Big Top, 1942; Sauce Tartare, 1949; Better Late, The Watergate Revues, 1956, and many other revues; author of Weeping Willow and A Word of Two Syllables, 1935; The House in the Square, 1940; Three Waltzes (from the French), 1945; Rain Before Seven, 1949; The White Eagles, 1950; After My Fashion (also produced as The Starcross Legend and in New York as The Starcross Story), 1952; Your Obedient Servant, 1959; Time to Kill, 1960; The Dark Stranger, The Judge's Story (with Clive Brook) from the novel by Charles Morgan, 1964; The Little Evenings, 1970; My Cousin Rachel (adapted), Everyman (children's version), 1979; devised Merely Players, 1949, 1950 and 1952; The Green Room Show, 1956, and Our Central School Show, 1957; contract writer at Ealing Studios; film credits include: A Run For Your Money, Poets Pub, etc; wrote Hand in Hand which won fourteen international awards; has scripted many television series (including: *Emergency Ward 10*), documentaries and radio plays; she has broadcast and appeared in television drama; author of the novels Delia, and Thomas the Fish.

Recreations: Cats, conversation and collecting china.
Address: c/o ML Representation Ltd, 194 Old Brompton Road, London SW5.

MORGAN, Gareth, director
b Carmarthen, South Wales, 15 Feb 1940; *s* of Gwyn Hughes Morgan and his wife Lily May (Williams); *e* the Royal Masonic Schools, Bushey, Herts; *m* Patricia England; trained for the stage at the Rose Bruford College.

Started in the profession as an actor with the BBC Drama Repertory Company; joined the Royal Shakespeare Company in 1961, playing at Stratford in Much Ado About Nothing, As You Like It, Hamlet, The Wars of the Roses, etc, and at the Aldwych in The Cherry Orchard, The Beggar's Opera and The Representative; his first professional production was The Miracles, Southwark Cathedral, Nov 1963; assistant director, Puntila, 1965; directed The Comedy of Errors (New Zealand), 1966; Director of Productions, Welsh Theatre Company, 1966–8; artistic director of the RSC Theatregoround Company, 1968–70; for the company he directed Room for Company (also devised), Waiting for Godot, Men-at-Arms, 1968; When Thou Art King (with John Barton), The Merry Month of May (also devised), The Trial and Execution of Charles I, The Two Gentlemen of Verona, 1969; Dr Faustus, When Thou Art King (with John Barton), 1970; appointed Artistic Director in 1971 and Theatre Director 1972–7, for the Tyneside Theatre Company, Newcastle upon Tyne, where his productions included the following premières, all directed by him: Prisoners of the War, Slip Road Wedding, 1971; Play Strindberg (also Hampstead), The Baker, the Baker's Wife and the Baker's Boy, 1972; The Faery Queen (also co-adapted), Peer Gynt, A Worthy Guest, 1973; Cyrano de Bergerac, Rock Nativity, 1974; since leaving Newcastle he has directed Small Change and Shifts (Theatre Yr Yuslon), Much Ado About Nothing (Nottingham), 1977; Relatively Speaking (Coventry), Ashes (Bristol), 1978; St Joan (Birmingham), 1979; has directed productions for drama schools including: LAMDA and the Guildhall; in 1969 directed the first Macedonian translation of Macbeth for the Dramski Teatar, Skopje, Yugoslavia; member of the Arts Council Drama Panel and Young People's Theatre Committee 1974–; Executive Committee, CORT, 1973–; a governor of the Rose Bruford College of Drama; work for television includes the Arts Series *Northern View*, and he is currently presenter of HTV's Image.

Address: 63 Church Road, Gosforth, Newcastle upon Tyne. *Tel:* 0632–855213.

MORGAN, Joan, actress and dramatic author
b London, 1 Feb 1905; *d* of Sidney Morgan and his wife Evelyn (Wood); *e* Ellerker College, Richmond, and privately; commenced her career, acting for the cinema stage, in 1913.

Made her first appearance on the stage at the Apollo Theatre, 21 Nov 1916, as the little girl in A Pierrot's Christmas; at the Comedy, May 1917, played in Bubbly; from 1917–24, appeared on the cinema stage; at the Apollo, Sept 1924, played Dilly Gilliam in The Fool; subsequently toured as Eva in Adam and Eva, and Aggie Lynch in Within the Law; Prince's, Dec 1925, Katie Pottlebury in When Knights Were Bold; Lyceum, May 1926, Estelle in The Padre; during 1926–7, toured as June in Mercenary Mary; subsequently returned to the cinema stage, and wrote several film scenarios, including: Contraband Love, The Call-Box Mystery, and adapted The Flag Lieutenant; author of the plays, This Was a Woman, 1944; Deep as a Well, 1947; Who Goes Home?, 1950; The Martin's Nest, 1951; The Valley and the Peak, Shadow on the Sun, The Honourable Member, 1952; Dr Jo, 1955; Square Dance, 1957; A Feather in His Cap, 1959; The Hours of Darkness, 1960; The Hanging Wood, 1969; has written a number of plays for television; she is also the author of thirteen novels, essays and a book on houses; during the War, from 1942–4, was engaged at the Ministry of Supply; committee member of various preservation societies.

Recreations: Reading, swimming, travel, and converting houses. *Address:* The Toll House, Ancastle Green, Henley on Thames, Oxon. *Tel:* 04912–4640.

MORGAN, Roger, lighting designer and theatre consultant
b New Kensington, Pa, 19 Dec 1938; *e* Carnegie Institute of Technology; *m* Ann Sachs.

Designed the lighting for his first New York Show. Witches' Sabbath, at the Madison Avenue Playhouse, 19 Apr 1962; since then has lit At Sea, Alcestis Come Back, We're Civilized?, 1962; The Knack, Kiss Mama, Othello, The Room, A Slight Ache, 1964; Mary Agnes Is 35, The River, Passport in a triple bill called Friday Night, The Great Western Union, Baal, Troubled Waters, Medea, 1965; Jonah!, Half Horse, Half Alligator, The Journey of the Fifth Horse, The World of Gunter Grass, The Long Christmas Dinner, Queens of France, The Happy Journey to Trenton and Camden, Who's Got His Own, Under the Weather, 1966; Fragments, The Basement, 1967; The Ceremony of

Innocence, I Only Want an Answer, Saturday Night, The Electronic Nigger, Clara's Ole Man, A So, Come Home, Endicott and the Red Cross, Sweet Eros, Witness, Brother to Dragons, The Sudden and Accidental Re-Education of Horse Johnson, 1968; Peace World War 2½, The Honest-to-God Schnozzola, The Leader, Papp, Mercy Street, 1969; Wilson in the Promise Land, Dr. Galley, Transfers, The Rooming House, Forensic and the Navigators, The Unseen Hand, The Last Straw, Duet for Solo Voice, The Nest, Colette, Gandhi, Saved, Sunday Dinner, The Castro Complex, One Night Stands of a Noisy Passenger, 1970; Do It Again!, Behold! Cometh the Vanderkellans, Jonny Johnson, Unlikely Heroes, The Last Analysis, F. Jasmine Addams, Fingernails Blue As Flowers, Lake of the Woods, 1971; Two If by Sea, Elizabeth I, Ring Round the Bathtub, The Web and the Rock, Older People Sleep, Metamorphosis, The Chickencoop Chinaman, Dude (with Eugene and Franne Lee), The Kid, 1972; The Enemy Is Dead, Welcome to Andromeda, Variety Obit, 42 Seconds from Broadway, The Karl Marx Play, The Children's Mass, Baba Goya, A Break in the Skin, Nourish the Beast, House Party, Lotta, 1973; Barbara Shore, Bread, Joan of Lorraine, Richard III, Where Do We Go from Here?, The Beauty Part, Saturday Sunday Monday, 1974; Black Picture Show, Rubbers, Yanks 3 Detroit 0 Top of the Seventh, Straws in the Wind, Gorky, The Soft Touch, 1975; Dracula, 1977; Spotlight (tour), The Crucifer of Blood ('Tony' award), First Monday in October, Gorey Stories, 1978; I Remember Mama, 1979; as a theatre consultant and/or lighting consultant he has served on projects including The American Place Theatre, NY, Center Stage, Baltimore, Ford's Theatre, Washington DC (Son et lumière), Kennedy Center, Washington DC, etc.

Address: United Scenic Artists, 1540 Broadway, New York, NY.

MORIARTY, Michael, actor
b Detroit, Michigan, 5 Apr 1941; *e* Dartford College; prepared for the stage at LAMDA.

Made his New York debut at the Delacorte, 13 Jun 1963, as Octavius Caesar in the New York Shakespeare Festival production of Antony and Cleopatra; same theatre, Jul 1973, Jack in As You Like It, and Aug 1963; Florizel in The Winter's Tale; Delacorte, Jun 1965, Longaville in Love's Labour's Lost, and Aug 1965, Helenus in Troilus and Cressida; appeared with the Minnesota Theatre Company, Minneapolis, 1966–67 season, and in June–Dec 1968 as a member of the chorus in The House of Atreus and as Ted Ragg, Charles Fish, and Ignatius Dullfeet in The Resistible Rise of Arturo Ui; repeated his parts in The House of Atreus and The Resistible Rise of Arturo Ui at the Billy Rose, Dec 1968; appeared for a season with the Charles Playhouse, Boston, Mass, 1969–70; University of the Streets, NY, May 1970, Man in Peanut Butter and Jelly; Alley Theatre, Houston, Texas, 1970, played Thoreau in The Night Thoreau Spent in Jail; Good Shepherd—Faith Church, NY, Mar 1971, took over as George Mische in The Trial of the Catonsville Nine; repeated this last part at the Lyceum, June 1971; Brooks Atkinson, Jan 1974; Julian Weston in Find Your Way Home, for which he received the Antoinette Perry (Tony) Award; Mitzi E. Newhouse, Oct 1974, title role in Richard III; played the piano in cabaret at Michael's Pub, NY, Apr 1975; Brooklyn Academy, Jan 1976, Edmund Tyrone in Long Day's Journey into Night; Delacorte, June 1976, Chorus in Henry V; Lake Forest, Chicago, Aug 1976, Scoutmaster Hennessey in Dirty Jokes; Playhouse, NY, Apr 1979, Micah in G R Point; St John's Cathedral NY, Sept 1979, directed

Love's Labour's Lost and Psalms to the Son of Man (Feb 1980) for The Potter's Field Theatre Company; has appeared in the films Bang the Drum Slowly, Report to the Commissioner, Shoot It: Black, Shoot It: Blue, etc.

Address: Actors Equity Association, 165 West 46th Street, New York, NY 10036.

MORLEY, Christopher, designer

His work includes: Edward II (Leicester and London), 1964; Their Very Own and Golden City, Three Men for Colverton, Macbeth, 1966; became an associate artist of the Royal Shakespeare Company, 1966, and has since designed the following productions for them: The Revenger's Tragedy, 1966; The Taming of the Shrew, The Relapse, 1967; King Lear, Much Ado About Nothing, 1968; The Winter's Tale, Twelfth Night, 1969; Hamlet, King John, The Tempest, 1970; Twelfth Night, 1971; Coriolanus, Julius Caesar, Antony and Cleopatra, Titus Andronicus, 1972; left to form Christopher Morley Associates, 1974, who have been responsible for a number of operas and for Liza of Lambeth, 1976; other productions include: As You Like It (Regent's Park), 1973; The Sunshine Boys, 1975; Sticks and Bones (New End), The Achurch Letters (Greenwich), Molly (Comedy), 1978; Mary Barnes (Royal Court), 1979; for Birmingham Rep, 1978–9, he designed The Merchant, The Beggar's Opera (co-designer) and St Joan; further productions for the RSC include The Merchant of Venice and Measure for Measure (Stratford 1978, London 1979); Cymbeline (Stratford), The White Guard (Aldwych), 1979; The Maid's Tragedy (Stratford), 1980.

Address: c/o Royal Shakespeare Theatre, Stratford-on-Avon, Warwicks.

MORLEY, Robert, CBE, actor and dramatic author

b Semley, Wilts, 26 May 1908; *s* of Major Robert Wilton Morley and his wife Gertrude Emily (Fass); *e* Wellington College and in Germany, France, and Italy; *m* Joan Buckmaster; originally intended for a diplomatic career; studied for the stage at the Royal Academy of Dramatic Art.

Made his first appearance on the stage at the Hippodrome, Margate, 28 May 1928, in Dr Syn; first appeared in London at the Strand Theatre, 26 Dec 1929, as a Pirate in Treasure Island; he then toured as assistant stage-manager of And So To Bed, and appeared at the Playhouse, Oxford, under the late J B Fagan, 1931; in 1933, appeared at the Festival, Cambridge, for a season under Norman Marshall; appeared at the Royalty, London, Nov 1933, as Oakes in Up In The Air; toured with Sir Frank Benson in H V Neilson's Shakespearean company; during 1934, toured as the Rev Vernon Isopod in Late Night Final and during 1935, as Gloucester in Richard of Bordeaux; in conjunction with Peter Bull established repertory at Perranporth, Cornwall, where he played a variety of parts; Gate Theatre, Sept 1936, played Oscar Wilde in the play of that name; Strand, May 1937, and New, June 1937, Alexandre Dumas in The Great Romancer; at the Old Vic, Sept 1937, played Henry Higgins in Pygmalion; made his first appearance on the New York stage at the Fulton Theatre, 10 Oct 1938, as Oscar Wilde; returned to England, 1939, and appeared at Perranporth, July 1939, as Henry in Springtime for Henry; Theatre Royal, Brighton, Feb 1941, played Decius Hess in Play with Fire (The Shop at Sly Corner); Savoy Theatre, Dec 1941, played Sheridan Whiteside in The Man Who Came to Dinner, which he continued to play in London, and on tour until 1943; toured, Feb 1944, as Charles in Staff Dance; New Theatre, July 1945, played the Prince Regent in The First Gentleman, which ran there and at the Savoy for over a year; His Majesty's, May 1947, Arnold Holt in Edward, My Son; at the Martin Beck Theatre, NY, Sept 1948, again played Arnold Holt in Edward, My Son; subsequently appeared in this part in Australia and New Zealand, July 1949–50; on returning to London, appeared at the Lyric, Aug 1950, as Philip in The Little Hut; next appeared in London, at the same theatre, Apr 1954, as Hippo in Hippo Dancing, which he adapted from the French of André Roussin; Globe, Mar 1956, presented (with H M Tennent, Ltd), and played Oswald Petersham in A Likely Tale; Drury Lane, Nov 1956, made his first appearance in a musical play, as Panisse in Fanny; Her Majesty's, Dec 1957, directed The Tunnel of Love; Piccadilly, Nov 1958, adapted, and also played Sebastian Le Boeuf in Hook, Line, and Sinker; New, July 1959, directed Once More, With Feeling; Phoenix, Mar 1960, played Mr Asano in A Majority of One; Royal, Windsor, Oct 1961, played the title-part in Mr Rhodes; Piccadilly, Apr 1962, played The Bishop in A Time to Laugh; 1966–7 toured Australia in one-man show The Sound of Morley; Queen's, London, Nov 1967, Sir Mallalieu Fitzbuttress in Halfway Up the Tree; Lyric, Aug 1970, Frank Foster in How the Other Half Loves; repeated this role in N America, 1972, and Australia, 1973; at the Savoy, Apr 1974, played Barnstable in A Ghost on Tiptoe, of which he was joint author (with Rosemary Anne Sisson); Savoy, Aug 1976, Pound in Banana Ridge; 1978, toured in his one man show Robert Morley Talks to Everyone; in the same year toured the provinces and Canada in Picture of Innocence (also co-author); Theatre Royal, Sydney, Mar 1980, Hilary in The Old Country; he has also written the plays Short Story, 1935; Goodness, How Sad, 1937; Staff Dance, 1944; Edward, My Son (with Noel Langley), 1947; The Full Treatment (with Ronald Gow); Six Months Grace (with Dundas Hamilton), 1957; his autobiography Responsible Gentleman (with Sewell Stokes), 1966; recent publications include Robert Morley's Book of Bricks, 1978; Book of Worries, 1979; entered films, 1937, and has appeared in Major Barbara, The African Queen, The Good Die Young, The Doctor's Dilemma, Oscar Wilde, Topkapi, The Loved Ones, Murder At The Gallop, Ladies Who Do, Genghis Khan, Finders Keepers, Cromwell, Doctor in Trouble, Scavenger Hunt, The Human Factor, etc; television appearances include the series: Charge; appeared in cabaret at the Mandarin, Hong Kong, Mar 1976; received the CBE, in the New Year Honours, 1957.

Recreations: Conversation and horse-racing. *Clubs:* Garrick and Buck's. *Address:* Fairmans Cottage, Wargrave, Berks.

MORLEY, Sheridan, drama critic and writer

b Ascot, 5 Dec 1941; *s* of the actor Robert Morley and his wife Joan (Buckmaster); *e* Sizewell Hall, Suffolk and Merton College, Oxford; *m* the novelist and critic Margaret Gudejko.

Deputy features editor, 1973–75, *The Times;* drama critic and arts editor, 1975– , Punch; writes regularly for the *Evening Standard,* London, *Tatler, Radio Times* etc; stage appearances include walking on in Edward My Son in Australasia at the age of nine, followed by an appearance at the Yvonne Arnaud, Guildford, Oct 1978, narrating Side By Side By Sondheim; published works include A Talent to Amuse, 1969; Review Copies, 1974; Oscar Wilde, 1975; Marlene Dietrich, 1976; Sybil Thorndike, 1977; Gladys Cooper, Noel Coward and His Friends, The Stephen Sondheim Songbook, all 1979; appears frequently on radio; for TV was an ITN newscaster, 1965–67, and an interviewer on Late Night Line-Up, BBC, 1967–72.

Recreations: Talking, drinking, eating, theatregoing, swimming. *Address:* c/o Punch, 23 Tudor Street, London EC4. *Tel:* 583 9199.

MORRIS, Mary, actress

b Suva, Fiji Islands, 13 Dec 1915; *d* of Herbert Stanley Morris *b* Suva, Fiji Islands, 13 Dec 1915; *d* of Herbert Stanley Morris and his wife Sylvia Ena (de Creft-Harford); *e* The Priory, Hayward's Heath, Sussex; studied for the stage at the Royal Academy of Dramatic Art.

Made her first appearance on the stage, as a child, 1925, at Barbados, BWI; first appeared in London, at the Gate Theatre, 12 Mar 1936, as the third Old Woman in Lysistrata; appeared with her own repertory company, Stranger Players, at Oxted, Surrey, Sept 1936–Apr 1937; spent six months in Hollywood, under contract with MGM Films, 1937–8; Vaudeville, Aug 1941, Antonia in Squaring the Circle; Westminster, Oct 1941, Glasha in Distant Point; toured, 1942, as Emmy Baudine in They Walk Alone, and 1943 Kathy in Wuthering Heights; Arts, Dec 1943, played Esther in On Life's Sunny Side, and Feb 1944, Anne Pedersdotter in The Witch; Lyric, June 1945, Abigail Sarclet in Duet for Two Hands; Embassy, Nov 1946, played Julia in The Day of Glory; Scala, Dec 1946, appeared as Peter Pan; Lyric, Hammersmith, July 1947, Lucie in Men Without Shadows; Embassy, Jan 1948, the Strange Lady in As You Desire Me; Feb 1949, Caesonia in Caligula; Q, Dec 1949, and Lyric, Hammersmith, May 1950, played Nina Moore in If This Be Error; Rudolf Steiner Hall, July 1950, Chorus in Pericles; at the Mercury, 1949, produced Beauty and the Beast; Embassy, Jan 1951, produced Celestina; New, Apr 1952, played Elizabeth Tudor in The Young Elizabeth; at the Arts, June 1954, and at the St James's, July 1954, appeared as the Step-Daughter in Six Characters in Search of an Author; Arts, June 1955, played Lavinia Mannon in Mourning Becomes Electra; Oxford Playhouse, Oct 1956, played the title-part in Electra by Jean Giraudoux; 1964, toured in The Maids; has also broadcast, and appeared frequently on television, including An Unofficial Rose, The Spread of the Eagle, Richard II, Anna Karenina, and The Velvet Glove; first appeared in films 1938, in Prison Without Bars; other films include: Pimpernel Smith and The Thief of Bagdad.

Favourite parts: Saint Joan, Cleopatra, and Juliet. *Recreation:* Painting. *Club:* The Ski Club of Great Britain. *Address:* c/o Larry Dalzell, 3 Goodwin's Court, St Martin's Lane, London WC2. *Tel:* 01–240 3086.

MORRIS, Phyllis, dramatic author and actress
b London, 18 July 1894; *d* of Alfred Morris and his wife Helen (Matthews); *e* Cheltenham College; formerly engaged in journalism.

Made her first appearance on the stage, touring in Shaw repertory under the management of Charles Macdona; at Wyndham's, Oct 1932, played Mrs Munsey in Service; His Majesty's, May 1933, Anna in Music in the Air; New, Apr 1934, Miss Casson in The Laughing Woman; Q, Oct 1934, Miss Pendlebury in Courtship Dance; Comedy, Feb 1935, Emma Hodges in Mrs Nobby Clark; Globe, Oct 1935, Mrs Milson in Call It a Day; Gate, Mar 1937, Mabel Rudge in Out of Sight; Apollo, Apr 1937, Mrs Guffy and Jeannie Dean in London After Dark; St James's, Dec 1939, Emily Creed in Ladies in Retirement; toured for the Old Vic company, 1940–1, in Wales and in mining areas; Arts, Dec 1942, played Ku in Holy Isle, and Agnes Dowton in The Drunkard; Apollo, 1943, Mrs Oakes in Flare Path; Scala, Dec 1943, the Duchess in Alice in Wonderland; subsequently appeared with the BBC repertory company; appeared in films in Hollywood, 1946–51; returned to London and at the Lyric, Hammersmith, Sept 1951, appeared as Anna in Thor, With Angels; Ambassadors', Nov 1952, played Emmie in Murder Mistaken; Duchess, Sept 1955, played Mrs Twigg in Mr Kettle and Mrs Moon; Royal Court, June 1958, played the Maid in The Lesson; returned to the stage after temporary

retirement, at the Arts, Ipswich, Aug 1968, as the Housekeeper in The Innocents; Ambiance, Oct 1968, played Mother in Why Bournemouth?; Playhouse, Oxford, Apr 1969 and tour, Vassilyevna in Uncle Vanya; Royal Court, Feb 1970, Mrs Dobey in The Big Romance; has appeared in numerous television plays since 1952, including the serial: Great Expectations, and the *Probation Officer* series; has appeared in British films since 1935, and her pictures include: Mandy, Top Secret, The Devil's Disciple, etc; is the author of the following plays: The Rescue Party, 1926; Made in Heaven, 1926; Tinker, Tailor . . . (adapted from the German), 1928; A-Hunting We Will Go, 1931; she is the author of several children's books, and has exhibited her paintings in several London galleries.

Address: Denville Hall, 62 Ducks Hill Road, Northwood, Middlesex.

MORRISON, Hobe, author and critic
b Germantown, Pennsylvania, 24 Mar 1904; *s* of J I Morrison and his wife Agnes (Millar); *e* public school in Philadelphia; *m* (1) Elizabeth Augur (mar dis); (2) Toni Darnay.

Entered journalism as the drama editor and second-string critic of *The Record*, Philadelphia, 1932, and held these positions until 1937; joined the staff of *Variety*, Feb 1937, where he currently serves as drama editor and as critic of Broadway shows; writes a daily column for the Passaic (NJ) Herald News; is a free-lance writer on theatrical subjects.

Recreations: Walking, bird-watching, crossword puzzle solving. *Clubs:* The Players, New York Drama Critics Circle, Coffee House. *Address:* 7 West 16th Street, New York, NY, 10011, or c/o *Variety*. *Tel:* 212–582 2700.

MORRISON, Jack, theater educator and administrator, actor and director
b Santa Barbara, California, 17 Dec 1912; *s* of Charles Pacific Morrison and his wife Anna Marie; *e* UCLA and University of Southern California; *m* (1) Martha Godfrey (mar dis); (2) the actress Jeanne Cagney (mar dis).

After nine years as director of theatre activities, 1938–47, became a founding member of the theatre arts department, UCLA, later serving as associate professor; directed many student productions there; dean of the College of Fine Arts, Ohio University, 1966–71; presently executive director, American Theatre Association; author of The Rise of the Arts on the American Campus, 1973, as well as numerous articles etc.

Club: Players. *Address:* American Theatre Association, 1000 Vermont Avenue NW, Washington DC 20003. *Tel:* 202-628 4634.

MORSE, Robert, actor and singer
b Newton, Mass, 18 May 1931; *s* of Charles Morse and his wife May (Silver); *e* Newton, Mass, High School; *m* Carole Ann D'Andrea; served in the US Navy, 1951.

Directed and played in a school production of Sing Out, Sweet Land, 1951; made his professional debut with the Peterborough, NH, Players in Our Town, 1949; made his New York debut at the Royale, 5 Dec 1955, as Barnaby Tucker in The Matchmaker, playing for over a year, and then toured in the part; ANTA, Apr 1958, played Ted Snow in the musical Say, Darling; Shubert, Oct 1959, Richard Miller in Take Me Along; 46th Street, Oct 1961, J Pierpont Finch in How to Succeed in Business Without Really Trying, and played the part for nearly two years; played in films for some years, then reappeared in NY at the Majestic, Apr 1972, as Jerry in Sugar; Waldorf-Astoria, Jun 1973, appeared in the revue Milliken Breakfast Show; Meadowbrook Dinner, Cedar Grove, NJ, Nov 1973, Mr Applegate in Damn Yankees; Dorothy Chandler Pavilion, Los Angeles, Cal., Sept 1974, again played Jerry in Sugar; same theatre, May 1975, directed and played J Pierpont Finch in How to Succeed in Business Without Really Trying; Harkness, NY, Apr 1976, David in So Long, 174th Street; first appeared in films in The Proud and Profane, 1956, and has since played in The Matchmaker, How to Succeed in Business Without Really Trying, The Loved One, Oh Dad, Poor Dad, Mama's Hung You in the Closet and I'm Feelin' So Sad, etc.; has appeared frequently on Television in *Naked City*, the *Jack Paar Show*, and his series *That's Life*.

Recreations: Sports, cooking, photography. *Address:* Actors Equity Association, 165 West 46th Street, New York, NY 10036.

MORTIMER, John, dramatic author
b Hampstead, London, 21 Apr 1923; *s* of Clifford Mortimer and Kathleen May (Smith); *e* Harrow, and Brasenose College, Oxford; *m* (1) Penelope Fletcher (mar dis); (2) Penelope Jollop; is, by profession, a barrister.

During the war, worked with the Crown Film Unit as a script writer; his first play The Dock Brief (originally written for sound radïo) was broadcast May 1957, later televised, and subsequently presented in a double bill with What Shall We Tell Caroline? at the Lyric, Hammersmith, Apr 1958, transferring to the Garrick, May 1958; The Dock Brief won the Italia prize, 1957; both plays have since been performed in the USA, Italy, France, Yugoslavia, Germany, Poland, and also on television in America; author of I Spy, produced in a triple bill at the Palm Beach Playhouse, Florida, Mar 1959; The Wrong Side of the Park, Cambridge, Feb 1960; Lunch Hour (one-act), in the triple-bill Three, Arts and Criterion, 1961; Two Stars for Comfort, Garrick, 1962; translated A Flea in Her Ear (La Puce à l'Oreille), National Theatre Company, 1966; The Judge, 1967; translated A Cat Among the Pigeons, 1969; Come As You Are, A Voyage Round My Father, 1970; translated The Captain of Köpenick, 1971; I Claudius, 1972; Collaborators, 1973; Heaven and Hell (double-bill), 1976, revised as The Bells of Hell, 1977; translated The Lady from Maxims, National, 1978; author of the script for *Son et Lumière*, Hampton Court, 1964; has contributed material to various revues; his film scripts include: John and Mary; numerous television plays include the award-winning Voyage Round My Father, and Married Alive; creator of the series *Rumpole of the Bailey*; author of six novels and one book of travel.

Recreations: Working, cooking, and going to the theatre. *Address:* Turville Heath Cottage, Henley on Thames, Oxon.

MOSES, Gilbert, III; director
b Cleveland, Ohio, 20, Aug 1942; *s* of Gilbert Moses, Jr, and his wife Bertha Mae (Jones); *e* Oberlin, Ohio, College; formerly a journalist.

Directed his first play, Roots, at the Free Southern Theatre, New Orleans, La, Sept 1964; directed his first play in New York, LeRoi Jones's (Imanu Amiri Baraka's) Slaveship, at the Chelsea, Brooklyn, Oct 1970, which later transferred to Manhattan; for the American Conservatory Theatre, San Francisco, Cal, Directed Bloodknot; for the Arena Stage, Washington, DC, directed Mother Courage and No Place to Be Somebody; Jerry Adler directed Charlie Was Here and Now He's Gone (NY), and directed Aint Supposed to Die a Natural Death, all 1971; since then has directed The Duplex, Don't Let It Go to Your Head, 1972; The Taking of Miss Janie, 1975; with George Faison directed 1600 Pennsylvania Avenue, 1976; received the Obie Award for Slaveship and the Drama Desk Award for Aint Supposed to Die a Natural

Death; directed and wrote music for the film Willie Dynamite, 1973.

Address: 6740 Milner Road, Los Angeles, Calif 90068.

MOSS, Arnold, actor
b Brooklyn, New York, 28 Jan 1910; *s* of Jack Moss and his wife Essie (Joseph); *e* City College, NYC, Columbia University (MA), and New York University (PhD); *m* Stella Reynolds.

Made his first appearance in NY, with the Civic Repertory company, 1929, and remained with the company until 1931; Alvin, Oct 1931, appeared in Wonder Boy; Alvin, Mar 1940, played Antonio in The Fifth Column; Shubert, Sept 1940, Fernando in Hold On to Your Hats; National, Oct 1940, Ishmael in Journey to Jerusalem; Guild, Dec 1940, Howard Ingraham in Flight to the West; Music Box, Oct 1941, Count Czarniko in The Land Is Bright; Alvin, Jan 1945, played Prospero in The Tempest; Royale, Sept 1946, Walter Burns in The Front Page; Empire, Oct 1949, Malvolio in Twelfth Night; National, Dec 1950, Gloucester in King Lear; toured in one-man show called The Seven Ages of Man, 1952; ANTA Playhouse, Feb 1955, played Col Janik in The Dark Is Light Enough; Paris, June 1955, Creon in Medea in a Salute to France programs; American Shakespeare Festival, Stratford, Connecticut, June 1956, King of France in King John, and Duke of Vienna in Measure for Measure; Phoenix, NY, Jan 1957, again played the Duke in Measure for Measure; toured, 1957, and Ambassador, NY, Mar 1958, as George Bernard Shaw in Back to Methuselah, which he also co-produced and adapted; Brussels World Fair, Oct 1958, the Society Man in The Time of Your Life; toured the United States in 1959 with the Shakespeare Festival Players as Prospero in The Tempest and Duke of Vienna in Measure for Measure; produced and appeared annually at the Library of Congress, Washington, DC, 1955–75, toured as Theatre Specialist for the US State Department, Latin America, 1961; Paris and Africa, 1964; at various times has also toured the US in a one-man concert reading Seven Ages; toured US colleges, 1964, lecturing on Shakespearean production; Artist-in-Residence at Otterbein College, Ohio, where he directed and played Don Armado in Love's Labour's Lost (1964); and Shylock in The Merchant of Venice (1979); University of Kansas, Mar 1964, played Prospero in The Tempest; University of Hawaii, 1965, played Lear in King Lear; University of Kentucky, 1966, again played Lear; Kent State University, 1969, Willy Loman in Death of a Salesman; Trenton, New Jersey, State College, 1970, again played Lear; Winter Garden, Mar 1971, Dimitri Weissman in Follies; Carnegie Hall, Oct 1975, appeared as MC with Molly Picon; played Milton and Voice of God in Chicago Lyric Opera's Paradise Lost, 1979, appearing in the same production at La Scala, Milan, followed by a command performance for Pope John Paul II at the Vatican, also 1979; was visiting professor, University of Connecticut, 1973–4; College of William and Mary, 1977; Purdue University, 1977; awarded the James K Hacket medal of CCNY, 1968, for outstanding achievement in dramatic arts; Townsend Harris Medal of CCNY, 1978; first appeared in films in Temptation, 1946, and has since played in The Loves of Carmen, Kim, My Favorite Spy, Viva Zapata! etc; played for various radio programs in the 1930s and 1940s; has appeared on major dramatic television programs; author, The Professional Actor as Performing Guest Artist at American Colleges and Universities.

Address: c/o Actors Equity Association, 165 West 46th Street, New York, NY 10036.

MOSTEL, Zero (*né* Samuel Joel), actor
b Brooklyn, New York, 28 Feb 1915; *s* of Israel Mostel and

his wife Zina (Druchs); *e* College of the City of New York; *m* Kathryn Harkin; formerly a painter.

First appeared on the stage in NY at the Café Society Downtown in 1942, in a cabaret act; first appeared on Broadway at the 44th Street Theatre, Apr 1942, in Keep 'Em Laughing; next appeared at the Ziegfeld, June 1945, in the revue Concert Varieties; Broadway, Dec 1946, played Hamilton Peachum in Beggar's Holiday; Music Box, Mar 1952, played Glubb in Flight into Egypt; made his first appearance in London at the Palladium in 1953, in his cabaret and vaudeville act; Downtown National, NY, Oct 1954, played Maxie Fields in A Stone for Danny Fisher; Phoenix, off-Broadway, Dec 1956, Shu Fu in The Good Woman of Setzuan; Belasco, Mar 1957, Doc Penny in Good as Gold; Rooftop, June 1958, played Leopold Bloom in Ulysses in Nighttown; toured Europe in the last play appearing at the Arts Theatre, London, May 1959, at the International Festival, Paris, July 1959, at the Holland Festival, Amsterdam, and The Hague, July 1959; Longacre, Jan 1961, played John in Rhinoceros; Longacre, Sept 1961, again played John in Rhinoceros, subsequently touring the USA with the production; Alvin, May 1962, played Pseudolus and Prologus in A Funny Thing Happened on the Way to the Forum, in which he appeared for nearly two years; Imperial, Sept 1964, played Tevye in Fiddler on the Roof, receiving the New York Drama Critics Award for this performance, 1965; Kalita Humphreys, Dallas Texas, Mar 1968, played the title-role in The Latent Heterosexual, Westbury, Long Island, Music Fair, Oct 1971, Tevye in Fiddler on the Roof, and Nov 1973, Pseudolus and Prologus in A Funny Thing Happened on the Way to the Forum; Winter Garden, Mar 1974, Leopold Bloom in a revival of Ulysses in Nighttown; toured, 1976, as Tevye in Fiddler on the Roof also playing at the Winter Garden, NY; first appeared in films in 1941, and subsequently appeared in Dubarry Was a Lady, Sirocco, Panic in the Streets, Zero, A Funny Thing Happened on the Way to the Forum, The Producers, Rhinoceros (1974), etc; has appeared frequently on television in such programs as Cavalcade, *The Ed Sullivan Show,* and in the productions Waiting for Godot, The World of Sholem Aleichem, in the title-role of the opera Gianni Schichi (1975), etc; received the International Critics Award as the Best Actor, 1959, and three Tony Awards as Best Dramatic Actor, 1961, and Best Musical Comedy Actor, 1963 and 1965; Hon DLitt, Middlebury College, 1974.

(*Died 8 Sept 1977, while on a pre-Broadway tour of* The Merchant.)

MOTLEY, designers
Firm originally composed of three women, Audrey Sophia Harris, Margaret F Harris (dec), and Elizabeth Montgomery (*qv*).

Have designed settings and costumes for numerous productions, including Romeo and Juliet, OUDS, Feb 1932; Men About the House, Globe; Strange Orchestra, St Martin's; Merchant of Venice, Old Vic, 1932; Richard of Bordeaux, New; A Midsummer Night's Dream, Open Air, Regent's Park Ball at the Savoy, Drury Lane, 1933; tour of Jack and Jill, 1933; Spring 1600, Shaftesbury; The Haunted Ballroom (ballet), Sadler's Wells; Hamlet, New, 1934; The Old Ladies, Noah, and Romeo and Juliet, New; Dusty Ermine, Comedy; Aucassin and Nicolette, Duke of York's, 1935; Richard II, OUDS; Happy Hypocrite, His Majesty's; Farewell Performance, and Charles the King, Lyric; The Witch of Edmonton, Old Vic, 1936; Henry V, Old Vic; He Was Born Gay, Queen's; Great Romancer, New; Macbeth, Old Vic; Richard II, School for Scandal, Queen's, 1937; Merchant of Venice,

Three Sisters, Dear Octopus, Queen's, 1938; Marriage of Blood, Savoy; Scandal in Assyria, Globe; Weep for the Spring, tour; Rhondda Roundabout, Globe, The Importance of Being Earnest, Great Expectations, 1939; The Beggar's Opera, 1940; The Cherry Orchard, 1941; The Doctor's Dilemma, Watch on the Rhine, 1942; The Wind of Heaven, A Month in the Country, 1945; Antony and Cleopatra, The King Stag, 1946; The Shoemaker's Holiday, 1947; The Snow Queen, 1947; The Heiress, Marriage Story, Antigone, 1949; For Love or Money, Bartholomew Fair, 1950; Hassan (revival), Othello, Colombe, 1951; The Happy Time, The Innocents, The River Line, 1952; Paint Your Wagon, Richard III, Antony and Cleopatra, King John, 1953; Charley's Aunt, I Capture the Castle, Wedding in Paris, Nelson (opera), Hedda Gabler, Can-Can, A Midsummer Night's Dream, Romeo and Juliet, 1954; The Merry Wives of Windsor, 1955; A Likely Tale, The Mulberry Bush, The Crucible, Othello (Stratford-on-Avon), Cards of Identity, The Seagull, The Country Wife, 1956; Eugene Onegin (Sadler's Wells), The Magic Flute (Sadler's Wells), As You Like It, and Julius Caesar (Stratford-on-Avon), Requiem For a Nun, 1957; Major Barbara, Hamlet (Stratford-on-Avon), 1958; The Magistrate, The Aspern Papers, Rosmersholm, 1959; The Naming of Murderer's Rock, Ross, A Man For All Seasons, King Lear (Stratford-on-Avon), Waiting in the Wings, Toys in the Attic (costumes only), 1960; The Lady From the Sea, Dazzling Prospect, You in Your Small Corner, 1961; Playing With Fire (one-act, costumes only), Vanity Fair (costumes only), The Tulip Tree, 1962; Where Angels Fear to Tread, The Doctor's Dilemma, 1963; Hobson's Choice (National), The Right Honourable Gentleman, Faust (Sadler's Wells), A Cuckoo in the Nest (costumes only), Hay Fever (National), 1964; A Masked Ball (Sadler's Wells), Spring Awakening (costumes only), Trelawny of the 'Wells' (National), 1965; You Never Can Tell, 1966; since 1941, the organization has designed settings and costumes for the following productions in America; The Doctor's Dilemma, 1941; The Three Sisters, 1942; Richard III, Lovers and Friends, 1943; The Cherry Orchard, A Highland Fling, A Bell for Adano, 1944; The Tempest, Hope for the Best, You Touched Me, Carib Song, Skydrift, Pygmalion, 1945; He Who Gets Slapped, Second Best Bed, 1946; The Importance of Being Earnest, 1947; Anne of a Thousand Days, 1948; South Pacific, Miss Liberty, 1949; Happy as Larry, The Innocents, The Liar, Peter Pan, and Captain Carvallo, 1950; Paint Your Wagon, The Grand Tour, 1951; Candida, To Be Continued, 1952; Mid-Summer, Can-Can, 1953; Mademoiselle Colombe, The Immoralist, Peter Pan, 1954; The Honeys, South Pacific (revival), The Young and Beautiful, The Island of Goats, 1955; Middle of the Night, The Most Happy Fella, Long Day's Journey Into Night, 1956; Shinbone Alley, The First Gentleman, South Pacific, Look Back in Anger, Look Homeward, Angel, The Country Wife, 1957; Love Me Little, Asmodée, Jane Eyre, The Cold Wind and the Warm, 1958; The Rivalry, Requiem For a Nun, A Majority of One, 1959; Becket (costumes), 1960; Il Trovatore (Metropolitan), Martha (Metropolitan, costumes), As You Like It, Macbeth, Troilus and Cressida (last three productions at Stratford, Conn), Kwamina (costumes), The Complaisant Lover, A Man For All Seasons, Ross, 1961; We Take the Town (costumes), Richard II (costumes), Henry IV, Part I (costumes, last two productions at Stratford, Conn), 1962; Tovarich (costumes), Lorenzo, Mother Courage and Her Children (costumes), 110 in the Shade (costumes), 1963; Ben Franklyn in Paris (costumes), 1964; Baker Street (costumes), The Devils (costumes), 1965; they have since designed, in London unless otherwise stated, productions including The Clandestine Marriage and The

Fighting Cock (both Chichester, costumes), Don't Drink the Water (New York, costumes), The Rivals, 1966; 110 In the Shade (costumes), The Dance of Death (Old Vic and Canadian tour), Brother and Sister (tour), The Unknown Soldier and His Wife (NY), The Merchant of Venice, Wise Child, 1967; The Bells, Hay Fever, 1968; Three, The Heretic (costumes), The Wild Duck, 1970; The Unknown Soldier and His Wife (London), 1973; authors of books on Stage Costume and Stage Properties.

MOUNT, Peggy, actress

b Southend-on-Sea, 2 May 1916; d of Alfred Mount and his wife Rose (Penny); e Leigh North Street School; studied for the stage privately under Phyllis Reader.

First appeared in wartime concert party, and made her first appearance in a straight part at the Hippodrome, Keighley, 1944, in Hindle Wakes; from 1945 spent three years with the Harry Hanson Court Players; 1948–54 continued in repertory at Colchester, Preston, Dundee, Wolverhampton and Liverpool, etc; at the Strand, 16 Feb 1955, appeared as Emma Hornett in Sailor, Beware! for more than 1000 performances; at the Lyric, Mar 1957 (for the Repertory Players), played the Charwoman in Man on Trial; Garrick, June 1959, played Florence Povis in Farewell, Farewell, Eugene; Old Vic, autumn, 1960, played the Nurse in Romeo and Juliet and Mrs Hardcastle in She Stoops To Conquer; Bristol Old Vic, Oct 1962, played Queenie Hesseltine in All Things Bright and Beautiful, subsequently appearing at the Phoenix, London, Dec 1962, in the same play; Globe, Mar 1964, played Mrs Spicer in Mother's Boy; Arts, Ipswich, Sept 1964, Mrs Wolff in The Beaver Coat; Alexandra, Birmingham, May 1965, played Gladys in Did You Feel It Move?; Mermaid, Mar 1966, again played Ma Wolff in The Beaver Coat; Lyric, Aug 1968, Dame Daphne Winkworth in Oh, Clarence!; Mermaid, Oct 1969, played Mrs Botterill in The Band-wagon, touring Australia in the part in 1970; Arnaud, Guildford, Sept 1970, Clara Soppitt in When We Are Married, playing the same part at the Strand, Nov 1970; toured, Aug 1971, as Emma Hornett in Sailor Beware; toured, Feb 1972, as Mrs Malaprop in The Rivals; toured, July 1972, as Lady Catherine Champion-Cheney in The Circle; toured, Feb 1973, as Sally Blunt in Fiddlers Three; at the Palace, Westcliffe, 1973, appeared in All Things Bright and Beautiful, Sept, and Jacks and Knaves, Dec; Theatre Royal, Brighton, Dec 1973, the Queen in Alice in Wonderland; Chichester Festival, May 1974, Mrs Amlet in The Confederacy; Criterion, Oct 1974, Daphne Drummond in There Goes the Bride; Comedy, June 1976, Madame Jambart in Signed and Sealed; Olivier, Oct 1976, Donna Pasqua in the National Theatre's Il Campiello; Birmingham Rep, Oct 1977, title-role in Mother Courage; National Theatre, May 1978, Mrs Hewlett in Plunder; Birmingham Rep, June 1979, Mrs Leverett in Rookery Nook; Cottesloe (NT), Oct–Nov, 1979, played Mrs Spicer and Old Sally in Lark Rise, and Mrs Gubbins and Cinderella Doe in Candleford; she has appeared in numerous films including: Sailor Beware, Hotel Paradiso, Oliver!, One Way Pendulum, Ladies Who Do, etc; television appearances include: Lollipop Loves Mr Mole, You're Only Young Twice, and *The Larkins*.

Favourite parts: Emma Hornett in Sailor, Beware!, and the Nurse in Romeo and Juliet. *Recreations:* Knitting, reading, and horse-riding. *Address:* c/o Richard Stone, 18–20 York Buildings, London, WC2.

MROZEK, Slawomir, dramatist

b Borzecin, Poland, 26 June 1930; s of Antoni Mrozek and his wife Zofia (Keozior); formerly a cartoonist.

His first play was The Police, 1958; since then his works have been performed all over the world; other plays include: Let's Have Fun, What A Lovely Dream!, Tango, Enchanted Night, Out At Sea, Charlie, Striptease, Vatzlav: a Play in 77 Scenes, and Emigrés; is also the author of The Elephant, 1957, and other books of short stories.

Address: U1, Pickarska 4/5, Warsaw.

MULDOON, Roland, writer, actor, director and comedian

b Weybridge, 12 Apr 1941; s of William Edmund Muldoon and his wife Mary (Clifford); e St James Church of England Secondary School, Weybridge; m actress/director Claire Burnley; trained in stage management at Bristol Old Vic School; formerly a con-man, labourer, electrician's mate, photo researcher, and photographer's agent.

Made his debut at Unity theatre, 1964, as the Mad Poet in Squaring the Circle; in 1965 with his wife founded CAST, the Cartoon Archetypical Slogan Theatre group, with which he has featured as actor, writer and director in a series of productions; these include John D Muggins Is Dead, Trials of Horatio Muggins, Mr Oligarchy's Circus, Muggins Awakening, Harold Muggins Is a Martyr (written by CAST and John Arden), Come In Hilda Muggins, Sam the Man, Goodbye Union Jack, What Happens Next?, and Confessions of a Socialist; made his NY debut in a one-man show, Full Confessions of a Socialist, at the Labor Theatre, Jan 1980, for which he received an Obie; films include Planet of the Mugs, 1971.

Favourite parts: Harold Percival Muggins and Sam the Man. *Address:* PO Box 294, London NW1 5BH.

MULLEN, Barbara, actress

b Boston, Mass, USA, 9 June 1914; d of Patrick Mullen and his wife Bridget (McDonough); e SS Peter and Paul's School, Boston; m John Taylor.

Made her first appearance on the stage as a small child dancer of three, at Boston, Mass; appeared as a dancer and singer in variety theatres from 1917–34, when she left America; on coming to London, studied at the Webber-Douglas Drama School; made her first appearance in London at the Chanticleer Theatre, Apr 1939, as Percy in Bar Sinister; subsequently toured in Anna Christie and They Walk Alone; Players', Dec 1939, played Alice in Dick Whittington; at the Torch, Jan 1940, played Jancy Fitzpatrick in Killicregs in Twilight, and Feb 1940, Jeannie in the play of that name, and transferred to Wyndham's Theatre, Apr 1940; Queen's, July 1940, succeeded Celia Johnson as Mrs de Winter in Rebecca; toured in 1941, in Rebecca; Adelphi, Dec 1941, appeared as Peter Pan; Q, Nov 1942, played Margaret Cluny in Dust Before the Wind; Lyric, Mar 1943, Maggie Wylie in What Every Woman Knows; toured, autumn 1945, as Jennifer Trelawny in So Brief the Spring; Q, July, and Comedy, Sept 1946, appeared as the Widow Brant in Mother of Men; Strand, July 1947, played Mary in My Wives and I; Playhouse, Dec 1949, Miss Marple in Murder at the Vicarage; toured 1957, as Mrs Gibbons in Mrs Gibbons' Boys; Lyric (Repertory Players'), Feb 1961, played Penny in Out of Season; Olympia, Dublin, Sept 1961, Mrs Mac in The Temptation of Mr O; Savoy, July 1975, again played Miss Marple in Murder at the Vicarage; Whitehall, May 1977, Abby Brewster in Arsenic and Old Lace; first appeared in films, 1941, in Jeannie, and, since 1953, has appeared in Innocent Sinners, The Challenge, Kidnapped, etc; television appearances include: Juno and the Paycock, *The Danny Thomas Show*, and Janet in the series *Dr Finlay's Casebook*, Director of Pilot Films, Ltd, since 1954, and Falcon Productions, Ltd; published a book of reminiscences, Life is My Adventure, 1938.

(*Died Mar 1979.*)

MULLIGAN, Richard, actor
b The Bronx, NY, 13 Nov 1932.

Made his NY debut at the Belasco, 30 Nov 1960, as an understudy to Arthur Hill and Tom Wheatley in all the Way Home; Lyceum, Dec 1963, played Phil Matthews in Nobody Loves an Albatross; Colonial, Boston, Dec 1964, Max in Everybody Out, The Castle Is Sinking; The Playhouse, 1965, took over as Charlie in Never Too Late; Eugene O'Neill, Nov 1965, Roger MacDougall in Mating Dance; The American Place, 1966, took over as Matthew Stanton in Hogan's Goat; Mechanic, Baltimore, Md, Jan 1968, Joe Grady in The Only Game in Town; played with the Repertory Theatre New Orleans, 1970 season; Royale, Mar 1971, Bob Phillips in How the Other Half Loves; Martin Beck, Apr 1972, Dan Train in Ring Round the Bathtub; Broadhurst, Apr 1974, Martin Cramer in Thieves; has appeared in the films From the Mixed-up Files of Mrs Basil E Frankweiler, Irish Whiskey Rebellion, Visit to a Chief's Son (1974), etc.

Address: Actors Equity Association, 165 West 46th Street, New York, NY 10036.

MUNRO, Nan, actress
b Potgietersrust, South Africa, 24 June 1905; *d* of Donald Mackay Munro and his wife Ann Galbraith (Murdoch); *e* Pretoria, South Africa; *m* (1) Cullis William Gau (dec); (2) Rayne Kruger (mar dis); formerly a teacher of physical training and masseuse; studied for the stage at the Royal Academy of Dramatic Art.

Made her first appearance on the stage at the Pavilion, Weymouth, 1931, as Mrs Woodman in The Crime at Blossoms; toured 1931–2, as Julia in The Young Idea and Lady Higgins in Out of the Bottle; made her first appearance in London at the Grand Theatre in London at the Grand Theatre, Croydon, 25 Jan 1932, as Diana Rump in Room for Two; spent two years with the Repertory Company at Croydon; at the Westminster, Feb 1934, played Isobel in Private Room; Sept 1934, Aunt Colomba in The Moon in the Yellow River and Oct 1934, Fräulein von Nordeck in Children in Uniform; Haymarket, Nov 1934, again played in The Moon in the Yellow River; Whitehall, May 1935, played Caroline Percival in Golden Arrow; Arts, May 1936, Oline in Too Famous for Words; Queen's, July 1937, Sandra in Women of Property; New, Mar 1938, Miss Driver in The Painted Smile; Queen's, Sept 1938, Hilda Randolph in Dear Octopus, and toured in this, 1939–40; returned to South Africa, 1941; toured there, 1942, in Jeannie; in 1943, formed the Munro-Inglis Company and toured the Military Camps until 1944; subsequently toured as Ruth Sherwood in My Sister Eileen; 1945–6, toured South Africa and Rhodesia as Frynne Rodney in Full House, Mistress Knight in And So To Bed, Eliza Doolittle in Pygmalion, and Tracy Lord in The Philadelphia Story; toured again in South Africa, 1947, as Catherine Winslow in The Winslow Boy, and in Lady Frederick; reappeared in London at the Chepstow, Dec 1948, as Dr Barry in The Green Box; Comedy (for the Repertory Players), Dec 1949, played Maisie Sedge in The Mountain; Lyric, Hammersmith, Jan 1950, appeared as Mrs Bland in Shall We Join the Ladies? and Chorus in The Boy With a Cart; subsequently toured as Consuelo Howard in Treasure Hunt; Haymarket, Apr 1951, played Mrs Daly in Waters of the Moon; Vaudeville, Sept 1953, Mrs O'Connor in Trial and Error; Wyndham's (for Repertory Players), Apr 1954, played Mavis Maxwell in The Sultan's Turret; Comedy, Dec 1955,

Esther Crampton in Morning's At Seven, transferring to the Westminster, Feb 1956; Apollo, Mar 1958, Mrs Dix in Beth; toured Oct 1958, as the Widow in The Broken Jug; Westminster, Jan 1959, played Sophie Trelian in The Woman on the Stair; Piccadilly, May 1959, Lady Cartmichael in Caught Napping; Royal Court, June 1961, played Lady Patricia in Empress With Teapot in a production without décor; Adelphi, 1961, played the part of Eulalie Mackechnie Shinn in The Music Man; Haymarket, Nov 1962, Mary Weldon in The Tulip Tree; New Arts, June 1963, played Harriet Herriton in Where Angels Fear to Tread, transferring with the production to the St Martin's, July 1963; Haymarket, 1964, took over the part of Maud Lowder in The Wings of the Dove; Royal Court, Oct 1964, played Mrs Bone in A Cuckoo in the Nest; at the same theatre, Nov 1964, Calpurnia in Julius Caesar; Garrick, Oct 1965, took over Mrs Mopply in Too True to be Good; Close, Glasgow, Apr 1966, The Woman in Lunchtime Concert; Playhouse, Oxford, Sept 1966, played Lady Politick Would-be in Volpone, and at the Garrick, Jan 1967; Hampstead Theatre Club, Apr 1967, Mrs Probert in Studies of the Nude; South African National Theatre, Mar 1968, Lady Bracknell in The Importance of Being Earnest; Chichester Festival, 1968 season, Julia in The Cocktail Party and the Fortune Teller in The Skin of Our Teeth, repeating the role of Julia at Wyndham's, Nov 1968, and the Haymarket, Feb 1969; Hampstead Theatre Club, Oct 1969, Mother in This Space is Mine; toured, Nov 1970, as Veta Louise Simmonds in Harvey; Thorndike, Leatherhead, Sept 1972, La Duchesse Dupont-Dufort in Traveller Without Luggage; Orange Tree, Richmond, Apr 1974, Dewey in Beach Games; Maximus Actors' Arena, Aug 1975, Mrs Justice Credulous in The Scheming Lieutenant; English Theatre, Vienna, Mar 1976, Mrs Culver in The Constant Wife; Mar 1977, toured as the Duchess of Bonnington in Quadrille; New End, Hampstead, July 1978, Mrs Baker in The Singular Life of Albert Nobbs; entered films, 1938, in Black Limelight, and has recently appeared in Morgan: A Suitable Case for Treatment, Song of Norway, Games that Lovers Play and Jane Eyre; her numerous television appearances include: The Picture of Dorian Gray, Rumpole of the Bailey, and The Prince Regent.

Hobby: Home Life. *Address:* 42 Airlie House, Airlie Gardens, London, W8. *Tel:* 01–727 4000.

MURCELL, George, actor and director
b Naples, Italy, 30 Oct 1925; *s* of Chesley Gordon Murcell and his wife Lucy Victoria (Bougeia); *m* (1) Josephine Tweedie (mar dis); (2) Elvi Hale.

Began career as a child singer and musician in Italy; educated in Italian and English schools and at Surrey County Technical College; trained for the stage at RADA; made his professional début at the Embassy, Mar 1949, as Poet in Caligula; Fortune, Dec 1949 and tour, Black Dog in Treasure Island; toured, 1950–1 with Donald Wolfit's company, playing many roles in nine classical plays; joined the Old Vic company, Sept 1951, playing Menaphon in Tamburlaine the Great; subsequent appearances with the company include: Gregory in Romeo and Juliet, Sept 1952; Morocco in The Merchant of Venice, 1953; Aldwych, Apr 1954, played Beppy in The Dark is Light Enough; Lyric, Hammersmith, May 1955, La Hire in The Lark; Royal Court, Feb, and Aldwych, Mar 1956, Readymoney Matt in The Threepenny Opera; after a period in films returned to the Royal Court, Oct 1960, to play Osip in Platonov; Oxford Playhouse, Feb 1961, Bhabani in The Guide; with the Royal Shakespeare Company, 1961–2, his parts included: First Baron and Cardinal in Becket, July 1961, Hortensio in The Taming of the

Shrew, Sept 1961, and Lopahin in The Cherry Orchard, Dec 1961, all at the Aldwych; 1964, for Welsh National Theatre, played the title-role in Macbeth; Arts, Apr 1965, Gudinszki in The Game as Played; Royal Court, June 1965, Colonel Oblensky in A Patriot for Me; Edinburgh Festival, Aug 1966, appeared in The Little Men at the Church Hill Hall; Wyndham's, 1970, took over Gilles de Vannes in Abelard and Heloise; entered management, 1967, and directed his own productions of The Spies at Richmond and She Stoops to Conquer at the Ashcroft, Croydon; Artistic Director, St George's Elizabethan Theatre Ltd, which he formed in 1968 with the object of rebuilding Shakespeare's Globe Theatre in London; the St George's Theatre, Islington, opened under his direction on 21 Apr 1976; here he directed Romeo and Juliet, May, and played Buckingham in Richard III, July; played Shylock in The Merchant of Venice, Falstaff in The Merry Wives, and Claudius in Hamlet, 1977; directed Richard II and As You Like It, 1979; has appeared frequently over the years in films and on television.

Recreations: Traditional jazz, messing about in boats. *Address:* 44 Bushwood Road, Kew Green, Richmond, Surrey.

MURDOCH, Richard, actor
b Keston, Kent, 6 Apr 1907; *s* of Bernard Murdoch and his wife Amy Florence (Scott); *e* Charterhouse and Pembroke College, Cambridge; *m* Peggy Rawlings.

Made his first appearance on the stage at the King's Theatre, Southsea, 14 Mar 1927, in the chorus of The Blue Train; first appeared in London at the Prince of Wales's, 10 May 1927, in the same piece; toured, 1929, as Philip Brown in Oh, Letty!; London Hippodrome, Mar 1929, played Ronnie Webb in The Five O'Clock Girl; London Pavilion, Mar 1930, appeared in Cochran's 1930 Revue; Hippodrome, Mar 1931, played Percy Pim in Stand Up and Sing; Comedy, Dec 1932, played in Ballyhoo; toured, 1933, as Paul Daventry in Mother of Pearl; Vaudeville, from Mar 1935–6, appeared in Charlot's Char-a-Bang!, Stop-Go!, The Sleeping Beauty, and The Town Talks; toured, 1936, as Guy Holden in Gay Divorce; Saville, Sept 1936, played Sergeant Oliver in Over She Goes; toured, 1938, in Band Waggon, and appeared in the same show at the Palladium, July 1939; during the War, served with the Royal Air Force, 1939–45; toured, 1946, in Strike a New Note; Casino, Dec 1949, played Queen Hysteria in Little Miss Muffet; Wimbledon, Dec 1952, Buttons in Cinderella; Grand, Blackpool, Apr 1953, played Bobby Denver in As Long As They're Happy; toured, Sept 1961, as Tommy Towers in Tax Free; Belgrade, Coventry, Mar 1962, appeared in the revue Happy Returns; Harrogate Festival, Aug 1966, General de la Petadière-Frenouillou in The General's Tea Party, and at the Jeannetta Cochrane, Nov 1966; May Fair, Dec 1968, Aubrey Allington in Tons of Money; Niagara on the Lake (Shaw Festival), and tour of US and Canada, 1973, William in You Never Can Tell; toured S Africa, 1974, as Col Barstow in Not in the Book; toured, 1976, as Farmer in Birds of Paradise; 1977, toured as Sir William Boothroyd in Lloyd George Knew My Father; Athenaeum, Plymouth, 1979, Ernest in Bedroom Farce; has appeared in summer shows and toured regularly in Britain; has also appeared as Dame in pantomimes in Canterbury, Bromley, Eastbourne, Norwich, Hull, Torquay etc; a well-known broadcaster, in Band Waggon, Much Binding-in-the-Marsh, The Men from the Ministry, and, during the War, in various Service programmes; broadcast for the Australian Broadcasting Commission, 1954; recent television includes *Rumpole of the Bailey, The New Avengers, In the Looking Glass,* and *The Three Kisses;* first appeared in films, 1934; Captain of the Stage Golfing Society, 1953 and 1965.

Favourite Parts: William in You Never Can Tell, Ernest in Bedroom Farce and Sir William Boothroyd. *Recreations:* Golf and sailing. *Clubs:* RAC, Stage Golfing Society. *Address:* The End Cottage, Walton-on-the-Hill, Tadworth, Surrey. *Tel:* Tadworth 3431.

MURPHY, Rosemary, actress
b Munich, Germany, 13 Jan 1927; *d* of Robert D Murphy and his wife Mildred Taylor; *e* Convent of the Sacred Heart, New York, and Notre Dame de Sion, Kansas City, Missouri; prepared for the stage at the Neighborhood Playhouse School of the Theatre and at the Actors Studio, of which she has been a member since 1954.

Made her stage début at the Schlosspark Theatre, Berlin, Germany, 1949, as the Woman in Green in Peer Gynt; made her US début at the Flatbush, Brooklyn, June 1950, as Mary Boleyn in Anne of the Thousand Days, and subsequently toured; ANTA, Nov 1950, played One of the Townspeople in The Tower Beyond Tragedy, marking her NYC début; Memphis, Tennessee, Arena, 1952, played Jane Pugh in Clutterbuck and Liserle in Candle Light; played in stock in Red Sky at Morning, The Women, Lizzie Curry in The Rainmaker, and Rosemary Sidney in Picnic, 1953–5; Davenport, NY, Feb 1955, played Lady Isabel Welwyn in The Ascent of F6; Rooftop, Oct 1955, Lady Macduff in Macbeth; toured, 1956, as Olivia in The Chalk Garden; Ethel Barrymore, Nov 1957, Helen Gant Barton in Look Homeward, Angel; Festival of the Two Worlds, Spoleto, Italy, July 1959, Hannah Jelkes in The Night of the Iguana; Helen Hayes, Nov 1960, Dorothea Bates in Period of Adjustment; Theatre de Lys, June 1962, took over the roles of Viveca Lindfors in the revue Brecht on Brecht; American Shakespeare Festival, Stratford, Connecticut, June 1963, Goneril in King Lear, and a Courtesan in Comedy of Errors; Music Box, Feb 1964, Dorothy Cleves in Any Wednesday; Martin Beck, Sept 1966, Claire in A Delicate Balance, for which she received the New York Critics Poll Award; toured, 1966–7, in this last part; Broadhurst, Mar 1968, Estelle MacGruder in Weekend; made her London début at the New, June 1968, when she played Harriet, Edith, and Muriel in You Know I Can't Hear You When the Water's Running; Billy Rose, Oct 1968, The Nurse in The Death of Bessie Smith; Booth, Oct 1970, took over from Eileen Heckart as Mrs Baker in Butterflies Are Free; Stratford, Conn, July 1973, Lady Macbeth in Macbeth; Ahmanson, LA, Apr 1975, appeared in Ring Round the Moon; Goodman, Chicago, Jan 1976, in Mourning Becomes Electra; Martin Beck, Apr 1977, Joanne Remington in Ladies at the Alamo; Biltmore, Jan 1978, Monica in Cheaters; Promenade, Dec 1978, guest appearance as Lillian Hellman in Are You Now Or Have You Ever Been?; entered films in Berlin Express, 1948, and has since played in Der Ruf (Germany, 1949), The Night, To Kill a Mockingbird, Forty Carats, etc; played on the television production of The Long Way Home, 1956, and has since played on *Thriller, The Virginian, Wide Country,* A Case of Rape, etc.

Address: c/o Hesseltine-Baker Associates, 119 West 57th Street, New York, NY 10019.

MURRAY, Barbara, actress
b London, 27 Sept 1929; *d* of Frederick Murray and his wife Petronella; *m* (1) John Justin (mar dis); (2) Bill Holmes.

Hippodrome, Golders Green, Apr 1952, played Penelope Blessington in Adam's Apple; Duchess, Jan 1954, Joanna Winter in No Other Verdict; Her Majesty's, Dec 1957, and later Apollo, Isolde Poole in The Tunnel of Love; Aldwych,

June 1962 (for RSC), Stella in The Collection; made her New York début at the Biltmore, Dec 1962, as Madeline Hanes in In the Counting House; Savoy, Mar 1963, the Woman in Trap for a Lonely Man; toured, June 1965, as Orinthia in The Apple Cart; Strand, Jan 1967, took over Susy Henderson in Wait Until Dark; St Martin's, Jan 1968, Ruth Honeywill in Justice; Oxford Playhouse, Aug 1974, Mrs Jelliwell in Springtime for Henry; same theatre, July 1976, Catherine Petkoff in Arms and the Man; in the same year, toured with the Actor's Company in England and in Jamaica, Mexico and South America, as Beth in Landscape and Fiona Foster in How the Other Half Loves; Theatre Royal, Windsor, 1977, appeared in Separate Tables; at the Chichester Festival appeared as Mrs Allonby in A Woman of No Importance, 1978, and in 1979, as Lorraine Sheldon in The Man Who Came to Dinner; has appeared in numerous films since her first, Passport to Pimlico; television appearances include the series: *The Power Game* and *Never a Cross Word*.

Address: c/o ICM Ltd, 22 Grafton Street, London W1.

MURRAY, Braham (*né* Goldstein), director
b London, 12 Feb 1943; *s* of Samuel Goldstein and his wife Gertrude (Prevezer); *e* Clifton College and University College, Oxford; *m* (1) Lindsay Stainton (mar dis); (2) Johanna Bryant, theatrical designer.

While still at Oxford co-wrote and directed Hang Down Your Head and Die, which was presented at the Comedy, London, Mar 1964 and in New York at the Mayfair, Oct 1964; directed Chaganog (London) and The Winter's Tale (Birmingham), 1965; artistic director, Century Theatre, 1966, where his productions included: Loot, Uncle Vanya, Little Malcolm, The Ortolan, The Saviour (première), Waiting for Godot, Romeo and Juliet etc; a founding artistic director of the 69 Theatre Company, Manchester, 1968; many of his productions here have transferred to London: She Stoops to Conquer, 1969; 'Erb, Catch My Soul, 1970; Charley's Aunt, 1971; Mary Rose, 1972; Endgame, 1973; artistic director, Royal Exchange Theatre Company, 1976, Resident AD, 1978: directed the company's opening production, The Rivals; he has since directed the following plays there: What the Butler Saw, 1976; Leading Finger, 1977; The Dybbuk, The Winter's Tale (also European tour), 1978; The Three Musketeers (co-author), The Lower Depths, 1979; other productions, in London unless otherwise stated, include: Antigone (Nottingham), 1971; Othello Story (Paris), 1972; The Good Companions, 1974; The Black Mikado, 1975; Fire Angel, 1977; has taught at Central School, LAMDA, and the theatre design department of Wimbledon College of Art.

Recreations: Reading, music, good food. *Club:* Savile.
Address: Royal Exchange Theatre, St Anne's Square, Manchester. *Tel:* 061–833 9333.

MURRAY, Brian (*né* Bell), actor
b Johannesburg, South Africa, 10 Sept 1937; *s* of Alfred Bell and his wife Mary Dickson (Murray); *e* King Edward VII School, Johannesburg.

Made his first appearance on the stage at the Hofmeyer Theatre, Cape Town, July 1950, as Taplow in The Browning Version; appeared as a child actor in Johannesburg, 1950–4, and continued on the South African stage until 1957, playing such parts as Bo Decker in Bus Stop, Bruno in Dear Charles, Peter in The Diary of Anne Frank and Father Oros in The Strong are Lonely; following a period in radio as announcer, editor, and director, he made his first appearance in London at the Lyric, Hammersmith, Nov 1959, as Harry Lomax in Last Day in Dreamland; Westminster, Feb 1960, played Conrad Mayberry in Visit From a Small Planet and, May,

Wade in Roger the Sixth; joined the Royal Shakespeare Theatre Company, Stratford-on-Avon, Apr 1961, to play the following parts: Horatio in Hamlet, Earl of Richmond in Richard III, Romeo in Romeo and Juliet, Cassio in Othello, and Lysander in A Midsummer Night's Dream 1961; Malcolm in Macbeth, Guiderius in Cymbeline, Edgar in King Lear, 1962; Aldwych, June 1962, again played Lysander in The Dream, and also, in Dec, Edgar in King Lear, appearing in the same production at the Théâtre Sarah-Bernhardt, Paris, May 1963, during the International Festival; toured with the Royal Shakespeare Company with the same production, Feb–June 1964, visiting Europe, USSR, Canada, and making his first appearance in New York, at the State Theatre, May 1964; New, NY, June 1964, Tolen in The Knack; Royale, NY, Feb 1965, played Arthur Fitton in All in Good Time; Bristol Old Vic, Sept 1965, Philip in The Spiral Bird, and, Oct Bassanio in The Merchant of Venice; same theatre, Mar 1966, Claudio in Measure for Measure; Strand, July 1966, Mike in Wait Until Dark; Alvin, NY, Oct 1967, played Rosencrantz in Rosencrantz and Guildenstern are Dead, transferring to the Eugene O'Neill where it ran until Nov 1968, and touring in the same production Jan–June 1969; toured in England, Apr 1970, as Donny in A Present from Harry; Music Box, NY, Mar 1973, took over as Milo Tindle in Sleuth; Goodman, Chicago, Feb 1975, Philip in The Philanthropist; Long Wharf, New Haven, Oct 1975, Gibson McFarland in Artichoke; Goodman, May 1976, in The Devil's Disciple; same theatre, Oct 1976, in Design for Living; Manhattan Theatre Club, Oct 1976, and Public/Anspacher, Jan 1977, Colin in Ashes; Hudson Guild, Mar 1978, transferring to the Morosco, May 1978, Charlie Now in Da; Manhattan Downstage, NY, Nov 1979, played Albie in The Jail Diary of Albie Sachs; Brooklyn Academy, Apr 1980, Monakhov in Barbarians; directed his first production, Civic Theatre, Torquay, Dec 1965, with Beauty and the Beast, followed by Ruffian on the Stair (NY), the double-bill, Mephistopheles Smith and Pigeons (NY), 1968; The Private Ear and The Public Eye (Sullivan, Illinois), A Scent of Flowers (NY), the double-bill A Slight Ache and Oldenburg (Cincinnati), 1969; A Place Without Doors (NY), 1970; Bedtime and Butter, Charley's Aunt (London), 1971; Ride a Cock-Horse (London), 1972; The Waltz of the Toreadors (NY), Fanny's First Play (Niagara-on-the-Lake), 1973; The Ruffian on the Stair (NY), 1974; Downriver (NY), 1975; two plays in The Old Glory (NY), 1976; The Dream Watcher (Seattle), 1977; Hobson's Choice (Phila), 1978; Stevie (NY), 1979; entered films, 1959, appearing in The Angry Silence, The League of Gentlemen, etc; first appeared on television, Feb 1959, and principal performances include the title-part in Kipps, Jed in Shadow of a Pale Horse, etc.

Favourite parts: Edgar, Romeo, and Rosencrantz. *Recreations:* Music of every sort, writing, travelling and thinking.
Address: c/o ICM, 22 Grafton Street, London W1.

MURRAY, Peg, actress
b Denver, Colorado: *e* Western Reserve University.

First appeared in New York at the Coronet, 4 Jan 1956, as Vlasta Habova in The Great Sebastians, with the Lunts; toured in this part, beginning Oct 1956; Downtown, 1959, took over in the revue Diversions; Broadway, 21 May 1959, Miss Cratchitt in Gypsy; Wollman Memorial Skating Rink, June 1961, Hippolyta in A Midsumer Night's Dream, in the Joseph Papp production; Morosco, Oct. 1961, Mrs Bucci in Blood, Sweat and Stanley Poole; Phoenix, Feb 1962, was Standby in Oh Dad, Poor Dad, Mama's Hung You in the Closet and I'm Feelin' So Sad; Eugene O'Neill, 23 Apr 1963, played various parts in She Loves Me; Majestic, Apr 1964,

Mrs Schroeder in Anyone Can Whistle; Royale, May 1964, understudied Irene Dailey as Nettie in The Subject Was Roses; Eugene O'Neill, Nov 1964, Mrs Ferenzi in Something More!; Broadhurst, Nov 1966, Fraulein Kost in Cabaret, for which she recived the Antoinette Perry (Tony) Award, and also played the part of Fraulein Schneider in this production during the illness of Lotte Lenya; Majestic, 1969, took over as Golde in Fiddler on the Roof; played this part for several years; Theatre Four, Nov 1973, Cassie in The Enclave; appeared with the Hartford Stage Company, 1972–73 season; New, Jun 1972, took over as Leona Dawson in Small Craft Warnings; Arena Stage, Washington, 1974, Martha in Who's Afraid of Virginia Woolf?; Helen Hayes, June 1976, took over as Kitty Dean in The Royal Family; Academy Festival Theater, Lake Forest, Ill, July 1977, and Public/Newman, NY, Sept 1977, Rosalie in Landscape of the Body; Hudson Guild, Jan 1979, Bodey in A Lovely Sunday for Creve Coeur; appeared in the film Some of My Best Friends are . . ., 1971; TV work includes *The Nurses* and *Love of Life*.

Address: c/o Bret Adams, 36 East 61st Street, New York, NY.

MURRAY, Stephen, actor

b Partney, Lincs, 6 Sept 1912; *e* Brentwood; *m* Joan Butterfield; studied for the stage at the Royal Academy of Dramatic Art.

Made his first appearance on the stage at the Memorial Theatre, Stratford-on-Avon, Apr 1933, in Much Ado About Nothing; made his first appearance in London, at the Ambassadors' Theatre, 21 Nov 1933, as Captain Odderedi in Cabbages and Kings; during 1934–5, appeared with the Birmingham Repertory Company; at the Malvern Festival, July–Aug 1934, played Sloth in Doctor Faustus, De Biaufort in Saint Bernard and Corporal Saunders in Mutiny; Malvern Festival, July–Aug 1935, Hammingtap in The Simpleton of the Unexpected Isles, Mosca in Volpone, Gunner in Misalliance, and in 1066 and All That; Sept 1935, returned to Birmingham Repertory Company, for the season, playing leading parts, including Hamlet in modern dress; Malvern Festival, 1936, played the Prime Minister in On the Rocks, Dunois in Saint Joan, Brush in The Clandestine Marriage, Branwell Brontë in The Brontës of Haworth Parsonage and Hsieh Ping Kuei in Lady Precious Stream; Westminster, Sept 1936–Feb 1937, played Aleksie Bieliaev in A Month in the Country, Walter Kent in Waste, Helmy in Crooked Cross; People's Palace, Mar 1937, Othello; Old Vic, Apr–Oct 1937, the Dauphin in Henry V, Freddy Eynsford-Hill in Pygmalion, Vincentio in Measure for Measure; Vaudeville, Nov 1937, Pastor Manders in Ghosts; Old Vic, Dec 1937–May 1938, Lysander in A Midsummer Night's Dream, Roderigo in Othello, Mr Lovat in The King of Nowhere, Sicinius Velutus in Coriolanus; Open Air Theatre, Aug 1938, Raguel in Tobias and the Angel; Westminster, Sept 1938–June 1939, Thersites in Troilus and Cressida (in modern dress), Charles Stanton in Dangerous Corner, Nicolo Polo in Marco Millions, Philip Ross in The Will, Sir Patrick Cullen in The Doctor's Dilemma, Hugh O'Neill and subsequently Stephen Moore in Bridge Head; toured, 1939, in Holland, in Dangerous Corner; Westminster, Oct 1939 to Aug 1940, played Nicholas Lengel and Tom in Music at Night, Andrew Undershaft in Major Barbara, Eben in Desire Under the Elms, Lincoln in Abraham Lincoln, and Cornelius in the play of that name; joined the Army, Jan 1941, was commissioned 1944; Playhouse, Feb 1944, played Sergeant Ben Joseph in Desert Highway; demobilized, Mar 1946; from 1946–9, mainly engaged in films and radio; Ambassadors', July 1949, Gregory Black in The Late Edwina Black; Lyric, Hammer-

smith, Nov and Duke of York's, Dec 1950, M Henri in Point of Departure; Arts, Sept 1951, directed many plays, including: Saint's Day; toured Europe, 1952, as Lear, playing this part at the Old Vic, Mar 1952; Arts, July 1952, directed The Way to Keep Him, and Oct 1952, directed Lord Arthur Savile's Crime; Embassy, Mar 1953, Doc in The Doctor in Bean Street; at the Q, Sept 1953, directed Uncertain Joy, in which he appeared as Stephen Leigh; Arts, Mar 1955, directed Sacrifice to the Winds, and also appeared as the Professor in The Lesson; at the Q, Feb 1956, played Harry in Who Cares?; Winter Garden, May 1957, David Mischler in The Best Damn Lie; Piccadilly, Oct 1958, Erno Gero in Shadow of Heroes; Fortune, June 1959, Antoine in Détour After Dark; May Fair, Aug 1963, took over the Father in Six Characters in Search of an Author; Ashcroft, Croydon, Nov 1963, played Gustave in Creditors, and directed and played the Professor in The Lesson; toured, Apr 1964, as Shylock in The Merchant of Venice; Richmond, Sept 1964, played Teddy in The Poker Session; Gate, Dublin, Feb 1965, Ansgar in Forrests of the Night; Haymarket, Sept 1965, succeeded Michael Denison as Simon Crawford in Hostile Witness; Savoy, Apr 1967, Gustave Kummer in The Deadly Game; Arnaud, Guildford, Apr 1968, played the Cardinal in The Prisoner; Lyceum, Edinburgh, June 1968, George in Who's Afraid of Virginia Woolf?; Watford, Nov 1968, Bill Maitland in Inadmissible Evidence; Stratford Festival, Ontario, summer, 1970, Sir Peter Teazle in The School for Scandal and Macey in The Friends; Thorndike, Leatherhead, Mar 1975, Jack in Home; Mermaid, Aug 1975, the Prime Minister in On the Rocks; appeared in a number of films, 1946–51; his several hundred television appearances range from Macbeth and Svengali to serials; on radio his several thousand performances include a large number of the great classical roles, as well as *The Navy Lark*.

Favourite part: George in Who's Afraid of Virginia Woolf? *Address:* c/o *The Spotlight,* 42–43 Cranbourn Street, London WC2.

MUSSER, Tharon, lighting designer

b Roanoke, Va, 8 Jan 1925; *d* of George C Musser and his wife Hazel (Riddle); *e* Berea College (BA 1946), Yale University School of the Drama (MFA 1950).

Designed her first lighting professionally at the Provincetown Playhouse, NY, 19 Jul 1949, for The Father; then designed the lighting for Naked, Lucky Sam McCarver, 1950; lighting designer for dance events at the YMHA, NY, 1950–51; toured with Jose Limon, US and Buenos Aires, Argentina, as lighting director and stage manager, 1953–54; lighting for Long Day's Journey into Night, 1956; Shinbone Alley, Much Ado About Nothing (Stratford, Conn), Monique, The Makropoulos Secret, 1957; The Chairs, The Lesson, The Infernal Machine, The Firstborn (NY and Tel Aviv, Israel), The Entertainer, The Shadow of a Gunman, A Midsummer Night's Dream (Stratford, Conn), Murder in the Cathedral, JB, 1958; The Beaux' Stratagem, The Rivalry, Once upon a Mattress, Romeo and Juliet, A Midsummer Night's Dream, The Merry Wives of Windsor (last three in Stratford, Conn), The Great God Brown, Only in America, Five Finger Exercise, 1959; Peer Gynt, The Long Dream, The Tumbler, Twelfth Night, the Tempest, Antony and Cleopatra (last three for Stratford, Conn), 1960; As You Like It, Macbeth (last two for Stratford, Conn), The Garden of Sweets, The Turn of the Screw, Anatol, Elizabeth the Queen (last three in Boston for the American Festival), Advise and Consent (tour), the National Repertory Theater's tour of Mary Stuart and Elizabeth the Queen, and the American Repertory Company's State Dept sponsored tours of The Skin of Our Teeth, The Glass Menagerie, and The Miracle Worker, 1961; Giants, Sons of Giants, Calculated Risk, Nowhere to Go But Up, HMS Pinafore, Androcles and the Lion (last two in Boston), 1962; Andorra, Mother Courage and Her Children, King Lear, The Comedy of Errors, Henry V (last three for Stratford, Conn), Here's Love, Marathon '33, and the National Repertory Theater's tours of Ring Round the Moon, The Seagull, and The Crucible, 1963; Any Wednesday, Much Ado About Nothing, Richard III, Hamlet (last three for Stratford, Conn), Golden Boy, Alfie, Hedda Gabler, Liliom, She Stoops to Conquer (NRT tour), 1964; Kelly, All in Good Time, Flora, The Red Menace, Coriolanus, Romeo and Juliet, The Taming of the Shrew, King Lear (last four for Stratford, Conn), Mais Oui (Beirut, Lebanon), Minor Miracle, and the National Repertory Theater's tours of The Rivals, The Madwoman of Chaillot, and The Trojan Women, 1965; Malcolm, The Great Indoors, The Lion in Winter, Mame, Falstaff, Murder in the Cathedral, Twelfth Night, Julius Caesar (last four for Stratford, Conn), A Delicate Balance, the National Repertory Theater's tours of Tonight at 8.30, A Touch of the Poet, and The Imaginary Invalid, 1966; Hallelujah, Baby!, A Midsummer Night's Dream, Antigone, The Merchant of Venice (last three for Stratford, Conn), The Birthday Party, After the Rain, The Promise, Everything in the Garden, and the National Repertory Theater's tours of John Brown's Body and The Comedy of Errors, 1967; House of Flowers, Catch My Soul (Los Angeles), Man and the Universe at the Hemis Fair Exhibit, San Antonio, Tex, Golden Boy (Palladium, London), As You Like It, Androcles and the Lion (last two for Stratford, Conn), The Lovers, Maggie Flyn, 1968; The Fig Leaves Are Falling, The Gingham Dog, Spofford (tour), Mame (Drury Lane, London), Fedora (Dallas, Tex, Civic Opera), 1969; Blood Red Roses, Applause, The Boy Friend, The Dream on Monkey Mountain, Rosebloom (last two in Los Angeles), The Merry Widow, Madama Butterfly, Il Tabarro, and Carmina Burana (all for the Dallas Civic Opera), L.A. under Siege, The Trial of the Catonsville Nine (Los Angeles), 1970; Follies, The Trial of the Catonsville Nine, Who Wants to be the Lone Ranger (Los Angeles), On the Town, The Prisoner of Second Avenue, Major Barbara (Los Angeles), Fidelio (Dallas Civic Opera), 1971; Night Watch, The Creation of the World and Other Business, The Great God Brown, Don Juan, The Sunshine Boys, Old Times (Los Angeles), The Dream on Monkey Mountain (Munich Germany), Applause (Her Majesty's, London), 1972; A Little Night Music, Forget Me Not Lane (Los Angeles), Sondheim: A Musical Tribute, The Orphan, The Good Doctor, Andrea Chenier (Dallas Civic Opera), 1973; Candide, Saint Joan, The Charlatan (last two in Los Angeles), God's Favorite, Mack and Mabel, Good News, The Pearl Fishers (Miami, Fla, Opera Guild), Lucrezia Borgia, Mignon (Dallas) 1974; The Wiz, Same Time, Next Year, A Chorus Line, Me and Bessie, The Tables of Hoffman (Dallas), The Flying Dutchman (Miami) 1975; Pacific Overtures, Othello (Miami), 1600 Pennsylvania Avenue, California Suite, A Chorus Line (London), Hooray USA! (Miami Bicentennial Pageant), 1976; The Act, Chapter Two, A Chorus Line (Australia), Travesties, and The Importance of Being Earnest (LA), 1977; Tribute, Ballroom, Black Angel (LA), 1978; They're Playing Our Song, Whose Life Is It Anyway?, 1940's Radio Hour, Romantic Comedy, Terra Nova (LA), Last Licks, 1979; has been a lecturer at the Bridgeport University, 1967, Yale University, 1962 and 1969, State University of NY, 1969, Bucknell University, 1973, Harvard University, 1974–76, Pennsylvania State University, 1977, Smith College, Harvard College, 1978, etc; received the Antoinette Perry (Tony) Award for Follies and A Chorus Line, the last while competing against herself for Pacific Overtures; received the USITT Art and Technology Award, 1976; Berea College Distinguished Alumnus Award, 1973; hon DFA, 1979; has served as design consultant to Webb and Knapp, Radcliffe College, American Academy of Dramatic Arts, The NY Council on the Arts, etc; designed the lighting for the television special on the re-opening of Ford's Theater, Washington, DC, 1968.

Recreation: Travel. *Address:* 21 Cornelia Street, New York, NY 10014. *Tel:* CH 3–9076.

MYERS, Paul, librarian

b New York, 5 Mar 1917; *s* of J Franklyn Myers and his wife Miriam (Heimerdinger); *e* New York University (BFA 1937) and Pratt Institute (MLS 1957); *m* Elizabeth Burke.

Began his career as an actor with various troupes, including a season's tour with the James Hendrickson – Claire Bruce Shakespearean Repertory Co; worked on Stage Magazine, NY, during its short life, Nov 1940–Feb 1941; joined the staff of the theatre collection, New York Public Library, 1945; curator since 1967 of the collection, now known as the Billy Rose Collection; retired July 1980; author (with Roy Stallings) of A Guide to Theatre Reading.

Club: Players. *Address:* R.D. 1, Millbrook, NY 12545.

N

NADEL, Norman, critic and author
b Newark, New Jersey, 19 June 1915; *s* of Louis D Nadel and his wife Sara (Fiverson); *e* Denison University (AB in psychology, 1938), University of Chicago (1943); *m* Martha Smith.

Founded, was member of board, and played trombone for the Columbus, Ohio, Philharmonic Orchestra, 1940; taught journalism at the Ohio State University; joined the Columbus *Citizen* as make-up editor in 1939, and become successively radio columnist, 1940, music critic, 1942, and drama, movie, and music critic and theatre editor, 1947–61; while holding these posts organized a plane and train tour to the theatres of New York (24 separate tours) and Europe (two tours), serving as general manager and host under the sponsorship of the *Citizen*; has lectured extensively throughout the US on the theatre; has written articles for *The New York Times, Saturday Review, Bravo, Theatre Arts,* etc; appointed drama critic for the *New York World-Telegram and Sun,* 1961, and, Mar 1963, appointed entertainment editor; drama critic, *World Journal Tribune,* 1966–7; cultural affairs writer, Scripps-Howard Newspapers, 1967–; critic-at-large, Newspaper Enterprise Association, 1977–; president, 1966–7, New York Drama Critics Circle; consultant to the Theatre Guild, 1967–; co-founder, 1968, National Critics Institute, and a regular faculty member; member, board of directors, American Theatre Association; arbiter since 1968 of disputes between Actors Equity and the League of New York Theatres over the employment of foreign actors; critic in residence, University of Calgary, 1979; Florida State University, 1980; publications include A Pictorial History of the Theatre Guild, 1970; recipient of the *Variety* Spotlight Award; Denison University Alumni Citation, 1963; hon DHL, Denison, 1967.

Recreations: Sailing, canoeing, photography. *Address:* 234 College Avenue, Staten Island, NY 10314. *Tel:* 727 3693.

NAISMITH, Laurence (*né* Johnson), actor
b Thames Ditton, Surrey, 14 Dec 1908; *s* of Bernard Johnson and his wife Beatrice (Lawrence); *e* All Saints Choir School, Margaret Street, London; *m* Christine Bocca; formerly a merchant seaman.

Made his first appearance on the stage at His Majesty's, 21 Sept 1927, in the chorus of Oh! Kay!; subsequently engaged as assistant stage manager with Bristol Repertory Company, 1930; later appeared with repertory and touring companies, and managed his own repertory companies; served in the Royal Artillery, 1939–46, becoming Acting Battery Commander; after returning to the stage, made his first appearance in the West End at the St Martin's, 20 Mar 1948, as The Salesman in Rocket to the Moon; Duke of York's, Feb 1950, played Wilson in Larger Than Life; New, Dec 1951, Lagarde in Colombe; Haymarket May 1953, Proteus in The Apple Cart; Apollo, Jan 1954, appeared as Montagu Winthrop in The Burning Glass; Lyric, Hammersmith, May 1955, played Cauchon, Bishop of Beauvais, in The Lark; Princes, Feb 1956, played Dvořák in Summer Song; Saville, Apr 1959, Dr Pangloss and Martin in Candide; Haymarket, Apr 1962, played Sir Oliver Surface in The School for Scandal, subsequently making his first appearance in New York at the Majestic, Jan 1963, in the same production; Shubert, NY,

Oct 1963, played Kris Kringle in Here's Love, subsequently touring the US with the production, Aug 1964; Broadway, NY, May 1966, played Gwillym Morgan in A Time for Singing; toured England, Apr 1967, as Newton Reeves in Brother and Sister; Billy Rose, NY,ed in films, 1947, in High Treason, and has since played in more than fifty films, including: Richard III, The Angry Silence, Camelot, Scrooge, etc; recent TV includes Romeo and Juliet, 1979.

Hobby: His home and family. *Recreations:* Swimming, bridge, and horse-racing. *Address:* c/o London Management, 235–241 Regent Street, London, W1.

NAPIER, John, designer
b London, 1 Mar 1944; *s* of James Edward Thomas Napier and his wife Florence (Godbold); *e* Hornsey College of Art; *m* Andreane Neofitou; trained as a designer at the Central School of Arts and Crafts.

Designed his first production, A Penny for a Song, for the Phoenix, Leicester, July 1967; subsequently designed a number of productions at the Phoenix, 1967–8; first West End production, Fortune and Men's Eyes, Comedy, 22 Oct 1968; London productions which he has since designed include The Ruling Class, The Fun War, Muzeeka, George Frederick (Ballet Rambert), La Turista, 1969; Cancer, Isabel's a Jezebel, 1970; Mister, The Foursome, The Lovers of Viorne, Lear (Edward Bond), 1971; Jump, Sam Sam, Big Wolf, 1972; The Devils (English National Opera), Equus, The Party (both National Theatre), 1973; Knuckle, 1974; Kings and Clowns, The Travelling Music Show, 1978; George Friedric (Ballet Rambert), The Devils of Loudon (Sadler's Wells), Lohengrin (Royal Opera); for RSC, King John, Richard II, Cymbeline, Macbeth, Richard III, 1974; Hedda Gabler, (Aldwych), 1975; Much Ado About Nothing, The Comedy of Errors, King Lear, 1976; Macbeth, A Midsummer Night's Dream, As You Like It, 1977; The Merry Wives of Windsor, Twelfth Night, Three Sisters (Other Place), Once In A Lifetime (Aldwych), 1979; The Greeks, Nicholas Nickleby (both Aldwych), 1980; co-designed Stratford permanent set, season 1976; has designed productions for theatres in Austria, France, Germany, Italy, S. Africa, Sweden and the USA, including six stagings of Equus and several of Charles Marowitz's collages of Shakespeare; designed the independent television productions of Macbeth and The Comedy of Errors; also designed the costumes for the film of Hedda Gabler.

Recreation: Photography, football. *Address:* c/o ML Representation, 194 Old Brompton Road, London SW5 0AS. *Tel:* 01–373 1161.

NASH, N. Richard (né Nathaniel Richard Nusbaum), dramatic author
b Philadelphia, Pa, 8 Jun 1913; *s* of Shael Leonard Nusbaum and his wife Jenny (Singer); *e* University of Pa (BS 1934); *m* (1) Helena Taylor (mar dis), (2) Katherine Copeland.

First play to be produced in NY was Second Best Bed, presented at the Ethel Barrymore, 3 June 1946, which he also directed; since then has written The Young and Fair, 1948; See the Jaguar, 1952; The Rainmaker, 1954; Girls of Summer, 1956; Handful of Fire, 1958; Wildcat (musical), 1960;

110 in the Shade (musical based on his The Rainmaker), The Happy Time (musical), 1968; Echoes, produced in Seattle, Wash, 1972; co-produced Wildcat, 1960; co-author of the screenplay for Welcome Stranger, 1947, and has since written Nora Prentiss, Porgy and Bess, Vicious Years, The Rainmaker, Sainted Sisters, Dear Wife, etc; for television has written extensively for the *US Steel Hour, General Electric Theater, Television Playhouse, Philco Playhouse, Theater Guild of the Air*, etc; author of two novels: East Wind, Rain and The Last Magic; has taught philosophy and drama at a number of colleges and universities including Bryn Mawr and Princeton; has received various awards, notably the Maxwell Anderson Verse Drama Award for his verse play Parting at Imsdorf, 1940, The International Drama Award at Cannes, France, and the Prague, Czechoslovakia, Award, etc.

Recreation Furniture making. *Address:* 850 Seventh Avenue, New York, NY 10019. *Tel:* 582–0285.

NATWICK, Mildred, actress

b Baltimore, Maryland, 19 June 1908; *d* of Joseph Natwick and his wife Mildred Marion (Dawes); *e* Bryn Mawr School, Baltimore, and Bennett School, Millbrook.

As an amateur made her first appearance at the Vagabond Theatre, Baltimore, 1929, in The Playboy of the Western World, and also played with the National Junior Theatre Company, Washington; made her first appearance on the professional stage at the Biltmore, New York, 29 Oct 1932, as Mrs Noble in Carry Nation; made her first appearance on the London stage at the Globe Theatre, 12 May 1933, as Aunt Mabel in The Day I Forgot; Henry Miller, NY, Sept 1933, played Drusilla Thorpe in Amourette and Oct 1933, Pura in Spring in Autumn; Ritz, Feb 1934, Mrs McFie in The Wind and the Rain; Booth, Sept 1934, Mrs Venables in The Distaff Side; Booth, Nov 1935, May Beringer in Night in the House; Guild, Feb 1936, Mrs Wyler in End of Summer; Fulton, Sept 1936, Ethel in Love from a Stranger; Empire, Mar 1937, Proserpine Garnett in Candida, Sept 1937, Mrs Rutledge in The Star Wagon and Sept 1938, Widow Weeks in Missouri Legend; Majestic, Feb 1939, Bess in Stars in Your Eyes; Henry Miller, Dec 1939, Mother McGlory in Christmas Eve; Maxine Elliott, Jan 1941, Milly in The Lady Who Came to Stay; Morosco, Nov 1941, Madame Arcati in Blithe Spirit; Shubert, Apr 1942, again played Proserpine Garnett in Candida, and at the Cort, Apr 1946, again played the same part; Booth Theatre, Oct 1946, Widow Quin in The Playboy of the Western World; Martin Beck, Mar 1952, appeared as Dolly Talbo in The Grass Harp; Phoenix, Jan 1954, played Volumnia in Coriolanus; Coronet, Jan 1957, played Madame St Pé in The Waltz of the Toreadors; Belasco, Feb 1958, Kathie Morrow in The Day the Money Stopped; Coronet, Apr 1958, Miriam in The Firstborn; at the Plymouth, Mar 1960, played Marie-Paule's Mother, Angele, and Armand's Mother in The Good Soup; Ethel Barrymore, Dec 1960, played Charlotte Orr in Critic's Choice; Biltmore, Oct 1963–5, played Mrs Banks in Barefoot in the Park; Piccadilly, London, Nov 1965, again played Mrs Banks in Barefoot in the Park; ANTA, Nov 1969, Mrs Gibbs in Our Town; The Forum, Apr 1970, Beth in Landscape; Broadhurst, Apr 1971, played in the musical 70, Girls, 70; Brooks Atkinson, 1979, took over as Delia in Bedroom Farce; films in which she has appeared include The Long Voyage Home, 1940; The Enchanted Cottage, 1945; A Woman's Vengeance, 1947; The Quiet Man, 1952; The Court Jester, 1956; Barefoot in the Park, 1965; The Maltese Bippy, 1969, Daisy Miller, 1974, etc; she has also appeared on television, notably in Arsenic and Old Lace, Blithe Spirit, Eloise, as one of *The Snoop Sisters* (with Helen Hayes), 1973, etc.

Recreations: Swimming, tennis, reading, and going to the theatre. *Address:* 1001 Park Avenue, New York City, NY 10028. *Tel:* TR 9–6416.

NAUGHTON, Bill, dramatic author

b Ballyhaunis, Ireland, 12 June 1910; *s* of Thomas Naughton and his wife Maria (Fleming); *e* St Peter and Paul School, Bolton, Lancs; *m* Ernestine Pirolt; formerly a lorry driver, weaver, and coalbagger.

Author of the following plays: All in Good Time (London), 1963, (New York), 1965; Alfie (London), 1963, (NY), 1964; Spring and Port Wine, 1964; He Was Gone When They Got There, June Evening, 1966; Keep it in the Family (Spring and Port Wine), NY, 1967; Lighthearted Intercourse, 1971; plays for television include: June Evening; author of a series of radio documentary dramas, of which Wigan to Rome, June Evening, Alfie Elkins and His Little Life, were Italia Prize entries; he wrote the film-scripts for Alfie, The Family Way (each winning the Screen Writer's Guild Award), and Spring and Port Wine; his books include: One Small Boy, Late Night on Watling Street, Alfie and Alfie Darling.

Address: Ballasalla, Isle of Man. *Tel:* Castletown 2440.

NEAGLE, Dame Anna (cr 1969), CBE (1952), (née Florence Marjorie Robertson), actress

b Forest Gate, London, 20 Oct 1904; *d* of Herbert William Robertson and his wife Florence (Neagle); *e* St Albans, Herts; *m* Herbert Wilcox, CBE, (dec); studied dancing as a child, with Madame Espinosa and with Gwladys Dillon.

Made her first appearance on the stage as a child dancing, Ambassadors', 22 Dec 1917, in J B Fagan's The Wonder Tales; Duke of York's, June 1925, in the chorus of André Charlot's revival Bubbly; Prince of Wales's Theatre, Sept 1925, was in the chorus of Charlot's Revue; Drury Lane, Mar 1926, appeared in the chorus of Rose Marie; Drury Lane, Apr 1927, in chorus of The Desert Song; London Pavilion, Mar 1928, in chorus of This Year of Grace; during 1926–9, also appeared as a dancer in cabaret at the Trocadero Restaurant; London Pavilion, Mar 1929, appeared as a dancer in Wake Up and Dream; went to New York, where she made her first appearance, at the Selwyn Theatre, 30 Dec 1929, in the same show; at Southampton, Dec 1930, played Mary Clyde-Burkin in Stand Up and Sing, which opened at the London Hippodrome, Mar 1931; Open Air Theatre, May 1934, Rosalind in As You Like It, and Olivia in Twelfth Night; Palladium, Dec 1937, Peter Pan; during the war she toured for ENSA, in England and on the Continent, appearing in Victoria Regina, French Without Tears, etc; toured, 1944, as Emma Woodhouse in Emma, and played the same part at the St James's, Feb 1945; toured, 1952, as Carol Beaumont, Nell Gwynn, Victoria and Lilian Grey in The Glorious Days, and appeared in this production at the Palace, Feb 1953; Strand, Feb 1960, played Stella Felby in The More the Merrier; Lyceum, Edinburgh, July 1961, Ruth Peterson in Nothing is For Free; Pavilion, Bournemouth, Nov 1963, Jane Canning in Person Unknown; Adelphi, Dec 1965, Lady Hadwell in Charlie Girl, remaining with the production almost without interruption during its run of over 2000 performances; subsequently played the part in Melbourne, 1971, and Auckland, 1972; Drury Lane, May 1973, Sue Smith in No No Nanette; Duke of York's, 1975, took over as Dame Sibyl Hathaway in The Dame of Sark; Arnaud, Guildford, and tour, Mar 1976, Janet Fraser in The First Mrs Fraser; Theatre Royal, Windsor, Silver Jubilee, 1977, appeared in Most Gracious Lady; Shaftesbury, Oct 1977, Comtesse de la Brière in Maggie; English Theatre, Vienna,

1978, in Relative Values; Haymarket, Leicester and national tour, 1978, Mrs Higgins in My Fair Lady, opening at the Adelphi, Oct 1979; commenced film career 1930, and has appeared successfully in numerous pictures, including: Goodnight Vienna, Bitter Sweet, Nell Gwynn, Sixty Glorious Years, Nurse Edith Cavell, Irene, Spring in Park Lane, Odette, Lady with the Lamp, My Teenage Daughter; co-producer with Herbert Wilcox since 1947, first solo production These Dangerous Years, 1957; has received many film awards; Hon Ensign, FANY, 1950; member of the Executive Council of the King George VI Memorial Foundation, 1953; King George's Fund for Actors and Actresses; her autobiography, There's Always Tomorrow, was published in 1974.

Recreations: Travel, reading, swimming and walking. *Club:* FANY Regimental. *Address:* c/o Herbert de Leon, 13 Bruton Street, London, W1.

NEDERLANDER, James, producer and theater owner
b Detroit, Michigan, 31 Mar 1922; *s* of David Nederlander and his wife Sarah; *e* Detroit Institute of Technology, University of North Dakota; *m* Charlene Saunders; served in the US Army Air Force during World War II; father was a noted theater owner.

Made his New York debut while in the Air Force as a member of the staff producing Winged Victory at the 44th Street, 20 Nov 1943; many theaters, including the Alvin, Brooks Atkinson, Lunt–Fontanne, Mark Hellinger, Palace, Trafalgar and Uris in New York; the Fisher in Detroit, the Studebaker and the Arie Crown in Chicago, the Pantages and the Greek in Los Angeles, the Fox in San Diego, and the Curran and the Golden Gate in San Francisco; producer since 1968 of the New York State Theatre summer season; director and treasurer of the Independent Booking Office; entered production and presented the tours of On a Clear Day You Can See Forever, 1967, and in NY at the Biltmore, 6 Nov 1967, co-produced The Ninety-Day Mistress; the tour of George M!, 1969; the tour of Spofford!, Applause in NY, Not Now, Darling in NY, 1970; Abelard and Heloise, and the tours of Applause, Black Girl, The Effect of Gamma Rays on Man-in-the-Moon Marigolds, and Light up the Sky, 1971; Seesaw, NY, 1973; My Fat Friend, NY and tour, London Assurance, Sherlock Holmes, 1974; Treemonisha, Habeas Corpus, 1975; The D'Oyly Carte Company, 1976; Otherwise Engaged, Annie, Caesar and Cleopatra, 1977; Hello Dolly, Stop the World–I Want to Get Off, 1978; Whose Life Is It Anyway, Peter Pan, Night and Day, Oklahoma, Hello Dolly (London), 1979; has also presented engagements of many leading solo artists such as Sammy Davis Jr, Shirley MacLaine, Andy Williams, etc.

Address: 1564 Broadway, New York, NY 10036. *Tel:* 765–3906.

NEILSON, Perlita (*née* Margaret Sowden), actress
b Bradford, Yorks, 11 June 1933; *d* of Wilson Sowden and his wife Isabella (Gibson); *e* Escuela General Jose de San Martin, Buenos Aires; *m* Bruce Sharman (mar dis).

Made her first appearance on the stage in 1942, as a member of a Variety Group with the British Community Players, Buenos Aires; first appearance in London, Coliseum, June 1947, as Minnie in Annie Get Your Gun; Scala, Dec 1948, played Lisa in Peter Pan; Lyric, Apr 1949, played Anukta in The Power of Darkness; Scala, Dec 1949, again played Lisa in Peter Pan; Ambassadors', Dec 1950, Alexandra Carmichael in Lace on Her Petticoat; made her first appearance in New York, Booth, Sept 1951, in the same part; London, Arts, Apr 1954, Lucy in The Enchanted; at the same theatre, Apr 1954, played Meg in The Sun Room; joined the

Bristol Old Vic Company for the season, 1954–5, and played the following parts: Sophia Truelove in The Road To Ruin, Dido in Marching Song, Hero in Much Ado About Nothing, Nerissa in The Merchant of Venice, Mary Warren in The Crucible, Perdita and Mamillius in The Winter's Tale; Saville, Aug 1956, played Nina in The Seagull; Phoenix, Nov 1956, played the title-part in The Diary of Anne Frank; Dublin Festival, May 1957, Cecily Cardew in The Importance of Being Earnest; Nottingham Repertory, May 1958, played Patty O'Neil in The Moon is Blue; toured, Oct 1958, as Lesley Paul in Matilda Shouted Fire; Oxford Playhouse, Apr 1959, Pernette in The Green Years; Duke of York's, June 1960, Felicity in Will You Walk a Little Faster?; Pembroke, Croydon, Nov 1960, played A Girl in The Pleasure Garden; Playhouse, Oxford, Oct 1961, Ellie Dunn in Heartbreak House, subsequently appearing at Wyndham's, London, Nov 1961, in the same production; New, Cardiff, Nov 1963, played Natasha in War and Peace; joined the Birmingham Repertory Company, Apr 1965, to play Ellie Dunn in Heartbreak House, and Prossy in Candida, subsequently touring Europe with both plays; Strand, Dec 1965, played Miss Chiltern in An Ideal Husband; Strand, Apr 1967, Edith in Getting Married; Haymarket, Dec 1967, Fenny in Dear Octopus; Arnaud, Guildford, Aug 1968, Queen Victoria in My Dearest Angel; Open Air, Regent's Park, July 1969, Portia in The Merchant of Venice; Reardon Smith, Cardiff, Oct 1970, Kate in She Stoops to Conquer; Casson, Cardiff, Dec 1970, played the name part in Mary Rose; played the same part at the Arnaud, Guildford, 1971; in repertory at the Theatre Royal, York, 1972; Arnaud and tour, 1973, Judy in Flowering Cherry; Open Air, Regent's Park, July 1973, Celia in As You Like It; York, Apr 1974, Freda in Dangerous Corner; Thorndike, Leatherhead, Sept 1974, Duchess of York in Crown Matrimonial; again in repertory at York, 1975; June 1977, introduced and narrated Queen's Jubilee Concert, with Brighton Youth Orchestra; has appeared in the film She Didn't Say No; made her first appearance on television in Lace on Her Petticoat, in 1952, and has since been seen in many television plays, including: The Boy David and *Fall of Eagles*.

Recreations: Gardening and reading. *Address:* c/o John Hunter, Film Rights, 113–117 Wardour Street, London W1V 4EH.

NELLIGAN, Kate, actress
b London, Ontario, 16 Mar 1951; *d* of Patrick Joseph Nelligan and his wife Alice (Dier); *e* St Martin's Catholic School, London, Ont, and York University, Toronto; trained for the stage at the Central School of Speech ad Drama.

Made her first professional appearance at the Little Theatre, Bristol, Aug 1972, as Corrie in Barefoot in the Park; other parts played here and at the Theatre Royal for the Bristol Old Vic, 1972–3, include Hypatia in Misalliance, Stella Kowalski in A Streetcar Named Desire, Pegeen Mike in The Playboy of the Western World, Grace Harkaway in London Assurance, title role in Lulu, and Sybil Chase in Private Lives; made her first London appearance at the Comedy, 4 Mar 1974, as Jenny in Knuckle; joined the National Theatre Company at the Old Vic, Feb 1975, to play Ellie Dunn in Heartbreak House; Olivier, Jan 1977, Marianne in Tales from the Vienna Woods; for the RSC, Stratford, Sept 1977, played Rosalind in As You Like It; Lyttelton, Apr 1978, Susan Traherne in Plenty, for which she won the *Evening Standard* Award for Best Actress, 1978; films include The Romantic Englishwoman, and Dracula; TV includes Licking Hitler, Measure for Measure, Dreams of Leaving, and Thérèse Raquin.

Favourite part: Jenny in Knuckle. *Recreations:* Reading, cooking, gardening. *Address:* c/o Chatto & Linnit, Globe Theatre, Shaftesbury Avenue, London W1.

NELSON, Barry (*né* Robert Nielson), actor
b Oakland, California, 1925; *s* of Trygve Nielson and his wife Betsy (Christophsen); *e* University of California; *m* Teresa Celli (mar dis).

Made his first appearance on the New York stage at the 44th Street Theatre, 20 Nov 1943, as Bobby Grills in Winged Victory; Royale, Nov 1948, played Peter Sloan in Light Up the Sky; Ethel Barrymore, Dec 1949, Gus Hammer in The Rat Race; Henry Miller, Mar 1951, Donald Gresham in The Moon Is Blue; Ethel Barrymore, May 1956, Don Emerson in Wake Up, Darling; made his first appearance in London at Her Majesty's, Aug 1956, as Will Stockdale in No Time for Sergeants; Helen Hayes, NY, Mar 1961, Bob McKellaway in Mary, Mary, which he played until 1963; Lyceum, May 1964, took over from Robert Preston the role of Nat Bentley in Nobody Loves an Albatross; Royale, Dec 1965, Julian in The Cactus Flower; Plymouth, Nov 1967, Richard in Everything in the Garden; Broadhurst, May 1968, Joe Grady in The Only Game in Town, which he also directed; Broadhurst, Jan 1969, Harry Stone in The Fig Leaves Are Falling; Helen Hayes, May 1970, Walter Whitney in The Engagement Baby; toured, 1971, as Sam Nash, Jesse Kiplinger, and Roy Hubley in Plaza Suite; toured, 1972, in Conflict of Interest; Shubert, Philadelphia, Mar 1973, Detective McLeod in Detective Story; toured, 1974, in Lovers and Other Strangers; Shubert, Jan 1975, Charlie in Seascape; Shubert, Los Angeles, Apr 1975, again played Charlie in Seascape; Morosco, Dec 1975, Reg in the three plays with the overall title The Norman Conquests; Majestic, Oct 1977, Dan Connors in The Act; has appeared in films, notably in A Guy Named Joe, Winged Victory, Mary, Mary; Pete 'n' Tillie (1972); has also appeared on television in the series *The Hunter*, and *My Favorite Husband*.
Recreations: Reading, listening to music, and travelling. *Address:* c/o William Morris Agency, 151 El Camino Drive, Beverly Hills, Calif.

NELSON, Gene (*né* Leander Berg), actor, dancer, singer and director
b Seattle, Wash, 24 Mar, 1920; *e* Santa Monica, Cal, High School.

Began dancing and ice-skating while in high school; joined Sonja Henie and toured in her ice shows in 1940–41; made his NY debut as Gene Berg at the Center, 10 Oct 1940 in It Happens on Ice; same theater, Apr 1941, again appeared in it Happens on Ice; during World War II played in This is the Army, and appeared in this revue at the Broadway, 4 Jul 1942; after the war reappeared in NY at the National, 16 Dec 1948, in the revue Lend an Ear, under the name of Gene Nelson; went to Hollywood and made films for many years then reappeared in NY at the City Center, 19 Mar 1958, as Will Parker in Oklahoma!; toured in Hit the Deck, June 1960; returned to films, then, at the Winter Garden, 4 Apr 1971, played Buddy Plummer in Follies; Shubert, Century City, Cal, Jul 1972, again played Buddy Plummer in Follies; City Center, Apr 1974, appeared as Master of Ceremonies and performed in Music! Music!; St James, Dec 1974, Bill Johnson in Good News; first appeared in film musicals in The Daughter of Rosie O'Grady, 1950, and has since appeared in numerous others, including Tea for Two, Lullaby of Broadway, So This Is Paris, Oklahoma!, etc; directed the films of Kissin' Cousins, The Perils of Pauline, Harem Scarem, etc; has directed extensively on television, including *Mod Squad,*

Hawaii Five-O, Burke's Law, The Rifleman, The Donna Reed Show, etc.
Address: Actors Equity Association, 165 West 46th Street, New York, NY 10036.

NELSON, Kenneth, actor
b Rocky Mount, North Carolina, 24 Mar 1930; *s* of Frederick Nelson and his wife Rachel (Barro); *e* Brackenridge High School, San Antonio, Texas.

Studied acting with Paul Baker at Baylor University, 1950–1, with Uta Hagen, 1953–8, and singing with Keith Davis, 1958–70; made his New York début at the Broadhurst, 21 June 1951, as Willie Baxter in Seventeen; toured, 1953, in the title role of Solomon Grundy; Tempo Playhouse, Sept 1955, played the Twins in The Typewriter; Provincetown, Massachusetts, Playhouse, Jan 1957, played in the revue Kaleidoscope; Showplace, Apr, 1958, played in the revue Night-Cap; Sullivan Street Playhouse, May 1960, The Boy in The Fantasticks; Shubert, Oct 1962, was stand-by to Anthony Newley as Littlechap in Stop the World—I Want to Get Off, playing this role first in Feb 1963, and several times thereafter; took over from Joel Gray in the tour of this play, Sept 1963; Shubert, New Haven, Connecticut, Jan 1965, Bob in Royal Flush; toured, 1966, as Arthur Kipps in Half a Sixpence; Coconut Grove Playhouse, Miami, 1967, again played Arthur Kipps in Half a Sixpence; Theatre Four, Apr 1968, Michael in The Boys in the Band; made his London début at Wyndham's, Feb 1969, when he again played Michael in The Boys in the Band; Majestic, NY, Dec 1970, Sakini in Lovely Ladies, Kind Gentlemen; Adelphi, London, July 1971, Frank in Show Boat; St Martin's, Mar 1973, Terry Cleaves in Lover; Mermaid, July 1974, appeared in the revue Cole; Quaglino's, Sept 1975, appeared in the revue Curtain Up on Coward; toured July 1976 as Don Patterson in Once More With Music; Mermaid, London, Apr 1977, appeared in Oh Mr Porter; Regent, London, Dec 1977, played Bernard Litko in Sexual Perversity in Chicago; Victoria Palace, May 1978, took over Rooster Hannigan in Annie; made his film début as Michael in The Boys in the Band, 1970; made his television début as Henry Aldrich in the series *The Aldrich Family,* 1952, and since has appeared on various dramatic series.
Recreation: Gardening. *Address:* CCA Personal Management, White House, 29 Dawes Road, London SW6.

NELSON, Ruth, actress
b Saginaw, Michigan, 2 Aug 1905; *d* of Sanford Leroy Nelson and his wife Eva (Mudge); *e* Immaculate Heart College, Hollywood; *m* John Cromwell (dec); prepared for the stage with Richard Boleslavsky.

First appeared on the stage at the Lobero, Santa Barbara, California, 1926, as Sorel in Hay Fever; first appeared in New York at the American Laboratory Theatre, 1928, in the title-role of Martine; joined the Group Theatre, in 1931 and remained with it until 1941, when it disbanded; Martin Beck, Mar 1952, played Verena Talbo in The Grass Harp; Helen Hayes, Nov 1956, understudied Florence Eldridge in Long Day's Journey into Night, and toured, Dec 1957–May 1958, as Mary Tyrone in this play; joined the Tyrone Guthrie Theatre Company in Minneapolis, 1963, and played the Player Queen in Hamlet and Anfisa in The Three Sisters, 1963; Mistress Quickly in Henry V, Amanda Wingfield in The Glass Menagerie, and Lady Politic Wouldbe in Volpone, 1964; Duchess of York in Richard III, Charlotta in The Cherry Orchard, and various parts in The Caucasian Chalk Circle, 1965; Ellen Stewart, NY, Oct 1970, played Sido in Colette; Long Wharf, New Haven, Mar 1971, Mrs Potter in

Double Solitaire and Madam in Solitaire in a double bill of the premiere of Robert Anderson's plays; John Golden, Sept 1971, repeated these last parts; Long Wharf, Nov 1971, Old Mrs Ewbank in The Contractor; Shaw Festival, Niagara-on-the-Lake, Ontario, June 1972, Fanny Cavendish in The Royal Family; New Theater for Now, Los Angeles, 1973, played in Tadpole; Eisenhower, Washington, DC, May 1974, Anna Riabovska in Headhunters; entered films in 1943, and has since appeared in North Star, The Eve of St Mark, Wilson, A Tree Grows in Brooklyn, Sea of Grass, Three Women, A Wedding (1977), etc.

Favourite part: Mary Tyrone in Long Day's Journey into Night. *Address:* 272 South Lasky Drive, Beverly Hills, Calif 90212.

NESBITT, Cathleen, CBE (1977), actress
b Cheshire, 24 Nov 1888; *d* of Thomas Nesbitt and his wife Catherine (Parry); *e* Victoria College, Belfast, and at Lisieux, France; *m* C B Ramage; studied with Rosina Filippi.

Made her first professional appearance at the Royalty, Apr 1911, as Miss Borlasse in The Master of Mrs Chilvers; she then joined the Irish Players and went with them to America, making her first appearance in New York, Dec 1911, as Molly Byrne in The Well of the Saints; also played Honor Brady in The Playboy of the Western World, and Nora Burke in The Shadow of the Glen; at the Abbey, Dublin, Mar 1912, played Mrs Carragher in The Family Failing; at the Prince of Wales's Theatre, 1912, played in The Workhouse Ward, and at the Court, June 1912, appeared as Marcelle de Rochefort in The Escape, and as Vivien in The Temptation of Sir Galahad; at the Savoy, Sept 1912, played Perdita in The Winter's Tale; at the Kingsway, Nov 1912, Freda in The Eldest Son; at the Haymarket, Dec 1912, Euphemia in The Waldies; at the Apollo, Jan 1913, Mary Ellen in General John Regan, and June 1913, Madge Cray in The Perfect Cure; appeared in Paris, June 1913, as Viola in Twelfth Night; at the Little Theatre, Deirdre in Deirdre of the Sorrows; at the St James's, Sept 1913, played Alice Whistler in The Harlequin-ade; at the Duke of York's, Nov 1913, Phoebe Throssell in Quality Street; at the King's Hall, Covent Garden, Mar 1914, Mrs Denbigh in Daughters of Ishmael; in Aug 1914, toured as Peggy in A Butterfly on the Wheel; at the Little Theatre, May 1915, played Martha in Exchange; at the Playhouse, June 1915, Mary Dean in Mater; at the Court, Liverpool, Sept 1915, played Mabel Dredge in Quinneys, and went to America, to play the same part, Oct 1915, at Maxine Elliott Theatre; at the Candler Theatre, Apr 1916, played Ruth Honeywill in Justice; at the Little Theatre, NY, Oct 1916, Julie Laxton in Hush; at the Princess', NY, Nov 1916, Leslie Crankshaw in Such is Life; at Maxine Elliott Theatre, Jan 1917, appeared as The Queen in The Queen's Enemies, and Varinka in Great Catherine; Feb 1917, as Patricia Carleon in Magic; at the Belasco, Apr 1917, as Kathleen in The Very Minute, subsequently, at Chicago, played Nan Carey and Ruth Brockton in Cheating Cheaters, and at the Playhouse, Chicago, July 1918, appeared in The Garden of Paradise; she then toured in the United States as Betty in General Post; at the Empire, NY, Sept 1918, played Susan Blaine in The Saving Grace; returned to England in 1919 and appeared at the Court, Oct 1919, as Jessica in The Merchant of Venice; at the Lyric, Hammersmith, Nov 1919, played the title-role in a revival of The Duchess of Malfi, and Feb 1920, Doralice in a revival of Marriage à la Mode; at the Ambassadors, Mar 1920, played Pamela in a revival of Grierson's Way, and Apr 1920, Marjorie Corbett in The Grain of Mustard Seed; at the Playhouse, Nov 1920, appeared as Melisande in The Romantic Age; at the Lyric, Hammersmith, Nov 1920, as Belvidera

in a revival of Venice Preserved; at the New Theatre, Oxford, for the OUDS, Dec 1920, played Cleopatra in Antony and Cleopatra; at the Shaftesbury, May 1921, as Audrey in Sweet William; at the Comedy, Sept 1921, Ginevra in The Love Thief; at the Shaftesbury, Jan 1922, Myrtle Carey in The Rattlesnake; at the St Martin's, Mar 1922, Margaret Orme in Loyalties; at the Everyman Theatre, Apr 1923, Mrs Dubedat in The Doctor's Dilemma; at the Shaftesbury (for the Phoenix Society), June 1923, Amarillis in The Faithful Shepherdess; at the New Theatre, Aug 1923, Hilda Norbury in The Eye of Siva; at His Majesty's, Sept 1923, Yasmin in Hassan; at the Comedy, May 1924, Vera Farington in This Marriage; in Sept 1924, toured as Emma Hunter in The Blue Peter, and played the same part at the Princes Theatre, Oct 1924; St Martin's, Jan 1925, played Mona in Spring Cleaning; Ambassadors', Nov 1925, Jessica Madras in The Madras House; Court (for the 300 Club), July 1926, Julia Dwyer in Confession; Prince's, July 1926, Malia in Down Hill; New, Sept 1926, Florence Churchill in The Constant Nymph; went to NY, and at the 49th Street Theatre, Jan 1928, played Rayetta Muir in Diversion; on returning to London, appeared at the Q, Sept 1928, as Lily Shane in The House of Women; Arts, Sept 1928, and Little, Oct 1928, again played Rayetta in Diversion; St James's, Feb 1929, Lady Myrtle in Fame; Scala (for the Venturers), May 1929, Mother Goddam in The Shanghai Gesture; St Martin's, July 1929, Margaret Fairfield in A Bill of Divorcement; Wyndham's, Sept 1929, Lady Panniford in The Calendar; Arts, Mar 1930, Greta in After All; Kingsway, Apr 1930, Stella de Gex in His Excellency the Governor; Duke of York's, June 1930, Lady Porter in The Way to Treat a Woman; Whitehall, Feb 1931, Cora Drew in Good Losers; Wyndham's, Aug 1931, Lady Lebanon in The Case of the Frightened Lady; Comedy, Feb 1932, Lady Pauline in Sentenced; Garrick, Mar 1932, Eloise Fontaine in Marriage by Purchase; St Martin's, May 1932, Eunice Malvinetti in Somebody Knows; Garrick, Aug 1932, Margaret Orme in Loyalties; Duchess, Oct 1932, Fräulein von Nordeck in Children in Uniform; Daly's, Oct 1933, Lucie Brignac in Maternité; Playhouse, Nov 1933, Enid Deckle in The World of Light; Arts, Apr 1934, Manuella in Secret Orchard; Open Air Theatre, June 1934, Elizabeth in King Richard III; at Sadler's Wells, Jan 1935, appeared as Katherine in The Taming of the Shrew; Garrick, Jan 1935, Mrs Hardcastle in Love on the Dole; Shaftesbury, Mar 1935, Hilda Lester in Ringmaster; Garrick, Mar 1936, succeeded Louise Hampton as Harriet in The Two Mrs Carrolls; Apollo, Apr 1937, played Mrs Morant in London After Dark; Westminster, Feb 1938, Judith in Land's End; Lyceum, May 1938, Madame Gautier in Money Talks; Garrick, June 1938, Countess Isabel in Trumpeter, Play!; Playhouse, Aug 1938, Thérèse Raquin in Thou Shalt Not . . .; toured, Oct 1938, as Miss Rimmer in The King of Nowhere; toured, Jan–Apr 1939, with the Old Vic company on the Continent and in Egypt, playing the Queen in Hamlet, Queen of France in Henry V, Lady Loddon in Libel etc; Open Air, June 1939, Beatrice in Much Ado About Nothing, and Dionyza in Pericles; Richmond, Mar 1940, Alinda Howard in Under One Roof; Old Vic, Apr 1940, Goneril in King Lear; New, Aug 1940, Mrs Cliveden-Banks in Outward Bound; Aldwych, Feb 1942, Mrs Wislack in On Approval; Q, Aug 1942, Mrs Gordon in We Are the People; Lyric, Mar 1944, Delia Channing in A Murder for a Valentine; toured, 1944–5, in The Case of the Frightened Lady, The Calendar, The Frog, and The Ringer; St Martin's, Apr 1945, Mathilde Heiss in The Shop at Sly Corner, which she played for a year; Playhouse, Oct 1946, played Principessa della Cercola in Our Betters; Covent

Garden, July 1948, appeared as Discretion in The Pilgrim's Progress; Globe, Sept 1948, the Nurse in Medea; Duke of York's, Jan 1949, Mrs Mannering in Breach of Marriage; Henry Miller Theatre, NY, Jan 1950, played Julia in The Cocktail Party, which ran for a year; Fulton, Nov 1951, Alicia de St Ephlam in Gigi; returned to England and at the Royal Court, Liverpool, Aug 1952, played Margaret, Dowager Duchess of Burgundy in The Player King; St James's, London, May 1953, played Lady Lannion in The Uninvited Guest; at the National, NY, Nov 1953, appeared as Maude Larrabee in Sabrina Fair; Palace, London, Aug 1954, again played Maude in Sabrina Fair; ANTA Playhouse, NY, Dec 1954, appeared as Countess Gemini in Portrait of a Lady; Lyceum, NY, 1955, took over the part of the Dowager Empress from Eugénie Leontovitch in Anastasia; Mark Hellinger, Mar 1956, Mrs Higgins in My Fair Lady; Coronet, Nov 1956, the Grand Duchess in The Sleeping Prince; toured US in 1957 as Mrs St-Maugham in The Chalk Garden; toured the US in the 1958–9 seasons as Mrs Venable in Suddenly, Last Summer, the Duchess in Time Remembered, and Amanda in The Glass Menagerie; Eugene O'Neill, NY, Apr 1960, Clara in The Second String; in summer theatre, June 1960, played Ex-Queen Sophia in Royal Enclosure; Music Box, Jan 1962, played Julia in Romulus; Playhouse-in-the-Park, Philadelphia, June 1962, Juliana Bordereau in A Garden in the Sea; Comedy, London, Jan 1964, The Dowager Lady Headleigh in The Claimant; Mendelsohn, Ann Arbor, Dec 1967, played the Mother in Amazing Grace; Arnaud, Guildford, Mar 1968, Amy in The Family Reunion; O'Keefe, Toronto, 1971, again played Mrs St. Maugham in The Chalk Garden; Goodman, Chicago, Jan 1972, Fanny Cavendish in The Royal Family; toured, 1972, in Sabrina Fair; Royal, Brighton, Mar 1973, The Countess in What Every Woman Knows; Circle in the Square, NY, June 1973, Mrs Voinitsky in Uncle Vanya; Los Angeles, 1975, appeared in The Opening of a Door; Chichester Festival Season, 1978, played Juliana Bordereau in The Aspern Papers; has appeared in 37 films since 1922, notably Canaries Sometimes Sing, The Case of the Frightened Lady, So Long at the Fair, Staircase, The French Connection, An Affair to Remember, etc; has made many television appearances including *The Farmer's Daughter* series in America, and, in England, *Upstairs Downstairs*, Abide With Me, and The Old Crowd among many plays; has published her autobiography, A Little Love and Good Company.

Favourite parts: Mrs St-Maugham in The Chalk Garden and Mona in Spring Cleaning. *Address:* c/o ICM, 22 Grafton Street, London, W1.

NESBITT, Robert, dramatic author and director
b London, 11 Jan 1906; s of Robert Nesbitt and his wife Ada Isobel (Nesbitt); e Repton; m Iris Lockwood.

Formerly engaged in advertising and also as a lyric writer; has directed the following revues and musical plays: Ballyhoo, 1932; Here's How, Hi-Diddle-Diddle, 1934; Char-a-Bang! Shall We Reverse? Stop—Go! The Sleeping Beauty, or What a Witch, 1935; The Town Talks, 1936; And On We Go, Take It Easy, Aladdin, 1937; Maritza, Pélissier's Follies of 1938, 1938; Black and Blue, The Little Dog Laughed, Black Velvet, 1939; Up and Doing, Garrison Theatre, Top of the World, 1940; Black Vanities, Get a Load of This, Gangway, 1941; Happidrome, Fine and Dandy, No Orchids for Miss Blandish, Wild Rose, Best Bib and Tucker, Blossom Time, 1942; Strike a New Note, The Vagabond King, Magic Carpet, 1943; Happy and Glorious, 1944; The Night and the Music, Fine Feathers, 1945; High Time, The Night and the Laughter, 1946; Here, There and Everywhere, Starlight

Roof, 1947; High Button Shoes, 1948; Latin Quarter, 1949; in the following year he directed, at the Casino, Latin Quarter, 1950, which was his fiftieth production; Casino, Mar 1951, directed Latin Quarter of 1951; Stoll, Sept 1951, directed Rainbow Square; subsequently directed Excitement, 1952; The Glorious Days, Three Cheers, 1953; at the Plymouth, New York, Sept 1955, was responsible for production of the revue Catch a Star!; in London, directed Rocking the Town, 1956; Plaisirs de Paris, We're Having a Ball, 1957; Large as Life, 1958; Swinging Down the Lane, 1959; Stars in Your Eyes, 1960; Let Yourself Go, 1961; Every Night at the Palladium, 1962; Swing Along, 1963; Doddy's Here, 1965; London Laughs, 1966; since 1956, has devised and directed new versions of the following pantomimes, The Wonderful Lamp, 1956; Robinson Crusoe, 1957; The Sleeping Beauty, 1958; Humpty Dumpty, 1959; Turn Again, Whittington, 1960; Little Old King Cole, 1961; Puss in Boots, 1962; The Man in the Moon, 1963; was appointed Managing Director of Bernard Delfont Television Productions, Oct 1955; designed and built in conjunction with Bernard Delfont and Charles Forte The Talk of the Town and produced and directed subsequent revues there to date (1979); part-author of Here's How, Hi-Diddle-Diddle, The Sleeping Beauty, Take It Easy (revised version), and No Orchids for Miss Blandish; author of Excitement, The Glorious Days; he also devised Latin Quarter, 1949; Latin Quarter, 1950; Latin Quarter of 1951; staged and directed 23 Royal Variety Performances between 1945 and 1979, at the Palladium, Coliseum and Prince of Wales Theatre.

Address: Talk of the Town, London, WC2.

NETTLETON, John, actor
b Sydenham, London, 5 Feb 1929; s of Alfred Nettleton and his wife Dorothy (Pratt); e St Dunstan's College, Catford; m Deirdre Doone; trained for the stage at RADA.

Made his first professional appearance at the St James's, Dec 1951, walking on in Snow White and the Seven Dwarfs; joined the Shakespeare Memorial Theatre Company, 1952, playing small parts and touring New Zealand and Australia with them in 1953; toured, 1954, with the Elizabethan Theatre Company, as Aguecheek in Twelfth Night and Morocco and the Duke in The Merchant of Venice; in repertory at Nottingham, 1955; Sept 1955, Peasant in The Burnt Flower Bed at the Arts; Royal Court, Oct 1956, Husband in The Good Woman of Setzuan; Phoenix, Apr 1957, Lord Mulligan in Camino Real; Arts, Sept 1957, Harry in All Kinds of Men; Piccadilly, Oct 1958, Doctor in Shadow of Heroes; Strand, Oct 1959, Albert in Rollo; Comedy, Apr 1960, Mr McBryde in A Passage to India; joined the Royal Shakespeare Company, 1961, remaining with them until Jan 1966; in that time his parts, at the Aldwych unless otherwise stated, included Bubnov in The Lower Depths, (Arts), Mannoury in The Devils, Agamemnon in Troilus and Cressida, Gilbert Foliot in Curtmantle, 1962; Snug in A Midsummer Night's Dream, Archbishop Orsenigo in The Representative, 1963; Taffy in Afore Night Come, General Lonsegur in Victor, Barnadine in The Jew of Malta, Sir Hugh Evans in The Merry Wives of Windsor, 1964; Fluellen and Archbishop of Canterbury in Henry V, 1965; for the company he toured the USA and Canada, 1964, in The Hollow Crown, also performing it in London; toured, 1970, as Subtle in the Cambridge Theatre Company's The Alchemist; Greenwich, Nov 1970, played the Headmaster in A Voyage Round My Father; toured, Feb 1972, as Oliver in Me Times Me; Greenwich, May 1973, Dr Kroll in Rosmersholm; Aldwych, Oct 1973, for RSC, Sicinius Velutus in Coriolanus; toured N America, July–Dec 1974 as Jaques in the National Theatre's all-male As You Like It; Olivier, Oct 1976, Agydas in Tamburlaine the Great Part I and Sigismund in Part II; Old Vic, May 1977, Polonius in Hamlet; Old Vic, July 1977, Serapion in All for Love, and Lepidus in Antony and Cleopatra; Windsor, Sept 1978, Lord Summerhays in Misalliance; Hampstead, May 1979, Fenwick in Then and Now; first film, A Man for All Seasons, 1966; recent appearances include And Soon the Darkness and Black Beauty; television, since 1956, includes The Country Wife, Henry VIII and The Tempest.

Favourite parts: Jaques and Polonius. *Recreations:* Listening to music and making bread. *Address:* 24 The Avenue, St Margarets, Twickenham, Middlesex. *Tel:* 01–892 2993.

NETTLETON, Lois, actress
b Oak Park, Illinois; *d* of Edward L. Nettleton and his wife Virginia (Schaffer); *e* Senn High School, Chicago; prepared for the stage at the Goodman Memorial Theater, Chicago, and Actors Studio (1951); *m* Jean Shepherd.

Made her debut at age 11 as the Father in Hansel and Gretel at the Greenbriar Community Center, Chicago; first appeared in New York at the Mansfield, 30 Mar 1949, as Laurie Hutchins in The Biggest Thief in Town; Alvin, 1951, took over from Kim Hunter as Luba in Darkness at Noon; toured in this last part from Sept 1951; Morosco, Mar 1955, understudied Barbara Bel Geddes as Maggie in Cat on a Hot Tin Roof and played the part on occasion; American Shakespeare Festival, Stratford, Conn, Jun 1957, Nerissa in The Merchant of Venice, and, Aug 1957, Hero in Much Ado About Nothing; 54th Street, Feb 1959, played Shelagh O'Connor in God and Kate Murphy; Morosco, Dec 1959, Janet in Silent Night, Lonely Night; 46th Street, Jan 1966, Julia Stevens in The Wayward Stork; Shubert, New Haven, Feb 1967, Catherine, Diane, Dorothy, and Maria in The Hemingway Hero; Arlington Park, Ill, 1972, played in The Only Game in Town; St James, Oct 1973, Blanche du Bois in A Streetcar Named Desire; Playhouse, Jan 1976, Amy in the Phoenix production of They Knew What They Wanted; Chicago, 1978, appeared in Compliments of Cole; John Golden, Mar 1979, Dorothy Thompson in Strangers; made her film debut in Period of Adjustment in 1962, and has since played in Come Fly with Me, Mail Order Bride, Dirty Dingus Magee, The Honkers, Echoes of a Summer (1975), etc; first appeared on television in The Brighter Day in 1954 and has since played in Portrait of Emily Dickinson, Duet for Two Hands, The Hidden River, *Gunsmoke, Dr Kildare,* and numerous other dramatic shows, recently Dolly and the Great Little Madisons, 1979; received the Clarence Derwent Award for God and Kate Murphy.

Address: Actors Equity Association, 165 West 46th Street, New York, NY 10036.

NEVILLE, John, OBE, actor, director
b Willesden, London, 2 May 1925; *s* of Reginald Daniel Neville and his wife Mabel Lillian (Fry); *e* Willesden, and Chiswick County Schools; *m* Caroline Hooper; formerly a stores clerk; studied for the stage at the Royal Academy of Dramatic Art.

First appeared at the New, 23 Apr 1947, walking-on in Richard II; Open Air Theatre, season 1948, played Lysander in A Midsummer Night's Dream and Chatillon in King John; appeared in repertory at Lowestoft, 1948, and with Birmingham Repertory Company, Jan 1949–Mar 1950; played three consecutive seasons with the Bristol Old Vic Company, Sept 1950–June 1953; joined the Old Vic Company in London for the season 1953–4, playing, among other parts, Fortinbras in Hamlet, Bertram in All's Well That Ends Well,

and Ferdinand in The Tempest; remained with the company and during the season 1954–5 appeared as Macduff, Richard II, Berowne in Love's Labour's Lost, Orlando in As You Like It, and Henry Percy in Henry IV (Part I); during the 1955–6 season played Marc Antony in Julius Caesar, Autolycus in The Winter's Tale, alternated with Richard Burton in the parts of Othello and Iago, played Troilus in Troilus and Cressida (in a modern dress production), Romeo in Romeo and Juliet, and the title-part in Richard II; made his first appearance in New York, with the same company, at the Winter Garden Theatre, Oct 1956, when he played Romeo, followed by Richard II, Macduff in Macbeth, and Thersites in Troilus and Cressida; after touring in the United States, he returned to the Old Vic for the 1957–8 season, when he appeared as Hamlet, Angelo in Measure For Measure, and Sir Andrew Aguecheek in Twelfth Night; Sept 1958–Feb 1959 again toured the United States with the Old Vic Company, playing Hamlet and Sir Andrew Aguecheek; on returning to London, he appeared at the New Theatre, July 1959, as Victor Fabian in Once More, With Feeling; Lyric, Oct 1959, succeeded Keith Michell as Nestor in Irma La Douce; Old Vic, May 1960, directed Henry V; Arts, Sept 1960, played Jacko in The Naked Island; Queen's, Mar 1961, played The Stranger in The Lady from the Sea; Palace, Watford, May 1961, the Evangelist in The Substitute; joined the Nottingham Playhouse Company, Sept 1961; appointed Associate Producer Dec 1961, and was joint Theatre Director 1963–7; while with the Company he played the title-part in Macbeth, Sir Thomas More in A Man for All Seasons (also appearing in both plays in Malta, Oct 1961), Petruchio in The Taming of the Shrew, 1962; Haymarket, Apr 1962, played Joseph Surface in The School For Scandal; left the cast to appear in the opening Chichester Festival, July 1962, as Don Frederick in The Chances, and Orgilus in The Broken Heart; returned to Nottingham Playhouse, Oct 1962, when he directed Twelfth Night; for the same company, Oct 1962, co-adapted and played D'Artagnan in a musical of The Three Musketeers; directed A Subject of Scandal and Concern, Nov 1962; toured West Africa, Feb 1963, for The British Council, with the Nottingham Playhouse Company, playing Macbeth; Mermaid, London, June 1963, played the title-part in Alfie, transferring with the production to the Duchess, July 1963; returned to Nottingham, to appear in the opening production of the new Playhouse, Dec 1963, as Coriolanus; subsequently appeared, in repertory, in the following parts: John Worthing in The Importance of Being Earnest (also co-directed), 1963; Bernard Shaw in The Bashful Genius, Memento Mori (directed), The Mayor of Zalamea (directed), Listen to the Knocking Bird (directed), Moricet in The Birdwatcher, the title-part in Œdipus the King, 1964; Richard in Richard II (also directed), Collapse of Stout Party (co-directed), Corvino in Volpone, Measure for Measure (directed), 1965; Saint Joan (directed), Barry Field in The Spies Are Singing, Moll Flanders (co-directed), Faustus in Doctor Faustus, Antony and Cleopatra (directed), Jack and the Beanstalk (directed), 1966; Willy Loman in Death of a Salesman, Kolpakov and others in Beware of the Dog (also at the St Martin's), Iago in Othello, 1967; Palace, Dec 1968, played Henry Gow in Mr and Alec Harvey in Mrs in the double-bill Mr and Mrs; Fortune, May 1969, directed Honour and Offer; Mermaid, Mar 1970, King Magnus in The Apple Cart; Edinburgh Festival, Aug 1970, for Prospect Productions, Garrick in Boswell's Life of Johnson, and Benedick in Much Ado About Nothing; US tour, Mar 1970, Humbert Humbert in Lolita; Chichester Festival, 1972, played Macheath in The Beggars' Opera, and Sir Colenso Ridgeon in The Doctor's Dilemma; also directed at Bristol

Old Vic; came to Canada in 1972, directed The Rivals and played Prospero in The Tempest at the National Arts Centre in Ottawa; played Judge Brack in Hedda Gabler, at the Manitoba Theatre Centre; became Theatre Director of the Citadel Theatre in Edmonton, Alberta, 1972, where he directed Romeo and Juliet, The Master Builder, Schweyk In The Second World War, and Antigone; he appeared in Oh Coward, Bethune, Pygmalion, and starred opposite Dame Peggy Ashcroft in Happy Days; became Theatre Director of the Neptune Theatre, Halifax, Nova Scotia, May 1978, where he appeared in Othello, and Staircase, and directed Les Canadiens, and The Seagull; films in which he has appeared include: Oscar Wilde, 1960; Billy Budd, 1961; Topaze, 1961; television appearances include: Henry V, 1957; Romeo and Juliet (NY), 1957; Hamlet (NY), 1959; received the OBE, in the Birthday Honours, 1965.

Favourite parts: Gregers Werle in The Wild Duck, Richard II, and Pistol in Henry IV (Part II). *Recreations:* Music and opera. *Address:* c/o Larry Dalzell Associates, 3 Goodwin's Court, St Martin's Lane, London, WC2.

NEWAY, Patricia, singer and actress
b New York City, 30 Sept 1919; *d* of Edward M Neway and his wife Mary (Stroh); *e* Notre Dame College for Women, Staten Island; *m* (1) Morris Gessel; (2) John Byrne.

Formerly a piano student and choral singer; toured the US, Apr–June 1946, in the chorus of Windy City; made her NY début at the Ziegfeld, 29 Dec 1948, alternating with Brenda Lewis as the Female Chorus in The Rape of Lucretia, the opera by Benjamin Britten; has since then divided her time between opera and the musical theatre; Ethel Barrymore, Mar 1950, played Magda Sorel in The Consul, which she has sung more than 700 times since; made her London début at the Cambridge, 7 Feb 1951, as Magda Sorel in The Consul; joined the New York City Opera Company, and at the City Center, 1951–2 season, sang Marie in Wozzeck, Santuzza in Cavalleria Rusticana, and Leah in The Dybbuk; at the Opéra-Comique in Paris, 1953, sang the title-role of La Tosca; Paris, 1954, sang in The Resurrection; New Orleans, Louisiana, Jan 1955, sang the Old Woman in Lord Byron's Love Letters; Sadler's Wells, Oct 1957, again sang Magda Sorel in The Consul; New York City Center, Apr 1958, Laura Gates in Tale for a Deaf Ear; also in Apr 1958, directed a workshop production of Chanticleer; New York City Center, May 1958, sang Madame Flora in The Medium; Martin Beck, Nov 1958, The Mother in Maria Golovin; New York City Center, Mar 1959, again sang The Mother in Maria Golovin; Apr 1959, Miriam in The Scarf; also Apr 1959, Nelly in Wuthering Heights; Lunt-Fontanne, Nov 1959, Mother Abbess in The Sound of Music; Kaufmann Auditorium, May 1960, directed her opera workshop in The Mother, A Hand of Bridge, and Goodbye to the Clown; New York City Center, Mar 1962, played the Governess in The Turn of the Screw; Phoenix, Oct 1963, The Mother in Morning Sun; NY State, July 1964, Lady Thiang in The King and I; New York City Center, Oct 1964, Herodias in Salome; same theatre, Dec 1966, Nettie Fowler in Carousel; Florida State University Apr, 1970, played the Queen in The Leper; has appeared on television in productions of opera, notably in The Dialogues of the Carmelites, Golden Child, The Consul, Maria Golovin, Macbeth, Wozzeck, Carousel (1967), and on various variety programs; received *Variety's* New York Drama Critics Poll Award and the Donaldson Award for The Consul; received the Antoinette Perry (Tony) Award for The Sound of Music.

Address: c/o Actors Equity Association, 165 West 46th Street, New York, NY 10036.

NEWLEY, Anthony, actor, author, composer, director
b Hackney, London, 24 Sept 1931; *s* of George Anthony Newley and his wife Frances Grace (Gardiner); *e* Manderville Street School, Clapton, E; *m* (1) Elizabeth Ann Lynn (mar dis), (2) Joan Collins; trained for the stage with Italia Conti.

Made his first appearance on the stage at the Colchester Repertory Theatre, Apr 1946, when he played Gwyn in The Wind of Heaven; first appeared in London at the New Watergate, Dec 1955, in the *revue* Cranks, transferring with the production to the St Martin's, Mar 1956; made his first appearance on Broadway at the Bijou, Nov 1956, in the same *revue*; on returning to England, toured with his own Variety Show; at the Queen's, July 1961, co-author and composer with Leslie Bricusse, of Stop the World—I Want to Get Off, which he also directed, and in which he played Littlechap; after a run of more than a year, he appeared in the American production of the same musical, at the Shubert, New York, Oct 1962, and Ambassador, Sept 1963, for over 500 performances; Royal, Nottingham, Aug 1964, co-author and directed of The Roar of the Grease Paint—the Smell of the Crowd; Shubert, New York, May 1965, again directed (and also played Cocky) The Roar of the Grease Paint—the Smell of the Crowd; Prince of Wales, London, Dec 1972, played Bubba and directed The Good Old Bad Old Days, of which he was co-author; Uris, NY, Oct 1974, appeared in an entertainment with Henry Mancini; first appeared in films, 1946, in The Adventures of Dusty Bates, and has since been seen in numerous pictures, including Oliver Twist, Cockleshell Heroes, Hieronymus Merkin, Quilp (1974), etc; made his first appearance on television, Mar 1958.

Recreations: Photography, painting, fishing. *Address* c/o The Taralex Corporation, Suite 1101, 9255 Sunset Boulevard, Los Angeles, Calif 90069.

NEWMAN, Phyllis, actress and singer
b Jersey City, New Jersey, 19 Mar 1935; *d* of Arthur Newman and his wife Rachael; *e* Western Reserve Univ, Columbia Univ; *m* Adolph Green, the writer and performer; prepared for the stage with Wynn Handman.

Made her New York debut at the Imperial, 25 June 1953, as Sarah in Wish You Were Here; Theatre de Lys, Oct 1954, appeared in the revue I Feel Wonderful; understudied Judy Holliday as Ella Peterson in Bells Are Ringing at the Shubert, 1956–7; Alvin, Mar 1959, Jane Bennett in First Impressions; Cort, Oct 1959, Sylvie in Moonbirds; St James, Dec 1961, Martha Vail in Subways Are for Sleeping, for which she received the Antoinette Perry (Tony) Award; Fisher, Detroit, Mar 1965, Sura in Pleasures and Palaces; Shubert, 1967, took over from Barbara Harris as Eve, Princess Barbara, Ella and Passionella in The Apple Tree; Imperial, Oct 1971, Claire in On the Town; Westbury, Long Island, Music Fair, June 1972, played in Last of the Red Hot Lovers; Eugene O'Neill, 2 Oct 1972, took over from Barbara Barrie as Edna Edison in The Prisoner of Second Avenue; Pfister, Milwaukee, Wis, Mar 1974, appeared in cabaret; American Place, Feb 1975, directed Straws in the Wind; Imperial, 9 Mar 1975, appeared in Gala Tribute to Joshua Logan; Hudson Guild, May 1978, wrote and appeared in a one-woman musical, My Mother Was a Fortune Teller; 22 Steps, June 1979, co-wrote and appeared in The Madwoman of Central Park West; appeared in the film Picnic in 1955, and has since played in The Vagabond King, Let's Rock, To Find a Man (1972), etc.

Address: Actors Equity Association, 165 West 46th Street, New York, NY 10036.

NICHOLS, Mike, actor, author, director
b Berlin, Germany, 6 Nov 1931; *s* of Nicholaievitch

Peschkowsky (Dr Paul Nichols) and his wife Brigitte (Landauer); *e* University of Chicago; *m* (1) Patricia Scot (mar dis); (2) Margot Callas (mar dis).

Toured in cabaret with Elaine May performing material of their own composition; first appeared on the stage at the Playwrights Theatre Club, at the Compass Theatre, Chicago, Illinois; first appeared in New York at the John Golden, Oct 1960, in An Evening with Mike Nichols and Elaine May; at the Walnut, Philadelphia, Sept 1962, played Howard Miller in A Matter of Position; directed his first production at the Biltmore NY, Oct 1963, with Barefoot in the Park, for which he received the Antoinette Perry (Tony) Award; ; he has since directed the following plays: The Knack, Luv, 1964; The Odd Couple, 1965; received the Antoinette Perry Award as the Best Director, 1964 and 1965; received the New York Drama Critics Award, as Best Director of 1964, for Luv, and The Odd Couple; The Apple Tree, 1966; The Little Foxes, 1967; Plaza Suite, 1968 (Tony Award); The Prisoner of Second Avenue (Tony Award), 1971; Uncle Vanya, which he also co-adapted, 1973; Streamers, Comedians, 1976; The Gin Game, 1977; Drinks Before Dinner, 1978; The Gin Game (London), 1979; Long Wharf, Apr 1980, played George in Who's Afraid of Virginia Woolf; producer of Annie, The Gin Game, 1977; Washington, DC, Jan 1965, appeared in The 1965 Inaugural Gala; has directed the films Who's Afraid of Virginia Woolf? 1965; The Graduate, 1968, receiving the Academy Award and the New York Film Critics Award; Catch 22, 1970; Carnal Knowledge, 1971; The Day of the Dolphin, 1973; The Fortune, 1975; first appeared on television in 1958 on *Omnibus* and appearances include: *Jack Paar Show*, The Fabulous Fifties, the American version of *That Was the Week That Was*, Nov 1963, etc.

Recreations: Movies and horses. *Address:* c/o Marvin B Meyer, Rosenfeld, Meyer and Sussman, 9601 Wilshire Boulevard, Beverly Hills, Calif, 90210. *Tel:* 213–271–9144.

NICHOLS, Peter, dramatist
b 31 July 1927; *s* of Richard George Nichols, and his wife Violet Annie (Poole); *e* Bristol Grammar School; *m* Thelma Reed.

Formerly a teacher and actor; is the author of the following plays: The Hooded Terror, 1965; A Day In the Death of Joe Egg (*Evening Standard* Best New Play, 1967); The National Health, 1969 (*Evening Standard* Best Play); Forget-me-not Lane, 1971; Chez Nous, The Freeway, Harding's Luck (adapted from E Nesbit), 1974; Privates on Parade, 1976 (won *Evening Standard* Best Comedy, Society of West End Theatre Best Comedy and Ivor Novello Best British Musical awards); Born in the Gardens, 1979; has written twenty TV plays since 1959; his film scripts include: Georgy Girl, Joe Egg, National Health, and Changing Places; visiting playwright, Guthrie Theatre, Minneapolis, 1976.

Address: c/o Margaret Ramsay, 14a Goodwin's Court, St Martin's Lane, London, WC2. *Tel:* 01–240 0691.

NIMMO, Derek, actor
b Liverpool, 19 Sept 1932; *s* of Harry Robert Nimmo and his wife Marjorie Sudbury (Hardy); *e* Quarry School; *m* Patricia Brown.

Made his first professional appearance at the Hippodrome, Bolton, Sept 1952, as Ensign Blades in Quality Street; after experience in repertory and variety, made his London début at the Criterion, 1957, when he took over the part of Gaston in Waltz of the Toreadors; Apollo, Apr 1958, played Joseph in Duel of Angels; Aldwych, Apr 1959, Hubert Shannon in

How Say You?; Saville, Dec 1959, Pte Willie Maltravers in The Amorous Prawn; Criterion, Apr 1961, Michael Vickers in The Irregular Verb to Love; Vaudeville, July 1964, Rev Lionel Toop in See How They Run; toured South Africa, Dec 1964–Mar 1965, in Bedtime Story; Adelphi, Dec 1965, played Nicholas Wainwright in Charlie Girl, remaining with the production throughout its run of over 2000 performances, 1965–71, and touring Australia and New Zealand, 1971–2; Palladium, Dec 1972, Rodney Fortescue in Babes in the Wood; Apollo, Dec 1973, George in Why Not Stay for Breakfast?, followed by tour of South Africa and Australia, 1975–6; Connaught, Worthing, 1976, Bertie Wooster in Carry on Jeeves, and 1977, George Harper in Who Gets the Curtains; played Philip Markham in Move Over Mrs Markham in Hong Kong; Prince of Wales, Apr 1977, took over the part of George in Same Time Next Year; toured again in Why Not Stay for Breakfast, New Zealand, Aug 1977, and Australia and Dubai, 1979; Bromley, Apr 1978, in A Little Bit of Fluff; Comedy, Melbourne, May 1980, Arthur Pullen in Shut Your Eyes and Think of England; films, since 1959, include Casino Royale, Joey Boy, and One of our Dinosaurs is Missing (for Walt Disney Productions); television, since 1958, includes leads in comedy series such as: *All Gas and Gaiters,* his own series: *If It's Saturday It Must Be Nimmo* and *Just a Nimmo,* and documentaries.

Recreations: Collecting pottery, bricklaying. *Club:* Garrick. *Address:* c/o The Garrick Club, Garrick Street, London, WC2.

NORGATE, Matthew, dramatic critic
b London, 10 May 1901; *s* of G Le Grys Norgate and his wife Edith (Hickman); *e* University College School; *m* (1) Peggy Evans (mar dis); (2) Phyllis M Berry.

Formerly an actor; was secretary of the Fellowship of Players, 1922–4; Phoenix Society, 1924–7; Incorporated Stage Society, 1924–9; Greek Play Society, 1925–7; contributed dramatic criticism to the *Nation and Athenaeum*, 1927–31; London dramatic critic, *Western Morning News*, 1928–34, and *Liverpool Post*, 1935–8; contributed weekly article on Cabaret and Variety to *New Britain*, 1933–4, and to the *Evening Standard*, 1934–9; was radio critic of the *Evening Standard*, 1936; dramatic critic, *Daily Express*, 1938; film critic, *Evening Standard*, 1938–9, and BBC, 1939–43; on staff of BBC, 1940–63, first as sub-editor, later as scriptwriter of Radio Newsreel; has broadcast over 1000 times on theatre, cinema and other topics; film critic, *Sunday Chronicle*, 1944–6, *Time and Tide* (intermittently), *Tribune*, 1947–56, and *Truth*, 1956–7; has written occasionally on films for the *Guardian, The Times, The Spectator, Films and Filming*, etc; since 1945 has made lecture tours in Czechoslovakia, France, and Finland (for the British Council), and has been a British delegate at Film Festivals in many countries; appeared as drama critic in the television programme *Town and Around* 1963–5; broadcast a weekly film review in various radio programmes, 1964–9; regular contributor to West End theatre programmes, 1973–, and to *Drama*, 1976–; President of the Critics Circle, 1947–8; Hon Secretary, 1952–64, 1975–; Hon Treasurer, 1964–9.

Club: Savage. *Address:* 7 Lloyd Square, London, WC1. *Tel:* 01–837 4379.

NORMINGTON, John, actor
b Dukinfield, Cheshire, 28 Jan 1937; *s* of John Normington, and his wife Annie (Taylor); *e* Crescent Road School, Dukinfield; trained as an opera singer at the Northern School of Music, Manchester.

First appeared on the stage Mar 1950, at the Repertory Theatre, Oldham, as Hopcroft Minor in The Happiest Days of Your Life; in repertory at the Library, Manchester, 1959–62; Oxford Playhouse, 1962; made his first London appearance at the Arts, Aug 1962, as Jerry Lassiter in Infanticide in the House of Fred Ginger; Criterion, Jan 1963, Gunner in Misalliance; joined the Royal Shakespeare Company as an associate artist, 1963, and played parts including: Mortimer, Simpcox and Young Clifford in The Wars of the Roses, Stratford, 1963; Bardolph in Henry IV (both parts), Stratford, 1964; Dean in Puntila, Sam in The Homecoming, Antipholus in The Comedy of Errors; and Oblong Fitz Oblong in The Thwarting of Baron Bolligrew, Aldwych, 1965; Glendower and Shallow in Henry IV, Osric and Player Queen in Hamlet, Stratford, 1966; made his New York début at the Music Box, Jan 1967, as Sam in The Homecoming; left the RSC, 1967; at the Royal Court, played Feste in Twelfth Night, Jan 1968 and Commander in The Houses by the Green, Oct 1968; Arnaud, Guildford, 1969, Harry in On Such A Night; Royal Court, Aug 1969, Adam Hepple in Revenge; Apollo, Mar 1970, Kenilworth in The Happy Apple; Soho Poly, Aug 1970, Old Man in History of a Poor Old Man; Phoenix, Leicester, Sept 1972, David in Me Times Me; Soho Theatre, London, May 1973, directed RIP; Summer Theatre, Southwold, July 1973, directed Hay Fever; Theatre Royal, Brighton, May 1974, Father Vernon in The Prodigal Daughter; Royal Court, Aug 1974, George in Taking Stock; Forum, Billingham, Dec 1974, Muller in Underground; Nottingham Playhouse, Aug 1975, also Edinburgh Festival, Jaques in As You Like It; Royal Court, Nov 1975, Parson and Napoleon in The Fool; Theatre Royal, Bath, Apr 1976, Sainsbury in Donkey's Years; repeated the part of Jaques in As You Like It for the opening of the Riverside Studios, May 1976; Bush, Jan 1977, Martin Jones in German Skerries; May 1977, joined the National Theatre to play Dzerzhinsky in State of Revolution at the Lyttelton; July 1977, W H Auden in Letter to Lord Byron, a solo Platform Performance for the National; Lyttelton, Oct 1977, Etienne in The Lady from Maxim's; Traverse, Edinburgh, Aug 1978, Thomas in Rooting; Hampstead, Nov 1978, Jimmy in Comings and Goings; Olivier, Aug 1979, Touchstone in As You Like It; followed by Clarence in Richard III, Oct 1979 and Emperor Joseph II in Amadeus, Nov 1979; took part in Protest, Platform Performance at the Lyttelton, Mar 1980; first film, 1967, Inadmissible Evidence; subsequent pictures include: Rollerball and The 39 Steps; television appearances, since 1966, include Will Shakespeare, The Chester Mystery Plays and John Vassall, Spy; television appearances, since 1966, include the series: Her Majesty's Pleasure.

Favourite parts: Feste, Uncle Sam, Martin in German Skerries. *Recreations:* Opera, travel, especially to Greek Islands. *Address:* 66 Redcliffe Gardens, London SW10. *Tel:* 01–373 2949.

NORTHEN, Michael, lighting designer
b London, 12 May 1921; s of Major Ernest Northen and his wife Helen Clara (Gazeley-Hocken); e Canford School.

Began his theatrical career in 1939 as an ASM; after war service in the RAF he returned to the theatre, working at the Memorial Theatre, Stratford, and Covent Garden as well as in London theatres; at Stratford he designed Measure for Measure (with Peter Brook), 1950; Macbeth (with John Gielgud), 1952; Titus Andronicus (with Peter Brook), Hamlet, 1955; The Tempest (with Peter Brook), 1957; since 1957 he has devoted himself exclusively to lighting, designing for over 180 productions including: ballet, opera, pantomime and plays; the latter include: The World of Paul Slickey, The

Music Man, Alfie, Charlie Girl, Wait Until Dark, Man In A Glass Booth, Canterbury Tales, The Great Waltz, The Card, The Exorcism, and Betzi.

Recreations: Gardening, breeding and showing donkeys. *Club:* Green Room. *Address:* The Pheasantry, Bramshill Park, Basingstoke, Hants. *Tel:* 0251–262343.

NORTON, Elliot, drama critic and lecturer
b Boston, Massachusetts, 17 May 1903; s of William Laurence Norton and his wife Mary Elizabeth (Fitzgerald); e Harvard College (AB); m Florence E Stelmach.

A news reporter for the *Boston Post*, 1926–34; drama critic for the newspaper, 1934–56; drama critic for the *Boston Daily Record* and *Boston Sunday Advertiser*, 1956–62; 1962–71 was drama critic for the *Boston Record American* and *Boston Sunday Advertiser*; since 1971 has been drama critic of *Boston Herald American*; moderator of the television program *Elliot Norton Reviews* in Boston since 1958, receiving the George Foster Peabody Award, 1962; gave his thousandth program, Oct 1978; author of Broadway Down East, 1978; has written articles for *Theatre Arts, Theater Annual, Shakespeare Quarterly, Boston Magazine,* etc; Lecturer in Dramatic Literature at Boston University, 1954–67, and, since 1967, Adjunct Professor of Dramatic Literature; has served at various times on the faculties of Boston College, Emerson College, and, in 1963, of the Harvard Summer School; has received numerous awards, including the Boston College Citation of Merit, 1947; the Connor Memorial Award of Phi Alpha Tau, 1956; the Rodgers and Hammerstein College Presidents' Award for the person who has done most for theatre in Boston, 1962; the George Jean Nathan Award for the best dramatic criticism of the theatrical year 1963–4; received a special Antoinette Perry (Tony) Award, 1971; received the Humanities Award of the National Council of Teachers of English, 1971; New England Theatre Conference Award, 1974; designated a Grand Bostonian, 1978; President of the Boston Press Club, 1950–1 and 1951–2; President of the New England Theatre Conference, 1951–2 and 1952–3; received the following honorary degrees: Doctor of Journalism from Suffolk University, 1956; Doctor of Literature from Emerson College, 1963; Northeastern University, 1966; Merrimack College, 1977; Doctor of Humane Letters from Fairfield University, 1964; Boston College, 1970; St Joseph's College, 1976; Assumption College, 1978; Doctor of Letters, St Francis College, 1970; honorary member of the National Theatre Conference; Fellow of the American Academy of Arts and Sciences; Vice Chairman of the Massachusetts Council on the Arts and Humanities 1966–72.

Recreation: Gardening. *Clubs:* Harvard, Boston; Players, New York. *Address:* 126 Church Street, Watertown, Mass. *Tel:* WA 4–7731.

NUNN, Trevor, CBE (1978), director
b Ipswich, Suffolk, 14 Jan 1940; s of Robert Alexander Nunn and his wife Dorothy May (Piper); e Northgate Grammar School, Ipswich, and Downing College, Cambridge; m Janet Suzman.

After directing undergraduate productions at Cambridge, joined the Belgrade Theatre, Coventry, in 1962; his productions here from 1962–4 included: The Caucasian Chalk Circle, A View From the Bridge, and Peer Gynt; his first London production was The Thwarting of Baron Bolligrew for the Royal Shakespeare Company at the Aldwych, Dec 1965; he has since directed the following plays for the company, at Stratford unless otherwise stated: Henry IV (co-directed both parts), Tango (Aldwych; also played

Arthur), Henry V (co-directed), The Revenger's Tragedy, 1966; The Taming of the Shrew (also Aldwych; Los Angeles, 1968), The Relapse (Aldwych), 1967; King Lear, Much Ado About Nothing (also Los Angeles; Aldwych, 1969), 1968; The Winter's Tale (also toured Japan and Australia; revived at the Aldwych, 1970), Henry VIII (revived at the Aldwych, 1970), 1969; Hamlet, 1970; The Romans, a season of Shakespeare's four Roman plays, 1972 (also Aldwych, 1973); Macbeth, 1974 (also Aldwych, 1975); Hedda Gabler (Australia and Aldwych: own adaptation), 1975; Romeo and Juliet, The Comedy of Errors, Macbeth (The Other Place) also main theatre and Warehouse, 1977), 1976; King Lear, 1976 (Aldwych, 1977); A Comedy of Errors, Romeo and Juliet (Aldwych), Every Good Boy Deserves Favour (Royal Festival Hall) (revived at Mermaid, 1978), The Alchemist (Other Place), As You Like It (also Aldwych, 1978), 1977; The Merry Wives of Windsor (also Aldwych, 1980), Three Sisters (Other Place: Warehouse, 1980), Once In A Lifetime (Aldwych), 1979; Nicholas Nickleby (Aldwych), 1980; directed Antony and Cleopatra for TV, 1974, and in 1979 wrote and presented Shakespeare Workshop; directed a film of his Hedda Gabler, 1975; Artistic Director and Chief Executive of the Royal Shakespeare Company, 1968–78; currently Chief Executive and Joint Artistic Director; received the CBE in June 1978.

Recreations: None. *Address:* c/o Royal Shakespeare Theatre, Stratford-upon-Avon, Warwicks. *Tel:* 296655.

NYE, Carrie, actress
e Stephens College and Yale Drama School; *m* Dick Cavett.

Acted professionally since the age of fourteen; made her New York début at the Eugene O'Neill, 13 Apr 1960, as Inez in A Second String; Equity Library Theatre, Apr 1961, played Ondine in the play of that name; Helen Hayes, 1962, took over from Betsy von Furstenberg as Tiffany Richards in Mary, Mary; American Shakespeare Festival, Stratford, Connecticut, 1961, Celia in As You Like It, Lady Macduff in Macbeth, and Cressida in Troilus and Cressida; Fourth Street, Sept 1961, Regina Engstrand in Ghosts; Madison Avenue Playhouse, Feb 1963, Cecily Cardew in The Importance of Being Earnest; American Shakespeare Festival, Stratford, Connecticut, 1963, Regan in King Lear, Adriana in The Comedy of Errors, and Cleopatra in Caesar and Cleopatra; Circle in the Square, Dec 1963, Cassandra in The Trojan Women; Broadhurst, April 1965, Helen Walsingham in Half a Sixpence; Belasco, Sept 1965, Ursula Bailey in A Very Rich Woman; Circle in the Square, Dec 1965, Vittoria Corombona in The White Devil; Stratford, Connecticut, 1967, played Lady Macbeth; Cort, Apr 1969, Margaret Ross-Hughes in Home Fires; Studio Arena, Buffalo, NY, 1969, Elinor of Aquitaine in The Lion in Winter; Theatre Four, Apr 1972, Thelma in After Magritte, and Cynthia in The Real Inspector Hound; Playhouse-in-the-Park, Cincinnati, Ohio, Mar 1973, Blanche du Bois in A Streetcar Named Desire; Goodman, Chicago, Oct 1976, Gilda in Design for Living; Williamstown Festival, Aug 1977, Anna Petrovna in Platonor; Stage West, Nov 1977, Regina Giddens in The Little Foxes; McCarter, Princeton, 1979, in No Time for Comedy; Williamstown, Aug 1979, Yelena in Children of the Sun.

Address: Actors Equity Association, 165 West 46th Street, New York, NY 10036.

NYE, Pat, OBE, actress
b London, 11 Feb 1908; *d* of Ralph Nye and his wife Elizabeth Innes Hall (Rose); *e* privately, Lausanne University and Lausanne Conservatoire of Music; studied for the stage at the Royal Academy of Dramatic Art.

Made her first appearance on the stage at the Repertory Theatre, Croydon, Mar 1933, as Frau Feldmann in Autumn Crocus; first appeared in London, at the Shaftesbury, 23 May 1933, as Martha Brown in Gallows Glorious; has been engaged in management ever since 1934; was managing director of the repertory company at the Theatre Royal, Margate, 1934–7; managing director, Park Theatre, Hanwell, 1937–8; managing director, Pier Theatre, Lowestoft, 1939; from Oct 1939, to April 1946, was with the WRNS, in which she was Chief Officer, and was awarded the OBE; after the War, appeared at the Aldwych, Nov 1946, as the Policewoman in And No Birds Sing; 1947–8, manager of the Repertory company, Bexhill-on-Sea; Lyric, Apr 1949, played the Neighbour in The Power of Darkness; was managing director of the Bedford Theatre, Camden Town, from Oct 1949; opened with a revival of Lady Audley's Secret, in which she played Lady Audley, and which was transferred to the Princes Theatre, Nov 1949; Oct 1949, played Mrs Pirbright in A Wind on the Heath; she appeared in a number of parts at the Bedford, Jan–June 1950, including: Mrs O'Kelly in The Shaughraun, Anna Halvorsen in The Leopard, Mrs Nixon in Craven House, Cornelia Carlyle in East Lynne, Tabitha in The Silver King, Catherine in The Bells, and Cowslip in Black-Eye'd Susan; Ambassadors', Aug 1950, played Mrs Playbill in For Love or Money; Arts, Nov 1950, Miss Stulkeley in Preserving Mr Panmure; at the Q, Feb 1951, played Minnie Simpson in A Dog for Delmonte; made her first appearance on the New York stage at the Ziegfeld, Dec 1951, as Ftatateeta in Caesar and Cleopatra, and an Attendant on Octavia in Antony and Cleopatra; Plymouth, NY, Oct 1956, Lysistrata in a revival of The Apple Cart; Martin Beck, NY, Nov 1960, played Hippobomene in The Rape of the Belt; returned to England, 1962; Savoy, Feb 1963, played the Nurse in Trap For a Lonely Man; Malvern Festival, July 1965, played Aunt Helen in The Living Room; Marlowe, Canterbury, Oct 1965, Medea in Face to Face; Chichester Festival, July 1971, Ftatateeta in Caesar and Cleopatra; also Countess von Stainz in Reunion in Vienna, which she repeated at the Piccadilly, Feb 1972; has also appeared in television plays in the US, and in England, including: Père Goriot, Little Women and Edna, the Inebriate Woman; first entered films, 1947.

Favourite parts: Agatha Payne in The Old Ladies and Lysistrata in The Apple Cart. *Recreations:* Swimming and motoring. *Address:* Box 1500, Sag Harbor, NY 11963.

NYPE, Russell, actor
b Zion, Illinois, 26 Apr 1924; *s* of William Nype and his wife Elizabeth (Huisinga); *e* Lake Forest College (BA 1943); *m* Diantha Lawrence.

Made his New York début at the 46th Street, 31 Oct 1949, as Leo Hubbard in Regina; Winter Garden, Mar 1950, Freddie in Great to Be Alive; Imperial, Oct 1950, Kenneth Gibson in Call Me Madam, for which he received the Antoinette Perry (Tony) Award; Alcazar, San Francisco, 1954, Bud Walters in Anniversary Waltz, and subsequently played this part at the Ritz in Los Angeles; toured, 1955, as Charlie Reader in The Tender Trap; Ethel Barrymore, May 1956, Deerfield Prescott in Wake Up, Darling; New York City Center, Sept 1957, Enoch Snow in Carousel; Lunt-Fontanne, Oct 1958, George Randolph Brown in Goldilocks, for which he received the Tony Award; 175 East Broadway Playhouse, Apr 1960, Stitch Allenstock in Brouhaha; Coconut Grove Playhouse, Miami, Florida, 1961, Albert Peterson in Bye, Bye Birdie; toured, 1962, as Hogan in Under the Yum-Yum Tree; New York City Center, Jan 1963, Jeff Douglas in Brigadoon; May 1964, Freddy Eynsford-Hill in

My Fair Lady; toured, 1965–6, as F Sherman in The Owl and the Pussycat; Booth, May 1967, Dr Alec Rice in The Girl in the Freudian Slip; New York City Center, Dec 1967, again played Jeff Douglas in Brigadoon; Coconut Grove Playhouse, 1968, again played Kenneth Gibson in Call Me Madam; Theatre de Lys, May 1968, Elyot Chase in Private Lives; St James, Mar 1970, took over as Cornelius Hackl in Hello, Dolly! with Ethel Merman as Dolly; toured, 1971, as Tyler Rayburn in Light Up the Sky; Goodman, Chicago, 1971, Robert Audley in Lady Audley's Secret, and repeated this part at the Washington, DC, Theater Club, Aug 1972, and at the Eastside Playhouse, NY, Oct 1972; John Drew, Easthampton, NY, July 1973, played in the revue The Great American Musical Comedy; appeared with the Hartford, Conn, Stage Company, 1973–4 season; toured, 1975, in Sabrina Fair; Los Angeles, 1979, Col Pickering in My Fair Lady; most recent film Can't Stop the Music, 1980; appeared regularly on the *Ed Sullivan Show,* 1950–8, and has played on the *Milton Berle Show*, in the mini-series *Dorothy*, 1979, etc; has also played extensively in cabaret in NY, Chicago, Las Vegas, etc.

Address: Actors Equity Association, 165 West 46th Street, New York, NY 10036.

O

O'BRIAN, Hugh (*né* Hugh Charles Krampe), actor
b Rochester, New York, 19 Apr 1925; *s* of Hugh John Krampe and his wife Edith; *e* Univ of Cincinnati and City College of Los Angeles; served as a drill instructor in the US Marine Corps.

Made his New York debut at the Imperial, summer 1959, when he took over from Andy Griffiths in the title role of Destry; Morosco, 25 Dec 1961, played Romain in First Love; Melodyland, Los Angeles, Cal, Oct 1963, played Sky Masterson in the musical Guys and Dolls; summer tour, 1965, repeated this last part, and again played it at the New York City Center, June 1966; Blackstone, Chicago, Ill., Oct 1967, Julian in Cactus Flower, and subsequently toured; Billy Rose, Mar 1972, co-produced The Country Girl; Arlington Park Playhouse, Arlington Heights, Ill, Jan 1972, played Murray Burns in A Thousand Clowns; toured, 1972, in 1776; Arlington Park Playhouse, 1973, played in The Desperate Hours; Huntingdon Hartford, Los Angeles, Jan 1974, Walter Burns in The Front Page; Drury Lane, Chicago, Jul 1974, Alan Baker in Come Blow Your Horn; Walnut Street, Philadelphia, Aug 1976, George Washington in The Decision; produced and directed a USO tour of Guys and Dolls to the Far East; made his film debut in Never Fear, 1950, and has since appeared in Little Big Horn, Broken Lance, There's No Business Like Show Business, in Harm's Way, Ten Little Indians, The Shootist, Game of Death (1979), and many others; made his television debut in *Arch Oboler's Mystery Theatre*, 1949, and has since appeared in many dramatic series, including six years as *Wyatt Earp*, Dial M for Murder, *Fantasy Island*, etc; has founded various producing companies, including HOB Inc; founded the Hugh O'Brian Annual Acting Awards at UCLA, 1965.

Recreations: Sailing, tennis, skindiving, swimming. *Address:* Actors Equity Association, 165 West 46th Street, New York, NY 10036.

O'BRIEN, Maureen, actress
b Liverpool, 29 June 1943; *d* of Leo O'Brien and his wife Eileen (Connolly); *e* Notre Dame High School, Liverpool; *m* Michael B Moulds; trained for the stage at the Central School of Speech and Drama.

Made her first appearance at the Everyman, Liverpool, Sept 1964, as Lady Mortimer in Henry IV (Part I); Hampstead, Dec 1965, played Beauty in Beauty and the Beast; Garrick, Jan 1967, Celia in Volpone; Chichester Festival, season 1967, Sibley Sweetland in The Farmer's Wife and Dorinda in The Beaux' Stratagem; season 1968, Miranda in The Tempest and Gladys in The Skin of Our Teeth; Haymarket, Oct 1968, Isabelle in Ring Round the Moon; Stratford, Ontario, Festival, season 1970, Portia in The Merchant of Venice and Imogen in Cymbeline; Theatre Royal, Windsor, 1972, Rana in Arms and the Man; Chichester, May 1973, Emilia in The Director of the Opera and Nina in The Seagull; again played Nina at Greenwich, Jan 1974; Basement Theatre, July 1974, played the Girl in a lunchtime production, Rape; ICA, Sept 1974, Molly in The Iron Harp; Crucible, Sheffield, 1975, Vivie in Mrs Warren's Profession; Young Vic, 1975, the Young Witch in Woodpainting; Crucible, Sheffield, 1976, Rosalind in As You Like It; Chichester

Festival, 1977, Evelyn Daly in Waters of the Moon; Belgrade, Coventry, Sept 1977, Leontine in 13 Rue de l'Amour, and Oct 1977, Ann in Treats; King's Head, Nov 1977, Beth in Confession Fever; Belgrade, Coventry, Oct 1978, Stepdaughter in Six Characters in Search of an Author, and Apr 1979, Levidulcia in The Atheist's Tragedy; first appeared on television in England in *Doctor Who* in 1965, and most recently in The Lost Boys and The Serpent Son; author of a children's play, The Great Gobstopper Show, 1977.

Favourite parts: Imogen, Rosalind. *Address:* c/o William Morris Agency, 149 Wardour Street, London W1.

O'BRIEN, Timothy, designer
b Shillong, Assam, India, 8 Mar 1929; *s* of Brian Palliser Tieghe O'Brien, and his wife Elinor Laura (Mackenzie); *e* Wellington College, Cambridge Univ, and Yale University.

Was Head of Design, ABC Television, from 1955–66; his designs for the stage include the following productions, in London unless otherwise stated: The Bald Primadonna and The New Tenant (double-bill), 1956; Hunter's Moon, Five Finger Exercise, 1958; The Darling Buds of May, 1959; Don't Shoot, We're English, 1960; Henry IV (Part I), Progress to the Park, 1961; Next Time I'll Sing to You, Licence to Murder, Luv, Poor Bitos, 1963; Hedda Gabler, Entertaining Mr Sloane, A Scent of Flowers, Poor Bitos (New York), Waiting for Godot, 1964; Travelling Light, A Scent of Flowers (Stuttgart), 1965; became an associate artist of the Royal Shakespeare Company, 1966, and designed for them in Stratford or London, Tango, Days in the Trees, Joey, Joey (not RSC), Staircase, 1966; All's Well That Ends Well, As You Like It, Romeo and Juliet, 1967; The Merry Wives of Windsor, Troilus and Cressida, The Latent Heterosexual, 1968; Pericles, Women Beware Women, Bartholomew Fair, 1969; Measure for Measure, 1970; work with Tazeena Firth includes, for RSC, The Merchant of Venice, Enemies, The Man of Mode, 1971; The Lower Depths, The Island of the Mighty, 1972; Richard II, Love's Labour's Lost, 1973; Summerfolk, 1974; The Merry Wives of Windsor, The Marrying of Ann Leete, 1975; The Zykovs, 1976; for National Theatre, Next of Kin, 1974, John Gabriel Borkman, 1975; Troilus and Cressida, Force of Habit, 1976; Tales from the Vienna Woods, Bedroom Farce, 1977; also designed Evita, London, 1978 and New York, 1979; for the Royal Opera, The Knot Garden, 1970, Peter Grimes, 1975, The Rake's Progress, 1979; for English National Opera, The Bassarids, 1974; work abroad (also with Miss Firth), includes: La Cenerentola, Oslo 1972; Pericles, Comédie Française, 1974; The Bassarids, Frankfurt, 1975; Wozzeck, Adelaide Festival, 1976; Falstaff, Berlin, 1977; Cunning Little Vixen, Gothenburg, and A Midsummer Night's Dream, Sydney, 1978; Peter Grimes, Gothenburg, 1979; Mr O'Brien designed the exhibition Trafalgar, at Madame Tussaud's, 1966, and Tussaud's in Amsterdam, 1970; designed the film Night Must Fall, 1964; joint winner of individual Gold Medal for set design, Prague Quadriennale, 1975.

Address: 33 Lansdowne Gardens, London, SW8. *Tel:* 01–622 5384.

O'CALLAGHAN, Richard, actor
b London, 4 Mar 1940; *s* of Valentine Ernest Cozens Brooks

and his wife Patricia Lawlor (Hayes); *e* Wimbledon College; *m* Juliet Elizabeth Alliston; trained for the stage at LAMDA.

His first professional appearance was at the Royal Court, 20 Apr 1965, as Moritz in Spring Awakening; at the same theatre, 1966, played four parts in Ubu Roi, July, Brother Ched in Three Men for Colverton, Sept, Fleance in Macbeth, Oct, and Ivan Cheprakov in A Provincial Life, also Oct; Swan, Worcester, 1969, Gerald Popkiss in Rookery Nook; Royal Court, Jan 1970, Alvin Hanker in Three Months Gone, transferring to the Duchess, Mar 1970; Criterion, Jul 1971, Joey Keyston in Butley; Theatre Upstairs, Dec 1972, Worsely in Owners; The Howff, Nov 1973, Peter in Kingdom Cottage; parts with the Young Vic, 1974–5, included Guildenstern in Rosencrantz and Guildenstern are Dead; Royal Court, Oct 1974, Eugene Grimley in The Great Caper; Criterion Aug 1975, again played Guildenstern in the Young Vic's Rosencrantz and Guildenstern Are Dead; Almost Free, Apr 1976, appeared in Dirty Linen; Derby Playhouse, June 1976, Konstantin in The Seagull, transferring with the production to the Duke of York's; Orange Tree, Richmond, Nov 1977, in Mr Whatnot; Open Space, Feb 1979, Martin Taylor in Brimstone and Treacle; films, since his first, The Bofors Gun, 1968, include Carry On Loving, Butley, and Galileo; TV, since 1965 includes Professional Foul, Born and Bred, Renoir My Father.

Favourite parts: Alvin Hanker, Joey Keyston, and Guildenstern. *Recreations:* Going to the movies, dropping in on friends. *Address:* c/o Duncan Heath Associates Ltd, The Studio, 57 Redcliffe Road, London SW10 9NQ. *Tel:* 01–351 4142.

O'CONNELL, Arthur, actor
b New York City, 29 Mar 1908; *s* of Michael O'Connell and his wife Julia (Byrne); *e* St John's High School and College, Brooklyn; *m* Anne Hall Dunlop; served in the US Army, 1941–45.

Made his debut at the Franklin Park, Dorchester, Mass, Dec 1929, in The Patsy; played in vaudeville in an act called Any Family, and later toured with Bert Lahr and other vaudeville comedians, 1931–34; made his London debut at the St James's, during 1938, when he took over as Pepper White in Golden Boy; made his New York stage debut at the 46th Street, 14 June 1943, as the Orderly in the one-act play Button Your Lip in a production called The Army Play by Play, which he also directed; while still in the Army performed with the Army Emergency Relief, including a performance for President Roosevelt and Queen Wilhelmina of the Netherlands on 19 June 1943; Lyceum, Dec 1945, directed Brighten the Corner; toured, Sept 1948–Apr 1949, with the Margaret Webster Shakespeare Company as Polonius in Hamlet and Banquo and Siward in Macbeth; Playhouse, NY, Dec 1949, played Fred Johnson in How Long Till Summer; Shubert, Boston, Nov 1951, Father John in Child of the Morning; New York City Center, Jan 1952, Postman in Anna Christie; ANTA Playhouse, Mar 1952, again played Pepper White in Golden Boy; Music Box, Feb 1953, Howard Bevins in Picnic; Broadhurst, Dec 1954, Will Harrison in Lunatics and Lovers; Ambassador, Nov 1958, Charlie Lawton in Come a Day; Locust, Philadelphia, Jan 1962, Cornelius V Stolts in The Umbrella; entered films for some years, then, at the Ahmanson, Los Angeles, Dec 1970, played Ray in Remote Asylum; made his film debut in England, 1938, in Murder in Soho, and has since appeared in numerous others, including Citizen Kane, Picnic, The Solid Gold Cadillac, Bus Stop, Anatomy of a Murder, Huckleberry Finn (1974); has also appeared extensively on television in various dramatic series.

Recreations: Horses, gardening, cooking, *Address:* Actors Equity Association, 165 West 46th Street, New York, NY 10036.

O'CONNOR, Kevin, actor, director, producer
b Honolulu, Hawaii, 7 May 1938; *e* Univ of Hawaii, Univ of California, and San Francisco State; prepared for the stage at the Neighborhood Playhouse.

Made his NY debut at the Cherry Lane, 10 Feb 1965, as Harry in Up to Thursday; Martinique, 11 Apr 1962, played Office Boy in Thank You, Miss Victoria, Frankie Basta in Birdbath, and appeared in This Is The Rill Speaking; 12 Apr played Younger Actor in War, Stu in Chicago in a production with the overall title 6 from LaMama; Cherry Lane, Feb 1967, Walter in The Rimers of Eldritch; Stage 73, Mar 1968, the title role of Tom Paine; St. Clement's Church, Feb 1969, Toby in Boy on a Straight-Back Chair; ANTA, Feb 1970, Julius Esperanza in Gloria and Esperanza; Gramercy Arts, Apr 1970, Alec Kooning in Dear Janet Rosenberg, Dear Mr Kooning, and Jake in Jakey Fat Boy; played with the Milwaukee, Wisconsin, Repertory Theatre in the 1970–71 season; Forum, Nov 1971, Douglas Two in Grail Green and Douglas in Three Street Koans in the double bill Kool Aid; Artistic Director, Theatre at St Clement's Church, 1972–75; here in June 1972 he played Abe in Eyes of Chalk; Nov 1972, played in The Funny Men Are in Trouble; Jan 1973, produced Moon Mysteries; Apr 1973, directed Whiskey; in addition to the above presented Of Mice and Men, Ceremony for a Murdered Black, Two by Paul Austin, 1972; The White Whore and the Bit Player (in both English and Spanish), The Golden Daffodil Dwarf, The Open Theatre in Nightwalk, Terminal, and The Mutation Show, The Richard Morse Mime Theatre, Secrets of the Citizens Correction Committee, the Theatre Asylum production of Babel— Babble, The Open Eye production of Moon Mysteries, The Greatest Fairy Story Ever Told, 1973; Chelsea Manhattan, Oct 1973, played Glendenning in The Contractor; St Clement's Church, Mar 1974, The Kid in Alive and Well in Argentina, which he also directed; Mar 1974, Man in Duet and Trio; also presented The Petrified Forest, Disquieting Muses, Theatre Laboratory of Denmark in Studio II, The Duo Theatre Company in La Ramera de la Cueva (The Harlot of the Cave), Bread and Puppet Theatre in First Garbagemen Cantata, Or the Grey Lady Cantata No 4, and The Meadow Green, In Our Time, Electra, 1974; Manhattan Theater Club, June 1974, played James in The Morning After Optimism; St Clement's Church, Oct 1974, played Man in Figures in the Sand; same theatre presented Nuts, The Fall and Redemption of Man, The Robber Bridegroom, The King of the United States, Enter a Free Man, Icarus's Mother, 1974; presented War Babies, Joe's Opera, Workers, The Medicine Show Theatre Ensemble in Frogs, Waking Up to Beautiful Things, The Red Blue-Grass Western Flyer Show, 1975; The Other Stage, Nov 1975, played Jesse James in Jesse and the Bandit Queen; St Clement's June 1976, directed Virility; appeared there in Memphis is Gone, Jan 1977; at the Theatre of the Open Eye appeared in Gauguin in Tahiti, Dec 1976, and Natures, May 1977; Theatre Genesis, Feb 1978, directed The Day Roosevelt Died; Perry Street, Mar 1978, appeared in Scenes from Country Life; appeared in the films Coming Apart, 1969, Let's Scare Jessica to Death, Welcome to the Club, 1971, etc.

Address: Leaverton Associates Ltd, 1650 Broadway, New York, NY 10019.

O'CONOR, Joseph, actor
b Dublin, Ireland, 14 Feb 1916; *s* of Daniel O'Conor and his

wife Frances (Call); *e* Cardinal Vaughan School, and London University; *m* Naita Moore; studied for the stage at the Royal Academy of Dramatic Art.

Made his first appearance on the stage at the Embassy Theatre, 29 Nov 1939, as Flavius, Trebonius and Titinius in Julius Caesar (in modern dress), playing the same parts at His Majesty's, Dec 1939; after the War, appeared at the Aldwych, Oct 1946, as Conrade in Much Ado About Nothing; Boltons, May 1947, Miles Forrester in Give Me the Sun; Q, Oct 1947, James Vane in The Picture of Dorian Gray; Playhouse, Feb 1948, Captain Ridley in Cockpit; Q, Apr 1948, Faust in a new version of the play of that name; Open Air Theatre, June–Sept 1948, played Orlando, Philip the Bastard, and Oberon; Bedford, Camden Town, Jan–June 1949, was with Donald Wolfit, and played Othello and Iago alternatively, and Hamlet; at Canterbury, for the Festival, July 1949, played Michael in Zeal of Thy House; Theatre Royal, Windsor, from Jan 1950, played the leading parts in the repertory company; at the Edinburgh Festival, 1950, appeared as King Malcolm in Saxon Saint; at the Q, Jan 1951, Alan Wainwright in Virtuoso; again appeared with the Windsor Repertory Company, 1951; at the York Festival of Arts, 1951, appeared as Christ in the Mystery Plays; at the Westminster, Oct 1951, played Sean Murphy in A Priest In the Family; New, Apr 1952, played Lord Thomas Seymour in The Young Elizabeth; toured, 1953, as the Second Workman in Purple Dust; Duke of York's, Jan 1954, Hank Teagle in The Big Knife; York Festival of Arts, 1954, again played Christ in the Mystery Plays; Citizens Theatre, Glasgow, 1954–5, appeared as Benedick in Much Ado About Nothing and Raphael in Tobias and the Angel; Arts, London, June 1955, played Capt Adam Brant in Mourning Becomes Electra; Citizen's, Glasgow, Sept 1955, Baron Nicholas de Balbus in The Wayward Saint; Guildford Repertory, Nov 1955, played Michael O'Riordan in his own play The Iron Harp; was member of the Bristol Old Vic Company, 1956–8, and played the following parts: Kent in King Lear, Georges Danton in The Empty Chair, Higgins in Pygmalion, Bottom in A Midsummer Night's Dream, Andrew Undershaft in Major Barbara, the title-part in Othello, Uncle Fritz in Oh! My Papa!, and Michael O'Riordon in The Iron Harp; in this last play he subsequently toured; Canterbury Festival, June 1958, played King Artaban in Christ's Comet; joined the Old Vic Company for their United States tour, 1958–9, to play Chorus in Henry V, and Polonius in Hamlet; Lincoln Cathedral, May 1959, played Becket in Murder in the Cathedral; Pembroke, Croydon, Apr 1960, Nicolas in The Lotus-Eaters; Globe, Sept 1960, took over the part of the Duke in A Man For All Seasons; Strand, June 1961, played Claudius in Hamlet; Glasgow Citizens', Sept 1961, the Inca Atahualpa in his own play Inca; Mermaid, Nov 1961, played Julian in The Long Sunset; Old Vic, Mar–July 1962, played Buckingham in Richard III, the title-part of Julius Caesar, Gonzalo in The Tempest, and also directed Inca; Empire, Sunderland, Feb 1963, directed Hamlet; St Martin's, Mar 1963, took over Father Arnall and The Preacher in Stephen D; Mermaid, Oct 1963, Stepan in The Possessed; Empire, Sunderland, Feb 1964, played the title-part in King Lear, and directed The Merchant of Venice, at the North-East Theatre Festival; Oxford Playhouse, Apr–May 1964, played Vershinin in The Three Sisters, and Nikolai Dor in The Twelfth Hour; Empire, Sunderland, Mar 1965, played Falstaff in Henry IV (Part I), directed The Winter's Tale and played Robert Wise in his own play The Third Picture; Director of North-East Theatre Festival, 1964 and 1965; Belgrade, Coventry, July 1965, Wally Cross in The Big Breaker; Thorndike, Leatherhead, Mar 1968, played the title-role in King Lear; Playhouse,

Oxford, Apr 1969, Prospero in The Tempest; Abbey, Dublin, Sept 1969, O'Neill in The O'Neill; Round House, Nov 1969, Pontius Pilate in Son of Man; Duke of York's, July 1970, co-directed The Heretic, playing the part of Prior Gabrielli; Thorndike, Leatherhead, Nov 1970, directed Hamlet; Richmond and tour, Feb 1971, Dr Sloper in The Heiress; at the Shaw, played Bert Careless in Slip Road Wedding, Oct 1971, and Capulet in Romeo and Juliet, Feb 1972; Thorndike, Leatherhead, Mar 1973, Sir Antony Absolute in The Rivals, also at Bucks County Playhouse, Pa; at the Howff, Dec 1973, directed Hamlet and played Claudius; Old Vic, 1974, appeared for the National Theatre as Alonso in The Tempest, Mar, and Herr Gabor in Spring Awakening, May; Maynardville, Cape Town, 1975, again played Claudius; Greenwich, 1975, played the King of France in All's Well That Ends Well, July, and the Duke in Measure for Measure, Aug; St George's; Islington, season 1976, playd in Apr, Toby Belch in Twelfth Night, June, Friar Laurence in Romeo and Juliet, July, George, Duke of Clarence and Cardinal Bouchier in Richard III; season 1977, May, directed Merchant of Venice, June, played Vicentio in Measure for Measure, July, Polonius in Hamlet, Aug, Shallow in The Merry Wives of Windsor; for the Welsh Drama Company, played Prospero in The Tempest, 1976; Lear, and More in A Man For All Seasons, 1977; for the Bristol Old Vic, 1978, his part included Duke Frederick and Duke Senior in As You Like It, Vermandero in The Changeling, Sorin in The Seagull; again at St George's, 1979, as Soothsayer in Julius Caesar, Apr, John of Gaunt in Richard II, May, and Duke Senior in As You Like It, June; Thorndike, Leatherhead, Sept 1979, directed Saint Joan; entered films, 1950; author of The Iron Harp (which received the Foyle Award for New Plays, 1956), Dagger's Point, 1958; Inca, 1961; The Tumble Stone (musical), 1962; A Lion Trap, 1963; The Third Picture, 1964.

Favourite parts: Lear and Falstaff. *Recreations:* Judo, cricket and guitar playing. *Address:* 18 Melville Road, Barnes, London, SW13. *Tel:* 01–748 4946.

O'DONOVAN, Desmond, director
b Burbage, Leicester, 2 Feb 1933; *s* of Charles O'Donovan, and his wife Mary (Allen); *e* Stonyhurst and Oxford University; formerly a Dominican friar.

His first production on the stage was in 1961 at the Playhouse, Salisbury, when he directed The Tiger and the Horse; in Nov 1962 at the Arts, London, he directed A Cheap Bunch of Nice Flowers; subsequent productions he has directed, in London unless otherwise stated, include: Spring Awakening, 1963; The Royal Hunt of the Sun (co-directed at Chichester and for the Old Vic), 1964; the Sleepers' Den, Spring Awakening, Trelawny of the 'Wells' (Chichester/Old Vic), Easter, 1965; The Knack, The Duchess of Malfi (Off-Broadway), The Clandestine Marriage (Chichester), Three Men for Colverton, The Lion and the Jewel, 1966; Chikamatzu Suicides, A View to the Common, 1967; Hamlet, The Tempest (both St John's, Smith Square), 1970.

Recreation: Talking. *Address:* 29 Wandsworth Common North Side, London, SW18.

OGILVIE, George, director and former actor
b Goulburn, New South Wales, 5 Mar 1931; *s* of Stewart Duthie Ogilvie and his wife Agnes Davidson (Murray): toured England in a fit-up company, 1953, in a number of roles; returned to Australia, 1956, as an actor with the Elizabethan Theatre Trust; joined the Union Theatre Com-

pany, 1958, (later Melbourne Theatre Company), appearing in a number of parts and making his debut as a director, 1958, with Blood Wedding; studied mime under Jacques Lecoq in Paris, 1960–2; with Julian Chagrin devised and appeared in the revue Chaganog, Lyceum, Edinburgh (for Festival), Aug 1964, subsequently at the Vaudeville, London, Dec 1964, and St Martin's, Apr 1965, taught for two years at the Central School, RSC Stratford and elsewhere; returned to Australia, 1966, as Associate Director, Melbourne Theatre Company; directed productions over five years including The Three Sisters, The Royal Hunt of the Sun, The Knack, The Country Wife, and Burke's Company (world premiere); study tour of Europe, 1970; on his return to Australia, directed productions including The Government Inspector, The Philanthropist, Conduct Unbecoming, Patate, 1971; Trelawny of the 'Wells', Uncle Vanya, The Alchemist, 1972; Artistic Director, South Australian Theatre Company, 1972–7, where his productions included Alpha Beta, The Comedy of Errors, Journey's End, Equus, The Winslow Boy, and Coriolanus (Festival of Arts, 1976); directed The Kingfisher (tour), 1978; has directed operas in South Australia and at the Sydney Opera House, including Don Giovanni, Sydney, 1978.

Address: 3 Fishburn Street, Red Hill, Canberra, ACT. *Tel:* 950735.

O'HORGAN, Tom, director and composer
b Chicago, Ill, 3 may 1926; *e* DePaul University.

Directed many plays off-off Broadway, most notably at the Cafe LaMama for Ellen Stewart, before directing his first production off-Broadway, 6 from LaMama, at the Martinique, 11 Apr 1966, the six plays performed on two consecutive evenings being Thank You, Miss Victoria, This Is the Rill Speaking, Birdbath (in Bill One), and War, The Recluse, and Chicago (in Bill Two); also composed the music for these plays; since then has directed Tom Paine (also music), 1967; directed the LaMama troupe in Tom Paine at the Edinburgh Festival, Sept 1967, and at the Vaudeville, London, Oct 1967; Times Square, Futz (also music), Hair (on Broadway and at the Shaftesbury, London), 1968; author of the play Massachusetts Trust produced in Sept 1968; directed and wrote the music for Lenny, conceived for the stage and directed Jesus Christ, Superstar, conceived for the stage, directed, and co-produced Inner City, 1971; directed Dude, 1972; directed Sergeant Pepper's Lonely Hearts Club Band on the Road, 1974; The Leaf People, 1975; The Architect and the Emperor of Abyssinia 1976, Hair (re-staged), 1977; directed The Tempest (also wrote music), Feb 1978.

OLAF, Pierre (*né* Pierre-Olaf Trivier), actor
b Cauderan, France, 14 July 1928; *s* of Pierre Alexis Trivier and his wife Anne Marie (Lenglet); *e* Bordeaux and Paris.

First appeared on the stage at the Théâtre de Poche, Paris, June 1947, as the Innkeeper and a Spanish Soldier in Les Espagnols au Danemark; Théâtre des Arts, Paris, 1948, played the Bellboy in The Skipper Next to God, and played this part in Brussels and Geneva, Feb–Mar 1949; Vieux-Colombier, Paris, 1949, Evariste in La Tour Eiffel Qui Tue; Athénée, 1949, played Damis in Tartuffe; La Bruyère, 1951, played in the revue Dugudu; Quartier Latin, 1953, played Jonathan in Folies Douces; Quartier Latin, 1954, again played Evariste in La Tour Eiffel Qui Tue; Théâtre des Variétés, 1954, played in the revue Jupon Volé; Renaissance, 1955, Phillippe in Orvet; made his London début at the Garrick, 3 Nov 1955, in the revue La Plume de Ma Tante; Théâtre de Paris, 1957, played in the revue Pommes à l'Anglaise; made his New York début at the Royale, 11 Nov 1958, in the revue La Plume de Ma Tante; Imperial, Apr

1961, played Jacquot in Carnival; Municipal Opera, St Louis, Missouri, and Starlight, Kansas City, Kansas, summer, 1963, played Passepartout in Around the World in 80 Days; Barter, Abingdon, Virginia, 1963, played The Golux in The 13 Clocks, which he also directed; Morosco, Mar 1964, Jerome Lahutte in A Murderer Among Us; Theatre Four, Sept 1964, Ferdinand Goddard in That Hat!; ANTA Washington Square, 1966, took over as Sancho Panza in Man of La Mancha; New York City Center, Dec 1968, Jacquot in Carnival; Ahmanson, Los Angeles, Mar 1970, Quillery in Idiots' Delight; Theatre des Variétés, Paris, Nov 1972, appeared in the revue Branquingnols; has also appeared in cabaret in Paris, notably at the Pigalle in sketches by Jacques Prévert, at La Rose Rouge in sketches by Tardieu, Billet-doux, and Van Parys, and at La Galérie 55 in a one-man act; first appeared in films in 1946 in Le Diable au Corps (Devil in the Flesh), and has since appeared in Les Trésors des Pieds Nickèles, 1949, Virgile, 1951, Miguette et Sa Mère, Trois Femmes, French Can-Can, The Art of Love, Camelot, Le Petit Theatre de Jean Renoir (1974), etc; has appeared on television in France, 1953, in Entrez dans la Danse, Christophe Colombe, Liliom, in London in The Jack Hylton Show, and in the US in He Who Gets Slapped, 1961, The Enchanted Nutcracker, and in *The Perry Como Show, The Jack Paar Show,* etc; author of the book The Fortune of the Verb To Be, 1971.

Recreations: Painting, writing. *Address:* 33 Tennessee Avenue, Long Beach, New York. *Tel:* GE 2–2358.

OLIVER, Anthony, actor and author
b Abersychan, Monmouthshire, 4 July 1923; *s* of George Oliver and his wife Florence (Le Blond); *e* Monmouth; served with the RAF, 1941–6.

Made his first appearance on the stage at the Q, 25 June 1946, as Sandy Tyrell in Hay Fever; Comedy, Sept 1946, played Paul Brant in Mother of Men; Arts, May 1947, Plato Cartwright in Boys in Brown; Boltons, Oct 1947, played Digby in The Hidden Years, and appeared at the Fortune, Jan 1948, in the same part; at the Phoenix, Sept 1948, in Terence Rattigan's Playbill, appeared as Peter Gilbert in The Browning Version and as Fred Ingram in A Harlquinade; Vaudeville, June 1949, Kit Neilan in a revival of French Without Tears; Aldwych, Sept 1950, Albert in Accolade; Piccadilly, June 1952, played Peter in The Gay Dog; Vaudeville, Apr 1953, Ken Wilson in Red-Headed Blonde; first appeared on the New York stage at the Playhouse, 28 Oct 1953, as Edward Bare in Gently Does It; following his return to London, appeared at the Vaudeville, Mar 1954, as Donald Gresham in the revival of The Moon Is Blue; Cambridge, May 1957, Tim Riley in A Month of Sundays; Saville, Jan 1958, Denis Lester in A Touch of the Sun; Ambassadors', Nov 1959, took over Det-Sergeant Trotter in The Mousetrap, for one year; Phoenix, May 1962, played Malcolm Rockhart in The Lizard on the Rock; Ambassadors', Nov 1963, again played Det-Sergeant Trotter in The Mousetrap; toured, Apr 1965, as Bill Smith in Heirs and Graces; Strand, Sept 1965, played the Doctor in Too True to be Good; Hampstead Theatre Club, Sept 1966, Captain Hunter in After the Rain, transferring to the Duchess, Jan 1967, and playing the same part at the Golden, NY, Oct 1967; first appeared in films 1948, and has since played in numerous productions; has also read his own stories on television; author of The Victorian Staffordshire Figure, the standard work on nineteenth-century theatre ceramics, and of a novel, The Pew Group.

Favourite parts: Digby in The Hidden Years, Albert in Accolade, and Edward Bare in Gently Does It. *Recreations:* Under-water swimming, collecting Staffordshire figures, and looking at cats. *Address:* c/o Oliver-Sutton Antiques, 34c Kensington Church Street, London, W8. *Tel:* 01–937 0633.

OLIVER, Edith (*née* Goldsmith), drama critic
b New York City, 11 Aug 1913; *d* of Samuel Goldsmith and his wife Maude (Biow); *e* Horace Mann High School, and Smith College (1931–3); studied acting with Mrs Patrick Campbell, Laura Elliott, and Frances Robinson Duff.
Began her career as a student of acting at the Berkshire Playhouse, Stockbridge, Massachusetts and later became assistant to the director, 1932–3; casting director for the Biow Agency, 1944–6; was an actress on the radio in Gangbusters, *True Detective, Crime Doctor, Philip Morris Playhouse*, etc, 1937–41; wrote the quiz show *True or False?* 1938; wrote and produced *Take It or Leave It, The $64 Dollar Question*, 1940–52; began her career in journalism when she joined the editorial staff of *The New Yorker*, 1948; became its off-Broadway theatre critic in 1961, a position she still holds; dramaturg since 1972 at the O'Neill Playwright's Conference, Waterford, Conn.
Club: The National Arts Club, The Cosmopolitan Club, The Coffee House. *Address: The New Yorker* Magazine, 25 West 43rd Street, New York, NY 10036. *Tel:* 840 3700.

OLIVIER, Laurence (*cr.* Baron, 1970; Kt, 1947), actor, director, and manager
b Dorking, 22 May 1907; *s* of the Rev Gerard Kerr Olivier and his wife Agnes Louis (Crookenden); *e* St Edward's School, Oxford; *m* (1) Jill Esmond (mar dis); (2) Vivien Leigh (mar dis); (3) Joan Plowright; studied with Elsie Fogerty.
Made his first stage appearance at the Shakespeare Festival Theatre, Stratford-on-Avon, Apr 1922, when he appeared in a special boys' performance, playing Katherine in The Taming of the Shrew; Century Theatre, Nov 1924, as the Suliot Officer in Byron; appeared at the Regent (for the Fellowship of Players), Feb 1925, as Thomas of Clarence and Snare in King Henry IV (Part II); at the Empire, Dec 1925, played in Henry VIII and The Cenci; appeared with the Birmingham Repertory Company, 1926–8, playing leading and other parts, and appeared at the Kingsway, Apr 1926, as the Minstrel in The Marvellous History of Saint Bernard; toured in July 1926, as Richard Coaker in The Farmer's Wife; he also appeared with the company at the Court, Jan–Apr 1928, as the Young Man in The Adding Machine, Malcolm in Macbeth (in modern dress), Martellus in Back to Methuselah, Harold in the play of that name, The Lord in The Taming of the Shrew (modern dress); at the Royalty, June 1928, played Gerald Arnwood in Bird In Hand; at the Apollo (for the Stage Society), Dec 1928, played Captain Stanhope in Journey's End; His Majesty's, Jan 1929, Michael (Beau) Geste in Beau Geste; New, Mar 1929, Prince Po in The Circle of Chalk; Lyric, Apr 1929, Richard Parish in Paris Bound; Garrick, June 1929, John Hardy in The Stranger Within; in Aug 1929, went to America, and made his first appearance there, at the Eltinge Theatre, 11 Sept 1929, as Hugh Bromilow in Murder on the Second Floor; returning to London, appeared at the Fortune Theatre, Dec 1929, as Jerry Warrender in The Last Enemy; Arts, Mar 1930, played Ralph in After All; Phoenix, Sept 1930, Victor Prynne in Private Lives, and played the same part at the Times Square Theatre, New York, Jan 1931; he then went to Hollywood; Playhouse, Apr 1933, Steven Beringer in The Rats of Norway; Cort Theatre, NY, Oct 1933, Julian Dulcimer in The Green Bay Tree; Globe, London, Apr 1934, Richard Kurt in Biography; New, June 1934, Bothwell in Queen of Scots; Lyric, Oct 1934, Anthony Cavendish in Theatre Royal; Shaftesbury,

Mar 1935, Peter Hammond in Ringmaster; Whitehall, May 1935, Richard Harben in Golden Arrow; New, Oct 1935, played Romeo in Romeo and Juliet, and in Nov 1935, Mercutio in the same production; at the Lyric, May 1936, in conjunction with Ralph Richardson, presented Bees on the Boatdeck, in which he appeared as Robert Patch; Old Vic, Jan–Nov 1937, appeared as Hamlet (in its entirety), Sir Toby Belch in Twelfth Night, King Henry in Henry V, and Macbeth; appeared at Kronborg Castle, Elsinore, June 1937, as Hamlet, with the Old Vic Company; New Theatre, Dec 1937, again played Macbeth; Old Vic, Feb–Apr 1938, Iago in Othello, Vivaldi in The King of Nowhere, and Caius Marcius in Coriolanus; Ethel Barrymore, NY, Apr 1939, Gaylord Easterbrook in No Time for Comedy; 51st Street Theatre, NY, May 1940, Romeo in Romeo and Juliet, which he directed; served with the RN Fleet Air Arm; in 1944, was appointed co-director of the Old Vic company; reappeared on the London stage, at the New Theatre, with the Old Vic company, Aug 1944, as the Button Moulder in Peer Gynt; during the season also played Sergius Saranoff in Arms and the Man, Duke of Gloster in Richard III, and Astrov in Uncle Vanya; during the season, 1945–6, appeared there as Hotspur in Henry IV (Part I), Justice Shallow in Henry IV (Part II), Œdipus in Œdipus Rex, and Puff in The Critic; appeared at the Comédie FranFFaise, July 1945, in Peer Gynt, Arms and the Man, and Richard III; at the Century Theatre, NY, May 1946, appeared in the five last-mentioned parts; at the New Theatre, with the Old Vic company, Sept 1946, played King Lear, also directing the play; toured Australia and New Zealand, Feb 1948, with an Old Vic company, where he appeared in The School for Scandal, Richard III, and The Skin of Our Teeth, in which he played Mr Antrobus; on returning to London, appeared at the New Theatre, with the Old Vic company, Jan–Feb 1949, as Richard III, Sir Peter Teazle in The School for Scandal, Chorus in Antigone, also directing the last two plays and The Proposal; at the St James's, Jan 1950, played the Duke of Altair in Venus Observed; St James's, May 1951, played Caesar in Caesar and Cleopatra and Antony in Antony and Cleopatra; subsequently appeared in these parts at the Ziegfeld, NY, Dec 1951; at the New Century, NY, Feb 1952, directed the production of Venus Observed; Phoenix, London, Nov 1953, appeared as the Grand Duke in The Sleeping Prince; at Stratford-on-Avon, during the 1955 season, appeared with the Shakespeare Memorial Theatre Company as Macbeth, Titus Andronicus, and Malvolio in Twelfth Night; Royal Court, Apr 1957, played Archie Rice in The Entertainer for the English Stage Company; in June 1957, toured Europe in the title-part of Titus Andronicus, playing in Paris, Venice, Belgrade, Zagreb, Vienna, and Warsaw, and subsequently appeared at the Stoll, July 1957 (the last production to be presented before that theatre was demolished); Palace, Sept 1957, again played Archie Rice in The Entertainer, and subsequently appeared in the same part on Broadway, at the Royale, NY, Feb 1958; Memorial Theatre, Stratford-on-Avon, July 1959, played the title-part in Coriolanus; Royal Court, Apr 1960, played Berenger in Rhinoceros, transferring to the Strand, July 1960; St James's, NY, Oct 1960, played the title-part in Becket, subsequently touring with the production, Mar 1961, when he played the part of Henry II, and appearing at the Hudson, NY, May 1961, in the same part; on returning to England at the opening Chichester Festival, July 1962, directed The Chances, directed and played the Prologue and Bassanes in The Broken Heart, and directed and played Astrov in Uncle Vanya; Saville, Dec 1962, played Fred Midway in Semi-Detached; Chichester Festival, July 1963, again directed and played Astrov in

Uncle Vanya; at the Old Vic, Oct 1963, directed the National Theatre Company's inaugural production of Hamlet, subsequently appearing as Astrov in his own production of Uncle Vanya, and Captain Brazen in The Recruiting Officer, 1963; played the title-part in Othello (also Chichester Festival), Halvard Solness in The Master Builder, 1964; directed The Crucible, 1965; visited Moscow and Berlin with the National Theatre Company, Sept 1965, appearing in Othello, and Love for Love; Old Vic, Oct 1965, played Tattle in Love for Love; directed Juno and the Paycock, 1966; played Edgar in The Dance of Death, directed The Three Sisters, 1967; toured Canada (including Expo '67) in Love for Love, The Dance of Death, and as Plucheux in A Flea in Her Ear, 1967; co-directed The Advertisement, directed Love's Labour's Lost, 1968; took over the part of A B Raham in Home and Beauty, directed The Three Sisters, 1969; Shylock in The Merchant of Venice, 1970; directed Amphitryon 38, 1971; in the same year played James Tyrone in Long Day's Journey into Night; Antonio in Saturday, Sunday, Monday, and John Tagg in The Party, 1973; directed Eden End, 1974; directed Filumena, NY, 1980; under his own management he has presented Golden Arrow, 1935; The Skin of Our Teeth, Phoenix, May 1945; Born Yesterday, Garrick, Jan 1947; A Streetcar Named Desire, Aldwych, Oct 1949; Venus Observed, St James's, Jan 1950; Captain Carvallo, St James's, Aug 1950; Caesar and Cleopatra and Antony and Cleopatra, St James's, May 1951; Othello, St James's, Oct 1951; The Happy Time (with Gilbert Miller), St James's, Jan 1952; Anastasia, St James's, Aug 1953; Waiting For Gillian, St James's, Apr 1954; Meet a Body, Duke of York's, July 1954; Double Image, 1956; Summer of the Seventeenth Doll, Titus Andronicus 1957; The Shifting Heart, 1959; The Tumbler (NY), A Lodging for a Bride (co-presented), Over the Bridge (co-presented), 1960; entered films, 1927, in Too Many Crooks, and has appeared in innumerable pictures, including: Wuthering Heights, Rebecca, Pride and Prejudice, Lady Hamilton, Henry V, which he also produced and directed, and Hamlet, which he also produced and directed, and which received the Academy (Oscar) Award, 1948–9; subsequently appeared in films of The Beggar's Opera, Richard III (British Film Academy Award, 1956), The Prince and the Showgirl (which he also directed), The Devil's Disciple, Spartacus, The Entertainer, Term of Trial, Othello, Khartoum, Oh! What a Lovely War, The Battle of Britain, Dance of Death, and Three Sisters (which he also directed), David Copperfield, Nicholas and Alexandra, Lady Caroline Lamb, Sleuth, The Betsy, The Boys from Brazil, A Little Romance (Filmex Award, 1978), Dracula, Inchon, etc; made his first television appearance in Nov 1958, as John Gabriel Borkman in the play by Ibsen; also appeared in The Moon and Sixpence, on American television (Emmy Television Award, 1960); recent appearances include: Long Day's Journey into Night (Emmy, 1973), The Merchant of Venice, Love Among the Ruins (Emmy, 1975), Cat on a Hot Tin Roof; appointed Director of Chichester Festival Theatre, 1961; Director Founder of the National Theatre of Great Britain, 1963–73; was Knighted in the Birthday Honours, 1947, and created Baron Olivier (Life Peer) for services to the Theatre, Birthday Honours, 1970; created Commander of the Order of Dannebrog, 1949; Officer of the Légion d'Honneur, 1953; Grand Officer of the Ordine al Merito della Republica, 1954; Order of the Yugoslav Flag with Golden Wreath, 1971; received the Selznick Golden Laurel Trophy, 1956, for contributions to international goodwill; received the Mask of Tragedy (Olympus Award), at the Taormina Film Festival, 1962; awarded a special Oscar, 1979; HonDLitt, Oxon, 1957; HonLLD, Edinburgh, 1964; LLD, Manchester, DLitt, London, 1968; Hon-

DLitt, Sussex, 1978; elected President of the Actors' Charitable Trust, 1956.

Recreations: Tennis, swimming and gardening. *Clubs:* Garrick, Green Room. *Address:* 33–4 Chancery Lane, London, WC2.

OMAN, Julia Trevelyan, RDI, Des RCA, FSIAD, designer *b* Kensington, 11 July 1930; *d* of Charles Chichele Oman and his wife Joan (Trevelyan); *e* Royal College of Art; *m* Roy Strong.

Designed settings and costumes for Brief Lives (London and New York), Country Dance, 1967; Enigma Variations (Royal Ballet), Forty Years On, 1968; The Merchant of Venice (National Theatre), 1970; Eugene Onegin (Covent Garden), Othello (Stratford), Getting On, 1971; Un Ballo in Maschera (Hamburg), 1973; La Bohème (Covent Garden), 1974; has also designed since 1966 for television productions including: Vote, Vote, Vote for Nigel Barton and Alice in Wonderland (Designer of the Year Award, 1967); designed Hay Fever for Danish television, 1979; film work includes: The Charge of the Light Brigade, Laughter in the Dark, Julius Caesar, and Straw Dogs; publications include: Street Children (with B S Johnson), 1964; Elizabeth R (with Roy Strong), 1971; Mary Queen of Scots (with Roy Strong), 1972; A Month in Country (Royal Ballet), The Importance of Being Earnest (Burgtheater, Vienna), 1976; Die Fledermaus (Covent Garden), 1977; Work for Exhibitions includes Samuel Pepys (National Gallery), 1970; Royal Scholar, 1953; RCA Silver Medal, 1955; Royal Designer for Industry, 1977.

Address: c/o London Management, 235–241 Regent Street, London, W1. *Tel:* 01–734 4192.

O'MARA, Kate, actress *b* Leicester, 10 Aug 1939; *d* of John Carroll and his wife Hazel (Bainbridge); *m* Jeremy Young (mar dis); formerly a teacher; trained for the stage at the Aida Foster School.

Made her first professional appearance at the Flora Robson Playhouse, Newcastle, 1963, as Jessica in The Merchant of Venice; appeared at the Shaftesbury, 1964, in a Shakespeare for Schools season; Welsh Theatre Company, 1965, Lydia Languish in The Rivals; Wyndham's, 1968, took over the part of Elsa in The Italian Girl; May Fair, Sept 1969, Fleda Vetch in The Spoils of Poynton; Arnaud, Guildford, 1969, Margaret in The Holly and the Ivy; Palace, Watford, 1970, Angelica in Love for Love; New, Bromley, 1970, Curley's wife in Of Mice and Men; Thorndike, Leatherhead, 1970, Tamala in The Silent House; Palace, Watford, 1971, Mrs Cheveley in An Ideal Husband; Prince of Wales, Aug 1971, Madame Gerda in The Avengers; Sadler's Wells, Mar 1972, Sybil Merton in Lord Arthur Savile's Crime; Fortune, June 1972, took over the part of Sheila Wallis in Suddenly at Home; Little, Bristol, Nov 1973, Elvira in Blithe Spirit, in that theatre's Golden Jubilee production; Arnaud, Guildford, and tour, Jan 1974, Gillian in Bell Book and Candle; Open Space, July 1974, Liza Moriarty in Sherlock's Last Case; toured, 1975, as Ann Marsh in Shock; Thorndike, Leatherhead, Jan 1977, played Louka in Arms and the Man, and subsequently at the Hong Kong Arts Festival; May, 1977, toured as Helen Galt in Double Edge; Thorndike, Leatherhead, Feb 1978, Rosaline in Love's Labour's Lost; toured as Cyrenne in Rattle of A Simple Man, 1978; played Katharina in Taming of the Shrew at the Ludlow Festival, 1978; Thorndike, Leatherhead, Apr 1979, Cleopatra in Antony and Cleopatra; Malvern Festival, May 1979, Lina Szczepanowska in Misalliance, and Monica Claverton Ferry in The Elder Statesman, subsequently touring in the latter part; Haymarket, Sept 1979, took over Irene St Claire in The

Crucifer of Blood; made her first film appearance in 1955 as a child actress; subsequent films include Great Catherine, The Desperados, and The Limbo Line; TV, since 1957, includes plays and series.

Favourite parts: Cleopatra, Katharina. *Recreations:* Music, prehistory. *Address:* c/o Barry Burnett, Suite 409, Princes House, 190 Piccadilly, London W1. *Tel:* 01–437 7048.

O'NEAL, Frederick, actor, director, lecturer, administrator *b* Brooksville, Mississippi, 27 Aug 1905; *s* of Ransome James O'Neal and his wife Ninnie Bell (Thompson); *e* St Louis public schools and correspondence courses; *m* Mrs Charlotte Talbot Hainey; was formerly engaged as a laboratory technician and as a cowhand, farmer, as an owner of advertising business as well as a valet service; studied for the stage at the New Theatre School, American Theatre Wing, and privately with Komisarjevsky.

Made his first professional appearance at St Louis, Mo, Oct 1927, as Silvius in As You Like It; founded the Aldridge Players, St Louis, 1927; made his first appearance in New York, at the Civic Repertory Theatre, 1936, in Twenty Million Others; in 1940, was one of the founders of the American Negro Theatre, and appeared in a number of productions for that organization; served with the US Armed Forces, 1942–3; first appeared on Broadway, at the Mansfield Theatre, 30 Aug 1944, as Frank in Anna Lucasta, for which he gained the Clarence Derwent Award, and the New York Drama Critics' Award, for the best supporting performance of the season; played the same part in Chicago, 1945; made his first appearance in London, at His Majesty's Theatre, 29 Oct 1947, in the same part, and repeated his previous success; at Westport, Conn, Sept 1950, played Henry Jackson in Head of the Family; subsequently appeared with the New York Philarmonic Orchestra, 1950, as Narrator in the Children's Concert Series; London, 1953, directed and again played in a revival of Anna Lucasta; Lyceum, NY, Sept 1953, played Lem Scott in Take a Giant Step; Playhouse, Feb 1954, Judge Samuel Addison in The Winner; Alvin, Dec 1954, appeared as The Houngan in House of Flowers; Cherry Lane, June 1956, Captain Bednar in The Man with the Golden Arm; Kaufmann Concert Hall, Mar 1958, a Slave in The Common Wind; City Center, Apr 1958, John Kumalo in Lost in the Stars; Cambridge Drama Festival, Boston, July 1959, Antonio in Twelfth Night; 41st Street, NY, Mar 1960, in Shakespeare in Harlem; played Willy Loman in the Clark College production of Death of a Salesman, 1963; Mayfair, NY, Oct 1963, Captain Neddie Boyce in Ballad for Bimshire; Prospect Park, Brooklyn, June 1965, played in An Afternoon of Langston Hughes; Arena Stage, Washington, DC, Mar 1968, appeared in The Iceman Cometh; Sokol, NY, Mar 1970, in The Madwoman of Chaillot; has also appeared in films and in radio and television plays, including the films Pinky, 1949, No Way Out, 1950, Something of Value, 1957, Anna Lucasta, 1958, Free, White, and 21, 1962, etc, and the television productions of God's Trombones, Simply Heavenly, Green Pastures, The Patriots, Profiles in Courage, In Darkness Waiting, and various series; has recorded Great American Negroes, Silhouettes in Courage, various books for the blind, and Prose and Poetry for Enjoyment, etc; author of The Negro in American Theatre; visiting Professor at the Southern Illinois University, 1962, and Clark College, Atlanta, 1963; additional theatrical honors include the Donaldson Award, 1944–5; Best Actor of Chicago Season, 1945–6; New England Theatre Conference Award for distinguished service to the American theatre, 1963; Ohio Community Theatre Association, 1964; Canada Lee Foundation Achievement Award for courage and leadership toward

integration in the performing arts; Motion Pictures Critics Award for performance in Anna Lucasta, etc; received honorary Doctor of Fine Arts from Columbia College, Chicago, June 1966; citation from Loeb Student Center of New York University, 1967; President, Associated Actors and Artists of America, 1970–1; Vice-President of AFL, CIO and Chairman of its Civil Rights Committee, 1969; Treasurer, Catholic Interracial Council; Vice-President, Catholic Actors Guild; Treasurer of the American Committee for World Festival of Negro Arts, Dakar, 1966; member of the Board of the following organizations: National Center for US/China Relations, League for Industrial Democracy, National Epilepsy Foundation, African-American Labor Center, International Communications University, A Phillip Randolph Institute, Foundation for the Extension and Development of the American Professional Theatre, Community Council of Greater New York, American Arbitration Association, Actors Fund of America, International Theatre Institute, Harlem Cultural Council, AFTRA, Institute for Advanced Studies in Theatre Arts; has received numerous other awards; President of Actors Equity Association, 1964 to May 1973; formerly President, Negro Actors' Guild of America, Inc (1961–3); Doctor of Humanities, Lincoln, Mo, Univ, 1976; Doctor of Fine Arts, Wooster Ohio, College, 1976.

Favourite parts: Frank in Anna Lucasta, and Henri Christophe in Black Majesty. *Clubs:* Lambs and Players. *Recreations:* Cooking, and outdoor sports. *Address:* Progressive Artists Agency, 400 South Beverly Drive, Beverly Hills, Calif 90212.

O'NEAL, Patrick, actor
b Ocala, Florida, 26 Sept 1927; *s* of Coke Wisdom O'Neal and his wife Martha (Hearn); *e* Ocala High School, Riverside Military Academy, and the University of Florida (BA); *m* Cynthia Baxter; prepared for the stage at the Actors Studio and at the Neighborhood Playhouse; served in the US Air Force for which he wrote and directed films.

First appeared on the stage at the PK Yonge Theatre, Gainesville, Florida, 1944, as Marchbanks in Candida; toured, summer 1951, in William Saroyan's The Violin Messiah; made his New York début at Henry Miller's, 1954, when he took over the role of Arthur Turner in Oh, Men! Oh, Women!; Spoleto Festival, Italy, July 1959, appeared as T Lawrence Shannon in Shannon, which was later called The Night of the Iguana; Shubert, New Haven, Conn, Sept 1960, played John Gilbert in Laurette; Music Box, Apr 1961, played Frederick Wohlmuth in A Far Country; Royale, Dec 1961, again played T Lawrence Shannon in The Night of the Iguana; Orpheum, Nov 1963, played Sebastian Dangerfield in The Ginger Man; first entered films, 1954, and has since appeared in A Fine Madness, The Secret Life of an American Wife, The Kremlin Letter, Assignment to Kill, King Rat, From the Terrace, The Cardinal, The 91st Day, The Way We Were, Stepford Wives (1974), etc; directed the film Circle Back, 1970; first appeared on television, 1949, and has since played in innumerable productions including the series: *Dick and the Duchess* and *Diagnosis: Unknown.*

Favourite parts: The Rev T Lawrence Shannon and Sebastian Dangerfield. *Recreations:* Boating and his restaurant, The Ginger Man. *Address:* Perry and Naidorf, 315 South Beverly Drive, Beverly Hills, Calif 90212.

O'NEIL, Colette, actress
b Glasgow; *d* of Neil McCrossan and his wife Mary (Ellis); *e* St Joseph's Convent, Girvan, and Notre Dame, Strathclyde; *m* Michael Ellis.

Made her first professional appearance at the Palace Court, Bournemouth, July 1956, as Monica in Mr Kettle and Mrs Moon; first London appearance, July 1958, Royal Court, as Anne Gascoyne in Gay Landscape; Theatre Royal Stratford E, Nov 1960, Mrs Keegan in Progress to the Park; Duchess, June 1961, May Becket in Celebration; Pitlochry Festival, 1963, title role in Hedda Gabler; for RSC, Stratford, 1964, played Lady Bona in Edward IV, and Duchess of Gloucester in Henry VI, in the trilogy The Wars of the Roses; Mermaid, May 1970, Lady Percy in parts 1 and 2 of Henry IV, and Doll Tearsheet in part 2; Criterion, July 1971, Anne Butley in Butley; Royal Court, Nov 1972, Josie in A Pagan Place; for Welsh National Theatre, 1975, played Lady Macbeth; Albery, Jan 1977, took over Dora Strang in the National Theatre Company's Equus; Watford Palace, Mar 1979, Constance in The Autumn Garden; Perth Festival, 1979, played the title-part in Candida; Dublin, Oct 1979, played Marianne in Close of Play for the National Theatre; films include A Smashing Bird I Used to Know, and Frankenstein Must Be Destroyed; TV includes plays and serials, notably, Blue Skies from Now On, Between the Covers, The Standard and The Spoils of War.

Address: c/o Joy Jameson Ltd, 7 West Eaton Place Mews, London SW1. *Tel:* 01–245 9551.

O'NEILL, Sheila, actress, dancer and choreographer
b Dulwich, London, 5 May 1930; *d* of Reuen O'Neill and his wife Marie (Long); *e* Arts Educational Trust, Tring; *m* Don Lawson; trained as a dancer by Madeleine Sharpe.

Her first professional appearance was at the Palace, London, July 1949, in the chorus of Song of Norway; danced in Brigadoon, Her Majesty's, 1949; Paint Your Wagon (in the part of Yvonne Sorel), Her Majesty's, Feb 1953; appeared in the revue Jokers Wild, Victoria Palace, Dec 1954; Kismet, Princes, June 1957; further revue work in One over the Eight, Duke of York's, Apr 1961; Six of One, Adelphi, Sept 1963, Chaganog, Vaudeville, Dec 1964, and St Martin's, Apr 1965; Prince of Wales, Oct 1967, played Fritzie in Sweet Charity, later taking over the title-part; Her Majesty's, Nov 1972, Sheila in Applause; Shaftesbury, Mar 1978, Princess of Ababu in Kismet; has appeared in four Command Performances; cabaret; in films such as Summer Holiday and Half a Sixpence and over one hundred times on television; adviser in movement to the National Theatre, 1970; choreography includes: Kiss Me Kate for Sadler's Wells, Coliseum, Dec 1970; The Beggars' Opera (Chichester), 1972; The King and I, 1973; Cockie, 1973; The Pajama Game (tour), 1974; Dad's Army, 1975; and productions at Coventry, Cambridge and Greenwich.

Favourite part: Charity. *Recreation:* Listening to jazz. *Address:* 14 Rushdene Avenue, East Barnet, Herts. *Tel:* 01–368 8450 or c/o agent at 01–352 2667.

OPATOSHU, David (Opatovsky), actor
b New York City, 30 Jan 1918; *s* of Joseph Opatovsky and his wife Adele (Opatoshu); *e* Morris High School, Bronx; *m* Lillian Weinberg; prepared for the stage with Benno Schneider; served in the US Army Air Force, 1942–45; formerly a silk-screen printer.

Made his stage debut at the Shubert, Newark, NJ, 19 Sept 1938, as Mr Carp in Golden Boy; made his NY debut at the Broadhurst, 22 Feb 1940, as the Sleeping Man and the Blind Man in Night Music; Mercury Theatre, 1940, played Dan in Clinton Street; National, 1941, Ralph in Man of Tomorrow; Apr 1942, appeared in Mexican Mural: Moonlight Scene; Belasco, Feb 1948, Mr Mendel in Me and Molly; Music Box, Mar 1952, Tewfik Bey in Flight into Egypt; Lyceum, Oct

1954, Denesco in Reclining Figure; Imperial, Feb 1955, Bibinski in Silk Stockings; Curran, San Francisco, Cal, Apr 1956, repeated this last part and subsequently toured; Philharmonic Auditorium, Los Angeles, Cal, July 1958, Luca in At the Grand, and subsequently toured; National, 15 Mar 1959, took over from Joseph Buloff as Maxwell Archer in Once More, With Feeling; Billy Rose, Oct 1960, Pan Apt in The Wall; Broadhurst, May 1962, Amedeo in Bravo Giovanni; Plymouth, Feb 1963, Filippo in Lorenzo; Mark Taper Forum, Apr 1967, played in The Devils; Belasco, Feb 1969, Dr Werner in Does a Tiger Wear a Necktie?; Eden, Oct 1972, Rabbi Reb Melech in Yoshe Kalb, performing in Yiddish; Eden, Oct 1974, Shimele Soroker in The Big Winner, performing in Yiddish, which he also directed; Alley, Houston, 1978, appeared in Scream; made his film debut in The Light Ahead in 1939, and has since played in Naked City, The Goldbergs, The Brothers Karamazov, Exodus, Enter Laughing, The Romance of a Horse Thief, etc; made his television debut as Mr Dutton in the series The Goldbergs, 1949, and has since appeared regularly in various dramatic programs; was a newscaster for radio station WEVD, NY, 1941, 1946–55.

Address: Actors Equity Association, 165 West 46th Street, New York, NY 10036.

ORBACH, Jerry, actor
b Bronx, New York, 20 Oct 1935; *s* of Leon Orbach and his wife Emily; *e* University of Illinois (1952–3) and Northwestern University (1953–5); studied acting with Herbert Berghof, Mira Rostova, Lee Strasberg, and singing with Mazel Schweppe; *m* (1) Marta Curro; (2) Elaine Cancilla.

Made his professional début at the Chevy Chase Tent Theatre, Wheeling, Illinois, June 1952, as the Typewriter Man in Room Service; Show Case, Evanston, Illinois, 1953–4, played in some forty or more productions; Grist Mill Playhouse, Andover, New Jersey, 1955, played in Picnic, The Caine Mutiny Court Martial; made his NY début at the Theatre de Lys, 20 Sept 1955, as the Streetsinger and Mack the Knife in Threepenny Opera; played in stock in The King and I, Harvey, Guys and Dolls, The Student Prince, etc, until 1959; Sullivan Street Playhouse, May 1960, played El Gallo in The Fantasticks; Imperial, Apr 1961, Paul in Carnival!; Shubert, Chicago, Nov 1963, again played Paul in Carnival!; Theatre Four, Nov 1964, Larry Foreman in The Cradle Will Rock; New York City Center, Apr 1956, Sky Masterson in Guys and Dolls; NY State, Aug 1965, Jigger Craigin in Carousel; NY State, May 1966, Charlie Davenport in Annie Get Your Gun, and played this part when the production transferred to the Broadway, Sept 1966; Longacre, Mar 1967, Malcolm in The Natural Look; The New, Oct 1967, Harold Wonder in Scuba Duba; Imperial, Nov 1968, Chuck Baxter in Promises, Promises, and received the Antoinette Perry (Tony) Award for this part; Helen Hayes, Oct 1972, Paul Friedman in 6 Rms Riv Vu; toured, 1973, in this last part; Walnut, Philadelphia, Nov 1973, played in The Rose Tattoo; Coconut Grove Playhouse, Miami, Fla, Feb 1974, appeared in the Neil Simon revue The Trouble with People . . . And Other Things; 46th Street, June 1975, Billy Flynn in Chicago; toured in the same role, 1977–8; toured, 1978–9, as George Schneider in Chapter Two; has appeared in the film Please Come Home, 1964; has appeared frequently on television variety programs and on The Nurses, Bob Hope Presents, etc.

Address: c/o David de Silva, 225 East 57th Street, New York, NY 10022.

ORNBO, Robert, lighting designer
b Hessle, Yorks, 13 Sept 1931; *s* of Karl Gerhardt Ornbo and

his wife Gwendoline Cicely (Fenner); *e* Hull University; *m* Rose Ornbo.

Since his first London production, Urfaust, in May 1959, he has lit numerous productions, including operas at Covent Garden, Glyndebourne and Sadler's Wells; plays for the National Theatre, West End theatres, and in Lebanon, Norway, Sweden and Switzerland; he was responsible for the lighting of the opening productions of the Sydney Opera House in Australia; London productions for which he has designed lighting include: A Funny Thing Happened on the Way to the Forum, Little Malcolm, A Patriot for Me, Cabaret, Little Murders, The Ruling Class, Cyrano, I and Albert, The Unknown Soldier and His Wife, Grease, Habeas Corpus, The Dirtiest Show in Town, There's a Girl in My Soup, Voyage Round My Father, Henry IV, Who Saw Him Die?, Travesties, Bloomsbury, Wild Oats, The Devil is an Ass, etc; his first New York production was Company, 1970; member, Society of British Theatre Lighting Designers, United Scenic Artists of America.

Recreations: Antiques, the opposite sex. *Address:* 10 Long Acre, London WC2. *Tel:* 01-240 5411.

ORR, Mary, actress, dramatic author, writer
b Brooklyn, New York, 21 Dec 1918; *d* of Chester Andrew Orr and his wife Jessica Hawks (Caswell); *e* Briarcliff, Ward Belmont, and Syracuse University; *m* Reginald Denham; prepared for the stage at the American Academy of Dramatic Art.

First appeared on stage at Syracuse University, 1934, as the ingenue in New Toys; made her professional début at the Ivoryton Playhouse, Connecticut, summer 1935, as Mary Norton in Seven Keys to Baldpate; National, Washington, DC, Dec 1936, played Mary Lou Gregg in Julie the Great; Ivoryton Playhouse, summer 1936, played Ollie Frey in A Church Mouse, Nancy Lee Faulkner in The Night of January 16th, Stonewall Jackson in Sailor Beware, and Claire in Co-Respondent Unknown; understudied the role of Curley's Wife in Of Mice and Men at the Music Box, NY, Nov 1937; made her NY début at the Morosco, 1 June 1938, when she took over the role of Rosemary in Bachelor Born; toured, 1939, as Curley's Wife in Of Mice and Men; Biltmore, Sept 1940, Jennie in Jupiter Laughs; Papermill Playhouse, Millburn, New Jersey, 1941, Blanche in Jeannie; Stony Creek, Connecticut, 1942, Corinee Mahon in Malice Domestic; also in stock, 1942, played Alda in Death Takes a Holiday, Alma Kent in Evening Rise, and Margaret in Play with Fire; Wilbur, Boston, Dec 1942, Hazel in The Wife Takes a Child; stock, 1943, played Ada in The Late Christopher Bean and Martha Ladd in Without Love; Cort, Jan 1944, Ruth Hennicut in Wallflower; Forrest, Dec 1944, Coral Platt in Dark Hammock; played in stock in 1948 as Ann Marvin in This Thing Called Love, Emily Blackman in Chicken Every Sunday, Liz Imbrie in The Philadelphia Story, and Anne Rogers in Goodbye Again; Elitch Gardens, Denver, Colorado, 1952, played Shirley in Love and Let Love, Alicia Christie in Black Chiffon, Maude Abbott in Glad Tidings, Alice in The Number, and Liz Kendall in Buy Me Blue Ribbons; New Century, NY, Oct 1953, Alice Dunbar in Sherlock Holmes; Ethel Barrymore, Feb 1955, Miss Swift in The Desperate Hours; John Drew, Easthampton, NY, 1958, Mrs Lincoln in Abraham Lincoln and Lucienne Ravinel in Monique; toured Australia and New Zealand, Apr–Sept 1964, as Edith Lambert in Never Too Late; toured US, June –Sept 1970, as Mrs Bradman in Blithe Spirit; Stage 73, NY, Jan 1976, played Elizabeth Avery Stern in her play Grass Widows; with Reginald Denham has written the following plays: Wall-

flower, Dark Hammock, 1944; Round Trip, 1945; The Platinum Set (produced in London), 1950; Sweet Peril (London), 1952; Be Your Age (NY), 1953; Minor Murder (London), 1967; author of the novels Diamond in the Sky, 1955, A Place to Meet, 1961, The Tejera Secrets, 1974, Rich Girl, Poor Girl, 1975; her short story The Wisdom of Eve, 1947, was the basis for the film All About Eve, 1950, and of the musical Applause, 1970 (London, 1972); first professionally performed as play at the Three Muses, Aug 1979, in an adaptation written with Reginald Denham; together they have written nearly fifty television scripts; has acted frequently on television, notably in Suspect, 1942, the first play presented on television, and on *Studio One, Philco Playhouse, Colgate Theatre,* etc; appeared first in films in 1971 in Pigeons.

Recreation: Travelling. *Address:* 100 West 57th Street, New York, NY. *Tel:* CI 7–1094.

OSBORNE, John, dramatic author, and actor
b London, 12 Dec 1929; *s* of Thomas Godfrey Osborne and his wife Nellie Beatrice (Grove); *e* Belmont College, Devon; *m* (1) Pamela Lane (mar dis); (2) Mary Ure (mar dis); (3) Penelope Gilliatt (mar dis); (4) Jill Bennett (mar dis); (5) Helen Dawson.

Began his theatrical career as an actor, appearing on the stage for the first time at the Empire, Sheffield, Mar 1948, as Mr Burrells in No Room at the Inn; he made his first appearance in London, with the English Stage Company, at the Royal Court, May 1956, as Antonio in Don Juan, and Lionel in The Death of Satan, and subsequently appeared in the following parts for the same company, also at the Royal Court; June 1956, as Dr Scavenger, Custodian, and An Aunt in Cards of Identity; Oct 1956, Lin To in The Good Woman of Setzuan; May 1957, the Commissionnaire in The Apollo de Bellac; June 1957, Donald Blake in The Making of Moo; Claude Hickett in A Cuckoo in the Nest, Oct 1964; directed Meals on Wheels, May 1965; he is the author of the following plays: Look Back in Anger, 1956; The Entertainer, 1957; Epitaph For George Dillon (co-author with Anthony Creighton), 1958; The World of Paul Slickey, 1959; Luther, 1961; Blood of the Bambergs and Under Plain Cover (Plays for England), A Subject of Scandal and Concern, 1962; Inadmissible Evidence, 1964; A Patriot for Me, 1965; A Bond Honoured (adapted), Time Present, The Hotel in Amsterdam (*Evening Standard* Drama Award for Best New Play), 1968; West of Suez, 1971; A Sense of Detachment, 1972; The End of Me Old Cigar, The Picture of Dorian Gray (from Wilde), A Place Calling Itself Rome (from Coriolanus), 1975; Watch It Come Down, 1976; author of the films Look Back in Anger, The Entertainer, and Tom Jones; author of the television plays A Subject of Scandal and Concern, 1960; The Right Prospectus, and Very Like A Whale, 1970; Almost a Vision, 1976; You're Not Watching Me, Mummy, and Try a Little Tenderness, 1978; has also appeared on television in The Parachute, First Night of Pygmalion and films of First Love; received the New York Drama Critics Award for the Best Play, 1957 and 1963; received the Film Academy (Oscar) Award for the screenplay Tom Jones, 1964; Hon Dr, Royal College of Art.

Clubs: Garrick. *Address:* c/o 18 Elm Tree Road, London NW8.

OSBORNE, Kipp, actor
b Jersey City, New Jersey, 17 Oct 1944; *e* Univ of Michigan; prepared for the stage at the Neighborhood Playhouse.

Toured, Oct 1967–Feb 1968, as Ricky Fleisher in The Impossible Years; made his NY debut at the Booth, 1970, when he took over from Keir Dullea as Don Baker in

Butterflies Are Free; Theatre de Lys, Jan 1973, played W S, The Salesman in Love Gotta Come by Saturday Night; Shubert, Philadelphia, Mar 1973, Arthur Kindred in Detective Story; Theatre de Lys, May 1973, Jimmy in The Children's Mass; Studio Arena, Buffalo, NY, 1973, again played Don Baker in Butterflies Are Free; Music Box, Oct 1973, The Young Man in Veronica's Room.; ircle in the Square, Mar 1976, Lyngstrand.

Address: c/o Jeff Hunter, 119 West 57th Street, New York, NY 10019.

OSTERMAN, Lester, producer
b New York City, 31 Dec 1914; *s* of Lester Osterman and his wife Adrienne (Pinover); *e* Columbia Grammar High School and the University of Virginia; *m* Marjorie Korn; a member of the New York Stock Exchange from 1945–59.

Began his theatrical career Mar 1956, at the Broadway Theatre, NY, when he co-produced Mr Wonderful with Jule Styne and George Gilbert; he has since produced or co-produced, among others, the following: Candide, 1956, Lonelyhearts, 1957, Brouhaha (London), Say Darling, 1958, A Loss of Roses, 1959, The Cool World, Face of a Hero, 1960, Isle of Children, 1962, High Spirits, Fade Out—Fade In, Something More, 1964; The Coffee Lover at Westport Country Playhouse, Conn, and Dinner at Eight, 1966; Weekend, A Mother's Kisses (tour), 1968; Hadrian VII, 1969; The Rothschilds, 1970; Butley, 1972; Crown Matrimonial, A Moon for the Misbegotten, 1973; Will Rogers' USA, Sizwe Banzi Is Dead, The Island, 1974; The Norman Conquests, Rockabye Hamlet, Rodgers and Hart, 1975 The Shadow Box 1977; Da, 1978; The Crucifer of Blood, Getting Out, 1979; The Lady from Dubuque, 1980; seven of these productions have won Tony awards; ; president of L O Management Corporation, which owns and operates the Morosco and Helen Hayes Theatres; president of Lester Osterman Productions, which has produced The Littlest Angel and Raggedy Ann on television.

Recreations: Football, harness racing, and baseball.
Address: 1650 Broadway, New York, NY.

OSTERWALD, Bibi, actress and singer
b New Brunswick, NJ, 3 Feb 1920; *d* of R August Osterwald and his wife Dagmar (Kvastad); *e* Catholic University, Washington, DC; *m* Ed Justin-Arndt; formerly a secretary; studied for the stage in the Drama Department at the Catholic University.

Made her first appearance on the stage at the New York Music Hall, June 1944, when she played Sal in Broken Hearts of Broadway; International, NY, Dec 1944, played Texas Guinan in Sing Out Sweet Land; Adelphi, Mar 1946, appeared in the revue Three to Make Ready; Martin Beck, May 1948, Lily Bedlington in Sally; Mansfield, Apr 1949, Maybelle in Magnolia Alley; Ziegfeld, Dec 1949, acted as a standby for Dorothy in the musical version of Gentlemen Prefer Blondes, later taking over the part of Lorelei Lee; Phoenix, Mar 1954, played Lovey Mars in The Golden Apple, for which she received the Outer Critics Award, transferring with this to the Alvin Theatre, Apr 1954; Winter Garden, Nov 1955, played Bessie Biscoe in The Vamp; Music Box, Mar 1955, took over as Grace in Bus Stop; 46th Street, 1957, played Marthy in New Girl in Town during the absence of Thelma Ritter; Ethel Barrymore, Nov 1957, played Madame Elizabeth in Look Homeward, Angel; Shubert, New Haven, Sept 1960, Elizabeth Cooney in Laurette; Billy Rose, Jan 1962, Miss Lumpe in A Family Affair; was stand-by for the role of Dolly Gallagher Levi in Hello, Dolly! and played the part frequently at the St James, between 1964–71; Paper

Mill Playhouse, Milburn, NJ, May 1975, Mrs O'Dare in Irene; Dorothy Chandler Pavilion, LA, June 1977, appeared in Annie Get Your Gun; films include Parrish, 1961; The World of Henry Orient, 1964; Tiger Makes Out, 1968; Bank Shot, 1974; first appeared on television, 1948, in Captain Billy's Mississippi Music Hall, and has since given numerous performances, including Mrs Gibbs in Our Town and in the serial Where the Heart Is, 1970–1; she has also appeared as a singer and comedienne in cabaret.

Recreations: Her son Christopher, boating, and music.
Address: Actors Equity Association, 165 West 46th Street, New York, NY 10036.

OSTROW, Stuart, producer, director, author
b New York City, 8 Feb 1932; *s* of Abe Ostrow and his wife Anna (Silverstein); *e* High School of Music and Art and the New York University School of Education; *m* Ann Gilbert.

Entered production at the Shubert, New Haven, Feb 1962, when he presented the musical We Take the Town; first NY production was Here's Love, presented and directed at the Shubert, Oct 1963; since then has produced the following plays: The Apple Tree, 1965; 1776, 1969; presented his first play in London at the New, 29 June 1970, when he produced 1776; Scratch, 1971; Pippin, 1972; Pippin (London: also directed), 1973; associate director, Chicago, 1975; author and producer of Stages, Belasco, Mar 1978; President of Stuart Ostrow Foundation, 1974 (Musical Theatre Lab), a workshop for development of original musical theatre works.

Address: Box 188, Pound Ridge, New York, NY 10576 *and* 245 West 52nd Street, New York, NY 10019. *Tel:* 914–764 4412 *and* 212–582 7263.

O'SULLIVAN, Maureen, actress
b Roscommon, Ireland, 17 Mar 1917; *d* of Major Charles Joseph O'Sullivan and his wife Mary Lovatt (Fraser); *e* Convents of the Sacred Heart in London, Dublin, and Paris; *m* John Villiers Farrow (dec).

First appeared on the stage at the Dury Lane Theatre, Chicago, Illinois, Nov 1961, as Nancy Fallon in A Roomful of Roses; first appeared in New York at The Playhouse, Nov 1962, as Edith Lambert in Never Too Late; first appeared in England at the Royal, Nottingham, as Edith Lambert in Never Too Late, when she assumed the role during the temporary indisposition of Joan Bennett; returned to NY and resumed her part in the same play; toured, 1965, in the same production; Helen Hayes, Sept 1965, took over the role of Nettie Cleary in The Subject Was Roses; toured, 1966–7, in the last play; Royal Poinciana Playhouse, Palm Beach, Fla, Mar 1967, Marian Plummer in The 5.07; Plymouth, Sept 1967, Daisy Brady in Keep It in the Family; Coconut Grove Playhouse, Miami, 1968, played the leads in You Know I Can't Hear You When the Water's Running; Brooks Atkinson, July 1970, Donna Lucia D'Alvadorez in Charley's Aunt; Ethel Barrymore, 1970, took over as Mrs Grant in The Front Page; toured, 1971, in The Pleasure of His Company; Ritz, Feb 1973, Eleanor Hunter in No Sex, Please, We're British; Strand, London, took over this part in the English production, 1973; toured, 1975, in Sabrina Fair; Cohoes Music Hall, Oct 1977, Amanda Wingfield in The Glass Menagerie; Ahmanson, LA, 1978, appeared in Pygmalion; Lyceum, NY, April 1980, Esther Crampton in Morning's at Seven; has played in many films since 1930, notably in the Tarzan films as Jane, Tugboat Annie, The Barretts of Wimpole Street, David Copperfield, Anna Karenina, A Day at the Races, A Yank at Oxford, Cardinal Richelieu, Never Too Late, etc; first appeared on television in 1946, and has since played in many dramatic productions, including *Playhouse 90, Screen Gems, Alcoa Presents,* The Crooked Hearts (1972), etc.

Recreations: Painting and acting. *Club:* Social Service Auxiliary. *Address:* International Creative Management, 40 West 57th Street, New York, NY 10019.

O'TOOLE, Peter, actor
b Ireland, 2 Aug 1932; *s* of Patrick Joseph O'Toole and his wife Constance Jane (Ferguson); *e* Leeds, Ireland, and Gainsborough; formerly a journalist; *m* Siân Phillips (mar dis); studied for the stage at the RADA.

Made his first appearance at the Civic Theatre, Leeds, 1949; joined the Bristol Old Vic company, Sept 1955, to play a Cabman in The Matchmaker, and remained as a member of the company until 1958, to play the following parts: Corvino in Volpone, 1955; Duke of Cornwall in King Lear, Hébert in The Empty Chair, Bullock in The Recruiting Officer, Peter Shirley in Major Barbara, Maupa in The Queen and The Rebels, Cardinal Malko Barberini in Lamp at Midnight, Lodovico in Othello, Baron Parsnip in The Sleeping Beauty, 1956; Mr Jaggers in Great Expectations, Alfred Doolittle in Pygmalion, Lysander in A Midsummer Night's Dream, Jimmy Porter in Look Back in Anger, Uncle Gustave in Oh, My Papa, the Angel in Sodom and Gomorrah, The General in Romanoff and Juliet, Mrs Millie Baba in Ali Baba and the 40 Thieves, 1957; John Tanner in Man and Superman, the title-part in Hamlet, Paddy in The Pier, Jupiter in Amphitryon 38, 1958; made his first appearance in London with the Bristol Old Vic company at the Old Vic, July 1956 as Peter Shirley in Major Barbara; at the Garrick, July 1957, played his original part of Uncle Gustave in Oh, My Papa! also with the Bristol Old Vic company; toured, Sept 1958, as Roger Muir in The Holiday; Royal Court, Jan 1959, played Private Bamforth in The Long and the Short and the Tall, transferring with the production to the New, April 1959; joined the Shakespeare Memorial Theatre Company, Stratford-on-Avon, 1960 season, to play Shylock in The Merchant of Venice, Petruchio in The Taming of the Shrew, and Thersites in Troilus and Cressida; Phoenix, Feb 1963, played the title-part in Baal; at the Old Vic, Oct 1963, played the title-part in the National Theatre Company's inaugural production of Hamlet; Piccadilly, June 1965, played Peter in Ride a Cock Horse; Gaiety, Dublin, Aug 1966, Captain Jack Boyle in Juno and the Paycock; same theatre, Oct 1969, John Tanner in Man and Superman; Abbey, Dublin, Dec 1969, Vladimir in Waiting for Godot; rejoined the Bristol Old Vic, Oct 1973, to play the title-role in Uncle Vanya, also appearing as D'Arcy Tuck in Plunder, Nov, King Magnus in The Apple Cart, Dec, and giving a solo reading of Justice, Jan 1974; Dublin Festival, Oct 1976, played three parts in Dead-Eyed Dicks; films in which he has appeared include: Lawrence of Arabia, Lord Jim, What's New Pussycat?, The Lion in Winter, Goodbye Mr Chips, The Ruling Class, Man of La Mancha, and Zulu Dawn (1978); TV includes Rogue Male, 1976.

Club: Garrick. *Address:* c/o Veerline Ltd, 54 Baker Street, London W1.

OTTAWAY, James, actor
b Chertsey, Surrey, 25 July 1908; *s* of William Harry Ottaway, and his wife Mary Ellen (Monney); *e* Owen's School, Islington, and Imperial College, London; *m* Anne Pichon; formerly a schoolmaster; trained for the stage at the Central School of Speech and Drama (Gold Medal 1937).

First appeared on the stage in July 1937, at the Q Theatre as the Club Waiter in The Island; Old Vic, Nov 1937, played a Messenger in Macbeth; again played the Club Waiter in The Island, at the Comedy, Feb 1938; toured with the Old Vic Company 1940–1, in parts including: Tony Lumpkin in She Stoops to Conquer, Launcelot Gobbo in The Merchant of Venice and Fabian in Twelfth Night; returned to the stage after war service (Capt, REME), and at the Saville, Jan 1948, played Joseph Taft in Four Hours to Kill; Bedford, Camden Town, 1949, appeared in a Shaw season in parts including the Inca in The Inca of Perusalem, and Adolphus Cossins in Major Barbara; St James's, Oct 1950, Mr Wingate in Top of the Ladder; same theatre, Feb 1951, Dr Jadin in The Madwoman of Chaillot; New, July 1951, Forshaw in His House In Order; played various parts with the Old Vic company, 1951–5, including a South African tour, 1952, as the Porter in Macbeth, and an Australian tour, 1955; Open Air, Regent's Park, 1962 season, played Quince in A Midsummer Night's Dream; and Sir Nathaniel in Love's Labour's Lost; St Martin's, Oct 1962, Dr Welling in Kill Two Birds; Strand, Mar 1963, The Gentleman in Devil May Care; Open Air, Summer, 1963, Verges in Much Ado About Nothing; Arts, July 1966, Murchison in The Waiting Game; Open Air, 1967 season, again played Quince, and Ragueneau in Cyrano de Bergerac; Phoenix, Mar 1968, Chaucer in Canterbury Tales; Thorndike, Leatherhead, Nov 1970, Polonius in Hamlet; Greenwich, Nov 1970, four parts in A Voyage Round My Father; Royal Court, Apr 1975, Kemp in Entertaining Mr Sloane, transferring to the Duke of York's, June 1975; has played various small parts in a number of films; has appeared frequently on television since his début in 1937.

Favourite parts: Tony Lumpkin and Adolphus Cossins. *Recreations:* Cricket, cookery, photography. *Address:* 29 Carroll House, Craven Terrace, London, W2 3PR. *Tel:* 01–262 8645.

OULTON, Brian, actor, writer and director
b Liverpool, 11 Feb 1908; *s* of William Harold Stowe Oulton and his wife Kate (Brunner); *e* Wantage; *m* Peggy Thorpe-Bates, actress; studied for the stage at the Royal Academy of Dramatic Art.

First appeared at the Regent, King's Cross, Apr 1928, as Stephani in Listeners; at Liverpool Playhouse, 1928–9; toured, 1929–30, as Hibbert in Journey's End; Arts, Oct 1930, played Peter Dubbin in Mr Eno, His Birth, Death, and Life; New, Jan 1931, Jarvis in To Account Rendered; Royalty, Apr 1933, G. H Lewes in The Brontës; Vaudeville, Jan 1934, played Kenneth Squire in The Man Who Was Fed Up; Lyceum, May 1934, Latour in King of the Damned; with Croydon Repertory, 1934, directed his own musical play Twenty-Four Hours; played at Little Theatre, Bristol, 1936–7; Vaudeville, Feb 1938, appeared as Mr Potteby in Mirabelle; Playhouse, Aug 1938, Camille Raquin in Thou Shalt Not . . .; Vaudeville, May 1940, Charles Vyse in Peril At End House; served in the Army, 1941–6; returned to the stage, 1946, playing leading parts at the Birmingham Repertory Theatre; Palladium, Dec 1947, Cyril Copley in More Just William; St Martin's, Sept 1950, appeared as Mr Raham in a revival of Home and Beauty; New, July 1951, Pryce Ridgeley in a revival of His House In Order; Wimbledon, May 1954, Chancellor in The Soldier and the Lady; Q, Sept 1954, Edwin Bland in Finishing School; New, Jan 1955, appeared as Toby Carter in Night of the Ball; Winter Garden, May 1955, played Camille Raquin in The Lovers; Q, Oct 1955, Mr Perry in Moonshine; New Lindsey, Feb 1956, Brother Traymark in Lead Me Gently; Lyric, Hammersmith, June 1956, Monsieur Héro in Love Affair; Leatherhead, Sept 1957, Sir Charles Critchley in Mathilda; Strand, June 1959, Armand Marescaud in All in the Family; Arts, Feb 1961,

played Captain Bootle in Stop It, Whoever You Are; Richmond, Apr 1961, Henry Fordyce in Goodnight, Mrs Puffin; Pembroke, Croydon, Oct 1961, directed The Second Mrs Tanqueray; Duchess, May 1962, for the Repertory Players, directed Out of Character; Haymarket, Nov 1964, played Mr Naylor in Hostile Witness; Vaudeville, Dec 1964, for the Repertory Players, directed Shadow of a Pale Horse; New Arts, Aug 1966, played Thaddeus Mortimore in The Thunderbolt, which he also adapted; Royal, Bury St Edmunds, 1968, Pastor Manders in Ghosts; Birmingham Repertory, Mar 1969, Voltore in Volpone, and Polonius in Hamlet (also 1970); Old Vic, for the National Theatre, Oct 1969, played Mackie in The National Health, and Dec, the Priest in The Travails of Sancho Panza; Hampstead Theatre Club, June 1970, Canon Cushion in Mr Kilt and the Great I Am; Birmingham Repertory, Aug 1970, the Headmaster in Forty Years On; Jan 1971, toured in For Entertainment Only (a recital of the plays of Pinero), which he also devised and directed; Arnaud, Guildford, Sept 1971, and tour, Hebble Tyson in The Lady's Not for Burning; Harrogate, Oct 1972, Rev Sydney Smith in his own play, Mr Sydney Smith Coming Upstairs; Coventry Cathedral, Nov 1972, wrote and appeared as Sydney Smith in A Sermon for Two Voices; Hackney Festival, Apr 1973, devised and appeared in Words Between Us; made a lecture and recital tour of S Africa, autumn 1973; Palace, Westcliff, June 1974, Gen Sir William Boothroyd in Lloyd George Knew My Father; Arnaud, Guildford, and tour, Aug 1974, Sir Francis Bacon in The Wisest Fool; Assembly Hall, Hackney, Jan 1975, devised and appeared in Births, Marriages and Deaths; Thorndike, Leatherhead, Mar 1975, Maingot in French Without Tears; Theatre at the Park, Bracknell, Oct 1975, Mr Candle in His First Wife; Key Theatre, Peterborough, Dec 1975, Sir Francis Chesney in Charley's Aunt; Leeds Playhouse, March 1976, Colonel Pickering in Pygmalion; Players', June 1976, Mr Caudle in Up All Night, which he also co-adapted; Stoke Newington Assembly Hall, Sept 1976, wrote and played Mr Caudle in Upstairs, Downstairs and in My Lady's Chamber; Orange Tree, Richmond, Nov 1976, wrote and appeared in For Entertainment Only; Playhouse, Liverpool, Mar 1977, Sir Peter Teazle in The School for Scandal; Thorndike, Leatherhead, June 1977, numerous parts in Sybil: Her Infinite Variety; Royal, Northampton, Sept 1977, Arthur Wicksteed in Habeas Corpus; Palace, Watford, June 1978, Rev Alfred Davidson in Rain; Everyman, Cheltenham, Sept 1978, Eggerson in The confidential Clerk; first appeared on television 1937, and in films 1938, and has since played in numerous productions; has also frequently broadcast, notably as Cyril in the Just William series, 1946–8.
Favourite parts: The Stage Manager in Our Town and the name-part in Mr Bolfry. *Club:* Garrick. *Address:* 43 Chester Close North, Regent's Park, London, NW1. *Tel:* 01–486 4290.

OWEN, Alun, dramatic author
b Liverpool, 24 Nov 1925; *s* of Sydney Owen and his wife Ruth (Davies); *e* Cardigan County School, Wales, and Oulton High School, Liverpool; *m* Mary O'Keefe.
Formerly an actor, beginning his career as an assistant stage-manager in repertory, 1942; appeared with the Birmingham Repertory Company, Sir Donald Wolfit's Company, the Old Vic Company, and the English Stage Company; he is the author of the following plays: Progress to the Park, The Rough and Ready Lot, 1958; A Little Winter Love, 1963; Maggie May (book of the musical), 1964; The Game, 1965; The Rose Affair, 1967; Norma, There'll Be Some Changes Made, 1969; The Male of the Species, 1974; his screenplays include: The Criminal, 1960, A Hard Day's Night, and Spare Time; he has also written numerous television plays including: No Trams to Lime Street, After the Funeral, Lena, Oh My Lena, The Ruffians, The Ways of Love, The Rose Affair, You Can't Win 'Em All, Dare to be a Daniel, The Hard Knock, The Stag, The Strain, A Local Boy, The Other Fella, Charlie, Stella, Time for the Funny Walk, Gareth, Park People, Macneil, Cornelius, Emlyn (these last three were seen in America as The Male of the Species); Giants and Ogres, Just the Job, Forget-Me-Not (series).
Address: c/o Felix de Wolfe and Associates, 61 Berkeley House, 15 Hay Hill, London, W1. *Tel:* 01–629 5713.

OWEN, Bill, MBE, actor
b Acton, London; *s* of William George Davenport Rowbotham and his wife Louise (Matthews); *e* Acton Central School; *m* (1) Edith Stevenson (mar dis); (2) Kate O'Donoghue; was formerly known as Bill Rowbotham.
Made his first appearance on the stage at Cambridge, in the repertory season of 1934; wrote and produced many plays and revues for Unity Theatre 1939–52, where he became Artistic Director; first appeared in the West End of London, at the Playhouse, Nov 1943, when he played Gunner Cohen in Mr Bolfry; directed and played in several plays, at the Unity Theatre; Adelphi, Apr 1945, played Trooper Bates in Desert Rats; Embassy, Jan 1946, Hughie in Now the Day is Over; Players, 1946, Albert Norton in The Amiable Mrs Luke; Lyric, Hammersmith, Nov 1946, and Duke of York's, Jan 1947, Sam Gerridge in Caste; Players', Dec 1947, appeared in the revue, Players Please; St Martin's, Sept 1948, in the revue, Sugar and Spice; made his first appearance in New York, Cort Theatre, 26 Jan 1950, as Touchstone in As You Like It; at the New Boltons, Jan 1951, directed The Christmas Tree, Embassy; Apr 1952, played Bill Moodie in The Magnificent Moodies; Duke of York's, July 1952, played Lorenz in The Trap; Lyric, Hammersmith, Oct 1952, appeared as Happy Coombes in The Square Ring; Garrick, June 1954, played Fred Slater in Where There's a Will . . .; Royal, Brighton, Mar 1955, directed The Art of Living; Royal, Windsor, Oct 1955, appeared as Sam Gerridge in a musical version of Caste, which he adapted from the play by T W Robertson, and for which he also wrote the lyrics and directed the musical numbers; Royal Court, and subsequently at the Aldwych, Feb–Mar 1956, appeared as Mack the Knife in the first British production of The Threepenny Opera; High Wycombe, Nov 1956, directed Money For Nothing; Connaught, Worthing, played Ernie Briggs in The Dream House; Belgrade, Coventry, Mar 1959, played Bill in the British première of his own play Breakout, and subsequently toured with the production; Breakout was first performed in Dutch at the Rotterdam State Theatre, 1957, and has since been played in Germany, Sweden, and Mexico; toured, July 1960, as Joe Scotswood in Love Locked Out; Paris and Holland Festivals, and Royal Court, London, July 1961, played Hans Luther in Luther, subsequently appearing at the Edinburgh Festival, Aug 1961, in the same production, returning with the play to the Phoenix, London, Sept 1961; Sadler's Wells, Nov 1962, played Ko-Ko in The Mikado; toured, Oct 1963, as Jim in The Importance of Being Dressed; New Lyric, Hammersmith, Oct 1964, played Zakhar in Oblomov, transferring to the Comedy, Dec 1964, when the play was re-titled Son of Oblomov; Wimbledon, Sept 1966, played George in Who's Afraid of Virginia Woolf; Arnaud, Guildford, May 1967, Tom in The Ballad of Queenie Swann, transferring with the production, re-named Queenie, to the Comedy, June 1967; Royal Court, Apr 1969, played Mr Shaw in In Celebration; same theatre, Oct 1969,

appeared as Ewbank in The Contractor, and later at the Fortune, Apr 1970; Royal Court, Dec 1969, Chief Officer Evans in Insideout; Royal Court, Mar 1974, Ernest in Runaway; Thorndike, Leatherhead, Apr 1976, Hal Lewis in Sunshine Boys, and subsequently at the New Theatre, Cardiff; Vanbrugh, 1977, Eddie Waters in Comedians; Churchill, Bromley, 1977, Baron Hardup in Cinderella; Arts Council tour, 1978, as Doolittle in Pygmalion; Cottesloe, Sept 1978 and Oct 1979, Old Price and Grandfather in Larkrise; Ashcroft, Croydon, 1978, Ald Fitzwarren in Dick Whittington; Cottesloe, Feb 1979, Cocky in The Long Voyage Home; Apr 1979 in The Passion; Nov 1979, Thomas Brown in Candleford; entered films, 1944; author of the following plays: Ragged Trousered Philanthropists (adaptation), 1952; Money For Nothing (with Ted Willis), 1956; Party for Jeremy, Breakout, 1959; Exercise, 1960; Fringe of Light, 1961; Off Guard (one-act), Autumn Romance (one-act), Double Act (one-act), 1963; Matchgirls (book and lyrics), 1964; Viva Viva; The Ragged School, The Laundresses (both one-act); Truth or Murder, Away from it All, 1975; Rehearsal (one-act), 1978; These Boots Ain't Made for Walking (one-act), 1979; he is also the author of a number of plays written for The Theatre of the Adolescent, a theatrical experiment recognized by the National Association of Boys Clubs; he has also written for television, and written lyrics for many leading singers; his numerous films include: The Square Ring, The Rainbow Jacket and In Celebration; work for TV includes: Passing Through, Three Piece Suite, and the series *Last of the Summer Wine* and *Sally Ann*; awarded the MBE in 1976.

Favourite parts: Mack the Knife in The Threepenny Opera, Ko-Ko in The Mikado, Mr Shaw in In Celebration, and Ewbank in The Contractor. *Recreations:* Theatre-going and fishing. *Address:* c/o Richard Stone, 18–20 York Buildings, London WC2.

OWENS, Rochelle (*née* Rochelle Bass), playwright
b Brooklyn, New York, 2 Apr 1936; d of Maxwell Bass and his wife Molly (Adler); e NY public schools; m George D Economou.
First play to be produced was The String Game, at the Judson Poets Theatre, NY, Feb 1965; Futz was produced by the Tyrone Guthrie Workshop in Minneapolis, Minnesota, Nov 1965; first play produced in London was at the Ambiance, 1966, under the title Homo; Futz was subsequently produced by the Cafe La Mama, NY, 1966, and later was performed at the Actors Playhouse and Theatre de Lys; Beclch, produced at the Theatre of the Living Arts, Philadelphia, 1967, and at the Gate, NY, Dec 1968; Istanbul, produced at the Actors Playhouse, NY, Mar 1971; He Wants Shih, Kontraption, 1971; The Karl Marx Play, 1973; Futz was made into a controversial film, 1969; Beclch was televised before its stage production; author of the radio play Sweet Potatoes, 1977; author of Futz and What Came After and The Karl Marx Play and Others, two volumes of her plays, as well as nine books of poetry; recipient of Guggenheim and Rockefeller fellowships, also from Yale School of Drama, CAPS, and the National Endowment for the Arts; founding member, New York Theatre Strategy; member, editorial board, Performing Arts Journal.
Hobbies and recreations: Swimming, sculpting, collage-making, painting, and archaeology. *Address:* 606 West 116th Street, New York, NY 10034. *Tel:* UN 4–4374.

P

PACINO, Al, actor
b New York City, 25 Apr 1940; prepared for the stage at The Actors Studio.

Appeared off-Broadway in Why Is A a Crooked Letter and The Peace Creeps; was a member of the Charles Playhouse, Boston, Mass, 1967–68 season; Astor Place, Jan 1968, played Murps in The Indian Wants the Bronx; Belasco, Feb 1969, played Bickham in Does a Tiger Wear a Necktie? for which he received the Antoinette Perry (Tony) Award; Actors Playhouse, Nov 1969, Graham in The Local Stigmatic; Vivian Beaumont, Jan 1970, Kilroy in Camino Real; Theatre Company of Boston, 1972, played lead in The Basic Training of Pavlo Hummel, and Feb 1973, the title role of Richard III; Charles Playhouse, Boston, May 1975, title role of Arturo Ui; Cort, June 1979, title role in Richard III; has also played in Hello Out There, The Connection, etc; first appeared in films in Panic in Needle Park, 1971, and has since played in The Godfather, Scarecrow, Serpico, Godfather II, Dog Day Afternoon, And Justice for All, etc.
Address: Actors Equity Association, 165 West 46th Street, New York, NY 10036.

PAGE, Anthony, director
b Bangalore, India, 21 Sept 1935; *s* of Frederick Charles Graham Page and his wife Pearl Valerie Montague (Hall); *e* Winchester and Magdalen College, Oxford; after directing a number of student productions at Oxford, trained at the Neighborhood Playhouse School of Theatre, New York; assistant director, Royal Court Theatre, 1958; in this capacity assisted on several productions and directed The Room, 1960; directed also at various reps, and a tour of The Long and the Short and the Tall, 1960; directed Coriolanus (Oxford), 1961; artistic director, Dundee Repertory Theatre, 1961–2; The Caretaker (Oxford), 1962, and two plays in the Royal Shakespeare Company's experimental season at the Arts, Nil Carborundum and Women Beware Women; artistic director, Royal Court, 1964–5, during which period he directed Inadmissible Evidence, A Cuckoo in the Nest, Waiting for Godot and a Patriot for Me; his first NY production was Inadmissible Evidence, 1965; returning to London, directed Diary of a Madman, 1967; Time Present, The Hotel in Amsterdam and Look Back in Anger, 1968; Uncle Vanya, 1970; Nottinghamn 1970 and London, 1971, Hamlet; The Rules of the Game (National), West of Suez, 1971; Alpha Beta, Hedda Gabler, 1972; Not I and Krapp's Last Tape (double-bill), Cromwell, King Lear (Connecticut), 1973; television productions, since 1963, include: Stephen D, The Parachute, The Hotel in Amsterdam, and The Missiles of October; films he has directed include: Inadmissible Evidence, Alpha Beta, I Never Promised You a Rose Garden, Absolution and The Lady Vanishes.
Recreations: Riding, music, travelling. *Address:* 68 Ladbroke Grove, London, W11.

PAGE, Geraldine, actress
b Kirksville, Missouri, 22 Nov 1924; *d* of Leon Elwin Page and his wife Edna Pearl (Maize); *e* Englewood High School, Chicago; *m* (1) Alexander Schneider (mar dis); (2) Rip Torn;

studied for the stage at the Goodman Theatre School, Chicago.

First appeared at the Englewood Methodist Church, Chicago, 1940, in Excuse My Dust; first appeared in New York at the Blackfriars Guild, 25 Oct 1945, as the Sophomore in Seven Mirrors; subsequently appeared at the Lake Zurich Summer Playhouse, 1945–8, the Woodstock Winter Playhouse, 1947–9, and the Shadylane Summer Theatre, 1950–1; at the Circle in the Square, 1951, played the Pagan Crone in Yerma, and Apr 1952, Alma in Summer and Smoke; Vanderbilt, 21 Jan 1953, Lily Barton in Midsummer; Royale, Feb 1954, Marcelline in The Immoralist; Cort, Oct 1954, Lizzie Curry in The Rainmaker, and toured in this part, Mar–May 1955; John Golden, Feb 1956, Amy McGregor in The Innkeepers; first appeared in London at the St Martin's, May 1956, as Lizzie Curry in The Rainmaker; Studebaker, Chicago, Oct–Dec 1956, played in a repertory of plays, including Abbie Putnam in Desire under the Elms, Natalia Islaev in A Month in the Country, and Marcelline in The Immoralist; Music Box, NY, July 1957, took over from Margaret Leighton as Mrs Shankland and Miss Railton-Bell in the double-bill Separate Tables, and subsequently toured in the production; Martin Beck, Mar 1959, Alexandra del Lago in Sweet Bird of Youth, for which she received the New York Drama Critics Award as Best Actress of the Year, and in which she subsequently toured; Locust, Philadelphia, Jan 1962, Sister Bonaventure in The Umbrella; Hudson, Mar 1963, Nina Leeds in a revival of Strange Interlude; Morosco, June 1964, Olga in The Three Sisters, and in Aug 1964, succeeded Kim Stanley in the role of Masha; Henry Miller's, Nov 1964, Julie Cunningham in PS I Love You; Eugene O'Neill, Feb 1966, Oriane Brice in The Great Indoors; Ethel Barrymore, Feb 1967, Baroness Lemberg in White Lies and Clea in Black Comedy; The Music Box, Oct 1969, Angela Palmer in Angela; toured, 1971, in Marriage and Money; Playhouse in the Park, Philadelphia, July 1971, played in The Marriage Proposal and The Boor; Playhouse, Jan 1973, Mary Todd Lincoln in Look Away; Circle in the Square, 29 Apr 1974, appeared in a Benefit Gala; Academy Festival, Lake Forest, Ill, July 1974, Regina Giddens in The Little Foxes, and also played this part at the Walnut, Philadelphia; Music Box, Oct 1974, Marion in Absurd Person Singular, and played this role for over a year; Lake Forest, Ill, June 1976, Blanche DuBois in A Streetcar Named Desire; Hudson Guild, Jan 1977, and Public/Newman, Apr, Tekla in Creditors; toured, summer 1979, in Slightly Delayed; has also received the Drama Critics Award, 1953, the Donaldson Award, 1953, Sarah Siddons Award, 1960; first appeared in films, 1947, in Out of the Night; other films include Taxi, 1953; Summer and Smoke, 1961; Sweet Bird of Youth, 1962; Toys in the Attic, 1963; Dear Heart, 1964; Whatever Happened to Aunt Alice?, Trilogy, 1969, J W Coop, Pete 'n' Tillie; Nasty, Habits, Interiors, Harry's War (1979), etc; has received three Golden Globe Awards of the Foreign Press for her films, as well as the Cinema Nuova Gold Plaque, Venice, the National Board of Review of Motion Pictures Award, and the Donatello Award of Italy, 1961, for Summer and Smoke; made her television début in Easter Story, 1946, and has since played in A Christmas Memory; 1967, and The

Thanksgiving Visitor, 1969, for both of which she received the Emmy Award, etc.

Favourite parts: Alma in Summer and Smoke, Sadie Thompson in Rain, Blanche Du Bois in A Streetcar Named Desire, and Mama in Papa Is All. *Recreation:* Studying acting. *Address:* c/o Stephen Draper, 37 West 57th Street, New York, NY 10019.

PAGET-BOWMAN, Cicely, actress
b Bedford Park, London, 13 Dec 1910; *d* of Paget John Merriman Bowman and his wife Sibyl Mary (Gilpin); *e* Roland House School, London.

Made her first appearance on the stage at Wyndham's Theatre, 30 Oct 1928, as the Girl in To What Red Hell; at the Gaiety, Dec 1928, played Kitty Verdun in Charley's Aunt; Arts, July 1929, Lady Cecily Brent in These Pretty Things; Ambassadors', Oct 1929, Ursula in A Girl's Best Friend; Lyric, Hammersmith, Sept 1930, the Maid in Marriage à la Mode; Fortune, May 1933, appeared in Heritage; in Feb 1935, joined the repertory company at the Theatre Royal, Brighton, playing leading parts, and from May 1937, fulfilled a similar engagement with the White Rose Players, at Harrogate; toured, Aug 1938, as Mary Charrington in Black Limelight; from June 1939, played lead with Messrs Howard and Wyndham's company at Edinburgh and Glasgow, and 1940, at the King's, Hammersmith, with Wilson Barrett's repertory company; in July 1940, joined the British Volunteer Ambulance Corps, and in Oct 1940, was posted to No 2 Commando, afterwards the First Parachute Battalion; toured, from Nov 1942, for ENSA, playing Olwen Peel in Dangerous Corner, and from Oct 1941–Sept 1944, with Henry Baynton's Shakespearean company, playing Desdemona, Portia, etc; Arts Theatre, Mar 1945, played Prola in The Simpleton of the Unexpected Isles; Open Air Theatre, May 1945, appeared as Rosalind in As You Like It, Portia in The Merchant of Venice, and Helena in A Midsummer Night's Dream; Granville, Walham Green, Oct 1945, appeared in Grand Guignol plays; Lyric, Hammersmith, Nov 1945, played Athena in The Trojan Women; Aug 1946, the Lady in Black in Fear No More; Players' Theatre, Sept 1946, Lady Joyce Lindley in The Amiable Mrs Luke; Haymarket, Feb 1947, Edith de Berg in The Eagle Has Two Heads; Aldwych, July 1948, Michal in Jonathan; Richmond, Jan 1949, Eve Blayne in The White Cliffs; Piccadilly, May 1949, Kitty Brett in Ann Veronica; Arts, Mar 1950, Ella Rentheim in John Gabriel Borkman; Mercury, May 1950, Lady Maria Stratton in Stratton; at the Q, Jan 1951, played Margot in Harvest Time; Strand, July 1951, Leonie in Intimate Relations; at the Q, Feb 1952, Olga Iliana Constantine in The Hungry God; Winter Garden, Mar 1952, played Errand's Wife and a Lady in The Constant Couple; at the Q, May 1952, Laura Merrall and Maude Reilly in Immortal Minute, and Jan 1953, Linda Marshall in The Golden Thread; Whitehall, Aug 1954, Mrs Wagstaff in Dry Rot; Strand (for Repertory Players), Oct 1955, appeared as Dr Susan Henlow in The Bandit's Hat; Strand, Mar 1956 (for Repertory Players), played Lady Millicent in Things That Go Bump; Strand, June 1957 (for Rep Players), Augusta Gordon in The Last Hero; Wyndham's, Mar 1958 (for Rep Players), played Julia van Alden in The Quiet Room; Strand, Sept 1958 (for Rep Players), the Magistrate in The Unloved; at the Guildford Theatre, Mar 1959, Diana in Members Only; Apollo, Sept 1960 (for Rep Players), Margaret Kingsley in Refer to Drawer; Savoy, May 1963, and Piccadilly, Sept 1963, played Mrs Royce in The Masters; Malvern Festival, Feb 1966, Lady Undershaft in Major Barbara; Bromley, Feb 1970, Ethel Fordyce in Goodnight

Mrs Puffin; same theatre, 1971, Mrs Pennyman in The Heiress; first appeared in films, 1936.

Recreations: Music, cooking, swimming, tennis, and walking. *Address:* Garden Flat, 25 Fitzjohn's Avenue, London, NW3. *Tel:* 01–794 5204.

PAGETT, Nicola (*née* Scott), actress
b Cairo, Egypt, 15 June, 1945; *d* of Herbert Wyndham Fitzgerald Scott and his wife Barbara Joan (Black); *e* Yokohama Convent, Japan, and The Beehive, Bexhill on Sea, Sussex; *m* Graham Swannell; trained for the stage at RADA.

Made her professional debut at the Connaught, Worthing, autumn 1964, in the title role of Cornelia; in repertory at the Citizens', Glasgow; toured, Apr 1965, as Carmela in La Contessa; Open Air, Regent's Park, June 1967, Hermia in A Midsummer Night's Dream; made her London debut at the Duchess, 19 Sept 1968, as Nora Lambert in A Boston Story; Playhouse, Nottingham, June 1969, and Royal Court, Apr 1970, Blanche in Widowers' Houses; again at Nottingham, Sept 1970, played Celimene in The Misanthrope; Haymarket, Aug 1971, Elizabeth in A Voyage Round My Father; Hampstead, Nov 1973, appeared in The Ride Across Lake Constance; Greenwich, for Company Theatre, 1974, played Regina Engstrand in Ghosts, Jan, Masha in The Seagull, Jan, and Ophelia in Hamlet, Mar; with the National Theatre company at the Old Vic, July 1974, played Suzanne in The Marriage of Figaro; Apollo, Apr 1975, Justine in A Family and a Fortune; Criterion, Mar 1976, Bella Manningham in Gaslight; Queen's, Oct 1976, Stella in Yahoo; film appearances include Anne of the Thousand Days, There's a Girl in My Soup, Operation Daybreak; TV, since 1964, includes, recently, The Sweeney, Anna Karenina, Aren't We All and Love Story.

Favourite parts: Jil Tanner in Butterflies Are Free; Celimene. *Recreations:* Gardening, cats, cooking. *Address:* Fraser and Dunlop Ltd, 91 Regent Street, London W1R 8RU. *Tel:* 01–734 7311–5

PAIGE, Janis (*née* Donna Mae Tjaden), actress and singer
b Tacoma, Washington, 16 Sept; *e* Stadium High School, Tacoma; *m* (1) Frank Martinelli (mar dis), (2) Arthur Stander (dec), (3) Ray Gilbert (dec).

Entered films in Hollywood Canteen, 1944, and remained in films for some years; toured extensively as a cabaret singer, performing in New York, Las Vegas, Los Angeles, Miami, etc; made her NY stage début at the Morosco, 3 Oct 1951, as Jody Revere in Remains to Be Seen; St James, May 1954, played Babe Williams in The Pajama Game; Shubert, Oct 1963, played Doris Walker in Here's Love; Winter Garden, 1968, took over from Angela Lansbury as Mame Dennis in Mame; Civic, Johannesburg, South Africa, Oct 1971, Margo Channing in Applause; toured, 1979, as Bea Asher in Ballroom; has played stock engagements as Adelaide in Guys and Dolls, as Annie Oakley in Annie Get Your Gun, in High Button Shoes, Gypsy, The Desk Set, Born Yesterday, The Gingerbread Lady, etc; has played in numerous films, including Of Human Bondage, Cheyenne, Silk Stockings, Please Don't Eat the Daisies, The Caretakers, Welcome to Hard Times, etc; has appeared frequently on television, notably in her own series *It's Always Jan*, 1955–6, and on Bob Hope Specials *Wagon Train*, *Eight is Enough*, *All in the Family*, etc.

Address: PO Box 5524, Beverly Hills, Calif 90210.

PALMER, Betsy (*née* Patricia Betsy Hrunek), actress
b East Chicago, Indiana, 1 Nov 1929; *d* of Vincent R Hrunek

and his wife Marie (Love); *e* Indiana Univ, De Paul Univ (BDA 1949); *m* Vincent J Merendino (mar dis); prepared for the stage at the Actors Studio; formerly engaged as a secretary in business.

Made her debut in stock, summer 1950, at Lake Geneva, Wisconsin; later played in stock at Woodstock, Ill (1950–51); made her NY debut at the Plymouth, 26 Jan 1955, as Kate Wilson in The Grand Prize; Ethel Barrymore, Apr 1956, played Sally MacKenzie in Affair of Honor; summer tour, Ohio, 1962, Lorelei Lee in Gentlemen Prefer Blondes; toured, 1963, in the title role of Maggie; toured, 1963, as Nellie Forbush in South Pacific; also toured, 1963, as Anna Leonowens in The King and I; Booth, May 1964, Lady Dungavel in Roar Like a Dove; New York City Center, June 1965, again played Nellie Forbush in South Pacific; Royale, 1967, took over from Lauren Bacall as Stephanie in Cactus Flower; Theater Venture '73, Beverly, Mass, May 1973, Nora in A Doll's House; Ivanhoe, Chicago, Ill, Apr 1974, played in The Dark at the Top of the Stairs; Imperial, NY, 9 Mar 1975, appeared in Gala Tribute to Joshua Logan; Studio Arena, Buffalo NY, Dec 1975, Nora in A Doll's House; Studio Arena, Oct 1976, and Morosco, Nov, Alma Winemiller in The Eccentricities of a Nightingale; Brooks Atkinson, Oct 1977, took over as Doris in Same Time Next Year, playing the part for a year; Studio Arena, 1978–9, title role in Countess Dracula; Charles Theatre, Boston, 1979, in The Shadow Box; toured in stock, summer 1979, in Wait Until Dark; entered films in The Long Gray Line, 1955, and has since appeared in The Last Angry Man, Mister Roberts, Queen Bee, Friday the Thirteenth (1980), etc; has appeared on television since 1951 in such dramatic shows as *Studio One, US Steel Hour,* Climax, *Kraft Theater,* and as a regular on *I've Got a Secret.*
Address: Kimble-Parsighian Associates, 250 West 57th Street, New York, NY 10019.

PALMER, Lilli, actress
b Germany, 24 May 1914; *d* of Dr Alfred Peiser and his wife Rose (Lissmann); *e* Berlin and Vienna; *m* (1) Rex Harrison (mar dis); (2) Carlos Thompson; studied for the stage at the Ilka Grüning School of Acting, Berlin.

Made her first appearance on the stage at the Rose Theater, Berlin, June 1932, as Rolly in Die eiserne Jungfrau; subsequently played in repertory companies and also appeared in cabaret; at the Moulin Rouge, Paris, Dec 1933, appeared in Viktoria et son Hussard; at Frankfurt, played Sylvia in The Gypsy Princess; came to London, 1935, and appeared in films; made her first appearance on the London stage at the Garrick Theatre, 24 Mar 1938, as Katia in Road to Gandahar; Apollo, Oct 1938, played Eve in The Tree of Eden; Strand, Feb 1939, Eve in Little Ladyship; Apollo, Dec 1939, Elsie Sorel-Easton in You, of all People; Lyric, Apr 1940, Felicity Van der Loo in Ladies into Action; Haymarket, Mar 1941, Amanda Smith in No Time for Comedy; made her first appearance on the New York stage at the Lyceum, 9 Feb 1949, as Christine Benoit-Benoit in My Name is Aquilon; subsequently appeared at the National, Dec 1949, as Cleopatra in Caesar and Cleopatra; Ethel Barrymore, Nov 1950, played Gillian Holroyd in Bell, Book and Candle; New Century, Feb 1952, Perpetua in Venus Observed; Shubert, Jan 1953, Beauty in The Love of Four Colonels; re-appeared on the London stage at the Phoenix, Oct 1954, when she again played Gillian in Bell, Book and Candle; Queen's, Apr 1966, played Carlotta in A Song at Twilight, Linda in Shadows of the Evening and Maud in Come Into the Garden, Maud (double-bill), the three plays being collectively titled

Suite In Three Keys; first appeared in films in England, 1935; in Hollywood, 1945; and in Germany, 1954; television includes *The Zoo Gang*; in 1976 published her autobiography, Change Lobsters and Dance.
Address: c/o John Redway & Associates, 5–11 Mortimer Street, London, W1.

PAPP Joseph (*né* Papirofsky), producer of the New York Shakespeare Festival, and director
b Brooklyn, NY, 22 June 1921; *s* of Samuel Papirofsky and his wife Yetta (Morris); *e* Eastern District High School, Brooklyn, and Actors Laboratory, Hollywood; *m* (3) Peggy Marie Bennion (mar dis); (4) Gail Merrifield.

Formerly a stage manager on Broadway; his first production was Telegram from Heaven for the Actors Laboratory, Hollywood, 1948; at Lake Arrowhead, NY, 1951, produced and directed plays for the One-Act Play Company; presented his first NY productions at the Yugoslav Hall, 1952, with Bedtime Story, Hall of Healing, and Time to Go; Equity Library Theatre, 1952, directed Deep Are the Roots; founded the Shakespeare Workshop, 1953, which formed the basis of the New York Shakespeare Festival; the performances through 1956 were given at the Emmanuel Presbyterian Church, and subsequently at the Belvedere Lake Theatre, the Heckscher, and the Wollman Memorial Rink, in Central Park; in 1962, a permanent theatre, the Delacorte, was built in Central Park for the Shakespeare Festival Company; he has produced and directed the following plays: Cymbeline, 1955; The Changeling, 1956; Twelfth Night, 1958; Antony and Cleopatra (in a concert reading), 1959; King Henry V, 1960; Romeo and Juliet, Much Ado About Nothing, 1961; Julius Caesar, The Merchant of Venice, King Lear, 1962; Antony and Cleopatra, Twelfth Night, 1963; Hamlet, 1964; Troilus and Cressida, Henry V, The Taming of the Shrew, 1965; All's Well That Ends Well, 1966; King John, 1967; Hamlet, Romeo and Juliet, 1968; Twelfth Night, 1969; has also produced the following plays: An Evening with Shakespeare and Marlowe, 1954; Shakespeare's Women, Much Ado About Nothing, As You Like It, Romeo and Juliet, Two Gentlemen of Verona, 1955; Much Ado About Nothing, Titus Andronicus, Julius Caesar, The Taming of the Shrew, 1956; Romeo and Juliet, Two Gentlemen of Verona, Macbeth, King Richard III, 1957; As You Like It, Othello, 1958; Julius Caesar, 1959; Measure for Measure, The Taming of the Shrew, 1960; A Midsummer Night's Dream, King Richard II, The Tempest, Macbeth, 1962; As You Like It, The Winter's Tale, 1963; Othello, Electra, A Midsummer Night's Dream, 1964; Love's Labour's Lost, Coriolanus, Romeo and Juliet (in Spanish), 1965; Measure for Measure, Macbeth, 1966; The Comedy of Errors, Titus Andronicus, Volpone, 1967; Henry IV, Part I and Part II, 1968; Peer Gynt, Electra, 1969; The Wars of the Roses, Part I, Part II, and Richard III, 1970; Timon of Athens, Two Gentleman of Verona (musical: later on Broadway, winning a 'Tony'), Cymbeline, 1971; Hamlet, Ti-Jean and His Brothers, Much Ado About Nothing, 1972; As You Like It (also directed), King Lear, Two Gentlemen (revival), 1973; Pericles, The Merry Wives of Windsor, What the Wine-Sellers Buy (Mobile production), 1974; Hamlet, The Comedy of Errors, 1975; Henry V, Measure for Measure, 1976; Threepenny Opera, Agamemnon, An Unfinished Woman (Mobile production), 1977; All's Well That Ends Well, The Taming of the Shrew, 1978; Julius Caesar, Coriolanus, 1979; in 1967 founded the Public Theatre, which consists of the Anspacher, Newman, Other Stage Theatres, Martinson Hall, and several galleries and workshops for photography, drama, and films, and where he produced Hair, Hamlet, 1967; Ergo, The

Memorandum (also directed), Huui, Huui (also directed), The Expressway, Romania . . . *That's* the Old Country, Untitled, 1968; Cities in Bezique, Invitation to a Beheading, No Place to Be Somebody, Sambo, Stomp, The Wonderful Years, Kumaliza, Play on the Times, 1969; Mod Donna, The Happiness Cage, Trelawny of the 'Wells', Jack MacGowran in the Works of Samuel Beckett, X Has No Value, Willie, Fuga, Coocooshay, 1970; Subject to Fits, Slag, Here Are Ladies, Blood, Candide, Underground, a double bill of The Life and Times of J Walter Smintheus and Jazznite, The Basic Training of Pavlo Hummel, Dance wi' Me or The Fatal Twitch, Nigger Nightmare, Sticks and Bones (which received the Tony Award as best play of the year when it transferred to Broadway), The Black Terror, The Wedding of Iphigenia, Iphigenia in Concert, 1971; Black Visions, That Championship Season (which received the Tony Award as best play when it transferred to Broadway), Older People, The Hunter, The Corner, Wedding Band (also co-directed), The Children, The Cherry Orchard, 1972; Siamese Connections, The Orphan, Lotta, 1973; More Than You Deserve, Barbary Shore, Short Eyes, The Emperor of Late Night Radio, Les Femmes Noires, The Killdeer, The Measures Taken, Where Do We Go from Here?, Sweet Talk, The Last Days of British Honduras, In the Boom Boom Boom, 1974; the Manhattan Project in Sea Gull, and Our Late Night, Kid Champion, Fishing (also directed), Time Trial, Ghosts, A Chorus Line (later on Broadway, winning a 'Tony'), Jesse and the Bandit Queen, So Nice, They Named It Twice, 1975; Jinx Bridge, Rich and Famous, Apple Pie, Woyzeck, For Colored Girls . . . (later on Broadway), Rebel Women, 1976; Marco Polo Sings a Solo, Ashes, Museum, Hagar's Children, On the Lock-In, The Stronger/Creditors, Miss Margarida's Way, Landscape of the Body, The Misanthrope, Tales of the Hasidim, The Mandrake, Where the Mississippi Meets the Amazon, The Dybbuk, A Photograph, The Water Engine, 1977; A Prayer for My Daughter, Curse of the Starving Class, Runaways (later on Broadway), Sganarelle, I'm Getting My Act Together . . ., Spring Awakening, Fathers and Sons, The Master and Margarita, Drinks Before Dinner, 1978; Julius Caesar, The Umbrellas of Cherbourg, New Jerusalen, Taken in Marriage, Coriolanus, Sancocho, Dispatches, The Woods, Happy Days, Leave It to Beaver Is Dead, Nasty Rumours and Final Remarks, Remembrance, Spell No 7, The Art of Dining, the Sorrows of Stephen, Salk Lake City Skyline, Marie and Bruce, Tongues, 1979; from 1973–7 assumed management control of the New York Shakespeare Festival at Lincoln Center where, at the Vivian Beaumont, and, the Forum, renamed the Mitzi E Newhouse, he presented Boom Boom Boom (also directed), Troilus and Cressida, The Au Pair Man, 1973; The Tempest, What the Wine-Sellers Buy, The Dance of Death, Macbeth, Short Eyes (transfer), Richard III, Mert and Phil (also directed), 1974; Black Picture Show, A Midsummer Night's Dream, A Doll's House, The Taking of Miss Janie, Little Black Sheep, Trelawny of the 'Wells', Hamlet, 1975; The Shortchanged Review, Mrs Warren's Profession, Streamers, Threepenny Opera (later on Broadway), 1976; The Cherry Orchard, Agamemnon, 1977; at the Peabody Institute, Baltimore, Maryland, 1962, directed an operatic version of Hamlet; adapted the libretto and directed Mozart's Idomeneo, 1963; produced the *Rebekah Harkness Foundation Dance Festival*, 1962–5; *Robert Joffrey Ballet*, 1965; the Newport Folk Festival, 1965; Adjunct Professor of Play Production, Yale University Drama School, 1966; for television he has directed The Merchant of Venice, 1962; Antony and Cleopatra, 1963, and Hamlet, 1964; presented Sticks and Bones and Much Ado About Nothing in his company's productions on televi-

sion, 1973; has received numerous awards, including the Obie, 1955–6; the Antoinette Perry (Tony) for Distinguished Service to Theatre, 1957–8; Brandeis University Creative Arts Award, and the New England Theatre Conference Award for Outstanding Creative Achievement in the American Theatre, 1963; the ANTA Annual Award for his outstanding contribution to the art of the living theatre, 1965; Honorary Doctor of Fine Arts, Northwestern University, 1972; City University of NY, 1974; Villanova Univ, Pa, 1976; Kalamazoo College, Mich, 1977; NYU, 1978; Princeton U, 1979; awarded the Pulitzer Prize, 1970, 1975; New York City's Handel Medallion, 29 June 1971; serves on the Advisory Committee to the NY State Education Dept of the English Language Arts, as a Director of the Harlem Cultural Committee, as a member of the Professional Panel of the Board of Directors of ANTA, etc.

Address: The Public Theatre, 425 Lafayette Street, New York, NY 10003. *Tel:* 598 7100.

PARFITT, Judy, actress

b Sheffield, Yorkshire, 7 Nov; *d* of Lawrence Hamilton Parfitt and his wife Catherine Josephine (Caulton); *m* Tony Steedman; trained for the stage at RADA.

Made her first professional appearance in Spring, 1954, at Amersham Rep as a bridesmaid in Fools Rush In; her first London appearance was at the Globe on 22 Mar 1956, as Ursula Budgeon in A Likely Tale; at the Royal Court, Mar 1967, played Minnie Gascoigne in The Daughter-in-Law; repeated the part in Mar 1968 at the same theatre, also playing the title-role in The Widowing of Mrs Holroyd; Royal Court, July 1968, Annie in The Hotel in Amsterdam, transferring to the New, Sept 1968 and the Duke of York's, Dec 1968; Round House, Mar 1969, Getrude in Hamlet; Royal Court, July 1969, Lady Touchwood in The Double Dealer; same theatre, Jan 1971, the title-part in The Duchess of Malfi; Piccadilly, Apr 1971, took over the part of Mary Queen of Scots in Vivat! Vivat Regina!; Theatre Royal, Bristol, Dec 1973, Orinthia in The Apple Cart; Theatre Upstairs, May 1975, Rachel in Echoes from a Concrete Canyon; Criterion, June 1976, Victoria Musgrave in The Family Dance; Riverside Studios, Jan 1978, Madame Ranevsky in The Cherry Orchard; first film, 1970, The Mind of Mrs Soames; subsequent films include Galileo; television includes *The Edwardians, Shoulder to Shoulder*, and Secret Orchards.

Favourite parts: Mrs Holroyd, Content Delville in The Marriage-Go-Round. *Recreations:* Interior decorating, swimming, gardening. *Address:* c/o Boyack and Conway, 8 Cavendish Place, London W1. *Tel:* 01–636 3916

PARSONS, Estelle, actress

b Lynn, Massachusetts, 20 Nov 1927; *d* of Eben Parsons and his wife Elinor (Mattson); *e* Oak Grove School for Girls, Vassalboro, Maine, 1945, Connecticut College for Women (BA 1949), and Boston University Law School (1949–50); *m* Richard Gehman (mar dis); held a political office in Marblehead, Mass.

Worked for NBC-TV's Today Show as production assistant, writer, feature producer, and commentator; appeared in two of Julius Monk's revues; appeared in Nightcap at the Showplace, 19 May 1958; made her Broadway début at the Majestic, 6 Dec 1956, as the Girl Reporter in Happy Hunting; North Shore, Beverly, Massachusetts, 1958, played Cleo in The Most Happy Fella; Upstairs at the Downstairs, 1959, played in the revues Demi-Dozen and Pieces of Eight; Martin Beck, Feb 1960, Ollie in Beg, Borrow, or Steal; Theatre de Lys, 1960, played Mrs. Coaxer in Threepenny Opera, and in the Los Angeles and San Francisco productions played Mrs. Peachum; Chautauqua, New York, 1961, Nellie Forbush in South Pacific; 41st Street, Nov 1961, Lasca in The Automobile Graveyard; Royal Poinciana Playhouse, Palm Beach, Florida, 1962, played in the *revue* Put It in Writing; Theatre by the Sea, Matunuck, Rhode Island, 1962, played Lula Roca in Hey You, Light Man!; Cherry Lane, Oct 1962, Mrs. Dally in Mrs. Dally Has a Lover; toured, 1963, for the Theatre Guild, as Polly Seedystockings in The Millionairess; Phoenix, Nov 1963, Lizzie in Next Time I'll Sing to You; Little Fox, Mar 1964, Gertrude Eastman-Cuevas in In the Summer House; Brooks Atkinson, Dec 1964, Felicia in Ready When You Are, C. B.!; Playhouse in the Park, Cincinnati, summer, 1965, played in Major Barbara and Summer of the Seventeenth Doll; Stage 73, N.Y., Mrs. Goldman in Suburban Tragedy and Shirley in Princess Rebecca Birnbaum in a production with the overall title Monopoly; Sam S S Shubert, Jan 1966, Laureen in Malcolm; Vivian Beaumont, Feb 1967, Doris in The East Wind; same theatre, Apr 1967, Virginia in Galileo; was a member of the Yale Repertory Theatre, 1967–8 season; Ethel Barrymore, Mar 1968, played Myrtle in The Seven Descents of Myrtle; Playhouse in the Park, Cincinnati, 1968, played in Honor and Offer; A.N.T.A., Jan 1969, played Janice Krieger in A Way of Life; Delacorte, July, 1969, Aase in Peer Gynt; Anderson, Apr 1970, Leocadia Begbick in Mahagonny; Morosco, Feb 1971, Catherine Reardon in And Miss Reardon Drinks a Little; Forum, Nov 1971, Milly in People Are Living There; Actors Studio, May 1974, in Oh Glorious Tintinnabulation; Beaumont, Oct 1974, Mert in Mert and Phil; Hartman, Stamford, Nov 1976, Edna Wrath in The Reason We Eat; Martin Beck, Apr 1977, Dede Cooper in Ladies at the Alamo; Public, July 1977, transferring to the Ambassador, Sept, title role in Miss Margarida's Way; Yale Rep, Feb 1978, appeared in Man is Man; Studio Arena, Buffalo, Apr 1978, Martha in Who's Afraid of Virginia Woolf?; Theatre at St Clement's, May 1978, directed Voices; Interart, May 1979, directed Antony and Cleopatra; first appeared in films in Ladybug, Ladybug, 1964, and since has played Blanche in Bonnie and Clyde (Academy Award, 1968), Rachel, Rachel, For Pete's Sake, etc; has appeared on television in The Gambling Heart, 1964, and on *The Nurses, The Verdict Is Yours, Faith for Today*, etc.

Address: Actors Equity Association, 165 West 46th Street, New York, NY 10036. *Tel:* 212–362 1289.

PASCO, Richard, CBE, 1977; actor
b Barnes, London, 18 July 1926; *s* of Cecil George Pasco and his wife Phyllis Irene (Widdison); *e* Colet Court, and King's College School, Wimbledon; *m* (1) Greta Watson (mar dis); (2) Barbara Leigh-Hunt; trained for the stage at the Central School of Speech and Drama (Gold Medal, 1950).
Made his first appearance on the stage at the Q Theatre, Feb 1943, when he played Diggory in She Stoops to Conquer; first appeared in London at the Lyric, June 1944, as the Sentry in Zero Hour; served in HM Forces, 1944–8; joined the Old Vic Company, Sept 1950, and remained for two seasons, playing the following parts: Curio in Twelfth Night, Bookholder in Bartholomew Fair, 1950; Gloucester in Henry V, Simple in The Merry Wives of Windsor, Agydas and Messenger in Tamburlaine the Great, 1951; Old Man in King Lear, Lucilius in Timon of Athens, 1952; Birmingham Repertory Theatre Company, 1952–5; toured Oct 1955, as Fortinbras in Hamlet, prior to appearing in Moscow in the same production, Nov 1955, and at the Phoenix, London, Dec 1955; Lyric, Hammersmith, Nov 1956, played Jimmy Porter in a revival of Look Back in Anger; joined the English Stage Company, at the Royal Court, Feb 1957, and played the

following parts: Jarvis in The Member of the Wedding, Jimmy in Look Back in Anger, Frank Rice in The Entertainer, Man from Bellac in The Apollo de Bellac, and the Orator in The Chairs (double-bill), 1957; Palace, Sept 1957, again played Frank Rice in The Entertainer; made his first appearance in New York, at the Royale, Feb 1958, in the same part and play; at the Moscow Youth Festival, 1959, again played Jimmy Porter in Look Back in Anger; at the Pembroke, Croydon, Oct 1960, played Ben Gant in Look Homeward, Angel; Queen's, Mar 1961, played Lyngstrand in The Lady From the Sea; Dublin Theatre Festival, Sept 1961, played Father Gracian in Teresa of Avila, subsequently appearing in the same production at the Vaudeville, London, Oct 1961; Phoenix, Apr 1962, again played Ben Gant in Look Homeward, Angel; Strand, Sept 1962, played Walter Luke in The New Men; Globe, June 1963, took over the part of Julian in The Public Eye, in the double-bill The Private Ear and the Public Eye; Bristol Old Vic, May 1964, played the title-part in Henry V, and Berowne in Love's Labour's Lost, prior to touring with both productions for 22 weeks in Austria, Scandinavia, Belgium, Germany, Holland, Israel, Jugoslavia and the Paris Festival; Old Vic, Sept 1964, appeared in the same productions, before appearing at the Venice Festival; Bristol Old Vic, Mar 1965, played the title-part in Hamlet; Phoenix, Sept 1965, Yevgeny Konstantinovitch in Ivanov; returned to Bristol Old Vic, 1966, where he played Angelo in Measure for Measure, Peer in Peer Gynt, John Tanner in Man and Superman, Lord Chamberlain and others in Sixty Thousand Nights and the title-role in Hamlet; 1967, toured North America (including Expo 67), and Europe with the Company, appearing as Angelo and Hamlet; again at Bristol, Nov 1967, Edmund in The Italian Girl, playing the same part at Wyndham's, Feb 1968; Ambiance Theatre Club, Feb 1969, Tremayne in The Window; May 1969, joined the Royal Shakespeare Company at Stratford-on-Avon, where he played the following parts: Polixenes in The Winter's Tale, Leantio in Women Beware Women, Proteus in The Two Gentlemen of Verona, Buckingham in Henry VIII; Jan–Apr 1970, toured with the Company to Japan (including Expo 70) and Australia and returned with them to the Aldwych, July 1970, to play Polixenes, Orsino in Twelfth Night, and Adolphus Cusins in Major Barbara; Aldwych, Dec 1970, again played Buckingham in Henry VIII; Stratford, 1971, played Richard II (for Theatregoround), Orsino, Don John in Much Ado About Nothing, Antonio in the Duchess of Malfi, and took part in Pleasure and Repentance; toured Japan, Feb–Mar 1972, as Orsino; Aldwych, 1972, played The Baron in The Lower Depths, June, Becket in Murder in the Cathedral, Aug, and Medraut in The Island of the Mighty, Dec; Stratford, Apr 1973, alternated the parts of Richard and Bolingbroke (with Ian Richardson), in Richard II, also playing Jaques in As You Like It, June; played Richard and Bolingbroke at the Brooklyn Academy of Music, Jan 1974; also Aldwych, Sept 1974, following the 1974 Stratford season in which he played these parts, and Philip the Bastard in King John; Aldeburgh Festival, June 1974, Manfred; The Place, Nov 1974, Aleister Crowley in The Beast; Aldeburgh Festival, June 1975, speaker in Jane Austen at Home; Aldwych, Sept 1975, Lord John Carp in The Marrying of Ann Leete; 1977 toured American universities; Malvern Festival, May 1977, Jack Tanner in Man and Superman, subsequently appearing in the part, after provincial tour, at the Savoy Theatre, Aug 1977; appeared in Poetry International, Pittsburgh, also touring USA, 1978; Theatre Royal, Bristol, Aug 1978, Trigorin in The Seagull; rejoined the RSC, 1980, to play the title role in Timon of Athens, Other Place, Oct; has appeared in many festivals in Britain, Europe and America, including Bath, Harrogate, Aldeburgh and Edinburgh; has made many broadcasts and recordings of both plays and verse; since his first TV appearance in 1954, has appeared in plays, series and serials including, most recently, Love Letters on Blue Paper, Ghosts, As You Like It, The British in Love, Sweet Wine of Youth, etc; his films include Room at the Top, Yesterday's Enemy, Rasputin, Hot Enough for June, etc; an associate artist of the RSC.

Favourite part: Thomas à Becket in Murder in the Cathedral. *Recreations:* Music, gardening and walking. *Address:* MLR, 194 Old Brompton Road, London SW5 0AS.

PATRICK, John, dramatic author
b Louisville, Kentucky, 17 May 1907; *e* Holy Cross College, New Orleans, Harvard Summer School, and Columbia University.

Commenced his career by writing broadcast scripts in San Francisco; subsequently engaged in writing for films; joined the American Field Service, 1942, and served overseas as a Captain with a British Ambulance Unit, in Egypt, India, Burma, and Syria; is the author of the following plays: Hell Freezes Over, 1935; The Willow and I, 1942; The Hasty Heart, 1945; The Story of Mary Suratt, 1947; The Curious Savage, 1950; Lo and Behold!, 1951; The Teahouse of the August Moon, 1953 (from Vern Sneider's Novel); the last-named was awarded the Pulitzer Prize and was voted the best American play of the Broadway season by the New York Drama Critics' Circle; Good as Gold (from Alfred Toombs' book), 1957; Juniper and the Pagans, 1959; Everybody Loves Opal, 1962; Everybody's Girl, 1967; Scandal Point, A Barrelful of Pennies, 1968; Love Is a Time of Day, 1969; Lovely Ladies, Kind Gentlemen, a musical based on The Teahouse of the August Moon, 1970; Opal Is a Diamond, 1971; Macbeth Did It, Dancing Mice, which he also directed at the Berea Summer Theatre, Cleveland, Ohio, 1972; A Bad Year for Tomatoes, 1974; Noah's Animals, Enigma, which he also directed at the last theater; Roman Conquest, produced at the Drury Lane South, Chicago, 1975; Divorce, Anyone?, Suicide, Anyone?, 1976; Girls of the Garden Club, Opal's Million Dollar Duck, 1979; he is also the author of some thirty screen plays, including: Three Coins in a Fountain, Love Is a Many-Splendored Thing, The Teahouse of the August Moon, High Society, Les Girls (for which he received the Screen Guild Award), The World of Suzie Wong, The Shoes of the Fisherman, etc; honorary Doctor of Fine Arts, Baldwin-Wallace College, 1972.

Address: The Dramatists Guild, 234 West 44th Street, New York, NY 10036, and Fortuna Mill Estate, Box 2386, St Thomas, US Virgin Islands 00801.

PATRICK, Nigel, actor and director
b London, 2 May 1913; *s* of Charles Aubrey Wemyss and his wife Dorothy (Turner); *e* privately; *m* Beatrice Campbell (dec).

Made his first appearance on the stage at the Regent Theatre, 9 Jan 1932, as the Young Man in The Life Machine; Apr 1932, played repertory at Birmingham and during 1933 toured as Ken Warwick in Night of the Garter; Victoria Palace, Dec 1933, played Jimmie McBride in Daddy-Long-Legs; toured in Egypt and the Near East, Mar 1934, subsequently playing repertory seasons at Worthing and Northampton; Whitehall, Oct 1934, played Ronnie in Immortal Garden; Aldwych, Dec 1934, Bill Hunnisett in Half-a-Crown; Shaftesbury, Mar 1935, Julian West in Ringmaster; Duke of York's, May 1935, Peter Harford in Roulette; Q, Feb 1936, and Ambassadors', Mar 1936, Martin in Children to Bless You; Criterion, July 1936, John Verney in The Lady

of La Paz; Wyndham's, Sept 1936, Maurice in Mademoiselle; Strand (for Repertory Players), Jan 1937 and Wyndham's, Feb 1937, Dudley in George and Margaret, which ran nearly two years; Criterion, Jan 1939, Tim Shields in Tony Draws a Horse; joined the Army, Sept 1939, in the King's Royal Rifle Corps; commissioned Feb 1940, in the same corps; served in the Middle East, North Africa, and Italy; demobilized, Jan 1946, with the rank of Lieut-Colonel; reappeared on the London stage, at the Lyric, Hammersmith, Mar 1946, as Alan Winter in To-Morrow's Child; Fortune, Jan 1947, played Joe in Fools Rush In; Saville, June 1947, Gorman in Noose; People's Palace, Nov 1948, Zeus in These Mortals; New, June 1949, David Normandy in Champagne for Delilah; Arts, Aug 1949, Hon Vere Queckett in The Schoolmistress; Vaudeville, Apr 1951, played Miles Cornwall in Who Goes There!; St James's, Jan 1953, John Hampden in Escapade; Criterion, Oct 1953, directed Birthday Honours; New, May 1955, appeared as Pa Pennypacker in The Remarkable Mr Pennypacker; Saville, Oct 1957, played Emile in The Egg; Criterion, Apr 1958, directed Not in the Book; Haymarket, Apr 1959, played Biddeford Poole in The Pleasure of His Company (which he also directed); Strand, Oct 1960, played Lonsdale Walsh in Settled Out of Court (which he also directed); Phoenix, Dec 1960, directed The Geese Are Getting Fat; Savoy, Apr 1964, played the Hon Vere Queckett in a revival of The Schoolmistress; St Martin's, June 1964, directed Past Imperfect; made his first appearance in the US at the Colonial, Boston, Dec 1964, as Jonathan Joy in Everybody Out, the Castle is Sinking; Queen's, Apr 1965, directed and played Garry Essendine in Present Laughter; Chichester Festival, July 1971, and Piccadilly, Feb 1972, played Rudolf Maximilian in Reunion in Vienna; in South Africa, May 1974, played Dr Arthur Wicksteed in Habeas Corpus; Comedy, Nov 1974, Max Forrester in his production of The Pay Off; Ambassadors', Oct 1976, Bernard in Dear Daddy, repeating the part in South Africa, Jan 1978; Shaftesbury, Dec 1978, Mr Darling and Captain Hook in Peter Pan; since 1966 he has directed the following plays in the West End, unless otherwise stated: Relatively Speaking, The Others, 1967; Avanti! (New York), Out of the Question, 1968; They Ride On Broomsticks (tour), Trio (The Will, Village Wooing and Ways and Means) (Guildford), 1969; Village Wooing (in the triple-bill Three), Best of Friends (also played Archer Connaught), Blithe Spirit, 1970; George and Margaret (tour), Finishing Touches, Night Must fall, 1973; The Pay Off, 1974; Suite in Two Keys (tour), 1978; has frequently appeared for the Repertory Players; films in which he has appeared include: Morning Departure, Trio, The Browning Version, Pickwick Papers, Sapphire, The League of Gentlemen, etc; television appearances include: Alan Garnett in the series *Zero One*.

Recreations: Reading and golf. *Club:* Garrick. *Address:* c/o ICM Ltd, 22 Grafton Street, London, W1.

PATRICK, Robert, playwright and director
b Kilgore, Texas, 27 Sept 1937; *s* of Robert Henderson O'Connor and his wife Beulah Adele (Goodson); *e* Eastern New Mexico University.

His first play to be produced was The Haunted Host, Caffe Cino, NY, 4 Oct 1964; has since written a large number of plays, most of them first produced off-off-Broadway; these include Lights, Camera, Action, 1966; Dynel, and Joyce Dynel, 1968–69; The Golden Circle, Play-by-Play, 1972; Mercy Drop, 1973; How I Came to Be Here Tonite, 1974; The Haunted House, 1975; My Cup Ranneth Over, 1977; Judas, T-Shirts, Mutual Benefit Life, 1978; his play Kennedy's Children, first produced NY 1973, was seen at the

King's Head, London, 1974, transferring to the Arts; subsequently produced on Broadway at the John Golden, 1975; has directed the first productions of many of his plays, and acted in his own and others' works at La Mama, Caffe Cino, Old Reliable etc.

Address: c/o La Mama, 74A East 7th Street, New York, NY 10003. *Tel:* 475 7710.

PATTERSON, Tom, journalist, and founder of the Stratford Shakespearean Festival of Canada

b Stratford, Ontario, Canada, 11 June 1920; *s* of Harry Murray Patterson and his wife Lucinda (Whyte); *e* Stratford, and University of Toronto; *m* (1) Dorothy W Patterson (mar dis); (2) Patricia Patterson.

After his university graduation, he became associated with a publishing company in Toronto as Associate Editor of a Civic Administration Magazine; in 1951, he approached the Mayor of Stratford with a scheme for an international theatre in Stratford, and with the co-operation of the Stratford City Council, a committee was formed, and he was authorized to ask Dr Tyrone Guthrie to act as Director; in Nov 1952, he was made general manager when the Festival Foundation was officially chartered; the first Stratford Shakespearean Festival was held in July 1953, and has since taken place annually; co-founder of Canadian Players, with Douglas Campbell, 1954; founder and president of Canadian Theatre Exchange, Ltd, 1959; consultant to West Indies Festival of the Arts, Trinidad, 1958; Founder of the Dawson City (Yukon) Gold Rush Festival.

Address: c/o Lockwood Patterson Associates, Suite 3212, 33 Harbour Square, Toronto, Canada M5J 2G2.

PAVLOW, Muriel, actress

b Lee, Kent, 27 June 1921; *d* of Boris Pavlow and his wife Germaine Caroline (Georget); *e* Colne Valley School, Rickmansworth; *m* Derek Farr.

Made her first appearance on the stage at the King's Theatre, Glasgow, 2 Mar 1936, as one of the children in The Old Maid; first appeared in London, at Covent Garden Theatre, 28 Sept 1936, as a daughter of Œdipus in Œdipus Rex; at the Lyric, June 1937, appeared in Victoria Regina; Royalty, Apr 1938, played Elsie in April Clouds; Queen's, Sept 1938, made a great success as Kathleen (Scrap) in Dear Octopus, and played the same part in the revival of the play at the Adelphi, July 1940; at the Globe, Jan 1941, played Margaret in Dear Brutus; Apollo, Dec 1941, Deirdre Drake in Old Acquaintance; Aldwych, Dec 1943, Eleni Rhalles in There Shall Be No Night; Globe, Dec 1944, succeeded Jane Baxter as Lady Elizabeth Randall in While the Sun Shines; Aldwych, Aug 1949, Catherine in The Return of Peter Grimm; Royal, Brighton, July 1951, played Mary Gainsborough in The Gainsborough Girls; Duke of York's, Dec 1951, played Laura Vining in The Day's Mischief; joined the Shakespeare Memorial Theatre Company, 1954, and during the season appeared as Titania in A Midsummer Night's Dream, Bianca in Othello, Bianca in The Taming of the Shrew, and Cressida in Troilus and Cressida; St Martin's, July 1957, played Jane Maxwell in Odd Man In; Strand, Mar 1959, Sally Calvert in Wolf's Clothing; toured Australia, and New Zealand, 1959–60, playing her original part in Odd Man In, and also Nell Nash in The Gazebo; on returning to England, appeared at the Vaudeville, Dec 1961, as Angela Ballantine in Critic's Choice; again toured Australia, 1963–4, as Mary in Mary, Mary; St Martin's, London, Mar 1965, played Valerie in Stranger in My Bed; Savoy, Sept 1967, Elizabeth Low in According to the Evidence; Savoy, Nov 1970, took over as Liz Walford in The Secretary Bird, playing

this part until June 1972; Theatre Royal, Windsor, Oct 1973, Ruth in Blithe Spirit; toured S Africa, Feb–Aug 1974, as Lydia in In Praise of Love; played the same part at Windsor, Mar 1975; toured, 1976, as Liz in There Goes the Bride; Fortune, May 1977, took over the part of Miss Marple in Murder at the Vicarage; first appeared in films, 1936, in A Romance in Flanders; and has since played in Doctor in the House, Simon and Laura, Reach For the Sky, Eyewitness, Doctor at Large, Rooney, Meet Miss Marple, etc; appeared on television recently in Emmerdale Farm.

Recreations: Riding and swimming. *Address:* c/o Larry Dalzell Associates, 3 Goodwin's Court, London WC2.

PAYN, Graham, actor and singer

b Pietermaritzburg, Natal, South Africa, 25 Apr 1918; *s* of Philip Francis Payn and his wife Sybil (Graham); *e* in South Africa and privately in England.

Made his first appearance on the stage, at the Palladium, 21 Dec 1931, as Curly in Peter Pan; Princes, Aug 1939, appeared in Sitting Pretty; Saville, Apr 1940, and again in May 1941, in Up and Doing; Apr 1942, in Fine and Dandy; Princes, May 1943, in Magic Carpet; His Majesty's, Apr 1944, played Elliston Deyn in The Lilac Domino; Palace, Dec 1944, the Mock Turtle and Tweedledum in Alice in Wonderland; Winter Garden, Mar 1945, appeared in The Gaieties; Piccadilly, Aug 1945, in Sigh No More; Drury Lane, Dec 1946, played Kerry Stirling in Pacific 1860; toured in the United States, 1947–8, and appeared at the National, New York, 20 Feb 1948, in To-night at 8.30; Cambridge, London, July 1950, played Harry Hornby in Ace of Clubs; Lyric, Hammersmith, May 1951, appeared in The Lyric Revue; Globe, July 1951, appeared in The Globe Revue; at the same theatre, Sept 1951, again played in The Lyric Revue; again at the Globe, June 1954, appeared as Mr Hopper in After the Ball; New Watergate, Feb 1955, played Johnny Wheelright in Love Is News; at the Aldwych, Jan 1959, took over the part of Stitch Allentock in Brouhaha; Duke of York's, Nov 1959, played Brian Lawson in And Suddenly It's Spring; at the same theatre, Sept 1960, appeared as Perry Lascoe in Waiting in the Wings; Savoy, Nov 1964, co-directed High Spirits; Queen's, Apr 1965, played Morris Dixon in Present Laughter; joint author, Noël Coward and His Friends, 1979; first appeared in films, 1932, as a boy soprano.

Recreation: Swimming. *Hobby:* Painting in oils. *Address:* c/o Personal Management Ltd, 15 Hay Hill, London, W1.

PAYTON-WRIGHT, Pamela, actress

b Pittsburgh, Pa, 1 Nov 1941; *e* Birmingham Southern College; prepared for the stage at the Royal Academy of Dramatic Art, London.

Made her first appearance in New York at the Lyceum, 5 Dec 1967, as Amy in The Show-Off, in the APA-Phoenix production; Jan 1968, played Juliette in Exit the King; Mar 1968, Anya in The Cherry Orchard, and subsequently toured with this company; Brooks Atkinson, Dec 1968, Constance Fry in Jimmy Shine; appeared with the Trinity Square Repertory, Providence, RI, 1969–70 season; Mercer O'Casey, Apr 1970, Tillie in The Effect of Gamma Rays on Man-in-the-Moon Marigolds; Vivian Beaumont, Apr 1972, Abigail Williams in The Crucible; Circle in the Square—Joseph E Levine, Nov 1972, Lavinia Mannon in Mourning Becomes Electra; appeared with the Long Wharf Theater, New Haven, Conn, 1973–74 season; Trinity Square Repertory, Providence, RI, Dec 1973, Aimee Semple McPherson in Aimee; Booth, Dec 1974, Millie in All Over Town; The Other Stage, Nov 1975, Belle in Jesse and the

Bandit Queen; Circle in the Square, Dec 1975, Laura in The Glass Menagerie; same theatre, Mar 1977, Juliet in Romeo and Juliet; Long Wharf, Nov 1977, Clare in The Lunch Girls; same theatre, Jan 1979, Kaleria in Summerfolk; appeared in the film Corky, 1972.

Address: Actors Equity Association, 165 West 46th Street, New York, NY 10036.

PEACOCK, Trevor, actor, composer and dramatic author
b Tottenham, London, 19 May 1931; *s* of Victor Edward Peacock and his wife Alexandria; *e* Enfield Grammar School, Middlesex; *m* (1) Iris Jones (mar dis); (2) Tilly Tremayne, actress.

First appeared on the London stage April 1956, at the Windmill as a comedian; 1962–3 played small parts at the Old Vic; Open Air, Regent's Park, July 1964, Grumio in The Taming of the Shrew; Royal Court, Feb 1967, Jimmy Beales in Roots; for the 69 Theatre Company, Manchester, played Estragon in Waiting for Godot, 1967, Horatio in Hamlet, 1968 (Edinburgh Festival), and Tony Lumpkin in She Stoops to Conquer, 1969, transferring in the last part to the Garrick, May 1969; Strand, Dec 1969, played the title-role in his own musical, Erb; Open Air, Regent's Park, June 1970, Bottom in A Midsummer Night's Dream; toured, Oct 1970 as Sgt Kite in the Cambridge Theatre Company's The Recruiting Officer; Royal Court, Mar 1971, played Sgt Charles Fairchild in Man Is Man; Round House, July 1971, title-role in Titus Andronicus; Hampstead, Nov 1971, the title-role in The Novelist; Young Vic, 1971, Petruchio in The Taming of the Shrew; University, Manchester, Oct 1972, Nathan Detroit in Guys and Dolls; Watford Palace, Feb 1973, Sir John Brute in The Provok'd Wife; Manchester, May 1973, and Shaw, July 1973, Clov in Endgame; joined the Royal Shakespeare Company at the Aldwych, Jan 1974, to play Sidney Prime in Sherlock Holmes, a part he also played on his New York début at the Broadhurst, Nov 1974; Aldwych, May 1974, Friar Mauro Tenda and Diego Lopez Duro in The Bewitched; Stratford, season 1975, Bishop of Ely and Fluellen in Henry V, Poins in both parts of Henry IV, Silence in Part 2, and Sir Hugh Evans in The Merry Wives of Windsor; repeated these performances at the Aldwych, Jan–Apr, 1976, member of the Royal Exchange Company, Manchester, in its opening season, 1976; playing Bob Acres in The Rivals, Colonel Kottwitz in The Prince of Homberg, the title-role in Zack, Police Sergeant in What the Butler Saw; Old Vic, Sept 1977, Mark Twain in White Suit Blue, repeating the part in Nottingham and Edinburgh, 1978; Haymarket, July 1978, Tom Price in A Family; Manchester Royal Exchange, June 1979, Aramis in The Three Musketeers; he is author of the play Collapse of Stout Party; wrote the lyrics for Passion Flower Hotel, 1965 and Saturday Night and Sunday Morning, 1966; book, lyrics and music for Erb, 1970; Leaping Ginger, 1977; book, lyrics and music for Cinderella, 1978; has appeared in films and television, also writing for both: recent television includes The Old Curiosity Shop, Twelfth Night and *Born and Bred*.

Favourite parts: Estragon and Lumpkin. *Recreations:* Cricket and soccer. *Address:* c/o Peter Crouch, 59 Frith Street, London W1V 5TA.

PEARSON, Richard, actor
b Monmouth, 1 Aug 1918; *s* of Cyril Hearne Pearson and his wife Dorothy (Clabburn); *e* Aymestrey Court, Worcester, and Monmouth School; *m* Patricia Dickson.

Made his first appearance on the stage at the Collins Music Hall, Islington, Mar 1937, as Dallis in The Ruined Lady; 1937–8, played in repertory at Westcliff, and toured as Flossie

in Housemaster; first appeared in the West End at the Gate, Oct 1938, as Unwin in Private History; Richmond, Feb 1939, played Dick Fortesque in Ill Blows the Wind; 1939, toured as Larry in They Walk Alone; served in HM Forces 1939–46; appeared for the Services Sunday Society at the Whitehall, Feb 1947, when he played Elwes in Quay South; 1947, toured in Lady From Edinburgh; Strand, Feb 1948, played Simon in Family Portrait; Embassy, May 1948, played John in Symphony in Violence; toured as Ewan in This is Where We Came In; at the Q Theatre, July 1949, played Ralph Tyler in The Town Bowl; Duchess, Dec 1949, Mac in The Philadelphia Story; for the Repertory Players, Phoenix, Apr 1950, played A B Tubs Brewster in Red Dragon; Embassy, Sept 1950, played Eric Grant in Soldier Boy; at the same theatre, Sept 1950, played the Chauffeur in Turn to Page Two; Q Theatre, Oct 1950, Edward Macey in A Pig in a Poke; Aldwych, Mar 1951, Rev John Caldecot in Macadam and Eve; Duke of York's Apr 1952, played Tom Thistleton in The Mortimer Touch; Comedy, Oct 1952, PC Potter in The Apples of Eve; Q Theatre, Dec 1952, Howard in To Christabel; and Jan 1954, Bob Carver in Birds of Sadness; at the Apollo, June 1954, played Mr Wilson in Both Ends Meet; Globe, Mar 1956, Gregory Lupton in A Likely Tale; Cambridge, Mar 1957, Collins in The Iron Duchess; Lyric, Hammersmith, May 1958, Stanley in The Birthday Party; at the Globe, May 1962, Charles Sidley in The Public Eye; Arts, Cambridge, Mar 1969, played Harry in Staircase; Hampstead Theatre Club, Sept 1969, Curio in Papp; Aldwych, Jan 1970, for the Royal Shakespeare Company, played the Cardinal in Tiny Alice; Chichester Festival, May 1970, appeared as William Cecil in Vivat! Vivat Regina! and again at the Piccadilly, Oct 1970; Young Vic, Feb 1972, Mr Hardcastle in She Stoops to Conquer; Chichester Festival, May 1973, Impossibile in The Director of the Opera, and Sorin in The Seagull; Cottesloe, Nov 1977, Francis Mallock in Half-Life, repeating the part at the Duke of York's, Mar 1978; first entered films in 1938, and has recently appeared in It Shouldn't Happen to a Vet, The Bluebird, and Tess; first appeared on television in 1947, and performances include: Love Among the Ruins, She Fell Among Thieves, Coming Out, and Thérèse Raquin.

Favourite parts: Pecksniff in Martin Chuzzlewit, and Stanley in The Birthday Party. *Recreation:* Reading and gardening. *Address:* c/o Representation Joyce Edwards, 8 Theed Street, London, SE1 8ST.

PEMBER, Ron, actor, writer and director
b Plaistow, London, 11 Apr 1934; *s* of William Henry Pember, and his wife Gladys Emily Martha (Orchard); *e* Eastbrook Secondary Modern, Dagenham, Essex; *m* Yvonne Tylee.

First appeared on the stage in Summer 1949, on a tour of the Durham Mining District, playing the part of Fabian in Twelfth Night; after seven years' repertory experience first appeared on the London stage Dec 1959, at the Mermaid, as Harry in Treasure Island; Adelphi, May 1962, played Bird in Blitz!; with the National Theatre Company, 1965–8, he played numerous smaller parts; his work at the Mermaid has included six productions of Treasure Island; Staff in a revival of Lock Up Your Daughters, which he directed in Mar 1969; Bernard in The Bandwagon, Oct 1969; Trinculo in The Tempest, June 1970; he has also directed Treasure Island twice at the Mermaid and once on tour, also in Canada and New York; The Goblet Game, 1968; Enter Solly Gold, Henry IV (both parts), Dick Turpin (also wrote), 1970; Royal Court, Sept 1971, played Third Workman in Lear; Savoy, Oct 1973, Bert Brown in At the End of the Day; for the Royal Shakespeare Company, played Feste in Twelfth Night, Porter in Macbeth, Stratford 1974 (where he also played the Sergeant in Macbeth) and Aldwych, 1975; Shaftesbury, June 1976, Fingers Philips in Liza of Lambeth; Mermaid, Sept 1976, co-directed King and Country; Mermaid, Dec 1976, co-adapted and directed The Point; Riverside Studios, Jan 1978, the Stranger in The Cherry Orchard; co-founded the CVI Theatre Company (Coventry), for which he wrote and co-directed the opening production, 1900 and Froze to Death, Aug 1978; directed his own musical, Jack the Ripper, Providence Rhode Island, 1979; Feb 1980, toured as Shylock in The Merchant of Venice; Aug 1980, appointed Artistic Director of CVI Theatre Company; composer and co-author of the musical, Jack the Ripper, London, 1974; has appeared in films since 1960, including Oh What a Lovely War, Young Winston, and Murder by Decree, and on television since the same date, recently appearing in Nicholas Nickleby and *Secret Army*.

Recreations: Chess, writing. *Address:* 11 Glencoe Drive, Dagenham, Essex.

PEMBERTON-BILLING, Robin, director and dramatist
b London, 5 Apr 1929; *s* of Noel Pemberton-Billing, MP and his wife Veronica; *e* KCS Wimbledon and Loughborough College of Education; *m* Margaret Hellewell; formerly a teacher and a lecturer in drama.

Director, 1967–71, of the Octagon Theatre, Bolton, which he helped design; his productions there include the premières of Annie and Fanny, 1967; Crompton's Mule and The Golden Cockerel (also wrote), 1968; Bolton Massacre and King Arthur and the Round Table (also wrote), 1969; In Place of Strife? 1971; apart from the four plays mentioned above he is the author of Teaching Drama.

Recreations: Sailing, water ski-ing, ceramics.

PENDLETON, Austin, actor, director
b Warren, Ohio, 27 Mar 1940; *e* Yale Univ.

Made his NY debut at the Phoenix, 26 Feb 1962, as Jonathan in Oh Dad, Poor Dad, Mama's Hung You in the Closet and I'm Feelin' So Sad; Imperial, Sept 1964, Motel in Fiddler on the Roof; toured with the American Conservatory Theatre, 1966–67, in Beyond the Fringe; Booth, NY, Nov 1966, Irwin Ingham in Hail Scrawdyke!; Vivian Beaumont, Oct 1967, Leo Hubbard in The Little Foxes, and transferred with this production to the Ethel Barrymore, Dec 1967; appeared with the Studio Arena, Buffalo, NY, in the 1968–69 season; Eastside Playhouse, Jan 1970, Isaac in The Last Sweet Days of Isaac; appeared with the Long Wharf, New Haven, Conn, 1971–72 season; Playhouse-in-the-Park, Cincinnati, Ohio, 1971, again played Isaac in The Last Sweet Days of Isaac; John Golden, Feb 1973, directed Shelter; Long Wharf, Oct 1973, directed The Master Builder; The New Dramatists, Inc, Nov 1973, Charles in American Glands; Circle in the Square—Joseph E Levine, Apr 1974, Prof Bobby Rudetsky in An American Millionaire; Playhouse-in-the-Park, Cincinnati, Oct 1974, title role in Tartuffe; Manhattan Theater Club, Dec 1974, directed The Runner Stumbles; Eisenhower, Washington, Aug 1975, directed The Scarecrow; Hartman, Stamford, Conn, Nov 1975, played in the Government Inspector; same theatre, Dec, again directed The Runner Stumbles (also on Broadway, May 1976); St C American Repertory, Feb 1976, appeared in The Sorrows of Frederick; American Place, Apr 1976, directed Benito Cereno; Lake Forest, Ill, Aug 1976, directed Misalliance; Hartman, Jan 1977, again played Tartuffe; Manhattan Theatre Club, Mar 1977, directed The Gathering; Brooklyn Academy, Apr 1977, Tusenbach in

Three Sisters; at the same theatre played Mark Antony in Julius Caesar, Apr 1978, and Estragon in Waiting for Godot, May; 78th Street, Mar 1979, directed Say Goodnight, Gracie; Quaigh, Sept 1979, Jack in The Office Murders; has also directed and appeared at the Williamstown Theatre Festival, recently After the Fall; teaches acting at the HB Studio; appeared in the films What's Up Doc?, 1972, Every Little Crook and Nanny, The Front Page, The Muppet Movie, Starting Over, etc.

Address: Actors Equity Association, 165 West 46th Street, New York, NY 10036.

PENDLETON, Wyman, actor
b Providence, Rhode Island, 18 Apr 1916; *s* of Wyman Pendleton and his wife Mildred (Chambers); *e* Brown University, 1938; was for several years a salesman and office manager for the Yale and Towne Manufacturing Co.

Made his first appearance on the stage while at Brown University, Providence, Rhode Island, 1937, at the Modern as the First Citizen in Orson Welles's Julius Caesar; made his New York début at the Cherry Lane, 11 Feb 1962, as the Prologue in Gallows Humor in a season of plays with the overall title Theatre of the Absurd; same theatre, 1963, took over as Daddy in The American Dream and Peter in Zoo Story; Oct 1963, played Malgai in Corruption in the Palace of Justice; summer 1964, again took over as Daddy in The American Dream; Nov 1964, played Arch-Druid Grigas in The Giant's Dance; Garrick, Dec 1964, Willard Owing in The Child Buyer; Billy Rose, Dec 1964, understudied Lawyer, Butler, and Cardinal in Tiny Alice; Cherry Lane, Sept 1965, played Willie in Happy Days in French, with Madeleine Renaud; Sam S Shubert, Jan 1966, Girard in Malcolm; Hopkins Center, Hanover, New Hampshire, summer 1965 and 1966, played Tartuffe, John of Gaunt in Richard II, and Julius Caesar; Cherry Lane, Oct 1966, A J Patterson in The Butter and Egg Man; Theatre Company of Boston, Jan 1967, played Cardinal in Tiny Alice; toured, spring 1967, as stand-by for Harry and Tobias in A Delicate Balance, and played Harry in Detroit; toured with the National Repertory Theatre, Oct–Dec 1967, and Ford's, Washington, Feb 1968, as Egeon in The Comedy of Errors, various roles in John Brown's Body, and Sir Charles Marlow in She Stoops to Conquer; Billy Rose, Sept 1968, Chairman Mao in Quotations from Chairman Mao-Tse Tung and, Oct 1968, Willie in Happy Days; American Shakespeare Festival, Stratford, Connecticut, 1969, played in Henry V, Much Ado About Nothing, and Hamlet; ANTA, Nov 1969, Ely and Charles VI in Henry V; Stratford, Connecticut, 1970, played in Othello, All's Well That Ends Well, and The Devil's Disciple; ANTA, Sept 1970, Duke of Venice in Othello; appeared with the Stratford Festival, Ontario, Canada, in 1971; Royale, Jan 1972, Jean in There's One in Every Marriage; appeared with the American Shakespeare Festival, Stratford, Conn, 1972; Stratford, Conn, 1973, played the Doctor in Macbeth, Escalus in Measure for Measure, and the title role of Julius Caesar; Virginia Museum, Richmond, Va, Feb 1974, Baron Jacobi in Democracy; Stratford, Conn, 1974, Lord Montague in Romeo and Juliet and Reverend Tooker in Cat on a Hot Tin Roof; repeated this last part at the ANTA, Sept 1974; Stratford, Conn, 1975, Doctor in King Lear, Professor Willard in Our Town, and Archidamus in The Winter's Tale; Roundabout Stage One, Oct 1975, Reverend Winemiller in Summer and Smoke; Richmond, Va, Jan 1976, in The Country Wife and The Mousetrap; Stratford, Conn, June 1976, in The Crucible, and The Winter's Tale; Stage West, Springfield, Dec 1976, in The Tooth of Crime, Hot L Baltimore, and You Can't Take it with You; Goodman,

Chicago, Sept 1977, in Saint Joan; Roundabout, Jan 1978, Brabantio and Gratiano in Othello; toured US and Far East, Sept 1978–June 1979, in Albee directs Albee, a program of 8 one-act plays; The Annex, Sept 1979, Wilke in Dance for Me, Simeon; entered films in Pigeons, 1970; recently in The Seduction of Joe Tynan, 1979; has appeared on television talk shows in the series *Toma*, 1973, *Edge of Night*, 1977–9, etc.

Favourite parts: Mao Tse-Tung, Polonius, John of Gaunt, Peter in Albee's The Zoo Story. *Recreations:* Music, swimming, reading. *Address:* 36 Bedford Street, New York, NY 10014. *Tel:* 861-7237.

PENN, Arthur, director
b Philadelphia, Pa, 27 Sept 1922; *e* Black Mountain College, and the Universities of Perugia and Florence, Italy; *m* Peggy Maurer; studied for the theatre with Michael Chekhov.

Began his stage career as an actor, and made his first appearance on the stage at the Neighborhood Playhouse, Philadelphia, in 1940; he directed his first Broadway production at the Booth Theatre, Jan 1958, with Two for the Seesaw, and directed his first London production at the Haymarket, Dec 1958, with the same play; Playhouse, New York, Oct 1959, directed The Miracle Worker; Hudson, Feb 1960, directed Toys in the Attic; John Golden, Oct 1960, directed An Evening with Mike Nichols and Elaine May; Belasco, Dec 1960, directed All the Way Home; he has since directed In the Counting House, 1962; Lorenzo, 1963; Golden Boy, 1964; Wait Until Dark, 1966; executive producer of the Actors Studio production of Clifford Odets's The Silent Partner, 1972; directed Felix, 1972; Sly Fox, 1976; Golda, 1977; directed many films including The Left-Handed Gun, 1957; The Miracle Worker, 1962; Bonnie and Clyde, 1968; Alice's Restaurant, 1969; Little Big Man, 1970; The Missouri Breaks, 1976; television productions include: Man on a Mountain Top, and The Miracle Workers; a director of the Actors Studio.
Address: 2 West 67th Street, New York, NY 10023.

PERKINS, Anthony, actor and director
b New York City, 4 Apr 1932; *s* of Osgood Perkins and his wife Janet Esselton (Rane); *e* Rollins College, Florida, and Columbia University; *m* Berinthia Berenson.

Made his first appearance on the NY stage, at the Ethel Barrymore Theatre, June 1954, when he took over the part of Tom Lee in Tea and Sympathy; at the same theatre, Nov 1957, played Eugene Gant in Look Homeward, Angel, which ran for more than a year; Alvin, Mar 1960, played Gideon Briggs in Greenwillow; Cort, Nov 1962, Harold Selbar in Harold; Plymouth, Dec 1966, Andy Hobart in The Star-Spangled Girl; Huntington Hartford, Los Angeles, Feb 1968, again played Andy Hobart in The Star-Spangled Girl and later toured in this production, which he also directed; Playhouse in the Park, Philadelphia, 1968, directed The Unknown Soldier and His Wife; Milwaukee Repertory, Wisconsin, 1968, directed The Imaginary Invalid and, 1969, directed The Burgermaster; Truck and Warehouse, NY, June 1970, played Tandy in Steambath, which he also directed; Shubert, 11 Mar 1973, appeared in Sondheim: A Musical Tribute; Eastside Playhouse, Oct 1974, directed The Wager; Plymouth, Oct 1975, took over from Anthony Hopkins as Martin Dysart in Equus, and continued in this part until Feb 1976; Plymouth, May 1976, took over from Richard Burton in this last play; Ethel Barrymore, Nov 1979, Jason Carmichael in Romantic Comedy; first entered films, 1953, in The Actress, and has since appeared in a number of pictures, including: The Matchmaker, On the Beach, Psycho, Goodbye Again, Friendly Persuasion, Lovin' Molly, Murder

on the Orient Express, Winter Kills, etc; with Stephen Sondheim wrote the screenplay of The Last of Sheila, 1973; made his first appearance on television, Oct 1953, in Joey, and has since appeared regularly in this medium.

Favourite part: Eugene Gant. *Recreations:* Piano, painting, and tennis. *Address:* Actors Equity Association, 165 West 46th Street, New York, NY 10036.

PERRYMAN, Jill, actress
b Melbourne, Victoria, 30 May 1933; *d* of William Thomas Perryman and his wife Dorothy (Duval); *e* Sydney Public Schools; *m* Kevan Johnston; trained for the stage by her family.

Her first stage appearance was in May 1935, at the King's Theatre, Melbourne, in White Horse Inn; at Her Majesty's, Melbourne, appeared in the chorus of Call Me Madam, Sept 1953; South Pacific, Oct 1954; played a Mormon's wife in Paint Your Wagon, Nov 1954; appeared in the Chorus of Can Can, Oct 1955, played Mabel in The Pajama Game, Feb 1957; from 1958–61 appeared at the Phillip Theatre, Sydney, in the revues Bats, 1958; Birthday Show, Hey Diddle Diddle, The Phillip Revue, 1959; Yes Please, and At It Again, 1960; Do You Mind, 1961; Her Majesty's, Melbourne, Oct 1962, played Rosalie in Carnival; Her Majesty's, Sydney, Mar 1965, Mrs Molloy in Hello Dolly; same theatre, Mar 1966, Fanny Brice in Funny Girl; Her Majesty's, Melbourne, Feb 1969, Agnes in I Do, I Do; Phillip, Sydney, 1970, appeared in the revue When We Are Married; St Martin's, Melbourne, Dec 1971, played four parts in the collection, The Two of Us; Her Majesty's, Melbourne, June 1972, Lucille in No No Nanette; Her Majesty's, Sydney, Nov 1973, Countess Malcolm in A Little Night Music; Music Loft, Sydney, Apr 1976, various characters in the revue Leading Lady, repeating the parts at St Martin's, Melbourne, Mar 1977; Theatre Royal, Sydney, Sept 1977, in Side by Side by Sondheim; Her Majesty's, Sydney, May 1979, Miss Hannigan in Annie; received the Erik award as best actress, 1966 and 1972, for her performances in Funny Girl and No No Nanette; TV includes Bellbird, Dynasty, and Perryman on Parade, 1973, for which she received the Television Society of Australia award as best variety entertainer.

Favourite parts: Fanny Brice, Agnes, Countess Malcolm; *Recreations*: Classical recorded music, reading. *Address:* 4 Hillside Crescent, Gooseberry Hill 6076, Western Australia. *Tel:* 931395.

PERSOFF, Nehemiah, actor
b Jerusalem, Israel, 14 Aug 1920; *s* of Samuel Persoff and his wife Puah (Holman); *e* Technical High School, Dramatic Workshop, and Actors Studio; *m* Tia Persov; formerly an electrician and a signal maintenance man; prepared for the stage with Stella Adler, Lee Strasberg, and Elia Kazan.

Made his New York stage début off-Broadway at the Heckscher Foundation, 1940, as the Minister of State in The Emperor's New Clothes; at the Haverhill, Mass, Playhouse, 1947, played Candy in Of Mice and Men, Dean Damon in The Male Animal, Dick Dudgeon in The Devil's Disciple, and in Hay Fever; President, Apr 1947, played the Tutor in The Flies; Maxine Elliott, Dec 1947, played Andrea in Galileo; Belasco, Sept 1948, Cecil in Sundown Beach; Booth, Feb 1949, Tyrell in Richard III; Fulton, Oct 1949, Antonanzas in Montserrat; Imperial, Apr 1950, Cecco in Peter Pan; National, Dec 1950, Duke of Cornwall in King Lear; ANTA, Feb 1951, Ingrid's Father and the Troll King in Peer Gynt; Broadhurst, May 1951, Fowzi The Younger Arab, in Flahooley; Chamber Theatre, Tel-Aviv, Israel, 1951, played Tom in The Glass Menagerie and Mosca in Volpone;

National, Mar 1953, Street Cleaner in Camino Real; Playhouse in the Park, Philadelphia, 1953, played in The Detective Story and The Road to Rome; Longacre, Jan 1954, Hairdresser in Mademoiselle Colombe; Playhouse in the Park, Philadelphia, 1954, Eddie Fuseli in Golden Boy; Lyceum, Oct 1954, Dr Hickey in Reclining Figure; Plymouth, Oct 1955, a Topman in Tiger at the Gates; Cort, Nov 1959, Harry Golden in Only in America; reappeared on the stage at the Mark Taper Forum, Los Angeles, Oct 1970, when he played Harry in Rosebloom; Oxford, Los Angeles, Aug 1971, appeared in the one-man show Aleichem Sholem— Sholem Aleichem, for which he received the Los Angeles Critics Circle Award; toured the US, 1974, as John in Snowangel and Man in Epiphany in a double-bill called Cages, later renamed Last of the Great Jelly Bellies; Mark Taper Forum, Los Angeles, 1975, Rabbi Azrielke in The Dybbuk, for which he again received the Los Angeles Critics Circle Award; has also appeared in stock, including Fagin in Oliver; entered films in 1948, in Naked City, and has since appeared in On the Waterfront, The Harder They Fall, Men in War, Some Like It Hot, Never Steal Anything Small, The Greatest Story Ever Told, Mrs Pollifax, Spy, Red Sky at Morning, Voyage of the Damned, In Search of the Historic Jesus (1979), and many others; TV, since 1953, includes over three hundred appearances in plays, series and serials.

Favourite parts: Tom in The Glass Menagerie, and Jerry in Clash by Night. *Recreations:* Tennis, gardening, and playing with his children. *Address:* Actors Equity Association, 165 West 46th Street, New York, NY 10036.

PERTWEE, Jon, actor

b Chelsea, London, 7 July 1919; *s* of Roland Pertwee and his wife Avice (Scholtz); *e* Sherborne and Frensham Heights; *m* (1) Jean Marsh, actress; (2) Ingeborg Rhoesa; trained for the stage at RADA.

Made his first professional appearance at the West Pier, Brighton, 1936, as Marchbanks in Candida; first London appearance, Aldwych, 1939, as Esmond Proust in Independence; at the Strand, Feb 1958, played Ogleby in Touch It Light; Duchess, Mar 1963, appeared in the revue See You Inside; Strand, Oct 1963, Lycus in A Funny Thing Happened on the Way to the Forum; Globe, June 1966, Andrew in There's A Girl In My Soup, making his New York début in the same part at the Music Box, Oct 1967; Lyric, London, Aug 1968, Sir Gregory Parsloe-Parsloe in Oh, Clarence!; Royalty, Sept 1974, Pat Plummer in The Bedwinner; toured, 1975, in So Who Needs Marriage?; toured, Nov 1975, as Sir William Mainwaring-Brown in Don't Just Lie There, Say Something!; Richmond, Dec 1975, Abanazar in Aladdin; Adelphi, June 1976, Madame Lucy in Irene; films, since 1939, include several of the Carry On series, One of Our Dinosaurs Is Missing, and Africana 2000; television, since 1945, includes *Dr Who* and *Worzel Gummidge*.

Favourite parts: Andrew and Lycus. *Club:* Water Rats. *Recreations:* Water sport, motor-cycling, folk music. *Address:* c/o Richard Stone, 18–20 York Buildings, Adelphi, London, WC2.

PERTWEE, Michael, dramatic writer

b London, 24 Apr 1916; *s* of Roland Pertwee and his wife Avice (Scholtz); *e* Sherborne; *m* Maya Pertwee.

Author of several plays, of which the following have been presented in London: Death on the Table (also New York), 1938; The Paragon (co-author), 1948; It's Different for Men (co-author), 1955; The Four Musketeers (book), 1967; She's Done It Again! 1969; Don't Just Lie There, Say Something!, 1971; A Bit Between the Teeth, Birds of Paradise (adapta-

tion), 1974; Sextet, 1977; Find the Lady, 1979; has also written numerous film scripts, since 1939, and for television since 1950.

Recreations: Golf. *Address:* 34 Aylestone Avenue, London, NW6 7AA. *Tel:* 01–459 3353.

PETERS, Bernadette, actress and singer

b Ozone Park, Long Island, New York, 28 Feb 1948; *d* of Peter Lazzara and his wife Marguerite (Maltese); *e* Public School 58, Queens, NY and Quintano School for Young Professionals, NY.

Made her first appearance in NY at the New York City Center, 10 Feb 1959, as Tessie in The Most Happy Fella; Stage 73 Theatre, 26 Dec 1966, played Cinderella in The Penny Friend; Booth, May 1967, was an understudy in The Girl in the Freudian Slip; Cort, Oct 1967, Bettina in Johnny No-Trump; Bert Wheeler, Nov 1967, Alice in Curley McDimple; Palace, Apr 1968, Josie Cohan in George M!; Bouwerie Lane, Dec 1968, Ruby in Dames at Sea and scored a great personal success and received the Drama Desk Award; Lunt-Fontanne, Dec 1969, Gelsomina in La Strada; toured, 1971, as Carlotta Monti in WC; Lambs Club, Mar 1971, Consuelo in Nevertheless They Laugh; Imperial, Oct 1971, Hildy in On the Town; Walnut Street, Philadelphia, Nov 1972, Dorine in Tartuffe; Majestic, Oct 1974, Mabel Normand in Mack and Mabel; appeared in the film The Longest Yard, 1974, and subsequently in Silent Movie, The Jerk, Tulips (1980), etc; has appeared on television, notably on *The Carol Burnett Show*, 1970–5, *All's Fair*, and The Martian Chronicles (1980); has made frequent cabaret appearances in Las Vegas, Atlantic City, etc.

Recreations and hobbies: Piano, guitar, old songs, old jewellery. *Address:* Actors Equity Association, 165 West 46th Street, New York, NY 10036.

PETHERBRIDGE, Edward, actor and director

b Bradford, Yorkshire, 3 Aug 1936; *s* of William Petherbridge and his wife Hannah (Harrison); *e* Grange GS, Bradford; *m* Louise Durant Harris (mar dis); trained at the Northern Theatre School, Bradford.

Made his first stage appearance in 1956 at the Ludlow Festival as Gaveston in Edward II; after varied experience in provincial repertory and touring, made his first London appearance June 1962 at the Open Air, Regent's Park as Demetrius in A Midsummer Night's Dream; Mermaid, March 1963, played Geoffrey Fitton in All In Good Time, transferring to the Phoenix in April; member of the National Theatre Company from 1964 to 1970, playing fifteen parts from walk-ons upwards, including: Ferdinand Gadd in Trelawny of the Wells, 1965; Guildenstern in Rosencrantz and Guildenstern Are Dead, 1967; Voltore in Volpone, Spencer in Edward II, and Lorenzo in The Advertisement, 1968; Harlequin and Piérrot in Scrabble, Waitwell in The Way of the World and Lodovico in The White Devil, 1969; Bath Festival, 1968, played the soldier in The Soldier's Tale; Playhouse, Nottingham, Sept 1970, Alceste in The Misanthrope; Royal Court, Dec 1970, Alwa in Lulu, transferring to the Apollo, Jan 1971; Theatre Upstairs, Jan 1971, Laurence Caldecott in Morality; Mermaid, May 1971, Laurence Doyle in John Bull's Other Island; at the opening of the Crucible, Sheffield, Nov 1971, played Nikita in Swan Song; Arts, May 1972, gave a solo performance, Who Thought It?; founder member of the Actors' Company, playing Soranzo in 'Tis Pity She's a Whore at the Edinburgh Festival, Sept 1972; Northcott, Exeter, Apr 1973, Prospero in The Tempest; again with the Actors' Company, he directed Flow, and Knots (double-bill), appearing in the latter, which he also devised (from R D Laing), Edinburgh Festival, Sept 1973, and tour; also played Fool in King Lear; to the last two parts he added Simon in The Wood Demon, and Mirabell in The Way of the World, at Brooklyn Academy of Music, Jan 1974; Wimbledon, Mar–May 1974, played Soranzo, Fool, Simon, also Hotel Manager in Ruling the Roost; Edinburgh Festival, Aug 1974, played Valère in Tartuffe, and Teiresias in The Bacchae, which he also directed; in the Actors' Company, second Wimbledon season, June–Aug 1975, played Erik in The Phantom of the Opera, title-role in Tartuffe, directed The Bacchae and The Beanstalk (double-bill), playing the Ring Master in the latter; 1976, toured in Australia and New Zealand with the RSC, in The Hollow Crown and Pleasure and Repentance; 1977, toured with the Cambridge Theatre Company as Dobson in Dog's Dinner and directed Uncle Vanya; Actors' Company tour and Round House, Dec 1977–Jan 1978, directed and played The Compere and Museum Attendant in his own adaptation of R D Laing's Do You Love Me?, and played Dr Chasuble in The Importance of Being Earnest; June 1978, toured as The Brigadier in Game of Kings; Nov 1978, in RSC's first small-scale tour, playing Orsino in Twelfth Night, Vershinin in The Three Sisters, and appearing in the anthology Is there Honey still for Tea?; Haymarket, Mar 1979, Captain St Clare in The Crucifer of Blood; Other Place, Stratford, Sept 1979, again played Vershinin for the RSC; Aldwych, June 1980, Newman Neggs in Nicholas Nickleby; has held teaching workshops and demonstrations of mime, which he studied with Claude Chagrin, his many television appearances, since 1961, include The Soldier's Tale, After Magritte, and recently, A True Patriot, Schubert, and Pyramid of Fire; appeared in the film version of Knots, 1975.

Recreations: Listening to music; the countryside, photography. *Address:* c/o French's, 26 Binney Street, London, W1.

PHETHEAN, David, director and former actor
b Worsley, Lancashire, 6 July 1918; *s* of Charles Phethean and his wife Mabel Alice (Yates); *e* Wrekin College; *m* Eleanor Warwick Gibson; trained as an actor at RADA, 1936–7.

Made his first London appearance at His Majesty's, June 1939, as Wagner in The Devil to Pay; after a career as an actor which included plays in the West End and provincial rep, as well as films and television, directed his first play at Nottingham Playhouse, 1956; Director of Productions, Queen's, Hornchurch, 1960–3; assistant director, Bristol Old Vic, 1963–4, in charge of Little Theatre; directed a new London production of Beyond the Fringe, 1965; directed tour of Oliver! 1965; new London production, 1967; Tokyo production, 1968; returned to Bristol Old Vic, 1969, as Associate Director; numerous subsequent plays directed include: The Iceman Cometh, 1971; Misalliance, 1972; Journey's End, 1973; Vivat! Vivat Regina!, 1974; Lock Up Your Daughters, 1975; A Flea in Her Ear, 1976; Round and Round the Garden, Absurd Personal Singular, 1977; has directed student productions at RADA since 1965.

Address: c/o Bristol Old Vic Co, Theatre Royal, King Street, Bristol BS1 4ED.

PHILLIPS, Leslie, actor and director
b Tottenham, London, 20 Apr 1924; *s* of Frederick Samuel Phillips and his wife Cecelia Margaret (Newlove); *e* Chingford School; *m* Penelope Bartley (mar dis); studied for the stage at the Italia Conti Stage School.

Made his first appearance at the Palladium, 26 Dec 1935, as a wolf in Peter Pan; as a child, appeared in London productions of The Zeal of Thy House and Dear Octopus; later appeared in repertory at York, Dundee, Watford, Buxton, Croydon, etc; at the Haymarket, 1942, appeared in The

Doctor's Dilemma; during the war served in the Durham Light Infantry as a Lieutenant; after returning to the stage appeared at the Comedy, Dec 1948, as Jimmy McBride in Daddy Long-Legs; Embassy, Apr 1949, played Jerry Winterton in On Monday Next, and appeared in this part at the Comedy, June 1949, where the play ran for over a year; Saville, Dec 1950, played Lord Fancourt Babberley in Charley's Aunt; Comedy, Dec 1952, Tony in For Better, For Worse . . ., which ran for eighteen months; Arts, Sept 1954, played Lupin Pooter in The Diary of a Nobody; Garrick, June 1955, Scruffy Pembridge in The Lost Generation; Aldwych, Oct 1955, Carliss in The Whole Truth; Aldwych, July 1958, played Peter Croone in Three-Way Switch; Princes, Feb 1962, played Peter Cadbury in The Big Killing; Ashcroft, Croydon, Apr 1963, Alfred Trapp in the Deadly Game; Apollo, Apr 1963, took over the part of Robert in Boeing-Boeing; Feb 1966, toured as Clancy Pettinger in On the Level; Savoy, Apr 1967, played Alfred Trapp in his own production of The Deadly Game; Vaudeville, July 1968, played Victor Cadwallader in his own production of The Man Most Likely to . . . for twenty months, touring South Africa and Australia with the play in 1970; Duke of York's, Oct 1973, returned as Victor Cadwallader, making another tour of Australia, 1974; again at the Duke of York's, Oct 1975, played Roger in Roger's Last Stand; Criterion, Apr 1977, Phillip in Sextet; toured, Feb 1979, as Geoffrey Lymes in Canaries Sometimes Sing; Savoy, Nov 1979, Gilbert Bodley in Not Now Darling; has directed various repertory companies since 1950, and also for The Repertory Players; first London production, Westminster, May 1960, when he directed Roger the Sixth; directed The Avengers, 1971; first appeared in films 1936, in The Citadel.

Favourite parts: Toni Rigi in To Dorothy, A Son, Trapp in The Deadly Game, and Tony in For Better, For Worse . . .
Recreations: Racing, golf, chess, weaving, collecting antique jewellery. *Address:* c/o ICM Ltd, 22 Grafton Street, London, W1. *Tel:* 01–629 8080.

PHILLIPS, Margaret, actress
b Cwmgwrach, South Wales, 6 July 1923; studied for the stage in London, before leaving for the United States, 1939; continued her studies at the Woodstock Summer Theatre and appeared there and at the Barter Theatre, Abingdon, Va.

Made her first appearance in New York at the Morosco Theatre, 25 Dec 1942, as Sue in Proof Through the Night (Cry Havoc); Lyceum, Nov 1944, played Agnes Willing in The Late George Apley; Fulton, Nov 1946, Birdie Bagtry in Another Part of the Forest; this performance gained the Clarence Derwent Award for the best performance in a supporting role, 1946–7; Music Box, Oct 1948, Alma Winemiller in Summer and Smoke; Henry Miller, June 1950, succeeded Irene Worth as Celia Copplestone in The Cocktail Party; Morosco, Jan 1951, Miranda Bolton in Second Threshold; in summer theatres, 1951, played Jeannie in A Case of Scotch; summer theatres, 1952, appeared in The Lady's Not for Burning and Venus Observed; New York City Center, Mar 1953, appeared as Portia in The Merchant of Venice; Playhouse, Jan 1956, played Jane Danbury in Fallen Angels; at the Carnegie Hall Playhouse, NY, Feb 1957, Alison in The Lady's Not for Burning; Cricket, off-Broadway, Mar 1960, played the Queen in Under the Sycamore Tree; American Shakespeare Festival, Stratford, Conn, June 1960, Olivia in Twelfth Night; toured US 1960–1, as Titania in A Midsummer Night's Dream; Stratford, Conn, Aug 1961, took over from Jessica Tandy as Lady Macbeth in Macbeth; Orpheum, NY, Nov 1963, Marion Dangerfield in The Ginger Man; American Shakespeare Festival, Stratford, Conn, summer

1964, Queen Margaret in Richard III and Gertrude in Hamlet; Kauffman Auditorium, NY, Jan 1966, appeared in the concert reading The White Rose and the Red; Paper Mill Playhouse, Millburn, New Jersey, Aug 1966, Jane Danbury in Fallen Angels; toured, 1968, as Queen Eleanor in The Lion in Winter; Studio Arena, Buffalo, 1968, played in Blithe Spirit; Center Stage, Baltimore, 1970–1 season, appeared in The Collection; Seattle, Washington, Repertory, 1971, played in Getting Married; toured, Apr 1972, as Gladys Wagner in Keep Off the Grass; Arlington Park, Ill, 1972, Mrs Manningham in Angel Street; Indianapolis, Indiana, Repertory, Nov 1974, Regina Giddens in The Little Foxes; played the same part at the Syracuse Stage, Mar 1975; Hartford Stage, Conn, Dec 1976, appeared in The Waltz of the Toreadors; Indianapolis, Feb 1978, in The Seagull; made film début in 1950 in A Life of Her Own, and has since appeared in The Nun's Story; has appeared on television as Juliet in Romeo and Juliet, as Regan in King Lear, and on various dramatic programs.

Address: Actors Equity Association, 165 West 46th Street, New York, NY 10036.

PHILLIPS, Robin, director and actor
b Haslemere, Surrey, 28 Feb 1942; *s* of James William Phillips and his wife Ellen Anne (Barfoot); *e* Midhurst Grammar School, Sussex; trained for the stage under Duncan Ross at the Bristol Old Vic Theatre School.

Made his first professional appearance for the Bristol Old Vic Company at the Theatre Royal, Bristol, June 1959, as Mr Puff in The Critic; at Bristol, 1959–60, his roles included: Romeo, Konstantin in The Seagull and Geoffrey in A Taste of Honey; associate director, Bristol Old Vic, 1960–1; Lyric, Hammersmith, Apr 1961, played Eric MacClure in South; Chichester Festival, July 1962, Curio in The Chances and Prophilus in The Broken Heart; May Fair, 1963, took over as the son in Six Characters in Search of an Author; with the Oxford Playhouse company, 1964; assistant director with the Royal Shakespeare Company, Stratford, 1965, working on Timon of Athens and Hamlet; Hampstead, Dec 1966, directed The Ballad of the False Barman; associate director, Northcott Theatre, 1967–8; Thorndike, Leatherhead, Nov 1969, directed The Seagull; Aldwych, Jan 1970, for RSC, Tiny Alice; Greenwich, Feb 1970, later Garrick, Sing A Rude Song; Wyndham's, May 1970, Abelard and Heloise; Stratford, July 1970, later Aldwych, The Two Gentlemen of Verona, his first New York production was Abelard and Heloise, Brooks Atkinson, Dec 1970; directed Dear Antoine (Chichester and London), Caesar and Cleopatra (Chichester), Miss Julie (London), 1971; Notes on a Love Affair (London), The Beggars' Opera, The Lady's Not for Burning (both Chichester: also played Louis Dubedat in The Doctor's Dilemma), 1972; artistic director of Company Theatre, Greenwich, 1973, for whom he directed Three Sisters, The House of Bernarda Alba, Rosmersholm, Catsplay, Zorba, Not Drowning But Waving, all 1973; appointed artistic director, Stratford Festival, Ontario, Canada, 1974; in Feb 1975 co-directed The Comedy of Errors and The Two Gentlemen of Verona in a national tour for the company, adding his own productions of Measure for Measure, Trumpets and Drums, and The Importance of Being Earnest to the Festival Season; season 1976, directed Antony and Cleopatra, A Midsummer Night's Dream and The Way of the World, co-directed Hamlet and The Tempest, and restaged Measure for Measure and The Importance of Being Ernest ; directed The Guardsman in Los Angeles, 1976; 1977 season, re-staged A Midsummer Night's Dream and The Guardsman, and directed Richard III, As You Like It, and Hay Fever;

directed Long Day's Journey into Night, Theatre London, 1977; 1978 season, co-directed Macbeth, The Winter's Tale, Uncle Vanya, Private Lives, and directed Judgement, and The Devils; 1979 season, co-directed Love's Labour's Lost, re-staged The Importance of Being Earnest, and directed King Lear; 1980 season, directed The Beggar's Opera, Virginia, Much Ado About Nothing, Foxfire, The Seagull, and Long Day's Journey into Night; films, since 1967, include leads in Decline and Fall and David Copperfield; television performances include: The Seagull.

Recreation: Painting. *Address:* c/o Stratford Shakespeare Festival, Box 520, Stratford, Ontario, Canada.

PHILLIPS, Siân, actress
b Bettws, Carmarthenshire, Wales; *d* of David Phillips and his wife Sally (Thomas); *e* Pontardawe Grammar School, and University of Wales; *m* Peter O'Toole (mar dis).

Began her professional career at the age of eleven, broadcasting for the BBC in Wales; toured extensively for the Arts Council in Wales in original Welsh plays and also in translations from the English Classics; in 1957, she was awarded a Bursary by the Arts Council, and entered the RADA; toured the English provinces, June 1957, as Margaret Muir in The Holiday; made her first London appearance in a special charity matinée at the Duke of York's, Dec 1957, as Hedda in Hedda Gabler; Belgrade, Coventry, May 1958, played Joan in Saint Joan; Nottingham Playhouse, 1958, played Masha in The Three Sisters; at the opening of the Hampstead Theatre Club 1959, played Princess Siwan in King's Daughter; Oxford Playhouse, 1960, played Katherine in The Taming of the Shrew; at the Aldwych, Dec 1960, played Julia in The Duchess of Malfi, and Jan 1961, Bertha in Ondine, in the first London repertory season of the Royal Shakespeare Company; Phoenix, May 1962, Arlow in The Lizard on the Rock; Queen's, Nov 1963, Penelope in Gentle Jack; at the same theatre, Dec 1964, played Yolande in Maxibules; Ashcroft, Croydon, Feb 1965, played Hannah Jelkes in Night of the Iguana, transferring with the production to the Savoy, Mar 1965; Piccadilly, June 1965, played Myra in Ride a Cock Horse; New Arts, Nov 1965, Ann Whitefield in Man and Superman, transferring to the Vaudeville, Jan 1966, and to the Garrick, Feb 1966; Mermaid, Sept 1966, played the Strange Lady in The Man of Destiny; Vaudeville, Feb 1967, Edwina in The Burglar; Arnaud, Guildford, Oct 1967, Alma Winemiller in The Eccentricities of a Nightingale; same theatre, Feb 1969, Queen Juana in The Cardinal of Spain; Young Vic, Dec 1972, Ruth Gray in Epitaph for George Dillon; Palace, Watford, 1973, in Alpha Beta; Hampstead, 1974, played Virginia Woolf in A Nightingale in Bloomsbury Square; Albery, June 1975, Duchess of Strood in The Gay Lord Quex; Duke of York's, Jan 1978, Myra Evans in Spinechiller; Chichester Festival, 1978, Mrs Arbuthnot in A Woman of No Importance, and The Countess in The Inconstant Couple; Lyric, Hammersmith, Oct 1979, Mrs Clandon in You Never Can Tell; films in which she has appeared include: Becket, Laughter in the Dark, Goodbye Mr Chips, Murphy's War, and Clash of the Titans; made her first television appearance in 1951, and has since played leading parts in many productions including: How Green Was My Valley, I, Claudius, The Oresteia of Aeschylus, Crime and Punishment, The Achurch Papers and Lady Windermere's Fan; she is a Member of the Welsh Arts Council and a Governor of the National Theatre of Wales; at the National Eisteddfod of Caernarvon, she was elected to The Honorary Order of Druids in recognition of her services to Welsh Drama.

Recreations: Reading and gardening. *Address:* c/o Saraband Associates, 348a Upper Street, London N1.

PHILLPOTTS, Ambrosine, actress

b London, 13 Sept 1912; *d* of Admiral Edward Montgomery Phillpotts, CB, and his wife Violet Selina (Cockburn); a niece of Eden Phillpotts, dramatic author; *e* Old Palace School, Bromley, and Manor House, Brondesbury; *m* John Anthony Reiss (mar dis); studied music in Paris, and for the stage, at the Royal Academy of Dramatic Art.

Made her first appearance on the stage at the Q Theatre, 1930, as Cora Ann in The Ringer; played repertory at Reading and Playhouse, Oxford, 1930; toured, 1931–3, with Ben Greet's company, playing Portia, Lady Macbeth, Rosalind, etc; Adelphi, Mar 1934, appeared in Magnolia Street; at the Hull Repertory Theatre, 1935–7, playing leading parts; Players' Theatre, May 1937, played Shirley in Out She Goes; Daly's, June 1937, Madeleine in No Sleep for the Wicked; played leading parts at the Playhouse, Liverpool, 1937–8; at Richmond, Nov 1938, played Susan in Chain Male, and Mrs Squirrel in Weights and Measures; Criterion, Mar 1939, Kitty Cranston in Sugar Plum; toured, July 1939, in Goodness, How Sad!; subsequently appeared in repertory, at the King's, Hammersmith; Richmond, Apr 1940, played Anna Portal in Blue Goose; at Edinburgh and Glasgow, May 1940, Marion Froude in Biography; toured, 1941, as Joan Deal in Play With Fire (The Shop at Sly Corner); Globe, Dec 1941, played Wanda Baring in The Morning Star; Savoy, July 1943, succeeded Coral Brown as Maggie Cutler in The Man Who Came to Dinner, subsequently touring in the same part; toured, 1944, in Western Europe, with Emlyn Williams, in Blithe Spirit; subsequently toured as Mrs Elton in Emma, and played the same part at the St James's, Feb 1945; toured, 1946, as Helen Dugdale in A Play for Ronnie; Duke of York's, Mar 1947, played Kay in The Anonymous Lover; Embassy, Sept 1947, Hilda James in Point Valaine; Comedy, June 1948, Aunt Cora in Wonders Never Cease; Q, Dec 1948, Judith MacKinder in Madeline; Arts, Mar 1949, Isabella Trench in Caroline; during 1949, toured as the Duchess of Fernyrigg in Master of Arts, and Lady Isobel in The Day After To-morrow; Q, Sept 1949, Amanda Carrington in Marriage Playground; Bedford, Camden Town, Feb 1950, Mabel Pitchforth in Primrose and the Peanuts; Wyndham's, Mar 1951, played Marion Butterworth in Count Your Blessings; at the Q, May 1952, Augusta Winterton in And If I Laugh, Nov 1952, Laura Hammond in It's Never Too Late, and Feb 1953, Hattie Aladin in The Full Treatment; Royal, Windsor, Apr 1953, Mrs Frobisher in Spring Model; King's, Glasgow, Nov 1953, Marjory Leland in A Sense of Guilt; Royal, Windsor, Mar 1954, Mrs Wagstaff in Dry Rot; Q, Apr 1955, Mrs Salesby in Lucky Strike; Cambridge Theatre, London, May 1955, Mabel Crosswaite in The Reluctant Debutante; Apollo, Sept 1955, again played Mrs Salesby in Lucky Strike; toured, Jan 1957, as Juliette Dulac in The Head of the Family; Saville, Oct 1959, played Lucy in The Edwardians; Pembroke, Croydon, Oct 1961, played Mrs Cortelyon in The Second Mrs Tanqueray; St Martin's, May 1963, Kitty in The Hot Tiara; Ashcroft, Croydon, Jan 1964, Mrs Shuttleworth in Home and Beauty; Oxford Playhouse, Oct 1964, played Judith Bliss in Hay Fever, and Nov 1964, Lady Fidget in The Country Wife; Royal Court, Apr 1965, played Mrs Gabor in Spring Awakening; Yvonne Arnaud Theatre, Guildford, July 1965, and Garrick, London, Aug 1965, played Lady Benbow in Thark; St Martin's, July 1966, took over as Mrs Mercy Croft in The Killing of Sister George; Whitehall, Aug 1967, played the Matron in Sign Here Please; Queen's, Nov 1967, Lady Fitzbuttress in Halfway Up the Tree; Sept 1970, toured as Kate in Eat Your Cake and Have It; toured, 1971, as Mrs Culver in The Constant Wife; Phoenix, Leicester, Aug 1971, Emma Gray in Me Times Me

Times Me; Oxford Playhouse, Oct 1973, the Lady in Violet in Dr Knock; Savoy, Apr 1974, Nora Barnstable in A Ghost on Tiptoe; Apollo, Jan 1977, Lady Matheson in Separate Tables; Chichester Festival, 1978, Lady Hunstanton in A Woman of No Importance; she has also appeared in such films as Room at the Top, Expresso Bongo, Ooh, You Are Awful, etc, and in many television productions, including: *Hadleigh, Follyfoot,* and *Doctor at Large.*

Recreation: Bridge, gardening. *Address:* c/o Leading Artists, 60 St James's Street, London SW1.

PIAZZA, Ben, actor

b Little Rock, Arkansas, 30 July 1934; *s* of Charles Piazza and his wife Elfreida (Spillman); *e* Princeton University; *m* Dolores Dorn-Heft; prepared for the stage at the Actors Studio.

Made his first appearance on the stage at the Theatre Intime, Princeton, NJ, spring, 1952, as a Venetian Senator in Othello; made his New York début at the National, Feb 1958, as George Willard in Winesburg, Ohio; Ambassador, NY, Apr 1959, played Alvin in Kataki; Eugene O'Neill, Apr 1960, Paul in A Second String; York Playhouse, Jan 1961, played the Young Man in The American Dream, transferring with the production to the Cherry Lane, off-Broadway, May 1961; toured South America, summer, 1961, as Isherwood in I Am a Camera, Jerry in The Zoo Story, and Chance Wayne in Sweet Bird of Youth; Cherry Lane, off-Broadway, Feb 1962, appeared in the repertory season Theatre of the Absurd, playing Clov in Endgame, Green Eyes in Deathwatch, the Young Man in The American Dream, and Jerry in The Zoo Story; again toured South America, summer 1962, as Christopher Isherwood in I Am a Camera; Lyceum, NY, Oct 1962, played Leopold in The Fun Couple; Billy Rose, Feb 1963, took over the part of Nick in Who's Afraid of Virginia Woolf?; Playhouse, Paramus, NJ, Aug 1964, played in One in a Row; Cherry Lane, June 1965, again appeared in The Zoo Story; ANTA, Sept 1967, Alfredo in The Song of the Grasshopper; Coconut Grove Playhouse, Miami, 1968, played in the four-part You Know I Can't Hear You When the Water's Running; Billy Rose, Oct 1968, The Intern in The Death of Bessie Smith and Jerry in The Zoo Story; his plays Lime Green and Khaki Blue produced at the Provincetown Playhouse, Mar 1969; Repertory Theatre, New Orleans, June 1970, Stanley Kowalski in A Streetcar Named Desire; Ivanhoe, Chicago, Aug 1970, Buck in Bus Stop; Ivanhoe, 1971, played in Who's Afraid of Virginia Woolf?; Mark Taper Forum, Los Angeles, Aug 1974, Mark Crawford in Savages; entered films, 1959, in Dangerous Age, subsequently appearing in The Hanging Tree, No Exit, Tell Me That You Love Me, Junie Moon, and The Outside Man (1973), first appeared on television, 1957, and principal programs in which he has appeared include *Ben Casey, The Defenders, Naked City, Kraft Theatre,* etc; he is also the author of the novel The Exact and Very Strange Truth, 1964.

Address: 300 East 59th Street, New York, NY 10022.

PICKUP, Ronald, actor

b Chester, 7 June 1941; *s* of Eric Pickup and his wife Daisy (Williams); *e* King's School, Chester, Leeds University; *m* Lans Traverse; trained for the stage at RADA.

First appeared on the stage 14 Sept 1964, at the Phoenix Theatre, Leicester as Sir John Friendly in Virtue in Danger; his first London appearance was as Octavius in Julius Caesar at the Royal Court, Nov 1964; played a number of small parts for the National Theatre at the Old Vic, 1965, returning to the Royal Court, Oct 1965, to play the title-part in Shelley; there also he played Pete in Saved, Nov 1965; Private Hurst in Serjeant Musgrave's Dance, Dec 1965; Sir Oliver Kix in A Chaste Maid in Cheapside, Jan 1966, and Simon in Transcending, also Jan 1966; rejoined the Old Vic, and his parts have since included: Johnny Boyle in Juno and the Paycock, Jeremy in Love for Love, and Don John in Much Ado About Nothing, 1966 season; Fedotik in Three Sisters, Rosalind in an all-male As You Like It, 1967; Messenger in Seneca's Œdipus, Me in In His Own Write, and Don Armado in Love's Labour's Lost, 1968; Joaquin and others in Macrune's Guevara, Tusenbach in Three Sisters, Haslam in Part I and Pygmalion in Part II of Back to Methuselah, Aimwell in The Beaux' Stratagem, 1969; Guildenstern in Rosencrantz and Guildenstern Are Dead, Ippolit in The Idiot, Œdipus in Sophocles' Œdipus (Young Vic), and Frank Gardner in Mrs Warren's Profession, 1970; Dr Jellinek, Field Marshal, and Rosencrantz in The Captain of Köpenick, Angelo in Measure for Measure (Mobile production), St Just in Danton's Death, and Edmund in Long Day's Journey into Night, 1971; title-role in Richard II, Joseph Surface in The School for Scandal, and Malcolm in Macbeth, 1972; Joe Shawcross in The Party, 1973; at the Globe, Sept 1975, took over as Norman in The Norman Conquests; Royal Court, May 1976, Man in Play; Olivier, Mar 1977, Caius Cassius in Julius Caesar; Olivier, June 1977, Philip Madras in The Madras House; first film, 1970, the National Theatre's Three Sisters; subsequent films include: The Day of the Jackal, The Thirty-Nine Steps, and Zulu Dawn; television, since 1964, includes: *Jennie, The Fight Against Slavery, Tropic,* and The Life of Verdi.

Recreations: Painting, listening to music, reading. *Address:* c/o London Management, 235–41 Regent Street, London W1A 2JT. *Tel:* 01–734 4192.

PICON, Molly, actress and author
b New York City, 1 June 1898; *d* of Lewis Picon and his wife Clara (Ostrow); *e* Philadelphia; *m* Jacob Kalich (dec).

Made her first appearance on the stage in Philadelphia, 1904, under the management of Michael Thomashefsky; in Yiddish repertory, Philadelphia, appeared in Gabriel, The Silver King, Sappho, Uncle Tom's Cabin, Shulamite, 1904–7; at the Arch Street, Philadelphia, 1908–12, played in Girl of the Golden West, God of Revenge, Medea, King Lear, The Kreutzer Sonata etc; appeared in cabaret, 1912–15; at the Chestnut, Philadelphia, 1915, played in Broadway Jones and Bunty Pulls the Strings; toured in a vaudeville act called Four Seasons, 1918–19; appeared in Yiddish repertory with her husband's troup at the Boston Grand Opera, 1919–20, and toured with the company in European theatres, 1920–2; on returning to NY, 1923, appeared at Kessler's Theatre, in Yankele; she remained at that theatre, playing leading parts for several years, in Zipke, Shmendrik, 1924; Mamele, Gypsy Girl, 1925; Molly Dolly, Rabbi's Melody, Little Devil, 1926; Kid Mother, Little Czar, Raizelle, 1927; Mazel Brocke, Hello, Molly! 1928; at the Molly Picon, Sept 1931, played in Girl of Yesterday; Palace, and US tour, 1931, played in vaudeville; Molly Picon, Dec 1931, played in Love Thief; toured, with her husband, in Europe, the Near East, South Africa, and Argentina, until 1935; returned to NY, and in 1936, appeared in Kale Loift; appeared in vaudeville, 1937; at the Longacre Theatre, NY, Apr 1940, played Becky Felderman in Morning Star; Molly Picon Theatre, Oct 1942, Molly in Oy Is Dus a Leben; toured US and Canada in vaudeville, 1943; toured in US military camps and DP Camps in Europe, 1944–6; in 1947, toured in South Africa; Belasco, NY, Nov 1948, Mrs Rubin in For Heaven's Sake; 2nd Avenue Theatre, Jan 1949, Sadie in Sadie Is a Lady; toured, 1950, in Abi Gezunt; 2nd Avenue Theatre, NY, Sept 1950, Molly in Mazel Tov Molly; Dec 1950, Sarah in Take It Easy; toured Korea

and Japan for the USO, 1951; toured US and Canada for Israeli Bonds, 1953; appeared in vaudeville at the Alhambra, Paris, Mar 1953; Walnut St, Philadelphia, summer 1953, played in Make Momma Happy; toured in Yiddish plays in London, Israel, and NY State, 1955; Palace, Brooklyn, Sept 1956, played in Farblonjet Honeymoon; Anderson, NY, Oct 1959, Peppy in The Kosher Woman; Phoenix, London, Mar 1960, Mrs Jacoby in A Majority of One, and subsequently toured; Martin Beck, NY, Oct 1961, Clara Weiss in Milk and Honey; in Nov 1962, after an absence of ten weeks, returned to the cast of this last musical and toured US, 1963–4, in the same part; Royal Poinciana Playhouse, Palm Beach, Fla, Mar 1965, again played Mrs Jacoby in A Majority of One; Playhouse-in-the-Park, Philadelphia, June 1965, Libby Hirsch in Dear Me, The Sky Is Falling; Westport Country Playhouse, Aug 1965, Matilda Mousse in Madame Mousse; Roosevelt Playhouse, Miami, Fla, Feb 1966, again played in Majority of One; Westbury Music Fair, May 1967, played in The Rubaiyat of Howard Klein; Hudson, Dec 1967, played in the revue How to Be a Jewish Mother; Brooks Atkinson, Jan 1970, Hortense Brand in Paris Is Out!; Ethel Barrymore, 1970, took over from Helen Hayes as Mrs Grant in The Front Page; toured, 1971, as Dolly Gallagher Levi in Hello, Dolly! and as Hortense Brand in Paris Is Out!; White Barn, Westport, Conn, July 1975, played in How Do You Live with Love?; Carnegie Hall, Oct 1975, appeared in revue; Morosco, Jan 1977, played Laura Curtis in Something Old, Something New, playing the same role in dinner theatres, Jan 1978, when the play was retitled Second Time Around; Queen's College, Flushing, Apr 1979, gave a one-woman show in Yiddish, Hello Molly; author of a family biography So Laugh a Little, 1962; co-author of an autobiography, The Sound of Laughter, 1979; has appeared on the variety stage in London and Paris; films include Yiddle and His Fiddle, in Poland, 1936; Mamale, in Poland 1938; Come Blow Your Horn, 1963, Fiddler on the Roof, 1972, For Pete's Sake, 1974, etc; she has also appeared frequently on television.

Address: Actors Equity Association, 165 West 46th Street, New York, NY 10036.

PIDGEON, Walter, actor
b East St John, New Brunswick, Canada, 23 Sept 1897; *e* University of New Brunswick, 1914–15; *m* (1) Edna Pickles (dec); (2) Ruth Walker; served in World War I in the Royal Canadian Army.

Made his first appearance on the stage in Boston, Massachusetts, 1924, with the Copley Players in You Never Can Tell; made his New York début at the Fulton, 2 Feb 1925, in the revue Puzzles of 1925; made his London début in 1925 in At Home; played in films for several years; re-appeared on the stage at the Morosco, NY, 3 Sept 1934, as Sheridan Warren in No More Ladies; Morosco, Apr 1935, Herbert Gray in Something Gay; Ambassador, Sept 1935, Guts Regan in The Night of January 16; Cort, Oct 1935, Leon Nordoff in There's Wisdom in Women; re-entered films for twenty years, then, at the Lyceum, Nov 1956, played Anthony J Drexel Biddle in The Happiest Millionaire, and toured in this part Oct 1957–May 1958; Shubert, Oct 1959, Nat Miller in the musical Take Me Along; toured, 1964, as Frank Michaelson in Take Her, She's Mine; toured, 1965, in The Happiest Millionaire and Take Her, She's Mine; Alvin, Sept 1966, Oliver Jordan in the revival of Dinner at Eight; entered films in Mannequin, 1926, and has made many notable films since then, including Saratoga, The Girl of the Golden West, Nick Carter, Master Detective, Man Hunt, How Green Was My Valley, Mrs Miniver, Madame Curie, White Cargo, Command Decision, Forbidden Planet, Voyage to the Bottom of the Sea, Advise and Consent, Warning Shot, The Neptune Doctor, Harry in Your Pocket (1973), etc; has appeared on television in Swiss Family Robinson, 1958, Meet Me in St Louis, 1959, The Vanishing 400, 1962, The Lindbergh Kidnapping Case, 1976, etc.

Address: 230 Strada Corta, Los Angeles, Calif.

PILBROW, Richard, lighting designer, theatre consultant, and producer

b Beckenham, Kent, 28 Apr 1933; *s* of Arthur Gordon Pilbrow and his wife Marjorie (Haywood); *e* Cranbrook School; *m* (1) Viki Brinton (mar dis); (2) Molly Friedel; studied stage-management at the Central School of Speech and Drama.

Assistant stage-manager at Her Majesty's Theatre, Apr 1954, for The Teahouse of the August Moon; in 1957, he founded Theatre Projects Ltd, to provide a unique service, embracing design, technical planning, equipment supply and production for the theatre and associated fields; through this company's work and research at home and abroad, many new techniques have since been introduced; lighting designer for Lady at the Wheel, at the Lyric, Hammersmith, Jan 1958; he has since acted as lighting designer for many productions, including: Brand, Danton's Death, Richard II (Old Vic), Pieces of Eight, 1959; Inherit the Wind, Platonov, 1960; The Tenth Man, One Over the Eight, Richard III, As You Like It (last two productions at Stratford-on-Avon), 1961; Blitz, Peer Gynt, The Merchant of Venice, The Alchemist (Old Vic), 1962; Othello (Old Vic), Baal, Half-a-Sixpence, How To Succeed in Business Without Really Trying, Measure for Measure (Old Vic), Uncle Vanya, Saint Joan, The Work-house Donkey (last three productions at Chichester Festival), Hamlet, The Recruiting Officer (last two for the National Theatre at the Old Vic), 1963; Camelot, Our Man Crichton, 1964; Armstrong's Last Goodnight, Miss Julie, and Black Comedy (double-bill) (last three plays at Chichester Festival), Love for Love, 1965; Juno and the Paycock, Rosencrantz and Guildenstern (National Theatre, London, and New York), The Prime of Miss Jean Brodie, Jorrocks, 1966; The Storm, Wise Child, Fiddler on the Roof, 1967; The Three Sisters, Love's Labour's Lost, Zorba (NY), 1968; The Travails of Sancho Panza, 1969; Oh! Calcutta! The Roths-childs (NY), 1970; Showboat 1971; Gone with the Wind, The Threepenny Opera, 1972; Shelter (NY), 1973; The Story of Vasco, A Street Car Named Desire, Eden End, 1974; Heart-break House, 1975; Irene, Blithe Spirit (National), 1976; Kings and Clowns, The Travelling Music Show, Annie, 1978; Joking Apart, 1979; he has also been scene projection consultant for the following productions: One Over the Eight, 1961; Peer Gynt, and The Merchant of Venice, 1962; A Funny Thing Happened on the Way to the Forum (NY), 1963; Golden Boy (NY), 1964; he has co-produced the following productions: A Funny Thing Happened on the Way to the Forum, 1963; She Loves Me, A Scent of Flowers, 1964; Fiddler on the Roof, 1967; Cabaret, The Beggar's Opera, 1968; She Stoops to Conquer, 1969; Edward II and Richard II, Erb, Catch My Soul, 1970; Company, 1972; I and Albert, 1973; The Good Companions, 1974; A Little Night Music, 1975; Carte Blanche, 1976; Kismet, 1978; Film Producer, Swallows and Amazons, 1973; TV Executive Producer, All You Need Is Love—The Story of Popular Music, 1975; directed Mister (Edinburgh, 1970, London, 1971); Theatre Projects Consultants Ltd, have been technical consultants for the planning of many theatres, including the Thorndike, Leatherhead; New National Theatre of Great Britain; Barbican Theatre and the Guildhall School; Birmingham Repertory; Sheffield Playhouse, Royal Opera Covent Garden,

Gulbenkian Foundation Auditorium Lisbon, Royal Exchange Manchester, Glasgow Arts Centre, Hong Kong Arts Centre, Sherman Theatre Cardiff; Director 69 Theatre Company, New Shakespeare Theatre Company, council of LAMDA, National Youth Theatre, Member Drama Panel of Arts Council 1968–70; Founder member of the Association of British Theatre Technician's, Society of British Theatre Designers (chairman), Society of Theatre Consultants; author of Stage Lighting, 1971; Fellow, Royal Society of Arts.

Club: Garrick. *Recreations:* Retreating to the Hebrides, cooking, photography and basset hounds. *Address:* Theatre Projects Ltd, 10 Long Acre, London, WC2. *Tel:* 01–240 5411.

PINTER, Harold, CBE, dramatic author, director, and actor

b Hackney, London, 10 Oct 1930; *s* of Hyman Pinter and his wife Frances (Mann); *e* Hackney Downs Grammar School; *m* Vivien Merchant.

Began his career as an actor; author of the following plays: The Birthday Party, 1958; The Room (one-act), The Dumb Waiter (one-act), The Hothouse, The Caretaker, 1960; A Slight Ache (one-act), 1961; A Night Out (one-act), 1961; The Collection (one-act, also co-directed), 1962; The Lover (one-act), The Dwarfs (one-act, also directed), 1963; The Homecoming, 1965; Landscape, 1968; Silence, 1969; Old Times, 1971; Monologue; No Man's Land, 1975; Betrayal, 1978; The Caretaker received the *Evening Standard* Award as the best new play of 1960; at the Duchess, Feb 1961, he took over the part of Mick in The Caretaker; Aldwych, June 1964, directed The Birthday Party; directed The Man in the Glass Booth (also New York, 1968), 1967; Exiles, 1970; Butley, Exiles (for RSC), 1971; Next of Kin (National), 1974; Otherwise Engaged, 1975; Blithe Spirit (National), The Innocents (NY), 1976; The Rear Column, 1978; Close of Play (National), 1979; The Hothouse (first production), 1980; he is also the author of a number of revue sketches, notably in One to Another, and Pieces of Eight, 1959; screenplays include The Servant, The Pumpkin Eater, The Quiller Memorandum, Accident, The Go-Between, The Last Tycoon, A la Recherche du Temps Perdu, The French Lieutenant's Woman, etc; television plays include: A Night Out, 1959, Night School, 1960, The Collection, The Lover, Tea Party, The Basement, etc; directed Butley and The Rear Column for BBC TV; author of the radio plays A Night Out, 1959, and The Dwarfs, 1960; published a volume of poems and prose, 1978; associate director, National Theatre, 1973–; received the CBE in 1966 Birthday Honours.

Recreation: Watching cricket. *Address:* c/o Emmanuel Wax, 16 Cadogan Lane, London, SW1.

PITHEY, Wensley, actor

b Cape Town, South Africa, 20 Jan 1914; *s* of Nelson Ivan Pithey, and his wife Helen Marguerite (Hogg); *e* South African College School and University of Cape Town; *m* Ingrid Hedwig Anna Rosengarten; trained for the stage at the College of Drama, University of Cape Town, and University Little Theatre, where he was the first Director, 1939; previously an announcer/producer for South African Broadcasting Corporation.

First appeared on the stage July 1925, at the Old Tivoli Theatre, Cape Town, as Hubert in King John; as a child actor, he gave excerpts from Shakespeare in variety; after various touring parts in South Africa, 1945–7, during which period he also ran his own company, came to London in 1947; first London appearance, St Martin's, Mar 1948, as Phil Cooper in Rocket to the Moon; in repertory at the Library Theatre, Manchester, 1948–9, appearing in the Library production of The Rising Wind at the Embassy, May 1949; with the Bristol Old Vic, 1949–50, appearing at the Lyric, Hammersmith, June 1950, in their production of Tartuffe, as M Orgon; Cambridge, May 1951, played the Chief of Police in Hassan; Mermaid, Sept 1951, Stephano in The Tempest; Duchess, Jan 1952, Dr Buchanan in Summer and Smoke; Westminster, May 1952, Mr Weller in The Trial of Mr Pickwick; Q, Jan 1953, Judge Cato in Star Witness; Duchess, Apr 1955, Sir Roderick Fletcher in It's Different for Men; Duke of York's, June 1955, Middle Aged Actor in Moby Dick; Garrick, Sept 1955, Maître Galuchon in The Count of Clérambard; Globe, Dec 1955, Stephen Spettigue in Charley's Aunt; Arts, Mar 1957, Old Man Devius in The Wit to Woo; for the next few years concentrated on television work, returning to the stage as Sam Elderly in Photo Finish, Saville, Apr 1962; Mermaid, Jan 1966, Col Craven in The Philanderer; Royal, Bury St Edmunds, Feb 1967, again played Spettigue in the fiftieth anniversary production of Charley's Aunt at its original theatre; St Martin's, July 1968, took over as Rafe Crompton in Spring and Port Wine; Vaudeville, Sept 1970, Lord Green in The Jockey Club Stakes; Arnaud, Guildford, July 1972, Maj-Gen Sir Charles Arbuthnot-Green in The Brass Hat; Birmingham Rep, June 1973, Sir Toby Belch in the tenth anniversary production of Twelfth Night; Arnaud, Nov 1974, Lord Porteous in The Circle, also Charley in Death of a Salesman, Jan; played both these parts at the Hong Kong Festival, Feb 1975; toured, June 1975, as Brad Morris in The Gentle Hook; Shaw Theatre, Ontario, May 1976, Earl of Loam in The Admirable Crichton and Sir George Croft in Mrs Warren's Profession; Sept 1977, toured as Duke of Newcastle in A Perfect Gentleman; Dec 1977, played Simeonov-Pishchik in Riverside Studios' opening production, The Cherry Orchard; first appeared in films, 1947, and has since appeared in pictures including: Oliver!, The Knack, Oh! What A Lovely War and One of Our Dinosaurs is Missing; television, since 1949, includes series such as *Special Branch*, *Ike*, *Edward and Mrs Simpson* and Suez.

Favourite parts: Stephen Spettigue, Falstaff and Winston Churchill. *Recreations:* Music, swimming, motoring. *Address:* c/o London Management, 235–241 Regent Street, London W1A 2JT.

PITKIN, William, designer

b Omaha, Nebraska, 15 July 1925; s of Loren H Pitkin and his wife Letha M (Wimmer); e Universidad Nacional de Mexico, 1941, University of Texas, 1942–3, University of New Mexico, 1943, Bard College, Annandale-on-Hudson (BA 1949); served in the United States Army Air Force, 1943–6; studied in Paris with Christian Bérard and at the Ecole Paul Colin.

Staff designer for Raymond Loewy Associates, 1953; designed his first work for the theatre for the Maverick Theatre, Woodstock, New York, production of Thunder Rock, 1947, and designed nine other shows for that troupe in the same season; went to Italy and for the Theatre Guild designed the Rome productions of Born Yesterday and Napoleone, Unico in 1950; Brainerd, Minnesota, 1951, designed ten productions for the Paul Bunyan Drama Festival; designed his first NY production at the Theatre de Lys, 10 Mar 1954, for The Threepenny Opera; has since designed the décor for La Ronde, 1954; Child of Fortune, The Potting Shed, 1956; A Moon for the Misbegotten, The Cave Dwellers, 1957; The Marriage of Figaro (Washington Opera Society), 1958; The Good Soup, Invitation to a March (with Jean Rosenthal), 1960; The Conquering Hero, The Glass Menagerie (for a European and South American tour), 1961; Something About a Soldier, Seidman and Son, The Beauty Part, 1962; the American Shakespeare Festival production of Henry V

(also the costumes), Gentlemen, Be Seated (NYC Opera), 1963; The Impossible Years, The Taming of the Shrew (Stratford, Connecticut), 1965; The Impossible Years (first London design), 1966; for the National Repertory Theatre designed The Comedy of Errors, John Brown's Body, and She Stoops to Conquer, 1967; The Guide, Adaptation and Next, 1968; The Chinese and Dr Fish, Hamlet (National Shakespeare Company), 1970; Memphis Store-Bought Teeth (costumes), 1971; Comedy (Boston), Buy Bonds Buster!, Dear Oscar, 1972; 42 Seconds from Broadway, 1973; for the Syracuse Stage Company, Waiting for Lefty, Noon, Of Mice and Men, 1973–4 season; Souvenir (Los Angeles), 1975; has also designed extensively for ballet companies, including Coppelia for the American Ballet Theater, 1968; The Maids for Eliot Feld's Ballet, 1970; and, for the City Center Joffrey Ballet, Contretemps, Le Bal, 1958, Whirlygig, 1959, La Fille Mal Gardée, 1962, Pas de Dix, 1964, These Three, Cakewalk, Donizetti Variations, 1966, The Green Table, Scotch Symphony, 1967, Konservatoriet, 1968, The Three-Cornered Hat (from designs by Pablo Picasso); La Fille Mal Gardée for Le Ballet de Wallonie, Belgium, produced in Paris, Jan 1976; Romeo and Juliet for the San Francisco Ballet, Jan 1976; Swan Lake, Houston 1977; Coppelia, Dallas 1979; has also designed the operas Fledermaus for the NY Opera and Madame Butterfly for the Washington Opera Society; for the Children's Theatre and Nicolo Marionettes designed Hansel and Gretel, Aladdin, Pinocchio, Jack and the Beanstalk, The Jungle Book, The Wizard of Oz, The Magic Flute, Sleeping Beauty; for the Berkshire Theatre Festival designed A Matter of Position, Adaptation, Next, 1968, and Hunger and Thirst, Encounters, 1969; designed a permanent portable stage for the National Shakespeare Company, 1967, which is still in use by that troupe; Emmy award, 1978, for his costumes for the PBS production of Romeo and Juliet.

Recreations: Archaeology and Egyptology. *Address:* 799 Lexington Avenue, New York, NY 10021. *Tel:* PL 8–2545.

PLATER, Alan, dramatic author

b Jarrow-on-Tyne, 15 Apr 1935; s of Herbert Richard Plater and his wife Isabella Scott (Plunkett); e Kingston High School, Hull and King's College, Newcastle (Durham Univ); m Shirley Johnson; formerly an architect.

Author of the following plays: The Referees, The Mating Season (double-bill), 1962; Ted's Cathedral, 1963; A Smashing Day, 1965; Hop, Step and Jump, 1967; Close the Coalhouse Door, Charlie Came to Our Town, 1968; Don't Build a Bridge, Drain the River, Simon Says, And a Little Love Besides, 1970; The Tigers Are Coming, OK?, 1972; Swallows on the Water, 1973; Trinity Tales, Tales of Humberside, 1975; Our Albert, The Fosdyke Saga, 1976; Drums along the Ginnel, Fosdyke II, 1977; Well Good Night Then . . ., 1978; screenplays for films including The Virgin and The Gypsy, It Shouldn't Happen to a Vet, Juggernaut; work for television includes Willow Cabins, Night People and the serialization of *The Good Companions*; co-founder of Humberside Theatre (formerly Hull Arts Centre); a member of the BBC General Advisory Council; member of the Writers' Guild of Great Britain.

Recreations: Reading, jazz, watching soccer. *Address:* 5 Hull Road, Cottingham, North Humberside HU16 4PA. *Tel:* 0482 847435.

PLEASENCE, Angela, actress

b Chapeltown, Yorkshire; d of Donald Pleasance and his wife Miriam (Raymond); m Michael Cadman (mar dis); trained for the stage at RADA.

Made her professional début at Birmingham Repertory Theatre, 1964, as Titania in A Midsummer Night's Dream; toured, 1967, in The Hollow Crown; Lyceum, Edinburgh, Nov 1967, played Josephine in The Ha-Ha; repeated this performance at Hampstead, June 1968; Lyceum, Edinburgh, Dec 1968, Irina in The Three Sisters; Ludlow Festival, Mar 1969, Juliet in Romeo and Juliet; Mermaid, June 1970, Miranda in The Tempest; Mermaid, Sept 1970, the title-part in Saint Joan; Playhouse, Nottingham, Feb 1973, Mollser in The Plough and the Stars; Theatre at New End, Apr 1974, Electra in You Were So Sweet When You Were Little; Greenwich, Dec 1974, Jean Rice in The Entertainer; Round House, Mar 1976, appeared in The Journey; Theatre at New End, June 1976, in The Bitter Tears of Petra von Kant; Shaw, Oct 1976, Juliet in Romeo and Juliet; King's Head, 1976, Water Sprite in Better Days Better Knights; New End, Apr 1979, Girl in The Square; Hampstead, Apr 1980, Miss Cutts in The Hothouse; first film, Here We Go Round the Mulberry Bush, 1967; subsequent films include: Hitler—The Last Ten Days, and Les Miserables; television includes: The Six Wives of Henry VIII, Marching Song, Breath, and Murder at the Wedding.

Address: c/o Joyce Edwards, 8 Theed Street, London, SE1. Tel: 01–261 1488.

PLEASENCE, Donald, actor
b Worksop, Notts, 5 Oct 1919; s of Thomas Stanley Pleasence and his wife Alice (Armitage); e Ecclesfield Grammar School; m (1) Miriam Raymond (mar dis); (2) Josephine Crombie; (3) Meira Shore.

Made his first appearance on the stage at the Playhouse, Jersey, May 1939, as Hareton in Wuthering Heights; first appeared in London at the Arts, June 1942, as Valentine in Twelfth Night; served with the RAF, 1942–6, and was prisoner-of-war, 1944–6; returned to the stage at the Lyric, Hammersmith, June 1946, as Mavriky in The Brothers Karamazov; Scala, Dec 1946, played Starkey in Peter Pan; Birmingham Repertory Theatre, 1948–50; Bristol Old Vic Company, 1951; Arts, Aug 1951, played Sherman in Right Side Up; Sept 1951, Rev Giles Aldus in Saints Day; first appeared in New York, at the Ziegfeld, Dec 1951, with Sir Laurence Olivier's company in Caesar and Cleopatra and Antony and Cleopatra; Arts, June 1952, played William Mossop in Hobson's Choice; at the Edinburgh Festival, 1952, appeared as Huish in his own play, Ebb Tide, and at the Royal Court, London; appeared at the Memorial Theatre, Stratford-on-Avon, 1953 season, and at the Princes, London, Nov 1953, played Lepidus in Antony and Cleopatra; Arts, May 1954, played Maccario in The Impresario From Smyrna; Jan 1955, Leone Gola in The Rules of the Game; Lyric, Hammersmith, May 1955, appeared as the Dauphin, in The Lark; Lyric, Hammersmith, Feb 1956, Gunner in Misalliance; St James's, May 1957, Monsieur Tarde in Restless Heart; Arts, Apr 1960, played Davies in The Caretaker, subsequently transferring to the Duchess, May 1960; Lyceum, NY, Oct 1961, again played Davies in The Caretaker; New Arts, Nov 1963, and Duke of York's, Jan 1964, played Bitos in Poor Bitos, subsequently leaving the cast to appear in the same play at the Cort, NY, Nov 1964; St Martin's, July 1967, played Arthur Goldman in The Man in the Glass Booth (London Variety Award for Stage Actor of the Year, 1968), appearing in that part at the Royale, NY, Sept 1968; Duchess, Sept 1970, Law in The Basement and Disson in Tea Party in a Pinter double-bill; Helen Hayes, NY, Feb 1972, Mrs Artminster in Wise Child; Haymarket, Mar 1980, George Greive in Reflections; films in which he has appeared include: The Great Escape, The Caretaker, Will Penny, Cul de Sac,

Soldier Blue, Dracula, etc; since 1946, he has also appeared in many television productions, including: Occupations, Call Me Daddy (American Emmy Award), Shades of Greene, The Captain of Köpenick, Mrs Colombo, The Ghost Sonata; named television Actor of the Year, 1958; produced his own series Armchair Mystery Theatre, 1960.

Favourite parts: Gunner in Misalliance, and Davies in The Caretaker. Recreation: Talking too much. Club: White Elephant. Address: c/o Joy Jameson Ltd, 7 West Eaton Place Mews, London, SW1.

PLOUVIEZ, Peter, General Secretary, British Actors' Equity
b 30 Jul 1931; s of Charles Alexander William Plouviez and his wife Emma Alice; e Hastings Grammar School; m (1) Nairne Angela Cardew (mar dis); (2) Alison Dorothy MacRae; formerly an organiser for NUBE.

Assistant secretary, Equity, 1960; assistant general secretary, 1964; general secretary since 1974; member, Cinematograph Films Council; trustee, Theatres Trust; Chairman, 1974–present, Radio and Television Safeguards Committee; Secretary, Federation of Theatre Unions, 1974–present; vice-chairman, Confederation of Entertainment Unions, 1974–present.

Address: 8 Harley Street, London W1.

PLOWRIGHT, Joan, CBE, actress
b Brigg, Lincs, 28 Oct 1929; d of William Ernest Plowright and his wife Daisy Margaret (Burton); e Scunthorpe Grammar School; m (1) Roger Gage (mar dis); (2) Lord Olivier; studied for the stage at the Old Vic Theatre School, with Michel St Denis, Glen Byam Shaw, and George Devine.

Made her first appearance on the stage in repertory at the Grand Theatre, Croydon, July 1951, as Hope in If Four Walls Told; appeared in repertory at the Bristol Old Vic, and was a member of the Old Vic Company during their tour of South Africa, 1952; first appearance in London, Westminster, July 1954, when she played Donna Clara in The Duenna; Duke of York's, June 1955, played the Young Actress in Moby Dick; following a season of playing leading parts at the Nottingham Playhouse, 1955–6, she joined the English Stage Company, Royal Court, Apr 1956, to play Mary Warren in The Crucible; subsequently Baptista in Don Juan, and the Receptionist in The Death of Satan; Miss Tray in Cards of Identity; and Mrs Shin in The Good Woman of Setzuan; at the same theatre, Dec 1956, made a great success in her first leading part with the English Stage Company, as Margery Pinchwife in a revival of The Country Wife, and transferred with the production to the Adelphi, Feb 1957; returned to the Royal Court, May 1957, to play the Old Woman in The Chairs, and Elizabeth Compton in The Making of Moo; at the Palace, Sept 1957, played Jean Rice in The Entertainer; made her first appearance in New York in a double-bill at the Phoenix Theatre, Jan 1958, when she played the Old Woman in The Chairs, and the Pupil in The Lesson; Royale, NY, Feb 1958, played Jean Rice in The Entertainer; on returning to London, Royal Court, June 1958, she again played in The Chairs and The Lesson; at the same theatre, Aug 1958 played the title-part in Major Barbara; Piccadilly, Nov 1958, played Arlette in Hook, Line, and Sinker; Belgrade, Coventry, May 1959, played the leading part of Beatie Bryant in Roots; subsequently appeared in the same play at the Royal Court, June 1959, and transferred to the Duke of York's, July 1959; Royal Court, Apr 1960, played Daisy in Rhinoceros; at the Lyceum Theatre, NY, Oct 1960, played Josephine in A Taste of Honey, receiving the New York Drama Critics Award, 1961, for this performance; on returning to England, she

appeared in the opening Chichester Festival, July 1962, as Another Constantia in The Chances, and as Sonya in Uncle Vanya; Chester Festival, June 1963, played the title-part in Saint Joan, and also Sonya in Uncle Vanya; Edinburgh Festival, Sept 1963, played the title-part in Saint Joan; joined the first National Theatre Company at the Old Vic, Oct 1963, where she appeared in repertory as Joan in Saint Joan, and Sonya in Uncle Vanya, 1963; Maggie Hobson in Hobson's Choice, Hilda Wangel in The Master Builder, 1964; took over Beatrice in Much Ado About Nothing, played Maria Sergueevna in The Three Sisters and Dorine in Tartuffe, 1967; Teresa in The Advertisement, Rosaline in Love's Labour's Lost, 1968; Voice of Lilith in Back to Methuselah Part II, 1969; Portia in The Merchant of Venice, 1970; Mistress Anne Frankford in A Woman Killed with Kindness, Silla in The Rules of the Game, 1971; Chichester Festival, 1972, played Jennifer Dubedat in The Doctor's Dilemma, May, and Katharina in The Taming of the Shrew, July; Greenwich, May 1973, Rebecca West in Rosmersholm; returned to the Old Vic to play Rosa in Saturday, Sunday, Monday, 1973, and Stella Kirby in Eden End, 1974; Queen's, Oct 1974, Rosa in Saturday, Sunday, Monday; joined the Lyric Theatre Company, Oct 1975, to play Irena Arkadina in The Seagull, alternating in repertory from Dec 1975 with the part of Alma in The Bed Before Yesterday; Lyric, Nov 1977, Filumena Marturano in Filumena, and at the St James, NY, Feb 1980; also for the National Theatre, co-directed An Evasion of Women and The Travails of Sancho Panza, and directed Rites, 1969; films include: Moby Dick, The Entertainer and Three Sisters; television appearances include: Odd Man In, The Secret Agent, and The School For Scandal; received the CBE in 1970 New Year Honours.
Address: 33–4 Chaucer Lane, London, WC2.

PLUMMER, Christopher (Arthur Christopher Orme Plummer), actor
b Toronto, Ontario, Canada, 13 Dec 1927; *s* of John Plummer and his wife Isabella Mary (Abbott); *e* Canadian public and private schools; *m* (1) Tammy Lee Grimes (mar dis); (2) Patricia Audrey Lewis (mar dis); (3) Elaine Taylor.
Began his professional career as an actor with the Canadian Repertory Theatre, Ottawa, Ontario, in 1950, when he played Faulkland in The Rivals; remained with the company until 1952, by which time he had played nearly 100 roles; Bermuda Repertory Theatre, winter, 1952, played Old Mahon in The Playboy of the Western World, Gerard in Nina, Anthony Cavendish in The Royal Family, Ben in The Little Foxes, Duke Manti in The Petrified Forest, Father in George and Margaret, Hector Benbow in Thark, and Bernard Kersal in The Constant Wife; made his first appearance in New York at the Royale Theatre, Jan 1954, as George Phillips in The Starcross Story; Booth, NY, Sept 1954, Manchester Monaghan in Home Is the Hero; ANTA, Feb 1955, Count Peter Zichy in The Dark Is Light Enough; Sarah Bernhardt Theatre, Paris, June 1955, played Jason in Medea, in a Salute to France Programme; Stratford Festival, Conn, July 1955, appeared as Mark Antony in Julius Caesar, and Ferdinand in The Tempest; Longacre, NY, Nov 1955, played the Earl of Warwick in The Lark; Shakespeare Festival, Stratford, Ontario, June 1956, played the title part in Henry V, and appeared in the same production at the Assembly Hall, Edinburgh Festival, Aug 1956; Playhouse, NY, Dec 1956, played Lewis Rohnen in Night of the Auk; Shakespeare Festival, Stratford, Ont, July 1957, played the title part in Hamlet, and Sir Andrew Aguecheek in Twelfth Night; June 1958, played Benedick in Much Ado About Nothing, Leontes in The Winter's Tale, and Bardolph in Henry IV, Part I;

ANTA, NY, Dec 1958, played Nickles in JB; Stratford Shakespeare Festival, Ontario, June 1960, played The Bastard in King John and Mercutio in Romeo and Juliet; Royal Shakespeare, Stratford-on-Avon, Apr 1961, Benedick in Much Ado About Nothing, and, May 1961, the title-role in Richard III; Aldwych, London, July 1961, King Henry in Becket, transferring to the Globe, Dec 1961; returned to Stratford, Ontario, July 1962, where he played the title-roles in Cyrano de Bergerac and Macbeth; Lunt-Fontanne, NY, Nov 1963, played the title-role in Arturo Ui; ANTA, Oct 1965, Francisco Pizarro in The Royal Hunt of the Sun; Stratford, Ontario, July 1967, Mark Antony in Antony and Cleopatra; joined the National Theatre Company, London, 1971 and at the New, London, June 1971, played Jupiter and Amphitryon in Amphitryon 38, and Aug 1971, Danton in Danton's Death; Palace, NY, May 1973, Cyrano de Bergerac in a musical Cyrano, and received the Antoinette Perry (Tony) Award as best actor in a musical; Eugene O'Neill, Nov 1973, Anton Chekov in The Good Doctor; Opera House of the Kennedy Center, Washington, DC, Sept 1975 devised and appeared with Zoë Caldwell in Love and Master Will; Public/Newman, Nov 1978, Edgar in Drinks Before Dinner; first entered films, 1957, and principal films include Stage Struck, The Fall of the Roman Empire, The Sound of Music, Inside Daisy Clover, Œdipus the King, Royal Hunt of the Sun, Lock Up Your Daughters, Waterloo, Across the Everglades, The Return of the Pink Panther, International Velvet (1978); made his first television appearance in 1951, and has since starred in Œdipus Rex, The Lady's Not for Burning, The Doll's House, The Prince and the Pauper, Little Moon of Alban, Captain Brassbound's Conversion, Cyrano de Bergerac, Prisoner of Zenda, Time Remembered, Macbeth, Hamlet (Elsinore), After the Fall, Jesus of Nazareth (1977), etc; received the *Evening Standard* Award, 1961, for his performance in Becket; on 25 Sept 1970, made a Companion of the Order of Canada, the highest civilian award.
Recreations: Ski-ing, tennis and the piano. *Club:* Players, New York. *Address:* c/o Stanley, Gorrie, Whitson & Co, 9 Cavendish Square, London W1. *Tel:* 697–8044.

POITIER, Sidney, actor
b Miami, Florida, 20 Feb 1924; *s* of Reginald Poitier and his wife Evelyn (Outten); *e* Governor's High School, Nassau, British West Indies; *m* Juanita Hardy; prepared for the stage with Paul Mann and Lloyd Richards.
Made his professional début with the American Negro Theatre, New York, 1945, in Days of Our Youth and subsequently played roles in On Striver's Row, Rain, Freight, You Can't Take It with You, The Fisherman, Hidden Horizon, Sepia Cinderella, and Riders to the Sea; made his Broadway début at the Belasco, 17 Oct 1946, as Polydorus in Lysistrata; National, Sept 1947, played Lester in a revival of Anna Lucasta; Ethel Barrymore, Mar 1959, played Walter Lee Younger in A Raisin in the Sun; John Golden, Feb 1968, directed Carry Me Back to Morningside Heights; entered films in a US Army documentary, From Whom Cometh Help, 1949, and made his first theatrical film, No Way Out, 1950; subsequent films include Cry the Beloved Country, The Blackboard Jungle, Something of Value, The Defiant Ones, Porgy and Bess, A Raisin in the Sun, Lilies of the Field, for which he received the Academy Award, In the Heat of the Night, Uptown Saturday Night, (also directed) The Wilby Conspiracy, Let's Do It Again (also directed, 1976), etc; has also received the Venice Film Festival Giorgio Cine Award for Something of Value and the Berlin Film Festival Award for The Defiant Ones; appeared on television in A Man Is Ten Feet Tall, 1955.

Address: Actors Equity Association, 165 West 46th Street, New York, NY 10036.

POLIAKOFF, Stephen, playwright
b London, 1952.

Author of plays including Granny, produced 1969; Bambi Ramm, 1970; A Day with My Sister, 1971; Pretty Boy, 1972; Theatre Outside, Berlin Days, The Carnation Gang, all 1973; Clever Soldiers, 1974; Heroes, Hitting Town, City Sugar, Join the Dance (NY), 1975; Strawberry Fields (National Theatre), 1977; Shout Across the River (RSC), 1978; American Days, 1979; The Summer Party, 1980; contributor to Lay By, 1971.

Address: c/o Margaret Ramsay, 14A Goodwin's Court, St Martin's Lane, London WC2.

POLLOCK, Ellen, actress and director
b Heidelberg, Germany, 29 June 1903; *e* St Mary's College, London, and Convent of the Blessed Sacrament, Brighton; *m* (1) Captain Leslie Frank Hancock, RE; (2) James Proudfoot, RP, ROI.

First appeared on the stage at the Everyman Theatre, 18 Nov 1920, as a page in Romeo and Juliet; at the same theatre, Dec 1920, played the Baroness in The Melting Pot, the Big-eared Goblin and the Fairy Doll in Through the Crack, and Herod's son in an Old English Nativity Play, in which she appeared with the late Ellen Terry; Globe, Apr 1921, played in The Knave of Diamonds; subsequently toured in The Eleventh Commandment; in 1923, toured in a repertory of Bernard Shaw's plays, and in Mr Garrick; in the same year accompanied Gertrude Elliott on her South African tour, appearing in Woman to Woman, The Sign on the Door, Paddy the Next Best Thing; on returning to England, toured in The Cabaret Girl, and in 1924, toured as Louise in Tons of Money; in 1925, toured as Tondeleyo in White Cargo; at Chelsea Palace, Dec 1925, played the Good Fairy in Bluebell in Fairyland; Regent, Mar 1926, the Salvation Lass in From Morn to Midnight; later in 1926, sailed for Australia, with Maurice Moscovitch, playing lead in They Knew What They Wanted, Trilby, The Outsider, and The Fake; on her return, appeared at the London Hippodrome, Nov 1927, as Rita in Hit the Deck; in Sept 1928, toured with Billy Merson, as Lady Fandon in The Lad; Everyman, Mar 1929, played Topsy in The Pleasure Garden; Garrick, Mar 1930, Esther in The Lady of the Camellias; Everyman, June 1930, the Girl in Yellow in Long Shadows; Lewisham, Aug 1930, Vivian Leiter in Her First Affaire; Kingsway, Sept 1930, Susanne in the same play; Everyman, Mar 1931, Jean Somers in Phoenix; His Majesty's, May 1931, Elsie and Effie Longstaffe in The Good Companions; New, Apr 1932, Hortense in Napoleon; Phoenix (for the G Club), May 1932, Jimmie Franklin in Rings on Her Fingers; at the Malvern Festival, Aug 1932, Charlotte Welldon in Oroonoko, The Dancer in Tom Thumb, and the Nurse in Too True to be Good, appearing in the last-mentioned part when the play was reproduced at the New Theatre, Sept 1932; Gaiety, Nov 1932, Ruth Goldman in Potash and Perlmutter; Garrick, Apr 1933, Mrs Henderson in Beggars in Hell; Embassy, June 1933, Elizabeth Barrie in Fly Away Peter; Sept 1933, Countess Upsala in Bastos the Bold; Fulham, Oct 1933, Connie in Finished Abroad; Winter Garden, Nov 1933, Aloysia Brollikins in On the Rocks; Savoy, Mar 1934, Connie in Finished Abroad; Westminster, July 1934, Leonora Hutt in French Salad; Arts, Sept 1934, Guinevere in Fire in Amsterdam; Embassy, Dec 1934, and Shaftesbury, Jan 1935, Gwen Clayton in The Dominant Sex, which ran for eighteen months; Duke of York's, Sept 1936, Madame Geneviève Dumontier in No Ordinary Lady; Em-

bassy, May 1937, Lady Sneerwell in The New School for Scandal; Ambassadors', Sept 1937, Julia Britton in People in Love; Garrick, Nov 1937, Alice Peabody in It's a Wise Child; Duke of York's, Apr 1938, Lady Bramber in Three Blind Mice; Open Air, July–Aug 1938, Kalonike in Lysistrata, and Audrey in As You Like It; toured, Oct 1938, as Mary Carlton in The Middle Watch; Richmond, Apr 1939, and subsequently at the Comedy, Jan 1940, Julia Foster in The Bare Idea; Golder's Green, June 1941, Sophie Battersby in No Name in the Visitor's Book; Piccadilly, Jan 1943, Freda Tunbridge in Sleeping Out; Comedy, Nov 1943, Florence Beaudouin in This Time It's Love; Lyric, Hammersmith, Oct–Dec 1944, appeared as the Nurse in Too True to be Good, Candida, Z in Village Wooing, Eliza in Pygmalion, and directed each of these productions; Granville, Walham Green, May–Sept 1945, appeared in a season of Grand Guignol plays, which she directed in conjunction with Hugh Miller and John Hanau; Lindsey Theatre, Nov 1945, played Vera in To-morrow Will be Different; Granville, Walham Green, May 1946, Jane in The 19th Hole of Europe; Winter Garden, Dec 1946, Wilma in The Wizard of Oz; Q, Apr 1947, Mrs Val Stratheden in Quiet in the Forest; Oct 1947, played the Woman in The Picture of Dorian Gray; Nov 1947, Charmian Daly in Reluctant Lady, which she also directed; Strand, Feb 1948, Selima in Family Portrait; Playhouse, Sept 1948, Lady Geviphie in The Perfect Woman; Comedy, Mar 1949, directed Summer in December; St Martin's, May 1949, directed Miss Turner's Husband; Duke of York's, June 1949, directed The Third Visitor; Whitehall (for Sunday Theatre, Ltd), Oct 1949, directed Old Hickory; New Chepstow, Nov 1949, played Fanny Cornforth in Rossetti, and directed the play; toured in Germany, 1950, with The Third Visitor, and on her return toured in Dark Enchantment, and A Guardsman's Cup of Tea; Watergate, Sept 1950, appeared as Rose and the Teacher in Farfetched Fables; St Martin's, Apr 1951, appeared as Queen Elizabeth in The Dark Lady of the Sonnets, which she also directed, together with the The Man of Destiny and Village Wooing; Watergate, July 1951, played Delta in Sex and Seraphim; Comedy, July 1951, directed Storks Don't Talk; Court, July 1952, played Lady Eastlake in The Bride of Denmark Hill; in the same month at this theatre also played Z in Village Wooing, which she directed, together with Bernard Shaw In Heaven; Comedy, Aug 1952, again played Lady Eastlake in The Bridge of Denmark Hill; joined the Donald Wolfit Company at the King's, Hammersmith, 1953, and during the year appeared there as Jocasta in Œdipus, Audrey in As You Like It, Regan in King Lear, Maria in Twelfth Night, Judith in The Wandering Jew, Mistress Candour in The School for Scandal, Mistress Quickly in Henry IV, and Mrs Heidelberg in The Clandestine Marriage; New Lindsey, Nov 1954, played Dorothy Foster in The Lost Generation, which she directed in association with Leslie Linder; at Peterborough Cathedral, May 1955, appeared as Katherine of Aragon in a dramatic chronicle, Upon This Rock; at the Royal Court, London, at three matinées given in celebration of the G B Shaw centenary, July 1956, played Mrs Warren in Mrs Warren's Profession; Victoria Palace, Dec 1960, directed Billy Bunter's Swiss Roll; at the Pembroke, Croydon, Jan 1961, played Agata in Crime on Goat Island; at the same theatre, May 1961, directed As You Like It; Arts, Oct 1961, played Yana Latore in Ducks and Lovers; May Fair, June 1963, played Madame Pace in Six Characters in Search of An Author; Ashcroft, Croydon, Apr 1964, directed and played Rozalia in Fata Morgana; Comedy, Apr 1965, for the Repertory Players, played Lady Stanford-Jones in Love by Appointment; Malvern Festival, Apr 1967, directed Fallen Angels; Palace, Watford, Feb 1969, played

Mother in The Guardsman; Royal, Brighton, June 1969, directed The Murder Game; Detroit, USA, Oct 1969, directed Pygmalion; Vaudeville, June 1970, and Duke of York's, Madame Claude in Lady Frederick; Her Majesty's, Oct 1971, Gloriani in Ambassador; Albery, May 1974, Mrs Higgins in Pygmalion; Olivier, Jan 1977, Baroness in Tales from the Vienna Woods; Theatre Royal, Bromley, Aug 1978, Queen Mary in The Woman I Love; has directed a number of productions for the Repertory Players; has also directed two seasons of Grand Guignol at the Irving and Embassy, the former in conjunction with Kenneth Tynan; has also acted in television plays and series including: *The Forsyte Saga, The Pallisers,* and Chéri; commenced film career 1927, in Moulin Rouge, and has since appeared in numerous pictures; elected President of the Shaw Society, in 1949; Professor at the RADA, for twelve years.

Recreations: Running an antique stall. *Address:* 9 Tedworth Square, London, SW3. *Tel:* 01–352 5082.

POND, Helen, designer
b Shaker Heights, Cleveland, Ohio, 26 Jun 1924; *d* of Ralph Herbert Pond and his wife Charlotte Ann (Waters); *e* Ohio State U.

Her first designs for NY were for House of Connelly, 2 Nov 1955; since then has designed the decor for Liliom, The Beaver Coat, 1956; Idiot's Delight, Right You Are If You Think You Are, A Palm Tree in a Rose Garden, 1957; Oklahoma!, Ardele, Hamlet of Stepney Green, 1958; She Shall Have Music, Time of Vengeance, 1959; Gay Divorce, La Ronde, The Idiot, Man and Superman, Emmanuel, 1960; Montserrat, Five Posts in the Market Place, Smiling the Boy Fell Dead, Oh Marry Me, 1961; The Merchant of Venice, Can-Can, 1962; I Got Shoes, The Boys from Syracuse (also UK début, Theatre Royal, Drury Lane), Double Dublin, 1963; What Makes Sammy Run?, Roar Like a Dove, 1964; Great Scot!, 1965; By Jupiter, The Peddler, The Dodo Bird, 1967; Private Lives, 1968; Trevor, The Coffee Lace, 1969; The Divorce of Judy and Jane, 1971; Berlin to Broadway with Kurt Weill, Oh Coward, 1972; No Sex, Please, We're British, 1973; A Community of Two (tour), 1974; Much Ado About Nothing (Chicago, Princeton, Stratford, Conn), At the Old Bull and Bush (Huntington), 1978; has also designed for the Paper Mill Playhouse, NJ, and for 23 seasons at the Cape Playhouse, Dennis, Mass; has designed over 40 productions since 1970 as principal designer for the Opera Company of Boston; also for NY City Opera, etc; designed the lighting for many of these productions, and designed most of them in partnership with Herbert Senn.

Address: 316 West 51st Street, New York, NY. *Tel:* CO 5–3728.

POPPLEWELL, Jack, dramatic author
b Leeds, Yorks, 22 Mar 1911; *s* of Walter Popplewell and his wife Beatrice Maud (Hudson); *e* Kirkham Grammar School; *m* Betty Bryant.

Formerly a farmer, composer, and lyric writer; he is the author of the following plays: Blind Alley, 1953; Dead on Nine, 1955; Breakfast in Bed; The Vanity Case, Dear Delinquent, 1957; The Last Word, A Day in the Life Of . . ., 1958; And Suddenly It's Spring, 1959; Hocus Pocus, 1961; Policy For Murder, 1962; Dear Children, 1962; Every Other Evening (adapted from the French of François Campaux), Boomerang, Busybody, 1964; Dear Children, Mississippi, 1969; High Infidelity, Darling, I'm Home, 1970; Dead Easy, 1973; The Queen's Favourites, 1975; Travellers' Tales, 1979; his plays have been produced throughout Europe, in Israel, Australia, South Africa and the United States; he is also the

author of the film Tread Softly, Stranger (adapted from his play Blind Alley); eight of his plays have been performed on television; four have been filmed; he is also the composer of the songs If I Should Fall in Love Again and My Girl's an Irish Girl; author of novels, Operation Globesaver and The Blue Lake.

Recreations: Music and travel. *Address:* Great Batchelors, Sissinghurst Road, Biddenden, Kent. *Tel:* Biddenden 291331.

PORTER, Don, actor
b Miami, Oklahoma, 24 Sept 1912; *s* of Jesse Bradley Porter and his wife Hazel Margaret (Wills); *e* Oregon Institute of Technology; *m* Peggy Converse; trained for the stage with Bess Whitcomb; formerly a bank teller, office manager, salesman, and reporter.

Made his stage début at the Civic Theatre, Portland, Oregon, 1936, as the Messenger in Elizabeth the Queen; remained in repertory until entering films in 1939 in The Mystery of the White Room; reappeared on the stage at the 18 Actors, Inc, Los Angeles, 1954, when he played Aubrey Piper in The Show-Off; toured the Western US, 1958, as J Malcolm and Major Pollock in Separate Tables; toured, 1962, as William Russell in The Best Man; made his New York début at the Ambassador, Winter, 1962, when he took over from Roland Winters as Malcolm Turnbull in Calculated Risk; The Music Box, Feb 1964, John Cleves in Any Wednesday; toured, 1966–7, as Jim Bolton in Generation; Ethel Barrymore, May 1969, McCue in The Front Page; Plymouth, Fall, 1969, took over as Sam Nash, Jesse Kiplinger, and Roy Hubley in Plaza Suite; toured, 1971, in Plaza Suite; toured, 1974, in Winning Is Better; 1977, in How to Succeed in Business Without Really Trying; 1979, in Harvey; among his films may be mentioned 711 Ocean Drive, Youngerblood Hawke, Bachelor in Paradise, Madame Spy, Because You're Mine, Forty Carats, Mame, The Candidate, etc; first appeared on television in 1953 and since has played regularly in *Private Secretary* for four years, *The Ann Sothern Show* for three years, on *Mod Squad, Love American Style, Gidget, The Bionic Woman, The Paper Chase, Three's Company,* etc.

Favourite parts: Petruchio in The Taming of the Shrew, Ben in Another Part of the Forest, and the roles in Plaza Suite. *Hobby:* Photography. *Recreation:* Golf. *Address:* 1900 Avenue of the Stars, Suite 2270, Los Angeles, Calif 90067. *Tel:* 277–1900.

PORTER, Eric, actor
b London, 8 Apr 1928; *s* of Richard John Porter and his wife Phoebe Elizabeth (Spall); *e* elementary school, and Wimbledon Technical College.

Made his first appearance on the stage at the Arts Theatre, Cambridge, Feb 1945, when he walked on in the Shakespeare Memorial Theatre Company's production of Twelfth Night; after remaining for a season with the same company at Stratford-on-Avon, he joined the Travelling Repertory Theatre Company, autumn 1945, and made his first appearance in London at the King's Theatre, Hammersmith, Mar 1946 as Dunois' Page in Saint Joan; King's, Hammersmith, May 1946, played Dillan in In Time To Come; 1946–7, on National Service with the RAF; on returning to the theatre, he toured Britain and Canada with Sir Donald Wolfit's Company, followed by two seasons with Sir Barry Jackson's Company at the Birmingham Repertory Theatre, 1948–50; Lyric, Hammersmith, Mar 1951, he took over the part of Jones in The Silver Box; Aldwych, May 1951, played Solyoni in a revival of The Three Sisters; Lyric, Hammersmith, Sept 1951, played the Messenger in Thor, With Angels; Lyric,

Hammersmith, Jan 1952, Jeff Smith in The Same Sky; Aldwych, Apr 1952, Boy in Under the Sycamore Tree; Lyric, Hammersmith, Dec 1952 joined the John Gielgud Season, to play Bolingbroke in Richard II, Feb 1953, Fainall in The Way of the World, May 1953, Reynault in Venice Preserv'd; Bristol Old Vic, 1954, played leading parts as a member of the company, including Becket in Murder in the Cathedral and Father Browne in The Living Room; joined the Old Vic Company, opening Sept 1955, as Banquo in Macbeth, subsequently playing Navarre in Love's Labour's Lost, Christopher Sly in The Taming of the Shrew, Bolingbroke in Richard II, Jaques in As You Like It, and King Henry in Henry IV, Parts I and II; returned to the Bristol Old Vic for the season 1955–6, to play, among other parts, Horace Van der Gelder in The Matchmaker, and the title-parts in Uncle Vanya, Volpone, and King Lear; Piccadilly, July 1956, took over the part of Vadim Romanoff in Romanoff and Juliet, on the death of Frederick Valk; Edinburgh Festival, Aug 1957, played Herr Compass in A Man of Distinction, and subsequently at the Princes, Oct 1957; Theatre Royal, Brighton, Dec 1957, played the Burgomaster in Time and Again, and toured with the production in England, before making his first appearance in New York in the same play (renamed The Visit), at the opening of the Lunt-Fontanne Theatre, May 1958; toured England, Jan 1959, as Jansen in The Coast of Coromandel; Royal Court, Nov 1959, played Rosmer in Rosmersholm, and transferred with the production to the Comedy, Jan 1960; he won the *Evening Standard* Award as Best Actor of 1959 in this part; Shakespeare Memorial Theatre, Stratford-on-Avon, 1960 season, played Malvolio in Twelfth Night, Duke of Milan in The Two Gentlemen of Verona, Ulysses in Troilus and Cressida, and Leontes in The Winter's Tale; became a long-term contract player with the same company (re-named Royal Shakespeare Company), Dec 1960, to appear in repertory both at Stratford-on-Avon and the Aldwych, London, for whom he has since played the following parts: Ferdinand in The Duchess of Malfi, Malvolio in Twelfth Night, 1960; Lord Chamberlain in Ondine, Duke of Buckingham in Richard III, Thomas Becket in Becket (transferring with the last production to the Globe Theatre, Dec 1961), 1961; the title-part in Macbeth, Iachimo in Cymbeline, 1962; took over Pope Pius XII in The Representative, 1963; Bolingbroke in Richard II, King Henry in King Henry IV (Parts I and II), Chorus in Henry V, the Earl of Richmond in Richard III, 1964; Barabas in The Jew of Malta, Shylock in The Merchant of Venice, Chorus in Henry V, 1965; Ossip in The Government Inspector, 1966; title-roles in King Lear and Dr Faustus, 1968; US tour with RSC, Dr Faustus, 1969; Fortune, Oct 1969, directed and played Paul Thomsen in My Little Boy, My Big Girl; Gardner Centre, Brighton, May 1971 (for Brighton Festival), title-role in The Protagonist; Coliseum, Dec 1971, Mr Darling and Captain Hook in Peter Pan; St George's, Islington, Apr 1976, Malvolio in Twelfth Night; films in which he has appeared include: Nicholas and Alexandra, The Day of the Jackal, The Belstone Fox, and The Thirty-Nine Steps; made his first appearance on television, 1945, as Dunois' Page in Saint Joan, and has since played leading roles in numerous productions, including *The Forsyte Saga*, Cyrano de Bergerac, Man and Superman, Separate Tables, The Statue and the Rose, Anna Karenina, and Why Didn't They Ask Evans?.

Favourite parts: King Lear and Uncle Vanya. *Recreations:* Reading, walking. *Address:* c/o London Management Ltd, 235–241 Regent Street, London, W1.

PORTER, Stephen, director and producer
b Ogdensburg, New York, 24 July 1925; s of Charles Talbot Porter and his wife Anna Martin (Newton); e Yale University and the Yale School of the Drama; formerly engaged as an assistant professor at McGill University, Montreal, Canada.

Directed his first play, The Misanthrope, which he also produced, at the Theatre East, NY, 12 Nov 1956; produced, directed, and designed The Country Wife at the Renata, June 1957; since then has directed Two Philoctetes and, with Ellis Rabb, adapted the play from Sophocles, 1959; joined the Association of Producing Artists during its first year, 1960, and for that organization directed Scapin, which he translated with Ellis Rabb, 1960; King Lear, Twelfth Night, 1961; A Phoenix Too Frequent, Right You Are (If You Think You Are), 1963; Impromptu at Versailles, which he also translated, Man and Superman, 1964; The Wild Duck, 1966; The Show-Off, 1967; The Misanthrope, 1968; Krapp's Last Tape, The Hostage, Private Lives, 1969; Harvey, 1970; School for Wives, 1971; for other managements has directed The Alchemist, 1964; Phaedra for the Theatre of the Living Arts, Philadelphia, 1967; As You Like It for the American Shakespeare Festival, Stratford, Connecticut, Thieves' Carnival, and The Master Builder for the Tyrone Guthrie, Minneapolis, 1968; The Wrong Way Light Bulb, Chemin de Fer for the Mark Taper Forum, Los Angeles, 1969; Richard II for the Old Globe, San Diego, Calif, 1970; The Italian Straw Hat for the Stratford, Ontario, Festival, 1971; directed the tour of Harvey for the Phoenix Repertory and The School for Wives (NY), 1971; directed Captain Brassbound's Conversion, 1972; joined the New Phoenix Repertory Company as Artistic Director, 1972, which has since presented The Great God Brown, A Meeting by the River, Don Juan (also adapted and directed), 1972; Strike Heaven on the Face, Games, After Liverpool, The Government Inspector, The Visit, Chemin de Fer (also directed), Holiday, and, for other managements, directed The Enchanted and The Prodigal Daughter in Washington, DC, 1973; The Removalists, Love for Love, In the Voodoo Parlor of Marie Leveau, Pretzels, the Rules of the Game (also directed), 1974; The Member of the Wedding, Knuckle, Dandelion Wine, Meeting Place, and at the John Drew, Easthampton, NY, End of Summer and for the tour, directed Present Laughter, 1975; directed They Knew What They Wanted, Days in the Trees, 1976; for the Circle-in-the-Square, NY, has directed The Importance of Being Earnest, Tartuffe, 1977; Man and Superman, 1978; directed The Circle for ACT, San Francisco, 1978; Absurd Person Singular, Ahmanson, LA, Feb 1978; has also directed productions of the Cincinnati Playhouse-in-the-Park, the Milwaukee Repertory Theatre, the McCarter Theatre of Princeton, NJ, and the Studio Arena, Buffalo, NY.

Address: 44 Gramercy Park North, New York, NY 10010.

POSTON, Tom, actor
b Columbus, Ohio, 17 Oct 1921; s of George Poston and his wife Margaret; e Bethany College, 1938–40; m Jean Sullivan; prepared for the stage at the American Academy of Dramatic Arts.

First appeared on the stage as a tumbler with a troupe called The Flying Zebleys, 1930; made his New York acting début at the Alvin, in 1947, when he succeeded to a part in Jose Ferrer's production of Cyrano de Bergerac; City Center, June 1948, played Otakar in The Insect Comedy; National, Dec 1950, played the Herald in King Lear; President, Feb 1954, played Private Turnipseed in Stockade; Plymouth, Jan 1955, Edward Martin in The Grand Prize; Belasco, 1955, took over from Orson Bean as George MacCauley in Will Success Spoil Rock Hunter?; Helen Hayes, Apr 1956, Arthur Westlake in Goodbye Again; Forrest, Philadelphia, Feb

1957, Hermes in Maiden Voyage; Carnegie Hall Playhouse, Sept 1957, appeared in the revue The Best of Burlesque; Plymouth, June 1958, took over from Peter Ustinov as the General in Romanoff and Juliet; 54th Street, Oct 1958, Miles Pringle in Drink to Me Only; Henry Miller's, Oct 1959, Ferguson Howard in Golden Fleecing; York Playhouse, Apr 1959, Cornelius in Come Play with Me; ANTA, Jan 1961, Woodrow Truesmith in The Conquering Hero; toured, summer 1961, as Destry in Destry Rides Again; Brooks Atkinson, July 1962, took over as Alan Baker in Come Blow Your Horn; Helen Hayes, Nov 1962, took over from Barry Nelson as Bob McKellaway in Mary, Mary; Yonkers Playhouse, Feb 1964, played in Easy Does It; Coconut Grove Playhouse, June 1966, Jeremy Troy in The Well-Dressed Liar; toured, 1967, in Any Wednesday; Henry Miller's, Feb 1969, Walter London in But, Seriously . . .; Morosco, 1970, took over the part of Billy Boylan in Forty Carats; toured, 1971, as F Sherman in The Owl and the Pussycat; toured, 1971, as Sam Nash, Jesse Kiplinger, and Roy Hubley in Plaza Suite; Falmouth, Mass, Playhouse, July 1971, appeared in Play It Again, Sam; Lunt-Fontanne, Aug 1972, took over from Phil Silvers as Prologus and Pseudolus in A Funny Thing Happened on the Way to the Forum; Bucks County Playhouse, New Hope, Pa, 1972, title-role in Cyrano de Bergerac, and also appeared in Anything Goes, 1972; same theater, Oct 1973, Nick in The Inn People; toured, 1973, in Lovers and Others Strangers; McCarter, Princeton, NJ, Feb 1975, Chaplain in Mother Courage; has appeared in the films The City That Never Sleeps, Zotz, The Old Dark House, Cold Turkey, The Happy Hooker (1975), etc; on television served as the Master of Ceremonies for the series *Entertainment*, 1955, and has since played in You Sometimes Get Rich, The Tempest, *The Steve Allen Show* (1956–8), *To Tell the Truth* (regular panelist), etc; received an Emmy for his appearances on *The Steve Allen Show*, 1959.

Address: c/o Jack Rollins, 130 West 57th Street, New York, NY 10019.

POTTER, Dennis, dramatic author
b Forest of Dean, Glos, 17 May 1935; s of Walter Edward Potter and his wife Margaret Constance (Wale); e Bell's G S, Coleford, St Clement Dane's G S, London, and New College, Oxford; m Margaret Morgan; formerly a journalist.

His first play to be performed on stage was Vote Vote Vote for Nigel Barton, 1968; subsequently Son of Man, 1969; Only Make Believe, 1974; Brimstone and Treacle, 1977; television critic of the *Sunday Times*, 1976–; a prolific television writer, his plays for this medium include the above, and more than twenty others, as well as the series *Casanova*, the serial Pennies From Heaven, and Blue Remembered Hills; Writers Guild Writer of the Year, 1966.

Address: Morecambe Lodge, Duxmere, Ross-on-Wye, Herefordshire. *Tel:* Ross 3199.

POTTS, Nancy, costume designer
First designs for New York were the costumes for Right You Are (If You Think You Are), produced by the Phoenix, 4 Mar 1964; since then has designed costumes for The Tavern, Scapin, Impromptu at Versailles, The Lower Depths, Man and Superman, 1964; War and Peace, Judith, You Can't Take It with You, 1965; The School for Scandal, We Comrades Three, 1966; The Wild Duck, Pantagleize, The Show-Off, 1967; Exit the King, The Cherry Orchard, Hair (first designs for London at the Shaftesbury, Sept), The Cocktail Party, The Misanthrope, 1968; Horseman, Pass By, Cock-a-Doodle Dandy, Hamlet, La Strada, 1969; Harvey, The Criminals, The Persians, Early Morning, 1970; The

School for Wives, The Grass Harp, 1971; The Selling of the President, Don Juan, Rainbow, 1972; Medea, Detective Story (Philadelphia), A Streetcar Named Desire, Veronica's Room, Chemin de Fer, Holiday, 1973; Who's Who in Hell, The Rules of the Game, 1974; Present Laughter (tour), Edward II, The Time of Your Life, 1975; Porgy and Bess, 1976; The New York Idea, Three Sisters, 1977; The Play's the Thing, King Lear, 1978; The Most Happy Fella, 1979.

Address: 442 East 75th Street, New York, NY. *Tel:* 794–0392.

POWELL, Robert, actor
b Salford, Lancs, 1 June 1944; s of John Wilson Powell and his wife Kathleen (Davis); e Manchester GS and Manchester U; m Barbara Lord.

Began his professional career at the Victoria, Stoke-on-Trent, 1964; appeared at the Royal Court, July 1966, as various messengers and guests in Ubu Roi; Leeds Playhouse, 1971, played Hamlet; Greenwich, Apr 1971, Lyngstrand in The Lady from the Sea; Theatre Upstairs, Dec 1971, Jean Misson in Pirates; Arnaud, Guildford, Nov 1972, Scythrop Glowery in Nightmare Abbey; University, Newcastle, 1973, Oberon in The Fairy Queen; Westminster, July 1973, Branwell Brontë in Glasstown; Aldwych, for RSC, May 1975, Tristan Tzara in Travesties, later playing the same part at the Albery; films, since his first appearance in 1968, include Mahler, Tommy, Jesus of Nazareth, The Thirty-Nine Steps, and Harlequin; TV includes *Doomwatch*, Jude the Obscure, and Looking for Clancy.

Address: c/o Boyack and Conway, 15 Hay Hill, London W1. *Tel:* 01–493 9744.

POWERS, John, dramatic author
b Melbourne, Victoria, 12 Jan 1935; s of John Powers and his wife Henrietta (McGuigan); e Xavier College, Melbourne; m Carmel Dunn; formerly in publishing and bookselling.

His first play to be performed was The Hot Centre of the World, St Martin's Melbourne, 18 Oct 1970; has subsequently written The Last of the Knucklemen, 1973; Shindig, 1975; The Hot Centre of the World was also filmed.

Recreations: Weightlifting, films, reading. *Address:* 24 Hambledon Road, Hawthorn, Victoria. *Tel:* 81–6316.

PREECE, Tim, actor
b Shrewsbury, Shropshire, 5 Aug 1938; s of Denis Goodwin Preece and his wife Dorothy (Mann); e Priory Grammar School, Shrewsbury, and Bristol University; m Gilly Wray; trained for the stage at the Bristol Old Vic Theatre School, 1960–1.

First appeared on the stage 4 Aug 1960, at the Spa Theatre, Whitby, as Inspector Malcolm in Not in the Book; first appeared on the London stage 2 Oct 1962, at the New Arts, as Charlie Weston in Doctors of Philosophy; Phoenix, Feb 1963, played Johannes in Baal; York, June 1963, John the Baptist in the York Mystery Plays; Arts, Oct 1963, played Hoskinson and Garibaldi in the triple-bill Cockade; Old Vic, 1964, took over Ragnar in the National Theatre production of The Master Builder; Queens, Dec 1964, Celestin in Maxibules; Garrick, Feb 1966, Nipple in Little Malcolm and his Struggle Against the Eunuchs; Arts, Oct 1966, Bertrand in The Swallows; made his New York début, Nov 1966, as Nipple in Hail Scrawdyke! (American title of Little Malcolm) at the Booth; Jeannetta Cochrane, London, June 1967, Church in The Mighty Reservoy; toured India and Pakistan for Prospect Productions, Oct 1967–Feb 1968, playing Stanley in The Birthday Party and Gunner in Misalliance; Arts, June 1968, The Press in The Foundations; Manchester, 1969, for 69 Theatre Co, Pierre Maurice in The Trial of Joan of Arc; LAMDA, Sept 1969, Thagney in K D Dufford; University, Newcastle, Nov 1970, Bartholomew Cokes in Bartholomew Fair; Perth, Sept 1971, Bluntschli in Arms and the Man; Arts, Cambridge, Feb 1972, Travelling Salesman in You and Your Clouds; Perth, Mar 1972, Strom in A Spell for Green Corn; Act Inn Theatre Club, May 1972, Frank in Bad Bad Jo Jo; Forum Theatre, Billingham, June 1972, General Stephens in Never Say Die; Greenwich, Sept 1972, Captain Hawtree in Caste; Shaw, Oct 1973, Malcolm in Macbeth; Traverse, Edinburgh, June 1973, directed Plat du Jour; television, since 1964, includes: Glittering Prizes, The Fall and Rise of Reginald Perrin and The Kilvert Diaries; author of play Father's Day, 1979.

Favourite part: Nipple. *Recreations:* Building, gardening. *Address:* c/o Crouch Associates, 59 Frith Street, London W1V 5TA.

PRESTON, Robert (*né* Meservey), actor
b Newton Highlands, Massachusetts, 8 June 1918; *s* of Frank W Meservey and his wife Ruth (Rea); *e* Lincoln High School, Los Angeles; *m* Catherine Feltus.

First appeared on the stage in Los Angeles, 1932, in Kearney from Killarney; Los Angeles, 1936, appeared in Julius Caesar with the Patia Power Company; Pasadena Playhouse, 1936–8, played in Shakespearean repertory and in Montezuma, Murder in the Cathedral, Night over Taos, Ethan Frome, Knights of Song, Idiots' Delight, Star of Navarre, and The Girl of the Golden West; made his first appearance in New York at the Fulton Theatre, 1951, when he took over from José Ferrer as Oscar Jaffe in 20th Century; City Center, NY, Apr 1952, played Joe Ferguson in The Male Animal, subsequently transferring with the production to the Music Box, May 1952; 48th Street, Apr 1953, Peter Hogarth in Men of Distinction; 48th Street, Jan 1954, Clem Scott in His and Hers; Booth, Apr 1954, played George Wilson in The Magic and the Loss; Longacre, Oct 1954, appeared as Joe McCall in The Tender Trap; Plymouth, Nov 1955, played Gil in Janus; Playhouse, Jan 1957, played Jean Monnerie in The Hidden River; Majestic, Dec 1957–60, played Harold Hill in The Music Man (Antoinette Perry 'Tony' Award and New York Drama Critics Award for Best Male Lead in a Musical, 1958, for this performance); Shubert, New Haven, Conn, Feb 1962 Pancho Villa in We Take the Town; 54th Street, Mar 1963, The Burglar in a revival of Too True to Be Good; Lyceum, Dec 1963, Nat Bently in Nobody Loves an Albatross; Lunt-Fontanne, Oct 1964, Benjamin Franklin in Ben Franklin in Paris; Ambassador, Mar 1966, King Henry II in The Lion in Winter; 46th Street, Nov 1966, Michael in I Do! I Do! for which he received the Antoinette Perry (Tony) Award and the New York Drama Critics Award; toured, 1968, in the last part; Majestic, Oct 1974, Mack Sennett in Mack and Mabel; Broadhurst, May 1977, took over from George C Scott as Foxwell J Sly in Sly Fox; first entered films, 1938, and has since appeared in numerous pictures, including Union Pacific, Typhoon, Northwest Mounted Police, Reap the Wild Wind, This Gun for Hire, Wake Island, Beau Geste, The Macomber Affair, The Sundowners, The Dark at the Top of the Stairs, The Music Man, All the Way Home, Junior Bonner, Child's Play, Mame, Semi-Tough (1977), etc; first appeared on television, 1951, since which time he has performed in many programs, including: *Playhouse 90, Omnibus,* The Man That Corrupted Hadleyburg, etc.

Favourite parts: Joe Ferguson in The Male Animal, and Harold Hill in The Music Man. *Recreation:* Acting. *Club:* Players. *Address:* 436 North Bristol Avenue, Los Angeles, Calif 90049.

PRICE, Vincent, actor
b St Louis, Missouri, 27 May 1911; *s* of Vincent Leonard Price and his wife Marguerite Cobb (Willcox); *e* St Louis Country Day School, Yale University, University of London, and California College of Arts and Crafts; *m* (1) Edith Barrett (mar dis); (2) Mary Grant; (3) Coral Browne; formerly taught at Riverdale Country School, New York; studied Art at the Courtauld Institute in London.

Made his first appearance on the stage at the Gate Theatre, 13 Mar 1935, as Charles Murdock and the Judge in Chicago, and appeared at the same theatre, May 1935, as Prince Albert in Victoria Regina; Oct 1935, played Max in Anatol; he then returned to America, and made his first appearance in NY, at the Broadhurst Theatre, 26 Dec 1935, as Prince Albert in Victoria Regina, which he continued to play until June 1937; in summer theatres, 1937, played the leading parts in What Every Woman Knows, Elizabeth the Queen, Parnell, The Wild Duck, The Passing of the Third Floor Back, Romance, Eden End, Turandot, The Lady of La Paz; Longacre, Sept 1937, played Jean in The Lady Has a Heart; Mercury, Jan 1938, Master Hammon in The Shoemaker's Holiday, and Apr 1938, Hector Hushabye in Heartbreak House; Playhouse, Dec 1938, Rev William Duke in Outward Bound; Biltmore, Los Angeles, Sept 1941, Saint in Mamba's Daughters; Golden, Dec 1941, Mr Manningham in Angel Street; Las Palmas, California, Playhouse, Nov 1950, Arthur Winslow in The Winslow Boy; at the Curran, San Francisco, Oct 1951, appeared in The Cocktail Party; toured, 1952, in Goodbye Again; at La Jolla Playhouse, California, Aug 1952, played Thomas Mendip in The Lady's Not for Burning; in San Francisco, Sept 1952, succeeded Charles Laughton in the dramatic readings of Don Juan in Hell; New York City Center, Dec 1953, played the Duke of Buckingham in Richard III; Playhouse, Dec 1954, played Dr Nicholas Marsh in Black-Eyed Susan; reappeared in NY at the George Abbott, Jan 1968, as Priam Farel in the musical Darling of the Day; Queen's, London, June 1975, played The Count in Ardèle; Dallas, Texas, Music Fair, Aug 1976, again played Fagin; toured, Nov 1976, in Charley's Aunt; Marines, San Francisco, July 1977, followed by tour, and Eugene O'Neill, NY, Apr 1978, appeared as Sebastian Melmoth in a one-man show about Oscar Wilde, Diversions and Delights; has appeared as narrator with various symphony orchestras, including the opera Moses, Peter and the Wolf, and A Lincoln Portrait; member of the Board of the Archives of American Art; the Whitney Museum Friends of American Art; the Royal Academy of Arts; the Fine Arts Commission for the White House; etc; Commissioner of the US Indian Arts and Crafts Board; author of I Like What I Know, 1958, Book of Joe, 1960, Michelangelo Bible, 1964 (with Mary Grant Price), A Treasury of Great Recipes, 1965, A National Treasury of Cookery, 1967; has broadcast in *The Saint, Lux Radio Theatre,* and *CBS Playhouse,* and has appeared frequently on television; entered films, 1938, and has since appeared in 100 films, including: House of Wax, The Fall of the House of Usher, and Theatre of Blood.

Recreations: Swimming and hiking. *Hobby:* Collecting drawings and paintings. *Clubs:* Elizabethan, Yale. *Address:* 580 North Beverly Glen Boulevard, Los Angeles, Calif 90024. *Tel:* 213–274–2883.

PRIDE, Malcolm, designer
b London, 5 July 1930; *s* of Alan Pride; *e* Bryanston School, Dorset; trained for the stage at the Old Vic Theatre School.

Designed his first stage production for an Arts Council Tour of The Merchant of Venice; 1951, designer for the West of England Theatre Company, Exmouth; designed his first

London production at Sadler's Wells Theatre, 1952, with Cavalleria Rusticana; he has since designed the following productions: Volpone (Stratford-on-Avon), 1952; Romeo and Juliet (Sadler's Wells Opera), 1953; Troilus and Cressida (Stratford-on-Avon), Troilus and Cressida (opera costumes) (Covent Garden), 1954; Twelfth Night (Stratford-on-Avon), 1955; The Marriage of Figaro, Il Trovatore, Fidelio (last three productions at Sadler's Wells), 1956; The Crystal Heart, The Rape of the Belt, The Telephone and Bluebeard's Castle (Sadler's Wells), 1957; Little Eyolf, 1958; Danton's Death, Creditors and The Cheats of Scapin (double-bill), The Rough and the Ready Lot, As You Like It (Old Vic), Man On Trial, 1959; Orpheus in the Underworld (Sadler's Wells), 1960; La Vie Parisienne (Sadler's Wells), 1961; A Gazelle in Park Lane, Two Stars for Comfort, The Chances (opening of the Chichester Festival), 1962; The Merchant of Venice (Old Vic), 1962; Measure for Measure (final production of the Old Vic Company), Portrait of Murder, The Yes-Yes-Yes Man, 1963; The Father, March Hares, Robert and Elizabeth, 1964; On the Level, 1966; Hamlet (Edinburgh), Il Seraglio and The Impresario (Bath Festival), 1968; Two Cities (sets only), 1969; Albert Herring (Chester Festival), Catch My Soul, 1970; Amphitryon 38 (National), Charley's Aunt (costumes), 1971; Pull Both Ends, 1972; The Card, 1973; The Good Companions, The Englishman Amused, 1974; Maggie, 1977; La Spinalba (Camden Festival), 1978; entered television Jan 1958, designing the costumes for Women of Troy; he has since designed the following: Moon on a Rainbow Shawl (costumes only), Hay Fever, Private Potter, Cliff Sings Scots (costumes only), etc; since 1973 Head of Theatre Design, Wimbledon School of Art.

Recreations: Films, travel, reading, sociological research. *Address:* c/o Felix de Wolfe, 1 Robert Street, Adelphi, London, WC1.

PRIESTLEY, J B, OM 1977, MA LLD, DLitt (*né* John Boynton Priestley), dramatic author, novelist and essayist *b* Bradford, 13 Sept 1894; *s* of Jonathan Priestley; *e* Bradford and Trinity Hall, Cambridge (MA); *m* (1) Patricia Tempest (*d* 1925); (2) Mrs Mary Wyndham Lewis (mar dis); (3) Jacquetta Hawkes; during the War, served with the Duke of Wellington's and Devon Regiments (1914–19).

Began his career as a writer, while still at Cambridge, with Brief Diversions; author of the following plays: The Good Companions (with Edward Knoblock), 1931; The Roundabout, Dangerous Corner, 1932; Laburnum Grove, 1933; Eden End, 1934; Duet in Floodlight, Cornelius, 1935; Bees on the Boatdeck, 1936; Time and the Conways, I Have Been Here Before, People at Sea; Music at Night, When We Are Married, 1938; Johnson Over Jordan, 1939; associated in the management of the Duchess Theatre, 1934–5, where Eden End and Cornelius were produced; also at the Duchess, 1937 (Time and the Conways); Royalty, 1937 (I Have Been Before); St Martin's 1938 (When We Are Married), also at the Princes, 1939; Saville, 1939 (Johnson Over Jordan); a director of the Mask Theatre, which operated at the Westminster, 1938–9; has since written The Long Mirror, 1940; Goodnight, Children, 1942; They Came to a City, Desert Highway, 1943; How Are They at Home? 1944; An Inspector Calls, 1945; Ever Since Paradise, 1946; The Linden Tree, 1947; Home Is To-Morrow, 1948; Summer Day's Dream, 1949; Dragon's Mouth (with Jacquetta Hawkes), Treasure On Pelican, 1952; The White Countess (with Jacquetta Hawkes), 1954; Mr Kettle and Mrs Moon, The Golden Entry, 1955; These Our Actors, 1956; The Thirty-First of June, and The Glass Cage (written for Crest Theatre, Toronto), 1957; A Severed Head (with Iris Murdoch), The

Pavilion of Masks, 1963; his 80th birthday was celebrated by the National Theatre with a production of Eden End, 1974; in the same year The Good Companions was adapted as a musical; has written several screen plays, notably The Foreman Went to France and Last Holiday, also many novels, volumes of essays and autobiography; a well-known broadcaster, especially for his Postscripts during World War II, and has appeared on television; Chairman of International Theatre Conferences at Paris, 1947, and Prague, 1948; first President of International Theatre Institute; Chairman of British Theatre Conference, 1948.

Recreations: Reading, music, and painting. *Club:* Savile. *Address:* Kissing Tree House, Alveston, Stratford-on-Avon, Warwickshire.

PRIMROSE, Dorothy, actress
b Edinburgh, Scotland, 19 Apr 1916; *d* of Frank Buckley and his wife Alice (Jennings); *e* Oakham; *m* Laurence Howe Bear.

Made her first appearance at the Lyceum Theatre, Edinburgh, 1916, being carried on in The Manxman; first appeared in London, at the St James's Theatre, 21 June 1939, walking-on in After the Dance; first appeared in New York, at the Henry Miller Theatre, 30 Jan 1940, in Geneva; at Wimbledon, Oct 1942, played Eva Wiltshire in Lottie Dundass; Arts Theatre Mar 1943, Bridie in The Well of the Saints, and the Nurse in Beyond; Scala, May 1943, Ethel Chichester in Peg O' My Heart; Arts, July–Nov 1943, Angelica in The Constant Couple, Lydia Languish in The Rivals, and Sybil in The Watched Pot; at the Scala, Feb–Apr 1944, with Donald Wolfit's company, Nerissa in The Merchant of Venice, and Maria in Twelfth Night; St Martin's, Nov 1944, played Beatie Tomlinson in The Magistrate; Arts, Sept–Oct 1945, Leo in Getting Married, Louisa in The Thunderbolt, Maria in The School for Scandal, Angelica in The Constant Couple, and Ophelia in Hamlet; Arts, Aug 1946, Princess Alice in The Apple Cart; toured, 1946–7, for the British Council European tour, in Hamlet, and Othello; during 1948, was with the Glasgow Citizen's Theatre; appeared at the Edinburgh Festival, 1949, as the Princess Christina in The Saxon Saint, and 1950, as Hecemede in The Queen's Comedy, and Mrs Thistleton in The Atom Doctor; Arts, Dec 1950, played Silver Stream in Lady Precious Stream; Arts, July 1952, Lady Constant in The Way To Keep Him; at the Studio Theatre, Nairobi, Nov 1954, appeared in The Heiress; Vaudeville, 1957–60, played Lady Raeburn in Salad Days; again appeared at the Donovan Maule Theatre, Nairobi, 1961–2; Nottingham Playhouse, Apr 1962, played Meg in The Birthday Party; Queen's, Feb 1965, Margaret Ainsley in Ring of Jackals; Prince of Wales, Jan 1966, Edna Swithinbank in Doctor at Sea; Haymarket, Dec 1967, Margery Harvey in Dear Octopus, transferring to the Piccadilly, Feb 1968, and the Strand, Apr 1968 toured US, Aug 1968, with the Theatre Royal Windsor Company, as Lady Markby in An Ideal Husband and Lady Bountiful in The Beaux' Stratagem; Royal Court, Theatre Upstairs, July 1969, played Madame in Poet of the Anemones and Mrs Blim in Blim at School (double-bill); Dublin Festival, Sept 1969, and tour, Hilda Hanways in On the Rocks; Royal Court, Liverpool, Mar 1970, played the Marchioness in the pre-London tour of Lady Frederick, until forced to withdraw by a broken ankle; Hampstead, May 1971, Mrs Hutcheson in Disabled; Everyman, Cheltenham, Sept 1971, Mother in Top of the Ladder; same theatre, Sept 1972, Emmie Gurney in Gathering of the Clan; Cambridge Festival, July 1976, Mrs Higgins in Pygmalion; Theatre Royal, York, Aug 1977, Miss Fiske in Ladies in Retirement; Thorndike, Leatherhead, Sept 1979, Mrs Bradman in Blithe Spirit; joined the staff of the Royal College of Music and Drama, 1973, as associate drama director; first appeared in films, 1943, in SS San Demetrio.

Address: 16 St George's Drive, London, SW1.

PRINCE, Harold S, producer and director
b New York City, 30 Jan 1928; *s* of Milton A Prince and his wife Blanche (Stern); *e* University of Pennsylvania; *m* Judith Chaplin.

Formerly a stage manager; with Robert E Griffith, presented his first production, The Pajama Game at the St James's Theatre, NY, May 1954; he has since produced or co-produced and/or directed the following: Damn Yankees, 1955; New Girl in Town, West Side Story, 1957; A Swim in the Sea, West Side Story (London), 1958; Fiorello! 1959; Tenderloin, 1960; A Call on Kuprin, Take Her, She's Mine, A Funny Thing Happened on the Way to the Forum (also London, 1963), A Family Affair (directed), 1962; She Loves Me (also directed), She Didn't Say Yes (also directed), 1963; She Loves Me (also directed, London), Fiddler on the Roof, Poor Bitos (NY), 1964; Baker Street (directed), Flora, the Red Menace, 1965; It's a Bird . . . It's a Plane . . . It's Superman (also directed), 1966; at the US Embassy, London, 12 June 1966, narrated a revue in the Festival of American Arts and Humanities; Cabaret (also directed), Fiddler on the Roof (London), 1967; Zorba (also directed), Cabaret (London, also directed), The Beggar's Opera (London), 1968; Company (also directed), 1970; produced, and directed with Michael Bennett, Follies, 1971, for which he received the Antoinette Perry (Tony) Award, 1971; Company (London), 1972; joined the New Phoenix Repertory Company as Artistic Director, 1972, which has since presented The Great God Brown (also directed), Don Juan, A Meeting by the River, 1972; Strike Heaven on the Face, Games, After Liverpool, The Government Inspector, The Visit (also directed), Chemin de Fer, Holiday, 1973; also co-produced and directed A Little Night Music, for which he received the Tony Award for best musical, 1973; for the New Phoenix presented The Removalists, In the Voodoo Parlor of Marie Leveau, Pretzels, The Rules of the Game, Love for Love (also directed), 1974; co-produced and directed Candide, for which he received the Tony Award, 1974; A Little Night Music (London), and for the New Phoenix presented The Member of the Wedding, Knuckle, Dandelion Wine, Meeting Place, 1975; co-produced and directed Pacific Overtures, 1976; co-produced Side by Side by Sondheim, 1977; directed On the Twentieth Century, Evita (London), 1978; Sweeney Todd, the Demon Barber of Fleet Street, for which he received a Tony Award, Evita (Broadway), 1979; Evita (Vienna), Sweeney Todd (London), 1980; directed opera Ashmedai for New York City Opera, 1976; The Girl of the Golden West for the Chicago Lyric Opera, 1978, and the San Francisco Opera, 1979; Silverlake for the New York Opera, 1980; author of Contradictions: Notes on 26 Years in the Theatre, 1975; has also received Tony Awards for The Pajama Game, Damn Yankees, A Funny Thing Happened on the Way to the Forum, Fiddler on the Roof, Cabaret (two Awards), Company (two Awards); his productions have won twelve Tony Awards as of 1979, and he has received five as best director; has also received various other awards, including the New York Drama Critics Circle Award for many of these same musicals; President of League of New York Theatres, 1964–5; films with which he has been associated include: The Pajama Game, Damn Yankees, West Side Story, Something for Everyone, A Little Night Music, etc.

Address: 1270 Avenue of the Americas, New York, NY 10020. *Tel:* 399 0960.

PRINCE, William, actor
b Nichols, New York, 26 Jan 1913; *s* of Gorman Prince and his wife Myrtle (Osborne); *e* Cornell University; *m* (1) Dorothy Huass (mar dis); (2) Augusta Dabney; studied acting with Tamara Daykarhanova.

Made his first appearance on the NY stage, at the Manhattan Opera House, 7 Jan 1937, walking-on in The Eternal Road; he was then engaged by Maurice Evans and remained with him for three years, appearing at the St James Theatre, Sept 1937, as the Servant to York in Richard III Oct 1938, the Page in Hamlet; Jan 1939, John of Lancaster in King Henry IV (Part I); was subsequently engaged as a radio announcer with National Broadcasting Corporation; at the Guild Theatre, Oct 1941, played Richard in Ah! Wilderness; Plymouth, Feb 1942, Dan Proctor in Guest in the House; Belasco, Aug 1942, Callaghan Mallory in Across the Board on To-Morrow Morning; Cort, Oct 1942, Private Quizz West in The Eve of St Mark; then went to Hollywood, 1943, and remained there until 1947; Booth, Feb 1947, John Lawrence in John Loves Mary; 48th Street, Jan 1949, David Gibbs in Forward the Heart; Cort, Jan 1950, Orlando in As You Like It; Empire, Nov 1951, Christopher Isherwood in I Am a Camera; Ethel Barrymore, Apr 1956, Capt Tom Cochran in Affair of Honor; Ambassador, Dec 1958, Dr Lockwood in Third Best Sport; Longacre, Nov 1959, Dr Robert Leigh in The Highest Tree; Morosco, Apr 1962, Alec Grimes in Venus at Large; Hudson, Mar 1963, Charles Marsden in a revival of Strange Interlude; Martin Beck, Oct 1963, Henry Macy in The Ballad of the Sad Café; toured the US, 1964, as Bob McKellaway in Mary Mary, and took over this role at Helen Hayes, NY, June 1964; East 74th Street, Sept 1967, Father Arnall and Preacher in Stephen D; Vivian Beaumont, Oct 1967, William Marshall in The Little Foxes; St Clements' Church, Oct 1969, Arthur in Mercy Street; Center Stage, Baltimore, Maryland, 1970, James Tyrone in Long Day's Journey into Night; Actors Studio, May 1972, Gracie in The Silent Partner; Goodman, Chicago, Jan 1973, appeared in In the Matter of J Robert Oppenheimer; Roundabout, July 1973, Davies in The Caretaker; Shubert, Los Angeles, Apr 1975, took over as Charlie in Seascape; Hartford Stage, Conn, Jan 1977, He in Counting the Ways and Man in Listening; first appeared in films, 1943, in Destination Tokyo and has since appeared in The Heartbreak Kid (1972), Blade (1973), etc; on television appeared as Jerry Malone in the series *Young Dr Malone,* 1958–63.

Address: c/o Fred Amsel and Associates, 321 South Beverly Drive, Beverly Hills, Calif 90212.

PSACHAROPOULOS, Nikos, director and professor
b Athens, Greece, 18 Jan 1928; *s* of Constantine Psacharopoulos and his wife Helen (Mitsakas); *e* Oberlin College and Yale School of Drama (MFA); trained for the stage at Actors Studio.

Helped to establish the Williamstown Theatre Festival, Williamstown, Mass, in 1955, and has been its artistic/executive director since 1956, directing over sixty plays including Heartbreak House, Peer Gynt, Cyrano de Bergerac, Saint Joan, Enemies, The Three Sisters, Misalliance, and The Seagull; staged The Play of Daniel at the Cloisters, NY, 1956, and subsequently all over the US and Europe; staged The Play of Herod, Cloisters, 1963; on Broadway, directed Tambourines to Glory at the Little, Nov 1963; has directed Androcles and the Lion for the American Shakespeare Festival, Stratford, Conn, 1968, and in regional theatres including Studio Arena etc; opera direction includes a number of assignments with the NY City Opera; teaches at Yale, Circle in the Square, and privately; Hon DHL, Williams College, 1974.

Address: c/o Williamstown Theatre Festival, Williamstown, Mass 01267. *Tel:* 413-458 8146.

PURNELL, Louise, actress

b Purley, Surrey, 29 May 1942; *d* of Douglas Southey Purnell and his wife Jeanne Marie (de Guingand); *e* Coloma Convent and Royal Ballet School; *m* Andrew Robertson (actor); trained for the stage at Italia Conti Stage School.

First appeared on the stage 26 Dec 1959, at the New Theatre, Oxford as one of The Normandy Singers in Puss in Boots; first appeared on the London stage 20 Sept 1960, at the Adelphi, as Lady Mabelle in Once Upon A Mattress; Piccadilly, Oct 1962, played Sophie in Fiorello!; joined the National Theatre company at the Old Vic, 1963, for whom she has appeared regularly in parts including the following: Sorel Bliss in Hay Fever, 1964; Abigail in The Crucible, Rose in Trelawny of the Wells, 1965; Carol Melkett in Black Comedy, 1966; Irina in Three Sisters, Mariane in Tartuffe, 1967; Manto in Seneca's Œdipus, Elena in The Advertisement, Princess of France in Love's Labour's Lost, 1968; Eve, Zoo and Cleopatra in Back to Methuselah, 1969; Aglaya in The Idiot, 1970; Lady Byron in Byron, the Naked Peacock (Young Vic), Susan Mountford in A Woman Killed with Kindness, Lady in Danton's Death, Juliet in Romeo and Juliet (Young Vic), 1971; Lady Teazle in The School for Scandal, Lady Macduff in Macbeth, 1972; Viola in Twelfth Night (mobile production), Dunyasha in The Cherry Orchard, Guilianella in Saturday, Sunday, Monday, 1973; at the Shaw, Mar 1974, played Cecily Cardew in The Importance of Being Earnest; same theatre, Jan 1976, Mrs Dangerfield in The Ginger Man; Old Vic, Nov 1976, Julie Price in The Ghost Train; Open Air Theatre, Regent's Park, 1977, Rosaline in Love's Labours Lost, and Princess Katherine in Henry V; for the Prospect Theatre Co at the Old Vic, Apr 1978, Olivia in Twelfth Night, and Aug 1978, Anna Petrovna in Ivanov; first film, 1970, the National Theatre's Three Sisters; television, since 1961, includes The Bear, Clayhanger and Cork and Bottle.

Recreations: Music, travel. *Address:* c/o Peter Crouch, 60–66 Wardour Street, London, W1.

Q

QUAYLE, Anna, actress

b Birmingham, 6 Oct 1937; *d* of John Douglas Stuart Quayle and his wife Kathleen (Parke); *e* Convent of Jesus and Mary, Harlesden; *m* Don Baker; trained for the stage at RADA.

Appeared many times as child with her father; Edinburgh Festival, Aug 1956, played various parts in the Fringe revue, Better Late; Players', 1958 appeared in Ridgeway's Late Joys; toured, Sept 1958, as Lucie in A Fig for Glory; Palladium, Edinburgh, 1959, appeared in the revue, Do You Mind?; Fortune, June 1960, made her West End début in the revue Look Who's Here!; this was followed at the same theatre in Oct 1960, by And Another Thing; Queen's, July 1961, played female lead in Stop the World—I Want to Get Off; made her New York début in the same roles at the Shubert, Oct 1962, winning the Tony for Best Supporting Actress, 1962, as well as the London Critics Circle award, for these performances; Globe, London, June 1965, played Doris in Homage to T S Eliot; Apollo, Dec 1970, appeared in her one-woman show, Full Circle, which she also wrote; Bristol Old Vic, Dec 1973, Miss Dyott in Out of Bounds; Edinburgh Festival, Sept 1976, Melba in the Oxford Playhouse production of Pal Joey; Phoenix, Mar 1978, Anne of Cleves in Kings and Clowns; Her Majesty's, Sept 1979, Lady Tremurrain in The Case of the Oily Levantine; films, since 1964, include Chitty Chitty Bang Bang, The Seven Per Cent Solution and The Sinking of the Titanic; television, since 1960, includes regular appearances in variety programmes, in Britain and the US, most recently in Brideshead Revisited and Henry V.

Recreations: Reading, music and Siamese cats. *Address:* 2 St Nicholas Road, Brighton, Sussex.

QUAYLE, Anthony, CBE, actor

b Ainsdale, Lancashire, 7 Sept 1913; *s* of Arthur Quayle and his wife Esther (Overton); *e* Rugby; *m* (1) Hermione Hannen (mar dis); (2) Dorothy Hyson; studied for the stage at the Royal Academy of Dramatic Art.

Made his first appearance on the stage at the Q Theatre, 28 Dec 1931, as Richard Cœur de Lion and Will Scarlett in Robin Hood; then appeared at the Festival Theatre, Cambridge, as Hector in Troilus and Cressida; New, June 1932, played Aumerle in Richard of Bordeaux; Westminster, July 1932, Ferdinand in Love's Labour's Lost; joined the Old Vic company, Sept 1932, and played small parts during the season; during 1933 played in Shakespearean season at the Chiswick Empire; Adelphi, Mar 1934, Bennie Edelman in Magnolia Street; Imperial Institute, July 1934, Matt Burke in Anna Christie; subsequently appeared at the Embassy; New, Nov 1934, Guildenstern in Hamlet; Ambassadors', Oct 1935, Captain Courtine in The Soldier's Fortune; Old Vic, Feb 1936, St Denis in St Helena; St James's, Feb 1936, Mr Wickham in Pride and Prejudice; made his first appearance in New York at the Henry Miller Theatre, Dec 1936, as Mr Harcourt in The Country Wife; with the Old Vic company, appeared at Elsinore, June 1937, as Laertes in Hamlet; Westminster, July 1937, Horatio in Hamlet; Queen's, Sept 1937, Duke of Surrey in Richard II; St James's, Nov 1937, Beppo in The Silent Knight; Old Vic, Dec 1937–Feb 1938, Demetrius in A Midsummer Night's Dream, and Cassio in

Othello; Gate, Mar and Haymarket, Apr 1938, Earl of Essex in Elizabeth, La Femme Sans Homme; returned to the Old Vic, Sept–Dec 1938, playing Ferdinand in Trelawny of the Wells, Laertes, John Tanner in Man and Superman, Captain Absolute in The Rivals; Jan–Apr 1939, toured with the Old Vic company on the Continent and in Egypt, where he also played the King in Henry V; during the War, served from 1939–45, in the Royal Artillery; demobilized, 1945, with the rank of Major; reappeared on the stage at the Criterion, Sept 1945, as Jack Absolute in The Rivals; directed Crime and Punishment at the New Theatre, June 1946; Piccadilly, Dec 1946, played Enobarbus in Antony and Cleopatra; Mar 1947, Iago in Othello; at the Lyric, Hammersmith, Dec 1947, and Phoenix, Jan 1948, directed The Relapse; in 1948, joined the Shakespeare Memorial Theatre Company, Stratford-on-Avon, as director and actor, appearing during the season as Iago, Claudius and Petruchio; was appointed Director of the Theatre, Oct 1948; at the Prince of Wales's, Jan 1949, directed Harvey; continued his association with the Shakespeare Memorial Theatre through the seasons 1949–50, and also took the company to Australia and New Zealand, Oct 1949–Feb 1950, performing Macbeth, Much Ado About Nothing, Henry VIII; Criterion, London, Oct 1950, directed Who Is Sylvia?; at Stratford-on-Avon, 1951, directed and played Falstaff in the Cycle of Histories; returned to Australia and New Zealand with the Shakespeare Memorial Theatre Company, Jan–Oct 1953, with productions of As You Like It, Henry IV (Pt I), and Othello; at Stratford-on-Avon, during the 1954 season, directed and played Othello, and appeared as Bottom in A Midsummer Night's Dream and Pandarus in Troilus and Cressida; during the 1955 season, played Falstaff in The Merry Wives of Windsor and Aaron in Titus Andronicus; Winter Garden, NY, Jan 1956, played the title-part in Tamburlaine the Great; Memorial Theatre, Stratford, Aug 1956, directed Measure for Measure; resigned from directorship of Shakespeare Memorial Theatre, July 1956; Comedy, Oct 1956, played Eddie in A View From the Bridge; Paris Festival, May 1957, played Aaron in Titus Andronicus, subsequently visiting Venice, Belgrade, Zagreb, Vienna, and Warsaw, with the production, before appearing at the Stoll, London, July 1957, in the same play; Coronet, NY, Apr 1958, played Moses in The Firstborn (which he also directed), subsequently appearing in the same production at the Habimah Theatre, Tel-Aviv, July 1958; Edinburgh Festival, Sept 1958, played James Tyrone in Long Day's JLook After Lulu, transferring with the production to the New, Sept 1959; Wyndham's, Nov 1960, played Cesareo Grimaldi in Chin-Chin; Garrick, Sept 1963, co-directed and played Nachtigall in Power of Persuasion; Her Majesty's, May 1964, Sir Charles Dilke in The Right Honourable Gentleman; Phoenix, Jan 1966, Leduc in Incident at Vichy; Phoenix, Oct 1966, directed Lady Windermere's Fan; Vivian Beaumont, NY, Apr 1967, played the title-part in Galileo; Atkinson, NY, Nov 1967, General Fitzbuttress in Halfway Up the Tree; St Martin's, Feb 1970, played Andrew Wyke in Sleuth, and at the Music Box, NY, Nov 1970; for the National Theatre at the Old Vic, July 1970, directed The Idiot; Prince of Wales, Apr 1975, directed Harvey; Aldwych, Oct 1976, for RSC, played Rodion Nikolayevich in Old World; 1977, toured US playing Rodion Nikolayevich in Do You Turn Somersaults (retitled from Old World), and then at 46th Street Theatre, NY, Jan 1978; Queen's, June 1978, took over the part of Hilary in The Old Country; Old Vic, Sept 1978, directed and played Sir Anthony Absolute in The Rivals; Old Vic, Oct 1978, played title-role in King Lear; has also appeared in numerous films, including: Hamlet, The Battle of the River Plate, Woman in a Dressing Gown, Ice Cold in Alex, The Guns of Navarone, Lawrence of Arabia, Anne of the Thousand Days, The Tamarind Seed, etc; television appearances include: Strange Report, QB VII, Moses the Lawgiver, Ice Age, Henry IV (Parts I & II), Masada; created CBE, 1952; guest professor, University of Tennessee, 1974, lecturing on drama; is the author of the books Eight Hours from England and On Such a Night.

Recreation: Sailing. *Club:* Garrick. *Address:* c/o ICM Ltd, 22 Grafton Street, London W1.

QUILLEY, Denis, actor

b London, 26 Dec 1927; *s* of Clifford Charles Quilley and his wife Ada Winifred (Stanley); *e* Bancroft's School, Woodford Green, Essex; *m* Stella Chapman.

Made his first appearance on the stage with the Birmingham Repertory Theatre Company, during the season, 1945, appearing, among other parts, as Lyngstrand in The Lady From the Sea; at the Globe Theatre, London, Jan 1950, took over the part of Richard in The Lady's Not For Burning; Phoenix, Apr 1950, played Leading Seaman Kendall in Red Dragon; joined the Old Vic Company for a British Council Tour of Italy, 1950, playing Fabian in Twelfth Night; with the Young Vic Company, Old Vic, Dec 1950, played Richard Shelton in Black Arrow, and Jan 1951, Gratiano in The Merchant of Venice; Duke of York's, 1951, took over the part of Mathias in Point of Departure; Nottingham Repertory Theatre, 1952; at the Royal Court, Apr 1953, appeared in the revue Airs on a Shoestring, which ran for more than 700 performances; Duke of York's, July 1955, played his first leading part in the West End as Geoffrey Morris in Wild Thyme; Piccadilly, Dec 1955, played Laurie in A Girl Called Jo; Lyric, Hammersmith, Nov 1956, Tom Wilson in Grab Me a Gondola, subsequently transferring with the production to the Lyric, W1, Dec 1956, and running for over 600 performances; at the Bristol Old Vic, Sept 1958, played Captain Brassbound in Captain Brassbound's Conversion and Orlando in As You Like It; Saville, Apr 1959, played the title-part in Candide; Piccadilly, May 1960, Mike Polaski in Bachelor Flat; Everyman, Cheltenham, Sept 1960, played Mark Raven in Wildest Dreams; Lyric, 1960, took over the part of Nestor-le-Fripe in Irma La Douce; left the London company to make his first appearance in New York, at the Plymouth Theatre, June 1961, when he again took over the part of Nestor-le-Fripe in Irma La Douce, subsequently touring the US with the production, Jan 1962; on returning to England, he appeared at the Open Air Theatre, Regent's Park, June 1963, as Benedick in Much Ado About Nothing; Drury Lane, Nov 1963, played Antipholus of Ephesus in The Boys From Syracuse; Savoy, Nov 1964, Charles Condamine in the musical High Spirits; Apr 1966, played Robert Browning in Robert and Elizabeth in Melbourne and Sydney; on return, Jan 1969, at the Playhouse, Nottingham, played Archie Rice in The Entertainer and took over the title-role in Macbeth; Gardner Centre, Sussex University, Jan 1970, played Krogstad in A Doll's House; Greenwich, Feb 1970, Alec Hurley in Sing a Rude Song, transferring to the Garrick, May 1970; Mar 1971, joined the National Theatre to play Aufidius in Coriolanus; he subsequently played Scofield in Tyger, Jamie in Long Day's Journey into Night, 1971; Henry

Bolingbroke in Richard II, Crabtree in The School for Scandal, Hildy Johnson in The Front Page, Banquo in Macbeth, 1972; took over as Macbeth, 1973, also playing Lopakhin in The Cherry Orchard, Luigi Ianiello in Saturday, Sunday, Monday, and Andrew Ford in The Party; 1974, played Caliban in The Tempest; Arnaud, Guildford, Aug 1975, John Tanner in Man and Superman; Old Vic, Dec 1975, Claudius in Hamlet, playing the same part in the opening production at the Lyttelton, Mar 1976; Young Vic, June 1976, Hector in Troilus and Cressida; Olivier, Oct 1976, Bajazeth and Callapine in Tamburlaine the Great; Aldwych, Feb 1977, Cpt Terri Dennis in Privates on Parade, and again at the Piccadilly, Feb 1978; Albery, June 1977, Morell in Candida; Garrick, Oct 1978, Sidney Bruhl in Deathtrap; Drury Lane, July 1980, title-role in Sweeney Todd; appeared in the films Life at the Top, Anne of the Thousand Days, and Murder on the Orient Express; has also played leading parts in the following television plays and series: The Father, Henry IV (Pirandello), Murder in the Cathedral, *Clayhanger,* etc.

Favourite parts: Jamie, and Hildy Johnson. *Recreations:* Playing the flute and cello. *Address:* c/o NEMS Management, 29–31 King's Road, London SW3.

QUINN, Anthony, actor

b Chihuahua, Mexico, 21 Apr 1915; *s* of Frank Quinn and his wife Manuela (Oaxaca); *e* Polytechnic High School, Los Angeles, Cal; *m* (1) Katherine de Mille (mar dis), (2) Yolanda Addolari; formerly a boxer, electrician, carpenter, painter, writer, factory worker, etc.

Made his New York debut at the Mansfield, 9 Dec 1947, as Stephen S Christopher in The Gentleman from Athens; Harris, Chicago, and tour, 1948–49, played Stanley Kowalski in A Streetcar Named Desire; toured, 1949–50, as Harry Brock in Born Yesterday; New York City Center, May 1950, again played Stanley Kowalski in A Streetcar Named Desire; Fulton, Aug 1950, Texas in Borned in Texas; Playhouse, Wilmington, Del, Mar 1951, Alvin Connors in Let Me Hear the Melody; St James, Oct 1960, Henry II in Becket; Plymouth, Oct 1962, Caesario Grimaldi in Tchin-Tchin; Shubert, Boston, June 1975, King Del Rey in The Red Devil Battery Sign; first appeared in films in The Plainsman, 1937, and since then has played in Blood and Sand, They Died with Their Boots On, The Ox-Bow Incident, Viva Zapata! (for which he received the Academy Award, 1952), Lust for Life (Academy Award, 1956), Lawrence of Arabia, The Visit, The Don Is Dead, and many others; recent TV includes Jesus of Nazareth, 1977.

Address: c/o ICM, 40 West 57th Street, New York, NY 10019.

QUINTERO, José, director

b Panama City, Panama, 15 Oct 1924; *s* of Carlos Rivira Quintero and his wife Consuelo (Palmorala); *e* Los Angeles City College; University of Southern California.

Directed his first production at Woodstock Summer Theatre, New York, 1949, with The Glass Menagerie and Riders to the Sea; has been associated with Circle-in-the-Square, off-Broadway, as director of Dark of the Moon, 1950; Bonds of Interest, The Enchanted, Yerma, Burning Bright, 1951; Summer and Smoke, 1952; The Grass Harp, American Gothic, 1953; The Girl on the Via Flaminia, 1954; La Ronde, The Cradle Song, 1955 (both of which he also co-produced); The Iceman Cometh, 1956; Children of Darkness, The Quare Fellow, 1958, both of which he also co-produced; Our Town, 1959; The Balcony, 1960; Under Milkwood, 1961; Plays for

Bleecker Street, Pullman Car Hiawatha (both of which he also co-produced), 1962; Desire Under the Elms (which he also co-produced), 1963; for other managements he has also directed the following plays: In the Summer House, 1953; The Girl on the Via Flaminia, Portrait of a Lady, 1954; The Innkeepers, Long Day's Jouney into Night, 1956; made his London début by directing the last play at the Globe, Sept 1958; also directed Lost in the Stars, 1958; The Triumph of Saint Joan (opera), Macbeth (Cambridge Drama Festival, Mass), 1959; Camino Real, Laurette, 1960; Look, We've Come Through, 1961; Great Day in the Morning, 1962; Strange Interlude, 1963; Marco Millions, Hughie, 1964; Diamond Orchid, Matty and the Moron and the Madonna, 1965; directed Pagliacci and Cavalleria Rusticana for the Metropolitan Opera Co; directed Pousse Café, 1966; More Stately Mansions, 1967; The Seven Descents of Myrtle, 1968; Gandhi, 1970; Johnny Johnson, The Big Coca-Cola Swamp in the Sky (Westport, Conn), 1971; A Moon for the Misbegotten, for which he received the Tony Award, 1973; wrote the book and directed Gabrielle at the Studio Arena, Buffalo, NY, 1974; The Skin of Our Teeth, 1975; Knock, Knock, Hughie (Lake Forest), 1976; Anna Christie, A Touch of the Poet, 1977; The Human Voice (also Melbourne), 1978; Faith Healer, 1979; Public, Oct 1979, appeared in O'Neill and Carlotta; directed the film The Roman Spring of Mrs Stone, 1961; has also directed plays for television, notably Medea and Our Town, 1959; author of an autobiography, If You Won't Dance, They Beat You.

Address: Society of Stage Directors and Choreographers, 1501 Broadway, New York, NY.

R

RABB, Ellis, actor, director, producer
b Memphis, Tennessee, 20 June 1930; *s* of Clark Williamson Rabb and his wife Mary Carolyn (Ellis); *e* University of Arizona, Carnegie Institute of Technology (BFA 1953), Yale University; *m* Rosemary Harris (mar dis).

Made his stage début at the Antioch Arena Theatre, Yellow Springs, Ohio, 1952, as the Dauphin in King John, and also played the Duke of York in Richard II, Earl of Worcester in Henry IV, Part I, Shallow in Henry IV, Part II, Archbishop of Canterbury and Lewis in Henry VI, Parts I, II, and III, a Murderer in Richard III, and Cardinal Wolsey in Henry VIII, Troilus in Troilus and Cressida, a Citizen in Coriolanus, Ventidius in Timon of Athens, Lysimachus in Pericles, Cassius in Julius Caesar, Eros in Antony and Cleopatra, 1953; Gremio in The Taming of the Shrew, Speed in Two Gentlemen of Verona, Herald in Othello, Bassanio in The Merchant of Venice, Palemon in Two Noble Kinsmen, Ariel in The Tempest, 1954; Leontes in The Winter's Tale, Lucius in Titus Andronicus, Sir Andrew Aguecheek in Twelfth Night, First Lord in Cymbeline, Old Man in Macbeth, 1955; Benedick in Much Ado About Nothing, title-role in King Lear, 1956; Malvolio in Twelfth Night, and directed Measure for Measure, A Midsummer Night's Dream, and Julius Caesar, and served as the Artistic Director, 1957; made his New York début at the Jan Hus House, 13 Jan 1956, as Starveling in A Midsummer Night's Dream; Theatre East, Nov 1956, Alceste in The Misanthrope; Phoenix, Oct 1957, Sir William Davidson in Mary Stuart; American Shakespeare Festival, Stratford, Connecticut, 1958, Player King in Hamlet, Starveling in A Midsummer Night's Dream, and Camillo in The Winter's Tale; toured, 1958, as Verges and Don Pedro in Much Ado About Nothing; Henry Miller's, Mar 1959, General Koschnadieff in Look After Lulu; joined Group 20, Wellesley, Massachusetts, 1959, and directed Much Ado About Nothing, A Streetcar Named Desire, and played Octavius in Man and Superman, Smee in Peter Pan, and Tiresias in Œdipus Rex; Longacre, NY, Dec 1959, Reverend Furze in Jolly's Progress; founded and became Artistic Director of the APA (Association of Producing Artists), 1960, and toured with it in the US and Bermuda; APA first performed in NY at the Folksbiene, 17 Mar 1962, in repertory, for which he directed The School for Scandal, The Tavern, and The Seagull; toured and appeared in NY annually, until its disbandment in 1970; for APA staged Anatol, The Seagull, and played John Tanner and Don Juan in Man and Superman, Gremio in The Taming of the Shrew, Matthew Skips in The Lady's Not for Burning, The Vagabond in The Tavern, Algernon Moncrieff in The Importance of Being Earnest, and, in addition to these, presented Right You Are (If You Think You Are), Box and Cox, The Cat and the Moon, Scapin, 1960; played King Lear, William in As You Like It, Malvolio in Twelfth Night, Robin Starveling in A Midsummer Night's Dream, The Vagabond in The Tavern, and Mr Tiffany in Fashion, directed Hamlet, The Tavern, The School for Scandal, A Midsummer Night's Dream, The Seagull, and also presented As You Like It, 1961; played Joseph Surface in The School for Scandal, The Vagabond in The Tavern, directed a Penny for a Song, We, Comrades Three, and presented The Seagull, Ghosts, 1962; played Oberon in A Midsummer Night's Dream, Richard II, Benedick in Much Ado About Nothing, Geronte in Scapin, The Baron in The Lower Depths, directed Richard II, and presented The Merchant of Venice, A Phoenix Too Frequent, Right You Are, 1963; this troupe combined with the Phoenix Theatre, 1964, to form APA at the Phoenix, for which he played the Governor of the Province in Right You Are, repeated The Vagabond in The Tavern, Geronte in Scapin, La Thorilliere in Impromptu at Versailles, The Baron in The Lower Depths, and Jack Tanner in Man and Superman, 1964; directed War and Peace, Judith, You Can't Take It with You, 1965; played Joseph Surface in The School for Scandal, which he also directed, and presented Right You Are, We, Comrades Three, 1966; played the title-role in Pantagleize, which he co-directed with John Houseman, and presented Exit the King, The Cherry Orchard, Show-Off, 1967; played Pantagleize and presented Exit the King, The Cherry Orchard, The Show-Off, The Cocktail Party, The Misanthrope, 1968; played Shanaar in Cock-a-Doodle Dandy, the title-role of Hamlet, which he also directed, 1969; also directed for other managements during this time, notably Antony and Cleopatra for the American Shakespeare Festival, 1963, A Midsummer Night's Dream for the Old Globe, San Diego, California, 1963, the opera Orpheus in the Underworld for the Kansas City Opera, 1967, and Hamlet for the Old Globe, 1968; directed The Grass Harp, 1971; Twelfth Night, Enemies, 1972; The Merchant of Venice, A Streetcar Named Desire, Veronica's Room, 1973; Who's Who in Hell, 1974; Edward II, The Royal Family, 1975; took over the role of Tony Cavendish from George Grizzard in this last play at the Helen Hayes, Jan 1976; directed Caesar and Cleopatra, 1977; de Lys, Oct 1977, played Robert in A Life in the Theater; played in Bartleby, the Scrivener, for television, 1958; received the Clarence Derwent Award for his role in The Misanthrope; received the Obie and Vernon Rice Awards for his off-Broadway season with the APA, 1962–3; received the Antoinette Perry (Tony) Award for direction, 1976.
Address: Actors Equity Association, 165 West 46th Street, New York, NY 10036.

RABE, David, playwright
b Dubuque, Iowa, 10 Mar 1940; *s* of William Rabe and his wife Ruth (McCormick); *e* Loras College (BA, English); *m* (1) Elizabeth Pan (mar dis); (2) Jill Clayburgh; formerly a bellhop, parking lot attendant, substitute teacher, etc.

First play to be produced in New York was The Basic Training of Pavlo Hummel, at the Estelle Newman for the New York Shakespeare Festival, 19 May 1971; since then has written Sticks and Bones, produced both on and off Broadway and televised, and for which he received the Antoinette Perry (Tony) Award, 1971; The Orphan, Boom Boom Room, 1973; last play revised and produced as In the Boom Boom Room, Burning, 1974; Streamers, 1976; also received the Obie Award, the Drama Desk Award, and the Variety Critics Poll for The Basic Training of Pavlo Hummel, and the Outer Circle Critics Award and the New York Drama Critics Citation for Sticks and Bones.
Address: Public Theater, 425 Lafayette Street, New York, NY 10003.

558

RAE, Charlotte (*née* Lubotsky), actress and singer
b Milwaukee, Wisconsin, 22 Apr 1926; *d* of Meyer Lubotsky and his wife Esther (Ottenstein); *e* Northwestern University (BS); *m* John Strauss.

Made her New York début at the Mark Hellinger, 21 Mar 1952, as Tirsa Shanahan in Three Wishes for Jamie; Theatre de Lys, Mar 1954, Mrs Peacham in The Threepenny Opera; Alvin, Apr 1954, Mrs Juniper in The Golden Apple; Phoenix, May 1956, played in The Littlest Revue; St James, Nov 1956, Mammy Yokum in Li'l Abner; New York City Center, Mar 1957, Molly Brazen in The Beggars Opera; Music Box, Dec 1962, Gloria Krumgold, Mrs Younghusband, Rowena Inchcape, and Mrs Lafcadio Mifflin in The Beauty Part; Writers Stage, May 1964, the Caretaker in The New Tenant and Madeleine in The Victims of Duty; Curran, San Francisco, California, Apr 1965, Mrs Bardell in Pickwick, and subsequently toured; 46th Street, Oct 1965, repeated her role in Pickwick; Delacorte, for the New York Shakespeare Festival, June 1968, Hostess Quickly in Henry IV, Parts I and II, and, Aug 1968, the Nurse in Romeo and Juliet; Henry Miller's, Nov 1968, Gertrude in Morning, Beryl in Noon, and Filigree Bones in Night; Ethel Barrymore, Mar 1970, Charlotte Mendelssohn in Dr Fish; Playhouse-in-the-Park, Cincinnati, Ohio, 1970, Lola in Come Back, Little Sheba; Shubert, Boston, Feb 1971, Mother Sweet in Prettybelle; St Clement's, Apr 1973, Tia Maria in Whiskey; Ahmanson, Apr 1974, played in The Time of the Cuckoo; New Las Palmas, LA, May 1978, Juno in Heaven Sent; has performed extensively in cabaret as a singer and comedienne, notably in NY at The Village Vanguard, The Blue Angel, Cafe Society, Bon Soir, Sherry-Netherland, in Chicago at the Empire Room of the Palmer House, 1957, etc; has appeared in the films Hello Down There, Jenny, Hot Rock, Bananas, 1971, etc; has appeared on television in Harvey, The World of Sholem Aleichem, and on various comedy, dramatic, music, and variety shows.
Address: c/o ICM, 40 West 57th Street, New York, NY 10019.

RAEDLER, Dorothy, director and producer
b New York City, 24 Feb 1917; *d* of Charles Conrad Raedler and his wife Florence Elizabeth (Radley); *e* Hunter College (BA 1942).

Has been engaged in the theatre in various capacities since the age of six; while in her teens organized a neighborhood theatrical troupe in NY; produced and directed shows in high school and college; organized the semi-professional troupe, The Masque and Lyre Gilbert and Sullivan Company, in 1939; first NY season for the troupe was at the Jan Hus House in Aug 1949, when she produced and directed The Mikado, HMS Pinafore, The Pirates of Penzance, Iolanthe, and The Gondoliers; since then has produced and directed the entire Gilbert and Sullivan repertory as founder of the professional company, The American Savoyards, which has toured regularly in the US and Canada since 1952, including annual engagements in NY until 1968; was producer, director, and manager of several theatres, including the Festival in Monmouth, Maine, for seven years; the Phillipe Park Amphitheatre, Safety Harbor, Florida; Las Palmas, Hollywood, California; Jan Hus House, NY; President, Shakespearewrights, Sullivan Street, and Greenwich Mews, all NY; has directed operas and operettas at other theatres on a guest basis, notably Coconut Grove Playhouse, Carter-Barron Amphitheatre (Washington, DC), Toledo University, Toronto Music Tent, St John Terrell's Music Tent in Lambertville, New Jersey, Harris Theatre in Chicago, National Theatre in Washington, and Goodspeed Opera House in East Haddam,

Connecticut; was stage director, New York City Opera Company, for seven years; was Production Co-ordinator and principal stage director of the City Center Gilbert and Sullivan Opera Company; has also produced and directed at many other summer and winter stock companies in US and Canada; has directed Cavalleria Rusticana, I Pagliacci, La Boheme, Madame Butterfly, Abduction from the Seraglio, Carmen, La Traviata, La Perichole, Gallantry, and six contemporary one-act operas; was stage director of the Baltimore Opera Company for two years; among the operettas and musical comedies directed are The Student Prince, The Boy Friend, Bittersweet, The Vagabond King, The Firefly, The Merry Widow, Naughty Marietta, Sweethearts, Little Mary Sunshine, Once upon a Mattress, etc; has lectured extensively throughout the US and Canada; received the Show Business Award for her direction in 1951 and 1954; moved to St Croix in 1968, where she became the Associate Director of the Virgin Island Council on the Arts; is Director and President of the St Croix School of the Arts, US Virgin Islands; is an honorary member of the New York Gilbert and Sullivan Society.
Recreations and hobbies: Cooking, gardening, swimming, horseback riding. *Address:* PO Box 1086, Christiansted, St Croix, US Virgin Islands 00820.

RAIN, Douglas, actor
b Winnipeg, Canada; studied for the stage at the Banff School of Fine Arts, and the Old Vic Theatre School.

After early appearances at the Jupiter Theatre and Royal Alexandra Theatre, Toronto, he joined the original Stratford Festival Company, Stratford, Ontario, July 1953, where he understudied Alec Guinness as Richard III and also played the Marquis of Dorset and Tyrrel; at subsequent Stratford Shakespearean Festivals he has played the following parts: Claudio in Measure for Measure, Biondello in The Taming of the Shrew, and the Messenger in King Œdipus, 1954; Decius Brutus and Titinius in Julius Caesar, 1955; Michael Williams in Henry V, and Simple in The Merry Wives of Windsor, 1956; First Player in Hamlet, and Malvolio in Twelfth Night, 1957; Prince Hal in Henry IV, Part I, and the Clown in The Winter's Tale, 1958; Iago in Othello and Silvius in As You Like It, 1959; the title-part in King John and Tybalt in Romeo and Juliet, 1960; Wolsey in Henry VIII, Boyet in Love's Labour's Lost, Grandad in The Canvas Barricade, 1961; Ragueneau in Cyrano de Bergerac, 1962; Ulysses in Troilus and Cressida, Dromio of Syracuse in The Comedy of Errors, Apemantus in Timon of Athens, 1963; Monsieur Jourdain in Le Bourgeois Gentilhomme, Edgar in King Lear, Pinchwife in The Country Wife, 1964; Prince Henry in Henry IV (Parts I and II), 1965; the name part in Henry V, Sir Toby Belch in Twelfth Night, 1966; Orgon in Tartuffe, D'Artagnan in The Three Musketeers, 1968; at the Winter Garden, New York, Jan 1956, he played Bajazeth and Almeda in Tamburlaine the Great, directed by Tyrone Guthrie; he has also toured with the Festival company as Speed in The Two Gentlemen of Verona and as Huish in The Broken Jug, 1957–8; at the Crest Theatre, Toronto, he appeared as Tony Lumpkin in She Stoops to Conquer, 1957, and as Higgins in Pygmalion, 1958; toured universities in Canada and the US, 1962, in Two Programs of Shakespearean Comedy; Lyceum, NY, Nov 1963, appeared in the concert reading The Golden Age; Chichester Festival Theatre, England, Apr 1964, appeared with the Stratford (Ontario) Company, as Holofernes in Love's Labour's Lost, Monsieur Jourdain in Le Bourgeois Gentilhomme, and Apemantus in Timon of Athens; Manitoba Theatre Center, Winnipeg, Dec 1964, appeared in Mother Courage; Central Library Theatre, Toronto, Oct

1965, Christopher Mahon in The Playboy of the Western World; Nov 1965, Gottlieb Biedermann in The Firebugs; Mermaid, London, Nov 1968, took over Father William Rolfe in Hadrian the Seventh; Duke of York's, July 1970, played Giovanni Mocenigo in The Heretic; Thorndike, Leatherhead, Nov 1970, Claudius in Hamlet; Arena Stage, Washington, Jan 1971, 14th Earl of Gurney in The Ruling Class; Stratford, Ont, season 1971, Mosca in Volpone; Broadhurst, NY, Jan 1972, Cecil in Vivat! Vivat! Regina!; Festival Lennoxville, 1972, played the lead in The Ottawa Man; Manitoba Theatre Centre, 1972, Tesman in Hedda Gabler and Andrew Wyke in Sleuth, touring in the latter role; at the same theatre directed Rosencrantz and Guildenstern are Dead, 1973; Stratford, 1973, Iago in Othello and Lysimachus in Pericles; 1974, again played Lysimachus, and Philip the Bastard in King John; associate director, Avon Stage, 1974; Danforth in The Crucible, 1975; Angelo in Measure for Measure, 1976; Jean in Miss Julie, 1977; De La Rochepozay and Prince de Condé in The Devils, and performed the monologue From an Abandoned Work, 1978; King Henry IV in Henry IV, Parts I and II, and Gloucester in King Lear, 1979; season 1980 appeared in Henry V, as Weller in The Gin Game, Gloucester in King Lear, and as John Aubrey in Brief Lives; appeared in numerous television plays in Canada, including the title-part in Henry VI and leading parts in The Crucible, Hedda Gabler, The Circle, Talking to a Stranger, etc; Head of the English Section of the National Theatre School, Montreal.
Address: c/o Elspeth Cochrane Agency, 1 The Pavement, London, SW4.

RAINBOW, Frank, theatre press representative
b London, 29 Dec 1913; *s* of Ernest Albert Rainbow and his wife Harriet Amelia (Tebbitt); *e* London; *m* Elsie Booth.

Formerly engaged in film production and publicity for overseas distribution, and also in the production of European films; appointed press representative for the English Stage Company at the Royal Court Theatre, 1960–3; has also acted as press representative for Jack Hylton, David Conville, Charles Ross, Henry Sherwood, Michael White, Ray Cooney and, since 1968, The New Shakespeare Company at the Open Air Theatre, Regent's Park; appointed chairman, ALTPR, 1970.
Recreations: Photography and golf. *Club:* Green Room. *Address:* 32 Hyde Gardens, Eastbourne, Sussex. *Tel:* 0323 2699.

RAITT, John, actor and singer
b Santa Ana, California, 19 Jan 1917; *s* of Archie John Raitt and his wife Stella Eulalie (Walton); *e* University of Redlands, California; *m* (1) Marjorie Geraldine Haydock; (2) Kathy Landry; studied voice production with Richard Cummings.

Curran, San Francisco, appeared in the chorus of HMS Pinafore with the Los Angeles Civic Light Opera Company, 1940; at the Pasadena Civic Auditorium, 1941, appeared as Figaro in The Barber of Seville, Count Almaviva in The Barber of Seville, and Escamillo in Carmen; Erlanger, Chicago, May 1944, played Curly in Oklahoma!; made his first appearance on the New York stage at the Majestic, 19 Apr 1945, as Billy Bigelow in Carousel, and gained the New York Drama Critics' Award, and the Donaldson Award, for the best performance in a musical production; Ziegfeld, Sept 1948, played Pedro in Magdalena; Creek, Los Angeles, July 1949, Robert in New Moon; Mark Hellinger, Mar 1952, played Jamie McRuin in Three Wishes for Jamie; Century, Sept 1953, appeared as The Duke in Carnival in Flanders; St

James, May 1954, played Sid Sorokin in The Pajama Game; Stadium, Pittsburgh, July 1957, again played in The Pajama Game; San Francisco and Los Angeles, Aug 1957, played Frank Butler in Annie Get Your Gun; toured, 1960, in Destry Rides Again, Carousel, and Oklahoma!; toured, 1961–2, in The Pajama Game, Oklahoma! and Carousel; Curran, San Francisco, Apr 1963, Billy Bigelow in Carousel; St Paul Civic Opera, Jan 1964, Sid Sorokin in The Pajama Game, in which he also toured, summer 1965; summer tour, 1964, as Curly in Oklahoma!; NY State, Aug 1965, again played Billy Bigelow in a revival of Carousel and subsequently toured; Mark Hellinger, Dec 1966, Shade Motley in A Joyful Noise; toured, 1967 and 1968, as Dr Mark Buckner in On a Clear Day You Can See Forever; Music Theatre, Houston, May 1967, again played in Carousel; Westbury Music Fair, Long Island, Oct 1970, title-role in Zorba; toured, 1971, as Hajj in Kismet; Royal Alexandra, Toronto, Canada, May 1972, Billy Bigelow in Carousel; toured, 1973, in 1776; St James, Nov 1975, played in the revue A Musical Jubilee; toured, 1976–7, as Charlie Anderson in Shenandoah; toured, 1978, in the title-role of Man of La Mancha; films in which he has appeared include Flight Command, 1940; Ziegfeld Girl, 1941; and The Pajama Game, 1957; has also appeared on television as Frank in Annie Get Your Gun, as the star of the *Chevy Show*, 1958–9, and as guest on the *Bell Telephone Hour*, etc.
Recreations: Golf, water ski-ing. *Address:* James Fitzgerald Enterprises Inc, 1061 Ravoli Drive, Pacific Palisades, Calif 90272.

RAMSAY, Remak, actor
b Baltimore, Md, 2 Feb 1937; *s* of John Breckinridge Ramsay Jr and his wife Caroline Voorhees (Remak); *e* Princeton Univ (BA 1958); trained for the stage at the Neighborhood Playhouse and with David Craig.

After work in summer theatres, 1963–4, made his New York debut at the Mayfair, 18 Oct 1964, in the revue Hang Down Your Head and Die; Broadhurst, Aug 1965, took over as Young Walsingham in Half a Sixpence; toured, summer 1967, as Ken Powell in Generation; toured, 1967–8, as Norman Cornell in The Star-Spangled Girl; appeared at the Charles Playhouse, Boston, Mass, during the 1968–9 season, as Jack in Everything in the Garden; toured, summer 1969, as Gordon Lowther in The Prime of Miss Jean Brodie; Helen Hayes, Jan 1970, Edward Snelling in Sheep on the Runway; Majestic, Dec 1970, Capt McLean in Lovely Ladies, Kind Gentlemen; Imperial, Oct, 1971, Ozzie in a revival of On the Town; Theatre Four, Apr 1972, Foot in After Magritte and Magnus in The Real Inspector Hound; toured, Jan 1973, as Chrysalde in School for Wives, and in Oct 1973, as Hysterium in A Funny Thing Happened on the Way to the Forum; Billy Rose, Apr 1974, Archie in Jumpers; 46th Street, Feb 1975, Victor Prynne in Private Lives; with Phoenix at the John Drew, Easthampton, summer 1975; Williamstown, Mass, Summer 1976, Hector Hushabye in Heartbreak House; John Golden, Jan 1977, Cocklebury-Smythe in Dirty Linen; Public/Newman, Sept 1977, Durwood Peach in Landscape of the Body; Delacorte, June 1978, King of France in All's Well That Ends Well; toured, Aug 1978, as the Doctor in Every Good Boy Deserves Favour; Manhattan Theatre Club, Nov 1978, Bartellot in The Rear Column; Eisenhower, Washington DC, June 1978, Maj Frederick Lowndes in Home and Beauty; Metropolitan Opera, July 1979, again played the Doctor in Every Good Boy Deserves Favour; appeared in the film The Tiger Makes Out, 1967; subsequently The Great Gatsby, The Front, Simon, etc.

Favourite part: Bartellot. *Address:* 115 Central Park West, New York, NY 10023.

RAMSDEN, Dennis, actor and director

b Leeds, 7 Nov 1918; *s* of Laurie Balfour Ramsden, and his wife Mabel Georgiana (Hawson); *e* Leeds Grammar School; *m* Christine Mary Russell.

First appeared on the stage Jan 1946, at the Repertory Theatre, Dundee, as Finch McComas in You Never Can Tell; first appeared on the London stage, 1948, at the Apollo, when he took over as Rupert Billings in The Happiest Days of Your Life; at the Phoenix, Jan 1950, played Det-Sgt Fleming in The Non-Resident; Whitehall, July 1964, Mr Laver in Chase Me, Comrade; at the Garrick, played Hubert Wooley in Stand By Your Bedouin, Mar 1967; David Prosser in Uproar in the House, Apr 1967 and Willie Kitson in Let Sleeping Wives Lie, July 1967; Academy Theatre, Johannesburg, Nov 1970, played Mr Laver in Stand By Your Bedouin (also directed); Strand, June 1971, Mr Needham in No Sex Please, We're British; Vaudeville, June 1973, Bob Gilchrist in Signs of the Times; Theatre Royal, Brighton, Jan 1974, March Hare and Mock Turtle in Alice in Wonderland; toured, Apr 1974, as Hubert Boothroyd in Lloyd George Knew My Father, subsequently directing and playing the same part at the Academy, Johannesburg; National Arts Centre, Ottawa and Toronto, Dec 1974, the Baron in Cinderella; toured S Africa, Mar 1975, as Claude Philby in A Bedfull of Foreigners, playing the same part at the Victoria Palace, Apr 1976, transferring to the Duke of York's, Oct 1976; Arnaud, Guildford and tour, 1978, Colonel Pickering in Pygmalion; Apollo, 1978–9, took over Sir Justin Holbrook in Shut Your Eyes and Think of England; Strand, 1980, returned to No Sex Please We're British as Mr Needham, the part he played from 1971–3; as a director, he directed productions at Dundee, 1954–5; tours for Howard and Wyndham Ltd, 1956–62; London productions include: Music at Midnight, 1962; new productions of The Mousetrap, 1964–7; Uproar in the House (revival), 1967; There Was a Man, 1968; television appearances, since 1956, include several farces.

Favourite parts: David Prosser, Arnold Needham. *Club:* Green Room. *Address:* c/o Richard Stone, 18 York Buildings, Adelphi, London WC2. *Tel:* 01–839 6421.

RANDALL, Leslie, actor

b South Shields, Co Durham, 19 Oct 1924; *s* of Charles Randall and his wife Mary Richardson (Proud); *e* some fifteen day schools; *m* Joan Reynolds (mar dis); formerly a journalist; studied for the stage at the New Era Academy (London) and film production at the University of Southern California.

Made his first stage appearance while serving with the RAF in a service production of The Ghost Train; between 1948–49, appeared in repertory at Norwich, Yarmouth, Redcar, and Darlington; subsequently toured, Aug 1949, as Dick Pentwick in Love's a Luxury; made his first London appearance at the Gateway Theatre, Jan 1951, as one of two comedians in Late Night Revue; toured Feb–Jun, 1951, in variety; at the Windmill Theatre, Jan 1952, appeared in Revuedeville; London Palladium, Aug 1952, appeared as solo comedian; Prince of Wales, Dec 1952, took over from Norman Wisdom in the *revue* Paris to Piccadilly; from 1953–58, toured in variety, and also appeared on television in his own series; at the Piccadilly, May 1959, played Gordon Whiting in the farce Caught Napping; toured, Oct 1960, as Arnold in Lock, Stock, and Barrel; toured, June 1961, in Fol de Rols of 1961; Palace, Westcliff, May 1965, played Val Corbett in I Found April; Pavilion, Torquay, summer, 1966,

the Corporal in The Amorous Prawn; went to California, 1967–69, and played Chitterlow in a West Coast tour of Half-a-Sixpence; in Australia 1969–70 as a director of TV programme development; toured S Africa with Joan Reynolds, 1972, in the revue Me and the Fella; subsequently toured UK, 1973; in pantomime at Camberley, 1974, Whitehaven, 1975; toured, 1975–76, in his one-man show, Laughs; at the Comedy, Feb 1979, played Murray in his own play, Forty Love; toured UK, 1979, in Shut Your Eyes and Think of England; toured S Africa, 1979, in Forty Love; has played in cabaret worldwide; films, since his first in 1948, include The Small Back Room, Billy Liar, etc; TV, since 1950, in the UK and the US, includes several of his own series, recently Husband of the Year; wrote the US series *The Go Between*.

Recreations: Golf and poker. *Club:* Savage. *Address:* 23 Phoenix House, 110 Charing Cross Road, London WC2. *Tel:* 240 3800.

RANDALL, Tony, actor

b Tulsa, Oklahoma, 26 Feb 1920; *e* Northwestern Univ, Columbia Univ; prepared for the stage at the Neighborhood Playhouse School of the Theatre, 1938–40; served in the US army 1942–46 as Lieutenant.

First appeared on the stage as Anthony Randall at the Upper Ferndale, NY, Country Club, summer 1939; made his NYC début at the New School for Social Research, spring 1941, as the Brother in The Circle of Chalk; North Shore Players, Marblehead, Mass, Aug 1941, played Marchbanks in Candida; toured the NYC Subway Circuit, July 1942, as a Miner in The Corn Is Green; joined the Olney, Md, Theatre after the War, acting and directing; toured, May 1947, as Octavius Moulton-Barrett in The Barretts of Wimpole Street; made his Broadway debut at the Martin Beck, 26 Nov 1947, as Scarus in Antony and Cleopatra, with Katharine Cornell; New Stages, Apr 1948, Adam in To Tell the Truth; National, Dec 1949, Major Domo in Caesar and Cleopatra; as Tony Randall, Henry Miller's, July 1954, took over from Gig Young as Arthur Turner in Oh, Men! Oh, Women!; National, Apr 1955, E K Hornbeck in Inherit the Wind; Alvin, Feb 1958, Capt Henry St James in Oh, Captain!; toured in Arms and the Man, 1960, and in Goodbye Again, 1961; Helen Hayes, Jan 1966, J Francis Amber in UTBU; toured, summers 1970 to 1976, as Felix Unger in The Odd Couple; toured, summer 1978, in The Music Man; worked in radio as an announcer in Worcester, Mass, 1941–42, and as an actor, 1946–55; made his film debut in Oh, Men! Oh, Women!, 1957, and has since appeared in Will Success Spoil Rock Hunter?, The Mating Game, Pillow Talk, Scavenger Hunt, and many others; first appeared on television in *One Man's Family,* 1949, and has played regularly since in the series *Mr. Peepers,* 1952–55, as Felix Unger in the long-running series *The Odd Couple,* 1970–75, *The Tony Randall Show,* 1976; is a member of the Association of the Metropolitan Opera Company.

Recreations: Opera, appearing frequently as a guest on the radio intermission feature of the Metropolitan Opera broadcasts called *Opera Quiz. Address:* 145 Central Park West, New York, NY 10023.

RANDELL, Ron, actor

b New South Wales, Australia, 8 Oct 1923; *s* of Ernest B Randell and his wife Louisa Maria (Castello); *e* St Mary's College, Sydney; *m* Laya Raki.

Made his first appearance on the stage in Sydney, Australia, in 1943, when he played Sgt Mulraney in While the Sun Shines; between 1943–6, he appeared in Melbourne and Sydney in a number of plays, including: Of Mice and Men,

Dangerous Corner, and The Voice of the Turtle; made his first appearance on Broadway at the Coronet Theatre, Oct 1949, when he played Frank Hunter in The Browning Version, and Jack Wakefield in Harlequinade (double-bill entitled Playbill); National, New York, Apr 1952, played the Rev James Morell in a revival of Candida; made his first appearance in London at the St James's, Dec 1952, when he played Chester Ames in Sweet Peril; Cambridge, Feb 1954, played Johnny Goodwin in The Fifth Season; Palace, Aug 1954, played Linus Larrabee, Jnr, in Sabrina Fair; Broadhurst, NY, Oct 1958, played Ben Jeffcoat in The World of Suzie Wong; Queen's, London, Feb 1963, played Dirk Winston in Mary, Mary; Cambridge, Aug 1966, Leo Messner in A Share in the Sun; Royal, Nottingham, Nov 1968, David Morgan in The Button; Wimbledon, Apr 1969, Victor Lance in The Passionate Husband; Broadhurst, Feb 1975, took over as James Larrabee in Sherlock Holmes; Vivian Beaumont, Feb 1976, Praed in Mrs Warren's Profession; Delacorte, July 1976, Escalus in Measure for Measure; Hartford Stage, Conn, Mar 1978, appeared in Holiday; Hartman, Stratford, 1978–9 season, appeared in Absurd Person Singular; American Place, May 1979, Fumio in Tunnel Fever; New Apollo, Dec 1979, Captain in Bent; films in which he has appeared include: Pacific Adventure, I Am a Camera, King of Kings, etc; television appearances include American Heritage, etc.

Address: 201 West 70th Street, #23H, New York, NY 10023.

RANDOLPH, Elsie, actress and singer
b Stockwell, London, 9 Dec 1904; *d* of James Randolph and his wife Elizabeth Ann (née Thurston); *e* Stockwell College; *m* Leopold Vernon Page (dec).

Made her first appearance on the stage at the age of twelve in the provinces; first appeared in London, at the Duke of York's Theatre, 23 Sept 1919, as a Model in The Girl for the Boy; at the Adelphi, Oct 1920, played Bibi in The Naughty Princess; Queen's, Aug 1921, a Schoolgirl in My Nieces; Gaiety, Apr 1922, a Guest in His Girl; subsequently appeared in The Follies Cabaret at the Queen's Hall; at the Adelphi, Mar 1923, played the Flapper in Battling Butler; at the Shaftesbury, May 1924, played Folly in Toni; Daly's, 1924, for a time, played Madeleine in Madame Pompadour; Empire, Mar 1925, Clematis Drew in Boodle; London Hippodrome, Oct 1926, Weenie Winters in Sunny; Daly's, July 1927, Alice Frost in Peggy-Ann; London Hippodrome, June 1928, Joy Dean in That's a Good Girl; Dominion, Oct 1929, Ruth Vanning in Follow Through; London Hippodrome, Apr 1930, appeared with The Co-Optimists of 1930; Savoy, Dec 1930, played Inez in Wonder Bar; London Hippodrome, Mar 1931, Ena in Stand Up and Sing; London Hippodrome Feb 1934, Betty Trotter in Mr Whittington; Vaudeville, Apr 1935, appeared in Charlot's Char-a-Bang!; during 1935–6, toured as Bobbie Rivers in This'll Make You Whistle, appearing at the Palace, Sept 1936, in the same part; Adelphi, Dec 1937, played Aladdin in the pantomime; Comedy, Sept 1938, Clare Broden in Room for Two; toured, Apr–Nov 1940, in the revue Top Hat and Tails; also toured, from Nov 1940, in The Body Was Well Nourished; Coliseum, Apr 1942, Vittoria in The Maid of the Mountains; Winter Garden, July 1943, Marian Kane in It's Time to Dance; Playhouse, Mar 1945, Mrs Mott in Great Day; Duke of York's, July 1945, Yvonne Vining in Is Your Honeymoon Really Necessary?, which she played for over a year; Duchess, Jan 1954, appeared as Susan Barclay in No Other Verdict; Garrick, June 1955, played Dorothy Foster in The Lost Generation; Pier, Bournemouth, June 1965, appeared with Arthur Askey in What a Racket, and Second Honeymoon; Palace, Westcliff, July 1966, Judith

Bliss in Hay Fever; same theatre, July 1967, Lady Fitzadam in The Amorous Prawn; Ashcroft, Croydon, Sept 1968, Lady Clementina Beauchamp in Lord Arthur Savile's Crime, in which she toured, appearing in the same role at Sadler's Wells, Mar 1972; Churchill, Bromley, Sept 1978, Mrs Dorbell in The Cure for Love; first appeared in films, 1932, in Rich and Strange, and has since appeared in many others, including Riders in the Sky (1968), Frenzy (1972), and Charleston (1977); recent television drama performances include: *Z-Cars, Within These Walls*, The Coffee Lace, and Edward and Mrs Simpson (1978).

Address: High Hedge, The Drive, Angmering-on-Sea, Sussex. *Tel:* Rustington 4456.

RANDOLPH, Robert, designer
b Centerville, Iowa, 9 Mar 1926; *s* of Charles W Randolph and his wife Saide M (Walker); *e* State University of Iowa (BFA 1950, MA 1953).

Formerly engaged as an architectural and industrial designer and as an instructor at the State University of Iowa; first New York production was at the Broadway, 27 Dec 1954, when he designed the scenery and costumes for The Saint of Bleecker Street; since then has designed, principally décor, for the following productions: The Desperate Hours, 1955; Bye Bye Birdie, 1960; How to Succeed in Business Without Really Trying, 1961; Bravo, Giovanni, Calculated Risk, Little Me, 1962; Sophie, 1963; Foxy, Any Wednesday, Funny Girl, Something More! 1964; Pleasures and Palaces, Minor Miracle, Xmas in Las Vegas, Skyscraper, Anya, 1965; Sweet Charity, It's a Bird . . . It's a Plane . . . It's Superman, Walking Happy, 1966; Sherry, Sweet Charity (London), Henry, Sweet Henry, How to Be a Jewish Mother, 1967; Golden Rainbow, 1968; A Teaspoon Every Four Hours, Angela, 1969; Applause, 1970; Ari, 70, Girls, 70 (also lights), 1971; Applause (London), 1972; No Hard Feelings (also lights), Gypsy (London), Good Evening, The Enclave (also lights), 1973; Words and Music, Sammy Cahn's Songbook (London), Gypsy, The King and I (Los Angeles), 1974; We Interrupt This Program, How to Succeed in Business Without Really Trying, Wonderful Town (last two Los Angeles, and also lights), The Norman Conquests, 1975; Porgy and Bess, Hellzapoppin (tour), 1976; Annie Get Your Gun (LA), 1977; Spotlight (Washington), 1978.

Address: 100 West 57th Street, New York, NY 10019. *Tel:* JU 6–2873.

RATTIGAN, Sir Terence (*cr* 1971), CBE, dramatic author
b London, 10 June 1911; *s* of William Frank Arthur Rattigan, CMG, and his wife Vera (Houston); *e* Harrow (Scholar), and Trinity College, Oxford (Scholar in Modern History).

Author of First Episode, 1934, and French Without Tears, 1936, which ran over a thousand performances; After the Dance, 1939; Follow My Leader (with Anthony Maurice), 1940; Grey Farm (with Hector Bolitho), 1940; Flare Path, 1942, which ran for 670 performances; While the Sun Shines, 1943, which ran for 1154 performances; Love in Idleness (O Mistress Mine), 1944; The Winslow Boy, 1946; the last-named play received the Ellen Terry Award for the best play produced on the London stage during 1946, and the following year won the New York Critics' Award for the best foreign play produced in NY during 1947; Playbill (The Browning Version, and Harlequinade), 1948; The Browning Version, also received the Ellen Terry Award for 1948; Adventure Story, 1949; Who Is Sylvia?, 1950; The Deep Blue Sea, 1952; The Sleeping Prince, 1953; Separate Tables (The Window Table and Table Number Seven), 1954; Variation on a Theme, 1958; Ross, Joie de Vivre, 1960; Man and Boy, 1963;

A Bequest to the Nation, 1970; In Praise of Love (Before Dawn, and After Lydia), 1973; Cause Célèbre, 1977; also the author of the following films: French Without Tears, Quiet Wedding, The Day Will Dawn, Way to the Stars, While the Sun Shines, The Winslow Boy, The Browning Version, The Sound Barrier, The Final Test, The Deep Blue Sea, The Prince and the Showgirl, Separate Tables, The VIP's, The Yellow Rolls-Royce, and Goodbye, Mr Chips; television plays include: The Final Test, Heart to Heart, and Nelson; during the War served in the RAF as an air-gunner; received the CBE in the Birthday Honours, 1958; Knighted in the Birthday Honours, 1971.
(*Died 30 Nov 1977.*)

RAWLINGS, Margaret, actress
b Osaka, Japan, 5 June 1906; *d* of the Rev George William Rawlings and his wife Lilian (Boddington); *e* Oxford High School and Lady Margaret Hall, Oxford; *m* (1) Gabriel Toyne (mar dis); (2) (Sir) Robert Barlow (Kt 1943; dec).

First professional engagement, 1927, with the Macdona Players in a Shaw repertory on tour; first appearance on the London stage, Strand Theatre (for the Venturers), 22 Jan 1928, as Louise in Jordan; Embassy, Oct 1928, Vivian Mason in The Seventh Guest, and Moya in The Shadow; 1929–30, toured in Canada and the United States with Maurice Colbourne; New Theatre, London, May 1930, Nora Tanner in The Last Chapter; went to Paris, and played Minn Lee in On the Spot; Little Theatre, London, 1931, played in Caviare, and Bianca Capello in The Venetian also Masque, New York; Gate, May 1931, title-part in Salome; Australia and New Zealand, 1932, Elizabeth in The Barretts of Wimpole Street; on returning to London, appeared at the Gate, Feb 1933, in I Hate Men; Shilling, Fulham, May 1933, Ricciarda in Night's Candles; Lyric, Oct 1933, Mary Fitton in This Side Idolatry; Queen's, Dec 1933, Liza Kingdom in The Old Folks at Home; Embassy, Sept 1934, Josephine in Napoleon; Duke of York's, Nov 1934, Jean in The Greeks Had a Word for It; Cambridge, Aug 1935, rejoined the Macdona Players, playing Ann Whitefield in Man and Superman, and Eliza Doolittle in Pygmalion; Ethel Barrymore, NY, Nov 1935, played Katherine O'Shea in Parnell and, 1936, at the Gate, London; New, Oct 1936 Charmian in Antony and Cleopatra; New, Nov 1936, again played Katherine in Parnell; at Oxford, for the OUDS, Feb 1937, played Lady Macbeth; Q and St James's, Apr 1937, Mary Charrington and Lily James in Black Limelight; Adelphi, Dec 1937, Helen in The Trojan Women; Lyric, Sept 1938, Karen Selby in The Flashing Stream, and at the Biltmore, NY, Apr 1939; Embassy, May and Haymarket, June 1939, Eliza Doolittle in Pygmalion; Apollo, Dec 1939, Stephanie Easton in You, of all People; St Martin's, Apr 1940, Verna Mountstephan in A House in the Square; Globe, Jan 1941–2, Mrs Dearth in Dear Brutus; Haymarket, Apr 1946, Gwendolen in The Importance of Being Earnest; Covent Garden, Dec 1946, Titania in The Fairy Queen; Duchess, Mar 1947, Vittoria Corombona in The White Devil; Arts, Feb 1949, Marceline in The Unquiet Spirit; Embassy, Apr 1949, Germaine in A Woman in Love; Piccadilly, Feb 1950, the Countess in The Purple Fig-Tree; Arts, June 1950, Lady Macbeth; same theatre, Feb 1951, Anna Sergievna in Spring at Marino; Old Vic, Sept 1951, Zabrina in Tamburlaine the Great; Haymarket, May 1953, Lysistrata in The Apple Cart; 1955, Arts, Salisbury, and Royal, Windsor, the Countess in The Dark is Light Enough; Old Vic, 1955–6 season, Mistress Ford in The Merry Wives of Windsor, and Paulina in The Winter's Tale; Theatrein-the-Round, Nov 1957, and tour, title-part in Phèdre; Edinburgh Festival, Aug 1961, title-part in Sappho; Royal, Windsor,

May 1962, Alex Bliss in Ask Me No More; Arts, Cambridge, May 1963, title-part in her own translation of Phèdre; Duchess, Dec 1963, played Ella Rentheim in John Gabriel Borkman; Nottingham Playhouse, Nov 1964, Jocasta in Œdipus the King; Ludlow Festival, July 1965, Gertrude in Hamlet; Yvonne Arnaud, Guildford, Oct 1965, Ursula-Maria Torpe in Torpe's Hotel; Strand, Apr 1967, Mrs Bridgenorth in Getting Married; 1968, Carlotta in A Song At Twilight; Greenwich, Oct 1973, Giza in Catsplay; King's Head, 1977, appeared in Mixed Economy; Cambridge Festival, July 1978, gave a one-woman performance as Empress Eugenie, also touring in the role and appearing at the May Fair and Vaudeville Theatres, Feb 1979, the Arnaud, July 1979, and the Dublin Festival, Oct 1979; for 30 years a member of the Council of Equity, of which she was Vice-President, 1973–4 and 1975–6; films include: Roman Holiday, Beautiful Stranger, and No Road Back; has also appeared in numerous television programmes including: *Somerset Maughan Hour, The Plane-makers,* Wives and Daughters, etc; she has also broadcast in innumerable radio programmes and recorded drama, poetry and prose.
Favourite parts: Katy O'Shea in Parnell, and Vittoria Corombona. *Recreations:* Poetry and preservation of the countryside. *Club:* Arts. *Address:* Rocketer, Wendover, Bucks. *Tel:* Wendover 622234.

RAWLINS, Lester, actor
b Sharon, Pennsylvania, 24 Sept 1924; *s* of Leona Verier; *e* Carnegie-Mellon University (BFA in drama); formerly engaged as a waiter, salesman, file clerk, etc; prepared for the stage with Mary Morris, Henry Boettcher, Lawrence Carra, and Edith Skinner.

First appeared on the stage at the Farrell, Pennsylvania, Auditorium, in 1930, as a Hunchback Dwarf in Birthday of the Infanta; same theatre, 1935, played Scrooge in Christmas Carol; Chapel Playhouse, Guildford, Connecticut, 1948, played Maxie in June Moon; was stage manager for this theatre, and appeared in its productions, 1949; charter founder and member of the Arena Stage, Washington, DC, 1950, appearing there in a wide variety of roles, 1950–5; Pasadena, California, Playhouse, 1953, played the Nephew in The Golden State; Brattle, Cambridge, Massachusetts, summer 1955, played Lodovico in Othello, Conrade in Much Ado About Nothing, and Worcester in Henry IV, Part I; made his New York début at the City Center, 18 Sept 1955, as Lodovico in Othello; Sept 1955, Worcester in Henry IV, Part I; Jan Hus House, Dec 1955, Lennox in Macbeth; City Center, Jan 1956, Gloucester in King Lear in the Orson Welles production; Jan Hus House, Feb 1956, Friar Lawrence in Romeo and Juliet; Martin Beck, May 1956, Escavalon in The Lovers; Antioch, Ohio, Shakespeare Festival, Sept 1956, Dogberry in Much Ado About Nothing, Angelo in Measure for Measure, and Gloucester in King Lear; Shakespearewrights, NY, Oct 1956, Polonius in Hamlet; Arena Stage, Washington, DC, The Cardinal in The Prisoner; in summer stock, Flint and Detroit, Michigan, 1957, Pop in Pajama Game, the Artist in Can-Can, Mr Moon in Anything Goes, Jeff in Brigadoon, Mr Applegate in Damn Yankees, and Luther Billis in South Pacific; Heckscher, for the New York Shakespeare Festival, Nov 1957, Clarence in Richard III; Cherry Lane, Jan 1958, Hamm in Endgame; toured, summer 1958, as Mr Applegate in Damn Yankees; Circle in the Square, Nov 1958, Regan in The Quare Fellow; Library of Congress, Washington, DC, Apr 1959, Sir Nathaniel in Love's Labour's Lost; toured, 1959, as Jack Jordan in Say, Darling and Papa in Happy Time; St Mark's Playhouse, May 1960, Lord Byron in Camino Real; in stock, 1960, played

Poppet in Redhead, Bennie in The Desert Song, Fender in The Bespoke Overcoat, Grigson in Shadow of a Gunman, title role in Richard III, and the Beggar in Electra; 4th Street, Nov 1960, Tesman in Hedda Gabler; ANTA, Nov 1961, Cranmer in A Man for All Seasons; Shubert, New Haven, Connecticut, Feb 1962, Don Felipe in We Take the Town; American Shakespeare Festival, Stratford, Connecticut, June 1963, the Fool in King Lear, Fluellen in Henry V, and Angelo in Comedy of Errors; Lyceum, Nov 1963, played in the concert reading The Golden Age; Stratford, Conn, 1964 played Hamlet; artist in Residence at the Festival of the Two Worlds, Spoleto, Italy, 1964; American Place, Nov 1964, Capt Amasa Delano in Benito Cereno; Garrick, Dec 1964, Wissey Jones in The Child Buyer; Jan Hus Playhouse, Feb 1966, Trock in Winterset; Eastside Playhouse, May 1969, Leonard in In the Bar of a Tokyo Hotel; St Mark's Playhouse, Sept 1969, Governor in The Reckoning; Playhouse-in-the-Park, Cincinnati, Sept 1970, He in He Who Gets Slapped; Van Dam, Dec 1971, Jon Bristow in Nightride; Palace, Nov 1976, Count Paul Nevlinski in Herzl; Circle-in-the-Square, Mar 1977, Capulet in Romeo and Juliet; Hudson Guild, Mar 1978, and Morosco, May 1978, Drumm in Da, receiving a 'Tony' as best featured actor; has received a number of other awards, including three Obies; entered films in Mr Congressman, 1951, and has since played in Within Man's Power, Diary of a Mad Housewife, They Might Be Giants, etc; first appeared on television in 1953 on *The Dinah Shore Show,* and has since played in Salome, The Life of Samuel Johnson, The serials *Secret Storm* and *Edge of Night, The Nurses, The Defenders, The Snoop Sisters, Banacek, Starsky and Hutch,* etc.

Recreations: Reading, cooking, driving, and being a foster father. *Club:* The Players. *Address:* Richard Astor Agency, 119 West 57th Street, New York, NY, 10019. *Tel:* 212–581 1970.

RAWLS, Eugenia, actress
b Macon, Georgia, 11 Sept; *d* of Hubert Fields Rawls and his wife Louise (Roberts); *e* Wesleyan Conservatory, 1932, Univ of North Carolina, 1933; *m* Donald Seawell, the producer and publisher; prepared for the stage with Anne Chenault Wallace and Edna West.

Member of the Clare Tree Major's Children's Theatre, NY, 1933–34; Maxine Elliott's, 20 Nov 1934, played Peggy in The Children's Hour; toured as Jane Bennett in Pride and Prejudice; Guild, Oct, 1937, Tomasa in To Quito and Back; Fulton, Jan 1938, Dene Horey in Journeyman; Westport, Conn, Country Playhouse, summer 1938, played in Susannah and the Elders and in The Inner Light; NY World's Fair, Apr–July 1939, played Celia in As You Like It, Titania in A Midsummer Night's Dream, Bianca in The Taming of the Shrew, and in The Comedy of Errors, with Margaret Webster's Shakespeare Company; National, Oct 1939, took over as Alexandra in The Little Foxes, and toured in this part Feb 1940–Apr 1941; in stock played Ellean in The Second Mrs Tanqueray, june 1940; Univ of Syracuse, NY, Nov 1942, title-role in Harriet; Plymouth, 1942, took over as Evelyn Heath in Guest in the House, and subsequently toured; Studebaker, Chicago, Ill, Feb 1943, Connie in Cry Havoc; toured, 1944–45, as Mrs de Winter in Rebecca; Forrest, Nov 1944, Hester Falk in The Man Who Had All the Luck; Royale, Nov 1945, Harriet Harris in Strange Fruit; Cort, May 1952, took over from Judith Evelyn as Ann Downs in The Shrike; ANTA, Jan 1956, Mrs Czerney in The Great Sebastians; Playhouse-in-the-Park, Philadelphia, Pa, July 1961, Catherine in All the Way Home; Playhouse-in-the-Park, Cincinatti, Ohio, Aug 1965; Amanda Wingfield in The Glass

Menagerie; Repertory Theatre of New Orleans, 1966–67 season, played in Our Town; Playhouse-in-the-Park, Cincinnati, Ohio, Aug 1965, Martinique, Sept 1967, Mrs Beavis in The Poker Session; toured, 1967–8, as Mrs Casside in Pictures in the Hallway; made her London debut at the Arts, 1969, in her one-woman show Fanny Kemble; Library and Museum of the Performing Arts, NY, Jan and Apr 1971, played Tallulah Bankhead in her one-woman show, Tallulah, A Memory; repeated this last show at the American Embassy, London, 1974; Brooklyn Academy of Music, 3 Dec 1975, Aunt Nonnie in Sweet Bird of Youth, and transferred with this part to the Rebekah Harkness, 29 Dec 1975; John F Kennedy Center for the Performing Arts, July 1976, performed in three one-woman shows; Opera New England, 1978, Duchess of Krakentorp in The Daughter of the Regiment; Hudson Guild, July 1978, Charlotte Keller in Just the Immediate Family; Joseph Jefferson Company, NY, 1979, repeated Tallulah, A Memory; Queen's hall, Edinburgh, May 1980, again appeared as Fanny Kemble; has recorded talking books for the blind; has appeared on television as Mrs Elvsted in Hedda Gabler, 1954, on *Armstrong Circle Theatre, DuPont Show of the Month,* in The Great Sebastians, *The Doctors, The Nurses,* and various others; Artist-in-Residence Denver Univ, 1967–68, Univ of Tampa, 1970, Univ of North Carolina, 1971–73; received the Gold Chair Award of the Central City Opera Association; Tallulah, A Memory, published 1979; Hon DHL, University of Northern Colorado, 1979.

Recreations: Her farm in Maryland, travelling. *Address:* 510 East 84th Street, New York, NY 10028.

RAY, James, actor
b Calgra, Oklahoma, 1 Jan 1932; *s* of Sherman Gentry Ray and his wife Ora Catherine (Mitchell); *e* Oklahoma A and M; prepared for the stage with Uta Hagen, 1957–60, and Fanny Bradshaw, 1958–61.

Made his début at the Margo Jones Theatre, Dallas, Texas, 1949, as Friar John in Romeo and Juliet; made his New York début at Circle in the Square, Dec 1950, as the Witch Boy in Dark of the Moon; same theatre, Apr 1952, Vernon in Summer and Smoke; Ambassador, Oct 1957, Lyman in Compulsion; toured 1959–60, as The Roustabout in J B; Belvedere Lake, for the New York Shakespeare Festival, June 1960, title-role in Henry V; Billy Rose, Oct 1960, Katz in The Wall; American Shakespeare Festival, Stratford, Connecticut, 1961, played Malcolm in Macbeth, Diomedes in Troilus and Cressida, and Oliver in As You Like It; Mermaid, Jan 1962, Adolf in The Creditors; Stratford, Connecticut, 1962, title-role of Henry IV, Part I, and Mowbray in Richard II; Cherry Lane, Nov 1962, James in The Collection; Stratford, Connecticut, 1963, Edgar in King Lear, Henry V, and Apollodorus in Caesar and Cleopatra; Plymouth, Jan 1964, Brinnin in Dylan; Phoenix, Oct 1964, Mephistophilis in The Tragical Historie of Doctor Faustus; Delacorte, for the New York Shakespeare Festival, June 1965, Ferdinand in Love's Labour's Lost; Delacorte, June 1968, title-role in Henry IV, Parts I and II; Eastside Playhouse, Oct 1968, Stott in The Basement; The Forum, Jan 1970, William Cherry in The Disintegration of James Cherry; The Forum, May 1970, Mercury in Amphitryon; Theatre Four, Oct 1970, Lord Capulet in Sensations; Martin Beck, Mar 1971, The Son in All Over; toured Canada and the USA, Sept–Nov 1971, as Dr Rank in A Doll's House; Alliance, Atlanta, Ga, Jan 1972, Chris in This Way to the Rose Garden; Walnut Street, Philadelphia, Nov 1972, Cleante in Tartuffe; Cincinnati, Ohio, Playhouse, 1973, Deeley in Old Times; same theatre, Nov 1974, George in Who's Afraid of Virginia Woolf?; Mark

Taper Forum, Apr 1976, Man in Ashes; Seattle Rep, Mar 1977, Dysart in Equus; has appeared on television in various dramatic programs.

Address: Arcara, Bauman and Hiller, 9220 Sunset Boulevard, Los Angeles, Calif.

RAYE, Martha (*née* Margaret Theresa Yvonne Reed), actress, singer

b Butte, Montana, 27 Aug 1916; *d* of Peter Reed and his wife Mabelle (Hooper), vaudevillians; *e* Professional Children's School, New York; *m* (1) Hamilton Buddy Westmore (mar dis); (2) David Rose (mar dis); (3) Neal Lang (mar dis); (4) Nick Condos (mar dis); (5) Edward Thomas Begley (mar dis); (6) Robert O'Shea.

Made her stage début as a member of her parents' vaudeville act in 1919; toured extensively in vaudeville, 1919–29, with the Benny Davis Revue, the Ben Blue Company, and the Will Morrissey Company; made her NY début at Loew's State, 1934, in vaudeville; made her Broadway début at the Hollywood, 13 Dec 1934, in the revue Calling All Stars; Winter Garden, June 1935, played in the revue Earl Carroll's Sketchbook; Shubert, Sept 1940, Mamie in Hold on to Your Hats; Loew's State, Nov 1941, again played Mamie in Hold on to Your Hats; toured with the USO during World War II; made her London début at the Palladium, 29 Mar 1948, in variety; in Miami Beach, Florida, summer 1952, played Annie Oakley in Annie Get Your Gun; Drury Lane, Chicago, Dec 1960, Laura Partridge in The Solid Gold Cadillac; Sombrero Playhouse, Phoenix, Arizona, Feb 1961, Carole Arden in Personal Appearance; toured, 1961, as Pam in Separate Rooms; Pittsburgh Light Opera Company, 1961, played Calamity Jane, in a musical of that name; toured, 1962, in the title-role of Wildcat; toured, 1963, as Sally Adams in Call Me Madam; toured, 1965, as Opal in Everybody Loves Opal; St James, NY, 27 Feb 1967, took over from Ginger Rogers as Dolly Gallagher Levi in Hello, Dolly!; Shamrock Hotel, Houston, Texas, July 1972, appeared in cabaret; toured in Minsky's Burlesque theaters, Oct 1972; 46th Street, Nov 1972, took over as Pauline in No, No, Nanette; Sardi Dinner Theater, Franklin Square, Long Island, Jan 1975, Opal in Everybody Loves Opal, and subsequently toured; first appeared in films in 1934 in short subjects, and has since played in Rhythm on the Range, Artists and Models, The Big Broadcast of 1938, The Boys from Syracuse, Hellzapoppin, Four Jills in a Jeep, Monsieur Verdoux, Jumbo, Concorde Airport '79, etc; has appeared extensively on radio, and in television has performed on the *All Star Revue, Milton Berle Show, Martha Raye Show* (1954–6), *Carol Burnett Show* (1968–75), *MacMillan and Wife*, Gossip Columnist (1980), etc; has played in cabaret as a singer and comedienne since 1929, notably with Nick Condos at the Five O'Clock Club, Miami Beach, Florida, 1949–53; toured annually in Vietnam until the American withdrawal in 1974.

Address: Actors Equity Association, 165 West 46th Street, New York, NY 10036.

RAYMOND, Gene (*né* Raymond Guion), actor, director, producer

b New York City, 13 Aug 1908; *s* of Leroy Guion and his wife Mary (Smith); *e* Professional Children's School, NY; *m* (1) Jeanette MacDonald (dec); (2) Nel Bentley Hees; known as Raymond Guion until 1931.

Made his first appearance on the stage as a small child in 1913; at the Fulton Theatre, 19 Mar 1920, appeared as one of the children in The Piper; Greenwich Village, Feb 1921, played the Shepherd Boy in Eyvind of the Hills; 48th Street,

Dec 1922, Billy Thompson in Why Not?; Plymouth, Dec 1923, Bill Potter in The Potters; Music Box, Sept 1925, Oscar Nordholm in Cradle Snatchers; Belmont, Nov 1927, Bud Weaver in Take My Advice; Forrest, Jan 1928, Calvin Trask in Mirrors; Cosmopolitan, Feb 1928, Billy in Sherlock Holmes; Morosco, June 1928, Michael Graham in Say When; National, Sept 1928, Sid Swanson in The War Song; Bijou, Apr 1929, Wilbur Jones in Jonesy; Morosco, Nov 1929, Gene Gibson in Young Sinners; in 1931 went to Hollywood and under the name of Gene Raymond appeared in innumerable pictures; re-appeared on the regular stage in Dennis, Mass, Aug 1946, in The Man in Possession; Chicago, 1947, played in The Greatest of These; 1950–1, toured as the Actor in The Guardsman; toured, 1952, in The Voice of the Turtle, Angel Street, and The Petrified Forest; Dallas, Aug 1952, appeared in Call Me Madam; toured in Private Lives, The Moon Is Blue, Be Quiet, My Love, 1953; in The Detective Story and The Devil's Disciple, 1954; toured California in The Fifth Season, 1955, and Will Success Spoil Rock Hunter? 1956; Community Playhouse, Pasadena, California, 1957, Mercutio in Romeo and Juliet; ANTA, NY, Dec 1957, Horace Smith in A Shadow of My Enemy; Drury Lane, Chicago, 1959, played in Holiday for Lovers; toured, Aug 1960, as Joseph Cantwell in The Best Man; stock and other appearances, 1961–3; Playhouse in the Park, Philadelphia, Aug 1963, Edward Burgeon in Madly in Love; Ogunquit Playhouse, Maine, Aug 1965, played in Diplomatic Relations; has also appeared in numerous other stock productions, such as Candida, Mr Roberts, Kiss Me, Kate, Write Me a Murder, A Majority of One, etc; entered films, 1931, in Personal Maid, and more recent films include Hit the Deck, 1955; The Best Man, I'd Rather Be Rich, 1964; Five Bloody Graves, 1971; author of the television play Prima Donna, and of a number of published songs; has appeared frequently on variety and dramatic television programs since 1951.

Recreations: Tennis, swimming, and golf. *Clubs:* Players, New York, Bel Air Country Club, Los Angeles Tennis Club. *Address:* 9570 Wilshire Boulevard, Beverly Hills, Calif 90212.

RAYMOND, Paul, producing manager

Former lessee of the Royalty and currently proprietor of the Whitehall and Windmill Theatres, London; has presented shows including Pyjama Tops, 1969, which ran for 2498 performances; The Bed, 1970; Let's Get Laid, 1974; Come into My Bed, Rip Off, 1976; Wot, No Pyjamas?, 1980; proprietor of the Raymond Revuebar, where his Festival of Erotica is in its twenty-third year, 1980; publisher of Men Only, Club, and other adult magazines; managing director, the Paul Raymond Organization.

Address: 2 Archer Street, London W1.

READER, Ralph, CBE, MBE, actor and director

b Crewkerne, Somerset, 25 May 1903; *s* of William Henry Reader and his wife Emma (Frost); *e* Crewkerne, and St John's Cardiff; originally intended for the Church.

Appeared at the Winter Garden, New York, 3 Sept 1924, in The Passing Show of 1924; at the same theatre, Jan 1925, played in Big Boy; Astor, Aug 1925, in June Days; directed dances in revues and musical plays, notably Bad Habits of 1926; Yours Truly, 1927; Greenwich Village Follies, 1928; Sunny Days, 1928; he then returned to England, and in 1929 toured as Tom Marlowe in Good News; subsequently specialized in the production of dances, etc, and has been associated with Virginia, Merry Merry, Hold Everything, 1929; Dear Love, Silver Zings, The Cochran Revue of 1930; Sons O' Guns, 1930; Song of the Drum, Tommy Tucker, The

Hour Glass, 1931; directed Viktoria and Her Hussar at the Palace, Theatre, 1931; presented Yes Madam, London Hippodrome, 1934; directed Please Teacher! (with Jack Waller), London Hippodrome, 1935; Rise and Shine, Drury Lane; Certainly, Sir! London Hippodrome, 1936; Big Business, London Hippodrome, 1937; devised and arranged the dances in Crest of the Wave, Drury Lane, 1937; London Hippodrome, Aug 1938, played Lieut Jack Prentice in The Fleet's Lit Up; arranged the dances and ensembles in Babes in the Wood, Drury Lane, 1938; author and director of The Gang Shows, 1932–8, and of the Royal Albert Hall pageants, Boy Scout, and Battle for Freedom; the British Legion Festival; Heart of Oak (for the Admiralty), and Per Ardua ad Astra (for the Air Ministry); Stoll Theatre, May 1946, directed and appeared in The Gang Show; Lewisham Hippodrome, Dec 1947, played Buttons in Cinderella; Covent Garden, July 1948, directed The Pilgrim's Progress; Granada, Tooting, Dec 1948, and other theatres on this circuit, appeared as Wishee-Washee in Aladdin; Empire, Croydon, Dec 1949, played Simple Simon in The Babes in the Wood, and has subsequently starred in his own pantomime productions; he formed the National Light Opera Company (with Ralph Reader, Ltd), 1950, producing Chu Chin Chow, Merrie England, and The Lilac Domino; at the King's Theatre, Hammersmith, Dec 1950, he revived his Gang Show, with great success, and continued to write and direct these productions until the last in Oct 1974; his twenty-second Gang Show, in 1954, was attended by Her Majesty the Queen; Hippodrome, May 1956, directed Wild Grows the Heather; 1958–60, directed Gang Show in Chicago and Pittsburgh, USA; Open Air Theatre, Scarborough, Yorks, summer 1960, presented his own musical play Summer Holiday; in Remembrance Festival, 1960, he directed his 100th production at the Royal Albert Hall; wrote and directed The Pathfinders, Toronto 1965; The Torch Bearers, Los Angeles, 1972; toured with a variety programme, Stars of Tomorrow, 1973–5; Royal Albert Hall, 1974, directed A Night with the Stars; 1975, directed his 146th production at the Albert Hall with the Festival of Remembrance; previous presentations have included the Burma and El Alamein Reunions and Old Contemptibles Presentation; ran a television series, *It's a Great Life*, 1954–5; published his autobiography, It's Been Terrific, 1954, This is the Gang Show, 1960, and a further autobiography, Ralph Reader Remembers, 1974; received the CBE in the Birthday Honours, 1957; Hon Citizen, State of Illinois, 1961; Bronze Wolf (World Scout Association), 1975; Member, Grand Order of Water Rats.

Recreations: Motoring, football, writing and presenting amateur shows. *Address:* Round Corners, Hedsor Road, Bourne End, Bucks. *Tel:* Bourne End 25586.

REDGRAVE, Corin, actor

b London, 16 July 1939; *s* of Sir Michael Redgrave and his wife Rachel (Kempson); *e* Westminster and King's College, Cambridge; *m* Deirdre Hamilton-Hill.

After appearances with the ADC, the Marlowe Society and others at Cambridge, joined the English Stage Company at the Royal Court, where he directed a Sunday-night production of The Scarecrow, Dec 1961; made his first professional appearance there, Jan 1962, as Lysander in A Midsummer Night's Dream; Feb 1962, played Sebastian in a production without décor of Twelfth Night; Apr 1962, played the Pilot Officer in Chips with Everything, transferring with the production to the Vaudeville, June 1962, and in Oct 1963, making his New York début in the same part at the Plymouth; returning to London, May 1964, played Mr Bodley in The Right Honourable Gentleman at Her Majesty's;

Phoenix, Oct 1966, Mr Cecil Graham in Lady Windermere's Fan; Wyndham's, May 1971, took over Abelard in Abelard and Heloise; Stratford, season 1972, played Octavius Caesar in Julius Caesar and in Antony and Cleopatra, as well as Antipholus of Ephesus in The Comedy of Errors; repeated the two Octavius roles at the Aldwych, July 1973; Forum, Wythenshaw, 1976, played Norman in The Norman Conquests; films, since 1963, include: A Man for All Seasons, Oh! What a Lovely War!, Between Wars and David Copperfield; television, since 1963, includes: Hassan, and The Governor (New Zealand, 1977).

Recreation: Music. *Address:* c/o Sandra Marsh, 50 Glebe Road, London SW13. *Tel:* 01–878 4864.

REDGRAVE, Lynn, actress

b London, 8 Mar 1943; *d* of Sir Michael Redgrave and his wife Rachel (Kempson); *m* John Clark; *e* Queen's Gate School, London; studied for the stage at the Central School of Speech and Drama.

Made her first appearance on the stage at the Royal Court Theatre, London, Jan 1962, as Helena in A Midsummer Night's Dream; made her first West End appearance at the Haymarket, Nov 1962, as Sarah Elliott in The Tulip Tree; joined the National Theatre Company, Oct 1963, and appeared as a Court Lady in the inaugural production of Hamlet; subsequently playing the following parts, in repertory, with the same company: Court Lady in Saint Joan; Rose in The Recruiting Officer, 1963; Barblin in Andorra, Jackie Coryton in Hay Fever, 1964; Margaret in Much Ado About Nothing, Kattrin in Mother Courage, Miss Prue in Love for Love, 1965; appeared with the National Theatre Company in Moscow and Berlin, Sept 1965; first appearance in New York, Feb 1967, at the Ethel Barrymore, as Carol Melkett in Black Comedy; Edinburgh Festival, Sept 1969, Mave in Zoo, Zoo Widdershins Zoo; Garrick, July 1970, played six parts in The Two Of Us; Royal Court, May 1971, Joanne in Slag; Gate, Dublin, Oct 1972, presented and appeared in A Better Place, directed by her husband; Greenwich, Apr 1973, Billie Dawn in Born Yesterday; Brooks Atkinson, NY, Mar 1974, Vicky in My Fat Friend; also toured the US in this part; summer 1975, presented with her husband and toured the US in The Two of Us; Beaumont, NY, Feb 1976, Vivie in Mrs Warren's Profession; Biltmore, NY, June 1976, Joan in Knock Knock; Lake Forest, Ill, Aug 1976, appeared in Misalliance; toured, Nov 1976, in Hellzapoppin; Goodman, Chicago, Sept 1977, and Circle-in-the-Square, Nov, title-role in Saint Joan; Stratford, Conn, July 1978, Viola in Twelfth Night; first appeared in films in Tom Jones, 1963; subsequent appearances include: Georgy Girl, The Virgin Soldiers, and The Happy Hooker; first television appearance, 1963, in Power and Glory; has also appeared in numerous other television dramas, and as hostess of *Not For Women Only*, 1977.

Favourite parts: Myrtle in Blood Kin, Billie Dawn, and Xaviera Hollander in The Happy Hooker. *Recreations:* Gardening, cooking. *Address:* c/o International Clients' Servicing, Balscadden Bay, Howth, Dublin, Eire and 200 W 57th Street, New York, NY 10019.

REDGRAVE, Sir Michael (*cr* 1959), CBE, MA, actor, author, director, manager

b Bristol, 20 Mar 1908; *s* of Roy Redgrave and his wife Margaret (Scudamore); *e* Clifton College, and Magdalene College, Cambridge; *m* Rachel Kempson; formerly a schoolmaster at Cranleigh School.

Made his first professional appearance at the Playhouse, Liverpool, 30 Aug 1934, as Roy Darwin in Counsellor-at-Law; spent two years with the Liverpool repertory company; he first appeared professionally in London at the Old Vic, 14 Sept 1936, as Ferdinand in Love's Labour's Lost; during the season 1936–7, played Mr Horner in The Country Wife, Orlando in As You Like It, Warbeck in The Witch of Edmonton, and Laertes in Hamlet; at the New Theatre, Feb 1937, played Orlando in As You Like It; Embassy, Mar 1937, Anderson in The Bat; Old Vic, Apr 1937, succeeded Marius Goring as Chorus in Henry V; St Martin's, May 1937, Christopher Drew in A Ship Comes Home; Embassy, June 1937, Larry Starr in Three Set Out; joined John Gielgud's company at the Queen's Theatre, Sept 1937–Apr 1938, appearing as Bolingbroke in Richard II, Charles Surface in The School for Scandal, and Baron Tusenbach in The Three Sisters; Phoenix, Oct 1938, Alexei Turbin in The White Guard, and, Dec 1938, Sir Andrew Aguecheek in Twelfth Night; Westminster, Mar 1939, played Harry, Lord Monchensey, in The Family Reunion; toured, 1939, as Henry in Springtime for Henry; Haymarket, Mar 1940, Captain Macheath in The Beggar's Opera; Neighbourhood, June, and Globe, July 1940, played Charleston in Thunder Rock; entered the Royal Navy as an Ordinary Seaman, July 1941; released to Reserve, 1942; finally discharged on medical grounds, Nov 1942; Duchess, July 1942, directed Lifeline; St James's, Oct 1942, played Gribaud in The Duke in Darkness, which he also directed; St James's, Mar 1943, played Rakitin in A Month in the Country, and in June 1943, directed, and played Lafont in matinées of Parisienne; Playhouse, Aug 1943, directed Blow Your Own Trumpet, and Phoenix, Sept 1943, The Wingless Victory; Garrick, Mar 1944, directed (with William Armstrong), and played the title-role in Uncle Harry; Piccadilly, June 1945, directed, and played Colonel Stjerbinsky in Jacobowsky and the Colonel; Aldwych, Dec 1947, played Macbeth; first appeared on the New York stage at the National, 31 Mar 1948, as Macbeth; Embassy, London, Nov 1948, appeared as the Captain in The Father, subsequently playing the same part at the Duchess, Jan 1949; Embassy, Apr 1949, played Etienne in A Woman in Love, which he also directed; joined the Old Vic company, at the New Theatre, and during the 1949–50 season appeared as Berowne in Love's Labour's Lost, Marlow in She Stoops to Conquer, Rakitin in A Month in the Country, and as Hamlet; at the Zürich Festival, the Holland Festival, and at Kronborg Castle, Elsinore, June 1950, he again played Hamlet; joined the Shakespeare Memorial Theatre Company, Stratford-on-Avon, 1951, and during the season appeared as Richard II, Hotspur, and Chorus in the Cycle of Histories, of which he directed Henry IV (Pt II); during this season he also played Prospero in The Tempest; at the St James's, Apr 1952, appeared as Frank Elgin in Winter Journey; rejoined the Shakespeare Memorial Theatre Company for the 1953 season, appearing as Shylock, King Lear, and Antony in Antony and Cleopatra; appeared as Antony in this production when the Company transferred to the Princes, London, Nov 1953; played the same part, Jan 1954, when the Company toured Holland, Belgium and Paris; Apollo, June 1955, played Hector in Tiger at the Gates; appeared in the same part at the Plymouth, NY, Oct 1955, and received the New York Critics Award for this performance; Phoenix, NY, Apr 1956, directed A Month in the Country; Coronet, NY, Nov 1956, directed and played the Prince Regent in The Sleeping Prince; Saville, London, Jan 1958, Philip Lester in A Touch of the Sun; rejoined the Shakespeare Memorial Theatre Company, June 1958, to play Hamlet, and Benedick, and, with the same company, played Hamlet in Leningrad and Moscow, 1958–9; Queen's, London, Aug 1959, played HJ in his own adaptation of The Aspern Papers; Queen's, Aug 1960, played Jack Dean in The Tiger and the Horse; Ethel

Barrymore, NY, Nov 1961, played Victor Rhodes in The Complaisant Lover; at the opening Chichester Festival, England, July 1962, played the title-part in Uncle Vanya; Wyndham's, Nov 1962, Lancelot Dodd in Out of Bounds; Chichester Festival, July 1963, again played Uncle Vanya; Old Vic, Oct 1963, played Claudius in the National Theatre Company's inaugural production of Hamlet, subsequently appearing as Uncle Vanya, Nov 1963; Henry Hobson in Hobson's Choice, Jan 1964; Halvard Solness in The Master Builder, June 1964; director of the opening Festival of the Yvonne Arnaud Theatre, Guildford, May–June 1965: directing and playing Rakitin in A Month in the Country, and Samson in Samson Agonistes; Cambridge, London, Sept 1965, again played Rakitin and directed A Month in the Country; Glyndebourne Festival Opera, directed Werther, 1966, and La Boheme, 1967; Mermaid, July 1971, Mr Jaraby in The Old Boys; Haymarket, Apr 1972, took over the part of the Father in A Voyage Round My Father, also touring Canada and Australia in the role, 1972–3; toured the US and Australia for the RSC, 1974–5, in The Hollow Crown; he has also appeared in solo performances of Shakespeare or Hans Andersen in Holland, Budapest, the US, and the Bath Festival; under his own management he has presented Parisienne, 1943; and co-presented The Aspern Papers, My Friend Judas, 1959; The Tiger and the Horse, Waiting in the Wings, The Importance of Being Oscar, 1960; Out of Bounds, 1962; received the *Evening Standard* Award, 1958 and 1963, for his performances in A Touch of the Sun and Uncle Vanya, also receiving the Variety Club of Great Britain Actor of the Year Awards, in those years; 1976–7, toured South America, Canada and the UK in the anthology, Shakespeare's People; Lyttleton (National Theatre), May 1979, Jasper in Close of Play; entered films 1938, and has appeared in The Lady Vanishes, Kipps, The Way to the Stars, Dead of Night, The Captive Heart, The Browning Version, The Importance of Being Earnest, The Dam Busters, The Quiet American, Law and Disorder, Oh! What a Lovely War, The Go-Between, etc; first appeared on television at the Alexandra Palace, 1937, in scenes from Romeo and Juliet; notable television performances include the *Great War* and *Lost Peace* series; is the author of several plays, among them, The Seventh Man and Circus Boy, both performed at the Playhouse, Liverpool, 1935, and adapted Amoureuse (A Woman in Love), and The Aspern Papers; also author of The Actor's Ways and Means, published 1955; Mask or Face, 1958; The Mountebank's Tale, 1959; received the CBE in 1952; Commander of the Order of the Dannebrog, Denmark, 1955; Knighted in the Birthday Honours, 1959; First President of the English Speaking Board, 1953; President of the Questors, Ealing, since 1958; Hon DLitt (Bristol), 1966.

Club: Garrick. *Address:* Wilks Water, Odiham, Hampshire.

REDGRAVE, Vanessa, CBE, actress
b London, 30 Jan 1937; *d* of Sir Michael Redgrave and his wife Rachel (Kempson); *e* Queensgate School, London; *m* Tony Richardson (mar dis); studied for the stage at the Central School of Speech and Drama.

Made her first appearance on the stage at the Frinton Summer Theatre, July 1957, when she played Clarissa in The Reluctant Debutante; Arts, Cambridge, Sept 1957, played Mrs Spottsworth in Come On, Jeeves; first appeared in London at the Saville Theatre, 31 Jan 1958, as Caroline Lester in A Touch of the Sun (in which Sir Michael Redgrave played her father); Royal Court, 28 Aug 1958, played Sarah Undershaft in Major Barbara; Leatherhead, Dec 1958, played the Principal Boy in Mother Goose; joined the

Shakespearean Memorial Theatre Company, at Stratford-on-Avon, for the season, 1959, to play Helena in A Midsummer Night's Dream, and Valeria in Coriolanus; Comedy Theatre, Mar 1960, played Rose Sinclair in Look on Tempests; Queen's, Aug 1960, played Stella Dean in The Tiger and the Horse; Queen's, Mar 1961, played Boletta in The Lady From the Sea; joined the Royal Shakespeare Company, Stratford-on-Avon, July 1961, to play Rosalind in As You Like It and Aldwych, Sept 1961, Katharina in The Taming of the Shrew; Aldwych, Jan 1962, played Rosalind in As You Like It; Stratford, Apr 1962, Katharina in The Taming of the Shrew, and July 1962, Imogen in Cymbeline; Queen's, Mar 1964, played Nina in The Seagull; Wyndham's, May 1966, Jean Brodie in The Prime of Miss Jean Brodie; University Theatre, Manchester, Jan 1969, Gwendolen Harleth in Daniel Deronda; Young Vic, Nov 1971, Susan Thistlewood in Cato Street; Prince of Wales, Feb 1972, Polly Peachum in The Threepenny Opera; Shaw, May 1972, Viola in Twelfth Night; Bankside Globe, Aug 1973, Cleopatra in Antony and Cleopatra; Phoenix, Nov 1973, Gilda in Design for Living; Circle in the Square, NY, Mar 1976, Ellida in The Lady from the Sea; Royal Exchange, Manchester, 1978, again played Ellida, and also at the Round House, May 1979; received the *Evening Standard* Award, 1961 and 1967, as Actress of the Year; films include: Murder on the Orient Express, Julia (Golden Globe and Academy Award, 1977), Agatha, Yanks and Bear Island; made her first appearance on television, 1958, and performances include Helena in A Midsummer Night's Dream, Rosalind in As You Like It, 1962; Maggie, Sally, 1964; received the CBE in the Birthday Honours, 1967.

Favourite part: Rosalind in As You Like It. *Address:* Marina Martin Management Ltd, 7 Windmill Street, London W1P 1HF. *Tel:* 01–323 1216.

REDMAN, Joyce, actress
b Co Mayo, Ireland, 1918; studied for the stage at the Royal Academy of Dramatic Art; *m* Charles Wynne Roberts.

Made her first appearance at the Playhouse, London, 23 Dec 1935, as the First Tiger Lily in Alice Through the Looking Glass; at the Little, June 1936, played Mrs Cricket in The Insect Play and Nov 1936, Precious Stream in Lady Precious Stream; St Martin's, June 1937, Katherine Carew in The King's Pirate; Playhouse, Apr 1938, Mrs Cricket in The Insect Play; Aug 1938, Suzanne in Thou Shalt Not . . .; Little, Oct 1938, Hsiang Fei in The Fragrant Concubine; Torch, Dec 1938, Hung Niang in The Western Chamber; Q, Dec 1938, Alice in Alice in Wonderland and Through the Looking Glass; Gate, Feb 1939, Emanuelle in Asmodée; Mar 1939, toured as Laura in Drawing Room; and appeared in this part at Streatham Hill, May 1939; Kingsway, Dec 1939, again played in Lady Precious Stream; Piccadilly, July 1940, Essie in The Devil's Disciple; Arts, June 1942, Maria in Twelfth Night; Wimbledon, Oct 1942, Rose in Lottie Dundass; Orpheum, Golder's Green, Oct 1942, Roberta in The House of Jeffreys; Winter Garden, Dec 1942, Wendy in Peter Pan; Duke of York's, May 1943, scored a big success when she played Brigid in Shadow and Substance; St Martin's, July 1943, succeeded Pamela Brown as Claudia in the play of that name, and toured in this 1943–4; joined the Old Vic company at the New Theatre, Aug 1944, and during the season, played Solveig in Peer Gynt, Louka in Arms and the Man, Lady Anne in Richard III, and Sonya in Uncle Vanya; appeared with the company at the Comedie Française, July 1945; at the New, Oct 1945–Apr 1946, played Doll Tearsheet in Henry IV (Part II), Jocasta's Attendant in Œdipus Rex, and the Confidante in The Critic; went with the company to New York,

May 1946, and made her first appearance there, at the Century Theatre, 7 May 1946, as Doll Tearsheet in Henry IV (Part II); with the Old Vic company, at the New Theatre, during the 1946–7 season, appeared as Cordelia in King Lear, Dol Common in The Alchemist; Strand, June 1947, played Valentine North in Angel; Booth, Theatre, NY, Oct 1947, appeared as Abigail Sarclet in Duet for Two Hands; Lyric, Hammersmith, June, and Garrick, Aug 1948, played Jessica in Crime Passionnel; Shubert, NY, Dec 1948, played Anne Boleyn in Anne of the Thousand Days; Wyndham's, Mar 1951, appeared as Gay Butterworth in Count Your Blessings; New, Dec 1951, played the title-role in Colombe; Cambridge Theatre, Aug 1952, appeared as Irene Elliott in Affairs of State; joined the Shakespeare Memorial Theatre Company, Stratford-on-Avon, 1955, and during the season played Helena in All's Well That Ends Well and Mistress Ford in The Merry Wives of Windsor; St James's, Aug 1956, played Fay Edwards in The Long Echo; Old Vic, Dec 1957, Titania in A Midsummer Night's Dream; New, May 1958, played Frances Brough in The Party; Martin Beck, NY, Nov 1960, played Hippolyte in The Rape of the Belt; Criterion, Sept 1961, succeeded Joan Greenwood as Hedda Rankin in The Irregular Verb to Love; Garrick, Sept 1963, played Therese in Power of Persuasion; Piccadilly, Jan 1964, Laura in The Father; joined the National Theatre Company at the Old Vic, Apr 1964, to play Emilia in Othello, subsequently appearing as Crispinella in The Dutch Courtesan (also Chichester Festival); Elizabeth Proctor in The Crucible, Mrs Frail in Love for Love, 1965; visited Moscow and Berlin, Sept 1965, with the National Theatre Company in Othello and Love for Love; Juno Boyle in Juno and the Paycock, Mrs Frail in Love For Love (Queen's), 1966; Lyric, Nov 1969, appeared as Vivian Fairleigh in The Lionel Touch; Lyric, June 1969, played three parts in Plaza Suite; Chichester Festival, May 1971, Estelle in Dear Antoine; Olivier (National Theatre), March 1979, The Mistress in The Fruits of Enlightenment and, June 1979, Mrs Von Aigner in Undiscovered Country; films include: Tom Jones, Prudence and the Pill, and Othello.

Address: c/o ICM, 22 Grafton Street, London W1.

REDMOND, Liam, actor
b Limerick, Ireland, 27 July 1913; *s* of Thomas Redmond and his wife Eileen (McAllister); *e* National University; *m* Barbara MacDonagh.

Made his first appearance on the stage at the Abbey Theatre, Dublin, 1935, in The Silver Tassie; at the Abbey Theatre, he acted and produced for some years, appearing in over fifty and producing ten plays; made his first appearance in New York, at the Cort Theatre, 10 Jan 1939, as Denis Dillon in The White Steed; first appeared in London, at the Embassy, 3 Mar 1947, as Canon Matt Lavelle in the same play, which was transferred to the Whitehall Theatre, in the same month; Mercury, Sept, and Criterion, Dec 1947, played Larry in Happy as Larry, and at the Mercury, Mar 1948, Christopher Mahon in The Playboy of the Western World; Westminster, Nov 1948, Burke in The Anatomist; Lyric, Hammersmith, Aug 1949, Gaisceen Brehony in The King of Friday's Men; Embassy, July, and Phoenix, Aug 1950, Owney Tubridy in They Got What They Wanted; Scala, June 1951, played Dr Baring in Breach of Marriage; Lyric, Hammersmith, Oct 1952, Danny Felton in The Square Ring; Embassy, Jan 1953, Sgt Whistler in The Devil Came From Dublin; Royal, Glasgow, Apr 1953, the First Workman in Purple Dust; at the Cort, New York, Feb 1955, appeared as Canon Daniel McCooey in The Wayward Saint, this performance gaining the George Jean Nathan Award for the 1954–5 season; St James's, London, June 1957, played Hurst in It's The Geography That Counts; Haymarket, May 1963, Sir Patrick Cullen in The Doctor's Dilemma; Helen Hayes, NY, Oct 1967, Harry in The Loves of Cass Maguire; Biltmore, NY, Mar 1968, McLeavy in Loot; Opera House, Manchester, Sept 1969, Mr Hipney in On the Rocks; joined the National Theatre company to play Michael James Flaherty in The Playboy of the Western World, Old Vic, Oct 1975; first appeared in films, 1947, in I See a Dark Stranger, and has appeared frequently on television.

Address: c/o William Morris Agency, 149 Wardour Street, London W1.

REDMOND, Moira, actress

m (1) Anthony Hughes (mar dis); (2) Herbert Wise (mar dis).

Made her first appearances on stage, 1957, understudying Vivien Leigh and walking on in the Shakespeare Memorial Theatre Company's tour of Titus Andronicus, and her London début at the Stoll, July 1957, in the same production; Strand, May 1958, played Helen Rollander in Verdict; toured, Oct 1958, as Peggy Thompson in Matilda Shouted Fire; Fortune, June 1959, Chris in Detour After Dark; in repertory at Leatherhead and Nottingham, 1962–5; Edinburgh Festival, Aug 1966, for Pop Theatre, played Hermione in The Winter's Tale and Helen in The Trojan Women, repeating the former part at the Cambridge, Aug 1966, and at the Venice Festival; Mermaid, Jan 1967, played three parts in Trifles and Tomfooleries, a Shaw triple-bill; Comedy, May 1967, Mavis Pritchard in Horizontal Hold; Royal Court, Oct 1967, Katerina Prolomnaya in Journey of the Fifth Horse; same theatre, Apr 1968, Queen Victoria in Early Morning; after more repertory appearances, 1968, including Lady Claire Gurney in The Ruling Class, Nottingham, Oct, again played Queen Victoria in Early Morning, Royal Court, Mar 1969; toured, 1969, as Amanda Estriss in The Passionate Husband; Criterion, May 1970, Esme in Flint; Mermaid, Dec 1970, Mrs Peter Vulpy in The Watched Pot; Queen's, June 1971, Grainne Gibbon in The Patrick Pearse Motel; Thorndike, Leatherhead, Oct 1971, Mrs Holroyd in The Widowing of Mrs Holroyd; joined the original Actors' Company to appear at the Edinburgh Festival, Sept 1972, in Ruling the Roost, and at the Arts, Cambridge, Oct 1972, in The Three Arrows; Soho Poly, Feb 1973, Amelia in a lunchtime production, Ag and Fish; Bush, June 1973, Faded Lady in a late-night production, Good Times; Thorndike, Leatherhead, Jan 1975, Blanche Cook in Night Watch; with the Bristol Old Vic, Sept–Nov 1975, played Sister McPhee in The National Health, Ariadne Utterword in Heartbreak House, and Muriel Wicksteed in Habeas Corpus; Mermaid, July 1976, Mme Colombot in Some of My Best Friends are Husbands; Young Vic, Sept 1976, Paula Tax in They Are Dying Out; toured South America with the Oxford Playhouse Company, as Mrs Wicksteed and Hesione Hushabye in Heartbreak House; Greenwich, May 1978, Florence Farr in The Achurch Letters; toured, Feb 1979, as Romaine in Witness for the Prosecution; films, since 1957, include Nightmare, Jigsaw and Kill or Cure; television, also since 1957, includes plays and the serials I Claudius, and Edward VII.

Favourite parts: Constance in King John, Mrs Wicksteed and Hesione Hushabye. *Recreations:* Music, ballet, opera, foreign films and cats. *Address:* c/o Nems Management Ltd, 31 King's Road, London SW3. *Tel:* 01–730 9411.

REES, Llewellyn, actor, manager, and Hon President of the International Theatre Institute

b Charmouth, Dorset, 18 June 1901; *s* of Walter Francis Rees, MA, and his wife Mary Gwendoline (Naden); *e* King Edward's School, Birmingham, and Keble College, Oxford (MA); *m*

Madeleine Newbury; studied for the stage at the Royal Academy of Dramatic Art; was engaged as a private tutor from 1923–6.

Subsequently became an actor, and made his first appearance on the stage at the Empire Theatre, Nottingham, Apr 1928, as Inspector Garrett in The Joker; subsequently toured in several plays, and appeared in repertory, 1930–2, at Newcastle upon Tyne, Cardiff, Whitley Bay, and Leeds; first appeared in London at the Embassy Theatre, 21 Sept 1932, in Miracle at Verdun, and also appeared in the same play at the Comedy, Oct 1932; Arts, and Westminster, Mar 1933, played Arthur Carrington in The Lake; during 1934, appeared with the Greater London Players; Comedy, Feb 1935, played Eustace in Mrs Nobby Clark; His Majesty's, May 1935, George in Hervey House; during 1935–6, acted and produced for the Scottish National Players; Strand, June 1937, played Malinov in Judgment Day; was stage-director for George and Margaret, Morosco Theatre, New York, Sept 1937; general secretary of British Actors' Equity, 1940–6; joint-secretary of London Theatre Council, 1940–6; joint-secretary of the Provincial Theatre Council, 1942–6; secretary of the Federation of Theatre Unions, 1944–6; Governor of the Old Vic, 1945–6; Drama Director of the Arts Council of Great Britain, 1947–9; Chairman of the Executive Committee of the International Theatre Institute, 1948–51; was Administrator of the Old Vic, from 1949–51; Administrator of the Arts Theatre, 1951–2; Administrator for Donald Wolfit, 1952–3; Member of British Council Drama Committee 1952–75; Hon Counsellor, Council of Regional Theatre, 1952–7; after an absence of seventeen years, reappeared on the stage at the Playhouse, Oxford, Nov 1954, as Montane in The Public Prosecutor; at the Q, Jan 1955, played Mr Justice Rutland in The Evidence I Shall Give; same theatre, Feb 1955, Dr Farley and the Prison Governor in The Crime of Canon Wayd; Haymarket, Jan 1956, played the Bishop of Buenos Aires in The Strong are Lonely; Lyric, Hammersmith, Feb 1957, Don Fernando de Olmeda in The Master of Santiago; Bristol Old Vic, Apr 1958, Polonius in Hamlet; Arts, Oct 1959, Dean in My Friend Judas; Strand, Oct 1960, Charles Brandy in Settled Out of Court; Mermaid, May 1962, played Worthy in Lock Up Your Daughters, transferring with the production to Her Majesty's, Aug 1962; at the same theatre, May 1964, played Sir Henry James, QC, in The Right Honourable Gentleman; Greenwich, Sept 1970, Father Ambrose in The Servants and the Snow, and Feb 1971, Duncan in Macbeth; Savoy, 1978, took over Mr Justice Millhouse in Whose Life Is It Anyway?; has also appeared in films and on television, most recently in Holocaust; director and administrator, Travelling Playhouse Ltd.

Address: 30 Ullswater Road, London SW13 9NP.

REES, Roger, actor

b Aberystwyth, Wales, 5 May 1944; *s* of William John Rees and his wife Doris Louise (Smith); *e* Balham Secondary Modern School, Camberwell School of Art, and Slade School of Fine Art.

After an appearance in the chorus of the Ralph Reader Gang Show, Golder's Green Hippodrome, Oct 1963, made his professional debut at Wimbledon, 1964, as Alan in Hindle Wakes; at Pitlochry, 1965, played Yasha in The Cherry Orchard; joined the RSC, Stratford, 1967, to play small parts in The Taming of the Shrew and As You Like It; visited Los Angeles with these productions, 1968; season 1968, his parts included Volumnius in Julius Caesar, Fenton in The Merry Wives of Windsor; repeated the latter role, 1969, also playing Patchbreech in Pericles, Curio in Twelfth Night, Guildford in Henry VIII, and appearing in The Winter's

Tale; toured Japan in The Merry Wives and The Winter's Tale, and Australia in The Winter's Tale and Twelfth Night, 1970; Aldwych, summer 1970, again appeared in The Winter's Tale and Twelfth Night, and played Damaschke in The Plebeians Rehearse the Uprising, July; Stephen Undershaft in Major Barbara, Oct; Stratford, 1971, parts included Claudio in Much Ado About Nothing, Roderigo in Othello; repeated these parts at the Aldwych, 1971–2, also playing Gratiano in The Merchant of Venice, and Balin in The Island of the Mighty; Neptune, Halifax, Nova Scotia, Apr 1973, Marchbanks in Candida; toured with the Cambridge Theatre Company, 1973–4, in parts including Fabian in Twelfth Night, Pierre in Aunt Sally or the Triumph of Death, Young Marlowe in She Stoops to Conquer, the Brother in Fear and Misery in the Third Reich, and Simple Simon in Jack and the Beanstalk; toured the US, 1974–5, as Charles Courtly in the RSC's London Assurance, making his New York debut in this part at the Palace, 5 Dec 1974; Theatre Upstairs, 1975, played Vosco in Paradise, and Q in Moving Clocks Go Slow, June; with Cambridge Theatre Company, 1975, toured as Algernon Moncrieff in The Importance of Being Earnest, and Stanley in The Birthday Party; returned to the RSC, Stratford season, 1976, to play Benvolio in Romeo and Juliet, Young Shepherd in The Winter's Tale, Malcolm in Macbeth (Other Place), Antipholus of Syracuse in The Comedy of Errors; Other Place, May 1977, Ananias in the Alchemist; Aldwych, summer 1977, again played Benvolio and Antipholus, also repeating Malcolm at the Warehouse, Sept, and playing Nazzer in Factory Birds at the same theatre; Aldwych, Dec 1977, played Ananias, and, Jan 1978, Petulant in The Way of the World; took part in the RSC's first small-scale tour, 1978, playing, Sir Andrew in Twelfth Night, Tusenbach in The Three Sisters, and devised the recital Is There Honey Still for Tea?; Stratford, 1979, played Posthumus in Cymbeline, and at the Other Place, repeated Tusenbach and played Semyon Podsekalnikov in The Suicide; played the last two parts in Newcastle, and at the Warehouse, 1980, and at the Aldwych, June 1980, played the title-role in Nicholas Nickleby; is an associate artist of the RSC; TV includes A Bouquet of Barbed Wire, The Comedy of Errors, Macbeth (both RSC), and The Voysey Inheritance.

Recreations: Horse riding, tap dancing. *Address:* c/o ICM, 22 Grafton Street, London W1. *Tel:* 01–629 8080.

REEVES, Geoffrey, director
b London, 21 Apr 1939; *s* of Cecil Reeves, and his wife Winifred Mary Elizabeth (Denby); *e* Dulwich College, St Catharine's College, Cambridge, and Bristol University; *m* Rosemary Joyce; formerly a university lecturer in Drama at Birmingham.

Gained directing experience at Cambridge, and with the National Youth Theatre as associate director, 1964–5; directed his first professional production in London, Dingo, Royal Court, Oct 1967; he has since directed, in London unless otherwise stated, God Bless (RSC), 1968; H, or Monologues at the Front of Burning Cities (National Theatre), Erogenous Zones, Purple Dust (Tel Aviv), Song of the Lusitanian Bogey (Copenhagen), The Ruling Class (Düsseldorf and Zürich), 1969; After Magritte, Measure for Measure (Amsterdam), 1970; has directed several productions for the National Youth Theatre; has assisted Peter Brook on productions including US and Seneca's Œdipus, 1968, Orghast (Persepolis), 1971; co-director, with him, of the CIRT, Paris, 1970–1; Troilus and Cressida (Tokyo), You Can't Take It with You, Plugged In (both Cologne), Straight Up (Darmstadt), 1972; Heartbreak House, The Glambays (both Düsseldorf), Amleth (tour), 1973; director, Northcott

Theatre, Exeter 1974–7, where his many productions have included The Maids, Arms and the Man, For Services Rendered, 1974; The Measures Taken, Coriolanus (Liverpool), The Provok'd Wife, Hamlet, 1975; The Italian Straw Hat, All's Well That Ends Well, Major Barbara, Antony and Cleopatra (tour), 1976; The Rivals, A Midsummer Night's Dream, Othello, 1977; directed The Devil is an Ass (Düsseldorf), 1977, and Has Washington Legs? (National Theatre), 1978; director, Nottingham Playhouse, 1978–, where his productions include: Funny Peculiar, Around the World in 80 Days, Henry V, Jumpers, The Strongest Man in the World, 1978; Comings and Goings, Heartbreak House, Toads, Antonio (co-director), Round Heads and Pointed Heads, Hotel Paradiso, Rich and Rich, 1979; director, Cologne State Theatre, 1972–3; worked on the film Tell Me Lies, 1967.

Recreation: Cooking. *Club:* MCC. *Address:* Playtime, South Road, Chorleywood, Herts.

REID, Beryl, actress
b Hereford, 17 June 1920; *d* of Leonard Reid and his wife Anne Burton (Macdonald); *e* Lady Barne House School, Withington High School, and Levenshulme High School, Manchester; *m* (1) Bill Worsley (mar dis); (2) Derek Franklin (mar dis).

First appeared on the stage in concert party at the Floral Hall, Bridlington, May 1936; made her reputation on radio as Monica in the series *Educating Archie*, the programme running for four years; made her first appearance on the London stage at the St Martin's, Apr 1951, in the revue After the Show; at the New Watergate, Mar–Nov 1954, appeared in three revues: First Edition, Second Edition, and Autumn Revue; at the Palladium, May 1956, appeared in her own act and other sketches in Rockin' the Town; Lyric, Hammersmith, July 1959, appeared in the revue One To Another, transferring with the production to the Apollo, Aug 1959; Globe, June 1961, appeared in the revue On the Avenue; toured in Manchester and Birmingham, 1961, in her own act and in sketches with Jimmy Edwards; Vaudeville, Apr 1963, appeared in the revue All Square; Golder's Green, Dec 1964, Marlene in Dick Whittington; Bristol Old Vic, Apr 1965, played June Buckridge (Sister George) in The Killing of Sister George, transferring with the production to the Duke of York's, London, June 1965; played the same part in New York, at the Belasco, Oct 1966 (1967, Tony Award for Best Actress); Arnaud, Guildford, June 1970, Madame Arcati in Blithe Spirit, and at the Globe, July 1970; also O'Keefe, Toronto, Jan 1971; Old Vic, May 1974, and tour, for National Theatre, played Frau Bergmann in Spring Awakening; Nurse in Romeo and Juliet, Old Vic and Mobile tour, July 1974; Royal Court, Apr 1975, Kath in Entertaining Mr Sloane, transferring to the Duke of York's, June; joined the National Theatre to play Donna Katherina in Il Campiello, and She in Counting The Ways, 1976; for the Royal Shakespeare Company, Aldwych, Jan 1978, played Lady Wishfort in The Way of the World; Bristol Old Vic, Sept 1979, and Globe, Jan 1980, Maud in Born in the Garden; between 1955–62, appeared in three pantomimes in the provinces; she has also starred in a number of revivals at the Theatre Royal, Windsor; entered films in The Belles of St Trinians, 1954, and recent pictures include Star, The Killing of Sister George, Entertaining Mr Sloane, No Sex Please, We're British, and The Dock Brief; first appeared on television, 1952, and has been seen in her own series (four times), The Rivals, The Goodies, When We Are Married, Flint, Tinker, Tailor, Soldier, Spy, etc; radio performances include her own series.

Recreations: Gardening and cooking. *Clubs:* Lady Ratlings, Pickwick. *Address:* Honeypot Cottage, Old Ferry Drive, Wraysbury, near Staines, Middlesex.

REID, Kate, actress

b London, England, 4 Nov 1930; *d* of Walter Clark Reid and his wife Helen Isabel (Moore); *e* Havergal College, Toronto, Canada, and University of Toronto; *m* Austin Willis (mar dis); trained for the stage with Uta Hagen at the Herbert Berghof Studio, New York.

Made her first appearance on the stage as a student, at the Hart House Theatre, University of Toronto, as Daphne in The Damask Cheek; appeared for several seasons in summer stock companies in Canada, and also in Bermuda, before making her first appearance on the English stage at the St Martin's Theatre, London, May 1956, as Lizzie in The Rainmaker; at the same theatre, Nov 1958, played Catherine Ashland in The Stepmother; joined the Stratford Shakespearean Festival Company, Ontario, June 1959, to play Celia in As You Like It, and Emilia in Othello; rejoined the Festival Company, 1960, to play the Nurse in Romeo and Juliet, and Helena in A Midsummer Night's Dream; at subsequent Stratford Shakespearean Festivals she has played the following parts: Katherine in Henry VIII, Jacquenetta in Love's Labour's Lost, and Elly Cassidy in The Canvas Barricade, 1961; Lady Macbeth in Macbeth, and Katharine in The Taming of the Shrew, 1962; Cassandra in Troilus and Cressida, Adriana in The Comedy of Errors, and Lisa and Sister Marthe in Cyrano de Bergerac, 1963; Portia in Julius Caesar, Madame Ranevsky in The Cherry Orchard, 1965; Canadian Universities Tour, Feb 1962, appeared in Two Programmes of Shakespearean Comedy; Billy Rose, NY, Nov 1962, played Martha in Who's Afraid of Virginia Woolf? (matinées only); Plymouth, NY, Jan 1964, played Caitlin Thomas in Dylan; Manitoba Theatre Centre, Winnipeg, Apr 1965, Martha in Who's Afraid of Virginia Woolf?, Stratford, Ontario, summer 1965, Portia in Julius Caesar; Longacre, NY, Feb 1966, Celeste in The Mutilated and Molya in The Gnadiges Fraulein in a double-bill called Slapstick Tragedy; Confederation Memorial Centre, Charlottetown, Prince Edward Island, July 1966, the Medical Officer in The Adventures of Private Turvey and The Mayor's Wife in The Ottawa Man; Shubert, New Haven, Conn, Mar 1967, the Writer's Wife in What Do You Really Know About Your Husband?; Morosco, NY, Feb 1968, Esther Franz in The Price; Duke of York's, London, Mar 1969, again played Esther Franz in The Price; Stratford, Connecticut, 1969, played Gertrude in Hamlet and in The Three Sisters; Stratford, Ontario, season 1970, played Esther in The Friends, and Mrs Bat in Vatzlav; Walnut, Philadelphia, 1973, Juno Boyle in Juno and the Paycock; Vancouver, Nov 1973, appeared in Leaving Home; Alvin, NY, Feb 1974, Lily in The Freedom of the City; Stratford, Conn, summer 1974, Nurse in Romeo and Juliet and Big Mama in Cat On a Hot Tin Roof; repeated this last part at the ANTA, Sept 1974; Shaw Festival, Niagara-on-the-Lake, 1976, appeared in Mrs Warren's Profession and The Apple Cart; Alley, Houston, Jan 1977, appeared in The Corn is Green; Shaw Festival, 1978, Rummy Mitchens in Major Barbara; Long Wharf, Dec 1978, Gwyneth Price in I Sent a Letter to My Love; Longacre, May 1979, Henny in Bosoms and Neglect; repeated this part at Stratford, Ont, season 1980, where she also appeared in Twelfth Night and as Fonsia in The Gin Game; has also appeared frequently at the Crest Theatre, Toronto; films in which she has appeared include Arch Oboler's One Plus One; made her first television appearance, 1953, and performances include Candida, A Month in the Country, The Three Sisters, Salt of the Earth,

Queen After Death, Hamlet, etc; Officer of the Order of Canada, 1976; Hon PhD, York University.

Favourite parts: All played. *Address:* 14 Binscarth Road, Toronto, Canada. *Tel:* WA 4–5015.

REILLY, Charles Nelson, actor

b New York City, 13 Jan 1931; *s* of Charles Joseph Reilly and his wife Signe Elvera (Nelson); *e* University of Connecticut, prepared for the stage with Herbert Berghof and Uta Hagen at HB Studio, and studied singing with Keith Davis; formerly engaged as a mail clerk, hospital orderly, usher, stock boy, etc.

Made his début in school plays in the Bronx, NY; made his professional début with the Tiverton, Rhode Island, Metropolitan Players, 1950, as the Detective in The Broken Dishes; performed in stock at the Newport, Rhode Island, Casino, the Starlight in Kansas City, Missouri, Playhouse on the Mall, Paramus, New Jersey, the Woodstock, NY, Playhouse, and the Matunuck, Rhode Island, Theatre, 1951–64; made his NY début at the Lenox Hill Playhouse, 22 Feb 1956, in the Equity Library Theatre production of Best Foot Forward; York Playhouse, Feb 1959, played Virgil Cicero Tubbs in The Saintliness of Margery Kempe; Renata, May 1959, played in the revue Fallout; Renata, Sept 1959, played in the revue Lend an Ear; Carnegie Hall Playhouse, Oct 1959, in The Billy Barnes Revue; Players, Jan 1960, in the revue Parade; Equity Library Theatre, 1960, played in The Inspector General; Martin Beck, Apr 1960, Mr Henkel in Bye Bye Birdie; in this last production understudied Dick Van Dyke as Albert Peterson and Paul Lynde as Mr MacAfee, and played their roles on numerous occasions; 46th Street, Oct 1961, Bud Frump in How to Succeed in Business Without Really Trying; St James, Jan 1964, Cornelius Hackl in Hello, Dolly!; Lunt-Fontanne, Nov 1965, Roger Summerhill in Skyscraper; Eugene O'Neill, Dec 1974, Sidney Lipton in God's Favorite; directed Julie Harris in The Belle of Amherst, NY, 1976 (and tour), including London, 1977; staged Paul Robeson, 1978; directed Break a Leg, 1979; opera productions he has directed include La Traviata, San Diego, 1979; first appeared in films in A Face in the Crowd, 1957, and has since played in Two Tickets to Paris, The Tiger Makes Out, etc; has appeared on television in The Broadway of Lerner and Loewe, *The Sid Caesar Show, The Ed Sullivan Show,* as Claymore Gregg in *The Ghost and Mrs Muir,* 1968–70, *The Dean Martin Show* as a regular, 1970–1, *The Gold Diggers* as a regular, 1970–1, as Hoo Doo in the children's series *Lidsville,* etc; has performed in cabaret at the Showplace, 1958, in the revue Nightcap, and in Brennan and Reilly, teamed with Eileen Brennan, etc; received the Antoinette Perry (Tony) Award for How to Succeed in Business Without Really Trying and the *Variety* New York Drama Critics Poll for Hello, Dolly!; founded the drama school, The Faculty, in Los Angeles, where he teaches currently.

Address: AFTRA, 724 Fifth Avenue, New York, NY.

REINKING, Ann, dancer and actress

b Seattle, Wash, 10 Nov 1949; *d* of Walton F Reinking and his wife Frances; *e* Bellevue H S; trained for three years with the San Francisco Ballet Co.

Made her Broadway debut Jun 1969 at the Broadway, when she joined the company of Cabaret, as Lulu; appeared at the Mark Hellinger, Dec 1969, in Coco, and at the Lyceum, Dec 1971, in Wild and Wonderful; at the Imperial, Oct 1972, was a Player in Pippin; Shubert, Mar 1974, Maggie in Over Here!; Palace, Mar 1975, played Joan of Arc in Goodtime Charley; Shubert, Mar 1976, took over as Cassie in A Chorus Line; 46th Street, Feb 1977, took over the part of Roxie Hart in Chicago; Broadhurst, Mar 1978, appeared in Dancin'; films include Movie, Movie, and All That Jazz; seen on TV in *Ellery Queen*.

Favourite parts; Joan of Arc, Roxie Hart. *Address:* c/o Hesseltine-Baker Associates, 119 West 57th Street, New York, NY 10019.

REVILL, Clive (Selsby), actor
b Wellington, New Zealand, 18 April 1930; *s* of Edward Malet Barford Revill and his wife Eleanor May (Neel); *e* Rongotai College, and Victoria University, Wellington, NZ; *m* Valerie Nelson; began training as an accountant.

Made his first appearance on the stage in Auckland, NZ, 1950, as Sebastian in Twelfth Night; 1950–2 studied at the Old Vic School, London; first appeared in New York at the Plymouth Theatre, Sept 1952, as Sam Weller in Mr Pickwick; returning to England he joined the Ipswich Repertory Theatre, and remained with the company 1953–5; made his first appearance in London, Arts Theatre, Dec 1955, when he played Pearson in Listen to the Wind; joined the Shakespeare Memorial Theatre Company, Stratford-on-Avon, 1956, and remained for two seasons, appearing in The Merchant of Venice, Hamlet, Love's Labour's Lost, Measure for Measure, King John, Julius Caesar, Cymbeline and The Tempest (also playing Trinculo in the latter production, Drury Lane, Dec 1957); played Ratty in Toad of Toad Hall between seasons; appeared in the last production at Drury Lane, Dec 1957; Lyric, July 1958, played Bob Le Hotu in Irma La Douce; after nearly two years, he left the London production to appear in the same part at the Plymouth, NY, Sept 1960 and was nominated for a Tony Award; left the cast to appear in Las Vegas, Jan 1961, in the same musical; on returning to London, appeared at Sadler's Wells, May 1962, as Ko-Ko in The Mikado; Fagin in Oliver! at the Imperial, NY, Jan 1963, and was again nominated for a Tony; joined the Royal Shakespeare Company, and appeared at the Aldwych, London, Aug 1964, as Jean-Paul Marat in The Marat/Sade, and Oct 1964, as Barabas in The Jew of Malta; Alvin, NY, Mar 1967, Sheridan Whiteside in Sherry; returned for the Chichester Festival Season, May 1968, to play the General in The Unknown Soldier and His Wife, Caliban in The Tempest and Mr Antrobus in The Skin of Our Teeth; Royal Court, Theatre Upstairs, Nov 1969, appeared in A Who's Who of Flapland; Royale, NY, Oct 1971, Max Beerbohm in The Incomparable Max; Broadhurst, 1975, took over the part of Moriarty in Sherlock Holmes; first performance in films 1965, and appearances since then include The Little Prince, One of Our Dinosaurs is Missing, and Galileo; made his first appearance on London television, 1955, NY, 1961.

Recreations: Golf, driving and flying. *Clubs:* Stage Golfing Society, Macready's (founder member and director). *Address:* c/o William Morris Agency, 147–149 Wardour Street, London, W1. *Tel:* 01–784 9361.

RIBMAN, Ronald, playwright
b New York City, 28 May 1932; *s* of Samuel M Ribman and his wife Rose (Lerner); *e* University of Pittsburgh (BBA, MLitt, PhD); *m* Alice Rosen; formerly an assistant professor of English, Otterbein College, Ohio.

First play to be produced in NY was Harry, Noon and Night, at the American Place, 1965; since then has written The Journey of the Fifth Horse, 1966; which received the Obie Award as best play; The Ceremony of Innocence, 1968; Passing Through from Exotic Places, 1969; Fingernails Blue as Flowers, 1971; A Break in the Skin (Yale Repertory),

1972; The Poison Tree, 1973 (produced in NY in 1976); Cold Storage, 1977; wrote his first film, The Angel Levine, 1970; wrote the television play The Final War of Olly Winter, produced by the CBS Playhouse, 1967; is a member of the Writers Guild of America has received fellowships from the Rockerfeller Foundation, Guggenheim Foundation, and the National Foundation for the Arts.

Address: Dramatists Guild, 234 West 44th Street, New York, NY 10036.

RICE, Peter, designer
b Simla, India, 13 Sept 1928; *s* of Cecil Morrish Rice and his wife Ethel (Blacklaw); *e* St Dunstan's College, Reigate, Surrey and Royal College of Art; *m* Pat Albeck.

Designed his first professional production, Sex and Seraphim, at the Watergate, July 1951; subsequent productions include: Time Remembered, 1954; The Taming of the Shrew, The Winter's Tale, Much Ado About Nothing (all Old Vic), 1956; Living for Pleasure, A Day in the Life Of . . ., 1958; On the Avenue, The Lord Chamberlain Regrets, 1961; Castle in Sweden, Talking to You and Across the Board on Tomorrow Morning (double-bill), Rule of Three, 1962; Madigan's Lock, The Wood of the Whispering, 1963; Mr Whatnot, 1964; Pickwick (New York), As You Like It, 1965; The Farmer's Wife, The Beaux' Stratagem, Heartbreak House, An Italian Straw Hat (all Chichester), The Two-Character Play, 1967; The Duel, 1968; Ann Veronica, On a Foggy Day, His, Hers and Theirs, 1969; The Happy Apple, Flint, Arms and the Man, The Proposal (both Chichester), 1970; Move Over, Mrs Markham, Ambassador, 1971; Œdipus Now, 1972; Say Goodnight to Grandma, 1973; The Vortex, 1975; The Bells of Hell, Shut Your Eyes and Think of England, 1977; Murder Among Friends, 1978; Happy Birthday, 1979; has designed many productions for Greenwich Theatre, including, from 1976: Heaven and Hell, Miss Julie; 1977: The Admirable Crichton, Singles, Pinch-Me-Not; 1978: Don Juan, An Audience Called Edouard, See How They Run (also Royal Exchange, Manchester); 1979: Semi-Detached, The Passing-Out Parade, I sent a Letter to my Love; has designed productions of Toad of Toad Hall since 1961; has also designed operas and ballets for Aldeburgh, Covent Garden, Glyndebourne, Sadler's Wells and abroad.

Recreations: Ancient films and making shell grottos. *Address:* 4 Western Terrace, London, W6. *Tel:* 01–748 3990.

RICE, Tim, lyricist
b Amersham, Bucks, 10 Nov 1944; *s* of Hugh Gordon Rice and his wife Joan Odette (Bawden); *e* Lancing College; *m* Jane McIntosh.

Wrote the lyrics for Joseph and the Amazing Technicolour Dreamcoat, 1968, which was presented in London at the Albery, 1973; Jesus Christ Superstar, Mark Hellinger, New York, 1971, Palace, London 1972; Evita, Prince Edward, 1978, and Broadway, NY, 1979; also a frequent broadcaster and disc jockey.

Recreations: Cricket, history of popular music. *Clubs:* MCC, Rick Nelson International. *Address:* c/o David Land, 118 Wardour Street, London W1. *Tel:* 01–437 3224.

RICHARDS, Angela, actress
b 18 Dec, 1944; trained for the stage at RADA.

On leaving RADA made her West End debut at the Lyric, 20 Oct 1964, as Henrietta in Robert and Elizabeth; Saville, Apr 1966, played Kathie in On the Level; Westminster, July 1967, Millie Jackson in Annie; Apollo, Sept 1968, Jenny Diver in the Prospect company's The Beggar's Opera; Nottingham Playhouse, 1970, Sally in a musical version of Love on the Dole; Bristol Old Vic, 1971, Titania in A Midsummer Night's Dream, and Countess Sophia in A Patriot for Me; Nottingham, July 1971, Angele in A Close Shave and Eurydice in Antigone; Hampstead, Jan 1972, Fanny in Ride a Cock-horse; Chichester Festival, 1972, Lucy Lockit in The Beggar's Opera, and Minnie Tinwell in The Doctor's Dilemma, also taking over from Joan Plowright as Jennifer Dubedat; Her Majesty's, Nov 1972, Eve Harrington in Applause; Greenwich, Nov 1973, the Widow in Zorba; Mermaid, July 1974, appeared in Cole; Oxford Playhouse, 1975, Celia in As You Like It, Apr, and Lieut Lillian Holliday in Happy End, May, transferring with the latter production to the Lyric, Aug 1975; Shaftesbury, June 1976, title-role in Liza of Lambeth; 1980, toured as Catherine Winslow in The Winslow Boy; has made numerous TV appearances in plays and series, recently in *Women—Which Way Now?*, King of the Castle, and three series of *Secret Army*, for which she wrote and sang the songs.

Address: c/o Bryan Drew, 81 Shaftesbury Avenue, London W1. *Tel:* 01–437 5217.

RICHARDSON, Ian, FRSAMD, actor

b Edinburgh, Scotland, 7 Apr 1934; *s* of John Richardson and his wife Margaret (Drummond); *e* Tynecastle School, Edinburgh; *m* Maroussia Frank; studied for the stage at the College of Dramatic Art, Glasgow, where he received the James Bridie Gold Medal, 1957.

Joined the Birmingham Repertory Theatre Company, Aug 1958, where he played a variety of parts including Hamlet, John Worthing in The Importance of Being Earnest, and Adolph in Creditors; joined the Shakespeare Memorial Theatre Company, Stratford-on-Avon, Jan 1960, to play Arragon in The Merchant of Venice, and Sir Andrew Aguecheek in Twelfth Night; became a long-term contract player with the same company, Nov 1960 (re-named Royal Shakespeare Company, Jan 1961), and made his first appearance in London at the Aldwych, Dec 1960, as Count Malatesti in The Duchess of Malfi; he has since played the following parts for The Royal Shakespeare Company; Don John in Much Ado About Nothing, 1961; Oberon in A Midsummer Night's Dream, Tranio in The Taming of the Shrew, Antipholus of Ephesus in The Comedy of Errors, 1962; Doctor in The Representative, 1963; Southwark Cathedral, Nov 1963, played Herod in The Miracles; Aldwych, Dec 1963, again played Antipholus of Ephesus in The Comedy of Errors, and Feb 1964, played Edmund in King Lear, prior to touring both plays in Europe, the USSR, and making his first appearance in New York, at the State Theatre, May 1964, as Antipholus of Ephesus in The Comedy of Errors, and subsequently in King Lear; Aldwych, London, Aug 1964, played the Herald in Marat/Sade; Oct 1964, played Ithamore in The Jew of Malta; Dec 1964, played Ford in The Merry Wives of Windsor; Royal Shakespeare, May 1965, Antipholus of Syracuse in The Comedy of Errors; Aldwych, July 1965, Eino Silakka in Squire Puntila and His Servant Matti; same theatre, Nov 1965, played Marat in Marat/Sade; also at the Martin Beck, NY, Dec 1965; since then, he has appeared for the Company in repertory, as the Chorus in Henry V, Vendice in The Revenger's Tragedy, 1966; the title-role in Coriolanus, Vendice in The Revenger's Tragedy, Bertram in All's Well That Ends Well, Malcolm in Macbeth, 1967 (also playing the latter two parts at the Aldwych, Jan 1968); Cassius in Julius Caesar and Ford in The Merry Wives of Windsor (also at the Aldwych), 1968; the title-role in Pericles, Ford in The Merry Wives of Windsor, Vendice in The Revenger's Tragedy (Aldwych), 1969; toured Japan with the

Company, Jan 1970; Angelo in Measure For Measure, Buckingham in Richard III, Proteus in The Two Gentlemen of Verona (later at the Aldwych), Prospero in The Tempest, 1970; Sadler's Wells, June 1972, and Prince of Wales, Aug 1972, played Tom Wrench in Trelawny; returning to Stratford, 1973, he alternated the parts of Richard II and Bolingbroke in Richard II (with Richard Pasco), Apr 1973 (also Brooklyn Academy, Jan 1974) and played Berowne in Love's Labour's Lost, Aug 1973; Stratford, season 1974, again played Richard and Bolingbroke, Apr, Iachimo in Cymbeline, May; Aldwych, 1974, played Shalimov in Summerfolk, Aug (also Brooklyn), Richard and Bolingbroke, Sept, Ernst Scholz in The Marquis of Keith, Nov, Iachimo, Dec; Aldwych, Apr 1975, Berowne in Love's Labour's Lost; Stratford, Aug 1975, played Ford in The Merry Wives of Windsor, also the title-role in Richard III (at The Other Place); St James's, NY, Mar 1976, Higgins in My Fair Lady; 1977, Jack Tanner in Man and Superman (including Don Juan in Hell), and the Doctor in The Millionairess, at the Shaw Festival Theatre, Niagara-on-the-Lake, Ontario; Old Vic, 1979, played Mercutio in Romeo and Juliet, Khlestakov in The Government Inspector, and David Garrick in The Undisputed Monarch of the English Stage; first appeared on television, Dec 1962, in As You Like It; recent appearances include Ike, Tinker, Tailor, Soldier, Spy, Churchill and the Generals, and Charlie Muffin; films include The Darwin Adventure, and Man of La Mancha.

Favourite parts: Richard II, Cassius, Prospero, Richard III. *Recreations:* Music, cine-photography. *Address:* c/o London Management, 235–241 Regent Street, London, W1A 2JT.

RICHARDSON, Sir Ralph (cr 1947), actor

b Cheltenham, Gloucestershire, 19 Dec 1902; *s* of Arthur Richardson and his life Lydia (Russell); *m* (1) Muriel Hewitt (dec); (2) Meriel Forbes.

Began his career with Frank R Growcott's St Nicholas Players, St Nicholas Hall, Brighton, Dec 1920; made his first professional appearance at the Marina Theatre, Lowestoft, Aug 1921, with Charles Doran's Company, as Lorenzo in The Merchant of Venice; toured the provinces for four years, before joining the Birmingham Rep, Jan 1926; first appearance on the London stage at the Scala Theatre (for the Greek Play Society), 10 July 1926, as the Stranger in Œdipus at Colonus; Haymarket, Nov 1926, Arthur Varwell in Yellow Sands; at the Court, Mar 1928, played Zazim and Pygmalion in Back to Methuselah, and Apr 1928, Gurth in Harold, and Tranio in The Taming of the Shrew (in modern dress); Arts, June 1928, played Hezekiah Brent in Prejudice; Court, Aug 1928, Ben Hawley in Aren't Women Wonderful?; Garrick, Nov 1928, James Jago in The Runaways; during 1929 toured in South Africa; Dominion, Feb 1930, played Gilbert Nash in Silver Wings; Savoy, May 1930, Roderigo in Othello; joined the Old Vic company, opening in Sept 1930, as the Prince of Wales in Henry IV (Part I); subsequently played Sir Harry Beagle in The Jealous Wife, Caliban, Bolingbroke, and Enobarbus; re-opening of Sadler's Wells Theatre, Jan 1931, played Sir Toby Belch in Twelfth Night; other parts at the Old Vic and Wells, included: Bluntschli in Arms and the Man, Don Pedro in Much Ado About Nothing, Earl of Kent in King Lear; Malvern Festival, Aug 1931, Nicholas in A Woman Killed With Kindness, Courtall in She Would if She Could, and Viscount Pascal in The Switchback; returned to the Vic-Wells company for the 1931–2 season, playing Philip Faulconbridge in King John, Petruchio, Bottom, Henry V, Ralph in The Knight of the Burning Pestle, Brutus, General Grant in Abraham Lincoln, Iago, and the Ghost and First Gravedigger in Hamlet; Malvern Festival, Aug 1932, played

Merrygreek in Ralph Roister Doister, Face in The Alchemist, Oroonoko, and Sergeant Fielding in Too True to be Good; at the New, Sept 1932, again played the last-mentioned part; Globe, Nov 1932, played Collie Stratton in For Services Rendered; Queen's, Feb 1933, Dirk Barclay in Head-On Crash; Apollo, May 1933, Arthur Bell Nicholls in Wild Decembers; Wyndham's, Sept 1933, the title-role in Sheppey; Palladium, Dec 1933, Mr Darling and Captain Hook in Peter Pan; Globe, Feb 1934, John MacGregor in Marriage is No Joke; Duchess, Sept 1934, Charles Appleby in Eden End; Mar 1935, Cornelius in the play of that name; toured America, Oct 1935, as Mercutio in Romeo and Juliet, making his first appearance in New York, at the Martin Beck Theatre, 23 Dec 1935, as Chorus and Mercutio in the same play; Shaftesbury, London, Feb 1936, played Emile Delbar in Promise; Lyric, in conjunction with Laurence Olivier, May 1936, directed Bees on the Boat Deck, and appeared as Sam Gridley; Haymarket, Aug 1936, played Dr Clitterhouse in The Amazing Dr Clitterhouse; St James's, Nov 1937, Peter Agardi in The Silent Knight; Old Vic, Dec 1937, Bottom in A Midsummer Night's Dream, and Feb 1938, Othello; New, Feb 1939, Robert Johnson in Johnson Over Jordan; on the outbreak of War, joined the Fleet Air Arm, and served until 1944, retiring with rank of Lieut Commander (A); joined the Old Vic company at the New Theatre as joint-director, Aug 1944, and played Peer in Peer Gynt, Bluntschli in Arms and the Man, Richmond in Richard III, and Uncle Vanya; subsequently, 1945, toured with the company in Germany, and also appeared at the Comédie Française; reopened at the New, Sept 1945, and during the season, played Falstaff in Henry IV (Parts I and II), Tiresias in Œdipus Rex, and Lord Burleigh in The Critic; went with the company to NY, May 1946, and appeared at the Century Theatre, playing the four last-mentioned parts; after returning to England, again appeared at the New Theatre, with the Old Vic company 1946–7 season, playing Inspector Goole in An Inspector Calls, Cyrano de Bergerac, Face in The Alchemist, and John of Gaunt in Richard II, also producing the last play; Wyndham's, Apr 1948, played Marcus in Royal Circle, which he produced; Haymarket, Feb 1949, Dr Sloper in The Heiress; Wyndham's, Mar 1950, played David Preston in Home at Seven; Aldwych, May 1951, Vershinin in Three Sisters; joined the Shakespeare Memorial Theatre Company, Stratford-on-Avon, 1952, and appeared as Prospero in The Tempest, and Volpone; Globe, Mar 1953, played John Greenwood in The White Carnation; Haymarket, Nov 1953, appeared as Dr Farley in A Day By the Sea; toured Australia, 1955, in Separate Tables, in which he played Mr Martin in The Window Table and Major Pollock in Table Number Seven, also appearing as the Grand Duke in The Sleeping Prince; Old Vic, Sept 1956, played the title-part in Timon of Athens; Coronet, NY, Jan 1957, General St Pé in The Waltz of the Toreadors; Haymarket, London, Nov 1957, appeared as Cherry in Flowering Cherry, which ran for over 400 performances, and in which he subsequently toured; Globe, June 1959, played Victor Rhodes in The Complaisant Lover; Phoenix, Sept 1960, Edward Portal in The Last Joke; Haymarket, Apr 1962, Sir Peter Teazle in The School for Scandal, touring the US, with the same production, Nov–Jan 1962, and appearing at the Majestic, NY, Jan 1963; appeared in the opening production at the May Fair Theatre, London, June 1963, as the Father in Six Characters in Search of an Author; at the Royal, Brighton, Feb 1964, played Shylock in The Merchant of Venice, and Bottom in A Midsummer Night's Dream, prior to appearing in both productions in the British Council's Shakespeare Quatercentenary Tour to South America and Europe, Mar–May 1964; Haymarket,

Sept 1964, played Father in Carving a Statue; Haymarket, Jan 1966, the Waiter in You Never Can Tell; Haymarket, Sept 1966, Sir Anthony Absolute in The Rivals; Haymarket, Sept 1967, Shylock in The Merchant of Venice; Queen's, Mar 1969, Dr Rance in What the Butler Saw; Royal Court, June 1970, Jack in Home, transferring to the Apollo, July and to the Morosno, NY, Nov 1970; Royal Court, Aug 1971, and Cambridge Theatre, Oct 1971, Wyatt Gilman in West of Suez; Savoy, July 1972, Gen Sir William Boothroyd in Lloyd George Knew My Father, afterwards touring Australia, 1973, and N America, 1974, in the role; Old Vic, Jan 1975, joined the National Theatre company to play the title-role in John Gabriel Borkman; also played Hirst in No Man's Land, Apr 1975, transferring with this production to the Wyndham's, July 1975; Old Vic, Feb 1976, appeared in Tribute to a Lady; Lyric, May 1977, Cecil in The Kingfisher; Olivier (NT), Feb 1978, Firs in The Cherry Orchard; Savoy, May 1978, Col White in Alice's Boys; Olivier, Sept 1978, Lord Touchwood in The Double Dealer, Mar 1979, The Master in The Fruits of Enlightenment, and Dec 1979, Old Ekdal in The Wild Duck; Cottesloe (NT), Apr 1980, Kitchen in Early Days; entered films, 1933, in The Ghoul; has played in Anna Karenina, The Fallen Idol, The Heiress, The Sound Barrier, Richard III, Our Man in Havana, Dr Zhivago, The Battle of Britain, Oh! What a Lovely War, David Copperfield, etc; television appearances include Judge Brack in Hedda Gabler, Sir Toby in Twelfth Night, and Lord Emsworth in the *Blandings Castle* series; received the Norwegian Order of St Olaf, 1950; Hon DLitt Oxon, 1969.

Hobby: Drawing. *Clubs:* Athenæum, Beefsteak, and Savile. *Address:* 1 Chester Terrace, London, NW1. *Tel:* 01–486 5063.

RICHARDSON, Tony, director and producer
b Shipley, Yorks, 5 June 1928; *s* of C A Richardson and his wife Elsie (Campion); *e* Ashville College, Harrogate, and Wadham College, Oxford; *m* Vanessa Redgrave (mar dis).

While at the university, he directed a number of productions for the OUDS (President, 1949–51), including: The Duchess of Malfi, Peer Gynt, Romeo and Juliet and King John; began his career with BBC Television, and directed, among other plays, Othello and Dostoievsky's The Gambler; Royal, Stratford, June 1955, directed The Country Wife; appointed Associate Artistic Director of The English Stage Company, 1955, and directed the following plays at the Royal Court Theatre: Look Back in Anger, Cards of Identity, 1956; The Member of the Wedding, The Entertainer, The Chairs, and The Making of Moo, 1957; following the successful transfer of The Entertainer to the Palace Theatre, Sept 1957, he directed his first Broadway production at the Lyceum, New York, Oct 1957, with Look Back in Anger; he has since directed the following plays: Requiem For a Nun, 1957; The Chairs and The Lesson (double-bill), (Phoenix, NY), The Entertainer (Royale, NY), Flesh To a Tiger, Pericles (Shakespeare Memorial Theatre), 1958; Requiem For a Nun (John Golden, NY), Othello (Shakespeare Memorial Theatre), Orpheus Descending, Look After Lulu, 1959; co-directed A Taste of Honey (Lyceum, NY), 1960; The Changeling, Luther (also Paris, Holland and Edinburgh Festivals), 1961; A Midsummer Night's Dream, Semi-Detached, 1962; Natural Affection (Booth, NY), Arturo Ui (Lunt-Fontanne, NY), The Milk Train Doesn't Stop Here Any More (Brooks Atkinson, NY), 1963; The Seagull, St Joan of the Stockyards, 1964; Hamlet (also Lunt-Fontanne, NY), 1969; The Threepenny Opera, I Claudius, 1972; Antony and Cleopatra, 1973; The Lady From the Sea (Circle-in-the-Square, NY), 1976; As You Like It (Long Beach Festival), 1979; he has produced and/or directed films including Momma Don't Allow, Look Back in Anger, The Entertainer, Saturday Night and Sunday Morning, A Taste of Honey, The Loneliness of the Long Distance Runner, Tom Jones (Film Academy Award as Best Director 1963), Girl With Green Eyes, The Loved One, Laughter in the Dark, The Charge of the Light Brigade, Hamlet, Ned Kelly, A Delicate Balance, Dead Cert, Joseph Andrews, A Death in Canaan.

Address: c/o 23 Albemarle Street, London, W1.

RIDLEY, Arnold, actor and dramatic author
b Bath, 7 Jan 1896; *s* of William Robert Ridley and his wife Rosa (Morrish); *e* Bath, and Bristol University; *m* (1) Hilda Mary Cooke (mar dis); (2) Isola Strong (mar dis); (3) Althea Parker.

Originally an actor, making his first appearance at the Theatre Royal, Bristol, in Prunella, 1914; served in the Army, but was discharged, wounded, in 1917; appeared with the Birmingham Repertory Company, 1918–20, where he played over forty parts; was with the Plymouth Repertory Company, 1920–1; retired from the stage in consequence of ill-health, caused by War injuries; reappeared at the Garrick, Apr 1927, as Saul Hodgkin in The Ghost Train; rejoined the army, Oct 1939, and served with the BEF in France; he also appeared at the Q, Mar 1948, as Philip Stafford in his own play, Easy Money; Gateway, Apr 1950, played John Hengist in Marshall's Aid; at the Royal, Birmingham, Sept 1953, appeared as Walter Gabriel in The Archers; Queen's, July 1964, played Juror No 9 in 12 Angry Men; Arnaud, Guildford, Nov 1971, played the Station Master in his play, The Ghost Train; Shaftesbury, Oct 1975, Private Godfrey in a stage adaptation of Dad's Army; television appearances include: Crossroads and Dad's Army; he has also broadcast as Doughy Hood in The Archers; is the author of The Brass God, 1921; The Ghost Train, 1925; The God o' Mud, 1926; The Wreckers (with Bernard Merivale), 1927; Keepers of Youth, The Flying Fool (with Merivale), Third Time Lucky, 1929; Recipe for Murder, 1932; Headline, Half-a-Crown (with Douglas Furber), 1934; Glory Be!, 1935; Needs Must, 1938; Out Goes She (with Merivale), 1939; Peril at End House (adaptation), 1940; Murder Happens, 1945; Easy Money, 1947; East of Ludgate Hill, 1950; Trifles Light As Air (with St Vincent Troubridge), The Dark Corridor (with Richard Reich), 1951; Beggar My Neighbour, 1952; Happy Holiday (with Eric Maschwitz), 1954; The Running Man (with Anthony Armstrong), 1955; You, My Guests, Shadows on the Sand (with Mary Cathcart Borer), Tabitha (with Mary Cathcart Borer), 1956; Bellamy (with Anthony Armstrong), 1959; Amongst Those Present, 1960; High Fidelity (with Cedric Wallis), 1964; Festive Board, 1970; as a director, has staged Sunshine House, Will You Play With Me?, 1933; Rude Awakening, 1934; Needs Must, Flood Tide, 1938; Beggar My Neighbour, 1952; The Cat and the Canary (tour), 1966; was director of productions of the Malvern company, 1942–4; is a Past President and Life Member of Bath Rugby Football Club.

Recreations: Rugby football and cricket. *Address:* c/o Hughes Massie & Co, 69 Great Russell Street, London WC1.

RIETTY, Robert, actor, director, and author
b London, 8 Feb 1923; *s* of Victor Rietti and his wife Rachel Leah (Rosinay); *e* London; *m* Albertine Shalom; studied for the stage under his father, and at the Royal Academy of Dramatic Art.

Made his first appearance on the stage, 1932, in Mysterious Currents; Fortune Theatre, 1935, played the title-part in Poil de Carotte; Little, June 1936, played the Chrysalis in The Insect Play, and His Majesty's, Dec 1936, Jonathan in The Boy David; Arts, Apr 1937, Mishel in Thou Art the Man; during 1940, was with the Oxford Repertory Theatre, and 1941, at Colchester; toured, 1941, for ENSA, as Joe Varwell in Yellow Sands; at the Mercury Theatre, Aug 1941, played the Baron in L'Enfant Prodigue; was subsequently engaged with the BBC European Section; toured, 1942, as Eben in Desire Under the Elms, and then joined the Army, first serving with the Rifle Brigade; subsequently transferred to the Central Pool of Artists, touring Germany, Italy, and Austria at the end of the War; from 1946–8, engaged with the BBC Repertory Company; at the Edinburgh Festival, 1948, played Shendi in The First Born, subsequently touring with this play; Arts Theatre, Jan 1949, played Percy Goldfinch in A Pair of Spectacles; Torch, Aug 1949, Professor Boffles in Nuts in May; New Lindsey, May 1950, Arthur Marr in The Dark Corridor; Saville, Sept–Oct 1950, Sidney Kurtz in Spring Song, and Beau Belasco in The King of Schnorrers; Rudolf Steiner Hall, Oct–Nov 1950, appeared in a series of plays, adapted from the Italian, presented by his father and himself; Arts, Jan 1951, played Eilert Lovborg in Hedda Gabler; Cambridge Theatre, May 1951, played Selim in the revival of Hassan; also, 1951, appeared in a further series of plays presented at Rudolph Steiner Hall, and at the Royal, Bristol, played Maso in To Live In Peace; Winter Garden, Jan 1952, played Shendi in The Firstborn; Rudolph Steiner Hall, Sept–Nov 1953, appeared in three plays presented during the International Theatre season; in Dublin, and subsequently at the Richmond Theatre, Apr 1954, appeared as Mario in If It's a Rose; Q, and Embassy, 1955, played Eben in Desire Under the Elms, and at the Rudolph Steiner Hall played in He, She and the Other and The Shadow of Mart; Lyric, Mar 1957, played John in Man on Trial, for the Repertory Players; York Festival, 1957, appeared as Satan in The York Mystery Play; at the Rudolph Steiner, 1958, appeared as Giulio in The Little Saint; Royal Court, May 1959, played Don Landolina in the International Theatre production of The Shameless Professor; Arts, July 1959, played Dr Jacobson in The Rope Dancers; Pembroke, Croydon, Apr 1961, played Jon Pinedus in The Pinedus Affair; toured, Mar 1962, as Leo in The Magnificent Gourmet; Canterbury Festival, Sept 1970, played Fourth Tempter and Knight in the first performance in the Cathedral of Murder in the Cathedral; narrated Laborinthus, Covent Garden, Nov 1972 (for Royal Ballet); 1962–5, directed and took part in a series of Studio Performances of International Plays at the Institute of Contemporary Arts; has appeared in many films, including The Bible, Joseph and His Brothers, The Scarlet Blade, and The Omen; has directed the English versions of many continental films, including October Revolution, The Red Tent, The Night Porter, and The Sorrow and the Pity, and regularly dubs the voices of leading foreign artists; has made over six thousand broadcasts; is author of the plays If It's a Rose (with Dario Niccodemi), 1954; translated Pirandello's The Rules of the Game (with Noel Cregeen), and The Slapstick Angels; adapted Yours Faithfully, Romantic Chapter, 1955; A Candle to the Madonna, 1958; A Gust of Wind, The Little Saint (with V Rietti), 1958; Corina, Strange Meeting, 1959; Una Bella Domenica di Settembre, The Pinedus Affair, 1960; Editor of the International Drama Quarterly *Gambit*; has also contributed to a number of theatre journals; writes regularly for religious and domestic radio programmes; received the honour of Cavaliere al Merito (Knight of Merit), for services to the Italian Theatre, 1960.

Recreation: Piano playing. *Address:* 40 Old Church Lane, London, NW9 5TA. *Tel:* 01–205 3024.

RIGBY, Harry, producer

b Pittsburgh, Pa, 21 Feb 1925; *s* of Howard Rigby and his wife Anne (Halpen); *e* Haverford School and U of North Carolina.

Co-producer of Make a Wish, 1951; has since produced or co-produced John Murray Anderson's Almanac, 1953; Half-a-Sixpence, 1965; Hallelujah, Baby, 1967 (Tony award); Riot, 1968; conceived the revival of No, No, Nanette, 1971; adapted and co-produced Irene, 1973; produced Good News, 1974; with Terry Allen Kramer produced Knock, Knock, 1976; I Love My Wife, 1977; Sugar Babies, 1979 (also co-author); produced the film Pound, 1970.

Address: 1650 Broadway, New York, NY 10019. *Tel:* 757 3903.

RIGG, Diana, actress

b Doncaster, Yorks, 20 July 1938; *d* of Louis Rigg and his wife Beryl (Helliwell); *e* Fulneck Girls School, Pudsey; *m* Menachem Gueffen (mar dis); trained for the stage at the Royal Academy of Dramatic Art.

Made her first appearance on the stage in a RADA production in the York Festival, at the Theatre Royal, York, summer 1957, when she played Natella Abashwili in The Caucasian Chalk Circle; after appearing in repertory in Chesterfield and in York she joined the Royal Shakespeare Company, Stratford-on-Avon, 1959, and made her first appearance in London at the Aldwych Theatre, Jan 1961, when she played 2nd Ondine and Violanta in Ondine; at the same theatre, in repertory, she played the following parts: Phillipe Trincante in The Devils; Gwendolen in Becket; Bianca in The Taming of the Shrew, 1961; Madame de Touruel in The Art of Seduction, 1962; Royal Shakespeare, Stratford-on-Avon, Apr 1962, played Helena in A Midsummer Night's Dream; Bianca in The Taming of the Shrew, Lady Macduff in Macbeth, Adriana in The Comedy of Errors, and Cordelia in King Lear, subsequently appearing in the last production at the Aldwych, Dec 1962, followed by Adriana in The Comedy of Errors; Aldwych, Jan 1963, played Monica Stettler in The Physicists; toured the provinces, spring, 1963, in A Midsummer Night's Dream, subsequently appearing at the Royal Shakespeare, Stratford, and at the Aldwych, in The Comedy of Errors, Dec 1963; Aldwych, Feb 1964, again played Cordelia in King Lear prior to touring with both plays for the British Council, in Europe, the USSR, and the US; during this tour she made her first appearance in New York at the State Theatre, May 1964, in the same plays; Stratford, June 1966, Viola in Twelfth Night; Wyndham's, May 1970, played Heloise in Abelard and Heloise, also at the Brooks Atkinson, NY, Mar 1971; for the National Theatre, played Dottie in Jumpers, Lady Macbeth in Macbeth, 1972; Célimène in The Misanthrope, 1973; Albery, May 1974, Eliza Doolittle in Pygmalion; toured the US as Célimène, including the St James's, NY, Mar 1975, returning to the Old Vic in this part and as the Governor's Wife in Phaedra Britannica, Sept; Lyttleton (NT), Jan 1978, Ilona in The Guardsman; Phoenix, Nov 1978, Ruth Carson in Night and Day; films include Assassination Bureau, On Her Majesty's Secret Service, Julius Caesar; The Hospital, Theatre of Blood, A Little Night Music; first appeared on television, Jan 1964, as Adriana in The Comedy of Errors and subsequently in *The Avengers*, Married Alive, In This House of Brede (US), Three Piece Suite, etc.

Favourite parts: Helena and Cordelia. *Recreations:* Reading and trying to get organized. *Address:* c/o John Redway Ltd, 16 Berners Street, London W1.

RITCHIE, June, actress

m Marcus Turnbull; trained for the stage at RADA.

After considerable repertory experience, made her West End debut at the Strand, 22 Sept 1965, as Miss Mopply in Too True to be Good; Prince of Wales, Feb 1966, Doreen in Saturday Night and Sunday Morning; Duke of York's, Apr 1966, Shirley in The Anniversary; Arnaud, Guildford, Oct 1971, and tour, Becky Sharp in Vanity Fair; Hampstead, Dec 1971, Emily in His Monkey Wife; Drury Lane, May 1972, Scarlett O'Hara in Gone With the Wind; Chichester, May 1974, appeared in Tonight We Improvise; at the Gardner Centre, Brighton, Oct–Nov 1974, played Lady Macbeth, Dotty in Jumpers, and Ruth in The Homecoming; Arnaud, Guildford, Apr 1976, and Cambridge Theatre, June, Natasha in The Three Sisters; Bristol Old Vic, May 1977, Mrs Kopecka in Schweyk in The Second World War; 1979, toured as Beverly in The Shadow Box; films, since her first, A Kind of Loving, 1961, include Live Now, Pay Later, and This is My Street; TV includes plays and serials.

Address: c/o Fraser and Dunlop, 91 Regent Street, London W1.

RITMAN, William, designer

Designed the decor and lighting for a revival of On the Town, 13 Feb 1959, and has since designed the decor for The Zoo Story, Krapp's Last Tape, Russell Patterson's Sketch-Book (also costumes), The Killer (all also lighting); Kukla, Burr and Ollie, 1960; The Sudden End of Anne Cinquefoil, Bartleby, The American Dream, The Death of Bessie Smith (all also costumes and lighting), Gallows Humor, Happy Days, 1961; Fortuna (also lights), End Game, Mrs Dally Has a Lover, Whisper into My Good Ear, Who's Afraid of Virginia Woolf?, The Dumb Waiter, The Collection, King of the Whole Damned World (lighting only), 1962; The Riot Act, Corruption in the Palace of Justice, 1963; The Lover, Play, Funnyhouse of a Negro, Dutchman, The Two Executioners, A Midsummer Night's Dream, The Giant's Dance, Tiny Alice, The Place for Chance, Absence of a Cello (last two also lighting), 1964; Do Not Pass Go, Entertaining Mr Sloane, Play That on Your Old Piano, 1965; Malcolm, A Delicate Balance, Night of the Dunce, 1966; Come Live with Me (also lighting), The Rimers of Eldritch, The Birthday Party (also costumes), Johnny No-Trump (also costumes and lighting), The Promise, Everything in the Garden, 1967; Box-Mao-Box (a double bill of Box and Quotations from Chairman Mao-Tse-Tung, also lighting and costumes), Loot, We Bombed in New Haven, Lovers: Winners, Lovers: Losers, The American Dream, The Death of Bessie Smith, Krapp's Last Tape, The Zoo Story, Happy Days (last five also lighting), 1968; Play It Again, Sam, The Gingham Dog, The Three Sisters, Hello and Goodbye, The Penny Wars, The Ruffian on the Stair, The Erpingham Camp, The Mundy Scheme (also lighting), 1969; Nature of the Crime, How Much, How Much? (also lighting), What the Butler Saw, Sleuth (lighting only), Bob and Ray: The Two and Only, The Devil's Disciple (Stratford, Conn), 1970; Waiting for Godot, 1971; The Sign in Sidney Brustein's Window, Moonchildren, The Real Inspector Hound, After Magritte, An Evening with Richard Nixon and . . ., 6 Rms Riv Vu, The Last of Mrs Lincoln (also lighting), 1972; Measure for Measure (Stratford, Conn), Detective Story (Philadelphia), Milliken Breakfast Show, 1973; The Madness of God (Washington, DC), Find Your Way Home, Noel Coward in Two Keys (also lighting), My Fat Friend, God's Favorite, 1974; Same Time, Next Year, P.S. Your Cat Is Dead! (also lighting), 1975; California Suite, 1976; Chapter Two, 1977; Deathtrap, Tribute, 1978; Once a Catholic, Last Licks, 1979.

Address: 325 West 89th Street, New York, NY.

RIVERA, Chita (*née* Concita del Rivero), actress and singer

b Washington, DC, 23 Jan 1933; *d* of Pedro Julio Figueroa del Rivero; *e* Taft High School, New York City; *m* Anthony Mordente; trained as a dancer at the American School of Ballet.

Made her début at the Imperial Theatre, NY, in 1952, in Call Me Madam, subsequently touring the US as Principal Dancer in the same production; 46th Street, 1953, in the chorus of Guys and Dolls; Shubert, 1954, appeared in Can-Can; at the President Theatre, Feb 1955, appeared in the Shoestring Revue; ANTA, May 1955, played Fifi in Seventh Heaven; Broadway, Mar 1956, played Rita Romano in Mr Wonderful; at the same theatre, Apr 1957, stood-in for Eartha Kitt in Shinbone Alley; Winter Garden, Sept 1957, played Anita in West Side Story, subsequently leaving the cast to make her first appearance in London, at Her Majesty's, Dec 1958, in the same part; after a run of more than a year, she appeared at the Martin Beck, NY, Apr 1960, as Rose Grant in Bye Bye, Birdie; Her Majesty's, London, June 1961, again played Rose in Bye Bye, Birdie; toured the US, Aug 1962, as Rose in Bye Bye, Birdie; Curran, San Francisco, Cal, Aug 1963, Athena Constantine in Zenda; Shubert, NY, Nov 1964, played Anyanka in Bajour; Mineola, Long Island, Sept 1966, Jenny in The Threepenny Opera; Melody Top, Milwaukee, Wisconsin, summer 1966, played in Flower Drum Song; toured US and Canada, 1967–8, as Charity in Sweet Charity; Westbury Music Fair, Oct 1970, played in Zorba; Walnut St, Philadelphia, 1972, Billie Dawn in Born Yesterday; Waldorf-Astoria, June 1972, appeared in the revue Milliken Breakfast Show; toured, 1972, in Jacques Brel Is Alive and Well and Living in Paris; Shubert, 11 Mar 1973, appeared in Sondheim: A Musical Tribute; toured, 1974, as Lilli Vanessi and Katherine in Kiss Me, Kate; Ivanhoe, Chicago, 1974, played in Father's Day; 46th St, June 1975, Velma Kelly in Chicago; first appeared on television 1956, and has since made numerous appearances, including playing the Neighbor on The New Dick Van Dyke Show, 1973–4.

Favourite parts: Anita in West Side Story, and Rose Grant in Bye Bye, Birdie. *Recreations:* Cooking, bowling, riding, tennis, swimming. *Address:* 15 West 75th Street, New York, NY 10023.

RIX, Brian, CBE, actor and manager
b Cottingham, Yorkshire, 27 Jan 1924; *s* of Herbert Dobson Rix and his wife Fanny (Nicholson); *e* Bootham School, York; *m* Elspet Gray.

First appeared on the stage at the Prince of Wales, Cardiff, 24 Aug 1942, as a Courtier in King Lear; played with the Donald Wolfit Company, Aug 1942–Apr 1943, during which period he made his first appearance in London, at the St James's, 27 Jan 1943, as Sebastian in Twelfth Night; appeared with the White Rose Players, Harrogate, May 1943–July 1944; served in the RAF, 1944–7; after his release became actor-manager of Rix Theatrical Productions, his own repertory company at Ilkley, Mar 1948, and at Bridlington, Nov 1948; he formed a second company at the Hippodrome, Margate, in Jan 1949; in 1950, presented Reluctant Heroes on tour subsequently presenting this play at the Whitehall Theatre, 23 Sept 1950, where it ran for nearly four years, and in which he appeared as Gregory; in March 1953, in association with Colin Morris, presented Long March (originally entitled Desert Rats); in April 1953, presented Tell the Marines, which he also directed; Whitehall, Aug 1954, presented Dry Rot, which also ran for nearly four years, and in which he played the part of Fred Phipps; Whitehall, Mar 1958, presented, and played Percy Pringle, in Simple Spymen, which ran for over three years; Whitehall, Aug 1961,

presented and played Hickory Wood in One For the Pot, which ran for nearly three years; Whitehall, July 1964, presented and played Gerry Buss in Chase Me Comrade; 1967, moved to the Garrick and from March, presented a repertoire of farce, as well as appearing himself as Fred Florence in Stand By Your Bedouin, Nigel Pitt in Uproar in the House, and Jack in Let Sleeping Wives Lie; the latter production continued to run alone from Sept 1967–Apr 1969; Garrick, Oct 1969, presented She's Done It Again in which he played Hubert Porter; toured, spring 1971, in six Vernon Sylvaine farces adapted by Michael Pertwee (also televised); Garrick, Sept 1971, presented Don't Just Lie There, Say Something, in which he played Barry Ovis; New, Cardiff, Dec 1973, appeared in his first pantomime, Robinson Crusoe, as Billy; Cambridge Theatre, Sept 1974, presented A Bit Between the Teeth, playing Fogg; Whitehall, 1976, co-presented Fringe Benefits, playing Colin Hudson; Astoria, Oct 1979, co-presented Beatlemania; Shaftesbury, Nov 1979, presented Lunatic Fringe; in Apr 1961, he broke the Aldwych Theatre Farce record of over ten years continuous presentation of farce by one management in one theatre; he has also co-presented the following productions: You, Too, Can Have a Body, 1958; Instant Marriage, Diplomatic Baggage, 1964; Come Spy with Me, 1966; Close the Coalhouse Door, 1968; from Jan 1956, presented farce and appeared in over 70 leading parts on television, from the stage of the Whitehall Theatre and the Garrick; these television productions include: Reluctant Heroes, You, Too, Can Have a Body, Thark, Doctor in the House, High Temperature, All For Mary, Women Aren't Angels, and Six of Rix; also appeared in *Men of Affairs* and *A Roof Over My Head*, and presents the series *Let's Go*, for the mentally handicapped; first appeared in films 1951, as Gregory in Reluctant Heroes, and he has since produced and appeared in many film farces; published his autobiography, My Farce from My Elbow, 1975; retired from acting and became a Director of the Cooney-Marsh Group, 1977; awarded the CBE in the Jubilee Honours List, 1977, for services to the handicapped.

Hobbies: Amateur radio transmission and gardening. *Recreation:* Cricket. *Clubs:* MCC, Lord's Taverners. *Address:* 3 St Mary's Grove, Barnes Common, London SW13. *Tel:* 01–785 9626.

ROBARDS, Jason, Jnr, actor
b Chicago, Illinois, 26 July 1922; *s* of Jason Robards, Snr and his wife Hope Maxine (Glanville); *e* Hollywood High School; *m* (1) Eleanor Pitman (mar dis); (2) Rachel Taylor (mar dis); (3) Lauren Bacall (mar dis); (4) Lois O'Connor; formerly a sailor; studied for the theatre at the American Academy of Dramatic Arts.

Made his first appearance on the stage at the Delyork Theatre, Rehoboth Beach, Delaware, July 1947, in Out of the Frying Pan; made his first appearance in New York, at the Children's World Theatre, Oct 1947, as the rear end of The Cow in Jack and the Beanstalk; Century, NY, Dec 1947, walked on in The Mikado; followed by Iolanthe, and The Yeoman of the Guard; 48th Street Theatre, NY, May 1951, understudied (and was assistant stage manager) in Stalag 17; after a run of 473 performances, he toured for nearly a year as Witherspoon in the same play; Playhouse, Apr 1952, assistant stage manager for The Chase; Circle-in-the-Square, NY, 1953, played Ed Moody in American Gothic; at the same theatre, May 1956, Hickey in The Iceman Cometh; Helen Hayes, Nov 1956, Jamie in Long Day's Journey into Night (winning the New York Drama Critics Award for Most Promising Actor, 1956–7); joined the Stratford Festival Company, Stratford, Ontario, June 1958, to play Hotspur in

Henry IV, Part I, and Polixenes in The Winter's Tale; Coronet, NY, Dec 1958, Manley Halliday in The Disenchanted (for which performance he won the New York Drama Critics Award, 1958–9, and the Antoinette Perry Award); Cambridge, Massachusetts, Aug 1959, the title-part in Macbeth; Hudson, Feb 1960, Julian Berniers in Toys in the Attic (receiving the New York Drama Critics Award, 1959–60); ANTA, Mar 1961, William Baker in Big Fish, Little Fish; Eugene O'Neill, Apr 1962, Murray Burns in A Thousand Clowns; ANTA, Washington Square, Jan 1964, Quentin in After the Fall; same theatre, Mar 1964, played Seymour Rosenthal in But for Whom Charlie, alternating the two plays in repertory; Royale, Dec 1964, Erie Smith in Hughie, in which he also toured California, 1965; Broadway, NY, Nov 1965, Vicar of St Peters in The Devils; Ambassador, Oct 1968, Capt Starkey in We Bombed in New Haven; Billy Rose, Mar 1972, Frank Elgin in The Country Girl; Morosco, Dec 1973, James Tyrone, Jr, in A Moon for the Misbegotten; repeated this part at the Ahmanson, Los Angeles, Nov 1974; Zellerbach Auditorium, Los Angeles, 28 June 1975, Erie Smith in Hughie; Brooklyn Academy of Music, Feb 1976, James Tyrone in Long Day's Journey into Night, a production which he also directed; Lake Forest, Ill, July 1976, again played Eric Smith; Helen Hayes, Dec 1977, Cornelius Melody in A Touch of the Poet; Public, Oct 1979, appeared in O'Neill and Carlotta; first appeared in films, 1958, in The Journey and has since appeared in Long Day's Journey into Night, By Love Possessed, Tender Is the Night, A Thousand Clowns, Act One, Pat Garrett and Billy the Kid, All the President's Men, Julia (1977), etc; made his first television appearance in May 1948, and performances include Hickey in The Iceman Cometh, Dr Rank in The Doll's House, and Robert Jordan in For Whom the Bell Tolls.

Favourite parts: Hickey, Macbeth, Jamie, Hotspur, Halliday. *Recreations:* Guitar, banjo. *Hobby:* Photography. *Club:* Players. *Address:* STE Representation, 888 Seventh Avenue, New York, NY 10019.

ROBBINS, Carrie Fishbein, costume designer
b Baltimore, Maryland, 7 Feb 1943; *d* of Sidney W Fishbein and his wife Betty A (Berman); *e* Pennsylvania State Univ, Yale Univ School of Drama (MFA); *m* Richard D Robbins, MD.

First design for the stage was decor for Bells Are Ringing, at the Schwab Auditorium, University Park, Pa, 1962; first designs for NY were costumes for Leda Had a Little Swan at the Cort, 29 Mar 1968; subsequent Broadway and off-Broadway designs have included Look to the Lilies, 1970; Grease (also tours and London), The Hostage, The Secret Affairs of Mildred Wild, 1972; Let Me Hear You Smile, Molly, The Iceman Cometh, The Beggar's Opera, 1973; Over Here, Yentl, 1974; Truckload, 1975; Happy End, 1977; Broadway (try out), 1978; for the Repertory Theatre of Lincoln Center, 1969–73, designed costumes for Inner Journey, The Year Boston Won the Pennant, The Time of Your Life, The Good Woman of Setzuan, An Enemy of the People, Narrow Road to the Deep North, The Crucible, and The Plough and the Stars; for Chelsea Theatre Centre has designed Sunset, The Beggar's Opera, 1972, Yentl the Yeshiva Boy, 1974, Polly, 1975, The Boss, 1976, and Happy End, 1977; for the New York Shakespeare Festival, has designed The Merry Wives of Windsor, 1974, Rebel Women, 1976, Creditors/The Stronger, The Misanthrope, 1977; regional work includes designs for Center Stage, Baltimore; Studio Arena, Buffalo; Inner City Repertory (resident) and Mark Taper Forum, LA; Guthrie, Minneapolis; Long Wharf, New Haven; McCarter, Princeton; ACT, San Francisco; Seattle

Rep; Kennedy Center, Washington, DC; and the Williamstown Festival; has also designed for The Opera Company of Boston, Hamburg State Opera, etc; her renderings have been exhibited at Yale, The Cooper-Hewitt Museum, NY; for television has designed The Seagull, In Fashion, and The Beggar's Opera; received the Drama Desk Award for Grease and The Beggar's Opera, etc; is a faculty member of the New York Univ Theatre Design Dept; has also given guest lectures, and was visiting lecturer in advanced costume design, U of Illinois, 1977–8; is a member of Phi Beta Kappa Society.

Recreations: Looking, tap-dancing, fighting insomnia and workaholism. *Address:* 22 East 36th Street, New York, NY 10016. *Tel:* 532–5291.

ROBBINS, Jerome, director and choreographer
b New York City, 11 Oct 1918; *s* of Harry Rabinowitz and his wife Lena (Rips); *e* Weehawken, NJ, and New York University.

Began his career as a dancer, appearing with the Sandor-Sorel Dance Center, 1937, and subsequently with the Ballet Theatre, for which he choreographed and danced Fancy Free, 1944; he has since arranged the choreography for many notable productions, including On the Town (which he also devised), 1944; created ballet and danced Interplay in Concert Varieties, Billion Dollar Baby, 1945; High Button Shoes, 1947; co-author, directed, and choreographed Look Ma, I'm Dancin', directed That's the Ticket, 1948; Miss Liberty, 1949; Call Me Madam, 1950; The King and I, 1951; Two's Company, 1952; Wonderful Town, 1953; he also directed the plays The Pajama Game, and Peter Pan, and the opera The Tender Land, 1954; directed and arranged the choreography for Bells Are Ringing, 1956; devised, directed, and arranged the choreography for West Side Story, 1957 (London, 1958); directed and arranged the choreography for Gypsy, 1959; directed Oh Dad, Poor Dad, Mama's Hung You in the Closet and I'm Feelin' So Sad, 1962; co-produced and directed Mother Courage and Her Children, 1963; supervised the production of Funny Girl and directed and choreographed Fiddler on the Roof, 1964; at the Nissei, Tokyo, Japan, Nov 1964, supervised the production of West Side Story; choreographed and directed London production of Fiddler on the Roof, 1967; since 1949 Associate Artistic Director, New York City Ballet; he has also been the choreographer for many ballet companies, including Ballet Theater, Ballet Russe, The Royal Danish Ballet, New York City Ballet, The Royal Ballet, and his own company Ballet: USA, the last-named being seen at the Edinburgh Festival, prior to its appearance in London, at the Piccadilly Theatre, Sept 1959 and 1961; for the New York City Ballet and The Royal Ballet choreographed Dances at a Gathering, 1970; for the former, Goldberg Variations, and In the Night, 1971; Watermill, choreographed and danced the Ring Master in Circus Polka, and choreographed with George Balanchine and danced in Pulcinella, 1972; An Evening's Waltzes, Four Bagatelles, 1973; Dybbuk, 1974; choreographed The Concert for Royal Ballet Covent Garden, 1975; choreographed In G Major, Introduction and Allegro for Harp, Mother Goose, Und Barque Sur L'Ocean, Chansons Madecasses for New York City Ballet Ravel Festival, 1975; choreographed Other Dances for American Ballet Theater, 1976; choreographed (with Peter Martins and Jean-Pierre Bonnefous) Tricolore, 1978; choreographed The Four Seasons and Opus 19 for New York City Ballet, 1979; has danced with various ballet companies from 1937–51; arranged the choreography for the film The King and I, 1956; co-directed and choreographed West Side Story, 1960 (two Academy Awards, 1961); he has also acted as choreographer for many notable television productions, including Ford 50th Anniversary Show, 1953, and Peter Pan, 1956 and 1960; he received the Donaldson Award for Billion Dollar Baby, 1946, High Button Shoes (also New York Drama Critics Award), 1948, and The King and I, 1951; received the Emmy Television Award for Peter Pan, 1957; the *Evening bstandard* Award for the best musical with West Side Story, 1959; two Antoinette Perry (Tony) Awards for Fiddler on the Roof, 1966; Chevalier des Arts Award, 1964; Handel Medallion of the City of New York, 1976; American–Israel Arts, Sciences and Humanities Award, 1979; member of Theatre Advisory Group of the Hopkins Center at Dartmouth College; served on National Council of the Arts, 1974–9, and New York State Council on the Arts Dance Panel, 1973–7.

Address: Society of Stage Directors and Choreographers, 1501 Broadway, New York, NY 10036.

ROBERTS, Doris, actress
b St Louis, Missouri, 4 Nov 1930; *d* of Ann Meltzer; *e* New York Univ; *m* William Goyen, the novelist; prepared for the stage at the Neighborhood Playhouse with Sanford Meisner and at the Actors Studio with Lee Strasberg; formerly engaged as a typist.

First appeared on the stage at the New York City Center, 19 Jan 1955, as a Prostitute in The Time of Your Life; Broadhurst, Oct 1955, played Miss Rumple in The Desk Set; York Playhouse, Jan 1961, The Nurse in The Death of Bessie Smith, and occasionally played the part of Mommy in The American Dream; Cherry Lane, Sept 1971, played this last part; Writers' Stage, Sept 1963, played in Color of Darkness, and Cracks; ANTA, Dec 1963, Rae Wilson in Marathon '33; Shubert, Jan 1966, understudied Madame Girard and Eloisa in Malcolm; Henry Miller's, Apr 1966, Miss Punk in The Office; Longacre, Mar 1967, Edna in The Natural Look; Eugene O'Neill, Dec 1969, Jeanette Fisher in Last of the Red Hot Lovers; Actors Studio, Feb 1972, May in Felix; summer tour, 1972, Claudia in The Opening; Ambassador, Nov 1972, Miss Manley in The Secret Affairs of Mildred Wild; Astor Place, Feb 1974, Dolly Scupp in Ravenswood and Becky Hedges in Dunelawn in the double bill called Bad Habits; transferred with these parts to the Booth, May 1974; Actors Studio, May 1975, Dede in Ladies at the Alamo; toured, 1976, in Morning's at Seven; Biltmore, Jan 1978, Grace in Cheaters; has appeared in the films A New Leaf, No Way to Treat a Lady, The Honeymoon Killers, Little Murders, The Taking of Pelham 123, Hester Street, The Rose, Such Good Friends, etc; first appeared on television in 1952 and has since played in Look Homeward, Angel, Four by Tennessee Williams, and in a number of series including Angie.

Hobbies and recreations: Painting, re-doing old furniture, needlepoint. *Address:* c/o William Morris Agency, 151 El Camino Drive, Beverly Hills, Calif 90212.

ROBERTS, Ewan, actor
b Edinburgh, Scotland, 29 Apr 1914; *s* of Frederick James Simpson Hutchison and his wife Nora (McEwan); *e* Edinburgh Institution (Melville College), and Peebles High School; *m* Margery Vosper; formerly a tweed designer.

Made his first appearance on the stage, at the Lyceum, Edinburgh, Sept 1935, as Lord Hastings in The Scarlet Pimpernel with the Jevan Brandon-Thomas company; 1936–40, with repertory companies at Colwyn Bay, Warrington, Gourock, Hoylake and Jesmond, Newcastle upon Tyne; served with the RNVR, 1941–6; joined the Old Vic company, at the New Theatre, for the 1946–7 season, playing in King Lear, Cyrano de Bergerac, The Alchemist, and Richard II, and understudying Sir Ralph Richardson as

Inspector Goole in An Inspector Calls, which he also played; toured, 1947–8, in the Middle East, as Richard Halton in On Approval; Wyndham's, Apr 1948, played the Usher in Royal Circle; toured, 1948, as Willie Murray in Thanks a Million; Jan 1949, Gateway, the Man from the Sea in Granite; in 1949, was engaged with the Tennent Players, playing Sir John Fletcher in Love in Idleness, Orsino in Twelfth Night, and Estaban in The Marquise; Adelphi, Dec 1949, Menzies in Castle in the Air; Strand (for Repertory Players), Dec 1950, Archie Windust in Guest of Honour; Embassy, Feb 1951, Bruce McRae in The Late Christopher Bean; at the Q, Mar 1951, Stephen Tallys in Two's Company, and Apr, Mr Preston in Home at Seven; New, Feb 1952, succeeded David Horne as Desfournettes in Colombe; Richmond, Feb 1953, Sir Francis Brittain in The Hanging Judge; Strand (for Repertory Players), Oct 1953, Inspector Thornton in The Secret Tent, subsequently touring in this part; at the Q, Jan 1955, played Sam Curtis in The Visiting Moon; Royal, Windsor, Mar 1955, John Pym in The Conscience of the King; Opera House, Manchester, July 1955, and subsequently on tour, appeared as The Man Called Gray in The Delegate; at the Q, Dec 1955, appeared in Call Me a Gondola; Richmond, Apr 1956, played Porphyrius Petrovitch in Three Thousand Roubles; Phoenix, Sept 1957, Mackintosh in Roar Like a Dove, which ran for more than a thousand performances, and in which he subsequently toured; Duke of York's, Oct 1962, played Mark Malcolm in Fit to Print; St Martin's, June 1964, McVitie in Past Imperfect; Arnaud, Guildford, Apr 1966, and tour, Dr Harvester in The Sacred Flame; Vaudeville, Nov 1966, Alastair MacLeod in Justice is a Woman; Arnaud, Guildford, 1969, Sir Wilfrid Robarts QC, in Witness for the Prosecution; Haymarket, Sept 1970, George Matcham Snr in A Bequest to the Nation; Leeds Playhouse, Jan 1972, played Capulet in Romeo and Juliet and Billie Rice in The Entertainer; toured, Oct 1972, as Mr Palmer in Death on Demand; Arnaud, Guildford, May 1974, Ralph Seymour in The Sacking of Norman Banks, which transferred to the Ambassadors', July 1974, under the title The Sack Race; toured, Jan 1975, as Dr Stoner in Verdict; Royal Court, Aug 1975, the Judge in a Sunday night production, Soul of the Nation; Gardener Centre, Nov–Dec 1975, Inspector Grimes in Jack in the Box; Walter Parrow in Raven, and appeared in The Plotters of Cabbage Patch Corner; toured, Feb 1976, as Dr Stoner in Verdict; Fortune, Oct 1976, took over as Rev Clement in Murder at the Vicarage; Strand, Jan 1977, took over as Arnold Needham in No Sex Please, We're British; Mar 1978, toured as Mr Birkett in Donkey's years; Vaudeville, Mar 1979, Mr Craddock in A Murder Is Announced; he has also appeared for the Repertory Players on numerous occasions; first appeared in films, 1946, since when he has worked as dialogue director on several pictures; first television appearance, 1953.

Favourite Parts: The one I'm playing. *Hobbies:* Lampshade making, DIY, Bulb growing. *Address:* c/o Film Rights Ltd, 113–117 Wardour Street, London, W1.

ROBERTS, Rachel, actress
b Llanelli, Wales, 20 Sept 1927; *d* of the Reverend Richard Rhys Roberts and his wife Rachel Ann (Jones); *e* University of Wales (BA); *m* (1) Alan Dobie (mar dis); (2) Rex Harrison (mar dis); trained for the stage at the Royal Academy of Dramatic Art, where she received the Athene Seyler Award for Comedy.

Joined the Shakespeare Memorial Theatre, Stratford-on-Avon, 1951, when she played Ceres in The Tempest; made her first appearance in London at the Watergate Theatre, Sept 1953, when she played Mrs Winterton in The Buccaneer; Lyric, Hammersmith, Dec 1953, appeared in the revue At the Lyric, subsequently transferring with the production to the St Martin's, May 1954, under the title Going to Town; joined the Old Vic Company, Sept 1954, where she remained for two years to play a variety of parts including: First Witch in Macbeth, Jacquenetta in Love's Labour's Lost, Mistress Quickly in Henry IV (Parts I and II), Bianca in Othello, Mistress Quickly and Alice in Henry V, and Cassandra in the modern-dress production of Troilus and Cressida; Bristol Old Vic Company, Nov 1956–Apr 1957, played a number of leading parts including: Melinda in The Recruiting Officer, Argia in The Queen and the Rebels, Emilia in Othello, Prince Florizel in The Sleeping Beauty, and Iduna in Oh! My Papa!; Garrick, London, July 1957, again played Iduna in Oh! My Papa!; at the Apollo, Feb 1958, played Mabel Gibbs in Keep Your Hair On; Theatre Royal, Stratford, E, Apr 1959, played Mary Faugh in The Dutch Courtesan; Criterion, Dec 1959, Ann Patten in A Clean Kill; Royal Court, Sept 1960, Mrs Letouzel in The Happy Haven; Royal Court, Oct 1960, Anna Petrovna in Platonov, for which she received the Clarence Derwent Award for the best supporting actress, 1960; Edinburgh Festival, Sept 1961, played Mrs Fulton in August for the People, subsequently appearing in the same production at the Royal Court, Sept 1961; Adelphi, Sept 1964, played the title-part in the musical Maggie May; Theatre Royal, Bath, Sept 1969, Martha in Who's Afraid of Virginia Woolf; Royal Court, Dec 1969, Madame de Winter in The Three Musketeers Ride Again; Los Angeles, Autumn 1971, Beatrice in The Effect of Gamma Rays on Man-in-the-Moon Marigolds; Royal Court, Jan 1972, Mrs Elliot in Alpha Beta, also at the Apollo, Mar 1972; Barrymore, New York, Nov 1973, appeared in repertory as Clara Zachanassian in The Visit, and Francine in Chemin de Fer; Greenwich, Jan 1975, Lady Regine Frimley in The End of Me Old Cigar; Helen Hayes, NY, Oct 1979, Mother Peter in Once A Catholic; notable films in which she has appeared include The Weak and the Wicked, Our Man in Havana, Saturday Night and Sunday Morning (British Film Academy Award for Best British Actress, 1960), This Sporting Life (British Film Academy Award, 1963, as Best Actress of the Year), O Lucky Man, Murder on the Orient Express, etc; television appearances include Yvette Guilbert in The Young Yvette, Lizzie Hexham in the serial Our Mutual Friend, Catherine Bailey in Release, etc.

Address: c/o ICM Ltd, 22 Grafton Street, London, W1.

ROBERTS, Tony (David Anthony Roberts), actor
b New York City, 22 Oct 1939; *s* of Kenneth Roberts and his wife Norma; *e* Northwestern Univ; *m* (mar dis).

First appeared in NY at the Ambassador, 4 Jan 1962, as an Air Cadet in Something About a Soldier; Biltmore, 1962, took over as Richard Gluck in Take Her, She's Mine; Belasco, Oct 1964, played Max in The Last Analysis; The Playhouse, 1964–65, took over as Charlie in Never Too Late; Biltmore, 1965, took over as Paul Bratter in Barefoot in the Park; Morosco, Nov 1966, Axel Magee in Don't Drink the Water; Lunt-Fontanne, Dec 1967, Charley in the musical How Now, Dow Jones; Broadhurst, Feb 1969, Dick Christie in Play It Again, Sam; US tour, commencing in San Diego, Cal, May 1970, Chuck Baxter in Promises, Promises, then took over this part from Jerry Orbach at the Shubert, NY, 1971; Majestic, Apr 1972, Joe in Sugar, having changed his stage name to Tony Roberts; appeared with the Yale Repertory, New Haven, Conn, 1973–74 season; Music Box, Oct 1974, Geoffrey in Absurd Person Singular; Otterbein U,

Ohio, 1976, title-role in Hamlet; Alliance, Atlanta, Petruchio in The Taming of the Shrew; Lake Forest, Ill, 1978, in Serenading Louie; John Golden, May 1979, Mitchell Lavell in Murder at the Howard Johnson's; Manhattan Theatre Club, Sept 1979, Todd in Losing Time; Imperial, Dec 1979, took over as Vernon Gersch in They're Playing Our Song; appeared in the films $1,000,000 Duck (1971), Star-Spangled Girl, Play It Again, Sam, Serpico, The Taking of Pelham One Two Three, Annie Hall, Just Tell Me What You Want (1977), etc; TV work includes Rossetti and Ryan, The Lindbergh Kidnapping Case, etc.

Address: c/o ICM, 40 West 57th Street, New York, NY 10019.

ROBERTSON, Malcolm, director, actor and writer
b Roseville, New South Wales, 16 Mar 1933; *s* of Victor Norman Robertson and his wife Gwynneth Addieleigh (Garnett); *e* North Sydney Boys' HS; *m* Wendy Elizabeth Hamilton.

After early experience 1951–2 with the John Alden company, joined the Union Theatre Repertory Company (now Melbourne Theatre Company) in their inaugural seasons; appeared for the Elizabethan Theatre Trust, 1955–7; rejoined Union Theatre Company, 1961–9, during which time he made his debut as a director, with a touring production of Pygmalion, Mar 1962, and directed a number of other plays; Theatre Consultant, 1970–1, Australia Council for the Arts; formed Stable Productions Pty, 1971, presenting and directing The Trial of the Catonsville Nine; associate director, Melbourne Theatre Company, 1972–5, for whom he has directed frequent productions including Macquarie, Jugglers Three, The Old Familiar Juice, Tom (all world premières), 1972; Annie Storey (première), 1974; How Does Your Garden Grow, 1975; co-ordinator, 1975–, Alternative Theatre Project at La Mama, Carlton; Adelaide Festival Centre, 1976, presented his own production of You Want it, Don't You, Billy, also playing Bill; since then he has directed the following plays, in Melbourne, unless otherwise stated: Absurd Person Singular (Hobart), Summer and Smoke (Brisbane), What the Butler Saw, 1976; Agamemnon (Victoria State Opera), Yamashita (also played Chow), 1977; Innocent Bystanders (also played Lugar), Bullsh (world première), 1978; Measure for Measure, Bertolt Brecht leaves Los Angeles (world première), his own adaptation of Chekhov's Notes from an Old Man's Diary (also toured), 1979; Alexander Theatre Company, Melbourne, 1977, played Gaev in The Cherry Orchard; Playbox, Melbourne, 1978, Royce in Freaks; Playboy, Jan 1980, Vukhov in Judgement; took part in the first Australia Theatre People's Tour of China, 1978; drama panel, Australia Council, 1973–5; has also worked as an adjudicator and tutor; first film appearance in The Last Wave, 1977.

Recreations: Walking, swimming. *Address:* 120 Page Street, Albert Park, Victoria, 3206 Australia. *Tel:* 03–699 3049.

ROBERTSON, Toby (Sholto), OBE, 1978; director
b Chelsea, London, 29 Nov 1928; *s* of David Lambert Robertson and his wife Felicity Douglas (Tomlin); *e* Stowe and Trinity College, Cambridge; *m* Jane McCulloch.

Formerly an actor; directed his first professional production, The Iceman Cometh, at the New Shakespeare, Liverpool, May 1958; in London directed The Buskers, 1959; The Lower Depths (for RSC), 1960; Pitlochry, 1962, Henry IV (Pirandello), Muir of Huntershill; Richmond, Yorkshire and London, 1963, The Provok'd Wife; artistic director, Prospect Theatre Company, 1964–79, for whom he directed

over fifty productions, including: The Soldier's Fortune, You
Never Can Tell, The Confederacy, The Importance of Being
Earnest, 1964; The Square, Howard's End, The Man of
Mode, 1965; Macbeth, The Tempest, The Gamecock, 1966;
A Murder of No Importance, A Room with a View (Edin-
burgh Festival), 1967; Twelfth Night, No Man's Land, The
Beggar's Opera (also Edinburgh and London), The Servant
of Two Masters (London, for Michael Codron), 1968; Edward II (also Edinburgh and London), 1969; Much Ado
About Nothing (also Edinburgh), Boswell's Life of Johnson
(also Edinburgh), Venice Preserved, 1970; King Lear, Love's
Labour's Lost (both including Edinburgh, Australian tour,
and London), Alice in Wonderland (Ashcroft, Croydon),
1971; Richard III, Ivanov, The Beggars' Opera (for Phoenix
Opera), 1972; The Grand Tour, Pericles, The Royal Hunt of
the Sun, Twelfth Night, 1973 (these three productions were
seen on a tour embracing several international festivals,
Moscow, Leningrad and Hong Kong); The Pilgrim's Progress, A Month in the Country (for Chichester Festival),
1974; Circle of Glory (not Prospect), Pilgrim (including
Edinburgh and Round House), A Room With a View (co-
directed), A Month in the Country (these two for a London
season), 1975; for Prospect at the Old Vic (the Old Vic
Company, 1978–9), he directed: War Music, Hamlet, Buster,
Antony and Cleopatra, 1977; Twelfth Night, Great English
Eccentrics (triple bill), Ivanov, King Lear, 1978; Hamlet,
Romeo and Juliet, The Government Inspector, The Padlock,
The Trial of Queen Caroline, 1979; Great English Eccentrics
has been presented worldwide, including Moscow, Hong
Kong and Australia; other overseas productions for Prospect
include Hamlet at Elsinore, and the first Western theatre tour
of China, 1979; directed Next Time I'll Sing to You, 1980;
opera productions include: A Midsummer Night's Dream,
1972, Hermiston, 1975, and The Marriage of Figaro, 1977
(both Scottish Opera); assistant director for the film Lord of
the Flies, 1961; has directed more than twenty-five television
productions including The Beggar's Opera, Richard II and
Edward II; gave the Wilson Memorial Lecture, Cambridge
University, 1974.

Recreations: Painting, sailing. *Club:* Bunbury. *Address:* 5
Spencer Park, London, SW18. *Tel:* 01–870 3558.

ROBSON, Dame Flora, DBE, (*cr* 1960); CBE; Hon LittD
(Durham, Wales, London, Oxford); actress
b South Shields, Durham, 28 Mar 1902; *d* of David Mather
Robson and his wife Eliza (McKenzie); *e* Palmer's Green
High School; studied for the stage at the Royal Academy of
Dramatic Art, where she gained the Bronze Medal, 1921.

Made her first appearance on the stage at the Shaftesbury
Theatre, 17 Nov 1921, as Queen Margaret, one of the
Shadows, in Will Shakespeare; during 1922, played in Shake-
spearean repertory with Ben Greet; 1923, played in repertory
at the Oxford Playhouse, under J B Fagan; Ambassadors',
Sept 1924, played Annie in Fata Morgana; she then left the
stage for four years; reappeared, Oct 1929, when she joined
Anmer Hall's company at the Festival Theatre, Cambridge,
remaining for one year; Little, London, Jan 1931, played
Tatiana in Betrayal; Gate, Feb 1931, Abbie Putnam in Desire
Under the Elms; May 1931, Herodias in Salome; Westminster, Oct 1931, played Mary Paterson in The Anatomist; Feb
1932, played the Stepdaughter in Six Characters in Search of
an Author; St James's, Apr 1932, Bianca in Othello; Lyric,
May 1932, Olwen Peel in Dangerous Corner; St Martin's (for
the Sunday Players), June 1932, Mercia in The Storm Figh-
ter; Globe, Nov 1932, Eva in For Services Rendered; Arts,
Jan 1933, Lady Audley in Lady Audley's Secret; Queen's,
Feb 1933, Penelope Otto in Head-on Crash; Embassy, Mar

1933, Ella Downey in All God's Chillun; July 1933, Narouli
Karth in Vessels Departing; joined the Old Vic–Sadler's
Wells Company, Oct 1933, and during the season played
Varya in The Cherry Orchard, Queen Katharine in Henry
VIII, Isabella in Measure for Measure, Gwendolen Fairfax in
The Importance of Being Earnest, Mrs Foresight in Love for
Love, Ceres in The Tempest, and Lady Macbeth in Macbeth;
at the Haymarket, May 1934, played Elizabeth Enticknap in
Touch Wood; His Majesty's, Nov 1934, Mary Read in the
play of that name; Embassy, June 1935, and Haymarket, July
1935, Liesa Bergmann in Close Quarters; Playhouse, Dec
1935, Mary Tudor in a play of that name; Westminster, Apr
1937, Anna Christopherson in Anna Christie; Shaftesbury,
June 1937, Mrs Ellen de Meyer in Satyr; St Martin's, Oct
1937, Lady Catherine Brooke in Autumn, and Aug 1938,
Anya in Last Train South; subsequently went to America;
appeared in films in Hollywood from 1939; she also appeared
at the Henry Miller Theatre, New York, Mar 1940, as Ellen
Creed in Ladies in Retirement; St James, Oct 1941, the
Duchess of Marlborough in Anne of England; toured in
summer theatres, 1942, as Elizabeth in Elizabeth the Queen;
Playhouse, NY, Oct 1942, played Rhoda Meldrum in The
Damask Cheek; Belasco, Los Angeles, June 1943, appeared
in Grand Guignol plays; she then returned to England;
reappeared, at the Lyric, Hammersmith, Apr 1944, as
Thérèse Raquin in Guilty; toured, Feb 1945, as Ethel Fry in a
play of that name; toured, Oct 1945, as Agnes Isit in A Man
About the House, and appeared in this at the Piccadilly, Feb
1946; Westminster, Aug 1946, played Margaret Hayden in
Message for Margaret; at the National Theatre, NY, Mar
1948, played Lady Macbeth; returned to England, and at the
Theatre Royal, Windsor, July 1948, and Lyric, Hammers-
mith, Oct 1948, played Lady Cicely Waynflete in Captain
Brassbound's Conversion; Westminster, May 1949, Alicia
Christie in Black Chiffon; 48th Street Theatre, NY, Sept
1950, again appeared as Alicia in Black Chiffon; after return-
ing to England, appeared at the Q, Apr 1951, as Lady
Brooke in a revival of Autumn; Phoenix, June 1951, played
Paulina in The Winter's Tale; Her Majesty's, July 1952,
played Miss Giddens in The Innocents; Duchess, Nov 1953,
Sister Agatha in The Return; toured, 1954, as Rachel Lloyd
in No Escape; Duchess, Feb 1955, played Sarah Ashby in A
Kind of Folly; Duke of York's, May 1956, Janet in The
House by the Lake, which ran for more than 700 perfor-
mances; Old Vic, Nov 1958, played Mrs Alving in Ghosts,
transferring with the production to the Princes, Apr 1959;
Queen's, Aug 1959 appeared as Miss Tina in The Aspern
Papers, for which performance she received the *Evening
Standard* Award, 1960; toured South Africa, Aug–Dec 1960,
in The Aspern Papers; St Martin's, May 1961, played Grace
Rovarte in Time and Yellow Roses; Connaught, Worthing,
Nov 1961, played Miss Moffat in The Corn is Green, prior to
touring South Africa, Jan 1962, in the same play; on return-
ing to England appeared at the Flora Robson Playhouse,
Newcastle upon Tyne, Oct 1962, in the same play; toured,
Feb 1963, as Liesa Bergmann in Close Quarters; Duchess,
Dec 1963, played Gunhild Borkman in John Gabriel Borkman; Flora Robson Playhouse, Newcastle, 1964, Lady Bracknell in The Importance of Being Earnest; Edinburgh Festival,
1966, Hecuba in The Trojan Women; Apr 1967, toured as
Winifred Brazier in Brother and Sister; Haymarket, Feb
1968, Miss Prism in The Importance of Being Earnest; same
theatre, Oct 1968, the Mother in Ring Round the Moon;
Westminster, Nov 1969, Agatha Payne in The Old Ladies,
transferring to the Duchess in Dec; Edinburgh Festival, Aug
1970, appeared in the title-role in Elizabeth Tudor, Queen of
England; Brighton Festival, May 1974, narrated Peter and

the Wolf; entered films, 1931, appeared in Catherine the Great, 1933; more recent appearances include 55 Days at Peking, Young Cassidy, Guns at Batasi, Those Magnificent Men in Their Flying Machines, Seven Women, Les Miserables, A Search for Eden, and The Clash of Titans; was created CBE, 1952, and received the DBE in the Birthday Honours, 1960.

Recreation: Making tapestry. *Address:* c/o Film Rights, Ltd, 113 Wardour Street, London, W1.

RODD, Marcia, actress and singer
b Lyons, Kansas, 8 July 1940; *d* of Charles C Rodd and his wife Rosetta (Thran); *e* Northwestern University; *m* Dale W Hagen; prepared for the stage with Alvina Krause.

First appeared on the stage while at school, on Thanksgiving Day, 1948, at Eliot Grade School, Tulsa, Oklahoma, as Priscilla Alden in a pageant; made her New York début at the Provincetown Playhouse, 8 Oct 1962, as One of the Girls in Oh Say Can You See!; at the Broadhurst, in 1964, took over various parts in the revue Oh! What a Lovely War; Square East, Oct 1964, played in the revue Cambridge Circus; New, Jan 1966, took over various parts in the revue The Mad Show; toured, summer 1966, as Dorothy in Gentlemen Prefer Blondes; New Locust, Philadelphia, Nov 1966, played Lotte in Chu Chem; Brooks Atkinson, Feb 1967, Bea in Love in E-Flat; toured, 1967, as Daisy Gamble in On a Clear Day You Can See Forever; Sheridan Square Playhouse, Jan 1968, Viola in Love and Let Love; Orpheum, 1968, took over as Olivia in Your Own Thing, played this part at the Huntington Hartford, Los Angeles, California, Aug 1968, and made her début in London at the Comedy, 6 Feb 1969, in this same part; Eugene O'Neill, Dec 1969, Bobbi Michele in Last of the Red Hot Lovers, which she played for more than a year; toured, 1971, as Aldonza in Man of La Mancha; John Golden, Feb 1973, Maud in Shelter; toured, 1973, as Anne Miller in 6 Rms Riv Vu; Delacorte, July 1974, Mistress Margaret Page in The Merry Wives of Windsor; Mark Taper Forum, Los Angeles, July 1975, May Daniels in Once in a Lifetime; Circle, LA, Mar 1977, K C Wofford in And If That Mockingbird Don't Sing; Center Stage, Baltimore, appeared in The Goodbye People, Nov 1977, and directed Blithe Spirit, May 1978; first appeared in films as Patsy Newquist in Little Murders, 1971; first played on television in Sept 1965, and since has appeared on *The Ed Sullivan Show, The Tonight Show, My Friend Tony,* Pioneer Spirit, The Peter Ustinov Report, *The David Frost Show, The Dick Van Dyke Show,* etc.

Hobbies and *recreations:* Tennis, carpentry, painting, needle-point, crossword puzzles, reading mysteries, and card games. *Address:* STE Representation, 888 Seventh Avenue, New York, NY 10019.

RODGERS, Anton, actor and director
b Wisbech, Cambridgeshire, 10 Jan 1933; *s* of William Robert Rodgers and his wife Leonore Victoria (Wood); *e* Westminster City School; *m* Morna Eugenie Watson; trained for the stage at Italia Conti and LAMDA.

Made his first West End appearance 1947, aged 14, in Carmen at the Royal Opera House, Covent Garden; followed this with a tour, 1948, of Great Expectations, playing Pip, and in 1949 toured in the title-part of The Winslow Boy; after repertory experience at Birmingham, Northampton and Hornchurch, trained at LAMDA; returning to London in Nov 1957, joined the cast of The Boy Friend, Wyndham's; at the Cambridge, Sept 1959, played Fingers in The Crooked Mile; Fortune, Oct 1960, appeared in the revue And Another Thing; Arts, Feb 1962 and Edinburgh Festival, appeared in

Twists; Royal Court, July 1962, Withers and Tim in Plays for England; Saville, July 1963, Jingle in Pickwick, making his New York début in the same part at the 46th Street, Oct 1965; Criterion, London, Feb 1966, Felix in The Owl and the Pussycat; Chichester Festival, season 1967, Francis Archer in The Beaux' Stratagem, Randall Utterword in Heartbreak House and Fadinard in An Italian Straw Hat; Belgrade, Coventry, Mar 1968, played the title-role in Henry V; University Theatre, Manchester, 1968, Vladimir in Waiting for Godot; in the same year, at Leatherhead, directed A Piece of Cake and Grass Roots; Hampstead, Feb 1969, devised and co-directed We Who Are About To . . ., which was later presented in a modified form at the Comedy as Mixed Doubles; Harrogate, Aug 1969, Dr Stockmann in An Enemy of the People; Hampstead, May 1970, directed The Fantasticks; took this production and The Rainmaker to the Ibiza Festival, returning to direct Roses of Eyam and The Taming of the Shrew at the Northcott, Exeter; Hampstead, Jan 1971, played Gerald in The Formation Dancers; Greenwich, later Apollo, Apr 1971, Frank in Forget-Me-Not Lane; Stratford Festival, Ontario, 1972, Macheath in The Threepenny Opera; Criterion, Feb 1973, Dr Rank in A Doll's House; toured Australia, 1974, for National Theatre, as Hildy Johnson in The Front Page; Greenwich, Feb 1975, Lord Henry Wotton in The Picture of Dorian Gray; for the Oxford Playhouse, 1975, directed Death of a Salesman, Oct, and played Astrov in Uncle Vanya, Dec; Criterion, Mar 1976, Jack Manningham in Gaslight; Bush, June 1977, directed Are You Now or Have You Ever Been . . .?; New End, Dec 1978, and Mayfair, Feb 1979, directed Flashpoint; Globe, July 1979, appeared in Songbook; his films include Rotten to the Core, The Man Who Haunted Himself and Scrooge; television, since 1958, includes plays and series, recently The Flaxborough Chronicles, Lily Langtry and Disraeli.

Favourite parts: Vladimir, Henry V. *Recreation:* Fly fishing. *Clubs:* Savile, Players, RAC. *Address:* RAC Club, Pall Mall, London SW1.

RODGERS, Mary, composer, author and screenwriter
b New York, 11 Jan 1931; *d* of the composer Richard Rodgers and his wife Dorothy (Feiner); *e* Wellesley College; *m* (1) Julian B Beaty, Jr (mar dis); (2) the film executive Henry Guettel.

Composed the music for Once Upon a Mattress, 1959; Hot Spot, 1963; The Mad Show, 1966; also music for Bil Baird's marionette shows Davy Jones' Locker, 1959, and Pinocchio, 1973; author of books including Freaky Friday, for the film of which she wrote the screenplay, and A Billion for Boris; wrote a monthly column for *McCall's* with her mother, entitled Of Two Minds.

Club: Cosmopolitan. *Address:* 115 Central Park West, New York, NY 10023.

RODGERS, Richard, composer and producer
b New York City, 28 June 1902; *s* of William Rodgers and his wife Mamie (Levy); *e* Columbia University, and Juilliard School of Music; *m* Dorothy Feiner.

His first contribution to a professional production was in conjunction with the late Lorenz Hart, A Lonely Romeo, produced at the Shubert Theatre, NY, June 1919; composed the scores of Fly with Me, The Poor Little Ritz Girl, 1920; You'll Never Know, 1921; Melody Man, 1924; Garrick Gaieties, Dearest Enemy, 1925; The Fifth Avenue Follies, Peggy-Ann, Betsy, Lido Lady, The Girl Friend, Garrick Gaieties, 1926; One Dam Thing After Another, A Connecticut Yankee, 1927; She's My Baby, Present Arms (co-author),

Chee-Chee, 1928; Spring Is Here, Heads Up!, 1929; Simple Simon, Ever Green, 1930, America's Sweetheart, 1931; Jumbo, 1935; On Your Toes (of which he was also part-author), 1936; Babes in Arms, I'd Rather Be Right, 1937; I Married an Angel (also part-author), The Boys from Syracuse, 1938; Too Many Girls, 1939; Higher and Higher, Pal Joey, 1940; By Jupiter, 1942; Oklahoma! (which was awarded a Pulitzer Prize), 1943; Carousel (which received the New York Drama Critics Award), 1945; Allegro, 1947; South Pacific, 1949; The King and I, 1951; Me and Juliet, 1953; Pipe Dream, 1955; Cinderella (Coliseum, London), 1958; Flower Drum Song, 1958; The Sound of Music, 1959; No Strings, 1962; Do I Hear a Waltz? 1965; Two by Two, 1970; Imperial, 26 Mar 1972, appeared in A Celebration of Richard Rodgers; Rodgers and Hart, a revue presented at the Helen Hayes, May 1975; Rex, 1976; I Remember Mama, 1979; received a special Antoinette Perry (Tony) Award, 1972; Laurence Langner Award, 1979; presented By Jupiter, 1942 (with Deere Dwight Wiman); A Connecticut Yankee, 1943; I Remember Mama (with Oscar Hammerstein II), 1944; Annie Get Your Gun (with Oscar Hammerstein II), Happy Birthday (with Hammerstein), 1946; John Loves Mary (with Oscar Hammerstein II), 1947; South Pacific (with Oscar Hammerstein II, Leland Hayward and Joshua Logan), 1949, which received the New York Drama Critics Award 1948–9, and the Pulitzer Prize, 1949–50; The Happy Time (with Hammerstein), Burning Bright (with Hammerstein), 1950; The King and I (with Hammerstein), 1951; Me and Juliet (with Hammerstein), 1953; Pipe Dream (with Hammerstein), 1955; Flower Drum Song (with Hammerstein), 1958; The Sound of Music (with Hammerstein, L Hayward, and R Halliday), 1959; No Strings, 1962; Do I Hear a Waltz? 1965; Avanti! 1968; Two by Two, 1970; in 1962 was appointed President and Producing Director The Music Theatre of Lincoln Center, where he produced The King and I and The Merry Widow, 1964, Kismet and Carousel, 1965; Annie Get Your Gun, Showboat, 1966; South Pacific, 1967; West Side Story, 1968; Oklahoma! 1969; the following musicals have been adapted for films: Present Arms, Spring is Here, Heads Up!, 1930; Ever Green, 1934; On Your Toes, Babes in Arms, 1939; The Boys from Syracuse, Too Many Girls, 1940; I Married An Angel, 1942; Higher and Higher, 1943; Oklahoma! (also produced), 1955; Carousel, The King and I, 1956; Pal Joey, 1957; South Pacific (also produced), 1958; Flower Drum Song, 1961; Jumbo, 1962; The Sound of Music, 1965; original film scores are The Hot Heiress (1931), Love Me Tonight, The Phantom President (1932), Hallelujah! I'm a Bum! (1933), Hollywood Party (1934), Mississippi (1935), Dancing Pirate (1936), Fools for Scandal (1938), They Met in Argentina (1941), State Fair (1945); subject of the film-biography Words and Music, 1948; his autobiography, Musical Stages, published 1975; composed the background music for the television documentaries Victory at Sea, 1952, and Winston Churchill, The Valiant Years, 1960; composed scores of television productions of Cinderella, 1957, and Androcles and the Lion, 1967.

(*Died 30 Dec 1979.*)

RODWAY, Norman, actor
b Dublin, Eire, 7 Feb 1929; *s* of Frank Rodway and his wife Lilian Sybil (Moyles); *e* High School, and Trinity College, Dublin; *m* (1) Pauline Delany (mar dis); (2) Mary Selway (mar dis); (3) Sarah Callaby (*née* Fitzgerald); formerly a schoolmaster, university lecturer, and cost accountant.

Made his first appearance on the stage at the Opera House, Cork, May 1953, as Mannion in The Seventh Step; since 1955, has appeared frequently at the Gaiety, Gate, and

Olympia Theatres in Dublin, where he has played many parts, including: Christopher in I Am a Camera, George in Epitaph for George Dillon, Jerry Ryan in Two for the Seesaw, Parke Ballantyne in Critic's Choice, and Clive Root in The Complaisant Lover; at the Globe, Dun Laoghaire, Eire, Oct 1958, played Giovanni in The Burnt Flower-Bed; first appeared in London, at the Royal Court, Sept 1959, when he played The Messenger in Cock-A-Doodle-Dandy; at the Eblana, Dublin, May 1960, played Brick in Cat on a Hot Tin Roof; at the Dublin Festival, Gate, Oct 1962, played the title-part in Stephen D, subsequently appearing at the St Martin's, London, Feb 1963, in the same part; Dublin Festival, Sept 1963, played Billy Beavis in The Poker Session, subsequently appearing in the same part at the Globe, London, Feb 1964; Nottingham Playhouse, Mar 1965, played Lopahkin in The Cherry Orchard; joined the Royal Shakespeare Company, Apr 1966, and has since played the following parts: at the Royal Shakespeare, Stratford-on-Avon, 1966 season, Henry Hotspur in Henry the Fourth Part I, Pistol in Henry the Fourth, Part II, Feste in Twelfth Night, Spurio in The Revenger's Tragedy; 1967, Mercutio in Romeo and Juliet; 1968 season, Edmund in King Lear, Thersites in Troilus and Cressida, Don Pedro in Much Ado About Nothing (US tour, 1969); at the Aldwych, 1969 season, Thersites in Troilus and Cressida, Bates in Silence (in the double-bill Landscape and Silence), Tom Quar'lous in Bartholomew Fair, Spurio in The Revenger's Tragedy; Stratford, 1970 season, played the title-part in Richard the Third, Philip the Bastard in King John, Snout in A Midsummer Night's Dream, Trinculo in The Tempest; Olympia, Dublin, Apr 1971, played James Usheen in the festival production, The Patrick Pearse Motel, transferring to the Queen's, London, June 1971; Olympia, Mar 1972, George in the Dublin Festival production, Stag Party; Albery, Aug 1972, Dazzle in London Assurance; Greenwich, Jan 1973, Andrey in Three Sisters; Palace, Watford, Sept 1973, title-role in Butley; Aldwych, Aug 1974, Bassov in Summerfolk, subsequently touring the US in this production, Feb–Mar 1973; returning to London, played Holofernes in Love's Labour's Lost, Aldwych, Apr 1975; Aldwych, 1976, Muratov in The Zykovs, Apr, Harry Hope in The Iceman Cometh, May, and Lebedev in Ivanov, Sept; Aldwych, Dec 1976, and Piccadilly, Apr 1977, played Sir George Thunder in Wild Oats, and also in the revival, Aldwych, June 1979; same theatre, Oct 1979, Protasson in Children of the Sun; Other Place, Stratford, Apr 1979, Seamus Shields in The Shadow of a Gunman; entered films, 1958, and notable pictures include: The Quare Fellow, This Other Eden, A Question of Suspense, Four in the Morning, Chimes at Midnight, The Penthouse, I'll Never Forget What's 'Is Name, etc; first appeared on television, Feb 1962, and recent performances include Danton in Danton's Death, St Joan, Out, Tycoon, etc.

Favourite parts: Richard the Third, Butley, Bassov. *Recreations:* Friends, family, wine and Mozart. *Club:* Gerry's. *Address:* 25 Shandon Road, London, SW4. *Tel:* 01–673 5387.

ROEBLING, Paul, actor
b Philadelphia, Pennsylvania, Mar 1934; *s* of Siegfried Roebling and his wife Mary (Gindhart); *e* Episcopal Academy, Philadelphia; Valley Forge, Pennsylvania, Military Academy; and Columbia University (1952); prepared for the stage at the HB Studio and with Beatrice Desfosses; *m* Olga Bellin.

Made his stage début at the Intime, Princeton, New Jersey, July 1949, as a Newsboy in Scott Fitzgerald's play The Vegetable; played several seasons of stock with this company, with the Ivy Tower Playhouse, and with the Royal Poinciana Playhouse, Palm Beach, Florida; made his New York début at the Royale, 29 Oct 1953, as an understudy in A Girl Can Tell; first appeared on the stage in NY at the Theatre de Lys, June 1954, in The Homeward Look; ANTA, Feb 1955, played Stefan in The Dark Is Light Enough; John Golden, Mar 1959, played Sir Mark Grahame in A Desert Incident; Heckscher, for the New York Shakespeare Festival, Dec 1960, Romeo in Romeo and Juliet; Vancouver, Canada, International Festival, Aug 1961, the Angel in Men, Women, and Angels; Sheridan Square Playhouse, Feb 1962, Amory in This Side of Paradise; Festival of the Two Worlds, Spoleto, Italy, at the Teatro Nuovo, June 1962, Christopher Flanders in The Milk Train Doesn't Stop Here Anymore, which he repeated at the Morosco, NY, Jan 1963; Theatre Four, Mar 1968, Adam in The Four Seasons; appeared with the Seattle, Washington, Repertory in the 1973–4 seasons; has appeared on television in Mrs Miniver, 1962, Romeo and Juliet, 1964, etc; received the Obie Award for This side of Paradise.

Address: c/o Diana Hunt, 246 West 44th Street, New York, NY 10036. *Tel:* BR 9–0069.

ROERICK, William (né Roehrich), actor and author
b Hoboken, New Jersey, 17 Dec 1912; *s* of William George Roehrich and his wife Josephine (Clark); *e* Hamilton College (BS) and honorary Doctor of Humane Letters, 1971; trained to be an English teacher but began acting in college; trained for the stage at the Berkshire Playhouse Drama School.

First appeared on the stage at the Berkshire Playhouse, Stockbridge, Massachusetts, Aug 1935, as Count Paulo del Magiore in Déclassée, with Ethel Barrymore; first appeared in New York at the Martin Beck, 23 Dec 1935, as Balthasar in Romeo and Juliet with Katharine Cornell and Maurice Evans; same theatre, Mar 1936, played Giles de Rais in Saint Joan with Miss Cornell, and subsequently toured; Empire, Oct 1936, Guildenstern in Hamlet with John Gielgud, later took over as Laertes, and toured in this latter part; Henry Miller's, Feb 1938, played the Baseball Player in Our Town and subsequently toured as George in the same play; toured, 1939, in Easy Virtue; Vanderbilt, Jan 1939, Algernon Moncrieff in The Importance of Being Earnest; Music Box, Oct 1941, Theodore Kincaid in The Land Is Bright; Royale, Feb 1942, Bob Ferguson in Autumn Hill; joined the US Infantry, 1942; appeared at the Broadway, 4 July 1942, in the revue This Is the Army, toured in this production, 1942–3, and made his London début in it at the Palladium, Winter, 1943; toured Great Britain, and continued touring in it in North Africa, Italy, Egypt, Iran, India, Australia, New Guinea, The Philippines, and the Pacific Islands, 1943–5; Royale, NY, Jan 1946, Mr Palmer in The Magnificent Yankee; Princess, Mar 1947, John in The Great Campaign; toured, 1948, with Gertrude Lawrence in Tonight at 8.30; National, Feb 1948, played in Tonight at 8.30; Biltmore, June 1948, took over as Morriss in The Heiress and subsequently toured as Arthur in this play; Phoenix, Dec 1953, Father Christy in Madam Will You Walk; Longacre, Mar 1954, Gerry Hardlip in The Burning Glass; Morosco, 1955, took over as Jeffrey in Dear Charles and subsequently toured with Tallulah Bankhead; toured, 1962–3, with Dame Judith Anderson, as Jason in Medea and as Macbeth; Charles Street, Boston, 1964, Roebuck Ramsden in Man and Superman; Billy Rose, Oct 1965, Joseph Camberlain in The Right Honourable Gentleman; Majestic, Jan 1967, Marquis de Sade in Marat/Sade; Music Box, May 1967, took over from Paul Rogers as Max in The Homecoming, and toured in this part, 1967–8; Studio Arena, Buffalo, 1968, again played Max in The Homecoming; Ambassador, Oct 1968, played The Major in We Bombed in New

Haven; Theatre de Lys, Oct 1970, played in A Passage to E M Forster, which he compiled with Thomas Coley, and which he directed; played in this last production at the Berkshire Theater Festival and at the McCarter Theatre, Princeton, New Jersey, 1971; Circle in the Square—Joseph E Levine, Sept 1973, Dr Bonfant in Waltz of the Toreadors; toured in this part, Jan–Apr 1974; Goodman, Chicago, Oct 1974, Gaev in the Cherry Orchard; Playhouse on the Hill, Clinton, NJ, directed The Importance of Being Earnest, 1974, Charley's Aunt, 1975, The Showoff, 1976; Roundabout, Apr 1976, again played Gaev; Circle in the Square, Dec 1976, Nonno in The Night of the Iguana; Plymouth, Nov 1977, Girolamo Privli in The Merchant; McCarter, Princeton, Mar 1978, in Much Ado About Nothing; Ahmanson, LA, 1979, in Pygmalion; at the same theatre in Cause Celebre; Morosco, Apr 1980, Edward Sefon in Happy New Year; author, with Thomas Coley, of the play The Happiest Years, produced at the Lyceum, 25 Apr 1949; first appeared in films in This Is the Army, 1943, and has since played in The Harder They Fall, Flight to Hong Kong, Not of This Earth, The Sporting Club, The Love Machine, A Separate Peace, 1972, etc; has appeared frequently on television in Climax, Playhouse 90, as Colonel Adams in the series Clear Horizon, in Hard Travelin', Realities, etc; is author with Thomas Coley of scripts for Mama, Claudia, Casey, Crime Photographer, The Billy Rose Show, Climax, etc; author of the essay Forster and America in Aspects of E M Forster, 1969; has played extensively in summer stock, notably in Criminal at Large, Glad Tidings, The Time of the Cuckoo, and Janus; is a member of the Emerson Literary Society and is on the Board of the Edward Root Art Center, Clinton, New York.

Favourite parts: Fancourt Babberly in Charley's Aunt and Max in The Homecoming. *Recreation:* Holding a 200-year-old house together. *Address:* Lost Farm, Tyringham, Massachusetts 01264. *Tel:* 413–243–2579.

ROGERS, Anne, actress and singer
b Liverpool, 29 July 1933; *e* at St John's School, Winsford, Cheshire; *m* Mike Hall; studied at the School of Dancing, Hanley, and also with Beryl Cooper.

First appearance on the stage, Burnley, Lancs, Aug 1950, as Snow White in Snow White and the Seven Dwarfs; and toured with this production, 1950–3; Wyndham's, Jan 1954, played Polly Browne in The Boy Friend; remained in this success until she went to America, where she appeared for the first time, Philharmonic, Los Angeles, Apr 1957, as Eliza Doolittle in My Fair Lady; played in the same production at the Shubert, Chicago, Dec 1958, returning to England, to take over the same part, Theatre Royal, Drury Lane, Aug 1959, in the London production of My Fair Lady, which she played until 1962; San Francisco and Hollywood, Aug 1963, played the Princess Flavia in Zenda; Lyric, London, Apr 1964, played Amalia Balash in She Loves Me; Yvonne Arnaud Theatre, Guildford, June 1965, Clarissa in Lionel and Clarissa; Los Angeles, Sept 1966, co-starred in Half-a-sixpence; Lunt-Fontanne, New York, Apr 1967, took over Maggie in Walking Happy; Lyric, May 1968, played Agnes Hobson in I Do! I Do!; toured Feb 1969, as Veronica Hillyer in They Ride on Broomsticks; Ivanhoe, Chicago, May 1970, appeared in A Shot in the Dark; toured the UK, 1973, in The Sweetest Sounds; Shubert, Chicago, 1973, Lucille Early in No, No, Nanette, subsequently playing the same part at the Theatre Royal, Drury Lane, May 1973; Duke of York's, Sept 1974, Imogen in The Turning Point; Johannesburg, 1975, Blanche Du Bois in A Streetcar Named Desire; San Francisco, 1975, Guinevere in Camelot; Norwich Festival, 1976, Blanche Dubois in A Streetcar named Desire; 1977, toured in

Quadrille; 1978–9, toured USA as Eliza in My Fair Lady; television; since her first appearance in 1953, includes *Birds on the Wing*, and Song of Songs.

Favourite parts: Polly Browne, Eliza Doolittle, and Blanche Du Bois. *Club:* The Players' Theatre. *Address:* c/o Felix De Wolfe, 1 Robert Street, London WC2.

ROGERS, Ginger (neé Virginia Katherine McMath), actress, singer, dancer

b Independence, Missouri, 16 July 1911; *d* of William Eddins McMath and his wife Lela Emogen (Owens); *e* Benton Blvd Elementary School, Kansas City, Mo, 6th Ward Elementary School, Fort Worth, Tex (1920–26); prepared for the stage with her mother, a manager, coach, and producer; *m* (1) Jack Edward Culpepper (mar dis), (2) Lew Ayres (mar dis), (3) Jack Briggs (mar dis), (4) Jacques Bergerac (mar dis), (5) William Marshall (mar dis).

Won a Charleston contest in Texas, which led to vaudeville engagements; first appeared in a legitimate play in Fort Worth, Tex, 1924, as Mme St Dennis in The Death of St Dennis, produced by her mother; Majestic, Fort Worth, 1926, played mistress of ceremonies in vaudeville; appeared as a song and patter performer at the Paramount, Brooklyn, 1928; made her Broadway debut at the 46th Street, 25 Dec 1929, as Babs Green in Top Speed; Alvin, Oct 1930, Mollie in Girl Crazy, and was a great success; entered films for 20 years then re-appeared in NY at the Ziegfeld, 6 May 1951, in the revue ANTA Album; Plymouth, Oct 1951, Valerie King and Ruth Gage in Love and Let Love; Alcazar, San Francisco, Oct 1959, Tess Jackson in Pink Jungle, and subsequently toured; toured, 1960, as Annie Oakley in Annie Get Your Gun, 1961 as Gillian Holroyd in Bell, Book, and Candle, and 1963 as Molly in The Unsinkable Molly Brown; St James, Aug 1965, took over from Carol Channing as Dolly Gallagher Levi in Hello, Dolly!; 1966–67, in national touring production of Hello, Dolly!; made her London stage debut at the Drury Lane, 20 Feb 1969, as Mame Dennis in Mame; toured US, 1971, as Coco Chanel in Coco; opened the Drury Lane East, Chicago, Ill, Dec 1974, as Ann Stanley in 40 Carats; Empire Room, Waldorf-Astoria, Mar 1976, appeared in cabaret and subsequently in other cities; Radio City Music Hall, May 1980, appeared in A Rockette Spectacular; first appeared in films in Young Man of Manhattan, 1930, and later played in some 80 others, notably the series of musicals with Fred Astaire including The Gay Divorce, Roberta, Top Hat, Follow the Fleet, Swingtime, Shall We Dance, The Barkleys of Broadway, and dramatic films like Kitty Foyle, Tom, Dick, and Harry, Roxie Hart, The Major and the Minor, Oh, Men!, Oh, Women!, Harlow, etc; won the Academy Award for her performance in Kitty Foyle (1940); has performed on television in her own "spectaculars" and with various others such as Bob Hope, Perry Como, Dinah Shore, Steve Allen, Ed Sullivan, Jack Benny, etc.

Recreations: Dancing, tennis, sculpture, painting. *Address:* Actors Equity Association, 165 West 46th Street, New York, NY 10036.

ROGERS, Paul, actor

b Plympton, Devon, 22 Mar 1917; *s* of Edwin Rogers and his wife Dulcie Myrtle (Collier); *e* Hooe, Plympton, and Newton Abbot; *m* (1) Jocelyn Wynne (mar dis); (2) Rosalind Boxall; studied for the stage at the Michael Chekhov Theatre Studio, Dartington Hall.

Made his first appearance at the Scala, 1938, as Charles Dickens in Bird's-Eye View Of Valour, also playing two smaller parts; at Stratford-on-Avon, 1939, and also appeared in a concert party at Colchester during the same year; in repertory at Colchester, 1940; served in the Navy during the war; returned to the stage, again in repertory at Colchester, 1946; Piccadilly, May 1947, appeared as Jonathan Kail and the Shepherd in Tess of the D'Urbervilles; joined the Bristol Old Vic Company, Sept 1947, playing a wide variety of parts; played a second season with this company, from Sept 1948, appearing as Sir Anthony Absolute, Tybalt, Bottom, Esdras in Winterset, Lord Porteous in The Circle, etc; joined the Old Vic Company, London, at the New, for the 1949–50 season, appearing as Don Armado, Dull in Love's Labour's Lost, First Player and Osric in Hamlet, Schaaf in A Month in the Country, La Flèche in The Miser; Old Vic, 1950–1 season, appeared as Malvolio, Dr Caius, Trouble-all in Bartholomew Fair, Aegisthus in Electra, Revunov-Karaulov in The Wedding, etc; Old Vic, 1951–2 season, appeared as Iago, Bottom, and William Villon in The Other Heart, receiving the Clarence Derwent Award for his performance in the last-named part; toured South Africa, 1952, playing Iago, Bottom, and 3rd Witch in Macbeth; Old Vic, 1952–3 season, played Shylock, Henry VIII, and 1st Knight in Murder in the Cathedral; at the Edinburgh Festival, 1953, appeared as Sir Claude Mulhammer in The Confidential Clerk, and played the same part at the Lyric, Sept 1953; at the Edinburgh Festival, 1954, appeared as Macbeth; Old Vic, 1954–5 season, again played Macbeth, and also appeared as Petruchio, Touchstone, Sir John Falstaff in Henry IV, Parts I and II, and Don Adriano de Armado in Love's Labour's Lost; Old Vic, 1955–6 season, appeared as Sir John Falstaff in The Merry Wives of Windsor, Leontes in The Winter's Tale, the title-role in Macbeth, Mercutio in Romeo and Juliet, and John of Gaunt in Richard II; made his first appearance on Broadway at the Winter Garden, New York, Oct 1956, with the Old Vic Company, as John of Gaunt in Richard II, subsequently playing Mercutio, Macbeth, and also Pandarus in Troilus and Cressida; toured Australia, Mar–Nov 1957, with the Australian Elizabethan Theatre Trust Drama Co, playing the title-role in Hamlet, and Lord Foppington in The Relapse; on his return to England, he appeared at the Old Vic, Feb 1958, in the title-role of King Lear; Edinburgh Festival, Aug 1958, played Lord Claverton in The Elder Statesman, and appeared in the same part at the Cambridge Theatre, Sept 1958; Piccadilly, Apr 1959, played Cecil Fox in Mr Fox of Venice; Duke of York's, Oct 1959, Johnny Condell in One More River, subsequently transferring to the Westminster, Nov 1959; Duchess, Apr 1960, played Richard Medway in A Shred of Evidence; Old Vic Company, Sept 1960, again toured as Macbeth, and Cauchon in Saint Joan; Phoenix, Mar 1961, played Nickles in JB; Saville, Apr 1962, Reginald Kinsale in Photo Finish, subsequently taking over the part of Sam Old in the same production, Aug 1962; Brooks Atkinson, NY, Feb 1963, again played Reginald Kinsale in Photo Finish; Queen's, London, Mar 1964, played Sorin in The Seagull; at the same theatre, Sept 1964, Oscar Portman in Season of Goodwill; Leatherhead, Nov 1964, played Harry in Honey, I'm Home; joined the Royal Shakespeare Company at the Aldwych, June 1965, to play Max in The Homecoming; Royal Shakespeare, Stratford-on-Avon, July 1965, Apemantus in Timon of Athens, appearing in both productions in repertory; Aldwych, Jan 1966, The Mayor in The Government Inspector; Stratford, Apr 1966, Falstaff in Henry the Fourth, Parts I and II; Music Box, NY, Jan 1967, again played Max in The Homecoming (1967 Tony Award for Best Actor in a Drama); Billy Rose, NY, Jan 1968, Adam Trask in Here's Where I Belong; Aldwych, 1968, appeared in RSC Theatre-go-round's Room for Company; Lyric, Feb 1969, played Sam Nash in Visitor from Mamaroneck, Jesse Kiplinger in Visitor from Hollywood, and Roy Hubley in Visitor from Forest Hills, in the triple-bill Plaza Suite; Apollo, Mar 1970, played Charles Murray in The Happy Apple; St Martin's, Sept 1970, took over as Andrew Wyke in Sleuth; went to NY, Sept 1971, to play the role at the Music Box; toured, spring 1973, as Maurice Fisher in The Starving Rich; Apr 1974, played Othello for the Bristol Old Vic; joined the National Theatre Company at the Old Vic, 1974, to play Les in The Freeway, Oct, Major Henry in Grand Manoeuvres, Dec, and Boss Mangan in Heartbreak House, Feb 1975; Aldwych, for RSC, played Carnaby Leete in The Marrying of Ann Leete, Sept, and Mr Portland in The Return of A J Raffles, Dec 1975; Antipa Zykov in The Zykovs, Apr 1976; National Theatre Company, Olivier, 1977, The Zauberkönig in Tales from the Vienna Woods, Jan, Voltore in Volpone, Apr, Henry Huxt-able in The Madras House, June, and Cottesloe, Nov, Jones in Half-Life; Royal Court, Aug 1978, Trevelyan in Eclipse; for Birmingham Rep, Feb 1979, Shylock in The Merchant of Venice, and May, John Tarleton in Misalliance and Lord Claverton in The Elder Statesman, at the Malvern Festival; Lyric, Hammersmith, Oct 1979, Waiter in You Never Can Tell; first appeared in films, 1950 and films include Billy Budd, The Looking Glass War, The Homecoming, etc; television appearances include The Three Sisters, The Skin Game, A Tragedy of Two Ambitions.

Favourite parts: Iago, Bottom, Falstaff, Lord Claverton, Andrew Wyke. *Hobbies:* Reading and music. *Recreations:* Swimming and walking. *Address:* c/o London Management, 235–241 Regent Street, London, W1.

ROLLE, Esther, actress
b Pompano Beach, Florida; *e* Hunter College.

First appeared in New York at the St Marks Playhouse, 1962, when she took over as Felicity Trollop Pardon in The Blacks; ANTA, 1964, took over a role in Blues for Mister Charlie; Ethel Barrymore, 1965, played in The Amen Corner; St Mark's Playhouse, Nov 1965, played Ellie in Happy Ending and Clubwoman in Day of Absence; appeared with the Arena Stage, Washington, DC, 1966–67 season; St Mark's Playhouse, Feb 1968, for the Negro Ensemble Company, played Pearl Cunningham in Summer of the Seventeenth Doll; Dec 1968, Cannibal in God Is a (Guess What?), Apr 1969, Mrs Beverly in String and Katy Jones in Contribution; made her London debut with the Negro Ensemble Company in a World Theatre season at the Aldwych, 5 May 1969, as Cannibal in God Is a (Guess What?), and on 8 May 1969 played in Song of the Lusitanian Bogey; St Mark's Playhouse, July 1969, Alice Sugar in Man Better Man; Mar 1970, First Operator and Aide in Day of Absence; May 1970, played in the revue Akokawe (Initiation); Theatre Company of Boston, Mass, 1969–70 season, played in The Blacks; Mark Taper Forum, Los Angeles, Cal, 1970, Market Wife in The Dream on Monkey Mountain; St Mark's Playhouse, Jan 1971, Maybelle Johnson in Rosalee Pritchett; Mar 1971, again played Market Wife in The Dream on Monkey Mountain; May 1971, Faye in Ride a Black Horse; Mar 1972, Shouter Woman in A Ballet Behind the Bridge; Ethel Barrymore, May 1972, Mis Maybell in Don't Play Us Cheap; Jacksonville, Fla, 1976, the Mother in The Newlyweds; New Federal, May 1977, Lady Macbeth in Macbeth; appeared in the film Cleopatra Jones, 1973; has appeared on television as Florida in the series *Maude*, 1972–74, and in her own series *Good Times* since 1973.

Address: Actors Equity Association, 165 West 46th Street, New York, NY 10036.

ROOSE-EVANS, James, director
b London, 11 Nov 1927; *s* of John Roose-Evans and his wife Catherina (Primrose); *e* various schools, and St Benet's Hall, Oxford (MA); formerly a teacher.

Began his career in the theatre as an actor in repertory; resident director at the Maddermarket Theatre, Norwich, 1954–5; member of the faculty at the Juilliard School of Music, New York, 1955–6; member of the staff at the Royal Academy of Dramatic Art, 1957–61; Belgrade, Coventry, 1957–9; directed the tour, June 1959, of Nothing to Declare; directed his first London production at the Royal Court, Mar 1960, with The Dumb Waiter; director of the tenth Pitlochry Festival, 1960; Lyric, Hammersmith, Aug 1961, directed Under Milk Wood; for the Hampstead Theatre Club he has directed the following productions: The Seagull, 1962; In at the Kill, Private Lives, The Square, Cider With Rosie, The Singing Dolphin, 1963; The Cloud, The Tower, The Little Clay Cart (also co-adapted), The Corn is Green, He Who Gets Slapped, 1964; Hippolytus, 1965; Adventures in the Skin Trade, Flashing into the Dark, Letters from an Eastern Front (also designed), 1966; Country Dance (later at the Edinburgh Festival), The Happy Apple, Nathan and Tabileth and Oldenburg (double-bill), The Two Character Play, 1967; Spitting Image, 1968; the following plays transferred to the West End: Private Lives, Cider with Rosie, 1963; Spitting Image, 1968; The Happy Apple (new production), 1970; Strand, Dec 1965, directed An Ideal Husband, also Garrick, Dec 1966; has also directed the Chester Mystery Plays, 1973; Under Milk Wood, The Taming of the Shrew (both Shaw), 1974; A Streetcar Named Desire (S Africa), The Vortex, Fallen Angels (both Greenwich), 1975; Romeo and Juliet (Shaw), 1976; An Inspector Calls (Shaw), 1978; has directed productions at Aldeburgh, King's Lynn, and other Festivals; founded Hampstead Theatre Club, 1959, of which he was Artistic Director for its first ten years; founded Stage Two Theatre Workshop, 1969; author of Experimental Theatre (3rd edition, revised, 1980), Directing A Play, London Theatre, etc; an established childrens author, and has written a number of documentaries for the BBC; a reviewer for the *Times Educational Supplement* and other journals; conducts theatre workshops and lectures in the US and adjudicates in Britain and abroad; became first Reader in Drama at Middlesex Polytechnic, 1979.

Club: Garrick. *Address:* c/o David Higham Associates, 5–8 Lower John Street, Golden Square, London, W1.

ROSE, George, actor
b Bicester, 19 Feb 1920; *s* of Walter John Alfred Rose and his wife Eva Sarah (Rolfe); *e* privately and Oxford High School; formerly a secretary and farmer; studied for the stage at the Central School of Speech and Drama.

First appeared at the New Theatre, 31 Aug 1944, with the Old Vic Company, in Peer Gynt, remaining as a member of the company, 1944–8, during which period he played, among other parts, Sir Christopher Hatton in The Critic, Montfleury in Cyrano de Bergerac, Kastril in The Alchemist, Lucentio in The Taming of the Shrew, The English Soldier in Saint Joan, Zemlyanika in The Government Inspector; made his first appearance in New York, with this company, at the Century, 6 May 1946, as Peto in Henry IV (Part I); at Wyndham's, June 1948, played Dickie Miles in People Like Us; appeared at the Shakespeare Memorial Theatre, Stratford-on-Avon, 1949–50, playing Lennox in Macbeth, Snug in A Midsummer Night's Dream, Dogberry in Much Ado About Nothing, Belarius in Cymbeline, Brabantio in Othello, Pompey in Measure for Measure, Oswald in King Lear, etc; Haymarket, Mar 1951, William Humpage in A Penny for a Song; Phoe-nix, June 1951, Autolycus in The Winter's Tale; same theatre, Jan 1952, Dogberry in Much Ado About Nothing; Lyric, Hammersmith, Oct 1952, Sailor Johnston in The Square Ring; Haymarket, May 1953, Boanerges in a revival of The Apple Cart; Lyric, Hammersmith, Sept 1953, Nils Krogstad in A Doll's House; Royal, Brighton, Jan 1955, Jules in My Three Angels, and appeared in this part at the Lyric, May 1955; Haymarket, Apr 1956, Maitland in The Chalk Garden; Garrick, July 1958, appeared in the revue Living for Pleasure; Royal Court, Apr 1959, the Magistrate in The Trial of Cob and Leach, a Sunday night production for the English Stage Company; at the Cambridge (Mass) Drama Festival, Aug 1959, Dogberry in Much Ado About Nothing, subsequently appearing in the same part at the Lunt-Fontanne Theatre, NY, Sept 1959; Royalty, London, June 1960, Burgomaster in The Visit; Royal Court, Nov 1960, Creon in Antigone, and the Magistrate in The Trial of Cob and Leach (double-bill under the title of Trials by Logue); Globe, Jan 1961, took over the part of the Common Man in A Man for All Seasons; Globe, June 1961, appeared in the revue On the Avenue; ANTA, NY, Nov 1961, again played the Common Man in A Man for All Seasons, subsequently touring the US with the production; Lunt-Fontanne, NY, Apr 1964, the First Gravedigger in Hamlet; Plymouth, NY, Nov 1964, Glas in Slow Dance on the Killing Ground; ANTA Playhouse, Oct 1965, Martin Ruiz in The Royal Hunt of the Sun; Lunt-Fontanne, Nov 1966, Henry Horatio Hobson in Walking Happy; Biltmore, Mar 1968, Truscott in Loot; City Center, June 1968, Alfred P Doolittle in My Fair Lady; Artist in Residence, Mankato University, Apr 1968, also playing Mr Peachum in The Threepenny Opera; Ahmanson, Los Angeles, 1968, Rev Leslie Rankin in Captain Brassbound's Conversion; Eugene O'Neill, Feb 1969, Steward, Carpenter, and January in Canterbury Tales; Mark Hellinger, Dec 1969, Louis Greff in Coco; toured in this part, 1971; Helen Hayes, Jan 1972, Mr Booker in Wise Child; toured, Sept 1972–Mar 1973, as Andrew Wyke in Sleuth, and took over this part at the Music Box, Apr 1973; toured, summer 1973, as Lutz in The Student Prince; Brooks Atkinson, Mar 1974, Henry in My Fat Friend, and toured in this part in 1975; St James, Mar 1976, Alfred P. Doolittle in My Fair Lady, for which he received the Antoinette Perry (Tony) Award, and the Drama Desk Award; for BAM Theater Company, Brooklyn Academy, 1978, played General Burgoyne in The Devil's Disciple and Almady in The Play's the Thing, Feb, and the title-role in Julius Caesar, Apr; Biltmore, Dec 1978, Hawkins in The Kingfisher; Lunt-Fontanne, Sept 1979, Mr Darling and Captain Hook in Peter Pan; first appeared in films, 1952, in The Pickwick Papers; films include No Love for Johnnie, A New Leaf and From the Mixed-up Files of Mrs Basil E Frankweiler (1973), etc; he has also made numerous television appearances in England and the United States, recently in *Beacon Hill* and Holocaust.

Recreations: Collecting gramophone records, reading, and cats. *Address:* c/o International Famous Agency, Inc, 1301 Avenue of the Americas, New York, NY.

ROSE, Philip (*né* Rosenberg), producer, director
b New York City, 4 July 1921; *s* of Max Rosenberg and his wife Esther; *e* Seward Park High School; *m* Doris Belack.

Began his theatrical career as a singer, and performed with the St Louis Municipal Opera, summer 1945; first NY production, A Raisin in the Sun, was presented in partnership with David J Cogan at the Ethel Barrymore, 11 Mar 1959; has since produced and/or directed the following: Semi-Detached, 1960; Purlie Victorious, Bravo, Giovanni, 1962; Nobody Loves an Albatross, 1963; Cafe Crown, The Owl and the Pussycat, 1964; Nathan Weinstein, Mystic, Connecticut,

1966; The Ninety-day Mistress, 1967; Does a Tiger Wear a Necktie? 1969; Purlie, 1970; a revival of Purlie, 1972; Shenandoah, also co-adapted and wrote the book, for which he received the Antoinette Perry (Tony) Award, 1975; The Trip Back Down, 1977; Angel, 1978; My Old Friends, Comin' Uptown (also co-author), 1979.

Address: 157 West 57th Street, New York, NY. *Tel:* CI5–2255.

ROSS, Annie, actress and singer
b Mitcham, Surrey, 25 July 1930; *d* of Jack Short and his wife May Dalziel (Allan); *e* Beverly Hills, Calif; *m* Sean Lynch (mar dis); trained for the stage at the American Academy of Dramatic Arts, NY.

First appeared on stage in Scotland, 1932, in her parents' show; London debut 25 Feb 1948, as Cuddles in Burlesque, at the Prince's; made her name as a singer in the trio Lambert, Hendricks and Ross; St Martin's, Mar 1956, appeared in the revue Cranks, making her NY stage debut in the same production at the Bijou, 26 Nov 1956; Hampstead, 1971, gave a one-woman show, Annie Ross; Prince of Wales, Feb 1972, Jenny in The Threepenny Opera, transferring to the Piccadilly, Apr 1972; Chichester Festival, 1974, the Italian Singer in Tonight We Improvise; Palace, Watford, 1975, Hedda Louella in Hello Hollywood Hello; Arts, Apr 1975, Carla in Kennedy's Children; Westminster, Mar 1977, Monica in Fire; first film appearance as a child, 1935, in Our Gang; more recently in Yanks; television includes Charles Endell Esq, and frequent appearances as a singer.

Favourite parts: Jenny, Carla. *Recreations:* Cooking, fishing, ballet. *Clubs:* Gerry's, Macready's. *Address:* c/o Peter Campbell, NEMS, 29–31 King's Road, London SW3.

ROSS, Charles Cowper, actor, director and producing manager
b London, 30 June 1929; *s* of Charles Edward Ross, and his wife Evelyn Daisy (Donnelly); *e* Repton; *m* (1) Elizabeth Wallace (mar dis); (2) Lisette Lecat.

First professional appearance, Watergate, 1950, in the revue Midcentury Madness; Royal Court, 1953, appeared in Airs on a Shoestring; since 1955 he has presented plays and revues, alone or in association with others, including: Harmony Close, 1957, which he also wrote and directed; Double Cross, 1958; Look Who's Here (also directed), And Another Thing (also directed), 1960; Four to the Bar (also directed), 1961; The Big Killing, The Gimmick (also directed), 1962; See You Inside (also directed), 1963; The First Fish (also directed), Toad of Toad Hall (with David Conville), 1964 and succeeding years; Ten Years Hard (also directed), 1970; Romance (also wrote music and lyrics and directed), 1971; Who Killed Jack Robin? (tour), 1973; Who Saw Him Die? (same play), 1974; Roger's Last Stand (also directed), 1975; Castle In the Air (tour), 1977; Bird in the Hand (tour and directed), 1977; East, 1978; Let the Good Stones Roll, 1979; directed Night & Day in New Zealand, 1979; directed 28th year of The Mousetrap in London, 1979; member, Society of West End Theatre.

Recreations: Squash, golf and starting businesses. *Club:* Garrick. *Address:* 12 St Paul's Crescent, London NW1. *Tel:* 01-267 4773.

ROSS, George I, dramatic author
b Johannesburg, South Africa, 29 July 1907; *s* of Maurice Ross and his wife Rebecca (Suskin); *e* Marist Brothers College, Uitenhage, and Witwatersrand University, Johannesburg; *m* Eileen Maud Arnold; formerly a chartered accountant in South Africa.

Co-author, with Campbell Singer, of the following plays: The Friendship of Stephen Haslett, 1944; Two Into One, 1949; Mercury and Gold, 1952; Any Other Business, 1957; The Will to Kill, 1958; Refer to Drawer, 1960; Guilty Party, 1961; Difference of Opinion, 1963; The Sacking of Norman Banks, 1969 (seen in London as The Sack Race, 1974); Calculated Risk (New York), 1962, was based on Any Other Business; first play to be seen on television Any Other Business, May 1961.

Address: 26 St Stephens Avenue, Ealing, London, W13. *Tel:* 01–997 7534.

ROSSITER, Leonard, actor
b Liverpool, 21 Oct 1926; *s* of John Rossiter, and his wife Elizabeth (Howell); *e* Liverpool Collegiate School; *m* (1) Josephine Tewson (mar dis); (2) Gillian Raine; formerly an insurance clerk.

First appeared on the stage Sept 1954, at the Repertory Theatre, Preston, as Bert in The Gay Dog; after a year in repertory at Wolverhampton, made his first London appearance in Free As Air at the Savoy, as John and a Reporter; with Bristol Old Vic Company, 1959–61; Mermaid, Oct 1962, played Brennan o' the Moor in Red Roses for Me; made his début on Broadway at the Music Box, Oct 1963, as Fred Midway in Semi-Detached; Garrick, London, Jan 1967, played Corvino in Volpone; Hampstead Theatre Club, Nov 1968, Martin Richter in The Strange Case of Martin Richter; Edinburgh Festival, Aug 1968, Arturo Ui in The Resistible Rise of Arturo Ui; at the Saville, July 1969, repeated this performance, for which he gained the London Critics' and the Variety Club's Best Actor awards, 1969; Duke of York's, June 1970, played Giordano Bruno in The Heretic; Nottingham Playhouse, Oct 1971, title-role in Richard III; Mermaid, Mar 1972, Davies in The Caretaker; Hampstead, May 1973, Rooksby in The Banana Box, transferring to the Apollo; Hampstead, Oct 1974, Brian in The Looneys; Old Vic, Oct 1976, Follovoine in the Purging, and Dhuring in The Singer, in a double-bill entitled Frontiers of Farce; Greenwich, Dec 1976, title-role in Tartuffe; Mermaid, Nov 1977, title-role in The Immortal Haydon; Greenwich, Feb 1979, co-directed and played Fred Midway in Semi-Detached; Lyric, Hammersmith, Apr 1980, Garrard in Make and Break, transferring to the Haymarket, Apr; films, since A Kind of Loving in 1961, include Billy Liar, This Sporting Life, Oliver, 2001 and Otley; his television appearances since 1956 have been numerous, including recently *Rising Damp* (also filmed, 1980), and The Rise and Fall of Reginald Perrin.

Favourite parts: Arturo Ui, Fred Midway. *Recreations:* Football, squash. *Address:* c/o ICM Ltd, 22 Grafton Street, London, W1.

ROTH, Ann, costume designer
First designs for NY were for Maybe Tuesday at the Playhouse, 29 Jan 1958; since then has designed the costumes for Edward II, Make a Million, The Disenchanted, 1958; A Desert Incident, 1959; The Cool World, Gay Divorce, Ernest in Love, Face of a Hero, 1960; A Far Country, Purlie Victorious, Look: We've Come Through, 1961; This Side of Paradise, Isle of Children, Venus at Large, A Portrait of the Artist as a Young Man, The Barroom Monks, 1962; Natural Affection, Hey You, Light Man!, Children from Their Games, A Case of Libel, 1963; In the Summer House, The Last Analysis, Slow Dance on a Killing Ground, I Had a Ball, 1964; The Odd Couple, Romeo and Juliet, The Impossible Years, 1965; The Wayward Stork, The Star-Spangled Girl, 1966; The Deer Park, The Beard, Something Different, 1967; Happiness Is Just a Little Thing Called a Rolls Royce, 1968;

Play It Again, Sam, My Daughter, Your Son, Tiny Alice, The Three Sisters, 1969; Gantry, Purlie, What the Butler Saw, The Engagement Baby, 1970; Father's Day, Prettybelle (Boston), 1971; Fun City, Rosebloom, Twelfth Night, Children! Children!, 6 Rms Riv Vu, Enemies, Purlie (revival), 1972; The Merchant of Venice, Seesaw, The Women, 1973; The Royal Family, 1975; The Heiress, 1976; The Importance of Being Earnest, 1977; Do You Turn Somersaults, The Best Little Whorehouse in Texas, The Crucifer of Blood, First Monday in October, 1978; They're Playing Our Song, Strangers, 1979; also designed the decor for We Comrades Three, 1962; has designed costumes for the American Conservatory Theater, San Francisco, the Kennedy Center, Washington DC, etc; has also designed extensively for films, including Up the Down Staircase, Pretty Poison, Midnight Cowboy, The Owl and the Pussycat, Klute, They Might Be Giants, The Pursuit of Happiness, The Valachi Papers, Murder by Death, Hair, California Suite, The Island, etc.

Address: United Scenic Artists, 1540 Broadway, New York, NY.

ROTH, Lillian, actress and singer
b Boston, Mass, 13 Dec 1910; *d* of Arthur Roth and his wife Kate (Silverman); *e* Professional Children's School, NY, 1923, and Clark School of Concentration, 1924; *m* (1) William Scott (mar dis), (2) Ben Shalleck (mar dis), (3) Mark Harris (mar dis), (4) Edward Leeds (mar dis), (5) Burt McGuire (mar dis).

In vaudeville from age eight with her sister in the act called Lillian Roth and Company and, later, The Roth Kids; later appeared in a solo act, notably at the Palace, NY, and on tour; Lyric, NY, 1917, took over a role in The Inner Man; Globe, Sept 1918, appeared in Penrod; Shubert, Nov 1918, Tyltyl's Grandchild in The Betrothal; Knickerbocker, Feb 1920, Barbara Armstrong in Shavings; Shubert, Chicago, Ill, 1925, appeared in the revue Artists and Models; Shubert, NY, July 1927, in the revue Padlocks of 1927; Earl Carroll, Aug 1928, in the revue Vanities; New Amsterdam Roof, 1928, appeared in Midnight Frolics; Earl Carroll, Aug 1931, appeared in a new edition of Vanities; Oct 1934, appeared in the revue Revels of 1935; retired from the stage for many years and then, at the Starlight, Kansas City, Mo, summer 1957, played Lottie Gibson in By the Beautiful Sea; summer theaters, 1957, played Emma Wallace in The Primrose Path; Westbury, Long Island, Music Fair, Aug 1958, Ruth in Wonderful Town; reappeared in NY at the Shubert, 22 Mar 1962, as Mrs Bogen in I Can Get It for You Wholesale; Dallas, Tex, State Fair, Oct 1965, Mrs Brice in Funny Girl, and subsequently toured; Broadhurst, Apr 1971, appeared in 70, Girls, 70; toured, Han 1973, as Catherine Reardon in And Miss Reardon Drinks a Little; Playhouse in the Ansonia, May 1974, appeared in The Cosmopolites; appeared in cabaret at the Grand Finale, 1974, Soerabaja, Riverboat and Reno Sweeney's, 1975; appeared in films since childhood, and among her sound films are The Love Parade (1929), The Vagabond King, Animal Crackers (1930), Madame Satan (1930), Take a Chance (1934), The Communion (1976), Anna (1980); her autobiography I'll Cry Tomorrow turned into a film in 1955; also wrote Beyond My Worth, 1958; also appeared on television in Outcast, 1955, *Playhouse 90, Matinee Theatre, Ed Sullivan Show*, etc.

(Died 12 May 1980.)

ROTHA, Wanda, actress
b Vienna; *d* of Paul Rotha and his wife Rosa (Brauer); *e* Vienna; *m* (1) Karel Stepanek (mar dis); (2) Manning Whiley (mar dis); studied for the stage at the Academy of Dramatic Art, Vienna.

Made her first appearance on the stage at the Deutsches Volks Theater, Vienna, Dec 1926, as the child in Six Characters in Search of An Author; made her first appearance on the London stage at the Duke of York's Theatre, 9 Feb 1937, when she succeeded Nora Swinburne as Luise Drexler in The Astonished Ostrich, subsequently touring in the same part; Westminster (for Stage Society), May 1937, played The Lady in The Road to Damascus and Nov 1937 (for Stage Society), Queen Christina in the play of that name; Garrick, Nov 1938, played Elisabeth in Elisabeth of Austria; Q, Mar 1942, Maria Krasnova in Once There Was Music; St Martin's, June 1942, Sadie Thompson in Rain, in which she subsequently toured; Phoenix, Sept 1943, played Princess Oparre in The Wingless Victory; toured, Mar 1944, as Anna in Anna Christie; Q, June 1945, Steffy Millington in The Third Visitor, subsequently touring in this; New Lindsey, Nov 1946, played Henriette in There Are Crimes and Crimes; toured, Sept 1949, in Until the Thaw; New Theatre, Feb 1950, with the Old Vic company, appeared as Gertrude in Hamlet, and in June 1950, played the part at Kronberg Castle, Elsinore; New, Bromley, Nov 1952, played the Woman in Make Believe; at the same theatre, Sept 1953, Madeleine Rousset in That Frenchwoman; 1959–60, toured Germany, Austria, Italy, France, and Luxembourg, in the title-part of Schiller's Maria Stuart; Belgrade, Coventry, Aug 1960, played the title-role in Filumena; Bavaria, Germany, 1962, appeared in The Eagle Has Two Heads; Germany, 1963, appeared in The Irregular Verb to Love; Vienna, Austria, 1964, played Martha in Who's Afraid of Virginia Woolf?, subsequently touring Switzerland with the production; Basle, 1966, appeared in The Rose Tattoo, and again toured Switzerland and Germany; Arnaud, Guildford, June 1968, played Madame de Lery in Caprice and She in Frenzy for Two or More, in the double-bill, Teacups and Handgrenades; Hamburg, 1969, appeared in Landscape; Arnaud, Guildford, Apr 1969, played the Queen in The Eagle Has Two Heads, Royal Court, Aug 1972, Teresa in The Old Ones; she has also appeared in television plays and films, notably Délire à Deux, on the continent, and a series in America.

Recreation: Music. *Address:* c/o Fraser and Dunlop, 91 Regent Street, London W1.

ROUTLEDGE, Patricia, actress and singer
b Birkenhead, Cheshire, 17 Feb 1929; *d* of Isaac Edgar Routledge and his wife Catherine (Perry); *e* Birkenhead High School, and University of Liverpool; studied at the Bristol Old Vic Theatre School.

Made her first appearance on the stage at the Liverpool Playhouse, Aug 1952, as Hippolyta in A Midsummer Night's Dream, and remained a member of the Repertory Company for one year; subsequent wide repertory experience included seasons at Guildford, Worthing and Windsor, and appearances as Principal Boy; first appeared in London at the Westminster Theatre, July 1954, as Carlotta in the musical The Duenna; Arts, Mar 1956, played Adriana in the musical version of The Comedy of Errors; Saville, Apr 1957, played Aunt Mabel in Zuleika; Piccadilly, Oct 1959, played Henrietta Argan in The Love Doctor; Vaudeville, Mar 1960, Mrs Gilchrist in Follow That Girl; Lyric, Hammersmith, Nov 1961, appeared in the revue Out of My Mind; Comedy, May 1962, played the title-part of Mary in Little Mary Sunshine; Mermaid, Apr 1963, played Berinthia in the musical Virtue in Danger, subsequently transferring with the production to the Strand, June 1963; Ashcroft, Croydon, Jan 1964, played Victoria in Home and Beauty; Hampstead Theatre Club, Aug 1965, played Violet, Nell, and Rover in How's the World Treating You?, subsequently appearing at the New

Arts, Jan 1966, in the same production transferring to Wyndham's, Jan 1966, and to the Comedy, May 1966; made her Broadway début in Oct 1966, at the Music Box Theatre in the same play; returned to play Alice Challice in the musical Darling of the Day at the George Abbott Theatre, Jan 1968, receiving The Antoinette Perry Award for the Best Musical Actress 1968; Ahmanson, Los Angeles, Dec 1968, played Victoria in Love Match; Chichester Festival, 1969, played the Mother-in-Law in The Caucasian Chalk Circle, Lady Fidget in The Country Wife and Agatha Posket in The Magistrate, transferring with the latter production to the Cambridge Theatre, Sept 1969; at the opening of the new Birmingham Repertory Theatre, Nov 1971, played Mrs Bennet in First Impressions; Mermaid, July 1972, appeared in Cowardly Custard; Chichester Festival, July 1973, Georgiana Tidman in Dandy Dick, transferring with the production to the Garrick, Oct; Theatre Royal, Bristol, May 1975, with the Bristol Old Vic company, played Madame Ranevsky in The Cherry Orchard; again at Chichester, 1975, played Emilia in Othello, May, and Martha Avon in Made in Heaven, July; Mark Hellinger, NY, May 1976, played the Presidents' wives in 1600 Pennsylvania Avenue; Royal Exchange, Manchester, Sept 1976, Mrs Malaprop in The Rivals, and Nov, Mrs Munnings in Zack; Vaudeville, June 1977, Maria Wislack in On Approval; Camden Festival, Mar 1978, made her operatic début in Offenbach's The Grand Duchess of Gerolstein; Eisenhower Theater, Washington, DC, May 1978, Daisy Tuttle in Gracious Living and, Oct, Julia in Semmelweiss; Royal Exchange, Manchester, Feb 1979, Miss Dyott in The Schoolmistress; Queen's, July 1979, Peggy Stott in And a Nightingale Sang; first film appearance, 1966, in To Sir With Love; first appeared on television in 1954, recent productions include When We are Married, The Years Between, Doris and Doreen, and Nicholas Nickleby; radio work includes straight plays, Gilbert and Sullivan and The Beggar's Opera; recordings include Cowardy Custard, and Presenting Patricia Routledge.

Address: c/o Larry Dalzell Associates, 3 Goodwin's Court, St Martin's Lane, London, WC2. *Tel:* 01–240 3086.

ROWLAND, Toby, producing manager
b Libby, Montana, USA, 19 Oct 1916; *s* of Morris Downs Rowland, and his wife Alberta Louella (Allis); *m* Mildred Virginia Landstrom (Martha Downs).

His first production was The Infernal Machine, at the Playroom Club, New York, 1938; his first London production was The Desperate Hours, 1955; he has since presented or co-presented, in London unless otherwise stated, Summertime, 1955; The Crystal Heart, Camino Real, Janus, It's the Geography that Counts, 1957; Keep Your Hair On, Come Rain, Come Shine (tour), Brouhaha, Suddenly, Last Summer, Shadow of Heroes, 1958; Traveller Without Baggage and Madame de, Dark Halo, Change of Tune, Detour After Dark, The Sound of Murder, Make A Million (tour), 1959; Watch It, Sailor, Will You Walk A Little Faster? 1960; Pools Paradise, The Fantasticks, 1961; Rock-a-Bye, Sailor, 1962; Wait A Minim!, 1964; Nymphs and Satires, 1965; Wait a Minim! (NY), 1966; Forty Years On, 1968; The Stiffkey Scandals of 1932, 1969; Getting On, 1971; Saturday, Sunday, Monday (in association with the National Theatre), 1974; The Matchmaker, 1978; Songbook, 1979; President, Society of West End Theatre, 1970; joint managing director, Stoll Moss Theatres Ltd, managing director, Associated Theatres Properties Ltd.

Recreations: Gardening and riding. *Club:* Garrick. *Address:* Cranbourn Mansions, Cranbourn Street, London WC2H 7AG. *Tel:* 01–437 2274.

ROWLANDS, Patsy, actress

b Palmers Green, London, 19 Jan 1935; *d* of Albert Edward Rowlands and his wife Amy Beatrice Lydia (Shillinglaw); *e* Convent of the Sacred Heart, Whetstone; *m* Malcolm Sircom (mar dis); trained for the stage at the Guildhall School of Music and Drama.

First professional appearance, 1951, in the chorus for a tour of Annie Get Your Gun; Lyric, Hammersmith, Oct 1958, played Thetis Tooke in Valmouth, making her first London appearance in the same part at the Saville, Jan 1959; Criterion, Dec 1959, Sylvia Groomkirby in One-Way Pendulum; Saville, Mar 1962, Avril Hadfield in Semi-Detached; Vaudeville, Dec 1964, appeared in the revue Chaganog; Mermaid, Apr 1966, Toinette in The Imaginary Invalid and Frosine in The Miser, in a double-bill; Duke of York's, Dec 1972, appeared in Once Upon a Time; Lyric, Dec 1975, Lolly Tucker in The Bed Before Yesterday; Apollo, Nov 1977, Mrs Joyce Pullen in Shut Your Eyes and Think of England; films, since 1960, include Tom Jones and Carry On Loving; her frequent television appearances include plays, serials and series, recently, The History of Mr Polly.

Favourite part: Sylvia Groomkirby. *Recreations:* Cooking, driving, hairdressing. *Address:* Flat 4, 12 St George Street, London W1R 9DF. *Tel:* 01–499 8317/9.

ROWLES, Polly, actress

b Philadelphia, Pa, 10 Jan 1914; *d* of Ralph Rowles and his wife Mary (Dick); *e* Carnegie Institute of Technology; *m* Franklin Snyder (mar dis); studied acting with Ben Iden Payne, Elizabeth Kimberly, Chester Wallace, and E Hickman.

Made her New York début at the Mercury, Apr 1938, when she took over Calpurnia in Julius Caesar; Shubert, New Haven, Jan 1947, played Ronnie James in Carrot and Club; made her first London appearance at the Strand, Mar 1948, as Natasha Rapanovich in Dark Eyes; Booth, Feb 1949, played Queen Elizabeth in Richard III; Booth, Feb 1950, understudied Shirley Booth in Come Back, Little Sheba; Fulton Nov 1950, played Sophie Kressner in The Golden State; National, Feb 1951, Lucy McLean in The Small Hours; Plymouth, Jan 1952, Candida Kaufman in Gertie; Lyceum, Nov 1952, Agnes Carol in Time Out for Ginger; American Shakespeare Festival, Stratford, Conn, July 1955, Calpurnia in Julius Caesar; Booth, Oct 1955, Clara Dennison in The Wooden Dish; Helen Hayes, Apr 1956, Anne Rogers in Goodbye Again; Broadhurst, Oct 1956, Vera Charles in Auntie Mame, which she played for 637 performances; Henry Miller's, Mar 1959, Claire in Look After Lulu; Cort, Jan 1960, Phyllis Clyde in A Mighty Man Is He; 54th Street, Mar 1962, Mollie Plummer in No Strings; Westport Country Playhouse, Aug 1965, Mrs Jane Wharton Bondry in A Remedy for Winter; Brooks Atkinson, Mar 1966, Evelyn Hopper in The Best Laid Plans; Belasco, Oct 1966, Madame Xenia in The Killing of Sister George; toured the US, 1967–8, in the last part; Morosco, Dec 1968, Mrs Margolin in Forty Carats; Anspacher, May 1972, appeared in Older People; 46th Street, Apr 1973, Miss Curtis and Lucy in The Women; Meadow Brook, Rochester, Mar 1977, Mrs Fisher in The Show-Off; National, Washington, DC, Jan 1978, Louise Pembley in Spotlight; Roundabout, May 1978, again played Mrs Fisher; has appeared on television in various dramatic programs such as *Playhouse 90, US Steel Hour, Jamies* (1954–6), *The Nurses,* etc.

Address: Agency for the Performing Arts, 120 West 57th Street, New York, NY 10019.

RUBY, Thelma (*née* Wigoder), actress

b Leeds, Yorkshire, 23 Mar 1925; *d* of Louis Ely Wigoder, MA, BDS, JP, and his wife Paula Ruby (Lubelski); *e* Leeds Girls High School; Alexandra School, Dublin; Finch College, New York; *m* Peter Frye; formerly a teacher; trained for the stage at Yale Drama School.

Made her first appearance on the stage at the Opera House, Manchester, 1945, in The Three Waltzes; made her first appearance in London at the Duchess Theatre, Mar 1947, as Matrona in The White Devil; Saville, Jan 1948, played the First Girl in Four Hours to Kill; Phoenix, Sept 1948, played Muriel Palmer in Harlequinade (in the double-bill entitled Playbill); Hippodrome, May 1953, appeared in the revue High Spirits; New Watergate, May 1955, appeared in the revue Happy Returns; Lyric, Hammersmith, Sept 1955, played Mrs Winterton in The Buccaneer, transferring with the production to the Apollo, Feb 1956; Apollo, June 1956, appeared in the revue For Amusement Only; following the long run of performances, she next appeared at the Lyric, Hammersmith, July 1958, when she played Bessie Levy in The Hamlet of Stepney Green; Palladium, Dec 1958, played The Queen in The Sleeping Beauty; Gaiety, Dublin, Mar 1960, played Mistress Quickly in Chimes at Midnight (Orson Welles version of Henry IV, Parts I and II); Adelphi, Sept 1960, played The Queen in Once Upon a Mattress; Palladium, Dec 1960, played the Empress of Morocco in Turn Again Whittington; Queen's, Sept 1962, followed Anna Quayle in Stop the World—I Want to Get Off; Royal, Stratford, E, Dec 1964, played Countess Gruffanuff in The Rose and the Ring; Yvonne Arnaud, Guildford, Dec 1965, again played Countess Gruffanuff in The Rose and the Ring; New, Aug 1966, Mrs Jorrocks in Jorrocks; Royal Court, June 1967, Mumsie Doll in A View to the Common; Palace, Aug 1968, took over as Fraulein Schneider in Cabaret; Edinburgh Festival, Sept 1969, played Lady Emma Hamilton in The Hero Rises Up, and at the Nottingham Playhouse, Oct 1969, where she also appeared as Goneril in King Lear, in which production she went to the Old Vic, Feb 1970; Apr 1970, toured as Golde in Fiddler On the Roof; Leeds Playhouse, Sept 1971, Lavinia Featherways in Family Album, and Julia Sterroll in Fallen Angels, in a double-bill; Citizens', Glasgow, June 1972, appeared in Me; Greenwich, Dec 1972, Countess Gruffanuff in The Rose and The Ring; toured, 1973, in Cowardy Custard; toured, Mar 1974, as Domina in A Funny Thing Happened on the Way to the Forum; New London, Oct 1976, Mrs Lewis in So Who Needs Men?; Pretoria and Johannesburg, South Africa, June–Sept 1978, Golda Meir in Golda; Birmingham Rep and tour, Sept 1979, Mrs Peachum and Mrs Trapes in The Beggar's Opera; first entered films, 1955, and notable pictures include Room at the Top, Live Now, Pay Later, etc; first appeared on television, 1951, in Cranford, subsequently appearing in the series Before the Fringe, and in Nicholas Nickleby, etc.

Favourite parts: Mrs Winterton in The Buccaneer, the Empress of Morocco, the leading female role in Stop the World—I Want to Get Off, and Fraulein Schneider in Cabaret. *Recreations:* Cooking and entertaining. *Address:* c/o David Preston Associates. *Tel:* 01–629 5205.

RUDD, Paul, actor

b Boston, 15 May 1940; *s* of Frank Rudd and his wife Kathryn (Ryan); *e* Fairfield University and Fordham University; *m* Joan Mannion; formerly an advertising executive.

Made his professional debut at the Delacorte, 11 Jun 1968, walking on in part 1 of Henry IV; played a messenger in part 2; with the Repertory Theatre of Lincoln Center, 1968–69, played small parts including the Herald in King Lear; at the Long Wharf, Nov 1972, played Copley in The Changing

Room; same theatre, Jan 1974, Caimi in A Pagan Place; played Ken in the Long Wharf production of The National Health, transferring to the Circle in the Square, Oct 1974; Arena Stage, Washington DC, Mar 1975, Skip Hampton in The Last Meeting of the Knights of the White Magnolia; at Circle in the Square, 1975, played Arthur Miller in Ah, Wilderness, Mar, and Jim in The Glass Menagerie, Dec; Mitzi E Newhouse, Apr 1976, Billy in Streamers; Circle in the Square, Mar 1977, Romeo in Romeo and Juliet; Delacorte, Jun 1976, title role in Henry V; Hudson Guild, Mar 1978, Oliver in Da; Roundabout, Apr 1978, Aubrey Piper in The Show-Off; Longacre, May 1979, Scooper in Bosoms and Neglect; in Canada, 1979, played Charlie Gordon in Flowers for Algernon; other work outside New York includes the national tour of The Boys in the Band, and appearances at the Goodman, Chicago, Hartford Stage, Conn, and American Shakespeare Festival, San Diego; films include The Betsy; TV work includes Beacon Hill, and A Connecticut Yankee in King Arthur's Court.
Address: 145 West 55th Street, New York, NY 10019.

RUDDOCK, John, actor
b Lima, Peru, 20 May 1897; *s* of William Warren Ruddock and his wife Maud Eleanor (Davis); *e* University College School, Hampstead, and St Lawrence College Ramsgate; *m* (1) Avril Edythé Voules (mar dis); (2) Elizabeth Rudder; after leaving the Army, studied at the Royal Academy of Music, under the late Acton Bond.

First appeared on the stage at the Empire Theatre, Kingston, Jan 1922, in Brown Sugar; appeared with various repertory companies, and in Shakespeare with Henry Baynton's company, and Ben Greet's company; 1931–2, with the Shakespeare Memorial Theatre, Stratford-on-Avon, touring the USA with the company, 1931; made his first appearance in London, at the Prince of Wales, 11 Feb 1931, as a Chinese in The Ninth Man; Kingsway, Oct 1932, Prime Minister Hughes in Versailles; Royalty, Apr 1934, Tito in The Mask and the Face; 1936–9, in John Clements' productions at the Intimate, Palmers Green; Richmond, Aug 1937, Len Griffin and Fullergrave in Poison Pen; New, Mar 1939, Gibson in The Man in Half-Moon Street; with the Old Vic Company, Nov 1940–Apr 1941, Feste in Twelfth Night, and Rev Thomas Bagot in Trilby; Arts, May–Dec 1942, Myron Berger in Awake and Sing, Admiral Papanin in The House of Regrets, and Mr Rencelaw in The Drunkard; St James's, Feb 1943, Bolshintsov in A Month in the Country, subsequently playing the Doctor; Arts, Jan 1944, Don Abel in Don Abel Wrote a Tragedy; St James's, Dec 1944, the Father in The Glass Slipper, Memorial Theatre, Stratford-on-Avon, 1947 season, played John of Gaunt in Richard II, Gonzalo in The Tempest, Boyet in Love's Labour's Lost, Shylock in The Merchant of Venice, and Friar Laurence in Romeo and Juliet; His Majesty's, Oct 1947, played Gaunt and Friar Laurence; Cambridge, Nov 1948, Professor Chu in Home is To-Morrow; Arts, Feb 1949, Cokane in Widower's Houses; Duke of York's, June 1949, George Hewson in The Third Visitor; New Boltons, Mar 1951, Ghost in Hamlet; Embassy, June 1951, Jacob Engstrand in Ghosts; Mermaid, Sept 1951, Gonzalo in The Tempest; Arts, Dec 1951, Father Looe and Mr Texel in The Great Adventure; Arts, May 1952, Peacey in The Voysey Inheritance; Old Vic (for Bristol Old Vic Company), June 1953, Exeter in Henry V; Duke of York's, Apr 1959, Harry in Gilt and Gingerbread; Mermaid, Dec 1959, Ben Gunn in Treasure Island; Yvonne Arnaud Theatre, Guildford, Sept 1965, Titus Dudgeon in The Devil's Disciple; same theatre, Mar 1966, Peter Bernadone in The Door; Mermaid, Sept 1967, Friar in Nathan the Wise; Mar 1969,

Dabble in Lock Up Your Daughters; first appeared in films, 1938, in Lancashire Luck, and has since appeared in many films, including Quo Vadis, Lawrence of Arabia, Cromwell, etc; television productions include *Elizabeth R*, *Churchill's People*, The Harbourer, The First Christmas, etc; member of the BBC Drama Repertory Company, 1954–5, 1957–8, 1963–5, 1971–3; since 1973 has taught at Guildford School of Acting.
Favourite parts: John of Gaunt, Papinin in The House of Regrets and Polonius in Hamlet. *Recreations:* Music, gardening and photography. *Address:* 17 Cheselden Road, Guildford, Surrey.

RUDKIN, David, dramatic author
b 1936; *s* of David Jonathan Rudkin and his wife Anne Alice (Martin); *e* King Edward's School, Birmingham and St Catherine's, Oxford; *m* Sandra Margaret Thompson; formerly a schoolteacher.

His first stage play, Afore Night Come, written in 1960, was performed by the Royal Shakespeare Company at the New Arts, London, 7 June 1962; subsequent plays, Burglars, a play for children, performed 1968; The Filth Hunt, 1972; Cries from Casement As His Bones Are Brought to Dublin, 1973; Ashes, No Title, 1974; The Sons of Light, 1976; Sovereignty under Elizabeth, 1978; Hippolytus (adapted), 1979; has also translated the opera Moses and Aaron, 1965; libretto for the opera The Grace of Todd, 1966; libretto for Sabbatai Zevi, 1973; TV work includes The Stone Dance, 1963; Children Playing, 1967; House of Character, 1968; Blodwen, Home from Rachel's Marriage, 1969; Penda's Fen, 1974; collaborator with François Truffaut on the screenplay for Fahrenheit 451, 1966; work for radio includes translations from Aeschylus and Euripides; Cries from Casement was originally a radio play, 1973.
Recreations: Music, bridge, languages, anthropology. *Address:* c/o Margaret Ramsay Ltd, 14a Goodwin's Court, St Martin's Lane, London WC2.

RUDMAN, Michael, director
b Tyler, Texas, 14 Feb 1939; *s* of M B Rudman and his wife Josephine (Davis); *e* St Mark's School of Texas, Oberlin College (BA Goverment), St Edmund Hall, Oxford (MA); *m* Veronica Anne Colburn Bennett.

Stage manager for the Living Theatre on a tour of Europe, 1961; while at Oxford, where he was President of the OUDS, directed a number of productions in Oxford Playhouse and also on the Edinburgh Festival fringe; his first London production was A Spring Song, originally seen at the Edinburgh Festival, which opened at the Mermaid on 28 Sept 1964; 1964–8, assistant director, subsequently Associate Producer, Nottingham Playhouse, where his productions included Changing Gear (revue: also devised), Schweik in the Second World War, Julius Caesar, A Man for All Seasons (British Council tour of Malaysia and the Philippines), Death of a Salesman, and wrote Moll Flanders (musical adaptation); with the RSC 1968, directing Volpone for Theatregoround; in 1969 directed An Evening for Merlin Finch, and Black Comedy, Coventry; Look Back in Anger, Watford; The Country Wife, Bath; A Delicate Balance, Glasgow; Henry IV, part 1, Sheffield, 1970; Director of the Traverse, Edinburgh, 1970–3, directing numerous productions there, as well as A Game Called Arthur, Curtains, Straight Up, all transferring to London, 1971; The Changing Room, Long Wharf, New Haven, 1972; made his Broadway debut with this production at the Morosco, Mar 6 1973; Artistic Director, Hampstead Theatre 1973–9, where his productions included The Ride Across Lake Constance, 1973, which transferred to the Mayfair; The Black and White Minstrels, The Show-Off, The Connection, 1974; Alphabetical Order, 1975, which transferred to the Mayfair; Cakewalk, Clouds, 1976; also in 1975 directed Hamlet for the New York Shakespeare Festival in Central Park and subsequently at the Vivian Beaumont, Lincoln Center; directed Donkeys' Years, Globe, 1976; Clouds, Duke of York's, 1978; Gloo Joo, Criterion, 1978; became Director of the Lyttelton Theatre at the National Theatre, July 1979; productions there are For Services Rendered, 1979, and Death of a Salesman, 1979; Thee and Me, The Browing Version/Harlequinade, 1980; among the new plays produced during the period he was Artistic Director of the Hampstead Theatre were: Little Ocean, Other People, Clever Soldiers, A Man's A Man, Dusa, Fish, Stas and Vi, Abigail's Party, Pictorial Smash, The Elephant Man, and Bodies.

Recreations: Golf, Tottenham Hotspur, tennis. *Club:* Oxford and Cambridge United Universities Club. *Address:* c/o Peter Murphy, Spokesmen, 1, Craven Hill, W2 3EW.

RULE, Janice (*née* Mary Janice Rule), actress
b Norwood, Ohio, 15 Aug 1931; *d* of John Christopher Rule and his wife Kathleen Frances (Forbes); *e* Glenbard High School, Glen Ellyn, Ill; *m* Ben Gazzara, the actor; prepared for the stage at the Chicago, Ill, Professional School.

First appeared in NY at the Imperial, 15 July 1949, as a dancer in Miss Liberty; Winter Garden, Mar 1950, danced in the chorus and understudied Bambi Lynn as Bonnie in Great to Be Alive!; made her dramatic debut at the Music Box, 19 Feb 1953, as Madge Owens in Picnic; Belasco, Dec 1954, played Rachel in The Flowering Peach; Olney, Md, Playhouse, summer 1955, played in Ondine; also in 1955 played Cherie in Bus Stop; at the Westport, Conn, Country Playhouse, 1955, played in The Minotaur; Phoenix, NY, Oct 1955, Princess in The Carefree Tree; John Golden, Dec 1958, Daphne Bau in Night Circus; Martin Beck, Apr 1961, Diana in The Happiest Girl in the World; played with the Pittsburgh, Pa, Playhouse, 1966–67 season; Bijou, May 1971, Ruth in The Homecoming; first appeared in films in Goodbye, My Fancy, 1951, and has since played in Invitation to a Gunfighter, Welcome to Hard Times, Kid Blue (1973), etc; has played on television since 1951 in the major dramatic series; appeared as a dancer at the Chez Paree, Chicago, 1946, and later at the Copacabana and the Riviera, NY, 1947.

Address: c/o Jay Julien, 9 East 41st Street, New York, NY 10016. *Tel:* 586–5100.

RUSSELL, Iris, actress
b Kuala Lumpur, FMS, 22 Feb 1922; *d* of William Roy Russell and his wife Elizabeth (Haddow); *e* St Denis School, Edinburgh; *m* (1) Nigel Harvie Bennet (mar dis); (2) W G Chapman (dec); studied at the Glover-Turner Robertson School of Dramatic Art, Edinburgh.

Made her first appearance on the stage at the Theatre Royal, Bath, 5 May 1941, as the Viscomte de Tournai in The Scarlet Pimpernel; toured, 1941–3, with Donald Wolfit's company; first appeared in London, at the Strand, 24 Dec 1941, as Hermia in A Midsummer Night's Dream, and subsequently appeared there, Jan–Feb 1942, as Jessica in The Merchant of Venice, the Prince of Wales in Richard III, and Anne Page in The Merry Wives of Windsor; St James's, Dec 1942, Kitty Clive in The Romance of David Garrick; Jan 1943, Goneril in King Lear, and Maria in Twelfth Night; during 1943–4, toured for ENSA, as Mary in Without the Prince; during 1944–5, played in repertory at Wolverhampton, and Alexandra Theatre, Birmingham, and toured in Italy, as Susan in The Late Christopher Bean; Lindsey

Theatre, Sept 1945, played Jalline in Winter of Our Discontent; toured, 1946, as Masha in Redemption; Lyric, Hammersmith, Nov 1946, and Duke of York's, Jan 1947, Esther Eccles in Caste; Mercury, Aug 1947, Mary Godwin in The Shelley Story; during 1948, appeared in several productions at the Q Theatre; Winter Garden, Oct 1948, Princess Nieou-chi in Lute Song; also played repertory at the Regent Theatre, Hayes, 1948; Phoenix, May 1949, Dorinda in The Beaux' Stratagem, which ran over a year; Q, Aug 1950, played Ilona Szapary in Give Me Yesterday; during 1951 appeared at the Glasgow Citizen's Theatre as Perpetua in Venus Observed and Mrs Maclehose in The Other Dear Charmer, and at the Edinburgh Festival as the Countess of Buchan in King of Scots; at the Q, Oct 1951, played Elizabeth in Cry For the Moon; toured, 1952, as Linda Bryant in Shadow of a Man and appeared at the Edinburgh Festival as Nanny in Highland Fair; played leading parts at the Glasgow Citizens' Theatre during the seasons 1952–3 and 1953–4; at the Royal Princesses', Glasgow, Nov 1952, Louisa Temple in A Masque of Summer; Edinburgh Festival, 1953, again appeared in Highland Fair; Edinburgh Festival, 1954, again appeared as Mrs Maclehose in The Other Dear Charmer; toured, 1963, as Stella in Photo Finish with the Oxford Playhouse Company; Royal, Windsor, 1967, appeared in The Killing of Sister George; has appeared in many films; has appeared in over 200 television productions since The Other Dear Charmer, 1953, including recently, Tobias and The Angel, and the series *General Hospital* and *Crown Court*.

Favourite parts: Esther Eccles in Caste and Stella in Photo Finish. *Address:* 6 Wentworth Road, Oxford. *Tel:* Oxford 56173.

RUTHERFORD, Mary, actress
b Toronto, Ontario, 19 May, 1945; *d* of David Edward Rutherford and his wife Margaret Eleanor (McLaughlin); trained for the stage at Drama Centre, London.

Made her first professional appearance at the Royal Court, London, 13 Oct 1968, as Fraulein Rabenjung in The Tutor; at the Round House, Nov 1968, played several parts in The Hero Rises Up; Mermaid, Jan 1969, Glumdalclitch in Gulliver's Travels; Mercury, May 1969, Haze Cook in And These Is Not All; joined the Royal Shakespeare Company and played Alice in Bartholomew Fair, Aldwych, Oct 1969; Stratford, season 1970, Princess Elizabeth in Richard III, Juliet in Measure for Measure, and Hermia in A Midsummer Night's Dream, touring in the latter part and making her first New York appearance at the Billy Rose, 18 Jan 1971; repeated the role at the Aldwych, June 1971, also playing Nadya in Enemies, July, and the Thief in The Balcony, Nov; for the Welsh Theatre Company, Apr 1972, Lika in The Promise; University Theatre, Newcastle, Feb 1973, Ingrid, the Green Woman and Anitra in Peer Gynt; again at the Aldwych, 1973, Calphurnia in Julius Caesar, and Octavia in Antony and Cleopatra (both June), and Alice Faulkner in Sherlock Holmes, Jan 1974; Stratford, Aug 1974, and Aldwych, Feb 1975, Olivia in Twelfth Night; Haymarket, Leicester, Sept 1975, Juliet in Romeo and Juliet; Crewe Theatre, Oct 1976, Polly Eccles in Caste; Roundhouse, Mar 1977, and Young Vic, July 1977, Dymphna Pugh-Gooch in A Last Belch for the Great Auk; with the London Theatre Group, May–Nov, 1977, Cottesloe, Collegiate and New London Theatres and on tour, played Greta in Metamorphosis; TV work includes Antony and Cleopatra.

Recreations: Singing, bicycling, Mozart. *Address:* c/o Jean Diamond, London Management, 235 Regent Street, London W1. *Tel:* 01–734 4192.

RYAN, Madge, actress
b Townsville, Australia, 8 Jan 1919; *d* of Michael Edward

Ryan and his wife Sarah Josephine (Brady); *e* St Patrick's College, Townsville, Queensland; *m* Michael Rumble (mar dis).

Began her career in the theatre as an amateur, making her first appearance as a professional actress at the Independent Theatre, North Sydney, Nov 1945, as Birdie in The Little Foxes; subsequent performances at the same theatre included Lavinia in The Cocktail Party, and Smilja in Captain Carvallo; at the National Theatre, Sydney, Jan 1956, played Pearl in Summer of the Seventeenth Doll; made her first appearance in London at the New Theatre, Apr 1957, as Pearl in Summer of the Seventeenth Doll, subsequently appearing in the same part at the Coronet, New York, Jan 1958; Duke of York's, London, Sept 1959, played Leila Pratt in The Shifting Heart; Pembroke, Croydon, Nov 1960, Dolly in The Pleasure Garden; Pembroke, Croydon, Feb 1961, played Lottie Lacey in Dark at the Top of the Stairs; St Martin's, May 1961, the Nurse in Time and Yellow Roses; Royal, Bath, Apr 1962, Sarah in The Glad and the Sorry Season; Wyndham's, June 1964, played Kath in Entertaining Mr Sloane; Old Vic (National Theatre Company), May 1965, played the title-part in Mother Courage, followed by Mrs Foresight in Love For Love; appeared with the National Theatre Company in Moscow and Berlin, Sept 1965, in the last production; returned to the Old Vic, Apr 1966, as Mrs Maisie Madigan in Juno and the Paycock; City Centre, NY, Feb 1967, for the Bristol Old Vic Company, played Gertrude in Hamlet, Mistress Overdone in Measure for Measure and the Nurse in Romeo and Juliet, touring the US, Europe and Israel in these parts; Lyric, London, Sept 1967, played Lizzy Sweeny in Philadelphia, Here I Come!; Sydney and Melbourne, Australia, 1968, appeared as Mrs Furnival in Black Comedy and the Fortune Teller in White Liars (double bill); Citizens', Glasgow, 1970, played Madame Alexandra in Colombe; Hampstead, July 1971, Marjorie in A Hearts and Minds Job; Thorndike, Leatherhead, Sept 1972, Mme Renaud in Traveller Without Luggage; Young Vic, Dec 1972, Mrs Elliot in Epitaph for George Dillon; St Martin's, Mar 1973, Mrs Weston in Say Goodnight to Grandma; played the same part at Leeds, May 1974; Northcott, Exeter, Sept 1974, Mme Arkadina in The Seagull; Birmingham Rep, 1975, Mrs Warren in Mrs Warren's Profession, Apr, and Lady Bracknell in The Importance of Being Earnest, May; Old Vic, July 1976, Cornelia in The White Devil; Jan 1979, toured with Cambridge Theatre Company as Felicity in The Shadow Box; first film appearance, Apr 1960, in Upstairs and Downstairs; recent films include Too Many Cooks, The Lady Vanishes and SOS Titanic; made her first appearance on television Dec 1958, and notable productions in which she has appeared include Anna Christie, One Day of the Year, Sherlock Homes, The Rainbirds, etc.

Favourite parts: Gertrude in Hamlet, Birdie, Pearl, Kath, and Lavinia. *Recreations:* Swimming, riding, cooking, reading. *Club:* Pickwick. *Address:* 54 Blenheim Terrace, St John's Wood, London, NW8. *Tel:* 01–624 8566.

RYDER, Alfred (*né* Alfred Jacob Corn), actor and director
b New York City, 5 Jan 1919; *s* of Max Corn and his wife Zelda (Baruchin); *e* Professional Children's School; *m* Kim Stanley; prepared for the stage with Benno Schneider, Robert Lewis, and Lee Strasberg.

First appeared on the stage at Public School 70 in a recitation of Hiawatha; first appeared on the professional stage, billed as Alfred Corn, at the Civic Repertory, 26 Nov 1928, in Eva Le Gallienne's production of Peter Pan, playing Curly; toured in this part, 1929; Belasco, Jan 1932, played

Benny Solomon in East of Broadway; Vanderbilt, Mar 1934, Etienne Du Bois in Another Love; Plymouth, May 1934, Billy Harrison in Come What May; as Alfred Ryder appeared at the Henry Miller's, Feb 1938, as a Baseball Player in Our Town; Fulton, Mar 1938, Alec Jenkins in All the Living; Guild, Feb 1939, Baruch in Jeremiah; 48th Street, Mar 1939, Ralphie in a revival of Awake and Sing; Belasco, Apr 1939, played in Quiet City; New Yorker, Apr 1940, Dr Young in Medicine Show; Belasco, Apr 1942, Knight Templar in Nathan the Wise; 44th Street, Nov 1943, Milhauser in Winged Victory; Belasco, Nov 1944, played in The Man with Blonde Hair; Belasco, Nov 1945, Sergeant Robert A Kane in Skydrift; during 1946–7 taught at the Actors Laboratory, Las Palmas, California, where he directed Mooney's Kid Don't Cry, The Long Goodbye, played Ralphie in Awake and Sing and Mosca in Volpone; International, NY, Feb 1947, Jesse W Lazear in Yellow Jack; Cort, Feb 1948, Oswald Alving in Ghosts; toured, Sept 1948–Apr 1949, as Hamlet and Malcolm in Macbeth with the Margaret Webster Shakespeare Company; Shubert, New Haven, Connecticut, Nov 1949, Alfredo in Signor Chicago; The Arena, NY, June 1950, Mark Antony in Julius Caesar; ANTA, Dec 1950, Orestes in The Tower Beyond Tragedy; Fourth Street, 30 June 1956, took over from Franchot Tone as Astroff in Uncle Vanya; Rooftop, Jan 1957, Mosca in Volpone; Theatre de Lys, Apr 1959, D H Lawrence in I Rise in Flames, Cried the Phoenix and directed Sweet Confession; Ambassador, NY, Mar 1960, Sewell in One More River, and subsequently directed the national tour; Festival of the Two Worlds, Spoleto, Italy, summer 1960, again played D H Lawrence, and also Laurence and The Writer in The Lady of Larkspur Lotion; Music Box, Apr 1961, directed A Far Country; toured, 1961, as Berenger in Rhinoceros, also playing this part at the Longacre, NY; Mayfair, Mar 1963, directed Hey You, Light Man! in which he also played Ashley Knight; Little Fox, Mar 1964, directed a revival of In the Summer House; Delacorte, for the New York Shakespeare Festival, June 1964, played Hamlet, but withdrew from the cast after opening night owing to illness; Schoenberg Hall, University of California at Los Angeles, June 1965, directed Windows; John Golden Apr 1968, directed The Exercise; Ritz, Apr 1971, directed Dance of Death; Center Stage, Baltimore, Md, 1971, played in Staircase; for LA Free Shakespeare Festival, 1973, directed As You Like It; first appeared in films in Winged Victory, 1944, and since has played in T-Men, Story on Page One, Invitation to a Gunfighter, Hotel, 1968, The Stone Killer, 1973, Who Fears the Devil, W (both 1974); etc; on radio played Sammy in *The Rise of the Goldbergs*, 1930–3, and continued to play various roles on radio for ten years; first played on television in 1950, and has since played Iago, Tiberius, Mark Antony, John Wilkes Booth, Claggart in Billy Budd, I Rise in Flames, Cried the Phoenix, The Lady of Larkspur Lotion, and many other classic roles; taught acting at the Dramatic Workshop, 1958–60.

Address: Actors Equity Association, 165 West 46th Street, New York, NY 10036.

RYLANDS, George, CBE, MA, LittD, director
b Tockington, near Bristol, 23 Oct 1902; *s* of Thomas Kirkland Rylands and his wife Betha Nisbet Wolferstan (Thomas); *e* Eton College and King's College, Cambridge; University lecturer, Fellow and sometime Dean, Bursar, and Director of Studies of King's College, Cambridge; a Governor of the Old Vic for thirty years; Council Member, RADA.

Director and trustee of Arts Theatre, Cambridge, to 1946, when he succeeded the late Lord Keynes as Chairman; directed many plays for the ADC, and the Marlowe Society at Cambridge; directed Hamlet at the Haymarket, Oct 1944, and

The Duchess of Malfi, Apr 1945; devised the solo-recital The Ages of Man, 1959, and the dramatic anthology The World's A Stage, 1970; with Douglas Allen, directed the television production of Troilus and Cressida, Sept 1954; Director of LP Recording of the whole Shakespeare canon (uncut), by professional actors with the Marlowe Society, for the British Council; also of his selection of the English Poets from Chaucer to Yeats; was a Director of Tennent Productions, Ltd, and Chairman of the Apollo Society; author of Words and Poetry; Shakespeare, the Poet (in Companion to Shakespeare Studies); Shakespeare's Poetic Energy (British Academy Lecture), 1951; toured Australia for the British Council, 1964, giving a series of lectures on Shakespeare; received the CBE in the Birthday Honours, 1961.

Clubs: Athenaeum and Reform. *Address:* King's College, Cambridge. *Tel:* Cambridge 350411.

S

SACHS, Leonard, actor and director
b Roodeport, Transvaal, South Africa, 26 Sept 1909; *s* of Jacob Sachs and his wife Bessie (Channoch); *e* Jeppe High School and Witwatersrand University; *m* Eleanor Summerfield.

Made his first appearance on the stage at His Majesty's Theatre, Johannesburg, 1926, as Jim Hawkins in Treasure Island; first appeared in London, Mar 1929, as the Poet in The Circle of Chalk; at the Grafton Theatre, 1930, appeared in Highbrow Variety; Globe, Sept 1930, played Samuel Kaplan in Street Scene; toured, 1931, with the Brandon Thomas company; during 1932–3, with the Windsor and Croydon repertory companies; Arts, Feb 1936, played Joseph Severn in Bright Star; Embassy, June, and Phoenix, July 1936, Dr Oskar Bernhardi in Professor Bernhardi; New, Sept 1936, Dr Tiring and Nando in Girl Unknown; Old Vic, Dec 1936, Somerton in The Witch of Edmonton; with Peter Ridgeway, founded the Players' Theatre, 1936, and with the exception of Army service, continued to direct and produce at this theatre until 1947; New Lindsey, July 1948, played Tom Sully in Georgia Story; Richmond, Sept 1948, Albert Blondel in La Jalousie; Embassy, Mar 1949, Helicon in Caligula, and Sept 1949, Harry Engel in The Golden Door; Festival Gardens, Battersea, 1951, performed in Mr Sachs's Song Saloon, and subsequently toured the Moss Empires circuit; Duchess, Mar 1955, played Dr Vince in Misery Me; toured, Oct 1962, as Morry Schwartz in Enter Solly Gold; Royal Court, Sept 1966, Mr Dole in Three Men for Colverton; Phoenix, Leicester, 1968, Chorus in Henry the Fifth; Playhouse, Oxford, Jan 1969, Peter Stockman in An Enemy of the People; in 1969, for the '69 Theatre Company, Manchester, appeared as Stanley Fender in Country Matters; has appeared on television, notably as the Chairman in *The Good Old Days*, and in The Glittering Prizes; first appeared in films, 1936.

Favourite parts: Peter Standish in Berkeley Square, Chris in Anna Christie, and Vershinin in The Three Sisters. *Recreations:* Walking and dancing. *Address:* Miller Management, 248–250 Lavender Hills, London SW11.

SADDLER, Donald, choreographer, director
b Van Nuys, Cal, 24 Jan 1920; *s* of Elmer Edward Saddler and his wife Mary Elizabeth (Roberts); *e* David Starr Jordan High School, Los Angeles, and Los Angeles City College; served as Sergeant in US Army, 1943–45.

Formerly a dancer, and made his first appearance at the Hollywood Bowl, 1937, in Grand Canyon Suite; member of the Ballet Theatre, 1940–43, and 1946–47, performing in Romeo and Juliet, Billy the Kid, Bluebeard, Swan Lake, Les Patineurs, Peter and the Wolf, Lilac Garden, etc; made his first appearance on the musical comedy stage in NY at the Century, 1 Nov 1947, when he took over as Uncle Willie in High Button Shoes; Royale, Jan 1950, danced in Dance Me a Song; Mark Hellinger, Dec 1950, principal dancer in Bless You All; State Fair Music Hall, Dallas, Texas, Aug 1951, danced in The Song of Norway; first choreography was for Blue Mountain Ballads, produced by the Alicia Markova—Anton Dolin Dance Company, 1948; first musical comedy was Wonderful Town at the Winter Garden, NY, 25

Feb 1953, for which he received the Antoinette Perry (Tony) Award; choreographed John Murray Anderson's Almanac, 1953; Tobia la Candida Spia (Rome, Italy), for which he received the Maschera d'Argento, 1954; La Patrona di Raggio di Luna (Rome), and made his London debut as choreographer at the Prince's, 24 Feb 1955, with Wonderful Town, also in Los Angeles in July, 1955; Shangri-La, Buona Notte, Bettina (Milan), 1956; L'Adorabile Giulio (Rome), 1957; directed the State Fair Music Hall, Dallas, musicals in 1957 and 1959; Un Trapezio per Lisistrata (Rome), and as head of his own dance company at Jacob's Pillow, Mass, choreographed This Property Is Condemned and choreographed and danced in Winesburg, Ohio, choreographed When in Rome (London), 1959; Jacob's Pillow, danced in Macbeth and Other Voices, Other Rooms, 1960; Boston, Mass, Arts Festival, danced in The Castle Period, choreographed Dreams of Glory (for the Robert Joffrey Ballet Company), Milk and Honey, 1961; Sophie, Morning Sun, 1963; To Broadway with Love (NY World's Fair), 1964; became assistant artistic director of the Harkness Ballet, 1964; choreographed Knickerbocker Holiday (San Francisco), No, No, Nanette, 1971; Much Ado About Nothing, Berlin to Broadway with Kurt Weill, 1972; Tricks, Good News (tour), No, No, Nanette (London), 1973; The Merry Wives of Windsor, Miss Moffat (Philadelphia), 1974; A Midsummer Night's Dream, Gala Tribute to Joshua Logan, Rodgers and Hart, The Robber Bridegroom, 1975; Hellzapoppin (tour), 1976; The Grand Tour, 1979; Happy New Year, 1980; choreographed the film By the Light of the Silvery Moon, 1953, and since then Young at Heart, Main Attraction, etc; for television has choreographed for *Holiday Hotel*, 1950, *Bell Telephone Hour*, 1961–64, for programs in Rome, 1959–60, etc.

Address: Society of Stage Directors and Choreographers, 1501 Broadway, New York, NY 10036.

SAINT-SUBBER, Arnold, producer
b Washington, DC, 18 Feb 1918; *s* of Saul Saint-Subber and his wife Rose (Wesser); *e* New York University; studied for the stage with John Murray Anderson.

Assistant stage manager for Hellzapoppin, 1938; assistant to John Murray Anderson for Billy Rose's Aquacade, NY, World's Fair, 1939; Ringling Brothers Circus, 1942; Ziegfeld Follies, 1943; Firebrand of Florence, 1945; supervised the production Hollywood Pinafore, Alvin, May 1945, also Park Avenue, Century, NY, Nov 1946; has presented or co-presented the following productions on Broadway; Kiss Me, Kate, 1948; Out of This World, 1950; The Grass Harp, 1952; My Three Angels, 1953; House of Flowers, 1954; The Square Root of Wonderful, The Dark at the Top of the Stairs, 1957; A Loss of Roses, The Tenth Man, 1959; Look! We've Come Through, 1961; Harold, 1962; Barefoot in the Park, 1963; Rich Little Rich Girl (Philadelphia), 1964; The Odd Couple, 1965; The Odd Couple (London), The Star-Spangled Girl, 1966; Dr Cook's Garden, There's a Girl in My Soup, The Little Foxes, 1967; Plaza Suite, Carry Me Back to Morningside Heights, Weekend, House of Flowers, 1968; Last of the Red Hot Lovers, 1969; The Gingerbread Lady, 1970; The Prisoner of Second Avenue, 1971; Gigi, 1973; 1600 Pennsylvania Avenue, 1978.

Address: 116 East 64th Street, New York, NY 10021. *Tel:* TE 8–3020.

SAKS, Gene, actor and director

b New York City, 8 Nov 1921; *s* of Morris J Saks and his wife Beatrix (Lewkowitz); *e* Cornell University (AB 1943); *m* Beatrice Arthur; prepared for the stage at the Actors Studio with Lee Strasberg, Sanford Meisner, and David Pressman, and at the Dramatic Workshop.

Made his stage début in a high school production of Charley's Aunt, 1939, playing Lord Fancourt Babberley; made his professional début at the Cherry Lane, NY, June 1947, as Joxer in Juno and the Paycock; July 1947, Vicar and Poet in The Dog Beneath the Skin; Aug 1947, the Engineer in Gas; Sept 1947, Henry IV in the Pirandello play of that name, Oct 1947, Rene St Gall in The Watched Pot; Morosco, Dec 1947, The Butler in Topaze; Provincetown Playhouse, June 1948, Old Shepherd in The Infernal Machine; June 1948, Park Attendant in Within the Gate; June 1948, the Doctor in him; Cherry Lane, June 1949, the German in Yes Is for a Very Young Man; Aug 1949, Professor of Religion in Too Many Thumbs; Sept 1949, Monsieur Jordan in The Bourgeois Gentleman; Mansfield, Feb 1950, Second Discusser, Marty's Double, and Sam in All You Need Is One Good Break; toured, 1950–1, as Stefanowski in Mister Roberts; Circle, Atlantic City, New Jersey, summer 1951, played the Chauffeur in Personal Appearance, Bill Page in The Voice of the Turtle, Wilbur in For Love or Money, and in Missouri Legend; Majestic, NY, in 1951, took over as the Professor in South Pacific; Phoenix, Jan 1954, Citizen and a Servant in Coriolanus; Westport Country Playhouse, Connecticut, 1954, Wicked Duke in The Thirteen Clocks; Westchester, NY, Playhouse, Aug 1954, Billy Gordon in Late Love; Phoenix, Mar 1955, Ragnar Brovik in The Master Builder; City Center, May 1955, Professor in South Pacific; Westchester Playhouse, Aug 1955, Charlie Reader in The Tender Trap; June 1956, Richard Sherman in The Seven Year Itch; Westport Country Playhouse, Connecticut, July 1956, Del Rio in The Gimmick; Carnegie Hall Playhouse, Oct 1956, various roles in Johnny Johnson; Phoenix, Dec 1956, First God in The Good Woman of Setzuan; ANTA, Feb 1957, took over from Martin Balsam as the Son-in-Law in Middle of the Night; Phoenix, Feb 1958, Captain in The Infernal Machine; 46th Street, Sept 1958, The Professor in Howie; Festival of the Two Worlds, Spoleto, Italy, 1959, played various roles in Album Leaves; Booth, Nov 1959, Rabbi in The Tenth Man; Martin Beck, Dec 1960, Norman Yarrow in Love and Libel; Booth, Oct 1961, Morestan in A Shot in the Dark; Eugene O'Neill, Apr 1962, Leo Herman in A Thousand Clowns; turned to directing and, at the Henry Miller's, Mar 1963, directed his first Broadway play, Enter Laughing; has since directed The Millionairess (tour), Nobody Loves an Albatross, 1963; Half a Sixpence, Generation, 1965; Mame, 1966; A Mother's Kisses, 1968; Sheep on the Runway, 1970; How the Other Half Loves, 1971; at the Berkshire Theater Festival, Stockbridge, Mass, July 1971, played in The Goodbye People; directed Same Time, Next Year, 1975; California Suite, 1976; I Love My Wife (Tony Award), 1977; The Prince of Grand Street (tour), 1978; played Leo in the film of A Thousand Clowns, 1966, and directed Barefoot in the Park, 1968, The Odd Couple, Cactus Flower, 1969, Last of the Red Hot Lovers, Mame, and appeared as an actor in The Prisoner of Second Avenue (1974), etc; has appeared frequently on the various dramatic television programs, notably the *Actors Studio Series*, 1949, *US Steel Hour, You Are There, Playwright '55 and '56*, etc.

Address: 271 Central Park West, New York, NY.

SALBERG, Derek S, CBE 1977 (OBE 1965), JP, manager

b Birmingham, Warwickshire, 30 July 1912; *s* of Leon Salberg and his wife Janie (Thomas); *e* Chigwell House School, Birmingham, and Clifton College; *m* Joan Horstead (dec).

Joined the Alexandra Theatre, Birmingham, 1932, as stage manager, subsequently appointed assistant manager, and appointed General Manager of the theatre in 1936; Managing Director and Licensee, 1937–77; member of the Drama Panel of the Arts Council of Great Britain 1953–61; two terms as director on the Sadler's Wells Theatre Trust Ltd; original member of the Board of the National Theatre, 1963–5; 1977, appointed to serve a second term on Board of Birmingham Repertory Theatre; awarded the Gold Medal of the Birmingham Civic Society, 1961; 1978, Consultant to Old Vic Trust, becoming Secretary, 1979; created Justice of the Peace, 1961; served in the Royal Corps of Signals in World War II, subsequently being transferred to RASC/EFI for service with ENSA.

Recreation: Cricket. *Clubs:* Warwickshire CCC, Press (Birmingham), and Midland (Birmingham). *Address:* 28 St Peter's Road, Harborne, Birmingham B17 0AY. *Tel:* 021–427 6486.

SALLIS, Peter, actor and dramatic author

b Twickenham, 1 Feb 1921; *s* of Harry Sallis and his wife, Dorothy Amea Frances (Barnard); *e* Minchenden Grammar School, Southgate; *m* (1) Elaine Usher (mar dis); (2) Elaine Usher; was formerly employed as a bank clerk; studied for the stage at the RADA.

Made his first appearance on the professional stage, Arts, Sept 1946, as a Soldier and Servant in The Scheming Lieutenant; after three years in various repertory theatres, and appearing on tour, he returned to London, Aldwych, May 1951, as Fedotik in a revival of The Three Sisters; Lyric, Hammersmith, Nov 1951, Roger Doremus in Summer and Smoke, and transferred with this to the Duchess, Jan 1952; Old Vic, May 1952, played the Jeweller in Timon of Athens; Mermaid, Sept 1952, played the Porter and Doctor in Macbeth; Mermaid, Oct 1952, played Hoard in A Trick to Catch the Old One; during John Gielgud's season at the Lyric, Hammersmith, Dec 1952–May 1953, appeared as Waitwell in The Way of the World, and Retrosi in Venice Preserved; Aldwych, Apr 1954, 1st Soldier in The Dark is Light Enough; Haymarket, Nov 1954, played Joe Scanlon in The Matchmaker; Globe, May 1955, Virgil Penny in Into Thin Air; Duke of York's, June 1955, Stage Manager in Orson Welles's adaptation of Moby Dick; Garrick, Sept 1955, Priest in The Count of Clérembard; Saville, Feb 1956, played Fag in a revival of The Rivals; Fortune, Dec 1956, played JG in Who Cares?; Aldwych, Apr 1957, Denny in Janus; Winter Garden, Dec 1957, Frank Braddock in Be My Guest; Lyric, Hammersmith, Jan–Apr 1959, appeared as Simon and Barère in Danton's Death, Thrifty in The Cheats of Scapin; and Doctor and Provost in Brand; Royal Court, July 1959, Gigot in Look After Lulu; New, Sept 1959, took over the part of Van Putzeboom in the same play; Royal Court, Apr 1960, played Bottard in Rhinoceros, transferring to the Strand, June 1960; Arts, Aug 1960, played Peter in The Zoo Story; Royalty, Jan 1961, played Phillip Vanderkamp in Masterpiece; Garrick, Apr 1962, Mr Moxer in Two Stars For Comfort; Lyric, May 1963, Morestan in A Shot in the Dark; Lyric, Apr 1964, Ladislav Sipos in the musical She Loves Me; made his first appearance in New York at the Broadway Theatre, Feb 1965, as Dr Watson in Baker Street; Belasco, NY, Dec 1965, Hudson in Inadmissible Evidence; Strand, July 1966, Roat in Wait Until Dark; Palace, Feb 1968, Herr Schultz in Cabaret; Comedy, Nov 1972, Edwin Palmer in The Pay-Off; author of the stage play End of Term, and three radio plays; made his first appearance in films, 1952, and played in the following films: Anastasia, The Doctor's Dilemma, The Scapegoat, Saturday Night and Sunday Morning, The VIP's, Full Circle, Someone is Killing the Great Chefs of Europe; first appeared on television, 1948, and has since appeared frequently, including: The Diary of Samuel Pepys, and *Last of the Summer Wine.*

Favourite parts: Roat in Wait until Dark, and Sipos in She Loves Me. *Recreations:* Painting and gardening. *Club:* Garrick. *Address:* c/o London Management, 235–241 Regent Street, London, W1.

SAND, Paul (*né* Sanchez), actor
b Los Angeles, Cal, 5 Mar; *s* of Ernest Rivera Sanchez and his wife Sonia Borodiansky (Stone); *e* Los Angeles high schools and City College; prepared for the stage with Viola Spolin at the Young Actors Company Repertory Company, Los Angeles.

First appeared on the stage at age ten with the Spolin troupe at the Circle, Los Angeles; played numerous roles for this company; as Paul Sanchez joined the Marcel Marceau mime troupe and made his New York debut at the NY City Center, 1 Feb 1956; joined the Second City improvisational troupe in Chicago, Ill, and next appeared in NY, as Paul Sand, at the Royale, 26 Sept 1961, in the revue From the Second City; Second City at Square East, Apr 1963, played in the revue To the Water Tower; made his London debut at the Prince Charles, 23 Apr 1963, with the Second City troupe in Looking for the Action; Spoleto, Italy, Festival of the Two Worlds, summer 1963, appeared in Luis, which he also wrote; Theatre de Lys, NY, Nov 1963, appeared in his first straight play as Arthur in Journey to the Day; Renata, Apr 1965, appeared in the revue Wet Paint; East 74th Street, Oct 1965, Maxime in Hotel Passionato; The New, Jan 1966, appeared in the revue The Mad Show, and subsequently played in it in Los Angeles at the PJ Theatre; Plymouth, Aug 1967, took over a part in The Star-Spangled Girl; Ambassador, Oct 1970, played in Paul Sills' Story Theatre, and received the Antoinette Perry (Tony) Award; Ambassador, Apr 1971, played in Ovid's Metamorphoses; Mark Taper Forum, Los Angeles, Cal, June 1971, again played in Story Theatre, and subsequently at the John F. Kennedy Center for the Performing Arts, Washington, DC; Mark Taper Forum, LA, Apr 1977, in Angel City; Public/Martinson Hall, Nov 1977, appeared in Paul Sills' Tales of the Hasidim; has appeared in the films Hot Rock, 1971, The Main Event, Can't Stop the Music, 1980, etc; on television has appeared on the *Carol Burnett Show,* 1971–73, *Mary Tyler Moore Show,* 1972, on *Ed Sullivan's Show,* Jack Paar's show, on Dick Cavett's show, in *Story Theatre,* in his series *Friends and Lovers,* etc.

Hobbies and recreations: Reading, writing, theatre- and movie-going, body surfing. *Address:* 2409 Panorama Terrace, Los Angeles, Cal.

SANDS, Dorothy, actress
b Cambridge, Mass, 5 Mar 1893; *d* of Frank Edgar Sands and his wife Lydia Reynolds (Phipps); *e* Radcliffe College; formerly a teacher; studied for the stage at the Curry School of Expression, Boston, at the Central School of Speech and Drama, London, and with George Pierce Baker at the 47 Workshop, Harvard.

Wrote and directed the pageant The Spirit of Niagara Falls, at Niagara Falls, New York, July 1919; made her first professional appearance on the stage at the Studebaker Theatre, Chicago, Dec 1923, as Jane in The Children of the Moon; first appeared in New York, at the Belmont Theatre, 1924, when she played Nautcha in Catskill Dutch; joined the Neighborhood Playhouse Repertory Company, appearing in Grand Street Follies of 1924, and remained a member of this company until 1927; during this period she played in a variety of plays, including: The Little Clay Cart, 1924; The Critic, The Legend of the Dance, and The Dybbuk, 1925; The Romantic Young Lady and The Lion Tamer, 1926; Pinwheel, 1927; also appearing annually in her impersonations of stage and screen stars in the production Grand Street Follies; Bijou, Nov 1927, Clothilde in The Stairs; Booth, NY, May 1928, appeared in Grand Street Follies of 1928; Comedy, Apr 1929, Madame Arkadina in The Seagull; Booth, May 1929, The Grand Street Follies; Plymouth, Dec 1929, Helena Grey in Half-Gods; Little, Feb 1930, Emily Coster in Many-a-Slip; Royale, Feb 1931, Winifred Dexter in Rock Me, Julie; Shubert-Riviera, Apr 1931, Julie Cavendish in The Royal Family; between 1932–9, gave one-woman recitals Styles in Acting, and Our Stage and Screen at the Booth Theatre, NY, and also on a coast to coast tour of the United States; played stock engagements, 1931–42; toured, 1939, as Proserpine Garnett in Candida; Guild Theatre, NY, Jan 1942, played Mrs Yoder in Papa Is All; Longacre, NY, May 1942, played Josephine Bender in All the Comforts of Home; Ethel Barrymore, Apr 1943, Jessie Frame in Tomorrow the World; Biltmore, Jan 1946, Tina in A Joy Forever; again played stock, 1946–9; under the auspices of the American State Department, 1949, toured Germany, with her own entertainment American Theatre Highlights and appeared in this at the Mercury, London, June 1949; ANTA, NY, Dec 1950, played Maud Mayo in The Cellar and the Well; toured US, 1951–2, as Aunt Queenie in Bell, Book, and Candle; City Center, NY, Feb 1953, and Ethel Barrymore, 1953, played Mrs Tarleton in Misalliance; Coronet, NY, Nov 1954, played Lady Bonnington in Quadrille; Belasco, NY, Apr 1957, Cornelia Knight in The First Gentleman; Phoenix, NY, Oct 1957, Ivy in The Family Reunion; Morosco, Jan 1958, took over from Helen Hayes as the Duchess in Time Remembered; Phoenix, Oct 1958, played Hannah Kennedy in Mary Stuart; on a Rockfeller Foundation Grant, she visited Istanbul and Ankara, 1958, to give her one-woman entertainment Styles in Acting, also directing the play, Ah, Wilderness! at the Turkish National Theatre, Ankara; Cort, NY, Oct 1959, played Madame Bobignot in Moonbirds; Players, off Broadway, Nov 1960, played Little Pigeon in Whisper to Me; toured Europe, Middle East, and South America with the American Repertory Company for the US State Department, 1961, as the Fortune Teller in The Skin of Our Teeth and Aunt Ev in The Miracle Worker; Charles Playhouse, Boston, Apr 1962, appeared in The Autumn Garden; Westport Country Playhouse, Conn, Oct 1963, Mrs Vissershooft in The Moments of Love; Booth, Nov 1963, Mrs Goolsby in Once for the Asking; City Center, May 1964, Mrs Pearce in My Fair Lady; toured, Mar–Aug 1965, as Madame Alvarez in Gigi; Greenwich Mews, Mar 1966, took over as Oenone in Phèdre, and played this part in Denver and Aspen, Colorado, Aug 1966; Bonfils, Denver, July 1967, Martha Brewster in Arsenic and Old Lace; Théâtre de Lys, Dec 1967, Mrs Miles in The Club Bedroom; University of Denver, Apr 1968, Mrs Hardcastle in She Stoops to Conquer; Lunt-Fontanne, Mar 1969, Mrs Meserve in Come Summer; Brooks Atkinson, Jan 1970, Hattie Fields in Paris Is Out!; Roundabout, Oct 1972, Signora Frola in Right You Are . . . If You Think You Are; first appeared on television, 1948, and has played in Morning's at Seven, Pygmalion, and the title-role in Colette; teacher of Classic Acting at the American Theatre Wing (Professional Training Program), and received the Tony Award for Teaching, 1959; member of the Council of the Actors Equity Association; member of the Advisory Board of IASTA; Hon Phi Beta Kappa from Radcliffe College.

Favourite parts: Prossy in Candida, Madame Arkadina in The Seagull, and Mrs Tarleton in Misalliance. *Recreations:* Gardening and travelling. *Clubs:* Cosmopolitan, and Radcliffe. *Address:* The Ruxton, 50 West 72nd Street, New York, NY 10023. *Tel:* SU 7-0500.

SANDS, Leslie, actor and dramatic author
b Bradford, Yorkshire, 19 May 1921; *s* of Albert Edward Sands, and his wife Alice (Riley); *e* Hanson High School, Bradford, and Leeds University; *m* Pauline Williams.

First appeared on the stage singing comic songs at the age of seven; first appeared on professional stage, 14 July 1941, at the Lyceum, Sheffield, as Peter Storm in Do You Remember?; first appeared on the London stage, 18 Dec 1946, at the Piccadilly, as Silius in Antony and Cleopatra; Aldwych, Dec 1947, played Menteith and first murderer in Macbeth; after a season at Bristol Old Vic, 1948–9, and an Australian tour, 1950–1, appeared in repertory at the Alexandra, Birmingham, 1951–6; Theatre Royal, York, June 1963, Sir Giles Overreach in A New Way to Pay Old Debts; Aldwych, Feb 1970, for RSC, Mr Link in After Haggerty; Aug 1970, same theatre, Sir Toby Belch in Twelfth Night; Criterion, Feb 1971, again played Mr Link; Phoenix, Leicester, Feb 1972, narrated Open House, which he also devised; joined the National Theatre company at the Old Vic, Apr 1974, to play Dr Kirby in Eden End; Arnaud, Guildford, Aug 1975, Henry Hobson in Hobson's Choice; Albery, June 1977, Burgess in Candida; Lyttelton, May 1979, Leonard Ardsley in For Services Rendered; Lyttelton, Dec 1979, Alderman Helliwell in When We Are Married; films, since 1960, include: The Deadly Affair, One More Time and The Ragman's Daughter; television, since 1955, includes: Where the Difference Begins, The Lump and the series *Cluff*; is the author of six stage plays and has written extensively for television.
Favourite part: Coriolanus. *Recreations:* Dogs, gardening. *Address:* c/o Fraser and Dunlop Ltd, 91 Regent Street, London W1. *Tel:* 01-734-7311.

SARANDON, Chris, actor
b Beckley, West Virginia, 24 Jul 1942; *e* West Virginia University (BA) and Catholic University (MFA).

Made his professional debut 1965–66 as Jack Hunter in The Rose Tattoo; Broadway debut, Lunt-Fontanne, 19 Oct 1970, as Jacob in The Rothschilds, later taking over the role of Nathan in the same show; St James, Nov 1972, took over as Proteus in Two Gentlemen of Verona; at the Public, Jan 1977, played Tom Wintermouth in Marco Polo Sings a Solo; in Sept 1977 appeared there in a workshop production of Prayer for My Daughter; Ahmanson, LA, Dec 1977, and Brooklyn Academy, Feb 1978, Dick Dudgeon in The Devil's Disciple; Wilbur, Boston, Apr 1978, Steve Crandall in a try-out of Broadway; Public, Apr 1979, Nick in The Woods; regional work includes a season with Long Wharf, and appearances at Hartford Stage, the McCarter, Princeton, and the Shaw Festival, Niagara-on-the-Lake, Ont; films include Dog Day Afternoon, Lipstick, The Sentinel, and Cuba; recent TV includes The Day Christ Died, 1980.
Address: c/o Andrews Management, 488 Madison Avenue, New York, NY 10022. *Tel:* 759-1780.

SARONY, Leslie, actor and vocalist
b Surbiton, 22 Jan 1897; *s* of William Rawstone Frye and his wife Mary (Sarony); *e* Twickenham; *m* Anita Eaton.

First appearance on the stage in a music-hall act in 1911, and was subsequently one of Park's Eton Boys; appeared at the Hippodrome, Dec 1913, in Hullo, Tango; after some concert party engagements, joined the London Scottish in 1915, and served in the Army in France and Salonica until 1919; after the War appeared at the King's, Hammersmith, Dec 1919, as the Baron in Cinderella; at the Hippodrome, Apr 1921, played in The Peep Show, and at the Gaiety, Apr 1922, in His Girl; subsequently toured in South America; appeared at the London Pavilion, 1923, in Dover Street to Dixie; at the London Hippodrome, 1923, in Brighter London; Palladium, Mar 1924, in The Whirl of the World; in 1925 toured in Rat-a-Tat; subsequently appeared in cabaret at the Café de Paris, and in the music-halls in We; Adelphi, Aug 1927, played Hyacinth in Up With the Lark; at Drury Lane, May 1928, Frank in Show Boat; Prince Edward, Apr 1930, Chic Bean in Rio Rita; in May 1932, toured in Between Ourselves; with Leslie Holmes created the music hall act The Two Leslies, and appeared in it for many years, including a Royal Variety Performance, and tours to entertain the troops during World War II; in his seventies, began a new career as a straight actor in Echoes from a Concrete Canyon, Theatre Upstairs, 1975; Nottingham Playhouse, also Edinburgh Festival, Sept 1975, played Adam in As You Like It; again at Nottingham Jan 1976, played Kemp in Entertaining Mr Sloane; Royal Court, May 1976, Nagg in Endgame; Churchill, Bromley, 1977, Uncle Pestemon in Mr Polly; Royal Court, Feb 1978, Luka in The Bear; Churchill, 1979, the Butler in Dandy Dick; his films include Chitty Chitty Bang Bang and, most recently, Yanks; TV includes plays and series such as I Didn't Know You Cared; author and composer of many hit songs.
Favourite parts: Buttons in Cinderella, Frank in Show Boat. *Address:* c/o Spotlight, 42–43 Cranbourn Street, London WC2.

SAROYAN, William, dramatic author and novelist
b Fresno, California, 31 Aug 1908; *s* of Armenag Saroyan and his wife Takoohi (Sarovan); *e* Fresno; *m* Carol Marcus (mar dis); formerly a telegraph messenger, newspaper reporter, and postal employee.

Entered on the management of the Lyceum Theatre, New York, 1941, where he staged his own play, The Beautiful People; at the Belasco, 1942, staged Across the Board on Tomorrow Morning and Talking to You; at the Theatre Royal, Stratford, London, Apr 1960, directed his own play, Sam, the Highest Jumper of Them All; also author of the following plays: My Heart's in the Highlands, 1939; The Time of Your Life, 1939, which gained the New York Critics Circle Award and the Pulitzer Prize, 1940; Love's Old Sweet Song, Sweeney Among the Trees, Hero of the World, Something About a Soldier, 1940; Hello, Out There, Afton Water, Razzle-Dazzle (a collection of short plays), 1942; Get Away Old Man, 1943; The Hunger, Ping Pong Players, 1945; Don't Go Away Mad, 1949; The Son, 1950; Jim Dandy, The Violin Messiah, 1951; Opera, Opera, 1955; Once Around the Block, 1956; The Cave Dwellers, Ever Been in Love with a Midget? (Berlin), 1957; Parisian Comedy, Settled Out of Court (co-author), Sam, the Highest Jumper of Them All, 1960; High Time Along the Wabash, a trilogy produced at Purdue University, 1961; The Rebirth Celebration of the Human Race at Artie Zabala's off-Broadway Theater, produced at the Shirtsleeve, NY, July 1975; wrote a ballet, The Great American Goof, produced at the Ballet Theatre, NY, 1940; films include: The Human Comedy (Academy (Oscar) Award, 1943), and The Time of Your Life; wrote Ah Sweet Mystery of Mrs Murphy and The Unstoppable Gray Fox for television; wrote the text for the cantata Ah Man, performed at the Aldeburgh Festival, 1962; author of The Daring Young Man on the Flying Trapeze, 1934, My Name Is Aram, 1939, Dear Baby, 1944, The Adventures of Wesley Jackson, 1946,

Papa You're Crazy, 1957, Here Comes, There Goes, You Know Who, 1961, Boys and Girls Together, 1963, Not Dying, 1963, and other novels and short story collections.

Address: c/o Harcourt, Brace, Jovanovich Inc, 750 Third Avenue, New York 10017.

SARTRE, Jean-Paul, dramatic author
b Paris, 5 June 1905; *e* La Rochelle and Paris; after concluding his military service, went to Le Havre as a teacher of philosophy.

Commenced writing, 1936; first attracted attention with a semi-autobiographical novel, La Nausée; served in the Army from Sept 1939, taken prisoner during 1940, and was a prisoner-of-war 1940–1, when he was released, owing to ill-health; subsequently lectured on Greek Drama at the Charles Dullin School of Acting; is the author of the following plays: Les Mouches (The Flies), 1942; Huis Clos (No Exit, 1943, and Vicious Circle, 1946); Morts sans Sépulture (Men Without Shadows, 1947); La Putain Respectueuse (The Respectable Prostitute, 1947); Crime Passionnel, 1948; Les Mains Sales, (Crime Passionel 1948); Le Diable et le Bon Dieu, 1950; Nekrassov, 1957; Les Séquestrés d'Altona (Altona), 1959; Kean (adaptation from a play by Dumas), 1961; he was the founder and editor of the newspaper, *Les Temps Modernes*; author of several novels and works on existentialism and ethics, as well as a biography of Jean Genet.

(Died 15 Apr 1980.)

SAUNDERS, James, dramatic author
b Islington, London, 8 Jan 1925; *s* of Walter Percival Saunders and his wife Dorcas Geraldine (Warren); *e* Wembley County School, Southampton University; *m* Audrey Cross.

Author of the following plays: Moonshine, 1955; Alas, Poor Fred (one-act), The Ark, 1959; Committal (one-act), Barnstable (one-act), Return to a City (one-act), 1960; A Slight Accident (one-act), 1961; Double Double, Next Time I'll Sing to You, 1962; Next Time I'll Sing to You (revised), The Pedagogue (one-act), Who Was Hilary Maconochie? (one-act), Next Time I'll Sing to You (New York), 1963; A Scent of Flowers, Neighbours (one-act), 1964; The Italian Girl (co-author), 1968; A Man's Best Friend, Haven, The Borage Pigeon Affair, The Travails of Sancho Panza, 1969; After Liverpool (one-act), 1970; Games, Savoury Meringue (both one-act), 1971; Hans Kohlhaas, 1972; Bye Bye Blues (one-act), 1973; The Island, A Journey to London (co-author), 1975; Bodies, 1977; Birdsong (one-act), 1979; Random Moments in a May Garden, 1980; plays for television include: Watch Me I'm a Bird, 1964, and the series *Bloomers*, 1979; Most Promising Playwright (with Charles Wood) in *Evening Standard Award,* 1963.

Address: c/o Margaret Ramsay Ltd, 14a Goodwin's Court, St Martin's Lane, London, WC2.

SAUNDERS, Peter, producing manager and theatre owner
b London, 23 Nov 1911; *s* of Ernest Saunders; *e* Oundle; *m* (1) Ann Stewart (dec); (2) Catherine Baylis (Katie Boyle).

Formerly a film cameraman, film director, journalist and subsequently a press agent; during the war he was 6 years in the army rising from the ranks to Captain; has presented the following plays, either alone or in association with others; Fly Away Peter (St James's), 1947; The Perfect Woman (Playhouse), 1948; Breach of Marriage (Duke of York's), My Mother Said (Fortune), Wanted on Voyage (tour), The Ex-Mrs Y (tour), 1949; The Poison Belt (tour), Murder At The Vicarage (tour), Flowers For The Living (tour), Castle In The Air (tour), Black Coffee (tour), 1950; Daddy Wore Velvet Gloves (tour), The Hollow (Fortune), Say It With

Flowers (tour), 1951; To Dorothy A Son (tour), 1952; The Mousetrap, 1952, produced at the Ambassadors' and after 8 years at the same theatre, on 25 Aug 1960, achieved the Long Run Record (in London and New York) of 3214 performances; on 23 Dec 1970, became the World's Longest Run beating The Drunkard with 7511 performances; on 25 Mar 1974 transferred to the St Martin's and still continues, Nov 1976; Witness For The Prosecution (Winter Garden), 1953; The Manor of Northstead (Duchess), Spider's Web (Savoy), 1954; in NY, with Gilbert Miller, presented Witness For The Prosecution, 1954; in England, presented The Water Gipsies (Winter Garden), The Bride and the Bachelor (Duchess), 1956; Subway In The Sky (Savoy), 1957; Verdict (Strand), The Trial of Mary Dugan (Savoy), The Unexpected Guest (Duchess), A Day In The Life Of . . . (Savoy), 1958; Murder On Arrival (tour), And Suddenly It's Spring (Duke of York's), 1959; Go Back For Murder (Duchess), The More The Merrier (tour), 1960; Milk and Honey (tour), You Prove It (St Martin's), 1961; Fit To Print (Duke of York's), Rule of Three (Duchess), 1962; Alfie (Duchess), 1963 which was also produced on Broadway; The Reluctant Peer (Duchess), Hostile Witness (Haymarket) which was also produced on Broadway, Every Other Evening (Phoenix), 1964; Return Ticket (Duchess), 1965; Arsenic And Old Lace (Vaudeville), Justice Is A Woman (Vaudeville), 1966; As You Like It (Vaudeville), 1967; Oh Clarence! (Lyric), 1968; On A Foggy Day (St Martin's), 1969; The Jockey Club Stakes (Vaudeville), 1970; Move Over Mrs Markham (Vaudeville), 1971; Lover (St Martin's), Cockie (Vaudeville), 1973; Double Edge (Vaudeville), 1975; in 1971 acquired Volcano Productions Ltd, whose productions include: No Sex Please, We're British (Strand), 1971; The Mating Game (Apollo), Lloyd George Knew My Father (Savoy), Parents Day (Globe), Stand And Deliver (Roundhouse), 1972; At The End Of The Day (Savoy), Signs Of The Times (Vaudeville), Birds Of Paradise (Garrick), 1973; Touch Of Spring (Comedy), Betzi (Haymarket), No Room for Sex (tour), 1975; Out on a Limb (Vaudeville), 1976; In the Red (tour), Cause Célèbre (Her Majesty's), A Murder is Announced (Vaudeville), 1977; The Family Reunion (Vaudeville), 1979; operated repertory at the Royal Artillery Theatre, Woolwich, 1951; also at the Prince of Wales Theatre, Cardiff, 1956; in 1958, took over a long lease of the Ambassadors'; bought the freehold of the Duchess Theatre, 1961, and sold it in 1968; acquired a long lease of the St Martin's Theatre, 1968; bought the freehold of the Vaudeville Theatre, 1969, and of the Duke of York's, 1976, selling it in 1979 to Capital Radio on condition that it remained a live theatre in perpetuity; has produced more than 1500 programmes for Radio Luxembourg, and has also presented a series of plays of his own choice for television, including The Manor of Northstead on A E Matthews' 90th Birthday, 1959; received the Variety Club of Great Britain's Silver Heart for the Theatrical Manager of the Year, 1955; has been a member of the Executive Council of the Society of West End Theatre since 1954 (President, 1961–2 and again 1967–9); member of the Council of the Theatrical Managers' Association 1958–64; President of the Stage Golfing Society, 1963; President of the Stage Cricket Club from 1956–65; was one of the Consortium that bid successfully for Yorkshire Television and was a director of the first Board, 1967; member of the Editorial Board of *Who's Who In The Theatre* since 1970; Vice President of the Actors' Benevolent Fund since 1972; Vice President of the Theatres Investment Fund since 1973; member of the Consortium awarded London General Radio Station by IBA 1973; publication The Mousetrap Man (autobiog) 1972; author of the play Scales of Justice, produced in 1978; served on the Board of the US

Bicentennial World Theatre Festival 1976; chairman and managing director of Peter Saunders Ltd, Peter Saunders Theatres Ltd, Peter Saunders Properties, Volcano Productions Ltd and Hampdale Ltd; Director of Dominfast Investments Ltd, West End Theatre Managers Ltd, Kroy Investments Ltd, Theatre Investment Fund Ltd, Theatre Investment Finance Ltd and The Duke of York's Theatre Ltd.

Recreations: Cricket, bridge, the music of George Gershwin and telephoning. *Address:* Vaudeville Theatre, Strand, London, WC2R 0NH. *Tel:* 01–240 3177.

SAVORY, Gerald, actor and dramatic author
b London, 17 Nov 1909; *s* of Kenneth Douglas (Savory) and his wife Grace Mabel (Lane); *e* Bradfield College; *m* (1) Teo Dunbar; (2) Althea Murphy; (3) Annette Carell; (4) Sheila Brennan.

Made his first appearance on the stage at the Savoy Theatre, 12 Jan 1926, as the Earl of Loam in the juvenile performance of The Admirable Crichton; subsequently engaged as a stockbroker's clerk, made his first appearance, professionally, at the Playhouse, Whitley Bay, 30 Apr 1931, as Mr Smith in It Pays to Advertise; Ambassadors', London, Feb 1932, played Laker in The Queen's Husband; toured in Canada, with Barry Jones's company, 1932; appeared with the Hull repertory company, 1932–3; toured in Australia with his mother, 1933–4; played in repertory companies at Brighton and Bournemouth, 1934–5, and at Perth, 1936; appeared at the New, London, 1936, in Girl Unknown and Savoy, Nov 1936, in Young Madame Conti; subsequently went to America; at the Cort Theatre, New York, Dec 1941, played Norman in Golden Wings; Henry Miller, Dec 1942, Sergeant Miller in Flare Path; Playhouse, Apr 1944, Bradley in Sheppey; author of George and Margaret, 1937, which ran for two years; Good and Proper, 1938; String Quartet, 1939; Hand in Glove (with Charles Freeman), 1944; Now the Day is Over, 1945; The Quick and the Dead, 1946; Marriage Aforethought, 1948; A Likely Tale, 1956; A Month of Sundays, 1957; So Many Children, Come Rain, Come Shine, 1958; Hilary, 1959; Cup and Saucer, 1961; The Twinkling of an Eye, 1965; author of a novel, Behold This Dreamer, 1943; Executive Producer of Granada Television, 1964; head of plays, BBC television, 1965–72; author of Count Dracula, BBC2, 1976; produced the series *Churchill's People*, 1975, and Love in A Cold Climate, 1978–80.

Recreation: Reading. *Address:* 20 Charles Street, London W1.

SCALES, Prunella (*née* Illingworth), actress
b Sutton Abinger, Surrey; *d* of John Richardson Illingworth, and his wife Catherine (Scales); *e* Moira House, Eastbourne; *m* Timothy West; trained for the stage at the Old Vic School, London, and Herbert Berghof Studio, New York (under Uta Hagen).

First appeared on the stage in Sept 1951, at the Theatre Royal, Bristol, as the Cook in Traveller Without Luggage; first appeared on the London stage in May 1954, at the Arts, as Lucrezia in The Impresario from Smyrna, and later that year was in the revue Reprise at the Watergate; made her Broadway début at the Royale, Dec 1955, as Ermengarde in The Matchmaker; Shakespeare Memorial, Stratford, 1956, appeared as Nerissa in The Merchant of Venice, Jacquenetta in Love's Labour's Lost, and Juliet in Measure for Measure; Oxford Playhouse, 1957, played the pupil in The Lesson, Alice Arden in Frost at Midnight, and Myrrhine in Lysistrata; Prince's, Oct 1957, Aline in The Man of Distinction; Arts, Jan 1958, and later at the Winter Garden, Margie in The Iceman Cometh; Players', Dec 1958, Nelly Denver in The

Silver King; toured Europe in 1959 with the Oxford Playhouse Company, as Olivia in Twelfth Night, and Hermia in A Midsummer Night's Dream; Bromley Little Theatre, Nov 1960, played Anna Bowers in All Good Children; Oxford, Aug 1961, Marita in Whiteman; Garrick, Feb 1962, appeared in the revue Not To Worry; Arts, May 1963, played Mabel in The Trigon; Birmingham Repertory, 1965, Hermione in The Winter's Tale; Hampstead Theatre Club, Jan 1966, Leontine in The Birdwatcher; Arnaud, Guildford, Oct 1966, appeared in the revue, Night is for Delight; Vaudeville, Jan 1967, Valerie in Say Who You Are; Chichester Festival, June 1967, Cherry in The Beaux' Stratagem; Fortune, 1967, took over the part of Lika in The Promise; Duke of York's, Feb 1968, played Jackie Coryton in Hay Fever; Chichester Festival, May 1968, the Wife in The Unknown Soldier and His Wife; Mermaid, Sept 1969, Emma Partridge in Children's Day; Wyndham's, Jan 1970, Esther Goonahan in It's a Two Foot Six Inches Above the Ground World; appeared in the Ambiance lunchtime productions, After Magritte (Apr 1970), and Have You Met Our Rabbit? (Dec); Hampstead, June 1971, played Mabel and Susan in the double-bill, Bedtime and Butter; Arts, Cambridge, and tour, Oct 1971, Natasha in Three Sisters and Avonia Bunn in Trelawny of the 'Wells'; toured Australia with Prospect Theatre Company, spring 1972, in King Lear, Love's Labour's Lost, and Endgame; Arnaud, Guildford, Aug 1972, Hilary Plummer in That's No Lady—That's My Husband; Watford Palace, Feb 1973, Lady Brute in The Provok'd Wife; Playhouse, Nottingham, Sept 1973, Katharina in The Taming of the Shrew; Soho Poly, Dec 1973, Joyce in The Ruffian on the Stair; Open Space, Feb 1976, played six parts in Anatol; Round House, Dec 1976, appeared in The Pelican; Mermaid, Mar 1977, Henrietta Barnett in It's All Right If I Do It; Whitehall, Nov 1977, Betty in Breezeblock Park; Old Vic, June 1978, in Smith of Smiths (part of triple bill Great English Eccentrics); Bristol Old Vic, May 1979, Natalya Petrovna in A Month in the Country; for the re-formed Old Vic Company, played Tag in Miss in Her Teens, Sept 1979; Mrs Prentice in What the Butler Saw, Oct 1979; and Queen Caroline in The Trial of Queen Caroline, Nov 1979; Lyric, Hammersmith, Mar 1980, transferring to Haymarket, Apr, Mrs Rogers in Make and Break; films, since 1952, include: Waltz of the Toreadors, The Boys from Brazil and The Hound of the Baskervilles; first television performance also 1952, in Pride and Prejudice and appearances include: Ghosts, and the series *Marriage Lines* and *Fawlty Towers.*

Favourite parts: Natalya Petrovna and Cherry. *Recreations:* Growing vegetables, listening to music, reading in English and French. *Address:* c/o Boyack and Conway, 8 Cavendish Place, London W1.

SCHAEFER, George, director and producer
b Wallingford, Conn, 16 Dec 1920; *s* of Louis Schaefer and his wife Elsie (Otterbein); *e* Oak Park High School, Illinois; Lafayette College (BA) and Yale Drama School; *m* Mildred Trares.

Directed his first production for the stage with the Pastime Players, Oak Park, 1937, in Leave It to Psmith; for the US Army Special Services, Honolulu, Hawaii, 1942–5, directed more than fifty productions; directed his first New York production at the Columbus Circle Theatre, 14 Dec 1945, when he staged Hamlet; City Center, June 1946, again directed Hamlet; McCarter Theatre, Princeton, NJ, Jan 1947, co-directed Darling, Darling, Darling; Alvin, Oct 1947, co-directed Man and Superman; Music Box, Mar 1948, directed The Linden Tree; at the City Center has served as executive producer, artistic director, or director of the following plays: Man and Superman, She Stoops to Conquer, 1949; The Corn Is Green, The Heiress, The Devil's Disciple, Captain Brassbound's Conversion, 1950; The Royal Family, Richard II, The Taming of the Shrew, Dream Girl, Idiot's Delight, The Wild Duck, 1951; Anna Christie, Come of Age, The Male Animal, Tovarich, First Lady, 1952; Martin Beck, Oct 1953, co-produced The Teahouse of the August Moon; made his London début as director at Her Majesty's, Apr 1954, with The Teahouse of the August Moon; he has since directed The Southwest Corner; Kiss Me, Kate, 1955; The Apple Cart, 1956; The Body Beautiful, 1958; Write Me a Murder, 1961 (London, 1962); directed Zenda (also co-produced), 1963; at the New York World Fair, 1964, produced To Broadway with Love; directed The Great Indoors, 1966; directed The Last of Mrs Lincoln, 1972; directed the tour of The Student Prince, 1973; directed the tour of Ah, Wilderness!, 1975; between 1952–8, directed over 25 musicals at the State Fair, Dallas, Texas; directed his first film, Macbeth, 1960, and subsequently directed An Enemy of the People, Pendulum, Generation, Doctors' Wives, Once upon a Scoundrel; since 1954, he has both produced and directed innumerable television plays and musicals; including: Hamlet, Richard II, and Macbeth, One Touch of Venus, Alice in Wonderland, The Devil's Disciple, Dream Girl, The Corn Is Green, The Good Fairy, The Taming of the Shrew, and The Cradle Song, 1955–6; Born Yesterday, Man and Superman, The Little Foxes, The Lark, There Shall Be No Night, and The Yeoman of the Guard, 1956–7; Green Pastures, On Borrowed Time, Little Moon of Alban, and Dial M for Murder, 1957–8; Harvey, Gift of the Magi, Meet Me in Saint Louis, Johnny Belinda, Kiss Me, Kate, Berkeley Square, and Green Pastures, 1958–9; Winterset, A Doll's House, Christmas Festival—The Borrowed Christmas, The Tempest, The Cradle Song, Captain Brassbound's Conversion, and Turn the Key Deftly, 1959–60; Shangri-La, Time Remembered, Give Us Barabbas, The Joke and the Valley, and Golden Child, 1960–1; Victoria Regina, Hour of the Bath, and Arsenic and Old Lace, 1961–2; The Teahouse of the August Moon, Cyrano de Bergerac, Pygmalion, The Invincible Mr Disraeli, and The Hands of Danofrio, 1962–3; The Patriots, A Cry of Angels, Abe Lincoln in Illinois, and Little Moon of Alban, 1963–4; The Fantasticks, The Magnificent Yankee, The Holy Terror, 1964–5; Gideon, USA, 1970–71; F Scott Fitzgerald and the Last of the Belles, 1973; Sandburg's Lincoln, 1974; In This House of Brede, Truman at Potsdam, The Last of Mrs Lincoln, Amelia, 1975, Blind Ambition, 1979, etc; in 1959 formed Compass Productions, Inc, serving as president; President, Directors' Guild of America; member of the Phi Beta Kappa Society and has received a DLitt, *honoris causa,* from Lafayette College, 1963, Doctor of Humane Letters, Coker College, 1973; received numerous awards for his television work, including eight Emmy Awards, the Sylvania Award, three Radio Television Daily Awards, and three Directors Guild of America Awards.

Recreations: Theatre and film going, and duplicate bridge. *Club:* Players. *Address:* 1801 Avenue of the Stars, Los Angeles, Calif 90067. *Tel:* 553–6205.

SCHARY, Doré, dramatic author, director, and producer
b Newark, New Jersey, 31 Aug 1905; *s* of Herman Hugo Schary and his wife Belle (Drachler); *e* Central High School, Newark; *m* Miriam Svet.

Began his career in the theatre as an actor, and made his first appearance in New York at the Sam H Harris Theatre, Feb 1930, when he played Jake in The Last Mile; after more than twenty years as a writer and producer of films, he returned to NY, Cort Theatre, Jan 1958, where he co-

produced (with the Theatre Guild) his own play Sunrise at Campobello, which won five Antoinette Perry (Tony) Awards; (with the Theatre Guild), Shubert, Feb 1959, co-produced and directed A Majority of One; Playhouse, Apr 1959, produced Triple Play; Longacre, Nov 1959, co-produced and directed his own play The Highest Tree; Winter Garden, Nov 1960, co-produced and directed The Unsinkable Molly Brown; Billy Rose, Mar 1961, produced and directed his adaptation of The Devil's Advocate; Ambassador, Jan 1962, co-produced and directed Something About a Soldier; Forrest, Philadelphia, Sept 1962, directed his own play Banderol; Music Box, Dec 1963, produced and directed Love and Kisses; Belasco, Dec 1964, produced and directed his own play One by One; Cort, NY, Nov 1965, co-presented and directed The Zulu and the Zayda; John Golden, Jan 1970, wrote Brightower; Mercer-O'Casey, June 1973, co-produced Antiques; produced and co-wrote Harzl, Palace, NY, 1976; author of a one-man show, FDR, 1977; Professor in Residence, University of Illinois, 1966; appointed NYC's first Commissioner on Cultural Affairs, 25 Feb 1970, and resigned in Apr 1971; author of forty films, including Boys Town (Academy [Oscar] Award), 1938; and Young Tom Edison, 1940; executive producer of over 300 films for MGM and RKO; from 1948–57, Vice President in charge of production at MGM; President of Schary Productions Inc, and Schary Television Productions Inc, 1959; president and chief executive officer of Theatre Vision, Inc, 1972, and Schary Productions, Inc, 1973; first appeared on television, 1954, when he played in Ed Sullivan's program MGM Story; received Hon DHL from College of the Pacific, and Wilberforce University, 1951; Hon DFA from Lincoln College, 1960; author of the books Case History of a Movie, 1950, For Special Occasions, 1962, Storm in the West (with Sinclair Lewis), 1963, and his autobiography, Heyday, 1979.

Address: 50 Sutton Place South, New York, NY 10022.

SCHECHNER, Richard, director, editor, teacher
b Newark, New Jersey, 23 Aug 1934; *s* of Sheridan Schechner and his wife Selma Sophia (Schwarz); *e* Cornell University (BA 1956), Johns Hopkins University, State University of Iowa (MA 1958), Tulane University (PhD 1962); studied under Joan MacIntosh.

Editor of the *Tulane Drama Review,* 1962–9; contributing editor, The Drama Review, 1969–present, and has contributed articles to other publications, including the *Educational Theatre Journal, Salmagundi* and the *Yale French Studies;* for the East End Players, Provincetown, Massachusetts, 1958–61, produced and directed Miss Julie, The Lesson, The Woman of Paris, Philoctetes, Riders to the Sea, Purgatory, and When We Dead Awaken; his play Blessing of the Fleet was produced by this company in 1958 and in New Orleans in 1961; also author of Briseis and the Sergeant, produced by Tulane University, 1962; directed The Maids at Tulane, 1963; co-producing Director of the Free Southern Theatre, an integrated troupe that toured the Southern states, and directed its production of Purlie Victorious in 1964; a director of the New Orleans Group, 1965–7, and directed Victims of Duty for them, 1967; founded Performance Group, NY, 1968, for whom he has directed Dionysus in '69, 1968; Makbeth, 1969; Government Anarchy (performed at the Electric Circus), Commune, 1970; The Tooth of Crime, 1973; Mother Courage and Her Children, The Marilyn Project, 1975; Oedipus, 1977; Cops, 1978; The Balcony, 1979; author of Public Domain, 1968; Environmental Theatre, 1973; Essays on Performance Theory, 1976; Professor of Drama, New York University, 1967–present.

Address: The Performance Group, PO Box 654, Canal Street Station, New York, NY 10013. *Tel:* 212–966 9796.

SCHEEDER, Louis W, director and producer
b 26 Dec 1946; *s* of Louis W Scheeder and his wife Julia (Callery); *e* Regis High School, New York City, Georgetown University and Columbia University School of the Arts; *m* Donna Wills.

Made his professional debut as an actor at the Gate, NY, Jun 1966, as the Boy in The Rapists; on leaving university worked as an ASM at the Arena Stage, Washington DC, 1969–70; director of new play readings for the Washington Theatre Club, 1970; associate artistic director, Folger Theatre Group, Washington, 1970–73, and in this post directed Happy Days, The Promise, Landscape/Silence, The Revenger's Tragedy, The Winter's Tale, and Total Eclipse; producer for the group, 1973–present, and among Folger productions in that period he has himself directed Creeps, 1973 (also NY); The Farm, 1974; The Collected Works of Billy the Kid, 1975; Henry V, The Fool, 1976; Mummer's End, Teeth 'n' Smiles, Two Gentlemen of Verona, 1977; Mackerel, Black Elk Speaks (tour), Richard III, Whose Life Is It, Anyway?, Richard II, 1978; As You Like It, Custer, 1979.
Address: Folger Theatre Group, 201 East Capitol Street, SE, Washington DC 20003. *Tel:* 202-547 3230.

SCHISGAL, Murray, playwright
b New York City, 25 Nov 1926; *e* Brooklyn Law School (LIB 1953), New School of Social Research (BA 1959); *m* Renee Shapiro; formerly a lawyer, musician, and teacher.

First produced plays were a series of one-acters, The Typists, The Postman, and A Simple Kind of Love Story, presented at the British Drama League, London, Dec 1960; since then has written Ducks and Lovers produced at the Arts, London, Oct 1961; The Tiger, produced on a double-bill with The Typists, Knit One, Purl Two (Boston), 1963; Luv, 1964; Windows (Los Angeles), 1965; Basement, Fragments, 1967; Jimmy Shine, 1968; A Way of Life, 1969; The Chinese, Dr Fish, 1970; An American Millionaire, All over Town, 1974; Popkin (Dallas), 1978; The Pushcart Peddlers (one-act), 1979; The Downstairs Boys (Cincinnati), 1980; his plays Ducks and Lovers and The Tiger were filmed, the last under the title The Tiger Makes Out; The Typists produced on television in England and Canada; wrote The Love Story of Barney Kempinski, 1966, and Natasha Kovolina Pipishinsky, 1976, for American television; author of the novel Days and Nights of a French Horn Player, 1980; received the Vernon Rice Award, the Outer Circle Critics Award, etc, for The Tiger.
Address: The Dramatists Guild, 234 West 44th Street, New York, NY 10036.

SCHLESINGER, John, CBE, director
b London, 16 Feb 1926; *s* of Bernard Edward Schlesinger and his wife Winifred Henrietta (Regensburg); *e* Uppingham and Balliol College, Oxford.

His first stage production was No Why, in the RSC's Expeditions One, Aldwych, July 1964; has since directed, for the same company, Timon of Athens, Stratford, 1965; Days in the Trees, 1966; directed I and Albert, 1972; Associate Director, National Theatre, 1973, for whom he directed Heartbreak House, 1975; Julius Caesar, 1977; films he has directed, since Terminus in 1961, include: A Kind of Loving, Billy Liar, Darling, Midnight Cowboy (Oscar 1968), Sunday, Bloody Sunday, The Day of the Locust, Marathon Man, Yanks (1978).
Address: c/o Michael Oliver, 40 Piccadilly, London W1.

SCHMIDT, Douglas W, designer
b Cincinnati, Ohio, 4 Oct 1942; *s* of Robert W Schmidt and his

wife Amy Jean (Murdoch); *e* High Mowing School, Wilton, New Hampshire, and Boston University.

First design for the stage was the décor for The Caretaker, produced at the Playhouse-in-the-Park, Cincinnati, July 1964; designed twenty productions for the Playhouse, 1964–8; first designs for a New York production were the décor of La Bohème, presented by the Juilliard Opera Theatre, Mar 1965; designed six productions for the Juilliard Opera Theatre, including the world premières of The Losers and Huckleberry Finn, 1971, and two for the Juilliard Dance Company, 1965–71; designed The Ox Cart, 1966, To Bury a Cousin, Father Uxbridge Wants to Marry, 1967; for the New York Shakespeare Festival designed King John, 1967, The Memorandum, Huui-Huui, 1968, and Twelfth Night, 1969; for the Tyrone Guthrie Theatre, Minneapolis, Minnesota, 1969, designed Julius Caesar and The Homecoming; Resident Designer of the Repertory Theater of Lincoln Center, 1969–73; designed for this and other managements, more than 100 productions, including The Time of Your Life, 1969, The Good Woman of Setzuan, Operation Sidewinder, Landscape and Silence in a double-bill for which he also designed the costumes, The Disintegration of James Cherry, Paris Is Out! 1970, Playboy of the Western World, An Enemy of the People, Antigone, Play Strindberg, The Merry Wives of Windsor (Stratford, Conn), Landscape, Silence, Pictures in the Hallway, Mary Stuart, People Are Living There, The Wedding of Iphigenia, Iphigenia in Concert, 1971; Narrow Road to the Deep North, Twelfth Night, The Love Suicide at Schofield Barracks, Grease, The Country Girl, The School for Scandal, The Hostage, Women Beware Women, Lower Depths, Enemies, Happy Days, Act Without Words I, Krapp's Last Tape, Not I, 1972; Macbeth (Stratford, Conn), The Plough and the Stars, A Streetcar Named Desire, A Breeze from the Gulf, Veronica's Room, The Three Sisters, Measure for Measure, 1973; Over Here!, An American Millionaire, Fame, Kid Champion, Who's Who in Hell, 1974; Our Late Night, The Robber Bridegroom, Edward II, The Time of Your Life, The Three Sisters, Angel Street, Truckload, 1975; Threepenny Opera, Let My People Come, Herzl, 1976; The Crazy Locomotive, Agamemnon, Sunset (LA), 1977; Stages, Runaways, 1978; They're Playing Our Song, The Most Happy Fella, Romantic Comedy, 1979; has designed frequently for WNET, including Enemies and The Time of Your Life.
Recreation: Body building. *Address:* 607 West End Avenue, New York, NY 10024. *Tel:* TR 3–5565.

SCHMIDT, Harvey, composer
b Dallas, Texas, 12 Sept 1929; *s* of the Reverend Emmanuel Carl Schmidt and his wife Edna (Wieting); *e* University of Texas; formerly in the United States Army.

With Tom Jones as lyricist, contributed music to Shoestring '57, Barbizon-Plaza, Nov 1956, and to Kaleidoscope, 1957; music for The Fantasticks, which opened at the Sullivan Street Playhouse on 3 May 1960 and has run ever since, becoming the world's longest-running musical; has since written music for 110 in the Shade, 1963; I Do! I Do!, 1966; Celebration, 1969; incidental music for Colette, 1970; ballet music for Texas Fourth, 1973; music for The Portfolio Revue, 1974; Philemon, Celebration (revised), The Bone Room, all 1975; film work includes the scores for A Texas Romance, 1909 (1965) and Bad Company (1972); for TV wrote the music for New York Scrapbook, 1961; also a graphic artist, his illustrations have appeared in a number of major magazines.
Address: 313 West 74th Street, New York, NY. *Tel:* 873–7995.

SCHNABEL, Stefan, actor
b Berlin, Germany, 2 Feb 1912; *s* of Artur Schnabel, the pianist and musician; *e* Bonn Univ and the Old Vic, London.

Made his NY debut at the Orson Welles—John Houseman Mercury Theatre, 11 Nov 1937, in Julius Caesar; Mercury, Jan 1938, played in Shoemaker's Holiday; Booth, Nov 1940, played Nicholas Jorga in Glamour Preferred; played in Everyman, May 1941; Belasco, Sept 1943, Lieutenant Werner in Land of Fame; National, Jan 1944, Lopahin in The Cherry Orchard; Adelphi, May 1946, Avery Jevity in Around the World; played in Faust, Nov 1947; Broadhurst, Mar 1950, M Hufnagel and Don Modesto in Now I Lay Me Down to Sleep; New York City Center, May, 1951, Dr Waldersee in Idiot's Delight; Shubert, Jan 1953, Colonel Alexander Ikonenko in The Love of Four Colonels; Mark Hellinger, Jan 1955, Papa Yoder in Plain and Fancy; Ethel Barrymore, Jan 1957, General Graf von Donop in Small War on Murray Hill; Mar 1965, appeared in Die Dreigroschenoper; Belasco, Sept 1965, Supervisor in A Very Rich Woman; Pocket, Jan 1969, Stomil in Tango; Vivian Beaumont, Mar 1969, Hans Bethe in In the Matter of J Robert Oppenheimer; Imperial, Oct 1969, General Conrad von Hotzendorf in A Patriot for Me; Anspacher, May 1972, Brother in Older People; Vivian Beaumont, Nov 1972, General Pechenegov in Enemies; Roundabout/Stage Two, Dec 1974, Ulrik Brendel in Rosmersholm; Vivian Beaumont, May 1975, Willie Schmidt in Little Black Sheep, Cherry Lane, Mar 1978, took over as Professor van Helsing in The Passion of Dracula; Alaska Rep, Anchorage, 1979, Glas in Slow Dance on the Killing Ground; PAF Playhouse, Huntington, 1979, appeared in Goodnight, Grandpa; Brooks Atkinson, Dec 1979, Rabbi in Teibele and Her Demon; Manhattan Theatre Club, Mar 1980, appeared in Biography; TV includes *Guiding Light.*

Address: Hesseltine–Baker Associates, 117 West 57th Street, New York, NY 10019.

SCHNEIDER, Alan, director
b Kharkov, Russia, 12 Dec 1917; *s* of Leo Victor Schneider and his wife Rebecka (Malkin); *e* University of Wisconsin (BA), Cornell University (MA), and Johns Hopkins University; *m* Eugenie Muckle; formerly a teacher and journalist.

Made his début as director at the Catholic University Theatre, Washington, DC, Oct 1941, when he staged William Saroyan's Jim Dandy; continued to direct plays for the University until 1952; made his début as an actor at the Belasco, New York, Jan 1944, when he played Winkle in Storm Operation; directed at the Cain Park Theatre, Cleveland Heights, Ohio, 1947–8; directed his first NY production at the Maxine Elliott, Feb 1948, with A Long Way from Home; at the Barn, Dartington Hall, England, July 1949, directed My Heart's in the Highlands; returned to America and directed plays in Washington, DC, Massachusetts summer theatres, Houston, Texas, etc; directed Pullman Car Hiawatha for the Neighborhood Playhouse, NY, Jan 1952, and Hide and Seek, Apr 1953; he has since directed the following plays: The Remarkable Mr Pennypacker, 1953; All Summer Long, Anastasia, 1954; The Skin of Our Teeth (also in the *Salute to France* program, Paris), Tonight in Samarkand, 1955; Waiting for Godot (Miami), Little Glass Clock, The Trip to Bountiful (London), The Glass Menagerie (revival), 1956; The Circus of Dr Lao (Chicago), Miss Lonelyhearts, 1957; Endgame, 1958; Kataki, Summer of the Seventeenth Doll (revival), 1959; Krapp's Last Tape, Measure for Measure (New York Shakespeare Festival), 1960; The American Dream, Happy Days, The Caucasian Chalk Circle (Arena, Washington, DC), 1961; Endgame (revival), Uncle

Vanya (Arena, Washington, DC), Who's Afraid of Virginia Woolf?, The Pinter Plays (double-bill, consisting of The Collection and The Dumb Waiter) 1962; The Threepenny Opera (Arena, Washington, DC), The Ballad of the Sad Cafe, 1963; Play and The Lover (double-bill), Who's Afraid of Virginia Woolf? (London), The Glass Menagerie (Tyrone Guthrie Theatre, Minneapolis), Tiny Alice, 1964; Do Not Pass Go, The Zoo Story and Krapp's Last Tape (double-bill), The Mutilated and The Gnadiges Fraulein (double-bill), Entertaining Mr Sloane, Herakles (Ann Arbor), Happy Days, 1965; Malcolm, Slapstick Tragedy, The Cherry Orchard (Tel Aviv), A Delicate Balance, 1966; You Know I Can't Hear You When the Water's Running, The Birthday Party, 1967; I Never Sang for My Father, Box, Quotations from Chairman Mao Tse-Tung, Krapp's Last Tape, Happy Days, 1968; The Watering Place, The Gingham Dog, La Strada, 1969; Blood Red Roses, Inquest, Saved, 1970; Waiting for Godot, 1971; The Foursome (Arena Stage), The Sign in Sidney Brustein's Window, Moonchildren, Happy Days, Act Without Words I, Not I, Krapp's Last Tape, Our Town (Arena Stage), 1972; toured Soviet Union, 1973; The Madness of God (Arena Stage), 1974; A Texas Trilogy (Arena Stage), 1975; The Madness of God, A Texas Trilogy (both NY), 1976; Footfalls/That Time, 1978; Loose Ends, 1979; The Lady from Dubuque, 1980; since 1951 has directed many other plays for The Arena Stage in Washington, DC; received the Antoinette Perry Award for Who's Afraid of Virginia Woolf?, 1962–3; received the off-Broadway (Obie) Award for The Pinter Plays, 1962–3; directed his first film with Samuel Beckett's Film (NY), 1964, starring Buster Keaton; directed his first television production, Pullman Car Hiawatha, 1951; subsequent productions include: Œdipus the King, The Life of Samuel Johnson, Waiting for Godot, and The Years Between; served as Director of the Drama Division of the Juilliard School, 1976–9; Professor of Drama, University of California, San Diego, 1979–; executive vice-president, Society of Stage Directors and Choreographers, 1976–; served as drama critic for *The New Leader,* resigning this post 1965; author of numerous articles on the theatre in *Saturday Review, Theatre Arts, The New York Times,* etc.

Recreations: Music, reading history, walking, the family. *Address:* 41 Gingerbread Lane, East Hampton, NY. *Tel:* 324–4267.

SCHULTZ, Michael A, director
b Milwaukee, Wisconsin, 10 Nov 1938; *s* of Leo Schultz and his wife Katherine Frances (Leslie); *e* University of Wisconsin and Marquette University; *m* Lauren Jones.

Directed his first play, Waiting for Godot, at the McCarter Theatre, Princeton, New Jersey, 1966; directed his first New York production, Song of the Lusitanian Bogey, for the Negro Ensemble Company, with which troupe he has been closely identified, 1968; has since directed Kongi's Harvest, God Is a (Guess What?) and his first London production, Song of the Lusitanian Bogey, 1968; Does a Tiger Wear a Necktie? The Reckoning, Every Night When the Sun Goes Down and plays of new playwrights at Eugene O'Neill Memorial Theatre, 1969; Operation Sidewinder, Dream on Monkey Mountain (Mark Taper Forum, Los Angeles, California), Woyzeck, 1970; Dream on Monkey Mountain (Negro Ensemble), 1971; The Three Sisters, Thoughts, The Poison Tree (Westport, Conn, Country Playhouse), 1973; What the Wine-Sellers Buy, and directed at the New Theater for Now, Los Angeles, 1974; directed his first film, To Be Young, Gifted and Black, 1971, and subsequently directed Billie Holiday and Honeybaby, Honeybaby (1974); directed his first television production, July 1971, also To Be Young, Gifted and Black.

Address: 127 West 80th Street, New York, NY 10024. *Tel:* 874–2798.

SCHWARTZ, Arthur, composer

b Brooklyn, New York, 25 Nov 1900; *s* of Solomon S Schwartz and his wife Dora (Grossman); *e* Boys' High School, Brooklyn, New York University (AB, JD), and Columbia University (MA); *m* (1) Katherine Carrington (dec); (2) Mary O'Hagan; originally a teacher of English literature in NY High Schools, subsequently admitted to NY bar, and practiced 1924–8.

Composed music for Grand Street Follies, 1926; The New Yorker, 1927; The Little Show, Grand Street Follies, 1929; The Second Little Show, Princess Charming, The Co-Optimists of 1930, Three's a Crowd, Here Comes the Bride, 1930; The Band Wagon, 1931; Flying Colors, 1932; Nice Goings On, 1933; Revenge with Music, 1934; At Home Abroad, 1935; Follow the Sun, 1936; Virginia, Between the Devil, 1937; Stars in Your Eyes, 1939; American Jubilee, 1940; Park Avenue, 1946; Inside USA which he also produced, 1948; at the Coronet, Nov 1950, presented Hilda Crane; composed A Tree Grows in Brooklyn, 1951; By the Beautiful Sea, 1954; The Gay Life, 1961; Jennie, 1964; That's Entertainment, 1972; Nicholas Nickleby (lyrics and music), 1975; an anthology of his work, Dancing in the Dark, produced at the Manhattan Theatre Club, 1979; elected Treasurer of The Dramatists Guild, 1964; member of the Board of Directors of ASCAP, 1958 to present; has written numerous scores for films, including: Under Your Spell, That Girl from Paris, 1936, Navy Blues, 1941, Thank Your Lucky Stars, 1943, The Time, the Place, and the Girl, 1946, Excuse My Dust, 1951, Dangerous When Wet, The Band Wagon, 1953, You're Never Too Young, 1955, and also produced Cover Girl, 1944, and Night and Day, 1946.

Address: ASCAP, 1 Lincoln Center Plaza, New York, NY 10023.

SCHWARTZ, Stephen L, composer

b New York City, 6 Mar 1948; *s* of Stanley L Schwartz and his wife Sheila (Siegal); *e* Carnegie Institute of Technology; *m* Carole Piasecki.

First work for the stage was for the New London, NH, Playhouse, summer 1966, for which he directed various works; first NY production was the title song for Butterflies Are Free, Booth, 21 Oct 1969; since then has composed the music and written new lyrics for Godspell, May 1971; first London production was Godspell at the Roundhouse, 17 Nov 1971; English texts (with Leonard Bernstein) for Mass, music and lyrics for Pippin, Oct 1972; Pippin produced at Her Majesty's, London, Oct 1973; music and lyrics for The Magic Show, May 1974; music and lyrics for The Baker's Wife, 1976; adapted, directed and wrote music and lyrics for some songs in Working, May 1978; was the only composer lyricist to have three shows running simultaneously on Broadway, which were Pippin, The Magic Show, and Godspell; composed the film of Godspell, 1972; author of a children's book, The Perfect Peach, 1977.

Recreations: Bridge, tennis. *Address:* Paramuse Associates, 1414 Avenue of the Americas, New York, NY 10019. *Tel:* PL 8-5055.

SCOFIELD, Paul, CBE, actor

b Hurstpierpoint, Sussex, 21 Jan 1922; *e* Varndean School for Boys, Brighton; *m* Joy Parker; studied for the stage at the London Mask Theatre School, in connection with the Westminster Theatre.

Made his first appearance on the stage at the Theatre Royal, Brighton, while still at school, 1936, as one of the crowd in The Only Way; first appeared, professionally, at the Westminster Theatre, Jan 1940, in Desire Under the Elms, and subsequently, Apr 1940, as the Third Clerk and the First Soldier in Abraham Lincoln; joined the Bideford Repertory Theatre Company, spring, 1941, where he played a variety of leading parts; toured for ENSA, autumn, 1941, as Vincentio and subsequently Tranio in The Taming of the Shrew; Birmingham Repertory Theatre, Sept–Oct 1942, played Stephen Undershaft in Major Barbara, and Horatio in Hamlet, with the Travelling Repertory Theatre Company; Whitehall, June 1943, played Alex Morden in The Moon is Down; played two seasons, 1944–6, with the Birmingham Repertory Theatre, appearing, among other parts, as Reginald in Getting Married, the Prince in The Circle of Chalk, the Clown in The Winter's Tale, Valentine in Doctor's Delight, Young Marlow in She Stoops to Conquer, Konstantin in The Seagull, John Tanner in Man and Superman, and Philip, The Bastard in King John; played two seasons, 1946–7, at the Shakespeare Memorial Theatre, Stratford-on-Avon, appearing as Henry V, Don Armado in Love's Labour's Lost, Malcolm in Macbeth, Lucio in Measure for Measure, Mercutio, Sir Andrew Aguecheek, Cloten in Cymbeline, Pericles, and as Mephistophilis in Marlowe's Faust; Arts Theatre, Nov 1946, played Tegeus-Chromis in A Phoenix Too Frequent; His Majesty's, Oct 1947, Mercutio in Romeo and Juliet, and Sir Andrew in Twelfth Night; Lyric, Hammersmith, Dec 1947, and Phoenix, Jan 1948, Young Fashion in The Relapse; returned to Stratford-on-Avon, for the 1948 season, playing the Bastard in King John, Bassanio, Hamlet, the Clown in The Winter's Tale, Troilus in Troilus and Cressida and Roderigo in Othello; St James's, Mar 1949, Alexander in Adventure Story; Lyric, Hammersmith, Oct, and St James's, Nov 1949, Konstantin in The Seagull; Globe, Jan 1950, Hugo and Frederic in Ring Round the Moon; Rudolf Steiner Hall, July 1950, Pericles in his own production of the play of that name; Phoenix, Jan 1952, played Don Pedro in Much Ado About Nothing; at the Edinburgh Festival, 1952, played Philip Sturgess in The River Line, and subsequently appeared in this part at the Lyric, Hammersmith, Sept 1952, and Strand, Oct 1952; during Sir John Gielgud's season at the Lyric, Hammersmith, Dec 1952–July 1953, appeared as Richard II, Witwoud in The Way of the World, and Pierre in Venice Preserved; Piccadilly, Dec 1953, played Paul Gardiner in A Question of Fact; Lyric, Hammersmith, Dec 1954, and New, Apr 1955, played Prince Albert Troubiscoi in Time Remembered; toured, Oct–Nov 1955, as Hamlet, prior to playing this part in Moscow, and then appearing in the same production at the Phoenix, London, Dec 1955; in the same season at the Phoenix, Apr 1956, he played the Priest in The Power and the Glory (for which performance he won the 1956 *Evening Standard* Drama Award), and June 1956, appeared as Harry in a revival of The Family Reunion; Piccadilly, May 1957, played Fred Dyson in A Dead Secret; Saville, Apr 1958, made his first appearance in a musical, as Johnnie in Expresso Bongo; Globe, June 1959, Clive Root in The Complaisant Lover; Globe, July 1960, played Sir Thomas More in A Man For All Seasons; at the Stratford Shakespearean Festival, Stratford, Ontario, June–Sept 1961, played the title-part in Coriolanus, and Don Armado in Love's Labour's Lost; made his first appearance on Broadway at ANTA, Nov 1961, as Thomas More in A Man For All Seasons (Antoinette Perry Award, 1962); Royal Shakespeare Theatre, Stratford-on-Avon, Nov 1962, played the title-part in King Lear (*Evening Standard* Award, 1962) subsequently appearing in the same production at the Aldwych, Dec 1962, and at the Théâtre Sarah-Bernhardt, Paris, May 1963, during the *Théâtre des Nations* 10th season; with the Royal Shakespeare Company, toured Berlin, Prague, Budapest, Belgrade, Bucharest, Warsaw, Helsinki, Leningrad, and Moscow with King Lear, Feb–May 1964, subsequently appearing at the State Theatre, New York, May 1964, with the production; Royal Shakespeare, Stratford-on-Avon, July 1965, played the title-part in Timon of Athens; Aldwych, Jan 1966, Ivan Alexandrovitch Khlestakov in The Government Inspector; Aldwych, Nov 1966, Charlie Dyer in Staircase; same theatre, Dec 1966, the Dragon in The Thwarting of Baron Bolligrew; Stratford, Aug 1967, played name-part in Macbeth, touring Finland and Russia in the part, Nov–Dec, and appearing at the Aldwych, Jan 1968; Royal Court, July 1968, played Laurie in The Hotel in Amsterdam, transferring to the New, Sept, and the Duke of York's, Dec; Royal Court, Feb 1970, played the title-role in Uncle Vanya; for the National Theatre, Old Vic, Mar 1971, Wilhelm Voigt in The Captain of Kopenick, and Leone in The Rules of the Game, New Theatre, June 1971; Royal Court, Apr 1973, Alan West in Savages, transferring to the Comedy; Leeds Playhouse, Nov 1974, Prospero in The Tempest, transferring to the Wyndham's in this production, Feb 1975; Nottingham Playhouse, Apr 1976, and Comedy, May, title part in Dimetos; Olivier, Apr 1977, title-role in Volpone, and June 1977, Constantine Madras in The Madras House; Royal Exchange, Manchester, May 1978, Freddie Kilner in A Family, transferring to the Haymarket, July 1978; Olivier, Nov 1979, Salieri in Amadeus; Olivier, Mar 1980, title-role in Othello; entered films, 1954, in Carve Her Name with Pride, subsequent films include: That Lady, The Train, A Man For All Seasons (Academy Award 'Oscar'), London Film Academy Award, New York Critics' Award, and the Saint Genesius Gold Medal (Rome), for his performance as Thomas More), King Lear (Danish Bodil Award), Bartleby, Scorpio; Member Royal Shakespeare Directorate, 1966–8; joined the National Theatre as an Associate Director, 1970–2; received the CBE in the New Year Honours, 1956; Hon LLD, Glasgow, 1968; Hon DLitt, Kent, 1973.

Address: The Gables, Balcombe, Sussex. *Tel:* Balcombe 378.

SCOTT, George C, actor and director
b Wise, Virginia, 18 Oct 1927; *e* University of Missouri; *m* (1) Colleen Dewhurst (mar dis); (2) Colleen Dewhurst (mar dis); (3) Trish Van Devere.
Played more than 150 parts in stock companies before he made his New York début at the Heckscher, for the New York Shakespeare Festival, Nov 1957, when he played Richard, Duke of Gloucester, in Richard III, and, Jan 1958, Jacques in As You Like It; Circle-in-the-Square, Feb 1958, Lord Wainwright in Children of Darkness; Ambassador, Nov 1958, Tydings Glenn in Comes a Day; Heckscher, Jan 1959, Antony in Antony and Cleopatra; Henry Miller's, Dec 1959, Lt Col N P Chipman in The Andersonville Trial; Salt Lake City, Utah, 1960, Shylock in The Merchant of Venice; Billy Rose, Oct 1960, Dolek Berson in The Wall; Lyceum, Feb 1962, the title-role in General Seeger (which he also directed and co-produced); Henry Miller's, Mar 1962, co-produced Great Day in the Morning; New York Shakespeare Festival, Aug 1962, played Shylock in The Merchant of Venice; Circle-in-the-Square, Jan 1963, Ephraim Cabot in Desire Under the Elms; made his London début with the Actors Studio, at the Aldwych, May 1965, as Vershinin in The Three Sisters, in a World Theatre season; Vivian Beaumont, Oct 1967, Benjamin Hubbard in The Little Foxes; Plymouth, NY, Feb 1968, Sam Nash, Jesse Kiplinger, and Roy Hubley in

Plaza Suite; Circle in the Square—Joseph E Levine, June 1973, Michael Astrov in Uncle Vanya; Walnut St, Philadelphia, Feb 1974, directed Death of a Salesman; Circle in the Square, Mar 1975, directed All God's Chillun Got Wings; Circle in the Square, June 1975, directed and played Willy Loman in Death of a Salesman; Broadhurst, Dec 1976, Foxwell J Sly in Sly Fox; films in which he has appeared include The Hustler, Dr Strangelove, The List of Adrian Messenger, Anatomy of a Murder, The Flim Flam Man, Patton, etc; refused the 1971 Academy Award (Oscar) voted him for this last performance; The New Centurions, Rage (also directed, 1972), The Day of the Dolphin, Bank Shot, The Savage Is Loose (also directed, 1974), The Prince and the Pauper, The Changeling (1980), etc; has also appeared in the television series *East Side/West Side*, 1964–5.

Address: c/o Actors Equity Association, 165 West 46th Street, New York, NY 10036.

SCOTT, Jay Hutchinson, designer
b Stakeford, Northumberland, 1 Aug 1924; *s* of Matthew Scott and his wife Alice Hutchinson (Elliot); *e* Edward VII School of Art, University of Durham; received further training as a member of the People's Theatre, Newcastle upon Tyne.
First London production, Arts, Aug 1945, designed the setting and costumes for The Circle of Chalk; resident designer of the Oxford Playhouse, 1945–8; Bristol Old Vic, 1949–53; London productions include: Penny Plain, 1951; Dear Charles, 1952; Escapade, The Confidential Clerk, 1953; A Girl Called Jo, The Reluctant Debutante, Misery Me, 1955; Misalliance, Plaintiff in a Pretty Hat, 1956; Dear Delinquent, 1957; The Iceman Cometh, Not in the Book, The Birthday Party, The Elder Statesman, Hot Summer Night, The Grass is Greener, 1958; The Rose Tattoo, The Marriage-Go-Round, 1959; The More the Merrier, Double Yoke, Follow That Girl, Horses in Midstream, And Another Thing, Strip the Willow, 1960; The Irregular Verb to Love, The Bird of Time, Teresa of Avila (also Dublin Festival), 1961; Boeing-Boeing, Look Homeward, Angel, The Lower Depths, Gentlemen Prefer Blondes, A Touch of the Poet (Dublin and Venice Festivals), The New Men, Doctors of Philosophy, Out of Bounds, 1962; Devil May Care, The Hot Tiara, The Masters, Windfall, The Diplomats, 1963; The Fourth of June, The Claimant, Amber for Anna, I Love You, Mrs Patterson, Past Imperfect, Monique, The Love Game, High Spirits, 1964; Boeing-Boeing (New York), Present Laughter, The Apple Cart (tour), The Creeper, Dual Marriageway (tour), Comfort Me with Apples, Say Who You Are, The Platinum Cat, 1965; A Friend Indeed, Doctor's Dilemma, Doctor Faustus (Oxford University Dramatic Society), Cyrano de Bergerac (Belgrade, Coventry), The Anniversary, There's A Girl in My Soup (also NY), Public and Confidential, A Share in the Sun, 1966; Volpone, Spring and Port Wine, Relatively Speaking, Queenie, The Flip Side (also NY), The Others, The Cherry Orchard (also Edinburgh Festival), Number 10 (also Toronto), 1967; Little Boxes, Not Now Darling (also NY), The Real Inspector Hound and The Audition (double-bill), Out of the Question, The Secretary Bird, They Don't Grow on Trees, 1968; Dead Silence, What the Butler Saw, Highly Confidential, The Country Wife (Chichester), Birds On the Wing (also Toronto), My Little Boy . . . My Big Girl, 1969; Play on Love, Best of Friends, Lie Down, I Think I Love You, 1970; Meeting at Night, No Sex Please—We're British, The Chalk Garden, The Douglas Cause, 1971; The Mating Game, Parents' Day, Who's Who, The Three Arrows (Actors' Company), 1972; A Private Matter, Signs of the Times, Two and Two Make Sex, Why

Not Stay for Breakfast?, 1973; Snap, Springtime for Henry (Oxford), The Turning Point, Robin Redbreast (Guildford), The Little Hut, There Goes the Bride, The Gentle Hook, 1974; The Case in Question, Night Must Fall, Norman Is That You?, Betzi, 1975; Getting Away With Murder, Dear Daddy, Out on a Limb, 1976; Sextet, The Dragon Variation, Laburnum Grove, 1977; also designed for the Old Vic, Memorial Theatre, Stratford-on-Avon, the Glyndebourne Festival and The Royal Theatre, The Hague, Holland; founder member of the Crest Theatre, Toronto, Canada, for whom he designed several productions, including: The Cherry Orchard, As You Like It, The Devil's Disciple, Caesar and Cleopatra, Four Faces, The Provok'd Wife; also designed for television and films.

(*Died 14 Sept 1977.*)

SCOTT, Margaretta, actress
b London, 13 Feb 1912; *d* of Hugh Scott and his wife Bertha Eugenie (Casano); *e* Convent of the Holy Child, Cavendish Square; *m* John de Lacy Wooldridge, DSO, DFC and Bar, DFM (dec); studied for the stage with Rosina Filippi and at the Royal Academy of Dramatic Art.

Made her first appearance on the stage at the Strand Theatre (for the Fellowship of Players), 12 Dec 1926, as Mercutio's Page in Romeo and Juliet; at the Repertory Theatre, Hull, 13 Aug 1928, played Catherine in The Lilies of the Field; appeared at the Criterion Theatre, 7 Feb 1929, as Hebe in Her Shop; at the Haymarket, July 1929, played Alice Fraser in The First Mrs Fraser; Apr 1930, the Player Queen in the all-star revival of Hamlet; Strand (for Repertory Players), May 1930, Suzanne in How to be Healthy Though Married; St James's, Nov 1930, Lady Jasper in A Murder Has Been Arranged; Haymarket, Mar 1931, the Player Queen in Hamlet, and subsequently succeeded Fay Compton as Ophelia; Arts, Apr 1931, played Eve Palliser in To-Morrow; with the OUDS, June 1931, Beatrice in Much Ado About Nothing; Cambridge, Sept 1931, Princess Isabella in Elizabeth of England; Savoy (for Repertory Players), Dec 1931, Mary in The Traveller in the Dark; Aldwych, Mar 1932, Leonora Stafford in Dirty Work; Savoy (for Repertory Players), Apr 1932, Diana Treherne in Red Triangle; New, Aug 1932, Viola in Twelfth Night; Garrick, Sept 1932, Mabel Dancy in Loyalties, and Ruth Honeywell in Justice; during 1932, for the BBC, played Ophelia in Hamlet and Juliet in Romeo and Juliet; Ambassadors', Dec 1932, Alida Bloodgood in The Streets of London; Open Air Theatre, June–Sept 1933, Viola and Olivia (alternately) in Twelfth Night, Celia in As You Like It, Hermia in A Midsummer Night's Dream, Miranda in The Tempest; Cambridge, Feb 1934, Lallah in Birthday; Ambassadors', Mar 1934, Alithea in The Country Wife; again appeared at the Open Air Theatre, 1934, playing Celia, Viola, Adriana in The Comedy of Errors, Hermia, Lavinia in Androcles and the Lion, and Juliet in Romeo and Juliet; at the Shaftesbury, Nov 1934, Beatrice Portinari in For Ever; St Martin's (for RADA Players), Feb 1935, Gioconda Dianti in Gioconda; Victoria Palace, May 1935, Helena in The Miracle Man; Victoria Palace, Jan 1936, Germaine in The Man in Dress Clothes; Embassy, Apr 1936, Lady Hamilton in England Expects . . .!, Open Air Theatre, 1936 season, Rosalind, Hermia, and Viola; Old Vic, Sept 1936, Rosaline in Love's Labour's Lost; Mercury, Nov 1936, Ann Groat in The Dumb Wife and Ione in Panic; Ring, Blackfriars, Jan 1937, Beatrice in Much Ado About Nothing; Open Air, Aug 1937, Viola in Twelfth Night; St James's, Nov 1937, Beatrice in The Silent Knight; Vaudeville, Dec 1937, Katinka in A Lady's Gentleman; Phoenix, Mar 1938, Janet Tarrant in Flood Tide; Duke of York's, Nov 1938, Peg Clement in Traitor's Gate;

Aldwych, June 1939, Ruth Henley in To Kill a Cat; Wyndham's, July 1939, Elsa Brandt in Alien Corn; Whitehall, Dec 1939, Prince Charming in Who's Taking Liberty?; Apollo, Aug 1940, Sophie Baumer in Margin for Error; Stratford-on-Avon Memorial Theatre, 1941 season, played Juliet, Viola and Portia, and Jennifer Dubedat in The Doctor's Dilemma, and 1942 season Lady Macbeth and Rosalind; at the Birmingham Repertory Theatre, Oct 1942, Barbara in Major Barbara; Arts Theatre, London, Dec 1942, Queen Margause in Holy Isle; Aldwych, Feb 1943, succeeded Valerie Taylor as Martha de Brancovis in Watch on the Rhine; toured in North Africa and Italy, Feb 1944, for ENSA, playing Marcia Brent in Quiet Week-End; toured, Apr 1945, as Madame Tallien in Ah, Josephine; Aldwych, Aug 1945, played Sister Margaret in The Hasty Heart; Garrick, July 1948, Connie in Written for a Lady; at the Glasgow Citizens Theatre, 1949, played Lady Macbeth; Richmond, Nov 1949, Lorna in The Foxes of Kildorgan; Cambridge Theatre (for Repertory Players), Dec 1951, and at the New, Apr 1952, played Katherine Parr in The Young Elizabeth; Cambridge Theatre, Aug 1953, succeeded Coral Browne as Constance Russell in Affairs of State; Duke of York's, Dec 1953, appeared as Consuelo Dolores Koukowsko in Thirteen For Dinner; Cambridge Theatre, Oct 1954, played Marcia Wentworth in Book of the Month; Saville, Dec 1956, played Mrs Marwood in The Way of the World; at the Bristol Old Vic, Apr 1958, played the Queen in Hamlet; Fortune, Nov 1959, Cecilia Ryan in Aunt Edwina; Richmond, May 1961, played Laura Wilding in This Is My Life; Her Majesty's, July 1965, took over the part of Mrs Rossiter in The Right Honourable Gentleman; Arnaud, Guildford, Mar 1966, Ortolana in The Door; toured, 1968, in Lord Arthur Savile's Crime; Belgrade, Coventry, Apr 1971, Mary Portman and Cornelia in Confrontation, also at the Round House; toured S. Africa, 1971, as The Reverend Mother in Heloise and Abelard; Birmingham Rep, May 1972, Jocasta in Œdipus Rex; Piccadilly, Feb 1973, Mother Josephine in Mistress of Novices; Thorndike, Leatherhead, Apr 1974, Lady Hunstanton in A Woman of No Importance; Crucible, Sheffield, Oct 1974, Lady Bracknell in The Importance of Being Earnest and Hester Saloman in Equus; Theatre Upstairs, July 1975, Officer PX9968WN in Mean Time; Watford Palace, Jan 1976, played Mrs Higgins in Pygmalion, also touring South East Asia for the British Council; Nov 1976–Jan 1977, toured England and Canada as Lady Markby in An Ideal Husband; Chichester Festival, May 1978, Lady Pontefract in A Woman of No Importance; toured Canada, Jan 1979, as The Duchess of Berwick in Lady Windermere's Fan; for the Cambridge Theatre Company, Feb 1979, played Mrs Culver in The Constant Wife; has also appeared in a number of television productions, including The Duchess of Duke Street, What Every Woman Knows, and All Creatures Great and Small; entered films, 1934, and has appeared successfully in numerous pictures.
Recreation: Her family. *Address:* 30 Molyneux Street, London, W1.

SCOTT, Martha, actress, producer
b Jamesport, Missouri, 22 Sept; *d* of Walter Scott and his wife Letha (McKinley); *e* University of Michigan; *m* (1) Carleton Alsop (mar dis); (2) Mel Powell.

Gained her early experience in Eastern theatres; joined the Globe Theatre at the World's Fair, Chicago, 1934, and played in several condensed Shakespeare plays; first appeared in New York, at the Henry Miller Theatre, 4 Feb 1938, as Emily Webb in Our Town, scoring an instantaneous success; Belasco, Dec 1939, played the Girl in Foreigners; spent the next three years in Hollywood, in films; Windsor,

NY, Dec 1942, played Mara Sutro in The Willow and I; City Center, Jan 1944, again played Emily in Our Town; Golden Theatre, Oct 1944, played Katherine Rogers in Soldier's Wife; Morosco, Aug 1945, Sally Middleton in The Voice of the Turtle; Biltmore, Feb 1947, Connie Frazier in It Takes Two; in summer theatres, 1947, played Elizabeth Barrett in The Barretts of Wimpole Street; Mansfield, Jan 1950, Margaret Clitherow in Design for a Stained Glass Window; summer theatres, 1950, Stella Hallam in Another Language; Morosco, July 1951, took over as Nancy Willard in Gramercy Ghost; Biltmore, NY, Oct 1951, played Sylvia in The Number; City Center, Apr 1952, Ellen Turner in The Male Animal, and subsequently toured; Coronet, Dec 1953, Ma Pennypacker in The Remarkable Mr Pennypacker; Golden, Feb 1958, Mary Reece in Cloud 7; Eugene O'Neill, Jan 1960, Lucy Greer in A Distant Bell; Helen Hayes, Feb 1960, Nina in The Tumbler; Ambassador, Oct 1960, Fanny Lowe in The 49th Cousin; Cape Playhouse, Dennis, Mass, July 1961, Lillian Hudson in Future Perfect; Pasadena Playhouse, Apr 1963, played Mattie Martin in Open Book; Playhouse, NY, Apr 1964, took over as Edith Lambert in Never Too Late; Helen Hayes, NY, June 1965, took over Nettie Cleary in The Subject Was Roses, and subsequently toured; at the ANTA, Nov 1969, co-produced with the Plumstead Playhouse a revival of Our Town; Mark Hellinger, Sept 1975, Mrs Antrobus in The Skin of Our Teeth; for Plumstead Theater Society, 1978, co-presented First Monday in October, in Washington and on Broadway; first appeared in films, 1940, in Our Town, gaining an Academy Award nomination, and pictures since that date include The Ten Commandments, Sayonara, Ben Hur; Airport 1975, The Turning Point (1979), etc; played in radio programs, 1936–8; has appeared on television in many dramas and dramatic series, including hostess of *Modern Romances,* 1954–7, and *The Nurses, Columbo, The Bionic Woman, The Bob Newhart Show,* etc.

Address: c/o Bresler, Wolf, Cota, Livingston, 190 North Canon Drive, Beverly Hills, Calif. *Tel:* 278–3200.

SCOURBY, Alexander, actor

b Brooklyn, New York, 13 Nov 1913; *s* of Constantine Scourby and his wife Bessie; *e* University of West Virginia; *m* Lori March; served his apprenticeship with the Civic Repertory Theatre, 1932.

Made his NY début at the Imperial, 10 Nov 1936, as the Player King in Hamlet, with Leslie Howard; Cape Playhouse, Dennis, Massachusetts, again played this part in Eva Le Gallienne's production of Hamlet; St James, Oct 1938, played Rosencrantz in Hamlet, with Maurice Evans; St James, Jan 1939, Earl of Westmoreland in Henry IV, Part I; St James, Apr 1940, Green in Richard II; Alvin, 1946, took over from Ruth Chatterton as the Speaker in A Flag Is Born; Henry Street Playhouse, Mar 1947, Jacques Dubois in The Deputy of Paris; National, Dec 1947, Dmitri Razoumikhin in Crime and Punishment; Hudson, Mar 1949, Tami Giacopetti in Detective Story; Alvin, Jan 1951, Ivanoff in Darkness at Noon; Cort, Oct 1951, Peter Cauchon in Saint Joan, with Uta Hagen; Morosco, Feb 1955, Paul Tabourier in Tonight in Samarkand; Phoenix, Apr 1956, Rakitin in A Month in the Country; Phoenix, 1956, took over from Ian Keith as Peter Cauchon in Saint Joan, with Siobhan MacKenna; Phoenix, Mar 1961, Claudius in Hamlet; Broadway, Mar 1963, Gorotchenko in Tovarich; Gramercy Arts, Oct 1966, Walt Whitman in A Whitman Portrait; Broadhurst, Jan 1972, John Knox in Vivat! Vivat! Regina; St Thomas's Church, 20 Nov 1974, appeared in a reading, The Romance of Elizabeth Barrett and Robert Browning—Their Letters and Poems; for Hartford Stage Co, 1979, played the title-role in Galileo,

Feb, and Rodion Nikolayevich in Old World, Oct; first appeared in films, 1952, in Affair in Trinidad, and has since played in The Big Heat, The Silver Chalice, Giant, Seven Thieves, The Big Fisherman, Confession of a Counterspy, etc; has appeared frequently on television, acting and narrating in various dramatic programs, notably The World of Maurice Chevalier, The World of Jacqueline Kennedy, The World of Bob Hope, The World of Sophia Loren, The World of Benny Goodman, The Death of the Hired Man, and *The Body Human,* 1978–9; has recorded nearly 500 books for the blind, since 1937, including The Bible, War and Peace, Les Miserables; for his work for the blind received the Certificate of Merit from the American Foundation for the Blind.

Address: c/o Actors Equity Association, 165 West 46th Street, New York, NY 10036.

SEAL, Elizabeth, actress and dancer

b Genoa, Italy, 28 Aug 1933; *d* of Frederick George Seal and his wife, Alice Muriel (Read); *e* Harvington School, Ealing; *m* (1) Peter Townsend (mar dis); (2) Zack Matalon (mar dis); (3) Michael Ward; trained as a dancer, at the Royal Academy of Dancing (Idjikovski), with Karsavina, Margaret Clarke, Molly Radcliff and others.

First appeared in London, Saville, Feb 1951, in Gay's the Word; Coliseum, Oct 1955, played Gladys in The Pajama Game; Phoenix, Apr 1957, played Esmeralda in Camino Real; Coliseum, June 1957, took over the part of Lola in Damn Yankees; at the Lyric, July 1958, played the leading part of Irma in Irma La Douce; after nearly two years, she left the London production to make her first appearance in the United States in the same part, at the National Theatre, Washington, Sept 1960, subsequently appearing on Broadway at the Plymouth Theatre, Sept 1960; received the Antoinette Perry (Tony) Award for her performance of Irma La Douce, 1961; toured the US, Oct 1962–3, as Josefa Lantenay in A Shot in the Dark; Arts, Cambridge, England, Aug 1965, appeared with Zack Matalon in the entertainment Have Bird, Will Travel; Prince of Wales, Apr 1969, Lucette in Cat Among the Pigeons; Greenwich, July 1972, Connie Kate Culpeper in Liberty Ranch; in the opening season of the Haymarket, Leicester, Oct 1973, played Sylvia in The Recruiting Officer and Sally Bowles in Cabaret; Ipswich, Sept 1974, Martha in Who's Afraid of Virginia Woolf?; toured, spring 1975, as Myra Arundel in Hay Fever; Mermaid, Oct 1975, appeared in Farjeon Reviewed; Duke of York's, Apr 1976, appeared in Salad Days; Chichester Festival, 1977, played several parts in In Order of Appearance; Cambridge, Jan 1980, took over as Roxie Hart in Chicago; films, since her first in 1955, include: Town on Trial, and Cone of Silence; TV includes: Trelawny of the "Wells", Philby, Burgess and Maclean, Supernatural, My Son, My Son, etc.

Address: c/o Plunket Greene, 91 Regent Street, London W1. *Tel:* 01–734 7311.

SEALE, Douglas, director

b London, 28 Oct 1913; *s* of Robert Henry Seale and his wife Margaret (Law); *e* Rutlish; *m* (1) Elaine Wodson (mar dis); (2) Joan Geary; formerly an actor, having studied for the stage at the Royal Academy of Dramatic Art.

First appeared at the Embassy, 2 Apr 1934, as Starling in The Drums Begin; New, June 1934, played D'Amville in Queen of Scots; appeared in repertory, 1934–40, at Brighton, Croydon, Edinburgh, Glasgow, and Perth; his first experience as a director was The Queen Was In the Parlour, at Perth in Jan 1940; served in the Army 1940–6, being commissioned in the Royal Signals; following demobilization, joined the Shakespeare Memorial Theatre Company, Stratford-on-Avon, as an actor, remaining for two seasons; Fortune, Jan 1948, played Mr Ireland in The Hidden Years; later in the same year, at the Birmingham Repertory Theatre, directed The Comedy of Errors; at the Bedford, Camden Town, under Donald Wolfit's management in 1949, directed six plays in a Bernard Shaw season; also directed The Romantic Young Lady, at Birmingham Repertory Theatre in the same year; appointed Director of Productions at Birmingham Repertory Theatre, Jan 1950, where he directed the plays of Shakespeare, Chekhov, Turgenev, Ibsen, etc; his production of Henry VI (Part III), with the original Birmingham company, was presented at the Old Vic in July 1952; his production of the complete Trilogy of Henry VI at Birmingham, in June 1953, was also presented with the original company at the Old Vic in July 1953; at Amsterdam, Feb 1954, directed Shaw's St Joan, in Dutch; at the Old Vic, 1955, directed Henry IV (Parts I and II) and The Merry Wives of Windsor; he has since directed the following plays and operas: The Marriage of Figaro (Sadler's Wells), Henry V (Cambridge Festival, Mass), Caesar and Cleopatra (Paris Festival, and Old Vic, with the Birmingham Repertory Company), Fanny's First Play (Edinburgh Festival), Fidelio (Sadler's Wells), 1956; King John (Stratford-on-Avon), Richard III (Old Vic), Henry VI, Parts I, II, III (Old Vic), 1957; King Lear (Old Vic), School, Much Ado About Nothing (Stratford-on-Avon), Richard II (Amsterdam, in Dutch), World of the Wonderful Dark (first Vancouver Festival), Julius Caesar (Old Vic), Macbeth (Old Vic), 1958; Tartuffe (Old Vic), The Magistrate (Old Vic), The Tempest, or The Enchanted Island (Old Vic), 1959; Saint Joan (Old Vic), She Stoops to Conquer (Old Vic), 1960; Once There Was a Russian (New York), One Way Pendulum (NY), 1961; Saint Joan (NY), Henry IV, Part I (Stratford, Conn), 1962; The Comedy of Errors and Henry V (Stratford, Conn), The Importance of Being Earnest (NY), 1963; The Choice Is Murder (US), 1964; The Chinese Wall (Baltimore), Lady Audley's Secret (Baltimore, also book), 1966; at the Goodman, Chicago, his productions included: Soldiers, 1969; The Tempest, The Man in the Glass Booth, Heartbreak House, The Threepenny Opera, Twelfth Night, 1970; Marching Song, The Importance of Being Earnest, 1971; also directed A Doll's House (Cleveland), 1971; Lady Audley's Secret (own adaptation: Washington and Eastside Playhouse, NY, where he played Sir Michael Audley), 1972; Look Back in Anger (Cleveland), Getting Married (Hartford), 1973; Seattle, Jan 1974, played Oliver Seaton in A Family and a Fortune; Artistic Director, 1975–9, Philadelphia Drama Guild, for whom he directed The Royal Family, 1975; The Birthday Party, The Miser, Heartbreak House, 1976; Five Finger Exercise, Blithe Spirit, Hamlet, Travesties, 1977; Saint Joan, Uncle Vanya, 1978; the Guild's productions, 1978–9, included Arms and the Man, Private Lives, and The Night of the Iguana, in which he played the Rev Shannon; associate director of the Old Vic, Apr 1958–July 1959.

Address: Philadelphia Drama Guild, 220 South 16th Street, Philadelphia, PA 19102.

SEALE, Kenneth, director, *The Spotlight*
b London, 16 Feb 1916; *s* of Francis Vernon Holford Seale and his wife Rosa (Horn); *e* Dulwich College; *m* Elizabeth Hindle.
Served in the Army 1939–46, retiring with the rank of Major; joined *The Spotlight* in 1946, being appointed a director in 1947.
Recreations: Cricket, golf. *Clubs:* Green Room, Lords' Taverners, Stage Golfing Society. *Address:* The Spotlight, 43 Cranbourn Street, London WC2H 7AP. *Tel:* 01–437 7631.

SEARS, Heather, actress
b Whitechapel, 28 Sept 1935; *d* of William Gordon Sears and his wife Eileen (Gould); *e* St Winifred's, Llanfairfechan, and Wentworth School, Bournemouth; *m* Tony Masters; trained for the stage at the Central School of Speech and Drama.
Made her first professional appearance at the Theatre Royal, Windsor, 25 July 1955, as Rose in The Love Match; her first London appearance was at the Royal Court, 11 Mar 1957; as Alison in Look Back in Anger; same theatre, May 1957, played Agnes in The Apollo de Bellac; toured, Oct 1959, as Amy Kittridge in The Sea Shell; Lyric, Hammersmith, Apr 1961, Regina in South; Yvonne Arnaud, Guildford, Mar 1966, Clare in The Door; Chichester Festival, Mar 1969, Grusha in The Caucasian Chalk Circle; Lyric, Aug 1970, Terry Phillips in How the Other Half Loves; King's Head, Islington, Dec 1971, played the Woman in The Love Songs of Martha Canary; at the Haymarket, Leicester, played Lucy in The Recruiting Officer, Oct 1973, Grusha in The Caucasian Chalk Circle, Mar 1974, Terry in How the Other Half Loves, Nov 1974; since then her many major roles at the Haymarket include: Alma Rattenbury in Cause Célèbre (also tour), Antigone, as title-role and in Oedipus at Colonnus, Dunya in Crime and Punishment, Kate in She Stoops to Conquer, Fish in Dusa Fish, Stas and Vi, Nora in A Doll's House, Lady Macbeth in Macbeth, the title-role in Electra, and a solo show as Virginia Woolf; New End, Hampstead, Apr 1980, Tekla in the Haymarket production of Creditors; films, since The Story of Esther Costello, 1956, include: Room at the Top and Sons and Lovers; television, also since 1956, includes: Our Town and Ring Round the Moon.
Favourite parts: Antigone, Nora, Lady Macbeth and Electra. *Recreations:* Painting, pre-war cars, and classical music. *Address:* The Woodlands, 112 Manor Road North, Esher, Surrey.

SEAWELL, Donald R, producer and publisher
b Sanford, NC; *s* of Justice A A F Seawell and his wife Bertha (Smith); *e* University of North Carolina (AB 1933, JD 1936); *m* Eugenia Rawls.
Chairman of the Board of The American National Theatre and Academy, 1965 to present; President, Publisher and Chairman of the Board, *The Denver Post,* the newspaper; Chairman and Founder, Denver Center for the Performing Arts; Chairman, Bonfils Theatre; President, Denver Opera Foundation; has produced or co-produced on Broadway The Great Sebastians, 1955; A Thurber Carnival, 1960; Sail Away, 1961, The Affair, 1962; The Hollow Crown, The Beast in Me, 1963; The Royal Shakespeare Company for the opening of the New York State Theatre with King Lear and The Comedy of Errors, and The Last Analysis, Slow Dance on a Killing Ground, Beekman Place, 1964; in London has produced A Thurber Carnival, 1961, and Sail Away, 1962; produced the US touring companies of The Great Sebastians and The Hollow Crown; co-produced in Cheesman Park (Denver) outdoor theatre, The Sound of Music, 1967 and 1968, Camelot, 1969, Hello, Dolly! 1970, Guys and Dolls, 1971; is a Director of The American Academy of Dramatic Arts, Denver Symphony Association, Central City Opera House, Institute of Outdoor Drama, Theatre Panel of the National Endowment for the Arts; is Partner, Bonfils-Seawell Enterprises, New York; Director of Swan Productions (motion pictures, London); received a DHL from the University of Northern Colorado, 1978.
Clubs: Players, New York; Bucks, London; Dutch Treat, New York; Cherry Hills Country Club, Denver; The Denver Country Club, and the Denver Club. *Address:* 510 East 84th

Street, New York, NY 10028, and 650 Fifteenth Street, Denver, Colo 80202.

SECOMBE, Harry, CBE, actor and singer
b Swansea, Wales, 8 Sept 1921; *s* of Frederick Ernest Secombe and his wife Nellie Jane Gladys (Davies); *e* Dynevor Secondary School, Swansea; *m* Myra Joan Atherton; formerly a clerical worker.

Made his first appearance on the stage at the Windmill Theatre, London, Oct 1946, in Revuedeville; has appeared at the London Palladium in the following variety shows: Rocking the Town, May 1956; Large As Life, May 1958; Let Yourself Go, May 1961; Palladium, Dec 1959, played the title-part in Humpty Dumpty; at the Saville, July 1963, played the title-part in the musical Pickwick; made his first appearance in the US, at the Curran, San Francisco, Apr 1965, in the title-part of Pickwick, and after a short tour, appeared at the 46th Street Theatre, New York, Oct 1965, in the same musical; Palladium, May 1966, starred in London Laughs; Drury Lane, Dec 1967, D'Artagnan in The Four Musketeers; Prince of Wales, Oct 1975, Paul Schippel in The Plumber's Progress; has appeared in nine Royal Variety Performances; entered films, 1949, and notable pictures include: Oliver! Song of Norway, The Bed Sitting Room, and Sunstruck; first appeared on television, Dec 1946, and principal appearances include several series; radio performances include: *The Goon Show*; author of two novels, Twice Brightly, 1974, Welsh Fargo, 1976, a book of short stories, Goon for Lunch, 1975, and a children's book, Katy and the Nurgla, 1978; regular contributor to *Punch;* received the CBE, 1963; Queen's Silver Jubilee Medal, 1977.

Favourite parts: Humpty Dumpty and Pickwick. *Recreations:* Photography, golf, cricket, writing and reading. *Clubs:* Savage, RAC, Lords' Taverners. *Address:* 46 St James's Place, London, SW1. *Tel:* 01–629 2768.

SELBY, Nicholas, actor
b Holborn, London, 13 Sept 1925; *m* Kathleen Rayner; trained for the stage at the Central School of Speech and Drama, 1948–50.

First appeared on the stage Oct 1943, for ENSA, near Preston, as Gordon in Dangerous Corner; after war service and the Central School, spent nine years in repertory at Liverpool, Birmingham, Coventry, York, Guildford, Hornchurch, Cambridge, etc, and on tour, making his first London appearance at the Fortune, Nov 1959, as Bernardo in Aunt Edwina; for the English Stage Company at the Royal Court, 1960, played Ben in The Dumb Waiter, Mar; Sullivan in The Naming of Murderer's Rock, Apr; Hardrader in The Happy Haven, Sept, and Vengerovich in Platonov, Oct; Pembroke, Croydon, Nov 1960, Bluntschli in Arms and the Man; Royalty, Jan 1961, Joseph Engleman in Masterpiece; Royal Court, Nov 1961, Surrey in That's Us; Arts, Cambridge, Dec 1961, Mosbie in the ESC's Arden of Faversham; Playhouse, Liverpool, Sept 1962, Lord Byron in An Elegance of Rebels; Mermaid, Dec 1962, Richard Warboys in Rockets in Ursa Major; joined the Royal Shakespeare Company as an associate artist, 1963, and has since played numerous parts at Stratford and the Aldwych, including: Antonio in The Tempest, Casca in Julius Caesar, Winchester in Henry VI, Stratford, 1963; Lord Chief Justice in Henry IV (Part II), Stratford, Rev Mort in Eh? Aldwych, 1964; Duke Solinus in The Comedy of Errors, French King in Henry V, Aldwych, 1965; The Great Muheim in The Meteor, Squire Blackheart in The Thwarting of Baron Bolligrew, Aldwych, 1965 and 1966; Junius Brutus in Coriolanus, the Duke in The Revenger's Tragedy, Capulet in Romeo and Juliet, Stratford, 1967;

Lafeu in All's Well that Ends Well, Aldwych (also Paris), 1968; Camillo in The Winter's Tale, Hippolito in Women Beware Women, Lord Chamberlain in Henry VIII, Stratford, 1969; Camillo, Lord Chamberlain, and Erwin in The Plebeians Rehearse the Uprising, Aldwych, 1970; Royal Court, Aug 1971, and Cambridge Theatre, Oct 1971, Owen Lamb in West of Suez; Birmingham Repertory Theatre, 1972, played Foot in After Magritte and Birdboot in The Real Inspector Hound, June, God Ra in Caesar and Cleopatra, Garry Essendine in Present Laughter, Sept; Theatre Upstairs, Apr 1973, Carter in Captain Oates' Left Sock; Open Space, June 1973, Eric in The Houseboy; The Place, Oct 1973, for RSC, Asquith in Cries from Casement; Aldwych, Oct 1973, Cominius in Coriolanus; same theatre, Jan 1974, James Larrabee in Sherlock Holmes, playing this part at the Kennedy Center, Washington, Oct, and the Broadhurst, NY, Nov 1974; Aldwych, May 1974, Almirante de Castilla in The Bewitched; Royal Court, Nov 1975, Lord Milton in The Fool; Open Space, Mar 1976, Max in Anatol; Young Vic (National Theatre Company), June 1976, Nestor in Troilus and Cressida; Olivier, Oct 1976, Meander in Tamburlaine the Great; has since played the following roles for the National Theatre Company, at the same theatre: The Captain in Tales from the Vienna Woods, Jan 1977, First Avocatore in Volpone (also at the Hippodrome, Bristol), Apr, Quack in The Country Wife, Nov; The Dean in Brand, Apr 1978, Duncan in Macbeth, June, Lord Froth in The Double Dealer, Sept, William Scantlebury in Strife, Nov; The Professor in The Fruits of Enlightenment, Mar 1979, Duke Frederick in As You Like It, Aug, Baron Von Swieten in Amadeus, Nov; Lodovico in Othello, Mar 1980; films include: A Midsummer Night's Dream and Macbeth; since 1956, has made over 100 television appearances, and broadcasts frequently.

Recreations: Music, books, architecture. *Address:* c/o John Cadell Ltd, 2 Southwood Lane, London, N6 5EE. *Tel:* 01–348 1914.

SELBY, Tony, actor
b Westminster, 26 Feb 1938; *s* of Samuel Joseph Selby and his wife Annie Elizabeth; *e* Buckingham Gate Secondary Modern School, London; *m* Jacqui Milburn; trained as a child at the Italia Conti Stage School.

Made his first professional appearance as Curly in Peter Pan at the Scala, Dec 1949; first adult appearance, July 1956, at the Comedy, as Schol in The Quare Fellow; Garrick, July 1958, appeared in the revue Living for Pleasure; Globe, June 1961, in On the Avenue; 1954–5, Old Time Music Hall at the Players'; Royal Court, Nov 1965, played Fred in Saved; at the same theatre, Jan 1966, Touchwood Senior in A Chaste Maid in Cheapside; Fortune, June 1969, Christopher Budgett in Sometime Never; Saville, Dec 1969, Ken in Enemy; Theatre Upstairs, Nov 1971, Eric in Friday; New End, Dec 1978, and May Fair, Feb 1977, Carter in Flashpoint; Wyndham's, Oct 1979, Cullin in Tishoo; films include: Alfie, Villain, and Witchfinder General; television appearances include: Silent Song, *Get Some In*, A Touch of the Tiny Hacketts, and *Minder.*

Recreations: Charity football; swimming, with his children. *Address:* c/o Morris Aza, 652 Finchley Road, London NW11.

SELDES, Marian, actress
b New York City, 23 Aug 1928; *d* of Gilbert Seldes and his wife Alice (Hall); *e* Dalton School; *m* Julian Claman (mar dis); prepared for the stage at the School of the American Ballet, and the Neighborhood Playhouse.

First appeared on the stage at the Metropolitan Opera House, NY, with the Ballet Theatre in Petrouchka; made her professional acting début at the National, Oct 1947, as an Attendant in Medea, at the same theatre, Dec 1947, played Dounia in Crime and Punishment; City Center, May 1949, Second Woman of Corinth in Medea; Martin Beck, Nov 1949, Anichu in That Lady; ANTA Playhouse, Nov 1950, played Electra in The Tower Beyond Tragedy; 48th Street, Feb 1951, Nurse Phillips in The High Ground; Hebbel, Berlin, Germany, Sept 1951, First Woman of Corinth in Medea; City Center, Jan 1952, A Close Friend in a revival of Come of Age; Empire, May 1953, Nancy in Oliver Twist in the programme Highlights of the Empire; 46th Street, Feb 1954, Bertha in Ondine; Ethel Barrymore, Oct 1955, Olivia in The Chalk Garden; at the Carthay Circle, Los Angeles, 1956, played Rachel in The Flowering Peach; at the La Jolla Playhouse, 1957, Sara in The Potting Shed; Player's Ring, Los Angeles, Dec 1957, Romaine in Witness for the Prosecution; returned to NY and at the Billy Rose, Oct 1960, played Symka Berson in The Wall, taking over the part of Rachel for four months; Mermaid, Oct 1961, Mag in The Long Voyage Home; at the same theatre, Oct 1961, played Emma Crosby in Diff'rent; Gramercy Arts, 1961, took over as Mrs Patrick Campbell in A Fig Leaf in Her Bonnet; Ethel Barrymore, Feb 1962, Susan Loring in A Gift of Time; Orpheum, Nov 1963, Miss Frost in The Ginger Man; Brooks Atkinson, Jan 1964, Blackie in a revised version of The Milk Train Doesn't Stop Here Anymore; Gate, NY, Jan 1965, played the Postmistress in All Women Are One; Billy Rose, Apr 1965, played Alice in Tiny Alice for some performances; Valley Music Theatre, Los Angeles, Oct 1965, the Nurse in Medea; American Place, NY 1965, Juana in Juana la Loca; Martin Beck, Sept 1966, Julia in A Delicate Balance, for which she received the Antoinette Perry (Tony) Award; Henry Miller's, Jan 1968, Sylvia in Before You Go; Felt Forum, Mar 1968, The Woman in Final Solutions; toured, summer 1968, as Mary in Who's Happy Now?; Theatre de Lys, Feb 1969, in the revue An Evening with James Agee; American Shakespeare Festival, Stratford, Conn, June 1969, Olga in The Three Sisters; St Clement's Church, Oct 1969, Daisy in Mercy Street; Berkshire Theatre Festival, Mass, 1970, Gretchen in Other People; John Golden, Mar 1971, Marian in Father's Day; Hedgerow, Aug 1971, Constance in The Celebration; Westport, Conn, Country Playhouse, Aug 1972, Katherine Carney in Remember Me; Good Shepherd—Faith Church, Oct 1972, directed Next Time I'll Sing to You, and directed it again 1974; Alvin, Apr 1973, The Witness in Martha Graham's Ballet Mendicants of Evening; Trinity Square Repertory, Providence, RI, 1974, appeared in For the Use of the Hall; Plymouth, Oct 1974, Hester Salomon in Equus, and continued in this part until June 1976, when she took over from Frances Sternhagen as Dora Strang in the same play; American Place, Jan 1977, Isadora in Isadora Duncan Sleeps with the Russian Navy; Plymouth, Nov 1977, Rivka in The Merchant; Music Box, Feb 1978, Myra Bruhl in Deathtrap; since 1945, has appeared with numerous summer stock companies in such plays as Night Must Fall, The Late George Apley, Peg O' My Heart, The Little Foxes, The Glass Menagerie, The Silver Cord, Angel Street, Pygmalion, The Importance of Being Earnest, Lady in the Dark, Show Boat, Dream Girl, etc; artist-in-residence at Stanford University, California, 1955; joined the faculty of the Drama Division of the Juilliard School, 1969, as director and teacher, and joined the Dance Division, 1972; member of the board of the Neighborhood Playhouse and of The Acting Company; first entered films, 1951, in the documentary The Lonely Light and has since appeared in Mr Lincoln, The Big Fisher-

man, The Greatest Story Ever Told, Fingers, etc; first appeared on television, 1949, in Macbeth; since Nov 1974 has appeared weekly on CBS Radio Mystery Theater; author of The Bright Lights: a theatre life, 1978.

Address: 125 East 57th Street, New York, NY 10022. *Tel:* PL 3–4595.

SELL, Janie, actress and singer
b Detroit, Mich, 1 Oct 1941; e Univ of Detroit.

Made debut in NY in 1966 in the revue Mixed Doubles; Upstairs at the Downstairs, 30 Dec 1967, appeared in the revue Dark Horses; Palace, Apr 1968, played Mme Grimaldi and Mrs Baker in George M!; Bouwerie Lane, Dec 1968, stand-by for Bernadette Peters as Ruby in Dames at Sea, and took over this part in Jan 1970; Plaza 9 Music Hall, Sept 1970, played Mona Kent in Dames at Sea; Minskoff, Mar 1973, Jane Burke in Irene; Shubert, Mar 1974, Mitzi in Over Here!; Chelsea Westside, Nov 1975, played in the revue By Bernstein; Circle-in-the-Square, June 1976, Gladys in Pal Joey; Martin Beck, June 1977, took over as Lt Lillian Holliday in Happy End; Ethel Barrymore, 1979, took over as Monica in I Love My Wife; Entermedia, Oct 1979, Sylvia Rosewater in God Bless You Mr Rosewater.

Address: Actors Equity Association, 165 West 46th Street, New York, NY 10036.

SELLARS, Elizabeth, actress
b Glasgow, 6 May 1923; d of Stephen Macphee Sellars and his wife Jean (Sutherland); e Queenswood, Hatfield, Herts; m Francis Henley; studied at the Royal Academy of Dramatic Art.

Made her first appearance at Bridlington, 1938, in When We Are Married; appeared with the Wilson Barrett Company, 1939, and subsequently toured for ENSA, in Jeannie; also appeared at Salisbury, for Southern Command, in Love From A Stranger; first appeared in London at the Lyric, Hammersmith, 4 June 1946, as Grushenka in The Brothers Karamazov; Comedy, Aug 1946, Marie von Leyde in The Other Side; appeared with the Bristol Old Vic Company, 1947–8; Cambridge, May 1951, played Yasmin in the revival of Hassan; toured, 1953, in Angels In Love; New, May 1955, appeared as Ma Pennypacker in The Remarkable Mr Pennypacker; Lyric, Aug 1956, followed Vivien Leigh as Lady Alexandra in South Sea Bubble; Comedy, Apr 1957 (for the New Watergate Theatre Club), played Laura Reynolds in Tea and Sympathy; Oxford Playhouse, Mar 1958, Helen in Paris Not So Gay; Royal Court, Liverpool, Aug 1958, Sister Grace in The Deserters; Arts, Jan 1959, the title-part in Madame De . . ., and Valentine Renaud in Traveller Without Luggage; Aldwych, Aug 1959, Anne Norbury in The Sound of Murder; joined the Shakespeare Memorial Theatre Company, Stratford-on-Avon, 1960–1, to play Helen in Troilus and Cressida, Bianca in The Taming of the Shrew, Hermione in The Winter's Tale, Gertrude in Hamlet, and Queen Elizabeth in Richard III; Oxford Playhouse, Apr 1964, played Olga in The Three Sisters; Yvonne Arnaud, Guildford, Nov 1965, Titania in A Midsummer Night's Dream; Cambridge, Apr 1966, Rosie Butterfield in A Friend Indeed; Wyndham's, Apr 1967, took over as Jean Brodie in The Prime of Miss Jean Brodie; same theatre, Feb 1968, Isabel in The Italian Girl; Lyceum, Edinburgh, Oct 1970, Margaret Cragg in The Hero; Playhouse, Bournemouth, Oct 1971, Grace Winslow in The Winslow Boy; first appeared in films, 1949, in Floodtide, and films include 55 Days in Peking, The Chalk Garden, The Hireling, etc; has also appeared in a number of plays on television including The Three Fat Women of Antibes and Repent at Leisure, and the series *Shades of Greene* and *Beasts*; is a member of the Hon Society of Lincoln's Inn, and a Fellow of the Zoological Society of London.

Recreations: Travel, reading for the Bar, and animals. *Address:* c/o Larry Dalzell Associates Ltd, 3 Goodwin's Court, St Martin's Lane, London WC2.

SENN, Herbert, designer
b Ilion, NY, 9 Oct 1924; *s* of Robert Charles Senn and his wife Elizabeth (Deutsch); *e* Columbia U.

First designs for NY were for the decor of House of Connelly, for Equity Library Theater, 2 Nov 1955; since then has designed Liliom, The Beaver Coat, 1956; Idiot's Delight, Right You Are (If You Think You Are), The Brothers Karamazov, 1957; Oklahoma!, Ardele, Hamlet of Stepney Green, 1958; She Shall Have Music, Time of Vengeance, 1959; Gay Divorce, La Ronde, The Idiot, Man and Superman, Emanuel, 1960; Montserrat, Five Posts in the Market Place, Smiling the Boy Fell Dead, O Marry Me (also lighting), 1961; The Merchant of Venice, 1962; I Got Shoes, The Boys from Syracuse (London debut 7 Nov 1963, Drury Lane), Double Dublin (also lighting), 1963; What Makes Sammy Run?, Roar Like a Dove (both also lighting), 1964; Great Scot!, 1965; By Jupiter, The Dodo Bird, The Peddler, 1967; Private Lives, 1968; Little Boxes, a double-bill consisting of Trevor and The Coffee Lace, 1969; The Divorce of Judy and Jane, 1971; Berlin to Broadway with Kurt Weill, Oh Coward, 1972; No Sex, Please, We're British, 1973; A Community of Two (tour), 1974; A Musical Jubilee, Oh Coward (London), 1975; has designed 23 seasons of summer stock at the Cape Playhouse, Denver, Mass; principal designer since 1970 for the Opera Company of Boston, for over 40 operas including, recently, The Ice Break, 1979; designs for the NY City opera include Ariadne and Naxos, 1975; designed most of these productions in partnership with Helen Pond.

Address: 316 West 51st Street, New York, NY. *Tel:* CO 5-3728.

SERBAN, Andrei, theatre director
b Bucharest, Romania, 21 Jun 1943; *s* of George Serban and his wife Elpis (Lichardopu); *e* University of Bucharest.

Came to the US to work at La Mama, where he directed Arden of Faversham, 1970; worked with Peter Brook in Paris, 1973; at La Mama 1974–76, where he directed and adapted a Greek trilogy consisting of The Trojan Women, Medea and Electra, also touring worldwide with these productions; for the same company directed The Good Woman of Setzuan, 1975, and As You Like It, in Brittany, 1976; at the Vivian Beaumont, directed The Cherry Orchard, 1976, and his adaptation of Agamemnon, 1977, later at the Delacorte; visiting professor at Yale, 1977–78, where he directed The Ghost Sonata and An Evening of Molière Farces for Yale Rep; at the Public, NY, directed his adaptation of The Master and Margarita, 1978; The Umbrellas of Cherbourg, Happy Days, 1979; London debut, Phoenix, May 1980, directing The Umbrellas of Cherbourg; Public, NY, 1980, directed The Sea Gull; opera work includes Eugene Onegin for the Welsh National Opera, 1980.

Address: c/o New York Shakespeare Festival, 425 Lafayette Street, New York, NY 10003. *Tel:* 598 7100.

SEYMOUR, Alan, playwright
b Perth, W Australia, 6 Jun 1927; *s* of Herbert Augustus Seymour and his wife Louise Mary; *e* Fremantle State School and Perth Modern School.

His first play to be produced was Swamp Creatures, seen at Canberra Rep in 1957; has since written The One Day of the Year, produced Sydney, 1961, also London 1961; The Gaiety of Nations, 1965; A Break in the Music, 1966; The Pope and the Pill, 1968; Oh Grave, Thy Victory, 1973; Structures, 1974; The Floet, 1980; plays for television include The Runner, 1962, and various adaptations including Eustace and Hilda; author of the novel The Coming Self-Destruction of the USA, 1969; theatre critic, 1963–65, The London Magazine.

Recreations: Music, travel. *Address:* c/o Laurence Fitch, Film Rights Ltd, 113 Wardour Street, London W1.

SHAFFER, Anthony, dramatic author
b Liverpool, 15 May 1926; *s* of Jack Shaffer and his wife Reka (Fredman); *e* St Paul's and Trinity College, Cambridge; *m* Carolyn Soley; formerly a barrister.

Author of the plays The Savage Parade, 1963, revised 1967; Sleuth, 1970; Murderer, 1975; The Case of the Oily Levantine, 1979; Sleuth was performed both in London and on Broadway, where it won the Tony award for the best play of 1970; film scripts include: Forbush and the Penguins, Frenzy, The Wicker Man, and Death on the Nile; television work, since 1969, includes: Pig in the Middle.

Recreation: Dilettante country living. *Address:* Apt 10d, 300 Central Park West, New York, NY.

SHAFFER, Peter, dramatic author
b Liverpool, 15 May 1926; *s* of Jack Shaffer and his wife Reka (*née* (Fredman); *e* St Paul's School, London, and Trinity College, Cambridge; formerly a coalminer (Bevin Boy), 1944–7, and a librarian in the New York Public Library.

His first play to be produced was Five Finger Exercise, at the Comedy Theatre, London, in July 1958; following a year's run, the London company gave place to a new production of the play with a different company, the original company and production appearing at the Music Box, New York, Dec 1959; he is also the author of the following plays: The Private Ear and the Public Eye (double-bill), 1962 (NY, 1963); The Merry Roosters Panto (with Joan Littlewood and Theatre Workshop), 1963; The Royal Hunt of the Sun, 1964 (NY, 1965); Black Comedy (one-act), 1965 (NY, 1966); The White Liars (one-act), 1967; The Battle of Shrivings, 1970; Equus, 1973/(NY, 1976); Amadeus, 1979; received the *Evening Standard* Award for the Best Play of 1958; received the New York Drama Critics Award for the Best Foreign Play, 1959–60; filmscripts include: The Lord of the Flies; Equus was filmed in 1977; television plays he has written since 1955 include: The Salt Land, 1955; Balance of Terror, 1957; he is also the author of a radio play, The Prodigal Father.

Recreations: Music, architecture, and travel. *Club:* Dramatists'. *Address:* 18 Earl's Terrace, London, W8. *Tel:* 01–602 6892.

SHANGE, Ntozake (*née* Paulette L Williams), playwright, director, and actress
b Trenton, NJ, 18 Oct 1948; *d* of Paul Williams and his wife Eloise; *e* Barnard College (BA 1970) and University of Southern California (MA 1973).

Appeared as the Lady in Yellow in her poem-play For Colored Girls Who Have Considered Suicide/When the Rainbow Is Enuf, at the Public/Anspacher, Jun 1976, transferring with the production and making her Broadway debut at the Booth on 15 Sept 1976; at the Public, Dec 1977, appeared in Where the Mississippi Meets the Amazon, which she co-wrote; author of A Photograph: A Study in Cruelty,

1977; Spell #7, 1979; Boogie-Woogie Landscapes, 1980; translated Mother Courage, 1980; directed The Mighty Gents, for the New York Shakespeare Festival's Mobile Theatre, and A Photograph, for Equinox Theatre, 1979; her published poetry includes Sassafrass, 1976, and Nappy Edges, 1978; performing member of the dance company Sounds in Motion, and a regular teacher and lecturer; has written for a Diana Ross TV special and appeared in a PBS documentary about her own work.

Recreations: Violin, collecting Black memorabilia. *Address:* c/o Zaki Pony, 1270 Broadway, Suite 503, New York, NY 10001. *Tel:* 564—1324.

SHANKS, Alec, director
b Birmingham; *s* of David Shanks, JP, and his wife Christina (Robertson); *e* King Edward's School, Birmingham; *m* Jay Mann.

From 1930 designed Paris Revues, at the Folies Bergère, Moulin Rouge, Théâtre du Chatelet, etc; his first London production was at the Prince of Wales, 28 Nov 1944, when he designed and staged the revue Strike It Again; has since staged the following productions: Cinderella (Adelphi), 1945; Piccadilly Hayride, 1946; Together Again, 1947; Knights of Madness, 1949; London Laughs, 1951; Ring Out the Bells, 1952; You'll Be Lucky (with Joan Davis), The Talk of the Town (with Joan Davis), Jokers Wild (with Charles Henry), 1954; at the Stoll, Apr 1955, arranged the lighting for Kismet; directed These Foolish Kings, and La Plume de Ma Tante (also New York), 1956; co-directed Clown Jewels, 1959; directed Young in Heart, 1960; Drury Lane, 1964, assembled the production of Camelot and produced The Diamond Fair (NY); Drury Lane, 1965, produced The Stars Shine for Jack; designed costumes for Enter Solly Gold, 1970; décor for The Maid of the Mountains, 1972; in addition to the above London productions has directed most of the annual summer revues at Blackpool since 1945, either alone or with Joan Davis; in Paris, directed Histoires d'Eve, 1949, and Filles d'Eve, 1950; also at the Coliseum, 1949, directed the Royal Variety Performance in aid of the Variety Artists' Benevolent Fund.

Address: 14 Wellington House, Eton Road, London, NW3. *Tel:* 01-586 0911.

SHARAFF, Irene, designer
b Boston, Mass, studied at Art Student's League, the New York School of Fine and Allied Arts, and at the Grande Chaumière, in Paris.

Began theatrical career as assistant to Aline Bernstein at Civic Repertory Theatre company for three years, 1928-30; designed costumes for Alice in Wonderland (also scenery), 1932; As Thousands Cheer, 1933; Life Begins at 8:40, The Great Waltz, 1934; Crime and Punishment (also scenery), Parade, Jubilee, Rosmersholm (also scenery), 1935; Idiot's Delight, On Your Toes, White Horse Inn, 1936; Virginia, I'd Rather Be Right, 1937; The Boys from Syracuse, 1938; The American Way, Streets of Paris, Gay New Orleans, 1939; Boys and Girls Together, All in Fun, 1940; Lady in the Dark, The Land Is Bright, Sunny River, Banjo Eyes, 1941; By Jupiter, Star and Garter, Count Me In, 1942; Billion Dollar Baby, 1945; The Would-be Gentleman, G I Hamlet, 1946; Bonanza Bound, Magdalena, 1948; Montserrat, 1949; Dance Me A Song, Mike Todd's Peep-show, 1950; The King and I, A Tree Grows in Brooklyn, 1951; Of Thee I Sing, 1952; Me and Juliet, The King and I (London), 1953; By the Beautiful Sea, On Your Toes, 1954; Shangri-La, Candide, Happy Hunting, 1956; Small War on Murray Hill, West Side Story, 1957; Flower Drum Song, 1958; Juno, 1959; Do Re Mi, 1960;

Jenny, The Girl Who Came to Supper, The Boys from Syracuse (London), 1963; Funny Girl, The King and I (revival), 1964; Sweet Charity, 1965; Hallelujah, Baby!, 1967; Irene (costumes for Debbie Reynolds), 1972; has also designed for the Ballet Russe de Monte Carlo, American Ballet Theatre, New York City Ballet, Joffrey Ballet, Royal Ballet, etc; her designs for films have included fifteen nominations for Academy Awards, of which 'Oscars' were won by An American in Paris, 1951; The King and I, 1956; West Side Story, 1961; Cleopatra, 1963; Who's Afraid of Virginia Woolf?, 1966; television includes Aladdin, 1958; author of Broadway and Hollywood: Costumes Designed by Irene Sharaff, 1976.

Address: United Scenic Artists, 268 West 47th Street, New York, NY 10036.

SHARP, Anthony (Dennis Anthony John Sharp), actor, director, and dramatic author
b Highgate, 16 June 1915; *s* of Wilfrid Leo Sharp and his wife Florence Emily (Sherlock); *e* St Mary's, Canterbury; *m* Margaret Wedlake; formerly employed as an insurance policy draughtsman; studied for the stage at the London School of Dramatic Art.

First appeared at the De La Warr Pavilion, Bexhill-on-Sea, Feb 1938, as the Sergeant in Macbeth, with H V Neilson's Shakespearean Touring Company; toured 1938-9, and appeared in repertory at Wigan, Hastings, Peterborough, and Liverpool; in the Royal Artillery, 1940-6, serving in North Africa, Austria, and Italy, where he ran the Forces Radio Stations in 1946; returned to the stage at the Mercury, Sept 1946, as Hansell in Tangent; appeared with the Bristol Old Vic Company, 1946-7; Strand, Feb 1948, played Rabbi Samuel in Family Portrait; New Lindsey, Apr 1948, State Attorney Seyffert in The Burning Bush; toured, Aug 1948, as Rex in The Linden Tree; Boltons, Sept 1949, Bishop Elphinstone in The Thistle and the Rose; Vaudeville, Apr 1950, William Hampton in Cry Liberty; Vaudeville, Apr 1951, Guy Ashley in Who Goes There!; Whitehall, Oct 1951, in a season of matinées, appeared as Ambrose Applejohn in Ambrose Applejohn's Adventure; toured, Apr 1952, as Commander Trout in Treasure on Pelican; Comedy, Dec 1952, played Peter Debenham in For Better, For Worse . . .; Royal, Newcastle, Sept 1954, Mr Finch in The Jolly Fiddler; Royal, Windsor, Mar 1955, appeared as John Hampden in his own play The Conscience of the King; St Martin's, Oct 1955, Mr Finch in Small Hotel; King's, Glasgow, Feb 1956, played Henry Watson-Smith in The Gay Deceiver; Her Majesty's, Aug 1956, the Psychiatrist in no time for sergeants; Chiswick Empire, Apr 1958, played Benedìck in Much Ado About Nothing, toured with the production, and also played Hotspur and Justice Shallow in Henry IV, Parts I and II on tour; Open Air Theatre, Regent's Park, June 1958, again played Benedick; at the same theatre, June, and July 1959, played Malvolio in Twelfth Night, and Quince in A Midsummer Night's Dream; Saville, Oct 1959, played Lord Roehampton in The Edwardians; Royal, Brighton, Feb 1964, played the Duke of Venice in The Merchant of Venice, and Quince in A Midsummer Night's Dream, prior to touring Latin America and European capitals with both productions for the British Council and H M Tennent, Ltd; Garrick, Oct 1969, played the Bishop of Upton in She's Done It Again; Sadler's Wells, May 1972, Sir Anthony Absolute in The Rivals; Opera House, Manchester, Dec 1972, Mr Darling and Capt Hook in Peter Pan; Mermaid, Apr 1973, Lord Summerhayes in Misalliance; Devonshire Park, Eastbourne, Nov 1973, the Monsignor in I Want to Be a Father, Madam; Open Air, Regent's Park, Quince in A Midsummer Night's Dream, also appearing in Sweet Mr Shakespeare, July 1975, Don Armado in Love's Labour's Lost, 1976, and Quince in A Midsummer Night's Dream, 1978; Regal, Perth, W Australia, played Leslie Bromhead in No Sex Please . . . We're British; Arnaud, Guildford, Nov 1978, Gilbert Waynward in Murder in a Bad Light, also touring, spring 1979; Regent's Park, May 1979, again played Quince, and also Malvolio in Twelfth Night; he has also directed the following plays: Any Other Business (Repertory Players), 1957, (Westminster) 1958; Wolf's Clothing, Caught Napping, Billy Bunter Flies East, 1959; The Gazebo, Refer to Drawer (Repertory Players), 1960; Milk and Honey (tour), Guilty Party, The Marriage Game (tour), Critic's Choice, 1961; Act of Violence (tour), 1962; Devil May Care, Difference of Opinion, 1963; Hostile Witness, 1964; Difference of Opinion (Australia), 1965; The Importance of Being Earnest (Hong Kong), Wait Until Dark, Justice is a Woman, 1966; Sign Here Please, 1967; Justice, 1968, and in the same year Private Lives and Present Laughter in Australia; in South Africa, An Ideal Husband, 1969, and Oh! Clarence, 1970; Harvey (English tour), 1970; Who Killed Santa Claus? (S Africa), 1971; The Dragon Variation (tour), Wait Until Dark (S Africa), 1972; Double Edge (Vaudeville, 1975, S Africa, 1976, and tours, 1977-8); Peter Pan (S Africa), 1977; In Praise of Love (W Australia), 1978; is author of the plays Nightmare Abbey, and adaptation of Peacock's novel, produced at the Westminster, 1952; Tale of a Summer's Day, 1959; has appeared in a number of Sunday night productions with the Repertory Players and the Under-Thirty Theatre Group; film appearances include: A Clockwork Orange, Gawain and the Green Knight, and The Confessional; has also made several hundred appearances on television.

Favourite part: Malvolio. *Recreations:* Cricket, music and old churches. *Address:* c/o Richard Stone, 18–20 York Buildings, London, WC2.

SHATNER, William, actor
b Montreal, Canada, 22 Mar 1931; *s* of Joseph Shatner and his wife Anne; *e* McGill Univ; *m* Gloria Rosenberg.

First appeared on the stage at the Children's Theatre in Montreal as Tom Sawyer in the play of that name; toured Canada in various stock and repertory companies, notably the Canadian Repertory Theatre of Ottawa; joined the Stratford, Ontario, Shakespeare company in 1954, appearing, from June to Aug, as A Young Lord in Measure for Measure, Lucentio in The Taming of the Shrew, and in the Chorus of Oedipus Rex; at Stratford, Ontario, June–Aug 1955, appeared as Lucius in Julius Caesar, Gratiano in The Merchant of Venice, and in the Chorus of King Oedipus; made his NY debut at the Winter Garden, Jan 1956, as Usumcasame in Tamburlaine the Great; Stratford, Ontario, June–Aug 1956, played Fenton in The Merry Wives of Windsor and the Duke of Gloucester in Henry V; Broadhurst, Oct 1958, played Robert Lomax in The World of Suzie Wong, which ran for 508 performances; Booth, Oct, 1961, played Paul Sevigne in A Shot in the Dark; reappeared on the stage at the Ahmanson, Los Angeles, 1971, as Tom in Remote Asylum; toured, Aug 1977, in Tricks of the Trade; received the Tyrone Guthrie Award for most promising actor in 1957; first appeared in films in 1956 and has since played in The Brothers Karamazov, The Intruder, The Outrage, Big Bad Mama, Dead of Night, Star Trek (1979), etc; first appeared on television in 1954 and has since played frequently in the major dramatic programs including playing Captain James Kirk on Star Trek, 1966–69.

Favourite part: Henry V. *Recreations:* Riding, archery, photography, writing. *Address:* 15408 Stonewood Terrace, Sherman Oaks, California. *Tel:* 783–1537.

SHAW, Glen Byam, CBE, actor and director
b London, 13 Dec 1904; *s* of J Byam Shaw, RI, and his wife Evelyn (Pyke-Nott); *e* Westminster School; *m* Angela Baddeley.

Made his first appearance on the stage at the Pavilion Theatre, Torquay, 1 Aug 1923, as Colin Langford in At Mrs Beam's; made his first appearance in London, at the Lyric Theatre, Hammersmith, 25 May 1925, as Yasha in The Cherry Orchard; in 1926, played repertory at J B Fagan's Oxford Playhouse; Queen's, June 1926, played Tim Wakely in Down Hill; then returned to Oxford Playhouse; Globe, June 1927, played the Student in The Spook Sonata; went to America, and made his first appearance in New York, at the Shubert Theatre, 9 Nov 1927, as Pelham Humfrey in And So To Bed; at the Bijou, NY, Mar 1928, Peter Trophimof in The Cherry Orchard; returned to London, and at the Globe, Oct 1928, played Lord Straffield in The Truth Game; Apollo, Nov 1928, Lyngstrand in The Lady from the Sea; subsequently appeared with the Masque Theatre company at Edinburgh; at the Arts, July 1929, played Charles in The Hell Within; Q, Aug 1929, Lionel and Anthony Bramber in Portrait of a Lady; Fortune, Sept–Oct 1929, Konstantin Treplev in The Seagull, and Baron Tusenbach in The Three Sisters; Garrick, Mar 1930, Armand Duval in The Lady of the Camellias; Lyric, Hammersmith, Oct 1930; Leonidas in Marriage à la Mode; went to South Africa with his wife, Aug 1931, and toured there in Marigold, Autumn Crocus, and The Truth Game; on his return, appeared at the Globe, Feb 1932, as the Young Actor in Punchinello; Lyceum, Apr 1932, played the Cripple and the King's Son in The Miracle; in Sept 1932, toured in the same parts; Lyric, Hammersmith, June 1933, Percinet in The Fantasticks; Gate, Sept 1933, Alfredo in As You Desire Me; Lyric, Oct 1933, appeared as the Earl of Southampton in This Side Idolatry; New, Nov 1933, in the absence of John Gielgud, played Richard in Richard of Bordeaux; Jan 1934, toured as Richard in Richard of Bordeaux; New, June 1934, played Darnley in Queen of Scots; Nov 1934, Laertes in Hamlet; Little, July 1935, Oswald Alving in Ghosts; New, Oct 1935, Benvolio in Romeo and Juliet; New, Nov 1936, Captain O'Shea in Parnell; toured, Feb 1937, as D'Arcy in Pride and Prejudice; Queen's, May 1937, Lewis Dell in He was Born Gay; Queen's, Sept 1937–June 1938, Duke of Norfolk and Sir Stephen Scroop in Richard II, Sir Benjamin Backbite in The School for Scandal, Solyony in Three Sisters, and Gratiano in The Merchant of Venice; Phoenix, Oct 1938, Alexander Studsinsky in The White Guard; Lyceum, June 1939, Horatio in Hamlet, and subsequently played the same part at Kronborg Castle, Elsinore; served in the Royal Scots, 1940–5; directed Richard II (with John Gielgud), for OUDS, 1935; The Island, 1938; The Merchant of Venice (with John Gielgud), 1938; Dear Octopus (with Dodie Smith), 1938; Rhondda Roundabout, 1939; The Winslow Boy, 1946; Antony and Cleopatra, 1946; The Winslow Boy (NY), 1947; As You Like It, Old Vic (for Young Vic Company), 1949; Accolade, 1950; The Merchant of Venice, Old Vic (for Young Vic Company), 1950; at the Old Vic, Jan 1951, directed Henry V; at the Shakespeare Memorial Theatre, Stratford-on-Avon, 1952, directed Coriolanus and As You Like It; in 1952 was appointed co-director, with Anthony Quayle, of the Shakespeare Memorial Theatre, and in that year directed Richard III and Antony and Cleopatra; directed Romeo and Juliet, Troilus and Cressida, 1954; Macbeth and The Merry Wives of Windsor, 1955; on Anthony Quayle's resignation, 1956, he became sole director of the Shakespeare Memorial Theatre, and directed the following plays: Othello, 1956; As You Like It, Julius Caesar, 1957; Romeo and Juliet, Hamlet, 1958; King Lear, 1959; resigned his position as director of the Memorial Theatre,

Joke, 1960; The Lady From the Sea, The Complaisant Lover (NY), Ross (NY), 1961; The Tulip Tree, 1962; Where Angels Fear to Tread, 1963; The Right Honourable Gentleman, 1964; You Never Can Tell, 1965; The Rivals, 1966; The Dance of Death (National Theatre and Canadian tour), The Merchant of Venice, 1967; The Wild Duck, 1970; appointed Director of Productions at Sadler's Wells Theatre, Mar 1962, where he directed the following operas: The Rake's Progress, Idomeneo, 1962; Cosi Fan Tutti, Der Freischütz, Hänsel and Gretel, 1963; Faust, 1964; A Masked Ball, 1965; Die Fledermaus, 1966; for the English National Opera has directed Duke Bluebeard's Castle, 1972; The Ring Cycle (with John Blatchley), 1973, etc; was appointed Director of the Old Vic School, and Director of the Old Vic Theatre Centre, 1947; Director of the English Opera, 1968; received the HonDLitt, University of Birmingham, 1959; created CBE, 1954.

Club: Reform. *Address:* c/o The Coliseum Theatre, St Martin's Lane, London WC2 4ES.

SHAW, Irwin, dramatic author and novelist
b New York City, 27 Feb 1913; *s* of William Shaw and his wife Rose (Tompkins); *e* Brooklyn College (BA); *m* Marian Edwards (mar dis).

Has written the following plays: Bury the Dead, 1936; Siege, 1937; Quiet City, The Gentle People, 1939; Retreat to Pleasure, 1940; Sons and Soldiers, 1943; The Assassin, 1945; The Survivors (with Peter Viertel), 1948; adapted Patate, 1958; author of A Choice of Wars, a double-bill produced at the Citizens', Glasgow, 1958; Children from Their Games, 1963; author of the original novel for the play Lucy Crown, produced in France, 1958; Bury the Dead was adapted by Vinette Carroll as Step Lively, Boy, 1973; drama critic of *New Republic,* NY, 1947; has also written several screen-plays; among his novels are The Young Lions, 1948, Two Weeks in Another Town, 1960, Voices of a Summer Day, Rich Man, Poor Man, 1970, Evening in Byzantium, 1973, Nightwork, 1975, Beggarman, Thief, 1977; short story collections include: Mixed Company, 1950, Tip on a Dead Jockey and Other Stories, 1957, Love on a Dark Street, 1965; also author of the travel books In the Company of Dolphins, 1964, Paris! Paris!, 1976; Rich Man, Poor Man, and Beggarman, Thief adapted for television, 1979.

Address: c/o Hope, Laresche and Sayle, 11 Jubilee Place, London SW3.

SHAW, Sebastian, actor
b Holt, Norfolk, 29 May 1905; *s* of Dr Geoffrey Shaw; *m* Margaret Delamere (dec); studied for the stage at the Royal Academy of Dramatic Art.

Made his first appearance on the stage, at the Court Theatre, 1 Jan 1914, as one of the Juvenile Band in The Cockyolly Bird; after leaving the Academy, he appeared at the Bristol Repertory Theatre; subsequently played at Strat-ford-on-Avon, Liverpool Repertory, and Hull Repertory Theatres; made his first appearance in London, at the Regent Theatre, 3 May 1925, as the Archangel in The Sign in the Sun; subsequently toured as Lewis Dodd in The Constant Nymph; at the New Theatre, Apr 1928, played Martin in Come With Me; Strand (for the Play Actors), June 1928, Stephen Rolf in The Comic Artist; Garrick, Aug 1928, Dick Hetherington in The Moving Finger; Sept 1928, Major Rob-ert Mainwaring in The Constant Nymph; Arts, Jan 1929, Nils in The Age of Unreason; Playhouse, Feb 1929, Colin Tabret in The Sacred Flame; Strand (for Repertory Players), Mar 1929, Wyndham Brandon in Rope; then went to New York,

and made his first appearance at the Masque Theatre, 19 Sept 1929, in the same part; on his return, appeared at the Gate, Apr 1930, as Lieut Marrien in Oktobertag; Everyman, May 1930, George Cruise in The Blue Coast; Apollo, Oct 1930, Basil Owen in The Outsider; Embassy, Dec 1930, Tony in Carpet Slippers; Everyman, Jan 1931, Paul Stark in Danger! High Tension; New, Feb 1931, Captain Hamilton in Who Goes Next?; Royalty, Mar 1931, Bill Hamblin in The World of Light; Fortune, July 1931, Claudio in Measure for Measure; went to NY, and at the Maxine Elliott, Oct 1931, played Pierre Belcroix in Melo; on his return, appeared at the Embassy, Jan–Feb 1932, as Philip in Full Fathom Five, and Romeo in Romeo and Juliet; St Martin's, Mar 1932, Kester Woodseaves in Precious Bane; Strand, May 1932, Sir Philip Bay-Clender in Party; Globe, May 1933, Andrew and Jacko in The Day I Forgot; Queen's, Nov 1933, Rollo in Sunshine Sisters; Globe, Mar 1934, Dr John Sully in Double Door; Playhouse, Nov 1934, Richard Deval in Hurricane; His Majesty's, May 1935, Gareth Evans in Hervey House; toured, Mar 1936, as Joseph Ralston in The Old Maid; Vaudeville, May 1936, played Michael Fraser in Green Waters; Phoenix, Dec 1937, the Policeman in A Kiss for Cinderella; Q, Feb 1938, Andrew Mayo in Beyond the Horizon; Apollo, Oct 1938, Dick Reeves in Tree of Eden; Q, Jan 1939, Joe Burch in The Ship's Bell (of which he was part-author with Margaret Delamere); Vaudeville, Apr 1939, Robert Maine in Goodness, How Sad!; Q, Dec 1940, Stanley in A Lass and a Lackey; Embassy, Nov 1945, directed The Gambler; Lyric, Hammersmith, May 1946, played Heracles in The Thracian Horses; Mercury, July 1947, Mr Hern-Lawrence in I Said to Myself; Arts, Oct 1947, Thomas Freeman in Smith; Prince's, May 1950, Sir James Kirkman in His Excellency; New, July 1951, played Filmer Jesson, MP, in His House In Order; Criterion, Mar 1952, appeared in Third Person; St Martin's, Jan 1953, Sir David Crossley in The Gift; toured, May 1953, in Third Person; at Lichfield Cathedral, Sept 1953, appeared as King Wulfhere in St Chad of the Seven Wells; Ludlow Festival, July 1956, the title-part in the first English production of Hugo von Hofmansthal's Everyman; Playhouse, Oxford, Nov 1956, played the Keeper in The Numbered; at the same theatre, Dec 1956, He in Lock and Key; Shrewsbury Festival, June 1957, Lucifer in Brother Lucifer; Edinburgh Festival, Aug 1957, Borrazzo in The Hidden King; Winter Garden, Feb 1958, Roger and Dr Seaton in Hunter's Moon; Mermaid, Apr 1961, wrote, directed, and played the Detective in Take A Life; Royal Court, June 1961, played Sir Desmond in Empress With Teapot, in a Production without Décor; Dublin Festival, Sept 1961, played Sir George Crofts in Mrs Warren's Profession, and Morell in Candida, subsequently touring Europe with both plays; Pembroke, Croydon, May 1962, Dr Washburn in The Summer People; Ashcroft, Croydon, Feb 1963, Dr Tom Lilly in The Poison Tree; Queens', Hornchurch, Apr 1963, Ephraim in Desire Under the Elms; Birmingham Repertory, May 1963, played Sam Turner in Two Stars For Comfort; Hampstead Theatre Club, Feb 1964, Sir Rodney Haviland in The Tower; Royal Court, June 1965, General Conrad von Hotzendorf in A Patriot For Me; Royal Court, Oct–Dec 1965, played Older Man, Coplestone, Godwin, and Lord Eldon in Shelley; Sir Francis Harker in The Cresta Run, and Private Attercliffe in Serjeant Musgrave's Dance; Royal Court, 1966, appeared as Sir Walter Whorehound in A Chaste Maid in Cheapside (Jan), Mr Voysey in The Voysey Inheritance (Apr), and as Jake Latham and Reginald Mait-land in Their Very Own and Golden City (May); Nov 1966, joined the Royal Shakespeare Company at the Aldwych to play Sir Gerald Catesby in Belcher's Luck, and Sir Oblong

Fitz Oblong in the Thwarting of Baron Bolligrew, 1966; since then he has played the following parts at Stratford: Friar Laurence in Romeo and Juliet, the King of France in All's Well That Ends Well, Duncan in Macbeth, 1967 (also appearing at the Aldwych, 1968, after a tour of Finland and Russia in the latter two parts); Gloucester in King Lear, Ulysses in Troilus and Cressida, Leonato in Much Ado About Nothing, 1968; also toured the USA in the latter production and returned to play the same parts at the Aldwych, together with that of Justice Adam Overdo in Bartholomew Fair, June–Oct 1969; Stratford, 1970, Vincentio in Measure for Measure, Polonius in Hamlet, and Sir Eglamour in The Two Gentlemen of Verona, repeating the latter part at the Aldwych, Dec 1970; Theatre Royal, Windsor, Feb 1971, Capt Shotover in Heartbreak House; Criterion, May 1971, Mr Link in After Haggerty; Aldwych, July 1971, General Pechenegov in Enemies; The Place, Oct 1971, Valletta in Occupations; Aldwych, Jan 1972, the Best Friend in All Over; toured, Sept 1972, in Eden End; Stratford, season 1973, played Duke of York in Richard II and Boyet in Love's Labour's Lost, repeating the former role at the Brooklyn Academy, Jan 1974, Stratford, Apr 1974, Aldwych, Sept 1974; Stratford, June 1974, and Aldwych, Dec 1974, title-role in Cymbeline; Aldwych, Aug 1974, Dvoetochie in Summerfolk, touring the US in this part, 1975; Arnaud, Guildford, 1976, Chebutykin in Three Sisters, transferring to the Cambridge, June; Aldwych, Sept 1976, Shabelsky in Ivanov; Oct–Nov, 1977 and 1978, took part in 'Actors in Residence' tour of American universities, teaching and giving recitals; Mermaid, Mar 1978, Mr Justice Millhouse in Whose Life Is It Anyway?, transferring to the Savoy, June 1978; he is an Associate Artist of the Royal Shakespeare Company; has appeared in numerous films and radio plays; latest television performance, The Old Curiosity Shop; he is also the author of a play, The Cliff Walk, 1969, and a novel, The Christening, 1975.

Address: c/o Lloyds Bank, Ltd, 16 St James's Street, London SW1A 1EY.

SHAWN, Dick (*né* Richard Schulefand), actor
b Buffalo, NY, 1 Dec; *e* Univ of Miami.

First appeared in New York at the Belasco, 16 Nov 1948, as Milton Rubin in For Heaven's Sake, Mother!, acting under the name Richy Shawn; became a comedian and toured in cabaret, then appeared at the Palace, Oct 1953, in Betty Hutton and Her All-Star International Show, as chief comic; again played in cabaret, then, at the Cort, Jan 1962, played Emile Magis in The Egg; Majestic, 1964, took over from Jerry Lester as Pseudolus and Prologus in A Funny Thing Happened on the Way to the Forum; Longacre, Jan 1965, Peter in Peterpat; Mark Hellinger, Feb 1965, Byron Prong in Fade Out—Fade In; Mark Hellinger, Apr 1968, Yoni and Solomon in I'm Solomon; Edison, May 1970, took over from Ron Leibman as Gordon Miller in Room Service; Truck and Warehouse, May 1970, Tandy in Steambath, but did not open in this role; Yale Repertory, New Haven, Conn, 1971, played in The Big House; Bucks County Playhouse, Pa, Sept 1972, played in Halloween; St James, Nov 1975, appeared in A Musical Jubilee; Hartman, Stamford, May 1976, Major Upshaw in Stag at Bay; Roundabout, June 1976, Mendel in The World of Sholem Aleichem; Westport Country Playhouse, Conn, Aug 1976, appeared in the revue Bananas and Drums; Promenade, June 1977, appeared in his one-man show, The 2nd Greatest Entertainer in the Whole Wide World; has appeared in the films It's a Mad Mad Mad Mad World, Wake Me When It's Over, The Producers, The Happy Ending, etc; has appeared on television in Max Liebman TV Spectaculars and on various dramatic and comedy programs.

Address: Actors Equity Association, 165 West 46th Street, New York, NY 10036.

SHEEN, Martin (*né* Ramon Estevez), actor
b Dayton, Ohio, 3 Aug 1940; *s* of Francisco Estevez and his wife Mary Ann (Phelan); *m* Janet Sheen.

Made his New York début as a member of the Living Theatre, in 1959, when he took over the role of Ernie in The Connection; Living Theatre, 1960, played Hyllos in Women of Trachis and the Third Soldier in Cavalry; in 1961 played Horace in Many Loves and The Man with the Turned-Up Nose in In the Jungle of Cities; left the Living Theatre, and, at the Eugene O'Neill, 29 Mar 1964, played Mike in Never Live over a Pretzel Factory; Royale, May 1964, played Timmy Cleary in The Subject Was Roses, and continued in this part for more than a year; toured in this part, 1965–6; Orpheum, Jan 1967, Vasco in The Wicked Cooks; Anspacher, Dec 1967, for the New York Shakespeare Festival, played Hamlet in a modern adaptation of that play; Delacorte, Aug 1968, Romeo in Romeo and Juliet; Sheridan Square Playhouse, Sept 1969, Johnny in Hello and Goodbye; The Other Stage, Feb 1970, Reese in The Happiness Cage; Circle in the Square, Aug 1975, took over as Happy in Death of a Salesman; first appeared in films in The Subject Was Roses, 1969, and has since played in The Incident, Rage, Badlands, The Legend of Earl Durand, Eagle's Wing, Apocalypse Now (1979), etc; has appeared on television in That Certain Summer (1974), Letters for Three Lovers, The Execution of Private Slovik, Catholics, The California Kid, No Drums No Bugles, etc.

Address: 29081 PCH, Malibu, California.

SHELLEY, Carole, actress
b London, 16 Aug 1939; *d* of Curtis Shelley and his wife Deborah (Bloomstein); *e* private schools, Arts Educational School, and the Royal Academy of Dramatic Art; *m* Al Woods (dec); previously engaged as a milliner; prepared for the stage with Iris Warren and Eileen Thorndike.

First appeared on the stage at the George Inn, Southwark, 1950, as Little Nell in The Old Curiosity Shop; first appeared on the stage in London at the Apollo, 1955, as Angela in Simon and Laura; Lyric, Hammersmith, 1959, appeared in the revue New Cranks; Criterion, Aug 1960, appeared in the revue The Art of Living; Apollo, Feb 1962, Jane in Boeing-Boeing; Queen's, during 1963, took over as Mary McKellaway in Mary, Mary, and subsequently toured in this part; came to America and at the Plymouth, New York, 6 Mar 1965, played Gwendolyn Pigeon in The Odd Couple; Helen Hayes, Jan 1967, played Barbara in The Astrakhan Coat; Biltmore, Mar 1968, Fay in Loot; Ethel Barrymore, Sept 1968, played in the revue Noel Coward's Sweet Potato, and played in it again when it was revived at the Booth, Nov 1968; Circle in the Square, Mar 1969, took over as Patsy Newquist in Little Murders; Helen Hayes, Nov 1970, Jackie Coryton in a revival of Hay Fever; Niagara-on-the-Lake, Canada, Shaw Festival, July 1971, appeared in Tonight at 8.30, Press Cuttings, and War, Women, and Other Trivia; Stratford Festival, Ontario, Canada, summer 1972, Rosalind in As You Like It, Constance Neville in She Stoops to Conquer, and Regan in King Lear; toured Denmark, Holland, Poland, and Russia with this troupe as Regan in King Lear and Bianca in The Taming of the Shrew; American Shakespeare Festival, Stratford, Conn, July 1973, First Witch in Macbeth and Margery Pinchwife in The Country Wife; Goodman, Chicago, Nov 1973, Nora in A Doll's House, Stratford, Conn, June 1974, Lady Capulet in Romeo and Juliet; Westport, Conn, Country Playhouse, Aug 1974, Jane in Absurd Person Singular, and repeated this part at the Music Box, Oct 1974; Morosco, Dec 1975, Ruth in The Norman Conquests; toured, 1975–66, as Julie Cavendish in The Royal Family; Shaw Festival, Niagara-on-the-Lake, 1977, played Ann Whitefield in Man and Superman and Epifania in The Millionairess; Ahmanson, LA, Dec 1977, Judith Anderson in The Devil's Disciple, also at Brooklyn Academy, Feb 1978, where she went on to play Ilona Szabo in The Play's the Thing, Feb; played Lady Driver in the US première of Donkey's Years, 1978; Theatre of St Peter's Church, Jan 1979, Madge Kendal in The Elephant Man, transferring with the production to the Booth, Apr, and winning a 'Tony' for her performance; first appeared in films in Little Nell, 1942, and has since played in It's Great to Be Young, Give Us This Day, The Odd Couple, The Boston Strangler, Robin Hood (animated, voice only), 1973, etc; appeared on television in England in many of the Brian Rix farces, and in America played Gwendolyn Pigeon in the series *The Odd Couple*, 1970–1; appointed to the Board of Trustees of the American Shakespeare Theatre, Stratford, Conn, 1976.

Recreations: Needlepoint, dressmaking, cooking, and reading. *Address:* c/o Lionel Larner Inc, 850 Seventh Avenue, New York, NY 10019. *Tel:* 246–3105.

SHEPARD, Sam (*né* Samuel Shepard Rogers), playwright and musician

b Fort Sheridan, Ill, 5 Nov 1943; *s* of Samuel Shepard Rogers and his wife Jane (Schook); *e* Duarte HS, Calif; *m* O-Lan Johnson, the actress; formerly an actor with Bishop's Company Repertory Players, a waiter at the Village Gate, NY, "horseshit remover and hot walker" at Santa Anita Race Track, etc.

Author of the following plays, which have been produced at various avant-garde and other theatres in NY, London, and throughout the world: Cowboys, Rock Garden (a short play later included in the revue Oh! Calcutta!), Up to Thursday, Dog, Rocking Chair, 1964; Chicago, Icarus's Mother, 4-H Club, 1965; Fourteen Hundred Thousand, Red Cross, La Turista, 1966; Forensic and the Navigators, Melodrama Play, 1967; Shaved Splits, 1968; Operation Sidewinder, The Unseen Hand (for which he wrote and performed music when produced in NY at the Astor Place, Apr), 1970; Mad Dog Blues, Cowboy Mouth (with Patti Smith), Back Bog Beast Bait, The Holy Ghostly, 1971; The Tooth of Crime (produced at the Open Space, London), 1972; Blue Bitch, Nightwalk (with Jean-Claude Van Itallie and Megan Terry), 1973; Little Ocean, Geography of a Horse Dreamer, Action, 1974; Killer's Head, 1975; Angel City, Curse of the Starving Class, Suicide in B Flat, 1976; Seduced, Buried Child, 1978; Tongues/Savage Love (co-author), 1979; author of the screenplay Zabriskie Point, with Michelangelo Antonioni and others, 1969; has received the Obie Award eight times for distinguished playwriting; awarded a Rockefeller Foundation and a Guggenheim Foundation Fellowship; Pulitzer Prize for Buried Child, 1979.

Address: c/o Toby Cole, 234 West 44th Street, New York, NY 10036.

SHEPHERD, Jack, actor

b Leeds, Yorkshire, 29 Oct 1940; *s* of Thomas William Shepherd and his wife Violet Mary (Hodgson); *e* Roundhay School, and King's College, Newcastle; *m* (1) Judith Harland (mar dis); (2) Ann Scott; trained for the stage at the Drama Centre, London; previously an art teacher and jazz musician.

First appeared on the London stage Jan 1966, at the Royal Court, as an Officer of Dragoons in Serjeant Musgrave's Dance; subsequently played numerous parts at the same

theatre, among them Paul Dobson in Their Very Own and Golden City, May, Mère Ubu in Ubu Roi, July, Brother Droman in Three Men for Colverton, Sept 1966; Frankie Bryant in Roots, Feb, Vassily Solyony in Three Sisters, Apr, Arnold Middleton in The Restoration of Arnold Middleton (also Criterion: for this performance he received the *Plays and Players* London Critics' Award as most promising actor of the year), July, Henry in The Dragon, Dec 1967; Malvolio in Twelfth Night, Jan Gladstone in Early Morning, Apr 1968; Shogo in Narrow Road to the Deep North, Feb, Prince Arthur in Early Morning, Mar 1969; at the Gardner Centre, Brighton, Aug 1970, played Benjamin Mandelstam in Bloomers; Traverse, Edinburgh, Oct 1970, directed Disaster Strikes the Home; Royal Court, Dec 1970, Jacques in Pirates; toured, for Cambridge Theatre Company, Jan 1971, as Maitland in Inadmissible Evidence; Theatre Upstairs, May 1971, Lomax in Corunna, also tour; Lyceum, Edinburgh, Aug 1971, for Edinburgh Festival, Gil Martin in Confessions of a Justified Sinner; Lyceum, Edinburgh, Oct 1971, Alceste in The Misanthrope; Cockpit, Nov 1971, directed his adaptation of Under the Hill (from Beardsley); founder member of the Actors' Company, playing Vasques in 'Tis Pity She's a Whore, Inspector of Police in Ruling the Roost (Edinburgh Festival and tour), Sept 1972, and Okano in The Three Arrows, Arts, Cambridge, Oct 1972; King's Head, Islington, Dec 1972, Ben in Let's Murder Vivaldi; Bush, Jan 1973, title-role in Dracula, also collaborating in the writing; Edinburgh Festival, Sept 1973 (Traverse Theatre), directed Sleep of Reason (also co-author); University, Newcastle upon Tyne, Feb 1974, title-role in Hamlet; toured as Sloman in the National Theatre's mobile production of The Party, Sept 1974; directed a new version of Dracula at the University, Newcastle upon Tyne, Apr 1975, again playing Dracula and collaborating in the writing; Royal Court, Sept 1975, Arthur in Teeth 'n' Smiles; Old Vic, July 1976, Flamineo in The White Devil; Theatre Upstairs, June 1977, Carver in The Winter Dancers; for the National Theatre at the Cottesloe he has played the following: Teach in American Buffalo, June 1978, Judas in The Passion, Aug, Boamer in Lark Rise, Sept, Thomas Clarkeson in The World Turned Upside Down, Nov; Smitty in The Long Voyage Home, Jan 1979, The Correspondent in Dispatches, June 1979; Hickey in The Iceman Commeth, Mar 1979; films, since 1969, include: The Virgin Soldiers; television, since 1967, includes: Occupations, Bill Brand, and Ready When You Are Mr MacGill (both gaining RTS Award, 1976), Nina (TV film), and Underdog.

Address: c/o Green and Underwood, 3 The Broadway, Gunnersbury Lane, London W3 8HR. *Tel:* 01–993 6183.

SHERIDAN, Dinah, actress

b Hampstead Garden Suburb, 17 Sept 1920; *d* of James Archer Mec and his wife Lisa Charlotte Everth; *m* (1) Jimmy Hanley (mar dis); (2) John Davis (mar dis); trained for the stage by Italia Conti.

First professional engagement, Holborn Empire, Dec 1932, when she understudied the part of Rosamund in Where the Rainbow Ends; in repertory 1940–2; in films until 1952, when she retired until 1967, returning to the stage in Oct of that year as Rose Craig in Let's All Go Down the Strand, at the Phoenix; Duchess, Sept 1968, Isobel Keith in A Boston Story; St Martin's, 1969, took over the part of Celia Pilgrim in Out of the Question; Thorndike, Leatherhead, Feb 1972, Katie Weiner in A Touch of Purple; Vaudeville, June 1972, took over the part of Mrs Markham in Move Over Mrs Markham; Queens, Aug 1973, took over as the Countess of Chell in The Card; Arnaud, Guildford, Oct 1974, Stacey Harrison in The Gentle Hook, transferring to the Piccadilly,

Dec; Phoenix, July 1976, Katharine Dougherty in The Pleasure of His Company; Whitehall, Mar 1977, Susan Clifton in In the Red; Vaudeville, Sept 1977, Letitia Blacklock in A Murder is Announced; Nov 1978, toured in Half Life, also visiting Toronto, Canada; first film lead, Irish and Proud of It, 1936; subsequent films include Where No Vultures Fly, Sound Barrier, Genevieve, and The Railway Children; has made numerous television appearances since her first in 1936; has her own company, Sheridan-Hanley Enterprises Ltd.

Favourite parts: Costume ones. *Recreations:* Tapestry, gardening, dried flower collage. *Address:* c/o John Mahoney, 30 Chalfont Court, Baker Street, London NW1. *Tel:* 01–486 2957.

SHERIN, Edwin, actor and director
b Harrisburg, Pa, 15 Jan 1930; *s* of Joseph Sherin and his wife Ruth (Berger); *e* Brown Univ; *m* (1) Pamela Vevers (mar dis); (2) Jane Alexander, the actress; served in the US Naval Reserve, 1952–55; prepared for the stage with Paul Mann's Actors Workshop and with John Houseman at the American Shakespeare Festival Academy.

Began his career as an actor, with the Houseman troupe at the Phoenix, 22 Jan 1957, as a Citizen in Measure for Measure; June, 1957, joined the New York Shakespeare Festival, and appeared as Tybalt in Romeo and Juliet, and Aug 1957, Malcolm in Macbeth; at the Heckscher, Jan 1958, played Hymen in As You Like It; Belvedere Lake, Aug 1958, played Cassio in Othello and Sebastian in Twelfth Night; John Golden, Mar 1959, understudied Paul Roebling as Sir Mark Grahame in A Desert Incident; Gate, 14 Oct, 1959, directed his first play, Deirdre of the Sorrows; Phoenix, Nov 1959, played Philourgos in Lysistrata; Mar 1960, Prince Hal in Henry IV, Part I and Part II; Jan 1959, Octavius in Antony and Cleopatra; June 1959, played in Dr Willy-Nilly; Eugene O'Neill, Oct 1960, played Jonathan Spring in Face of a Hero; Mermaid, Oct 1961, played in Diff'rent; Music Box, Jan 1962, Theodoric in Romulus; resumed his career as a director in 1961, and has since directed Joan of Lorraine, 1961; Mister Roberts, 1962; The Wall, for the Arena Stage, Washington, DC, where he became assistant producing director and staged some 18 productions before 1968, including Galileo, Saint Joan, The Inspector General, Billy Budd, The Andersonville Trial, Major Barbara, The Iceman Cometh, Serjeant Musgrave's Dance, The Lonesome Train, Hard Traveling, Project Immortality, The Great White Hope, King Lear, etc; in NY directed Look at Any Man, 1963; The White Rose and the Red, 1964; The Great White Hope, Glory! Hallelujah! (for the ACT, San Francisco, Cal), 1968; Cosi Fan Tutte (NY City Opera), The Time of Your Life (Washington, DC), 1971; An Evening with Richard Nixon and . . ., Major Barbara (Stratford, Conn), 6 Rms Riv Vu, 1972; Baba Goya, King Lear, Nourish the Beast, 1973; Find Your Way Home, directed his first play in London, at the Piccadilly, 14 Mar, A Streetcar Named Desire, Of Mice and Men (NY), 1974; The Red Devil Battery Sign (Boston), Sweet Bird of Youth, 1975; Rex, The Eccentricities of a Nightingale, 1976; Do You Turn Somersaults?, Semmelweiss (Washington DC), 1977; First Monday in October, 1978; Losing Time, 1979; Goodbye Fidel, 1980; directed his first film, Valdez Is Coming, 1969, and has since directed My Old Man's Place and others; first acted on television in 1956, continuing for eight years on such programs as *Omnibus, Playhouse 90, Studio One, East Side/West Side,* etc; has directed on television since 1959, including Deirdre of the Sorrows, King Lear, An American Christmas in Words and Music, etc.

Recreations: Ocean racing, backpacking, tennis. *Address:* Gordon Road, RD #2, Carmel, NY 10512. *Tel:* 212–759–8730.

SHERMAN, Hiram, actor
b Boston, Mass, 11 Feb 1908; *s* of Clifford Sherman and his wife Gwendolen (Lawrence); *e* Springfield, Ill, and University of Illinois; studied for the stage with the Goodman repertory company, Chicago.

Made his first appearance, Oct 1927, as the Murderer in Le Tour de Nesle; first appeared in New York, at the Maxine Elliott Theatre, Oct 1936, as Robbin in Horse Eats Hat, with the Federal Theatre Project; Venice Theatre, NY, June 1937, played Rev Salvation and Junior Mister in The Cradle Will Rock; at the Mercury Theatre, Nov 1937, played Casca in Julius Caesar, subsequently appearing as Firk in The Shoemaker's Holiday; Music Box, Sept 1938, in the revue, Sing Out the News; New York World's Fair (Globe Theatre), Apr 1939, Bottom in A Midsummer Night's Dream, and Touchstone in As You Like It; Alvin, Nov 1939, played Ogden Quiler in Very Warm for May; Booth, Oct 1940, Rev Ernest Dunwoody in Boyd's Daughter; Belmont, Dec 1940, Copmère in Mum's the Word; Henry Miller, Mar 1941, Cy Blodgett in The Talley Method; during the War, served in the US Navy, 1941–6; reappeared on the NY stage, at the Alvin, Oct 1946, as Ragueneau in Cyrano de Bergerac; City Center, June 1948, played Kastril in The Alchemist; National, Sept 1948, Pete Murray in Town House; subsequently went to England, and made his first appearance at the Opera House, Manchester, 23 Mar 1949, as Jeff in Brigadoon, making his first appearance in London, at His Majesty's, 14 Apr 1949, in the same part; on his return to America, appeared extensively in television; 48th Street, NY, Jan 1951, played Philip Dupre in Four Twelves Are 48; at Fair Park Auditorium, Dallas, Aug 1951, played Harry in I Married an Angel and Baron Popoff in The Merry Widow; toured, 1951–2, as David Slater in The Moon Is Blue, and appeared in this part at the Harris Theatre, Chicago, June 1952; Fair Park Auditorium, Dallas, Aug 1952, played the Cowardly Lion in The Wizard of Oz; Alvin, NY, Dec 1952, appeared in the revue Two's Company; in summer theatres, 1953, appeared as Charles Belden in The Frogs of Spring, and played this part at the Broadhurst, NY, Oct 1953; New Parsons Theatre, Hartford, Dec 1953, played Edward in Dear Charles; Ann Arbor, June 1954, played Philip in The Little Hut, and subsequently toured in this part; at the Plymouth, NY, Apr 1955, acted as compère in the revue Three for Tonight; Helen Hayes, Apr 1956, Harvey Wilson in Goodbye Again; American Shakespeare Festival Theatre, Stratford, Connecticut, June 1956, played Pompey in Measure for Measure and Hubert de Burgh in King John; City Center, Sept 1956, Jupiter in Orpheus in the Underworld; Phoenix, Jan 1957, again played Pompey in Measure for Measure; State Fair Auditorium, Dallas July 1957, Panisse in Fanny; Congress Hall, Berlin, Germany, Sept 1957, played in a dedicatory programme of one-act plays by William Saroyan and Thornton Wilder; City Center, Oct 1957, Baron Popoff in The Merry Widow, in which he subsequently toured; Bijou, Mar 1958, appeared as compère in a revue International Soirée; returned to Stratford, Conn, June–July 1958, to play Polonius in Hamlet, Bottom in A Midsummer Night's Dream, and a Shepherd and the Third Gentleman in The Winter's Tale; Stratford, Conn, June–July 1959, played Friar Laurence in Romeo and Juliet, Ford in The Merry Wives of Windsor, and Sergeant in All's Well That Ends Well; Seven Arts Center, NY, Mar 1960, Berenger in The Killer; returned to England, and at the Criterion, London, Aug 1960, appeared in the revue The Art of Living; Stratford, Conn, Apr–Oct 1961, played Touchstone in As You Like It, Porter in Macbeth, and Pandarus in Troilus and Cressida; appeared in the last two roles and served as Master of Ceremonies for the American Shakespeare Festival Performance at the White House, Oct 1961; Carnegie Hall, Mar 1962, Narrator for Die Lustige Witwe;

toured US, 1962–3, as Oscar Nelson in Mary, Mary, and took over this part at the Helen Hayes, NY, May 1963; Philharmonic Hall, Apr 1964, Rev Salvation in a revival of The Cradle Will Rock; in summer theatres, 1964, Harbour Gage in Heart's Delight; Colonial, Boston, Dec 1964, Albert Denison in Everybody Out, The Castle Is Sinking; Westport, Conn, July 1965, played Pinky in Family Things Etc; Billy Rose, Mar 1966, again played Pinky when the play was renamed Where's Daddy?; Lunt-Fontanne, Dec 1967, Wingate in How Now, Dow Jones; New, London, Apr 1969, Matthew Cuthbert in Anne of Green Gables; Niagara-on-the-Lake, Ontario, Shaw Festival, July 1971, played in War, Women, and Other Trivia; played at the Goodman, Chicago, in the 1971–2 season; is the author of several plays; first appeared in films, 1938, in One Third of a Nation, and has since appeared in The Solid Gold Cadillac, Mary, Mary, Oh Dad, Poor Dad, Mama's Hung You in the Closet and I'm Feelin' So Sad.

Address: Actors Equity Association, 165 West 46th Street, New York, NY 10036.

SHERRIN, Ned, producer, director, performer and dramatic author
b Low Ham, Somerset, 18 Feb 1931; *s* of Thomas Adam Sherrin and his wife Dorothy Finch (Drewett); *e* Sexey's, Bruton, Exeter College, Oxford, and Grays Inn; a barrister.

He is the author, with Caryl Brahms, of stage shows including: No Bed for Bacon, 1959; Cindy-Ella, or I Gotta Shoe, 1962; The Spoils, 1968; Nicholas Nickleby, 1969; Sing A Rude Song, 1970; Fish Out of Water, 1971; Liberty Ranch, 1972; Nickleby and Me, 1975; Hush and Hide, 1978; Beecham, 1979; directed Come Spy With Me, Whitehall, 1966; Nickleby and Me, Theatre Royal, Stratford E, 1976; narrator, director and book writer of Side by Side by Sondheim, which transferred to the Wyndham's, July: made his New York début in the show, Music Box, Apr 1977; Criterion, 1977, directed I Gotta Shoe; Round House, 1980, devised and co-directed Only in America; first film production (with Leslie Gilliat) The Virgin Soldiers, 1969, followed by Every Home Should Have One and Up Pompeii; his work for television includes production and direction of TW3, which he also created; most recent appearances in The Rather Reassuring Programme, his own production Song By Song, and, in New York, in his own series We Interrupt This Week; received Awards for TW3, 1963 and 1964, and for Not So Much A Programme, 1965; author (with Caryl Brahms) of novels including I Gotta Shoe and Benbow Was His Name, and of short stories.

Recreation: Appearing on television. *Address:* c/o Margaret Ramsay, 14a Goodwin's Court, London WC2.

SHERWOOD, Henry, presenting manager and theatre director
b Leeds, Yorkshire, 5 July 1931; *s* of James Peter Sherwood and his wife Phyllis (Anderson); *e* Leeds Grammar School; *m* Brenda Walsh; trained as a stage manager, 1948.

First stage appearance, Isle of Man, 1949, in a summer season; after national service in the RAF, joined his father; with him and Edward Reid, 1961, formed Sherwood and Reid Ltd (for details of this company's productions, *see* James P Sherwood, *15th Edition*); formed Henry Sherwood Productions Ltd, 1969, and has since presented or co-presented A Woman Named Anne, Lady Frederick, The High Bid, 1970; Meeting at Night, Romance, The Douglas Cause, 1971; Relative Values (tour), Eden End (tour), 1972; The Hollow (tour), Relative Values, 1973; Oh! Kay, The Turning Point, The Little Hut, 1974; Kennedy's Children,

Tarantara Tarantara, 1975; joined the board of ATS Management in 1977 with Stanley and Michael Joseph and this company presented Say Who You Are, The Charlie Williams Show, 1978; Grand National Night, and Bring Judy and Friends (which he compiled and narrated), 1979; Director of the Birmingham Hippodrome, 1979–present.

Recreations: Cricket and racing. *Club:* Lord's Taverners. *Address:* Birmingham Hippodrome, Hurst Street, Birmingham.

SHERWOOD, Madeleine (*née* Thornton), actress
b Montreal, Canada, 13 Nov 1922; *d* of Laurence Holmes Thornton and his wife Yvonne Madeleine (Villard); *e* Montreal West High School; *m* Robert M Sherwood (mar dis); prepared for the stage at the Yale University Dramatic Workshop, the Montreal Repertory Theatre, and the Actors Studio.

Made her Broadway début at the Martin Beck, Jan 1953, as Abigail Williams in The Crucible; Morosco, Mar 1955, played Mae in Cat on a Hot Tin Roof, which ran for 692 performances; toured the US, 1956–7, in the same play; Martin Beck, Mar 1959, played Miss Lucy in Sweet Bird of Youth; Music Box, Oct 1960, Lily Brown in Invitation to a March; ANTA, Oct 1961, played Ida in The Garden of Sweets; Majestic, 1961, took over the role of Morgan la Fay in Camelot; Mayfair, Mar 1962, Lula Roca in Hey, You, Light Man!; Theatre de Lys, 1962, appeared in the programme Brecht on Brecht; Royale, Sept 1962, took over the role of Maxine Faulk in Night of the Iguana; Lunt-Fontanne, Nov 1963, played Betty Dullfeet in Arturo Ui; 46th Street, Mar 1965, played Mrs McIlhenny in Do I Hear a Waltz?; Belasco, Dec 1965, Mrs Garnsey in Inadmissible Evidence; Martin Beck, Mar 1971, The Daughter in All Over; Provincetown Playhouse, Oct 1971, Teresa in Friends and Nita Moon in Relations; Anspacher, May 1972, appeared in Older People; Actors Studio, May 1974, Epic in O Glorious Tinntinnabulation; received the Obie Award for her performance in Hey, You, Light, Man!, 1962; Marymount, Manhattan, Oct 1978, later Theatre de Lys, Mother in Getting Out; first entered films, 1956, in Baby Doll; recent films include Cat on a Hot Tin Roof, Sweet Bird of Youth, The 91st Day, Hurry Sundown, Pendulum, Wicked, Wicked, The Changeling (1979), etc; television appearances include Double Indemnity (London), the Mother Superior in *The Flying Nun*, 1966–70, Rich Man, Poor Man; studied at GROW Institute, 1970–1, to become psychotherapist and group counsellor.

Favourite parts: Lula Roca, Abigail Williams, and Betty Dullfeet. *Recreation:* Her house on Lac Cornu in the Laurentian mountains. *Address:* c/o Susan Smith Agency, 850 Seventh Avenue, New York, NY.

SHEVELOVE, Burt, director, playwright
b Newark, New Jersey, 19 Sept 1915; *s* of Jacob J Shevelove and his wife Betty (Lessner); *e* Brown University (AB 1937), Yale University.

Began his professional theatrical career at the Coronet, New York, 15 Sept 1948, when he directed Small Wonder, a revue to which he also contributed material and in which he played, under the name Billings Brown; directed the revival of Kiss Me, Kate, at the New York City Center, May 1956; co-librettist, with Larry Gelbart, of A Funny Thing Happened on the Way to the Forum, produced at the Alvin, May 1962; adapted the Phoenix production of Too Much Johnson from the farce by William Gillette, and directed it Jan 1964; since then has concentrated on directing, notably The Butter and Egg Man, 1966; People Is the Thing That the World Is Fullest of for Bil Baird's Puppet Theatre, Hallelujah, Baby,

1967; Rockefeller and the Red Indians, 1968; No, No, Nanette, 1971; the revival of A Funny Thing Happened on the Way to the Forum, 1973; Sondheim: A Musical Tribute, No, No, Nanette (Drury Lane, London), 1973; adapted and directed The Frogs at the Yale Repertory, New Haven, Conn, 1974; Rodgers and Hart, 1975; adapted and directed Happy New Year, Stratford, Ontario, 1979 and NY, 1980; has produced and directed the Art Carney Specials on television, 1950–60, and has directed *The Bell Telephone Hour,* 1960–5, *The Judy Garland Show, The Jack Paar Show, Victor Borge Show,* An Evening with Richard Rodgers, etc; received the Antoinette Perry (Tony) Award for A Funny Thing Happened on the Way to the Forum.

Address: Society of Stage Directors and Choreographers, 1501 Broadway, New York, NY 10019.

SHINE, Bill (*né* Wilfred William Dennis Shine), actor
b London, 20 Oct 1911; *s* of the late Wilfred E Shine and his wife Amy Elizabeth (Procter); *e* privately; *m* (1) Julia Sybil Lang; (2) Diana Cecil (née Manship).

Made his first appearance on the stage at the Winter Gardens, New Brighton, 26 Dec 1917, as a Stork in Princess Posy; first appeared in London at the Q, 15 Feb 1926, as the Butcher's Boy in The Mother; Arts, Apr 1928, Jack Thornley in The Making of an Immortal; from 1929–39, appeared mainly in films, although at intervals he appeared at the Richmond Theatre in various productions; Strand Theatre, Mar 1938, played George in Death on the Table; from 1941 to 1943, toured all over England with the Market Theatre (CEMA) in The Man of Destiny, Suitable Suitors, The Lover, etc; returned to London, 1943, and from May–Aug 1943, appeared at the Arts Theatre, playing Dan in The Old Foolishness, Sir Lucius O'Trigger in The Rivals, Clincher in The Constant Couple, Horace Vale in The Magistrate, and Lord Summerhays in Misalliance; at the Cambridge, Oct 1944, played Private Reynolds in Happy Few; St Martin's, Nov 1944, again played Horace Vale in The Magistrate; Arts, Mar 1945, the Angel in The Simpleton of the Unexpected Isles; Birmingham Repertory Theatre, 1945, played Joxer Daly in Juno and the Paycock; Lyric, Hammersmith, Aug 1946, played Mr McCrossan and Mr Alderton in Fear No More; Players' Theatre, Sept 1946, Freddie Lloyd Lacey in The Amiable Mrs Luke; Dec 1946, the Baron in Cinderella; Dec 1948, Larry O'Log in The Sleeping Beauty in the Wood; Bedford, Camden Town, Oct, and Princes, Nov 1949, George Tallboys in Lady Audley's Secret; Bedford, Camden Town, Jan–June 1950, appeared as Conn in The Shaughraun, Archibald Carlyle in East Lynne, Sandy in Trilby, Hans in The Bells, William in Black Eyed Susan; toured, 1950, in The Chuckeyhead Story; St James's, Feb 1951, played the Sewer man in The Madwoman of Chaillot; Gaiety, Dublin, 1951, appeared as King Phillip II of Spain in That Lady; at the Q, Dec 1952, played S/Ldr the Rev Bill Hooker in Rumpus on the River; New Lindsey, Sept 1954, Jack Brent in Fortune's Finger; Prince of Wales's, Mar 1955, Henry Westby in Room For Two; appeared in the tours of The Gay Deceiver, 1956, and in Short, Back and Sides, 1957; toured, Jan 1961, as Squadron-Leader Pat Brophy in The Angry Deep; Royal, Windsor, Aug 1963, played Major Randolph in Meet Me on the Fence, subsequently touring in the play, when it was retitled The Yes–Yes–Yes Man; toured, Jan 1966, as Lord Ryall in The Grass Is Greener; York Festival, June 1966, played Lord Foppington in Virtue In Danger and The Earl of Warwick in St Joan; North East Theatre Festival, Feb 1967, Montano in Othello and Colonel Pickering in Pygmalion; Harrogate Festival, Sept 1967, Mr Justice Squeezum in Lock Up Your Daughters; Royal, Bury, St Edmunds, Dec 1967,

the Chief Constable in Aladdin; May 1968, toured as General Boganovich in The Merry Widow, opening at the Cambridge in that production, Feb 1969; Bournemouth, summer season 1969, played Sir Lindsay Cooper in Uproar in the House; Bromley, Dec 1969, The Squire in Jack and the Beanstalk; Opera House, Scarborough, Summer season 1971, Sir Lindsay Cooper in Uproar in the House and the Commander in Not Now, Darling; toured, Jan–July 1972, as Chief Insp Hubbard in Dial M for Murder; toured, Aug 1972, as Maxwell Davenport in The Late Christopher Bean; Kenton Theatre, Henley-on-Thames, May–July 1973, played Tom Kemp in The Mollusc and Wallace Stothard in When All the World is Young, Lad; toured, Oct 1973, as Hugo Birch in Spider's Web; toured, Jan 1974, again playing the Commander in Not Now, Darling; Kenton, Henley, June 1974, Joxer Daly in Juno and the Paycock; Summer Theatre, Frinton, July 1974, General Boothroyd in Lloyd George Knew My Father; Thorndike, Leatherhead, Oct 1974, Lord Littlehampton in Maudie!; same theatre, Sept 1975, Walter Pangbourn in Move Over, Mrs Markham; Theatre Royal, Stratford E, Nov 1975, Rev Jenkins in Cranford; Summer Theatre, Frinton, 1977, Hucklebee in The Fantasticks, The Earl of Lister in The Chiltern Hundreds, and directed Suddenly at Home; English Theatre, Vienna, Mar 1978, the Admiral in Relative Values; Aug–Dec 1979, toured as Brad in The Gentle Hook; has also appeared on television; first appeared in films in 1929, in Under the Greenwood Tree.

Favourite parts: Conn in The Shaughraun. *Recreations:* Gardening, fishing, riding, and horse-racing. *Clubs:* Savage and Players'. *Address:* The Garden Flat, 36 Harcourt Terrace, London, SW10. *Tel:* 01–373 3915.

SHIPLEY, Joseph T, dramatic critic and lecturer
b Brooklyn, New York, 19 Aug 1893; *s* of Jay R Shipley and his wife Jennie (Fragner); *e* City College of New York, Columbia University (MA, PhD); *m* (1) Helen Bleet; (2) Ann Ziporkes.

Instructor in English, Stuyvesant High School from 1914, and its Senior Advisor, 1940–56; drama critic for *The Call,* 1919–22; *The Leader,* 1922–3; drama critic of *New Leader,* NY, 1922–62; drama critic on radio WEVD, since 1940; editor of *American Bookman*; writes monthy column on NY theatre for European and Asian periodicals; has written many books on poetry and the drama, including: Five Major Plays of Ibsen, Guide to Great Plays, The Art of Eugene O'Neill, and Guides to 14 Plays of Shakespeare; Vice-President for the USA of the Association Internationale des Critiques du Théâtre; is a member of the New York Drama Critics' Circle, was President 1952–4, and Secretary since 1965; is an Hon Overseas Member of The Critics' Circle (London); has taught literary and dramatic criticism in the graduate schools of New York City College and Brooklyn College; conducted seminars for professional playwrights; has lectured on the American theatre extensively in the USA, Europe, and Asia.

Address: 29 West 46th Street, New York, NY 10036.

SHULL, Leo, publisher, producer, and columnist
b Milwaukee, Wisconsin, 8 Feb 1913; *s* of David Shull and his wife Anne (Rosenkrantz); *e* University of Pennsylvania (BS 1934), Temple University (MA 1936), New School for Social Research, New York Law School; *m* Claire Klar.

Has produced some thirty plays off-Broadway and off-off-Broadway, including The Virtuous Island and The Apollo of Bellac at the Carnegie Hall Playhouse, Apr 1957; on-Broadway has produced Genius Inc, Norman Corwin Plays, 1943, and Political Revue, 1946; has published the weekly trade paper Show Business, in which he also writes a column, since 1941; also publishes fourteen books and guides stemming from this publication, notably Summer Theatre Guide, Angels, Model's Guide, Who's Where, Dancer's Guide, Production Directory, Casting Guide, Playwriting for Broadway, Geographic Casting Guide, Show Guide, Show Business Syndicate, etc; produced the film New York Town, 1948; produced *The Leo Shull Show* on television, 1951; is a member of the Drama Desk, the Dramatists Guild, and Genius Inc.

Address: Show Business, 136 West 44th Street, New York, NY 10036. *Tel:* 586–6900.

SHULMAN, Milton, dramatic critic and author
b Toronto, Canada, 1 Sept 1913; *e* University of Toronto and Osgood Hall; *m* Drusilla Beyfus.

Formerly a barrister, and also a television producer; film critic of the *Evening Standard,* 1948–53; book critic of the *Sunday Express,* 1953–4; theatre critic of the *Evening Standard,* 1953–; television critic of the *Evening Standard,* 1964–72; commentator on arts and current affairs, *Daily Express,* 1973–4, *Evening Standard,* 1972–; film critic, *Vogue,* 1975–; received the IPA Award as Critic of the Year, 1966; Executive Producer of Granada Television, 1958–62; Assistant Controller of Programmes, Rediffusion Television, 1962–4; programmes produced include: Animal Story, Who Goes Next?, In My Opinion, Head On (Granada Television), Decision (Rediffusion Television); scripted the film: Every Home Should Have One (with Herbert Kretzmer); author of the television play Kill Three; author of books including: Defeat in the West, How to be a Celebrity, The Ravenous Eye, The Least Worst Television in the World, and the Preep series of children's books.

Recreations: Tennis, conversation, and modern art. *Club:* Savile. *Address:* Flat G, 51 Eaton Square, London, SW1. *Tel:* 01–235 7162.

SHUMLIN, Herman E, producer and director
b Atwood, Colorado, 6 Dec 1898; *s* of George Shumlin and his wife Rebecca (Slavin); *e* Newark, NJ; *m* (1) Rose Keane Caplan (mar dis); (2) Carmen Winckelman; (3) Diana Green Krasny.

Was a reporter on the *New York Clipper,* 1924–5, and *The Billboard,* 1924–5; in 1926, was press-representative for Schwab and Mandel; in 1927, manager for Jed Harris; since 1927, responsible for the production of the following plays in New York: Celebrity (with Paul Streger), 1927; The Command Performance and To-Night at Twelve, 1928; Button, Button (with Haight and Potter), 1929; The Last Mile and Grand Hotel (with Harry Moses), 1930; Clear All Wires, 1932; The Bride of Torozko (with Gilbert Miller), The Children's Hour, 1934; Sweet Mystery of Life, 1935; Days to Come, 1936; The Merchant of Yonkers, 1938; The Little Foxes, 1939; The Male Animal, The Corn Is Green, Watch on the Rhine, 1940; The Great Big Doorstep, 1942; The Searching Wind, The Visitor, 1944; Feb, 1946; Daphne Laureola (with Leland Hayward), 1950; Lace on Her Petticoat, To Dorothy, A Son, 1951; Gertie, 1952; Inherit the Wind (with Margo Jones), 1955; Only in America, 1959; Bicycle Ride to Nevada (with Roger L Stevens), 1963; The Deputy, 1964; Soldiers, 1968; Transfers, 1970; Flowers, As You Like It (with Hurok), 1974; also directed Wine of Choice for the Theatre Guild, 1938; Kiss Them for Me, 1945; The Biggest Thief in Town, 1949; The High Ground, 1951; Candida, The Gambler, 1952; Regina, 1953; Wedding Breakfast, 1954; Tall Story, 1959; Little Moon of Alban, 1960; Dear Me, The Sky Is Falling, 1963; Spofford, which he also

wrote, 1967; films he directed include Watch on the Rhine, and The Confidential Agent.
(*Died 4 June 1979.*)

SHYRE, Paul, director, producer, dramatic author, and actor
b New York City, 8 Mar 1929; *s* of Louis Philip Shyre and his wife Mary (Lee); *e* University of Florida and the American Academy of Dramatic Arts.

First production was at the Westport Country Playhouse, Connecticut, 1953, when he directed USA, which he adapted from the novel by John Dos Passos; first production in NY was at the Playhouse, 1956, when he co-produced and acted in the concert reading Pictures in the Hallway, which he adapted from the autobiography of Sean O'Casey; also in 1956 co-produced Purple Dust, in which he played Basil Stoke, Cherry Lane, Dec 1956; Belasco, Sept 1957, co-produced, directed, and acted in the concert reading I Knock at the Door, which he also adapted from the autobiography of Sean O'Casey; Belvedere Lake, Aug 1958, played Roderigo in Othello; Carnegie Hall Playhouse, Nov 1958, played Shanaar in Cock-a-Doodle Dandy, which he also co-produced; Martinique, Oct 1959, directed USA, of which he was co-author and in which he later took over one of the parts; Cherry Lane, Oct 1960, directed and produced Drums Under the Windows, which he adapted from the autobiography of Sean O'Casey; Mermaid, Oct 1961, co-produced and directed The Long Voyage Home and Diff'rent, and, in Jan 1962, The Creditors; Cort, Feb 1964, directed A Fair Game for Lovers; Theatre de Lys, 1964, directed and played in I Knock at the Door and Pictures in the Hallway; Theatre Four, Feb 1965, directed The Queen and the Rebels; also in 1965 adapted The Child Buyer from the novel of John Hersey, which was produced at the Garrick; his first London production was of Pictures in the Hallway, at the Mermaid, Sept 1966; adapted and directed A Whitman Portrait, produced at the Gramercy Arts, NY, Oct 1966; The Forum, for the Lincoln Center Repertory Theater, Apr 1971, directed and played in Pictures in the Hallway; adapted and directed An Unpleasant Evening with H L Mencken, 1972; adapted and directed Will Rogers' USA, 1972, performed in NY in 1974; Hartford, Conn, Stage Company, 1973, directed Juno and the Paycock; Olympia, Dublin, Eire, 1974, directed The Morgan Yard; Cherry Lane, Jan 1975, wrote and played H L Mencken in the one-man show Blasts and Bravos: An Evening with H L Mencken; Music Box, May 1975, took over from Larry Blyden in Absurd Person Singular; toured, 1977, as Sidney in Absurd Person Singular; Circle-in-the-Square, Nov 1977, Beauvais in Saint Joan; adapted and directed Paris Was Yesterday (from Janet Flanner), for stock, 1978; Seattle Rep, 1978, narrated Side by Side by Sondheim; Paris was Yesterday presented at the Harold Clurman, NY, Dec 1979; was Artistic Director for the Fred Miller Theatre, Milwaukee, Wisconsin, 1962–3; has received the New York Drama Desk Award, the Brandeis University Theatre Arts Award, the Obie Award, etc; in 1960 directed Juno and the Paycock for television.

Hobby and recreation: Music and swimming. *Club:* Players. *Address:* 162 West 56th Street, New York, NY 10019. *Tel:* JUdson 2–5379.

SIDNEY, Sylvia (*née* Sophia Kosow), actress
b New York City, 8 Aug 1910; *d* of Victor Kosow and his wife Rebecca (Saperstein); *e* NY, and at the Theatre Guild School with Rouben Mamoulian, Alfred Lunt, Lynn Fontanne, the Langners, etc; *m* (1) Bennett A Cerf (mar dis); (2) Luther Adler (mar dis); (3) C W Alsop (mar dis).

Made her first appearance on the stage at the Garrick, 15 June 1926, as Prunella in a play of that name; Poli's Theatre, Washington, 11 Oct 1926, played in The Challenge of Youth; 48th Street Theatre, 3 Jan 1927, succeeded Grace Durkin as Anita in The Squall; Eltinge Theatre, Feb 1927, played Annabelle Porter in Crime; Forrest, Jan 1928, Mary Norton in Mirrors; Klaw, Apr 1928, Amy in The Breaks; at the Little, Oct 1928, Rosalie in The Gods of the Lightning; she then went to Denver, where she played in stock for three months, and after making a picture in Hollywood, went to Rochester, NY, for a further stock engagement; at the Longacre, NY, June 1929, played Elizabeth Girard in Nice Women; Morosco, Nov 1929, Patricia in Cross-Roads; Little, Feb 1930, Patsy Coster in Many a Slip; Hudson, Oct 1930, Dot in Bad Girl; Guild Theatre, NY, Oct 1937, played Lola Hobbs in To Quito and Back; during 1938, appeared in summer theatres as Eliza Doolittle in Pygmalion and in Tonight at 8.30; Belasco, NY (Group Theatre), Jan 1939, played Stella Goodman in The Gentle People; toured, 1941, as Linda Brown in Accent on Youth; 1942, as Mrs Manningham in Angel Street, and Eliza in Pygmalion; 1943, as Jane Eyre; Madison Square Garden, Mar 1943, appeared in the pageant, We Will Never Die; in summer theatres, 1947, appeared in Joan of Lorraine; summer theatres, 1948, in Kind Lady; summer theatres, 1949, in The Two Mrs Carrolls, Pygmalion, O Mistress Mine; summer theatres, 1950, in Goodbye, My Fancy, Anne of the Thousand Days, and also toured in The Innocents; toured, 1951, as Alicia Christie in Black Chiffon; at the Falmouth Playhouse, Coonamessett, Aug 1952, played Fanny Benton in The Gypsies Wore High Hats; Golden, NY, Dec 1952, succeeded Sylvia Field as Agnes in The Fourposter; Playhouse, Nov 1956, played Anna in A Very Special Baby; toured, 1958–9, in the title-role of Auntie Mame; Henry Miller's, Mar 1963, Mrs Kolowitz in Enter Laughing; Theatre de Lys, Feb 1964, Beatrice Wright in Damn You, Scarlet O'Hara and Leslie Ross in All My Pretty Little Ones, in a double-bill under the title Riverside Drive; summer tours, 1964, as Mrs Manningham in Angel Street and in The Silver Cord and Kind Lady; toured with the National Repertory Theatre, 1965–6, in Trojan Women, The Rivals, and The Madwoman of Chaillot; toured, 1966, as Regina in The Little Foxes; Oakland, Cal, National Repertory, Dec 1966, Lady Bracknell in The Importance of Being Earnest; Biltmore, Apr 1967, took over from Ilka Chase as Mrs Bank in Barefoot in the Park, and subsequently toured; Ford's, Washington, DC, for National Repertory, 1968, played Mrs Hardcastle in She Stoops to Conquer; toured US and Canada, 1968–9, as Mrs Baker in Come Blow Your Horn; Seattle, Washington, Repertory, Jan 1974, Matty Seaton in A Family and a Fortune; toured, 1974, in Arsenic and Old Lace; John Golden, Mar 1976, Tessie in Me Jack, You Jill; St James, May 1977, Mrs Wire in Vieux Carré; commenced film career, 1929, and appeared in Thru Different Eyes, Street Scene, Madame Butterfly, Jennie Gerhardt, Trail of the Lonesome Pine, Fury, Love from a Stranger, Les Misérables, Summer Wishes, Winter Dreams (1973), etc.

Address: c/o Actors Equity Association, 165 West 46th Street, New York, NY 10036.

SILLMAN, Leonard, producer, actor

b Detroit, Michigan, 9 May 1908; *s* of Morton Sillman and his wife Marion (Grosslight); *e* Northern High School, Detroit.

Formerly a singer and dancer and made his theatrical début as such in an act with Lew Fields in 1924; made his New York début at the Palace, 1926, with Imogene Coca in the vaudeville act called Sillman and Coca; toured in this act until 1927; made his début in a book musical when he played Dick

Trevor in the tour of Lady Be Good, 1926; toured in The Greenwich Village Follies, 1927; 52nd Street, NY, Mar 1927, played Josephus in Loud Speaker; Klaw, May 1927, appeared as the juvenile in Merry-Go-Round; Mayan, Los Angeles, California, 1930, appeared in the revue Temptation of 1930; Hollywood, 1930, produced, directed, and played in The 11.15 Revue; Pasadena (California) Community Playhouse, 1931, appeared in the revue Hullaballoo; same theatre, July 1933, produced and played in Low and Behold, which he transferred to the Music Box in Hollywood; produced his first NY show, New Faces of 1934, at the Fulton, 15 Mar 1934; since then has concentrated on production, making occasional appearances, as follows: Fools Rush In (also appeared in), 1934; New Faces of 1936, which he also directed, Up to the Stars (ann Arbor, Michigan, which he also directed and appeared in), 1936; Periphery (Pasadena), 1937; Who's Who, which he also directed and to which he contributed sketches, 1938; They Knew What They Wanted, Journey's End, both for the New York Drama Festival, 1939; All in Fun, which he also directed, 1940; New Faces of 1943, which he also directed and appeared in, 1942; If the Shoe Fits, 1946; Happy as Larry, 1950; New Faces of 1952, 1952; Mrs Patterson, 1954; New Faces of 1956, 1956; Mask and Gown, Miss Isobel, 1957; A Second String, 1960; New Faces of 1962, which he also directed, 1962; The Family Way, 1965; New Faces of 1966 (Philadelphia), 1966; New Faces of 1968, which he also directed and in which he appeared at the Booth, May 1968; The American Hamburger League, 1969; Hay Fever, 1970; at the Sokol, NY, Mar 1970, played the Prospector in a revival of The Madwoman of Chaillot; produced the cabaret revue Come as You Are at the Versailles, NY, 1956; first appeared in films in Goldie Gets Along, 1933, subsequently playing in Whistling in the Dark, and Bombshell; first produced a film Angel Comes to Broadway, 1945, and since produced New Faces, 1954; produced the radio show *New Faces on the Air,* 1948; produced and directed the television show The Best of New Faces, 1960, and has appeared on various talk shows, notably on Jack Paar's program; published his autobiography Here Lies Leonard Sillman, Straightened Out At Last, 1961.

Address: Apt 25K, 30 Lincoln Plaza, New York, NY 10023. *Tel:* 757–1922.

SILLS, Paul, director

b Chicago, Ill; *e* U of Chicago and Bristol U; married three times; studied improvisational theatre with his mother, Viola Spolin.

Co-founder, around 1953, of the Improvisational Playwrights' Theatre Club, Chicago, which grew into The Second City, 1957; made his NY debut at the Royale, Sept 1961, as director of From the Second City, later seen at Square East, where he also co-directed Seacoast of Bohemia, Alarums and Excursions, 1962, and directed To the Water Tower, and When the Owl Screams, 1963; Open Season at the Second City, 1964; co-directed Dynamite Tonite, 1964, and directed its revival, 1967; conceived Metamorphoses (from Ovid), seen at Yale Rep 1969, Mark Taper Forum, 1971, and in repertory at the Ambassador, NY, 1971, with his Story Theatre, based on Grimm and first seen at the Mark Taper Forum, 1970; co-author with Arnold Weinstein and director of The American Revolution, Part 1, Washington 1973; directed Sweet Bloody Liberty, 1975; Public, NY, Dec 1977, adapted and directed Tales of the Hasidim; won a Tony award for his direction of Story Theatre, 1971.

Address: c/o New York Shakespeare Festival, 425 Lafayette Street, New York, NY 10003.

SILVER, Joe, actor and director

b Chicago, Ill, 28 Sept 1922; *s* of Morris Silver and his wife

Sonja; *e* East High School, Green Bay, Wisc, Univ of Wisconsin, 1940–42; *m* Chevi Colton; prepared for the stage at the American Theatre Wing, 1946–47; served in US Army Signal Corps, 1944–46.

Made his NY debut at the Forrest, 5 Sept 1942, as Lov Bensey in Tobacco Road; Adams, Newark, NJ, appeared in See My Lawyer and in Boy Meets Girl, July 1943; Theatre Showcase, NY, Aug 1943, appeared in The Goldfish Bowl; toured, Sept 1943, as the Bellboy in The Doughgirls; Cort, May 1947, Burton Snead in Heads or Tails; New Stages, Dec 1947, Aldobrandini in Lamp at Midnight; Carnegie Hall, 1948, appeared in The Terrorists; New Stages, Jan 1949, Dubois in The Victors; Feb 1949, A Man in Blood Wedding; Mar 1949, Gad in The Sun and I; entered television, then reappeared on the stage in Mar 1957 in Annie Get Your Gun; Coronet, Oct 1957, Waiter in Nature's Way; Broadway, May 1959, Weber in Gypsy; Gate, Oct 1961, Squire Hardcastle in O Marry Me!; Lyceum, Feb 1963, Phil Barr in The Heroine; Cort, Nov 1965, Harry Grossman in The Zulu and the Zayda; Ambassador, Mar 1967, Herb Miller in You Know I Can't Hear You When the Water's Running; took over from Martin Balsam as Richard Pawling, George, and Chuck in this play, 1968; Village Gate, 1969–70 season, played in Jacques Brel Is Alive and Well and Living in Paris; Mercury, Jan 1971, Julius Katz in The Shrinking Bride; Equity Library Theatre, Mar 1971, directed Shoe Store; Brooks Atkinson, May 1971, Sherman Hart in Lenny, and played in this part for over a year; New Dramatists, Feb 1974, directed The Rabinowitz Gambit; Manhattan Theatre Club, Nov 1974, Narration for Bits and Pieces; New Dramatists, Jan 1975, Moe in Cakes with the Wine; appeared in the films Diary of a Bachelor, 1963, Rhinoceros, The Apprenticeship of Duddy Kravitz, Boardwalk, etc; first appeared on television as a panelist on What's It Worth?, 1947, and has since played in nearly 900 shows, including Red Buttons' program (1953–55) and his own series, *Captain Jet, Space Funnies,* etc; has also appeared in cabaret in the act called The Wry Guys, 1946 and later.

Recreations: Refinishing antiques, gardening, cooking, fishing. *Address:* Actors Equity Association, 165 West 46th Street, New York, NY 10036.

SILVERS, Phil, actor and comedian
b Brooklyn, NY, 11 May 1911; *s* of Saul Silver and his wife Sarah; *e* New Utrecht High School, Brooklyn; *m* (1) Jo Carroll Dennison (mar dis), (2) Evelyn Patrick; formerly a sports announcer and reporter.

First performed as a singer in amateur "kiddie" shows, Apr 1922; first appeared professionally at the Earle, Philadelphia, Pa, July 1925, as a singer in the Gus Edwards Revue; toured in vaudeville with Morris and Campbell; toured, 1934–39, with the Minsky Burlesque Troupe; made his Broadway debut at the Majestic, 6 July 1939, as Punko Parks in Yokel Boy; during World War II toured the Mediterranean with the USO; entered films, then returned to the stage at the Century, Oct 1947, as Harrison Floy in High Button Shoes; Winter Garden, Nov 1951, played Jerry Biff in Top Banana, and received the Antoinette Perry (Tony) Award; St James, Dec 1960, Hubert Cram in Do Re Mi; O'Keefe Center, Toronto, Canada, Jan 1962, repeated this last part, and subsequently toured; Royale, Mar 1971, Frank Foster in How the Other Half Loves; Ahmanson, Los Angeles, Oct 1971, Prologus and Pseudolus in A Funny Thing Happened on the Way to the Forum; Lunt-Fontanne, Mar 1972, repeated these parts, and received the Antoinette Perry (Tony) Award; author of the autobiography The Laugh Is on Me, 1974; made his film debut in Hit Parade of 1941 (1940), and has since

played in numerous pictures, including You're in the Army Now, Roxie Hart, Cover Girl, Something for the Boys, Summer Stock, Top Banana, Won Ton Ton (1976), etc; has appeared frequently on television, notably on his own series The Phil Silvers Show as Sergeant Bilko, for which he received three Emmy Awards and the Television Showman Award (1956); is also a noted club and cabaret performer.

Recreations: Various sports. *Address:* Actors Equity Association, 165 West 46th Street, New York, NY 10036.

SIMMS, Hilda, actress
b Minneapolis, Minnesota, 15 Apr 1920; *d* of Emil George Moses and his wife Lydia (Webber); *e* St Martin's Academy, University of Minnesota, Hampton Institute, Hampton, Va, and the Sorbonne, Paris, 1950–2; *m* Richard Angarola (mar dis); formerly in a girl's settlement, where she officiated as Supervisor, drama and dance assistant, and for two years modelled for portrait classes at the Minneapolis Art Institute, University of Minnesota; was subsequently publicity assistant, and was for eight months with the US Office of War Information.

Made her first appearance on the stage at the Edythe Bush Playhouse, St Paul, Minn, 1937, as the Maid in Kiss the Boys Goodbye; first appeared in New York, at the Lafayette Theatre, June 1943, as Marion in Three's a Family; Mansfield Theatre, Aug 1944, scored a great success when she appeared as Anna Lucasta in the play of that name, and which ran for two years; she then studied at Carnegie Hall, under Betty Chasman; made her first appearance on the London stage, at His Majesty's Theatre, 29 Oct 1947, as Anna Lucasta; at the Rudolf Steiner Hall, London, Feb 1950, appeared in Picasso's play Desire Caught by the Tail; Embassy, Apr 1950, played Stella Goodman in The Gentle People; Cambridge Theatre, May 1951, appeared as Pervaneh in Hassan; at the Eugene O'Neill, NY, Feb 1960, played Miss Dewpont in The Cool World; Red Barn, Northport, NY, July 1961, starred in The Captain's Paradise and Black Monday; has toured frequently since 1961 in a one-woman show Love Letters of Famous Courtesans; Little, Nov 1963, Laura Wright Reed in Tambourines to Glory; Sokol, NY, Mar 1970, Therese in The Madwoman of Chaillot; films include: The Joe Louis Story, 1953; had her own radio program, *Ladies' Day with Hilda Simms,* 1954–7; on television has appeared on various dramatic programs and the series The Nurses, 1962 and several seasons thereafter.

Favourite parts: Saint Joan, and Juliet. *Recreations:* Swimming, reading, music, fencing, and window-shopping. *Address:* Actors Equity Association, 165 West 46th Street, New York, NY 10036.

SIMON, John, critic
b Subotica, Yugoslavia, 12 May 1925; *s* of Joseph Simmon and his wife Margaret (Reves); *e* Harvard University (AB 1946, AM 1948, PhD 1959), and attended University of Paris, 1949–50; *m* Cheryle Brown (mar dis); taught at Harvard University, University of Washington, Massachusetts Institute of Technology, Bard College, principally comparative literature; received a Fulbright Fellowship, 1949–50, and a Rockefeller Foundation grant, 1964.

Film critic of *The New Leader* since 1962; drama critic of the *New York Magazine,* 1969–75, 1977–present, and of *The Hudson Review* since 1960; film critic of *New York Magazine* 1975; is a frequent contributor to *The New York Times* on drama, books, and films; is the author of Acid Test, 1963, Private Screenings, 1967, Film 67/68 (editor), 1968, Fourteen for Now (editor), 1969, Movies into Film, 1971, Ingmar Bergman Directs, 1972; Singularities, Uneasy Stages, 1976; is a member of the New York Drama Critics Circle, the New York Film Critics Circle, and of the PEN; received the George Jean Nathan Award for Drama Criticism, 1969–70, the George Polk Memorial Award (for film criticism), 1968, and the Literary Award of the National Academy of Arts and Letters, 1976.

Recreations and hobbies: Art exhibitions, concerts, opera, ballet, reading, walking. *Address:* 200 East 36th Street, New York, NY 10016. *Tel:* MU 5–8413.

SIMON, Louis M, director, public relations, Actors Fund of America

b Salt Lake City, Utah, 25 Oct 1906; *s* of Adolph Simon and his wife Stella (Furchgott); *e* Harvard and Yale Universities; *m* Edith Morrissey.

Engaged as stage-manager with Doris Keane, 1929, producing The Pirate, at the Belasco Theatre, Los Angeles, Apr 1929; subsequent productions were Red Rust, for the Theatre Guild, New York, Jan 1930; Garrick Gaieties, for the Guild, May 1930; Run, Little Chillun', Lyric, NY, Mar 1933; was supervisor for the Federal Theatre, New Jersey, 1934–5, and in NY, 1936–7; during the War, served with the Armed Forces, 1940–5, retiring with the rank of Major; was Executive Director of the Veteran's Hospital Camp Shows Inc; was Executive Secretary of Actors Equity Association, 1949–52; director, Professional Training Program, American Theatre Wing, 1952–59.

Recreations: Gardening and carpentry. *Address:* 1501 Broadway, New York, NY 10036. *Tel:* 869–8530.

SIMON, Neil (*né* Marvin Neil Simon), playwright

b New York City, 4 July 1927; *s* of Irving Simon and his wife Mamie; *e* New York University, 1946; *m* (1) Joan Simon (dec); (2) Marsha Mason.

Began his writing career by supplying sketches and other material for the *Phil Silvers Arrow Show*, produced on television in 1948; wrote material for *The Tallulah Bankhead Show,* 1951; wrote his first material for the theatre when he contributed sketches to the Tamiment (Pa) Revue, 1952–3; first Broadway show was Catch a Star, produced at the Plymouth, 6 Nov 1955, to which he contributed sketches written with his brother Daniel; wrote sketches for New Faces of 1956, 1956; wrote his first full-length Broadway show, Come Blow Your Horn, produced at the Brooks Atkinson, 22 Feb 1961; since then has written the book of the musical Little Me, 1962; Barefoot in the Park, 1963; The Odd Couple, 1965; the book of the musical Sweet Charity, The Star-Spangled Girl, 1966; Plaza Suite, which consists of three one-act plays entitled Visitor from Mamaroneck, Visitor from Hollywood, and Visitor from Forest Hills, and the book of the musical Promises, Promises, 1968; Last of the Red Hot Lovers, 1969; The Gingerbread Lady, 1970; The Prisoner of Second Avenue, 1971; The Sunshine Boys, 1972; The Good Doctor (adapted from short stories of Chekhov), 1973; God's Favorite, 1974; California Suite, 1976; Chapter Two, 1977; They're Playing Our Song (book), 1978; I Ought to Be in Pictures, 1980; for television has also written for *The Garry Moore Show,* 1959–60, *The Phil Silvers Show,* 1958–9, *The Sid Caesar Show,* 1957–8, etc; wrote five sketches for television called The Trouble with People, 1972; received a Special Antoinette Perry (Tony) Award, 1975; besides the films of his plays has also written the screenplay for After the Fox, 1976, The Out-of-Towners, 1970, The Heartbreak Kid, 1973, Murder by Death, 1976, The Goodbye Girl, 1977, and The Cheap Detective, 1978; is the only playwright in history to have had four plays running simultaneously on Broadway.

Address: The Dramatists Guild, 234 West 44th Street, New York, NY 10036.

SIMPSON, N F, dramatic author

b London, 29 Jan 1919; *s* of George Frederick Simpson and his wife Elizabeth (Rossiter); *e* Emanuel School, and London University; *m* Joyce Bartlett.

His first play to be produced was A Resounding Tinkle at the Royal Court, Dec 1957; he is also the author of The Hole (one-act), 1958; One Way Pendulum, 1959; The Form (one-act), 1961; The Cresta Run, 1965; Was He Anyone, 1972; he has also contributed to various revues; author of the film One Way Pendulum, 1964; first television production, July 1961; plays produced on television include: One Way Pendulum and A Resounding Tinkle; other television writing includes: the series World in Ferment; author of the novel, Harry Bleachbaker, 1976.

Address: c/o Deborah Rogers, 5–11 Mortimer Street, London W1.

SIMS, Joan (Irene Joan Marian Sims), actress

b Laindon, Essex, 9 May 1930; *d* of John Henry Sims and his wife Gladys Marie (Ladbrooke); *e* St John's School, Billericay, Essex, and County High School, Brentwood, Essex; studied for the stage at the Royal Academy of Dramatic Art, London.

Made her first appearance on the stage at the Repertory Theatre, Chorlton-cum-Hardy, 1950; after a season of plays, she made her first appearance on the London stage at the Players Theatre; Irving, July 1952, appeared in the revue Just Lately, and subsequently joined the cast of Bells of St Martin's at the St Martin's; New Lindsey, Dec 1952, appeared in the revue Intimacy at Eight; London Hippodrome, Mar 1953, appeared in the revue High Spirits; New Lindsey, Dec 1953, played in the revue sequel More Intimacy at Eight; Criterion, Apr 1954, appeared in Intimacy at 8.30; Aldwych, June 1956, played Jubilee in Man Alive!; Cambridge, Mar 1958, played Lily in Breath of Spring; Saville, Aug 1961, appeared in the revue The Lord Chamberlain Regrets . . .; Piccadilly, Aug 1964, played Lavinia in Instant Marriage; Whitehall, Oct 1967, Melanie Sinclair in Uproar in the House; Theatre Royal, Bath, Aug 1969, for Bristol Old Vic, Lady Fidget in The Country Wife; Birmingham Rep, Dec 1971, Queenie in Good Time Johnny; Chichester Festival Theatre, 1977 season, took part in In Order of Appearance; first appeared in films Oct 1952, and has since been in numerous pictures, including many of the Carry On . . . films; One of Our Dinosaurs is Missing, and Love Among the Ruins; made her first appearance on television in 1952; recent performances include: Iolanthe, Worzel Gummidge, In Loving Memory, and Born and Bred; has broadcast regularly in *The Floggits, London Lights, Stop Messing About,* etc.

Recreation: Cooking. *Address:* c/o Peter Eade, Ltd, 9 Cork Street, London W1. *Tel:* 01–734 2858 and 01–734 7409.

SINCLAIR, Barry, actor and singer

b London, 15 Jan 1911; *s* of Robert Sinclair and his wife Louise (Stanley); *e* Halstead Grammar School and St Paul's Cathedral Choir School; *m* (1) Nicolette Roeg; (2) Jennifer Wood; formerly engaged with an advertising agency.

Made his first appearance on the stage at the Holborn Empire, 24 Dec 1928, in Where the Rainbow Ends; Haymarket, Feb 1929, walked on in Quality Street; later in 1929, toured as Jack Chesney in Charley's Aunt and as Young Woodley; was a member of the Bristol Repertory company, 1929–33, and appeared with that company at the Garrick

Theatre, Mar 1933, as John Cameron in She Had to Come Back; Adelphi, Mar 1934, played Max Emanuel in Magnolia Street; Fulham, May 1934, Jim in Forsaking All Other; Arts, May 1934, Colonel Parke in Viceroy Sarah; Piccadilly, Aug 1934, Maurice Appleton Myers in Queer Cargo; Fortune, May 1935; Martin Trent in Double Error; toured 1936, as Anthony Allen in Glamorous Night, appearing in that part at the Coliseum, May 1936, and again toured in the part and that of Michael in Careless Rapture, until 1938; at Wyndham's, Aug 1938, played Harry L'Estrange in She, Too, Was Young; toured, Jan 1940, as John in Full House, and appeared in this at Streatham Hill, Apr 1940; toured, 1940–1, as Franzel in The Dancing Years, and appeared in this part at the Adelphi Theatre, May 1942, sharing the performances with Ivor Novello; he then joined the Army and was not demobilized until Apr 1946; he then resumed touring as Rudi in The Dancing Years, and he appeared at the Casino, Mar 1947, in the same part; at the London Hippodrome, Dec 1946, he replaced Ivor Novello as Sir Graham Valentine and Bay in Perchance to Dream, for 10 weeks; toured again in The Dancing Years, until Apr 1949; toured, 1949–50, as Michael in Careless Rapture, and Aug–Sept 1950, toured in Castle in the Air; Palace, Dec 1950, played the King in King's Rhapsody, for seven weeks; toured, Apr 1951, as Charles Dyer in Who On Earth!; toured, Sept 1951, in King's Rhapsody, subsequently touring South Africa in this production, 1952; after returning to England, toured, Nov 1952, as Oliver in To Christabel; St Martin's, Dec 1952, played Michael Barry in Friendly Relations; toured, Mar 1954, in Escapade; New Watergate, Nov 1954, appeared in Autumn Revue; at the Q, Apr 1955, played Arnold Debrett in By Kind Permission; Embassy, June 1955, played Freddie Martin in The Lion In the Lighthouse; at the Royal, Bath, May 1956, played Bruce Phillips in Sight Unseen; Connaught, Worthing, Dec 1956, Capt Robert Hetherington in Something About a Sailor; Chelsea Palace, Dec 1956, played the Caterpillar, March Hare, and King of Hearts in Alice in Wonderland; Princes, Nov 1957, the Chamberlain in Royal Suite; Devonshire Park, Eastbourne, Mar 1958, played Captain Alan Langdon in Act of War; Harrogate White Rose Company, June 1961, appeared as Guest Artist as the Earl of Hewlyn in Plaintiff in a Pretty Hat; Oxford Playhouse, Oct 1961, played Randall Utterwood in Heartbreak House, subsequently appearing in the same production at Wyndham's, Nov 1961; toured, Dec 1962, in No Time For Love; Richmond, Apr 1963, played Paul Trescott in All About Love; toured, June 1963, in The Tulip Tree; Arts, Cambridge, Feb 1964, and subsequent tour, Edward Rochester in Jane Eyre; New Lyric, Hammersmith, June 1965, appeared in The French Mistress; Hippodrome, Golders Green, July 1967, Andrew in Something in the Family; at the Cambridge, Feb 1969, Baron Mirko Popovski in The Merry Widow; Hippodrome, Bristol, Aug 1969, the Director in Rumour About Romeo; Congress, Eastbourne, Feb 1970, and tour, Lord Shane in Bitter Sweet; toured, July 1970, as Edward in Roar Like a Dove; toured, Sept 1970, as Sir Hamish Fitzadam in The Amorous Prawn; toured, July 1971, as Sellars in The Grass is Greener; Playhouse, Bournemouth, Dec 1971, Mr Fezziwig in A Christmas Carol; toured Britain, the US and Canada, Jan 1972, as Esteban in The Marquise; Playhouse, Weston-super-Mare, July 1972, appeared in The Sound of Murder; Civic, Darlington, Oct 1972, Charles Prestwick in Love's a Luxury; Theatre Royal, Bath, Nov 1972, Prof Higgins in Pygmalion; Ashton Theatre, St Anne's, June 1973, Hugh Walford in The Secretary Bird; Belgrade, Coventry, Aug 1973, and tour, Billy Rice in The Entertainer; Adeline Genée, E Grinstead, Aug 1974, the Duke in Magic;

Thames-side, Gray's, May 1975, Sebastian Crutwell in In Praise of Love; Shaftesbury, Oct 1979, Mr Venables in Maggie; has appeared all over Britain in concerts of the works of Ivor Novello; since 1975 has given his own one-man show, My Novello Story.

Club: Savage. *Address:* 8 Fernwood Rise, Brighton BN1 5EP.

SINDEN, Donald, CBE 1979, actor

b Plymouth, Devon, 9 Oct 1923; *s* of Alfred Edward Sinden and his wife Mabel Agnes (Fuller); *m* Diana Mahony, actress.

Made his first appearance on the stage in the Mobile Entertainments Southern Area (Charles F Smith's Company), Jan 1941, when he played Dudley in George and Margaret; remained with the company for four years, to play modern comedies in one-night-stands, for the Forces; studied for two terms at the Webber-Douglas School of Dramatic Art, 1944; returned to MESA for a tour of France, Belgium, Germany, India, and Burma, with The Normandy Story; became a member of the Leicester Repertory Company, winter 1945, before joining the Shakespeare Memorial Theatre Company, Stratford-upon-Avon, Apr 1946; during this season he played among other parts, Dumain in Love's Labour's Lost, Arviragus in Cymbeline, and Pride in Dr Faustus; 1946–7, he toured with John Harrison in their own Shakespearean Recital; rejoined the Shakespeare Memorial Theatre, Apr 1947 to play Paris in Romeo and Juliet, Adrian in The Tempest, Aumerle in Richard II, and Lorenzo in The Merchant of Venice, in addition to parts already played the previous season; His Majesty's, Oct 1947, made his first appearance in London, as Aumerle in Richard II, subsequently appearing as Romeo in Romeo and Juliet; joined the Bristol Old Vic Company, 1948, and appeared with them, at the St James's, July 1948, as Rosencrantz in Hamlet; New, Sept–Oct 1948, with the Old Vic Company, played Sebastian in Twelfth Night, and Envy and the Scholar in Dr Faustus; Haymarket, Jan 1949, appeared as Arthur Townsend in The Heiress, which ran for 644 performances; rejoined the Bristol Old Vic Company, 1950, playing in The Lady's Not For Burning, The Good Natured Man, The Merry Wives of Windsor, and Puss in Boots; Garrick, Feb 1952, played Manuel Del Vega in Red Letter Day; through this performance, he entered films with the Rank Organization, 1952 and was under contract for eight years; St Martin's, July 1957, he returned to the theatre, to play Mervyn Browne in Odd Man In; Cambridge, Dec 1958, Bob Brewster in Who's Your Father?; Strand, June 1959, played Frank Marescaud in All in the Family; Queen's, July 1960, played Brian Curtis in Joie De Vivre; Scala, Dec 1960, Captain Hook and Mr Darling in Peter Pan; Phoenix, Mar 1961, played the title-part in JB; St Martin's, Aug 1961, Edward Bromley in Guilty Party; joined the Royal Shakespeare Company, Stratford-upon-Avon, Apr 1963, to play Sebastian in The Tempest, Solinus in The Comedy of Errors, and Richard Plantaganet in Henry VI and Edward IV (in the trilogy The Wars of the Roses); Aldwych, Dec 1963, again played Solinus in The Comedy of Errors, and Jan 1964, Richard Plantaganet in The Wars of the Roses, subsequently returning to the Royal Shakespeare, Stratford-upon-Avon, July 1964, to appear in The Wars of the Roses during the Shakespeare Quatercentenary season; Aldwych, Oct 1964, played Mr Price in Eh?; 1965, toured South America for the British Council, appearing as George Bernard Shaw in Dear Liar and Willie in Happy Days; Globe, June 1966, played Robert Danvers in There's A Girl in My Soup; Aldwych, Aug 1967, for the Royal Shakespeare Company, played Lord Foppington in

The Relapse; 1968, directed Relatively Speaking (tour); Strand, June 1968, played Gilbert Bodley in Not Now, Darling; returned to Stratford in Aug 1969 to play Malvolio in Twelfth Night and the name part in King Henry the Eighth, touring Japan and Australia in the former role Jan 1970, and repeating both at the Aldwych, 1970–1 Season, when he also played Sir William Harcourt Courtly in London Assurance; New, Apr 1972, again played Sir Harcourt Courtly in London Assurance; Duchess, Sept 1973, Baron Scarpia in Before Dawn and Sebastian Crutwell in After Lydia, in the double-bill, In Praise of Love; toured the US in London Assurance, Sept 1974, appearing at the Palace, NY, Dec 1974; Chichester Festival, May 1975, Dr Stockmann in Enemy of the People; Martin Beck, NY, Nov 1975, Arthur Wicksteed in Habeas Corpus; Stratford, season 1976, Benedick in Much Ado About Nothing, and title-role in King Lear, repeating both at the Aldwych, 1977; Apollo, Nov 1977, Arthur Pullen in Shut Your Eyes and Think of England; RSC, Stratford, Aug 1979, played the title-role in Othello; since 1952 has appeared in 29 films including: The Cruel Sea, Mogambo, Doctor in the House, The Island at the Top of the World, etc; since his first TV appearance in 1948 he has played leading parts in a number of plays and series such as *Our Man at St Mark's*, The Organisation, and Discovering English Churches; Fellow of the Royal Society of Arts; Member of Advisory Council, Victoria and Albert Museum; Chairman, the Theatre Museum Advisory Council; Chairman, British Theatre Museum Association, 1971–7; Council Member, British Actors' Equity, 1966–75; Member, Arts Council Drama Panel, 1973–7; Council Member, LAMDA, 1975– ; President, Federation of Playgoers' Societies; Vice-president, London Appreciation Society, 1960.

Recreations: Theatrical history, London, architecture, ecclesiology. *Clubs:* Garrick, Beefsteak, MCC. *Address:* 60 Temple Fortune Lane, London NW11.

SKALA, Lilia, actress
b Vienna, Austria; e Univ of Dresden; early stage experience in Europe, including tours with Max Reinhardt.

First appeared in New York at the Cort, 23 Dec 1941, as Margarethe in Letters to Lucerne; Dec 1947, appeared in Many Moons; Mar 1948, appeared in Rumplestiltskin; Jan 1949, appeared in The Indian Caper; Lyceum, Apr 1950, played Anna in With a Silk Thread; Imperial, Oct 1950, Grand Duchess Sophie in Call Me Madam; Cort, 1955, took over as Mrs Frank in The Diary of Anne Frank, 1958; toured in the same part, 1958; Music Box, Feb 1961, understudied Françoise Rosay as Catherine the Great in Once There Was a Russian; New York City Center, Mar 1965, appeared in Die Dreigroschenoper; Ethel Barrymore, Mar 1969, Rose Hartman in Zelda; Westbury Music Fair, 1970, Fraülein Schneider in Cabaret; Morosco, 1970, took over as Maud Hayes in Forty Carats, and subsequently toured; Studio Arena, Buffalo, NY, Oct 1972, title role in Roberta; Mesa College, Grand Junction, Colo, Mar 1973, Mrs Malaprop in The Rivals; Little, Oct 1974, Nurse in Medea and Jason; American Place, Nov 1975, Grandma in Gorky; Mesa College, 1976, the Mother in Sabrina Fair; has appeared in the films Ship of Fools, Charly, Caprice, Deadly Hero (1976), etc; has also appeared on television, since 1948.

Address: c/o William Morris Agency, 1350 Avenue of the Americas, New York, NY 10019.

SKELTON, Thomas, lighting designer; formerly a stage manager
First designs in New York were for the lighting of The Enchanted, Renata, 22 Apr 1958; since then has designed lighting for Calvary, Santa Claus, Escurial, 1960; Misalliance,

1961; Oh Dad, Poor Dad, Mamma's Hung You in the Closet and I'm Feelin' So Sad, 1962 and 1963; In the Summer House, Wiener Blut, Zizi, 1964; Sing to Me Through Open Windows, The Day the Whores Came Out to Play Tennis, 1965; Your Own Thing, Mike Downstairs, Jimmy Shine, Big Time Buck White, 1968; Does a Tiger Wear a Necktie?, Come Summer, Henry V, Much Ado About Nothing, Hamlet, The Three Sisters, A Patriot for Me, Indians, Coco, 1969; Purlie, Mahagonny, Bob and Ray—The Two and Only, Lovely Ladies, Kind Gentlemen, 1970; The Survival of St Joan, Remote Asylum, Design for Living (last two in Los Angeles, Cal), 1971; The Selling of the President, Rosebloom, The Lincoln Mask, The Secret Affairs of Mildred Wild, Purlie (revival), 1972; Status Quo Vadis, Gigi, Waltz of the Toreadors, 1973; Brainchild (Philadelphia), Where's Charley?, Absurd Person Singular, 1974; Shenandoah, All God's Children, Got Wings, Death of a Salesman, A Musical Jubilee, The Glass Menagerie, 1975; A Matter of Gravity, Guys and Dolls, Days in the Trees, 1976; Caesar and Cleopatra, Romeo and Juliet, The King and I, 1977; The November People, The Kingfisher, 1978; Peter Pan, Oklahoma!, 1979; also designed the decor for Tio Ch'an, The Beautiful Bait, 1962; work for ballet includes sets and lighting for Astarte (Joffrey), Dances at a Gathering (NY City Ballet), etc.

Address: United Scenic Artists, 1540 Broadway, New York, NY 10036.

SLADE, Julian, actor, author, and composer
b London, 28 May 1930; s of George Penkivil Slade and his wife Mary Albinia Alice (Carnegie); e Eton and Trinity College, Cambridge; studied for the stage at the Bristol Old Vic Drama School.

Made his first appearance on the stage at the Theatre Royal, Bristol, Sept 1951, as a Flunkey in The Prodigious Snob; first appeared in London at the Old Vic, June 1952, as a Musician in The Two Gentlemen of Verona; collaborated with James Cairncross and Dorothy Reynolds in writing Christmas in King Street, 1952; appointed musical director of the Bristol Old Vic, 1953, and wrote music for The Duenna, Love for Love, and She Stoops to Conquer; he has since composed incidental music for The Merchant of Venice (Shakespeare Memorial Theatre), 1953; composed music for the adaptation of The Comedy of Errors for television, 1954, which was subsequently produced at the Arts Theatre, 1956; collaborated with Dorothy Reynolds in the following musicals; The Merry Gentleman, 1953; Salad Days, 1954; Free As Air, 1957; Hooray For Daisy, 1959; Follow That Girl, and Wildest Dreams, 1960; composed music for Vanity Fair, 1962, and Sixty Thousand Nights (Theatre Royal, Bristol's Bicentenary Production), 1966; wrote the book and lyrics, and composed music for Nutmeg and Ginger (Cheltenham), 1963; and adapted The Pursuit of Love (Bristol), 1967; composed music for songs in As You Like It (Bristol), A Midsummer Night's Dream and Much Ado About Nothing (Regent's Park), 1970; adapted and composed additional music for Winnie the Pooh (Phoenix), 1970; lyrics and music for Trelawny, 1972; book, lyrics and music for Out of Bounds (Bristol), 1973; Salad Days, which ran for 2288 performances in London, has also been presented in Paris, the United States, Canada, South Africa, Australia, New Zealand, and Scandinavia; it was successfully revived in London, 1976; composed the music for the TV series Love a Cold Climate, 1980.

Recreations: Drawing, going to the theatre and cinema. *Address:* 3 Priory Walk, London SW10. *Tel:* 01–370 4859.

SLEZAK, Walter, actor
b Vienna, Austria, 3 May 1902; s of Leo Slezak, the operatic

tenor, and his wife Elsa (Wertheim); *e* Theresianum, Vienna, Maximilians Gymnasium, Munich, and the University of Vienna; *m* Johanna Van Rijn; originally studied medicine, but abandoned it and became a bank clerk.

First appeared on the stage in Berlin; made his New York début at the Shubert, 30 Dec 1930, as Eric Molinar in Meet My Sister; Alvin, Nov 1932, played Karl Reder in Music in the Air; Erlanger, Philadelphia, Pennsylvania, Oct 1934, Arno in Love! Out of the Window; Lyceum, Oct 1934, the Policeman in Ode to Liberty; St James, Dec 1935, Professor Johann Volk in May Wine; Central City, Colorado, July 1937, Thorvald Helmer in A Doll's House; Shubert, May 1938, Harry Mischka in I Married an Angel; John Golden, Nov 1941, Emil Onzain in Little Dark Horse; entered films and continued in Hollywood for more than ten years; re-appeared on the stage at the Morosco, Mar 1953, as Joseph in My Three Angels; toured, Feb–May 1954, as Joseph in My Three Angels; Majestic, Nov 1954, Panisse in Fanny, for which he received the Antoinette Perry (Tony) Award; Belasco, Apr 1957, Prince Regent in The First Gentleman; Lyceum, Dec 1958, Elliott Nash in The Gazebo; Metropolitan Opera House, 25 Nov 1959, made his operatic début as Szupan in The Gypsy Baron; toured, summer 1966, as Fagin in Oliver!; toured, 1968, as Henry II in The Lion in Winter; San Francisco Opera House, Sept 1973, Frosch in Die Fledermaus; Imperial, 9 Mar 1975, appeared in A Gala Tribute to Joshua Logan; first American film was Once upon a Honeymoon, 1942, and since has played in Lifeboat, Cornered, Sinbad the Sailor, The Pirate, The Inspector General, Call Me Madam, Emil and the Detective, A Very Special Favor, Treasure Island (1972), and many others; has appeared on more than 200 radio dramas; on television has played in The Good Fairy, The Borrowed Christmas, *Playhouse 90, Studio One,* etc; published his autobiography, What Time's the Next Swan? in 1962.

Recreations: Painting and golf. *Address:* Actors Equity Association, 165 West 46th Street, New York, NY 10036.

SMITH, Alexis (*née* Gladys), actress
b Penticton, Canada, 8 Jun 1921; *e* Los Angeles City College, Cal; *m* Craig Stevens, the actor.

Appeared in films since 1940; made her New York debut at the Winter Garden, 4 Apr 1971, as Phyllis Rogers Stone in the musical Follies, for which she received the Antoinette Perry (Tony) Award; Shubert, Century City, Cal, July 1972, repeated this role; 46th Street, Apr 1973, played Sylvia (Mrs Howard Fowler) in a revival of The Women; ANTA, Oct 1975, Rosemary Sydney in Summer Brave, the original version of William Inge's Picnic; Studio Arena, Buffalo, Sept 1977, Lila Halliday in Sunset; Mark Hellinger, Nov 1978, Lila Halliday in Platinum; first appeared in films in Lady with Red Hair, 1940, and has since played in numerous pictures, including Dive Bomber, Gentleman Jim, Thank Your Lucky Stars, The Constant Nymph, The Adventures of Mark Twain, The Doughgirls, Rhapsody in Blue, Night and Day, Of Human Bondage, Beau James, Once Is Not Enough, Casey's Shadow (1977), etc; has also appeared on television, and played in stock in British Columbia, Canada, and in college productions.

Address: Actors Equity Association, 165 West 46th Street, New York, NY 10036.

SMITH, Derek, actor
b Tooting, London, 15 June 1927; *s* of Wilfred James Smith and his wife Constance Alice (Betambeau); *e* Beckenham and Penge CGS; *m* Lilian Box; previously in a variety of jobs.

Made his professional debut as Baron Hardup in the pantomime Cinderella, at the Capitol, St Austell, Dec 1956; after experience with various repertory companies won a Leverhulme scholarship to RADA, where he won the Bancroft Gold Medal in 1960; joined the Old Vic Company to play Medvedenko in The Seagull at the Edinburgh Festival and the Old Vic (London debut), Sept 1960; in the same season played Chorus in Romeo and Juliet, Egeus in A Midsummer Night's Dream, and Fabian in Twelfth Night; at the Bristol Old Vic, 1961–2, his parts included Pierre Bezhukov in War and Peace, which was seen at the Old Vic, June 1962, and transferred to the Phoenix in the same month; Bristol, Sept 1962, title-role in Fiorello!, transferring to the Piccadilly, Oct; joined the RSC at Stratford, 1963, playing Stephano in The Tempest, Pinch in The Comedy of Errors, and Talbot and Jack Cade in The Wars of the Roses; toured Europe, 1965, as Boss Mangan in Heartbreak House and Burgess in Candida; Phoenix, Jan 1966, Professor in Incident at Vichy; again with the RSC, July 1967, played Carol Newquist in Little Murders, Aldwych; Fortune, Dec 1967, Toad in Toad of Toad Hall; at Stratford, season 1968, played Casca in Julius Caesar, and Caius in The Merry Wives of Windsor, appearing in both of these productions at the Aldwych later in the year and playing the President in Indians, and Bull in The Relapse; Stratford, 1969, Autolycus in The Winter's Tale, Simonides in Pericles, and Guardiano in Women Beware Women, also repeating the part of Caius; toured Japan, 1970, in The Winter's Tale and The Merry Wives, followed by The Merry Wives in Australia; Aldwych, June 1970, Meddle in London Assurance; Dec 1970, Bishop Gardiner in Henry VIII; Duke of York's, Dec 1971, again played Toad; Greenwich, Feb 1972, Chief of Police in The Feydeau Farce Festival of 1909; New April 1972, again played Meddle; returned to Stratford, season 1973, to play Touchstone in As You Like It, Holofernes in Love's Labour's Lost, and Baptista in The Taming of the Shrew, also Toad at Christmas; Manitoba Theatre Centre, Winnipeg, 1974, Fluther Good in The Plough and the Stars; Stratford, 1975, again played Caius, also Archbishop of Canterbury and Gower in Henry V; at The Other Place in the same season appeared in Mouth Organ, which he also co-wrote; Hampstead, Apr 1976, Scheidecker in Lenz; Her Majesty's, Mar 1977, Joe Diamonds in Fire Angel; Crucible, Sheffield, 1977, Herr Schultz in Cabaret; films, since Alfie Darling, 1975, include Too Many Chefs, and Recluse; frequent television appearances, since 1960, include The Chester Mystery Plays, Pinocchio, Crime and Punishment, and The Further Adventures of Oliver Twist; an associate artist of the RSC since 1969; a working member of Actorum (21 Tower Street, WC2), the first theatrical agency run to tally by actors for actors.

Favourite parts: Autolycus, Pierre Bezhukov, Holofernes.
Recreations: Going to the theatre and cinema. *Address:* 63 Elstree Road, Bushey, Heath, Herts. *Tel:* 01–950 5471.

SMITH, Dodie, dramatic author, novelist, and former actress
b Whitefield, Lancs; *d* of the late Ernest Smith and his wife Ella (Furber); *e* Manchester and St Paul's Girls' School, London; *m* Alec Macbeth Beesley; studied for the stage at the Royal Academy of Dramatic Art.

While still at the Academy she wrote a screen play, Schoolgirl Rebels, under the pseudonym of Charles Henry Percy; made her first appearance on the stage in a sketch, Playgoers, at Tottenham Palace in 1915; after several years of touring (for details see the Fourteenth Edition of this book), she left the stage and entered on a business career as buyer for Heal's of London; her first play, to be produced, was entitled British Talent, and was performed at the Three Arts Club, 1923; her first play in the professional theatre, Autumn Crocus, was produced at the Lyric Theatre, Apr 1931, and was an immediate success; has since written Service, Wyndham's, 1932; Touch Wood, Haymarket, 1934; Call It a Day, Globe, 1935; Bonnet Over the Windmill, New, 1937; Dear Octopus, Queen's, 1938 (revived, Haymarket, 1967); Lovers and Friends, Plymouth, New York, 1943; Letter From Paris, Aldwych, London, 1952; subsequently wrote I Capture the Castle (adapted from her own novel), Aldwych, 1954; These People, Those Books, Grand, Leeds, 1958; Amateur Means Lover, Liverpool Playhouse, 1961; is also the author of six novels: I Capture the Castle, 1949; The New Moon with the Old, 1963; The Town in Bloom, 1965; It Ends with Revelations, 1967; A Tale of Two Families, 1970; The Girl From the Candle-lit Bath, 1978; and three books for children, The Hundred and One Dalmatians, 1956, The Starlight Barking, 1967, and The Midnight Kittens, 1978; her autobiography has been published in three parts: Look Back With Love, 1974; Look Back With Mixed Feelings, 1978; Look Back With Astonishment, 1979; until 1935 wrote all her plays under the pseudonym of C L Anthony.

Recreations: Reading, music, television, and dogs. *Address:* The Barretts, Finchingfield, Essex. *Tel:* Great Dunmow 810 260.

SMITH, Kent, actor
b New York City, 19 Mar 1907; s of James E Smith and his wife Charlotte; e Exeter and Harvard University; m (1) Elizabeth Gillette (mar dis); (2) Edith Atwater.

Co-founder of University Players Guild, West Falmouth, Mass, and appeared with them as leading man, 1928–32; Ford's, Baltimore, Aug 1929, played a juvenile in Blind Window; first appeared in NY, at the Lyceum Theatre, 14 Oct 1932, as Lieut Chase in Men Must Fight; Booth, Sept 1933, played in Heat Lightning; Henry Miller, Oct 1933, played Juan Lorenzana in Spring in Autumn; Shubert, Nov 1933, Karl Hoffman in The Drums Begin; Shubert, Feb 1934, Kurt von Obersdorf in Dodsworth; Martin Beck, Mar 1936, Dunois in Saint Joan; Henry Miller, Sept 1936, Bob Winthrop in Seen But Not Heard; Empire, Dec 1936, Rev Phineas McQuestion in The Wingless Victory; Mar 1937, James Mavor Morell in Candida; Sept 1937, Duffy in The Star Wagon; Broadhurst, Dec 1937, Thorvald Helmer in A Doll's House; Martin Beck, Feb 1938, Matt Grogan in How to Get Tough About It; at Elitch's Gardens, Denver, Aug 1938, played in Once Is Enough and Tovarich; Oct 1938, toured with Katharine Cornell as Titus in Herod and Mariamne; Guild, NY, Feb 1939, played the title-role in Jeremiah; Playhouse, May 1939, Rev Mr Duke in Outward Bound; Henry Miller, Dec 1939, Peter Tor in Christmas Eve; Ethel Barrymore, Apr 1940, Hank Rogers in An International Incident; Morosco, Dec 1940, Rudd Kendall in Old Acquaintance; reappeared on the NY stage at the Henry Miller Theatre, Feb 1947, as Reverdy Johnson in The Story of Mary Surratt; in summer theatres, 1947, played the Actor in The Guardsman; Martin Beck, Nov 1947, played Enobarbus in Antony and Cleopatra; Mar 1950, Yancy Loper in The Wisteria Trees; Broadhurst, Oct 1950, Joe Saul in Burning Bright; City Center, Jan 1951, Henry Bolingbroke in King Richard II; Coronet, Mar 1951, Edward Crossman in The Autumn Garden; City Center, Dec 1951, played Gregers Werle in The Wild Duck; at the Shubert, New Haven, Mar 1952, played Olaf Ecklund in Salt of the Earth; Opera House, San Francisco, July 1952, appeared in Call Me Madam; City Center, Dec 1953, played Col Sir Francis Chesney in Charley's Aunt; opened Huntington Hartford Theatre, Holly-

wood, subsequently toured, and at the New York City Center, Dec 1954, played John Shand in What Every Woman Knows; at the Music Box, Jan 1956, took over the part of Dr Gerald Lyman in Bus Stop; Shakespeare Festival, Stratford, Conn, June 1956, played Angelo in Measure for Measure; Cambridge Drama Festival, Mass, Aug 1956, played Warwick in Saint Joan, subsequently appearing in the same part at the Phoenix, NY, Sept 1956; Shubert, New Haven, Dec 1959, played Jamie Garland in Sweet Love Remember'd; US tour, Nov 1961, took over from Melvin Douglas the part of William Russell in The Best Man; summer stock, 1962, appeared as Senator Mansfield in The Child Buyer; Pasadena, California, Playhouse, 1967, played in Ah, Wilderness!; Mark Taper Forum, Laboratory, Oct 1977, appeared in MGMT; films in which he has appeared, since 1936, include Cat People, The Spiral Staircase, The Damned Don't Cry, The Badlanders, Pete 'n' Tillie (1972), etc; first appeared on television in Death Takes a Holiday, Sept 1939, and has since played in Richard II, 1954, the series Peyton Place and The Invaders, Charles Evans Hughes in Profiles in Courage, etc.

Address: The Barskin Agency, 8730 Sunset Boulevard, Los Angeles, Calif 90069.

SMITH, Lois (*née* Humbert), actress
b Topeka, Kansas, 3 Nov 1930; d of William Oran Humbert and his wife Carrie Davis (Gottshalk); e Univ of Washington; m Wesley D Smith (mar dis); prepared for the stage with Donal Harrington at the Univ of Wash and with Lee Strasberg at the Actors Studio.

First appeared on the professional stage at the Wilmington, Del, Playhouse, Nov 1952, as Jeannie in Time Out for Ginger; made her New York debut at the Lyceum, 26 Nov 1952, in the same part; Locust, Philadelphia, Pa, Jan 1954, played Cathy in Mardi Gras; New York City Center, Feb 1955, Antoinette in The Wisteria Trees; Longacre, Oct 1955, Josephine Perry in The Young and Beautiful; made her London debut at the Arts, 15 Aug 1956, in the same part; New York City Center, Nov 1956, Laura Wingfield in The Glass Menagerie; Martin Beck, Mar 1957, Carol Cutrere in Orpheus Descending; 46th Street, Nov 1958, Mary Devlin in Edwin Booth; Cort, Sept 1963, Lucha Moreno in Bicycle Ride to Nevada; ANTA, 1964, took over as Jo Britten in Blues for Mr Charlie; Playhouse in the Park, Philadelphia, 1963, Sheila Knight in Time of Hope; 1965, Virginia in Galileo, Andromache in Tiger at the Gates, Celimene in The Misanthrope, Yelena in Uncle Vanya, Confidante in The Critic; 1966, Julie in Miss Julie, Pamela in The Last Analysis; 1967, Mary L in The Time of Your Life, Preacher Woman in Bechlch; Mark Taper Forum, Los Angeles, Cal, 1969, Sonya in Uncle Vanya; St Clement's Church, for the American Place Theatre, Nov 1970, Mary in Sunday Dinner; Sheridan Square Playhouse, July 1972, various roles in Present Tense; Actors Studio, May 1973, Mission Control Voice in A Break in the Skin; Joseph E Levine—Circle in the Square, Dec 1973, Cora in The Iceman Cometh; Olney, Md, Playhouse, Aug 1974, Trina Halvey in Summer; repeated this part at the John F Kennedy Center for the Performing Arts, Washington, DC, and at the Ivanhoe, Chicago; Harvard U, Feb 1975, Woman in Eh, Joe?; Circle Repertory Company, May 1975, Gabby in Harry Outside; Belasco, Mar 1978, played five roles in Stages; American Place, Dec 1978, the three women in Touching Bottom; Actors Studio, Feb, and Long Wharf, New Haven, Apr 1979, Denise in Hillbilly Women; Ensemble Studio, Nov 1979, Old Woman in Tennessee; St Clement's, Jan 1980, Emily in Deer Season; first appeared in films in East of Eden, 1955, and has since played in Five Easy

Pieces, receiving the National Society of Film Critics Award for this part, Strange Lady in Town, The Way We Live Now, Up the Sandbox, Resurrection (1980), etc; first appeared on television in The Apple Tree on *Kraft Television Theater*, 1953, and has since played in Miss Julie, The Master Builder, Tennessee Williams's Talk to Me Like the Rain and Let Me Listen, Particular Men, The Jilting of Granny Wetherall, The House of Mirth (1980), etc.

Favourite parts: Sonya and Yelena in Uncle Vanya, Carol Cutrere in Orpheus Descending, and Josephine Perry in The Young and Beautiful. *Address:* Actors Equity Association, 165 West 46th Street, New York, NY 10036. *Tel:* JU2 4240.

SMITH, Maggie, CBE, actress
b Ilford, Essex; *d* of Nathaniel Smith and his wife Margaret Little (Hutton); *e* Oxford High School for Girls; *m* (1) Robert Stephens (mar dis); (2) Beverley Cross; studied for the stage at the Oxford Playhouse School.

Made her first appearance on the stage with the OUDS, June 1952, as Viola in Twelfth Night; first appeared in New York at the Ethel Barrymore Theatre, June 1956, as a comedienne in New Faces '56 Revue; Lyric, Hammersmith, Aug 1957, appeared as the leading comedienne in the revue Share My Lettuce, transferring with the production to the Comedy, Sept 1957; St Martin's, Nov 1958, played Vere Dane in The Stepmother; joined the Old Vic Company, and during the season 1959–60, played Lady Plyant in The Double Dealer, Celia in As You Like It, the Queen in Richard II, Mistress Ford in The Merry Wives of Windsor, and Maggie Wylie in What Every Woman Knows; Strand, June 1960, played Daisy in Rhinoceros; toured, Oct 1960, as Kathy in Strip the Willow; Royal, Bristol, Mar 1961, played Lucile in The Rehearsal, subsequently appearing in the same production at the Globe, London, Apr 1961, Queen's, May 1961, Globe, July 1961, and Apollo, Dec 1961; Globe, May 1962, played Doreen in The Private Ear and Belinda in The Public Eye (double-bill), receiving the *Evening Standard* Award as the Best Actress of 1962, for her performances; Mermaid, Sept 1962, appeared in a reading of Pictures in the Hallway; Queen's, Feb 1963, played Mary in Mary, Mary, receiving the Variety Club Award as the Best Actress of 1963, for this performance; joined the National Theatre Company, Old Vic, Dec 1963, to play the following parts: Silvia in The Recruiting Officer, 1963; Desdemona in Othello (also Chichester Festival), Hilde Wangel in The Master Builder, Myra in Hay Fever, 1964; Beatrice in Much Ado About Nothing, Clea in Black Comedy and the title-part in Miss Julie (double-bill, Chichester Festival), 1965, also at the Old Vic, 1966; same year, Marcela in A Bond Honoured; Margery Pinchwife in The Country Wife (Chichester), 1969; Mrs Sullen in The Beaux' Stratagem (having already appeared in the part with the National Theatre Company in Los Angeles, Jan 1970, and also as Masha in The Three Sisters); Hedda in Hedda Gabler, 1970; Queen's, Sept 1972, played Amanda Prynne in Private Lives, again receiving the Variety Club's Best Actress Award; transferred with the production to the Globe, July 1973; Coliseum, Dec 1973, title-role in Peter Pan; Vaudeville, Mar 1974, Connie Hudson in Snap; again played Amanda in Los Angeles, 1974, and at the 46th Street, NY, Feb 1975; Stratford, Ontario, season 1976, played Cleopatra in Antony and Cleopatra, Millamant in The Way of the World and Masha in The Three Sisters; Ahmanson, Los Angeles, 1976, played The Actress in The Guardsman; returned to Stratford, Ontario, to play the following parts: Titania/Hippolyta in A Midsummer Night's Dream, Queen Elizabeth in Richard III, The Actress in The Guardsman, Judith Bliss in Hay Fever, 1977; Rosalind in As You

Like It, 1977 and 1978; Lady Macbeth in Macbeth, Amanda in Private Lives, 1978; Phoenix, London, 1979, took over Ruth Carson in Night and Day, later playing the part in Washington and at the ANTA, NY, Nov 1979; Stratford, Ontario, 1980 season, her parts included Virginia Woolf in Virginia, Beatrice in Much Ado About Nothing, and Masha in The Seagull; first appeared in films, 1957, subsequently in Oh! What A Lovely War, Othello, The Prime of Miss Jean Brodie (receiving an Oscar, 1969, for her performance as Jean Brodie; also the Society of Film and TV Arts Award, 1970, as Best Actress of the Year); more recent appearances include Death on the Nile, Clash of the Titans and California Suite (Golden Globe Award, 1979, and Oscar for Best Supporting Actress); has made numerous television appearances, including: Much Ado About Nothing, Man and Superman, On Approval and Home and Beauty; received the CBE in the New Year Honours, 1970.

Recreation: Reading. *Address:* c/o Fraser and Dunlop, 91 Regent Street, London W1. *Tel:* 01–734 7311.

SMITH, Oliver, designer and producer
b Wawpawn, Wisconsin, 13 Feb 1918; *s* of Larue F Smith and his wife Nina (Kincaid); *e* Pennsylvania State College.

First professional stage design at Metropolitan Opera House, 1941, Saratoga; has since designed the following productions: Rodeo, Rosalinda, 1942; The New Moon, The Perfect Marriage, Rhapsody, On the Town (also co-produced), 1944; Billion Dollar Baby (also co-produced), 1945; Twilight Bar, No Exit (also co-produced), Beggar's Holiday, 1946; Brigadoon, High Button Shoes, Topaze, 1947; Look, Ma, I'm Dancin'!, Me and Molly, Fall River Legend (ballet), 1948; Along Fifth Avenue, Miss Liberty, No Exit, Bless You All, Gentlemen Prefer Blondes (also co-produced), 1949; Paint Your Wagon, 1951; Pal Joey, 1952; Carnival in Flanders, At Home with Ethel Waters, In the Summer House, 1953; The Burning Glass, On Your Toes, 1954; Will Success Spoil Rock Hunter? 1955; Mr Wonderful, My Fair Lady, Auntie Mame, The Amazing Adele, Candide, 1956; A Clearing in the Woods (also co-produced), Eugenia, Visit to a Small Planet, The Saturday-Night Kid (co-produced), Carousel (revival), The Carefree Heart, West Side Story, Jamaica, Time Remembered, Nude with Violin, La Traviata for the Metropolitan Opera, 1957; Present Laughter, Winesburg, Ohio, My Fair Lady (his first design for the London stage, Drury Lane Theatre), Say Darling, Flower Drum Song, West Side Story (London), 1958; Juno (also co-produced), Destry Rides Again, Chéri, Take Me Along, The Sound of Music, Five Finger Exercise, Juniper and the Pagans, Goodbye, Charlie, 1959; Flower Drum Song (London), A Taste of Honey (New York), Becket, The Unsinkable Molly Brown, Under the Yum-Yum Tree, Camelot, 1960; Martha (Metropolitan Opera), Show Girl (also co-produced), Mary, Mary, The Sound of Music (London), Oh Dad, Poor Dad, Mama's Hung You in the Closet and I'm Feelin' So Sad (London), The Night of the Iguana, Sail Away, The Gay Life, Daughter of Silence, 1961; Romulus, Sail Away (London), Come on Strong, Lord Pengo, Tiger, Tiger, Burning Bright (also co-produced), 1962; Natural Affection (also co-produced), Children from Their Games, On the Town (London, also co-produced), The Time of the Barracudas, 110 in the Shade, Barefoot in the Park, The Girl Who Came to Supper, 1963; The Chinese Prime Minister, Hello, Dolly! (also National and International Companies and Australian production), Dylan, In the Summer House (revival), Beekman Place, Ben Franklin in Paris, I Was Dancing, Luv, Bajour, Slow Dance on a Killing Ground, Poor Richard, 1964; Kelly, Baker Street, The Odd Couple,

The Great Waltz, On a Clear Day You Can See Forever, Hot September, Cactus Flower, Barefoot in the Park (London), Hello, Dolly! (London), Cactus Flower, 1965; The Best Laid Plans, This Winter's Hobby, Show Boat, I Do! I Do!, The Star-Spangled Girl, The Odd Couple (London), 1966; 110 in the Shade (London), Cactus Flower (London), Illya Darling, A Certain Young Man (co-produced), Stephen D (co-produced), The Niggerlovers (co-produced), Song of the Grasshopper, How Now, Dow Jones, 1967; Darling of the Day, Plaza Suite, Weekend, The Exercise (also co-produced), I Do! I Do! (London), Collision Course (co-produced), 1968; Dear World, But Seriously . . ., Come Summer, Adaptation and Next (co-produced), A Patriot for Me, Indians (also co-produced), Jimmy, Last of the Red Hot Lovers, 1969; Alice in Wonderland (co-produced), Lovely Ladies, Kind Gentlemen, 1970; Four on a Garden, and the tours of Prettybelle, Candide, 1971; Lost in the Stars, The Little Black Book, Leonard Bernstein's Mass, The Time of Your Life (Washington, DC), and co-produced Doctor Selavy's Magic Theatre, The Mother of Us All, 1972; Tricks, The Women, Gigi, 1973; co-produced Alice in Wonderland, Endgame, Perfect Pitch (Washington, DC), décor for All Over Town, 1974; décor for Present Laughter (tour), Don't Call Back, Hello, Dolly!, The Royal Family, 1975; The Heiress, 1976; Do You Turn Somersaults?; First Monday in October, 1978; Carmelina, 1979; clothes for Summer Hotel, 1980; his designs for NY City Opera include Naughty Marietta; as co-director with Lucia Chase of The American Ballet Theatre, has been responsible for the New York seasons and European tours of this company, most recently in NY, 1976; Member of the National Council for the Arts, 1965–70; teaches a master class in scene design at New York University; has designed several films, including Band Wagon, Oklahoma, Guys and Dolls, Porgy and Bess, etc; has received the New York Drama Critics Award for his designs of the following productions: My Fair Lady, 1956; Candide, 1957; Destry Rides Again, 1959; Camelot, 1960; Hello, Dolly!, 1964; has received the Antoinette Perry (Tony) Award for his designs for West Side Story, Baker Street, My Fair Lady, The Sound of Music, Becket, Camelot, Hello, Dolly!; received the Donaldson Award for Brigadoon, High Button Shoes, Gentlemen Prefer Blondes, Pal Joey; has also received the Sam S Shubert Award for Achievement in the Theatre and New York City's Handel Medallion, 1975.

Recreations: Travel and easel painting. *Address:* 70 Willow Street, Brooklyn, New York, NY 11201.

SOBOLOFF, Arnold, actor

b New York City, 11 Nov 1930; s of Morris Soboloff and his wife Sarah (Artmann); e Cooper Union; m Suzanne Kauffman Romm; prepared for the stage with Herbert Berghof, Harold Clurman, and Mira Rostova; served in the US Army Air Force, 1951–54; formerly a commercial artist.

Made his stage debut at PS 94, New York, Apr 1940, as Aladdin; made his professional debut at the Tempo Playhouse, 2 Oct 1956, as the Monk in Escurial, also serving as stage manager for this play and for The Lesson; Theatre de Lys, May 1957, took over as the Policeman in The Threepenny Opera; Seventh Avenue South, May 1957, took over as Jack Goldman in Career; Gate, Dec 1957, Perhotin in The Brothers Karamazov; Cricket, Sept 1959, Dr Gachet in Vincent; toured, summer 1959, as Dr Kitchell in Bells Are Ringing; toured Europe, Sept 1960–Jan 1961, in the revue Broadway USA; Lyceum, May 1961, Neri in Mandingo; Cort, Jan 1962, various roles in The Egg; Broadhurst, May 1962, Moscolito in Bravo Giovanni; Music Box, Dec 1962, various roles in The Beauty Part; toured, summer, 1963, as

Boris in Can-Can; Cort, Nov 1963, Ellis in One Flew Over the Cuckoo's Nest; Majestic, Apr 1964, Treasurer Cooley in Anyone Can Whistle; Theatre de Lys, Oct 1964, Comte de la Ferrontière in Gogo Loves You; Palace, Jan 1966, Daddy Johann Sebastian Brubeck in Sweet Charity; Hudson, Apr 1968, Patsy in Mike Downstairs; The Forum, Dec 1968, A Ripe Banana in Bananas; St Clement's Church, for the American Place, May 1969, Curio in Papp; Avon, Stratford, Ontario, July 1969, Julius Proculus in The Satyricon; Vivian Beaumont, Jan 1970, Nursie in Camino Real; Edison, Mar 1970, Aaron in Show Me Where the Good Times Are; Avon, Stratford, Ontario, July 1970, The Emperor of Assyria in The Architect and the Emperor of Assyria; appeared with the Philadelphia Drama Guild, 1971–72 Season; Palace, May 1973, Ragueneau in Cyrano; Theatre of the Riverside Church, Dec 1973, Lionel Stander/Louis Mandel in Are You Now Or Have You Ever Been; New York City Center, Apr 1974, appeared in the revue Music! Music!; Manhattan Theatre Club, Mar 1975, Evens in The Sea; Mark Taper Forum, Los Angeles, Cal, July 1975, Rudolph Kammerling in Once in a Lifetime; Majestic, Oct 1977, Nat Schreiber in The Act; Circle-in-the-Square, Sept 1978, Khlopov in The Inspector General; Lunt-Fontanne, Sept 1979, Smee in Peter Pan; appeared on television since 1957 in The Day the Earth Stood Still, The Phil Silvers Show (1958), Ninotchka, and many dramatic series and specials; films include Silent Movie, Nickelodeon.

(Died 28 Oct 1979.)

SOFAER, Abraham, actor

b Rangoon, Burma, 1 Oct 1896; s of Isaac Sofaer and his wife Rahma (Solomon); e Diocesan Boy's High School, Rangoon; m Psyche Angela Christian; was formerly engaged as a schoolmaster in Rangoon, and in London.

Made his first appearance on the stage at the Palace Theatre, Newark-on-Trent, 4 Apr 1921, walking-on in The Merchant of Venice with Charles A Doran's company, with which he remained three years; subsequently toured with Alexander Marsh, and with Harold V Neilson's company, and in four years played nearly one hundred Shakespearean parts, including Othello, Shylock, Brutus, Malvolio, etc; in June 1925, toured as the Rajah of Rukh in The Green Goddess; made his first appearance in London, at the Little Theatre, 8 Dec 1925, as the Bishop of Avila in Gloriana, also playing three other parts in the same piece; St Martin's, Jan 1926, played Claude Montague in Scotch Mist; at the Shaftesbury (for Stage Society), May 1926, Zasha in The Mountain; Court (for Renaissance Society), Nov 1926, Bazilio in The Marriage of Figaro; in Jan 1927, toured as Leon in Dawn; Everyman, Oct 1927, Comte de Sallaz in Israel; in Jan 1928, toured as Dr Chan Fu in The Silent House; Strand, Oct 1928, played the Arab in The Beetle; Jan 1929, toured as De Levis in Loyalties, and Hector Frome in Justice; Arts, Feb 1929, played The Pack Pedlar in Black Velvet; Lyceum, Mar 1929, Odderitto in The Man in Dress Clothes; Little, Apr 1929, Professor Fell in Before Midnight; Royalty, May 1929, Isaac Cohen in The Matriarch; went to America, and made his first appearance in New York, at the Longacre, 18 Mar 1930, in the same part; on his return, appeared at the Embassy, June 1930, as Feste in Twelfth Night, and Claudius in Hamlet; Globe, Sept 1930, played Abraham Kaplan in Street Scene; Arts, Feb 1931, Ali and Ben Hussein in If; Embassy, Sept 1931, Piderit in Twelve Thousand, and Count Mario Grazia in The Mask and the Face; Garrick, Jan 1932, Leone in Volpone; His Majesty's, Feb 1932, Decius Brutus in Julius Caesar; Westminster, July 1932, Biron in Love's Labour's Lost; Comedy, Oct 1932, Chief Rabbi Forbach in Miracle at

Verdun; Garrick, Oct 1932, Leonti Levine in The Bear Dances; Saville, Mar 1933, Dr Zodiac in He Wanted Adventure; Oct 1933, Vasco in Command Performance; Fulham, Jan 1934, and Cambridge, Feb 1934, Rufus Sonnenberg in Success Story; he then joined the Old Vic–Sadler's Wells company, Sept 1934, and during the season appeared as the Messenger in Antony and Cleopatra, Bolingbroke in Richard II, Don Pedro in Much Ado About Nothing, the Bishop of Beauvais in Saint Joan, Gremio in The Taming of the Shrew, Othello, Theseus in Hippolytus (of Euripides), King Henry in Henry IV (Part II), Claudius in Hamlet; St Martin's, Apr 1936, Count de Reinach in The Great Experiment; Embassy, June, and Phoenix, July 1936, Professor Bernhardi in the play of that name; Broadhurst, NY, Aug 1936, Disraeli in Victoria Regina, subsequently touring in the same part, which he played over 750 times; during the tour, directed Helen Hayes' revival of The Merchant of Venice, and appeared as Shylock; Martin Beck, NY, Oct 1938, again played in Victoria Regina; after returning to London, appeared at the Strand, July 1939, as Jonah Goodman in The Gentle People; toured, 1940, as Macduff with Dame Sybil Thorndike; toured, 1941, and appeared at the New, July 1941, with the Old Vic Company, as the King of France in King John, and Jason in Medea; Piccadilly, July 1942, Ross in Macbeth; Stratford-on-Avon, 1943 season, played King Lear, Othello, Iago, Leontes, etc; Arts, Feb 1944, Master Absolon Beyer in The Witch; toured, 1944, as Dr Gortler in I Have Been Here Before; Haymarket, 1945, for a time, played Claudius in Hamlet; Embassy, Nov 1945, the Rabbi in Skipper Next to God; Winter Garden, Jan 1946, Nils Krogstad in A Doll's House; New Lindsey, Sept 1946, Ernesti in The Silver Trumpets; Boltons, Feb 1948, appeared as Edward Max in Native Son; Strand, Apr 1948, Kurt Auerbach in The Least of These; Covent Garden, July 1948, Evangelist in The Pilgrim's Progress; Bedford, Camden Town, Apr 1950, Svengali in Trilby; at St Martin-in-the-Fields, May 1951, appeared as Samson in Samson Agonistes; New, Nov 1951, played Zeus in The Flies, a Group Theatre production; Mark Taper Forum, Los Angeles, 1967–8, played in In the Matter of J Robert Oppenheimer; has also broadcast extensively since 1926, and appeared on television since 1939; has played in many films since 1931; since 1955 has lived in California, and worked in films and on television.

Club: Green Room. *Address:* 30473 Mulholland Highway, Agoura, Calif 91301.

SONDERGAARD, Gale (*née* Edith Holm Sondergaard), actress
b Litchfield, Minnesota, 1901; *d* of Hans T Sondergaard and his wife Kirstine (Holm); *e* University of Minnesota (BA 1921); *m* (1) Neill O'Malley (mar dis); (2) Herbert Biberman; prepared for the stage at the Minneapolis School of Dramatic Arts.

First appeared on the stage while in high school; toured in a Chatauqua circuit, 1920, as an ingenue in various plays; joined the John Keller Shakespeare Company, and toured the USA and Canada as Gertrude in Hamlet, Jessica in The Merchant of Venice, Calpurnia in Julius Caesar, and a Witch in Macbeth, 1921–2; made her New York début at the 49th Street, Nov 1923, when she took over as Edith Somers in What's Your Wife Doing?; joined the Jessie Bonstelle Stock Company in Detroit, Michigan, 1925, and remained with it until 1927; Guild, NY, Oct 1928, played a Witch in Faust; Nov 1928, Sarah Undershaft in Major Barbara; John Golden, Dec 1928, took over from Judith Anderson as Nina Leeds in Strange Interlude; Guild, Oct 1929, Marie in Karl and Anna; Martin Beck, Dec 1929, Nina in Red Dust; Civic Repertory, May 1931, took over from Eva Le Gallienne as Elsa in

Alison's House; Guild, Feb 1933, Lydia Kimball in American Dream; Playhouse, Nov 1933, Anna in Doctor Monica; Masque, May 1934, Lorinda Channing in Invitation to a Murder; entered films, then re-appeared on the stage at the Royale, Dec 1940, as Frances Chapman in Cue for Passion; stock, 1948–50, played in No Time for Comedy, The Corn Is Green, Ladies in Retirement, Henry IV; Playhouse-in-the-Park, Philadelphia, 1956, Empress of Russia in Anastasia; toured intermittently in a one-woman show called Woman, 1955–8; Gramercy Arts, NY, Oct 1965, appeared in her program Woman, which she arranged from works by Congreve, Ibsen, Houghton, Sierra, and Corwin; Gramercy Arts, Jan 1967, Mrs Kane in Kicking the Castle Down; Mark Taper Forum, Los Angeles, California, 1969, played in Uncle Vanya; Ahmanson, Los Angeles, Dec 1972, played in The Crucible; Seattle, Washington, Repertory, Jan 1974, Blanche Gaveston in A Family and a Fortune; Roundabout, Dec 1976, Gunhild Borkman in John Gabriel Borkman; stock tour, 1977, in The Royal Family; Ambassador, Apr 1980, Prudencia in Goodbye Fidel; entered films in Anthony Adverse, 1936, for which she received the Academy Award, and has since played in The Life of Emile Zola, The Cat and the Canary, The Bluebird, The Letter, The Mark of Zorro, Spider Woman, The Invisible Man's Revenge, Anna and the King of Siam, Road to Rio, East Side, West Side, and many others.

Address: 1924 Lake Shore Avenue, Los Angeles, Calif 90039.

SONDHEIM, Stephen, composer and lyricist
b New York City, 22 Mar 1930; *s* of Herbert Sondheim and his wife Janet (Fox); *e* George School and Williams College.

Composed his first music for the stage, with incidental music for Girls of Summer, at the Longacre, Nov 1956; has since written the lyrics for West Side Story, 1957; Gypsy, 1959; incidental music for Invitation to a March, 1960; music and lyrics for A Funny Thing Happened on the Way to the Forum, 1962; music and lyrics for Anyone Can Whistle, 1964; lyrics for Do I Hear a Waltz? 1965; music and lyrics for Company, 1970 for which he received the Antoinette Perry (Tony) Award; Follies, 1971, for which he received the Tony Award; appeared at the Kaufmann Auditorium, YMHA, 2 May 1971, in the series Lyrics and Lyricists; music and lyrics for A Little Night Music, for which he received the Tony Award, 1973; appeared at the Shubert, 11 Mar 1973, in Sondheim: A Musical Tribute; wrote incidental music for The Enclave, 1973; lyrics and music for The Frogs, at the Yale Repertory, New Haven, Conn, 1974; co-lyricist for revival of Candide, 1974; lyrics and music for Pacific Overtures, 1976; Sweeney Todd, 1979 (Tony Award); author of some scripts for the television series Topper, 1953, and music and lyrics for Evening Primrose, 1966; co-author with Anthony Perkins of the screenplay The Last of Sheila, 1973; composed score of film Stavisky, 1974.

Address: c/o Flora Roberts, 65 East 55th Street, New York, NY 10022.

SORVINO, Paul, actor, director
b New York City, 1939; prepared for the stage at the Academy of Musical and Dramatic Arts.

Made his New York debut at the Shubert, 23 Nov 1964, as a Patrolman in Bajour; Eugene O'Neill, Nov 1965, played Officer Lynch in Mating Dance; Lunt-Fontanne, Nov 1965, Francesco in Skyscraper; Newman, May 1972, Phil Romano in That Championship Season; Booth, Sept 1972, repeated this role; Delacorte, July 1973, Gloucester in King Lear; Joseph E Levine—Circle in the Square, Apr 1974, Nathaniel

Schwab in An American Millionaire; Westport, Conn, Country Playhouse, July 1975, Lionel Lane in For My Last Number; toured, summer 1975, in We'll Get By, and also toured in Philemon; toured, May 1976, as Aimable in The Baker's Wife; made his Broadway directing debut 11 Oct 1976, with Wheelbarrow Closers; appeared in the films Panic in Needle Park, Made for Each Other, The Day of the Dolphin, A Touch of Class, The Gambler, I Will, I Will . . . for Now (1976), etc; has also appeared on television in various dramatic shows, notably in The Queen of the Star Dust Ballroom, and the series Bert D'Angelo, 1975.

Address: Gage Group Inc, 1650 Broadway, New York, NY 10019.

SPARER, Paul, actor

b Boston, Mass; *e* Harvard U; *m* Nancy Marchand, the actress.

Made his New York debut at the New York City Center, 4 Feb 1953, as Dumain in Love's Labour's Lost; Mar 1953, played Salanio in The Merchant of Venice; Apr 1955, played in Moby Dick; Sept 1955, Cassio in Othello; Sept 1955, Owen Glendower and Sir Walter Blunt in Henry IV, Part I; Phoenix, Sept 1956, Gilles de Rais and The Executioner in Saint Joan, with Siobhan McKenna; The Players, Jan 1959, Earl of Gloucester in King Lear; Theatre de Lys, Jan 1959, Heracles in Philoctetes; Lunt-Fontanne, Sept 1959, Borachio in Much Ado About Nothing, in the Gielgud production; Ambassador, Feb 1960, John Brown in Cut of the Axe; Gramercy Arts, Dec 1960, Leone Gala in The Rules of the Game; American Shakespeare Festival, Stratford, Conn, June 1961, Lennox in Macbeth, July 1961, Ulysses in Troilus and Cressida, and Corin in As You Like It; The Playhouse, Oct 1961, Prosecuting Captain in A Cook for Mr General; Eugene O'Neill, Dec 1961, Auda Abu Tayi in Ross; Folksbiene Playhouse, for the AAP, Mar 1962, Boris Trigorin in The Seagull, and Apr 1962, Tom Allen in The Tavern; Phoenix, Mar 1964, repeated this last part, played Lamberto Laudisi in Right You Are If You Think You Are, Moliere in Impromptu at Versailles, and Satin in The Lower Depths; Phoenix, Dec 1964, Mendoza and The Devil in Man and Superman, Jan 1965, Dolokhov in War and Peace, Mar 1965, Holofernes in Judith; Orpheum, Oct 1965, Mead in The Pedestrian, David McLean in The Veldt, and The Stranger in To the Chicago Abyss, in a bill with the overall title The World of Ray Bradbury; American Shakespeare Festival, Stratford, Conn, June 1966, Robert Shallow in Falstaff, Sir Reginald Fitz Urse in Murder in the Cathedral, Cassius in Julius Caesar; John Golden, Oct 1967, The Lecturer in After the Rain; Eastside Playhouse, Oct 1968, Disley in Teaparty; Vivian Beaumont, June 1969, J Robert Oppenheimer in In the Matter of J Robert Oppenheimer; Mar 1970, General Browser in Operation Sidewinder; Delacorte, June 1970, Richard Plantagenet in Henry VI, Part I and Part II; Estelle Newman, Oct 1970, General in The Happiness Cage; Roundabout, Oct 1971, Halvard Solness in The Master Builder; Brooklyn Academy of Music, May 1972, Albert Valpor in The Water Hen; Winter Garden, 1973, took over as Leonato in Much Ado About Nothing; Hartford, Conn, Stage Company, 1973, Captain Melody in A Touch of the Poet; Roundabout, July 1974, Giovanni in The Burnt Flowerbed; St Clement's Church, Oct 1975, Emil Varec in Duck Variations; Lyceum, Mar 1976, Chairman of Council in Zalmen; Williamstown Festival, 1976, appeared in Heartbreak House; Ethel Barrymore, Oct 1976, several parts in Poor Murderer; American Place, Mar 1977, Friedrich Reisen in Cold Storage; St Clement's, Sept 1977, appeared in The Sponsor; Circle in the Square, Nov 1977, Inquisitor in Saint Joan, Queen's

Festival, May 1978, in Awake and Sing; Chelsea Westside, Apr 1979, Recorder in Biography: a Game.

Address: Arcasa, Bauman and Hiller, 850 Seventh Avenue, New York, NY 10019.

SPENCER, Marian, actress

b London, 2 Oct 1905; *d* of Edwin Spencer and his wife Edith (Stranack); *m* (1) R Steuart West (dec); (2) Basil Unite; studied for the stage at the Royal Academy of Music and at the Royal Academy of Dramatic Art.

Made her first appearance on the stage at the first Malvern Festival, 24 Aug 1929, in Caesar and Cleopatra; was engaged at the Bristol Little Theatre, Sept 1931–Dec 1933; made her first appearance in London at the Garrick Theatre, 28 Mar 1933, as Lady Joyce in She Had to Come Back; toured in South Africa, from Jan 1934, in The Barretts of Wimpole Street, Road House, While Parents Sleep, and Mother of Pearl; on returning to England, toured as Sylvia in Touch Wood, and appeared with the Worthing Repertory company; at the Playhouse, May 1935, played Mrs Jackman in The Skin Game; Lyric, Hammersmith, Dec 1935, played two parts in The Magic Marble; then spent nearly three years in various films; at Drury Lane, 1938, appeared in The Sun Never Sets; Duke of York's, Feb–Apr 1939, played Mrs Linden in Nora, Suzanna Bennett in Lady Fanny, and Eve O'Hara in Nina; Wyndham's, May 1939, Mademoiselle in The Intruder, and July 1939, Muriel Conway in Alien Corn; St Martin's, Apr 1940, Miss Brown in A House in the Square; Richmond, June 1940, Elinor in Here and Now; Apollo, Dec 1941, Mildred Drake in Old Acquaintance; at the Phoenix, Apr 1943, played Mrs Foresight in Love for Love, which ran for a year; with John Gielgud's company at the Haymarket Theatre, Oct 1944–July 1945, played Mrs Foresight, the Queen in Hamlet, Helena in A Midsummer Night's Dream, and Julia in The Duchess of Malfi; went to the Far East with John Gielgud, in the autumn of 1945, playing the Queen in Hamlet, Ruth in Blithe Spirit; after her return to England appeared at the New Theatre, Oct 1946, as Sheila Birling in An Inspector Calls; made her first appearance on the New York stage at the Royale, 26 May 1947, as Mrs Foresight in Love for Love; Apollo, London, Dec 1947, played Lady Brasted in The Blind Goddess; St Martin's, May 1949, Gwen Barrie in Miss Turner's Husband; Boltons, June 1949, Sylvia Strachan in The Deluded; Embassy, Sept 1949, Eve Masters in Rain Before Seven; Wyndham's, Mar 1950, Mrs Preston in Home at Seven; Duke of York's, Oct 1951, played Daisy Manifold in All the Year Round; Westminster, Jan 1952, Mrs Olney in Sunset in Knightsbridge; Phoenix, Sept 1952, Mrs Axel Diensen in Quadrille; Criterion, Oct 1953, appeared as Mary Titheradge in Birthday Honours; Globe, Aug 1955, played Mrs Gregson in Mrs Willie; Duchess, July 1956, Emily Wigsley Pearson in Someone to Talk To; Adelphi, Mar 1957, Lady Fidget in The Country Wife; Comedy, Dec 1958, took over the part of Louise Harrington for two months, in Five Finger Exercise; Piccadilly, Apr 1959, Theadora Sheridan in Mr Fox of Venice; Westminster, Oct 1959, Maud Hopkinson in The Kensington Squares; Phoenix, Apr 1961, Mrs Mills in The Landing Place, for the Repertory Players; Hampstead Theatre Club, Apr 1964, Cissy Bowers in All Good Children; Arts, Cambridge, Nov 1964, played Lady Bracknell in The Importance of Being Earnest; Ashcroft, Croydon, Mar 1965, again appeared in The Importance of Being Earnest; Wimbledon, May 1966, Mrs Violet Deakin in The Carib Sands; Arts, Cambridge, Oct 1966, Miss Anna Seward and Mrs Pritchard in Madam . . . Said Dr Johnson; Manchester, Royal Exchange, Oct 1973, Amy in the 69 Theatre Company's The Family Reunion; her frequent television appearances include: A Woman of No Importance, The Lovely Crime, the serials Dombey and Son and Persuasion, and numerous series; she has also broadcast in many sound radio programmes; first appeared in films, 1937, as Mary Livingstone in The Life of David Livingstone, and recent pictures include Gulliver's Travels, The World of Suzie Wong, The Doctor of Seven Dials, Seance on a Wet Afternoon, etc.

Recreations: Swimming, reading, and designing fabrics. *Address:* Mill House Farm, Bell Common, nr Epping, Essex.

SPIGELGASS, Leonard, playwright
b Brooklyn, New York, 26 Nov; *s* of Abraham Spigelgass and his wife Rebecca (Ratner); *e* New York University.

Began his career as a reader and story editor in Hollywood, 1930, and wrote his first screenplay, Princess O'Hara, which he also produced, 1935; wrote his first play produced on Broadway, A Majority of One, in 1959; A Majority of One produced in London in 1960, and subsequently in twenty-one countries; since then has written Dear Me, The Sky Is Falling, 1963; A Remedy for Winter, 1965; The Wrong Way Light Bulb, 1969; the book of the musical Look to the Lilies, adapted from the film The Lilies of the Field, 1970; original idea for the book of the musical Mack and Mabel, 1974; among his other screenplays are Letter of Introduction, 1938; Boys from Syracuse, 1940; Tight Shoes, 1941; Butch Minds the Baby, Big Street, All Through the Night, 1942; The Perfect Marriage, 1946; So Evil, My Love, 1947; I Was a Male War Bride, 1949; Because You're Mine, 1952; Deep in My Heart, 1954; Silk Stockings, 1957; Pepe, 1960; Gypsy, 1962, etc; first wrote for television in 1955, and has since written Eloise for *Playhouse 90,* and The Helen Morgan Story, also for *Playhouse 90,* etc; author of Scuttle under the Bonnet, 1962, Fed to the Teeth, 1964, and All My Yesterdays (with Edward G Robinson), 1973.

Address: The Dramatists Guild, 234 West 44th Street, New York, NY 10036.

SPINETTI, Victor, actor
b Cwm, Monmouthshire, 2 Sept 1933; *s* of Giuseppe Spinetti and his wife Lily (Watson); *e* Monmouth School; studied for the stage at the College of Music and Drama, Cardiff.

Began his career in 1953, in a concert party in Wales; after appearing in revue at the Irving Theatre, London, 1956, he appeared at the Saville, Apr 1958, as Leon, Fleet Street Editor, Psychiatrist, Parson, and Head Waiter in Expresso Bongo; at the same theatre, Apr 1959, played the First Inquisitor and Marquis Milton in Candide; Theatre Royal, Stratford, E, Oct 1959, played Sweeting in Make Me An Offer, subsequently appearing in the same production at the New, Dec 1959; Theatre Royal, Stratford, E, July 1960, played Brain-Worm in Every Man in His Humour; made his first appearance in New York at the Cort, Sept 1960, as IRA Officer in The Hostage; Garrick, 1961, took over the part of Tosher in Fings Ain't Wot They Used T' Be; Theatre Royal, Stratford, E, Mar 1963, played one of the leading parts in Oh, What a Lovely War!, transferring with the production to Wyndham's, June 1963; at the same theatre, Dec 1963, played Eartha in Merry Roosters Panto (matinées); Edinburgh Festival, Aug 1964, played Owen Glendower and Poins in Joan Littlewood's production of Henry IV; Broadhurst, NY, Sept 1964, again appeared in Oh, What a Lovely War! for which he received a Tony award; Fisher, Detroit, Sept 1965, Roger Summerhill in Skyscraper; 54th Street, NY, Dec 1965, M Cheri in La Grosse Valise; Queen's, London, Oct 1966, Felix Ungar in The Odd Couple; for the National Theatre, at the Old Vic, June 1968, co-adapted and directed In His Own Write; Prince of Wales, Apr 1969, General

Irrigua in Cat Among the Pigeons; Arts, Aug 1969, directed *Shirley Abicair's Evening;* Royalty, June 1970, directed The Bed; Arts, Nov 1970, assisted in the production of Cocky; 1970, directed various foreign productions of Hair; Ethel Barrymore, NY, Mar 1971, Braham in The Philanthropist; directed Jesus Christ Superstar for the TNP, Paris, Jan 1972; Bankside Globe, July 1973, Banquo in Macbett; Belgrade, Coventry, Nov 1973, Samuel Sleary in Hard Times; Arts, June 1974, devised and directed Off the Peg; Windmill, Sept 1974, directed Let's Get Laid; New London, Dec 1974, directed Déjà Revue; Whitehall, Feb 1976, directed Come Into My Bed; Shaftesbury, Dec 1976, Wizard and Sheriff of Nottingham in Emu in Pantoland; directed Don't Bother to Dress, 1977; Yes We Have No Pyjamas, 1979; films include: Help, The Taming of the Shrew, Under Milk Wood, and The Return of the Pink Panther; recent television includes Take My Wife, The Sea, and many guest appearances.

Favourite part: The Drill Sergeant Major in Oh, What a Lovely War! *Recreations:* Writing, talking, and occasionally listening. *Clubs:* Arts and Buckstone. *Address:* c/o Fraser and Dunlop Ltd, 91 Regent Street, London W1.

SPRIGGS, Elizabeth, actress
m (1) Marshall Jones; (2) Murray Manson; trained for opera at the Royal School of Music.

Early repertory experience including Bristol Old Vic and Birmingham Repertory, for whom her parts included Cleopatra in Antony in Cleopatra, Madame Ranevsky in The Cherry Orchard, 1958; joined the Royal Shakespeare Company, 1962, and at the Aldwych, season 1963–4 played Mrs Vixen in The Beggar's Opera, Mother in The Representative, Ida Mortemarte in Victor, and Rossignol in The Marat/Sade; Stratford, 1965, Courtezan in The Comedy of Errors, Phrynia in Timon of Athens, and Gertrude in Hamlet; Aldwych, 1965–6, Chairman Maudsley in The Governor's Lady, Locksmith's Wife in The Government Inspector, and again played Gertrude; Stratford, 1966, once again played Gertrude, also Mistress Quickly in Henry IV and Hostess in Henry V; Widow in All's Well That Ends Well, Witch in Macbeth and Nurse in Romeo and Juliet; played the two latter parts on tour to Helsinki, Leningrad and Moscow, 1967, and at the Aldwych, Jan 1968; Stratford, 1968, Portia in Julius Caesar, Mistress Ford in The Merry Wives of Windsor; Aldwych, Jan 1969, Claire in A Delicate Balance; Stratford, 1969, again played Mistress Ford, also Livia in Women Beware Women; toured as Mistress Ford to Japan and Australia, where she also played Paulina in The Winter's Tale and Maria in Twelfth Night; Aldwych, 1970, Lady Gay Spanker in London Assurance, Paulina in The Winter's Tale, Maria in Twelfth Night, and Lady Britomart in Major Barbara; Stratford, 1971, Maria in Twelfth Night, Emilia in Othello, Duchess of York in Richard II (for Theatregoround), and Beatrice in Much Ado About Nothing, repeating the latter at the Aldwych, Dec; New, Apr 1972, Lady Gay Spanker in London Assurance; Aldwych, 1974, Eleanor Jimenez in Duck Song, Queen Mariana in The Bewitched; made her New York debut at the Palace, Dec 5 1974, as Lady Gay Spanker; joined the National Theatre Company, June 1976, to play Madame Arcati in Blithe Spirit, at the Lyttleton; and at the Olivier, Valerie in Tales from the Vienna Woods; Lady Wouldbe in Volpone, Lady Fidget in The Country Wife, all in 1977; Cottesloe, Feb 1978, Sonia Marsden in Love Letters on Blue Paper (SWETM Best Supporting Actress Award, 1978); Olivier, June, a Witch in Macbeth; films include Work Is a Four-Letter Word, 1967; her many appearances on television include: Victorian Scandals, The Glittering Prizes, Wings of a Dove, The Dybbuk, and *Fox.*

Address: c/o Harbour and Coffey, 9 Blenheim Street, London W1.

SQUIRE, Katherine, actress
b Defiance, Ohio, 9 Mar 1903; *d* of Virgil Squire and his wife Mary (Haag); *e* Ohio Wesleyan University; *m* (1) Byron McGrath (mar dis); (2) George Mitchell; prepared for the stage with Richard Boleslavsky and Maria Ouspenskaya, at the American Laboratory Theatre, and the Cleveland Playhouse.

First appeared on the professional stage at the American Laboratory Theatre, Nov 1927, as a Witch in Macbeth; later played Natalia Hovind in At the Gate of the Kingdom; Cleveland Playhouse, 1927–9, played Maria in Twelfth Night, Hedvig in The Wild Duck, Serena Blandish in the play of that name, and Tessa in The Constant Nymph; first appeared in New York at the Sam Harris, Jan 1932, as Mona in Black Tower; Masque, Dec 1932, played Julie Wilson in Goodbye Again; Maxine Elliott, Oct 1934, played Helen Tyson in Hipper's Holiday; Playhouse, Jan 1935, Audry in Three Men on a Horse; Mansfield, Mar 1935, Winifred Shaw in Lady of Letters; Broadhurst, 1935, Hanna Priest in Life's Too Short; Martin Beck, 1937, took over Lise from Peggy Ashcroft in High Tor; Biltmore, Oct 1937, Mrs Roberts in Many Mansions; Biltmore, 1938, took over as Miss Wheeler in What a Life; at the New York World's Fair, 1939, appeared in a Shakespearean repertory; toured the US, 1940, as Mrs Elvsted in Hedda Gabler, with Eva Le Gallienne; Shubert, 1941, played Nurse Cotton in Liberty Jones; Windsor, Mar 1943, Anna Petrovna Chernov in The Family; Henry Miller's, Apr 1944, Miss Sally in Chicken Every Sunday; toured Italy, 1944–5, in a USO production of Ten Little Indians; toured the Pacific, 1945–6, as Madame Arcati in Blithe Spirit; Shubert, New Haven, Conn, Apr 1947, played Bernice Desor in Three Indelicate Ladies; appeared with the Margo Jones Theatre Company, in Dallas, Texas, 1947–8, as Kate in The Taming of the Shrew, subsequently in Portrait of a Madonna, etc; Lenox Hill Playhouse, NY, Feb 1949, played Mom in Cock-a-Doodle Doo; Playhouse, Oct 1954, Sitter Mavis in The Travelin' Lady; Phoenix, Dec 1955, played The Mother in Six Characters in Search of an Author; Cort, Mar 1957, Brigid Muldoon in The Sin of Pat Muldoon; Bijou, Nov 1958, Mrs Gallagher in The Shadow of a Gunman; Mayfair, Mar 1961, Mrs Bryant in Roots; appeared at the Charles Playhouse, Boston, 1964, as Mrs Malaprop in The Rivals, and Nora in A Touch of the Poet; Theatre 80 St Marks, Nov 1966, Julie in This Here Nice Place; Lydia Mendelssohn, Ann Arbor, Michigan, Dec 1966, Herman's Mother in Wedding Band; Tyrone Guthrie, Minneapolis, Minnesota, June 1967, Mary Brown in Harper's Ferry and Lady Hurf in Thieves' Carnival; St Clement's Church, NY, Feb 1969, Stella in Boy on the Straight-Back Chair; played at the Studio Arena, Buffalo, NY, in the 1969–70 season; played with the Meadow Brook troupe in Rochester, Mich, 1972–3 season; Arena Stage, Washington, DC, May 1974, Mrs Shaw in In Celebration; Arena Stage, Mar 1977, Giza in Catsplay; played the same part at the Manhattan Theatre Club, Apr 1978; Long Wharf, New Haven, Apr 1979, appeared in Hillbilly Women; first entered films, 1959, in Clifford Odets' Story on Page One, and has subsequently appeared in Song Without End and in Lolly-Madonna War, 1973, etc; first appeared on television, 1949, on *Studio One,* and has since appeared on *Playhouse 90, Alfred Hitchcock, Dr Kildare, The Virginian,* etc.

Favourite parts: Mrs Malaprop, Kate, and Mrs Bryant in Roots. *Recreations:* Photography and writing; *Address:* Actors Equity Association, 165 West 46th Street, New York, NY 10036.

SQUIRE, William, actor
b Neath, Wales, 29 Apr 1920; *s* of William Squire and his wife Martha (Bridgeman); *m* (1) Elizabeth Dixon (mar dis); (2) Juliet Harmer (mar dis); formerly a bell founder; studied for the stage at the Royal Academy of Dramatic Art (LCC Scholar).

Made his first appearance on the stage as a member of the Old Vic Company, New Theatre, Sept 1945, and remained with the company until 1947, making his first appearance in New York with them at the Century, May 1946; Boltons, London, Aug 1947, played Benvolio in Romeo and Juliet; and at the same theatre, Nov 1947, Dick in The Patched Cloak; Mercury, Jan 1948, the Knave in The Dragon and the Dove; joined the Shakespeare Memorial Theatre Company, Stratford-on-Avon, Apr 1948, to play the following parts: Citizen in King John, Laertes in Hamlet, Time in The Winter's Tale, Ulysses in Troilus and Cressida, and the Duke in Othello; Memorial Theatre, Dec 1948, played Ratty in Toad of Toad Hall; Shakespeare Memorial Theatre Company, Apr 1949, played the following parts: Verges in Much Ado About Nothing; Oberon in A Midsummer Night's Dream, Cloten in Cymbeline, Lord Chamberlain in Henry VIII; Birmingham Repertory Theatre, 1950, played Dawlish in Summer Day's Dream, Tommy Turner in The Male Animal and the Cat in The Blue Bird; Shakespeare Memorial Theatre, 1951, played the following parts: Exton in Richard II, Rumour and Silence in Henry IV, Part II, Chorus in Henry V, Sebastian in The Tempest, and First Witch in Macbeth; Shakespeare Memorial Theatre, Dec 1951, again played Ratty in Toad of Toad Hall; joined the Bristol Old Vic Company, 1952, where he played the following parts: The Duke in The Two Gentlemen of Verona, Vezinet in The Italian Straw Hat, Banquo in Macbeth, the Wicked Fairy in The Love of Four Colonels, and Timothy in A Penny For A Song; Old Vic, London, Sept 1952–4, played the following parts: Benvolio in Romeo and Juliet, Vezinet in The Italian Straw Hat, 1952; Gratiano in The Merchant of Venice, Casca in Julius Caesar, Cranmer in Henry VIII, 1st Tempter in Murder in the Cathedral, Horatio in Hamlet, Lafeu in All's Well That Ends Well, King of France in King John, 1953; Sir Andrew Aguecheek in Twelfth Night, Menenius in Coriolanus, 1954; Princes, Dec 1954, played Ratty in Toad of Toad Hall; Criterion, Sept 1955, took over Vladimir in Waiting for Godot; New, Sept 1956, played Captain Cat in Under Milk Wood; Edinburgh Festival, Aug 1958, and Cambridge, Sept 1958, played Federico Gomez in The Elder Statesman; Mermaid, June 1961, played Otis H Baker in The Andersonville Trial; at the Majestic, NY, 1961, took over the part of Arthur in Camelot, subsequently touring the US with the production, Jan 1963; Hampstead Theatre Club, London, Sept 1963, played the Narrator in Cider With Rosie, transferring with the production to the Garrick, Oct 1963; joined the Royal Shakespeare Company, Stratford, Apr 1964, to play the following parts: Thomas Mowbray in Richard II, Owen Glendower in Henry IV (Part I), Charles VI in Henry V, Suffolk in Henry VI, Duke of Buckingham in Edward IV, Buckingham in Richard III (the last three plays comprising The Wars of the Roses), 1964; Royal Shakespeare, Stratford-on-Avon, Aug 1965, played the Player King in Hamlet; Wyndham's, May 1966, Teddy Lloyd in The Prime of Miss Jean Brodie; Sherman, Cardiff, Oct 1973, the Mayor in The Government Inspector; joined the National Theatre company at the Old Vic, 1974, playing Sebastian in The Tempest, Mar and Headmaster Sunstroke in Spring Awakening, May; Criterion, 1976, Player in Rosencrantz and Guildenstern are Dead; St George's, Islington, Apr 1976, Sir Toby Belch Twelfth Night; Her Majesty's, Sept 1979, Rear Admiral

Knatchbull-Folliatt in The Case of the Oily Levantine; principal films in which he has appeared include: The Battle of the River Plate, Where Eagles Dare, and Anne of the Thousand Days; more recently seen in Les Miserables and The Thirty Nine Steps, and to be heard as Gandalf in The Lord of the Rings; first appeared on television, 1954, and has played in numerous programmes including *Callan*.

Recreation: Gardening. *Address:* c/o London Management, 235–241 Regent Street, London W1A 2JT.

STADLEN, Lewis J, actor
b Brooklyn, NY, 7 Mar 1947; prepared for the stage with the Neighborhood Playhouse; *m* Kathleen W Gray.

Toured US, commencing 1966, when he took over as Mendel in Fiddler on the Roof and continued in this part until 1968; made his New York debut at the Imperial, 26 Mar 1970, as Julie Marx (Groucho) in Minnie's Boys; rejoined the tour of Fiddler on the Roof, again as Mendel; Estelle Newman, Oct 1970, Reese in The Happiness Cage; Eisenhower, Washington, DC, Jan 1972, Harry in The Time of Your Life; Bucks County Playhouse, New Hope, Pa, Aug 1972, played in Play It Again, Sam; Broadhurst, Dec 1972, Ben Silverman in The Sunshine Boys; Broadway, Mar 1974, Dr Voltaire, Dr Pangloss, Governor, Host, Sage in Candide; Bert Wheeler, Mar 1976, directed The Big Apple; McCarter, Princeton, Mar 1977, Wheeler in Angel City; Studio Arena, Buffalo, Nov 1977, also Washington DC, title-role in Semmelweiss; has appeared in the films Portnoy's Complaint, Savages, Parades (all 1972), Serpico, etc.

Address: Actors Equity Association, 165 West 46th Street, New York, NY 10036.

STAFFORD-CLARK, Max, director
b Cambridge, 17 Mar 1941; *s* of Dr David Stafford-Clark, and his wife Dorothy Crossley (Oldfield); *e* Felsted School, Riverdale Country Day School, New York City, and Trinity College, Dublin; *m* (1) Carole Hayman (mar dis); (2) Ann Pennington.

His first professional production was Oh Gloria! at the Traverse, Edinburgh, Aug 1965; first London production, Dublin Fare, Arts, Oct 1965; associate director, Traverse, Sept 1966; after a visit to NY, Jan 1968, working with the La Mama troupe, returned to the Traverse as artistic director, Apr 1968; productions here included: The Lunatic, the Secret Sportsman and the Woman Next Door (also London), 1968; Dear Janet Rosenberg, Dear Mr Kooning (also London), Sawney Bean and Dracula, 1969; resigned as artistic director, Apr 1970, becoming director of the Traverse Workshop Company; with them he directed productions including: Mother Earth and Our Sunday Times, 1970; Sweet Alice, In the Heart of the British Museum, 1971; Hitler Dances, Amalfi, 1972; Shivvers, X, 1974; founded Joint Stock Theatre Group with William Gaskill in 1974; for the Group he has co-directed: The Speakers, 1974; Fanshen, 1975; Yesterday's News, 1976; and directed: Light Shining in Buckinghamshire, 1976; Epsom Downs, 1977, Cloud Nine, 1979; his other principal work has been for the Royal Court Theatre of which he is an Associate Director; productions include Slag, 1971, Magnificence, 1973, The Glad Hand, Prayer for my Daughter, Wheelchair Willie, 1978; Sergeant Ola and his Followers, 1979; he has also directed Tea Sex and Shakespeare (Abbey, Dublin), 1976, A Thought in Three Parts (ICA), A Mad World My Masters (co-directed, Young Vic), 1977; and at the New York Shakespeare Festival Public Theatre, 1978, for Joseph Papp, he directed Museum.

Recreations: Rugby, travel and horror movies. *Address:* 7 Gloucester Crescent, London NW1. *Tel:* 01–485 9911 *and* Royal Court Theatre, Sloane Square, London SW1. *Tel:* 01–730 5174.

STANDING, John (*né* Leon), actor
b London, 16 Aug 1934; *s* of Sir Ronald George Leon, Bt and his wife Dorothy Katherine (Standing) (Kay Hammond); *e* Eton and Millfield; *m* Jill Melford; formerly an art student.

Made his first professional appearance at the Sarah Bernhardt, Paris, playing small parts in the Shakespeare Memorial Theatre Company's Titus Andronicus; first London appearance, Saville, Sept 1959, as Mr Charlton in The Darling Buds of May; appeared with the Bristol Old Vic company, season 1960; Criterion, Apr 1961, played Andrew Rankin in The Irregular Verb To Love; Duchess, May 1962, the name part in Norman; Vaudeville, Sept 1963, appeared in the revue So Much To Remember; same theatre, July 1964, Clive Winton in See How They Run; Chichester Festival, 1966, played Sir John Melvil in The Clandestine Marriage, Lennox in Macbeth, Yepihodov in The Cherry Orchard and Mendigales in The Fighting Cock, repeating the last part at the Duke of York's, Oct 1966; Chichester, 1967, George Smerdon in The Farmer's Wife, Aimwell in The Beaux' Stratagem and Emile Tavernier in An Italian Straw Hat; Haymarket, Feb 1968, Algernon Moncrieff in The Importance of Being Earnest; same theatre, Oct 1968, Hugo and Frederick in Ring Round the Moon; Apollo, Feb 1970, Lorn Mason in Girlfriend; Chichester, 1970, Dapper in The Alchemist and Bluntschli in Arms and the Man; Globe, Aug 1972, Clive Popkiss in Popkiss; Royal Court, Dec 1972, Chap in A Sense of Detachment; Queen's, Apr 1973, took over the part of Elyot Chase in Private Lives; Oxford Festival, Sept 1974, Dauphin in Saint Joan; Los Angeles, Nov 1974, and 46th Street, NY, Feb 1975, again played Elyot Chase; Aldwych, Aug 1975, for RSC, George in Jingo; Gaiety, Dublin, Oct 1976, Dr Watson in the Festival production, Dead-Eyed Dicks; for the National Theatre Company at the Lyttleton, May 1978, played Freddy Malone in Plunder; Sept 1978, Dr Paramore in The Philanderer; May 1979, Benedict in Close of Play; films, since 1961, include: King Rat, All the Right Noises and X, Y and Zee; television, also since 1961, includes classic revivals and the series *The First Churchills*.

Favourite part: Algernon Moncrieff. *Recreations:* Painting and ski-ing. *Address:* 98 Ebury Street, London SW1. *Tel:* 01–730 1965.

STANLEY, Florence, actress
b Chicago, Ill, 1 July; *d* of Jack Schwartz and his wife Hanna (Weil); *e* Northwestern Univ; *m* Martin Newman.

Made her NY debut at the Gate, 7 Apr 1960, as Mother in Machinal; Delacorte, Aug 1964, Clytemnestra in Electra; Brooks Atkinson, May 1965, stand-by for Maureen Stapleton as Amanda Wingfield in The Glass Menagerie; Imperial, June 1965, took over from Beatrice Arthur as Yente in Fiddler on the Roof; played this last part steadily until 1971; Eugene O'Neill, Nov 1971, Pearl in The Prisoner of Second Avenue; Ambassador, Nov 1972, Bertha Gale in The Secret Affairs of Mildred Wild; New Dramatists, May 1974, Housemother in A Safe Place; has appeared in the films Up the Down Staircase, The Day of the Dolphin, The Prisoner of Second Avenue, The Fortune, etc; has also appeared on television, recently in the series Fish for ABC.

Address: Actors Equity Association, 165 West 46th Street, New York, NY 10036.

STANLEY, Kim, actress (*née* Patricia Reid)
b Tularosa, New Mexico, 11 Feb 1921; *d* of Dr J T Reid and

his wife Ann (Miller); *e* Texas State University and University of New Mexico; *m* (1) Bruce Hall (mar dis); (2) Curt Conway (mar dis); (3) Alfred Ryder.

First acted with stock companies in Louisville, Kentucky, and Pompton Lakes, New Jersey; went to New York, where she worked as a fashion model and a waitress; then joined the Actors Studio and studied with Elia Kazan and Lee Strasberg; Carnegie Recital Hall, Dec 1948, played Iris in The Dog Beneath the Skin; in 1949 appeared at the Provincetown Playhouse in him, at the Cherry Lane, in Yes Is for a Very Young Man, and at the Equity Library, in the title-role of Saint Joan; while in the last play, she was offered her first Broadway role by Kermit Bloomgarden at the Fulton, Dec 1949, as a replacement for Julie Harris in the role of Felisa in Montserrat; ANTA, Jan 1951, Adela in The House of Bernarda Alba; Playhouse, April, 1952, Anna Reeves in The Chase; Music Box, Feb 1953, Millie Owens in Picnic, for which she won the New York Drama Critics Award; Playhouse, Oct 1954, Georgette Thomas in The Travelling Lady; Madison Square Garden, Dec 1954, Mrs Theodore Herzl in The Great Dreamer; Music Box, March, 1955, Cherie in Bus Stop and won both the Donaldson Award and the New York Drama Critics Poll Award for her performance; Belasco, Jan 1957, Virgina in A Clearing in the Woods; first appearance on the London stage was at the Comedy, Jan 1958, as Margaret in Cat on a Hot Tin Roof; Helen Hayes, NY, Oct 1958, Sara Melody in A Touch of the Poet; Morosco, Oct 1959, Les de Lonval in Chéri; Music Box, Apr 1961, Elizabeth von Ritter in A Far Country; Booth, Jan 1963, Sue Barker in Natural Affection; Morosco, June 1964, played Masha in the Actors Studio production of The Three Sisters; again played Masha at the Aldwych, London, May 1965, when the Actors Studio made its London début in the World Theatre Season; entered films, 1958, in The Goddess, and has since played in Seance on a Wet Afternoon; has played frequently on television, notably in Clash by Night, The Travelling Lady, and as Cleopatra and Joan of Arc on *You Are There* programs, and received an Emmy for her performance in A Cardinal Act of Mercy, 1963.

Address: c/o Lucy Kroll Agency, 390 West End Avenue, New York, NY. *Tel:* TR 7–0627.

STAPLETON, Jean (*née* Jeanne Murray), actress
b New York City, 19 Jan; *d* of Joseph E Murray and his wife Marie (Stapleton); *e* Wadleigh High School, NY, Hunter College; *m* William H Putch; prepared for the stage with Carli Laklan at the American Apprentice Theatre, with James Rose and William Hansen at the American Actors Company, with Joseph Anthony and Peter Frye at the American Theatre Wing, and with Harold Clurman; formerly a secretary.

Sang with the Robert Shaw Chorale, then toured the women's club circuits performing Double Dozen Double Damask Dinner Napkins, 1940; made her legitimate debut at the Greenwood Playhouse, Peaks Island, Maine, 1941, in stock, later appearing in stock at Peterborough, NH, Playhouse, the Whitefield, NH, Chase Barn Playhouse, etc, 1947–48; first appeared in New York at the Equity Library Theater, 4 Feb 1948, as Mrs Watty in The Corn Is Green; toured, 1948–49, as Myrtle Mae in Harvey; toured, 1949–50, in this same part; toured, 1950–51, as Mrs Coffman in Come Back, Little Sheba; repeated this part in stock theatres, 1950–53; Circle in the Square, Nov 1953, played Mother in America Gothic; Playhouse, Dec 1953, Inez in In the Summer House; 46th Street, May 1955, Sister in Damn Yankees; Shubert, Nov 1956, Sue in Bells Are Ringing; began her long

association with her husband's theatre, the Totem Pole Playhouse, Fayettesville, Pa, summer 1958, as Woody in Goodbye, My Fancy, Miss Cooper in Separate Tables, Mother in Charm, Grace in Bus Stop, and Mme St-Pé in Waltz of the Toreadors; Walnut Street, Philadelphia, Pa, Sept 1958, Swart Petry in A Swim in the Sea; Winter Garden, NY, Mar 1959, Maisie Madigan in Juno; Totem Pole Playhouse, 1959, Sally Adams in Call Me Madam, and 1960, Laura Partridge in The Solid Gold Cadillac; Longacre, Jan 1961, Mrs Ochs in Rhinoceros, and subsequently toured California in this part; Totem Pole Playhouse, 1962, Mrs Keller in The Miracle Worker, Emma in Apple in the Attic, the revue A Thurber Carnival, Opal in Everybody Loves Opal, and Aunt Eller in Oklahoma!; 1963, Mrs Baker in Come Blow Your Horn, Mrs Spofford in Gentlemen Prefer Blondes, and Nannie in All for Mary; Winter Garden, Mar 1964, Mrs Strakosh in Funny Girl; Totem Pole Playhouse, 1964, Brewster in A Rainy Day in Newark, Rosemary in Picnic, Annabelle in George Washington Slept Here, Mrs Walworth in Speaking of Murder, Mrs Pearce in My Fair Lady, Mrs Yoder in Papa Is All, and the Mother Abbess in The Sound of Music; later played Anna Leonowens in The King and I, Bloody Mary in South Pacific, Lottie in The Dark at the Top of the Stairs; 1971, Dolly Gallagher Levi in Hello, Dolly!; 1972, Mrs Baer in Butterflies Are Free, Lola in Come Back, Little Sheba, Opal in Everybody Loves Opal; Ahmanson, Los Angeles, Cal, Apr 1974, appeared in The Time of the Cuckoo; Totem Pole, 1975, title role in The Secret Affairs of Mildred Wild; in Hay Fever and The Late Christopher Bean, 1976; The Reluctant Debutante and The Show-Off, 1977; The Great Sebastian's, Daisy Mayne (title role), Little Mary Sunshine, 1978; A Murder is Announced (as Miss Marple?, Papa is All, 1979; toured, 1979–80, in the title role of Daisy Mayme; first appeared in films in Damn Yankees, and has since played in Bells Are Ringing, Something Wild, Cold Turkey, Klute, etc; has appeared on television in *Omnibus, Camera Three, Naked City,* You Can't Take It With You, Aunt Mary, etc; has played Edith Bunker in the series *All in the Family* since 1971, winning three Emmy Awards for this role; holder of honorary degrees from Emerson College, Boston, Hood College, Frederick, Md, and Monmouth College, NJ.

Recreations: Swimming, singing, reading. *Address:* Columbia Broadcasting System, 4024 Radford Avenue, North Hollywood, Calif 91604.

STAPLETON, Maureen, actress
b Troy, New York, 21 June 1925; *d* of John P Stapleton and his wife Irene (Walsh); *e* Troy High School; *m* (1) Max Allentuck (mar dis); (2) David Rayfiel (mar dis); studied for the stage at the Herbert Berghof Acting School (Evening).

Made her first appearance in NY, at the Booth, Oct 1946, as Sarah Tansey in The Playboy of the Western World; Martin Beck, Nov 1947, played Iras in Antony and Cleopatra; Hudson, Mar 1949, played Miss Hatch in Detective Story; Coronet, Feb 1950, Emily Williams in The Bird Cage; Martin Beck, Feb 1951, Serafina delle Rose in The Rose Tatto, and received both the Antoinette Perry (Tony) and Peabody Awards for this performance; at the same theatre, Jan 1953, took over the part of Elizabeth Proctor in The Crucible; Ethel Barrymore, Feb 1953, Bella in The Emperor's Clothes; City Center, Dec 1953, Anne in Richard III, with José Ferrer; Phoenix, May 1954, Masha in The Seagull; Playhouse, Apr 1955, Flora in Twenty-Seven Wagon's Full of Cotton; Martin Beck, Mar 1957, Lady Torrance in Orpheus Descending; Morosco, Dec 1958, Ida in The Cold Wind and the Warm; Hudson, Feb 1960, Carrie in Toys in the Attic;

Brooks Atkinson, May 1965, Amanda Wingfield in a revival of The Glass Menagerie; City Center, Oct, and Billy Rose, Nov 1966, Serafina delle Rose in The Rose Tattoo; Plymouth, Feb 1968, Karen Nash, Muriel Tate, and Norma Hubley in Plaza Suite; Lyceum, Feb 1970, Beatrice Chambers in Norman, Is That You?; Plymouth, Dec 1970, Evy Meara in The Gingerbread Lady; Billy Rose, Mar 1972, Georgie Elgin in The Country Girl; Ambassador, Nov 1972, Mildred Wild in The Secret Affairs of Mildred Wild; Walnut, Philadelphia, Nov 1973, Serafina Delle Rose in The Rose Tattoo; Circle in the Square, 27 Apr 1974, appeared in a Benefit Gala; Mark Taper Forum, Los Angeles, Nov 1974, Juno Boyle in Juno and the Paycock; Circle in the Square, Dec 1975, Amanda Wingfield in The Glass Menagerie; John Golden, 1978, took over as Fonsia Dorsey in The Gin Game; appeared in her first film, 1960, in Lonelyhearts, and has since appeared in The Fugitive Kind, A View from the Bridge, Bye, Bye Birdie, Interiors, The Runner Stumbles, etc; has made numerous television appearances, including For Whom the Bell Tolls, All the King's Men, Tell Me Where It Hurts, Queen of the Stardust Ballroom, Cat on a Hot Tin Roof, etc; received an Emmy Award for her role in Save Me a Place at Forest Lawn, 1967.

STARKIE, Martin, director, dramatic author and presenting manager
b Burnley, Lancashire, 25 Nov 1925; *s* of Henry Starkie and his wife Pauline Anne (Martin); *e* Burnley Grammar School and Exeter College, Oxford; trained for the stage at LAMDA.

He was an actor from 1947–64, playing in repertory at Shanklin and appearing in two Canterbury Festivals, 1949 and 1951; began his career as a director at the Watergate, July 1950, with a triple-bill of The Shadow of the Glen, Riders to the Sea and The Tinker's Wedding; Playhouse, Oxford, Oct 1959, presented (for Classic Presentations) his adaptation of The Torrents of Spring, in which he played Sanin; Oxford, Oct 1964, adapted, directed and produced Canterbury Tales; directed A Beach of Strangers, Criterion, Dec 1967; Phoenix, Mar 1968, presented and co-directed Canterbury Tales, in a version with book by himself and Nevill Coghill; made his Broadway début as director of the same production at the Eugene O'Neill, 1969; production consultant to various overseas productions of Canterbury Tales, 1969–75; presented Holy Bedroc, 1974; wrote, with Nevill Coghill, More Canterbury Tales, and directed the première of this at Her Majesty's, Melbourne, Oct 1976; produced and directed the Nevill Coghill Eightieth Birthday production of The Canterbury Tales, at the Shaftesbury, Apr 1979; television appearances, from 1949, included; L'Aiglon and Saint Joan; also adapted The Torrents of Spring and The Bostonians for the medium; Chairman, Classic Presentations Ltd; Managing Director, Chanticleer Productions Ltd.
Recreations: Music, travel. *Address:* c/o Spotlight, 47 Cranbourn Street, London WC2. *Tel:* 01–437 7631.

STEADMAN, Alison, actress
b Liverpool, 26 Aug 1946; *d* of George Percival Steadman and his wife Marjorie (Evans); *e* Childwall Valley High School; trained at East-15 Acting School (1966–69); *m* Mike Leigh; formerly a secretary in the Liverpool Probation Service.

First professional appearance in The Prime of Miss Jean Brodie at the Theatre Royal, Lincoln, 1969, where she also played Ophelia; subsequently in repertory at Bolton, Worcester (where she was in the original production of The Plotters of Cabbage Patch Corner), Exeter, the Traverse

Theatre, Edinburgh (in Mike Leigh's The Jaws of Death), and Nottingham, where she played Desdemona; her London appearances began with Mike Leigh's Wholesome Glory at the Theatre Upstairs, 1973, where she was also seen as Sylvia in The Sea Anchor, Jul 1974; she was in The Pope's Wedding, Bush, 1973, Guinevere in The King, Shaw, May 1974; Anthea in Joking Apart, Globe, Mar 1979; at Hampstead she was Abigail in Abigail's Party, for which she won the Evening Standard and Plays and Players Best Actress Awards for 1977, and Sonya in Uncle Vanya, Nov 1979; television work includes Hard Labour, 1973, Nuts in May, 1976, and Abigail's Party, 1977, all devised by Mike Leigh, also Through the Night, 1979, and Pasmore, 1980.
Address: c/o Bill Horne, 15 Little Newport Street, London WC2.

STEELE, Tommy (*né* Hicks), actor
b Bermondsey, London, 17 Dec 1936; *s* of Thomas Walter Hicks and his wife Elizabeth Ellen (Bennett); *e* Bacon's School for Boys, Bermondsey; *m* Ann Donoughue; formerly a merchant seaman.

Made his first appearance on the stage at the Empire Theatre, Sunderland, Nov 1956, in variety; first appeared in London, at the Dominion Theatre, May 1957, also in variety; first London appearance in pantomime at the Coliseum, Dec 1958, as Buttons in Cinderella (Rodgers and Hammerstein); at the Old Vic, Nov 1960, played Tony Lumpkin in She Stoops to Conquer; Cambridge, Mar 1963, played Arthur Kipps in Half-a-Sixpence; following a run of twenty months he made his first appearance in New York at the Broadhurst, Apr 1965, in the same musical; Queen's, Dec 1968, played Truffaldino in The Servant of Two Masters; Palladium, Dec 1969, Dick in Dick Whittington; after a season in Las Vegas, appeared at the Adelphi, Apr 1971, in Meet Me in London; Palladium, Apr 1973, appeared in variety; same theatre, Dec 1974, title-role in Hans Andersen; toured, Sept 1976, in The Tommy Steele Anniversary Show; Palladium, Dec 1977, directed and again played Hans in the revival of Hans Andersen; Prince of Wales, 1979, An Evening With Tommy Steele; appeared at the Royal Variety Performance, Nov 1957, and Nov 1963; entered films, Oct 1956, in Kill Me Tomorrow, and subsequent pictures include: The Tommy Steele Story, The Happiest Millionaire, Half A Sixpence, Finian's Rainbow and Where's Jack?; first appeared on television Oct, 1956, in Off The Record; devised for television and appeared in Quincy's Quest, 1979; in 1974 composed and recorded his musical autobiography, My Life, My Song.
Address: c/o Talent Artists Ltd, 13 Bruton Street, London W1X 8JY. *Tel:* 01–493 0343.

STEIN, Joseph, playwright
b New York City, 30 May; *s* of Charles Stein and his wife Emma (Rosenblum); *e* College of the City of New York (BSS 1934), Columbia University, 1935–7; *m* (1) Sadie Singer; (2) Elisa Loti, actress; formerly engaged as psychiatric social worker.

With Will Glickman wrote sketches for his first NY show, Lend an Ear, produced at the National, 16 Dec 1948; with Will Glickman wrote Mrs Gibbons' Boys, 1949; sketches for Alive and Kicking, 1950; Inside USA, 1951; Plain and Fancy, 1955; Mr Wonderful, 1956; The Body Beautiful, 1958; Juno, Take Me Along, 1959; Enter Laughing, 1963; Fiddler on the Roof, for which he received the Antoinette Perry (Tony) Award and New York Drama Critics Award, and which is the longest-running musical in NY history, 1964; Zorba, 1968; co-produced We Bombed in New Haven, 1968; with Hugh

Wheeler revised the book of Irene, 1973; book for King of Hearts, 1978; Carmelina, 1979 (with Alan Jay Lerner); wrote the screenplays for Enter Laughing, 1967, and Fiddler on the Roof, 1971; wrote many radio scripts, notably for Henry Morgan, 1946–9; for television has written many shows, notably for *NBC Comedy Hour*, 1950–2, *Your Show of Shows*, 1952–3, *The Sid Caesar Show*, 1953–4, etc; council member, 1970–79, The Dramatists' Guild.

Address: 250 West 57th Street, New York, NY 10019. *Tel:* 246–9709.

STEPHENS, Robert, actor and director
b Bristol, 14 July 1931; *s* of Rueben Stephens and his wife Gladys (Deverell); *e* Bristol; *m* (1) Tarn Bassett (mar dis); (2) Maggie Smith (mar dis); trained for the stage at the Bradford Civic Theatre School.

Began his career with Caryl Jenner Mobile Theatre Company; made his first appearance in London, as a member of the English Stage Company, at the Royal Court, Apr 1956, when he played Judge Haythorne in The Crucible; and subsequently played the following parts: Don Luis Meija in Don Juan and Lord Byron in The Death of Satan (double-bill), an Aunt, a Radio Commentator, and Bank Manager in Cards of Identity, 3rd God in The Good Woman of Setzuan, Mr Dorilant in The Country Wife, 1956; transferred with the last production, to the Adelphi, Feb 1957, when he played Quack; returned to the Royal Court, May 1957, to play M Lepedura in The Apollo de Bellac, followed by Jim in Yes—and After (in a Production without Décor), 2nd Native and Mr Fosdick in The Making of Moo, and Alexander in How Can We Save Father?; Krank in The Waters of Babylon (in a Production without Décor), 1957; Palace, Sept 1957, played Graham in The Entertainer; Royal Court, Feb 1958, played George Dillon in Epitaph for George Dillon, transferring with the production to the Comedy, May 1958, under the title George Dillon; made his first appearance in New York at the Golden, Nov 1958, in the same part and play (under the original title of Epitaph for George Dillon) and after a short break, re-opened at the Henry Miller, Jan 1959; Royal Court, July 1959, played Phillipe de Croze in Look After Lulu, transferring with the production to the New, Sept 1959; Royal Court, Sept 1959 (in a Production without Décor), played Peter in The Kitchen; Cambridge, Feb 1960, played Miller in The Wrong Side of the Park; Royal Court, June 1961, again played Peter in The Kitchen; at the same theatre, Dec 1962, played Colin Broughton in The Sponge Room, and Jonathan Pearce in Squat Betty (double-bill); Chichester Festival, June 1963, and Edinburgh Festival, Sept 1963, played the Dauphin in Saint Joan; joined the National Theatre Company to appear at the Old Vic, Oct 1963, as Horatio in the inaugural production of Hamlet; he has since played the following parts with the National Theatre Company: Dauphin in Saint Joan, Captain Plume in The Recruiting Officer, 1963; Father Benedict in Andorra, Man in Play, Atahuallpa in The Royal Hunt of the Sun (also Chichester Festival), Sandy Tyrell in Hay Fever, 1964; Benedick in Much Ado About Nothing, Sir David Lindsay in Armstrong's Last Goodnight and Tom Wrench in Trelawny of the Wells (also Chichester Festival), 1965; Old Vic, Nov 1965, again played Tom Wrench in Trelawny of the Wells; played Leonido in A Bond Honoured and took over Harold Gorringe in Black Comedy in a double-bill, 1966; Kurt in The Dance of Death, Vershinin in The Three Sisters, Jacques in As You Like It, the title-role in Tartuffe, 1967; Most Unwarrantable Intrusion (directed in Triple Bill), Frederick Lowndes in Home and Beauty, 1968; Macrune and other parts in Macrune's Guevara (also co-directed), 1969; Francis Archer in

The Beaux' Stratagem (also Los Angeles), Vershinin in The Three Sisters (Los Angeles only), Ejlert Loevborg in Hedda Gabler, 1970; became an Associate Director of the National Theatre in 1969; Queen's, Sept 1972, Elyot Chase in Private Lives; Chichester, season 1973, played Trigorin in The Seagull, May; Open Space, Nov 1973, directed Apropos of Falling Sleet, playing Apollon; Greenwich, Jan–Mar 1974, played Pastor Manders in Ghosts, Trigorin in The Seagull, and Claudius in Hamlet; Garrick, Mar 1975, appeared in Murderer; Open Air, Regent's Park, July 1975, appeared in Zoo Story; Broadhurst, NY, Aug 1975, took over the title-role in Sherlock Holmes; Open Air, Regent's Park, season 1976 and 1977, played Othello; for the National Theatre Company, Olivier, Feb 1978, Gayev in The Cherry Orchard, Apr, the Mayor in Braud; Sept Maskwell in The Double Dealer; and Cottesloe, Nov 1978, Sir Flute Parsons in Has 'Washington' Legs?; since 1960, has appeared in films including: A Taste of Honey, Cleopatra, Travels With My Aunt, The Prime of Miss Jean Brodie, QB VII, etc; television performances include: Fairy Tales of NY, June Fall (USA), Vienna 1900, etc.

Favourite parts: George Dillon, Biff in Death of a Salesman, and Iago. *Recreations:* Cooking, gymnastics, and swimming. *Address:* c/o Film Rights Ltd, 113–117 Wardour Street, London W1.

STERLING, Jan (*née* Jane Sterling Adriance), actress
b New York City, 3 Apr 1923; *d* of William Allen Adriance; *m* (1) John Merivale (mar dis), (2) Paul Douglas (dec); prepared for the stage at the Fay Compton Dramatic School, London.

Made her New York debut under the name Jane Sterling at the Morosco, 25 Jan 1938, as Chris Faringdon in Bachelor Born; Lyceum, Dec 1939, played Nancy Holmes in When We Were Married; Hudson, May 1940, Judith Weaver in Grey Farm; 46th Street, 1941, took over from Virginia Field as Florrie in Panama Hattie; Longacre, Feb 1943, Margaret Stanley in This Rock; Music Box, 1944, took over from Beatrice Pearson as Jan Lupton in Over 21; as Jan Sterling appeared at the Plymouth, Nov 1945, as Edith Bowsmith in The Rugged Path; John Golden, Dec 1945, Zelda Rainier in Dunnigan's Daughter; Belasco, Apr 1946, Janet Alexander in This Too Shall Pass; Plymouth, Oct 1946, Daphne Stillington in Present Laughter; Erlanger, Chicago, Ill, 1947, Billie Dawn in Born Yesterday, and took over from Judy Holliday in this part at the Lyceum, May 1949; toured as Mary in John Loves Mary; Cort, Mar 1949, Karen Norwood in Two Blind Mice; Ethel Barrymore, Jan 1957, Marry Murray in Small War on Murray Hill; Chicago, Aug 1958, played in The Spider's Web; Cort, Oct 1962, Ann in The Perfect Setup; Booth, Nov 1963, Madelaine Robbins in Once for the Asking; Pocket, Feb 1965, Terry in Friday Night and Mary in Mary Agnes Is 35; toured, Feb 1969, as Sophie, the Baroness Lemberg in White Lies, and Clea in Black Comedy; Ethel Barrymore, 1970, took over from Peggy Cass as Mollie Molloy in The Front Page; Queens Playhouse, Aug 1974, Lola in Come Back, Little Sheba, and repeated this part at the Studio Arena, Buffalo, NY, winter 1974; Royal Alexandra, Toronto, Canada, July 1975, played in Hot 1 Baltimore; Billy Rose, Jan 1978, Mary in The November People; first appeared in films in Johnny Belinda, 1948, and has since played in Union Station, Caged, The High and the Mighty, The Harder They Fall; 1984, Sammy Somebody, etc; has appeared on television in various dramatic shows, including *The Guiding Light*.

Address: Actors Equity Association, 165 West 46th Street, New York, NY 10036.

STERNHAGEN, Frances, actress

b Washington, DC, 13 Jan 1930; *d* of John Meyer Sternhagen and his wife Gertrude (Hussey); *e* Maderia School, Virginia, and Vassar College (BA 1951); *m* Thomas A Carlin; prepared for the stage with Sanford Meisner at the Neighborhood Playhouse, at the Perry-Mansfield School of Theatre, and the Vassar College Drama Dept; formerly a teacher at the Milton Academy, Massachusetts.

First appeared on the professional stage at Bryn Mawr, Pennsylvania, Summer Theatre, 1948, as Laura in The Glass Menagerie and Mrs Manningham in Angel Street; at the Arena Stage Washington, DC, Jan 1953, played Margery Pinchwife in The Country Wife, Feb 1953, Mrs Webb, in Our Town, May 1953, Nancy Stoddard in The Country Girl, Sept 1953, Phyllis Carmichael in My Heart's in the Highlands, Oct 1953, Juliette in Thieves' Carnival, Nov 1953, Doto in A Phoenix Too Frequent and Ma Kirby in The Happy Journey from Trenton to Camden, Jan 1954, Muriel McComber in Ah, Wilderness! and, Apr 1954, Elvira in Blithe Spirit; for the summer 1954 season joined the Olney, Maryland, Theatre, and played Lavinia Chamberlayne in The Cocktail Party, Ann in Outward Bound, Georgie Elgin in The Country Girl, and Lady Ariadne Utterword in Heartbreak House; made her New York début at the Cherry Lane, 1 Feb 1955, as Eva in Thieves' Carnival; Sarah Bernhardt, Paris, June 1955, played Miss T Muse in The Skin of Our Teeth, toured the US in this part, and repeated it at the ANTA, NY, Aug 1955; Phoenix, Oct 1955, Widow Yang in The Carefree Tree; Cherry Lane, Feb 1956, Lydia Carew in The Admirable Bashville; Renata, June 1957, Margery Pinchwife in The Country Wife; toured, 1958, as Opal in The Isle of Cipango and the Postmistress in A Pound on Demand; Rooftop, Sept 1958, took over as the Nymph in Ulysses in Night Town; York, Feb 1959, title-role in The Saintliness of Margery Kempe; Longacre, Apr 1960, Dee Jones in Viva Madison Avenue!; toured, July 1960, as Miss Madrigal in The Chalk Garden; Provincetown Playhouse, July 1960, took over as Selma Chargesse in Red Eye of Love; McCarter, Princeton, New Jersey, 1960, Gwendolyn Fairfax in The Importance of Being Earnest; Sheridan Square, Sept 1961, Hypatia Tarleton in Misalliance; Henry Miller's, Mar 1962, Alice McAnany in Great Day in the Morning; Olney, Maryland, Aug 1962, Mrs Levi in The Matchmaker; Brandeis, Waltham, Massachusetts, June 1963, Sabina in The Skin of Our Teeth; East End, NY, Oct 1963, Lois in A Matter of Like Life and Death; Cherry Lane, Jan 1964, was in Play; Writers Stage, Dec 1964, Rose in The Room, and Flora in A Slight Ache, in a double-bill with the overall title The New Pinter Plays; Billy Rose, Oct 1965, Mrs Ashton Dilke in The Right Honourable Gentleman; St Clement's Church, Dec 1966, Mrs Hopewell in The Displaced Person; Lyceum, for APA-Phoenix, Oct 1968, Lavinia Chamberlayne in The Cocktail Party, and Jan 1969, Loreleen in Cock-a-Doodle Dandy; Vivian Beaumont, Feb 1971, Widow Quin in The Playboy of the Western World; Longacre, Jan 1972, Mavis Parodus Bryson in The Sign in Sidney Brustein's Window; Vivian Beaumont, Nov 1972, Paulina in Enemies; Eugene O'Neill, Nov 1973, played various parts in The Good Doctor, and won the Antoinette Perry (Tony) Award for this performance; Plymouth, Oct 1974, Dora Strang in Equus, and continued in this part until June 1976; Minskoff, May 1978, Eliza Gant in Angel; New Apollo, Feb 1979, Ethel Thayer in On Golden Pond, transferring to the Century, Sept 1979; well over a year; entered films in 1967 in Up the Down Staircase, and has since played in The Tiger Makes Out, 1970, The Hospital, 1971, Two People, 1973, Fedora, 1977, Starting Over, 1979; since 1956 has appeared frequently on television in dramatic programs,

as Toni in the serial *Love of Life,* 1968, and as Phyllis Corrigan in *Doctors,* 1970, etc; received the Clarence Derwent and Obie Awards for The Admirable Bashville and the Obie for The New Pinter Plays.

Favourite parts: Margery Pinchwife, Sabina, Dora in Equus, and Ethel in On Golden Pond. *Recreations:* Caring for her six children, singing, painting. *Address:* 152 Sutton Manor Road, New Rochelle, NY 10805. *Tel:* 914–632–5696.

STEVENS, Roger L, producer

b Detroit, Michigan, 12 Mar 1910; *e* Choate School, Wallingford, Conn, and University of Michigan; *m* Christine Gesell.

Has produced or co-produced the following: Twelfth Night, 1949; The Cellar and the Well, Peter Pan, 1950; Peer Gynt, The Fourposter, Barefoot in Athens, The Grand Tour, 1951; Mr Pickwick, 1952; The Emperor's Clothes, Escapade, Tea and Sympathy, In the Summer House, The Remarkable Mr Pennypacker, Sabrina Fair, 1953; Ondine, The Golden Apple, All Summer Long, The Travelling Lady, The Confidential Clerk, The Bad Seed, Flowering Peach, The Winner, 1954; The Dark Is Light Enough, Bus Stop, Cat on a Hot Tin Roof, Once upon a Tailor, Island of Goats, Tiger at the Gates, 1955; Tamburlaine the Great, Major Barbara, Separate Tables, The Sleeping Prince, The Lovers, The Ponder Heart, 1956; A Clearing in the Woods, The Waltz of the Toreadors, The Sin of Pat Muldoon, Small War on Murray Hill, Orpheus Descending, A Hole in the Head, West Side Story, Nude with Violin, The Rope Dancers, Under Milk Wood, The Country Wife, A Boy Growing Up, Time Remembered, 1957; Present Laughter, Summer of the Seventeenth Doll, The Firstborn, Howie, The Visit, A Handful of Fire, Joyce Grenfell Requests the Pleasure, The Gazebo, A Touch of the Poet, The Pleasure of His Company, Goldilocks, The Cold Wind and the Warm, Cue for Passion, The Man in the Dog Suit, Edwin Booth, 1958; Look After Lulu, Juno, Much Ado About Nothing, Chéri, The Flowering Cherry, Five Finger Exercise, Silent Night, Lonely Night, 1959; The Tumbler, The Best Man, Duel of Angels, Rosemary, The Alligators, Under the Yum-Yum Tree, 1960; Conquering Hero, A Far Country, Julia, Jake, and Uncle Joe, Midgie Purvis, Mary, Mary, The Importance of Being Oscar, Oh Dad, Poor Dad, Mama's Hung You in the Closet and I'm Feelin' So Sad (London), The Caretaker, Blood, Sweat, and Stanley Poole, Everybody Loves Opal, A Man for All Seasons, First Love, 1961; Romulus, Tender Loving Care (Palm Beach), The Magnificent Gourmet (England), Judith (London), Banderol (Philadelphia), Step on a Crack, Calculated Risk, Tiger, Tiger, Burning Bright, 1962; The Milk Train Doesn't Stop Here Anymore, Andorra, Mary, Mary (London), Children from Their Games, On the Town (London), Oh Dad, Poor Dad, etc, A Case of Libel, The Private Ear and the Public Eye, Bicycle Ride to Nevada, The Time of the Barracudas (California), A Rainy Day in Newark, 1963; The Chinese Prime Minister, Double-talk (a double-bill entitled The Dirty Old Man and Sarah and the Sax), The Last Analysis, Beekman Place, The Physicists, Slow Dance on a Killing Ground, Poor Richard, 1964; Diamond Orchid, Half a Sixpence, The Chinese Prime Minister (London), The Homecoming (London), 1965; Indians, 1969; Sheep on the Runway, Conduct Unbecoming, 1970; the Royal Shakspeare Company's production of Old Times, 1971; The Country Girl, The Pleasure of His Company, Captain Brassbound's Conversion, Lost in the Stars, Leonard Bernstein's Mass, 1972; The Jockey Club Stakes, Finishing Touches, The Enchanted, 1973; The Prodigal Daughter, Jumpers, London Assurance, Headhunters, Perfect Pitch, 1974; Present Laughter, The Scarecrow, The Skin of Out Teeth, Summer Brave, Sweet Bird of Youth, The Royal Family, 1975; A Matter of Gravity, The Heiress, Legend, A Texas Trilogy, No Man's Land, 1976; Annie, 1977; Deathtrap, 1978; Bedroom Farce, Carmelina, The Last of Mrs Cheyney (tour), Night and Day, 1979; Betrayal, West Side Story, 1980; President of Producers' Theatre during its existence; past President of the Phoenix Theatre; past President of the New Dramatists Committee; Member of the Board of Directors of ANTA; Member of the Executive Committee, and an original trustee of the American Shakespeare Festival Theatre and Academy; member of the Board of the Metropolitan Opera Company; former General Administrator of the Actors Studio Theatre; Special Assistant to President Lyndon B Johnson on the Arts; past Chairman, National Council on the Arts; past Chairman of the Board of Trustees of the John F Kennedy Center for the Performing Arts; Chairman of the Board of the American Film Institute; holds the degrees of Hon D Hum, Wayne State University, Hon LHD, Tulane University, and Hon D Humane Letters, University of Michigan.

Clubs: Century, Racquet, and Tennis, Bohemian, Phi Gamma Delta, The Pilgrims of the US. *Address:* 1501 Broadway, New York, NY 10036. *Tel:* 354–8350.

STEVENS, Ronnie, actor
b London, 2 Sept 1925; *s* of Henry Edward Stevens, and his wife Fanny Elizabeth (Carpenter); *e* Peckham Central School and Camberwell School of Art; *m* Ann Bristow; trained for the stage at PARADA.

First appeared on the stage in 1948 at the Chepstow Theatre Club, London, in the revue Ad Lib; appeared from 1948 to 1953 in revues at the Chepstow and other little theatres; made his first West End appearance at the Hippodrome, 1953, in the revue High Spirits followed by Intimacy at 8.30, Criterion, Apr 1954; For Amusement Only, Apollo, June 1956; Royal Court, Jan 1960, played five parts in The Lily White Boys; Lyric, Hammersmith, Apr 1960, appeared in The Billy Barnes Revue; Victoria Palace, Aug 1960, Hard-Boiled Herman in Rose Marie; Saville, Aug 1961, appeared in The Lord Chamberlain Regrets; Prince Charles, Apr 1963, in Round Leicester Square; Arts, Aug 1964, Cecil in Mr Whatnot; toured, Sept 1965, for Prospect Theatre Company, as Sir Fopling Flutter in The Man of Mode; also as Feste in Twelfth Night, Jan 1968, and as Moricet in The Birdwatcher, 1969; at the Open Air, Regent's Park, played Speed in Two Gentlemen of Verona and Launcelot Gobbo in The Merchant of Venice, 1969; Quince in A Midsummer Night's Dream and Leonato in Much Ado About Nothing, 1970; Nov 1970, for Prospect, again toured in a programme of dramatic readings, The World's a Stage; has appeared as dame in several pantomimes, since 1963; July 1971 for Prospect Productions played The Fool in King Lear and Sir Nathaniel in Love's Labour's Lost at the Edinburgh Festival followed by Australian tour, February 1972, and season at the Aldwych Theatre, June 1972; July 1972, founder member of The Actors' Company; played Pontagnac in Ruling The Roost, Richardetto in 'Tis Pity She's A Whore and Three Arrows; February 1973, Sparkish in The Country Wife for Prospect Productions; March 1973, also for Prospect, played Feste in Twelfth Night, Estete in Royal Hunt Of The Sun and Gower in Pericles, at Edinburgh Festival, Round House season and extensive Middle East, European, Russian and Hong Kong tours; Her Majesty's, June 1974, Gower in Pericles; September 1974, season at the Leeds Playhouse, playing Davies in The Caretaker, Joseph And The Amazing Technicolour Dreamcoat and Trinculo in The Tempest,

Quangle Wangle in Owl and the Pussycat; Wyndhams, February 1975, Trinculo in The Tempest; August 1975, season with the Bristol Old Vic, playing Loach in The National Health, Bargee in Sgt Musgrave's Dance, Sir Percy Shorter in Habeas Corpus, Mr Gradgrind in Hard Times and Fred Phipps in Dry Rot; same theatre, Mar 1976, Chandebise in A Flea in Her Ear; St George's Elizabethan Theatre, 1976 season: Feste in Twelfth Night, Peter in Romeo and Juliet, Bishop of Ely and Tyrrel in Richard III; 1977: Antonio in The Merchant of Venice, Pompey in Measure for Measure, Osric in Hamlet and Doctor Cains in The Merry Wives of Windsor; Old Vic, Christmas 1977, Herr Von Cuckoo in The Gingerbread Man; Old Vic, 1978, for Prospect Productions: The Dauphin in St Joan, Sir Andrew in Twelfth Night, Skipps in The Lady's Not For Burning; and for the Old Vic Company, Aug–Dec 1979, Friar Laurence in Romeo and Juliet, Bobchinsky in The Government Inspector and Major Lloyd in The 88; films, since 1952, include: I'm All Right Jack, A Home of Your Own, Goodbye Mr Chips, and SOS Titanic; television, since 1949, includes plays, and several comedy and musical series.

Recreations: Music, painting. *Address:* c/o Ronnie Waters, International Creative Management Ltd, 22 Grafton Street, London W1X 3LD. *Tel:* 01–629 8080.

STEVENSON, Margot, actress
b New York City, 8 Feb 1914; *d* of Charles A Stevenson and his wife Frances Anderson (Riley); *e* Brearley School, NY; *m* (1) Robert Russell (mar dis); (2) Val Avery; prepared for the stage with Laura Eliot, Mary Tarcai, and Don Richardson.

Made her first appearance on the stage at the Empire Theatre, NY, 21 Nov 1932, as Alice in Firebird, with Judith Anderson; Selwyn, Jan 1933, played a Guest in Evensong; Playhouse, Aug 1933, Lady Bay-Clender in A Party; Martin Beck, Feb 1935, Bella Hedley in The Barretts of Wimpole Street; Cort, Apr 1935, Estelle in Symphony; 49th Street, Jan 1936, Berna Bowen in Truly Valiant; Morosco, June 1936, Vera in Call It a Day; at Centerville, Mass, July–Aug 1936, appeared in A Family Man, Carry Me Back, etc; Music Box, Oct 1936, played Kendall Adams in Stage Door; Booth, Dec 1936, Alice in You Can't Take It with You, which she continued to play until 1938; Ivoryton, Conn, 1941, played Ellen Turner in The Male Animal; Cort, NY, Dec 1941, played Pam in Golden Wings; City Center, Dec 1944, Meg in Little Women; Plymouth, Nov 1945, took over as Edith Bowsmith in The Rugged Path; National, Oct 1948, Maudie in The Leading Lady; made her first appearance on the London stage at the St James's, 3 Dec 1952, as Marianne Ames in Sweet Peril; Aldwych, May 1953, Alice Sherman in The Seven Year Itch; at the Longacre, NY, Oct 1955, played Mrs Perry in The Young and Beautiful; Plymouth, Feb 1957, and toured, Mar–June 1957, as Amanda in The Apple Cart; toured, Oct 1957, as Mrs Anthony J Drexel Biddle in The Happiest Millionaire; Playhouse, NY, Apr 1959, played the Nurse in Portrait of a Madonna, and Girl in Charge in A Pound on Demand (in Triple Play); toured with the APA, 1961, as Mrs Candour in The School for Scandal, The Woman in The Tavern, and Paulina in The Sea Gull; Royale, 1963, succeeded Agnes Moorehead as Miss Swanson in Lord Pengo; Belasco, Dec 1964, Grace Sample in One by One; Music Box, Feb 1966, Lady Gregory in Hostile Witness; John Drew, Easthampton, NY, June 1975, played in End of Summer; Helen Hayes, Jan 1976, took over from Eva LeGallienne as Fanny Cavendish in The Royal Family for a time during Miss LeGallienne's illness; Manhattan Theatre Club, Feb 1977, and Stage West Two, West Springfield, Apr 1977, in Quail Southwest; Ensemble Studio, Jan 1978, in

Mama Sang the Blues; entered films in Smashing the Money Ring, 1939, and has since appeared in Castle on the Hudson, 1940, Valley of the Dolls, 1967, The Brotherhood and Rabbit Run, 1970, etc; has performed on television in *The Nurses, The Defenders, Philco Television Playhouse,* etc.

Address: 84 Grove Street, New York, NY 10014.

STEWART, Ellen, producer, manager, director
b Louisiana; *e* Arkansas State U; married five times; formerly an elevator operator at Saks Fifth Avenue, then a clothing designer.

Opened a combination boutique-theater in a tenement basement on East 9th Street, New York City, and presented Tennessee Williams's One Arm on 27 July 1962; since then has steadily produced and directed plays by Eugene O'Neill, Fernando Arrabal, Leonard Melfi, Andre Gide, Shaw, Saroyan, Jean Anouilh, Gertrude Stein, Ionesco, Buchner, Paul Foster, Lanford Wilson, Tom Eyen, Jean Genet, Sam Shepard, Jean-Claude van Itallie, Tom O'Horgan, H M Koutoukas, Megan Terry, Brecht, Rochelle Owens, Ben Piazza, Ross Alexander, Israel Horovitz, Julie Bovasso, John Gruen, Maria Irene Fornes, Adrienne Kennedy, Alfred Jarry, Charles Ludlam, Slawomir Mrozek, Samuel Beckett, Wilford Leach, Ed Bullins, Peter Weiss, Edward Bond, Antonin Artaud, Robert Patrick, Eric Bentley, Andy Warhol, Jackie Curtis, Shakespeare, Terrence McNally, Strindberg, Moliere, and many other international, avant garde, and young American playwrights and composers; her troupes, called La Mama, Cafe La Mama, and La Mama ETC (Experimental Theater Club) have travelled extensively and have had a profound effect on theater throughout the world; has also presented the works of visiting troupes, such as the Open Theatre, American Indian companies, Los Grillos Company from Peru, Tokyo Kid Brothers, Ridiculous Theater, Le Grand Cirque de Magique de Paris, Esta Noche Teatro from South America, Otrabunda Company of the Virgin Islands, Asian American Repertory Company—La Mama Chinatown, Andrei Serban's troupe, and others; the La Mama troupe toured Europe under the direction of Tom O'Horgan in 1966; appeared at the Vaudeville, London, 17 Oct 1967, in Tom Paine, after performing this play at the Edinburgh Festival; Arts, London, June–July 1969, performed The Last Chance Saloon and Woyzeck; Royal Court, May 1970, presented Cinque, Rat's Mass, and June 1970, Ubu Roi, Arden of Faversham; toured Europe in 1970; opened Dubrovnik, Yugoslavia, Festival, Aug 1971 with Emer, Renard, then toured West Berlin and Copenhagen; founded branches of La Mama in Boston, Amsterdam, Bogota, Israel, London, Melbourne, Morocco, Munich, Paris, Tokyo, Toronto, Vienna; served as cultural ambassador to the Philippine Republic, for UNESCO, 1971; honorary doctorate from Colby College; has received grants from the Rockefeller Foundation, Ford Foundation, National Arts Council, New York State Council on the Arts, The Kaplan Fund, etc.

Address: La Mama ETC, 74A East 4th Street, New York, NY 10003. *Tel:* 475–7710.

STEWART, James, actor
b Vinegar Hill, Pa, 20 May 1908; *s* of Alexander Maitland Stewart and his wife Elizabeth Ruth Jackson; *e* Mercersburg, Pa, Academy, Princeton Univ (BS 1932); *m* Gloria Hatrick McLean; prepared for the stage with Joshua Logan; served in the US Army Air Force, 1942–45.

First appeared on the stage at the University Players, Falmouth, Mass, summer 1932, as the Chauffeur in Goodbye Again; made his New York debut at the Biltmore, 20 Oct 1932, as Constable Gano in Carrie Nation; Masque, Dec 1932, again played the Chauffeur in Goodbye Again; Henry Miller's, Oct 1933, Jack Breenan in Spring in Autumn; Henry Miller's, Dec 1932, Johnny Chadwick in All Good Americans; Martin Beck, Mar 1934, Sergeant O'Hara in Yellow Jack; Ethel Barrymore, Oct 1934, Teddy Parrish in Divided by Three; Mansfield, Nov 1934, Ed Olsen in Page Miss Glory; Shubert, Apr 1935, Carl in A Journey by Night; entered films for many years then reappeared on the stage at the 48th Street, in 1947, when he succeeded Frank Fay as Elwood P Dowd in Harvey; re-entered films, then at the ANTA, Feb 1970, again played in Harvey; Circle in the Square at Ford's Washington, DC, 1970, played in Festival at Ford's; Imperial, 9 Mar 1975, played in Gala Tribute to Joshua Logan; made his London debut at the Prince of Wales, 10 Apr 1975, as Elwood P Dowd in Harvey; entered films in The Murder Man, 1935, and has since appeared in Rose Marie, Born to Dance, in which he sang a score by Cole Porter, Seventh Heaven, You Can't Take It with You, Mr Smith Goes to Washington, The Philadelphia Story, It's a Wonderful Life, Call Northside 777, Broken Arrow, The Greatest Show on Earth, The Glenn Miller Story, Rear Window, Vertigo, Anatomy of a Murder, The Man Who Shot Liberty Valance, Shenandoah, Airport 77, and numerous others; won the Academy Award for his role in The Philadelphia Story, 1940; has also appeared in the title-role of the television series *Hawkins,* 1973.

Address: Actors Equity Association, 165 West 46th Street, New York, NY 10036.

STEWART, Michael (*né* Rubin), playwright
b New York City, 1 Aug 1929; *s* of William E Rubin and his wife Kate (Dunitz); *e* Yale Univ (MFA 1953).

First work for the theatre was lyrics and sketches for Shoestring Revue, produced at the President, NY, 28 Feb 1955; since then has written material for Shoestring '57; wrote the book for the musical Bye Bye Birdie, 1960; Carnival!, 1961; adapted Thornton Wilder's The Matchmaker into the musical Hello, Dolly!, 1964; wrote Those That Play the Clowns, 1966; George M!, 1968; Mack and Mabel, 1974; book and lyrics for I Love My Wife, 1977; book (with Mark Bramble) for The Grand Tour, 1979; contributed material to the television series *Caesar's Hour,* 1955–59.

Address: Dramatists Guild, 234 West 44th Street, New York, NY.

STEWART, Patrick, actor
b Mirfield, Yorkshire, 13 July 1940; *s* of Alfred Stewart, and his wife Gladys (Baraclough); *e* Mirfield Secondary Modern School; *m* Sheila Falconer; trained for the stage at Bristol Old Vic Theatre School.

First appeared on the stage in Aug 1959, at the Theatre Royal, Lincoln, as Morgan in Treasure Island; in repertory at Sheffield, Manchester (Library) where his parts included: Henry V, and Aston in The Caretaker, 1963, Playhouse, Liverpool, 1963–4 and Bristol Old Vic Company, 1965, playing parts including: Goldberg in The Birthday Party, the title-role in Galileo and Shylock in The Merchant of Venice; made his London début with the Royal Shakespeare Company at the Aldwych, Feb 1966, as Witness Two in The Investigation, and became an Associate Artist in 1967; his appearances for the company include the Dauphin in Henry V, Hippolito in The Revenger's Tragedy, Stratford, 1966; Grumio in The Taming of the Shrew, Stratford and Aldwych, Worthy in The Relapse, Aldwych, 1967; Grumio (US tour), Cornwall in King Lear, Touchstone in As You Like It, Hector in Troilus and Cressida, Stratford, 1968; Hector,

Teddy Foran in The Silver Tassie, Hippolito, Aldwych, 1969; Edward IV in Richard III, the title-role in King John, Launce in The Two Gentlemen of Verona, Stephano in The Tempest, Stratford, 1970 (Launce also Aldwych); made his New York début, Jan 1971, at the Billy Rose, as Snout in Peter Brook's production of A Midsummer Night's Dream; repeated the part at the Aldwych, June 1971; also played Mikhail Skrobotov in Enemies, July; Kabac in Occupations (The Place), Oct; Stratford, season 1972, played Tullus Aufidius in Coriolanus, Cassius in Julius Caesar, Enobarbus in Antony and Cleopatra, and Bassianus in Titus Andronicus, repeating Enobarbus and Cassius at the Aldwych, July 1973, and playing Aaron in Titus Andronicus, Aug; The Other Place, Stratford, Dec 1974, Astrov in Uncle Vanya; toured US and Australia for RSC, Feb 1975, as Eilert Lövborg in Hedda Gabler, also Aldwych, July 1975; same theatre, June 1976, Larry Slade in The Iceman Cometh; Stratford, May 1977, and Aldwych, June, Oberon in A Midsummer Night's Dream; Festival Hall, July 1977, the Doctor in Every Good Boy Deserves Favour; Warehouse (RSC), July 1977, Knatchbull in That Good Between Us; Aug, Shakespeare in Bingo; Dec, Basho in The Bundle; Stratford, 1978, Enobarbus in Antony and Cleopatra; the Other Place, Shylock in The Merchant of Venice (May), and The King in Hippolytus (Nov); Warehouse, May 1979, repeated Shylock, and at the Aldwych, played Viktor Myshlaevsky in The White Guard, and repeated Enobarbus (July); an actor/administrator of Actors in Residence, based in the University of California, and devoted to the teaching and performance of Shakespeare and other dramatists in American universities and colleges; author of The Loving Voyage, a Shakespeare anthology, films include Hennessy and Hedda Gabler; first television appearance, 1964; recent TV work includes When the Actors Come, Oedipus Rex, Tolstoy, and Tinker, Tailor, Soldier, Spy.

Favourite parts: Aston, Galileo, Hector, Shakespeare and Shylock. *Recreations:* Cinema, fell-walking, squash, motor-caravanning. *Address:* c/o Boyack and Conway, 8 Cavendish Place, London W1.

STICKNEY, Dorothy, actress
b Dickinson, North Dakota, 21 June 1900; *d* of Dr Victor Hugo Stickney and his wife Margaret (Hayes); *e* La Salle Seminary, Auburndale, Mass, and St Catherine's College, St Paul, Minn; *m* Howard Lindsay (dec); studied for the stage at the North Western Dramatic School, Minneapolis.

Made her first appearance on the stage at the Minot Theatre, North Dakota, May 1921, giving recitations with The Southern Belles' Concert Party; first appeared in New York, in vaudeville, 1921; her first appearance on the regular stage, was in the autumn of 1921, when she toured with Leo Ditrichstein in Toto; she then spent nearly five years in various stock companies; made her first appearance in NY at the 48th Street Theatre, 11 Nov 1926, as Anita in The Squall; Music Box, Dec 1926, played Liz in Chicago; Little, Apr 1928, Claudia Kitts in March Hares; Hampden's, June 1928, Cherry in The Beaux' Stratagem; Times Square, Aug 1928, Mollie Molloy in The Front Page; Empire, June 1930, Rose Sibley in Milestones; Biltmore, Jan 1931, Miss Krail in Phillip Goes Forth; Guild, June 1931, Mincing in The Way of the World; Booth, Apr 1932, Stella Hallam in Another Language; National (for Players' Club), May 1936, Lorena Watkins in The County Chairman; West Falmouth, Aug 1936, Anne Sawyer in Lovers' Meeting; Longacre, Feb 1938, Granny in On Borrowed Time; Empire, Nov 1939, played Vinnie in Life with Father, which she continued to play until 1944; Empire, Oct 1948, played Vinnie in Life with Mother;

at the National, Feb 1951, played Laura Mitchell in The Small Hours; Booth, Apr 1952, appeared as Dolly in To Be Continued; Alvin, Nov 1953, Margaret Munson in Kind Sir; Longacre, Apr 1955, played Maggie in The Honeys; Barter, Abingdon, Virginia, Sept 1958, Hudson, NY, Feb 1960, and Globe, London, June 1960, appeared in A Lovely Light, a one-woman show adapted by herself from the writings of Edna St Vincent Millay; Cort, NY, Mar 1963, Katie Delaney in The Riot Act; Mayfair, Jan 1964, again played in A Lovely Light; Westport Country Playhouse, July 1965, Mrs Bigelow in Family Things Etc; New York City Center, Oct 1967, again played Vinnie in Life with Father; Royale, Dec 1969, Mrs Ryan in The Mundy Scheme; Imperial, June 1973, took over from Irene Ryan as Charlemagne's Mother in Pippin; Imperial, 9 Mar 1975, appeared in a Gala Tribute to Joshua Logan; entered films in 1931 in Working Girls and since has played in The Little Minister, 1934, What a Life, 1939, The Remarkable Mr Pennypacker, 1959, I Never Sang for My Father, 1970; etc; has appeared on television in Arsenic and Old Lace, Cinderella, A Lovely Light, etc.

Hobbies: Collecting musical-boxes and gardening. *Recreation:* Dancing. *Address:* 13 East 94th Street, New York, NY 10028. *Tel:* Sacramento 2–4428.

STOCK, Nigel, actor
b Malta, 21 Sept 1919; *s* of Capt W H Stock, RE, and his wife Margaret Marion (Munro); *e* St Paul's School; *m* (1) Sonia Williams; (2) Richenda Carey; studied for the stage at the Royal Academy of Dramatic Art, where he gained the Leverhulme Exhibition, Northcliffe Scholarship, and the Principal's Medal.

Made his first appearance on the stage at the Savoy Theatre, 6 Dec 1931, as the boy Dan in The Traveller in the Dark; Old Vic, and Sadler's Wells, Apr 1932, played Mamilius in The Winter's Tale; Westminster, Dec 1932, Thomas in Alice, Thomas and Jane, playing the same part there in Dec 1933; Old Vic, Apr 1934, Young Macduff in Macbeth; Arts, May 1936, Brownie in Little Ol' Boy; Lyric, Sept 1936, the Assistant Stage Manager and Boots in Farewell Performance; Victoria Palace, Dec 1936, Jimmy in Adventure; Gate, Apr 1937, Lord Adrian in the play of that name, and May 1937, Dude Lester in Tobacco Road; Q, Nov 1937, Teddie in Jenny Frensham; Royalty, Apr 1938, Steve in April Clouds; Royalty, July 1938, Jerry Morris in Little Stranger; Shaftesbury, Sept 1938, Redbrooks and Colley in Goodbye, Mr Chips; Garrick, Mar 1939, Peter in The Mother; Richmond, June 1939, Alfred in Rolling Stone; served in the Army, with the London Irish Rifles, 1939–41, and with the Assam Regiment, Indian Army, 1941–5, in Burma, China and Kohima; demobilized 1945, with the rank of Major; reappeared on the stage at the Aldwych, Nov 1946, as Kenneth Tweedie in And No Birds Sing; Arts, May 1947, played Jackie Knowles in Boys in Brown; Strand, Nov 1947 (for Repertory Players), played Dick Tassell in The Happiest Days of Your Life; Mercury, Dec 1947, Alexander Montgomerie in Kate Kennedy; made his first appearance on the New York stage at the Martin Beck Theatre, 16 Mar 1948, as Philip in You Never Can Tell; appeared with the Bristol Old Vic Company, Aug 1948–June 1949; Embassy, London, July 1949, played Miller in Wilderness of Monkeys; at the New Theatre, Oct–Nov 1949, with the Old Vic Company, appeared as Dumaine in Love's Labour's Lost, Tony Lumpkin in She Stoops to Conquer, Beliayev in A Month in the Country; Apollo, June 1950, played Able Seaman Sims in Seagulls Over Sorrento; Lyric, May 1955, appeared as Albert in My Three Angels; at the Apollo, Dec 1955, took over the part of Alberto in Summertime; London Hippodrome, June 1956, played Lieut Stephen

Maryk in The Caine Mutiny Court-Martial; Savoy, Feb 1957, played Gene Grierson in Subway in the Sky; Criterion, Dec 1957, Daniel in Paddle Your Own Canoe; Duchess, Aug 1958, Michael Starkwedder in The Unexpected Guest; Royal Court, Apr 1961, played Werner in Altona, transferring with the production to the Saville, June 1961; Vaudeville, Feb 1963, Detective-Sergeant Brown in How Are You, Johnnie?; Piccadilly, Jan 1964, played the Doctor in The Father; toured, Apr 1967, as Barret in Brother and Sister; Hampstead Theatre Club, Feb 1969, appeared as four characters in a group of playlets under the overall title We Who Are About To . . . transferring to the Comedy, Apr 1969, in the production (renamed Mixed Doubles); Gaiety, Dublin, Oct 1969, Roebuck Ramsden in Man and Superman; at the Theatre Royal, Bristol, Sept 1973–Feb 1974, his parts included: Serebryakov in Uncle Vanya, Prime Minister in The Apple Cart, Oswald Veal in Plunder; toured, Apr 1974, as Sir Winston Churchill in A Man and His Wife; Haymarket, Nov 1975, Sir Hudson Lowe in Betzi; King's Head, Islington, Dec 1975, appeared in Carol's Christmas, adding the part of Andrew Crocker-Harris in The Browning Version, Jan 1976; Oxford Festival, Aug 1976, Major Petkoff in Arms and the Man, also touring, and at the Hong Kong Arts Festival, 1977, where he also appeared in Sleuth; Chichester Festival, 1977, and Phoenix, Nov, Proteus in The Apple Cart; Chichester, 1978, and Haymarket, Oct, Her van Putzeboum and Inspector in Look after Lulu; Vaudeville, Nov 1979, Widdecome in Stage Struck; entered films, 1934, and has appeared in numerous pictures; recent films include: Cromwell, Seven Men at Daybreak, Russian Roulette, etc; television performances include: Dr Watson in *Sherlock Holmes*.

Recreations: Ornithology and philately. *Address:* c/o Derek Glynne, 17 Wilton Place, London SW1.

STODDARD, Haila, actress, writer, and producer
b Great Falls, Montana, 14 Nov 1913; *d* of George Ogden Stoddard and his wife Ivy (Leavitt); *e* University of Southern California (BS Speech); *m* (1) Jack Kirkland (mar dis); (2) Harald Bromley (mar dis); (3) Whitfield Connor.

Made her first appearance on the stage at the Belasco, Los Angeles, 1934, in Merrily We Roll Along; subsequently toured for fifteen months, as Pearl in Tobacco Road, with Henry Hull; during 1936–7, played leading parts in the stock company at Ivoryton, Conn; made her first appearance in New York, at the Playhouse, Sept 1937, when she succeeded Peggy Conklin as Ellen Murray in Yes, My Darling Daughter; National, Oct 1938, played Nina in A Woman's a Fool—To Be Clever; Hudson, Nov 1939, Rita in I Know What I Like; Maxine Elliott, Dec 1939, Agnes Keefe in Kindred; Bucks County Playhouse, New Hope, Pa, 1940, played in 20 productions; Morosco, Oct 1940, Sister Suzanna in Suzanna and the Elders; Shubert (for the Guild), Jan 1942, played Lydia Languish in The Rivals, in which she subsequently toured; Morosco, Feb 1943, Maria Meade in The Moon Vine; Morosco, Sept 1943, Elvira in Blithe Spirit, in which she also toured; during 1944, toured as Loraine Sheldon with USO company, in The Man Who Came to Dinner; Coronet, 1946, succeeded Betty Field as Georgina Allerton in Dream Girl; in summer theatres, 1947, appeared as Joan in Joan of Lorraine; City Center, NY, July 1947, played Katie in Rip Van Winkle; Los Angeles, 1947–8, Sally Middleton in The Voice of the Turtle, and Georgina in Dream Girl; Booth, Feb 1948, Lee Manning in Dr Social; in summer theatres, 1949, Simone in Her Cardboard Lover; in summer theatres, 1950, appeared in 20th Century; at the Golden, NY, Mar 1951, played Mrs Jelliwell in Springtime for Henry; Lyceum, Oct 1951, appeared as Ethel Nash in Glad Tidings; toured,

1952–3, as Irene Elliott in Affairs of State; Broadhurst, NY, Oct 1953, played Kay Allen in The Frogs of Spring; at the Vanderbilt, Dec 1953, in association with Harald Bromley, presented Dead Pigeon; at the Bijou, Nov 1954, presented One Eye Closed; at the Broadhurst, Dec 1954, appeared as Marian Harrison in Lunatics and Lovers; and directed a touring production in 1956; Henry Miller's, Oct 1958, Edith Rollo in Patate; York, Feb 1959, adapted and co-produced Come Play with Me; ANTA, Feb 1960, co-produced A Thurber Carnival; Billy Rose, Sept 1963, took over the part of Martha in Who's Afraid of Virginia Woolf?; Actors Playhouse, May 1964, Charlotte in Dark Corners; in 1960 formed Bonard Productions Inc in partnership with Helen Bonfils, and has since produced Sail Away, 1962; The Affair and The Hollow Crown, 1963; at the opening of the New York State Theatre, 1964, presented the Royal Shakespeare Company in King Lear and The Comedy of Errors; co-produced The Birthday Party, 1967; Private Lives, 1968; The Gingham Dog, 1969; The Last Sweet Days of Isaac, The Lemon Sky, 1970; The Survival of Saint Joan, 1971; Lady Audley's Secret, 1972; associate producer since 1963, Elitch Gardens Theatre, Denver, Colo; adapted Men, Women, and Less Alarming Creatures from works of James Thurber for television series, 1965; author of the play Zellerman, Arthur, 1979; has appeared extensively in all major dramatic television programs, including 16 years as Pauline in *Secret Storm*.

Favourite part: Martha in Who's Afraid of Virginia Woolf? *Hobby:* Cooking and testing for her company, Carriage House Comestibles. *Address:* Ladder Hill South, Weston, Conn.

STONE, Alix, designer
trained in design under Jeannetta Cochrane at the Central School of Arts and Crafts.

Designs include: Twelfth Night, Old Vic, The Taming of the Shrew, Stratford, Measure for Measure (costumes only), Stratford, A Penny for a Song, 1962; Virtue in Danger, 1963; The Professor, A Month in the Country, 1965; The Promise, 1966; The Wolf, 1974; Othello, On Approval, 1975; A Man for All Seasons, Tobias and the Angel, 1976; Romeo and Juliet, The Importance of Being Earnest, 1977; Waiting for the Parade, 1979; designs outside London include work for the Arnaud, Guildford, and Playhouse, Oxford; has also designed opera for Aldeburgh, the Royal Opera, Sadler's Wells, English National Opera, Scottish Opera and elsewhere; designed the costumes for the television productions of Don Pasquale and The Magic Box.

Recreation: Gardening. *Address:* The Stables, Haydown, Elvendon Road, Goring on Thames, Oxon. *Tel:* 049–14 3402.

STONE, Paddy, former dancer, choreographer and director
b Winnipeg, Canada, 16 Sept 1924; *s* of Isadore Stone and his wife Lottie (Setnor); *e* Winnipeg; trained as a dancer with the Royal Winnipeg Ballet and the American School of Ballet.

Made his first appearance on the stage in a dance recital at the Winnipeg Playhouse, 1936; *Premier Danseur* at the Winnipeg Ballet, 1938–46; made his first appearance in New York at the Imperial, May 1946, in the chorus of Annie Get Your Gun; first appeared in London at the Royal Opera House, Nov 1946, in the *corps de ballet* of Coppelia, remaining as a principal dancer with the Royal Ballet, 1946–7; Coliseum, June 1947–8, Wild Horse Ceremonial dancer in Annie Get Your Gun; Her Majesty's, Apr 1949, a principal dancer in Brigadoon; Fortune, June 1954, a principal dancer in Joyce Grenfell Requests the Pleasure, appearing in the same programme at the Bijou, NY, Oct 1955; Prince of Wales, Oct 1958, choreographer for Mister Venus; Arts, May

1959, played six parts in Ulysses in Nighttown; Apollo, Sept 1959, directed and choreographer for Pieces of Eight; Piccadilly, May 1960, directed and choreographer for The Golden Touch; Cambridge, June 1960, directed Don't Shoot—We're English; Duke of York's, Apr 1961, directed and choreographer for One Over the Eight; Comedy, May 1962, directed and choreographer for Little Mary Sunshine; Adelphi, Sept 1964, choreographer for Maggie May; Palace, Manchester, Nov 1965, choreographer for Twang!; choreographer, Cliff Richard at the Palladium, 1968; choreographer and assistant director, The Good Old Bad Old Days, Prince of Wales, Dec 1972; same theatre, 1976, choreographed Mardi Gras; choreographed Julie Andrews at the Palladium, and at Caesar's Palace, Las Vegas, 1976; also The Two Ronnies at the Palladium, 1978; director and choreographer for shows in Amsterdam, 1971, 1973, 1975, 1977–9; choreographer and director for Takarazuka Revue Company, 1965–8, 1970–2, 1976–7; he has also been the choreographer for the ballets Classico (Winnipeg), 1954, Octetto (Festival Ballet), 1958, Variations on Strike Up the Band (Winnipeg), 1969; The Hands (Winnipeg), 1975; Bolero (Winnipeg), 1978; films in which he has appeared include: As Long As They're Happy, Value for Money, Invitation to the Dance, and The Good Companions; choreographer for Great Catherine and Scrooge; has appeared on television in NY, London, Vienna, Paris, Berlin, and Rome; choreographer for several British and American television series; appeared in cabaret in London, Paris, NY, Chicago, Monte Carlo, 1953–6, in the act Three's Company.

Recreation: Poker. *Address:* 22 Eaton Place, London SW1. *Tel:* 01–235 7481.

STONE, Peter H, playwright

b Los Angeles, California, 27 Feb 1930; *s* of John Stone and his wife Hilda (Hess); *e* Bard College (BA 1951 and DLitt, 1971), Yale University Graduate School of the Drama (MFA 1953); *m* Mary O'Hanley.

First produced play was Friend of the Family, presented at the Crystal Palace, St Louis, Missouri, 9 Dec 1958; first New York show was the book for the musical Kean, produced at the Broadway, 2 Nov 1961; wrote the book for Skyscraper, 1965; 1776, which received the Antoinette Perry (Tony) Award, the New York Drama Critics Circle Award, and the Drama Desk Award, 1969; 1776 produced in London at the New, 16 June 1970; Two by Two, NY, 1970; Sugar, 1972; adapted Erich Maria Remarque's Full Circle, 1973; adapted Harvey Jacobs's Summer on a Mountain of Spires, 1975; first wrote for films in 1962, when his film play Charade won the Mystery Writers of America Edgar Award; has since written the screenplays for Father Goose, which received the Academy Award, Mirage, Arabesque, Sweet Charity, Skin Game, 1776, The Taking of Pelham One Two Three, Who Is Killing the Great Chefs of Europe?, Why Would I Lie?, etc; has written plays for television, notably for *Studio One, Brenner, Espionage, The Defenders, Asphalt Jungle,* and the book for the musical version of Androcles and the Lion; has received an Emmy Award for one of his *Defenders* scripts, and a Writers Guild of America Award for his television play The Benefactor, 1962; member of the Executive Council of The Dramatists Guild and of The Authors League of America.

Address: 160 East 71st Street, New York, NY 10021, and Stony Hill Road, Amagansett, NY 11930. *Tel:* 288–1099 (NY) and 516–267 3739.

STOPPARD, Tom, dramatist and critic

b Zlin, Czechoslovakia, 3 July 1937; *s* of Eugene Straussler

and Martha Stoppard; *e* Pocklington, Yorkshire; *m* (1) Jose Ingle (mar dis); (2) Dr Miriam Moore-Robinson; formerly a journalist.

Author of the following plays: Rosencrantz and Guildenstern Are Dead, 1966; Enter a Free Man, The Real Inspector Hound, 1968; If You're Glad I'll be Frank, Albert's Bridge, 1969; After Magritte, Where Are They Now? 1970; Jumpers, Travesties, 1974; Dirty Linen and New Found Land, 1976; Every Good Boy Deserves Favour (music-theatre, with André Previn), 1977; Night and Day, 1978; Dogg's Hamlet and Cahoot's Macbeth, 1979; adapted Tango, 1966; The House of Bernarda Alba, 1973; Undiscovered Country, 1979; Rosencrantz and Guildenstern Are Dead, originally produced at the Edinburgh Festival, 1966, was subsequently produced by the National Theatre at the Old Vic, Apr 1967 (London *Evening Standard* award for most promising playwright of 1967) and in New York at the Alvin, Oct 1967 (Tony award for best play); directed Born Yesterday, Greenwich, Apr 1973; directed Every Good Boy Deserves Favour, Metropolitan Opera, NY, July 1979; scripted the film The Engagement, 1969; television writing includes: A Walk on the Water, A Separate Peace, Neutral Ground, Boundaries and Professional Foul; If You're Glad I'll be Frank, Albert's Bridge and Where Are They Now? were originally written for radio; also co-author (with T Wiseman) of the filmscripts, The Romantic Englishwoman, and Despair.

Recreations: Fishing, cricket. *Address:* c/o Fraser and Dunlop, 91 Regent Street, London W1.

STORCH, Arthur, actor and director

b Brooklyn, New York, 29 June 1925; *s* of Sam Storch and his wife Bessie (Goldner); *e* Brooklyn College, New School for Social Research (BA 1949); *m* Virginia Kiser; prepared for the stage at Erwin Piscator's Dramatic Workshop and at the Actors Studio, of which he is a member of the Actors Unit, the Directors Unit, and the Playwriting Unit, and in which Units he has taught since 1963; also taught at the Stella Adler Studio, 1962–4.

First appeared on the stage in a stock company production in Deertrees, Maine, 1951; made his NY debut at the Theatre de Lys, 15 Sept 1953, as Maurice Maynall Simmons in End As a Man, and transferred with it to the Vanderbilt in Oct 1953; Booth, Jan 1956, played Lt Mike Livingston in Time Limit!; Longacre, Nov 1956, Gene Mitchell in Girls of Summer; Ethel Barrymore, Nov 1957, Luke Gant in Look Homeward, Angel; Booth, Dec 1958, the Businessman in Night Circus; Ambassador, Feb 1960, Mr McWilliams in The Long Dream; turned to directing in 1961, and directed his first production, Two by Saroyan, at the East End, 21 Oct 1961; Maidman Playhouse, NY, Feb 1962, directed Three by Three; made his London début as a director at the Duke of York's, 4 Oct 1962, with the double-bill Talking to You and Across the Board on Tomorrow Morning; since then has directed The Typists, The Tiger, 1963; The Owl and the Pussycat, 1964; The Impossible Years, 1965; Under the Weather, 1966; Golden Rainbow, Waiting for Godot (Charles Playhouse, Boston), 1968; The Local Stigmatic, The Rose Tattoo (Hartford, Connecticut), Hunger and Thirst (Berkshire Theatre Festival), 1969; The Chinese, Dr Fish, Hay Fever (Seattle Repertory), 1970; The Gingerbread Lady (Studio Arena, Buffalo, NY), Natural Ingredients (tour), 1971; Promenade, All!, The Milliken Breakfast Show, 1972; Bijou, Jan 1973, played Emmett in The Enemy Is Dead; directed 42 Seconds from Broadway, 1973; Tribute, 1978; appointed Producing-Artistic Director of Syracuse Stage, NY, and Chairman of the Syracuse University Drama Department, 1973; Shubert Chair in Theatre, 1977; at Syracuse Stage, season 1974, directed Waiting for Lefty, Noon, and Of Mice and Men; 1974–5, La Ronde (also adapted) and The Butterfingers Angel; Morning's at Seven, Dynamo, 1975–6; A Quality of Mercy, The Seagull, 1976–7; Love Letters on Blue Paper, The End of the Beginning, 1977–8; The Butterfingers Angel, Loved, 1978–9; Naked, 1979–80; first appeared in films in The Strange One, 1957, and other films include The Mugger, Girl of the Night, and The Exorcist; first directed for television in 1965, and since has directed the Harry Belafonte Special, 100 Years of Laughter, and the Robert Brustein Theatre, which presented George Washington Crossing the Delaware and The Exhaustion of Our Son's Love; directed *Calucci's Department* on television, 1973; TV appearances include Sharon: Portrait of a Mistress, 1978.

Address: Syracuse Stage, 820 East Genesee Street, Syracuse, New York, NY 13210.

STOREY, David, dramatist
b Wakefield, Yorkshire, 13 July, 1933; *e* QEGS, Wakefield, and Slade School of Art, London.

Author of the plays The Restoration of Arnold Middleton, 1967; In Celebration, 1969; The Contractor, 1969; Home, 1970; The Changing Room, 1971; associate artistic director, Royal Court Theatre, 1972–4; wrote Cromwell, The Farm, 1973; Life Class, 1974; Mother's Day, 1976; Sisters, 1978; Early Days (National Theatre), 1980; his novels include: This Sporting Life, 1959; Flight into Camden, 1960; Radcliffe, 1963; Pasmore, 1972; A Temporary Life, 1973; Saville, 1976; he scripted the film of This Sporting Life; author of the television play Grace, 1974.

Address: c/o Jonathan Cape Ltd, 30 Bedford Square, London WC1.

STRACHAN, Alan, director
b Dundee, Scotland, 3 Sept 1946; *s* of Roualeyn Robert Scott Strachan and his wife Ellen (Graham); *e* Morgan Academy, St Andrews Univ and Merton College, Oxford; *m* Jennifer Piercey.

Directed for OUDS and the ETC at Oxford, writing various revues for the latter; assistant director, Mermaid Theatre, for The Tempest, Apr 1970; literary editor for the same theatre, 1970–4; associate director, 1971– ; directed his first London production there in Sept 1970, the children's play OK for Sound; subsequently directed The Watched Pot, 1970; John Bull's Other Island, The Old Boys (also tour), 1971; Misalliance, 1973; Children, 1974; also co-devised for the Mermaid the musical compilations Cowardy Custard, 1972, and Cole, 1974, co-directing the latter; directed his first West End production, A Family and a Fortune, Apr 1975; subsequently directed (in London unless otherwise stated) Confusions, Yahoo (also co-devised) 1976; devised and directed Shakespeare's People, which toured S Africa, USA, UK and Europe, 1975–8; Just Between Ourselves, The Immortal Hayden, 1977; Bedroom Farce (Amsterdam), 1978; Artistic Director, Greenwich Theatre, 1978– , where his productions include An Audience Called Edouard, 1978; Semi-detached, The Play's the Thing, I sent a Letter to my Love, 1979; Private Lives, 1980.

Recreations: Reading, Travel, Music. *Address:* c/o Boyack and Conway, 8 Cavendish Place, London W1. *Tel:* 01–636 3916.

STRAIGHT, Beatrice, actress
b Old Westbury, Long Island, New York, 2 Aug 1918; *d* of Major Willard Dickerman Straight and his wife Dorothy (Whitney); *e* Lincoln School, NY, and Dartington Hall, Devonshire, England; *m* Peter Cookson; prepared for the stage with Tamara Daykarhanova and Michael Chekhov.

Made her first appearance on the stage at the Lyceum Theatre, NY, 11 Feb 1935, as one of the Spinning Girls in Bitter Oleander; appeared with the Dartington Hall Players, under Michael Chekhov, at Ridgefield, Conn, as Viola in Twelfth Night, and Goneril in King Lear; Lyceum, NY, Oct 1939, played Lisa in The Possessed; at the St James, 1941, played Viola in Twelfth Night; Belasco, Sept 1943, played Angela in Land of Fame; Princess (for the Experimental Theatre), Feb 1947, Felina in The Wanhope Building; Royale, Nov 1947, Emily Dickinson in Eastward in Eden; National, Mar 1948, Lady Macduff in Macbeth, with Michael Redgrave and Flora Robson; Biltmore, May 1948, succeeded Wendy Hiller as Catherine Sloper in The Heiress; Playhouse, Feb 1950, played Miss Giddens in The Innocents; Martin Beck, Dec 1951, Nell Valentine in The Grand Tour; Brattle Theatre, Cambridge, May 1952, played Hesione Hushabye in Heartbreak House; Martin Beck, NY, Jan 1953, Elizabeth Proctor in The Crucible; Phoenix, Oct 1954, Christine Collinger in Sing Me No Lullaby; at the Carnegie Hall Playhouse, NY, Jan 1957, played Marie Chassaigne in The River Line; Greenwich Mews, Feb 1966, played the title-role in Phèdre; US Embassy, London, June 1966, again played Phèdre; toured Great Britain in this role; Plymouth, NY, Nov 1967, Mrs Trothe in Everything in the Garden; was a member of the Long Island Festival Repertory Company in 1968; toured, 1969–70, as Blanche Du Bois in A Streetcar Named Desire; toured, 1971, in The Right Honourable Gentleman; Roundabout, Apr 1973, Helene Alving in Ghosts; Roundabout Stage One, Oct 1974, Kate Keller in All My Sons; Lake Forest, Ill, Aug 1977, Kate in Old Times; Circle Rep, Dec 1979, Gertrude in Hamlet; received the Antoinette Perry (Tony) Award for The Crucible, 1953; co-founder of Theatre, Inc, which presented Pygmalion, 1945, Playboy of the Western World, 1946, and the US visit of the Old Vic Company, 1946; films in which she has appeared include Call from a Stranger, The Nun's Story, The Young Lovers, Network, Bloodline, The Promise, etc; TV includes *Beacon Hill*, and The Dain Curse.

Recreation: Painting. *Addresses:* East Indies Farm, RFD, Canaan, Conn, and 156 East 62nd Street, New York City.

STRASBERG, Lee, actor, producer, director, teacher, coach, and Director of the Actors Studio
b Budanov, Austria-Hungary, 17 Nov 1901; *s* of Baruch Meyer Strasberg and his wife Ida (Diner); *m* (1) Nora Z Krecaun (dec); (2) Paula Miller (dec); (3) Anna Mizrahi; prepared for the stage with Richard Boleslavsky and Maria Ouspenskaya at the American Laboratory Theatre, New York.

Began his theatrical career as an assistant stage manager for The Guardsman, at the Garrick, NY, 13 Oct 1924; was actor and director at the Chrystie Street Settlement House, NY, 1925; Garrick, Jan 1925, made his NY stage début as the First Soldier in Processional; June 1925, appeared in The Garrick Gaieties; Guild, Jan 1926, played in Goat Song, and, Mar 1926, in The Chief Thing; stage manager for the second Garrick Gaieties, May 1926; Golden, Sept 1927, played Nick in Four Walls; Martin Beck, Dec 1929, Pimples in Red Dust; Guild, Sept 1930, took over in The Garrick Gaieties; Jan 1931, Ali Hakim in Green Grow the Lilacs; co-founded The Group Theatre and, with Cheryl Crawford, directed its production of The House of Connelly, and directed 1931,

1931; directed Night over Taos, Success Story, 1932; directed Hilda Cassidy, and, for the Group, Men in White, 1933; Gentlewoman, Gold Eagle Guy, 1934; The Case of Clyde Griffiths, Johnny Johnson, 1936; Many Mansions, 1937; Roosty, All the Living, Dance Night, 1938; Summer Night, 1939; The Fifth Column, 1940; Clash by Night, 1941; RUR, 1942; Apology, which he also produced, South Pacific (drama), 1943; Skipper Next to God, 1948; The Big Knife, The Closing Door, 1949; Peer Gynt, 1951; supervised Marathon '33, 1963; The Three Sisters, 1964; made his London début as director at the Aldwych, May 1965, in a World Theatre Season, when he directed the Actors Studio production of The Three Sisters; supervised The Country Girl, 1966; at the Actors Studio has produced the following plays: Felix, the American première of Clifford Odet's The Silent Partner, Siamese Connections, The Masque of St George and the Dragon, 1972; Virility, Othello, The Effect of Gamma Rays on Man-in-the-Moon, Marigolds, A Break in the Skin, Long Day's Journey into Night, The Masque of St George and the Dragon, 1973; People of the Shadows, American Night Cry, O Glorious Tintinnabulation, 1974; founder of Lee Strasberg Institute, New York City and Hollywood, Cal; taught a seminar with Paula Strasberg at Spoleto, Italy, 1962; conducted seminars in Mar del Plata and Buenos Aires, Argentina; Paris, France; at University of Wisconsin, Nebraska, NCLA; lectured on Stanislavsky in Paris, France, June–July 1967; has lectured at Harvard, Brown, Brandeis, and Northwestern Universities; Whittier College, New School for Social Research in New York City; also in Germany and Japan; film appearances include Godfather II, Boardwalk, and Justice for All, Going in Style (1979), etc; TV includes The Last Tenant, 1978; his influence on modern acting and directing techniques as espoused at the Actors Studio has had a profound worldwide effect.

Address: c/o John Springer Associates, 667 Madison Avenue, New York, NY 10021.

STRATTON, John, actor

b Clitheroe, Lancs, 7 Nov 1925; *s* of James Stratton and his wife Hilda Alice (Wilson); *e* Royal Grammar School, Clitheroe.

Made his first appearance on the stage at the Empire Theatre, Dewsbury, 19 July 1943, as Freddie Eynsford-Hill in Pygmalion; appeared with the Court Players, in repertory, 1943–4; during the War joined the Royal Navy, and served from 1944–7; after demobilization, Aug 1947, toured for six months, as Fred in Present Laughter; in Jan 1948, played with the Dundee Repertory company; made his first appearance in London, at the St James's Theatre, 27 July 1948, as Tommy Gold in No Trees in the Street; New Lindsey, Nov 1948, played Tony Hill in Honour Thy Father; toured in England and Germany, Jan–Apr 1949, as Morgan Evans in The Corn is Green; Aldwych, Sept 1950, played Harold in Accolade; toured, Mar 1951, in Here We Come Gathering; New, Dec 1951, played Paul in Colombe; toured, Apr 1953, as Edward Bare in Murder Mistaken; Globe, Nov 1953, played Martin in Someone Waiting; at the Sarah Bernhardt Theatre, Paris, July 1954, appeared as B Kaghan in The Confidential Clerk, subsequently touring in this part; at the Fortune, London, Dec 1954, played Puss in The Marvellous Story of Puss in Boots; at the Q, May 1955, played Rapcev in An Act of Madness, and again appeared in this part at the Edinburgh Festival, Aug 1955; St James's, June 1957, played James Armitt in It's the Geography that Counts; Oxford Playhouse, Mar 1958, played Menelaus and Paris in Paris Not So Gay, and subsequently toured in the production; Lyric, Hammersmith, May 1958, appeared as McCann in The Birthday Party;

toured, Sept 1958, as Tom Geaver in The Holiday; Cambridge, Apr 1959, played André Monnerie in The Hidden River; Strand, Oct 1960, played Douglas Broadwater in Settled Out of Court; Oxford Playhouse, Dec 1961, the White Rabbit in Alice's Adventure in Wonderland; Nottingham Playhouse, Apr 1962, Stockmann in An Enemy of the People; Queen's, Nov 1962, played Joseph Sedley and the Prince Regent in Vanity Fair; Century Mobile Theatre, Oxford, May 1963, Duchatel in The Birdwatcher; Garrick, Nov 1963, Henry Prosser in Difference of Opinion; Hampstead Theatre Club, Sept 1965, Saint-Claude in The Marriage of Mr Mississippi; Hampstead Theatre Club, Apr 1967, Eric Bassett in Studies of the Nude; has also played in many films and television productions, including When We Are Married, Forget Me Not, Backs to the Wall, Just William.

Favourite parts: Paul in Colombe and Rapcev in An Act of Madness. *Recreations:* Tennis, travel, reading, and shop-window gazing. *Address:* c/o Larry Dalzell Associates Ltd, 3 Goodwin's Court, St Martin's Lane, London WC2. *Tel:* 01–240 3086.

STREEP, Meryl, actress

b Summit, NJ, 22 Sept; *e* Vassar (BA) and Yale (MFA).

Made her debut in New York at the Vivian Beaumont, 15 Oct 1975, as Imogen Parrott in Trelawny of the 'Wells'; for Phoenix, 1976, played Flora Meighan in 27 Wagons Full of Cotton, and Patricia in A Memory of Two Mondays, Jan, and Edith Varney in Secret Service, Apr; at the Delacorte, also 1976, played Katherine in Henry V, Jul, and Isabella in Measure for Measure, Aug; Vivian Beaumont, Feb 1977, Dunyasha in The Cherry Orchard; Chelsea Theatre Center, Mar 1977, Lillian Holliday in Happy End, transferring to the Martin Beck, May 1977; Delacorte, Jul 1978, Katherina in The Taming of the Shrew; Public, Dec 1978, Alice in a workshop production, Wonderland in Concert; same theatre, Feb 1979, Andrea in Taken in Marriage; films include Julia and Kramer vs Kramer.

Address: c/o Actors Equity Association, 165 West 46th Street, New York, NY 10036.

STREISAND, Barbra, actress and singer

b Brooklyn, NY, 24 Apr 1942; *d* of Emanuel Streisand and his wife Diana (Rosen); *e* PS 89, Erasmus Hall High School, and Yeshiva of Brooklyn; *m* Elliott Gould (mar dis).

First made a success in cabaret appearing in NY, San Francisco, Las Vegas, Los Angeles, etc; made her NY theatre début off-Broadway at the Gramercy Arts, Oct 1961, in the revue Another Evening with Harry Stoones; Shubert, Mar 1962, played Miss Marmelstein in I Can Get It for You Wholesale, and received the New York Critics (Variety) Award; in the summer of 1963 appeared with Sammy Davis, Jr, at the Hollywood Bowl; Winter Garden, Mar 1964, played Fanny Brice in Funny Girl; in the summer of 1964 and 1965, appeared in concert at the Forest Hills Stadium, NY; Washington, DC, Jan 1965, appeared in the Inaugural Gala; Prince of Wales's, London, Apr 1966, Fanny Brice in Funny Girl, for which she received the London Critics Poll and the Anglo-American Award; US Embassy, London, 12 June 1966, appeared in a revue for the Festival of American Arts and Humanities; Central Park, NY, summer 1968, played in concert to 135,000 people, the largest crowd ever assembled for a solo performance; has appeared in cabaret at venues such as the Riviera, Las Vegas, 1970, The Hilton International, Las Vegas, 1972; recreated her performance as Fanny Brice for film and won the Academy Award; has also appeared in Hello, Dolly!, On a Clear Day You Can See Forever, The Owl and the Pussycat, 1970, What's Up, Doc?,

Up the Sandbox, 1972, The Way We Were, 1973, Funny Lady, 1975, A Star Is Born, 1976, The Main Event, 1979, etc; has appeared frequently on television in the *Gary Moore Show, Tonight, Judy Garland Show, Dinah Shore Show,* the *Ed Sullivan Show,* etc, and in 1965, received five Emmy Awards for her solo program My Name Is Barbra.

Address: Solters and Sabinson, Inc, 62 West 45th Street, New York, NY 10036. *Tel:* TN 7–8500.

STRIDE, John, actor

b London, 11 July 1936; *s* of Alfred Teneriffe Stride and his wife Margaret (Prescott); *e* Alleyns School, Dulwich; *m* Virginia Thomas (mar dis); (2) April Wilding; trained for the stage at the Royal Academy of Dramatic Art.

Made his first appearance on the stage at the Liverpool Playhouse, Aug 1957, as Professor Dingley in Goodbye, My Fancy, and remained for the season appearing in repertory; toured Sept 1958, as Tom Shulford in These People, Those Books; toured, Jan 1959, as Richard in The Coast of Coromandel; made his first appearance in London at the Comedy, Apr 1959, when he took over the part of Clive in Five Finger Exercise; joined the Old Vic Company, Sept 1959, to play Silvius in As You Like It, followed by the Duke of Aumerle in Richard II, Brother Martin in Saint Joan, and the Chorus in Henry V; Old Vic, Oct 1960–May, 1961, played Romeo in Romeo and Juliet, Lysander in A Midsummer Night's Dream, Prince Henry in Henry IV (part I), and Gratiano in The Merchant of Venice; at the Phoenix, Apr 1961, played Angel Mills in The Landing Place for the Repertory Players; toured with the Old Vic Company in England, autumn, 1961; made his first appearance in New York with the Old Vic Company at the City Center, Feb 1962, as Malcolm in Macbeth, followed by Romeo in Romeo and Juliet, subsequently touring the United States with the same productions, Mar–June 1962; toured Europe and the Middle East, with the same company, June–Aug 1962; Winter Garden, NY, Mar 1963, played Armand Duval in The Lady of the Camellias; Haymarket, London, Aug 1963, Valerius Catullus in The Ides of March; joined the National Theatre Company to appear at the Old Vic, Oct 1963, as Fortinbras in the inaugural production of Hamlet; he has since played the following parts with the same company: Dunois in Saint Joan, Costar Pearmain in The Recruiting Officer, 1963; Neoptolemus in Philoctetes, Young Freevil in The Dutch Courtesan (also Chichester Festival), 1964; with the National Theatre Company visited Moscow and Berlin, Sept 1965, appearing as Cassio in Othello and Valentine in Love for Love, subsequently appearing in the last play at the Old Vic, Oct 1965; he went on to appear for the Company as Romain Tournel in A Flea in Her Ear, Valentine in Love for Love, Tikhon Ivanich Kabanov in The Storm, 1966 (later touring Canada with the Company as Romain and Valentine, Oct–Nov 1967); played Rosencrantz in Rosencrantz and Guildenstern are Dead, and took over the part of Audrey in As You Like It, 1967; took over as Andrei in The Three Sisters, and appeared in the name part in Edward the Second, 1968; Arnaud, Guildford, Oct 1971, Michel Cayre in Suzanna Andler; Phoenix, Nov 1973, Leo in Design for Living; Oxford Playhouse, July 1976, Bluntschli in Arms and the Man; Old Vic, Oct 1976, Gerardo in The Singer; Mermaid, Mar 1977, Tony Barnett in It's All Right If I Do It; first appeared in films, Aug 1959, in Sink the Bismarck and recently in Macbeth, Juggernaut, The Omen, and A Bridge Too Far; first television appearance, 1959, in A Touch of the Sun, and has appeared in *The Main Chance* and *Wilde Alliance.*

Favourite parts: Good ones. *Recreation:* Music. *Address:* c/o William Morris Agency, 147 Wardour Street, London W1.

STRITCH, Elaine, actress and singer

b Detroit, Michigan, 2 Feb 1926; *d* of George Joseph Stritch

and his wife Mildred (Jobe); *e* Sacred Heart Convent, Detroit, and Duschesne Residence Finishing School; *m* John M Bay; prepared for the stage by Erwin Piscator at the Dramatic Workshop of the New School.

Made her first appearance on the stage at the New School, Apr 1944, as a Tiger and a Cow in the children's show Babino; City College Auditorium, New York, June 1945, played the Parlor Maid in The Private Life of the Master Race; Biltmore, Oct 1946, Pamela Brewster in Loco; Henry Miller's, 1946, took over the role of Miss Crowder in Made in Heaven; Shubert, New Haven, Conn, Apr 1947, appeared as Roberts in Three Indelicate Ladies; Rooftop, NY, Oct 1947, Regina Giddens in The Little Foxes; Coronet, Dec 1947, appeared in the revue Angel in the Wings; Booth, Oct 1949, played June Farrell in Yes M'Lord; Broadhurst, Jan 1952, Melba in a revival of Pal Joey; US tour, 1953, took over the role of Sally Adams in Call Me Madam; 46th Street, NY, Oct 1954, played Peggy Porterfield in a revival of On Your Toes; Music Box, Mar 1955, Grace in Bus Stop; Cort, Mar 1957, Gertrude Muldoon in The Sin of Pat Muldoon; Lunt-Fontanne, Oct 1958, Maggie Harris in Goldilocks; Broadhurst, Oct 1961, Mimi Paragon in Sail Away!, appearing in the same role in her London début at the Savoy, June 1962; Billy Rose, Apr 1963, took over the role of Martha, in the matinée performances of Who's Afraid of Virginia Woolf?; Curran, San Francisco, and California tour, Oct 1963, played Stella in The Time of the Barracudas; US tour, 1965, again played Martha in Who's Afraid of Virginia Woolf?; toured, 1965, as Anna Leonowens in The King and I; Trinity Square, Providence, Rhode Island, Dec 1966, Babylove Dallas in The Grass Harp; City Center, NY, May 1967, Ruth in Wonderful Town; toured, 1967, in Any Wednesday; Theatre de Lys, May 1968, Amanda Prynne in Private Lives; toured, 1968, as Vera Charles in Mame and later succeeded to the title-role; Alvin, Apr 1970, Joanne in Company; played this role in Los Angeles, May 1971, and at Her Majesty's, London, Jan 1972; Hampstead, and Comedy, Mar 1973, Leona Dawson in Small Craft Warnings; Phoenix, Oct 1974, Evy Meara in The Gingerbread Lady; first entered films in 1954, and has appeared in The Scarlet Hour, Three Violent People, A Farewell to Arms, etc; first appeared on television 1949, in the series *The Growing Paynes,* and has since appeared in *The Honeymooners, My Sister Eileen, The Trials of O'Brien, Two's Company, Pollyanna, Shades of Greene, Song By Song* and *Tales of The Unexpected.*

Favourite parts: Grace in Bus Stop, Martha in Who's Afraid of Virginia Woolf?, and Melba in Pal Joey. *Recreations:* Cooking and people. *Address:* Savoy Hotel, Strand, London WC2 *and* c/o Leading Artists, 60 St James's Street, London SW1.

STROUSE, Charles, composer

b New York City, 7 June 1928; *s* of Ira Strouse and his wife Ethel Newman; *e* Eastman School of Music (BM 1947); *m* Barbara Siman; studied composition with David Diamond, Aaron Copland, Nadia Boulanger, Arthur Berger, and others.

Began his theatrical musical career by supplying the scores for several stock productions at the Green Mansions Theatre, Warrensburg, NY, 1952–5; first NY score was for Shoestring Review, produced at the President, 28 Feb 1955; since then has written the music for Shoestring '57, A Pound in Your Pocket, 1956; Bye, Bye Birdie, 1960; All American, 1962; Golden Boy, 1964; It's a Bird . . . It's a Plane . . . It's Superman, 1966; Applause, 1970; book, lyrics, and music for Six, 1971; music for I and Albert, produced at the Piccadilly,

London, Nov 1972; Applause also produced in London, 1972; The Member of the Wedding, 1975; Annie, 1977 (London, 1978); A Broadway Musical, 1978; Flowers for Algernon (London), 1979; wrote the score for the films The Mating Game, 1959, Bonnie and Clyde, 1968, The Night They Raided Minskys, 1969, There Was a Crooked Man, 1970, Just Tell Me What You Want, 1979.

Address: c/o Linden & Deutsch, 110 East 59th Street, New York, NY 10022. *Tel:* CO 5–1459.

STRUDWICK, Shepperd, actor
b Hillsboro, North Carolina, 22 Sept 1907; *s* of Shepperd Strudwick and his wife Susan Nash (Read); *e* University of North Carolina (AB); *m* (1) Helen Wynn (mar dis); (2) Jane Straub (mar dis); (3) Margaret O'Neill; prepared for the stage with the Carolina Playmakers, and studied with Leo Bulgakov, Samuel Rosen, and Lee Strasberg.

First appeared on the stage at the Charles Coburn Theatre in New York, Oct 1928, in a revival of The Yellow Jacket; at the Royale, Mar 1933, played Alan McClain in Both Your Houses; toured for the Theatre Guild, 1934, with Ina Claire in Biography; Broadhurst, Nov 1935, John McChire in Let Freedom Ring; Guild, NY, Feb 1936, played Will Dexter in End of Summer and subsequently toured in this part; Ritz, Oct 1937, Orlando in As You Like It; Longacre, Oct 1939, Vershinin in The Three Sisters; Music Box, Nov 1946, played Mr Blake in Christopher Blake; Royale, Sept 1950, George Henderson in Affairs of State; National, Jan 1953, played Anderson in a revival of The Bat; Longacre, Oct, 1953, Charles Nichols in The Ladies of the Corridor; Phoenix, Jan 1955, Sir Colenso Ridgeon in The Doctor's Dilemma; 4th Street, Oct 1956, played Boris Tirgorin in The Seagull; John Golden, Dec 1958, The Father in The Night Circus; John Golden, Mar 1959, Dr Basil Ashley in A Desert Incident; Cort, Nov 1959, Lucius Whitmore in Only in America; US tour, 1960–1, appeared in the title-role of JB; 4th Street, Nov 1961, took over the part of Pastor Manders in Ghosts; Billy Rose, Oct 1962, played George in the matinée performances of Who's Afraid of Virginia Woolf?, and toured in this part 1963–4; Theatre de Lys, 1965, Abraham Lincoln in The Last Days of Lincoln; Broadway, Nov 1965, De la Rochepozay in The Devils; Delacorte, July 1966, the Duke in Measure for Measure; Vivian Beaumont, Apr 1967, Cardinal Inquisitor in Galileo; same theatre, 1968, took over as John Lonsdale in In the Matter of J Robert Oppenheimer; Duke of York's, London, Mar 1969, Walter Franz in The Price; toured the US, Sept 1969–Apr 1970, as Walter Franz in The Price; Arena Stage, Washington, DC, Mar 1971, Commander Lloyd Mark Bucher in Pueblo; Delacorte, June 1971, Timon in Timon of Athens; Goodman, Chicago, Oct 1971, Defense Attorney in Assassination, 1865; Shaw Festival, Niagara on the Lake, Ontario, Canada, June 1972, Oscar Wolfe in The Royal Family; taught at the University of Detroit's Mary-grove College, Mich, and acted in The Tempest, Child's Play, and Lysistrata, 1972; Arena Stage, Feb 1973, title-role in A Public Prosecutor Is Sick of It All; Uris, Sept 1973, General Birabeau in The Desert Song; Alley, Houston, Texas, Oct 1974, title-role in Wilson; Studio Arena, Buffalo, Oct 1976, and Morosco, Nov, Rev Winemiller in The Eccentricities of a Nightingale; Eisenhower, Washington DC, June 1977, appeared in The Master Builder; Studio Arena, Nov 1977, Rokitansky in Semmelweiss; Yale Reportory, Apr, Apr 1978, in Hankon Werle in The Wild Duck; has appeared in many films, including Joan of Arc, All the King's Men, A Place in the Sun, The Red Pony, Cops and Robbers (1973), etc; first appeared on television in Los Angeles, in 1948, and has since played more than 100 parts, including Cassius in

Julius Caesar, Tiresias in Antigone, etc; member of The Actors Studio.

Favourite parts: George in Who's Afraid of Virginia Woolf? and Abraham Lincoln. *Recreations:* Music, travel, history, and manual labour. *Address:* c/o ICM, 40 West 57th Street, New York, NY 10019.

STUBBS, Una, actress and dancer
b London, 1 May 1937; *d* of Clarrie Stubbs and his wife Angela; *m* (1) Peter Gilmore (mar dis); (2) Nicky Henson (mar dis); trained for the stage at the La Roche Dancing School, Slough.

Made her first professional appearance as a child, playing Peaseblossom in A Midsummer Night's Dream at the Theatre Royal, Windsor; early experience included the chorus at the Palladium, and an appearance in Grab Me A Gondola, Lyric, 1957; Princes, Apr 1961, appeared in the revue On the Brighter Side; Palladium, Apr 1964, Princess Balroubadour in Aladdin; joined the Young Vic Company, 1970, playing Nancy in The Knack and the Princess in The Soldier's Tale, at the Edinburgh Festival and in London; Mermaid, July 1972, appeared in Cowardy Custard; same theatre, July 1974, appeared in Cole; Watford Palace, 1975, title-role in Irma la Douce; Richmond, Dec 1975, again played Balroubadour; Vaudeville, June 1976, Ann in Baggage; Mermaid, Apr 1977, appeared in Oh, Mr Porter; film appearances include Summer Holiday and Wonderful Life; has made numerous TV appearances, in light entertainment shows such as the Cliff Richard series, in the series *Till Death Us Do Part, Give Us A Clue* and Worzel Gummidge.

Recreation: Embroidery. *Address:* c/o Richard Stone, 18–20 York Buildings, London WC2.

STYNE, Jule, composer and producer
b London, 31 Dec 1905; *s* of Isadore Stein and his wife Anna (Keitman); *e* Chicago Public; *m* (1) Ethel Rubenstein (mar dis); (2) Margaret Brown.

Was a child prodigy as a pianist, appearing with the Chicago Symphony Orchestra at age 8; was a motion picture theatre manager, Chicago; later a vocal coach; composed the scores of Glad to See You, 1944; High Button Shoes, 1947; Gentlemen Prefer Blondes, 1949; Two on the Aisle, 1951; Hazel Flagg, 1953; Peter Pan (in part), 1954; The Bells Are Ringing, 1956; Say, Darling, 1958; Gypsy, 1959; Do-Re-Mi, 1960; Subways Are for Sleeping, 1961; Gentlemen Prefer Blondes (London), 1962; Arturo Ui, 1963; Funny Girl, Fade Out—Fade In, 1964; Hallelujah, Baby, for which he received the Antoinette Perry (Tony) Award, 1967; Darling of the Day, 1968; Look to the Lilies, 1970; Prettybelle (Boston), 1971; Sugar, 1972; Lorelei or Gentlemen Still Prefer Blondes, 1974; Hellzapoppin, 1976; as a producer has presented or co-presented the following in NY: Make a Wish, 1950; Pal Joey, In Any Language, 1952; Hazel Flagg, 1953; Will Success Spoil Rock Hunter? 1955; Mr Wonderful, 1956; Say, Darling, 1958; Fade Out—Fade In, High Spirits, Something More (also directed), 1964; Jockeys, 1977; Teibele and Her Demon, 1979; films in which he has collaborated in composing songs, etc, include Sailors on Leave, Follow the Boys, The Kid from Brooklyn, The West Point Story, Anchors Aweigh, Tars and Spars, Three Coins in the Fountain (Academy Award for title-song), My Sister Eileen, etc; television shows for which he has composed music include The Ruggles of Red Gap, 1957, Mr Magoo's Christmas Carol, The Dangerous Christmas of Red Riding Hood . . . or Oh Wolf, Poor Wolf, 1965; has produced on television Anything Goes, Panama Hattie, The Best of Broadway,

1957, *The Eddie Fisher Show,* 1959, etc; received the Anglo-American Award, 1966, specifically for Funny Girl.

Address: 237 West 51st Street, New York City, NY 10019.

SUMNER, Geoffrey, actor
b Ilfracombe, Devon, 20 Nov 1908; *s* of Edmund Sumner and his wife Kathleen Marion (Brook); *e* Clifton College and Tarka Training Farm; *m* Gwen Williams Roberts; formerly a pigbreeder in South Africa, and sometime international bobsleigh racer and mountaineer.

First appeared on the stage in 1931 at the Q as Algie in Sport of Kings; toured, 1932, as Jerry in While Parents Sleep; his first London appearance was at the Shaftesbury in 1933, as the Flag Lieutenant in Admirals All; Queens, 1935, later Savoy, took over Gilbert in The Wind and the Rain; Drury Lane, May 1936, Alec Merton in Rise and Shine; Q, June 1937, and Vaudeville, Feb 1938, Capt Corrie in Mirabelle; Lyceum, May 1938, Armand de Perlichon in Money Talks; Comedy, Sept 1938, Henry Westby in Room for Two; Criterion, 1939, took over Tim Shields in Tony Draws a Horse; after war service (Colonel, Royal Artillery) returned to the stage, Jan 1948, as George Beesdale in Mountain Air at the Comedy; worked largely in films and television until Oct 1967, when he played Sir Lindsay Cooper in Uproar in the House at the Whitehall; toured South Africa, 1968–9, as Gilbert Bodley in Not Now, Darling; toured UK, May 1970, as Sir Tristram Marden in Dandy Dick; Vaudeville, Sept 1970, Lord Coverley de Beaumont in The Jockey Club Stakes, transferring to the Duke of York's, Mar 1971; directed the same play in S Africa, 1972, playing the Marquis of Candover; again played Coverley de Beaumont in the US, 1972–3, including the Cort, NY; Palace, Westcliff, June 1973, Dr Gerald Drimmond in Come Back to My Place; toured, 1974, as Sir William Boothroyd in Lloyd George Knew My Father; Criterion, Oct 1974, Dr Gerald Drimmond in There Goes the Bride, transferring to the Ambassadors'; Redgrave, Farnham, Oct 1975, again played Sir William Boothroyd; films, since his first in 1938, include: Top Secret, Cul de Sac, Mine Own Executioner, and There Goes the Bride; television since 1947 includes plays such as: Home and Beauty, series such as: *The Army Game,* and serials such as: Strictly Personal.

Recreations: Growing fuchsias and asparagus, collecting china and glass. *Address:* La Retraite, 24 High Street, Alderney, CI. *Tel:* 048–182 2445.

SUMNER, John, CBE, 1971; director
b London, 27 May 1924; *s* of Thomas Hackman Sumner and his wife Alice Gertrude (Stock); *e* London Choir School and University of Southampton; *m* Margaret Ann Parker.

After serving in the Merchant Navy during the Second World War, entered the theatre as an ASM in Dundee, where he also made his debut as a director with The Lady from Edinburgh, 1947; stage director for H M Tennent; left to manage the Union Theatre, University of Melbourne, 1952; founded the Union Theatre Repertory Company, Australia's first fully professional repertory company, 1953; General Manager, Elizabethan Theatre, Sydney, 1955–7; returned to Melbourne, 1957, as manager for Victoria of the Australian Elizabethan Theatre Trust, also Administrator, Union Theatre Repertory Company, 1959, becoming fulltime Director/Administrator of the latter in 1962; the company was renamed the Melbourne Theatre Company in 1968, and now performs the year round at three theatres, the Athenaeum, Athenaeum 2, and the Russell Street, with a touring programme; for the company he has directed innumerable plays, including Summer of the Seventeenth Doll,

1955, which he subsequently directed in London, 1957, and New York, 1958; recent productions include The Cherry Orchard, Sticks and Bones, 1972; Batman's Beach-Head, The Play's the Thing, 1973; The Removalists, Pericles, The Doctor's Dilemma, Coralie Lansdowne Says No, 1974; Much Ado About Nothing, Kid Stakes, 1975; Martello Towers, 1976; 'The Doll' Trilogy, The Wild Duck, 1977; Breaker Morant, 1978; Macbeth, 1979; Betrayal, 1980; has directed plays for Australian television since 1960; received the Britannica Award for Art, 1973.

Address: 211 Beaconsfield Parade, Albert Park, Victoria 3206, Australia. *Tel:* 699 6972.

SUZMAN, Janet, actress
b Johannesburg, S Africa, 9 Feb 1939; *d* of Saul Suzman and Betty Suzman; *e* Kingsmead College and University of Witwatersrand, Johannesburg; *m* Trevor Nunn; trained for the stage at LAMDA.

First appeared on the stage 30 Apr 1962, at the Tower Theatre, Ipswich, as Liz in Billy Liar; joined the Royal Shakespeare Company, Dec 1962, and made her London début at the Aldwych in The Comedy of Errors, playing Luciana; has since played Iris in The Tempest, Joan la Pucelle in Henry VI, Lady Anne in Richard III, Stratford, 1963; Lady Percy in Henry IV (both parts), Stratford, Lulu in The Birthday Party, Aldwych, 1964; Rosaline in Love's Labour's Lost, Portia in The Merchant of Venice, Stratford, Ophelia in Hamlet, Aldwych, 1965; at the Playhouse, Oxford, 1966–7 played Kate Hardcastle in She Stoops to Conquer, and Carmen in The Balcony; again for the RSC, 1967, played Katharina in The Taming of the Shrew and Celia in As You Like It, Stratford (also Aldwych and US tour, 1968), and Berinthia in The Relapse, Aldwych; Rosalind in As You Like It, Beatrice in Much Ado About Nothing, Stratford, 1968 (the latter part also Aldwych and US tour, 1969); appeared in the RSC's Pleasure and Repentance, Edinburgh Festival, Aug 1970; Stratford, season 1972, played Cleopatra in Antony and Cleopatra, Aug, and Lavinia in Titus Andronicus, Oct; King's Head, Islington, Mar 1973, Hester in Hello and Goodbye; Aldwych, July 1973, again played Cleopatra (*Evening Standard* Award, Best Actress of 1973); The Place, Oct 1973, again played Hester; Cambridge Theatre, June 1976, Masha in Three Sisters; (*Evening Standard* and Plays and Players Awards for Best Actress, 1976); Duke of York's, June 1977, and Edinburgh Festival played Hedda in Hedda Gabler; Royal Court, Oct 1977, Shen Te in The Good Woman of Setzuan; Opera Space, July 1978, Minerva in Boo Hoo; toured, 1979, in The Duchess of Malfi; Aldwych, Jan 1980, played Clytemnestra in The War, Helen in The Murders and Chorus in The Gods, in the RSC production, The Greeks; films include A Day in the Death of Joe Egg and Nicholas and Alexandra; television, since 1966, includes: The Three Sisters, Hedda Gabler, Twelfth Night, Miss Nightingale, and Clayhanger; Council member, LAMDA.

Address: c/o William Morris, 147–149 Wardour Street, London W1. *Tel:* 01–734 9361.

SVOBODA, Prof Josef, designer
b Caslav, Czechoslovakia, 10 May, 1920; trained at the special school for interior architecture and the Academy of Applied Arts, Prague; *m* Libuse Svobodova.

Chief designer, National Theatre, Prague, since 1948; his designs have been seen in theatres and opera houses all over the world, including Covent Garden, the Metropolitan Opera, NY, Bayreuth, etc; his first design for the English theatre was The Storm, for the National Theatre at the Old Vic, 18 Oct 1966; for the same theatre designed The Three

Sisters, 1967; The Idiot, 1970; he is noted for his work with Laterna Magika, seen at Expo 58 in Brussels; Chief of Laterna Magika, 1973– ; inventor of the Polyecran system of simultaneous projection; National Artist of the CSSR, 1968; Professor of Academy of Applied Arts, 1968; Hon RA, London, 1969.

Address: Filmarská 780, 1500 00 Prague 5, CSSR.

SWADOS, Elizabeth, writer, director and composer
b 5 Feb 1951; *d* of Robert Orville Swados and his wife Sylvia (Maisel); *e* Bennington College.

Began her collaboration with Andre Serban at La Mama, 1974, where she wrote the music for his Greek trilogy, The Trojan Woman, Electra, and Medea; wrote music for his New York Shakespeare Festival productions of The Cherry Orchard, 1976, and Agamemnon, 1977; directed and wrote music for Nightclub Cantata, Village Gate, 1976; music for Ghost Sonata, Yale, 1977; wrote and directed Runaways, seen at the Public, Mar 1978, and making her Broadway debut as director/composer when it moved to the Plymouth, May 1978; music, adaptation and direction for Wonderland in Concert, 1978, Dispatches, 1979, Haggadah, 1980, all at the Public; also wrote The Incredible Feeling Show, a children's musical adapted from her own book, 1979; music for As You Like It, La Mama, 1979; wrote and appeared in the film The Girl with the Incredible Feeling, 1979; other film work includes scores for Step by Step, 1978, and Sky Dance, 1979; has written music for the PBS American Short Story series and various TV specials.

Address: c/o New York Shakespeare Festival, 425 Lafayette Street, New York, NY 10003.

SWANN, Donald, composer and songwriter
b Llanelli, Wales, 30 Sept 1923; *s* of Herbert William Swann and his wife Naguimé Sultan (Pistsov); *e* Westminster School and Christ Church, Oxford; *m* Janet Mary Oxborrow.

Began his career by contributing music to revues, Penny Plain, 1951; Airs on a Shoestring, 1953; Pay the Piper, 1954; Duke of York's, July 1955, collaborated with Philip Guard in a musical play, Wild Thyme; Comedy, Jan 1956, collaborated with Michael Flanders in the revue Fresh Airs; New Lindsey, Dec 1956, made his first appearance on the stage, with Michael Flanders, in their two-man entertainment At the Drop of a Hat, and transferred with this to the Fortune, Jan 1957, where it ran for 759 performances; Lyceum, Edinburgh, Sept 1959, appeared for one week of late night performances at the Edinburgh Festival, in the same entertainment, under the title of At the Drop of a Kilt; appeared for the first time on the New York stage at the John Golden, Oct 1959, in At the Drop of a Hat, subsequently touring Canada and the US, 1960–1; with the same show toured Great Britain and Eire, 1962–3; Haymarket, London, Oct 1963, appeared in a new edition At the Drop of Another Hat; toured Australia, New Zealand, and Hong Kong, 1964–5, with both editions of the same entertainment; Globe, London, Sept 1965, again appeared in At the Drop of Another Hat, also at the Booth, NY, Dec 1966; since 1955, has broadcast and appeared frequently on television in Great Britain, the US, Canada, Australia, etc, in excerpts from the same shows; since 1967 has performed concert/entertainments—Set by Swann, his settings of 18 poets; An Evening in Crete, an impression of Crete in words and music devised by himself and Lilli Malandraki; and musical autobiography Between the Bars; has written two books, The Space Between the Bars, a book of reflections, and Swann's Way Out, a posthumous reflection; has composed satirical music for the poet Henry Reed, under the pseudonym Hilda Tablet, for the

BBC Third Programme; an opera, Perelandra, based on C S Lewis; Requiem for the Living, to the libretto of C Day Lewis; three books of new carols; a songbook, The Road Goes Ever On, with J R R Tolkien; Baboushka, a musical fable for Christmas, with Anton Scholey, 1978; with Alec Davison, The Yeast Factory, a musical play for Cockpit Youth Theatre, 1979; President of the Pacifist Fellowship Party.

Recreation: Living in Suffolk. *Address:* 13 Albert Bridge Road, London SW11. *Tel:* 01–622 4281.

SWANSON, Gloria (Josephine May), actress
b Chicago, Ill, 27 Mar 1899; *d* of Joseph Swanson and his wife Adelaide (Klanowski); *e* Chicago public schools; *m* (1) Wallace Beery, the actor (mar dis), (2) Herbert K Somborn (mar dis), (3) Marquis de la Falaise de la Coudray (mar dis), (4) Michael Farmer (mar dis), (5) William N Davey (mar dis), (6) William Dufty; she was formerly a columnist for the United Press.

First appeared on the stage when a child in Key West, Fla; had a long career in silent and sound films before reappearing on the stage in a tour of Reflected Glory, 1942; toured, 1943, in Let Us Be Gay; made her NY debut at the Playhouse, 23 Jan 1945, as Katherine in A Goose for the Gander; ANTA Playhouse, Dec 1950, played Lily Garland in Twentieth Century; Royale, Dec 1951, title-role in Nina; Newport, RI, Casino, summer 1959, played in Red Letter Day; Westport, Conn, Country Playhouse, July 1961, played in Between Seasons; Ziegfeld, 6 May 1951, did her imitation of Charlie Chaplin in ANTA Album; Studebaker, Chicago, Ill, July 1970, Mrs Baker in Butterflies Are Free, and toured in this until May 1971; Booth, Sept 1971, took over as Mrs Baker in Butterflies Are Free; entered films in Elvira Farina, 1913, and has since played in innumerable pictures, including Teddy at the Throttle, Don't Change Your Husband, Male and Female, Why Change Your Wife?, Love of Sunya, Sadie Thompson, Queen Kelly, Music in the Air, Sunset Boulevard (1950), Airport 1975, etc; has appeared on television in *The Gloria Swanson Show*, 1948, and on various dramatic shows; is a dress designer of note, and an authority on diet and food.

Recreations: Painting, sculpture. *Address:* Gloria Swanson Enterprises, Inc, 920 Fifth Avenue, New York, NY 10021.

SWASH, Bob, producing manager
b Margate, Kent, 14 Sept 1929; *s* of Walter Swash and his wife Elisse (Relnah); *e* Raynes Park GS.

Has produced or co-produced Belle, South, 1961; Chips with Everything, 1962; Portrait of Murder, The Provok'd Wife, Clap Hands, Let's Make an Opera, 1963; Woman in a Dressing Gown, Everybody Loves Opal, The Four Seasons, 1964; Stranger in My Bed, A Heritage and Its History, 1965; presented the Lyric Hammersmith Company's season at Bath, 1969; Three Months Gone, Sing a Rude Song, 1970; The Dirtiest Show in Town, 1971; joined the Robert Stigwood Organisation, 1972, to head their live theatre division; in this capacity he has presented Jesus Christ Superstar, Joseph and the Amazing Technicolor Dreamcoat, 1972; Pippin, 1973; The Golden Pathway Annual, John, Paul, George, Ringo . . . and Bert, 1974; Aspects of Max Wall, Jeeves, Happy End, 1975; Evita, Paul Robeson, 1978.

Address: 67 Brook Street, London W1. *Tel:* 01–629 9121.

SWENSON, Inga, actress and singer
b Omaha, Nebraska, 29 Dec 1934; *d* of A C R Swenson and his wife Geneva (Seeger); *e* Northwestern University, Evanston, Illinois, where she majored in theatre studies under

Alvina Krause; *m* Lowell M Harris; prepared for the stage at the Actors Studio.

Played in stock, 1949–54, in The Swan, The Merchant of Yonkers, Othello, The Medium, The Cherry Orchard, The Lady's Not for Burning, The Cocktail Party, etc; made her New York début at the Jan Hus Auditorium, Nov 1954, as Olivia in Twelfth Night; Ethel Barrymore, June 1956, appeared in the revue New Faces of 1956; Belasco, Apr 1957, played Princess Charlotte in The First Gentleman; Shakespeare Festival, Stratford, Conn, summer 1958, played Ophelia in Hamlet, Helena in A Midsummer Night's Dream, and Perdita in The Winter's Tale; Walnut, Philadelphia, Sept 1958, Amy Kittridge in A Swim in the Sea; Shakespeare Festival, Stratford, Conn, summer 1959, played Juliet in Romeo and Juliet; Phoenix, Jan 1960, Solveig in Peer Gynt; Arena Stage, Washington, DC, spring 1963, Desdemona in Othello; Broadhurst, Oct 1963, Lizzie Currie in 110 in the Shade, subsequently touring in the same production; Broadway, Feb 1965, played Irene Adler in Baker Street; made her London début at the Palace, Feb 1967, when she played Lizzie Currie in 110 in the Shade; Parker Playhouse, Fort Lauderdale, Fla, Nov 1967, Mary Stuart in Mary; New York City Center, June 1968, Eliza Doolittle in My Fair Lady; Ahmanson, Los Angeles, Dec 1972, played in The Crucible; same theatre, Feb 1979, Lady More in A Man for All Seasons; has appeared frequently in stock since 1960, and in a number of productions at the New Stage, Jackson, Miss, including The Four Poster, 1979; cabaret appearances include the Brothers and Sisters, NY, 1975; first appeared in films 1963, as Mrs Keller in The Miracle Worker, and has since played in Advise and Consent; first appeared on television in Canada 1957, and has since appeared frequently in plays and series, including recently seasons of *Soap*, and *Benson*.

Favourite part: Lizzie Currie. *Address:* 48 Paloma Avenue, Venice, Calif 90291.

SWENSON, Swen, actor, singer and dancer
b Inwood, Iowa, 23 Jan 1932; *s* of Swen L Swenson and his wife Myrtle (Knutson); *e* Sioux Falls, South Dakota; formerly a bank clerk, model, clothing salesman, farmer; studied for the stage with Mira Rostova, Keith Davis, and with the American School of Ballet.

Made his first professional appearance on the stage at the Winter Garden, New York, Mar 1950, as a dancer in Great to Be Alive; Mark Hellinger, Dec 1950, appeared as a dancer in Bless You All; ANTA, 1952, Jewel in As I Lay Dying; toured in concert as a mime with Mata and Hari; played in summer theatres in Annie Get Your Gun, Plain and Fancy, Guys and Dolls, Kiss Me Kate, etc; Library of Congress, Washington, DC, 1958 played the Poet-Prince in the première of Menotti's The Unicorn, the Manticore, and the Gorgon; Rooftop, June 1958, played Blazes Boylan, Navvy, Dark Mercury, Hobgoblin, Professor Maginni, and Watch, in Ulysses in Nighttown; Imperial, Apr 1959, played Bugs Watson in Destry Rides Again, which ran for 472 performances; Alvin, Dec 1960, Oney Tate in Wildcat; York Playhouse, Feb 1962, played Hector Charybdis in The Golden Apple; Lunt-Fontanne, Nov 1962, played George Musgrove in Little Me; toured the US, 1963, as Joey in Pal Joey; toured the US, 1964, as George Musgrove in Little Me; made his first appearance in London at the Cambridge, Nov 1964, in his original part in Little Me; Mark Hellinger, Dec 1966, Bliss Stanley in A Joyful Noise; Mineola, Long Island, 1967, the Devil in The Apple Tree; Bouwerie Lane, Oct 1969, co-produced And Puppy Dog Tails; Music Hall, Dallas, Texas, Oct 1972, Billy·Early in No, No, Nanette, and subsequently toured until Aug 1973

in this part; Alvin, Nov 1973, Michael Stone in Molly; Winter Garden, Mar 1974, choreographed and played Bella-Bellow in Ulysses in Nighttown; in Boston, 1974, played Professor Harold Hill in The Music Man; summer tour, 1976, Richard Henry Lee in 1776; Ford's, Washington, 1978 and 1979, appeared in The American Dance Machine; Curran, San Francisco, and Shubert, Los Angeles, 1978–9, Rooster Hannigan in Annie; produced Do You Think the Rain Will Hurt the Rhubarb, Hollywood, 1979; has performed in cabaret, including one year at the Lido in Paris, and as a solo dancer at the Radio City Music Hall in NY, 1963; films include: Nez de Cuir, Monte Carlo Baby, What's the Matter with Helen?, Ten from Your Show of Shows, 1972, etc; television appearances include: *The Ed Sullivan Show, Inside USA, Show of Shows, Perry Como Show, Martha Raye Show, Hit Parade,* etc.

Favourite parts: George Musgrove in Little Me, Joey in Pal Joey, Harold Hill in The Music Man, The Devil in The Apple Tree, and Blazes Boylan and Bella Bellow Cohen in Ulysses in Nighttown. *Recreations:* Breeding and showing Italian greyhounds and Yorkshire terriers; collecting giant woodcarvings. *Addresses:* 16 Minetta Lane, New York, NY 10012 and 1366 Angelo Drive, Beverly Hills, Calif 90210.

SWIFT, Clive, actor
b Liverpool, 9 Feb 1936; *s* of Abram Sampson Swift and his wife Lily Rebecca (Greenman); *e* Clifton College and Caius College, Cambridge; *m* Margaret Drabble (mar dis).

After appearing with the ADC and the Marlowe Society at Cambridge in parts including: Falstaff in Henry IV (both parts), he made his first professional appearance in Sept 1959 as Dr Bushtact in Take the Fool Away at the Playhouse, Nottingham; joined the Royal Shakespeare Company 1960 and remained with them until 1968, graduating from minor roles to parts which included: Cloten in Cymbeline, Pompey in Measure for Measure, Fluellen in Henry V, Falstaff in The Merry Wives of Windsor, Parolles in All's Well that Ends Well, the Porter in Macbeth, Oswald in King Lear, Inspector Voss in The Physicists, and the Sewerman in The Devils; Belgrade, Coventry, 1965, for Prospect, played Elvet Cross in The Big Breaker; Arts, Nov 1965, later Vaudeville and Garrick, Henry Straker in Man and Superman; Chichester Festival, June 1966, played Canton in The Clandestine Marriage and Michepain in The Fighting Cock; toured, 1966, for Prospect as Caliban in The Tempest, and Isaac Hooker in The Gamecock; Duchess, July 1969, Winston in The Young Churchill; at LAMDA, July 1970, directed The Wild Goose Chase and his own adaptation of The Lower Depths; Chichester, 1971, played Bob Acres in The Rivals, and Lapinet in Dear Antoine, transferring in the latter role to the Piccadilly; Jeannetta Cochrane, 1975, presented and played Robert in The Two of Me; toured US, 1975, for RSC, in The Hollow Crown; Arts, 1976, took over as The Chairman in Dirty Linen; Royal Court, Sept 1978, Hudson in Inadmissible Evidence; Royal Exchange, Manchester Dec 1978, Baron Hardup in Cinderella; Haymarket, Leicester, 1979, James Turney in All Together Now (also, co-devisor); films include: Catch Us If You Can, Frenzy, and The National Health; since 1961 has appeared in numerous television plays and series, notably *Waugh on Crime*, Clayhanger, The Exorcist, Home Movies, etc; is a frequent broadcaster; has taught and directed since 1970 at RADA and LAMDA; author of the Job of Acting, 1976; founder of the Actors' Centre, 1979.

Recreations: Music and sports. *Address:* c/o ICM, 22 Grafton Street, London W1.

SWINBURNE, Nora, actress
b Bath, 24 July 1902; *d* of Henry Swinburne Johnson and his

wife Leonora Tamia (Brain); *e* Rosholme College, weston-super-Mare; *m* (1) Francis Lister (mar dis); (2) Edward Ashley-Cooper (mar dis); (3) Esmond Knight; studied for the stage at the Royal Academy of Dramatic Art.

She was a member of Clive Currie's Young Players in 1914, and appeared at the Grand, Croydon, Court, and Little Theatres, during that year; while still a student at the Academy, appeared at the New Theatre, 11 Apr 1916, as The Wild Flowers in Paddly Pools; appeared at the Comedy Theatre, Sept 1916, as a dancer in This and That, and Oct 1916, appeared in Samples; at the Globe, Mar 1917, played Gabrielle in Suzette; Prince of Wales's, Dec 1917, Lulu in Yes, Uncle!; at the Strand, Dec 1918, played Regina Waterhouse in Scandal; at the Apollo, 1919, played Tilly in Tilly of Bloomsbury, for about six weeks; at the Gaiety, Jan 1921, Roselle in The Betrothal; at the St James's, Jan 1922, Miss Dale Ogden in The Bat; the following year went to America, and at the Lyceum, New York, May 1923, played Evadne in The Mountebank; at the Belasco, NY, Sept 1923, Sheila in Mary, Mary, Quite Contrary; on returning to England, appeared at the St Martin's, June 1924, as Lorna Webster in In the Next Room; at the Little Theatre, Dec 1924, played Veronica Duane in You and I; at the Vaudeville, Mar 1925, Joan Lee Tevis in Tarnish; New, Aug 1925, Nora in No 17; Lyric, Mar 1926, Marion Lennox in The Best People; Prince of Wales's, Jan 1928, Lady Blair in Regatta and Ann in Outward Bound; Haymarket, Feb 1928, Susan Cunningham in The Fourth Wall; Criterion, Dec 1928, Hyacinth in Out Goes She; St James's, Feb 1929, Sonia in Fame; Lyric, June 1929, Sylvia Armitage in Murder on the Second Floor; went to NY, and at the Booth Theatre, Apr 1930, played Yolande Probyn in Lady Clara; on returning to London, at the Comedy, Oct 1930, played Betty Mainwaring in Lucky Dip; Prince of Wales's, Feb 1931, Laurel Prescott in The Ninth Man; Grafton, July 1931, Helen in Disturbance; Whitehall, Dec 1931, Fay d'Allary in The Gay Adventure; Phoenix, Oct 1932, Lady Moynton in Never Come Back; Daly's, Feb 1933, Anne Vernon in It's You I Want; Queen's, Dec 1933, Sybil Kingdom in The Old Folks at Home; Vaudeville, Oct 1934, Helen Storer in Lovers' Leap; Criterion, Apr 1935, Phyllis Manton in All Rights Reserved; Westminster (for the Charta Theatre), May 1935, Helen Westdrake in Disturbance; St Martin's, Jan 1936, Marie in Sauce for the Gander; Daly's, May 1936, Judith Godfrey in The King's Leisure; Duke of York's, Dec 1936, Louise Dexter in The Astonished Ostrich; Lyric, Feb 1937, Tony Campion in Wise To-Morrow; Daly's, May 1937, Lady Hazel in African Dawn; Adelphi, Oct 1937, Maryka in The Laughing Cavalier; Palace, Feb 1938, Edith Cartwright in Dodsworth; Duke of York's (for London International Theatre), Apr 1938, Dinah Lot in Lot's Wife, which she reproduced under her own management at the Whitehall, June 1938, subsequently transferring to the Aldwych and Savoy; King's, Hammersmith, Apr 1939, played Fanny Grey in Autumn Crocus; St Martin's, May 1939, Ann Mordaunt in Third Party Risk; Aldwych, Nov 1939, Mrs Oswald Pink in Married for Money; Duke of York's, May 1940, Frances Courtenay in The Peaceful Inn; Globe, Jan 1941, Mrs Purdie in Dear Brutus; Apollo, Nov 1941, Sorel Tree in Ducks and Drakes; Palace, Apr 1942, Carole Markoff in Full Swing; St James's, Aug 1943, succeeded Valerie Taylor, as Natalia Petrovna in A Month in the Country; Aldwych, Oct 1943, succeeded Diana Wynyard as Sara Muller in Watch on the Rhine; Wyndham's, Jan 1945, Diana Wentworth in The Years Between, which ran over a year; Embassy, June 1947, played Lady Clare Marten in Miranda; Saville, Nov 1947, Elsa Meredith in Honour and Obey; Arts, Mar 1949, Caroline Ashley in Caroline; Garrick,

Feb 1952, played Jane Cooper in Red Letter Day; Savoy, Feb 1953, Mrs Arbuthnot in A Woman of No Importance; Grand, Blackpool, Oct 1954, Naomi Martyn in The Secret Tent; Garrick, London, June 1955, Mrs Astley in The Lost Generation; Royal, Nottingham, Oct 1955, Adelaide Lovell in The Call of the Dodo; Apollo, Apr 1959, Catherine Hayling in Fool's Paradise; Everyman, Cheltenham, June 1960, Diana in I Seem To Know Your Face; Westminster, May 1962, played the Chief Minister's Wife in Music at Midnight, subsequently touring the US, Jan 1963, with the same production; Hampstead Theatre Club, Apr 1964, Liz in All Good Children; for 69 Theatre Co, Manchester, played Violet in The Family Reunion, Oct 1973, and Julia Shuttlethwaite in The Cocktail Party, Sept 1975; commenced film career in 1921 and has appeared in numerous productions, including: Conspiracy of Hearts, Decision at Midnight, A Man Could Get Killed, Interlude, and Anne of the Thousand Days; recent television appearances include: Fall of Eagles, George Sand, and The Early Life of Stephen Hind.

Recreation: Gardening. *Address:* c/o Peter Eade Ltd, 9 Cork Street, London, W1.

SYMONDS, Robert, actor, producer, and director
b Bristow, Oklahoma, 1 Dec 1926; *s* of Walter Stout Symonds and his wife Nellie (Barry); *e* University of Texas, 1943–4, 1948–54 and University of Missouri, 1944–5; *m* Jan Kaderli; studied with Ben Iden Payne.

In 1954 became affiliated with the Actors Workshop in San Francisco as actor and director; acted in, among other plays, Waiting for Godot, in which he played Estragon at the Marines, San Francisco, Mar 1957; made his New York début in this part at the York, Aug 1958, and played it in Brussels, Belgium, at the World's Fair, Sept 1958, and at the Seattle World's Fair, July 1962; played Archie Rice in The Entertainer, Feb 1959, Hamm in Endgame, May 1959; War Memorial Opera House, San Francisco, Oct 1959, played the Major Domo in Ariadne auf Naxos; Krapp in Krapp's Last Tape, Feb 1961; directed The Maids, Mar 1961; played Galileo in the play of that name, Dec 1962; directed and played Volpone, Feb 1963; directed The Taming of the Shrew, Oct 1963; played Davies in The Caretaker, Nov 1963; directed The Night of the Iguana, Apr 1964; joined the Repertory Theater of Lincoln Center and, at the Vivian Beaumont, Oct 1965, played Robespierre in Danton's Death; Mr Sparkish in The Country Wife, which he also directed, Dec 1965; a Judge and Azdak in The Caucasian Chalk Circle, Mar 1966; became Associate Director of the Repertory Theatre of Lincoln Center in 1966; played Jeremy Butler in The Alchemist, Oct 1966; directed The East Wind, Feb 1967; played Federzoni in Galileo, Apr 1967; Chaplain de Stogumber in Saint Joan, Jan 1968; Demokos in Tiger at the Gates, Feb 1968; Cyrano in Cyrano de Bergerac, Apr 1968; Kemp in A Cry of Players, Nov 1968; at the Forum, Dec 1968, directed Bananas; played Dominic Christian in The Inner Journey, Mar 1969; Vivian Beaumont, May 1969, Harpagon in The Miser; Ward V Evans in In the Matter of J Robert Oppenheimer, June 1969; Kit Carson in The Time of Your Life, Nov 1969; The Forum, Jan 1970, Mendacious Porpentine in The Disintegration of James Cherry; Duff in Landscape, Rumsey in Silence, Apr 1970; directed Amphitryon, May 1970; Vivian Beaumont, directed The Good Woman of Setzuan, Nov 1970; played Lord Mulligan in Camino Real; Jan 1971, associate director of The Playboy of the Western World; Forum, Feb 1971, Goldberg in The Birthday Party, Rumsey in Silence, and Duff in Landscape; Mar 1971, played in Scenes from American Life; June 1971, Edgar in Play

Strindberg; Vivian Beaumont, Nov 1971, Sir Amias Paulet in Mary Stuart; Jan 1972, Basho in Narrow Road to the Deep North; Studio Arena, Buffalo, NY, 1972, Edgar in Play Strindberg; Olney, Md, Playhouse, Aug 1972, Fintan Kinmore in Patrick Pearse Motel; Vivian Beaumont, Nov 1972, Zekhar Bardin in Enemies; Mar 1973, Duke of Venice in The Merchant of Venice; left the Repertory Theater of Lincoln Center and toured, summer 1973, as the Prime Minister in The Student Prince; Alley, Houston, Texas, Feb 1974, Edgar in Comedy of Marriage; Mark Taper Forum, LA, July 1974, four parts in The Death and Life of Jesse James; Ambassador, Jan 1976, Sergeant Coyne in The Poison Tree; Alley, Apr 1976, appeared in The Show-Off; same theatre, 1977, directed Endgame, Mar, and appeared in How the Other Half Loves, Apr; 1978, directed Root of the Mandrake, Jan, Absurd Person Singular, Apr, and appeared in The Shadow Box, Mar; in 1979 appeared in Artichoke, Don Juan in Hell and Side by Side by Sondheim; McCarter, Princeton, 1979, appeared in A Month in the Country; was a member of the faculty of the University of California Extension, 1964–5.

Address: c/o Hesseltine-Baker Associates, 119 West 57th Street, New York, NY 10019.

SYMPSON, Tony, actor

b London, 10 July 1906; *s* of George Percy Sympson and his wife Hilda Clara (Goodwin); *e* St Clement Danes Grammar School, London; *m* Jill Kettle; trained for the stage at the Etlinger Theatre School, London; formerly an insurance inspector.

Contracted to Maurice Browne who sublet him for his first appearance at the Royal Birmingham, Oct 1929, as a speciality dancer in Dear Love, and first appeared in London at the Palace, 14 Nov 1929, in the same production; Duchess, Mar 1930, appeared in The Intimate Revue; London Hippodrome, June 1930, played in Sons O'Guns; Comedy, Apr 1933, appeared in the revue How D'You Do?; toured, 1934, as Jim in Mr Cinders; Queen's, Mar 1936, played The Pioneer in Red Night; Comedy, Oct 1936, played Andy Hardy in All-In Marriage; His Majesty's, Sept 1938, played Jarvis in Paprika toured for ENSA, at home and in the Middle East, 1940–4; played with the New London Opera Company in seasons at the Cambridge and Stoll theatres, 1946–8; New, Oct 1951, played Pelling in the musical version of And So To Bed; Arts, Sept 1953, appeared as The Patient in Penelope; Palladium, Dec 1953, played Buttercup, one of the Ugly Sisters, in Cinderella; Stoll, Dec 1954, The Saucepan Man in Noddy In Toyland; Rudolf Steiner, Mar 1955, the Notary in Chestnuts in Soho; Princes, Dec 1955, again played the Saucepan Man in Noddy in Toyland; Strand (for the Repertory Players) Mar 1956, Sylvester Crumb in Things That Go Bump; Stoll, Dec 1956, the Saucepan Man in Noddy in Toyland; Players', Dec 1958, Daniel Jaikes in The Silver King; Palace, May 1959, George in The World of Paul Slickey; Piccadilly, Oct 1959, Dr Bahys in The Love Doctor; Princes, Dec 1959, Saucepan Man in Noddy in Toyland; Players', Dec 1961, Baron Balderdash and Pantaloon in Cinderella; Comedy, May 1962, played Fleet Foot in Little Mary Sunshine; at the Flora Robson Playhouse, Newcastle upon Tyne, Sept 1962, Grandad in Azouk; London Palladium, Dec 1962, The Cobbler in Puss in Boots; Saville, July 1963, Fogg in Pickwick, subsequently making his first appearance in the US, at the Curran, San Francisco, Apr 1965, in the same musical; 46th Street, New York, Oct 1965, again played Fogg in Pickwick; Palladium, May 1966, Guy Fawkes in London Laughs; Her Majesty's, Feb 1967, Mordcha in Fiddler on the Roof; Cambridge Theatre, May 1972, Mr Lee in Tom Brown's Schooldays; Theatre Royal, Windsor, 1973, Sir George Lancaster in Mr Cinders; Her Majesty's, Feb 1974, Giovanni in Henry IV; Chichester, 1974, Shepherd in Œdipus Tyrannus; Coliseum, Dec 1974, Smee in Peter Pan; played the same part at the Palladium, Dec 1975, at the London Casino, 1977, and at the Shaftesbury, 1978; has appeared in films since 1930; and also television productions, council member, British Actors' Equity, 1975–6; Actors' Church Union, 1953–; Royal General Theatrical Fund, 1954–.

Favourite parts: Pappacoda in A Night In Venice, Jaikes in The Silver King, and Smee. *Recreations:* Gardening and music. *Club:* Green Room. *Address:* 24 Bedfordbury, London, WC2N 4BL. *Tel:* 01–836 4539.

T

TABORI, George, playwright

b Budapest, Hungary, 24 May 1914; *s* of Cornelius Tabori and his wife Elsa (Ziffer); *e* Zrinyl Gymnasium; *m* Viveca Lindfors (mar dis); during the Second World War served in the British Army as an Intelligence officer; formerly a waiter and cook, foreign correspondent, etc.

First play produced in New York was Flight into Egypt, at the Music Box, 18 Mar 1952; since has written The Emperor's Clothes, 1953; adapted Miss Julie, 1956; wrote Brouhaha, produced at the Aldwych, London, Aug 1958; adapted and arranged Brecht on Brecht, 1962; adapted Max Frisch's Andorra and Brecht's Arturo Ui for NY productions, 1963; with his wife formed a five-member company called The Strolling Players, 1966, which toured in various plays, notably Brecht on Brecht; wrote The Niggerlovers, which consists of two one-act plays entitled The Demonstration and Man and Dog, 1967; The Cannibals, 1968; adapted from Brecht The Guns of Carrar, 1968; wrote Pinkville, produced by the Berkshire Theatre Festival, Stockbridge, Massachusetts, 1970; moved to West Germany, 1971, where he has since been active as playwright and director; founder of the experimental group Bremen Theater Labor, 1975–8; resident director, Munich Kammerspiele, 1978–; author of the play Talk Show; wrote the screenplay for Young Lovers, produced by J Arthur Rank in 1952, and received the Academy Award for it; also wrote the screenplays for I Confess, directed by Alfred Hitchcock, 1953, The Journey, 1959, No Exit, 1962, Secret Ceremony, 1969, Parades, 1972, etc; directed the film White Christmas, 1980; received the Prix Italia, 1978, for his radio play Weisman and Copperhead; is the author of a number of novels and short stories, notably Beneath the Stone, Companions of the Left Hand, Original Sin, The Caravan Passes, The Good One, Sons and Bitches (1980), etc.

Recreation: Chess. *Address:* Kammerspiele, Hildegard-strasse 1, Munich. *Tel:* 22 53 71.

TAGG, Alan, designer

b Sutton-in-Ashfield, 13 Apr 1928; *s* of Thomas Bertram Tagg, and his wife Edith Annie (Hufton); trained for the stage at the Old Vic Theatre School.

His first stage designs were for The River Line, London, 1952; he has since designed numerous plays, principally in London, including: The Burning Glass, Waiting for Gillian, Both Ends Meet, Bell Book and Candle, Simon and Laura, 1954; Julius Caesar (Old Vic—costumes only), 1955; The Merchant of Venice (Stratford), Look Back in Anger, Cards of Identity, 1956; The Member of the Wedding, Look Back in Anger (New York), The Entertainer, 1957; Live Like Pigs, The Entertainer (NY), 1958; The Long and the Short and the Tall, One More River, 1959; A Majority of One, Billy Liar, The Geese Are Getting Fat, 1960; JB, Time and Yellow Roses, The American Dream and The Death of Bessie Smith (double-bill), The Fire Raisers, 1961; Play with a Tiger, England, Our England, Plays for England, 1962; Trap for a Lonely Man, Kelly's Eye, The Albatross, 1963; All in Good Time (NY), A Cuckoo in the Nest, 1964; Meals on Wheels, Trelawny of the Wells (Chichester), 1965; Black Comedy (National Theatre, later NY), The Fighting Cock, The Clan-

destine Marriage, The Cherry Orchard, Macbeth (all Chichester), Belcher's Luck, 1966; Halfway Up the Tree, 1967; Spitting Image, Mr and Mrs 1968; Come as You Are, After Haggerty, London Assurance, How the Other Half Loves, Mrs Warren's Profession, 1970; Dear Antoine (also Chichester), Straight Up, 1971; Alpha Beta, Hedda Gabler, Time and Time Again, 1972; The Cherry Orchard (National), The Director of the Opera (Chichester), Absurd Person Singular, Dandy Dick (also Chichester), The Constant Wife (also NY), 1973; London Assurance (NY), 1974; Alphabetical Order, The Gay Lord Quex, The Bed Before Yesterday, The Seagull, The Return of A J Raffles, 1975; Confusions, Donkey's Years, Same Time Next Year, 1976; Candida, Waters of the Moon, The Kingfisher (also New York, 1978), 1977; Whose Life is it Anyway? (also New York, 1979), The Millionairess, Alice's Boys, 1978; Joking Apart, Bent (London and New York), Middle Age Spread, Not Now Darling, 1979; has also designed in Europe and Australia.

Address: 54 Bradbourne Street, London, SW6.

TANDY, Jessica, actress

b London, 7 June 1909; *d* of Harry Tandy and his wife Jessie Helen (Horspool); *e* Dame Owen's Girls' School; *m* (1) Jack Hawkins (mar dis); (2) Hume Cronyn (Young); studied for the stage at the Ben Greet Academy of Acting.

Made her first appearance on the stage at Playroom Six, 22 Nov 1927, as Sara Manderson in The Manderson Girls; appeared at the Birmingham Repertory Theatre, in 1928, as Gladys in The Comedy of Good and Evil, also appearing there as Ginevra in Alice Sit-by-the-Fire; subsequently toured as Lydia Blake in Yellow Sands; made her first appearance in London, at the Court Theatre, 21 Feb 1929, as Lena Jackson in The Rumour; Arts, Apr 1929, played the Typist in The Theatre of Life; Little, June 1929, Maggie in Water; Haymarket, Nov 1929, Aude in The Unknown Warrior; she then went to New York, where she made her first appearance at the Longacre Theatre, Mar 1930, as Toni Rakonitz in The Matriarch; returned to London, and in the summer, played Olivia in Twelfth Night, for the OUDS, at Oxford; returned to NY, and appeared at the Shubert Theatre, Oct 1930, as Cynthia in The Last Enemy; on returning to London, appeared at the St Martin's Theatre, Jan 1931, as Fay in The Man Who Pays the Piper; Lyric, Apr 1931, Audrey in Autumn Crocus; Wyndham's, Nov 1931, Ruth Blair in Port Said; Arts, Nov 1931, Anna in Musical Chairs; Repertory Players, Jan 1932, played in Below the Surface; Phoenix, Feb 1932, played in Juarez and Maximilian; from Apr–June 1932, played leads at the Cambridge Festival Theatre, including Troilus and Cressida, See Naples and Die, The Witch, Rose Without a Thorn, The Inspector General, and The Servant of Two Masters; St Martin's (for the Sunday Players), July 1932, played Carlotta in Mutual Benefit; Duchess, Oct 1932, Manuela in Children in Uniform; Arts, Jan 1933, Alicia Audley in Lady Audley's Secret; Embassy, May 1933, Marikke in Midsummer Fires; Open Air Theatre, July 1933, Titania in A Midsummer Night's Dream; at the Haymarket, Nov 1933, succeeded Maisie Darrell as Betty in Ten Minute Alibi; Cambridge, Feb 1934, Rosamund in Birthday; Duke of York's, Oct 1934, Eva Whiston in Line Engaged; Manchester, Hippodrome, Apr–May 1934, Viola in Twelfth Night, and Anne Page in The Merry Wives of Windsor; New, Nov 1934, Ophelia in Hamlet; July 1935, Ada in Noah; Whitehall, Nov 1935, Anna Penn in Anthony and Anna; Queen's, Aug 1936, Marie Rose in The Ante-Room; Criterion, Nov 1936, Jacqueline in French Without Tears; Arts, Dec 1936, Pamela March in Honour Thy Father; Old Vic, Feb–Apr 1937, Viola and Sebastian in Twelfth Night, and Katherine in Henry V; St James's, June 1937, Ellen Murray in Yes, My Darling Daughter; Ritz, NY, Jan 1938, Kay in Time and the Conways; Duchess, London, May 1938, Leda in Glorious Morning; Cort, NY, Jan 1939, Nora Fintry in The White Steed; on returning to London, appeared at the Open Air Theatre, July 1939, as Viola in Twelfth Night; toured in Canada, Sept 1939, with Maurice Colbourne and Barry Jones in Charles the King, Geneva and Tobias and the Angel; Henry Miller, NY, Jan 1940, the Deaconess in Geneva; returned to London, and appeared at the Old Vic, Apr–May, 1940, playing Cordelia in King Lear, and Miranda in The Tempest; Biltmore, NY, Sept 1940, Dr Mary Murray in Jupiter Laughs; St James, Oct 1941, Abigail Hill in Anne of England; Guild, Apr 1942, Cattrin in Yesterday's Magic; at Los Angeles, 1946, appeared in Portrait of a Madonna; Ethel Barrymore, NY, Dec 1947, Blanche Dubois in A Streetcar Named Desire, for over two years, and subsequently toured in the same part, and won the Twelfth Night Club Award and the Antoinette Perry Award of 1948; Brattle, Cambridge, Mass 1950, played in The Little Blue Light; Coronet, NY, Nov 1950, appeared as Hilda Crane in the play of that name; at the Ethel Barrymore, Oct 1951, Agnes in The Fourposter, for which performance she received the Comoedia Matinee Club Bronze Medallion, subsequently touring extensively in this part; Phoenix, Dec 1953, Mary Doyle in Madame, Will You Walk; US tour, 1954, with Hume Cronyn in concert readings Face to Face; New York City Center, Jan 1955, again appeared as Agnes in The Fourposter; Longacre, Apr 1955, Mary in The Honey's; ANTA Playhouse, Sept 1955, Frances Farrar in A Day by the Sea; US tour with Hume Cronyn, summer 1958, in Triple Play; Coronet, NY, Oct 1958, Martha Walling in The Man in the Dog Suit; Palm Beach Playhouse, Mar 1959, Mrs Morgan in I Spy, Angela Nightingale in Bedtime Story and Innocent Bystander in A Pound on Demand in a programme entitled Triple Play; Playhouse, NY, Apr 1959, again played the same parts in Triple Play, excepting I Spy but with the addition of Miss Collins in Portrait of a Madonna; Music Box, Dec 1959, Louise Harrington in Five Finger Exercise, subsequently touring in the production, 1960; American Shakespeare Festival, Stratford, Conn, 1961, Lady Macbeth and Cassandra in Troilus and Cressida; Duke of York's, London, Sept 1962, Edith Maitland in Big Fish, Little Fish; Tyrone Guthrie, Minneapolis, Minn, summer 1963, Gertrude in Hamlet, Olga in The Three Sisters, and Linda Loman in Death of a Salesman; Martin Beck, NY, Oct 1964, Doktor Mathilde von Zahnd in The Physicists; Tyrone Guthrie, Minneapolis, summer 1965, Lady Wishfort in The Way of the World, Madame Ranevskaya in The Cherry Orchard, and the Mother-in-Law in The Caucasian Chalk Circle; on 2 Feb 1965, at the invitation of President Johnson, she performed with her husband at the White House in Hear America Speaking; Martin Beck, Sept 1966, Agnes in A Delicate Balance, for which she received the Leland Powers Honor Award and in which she toured Jan–June 1967; Mark Taper Forum, Mar 1968, Frosine in The Miser; for the Shaw Festival, Niagara-on-the-Lake, Ontario, July 1968, Hesione Hushabye in Heartbreak House; Ivanhoe, Chicago, Oct 1969, Pamela

Pew-Pickett in Tchin-Tchin; Vivian Beaumont, Jan 1970, Marguerite Gautier in Camino Real; Morosco, Jan 1971, took over from Dandy Nichols as Marjorie in Home; Martin Beck, Mar 1971, The Wife in All Over; Forum, Nov 1972, Winnie in Happy Days and Mouth in Not I, for which she received the Obie and Drama Desk Awards; toured, summer 1972 and winter 1973, in Promenade All!; Ethel Barrymore, Feb 1974, Anna-May Conklin in Come into the Garden, Maude, and Hilde Latymer in A Song at Twilight in the double-bill Noel Coward in Two Keys, and subsequently toured; toured, Oct 1974 and subsequently, in the dramatic reading The Many Faces of Love; Stratford, Ontario, Festival, 1976 played Lady Wishfort in The Way of the World, Hippolyta/Titania in a Midsummer Night's Dream, and Eve in Eve; Theatre London, Ontario, 1977, Mary Tyrone in Long Day's Journey into Night; John Golden, Oct 1977, Fonsia Dorsey in The Gin Game (Tony Award), subsequently touring in the part, including the Lyric, London, July 1979, and Russia, autumn 1979; Stratford, Ontario, season 1980, appeared in Foxfire, and again played Mary Tyrone; made her film début in England in 1932 when she appeared in The Indiscretions of Eve; subsequently appeared in American films, including: The Seventh Cross, Valley of Decision, Dragonwyck, The Birds, etc; has appeared on television frequently since 1948, including: Portrait of a Madonna, the *Alfred Hitchcock Program, Hallmark Hall of Fame,* and with Sir Laurence Olivier in The Moon and Sixpence, 1959; with her husband appeared in the radio series The Marriage, which was televised in 1954; became a naturalized American citizen, 1954; Branden's University Creative Arts Award, 1978; Hon LLD, U of Western Ontario, 1974.
Club: Cosmopolitan. *Address:* Box 85A, RR 2 Pound Ridge, New York, NY 19576.

TANNER, Tony, actor, director, singer, dancer and writer *b* Hillingdon, 27 Jul 1932; *s* of Herbert Arthur Tanner and his wife Frances Rosina; *e* Bishopshalt Grammar School, Middlesex; trained for the stage at Webber Douglas School.

After National Service, made his stage debut at Oldham, 1953, in repertory; later at Sheffield, where he contributed book and lyrics to a musical version of The Snow Queen; made his London debut at the Lyric, Hammersmith, 15 Jul 1959, in the revue One to Another, which transferred later to the Apollo; contributed to the revue Fine Fettle at the Palace, Aug 1959; Fortune, Jan 1960, appeared in the revue Look Who's Here, to which he contributed lyrics and sketches; Lyric Hammersmith, Apr 1962, Barry Paice in The Last Enemy; Queen's, Oct 1962, took over from Anthony Newley as Littlechap in Stop the World — I Want to Get Off; Arts, Oct 1963, devised, directed and appeared in Four and a Tanner; at the Oxford Playhouse in 1964 directed Hay Fever, Romeo and Jeannette, and Who's Afraid of Virginia Woolf?; made his New York debut at the Broadhurst, 1965, when he took over from Tommy Steele as Kipps in Half-a-Sixpence; Stage 73, Feb 1968, directed I Only Want an Answer; Bouwerie Lane, Sept 1968, directed The Happy Hypocrite; New, NY, Dec 1969, played Sonny in The Coffee Lace, and the title role in Trevor, in the double-bill Little Boxes; Bijou, May 1971, Lenny in The Homecoming; Ritz, Feb 1973, Brian Runnicles in No Sex, Please — We're British; Broadhurst, Feb 1975, took over as Sidney Prince in Sherlock Holmes; made his Broadway directing debut with Something's Afoot, Lyceum, 1976, and has since directed Something's Afoot, and The Club, London 1977; Gorey Stories, NY, 1977; Class Enemy, NY, 1979; has acted outside New York on tours and in regional theatres, and has directed opera in Chicago; other writing for the stage includes a musical adaptation of Thieves'

Carnival, seen at the Belgrade, Coventry, and the revue Words, New Jersey, 1980; films include Stop the World — I Want to Get Off, and Strictly for the Birds; TV includes plays, the revue series *Call It What You Like* etc.

Favourite parts: Iago, Puck, Charley in Where's Charley?
Address: 317 West 93rd Street, New York, NY 10025.

TAVEL, Ronald, playwright, scenarist, lyricist, essayist, poet, novelist
b Brooklyn, New York, May 1941; *s* of George Tavel and his wife Florence (Sterns); *e* Brooklyn College and the University of Wyoming; previously engaged as a tutor.

First published play was Christina's World, a three-act verse play, 1958; has since written the following plays: Tarzan of the Flicks, 1963; Screen Test, The Life of Juanita Castro, Shower, the last two being his first plays produced in NY, at the Saint Mark's Playhouse, 29 July 1965, Vinyl, 1965; The Life of Lady Godiva, Indira Gandhi's Daring Device, 1966; Kitchenette, Gorilla Queen, 1967; Canticle of the Nightingale, performed in Stockholm, Sweden, Cleobis and Bito, a one-act Oratorio produced by The Extension, NY, Arenas of Lutetia, 1968; Boy on the Straight-Back Chair, a musical which received the Obie Award, 1969; Vinyl Visits an FM Station, Bigfoot, 1970; Secrets of the Citizens Correction Committee, How Jacqueline Kennedy Became Queen of Greece, 1973; The Last Days of British Honduras, 1974; Playbirth, The Clown's Tail (for children), 1976; Gazelle Boy, The Ovens of Anita Orangejuice, 1977; The Ark of God, 1978, premiere 1979; The Nutcracker in the Land of Nuts, 1979; has written the scenarios of various films produced and directed by Andy Warhol, notably Harlot, Philip's Screen Test, Suicide, Horse, Space, 1965; Hedy, or the 14-Year Old Girl, Withering Sights, The Chelsea Girls, 1966, and the films of his plays; founded and named the Theatre of the Ridiculous Movement, July 1965; founding member of the New York Theatre Strategy, 1971–9; his plays have been produced by leading avant-garde troupes throughout the world, among them the Caffe Cino, Theatre of the Ridiculous, American Place Theater, No Exit Cafe in Chicago, in Rotterdam, Copenhagen, Sweden, and by Yale, Columbia, Rutgers, Judson Memorial Church, etc; was Playwright in Residence at Actors Studio in 1972, Playhouse of the Ridiculous, 1965–7, Theatre of the Lost Continent, 1971–3, Yale Divinity School, 1975 and 1977, Williamstown Theatre Festival, 1977, O'Neill Playwrights Conference, 1977, New Playwrights' Theatre, Washington DC, 1978–9; is a noted critic of films and has published articles and essays on film in *Graffiti, Aspen, Tri-Quarterly, Film Culture, Filmwise, The New American Cinema, Inter/View*, etc; has published poetry extensively in some of the same periodicals and in *The Lyric, Fuck You, Poets at Le Metro, Chicago Review, Wormwood*, etc; his novel Street of Stairs published in English, 1968, and in German, 1969; is a Lecturer for the New York State Council on the Arts; has received Rockefeller Foundation, John Simon Guggenheim Memorial Foundation, and National Endowment for the Arts Fellowships, etc.

Hobbies and recreations: Travelling, swimming, acting.
Address: 1095 East 53rd Street, Brooklyn, NY 11234. *Tel:* 226–4725.

TAYLOR, Cecil P, dramatist
b Glasgow, Scotland, 6 Nov 1929; *s* of Max George Taylor and his wife Frances (Leventhal); *e* Queen's Park School, Glasgow; *m* (1) Irene Diamond (mar dis); (2) Elisabeth Screen; formerly a television engineer.

His plays include Ae Went to Blaydon Races, 1962; Fable, Happy Days are Here Again, 1964; Allergy, Bread and Butter, 1966; Who's Pinkus? Where's Chelm? 1967; Thank U

Very Much, 1968; What Can a Man Do? Brave, Lies about Vietnam and Truth about Sarajevo (double-bill), 1969; Em'n Ben, Brave, 1970; The Cleverness of Us, The Grace Darling Show, 1971; Me, The Black and White Minstrels, Happy Anniversary, 1972; You Are My Heart's Delight, The Grand Adultery Convention, Next Year in Tel Aviv, Oil and Water, Apples, Columba, 1973; Carol O K, Schippel (from Sternheim), So Far So Bad, The Spital Tongues Plays, 1974; Gynt (from Ibsen), Pilgrim (from Bunyan), The Killingworth Play, 1975; in the same year Schippel was seen in London under the title The Plumber's Progress; Bandits, Walter, Ophelia, Some Enchanted Evening, Give Us a Kiss, Open the Big Box, Peter Pan and Emily, The Longhorsley Nativity, 1977; Withdrawal Symptoms, The Magic Island, Cyrano, 1978; Operation Elvis, Peter Pan Man, And a Nightingale Sang, 1979; Literary Associate, Tyneside Theatre Company; Literary Adviser, Northumberland Association of Youth Theatres; Director, North E Writers' Workshop; Regional Theatre Adviser, in association with Northern Arts; long-term involvement in drama for the young and the mentally handicapped; has written frequently for television, since 1966, including the trilogy Revolution, Wings of Song, Great Expectations, etc; author of the book Making a Television Play, 1971.

Recreations: Natural history, walking, music, reading.
Address: 2 Smallburn Road, Longhorsley, Morpeth, Northumberland. *Tel:* Capheaton 259.

TAYLOR, Clarice, actress
b Buckingham County, Virginia, 20 Sept 1927; *d* of Leon B Taylor, Sr, and his wife Ophelia (Booker); *e* Madleigh High School, Columbia Univ; *m* Claude Banks, Jr (mar dis); prepared for the stage at the American Negro Theatre, of which she was a co-founder, the Harlem, NY, YMCA theater group, The New Theatre School, and the Negro Ensemble Company.

First appeared on the stage in NY at the American Negro Theatre, 1942, as Sophie Slow in On Strivers' Row; also appeared in Juno and the Paycock, John Henry, Hits Bits and Skits; Dec 1945, played Ann Drake in Home Is the Hunter; Nov 1946, Sister Maloney in The Peacemaker; Feb 1948, played in Rain; joined the Committee for the Negro in the Arts and played in Simple Speaks His Mind, A Medal for Willie, Gold Through the Trees, which she also directed; Greenwich Mews, Oct 1954, played in In Splendid Error, and also in Major Barbara; Nov 1955, played Willetta in Trouble in Mind, which she also co-directed; Nov 1957, played in The Twisting Road; Sept 1958, played in The Egg and I; during this time also appeared in The Doctor in Spite of Himself, in a street theatre production; Casa Galicia, Nov 1960, played Naomi in Nat Turner; joined the Negro Ensemble Company as an original member, and at the St Mark's Playhouse, 20 Feb 1968, played Emma Leech in Summer of the Seventeenth Doll; Apr 1968, Sarumi in Kongi's Harvest; June 1968, Annie in Daddy Goodness; Dec 1968, Reba in God Is a (Guess What?); Apr 1969, Mrs Rogers in String and Mrs Grace Love in Contribution, in a bill with the overall title An Evening of One Acts; made her London debut as a member of the troupe at the Aldwych, 5 May 1969, in Song of the Lusitanian Bogey, and on 8 May 1969 played Reba in God Is a (Guess What?), in the World Theatre Season; Teatro Pariola, Rome, Italy, June 1969, repeated these parts; St Mark's Playhouse, July 1969, Village Woman in Man Better Man; Mar 1970, Clubwoman in Day of Absence; May 1970, played in Akokawe (Initiation); St Clement's Church, Jan 1970, Mrs Brooks in Five on the Black Hand Side; St Mark's Playhouse, Jan 1971, Dolly Mae

Anderson in Rosalee Pritchett; Nov 1971, Weedy in The Sty of the Blind Pig; The Forum, Mar 1972, Mamma in The Duplex; Estelle Newman, Oct 1972, Fanny Johnson in Wedding Band; Munich, Germany, during the Summer Olympics, 1972, appeared at the Kammerspiele as Weedy in The Sty of the Blind Pig; toured USA, 1972, in To Be Young, Gifted, and Black; Majestic, Jan 1975, Addaperle in The Wiz, and played this part until the show closed in Jan 1979; has appeared in the films Change of Mind, 1969, Tell Me That You Love Me, Junie Moon, Play Misty for Me, Such Good Friends, Willie Dynamite, Five on the Black Hand Side, etc; has appeared on television in *Ironside, Owen Marshall, The Doctors, Sanford and Son*, and in various specials, including Wedding Band, A Friend to Freedom, Light in the Southern Sky, etc.

Favourite parts: Mrs Brooks in Five on the Black Hand Side, Mrs Grace Love in Contribution. *Recreations:* Her children, and life in general. *Address:* 8715 Sunset Plaza Terrace, Los Angeles, Calif 90069. *Tel:* 659–5804.

TAYLOR, John Russell, author and critic
b Dover, Kent, 19 June 1935; *s* of Arthur Russell Taylor and his wife Kathleen Mary (Picker); *e* Dover Grammar School, Jesus College, Cambridge and the Courtauld Institute of Art.

Film critic of *The Times* 1962–73; writer of theatre criticism for *Plays and Players*, etc; Professor of Cinema, Division of Performing Arts, University of Southern California, 1972–8; Art Critic of *The Times*, 1978–; his books include: Anger and After: a Guide to the New British Drama, 1962; The Penguin Dictionary of the Theatre, 1966; The Rise and Fall of the Well-Made Play, 1967; Look Back in Anger: a Casebook, 1968; Harold Pinter, 1969; The Second Wave: British Dramatists for the Seventies, 1971; David Storey, 1974; Directors and Directions, Peter Shaffer, 1975; Cukor's Hollywood, 1979; member, Critics Circle.

Recreations: Buying books, talking to strange dogs. *Address:* c/o The Times, Gray's Inn Road, London W1X 8EZ.

TAYLOR, Noel, costume designer
b Youngstown, Ohio, 17 Jan 1917; *s* of Harold A Taylor and his wife Margery (Clark); *e* Paris, France.

First designs for a New York production were the costumes for Alice in Wonderland, produced at the International, 5 Apr 1947; has since designed the costumes for Twentieth Century, 1950; Stalag 17, The Wild Duck, 1951; One Bright Day, The Male Animal, Bernardine, Dial M for Murder, 1952; The Teahouse of the August Moon, The Ladies of the Corridor, In the Summer House, 1953; The Burning Glass, The Teahouse of the August Moon (London), 1954; Festival, No Time for Sergeants, 1955; Time Limit!, The Apple Cart, Auntie Mame, 1956; Good as Gold, The Square Root of Wonderful, 1957; The Body Beautiful, 1958; Tall Story, 1959; The Wall, 1960; A Shot in the Dark, Write Me a Murder, The Night of the Iguana, 1961; Great Day in the Morning, 1962; Desire Under the Elms, Strange Interlude, One Flew over the Cuckoo's Nest, Marathon '33, 1963; What Makes Sammy Run?, Hughie, 1964; Matty and the Moron and Madonna, Baal, Play That on Your Old Piano, The White Devil, 1965; The Great Indoors, Slapstick Tragedy, The Loves of Cass McGuire, We have Always Lived in the Castle, 1966; Dr Cook's Garden, Song of the Grasshopper, 1967; We Bombed in New Haven, Possibilities, Lovers, 1968; The Mundy Scheme, 1969; Brightower, 1970; The Caine Mutiny Court Martial (Los Angeles), Ovid's Metamorphoses, 1971; The Crucible (LA), A Funny Thing Happened on the Way to the Forum, Mourning Becomes Electra, The

Last of Mrs Lincoln, 1972; The Mind with the Dirty Man (LA), The American Revolution (Washington, DC), 1973; Hamlet (LA), 1974; The Night of the Iguana (LA), The Norman Conquests, 1975; The Magnificent Yankee (Washington, DC), The Night of the Iguana, 1976; Merton of the Movies (LA), FOR (Washington, DC), Chapter 2, 1977; Absurd Person Singular (LA), Paul Robeson (also London), Diversions and Delights, 1978; designed the film Rhinoceros, 1974; has designed extensively for television, notably for *The Hallmark Hall of Fame,* the NBC Opera Company productions, *Dupont Show of the Week,* The Turn of the Screw, Boswell's Life of Johnson, etc.

Address: 8952 Norma Place, Los Angeles, Calif 90069. *Tel:* 272–4885.

TAYLOR, Samuel, dramatic author
b Chicago, Illinois, 13 June 1912; *e* University of California, Berkeley; *m* Suzanne Combes.

Author of the following plays: The Happy Time, 1950; Nina (an adaptation from the French of André Roussin), 1951; Sabrina Fair, 1953; The Pleasure of His Company (co-author with Cornelia Otis Skinner), 1958; First Love, 1961; No Strings, a musical (which he also co-produced with its composer, Richard Rodgers), 1962; Beekman Place (also directed and co-produced), 1964; Avanti! 1968; Perfect Pitch, 1974; Avanti! (produced as A Touch of Spring) at the Comedy, London, 1975; Legend, 1976; Gracious Living, 1978; Avanti was filmed in 1972; is President of the Dramatists Play Service, Inc.

Address: East Blue Hill, Maine. *Tel:* 374–9948.

TAYLOR, Valerie, actress
b Fulham, 10 Nov 1902; *d* of Major Frederick Edward Verney Taylor and his wife Florence Julia (Robarts); *e* Hamilton House, Tunbridge Wells, and Abbey House, Netley; *m* (1) Hugh Sinclair (mar dis); (2) Desborough William Saunders; studied for the stage at the RADA, receiving a two years' scholarship in 1920.

Made her first appearance on the stage at the Casino Theatre, Mentone, Jan 1922, in an English repertory, playing Juliet in French Leave, Isabella in Caroline, Miss Roberts in The Mollusc; returned to London to understudy Audrey Carten in The Dancers, at Wyndham's, 1923; made her first appearance on the London stage at the Royalty Theatre, Oct 1924, when she played the title-part in Storm in the absence of Elissa Landi; next toured as Violet Deering in Havoc; joined the Birmingham Repertory Company, Apr 1925, and played Rosario in The Romantic Young Lady and the Madonna in The Marvellous History of Saint Bernard; at the St Martin's, July 1925, played a Lady in The Show, subsequently playing Anne Morecombe in the same play; Garrick, Aug 1925, Judith in Cobra; Little, Oct 1925, Nina Zaretchny in The Seagull; joined the Macdona Players at the Regent, Dec 1925, and played Feemy Evans in The Shewing-Up of Blanco Posnet and Lavinia in Androcles and the Lion; same theatre, Mar 1926 (for the Repertory Players), played Hermione Gordon in The Rescue Party; Kingsway, Apr 1926, again played the Madonna in The Marvellous History of Saint Bernard; St Martin's, Oct 1926, Miss Pettigrew in Berkeley Square; Dec 1926, Lady Trevor in Behind the Beyond; Fortune, Apr 1927, Helen Hayle in On Approval; Vaudeville, May 1928, Betty Harlowe in The House of the Arrow; Lyric, Mar 1929, Kate Pettigrew in the revival of Berkeley Square; Fortune, Sept 1929, again played Nina in The Seagull; made her first appearance in New York, at the Lyceum Theatre, 4 Nov 1929, as Kate Pettigrew in Berkeley Square; Empire, Dec 1930, played the Countess of Darnaway in Petticoat Influence; Shubert, Apr 1931, Mrs Deane in Peter Ibbetson; 44th Street, Oct 1931, Elizabeth Trant in The Good Companions; at Magnolia, Mass, June 1932, Crystal Weatherley in The Man in Possession; at the Cort, NY, Dec 1932, appeared as Mary Fanshawe in Red Planet; Westminster, London, Sept 1933, the Lady in The Man with a Load of Mischief; Arts, June 1934, Irène de Montcel in La Prisonnière; Globe, Oct 1935, Beatrice Gwynne in Call It a Day; which ran until Jan 1937; Gate, Nov 1936, played Martha Dobie in The Children's Hour; St James's, Feb 1937, Hilda McKenna in The Orchard Walls; John Golden, NY, Dec 1937, Vere Malcolm in Love of Women; Ambassadors', Feb 1938, Anita Karsten in Surprise Item; Queen's, Sept 1938, Cynthia Randolph in Dear Octopus; Q, Apr 1940, Helen Gordon in A Lady Reflects; Adelphi, July 1940, again played Cynthia in Dear Octopus; Duchess, Mar 1942, Myrtle Valentine in Skylark; Aldwych, Aug 1942, succeeded Judy Campbell as Marthe de Brancovis in Watch on the Rhine; St James's, Feb 1943, played Natalia in A Month in the Country; toured, 1944, in the play Claudia, and as Fiona Merril in I'll See You Again; St James's, Aug 1945, succeeded Diana Wynyard as Dilys Parry in The Wind of Heaven; Stratford-on-Avon, Memorial Theatre, 1946 season, played Imogen in Cymbeline, Lady Macbeth, and the Princess of France in Love's Labour's Lost; Duke of York's, Mar 1947, Marion in The Anonymous Lover; St James's, Apr 1948, Naomi Wright in Happy with Either; Wyndham's, Nov 1948, succeeded Pamela Brown as Janet Spence in The Gioconda Smile; St James's, Jan 1950, Rosabel Fleming in Venus Observed; Lyceum, NY, Oct 1950, again played Janet Spence in The Gioconda Smile; at the Lyceum, Edinburgh, Nov 1952, played Lady Crossley in The Gift; at the same theatre, Feb 1953, and at Wyndham's, London, Apr 1953, appeared as Mrs Dennis in The Living Room; Criterion (for the Under Thirty Group), Dec 1953, played Ruth in Facts of the Heart; Royal, Brighton, Mar 1955, appeared as Jessie in The Art of Living; Garrick, London, Sept 1955, played the Comtesse Louise de Clérembard in The Count of Clérembard; at the Fortune, Dec 1956, played Felicia in Who Cares?; Royal, Brighton, Oct 1957, Mam'selle in Father's Match, subsequently appearing in the same part at the Westminster, Dec 1957, when the play was re-named The Happy Man; Royal Court, Mar 1958 (in a Production Without Décor for the English Stage Co), Myra Bolton in Each His Own Wilderness; Globe, Jan 1959, Blanche Carrell in Eighty in the Shade; joined the Old Vic Company, Sept 1960, to tour as Lady Bracknell in The Importance of Being Earnest, subsequently visiting Moscow and Leningrad with the production, 1961; Old Vic, Oct 1960, played Queen Elizabeth in Mary Stuart; Savoy, May 1963, Alice Jago in The Masters; July 1966, for Prospect Productions, toured as Anna Seward and Mrs Pritchard in From China to Peru, and Lady Hurf in Thieves' Carnival; toured, Jan 1967, as the Mother in The Constant Wife; Arnaud, Guildford, Mar 1968, Aunt Agatha in The Family Reunion; Royal Court, May 1968, played Edith in Time Present, transferring to the Duke of York's in July; University Theatre, Manchester, Apr 1970, Amanda Wingfield in The Glass Menagerie; has also appeared in films and numerous television plays; co-author of the film Take My Life, and author of the radio play Persons Unknown.

Favourite parts: Imogen, Nina in The Seagull, and Lady Bracknell. *Recreations:* Sunbathing, writing and reading. *Address:* Flat 1, 74 Elm Park Gardens, London, SW10.

TEITEL, Carol (*née* Carolyn Sally Kahn), actress
b Brooklyn, New York, 1 Aug; *d* of Henry Kahn and his wife Blanche (Reisman); *m* Nathan R Teitel; prepared for the stage with Leo Bulgakov, on a scholarship at the American Theatre Wing, with William Hansen, and with Lee Strasberg.

Made her début at the Cedarhurst, Long Island, Playhouse, July 1941, as Little Mary in Stage Door; made her NY début at the Master Institute, 1942, as Anyutka in The Power of Darkness; toured in Theatre As You Like It; Carnegie Hall, Dec 1952, played in Billy the Kid; Cherry Lane, Oct 1954, took over as Foible in The Way of the World; Royale, Mar 1957, played Beatrice in The Anatomist; Adelphi, Nov 1957, was stand-by to Julie Harris as Margery Pinchwife in The Country Wife; Royale, Feb 1958, stand-by to Joan Plowright as Jean Rice in The Entertainer; stock, June 1958, played Princess Pavlikov in Nude with Violin; Arena Stage, Washington, DC, Dec 1958, Lady Angatell in The Hollow; Provincetown Playhouse, NY, Mar 1959, played in a Shaw repertory season of Getting Married, The Dark Lady of the Sonnets, Passion, Poison, and Petrifaction, and The Shewing Up of Blanco Posnet; Greenwich Mews, May 1960, Alexandra Ivanovna Platunov in A Country Scandal; Circle in the Square, Mar 1961, played various roles in Under Milk Wood; Charles Playhouse, Boston, Massachusetts, Nov 1961, Claire in The Maids; McCarter, Princeton, New Jersey, 1962, Dame Pliant in The Alchemist and Jessica in The Merchant of Venice; Circle in the Square, Dec 1962, again played in Under Milk Wood and played a Maiden in Pullman Car Hiawatha, subsequently touring in these plays; Kauffman Auditorium, Dec 1962, played in the concert reading An Evening with Ring Lardner; McCarter, Princeton, New Jersey, 1963, Nicole in Le Bourgeois Gentilhomme and Virginia in Galileo; Dartmouth College, Hanover, New Hampshire, 1963, Margery Pinchwife in The Country Wife, Hero in Much Ado About Nothing, and Ann Whitefield in Man and Superman; Lunt-Fontanne, Apr 1964, standby to Eileen Herlie as Gertrude in Hamlet; American Place, June 1964, title-role in Juana La Loca; Garrick, Feb 1965, title-role in Colombe; a founding member of the American Conservatory Theatre, under the direction of William Ball, and appeared with it in Pittsburgh, Chicago, San Francisco, etc in Death of a Salesman, Uncle Vanya, Six Characters in Search of An Author, Noah, In White America, Arsenic and Old Lace, Misalliance, A Flea in Her Ear, The Hostage, and other plays until 1969; Majestic, NY, Jan 1967, played one of the patients in The National Players Company production of Marat/Sade; Gramercy Arts, Mar 1968, Bettina in The Bench; ANTA, Oct 1969, Yvonne Chandel in the American Conservatory Theatre production of A Flea in Her Ear; Circle in the Square, Dec 1969, Mrs Charpolsky in Seven Days of Mourning; Seattle Repertory Theatre, 1970, played in her husband's play The Initiation; Promenade, NY, June 1971, took over from Geraldine Fitzgerald as Mary Tyrone in Long Day's Journey into Night; Long Wharf, New Haven, Conn, Nov 1971, Mrs Ewbank in The Contractor; and, also 1971, Olga in You Can't Take It With You; Williamstown, Mass, 1972, Elizabeth in Mary Stuart; Actors Theatre, Louisville, Ky, 1973, played Lady Macbeth; Dallas Theater Center, Texas, 1973, played in The Happy Hunter; St Clement's Church, Mar 1974, Woman in Duet & Trio, and again played these parts there in Oct 1974, when it was renamed Figures in the Sand; The Lambs, 1974, Teresa in The Old Ones; Williamstown, Mass, 1975 Essie Miller in Ah, Wilderness! and played Mrs Tancred in Juno and the Paycock; 1975 played in Mother in Six Characters in Search of an Author; Booth, Dec 1975, Beebee Morris in All Over Town; Roundabout, June 1976, played in The World of Sholem Aleichem; St Lawrence Center for the Performing Arts, Toronto, Canada, Sept 1976, Amanda Wingfield in The Glass Menagerie; Hartman, Stamford, Dec 1976, in Arsenic and Old Lace; same theatre, Mar 1977, Linda Loman in Death of a Salesman; Williamstown, July 1977, Mrs Tarleton in Misalliance; Manitoba Theater

Center, Winnipeg, Feb 1978, Hannah in The Night of the Iguana; Joseph Jefferson, NY, 1978, Phoebe in The Entertainer; Pittsburgh Public Theatre, 1978–79, Lady Bracknell in The Importance of Being Earnest; played the Teacher in Every Good Boy Deserves Favour, Kennedy Center and tour, 1978, and again at Kennedy and the Metropolitan Opera, NY, July 1979; for Phoenix, Apr 1979, Inga in Big and Little; toured, 1979, in her one-woman show, Faces of Love; has also played with the Association of Producing Artists in 1965 in Judith and Man and Superman; has played in stock in Harvey, opposite Joe E Brown, as Laura in The Glass Menagerie, Celia Pope in A Hatful of Rain, and Ann and Sibyl in Separate Tables; first appeared on television on *Kraft Theatre,* 1959, and since has played in The Little Moon of Alban, A Country Scandal, Misalliance, Under Milk Wood, and in the serials *Edge of Night, The Guiding Light, The Verdict Is Yours, Lamp unto My Feet,* Interrogation in Budapest, My Old Man (1979), etc.

Favourite parts: Sonya in Uncle Vanya, Mary Tyrone, and Margery Pinchwife. *Recreations:* Museum-going, gardening, cookery, architecture. *Address:* 365 West 25th Street, New York, NY 10001. *Tel:* AL 5–9376.

TENNENT LTD H M, and Tennent Productions Ltd, producing managers

The firm was founded by the late H M Tennent in 1936, and their first production was The Ante-Room, at the Queen's Theatre, 14 Aug 1936; since that date they have presented, either on their own account or in association with others, the following: Farewell Performance, Follow Your Saint, Mademoiselle, Charles the King, Heart's Content, 1936; Candida, Retreat from Folly, George and Margaret, The Constant Wife, They Came by Night, Bonnet Over the Windmill, Blondie White, Robert's Wife, You Can't Take It With You, 1937; Plan for a Hostess, Operette, People of Our Class, Spring Meeting, She Too Was Young, Dear Octopus, 1938; Design for Living, Sugar Plum, We at the Crossroads, Rhondda Roundabout, Hamlet, The Importance of Being Earnest, 1939; All Clear, The Light of Heart, Cousin Muriel, Rebecca, The Devil's Disciple, Thunder Rock, 1940; No Time for Comedy, Dear Brutus, The Nutmeg Tree, Blithe Spirit, Ducks and Drakes, Old Acquaintance, The Morning Star, 1941; Macbeth, On Approval, Watch on the Rhine, The Doctor's Dilemma, Skylark, Flare Path, The Little Foxes, The Petrified Forest, 1942; They Came to a City, A Month in the Country, Uncle Harry, Heartbreak House, Love for Love, Landslide, While the Sun Shines, There Shall Be No Night, 1943; The Druid's Rest, *Françoise Rosay,* The Cradle Song, Crisis in Heaven, The Last of Summer, Private Lives, *Ballets Jooss,* Hamlet, Love for Love, The Circle, A Midsummer Night's Dream, The Duchess of Malfi (Haymarket Repertory), Another Love Story, Love in Idleness, 1944; The Years Between, The Wind of Heaven, The Skin of Our Teeth, Lady Windermere's Fan, Sigh No More, The Rivals, A Bell for Adano, 1945; A Man About the House, Grand National Night, The Guinea-Pig, The Winslow Boy, Portrait in Black, Our Town, Crime and Punishment, The Gleam, Antony and Cleopatra, 1946; Jane, The Eagle has Two Heads, Othello, Candida, Present Laughter, The Play's the Thing, Angel, Deep Are the Roots, Trespass, Peace in Our Time, Tuppence Coloured, Dark Summer, Macbeth, 1947; The Relapse, I Remember Mama, The Happiest Days of Your Life, Traveller's Joy, All My Sons, The Glass Menagerie, Crime Passionnel, Medea, The Return of the Prodigal, September Tide, 1948; Oranges and Lemons, The Heiress, Adventure Story, Dark of the Moon, The Lady's Not For Burning, Love in Albania, Death of a Salesman, Treasure

Hunt, A Streetcar Named Desire, The Seagull, 1949; Ring Round the Moon, Home At Seven, The Holly and the Ivy, Seagulls Over Sorrento, Mister Roberts, The Little Hut, The Second Mrs Tanqueray, Accolade, Who is Sylvia?, Point of Departure, 1950; A Penny for a Song, Waters of the Moon, Three Sisters, The Lyric Revue, The Winter's Tale, Figure of Fun, Summer and Smoke, Charles Dickens, Relative Values, Indian Summer, Colombe, Let's Make An Opera, Nina (New York), 1951; Much Ado About Nothing, The Same Sky, The Vortex, The Deep Blue Sea, The Mortimer Touch, Montserrat, Under the Sycamore Tree, The Gay Dog, Trelawny of the 'Wells', The Millionairess (London and NY), The Globe Revue, Emlyn Williams in Bleak House, The River Line, Quadrille, Letter From Paris, The Square Ring, Richard II, 1952; A Woman of No Importance, The Way of the World, The White Carnation, The Apple Cart, the seven year itch, Venice Preserved, The Private Life of Helen, Aren't We All?, A Doll's House, The Sleeping Prince, The Little Hut (NY), Someone Waiting, A Day By the Sea, A Question of Fact, At the Lyric, 1953; Charley's Aunt, The Burning Glass, Hippo Dancing, Marching Song, The Prisoner, The Dark is Light Enough, Going To Town, The Cherry Orchard, Both Ends Meet, After the Ball, Hedda Gabler, Bell, Book and Candle, Simon and Laura, The Matchmaker, An Evening With Beatrice Lillie, Quadrille (NY), Time Remembered, 1954; The Bad Seed, The Lark, My Three Angels, Into Thin Air, *Ruth Draper,* Emlyn Williams in his solo performance as Dylan Thomas Growing Up, Nina, Mrs Willie, The Buccaneer, A Life in the Sun (Edinburgh Festival), Anniversary Waltz, Hamlet (Moscow and London), Charley's Aunt, 1955; A Likely Tale, Misalliance, The Power and the Glory, The Chalk Garden, South Sea Bubble, Hotel Paradiso, The Family Reunion, Man Alive!, *Ruth Draper,* A River Breeze, A View From the Bridge, Nude With Violin, The Devil's Disciple, The Diary of Anne Frank, 1956; The Glass Cage (Crest Theatre, Toronto company), A Dead Secret, Six Months Grace, Meet Me By Moonlight, Flowering Cherry, 1957; Cat on a Hot Tin Roof, A Touch of the Sun, The Potting Shed, Where's Charley?, Duel of Angels, My Fair Lady, Variations on a Theme, The Big Tickle, Living For Pleasure, Five Finger Exercise, Irma La Douce, Emlyn Williams in A Boy Growing Up, Long Day's Journey Into Night, Moon on a Rainbow Shawl, West Wide Story, Two For the Seesaw, 1958; Eighty in the Shade, The Pleasure of His Company, The Complaisant Lover, Farewell, Farewell, Eugene, Ages of Man (John Gielgud's Shakespeare Recital), Look After Lulu, 1959; Look on Tempests, A Passage to India, The Most Happy Fella, Ross, A Lovely Light (Dorothy Stickney Recital), The Visit, Joie de Vivre, A Man For All Seasons, The Tiger and the Horse, The Last Joke, 1960; The Lady From the Sea, The Rehearsal, Dazzling Prospect, On the Avenue, Bye Bye, Birdie, Oh Dad, Poor Dad, Mama's Hung You in the Closet, and I'm Feelin' So Sad, Do-Re-Mi, Becket, 1961; HMS Pinafore, The Pirates of Penzance, *Joyce Grenfell* season, Write Me a Murder, The School For Scandal, The Private Ear and The Public Eye, Judith, The Tulip Tree, 1962; Carnival, Mary, Mary, Some Men and Women (recital), On the Town, The Doctor's Dilemma, Virtue in Danger (transfer to Strand only), Where Angels Fear to Tread, The Ides of March, Man and Boy (also NY), At the Drop of Another Hat, Gentle Jack, 1963; I Love You, Mrs Patterson, The Tiger and The Typists (double-bill), The Trigon, Season of Goodwill, Carving a Statue, *Marlene Dietrich* season, 1964; Ring of Jackals, *Joyce Grenfell* season, Present Laughter, The Chinese Prime Minister, At the Drop of Another Hat, Ivanov, The Cavern, The Glass Menagerie,

Hello, Dolly!, You Never Can Tell, 1965; Incident at Vichy, Suite in Three Keys, The Rivals, The Odd Couple, Lady Windermere's Fan, 1966; Cactus Flower, Horizontal Hold, Beware of the Dog, The Merchant of Venice, The Cherry Orchard, Heartbreak House, Halfway Up the Tree, 1967; The Importance of Being Earnest, The White Liars and Black Comedy (double-bill), I Do! I Do!, You Know I Can't Hear You When the Water's Running, Ring Round the Moon, The Cocktail Party, 1968; Your Own Thing, What the Butler Saw, Cat Among the Pigeons, Play It Again Sam, The Magistrate, Promises, Promises, 1969; Play On Love, The Battle of Shrivings, Blithe Spirit, A Bequest to the Nation, Vivat! Vivat Regina!, The Winslow Boy, Butterflies are Free, The Magistrate, 1970; Captain Brassbound's Conversion, The Patrick Pearse Motel, Dear Antoine, Godspell, 1971; Private Lives, Reunion in Vienna, 1972; A Private Matter, Suzanna Andler, No No Nanette, In Praise of Love, The Constant Wife, Design for Living, Gypsy, Dandy Dick, 1973; Bloomsbury, What If You Died Tomorrow?, The Ginger-bread Lady, The Pay-Off, Billy, The Tempest, 1974; Emlyn Williams as Charles Dickens, The Tempest, Lenny, The Clandestine Marriage, Oh Coward, Godspell, The Seagull, The Bed Before Yesterday, 1975; Thomas and the King, Signed and Sealed, I Gotta Shoe, The Husband In-Law, The Family Dance, 1976; Banana Ridge, Side By Side By Sondheim; St Mark's Gospel, Molly, 1978; Brimstone & Treacle, 1979; they have also toured the following: A Thing Apart, 1938; I Lived With You, Fumed Oak, The Millionairess, Plays and Music, On Approval, 1940; The First Mrs Fraser, 1941; To Dream Again, Stranger's Road, Play Parade, 1942; Pen Don, 1943; Night Must Fall, Staff Dance, Fighters Calling, I'll See You Again, 1944; Dandy Dick, 1945; A Play for Ronnie, 1946; Runaway Victory, 1949; Time and Again, 1957; Ride A Cock Horse, 1958; The Coast of Coromandel, 1959; Irma La Douce, A Touch of the Poet (also Dublin and Venice Festivals), 1962; My Fair Lady, 1963; My Fair Lady (Southern Co.), Latin American and European tour of The Merchant of Venice and A Midsummer Night's Dream (Shakespeare Quatercentenary Celebrations), The Photographer, 1964; La Contessa, The Elephant's Foot, Marlene Dietrich season, 1965–6; George and Margaret, 1973; Godspell, 1974; Emlyn Williams as Charles Dickens, 1975; Dead Eyed Dicks, 1976.

Directors of H M Tennent Ltd: Arthur Cantor, Nick Salmon (*Joint Managing*), Bernard Gordon, Waring Jones (*USA*), Bernard Sandler.

Address: Globe Theatre, Shaftesbury Avenue, London W1. *Tel:* 01–437 3647–8.

TER-ARUTUNIAN, Rouben, designer
b Tiflis, 24 July 1920; *s* of Guegam Ter-Arutunian and his wife Anaida (Seylanian); *e* Friedrich-Wilhelm University, Berlin, 1941–2, University of Vienna, 1944–5, and École des Beaux-Arts, Paris, 1947–50.

His first designs were for costumes for The Bartered Bride, at the Dresden Opera House, 1941; designed the costumes for the Vienna Opera House production of Salome, 1944; designed the scenery and costumes for the Opéra-Comique, Paris, production of the ballet Concerto, 1950; first designs in America were for television in 1951, since which time his activity has been mainly confined to the United States; designed the stage for the American Shakespeare Festival Theatre at Stratford, Connecticut, as well as the scenery and costumes for King John, Measure for Measure, Othello, The Merchant of Venice (sets only), and Much Ado About Nothing, 1956–7 seasons; first Broadway assignment, scenery and costumes for New Girl in Town, 1957; scenery only for

Who Was That Lady I Saw You With?, At the Grand (LA), 1958; scenery and costumes for Redhead, 1959; designed the new permanent stage, the scenery and costumes for Twelfth Night and Antony and Cleopatra (Stratford, Conn), and the scenery for Advise and Consent, 1960; Donnybrook, and The Merry Widow (Los Angeles), 1961; A Passage to India, The Umbrella, 1962; Hot Spot, Arturo Ui, Save Me a Place at Forest Lawn and The Last Minstrel (double-bill), The Play of Herod (New York Cloisters), 1963; The Milk Train Doesn't Stop Here Anymore, The Deputy, 1964; Ivanov (London), The Devils, 1965; Ivanov (NY), Eh?, Medea (Rome), 1966; The Party on Greenwich Avenue, Macbeth (Stratford); Exit the King, 1967; I'm Solomon, 1968; The Dozens, Promenade, 1969; All Over, 1971; Schnitzler's Liebelei for the Vienna Burgtheater, 1972; Anatol (Vienna), 1974; Goodtime Charley, 1975; The Lady from the Sea, Days in the Trees, 1976; As You Like It (Long Beach), 1979; has designed for almost all the leading US ballet companies, especially the New York City Ballet, and for overseas companies such as the Royal Ballet, Royal Danish Ballet, Stuttgart Ballet, Royal Swedish Ballet, etc; has designed operas for NY City Opera, La Scala, Milan, and in Rome, Venice, Turin, Monte Carlo, Vienna, etc; designed the films The Loved One, 1964, and Such Good Friends, 1971; has also designed productions for television including The Would-Be Gentleman, Ariadne auf Naxos, 1955; The Magic Flute, 1956; Antigone, The Taming of the Shrew, The Flood, Twelfth Night, and The Tempest, 1960, La Cubana, 1973, etc; received the Emmy Award for his art direction of Twelfth Night, and the Antoinette Perry (Tony) Award for his designs for costumes for Redhead, 1959.

Address: 360 East 55th Street, New York, NY 10022. *Tel:* Plaza 5–4619.

TERRY, Megan, playwright
b Seattle, Washington, 22 July 1932; *e* Univ of Washington (BEd), Univ of Alberta, Banff School of Fine Arts, Yale Univ; formerly an actress with the Seattle Repertory Theatre, decor and costume designer, director, teacher of art; founding member of the Open Theatre (1963).

Author of the following plays: Ex-Miss Copper Queen on a Set of Pills, 1958; The Magic Realist, 1962; People vs Ranchman, 1963; The Gloaming, Oh My Darling, Calm Down, Mother, Keep Tightly Closed in a Cool, Dry Place, 1965; Viet Rock, Comings and Goings, 1966; Jack-Jack, Key is on the Bottom, 1967; Massachusetts Trust, Home, 1968; The Tommy Allen Show, One More Little Drinkie, 1969; Approaching Simone (which received the Obie Award as Best Play), 1970; Frankenstein, Pro Game, 1971; Choose a Spot on the Floor (with JoAnn Schmidman), Grooving, Brazil, Fado: You're always with Me, Don Juan, Madwoman with Carrot, 1972; Thoughts (lyrics only), 1973; Nightwalk (with Jean-Claude van Itallie and Sam Shepard, for The Open Theatre), 1973; Hothouse, 1974; Attempted Rescue on Avenue B, The Mother Jones and Mollie Bailey Family Circus, 1975; founding member of Women's Theatre Council and New York Theatre Strategy, 1971.

Recreations: Study of the living American language, fishing. *Address:* c/o Elisabeth Marton, 96 Fifth Avenue, New York, NY 10011.

TERSON, Peter, dramatic author
b Newcastle-upon-Tyne, 1932; formerly a teacher.

His first play to be produced was A Night to Make the Angels Weep, Victoria, Stoke-on-Trent, 1965; he has since written numerous plays, principally for the Stoke company and for the National Youth Theatre, including All Honour

Mr Todd, I'm in Charge of These Ruins, Jock-on-the-Go, The Ballad of the Artificial Mash, The Mighty Reservoy, Mooney and His Caravans, The Apprentices, Zigger Zagger, Cadmium Firty, Spring-Heeled Jack, Slip Road Wedding, Geordie's March, The Bread and Butter Trade, Love Us and Leave Us, double-bill: Family Ties (Wrong First Time, and Never Right, Yet Again), England My Own, Soldier Boy; his writing for television includes a trilogy.

Address: c/o Margaret Ramsay, 14a Goodwin's Court, St Martin's Lane, London WC2.

THAW, John, actor
b Manchester, 3 Jan 1942; *s* of John Edward Thaw and his wife Dorothy (Abblott); *e* Ducie Technical High School, Manchester; *m* Sheila Hancock; trained for the stage at RADA, winning the Vanbrugh Award and Liverpool Playhouse Award.

First appeared on the professional stage Aug 1960 at the Playhouse, Liverpool, as The Inspector in A Shred of Evidence; first appeared in London, Dec 1961 at the Royal Court, as The Professor in The Fire Raisers; Arts, July 1962, played Sordido in Women Beware Women; Saville, Dec 1962, Robert Freeman in Semi-Detached; Criterion, Sept 1969, Dicky in So What About Love?; Edinburgh Festival, Sept 1970, Jimmy in Random Happenings in the Hebrides; Greenwich, Apr 1971, Stranger in The Lady from the Sea; Theatre Upstairs, Nov 1971, George in Friday: Duchess, July 1973, took over as Sam Brown in Collaborators; toured, Jan 1976, in Absurd Person Singular; Royal Court, June 1977, Leary in Fair Slaughter; Phoenix, Nov 1978, Dick Wagner in Night and Day; films, since 1962, include the Bofors Gun and The Last Grenade; television, since 1961, includes Nil Carborundum and Macbeth, as well as the series *Redcap* and *The Sweeney.*

Favourite part: Mephistopheles in Goethe's Faust.
Recreations: Music, reading. *Address:* c/o John Redway Ltd, 16 Berners Street, London W1P 3DD. *Tel:* 01–637 1612/5.

THAXTER, Phyllis, actress
b Portland, Maine, 20 Nov 1920; *d* of Sidney St F Thaxter and his wife Marie Phyllis (Schuyler); *e* Deering High School, Portland, and Ste Géneviève School, Montreal, Canada; *m* (1) James T Aubrey (mar dis); (2) Gilbert Lea; prepared for the stage at the Montreal Repertory Theatre.

First appeared on the stage at the Ogunquit Playhouse, Ogunquit, Maine, as Daphne, with Laurette Taylor in the latter's play At the Theater; first appeared in New York at the Biltmore in 1938, when she took over the role of a schoolgirl in the long-running What a Life; Alvin, Apr 1940, played Lempi in There Shall Be No Night, a role she played again when the play was revived in Sept 1940; Selwyn, Chicago, 1941, the title-role in Claudia; later followed Dorothy McGuire in the role at the Booth; went to Hollywood and appeared in many films; re-appeared on the stage at the Shubert, New Haven, Conn, Feb 1947, when she took over the role of Kate Bannion in Heartsong; Belasco, Sept 1948, Nancy in Sundown Beach; returned to the stage at the Biltmore, Dec 1961, as Anne Michaelson in Take Her, She's Mine; Ogunquit Playhouse, 1963, Agnes Carol in Time Out for Ginger; Paper Mill Playhouse, Millburn, New Jersey, Feb 1966, played in The Women; Royal Poinciana Playhouse, Palm Beach, Florida, Jan 1967, played in The Impossible Years; Memphis, 1974, in The Effect of Gamma Rays on Man-in-the-Moon Marigolds; Royal Poinciana, 1979, Birdie in The Little Foxes; Birmingham, Mich, Nov 1979, Fonsia Dorsey in The Gin Game; also Royal Poinciana, Jan 1980; films in which she has appeared since 1945 include Thirty

Seconds over Tokyo, Weekend at the Waldorf, Sea of Grass, Bewitched, The World of Henry Orient, Superman, 1979, etc; first appeared on television, 1953, and programs include *Wagon Train, Alfred Hitchcock, The US Steel Hour, Playhouse 90, General Electric Theatre, The Fugitive, Barnaby Jones,* etc.

Recreations: Needlepoint, painting, golf, tennis. *Address:* Actors Equity Association, 165 West 46th Street, New York, NY 10036.

THOMAS, Gwyn, dramatic author
b Porth, Wales, 6 July 1913; *s* of Walter Morgan Thomas and his wife Ziphorah (Davies); *e* Porth County School, St Edmund Hall, Oxford, and the University of Madrid; *m* Eiluned Thomas; formerly a schoolmaster (Modern Languages).

Author of the following plays: The Keep, 1961; Loud Organs, 1962; Jackie the Jumper, 1963; Sap, 1974; The Breakers, 1976; received the *Evening Standard* Award (jointly) as The Most Promising Playwright, 1961, with his play The Keep; television plays include: The Singers of Meadow Prospect, The Slip, The Dig, Faces of Wales, etc.

Recreations: Opera and reading. *Club:* Ponteanna TV Studio Club, Cardiff. *Address:* Cherry Trees, Wyndham Park, Peterston, Cardiff, Wales. *Tel:* Peterston-super-Ely 435.

THOMPSON, Eric, actor and director
b Sleaford, Lincs, 9 Nov 1929; *s* of George Henry Thompson and his wife Anne; *e* Collyers, Horsham, Sussex; *m* Phyllida Law; trained for the stage at the Old Vic Theatre School.

Joined the Old Vic Company direct from the theatre school and made his first professional appearance in Jan 1953 as Balthasar in The Merchant of Venice; in repertory at Manchester, Coventry and Bristol; returned to the Old Vic for the company's final season, 1962–3, playing parts including Lorenzo in The Merchant of Venice, Cassio in Othello, and Pertinax Surly in The Alchemist; Mermaid, June 1966, Bastien and Police Officer in Let's Get A Divorce, transferring to the Comedy, July; directed his first production, Journey's End, Manchester, Sept 1971; this transferred to London, 1972, where he has subsequently directed Time and Time Again, My Fat Friend, 1972; Collaborators, Absurd Person Singular, 1973; The Norman Conquests, Absurd Person Singular, (New York), 1974; Jeeves, Absent Friends, The Norman Conquests (NY), 1975; Noah (Chichester), Same Time Next Year, 1976; he has since directed The Bells (Greenwich), 1976; Singles (Greenwich), The Sunset Touch (Bristol Old Vic), 1977; Balmoral (Yvonne Arnaud, Guildford), Sisters (Royal Exchange, Manchester), 1978; Last of the Red Hot Lovers, also at Manchester, and then transferring to London, 1979; films include One Day in the Life of Ivan Denisovitch; TV includes the children's series *Magic Roundabout,* which he writes and narrates.

Recreations: Golf, fishing, writing. *Club:* MCC. *Address:* c/o St James's Management, 22 Groom Place, London SW1.

THOMPSON, Sada, actress
b Des Moines, Iowa, 27 Sept 1929; *d* of Hugh Woodruff Thompson and his wife Corlyss Elizabeth (Gibson); *e* Carnegie Institute of Technology; *m* Donald E Stewart.

Made her début at the Carnegie Institute, 1945, as Nick's Ma in The Time of Your Life; made her professional début at the University Playhouse, Mashpee, Massachusetts, 30 June 1947, as Harmony Blue-blossom in The Beautiful People; remained with this theatre for two seasons, playing Lady

Bracknell in The Importance of Being Earnest, Peg in Peg o' My Heart, Eileen in Where Stars Walk, Adamina Wood in Dawn from an Unknown Ocean, Leda in Amphitryon 38, Nina in The Seagull, etc; Pittsburgh Playhouse, Oct 1948, played Joan in Joan of Lorraine; joined the Henrietta Hayloft Theatre in Rochester, New York, 1949, and played Mrs Higgins in Pygmalion, Emily Creed in Ladies in Retirement, Mrs Montgomery in The Heiress, Emily Webb in Our Town, Raina in Arms and the Man, Madame Arcati in Blithe Spirit, and, in 1950, Billie Dawn in Born Yesterday, Muriel in Ah, Wilderness!, Annie Marble in Payment Deferred, Jackie Coryton in Hay Fever, Birdie in The Little Foxes, Dona Lucia D'Alvadorez in Charley's Aunt, Betty Logan in Heaven Can Wait, Hilda Manney in Room Service, etc; played other stock engagements before making her New York City début at the Kaufmann Auditorium, 14 May 1953, in a concert reading of Under Milk Wood; Provincetown Playhouse, Oct 1954, Mrs Heidelberg in The Clandestine Marriage; Kaufmann Auditorium, Dec 1954, played in a concert reading of Murder in the Cathedral; Phoenix, Mar 1955, Cornelia in The White Devil; Barter, Abingdon, Virginia, July 1955, Lavinia Chamberlayne in The Cocktail Party; Theatre East, Nov 1956, Eliante in The Misanthrope; Theatre de Lys, Dec 1956, Isadora Duncan and Eleanor Stoddard in USA; Carnegie Hall Playhouse, Jan 1957, Valerie Barton in The River Line; Arena Stage, Washington, DC, Apr 1957, Masha in The Three Sisters; American Shakespeare Festival, Stratford, Connecticut, June 1957, Emilia in Othello and Margaret in Much Ado About Nothing, subsequently touring in this latter part; Renata, Oct 1958, Babakina in Ivanov; Winter Garden, Mar 1959, Mrs Coyne in the musical Juno; American Shakespeare Festival, Stratford, Connecticut, July 1959, Mistress Quickly in The Merry Wives of Windsor and a Widow of Florence in All's Well That Ends Well; Stratford, 1960, Maria in Twelfth Night, Juno in The Tempest, and Octavia in Antony and Cleopatra; Circle in the Square, Mar 1961, again played in Under Milk Wood; Stratford, 1962, Duchess of York in Richard II and Lady Percy in Henry IV, Part I; toured, Oct–Nov 1962, as Mrs Molloy in The Matchmaker; Pocket, May 1963, Mrs Rhythm in The Last Minstrel; Delacorte, for the New York Shakespeare Festival, July 1964, Emilia in Othello; ANTA Washington Square, Jan 1965, Dorine in Tartuffe; Milwaukee, Wisconsin, Repertory Theatre, Mar 1966, Amanda Wingfield in The Glass Menagerie; joined William Ball's American Conservatory Theatre for the 1966–7 season; Cort, Oct 1967, Florence Edwards in Johnny No-Trump; Studio Arena, Buffalo, 1968, Agnes in A Delicate Balance; Billy Rose, Oct 1968, Mommy in The American Dream and Winnie in Happy Days; The Forum, Dec 1968, Mrs Darlene Finch in An Evening for Merlin Finch; San Diego, California, National Shakespeare Festival, summer 1969, Lady Macbeth in Macbeth; Mercer-O'Casey, NY, Apr 1970, Beatrice in The Effect of Gamma Rays on Man-in-the-Moon Marigolds; Stratford, Conn, summer 1971, Christine Mannon in Mourning Becomes Electra; Broadhurst, Nov 1971, Emily, Celia, Dorothy, and Ma in Twigs, received the Antoinette Perry (Tony) Award for these parts, toured in them Sept 1972–Mar 1973, and played them again at the Westport, Conn, Country Playhouse, July 1973; same theatre, Aug 1974, played in Shay and subsequently toured; American Conservatory Theater, San Francisco, 1974, Madame Ranevskaya in The Cherry Orchard; Martin Beck, Nov 1974, Rosa in Saturday, Sunday, Monday; Hartford Stage, Conn, 1978–9, appeared in The Matchmaker; first appeared in films in You Are Not Alone, 1961, and has since played in The Pursuit of Happiness, Desperate Characters, 1971; has appeared frequently on television since 1954 in various dra-

matic programs and series; received the Vernon Rice Award of The Drama Desk for The River Line and The Misanthrope, an Obie Award for her role in Tartuffe, and a Drama Desk Award and Obie Award for The Effect of Gamma Rays on Man-in-the-Moon Marigolds.

Address: Actors Equity Association, 165 West 46th Street, New York, NY 10036.

THORNTON, Frank, (*né* Ball), actor
b Dulwich, London, 15 Jan 1921; *s* of William Ernest Ball and his wife Rosina Mary (Thornton); *e* Alleyn's School, Dulwich; *m* Beryl Jane Margaret Evans; formerly an insurance clerk; trained for the stage at the London School of Dramatic Art.

Made his first professional appearance on All Fools' Day, 1 Apr 1940, at the Confraternity Hall, Thurles, Co Tipperary, as Brian Curtis in French Without Tears, on a fit-up tour; joined Donald Wolfit's company at the Strand, Feb 1941, to play Fenton and Bardolph in The Merry Wives of Windsor; toured with the same company, June 1941, as Dewhurst in The Scarlet Pimpernel; returned to the Strand, Dec 1941, to play five parts in a further Shakespeare season, including Lysander in A Midsummer Night's Dream and Laertes in Hamlet; St James's, Mar 1942, played Mosca in Volpone, again with the Wolfit company; Piccadilly, July 1942, Angus and a Scottish lord in Macbeth; Apollo, autumn 1942, took over Cpl Jones in Flare Path; after war service with the RAF joined Southsea Rep; toured, 1947–8, as Franzel in The Dancing Years; toured, 1950, as Gregory Throstle in One Wild Oat, having under-studied for the production at the Garrick, 1949; this was followed by various tours and small parts in the West End; Playhouse, Oxford, 1956, Mouche in The Empty Chair; Edinburgh Festival, 1957, Dom Joao de Castro in The Hidden King; Piccadilly, May 1960, Bishop Zog in The Golden Touch; Cambridge, June 1960, appeared in the revue Don't Shoot, We're English; Dublin Festival, 1960, Caliph in Hassan; Playhouse, Oxford, Nov 1960, Ludovico Nota in Naked; Aldeburgh Festival, 1962, appeared in Five Players in Four Plays; Royal Court, May 1965, Edward in Meals on Wheels; toured, 1965, as Philip in The Little Hut; Savoy, 1966, took over Empton QC in Alibi for a Judge; Piccadilly, Dec 1968, played Minnit and Procurio in The Young Visiters; Richmond, 1969, Charlie Dyer in Staircase; Strand, Nov 1970, Councillor Parker in When We Are Married; Phoenix, Dec 1971 and Dec 1972, Eeyore in Winnie-the-Pooh; Lyceum, Edinburgh, Jan 1974, Cdr Rogers in French Without Tears; joined the RSC to play Sir Andrew Aguecheek in Twelfth Night, Aug, and Duncan in Macbeth, Oct, in the 1974 Stratford season; played the same parts at the Aldwych, Feb and Mar 1975; Mermaid, Apr 1975, Sir Patrick Cullen in The Doctor's Dilemma; King's Head, Sept 1975, Actor No 1 in Play by Play; Winter Gardens, Blackpool, June 1976, Captain Peacock in Are You Being Served?; toured, Aug 1977, as Roger in Roger's Last Stand; toured as Sir Justin Holbrook in Shut Your Eyes and Think of England, and then played the part at the Apollo, Nov 1977; Theatre Royal, Windsor, Feb 1979, Ernest in Bedroom Farce; Thorndike, Leatherhead, Nov 1979, George in Jumpers; has also appeared with the Repertory Players; films, since 1954, include The Bed-Sitting Room and A Flea in Her Ear; has broadcast frequently on radio since 1942, and television, since 1950, includes many plays and series, notably It's A Square World and Are You Being Served?

Favourite parts: Mouche and Mosca. *Recreations:* Music, photography. *Club:* Green Room. *Address:* c/o Max Kester, Blue Cedar, Highlands Road, Reigate, Surrey. *Tel:* Reigate 44745; or c/o The Spotlight, 42–43 Cranbourn Street, London WC2H 7AP.

THORPE-BATES, Peggy, actress

b London, 11 Aug 1914; *d* of Thomas Thorpe Bates and his wife Edith Helena (Leech); *e* Heathfield; *m* Brian Oulton; studied for the stage at the Cone School of Dancing, and the Royal Academy of Dramatic Art.

First appeared at the Shakespeare Memorial Theatre, Stratford-on-Avon, 1934, as Isabel in Henry V; appeared in repertory at Harrogate, Southampton, Bristol, etc, 1935–8; made her first appearance on the West End stage at the Little, 9 Apr 1940, as Mrs Dainty Fidget in The Country Wife; toured, 1940–1, as Doris in Saloon Bar; appeared in leading parts at the Intimate Theatre, 1942, and at the Birmingham Repertory Theatre, 1946; made guest appearances at Worthing, Windsor, Oxford, etc, 1947–8; at the Cambridge, Dec 1951, for the Repertory Players, appeared as Mary Tudor in The Young Elizabeth, and played the same part at the New, Apr 1952, when the play ran for over a year; Arts, Mar 1955, played Clytemnestra in Sacrifice to the Wind; New Lindsey, Feb 1956, Mother Saybrook in Lead Me Gently; 1956–7, BBC Drama Repertory Company; Strand, June 1959, Gertrude Marescaud in All in the Family; Pembroke, Croydon, Sept 1960, Mrs Ann Summer in Lady Barker's Last Appearance; Pembroke, Croydon, Sept 1961, and subsequently toured as Joyce Glyn in Unfinished Journey; Guildford, July 1962, Mary Tyrone in Long Day's Journey Into Night; Birmingham Repertory (Golden Jubilee), July 1962, Mrs George in Getting Married; Richmond, Apr 1964, Charity Hannigan in Three Acts of Charity; Leatherhead, Mar 1965, Nurse in Romeo and Juliet; St Martin's, June 1965, took over Mrs Porter in A Public Mischief; Arts, Aug 1966, played Phyllis in The Thunderbolt; Whitehall, Mar 1969, Mrs Winifred Masters in Dead Silence; Edinburgh Festival, 1969, played the Duchess of York in Richard the Second for Prospect Productions, subsequently touring in the role and playing the part in seasons at the Mermaid and Piccadilly theatres, 1969–70; Birmingham Repertory, 1970, played Matron in Forty Years On; Jan 1971, toured in For Entertainment Only (a recital of the plays of Pinero); at the gala reopening of the Harrogate Theatre, Oct 1972, played Catherine Smith in Mr Sydney Smith Coming Upstairs; toured S Africa, 1973, as Queen Mary in Crown Matrimonial, also giving recitals; Palace, Westcliff, Mrs Weston in Say Goodnight to Grandma, Feb 1974, and Lady Boothroyd in Lloyd George Knew My Father, June 1974; Arnaud, Guildford, Aug 1974, and tour, Bess Raleigh in The Wisest Fool; Assembly Hall, Hackney, Jan 1975, appeared in a new recital, Births, Marriages and Deaths; Thorndike, Leatherhead, Sept 1975, Miss Smythe in Move Over Mrs Markham; Theatre at the Park, Bracknell, Oct 1975, Mrs Candle in His First Wife; Key Theatre, Peterborough, Dec 1975, Donna Lucia D'Alvadorez in Charley's Aunt; Leeds Playhouse, Mar 1976, Mrs Higgins in Pygmalion; Player's, June 1976, Mrs Caudle in Up All Night; Stoke Newington Assembly Hall, Sept 1976, Mrs Caudle in Upstairs, Downstairs and in My Lady's Chamber; Orange Tree, Richmond, Nov 1976, appeared in a Pinero recital, For Entertainment Only; Royal Exchange, Manchester, Feb 1977, Maman in Uncle Vanya, and Mar 1977, Lady Saltburn in Present Laughter; Thorndike, Leatherhead, June 1977, numerous parts in Sybil: Her Infinite Variety, a tribute to Sybil Thorndike; Everyman, Cheltenham Literary Festival, Sept 1978, Lady Elizabeth Mulhammer in The Confidential Clerk; has made many appearances for the Repertory Players; first appeared on television, 1947, and has since played numerous parts in plays and serials, notably, Sanctuary, Glittering Prizes and Rumpole of the Bailey; frequently broadcasts for the BBC; served on the Council of British Actors' Equity Association, 1956–62; Director, Council of Royal General Theatrical Fund, 1966–.

Favourite parts: Portia and Sanchia in Robert's Wife. *Hobbies:* Handicrafts, cookery, gardening, and the study of architecture. *Address:* 43 Chester Close North, Regent's Park, London, NW1. *Tel:* 01–486 4290.

TILTON, James F, designer

b Rochelle, Illinois, 30 July 1937; *s* of Norval B Tilton and his wife Magdeline (Ripplinger); *e* University of Iowa (BA 1959); *m* Helga Strang.

Designed his first production, the décor for Stage Door, at the West High School Auditorium, Rockford, Illinois, Feb 1954; served in the US Army Special Services Division, 1959–62, and during this time was Resident Designer at the Frankfurt Playhouse, Frankfurt am Main, West Germany; upon returning to America became the designer for the John Drew, East Hampton, Long Island, 1963, and designed the sets for Finian's Rainbow, Carousel, Brecht on Brecht, Come Blow Your Horn, Irma la Douce, Brigadoon, and Write Me a Murder; became Principal Designer for the APA Repertory Theatre, 1963–71, and for it designed his first New York production, Scapin, presented at the Phoenix, 9 Mar 1964; has since designed, principally for the APA and APA-Phoenix, the following plays: Right You Are If You Think You Are, The Lower Depths, Impromptu de Versailles, Herakles, and, for the Front Street Theatre, Memphis, Tennessee, Ah, Wilderness! The Seven Year Itch, My Fair Lady, Damn Yankees, The Country Wife, The Sound of Music, The Little Hut, The Taming of the Shrew, Misalliance, and My Three Angels, 1964; You Can't Take It with You, and, for the Front Street, The Tavern, A Midsummer Night's Dream, The Music Man, and Roberta, 1965; The School for Scandal, We, Comrades Three, and, for Front Street, Guys and Dolls, 1966; The Wild Duck, War and Peace, Pantagleize, The Show-Off, Exit the King (lighting), and, for the Professional Theatre Program, Ann Arbor, Michigan, Escurial, The Cat and the Moon, Sweet of You to Say So, The Flies, 1967; The Cherry Orchard, The Cocktail Party, The Misanthrope, Ballad for a Firing Squad, The Latent Heterosexual, 1968; Cock-a-Doodle Dandy, Hamlet, Private Lives, Oh! Calcutta! (NY, Los Angeles, and San Francisco), Love-In (Kansas City Opera), The Doctor's Dilemma, and, at Ann Arbor, Michigan, Chronicles of Hell, Macbeth, Play, 1969; Harvey, The Merchant of Venice (San Francisco), Siamese Connections, The Selling of the President, Antony and Cleopatra, Caesar and Cleopatra (last three for ACT, San Francisco), Charley's Aunt (Sarasota, Fla), 1971; Rainbow, The Matchmaker (Sarasota), and for the John Drew, Easthampton, The American Dream, The Long Christmas Dinner, What the Butler Saw, The Palace at 4 AM, Dudes, 1972; The Government Inspector, The Merchant of Venice (also lighting), and for National Theatre Company tours Butterflies Are Free, The Age of Shaw, A Connecticut Yankee in King Arthur's Court, 1973; Come Blow Your Horn, The Miracle Worker (tour), That Championship Season, Flint (both Studio Arena, Buffalo NY), 1974; Declaration (tour), End of Summer, The Private Ear and The Public Eye, The Rehearsal, Tonight at 8.30 (all for the Phoenix at the John Drew, Easthampton), Knuckle, Seascape, 1975; Shakespeare Is Alive and Well and Living in America, Chaplin and His Time (tours), Death of a Salesman (Buffalo), The Cat and the Fiddle (Cleveland), 1976; Vieux Carré, 1977; Galileo, 1978; The Auction Tomorrow (Hartman, Conn), Flying Blind, 1979; for Phoenix since 1975 he has designed Twenty-Seven Wagons Full of Cotton, A Memory of Two Mondays, They Knew What They Wanted, Boy

Meets Girl, Secret Service, 1975–6; Ladyhouse Blues, American Modern/Canadian Gothic, Marco Polo, A Sorrow Beyond Dreams, GR Point, Scribes, 1976–7; Hot Grog, Uncommon Women, The Elusive Angel, One Crack Out, City Sugar, 1977–8; Getting Out, Big and Little, Later, 1978–9; has also designed industrial shows, notably for Avon, Coca-Cola, Mobil Oil, Seven-Up, and Pontiac, designed his first film, Dear Dead Delilah, 1970.

Recreations: Painting, woodworking, reading. *Address:* 726 Eighth Avenue, New York, NY 10036. *Tel:* 212–575 1385.

TINKER, Jack, drama critic
b Oldham, 15 Feb 1938; *s* of Edward Smith Tinker and his wife Lily (Pierce); *e* The Hulme Grammar School for Boys, Oldham, *m* Mavis Ann Page (mar dis).

Film and theatre critic, *Brighton Evening Argus,* 1961–69; editor, *Daily Sketch* diary column, 1970–71; joined *Daily Mail* 1971; presently drama critic; author of a book, The TV Barons, 1980, and of a BBCTV documentary, All Change for Brighton, 1979.

Recreation: Attending first nights and Saturday matinees. *Address:* 18 Queen's Gardens, Brighton, Sussex.

TODD, Ann, actress, writer and producer
b Hartford, Cheshire; *d* of Thomas Todd and his wife Constance (Brooke); *e* St Winifred's School, Eastbourne; *m* (1) Victor Neill Malcolm (mar dis); (2) Nigel Tangye (mar dis); (3) David Lean (mar dis); studied for the stage at the Central School of Speech Training and Dramatic Art.

Made her first appearance on the stage at the Arts Theatre, 28 Jan 1928, as A Faery Child in The Land of Heart's Desire; at the New Theatre, Aug 1928, played Lady Prudence Willowby in A Damsel in Distress; Apr 1929, Oenone in Baa, Baa, Black Sheep, Shaftesbury, Aug 1929, Nancy Hewitt in The Middle Watch; Strand (for Repertory Players), Sept 1929, Suzette Wurtz in Azaïs; St James's, Oct 1929, Irene March in Heat Wave; St Martin's, Feb 1930, Ann Winter in Honours Easy; Playhouse, June 1930, Gorla Kentish in Cynara; Criterion, Dec 1931, Carol in Flat to Let; Lyric, Apr 1932, Nicole in The Heart Line; Wyndham's, Oct 1932, Caroline Service in Service; Lyric, Apr 1933, Mary Howard in When Ladies Meet; Daly's, Apr 1934, Joan Cobham in Dark Horizon; Wyndham's, Sept 1934, Diana Townsend in No More Ladies; St Martin's, Feb 1935, Katherine Lindon in Man of Yesterday; Lyric, Jan 1936, Doris Hardred in The Old and the Young; Shaftesbury, Feb 1936, Solange in Promise; Phoenix, Mar 1938, Margery Byrne in Flood Tide; Wyndham's, Aug 1938, Kate Treowain in She, Too, Was Young; New, Mar 1939, Betty Ryan in The Man in Half-Moon Street; St Martin's, Nov 1941, Pat in Love in a Mist; Winter Garden, Dec 1942, Peter in Peter Pan; Vaudeville, July 1943, Lottie in Lottie Dundass; Prince of Wales, Apr 1944, Madeleine Smith in The Rest is Silence; Princes, Mar 1951, played Francesca Cunningham in The Seventh Veil; Royal, Birmingham, Sept 1953, appeared as Celia Clive in Foreign Field; at the Edinburgh Festival, 1954, appeared with the Old Vic Company as Lady Macbeth; remained with the Old Vic Company during the 1954–5 season, playing Lady Macbeth, the Princess of France in Love's Labour's Lost, Katharina in The Taming of the Shrew, and Lady Percy in Henry IV (Pts I and II); Saville, Oct 1956, played Jennifer Dubedat in a revival of The Doctor's Dilemma; made her first appearance on Broadway, Cort, Sept 1957, as Davina Mars in The Four Winds; Apollo, London, Sept 1958, followed Claire Bloom as Lucile in Duel of Angels; Yvonne Arnaud, Guildford, Nov 1965, played Florence Lancaster in The Vortex; entered films in Keepers

of Youth, and has since appeared in numerous pictures, notably in South Riding, The Seventh Veil, The Passionate Friends, The Paradine Case, Sound Barrier, Time Without Pity, Taste of Fear, Son of Captain Blood, The Human Factor (1979), etc; 1965–76 appeared in, wrote and created a number of diary documentaries; has also appeared on television in London and New York.

Favourite parts: Francesca in The Seventh Veil, Lottie Dundass and Lady Macbeth. *Recreations:* Writing, painting, and gardening. *Address:* c/o A M Heath, 40 William IV Street, London WC2.

TODD, Richard, actor and producing manager
b Dublin, 11 June 1919; *s* of Andrew William Palethorpe-Todd and his wife Marvil Agar-Daly; *e* Shrewsbury and privately; *m* (1) Catherine Grant-Bogle (mar dis); (2) Virginia Mailer; trained for the stage at the Italia Conti School.

Made his first professional appearance at the Open Air Theatre, Regent's Park, 1936, as Curio in Twelfth Night; early repertory experience included a season with Dundee Repertory Company, 1938; war service 1939–46 with the King's Own Yorkshire Light Infantry and subsequently the Parachute Regiment; rejoined Dundee rep on demobilisation; after many years in films returned to the stage, Dec 1965, as Lord Goring in An Ideal Husband, at the Strand and subsequently on a tour of S Africa; Haymarket, Dec 1967, Nicholas Randolph in Dear Octopus; formed Triumph Theatre Productions, 1970, and has since appeared in numerous productions presented by them, in Britain and elsewhere in the world; these include a tour of the US, 1972, as the Comte in The Marquise; tour of Australia and New Zealand, 1972–3, as Andrew Wyke in Sleuth, tour of US and Canada, 1974, in Royal Shakespeare Company productions of The Hollow Crown and Pleasure and Repentance; Perth Festival, 1975, played Martin Dysart in Equus, for the Australian National Theatre Company; toured, 1975, as John in Miss Adams Will Be Waiting; toured, 1976, as Andrew Wyke in Sleuth; Civic, Johannesburg, July 1976, Duke of Bristol in On Approval; toured, 1977, as Sebastian Crutwell in In Praise of Love; Arnaud, Guildford, Feb 1980, Frank in This Happy Breed; has made over forty films since his debut, 1948, in For Them That Trespass, including The Hasty Heart, Robin Hood, The Dam Busters, Yangtse Incident, A Man Called Peter, etc; television work includes Wuthering Heights.

Favourite part: Martin Dysart in Equus. *Recreations:* Shooting and farming. *Club:* Army and Navy. *Address:* Chinham Farm, Faringdon, Oxon. *Tel:* 03677 294.

TOGURI, David, dancer, director, choreographer
b Vancouver, BC; *e* Harbord Collegiate, and Ryerson Institute of Technology, Toronto; trained in Canada with Boris Volkoff.

Made his West End début at the Palace, 24 Mar 1960, as principal dancer in Flower Drum Song, playing the Head Waiter; Prince of Wales, 1961, with the Sammy Davis Show; Adelphi, Sept 1963, danced in Six of One; Edinburgh Festival, Aug 1964, appeared in the revue Chaganog, subsequently at the Vaudeville, Dec, and in a revised version at the St Martin's, Apr 1965; Adelphi, Dec 1965, John Sasaki in Charlie Girl, which he played for three years; assistant director for the London production of Hair, Shaftesbury, 1968; director of the National tour and the Scottish production, 1970; choreography and movement work includes What a Way to Run a Revolution, 1971; The Island of the Mighty, 1972; Zorba, 1973; The Marquis of Keith, 1974; Censored Scenes from King Kong, 1977; Saratoga, 1978; co-directed

Cole, 1974; directed Farjeon Reviewed, The Comedy of Errors, Two Gentlemen of Verona, the last two at Stratford, Ont, with Robin Phillips, 1975; co-directed and choreographed I Gotta Shoe, 1976; productions outside London include Guys and Dolls and Kiss Me Kate for the Northcott, Exeter; The Servant of Two Masters, Nottingham Playhouse, 1976; extensive work for TV includes choreography for the series Rock Follies.

Address: c/o William Morris Agency, 147–9 Wardour Street, London W1.

TOMLINSON, David, actor

b Henley-on-Thames, 7 May 1917, *s* of Clarence Samuel Tomlinson and his wife Florence Elizabeth (Sinclair-Thomson); *e* Tonbridge School; *m* Audrey Freeman; first appeared as an amateur in 1935.

As a professional actor appeared in repertory, 1936–8, at Folkestone, Leeds, Croydon, Northampton; first appeared on the West End stage at the Queen's, 21 Apr 1938, walking-on in The Merchant of Venice; subsequently played leading parts in tours of Quiet Wedding, George and Margaret, Once A Crook, Counter Attraction, The Police Are Anxious; served with the RAF, as a pilot, 1941–7; reappeared on the London stage at the Lyric, Aug 1959, as Henry in The Little Hut; at the Duke of York's, Sept 1954, played Clive Norton in All For Mary; Westminster, June 1957, played David Warren in Dear Delinquent, subsequently transferring to the Aldwych, Dec 1957; Savoy, July 1959, Tom Gore in The Ring of Truth; Apollo, Feb 1962, played Robert in Boeing-Boeing; Globe, Mar 1964, played Ralph Spicer and directed Mother's Boy; Northampton Repertory, Nov 1964, appeared as guest artist as Bamber Wishart and directed Trouble With Father; Cambridge, Apr 1966, played Sir John Holt in A Friend Indeed, and Nov 1966, Dr Jack Kingsley in The Impossible Years; Dublin Festival, Oct 1969, the Prime Minister in On the Rocks; in S Africa, 1973, again played Sir John Holt in a tour of A Friend Indeed, directing this production and subsequently appearing in Johannesburg in Suite in Three Keys; Duke of York's, Sept 1974, directed and played Philip Fitzgerald in The Turning Point; first appeared in films 1939, and has since played in numerous productions.

Recreaction: Antiques. *Club:* Travellers'. *Address:* Brook Cottage, Mursley, Bucks. *Tel:* Mursley 213.

TOMS, Carl, OBE, designer

b Kirkby-in-Ashfield, 29 May 1927; *s* of Bernard Toms and his wife Edith (Mountain); *e* High Oakham School, Mansfield, Nottinghamshire, Mansfield College of Art, the Royal College of Art and the Old Vic School.

He designed his first stage production, The Apollo de Bellac, for the Royal Court, May 1957; subsequent designs for the theatre, in London unless otherwise stated, include Beth, Something to Hide, 1958; The Complaisant Lover, The Seashell (Edinburgh), No Bed for Bacon (Bristol), The Merry Wives of Windsor, 1959; New Cranks, A Midsummer Night's Dream, 1960; Camille (Old Vic World Tour), 1961; Write Me A Murder, A Time to Laugh, 1962; Who'll Save the Plowboy?, The Importance of Being Earnest (Nottingham), 1963; The Merchant of Venice and A Midsummer Night's Dream (British Council Tour), 1964; A Singular Man, Public Mischief, 1965; The Trojan Women, The Winter's Tale (both Pop Theatre), 1966; The Burglar, Fallen Angels, The Tricks of Scapin, A Midsummer Night's Dream, The Soldier's Tale (the last three for Pop Theatre), 1967; Edward II, Love's Labour's Lost (both National Theatre), 1968; The Magistrate (also Chichester), Antony and Cleopa-

tra (Chichester), 1969; Girlfriend, Sleuth (also New York—first play design—and Paris), Vivat! Vivat Regina! (also Chichester), The Alchemist (Chichester), Cyrano (National Theatre), 1970; The Rivals, Caesar and Cleopatra, Reunion in Vienna (all Chichester), 1971; Reunion in Vienna, The Beheading, 1972; Dear Love, Section Nine, 1973; Sherlock Holmes (also NY), The Waltz of the Toreadors, Travesties, 1974; Murderer, Travesties (NY), Habeas Corpus (NY), 1975; Long Day's Journey Into Night (Los Angeles), Man and Superman (Malvern Festival and London), 1977; The Devil's Disciple (Los Angeles), Look After Lulu (Chichester and London), Night and Day (also NY, 1979), 1978; For Services Rendered (National), Stage Struck, 1979; appointed first head of design for the Young Vic, Aug 1970, for whom he has designed several productions, including Scapino, The Taming of the Shrew, The Real Inspector Hound, If You'll be Glad, I'll be Frank, Antony and Cleopatra; in Vienna has designed Travesties, 1977; She Stoops to Conquer, Betrayal, 1978; The Guardsman, 1979; has designed operas and ballets for Aldeburgh, Covent Garden, Glyndebourne, Sadler's Wells, New York City Opera and Metropolitan Opera (NY), etc; has designed a number of films since She, 1965; television design, since 1959, includes Boule de Suif, The Sandcastle and Twelfth Night; was design consultant for the Investiture of HRH the Prince of Wales, July 1969, receiving the Order of the British Empire in the Investiture Honours, July 1969; received the Tony and the Drama Desk Award for the Best Set Design, London and New York, 1974–5, for the RSC's production of Sherlock Holmes.

Recreations: Gardening, travel and parrots. *Address:* The White House, Beaumont, Nr Wormley, Broxbourne, Herts EN10 7JQ.

TOONE, Geoffrey, actor

b Dublin, 15 Nov 1910; *s* of Wilfrid Parker Toone and his wife Hilda Maria (Webb); *e* Charterhouse and Christ's College, Cambridge.

Was a student at the Old Vic, 1931, where he made his first appearance, walking on; Sadler's Wells, Sept 1931, played Peter of Pomfret in King John; Westminster, Nov 1931, Lemesle in The Unquiet Spirit; toured, 1932, in After All; appeared in repertory, at the Oxford Playhouse, 1933; toured in the West Indies, 1933–4, with a repertory company, in twelve plays; at the Malvern Festival, Aug 1934, played David in A Man's House, Youth in An Interlude of Youth, Nicholas in Saint Bernard, Darrell Blake in The Moon in the Yellow River, and Lieut Pickering in Mutiny; at the New Theatre, Sept 1934, played David in A Man's House; Nov 1934, Fortinbras in Hamlet; and Oct 1935, Tybalt in Romeo and Juliet; appeared with the Liverpool Repertory company, 1936–7; Embassy, Nov 1937, appeared as Posthumus in Cymbeline; Palace, Feb 1938, played Kurt von Obersdorf in Dodsworth; served with the Royal Artillery, 1939–42, invalided out in 1942; toured, 1943, as David in The Watch on the Rhine, subsequently appearing at the Aldwych, in the same part; at the New Theatre, Feb 1944, played Laertes in Hamlet; Phoenix, June 1944, Tom in The End of Summer; Embassy, Feb 1945, Valentine Brown in Quality Street; Haymarket, Aug 1945, Lord Windermere in Lady Windermere's Fan; made his first appearance on the New York stage at the National, 31 Mar 1948, as Banquo in Macbeth; 1949, toured in Perchance to Dream; 1950, toured Italy for the Old Vic as Orsino in Twelfth Night; Lyric, London, Aug 1950, played the Stranger in The Little Hut; in Hollywood, 1953–7, appearing in films and on television; returned to London, and at the Adelphi, Sept 1958, played Beauregard in Auntie Mame; Bristol Old Vic, Feb 1964, played the Cardinal of

Milan in The Successor, and Aug 1964, the Constable of France in Henry V, appearing in the last part at the Old Vic, Sept 1964, and also touring Europe in the last production; Haymarket, Oct 1966, played Sir Lucius O'Trigger in The Rivals; Phoenix, Leicester, 1969, Judge Brack in Hedda Gabler; Queen's, June 1970, took over the part of Major Wimbourne, and later that of Colonel Strang in Conduct Unbecoming; Feb 1972, toured as The Colonel in End of Conflict; Bristol Old Vic, 1973, Colonel in Journey's End; Palladium, Nov 1974, Max Klaus in Hans Andersen, later touring in this part; Toronto, May 1977, Colonel Julian in Rebecca; Gardner Centre, Brighton, Sept 1976, Judge in The Chalk Garden, and Best Friend in All Over, touring in the latter part; Royal Alexandra, Toronto, May 1977, Colonel Julian in Rebecca; repeated the part of Max Klaus in Hans Andersen at the Palladium, Dec 1977; Northcott, Exeter, Apr 1978, Nikolayevich in Old World; Churchill Theatre, Bromley, Oct 1978, Earl of Caversham in The Ideal Husband and in The Beaux' Stratagem; Albery, Apr 1979, took over the part of Mr Brownlow in Olivier; first appeared in films in 1936 in The Luck of the Navy and has since appeared in Sword of Honour, The King and I, Captain Lightfoot, Zero Hour, The Entertainer, Terror of the Tongs, etc; has made many television appearances in England and America.

Favourite part: Nikolayevich in Old World. *Address:* c/o Coutts Bank, 162 Brompton Road, London SW3.

TORN, Rip (*né* Elmore Rual Torn), actor and director
b Temple, Texas, 6 Feb 1931; *s* of Elmore Rual Torn and his wife Thelma (Spacek); *e* Texas A and M College, University of Texas (BSFA 1953); *m* (1) Ann Wedgeworth (mar dis); (2) Geraldine Page; prepared for the stage with Alice Hermes, Sanford Meisner, Lee Strasberg, and at the Martha Graham School of the Dance; formerly an oilfield roustabout and an architectural draughtsman.

Made his New York début at the Morosco, June 1956, when he took over as Brick in Cat on a Hot Tin Roof; Coconut Grove Playhouse, Miami, Florida, Mar 1958, Val in Orpheus Descending; Sheridan Square Playhouse, Sept 1968, Bubba John in Chaparral; Martin Beck, Mar 1959, Tom Junior in Sweet Bird of Youth; Martin Beck, Jan 1960, took over from Paul Newman as Chance Wayne in this last play, and subsequently toured in this part; Music Box, Nov 1961, Carlo in Daughter of Silence; University of Texas, Austin, Apr 1962, played Macbeth; Circle in the Square, Jan 1963, Eban Cabot in Desire Under the Elms; Hudson, May 1963, took over from Ben Gazzara as Edmund Darrell in Strange Interlude; ANTA, Apr 1964, Lyle in Blues for Mr Charlie; 81st Street, June 1966, Peter in The Kitchen; New York City Center, Sept 1966, Bernie Dodd in The Country Girl; Theatre de Lys, Jan 1967, Marion Faye in The Deer Park, for which he received the Obie Award; Evergreen, Oct 1967, directed The Beard; Henry Miller's, Sept 1968, Roberto in The Cuban Thing; made his London début at the Royal Court, Nov 1968, when he directed The Beard; Gramercy Arts, Apr 1969, directed The Honest-to-God Schnozzola; Theatre de Lys, Dec 1969, Edward Morris in Dream of a Blacklisted Actor; Arena Stage, Washington, DC, 1970, Edgar in The Dance of Death; Ritz, Apr 1971, again played Edgar in Dance of Death; Playhouse in the Park, Philadelphia, July 1971, played in The Marriage Proposal and in The Boor; toured, summer 1971, in Marriage and Money; Playhouse, Jan 1973, directed Look Away; Anspacher, Jan 1974, William McLeod in Barbary Shore; Circle in the Square, 29 Apr 1974, appeared in a Gala Benefit Show; Theater of the Riverside Church, June 1974, Richard Nixon in Expletive Deleted; Academy Festival, Lake Forest, Ill, July 1974,

played in The Little Foxes, and subsequently at the Walnut, Philadelphia; Yale Repertory, New Haven, Conn, Mar 1975, Captain in The Father; Circle in the Square, Dec 1975, Tom in The Glass Menagerie; Lake Forest, Ill, June 1976, in A Streetcar named Desire; Hudson Guild, Jan 1977, and Public, Apr, directed and played Gustav in Creditors; American Place, Jan 1979, Henry Hackamore in Seduced; first appeared in films in Baby Doll, 1956, and has since played in Cat on a Hot Tin Roof, The Cincinnati Kid, Sweet Bird of Youth, Beach Red, Sol Madrid, Norman Mailer's Beyond the Law, Slaughter, Payday, Crazy Joe, The Man Who Fell to Earth (1976), etc; has appeared frequently on television since 1956 in Face of a Hero, Wetback Run, Johnny Belinda, and various dramatic series.

Address: Actors Studio, 432 West 44th Street, New York, NY 10036.

TOWB, Harry, actor
b Larne, Co Antrim, 27 July 1925; *s* of Jacob Towb and his wife Bessie Amelia (Sergai); *e* Belfast Technical College; *m* Diana Hoddinott; formerly a photographic enlarger and freelance journalist.

Made his first professional appearance at the Guildhall, Londonderry, Aug 1946, as Hugh O'Caghan in Professor Tim; came to England, June 1947, and after repertory experience made his first London appearance at the Arts, Aug 1950, at Matt Sullivan in The Gentle Gunman; Saville, Oct 1950, played Ralph Berger in Awake and Sing; Lyric, Hammersmith, Nov 1951, Archie Kramer in Summer and Smoke, transferring to the Duchess, Jan 1952; Duke of York's, Apr 1952, Private Soldier in The Mortimer Touch; Lyric, Hammersmith, Oct 1952, Watty in The Square Ring; Arts, Oct 1953, John Hegarty in Drama at Inish; same theatre, Apr 1959, Carl in Dark Halo; Pembroke, Croydon, Dec 1960, and Comedy, Jan 1961, played four parts in Fairy Tales of New York; Comedy, Feb 1962, Henry Rattner in My Place; Duke of York's, Sept 1962, Thomas Piper in Across the Board on Tomorrow Morning; Jeannetta Cochrane, May 1966, and Fortune, June 1966, Harry Faufil, Mr Pennington and Solomon Ithimar in The Bellow Plays, a triple bill; made his New York début at the Cort, Oct 1966, in these parts (the production was retitled Under the Weather); Royal Court, Feb 1968, played Harry Levin in a production without décor of Backbone, repeating the performance in a full production, May 1968; Abbey, Dublin, May 1969, Daniel Boyce in Macook's Corner; Greenwich, Feb 1970, Moss Mindlebaum and Colonel Oldmeadow in Sing A Rude Song; toured, Mar 1971, as Brock in Born Yesterday; Fortune, July 1971, Charlie Rosenthal in Look No Hands; Belgrade, Coventry, Mar 1972, Lou in Twigs; joined the RSC and played Adrian Mackenzie in Section Nine at the Place, Oct 1973, and the Aldwych, Jan 1974; John Forman in Sherlock Holmes, Aldwych, Jan 1974, and Broadhurst, NY, Nov 1974; Lenin in Travesties, Aldwych, May 1975, transferring to the Albery, Aug 1975, and repeating the part at the Ethel Barrymore, NY, Oct 1975; Aldwych, May 1976, Mosher in The Iceman Cometh; Malvern Festival, May 1977, played Hector Malone Snr in Man and Superman for the RSC, then touring in the part and transferring to the Savoy, Aug 1977; Manchester Opera House, Sept 1978, Victor Green in Barmitzvah Boy, transferring to Her Majesty's, Oct 1978; toured in There's A Small Hotel, Feb 1979; joined the National Theatre, July 1979, to play Charley in Death of A Salesman; National, Mar 1980, took part in platform performances of The Kugelmass Episode and Mr Big, and Death Knocks; has directed at the Central School and LAMDA; has appeared frequently in films, also on television, for which he has written several revue sketches, and has read some of his own short stories on radio.

Favourite parts: The trio in The Bellow Plays. *Recreations:* Yoga, gardening, giving up smoking. *Address:* c/o Jean Diamond, 235 Regent St, London W1 2JT.

TOWERS, Constance, actress and singer
b Whitefish, Montana, 20 May; *d* of Harry J Towers and his wife Ardath L (Reynolds); *e* Seattle, Washington, High School, Juilliard School of Music; *m* (1) Eugene C McGrath (mar dis); (2) John Gavin; prepared for the stage with David La Grant, Carl Pitzer, Lyn Masters, David Craig, and Carlos Noble, and at the American Academy of Dramatic Arts, and Juillard School of Music.

First appeared on the stage at the Civic Light Opera Company, Los Angeles, Cal, 1960, as Sarah Brown in Guys and Dolls; later toured in Camelot; first appeared in New York at the Ziegfeld, 29 Nov 1965, in the title role of the musical Anya; New York State, July 1966, played Julie in Show Boat; New York City Center, Dec 1966, Julie Jordan in Carousel; Apr 1967, Maria Rainer in The Sound of Music; Civic Light Opera, Los Angeles, July 1967, Marie in Dumas & Son; New York City Center, May 1968, Anna Leonowens in The King and I; Helen Hayes, May 1970, Vivian Whitney in The Engagement Baby, her first straight dramatic role; Jones Beach Marina, July 1971, again played Maria Rainer in The Sound of Music; Mark Hellinger, Jan 1971; Kitty Fremont in Ari; Jones Beach Marina, July 1971, Maria Rainer in The Sound of Music; same theatre, July 1972, Anna Leonowens in The King and I; Chateau de Ville, Saugus, Mass, Nov 1972, Agnes in I Do! I Do!; State Fair Music Hall, Dallas, Texas, July 1973, again played Anna Leonowens in The King and I; Indianapolis, Aug 1973, Eliza Doolittle in My Fair Lady; Pittsburgh Civic Light Opera, Sept 1973, Maria in The Sound of Music; Springfield, Mo, Sept 1973, in Mame; Arlington Park, Ill, 1973, Eleanor Hilliard in The Desperate Hours; Westport, Conn, Country Playhouse, Aug 1974, played in the revue Oh Coward! and subsequently toured Cafe Lafitte, Philadelphia, Pa, Nov 1974, appeared in cabaret; Westwood, California, 1975, in Rodgers & Hart, and again at Arlington Park, Illinois, Oct 1976, and Detroit Civic Light Opera; toured, 1976, as Anna Leonowens in The King and I, and played this part at the Uris, May 1977; first appeared in films in Horse Soldiers, 1959, and has since played in Sergeant Rutledge, Fate Is the Hunter, Shock Corridor, Naked Kiss, The Spy, etc; first appeared on television on *The Ed Sullivan Show,* 1957, and has since played on *The Johnny Carson Show,* Love Is a Many Splendored Thing, Once in Her Life, Bob Hope Specials, The Tony Awards, Mike Douglas, Hawaii-Five-O.

Favourite parts: Maria Rainer in The Sound of Music and Julie in Show Boat. *Hobbies and recreations:* Needlepoint, swimming, painting, tennis. *Address:* Actors Equity Association, 165 West 46th Street, New York, NY 10036.

TOYE, Wendy, director and dancer
b London, 1 May 1917; *d* of Ernest Walter Toye and his wife Jessie Crichton (Ramsay); *e* privately; *m* Edward Selwyn Sharp (mar dis); studied dancing as a child.

First appeared at the Royal Albert Hall in 1921; produced a ballet at the Palladium when only ten years of age; made her first appearance on the stage at the Old Vic, 9 Dec 1929, as Mustard Seed in A Midsummer Night's Dream and from 1930 danced with Ninette de Valois' Vic-Wells Ballet Company; Lyric, Dec 1930, played Marigold in Toad of Toad Hall; Royal Albert Hall, 1931, appeared in Hiawatha; Savoy, Dec 1931, played Phoebe and The White Rabbit in Toad of

Toad Hall; Lyceum, Apr 1932, appeared in The Miracle; Royalty, Dec 1932, again played in Toad of Toad Hall; Gaiety, Oct 1933, played the Masked Dancer in Ballerina; Coliseum, Feb 1934, principal dancer in The Golden Toy; toured with Anton Dolin, 1934–5; Alhambra, Aug 1935, played Varel Naryshkinsky in Tulip Time; subsequently toured with Dolin and Alicia Markova, 1935, choreographing Aucassin and Nicolette for that Company; Globe, Feb 1937, appeared as Linda in Love, and How to Cure It; Adelphi, Dec 1937, principal dancer in Aladdin; as choreographer, produced Mother Earth at the Savoy, 1929, and The Legend of the Willow Pattern at the Lyceum, 1930; appeared in all Camargo Society Ballet performances and choreographed Frank Bridge's There is a Willow Grows Aslant the Brook, 1931; Cross Gartered, Mercury, 1937; arranged the dances for all George Black's productions for the next seven years, beginning with These Foolish Things, Palladium, 1938; Black and Blue, London Hippodrome, 1939; Shakespearean season, Open Air Theatre, 1939; Hiawatha, Royal Albert Hall, 1939; The Little Dog Laughed, Palladium, 1939; Black Velvet, London Hippodrome, 1939, and in Jan 1940, danced in the show; Who's Taking Liberty?, Whitehall, 1939; Black Vanities, Victoria Palace, 1941; Gangway, Palladium, 1941; It's About Time, Comedy, 1942; Best Bib and Tucker, Palladium, 1942; Hi-de Hi, Palace, 1943; The Lisbon Story, London Hippodrome, 1943; Strike a New Note, Prince of Wales's, 1943; Panama Hattie, Piccadilly, 1943; Jenny Jones, London Hippodrome, 1944; Strike It Again, Prince of Wales's, 1944, and also danced in the production; arranged the ballets for Gay Rosalinda, Palace, 1945; on tour, Aug 1945, and at His Majesty's, Oct 1945, Follow the Girls, in which she also appeared as Betty; on tour, and at the Adelphi, July 1946, directed the production of Big Ben, for Sir Charles Cochran; Prince's, Aug 1946, arranged the ballets in the revival of Gay Rosalinda; Prince's, Sept 1946, directed The Shephard Show; Alexandra, Birmingham, Dec 1946, played Principal Girl in the pantomime, Simple Simon; Adelphi, Apr 1947, directed the production of Bless the Bride, for Sir Charles Cochran; Coliseum, June 1947, played Winnie Tate in Annie Get Your Gun; in Sept 1948, sent her company, Ballet-Hoo de Wendy Toye, to Paris for a season; Adelphi, July 1949, directed the production of Tough at the Top for Sir Charles Cochran; at the Imperial, New York, Apr 1950, with John Burrell, directed Peter Pan; subsequently in London directed And So To Bed, New, 1951; Night of Masquerade, at the Q, 1952; Second Threshold, Vaudeville, 1952; arranged dances for Joyce Grenfell Requests the Pleasure, Fortune, 1954; directed Wild Thyme, Duke of York's, 1955; Sadler's Wells, Oct 1957, directed the one act operas Bluebeard's Castle and The Telephone; Lyric, Hammersmith, Jan 1958, directed Lady at the Wheel; Edinburgh Festival, 1958, choreography for Concerto for Dancers and also danced in it; Sadler's Wells, Feb 1959, directed Rusalka; Coliseum, Apr 1959, directed Fledermaus; Old Vic, Sept 1959, directed As You Like It; Phoenix, Mar 1960, directed A Majority of One; Sadler's Wells, May 1960, directed Orpheus in the Underworld; she has since directed the following productions: La Vie Parisienne (Sadler's Wells), 1961; Fledermaus (Sadler's Wells), 1962; Virtue in Danger, 1963; A Midsummer Night's Dream (Latin-American and European tour), Robert and Elizabeth (also choreography), 1964; Orpheus in the Underworld, 1965; On The Level, Saville, 1966; Il Seraglio for Phoenix Opera, The Soldier's Tale for Scottish Opera, Jack and The Beanstalk, Arnaud, Guildford, 1967; Boots with Strawberry Jam, Nottingham Playhouse, The Italian Girl in Algiers, Coliseum, The Impresario and Don Pasquale for Phoenix Opera, 1968; The Great

WHO'S WHO IN THE THEATRE

Waltz, Drury Lane, The Soldier's Tale for the Young Vic, 1970; Show Boat, Adelphi, 1971; Il Seraglio, Phoenix Opera, Orpheus in the Underworld, Coliseum, 1971; She Stoops to Conquer, Young Vic, Cowardy Custard, Mermaid, Stand and Deliver, Edinburgh Festival and Round House, 1972; R loves J, Chichester, 1973; The Confederacy, Chichester, The Englishman Amused, Young Vic, The Italian Girl in Algiers, Coliseum, Follow the Star, Chichester, 1974; Made in Heaven, Chichester, Follow the Star, 1975; Once More with Music (and choreography), Guildford and tour, The Englishman Amused By . . . (and 1977), 1976; Oh, Mr Porter, Mermaid; Orpheus in the Underworld for English National Opera North, 1978; La Cenerentola, Guildhall School of Music, The Merry Widow (ENO North), Dance for Gods (and choreography), 1979; since 1951 has directed films, productions including All For Mary, The Twelfth Day (also appearing in the last-named picture), The King's Breakfast (nominated British Entry Cannes Festival), The Stranger Left No Card (Winner of Best Short Film Award, Cannes Festival); has also directed for television including Cliff in Scotland, Girls Wanted, Istanbul, A Goodly Manor for a Song, and Follow the Star; received the Queen's Silver Jubilee Medal, 1977.

Address: c/o London Management, 235–241 Regent Street, London, W1.

TRAUBE, Shepard, producer and director
b Malden, Mass, 27 Feb 1907; *s* of William Traube and his wife Helen (Newhouse); *e* New York University; *m* Mildred Gilbert.

Formerly engaged as theatre press representative and was a director, and also acted with the Washington Square Players; at the Maxine Elliott Theatre, Oct 1930, was assistant stage-manager for Twelfth Night, with Jane Cowl; in Apr 1931, was associated with Walter Hart and Sidney Harmon, in the production of Precedent, at the Provincetown Playhouse and the Bijou Theatre; directed and co-produced No More Frontier, Provincetown Playhouse, Oct 1931; directed the production of A Thousand Summers, Selwyn, May 1932; presented and staged The Sophistocrats, at the Bijou, Feb 1933; But Not for Love, 1934; subsequently went to Hollywood, where he produced and directed films for five years; returned to NY, and was responsible for the production and staging of Angel Street, at the Golden Theatre, Dec 1941, which ran for three years; has since staged Winter Soldiers, and The Patriots, 1942; presented and staged The Stranger, 1945; The Gioconda Smile, 1950; Bell, Book, and Candle (tour), The Green Bay Tree, 1951; Time Out for Ginger, 1952; The Girl in Pink Tights, 1954; The Grand Prize, 1955; Goodbye Again, 1956; Holiday for Lovers, Monique, 1957; Blackstone, Chicago, Oct 1958, directed The Tunnel of Love; directed The Gay Felons, 1959, tour; Westport Country Playhouse (Conn), Aug 1961, directed Venus at Large; Shubert, New Haven, Feb 1963, co-presented and directed Memo; co-produced Undercover Man, 1966; co-produced, directed the tour of Keep Off the Grass, and at the Studebaker, Chicago, co-produced and directed Children of the Wind, 1973; co-produced and directed Children of the Wind, NY, 1973; produced and directed a revival of Angel Street, NY, 1975; elected President of the Society of Stage Directors and Choreographers in 1959; appointed Managing Director of Equity Library Theatre, July 1965; produced and directed several films, including Goose Step, 1939, Street of Memories, 1940, The Bride Wore Crutches, 1941, etc; is the author of So You Want to Go into the Theatre, and a novel, Glory Road.

Address: 168 West 86th Street, New York, NY 10024.

TRAVERS, Ben, CBE, dramatic author and novelist
b Hendon, 12 Nov 1886; *e* Charterhouse; *m* Violet Mouncey (dec).

Author of the following plays: The Dippers, 1922; The Three Graces (from the Hungarian), 1924; A Cuckoo in the Nest, 1925; Rookery Nook, 1926; Thark, 1927; Plunder, 1928; Mischief, 1928; A Cup of Kindness, 1929; A Night Like This, 1930; Turkey Time, 1931; Dirty Work, 1932; A Bit of a Test, 1933; Chastity, My Brother, O Mistress Mine, 1936; Banana Ridge, 1938; Spotted Dick, 1939; She Follows Me About, 1943; Outrageous Fortune, 1947; Wild Horses, 1952; Nun's Veiling (a revised version of O Mistress Mine), 1953; Corker's End, 1968; The Bed Before Yesterday, 1975; in Sept 1976 this play, Banana Ridge and Plunder were all running in London; Rookery Nook, 1979; After You With the Milk, 1980; is also the author of film adaptations of most of the above plays and of numerous original films including Fighting Stock, Stormy Weather, Foreign Affairs, Lady in Danger, Dishonour Bright, Pot Luck, For Valour, etc; adapted seven of his farces for television, 1970; is also the author of five novels and a large number of short stories; Prime Warden of the Worshipful Company of Fishmongers, 1946; served in the RNAS, 1914–18 (Air Force Cross), resigned, 1919; rejoined RAF, 1939; resigned 1943 with rank of Squadron-Leader; Vice-President of Somerset County Cricket Club; received the CBE in the Birthday Honours, 1976.

Recreation: Watching cricket. *Clubs:* Garrick, MCC, and Beefsteak. *Address:* c/o Fishmongers' Company, Fishmongers' Hall, London Bridge EC4R.

TREWIN, John Courtenay, FRSL, dramatic critic and author
b Cornwall, 4 Dec 1908; *s* of Captain John Trewin and his wife Annie (James); *e* Plymouth College; *m* Wendy Monk.

Dramatic critic to *The Western Independent*, Plymouth, 1928–32; deputy dramatic critic of *The Morning Post*, London, 1934–7; literary editor of *The Observer*, 1943–8; second dramatic critic of *The Observer*, 1943–53; dramatic critic of *Punch*, 1944–5; dramatic critic of *John o' London's Weekly*, 1945–54; of *The Illustrated London News*, since 1946; *The Sketch*, 1947–59; *The Lady*, since 1949; *The Birmingham Post*, since 1955; radio drama critic, *The Listener*, 1951–8, has contributed to the BBC, *The Times Literary Supplement*, *Drama*, *Plays and Players*; author of The Shakespeare Memorial Theatre (with M C Day), 1932; The English Theatre, 1948; Up From The Lizard, 1948; We'll Hear a Play, 1949; London-Bodmin (with H J Willmott), 1950; Stratford-upon-Avon, 1950; Drama, 1945–50, The Theatre Since 1900, Down to The Lion, The Story of Bath, Shakespeare's Country (editor), 1951; A Play Tonight (essays); An Evening at the Larches (with Harry Hearson and Ronald Searle), Printer to the House (with E M King), 1952; Dramatists of Today, The Stratford Festival (with T C Kemp), 1953; William Shakespeare and Stratford, Theatre Programme (editor), Edith Evans, 1954; Mr Macready: A Nineteenth-Century Tragedian, Sybil Thorndike, Verse Drama Since 1800, 1955; Paul Scofield, 1956; The Night Has Been Unruly, 1957; Alec Clunes, 1958; The Gay Twenties (with Raymond Mander and Joe Mitchenson), 1958; Benson and the Bensonians, 1960; The Turbulent Thirties: A Further Decade of the Theatre, 1960; A Sword for a Prince: Plays for a Young Company, 1960; John Neville, 1961; The Birmingham Repertory Theatre: 1913–63, 1963; Shakespeare on the English Stage: 1900–64, 1964; Drama in Britain, 1951–64, 1965; edited and completed Lamb's Tales, 1964; The Drama Bedside Book (with H F Rubinstein), 1966; edited the Journal of William Charles Macready, 1967; The Pomping

Folk, Robert Donat: A Biography, 1968; Portrait of Shakespeare's Country, Shakespeare's Plays Today (with Arthur Colby Sprague), 1970; Peter Brook: a Biography, 1971; Portrait of Plymouth, 1973; Tutor to the Tsarevitch, 1975; The Edwardian Theatre, 1976; revised and completed British Drama by Allardyce Nicoll, 1978; Going to Shakespeare, 1978; All Sail (edited memoirs of his father), Shakespeare, 1980; devised Farjeon Reviewed (with David Toguri), Mermaid, 1975; Editor of *The West Country Magazine*, 1946–52; The Year's Work in the Theatre (for the British Council), 1949–52; Plays of the Year (many volumes), since 1948; contributor to the Dictionary of National Biography (1931–40: 1951–60), to the *Enciclopedia Dello Spettacolo* (Rome), and to several miscellanies and anthologies, including GBS 90, An Experience of Critics, Theatrical Companion to Somerset Maugham, Eden Phillpotts, The American Imagination, Experimental Drama, and The Triple Bond; compiler of other anthologies, including: In Praise of the Theatre, The West Country Book, and Theatre Bedside Book; editor of Sir Walter Scott: A Prose Anthology, A Year in the Country (Beach Thomas), Sean, Eileen, etc; Lecturer for The British Council in Hungary, 1963, and Romania, 1973; lectured in Canada, 1977; President of The Critics Circle, 1964–5; Chairman of West Country Writers' Association, 1964–72; a Bard of the Gorsedd of Cornwall; awarded the degree of Master of Arts (Honoris Causa), University of Birmingham, 1978.

Club: Garrick. *Address:* 15 Eldon Grove, Hampstead, NW3. *Tel:* 01–435 0207.

TRILLING, Ossia, critic and journalist
b Belstock, 22 Sept 1913; *s* of Samuel Trilling and his wife Rachel (Kaplan); *e* St Paul's School, and St John's College, Oxford; *m* Marie-Louise Crichton-Foch.

While at the university, appeared with the OUDS and directed Cocteau's Orphée, 1935; Westminster, May 1937, co-directed Strindberg's The Road To Damascus, Part I, and at the same theatre, Nov 1937, Queen Christina (both British premières), for The Incorporated Stage Society; co-founder and stage director of the Chesham Repertory Theatre, 1939–40; began writing dramatic criticism 1937, and has since engaged in journalism, broadcasting, and lecturing on the theatre; editor, and drama and opera critic of *Theatre Newsletter*, 1946–51; regular contributor to *Theatre World*, 1954–65; editor of *Theatre News Agency* since 1946; drama and music correspondent to numerous British and overseas papers and periodicals; regular contributor to *The Financial Times*, The Stage, BBC, German, Swedish and Swiss Radio arts programmes; sometime member of the Council, Critics' Circle; Vice-President of the International Association of Theatre Critics, 1956–77; co-editor and contributor to *International Theatre*; member of the Board of Theatre Workshop, 1975–; council member, British Theatre Institute; Adviser to bitef, Yugoslavia; author, annual article on *Theatre*, Encyclopedia Britannica Yearbook; Literary Adviser to the Belgian National Theatre and Zürich Schauspielhaus; adapted Porché's The Peace and Tsar Lenin, and Ferrero's Angelica for The Incorporated Stage Society; Officer of the Royal Order of the North Star (Sweden), 1980.

Address: 9A Portland Place, London, W1N 3AA.

TRINDER, Tommy, CBE, 1975; comedian
b Streatham, London, 24 Mar 1909; *s* of Thomas Henry Trinder and his wife Jean (Mills); *e* St Andrew's, Holborn; *m* Violet Bailey.

Toured in South Africa, 1921; made his first appearance in London, at Collins's Music-hall, June 1922, and played continuously in variety theatres until 1939; toured, 1937, in the revues, Tune In and In Town To-Night; at the London Palladium, appeared in Band Waggon, 1939; Top of the World, 1940; Gangway, 1941; Best Bib and Tucker, 1942; Happy and Glorious, 1944–6; Here, There and Everywhere, 1947; toured in Australia, 1947–8; London Palladium, Dec 1948, played Buttons in Cinderella; toured in South Africa, 1949; London Palladium, Dec 1949, Miffins in Puss in Boots; Palladium, Sept 1950, appeared in Starlight Rendezvous; toured in South Africa, 1950, in pantomime; made his first appearance in New York, 1950, at the Latin Quarter Club; Prince of Wales's, London, May 1951, appeared in the revue Fancy Free; again visited South Africa, 1951, and appeared in the pantomime Cinderella; toured Canada, 1952; toured Australia and New Zealand, 1952–4; appeared in the ice-pantomime Cinderella On Ice, at the Empress Hall, London, 1954–5; Tooting Granada, Dec 1955, appeared as Buttons in Cinderella; Adelphi, Nov 1956, starred in the revue United Notions; returned to South Africa, 1957, with The Trinder Show; Bristol Hippodrome, Dec 1958, Muddles in The Sleeping Beauty; Streatham Hill, Dec 1961, Dame Horner in Jack and Jill; New, Cardiff, Dec 1965, appeared in Aladdin; Wimbledon, Dec 1967, played Abanazar in Aladdin; he has appeared in Command Performances at Windsor, Balmoral, and Buckingham Palace, and in several Royal Variety Performances; appeared in summer shows at Blackpool and Cliftonville; first appeared in films in Almost a Honeymoon; appeared on television, 1955, as compère of *Sunday Night at The London Palladium*, and has since starred in numerous television programmes, including The Trinder Box; radio programmes include *My Wildest Dream, Does the Team Think?*, etc.

Recreations: Football (Life President of Fulham Football Club). *Clubs:* Savage and Eccentric. *Address:* 27 Old Bond Street, London, W1. *Tel:* 01–493 6264.

TROOBNICK, Eugene, actor
b Boston, Mass, 23 Aug 1926; *s* of Maurice Troobnick and his wife Lallie (Rothenberg); *e* Ithaca College, Columbia Univ, Univ of Chicago; formerly an Associate Editor of *Playboy* magazine, and an announcer for radio stations WNYC in New York and NBC and WFMT, Chicago, Ill.

First appeared on the stage at the Community Players, Freeport, Long Island, NY, 1947, as The Man in Hello Out There, which he also directed; co-founded the Playwrights Theatre Club, Chicago, Ill, 1953, and played Mosca in Volpone; first appeared in NY at the Royale, 26 Sept 1961, in the improvisational revue From the Second City; Second City at the Square East, May 1962, appeared in the revue Seacoasts of Bohemia and Alarums and Excursions; Apr 1963, played in To the Water Tower, all these last three revues being also improvisational; made his London début at the Prince Charles, 23 Apr 1963, in the Second City improvisational revue Looking for the Action; Martinique, Mar 1967, Captain in Dynamite Tonite; Henry Miller's, Jan 1968, Man in Before You Go; American Shakespeare Festival, Stratford, Conn, June 1968, Androcles in Androcles and the Lion; joined the Yale Repertory, New Haven, Conn, and played Sganarelle in Don Juan; Vivian Beaumont, Nov 1969, Krupp in The Time of Your Life; Ambassador, 1971, took over parts in Paul Sills's Story Theatre and Ovid's Metamorphoses; Cherry Lane, Oct 1971, Stan in A Gun Play; Yale Repertory, Dec 1972, played in In the Clap Shack; Jan 1973, played in The Mirror; Apr 1973, Duncan in Eugene Ionesco's Macbett; Apr 1973, played also in Edward Bond's Lear; Nov 1975, Sganarelle in Don Juan; Dec 1975, Captain in Dynamite Tonite!; Jan 1976, Mr Browfield in Walk the Dog, Willie; Feb 1976, in General Gorgeous; Nov 1976, in Ivanov; Jan

1977, Howard Oates in The Durango Flash; Mar 1977, Judge in Puntila; Apr 1977, Father in White Marriage; Public, Nov 1977, in Tales of the Hasidim; Yale Rep, season 1978, appeared as Sganarelle in an evening of Molière farces, Jan, and as Hjalmar Ekdal in The Wild Duck, Apr; again appeared in the Molière programme at the Public/Newman, June 1978; Long Wharf, New Haven, 1978, appeared in Biography; first appeared in films in Harvey Middleman, Fireman (1965), and has since played in California Split, Funny Lady, etc; first played on television in 1960 and has performed in The Second City, *That Was the Week That Was*; *The Ed Sullivan Show*, *Hawaii 5-O*, *Story Theater*, etc.

Favourite parts: Sganarelle, Androcles, Duncan, Mosca, Macbeth, Iago, Richard III, Cyrano de Bergerac. *Hobbies:* Writing, cartooning. *Address:* Apt 1632, 2700 Neilson Way, Santa Monica, Calif 90405. *Tel:* 213–399–3508.

TROY, Louise, actress and singer
b New York City, 9 Nov; *d* of Seymour Troy and his wife Ella (Ziebel); *e* Friends Seminary; *m* Werner Klemperer; trained for the stage at the American Academy of Dramatic Arts, and with Stella Adler, Lee Strasberg, and Harold Clurman.

First appeared on the stage at the Club Theatre, NY, 1954, as the Sphinx in The Infernal Machine, for which she received the *Show Business* off-Broadway Award; Club, Jan 1955, Jessica in The Merchant of Venice; Shubert, Nov 1955, played Marjorie in the musical Pipe Dream; Barbizon-Plaza, Nov 1957, Sophie Otford in Conversation Piece; same theatre, 1958, took over as Lady Reyburne in Salad Days; toured, 1960, as Queen Natasha in Royal Enclosure; Village Gate, Jan 1961, appeared in the revue O, Oysters!; Cambridge Arts Center, Massachusetts, summer 1961, Annie in Anatol; Booth, Oct 1961, Dominique in A Shot in the Dark; Theatre Four, Feb 1963, Kristine Linde in A Doll's House; Broadway, Mar 1963, Natalia Mayovskaya in Tovarich; Alvin, Apr 1964, Ruth in High Spirits; Lunt-Fontanne, Nov 1966, Maggie Hobson in Walking Happy; Paper Mill Playhouse, Milburn, New Jersey, 1968, Sylvia in The Women; Circle in the Square, June 1971, Bella in The Last Analysis; Bijou, Apr 1972, Elaine in The Divorce of Judy and Jane; Walnut, Philadelphia, Jan 1973, Mlle de Ste-Euverte in Waltz of the Toreadors; Plymouth, June 1976, took over as Hester Salomon in Equus; with the Philadelphia Drama Guild, 1975–9, her parts included Julie in The Royal Family, Mrs Lenin in Travesties, Elvira in Blithe Spirit, Lady Utterwood in Heartbreak House, and Amanda in Private Lives; first appeared in films in The Swimmer, 1968, and since has played in Yours, Mine, and Ours; has appeared on television in *Dundee and Culhane, Run for Your Life, East Side/West Side, Hawaii Five-O, Hogan's Heroes, Lou Grant,* and as Sue Rollins in the serial *Love of Life*.

Favourite parts: Ruth in High Spirits (the musical version of Blithe Spirit) and Maggie Hobson in Walking Happy (the musical version of Hobson's Choice). *Address:* Actors Equity Association, 165 West 46th Street, New York, NY 10036.

TRUEMAN, Paula, actress
b New York City, 25 Apr 1907; *d* of Joseph Trueman and his wife Eva (Cohn); *e* Hunter College (AB); *m* Harold Sterner; prepared for the stage on a fellowship at the Neighborhood Playhouse School of the Theatre.

First appeared on the stage at the Hippodrome, 1922, as a dancer in Michel Fokine's production of The Thunderbird; Neighborhood Playhouse, 20 May 1924, appeared in the second Grand Street Follies; 5 Dec, 1924, made her dramatic début as Madanika in The Little Clay Cart; Mar 1925, Hostess in Legend of the Dance; May 1925, a Near Relative

in The Critic; June 1925, the third Grand Street Follies; Dec 1925, Gitl in The Dybbuk; Princess in A Burmese Pwe and Too Fie in Kuan Yin; May 1926, Irene in The Romantic Lady; June 1926, in the fourth Grand Street Follies; Nov 1926, Madanika in The Little Clay Cart; Dec 1926, Gitl in The Dybbuk; Feb 1927, the Lady Friend in Pinwheel; Apr 1927, Columbine in Commedia dell Arte; May 1927, played in the fifth Grand Street Follies, and transferred with this revue to the Little, also May 1927; Little, Sept 1927, Valerie in Loves and Enemies; Oct 1927, Liza in If; Comedy, Dec 1927, Maureen Milton in The Love Nest; Comedy, Feb 1928, Hermance in Maya; Booth, May 1928, played in the revue The Grand Street Follies of 1928; Booth, May 1929, in The Grand Street Follies of 1929; Chainin's 44th Street, Nov 1930, in Sweet and Low; toured, 1930, in Grand Hotel; Cort, Sept 1931, Tessie Wede in Ladies of Creation; Shakespeare, Nov 1932, Puck in A Midsummer Night's Dream, Jessica in The Merchant of Venice, and Margaret in Much Ado About Nothing; Imperial, Mar 1935, A Woman in Panic; Booth, Dec 1936, Essie in You Can't Take It with You; Lyceum, Oct 1940, Hester in George Washington Slept Here; Biltmore, Mar 1943, Mary Franklin in Kiss and Tell; Music Box, Dec 1943, Phoebe Fuller in Feathers in a Gale; Belasco, Oct 1944, Esther in Violet; toured during World War II in The Man Who Came to Dinner; Henry Miller's, Nov 1947, Mrs Tremaine in For Love or Money; Ziegfeld, Dec 1949, Mrs Spofford in Gentlemen Prefer Blondes; ANTA, Feb 1952, Sybil in Mrs McThing; toured in this last part, Jan–May 1953; Berkshire Playhouse, Stockbridge, Massachusetts, 1954, Laura Partridge in The Solid Gold Cadillac, and, 1955, played in The Book of Charm; Ethel Barrymore, May 1956, Juliet in Wake Up, Darling; Billy Rose, Jan 1962, Mrs Forsythe in A Family Affair; New York City Center, Feb 1963, Mrs Wade in Wonderful Town; Village South, Mar 1963, Little Mother in Like Other People; Morosco, May 1964, Mrs Mulligan in The Sunday Man, New York City Center, June 1965, Mrs Squires in The Music Man; Shubert, Boston, Sept 1965, Mrs Potts in Hot September; Cherry Lane, Sept 1966, Mother Bayard in The Long Christmas Dinner, Mme Pugeot in Queens of France, and Ma Kirby in The Happy Journey to Trenton and Camden, in an overall bill called Thornton Wilder's Triple Play; Alvin, Mar 1967, Harriet Stanley in Sherry!; Theatre de Lys, Dec 1967, Margaret in Postcards; Ethel Barrymore, Mar 1970, Mrs Fish in Dr Fish; Arena Stage, Washington DC, Mar 1977, Mousie in Catsplay; appeared in the film Homebodies, 1974, and The Outlaw Josey Wales, 1976; has appeared on television in various dramatic programs and soap operas, recently in *All My Children*.

Address: 340 East 63rd Street, New York, NY 10021. *Tel:* TE 8–4621.

TRUSSLER, Simon, editor and author
b 11 June 1942; *s* of John Trussler and his wife Margaret Joan (Ovenden); *e* Cranbrook School, Kent and University College, London; *m* Glenda Leeming.

London theatre critic of the *Tulane Drama Review*, later *The Drama Review*, 1965–70; theatre critic of *Tribune*, 1966–72, also contributing to *The Times, The Observer*, etc; co-founder 1971 and co-editor to 1977, *Theatre Quarterly*; sole editor since 1977; author of a number of books and monographs on theatre topics, including Theatre at Work (with Charles Marowitz), 1967; Eighteenth Century Comedy, 1969; the four 'assessments' of the plays of John Osborne, 1969, Arnold Wesker, 1971 (with Glenda Leeming), John Whiting, 1972, and Harold Pinter, 1973; and studies of Osborne and Bond for the series Writers and Their Work;

founder member, British Theatre Institute; associate director, British Centre of the International Theatre Institute; instrumental in setting up both of these; has taught and lectured in English and drama in association with British and American universities.

Address: Great Robhurst, Woodchurch, Ashford, Kent. *Tel:* 023-386 213.

TUCCI, Maria, actress
b Florence, Italy, 19 June 1941; prepared for the stage at the Actors Studio.

First appeared in New York at the Belvedere Lake, 6 Aug 1958, as a member of the cast of Othello; 7 Aug 1958, played in Twelfth Night; Theatre Marquee, Feb 1962, played Polly in The Jackhammer; Morosco, Jan 1963, played Angelina in The Milk Train Doesn't Stop Here Anymore; Village South, May 1963, Katia in Five Evenings; Cherry Lane, Oct 1963, Elena in Corruption in the House of Justice; Circle in the Square, Dec 1963, played in the Chorus of The Trojan Women; Brooks Atkinson, Feb 1964, A Girl in The Deputy; American Shakespeare Festival, June 1965, Virgilia in Coriolanus and Juliet in Romeo and Juliet; Circle in the Square, Dec 1965, Isabella in The White Devil, and later succeeded Carrie Nye as Vittoria Corombona in this production; New York City Center, Oct 1966, Rosa Delle Rose in The Rose Tattoo; Vivian Beaumont, Dec 1966, Maria in Yerma; Stratford, Conn, June 1967, title role of Jean Anouilh's Antigone, and Jessica in The Merchant of Venice; Vivian Beaumont, Oct 1967, Alexandra Giddens in The Little Foxes; Henry Miller's, Sept 1968, Alicia in The Cuban Thing; Fortune, Jan 1969, Timidity in Horseman, Pass By; Stratford, Conn, June 1969, Ophelia in Hamlet, and Aug 1969, played in The Three Sisters; toured, Sept 1969, as Eleanor Bachman in The Great White Hope; Fortune, May 1970, Teacher in The Shepherd of Avenue B; Lyceum, 1971, took over as Agnes in The School for Wives; Playwrights Horizon, Nov 1973, Annie/Susan in Sissie's Scrapbook; Long Wharf, New Haven, Conn, Feb 1974, Teacher in A Pagan Place; McCarter, Princeton, NJ, Oct 1974, Ruth Atkins in Beyond the Horizon; Feb 1975, Kattrin in Mother Courage and Her Children; Apr 1975, Juliet in Romeo and Juliet; Stratford, Conn, June 1975, Regan in King Lear; July 1975, Hermione and Perdita in The Winter's Tale; McCarter, Princeton, Feb 1976, Catherine Sloper in The Heiress; Stratford, June 1976, again played Hermione and Perdita; McCarter, Nov 1976, title role in Major Barbara; Long Wharf, Feb 1978, Kitty in Spokesong; Public/Newman, Nov 1978, Andrea in Drinks Before Dinner; Circle in the Square, Mar 1979, again played Kitty in Spokesong.

Address: Actors Equity Association, 165 West 46th Street, New York, NY 10036.

TUMARIN, Boris (*né* Tumarinson), actor, director, teacher
b Riga, Latvia, 4 Apr 1910; *s* of Joseph Tumarinson and his wife Hanna (Lifshitz); *e* Gymnasium, Riga, Academy of Arts, Riga, 1926–31, and Academy of Arts, Berlin, 1931–2; *m* Bertha Weinberg; prepared for the stage at the Drama Studio, Riga, with Michael Checkov, Michael Goz, Max Reinhardt Seminar in Berlin, Tamara Daykarhanova, and Audrey Jilinsky's Actors Workshop, New York; served in the Latvian Army, 1933.

Made his first appearance on the stage at the Riga Gymnasium, 1924, as Eli in Mottel; made his professional début in Kaunas, Lithuania, 1928, as the Pastor in The Father; joined the Jewish Labor Theatre, 1932, and played and directed plays for them until 1934; appeared with the Riga Jewish Repertory Theatre, touring in Europe, 1934–5; toured in a

one-man show in the Baltic States and Poland, 1934–7; came to the USA in 1939, and, at the Heckscher, Dec 1941, directed and played Ole in The Emperor's New Clothes; New School for Social Research, Nov 1942, played Karel in Erwin Piscator's production of Winter Soldiers; Windsor, Mar 1943, played Dr Isaacs in The Family; served in the US Army, 1943–5; Equity Library Theatre, Mar 1946, directed and played in A Checkov Carnival; Westchester Playhouse, Mount Kisco, New York, summer 1946, Captain in You Touched Me and Nick in The Time of Your Life; Equity Library Theatre, Feb 1947, General Assolant in Paths of Glory; Kingsmith, Washington, DC, summer 1947, Cradeau in No Exit; New Stages, Dec 1947, directed Lamp at Midnight; Dec 1948, played Canoris in The Victors; Feb 1949, directed Blood Wedding; Mar 1949, directed The Sun and I; ANTA, Jan 1951, co-produced and directed The House of Bernarda Alba; Broadhurst, Dec 1953, played Miroslav Babicka in The Prescott Proposals; President, Oct 1954, directed Sands of the Negev; Lyceum, Dec 1954, Chernov in Anastasia, and toured in this part in a production he directed, 1956; John Golden, Feb 1956, George Mainzer in The Innkeepers; Studebaker, Chicago, 1956, directed Desire Under the Elms; Gate, Dec 1957, directed and co-adapted with Jack Sydow The Brothers Karamazov; toured, 1958, as Mancini in He Who Gets Slapped; Fourth Street, Sept 1959, Solyony in The Three Sisters; Gate, Sept 1960, co-adapted and directed The Idiot; Jan 1961, directed Montserrat; Billy Rose, Mar 1961, Eugenio Cardinal Marotta in The Devil's Advocate; ANTA, Oct 1961, Father Athanasios in The Garden of Sweets; Gate, Feb 1962, directed and played Shylock in The Merchant of Venice; Morosco, Apr 1962, Mr Kronheim in Venus at Large; Cherry Lane, Oct 1962, Max in Whisper into My Good Ear; Maidman, Feb 1963, Gottlieb Biedermann in The Firebugs; Maidman, July 1963, Shpigelsky in A Month in the Country; ANTA, Sept 1964, Huspar in Traveller Without Luggage; Cherry Lane, Nov 1964, The King in The Giant's Dance; Mar 1966, Aleko, Old Peasant, Lawyer in Caucasian Chalk Circle; played Shylock in The Merchant of Venice with the Milwaukee Repertory Theatre, 1966–7; New York City Center, Nov 1967, Alper in The Tenth Man; Royale, Sept 1968, Presiding Judge in The Man in the Glass Booth; directed The Three Sisters for the Milwaukee Repertory, 1968–9, and A Midsummer Night's Dream, 1969–70 season; Plymouth, Nov 1977, played Abtalion de Modena in The Merchant; has appeared on television with the Lunts in The Great Sebastians, in Don Quixote, Ninotchka, *The Nurses, The Defenders, The Doctors, The Eternal Light,* and other dramatic programs; received the Obie Award for his co-adaptation of The Brothers Karamazov and the Vernon Rice Award of The Drama Desk for co-founding the Gate Repertory Company, 1961; taught acting at the American Theatre Wing, 1949–51, at the Dramatic Workshop, 1949–50, and the Actor's Workshop, which he directed, 1951–2; in 1970 joined the staff of the Drama Division of the Juilliard School, NY, where he taught and directed until his death.

(*Died 28 Jan 1979.*)

TUNE, Tommy, actor, director, choreographer and dancer
b Witchita Falls, Texas, 28 Feb 1939; *s* of Jim P Tune and his wife Eva M (Clark); *e* Lon Morris Junior College, Jacksonville, University of Texas at Austin and University of Houston (BFA).

Made his Broadway debut at the Broadway Theatre, 16 Feb 1965, in the chorus of Baker Street; appeared in Joyful Noise, Mark Hellinger, Dec 1966, and How Now Dow Jones, Lunt-Fontanne, Dec 1967; choreographer for the tour of

Canterbury Tales, 1969; won a Tony for his David in Seesaw, Uris, Mar 1973, and toured in the role, 1974; Circle in the Square, Oct 1976, directed The Club; Studio Arena, Buffalo, Sept 1977, directed Sunset; Entermedia, Apr 1978, co-directed and choreographed The Best Little Whorehouse in Texas, which transferred to the 46th Street, Jun 1979; direction and choreography (Tony) for A Day in Hollywood, A Night in the Ukraine, John Golden, May 1980; films include Hello Dolly and The Boyfriend.

Favourite part: David in Seesaw. *Address:* c/o ICM, 40 West 57th Street, New York, NY 10019.

TUPOU, Manu, actor
b Lomaloma, Lau, Fiji Islands, 5 Jan; *s* of Wilisoni Pau'u Fatafehi and his wife Waimoana (Kalolaini); *e* Univ of Hawaii, London School of Economics and Political Science (BA in Anthropology); trained for the stage with Uta Hagen, Herbert Berghof, Lee Strasberg, Elia Kazan, and Arthur Penn; formerly a writer and director of radio documentaries for Fiji Radio, and for the BBC Overseas Service.

First appeared on the stage at the Honolulu Community Theatre, Honolulu, Hawaii, June 1961, as the Recruiting Officer in Na'Au'Ao; at the American Academy of Dramatic Arts, Apr 1967, played King Creon in Antigone; made his New York professional début at the Brooks Atkinson, 13 Oct 1969, as Sitting Bull in Indians; Sokol, Mar 1970, played The Ragpicker in The Madwoman of Chaillot; Seattle Repertory, Washington, 1970–71 season, again played Sitting Bull in Indians, and repeated this part at the Bucks County Playhouse, New Hope, Pa; American Shakespeare Festival, summer 1971, played title role of Othello; Puerto Rican Traveling Theatre, Aug 1971, played in A Dramatized Anthology of Puerto Rican Short Stories; Public/Martinson Hall, Dec 1971, Agamemnon in The Wedding of Iphigenia and Iphigenia in Concert; Ethel Barrymore, Apr 1972, Sidi El Assif in Captain Brassbound's Conversion; Cathedral Church, May 1972, Creon Molina in The Passion of Antigona Perez; repeated this last part for the Puerto Rican Traveling Theater; Actors Studio, Feb 1973, again played Othello; appeared with the Center Stage, Baltimore, Md, 1972–73 season; American Place, Apr 1976, played Assawamset in Endecott and the Red Cross, and Ferryman in My Kinsman, Major Molineux, in the trilogy The Old Glory; first appeared in films in Hawaii, 1966, and has since played in A Man Called Horse, Castaway Cowboy, etc; has appeared on television in Hawaii 5-O, Quest in Paradise for BBC TV, etc.

Favourite parts: Othello, Sitting Bull, James Tyrone.
Recreations: Rugby, swimming, football, volleyball, reading.
Address: 11 West 69th Street, New York, NY 10023. *Tel:* 877–7122 or LO 4–3250.

TURNER, Bridget, actress
b Cleethorpes, Lincs, 22 Feb 1939; *d* of Eric Turner and his wife Phyllis Johanna (Blanchard); *e* Grimsby Wintringham Grammar School; *m* Frank Cox; trained for the stage at RADA.

Made her first appearance on the stage touring schools with the Welsh Children's Theatre, 1959, as Beatrice in The Servant of Two Masters; at the Belgrade, Coventry, June 1962, played Avril Hadfield in Semi-Detached; Hampstead, Dec 1962, Masha in The Seagull; same theatre, July 1963, The Girl in The Square; made her New York début in the same year at The Music Box, as Avril Hadfield in Semi-Detached; Royal Court, Feb 1967, played Beatie in Roots; with the 69 Theatre Company, Manchester, 1967, played Pegeen Mike in The Playboy of the Western World and Juliet in Romeo and Juliet; at Bristol, 1968, her parts with the Old

Vic included Nina in The Seagull and Muriel Rye in Brother and Sister; Fortune, June 1969, Bess Hogg in Sometime Never; Garrick, Sept 1969, took over as Kate Hardcastle in She Stoops to Conquer; Strand, Apr 1970, Louisa in Erb; Phoenix, Leicester, Aug 1971, Jenny in Me Times Me Times Me; Shaw, Dec 1971, Greenfly in The Plotters of Cabbage Patch Corner; Comedy, Aug 1972, Anna in Time and Time Again; Criterion, July 1972, Jane in Absurd Person Singular; Globe, Aug 1974, Ruth in The Norman Conquests; Royal Court, Nov 1975, Patty in The Fool; Nottingham, 1976/77 season, Emilia in Othello, Maggie Hobson in Hobson's Choice, and Mme Ranevsky in The Cherry Orchard; RSC tour, 1978, Olga in Three Sisters and Maria in Twelfth Night; Royal Exchange, Manchester, Apr 1979, Jeanette Fisher in Last of the Red Hot Lovers, transferring to the Criterion, Nov 1979; films, since her first in 1969, include The Walking Stick and Under Milk Wood; TV, since 1963, includes Resurrection, Slattery's Mounted Foot, Love Lies Bleeding, *Two People,* and *Jackanory..*

Recreations: Walking, listening to classical music. *Address:* 63 Elders Road, Ealing, London W13.

TURNER, David, dramatic author
b Birmingham, 18 Mar 1927; *s* of George Allen Turner and his wife Edith Marie (Ayres); *e* Moseley Grammar School and Birmingham University; *m* Joan Turner; formerly a teacher.

Is the author of Semi-Detached and The Bedmakers, 1962; The Antique Shop, 1963; Bottomley, 1965; The Prodigal Daughter, 1973; The Only True Story of Lady Godiva (co-author), 1974; The Girls, 1975; adapted The Beggars' Opera, 1967; The Servant of Two Masters, 1968; The Miser, 1973; wrote the book of the musical Quick, Quick, Slow, 1969; his writing for television, since 1961, includes plays such as The Train Set, Requiem for a Crown Prince, and Harold, as well as many dramatizations including Germinal, The Roads to Freedom, and Prometheus.

Recreation: Sailing. *Club:* Savage. *Address:* c/o Harvey Unna, 14 Beaumont Mews, London W1.

TURNER, Douglas. See Ward, Douglas Turner.

TURNER, Michael, actor
b Tabankulu, East Province, South Africa, 19 July 1921; *s* of Thomas Blake Turner, and his wife Irene Price (Edwards); *e* Durban, South Africa; *m* Monica Kirton; trained for the stage at the Central School of Speech and Drama.

First appeared on the stage in 1946, with the Old Vic Company, at the New Theatre, London, walking on in Cyrano de Bergerac; toured with the Young Vic, 1951, as Jasper in The Knight of the Burning Pestle; Memorial Theatre, Stratford, seasons 1952–3, his parts included Amiens in As You Like It and Solanio in The Merchant of Venice; at the Alexander, Johannesburg, 1957–8, his performances included the General in Romanoff and Juliet, Lt Maryk in The Caine Mutiny Court-Martial and Barney in The Summer of the Seventeenth Doll; South African Actor of the Year, 1958; Old Vic, Dec 1961, Macduff in Macbeth; Playhouse, Sheffield, 1963, the title part in King Lear; with the National Theatre Company, 1963–7 and 1969–72; Assistant Producer, 1970; his parts have included De Soto in The Royal Hunt of the Sun, 1964; Feraillon in A Flea in Her Ear, 1966 (also Queen's); Sir Wilfull Witwoud in The Way of the World, Innkeeper in The Travails of Sancho Panza, 1969; General Yepanchin in The Idiot, Pantaloon in The King Stag (Young Vic), 1970; Doss House Keeper and Police Inspector in The Captain of Köpenick, Rev Trussler and William

Shakespeare in Tyger, Cominius in Coriolanus, 1971; Lyceum, Edinburgh, Apr 1972, Dr Herdal in The Master Builder, also touring; Theatre Royal, Windsor, Aug 1975, appeared in The Pleasure of His Company; Staff Director for the National Theatre, 1976, on Tamburlaine and Force of Habit; Crucible, Sheffield, Judge Brack in Hedda Gabler, Nottingham Playhouse, Dr Chasuble in The Importance of Being Earnest and Ernest in Bedroom Farce, 1977; Belgrade, Coventry, Sept 1978, Bernard in Dear Daddy; first film, 1966, the National Theatre's Othello; subsequently, Battle of Britain; television, since 1951, includes leads in many plays and series.

Favourite part: Lear. *Recreations:* Golf, crossword puzzles. *Clubs:* Stage Golfing. *Address:* Sunny Cottage, Lower Chicksgrove, near Tisbury, Wiltshire.

TUSHINGHAM, Rita, actress
b Liverpool, 14 Mar 1942; *d* of John Tushingham and his wife Enid Ellen (Lott); *e* La Sagesse Convent, Liverpool; *m* Terence William Bicknell.

First appeared on the stage in Dec 1958 at the Liverpool Playhouse as a rabbit and the back legs of the Horse in Toad of Toad Hall; first appeared in London, in Feb 1961, at the Royal Court, as the Madwoman in The Changeling; at the same theatre, played third waitress in The Kitchen, Aug 1961; Hermia in A Midsummer Night's Dream, Jan, Maria in Twelfth Night, Feb, and Nancy in The Knack, Mar 1962; Garrick, Apr 1969, Daisy Wink in The Give-away; Greenwich, Sept 1970, Lorna in Lorna and Ted; Piccadilly, Feb 1973, Bernadette Soubirous in Mistress of Novices; films, since A Taste of Honey in 1961, include Girl With Green Eyes, The Knack, Dr Zhivago, The Human Factor, Black Journal, and The Incredible Mrs Chadwick; first appeared on television, 1964, recently in her own series, *No Strings*.

Recreation: Cooking. *Address:* c/o London Management, 235–241 Regent Street, London, W1. *Tel:* 01–734 4192.

TUTIN, Dorothy, CBE, actress
b London, 8 Apr 1930; *d* of John Tutin and his wife Adie Evelyn (Fryers); *e* St Catherine's, Bramley, Surrey; *m* Derek Waring; studied for the stage at PARADA and RADA.

Made her first appearance at The Boltons, 6 Sept 1949, as Princess Margaret of England in The Thistle and the Rose; joined the Bristol Old Vic Company, Jan 1950, appearing as Phebe in As You Like It, Anni in Captain Carvallo, Belinda in The Provoked Wife, etc; joined the Old Vic Company in London for the 1950–1 season, playing among other parts, Win-the-Fight Littlewit in Bartholomew Fair, Ann Page in The Merry Wives of Windsor, Princess Katharine in Henry V; Lyric, Hammersmith, Sept 1951, played Martina in Thor With Angels; Phoenix, Jan 1952, Hero in Much Ado About Nothing; at Wyndham's, Apr 1953, played Rose Pemberton in The Living Room; New, Mar 1954, played Sally Bowles in I Am a Camera; Lyric, Hammersmith, Mar 1955, played Joan in The Lark; Saville, Dec 1955, played Hedvig in The Wild Duck; toured, Sept 1956, as Caroline Traherne in The Gates of Summer; Royal Court, Apr 1957, played Jean Rice in The Entertainer; joined the Shakespeare Memorial Theatre Company, Stratford-on-Avon, Apr 1958, and appeared as Juliet in Romeo and Juliet, Viola in Twelfth Night, and Ophelia in Hamlet, subsequently playing the same parts, when the company visited Leningrad and Moscow, Dec 1958; New, London, July 1959, played Dolly in Once More, With Feeling; again joined the Shakespeare Memorial Theatre Company for the season, 1960, to play Portia in The Merchant of Venice, Viola in Twelfth Night, and Cressida in Troilus and Cressida; with the same company (re-named

Royal Shakespeare Company, Jan 1961) appeared at the Aldwych, Dec 1960, as Viola in Twelfth Night, and Feb 1961, as Sister Jeanne in The Devils; Royal Shakespeare, Stratford-on-Avon, Aug 1961, Juliet in Romeo and Juliet and Oct 1961, Desdemona in Othello; Aldwych, Dec 1961, played Varya in The Cherry Orchard; Edinburgh Festival, Sept 1962, again played Sister Jeanne in The Devils, and Cressida in Troilus and Cressida, prior to appearing in both plays in repertory at the Aldwych, Oct 1962; made her first appearance in New York at the Henry Miller Theatre, Jan 1963, in The Hollow Crown; Aldwych, London, July 1963, Polly Peachum in The Beggar's Opera; Festival Hall, Nov 1963, Beatrice in Beatrice et Benedict (concert version); Bristol Old Vic, Mar 1965, played Queen Victoria in Portrait of a Queen, transferring with the production to the Vaudeville, May 1965; Royal Shakespeare, Stratford-on-Avon, and Aldwych, summer 1967, played Rosalind in As You Like It, appearing in the same production at the Ahmanson, Los Angeles, Jan 1968; Henry Miller, NY, Feb 1968, Victoria in Portrait of a Queen; Belgrade, Coventry, Feb 1969, played the name part in Ann Veronica; St Martin's, Jan 1970, Francine in Play On Love; Roundhouse, Nov 1970, Royal Shakespeare Company's Theatregoround Festival, played Alice in Arden of Faversham; Aldwych, June 1971, Kate in Old Times; Coliseum, Dec 1971 and Dec 1972, title role in Peter Pan; toured, Mar 1972, as Maggie Wylie in What Every Woman Knows; Chichester, season 1974, Natalya in A Month in the Country; Albery, Nov 1974, again played Maggie Wylie; Albery, Nov 1975, for Prospect productions, again played Natalya in A Month in the Country, receiving the *Evening Standard* Best Actress Award for her performance; Arnaud, Guildford, Oct 1976, Lady Macbeth in Macbeth; Edinburgh, 1977, Cleopatra in Antony and Cleopatra, and at the Old Vic, Nov 1977; Olivier, Feb 1978, Madame Ranevsky in The Cherry Orchard; June 1978, Lady Macbeth in Macbeth; Sept 1978, Lady Plyant in The Double Dealer; June 1979, Genia Hofreiter in Undiscovered Country; Haymarket, Mar 1980, Mme Dubarry in Reflections; received the *Evening Standard* award, 1960, as the Best Actress, for her performance in Twelfth Night; first appeared in films, 1951, performances include The Importance of Being Earnest, The Beggar's Opera, A Tale of Two Cities, Cromwell, and Savage Messiah; TV includes The Six Wives of Henry VIII, South Riding, and Willow Cabins; received the CBE in the New Year Honours, 1967.

Recreations: Music and climbing mountains. *Address:* c/o Peter Browne Management, Pebro House, 13 St Martin's Road, London SW9. *Tel:* 01–737 3444.

TYNAN, Kenneth, FRSL, dramatic critic, author, and journalist
b Birmingham, 2 Apr 1927; *s* of Sir Peter Peacock and Letitia Rose Tynan; *e* at King Edward's School, Birmingham, and Magdalen College, Oxford; *m* (1) Elaine Dundy (mar dis); (2) Kathleen Halton.

Began his career in 1949 as director of the Lichfield Repertory Company; Lyric, Hammersmith, Feb 1950, directed Man of the World; Arts Council tour, 1950, directed Othello; New, May 1951, appeared as the First Player in Hamlet with Alec Guinness; New, Dec 1968, co-presented Soldiers; drama critic of *The Spectator*, 1951–2; *Evening Standard*, 1952–3; *Daily Sketch*, 1953–4, *The Observer*, 1954–8, *The New Yorker*, 1958–60, returned to *The Observer*, 1960–3; script editor for Ealing Films, 1956–8; editor of the television programme *Tempo*, 1961–2; film critic of *The Observer*, 1964; co-author of radio feature, The Quest for Corbett, 1956; author of He That Plays The King, 1950;

Persona Grata, 1953; Alec Guinness, 1953; Bull Fever, 1955; Curtains, 1961; Tynan Right and Left, 1969; A View of the English Stage, The Sound of Two Hands Clapping, 1975; devised the revue Oh! Calcutta!, 1968; Carte Blanche, 1976; Literary Manager of the National Theatre, 1963–9; Literary Consultant, 1969–73.

Recreations: Eating and watching bullfights. *Address:* 20 Thurloe Square, London, SW7.

TYSON, Cicely, actress
b New York City, 19 Dec.

First appeared in New York at the Longacre, 5 Dec 1959, when she understudied Eartha Kitt in the role of Jolly Rivers in Jolly's Progress; Eugene O'Neill, Feb 1960, played Girl in The Cool World; St Mark's Playhouse, May 1961, played Stephanie Virtue Diop in The Blacks; East 11th Street, Jan 1962, Mavis in Moon on a Rainbow Shawl; Booth, Dec 1962, Celeste Chipley in Tiger Tiger Burning Bright; Masque, Apr 1963, Joan in The Blue Boy in Black; Astor Place Playhouse, Dec 1963, Reverend Marion Alexander in Trumpets of the Lord; Longacre, Sept 1966, appeared in the revue A Hand Is on the Gates; John Golden, Feb 1968, Myrna Jessup in Carry Me Back to Morningside Heights; Brooks Atkinson, Apr 1969, again played Reverend Marion Alexander in Trumpets of the Lord; Cherry Lane, Jan 1969, played in To Be Young, Gifted, and Black; Playhouse in the Park, Cincinnati, Ohio, 1970–71 season, played in The Blacks; Academy Festival, Chicago, Ill, June 1974, Abbie Putnam in Desire Under the Elms; appeared in the film Sounder (1972); has also appeared on television, notably in The Autobiography of Miss Jane Pittman, for which she received the Emmy Award (1974), and Just an Old Sweet Song, 1976, etc.

Address: AFTRA, 1350 Avenue of the Americas, New York, NY.

TYZACK, Margaret, OBE, actress
d of Thomas Edward Tyzack, and his wife Doris (Moseley); *e* St Angela's Ursuline Convent, Forest Gate, London; *m* Alan Stephenson; trained for the stage at RADA.

First appeared on the stage Sept 1951 at the Chesterfield Civic Theatre, as a Bystander in Pygmalion; her first London appearance was at the Royal Court, Feb 1959, as Mag Keegan in Progress to the Park, in a production without décor; at the same theatre, also Feb 1959, played Miss Frost in The Ginger Man; Arts, May 1962, for RSC, played Vassilissa in The Lower Depths; Pembroke, Croydon, Nov 1963, again played Miss Frost; Open Space, May 1970, Jacqueline Harrison in Find Your Way Home; Piccadilly, Apr 1971, took over the part of Queen Elizabeth in Vivat! Vivat Regina!; for the RSC, Stratford season 1972, played Volumnia in Coriolanus, Apr, Portia in Julius Caesar, May, and Tamora in Titus Andronicus, Oct; repeated the parts of Portia, July 1973, and Volumnia, Oct 1973, at the Aldwych; Aldwych, Aug 1974, and Brooklyn Academy, Feb 1975, Maria Lvovna in Summerfolk; Stratford, Ontario, 1977 season, Countess of Rossillon in All's Well That Ends Well, Mrs Alving in Ghosts and Queen Margaret in Richard III; Royal Exchange, Manchester, Sept 1979, Milly in People are Living There; films, since 1957, include 2001, The Whisperers, A Touch of Love and A Clockwork Orange; her numerous television appearances include plays and series such as The Forsyte Saga, The First Churchills, Cousin Bette, Quatermass, and I Claudius; received the Order of the British Empire in the Birthday Honours, June 1970.

Address: c/o Representation Joyce Edwards, 8 Theed Street, London, SE1. *Tel:* 01–261 1488.

U

USTINOV, Peter, CBE, FRSA, actor, director, and dramatic author

b London, 16 Apr 1921; *s* of Iona Ustinov and his wife Nadia (Benois); *e* Westminster; *m* (1) Isolde Denham (mar dis); (2) Suzanne Cloutier (mar dis); (3) Helene du Lau d'Allemans; studied for the stage under Michel St Denis at the London Theatre Studio.

Made his first appearance on the stage at the Barn Theatre, Shere, 18 July 1938, as Waffles in The Wood Demon; first appeared in London, at the Players' Theatre Club, 30 Aug 1939, in his own sketch, The Bishop of Limpopoland; was with the Aylesbury Repertory company, Oct–Dec 1939, playing in White Cargo, Rookery Nook, Laburnum Grove, etc; Richmond, Jan 1940, played the Rev Alroy Whittingstall in First Night; Ambassadors', May 1940, appeared in Swinging the Gate; Threshold, Oct 1940, played M Lescure in Fishing for Shadows; Wyndham's, Oct 1940, appeared in Diversion, and Jan 1941, in Diversion No 2, in both revues writing his own material; at the Vaudeville, Aug 1941, directed Squaring the Circle; served in the Army (Royal Sussex Regiment), Jan 1942; demobilized, 1946; at the New Theatre, June 1946, played Petrovitch in Crime and Punishment; St Martin's, Apr 1948, played Caligula in Frenzy; Lyric, Hammersmith, June, and St James's, July, 1949, played Sergeant Dohda in Love in Albania, which he also directed; Wyndham's, May 1951, appeared as Carabosse in his own play, The Love of Four Colonels; Royal, Brighton, Oct 1952, directed A Fiddle at the Wedding; Savoy, Dec 1953, directed his own play, No Sign of the Dove; Piccadilly, May 1956, appeared as The General in his own play Romanoff and Juliet, which ran for nearly a year; at the Plymouth, New York, Oct 1957, again played the same part in the American production, subsequently touring the US in the same play; Saville, London, Apr 1962, co-directed and played Sam Old in his own play Photo Finish; Royal Opera, Covent Garden, June 1962, directed L'Heure Espagnole, Erwartung, and Gianni Schicci; Brooks Atkinson, NY, Feb 1963, co-directed and again played Sam Old in Photo Finish; Brooks Atkinson, Nov 1967, directed his own play Halfway Up the Tree; Chichester Festival, May 1968, directed and played the Archbishop in his own play The Unknown Soldier and His Wife; again directed the play and played the Arch-bishop at the New London, Jan 1973, in the theatre's opening production; Lunt-Fontanne, NY, Dec 1974, played Boris Vassilievitch in his play, Who's Who in Hell; Stratford, Ontario, Oct 1979, played the title-role in King Lear; repeated the role, Sept 1980; is the author of Fishing for Shadows (translation from the French), 1940; House of Regrets, 1942; Beyond, Blow Your Own Trumpet, 1943; The Banbury Nose, 1944; The Tragedy of Good Intentions, 1945; The Indifferent Shepherd, Frenzy (adapted), 1948; author of The Man in the Raincoat (produced at the Edinburgh Festival), 1950; The Love of Four Colonels, 1951; The Moment of Truth, 1951; High Balcony, 1952; No Sign of the Dove, 1953; Romanoff and Juliet, The Empty Chair, 1956; Paris Not So Gay, 1958; Photo Finish, 1962; The Life in My Hands (Nottingham Playhouse), 1963; The Unknown Soldier and His Wife, 1967; R Loves J (book), 1973; Who's Who in Hell, 1974; in NY, 1953, The Love of Four Colonels received the Donaldson Award as the best play of the Broadway season written by a new author; in 1957, he received the *Evening Standard* Drama Award for the Best New Play with Romanoff and Juliet; first entered films, 1940; co-author of the film The Way Ahead, 1943; author and director of the films School for Secrets, 1946; Vice-Versa, 1947; author, producer, director, and starred in Private Angelo, 1949; author, producer, director, and appeared in Romanoff and Juliet, 1960; director, producer, and appeared in Billy Budd, 1961; films in which he has appeared also include: Quo Vadis, We're No Angels, Topkapi, Death on the Nile; author of the novel The Loser, 1961; author of a book of cartoons, We Were Only Human, 1961; published his autobiography, Dear Me, 1977; television appearances include The Life of Samuel Johnson (NY), for which he received the Emmy Television Award, 1957–8; Member of the British Film Academy; received the Benjamin Franklin Medal, Royal Society of Arts, 1957; Rector, Dundee University, 1968–73; received the CBE in the Birthday Honours, 1976.

Favourite part: Old Chris in Anna Christie. *Recreations:* Tennis, squash and music. *Clubs:* Arts Theatre, RAC, Garrick, Queen's, Savage. *Address:* c/o William Morris (UK) Ltd, 147–149 Wardour Street, London W1V 3TB. *Tel:* 01–734 9361.

V

VACCARO, Brenda, actress
b Brooklyn, New York, 18 Nov 1939; *d* of Mario Vaccaro and his wife Christina (Pavia); *e* Thomas Jefferson High School, Dallas, Texas; prepared for the stage at the Neighborhood Playhouse School of the Theatre, 1960.

Made her début at the Ursuline Academy, Dallas, Texas, Apr 1946, playing an Old Woman in a school production of The Land of Dreams Come True; joined the Margo Jones Theatre, Dallas, and made her professional début there, 1961, as Angelina in The Willow Tree; made her NY début at the Longacre, 11 Oct 1961, as Gloria Gulock in Everybody Loves Opal; Westbury Music Fair, Long Island, June 1962, played Miss Novick in The Tunnel of Love; Henry Miller's, Sept 1962, Laura Howard in The Affair; Morosco, Apr 1963, Melissa Peabody in Children from Their Games; Royale, Dec 1965, Toni in Cactus Flower; Longacre, Mar 1967, Reedy Harris in The Natural Look; Lunt-Fontanne, Nov 1967, Cynthia in How Now, Dow Jones; Ethel Barrymore, Dec 1968, Nancy Scott in The Goodbye People; John Golden, Mar 1971, Louise in Father's Day; appeared in the films Midnight Cowboy, I Love My Wife, Going Home, Summertree, Once Is Not Enough (1976), etc; has appeared on television in The Greatest Show on Earth, *The Defenders, The Fugitive, Honor Thy Father, The Trial of Ethel and Julius Rosenberg,* played the title-role in the series *Sara,* 1976, etc.

Address: William Morris Agency, 151 El Camino, Beverly Hills, Calif 90212.

VALDEZ, Luis, playwright and director
b 26 Jun 1940; *s* of Francisco Valdez and his wife Armeda; *e* San Jose State University; *m* Guadalupe Valdez.

His play The Shrunken Head of Pancho Villa was first performed while he was at San Jose University in 1964; in 1966 made his professional debut at the Committee Theater, San Francisco, directing and playing the lead in Huelga; founded El Teatro Campesino, 1965, to perform for the United Farm Workers of America; the company toured the US in 1967 and 1968, winning an Obie in 1968; adapted and directed La Virgen del Tepeyac, first seen at the Mission San Juan Bautista, Calif, 1971; directed and co-wrote La Carpa de los Rasquachis, 1973, which toured Europe that year and was seen at the Chelsea Westside, NY, Oct 1974; wrote and directed El Fin del Mundo, 1976, touring the South-West; also in 1976 toured Europe in La Carpa; directed his play Zoot Suit at the Mark Taper Forum, LA, Apr 1978, and the Winter Garden, NY, Mar 1979; directed his play Tibercio Vasquez, 1980; has also worked with Peter Brook, in Conference of the Birds, Santa Cruz, 1973; television includes Los Vendidos, 1971, and El Corrido, an adaptation of La Carpa which he also directed, 1976; appeared in the film Which Way Is Up?, 1977; has taught theatre arts and Chicano history at campuses of the University of California.

Address: 705 Fourth Street, San Juan Bautista, CA 95045. *Tel:* 408–623 2340.

VAN, Bobby (*né* King), dancer, singer, actor
b New York City, 6 Dec 1930; *s* of Harry King and his wife Mina (Anapolsky); *e* NY public schools and the Metropolitan Vocational High School; *m* Elaine Joyce.

Made his stage début at the Winter Garden, NY, 17 Jan 1950, in the revue Alive and Kicking; Paramount, Los Angeles, Oct 1950, played in the revue Red, White, and Blue, and subsequently toured; 46th Street, NY, Oct 1954, played Junior in a revival of On Your Toes; made his first appearance in London at the Palladium, 1958, in a variety show for television; Civic Light Opera, Los Angeles, 1960, Will Parker in Oklahoma!; Circle Arts, San Diego, California, 1961, played Joey in Pal Joey; 46th Street, NY, Jan 1971, Billy Early in No, No, Nanette, and was a great success; Harrah's, Reno, Nevada, July 1974, appeared in cabaret; Westbury Music Fair, Oct 1974, appeared in variety with Totie Fields; Winter Garden, Mar 1975, Steve Anderson in Doctor Jazz; has also toured extenkirts Away, Small Town Girl, Dobie Gillis, Kiss Me Kate, The Night Crawlers, The Lost Flight, Lost Horizon (1973), etc; entered television in 1951 and has appeared on the major variety programs, such as *The Ed Sullivan Show, Kraft Music Hall, Hollywood Palace, Playhouse 90, The Jackie Gleason Show,* Yves Montand on Broadway, etc.

Favourite parts: Will Parker and Billy Early. *Address:* c/o Gloria Safier, 667 Madison Avenue, New York, NY 10021. *Tel:* TE 8–4868.

VANCE, Charles (*né* Goldblatt), actor, director and producing manager
b Belfast, Northern Ireland, 6 Dec 1929; *s* of Eric Goldblatt and his wife Sarah (Freeman); *e* Royal School, Dungannon and Queen's University, Belfast; *m* the Hon Imogen Moynihan; trained for the stage at the Ulster Group Theatre, Belfast; received mime training at the Marigny School, Paris.

After an early career as a broadcaster, made his acting début with the Anew MacMaster company at the Gaiety, Dublin, in 1949; subsequent roles have included leads in numerous national tours in the United Kingdom; directed his first production, The Glass Menagerie, at the Arts, Cambridge, Feb 1960; has since directed frequent touring productions; directed his adaptation of Wuthering Heights, 1972; Gardner Centre, Brighton, Sept 1973, directed The Glass Menagerie and The Merchant of Venice; devised and directed The Jolson Revue, 1974; wrote and staged four pantomimes, 1972–5; Greenwood, Nov 1975, played Sir Thomas More in A Man for All Seasons, and directed Oh! What a Lovely War; produced Stop the World—I Want to Get Off, 1976; with David Conville produced Salad Days, 1977; produced and directed In Praise of Love (tour), 1977; staged his Jolson Revue in Australia, 1978; produced and staged The Adventures of Paddington Bear, 1978; produced Witness for the Prosecution (tour), 1979; directed The Creeper (tour), 1979; produced and directed The Marriage Go-Round (tour), 1979; in all, he has been concerned as actor, director or entrepreneur in over 600 productions; founded the Civic Theatre, Chelmsford, 1962; as director of Charles Vance Productions, controlled repertory companies at Tunbridge Wells, Torquay, Whitby, Hastings, Eastbourne, and Folkestone; sold his theatre interests to Entertainment Investments, 1980, becoming executive producer, theatre division; advisor to the Government of Ghana on the building of a national theatre, 1969; President, Theatrical

Management Association, 1971–2, 1973–6; Executive Vice-President, 1976–9; member, Theatres National Committee, 1971–; Provincial Theatre Council, 1971–; Vice-Chairman, Theatres Advisory Council, 1974–; responsible to Theatres Advisory Council for theatres threatened by development; Director, Theatres Investment Fund, 1974; member of Drama Advisory Panel, South East Arts Association, 1974–9; Fellow of the Royal Society of Arts; founder, 1971, of Vance-Offord (Publications) Ltd, publishers of the *British Theatre Directory*.

Favourite parts: Sir Thomas More in A Man for All Seasons, Henry II in The Lion in Winter. *Recreations:* Sailing (crossed the Atlantic single-handed, 1956), cooking. *Club:* Hurlingham. *Address:* Quince Cottage, Bilsington, Ashford, Kent.

VANCE, Nina (*née* Whittington), director and producer
b Yoakum, Tex, 22 Oct; *d* of Calvin Percy Whittington and his wife Minerva (De Witt); *e* Texas Christian U (AB 1935); formerly a teacher of English and drama.

Producer and artistic director of the Alley Theatre, Houston, Tex, since she founded it in 1947; here she has herself directed well over a hundred productions ranging from new work to the American and European classics, including recently the world premieres of Wilson, 1974, and The Contest, 1975; directed The Cocktail Party, and Tiny Alice, season 1975–6; The Collection/The Dock Brief, 1976–7; Mary Stuart, 1977–8; Hon DLitt, University of St Thomas, 1969.

(Died 18 Feb 1980.)

VAN FLEET, Jo, actress
b Oakland, California, 1922, *d* of Roy H Van Fleet and his wife Elizabeth (Gardner); *e* College of the Pacific, Stockton, California; *m* William Bales; studied for the stage with Sanford Meisner at the Neighborhood Playhouse, New York.

Made her first professional appearance on the stage at the National Theatre, Washington, DC, 1944, as Miss Phipps in Uncle Harry, with Luther Adler; first appeared in NY at the Cort Theatre, Jan 1946, where she played Dorcas in a revival of The Winter's Tale; Biltmore, Mar 1947, played Major Anna Orlov in The Whole World Over; Empire, 1949, played Connie in The Closing Door; National, Dec 1950, Regan in King Lear; Music Box, Mar 1952, Miss Foster in Flight into Egypt; National, Mar 1953, Camille in Camino Real; Henry Miller, Nov 1953, Jessie Mae Watts in The Trip to Bountiful (Antoinette Perry Award); Ethel Barrymore, Nov 1957, Eliza Gant in Look Homeward, Angel (for which she received the New York Drama Critics Award, 1958); York Playhouse, Nov 1960, Frances Flint in The Alligators and Mrs Kittel in Rosemary (double-bill); Festival of Two Worlds, Spoleto, Italy, 1961, Frieda Lawrence in I Rise in Flame Cried the Phoenix and the title-role of The Lady of Larkspur Lotion; Phoenix, Feb 1962, Madame Rosepettle in Oh Dad, Poor Dad, Mama's Hung You in the Closet and I'm Feelin' So Sad; Brooks Atkinson, July 1965, took over from Maureen Stapleton the role of Amanda Wingfield in The Glass Menagerie; Studio Arena, Buffalo, NY, Beatrice in The Effect of Gamma Rays on Man-in-the-Moon Marigolds and Evy Meara in The Gingerbread Lady, 1971; Arlington Park, Ill, June 1972, Linda Loman in Death of a Salesman; made her first appearance in films, 1955, when she won the Academy Award for her performance in East of Eden; other films include The King and Four Queens, The Rose Tattoo, I'll Cry Tomorrow, Cool Hand Luke, Wild River, The Gang That Couldn't Shoot Straight, The Tenant (1976), etc; has appeared frequently on television, notably as Clara in Para-

dise Lost, 1971; in 1961, received an honorary Doctor of Fine Arts from the University of the Pacific, Stockton, California.
Address: Actors Equity Association, 165 West 46th Street, New York, NY 10036.

VAN GRIETHUYSEN, Ted (*né* Theodore André), actor, director, designer
b Ponca City, Oklahoma, 7 Nov 1934; *s* of Theodore André Van Griethuysen and his wife Treva Jane (Ogan); *e* University of Texas (BFA 1956), Yale University School of the Drama, 1957–8, and Aesthetic Realism with Eli Siegel, 1960 to present; *m* Rebecca Thompson; studied for the stage with Ben Iden Payne, at the Academy of Music and Dramatic Art, London, 1956–7, with William Hickey, Michael Howard, and Eli Siegel.

Made his début at the Four Arts, Houston, Texas, 24 Oct 1951, as the Lion in Androcles and the Lion; Houston, Jan 1952, played Sebastian in Twelfth Night, Apr 1952, Michael Brown in O, Mistress Mine, at the Alley, June 1953, Rudy Gibbons in My Dear Delinquents, and, Jan 1955, Orestes in The Flies; San Diego Shakespeare Festival, California, 1955, played Claudio in Measure for Measure, Gremio in The Taming of the Shrew, and Laertes in Hamlet; Oregon Shakespearean Festival, Ashland, Oregon, 1956, played Romeo, Clarence in Richard III, Guiderius in Cymbeline, and the King of Navarre in Love's Labour's Lost; made his London début in 1957 in LAMDA productions as Iago in Othello, Rameses in The First Born, and as Richard III; at the Drury Lane, 5 Dec 1957, was assistant to Peter Brook for the Shakespeare Memorial Theatre production of The Tempest; played in Williamstown, Massachusetts, 1958, as Pierre in The Madwoman of Chaillot and the Prince in Time Remembered; made his New York début at the Fourth Street, 5 Jan 1959, as the Rake in The Failures; New York City Center, Mar 1959, Li-Wang in The Lute Song; in Stockbridge, Massachusetts, summer 1959, Octavius in Man and Superman, Judd Steiner in Compulsion, John Worthing in The Importance of Being Earnest, Thomas Mendip in The Lady's Not for Burning, and Lord Brockhurst in The Boy Friend; Majestic, NY, 1959, Tom Lee in the Equity Library Theatre production of Tea and Sympathy; Theatre de Lys, Dec 1959, the Son in The Purification; designed the costumes for The Crystal Heart, produced at the East 74th Street, Feb 1960; Terrain Gallery, Dec 1960, appeared in a reading of Hamlet: Revisited; American Shakespeare Festival, Stratford, Connecticut, 1960, Florizel in The Winter's Tale, Adrian in The Tempest, and the Egyptian Messenger in Antony and Cleopatra; Phoenix, NY, Nov 1960, Mr Hastings in She Stoops to Conquer; Dec 1960, Sergeant Tinley in The Plough and the Stars; Jan 1961, Jules Thibodeaux in The Octoroon; Mar 1961, Laertes in Hamlet; Stratford, Connecticut, 1961, Monsieur Le Beau in As You Like It, Donalbain in Macbeth, and Troilus; Gate, Oct 1961, Young Marlow in O, Marry Me!; Greenwich Mews, Nov 1961, Ayamonn in Red Roses for Me; Music Box, Jan 1962, Aemilian in Romulus; Lyceum, Dec 1962, Oliver Brown in The Moon Besieged; Terrain Gallery, Jan 1963, directed and again played in Hamlet: Revisited; Stage 73, Mar 1963, Richard III in The White Rose and the Red; New York Shakespeare Festival, June 1964, Oberon in A Midsummer Night's Dream; Belasco, Nov 1965, Jones in Inadmissible Evidence; Actors Playhouse, Nov 1966, designed the costumes for Javelin; Vivian Beaumont, Apr 1967, Cardinal Bellarmine in Galileo; Eastside Playhouse, Oct 1968, Law in The Basement; Actors Playhouse, Jan 1970, directed and played Eilert Lovborg in Hedda Gabler; Artistic Director of The Opposites Company of the Theatre since 1968; has appeared on television in

Henry IV, Part I, 1960, and in *The Defenders, The Nurses, Frankenstein, The Patriot*, etc.

Address: 259 West 12th Street, New York, NY 10014. *Tel:* YU 9–0845.

VAN GYSEGHEM, André, actor and director

b Eltham, Kent, 18 Aug 1906; *s* of Georges Emil Van Gyseghem and his wife Minnie Evison (Offord); *e* Greenwich; *m* Jean Forbes-Robertson (dec); studied for the stage at the Royal Academy of Dramatic Art; was formerly engaged in a music-publishing business.

Made his first appearance on the stage at the Theatre Royal, Bognor, Sept 1927, as Peveril Leyburn in The Constant Nymph; in Jan 1928, toured as Lewis Dodd in The Constant Nymph; made his first appearance in London at the RADA Theatre, 6 May 1928, as Ashohal in A King's Daughter; Everyman, May 1928, played Professor John Rigby in The World's End; from Sept 1928–July 1930, was engaged at the Hull Repertory Theatre, playing a round of leading juvenile parts; at the Arts Theatre, July 1930, played Vitek in The Macropulos Secret; he then joined the Repertory Company at the Embassy Theatre, and remained there from Sept 1930–Oct 1934, played Ronny Instone in The House of Pretence, Phillip Barrett in Give a Dog —, Hon Robert Worth in Rich Man, Poor Man, Florindo in The Liar, Master Klaus in The Witch, Edward Raynor in Black Coffee, Karel Dengler in Lady in Waiting, Teddy Spearing in The Torchbearers, Claude Devenish in Belinda, Clark Storey in The Second Man, Val in Strange Orchestra, Martin in Twelve Thousand, Janek Prus in The Macropulos Secret, John in Rutherford and Son, Edgar Timbrell in Mary Broome, Augustus in Madame Pepita, Honey in This Woman Business, Nicholas in The Dover Road, Leonard Beebe in To the Ladies, etc; appeared at the St Martin's, Nov 1931, as Karel Dengler in Lady-in-Waiting; directed Black Coffee, 1930; The Nelson Touch, From the Four Winds, 1931; This Woman Business, Behind the Blinds, Stepdaughters of War, See Naples and Die, The Silver Cord, Dance With No Music, The Scion, Miracle at Verdun, The Cathedral, To the Ladies, 1932; The Young Huntress, The Blue Coast, The Glass Wall, All God's Chillun, The Age of Plenty, Bastos, the Bold, White Lies, Son of Man, The Tudor Wench, The Brontës of Haworth Parsonage, 1933; Genius at Home, Windfall, The Roof, Without Witness, Napoleon, 1934; Stevedore, Easter 1916, Goosefeather Bed, 1935; The Dangerous Age, Chu the Sinner, Cymbeline, A Lady's Gentleman, 1937; Gentleman's Agreement, Good and Proper, Profit and Loss, Open Verdict, 1938; Happy New Year, 1939; has also directed pageants at Johannesburg, 1936, Wembley Stadium, 1938, and South Wales, 1939; toured, and played in Scandinavian and Baltic States for Westminster Productions, 1938; Neighbourhood, Sept 1940, played Alec in To-Morrow; Vaudeville, Dec 1940, Peter Standish in Berkeley Square; Apollo, Sept 1941, Martin Radshaw in Forty-eight Hours Leave; toured 1942, with the Old Vic Company, as Gratiano in The Merchant of Venice, and in The Witch; Mercury, Feb, and Arts, June 1943, played John Loving in Days Without End; Comedy, June 1943, Patrick Graham in The Fur Coat; Phoenix, Sept 1943, Rev Phineas McQuestion in The Wingless Victory; Artistic Director of the Nottingham Playhouse, 1949–51; at Richmond, Sept 1953, played Charles Kemble in Nine Days Wonder; Arts, Apr 1954, Oliver Shield in The Sun Room; Hampstead Theatre Club, June 1960, played Jacques's Father in Jacques; Phoenix, Nov 1960, Colonel Thibon in Out of This World; Royalty, Jan 1961, Judge Karel Strengholt in Masterpiece; joined the Old Vic Company to make his first appearance in New York at the City Center,

Feb 1962, in the following parts: Duncan in Macbeth, Montague in Romeo and Juliet, and Peter Cauchon in Saint Joan, subsequently touring the US with the productions; Nottingham Playhouse, England, Apr 1963, John in The Zodiac in the Establishment; Bristol Old Vic, Feb 1964, Cardinal of Toledo in The Successor; in the Great Hall, Hampton Court Palace, June 1964, Malvolio in Twelfth Night; Hampstead Theatre Club, Mar 1965, Lord Pragnell in The Platinum People; 1969–70 appeared in various plays at the Stables Theatre Club, Manchester, including The Disorderly Women, Smashing All the Lovely Windows (also Edinburgh Festival), The People's Jack, The White Devil and Shakespeare Farewell; Cardiff, 1973, for Welsh National Theatre, played Serebryakov in Uncle Vanya; Birmingham Rep, Feb 1974, Judge Brack in Hedda Gabler; Oxford Playhouse, 1974, Luka in The Government Inspector, Oct, and the Doctor in Only Make Believe, Dec; joined the RSC, 1975, and played Polonius in Hamlet, at The Other Place, Feb, and the Archbishop of York in both parts of Henry IV at the Memorial Theatre, June; repeated Archbishop of York at the Aldwych, and Polonius at the Round House, Jan 1976; he has directed Forty-eight Hours Leave, and Distant Point, 1941; A Man With Red Hair, and Murder from Memory, 1942; The Blue Room Mystery, 1948; The Martin's Nest, A Priest In the Family, The Merchant of Yonkers, 1951; Husbands Don't Count, The Long Mirror, High Balcony, 1952; The Devil Came From Dublin, Five Philadelphia Physicians, The Gentle Maiden, 1953; The Pleasure Dome, Sailor Beware! (Worthing), Noddy in Toyland, 1954; The Mulberry Bush, 1955; Daughter of Desire (tour), Off the Mainland, The Famous Five, 1956; Daddy-O!, Justice in Heaven, Meet the Cousin, 1958; Night Without Sleep, 1959; Watch It, Sailor! (with Henry Kendall), 1960; Noddy in Toyland, 1962; The Zodiac in the Establishment (Nottingham), The Physicists (Glasgow), 1963; The Millionairess (Théâtre du Parc, Brussels), 1965; Doctor Faustus (Nottingham), Blithe Spirit (Bristol), 1966; Birmingham Rep, Oct 1978, Doge in The Merchant of Venice; recent television appearances include Prince Regent, Law and Order, Spy; author of Theatre in Soviet Russia, 1943; served with HM Forces, 1943–5.

Favourite part: Polonius in Hamlet.

(Died 13 Oct 1979.)

VAN HEUSEN, James (*né* Edward Chester Babcock), composer

b Syracuse, New York, 26 Jan 1913; *s* of Arthur E Babcock and his wife Ida May (Williams); *e* Cazenovia Seminary, 1929, Syracuse University, 1930–2.

First song to be performed in a stage production was Harlem Hospitality in the Cotton Club Revue, NY, Oct 1933; since then has written the scores for Swingin' the Dream, 1939; Billy Rose's Aquacade, 1940; Nellie Bly, 1946; Carnival in Flanders, which he also co-produced, 1953; Come on Strong, 1962; Skyscraper, 1965; Walking Happy, 1966; composed his first Hollywood score, Love Thy Neighbor, in 1940, and has since composed for films The Road to Zanzibar, Playmates, 1941; The Road to Morocco, 1942; Dixie, 1943; Lady in the Dark (additional songs), Going My Way, Belle of the Yukon, 1944; Road to Utopia, The Bells of St Mary's, 1945; Welcome Stranger, The Road to Rio, 1947; A Connecticut Yankee in King Arthur's Court, Top o' the Morning, 1949; Riding High, Mr Music, 1950; You Can Change the World, in which he also played a part, 1951; Road to Bali, 1952; Little Boy Lost, My Heart Goes Crazy, 1953; Not as a Stranger, Young at Heart, 1954; The Tender Trap, 1955; Anything Goes, Pardners, 1956; The Joker Is Wild, 1957; Paris Holiday, Some Came Running, 1958; Save One for Me,

A Hole in the Head, Journey to the Center of the Earth, Career, This Earth Is Mine, Night of the Quarter Moon, 1959; Let's Make Love, High Time, Oceans 11, Who Was That Lady?, Wake Me When It's Over, The World of Suzie Wong, Surprise Package, 1960; The Road to Hong Kong, A Walk on the Wild Side, Boy's Night Out, 1962; Papa's Delicate Condition, 1963; Thoroughly Modern Millie, 1968; Journey Back to Oz, 1974; composed the score for the television production of Our Town, 1955, and produced on television four Frank Sinatra specials, 1959–60; with Johnny Burke formed the music publishing firm Burke-Van Heusen Inc, of which he is the President; President of Van Heusen Music Corporation; has received· four Academy Award Oscars, and an Emmy Award; is active in various fund-raising and other humanitarian capacities, and has received awards from the US Treasury Department, Saints and Sinners, etc; made honorary citizen of Texas, 1958; Distinguished Alumnus Award from Cazenovia Seminary, 1961; etc.

Recreation: Piloting an airplane. *Clubs:* The Manuscript Society, Elks (Palm Springs, California), Thunderbird Golf Club, Racquet Club and Press Club. *Address:* Burke and Van Heusen, Inc, 309 West 57th Street, New York, NY 10019. *Tel:* CI 6–1280.

VAN ITALLIE, Jean-Claude, playwright
b Brussels, Belgium, 25 May 1936; *s* of Hugo Ferdinand van Itallie and his wife Marthe Mathilde Caroline (Levy); *e* Harvard University.

First play produced was written for the Playwrights Unit, called War, and was performed at the Vandam, New York, 22 Dec 1963; since then has written the following plays, principally for leading avant garde theatres, such as The Open Theatre, Cafe La Mama, etc; I'm Really Here, Motel, Pavane, 1964; Almost Like Being, Hunter and the Bird, 1965; War, Café La Mama, America Hurrah, 1966, produced in London at the Royal Court, June 1967; The Serpent, which had its première at the Teatro degli Arte, Rome, Italy, in a performance by The Open Theater, 1968; Thoughts on the Instant of Greeting a Friend on the Street (with Sharon Thie), 1968; Mystery Play, Nightwalk (with Megan Terry and Sam Shepard), 1973; The King of the United States, 1974; A Fable, 1975; Naropa, Bag Lady, 1979; has written English versions of The Seagull, 1975; The Cherry Orchard, 1977; Three Sisters, 1979; Uncle Vanya, 1980; Playwright in Residence at the McCarter Theater, Princeton, NJ, 1972–6; Visiting Mellon Professor at Amherst, Mass, 1976; taught at the Naropa Institute, Boulder, Colo, 1974–6; wrote Everything's OK with the Forbushers for television production, 1970, and his plays The Serpent, Pavane, Almost Like Being have been performed on television.

Recreations: Farming and sitting still. *Address:* Box 7, Charlemont, Massachusetts 01339; and 68 Jane Street, New York, NY, 10014.

VAN PATTEN, Joyce, actress
b New York City, 9 Mar 1934; *d* of Richard Van Patten and his wife Josephine (Acerno); *e* Lodge School, NY; *m* (1) Martin Balsam (mar dis); (2) Dennis Dugan; formerly a fashion model.

Made her first appearance on the stage at the age of two in July 1936, at the RKO Theatre, Richmond Hill, Staten Island, as winner of a Shirley Temple look-alike contest; made her Broadway début at the Plymouth, 1940, when she took over as Mae Yearlin in Love's Old Sweet Song; toured in this last part, 1940; 48th Street Playhouse, Feb 1941, played Marie Antoinette Benson in Popsy; Longacre, Feb 1943, Mary in This Rock; Ethel Barrymore, Apr 1943,

alternated with Nancy Nugent as Patricia Frame in Tomorrow the World; Elitch Gardens, Denver, Colorado, July 1944, again played Patricia Frame in Tomorrow the World; Ethel Barrymore, Oct 1944, Helen Williams in The Perfect Marriage; Booth, June 1945, Joan in The Wind Is Ninety; toured, 1946, as Judy in Junior Miss; Cort, Sept 1946, Ilka Morgan in The Bees and the Flowers; toured, 1947, as Miriam in Dear Ruth, and, 1948, as Monica in The Second Man; played for a season at Elitch Gardens, Denver, 1949; toured, 1953, as Pat in The Male Animal; Shubert, New Haven, Connecticut, Dec 1954, Joyce Reid in Put Them All Together; toured, 1955, in Spice of Life; Broadhurst, Oct 1955, Elsa in The Desk Set; Plymouth, Feb 1957, Shirl in A Hole in the Head; York, Feb 1960, Mary Magdalene in Between Two Thieves; co-founded Theatre West at the University of California at Los Angeles, 1961, and played several parts there, including Mary Magdalene in Between Two Thieves; Interlude Club, Hollywood, California, Nov 1962, wrote the sketches and appeared in the revue Wild Wicked World; Theatre West, May 1963, played various parts in Spoon River Anthology; Booth, Sept 1963, repeated these last roles in a production called Spoon River; The Theatre Group, Los Angeles, June 1965, Sarah in The Lover; New Theater for Now at the Mark Taper Forum, Los Angeles, 1971, played in Who Wants to Be the Lone Ranger; toured, 1971, as Karen Nash, Muriel Tate, and Norma Hubley in Plaza Suite; Mark Taper Forum, 1972, played in Volpone; New Theater for Now, 1973, played in 23 Years Later; toured, 1974, as Ellen Manville in Luv; for Los Angeles Actors Theatre, 1975, appeared in The Kitchen; Brooks Atkinson, 20 Oct 1975, took over from Ellen Burstyn as Doris in Same Time, Next Year, and subsequently toured; Mark Taper Forum, Sept 1977, Marianne in Gethsemane Springs; John Golden, May 1979, Arlene Miller in Murder at the Howard Johnson's; UCLA Theatre Company, July 1979, in Triptych; Eugene O'Neill, Apr 1980, Steffy in I Ought to Be in Pictures; first played in films in Reg'lar Fellers, 1941, and since has played in 14 Hours, The Goddess, I Love You, Alice B Toklas, Making It, 1970; Thumb Tripping, Something Big, Unreal, 1971, Mame, 1974, The Bad News Bears, 1976, etc; made her radio début in 1941 and played regularly in dramatic shows; has appeared regularly on television, notably in The Killers, 1959, the serial *Brighter Day,* 1961, on *Alfred Hitchcock Presents, Gunsmoke, The Defenders, The Good Guys* for two seasons, *The Mary Tyler Moore Comedy Hour, The Martian Chronicles* (1980), etc.

Recreations: Swimming, painting, cooking. *Address:* c/o Susan Smith, 850 Seventh Avenue, New York, NY 10019.

VAN PEEBLES, Melvin, actor, playwright, composer, lyricist, producer, director
b Chicago, Ill, 21 Aug 1932; *e* West Virginia State College and Ohio Wesleyan U (BA, 1953); was a navigator-bombardier in the USA Air Force; formerly a cable-car gripman in San Francisco, Cal.

First work produced in NY was Aint Supposed to Die a Natural Death, Ethel Barrymore, 20 Oct 1971, for which he wrote the book, music, and lyrics; wrote the book, music, lyrics for Don't Play Us Cheap, which he also produced and directed at the Ethel Barrymore, May 1972; Bottom Line, June 1974, appeared in cabaret/variety program; Shubert, Chicago, July 1975, appeared in his Don't Play Us Cheap; appeared in the film Sweet Sweetback's Baadasssss Song, 1971, which he also wrote, composed, produced, directed, and edited; directed the film Story of a Three-Day Pass, in France, 1968; directed and wrote the music for Watermelon Man, 1970; wrote the television play Just an Old Sweet Song,

Sept 1976; has also recorded albums of his music; author of A Bear for the FBI; Don't Play Us Cheap received the Belgian Festival first prize; also author of a photo-essay book on the San Francisco cablecars.

Address: The Dramatists Guild, 234 West 44th Street, New York, NY 10036, *and* Screen Directors Guild, Los Angeles, Calif.

VAUGHAN, Stuart, director, actor, and playwright
b Terre Haute, Indiana, 23 Aug 1925; *s* of John Harwood Vaughan and his wife Pauletta Rosalie (Walker); *e* Indiana State College (BS) and Indiana University (MA); *m* (1) Gladys Regier (mar dis); (2) Helen Quarrier (dec); (3) Anne Thompson; formerly an actor.

Made his first appearance on the stage at the Belfry, Williams Bay, Wisconsin, June 1945, as Fritz in Claudia; directed productions at the Little Theatre, St Augustine, Fla, and at the Belfry, 1948–9; played in stock in Erie, Pa, and Rochester, New York, 1950–2; played in stock and directed at the British Colonial Theatre, Nassau, Bahamas, 1953; made his NY début at the Broadhurst, Sept 1953, as the Sergeant in The Strong Are Lonely; Players (Provincetown Playhouse), Oct 1954, played Mr Lovewell in The Clandestine Marriage; Cherry Lane, Feb 1955, played Hector in Thieves' Carnival; Morosco, Feb 1954, understudy and assistant stage manager for The Confidential Clerk; Barrymore, Oct 1955, stage manager for The Chalk Garden; made his NY début as Artistic Director of the New York Shakespeare Festival, summer 1956, with The Taming of the Shrew and Julius Caesar; subsequently directing Romeo and Juliet, Two Gentlemen of Verona, Macbeth, Richard III, 1957; As You Like It, and Othello, 1958; Julius Caesar, 1959; he has also directed the following plays; at the Playhouse, Sept 1956, Pictures in the Hallway; Jan 1957, The River Line; Belasco, Sept 1957, I Knock at the Door; as Artistic Director of the Phoenix Theatre, directed The Power and the Glory, and The Family Reunion, 1958; The Beaux' Stratagem, The Great God Brown and Pictures in the Hallway, 1959; Peer Gynt, Henry IV (Parts I and II), She Stoops to Conquer, and The Plough and the Stars, 1960; The Octoroon and Hamlet, 1961; Antioch Area Theatre, Yellow Springs, Ohio, summer 1962, played Algernon and directed The Importance of Being Earnest and directed Medea; for the Studio Theatre, Buffalo, NY, Nov 1962, directed The Good Woman of Setzuan; at the Phyllis Anderson Theatre (Phoenix Theatre Company), Abe Lincoln in Illinois and The Taming of the Shrew, 1963; appointed the Artistic Director of the Seattle (Washington) Repertory Theatre, 1963, where he has directed King Lear, The Lady's Not for Burning, Shadow of Heroes, and The Firebugs, 1963–4; Twelfth Night, Man and Superman, and Hamlet, 1964–5; Julius Caesar, The Importance of Being Earnest, Heartbreak House, 1965–6; resigned this post in Jan 1966, and became founder and Producing Director of the Repertory Theatre, New Orleans, where he directed Charley's Aunt, Romeo and Juliet, Our Town, Saint Joan, The Rivals, 1966–7; The Crucible, A Midsummer Night's Dream, Saint Joan, Tartuffe, 1967–8; Arms and the Man, Twelfth Night, The Bald Soprano, 1968–9; resigned this post in 1969; for the New York Shakespeare Festival, 1970, edited and directed The Wars of the Roses and Richard III; Goodman, Chicago, Oct 1971, directed his play Assassination, 1865; Trinity Square Repertory, Providence, RI, Nov 1973, directed his play Ghost Dance; directed the tour of Come and Be Killed, 1975; Abbey, for the CSC Repertory, Oct 1975, played the Duke in Measure for Measure, The Chorus in Antigone, and directed and played Col Triletski in A Country Scandal; received a Fullbright Grant for study of repertory

theatre in England, 1949–50; received the Vernon Rice Award and the Obie Award for the Best Director, 1957–8 season; received a Ford Foundation Directors Grant for Travel in Europe, 1961; author of A Possible Theatre, 1969; Visiting Director, Loeb Drama Center, Harvard University, 1970–1; has been Guest Artist or Visiting Professor at Univ of Kansas, 1971–2; Ohio State, 1974; Univ of Georgia, 1975; Univ of South Carolina, 1976; directed the television production of The Lady's Not for Burning, 1958.

Recreation: Fencing. *Club:* Players. *Address:* 261 St John's Avenue, Yonkers, NY 10704.

VENUTA, Benay (*née* Venuta Rose Crooke), actress and singer
b San Francisco, California, 27 Jan 1911; *d* of Ernest Crooke and his wife Frances (Scalmanini); *e* Beaupré, Geneva, Switzerland; *m* (1) Kenneth Kelly (mar dis); (2) Armand S Deutsch (mar dis); (3) Fred Clark (mar dis).

Began her career as a dancer, and made her theatrical début at the Graumann's Egyptian, Hollywood, California, 1928, dancing in The Big Parade; toured California as a dancer in Tip Toes, 1928; toured in vaudeville theatres on the Franchon and Marco Circuit; made her Broadway début at the Alvin, 22 July 1935, when she took over from Ethel Merman as Reno Sweeney in Anything Goes; toured, 1936, in Anything Goes; Imperial, May 1937, played Lillian Mahoney in Orchids Preferred; Henry Miller's, Sept 1938, Myra Stanhope in Kiss the Boys Goodbye; Shubert, June 1942, Hippolyta in By Jupiter; Adelphi, Jan 1946, Battle Annie in Nellie Bly; Los Angeles, 1947–50, played in The Philadelphia Story, Personal Appearance, My Sister Eileen, Girl Crazy, etc; Las Palmas, Hollywood, 1950, Frances in Light Up the Sky; toured Korea, 1951, entertaining UN troops; Mark Hellinger, Feb 1953, Laura Carew in Hazel Flagg; La Jolla, California, Playhouse, 1954–6, played in Bus Stop, Liliom, The Time of the Cuckoo, etc; Martin Beck, Oct 1957, Estelle O'Shea in Copper and Brass; Civic Playhouse, Hollywood, 1958, Vera Simpson in Pal Joey; toured California, 1958, as Vera Charles in Auntie Mame; Riviera, Las Vegas, Nevada, July 1960, Rose in Gypsy; toured, 1962, as Mrs Baker in Come Blow Your Horn; toured, 1963, as Belle Poitrine, Today, in Little Me; Music Box, Apr 1964, took over as Mildred in Dear Me, The Sky Is Falling; New York State Theatre, Aug 1965, Mrs Mullin in Carousel; same theatre, May 1966, Dolly Tate in the slightly revised version of Annie Get Your Gun; Springfield, Mo, 1971, Lola in Come Back, Little Sheba; Broadway, Sept 1966, repeated her role in Annie Get Your Gun; Village Gate, Nov 1972, Wife in A Quarter for the Ladies Room; Royal Poinciana Playhouse, Palm Beach, Fla, 1974, Pearl in The Prisoner of Second Avenue, and Jan 1975, played in Janus; Brunswick Music Theatre, Maine, 1977, Mme Armfeldt in A Little Night Music; toured Florida, 1978, as the Grandmother in Pippin; Theatre by the Sea, Portsmouth, NH, 1978, Amanda Wingfield in The Glass Menagerie; first appeared in films in Trail of 98, 1928, and since has played in Kiki, Repeat Performance, Annie Get Your Gun, Call Me Mister, etc; member, advisory board, Dance Theatre of Harlem.

Recreations: Travel, painting, sculpture. *Address:* 50 East 79th Street, New York, NY. *Tel:* 288–3786.

VERDON, Gwen, actress, singer, and dancer
b Culver City, California, 13 Jan 1925; *d* of Joseph William Verdon and his wife Gertrude (Standring); *m* Robert Fosse (mar dis); studied dancing with her mother, and with E Belcher, Carmelita Marrachi, and Jack Cole.

At the Shubert, Philadelphia, Dec 1947, appeared as the Gambling Dancer in Bonanza Bound!; assistant choreographer to Jack Cole for Magdalena, Ziegfeld, Sept 1948; Winter Garden, New York, Jan 1950, appeared in the revue Alive and Kicking; Shubert, May 1953, played Claudine in Can-Can; 46th Street, NY, May 1955, played Lola in Damn Yankees, which ran for over 1000 performances; at the same theatre, May 1957, played Anna Christie in New Girl in Town; at the same theatre, Feb 1959, played Essie Whimple in Redhead, subsequently touring the US with the production, 1960; Palace, NY, Jan 1966, Charity Agnes Valentine in Sweet Charity; Library and Museum of the Performing Arts, 13 Dec 1971, appeared in a dance recital; Ritz, Mar 1972, Helen Giles in Children! Children!; Waldorf-Astoria, June 1973, appeared in the revue Milliken's Breakfast Show; Westbury, Long Island, Music Fair, June 1974, Lola in Damn Yankees; 46th Street, June 1975, Roxie Hart in Chicago; supervisor of production for the tour of Dancin, 1979–80; received two Donaldson Awards and the Antoinette Perry (Tony) Award for Can-Can, 1953, and Tony Awards for Damn Yankees; New Girl in Town, and Redhead; first appeared in films in 1951, and pictures include On the Riviera, David and Bathsheba, and Damn Yankees; has also appeared on television with her ex-husband, the dancer and choreographer.
Favourite parts: Charity, Roxie Hart, and Essie Whimple.
Address: 91 Central Park West, New York, NY 10023.

VEREEN, Ben, actor, singer, dancer
b Miami, Florida, 10 Oct 1946; *e* High School of the Performing Arts; married.
Made his New York début at the Greenwich Mews, Oct 1965, when he took over a role in The Prodigal Son; Caesar's Palace, Las Vegas, Nevada, Dec 1966, played Brother Ben in Sweet Charity, also touring; Shubert, Boston, Sept 1967, played Daddy Johann Sebastian Brubeck in Sweet Charity, and subsequently toured in this part, including an engagement at the O'Keefe, Toronto, Ontario, Can, Jan 1968; Auditorium, Chicago, Apr 1968, Flight Announcer and a member of the ensemble in Golden Boy; Biltmore, 1968, took over as Claude in Hair; Aquarius, Los Angeles, Cal, Nov 1968, played Hud in Hair, and later took over as Berger, then alternated these parts; National Shakespeare Company, Sept 1970, Johnny Williams in No Place to Be Somebody; Mark Hellinger, Oct 1971, Judas Iscariot in Jesus Christ Superstar; Imperial, Oct 1972, Leading Player in Pippin, which he played for several seasons and for which he received the Antoinette Perry (Tony) Award; has also appeared in cabaret, throughout the US; film appearances include Funny Lady, 1976; has appeared on television in specials, and recently in Roots; Hon DHL, Emerson College, 1977.
Address: 17200 Oak View Drive, Encino, Calif 91316.

VERNON, Richard, actor
b Reading, 7 Mar 1925; *s* of Evelyn Vernon and his wife Violet Mary Stuart (Foley); *e* Leighton Park and Reading School; *m* Benedicta Leigh Hoskyns; trained for the stage at Central School of Speech and Drama.
First appeared on the stage 30 May 1950 at the Mercury, as Hardwicke in Stratton; Scala, Dec 1953, played Mr Darling in Peter Pan; Westminster, Apr 1958, Charles Parkin MP in Any Other Business; Saville, Oct 1959, Sir Harry Tremayne in The Edwardians; Duchess, Apr 1960, Mr Bennett in A Shred of Evidence; Royal, Court, June 1963, Mr Brierly in Kelly's Eye; Royal, Windsor, Sept 1965, Sir John Holt in A Friend in Need; Duke of York's, Feb 1968, Richard Great-

ham in Hay Fever; Cambridge, June 1969, Austin in Highly Confidential; Arnaud, Guildford, Apr 1973, Malcolm Garth-Bender in George and Margaret; Queen's, Oct 1974, Antonio in Saturday, Sunday, Monday; toured, Sept 1975, as Jimmy Broadbent in The Reluctant Debutante; Dublin Festival, Oct 1976 and tour, Lord Bogmore in Dead Eyed Dicks; Queen's, Aug 1978, Cedric Seward in The Passion of Dracula; has appeared in many films, most recently in The Human Factor; TV appearances, since 1954, include the series *The Duchess of Duke Street* and Sextet.
Recreation: Sailing. *Address:* Leading Artists, 60 St James's Street, London W1.

VIDAL, Gore, dramatic author and novelist
b West Point, New York, 3 Oct 1925; *s* of Eugene L Vidal and his wife Nina (Gore); *e* Phillips Exeter Academy.
Author of the following plays: A Visit to a Small Planet, 1957, The Best Man, 1960, Romulus (adapted from the play by Friedrich Dürrenmatt), 1962, Weekend, 1968; An Evening with Richard Nixon and . . ., 1972; author of the following screenplays: The Catered Affair, 1956, I Accuse, The Scapegoat, 1958, Suddenly Last Summer (from the play by Tennessee Williams), 1959, Caligula, 1979; appeared in the film Fellini's Roma, 1972; has also written plays for television, including scripts for *Omnibus, Studio One, Philco Playhouse,* etc; has appeared frequently on television in various discussion programs; drama critic for *Reporter* magazine, 1959; and also for *Partisan Review*; has written the following novels: Williwaw, 1946, In a Yellow Wood, 1947; The City and the Pillar, 1948; The Season of Comfort, 1949; A Search for the King, Dark Green, Bright Red, 1950; The Judgment of Paris, 1952; Messiah, 1954; Julian, 1964; Washington DC, 1967; Myra Breckenridge, 1968; Two Sisters, 1970; Myron, 1973; Burr, 1974; 1876, 1976; author of the books of essays Rocking the Boat, 1962 and Sex, Death and Money, 1968; President of the Edgewater Publishing Company; founder of the newspaper *The Hyde Park Townsman,* 1960; editor of The Best Television Plays, 1956; ran as the Democratic-Liberal candidate for the US Congress, 1960; served with the AUS, 1943–6.
Club: New York Athletic. *Address:* The Dramatists Guild, 234 West 44th Street, New York, NY 10036.

VILLIERS, James, actor
b London, 29 Sept 1933; *s* of Eric Hyde Villiers, and his wife Joan Ankaret (Talbot); *e* Wellington College; *m* Patricia Donovan; trained for the stage at RADA.
First appeared on the stage 3 Aug 1953 at the Summer Theatre, Frinton, as William Blore in Ten Little Niggers; joined the Old Vic company, 1955, to play parts such as Trebonius in Julius Caesar, Antenor in Troilus and Cressida, and Bushy in Richard II; played the last two parts on the Old Vic tour of the US and Canada, 1956–7, making his New York début at the Winter Garden, Oct 1956, as Bushy; Lyric, Hammersmith, June 1960, played Richard Kerstin in Tomorrow—With Pictures, transferring with the production to the Duke of York's that month; Lyric, Mar 1962, Clive Rodingham in Write Me A Murder; Vaudeville, Apr 1964, Vic in Everybody Loves Opal; same theatre, Feb 1967, William in The Burglar; Apollo, Mar 1970, Freddy Mayne in The Happy Apple; Queen's, Sept 1972, Victor Prynne in Private Lives; Her Majesty's, Feb 1974, Tito Belcredi in Henry IV; New, Oxford, Sept 1974, Earl of Warwick in the Oxford Festival production of Saint Joan; in the same festival played Philip in The Little Hut, which transferred to the Duke of York's, Oct 1974; Mermaid, Apr 1975, Sir Ralph Bonnington in The Doctor's Dilemma; Old Vic, July 1976,

Bracciano in The White Devil; same theatre, Nov 1976, appeared in The Ghost Train; Queen's, Aug 1978, Lord Godalming in The Passion of Dracula; Shaftesbury, Dec 1979, Mr Darling and Captain Hook in Peter Pan; films, since 1963, include Otley, Half a Sixpence, The Ruling Class, and King and Country; first appeared on television in 1960.

Recreations: Cricket, football. *Address:* 29 Belsize Park, London NW3.

VOELPEL, Fred, designer

Designed the decor for Born Yesterday, Mar 1958; designed the costumes for On the Town, Feb 1959; first New York designs were the costumes, decor, and lighting for Fallout, at the Renata, 20 May 1959; since then has designed decor, costumes, lighting for From A to Z, and decor for Vintage '60, The Alligators, Rosemary, 1960; costumes for The Sudden End of Anne Cinquefoil, decor and costumes for Young Abe Lincoln; costumes for No Strings, 1962; The Milk Train Doesn't Stop Here Anymore, Sophie, 1963; Play, The Lover, A Murderer Among Us, Absence of a Cello, The Sign in Sidney Brustein's Window, The Giant's Dance, and decor for Hang Down Your Head and Die, 1964; costumes for Peterpat, Major Barbara, Drat! The Cat!, and costumes, decor and lighting for That Thing at the Cherry Lane, 1965; decor and costumes for South Pacific, 1967; costumes for Tiger at the Gates, Merton at the Movies, decor for The Indian Wants the Bronx, It's Called the Sugar Plum, South Pacific, 1968; costumes for Spitting Image, Oh! Calcutta!, decor for Gianni Schicchi, The Tale of Kasane, Blueprints, and decor and costumes for The Critic, Home Fires, Copout, 1969; costumes for Songs from Milk Wood, Two by Two, costumes and decor for The Memory Bank, Sganarelle, and decor for The Effect of Gamma Rays on Man-in-the-Moon Marigolds, 1970; decor for Carol Channing and Her Ten Stout-Hearted Men, at Drury Lane, Apr 1970; decor and costumes for Young Abe Lincoln, And Miss Reardon Drinks a Little, 1971; Small Craft Warnings, One for the Money, Two for the Show, Hurry, Harry, The Little Theatre of the Deaf, 1972; Smith, 1973; The Beauty Part, 1974; Dybbuk, Priscilla, Princess of Power, Cowboy (Goodspeed Opera House, East Haddam, Conn), costumes for Seascape, decor and lighting for Very Good Eddie, 1975; costumes for Ladyhouse Blues, 1976; decor for Winning Isn't Everything, 1978; Artichoke, Holiday (LA), The Wooden Boy (National Theatre of the Deaf), Crazy Horse, 1979; Director of National Theater Institute, 1975; associate professor, 1966–79, NYU School of Arts.

Address: 125 Christopher Street, New York, NY. *Tel:* WA 4-5594.

VOIGHT, Jon, actor

b Yonkers, NY, 29 Dec 1938; *e* Archbishop Stepinac High School, White Plains, Catholic Univ (BFA 1960); prepared for the stage at the Neighborhood Playhouse and privately with Sanford Meisner.

First appeared in New York at the Village Gate, 26 Jan 1961, in the revue O, Oysters!!!; Lunt-Fontanne, 1961, took over as Rolf Gruber in The Sound of Music; Sheridan Square Playhouse, Jan 1965, played Rodolpho in A View from the Bridge; San Diego, Cal, National Shakespeare Festival, June 1966, Romeo in Romeo and Juliet, Ariel in The Tempest, and July, 1966, Thurio in Two Gentlemen of Verona; Helen Hayes, NY, Mar 1967, Steve in That Summer—That Fall; Theatre Company of Boston, Nov 1967, played in The Dwarfs; Ahmanson, Los Angeles, Cal, Mar 1973, Stanley Kowalski in A Streetcar Named Desire, and repeated this part at the Studio Arena, Buffalo, NY, Nov 1973; Bijou, Jan

1975, co-produced The Hashish Club; Levin Theatre, Rutgers University, Sept 1976, title-role in Hamlet; first appeared in films in Frank's Greatest Adventure, 1967, and has since played in Midnight Cowboy, Catch-22, The Revolutionary, Deliverance, Conrack, The Odessa File, Coming Home, etc; has appeared on television in The Dwarf, and in *Gunsmoke, Cimarron Strip,* etc.

Address: Screen Actors Guild, 7750 Sunset Boulevard, Los Angeles, Calif 90046.

VON FURSTENBERG, Betsy (*née* Elizabeth Caroline Maria Agatha Felicitas Therese von Furstenberg-Hedringen), actress

b Neiheim Heusen, Germany, 16 Aug 1931; *d* of Count Franz-Egon von Furstenberg and his wife Elizabeth (Johnson); *e* Miss Hewitt's Classes and New York Tutoring School; *m* Guy Vincent de la Maisoneuve; prepared for the stage at the Neighborhood Playhouse with Sanford Meisner.

Made her stage début in NY at the Morosco, 2 Jan 1951, as Thankful Mather in Second Threshold; Royale, Feb 1952, played Lorraine in Dear Barbarians; toured, 1952, as Gabby in The Petrified Forest, Lisa in Jason, and in The Second Man; Playhouse, Wilmington, Delaware, Jan 1953, Josephine Perry in Josephine, and subsequently toured; Henry Miller's, Dec 1953, Myra Hagerman in Oh, Men! Oh, Women!; New York City Center, Dec 1954, Lady Sybil Tenterden in What Every Woman Knows; Ethel Barrymore, Oct 1955, Laurel in The Chalk Garden; toured, summer 1955, in Oh, Men! Oh, Women!; Royale, Nov 1956, Kate in Child of Fortune; Coronet, Oct 1957, Maggie Turk in Nature's Way; Rita Allen, June 1958, Elizabeth Compton in The Making of Moo; New York City Center, Feb 1959, Frankie Jordan in Say, Darling; New York City Center, Mar 1959, Helen in Wonderful Town; Barbizon-Plaza, Apr 1959, Cassandra Redwine in Season of Choice; Lunt-Fontanne, Sept 1959, Margaret in Much Ado About Nothing; Helen Hayes, Mar 1961, Tiffany Richards in Mary, Mary; Henry Miller's, Feb 1967, Sylvia Greer in The Paisley Convertible; New York City Center, May 1967, Helen in Wonderful Town; Theatre Four, Oct 1967, Cecile Jeanrenaud in Beyond Desire; Booth, Jan 1968, Helen Claiborne in Avanti!; Theatre de Lys, May 1968, Sybil Chase in Private Lives; Plymouth, Dec 1970, Toby Landau in The Gingerbread Lady; toured, Oct 1971–May 1972, in this last part; Ivanhoe, Chicago, July 1974, played in Status Quo Vadis; toured, 1975–6 in Absurd Person Singular; Wonderhorse, NY, Sept 1976, Polly Raisen in Does Anybody Here Do The Peabody?; appeared in the film Women Without Names, 1951; has appeared frequently on television since 1951 on *Playhouse 90, Alfred Hitchcock Presents, Kraft Television Theatre,* and various talk programs.

Recreations: Tennis, painting, riding. *Favourite parts:* Margaret in Cat on a Hot Tin Roof, Laurel in The Chalk Garden, and Toby Landau in The Gingerbread Lady. *Address:* c/o Hartig-Josephson Agency, 527 Madison Avenue, New York, NY 10022.

VON SCHERLER, Sasha (*née* Alexandra-Xenia Elizabeth Anne Marie Fiesola von Schoeler), actress

b New York City, 12 Dec 1939; *d* of Baron Walram-Voystingus Albert Alexander von Schoeler and his wife Ruth Hooper (Dayton); *e* in Detroit, Michigan, slum schools, Holy Name Convent, Windsor, Ontario, Canada, the Tokyo American School, Kingswood, Vassar, and the Yale School of the Drama, from which she was expelled for staging the first student sit-in in America; *m* Paul Avila Mayer; formerly engaged as a proof reader, a writer for horoscope magazines and as a fortune teller; prepared for the stage with her mother, who was trained by David Belasco, and with Mary V Heinlein and Constance Welch.

First appeared on the stage at the Cranbrook Summer Theatre, summer 1950, as Mitzi in Seven Sisters; first appeared in NY at the Cherry Lane, Feb 1956, as Lydia Carew in The Admirable Bashville, replacing Frances Sternhagen; Downtown, 24 Jan 1957, played Nell Gwynn in In Good King Charles's Golden Days; Barbizon-Plaza, Nov 1957, Martha James in Conversation Piece; Heckscher, for the New York Shakespeare Festival, Jan 1958, Phebe in As You Like It; Henry Miller's, Mar 1959, Yvonne in Look After Lulu; Coronet, Oct 1959, Mrs Brown in The Great God Brown; Phoenix, Nov 1959, Myrrhine in Lysistrata; Plymouth, Mar 1960, Irma in The Good Soup; Circle in the Square, Mar 1961, played in Under Milk Wood; Morosco, Dec 1961, Mariette in First Love; Circle in the Square, Aug 1962, Mrs Boker in Infancy; Morosco, Dec 1964, Flo in Alfie!; Theatre East, Mar 1966, Agnes in Ludlow Fair; Theatre de Lys, Feb 1967, Flo in Willie Doesn't Live Here Anymore; Province-town Playhouse, May 1967, Margaret in Sondra; Vivian Beaumont, Apr 1968, Orange Girl in Cyrano de Bergerac; Stage 73, Mar 1969, Gloria in the one-character play Laughs, Etc, in a bill with the overall title Stop, You're Killing Me; Delacorte, Aug 1969, Olivia in Twelfth Night; Astor Place, Oct 1969, Joyce in The Ruffian on the Stair and Lou in The Erpingham Camp in a bill with the overall title Crimes of Passion; The Other Stage, Feb 1970, Avonia Bunn in Trelawny of the 'Wells'; Delacorte, June 1970, Countess Auvergne in The Wars of the Roses—Part I; Anspacher, Oct 1970, again played Avonia Bunn in Trelawny of the 'Wells'; Brooklyn Academy of Music, Dec 1971, Vamp in The Screens; Stage 73, June 1972, November in Soon Jack November; Delacorte, June 1974, A Bawd in Pericles; Booth, Sept 1974, took over from Doris Roberts as Dolly Scupp and Becky Hedges in Bad Habits; Anspacher, Nov 1974, Mom in Kid Champion; Vivian Beaumont, Oct 1975, Avonia Bunn in Trelawny of the 'Wells'; Hartman, Conn, Nov 1975, Meg in The Hostage; Delacorte, June 1976, Mistress Quickly and Queen Isabel in Henry V; HB Studio, 1976, Mrs Fletcher in The Petrified Man; American Place, Nov 1976, Maggie in Camino Café; Public, 1977, several parts in a workshop production of Museum; Manhattan Theatre Club, Jan 1979, Zaira Marvuglia in Grand Magic; Stage One, Aug 1979, Mrs Champinsky (Mom) in Kid Champion; has appeared in the film Women, Women, Women, 1971, subsequently touring in Network, and The Last Embrace; first appeared on television on *Omnibus*, Sept 1955, and since has played as Sarah Hanley in the serial *Love Is a Many-Splendored Thing*, 1970–1, on *Camera Three*, in Mr Broadway, Under Milk Wood, *The Doctors*, The Last of the Belles, etc.

Recreation: Caring for her children, and studying the minutiae of large events. *Address:* 1290 Madison Avenue, New York, NY 10028. *Tel:* TE 1–2140.

VOSKOVEC, George, actor, producer, director, author
b Sazava, Czechoslovakia, 19 June 1905; *s* of Vaclav Voskovec and his wife Georgette (Pinkas); *e* Lycée Carnot, Dijon, University of Dijon (BA), and Charles University, Prague; *m* (1) Anne Gerlette (dec); (2) Christine McKeown; formerly a poet and journalist.

Made his first appearance on the stage at the Umělecká Beseda, Prague, Apr 1927, as Publius Ruka in Vest Pocket Revue; formed a partnership with Jan Werich and for the next eleven years V and W (as he and Jan Werich came to be known) wrote, produced and performed 26 productions for The Liberated Theatre of Prague; came to America and, at the Cleveland Playhouse, Mar 1940, wrote with Mr Werich and played the First Soldier in Heavy Barbara, and, Nov 1940, Taxidermes in The Ass and the Shadow; made his first appearance in New York at the Alvin Theatre, Jan 1945, as Trinculo in The Tempest; during the war years he and Werich wrote and broadcast numerous radio programmes for the Office of War Information (The Voice of America); between 1946–8, he returned to Prague, where he played Banjo in Werich's adaptation of The Man Who Came to Dinner, adapted and directed The Skin of Our Teeth, wrote, co-produced, directed and co-starred in Fist in the Eye, and adapted, co-produced, and directed Finian's Rainbow; went to Paris and founded the American Theatre of Paris, 1949, where he produced Three in One, Four in One, which he also directed, No Exit, Curly, Our Town, and Knickerbocker Holiday, which he also designed; on his return to the United States, he appeared at the Shubert, Jan 1953, as Colonel Frappot in The Love of Four Colonels, in which he subsequently toured; Phoenix, May 1954, Dr Dorn in The Seagull; Longacre, Jan 1955, Sasha Rostov in Festival; 4th Street, off-Broadway, Jan 1956, the title-part in Uncle Vanya for which he received the Obie Award; made his first appearance in London at the Phoenix, Nov 1956, as Mr Frank in The Diary of Anne Frank; at the Booth, New York, Nov 1959, played Mr Alper in The Tenth Man; ANTA, Mar 1961, played Paul Stumpfig in Big Fish, Little Fish; Broadhurst, May 1961, Professor V Kuprin in A Call on Kuprin; Billy Rose, Oct 1961, Dr Neuross in Do You Know the Milky Way?; Theatre de Lys, Jan 1962, appeared in the revue Brecht on Brecht; Stratford, Conn, summer 1963, played Caesar in Caesar and Cleopatra; Lunt-Fontanne, Apr 1964, played the Player King in John Gielgud's production of Hamlet; Martin Beck, Oct 1964, Ernst Heinrich Ernesti in The Physicists; Orpheum, Oct 1965, played in The World of Ray Bradbury; Vivian Beaumont, for the Lincoln Center Repertory Theatre, Oct 1966, Sir Epicure Mammon in The Alchemist, Feb 1967, Konarski in The East Wind, and Apr 1967, Cardinal Barberini in Galileo; Actors Playhouse, Feb 1968, Pop in Oh, Say, Can You See L A and Teddy in The Other Man; Imperial, June, 1968, took over as Herr Schultz in Cabaret; Royale, Oct 1969, Dr Wolf Axelrod in The Penny Wars; Mark Taper Forum, Los Angeles, Cal, Feb 1970, Dag Hammersjold in Murderous Angels; Sheridan Square Playhouse, May 1970, Glas in Slow Dance on the Killing Ground; Martin Beck, Mar 1971, The Best Friend in All Over; Public/Newman, Mar 1974, Otto Beethoven in The Killdeer; Eisenhower, Washington, DC, May 1974, Arthur Freeling in Headhunters; Beaumont, June 1977, Gayev in The Cherry Orchard, Feb, and Chorus Leader in Agamemnon, May; Manhattan Theatre Club, Jan 1979, Beethoven in Beethoven/Karl; Public/Newman, June 1979, Willie in Happy Days; first entered films, 1926 (in Czechoslovakia), and since 1952 in the USA principal films in which he has appeared include Affair in Trinidad, Twelve Angry Men, Butterfield 8, The Bravados, The Spy Who Came in from the Cold, The Boston Strangler, The Iceman Cometh, 1973, The Man on a Swing, 1974, Somewhere in Time, 1979, etc; first appeared on television, 1951, and performances include the title-part in Uncle Vanya (London), Judge Brack in Hedda Gabler (London), and various dramatic programs in the US, recently Roots II; served on the Secretariat of UNESCO in Paris as a program specialist in the fields of Press-Radio-Documentary Films, 1948–50; wrote and directed a documentary film for the International Refugee Organization, 1950; author of lyrics of some 300 popular songs.

Favourite parts: Clown work in Europe as part of V and W team, and Vanya in Uncle Vanya. *Address:* c/o Gage Group, 1650 Broadway, New York, NY 10019.

VOSS, Stephanie, actress and singer

b London, 17 Apr 1936; *d* of Louis Voss and his wife Edythe (Baum); *e* Minchenden Grammar School; *m* Frank Carson; studied ballet with Pauline Grant, and singing with Harold Miller.

Made her first appearance in London at the Casino Theatre, Dec 1951, in the chorus of Jack and Jill; Coliseum, May 1953, appeared as a Doll in Guys and Dolls; Criterion, Apr 1954, was a member of the company in Intimacy At 8.30; Palladium, Dec 1956, played Princess Yasmin in The Wonderful Lamp; Aldwych, Aug 1957, played Sarah in Meet Me By Moonlight; on the occasion of the opening of the Belgrade, Coventry, Mar 1958, played Cecily Cardew in Half In Earnest (a musical adaptation of Oscar Wilde's play The Importance of Being Earnest); Mermaid, May 1959, appeared as Hilaret in Lock Up Your Daughters, the opening play at the Mermaid; Palladium, Dec 1959, played Mary, Mary, Quite Contrary in Humpty Dumpty; Princes, Apr 1960, played Mary in Johnny the Priest; Victoria Palace, Aug 1960, played the title part in Rose Marie; Apollo, Sept 1961, played Luisa in The Fantasticks; Her Majesty's, Apr 1963, took over her original part of Hilaret in Lock Up Your Daughters!; Piccadilly, Aug 1964, Miranda in Instant Marriage; Civic, Johannesburg, Apr 1966, played Sarah Brown in Guys and Dolls; Drury Lane, London, Dec 1967, Constance in The Four Musketeers; toured with Brian Rix's company, spring 1971, in a number of Vernon Sylvaine farces; opening of Churchill, Bromley, 1977, appeared in The History of Mr Polly; toured, 1980, as Golde in Fiddler on the Roof; has appeared frequently at the Players' Theatre, and in cabaret; has appeared in a number of television and radio programmes, including Menotti's opera The Telephone, *Friday Night Is Music Night*, and *The Good Old Days*.

Recreations: Painting on glass and china, trying new cooking recipes. *Address:* c/o Mary Lambeth Associates, 22 Acol Road, London, NW3. *Tel:* 01–624 4858.

W

WADDINGTON, Patrick, actor

b York, 19 Aug 1901; *s* of William Henry Waddington and his wife Mary Louisa (Simpson); *e* Gresham's School, Holt, and St John's College, Oxford; while a member of the OUDS, of which he was secretary, 1923–4, he toured Scandinavia in John Galsworthy's Loyalties, directed by the author.

Made his first professional appearance at the Birmingham Repertory Theatre, 22 Nov 1924, as Valentine in The Two Gentlemen of Verona; same theatre, Dec, first sang as Don Antonio in The Duenna; made his first appearance in London at the Kingsway, Aug 1925, playing Rosencrantz in Hamlet (modern dress); at the Q Theatre, Mar 1926, played Freddie in The Master; Barnes, Mar 1926, in the Komisarjevsky season, played Fomin in Katerina; toured, Aug 1926, as Geoffrey in Mary, Mary, Quite Contrary; Little, Nov 1926, played Smith in The House of Cards; toured, Feb 1927, as John Whittaker in Easy Virtue; Arts, July 1927, Lundberg in Samson and Delilah; Globe, Sept 1927, Jerry Budd in The Golden Calf; toured, Jan 1928, as Lord Vail in The Luck of the Vails; Globe, May 1928, Sydney in Holding Out The Apple; Wyndham's, July–Dec 1928, appeared as Walter How in Justice, Charles Winsor in Loyalties, and Lord Anthony in The Love Lorn Lady; Arts, Apr 1929, played Pierrot in The Theatre of Life; Ambassadors', Apr 1929, Kenneth Raglan in Rope; St James's, Oct 1929, Nicholas Fayne in Heat Wave; Haymarket, Apr 1930, Guildenstern in Hamlet; Cambridge, Sept 1930, appeared in the revue Charlot's Masquerade; Haymarket, Feb 1931, again played Guildenstern; Daly's, Apr 1931, Harry Bronson in The Belle of New York; same theatre, Dec 1931, Lancelot in La Poupee; 1932, toured in variety; Dominion, May 1932, played Capt Gustl in The Land Of Smiles; Haymarket, Aug 1932, Duke of Brixham in Tomorrow Will Be Friday; toured, Nov 1932, as George in Prudence; Arts, Apr 1933, John Carslake in For Better, For Worse; Princes, Dec 1933, appeared in the revue On With The Show; Comedy, Jan 1934, David Lister in First Episode; Whitehall, May 1934, Toni Silver in No Way Back; first appeared in New York, at the Ritz, Sept 1934, as David Lister in First Episode, subsequently presented as College Sinners; His Majesty's, London, Feb 1935, played Prince Hal in Henry IV, Part I; Vaudeville, Dec 1935, Prince Florizel in The Sleeping Beauty; Royalty, Apr 1936, Dr Macrae in Glass Houses; toured, autumn 1936, in Private Lives and Man in Possession; Vaudeville, Dec 1936, again played in The Sleeping Beauty; Saville, May 1938, in Pelissier's Follies of 1938; Richmond, Nov 1938, Gerald Millett in Weights and Measures; toured, 1939, as Tony Radley in Good and Proper; Q, May 1946, George Osborne in Vanity Fair, subsequently touring in the same part, prior to appearing at the Comedy, Oct 1946; Embassy, Nov 1947, Sir John Mannering in Said The Spider! . . . ; St Martin's, May 1949, Geoffrey Temple in Miss Turner's Husband; Arts, June 1949, Mr Baxter in The Mollusc; Lyric, Hammersmith, Mar, and Duchess, May 1950, played Richard Wyndham in The Holly and the Ivy; Comedy, Feb 1952, Rhoderick Glyde in The Navy at Sea; 1952–6, served as full-time Administrator to the Actors' Orphanage Fund; toured the United States and Canada, 1959–60, as the Earl of Leicester in Mary Stuart; Comedy, New York, Apr 1961, played Louis Compass in The Magnificent Hugo; 4th

Street, May 1961, Professor Kroll in Rosmersholm; Broadway, Nov 1961, played the Count de Koeberg in Kean; Henry Miller, Sept 1962, Alec Nightingale in The Affair; Pocket, Mar 1963, Jean de Malestroit in A Darker Flower; returned to England, Mar 1964, to play the Colonel for 1,000 performances in the tour of My Fair Lady; New, Feb 1969, took over the part of General Sir Alan Brooke in Soldiers; entered films, 1926, and has appeared in numerous pictures, including Loyalties, Journey Together, Esther Waters, The Wooden Horse, School for Secrets, A Night to Remember, etc; has appeared in many television productions, also in cabaret, notably That Certain Trio, 1929–39.

Favourite parts: Harry in The Belle of New York, and Prince Hal in Henry IV, Part I. *Recreations:* Riding, sailing, and dancing. *Club:* Green Room. *Address:* c/o Midland Bank Ltd, 3a Carlos Place, London, W1.

WAGER, Michael (*né* Emanuel Weisgal), actor and director

b New York City, 29 Apr 1925; *s* of Meyer W Weisgal and his wife Shirley (Hirshfeld); *e* Harvard University (MA 1948); *m* (1) Mary Jo Van Ingen (mar dis); (2) Susan Blanchard Fonda (mar dis); prepared for the stage at the Actors Studio and with Herbert Berghof, Stella Adler, and Uta Hagen.

Made his début at the Brattle, Cambridge, Massachusetts, 1941, as the Boy in the Harvard Dramatic Club production of The Shoemaker's Prodigious Wife; served in the US Army, 1943–5; Westport, Connecticut, Country Playhouse, 1947, played Castro in The Girl of the Golden chusetts, of which he was also a director, where he played Cusins in Major Barbara and O'Connor in Shadow and Substance, 1948, among others; made his New York début at the Lenox Hill Playhouse, 12 Mar 1949, as Julian in Martine; Ethel Barrymore, Dec 1949, took over as the Young Collector in A Streetcar Named Desire; toured in this last part, 1950; National, Feb 1951, Peter Mitchell in The Small Hours; Playhouse, Oct 1952, Vernon Kinswood in Bernardine; New York City Center, Mar 1953, Lorenzo in The Merchant of Venice; Ethel Barrymore, Mar 1953, took over from Roddy McDowall as Bentley Summerhays in Misalliance; Coronet, Dec 1953, Wilbur Fifield in The Remarkable Mr Pennypacker; New York City Center, Sept 1955, Roderigo in Othello; same theatre, Sept 1955, Prince Hal in Henry IV, Part I; co-adapted with Tyrone Guthrie and played the Son in Six Characters in Search of an Author, at the Phoenix, Dec 1955; Phoenix, Sept 1956, Dauphin in Saint Joan and moved with this production to the Coronet, Dec 1956; Herodes Atticus, Athens, Greece, summer 1957, Hermes in Prometheus Bound; Coronet, Apr 1958; Shendi in The Firstborn, and repeated this role at the Habimah, Tel Aviv, Israel, May 1958; made his début in England at the Theatre Royal, Brighton, 1 Sept 1958, as Nick in The Deserters; Cambridge, Massachusetts, Drama Festival, 1959, Andrew Aguecheek in Twelfth Night and Malcolm in Macbeth; New York City Opera Company, Feb 1960, sang Sasha in The Cradle Will Rock; Theatre Marquee, June 1961, Mesa in Noontide; Theatre de Lys, Jan 1962, played in Brecht on Brecht; Theatre Club, Washington, DC, 1963, directed Brecht on Brecht; Morosco, Aug 1964, took over from Gerald Hiken as Andrei in The Three Sisters; Billy Rose, Mar 1966, produced Where's Daddy?; 81st Street,

May 1966, Benya Crick in Sunset; Stage 73, Dec 1966, sang Charles Bodie in The Penny Friend; Henry Miller's, Sept 1968, Carlos in The Cuban Thing; New, Mar 1969, directed Nag's Head; Anspacher, Oct 1970, Ferdinand Gadd in Trelawny of The Wells; Roundabout, Jan 1972, Petruchio in The Taming of the Shrew; Paper Mill Playhouse, Millburn, NJ, 1974, Dickenson in 1776; Mini-Met of the Metropolitan Opera, 1974, Thésée in Syllabaire pour Phèdre; Pittsburgh Playhouse, 1976, in The Interview; Lions Theater Club, 1977, William Burroughs in Visions of Kerouac; toured, Feb 1977, as James Browne in The Dream; La Mama, Mar 1977, in Songs at Twilight; toured Israel and Germany, 1978, with Leonard Bernstein and the Israel Philharmonic; Actors Studio, 1978, Buckingham in Richard III; Yale Rep, 1979, Trigorin in The Seagull; has also appeared with the Boston Symphony Orchestra as the Speaker in Stravinsky's Oedipus Rex (repeated on television), the Narrator in Berlioz's Lelio, Chamber Music Society of Lincoln Center in Stravinsky's Histoire du Soldat, etc; made his film début in the Israeli Hill 24 Does Not Answer, 1954, and since has played in Exodus, The King of Kings, etc; made his television début in 1948 and has played since in various dramatic programs.

Favourite parts: Dauphin, Prince Hal, Andrei, Mesa. *Recreations:* Barn restoration and collecting operatic recordings and pirated Callas tapes. *Club:* Signet Society. *Address:* 126 Fifth Avenue, New York, NY 10011 and Painter Hill Road, Roxbury, Conn.

WAGNER, Robin, designer
b San Francisco, California, 31 Aug 1933; *s* of Jens Otto Wagner and his wife Phyllis Edna Catherine (Smith); *e* California School of Fine Arts, 1952–4; *m* Joyce Marie Workman (mar dis).

First designs for the theatre were for the Golden Gate Opera Workshop, San Francisco, 1953, when he designed the sets for Don Pasquale, Amahl and the Night Visitors, and Zanetto; designed sets for the Theatre Arts Colony, San Francisco, 1954, both for the Contemporary Dancers wing and for Tea and Sympathy; at the Encore, San Francisco, designed the sets for The Immoralist and Dark of the Moon; for the Actors Workshop, San Francisco, designed Waiting for Godot, 1957, The Miser, The Ticklish Acrobat, 1958, The Plaster Bambino, 1959; décor and costumes for the San Francisco Ballet Company's The Filling Station and décor for the Sacramento Civic, The Guardsman, 1958; came to New York, and his first design was the décor of And the Wind Blows, presented at the St Mark's Playhouse, 28 Apr 1959; since then has designed a season of musical productions at Sacramento, California; off Broadway, designed The Prodigal, Between Two Thieves, Borak, 1960; A Worm in Horseradish, 1961; Entertain a Ghost, The Days and Nights of Beebee Fenstermaker, The Playboy of the Western World for the Irish Players, 1962; Cages, In White America, The Burning, 1963; The White Rose and the Red, and, for the Arena Stage in Washington, DC, Dark of the Moon and Galileo, 1964; A View from the Bridge, An Evening's Frost, 1965; The Condemned of Altona, 1966; Galileo (his first Broadway show), The Trial of Lee Harvey Oswald, A Certain Young Man, Love Match (Los Angeles), 1967; Hair, Lovers and Other Strangers, The Cuban Thing, The Great White Hope, Promises, Promises, and made his London début as designer at the Shaftesbury, 27 Sept, when he again designed Hair, 1968; The Watering Place, My Daughter, Your Son, Promises, Promises (London), 1969; Gantry, Mahagonny, The Engagement Baby, 1970; Lenny, Jesus Christ Superstar, Inner City, 1971; Sugar, Lysistrata, 1972; Seesaw, Full Circle, 1973; Mack and Mabel, Sergeant Pep-

per's Lonely Hearts Club Band on the Road, 1974; A Chorus Line, The Red Devil Battery Sign (Boston), The Rolling Stones' tour of America, 1975; Les Troyens, for the Vienna State Opera, Hamlet Connotations, for American Ballet Theatre, 1976; A Chorus Line (London), On the Twentieth Century, 1977; Julius Caesar (Stratford, Conn), West Side Story (Hamburg), 1978; Ballroom, Comin' Uptown, 1979; designed the film Glory Boy, 1970; designed Lulu for the National Opera Company; has designed many other plays for The Arena Stage and for various regional theatres; has received the Antoinette Perry (Tony) Award, Drama Desk Award, two NY Critics Circle Awards, the Lumen Award, three Joseph Maharam Awards, etc. for his designs.

Address: 101 West 12th Street, New York, NY. *Tel:* 475–1404.

WAISSMAN, Kenneth, producer
b Baltimore, 24 Jan 1943; *s* of Charles William Waissman and his wife Hilda (Shutz); *e* University of Maryland and New York University; *m* the theatrical producer Maxine Fox.

Produced and directed educational TV programs while with the Peace Corps in Bogota, Colombia, 1964–66; production assistant to George Abbott for The Education of Hyman Kaplan, 1968; produced Fortune and Men's Eyes at Stage 73, Oct 1969; with his wife co-produced And Miss Reardon Drinks a Little, 1971; Grease, 1972 (London 1973, 1979); Over Here!, 1974; the gala VIP Night on Broadway, 1979; his New York production of Grease ran for 3388 performances, a Broadway record.

Club: Players. *Address:* 108 East 38th Street, New York, NY 10016. *Tel:* 354–2900.

WALKEN, Christopher, actor
b Astoria, Long Island, New York, 31 Mar 1943; *s* of Paul Walker and his wife; *e* Hofstra University; married.

First appeared in New York at the ANTA, 1959, when he took over as David in J.B., playing under the name Ronnie Walken; as Ronald Walken appeared at the Stage 73, 2 Apr 1963, as Clayton "Dutch" Miller in Best Foot Forward; Alvin, Apr 1964, played in the chorus of High Spirits; Broadway, Feb 1965, played one of the Killers in Baker Street, under the name Christopher Walken, which he has used since; Ambassador, Mar 1966, Philip, King of France in The Lion in Winter; Delacorte, July 1966, Claudio in Measure for Measure; New York City Center, Oct 1966, Jack Hunter (The Sailor) in The Rose Tattoo; Vivian Beaumont, July 1967, Unknown Soldier in The Unknown Soldier and His Wife; Circle in the Square, Nov 1967, Achilles in Iphigenia in Aulis; Festival, Stratford, Ontario, Canada, summer 1968, played Romeo, Lysander in A Midsummer Night's Dream, and Felton in The Three Musketeers; San Diego, Cal, Shakespeare Festival, summer 1969, appeared in Julius Caesar; Oct 1969, played in The Chronicles of Hell; Playhouse, May 1970, Alan in Lemon Sky; Ivanhoe, Chicago, Ill, 1970, repeated this last part; Forum, Mar 1971, played in Scenes from American Life; Goodman, Chicago, 1971, title role in The Night Thoreau Spent in Jail; Delacorte, Aug 1971, Posthumus Leonatus in The Tale of Cymbeline; American Place, Apr 1972, Georg in The Judgment; Yale Repertory, New Haven, Conn, 1971–72, title role in Caligula; appeared with the Long Wharf, New Haven, 1972–73 season; Vivian Beaumont, Nov 1972, Sintsov in Enemies; Jan 1972, Jack Clitheroe in The Plough and the Stars; Mar 1973, Bassanio in The Merchant of Venice; Mitzi E Newhouse, Dec 1973, Achilles in Troilus and Cressida; Feb 1974, Antonio in The Tempest; Apr 1974, played Macbeth; Seattle, Wash, Repertory, Oct 1974, played Hamlet; Anspacher, Jan

1975, title role in Kid Champion; Brooklyn Academy of Music, 3 Dec 1975, Chance Wayne in Sweet Bird of Youth, and transferred to the Rebekah Harkness, 29 Dec 1975; Yale Rep, Apr 1978, Gregers Werle in The Wild Duck; appeared in the films The Anderson Tapes, The Happiness Cage, Roseland, The Dear Hunter (Oscar, 1979), Heaven's Gate, 1980, etc.

Address: c/o Bill Treusch Associates, 853 Seventh Avenue, New York, NY 10019.

WALKER, Nancy (*née* Anna Myrtle Swoyer), actress and singer

b Philadelphia, Pa, 10 May 1921; d of Dewey Stewart Swoyer, the comedian known as Dewey Barto, and his wife Myrtle (Lawler); e Bentley School, New York, and Professional Children's School, 1930–40; m (1) Gar Moore (mar dis); (2) David Craig.

Made her first appearance on the stage at the Ethel Barrymore Theatre, NY, 1 Oct 1941, as Blind Date in Best Foot Forward; she then went to Hollywood, appearing in the film of Best Foot Forward, followed by Girl Crazy and Broadway Rhythm; at the Adelphi, NY, Dec 1944, played Hilda in On the Town; Martin Beck, Apr 1947, Yetta Samovar in Barefoot Boy with Cheek; Adelphi, Jan 1948, Lily Malloy in Look, Ma, I'm Dancin'; Broadhurst, Jan 1949, appeared in the revue Along Fifth Avenue; in summer theatres, 1950, again appeared on On the Town; toured, 1951, as Moll in Roaring Girl; at the Shubert, Boston, Jan 1952, played Shirley Harris in A Month of Sundays; at the Broadhurst, NY, Dec 1952, succeeded Helen Gallagher as Gladys in Pal Joey; Phoenix, Apr 1953, appeared in the revue Phoenix '55; Playhouse, Jan 1956, Julia Starbuck in a revival of Fallen Angels; Martin Beck, Oct 1957, Katey O'Shea in Copper and Brass; City Center, Mar 1958, Ruth in Wonderful Town; Alvin, Nov 1959, starred in the revue The Girls Against the Boys; St James, Dec 1960, Kay Cram in Do-Re-Mi; Helen Hayes, Jan 1966, directed UTBU; stock, 1966, played Libby Hirsch in Dear Me, The Sky Is Falling and directed and played Julia Starbuck in Fallen Angels; toured, 1966, as Ellen Manville in Luv; Westbury Music Fair, May 1967, played in Bell, Book and Candle; Lyceum, for the APA Phoenix, Mar 1968, Charlotta Ivanovna in The Cherry Orchard, and Oct 1968, Julia in The Cocktail Party; Ahmanson, Los Angeles, 1971, Domina in A Funny Thing Happened on the Way to the Forum; Shubert, NY, 11 Mar 1973, appeared in Sondheim: A Musical Tribute; appeared in the films The World's Greatest Athlete and 40 Carats, 1973; directed Can't Stop the Music, 1980; has also appeared frequently on television, including playing Mildred in the long-running series *McMillan and Wife* (1972–6) and Mrs Ida Morgenstern in the series *Rhoda* (1974–6), as star of *The Nancy Walker Show* (1976–7), and broadcast in the radio serial *Lady Next Door*.

Address: 3702 Eureka Drive, Studio City, Calif 91604.

WALKER, Sydney, actor

b Philadelphia, Pa, 4 May 1921; s of Sydney Smith Walker and his wife Barbara Blakeley (Farrell); e Conservatoire Nationale de Musique, Paris; prepared for the stage with Jasper Deeter at the Hedgerow Repertory Theatre, Moylan, Pa.

First appeared on stage at the Hedgerow, Dec 1946, as Sir Andrew Aguecheek in Twelfth Night; first appeared in New York at the Rooftop, Apr 1957, when he took over as Corbaccio in Volpone; Shakespearewrights, Oct 1957, played Julius Caesar; The Players, Jan 1959, played King Lear; toured, Oct 1959–May 1960, as Sir Andrew Melvil in Mary Stuart; St James, Oct 1960, Archbishop of Canterbury in

Becket; subsequently toured in this part, and repeated it at the Hudson, May 1961; National Repertory tour, Oct 1961–Apr 1962, Captain Armin in Elizabeth the Queen and Earl of Leicester in Mary Stuart; 78th Street, Mar 1962, co-adapted Nathan the Wise; joined the APA (Association of Producing Artists) Repertory Company, and at the Univ of Michigan, Ann Arbor, 1963, played Theseus in A Midsummer Night's Dream, Mowbray and the Bishop of Carlisle in Richard II, Antonio in The Merchant of Venice, and Don Pedro in Much Ado About Nothing; East 74th Street, 1963–64 season, Luka in The Lower Depths, Freeman in The Tavern, Argante in Scapin, and Ponza in Right You Are; 1964–65 season, The Old Prince in War and Peace, Joachim in Judith, and, at the Lyceum, Mendoza and the Devil in Man and Superman; 1965–66, Paul Sycamore in You Can't Take It with You, and during this season also played at the Huntington Hartford, Los Angeles, Cal; Lyceum, 1966–67, Sir Peter Teazle in The School for Scandal, Walt in We, Comrades Three, in You Can't Take It with You, and Old Ekdal in The Wild Duck; also played at the Univ of Michigan and the Royal Alexandra, Toronto, Canada, during this season; Lyceum, 1967–68, Innocenti in Pantagleize, Semyonov-Pistchik in The Cherry Orchard, and appeared during the summer at Stanford Univ, Palo Alto, Cal; fall of 1967 appeared at Expo, Montreal, Canada in You Can't Take It with You and Right You Are; Lyceum, 1968–69, Sir Henry Harcourt-Reilly in The Cocktail Party, Philinte in The Misanthrope, and Michael Marthurin in Cock-a-Doodle-Dandy; left the APA and at the Martinique, Oct 1969, played Edgar in A Scent of Flowers; John Golden, Mar 1970, Fitzroy Somerset, Lord Raglan, Commander-in-Chief in Blood Red Roses; Cherry Lane, June 1970, played in The Nuns; joined the Repertory Theater of Lincoln Center, and at the Vivian Beaumont, Nov 1970, played a God in The Good Woman of Setzuan; Jan 1971, Michael James Flaherty in The Playboy of the Western World; Mar 1971, Morten Kiil in An Enemy of the People; May 1971, Teiresias in Antigone; Nov 1971, Earl of Shrewsbury in Mary Stuart; Jan 1972, Commodore in Narrow Road to the Deep North; Mar 1972, Sir Toby Belch in Twelfth Night; Apr 1972, Giles Corey in The Crucible; Olney, Md, Playhouse, Aug 1972, Hoolihan in The Patrick Pearse Motel; Vivian Beaumont, Nov 1972, Levshin in Enemies; Jan 1973, Bartender in The Plough and the Stars; Mar 1973, Shylock in The Merchant of Venice; Apr 1973, Mexican Man in A Streetcar Named Desire; Olney, Md, Aug 1974, title role in The Miser, and Stormy Loftus in Summer; repeated this last part at the John F Kennedy Center for the Performing Arts, Washington, DC; Eisenhower, Washington, DC, May 1974, Yakonov in The Headhunters; Olney Theatre, Md, Summer 1974, in Happy End, The Miser, and Summer; Geary, San Francisco, Cal, for the ACT, Nov 1974, Horatio Alger, Sr, in Horatio; same theatre, Mar 1975, in The Ruling Class; in Tiny Alice, Oct 1975; This Is, Jan 1976, playing an Ancient Dandy; Knock Knock, Jan 1977; Travesties, Mar 1977; Peer Gynt, Apr 1977; A Christmas Carol, Dec 1977; in 1978–79 appeared in Hotel Paradiso, The National Health, Travesties, etc; first appeared in films in The Way We Live Now, 1969, and has since played in Love Story, Puzzle of a Downfall Child, etc; has appeared extensively on television, notably in Enemies, *The Secret Storm* series, 1972–74, The Lower Depths, etc.

Favourite parts: The Old Prince in War and Peace, Luka in The Lower Depths. *Recreation:* Swimming. *Address:* Actors Equity Association, 165 West 46th Street, New York, NY 10036.

WALKER, Zena, actress

b Birmingham, 7 Mar 1934; d of George Walker and his wife

Elizabeth Louise (Hammond); *e* St Martin's, Solihull; *m* (1) Robert Urquhart (mar dis); (2) Julian Holloway (mar dis); (3) John French; trained at RADA.

Made her first professional appearance at the Alexandra, Birmingham in 1950 as a walk-on in Smooth-Faced Gentleman; at the Memorial Theatre, Stratford, played Miranda in The Tempest, 1952, and Juliet in Romeo and Juliet, 1954; first London appearance 1955, at the Arts, as Angelina in South; joined the Old Vic company, season 1955–6, playing Katharine in Henry V and Perdita in The Winter's Tale; Mermaid, Aug 1961, Annabella in 'Tis Pity She's A Whore; Arts, Nov 1965, Violet in Man and Superman, transferring to the Vaudeville, Jan 1966; Chichester Festival, 1966, played Varya in The Cherry Orchard, Lady Macduff in Macbeth and Aglae in The Fighting Cock, re-opening in the latter part at the Duke of York's in Oct; Comedy, July 1967, played Sheila in A Day in the Death of Joe Egg; made her first Broadway appearance in the same part at the Brooks Atkinson, Feb 1968; Hampstead, Oct 1968, June Elliott in It's All in the Mind; King's Head, Islington, June 1973, the Wife in Marriages; Haymarket, Feb 1974, Ghislaine de Ste Euverte in The Waltz of the Toreadors; ICA, Sept 1974, Susan in Away from It All; Haymarket, Mar 1975, Jenny Rastall in The Case in Question; Apollo, Jan 1977, Miss Cooper in Separate Tables; Lyttelton, May 1979, Jenny in Close of Play; first appeared in films 1967 and subsequent pictures include Sammy Going South, The Reckoning, and Cromwell; has made many television appearances since her first in 1951, including *Man at the Top*, Abide with Me, Telford's Change, That Crazy Woman, Write Away, etc; author of Wake, written for radio, 1976.

Favourite parts: Varya in The Cherry Orchard and Sheila in Joe Egg. *Recreations:* Home and family. *Address:* c/o French's, 26 Binney Street, London W1.

WALL, Max (*né* Maxwell George Lorimer), actor and dancer
b Brixton, London, 12 Mar 1908; *s* of Jack Lorimer and his wife Maud Clara (Mitcherson); *e* privately; *m* (1) Marian Pola (mar dis); (2) Jennifer Chimes (mar dis); (3) Christine Clements.

Made his first appearance on the stage, as a boy of fourteen, in Dec 1922, playing Jack in Mother Goose, with a travelling pantomime company, in Devon and Cornwall; first appeared in London, at the Lyceum Theatre, 2 Sept 1925, in The London Revue, as a speciality dancer; at the Adelphi, Sept 1926, played Sid Goyle in Merely Molly; London Pavilion, May 1927, appeared in One Dam Thing After Another; then appeared in variety; Sept 1930, toured as Jerry Wimpole in Silver Wings; London Hippodrome, Jan 1932, played in Bow Bells; went to America and made his first appearance in New York, at the Broadway Theatre, 27 Sept 1932, in Earl Carroll's Vanities; on returning to England, again appeared in variety; London Hippodrome, Dec 1936, played Jack in Mother Goose; toured, 1937, in variety, also in Tune Inn and In Town To-Night; toured, 1938, in Tops Everything; London Hippodrome, Mar 1939, in Black and Blue; toured, Dec 1939, in Band Waggon; Prince of Wales, May 1940, played Tom Carroway in Present Arms; toured, 1941, in the leading part in Funny Side Up; served in the Royal Air Force, 1941–3, when he was invalided out; Piccadilly, Nov 1943, played Eddy Brown in Panama Hattie, and again at the Adelphi, Jan 1945; Grand, Blackpool, June 1945, appeared in Hoopla!; Duchess, Mar 1946, appeared in Make It a Date, to which he also contributed several items; Hippodrome, Golder's Green, Dec 1947, played Muggles in Jack and the Beanstalk; engaged in variety and broadcasting,

1948–50; Empire, Swansea, Dec 1950, Billy Crusoe in Robinson Crusoe; Coliseum, Oct 1955, appeared as Hines in The Pajama Game; Richmond, May 1958, played Ernie Biggs in The Gypsy Warned Me; toured Australia in variety, 1958; toured South Africa, 1960; Adelphi, London, Sept 1960, played the Jester in Once Upon a Mattress; Royal Court, July 1966, Pere Ubu in Ubu Roi; Royal Court, Aug 1972, Emmanuel in The Old Ones; Vaudeville, Dec 1973, appeared in Cockie; Greenwich, Dec 1974, Archie Rice in The Entertainer; same theatre, Jan 1974, gave a solo entertainment, Aspects of Max Wall, which transferred to the Garrick, Feb 1975, and was followed by a number of one-man shows; Greenwich, Dec 1976 and Jan 1977, in the double-bill, Krapp's Last Tape and The Great Wall; Royal Court, June 1977, Old Gocher in Fair Slaughter; Old Vic, Sept 1977, in Buster; Greenwich, Mar 1977, Malvolio in Twelfth Night; Greenwich, Oct 1977, Davies in The Caretaker; Vaudeville, Feb 1979, devised and appeared in a further solo show, Aspects of Max Wall; television appearances include Waiting for Godot, Emmerdale Farm, Born and Bred; appeared in the films Jabberwocky and The Hound of the Baskervilles.

Address: c/o Peter Prichard, 19 West Eaton Place, Eaton Square, London SW1. *Tel:* 01–235 0977.

WALLACE, Hazel Vincent, Managing Director, Thorndike Theatre, Leatherhead, and Freelance Director
b Walsall, Staffordshire, 8 Dec 1919; *d* of George Liddel Wallace and his wife Beatrice Kate (Lazenbury); *e* Queen Mary's, Walsall, Staffordshire, and Birmingham University; gained Social Science Diploma, worked in personnel management.

As actress and singer worked with Combined Services Entertainment, then radio and television, West End and repertory; organising secretary and director of Under Thirty Theatre Group, 1946–52; founded the Buckstone Club, Haymarket, 1949; Managing Director, Leatherhead Theatre Club, 1951–; directed and acted there 1951–9; founded a theatre administrators' trainee scheme, 1958; raised £220,000 by public subscription to build the Thorndike Theatre, Leatherhead, opened Sept 1969; first woman Conference Chairman, Council of Repertory Theatres, 1970; received the Order of the British Empire in the New Year Honours, 1971; served on Training Committee, Arts Council of Great Britain, and of Arts Administration Working Party; member of Drama Panel, Arts Council of Great Britain, 1975–80, and of South East Arts Association; director, Young Theatre Ltd, Thorndike Theatre (Leatherhead) Ltd, and Leatherhead Green Room Ltd.

Address: 43 Mall Road, London, W6. *Tel:* 01–748 5604.

WALLACH, Eli, actor
b Brooklyn, New York, 7 Dec 1915; *s* of Abraham Wallach and his wife Bertha (Schorr); *e* University of Texas, and College of the City of New York; *m* Anne Jackson; studied for the stage at the Neighborhood Playhouse School of Theatre and with Lee Strasberg at the Actors Studio, of which he is a charter member, 1947.

First appeared in a boys' club performance in Brooklyn, Sept 1930; made his first appearance in NY at the Belasco, 8 Nov 1945, as the Crew Chief in Skydrift; subsequently appeared with the American Repertory Theatre on Broadway, 1947–8, in Androcles and the Lion, Henry VIII, Yellowjack, etc; Martin Beck, Nov 1947, Diomedes in Antony and Cleopatra with Katharine Cornell; at the Alvin, Jan 1949, succeeded Ted Kazanoff as Stefanowski in Mister Roberts; Martin Beck, Feb 1951, played Alvarro Mangiacavallo in The Rose Tattoo, and subsequently toured in this part; National, Mar 1953, played Kilroy in Camino Real; Theatre de Lys, July 1953, appeared as Dickson in Scarecrow; Longacre, Jan 1954, played Julien in Mademoiselle Colombe; made his first appearance on the London stage at Her Majesty's, 22 Apr 1954, as Sakini in The Teahouse of the August Moon; after his return to NY appeared at the Martin Beck, Feb 1955, when he again played Sakini, taking over the part from David Wayne; Martin Beck, Oct 1956, Bill Walker in Major Barbara; Phoenix, Jan 1958, the Old Man in The Chairs; Morosco, Dec 1958, Willie in The Cold Wind and the Warm; Longacre, Jan 1961, Berenger in Rhinoceros; Orpheum, Feb 1963, Ben in The Tiger and Paul XXX in The Typists; Globe, London, May 1964, again played in the last double-bill; returned to NY, and at the Booth, Nov 1964, played Milt Manville in Luv; toured US, 1966, in The Typists and The Tiger; Biltmore, Jan 1968, Charles Dyer in Staircase; toured, summer 1971, as Ollie H and Wesley in Promenade All!; Alvin, Apr 1972, repeated these last parts; Eisenhower, Washington, DC, July 1973, General St Pé in Waltz of the Toreadors; Circle in the Square—Joseph E Levine, Sept 1973, again played this last part and toured Jan–Apr 1974; Martin Beck, Nov 1974, Peppino in Saturday, Sunday, Monday; Peachtree Playhouse, Atlanta, Ga, Jan 1975, Arthur Canfield in The Sponsor; Long Wharf, Apr 1977, Colin in Absent Friends; toured in the same role, July 1977; Theatre Four, Dec 1978, Mr Frank in The Diary of Anne Frank, appearing with his wife and two daughters; Metropolitan Opera and tour, July 1979, Alexander in Every Good Boy Deserves Favour; entered films in 1956 in Baby Doll, for which performance he received the British Film Academy Award; has since appeared in Lord Jim, The Victors, How the West Was Won, The Misfits, The Magnificent Seven, Tiger Makes Out, Cinderella Liberty, Crazy Joe, The Sentinel (1977), etc; has also appeared in all the major television programs in the United States, including: *Playhouse 90, Studio One, Philco Playhouse,* and received an Emmy Award for his role in A Poppy Is Also a Flower.

Favourite parts: Kilroy in Camino Real and Mangiacavallo in The Rose Tattoo. *Hobbies:* Woodwork and the collection of antiques. *Recreations:* Tennis, baseball, swimming. *Address:* c/o William Morris Agency, 1350 Sixth Avenue, New York, NY 10019.

WALLER, David, actor

b Street, Somerset, 27 Nov 1920; *s* of Thomas Wright Waller and his wife Dorothy (Armitage); *e* Friends' Schools, Ackworth and Bootham, Yorkshire; *m* Elisabeth Vernon; trained for the stage under Eileen Thorndike at the Embassy School of Acting, 1937–8.

Made his first stage appearance at the Embassy, Oct 1937, as a Chinese beggar in Chu—The Sinner; joined the Sunderland Repertory, 1939, as an ASM; after war service, 1940–6, returned to the stage, playing with various repertories, 1947–8; played leading roles with the Citizens, York, 1948–51, at York and Scarborough; joined the Old Vic company, season 1951–2, playing Cosroe and Captain in Tamburlaine the Great, Sept 1951; Cornwall in King Lear, Mar 1952, and Lucius in Timon of Athens, May 1952; toured Europe with the company, 1952, as Cornwall; Mermaid, Sept 1952, played Lennox in Macbeth; rejoined the Old Vic, May, 1953, to play Brandon, and later Gardiner, Bishop of Winchester, in Henry VIII; Q, Jan 1954, Rodney in Birds of Sadness; with the Leatherhead Theatre company, 1954–5, where he also directed; Ipswich repertory, 1955–6; rejoined the Old Vic, 1957, to play parts including First Player in Hamlet, Sept; Bolingbroke, Clifford and Northumberland in the three parts of Henry VI, Oct; Barnadine in Measure for

Measure, Nov; Gardiner in Henry VIII, May 1958; toured Europe with the company in Hamlet and Henry VIII, 1958; St Martin's, Nov 1958, played Dr Powell in The Stepmother; again directed at Leatherhead, 1959; Arts, Mar 1960, Carter Winter in The Admiration of Life; toured, 1960, in Strip the Willow; Royalty, Mar 1961, the Doctor in The Miracle Worker, transferring with the production to Wyndham's; Arts, May 1962, Medvedev in The Lower Depths; Piccadilly, Oct 1962, Senator in Fiorello!; in repertory at the Belgrade, Coventry, 1963–4, his parts included Sir Toby Belch in Twelfth Night, Azdak in The Caucasian Chalk Circle, and the title role in Serjeant Musgrave's Dance; also directed The Private Ear and The Public Eye; joined the Royal Shakespeare Company, 1964, and at Stratford played parts including Northumberland in Richard II and both parts of Henry IV; season 1965, Friar Barnadine in The Jew of Malta, Dull in Love's Labour's Lost, Duke in The Merchant of Venice, First Gravedigger in Hamlet (also Aldwych), and Lucullus in Timon of Athens; Aldwych, Jan 1966, Schools Superintendent in The Government Inspector; Stratford, season 1966, Worcester in Henry IV, part I and Silence in part II, Fluellen in Henry V, the Duke in The Revenger's Tragedy, also repeating First Gravedigger; at the Aldwych, played Harry Belcher in Belcher's Luck, Nov 1966; Pastor Manders in Ghosts, June 1967; Sir Tunbelly Clumsy in The Relapse, Aug 1967; Stratford, 1968, Kent in King Lear, Pandarus in Troilus and Cressida, Dogberry in Much Ado About Nothing (also US tour, 1969), and read in The Hollow Crown; Aldwych, 1969, again played Pandarus, Duff in Landscape, Dogberry, Sylvester Heegan in The Silver Tassie, and once more the Duke in The Revenger's Tragedy; Stratford, 1970, played the title role in the Theatregoround production of Dr Faustus, Claudius in Hamlet, and Bottom in A Midsummer Night's Dream, making his Broadway début in the part when the production transferred to the Billy Rose, Jan 1971; after a short US tour he returned to the Aldwych, June 1971, playing Bottom, Levshin in Enemies, Old Bellair in The Man of Mode, and in Jan 1972 the Son in All Over; toured Britain and various European festivals, 1973, as Duff in Landscape and Edward in A Slight Ache, a double bill also seen at the Aldwych, Oct 1973; The Place, also Oct 1973, Senator Sinclair Caldwell in Section Nine, which transferred to the Aldwych, Jan 1974; at this theatre he played Herbert Shanklin in Duck Song, Feb, and Father Motilla in The Bewitched, May; Stratford, 1974 season, played Sir Toby Belch in Twelfth Night, and Escalus in Measure for Measure, repeating the former part at the Aldwych, Feb 1975; Stratford season, 1976, played Friar Lawrence in Romeo and Juliet (and Aldwych, July 1977), the Old Shepherd in The Winter's Tale, Pandarus in Troilus and Cressida (and Aldwych, Sept 1977), and Ben Jonson in Bingo at The Other Place (also Warehouse, Aug 1977); repeated all these parts in Newcastle; Aldwych, Aug 1977, Aune in Pillars of the Community; Warehouse, Dec 1977, Screw and Lord Plaistow in Frozen Assets; Lyric, Hammersmith, Oct 1979, Crampton in You Never Can Tell; is the author of the play, Happy Returns, Leatherhead, 1955, and radio and television plays; adapted Treasure Island (with Trevor Nunn), Coventry, 1963; first film experience in documentaries, 1956; more recently Work is a Four-Letter Word, Perfect Friday, and Landscape; television, since 1953, includes Heartbreak House, The Beaux' Stratagem, Edward and Mrs Simpson, The Tempest, etc.

Favourite parts: Sir Toby Belch, First Gravedigger, Ben Jonson. *Recreations:* Painting, writing, gardening, cooking. *Club:* Arts. *Address:* c/o Fraser & Dunlop, 91 Regent Street, London, W1.

WALSTON, Ray, actor

b New Orleans, Louisiana, 2 Nov 1917; *s* of Harry Walston and his wife Mittie (Kimball); *m* Ruth Calvert; formerly a printer and reporter.

Made his début at the Community Players, Houston, Texas, Sept 1938, when he played Buddy in High Tor; Cleveland, Ohio, Playhouse, Sept 1943, Hadrian in You Touched Me; made his New York début at the Columbus Circle, 13 Dec 1945, as an Attendant in the Maurice Evans production of Hamlet; Royale, Sept 1946, Schwartz of The Daily News in Front Page; Shubert, New Haven, Connecticut, Apr 1947, Sam Phelps in Three Indelicate Ladies; Playhouse, Jan 1948, One of the Townspeople in The Survivors; New York City Center, May 1948, Drugger in The Alchemist, May 1948, Davis in Moon of the Caribbees, and June 1948, Male Cricket and the Telegrapher in The Insect Comedy; Music Box, Oct 1948, Mr Kramer in Summer and Smoke; Booth, Feb 1949, Ratcliff in Richard III; Music Box, May 1949, Rodla Gibbons in Mrs Gibbons' Boys; Barrymore, Dec 1949, the Telephone Man in The Rat Race; toured and played for one year in Chicago, 1950–1, as Luther Billis in South Pacific; made his London début at the Drury Lane, 1 Nov 1951, as Luther Billis in South Pacific; Majestic, NY, May 1953, Mac in Me and Juliet; Alvin, Dec 1954, Captain Jona in House of Flowers; 46th Street, May 1955, Applegate (the Devil) in Damn Yankees; toured, 1956–7, in this last part and play; Martin Beck, Mar 1958, Michael Haney in Who Was That Lady I Saw You With?; Henry Miller's, Dec 1966, Eddie in Agatha Sue, I Love You; toured, Dec 1969–Apr 1970, as Steward in Canterbury Tales; Walnut, Philadelphia, 1972, Sir Lucius O'Trigger in The Rivals; in Aug 1973 took over from George Rose as Lutz in the tour of The Student Prince; Cleveland, Ohio, Playhouse, Oct 1973, Walter Burns in The Front Page; Westbury, Long Island, Music Fair, June 1974, Mr Applegate in Damn Yankees, and subsequently toured; toured, winter 1974, in The Drunkard; Imperial, 9 Mar 1975, appeared in Gala Tribute to Joshua Logan; toured, 1975, in the leading male roles in You Know I Can't Hear You When the Water's Running; Cleveland Play House, Oct 1977, in The Learned Ladies; made his film début in Kiss Them for Me, 1957, and since has appeared in Damn Yankees, The Apartment, Tall Story, Caprice, The Sting (1973), etc; appeared on television first in 1950 in *Suspense*, and since has played in The State of the Union, Uncle Harry, There Shall Be No Night, and the long-running series *My Favorite Martian*; received the Antoinette Perry (Tony) Award for Damn Yankees.

Clubs: Lambs, Players, Magic. *Address:* Actors Equity Association, 165 West 46th Street, New York, NY 10036.

WALTER-ELLIS, Desmond, actor

b London, 16 Sept 1914; *s* of Valentine Walter-Ellis and his wife Eileen (Kerin); *e* Sherborne School, Dorset; *m* Irene Gwynn; was a student at the Old Vic and Sadler's Wells, 1932–3.

Made his first appearance at the Grafton Theatre, 18 Dec 1932, as David Trevelyan in Fool's Music; then appeared at the Old Vic, Mar 1933, as the servant to Joseph Surface in The School for Scandal; Open Air Theatre, June 1933, played Curio in Twelfth Night; Old Vic, Dec 1933, Froth in Measure for Measure; Sadler's Wells, Jan 1934, Adrian in The Tempest; Palace, Sept 1934, appeared in the revue, Streamline, and during 1935, toured as Gilbert in The Wind and the Rain; Westminster, Jan 1936, was in The Dog Beneath the Skin, and Mar 1936, in Fulgens and Lucrece; toured, 1937–8, in Three Men on a Horse, and Bats in the Belfry; from 1938–40, engaged as leading comedian with the

Newcastle Repertory company; served in HM Forces, 1940–5, as Captain in the Royal Fusiliers; during 1945–6, was with the Central Pool of Artists, producing revues for the Middle East; from 1946–9, mainly engaged in television; Q, Dec 1947, played the Mad Hatter in Alice Through the Looking Glass; Princes, Apr 1949, Smirnov in The Bear; Prince of Wales's, May 1950, in the revue, Touch and Go; Embassy, Dec 1950, Teddy Deakin in The Ghost Train; appeared in cabaret at the Empress Rooms, Feb 1951; St Martin's, June 1951, appeared in the revue Penny Plain, and subsequently toured in this production; toured South Africa, Nov 1952–Apr 1953, as Dame in the pantomime Dick Whittington; after returning to England, toured, 1954, with Cicely Courtneidge, in the revue Bits and Pieces; at the Saville, London, Dec 1954, appeared in the revue Pay the Piper; toured, June 1955, as Tim Manners in Pardon My Claws; Chelsea Palace, Dec 1955, appeared as Tweedledee in Alice Through the Looking-Glass; Westminster, May 1956, Count Mogador in Albertine by Moonlight; White Rock, Hastings, summer season, 1958, starred in Out of the Blue; toured, Dec 1958–May 1959, as Peter Webster in Old Chelsea; toured, July 1959, as Benny in The Desert Song; Winter Garden, Dec 1959, played the Fish Footman, the March Hare, and the King of Hearts in Alice in Wonderland; toured, Oct 1960, as Peter Wilton in Lock, Stock and Barrel; Palladium, Dec 1960, played Jack Allright in Turn Again Whittington; toured, Mar–Dec 1962, as Benny in a revival of The Desert Song; Flora Robson Playhouse, Newcastle upon Tyne, Feb 1963, appeared in Two Stars For Comfort; toured Australia, Nov 1963–5, as King Pellinore in Camelot; Vaudeville, Feb 1966, played Teddy Brewster in Arsenic and Old Lace; Palace, Manchester, Dec 1966, Nurse Martha in Babes in the Wood; Civic, Newcastle, Feb 1968, guest star in Loot; Royal Court, Liverpool, Dec 1968, An Ugly Sister in Cinderella; Arnaud, Guildford, Dec 1969, and tour, the Cowardly Lion in The Wizard of Oz; toured, Feb 1970, as William Blore in Ten Little Niggers; Oxford Playhouse, Sept 1971, and tour, Pishchik in The Cherry Orchard; Victoria Palace, Dec 1971, Cowardly Lion in The Wizard of Oz; Ashcroft, Croydon, and tour, May 1972, Joseph in My Three Angels; Oxford Playhouse, Oct 1972, and tour, Oronte in The Misanthrope; Stratford, Dec 1972, and Theatre Royal, Brighton, Dec 1972, Mad Hatter in Alice in Wonderland; Palace, Westcliff, May 1974, Marquis of Candover in The Jockey Club Stakes; Richmond, Dec 1974, Squire in Mother Goose; Theatre Royal, Brighton, May 1975, and tour, the Hotel Manager in No Room for Sex; has appeared in films and on television.

Address: 10 Blithfield Street, London, W8.

WALTERS, Thorley, actor

b Teingrace, Devonshire, 12 May 1913; *s* of Prebendary Thomas Collins Walters and his wife Mary Francis (Swinstead); *e* Monkton Combe School, Bath; studied for the stage at the Old Vic School.

Made his first appearance when he walked-on at the Old Vic, 13 Feb 1933, in The Admirable Bashville, and remained until 1935; spent six months with the Manchester Repertory Theatre, from Aug 1935; from Feb 1936, appeared in several revivals at the Q Theatre; subsequently appeared at Daly's, as the Abbé Vignali in St Helena; at the Vaudeville, Sept 1936, in Gentle Rain, and Do You Remember; toured, May 1937, as Tom in Think of a Number; Haymarket, Feb 1938, played Edward Davis in Mary Goes to See; Arts, May 1938, Philip Hamilton in High Fever; Wyndham's, July 1940, and again in May 1941, played George Perrey in Cottage to Let; Lyric, Aug 1942, Lieut Fisher in Escort; St Martin's, Sept 1942, Jerry Seymour in Claudia, subsequently playing David

Naughton in the same play; Phoenix, Nov 1945, Tim Garrett in Under the Counter; first appeared in New York, at the Shubert Theatre, 3 Oct 1947, in the same part; toured 1948–9, in Australia and New Zealand, in the same part; London Hippodrome, June 1949, played Jimmy Denham in Her Excellency; toured Oct 1950, as Peter Lynton in Gay's the Word, and appeared in this part at the Saville, Feb 1951; Piccadilly, May 1953, appeared in the revue Over the Moon; toured, 1954, with Cicely Courtneidge in the revue Bits and Pieces; Gaiety, Dublin, Oct 1963, and Vaudeville, London, Jan 1964, played Johann Schneider in The Roses Are Real; Hampstead Theatre Club, Jan 1968, Mr Pim in Mr Pim Passes By; first appeared in films, 1934; recent TV includes Tinker, Tailor, Soldier, Spy, Henry V, and Malice Aforethought; is a Director of the Royal General Theatrical Fund.

Recreations: Swimming, surf-riding, and photography. *Address:* 808 Keyes House, Dolphin Square, SW1. *Tel:* 01–834 3800.

WALTON, Tony, (Anthony John), designer and producer
b Walton-on-Thames, Surrey, 24 Oct 1934; *s* of Lancelot Henry Frederick Walton and his wife Hilda Betty (Drew); *e* Radley College, City of Oxford School of Technology, Art and Commerce, and the Slade School of Fine Arts; *m* Julie Andrews (mar dis).

Designed for Peter Haddon's Company at Wimbledon Theatre, 1955–6; designed his first theatre production in New York at the Barbizon-Plaza, Nov 1957, with Conversation Piece; he has since designed sets and costumes for the following productions, in London unless otherwise stated: Valmouth (Lyric, Hammersmith), 1958; Fool's Paradise, The Pleasure of His Company (sets only), The Ginger Man, Pieces of Eight, 1959; Most Happy Fella, Valmouth (NY), 1960; Once There Was a Russian (NY), One Over the Eight, A Wreath for Udomo, 1961; A Funny Thing Happened on the Way to the Forum (NY), Cindy-Ella, 1962; The Love of Three Oranges (Sadler's Wells), The Rape of Lucretia (Edinburgh Festival, and subsequent English Opera Group tours), A Funny Thing Happened on the Way to the Forum, 1963; Caligula, Golden Boy (NY), The Rehearsal (NY, costumes only), 1964; Otello (Spoleto Festival), 1965; The Apple Tree (NY), 1966; Midsummer Marriage (Covent Garden), Golden Boy, 1968; for the National Theatre, The Covent Garden Tragedy, A Most Unwarrantable Intrusion, In His Own Write (triple-bill), 1968, and The Travails of Sancho Panza, 1969; Pippin (NY, sets only), Once Upon a Time, 1972; Pippin, Shelter, Uncle Vanya (all NY), 1973; The Good Doctor, 1974; Bette Midler's Clams on the Half Shell Revue (NY), Chicago (NY, sets only), The Cunning Little Vixen (Santa Fe), 1975; Streamers, 1976; The Act (NY) (sets only), 1977; Drinks Before Dinner (NY Shakespeare Festival), 1978; A Day in Hollywood, A Night in the Ukraine (NY), 1980; co-director of Spur Productions, presenting The Ginger Man, 1959; New Cranks, 1960; Fairy Tales of New York, 1961; Director of Theatre Projects Ltd since 1959, presenting A Funny Thing Happened on the Way to the Forum, 1963; She Loves Me, 1964; he has designed a number of films including Mary Poppins, Fahrenheit 451, The Seagull, The Boy Friend, Murder on the Orient Express, Equus, The Wiz, and All That Jazz (1980); has also designed three ballets for the San Francisco Ballet Co; designed his first television production, 1959, with *The Julie Andrews Show*.

Recreations: Travel, caricature, illustration, music. *Addresses:* c/o Theatre Projects Ltd, 10 Long Acre, London, WC2. *Tel:* 01–836 7879, *and* c/o The Sterling Lord Agency, 660 Madison Avenue, New York, NY 10021. *Tel:* PL1 2533.

WANAMAKER, Sam, actor, director, and producer
b Chicago, Ill, USA, 14 June 1919; *s* of Morris Wanamaker

and his wife Molly (Bobele); *e* Drake University; *m* Charlotte Holland; studied for the stage at the Goodman Theatre, Chicago.

Was an actor and director in Chicago summer theatres, 1936–9; joined the Globe Shakespearean Theatre group; in 1938, played a season with the Chicago Civic Repertory Theatre; made his first appearance in New York, at the Cort Theatre, 23 Jan 1942, as Lester Freed in Cafe Crown; Windsor, Feb 1943, played Kirichenko in Counterattack; served in the US Armed Forces, 1943–6; after demobilization appeared at the Belasco, Apr 1946, as Mac Sorrell in This, Too, Shall Pass; Alvin, Nov 1946, Jimmy Masters in Joan of Lorraine; Morosco, Nov 1948, Matt Cole in Goodbye, My Fancy, which he also staged; made his first appearance in London at the St James's, 3 Apr 1952, as Bernie Dodd in Winter Journey, which he also directed; at the Princes, London, Feb 1953, in association with Jack Hylton, he presented The Shrike, in which he appeared as Jim Downs; at the Royal, Glasgow, Apr 1953, directed Purple Dust; Royal, Birmingham, Sept 1953, directed Foreign Field; Duke of York's, London, Jan 1954, in association with Ralph Birch, presented The Big Knife, directing the play and appearing as Charles Castle; at Wimbledon, May 1954, directed The Soldier and the Lady; Embassy, Jan 1955, directed The World of Sholom Aleichem; Winter Garden, May 1955, in association with Jack de Leon, presented The Lovers, directing the play and appearing as Laurent; Royal Court, Feb 1956, directed The Threepenny Opera; Golder's Green, Apr 1956, co-directed (with Jack Minster), and played Bill Starbuck in The Rainmaker, subsequently appearing in the same production, St Martin's, May 1956; Princes, Mar 1957, played Polo Pope and also directed A Hatful of Rain; became Artistic Director of the New Shakespeare Theatre, Liverpool, Oct 1957, and directed and played in the following plays: A View from the Bridge, Tea and Sympathy, Finian's Rainbow, One More River, Cat on a Hot Tin Roof, The Potting Shed, Reclining Figure, King of Hearts, Bus Stop, and The Rose Tattoo; joined the Shakespeare Memorial Theatre Company, Stratford-on-Avon (100th season), Apr 1959, to play Iago in Othello; returned to NY and, at the Music Box, Apr 1961, played Dr Joseph Breuer in A Far Country; for summer theatres, Aug 1961, directed Ding Dong Bell; Coventry Festival, England, May 1962, directed the opera King Priam; Covent Garden, June 1962, again directed King Priam; Morosco, NY, Apr 1963, co-produced and directed Children from Their Games; Longacre, Oct 1963, directed A Case of Libel; Morosco, Mar 1964, directed A Murderer Among Us; Goodman, Chicago, Dec 1964, played Macbeth; Sydney, 1973, directed the opening production in the Opera House, War and Peace; directed the Southwark Summer Festival, and Shakespeare Birthday Celebrations, 1974; executive director, since 1970, of the Globe Playhouse Trust and World Centre for Shakespeare Studies, Southwark; films he has directed include: The Executioner, Catlow, and Sinbad and the Eye of the Tiger; a film director who has also appeared in numerous films, including Give Us This Day, Taras Bulba, Those Magnificent Men in Their Flying Machines, and recently, From Hell to Victory; also acts and directs in TV productions in Britain and the US, including Hawaii Five-O, and The Return of the Saint.

Address: 99 Aldwych, WC2B 4JY.

WARD, Douglas Turner, actor, playwright, director, producer; also known as Douglas Turner, when acting
b Burnside, Louisiana, 5 May 1930; *s* of Roosevelt Ward and

his wife Dorothy (Short); *e* Wilberforce University and the University of Michigan; *m* Diana Powell; formerly engaged as a journalist; trained for the stage with Paul Mann.

First appeared on the stage at the Circle in the Square, during 1957, when he took over as Joe Mott in the revival of The Iceman Cometh; New York City Center, 1958, Matthew Kumalo in Lost in the Stars; Ethel Barrymore, Mar 1959, played one of the Moving Men and understudied Sidney Poitier as Walter Younger and Lonne Elder III as Bobo in A Raisin in the Sun; toured in this play, 1960–1, succeeding to the part of Walter Younger; St Mark's Playhouse, Oct 1961–Mar 1962, Archibald in The Blacks; Circle in the Square, Dec 1962, A Porter in Pullman Car Hiawatha; Cort, Nov 1963, understudied Fredericks in One Flew over the Cuckoo's Nest; Cricket, 1964, took over as Zachariah Pieterson in The Blood Knot; Walnut Street, Philadelphia, Oct 1964, Fitzroy in Rich Little Rich Girl; Delacorte, July 1965, a Roman Citizen in Coriolanus; St Mark's Playhouse, Nov 1965, Arthur in Happy Ending and Mayor and Clan in Day of Absence, both of which he also wrote; co-founded, with Robert Hooks and Gerald S Krone, the Negro Ensemble Company, and serves as its Artistic Director; the premiére of the Company was at the St Mark's Playhouse, 2 Jan 1968, in a production of Peter Weiss's Song of the Lusitanian Bogey; during its first year the Company presented Summer of the Seventeenth Doll, Kongi's Harvest, in which he played Oba Danlola, and Daddy Goodness, which he directed and in which he played Thomas; Dec 1968, presented God Is a (Guess What?); Ceremonies in Dark Old Men, in which he played Russell B Parker, Feb 1969; An Evening of One Acts, consisting of String, Contribution, which he also directed, and Malcochon, Apr 1969; the Negro Ensemble Company made its London début in a World Theatre Season at the Aldwych, performing Song of the Lusitanian Bogey, 5 May 1969, and God Is a (Guess What?), 8 May 1969; St Mark's Playhouse, independently of the NEC, 4 Sept 1969, played Scar in his play The Reckoning; with the NEC presented Man Better Man, July 1969, which he also directed; The Harangues, in which he played a Black Man and Asura, Jan 1970; Brotherhood, which he also wrote and directed with a revival of his play Day of Absence, May 1970; Akokawe, May 1970; Ododo, June 1970; Jan 1971, directed Perry's Mission and produced Rosalee Pritchett; May 1971, directed Ride a Black Horse; Mar 1972, directed A Ballet Behind the Bridge; May 1972, played in Frederick Douglas . . . Through His Own Words; Dec 1972, directed and played Johnny Williams in The River Niger; Brooks Atkinson, Mar 1973, again directed and played in The River Niger; Walnut, Philadelphia, 1973, played Russell B Parker in Ceremonies in Dark Old Men; New Locust, Philadelphia, Oct 1973, directed and played Johnny Williams in The River Niger, and subsequently toured; for the Negro Ensemble Company at the St Mark's Playhouse, 1974, presented and directed The Great Macdaddy, Black Sunlight, and Nowhere to Run, Nowhere to Hide, and presented Terraces, Heaven and Hell's Agreement, In the Deepest Part of Sleep; Mar 1975, directed and played Harper Edwards in The First Breeze of Summer; May 1975, directed Waiting for Mongo; Mar 1976, presented Eden; June 1976, presented and directed Livin' Fat; Dec 1976, Mingo Saunders in The Brownsville Raid; Apr 1977, directed The Great Macdaddy; Nov 1977, Bob Tyrone in The Offering, directing this and Black Body Blues, Jan 1978, and The Twilight Dinner, Apr 1978; presented Nevis Mountain Dew, Dec 1978, A Season to Unravel, Jan 1979, Old Phantoms, Feb 1979, in which he played Jack Hamilton, The Michigan, Nov 1979, in which he played Flick Lacey, and Home, Dec 1979; transferred to Broadway, 1980; first ap-

peared in films in Man and Boy, 1971; first played in television in 1958, and since has played on such programs as *Studio One, East Side/West Side,* on the National Educational Television, produced and played in Ceremonies in Dark Old Men (1975), directed and played in The First Breeze of Summer (1976), etc.

Address: 222 East 11th Street, New York, NY 10003. *Tel:* AL 4–6524.

WARD, Simon, actor
b Beckenham, London, 19 Oct 1941; *s* of Leonard Fox Ward, and his wife Winifred; *e* Alleyn's School, Dulwich; *m* Alexandra Malcolm; trained for the stage at RADA.

First professional appearance, Oct 1963, at the Northampton Repertory Theatre, as Fred Beenstock in Hobson's Choice; first appeared in London, Jan 1964, at the St Martin's, as Tom Phillips in The Fourth of June; Ashcroft, Croydon, Mar 1964, played Alexander in Alexander's Death; at Birmingham Repertory, autumn 1964, his parts included Konstantin in The Seagull; Playhouse, Oxford, 1965–6, played roles including Abel Drugger in The Alchemist and Hippolytus in Phèdre; Jeannetta Cochrane, Sept 1966, and Criterion, Oct 1966, Dennis in Loot; Wyndham's, Oct 1967, Jerry in Wise Child; Chichester Festival, 1968, played the Unknown Soldier in The Unknown Soldier and His Wife, Ferdinand in The Tempest and Henry in The Skin of Our Teeth; Haymarket, Feb 1971, Donald in Spoiled; Shaw, Feb 1972, Romeo in Romeo and Juliet; toured, Feb 1973, for Cambridge Theatre Company, as Valentine in You Never Can Tell; Hampstead, Nov 1974, Teddy in Clever Soldiers; Young Vic, June 1976, Troilus in Troilus and Cressida; same theatre, Aug 1976, Harry in Four to One; Globe, Feb 1978, Ward in The Rear Column; toured, 1980, as Ken Harrison in Whose Life Is It Anyway?; a member of the National Youth Theatre from its foundation (as Youth Theatre) in 1956, he remained to play parts including Richard II and Hamlet; for them he co-directed part one of Henry IV, 1967; first film, Frankenstein Must Be Destroyed, 1969; also appeared in I Start Counting, Young Winston, etc; numerous television appearances, since 1964, include Bloomsday, Flowering Cherry, the serials The Black Tulip and The Roads to Freedom, and The Rear Column, 1980.

Recreations: Music, gardening, reading, badminton. *Address:* c/o IFA Ltd, 11–12 Hanover Street, London, W1. *Tel:* 01–629 8080.

WARDLE (John) Irving, dramatic critic
b Bolton, Lancashire, 20 July 1929; *s* of John Wardle and his wife Nellie (Partington); *e* Bolton School, Wadham College, Oxford and the Royal College of Music; *m* (1) Joan Notkin (mar dis); (2) Fay Vivian Crowder (mar dis); (3) Elizabeth Grist.

Formerly a sub-editor on the *Times Educational Supplement*; assistant theatre critic, *The Observer,* 1960–3; drama critic, *The Times,* 1963–; author of play The Houseboy, 1972, and of The Theatres of George Devine, 1978.

Recreations: Music, cooking. *Address:* 51a Richmond Road, New Barnet, Herts. *Tel:* 01–440 3671.

WARNER, David, actor
b Manchester, Lancs, 29 July 1941; *s* of Herbert Simon Warner; *e* Feldon School, Leamington Spa; formerly employed as a bookseller; studied for the stage at the Royal Academy of Dramatic Art, London.

Made his first appearance on the stage at the Royal Court, Jan 1962, as Snout in A Midsummer Night's Dream; at the Belgrade, Coventry, Mar 1962, played Conrade in Much Ado

About Nothing; New Arts, June 1962, played Jim in Afore Night Come; joined the Royal Shakespeare Company, Stratford-on-Avon, Apr 1963, to play Trinculo in The Tempest, Cinna, a poet, in Julius Caesar, and, in July 1963, played Henry VI in Henry VI, and Edward IV (an adaptation of Henry VI (Parts I, II, and III), which comprised the first two plays from the trilogy The Wars of the Roses); at the Aldwych, Jan 1964, played Henry VI in The Wars of the Roses; Aldwych, Feb 1964, appeared in an anthology The Rebel; Royal Shakespeare, Stratford-on-Avon, Apr 1964, played the title part in Richard II, subsequently appearing as Mouldy in Henry IV (Part II), and Henry VI in The Wars of the Roses; Aldwych, Oct 1964, played Valentine Brose in Eh?; Royal Shakespeare, Stratford-on-Avon, Aug 1965, played the title part in Hamlet, subsequently appearing in the same production at the Aldwych, Dec 1965; Aldwych, Jan 1966, played the Postmaster in The Government Inspector; Royal Shakespeare, 1966 season, again appeared as Hamlet, and also played Sir Andrew Aguecheek in Twelfth Night; Aldwych, Jan 1970, Julian in Tiny Alice; Hampstead, Feb 1972, Hammett in The Great Exhibition; Queen's, July 1972, Claudius in I, Claudius; first appeared in films, 1962, as Blifil in Tom Jones; subsequent films include Morgan, The Fixer, The Bofors Gun, Summer Rain, The Thirty-Nine Steps, Time after Time, Airport '79, etc; made his first appearance on television, Sept 1962, and subsequently in The Pushover, Clouds of Glory, Holocaust, etc.
    Address: c/o Leading Artists, 60 St James's Street, London SW1.

WARRE, Michael, actor, director, and designer
b London, 18 June 1922; *s* of Major Felix Warre, OBE, MC, and his wife Marjorie (Hamilton); *e* Eton College; *m* Isabel Herrin (formerly Bain); studied for the stage at the London Mask Theatre School under John Fernald.
    Made his first appearance on the stage at the Minack Theatre, Porthcurno, Cornwall, Aug 1939, as Albert Fernand in The Count of Monte Cristo; first appeared in London, at the Intimate Theatre, Palmer's Green, Aug 1940; at the Threshold Theatre, Oct 1940, played John in Fishing for Shadows; toured, Nov 1940, as Bill Stanton in It's a Wise Child, for ENSA, and Aug 1941, as Eben in Desire Under the Elms; at the Theatre Royal, York, Apr 1943, played Petruchio in The Taming of the Shrew; Playhouse, Aug 1943, Stanley Perrins in Blow Your Own Trumpet; Theatre Royal, York, Dec 1943, appeared as Hamlet; appeared at the Citizen's Theatre, Glasgow, Jan–Apr 1944; New Theatre, with the Old Vic company, Sept 1944, played Maas Moens in Peer Gynt, and Hastings in Richard III; toured, June 1945, with the Old Vic, CEMA company, as Romeo in Romeo and Juliet; New Theatre, Sept 1945, Prince Hal in Henry IV (parts I and II), and Oct 1945, Second Messenger in Œdipus Rex, and Sir Walter Raleigh in The Critic; went with the company to New York, Apr 1946, and appeared at the Century Theatre, May 1946, in the last-mentioned plays; again appeared at the New, during the Old Vic 1946–7 season, as Edgar in King Lear, Christian in Cyrano de Bergerac, Surly in The Alchemist, and Sir Pierce of Exton in Richard II; Phoenix, Apr 1948, succeeded Paul Scofield as Tom Fashion in The Relapse; toured, 1950, as Caliban in The Tempest, for the Glyndebourne Children's Theatre; Aldwych, May 1951, appeared as Andrey Sergueevitch Prozoroff in Three Sisters; St James's, Oct 1951, played Montano in Othello; joined the Shakespeare Memorial Theatre Company, Stratford-on-Avon, 1953, and during the season appeared as George, Duke of Clarence, in Richard III, Menas in Antony and Cleopatra, Christopher Sly in The Taming of

the Shrew, and the Duke of Albany in King Lear, also arranging the fights in the last-named production; appeared with the Shakespeare Memorial Theatre Company at the Princes, London, Nov 1953, as Menas in Antony and Cleopatra, subsequently playing the same part when the company visited Amsterdam, Brussels and Paris; Lyric, Hammersmith, Sept 1954, and subsequently at the Westminster, appeared as Eilert Lovborg in Hedda Gabler, and toured Holland, Copenhagen and Oslo, 1955, in this part; Arts, Nov 1955, played Augustus Peach in Komuso; Scala, Dec 1957, Mr Darling and Captain Hook in Peter Pan, afterwards touring in the play; Arts, Aug 1958, played Jerome Leprieur in Ariadne; Edinburgh Festival, Sept 1960, played Alex in The Dream of Peter Mann; appeared in the films Henry V and Reach for the Sky; has also made numerous television appearances; designed scenery for Fishing for Shadows, Holy Isle, 1942; Mr Bolfry, 1943; Scandal at Barchester, and It Depends What You Mean, 1944; The Simpleton of the Unexpected Isles, Romeo and Juliet, and Hamlet, 1945; designed scenery and costumes for Back to Methuselah, Othello, Richard II, Happy as Larry, St Joan, 1947; The Hidden Years, Cockpit, Twelfth Night, 1948; The Saxon Saint, Mrs Warren's Profession, 1949; The Firstborn, 1952; has directed (and designed) the following productions: Woyzeck, 1948; Power Without Glory, 1949; The Tempest, 1950; Peregrine Pickle, Early Rising, 1954; A Midsummer Night's Dream, 1957; and The Tempest, 1958 (Toneelgroep Theater, Arnhem); The Taming of the Shrew (Ensemble, Amsterdam), 1959; The Devil's Disciple (National, Brussels), The Aspern Papers (Toneelgroep, Amsterdam), 1961; Guilio Cesare (Handel Opera Society), 1963; Chichester Festival, 1968, designed The Unknown Soldier and His Wife, The Skin of Our Teeth, and The Cocktail Party, the latter play re-opening at Wyndham's, Nov 1968; The Doctor's Dilemma (Chichester), 1972; designed the new adaptable theatre for LAMDA (opened 1963); rebuilt interior of the Tower Theatre, Canonbury, 1968; member of the Society of Theatre Consultants; consultant for Northcott Theatre, Exeter, The Auditorium, University of Essex, and Billingham Sports Forum Theatre, Durham; author of Designing and Making Stage Scenery, 1965; teacher at LAMDA 1955–67, for whom he designed and directed many productions; lecturer and examiner in drama and theatre history for a number of bodies.
    Address: 1 Thornhill Grove, London N1, *and* Rue de la Forêt, L'Epine, France 85.

WARREN, Jeff (*né* Jones), actor, director, and teacher
b Wagner, South Dakota, 21 Jan 1921; *s* of Frank Jones and his wife Mary Frances (Strain); *e* University of Minnesota, Rutgers University (BA 1970), CUNY, Hunter College (MA 1971); studied for the stage at University and with James French.
    First appeared on the New York stage at the Broadway, 27 Feb 1943, as a soloist in Lady in the Dark; Imperial, Oct 1943, understudied role of Rodney Hatch in One Touch of Venus, and played the role for the month of Nov; subsequently played small parts in Follow the Girls, Hollywood Pinafore, The Day Before Spring; Ziegfeld, Mar 1947, played Sandy Dean in Brigadoon, subsequently taking over the part of Charlie Dalrymple; toured in the last part for USO, 1948, then toured Germany, Paris, Tripoli, the Azores as Tommy Albright in the same play; again played Charlie Dalrymple in the national touring company, 1949–50; Ziegfeld, May 1951, appeared in Gentlemen Prefer Blondes; Imperial, Aug 1951, played Kenneth Gibson in Call Me Madam; appeared in the same part at the London Coliseum,

15 Mar 1952; at the London Hippodrome, Apr 1954, played Paul Chandler in Wedding in Paris; Renata, NY, Sept 1959, played in a revival of the revue Lend an Ear; Eugene O'Neill, Jan 1961, stage manager for Showgirl; Actors Playhouse, June 1962, directed Down in the Valley; Playhouse, Ashtabula, Ohio, Nov 1962, directed Green Door Follies; Princess, Melbourne, Australia, Dec 1962, played the King in The King and I, and subsequently touring Australia and New Zealand in this production until Apr 1964; concert tour of the US, Apr–May 1965; Princess, Melbourne, Australia, June 1965, played Cass in Any Wednesday, and also directed the play; St Martin's, Melbourne, Dec 1965, directed Dear Me, The Sky Is Falling; Phillip, Sydney, Sept 1966, directed The Fantasticks; in summer stock has played the following parts: Caliph in Kismet and Lieutenant Cable in South Pacific, 1956; Tommy Keeler in Annie Get Your Gun, Mr Snow in Carousel, and Jack Chesney in Where's Charley?, 1957; Julio in Paint Your Wagon, and Herman in The Most Happy Fella, 1958; Kenneth in Call Me Madam, Charlie in Brigadoon, the Captain in Marietta (also author), and Sanford Stewart in Happy Hunting, 1959; at the Little Theatre, Sullivan, Illinois, directed the following summer stock productions: South Pacific, Pal Joey, Li'l Abner, West Side Story, Redhead, A Tree Grows in Brooklyn (also played Johnny), Carousel (also played Mr Snow), 1960; Paint Your Wagon, Bloomer Girl, Anything Goes, Brigadoon (also played Charlie), Flower Drum Song (also played Wang Ta), Take Me Along (also played Nat), The Merry Widow (also revised libretto and played Danilo), 1961; The Tunnel of Love, The Glass Menagerie, Bye Bye Birdie, Oklahoma!, Gypsy, The King and I (also played the King), The Music Man (also played Harold Hill), 1962; The Seven Year Itch, The Solid Gold Cadillac, The Sound of Music, The Pajama Game, My Fair Lady (also played Alfred P. Doolittle), 1964; Assistant Professor of Drama, West Virginia University, 1967–8 and 1970–1; while there directed Kiss Me Kate, 1967, and Who's Afraid of Virginia Woolf?, 1968; designed scenery for West Side Story, 1967; directed Cabaret, 1970, and Peace (also adapted book), 1971; Resident Director of St Martin's Theatre, Melbourne, and Principal, St Martin's Drama School, 1971; at St Martin's, directed The Servant, 1971; Salad Days, Dark of the Moon, Brecht on Brecht, 1972; Come Blow Your Horn, Yerma, The Insect Play, 1973; Uncle Vanya, Ondine, 1974; guest instructor, Hawkes Bay Performing Arts Centre, Napier, NZ, 1975; director, Jeff Warren School of Acting, 1975–7; directed Ladies in Retirement, 1976, and A Sleep of Prisoners, 1977, Temperance Hall Theatre; taught Mime and World Drama, Council of Adult Education, 1976–7; Theatre Manager of The Open Stage, 1976–present; the Reciter in Facade, Open Stage, 1978, and National Gallery, July 1979; American Colonel in Alice Alderson's Amazing War Relief Concert Party, Aug 1979; first appeared on television in July, 1943, and has since made numerous appearances in the United States, Australia, and Great Britain; four times member of the Council of Actors Equity Association (USA).

Favourite parts: The King in The King and I, and Rodney Hatch in One Touch of Venus. *Hobbies:* Writing, composing, photography, and collecting theatrical records, scripts, and scores. *Address:* 89 Raglan Street, South Melbourne, Victoria 3205, Australia. *Tel:* 699 2862.

WARRICK, Ruth, actress
b St Joseph, Missouri, 29 June 1916; *d* of Frederick R Warrick, Jr, and his wife Annie L (Scott); *e* Univ of Missouri at Kansas City; *m* (1) Erik Rolf (mar dis), (2) Carl Neubert (mar dis), (3) Robert McNamara (mar dis), (4) L Jarvis Cushing, Jr (mar dis); prepared for the stage with Antoinette Perry and Brock Pemberton.

First appeared on the stage in stock productions at the Univ of Missouri, 1933, and played, among others, Sister of the Dead Soldier in Bury the Dead at the Center Community Theater, Kansas City; remained with this stock company until 1936; entered films, then reappeared on the stage in the summer, 1955, as Margo Wendice in Dial M for Murder; made her New York début at the Provincetown Playhouse, 14 Feb 1956, in The Thorntons; made her Broadway début at the Music Box, 3 Oct 1957, as Mary Spain in Miss Lonelyhearts; Theatre Marquee, Apr 1959, played Dolores Dixon in Single Man at a Party; Shubert, 1960, took over from Una Merkel as Essie in Take Me Along; Music Fair, Toronto, Canada, 1960, Anna Leonowens in The King and I, and subsequently toured; Los Angeles, Cal, 1965, Martha in Who's Afraid of Virginia Woolf?, and subsequently toured; also in 1965 played Mary Tyrone in Long Day's Journey into Night in Los Angeles, then toured; Las Palmas, Los Angeles, 1966, Agnes in The Secret Life of Walter Mitty; Gate, NY, May 1971, Mrs Frodo, Anastasia in Any Resemblance to Persons Living or Dead; Roundabout, Mar 1972, Mrs John Tarleton in Misalliance; May 1972, Emily Doon in Conditions of Agreement; Minskoff, Mar 1973, Emmeline Marshall in Irene, and remained in this part through 1974; Westbury, Long Island, Music Fair, June 1976, played in Roberta; first appeared in films as Mrs Kane in Orson Welles's Citizen Kane, 1942, and has since played in Journey into Fear, China Sky, Guest in the House, The Iron Major, Forever and a Day, etc; first appeared on television in 1949, and has since played on major dramatic shows and on *As the World Turns*, Hannah Cord in *Peyton Place*, All My Children, etc.

Favourite parts: Anna Leonowens in The King and I, Martha in Who's Afraid of Virginia Woolf? *Recreations:* Swimming, skin-diving, walking, music, metaphysics, political activism. *Address:* International Famous Agency, 1301 Avenue of the Americas, New York, NY 10017.

WARRINER, Frederic, actor
b Pasadena, California, 2 June 1916; *s.* of Frederick Earl Warriner and his wife Hildreth Vivian (Vail); *e.* Pasadena City College; *m* Elinor Wright; prepared for the stage at the Pasadena College of Theatrical Arts.

First appeared on the stage at the Civic Auditorium, Riverside, California, 1928, as the villain's hoop-rolling pawn in The Drunkard; for five years was a member of the Pasadena Community Playhouse, for which he played in When Knighthood Was in Flower, 1932, Henry VI, Parts I, II, and III, in 1935, Cloten in Cymbelline, 1936, etc; played stock in New England, 1938–9; first appeared in New York at the Nora Bayes, 1939, in Speak of the Devil; at the Curran, San Francisco, 1940, played Eustace in Oscar Wilde; from Jan 1941, served in the US Army for five years, subsequently Entertainment Director of the XXIV Corps, playing various parts and becoming affiliated with Maurice Evans' Entertainment Section on Oahu, Hawaii, 1944; joined the Barter Theatre, Abingdon, Va, 1946, and remained with it until 1950, playing such roles as Spike McManus in State of the Union, Voltaire, Lachlen MacLachlen in The Hasty Heart, Fancourt Babberley in Charley's Aunt, Claudius in Hamlet, etc; toured Denmark and Germany as the Player King in Hamlet, 1949; Woodstock, NY, Sept 1950, The Dauphin in St Joan in the Margaret Webster production; at the National, NY, Dec 1950, played the King of France in King Lear; City Center, Apr 1951, played a Tailor in The Taming of the Shrew; ANTA, May 1951, the Reverend O C Soames in Getting Married, for which he received the Clarence Derwent Award; Cort, Oct 1951, Gilles de Rais and Thomas de

Courcelles in Saint Joan; Playhouse, Sept 1953, Captain Embury in A Pin to See the Peepshow; original member of the Group 20 of the Wellesley, Mass, 1953–8, as actor and director, notably in As You Like It; Provincetown Playhouse, Oct 1954, played Lord Ogleby in The Clandestine Marriage; Phoenix, Jan 1955, Redpenny in The Doctor's Dilemma; Cort, Feb 1955, Salambo in The Wayward Saint; Phoenix, Mar 1955, Count Lodovico in The White Devil, Oct 1955, Feng Chu in The Carefree Tree, and Dec 1955, Stage Manager in Six Characters in Search of an Author; Martin Beck, Oct 1956, played Stephen Undershaft in Major Barbara; Morosco, Nov 1957, Landlord in Time Remembered; Royal Playhouse, Jan 1959, Count Jolimaître in Fashion; American Shakespeare Festival Theatre, Stratford, Conn, May–Sept 1959, played Escalus in Romeo and Juliet, Starveling in A Midsummer Night's Dream, Slender in The Merry Wives of Windsor, and a French Lord in All's Well That Ends Well; 54th Street, Feb 1960, Major Domo in Caligula; Belvedere Lake, Central Park, NY, June–Aug 1960, played Archbishop of Canterbury in Henry V, Lucio in Measure for Measure, and Gremio in The Taming of the Shrew; at the Phoenix, 1960–1, appeared in the following roles: Sir Charles Marlow in She Stoops to Conquer, Peter Flynn in The Plough and the Stars, Mr Lafauche in The Octoroon, Rosencrantz in Hamlet, Caesar in Androcles and the Lion, and The Bearded Man in The Dark Lady of the Sonnets; toured, July–Dec 1962, as Mr Sowerberry in the original American company of Oliver; US tour, July 1963–May 1964, played Signor Chapuye in A Man for All Seasons, during which tour he appeared at the City Center, NY, Jan 1964; Stratford, Conn, June 1965, played Gremio in The Taming of the Shrew, and Sicinius Velutus in Coriolanus; Circle in the Square, Dec 1965, Camillo in The White Devil, later taking over as the Cardinal; Ypsilanti, Michigan, Greek Festival, June–Sept 1966, Aegisthus in The Oresteia and Neptune in The Birds; toured, Oct 1966–Jan 1967, as Fray Vincente de Valverde in The Royal Hunt of the Sun; Barter, Abingdon, Va, Mar–May 1967, Polonius in Hamlet and Fancourt Babberly in Charley's Aunt; New York Shakespeare Mobile Theatre, June 1967, Corbaccio in Volpone; Anspacher, Dec 1967, Ghost in a modern rock Hamlet; Henry Miller's, Feb 1968, Bishop of Durham and a Gentleman of the Press in Portrait of a Queen; Delacorte, Aug 1968, Prologue, Old Man, and Apothecary in Romeo and Juliet; Public, Mar 1969, Father-in-Law and the Minister of Opacity in Invitation to a Beheading; toured US and Canada, 1969–70, as Polonius and the Ghost in both Hamlet and Rosencrantz and Guildenstern Are Dead; Anspacher, Oct 1970, James Telfer in Trelawny of the 'Wells'; Studio Arena, Buffalo, NY, 1971, played Brabantio in Othello; Delacorte, July 1971, Friar Laurence and Antonio in Two Gentlemen of Verona, and repeated these parts at the St James, Dec 1971; joined the Yale Repertory, New Haven, Conn, and in Oct 1973 played Trinculo in The Tempest; Jan 1974, Claude Perkins in The Tubs; Mar 1974, Fingers in Geography of a Horse Dreamer; Mar 1975, Pastor in The Father; Apr 1975, Judge in The Shaft of Love; May 1975, Robin Starveling in A Midsummer Night's Dream; Nov 1975, Senor Domingo; Folger, Washington, Oct 1976, Lord Milton in The Fool; Feb 1977, Shooter O'Rourke in Mummer's End; Hartford Summer Stage, 1978, Argante in Scapino!, and Canon Chasuble in The Importance of Being Earnest; appeared in the film The Story of a Patriot as Thomas Jefferson; first appeared on television, 1951, in Lamp Unto My Feet, and has since appeared on *Omnibus, Armstrong Circle Theatre, Mr District Attorney,* etc.

Favourite parts: Shylock, Tybalt, Corbaccio, Fancourt Babberley, Lord Ogleby, and Androcles and Caesar in Androcles and the Lion. *Recreations:* Modelling historical figurines, and

renovating and restoring homes. *Address:* 548 La Guardia Place, New York, NY. *Tel:* GR 5-0791.

WASHBOURNE, Mona, actress
b Birmingham, 27 Nov 1903; d of Arthur Edmund Washbourne and his wife, Kate (Robinson); e Yardley Secondary School, Birmingham; m Basil Dignam; trained as a pianist at the Birmingham School of Music.

After some concert work and broadcasting, she made her first appearance on the stage at Yarmouth, 1924, with the Modern Follies concert party, as pianist and soubrette; subsequently toured with the Fol-De-Rols for three seasons in the same capacity; played a number of repertory seasons with various companies, including Harry Hanson's Court Players, Matthew Forsyth's Company, etc; made her first appearance in London at the Westminster, Nov 1937, as Minnie and Mrs Hills in Mourning Becomes Electra; during the war toured with the Malvern Company in a number of plays; Duchess, 1945, understudied and played Madam Arcati in Blithe Spirit; Lyric, May 1946, played Miss Barnes in The Winslow Boy; Arts, Oct 1947, Helen Poulter in Cupid and Mars; Saville, Nov 1947, Dorothy Pilkington in Honour and Obey; Duchess, Feb 1948, Mrs Poole in The Foolish Gentlewoman; Globe, Jan 1950, Mother in Ring Round The Moon; Duke of York's, Apr 1952, Mrs Bonamy in The Mortimer Touch; Lyric, Apr 1954, Mrs Osbourne in Hippo Dancing; Comedy, Dec 1955, Cora Swanson in Morning's At Seven; subsequently transferring to the Westminster, Feb 1956; Drury Lane, Nov 1956, Honorine in Fanny; made her first appearance in New York at the Belasco, Nov 1957, as Cherry-May Waterton in Nude With Violin; subsequently appeared in San Francisco and Hollywood for a season in the same play, alternating with Monica in Present Laughter; Cambridge, London, Sept 1960, played Alice Fisher in Billy Liar; Saville, Nov 1962, played Hilda Midway in Semi-Detached; Duke of York's, Apr 1966, Mum in The Anniversary; Nov 1967, with Prospect Productions, toured India, Pakistan and Ceylon for the British Council, as Mrs Tarleton in Misalliance; Royal Court, June, 1970, played Kathleen in Home, transferring to the Apollo in July, and to the Morosco, NY, Nov 1970; Queen's, Oct 1971, Enid Baker in Getting On; Prince of Wales, Apr 1975, Veta Louise Simmonds in Harvey; Vaudeville, Mar 1977, the Aunt in Stevie; principal films include The Winslow Boy, The Good Companions, Billy Liar, My Fair Lady, The Collector, Quilp, The Bluebird, Stevie, London Affair, etc; first appeared on television for Baird Television, 1929, subsequently playing in A Hundred Years Old, Dear Petitioner, Homecoming, Thérèse Raquin, etc.
Address: 15a Albert Court, London, SW7. *Tel:* 01-589 9767.

WATERHOUSE, Keith, dramatic author
b Leeds, Yorks, 6 Feb 1929; s of Ernest Waterhouse and his wife Elsie Edith (Spencer); e Leeds.

With Willis Hall was co-author of Billy Liar, which was produced at the Cambridge Theatre, London, Sept 1960; he is also the co-author (with Willis Hall) of the following plays: Celebration, 1961; England, Our England, All Things Bright and Beautiful, The Sponge Room (one-act), Squat Betty (one-act), 1962; Come Laughing Home, 1964; Say Who You Are, 1965; Joey, Joey, 1966; Children's Day, Whoops-A-Daisy, 1969; Who's Who, 1971; The Card (book), Saturday, Sunday, Monday (adaptation), 1973; Carte Blanche (contributor), 1976; Filumena (adaptation), 1978; the following plays have been produced in New York: Billy Liar, 1963; Squat Betty, The Sponge Room, 1964; and Help Stamp Out

Marriage (Say Who You Are), 1966; Saturday, Sunday, Monday, 1974; he has also written the following films: Whistle Down the Wind, A Kind of Loving, Billy Liar, Man in the Middle, etc.

Address: c/o London Management, 235 Regent Street, London W1.

WATERMAN, Dennis, actor
b Clapham, London, 24 Feb 1948; *s* of Harry Frank Waterman and his wife Rose Juliana (Saunders); *m* (1) Penny Waterman (mar dis); (2) Patricia Maynard; trained for the stage at the Corona Stage School.

First appeared as a child actor, May 1960, at the Shakespeare Memorial Theatre, Stratford-upon-Avon, as Mamillius in The Winter's Tale; first appeared on the London stage Mar 1961 at the Adelphi, as Winthrop Paroo in The Music Man; at the Haymarket, Sept 1964, played the Son in Carving a Statue; at the Royal Court, 1965–8, his parts included: Colin in Saved, Nov 1965; Nick in A Chaste Maid in Cheapside, Jan 1966; Potholer in The Performing Giant, 1966; Len in Early Morning, Apr 1968; Fabian in Twelfth Night, Jan 1968; Saville, Dec 1969; Paul in Enemy; Belgrade, Coventry, Feb 1976, title role in Alfie; Aldwych, Dec 1978, Robert Sackett in Saratoga; first film, 1959; other appearances include Up the Junction, My Lover, My Son, and Scars of Dracula; television, since Just William, 1960, includes: Sextet, The Sweeney (also filmed), Minder, and his own show—Dennis Waterman, With a Little Help from His Friends; has written and recorded his own songs.

Favourite part: Paul in Enemy. *Recreations:* Watching and playing football, music. *Address:* c/o ICM, 22 Grafton Street, London W1. *Tel:* 01–629 8080.

WATERS, Jan (Janet), actress and singer
b Bournemouth, 28 Jan 1937; *d* of Albert Edward Waters and his wife Florence May (Martin); *e* St Christopher's, Queensmount and Avonbourne Schools; *m* Peter Gilmore (mar dis); trained as a singer and appeared with the Bournemouth Symphony Orchestra.

Her stage début was as Cinderella in the pantomime of that name, Adelphi, 23 Dec 1960; at the Prince of Wales, Oct 1961, played Tilda Mullen in Do Re Mi; with the Bristol Old Vic company, 1962–3, played parts including Mary Grimaldi in Joey, Beatrice in Much Ado About Nothing, and Liz Rivet in Golden Rivet; Savoy, Nov 1964, Ruth Condomine in High Spirits; Bristol, May 1967, Linda in The Pursuit of Love; Apollo, Sept 1968, Polly Peachum in The Beggar's Opera; Piccadilly, Dec 1968, Miss Ethel Monticue in The Young Visiters; leading roles in repertory at Coventry and Edinburgh, 1969; toured, Feb 1970, for Cambridge Theatre Company as Doll Common in The Alchemist, and Eileen Midway in Semi-Detached; returned to Edinburgh, Apr 1970, to play Victoria in Trumpets and Drums; Garrick, Feb 1971, Vivien in Don't Start Without Me; Adelphi, Feb 1972, took over as Julie in Showboat; Shaw, Mar 1973, Eleanor in Only a Game; joined Prospect company, 1973, and toured as Oello in The Royal Hunt of the Sun, Maria in Twelfth Night, and Boult and Dionyza in Pericles, appearing in the latter production at Her Majesty's, June 1974; King's Head, Islington, Oct 1974, Carla in Kennedy's Children; Haymarket, Leicester, 1975, title role in Susanna Andler; spring 1976, toured Far East with Watford Palace Theatre playing Eliza in Pygmalion and Portia in Twelfth Night; Edinburgh Festival, 1977, played in Buster, transferring to the Old Vic, Sept 1977; Globe, Jan 1980, Queenie in Born in the Gardens; films, since Touch of Death in 1962, include Corruption; has appeared frequently on television since 1957, in plays and series.

Favourite parts: Polly Peachum and Victoria. *Recreation:* Tapestry. *Address:* c/o William Morris (UK) Ltd, 147–149 Wardour Street, London W1V 3TV.

WATERSTON, Samuel A, actor
b Cambridge, Massachusetts, 15 Nov 1940; *s* of George Chychele Waterston and his wife Alicia Tucker (Atkinson); *e* Groton School and Yale University; *m* Barbara Waterston (mar dis); (2) Lynn Woodruff; prepared for the stage at Yale and with John Berry at the American Actors Workshop in Paris, France, and with Herbert Berghof, Frank Corsaro, and at the Actors Studio.

First appeared on the stage at the Brooks Theatre, North Andover, Massachusetts, Winter, 1947, as the Page in Jean Anouilh's Antigone, in a production directed by his father; made his New York début at the Phoenix, 1962, when he took over as Jonathan in Oh Dad, Poor Dad, Mama's Hung You in the Closet and I'm Feelin' So Sad; Civic, Chicago, Apr 1963, again played Jonathan and subsequently toured; Morosco, NY, Apr 1963, again played Jonathan; Delacorte, July 1963, for the New York Shakespeare Festival, played Silvius in As You Like It; Gramercy Arts, Nov 1963, Wessey in Thistle in My Bed; New, 1964, took over from Roddy Maude-Roxby as Colin in The Knack, for which he was also stage manager, and repeated this part at the Huntington Hartford, Los Angeles; Circle in the Square, May 1966, Woodfin in Fitz; American Place, Mar 1967, Kent in La Turista; St Clement's Church, May 1967, Aburbio in Posterity for Sale; Playhouse in the Park, Cincinnati, Ohio, 1967, played in the American premiére of Henry Livings' Eh?; Brooks Atkinson, Nov 1967, Robert in Halfway up the Tree; Anspacher, Mar 1968, Aslan in Ergo; Provincetown Playhouse, Apr 1968, Jim in Red Cross and Jack Argue in Muzeeka; Delacorte, June 1968, Prince Hal in Henry IV, Parts I and II; Theatre de Lys, Mar 1969, Gary Rogers in Spitting Image; Brooks Atkinson, Oct 1969, John Grass in Indians; Chelsea, Brooklyn, and Brooklyn Academy of Music, Jan 1970, Phanocles in The Brass Butterfly; Lincoln Square, Apr 1970, Aaron in And I Met a Man; Helen Hayes, Nov 1970, Simon Bliss in Hay Fever; for the Phoenix Theatre, Jan 1971, Tom Lewis in The Trial of the Catonsville Nine; Lyceum, June 1971, again played Thomas Lewis in The Trial of the Catonsville Nine; Delacorte, Aug 1971, Cloten in The Tale of Cymbeline; Mark Taper Forum, Los Angeles, 1972, played in Volpone; New Theater for Now, Los Angeles, 1972, Oliver in A Meeting by the River; Delacorte, June 1972, Laertes in Hamlet and Aug 1972, Benedick in Much Ado About Nothing; Winter Garden, Nov 1972, again played Benedick in Much Ado About Nothing; Edison, Dec 1972, Oliver in A Meeting by the River; Mitzi E Newhouse, Feb 1974, Prospero in The Tempest; Vivian Beaumont, Mar 1975, Torvald Helmer in A Doll's House; Delacorte, June 1975, played Hamlet; Vivian Beaumont, Dec 1975, again played Hamlet; Delacorte, July 1976, Vincentio in Measure for Measure; Manhattan Theatre Club, Oct 1977, Phil in Chez Nous; Brooklyn Academy, May 1978, Vladimir in Waiting for Godot; first appeared in films in The Plastic Dome of Norma Jean, 1965, and since has played in Three, Fitzwilly, Generation, The Great Gatsby (1974), Rancho DeLuxe (1975), Sweet William (1979), etc; first appeared on television in 1964 and since has played on *NYPD, Dr Kildare,* Pound on *Camera Three,* Robert Lowell on Educational Television, The Good Lieutenant, Tom in The Glass Menagerie and Benedick in Much Ado About Nothing, 1973, etc.

Recreations: Ski-ing, guitar playing, poker. *Address:* Creative Management Associates, 600 Madison Avenue, New York, NY 10022. *Tel:* 935–4000.

WATFORD, Gwen, actress
b London, 10 Sept 1927; *d* of Percy Charles Watford and his wife Elizabeth (Cooper); *e* The Orchard School, St Leonards, Sussex; *m* Richard Bebb.

Made her first professional appearance at the White Rock Pavilion, Hastings, Mar 1944, as Florrie in Once A Gentleman; her London début was at the Embassy, Dec 1945, as Fenny in Dear Octopus; Winter Garden, May 1946, played Judith Drave in No Room at the Inn; St Martin's, Jan 1950, Jennifer in A Lady Mislaid; Haymarket, Oct 1955, Elisabeth in The Queen and the Rebels; Westminster, Jan 1959, Jane Pringle in The Woman on the Stair; Old Vic, season 1960–1, played the title role in Mary Stuart, Titania in A Midsummer Night's Dream, and Lady Percy in part one of Henry IV; Royal Court, June 1966, Mrs Evans in When Did You Last See My Mother?, transferring to the Comedy, July; New, Feb 1967, Margaret Schlegel in Howard's End; Fortune, Oct 1968, Violet Seedy in Come Sunday; toured, 1971, in The Constant Wife; Globe, July 1972, Emma Branksome in Parents' Day; Greenwich, Jan 1973, Masha in The Three Sisters; Thorndike, Leatherhead, Oct 1972, Helen Giles in Children! Children!; Palace, Watford, May 1974, Miss Moffatt in The Corn is Green; Greenwich, Oct 1974, Catherine de Troyes in Marching Song; Ludlow Festival, July 1976, Gertrude in Hamlet; Greenwich, June 1977, Mrs Baines in Singles; Hampstead, Feb 1978, Anne in Bodies, transferring to the Ambassadors, Apr 1979; has also played many leading roles in repertory; films, since 1961, include Cleopatra and The Very Edge; was twice named actress of the year for her work on television, which includes, recently, *Don't Forget to Write*.

Favourite parts: Mary Stuart, Margaret Schlegel. *Recreation:* The piano. *Address:* 22 Temple Fortune Lane, London, NW11. *Tel:* 01-455 5048.

WATLING, Dilys (*née* Rhys-Jones), actress
b Fulmer Chase, Buckinghamshire, 5 May 1946; *d* of Ian Rhys-Jones and his wife Patricia (Hicks); *e* St Mary's Convent, Woodford Green, Essex; *m* Bruce Charles Anderson (mar dis); trained for the stage at the Italia Conti Stage School.

First appeared on the stage in 1962 at the Hornchurch Repertory, Essex, as Tansy in Don't Tell Father; first appeared on the London stage in June 1963 at the Saville, as Mary in Pickwick; toured, Aug 1964, as The Girl in The Roar of the Greasepaint, the Smell of the Crowd; Shaftesbury, Dec 1964, Lady Agatha in Our Man Crichton; Sept 1965, Hilaret in the Bristol Old Vic's Lock Up Your Daughters; Her Majesty's, June 1967, took over Hodel in Fiddler On the Roof; made her New York début at the Winter Garden, Feb 1970, in the title role in Georgy; returning to London, took over Fran Kubelik in Promises, Promises at the Prince of Wales, Aug 1970; Her Majesty's, 1972, took over a part in Company; toured, Aug 1972, as Polly in She Was Only an Admiral's Daughter; toured S Africa, 1973, as Vicky in My Fat Friend; Hippodrome, Bristol, Dec 1973, played Aladdin; also Birmingham, Dec 1974; toured, Mar 1975, as Diana Lake in French Without Tears; toured Rhodesia and South Africa, 1977, in Rattle of a Simple Man; Phoenix, Mar 1978, Anne Boleyn in Kings and Clowns; Palladium, Dec 1978, title role in Aladdin; Quaglino's, July 1979, in Words and Music; Monte Carlo, Sept 1979, in Stepping Out with Mr Berlin; Bristol Old Vic, Dec 1979, Miss Adelaide in Guys and Dolls; television appearances include variety shows and series as well as plays.

Favourite parts: Georgy, Fran Kubelik. *Recreations:* Backing horses and cooking egg and chips. *Address:* c/o London Management, 235/241 Regent Street, London, W1. *Tel:* 01-734 4192.

WATLING, Jack, actor
b Chingford, Essex, 13 Jan 1923; *s* of Stanley Edward Watling and his wife Blanche Emily (Harnden); *m* Patricia Hicks; studied for the stage at the Italia Conti Stage School.

Made his first appearance at the Holborn Empire, Christmas 1935, as a Frog in Where the Rainbow Ends; at the same theatre, Christmas 1937, played William in the same play, and Christmas 1939, played St George; during 1940, played a season at Cambridge, with Donald Wolfit's company; New Theatre, Mar 1941, played Bill Hopkins in Once a Crook; Wyndham's, 1941, succeeded Thorley Walters as George Perrey in Cottage to Let; Apollo, Aug 1942, played Flight-Lieut Graham in Flare Path; during the latter part of the War, 1943–6, served in the RAF; Lyric, May 1946, appeared as Dickie Winslow in The Winslow Boy; Mercury, Aug 1947, played Percy Bysshe Shelley in The Shelley Story; subsequently engaged in films; reappeared on the stage at the Playhouse, Apr 1950, as Julian in The Green Bay Tree; first appeared in New York, at the Booth Theatre, 26 Oct 1950, as John in The Day After To-Morrow; at the Vaudeville, London, June 1951, appeared as Paul Tokarz in Come Live With Me; at the Q, Apr–May 1952, played Nicholas in Night of Masquerade, and Robert in And If I Laugh; Q, May 1953, John Fletcher in Shadow On the Sun; Royal, Brighton, Nov 1954, played Charlie Dover in Chandelier for Charlie; toured, July 1955, as Philip in Patience; Duchess, Mar 1956, played Martin Brentwood in Tabitha; at the Globe, May 1957 (for the Repertory Players), played Charles Brown in Cheque-Mate; toured, Nov 1958, as Roger Hewitt in Meet the Cousin; Palace, May 1959, played Michael Rawley in The World of Paul Slickey; toured, Sept 1959, as Lord Aldwych in Master of None; St Martin's, July 1962, Henry Walling in Brush With a Body; Royal, Windsor, Dec 1962, the title-part in Mother Goose; Sydney, Australia, Apr 1965, played Barry in Diplomatic Baggage; May 1967, toured in Waiting for Gillian; Leeds Festival, July–Aug 1968, directed The Game and Whose Baby?; Vaudeville, Mar 1970, took over Victor Cadwallader in The Man Most Likely To . . .; Savoy, May 1973, took over as Hubert Boothroyd in Lloyd George Knew My Father; Arnaud, Guildford, Oct 1974, and Piccadilly, Dec 1974, Philip Harrison in The Gentle Hook; directed a touring production of Two and Two Make Sex, Mar 1975; tour of She Won't Lie Down, Feb 1976; Arnaud, Guildford, July 1977, Brigadier Sir Hesketh de Langley in It Happened in Harrods; Belgrade, Coventry, Oct 1978, and tour as Philip in Six of One; has also presented seasons at Frinton, Walthamstow and elsewhere; first appeared in films, 1936, in Sixty Glorious Years; television appearances include The Power Game and The Cedar Tree.

Favourite part: Graham in Flare Path. *Club:* Green Room. *Address:* c/o Richard Stone, 18–20 York Buildings, London WC2. *Tel:* 01–839 6421.

WATSON, Douglass (*né* Larkin Douglass Watson III), actor
b Jackson, Georgia, 24 Feb 1921; *s* of Larkin Douglass Watson Jnr, and his wife Caroline (Smith); *e* University of North Carolina; *m* Eugenia Loaring-Clark; studied for the stage with Maria Ouspenskaya.

First appeared at the Harris Theatre, Chicago, May 1946, as Fenton in The Merry Wives of Windsor; toured, 1947, as Parritt in The Iceman Cometh; made his first appearance on the New York stage at the Martin Beck, 26 Nov 1947, as Eros in Antony and Cleopatra; Fulton, June 1948, took over the part of Captain Jenks in Command Decision; National, Oct 1948, Eugène in Leading Lady; Booth, Feb 1949, played Dorset in Richard III; Lyceum, Apr 1949, Richard Johnson in The Happiest Year; Martin Beck, Nov 1949, Rodrigo in

That Lady; Martin Beck, Mar 1950, Peter Whitfield in The Wisteria Trees; Broadhurst, Mar 1951, Romeo in Romeo and Juliet; at the Festival of Berlin, Sept 1951, appeared with Judith Anderson in Medea; ANTA Playhouse, NY, Jan 1952, Eban in a revival of Desire Under the Elms; Lyceum, Apr 1952, played Herbert Westman in The Brass Ring; Coronet, May 1952, Mike Decker in Sunday Breakfast; also toured, 1952, in Stalag 17; at the Central City Festival, Colorado, 1953, Don in The Time of the Cuckoo; Theatre de Lys, June 1953, played Lord Ravensbane in The Scarecrow; City Center, Nov 1953, Christian in Cyrano de Bergerac, and Dec 1953, Richmond in Richard III; Morosco, Feb 1954, played Colby Simkins in The Confidential Clerk; ANTA Playhouse, 1954, Ralph in Portrait of a Lady; Downtown National, Mar 1955, Valère in The Miser; Stanford University, June 1955, Hippolytos in The Cretan Woman and Kilroy in Camino Real; Longacre, Oct 1955, played Anthony Harker in The Young and Beautiful; John Golden, Mar 1956, played the Comte de Montfort in Little Glass Clock; at the Cambridge Drama Festival, Mass, July 1956, played the title-role in Henry V; Theatre de Lys, off Broadway, Feb 1957, played Golaud in Pelleas and Melisande, and Gregor in Metamorphosis (double-bill); in summer theatres, Sept 1957, appeared as the Narrator in Pale Horse, Pale Rider; at the Adelphi, NY, Dec 1957, took over the part of Mr Harcourt in The Country Wife; took over the part of Brian O'Bannion during the tour of Auntie Mame (Constance Bennett), 1958; at the Barbizon-Plaza, off Broadway, Apr 1959, played Jason Redwine in Season of Choice; toured, summer 1959, as Armand in Nina; Shakespeare Festival, Stratford, Conn, summer 1960, Leontes in The Winter's Tale and Canadius in Antony and Cleopatra; toured, Sept 1960–Feb 1961, as Lysander in A Midsummer Night's Dream and Leontes in The Winter's Tale; Stratford, Conn, Apr 1961, Orsino in Twelfth Night; San Diego Shakespeare Festival, June 1961, played the title-role in Richard III and Antonio in The Merchant of Venice; Gate, NY, Feb 1962, Bassanio in The Merchant of Venice; ANTA, June 1962, took over the part of Henry VIII in A Man for All Seasons; Stratford, Conn, summer 1963, Edmund in King Lear, Antipholus twins in The Comedy of Errors, and the Dauphin in Henry V; New York City Opera, Oct 1963, Brother Dominic in Jeanne d'arc au bûcher; Royale, Jan 1964, played Tarver in The Chinese Prime Minister; Stratford, Conn, summer 1964, Don Pedro in Much Ado About Nothing and the title-role in Richard III; University of Southern Florida, Nov 1964, Prospero in The Tempest; Billy Rose, Dec 1965, Arthur in Right Honourable Gentleman; Stratford, Conn, 1966, Brutus in Julius Caesar, Pistol in Falstaff, and a Knight in Murder in the Cathedral; Majestic, Jan 1967, Herald in Marat/Sade; University of Wisconsin, Feb 1967, Thomas More in A Man for All Seasons; Globe, San Diego, Cal, June 1967, Othello, and Parolles in All's Well That Ends Well; Helen Hayes, Jan 1968, Mr Perry and later, Teddy Lloyd in The Prime of Miss Jean Brodie; City Center, Apr 1968, Major-General Stanley in The Pirates of Penzance; toured, spring 1969, as Dylan Thomas in Dylan, and summer 1969, as Teddy Lloyd in The Prime of Miss Jean Brodie; Seattle Repertory, Oct 1969, Vershinin in The Three Sisters; toured, Jan–Apr 1970, as Victor in The Price; Mark Taper Forum, Los Angeles, July 1970, Dick in Los Angeles Under Siege; Seattle Repertory, Oct 1970, Buffalo Bill in Indians; Mark Taper Forum, June 1971, played in The Trial of the Catonsville Nine; Public Theater Annex, May 1972, Hunter in The Hunter; Delacorte, Aug 1972, Don Pedro in Much Ado About Nothing, and repeated this part at the Winter Garden, Nov 1972; Delacorte, June 1973, Duke Senior in As You Like It, and,

July 1973, Kent in King Lear; Shubert, Mar 1974, Norwin Spokesman in Over Here!; Circle Repertory, Dec 1975, Douglas North Wickstead in Dancing for the Kaiser; same theatre, Jan 1977, Wallace House in My Life; Eisenhower, Washington DC, Apr 1977, Marcus in The Archbishop's Ceiling; Hartman, Stamford, Jan 1978, Charles in The Middle Ages; Circle Repertory, Oct 1978, Frank in Glorious Morning; same theatre, Dec 1979, Claudius in Hamlet; has been guest lecturer at various universities, notably Connecticut in 1968 and Washington in 1970; first appeared in films 1952, in Julius Caesar, appeared in the films The Trial of the Catonsville Nine and Ulzana's Raid, 1972; appeared on television in Much Ado About Nothing, 1973, etc.

Favourite parts: Sefton in Stalag 17, André in Her Cardboard Lover, and Kilroy in Camino Real. *Hobby:* Collecting unusual recordings and sound effects.

WATTS, Richard, Jun, drama critic
b Parkersburg, W Virginia, 12 Jan 1898; *s* of Stephen Richard Watts and his wife Katharine (Reed); *e* Columbia University.

Commenced his career as a reporter on the Brooklyn *Times*, 1922–3; assistant night-editor *Herald-Sun* Syndicate, 1923–4; on the staff of the *New York Herald*, 1924; film critic to *New York Herald-Tribune*, 1924–36; drama critic *New York Herald-Tribune*, 1936–42; dramatic critic *Go*, 1945; drama critic *New York Post*, 1946–77; was press attaché of the US Legation in Dublin, 1942–3; editor-in-chief of the US Office of War Information in Chungking, China, 1943–4.

Address: 920 Fifth Avenue, New York, NY 10021.

WATTS, Stephen, author and dramatic critic
b Glasgow, 19 Sept 1910; *s* of William James Watts and his wife Isabella (Dickson); *e* North Kelvinside, Glasgow; *m* (1) Margaret Furse (dec); (2) Lady Helen Richards.

Film critic on *The Bulletin*, Glasgow, 1928–32; editor of *The Scottish Stage* magazine, 1931–4; critic and feature writer of *Film Weekly*, London, 1932–4; film and drama critic of the *Sunday Express*, London, 1934–9, and again 1945–9, the interval being occupied by war service (Major, King's Royal Rifle Corps); London film correspondent of the *New York Times*, 1949–69; television drama script editor (Rediffusion), 1960–2; consulting editor, The Bodley Head, 1970–present; author of Behind the Screen, 1938; The Pale Horse, 1943; The Sound of a Trumpet, 1946; Moonlight on a Lake in Bond Street, 1961; Sober and Properly Dressed, 1963; The Ritz, 1964; Chairman of the Film Section of the Critics' Circle, 1947–8; President of the Critics' Circle, 1953–4, and is a member of the Council.

Clubs: Savile, Garrick. *Address:* 20 Burton Court, London, SW3. *Tel:* 01–730 6484.

WAYNE, David (*né* Wayne James McMeekan), actor
b Traverse City, Michigan, 30 Jan 1914; *s* of David James McMeekan and his wife Helen (Mason); *e* Western Michigan College; *m* Jane Gordon Trix.

Made his first appearance on the stage with the Eldred Players, at the Globe Shakespearean Theatre, Cleveland Exposition, 1936, as Touchstone in As You Like It; first appeared in New York, at the 44th Street Theatre, 22 Apr 1938, walking-on in Escape This Night; Belasco, Oct 1938, played Harvey Bodine in Dance Night; Center, Jan 1939, Karl Gunther in The American Way; Fulton, Mar 1940, Jimmy Hanley in Scene of the Crime; Majestic, Aug 1943, Nish in The Merry Widow; Fulton, Feb 1944, Jonathan's Conscience in Peepshow; Shubert, Nov 1946, Mr Meacham in Park Avenue; 46th Street, Jan 1947, Og in Finian's Rainbow; Alvin, Feb 1948, Ensign Pulver in Mister Roberts;

Martin Beck, Oct 1953, Sakini in The Teahouse of the August Moon; Music Box, Feb 1956, Uncle Daniel Ponder in The Ponder Heart; Ambassador, Oct 1956, co-presented The Loud Red Patrick and also played Mr Finnegan; ANTA Playhouse, Apr 1958, Jack Jordan in Say, Darling; in summer theatre, Sept 1959, Felix in Marcus in the High Grass; toured, Dec 1959, as Juniper in Juniper and the Pagans; Morosco, Apr 1962, Sonny Stone in Venus at Large; 54th Street, Mar 1963, Private Meek in a revival of Too True to Be Good; State Fair, Dallas, Aug 1963, Bellac in Apollo and Miss Agnes; ANTA, Washington Square, Jan 1964, Chairman in After the Fall, Feb 1964, Kublai Khan in Marco Millions, Mar 1964, Brock Dunnaway in But for Whom Charlie, and Dec 1964, The Prince in Incident at Vichy; Alvin, Dec 1965, Ezra Baxter in The Yearling; Playhouse in the Park, Philadelphia, June 1966, Dr Jack Kingsley in The Impossible Years; NY State, July 1966, Captain Andy in Show Boat; Royal Poinciana Playhouse, Palm Beach, Florida, Jan 1967, again played in The Impossible Years; Broadway, Jan 1968, Grandpère Bonnard in The Happy Time; Ford's, Washington, DC, Mar 1972, appeared in the solo performance An Unpleasant Evening with H L Mencken; Bucks County Playhouse, New Hope, Pa, Sept 1972, Charlie Beddoes in Halloween; during the War, served as First Lieut, USARC, 1945–6; first appeared in films, 1946, in Portrait of Jenny; recent films include The Tender Trap, The Last Angry Man, The Big Gamble, Huckleberry Finn, and played Bensinger in The Front Page, 1974; first appeared on television in The Thousand Dollar Bill, 1948 and played Inspector Queen in the series *Ellery Queen,* 1975–6.

Recreations: Fishing, hunting, swimming, and horses. *Clubs:* Players, Lambs. *Address:* c/o Actors Equity Association, 165 West 46th Street, New York, NY 10036.

WEAVER, Fritz, actor

b Pittsburgh, Pa, 19 Jan 1926; *s* of John C Weaver and his wife Elsa Stringaro; *e* University of Chicago (BA 1952); studied at HB Studio, 1955–6; *m* Sylvia Short.

Joined the Barter Theatre, Abingdon, Va, and also toured with the company, 1952–4; in the summer of 1953 played with the Group 20 Players in Wellesley, Mass, in such roles as Petruchio in The Taming of the Shrew, Sir Francis Chesney in Charley's Aunt, Preacher in Dark of the Moon, Oberon in A Midsummer Night's Dream, Caesar in Androcles and the Lion, and Edward II in Carnival King; made his New York début at the Cherry Lane, off-Broadway, Oct 1954, where he played Fainall in The Way of the World; Phoenix, Jan 1955, a Secretary in The Doctor's Dilemma, and, Mar 1955, Flamineo in The White Devil; American Shakespeare Festival, Stratford, Conn, 1955, played Casca in Julius Caesar and Antonio in The Tempest; Ethel Barrymore, NY, Oct 1955, played Maitland in The Chalk Garden; Stratford, Conn, 1956, played Philip Faulconbridge in King John and Gremio in The Taming of the Shrew; Ambassador, NY, Dec 1956, Marc Bradley in Protective Custody; Music Box, Oct 1957, A Boy in Miss Lonelyhearts; Stratford, Conn, 1958, played Hamlet; Phoenix, off-Broadway, Oct 1958, played Harry, Lord Monchensey, in The Family Reunion, and, Dec 1958, The Priest in The Power and the Glory; Cambridge Drama Festival, Mass, June 1959, Malvolio in Twelfth Night; Coronet, Oct 1959, Dion Anthony in The Great God Brown; Phoenix, Jan 1960, the title-role in Peer Gynt, Mar 1960, the title-role of Henry IV (Part I), and Apr 1960, Henry IV (Part II); Cambridge Drama Festival, summer 1960, again played these last two roles; Queen Elizabeth, Vancouver, BC, Aug 1961, Mark in Men, Women and Angels; Winter Garden, Mar 1962, played Henderson in All American; Booth, sum-

mer 1962, took over from Walter Matthau as M Beaurevers in A Shot in the Dark; Plymouth, Feb 1963, Van Miessen in Lorenzo; Jones Beach Marine, summer 1963, Phileas Fogg in Around the World in 80 Days; Henry Miller, May 1964, played various parts in The White House; Broadway, Feb 1965, played Sherlock Holmes in the musical Baker Street; Mark Taper Forum, Los Angeles, June 1967, Frederick the Great in The Sorrows of Frederick; City Center, June 1968, Henry Higgins in My Fair Lady; Royale, Feb 1970, Jerome Malley in Child's Play, for which he received the Antoinette Perry (Tony) Award, the *Variety* Critics Poll, and the Drama Desk Award; Long Wharf, New Haven, Conn, May 1973, Patrick Power in Patrick's Day; Stratford, Conn, July 1973, played Macbeth; toured, summer 1974, as Father Day in Life with Father; Music Box, Mar 1975, took over from Richard Kiley as Ronald in Absurd Person Singular; Chelsea Theater Center, Nov 1976, appeared in a one-man play, Lincoln; Theater Four, May 1978, Sidney Kentridge in The Biko Inquest; Symphony Space, NY, Apr 1980, appeared in Dialogue for Lovers; has appeared in films, notably Fail-Safe, The Day of the Dolphin, Marathon Man (1977), etc; has appeared regularly on television since 1955, notably on *Kraft Television Theatre, US Steel Hour, Studio One,* in She Stoops to Conquer, A Tale of Two Cities, The Potting Shed, Jane Eyre, most recently in Holocaust, 1978, and The Martian Chronicles, 1980.

Address: Lucy Kroll Agency, 390 West End Avenue, New York, NY 10024.

WEBB, Alan, actor

b York, 2 July 1906; *s* of Major Thomas Francis Albertoni Webb and his wife Lili (Fletcher); *e* Bramcote School, Scarborough, and RN Colleges Osborne and Dartmouth; formerly in the Royal Navy.

Made his first appearance on the stage at the Century Theatre, Bayswater, Apr 1924, as Lawyer Hawkins in The Devil's Disciple, with the Lena Ashwell Players, with whom he remained until 1926; from 1926–8, was with J B Fagan's Oxford Players; in 1928, with the Masque Theatre Co, at Edinburgh and Glasgow; Strand, Nov 1928, played Dr Trewhawke in Out of the Sea, and Dec 1928, Doctor Parpalaid in Dr Knock; Queen's, Jan 1929, Ordulph in The Mock Emperor; from 1929–31, was engaged at the Liverpool Playhouse, with the Repertory Company; 1932–3, Croydon Repertory Company; Embassy, Apr 1933, played Marvin Holland in This One Man; Royalty, Apr 1933, Rev Arthur Bell Nicholls in The Brontës; Gate, Sept 1933, Bruno Pieri in As You Desire Me; Croydon Repertory, Oct–Dec 1933, Peter Mannoch in The Mannoch Family, and Edgar Linton in Wuthering Heights; Jan 1934, toured as the Earl of Oxford in Richard of Bordeaux; Sept 1934–May 1935, with the Old Vic-Sadler's Wells company; His Majesty's, May 1935, played Felix Cotton in Hervey House; Embassy, July 1935, Major Sergius Saranoff in Arms and the Man; at the Queen's, Aug 1935, for a time played Charles Tritton in The Wind and the Rain; in Oct 1935, toured with Noel Coward and Gertrude Lawrence in To-Night at 7.30, appearing in the group of one-act plays produced under that name; Phoenix, Jan 1936, appeared in the same plays when they were re-titled To-Night at 8.30, and also played in them at the National, New York, Nov 1936; Morosco, NY, Sept 1937, played Roger in George and Margaret; Haymarket, London, June 1938, Alan Crane in Comedienne; Wyndham's, Aug 1938, Dr Evan Jones in She, Too, Was Young; Savoy (for Repertory Players), Dec 1938, Caleb Deecie in Two Roses; Haymarket, Jan 1939, Ernest Friedman in Design for Living; served in HM Forces, 1940–5; reappeared on the London stage, at the Duchess, Nov 1945, when he took over the part of Charles Condomine in Blithe Spirit; Wyndham's, Apr 1946, appeared as Michael Wentworth in The Years Between; Lyric, Hammersmith, Mar 1947, directed The Rossiters; Lyric, July 1947, directed Peace In Our Time; Empire, NY, Oct 1947, played Arthur Winslow in The Winslow Boy, and toured in this in the United States from May–Dec 1948; Apollo, London, Sept 1949, played Hercules Ryall in Treasure Hunt; Haymarket, Mar 1951, appeared as Sir Timothy Bellboys in A Penny For a Song; New, May 1951, played Polonius in Hamlet; at the Edinburgh Festival, 1951, appeared as Henry Higgins in Pygmalion; at the Royale, NY, Dec 1951, played Adolphe in Nina; after returning to England, toured, 1952, as Henry Blessington in Adam's Apple; Morosco, NY, Nov 1952, played William Collyer in The Deep Blue Sea; at the Edinburgh Festival, Aug 1953, played Eggerson in The Confidential Clerk, and appeared in this part at the Lyric, London, Sept 1953; Apollo, June 1954, played Sir George Treherne in Both Ends Meet; joined the Shakespeare Memorial Theatre Company, Stratford-on-Avon, 1955, and during the season appeared as Sir Toby Belch in Twelfth Night, the King of France in All's Well That Ends Well, and Marcus Andronicus in Titus Andronicus; Lyric, Hammersmith, Feb 1956, Lord Summerhayes in Misalliance; Lyric, Apr 1956, Punalo Alani in South Sea Bubble; toured Europe, May 1957, as Marcus Andronicus in Titus Andronicus, subsequently appearing in the same part at the Stoll, London, July 1957; Henry Miller, NY, Dec 1957, played Dr Henry Maartens in The Genius and the Goddess; St Martin's, London, Apr 1958, Inspector Davies in Something to Hide; Royal Court, Aug 1958, Andrew Undershaft in Major Barbara; Piccadilly, Oct 1958, Janos Kadar in Shadow of Heroes; toured, Jan 1959, as Charles in The Coast of Coromandel; Criterion, Apr 1959, followed Wilfrid Hyde-White as Andrew Bennett in Not in the Book; Billy Rose, NY, Oct 1959, Mazzini Dunn in Heartbreak House; Royal Court, London, Apr 1960, Duddard in Rhinoceros; Royale, NY, Dec 1961, played Nonno in The Night of the Iguana; Royal Shakespeare, Stratford-on-Avon, Nov 1962, the Earl of Gloucester in King Lear, subsequently appearing in the same production at the Aldwych, Dec 1962; at the same theatre, with the Royal Shakespeare Company, Jan 1962, played Ernst Heinrich Ernesti in The Physicists; Sept 1963, Pope Pius XII in the Representative; Royale, NY, Jan 1964, played Bent in The Chinese Prime Minister; Globe, London, May 1965, again played Bent in The Chinese Prime Minister; Helen Hayes, NY, Jan 1966, William Uggins in UTBU; Barrymore, NY, Oct 1966, Uncle Julian in We Have Always Lived in the Castle; Royal Court, London, Apr 1967, Chebutykin in The Three Sisters; Longacre, NY, Jan 1968, Tom Garrison in I Never Sang For My Father; Royal Court, May 1973, Evens in The Sea; joined the National Theatre company, 1974, and played Willy in Happy Days; 1975, Foldal in John Gabriel Borkman; Lyric, Apr 1977, Hawkins in The Kingfisher; recent films include The Taming of the Shrew, Women in Love, Entertaining Mr Sloane, Nicholas and Alexandra, and The Last Great Train Robbery.

Recreations: Reading and gardening. *Address:* Shepherd's Cottage, 18 Shepherd's Hill, Haslemere, Surrey.

WEIDMAN, Jerome, playwright, librettist, novelist

b New York City, 4 Apr 1913; *s* of Joseph Weidman and his wife Annie (Falkovitz); *e* Washington Square College, College of the City of New York, New York University Law School; *m* Elizabeth Ann Payne; formerly an accountant; made his début as a dramatist, as co-librettist and co-author with George Abbott of Fiorello! presented at the Broadhurst,

23 Nov 1959, and for which he received the Pulitzer Prize, the Antoinette Perry (Tony) Award, and the New York Drama Critics Circle Award; with George Abbott wrote the book for Tenderloin, 1960; wrote the book for the musical I Can Get It for You Wholesale, which was based on his novel of the same name; wrote Cool Off! produced in Philadelphia, 1964; wrote the book for Pousse-Cafe, 1966; with James Yaffe wrote Ivory Tower, produced at the Lydia Mendelssohn, Ann Arbor, Michigan, 1967; wrote The Mother Lover, 1969; wrote his first film in 1950, and among his screenplays may be mentioned The Damned Don't Cry, House of Strangers, I Can Get It for You Wholesale; wrote the television series *The Reporter,* 1964; among his novels are What's in It for Me?, 1938, I'll Never Go There Any More, 1940, The Price Is Right, 1949, The Hand of the Hunter, 1950, Give Me Your Love, 1951, Before You Go, 1960, The Sound of Bow Bells, 1962, Word of Mouth, 1964, Other People's Money, 1969, Tiffany Street, 1974, A Family Fortune, 1978, Of Counsel, 1980, etc; is a prolific short story writer, and among his collections are The Horse That Could Whistle Dixie, 1939, The Captain's Tiger, 1950, My Father Sits in the Dark, 1961, The Nine Stories, 1964; author of the travel book Letter of Credit, 1940; wrote the books of essays Traveller's Cheque, 1951, and Back Talk, 1963; is President of the Authors League of America, Inc, 1969–75.

Addresses: 1390 South Ocean Boulevard, Pompano Beach, Florida 33062. *Tel:* 305–782–5481, *and* c/o Brandt and Brandt, 1501 Broadway, New York, NY 10036.

WEIDNER, Paul, director and producer

b 29 Mar 1934; *s* of Paul Russell Weidner and his wife Joanna (Powers); *e* College of Charleston (BA 1955), University of Besançon, France and Yale University School of Drama (MFA 1962).

Made his acting debut at the Martinique, 7 Mar 1963, in Six Characters in Search of an Author; gained early experience as actor and director in New York, and with the Asolo Theatre, Sarasota, Fla, and the Hartford Stage Company, Hartford, Conn, 1963–68; at Hartford, 1967, directed his translation of The Servant of Two Masters; Producing Director of Hartford Stage since 1968, where he had directed productions which include The Seagull, The Waltz Invention, A Delicate Balance, The Trial, Scapino (own translation), 1969; Rosencrantz and Guildenstern Are Dead, 1970; A Gun Play, The Boys in the Band, 1971; Rooted, Tiny Alice, Le Misanthrope, 1972; Nightlight, Old Times, My Sister, My Sister, 1973; Ubu Roi (also translated), A Touch of the Poet, School for Scandal, The Hot 1 Baltimore, The Cherry Orchard, 1974; Afternoon Tea, Room Service, All Over, 1975; The Estate, The Blood Knot, Waltz of the Toreadors, 1976; A History of the American Film, All the Way Home, Past Tense, 1977; Rain, Wedding Band, 1978; Galileo, Bonjour là Bonjour, 1979; My Sister, My Sister was produced on Broadway in 1974, where he again directed it; has also directed for the Williamstown Festival, Milwaukee Rep, etc; for WNET TV, 1975 directed, All Over.

Address: 17 Haynes Street, Hartford, CT 06103. *Tel:* 203–525 5601.

WEISS, Marc B, producer, director, stage manager and designer

Began his career in Washington DC, where his early work included scenery for the Washington Ballet and the Arena Stage; has since designed for regional and stock companies including the PAF Playhouse and Stage West; best known on Broadway as a lighting designer, he has been responsible for many productions including 6 rms riv vu, 1972; Find Your

Way Home, Cat on a Hot Tin Roof, Words and Music, 1974; Hughie/Duet, 1975; The Eccentricities of a Nightingale, 1976; Ladies at the Alamo, 1977; Deathtrap, 1978; Once a Catholic, 1979; has directed resident and stock productions including, recently, The Mousetrap, Stage West, 1979.

Address: 225 West 90th Street, New York, NY 10024. *Tel:* 877–6750.

WEISS, Peter, dramatic author
b Nowawes, Berlin, 8 Nov 1916; *s* of Eugen Weiss and his wife Frieda (Hummel); *e* Berlin, and the Art Academy, Prague; *m* Gunilla Palmstierna; formerly a painter.

His first play to be produced was Der Turm, Stockholm 1948; wrote Die Versicherung, 1952, produced in Göteborg, 1966; Nacht mit Gästen at the Schiller Theatre, Berlin, in Oct 1962; his play, Die Verfolgung und Ermordung Jean Paul Marats dargestellt durch die Schauspielgruppe des Hospizes zu Charenton unter Anleitung des Herrn de Sade, was also produced at the Schiller Theatre, Berlin, in 1964, subsequently being produced by the Royal Shakespeare Company at the Aldwych, London, Aug 1964, under the title of The Persecution and Assassination of Marat as Performed by the Inmates of the Asylum of Charenton under the Direction of the Marquis de Sade (Marat/Sade); author of The Investigation, 1965; Song of the Lusitanian Bogey, 1969; Hölderlin, 1971; Der Prozess (from Kafka) 1975; made a number of documentary and experimental films in Sweden, 1952–8, including The Mirage, 1958; radio scripts include Gespräch der Drei Gehenden (Talk of Three Walking Men).

Address: Suhrkamp Verlag, Lindenstr 29–35, 6 Frankfurt/Main, West Germany.

WELCH, Elisabeth, actress and singer
b New York City, 27 Feb 1909; *d* of John Wesley Welch and his wife Elisabeth (Kay); *e* New York public schools and Julia Richman High School; formerly engaged as a social worker.

Made her first appearance on the stage at the Liberty Theatre, New York, May 1928, in the revue Blackbirds of 1928, which was followed by an engagement at the Moulin Rouge, Paris; Broadway Theatre, NY, Jan 1931, appeared in The New Yorkers; made her first appearance in London, at the Leicester Square Theatre, June 1933, playing in the revue Dark Doings; Adelphi, Oct 1933, played Haidee Robinson in Nymph Errant; appeared at the Palladium, Mar 1934, and in variety theatres until Mar 1935; Drury Lane, May 1935, played Cleo Wellington in Glamorous Night; Victoria Palace, Sept 1936, in Let's Raise the Curtain; Saville, Nov 1937, in It's In The Bag; Opera House, Blackpool, June 1938, in All the Best; Haymarket, Mar 1941, played Clementine in No Time for Comedy; Phoenix, June 1942, appeared in Sky High; accompanied John Gielgud and company to Gibraltar and Malta, Jan 1943, entertaining HM Forces; Opera House, Blackpool, 1943 season, in We're All In It; Phoenix, Nov 1943, Josie in Arc de Triomphe; Palladium, Oct 1944–May 1946 appeared in Happy and Glorious; Lyric, Hammersmith, Sept and Globe, Oct 1947, appeared in the revue Tuppence Coloured; Lyric, Hammersmith, Nov 1948, and Globe, Jan 1949, appeared in the revue Oranges and Lemons; St Martin's, June 1951, in the revue Penny Plain; Saville, Dec 1954, in the revue Pay the Piper; toured the Middle East 1955, entertaining HM Forces; Cambridge, Sept 1959, appeared as Sweet Ginger in The Crooked Mile; Garrick, London, Dec 1962, played Mr Smith, Esmee, Lovable Fairy Godmammy, and Major Domo in Cindy Ella, or I Gotta Shoe; New Arts, Dec 1963, again played in Cindy-Ella (re-titled); Arnaud, Guildford, Oct 1966, appeared in Night Is for Delight; Wavendon Festival, 1970, took part in Tribute to Gershwin;

Hampstead Theatre Club, Dec 1970, appeared in her one-woman show A Marvellous Party; Arnaud, Guildford, Sept 1970, and tour, appeared in The Sweetest Sounds; Her Majesty's, Oct 1973, played Berthe in Pippin; Arnaud, May 1974, appeared in the revue, Now and Then; Criterion, Nov 1976, in I Gotta Shoe; Country Cousin Theatre Restaurant, July 1979, in Elisabeth Welch Gala evenings; Lyric, Hammersmith, Dec 1979, Fatimah in Aladdin; has frequently appeared in radio and television plays; commenced film career, 1934, in Death at Broadcasting House and has since appeared in numerous pictures, most recently in Revenge of the Pink Panther and The Tempest; has also appeared in cabaret in New York, Paris, Hong Kong and London.

Recreations: Reading, travel, and the theatre. *Address:* c/o Spotlight, 43 Cranbourn Street, London WC2H 7AP.

WELDON, Duncan Clark, Producing manager
b Southport, Lancs, 19 Mar 1941; *s* of Clarence Weldon and his wife Margaret Mary (Andrew); *e* King George V School, Southport; *m* (1) Helen Shapiro (mar dis); (2) Janet Mahoney; formerly a photographer.

Presented his first production, A Funny Kind of Evening with David Kossoff, at the Theatre Royal, Bath, Mar 1965; has since presented a large number of productions in London and on tour, in many parts of the world, principally with Triumph Theatre Productions, the company he founded in 1970 with Paul Elliott and Richard Todd; London productions include When We Are Married, 1970; The Chalk Garden, Big Bad Mouse, 1971; Bunny, 1972; Grease, The King and I, 1973; Dead Easy, Brief Lives (Broadway), 1974; The Case in Question, Hedda Gabler (with RSC), Dad's Army, Betzi, On Approval, 1975; 13 Rue de L'Amour, A Bedfull of Foreigners, Three Sisters, The Seagull, Fringe Benefits, The Circle, 1976; Separate Tables, Stevie, Hedda Gabler, On Approval, The Good Woman of Setzuan, Rosmersholm, The Apple Cart, Laburnum Grove, 1977; Waters of the Moon, King and Clowns, The Travelling Music Show, A Family, Look After Lulu, The Millionairess, 1978; The Crucifer of Blood, 1979; Reflections, 1980; co-producer of the film Hedda Gabler, 1975; first TV production, Big Bad Mouse, 1971.

Recreation: Photography. *Clubs:* Green Room, MacReady's. *Address:* The Griffins, Abinger Hammer, Surrey. *Tel:* Dorking 730444.

WELLER, Michael, playwright
b New York, 24 Sept 1942; *s* of Paul Weller and his wife Rosa (Rush); *e* Brandeis University, Massachusetts (BA 1965) and Manchester University.

Author of How Ho-Ho Rose and Fell (also music), produced at Manchester U, 1966; subsequent work includes Happy Valley, Edinburgh Festival fringe, 1969; The Body Builders, and Now There's Just the Three of Us (one-acts), Open Space, 1969; Cancer, Royal Court, Sept 1970, produced in the US as Moonchildren and seen on Broadway at the Royale, Feb 1972; Grant's Movie, Tira Tells Everything There Is to Know about Herself (one-acts), 1971; co-wrote lyrics (with Jim Steinman) for a musical, More than You Deserve, 1973; wrote Twenty-Three Years Later, produced LA 1973; Fishing, 1975; Split (one-act), 1978; Loose Ends, 1979; Dwarfman, 1980; his screenplays include Hair, 1979; Ragtime, 1980.

Address: c/o Howard Rosenstone, 850 Seventh Avenue, New York, NY 10019.

WENHAM, Jane, (*née* Figgins), actress
b Southampton, 26 Nov; *d* of Arthur Percival Figgins and his

wife Dorothy Mary (Wenham); *m* Albert Finney (mar dis); trained for the stage at the Central School of Speech and Drama, where she won a Gold Medal.

Made her first professional appearance with the Old Vic company at the New, Sept 1945, walking on in Henry IV, Part I; played other small parts that season, and made her New York début with the company at the Century, May 1946; Piccadilly, Sept 1946, Gladys in The Skin of Our Teeth; at Bristol, 1947–9, played juvenile leads with the Bristol Old Vic company, including Juliet, Ophelia, Desdemona and Vera in A Month in the Country; returned to the London Old Vic company at the New, to play Pimple in She Stoops to Conquer, Oct 1949; Katya in A Month in the Country, Nov 1949; Mariane in The Miser, Jan 1950; when the company returned to the Old Vic, she played Hermia in A Midsummer Night's Dream, Dec 1951, touring South Africa in the part, 1952, also playing second witch in Macbeth; Old Vic, Jan 1953, Nerissa in The Merchant of Venice; Westminster, July 1954, Donna Louisa in The Duenna; Duke of York's, July 1955, Ann in Wild Thyme; Arts, Mar 1956, Luciana in a musical Comedy of Errors; Lyric, Dec 1956, Margaret Kyle in Grab Me a Gondola; Stratford-upon-Avon, season 1957, played Celia in As You Like It, Calphurnia in Julius Caesar, and Iris in The Tempest; Mermaid, Apr 1963, Amanda in Virtue in Danger, transferring to the Strand, June 1963; Arts, Feb 1964, Mrs Elvsted in Hedda Gabler, transferring to the St Martins; Bristol Old Vic, 1967, played Sister Jeanne in The Devils and Maggie in The Italian Girl, transferring in the latter production to Wyndham's, Feb 1968; joined the National Theatre company at the Old Vic, 1968; her parts have since included Mrs Jones-Parry in H, Mrs Marwood in The Way of the World, Isabella in The White Devil, 1969; Mrs Yepanchin in The Idiot, Lise Ragueneau and Mother Superior in Cyrano, 1970; Tart and Frau Kessler in The Captain of Köpenick, Kate Blake in Tyger (New Theatre), Landlady in The Good-Natured Man, 1971; Young Vic, 1972, Jocasta in Oedipus; Haymarket, Oct 1972, The Princess Royal in Crown Matrimonial; returned to the National Theatre, Aug 1974, to take over the part of Dora Strang in Equus, repeating the part at the Albery, Apr 1976; Northcott, Exeter, Apr 1978, title role in Stevie, and May 1978, Catherine of Braganza in Good King Charles' Golden Days; Queen's, Apr 1980, Her Ladyship in The Dresser; films, since 1954, include An Inspector Calls, Make Me an Offer, and The Teckman Mystery; television, since 1950, includes Porridge, The Last of the Summer Wine, Enemy at the Door and Testament of Youth; spent two years with BBC Drama Repertory Company, 1965–7.

Favourite parts: Juliet, Desdemona, Sister Jeanne. *Recreation:* Sculpture. *Address:* c/o Michael Anderson, ICM, 22 Grafton Street, London W1X 3LD.

WESKER, Arnold, dramatic author
b Stepney, London, 24 May 1932; *s* of Joseph Wesker and his wife Leah (Perlmutter); *e* Upton House Central, Hackney; *m* Doreen Bicker; formerly a furniture-maker's apprentice, carpenter's mate, bookseller's assistant, plumber's mate, farm labourer, kitchen porter, and pastrycook; served in the RAF, 1950–2.

Author of the following plays: Chicken Soup With Barley, 1958; Roots, The Kitchen, 1959 (film script, 1961); I'm Talking About Jerusalem, 1960; Chips With Everything, The Nottingham Captain (play with music), 1962; Their Very Own and Golden City, 1964; The Four Seasons, 1965; The Friends, 1970; The Journalists (written), 1971; The Old Ones, 1972; The Wedding Feast, 1974; The Merchant, 1976;

Love Letters on Blue Paper (adapted from his own short stories), Fatlips (also book), 1978; has directed The Four Seasons, Havana, 1968; The Friends, Stockholm and London, 1970; The Old Ones, Munich, 1973; Their Very Own and Golden City (revised version), Aarhus, 1974; The Merchant, 1976; Love Letters on Blue Paper, London, 1978, Oslo, 1980; The Merchant, Canada, 1980; other work includes: two more books of short stories (Six Sundays in January, and Said the Old Man to the Young Man); the collection Fears of Fragmentation; the TV play Menace, and the television adaptation of Love Letters on Blue Paper; received the *Evening Standard* Award as the Most Promising British Playwright, 1960; received (with John Arden) the Encyclopedia Britannica Award, 1961; received the Marzotta Prize for the best unproduced play, 1964, with Their Very Own and Golden City; Artistic Director of Centre 42, 1961–70; Chairman of the International Theatre Institute (British Section), and Co-President of its International Playwrights Committee.

Address: c/o Robin Dalton, 91 Regent Street, London W1R 8RU.

WESLEY, Richard, playwright, and screenwriter
b Newark, New Jersey, 11 Jul 1945; *s* of George Richard Wesley and his wife Gertrude; *e* Howard University (BFA 1967) and Black Theatre Workshop, Harlem; *m* Valerie Wilson.

First play to be produced was The Black Terror, seen at the Public, NY, 1971; has since written The Past Is the Past, The Sirens, 1974; The Mighty Gents, 1977, presented at the Ambassador, NY, 1978; On the Road to Babylon (book), 1979; screenplays include Uptown Saturday Night, 1974, and Let's Do It Again, 1975.

Address: Apt 307, 70 South Munn Avenue, East Orange, NJ 07018.

WEST, Lockwood, actor
b Birkenhead, Cheshire, 28 July 1905; *s* of Henry Cope West and his wife Mildred (Hartley); *e* Colet Court School, and St Paul's School, London; *m* Olive Carleton-Crowe; formerly employed with Doncaster Collieries Association.

He made his first appearance on the stage at the Hippodrome, Margate, July 1926, as Lieut Allen in Alf's Button; for the next five years toured extensively, making his first appearance on the London stage at the Queen's Theatre, 1931, when for two weeks he played Henry Bevan in The Barretts of Wimpole Street; between 1932–9, appeared in repertory seasons at Bristol Little Theatre, Edinburgh, Coventry, etc; served in the Police War Reserve in Bristol, 1940–5; Westminster, Apr 1952, took over the part of Mr Toobad in Nightmare Abbey; Globe, Mar 1953, played Dr Macgregor in The White Carnation; Haymarket, Nov 1953, played Humphrey Caldwell in A Day by the Sea, which ran for nearly a year; Wimbledon, July 1955, played the Agent de Police in Nina, subsequently appearing in the same production at the Haymarket, July 1955; Winter Garden, Nov 1956, played Major Swindon in The Devil's Disciple; Globe, Feb 1958, John Callifer in The Potting Shed; at the same theatre, June 1959, played William Howard in The Complaisant Lover; Theatre Royal, Bristol, Mar 1961, played M Damiens in The Rehearsal, subsequently appearing in the same production at the Globe, London, Apr 1961, and later transferring with the play to the Queen's and Apollo theatres; Queen's, Feb 1963, played Oscar Nelson in Mary, Mary; Grand, Leeds, June 1964, played Ferguson in Wanted on the Voyage; Mermaid, July 1966, played Elliott in He Was Gone When They Got There; Royal, Windsor, 1969, appeared in

The Masters and The Right Honourable Gentleman; Shaw Festival, Niagara-on-the-Lake, 1973, the Emperor in The Brass Butterfly; Drury Lane, May 1974, Councillor Duxbury in Billy; Royal Exchange, Manchester, Sept 1976, Reggie in The Ordeal of Gilbert Penfold, and again at the Round House, Feb 1979; Cottesloe, 1978, took over Jones in Half-Life, repeating the part at the Duke of York's, Mar 1978, and then touring, including Toronto; Royal Exchange, Manchester, Mar 1980, Geoffrey Thornton in The Dresser, transferring to the Queen's Apr; entered films, 1948, and appearances include: Dandy in Aspic, Life at the Top, Bedazzled, and Jane Eyre; since 1948, has also appeared in numerous television productions including: *The Power Game, The Newcomers, Brett, No Hiding Place, Big Brother, The Pallisers*, Upstairs, Downstairs, Raffles, and Disraeli; since 1937, he has broadcast in nearly 3,000 radio programmes.

Favourite parts: Oscar Nelson in Mary, Mary, William in The Complaisant Lover, and Jones in Half-Life. *Recreations:* Motoring, cycling, walking. *Hobbies:* Paddle steamers. *Club:* Green Room. *Address:* Port Hall Cottage, 170A Dyke Road, Brighton, Sussex. *Tel:* 0273–551472.

WEST, Mae, actress and author

b Brooklyn, New York, 17 Aug 1892; *d* of John West and his wife Matilda (Delker-Doelger); *e* Brooklyn; *m* Frank Wallace (mar dis).

Has been on the stage from early childhood, and made her first professional appearance at the Gotham Theatre, Brooklyn, 1897, with Hal Clarendon's stock company; she appeared in various stock companies until 1903, playing such juvenile parts as Little Nell in Little Nell the Marchioness, Lovey Mary in Mrs Wiggs of the Cabbage Patch, the Angel Child in Ten Nights in a Bar Room, Willie Carlyle in East Lynne, Jessie in The Fatal Wedding, etc; subsequently spent several years in vaudeville; she appeared at the Folies Bergère, NY, Sept 1911, as Maggie O'Hara in A La Broadway; at the Winter Garden, Nov 1911, played Mdlle Angélique in Vera Violetta; Moulin Rouge, Apr 1912, La Petite Daffy in A Winsome Widow; San Francisco, July 1913, played Maria Tamburri in Such Is Life; in 1913, appeared on the vaudeville stage, where she remained some years; at the Shubert Theatre, Oct 1918, played Mayme Dean in Sometime; at the Capitol, Nov 1919, in Ned Wayburn's Demi-Tasse revue; at the Century Promenade, Aug 1921, played in The Mimic World; at Daly's, Apr 1926, played Margie La Mont in Sex; Nov 1927, Evelyn Carson in The Wicked Age; Royale, Apr 1928, Diamond Lil in her play of that name; Royale, Sept 1931, Babe Gordon in The Constant Sinner; reappeared on the NY stage, after thirteen years in Hollywood, at the Shubert Theatre, Aug 1944, as Catherine in Catherine Was Great; toured on the Pacific Coast, May 1946, in Ring Twice To-Night; made her first appearance in London at the Prince of Wales, 24 Jan 1948, as Diamond Lil, in her play of that name; Coronet, NY, Feb 1949, again played Diamond Lil, and toured in this, 1949–50; Broadway, NY, Sept 1951, again played Diamond Lil; in summer theatres, 1952, appeared as Carliss Dale in Come On Up . . . Ring Twice!; July 1961, toured as Marlo Manners in her play Sextet; Masquers Club, Hollywood, 14 Apr 1973, appeared in the one-woman show Mae Day; Saints and Sinners, Stardust Auditorium, Las Vegas, Nevada, Apr 1974, appeared in Sex Symbol Battle of the 30's; entered films, 1932, appearing in Night After Night; in 1933, she adapted and appeared in the screen version of Diamond Lil, under the film title She Done Him Wrong; subsequent pictures include I'm No Angel, 1933; Belle of the Nineties, 1934; Goin' to Town, 1935; Klondike Annie, 1936; Go West Young Man,

1936; Every Day's a Holiday, 1937; My Little Chickadee, 1940; The Heat's On, 1943; The Love Goddesses, 1965; Myra Breckenridge, 1970; Sextette, 1979; she has also appeared on television in Mister Ed, 1964; she is the author of Sex, 1926; The Wicked Age, The Drag, 1927; Diamond Lil, Pleasure Man, 1928; The Constant Sinner (from her own novel), 1931; I'm No Angel, 1933; Catherine Was Great, 1944; Sextet, 1961; part author of Clean Beds, 1939; her autobiography Goodness Had Nothing to Do With It, published 1959, revised, 1970; The Pleasure Man published as a novel, 1975; in 1954, 1955, 1956, and 1959, toured in cabaret; has produced several of her own plays and films.

Address: c/o William Morris Agency Inc, 151 El Camino, Beverly Hills, Calif.

WEST, Timothy, actor and director

b Bradford, Yorkshire, 20 Oct 1934; *s* of Harry Lockwood West, and his wife Olive (Carleton-Crowe); *e* John Lyon School and the Polytechnic, Regent Street; *m* Prunella Scales; formerly a recording engineer.

First appeared on the stage 12 Mar 1956, at the Wimbledon Theatre as The Farmer in Summertime; worked in repertory at Salisbury, Hull, Wimbledon and Northampton; first appeared in London, 22 May 1959 at the Piccadilly as Talky in Caught Napping; Mermaid, June 1960, played the Informer in The Life of Galileo; toured, 1961, as Colonel Gray-Balding in Simple Spymen; Arts, June 1962, Ginger in Afore Night Come; Queen's, Nov 1963, Hubert in Gentle Jack; Arts, May 1964, Arthur in The Trigon; joined the Royal Shakespeare Company, 1964, and at the Aldwych that year played Ginger in Afore Night Come, the Doctor in Victor, Schoolmaster in The Marat/Sade, Pilia-Borza in The Jew of Malta, Page in The Merry Wives of Windsor, and Sir Gilbert Boscoe in The Governor's Lady (Expeditions Two); at Stratford, season 1965, Sir Nathaniel in Love's Labour's Lost, Tubal in The Merchant of Venice, Pilia-Borza in The Comedy of Errors, and Lord Lucius in Timon of Athens; again at the Aldwych, 1966, Korobkin in The Government Inspector and Mulka in The Investigation; toured, autumn 1966, for Prospect, as Peterbono in Thieves' Carnival, Samuel Johnson in Madam, Said Doctor Johnson, Prospero in The Tempest, and Crabbe in The Gamecock; for the same company played Alderman Smuggler in The Constant Couple, New, June 1967; also Emerson in A Room With a View, Edinburgh Festival, 1967; Wyndham's, Feb 1968, Otto in The Italian Girl; toured for Prospect, 1969, as Bolingbroke in Richard II and Mortimer in Edward II; the productions were seen at Edinburgh, the Mermaid and the Piccadilly, also touring Europe; Wyndham's, Mar 1970, Gilles de Vannes in Abelard and Heloise; Edinburgh and tour (Prospect), Aug 1970, Don Pedro in Much Ado About Nothing and Samuel Johnson in Boswell's Life of Johnson; Mermaid, Nov 1970, Robert Hand in Exiles; Open Space, June 1971, Gilbert in The Critic as Artist; for Prospect played King Lear at the Edinburgh Festival and Venice Biennale of 1971; for the re-opening of the Theatre Royal, Bristol, Jan 1972, played Sir William Gower in Trelawny, before continuing as Lear and as Holofernes in Love's Labour's Lost on a tour of Australia and the UK and finally at the Aldwych; Bristol, Oct 1972, played Falstaff in both parts of Henry IV; appointed Artistic Director of the Forum Theatre, Billingham, spring 1973 season, directing We Bombed in New Haven, The National Health, and The Oz Trial, and playing Undershaft in Major Barbara; Open Space, June 1973, George Penny in The Houseboy; Chichester Festival, 1974, Shpigelsky in A Month in the Country; Gardner Centre, Brighton, autumn 1974, played the title role in Macbeth and

George in Jumpers, also directing The Homecoming; for the RSC, 1975, in Australia, USA and Canada, and at the Aldwych, July, played Judge Brack in Hedda Gabler; became co-director of the Prospect Theatre Co for their autumn 1975 season, again playing Shpigelsky, and Emerson in A Room with a View, on tour in Britain before coming to the Albery in November; Prospect Theatre Company tour, 1976, as Harry in Staircase; toured Germany, Middle East and UK, and at the Edinburgh Festival, and Old Vic, May 1977, playing Claudius in Hamlet, Storyteller in War Music and Enobarbus in Antony and Cleopatra; Royal Court, Jan 1978, Ivan/Gottlieb in Laughter!; Garrick, May 1978, Max in The Homecoming; Old Vic, June 1978, in Great English Eccentrics, followed by tour of Hong Kong and Australia, Feb 1979; Salisbury, July 1979, Sir Thomas Beecham in Beecham, and again played the part at the Apollo, Jan 1980; Old Vic, Nov 1979, directed and appeared in The Undisputed Monarch of the English Stage, and played Creeve in The Trial of Queen Caroline; Dec 1979, appointed Artistic Controller, Old Vic Theatre Company, responsible for its work in London, the regions and abroad; films, since The Deadly Affair, 1966, include Nicholas and Alexandra and Hedda; television, since 1959, includes Edward VII, Hard Times, Henry VIII, Crime and Punishment, and Churchill and the Generals; he is a frequent broadcaster, and has produced and appeared in recitals throughout the country; Member of the Arts Council Drama Panel 1974–6, and Touring Committee, 1978–; Board member of Platform Theatre Ltd, and the Apollo Society.

Favourite parts: Otto, Lear, Samuel Johnson. *Recreations:* Listening to music, travel, exploring old railways. *Address:* c/o Fraser and Dunlop Ltd, 91 Regents St, London, W1.

WESTBROOK, John, actor
b Teignmouth, Devon, 1 Nov 1922; *s* of Herbert Westbrook-St his wife Mabel Florence (Prudence); *e* Reigate Grammar School; *m* Beryl Hardy.

Made his first appearance on the stage at the Tonbridge Repertory Theatre, Dec 1939, as Edouard in Mademoiselle; at Tonbridge and at the Playhouse, Amersham, appeared in over two hundred plays; served for three years, 1943–6, in the RAF; made his first appearance in London at the Lyric, Hammersmith, 15 Oct 1946, as Lincoln's Ghost in The Assassin; at the Princes, July 1947, played The Emperor in The Nightingale; Q, Dec 1948, the Policeman and the Prince in A Kiss for Cinderella; Wyndham's, Feb 1949, Able-Seaman Owen Rivers in Sweethearts and Wives; Q, June 1949, Herr Punsch in Trifles Light as Air; St Martin's, Sept 1949, Christopher Dawlish in Summer Day's Dream; Gateway, Apr 1950, Geoffrey in Marshall's Aid; Q, May 1950, John in Forsaking All Others; toured, Feb 1951, as Larry Merrick in And Her Mother Came Too; New Bolton's, May 1951, appeared as Embury in A Pin to See the Peep Show; Lyric, Hammersmith, Apr 1952, played Lieut Zavala in Montserrat; at the Edinburgh Festival, 1952, played Major John Lang in The River Line, and appeared in this part at the Lyric, Hammersmith, Sept, and Strand, Oct 1952; at Ludlow Castle, June 1953, played the title-role in Comus; toured, Aug 1953, as Hans Wierck in The Gentle Rain; at the Q, Apr 1954, played Warwick in St Joan; Glyndebourne Opera House, Apr 1954, played St Richard in Like Stars Appearing; at the York Festival, June 1954, appeared in the York Mystery Plays; at the Q, Jan 1955, played David in The Evidence I Shall Give; at Ludlow Castle, July 1955, played Becket in Murder in The Cathedral; Lyric, Hammersmith, Feb 1956, played Joey Percival in Misalliance; at Ludlow Castle, July 1956, played the title-part in Edward II; Birmingham Repertory, July 1956, the title-part in Samson

Agonistes, subsequently playing the same part at the Edinburgh Festival, Aug 1956; Citizen's, Glasgow, Oct 1956, King Richard in Richard II; at the York Festival, June 1957, appeared in the York Mystery Plays; Ludlow Castle, July 1958 and 1959, played the title-part in Comus; Westminster Abbey, June 1960, Narrator in The Play of Daniel; Bristol Old Vic, Oct 1960, played Prospero in The Tempest; toured the US, Sept–Dec 1961, in the title-part of Coriolanus, and as Joseph Surface in The School For Scandal; Pro Musica Society of New York, Dec 1961, Narrator in The Play of Daniel; Lisner Theatre, Washington, DC, Jan 1962, Narrator in Stravinsky's Oedipus Rex; St George's Church, Stuyvesant Square, NY, Dec 1962, again appeared as the Narrator in The Play of Daniel, repeating his performance in Dec 1964, and subsequently appearing in the same play in Washington, DC, Jan 1965; Missenden Festival, Oct 1965, played the title part in Dr Faustus; York Festival, June 1966, Christ in the York Mystery Plays; Arnaud, Guildford, Mar 1967, Becket in Murder in the Cathedral; Festival Hall, May 1967, and Albert Hall, Aug, played the Evangelist in Penderecki's St Luke Passion; Mermaid, Feb 1968, the Narrator in The Black Girl in Search of God; Canterbury Festival, Sept 1970, again played Becket in Murder in the Cathedral; Lyceum, Edinburgh, Nov 1973, Don Pedro in Much Ado About Nothing; Library of Congress, Washington DC, Mar 1977, Speaker in An Oxford Elegy; has taken part in many poetry recitals all over the country, including his own solo programme The Ruling Passion; has made over two thousand broadcasts on sound radio and appeared in numerous television plays, and in films.

Favourite part: Samson. *Recreations:* Music and gardening. *Club:* Arts Theatre. *Address:* 43 Cleveland Square, London, W2.

WESTON, Jack, actor
Served in Europe in The US Army during World War II; prepared for the stage at the Cleveland, Ohio, Playhouse and at the American Theatre Wing, NY.

First appeared in New York at the Cort, 28 Sept 1950, as Michael Lindsey in Season in the Sun; Majestic, 1952, took over as Stewpot in South Pacific; Shubert, Nov 1956, played Francis in Bells Are Ringing; toured, Oct 1958–Jan 1959, as Rudy (Baby) Filbertson in Crazy October; Henry Miller's, Apr 1966, Pfancoo in The Office; National, Washington, DC, Sept 1970, Barney Cashman in Last of the Red Hot Lovers, and toured through 1971; Coconut Grove Playhouse, Miami Beach, Fla, Feb 1974, appeared in the Neil Simon revue The Trouble with People . . . And Other Things; Longacre, Jan 1975, Gaetano Proclo in The Ritz; Eugene O'Neill, June 1976, Marvin Michaels in Visitor from Philadelphia and Mort Hollender in Visitors from Chicago in the production with the overall title California Suite; Biltmore, Jan 1978, Sam in Cheaters; Palace, Apr 1979, Dietrich Merkenschrift in Break a Leg; has appeared in the films Wait Until Dark, Cactus Flower, April Fools, Fuzz, A New Leaf, The Thomas Crown Affair, Gator, The Ritz, Cuba (1979), etc; has appeared extensively on television on such shows as *Gunsmoke, Philco Playhouse, Studio One, Twilight Zone, The Untouchables, Carol Burnett Show*, in The Trouble with People, *79 Park Avenue*, etc.

Address: Actors Equity Association, 165 West 46th Street, New York, NY 10036.

WEXLER, Peter, designer
b New York City, 31 Oct 1936; *s* of S David Wexler and his wife Berda (Sarnoff); *e* Univ of Michigan, Yale Univ; *m* Constance Ross.

First appeared on the stage in All My Sons, produced at Chautauqua, NY, July 1947; first designs for NYC were for the decor, costumes, and lighting of the NY Shakespeare Festival production of Antony and Cleopatra, at the Hecksher, 13 Jan 1959; since then has designed decor, costumes, and lighting for The Big Knife, 1959; decor and lighting for Brecht on Brecht, decor for The Curate's Play, Tableaux, and the stage at the White House, Washington, DC, 1961; decor and lighting for Portrait of the Artist As a Young Man, The Barroom Monks, 1962; decor, costumes, and lighting for The Taming of the Shrew, decor and lighting for Abe Lincoln in Illinois, The Mystery of Elche, 1963; decor, costumes, and lighting for Venus and Adonis, Masque of Angels (Guthrie, Minneapolis, Minn), Capers (for the Robert Joffrey Ballet at the Bolshoi, Moscow), Dreams (ballet), and decor for the opera War and Peace, 1964; decor, costumes, lighting for La Boheme (opera), The Deputy (Los Angeles), decor and lighting for Lizzie Borden (NYC Opera), The Burnt Flower Bed, decor for The White Devil, and the interior for the NY Philharmonic Promenades at Philharmonic Hall, 1965; decor, costumes, and lighting for Candide (Los Angeles), Cosi Fan Tutte (Corpus Christi, Texas), decor and lighting for The Magic Flute (Washington Opera Society), A Joyful Noise, On a Clear Day You Can See Forever (tour), 1966; decor, costumes, lighting for The Devils, The Marriage of Mr Mississippi (both Los Angeles), 1967; decor for The Happy Time, In the Matter of J Robert Oppenheimer, decor and lighting for Camino Real (last two Los Angeles), 1968; decor for In the Matter of J. Robert Oppenheimer (NY), decor for Chemin de Fer (Los Angeles), Uncle Vanya (Los Angeles), and the State Dept tour of the Far East and Europe of the Mark Taper Forum, 1969; decor and costumes for Camino Real (NY), decor for Minnie's Boys, Murderous Angels (Los Angeles), costumes for Rosebloom (Los Angeles), 1970; decor for The Trial of the Catonsville Nine, The Trial of A Lincoln, Murderous Angels, Godspell (Los Angeles), 1971; The Web and the Rock, Curlew River (Central City, Colo, Opera), 1972; Leonard Bernstein's Mass (Los Angeles), decor, costumes, film for Les Troyens (Metropolitan Opera), Review of Reviews (Philharmonic Hall), Church Trilogy, 1973; decor and lighting for Hamlet (Los Angeles), Henry IV, Parts I and II (Chicago), 1974; The Philanthropist (Chicago), 1975; Le Prophete (Metropolitan Opera), 1976; Jockeys, Treats, 1977; A Broadway Musical, 1978; Un Ballo in Maschera (Metropolitan), 1979; has each year designed the Promenade Concerts and Rug Concerts at Avery Fisher Hall, NY; has also co-designed the Hollywood Bowl (1975), Stage B 20th Century Fox (Los Angeles, 1973), Upper West theatre complex (1970), Pittsburgh Public Theatre (1975), etc; designed the decor for the film Andy, 1964, and has since designed Watch the Birdie, The Trial of the Catonsville Nine, etc; has designed for television since 1962, notably the *Merv Griffin Show*, 1965; has exhibited his designs widely in galleries; taught and lectured at the Univ of Michigan, State Univ of NY, Univ of Arizona at Tucson, etc.
Adress: 277 West End Avenue, New York, NY 10023. *Tel:* 877-9494.

WHEATLEY, Alan, actor
b Tolworth, Surrey, 19 Apr 1907; s of William Henry Wheatley and his wife Rose Eva (Towers); e Tiffin's School, Kingston-on-Thames; formerly engaged in Industrial Psychology.
Made his first appearance on the stage at the Festival Theatre, Cambridge, Oct 1928, as Randal Utterword in Heartbreak House; played in repertory at the Festival, Cambridge, 1928–9; Little Theatre, Hull, 1929–30; Grafton, Lon-

don, 1930–1; toured, 1930, as Sir Roger Fairfax in Sweet Nell of Old Drury, with Fred Terry, and (1931) in The Quaker Girl, and with the Arts League Travelling Theatre; appeared at the Embassy and St Martin's, Nov 1931, as the Journalist in Britannia of Billingsgate; Embassy, Sept 1932, and Comedy, Oct 1932, played the Guide in Miracle at Verdun, Little, Feb 1933, Master Klaus in The Witch; Vaudeville, May 1933, Godfrey Perry in Wild Justice; appeared at the Malvern Festival, Aug 1933; Royalty, Feb 1934, the Gardener in Within the Gates; Westminster, Sept 1934, Earl of Gloucester in Rose and Glove; Oct 1934, Edgar in King Lear; was leading man at Croydon Repertory Theatre, for nine months, 1934–5; during 1935 appeared in several productions at the Embassy; Westminster, Dec 1935, played Count Lasca in The Impresario from Smyrna; Old Vic, Feb 1936, and Daly's, Mar 1936, Count Las Cases in St Helena; Phoenix, July 1936, Winkler in Professor Bernhardi; made his first appearance in New York at the Lyceum, 6 Oct 1936, as Las Cases in St Helena; People's Palace, London, Feb 1937, played Iago in Othello; Strand, June 1937, Vesnic in Judgment Day; subsequently toured in Scandinavia and adjoining countries, as Petkoff in Arms and the Man and Arnold in The Circle; Gate, Sept 1937, Earl of Beaconsfield in Mr Gladstone; Westminster, Jan 1938, Mosca in Volpone; Arts, Oct 1938, Frank Harris in Oscar Wilde; Q, Jan 1939, Sebastian in Walk in the Sun; Whitehall, May 1939, Sir Patrick Cullen in The Doctor's Dilemma; joined the BBC Drama Repertory company, Sept 1939; was an Overseas announcer, May 1940, and from Sept 1940 to Mar 1945, acted as principal announcer and newsreader in the BBC European service; toured, May 1945, on the Continent, for entertainment of BLA troops; toured, July 1945, with the Old Vic company, as Mercutio in Romeo and Juliet; toured, Sept 1945, as Squire Thornhill in The Vicar of Wakefield; Mercury, Dec 1945–June 1946, appeared in This Way to the Tomb, The Shadow Factory, The Resurrection, and A Phoenix too Frequent; Studio Champs-Elysées, Paris, July 1946, and Garrick, London, Sept 1946, again played Julian in This Way to the Tomb; Mercury, Oct 1946, Harry in The Family Reunion; June 1947, Smitty in SS Glencairn; Torch, Aug 1948, Andrew Shepley in The Haunted; Cambridge, Nov 1948, Louis Riberac in Home Is Tomorrow; Richmond, June 1949, appeared as Hamlet; at the Edinburgh Festival, Aug 1949, appeared as Mr Justice Moy in The Man in the Raincoat; Comedy (Repertory Players), Dec 1949, played the Man in The Mountain; toured, Feb 1950, as Mark Smeaton in The White Falcon; Embassy, Jan 1951, played Jerome in Celestina; at the Q, Feb 1951, played Fedor Bunyano in The Hungry God; New Boltons, Mar 1952, appeared as Reginald de Courcy in Lady Susan, and Cecil in The Constant Lover; at the same theatre, May 1952, played David Gillard in Desire Shall Fail, and appeared in the revue, Boltons Evening Party; Theatre Royal, Windsor, Feb 1959, played Edgar Marr in House Without Windows; Coliseum, Dec 1959, played Abanazar in Aladdin; Arnaud, Guildford, Feb 1970, Praed in Mrs Warren's Profession; has played on numerous occasions for the Stage Society, Repertory Players, etc; entered films, 1937, and has appeared in numerous pictures, and television appearances include the Sheriff of Nottingham in the series *Robin Hood*, and Holmes in the original *Sherlock Holmes* series.
Favourite parts: Richard II, and the Soldier in The Unknown Warrior. *Recreation:* Listening to music. *Address:* 6 Bryanston Square, London, W1. *Tel:* 01–262 3191.

WHEELER, Hugh, dramatic author
b Hampstead, London, 1912; s of Harold Wheeler and his

wife Florence (Scammell); *e* Clayesmore School and London Univ; came to America in 1934; served in the US Army during World War II.

First play produced was Big Fish, Little Fish, at the ANTA, 15 Mar 1961; since then has written Look, We've Come Through, 1961; first play produced in London was also Big Fish, Little Fish, at the Duke of York's, 18 Sept 1962; We Have Always Lived in the Castle, 1966; A Little Night Music (adapted from Ingmar Bergman's film Three Smiles of a Summer's Night), for which he received the Antoinette Perry (Tony) Award, the Drama Critics Circle Award, Drama Desk Award, etc, Irene (adapted from James Montgomery's play), 1973; Candide (from Voltaire's novel), for which he received the Tony, Drama Critics Circle Awards, etc; wrote the lyrics for Love for Love, 1974; co-wrote book for Pacific Overtures, 1976; book for Sweeney Todd, 1979, (Tony, Drama Critics Circle, Drama Desk, etc, awards); wrote the films Something for Everyone (1970), Travels with My Aunt (1972), Cabaret (1972), A Little Night Music (1977), Nijinsky (1980); first wrote for television in 1971 and has since written for *The Snoop Sisters* series; is a noted mystery story writer under the pseudonyms Q. Patrick, Patrick Quentin, and Johnathan Stagge in collaboration with Richard Wilson Webb, having published more than 30 titles.

Address: Twin Hills Farm, Monterey, Mass 01245. *Tel:* 413–528–0770.

WHITBY, Gwynne, actress

b Leamington, Warwickshire, 8 July 1903; *d* of the late Arthur Whitby and his wife Cissie (Saumarez); *e* Minehead; *m* Hugh Anthony Glanmôr Williams (mar dis); studied for the stage under her father and at the Royal Academy of Dramatic Art.

Made her first appearance on the stage as a small child at the Princes Theatre, 9 Feb 1912, as a Sprite in Shakespeare's Dream; at Stratford-on-Avon, 1916, played a Fairy in A Midsummer Night's Dream, and Martius in Coriolanus; her first grown-up appearance was made at the Theatre Royal, Worthing, Aug 1918, as Styles in Betty at Bay; appeared at His Majesty's, for a year, in Chu-Chin-Chow; at the Comedy, Aug 1920, played Doll Mortimer in The Ruined Lady; appeared at the New Theatre, Aug 1921, as the Third Lady in Christopher Sly; Dec 1921, as Mariana in Blood and Sand; Apr 1922, as Low Loong in Mr Wu, also understudying; at the Royalty, Dec 1922, played Amy Spettigue in Charley's Aunt; at the Ambassadors', June 1923, Violet in The Lilies of the Field, and understudied Edna Best as Catherine, in the same play; at the St Martin's, Nov 1923, played Suzanne in Fledglings; Jan 1924, succeeded Olga Lindo as Mrs Kemp in The Likes of Her, and Mrs Ross in The Will; at Drury Lane, June 1924, played Brunton and Miss Lacey in London Life; appeared at the St Martin's 1924, and subsequently toured as Lorna in In the Next Room; during 1925–6, played leading parts with the Liverpool Repertory Company; Duke of York's, Mar 1926, played Deborah Hinks in Life Goes On; joined the Old Vic Company, Sept 1926, and appeared there as Blanche in King John, Titania, Princess Katharine in Henry V, Miranda, Olivia, Perdita, Desdemona, etc; during 1927–8 toured in Australia, with Irene Vanbrugh and Dion Boucicault in The High Road, The Letter, Caroline, etc; at the Lyric, Hammersmith, June 1932, played Minnie Gilfillian in Sweet Lavender; at Stratford-on-Avon Memorial Theatre, from Apr 1934, played Miranda in The Tempest, Maria in Twelfth Night, Katharine in King Henry V, Maria in Love's Labour's Lost; Hermia in A Midsummer Night's Dream, Ursula in Much Ado About Nothing; from Apr

1935, appeared at Stratford-on-Avon Memorial Theatre, as Charmian in Antony and Cleopatra, Nerissa, Rosalind, Mistress Ford in The Merry Wives of Windsor, Lady Percy in King Henry IV (Part I), and Miranda; Lyric, Hammersmith, Dec 1935, in The Magic Marble; Q, Nov 1937, Martha in Jenny Frensham; New, May, 1938, Mildred Udall in People of Our Class; Wyndham's, Oct 1938, Marcia Brent in Quiet Wedding; toured, Nov 1939, as Mary in The Women, and played the part at the Strand Theatre, Apr 1940; during the autumn of 1940, appeared at Stratford-on-Avon in a season of modern plays, and at Dartington Hall, during the spring of 1941; Wyndham's, July 1941, played Marcia Brent in Quiet Week-End, and continued in this part until Sept 1944, including a short tour overseas; Piccadilly, May 1945, played Princess Caroline in The Gay Pavilion; Embassy, Nov 1946, Millicent Sanderson in The Day of Glory; Everyman, Dec 1947, Baroness Lehzen in Royal Romance; Ambassadors', Mar 1949, Ellen in Love's a Funny Thing; Embassy, Mar 1950, Laura Battelbridge in The Lady Purrs; toured, summer 1950, in Black Chiffon; toured, 1951, in Party Manners; at the Playhouse, Buxton, Sept 1951, appeared as Jane Leadbetter in Poison in Jest; Embassy, Oct 1951, played Laura in Women of Twilight, and appeared in this part at the Vaudeville, Nov 1951; at the Plymouth, New York, Mar 1952, again played Laura in Women of Twilight; on returning to London, repeated this part in a revival of the production at the Victoria Palace, June 1952; Comedy, Dec 1952, played Mrs Purves in For Better, For Worse . . . , continuing in this part for eighteen months; Grand, Blackpool, Oct 1954, played Miss Pearce in The Secret Tent; Cambridge Theatre, May 1955, appeared as Mrs Edgar in The Reluctant Debutante; Wyndham's, Apr 1956 (for the Repertory Players), played Mrs Feeney in Tolka Row; Aldwych, Dec 1956, Brenda Stanham in The Touch of Fear; Cambridge, Nov 1957, Mrs Drexel Biddle in The Happiest Millionaire; toured for 20 weeks, 1959, as Sheila Broadbent in The Reluctant Debutante; St Martin's, Feb 1960, played Miss Bennett in A Sparrow Falls, in the double-bill Double Yoke; Dublin Festival, Sept 1961, and Vaudeville, London, Oct 1961, played Sister Isabel in Teresa of Avila; Her Majesty's, Dec 1962, Mrs Titchburn and Grandma in Emil and the Detectives; Southern Company tour, Mar 1964, Mrs Higgins in My Fair Lady; Queen's, July 1969, played Mrs Strang in Conduct Unbecoming; appeared with the RSC in Richard II, Brooklyn Academy, Jan 1973; The Other Place, Stratford, Dec 1974, Madame Voinitsky in Uncle Vanya; has frequently broadcast and appeared on television; made her first appearance in films, 1945, in Quiet Week-End, and has since appeared in The Blue Lamp, I Believe In You, Mine Own Executioner, Turn the Key Softly, etc.

Favourite part: Viola in Twelfth Night. *Recreations:* Her grandchildren and theatre at Stratford. *Address:* 4 Cherry Street, Old Town, Stratford-upon-Avon. *Tel:* 2408.

WHITE, Jane, actress

b New York City, 30 Oct 1922; *d* of Walter White, the author and Executive Secretary of the NAACP, and his wife Gladys (Powell); *e* Fieldston Ethical Culture School, and Smith College (BA); *m* Alfredo Viazzi; prepared for the stage with Herbert Berghof, Peter Frye, Uta Hagen, studied voice with William Lawrence, Marjorie Schloss, Anna Hamlin, and dance with Hanya Holm.

Made her début at the Royale, New York, 29 Nov 1945, as Nonnie in Strange Fruit; Dramatic Workshop, June 1946, played Curley's Wife in Of Mice and Men; Greenwich Mews Playhouse, Mar 1947, The Woman in Green in Peer Gynt; American Negro Theater, Mar 1948, Mrs Lincoln in The

Washington Years; New York City Center, June 1948, a Butterfly and a Moth in The Insect Comedy; Hayloft, Allentown, Pennsylvania, July 1948, Elvira in Blithe Spirit; Blackfriars Guild, Feb 1949, Anna Velasquez in City of Kings; Hayloft, Allentown, Pennsylvania, July 1949, Katherine in The Taming of the Shrew and, Sept 1949, Barbara Allen in Dark of the Moon; Weidman Studio, May 1950, played in the revue Come What May; Arena, Feb 1951, played in the revue Razzle Dazzle; Martin Beck, Nov 1952, Ellen in The Climate of Eden; Lyceum, Sept 1953, Carol in Take a Giant Step; Greenwich Mews, Feb 1954, Mercy Wellman in Time of Storm; Kaufmann Auditorium, Nov 1956, the title-role of Hedda Gabler; Lenox Hill Playhouse, Dec 1956, title-role of Lysistrata; Belasco, May 1958, the Mad Wife in Jane Eyre; Phoenix, Dec 1958, Obregon's Wife in The Power and the Glory; Phoenix, May 1959, the Queen in Once upon a Mattress; Alvin, Nov 1959, repeated this last part; Belvedere Lake, for the New York Shakespeare Festival, Aug 1960, Katherine in The Taming of the Shrew; Cricket, May 1962, Margaret in Hop, Signor; Circle in the Square, Dec 1963, Helen of Troy in The Trojan Women; Delacorte, for the New York Shakespeare Festival, June 1965, Princess of France in Love's Labour's Lost, July 1965, Volumnia in Coriolanus, and Aug 1965, Helen in Troilus and Cressida; lived in Italy 1965–8, where she appeared as Mme Rosepettle in Oh, Dad, Poor Dad, Mama's Hung You in the Closet and I'm Feelin' So Sad, in Rome, 1966, and as Reverend Marion Alexander in Trumpets of the Lord in Rome, 1967, and in Paris at the Odeon Théâtre de France and the Gaité Montparnasse, 1967; Circle in the Square, Mar 1968, took over from Irene Pappas as Clytemnestra in Iphigenia in Aulis; Henry Miller's, Sept 1968, Barbara in The Cuban Thing; Ford's, Washington, DC, 1969, again played Clytemnestra in Iphigenia in Aulis; Delacorte, Aug. 1971, Queen in The Tale of Cymbeline; Roundabout, July 1974, Luisa in The Burnt Flowerbed, and Dec. 1974, Rebekka West in Rosmersholm; Stratford, Conn., June 1975, Goneril in King Lear; Blackstone, Chicago, Sept 1977, Tiy in Nefertiti; served as Technical Advisor for the film Pinky, 1949, and as Script Consultant for the film Lost Boundaries, 1949; co-founded Torchlight Productions, independent television producers, 1947–9; formed Jane White's Classes, Inc, for training of professional actors, 1960–4; made television début in 1950, and since has appeared in all major dramatic programs and in Once upon A Mattress, 1962, Trumpets of the Lord, 1968, Edge of Night, 1969, *Secret Storm*, 1971, *A World Apart*, 1971; winner of 1965 Obie Award as best actress of the year for The Princess of France in Love's Labours' Lost and Volumnia in Coriolanus; her film appearances have been in Le Dolce Signore and Non Scommettere con il Diavolo (Italy) and Klute (USA, 1971); appeared in cabaret at Alfredo's Settebello, NY, Sept 1976.

Address: 250 West 15th Street, New York, NY 10011. *Tel:* 929–1994.

WHITE, Joan, actress, producer, director, and teacher
b Alexandria, Egypt, 3 Dec 1909; *d* of Henry William George White and his wife Kathleen Mabel (Beach); *e* St Helen's School, Northwood, Middlesex; *m* (1) J V Beanes (mar dis); (2) A P Moore (mar dis); (3) Robert Grose (mar dis); studied for the stage at the Royal Academy of Dramatic Art.

Made her first appearance on the stage at the Festival Theatre, Cambridge, Sept 1930, as Azorah in Tobias and the Angel; made her first appearance in London, at the Little Theatre, 7 Jan 1931, as the Nurse in Betrayal; Ambassadors', June 1931, played Kate in A Knight Passed By; at the Westminster Theatre, Oct 1931–Jan 1933, played Janet in The Anatomist, Azorah in Tobias and the Angel, Margarita

in The Kingdom of God, Moth in Love's Labour's Lost, Euodias in Jonah and the Whale, Laurie in Follow Me, Assistant Stage Manager in Six Characters in Search of an Author; Royalty, Feb 1933, Eve in Synthetic Virgin; at the Fortune, Oct 1933, played Angela Knowle in Vacant Possession; Shaftesbury, Dec 1933, Joan Buckland in A Present from Margate; Coliseum, Feb 1934, Madanika in The Golden Toy; Mercury, July 1934, Charlotte in Charlotte's Progress; Piccadilly, Jan 1935, Bella Hedley in The Barretts of Wimpole Street; Bexhill, Sussex, summer 1935, directed Outward Bound and I'll Leave It to You; Shaftesbury, Oct 1935, Connie Windlestraw in The Black Eye; Arts, Jan 1936, Claudine in The Luck of the Devil; Ambassadors', Mar 1936, Tonie in Children to Bless You; Apollo, Nov 1936, Button Faringdon in Housemaster; Duke of York's (for London Int Theatre), Oct 1937, Susannah in Susannah and the Elders; Strand, Feb 1939, Judy Bingley in Little Ladyship; retired from the stage, 1939–43; reappeared at the Saville, Mar 1943, when she played Judy Graves in Junior Miss, in which she subsequently toured; Westminster, July 1945, played Janie Jenkins in The Cure for Love; Granville, July 1946, played Trixie in G I Brides at Sea; subsequently toured in This Desirable Residence; Arts, Nov 1946, Doto in A Phoenix Too Frequent; His Majesty's, May 1947, Lady Beatrice Willisder in Flat Spin, which she also directed; Piccadilly, June 1947, directed The Young May Moon; Torch, Sept 1948, Leah Barr in Ten Shilling Doll; joined the Birmingham Repertory Theatre company for a season, Jan 1949, playing the Duchess of York in Richard III, Madame Maniefa in Diary of a Scoundrel, Chorus Girl in A Cassilis Engagement, Spanish Dancer in The Romantic Young Lady, and in The Marvellous History of St Bernard, and A Modern Everyman; Sept 1949, played leading parts during a season at the Salisbury Arts Theatre, including Lady Kitty in The Circle, Mrs Goldfinch in A Pair of Spectacles, Mrs Malaprop in The Rivals, Fairy Queen in Aladdin, Penelope Toop in See How They Run; with the Bristol Old Vic company, Sept 1950, played Mistress Quickly, in The Merry Wives of Windsor, Mrs Posket in The Magistrate, Julia in The Cocktail Party, Margaret Devize in The Lady's Not for Burning, and Mrs Candour in The School for Scandal; at the Comedy, July 1951, played Gloria Cavendish in Storks Don't Talk; at the Q, Apr 1952, played Joanna in Night of Masquerade; Dundee, Scotland, fall, 1952, directed and played in The Queen's Husband, The Beaver Coat, The Hollow Crown; Arts, Salisbury, 1953, directed The Miser; Playhouse, Manchester, Nov 1953, Lady Kitty in The Circle and Yvonne in Les Parents Terribles; Arts, Dec 1953, Rosie and Maud Neville in A London Actress; Aldwych, Mar 1954, played Miss Marcy in I Capture the Castle; Cardiff, Wales, 1956, directed Quality Street, Angels in Love, Ten Little Indians; Crest, Toronto, Mar 1956, directed Present Laughter; Crest, May 1956, played Miss Marple in Murder at the Vicarage; in June 1956, was appointed director of the Trans-Canada Theatre Company, which opened in London, Ontario, with Dear Charles; subsequent productions included The Seven Year Itch, The Happiest Days of Your Life, When We Are Married, Sabrina Fair, All for Mary, and O Mistress Mine; Maple Leaf Theatre, London, Ont, July 1957, played Sheila Broadbent in The Reluctant Debutante; made her US début in Sept 1958, when she took over the part of Mrs Higgins in the touring company of My Fair Lady; re-opened the Berkshire Playhouse Drama School, 1960, and inaugurated a Playwriting Seminar; between 1960–4, at the Berkshire Playhouse, Mass, co-presented some fifty productions with Robert Grose, including three new plays, and her own musical (with Anna Russell) Lady Audley's Secret, or, Who Pushed

George?; Charles Playhouse, Boston, 1961, played Julia in The Cocktail Party; Master Theatre, New York, Nov 1961, Mrs Telfer in Trelawny of the Wells; Ambassador, NY, Jan 1962, Mrs Turton in A Passage to India; took over the direction of the Yarmouth Playhouse, Cape Cod, Mass, 1965; Colonial, Boston, Sept 1965, played Lady Insdale in On a Clear Day You Can See Forever; Theatre de Lys, NY, Mar 1966, played in Serjeant Musgrave's Dance; East 74th Street, Sept 1967, Mrs Dedalus in Stephen D; Theatre de Lys, Feb 1968, directed A Madrigal of Shakespeare; in 1968 was instrumental in taking the Trinity Square Repertory Theatre of Providence, Rhode Island, to the Edinburgh Festival in Years of the Locust; joined the Nottingham Playhouse, 1968, and played Eleanor in King John, Mrs Candour in The School for Scandal, and Paulina in The Seagull; returned to America and went to Seattle, Washington, where, in Sept 1969, she joined the faculty of the Drama School of the University of Washington and stayed until June 1975; directed The Seagull and a modern version of Love's Labour's Lost, 1969; Seattle Repertory, Dec 1969, played in Joe Egg; A Contemporary Theatre, Seattle, summer 1970, Meg in The Birthday Party; Seattle Repertory, also 1970 Frosine in The Miser, the Landlady in Hadrian VII, and Aunt Penniman in The Heiress; also directed a number of productions in Seattle; in association with the Adeline Greene Theatre of East Grinstead, Sussex, taught an English Summer Theatre School, a project of the University of Washington, 1970–75 which became affiliated with the Thorndike Theatre, Leatherhead, and played each year at the Edinburgh Festival Fringe; in 1975 formed the Joan White English Theatre School, Ltd, to continue these activities; made her first English television appearance in Tobias and the Angel, 1937, and later Cure for Love, 1954; made her American television début, 1959, in The Citadel, and has since appeared in Vanity Fair, The Invincible Mr Disraeli, etc, and has broadcast several of her own short stories.
Hobby: Writing. *Address:* PO Box 984, Ansonia Station, 1990 Broadway, New York, NY 10023.

WHITE, Michael Simon, producing manager
b Scotland, 16 Jan 1936; son of Victor White and his wife Doris (Cohen); e Lyceum Alpinum, Zuoz, Switzerland and the Sorbonne; m Sarah Hillsdon.

Began work in the theatre at the White Barn, Westport, Connecticut, 1956; assistant to Peter Daubeny, 1957–61; with him he presented his first London production, The Connection, 1961; subsequent productions and co-productions, in London unless otherwise stated, include The Secret of the World, The Scatterin', Jungle of the Cities, The Voice of Shem, 1962; The Blood Knot, Cambridge Circus, 1963; Hamp (Edinburgh), Son of Oblomov, 1964; Saint's Day, The Star Spangled Jack Show, Any Wednesday, 1965; Saturday Night and Sunday Morning, How's the World Treating You, The Trials of Brother Jero, Adam's Apple (tour), The Blood Knot, Breakdown (Dublin), Hogan's Goat (Dublin), Loot, 1966; The Burglar, America Hurrah, Philadelphia Here I Come, Tom Paine, Fanghorn, *The Paper Bag Players*, 1967; Summer, Fortune and Men's Eyes, The Beard, I Wonder, Soldiers, 1968; The Au Pair Man, The Resistible Rise of Arturo Ui, So What About Love, 1969; Sleuth (also New York—Tony Award), Widowers' Houses, Oh! Calcutta!, 1970; Hamlet, The Dirtiest Show in Town, As Time Goes By, Friday, 1971; The Threepenny Opera, Julius Caesar, I Claudius, Joseph and the Amazing Technicolor Dreamcoat, A Sense of Detachment, 1972; A Doll's House, Two Gentlemen of Verona, The Rocky Horror Show, The Ride Across Lake Constance, Judies, 1973; Snap, The Island,

Sizwe Bansi Is Dead, (these two also NY), That Championship Season, The Tooth of Crime, Play Mas, 1974; Murderer, Jeeves, Entertaining Mr Sloane, Loot, What the Butler Saw, Too True to Be Good, 1975; City Sugar, The Chairman, Housewife-Superstar, Baggage, A Chorus Line, Carte Blanche, 1976; Censored Scenes from King Kong, 1977; Sleuth, Annie, I Was Sitting On My Patio This Guy Appeared I Thought I Was Hallucinating, Dracula, Deathtrap, 1978; Ain't Misbehavin', Flowers for Algernon, 1979; films include Moviemakers, Monty Python and the Holy Grail, Rocky Horror Picture Show, Jabberwocky, and Rude Boys; he has also presented seasons of modern dance and contemporary music.
Recreations: Skiing, painting, racing. *Club:* Turf. *Address:* 13 Duke Street, St James's, London, SW1. *Tel:* 01–839 3971.

WHITE, Miles, costume designer
b Oakland, California, 27 July 1914; s of Carlos G White and his wife Verna (Edgren); e University of California, California School of Fine Arts, and the Arts Students League in New York.

First designs for the theatre were the costumes of Right This Way, presented at the 46th Street, 4 Jan 1938; since then has designed the costumes for Best Foot Forward, 1941; The Pirate, 1942; Ziegfeld Follies, Oklahoma!, Early to Bed, 1943; Bloomer Girl, Allah Be Praised! Dream with Music, 1944; Carousel, The Day Before Spring, 1945; Gypsy Lady, The Duchess of Malfi, 1946; High Button Shoes, 1947; That's the Ticket, Fall River Legend (American Ballet Theatre), 1948; Gentlemen Prefer Blondes, 1949; Bless You All, 1950; Pal Joey, Three Wishes for Jamie, Two's Company, 1952; Hazel Flagg, 1953; The Girl in Pink Tights, 1954; Ankles Aweigh, 1955; Strip for Action, 1956; Eugenia, Jamaica, Time Remembered, The Carefree Heart, 1957; Oh, Captain, 1958; Cheri, Show Business, 1959; Bye, Bye Birdie, The Unsinkable Molly Brown, 1960; Show Girl, Milk and Honey, 1961; Song of Norway (California tour), 1962; Zenda (California tour), 1963; Oklahoma! 1969; Candida, 1970; A Day in the Life of Just About Everyone, 1971; A Quarter for the Ladies Room, 1972; Tricks, 1973; Sleeping Beauty (American Ballet Theatre), 1974; Best Friend, 1976; Toller Cranston's The Ice Show, 1977; has also designed ten productions for the Ringling Brothers and Barnum and Bailey Circus, since 1944; three editions of Ice Capades, 1964–66 designed the films Up in Arms, 1944, The Kid from Brooklyn, 1946, The Greatest Show on Earth, 1952, There's No Business Like Show Business, 1954, Around the World in 80 Days, 1956, etc; received the Antoinette Perry (Tony) Award for Bless You All and Hazel Flagg, and the Donaldson Award for Bloomer Girl, High Button Shoes, Gentlemen Prefer Blondes, and Pal Joey.
Address: 360 East 55th Street, New York, NY. *Tel:* PL 3-3874.

WHITE, Onna, dancer, choreographer, director
b Nova Scotia, Canada; m Larry Douglas; made her professional début as a member of the corps de ballet of the San Francisco Opera Ballet Company.

Made her first appearance in New York dancing in the chorus of Finian's Rainbow at the 46th Street, 10 Jan 1947; made her London début as assistant to the choreographer Michael Kidd for Finian's Rainbow at the Palace, 21 Oct 1947; danced in the chorus of Guys and Dolls at the 46th Street, Nov 1950; Coliseum, London, May 1953, assistant to Michael Kidd in choreographing Guys and Dolls; Imperial, NY, Feb 1955, danced in the chorus of Silk Stockings; restaged the dances of Finian's Rainbow and Guys and Dolls in their New York City Center revivals, 1955; since then has choreographed the following musicals: Carmen Jones, 1956; The Music Man, 1957; Whoop-Up, 1958; Take Me Along, 1959; Irma la Douce, 1960; Let It Ride! 1961; I Had a Ball, 1964; Half a Sixpence, 1965; Mame, Illya Darling, 1967; A Mother's Kisses, 1968; 1776, 1969; Gantry, which she also directed, 1970; 70, Girls, 70, 1971; Gigi, 1973; Billy (Drury Lane, London), 1974; Goodtime Charley, 1975; I Love My Wife, 1977 (also London); choreographed the films The Music Man, 1962, Bye Bye Birdie, 1963, and Oliver!, 1968, for which she received the Academy Award, 1776, The Great Waltz, 1973, Mame, 1974, Pete's Dragon, 1976.

Address: Society of Stage Directors and Choreographers, 1501 Broadway, New York, NY 10019.

WHITEHEAD, Paxton, actor

b East Malling, Kent, 17 Oct 1937; *s* of Charles Parkin Whitehead and his wife Louise (Hunt); *e* Rugby School; *m* the actress Patricia Gage; trained for the stage at Webber-Douglas School.

Made his professional debut at the Devonshire Park, Eastbourne, Aug 1956, as Alphonse in All for Mary; on leaving drama school toured with the Anew McMaster company and worked in rep at Farnham, 1957; with the RSC at Stratford, season 1958, played minor roles including Francisco in Hamlet, visiting Russia with this production; toured UK in The Grass Is Greener, 1959, and as Freddie in Pygmalion in 1960; went to New York, 1960, and played various roles off-Broadway before making his Broadway debut at Henry Miller's, 20 Sept 1962, as Dawson-Hill in The Affair; Theatre Four, Feb 1963, played Torvald Helmer in A Doll's House; at the American Shakespeare Festival, Stratford, Conn, 1963, played Gower in Henry V and King of France in King Lear; toured US, Aug 1963, in Beyond the Fringe, and appeared at the John Golden, Jan 1964, in Beyond the Fringe 1964; played leads in regional theatres including Higgins in My Fair Lady, Memphis, and Jack Absolute in The Rivals, Boston, 1964; Archie Rice in The Entertainer, Hartford, Cusins in Major Barbara, Cincinnati, and three parts including Algernon Moncrieff in The Importance of Being Earnest, Winnipeg, 1965; at the Shaw Festival, Niagara-on-the-Lake, 1966 season, played Lord Summerhays in Misalliance and Magnus in The Apple Cart; artistic director of the festival, 1967–77 seasons; played Sergius in Arms and the Man, Cusins in Major Barbara, and directed The Circle, 1967; Hector Hushabye in Heartbreak House, Coustilliou in his adaptation (with Suzanne Grossmann) of The Chemmy Circle (La Main Passe), which he also directed, 1968; Dubedat in The Doctor's Dilemma, The Actor in The Guardsman, 1969; directed and played Tempest in Forty Years On, 1970; Charteris in The Philanderer, leading roles in Tonight at 8.30, 1971; directed Misalliance and Getting Married, 1972; Valentine in You Never Can Tell and Savoyard in Fanny's First Play, 1973; directed and played Fancourt Babberley in Charley's Aunt, 1974; also played Burgoyne in The Devil's Disciple, 1975; Sergius in Arms and the Man; Magnus in Apple Cart, Advian in The Millionairess, 1976; Ronnie Gamble in Thark, and directed Widowers' Houses, 1977; during this time he also acted and directed regularly in regional theatres including the Philadelphia Drama Guild, Playhouse, Vancouver (artistic director, 1971–73), Kennedy Center, Washington DC etc; roles in NY included The Emperor in The Brass Butterfly, Chelsea Theater Center, Jan 1970; Reverend Alexander Mill in Candida, Longacre, Apr 1970; his adaptation (again with Suzanne Grossmann) of Le Dindon, entitled There's One in Every Marriage, was seen at Stratford, Ont, 1971, and the

Royale, NY, 1972; at the Martin Beck, NY, Nov 1975, played Canon Throbbing in Habeas Corpus, later taking over the role of Arthur Wicksteed; Helen Hayes, Sept 1978, Sherlock Holmes in The Crucifer of Blood; at the Manitoba Theatre Centre, Winnipeg, 1979, played Henry Carr in Travesties; Citadel, Edmonton, 1979, Oscar Wilde in The Trials of Oscar Wilde; with the Philadelphia Drama Guild, 1980, played Ronnie Gamble in Thark and Malvolio in Twelfth Night; State, NY, Aug 1980, Pellinore in Camelot; his first TV appearance was in England in 1959; work for CBC in Canada includes Lady Windermere's Fan, The First Night of Pygmalion, and Riel, 1977; Hon LL D, Trent University.

Recreations: Tennis, skiing, cards. *Club:* The Players NY. *Address:* c/o Barna Ostertag, 501 Fifth Avenue, New York, NY 10017.

WHITEHEAD, Ted (E.A.), dramatic author

b Liverpool, 3 Apr 1933; *s* of Edward Whitehead and his wife Catherine (Curran); *e* St Francis Xavier's Jesuit College and Christ's College, Cambridge; *m* (1) Kathleen Horton; (2) Gwenda Bagshaw; formerly in advertising.

His first play to be produced was The Foursome, presented at the Royal Court's Theatre Upstairs, 17 Mar 1971; subsequent plays include Alpha Beta, 1972; The Sea Anchor, 1974; Old Flames, 1975; The Punishment, 1976; Mecca, 1977; joint winner of the George Devine Award, 1970; Resident dramatist, Royal Court, 1971–2; Evening Standard Award for Most Promising Playwright, 1971; Alpha Beta has been filmed; writing for TV includes Under the Age, and The Punishment; Fellow in Creative Writing, Bulmershe College, Reading, 1975–6; currently theatre and film reviewer for *The Spectator*.

Recreations: Pubs, soccer, music. *Address:* c/o Judy Daish Associates, Globe Theatre, Shaftesbury Avenue, London W1V 7AA.

WHITEHEAD, Robert, producer

b Montreal, Canada, 3 Mar 1916; *s* of William Thomas Whitehead and his wife Selena (Labatt); *e* Trinity College School, Lower Canada College; *m* (1) Virginia Bolen (dec); (2) Zoe Caldwell.

Formerly a commercial photographer, and also an actor; studied for the stage at the New York School of the Theatre with Benno Schneider; began acting career at the Barter Theatre, Abingdon, Virginia; appeared in NY at the Barrymore, Sept 1936, with Dame May Whitty and Emlyn Williams in Night Must Fall; after three and a half years with the American Field Service during World War II, he began his career as producer at the National Theatre, NY, Oct 1947, when he co-presented Medea, starring Judith Anderson; at the same theatre, Dec 1947, he co-presented Crime and Punishment; he has since produced or co-produced the following productions: The Member of the Wedding (Critics Circle Award), 1950; Night Music, 1951; Desire Under the Elms, Mrs McThing, Golden Boy, Four Saints in Three Acts, Sunday Breakfast (for ANTA), The Time of the Cuckoo, 1952; The Emperor's Clothes, The Remarkable Mr Pennypacker, 1953; The Confidential Clerk, Saint Joan (tour), The Flowering Peach, 1954; The Skin of Our Teeth (Salute to France Programme), Bus Stop, 1955; Tamburlaine the Great, Major Barbara, Separate Tables, The Sleeping Prince, 1956; The Waltz of the Toreadors (Critics Circle Award), A Hole in the Head, Orpheus Descending, 1957; The Day the Money Stopped, The Visit (Critics Circle Award), A Touch of the Poet, Goldilocks, The Cold Wind and the Warm, 1958; Much Ado About Nothing, 1959; The Conquering Hero, Midgie Purvis, A Man for All Seasons

(Critics Circle Award), 1961; Foxy (tour), Banderol, 1962; The Physicists, 1964; at the ANTA Washington Square Theatre for the Lincoln Center for the Performing Arts, co-presented After the Fall, Marco Millions, But for Whom Charlie, The Changeling, Incident at Vichy, 1964; The Prime of Miss Jean Brodie, The Price, 1968; Sheep on the Runway, Bequest to the Nation (London), 1970; The Creation of the World and Other Business, Old Times, 1972; Finishing Touches, The Prodigal Daughter (Washington, DC), 1973; A Matter of Gravity, 1975; No Mans Land, 1600 Pennsylvania Avenue, A Texas Trilogy, 1976; The Prince of Grand Street, Semmelweiss (Washington, DC), 1978; Bedroom Farce, Betrayal, 1979; Managing Director for ANTA, 1951; Executive Producer for Producers Theatre, 1953; Consultant to the Lincoln Center for Performing Arts, 1958; joint producing-director (with Elia Kazan) of the Center's Repertory Theatre, 1960–4; has served as President of the League of New York Theatres and as Treasurer, 1967; received the Sam S Shubert Foundation Gold Medal Award, 1973; principal television production, The Skin of Our Teeth.

Recreation: Fishing. *Clubs:* Century and Players. *Address:* 1501 Broadway, New York, NY 10036.

WHITELAW, Arthur, producer
b Brooklyn, NY, 7 Mar 1940; *s* of Fred F Neitlich and his wife Lenora (Whitelaw); *e* Roslyn HS, Bard College; trained for the stage at the American Academy of Dramatic Arts; formerly an actor.

First play produced in NY was Best Foot Forward at the Stage 73, 2 Apr 1963; since then has produced or co-produced Cabin in the Sky, 1964; A Woman and the Blues, 1966; You're a Good Man, Charlie Brown, which has been produced throughout the US, 1967; Butterflies Are Free, 1969; Minnie's Boys, 1970; 70, Girls, 70, a revival of You're a Good Man, Charlie Brown, 1971; The Gingerbread Lady (tour), Children! Children!, 1972; Thoughts, 1973; Snoopy!!!, which he also directed and co-adapted in its production at the Little Fox, San Francisco, Cal, 1975; directed Save the Seeds, Darling, produced Some of My Best Friends, 1977; The Utter Glory of Morrissey Hall, 1979; has produced for *Hallmark Hall of Fame*; leased and refurbished the Ritz Theatre, 1971; has also managed the Theatre 80 St Mark's, a filmhouse in NY dedicated to the revival of musical and other films from the past.

Address: 246 West 44th Street, New York, NY 10036.

WHITELAW, Billie, actress
b Coventry, 6 June; *d* of Gerry Whitelaw and his wife Frances Mary (Williams); *m* (1) Peter Vaughan (mar dis); (2) Robert Muller.

After early experience as an assistant stage manager in repertory, she made her first appearance on the stage at the Princes Theatre, Bradford, 1950, in Pink String and Sealing Wax; toured, Mar 1954, as June Hodge in Where There's a Will . . . ; first appeared on the London stage at the Winter Garden, May 1956, as Victoire in Hotel Paradiso; Theatre Royal, Stratford, E, Nov 1960, played Mag Keenan in Progress to the Park, subsequently appearing at the Saville, May 1961, in the same part and play; Princes, May 1962, starred in the revue England, Our England; Dublin and Venice Festivals, Sept–Oct 1962, played Sara Melody in A Touch of the Poet; joined the National Theatre Company, at the Old Vic, Apr 1964, to play the Second Woman in Play; with the same Company at the Chichester Festival, July 1964, played Franctschina in The Dutch Courtesan, also appearing at some performances in the same Festival as Desdemona in Othello; Old Vic, Oct 1964, again played Franctschina in

The Dutch Courtesan; Mar 1965, played Maggie Hobson in Hobson's Choice; Chichester Festival, July 1965, Avonia Bunn in Trelawny of the 'Wells'; visited Moscow and Berlin with the National Theatre Company, Sept 1965, appearing as Desdemona in Othello, and Maggie Hobson in Hobson's Choice; Old Vic, Nov 1965, again played Avonia Bunn in Trelawny of the 'Wells'; Criterion, Feb 1971, for the Royal Shakespeare Company, played Clare in After Haggerty; Royal Court, Jan 1973, and again in Jan 1975, Mouth in Not I; Hampstead, Mar 1975, Lucy in Alphabetical Order, transferring to the May Fair, Apr; Royal Court, May 1976, May in Footfalls; Comedy, Oct 1978, title role in Molly; Royal Court, June 1979, Winnie in Happy Days; Aldwych, Jan 1980, Andromache and Athene in The Greeks; entered films, 1955, and appearances include No Love for Johnny, Eagle In A Cage, Twisted Nerve, Charlie Bubbles (British Film Academy Award as best supporting actress, 1969), Gumshoe, Frenzy, Start the Revolution Without Me, The Omen, and The Water Babies; first appeared on television, 1952, and principal appearances include A World of Time, Sextet, The Withered Arm, Happy Days, and The Serpent Son; received the Variety Club Silver Heart Award for the Best Actress of the Year, 1961 and 1977, and also the SFTA Best Actress of the Year Award, 1960 and 1972.

Recreation: Do-It-Yourself. *Address:* c/o Joy Jameson Ltd, 7 West Eaton Place Mews, London, SW1.

WHITMORE, James, actor
b White Plains, NY, 1 Oct 1921; *s* of James Allen Whitmore and his wife Florence (Crane); *e* Choate School, Wallingford, Conn, Yale Univ (BA 1944); *m* (1) Nancy Mygatt (mar dis); (2) Alldra Lindley; prepared for the stage at the American Theater Wing, 1947.

Appeared with the Peterboro, New Hampshire, Players, summer, 1947; made his NYC debut at the Fulton, 1 Oct 1947, as Sergeant Harold Evans in Command Decision; entered films, then at the Univ of Cal at Los Angeles, 1953, played title role of Peer Gynt; La Jolla, Cal, 1954, played Starbuck in The Rainmaker; 1957, Mr Antrobus in The Skin of Our Teeth; Bucks County Playhouse, New Hope, Pa, 1958, Barney in Summer of the 17th Doll; National, NY, Feb 1958, Tom Willard in Winesburg, Ohio; Univ of Cal, 1959, Narrator in Under Milk Wood; Fresno State College, Cal, 1961, played title role in Brand; Playhouse on the Mall, Paramus, NJ, 1963, title role in Gideon; Music Box, Apr 1970, Emanuel Bloch in Inquest; Ford's, Washington, DC, Sept 1970, played Will Rogers in the one-man show Will Rogers' USA, and toured until Jan 1971; again toured, Sept 1971–Feb 1972, as Will Rogers in his one-man show; Helen Hayes, May 1974, again played Will Rogers, and subsequently toured; Ford's, Washington, DC, July 1975, President Harry S Truman in Give 'Em Hell Harry!, and subsequently toured; Eisenhower, Washington, DC, July 1976, appeared in The Magnificent Yankee; Forty-Sixth Street, Nov 1977, and tour, appeared as Theodore Roosevelt in a one-man show, Bully; toured the same year in Will Rogers' USA; first appeared in films in Battleground, 1949, and has since played in Black Like Me, Asphalt Jungle, Oklahoma!, Planet of the Apes, Chato's Land, Give 'Em Hell Harry (1975), etc; has also appeared on television in *The Law and Mr Jones*, etc; received the Antoinette Perry (Tony) Award for Command Decision.

Recreations: Gardening, fishing. *Address:* Actors Equity Association, 6430 Sunset Boulevard, Los Angeles, Calif 90028.

WHITROW, Benjamin, actor
b Oxford, 17 Feb 1937; *s* of Philip Benjamin Whitrow and his

wife Mary Alexandra (Flaunders); *e* Tonbridge; *m* Catherine Elizabeth Cook; trained for the stage at RADA.

Made his first professional appearance at the Empire, Belfast, 1959, as Hector Hushabye in Heartbreak House; worked extensively in repertory 1959–67; joined the National Theatre Company at the Old Vic, 1967, walking on in Love for Love and playing a Player in Rosencrantz and Guildenstern Are Dead; subsequently played Peregrine in Volpone, Chorus in Oedipus, Ensign Mullet in H, Camillo in The White Devil, 1968; took over Frederick Lowndes in Home and Beauty and Dr Finache in A Flea in Her Ear, 1969; played the Duke in The Merchant of Venice, Radomsky in The Idiot, 1970; Snake in The School for Scandal, the Trumpeter in Amphitryon 38 (New Theatre), also taking over two parts in The Captain of Köpenick and Arragon in The Merchant of Venice, 1971; Bensinger in The Front Page, Bushy in Richard II, also taking over Joseph Surface in The School for Scandal, 1972; Malvolio in a Mobile production of Twelfth Night, 1973, and took over as Inspector Bones in Jumpers; James Shanklin in Next of Kin, Dr Bartholo in The Marriage of Figaro, 1974; leaving the National, he played Canon Chasuble in The Importance of Being Earnest, Greenwich, Mar 1975; Wood in Otherwise Engaged, Queen's, July 1975; McTeazle in Dirty Linen, Arts, Sept 1976; Globe, Apr 1978, Donald in Ten Times Table; Arnaud, Guildford, Apr 1979, and tour, Hjalmar Ekdal in The Wild Duck; joined Prospect Theatre Company at the Old Vic, Sept 1979, to play Puff in Miss in Her Teens, Oct 1979, Dr Prentice in What the Butler Saw, and Nov 1979, Attorney General in The Trial of Queen Caroline; Chichester Festival, May 1980, appeared in The Last of Mrs Cheyney, and Terra Nova; TV work includes The Brontës, Two Sundays, King Lear, Fathers and Families, and Life at Stake.

Favourite parts: Malvolio, Surface and Chasuble *Recreations:* Reading, walking in the countryside. *Address:* c/o Ken McReddie, 4 Paddington Street, London W1. *Tel:* 01–935 2491.

WHITTAKER, Herbert, dramatic critic, columnist
b Montreal, Canada, 20 Sept 1911; *s* of George William Whittaker and his wife, Eleanor (Trappitt); *e* Strathcona Academy and Ecole des Beaux Arts, Montreal.

Formerly drama and film critic of *The Gazette*, Montreal; dramatic critic of *The Globe and Mail*, Toronto, 1949–75; Critic Emeritus, 1975–; has also reviewed for *The NY Times, NY Herald Tribune, The Christian Science Monitor,* and other papers; contributor to *The Culture of Canada* (Cornell University), *The Saturday Review, Theatre Arts, Encyclopaedia Americana*; author of *The Stratford Festival* (Canada), 1953–8; *Canada's National Ballet* (1951–67); has also directed the following plays: Galileo, Uncle Vanya, The Family Reunion, The Dybbuk, Electra (Giraudoux), The Lady's Not for Burning, The Glass Menagerie, In Good King Charles's Golden Days, The Living Room, The Prisoner, Every Bed Is Narrow, Jig for a Gypsy, Trumpets and Drums, The Three Sisters, The Caretaker, A Touch of the Poet, The Ecstasy of Rita Joe, Old Times, Back to Methuselah, The Critic, The Alcestiad, and others; twice awarded the Louis Jouvet Trophy for directing, in Dominion Drama Festival; also Sir Barry Jackson Award, Martha Allan Trophy, Bessborough Trophy, and Canadian Drama Award; Adjudicator, Canadian Playwriting Competition, 1954; Canada Medal, 1967; Governor of Dominion Drama Festival, 1949–69, and a member of its executive committee, 1957–69; has adjudicated drama festivals in British Columbia, Alberta, Western Ontario, and Nova Scotia; contributor to the Uni-

versities of Canada Shakespeare Seminar, Stratford, Ontario; DLitt (honoris causa), York University, 1971; founder and first chairman, The Drama Bench (Toronto), 1972; Life member, Canadian Actors' Equity Association, 1975; Officer of the Order of Canada, 1976; Trustee of National Arts Centre (1976–9, 1979–;) senior associate Drama Centre, University of Toronto, 1976–8; advisory board, George Brown College Theatre Department, 1978–; finals judge, Ontario Playwrights Showcase, 1979–80.

Address: 26 Chestnut Park Road, Toronto, Ontario M4W–IW6, Canada.

WICKHAM, Glynne, director and professor of drama
b Cape Town, South Africa, 15 May 1922; *s* of William Gladstone Wickham and his wife Catherine Agnes Mary (Simpson); *e* Winchester and New College, Oxford; *m* Marjorie Heseltine Mudford.

Acted and directed with OUDS at Oxford (President, 1946–7); has directed various classic productions at Bristol and in the USA; directed the American première of The Birthday Party, San Francisco, 1960; Professor of Drama, University of Bristol, since 1960; Ferens Visiting Professor of Drama, Hull University, 1969; Visiting Professor of Theatre History, Yale University, 1970; Killam Resident Professor, Dalhousie University, 1976–7; Governor, Bristol Old Vic Trust, 1963–; Chairman, National Council of Drama, 1970–; Chairman, National Drama Conference, 1970–6; President, Society for Theatre Research, 1976–; is the author of Early English Stages, 1300–1660; Vol I, 1958; Vol II (Part I), 1969; Vol II (Part II), 1971; Drama in a World of Science, 1962; Shakespeare's Dramatic Heritage, 1968; the Medieval Theatre, English Moral Interludes, 1975.

Recreations: Opera, gardening, ski-ing. *Club:* Garrick. *Address:* 6 College Road, Clifton, Bristol BS8 3JB. *Tel:* Bristol 34918.

WIDDOES, Kathleen, actress
b Wilmington, Delaware, 21 Mar 1939; *d* of Eugene Widdoes and his wife Bernice (Delapo); *m* Richard Jordan; studied mime at the Université au Théâtre des Nations, in Paris.

Made her professional début at the Robin Hood Playhouse, Wilmington, Delaware, Aug 1957, as Alma in Bus Stop and subsequently played Catherine in A View from the Bridge and in The Primrose Path; toured Canada, Dec 1957–Jan 1958, as Catherine in A View from the Bridge; first appeared in New York at the Coronet, 30 Mar 1958, as Teusret in The Firstborn; Habimah, Tel Aviv, Israel, May 1958, again played Teusret in The Firstborn; Broadhurst, Oct 1958, played a Tourist and understudied France Nuyen as Suzie Wong in The World of Suzie Wong; Fourth Street, Sept 1959, Irina in The Three Sisters; Theatre de Lys, Nov 1959, Sonja in Notes from the Underground; Jan 1960, again toured as Catherine in A View from the Bridge; Belvedere Lake, for the New York Shakespeare Festival, June 1960, Katherine in Henry V and, July 1960, Juliet in Measure for Measure; Gate, Sept 1960, Aglasia in The Idiot; New York Shakespeare Festival, July 1961, Titania in A Midsummer Night's Dream and, Aug 1961, the Queen in Richard II; Shubert, New Haven, Connecticut, Feb 1962, Teresa del Castillo in We Take the Town; Delacorte, for the New York Shakespeare Festival, July 1962, Miranda in The Tempest; Aldana, Nov 1963, Claire in The Maids; Lyceum, 1966, took over from Rosemary Harris as Alice in You Can't Take It with You; Sheridan Square Playhouse, Apr 1967, Ersilia Drei in To Clothe the Naked; as a member of the Yale Repertory Theater, New Haven, Connecticut, 1967–8, played in The Three Sisters and 'Tis Pity She's a Whore; Martinique, NY,

Mar 1969, The Woman in World War 2½; The Other Stage, Oct 1970, Mildred in Willie; Brooklyn Academy of Music, Mar 1972, Polly Peachum in The Beggar's Opera, and transferred with this production to the McAlpin Rooftop, May 1972; Delacorte, Aug 1972, Beatrice in Much Ado About Nothing; Winter Garden, Nov 1972, again played Beatrice in Much Ado About Nothing; Delacorte, June 1973, Rosalind in As You Like It; Kennedy Center, Washington, DC, Sept 1973, Desdemona, Juliet, and Titania in Shakespeare and the Performing Arts; Mitzi E Newhouse, Jan 1975, Titania in A Midsummer Night's Dream; Stratford, Ontario, Canada, June 1975, Viola in Twelfth Night and Mariana in Measure for Measure; Promenade, Feb 1977, appeared in Castaways; Circle in the Square, June 1977, Cecily Cardew in The Importance of Being Earnest; played in the films The Sea Gull and Petulia, 1969, Savages (1972); made her television début in 1957, and subsequently played Emily in Our Town, 1959, Colombe in the play of that name on Canadian television, 1960, title-role in Ondine, Joan in The Lark, in Canada, 1962, Beatrice in Much Ado About Nothing, 1973, etc; and in various dramatic series and programs.
Address: 71 Horatio Street, New York, NY 10014.

WILBUR, Richard, poet, critic, translator, and teacher
b New York City, 1 Mar 1921; *s* of Lawrence Lazear Wilbur and his wife Helen Ruth (Purdy); *e* Amherst College (AB 1942), Harvard University (MA 1947); *m* Charlotte Ward.

First work produced in the theatre was the translation of Molière's Le Misanthrope, presented by The Poets' Theater, Cambridge, Massachusetts, 25 Oct 1955; with Dorothy Parker and John La Touche wrote the lyrics for Leonard Bernstein's operetta Candide, produced at the Martin Beck, Dec 1956, and at the Saville, London, 30 Apr 1959; his verse translations of Molière have been widely performed, Tartuffe by the Lincoln Center Repertory, the Stratford, Ontario, Shakespeare Company, and the National Theatre of London, and The School for Wives by the Phoenix, NY, in 1971; The Learned Ladies, Williamstown Festival, 1977; Candide revived in 1974; his books of poetry include The Beautiful Changes and Other Poems, 1947, Ceremony and Other Poems, 1950, Things of This World, which received the Pulitzer Prize, 1956, Advice to a Prophet, 1961, Loudmouse, 1963, Walking to Sleep, 1969, etc; has edited the poems of Edgar Allan Poe, and Shakespeare for publication, in a series of which he was general editor; taught at Wellesley College, 1954–7, Harvard University, 1950–4, and Wesleyan University, Middletown, Connecticut, 1957 to date; writer in residence, Smith College, 1977 to date; has received two Guggenheim Fellowships (1952, 1963), the Prix de Rome of the American Academy of Arts and Letters (1954), the National Book Award (1956), Pulitzer Prize (1956), the Millay Prize (1956), a Ford Foundation Fellowship (1960), Bollingen Translation Prize (1963), Brandeis Creative Arts Award (1971), and other awards; honorary LHD from Lawrence College (1960) and Washington University (1964); DLitt from Amherst, 1967; President American Academy of Arts and Letters, 1974–6; Chancellor, Academy of American Poets.
Recreations: Tennis, herb gardening, walking. *Professional associations:* The Dramatists Guild, PEN: National Institute of Arts and Letters; American Academy of Arts and Sciences. *Address:* Dodwells Road, Cummington, Mass 01026. *Tel:* 634–5420.

WILDER, Clinton, producer
b Irvine, Pa, 7 July 1920; *s.* of Clinton Eugene Wilder and his

wife Frances (Kornreich); *e* Princeton University (BA 1942); served in the US Army and the US Army Air Force, 1942–5.

Served as stage manager for Arthur Laurents's Heartsong, and, at the Ethel Barrymore, New York, Dec 1947, for A Streetcar Named Desire; has since produced or co-produced the following plays: Regina, 1949; The Tender Trap, 1954; Six Characters in Search of an Author, 1955; A Visit to a Small Planet, 1957; The World of Suzie Wong (London), 1959; in association with Richard Barr, he formed a production company, Theatre 1960, and produced the following plays: The American Dream, Bartleby, *Valerie Bettis Dance Theatre,* The Death of Bessie Smith, Gallow's Humor, Happy Days, 1961; The Death of Bessie Smith, The American Dream, Who's Afraid of Virginia Woolf?, Whisper into My Good Ear, Mrs Dally Has a Lover, and the *Theatre of the Absurd Repertory,* consisting of Endgame, Bertha, Gallow's Humor, The Sandbox, Deathwatch, Picnic on the Battlefield, The Zoo Story, and The Killer, 1962; in 1963, Edward Albee joined the management of the company, and the following plays were produced: Like Other People, The American Dream, The Zoo Story, Corruption in The Palace of Justice, 1963; Play, The Lover, Funnyhouse of a Negro, Who's Afraid of Virginia Woolf? (London), The Two Executioners, The Dutchman, The Giant's Dance, Tiny Alice, 1964; Lovey, Hunting the Jingo Bird, Do Not Pass Go, That Thing at the Cherry Lane, Happy Days, Up to Thursday, Balls, Home Free, Pigeons, Conerico Was Here to Stay, 1965; Malcolm, The Long Christmas Dinner, Queens of France, The Happy Journey from Trenton to Camden, The Butter and Egg Man, Match Play, A Party for Divorce, Night of the Dunce, 1966; A Delicate Balance (Pulitzer Prize play), The Rimers of Eldritch, The Party on Greenwich Avenue, Johnny No-Trump, Everything in the Garden, Something Different, 1967; How Much, How Much? Home (with Alexander H Cohen), 1970; The Enclave, 1973; Seascape, 1975; received the Margo Jones Award for encouraging new playwrights, 1965.
Address: Quogue, NY 11959.

WILKINSON, Marc, composer, conductor
b Paris, France, 27 July 1929; *s* of Harold L Wilkinson and his wife Mireille (de Civrieux); *e* Columbia and Princeton Universities, USA and Conservatoire de Musique, Paris; *m* Fanny Yen.

Formerly a harpsichordist and lecturer; wrote incidental music for Richard III at Stratford-upon-Avon, 1962, and has since composed music for numerous productions, notably at the National Theatre, where he was director of music until 1974; recent music includes Knuckle, 1974; Too True to be Good (RSC), 1975; contributions to Carte Blanche, Wild Oats (RSC), 1976; Man and Superman (RSC), 1977; The Passion of Dracula, 1978; his music has also been used in productions at the Royal Court, the Chichester Festival, and in Brazil, France and the USA; has written music for drama recordings, and a record of his music for the National Theatre productions of As You Like It, Rosencrantz and Guildenstern are Dead, and The Royal Hunt of the Sun has been issued; film music includes If, The Royal Hunt of the Sun, and Eagle In A Cage; music for television includes Twelfth Night and The Lie.
Recreations: Driving, walking, gardening. *Address:* 21 St Ann's Terrace, London, NW8 6PH. *Tel:* 01–722 8514.

WILLIAM, David, (*né* Williams), actor and director
b London, 24 June 1926; *s* of Eric Hugh Williams and his wife Olwen (Roose); *e* Bryanston School, Dorset, and University College, Oxford.

While at the university appeared as Prospero, Richard II, and Hamlet for the OUDS; made his first professional appearance on the stage at the Old Vic, Sept 1953, as Rosencrantz in Hamlet, subsequently appearing in All's Well That Ends Well, and King John; directed his first London production at St Thomas's Church, Regent Street, Apr 1955, with Our Lady's Tumbler; Open Air Theatre, June 1955, directed The Tempest, and in Aug 1955, The Romanticks; Guildford Repertory, Nov 1955, directed The Iron Harp; joined the Shakespeare Memorial Company, Stratford-upon-Avon, for the 1956 season, to play Osric in Hamlet, Lorenzo in The Merchant of Venice, and Dumaine in Love's Labour's Lost; Lyric, Hammersmith, Mar 1958, directed Little Eyolf; Pembroke, Croydon, Oct 1960, played the title part in Hamlet; Royal Court, Feb 1961, Tomazo de Piracquo in The Changeling; Mermaid, Aug 1961, the Cardinal in 'Tis Pity She's a Whore; Citizens', Glasgow, Feb 1962, Sir Thomas More in A Man for All Seasons; at the Open Air Theatre, 1962, directed A Midsummer Night's Dream, and Love's Labour's Lost; Comedy, Dec 1962, directed Toad of Toad Hall; joined the Old Vic Company for their last season, 1962–3, to play the Thin Person in Peer Gynt, Prince of Arragon in The Merchant of Venice, and Ananias in The Alchemist; Royal Court, Apr 1962, directed Naked; Open Air Theatre, June–July 1962, Much Ado About Nothing, and A Midsummer Night's Dream (also played Oberon); Theatre Royal, Windsor, and tour, Sept 1963, directed Queen B; Associate Director, Mermaid Theatre 1964–6, during which time he directed The Canker and the Rose, The Shoemaker's Holiday, Left-Handed Liberty, and He Was Gone When They Got There; Founder and Artistic Director of the Ludlow Festival 1958–63, and there directed Comus, A Midsummer Night's Dream, Macbeth; Royal, Brighton, Feb 1964, directed The Merchant of Venice, which subsequently toured Latin America and Europe; toured Pakistan, India and Ceylon for the New Shakespeare Company as Richard in his own production of Richard II and also directed The Tempest; returned to London, and at the Royal, Stratford East, played Procathren in Saint's Day, May 1965, subsequently transferring to the St Martin's; Director of Productions, Citizens', Glasgow, 1965–6; directed Twelfth Night, Stratford, Ontario, and The Magistrate, Arena Stage, Washington, 1966; Hampstead Theatre Club, Apr 1967, directed Studies of the Nude; returned to Stratford, Ontario to direct The Merry Wives of Windsor and Albert Herring; subsequently directed operas including The Fairy Queen and Iphigénie en Tauride (for the Gulbenkian Festival, Lisbon) and Xerxes at Sadlers Wells; directed The Misanthrope for the American Conservatory Theatre, San Francisco, 1968; Artistic Director, National Theatre of Israel, 1968–70; directed The Misanthrope, Nottingham Playhouse, Sept 1970; directed the opening production of the Kreeger Theatre, Washington DC, Jan 1971, The Ruling Class; also What the Butler Saw, May; in the same year directed Volpone (Stratford, Ont), The Magistrate, The Owl on the Battlements (both Nottingham), and Swan Song, opening production of the Crucible, Sheffield; in 1972 directed A Life of the General (Nottingham), Richard II (Old Vic, for National Theatre), King Lear (Stratford, Ont and tour), Love's Labour's Lost, What the Butler Saw (these two Nottingham, as Artistic Director); Othello (Stratford, Ont), The Way of the World, King Lear (Actors' Company), 1973; Twelfth Night (Stratford, Conn), Iphigénie in Tauride (Lisbon), Albert Herring, (English Opera Group), 1974; Arnaud, Guildford, Oct 1974, played Mr Fisher in Robin Redbreast; in 1975 directed Il Re Pastore (Camden Festival), Pygmalion (Belgrade, Coventry); Chichester Festival, season 1975, played de

Guiche in Cyrano de Bergerac, and Roderigo in Othello, and subsequently appeared with the company in both these roles at the Hong Kong Festival; Greenwich, Oct 1975, played Pauncefort Quentin in The Vortex; Haymarket, Leicester, Nov 1975, directed Speak Now; Birmingham Rep, Mar 1976, played title role in Uncle Vanya; Oxford Festival, 1976, directed the premiere of Dear Daddy, which transferred to the Ambassadors, Oct 1976; also directed Peer Gynt (Lyceum, Edinburgh), Antigone (National Theatre School, Montreal), Romeo and Juliet (Stratford, Ontario), Albert Herring (English Music Theatre, Sadlers Wells), premiere of A Gentle Spirit and The Soldier's Tale (Bath and Cheltenham Festivals), The Queen of Spades (Welsh National Opera), 1976–7; returned to the stage, Oct 1977, to play M L'Abbe Pradeau de la Halle (or just Father Superior?) in The Fire that Consumes at the Mermaid; directed Sentenced to Life, The Aspern Papers (Chichester and national tour), Present Laughter (York), 1978; Fennimore and Gerda and Mavra (double-bill) (Camden Festival), The Eagle Has Two Heads (Chichester), Thérèse (Royal Opera House), 1979; has appeared frequently on television in productions including An Age of Kings, The Cruel Necessity, Troubleshooters; author of The Tempest on the Stage and Hamlet in the Theatre (both in Stratford-on-Avon Studies).

Recreation: Walking. *Address:* 3 Chesterford Gardens, London, NW3. *Tel:* 01–435 9265.

WILLIAMS, Billy Dee, actor
b New York City, 6 Apr 1937; *e* High School of Music and Art; prepared for the stage with Paul Mann and Sidney Poitier and at the National Academy of Fine Arts.

Made his first appearance on the stage at the Alvin, 22 Mar 1945, as the Page in The Firebrand of Florence; reappeared on the stage at the Eugene O'Neill, 22 Feb 1960, as Duke Custis in The Cool World; Lyceum, Oct 1960, played the Boy in A Taste of Honey; Masque, Apr 1963, Robert in The Blue Boy in Black; St Mark's Playhouse, 1964, took over in The Blacks; same theatre, 1966, took over from Robert Hooks as Junie in Happy Ending and John in Day of Absence; Martin Beck, 1967, took over from Robert Hooks as Clem in Hallelujah Baby; Martinique, July 1968, Willy Lee Irons in The Firebugs; Pocket, Apr 1969, Theopolis Parker in Ceremonies in Dark Old Men; Sheridan Square Playhouse, May 1970, Randall in a revival of Slow Dance on the Killing Ground; Ambassador, Sept 1976, Dr Martin Luther King in I Have a Dream; first appeared in films in The Last Angry Man, 1959; and has since played in The Out-of-Towners, The Final Comedown, Lady Sings the Blues (1972), etc; has played on television in various dramatic programs, including playing Gale Sayers in Brian's Song, The Glass House, and the series *Mod Squad*, etc.

Address: Actors Equity Association, 165 West 46th Street, New York, NY 10036.

WILLIAMS, Clarence III, actor
b New York City, 21 Aug 1939; *s* of Clarence Williams II; *m* Gloria Foster.

Made his NY début at the Ambassador, 17 Feb 1960, as Chris in The Long Dream; Greenwich Mews, Oct 1963, played Washington Roach in Walk in Darkness; Theatre de Lys, May 1964, played The Sax in Sarah and the Sax in a production with the overall title Doubletalk; Plymouth, Nov 1964, Randall in Slow Dance on the Killing Ground; Eugene O'Neill, Feb 1966, Hector Case in The Great Indoors; Brandeis University, 1966–7, was artist in residence and performed in Does a Tiger Wear a Necktie?; Cherry Lane, May 1967, Roosevelt in The Party on Greenwich Avenue;

Delacorte, for the New York Shakespeare Festival, July 1967, Hubert de Burgh in King John; New Federal, Oct 1979, Ray in Suspenders; ANTA, Nov 1979, President Mageeba in Night and Day; TV work includes *The Mod Squad*, 1968–73.

Address: Actors Equity Association, 165 West 46th Street, York, NY 10036.

WILLIAMS, Clifford, director
b Cardiff, Wales, 30 Dec 1926; *s* of George Frederick Williams and his wife Florence Maud (Gapper); *e* Highbury County Grammar School, London; *m* Josiane Peset.

Began his career as an actor at the Chanticleer Theatre, London, 1945, appearing in Larissa and More Than Science; People's Palace, Nov 1948, played Julius Caesar in These Mortals; between 1950–3, wrote and directed twenty mime plays for the Mime Theatre Company, which he also founded; Director of Productions at Marlowe Theatre, Canterbury, in 1956; Director of Productions at the Queen's Theatre, Hornchurch, 1957; directed his first London production at the Arts, July 1957, with Yerma; at the same theatre directed the following plays: Radio Rescue, Dec 1958; Dark Halo, Quartet For Five, The Marriage of Mr Mississippi, 1959; A Moon for the Misbegotten, The Shepherd's Chameleon, and Victims of Duty, 1960; at Llandaff Cathedral, June 1961, directed Race of Adam; joined the Royal Shakespeare Theatre Company, Oct 1961 (appointed Associate Director, 1963); for whom he has directed the following plays: Afore Night Come, 1962; The Comedy of Errors, 1962–3; The Tempest, The Representative, 1963; Richard II (co-directed), Henry IV (Parts I and II) (co-directed), The Comedy of Errors (overseas tour), Afore Night Come, The Jew of Malta, 1964; The Merchant of Venice, The Jew of Malta, The Comedy of Errors, 1965; also directed Our Man Crichton (London) in 1964, and The Gardener's Dog (Finnish National Theatre) in 1965; he has since directed the following productions: The Flying Dutchman (Covent Garden), The Meteor (London), Henry the Fourth (co-directed), and Twelfth Night (Stratford-upon-Avon), 1966; Volpone (Yale School of Drama), The Merry Wives of Windsor (Finnish National Theatre), an all male As You Like It (National Theatre), 1967; Soldiers (Toronto, New York, London), Dr Faustus (Stratford and US tour), Othello (Bulgarian National Theatre), 1968; directed A Winter's Tale (Yugoslav National Theatre), the two parts of Back to Methuselah (National Theatre), Dido and Aeneas (Windsor Festival) and Famine (English Stage Society), 1969; Sleuth (London, New York, Paris), Oh! Calcutta! (London, Paris), Major Barbara (Royal Shakespeare Company), 1970; The Duchess of Malfi (RSC), 1971; The Comedy of Errors (RSC), The Brass Hat (tour), 1972; The Taming of the Shrew (RSC), A Lesson in Blood and Roses (RSC), 1973; Henry IV (Pirandello: London and NY), Cymbeline (RSC), What Every Woman Knows, 1974; Murderer, The Mouth Organ (RSC: also co-devised), Too True To Be Good (RSC), 1975; Mardi Gras, Carte Blanche, Wild Oats, 1976; Stevie, The Old Country, Rosmersholm, Man and Superman (RSC), 1977; The Tempest (RSC), The Passion of Dracula, 1978; Threepenny Opera (Aalborg), Wild Oats (RSC revival), Richard III (Mexican National Theatre), Born in the Gardens, 1979; Lord Arthur Savile's Crime (tour), 1980; he has also directed plays for Arena Theatre, Birmingham, the Edinburgh Festival, Belgrade Theatre, Coventry, Theatre Workshop, Theatre-in-the-Round, the National Theatre of the Deaf, etc; author of the following plays: The Sleeping Princess, The Goose Girl, The Secret Kingdom, Stephen Dedalus, The Disguises of Arlecchino; Fellow of Trinity College, London; Chairman, British Theatre Association, 1977–.

Recreations: Motor sport, water ski-ing, and travelling.
Address: 43 Onslow Square, London, SW7.

WILLIAMS, Dick Anthony, actor, director, producer
b Chicago, Ill, 9 Aug 1938.

First appeared in New York at the Village South, 8 Dec 1968, as Big Time Buck White in the play of that name; American Place, May 1970, directed The Pig Pen; Henry Street Playhouse, Jan 1971, directed In New England Winter; Theatre de Lys, June 1971, co-produced Black Girl in association with Woodie King; Public/Other Stage, June 1971, played in Nigger Nightmare; Ethel Barrymore, Oct 1971, played in Aint Supposed to Die a Natural Death; Henry Street Playhouse, Mar 1962, played Omar Butler I in Jamimma; New Federal, Jan 1973, co-produced A Recent Killing; Vivian Beaumont, Feb 1974, Rico in What the Wine-Sellers Buy, and repeated this part at the New Theatre for Now, Los Angeles; Delacorte, summer 1974, again played this last part; Vivian Beaumont, Jan 1975, Alexander in Black Picture Show; Ambassador, Apr 1975, Al Seaver in We Interrupt This Program; Ambassador, Jan 1976, Bobby Foster in The Poison Tree; appeared in the films Who Killed Mary What's'ername?, The Anderson Tapes, Dog Day Afternoon, The Jerk (1979), etc; TV includes King, Brave New World, etc.

Address: 4075 West 29th Street, Los Angeles, Calif 90018.

WILLIAMS, Emlyn, CBE, MA (Oxon), LL D (Hon), actor, dramatic author and director
b Mostyn, Flintshire, Wales, 26 Nov 1905; *s* of Richard Williams and his wife Mary (Williams); *e* Holywell County School, St Julien, Switzerland, and Christ Church, Oxford; *m* Molly O'Shann (dec); a member of the OUDS, while at Oxford.

Made his first appearance on the stage at the Savoy Theatre, 4 Apr 1927, as Pelling's 'Prentice in And So To Bed; made his first appearance in New York, at the Shubert Theatre, 9 Nov 1927, as Pepys' Boy; on returning to London, appeared at the Arts Theatre, Oct 1928, as the Rev Yorke and Billy Saunders in The Pocket-Money Husband; Embassy, Dec 1928, played Jack in his own play Glamour, which was subsequently transferred to the Court Theatre; Wyndham's, Feb 1929, appeared as Camille in Thérèse Raquin (in French); Queen's, Feb–Mar 1929, played Beppo in Mafro, Darling, and Berthold in The Mock Emperor; Apollo, Oct 1929, the Trumpeter in The Silver Tassie; Duchess, Nov 1929, Captain Sandys in Tunnel Trench; Vaudeville, Jan 1930, Jules Marnier in French Leave; Arts, Mar 1930, Giovanni d'Amora in La Piccola (in Italian); Everyman, Mar 1930, the Usher in The Fire in the Opera House; Wyndham's, Apr 1930, Angelo in On the Spot; Arts, Sept 1930, Adolphe in Devant La Porte (in French); Wyndham's, Nov 1930, Commissar Neufeld in The Mouthpiece; St James's, Feb 1931, Etienne in the play of that name; Wyndham's, Aug 1931, Lord Lebanon in The Case of the Frightened Lady; Nov 1931, Youssef el Tabah in his own play, Port Said; Apollo, Mar 1932, the Young Frenchman in The Man I Killed; Garrick, May 1932, Jack in Man Overboard; at the Belasco, NY, Oct 1932, appeared as Lord Lebanon in Criminal at Large (The Case of the Frightened Lady); Apollo, May 1933, Patrick Branwell Brontë in Wild Decembers; Westminster, Sept 1934, Piers Gaveston in Rose and Glove; His Majesty's, Sept 1934, Eugene Beauharnais in Josephine; Duchess, May 1935, Dan in Night Must Fall, which ran over a year, and in which he also appeared at the Barrymore Theatre, NY, Sept 1936; Queen's, London, May 1937, played Lambert in He Was Born Gay; at Buxton, with the Old Vic Company, Aug 1937, played Oswald in Ghosts; Old Vic, Sept–Nov 1937, Angelo in Measure for Measure and the Duke of Gloucester in Richard III; Duchess, Sept

1938, Morgan Evans in The Corn is Green, which ran nearly two years; Globe, June 1941, played Maddoc Thomas in The Light of Heart, and Dec 1941, Cliff Parrilow in The Morning Star; toured, 1943, as Dan in Night Must Fall; toured in the Middle East, for Overseas Forces, Feb 1944, as Charles Condomine in Blithe Spirit, and in Night Must Fall, Flare Path, etc; St James's, Apr 1945, Ambrose Ellis in The Wind of Heaven; Lyric, May 1946, Sir Robert Morton in The Winslow Boy; Globe, July 1947, Saviello in Trespass; Fulton NY, Oct 1949, Izquierdo in Montserrat; Aldwych, London, Sept 1950, Will Trenting in Accolade; at the Lyric, Hammersmith, Oct 1951, he appeared as Charles Dickens, giving a solo performance of scenes from the novels; transferred to the Criterion, Nov 1951, and later to the Duchess, subsequently touring North America, Europe, and South Africa; at the Edinburgh Festival, Aug 1952, again appeared as Charles Dickens in a solo performance of Bleak House; subsequently appearing at the Ambassadors', London, Sept 1952; at the Bijou, NY, Apr 1953, again appeared as Dickens in Bleak House, and also in a mixed bill of scenes from the novels; at the National Eisteddfod of Wales, Aug 1953, appeared as Dickens in Welsh translation; at the Globe, London, Nov 1953, played Fenn in his own play, Someone Waiting; Globe, May 1955, appeared in a new solo performance, Dylan Thomas Growing Up; Saville, Dec 1955, played Hjalmar Ekdal in The Wild Duck; Shakespeare Memorial Theatre, Stratford-on-Avon, 1956 season, played Shylock, Iago, and Angelo; Longacre, NY, Oct 1957, Dylan Thomas in A Boy Growing Up; Apollo, London, Mar 1958, directed Beth; toured Australia and New Zealand, for five months, Mar 1958, in solo programmes; Globe, London, Sept 1958, for three weeks again appeared in A Boy Growing Up; Piccadilly, Oct 1958, played The Author in Shadow of Heroes; toured 59 cities in the US, Jan–May 1959, in A Boy Growing Up; Arts, London, and Criterion, Jan 1961, played The Man in Lunch Hour, Mr Chacterson in The Form, and Edward in A Slight Ache, in the triple-bill Three; Music Box, NY, Nov 1961, Ascolini in Daughter of Silence; ANTA, NY, June 1962, took over the part of Sir Thomas More in A Man For All Seasons; Brooks Atkinson, NY, Feb 1964, Pope Pius XII in The Deputy; toured 80 cities in the US and Canada, 1965, followed by a tour of the Far East, including Pakistan, India, and Japan, with Charles Dickens; Globe, London, Aug 1965, again appeared as Charles Dickens; Cambridge, Sept 1965, played Ignatyillyich in A Month in the Country; Apollo, Sept 1969 took over the part of the Headmaster in Forty Years On; 1970, Dickens Centenary World Tour as Charles Dickens, including Australia, Russia and the USA; Haymarket, Feb 1975, again appeared as Dickens; Apollo, Sept 1977, devised and acted in Emlyn Williams as Saki, which he performed at the Playhouse, NY, 1978, under the title The Playboy of the Weekend World; Arnaud, Guildford, July 1979, devised and appeared as Dylan Thomas Growing Up; played this role at the Ambassadors', Mar 1980; is the author of the following plays: Vigil, Glamour, 1928; Full Moon, 1929; A Murder Has Been Arranged, 1930; Port Said, 1931; The Late Christopher Bean (adaptation), Vessels Departing, 1933; Spring 1600, Josephine (adaptation), 1934; Night Must Fall, 1935; He Was Born Gay, 1937; The Corn is Green, 1938; The Light of Heart, 1940; The Morning Star, 1941; A Month in the Country (adaptation), 1943; The Druid's Rest, 1944; The Wind of Heaven, Spring 1600 (final version), 1945; Trespass, 1947; Accolade, 1950; Someone Waiting, Pen Don, 1953; Beth, 1958; The Master Builder (adapted), 1965; has directed many of his own plays, as well as Watch on the Rhine, and The Little Foxes, 1942; first appeared in films, 1932, in The Case of the Frightened Lady,

appearing since in The Last Days of Dolwyn (which he also wrote and directed), The Citadel, Major Barbara, Another Man's Poison, Ivanhoe, The Deep Blue Sea, I Accuse, Beyond This Place, The Wreck of the Mary Deare, The L Shaped Room, The Walking Stick, and David Copperfield, 1969; his play The Corn is Green, received the New York Drama Critics' Circle Award, for the best foreign play, 1941; author of George (autobiography), 1961; Beyond Belief, 1967; Emlyn (autobiography), 1973; received the Hon LL D (Bangor), 1949, and the CBE in the Birthday Honours, 1962.

Favourite part: Sir Robert in The Winslow Boy. *Recreations:* Reading and walking. *Address:* 123 Dovehouse Street, London, SW3. *Tel:* 01–352 0208.

WILLIAMS, Kenneth, actor
b London, 22 Feb 1926; *s* of Charles George Williams and his wife Louise Alexandra (Morgan); *e* Lyulph Stanley School, and Bolt Court, London; formerly a lithographic draughtsman.

Made his first appearance on the stage at the Newquay Repertory Theatre, Cornwall, May 1948, when he played Ninian in The First Mrs Fraser; appeared in various other repertory companies, before making his first appearance on the London stage, Scala, Dec 1952, as Slightly in Peter Pan; Arts, Sept 1954, played the Dauphin in a revival of Saint Joan, and repeated his performance in the same production, St Martin's, Feb 1955; Duke of York's, June 1955, played Elijah in Moby Dick; Lyric, Hammersmith, Sept 1955, played Montgomery in Sandy Wilson's The Buccaneer, and transferred with this to the Apollo, Feb 1956; Winter Garden, May 1956, played Maxime in Hotel Paradiso; Arts, Mar 1957, Kite in The Wit To Woo; Lyric, Hammersmith, Aug 1957, played Green in the revue Share My Lettuce, and transferred with this to the Comedy, Sept 1957, and again to the Garrick, Jan 1958; Coliseum, Dec 1958, played Portia, the Ugly Sister, in Cinderella; Apollo, Sept 1959, appeared in the revue Pieces of Eight; Duke of York's, Apr 1961, appeared in the revue One Over the Eight; Globe, May 1962, played Julian in The Public Eye in The Private Ear and The Public Eye; (double-bill), Queen's, Dec 1963, Jack in Gentle Jack; Arts, Cambridge, Feb 1965, played Truscott in Loot; Wyndham's, Nov 1965, Bernard in The Platinum Cat; Cambridge, Feb 1971, Drinkwater in Captain Brassbound's Conversion; Globe, Dec 1972, Henry in My Fat Friend; Comedy, June 1976, Barillon in Signed and Sealed; Greenwich, Sept 1979, The Undertaker in The Undertaking, transferring to the Fortune, Oct; made his first film in 1952, and has appeared in Trent's Last Case, The Seekers, Twice Round the Daffodils, and the Carry On . . . series of films; first appeared on television 1952, and has since made numerous appearances including the *Hancock's Half Hour* series, *International Cabaret*, and *The Kenneth Williams Show*; has broadcast regularly in *Round the Horne, Stop Messing About, Just A Minute,* etc.

Recreations: Calligraphy, reading, music, walking. *Address:* c/o Peter Eade Ltd, 9 Cork Street, London, W1X 1PD.

WILLIAMS, Michael, actor
b Manchester, 9 July 1935; *s* of Michael Leonard Williams and his wife Elizabeth (Mulligan); *e* St Edward's College, Liverpool; *m* Judi Dench; formerly an insurance clerk; trained for the stage at RADA.

His first stage appearance was at the Nottingham Playhouse, 28 Sept 1959, as Auguste in Take the Fool Away; first London appearance, 7 June 1961, as Bernard Fuller in Celebration, which came to the Duchess from Nottingham;

joined the Royal Shakespeare Company, 1963, and that year at the Aldwych played Puck in A Midsummer Night's Dream, Filch in The Beggar's Opera, and Adolf Eichmann in The Representative; Aldwych, 1964, Oswald in King Lear (also making his New York début in the part at the State Theater, Lincoln Center, May), Pinch in Comedy of Errors, Kokol in The Marat/Sade and Lodowick in The Jew of Malta; Aldwych, Feb 1965, a sergeant in Don't Make Me Laugh (Expeditions Two); at Stratford, 1965, played Dromio of Syracuse in The Comedy of Errors, a painter in Timon of Athens, and Guildenstern in Hamlet; Aldwych, Nov 1965, Herald in The Marat/Sade (also Martin Beck, NY, Dec 1965); returning to the Aldwych 1966, played Arthur in Tango; Stratford, season 1967, Petruchio in The Taming of the Shrew, and Orlando in As You Like It; season 1968, Fool in King Lear, Orlando and Troilus in Troilus and Cressida (also Aldwych, 1969); Aldwych, June 1970, Charles Courtly in London Assurance; appeared in the RSC's Theatregoround Festival, Round House, Oct 1970; Stratford, season 1971, Bassanio in The Merchant of Venice; Ferdinand in The Duchess of Malfi, and Henry V; Stratford, Jan 1972, Mole in Toad of Toad Hall; New, Apr 1972, again played Charles Courtly in London Assurance; Theatre Royal, York, Apr 1973, Stellio in Content to Whisper; Aldwych, Aug 1975, Ian in Jingo; University, Newcastle, Oct 1975, appeared in Scribes; Globe, Dec 1975, Private Meek in Too True to Be Good; Stratford, season 1976, title role in Schwek in the Second World War (The Other Place) (also Warehouse, Aug 1977), Dromio in The Comedy of Errors (also Aldwych, June 1977), Fool in King Lear (and Aldwych, May 1977), and Autolycus in The Winter's Tale; first film, 1966, The Marat/Sade, subsequently Eagle in a Cage and Dead Cert; television appearances include Elizabeth R, A Raging Calm, and The Hanged Man; has appeared on television in Comedy of Errors (with RSC), My Son, My Son, and Love in a Cold Climate; Chairman of Catholic Stage Guild, 1977–.

Favourite parts: Petruchio and Fool. *Recreation:* His family. *Club:* Garrick. *Address:* 4 Prospect Place, Holly Walk, London, NW3.

WILLIAMS, Tennessee (*né* Thomas Lanier Williams), dramatic author

b Columbus, Miss, 26 Mar 1911; *s* of Cornelius Coffin Williams and his wife Edwina (Dakin); *e* High School, St Louis, University of Missouri, Washington University (St Louis), and State University of Iowa (BA).

Author of several one-act plays, including Candles to the Sun, 1936, The Fugitive Kind, 1937, Spring Song, 1938, and Not About Nightingales, 1939; these four being produced in 1939, under the title of American Blues; author of the plays Battle of the Angels, Boston, 1940; Stairs to the Roof, The Glass Menagerie, Chicago, 1944, and New York, 1945; You Touched Me (with Donald Windham), 1945; A Streetcar Named Desire, 1947; Summer and Smoke, 1948; The Rose Tattoo, 1950; Camino Real, 1953; Cat on a Hot Tin Roof, Three Players of a Summer Game, 1955; Orpheus Descending, 1957; Garden District, a double-bill consisting of Something Unspoken and Suddenly Last Summer, 1958; Sweet Bird of Youth, Period of Adjustment (which he also co-directed at the Coconut Grove Playhouse, Miami, Florida), 1959; The Night of the Iguana, 1961; The Milk Train Doesn't Stop Here Anymore, 1963 (produced in a revised version in NY, 1964, and in a further revised version in San Francisco, 1965); The Mutilated and The Gnadiges Fraulein, produced under the overall title of Slapstick Tragedy, 1966; The Two-Character Play (produced at the Hampstead Theatre

Club, London), 1967; The Seven Descents of Myrtle, 1968; In the Bar of a Tokyo Hotel, 1969; Small Craft Warnings, and also occasionally played the role of Doc in this play at the Truck and Warehouse; Out Cry (a revised version of The Two Character Play), 1973; The Latter Days of a Celebrated Soubrette (a revised version of Gnadiges Fraulein), 1974; The Red Devil Battery Sign, 1975; This Is (an entertainment), The Eccentricities of a Nightingale (revision of Summer and Smoke), 1976; Vieux Carré, 1977; A Lovely Sunday for Greve Coeur, 1979; Clothes for a Summer Hotel, 1980; other short plays of his which have been produced include The Lady of Larkspur Lotion, The Purification (1940; also a ballet), This Property Is Condemned, I Rise in Flames, Cried the Phoenix, Portrait of a Madonna, 27 Wagons Full of Cotton, The Last of My Solid Gold Watches, Moony's Kid Don't Cry, Talk to Me Like the Rain, I Can't Imagine Tomorrow, Confessional (these last two produced in Bar Harbour, Maine, 1971), A Perfect Analysis Given by a Parrot (written 1958, produced in NY 1973), Purification given its NY début in Dec 1975, etc; several plays have been translated, including Le Tramway Nommé Désir (adaptation by Jean Cocteau) and La Chatte sur un Toit Brûlant (adaptation by André Obey); The Glass Menagerie gained the New York Drama Critics' Circle Award, 1944–5, and A Streetcar Named Desire received both the Drama Critics' Circle Award and the Pulitzer Prize, 1947–8; Cat on a Hot Tin Roof also gained the same two awards in 1955; received the Antoinette Perry Award and the New York Drama Critics Award for The Night of the Iguana, 1962; author of the screen plays for The Glass Menagerie, A Streetcar Named Desire, The Rose Tattoo, Baby Doll, Suddenly Last Summer, and The Fugitive Kind; author of the novels The Roman Spring of Mrs Stone, and Moise and the World of Reason; two books of poetry, Androgyne Mon Amour and In the Winter of Cities; Memoirs, 1975; received Rockefeller Fellowship Award, 1940; received Grant from National Institute of Arts and Letters, 1943; received Gold Medal for Drama from the National Institute of Arts and Letters, 1969.

Address: c/o Audrey Wood, c/o International Famous Agency, 1301 Avenue of the Americas, New York 10019.

WILLIAMSON, David, dramatic author

b Melbourne, Victoria, 24 Feb 1942; *s* of Edwin Keith Williamson and his wife Elvie May (Armstrong); *e* Melbourne and Monash Universities; *m* Kristin Ingrid Green; formerly a lecturer at Swinburne College of Technology.

His first play to be produced was The Removalists, at the Nimrod Street Theatre, Sydney, 13 Oct 1971; this was also seen at the Royal Court, London, 19 July 1973, and at Playhouse Two, NY, 23 Jan 1974; his other plays include Don's Party, Jugglers Three, 1972; What If You Died Tomorrow, 1973; The Department, 1974; A Handful of Friends, 1976; The Club, 1977 (seen as Players on Broadway, 1978); Travelling, 1979; film scripts include Stork, Petersen, and Eliza Fraser, as well as screen adaptations of The Removalists and Don's Party (Australian Film Institute's Best Screenplay Award); winner of the George Devine Award, 1973, and the *Evening Standard* Most Promising Playwright Award, 1973; visiting Professor of dramatic writing, University of Aarhus, Denmark, 1978.

Address: c/o Curtis Brown Pty Ltd, PO Box 19, Paddington, NSW, Australia 2021.

WILLIAMSON, Nicol, actor

b Hamilton, Scotland, 14 Sept 1938; *m* Jill Townsend (mar dis).

Began his career as an actor at the Dundee Repertory Theatre, where he remained for two seasons, 1960–1; at the Arts Theatre, Cambridge, Oct 1961, played I-ti in That's Us, prior to making his first appearance in London at the Royal Court, Nov 1961, in the same production; toured, Nov 1961, as Black Will in Arden of Faversham; Royal Court, Jan 1962, played Flute in A Midsummer Night's Dream; at the same theatre, Feb 1962, played Malvolio in Twelfth Night in a Production without Décor; joined the Royal Shakespeare Company at the New Arts, Apr 1962, to play SAC Albert Meakin in Nil Carborundum; May 1962, Satin in The Lower Depths; and July 1962, Leantio in Women, Beware Women; Royal Court, Apr 1962, played The Man at the End in Spring Awakening, in a Production without Décor; at the same theatre, June 1963, played Kelly in Kelly's Eye; Ashcroft, Croydon, Nov 1963, played Sebastian Dangerfield in The Ginger Man, transferring with the production to the Royal Court, Nov 1963; at the same theatre, Sept 1964, played Bill Maitland in Inadmissible Evidence; Oct 1964, Peter Wykeham in A Cuckoo in the Nest; Dec 1964, played Vladimir in Waiting for Godot; Wyndham's, Mar 1965, again played Bill Maitland in Inadmissible Evidence; Royal Court, Apr 1965, played Joe Johnson in Miniatures, in a Production without Décor; at the Globe Theatre, June 1965, appeared as Sweeney in Sweeney Agonistes in a Programme of Homage to T S Eliot; made his first appearance in New York at the Belasco, Dec 1965, as Bill Maitland in Inadmissible Evidence (NY Drama Critics Award 1965–6); Duchess, Mar 1967, Alexei Ivanovitch Poprichtchine in Diary of A Madman; Plymouth, NY, June 1968, took over three parts in Plaza Suite; Round House, Mar 1969, played the title role in Hamlet (*Evening Standard* Award for Best Actor, 1969); Lunt-Fontanne, NY, May 1969, again appeared as Hamlet in the same production, which subsequently toured the USA; Circle in the Square, NY, June 1973, title role in Uncle Vanya, also appearing in Nicol Williamson's Late Show; for the RSC, played Coriolanus, Oct 1973, at the Aldwych, also repeating Midwinter Spring, Nov; Stratford, Aug 1974, and Aldwych, Feb 1975, Malvolio in Twelfth Night; Macbeth, Stratford, Oct 1974, and Aldwych, Mar 1975; at the Other Place, 1975, directed Uncle Vanya, playing Vanya; Lunt-Fontanne, NY, Apr 1976, Henry VIII in Rex; Royal Court, Sept 1978, Bill Maitland in Inadmissible Evidence; films include The Reckoning, Laughter in the Dark, The Jerusalem File, and The Seven Per Cent Solution; television includes Terrible Jim Fitch, Arturo Ui, I Know What I Meant, and The Word.
Address: c/o ICM, 22 Grafton Street, London W1.

WILLIS, Ted (Edward Henry) (*cr* Baron, 1963), dramatic author
b Tottenham, Middlesex, 13 Jan 1918; *s* of John Alfred Willis; *e* Downhill, Central School; *m* Audrey Mary Hale; formerly a vehicle-builder.
His first play, Buster, was produced by the Unity Theatre Players at the Arts Theatre, July 1943; he has since written the following plays: No Trees in the Street, 1948; The Lady Purrs, 1950; The Blue Lamp (co-author with Jan Read), The Magnificent Moodies, 1952; Kid Kenyon Rides Again, 1954; Doctor in the House (adapted from the novel by Richard Gordon), 1956; Hot Summer Night, 1958; God Bless the Guvnor, Brothers-in-Law (co-author with Henry Cecil), Farewell Yesterday, (re-named The Eyes of Youth), 1959; Mother (adapted from the Novel by Gorky), 1961; Doctor at Sea (adapted from the Novel by Richard Gordon), Woman in a Dressing Gown, 1962; A Slow Roll of Drums, 1964; A Murder of Crows, 1965; Queenie, 1967; A Fine Day for

Murder, 1970; Dead on Saturday, 1971; The History of Mr Polly (musical), 1977; Doctor on the Boil, 1979; he has also written the following films: Holiday Camp, The Blue Lamp, It's Great to be Young, Woman in a Dressing Gown, No Trees in the Street, Flame in the Streets, Trouble in Store, Bitter Harvest, etc; he is the author of the television series *Dixon of Dock Green, Sergeant Cork, Mrs Thursday, Crimes of Passion, Hunter's Walk*, and of the television plays: The Young and the Guilty, Strictly for the Sparrows, Four Seasons of Rosie Carr, Look in Any Window, etc; autobiography, Whatever Happened to Tom Mix, 1970; director of World Wide Pictures, Capital Radio; member Sports Council, 1971–3; Fellow of the Royal Society of Arts; Fellow of the Royal Television Society; created Baron Willis of Chislehurst (Life Peer), Dec 1963.
Recreations: Tennis and badminton. *Address:* 5 Shepherd's Green, Chislehurst, Kent.

WILLMAN, Noel, actor and director
b Londonderry, Northern Ireland, 4 Aug 1918; *s* of Romain Willman and his wife Charlotte Ellis (O'Neil); *e* Londonderry and Strasbourg; studied for the stage at the London Theatre Studio under Michel St Denis.
Made his first appearance on the stage at the final production at the Lyceum Theatre, 28 June 1939, walking-on in Hamlet; Haymarket, Mar 1940, appeared as the Player in The Beggar's Opera; subsequently toured with the Old Vic company in The Witch, and The Merchant of Venice; Ambassadors', July 1942, played in Light and Shade; at the Arts, Oct 1942, played Grigori Tansmann in House of Regrets; New, Feb 1943, Lorenzo in The Merchant of Venice; for two seasons, 1943–5, engaged with the Old Vic company at the Playhouse, Liverpool, as actor and director; at the Winter Garden, Jan 1946, directed A Doll's House; played a season with the Bristol Old Vic, 1946; Lyric, Hammersmith, Sept 1946, played Baron Foehn in The Eagle Has Two Heads; was co-director of the Arts Theatre, with Beatrix Lehmann, Oct 1946–Mar 1947, and directed The Turn of the Screw, A Phoenix Too Frequent, and Back to Methuselah; toured in South Africa, Mar–Dec 1947; joined the Shakespeare Memorial Theatre company, Stratford-on-Avon, for the 1948 season, playing Robert Faulconbridge in King John, Antonio in The Merchant of Venice, Osric in Hamlet, Gremio in The Taming of the Shrew, Pandarus in Troilus and Cressida; St James's, Mar 1949, played Darius in Adventure Story; Lyric, Hammersmith, Jan 1950, Sir Joseph Wrathie in Shall We Join the Ladies?, and Old Tawn in The Boy with a Cart; Winter Garden, Apr 1950, the Stylish Young Man and the Prison Chaplain in The Trial; Aldwych, Sept 1950, Daker in Accolade; at the Plymouth, New York, Dec 1951, played Monsieur Henri in Legend of Lovers (Point of Departure); Lyric, Hammersmith, Apr 1952, played Col Izquierdo in Montserrat, and directed the play; Globe, Mar 1953, directed The White Carnation; Globe, Nov 1953, directed Someone Waiting; Globe, Apr 1954, appeared as the Interrogator in The Prisoner (for which performance he gained the 1955 Clarence Derwent Award); Westminster, Nov 1954, played Brack in Hedda Gabler; at the Shakespeare Memorial Theatre, Stratford-on-Avon, Apr 1955, directed All's Well That Ends Well; Winter Garden, Nov 1956, played General Burgoyne, and also directed The Devil's Disciple; St James's, June 1957, directed It's the Geography That Counts (last production before the theatre was demolished); Music Box, NY, Jan 1959, played the Husband in Rashomon; Globe, July 1960, directed A Man for All Seasons; joined the Royal Shakespeare Company, Stratford-on-Avon, Apr 1961, to play Don Pedro in Much Ado About Nothing and Claudius in Hamlet;

ANTA, NY, Nov 1961, directed A Man for All Seasons, receiving the Antoinette Perry Award for the Best Director, 1961–2; Cort, NY, Mar 1962, directed Isle of Children; Music Box, NY, Dec 1962, directed The Beauty Part; Queen's, London, Dec 1963, directed Gentle Jack; Walnut, Philadelphia, Oct 1964, directed Rich Little Rich Girl; he has since directed: The Lion in Winter (Ambassador, NY), 1966; Othello, Beware of the Dog (Nottingham Playhouse), Brother and Sister (tour), Beware of the Dog (St Martin's), 1967; Ring Round the Moon (Haymarket), Darling of the Day (George Abbott, NY), 1968; Lolita My Love (US tour), 1971; The Beheading (Apollo), The Three Arrows (Actors' Company), 1972; Oxford Festival, Sept 1974, played Peter Cauchon in Saint Joan; directed A Matter of Gravity (Broadhurst, NY), Feb, The Apple Cart (Niagara Shaw Festival), Aug 1976; The Inconstant Couple (Chichester), June, Heartbreak House, Aug 1978; has also made numerous television appearances, including Edward VII and Caesar and Cleopatra; recent films include The Odessa File and 21 Hours at Munich.

Recreation: Piano-playing. *Address:* c/o Larry Dalzell Associates, 3 Goodwin's Court, St Martin's Lane, London, WC2.

WILMER, Douglas, actor
b London, 8 Jan 1920; *s* of Harry Bradlaugh Wilmer and his wife Kate (Tavener); *e* King's School, Canterbury; *m* Elizabeth Melville (mar dis); formerly a student of architecture; trained for the stage at the Royal Academy of Dramatic Art.

Made his first appearance on the stage at the Repertory Theatre, Rugby, 1945, when he played Robert Browning in The Barretts of Wimpole Street; first appeared in London at the King's Theatre, Hammersmith, Mar–May 1946, with Basil C Langton's TRT Company, as Tybalt in Romeo and Juliet, Gilles de Rais in Saint Joan, Martyn Langley in The Wise Have Not Spoken, and Gordon in In Time To Come; Aldwych, Dec 1947, played Lennox in Macbeth; played as a member of the company at the Shakespeare Memorial Theatre, Stratford-on-Avon, 1948 season; Oxford Playhouse, 1949–50; Old Vic, Dec 1950–May 1951, played Tom Quarlous in Bartholomew Fair, Charles VI in Henry V, Redbrook in Captain Brassbound's Conversion, and Pistol in The Merry Wives of Windsor; Old Vic, season 1951–2, played Roderigo in Othello, Demetrius in A Midsummer Night's Dream, Rene de Montigny in The Other Heart; toured in South Africa with the Old Vic Company, 1952; St Martin's, Oct 1953, played Theobald Thin in Blind Man's Buff; New Lindsey, Feb 1954, directed The Grey Fedora; Arts, Sept 1954, Earl of Warwick in Saint Joan, subsequently transferring with the production to the St Martin's, Feb 1955; Saville, Dec 1956, Fainall in The Way of the World; Arts, Jan 1959, played Monsieur De, in Madame De . . . , and Maître Huspar in Traveller Without Luggage; Arts, July 1959, Narrator in Ulysses in Nighttown, later appearing in the same production at the Sarah Bernhardt, Paris, and at the Royal, Amsterdam; Arts, Sept 1959, played Mr Mississippi in The Marriage of Mr Mississippi; Royal Court, Dec 1959, played the Judge in One Way Pendulum, subsequently transferring with the same production to the Criterion, Feb 1960; Savoy, Sept 1967, Adam Low in According to the Evidence; Oxford Playhouse, Sept 1968, Morose in The Silent Woman; Nottingham Playhouse, Nov 1970, played Claudius in Hamlet, appearing in the same production at the Cambridge, Jan 1971; Apollo, 1971, took over a part in Lulu; Comedy, Mar 1974, Patrick Delafield in Knuckle; principal films in which he has appeared include: Richard III, El Cid, The Fall of the

Roman Empire, Cleopatra, One Way Pendulum, Patton, etc; first appeared on television Sept 1946 and performances include the title-part in the series *Sherlock Holmes*.

Favourite parts: Warwick in Saint Joan and the Judge in One Way Pendulum. *Recreations:* Wine and riding. *Club:* Garrick. *Address:* c/o Leading Artists Ltd, 60 St James's Street, London SW1.

WILSON, Elizabeth, actress
b Grand Rapids, Mich, 4 Apr 1925; *e* Grand Rapids Junior College; prepared for the stage at the Neighborhood Playhouse.

Made her first appearance in New York at the Music Box, 19 Feb 1953, as Christine Schoenwalder in Picnic; Broadhurst, Oct 1955, played Miss Warriner in The Desk Set; Royale, Feb 1957, Miss McCracken in The Tunnel of Love; ANTA, Mar 1961, Hilda Rose in Big Fish, Little Fish; Players, Mar 1963, Constance in Yes Is for a Very Young Man; Walnut Street, Philadelphia, Pa, Oct 1964, Liz Cantriss in Rich Little Rich Girl; Circle in the Square, Oct 1966, Mrs Murray in Eh?; Circle in the Square, Jan 1969, Marjorie Newquist in Little Murders; Helen Hayes, Jan 1970, Martha Wilkins in Sheep on the Runway; Mercer-Shaw Arena, Apr 1970, Mrs Summey in Dark of the Moon; Plymouth, 1970, took over from Maureen Stapleton for a week as Karen Nash, Muriel Tate, and Norma Hubley in Plaza Suite; Vivian Beaumont, Nov 1970, Mrs Shin in The Good Woman of Setzuan; Anspacher, Nov 1971, Harriet in Sticks and Bones, transferred with this play to the John Golden, Mar 1972, and received the Antoinette Perry (Tony) Award for the performance; Ambassador, Nov 1972, Helen Wild in The Secret Affairs of Mildred Wild; Joseph E Levine—Circle in the Square, June 1973, Sonya in Uncle Vanya; Beaumont, May 1976, Mrs Peachum in Threepenny Opera; Circle in the Square, June 1977, Lady Bracknell in The Importance of Being Earnest; Public, Apr 1978, appeared in a workshop production, The 75th; Delacorte, July 1978, Countess of Roussillon in All's Well That Ends Well; Public/Newman, Feb 1979, Aunt Helen in Taken in Marriage; Lyceum, Apr 1980, Aaronetta Gibbs in Morning's at Seven; has appeared in films in Little Murders, Day of the Dolphin, Man on the Swing (1974), etc; has also appeared on television in Sticks and Bones, in the series *Doc* (1975–76), etc.

Address: c/o STE Representation, 888 Seventh Avenue, New York, NY 10019.

WILSON, Lanford, playwright
b Lebanon, Missouri, 13 Apr 1937; *s* of Ralph Eugene Wilson and his wife Violetta Careybelle (Tate); *e* University of Chicago.

First play to be produced was So Long at the Fair, at the Caffé Cino, New York, 25 Aug 1963; since then has written the following plays, principally for the leading avant garde theatres in America and Great Britain: Home Free!, No Trespassing, Sand Castle, The Madness of Lady Bright, 1964; Ludlow Fair, Balm in Gilead, This Is the Rill Speaking, Days Ahead, Sex Is Between Two People, 1965; Wandering, The Rimers of Eldritch, 1966; The Gingham Dog, 1968; Lemon Sky, Serenading Louie, One Arm (adapted from Tennessee Williams), 1970; The Great Nebula in Orion, Sextet (yes), 1971; The Family Continues, The Victory on Mrs Dandywine's Island, 1972; The Hot 1 Baltimore, 1973; The Mound Builders, 1975 (televised in 1976); Serenading Louie, 1976; Brontosaurus (one-act), 1977; 5th of July, 1978; Talley's Folly, 1979; at the Circle Repertory, Apr 1974, played the title-role of e e cumming's him; wrote the libretto of the opera Summer and Smoke (from Tennessee William's play),

1971; his plays have been produced by Cafe La Mama, Mercury Theatre of London, Stables Theatre Club of Manchester, and most US regional theatre companies, as well as on Broadway; first television production was This Is the Rill Speaking, 1967, and since then has written for television The Sandcastle, Stoop, The Migrants, and Taxi!; is a member of the Dramatists Guild; co-founder and resident playwright, Circle Repertory Co, NY.

Address: Box 891, Sag Harbor, New York 11963.

WILSON, Robert, performance artist, director, and playwright
b Waco, Texas, 4 Oct 1941; *s* of D M Wilson and his wife Loree (Hamilton); *e* Pratt Institute, New York (BFA).

Studied painting with George McNeil in Paris, 1962; designed the set for America Hurrah, NY 1963; artistic director of the Byrd Hoffman Foundation Inc, NY, which has presented many of his works; these include the one-act Theater Activity, produced at the Bleecker Street Cinema, NY, 1967; Byrdwoman, 1968; The King of Spain, The Life and Times of Sigmund Freud, 1969, all seen in New York; Deafman Glance, Iowa, 1970, later produced in NY, Nancy, Rome, Paris and Amsterdam, 1971; Program Prologue Now, Overture for a Deafman, Paris 1971; Overture, seen in NY and Shiraz, and in Paris as a twenty-four hour continuous performance, 1972; KA Mountain and Guardenia Terrace, a seven-day continuous performance at Shiraz, 1972; King Lyre and Lady in The Wasteland, NY, The Life and Times of Joseph Stalin, Copenhagen and NY, 1973; A Mad Man A Mad Giant A Mad Dog A Mad Urge A Mad Face (Rome, Washington DC, Shiraz), The Life and Times of Dave Clark (Sao Paulo), A Letter for Queen Victoria (Spoleto, Belgrade, Zurich, French maisons de la culture and ANTA, NY), 1974; The $ Value of Man (Brooklyn Academy), To Street (solo: Bonn), Dia Log (NY), 1975; Einstein on the Beach (Avignon, European tour, Metropolitan, NY), an opera with music by Philip Glass, 1976; I was sitting on my patio this guy appeared I thought I was hallucinating, US tour 1977, European tour including UK debut at Royal Court, 1978; Death, Destruction and Detroit, Berlin 1979; Edison, Lyon etc 1979; has taught and lectured in the US and Europe, and exhibited his work as artist and sculptor in NY, Bonn, Milan etc; winner of numerous awards in the US and Europe for his theatre works including Rockefeller fellowship, 1975, and Grand Prize, International Festival of Nations, Belgrade, 1977.

Address: Byrd Hoffman Foundation, 147 Spring Street, New York, NY 10012. *Tel:* 966–1365.

WILSON, Sandy, dramatic author, composer, and lyric writer
b Sale, Cheshire, 19 May 1924; *s* of George Walter Wilson and his wife Caroline Elsie (Humphrey); *e* Elstree Preparatory School, Harrow, and Oriel College, Oxford (BA, Eng Lit).

Contributed items to Slings and Arrows, 1948, and Oranges and Lemons, 1949; sole author and composer of See You Later, 1951; See You Again, 1952; The Boy Friend, 1953, which, after presentation at the Players' and the Embassy, was produced at Wyndham's, Jan 1954, where it ran for more than five years; The Boy Friend was also produced on Broadway, New York, in 1954, where it ran for 15 months; a new production of the musical was presented off-Broadway, in Jan 1958, and ran for nearly two years; it has also been produced successfully in South Africa, and was revived, Dec 1967, at the Comedy, London, with the author directing; author and composer of The Buccaneer, 1955; author and composer of Valmouth, 1958; contributed material to the revue Pieces of Eight, 1959; author of the lyrics and composed music for Call It Love, 1960; author and composer of

Divorce Me, Darling!, 1965; composed music for As Dorothy Parker Once Said, 1966; devised and performed in Sandy Wilson Thanks the Ladies, 1971; author and composer of His Monkey Wife, 1971; author and composer of The Clapham Wonder, 1978; author of book, lyrics and music for Aladdin, 1979; published This is Sylvia (with own illustrations), 1954, The Boy Friend (with own illustrations), 1955; I Could Be Happy (autobiography), and Ivor, 1975; The Roaring Twenties, 1976.

Recreations: Travelling, cooking, and going to the cinema. *Club:* Players'. *Address:* 2 Southwell Gardens, London, SW7.

WILSON, Snoo, dramatic author and director
b Reading, Berks, 2 Aug 1948; *s* of Leslie Wilson and his wife Pamela Mary (Boyle); *e* Bradfield College and the University of East Anglia; *m* Ann Patricia McFerran.

While at University, wrote and directed the University revue Girl Mad As Pigs, 1968; his plays include Pignight, 1970; Blowjob, 1971; Boswell and Johnson on the Shores of the Eternal Sea, 1972; Vampire, 1973; The Pleasure Principle, The Beast, 1974; Reason, The Everest Hotel, 1975; The Soul of the White Ant, 1976; England—England, 1977; The Glad Hand, A Greenish Man, 1978; Flaming Bodies, 1979; co-author with six others of Layby, 1972, which he also directed; also of England's Ireland, 1973, which he co-directed with David Hare; directed Bodywork, 1974; wrote and directed Elijah Disappearing, 1977; contributed to the revue In At The Death, 1978; work for television includes Swamp Music, The Trip to Jerusalem, Don't Make Waves (with Trevor Griffiths), The Barium Meal, and A Greenish Man; joint winner of the John Whiting Award, 1978, for The Glad Hand.

Recreations: Beekeeping, tennis. *Address:* 41 The Chase, London SW4.

WINDSOR, Barbara (*née* Deeks), actress
b Whitechapel, 6 Aug 1937; *d* of John Henry James Deeks and his wife Rosealendra (Ellis); *e* Our Lady's Convent, Stamford Hill, London; *m* Ronald John Knight; trained for the stage at Aida Foster School.

First appeared on the stage, 24 Dec 1950, at the Golders Green Hippodrome as an Aida Foster Babe in Sleeping Beauty; first appeared on the London stage 25 Sept 1952 at the Saville, as Sadie Kate in Love From Judy; Theatre Royal, Stratford East, Dec 1959, played Rosie in Fings Ain't Wot They Used T'Be; transferred to the Garrick in this production, Feb 1960; her New York début was at the Broadhurst, Sept 1964, in Oh! What A Lovely War!; returning to London, played Delphina in Twang!, Shaftesbury, Dec 1965; Mavis Apple in Come Spy With Me, Whitehall, May 1966; Marie Lloyd in Sing A Rude Song, Greenwich, Feb 1970 and Garrick, May 1970; Prince of Wales, Feb 1972, Lucy Brown in The Threepenny Opera, transferring to the Piccadilly, Apr; toured, Sept 1972, as the Girl in The Owl and the Pussycat; Victoria Palace, Oct 1973, appeared in the spectacular, Carry On London; Richmond, Dec 1975, played Aladdin; Chichester Festival, June 1976, Maria in Twelfth Night; toured, autumn 1979, in the title role of Calamity Jane; Richmond, Dec 1979, played Dick Whittington; films, since The Belles of St Trinians, 1953, include Sparrers Can't Sing and a number of the Carry On films; television, also since 1953, includes *The Rag Trade, Wild, Wild Women* and *Carry on Laughing*.

Favourite parts: Marie Lloyd, Rosie. *Recreation:* Show business. *Address:* c/o Richard Stone, 18–20 York Buildings, London, WC2. *Tel:* 01–839 6421.

WINTERS, Marian, actress and playwright
b New York City, 19 Apr., 1924; *e* Erasmus Hall, Brooklyn, and Brooklyn College; *m* Jay H. Smolin.

Made début in 1940 in stock; at the Lenox Hill Playhouse, Nov., 1948, played Artemis in Hippolytus; Equity Library Theatre, 1949, played Constance in King John; at the Blackstone, Chicago, during the 1949–50 season, appeared in Detective Story; City Center, May, 1951, played Miriam and Arabella in The Dream Girl; Empire, Nov., 1951, Natalia Landauer in I Am a Camera; subsequently toured in the same production, 1952; Phoenix, off Broadway, Oct., 1954, played Maddy Hertzog in Sing Me No Lullaby; A.N.T.A., New York, Feb., 1955, Gelda in The Dark Is Light Enough; Sarah Bernhardt, Paris, June, 1955, in a Salute to France program, played First Women of Corinth in Medea; Broadhurst, Oct., 1956, Sally Cato MacDougal in Auntie Mame; Belasco, Jan., 1959, Myra Solomon in Tall Story; Ambassador, Oct., 1960, Tracy Lowe in The 49th Cousin; Theatre Four, off-Broadway, Nov., 1962, Madame Ranevsky in The Cherry Orchard; Lyceum, New York, Dec., 1963, Marge Weber in Nobody Loves an Albatross; Eugene O'Neill, Nov., 1965, Senator Lucia Barrett in Mating Dance; Delacorte, July, 1967, Constance in King John; Music Box, Feb 1978, Helga ten Dorp in Deathtrap; has written the following plays: Animal Keepers, 1967, which won two Emmy Awards; A Is for All, 1968, which is three one-act plays; All Saints' Day, which won the Provincetown Living Arts Award, and All Is Bright, which won the South-eastern Theatre Conference Award, 1970; Breadwinner, 1974; A New World! (musical), 1977; is a member of The New Dramatists, Inc; has received the Antoinette Perry (Tony) Award, The Donaldson Award, the New York Drama Critics Award, and the Variety Poll Award; first appeared on television, 1949, and has since played more than 300 rôles.
Favourite part: Constance in King John. *Recreations:* Cooking and gardening. *Address:* West Ridge Corners, Warwick, NY 10990. *Tel:* 914–986–2029.

WINTERS, Shelley (née Shirley Schrift), actress
b St Louis, Missouri, 18 Aug 1922; d of Jonas Schrift and his wife Rose (Winters); e St Louis and Brooklyn, New York; m (1) Mack P Mayer (mar dis); (2) Vittorio Gassman (mar dis); (3) Anthony Francioso (mar dis); formerly a model, and salesgirl; prepared for the stage at the Actors Studio.
First appeared on the stage in Jamaica, LI, NY, in 1930, as Edna in Clifford Odet's Waiting for Lefty; made her professional début at the Morosco, NY, Apr 1941, as Flora in Night Before Christmas; 44th Street, Oct 1942, played Fifi in the musical Rosalinda; Locust, Philadelphia, 1944, played a Danish Girl in Conquest in April; St James', NY, 1947–8, alternated with Celeste Holm as Ado Annie Carnes in Oklahoma!; Lyceum, Nov 1955, played Celia Pope in A Hatful of Rain; Longacre, Nov 1956, played Hilda Brookman in Girls of Summer; Westport Country Playhouse, Conn, Sept 1958, Mrs Topaz in The Saturday Night Kid; Royale, NY, Apr 1962, took over the role of Maxine Faulk in The Night of the Iguana; York Playhouse, off-Broadway, June 1963, played Connie in Cages, and Her in Snowangel (in the double-bill Cages); Westport Country Playhouse, June 1964, played Dolores Goodwin in Days of the Dancing; Coconut Grove, Miami, Florida, May 1965, Martha in Who's Afraid of Virginia Woolf?, subsequently touring with the production; Cort, Oct 1966, Flora Sharkey, Marcella Vankuchen, and Hilda in Under the Weather; Spoleto, Italy, Festival of the Two Worlds, July 1967, repeated her roles in Under the Weather; Imperial, Mar 1970, Minnie Marx in the musical Minnie's Boys; Actors Playhouse, Dec 1970, wrote three short plays called One Night Stands of a Noisy Passenger; Actors Studio, May 1973, Beatrice in The Effect of Gamma

Rays on Man-in-the-Moon Marigolds, and repeated this part at the Westchester Country Playhouse, Aug 1973; toured, 1974, as Connie in Snowangel and Woman in Epiphany in a double-bill called variously Cages and Last of the Great Jelly Bellies; Westwood Playhouse, LA, 1975, appeared in Cages; San Francisco, May 1976, took over as Wanda in Kennedy's Children; Biltmore, Mar 1978, Beatrice in The Effect of Gamma Rays on Man-in-the-Moon-Marigolds; has frequently appeared in summer stock in the following plays, Born Yesterday, Of Mice and Men, The Male Animal, Gentle People, The Rose Tattoo, A Streetcar Named Desire, Two for the Seesaw, Luv, etc; first entered films, 1943, in What a Woman! and has since appeared in many notable pictures including A Double Life, The Great Gatsby, A Place in the Sun, I Am a Camera, The Big Knife, The Chapman Report, The Balcony, The Diary of Anne Frank (Film Academy Award), A Patch of Blue (Academy Award), Bloody Mama, The Poseidon Adventure, Blume in Love, Diamonds, The Tenant (1976), etc; has appeared frequently on television in Sorry, Wrong Number, The Woman, the first Wagon Train, Two Is the Number (Emmy Award), etc; author of an autobiography, Shelley, 1980.
Favourite parts: Celia Pope, Connie, and Her. *Recreations:* Swimming, tennis, riding, politics, civic affairs. *Address:* Actors Equity Association, 165 West 46th Street, New York, NY 10036.

WISDOM, Norman, actor and comedian
b London, 4 Feb 1925; e various elementary schools; m Freda Simpson (mar dis); formerly in the Army.
Made his first appearance on the stage at Collins Music Hall, Dec 1946, as a comedian in variety; also appeared in variety at the London Casino, 1948; subsequently appeared in concert party at Scarborough, pantomime at Birmingham and Wolverhampton, and in the summer show Buttons and Bows, at Blackpool; at the Cambridge, Apr 1950, appeared in the revue Sauce Piquante; Prince of Wales's, Apr 1952, played in the revue Paris to Piccadilly; Palladium, May 1954, appeared in The 1954 Palladium Show; Palladium, Aug 1955, played in the revue Painting the Town; Palladium, Dec 1956, played Aladdin in The Wonderful Lamp; Palace, Feb 1958, played Charley Wykeham in Where's Charley?; Palladium, Dec 1960, Dick Whittington in Turn Again Whittington; Hippodrome, Bristol, Dec 1961, appeared in Robinson Crusoe; Empire, Liverpool, Dec 1963, again appeared in Robinson Crusoe; toured, Aug 1964, as Cocky in The Roar of the Grease Paint—The Smell of the Crowd; made his first appearance on Broadway, Nov 1966, at the Lunt-Fontanne, as Will Mossop in Walking Happy, winning two Broadway Awards; Brooks Atkinson, New York, Oct 1970, Arnold Crouch in Not Now Darling; toured in Norman Wisdom's Summer Show, 1975; has also appeared in the following Ice Shows: London Melody (Empress Hall, 1951); Sinbad the Sailor (Empress Hall, 1953); appeared in the Royal Variety Performances of 1952 and 1954; first appeared in films 1952, in the Academy Award-winning Trouble In Store, and subsequently in One Good Turn, Man Of The Moment, Up in the World, The Square Peg, Follow A Star, A Stitch in Time, and The Night They Raided Minsky's; has also broadcast and appeared on television, in England and the United States.
Recreations: Boxing, athletics, and sailing. *Address:* c/o Peter Elliott, 235–241 Regent Street, London, W1.

WISE, Herbert (né Weisz), director and former actor
b Vienna, Austria, 31 Aug 1924; s of Zsiga Weisz and his wife Juliska (Stern); e Oxted Secondary School, Surrey; m Moira Redmond (mar dis); formerly an analytical chemist.

Made his début as an actor at High Wycombe repertory, Oct 1949; directed his first production, While the Sun Shines, at Shrewsbury, Sept 1950; since 1952 exclusively a director, first as director of productions, Dundee, 1952–4; stage productions include So What About Love, Criterion, 1969; I Want to Marry a Goldwyn Girl, Manchester, 1970; has directed over 200 drama productions for BBC and ITC: notable productions since 1970 include Man of Straw, I Claudius, and The Norman Conquests.

Recreations: Watching football, chess, music. *Address:* Tim Corrie, Fraser and Dunlop, 91 Regent Street, London W1R 8RU.

WISEMAN, Joseph, actor

b Montreal, Canada, 15 May 1918; *s* of Louis Wiseman and his wife Pearl Rubin (Ruchwarger); *e* Montreal and New York City; *m* (1) Nell Kinard (mar dis); (2) Pearl Lang.

First appeared on the stage at the New Barn Theatre, Saugerties, NY, June 1936, as Moses in Three Men on a Horse; made his Broadway stage début at the Plymouth, 15 Oct 1938, as a Soldier in Abe Lincoln in Illinois; National, Oct 1940, played the Beggar and the Second Money Changer in Journey to Jerusalem; Shubert, Oct 1941, Corp Mueller in Candle in the Wind; Playhouse, Feb 1943, German Soldier in The Barber Had Two Sons; Ethel Barrymore, 1943, took over Andrei in The Three Sisters; Belasco, Jan 1944, Stefano in Storm Operation; Alvin, Nov 1946, played Champlain (Father Massieu) in Joan of Lorraine; Martin Beck, Nov 1947, Mardian in Antony and Cleopatra; Hudson, Mar 1949, Charlie in Detective Story; Martin Beck, Nov 1949, Juan de Escovedo in That Lady; National, Dec 1950, Edmund in King Lear; ANTA, Mar 1952, played Eddie Fuseli in a revival of Golden Boy; Longacre, Nov 1955, The Inquisitor in The Lark; Phoenix, Mar 1957, Ferdinand in The Duchess of Malfi; Westport Country Playhouse, Sept 1958, The Driver in The Saturday Night Kid; Shubert, New Haven, Conn, Dec 1959, Dr Rafael Taurez in Sweet Love Remembered; UCLA, Los Angeles, Calif, 1961, played The Father in Six Characters in Search of an Author; made his London début at the Royal Court, Apr 1963, as Ludovico Nota in Naked; joined the Lincoln Center Repertory Company in 1964, and at the ANTA Washington Square Theatre, Feb 1964, played Chu-Yin in a revival of Marco Millions; Dec 1964, Psychiatrist in Incident at Vichy; American Shakespeare Festival, Stratford, Conn, 1966, Thomas à Becket in Murder in the Cathedral; Mark Taper Forum, Los Angeles, 1968, J. Robert Oppenheimer in In the Matter of J Robert Oppenheimer; Vivian Beaumont, NY, Mar 1969, again played J Robert Oppenheimer; Mark Taper Forum, Los Angeles, 1969, Astrov in Uncle Vanya; Circle in the Square, June 1971, Bummidge in The Last Analysis; Vivian Beaumont, Nov 1972, Yakov Bardin in Enemies; Arena Stage, Washington, DC, May 1974, Rabbi in The Madness of God, which he repeated at the Lyceum, NY, 1976; Pittsburgh Public Theater, Dec 1977, Fyodor Balyasnikov in Balyasnikov; Harold Cluman, NY, Oct 1978, The Professor in The Lesson; has also appeared frequently in stock productions since 1936; first appeared in films in 1949 and has since played in Detective Story, Viva Zapata, Les Misérables, the title-role in Dr No, The Unforgiven, Bye Bye Braverman, The Night They Raided Minskys, The Lawman, The Apprenticeship of Duddy Kravitz, Journey into Fear (1975), etc; first appeared on television in 1950, and since has played in Darkness at Noon, Arrowsmith, Billy Budd, Macbeth, The Dybbuk, Antigone, etc.

Favourite part: The Father in The Diary of Anne Frank. *Address:* 382 Central Park West, New York, NY. *Tel:* UN 6-2680.

WITHERS, Googie (*née* Georgette Lizette Withers), actress

b Karachi, India, 12 Mar 1917; *d* of Captain Edgar Clements Withers, CBE, CIE, RIM, and his wife Lizette Catarina Wilhelmina (van Wageningen); *e* Fredville Park, Nonnington, Kent, and the Convent of the Holy Family, London; *m* John McCallum; studied for the stage with Italia Conti in London, Helena Lehmiski Academy, Birmingham, and at the Buddy Bradley school of dancing.

Made her first appearance on the stage, at the Victoria Palace, 26 Dec 1929, in The Windmill Man; Strand, Sept 1933, appeared in the chorus of Nice Goings On, and Duke of York's, May 1934, in Happy Week-end, in which she played her first speaking part; Apollo, June 1935, played Miss Worrall in Duet in Floodlight; Gate Theatre, Dec 1935, appeared in This World of Ours; Strand, May 1937, played Diana in Ladies and Gentlemen; Richmond, Nov 1937, Sally Pilgrim in Hand in Glove; Globe Theatre, Apr. 1943, played Alice Foster in They Came to a City; in 1944, joined Southern Command Entertainments, and played for the Troops in England and the BLA; Apollo, Nov 1945, succeeded Kay Hammond as Amanda Prynne in Private Lives; New, June 1949, played Lee in Champagne for Delilah; St James's, Apr 1952, appeared as Georgie Elgin in Winter Journey; Duchess, Dec 1952, succeeded Peggy Ashcroft as Hester Collyer in The Deep Blue Sea; St James's, Apr 1954, played Jill Manning in Waiting For Gillian; toured Australia and New Zealand, 1955, as Hester Collyer in The Deep Blue Sea and Laura Foster in Simon and Laura; returned to England, 1956; Aldwych, London, Apr 1957, played Jessica in Janus; Shakespeare Memorial Theatre, Stratford-upon-Avon, 1958 season, played Gertrude in Hamlet, and Beatrice in Much Ado About Nothing; toured Australia and New Zealand, 1959, as Emma in Roar Like a Dove; Comedy, Melbourne, Dec 1960, Georgie Elgin in Winter Journey, subsequently touring Australia and New Zealand, with the production, and also appearing as Constance in The Constant Wife; made her first appearance in New York at the Ethel Barrymore Theatre, Nov 1961, as Mary Rhodes in The Complaisant Lover; Comedy, Melbourne, Nov 1962, played Amy Preston in Woman in a Dressing Gown, subsequently touring with the play; Edinburgh Festival, and Royal Court, London, Sept 1963, Queen Marguerite in Exit the King; toured Australia and New Zealand, 1964, in The First Four Hundred Years, a programme of excerpts from Shakespeare, with Keith Michell; toured Australia, June 1965, as Lady Piper in Beekman Place; Comedy, Melbourne, Mar 1966, and tour, played Edith Cassidy in Desire of the Moth; Strand, London, Apr 1967, Mrs George in Getting Married; 1968, toured Australia in Relatively Speaking; 1969–70, toured Australia and New Zealand in Plaza Suite; for the Melbourne Theatre Co, 1972, played Madame Ranevsky in The Cherry Orchard, July, and Mrs Chevely in An Ideal Husband, Aug; Chichester season 1976, Lady Kitty in The Circle, repeating this part at the Haymarket, Oct 1978–9, toured Australia in The Kingfisher; Chichester Festival, July 1979, Lady Bracknell in The Importance of Being Earnest; first appeared in films, 1934, and has starred in over thirty, including One of our Aircraft is Missing, On Approval, Loves of Joanna Godden, White Corridors, and It Always Rains on Sunday; television includes Amphitryon 38, The Deep Blue Sea, and *Within These Walls*.

Recreations: Interior decorating, music and books. *Address:* c/o ICM Ltd, 22 Grafton Street, London, W1.

WITTOP, Freddy (*né* Fred Wittop Koning), designer, formerly a dancer

b Bussum, Holland, 26 July; *s* of Adriaan Wittop Koning and his wife Anna (Du Moulin); *e* in France.

Designed the costumes for the French Casino Folies, New York, 7 Jan 1937; since then has designed New Folies Bergere, NY, and his first London designs, Plaisirs de Paris, produced at the London Casino, 29 Apr 1938; Folies Bergere, San Francisco World's Fair, 1939; Ice Capades, 1940 and 1941; toured the US under the name Frederico Rey as a Spanish dancer-partner to Argentinita; 44th Street, NY, 29 May 1942, made his NY début dancing in Top-Notchers; designed the costumes for Beat the Band, 1942; served in the US Army, 1943–6; designed the Ballet Theatre productions of El Amor Brujo, Pictures of Goya, and Bolero, 1944; designed the décor and costumes for Madeleine Bastille, produced at the Alhambra, Paris, 1946; formed his own dance company and toured Europe and the USA with it 1951–8; designed the Latin Quarter Revues in NY, 1950–60; designed the costumes for Holiday on Ice tours, 1959–63; designed the costumes for Heartbreak House, 1959; Carnival, Subways Are for Sleeping, 1961; Judith (London), 1962; Hello, Dolly! for which he received the Antoinette Perry (Tony) Award, To Broadway with Love, Bajour, 1964; Kelly, The Roar of the Greasepaint—The Smell of the Crowd, Pleasures and Palaces, On a Clear Day You Can See Forever, 1965; 3 Bags Full, I Do! I Do! 1966; The Happy Time, George M!, I Do! I Do! (London), 1968; Dear World, A Patriot for Me, 1969; Lovely Ladies, Kind Gentlemen, 1970; for the Los Angeles Light Opera Association designed the costumes for The Great Waltz, Dumas and Son, Knickerbocker Holiday, Candide, 1971.

Address: United Scenic Artists, 268 West 47th Street, New York, NY 10036.

WITTSTEIN, Ed, designer

b Mount Vernon, New York, 7 Apr 1929; *s* of Nathan Harry Wittstein and his wife Miriam (Goldman); *e* Parson's School of Design, New York University (BS 1951), Cooper Union (1951–2); prepared for the theatre at Erwin Piscator's Dramatic Workshop, 1946–7.

First designs for the stage were for the Dramatic Workshop production of The Inspector General, 1947; resident designer for the Litchfield, Connecticut, Summer Theatre, 1958; designed sets for the Guildford, Connecticut, Summer Theatre, 1949, including Lady in the Dark; at the Cherry Lane, 6 June 1949, designed the sets for Gertrude Stein's Yes Is for a Very Young Man, and since then has designed the sets and costumes for the opera Ounga, Philadelphia, 1950; sets and costumes for the opera The Celebrated Jumping Frog of Calaveras County, produced at the La Fenice, Venice, Italy, 1953; The Transposed Heads, 1958; Dr Willy-Nilly, Legend of Lovers, 1959; The Fantasticks (which ran for more than 17 years), 1960; The Gondoliers, Kean, his first Broadway production, for which he also designed the costumes, 1961; Bravo Giovanni, La Belle, 1962; The Love Nest, Enter Laughing, Chips with Everything (supervision), A Rainy Day in Newark, The Ginger Man, Trumpets of the Lord, Opernhaus, Cologne, Germany, designed four ballets for Todd Bolender, Once in a Lifetime, The White House, The New Tenant, Victims of Duty, designed The New Theatre and its first production The Knack, The Tragical Historie of Doctor Faustus, The Room, A Slight Ache, décor and costumes for the Promenade Concerts at Philharmonic Hall, 1964; The Day the Whores Came Out to Play Tennis, Sing to Me Through Open Windows, And Things That Go Bump in the Night, The Yearling, The Marriage of Figaro for the New York City Opera Company, The Amen Corner, which opened in Vienna and toured Europe, playing in Edinburgh and London, 1965; Serjeant Musgrave's Dance, The Kitchen, The Long Christmas Dinner, Queens of France, The Happy

Journey from Trenton to Camden, Wedding Band, Ann Arbor, Michigan, The Office, Falstaff, for the Stratford, Connecticut, Shakespeare Festival Theatre, 1966; You Know I Can't Hear You When the Water's Running, The Natural Look, The Merchant of Venice for Stratford, Connecticut, 1967; Before You Go, The Man in the Glass Booth, Tea Party, The Basement, Richard II and As You Like It for Stratford, Connecticut, You Know I Can't Hear You When the Water's Running (London), The Miser and Honor and Offer (Cincinnati), 1968; Celebration, Little Murders, A Scent of Flowers, Much Ado About Nothing (Stratford, Connecticut), Volpone and The Good Woman of Setzuan (Cincinnati), 1969; The Last Sweet Days of Isaac, Blood Red Roses, Happy Birthday, Wanda June, I Dreamt I Dwelt in Bloomingdale's, He Who Gets Slapped (Cincinnati), 1970; The Soft Core Pornographer, Ring Round the Bathtub, Tough to Get Help, 1972; The Country Wife (Stratford, Conn), Echoes, 1973; Ulysses in Nighttown, 1974; Celebration, 1975; Eleanor (tour) 1976; The Dream Watcher (tour), 1977; The Torch-Bearers, The Aspen Papers (McCarter, Princeton), 1978; Grand Magic, King of Schnorrers, 1979; in partnership with Robert Miller has designed various interiors of restaurants, etc, in NY, notably the Plaza 9 Room of the Plaza Hotel, 1965, and four Schrafft Restaurants, 1970; designed the films Bananas, 1971; Play It Again, Sam, 1971; The Seven Ups, 1973; Fame, 1979; designed the cabaret revues Demi-Dozen, Pieces of Eight, and Dressed to the Nines, produced by Julius Monk at the Upstairs at the Downstairs cabaret; 1958; first designed for television for the *Armstrong Circle Theatre*, 1950, and designed for Italian experimental television, 1952–3, and designed the NBC TV Opera productions of La Boheme, which toured as a live production, 1957, Cosi Fan Tutte, Cavalleria Rusticana, Boris Godunov, The Love of Three Kings, 1957–62, the Esso Repertory Theatre productions of thirteen US repertory companies, 1965, Camino Real, The Confession, The Diary of Anne Frank, Blithe Spirit, 1966, Home, 1968, The Front Page, The Woody Allen Special, 1969, Sand Castle, 1970, A Memory of Two Mondays, 1971; production designer for the series *The Adams Chronicles*, 1975.

Recreations: Travelling, photography, drawing, food. *Address:* 339 East 87th Street, New York, NY 10023. *Tel:* 427–8725.

WOLSK, Eugene V, producer

b New York City, 16 Aug 1928; *s* of Isidore Wolsk and his wife Paulia (Pressman); *e* Allegheny College (BA, 1948), Yale Univ Drama School (1948–50); *m* (1) Cynthia Harris (mar dis); (2) Judith Licht.

First production in New York was The Father, at the Provincetown Playhouse, 19 July 1949; since then has produced or co-produced the following: Chaparral, 1958; The Lion in Winter, Mark Twain Tonight!, The Investigation, 1966; Something Different, 1967; Aint Supposed to Die a Natural Death, 1971; The Sunshine Boys, 1972; The Good Doctor, 1973; Scapino, Miss Moffat (Philadelphia), God's Favorite, 1974; Man of La Mancha, 1977; Back Country (Boston), 1978; Saravá, Last Licks, 1979; served as general manager of The Wiz, 1975, and more than a dozen other Broadway productions; produced The Investigation on television, 1967.

Address: 165 West 46th Street, New York, NY 10036. *Tel:* 354–3060.

WOOD, Charles, dramatic author

b St Peter Port, Guernsey, 6 Aug 1932; *s* of John Edward Wood and his wife Catherine Mae (Harris); *e* Chesterfield GS, Kidderminster GS, and Birmingham College of Art; served five years in the regular army.

After work in the theatre as a stage manager and scenic artist, including Theatre Workshop, 1957, became a full-time writer in 1963; in October of that year his three one-act plays Prisoner and Escort, John Thomas, and Spare, were presented at the New Arts under the Title Cockade; subsequent plays include Don't Make Me Laugh (one-act), Meals on Wheels, 1965; Fill the Stage with Happy Hours, Tie Up the Ballcock, 1966; Dingo, 1967; H, or Monologues at Front of Burning Cities (for National Theatre), 1969; Labour, 1971; Collier's Wood, 1971; Veterans, 1972; Jingo, 1975; The Script, 1976; Has 'Washington' Legs?, 1978; winner of the *Evening Standard* Awards for Most promising Playwright, 1963 (Cockade), and Best Comedy, 1972 (Veterans); work for television includes Drill Pig, Drums Along the Avon, Death or Glory Boys (trilogy), and two series of *Don't Forget to Write*; has also written a number of radio plays; screenplays include The Knack, Help!, How I Won the War, The Charge of the Light Brigade, and Cuba.

Club: Dramatists. *Address:* c/o Fraser and Dunlop Scripts, 91 Regent Street, London W1.

WOOD, David, actor and dramatic writer
b Sutton, Surrey, 21 Feb 1944; *s* of Richard Edwin Wood and his wife Audrey Adele (Fincham); *e* Chichester High School and Worcester College, Oxford; *m* (1) Sheila Dawson (mar dis); (2) Jacqueline Stanbury; at Oxford he acted with OUDS and the ETC.

Made his first London appearance in March 1964 at the Comedy in the ETC production of Hang Down Your Head and Die, which he also co-wrote; Mermaid, Sept 1964, played Geoff Manham in A Spring Song; OUDS, Feb 1966, Wagner in Dr Faustus with Richard Burton in the title role; Edinburgh Festival and Fortune Theatre, Sept 1966, appeared in Four Degrees Over, which he co-wrote; from 1966 to 1969 appeared in repertory at Worcester, Watford, Edinburgh, Windsor and Salisbury; Aldwych, Feb 1970, played Roger in the RSC's After Haggerty; Greenwich, Nov 1970, the Son in A Voyage Round My Father, a role he repeated in Toronto, Nov 1972; Criterion, 1971, again played Roger in After Haggerty; toured, Aug 1971, as James in Me Times Me; Thorndike, Leatherhead, May 1972, Frank in Mrs Warren's Profession; co-wrote and appeared in the revue Just the Ticket at the same theatre, May 1972; Greenwich, June 1973, Constant in The Provok'd Wife; Her Majesty's, Apr 1975, Bingo Little in Jeeves; Key, Peterborough, 1975, co-wrote and appeared in the revue Think of a Number; Haymarket, Leicester, Apr 1976, Cotton in The Flight of the Bumble Bee; Chichester 900 Festival, July 1976, appeared in Chi-Chestnuts; was responsible for music and lyrics for The Stiffkey Scandals of 1932, 1967; book, music and lyrics of The Tinderbox, 1967; The Plotters of Cabbage Patch Corner, 1970; Flibberty and the Penguin, 1971; The Papertown Paperchase, 1972; Hijack over Hygenia, 1973; Old Mother Hubbard, 1975; The Gingerbread Man (co-presented), Old Father Time, 1976; Tickle (re-write), Nutcracker Sweet, Mother Goose's Golden Christmas, 1977; Babes in the Magic Wood, 1978; There Was an Old Woman, 1979; co-author of Three to One On, The Owl and the Pussycat Went to See, 1968; Toytown, 1969; Maudie, Rock Nativity, 1974; Bars of Gould, 1977; The Luck of the Bodkins, 1978; while at Worcester directed various plays including The Knack, A Present from the Corporation (also lyrics), Flibberty and the Penguin; in London has directed The Owl and the Pussycat Went to See, 1969–71, 1973 (also Guildford, 1976, and Chichester, 1978), Larry the Lamb in Toytown (Toytown retitled), 1973; co-founder of WSG Productions Ltd, which produced the following plays in London and on tour, 1966–7:

Four Degrees Over, Three to One On, The Owl and the Pussycat Went to See . . ., John Gould's One Man Show, Betjemania, Flibberty and the Penguin, etc; co-founder with John Gould, 1979, of Whirligig Theatre for children; first film, If . . . , 1968; most recent films Sweet William and Esther, Ruth and Jennifer; wrote the screenplay for Swallows and Amazons; television appearances, since his first in 1964, include The Avengers, Van der Valk, Disraeli, Danger UXB, Enemy at the Door, etc.

Favourite part: Fool in King Lear. *Recreations:* Writing, conjuring and collecting old books. *Club:* Green Room. *Address:* c/o Miller Management, 82 Broom Place, Teddington, Middlesex, *and* c/o Margaret Ramsay, 14A Goodwin's Court, St Martin's Lane, London WC2.

WOOD, John, actor
b Derbyshire; *e* Bedford School and Jesus, Oxford; served as a lieutenant in the Royal Horse Artillery.

After acting at Oxford, where he was President of OUDS, worked with the Old Vic Company 1954—6, where his parts included Lennox in Macbeth, 1954; Bushy and Exton in Richard II, Sir Oliver Martext in As You Like It, Pistol in The Merry Wives of Windsor, 1955; Helenus in Troilus and Cressida, 1956; made his West End début at the Phoenix, 8 Apr 1957, as Don Quixote in Camino Real; Royal Court, June 1957, appeared in The Making of Moo; Aldwych, Aug 1958, The Wali in Brouhaha; Apollo, Sept 1961, Henry Albertson in The Fantasticks; made his New York début at the Alvin, 18 Oct 1967, as Guildenstern in Rosencrantz and Guildenstern Are Dead; Birmingham Rep, Mar 1970, Frederick II in The Sorrows of Frederick; Mermaid, Nov 1970, Richard Rowan in Exiles; joined the Royal Shakespeare Company and at the Aldwych, 1971, played Yakov Bardin in Enemies, July, Sir Fopling Flutter in The Man of Mode, Sept, Richard Rowan in Exiles, Oct, and Mark in The Balcony, Nov; Stratford, season 1972, Brutus in Julius Caesar, Antipholus of Syracuse in The Comedy of Errors and Saturninus in Titus Andronicus; Duchess, Apr 1973, Harry Winter in Collaborators; Aldwych, 1973, again played Brutus and Saturninus; The Place, Nov 1973; Monsieur Luc in A Lesson in Blood and Roses; Aldwych, Jan 1974, title role in Sherlock Holmes; June 1974, Henry Carr in Travesties; repeated these last two roles on Broadway, at the Broadhurst, Nov 1974, and the Ethel Barrymore, Oct 1975, respectively; for the Melbourne Theatre Co, Sept 1974, played Alceste in The Misanthrope; Aldwych, season 1976, General Burgoyne in The Devil's Disciple and the title part in Ivanov; Royal Festival Hall, July 1977, Ivanov in Every Good Boy Deserves Favour; Music Box, NY, Feb 1978, Sidney Bruhl in Deathtrap; US tour, Aug 1978, as Ivanov in Every Good Boy Deserves Favour; Olivier, June 1979, Friedrich Hofreiter in Undiscovered Country, and Oct 1979, Richard of Gloucester in Richard III; his many awards include the Antoinette Perry ('Tony'), 1976, for Henry Carr; television includes A Tale of Two Cities and Barnaby Rudge; films include Nicholas and Alexandra and Slaughterhouse Five.

Address: National Theatre, South Bank, London SE1.

WOOD, Peter, director
b Colyton, Devon, 8 Oct 1927; *s* of Frank Wood and Lucy Eleanor (Meeson); *e* Taunton, Somerset, and Downing College, Cambridge.

After some experience in amateur production at Cambridge, spent one year as resident director of the Oxford Playhouse, 1955–6; appointed the resident director of the Arts Theatre, London, 1956, and directed his first West End production at that theatre, Nov 1956, with the double-bill

The Bald Prima Donna and The New Tenant by Eugène Ionesco; Jan 1957, directed No Laughing Matter; Jan 1958, directed The Iceman Cometh, which transferred to the Winter Garden, Mar 1958; Lyric, Hammersmith, May 1958, directed The Birthday Party; Edinburgh Festival, Assembly Hall, Sept 1958, directed Schiller's Mary Stuart (for the Old Vic Company), the production subsequently being performed at the Old Vic, Sept 1958; Cambridge, Dec 1958, directed Who's Your Father?; at the Shakespeare Festival, Stratford, Ontario, Canada, June 1959, guest director for As You Like It; Comedy, London, Sept 1959, directed a new company in Five Finger Exercise, when the original company went to New York, following a run of more than a year; Shakespeare Memorial Theatre, Stratford-on-Avon, Aug 1960, directed The Winter's Tale; he has since directed the following productions: The Devils, Hamlet (Royal Shakespeare), 1961; The Private Ear and The Public Eye, 1962; The Beggar's Opera, The Private Ear and The Public Eye (NY), 1963; The Master Builder (National), Carving a Statue, Poor Richard (NY), 1964; Loot (tour), Love for Love (National), 1965; Incident at Vichy, The Prime of Miss Jean Brodie, 1966; Love for Love (Expo '67 and Toronto), 1967; The White Liars and Black Comedy (double-bill), 1968; Design for Living (Los Angeles), Rosencrantz and Guildenstern are Dead (Nottingham), 1971; Jumpers (National), 1972; Dear Love, Jumpers (Vienna), 1973; Jumpers (Washington and NY), Travesties (London), 1974; Macbeth (Los Angeles), Travesties (London and NY), 1975; Long Day's Journey Into Night (Los Angeles), 1977; became Assistant Director of the National Theatre, 1977, and has since directed for the Company, unless otherwise stated: The Guardsman, The Double Dealer, She Stoops to Conquer (Vienna), Night and Day (also NY, 1979), 1978; Undiscovered Country, 1979; directed two operas in Santa Fé, 1976–7, and for Glyndebourne, 1980; directed his first film In Search of Gregory, 1968; plays on television include Song of Songs, Long Day's Journey into Night, and Dear Love.

Recreation: Travel. *Address:* 11 Warwick Avenue, London, W9.

WOODMAN, William, director
b New York City, 1 Oct 1932; *s* of William E Woodman Sr and his wife Ruth; *e* Hamilton College, New York (BFA 1954) and Columbia University School of Dramatic Arts (MFA 1959); *m* the casting director Elizabeth Roberts.

Began his stage career as an ASM at the American Shakespeare Festival, Stratford, Conn, 1957; in stage management with the company for four seasons and two tours, 1957–61; co-producer and director, 1961–64, Robin Hood Theatre, Ardentown, Dela; directing experience 1964–68 with regional companies including Cleveland and Pittsburgh Playhouses, Hartford Stage etc; joined the new drama faculty at the Juilliard School, NY, as a founding member and administrative associate to John Houseman, 1968–73; during this time directed for the American Shakespeare Festival, Walnut Street, Philadelphia, etc; artistic director, 1973–78, Goodman Theatre, Chicago, Ill, directing productions including The Freedom of the City, 1973 (and on Broadway, 1974); The Sea, Henry IV Parts 1 and 2, 1974; Arturo Ui, 1975; Electra, The Devil's Disciple, Design for Living, 1976; Richard III, 1977; Much Ado About Nothing, Otherwise Engaged, 1978; in 1975 directed Dandelion Wine for Phoenix, NY; since 1978 has directed for a number of daytime TV series including *Another World*, *Guiding Light* and *The Doctors*.

Address: 320 West End Avenue, New York, NY 10023. *Tel:* 580–2838.

WOODTHORPE, Peter, actor
b York, 25 Sept 1931; *s* of Eric Henry Woodthorpe and his wife Hilda (Stembridge); *e* Archbishop Holgate's School, York and Magdalene College, Cambridge; while at the university, he made a number of appearances for the Marlowe Society, including the title part in King Lear; National Service in the Intelligence Branch of the Royal Navy.

He made his first professional appearance on the stage at the Arts Theatre Club, London, Aug 1955, as Estragon in Waiting for Godot, subsequently transferring with the production to the Criterion, Aug 1955; at the Royal Court, Oct 1956, played Wang, the Water Seller, in The Good Woman of Setzuan; Saville, Apr 1957, played Noaks in Zuleika; toured, Dec 1957, as Professor Muller in Time and Again, making his first appearance in New York, at the opening of the Lunt-Fontanne Theatre, May 1958, in the same part and play, re-named The Visit; on his return to England, joined the Shakespeare Memorial Theatre, Stratford-on-Avon, for the season 1959, and played the following parts: Flute in A Midsummer Night's Dream, Roderigo in Othello, and Junius Brutus in Coriolanus; Arts, Apr 1960, played Aston in The Caretaker, transferring with the production to the Duchess, May 1960, receiving the Clarence Derwent Award for this performance; at the opening of the Chichester Festival Theatre, July 1962, played The Clown in The Chances, Phulas in The Broken Heart, and Yefim in Uncle Vanya; Comedy, Dec 1962, played Toad in Toad of Toad Hall; Lyric, Hammersmith, Apr 1963, played Bob Acres in The Rivals; Glasgow Citizens, Feb 1964, Lord Foppington in The Relapse; Duke of York's, July 1964, took over the part of Bitos in Poor Bitos; Nottingham Playhouse, Oct 1964, Edward Kimberley in The Creeper; George Abbott, New York, Jan 1968, played Oxford in Darling of the Day; Arts, Cambridge, Feb 1970, Fred Midway in Semi-Detached; rejoined Royal Shakespeare Company, Stratford, Feb 1971, to play Dogberry in Much Ado About Nothing, the Dauphin in Henry the Fifth, and the Duke in The Merchant of Venice; Toad in Toad of Toad Hall, Stratford, Jan 1972, Arragon in The Merchant of Venice and The Actor in The Lower Depths, both Aldwych, June 1972; Criterion, Feb 1973, Nils Krogstad in A Doll's House; Royal Lyceum, Edinburgh, Sept, Sir Jolly Jumble in The Soldier's Fortune; Greenwich, June 1976, appeared in Heaven and Hell; Garrick, July 1977, Gavin Faber in The Bells of Hell; Apollo, Oct 1978, directed Emlyn Williams as Saki, also Playhouse, NY, Nov 1978, as Playboy of the Western World; Hampstead, May 1978, played August Strindberg in The Tribades; Collegiate, July 1979, Inspector in Cahoot's Macbeth (also 22 Steps, NY, Oct 1979), for the British American Repertory Company; his films include The Blue Max, The Charge of the Light Brigade, and The Evils of Frankenstein; television, since 1955, includes The Government Inspector, and The Fight Against Death.

Recreations: Gardening, reading and music. *Address:* 13 Greville Road, London, NW6.

WOODVINE, John, actor
b Tyne Dock, Co Durham, 21 July 1929; *s* of John Woodvine and his wife Rose (Kelly); *e* Lord William's Grammar School, Thame, Oxon; *m* Hazel Wright; formerly a laboratory assistant; trained for the stage at RADA.

First appeared on the stage May 1954, on tour of service establishments as Caspar Darde in Captain Carvallo; joined the Old Vic company, Sept 1954, walking on in Macbeth; in the same season played Vincentio in The Taming of the Shrew, Nov 1954; Duke (Senior) in As You Like It, Mar 1955; Vernon in Part I and Lord Chief Justice in Part II of Henry IV, Apr 1955; in 1956 his roles for the company included Tybalt in Romeo and Juliet and Roderigo in Othello; in 1959, Careless in The Double Dealer, Mowbray in Richard II, and Nym in The Merry Wives of Windsor; St Martin's, Mar 1960, Harry V Esterbrook in Inherit the Wind; at the Mermaid, his roles included General Lew Wallace in The Andersonville Trial, June 1961; Vasquez in 'Tis Pity She's A Whore, Aug 1961; Long John Silver in Treasure Island, Dec 1961; Pentheus in The Bacchae, Feb 1964; the title role in Macbeth, Apr 1964; Simon Eyre in The Shoemaker's Holiday, July 1964; Theseus in Oedipus at Colonus, May 1965; Comedy, June 1966, Cutler Walpole in The Doctor's Dilemma; same theatre, Dec 1966, Badger in Toad of Toad Hall; Fortune, Oct 1968, Jackie in Close the Coalhouse Door; Lyric, May 1970, Warrant Officer Ormsby in Poor Horace; University, Newcastle, and Greenwich, June 1971, Joe Wilson in a solo performance, Joe Lives!; for Prospect, Aug 1971, toured as Claudius in Hamlet; joined the Actors' Company, 1973, playing Sir Wilful Witwoud in The Way of the World (Edinburgh Festival), Orlovsky in The Wood Demon, Kent in King Lear, including appearances in all three parts at the Brooklyn Academy, New York, Jan 1974, and Wimbledon Theatre, Mar–May 1974, where he also played the Cardinal in 'Tis Pity She's A Whore, and Pontagnac in Ruling the Roost; Hampstead, Feb 1975, Staller in Stallerhof; Arnaud, Guildford, May 1975, Gerald in The Formation Dancers; Stratford, season 1976, played Duke of Cornwall in King Lear, Capulet in Romeo and Juliet, Dogberry in Much Ado About Nothing, Polixenes in The Winter's Tale, and Banquo in Macbeth (also at The Other Place, Aug 1976, and Warehouse, Sept 1977), repeating the roles of Dogberry and Capulet at the Aldwych, June–July 1977; also at the Aldwych, June 1977, played Dr Pinch in A Comedy of Errors; The Other Place, May 1977, Subtle in The Alchemist, repeating the part at the Aldwych, Dec 1977; Aldwych, Jan 1978, Fainall in The Way of the World; Mermaid, June 1978, Alexander in Every Good Boy Deserves Favour; Stratford season, 1979, played Sir John Falstaff in The Merry Wives of Windsor, Malvolio in Twelfth Night and the title role in Julius Caesar, also playing Malvolio and Falstaff at the Aldwych, 1980 season; films, since Darling, 1964, include: The Walking Stick and The Devils; television, since 1958, includes the series Z Cars, The Dustbinmen, and Elizabeth R.

Favourite parts: Simon Eyre, Othello, Jackie. *Address:* c/o Scott Marshall Ltd, 13 Queen's Gardens, London, W2. *Tel:* 01–723 4861.

WOODWARD, Charles, Jr, producer
First New York production was Johnny No-Trump, at the Cort, 8 Oct 1967, in association with Richard Barr and Clinton Wilder as Theater 1968; since then has produced or co-produced The Boys in the Band, 1968; The Front Page, 1969; Watercolor, Criss-Crossing, What the Butler Saw, 1970; All Over, Drat!, The Grass Harp, 1971; The Last of Mrs Lincoln, 1972; Detective Story (Philadelphia, Pa), 1973; Noel Coward in Two Keys, 1974; P.S. Your Cat Is Dead!, Seascape, 1975; Sweeney Todd, 1979.

Address: 404 West 22nd Street, New York, NY. *Tel:* 691–7163.

WOODWARD, Edward, OBE, 1978; actor
b Croydon, Surrey, 1 June 1930; s of Edward Oliver Woodward and his wife Violet Edith (Smith); e State schools, and Kingston Commercial College; m Venetia Mary Collett; formerly employed in the office of a sanitary engineer; studied for the stage at the Royal Academy of Dramatic Art.
Made his first appearance on the stage at the Farnham Repertory Theatre, Dec 1946, in A Kiss for Cinderella; was for some years a member of various repertory theatre companies,

including Perth, Oxford, and Guildford; toured India and Ceylon, appearing in Shakespeare and Shaw plays, 1951; first appeared on the London stage at the Garrick, June 1954, when he played Ralph Stokes in Where There's a Will; Piccadilly, Dec 1955, played John Brooke in A Girl Called Jo; Victoria Palace, July 1956, played John Evans in Doctor in the House; Guildford Repertory, May 1957, played John Mayfield in The Telescope; Lyric, Hammersmith, Nov 1957, played Sir Owen Tudor in The Queen and the Welshman; joined the Shakespeare Memorial Theatre Company, Stratford-on-Avon, Apr 1958, and played the following parts: Mercutio in Romeo and Juliet, Laertes in Hamlet, Thaliard in Pericles, and Claudio in Much Ado About Nothing; subsequently appeared with the same company on their visit to Leningrad and Moscow, 1958–9; Criterion, Aug 1960, appeared in the revue The Art of Living; Apollo (Repertory Players), Nov 1960, Dr Crippen in The Little Doctor; at the Alexandra Theatre, Johannesburg, Dec 1961, directed and played Percy in Rattle of a Simple Man; Adelphi, Mar 1962, played Haggis in Scapa; Garrick, Sept 1962, again played Percy in Rattle of a Simple Man; made his first appearance in New York at the Booth, Apr 1963, as Percy in Rattle of a Simple Man; Alvin, NY, Apr 1964, played Charles Condomine in High Spirits; Nottingham Playhouse, Sept 1965, Lucio in Measure for Measure; Walnut, Phila, Feb 1966, Jason Beckman in The Best Laid Plans, playing the same part at the Brooks Atkinson, NY, Mar 1966; Mermaid, London, Oct 1967, Captain Yule in The High Bid; Palace, Feb 1969, Sydney Carton in Two Cities (Variety Award for Best Performance in a Musical, 1969); 1969, joined the National Theatre to play Flamineo in The White Devil, and has since appeared as Cyrano de Bergerac in Cyrano, Oct 1970; Palladium, Dec 1972, Robin Hood in Babes in the Wood; Apollo, Oct 1973, George Szabo in the Oxford Playhouse production of The Wolf, transferring to the Queen's and the New London; Piccadilly, Oct 1974, Macneil, Sir Emlyn and Cornelius in The Male of the Species, followed by a tour of Australia and New Zealand; Haymarket, Dec 1975, Duke of Bristol in On Approval; Comedy, Aug 1978, Jaspar Tudor in The Dark House; Birmingham Rep, Sept 1979, co-directed and played Macheath in The Beggar's Opera, also touring; first appeared on television, Jan 1956, and has since appeared in over 200 productions including Major Barbara, A Dream Divided, the *Callan* series (1967–70), three of his own musical spectaculars, Saturday Sunday Monday, The Bass Player, and The Blonde (series); Television Actor of the Year Award, 1969, and the *Sun* Top Television Actor of the Year Award, 1969; has made a number of records, for which he received two Gold Discs; his films include Becket, Young Winston, Sitting Target, The Wicker Man, Stand Up Virgin Soldiers, and Breaker Morant.

Favourite parts: Mercutio, Drinkwater, and Percy in Rattle of a Simple Man. *Address:* c/o Eric Glass Ltd, 28 Berkeley Square, London, W1. *Tel:* 01–629 7162.

WOOLAND, Norman, actor
b Dusseldorf, Germany, 16 Mar 1905; e in Germany and at King Edward VI GS, Stratford-upon-Avon; m Jane Smith.
Made his first professional appearance at the Grand, Oldham, 11 Jan 1926, as Lorenzo in The Merchant of Venice, followed by six years in repertory; appeared at the Shakespeare Memorial Theatre, Stratford-upon-Avon, seasons 1933–7; first London appearance, Playhouse, 1937, in Night Club Queen; first New York appearance, Ritz, 1 March 1938, as Gerald in Time and the Conways; appeared at the Malvern Festival, 1938, and in 1939 as Mr Sheltie in What Say They?; Westminster, Aug 1940, Robert Murrison in Cornelius; Hay-

market, 1950, took over the part of Aubrey Tanqueray in The Second Mrs Tanqueray; St James's, May 1951, Enobarbus in Antony and Cleopatra; Winter Garden, May 1952, Matthew in Dragon's Mouth; Comedy, Apr 1960, Mr Fielding in A Passage to India; Playhouse, Oxford, 1967, Sgt Ruff in Gaslight; same theatre, 1968, Dr Stockman in Enemy of the People; appeared at the Haymarket, Oct 1969, in Hadrian VII; Criterion, Nov 1970, Haakon Werle in The Wild Duck; toured, Mar 1971, as Thomas More in A Man for All Seasons; toured, Jan 1972, as Col Strang in Conduct Unbecoming; Arnaud, Guildford, Sept 1972, the Father in Six Characters in Search of an Author; Globe, Nov 1972, took over as Max Weiner in A Touch of Purple; toured, 1973, as Gilles de Rais in Abelard and Heloise; Arnaud, Mar 1973, Bob Cherry in Flowering Cherry; Everyman, Cheltenham, Oct 1973, the Father in A Voyage Round My Father; Belgrade Studio, Coventry, Dec 1973, Wilson in The Butcher; toured, 1974, as Sgt Rough in Gaslight; Birmingham Rep, June 1975, George in Jumpers; toured, Sept 1975, as Mr Bennet in Pride and Prejudice; toured, Apr 1976, as Frank Strang in Equus; Harrogate Festival, Aug 1976, Capt Shotover in Heartbreak House; toured, 1977, playing Don Jerome in The Duenna; toured, 1978, as Sir Cecil in The Kingfisher; toured, 1979, as Old Ekdal in The Wild Duck; films, since Hamlet in 1947, include Richard III, The Fall of the Roman Empire, Saul and David, and International Velvet; recent TV includes Life at Stake and The Chief Mourner; wartime announcer and compere for BBC radio, 1941–6.

Recreations: Gardening and pottering about. *Address:* Wessex Cottage, Horsham Road, Handcross, Sussex.

WOOLFENDEN, Guy Anthony, composer and conductor
b Ipswich, Suffolk, 12 July 1937; *s* of Harold Arthur James Woolfenden and his wife Kathleen Nora Page (Groom); *e* Westminster Abbey Choir School, Whitgift School, Christ's College, Cambridge, Guildhall School of Music and Drama (LGSM); *m* Jane Aldrick.

Since 1962 Music Director to the Royal Shakespeare Company, for whom he has written over 70 scores, including award-winning Comedy of Errors, and The Greeks; has also composed four scores for the Comédie Française and two for the Burgtheater, Vienna; has written music for radio, TV and films, and arranged a ballet, Anna Karenina, for the Royal Australian Ballet; has conducted most of the major British symphony orchestras, also in Germany, France and Canada; conductor for Scottish Opera, 1979–80.

Address: Malvern House, Sibford Ferris, Banbury, Oxon. *Tel:* Swalcliffe 679.

WORDSWORTH, Richard, actor
b Halesowen Rectory, Worcestershire, 19 Jan 1915; *s* of Christopher William Wordsworth and his wife Ella Mary (Thompson); *e* Loretto, and Queen's College, Cambridge; *m* (1) Elizabeth Rundell Jeppe; (2) Sylvia Manning; studied for the stage under Eileen Thorndike, at the Embassy School of Acting.

Made his first appearance on the stage at the Old Vic, 11 Oct 1938, as Rosencrantz in Hamlet (in modern dress); next played two seasons at the Memorial Theatre, Stratford-on-Avon, playing, among other parts, Gratiano in The Merchant of Venice, Slender in The Merry Wives of Windsor, Silvius in As You Like It, etc; during 1940, appeared with the Brighton Repertory company; toured, 1940, with Donald Wolfit's company; Strand Theatre, Jan 1941, played The Cardinal in 'Tis Pity She's a Whore; rejoined the Old Vic Theatre company, at the Victoria Theatre, Burnley, in the spring of

1941, and subsequently toured as Bassanio in The Merchant of Venice and the Dauphin in King John; New Theatre, July 1941, played the last-mentioned part; toured 1942, as Roderigo in Othello and Slender in The Merry Wives of Windsor, playing the same parts at the New Theatre, July–Aug 1942; toured, 1942, under CEMA as leading actor in The Market Theatre; 1943, played leading parts with the Dundee Repertory company; Arts Theatre, Feb–May 1944, played Martin Beyer in The Witch, Leonard Charteris in The Philanderer, and Tom Fashion in A Trip to Scarborough; Wyndham's, Sept 1944; Reginald Hume-Banbury in The Banbury Nose; in the autumn of 1945, appeared at the Arts Theatre, Cambridge, in Androcles and the Lion, as Herod in Salome, Aubrey in The Second Mrs Tanqueray, etc; Lyric, Hammersmith, Mar 1946, Mr Walker in To-Morrow's Child; New, June 1946, played the Porter in Crime and Punishment; made his first appearance on the New York stage at the Royale, 3 Mar 1947, as Lane in The Importance of Being Earnest; at the same theatre, May 1947, played Jeremy in Love for Love; after returning to England, appeared at the Lyric, Hammersmith, Dec 1947, as Coupler in The Relapse, and played the same part at the Phoenix, Jan 1948; subsequently toured in this part; Arts, Dec 1948–Feb 1949, appeared as Mr Watt in Gog and MacGog, Lorimer in A Pair of Spectacles, and Antoine in The Unquiet Spirit; Piccadilly, May 1949, appeared in Ann Veronica; Apollo, Sept 1949, played Mr Walsh in Treasure Hunt, and toured in this, 1950; with the Shakespeare Memorial Theatre Company, Stratford-on-Avon, appeared as Pistol in the Histories during the season of 1951; Winter Garden, London, Mar 1952, played Smuggler in The Constant Couple; during Sir John Gielgud's season at the Lyric, Hammersmith, Dec 1952–May 1953, appeared as Edmund of Langley in Richard II, Petulant in The Way of the World, and Antonio in Venice Preserved, gaining the Clarence Derwent Award for the best supporting performance of 1953 in the last-named play; Arts, Feb 1954, played Mr Cattermole in The Private Secretary; Scala, Dec 1954, appeared as Mr Darling and Capt Hook in the Jubilee production of Peter Pan; joined the Old Vic Company, Sept 1955, and during the season appeared as Cassius in Julius Caesar, Ford in The Merry Wives of Windsor, Ulysses in Troilus and Cressida, Pistol in Henry V, and the First Witch and Porter in Macbeth; Old Vic American tour, Oct 1956, played Duke of York in Richard II, and Tybalt in Romeo and Juliet, in addition to the First Witch, and Ulysses; returned to the Old Vic, London, Apr 1958, to play Malvolio in Twelfth Night and the Duke of Norfolk in Henry VIII; Edinburgh Festival, Aug 1958, again played Malvolio in Twelfth Night, prior to appearing in the same part in the Old Vic American tour, 1958–9, in which he also played Pistol in Henry V; at the opening of the Mermaid Theatre, London, May 1959, played Justice Squeezum in Lock Up Your Daughters; Piccadilly, Oct 1959, Achille Diaforius in The Love Doctor; Scala, Dec 1959, played Captain Hook and Mr Darling in Peter Pan; Scala, Dec 1961, directed Peter Pan; Pembroke, Croydon, Jan 1962, played Mr Gruffwydd in Cry For Love; Mermaid, Mar 1962, Petkoff in Arms and the Man; at the same theatre, May 1962, directed a revival of Lock Up Your Daughters; Her Majesty's, Sydney, Australia, Aug 1962, played Ko-Ko in The Mikado, and the Duke of Plaza-Toro in The Gondoliers in the Gilbert and Sullivan Season, subsequently directing The Pirates of Penzance and Trial by Jury; Mermaid, London, Apr 1963, played Coupler in Virtue in Danger, transferring with the production to the Strand, June 1963; Bristol Old Vic, Feb 1964, Cardinal, Secretary-of-State in The Successor; Ashcroft, Croydon, Sept 1964, Sir Francis Bacon in No Bed For Bacon; toured Australia and New

Zealand, June 1965, in Beekman Place, and 1966–7 in his own production of Oliver! in which he played Fagin; Vaudeville, May 1968, Argan in The Imaginary Invalid; directed Peter Pan at the Scala, Dec 1968 (also playing Captain Hook), and at the New Victoria, Dec 1969; 1969–70 devised and directed his one-man show The Bliss of Solitude, touring England, Scotland and America as his great-great-grandfather, William Wordsworth; Mermaid, Dec 1970, played Mr Smears in Dick Turpin; at Nottingham Playhouse, 1971, played Sir Antony Absolute in The Rivals and Petey in The Birthday Party; Crucible, Sheffield, 1973, parts including Ashe in The National Health, Bill Broadhead in The Stirrings in Sheffield, the Archbishop in Facets on a Golden Image, and the Professor in Uncle Vanya; toured the US 1974, in The Bliss of Solitude; again in spring 1975, as Charles Lamb in The Frolic and the Gentle, and also in autumn 1975, in a Shakespeare anthology, Let Me Play the Lion, Too, and two Bicentennial programmes, Taxation No Tyranny, and An Interview with Thomas Jefferson; made further tours of The Bliss of Solitude, 1976–9, and lectured on the Romantic poets, also directing and performing Shakespeare at American universities; films include: The Man Who Knew Too Much and The Quatermass Experiment; his numerous television appearances include Dickens serials, The Trial of Roger Casement, and *The Regiment*.

Recreations: Gardening and croquet. *Address:* Melford House, 62 Portmore Park Road, Weybridge, Surrey. *Tel:* Weybridge 47557.

WORTH, Irene, Hon CBE, 1975; actress
b Nebraska, USA, 23 June 1916; *e* University of California, Los Angeles (Bachelor of Education); formerly a teacher.

Made her first appearance on the stage, 1942, as Fenella in Escape Me Never, touring with Elisabeth Bergner; made her first apperance in New York, at the Booth Theatre, 3 Aug 1943, as Cecily Harden in The Two Mrs Carrolls; went to London, 1944, and studied for six months with Elsie Fogerty; made her first appearance in London, at the Lyric Theatre, Hammersmith, 14 Feb 1946, as Elsie in The Time of Your Life; Mercury, Apr 1946, appeared in This Way to the Tomb; Embassy, June 1946, and Duchess, July 1946, played Annabelle Jones in Love Goes to Press; toured, Oct 1946, as Ilona Szabo in The Play's the Thing; Embassy, Dec 1946, played Donna Pascuala in Drake's Drum; Lyric, Hammersmith, Apr, and St James's, May 1947, Ilona in The Play's the Thing; toured, Oct 1947, in Return Journey; Q, Dec 1947, Olivia Brown in Love in Idleness, and Feb 1948, Iris in Pinero's play of that name; Boltons, Feb 1948, Mary Dalton in Native Son, and Apr 1948, Lucrece in a play of that name; Lyric, July 1948, succeeded Leueen McGrath as Eileen Perry in Edward My Son; subsequently toured as Lady Fortrose in Home Is To-Morrow, and appeared in this at the Cambridge, Nov 1948; New Theatre, June 1949, played Olivia Raines in Champagne for Delilah; Edinburgh Festival, Aug 1949, created Celia Coplestone in The Cocktail Party, and played the same part at the Henry Miller Theatre, NY, Jan 1950, and at the New Theatre, London, July 1950, when she succeeded Margaret Leighton; joined the Old Vic Company, appearing at the Berlin Festival, Oct 1951, as Desdemona in Othello; subsequently played the same part at the Old Vic, Oct 1951, followed by Helena in A Midsummer Night's Dream and Catherine de Vausselles in The Other Heart, 1951–2; toured South Africa with the Old Vic Company, 1953, in the same parts, and also appeared as Lady Macbeth; at the Old Vic Theatre, Jan 1953, played Portia in The Merchant of Venice; during the first season of the Shakespeare Festival Theatre, Stratford, Ontario, 1953, appeared as Helena in All's Well

That Ends Well and Queen Margaret in Richard III; Haymarket, London, Nov 1953, played Frances Farrar in A Day by the Sea; with the Midland Theatre Company, Coventry, Mar 1955, created the part of Argia in The Queen and the Rebels; at the Edinburgh Festival, 1955, played Alcestis in A Life in the Sun; Haymarket, London, Oct 1955, again played Argia in The Queen and the Rebels; Winter Garden, May 1956, played Marcelle in Hotel Paradiso; Phoenix, NY, Oct 1957, played the title-part in Schiller's Mary Stuart; Globe, London, Feb 1958, Sara Callifer in The Potting Shed; Assembly Hall, Edinburgh Festival, Sept 1958, again played the title-role in Mary Stuart, subsequently appearing in the same play at the Old Vic, Sept 1958; Shakespeare Festival, Stratford, Ontario, June 1959, played Rosalind in As You Like It; Hudson, NY, Feb 1960, Albertine Prine in Toys in the Attic; on returning to England, joined the Royal Shakespeare Company at the Aldwych, Mar 1962, to play the Marquise de Merteuil in The Art of Seduction (Les Liaisons Dangereuses); at the Royal Shakespeare, Stratford-on-Avon, June 1962, played Lady Macbeth in Macbeth, and Nov 1962, Goneril in King Lear; Aldwych, Dec 1962, again played Goneril in King Lear; Aldwych, Jan 1963, Doktor Mathilde von Zahnd in The Physicists; Haymarket, Aug 1963, played Clodia Pulcher in The Ides of March; Aldwych, Feb 1964, again appeared in King Lear with the Royal Shakespeare Company, prior to a British Council tour with the production to Europe, the USSR, and Canada, subsequently appearing with the company at the opening of the New York State Theatre, May 1964; Billy Rose, NY, Dec 1964, played Alice in Tiny Alice, receiving the Antoinette Perry (Tony) Award, 1965, for this performance; Queen's, London, Apr 1966, played Hilde Latymer in A Song at Twilight; Anne Hilgay in Shadows of the Evening, and Anna-Mary Conklin in Come into the Garden, Maud (double-bill), in Noël Coward's Suite in Three Keys (*Evening Standard* Award for Best Actress, 1966); Nov 1966, for the British Council toured South America and US universities in Men and Women of Shakespeare; Yale University, May 1967, played Io in Prometheus Bound; Chichester Festival, July 1967, Hesione Hushabye in Heartbreak House, also at the Lyric, Nov 1967; Old Vic, Mar 1968, Jocasta in Oedipus; Aldwych, Jan 1970, Miss Alice in Tiny Alice; Stratford, Ont, June 1970, Hedda in Hedda Gabler; Globe, London, Mar 1972, Dora Lang in Notes On A Love Affair; Chichester, May 1973, Irina Arkadina in The Seagull; played the same part at Greenwich, Jan 1974, also Mrs Alving in Ghosts, Jan, and Gertrude in Hamlet, Mar; Brooklyn Academy, NY, Dec 1975, Princess Kosmonopolis in Sweet Bird of Youth, transferring to the Harkness (Tony Award and Jefferson Award, 1975); Lincoln Center, Feb 1977, Mme Ranevskaya in The Cherry Orchard; Public/Newman, June 1979, Winnie in Happy Days; has also appeared at Lake Forest, Ill, in Misalliance, 1976, Old Times, 1977, After the Season, 1978; films include Orders to Kill (British Film Academy Award for the Best Actress, 1958); The Scapegoat, King Lear, and Nicholas and Alexandra; made her first television appearance, 1949, and performances include Stella in The Lake, Ellida Wangel in The Lady from the Sea, 1953; Candida, The Duchess of Malfi, Antigone, 1955; and Clytemnestra in Prince Orestes (NY, 1959); Rose Fish in Variations on a Theme, 1966; radio performances include The Cocktail Party, 1951; Major Barbara, All's Well That Ends Well, The Queen and the Rebels, 1954; The Merchant of Venice, 1958; Rosmersholm, 1959; Duel of Angels, 1964; received the *Daily Mail* National Television Award, 1953–4; Whitbread Anglo-American Award for outstanding actress, 1967; subsequent appearances in USA and Canada.

Recreations: Music, piano. *Address:* c/o ICM, Sixth Floor, Milton Goldman, 40 West 57th Street, New York, NY 10019.

WRIGHT, David, dramatic writer and director

b Chesterfield, 3 May 1941; *s* of Newport Victor Wright and his wife Mildred (Favell); *e* Latymer Upper School and Lincoln College, Oxford; *m* (1) Jennifer Argyle (mar dis); (2) Sue Rolfe.

Devised Hang Down Your Head and Die for ETC, Feb 1964; the production was subsequently presented at the Comedy, London, Mar 1964, and the Mayfair Theatre, New York, Oct 1964; has since written the following: Boswell in Scotland, A Life in Bedrooms, 1967; Would You Look At Them Smashing All the Lovely Windows?, Have You Seen Manchester?, 1968; The Stiffkey Scandals of 1932 (based on A Life in Bedrooms),1969; Deputy Director, Dolphin Theatre Company, 1971; The Stiffkey Scandals, as well as All the Lovely Windows, has also been performed on television; member, editorial board, *Drama*.

Recreation: Carpentry, wine tasting, and travel. *Address:* 2 Weston Road, London W4.

WRIGHT, Nicholas, director and dramatist

b Cape Town, S Africa, 5 July 1940; *s* of Harry Axon Wright and his wife Winifred Hannah (Smith); *e* Rondebosch Boys' HS.

Joined the Royal Court Theatre as casting director, 1967; Assistant Director, 1968, and in this year directed a Sunday-night production of his own play Changing Lines; Director, Theatre Upstairs, 1969–Apr 1971 and Aug 1972–Apr 1974; productions here included Poet of the Anemones, AC/DC (also at the Royal Court), Captain Jack's Revenge, Was He Anyone?, Owners, Captain Oates' Left Sock, Bright Scene Fading, Bird Child, and Paradise; at the Royal Court directed The Great Caper, 1974, T Zee, 1976; joint Artistic Director, Royal Court, Aug 1975–7; productions elsewhere include Play Strindberg, Biography, Drums in the Night, Uncle Vanya (all in S Africa); Sizwe Bansi Is Dead, The Sea (in Holland); returned to writing with Treetops, Riverside, 1978; The Gorky Brigade, Royal Court, 1979.

Recreation: Gossip. *Address:* c/o Barclay's Bank, Sloane Square, London SW1.

WRIGHT, Teresa, actress

b New York City, 27 Oct 1918; *d* of Arthur Wright and his wife Martha (Espy); *e* Columbia High School, Maplewood, New Jersey; *m* (1) Niven Busch (mar dis); (2) Robert Woodruff Anderson (mar dis); (3) Carlos Pierre (mar dis); (4) Robert Woodruff Anderson.

First appeared on the stage in a High School Production of Death Takes a Holiday, playing the role of Grazia, 1928; made her professional début in July 1938, as the Daughter in The Vinegar Tree; Wharf, Provincetown, Massachusetts, Aug 1938, played Blossom Trexel in Susan and God; made her NY début at the Henry Miller's, Oct 1938, when she joined the cast of Our Town in a small role and understudied Dorothy McGuire as Emily; subsequently toured as Rebecca in Our Town, and took over the role of Emily during the tour in the Spring of 1939; played a season of stock at Tanworth, New Hampshire, 1939; Empire, NY, Nov 1939, Mary in Life with Father; went to Hollywood to make films for some years, and reappeared on the stage at the Shubert, New Haven, Mar 1952, as Linnea Ecklund in Salt of the Earth; Sombrero Playhouse, Phoenix, Arizona, 1953, played in Bell, Book, and Candle; in Vancouver, Canada, 1953, played Georgie Elgin in The Country Girl; Palm Springs, California, 1954, played in The Heiress; La Jolla, California, Playhouse, 1954, Lizzie Curry in The Rainmaker; reappeared in NY at the Music Box, Dec 1957, as Cora Flood in The Dark at the

Top of the Stairs; toured, May–Aug 1962, as Mary McKellaway in Mary, Mary; toured, 1963, as Pamela Pew-Picket in Tchin-Tchin; toured, 1965, as Katherine Butler Hathaway in The Locksmith; Longacre, NY, Jan 1968, Alice in I Never Sang for My Father; Village South, Nov 1969, Mary Hallen in Who's Happy Now?; Theatre de Lys, Oct 1970, played in the concert reading A Passage to E M Forster; Hartford, Conn, Stage Company, 1971, Mary Tyrone in Long Day's Journey into Night; Shubert, New Haven, Conn, Oct 1972, Beatrice in The Effect of Gamma Rays on Man-in-the-Moon Marigolds; Walnut, Philadelphia, Feb 1974, Linda Loman in Death of a Salesman; Long Wharf, New Haven, Conn, Nov 1974, played in The Knight of the Burning Pestle; Long Wharf, Dec 1974, Lily Miller in Ah, Wilderness!; Circle in the Square, June 1975, Linda Loman in Death of a Salesman; same theater, Oct 1975, Lily Miller in Ah, Wilderness!; Eisenhower, Washington, DC, June 1977, appeared in The Master Builder; Hartford, Conn, Oct 1977, in All the Way Home; appeared at the Cleveland Playhouse, season 1978–9; Lyceum, Apr 1980, Cora Swanson in Morning's at Seven; made her film début as Alexandra in The Little Foxes, 1941, and later films include Mrs Miniver, Pride of the Yankees, Shadow of a Doubt, Casanova Brown, The Best Years of Our Lives, The Men, The Actress, etc; received the Academy Award for Mrs Miniver; has appeared on various television dramatic programs, notably as Annie Sullivan in The Miracle Worker, the title-role in The Louella Parsons Story, The Margaret Bourke-White Story, Big Deal in Laredo, on *Lux Video Theatre, Playhouse 90,* etc.

Address: Actors Equity Association, 165 West 46th Street, New York, NY 10036.

WYCKHAM, John (*né* Suckling), lighting designer and theatre consultant

b Solihull, Warwicks, 18 May 1926; *s* of Walter Scofield Suckling and his wife Garth Mary (Blackwell); *e* Repton; *m* (1) Mary Preston (mar dis); (2) Margaret Llewellyn.

Began his professional career as a stage manager, 1950; stage manager, later stage director, for Blackpool summer spectaculars, 1951–4, and for Emile Littler pantomimes in London and the provinces, 1951–61; began career as a lighting designer, 1955; lighting designer to the Royal Shakespeare Company, 1961, later technical administrator; left 1964; consultant and technical administrator, Sadler's Wells Opera at the Coliseum, 1968–71; the numerous productions he has lit, at Stratford, in London and abroad, include Beyond the Fringe (set and lighting, London and New York), The Devils, Oliver! (London and NY), King Lear (London and Paris), Robert and Elizabeth and The Shaughraun; founder member of the Society of Theatre Consultants (Chairman, 1974–9) and the Society of British Theatre Lighting Designers; Senior partner of John Wyckham Associates, Theatre Consultants, Epsom; Partner in charge of technical design for Stirling University (MacRobert Centre), Bangor University Theatre, Eden Court Theatre (Inverness), The New Pitlochry Festival Theatre, Dartford Civic Hall; Technical renovation design for Theatre Royal (Glasgow), Palace Theatre (Manchester), Grand Theatre (Blackpool).

Recreations: Fly fishing, reading, gardening, wine. *Address:* John Wyckham Associates, 119/121 High Street, Epsom, Surrey KT19 8DT. *Tel:* Epsom 27911.

WYNGARDE, Peter, actor and director

b Marseilles; formerly in advertising.

Early experience was repertory at Windsor, York and Nottingham; made his London début with the latter company at the Embassy, 28 June 1949, as Cassio in Othello; subsequently at the Bristol Old Vic, where his parts included Cyrano de Bergerac, and Petruchio in The Taming of the Shrew, and where he directed Long Day's Journey into Night; New, May 1951, Voltimand in Hamlet; Royal Court, Oct 1956; Yang Sun in The Good Woman of Setzuan; Apollo, Apr 1958, Marcellus in Duel of Angels, making his New York début in this part, 1960; Hampstead, Dec 1967, Felice in The Two-Character Play; Duke of York's, Apr 1968, Nikolay in The Duel; in Melbourne, 1972, played the title role in Butley; Hampstead, Apr 1973, Adam in Mother Adam; Adelphi, Oct 1973, The King of Siam in The King and I; toured, July 1974, as Gary Essendine in Present Laughter, which he also directed; Arnaud, Guildford, Dec 1975, directed Time and the Conways; Cambridge, Sept 1976, Prince Volkov in Anastasia; 1978, toured South Africa as Sidney Bruhl in Deathtrap; films include The Innocents, The Siege of Sidney Street and Flash Gordon; TV work includes over seventy plays and his own series *Department S* and *Jason King*.

Address: c/o ICM, 22 Grafton Street, London W1. *Tel:* 01–629 8080.

Y

YOUNG, Bertram Alfred, critic and author
b London, 20 Jan 1912; *s* of Bertram William Young and his wife Dora Elizabeth (Knight); *e* Highgate School.

Assistant editor, *Punch*, 1949–63; dramatic critic *Punch*, 1963–4; dramatic critic, *Financial Times*; President, Critics' Circle, 1978–80; is the author of a television play, Death of Uncle George, 1953, two novels and some 20 radio plays; member, Arts Council Theatre Writing Committee and British Council Drama Advisory Committee.

Recreations: Listening to music. *Club:* Garrick. *Address:* Flat 3, 28 Elm Park Gardens, London, SW10.

YOUNG, Joan, actress
b Newcastle upon Tyne, 1 Feb 1903; *d* of Charles Wragge and his wife, Nellie (Parker); *e* in convents in England and France; *m* John Young; both her parents were music-hall performers.

First appeared at the Woolwich Hippodrome, 1918, in variety, as a single turn; then, from 1934, worked exclusively in broadcasting; made her first appearance on the regular stage at the Playhouse, May 1944, when she played Mrs Gibbs in Our Town, for the American Army Drama Unit; Phoenix Theatre, May 1945, played Mrs Antrobus in The Skin of Our Teeth; Lyric, Hammersmith, Oct 1945, Amy Willard in The Shouting Dies, and Nov 1945, Ma Kirby in The Happy Journey to Trenton and Camden; Adelphi, July 1946, Alderman Busy in Big Ben; New Lindsey, Aug 1947, Sister Bessie in Tobacco Road; Lyric, Hammersmith, Mar 1948, Georgiana Tidman in Dandy Dick; Mar 1949, Conjur Woman and Mrs Allen in Dark of the Moon, and at Ambassadors', Apr 1949, played the same parts; Duchess, Aug 1949, Mrs Donnelly in Fading Mansion; New Lindsey, May 1950, Estelle in The Dark Corridor; toured, 1951, as Mrs Printing in And Her Mother Came Too; Lyric, Hammersmith, Nov 1951, and Duchess, Jan 1952, played Mrs Bassett in Summer and Smoke; at the Q, Nov 1952, appeared as Grannie in It's Never Too Late, and May 1953, as Mrs Boddington in Danger Line; Sadler's Wells, July 1954, played Cornelia in East Lynne, subsequently touring in this part; Arts, Mar 1955, played Mrs Strong in South; toured, Sept 1958, as Madame Hackenbutel in A Fig for Glory; toured, Dec 1958, as Mistress Murray in Old Chelsea; Arts, Aug 1961, Mrs Bolton in Lady Chatterley; Playhouse, Oxford, Oct 1961, and Wyndham's, London, Nov 1961, Nurse Guinness in Heartbreak House; Saville, Dec 1962, Garnet Hadfield in Semi-Detached; Shaftesbury, Oct 1966, played Lady Chesapeake in Big Bad Mouse, during its eighteen-month run, and at the Prince of Wales, Sept 1971, subsequently taking part in several tours including five of the UK, also South Africa, Canada, Australia (1974 and 1978), New Zealand, Rhodesia (1976), USA and Hong Kong, 1978; first appeared in films, 1943, in The Lamp Still Burns; has since appeared in numerous films, and also on television.

Recreations: Collecting antiques and china dogs, and cooking. *Address:* 4 Cable House, Lloyd Street, WC1X 9QT. *Tel:* 01–837 2211.

Z

ZEFFIRELLI, G Franco, director and designer
b 12 Feb 1923; *e* Florence.

Began his career as an actor under the direction of Visconti, subsequently becoming the latter's assistant in films; designed many sets and costumes for plays and operas in Italy, 1945–51; directed La Cenerentola at the Scala, Milan, 1953; has directed, and also designed, many plays in Italy, including: Troilus and Cressida, The Three Sisters, A Streetcar Named Desire, The She Wolf, After the Fall, and Who's Afraid of Virginia Woolf?; directed and designed his first play production in London at the Old Vic, Oct 1960, with Romeo and Juliet; at the Royal Shakespeare, Stratford-on-Avon, Oct 1961, directed and designed Othello; directed his first play in New York at the City Center, Feb 1962, with Romeo and Juliet; Winter Garden, NY, Mar 1963, directed and designed The Lady of the Camelias; Old Vic, Sept 1964, directed and designed Amleto (Proclemer-Albertazzi Company); Old Vic, Feb 1965, directed and designed Much Ado About Nothing (National Theatre Company); Aldwych, June 1969 (World Theatre Season), directed La Lupa; directed and designed Saturday, Sunday, Monday, National Theatre (Old Vic), 1973, NY 1974; directed Filumena, Lyric, 1977; directed and designed the films Romeo and Juliet, The Taming of the Shrew, Brother Sun, Sister Moon, and The Champ; he has also produced numerous operas at Covent Garden, Glyndebourne, the Metropolitan, NY, and in his native Italy; for TV directed Jesus of Nazareth, 1977.

Address: Via Due Macelli 31, Rome, Italy.

ZINDEL, Paul, playwright
b Staten Island, New York, 15 May 1936; *s* of Paul Zindel and his wife Betty (Frank); *e* Wagner College; *m* Bonnie Hildebrand; formerly a chemistry teacher.

His first produced play was The Effect of Gamma Rays on Man-in-the-Moon Marigolds, presented at the Mercer-O'Casey, 7 Apr 1970; this play was awarded the Pulitzer Prize for Drama, 1971; also received the New York Drama Critics Award and the Drama Desk Award; his play And Miss Reardon Drinks a Little produced at the Morosco, 25 Feb 1971; The Secret Affairs of Mildred Wild, 1972; Ladies at the Alamo, 1976; author of the television play Let Me Hear You Whisper, 1969; Marigolds produced on television four separate times; author of the novels The Pigman, My Darling, My Hamburger, I Never Loved Your Mind, etc.

Address: 60 East 8th Street, New York, NY 10003. *Tel:* 673–6226.

ZIPPRODT, Patricia, costume designer
b Evanston, Ill, 25 Feb 1925; *d* of Herbert Edward Zipprodt and his wife Irene (Turpin); *e* Wellesley College, Mass (BA Sociology), and Fashion Institute of Technology, NY.

First designs for New York were the costumes for The Potting Shed, at the Bijou, 29 Feb 1957; since then has designed the costumes for Visit to a Small Planet, The Virtuous Island, The Apollo of Bellac, Miss Lonelyhearts, The Rope Dancers, 1957; The Crucible, Back to Methuselah, The Night Circus, 1958; Our Town, The Gang's All Here, 1959; The Balcony, Camino Real, Period of Adjustment, 1960; The Blacks, The Garden of Sweets, Sunday in New York, Madame Aphrodite, 1961; Ah Dad, Poor Dad, Mama's Hung You in the Closet and I'm Feelin' So Sad, A Man's a Man, Step on a Crack, 1962; The Dragon, She Loves Me, Morning Sun, Next Time I'll Sing to You, 1963; Too Much Johnson, Fiddler on the Roof, The Tragical Historie of Dr Faustus, 1964; Anya, 1965; Pousse-Café, Cabaret, 1966; The Little Foxes, Fiddler on the Roof (London), 1967; Plaza Suite, Zorba, 1968; The Tale of Kasane, 1776, 1969; Georgy, 1970; Scratch, 1971; Pippin, The Mother of Us All (opera), 1972; Waiting for Godot (Minneapolis, Minn), Pippin (London), 1973; Dear Nobody, Mack and Mabel, 1974; All God's Chillun Got Wings, Chicago, The Leaves Are Fading (ballet), 1975; Poor Murderer, Four Saints in Three Acts (opera), Caprichos, Tres Cantos (ballets), 1976; Tannhäuser (Metropolitan Opera), 1977; Stages, King of Hearts, Naughty Marietta (NY City Opera), 1978; Swing, 1980; designed the costumes for the films The Graduate, Last of the Mobile Hotshots, 1776, etc.

Address: 45 University Place, New York, NY 10003. *Tel:* 677–3142.

ZORINA, Vera (*née* Brigitta Hartwig), actress, dancer and director
b Berlin, Germany, 2 Jan 1917; *d* of Fritz Hartwig and his wife Bille (Wimpelmann); *e* at private school in Berlin; *m* (1) George Balanchine (mar dis); (2) Goddard Lieberson; studied dancing under Nicholas Legat, and acting under Lina Abarbanell.

Made her first appearance on the stage at the Festival Hall, Kristiansund, Norway, 5 Dec 1923, as a Butterfly in a Flower Ballet; at the Grosses Schauspielhaus, Berlin, 1928, under the name of Brigitta, danced in Erik Charrell's production of Lilac Time; Deutsches Theater, Berlin, 1929, was the First Elf in Reinhardt's revival of A Midsummer Night's Dream, also appearing in his revival of The Tales of Hoffman, 1931; in June 1933, appeared at Oxford, England, in Reinhardt's production of A Midsummer Night's Dream; made her first appearance on the London stage, at the Gaiety, 10 Oct 1933, as Rosa in Ballerina; at the Alhambra, Oct 1933, appeared with the Ballets Russes company, in Choreartium; Savoy, June 1934, played Lydia Demurska in Precipice; in the same year, joined Col de Basil's company of the Monte Carlo Ballets Russes, when she appeared for the first time as Vera Zorina, and remained with the company until 1936, appearing at the Metropolitan Opera House, New York, 1934, and at Covent Garden, 1935 and 1936; at the Palace Theatre, London, Feb 1937, played Vera Baranova in On Your Toes, and the same part at the London Coliseum, Apr 1937; first appeared on the NY stage at the Shubert Theatre, 11 May 1938, as Angel in I Married an Angel; Imperial, May 1940, Marina Van Linden in Louisiana Purchase; Majestic, May 1944, Dina and Scheherezade in Dream with Music; Alvin, Jan 1945, Ariel in The Tempest; Maxine Elliott, Mar 1948, Suzette in A Temporary Island; at Dallas, Texas, July 1951, appeared in I Married an Angel; 46th Street Theatre, NY, Oct 1954, again played Vera Baranova in a revival of On Your Toes; Philharmonic Hall, 14 Jan 1964, narrated Persephone in French; Santa Fe Opera, New Mexico, 1964, directed

Daphne; Wesleyan University, Middleton, Conn, Dec 1964, played the title-role in Phaedra; Santa Fe Opera, 1966, directed Dialogues of the Carmelites and Capriccio; with the London Symphony Orchestra, June 1966, narrated Joan of Arc at the Stake; New York City Opera, 1968, directed Cavalleria Rusticana and I Pagliacci; appointed General Director and Artistic Administrator of the Norwegian Opera, Oslo, Aug 1977; entered films, 1938, in The Goldwyn Follies, subsequently appearing in On Your Toes, Louisiana Purchase, Follow the Boys, etc.

Recreations: Music, drawing and studying art. *Address:* c/o Norwegian Opera, Oslo, Norway.

ZWAR, Charles, composer
b Broadford, Victoria, Australia, 10 Apr 1914; *s* of Charles Henry Zwar and his wife Eliza Mary (Richards); *e* Trinity College, University of Melbourne (BA); *m* (1) Isobel Ann Shead (mar dis); (2) Diana Plunkett.

Began his career while still at the University, writing lyrics and composing music for University revues; his first professional work was the writing of the lyrics and composing the score of Blue Mountain Melody, Theatre Royal, Sydney, 1934; came to London, 1937; was musical director and pianist for the Gate Revues, Gate Theatre, 1938, and Ambassadors', 1939; during the War, served with the Royal Engineers, and later with the Australian Imperial Force; composed music for Gate Revue, 1939; Let's Face It, 1939; Swinging the Gate (most of the score and some lyrics), 1940; Sky High, 1942; Sweeter and Lower, 1944; Sweetest and Lowest (entire score), 1946; One, Two, Three, 1946; Four, Five, Six, 1947; A La Carte (entire score), 1948; The Lyric Revue, Penny Plain, 1951; Bet Your Life, The Globe Revue, 1952; Airs On a Shoestring, At the Lyric, 1953; Going to Town (a revised version of At the Lyric), 1954; From Here and There, 1955; Marigold, 1959; On the Avenue, 1961; All Square, 1963; Six of One, 1964; Is Australia Really Necessary? (Australia), 1964–5; The Stationmaster's Daughter (Guildford), 1968; contributed to Déjà Revue, 1975; he has also acted as musical director for many of the above productions; has also composed scores for several films.

Club: Chelsea Arts. *Address:* 18 Rossetti Gardens Mansions, Chelsea, London, SW3. *Tel:* 01-352 0252.

NAMES IN PREVIOUS EDITIONS

An index to the names of living persons (together with those *believed* to be living) whose biographies have appeared in previous issues. An asterisk * follows the names of a number of artists believed to be dead, but for whom no date of death has been traced. The figure indicates the Edition in which the biography last appeared.

NB Artists known to be dead are not listed here but in the appropriate Obituary listing.

A

B

C

D

E

F

I

J

K

OBITUARY

Please note that this is *not* a complete theatrical obituary. It is a listing of those deaths which have come to the editors' notice during the period 1 January 1976 to 31 July 1980 inclusive. The few earlier dates given here represent additions or amendments to the obituary listings in previous volumes of this book.

A full obituary listing to the end of 1965 appears in the Fourteenth Edition, and updates for the intervening period in the Fifteenth and Sixteenth Editions.

The figure given in parentheses after each name is the age, where known, at the date of death. Where a biography has appeared in *Who's Who in the Theatre*, the number of the last edition in which it appeared is given at the end of the entry in *italics*.

ADAM, Ronald, actor-manager and dramatic author, died 26 Mar 1979 (82), *16th*

ADDINSELL, Richard, composer, died 15 Nov 1977 (73), *16th*

ADDIS, Justus, director, died 26 Oct 1979 (62)

ADLER, Celia, actress, died 31 Jan 1979 (89)

ADLER, Jay, actor, died 23 Sept 1978 (82)

ALBERT, Kitty, actress, died 1977 (91)

ALBERY, Peter, playwright, died 22 Jun 1979 (66)

ALDEN, Hortense, actress, died 2 Apr 1978 (76), *10th*

ALLEN, A Hylton, actor, died 6 Feb 1975 (95), *12th*

ALSWANG, Ralph, designer, died 15 Feb 1979 (62), *17th*

ANDERSON, Eddie 'Rochester', comedian, died 28 Feb 1977 (71)

ANDERSON, Warner, actor, died 26 Aug 1976 (65)

ARBENINA, Stella, actress, died May 1976 (89), *10th*

ARDREY, Robert, playwright, died 14 Jan 1980 (71) *14th*

ARMSTRONG, Anthony (Anthony Armstrong Willis), playwright, died 10 Feb 1976 (79), *14th*

ASHLEY, Barbara, actress, died 1 Mar 1978 (50)

ASTOR, Gertrude, actress, died 9 Nov 1977 (90)

ATKINSON, Rosalind, actress, died 21 Feb 1977 (76), *16th*

AURTHUR, Robert Allan, dramatist, producer, died 20 Nov 1978 (56)

AYLMER, Sir Felix, actor, died 2 Sept 1979 (90), *15th*

AYRES, Queenie, actress, died 8 Oct 1976 (74)

BADDELEY, Angela, actress, died 22 Feb 1976 (71), *16th*

BADIA, Leopold, actor, died 2 July 1976 (74)

BAILEY, James, designer, died July 1980 (50's)

BAKER, George, actor, died 8 Jan 1976 (70), *14th*

BAKER, Josephine, singer and dancer, died 12 Apr 1975 (68), *16th*

BAKER, Sir Stanley, actor, died 28 Jun 1976 (48)

BANNERMAN, Margaret, actress, died 14 Jun 1976 (83), *15th*

BARBOUR, Joyce, actress, died Mar 1977 (75), *15th*

BARRETT, Edith, actress, died 22 Feb 1977 (64), *10th*

BARRIE, John, actor, died 24 Mar 1980 (63)

BARRIE, Wendy, actress, died 2 Feb 1978 (65)

BATES, Michael, actor, died 11 Jan 1978 (57), *16th*

BATSON, George, playwright, died 25 July 1977 (61)

BAXTER, Alan, died 8 May 1976 (67), *15th*

BAXTER, George, actor, died 10 Sept 1976 (72)

BEATON, Sir Cecil, designer, died 18 Jan 1980 (76), *16th*

BEATTY, Roberta, actress, died 1978, *9th*

BEAUMONT, Cyril, OBE, critic and author, died 24 May 1976 (84), *14th*

BECKINSALE, Richard, actor, died 19 Mar 1979 (31)

BECKLEY, Tony, actor, died Apr 1980 (50)

BEN-AMI, Jacob, Yiddish actor and director, died 2 July 1977 (86), *10th*

BENNETT, Dorothy Cheston, actress, died May 1977 (86)

BENNETT, Vivienne, actress, died 11 Nov 1978 (73), *16th*

BERGEN, Edgar, ventriloquist, died 30 Sept 1978 (75)

BERKELEY, Busby, actor, director, choreographer, died 14 Mar 1976 (80), *16th*

BETTS, Fred, actor, died 16 Mar 1977 (63)

BICKLEY, Samuel (Tony), actor, died 19 Jun 1976 (67)

BISSELL, Richard, dramatic author, died 4 May 1977 (63)

BLACKMAN, Don, actor, died 11 Sept 1977 (65)

BLONDELL, Joan, actress, died 25 Dec 1979 (70), *16th*

BLOOMGARDEN, Kermit, producer, died 20 Sept 1976 (71), *16th*

BOLES, Jim, actor, died 26 May 1977 (63)

BOLTON, Guy, dramatic author, died 5 Sept 1979 (96), *16th*

BONEHILL, Selina, music hall artiste, died 27 Sept 1976 (97)

BONN, Issy, comedian, died 21 Apr 1977 (74)

BOSWELL, Connee, singer, died 10 Oct 1976 (68)

BOURNEUF, Philip, actor, died 23 Mar 1979 (71), *16th*

BOVY, Berthe, actress, died Mar 1977 (90), *13th*

BOWLUS, Joan, Ziegfeld girl, died 2 July 1976 (86)

BOX, H Oldfield, writer, died 21 Feb 1978 (73)

BOYD, Stephen, actor, died 2 Jun 1977 (48)

BOYER, Charles, actor, died 26 Aug 1978 (78), *15th*

BRADFORD, Alex, composer and singer, died 15 Feb 1978 (51)

BRANDON-THOMAS, Jevan, actor and director, dramatic author, died Sept 1977 (79), *15th*

BREL, Jacques, Belgian singer-songwriter, died Oct 1978

BRENT, George, actor, died 26 May 1979 (75)

BRENT, Romney, actor, author, producer, died 24 Sept 1976 (74), *15th*

BRICKMAN, Miriam, RSC casting director, died 2 July 1977 (45)

BROGAN, Harry, actor, died 20 May 1977 (72)

BROOKES, Olwen, actress, died Oct 1976 (74)

BROOKS, Geraldine, actress, died 19 Jun 1977 (52)

BROUGH, Arthur, actor, died 28 May 1978 (73)

BROWN, A J, actor, died Feb 1978 (80)

BROWNE, E Martin, director and actor, died 27 Apr 1980 (80), *17th*

BRUNTON, Dorothy, actress, died 5 June 1977 (83), *10th*

BRUSTEIN, Norma, actress, died 9 Apr 1979 (50)

BURDICK, Harold P, actor and writer, died 12 Jun 1978 (84)

BURR, Donald (ne Edgar Lush), singer, actor, director, died 27 Feb 1979 (71)

BURTON, Martin, actor, died 4 Aug 1976 (71)

CABOT, Sebastian, actor, died 23 Aug 1977 (59)

CAMBRIDGE, Godfrey, comedian, died 29 Nov 1976 (43)

CAMPBELL, Flora, actress, died 6 Nov 1978 (67)

CARLETON, Moira, actress, died July 1978 (70)

CARLSON, Richard, actor, died 25 Nov 1977 (65)

CARNEY, Frank, dramatist, died Sept 1977 (73)

CARSON, Charles, actor, died Aug 1977 (92), *16th*

CARSTENS, Lina, German actress, died 1978

CASSIDY, Jack, actor, singer, dancer, died 12 Dec 1976 (49), *16th*

CAZALE, John, actor, died 12 Mar 1978 (42)

CECIL, Henry (Henry Cecil Leon), dramatic author, died 23 May 1976 (73), *16th*

CHAMBERLAIN, George, OBE, manager, died 15 May 1976 (85), *14th*

CHANDLER, Joan, actress, died 11 May 1979 (55)

CHAPLIN, Sir Charles, actor, died 25 Dec 1977 (88), *11th*

CHAPMAN, Edward, actor, died 9 Aug 1977 (75), *15th*

CHARDET, Anthony, producer and manager, died Dec 1976

CHARLES, Lewis, actor, died 9 Nov 1979 (63)

CHARLTON, Alethea, actress, died 11 May 1976 (43)

CHARNLEY, Elizabeth, director, died Nov 1976

CHASE, Ilka, actress and dramatic author, died 15 Feb 1978 (72), *16th*

CHITTY, Erik, actor, died Oct 1977 (70's)

CHRISTIE, Dame Agatha (Agatha Mary Clarissa Miller), dramatic author and novelist, died 12 Jan 1976 (85), *16th*

CLARK, Kathleen, assistant to Lilian Baylis, died 1977

CLARKE, Nigel, actor, died July 1976 (84), *12th*

COBB, Lee J, actor, died 11 Feb 1976 (64), *13th*

COE, Fred, producer and director, died 29 Apr 1979 (64), *16th*

COFFIN, Gene, costume designer, died 18 Oct 1977 (72)

COGNIAT, Raymond, designer, died Mar 1977 (80)

COLERIDGE, Ethel, actress, died 15 Aug 1976 (93), *11th*

COLOT, Ethel Barrymore, actress, died 22 May 1977 (65)

COMPTON, Fay, actress, died 12 Dec 1978 (84), *15th*

COMPTON, Jane, actress, died Dec 1979 (89)

CONSTANDUROS, Denis, writer, died Oct 1978 (68)

COOPER, Lilian Kemble, actress, died 4 May 1977 (85), *8th*

CORTEZ, Ricardo (Jack Kranze), actor, died 28 Apr 1977 (77)

COTSWORTH, Staats, actor, died 9 Apr 1979 (71), *16th*

COURTNEIDGE, Dame Cicely, actress, died Apr 1980 (87), *17th*

COUTAUD, Lucien, designer, died July 1977 (73)

CRABTREE, Paul, actor, writer, producer, director, died 21 Mar 1979 (60)

CRAIG, Edith, actress, died 2 Mar 1979 (71)

CRAVEN, Robin (Robin Henry Cohen), actor, died 15 May 1978 (71)

CRAWFORD, Joan, actress, died 10 May 1977 (69)

CROMWELL, John, actor, died 1 Sept 1979 (65)

CROMWELL, John, actor, died 1979 (92), *17th*

CROSBY, Bing, singer, died 14 Oct 1977 (76)

CROSS, Larry, actor, died 29 Jun 1976

CURZON, George, actor, died May 1976 (77), *14th*

CUZACK, Maureen, actress, died 18 Dec 1977 (57)

DAILEY, Dan, actor, singer and dancer, died 15 Oct 1978 (62), *16th*

D'ALBIE, Julian, actor, died 6 Apr 1978 (86)

DALY, James, actor, died 3 July 1978 (59), *16th*

DARLINGTON, William Aubrey, CBE, critic and author, died 24 May 1979 (89), *16th*

DARSEY, Herbert, producer and director, died 10 Oct 1976 (89)

DAUPHIN, Claude, actor, died 16 Nov 1978 (75), *16th*

DAVEY, Nuna, actress, died 11 Dec 1977 (74), *14th*

DAVID, Thayer, actor, died 17 July 1978 (51)

DAVIES, Rupert, actor, died 22 Nov 1976 (59)

DAVIS, Benny, songwriter and vaudevillian, died 20 Dec 1979 (84)

DAWN, Gloria, actress, died 2 Apr 1978 (49)

DAWSON, Beatrice, costume designer, died 16 Apr 1976 (68), *16th*

DEAN, Basil, actor and producer, died 22 Apr 1978 (89), *14th*

DECLERCQ, Aime, Belgian playwright and producer, died 24 July 1978 (79)

DE FILIPO, Peppino, Italian actor, producer, playwright, died 26 Jan 1980 (76)

DEHN, Paul, dramatic author and critic, died 30 Sept 1976 (63), *16th*

DE LEON, Herbert, agent, died 8 Dec 1979 (74)

DELYSIA, Alice, actress, died 10 Feb 1979 (89), *12th*

DE MARNEY, Derrick, actor, died 18 Feb 1978 (71), *14th*

DENNIS, Patrick (Edward E Tanner), playwright, died 6 Nov 1976 (55)

DENT, Alan, critic, died Dec 1978 (73), *16th*

DE RUYTER, Victor, director of the Flemish Theatre, Brussels, died 21 Aug 1976 (72)

DEVINE, Andy, actor, died 18 Feb 1977 (70)

DONOVAN, May Thompson, dancer, singer, actress, died 19 Nov 1978 (88)

DOUGLAS, Tom, actor, died 1978, *9th*

DOUGLASS, Amy, actress, died 5 Mar 1980 (77)

DOWLING, Eddie, actor, author, director, died 18 Feb 1976 (81), *15th*

DRESDEL, Sonia (Lois Obee), actress, died 18 Jan 1976 (67), *16th*

DUFFIELD, Brainerd, dramatist and actor, died 5 Apr 1979 (62)

DU GARDE, Barrie, actor and singer, died 28 Jun 1980 (93)

DUNCAN, Archie, actor, died Sept 1979 (65), *16th*

DUNLAP, Florence, actress, died 3 May 1977 (94)

DURANTE, Jimmy, comedian, died 29 Jan 1980 (86) *11th*

DYNELEY, Peter, actor, died Aug 1977 (56)

EASON, Myles, actor, died 8 Jan 1977 (61), *16th*

EDMONDSON, William, actor, died 28 May 1979 (76)

EDWARDS, Dorothy, actress, died 13 Aug 1979

EGLEVSKY, Andre, dancer and choreographer, died 4 Dec 1977 (60)

EMERY, Katherine, actress, died Feb 1980 (73), *11th*

ETTING, Ruth, singer and Ziegfeld girl, died 24 Sept 1978 (80), *9th*

EUSTRAL, Anthony, actor, died 2 July 1979 (76), *13th*

EVANS, Dame Edith, actress, died 14 Oct 1976 (88), *16th*

EVERETT, Tim, actor and choreographer, died 4 Mar 1977, (38)

FAIRMAN, Derek, actor, died 19 May 1979 (73)

FIELD, Betty, actress, died 13 Sept 1973 (55), *16th*

FIELDS, Gracie, entertainer, died 27 Sept 1979 (81), *11th*

FINCH, Peter, actor, died 14 Jan 1977 (60), *15th*

FINKLEHOFFE, Fred, producer and playwright, died 5 Oct 1977 (67)

FINN, Adelaide Raine, actress, died 20 Jan 1978 (84)

FITZGERALD, Walter, actor, died 20 Dec 1976 (80), *15th*

FLEMING, Kate, National Theatre voice coach, died 1978

FORD, Paul, actor, died 12 Apr 1976 (74), *16th*

FOREMAN, Marion, actress, died 1976

FOSTER, Norman, actor, died 7 July 1976 (72), *10th*

FOURNIER, Maurice, director and producer, died 9 Apr 1978 (61)

FRANK, Allan, actor, died 9 Aug 1979 (64)

FREEMAN, K Charles, critic, writer, director, died 1 Mar 1980 (79)

FRIEBUS, Beatrice, actress, died 4 Mar 1980 (94)

FRIZZELL, Lou, actor, died 17 Jun 1979 (59)

FULLER, Edward (Eddie), actor, died 22 Jan 1979 (67)

GABIN, Jean, French actor, died 15 Nov 1976 (72)

GALLICO, Paul, writer, died 16 July 1976 (78)

GALVIN, Gene, actor, died 24 Mar 1979 (63)

GARDINER, Reginald, actor, died 7 July 1980 (77), *10th*

GARGAN, William, actor, died 17 Feb 1979 (73), *10th*

GATESON, Marjorie, actress, died 17 Apr 1977 (86), *14th*

GEAR, Luella, actress, died 3 Apr 1980 (80)

GEER, Will, actor, died 22 Apr 1978 (76), *16th*

GERING, Marion, director and producer, died 19 Apr 1977 (73)

GENN, Leo, died 26 Jan 1978 (72), *16th*

GILBERT, Lou, actor, died 6 Nov 1978 (69), *17th*

GILKEY, Stanley, producer, died 3 Nov 1979 (79)

GILL, Tom, actor, died 22 July 1971 (55), *16th*

GIVNEY, Kathryn, actress, died 16 Mar 1978 (81)

GLUCKMAN, Leon, actor, director, author, producing manager, died 21 Feb 1978 (55), *16th*

GODFREY, Michael, actor, died Sept 1977

GOLDSTEIN, Shmulik, Yiddish comedian, died 23 Nov 1978 (70)

GOODLIFFE, Michael, actor, died 20 Mar 1976 (61), *16th*

GOODWIN, Clive, authors' agent, died Nov 1977 (45)

GORDON, Max, producer, died 2 Nov 1978 (86), *14th*

GRADE, Leslie, agent and producer, died 15 Oct 1979 (63)

GRAVES, Ralph, actor, died 18 Feb 1977 (75)

GREENWOOD, Charlotte, actress, died 18 Jan 1978 (87), *13th*

GRENFELL, Joyce, actress and writer, died 30 Nov 1979 (69), *16th*

GRESHAM, Edith, actress, died 31 Dec 1976 (79)

GRIBOV, Alexei, Russian actor, died 1977, *14th*

GRIFFIN, Norman, actor and vocalist, died Dec 1976 (89), *7th*

GRIFFITH, Corinne, actress, died 13 July 1979 (81)

GRIFFITH, Hugh, actor, died 14 May 1980 (67), *17th*

GROGAN, John, producer, died 26 Feb 1980 (67)

GWYNN, Michael, actor, died 29 Jan 1976 (59), *16th*

HAGEN, Jean, actress, died 28 Aug 1977 (54)

HALE, Lionel, critic and author, died 15 May 1977 (67), *16th*

HALEY, Jack, actor, died 6 Jun 1979 (79), *11th*

HALLIDAY, Hildegarde, actress, died 10 Oct 1967 (75)

HALOP, Billy, actor and Dead End Kid, died 9 Nov 1976 (56)

HAMMOND, Kay, actress, died 4 May 1980 (71), *14th*

HARE, J Robertson, actor, died 25 Jan 1979 (87), *16th*

HARRINGTON, Kate, actress, died 23 Nov 1978 (75)

HARRIS, Jed, producing manager, died 15 Dec 1979 (79), *14th*

HASSE, O E, German actor, died 12 Sept 1978 (75)

HAWLEY, William G, actor, died 22 Aug 1976 (66)

HAYES, Margaret (Maggie), actress, died 26 Jan 1977 (63)

HEARN, Julia Knox, actress, died 1 May 1976 (92)

HEARNE, Richard 'Mr Pastry', actor, died 23 Aug 1979 (70), *15th*

HENTSCHEL, Irene, actress, died 3 Aug 1979 (88), *14th*

HEPPNER, Rosa, theatre press representative, died 18 Sept 1979, *16th*

HERBERT, Annette, Ziegfeld girl, died 24 Apr 1978 (87)

HERON, Joyce, actress, died Apr 1980 (64), *17th*

HERRICK, Marguerite, actress and Ziegfeld girl, died 18 Jun 1979 (71)

HEWINS, Nancy, actress, died Jan 1978 (75)

HIGNETT, Mary, actress, died July 1980

HINNANT, Bill, actor, died 17 Feb 1978 (42)

HISLOP, Joseph, actor and singer, died May 1977 (93), *10th*

HOBBS, Carleton, actor, died July/Aug 1978 (82), *8th*

HOCTOR, Harriet, choreographer, died 9 Jun 1977 (74), *10th*

HOEY, Iris, actress, died 13 May 1979 (93), *13th*

HOFFMAN, Bern, actor, died 15 Dec 1979 (66)

HOLMES, Edward, actor, died 12 July 1977 (66)

HOLMES-GORE, Dorothy, actress, died 14 Oct 1977 (81), *9th*

HOMOLKA, Oscar, actor, died 27 Jan 1978 (79), *14th*

HOOD, Noel, actor, died 15 Oct 1979 (69)

HOPE-WALLACE, Philip, critic, died 3 Sept 1979 (67), *16th*

HOUSTON, Jane, actress, died 27 Sept 1979 (88), *7th*

HOUSTON, Renée, actress, died 9 Feb 1980 (77), *17th*

HUGHES, Julia, actress, died 31 July 1979

HULBERT, Jack, actor, died 25 Mar 1978 (85), *16th*

HULL, Henry, actor, died 8 Mar 1977 (86), *14th*

HURRY, Leslie, designer, died 20 Nov 1978 (69), *16th*

HUTCHESON, David, actor, died 18 Feb 1976 (70), *16th*

HUTCHINSON, Harry, actor, died 7 Mar 1980 (87), *16th*

HYLAND, Diana, actress, died 27 Mar 1977 (41)

HYLTON, Jane, actress, died 28 Feb 1979 (50)

HYMAN, Joseph M, producer, died 25 Feb 1977 (80), *11th*

IDZIKOWSKY, Stanislas, dancer, died 12 Feb 1977 (82), *11th*

ILLINGWORTH, David, playwright, died 1976

INESCOURT, Frieda, actress, died 21 Feb 1976 (75), *11th*

ISHAM, Sir Gyles, actor, died Jan 1976 (72), *11th*

IVES, Anne, actress, died 15 May 1979 (92)

JAMES, Sidney, actor, died 26 Apr 1976 (62)

JOHNSON, Nunnally, writer, died 25 Mar 1977 (79)

JONES, Preston, actor and playwright, died 19 Sept 1979 (43)

KALLOS, Nellie Knight, actress, died 10 Oct 1977 (80)

KARSAVINA, Tamara, dancer, died 26 May 1978 (93), *11th*

KASZNAR, Kurt, actor, died 6 Aug 1979 (65), *17th*

KEEGAN, Barry, actor, died Sept 1977 (55)

KEITH-JOHNSTON, Colin, actor, died 3 Jan 1980 (83), *14th*

KELLER, Greta, actress and singer, died 4 Nov 1977 (76)

KELTON, Richard, actor, died 11 Jan 1979 (35)

KEPPEL, Joe, vaudevillian, died Aug 1977 (82)

KERZ, Leo, actor, died 4 Nov 1976 (64)

KIDD, Robert, director, 17 July 1980 (37), *17th*

KILIAN, Victor, actor, died 11 Mar 1979 (88)

KING, Philip, playwright and actor, died Feb 1979 (74), *16th*

KONSTAM, Phyllis, actress, died 20 Aug 1976 (69), *10th*

KRELLBERG, Sherman S, producer, 10 Jan 1979 (87)

KRONENBERGER, Louis, writer and critic, died 30 Apr 1980 (75), *16th*

LACEY, Catherine, actress, died 23 Sept 1979 (75), *16th*

LAMBERT, Jack, actor, died Mar 1976 (76), *16th*

LANDON, Avice, actress, died 23 Jun 1976 (65), *16th*

LANDSTONE, Charles, critic, died Apr 1978 (87), *15th*

LATIMER, Sally, actress, died Jan 1977 (66), *14th*

LAURIE, John, actor, died 26 Jun 1980 (83), *17th*

LAWS, Gerald R (Jerry), actor, died 7 Sept 1976 (64)

LAWSON, John Howard, playwright, died 12 Aug 1977 (82), *11th*

LEHMANN, Beatrix, actress, died 31 July 1979 (76), *17th*

LEHMANN, Lotte, singer, died 26 Aug 1976 (88)

LEIGHTON, Margaret, actress, died 13 Jan 1976 (53), *16th*

LESLIE, Edgar, lyricist, died 22 Jan 1976 (90)

LESLEY, Cole, biographer of Noel Coward, died 4 Jan 1980 (70)

LEVITT, Saul, playwright, died 30 Sept 1977 (66)

LEWIS, Albert, producer, director, died 6 Apr 1978 (93)

LIEVEN, Tatiana, actress, died 30 Nov 1978 (69), *11th*

LIVESEY, Roger, actor, died 5 Feb 1976 (69), *16th*

LLOYD-DAVIES, Betty, actress and singer, died 25 Mar 1977 (84)

LOCKHART, Kathleen, actress, died 17 Feb 1978 (84)

LOMBARDO, Guy, bandleader, producer, died 5 Nov 1977 (75)

LORD, Basil, actor, died 3 Apr 1979 (70), *17th*

LOWRY, Judith, actress, died 29 Nov 1976 (86)

LUCKER, Leo, actor, died 1 Feb 1977 (64)

LUNT, Alfred, actor and director, died 3 Aug 1977 (84), *16th*

LYON, Ben, actor, died 22 Mar 1979 (78), *14th*

McCALLIN, Clement, actor, died Aug 1977 (64), *17th*

McCARTHY, Denis, actor, died May/Jun 1977

McCARTY, Mary, actress and singer, died 3 Apr 1980 (56), *17th*

McCOY, Tim, actor and cowboy, died 29 Jan 1978 (86)

McCULLOCK, Duff, actor, died 23 May 1979 (77)

McDERMOT, Rory, actor, died 7 July 1980 (66)

MacDERMOTT, Norman, producer and manager, died Dec 1977 (88), *13th*

McDEVITT, Ruth, actress, died 27 May 1976 (80), *16th*

MacDONNELL, Leslie, manager, died 1978, *15th*

McGINN, Walter, actor, died 31 Mar 1977 (40)

McGIVER, John, actor, died 9 Sept 1975 (61), *16th*

McGOWAN, Jack, actor and playwright, died 28 May 1977 (81)

McGRATH, Frank, playwright, died 24 Jan 1976 (72)

McGRATH, Paul, actor, died 13 Apr 1978 (74), *16th*

McGUIRE, Kathryn, actress, died 10 Oct 1978 (80's)

MACHIZ, Herbert, director, died 27 Aug 1976 (57), *16th*

MACLIAMMOIR, Micheál, actor, director, designer, author, died 6 Mar 1978 (78), *16th*

MacMANAMY, Sue, actress, died 10 Jun 1976 (84)

McMILLAN, Roddy, actor and playwright, died 9 July 1979 (56), *16th*

McNAMARA, Maggie, actress, died 18 Feb 1978 (48)

McQUADE, John, actor, died 24 Sept 1979 (63)

MALLIN, Tom, playwright, died Feb 1978 (50)

MANNHEIM, Lucie, actress, died 28 July 1976 (77), *14th*

MARMONT, Percy, actor, died Feb/Mar 1977 (93), *14th*

MARQUES, Rene, playwright, died 22 Mar 1979 (59)

MARQUET, Mary, actress, died 29 Aug 1979 (84), *14th*

MARRIOTT, John, actor, died 5 Apr 1977 (83)

MARSAN, Jean, dramatist, died Oct 1977 (57)

MARSHALL, Mort, actor, died 1 Feb 1979 (60)

MARX, Groucho, actor/comedian, died 19 Aug 1977 (86)

MARX, Gummo, actor, died 21 Apr 1977 (84)

MARX, Zeppo, actor, died 29 Nov 1979 (79)

MASSINE, Leonide, choreographer, died 16 Mar 1979 (83), *12th*

MATHEW, Ann, dancer, died 31 May 1976 (65)

MATRAY, Ernst, actor, director, playwright, died Nov 1978 (87)

MAUDE, Margery, actress, died 7 Aug 1979 (90), *16th*

MAY, Ada (Ada May Weeks), actress, died 25 Apr 1978 (80), *10th*

MEEHAN, Danny, actor, died 29 Mar 1978 (47)

MERCER, Johnny, songwriter, died 25 Jun 1976 (66), *16th*

MERRITT, George, actor, died Sept 1977 (86), *16th*

MERVYN, William, actor, died 6 Aug 1976 (64), *16th*

MESSEL, Oliver, artist and designer, died 13 July 1978 (74), *16th*

MIELZINER, Jo, designer, died 15 Mar 1976 (74), *15th*

MILAN, Frank, actor, died 8 Apr 1977 (71)

MILLER, Hugh, actor and director, died 1 Mar 1976 (87), *14th*

MILLER, Ruby, actress, died 2 Apr 1976 (86), *10th*

MILNE, Lennox, actress, died Jun 1980 (70)

MINEO, Sal, actor, director, died 12 Feb 1976 (37)

MITCHELL, Yvonne, actress and writer, died 24 Mar 1979 (53), *16th*

MONCRIEFF, Gladys, actress, died 8 Feb 1976 (83), *11th*

MONKMAN, Phyllis, actress and dancer, died 2 Dec 1976 (84), *11th*

MONTAGUE, Bertram, producer, died Oct 1977 (85), *13th*

MONTELEAGRE, Felicia, actress, died 16 Jun 1978 (56)

MOORE, Carroll B, playwright, died 5 Feb 1977 (63)

MOOREHEAD, Agnes, actress, died 20 Apr 1974 (67), *16th*

MORELL, Andre, actor, died Nov 1978 (69), *16th*

MORRIS, Margaret, dancer, died 29 Feb 1980 (88), *9th*

MOSTEL, Zero, actor, died on tour, 8 Sept 1977 (62), *17th*

MULLEN, Barbara, actress, died 9 Mar 1979 (64), *17th*

MURDOCH, Bryden, actor, died 1 May 1978 (53)

MURRAY, Sir William Patrick Keith, producer, died Nov 1977 (38)

MUSE, Clarence, actor, died 13 Oct 1979 (89)

MUSTIN, Burt, character actor, died 28 Jan 1977 (92)

MYERS, Peter, author and lyricist, died July 1978 (54), *16th*

MYERS, Richard, composer and producer, died 12 Mar 1977 (76), *15th*

MYRTIL, Odette, actress and singer, died 18 Nov 1978 (80), *14th*

NASH, Mary, actress, died 3 Dec 1976 (92)

NAUGHTON, Charlie, vaudevillian, died 1976

NEILSON-TERRY, Phyllis, actress, died 25 Sept 1977 (84), *14th*

NICOLL, Allardyce, theatre historian, died 17 Apr 1976 (81), *16th*

NICHOLLS, Anthony, actor, died Mar 1977 (69), *16th*

NORMAN, Maureen, actress, died Jun 1977 (62)

OAKIE, Jack, actor, died 23 Jan 1978 (74)

OBERON, Merle, actress, died 23 Nov 1979 (68)

O'BRIEN-MOORE, Erin, actress, died 3 May 1979 (77)

O'BRYEN, W J, manager, died Oct 1977 (79), *10th*

O'DEA, Denis, Irish actor, died 5 Nov 1978 (75), *14th*

O'FLYNN, Angela Newman, actress, died 14 Apr 1979 (49)

O'HALLORAN, Michael, actor, died 2 July 1976 (65)

O'HIGGINS, Brian, Irish actor, died 29 Mar 1980 (63)

O'MALLEY, Rex, actor, died 1 May 1976 (75), *15th*

O'NEILL, James T, actor, died 18 July 1977 (93)

OPPENHEIMER, George, critic and playwright, died 14 Aug 1977 (77)

ORCHARD, Julian, actor, died 20 Jun 1979 (49), *16th*

ORFALY, Alexander, actor, died 22 Jan 1979 (44)

PAGET, Peter, actor, died 8 Nov 1976 (92)

PARSONS, Donovan, lyricist, died 10 Jan 1980 (91), *9th*

PATRICK, Gail, actress died 6 July 1980 (69)

PAYNE, Ben Iden, director and scholar, died 6 Apr 1976 (94), *15th*

PAYNE, Virginia ('Ma Perkins'), actress, died 10 Feb 1977 (66)

PEARMAN, Vincent, theatre press representative, died Nov 1977 (74)

PEMBERTON, Reece, designer, died Sept 1977 (63), *16th*

PEISLEY, Frederick, actor, died 1976, *16th*

PEPPER, Jack, actor, died 31 Mar 1979 (76)

PETROVA, Olga (Muriel Harding), actress and playwright, died 30 Nov 1977 (93), *7th*

PHIPPS, Nicholas, actor, died 11 Apr 1980 (66), 16th

PICKFORD, Mary, actress, died 29 May 1979 (86), *11th*

PICKLES, Wilfred, actor, died Mar 1978 (73)

PIOUS, Minerva, actress, died 16 Mar 1979 (75)

POINDEXTER, H R, designer, died 24 Sept 1977 (41)

POLAN, Lou, actor, died 8 Mar 1976 (71), *16th*

POLLOCK, Nancy, actress, died 20 Jun 1979 (77), *16th*

POTTER, H C, director, died 31 Aug 1977 (73), *13th*

PRATT, Mike, actor, died 10 July 1976 (45)

PRESLEY, Elvis, entertainer, died 16 Aug 1977 (42)

PRINTEMPS, Yvonne, actress and singer, died 18 Jan 1977 (82), *14th*

PRUDHOE, John, professor of drama, died Jun 1977 (52)

PRYOR, Maureen, actress, died 5 May 1977 (52)

PUCK, Eva, actress, died 24 Oct 1979 (87)

PULASKI, Lillian, actress, died 29 Jan 1977 (95)

PURCELL, Harold, dramatic author and librettist, died 28 May 1977 (69), *14th*

QUENTIN, Robert, director and professor of drama, died 7 July 1979

RADD, Ronald, actor, died on tour 23 Apr 1976 (47), *16th*

RAMSKILL, Herbert, actor, died Jun 1977 (62)

RATTIGAN, Sir Terence, playwright, died 30 Nov 1977 (66), *16th*

REDFIELD, William, actor, died 17 Aug 1976 (49), *16th*

REED, Alan (Teddy Bergman), actor, died 14 Jun 1977 (69)

REED, Sir Carol, director, died 25 Apr 1976 (69), *11th*

REED, Daniel, actor, director, producer, died 9 Feb 1978 (86)

REID, Mary, actress, died Sept 1979 (83)

REMEY, Ethel, actress, died 28 Feb 1979

REVNELL, Ethel, comedienne, died Sept 1978 (83)

REYNOLDS, Dorothy, actress, died 7 Apr 1977 (63), *16th*

RHODES, Marjorie, actress, died 3 July 1979 (75), *16th*

RICHARDSON, Wells, actor, died 22 Feb 1979 (81)

RIGBY, Arthur, actor, died 25 Apr 1971 (70), *16th*

RITCHARD, Cyril, actor and director, died 18 Dec 1977 (80), *16th*

ROBERTS, John, producing manager, died Feb 1972 (55), *16th*

ROBESON, Paul, singer and actor, died 23 Jan 1976 (77), *14th*

ROBINSON, John, actor, died 6 Mar 1979 (70), *16th*

ROCKWELL, George 'Doc', vaudevillian, died 2 Mar 1978 (89)

RODGERS, Richard, composer, died 30 Dec 1979 (77), *17th*

RONAN, Robert, actor and director, died 6 Apr 1977 (41)

ROSE, Howard, actor, died Apr 1978 (95)

ROSE, Irving, dancer and actor, died 9 Sept 1977 (81)

ROSENTHAL, Andrew, playwright, died 11 Nov 1979 (61)

ROTH, Lillian, actress and singer, died 12 May 1980 (69), *17th*

ROUNSEVILLE, Robert, actor and singer, died 6 Aug 1974 (60), *16th*

ROYSTON, Roy, actor, died Oct 1976 (77), *13th*

RUPERT, Gene, actor, died 14 May 1979 (47)

RUSKIN, Shimen, actor, died 23 Apr 1977 (52)

RUSSELL, Rosalind, actress, died 28 Nov 1976 (64), *16th*

SAIDENBERG, Eleanor, producer, died 14 Feb 1978 (66)

SARTRE, Jean-Paul, author, playwright, died 15 Apr 1980 (74), *17th*

SCAIFE, Gillian, actress, died Oct 1976 (91), *11th*

SCHNITZER, Henriette, Yiddish actress, died 4 May 1979 (84)

SCHWARTZ, Samuel, producer, died 11 July 1977 (69)

SCOTT, Jay Hutchinson, designer, died 14 Sept 1977 (53), *17th*

SEGAL, Alex, director, died 22 Aug 1977 (62)

SEATON, Derek, actor, died 2 Sept 1979 (35)

SELLERS, Peter, actor, died 24 July 1980 (54)

SHAW, Robert, actor and writer, died 27 Aug 1978 (51), *16th*

SHERMAN, Charles, playwright and producer, died 25 Dec 1976 (77)

SHOEMAKER, Ann, actress, died 18 Sept 1978 (87), *16th*

SHREWSBURY, Lillian, actress, died 15 Jun 1979 (90)

SHUMLIN, Herman E, producer and director, died 4 Jun 1979 (80), *17th*

SHUTTA, Ethel, actress and singer, died 5 Feb 1976 (89), *15th*

SIM, Alastair, CBE, actor, died 19 Aug 1976 (75), *16th*

SIMPSON, Alan, Irish director and producer, died 15 May 1980 (59)

SINGER, Campbell, actor and playwright, died Mar 1976 (66), *16th*

SKINNER, Cornelia Otis, actress and writer, died 9 July 1979 (78), *16th*

SMITH, Queenie, actress, died 5 Aug 1978 (80), *10th*

SMITH, Sydney, actor, died 4 Mar 1978 (68)

SOBOLOFF, Arnold, actor, died 28 Oct 1979 (48), *17th*

SPEAIGHT, Robert, actor, died Nov 1976 (72), *16th*

STANITSIN, Victor, Russian actor, died Jan 1977 (79)

STARNES, R Leland, actor and director, died 14 May 1980 (58)

STEVENS, Onslow, actor, died 5 Jan 1977 (72), *14th*

STEWART, Hal D, playwright, stage director, actor, died Apr 1979 (80)

STEWART, Sophie, actress, died Jun 1977 (69), *16th*

STOKES, Sewell, writer, died 2 Nov 1979 (76), *11th*

STOKER, Willard, director, died Mar 1978 (72), *16th*

STUART, John, actor, died 17 Oct 1979 (81), *16th*

SUTCLIFFE, Berkeley, designer, died Dec 1979 (61)

SUTRO, Edward, first-nighter, died Jan 1978 (78)

SYRJALA, Sointu, designer, died 10 Apr 1979 (74)

TAFLER, Sydney, actor, died 7 Nov 1979 (63)

TALIAFERRO, Mabel, actress, died 24 Jan 1979 (91), *13th*

TEMPLETON, Olive, actress, died 29 May 1979 (96)

TETZEL, Joan, actress, died 31 Oct 1977 (56), *16th*

TAYLOR, Julia (Worsley), actress, died 4 Dec 1976 (98)

TEYTE, Dame Maggie, actress and singer, died 27 May 1976 (88), *13th*

THOMPSON, Frank, costume designer, died 4 Jun 1977 (57), *16th*

THOMPSON, May, actress, died 18 Nov 1978 (88)

THOMSON, Alden Gay, actress, died 1 Apr 1979 (80)

THORNDIKE, Dame Sybil, actress, died 6 Jun 1976 (93), *16th*

THORNTON, Sydney, actress, died July 1980 (87)

TOBIAS, George, actor, died Feb 1980 (78)

TREVOR, Austin, actor, died 22 Jan 1978 (80), *15th*
TROUTMAN, Ivy, actress, died 12 Jan 1979 (96), *11th*
TRUMAN, Ralph, actor, died Oct 1977 (77)
TRUMBO, Dalton, writer, died 10 Sept 1976 (79)
TUMARIN, Boris, actor, died 28 Jan 1979 (68), *17th*
TYNAN, Kenneth, critic, died 27 July 1980 (53) *17th*

URE, Joan, playwright, died Feb 1978 (58)
URQUHART, Molly, actress, died 6 Oct 1977 (71), *14th*

VALLI, Romolo, artistic director, Spoleto Festival, died 1 Feb 1980 (55)
VANCE, Nina, producer and director, died 18 Feb 1980 (65), *17th*
VANCE, Vivienne, actress, died 17 Aug 1979 (66)
VAN GYSEGHEM, Andre, actor and director, died 13 Oct 1979 (73), *17th*
VAZ DIAS, Selma, actress, died Sept 1977 (65), *15th*
VILLIERS, Mavis, actress, died 1976
VISCONTI, Luchino, director, died 17 Mar 1976 (69)
VYE, Murvyn, actor, died 17 Aug 1976 (63)

WALLACE, Regina, actress, died 13 Feb 1978 (86)
WALLACE, Robert, actor, died Apr 1977 (74)
WARREN, Beatrice, actress, died 1978 (86)
WATERS, Doris, comedienne, died Aug 1978 (74)
WATERS, Ethel, actress and singer, died 1 Sept 1977 (80), *16th*

WATKINS, Linda, actress, died 31 Oct 1976 (68), *11th*
WAYNE, Mabel, singer/songwriter, died 19 Jun 1978 (86)
WEDGE, Mawa K, actress, died 9 Nov 1979 (40)
WEISS, Rudolf, actor, died 6 Apr 1978 (77)
WELLS, Maurice, actor, died 26 Jun 1978 (76)
WENGER, John, scenic designer, died 24 Aug 1976 (89)
WHITE, Valerie, actress, died 3 Dec 1975 (59), *16th*
WILCOX, Herbert, producer, died 15 May 1977 (85)
WILDING, Michael, actor, died 9 July 1979 (66), *11th*
WILKINSON, Pitt, actor, died 1977
WILLIAMSON, Hugh Ross, writer, died 13 Jan 1978 (76), *14th*
WILMOT, Seamus, Irish playwright, director, died 21 Jan 1977 (75)
WINOGRADOFF, Anatol, actor, died 27 Apr 1980 (89)
WINTERS, Marian, actress, died 3 Nov 1978 (54), *16th*
WOOD, George ('Wee Georgie'), OBE, entertainer, died 19 Feb 1979 (83)
WOOD, Peggy, actress and singer, died 18 Mar 1978 (87), *16th*
WOOLGAR, Jack, actor, died July 1978 (64)
WORSLEY, T C, critic, died 23 Feb 1977 (69)
WORTH, Claude (Claude Holdsworth), actor and director, died 23 Nov 1976 (74)

YOUNG, Gig, actor, died 19 Oct 1978 (64), *16th*

ZAKHAVA, Boris, Russian director, died 1976
ZAVADSKY, Yuri, Russian actor/director, died May 1977 (82)
ZUCKMAYER, Carl, playwright, died 18 Jan 1977 (80), *16th*